BOOKS

HOCKEY REGISTER

2003-2004 EDITION

ON THE COVER: Top: Jean-Sebastien Giguere (photo by Albert Dixon/THE SPORTING NEWS); bottom left to right: John LeClair (Kent Smith for THE SPORTING NEWS), Jaromir Jagr (Bob Leverone/THE SPORTING NEWS), Brett Hull (Dilip Vishwanat/THE SPORTING NEWS); spine: Brett Hull (Dilip Vishwanat/THE SPORTING NEWS).

NHL statistics compiled by STATS, Inc., a News Corporation company; 8130 Lehigh Avenue, Morton Grove, IL 60053. STATS is a trademark of Sports Team Analysis and Tracking Systems, Inc.

Minor league statistics provided by SportsTicker.

ISBN: 0-89204-711-9

10 9 8 7 6 5 4 3 2 1

CONTENTS

EXPLANATION OF AWARDS

NHL AWARDS: Alka-Seltzer Plus Award: plus/minus leader. **Art Ross Trophy:** leading scorer. **Bill Masterton Memorial Trophy:** perseverance, sportsmanship and dedication to hockey. **Bud Light/NHL Man of the Year:** service to community; called Budweiser/NHL Man of the Year prior to 1990-91. **Budweiser/NHL Man of the Year:** service to community; renamed Bud Light/NHL Man of the Year in 1990-91. **Calder Memorial Trophy:** rookie of the year. **Conn Smythe Trophy:** most valuable player in playoffs. **Dodge Performance of the Year Award:** most outstanding achievement or single-game performance. **Dodge Performer of the Year Award:** most outstanding performer in regular season. **Dodge Ram Tough Award:** highest combined total of power-play, shorthanded, game-winning and game-tying goals. **Emery Edge Award:** plus/minus leader; awarded from 1982-83 through 1987-88. **Frank J. Selke Trophy:** best defensive forward. **Hart Memorial Trophy:** most valuable player. **Jack Adams Award:** coach of the year. **James Norris Memorial Trophy:** outstanding defenseman. **King Clancy Memorial Trophy:** humanitarian contributions. **Lady Byng Memorial Trophy:** most gentlemanly player. **Lester B. Pearson Award:** outstanding player as selected by NHL Players' Association. **Lester Patrick Trophy:** outstanding service to hockey in U.S. **Maurice "Rocket" Richard Trophy:** leading goal scorer. **Trico Goaltender Award:** best save percentage. **Vezina Trophy:** best goaltender; awarded to goalkeeper(s) having played minimum of 25 games for team with fewest goals scored against prior to 1981-82. **William M. Jennings Trophy:** goalkeeper(s) having played minimum of 25 games for team with fewest goals scored against.

MINOR LEAGUE AWARDS: Baz Bastien Trophy: top goaltender (AHL). **Bobby Orr Trophy:** best defenseman (CHL); awarded prior to 1984-85. **Bob Gassoff Award:** most improved defenseman (CHL); awarded prior to 1984-85. **Commissioner's Trophy:** coach of the year (IHL). **Dudley (Red) Garrett Memorial Trophy:** rookie of the year (AHL). **Eddie Shore Plaque:** outstanding defenseman (AHL). **Fred Hunt Memorial Award:** sportsmanship, determination and dedication (AHL). **Garry F. Longman Memorial Trophy:** outstanding rookie (IHL). **Governors Trophy:** outstanding defenseman (IHL). **Harry (Hap) Holmes Memorial Trophy:** goaltender(s) having played minimum of 25 games for team with fewest goals scored against (AHL); awarded to outstanding goaltender prior to 1983-84. **Jack Butterfield Trophy:** Calder Cup playoffs MVP (AHL). **Jake Milford Trophy:** coach of the year (CHL); awarded prior to 1984-85. **James Gatschene Memorial Trophy:** most valuable player (IHL). **James Norris Memorial Trophy:** outstanding goaltender (IHL). **John B. Sollenberger Trophy:** leading scorer (AHL); originally called Wally Kilrea Trophy, later changed to Carl Liscombe Trophy until summer of 1955. **Ken McKenzie Trophy:** outstanding U.S.-born rookie (IHL). **Ken McKenzie Trophy:** top rookie (CHL); awarded to scoring leader from 1992-93. **Leo P. Lamoureux Memorial Trophy:** leading scorer (IHL); originally called George H. Wilkinson Trophy from 1946-47 through 1959-60. **Les Cunningham Plaque:** most valuable player (AHL). **Louis A.R. Pieri Memorial Award:** top coach (AHL). **Max McNab Trophy:** playoff MVP (CHL); awarded prior to 1984-85. **N.R. (Bud) Poile Trophy:** playoff MVP (IHL); originally called Turner Cup Playoff MVP from 1984-85 through 1988-89. **Phil Esposito Trophy:** leading scorer (CHL); awarded prior to 1984-85. **Terry Sawchuk Trophy:** top goaltenders (CHL); awarded prior to 1984-85. **Tommy Ivan Trophy:** most valuable player (CHL); awarded prior to 1984-85. **Turner Cup Playoff MVP:** playoff MVP (IHL); renamed N.R. (Bud) Poile Trophy in 1989-90.

MAJOR JUNIOR LEAGUE AWARDS: Association of Journalists for Major Junior League Hockey Trophy: top pro prospect (QMJHL); renamed Michael Bossy Trophy in 1983-84. **Bill Hunter Trophy:** top defenseman (WHL); called Top Defenseman Trophy prior to 1987-88 season. **Bob Brownridge Memorial Trophy:** top scorer (WHL); later renamed Bob Clarke Trophy. **Bobby Smith Trophy:** scholastic player of the year (OHL). **Bob Clarke Trophy:** top scorer (WHL); originally called Bob Brownridge Memorial Trophy. **Brad Hornung Trophy:** most sportsmanlike player (WHL); called Frank Boucher Memorial Trophy for most gentlemanly player prior to 1987-88 season. **Dave Pinkney Trophy:** top team goaltending (OHL). **Del Wilson Trophy:** top goaltender (WHL); called Top Goaltender Trophy prior to 1987-88 season. **Des Instructeurs Trophy:** rookie of the year (QMJHL); awarded to top rookie forward since 1981-82 season; renamed Michel Bergeron Trophy in 1985-86. **Dunc McCallum Memorial Trophy:** coach of the year (WHL). **Eddie Powers Memorial Trophy:** scoring champion (OHL). **Emile (Butch) Bouchard Trophy:** best defenseman (QMJHL). **Emms Family Award:** rookie of the year (OHL). **Four Broncos Memorial Trophy:** most valuable player as selected by coaches (WHL); called Most Valuable Player Trophy prior to 1987-88 season. **Frank Boucher Memorial Trophy:** most gentlemanly player (WHL); renamed Brad Hornung Trophy during 1987-88 season. **Frank J. Selke Trophy:** most gentlemanly player (QMJHL). **F.W. (Dinty) Moore Trophy:** rookie goalie with best goals-against average (OHL). **George Parsons Trophy:** sportsmanship in Memorial Cup (Can.HL). **Guy Lafleur Trophy:** most valuable player during playoffs (QMJHL). **Hap Emms Memorial Trophy:** outstanding goaltender in Memorial Cup (Can.HL). **Jacques Plante Trophy:** best goaltender (QMJHL). **Jean Beliveau Trophy:** leading point scorer (QMJHL). **Jim Mahon Memorial Trophy:** top-scoring right winger (OHL). **Jim Piggott Memorial Trophy:** rookie of the year (WHL); originally called Stewart (Butch) Paul Memorial Trophy. **Leo Lalonde Memorial Trophy:** overage player of the year (OHL). **Marcel Robert Trophy:** top scholastic/athletic performer (QMJHL). **Matt Leyden Trophy:** coach of the year (OHL). **Max Kaminsky Trophy:** outstanding defenseman (OHL); awarded to most gentlemanly player prior to 1969-70. **Michael Bossy Trophy:** top pro prospect (QMJHL); originally called Association of Journalists for Major Junior League Hockey Trophy from 1980-81 through 1982-83. **Michel Bergeron Trophy:** top rookie forward (QMJHL); awarded to rookie of the year prior to 1980-81 season. **Michel Briere Trophy:** most valuable player (QMJHL). **Most Valuable Player Trophy:** most valuable player (WHL); renamed Four Broncos Memorial Trophy during 1987-88 season. **Raymond Lagace Trophy:** top rookie defenseman or goaltender (QMJHL). **Red Tilson Trophy:** outstanding player (OHL). **Shell Cup:** awarded to offensive player of the year and defensive player of the year (QMJHL). **Stafford Smythe Memorial Trophy:** most valuable player of Memorial Cup (Can.HL). **Stewart (Butch) Paul Memorial Trophy:** rookie of the year (WHL); renamed Jim Piggott Memorial Trophy during 1987-88 season. **Top Defenseman Trophy:** top defenseman (WHL); renamed Bill Hunter Trophy during 1987-88 season. **Top Goaltender Trophy:** top goaltender (WHL); renamed Del Wilson Trophy during 1987-88 season. **William Hanley Trophy:** most gentlemanly player (OHL).

COLLEGE AWARDS: Hobey Baker Memorial Award: top college hockey player in U.S. **Senator Joseph A. Sullivan Trophy:** outstanding player in Canadian Interuniversity Athletic Union.

OTHER AWARDS: Golden Puck Award: Sweden's Player of the Year. **Golden Stick Award:** Europe's top player. **Izvestia Trophy:** leading scorer (Soviet Union).

EXPLANATION OF FOOTNOTES AND ABBREVIATIONS

*	League leader.
†	Tied for league lead.
‡	Overtime loss/shootout loss.
§	Led or tied league lead, but total figure is divided between two different teams.
. . .	Statistic unavailable, unofficial or mathematically impossible to calculate.
—	Statistic inapplicable.

POSITIONS: C: center. **D:** defenseman. **G:** goaltender. **LW:** left winger. **RW:** right winger.

STATISTICS: A: assists. **Avg.:** goals-against average. **G:** goals. **GA:** goals against. **Gms.:** games. **L:** losses. **Min.:** minutes. **PIM.:** penalties in minutes. **+/-:** plus-minus. **PP:** power-play goals. **Pts:** points. **SH:** shorthanded goals. **SO:** shutouts. **SV%:** save percentage. **T:** ties. **W:** wins.

TEAMS: Bloom. Jefferson: Bloomington Jefferson. **Chem. Litvinov:** Chemopetrol Litvinov. **Chem. Litvinov Jrs.:** Chemopetrol Litvinov Juniors. **Culver Mil. Acad.:** Culver Military Academy. **Czech. Olympic team:** Czechoslovakian Olympic team. **Czech Rep. Oly. team:** Czech Republic Olympic team. **Czechosla. Jr. national:** Czechoslavakian Junior national team. **Det. Little Caesars:** Detroit Little Caesars. **Djur. Stockholm:** Djurgarden Stockholm. **Dynamo-Energ. Yek.:** Dynamo-Energiya Yekaterinburg. **Dyn.-Energiya 2 Yek.:** Dynamo-Energiya 2 Yekaterinburg. **Dynamo Ust-Kameno.:** Dynamo Ust-Kamenogorsk. **Fin. Olympic team:** Finnish Olympic team. **German Oly. team:** German Olympic team. **HC Ceske Bude.:** HC Ceske Budejovice. **HK 32 Lip. Mikulas:** HK 32 Liptovsky Mikulas. **IS Banska Byst.:** IS Banska Bystrica. **Kiek.-Karhut Jodusuu:** Kiekko-Karhut Jodusuu. **Krylja Sov. Moscow:** Krylja Sovetov Moscow. **Mass.-Lowell:** Massachusetts-Lowell. **Metal. Cherepovets:** Metallurg Cherepovets. **Metal. Magnitogorsk:** Metallurg Magnitogorsk. **Metallurg-2 Novok.:** Metallurg-2 Novokuznetsk. **MoDo Ornsk. Jrs.:** Modo Ornskoldsvik Jrs. **Motor Ceske Bude.:** Motor Ceske Budejovice. **N. Yarmouth Acad.:** North Yarmouth Academy. **N. Arizona Univ.:** Northern Arizona University. **N. Michigan Univ.:** Northern Michigan University. **NW Americans Jr. B:** Northwest Americans Junior B. **Poji. Pardubice Jrs.:** Pojistovna Pardubice Juniors. **Prin. Edward Island:** Prince Edward Island. **Rus. Olympic team:** Russian Olympic team. **Sault Ste. Marie:** Sault Sainte Marie. **Sever. Cherepovets:** Severstal Cherepovets. **Slovakian Oly. team:** Slovakian Olympic team. **Sov. Olympic team:** Soviet Olympic team. **Spisska N.V.:** Spisska Nova Ves. **Stad. Hradec Kralove:** Stadion Hradec Kralove. **Swed. Olympic team:** Swedish Olympic team. **Tor. Nizhny Nov.:** Torpedo Nizhny Novgorod. **Torpedo Ust-Kam.:** Torpedo Ust-Kamenogorsk. **Ukranian Oly. team:** Ukranian Olympic team. **Unif. Olympic team:** Unified Olympic team. **Univ. of New Hamp.:** University of New Hampshire. **Univ. of West. Ontario:** University of Western Ontario. **V. Frolunda Goteborg:** Vastra Frolunda Goteborg.

LEAGUES: AAHL: All American Hockey League. **ACHL:** Atlantic Coast Hockey League. **AHL:** American Hockey League. **AJHL:** Alberta Junior Hockey League. **AMHL:** Alberta Minor Hockey League. **AUAA:** Atlantic Universities Athletic Association. **BCJHL:** British Columbia Junior Hockey League. **CAHL:** Central Alberta Hockey League. **CAJHL:** Central Alberta Junior Hockey League. **Can. College:** Canadian College. **Can.HL:** Canadian Hockey League. **CCHA:** Central Collegiate Hockey Association. **CHL:** Central Hockey League. **CIS:** Commonwealth of Independent States. **CJHL:** Central Junior A Hockey League. **COJHL:** Central Ontario Junior Hockey League. **CPHL:** Central Professional Hockey League. **CWUAA:** Canada West University Athletic Association. **Conn. H.S.:** Connecticut High School. **Czech.:** Czechoslovakia. **Czech. Jrs.:** Czech Republic Junior. **Czech Rep.:** Czechoslovakia Republic. **ECAC:** Eastern College Athletic Conference. **ECAC-II:** Eastern College Athletic Conference, Division II. **ECHL:** East Coast Hockey League. **EEHL:** Eastern European Hockey League. **EHL:** Eastern Hockey League. **EURO:** Euroliga. **Fin.:** Finland. **Ger.:** Germany. **GWHC:** Great Western Hockey Conference. **Hoc. East:** Hockey East. **IHL:** International Hockey League. **Ill. H.S.:** Illinois High School. **Indiana H.S.:** Indiana High School. **Int'l:** International. **KIJHL:** Kootenay International Junior Hockey League. **Mass. H.S.:** Massachusetts High School. **Md. H.S.:** Maryland High School. **Met. Bos.:** Metro Boston. **Mich. H.S.:** Michigan High School. **Minn. H.S.:** Minnesota High School. **MJHL:** Manitoba Junior Hockey League. **MTHL:** Metro Toronto Hockey League. **NAHL:** North American Hockey League. **NAJHL:** North American Junior Hockey League. **N.B. H.S.:** New Brunswick High School. **NCAA-II:** National Collegiate Athletic Association, Division II. **N.D. H.S.:** North Dakota High School. **NEJHL:** New England Junior Hockey League. **NHL:** National Hockey League. **N.H. H.S.:** New Hampshire High School. **N.J. H.S.:** New Jersey High School. **Nia. D. Jr. C:** Niagara District Junior C. **NSJHL:** Nova Scotia Junior Hockey League. **N.S. Jr. A:** Nova Scotia Junior A. **N.Y. H.S.:** New York High School. **NYMJHL:** New York Major Junior Hockey League. **NYOHL:** North York Ontario Hockey League. **ODHA:** Ottawa & District Hockey Association. **OHA:** Ontario Hockey Association. **OHA Jr. A:** Ontario Hockey Association Junior A. **OHA Mjr. A:** Ontario Hockey Association Major Junior A. **OHA Senior:** Ontario Hockey Association Senior. **OHL:** Ontario Hockey League. **O.H.S.:** Ohio High School. **OJHA:** Ontario Junior Hockey Association. **OJHL:** Ontario Junior Hockey League. **OMJHL:** Ontario Major Junior Hockey League. **OPJHL:** Ontario Provincial Junior Hockey League. **OUAA:** Ontario Universities Athletic Association. **PCJHL:** Peace Caribou Junior Hockey League. **PEIHA:** Prince Edward Island Hockey Association. **PEIJHL:** Prince Edward Island Junior Hockey League. **Penn. H.S.:** Pennsylvania High School. **QMJHL:** Quebec Major Junior Hockey League. **R.I. H.S.:** Rhode Island High School. **Rus. Div II, III:** Russian Division II, III. **SAJHL:** Southern Alberta Junior Hockey League. **SJHL:** Saskatchewan Junior Hockey League. **Sask. H.S.:** Saskatchewan High School. **SOJHL:** Southern Ontario Junior Hockey League. **Swed. Jr.:** Sweden Junior. **Switz.:** Switzerland. **TBAHA:** Thunder Bay Amateur Hockey Association. **TBJHL:** Thunder Bay Junior Hockey League. **UHL:** United Hockey League. **USHL:** United States Hockey League. **USHS:** United States High School. **USSR:** Union of Soviet Socialist Republics. **V. Frolunda Goteborg:** Vastra Frolunda Goteborg. **Vt. H.S.:** Vermont High School. **W. Germany, W. Ger.:** West Germany. **WCHA:** Western Collegiate Hockey Association. **WCHL:** Western Canada Hockey League. **WHA:** World Hockey Association. **WHL:** Western Hockey League. **Wisc. H.S.:** Wisconsin High School. **Yukon Sr.:** Yukon Senior.

VETERANS AND TOP PROSPECTS

A

ABID, RAMZI   LW   PENGUINS

PERSONAL: Born March 24, 1980, in Montreal ... 6-2/207. ... Shoots left.

TRANSACTIONS/CAREER NOTES: Selected by Colorado Avalanche in second round (fifth Avalanche pick, 28th overall) of NHL entry draft (June 27, 1998). ... Returned to draft pool by Avalanche and selected by Phoenix Coyotes in third round (third Coyotes pick, 86th overall) of NHL entry draft (June 24, 2000). ... Traded by Coyotes with D Dan Focht and LW Guillaume Lefebvre to Pittsburgh Penguins for C Jan Hrdina and D Francois Leroux (March 11, 2003).

			REGULAR SEASON							PLAYOFFS				
Season Team	League	Gms.	G	A	Pts.	PIM	+/-	PP	SH	Gms.	G	A	Pts.	PIM
96-97—Chicoutimi	QMJHL	65	13	24	37	151	...	...	...	—	—	—	—	—
97-98—Chicoutimi	QMJHL	68	50	*85	*135	266	...	...	...	6	3	4	7	10
98-99—Chicoutimi	QMJHL	21	11	15	26	97	...	...	...	—	—	—	—	—
—Acadie-Bathurst	QMJHL	24	14	22	36	102	...	...	...	23	14	20	34	84
99-00—Acadie-Bathurst	QMJHL	13	10	11	21	61	...	...	...	—	—	—	—	—
—Halifax	QMJHL	59	57	80	137	148	...	...	...	10	10	13	23	18
00-01—Springfield	AHL	17	6	4	10	38	...	...	...	—	—	—	—	—
01-02—Springfield	AHL	66	18	25	43	214	...	...	...	—	—	—	—	—
02-03—Springfield	AHL	27	15	10	25	50	...	...	...	—	—	—	—	—
—Phoenix	NHL	30	10	8	18	30	1	4	0	—	—	—	—	—
—Pittsburgh	NHL	3	0	0	0	2	-5	0	0	—	—	—	—	—
NHL Totals (1 year)		33	10	8	18	32	-4	4	0					

ADAMS, BRYAN   LW

PERSONAL: Born March 20, 1977, in Fort St. James, B.C. ... 6-0/185. ... Shoots left.

TRANSACTIONS/CAREER NOTES: Signed as a non-drafted free agent by Atlanta Thrashers (July 1, 1999). ... Signed as free agent by Detroit Red Wings (August 5, 2002).

			REGULAR SEASON							PLAYOFFS				
Season Team	League	Gms.	G	A	Pts.	PIM	+/-	PP	SH	Gms.	G	A	Pts.	PIM
95-96—Michigan State	CCHA	42	3	8	11	12	...	...	...	—	—	—	—	—
96-97—Michigan State	CCHA	29	7	7	14	51	...	...	...	—	—	—	—	—
97-98—Michigan State	CCHA	31	9	21	30	39	...	...	...	—	—	—	—	—
98-99—Michigan State	CCHA	42	21	16	37	56	...	...	...	—	—	—	—	—
99-00—Orlando	IHL	64	16	18	34	27	...	...	...	4	0	1	1	6
—Atlanta	NHL	2	0	0	0	0	-1	0	0	—	—	—	—	—
00-01—Atlanta	NHL	9	0	1	1	2	-4	0	0	—	—	—	—	—
—Orlando	IHL	61	18	28	46	43	...	...	...	16	3	4	7	20
01-02—Chicago	AHL	64	10	17	27	25	...	...	...	5	0	0	0	2
02-03—Grand Rapids	AHL	74	8	17	25	37	...	...	...	—	—	—	—	—
NHL Totals (2 years)		11	0	1	1	2	-5	0	0					

ADAMS, CRAIG   RW   HURRICANES

PERSONAL: Born April 26, 1977, in Calgary ... 6-0/200. ... Shoots right.

TRANSACTIONS/CAREER NOTES: Selected by Hartford Whalers in the ninth round (ninth Whalers pick, 223 overall) in the 1996 Entry Draft (June 22, 1996). ... Whalers franchise moved to North Carolina and renamed Carolina Hurricanes for 1997-98 season; NHL approved move on June 25, 1997. ... Bruised chest (November 30, 2000); missed four games. ... Suspended 10 games by NHL for leaving bench to fight (February 13, 2002). ... Re-signed by Carolina (May 1, 2003).

			REGULAR SEASON							PLAYOFFS				
Season Team	League	Gms.	G	A	Pts.	PIM	+/-	PP	SH	Gms.	G	A	Pts.	PIM
95-96—Harvard University	ECAC	34	8	9	17	56	...	...	...	—	—	—	—	—
96-97—Harvard University	ECAC	32	6	4	10	36	...	...	...	—	—	—	—	—
97-98—Harvard University	ECAC	23	6	6	12	12	...	...	...	—	—	—	—	—
98-99—Harvard University	ECAC	31	9	14	23	53	...	...	...	—	—	—	—	—
99-00—Cincinnati	IHL	73	12	12	24	124	...	...	...	8	0	1	1	14
00-01—Carolina	NHL	44	1	0	1	20	-7	0	0	3	0	0	0	0
—Cincinnati	IHL	4	0	1	1	9	...	...	...	1	0	0	0	2
01-02—Carolina	NHL	33	0	1	1	38	2	0	0	1	0	0	0	0
—Lowell	AHL	22	5	4	9	51	...	...	...	—	—	—	—	—
02-03—Carolina	NHL	81	6	12	18	71	-11	1	0	—	—	—	—	—
NHL Totals (3 years)		158	7	13	20	129	-16	1	0	4	0	0	0	0

ADAMS, KEVYN   C   HURRICANES

PERSONAL: Born October 8, 1974, in Washington, D.C. ... 6-2/195. ... Shoots right.

TRANSACTIONS/CAREER NOTES: Selected by Boston Bruins in first round (first Bruins pick, 25th overall) of NHL entry draft (June 26, 1993). ... Signed as free agent by Toronto Maple Leafs (August 1, 1997). ... Selected by Columbus Blue Jackets in NHL expansion draft (June 23, 2000). ... Strained gluteal muscle (December 13, 2000); missed two games. ... Traded by Blue Jackets with fourth-round pick (RW Michael Woodford) in 2001 draft to Florida Panthers for LW Ray Whitney and future considerations (March 13, 2001). ... Traded by Panthers with D Bret Hedican, D Tomas Malec and conditional second-round draft pick in 2003 to Carolina Hurricanes for D Sandis Ozolinsh and C Byron Ritchie (January 16, 2002).

Season Team	League	REGULAR SEASON								PLAYOFFS				
		Gms.	G	A	Pts.	PIM	+/-	PP	SH	Gms.	G	A	Pts.	PIM
90-91—Niagara	NAJHL	55	17	20	37	24	...	...	...	—	—	—	—	—
91-92—Niagara	NAJHL	40	25	33	58	51	...	...	...	—	—	—	—	—
92-93—Miami of Ohio	CCHA	41	17	16	33	18	...	...	...	—	—	—	—	—
93-94—Miami of Ohio	CCHA	36	15	28	43	24	...	...	...	—	—	—	—	—
94-95—Miami of Ohio	CCHA	38	20	29	49	30	...	...	...	—	—	—	—	—
95-96—Miami of Ohio	CCHA	36	17	30	47	30	...	...	...	—	—	—	—	—
96-97—Grand Rapids	IHL	82	22	25	47	47	...	...	...	5	1	1	2	4
97-98—Toronto	NHL	5	0	0	0	7	0	0	0	—	—	—	—	—
—St. John's	AHL	58	17	21	38	99	...	...	...	4	0	0	0	4
98-99—St. John's	AHL	80	15	35	50	85	...	...	...	5	2	0	2	4
—Toronto	NHL	1	0	0	0	0	0	0	0	7	0	2	2	14
99-00—St. John's	AHL	23	6	11	17	24	...	...	...	—	—	—	—	—
—Toronto	NHL	52	5	8	13	39	-7	0	0	12	1	0	1	7
00-01—Columbus	NHL	66	8	12	20	52	-4	0	0	—	—	—	—	—
—Florida	NHL	12	3	6	9	2	7	0	0	—	—	—	—	—
01-02—Florida	NHL	44	4	8	12	28	-3	0	0	—	—	—	—	—
—Carolina	NHL	33	2	3	5	15	-2	0	0	23	1	0	1	4
02-03—Carolina	NHL	77	9	9	18	57	-8	0	0	—	—	—	—	—
NHL Totals (6 years)		290	31	46	77	200	-17	0	0	42	2	2	4	25

ADDUONO, JEREMY — RW — SABRES

PERSONAL: Born August 4, 1979, in Thunder Bay, Ont. ... 6-0/182. ... Shoots right.
TRANSACTIONS/CAREER NOTES: Selected by Buffalo Sabres in seventh round (eighth Sabres pick, 184th overall) of NHL entry draft (June 21, 1997).

Season Team	League	REGULAR SEASON								PLAYOFFS				
		Gms.	G	A	Pts.	PIM	+/-	PP	SH	Gms.	G	A	Pts.	PIM
95-96—Sudbury	OHL	66	15	22	37	14	...	...	...	—	—	—	—	—
96-97—Sudbury	OHL	66	29	40	69	24	...	...	...	—	—	—	—	—
97-98—Sudbury	OHL	66	37	69	106	40	...	...	...	10	5	5	10	10
98-99—Canadian nat'l team	Int'l	44	10	16	26	8	...	...	...	—	—	—	—	—
99-00—Rochester	AHL	51	23	22	45	20	...	...	...	21	6	11	17	2
00-01—Rochester	AHL	76	24	30	54	53	...	...	...	4	1	0	1	4
01-02—Rochester	AHL	79	15	20	35	38	...	...	...	1	1	0	1	0
02-03—Bridgeport	AHL	54	13	13	26	14	...	...	...	—	—	—	—	—

AEBISCHER, DAVID — G — AVALANCHE

PERSONAL: Born February 7, 1978, in Fribourg, Switzerland ... 6-1/192. ... Catches left. ... Name pronounced EH-bih-shuhr.
TRANSACTIONS/CAREER NOTES: Selected by Colorado Avalanche in sixth round (seventh Avalanche pick, 161st overall) of NHL entry draft (June 21, 1997). ... Suffered from pharyngitis (November 25, 2000); missed one game.

Season Team	League	REGULAR SEASON								PLAYOFFS							
		Gms.	Min	W	L	T	GA	SO	Avg.	SV%	Gms.	Min.	W	L	GA	SO	Avg.	SV%
96-97—Fribourg-Gotteron	Switzerland	10	577	...	...	...	34	...	3.54	—	3	184	1	2	13	0	4.24	—
97-98—Fribourg-Gotteron	Switzerland	1	60	...	...	...	1	0	1.00	—	4	240	...	...	17	...	4.25	—
—Hershey	AHL	2	80	0	0	1	5	0	3.75	—	—	—	—	—	—	—	—	—
—Chesapeake	ECHL	17	930	5	7	2	52	0	3.35	—	—	—	—	—	—	—	—	—
—Wheeling	ECHL	10	564	5	3	1	30	1	3.19	—	—	—	—	—	—	—	—	—
98-99—Hershey	AHL	38	1932	17	10	5	79	2	2.45	—	3	152	1	2	6	0	2.37	—
99-00—Hershey	AHL	58	3259	29	23	2	*180	1	3.31	—	14	788	7	6	40	2	3.05	—
00-01—Colorado	NHL	26	1393	12	7	3	52	3	2.24	.903	1	1	0	0	0	0	...	—
01-02—Colorado	NHL	21	1184	13	6	0	37	2	1.88	.931	1	34	0	0	1	0	1.76	.929
—Swiss Olympic team	Int'l	2	81	0	1	1	6	0	4.44	—	—	—	—	—	—	—	—	—
02-03—Colorado	NHL	22	1235	7	12	0	50	1	2.43	.916	—	—	—	—	—	—	—	—
NHL Totals (3 years)		69	3812	32	25	3	139	6	2.19	.917	2	35	0	0	1	0	1.71	.929

AFANASENKOV, DMITRY — LW — LIGHTNING

PERSONAL: Born May 12, 1980, in Arkhangelsk, U.S.S.R. ... 6-2/200. ... Shoots right. ... Name pronounced ah-fahn-ah-SEHN-kov.
TRANSACTIONS/CAREER NOTES: Selected by Tampa Bay Lightning in third round (third Lightning pick, 72nd overall) of NHL entry draft (June 27, 1998). ... Re-signed by Lightning (July 29, 2003).

Season Team	League	REGULAR SEASON								PLAYOFFS				
		Gms.	G	A	Pts.	PIM	+/-	PP	SH	Gms.	G	A	Pts.	PIM
95-96—Torpedo Yaroslavl	CIS Div. II	25	10	5	15	10	...	...	...	—	—	—	—	—
—Torpedo Yaroslavl	CIS Jr.	35	28	16	44	8	...	...	...	—	—	—	—	—
96-97—Torpedo Yaroslavl	Rus. Div. III	45	20	15	35	14	...	...	...	—	—	—	—	—
97-98—Torpedo-Yaroslavl	Russian	45	19	11	30	28	...	...	...	—	—	—	—	—
98-99—Moncton	QMJHL	15	5	5	10	12	...	...	...	—	—	—	—	—
—Sherbrooke	QMJHL	51	23	30	53	22	...	...	...	13	10	6	16	6
99-00—Sherbrooke	QMJHL	60	56	43	99	70	...	...	...	5	3	2	5	4
00-01—Detroit	IHL	65	15	22	37	26	...	...	...	—	—	—	—	—
—Tampa Bay	NHL	9	1	1	2	4	1	0	0	—	—	—	—	—
01-02—Springfield	AHL	28	4	5	9	4	...	...	...	—	—	—	—	—
—Grand Rapids	AHL	18	1	2	3	2	...	...	...	—	—	—	—	—
—Tampa Bay	NHL	5	0	0	0	0	-1	0	0	—	—	—	—	—
02-03—Springfield	AHL	41	4	9	13	25	...	...	...	—	—	—	—	—
NHL Totals (2 years)		14	1	1	2	4	0	0	0					

AFINOGENOV, MAXIM   RW   SABRES

PERSONAL: Born September 4, 1979, in Moscow, U.S.S.R. ... 6-0/190. ... Shoots left. ... Name pronounced ah-FEEN-o-gin-ov.
TRANSACTIONS/CAREER NOTES: Selected by Buffalo Sabres in third round (third Sabres pick, 69th overall) of NHL entry draft (June 21, 1997). ... Suffered from the flu (January 10, 2002); missed one game.

		REGULAR SEASON								PLAYOFFS				
Season Team	League	Gms.	G	A	Pts.	PIM	+/-	PP	SH	Gms.	G	A	Pts.	PIM
95-96—Dynamo Moscow	CIS	1	0	0	0	0	...	...	...	—	—	—	—	—
96-97—Dynamo Moscow	Russian	29	6	5	11	10	...	...	...	4	0	2	2	0
—Dynamo Moscow	Rus. Div. III	14	9	2	11	10	...	...	...					
97-98—Dynamo Moscow	Russian	35	10	5	15	53	...	...	...					
98-99—Dynamo Moscow	Russian	38	8	13	21	24	...	...	...	16	*10	6	†16	14
99-00—Rochester	AHL	15	6	12	18	8	...	...	...	8	3	1	4	4
—Buffalo	NHL	65	16	18	34	41	-4	2	0	5	0	1	1	2
00-01—Buffalo	NHL	78	14	22	36	40	1	3	0	11	2	3	5	4
01-02—Buffalo	NHL	81	21	19	40	69	-9	3	1	—	—	—	—	—
—Russian Oly. team	Int'l	6	2	2	4	4	...	...	...					
02-03—Buffalo	NHL	35	5	6	11	21	-12	2	0	—	—	—	—	—
NHL Totals (4 years)		259	56	65	121	171	-24	10	1	16	2	4	6	6

AHONEN, ARI   G   DEVILS

PERSONAL: Born February 6, 1981, in Jyvaskyla, Finland. ... 6-2/170. ... Catches left.
TRANSACTIONS/CAREER NOTES: Selected by New Jersey Devils in first round (first Devils pick, 27th overall) of NHL entry draft (June 26, 1999).

		REGULAR SEASON								PLAYOFFS							
Season Team	League	Gms.	Min	W	L	T	GA	SO	Avg.	SV%	Gms.	Min.	W	L	GA	SO	Avg.	SV%
97-98—JyP HT Jyvaskyla	Finland Jr.	31	1853	...	...	...	64	...	2.07	—	—	—	—	—	—	—	—	—
98-99—JyP HT Jyvaskyla	Finland Jr.	24	1447	...	...	...	70	0	2.90	—	—	—	—	—	—	—	—	—
99-00—HIFK Helsinki	Finland	24	1347	11	7	1	70	1	3.12	—	2	119	0	2	7	0	3.53	—
—HIFK Helsinki	Finland Jr.	11	658	...	...	...	22	0	2.01	—								
00-01—HIFK Helsinki	Finland Jr.	37	2101	18	13	4	97	2	2.77	—	5	395	2	3	9	1	1.37	—
01-02—Albany	AHL	36	2106	6	22	6	106	0	3.02	—	—	—	—	—	—	—	—	—
02-03—Albany	AHL	38	2171	13	20	3	110	1	3.04	—								

ALBAN, CHAD   G   STARS

PERSONAL: Born April 27, 1976, in Kalamazoo, Mich. ... 5-9/165. ... Catches right.
COLLEGE: Michigan State.
TRANSACTIONS/CAREER NOTES: Signed as non-drafted free agent by Dallas Stars (June 12, 2000).

		REGULAR SEASON								PLAYOFFS							
Season Team	League	Gms.	Min	W	L	T	GA	SO	Avg.	SV%	Gms.	Min.	W	L	GA	SO	Avg.	SV%
94-95—Michigan State	CCHA	13	636	8	2	0	29	0	2.74	—	—	—	—	—	—	—	—	—
95-96—Michigan State	CCHA	40	2286	26	13	1	117	0	3.07	—	—	—	—	—	—	—	—	—
96-97—Michigan State	CCHA	39	2272	23	11	4	103	3	2.72	—	—	—	—	—	—	—	—	—
97-98—Michigan State	CCHA	40	2438	31	4	5	64	*6	*1.58	—	—	—	—	—	—	—	—	—
98-99—Mobile	ECHL	34	1960	16	14	‡3	111	1	3.40	—	2	119	0	2	9	0	4.54	—
—Houston	IHL	5	284	1	3	‡1	14	0	2.96	—								
99-00—Mobile	ECHL	39	2334	27	13	1	114	0	2.93	—	5	299	2	3	20	0	4.01	—
—Utah	IHL	1	35	0	1	0	3	0	5.14	—								
00-01—Grand Rapids	IHL	3	180	2	1	‡0	4	1	1.33	—								
—Utah	IHL	11	597	2	4	‡4	23	0	2.31	—								
01-02—Utah	AHL	42	2102	17	15	1	103	2	2.94	—								
02-03—Grand Rapids	AHL	2	77	1	0	0	3	0	2.34	—								
—Kalamazoo	UHL	54	3083	21	25	5	175	1	3.41	—								

ALBELIN, TOMMY   D

PERSONAL: Born May 21, 1964, in Stockholm, Sweden ... 6-2/195. ... Shoots left. ... Name pronounced AL-buh-leen.
TRANSACTIONS/CAREER NOTES: Selected by Quebec Nordiques in eighth round (seventh Nordiques pick, 152nd overall) of NHL entry draft (June 8, 1983). ... Traded by Nordiques to New Jersey Devils for fourth-round pick (LW Niclas Andersson) in 1989 draft (December 12, 1988). ... Injured right knee (March 2, 1990); missed four games. ... Injured groin (November 21, 1992); missed two games. ... Suffered from urinary infection (1993-94 season); missed nine games. ... Bruised thigh (December 16, 1995); missed six games. ... Traded by Devils with D Cale Hulse and RW Jocelyn Lemieux to Calgary Flames for D Phil Housley and D Dan Keczmer (February 26, 1996). ... Strained groin (November 9, 1996); missed four games. ... Reinjured groin (November 25, 1996); missed two games. ... Strained abdominal muscle (December 7, 1996); missed five games. ... Suffered concussion (November 11, 1997); missed four games. ... Pulled groin (November 27, 1997); missed three games. ... Reinjured groin (December 9, 1997); missed four games. ... Injured ribs (February 2, 1998); missed three games. ... Strained groin (November 20, 1998); missed six games. ... Injured shoulder (January 6, 2000); missed final 41 games of season. ... Suffered concussion (October 27, 2000); missed five games. ... Signed as free agent by Devils (July 5, 2001).

Season Team	League	REGULAR SEASON Gms.	G	A	Pts.	PIM	+/-	PP	SH	PLAYOFFS Gms.	G	A	Pts.	PIM
82-83—Djurgarden Stockholm	Sweden	17	2	5	7	4	...	...	...	6	1	0	1	2
83-84—Djurgarden Stockholm	Sweden	37	9	8	17	36	...	...	...	4	0	1	1	2
84-85—Djurgarden Stockholm	Sweden	32	9	8	17	22	...	...	...	8	2	1	3	4
85-86—Djurgarden Stockholm	Sweden	35	4	8	12	26	...	...	...	—	—	—	—	—
86-87—Djurgarden Stockholm	Sweden	33	7	5	12	49	...	...	...	2	0	0	0	0
87-88—Quebec	NHL	60	3	23	26	47	-7	0	0	—	—	—	—	—
88-89—Halifax	AHL	8	2	5	7	4	...	...	...	—	—	—	—	—
—Quebec	NHL	14	2	4	6	27	-6	1	0	—	—	—	—	—
—New Jersey	NHL	46	7	24	31	40	18	1	1	—	—	—	—	—
89-90—New Jersey	NHL	68	6	23	29	63	-1	4	0	—	—	—	—	—
90-91—Utica	AHL	14	4	2	6	10	...	...	...	—	—	—	—	—
—New Jersey	NHL	47	2	12	14	44	1	1	0	3	0	1	1	2
91-92—New Jersey	NHL	19	0	4	4	4	7	0	0	1	1	1	2	0
—Utica	AHL	11	4	6	10	4	...	...	...	—	—	—	—	—
92-93—New Jersey	NHL	36	1	5	6	14	0	1	0	5	2	0	2	0
93-94—Albany	AHL	4	0	2	2	17	...	...	...	—	—	—	—	—
—New Jersey	NHL	62	2	17	19	36	20	1	0	20	2	5	7	14
94-95—New Jersey	NHL	48	5	10	15	20	9	2	0	20	1	7	8	2
95-96—New Jersey	NHL	53	1	12	13	14	0	0	0	—	—	—	—	—
—Calgary	NHL	20	0	1	1	4	1	0	0	4	0	0	0	0
96-97—Calgary	NHL	72	4	11	15	14	-8	2	0	—	—	—	—	—
97-98—Calgary	NHL	69	2	17	19	32	9	1	0	—	—	—	—	—
—Swedish Oly. team	Int'l	3	0	0	0	4	...	...	...	—	—	—	—	—
98-99—Calgary	NHL	60	1	5	6	8	-11	0	0	—	—	—	—	—
99-00—Calgary	NHL	41	4	6	10	12	-3	1	1	—	—	—	—	—
00-01—Calgary	NHL	77	1	19	20	22	2	1	0	—	—	—	—	—
01-02—Calgary	NHL	42	1	3	4	4	0	0	0	6	0	0	0	0
02-03—Albany	AHL	5	0	2	2	2	...	...	...	—	—	—	—	—
—New Jersey	NHL	37	1	6	7	6	10	0	1	16	1	0	1	2
NHL Totals (16 years)		**871**	**43**	**202**	**245**	**411**	**41**	**16**	**3**	**75**	**7**	**14**	**21**	**20**

ALEXEEV, NIKITA   RW   LIGHTNING

PERSONAL: Born December 27, 1981, in Murmansk, U.S.S.R. ... 6-5/225. ... Shoots left.
TRANSACTIONS/CAREER NOTES: Selected by Tampa Bay Lightning in first round (first Lightning pick, eighth overall) of NHL entry draft (June 24, 2000).

Season Team	League	REGULAR SEASON Gms.	G	A	Pts.	PIM	+/-	PP	SH	PLAYOFFS Gms.	G	A	Pts.	PIM
97-98—Krylja Sov. Moscow	Rus. Div. III	61	11	4	15	36	...	...	...	—	—	—	—	—
98-99—Erie	OHL	61	17	18	35	15	...	...	...	5	1	1	2	4
99-00—Erie	OHL	64	24	29	53	42	...	...	...	13	4	3	7	6
00-01—Erie	OHL	64	31	41	72	45	...	...	...	12	7	7	14	12
01-02—Tampa Bay	NHL	44	4	4	8	8	-9	1	0	—	—	—	—	—
—Springfield	AHL	35	5	9	14	16	...	...	...	—	—	—	—	—
02-03—Springfield	AHL	36	7	5	12	8	...	...	...	—	—	—	—	—
—Tampa Bay	NHL	37	4	2	6	8	-6	1	0	11	1	0	1	0
NHL Totals (2 years)		**81**	**8**	**6**	**14**	**16**	**-15**	**2**	**0**	**11**	**1**	**0**	**1**	**0**

ALFREDSSON, DANIEL   RW   SENATORS

PERSONAL: Born December 11, 1972, in Gothenburg, Sweden ... 5-11/199. ... Shoots right.
TRANSACTIONS/CAREER NOTES: Selected by Ottawa Senators in sixth round (fifth Senators pick, 133rd overall) of NHL entry draft (June 29, 1994). ... Strained abdominal muscle (January 29, 1997); missed six games. ... Injured right ankle (November 3, 1997); missed eight games. ... Fractured right fibula (December 11, 1997); missed 13 games. ... Tore medial collateral ligament in left knee (September 16, 1998); missed first nine games of season. ... Injured right eye (November 12, 1998); missed four games. ... Suffered from the flu (December 30, 1998); missed one game. ... Sprained medial collateral ligament in left knee (January 26, 1999); missed five games. ... Strained abdominal muscle (March 17, 1999); missed five games. ... Tore medial collateral ligament in right knee (October 21, 1999); missed 20 games. ... Sprained right knee (February 15, 2000); missed three games. ... Bruised left foot (March 31, 2000); missed one game. ... Strained hip flexor (October 19, 2001); missed 13 games. ... Injured right wrist (April 6, 2001); missed final game of regular season. ... Injured hip (December 8, 2001); missed four games.
STATISTICAL PLATEAUS: Three-goal games: 1995-96 (1), 2000-01 (1), 2001-02 (2). Total: 4.

Season Team	League	REGULAR SEASON Gms.	G	A	Pts.	PIM	+/-	PP	SH	PLAYOFFS Gms.	G	A	Pts.	PIM
91-92—Molndal	Sweden Dv. 2	32	12	8	20	43	...	...	...	—	—	—	—	—
92-93—Vastra Frolunda	Sweden	20	1	5	6	8	...	...	...	—	—	—	—	—
93-94—Vastra Frolunda	Sweden	39	20	10	30	18	...	...	...	4	1	1	2	...
94-95—Vastra Frolunda	Sweden	22	7	11	18	22	...	...	...	—	—	—	—	—
95-96—Ottawa	NHL	82	26	35	61	28	-18	8	2	—	—	—	—	—
96-97—Ottawa	NHL	76	24	47	71	30	5	11	1	7	5	2	7	6
97-98—Ottawa	NHL	55	17	28	45	18	7	7	0	11	7	2	9	20
—Swedish Oly. team	Int'l	4	2	3	5	2	...	...	...	—	—	—	—	—
98-99—Ottawa	NHL	58	11	22	33	14	8	3	0	4	1	2	3	4
99-00—Ottawa	NHL	57	21	38	59	28	11	4	2	6	1	3	4	2
00-01—Ottawa	NHL	68	24	46	70	30	11	10	0	4	1	0	1	2
01-02—Ottawa	NHL	78	37	34	71	45	3	9	1	12	7	6	13	4
—Swedish Oly. team	Int'l	4	1	4	5	2	...	...	...	—	—	—	—	—
02-03—Ottawa	NHL	78	27	51	78	42	15	9	0	18	4	4	8	12
NHL Totals (8 years)		**552**	**187**	**301**	**488**	**235**	**42**	**61**	**6**	**62**	**26**	**19**	**45**	**50**

ALLEN, BOBBY   D   OILERS

PERSONAL: Born November 14, 1978, in Braintree, Mass. ... 6-1/205. ... Shoots left.
TRANSACTIONS/CAREER NOTES: Selected by Boston Bruins in second round (second Bruins pick, 52nd overall) of NHL entry draft (June 27, 1998). ... Traded by Bruins to Edmonton Oilers for D Sean Brown (March 19, 2002).

Season Team	League	Gms.	G	A	Pts.	PIM	+/-	PP	SH	Gms.	G	A	Pts.	PIM
												REGULAR SEASON		
96-97—Cushing Academy	Mass. H.S.	36	11	33	44	28	...			—	—	—	—	—
97-98—Boston College	Hockey East	37	7	19	26	34	...			—	—	—	—	—
98-99—Boston College	Hockey East	43	9	23	32	34	...			—	—	—	—	—
99-00—Boston College	Hockey East	42	4	23	27	40	...			—	—	—	—	—
00-01—Boston College	Hockey East	42	5	18	23	30	...			—	—	—	—	—
01-02—Providence	AHL	49	5	10	15	18	...			—	—	—	—	—
—Hamilton	AHL	10	1	6	7	0	...			14	0	3	3	6
02-03—Hamilton	AHL	56	1	12	13	24	...			—	—	—	—	—
—Edmonton	NHL	1	0	0	0	0	0	0	0	—	—	—	—	—
NHL Totals (1 year)		1	0	0	0	0	0	0	0					

ALLEN, BRYAN   D   CANUCKS

PERSONAL: Born August 21, 1980, in Kingston, Ont. ... 6-4/220. ... Shoots left.
TRANSACTIONS/CAREER NOTES: Selected by Vancouver Canucks in first round (first Canucks pick, fourth overall) of NHL entry draft (June 27, 1998). ... Injured knee (September 15, 1999); missed first 57 games of season.

Season Team	League	Gms.	G	A	Pts.	PIM	+/-	PP	SH	Gms.	G	A	Pts.	PIM
95-96—Ernestown	Jr. C	36	1	16	17	71	...			—	—	—	—	—
96-97—Oshawa	OHL	60	2	4	6	76	...			18	1	3	4	26
97-98—Oshawa	OHL	48	6	13	19	126	...			5	0	5	5	18
98-99—Oshawa	OHL	37	7	15	22	77	...			17	0	3	3	30
99-00—Oshawa	OHL	3	0	2	2	12	...			3	0	0	0	13
—Syracuse	AHL	9	1	1	2	11	...			2	0	0	0	2
00-01—Kansas City	IHL	75	5	20	25	99	...			—	—	—	—	—
—Vancouver	NHL	6	0	0	0	0	0	0	0	2	0	0	0	2
01-02—Vancouver	NHL	11	0	0	0	6	1	0	0	—	—	—	—	—
—Manitoba	AHL	68	7	18	25	121	...			5	0	1	1	8
02-03—Manitoba	AHL	7	0	1	1	4	...			—	—	—	—	—
—Vancouver	NHL	48	5	3	8	73	8	0	0	1	0	0	0	2
NHL Totals (3 years)		65	5	3	8	79	9	0	0	3	0	0	0	4

ALLISON, JAMIE   D

PERSONAL: Born May 13, 1975, in Lindsay, Ont. ... 6-1/203. ... Shoots left.
TRANSACTIONS/CAREER NOTES: Selected by Calgary Flames in second round (second Flames pick, 44th overall) of NHL entry draft (June 26, 1993). ... Suffered concussion (December 20, 1996); missed three games. ... Fractured thumb (January 9, 1998); missed 11 games. ... Suffered concussion (March 28, 1998); missed 10 games. ... Traded by Flames with C/LW Marty McInnis and RW Erik Andersson to Chicago Blackhawks for C Jeff Shantz and C/LW Steve Dubinsky (October 27, 1998). ... Sprained wrist (November 17, 1998); missed 23 games. ... Strained groin (March 31, 1999); missed three games. ... Strained groin (December 26, 1999); missed four games. ... Injured muscle in rib cage (February 23, 2000); missed eight games. ... Suffered stiff neck (March 26, 2000); missed one game. ... Bruised foot (December 21, 2000); missed one game. ... Sprained knee (February 10, 2001); missed 13 games. ... Claimed by Flames from Blackhawks in NHL waiver draft (September 28, 2001). ... Injured groin (November 3, 2001); missed three games. ... Traded by Flames to Columbus Blue Jackets for RW Blake Sloan (March 19, 2002). ... Strained back (March 25, 2002); missed one game.

Season Team	League	Gms.	G	A	Pts.	PIM	+/-	PP	SH	Gms.	G	A	Pts.	PIM
90-91—Waterloo Jr. B	OHA	45	3	8	11	91	...			—	—	—	—	—
91-92—Windsor	OHL	59	4	8	12	52	...			4	1	1	2	2
92-93—Det. Jr. Red Wings	OHL	61	0	13	13	64	...			15	2	5	7	23
93-94—Det. Jr. Red Wings	OHL	40	2	22	24	69	...			17	2	9	11	35
94-95—Det. Jr. Red Wings	OHL	50	1	14	15	119	...			18	2	7	9	35
—Calgary	NHL	1	0	0	0	0	0	0	0	—	—	—	—	—
95-96—Saint John	AHL	71	3	16	19	223	...			14	0	2	2	16
96-97—Saint John	AHL	46	3	6	9	139	...			5	0	1	1	4
—Calgary	NHL	20	0	0	0	35	-4	0	0	—	—	—	—	—
97-98—Saint John	AHL	16	0	5	5	49	...			—	—	—	—	—
—Calgary	NHL	43	3	8	11	104	3	0	0	—	—	—	—	—
98-99—Saint John	AHL	5	0	0	0	23	...			—	—	—	—	—
—Chicago	NHL	39	2	2	4	62	0	0	0	—	—	—	—	—
—Indianapolis	IHL	3	1	0	1	10	...			—	—	—	—	—
99-00—Chicago	NHL	59	1	3	4	102	-5	0	0	—	—	—	—	—
00-01—Chicago	NHL	44	1	3	4	53	7	0	0	—	—	—	—	—
01-02—Calgary	NHL	37	0	2	2	24	-3	0	0	—	—	—	—	—
—Columbus	NHL	7	0	0	0	28	-4	0	0	—	—	—	—	—
02-03—Columbus	NHL	48	0	1	1	99	-15	0	0	—	—	—	—	—
NHL Totals (8 years)		298	7	19	26	507	-21	0	0					

ALLISON, JASON   C   KINGS

PERSONAL: Born May 29, 1975, in North York, Ont. ... 6-3/215. ... Shoots right.
TRANSACTIONS/CAREER NOTES: Selected by Washington Capitals in first round (second Capitals pick, 17th overall) of NHL entry draft (June 26, 1993). ... Injured ankle (February 15, 1997); missed one game. ... Traded by Capitals with G Jim Carey, C Anson Carter and third-round pick (RW Lee Goren) in 1997 draft to Boston Bruins for C Adam Oates, RW Rick Tocchet and G Bill Ranford (March 1, 1997). ... Injured hip (March 1, 1998); missed one game. ... Injured wrist (October 30, 1999); missed two games. ... Injured wrist (December 23, 1999); missed three games. ... Injured ligaments in left thumb (January 8, 2000) and underwent surgery; missed 15 games. ... Injured wrist (February 12, 2000) and underwent surgery; missed final 25 games of season. ... Missed first nine games of 2001-02 season due to contract dispute. ... Traded by Bruins with C/LW Mikko Eloranta to Los Angeles Kings for C Jozef Stumpel and RW Glen Murray (October 24, 2001).
STATISTICAL PLATEAUS: Three-goal games: 1997-98 (2), 1998-99 (1), 2000-01 (1). Total: 4.

		REGULAR SEASON								PLAYOFFS				
Season Team	League	Gms.	G	A	Pts.	PIM	+/-	PP	SH	Gms.	G	A	Pts.	PIM
91-92—London	OHL	65	11	18	29	15	...	...	...	7	0	0	0	0
92-93—London	OHL	66	42	76	118	50	...	...	...	12	7	13	20	8
93-94—London	OHL	56	55	87	*142	68	...	...	...	5	2	13	15	13
—Washington	NHL	2	0	1	1	0	1	0	0	—	—	—	—	—
—Portland	AHL	6	2	1	3	0	...	...	...	—	—	—	—	—
94-95—London	OHL	15	15	21	36	43	...	...	...	—	—	—	—	—
—Washington	NHL	12	2	1	3	6	-3	2	0	—	—	—	—	—
—Portland	AHL	8	5	4	9	2	...	...	...	7	3	8	11	2
95-96—Washington	NHL	19	0	3	3	2	-3	0	0	—	—	—	—	—
—Portland	AHL	57	28	41	69	42	...	...	...	6	1	6	7	9
96-97—Washington	NHL	53	5	17	22	25	-3	1	0	—	—	—	—	—
—Boston	NHL	19	3	9	12	9	-3	1	0	—	—	—	—	—
97-98—Boston	NHL	81	33	50	83	60	33	5	0	6	2	6	8	4
98-99—Boston	NHL	82	23	53	76	68	5	5	1	12	2	9	11	6
99-00—Boston	NHL	37	10	18	28	20	5	3	0	—	—	—	—	—
00-01—Boston	NHL	82	36	59	95	85	-8	11	3	—	—	—	—	—
01-02—Los Angeles	NHL	73	19	55	74	68	2	5	0	7	3	3	6	4
02-03—Los Angeles	NHL	26	6	22	28	22	9	2	0	—	—	—	—	—
NHL Totals (10 years)		486	137	288	425	365	35	35	4	25	7	18	25	14

AMONTE, TONY   RW   FLYERS

PERSONAL: Born August 2, 1970, in Hingham, Mass. ... 6-0/200. ... Shoots left. ... Full Name: Anthony Lewis Amonte. ... Name pronounced ah-MAHN-tee.
TRANSACTIONS/CAREER NOTES: Selected by New York Rangers in fourth round (third Rangers pick, 68th overall) of NHL entry draft (June 11, 1988). ... Traded by Rangers with rights to LW Matt Oates to Chicago Blackhawks for LW Stephane Matteau and RW Brian Noonan (March 21, 1994). ... Pulled groin (1993-94 season); missed three games. ... Played in Europe during 1994-95 NHL lockout. ... Signed as free agent by Phoenix Coyotes (July 12, 2002). ... Traded by Coyotes to Philadelphia Flyers for LW Guillaume Lefebvre, third-round pick in 2003 draft and second-round pick in 2004 draft (March 10, 2003).
STATISTICAL PLATEAUS: Three-goal games: 1991-92 (1), 1995-96 (1), 1996-97 (2), 1998-99 (2), 1999-00 (1). Total: 7.

		REGULAR SEASON								PLAYOFFS				
Season Team	League	Gms.	G	A	Pts.	PIM	+/-	PP	SH	Gms.	G	A	Pts.	PIM
86-87—Thayer Academy	Mass. H.S.	25	25	32	57	...	...	...	...	—	—	—	—	—
87-88—Thayer Academy	Mass. H.S.	28	30	38	68	...	...	...	...	—	—	—	—	—
88-89—Team USA Juniors	Int'l	7	1	3	4	...	...	...	...	—	—	—	—	—
—Thayer Academy	Mass. H.S.	25	35	38	73	...	...	...	...	—	—	—	—	—
89-90—Boston University	Hockey East	41	25	33	58	52	...	...	...	—	—	—	—	—
90-91—Boston University	Hockey East	38	31	37	68	82	...	...	...	—	—	—	—	—
—New York Rangers	NHL	—	—	—	—	—	—	—	—	2	0	2	2	2
91-92—New York Rangers	NHL	79	35	34	69	55	12	9	0	13	3	6	9	2
92-93—New York Rangers	NHL	83	33	43	76	49	0	13	0	—	—	—	—	—
93-94—New York Rangers	NHL	72	16	22	38	31	5	3	0	—	—	—	—	—
—Chicago	NHL	7	1	3	4	6	-5	1	0	6	4	2	6	4
94-95—Fassa	Italy	14	22	16	38	10	...	...	...	—	—	—	—	—
—Chicago	NHL	48	15	20	35	41	7	6	1	16	3	3	6	10
95-96—Chicago	NHL	81	31	32	63	62	10	5	4	7	2	4	6	6
96-97—Chicago	NHL	81	41	36	77	64	35	9	2	6	4	2	6	8
97-98—Chicago	NHL	82	31	42	73	66	21	7	3	—	—	—	—	—
—U.S. Olympic team	Int'l	4	0	1	1	4	...	...	...	—	—	—	—	—
98-99—Chicago	NHL	82	44	31	75	60	0	14	3	—	—	—	—	—
99-00—Chicago	NHL	82	43	41	84	48	10	11	5	—	—	—	—	—
00-01—Chicago	NHL	82	35	29	64	54	-22	9	1	—	—	—	—	—
01-02—Chicago	NHL	82	27	39	66	67	11	6	1	5	0	1	1	4
—U.S. Olympic team	Int'l	6	2	2	4	0	...	...	...	—	—	—	—	—
02-03—Phoenix	NHL	59	13	23	36	26	-12	6	0	—	—	—	—	—
—Philadelphia	NHL	13	7	8	15	2	12	1	1	13	1	6	7	4
NHL Totals (13 years)		933	372	403	775	631	84	100	21	68	17	26	43	40

ANDERSSON, CRAIG   G   BLACKHAWKS

PERSONAL: Born May 21, 1981, in Park Ridge, Ill. ... 6-2/174. ... Catches left.
TRANSACTIONS/CAREER NOTES: Selected by Calgary Flames in third round (third Flames pick, 77th overall) of NHL entry draft (June 26, 1999). ... Returned to draft pool by Flames and selected by Chicago Blackhawks in third round (fourth Blackhawks pick, 73th overall) of NHL entry draft (June 23, 2001).

Season Team	League	REGULAR SEASON									PLAYOFFS							
		Gms.	Min	W	L	T	GA	SO	Avg.	SV%	Gms.	Min.	W	L	GA	SO	Avg.	SV%
98-99—Chicago	NAHL	14	821	11	3	0	35	0	2.56	—	—	—	—	—	—	—	—	—
—Guelph	OHL	21	1006	12	5	1	52	1	3.10	—	3	114	0	2	9	0	4.74	—
99-00—Guelph	OHL	38	1955	12	17	2	117	0	3.59	—	3	110	0	1	5	0	2.73	—
00-01—Guelph	OHL	59	3555	30	19	*9	156	3	2.63	—	4	240	0	4	17	0	4.25	—
01-02—Norfolk	AHL	28	1567	9	13	4	77	2	2.95	—	1	21	0	1	1	0	2.86	—
02-03—Norfolk	AHL	32	1794	15	11	5	58	4	1.94	—	—	—	—	—	—	—	—	—
—Chicago	NHL	6	270	0	3	2	18	0	4.00	.856	—	—	—	—	—	—	—	—
NHL Totals (1 year)		6	270	0	3	2	18	0	4.00	.856								

ANDERSSON, JONAS   RW   PREDATORS

PERSONAL: Born February 24, 1981, in Lidingo, Sweden. ... 6-2/189. ... Shoots left.

TRANSACTIONS/CAREER NOTES: Selected by Nashville Predators in second round (second Predators pick, 33rd overall) of NHL entry draft (June 26, 1999).

Season Team	League	REGULAR SEASON								PLAYOFFS				
		Gms.	G	A	Pts.	PIM	+/-	PP	SH	Gms.	G	A	Pts.	PIM
97-98—AIK Solna	Sweden Jr.	33	14	16	30	32	...	...	...	—	—	—	—	—
98-99—AIK Solna	Sweden Jr.	16	3	7	10	18	...	...	...	—	—	—	—	—
99-00—North Bay	OHL	67	31	36	67	27	...	...	...	6	2	2	4	2
—Milwaukee	IHL	2	1	0	1	0	...	...	...	2	0	0	0	2
00-01—Milwaukee	IHL	52	6	7	13	44	...	...	...	5	0	0	0	2
01-02—Milwaukee	AHL	71	13	17	30	19	...	...	...	—	—	—	—	—
—Nashville	NHL	5	0	0	0	2	-2	0	0	—	—	—	—	—
02-03—Milwaukee	AHL	49	7	4	11	12	...	...	...	—	—	—	—	—
NHL Totals (1 year)		5	0	0	0	2	-2	0	0					

ANDREYCHUK, DAVE   LW   LIGHTNING

PERSONAL: Born September 29, 1963, in Hamilton, Ont. ... 6-4/220. ... Shoots right. ... Full Name: David Andreychuk. ... Name pronounced AN-druh-chuhk.

TRANSACTIONS/CAREER NOTES: Selected by Buffalo Sabres in first round (third Sabres pick, 16th overall) of NHL entry draft (June 9, 1982). ... Sprained knee (March 1983). ... Fractured collarbone (March 1985). ... Twisted knee (September 1985). ... Injured right knee (September 1986). ... Strained left knee ligaments (November 27, 1988). ... Fractured left thumb (February 18, 1990). ... Suspended two off-days and fined $500 by NHL for cross-checking incident (November 16, 1992). ... Traded by Sabres with G Daren Puppa and first-round pick (D Kenny Jonsson) in 1993 draft to Toronto Maple Leafs for G Grant Fuhr and fifth-round pick (D Kevin Popp) in 1995 draft (February 2, 1993). ... Injured knee (December 27, 1993); missed one game. ... Separated shoulder (December 2, 1995); missed five games. ... Suffered from the flu (December 27, 1995); missed one game. ... Underwent thumb surgery (January 15, 1996); missed two games. ... Traded by Maple Leafs to New Jersey Devils for second-round pick (D Marek Posmyk) in 1996 draft and third-round pick (traded back to New Jersey) in 1999 draft (March 13, 1996). ... Bruised left foot (October 23, 1997); missed six games. ... Bruised sternum (November 7, 1998); missed six games. ... Fractured right ankle (January 5, 1999); missed 21 games. ... Signed as free agent by Boston Bruins (July 28, 1999). ... Injured knee (January 11, 2000); missed two games. ... Traded by Bruins with D Ray Bourque to Colorado Avalanche for LW Brian Rolston, D Martin Grenier, C Samual Pahlsson and first-round pick (LW Martin Samuelsson) in 2000 draft (March 6, 2000). ... Signed as free agent by Sabres (July 13, 2000). ... Injured knee (February 13, 2001); missed two games. ... Signed as free agent by Tampa Bay Lightning (July 13, 2001). ... Re-signed by Lightning (June 26, 2003).

STATISTICAL PLATEAUS: Three-goal games: 1987-88 (3), 1988-89 (1), 1989-90 (1), 1991-92 (1), 1992-93 (1). Total: 7. ... Four-goal games: 1991-92 (1), 1992-93 (1), 1999-00 (1). Total: 3. ... Five-goal games: 1985-86 (1). ... Total hat tricks: 11.

Season Team	League	REGULAR SEASON								PLAYOFFS				
		Gms.	G	A	Pts.	PIM	+/-	PP	SH	Gms.	G	A	Pts.	PIM
80-81—Oshawa	OMJHL	67	22	22	44	80	...	...	...	10	3	2	5	20
81-82—Oshawa	OHL	67	58	43	101	71	...	...	...	3	1	4	5	16
82-83—Oshawa	OHL	14	8	24	32	6	...	...	...	—	—	—	—	—
—Buffalo	NHL	43	14	23	37	16	6	3	0	4	1	0	1	4
83-84—Buffalo	NHL	78	38	42	80	42	20	10	0	2	0	1	1	2
84-85—Buffalo	NHL	64	31	30	61	54	-4	14	0	5	4	2	6	4
85-86—Buffalo	NHL	80	36	51	87	61	3	12	0	—	—	—	—	—
86-87—Buffalo	NHL	77	25	48	73	46	2	13	0	—	—	—	—	—
87-88—Buffalo	NHL	80	30	48	78	112	1	15	0	6	2	4	6	0
88-89—Buffalo	NHL	56	28	24	52	40	0	7	0	5	0	3	3	0
89-90—Buffalo	NHL	73	40	42	82	42	6	18	0	6	2	5	7	2
90-91—Buffalo	NHL	80	36	33	69	32	11	13	0	6	2	2	4	8
91-92—Buffalo	NHL	80	41	50	91	71	-9	*28	0	7	1	3	4	12
92-93—Buffalo	NHL	52	29	32	61	48	-8	*20	0	—	—	—	—	—
—Toronto	NHL	31	25	13	38	8	12	*12	0	21	12	7	19	35
93-94—Toronto	NHL	83	53	46	99	98	22	21	5	18	5	5	10	16
94-95—Toronto	NHL	48	22	16	38	34	-7	8	0	7	3	2	5	25
95-96—Toronto	NHL	61	20	24	44	54	-11	12	2	—	—	—	—	—
—New Jersey	NHL	15	8	5	13	10	2	2	0	—	—	—	—	—
96-97—New Jersey	NHL	82	27	34	61	48	38	4	1	1	0	0	0	0
97-98—New Jersey	NHL	75	14	34	48	26	19	4	0	6	1	0	1	4
98-99—New Jersey	NHL	52	15	13	28	20	1	4	0	4	2	0	2	4
99-00—Boston	NHL	63	19	14	33	28	-11	7	0	—	—	—	—	—
—Colorado	NHL	14	1	2	3	2	-9	1	0	17	3	2	5	18
00-01—Buffalo	NHL	74	20	13	33	32	0	8	0	13	1	2	3	4
01-02—Tampa Bay	NHL	82	21	17	38	109	-12	9	1	—	—	—	—	—
02-03—Tampa Bay	NHL	72	20	14	34	34	-12	15	0	11	3	3	6	10
NHL Totals (21 years)		1515	613	668	1281	1067	60	260	9	139	42	41	83	148

ANTILA, KRISTIAN — G — OILERS

PERSONAL: Born January 10, 1980, in Vammala, Finland. ... 6-3/207. ... Catches left.
TRANSACTIONS/CAREER NOTES: Selected by Edmonton Oilers in fourth round (fourth Oilers pick, 113th overall) of NHL entry draft (June 27, 1998).

			REGULAR SEASON									PLAYOFFS						
Season Team	League	Gms.	Min	W	L	T	GA	SO	Avg.	SV%	Gms.	Min.	W	L	GA	SO	Avg.	SV%
96-97—Ilves Tampere	Finland Jr.	24	...	...	...	...	...	...	...	—	3	...	...	...	...	...	...	—
97-98—Ilves Tampere	Finland Jr.	11	564	...	...	...	28	0	2.98	—	—	—	—	—	—	—	—	—
98-99—Ilves Tampere	Finland	5	207	1	2	0	12	0	3.48	—	—	—	—	—	—	—	—	—
—Ilves Tampere	Finland Jr.	14	798	...	...	...	35	0	2.63	—	—	—	—	—	—	—	—	—
99-00—Ilves Tampere	Finland	25	1239	4	11	4	74	1	3.58	—	1	20	0	1	4	0	12.00	—
—Ilves Tampere	Finland Jr.	6	320	...	...	...	19	0	3.56	—	—	—	—	—	—	—	—	—
—Diskos	Finland Dv. 1	5	256	...	...	...	20	0	4.69	—	—	—	—	—	—	—	—	—
00-01—Assat Pori	Finland	42	2417	9	*27	7	*146	1	3.62	—	—	—	—	—	—	—	—	—
01-02—Assat Pori	Finland	35	1951	7	22	3	112	3	3.44	—	—	—	—	—	—	—	—	—
02-03—Hamilton	AHL	2	96	1	1	0	6	0	3.75	—	—	—	—	—	—	—	—	—
—Wichita	CHL	21	1147	10	7	2	70	0	3.66	—	—	—	—	—	—	—	—	—

ANTROPOV, NIK — LW — MAPLE LEAFS

PERSONAL: Born February 18, 1980, in Vost, U.S.S.R. ... 6-6/220. ... Shoots left. ... Full Name: Nikolai Antropov.
TRANSACTIONS/CAREER NOTES: Selected by Toronto Maple Leafs in first round (first Maple Leafs pick, 10th overall) of NHL entry draft (June 27, 1998). ... Suffered injury (November 27, 1999); missed seven games. ... Suffered injury (January 5, 2000); missed two games. ... Suffered injury (March 29, 2000); missed one game.
STATISTICAL PLATEAUS: Three-goal games: 1999-00 (1).

			REGULAR SEASON								PLAYOFFS				
Season Team	League	Gms.	G	A	Pts.	PIM	+/-	PP	SH		Gms.	G	A	Pts.	PIM
95-96—Torpedo Ust-Kam	CIS Jr.	20	18	20	38	30	...	...	...		—	—	—	—	—
96-97—Torpedo Ust-Kam	Rus. Div. II	8	2	1	3	6	...	...	...		—	—	—	—	—
97-98—Torpedo Ust-Kam	Rus. Div. II	42	15	24	39	62	...	...	...		—	—	—	—	—
98-99—Dynamo Moscow	Russian	30	5	9	14	30	...	...	...		11	0	1	1	4
99-00—St. John's	AHL	2	0	0	0	4	...	...	...		—	—	—	—	—
—Toronto	NHL	66	12	18	30	41	14	0	0		3	0	0	0	4
00-01—Toronto	NHL	52	6	11	17	30	5	0	0		9	2	1	3	12
01-02—Toronto	NHL	11	1	1	2	4	-1	0	0		—	—	—	—	—
—St. John's	AHL	34	11	24	35	47	...	...	...		—	—	—	—	—
02-03—Toronto	NHL	72	16	29	45	124	11	2	1		3	0	0	0	0
NHL Totals (4 years)		201	35	59	94	199	29	2	1		15	2	1	3	16

ARKHIPOV, DENIS — C — PREDATORS

PERSONAL: Born May 19, 1979, in Kazan, U.S.S.R. ... 6-3/210. ... Shoots left.
TRANSACTIONS/CAREER NOTES: Selected by Nashville Predators in third round (second Predators pick, 60th overall) of NHL entry draft (June 27, 1998). ... Re-signed by Predators (July 17, 2003).

			REGULAR SEASON								PLAYOFFS				
Season Team	League	Gms.	G	A	Pts.	PIM	+/-	PP	SH		Gms.	G	A	Pts.	PIM
94-95—Ak Bars Kazan	CIS Jr.	40	20	12	32	10	...	...	...		—	—	—	—	—
95-96—Ak Bars Kazan	CIS Jr.	40	15	8	23	30	...	...	...		—	—	—	—	—
—Ak Bars-2 Kazan	CIS Div. II	15	10	8	18	10	...	...	...		—	—	—	—	—
96-97—Ak Bars-2 Kazan	Rus. Div. III	50	17	23	40	20	...	...	...		—	—	—	—	—
—Ak Bars Kazan	Russian	1	1	0	1	0	...	...	...		—	—	—	—	—
97-98—Ak Bars Kazan	Russian	29	2	2	4	2	...	...	...		—	—	—	—	—
98-99—Ak Bars Kazan	Russian	34	12	1	13	22	...	...	...		9	2	3	5	6
99-00—Ak Bars Kazan	Russian	32	7	9	16	14	...	...	...		18	5	5	10	6
00-01—Milwaukee	IHL	40	9	8	17	11	...	...	...		—	—	—	—	—
—Nashville	NHL	40	6	7	13	4	0	0	0		—	—	—	—	—
01-02—Nashville	NHL	82	20	22	42	16	-18	7	0		—	—	—	—	—
02-03—Nashville	NHL	79	11	24	35	32	-18	3	0		—	—	—	—	—
NHL Totals (3 years)		201	37	53	90	52	-36	10	0						

ARMSTRONG, COLBY — RW — PENGUINS

PERSONAL: Born November 23, 1982, in Lloydminster, Sask. ... 6-1/180. ... Shoots right.
TRANSACTIONS/CAREER NOTES: Selected by Pittsburgh Penguins in first round (first Penguins pick, 21st overall) of NHL entry draft (June 23, 2001).

			REGULAR SEASON								PLAYOFFS				
Season Team	League	Gms.	G	A	Pts.	PIM	+/-	PP	SH		Gms.	G	A	Pts.	PIM
98-99—Red Deer	WHL	1	0	1	1	0	...	...	...		—	—	—	—	—
99-00—Red Deer	WHL	68	13	25	38	122	...	...	...		2	0	1	1	11
00-01—Red Deer	WHL	72	36	42	78	156	...	...	...		21	6	6	12	39
01-02—Red Deer	WHL	64	27	41	68	115	...	...	...		23	6	10	16	32
02-03—Wilkes-Barre/Scranton	AHL	73	7	11	18	76	...	...	...		—	—	—	—	—

PERSONAL: Born April 23, 1973, in Ottawa ... 6-0/195. ... Shoots right.
TRANSACTIONS/CAREER NOTES: Selected by New York Islanders in sixth round (fifth Islanders pick, 128th overall) of NHL entry draft (June 20, 1992). ... Suffered food poisoning (January 28, 1997); missed one game. ... Signed as free agent by Ottawa Senators (July 10, 1997). ... Signed as free agent by New York Rangers (July 20, 1998). ... Traded by Rangers to Los Angeles Kings for conditional pick in 2003 draft (July 16, 2002).

		REGULAR SEASON								PLAYOFFS				
Season Team	League	Gms.	G	A	Pts.	PIM	+/-	PP	SH	Gms.	G	A	Pts.	PIM
89-90—Hawkesbury	COJHL	48	8	10	18	30	...	...	...	—	—	—	—	—
90-91—Hawkesbury	COJHL	54	27	45	72	49	...	...	...	—	—	—	—	—
—Sudbury	OHL	2	0	2	2	0	...	...	...	—	—	—	—	—
91-92—Sudbury	OHL	66	31	54	85	22	...	...	...	9	2	2	4	2
92-93—Sudbury	OHL	66	44	62	106	56	...	...	...	14	9	10	19	26
93-94—Salt Lake City	IHL	76	23	35	58	61	...	...	...	—	—	—	—	—
94-95—Denver	IHL	59	13	18	31	65	...	...	...	6	0	2	2	0
95-96—Worcester	AHL	51	11	15	26	33	...	...	...	4	2	1	3	0
—New York Islanders	NHL	19	1	3	4	14	-6	0	0	—	—	—	—	—
96-97—New York Islanders	NHL	50	6	7	13	33	-8	0	0	—	—	—	—	—
—Utah	IHL	17	4	8	12	10	...	...	...	6	0	4	4	4
97-98—Detroit	IHL	10	0	1	1	2	...	...	...	—	—	—	—	—
—Hartford	AHL	54	16	30	46	40	...	...	...	15	2	6	8	22
—Ottawa	NHL	9	2	0	2	9	1	0	0	—	—	—	—	—
98-99—Hartford	AHL	59	29	51	80	73	...	...	...	7	5	4	9	10
—New York Rangers	NHL	3	0	0	0	0	0	0	0	—	—	—	—	—
99-00—Hartford	AHL	77	28	54	82	101	...	...	...	23	7	16	23	24
—New York Rangers	NHL	1	0	0	0	0	0	0	0	—	—	—	—	—
00-01—Hartford	AHL	75	32	*69	*101	73	...	...	...	5	0	6	6	6
—New York Rangers	NHL	3	0	0	0	0	0	0	0	—	—	—	—	—
01-02—Bern	Switzerland	44	17	36	53	62	...	...	...	6	3	5	8	8
02-03—Manchester	AHL	2	3	0	3	4	...	...	...	—	—	—	—	—
—Los Angeles	NHL	66	12	26	38	30	5	2	0	—	—	—	—	—
NHL Totals (7 years)		151	21	36	57	86	-8	2	0					

PERSONAL: Born March 16, 1979, in Oklahoma City ... 5-11/198. ... Shoots left.
TRANSACTIONS/CAREER NOTES: Selected by Chicago Blackhawks in sixth round (sixth Blackhawks pick, 183rd overall) of NHL entry draft (June 28, 1998).
STATISTICAL PLATEAUS: Three-goal games: 2002-03 (1).

		REGULAR SEASON								PLAYOFFS				
Season Team	League	Gms.	G	A	Pts.	PIM	+/-	PP	SH	Gms.	G	A	Pts.	PIM
96-97—Winnipeg	MJHL	56	35	30	65	18	...	...	...	—	—	—	—	—
97-98—Fargo	USHL	52	37	45	82	16	...	...	...	—	—	—	—	—
98-99—St. Cloud State	WCHA	38	14	17	31	16	...	...	...	—	—	—	—	—
99-00—St. Cloud State	WCHA	39	19	30	49	18	...	...	...	—	—	—	—	—
00-01—St. Cloud State	WCHA	41	28	28	56	14	...	...	...	—	—	—	—	—
01-02—Norfolk	AHL	60	26	30	56	42	...	...	...	—	—	—	—	—
—Chicago	NHL	21	3	1	4	4	-3	0	0	3	0	0	0	0
02-03—Chicago	NHL	82	19	20	39	20	7	3	0	—	—	—	—	—
NHL Totals (2 years)		103	22	21	43	24	4	3	0	3	0	0	0	0

PERSONAL: Born October 11, 1974, in Collingwood, Ont. ... 6-4/220. ... Shoots right. ... Name pronounced AHR-niht.
TRANSACTIONS/CAREER NOTES: Selected by Edmonton Oilers in first round (first Oilers pick, seventh overall) of NHL entry draft (June 26, 1993). ... Suffered from tonsillitis (November 3, 1993); missed one game. ... Bruised sternum (November 27, 1993); missed one game. ... Sprained back (December 7, 1993); missed one game. ... Underwent appendectomy (December 28, 1993); missed three games. ... Suffered from the flu (February 22, 1995); missed one game. ... Suffered concussion (March 23, 1995); missed two games. ... Strained knee (April 19, 1995); missed two games. ... Suspended one game by NHL for game misconduct penalties (April 22, 1995). ... Suffered concussion and lacerated face (October 8, 1995); missed seven games. ... Sprained knee (February 11, 1996); missed nine games. ... Strained knee (March 19, 1996); missed one game. ... Suffered inner ear infection (April 8, 1996); missed one game. ... Fractured ankle (December 27, 1996); missed seven games. ... Injured ankle (January 22, 1997); missed two games. ... Suffered from the flu (February 12, 1997); missed two games. ... Strained lower back (March 23, 1997); missed four games. ... Separated right shoulder (December 10, 1997); missed five games. ... Reinjured shoulder (January 2, 1998); missed two games. ... Traded by Oilers with D Bryan Muir to New Jersey Devils for RW Bill Guerin and RW Valeri Zelepukin (January 4, 1998). ... Suffered back spasms (March 21, 1998); missed one game. ... Bruised hip (April 8, 1998); missed three games. ... Reinjured hip (April 16, 1998); missed two games. ... Underwent offseason finger surgery; missed first game of 1998-99 season. ... Bruised thigh (December 28, 1998); missed one game. ... Suffered from the flu (January 15, 1999); missed two games ... Bruised foot (January 20, 1999); missed one game. ... Bruised hip (March 28, 1999); missed one game. ... Reinjured hip (April 4, 1999); missed two games. ... Suffered mouth injury (October 23, 1999); missed three games. ... Suffered from the flu (February 21, 2000); missed two games. ... Bruised ribs (March 17, 2000); missed one game. ... Missed first 18 games of 2000-01 season due to contract dispute. ... Injured back (February 16, 2001); missed six games. ... Suffered illness (December 20, 2001); missed two games. ... Injured back (March 10, 2002); missed five games. ... Traded by Devils with RW Randy McKay and first-round pick (traded to Columbus) in 2002 draft to Dallas Stars for C Joe Nieuwendyk and RW Jamie Langenbrunner (March 19, 2002). ... Strained groin (April 10, 2002); missed remainder of season.
STATISTICAL PLATEAUS: Three-goal games: 1994-95 (1), 1995-96 (1), 2001-02 (1), 2002-03 (1). Total: 4.

Season Team	League	REGULAR SEASON								PLAYOFFS				
		Gms.	G	A	Pts.	PIM	+/-	PP	SH	Gms.	G	A	Pts.	PIM
89-90—Stayner	Jr. C	34	21	31	52	12	...	...	...	—	—	—	—	—
90-91—Lindsay Jr. B..............	OHA	42	17	44	61	10	...	...	...	—	—	—	—	—
91-92—Oshawa...............	OHL	57	9	15	24	12	...	...	...	—	—	—	—	—
92-93—Oshawa...............	OHL	56	41	57	98	74	...	...	...	13	9	9	18	20
93-94—Edmonton	NHL	78	33	35	68	104	1	10	0	—	—	—	—	—
94-95—Edmonton	NHL	42	15	22	37	128	-14	7	0	—	—	—	—	—
95-96—Edmonton	NHL	64	28	31	59	87	-6	8	0	—	—	—	—	—
96-97—Edmonton	NHL	67	19	38	57	92	-21	10	1	12	3	6	9	18
97-98—Edmonton	NHL	35	5	13	18	78	-16	1	0	—	—	—	—	—
—New Jersey	NHL	35	5	10	15	21	-8	3	0	5	0	2	2	0
98-99—New Jersey	NHL	74	27	27	54	79	10	8	0	7	2	2	4	4
99-00—New Jersey	NHL	76	22	34	56	51	22	7	0	23	8	12	20	18
00-01—New Jersey	NHL	54	21	34	55	75	23	8	0	23	8	7	15	16
01-02—New Jersey	NHL	63	22	19	41	59	3	8	0	—	—	—	—	—
—Dallas.......................	NHL	10	3	1	4	6	-1	2	0	—	—	—	—	—
02-03—Dallas.......................	NHL	72	23	24	47	51	9	7	0	11	3	2	5	6
NHL Totals (10 years).........		670	223	288	511	831	2	79	1	81	24	31	55	62

ARVEDSON, MAGNUS — LW

PERSONAL: Born November 25, 1971, in Karlstad, Sweden ... 6-2/198. ... Shoots left. ... Name pronounced AHR-vihd-suhn.

TRANSACTIONS/CAREER NOTES: Selected by Ottawa Senators in fifth round (fourth Senators pick, 119th overall) of NHL entry draft (June 21, 1997). ... Strained groin (October 17, 1997); missed seven games. ... Strained groin (November 29, 1997); missed three games. ... Suffered concussion (December 16, 1997); missed five games. ... Strained left shoulder (January 11, 1998); missed one game. ... Strained groin (March 20, 1998); missed three games. ... Suffered back spasms (October 20, 1998); missed two games. ... Bruised hip (October 14, 1999); missed one game. ... Injured abdomen (January 20, 2000) and underwent surgery; missed 34 games. ... Strained buttocks (November 2, 2000); missed one game. ... Fractured left foot (November 16, 2000); missed 19 games. ... Sprained right knee (January 10, 2001); missed 10 games. ... Strained groin (April 6, 2001); missed final game of regular season and two playoff games. ... Injured groin (October 3, 2001); missed first six games of season. ... Suffered concussion (December 26, 2001); missed two games.

STATISTICAL PLATEAUS: Three-goal games: 1998-99 (1).

Season Team	League	REGULAR SEASON								PLAYOFFS				
		Gms.	G	A	Pts.	PIM	+/-	PP	SH	Gms.	G	A	Pts.	PIM
91-92—Orebro	Sweden Dv. 2	32	12	21	33	30	...	...	...	7	4	4	8	4
92-93—Orebro	Sweden Dv. 2	36	11	18	29	34	...	...	...	6	2	1	3	0
93-94—Farjestad Karlstad	Sweden	16	1	7	8	10	...	...	...	—	—	—	—	—
94-95—Farjestad Karlstad	Sweden	36	1	7	8	45	...	...	...	4	0	0	0	6
95-96—Farjestad Karlstad	Sweden	39	10	14	24	42	...	...	...	8	0	3	3	10
96-97—Farjestad Karlstad	Sweden	48	13	11	24	36	...	...	...	14	4	7	11	8
97-98—Ottawa	NHL	61	11	15	26	36	2	0	1	11	0	1	1	6
98-99—Ottawa	NHL	80	21	26	47	50	33	0	4	3	0	1	1	2
99-00—Ottawa	NHL	47	15	13	28	36	4	1	1	6	0	0	0	6
00-01—Ottawa	NHL	51	17	16	33	24	23	1	2	2	0	0	0	0
01-02—Ottawa	NHL	74	12	27	39	35	27	0	0	12	2	1	3	4
—Swedish Oly. team	Int'l	4	0	0	0	0	...	...	...	—	—	—	—	—
02-03—Ottawa	NHL	80	16	21	37	48	13	2	0	18	1	5	6	16
NHL Totals (6 years)...........		393	92	118	210	229	102	4	8	52	3	8	11	34

ASHAM, ARRON — RW — ISLANDERS

PERSONAL: Born April 13, 1978, in Portage-La-Prairie, Man. ... 5-11/196. ... Shoots right.

TRANSACTIONS/CAREER NOTES: Selected by Montreal Canadiens in third round (third Canadiens pick, 71st overall) of NHL entry draft (June 22, 1996). ... Injured back (October 23, 1999); missed one game. ... Suffered from the flu (December 27, 1999); missed one game. ... Strained groin (January 22, 2000); missed one game. ... Strained hip flexor (February 17, 2001); missed eight games. ... Suffered from the flu (March 19, 2001); missed one game. ... Traded by Canadiens with fifth-round pick (F Markus Pahlsson) in 2002 draft to New York Islanders for RW Mariusz Czerkawski (June 22, 2002). ... Re-signed by Islanders (July 20, 2003).

Season Team	League	REGULAR SEASON								PLAYOFFS				
		Gms.	G	A	Pts.	PIM	+/-	PP	SH	Gms.	G	A	Pts.	PIM
94-95—Red Deer....................	WHL	62	11	16	27	126	...	...	...	—	—	—	—	—
95-96—Red Deer....................	WHL	70	32	45	77	174	...	...	...	10	6	3	9	20
96-97—Red Deer....................	WHL	67	45	51	96	149	...	...	...	16	12	14	26	36
97-98—Red Deer....................	WHL	67	43	49	92	153	...	...	...	5	0	2	2	8
—Fredericton	AHL	2	1	1	2	0	...	...	...	2	0	1	1	0
98-99—Fredericton	AHL	60	16	18	34	118	...	...	...	13	8	6	14	11
—Montreal	NHL	7	0	0	0	0	-4	0	0	—	—	—	—	—
99-00—Montreal	NHL	33	4	2	6	24	-7	0	1	—	—	—	—	—
—Quebec	AHL	13	4	5	9	32	...	...	...	2	0	0	0	2
00-01—Quebec	AHL	15	7	9	16	51	...	...	...	7	1	2	3	2
—Montreal	NHL	46	2	3	5	59	-9	0	0	—	—	—	—	—
01-02—Quebec	AHL	24	9	14	23	35	...	...	...	—	—	—	—	—
—Montreal	NHL	35	5	4	9	55	7	0	0	3	0	1	1	0
02-03—New York Islanders.....	NHL	78	15	19	34	57	1	4	0	5	0	0	0	16
NHL Totals (5 years)...........		199	26	28	54	195	-12	4	1	8	0	1	1	16

ASKEY, TOM — G

PERSONAL: Born October 4, 1974, in Kenmore, N.Y. ... 6-2/185. ... Catches left.

TRANSACTIONS/CAREER NOTES: Selected by Mighty Ducks of Anaheim in eighth round (eighth Mighty Ducks pick, 186th overall) of NHL entry draft (June 26, 1993). ... Signed as free agent by Buffalo Sabres (August 8, 2001).

– 15 –

Season Team	League	REGULAR SEASON									PLAYOFFS							
		Gms.	Min	W	L	T	GA	SO	Avg.	SV%	Gms.	Min.	W	L	GA	SO	Avg.	SV%
92-93—Ohio State	CCHA	25	1235	2	19	0	125	0	6.07	—	—	—	—	—	—	—	—	—
93-94—Ohio State	CCHA	27	1488	3	19	4	103	0	4.15	—	—	—	—	—	—	—	—	—
94-95—Ohio State	CCHA	26	1387	4	19	2	121	0	5.23	—	—	—	—	—	—	—	—	—
95-96—Ohio State	CCHA	26	1340	8	11	4	68	0	3.04	—	—	—	—	—	—	—	—	—
96-97—Baltimore	AHL	40	2239	17	18	2	140	1	3.75	—	3	138	0	3	11	0	4.78	—
97-98—Cincinnati	AHL	32	1753	10	16	4	104	3	3.56	—	—	—	—	—	—	—	—	—
—Anaheim	NHL	7	273	0	1	2	12	0	2.64	.894	—	—	—	—	—	—	—	—
98-99—Cincinnati	AHL	53	2893	21	22	3	131	3	2.72	—	3	178	0	3	13	0	4.38	—
—Anaheim	NHL	—	—	—	—	—	—	—	—	—	1	30	0	1	2	0	4.00	.818
99-00—Kansas City	IHL	13	658	3	5	3	43	0	3.92	—	—	—	—	—	—	—	—	—
—Houston	IHL	13	727	5	7	1	33	0	2.72	—	—	—	—	—	—	—	—	—
00-01—Rochester	AHL	29	1671	15	8	4	71	1	2.55	—	—	—	—	—	—	—	—	—
01-02—Rochester	AHL	34	2048	16	15	3	86	3	2.52	—	1	58	0	1	4	0	4.14	—
02-03—Rochester	AHL	16	895	3	8	4	49	0	3.28	—	—	—	—	—	—	—	—	—
NHL Totals (2 years)		7	273	0	1	2	12	0	2.64	.894	1	30	0	1	2	0	4.00	.818

ASTASHENKO, KASPARS — D

PERSONAL: Born February 17, 1975, in Riga, U.S.S.R. ... 6-2/183. ... Shoots left. ... Name pronounced KAHS-phar ahs-tah-SHEHN-koh.
TRANSACTIONS/CAREER NOTES: Selected by Tampa Bay Lightning in fifth round (fifth Lightning pick, 127th overall) of NHL entry draft (June 26, 1999). ... Suffered concussion (April 8, 2000); missed final game of season. ... Traded by Lightning to Carolina Hurricanes for D Harlan Pratt (December 27, 2001).

Season Team	League	REGULAR SEASON								PLAYOFFS				
		Gms.	G	A	Pts.	PIM	+/-	PP	SH	Gms.	G	A	Pts.	PIM
93-94—Pardaugava Riga	CIS	4	0	0	0	10	...	...	...	—	—	—	—	—
94-95—Pardaugava Riga	CIS	25	0	0	0	24	...	...	...	—	—	—	—	—
95-96—CSKA Moscow	CIS	26	0	1	1	10	...	...	...	—	—	—	—	—
96-97—HC CSKA Moscow	Russian	41	0	0	0	48	...	...	...	2	0	1	1	4
97-98—HC CSKA Moscow	Russian	25	1	3	4	6	...	...	...	—	—	—	—	—
98-99—Cincinnati	IHL	74	3	11	14	166	...	...	...	3	0	2	2	6
—Dayton	ECHL	2	0	1	1	4	...	...	...	—	—	—	—	—
99-00—Detroit	IHL	51	1	10	11	86	...	...	...	—	—	—	—	—
—Long Beach	IHL	14	0	3	3	10	...	...	...	—	—	—	—	—
—Tampa Bay	NHL	8	0	1	1	4	-2	0	0	—	—	—	—	—
00-01—Detroit	IHL	51	6	10	16	58	...	...	...	—	—	—	—	—
—Tampa Bay	NHL	15	1	1	2	4	-4	0	0	—	—	—	—	—
01-02—Springfield	AHL	11	0	2	2	15	...	...	...	—	—	—	—	—
—Lowell	AHL	48	2	10	12	54	...	...	...	5	1	1	2	2
—Latvian Olympic team	Int'l	3	0	1	1	0	...	...	...	—	—	—	—	—
02-03—Lowell	AHL	47	6	11	17	60	...	...	...	—	—	—	—	—
NHL Totals (2 years)		23	1	2	3	8	-6	0	0					

AUBIN, JEAN-SEBASTIEN — G — PENGUINS

PERSONAL: Born July 17, 1977, in Montreal ... 5-11/180. ... Catches right. ... Name pronounced OH-ban.
TRANSACTIONS/CAREER NOTES: Selected by Pittsburgh Penguins in third round (second Penguins pick, 76th overall) of NHL entry draft (July 8, 1995). ... Strained hamstring (April 3, 1999); missed six games. ... Injured shoulder (November 23, 1999); missed two games. ... Sprained ankle (April 3, 2000); missed final three games of season. ... Injured knee and underwent surgery (December 3, 2000); missed 14 games.

Season Team	League	REGULAR SEASON									PLAYOFFS							
		Gms.	Min	W	L	T	GA	SO	Avg.	SV%	Gms.	Min.	W	L	GA	SO	Avg.	SV%
94-95—Sherbrooke	QMJHL	27	1287	13	10	1	73	1	3.40	—	3	185	1	2	11	0	3.57	—
95-96—Sherbrooke	QMJHL	40	2084	18	14	2	127	0	3.66	—	4	174	1	3	16	0	5.52	—
96-97—Sherbrooke	QMJHL	4	249	3	1	0	8	0	1.93	—	—	—	—	—	—	—	—	—
—Moncton	QMJHL	23	1311	9	13	0	72	1	3.30	—	—	—	—	—	—	—	—	—
—Laval	QMJHL	11	532	2	6	1	41	0	4.62	—	2	128	0	2	10	0	4.69	—
97-98—Syracuse	AHL	8	380	2	4	1	26	0	4.11	—	—	—	—	—	—	—	—	—
—Dayton	ECHL	21	1177	15	2	‡2	59	1	3.01	—	3	142	1	1	4	0	1.69	—
98-99—Kansas City	IHL	13	751	5	7	‡1	41	0	3.28	—	—	—	—	—	—	—	—	—
—Pittsburgh	NHL	17	756	4	3	6	28	2	2.22	.908	—	—	—	—	—	—	—	—
99-00—Wilkes-Barre/Scranton	AHL	11	538	2	8	0	39	0	4.35	—	—	—	—	—	—	—	—	—
—Pittsburgh	NHL	51	2789	23	21	3	120	2	2.58	.914	—	—	—	—	—	—	—	—
00-01—Pittsburgh	NHL	36	2050	20	14	1	107	0	3.13	.890	1	1	0	0	0	0	...	...
01-02—Pittsburgh	NHL	21	1094	3	12	1	65	0	3.56	.879	—	—	—	—	—	—	—	—
02-03—Wilkes-Barre/Scranton	AHL	16	919	8	6	1	29	3	1.89	—	—	—	—	—	—	—	—	—
—Pittsburgh	NHL	21	1132	6	13	0	59	1	3.13	.900	—	—	—	—	—	—	—	—
NHL Totals (5 years)		146	7821	56	63	11	379	5	2.91	.900	1	1	0	0	0	0	...	...

AUBIN, SERGE — LW — AVALANCHE

PERSONAL: Born February 15, 1975, in Val d'Or, Que. ... 6-1/200. ... Shoots left. ... Name pronounced AH-ban.
TRANSACTIONS/CAREER NOTES: Selected by Pittsburgh Penguins in seventh round (ninth Penguins pick, 161st overall) of NHL entry draft (June 29, 1994). ... Signed as free agent by Colorado Avalanche (December 18, 1998). ... Signed as free agent by Columbus Blue Jackets (July

11, 2000). ... Suffered from the flu (January 15, 2001); missed one game. ... Lacerated knee (November 25, 2001); missed two games. ... Bruised thigh (December 8, 2001); missed two games. ... Suffered concussion (January 26, 2002); missed two games. ... Suffered from the flu (March 14, 2002); missed one game. ... Suffered mouth injury (March 26, 2002); missed two games. ... Signed as free agent by Colorado Avalanche (August 27, 2002).

		REGULAR SEASON							PLAYOFFS				
Season Team	League	Gms.	G	A	Pts.	PIM	+/-	PP	SH	Gms.	G	A	Pts.	PIM
92-93—Drummondville	QMJHL	65	16	34	50	30	...	...	...	8	0	1	1	16
93-94—Granby	QMJHL	63	42	32	74	80	...	...	...	7	2	3	5	8
94-95—Granby	QMJHL	60	37	73	110	55	...	...	...	11	8	15	23	4
95-96—Cleveland	IHL	2	0	0	0	0	...	...	...	2	0	0	0	0
—Hampton Roads	ECHL	62	24	62	86	74	...	...	...	3	1	4	5	10
96-97—Cleveland	IHL	57	9	16	25	38	...	...	...	2	0	0	0	0
97-98—Syracuse	AHL	55	6	14	20	57	...	...	...	—	—	—	—	—
—Hershey	AHL	5	2	1	3	0	...	...	...	7	1	3	4	6
98-99—Hershey	AHL	64	30	39	69	58	...	...	...	3	0	1	1	2
—Colorado	NHL	1	0	0	0	0	0	0	0	—	—	—	—	—
99-00—Hershey	AHL	58	42	38	80	56	...	...	...	—	—	—	—	—
—Colorado	NHL	15	2	1	3	6	1	0	0	17	0	1	1	6
00-01—Columbus	NHL	81	13	17	30	107	-20	0	0	—	—	—	—	—
01-02—Columbus	NHL	71	8	8	16	32	-20	1	0	—	—	—	—	—
02-03—Colorado	NHL	66	4	6	10	64	-2	0	0	5	0	0	0	4
NHL Totals (5 years)		234	27	32	59	209	-41	1	0	22	0	1	1	10

AUCOIN, ADRIAN   D   ISLANDERS

PERSONAL: Born July 3, 1973, in Ottawa ... 6-2/214. ... Shoots right. ... Name pronounced oh-COYN.
TRANSACTIONS/CAREER NOTES: Selected by Vancouver Canucks in fifth round (seventh Canucks pick, 117th overall) of NHL entry draft (June 20, 1992). ... Sprained shoulder (January 10, 1997); missed six games. ... Strained groin (October 30, 1997); missed five games. ... Reinjured groin (November 12, 1997); missed 10 games. ... Sprained ankle (December 13, 1997); missed seven games. ... Injured groin (December 4, 1999); missed four games. ... Fractured finger (February 9, 2000); missed 20 games. ... Strained groin (November 4, 2000); missed nine games. ... Reinjured groin (November 9, 2000); missed three games. ... Traded by Canucks with second-round pick (C/LW Alexander Polushin) in 2001 draft to Tampa Bay Lightning for G Dan Cloutier (February 7, 2001). ... Traded by Lightning with RW Alexander Kharitonov to New York Islanders for D Mathieu Biron and second-round pick (traded to Washington) in 2002 draft (June 22, 2001). ... Injured heel (March 28, 2002); missed one game.

		REGULAR SEASON							PLAYOFFS				
Season Team	League	Gms.	G	A	Pts.	PIM	+/-	PP	SH	Gms.	G	A	Pts.	PIM
91-92—Boston University	Hockey East	33	2	10	12	62	...	...	...	—	—	—	—	—
92-93—Canadian nat'l team	Int'l	42	8	10	18	71	...	...	...	—	—	—	—	—
93-94—Canadian nat'l team	Int'l	59	5	12	17	80	...	...	...	—	—	—	—	—
—Can. Olympic team	Int'l	4	0	0	0	2	...	...	...	—	—	—	—	—
—Hamilton	AHL	13	1	2	3	19	...	...	...	4	0	2	2	6
94-95—Syracuse	AHL	71	13	18	31	52	...	...	...	—	—	—	—	—
—Vancouver	NHL	1	1	0	1	0	1	0	0	4	1	0	1	0
95-96—Syracuse	AHL	29	5	13	18	47	...	...	...	—	—	—	—	—
—Vancouver	NHL	49	4	14	18	34	8	2	0	6	0	0	0	2
96-97—Vancouver	NHL	70	5	16	21	63	0	1	0	—	—	—	—	—
97-98—Vancouver	NHL	35	3	3	6	21	-4	1	0	—	—	—	—	—
98-99—Vancouver	NHL	82	23	11	34	77	-14	18	2	—	—	—	—	—
99-00—Vancouver	NHL	57	10	14	24	30	7	4	0	—	—	—	—	—
00-01—Vancouver	NHL	47	3	13	16	20	13	1	0	—	—	—	—	—
—Tampa Bay	NHL	26	1	11	12	25	-8	1	0	—	—	—	—	—
01-02—New York Islanders	NHL	81	12	22	34	62	23	7	0	7	2	5	7	4
02-03—New York Islanders	NHL	73	8	27	35	70	-5	5	0	5	1	2	3	4
NHL Totals (9 years)		521	70	131	201	402	21	40	2	22	4	7	11	10

AUDETTE, DONALD   RW   CANADIENS

PERSONAL: Born September 23, 1969, in Laval, Que. ... 5-8/190. ... Shoots right. ... Name pronounced aw-DEHT.
TRANSACTIONS/CAREER NOTES: Selected by Buffalo Sabres in ninth round (eighth Sabres pick, 183rd overall) of NHL entry draft (June 17, 1989). ... Fractured left hand (February 11, 1990); missed seven games. ... Bruised thigh (September 1990). ... Bruised thigh (October 1990); missed five games. ... Tore ligaments in left knee (November 16, 1990); and underwent surgery. ... Sprained ankle (December 14, 1991); missed eight games. ... Injured knee (March 31, 1992). ... Underwent knee surgery prior to 1992-93 season; missed first 22 games of season. ... Tore knee cartilage (September 23, 1995); missed 11 games. ... Broke tip of right thumb (November 8, 1995); missed two games. ... Injured right knee (December 1, 1995); missed seven games. ... Underwent right knee surgery (January 26, 1996); missed remainder of season. ... Strained groin (October 26, 1996); missed five games. ... Suffered concussion (October 22, 1997); missed seven games. ... Missed first 25 games of 1998-99 season due to contract dispute. ... Traded by Sabres to Los Angeles Kings for second-round pick (RW Milan Bartovic) in 1999 draft (December 18, 1998). ... Suffered back spasms (April 8, 1999); missed one game. ... Suffered from the flu (April 18, 1999); missed one game. ... Sprained left ankle (January 6, 2000); missed 15 games. ... Traded by Kings with D Frantisek Kaberle to Atlanta Thrashers for RW Kelly Buchberger and RW Nelson Emerson (March 13, 2000). ... Strained groin (December 27, 2000); missed one game. ... Suspended four games by NHL for cross-checking incident (January 16, 2001). ... Suspended two games by NHL for delivering illegal blow to the head (March 12, 2001). ... Traded by Thrashers to Sabres for C Kamil Piros and fourth-round pick (traded to St. Louis) in 2001 draft (March 13, 2001). ... Signed as free agent by Dallas Stars (July 2, 2001). ... Traded by Stars with C Shaun Van Allen to Montreal Canadiens for LW Martin Rucinsky and LW Benoit Brunet (November 21, 2001). ... Lacerated forearm (December 1, 2001); missed 49 games.
STATISTICAL PLATEAUS: Three-goal games: 1994-95 (1), 1995-96 (1), 2000-01 (2). Total: 4.

Season Team	League	REGULAR SEASON								PLAYOFFS				
		Gms.	G	A	Pts.	PIM	+/-	PP	SH	Gms.	G	A	Pts.	PIM
86-87—Laval	QMJHL	66	17	22	39	36	...	...	...	14	2	6	8	10
87-88—Laval	QMJHL	63	48	61	109	56	...	...	...	14	7	12	19	20
88-89—Laval	QMJHL	70	76	85	161	123	...	...	...	17	*17	12	29	43
89-90—Rochester	AHL	70	42	46	88	78	...	...	...	15	9	8	17	29
—Buffalo	NHL	0	0	0	0	0	0	0	0	2	0	0	0	0
90-91—Rochester	AHL	5	4	0	4	2	...	...	...	—	—	—	—	—
—Buffalo	NHL	8	4	3	7	4	-1	2	0	—	—	—	—	—
91-92—Buffalo	NHL	63	31	17	48	75	-1	5	0	—	—	—	—	—
92-93—Buffalo	NHL	44	12	7	19	51	-8	2	0	8	2	2	4	6
—Rochester	AHL	6	8	4	12	10	...	...	...	—	—	—	—	—
93-94—Buffalo	NHL	77	29	30	59	41	2	16	1	7	0	1	1	6
94-95—Buffalo	NHL	46	24	13	37	27	-3	13	0	5	1	1	2	4
95-96—Buffalo	NHL	23	12	13	25	18	0	8	0	—	—	—	—	—
96-97—Buffalo	NHL	73	28	22	50	48	-6	8	0	11	4	5	9	6
97-98—Buffalo	NHL	75	24	20	44	59	10	10	0	15	5	8	13	10
98-99—Los Angeles	NHL	49	18	18	36	51	7	6	0	—	—	—	—	—
99-00—Los Angeles	NHL	49	12	20	32	45	6	1	0	—	—	—	—	—
—Atlanta	NHL	14	7	4	11	12	-4	0	1	—	—	—	—	—
00-01—Atlanta	NHL	64	32	39	71	64	-3	13	1	—	—	—	—	—
—Buffalo	NHL	12	2	6	8	12	1	1	0	13	3	6	9	4
01-02—Dallas	NHL	20	4	8	12	12	2	3	0	—	—	—	—	—
—Montreal	NHL	13	1	5	6	8	1	0	0	12	6	4	10	10
02-03—Hamilton	AHL	11	5	5	10	8	...	...	...	—	—	—	—	—
—Montreal	NHL	54	11	12	23	19	-7	4	0	—	—	—	—	—
NHL Totals (14 years)		684	251	237	488	546	-4	92	3	73	21	27	48	46

AUFIERO, PAT — D — RANGERS

PERSONAL: Born July 1, 1980, in Winchester, Mass. ... 6-2/186. ... Shoots right. ... Full Name: Patrick Aufiero.
TRANSACTIONS/CAREER NOTES: Selected by New York Rangers in third round (fifth Rangers pick, 90th overall) of NHL entry draft (June 26, 1999).

Season Team	League	REGULAR SEASON								PLAYOFFS				
		Gms.	G	A	Pts.	PIM	+/-	PP	SH	Gms.	G	A	Pts.	PIM
97-98—U.S. National	NAHL	56	10	11	21	111	...	...	...	—	—	—	—	—
98-99—Boston University	Hockey East	22	3	4	7	14	...	...	...	—	—	—	—	—
99-00—Boston University	Hockey East	38	3	20	23	37	...	...	...	—	—	—	—	—
00-01—Boston University	Hockey East	34	5	8	13	30	...	...	...	—	—	—	—	—
01-02—Boston University	Hockey East	26	2	10	12	16	...	...	...	—	—	—	—	—
02-03—Hartford	AHL	32	1	6	7	29	...	...	...	—	—	—	—	—
—Charlotte	ECHL	8	2	4	6	6	...	...	...	—	—	—	—	—

AULD, ALEXANDER — G — CANUCKS

PERSONAL: Born January 7, 1981, in Cold Lake, Alta. ... 6-4/200. ... Catches left.
TRANSACTIONS/CAREER NOTES: Selected by Florida Panthers in second round (second Panthers pick, 40th overall) of NHL entry draft (June 26, 1999). ... Traded by Panthers to Vancouver Canucks for second-round pick (traded to New Jersey) in 2001 draft and conditional pick in 2002 draft (May 31, 2001).

Season Team	League	REGULAR SEASON									PLAYOFFS							
		Gms.	Min	W	L	T	GA	SO	Avg.	SV%	Gms.	Min.	W	L	GA	SO	Avg.	SV%
97-98—North Bay	OHL	6	206	0	4	0	17	0	4.95	—	—	—	—	—	—	—	—	—
98-99—North Bay	OHL	37	1894	9	20	1	106	1	3.36	—	3	170	0	3	10	0	3.53	—
99-00—North Bay	OHL	55	3047	21	26	6	167	2	3.29	—	6	374	2	4	12	0	1.93	—
00-01—North Bay	OHL	40	2319	22	11	5	98	1	2.54	—	4	240	0	4	15	0	3.75	—
01-02—Manitoba	AHL	21	1103	11	9	0	65	1	3.54	—	1	20	0	0	0	0	...	—
—Columbia	ECHL	6	375	3	1	2	12	0	1.92	—	—	—	—	—	—	—	—	—
—Vancouver	NHL	1	60	1	0	0	2	0	2.00	.909	—	—	—	—	—	—	—	—
02-03—Manitoba	AHL	37	2208	15	19	3	97	3	2.64	—	—	—	—	—	—	—	—	—
—Vancouver	NHL	7	382	3	3	0	10	1	1.57	.939	1	20	0	0	1	0	3.00	.800
NHL Totals (2 years)		8	442	4	3	0	12	1	1.63	.936	1	20	0	0	1	0	3.00	.800

AULIN, JARED — C — KINGS

PERSONAL: Born March 15, 1982, in Calgary ... 6-0/192. ... Shoots right.
TRANSACTIONS/CAREER NOTES: Selected by Colorado Avalanche in second round (second Avalanche pick, 47th overall) of NHL entry draft (June 24, 2000). ... Traded by Avalanche to Los Angeles Kings (March 22, 2001); completing deal in which Kings traded D Rob Blake and C Steve Reinprecht to Colorado Avalanche for RW Adam Deadmarsh, D Aaron Miller, first-round pick (C David Steckel) in 2001 draft, a player to be named later and first-round pick in 2003 draft (February 21, 2001).

Season Team	League	REGULAR SEASON								PLAYOFFS				
		Gms.	G	A	Pts.	PIM	+/-	PP	SH	Gms.	G	A	Pts.	PIM
97-98—Kamloops	WHL	2	0	0	0	0	...	...	...	0	0	0	0	0
98-99—Kamloops	WHL	55	7	19	26	23	...	...	...	13	1	3	4	2
99-00—Kamloops	WHL	57	17	38	55	70	...	...	...	4	0	1	1	6
00-01—Kamloops	WHL	70	31	†77	108	62	...	...	...	4	0	2	2	0
01-02—Kamloops	WHL	46	33	34	67	80	...	...	...	4	1	2	3	2
02-03—Manchester	AHL	44	12	32	44	21	...	...	...	—	—	—	—	—
—Los Angeles	NHL	17	2	2	4	0	-3	1	0	—	—	—	—	—
NHL Totals (1 year)		17	2	2	4	0	-3	1	0					

AVERY, SEAN — C — KINGS

PERSONAL: Born April 10, 1980, in Pickering, Ont. ... 5-10/195. ... Shoots left.
TRANSACTIONS/CAREER NOTES: Signed as non-drafted free agent by Detroit Red Wings (September 21, 1999). ... Traded by Red Wings with D Maxim Kuznetsov, first-round pick in 2003 draft and second-round pick in 2004 to Los Angeles Kings for D Mathieu Schneider (March 11, 2003).

Season Team	League	Gms.	G	A	Pts.	PIM	+/-	PP	SH	Gms.	G	A	Pts.	PIM
95-96—Markham Waxers	OJHL	1	0	0	0	4	...	...	...	—	—	—	—	—
96-97—Owen Sound	OHL	58	10	21	31	86	...	...	...	4	1	0	1	4
97-98—Owen Sound	OHL	47	13	41	54	105	...	...	...	—	—	—	—	—
98-99—Owen Sound	OHL	28	22	23	45	70	...	...	...	—	—	—	—	—
—Kingston	OHL	33	14	25	39	88	...	...	...	5	1	3	4	13
99-00—Kingston	OHL	55	28	56	84	215	...	...	...	5	2	2	4	26
00-01—Cincinnati	AHL	58	8	15	23	304	...	...	...	4	1	0	1	19
01-02—Cincinnati	AHL	36	14	7	21	106	...	...	...	—	—	—	—	—
—Detroit	NHL	36	2	2	4	68	1	0	0	—	—	—	—	—
02-03—Grand Rapids	AHL	15	6	6	12	82	...	...	...	—	—	—	—	—
—Detroit	NHL	39	5	6	11	120	7	0	0	—	—	—	—	—
—Los Angeles	NHL	12	1	3	4	33	0	0	0	—	—	—	—	—
NHL Totals (2 years)		**87**	**8**	**11**	**19**	**221**	**8**	**0**	**0**					

AXELSSON, P.J. — LW — BRUINS

PERSONAL: Born February 26, 1975, in Kungalv, Sweden ... 6-1/175. ... Shoots left. ... Full Name: Per-Johan Axelsson. ... Name pronounced AK-sihl-suhn.
TRANSACTIONS/CAREER NOTES: Selected by Boston Bruins in seventh round (seventh Bruins pick, 177th overall) of NHL entry draft (June 8, 1995). ... Suffered concussion (October 28, 1998); missed one game. ... Suffered concussion (November 3, 1998); missed three games. ... Suffered from the flu (April 17, 1999); missed one game. ... Suffered from charley horse (October 23, 1999); missed one game. ... Strained shoulder (December 15, 2001); missed three games. ... Re-signed by Bruins (July 14, 2003).

Season Team	League	Gms.	G	A	Pts.	PIM	+/-	PP	SH	Gms.	G	A	Pts.	PIM
93-94—Frolunda	Sweden	11	0	0	0	4	...	...	...	4	0	0	0	0
94-95—Frolunda	Sweden	8	2	1	3	6	...	...	...	—	—	—	—	—
95-96—Frolunda	Sweden	36	15	5	20	10	...	...	...	13	3	0	3	10
96-97—Vastra Frolunda	Sweden	50	19	15	34	34	...	...	...	3	0	2	2	0
97-98—Boston	NHL	82	8	19	27	38	-14	2	0	6	1	0	1	0
98-99—Boston	NHL	77	7	10	17	18	-14	0	0	12	1	1	2	4
99-00—Boston	NHL	81	10	16	26	24	1	0	0	—	—	—	—	—
00-01—Boston	NHL	81	8	15	23	27	-12	0	0	—	—	—	—	—
01-02—Boston	NHL	78	7	17	24	16	6	0	2	6	2	1	3	6
—Swedish Oly. team	Int'l	4	0	0	0	2	...	...	...	—	—	—	—	—
02-03—Boston	NHL	66	17	19	36	24	8	2	2	5	0	0	0	6
NHL Totals (6 years)		**465**	**57**	**96**	**153**	**147**	**-25**	**4**	**4**	**29**	**4**	**2**	**6**	**16**

BABCHUK, ANTON — D — BLACKHAWKS

PERSONAL: Born May 6, 1984, in Kiev, U.S.S.R. ... 6-4/194. ... Shoots right.
TRANSACTIONS/CAREER NOTES: Selected by Chicago Blackhawks in first round (first Blackhawks pick, 21st overall) of NHL entry draft (June 22, 2002).

Season Team	League	Gms.	G	A	Pts.	PIM	+/-	PP	SH	Gms.	G	A	Pts.	PIM
01-02—Elektrostal	Russian Div. 1	40	7	8	15	90	...	...	...	—	—	—	—	—
02-03—St. Petersburg	Rus. Div. II	20	3	0	3	10	...	...	...	—	—	—	—	—

BACASHIHUA, JASON — G — STARS

PERSONAL: Born September 20, 1982, in Garden City, Mich. ... 5-11/167. ... Catches right.
TRANSACTIONS/CAREER NOTES: Selected by Dallas Stars in first round (first Stars pick, 26th overall) of NHL entry draft (June 23, 2001).

Season Team	League	Gms.	Min	W	L	T	GA	SO	Avg.	SV%	Gms.	Min.	W	L	GA	SO	Avg.	SV%
99-00—Chicago	NAHL	41	2432	20	19	2	118	2	2.91	—	2	103	0	2	12	0	6.99	—
00-01—Chicago	NAHL	39	2246	24	14	0	121	1	3.23	—	3	190	1	2	12	0	3.79	—
01-02—Plymouth	OHL	46	2688	26	12	7	105	*5	2.34	—	6	360	2	4	15	0	2.50	—
—Utah	AHL	1	60	0	1	0	3	0	3.00	—	—	—	—	—	—	—	—	—
02-03—Utah	AHL	39	2244	18	18	2	118	3	3.16	—	—	—	—	—	—	—	—	—

BACKMAN, CHRISTIAN — D — BLUES

PERSONAL: Born April 28, 1980, in Alingsas, Sweden ... 6-4/204. ... Shoots left.
TRANSACTIONS/CAREER NOTES: Selected by St. Louis Blues in first round (first Blues pick, 24th overall) of NHL entry draft (June 27, 1998).

Season Team	League	Gms.	G	A	Pts.	PIM	+/-	PP	SH	Gms.	G	A	Pts.	PIM
		REGULAR SEASON								**PLAYOFFS**				
96-97—Vastra Frolunda	Sweden Jr.	26	2	5	7	16	...	...	...	—	—	—	—	—
97-98—Vastra Frolunda	Sweden Jr.	28	5	14	19	12	...	...	...	2	0	1	1	4
98-99—Vastra Frolunda	Sweden	49	0	4	4	4	...	...	...	4	0	0	0	0
99-00—Vastra Frolunda	Sweden	27	1	0	1	14	...	...	...	5	0	0	0	0
00-01—Vastra Frolunda	Sweden	50	1	10	11	32	...	...	...	3	0	2	2	2
01-02—Vastra Frolunda	Sweden	44	7	4	11	38	...	...	...	10	0	0	0	8
02-03—Worcester	AHL	72	8	19	27	66	...	...	...	—	—	—	—	—
—St. Louis	NHL	4	0	0	0	0	-3	0	0	—	—	—	—	—
NHL Totals (1 year)		4	0	0	0	0	-3	0	0					

BALA, CHRIS — LW — WILD

PERSONAL: Born September 24, 1978, in Alexandria, Va. ... 6-1/180. ... Shoots left.
TRANSACTIONS/CAREER NOTES: Selected by Ottawa Senators in second round (third Senators pick, 58th overall) of NHL entry draft (June 27, 1998). ... Traded by Senators to Minnesota Wild (June 26, 2003).

Season Team	League	Gms.	G	A	Pts.	PIM	+/-	PP	SH	Gms.	G	A	Pts.	PIM
		REGULAR SEASON								**PLAYOFFS**				
96-97—The Hill School	USHS (East)	23	28	33	61	36	...	...	...	—	—	—	—	—
97-98—Harvard University	ECAC	33	16	14	30	23	...	...	...	—	—	—	—	—
98-99—Harvard University	ECAC	28	5	10	15	16	...	...	...	—	—	—	—	—
99-00—Harvard University	ECAC	30	10	14	24	18	...	...	...	—	—	—	—	—
00-01—Harvard University	ECAC	32	14	16	30	24	...	...	...	—	—	—	—	—
01-02—Grand Rapids	AHL	70	21	16	37	9	...	...	...	4	0	1	1	0
—Ottawa	NHL	6	0	1	1	0	1	0	0	—	—	—	—	—
02-03—Binghamton	AHL	51	6	18	24	20	...	...	...	—	—	—	—	—
NHL Totals (1 year)		6	0	1	1	0	1	0	0					

BALEJ, JOZEF — RW — CANADIENS

PERSONAL: Born February 22, 1982, in Ilava, Czechoslovakia. ... 5-11/170. ... Shoots right. ... Name pronounced BAH-lee..
TRANSACTIONS/CAREER NOTES: Selected by Montreal Canadiens in third round (third Canadiens pick, 78th overall) of NHL entry draft (June 24, 2000).

Season Team	League	Gms.	G	A	Pts.	PIM	+/-	PP	SH	Gms.	G	A	Pts.	PIM
		REGULAR SEASON								**PLAYOFFS**				
97-98—Dukla Trencin	Slovakia Jrs.	52	57	40	97	60	...	...	...	—	—	—	—	—
98-99—Thunder Bay Flyers	USHL	38	8	7	15	9	...	...	...	—	—	—	—	—
99-00—Portland	WHL	65	22	23	45	33	...	...	...	—	—	—	—	—
00-01—Portland	WHL	46	32	21	53	18	...	...	...	16	6	9	15	6
01-02—Portland	WHL	65	51	41	92	52	...	...	...	7	0	2	2	6
02-03—Hamilton	AHL	56	5	15	20	29	...	...	...	—	—	—	—	—

BALLANTYNE, PAUL — D — RED WINGS

PERSONAL: Born July 16, 1982, in Waterloo, Ont. ... 6-3/200. ... Shoots right.
TRANSACTIONS/CAREER NOTES: Selected by Detroit Red Wings in sixth round (eighth Red Wings pick, 196th overall) of NHL entry draft (June 24, 2000).

Season Team	League	Gms.	G	A	Pts.	PIM	+/-	PP	SH	Gms.	G	A	Pts.	PIM
		REGULAR SEASON								**PLAYOFFS**				
99-00—Sault Ste. Marie	OHL	58	4	15	19	60	...	...	...	—	—	—	—	—
00-01—Sault Ste. Marie	OHL	63	12	28	40	60	...	...	...	—	—	—	—	—
01-02—Sault Ste. Marie	OHL	68	4	24	28	40	...	...	...	6	1	1	2	8
02-03—Grand Rapids	AHL	7	0	0	0	8	...	...	...	—	—	—	—	—
—Toledo	ECHL	56	10	16	26	41	...	...	...	—	—	—	—	—

BANCROFT, STEVE — D — BLUES

PERSONAL: Born October 6, 1970, in Toronto. ... 6-1/214. ... Shoots left.
TRANSACTIONS/CAREER NOTES: Selected by Toronto Maple Leafs in first round (third Maple Leafs pick, 21st overall) of NHL entry draft (June 17, 1989). ... Traded by Maple Leafs to Boston Bruins for LW Rob Cimetta (November 9, 1990). ... Traded by Bruins with 11th-round pick in 1993 draft (traded to Winnipeg Jets who selected LW Russell Hewson) to Chicago Blackhawks for 11th-round pick in 1992 draft (LW Yevgeny Pavlov) and 12th-round pick in 1993 draft (January 8, 1992). ... Traded by Blackhawks with undisclosed pick in 1993 draft to Jets for C Troy Murray (February 21, 1993); Jets received 11th-round pick in 1993 draft (LW Russell Hewson) to complete deal. ... Selected by Florida Panthers in NHL expansion draft (June 24, 1993). ... Signed as free agent by Pittsburgh Penguins (August 2, 1993). ... Signed as free agent by Carolina Hurricanes (August 4, 1999). ... Signed as free agent by San Jose Sharks (August 10, 2000). ... Signed as free agent by St. Louis Blues (July 16, 2002).

Season Team	League	Gms.	G	A	Pts.	PIM	+/-	PP	SH	Gms.	G	A	Pts.	PIM
		REGULAR SEASON								**PLAYOFFS**				
86-87—St. Catharines Jr. B	OHA	11	5	8	13	20	...	...	...	—	—	—	—	—
87-88—Belleville	OHL	56	1	8	9	42	...	...	...	—	—	—	—	—
88-89—Belleville	OHL	66	7	30	37	99	...	...	...	5	0	2	2	10
89-90—Belleville	OHL	53	10	33	43	135	...	...	...	11	3	9	12	38
90-91—Newmarket	AHL	9	0	3	3	22	...	...	...	—	—	—	—	—
—Maine	AHL	53	2	12	14	46	...	...	...	2	0	0	0	2

Season Team	League	Gms.	G	A	Pts.	PIM	+/-	PP	SH	Gms.	G	A	Pts.	PIM
		REGULAR SEASON								**PLAYOFFS**				
91-92—Maine	AHL	26	1	3	4	45	...	...	...	—	—	—	—	—
—Indianapolis	IHL	36	8	23	31	49	...	...	...	—	—	—	—	—
92-93—Indianapolis	IHL	53	10	35	45	138	...	...	...	—	—	—	—	—
—Chicago	NHL	1	0	0	0	0	0	0	0	—	—	—	—	—
—Moncton	AHL	21	3	13	16	16	...	...	...	5	0	0	0	16
93-94—Cleveland	IHL	33	2	12	14	58	...	...	...	—	—	—	—	—
94-95—Fort Wayne	IHL	50	7	17	24	100	...	...	...	—	—	—	—	—
—Detroit	IHL	6	1	3	4	0	...	...	...	—	—	—	—	—
—St. John's	AHL	4	2	0	2	2	...	...	...	5	0	3	3	8
95-96—Los Angeles	IHL	15	3	10	13	22	...	...	...	—	—	—	—	—
—Chicago	IHL	64	9	41	50	91	...	...	...	9	1	7	8	22
96-97—Chicago	IHL	39	6	10	16	66	...	...	...	—	—	—	—	—
—Las Vegas	IHL	36	9	28	37	64	...	...	...	3	0	0	0	2
97-98—Las Vegas	IHL	70	15	44	59	148	...	...	...	—	—	—	—	—
—Saint John	AHL	9	0	4	4	12	...	...	...	19	2	11	13	30
98-99—Saint John	AHL	8	1	4	5	22	...	...	...	—	—	—	—	—
—Providence	AHL	62	7	34	41	78	...	...	...	15	0	6	6	28
99-00—Cincinnati	IHL	39	6	14	20	37	...	...	...	—	—	—	—	—
—Houston	IHL	37	2	18	20	47	...	...	...	10	2	6	8	40
00-01—Kentucky	AHL	80	23	50	73	162	...	...	...	3	0	2	2	8
01-02—Cleveland	AHL	72	6	38	44	226	...	...	...	—	—	—	—	—
—San Jose	NHL	5	0	1	1	2	-2	0	0	—	—	—	—	—
02-03—Worcester	AHL	21	4	6	10	32	...	...	...	—	—	—	—	—
—Binghamton	AHL	29	1	11	12	40	...	...	...	—	—	—	—	—
NHL Totals (2 years)		6	0	1	1	2	-2	0	0	—	—	—	—	—

BANHAM, FRANK   RW   COYOTES

PERSONAL: Born April 14, 1975, in Calahoo, Alta. ... 6-0/210. ... Shoots right.
TRANSACTIONS/CAREER NOTES: Selected by Washington Capitals in sixth round (fourth Capitals pick, 147th overall) of NHL entry draft (June 26, 1993). ... Signed as free agent by Mighty Ducks of Anaheim (January 22, 1996). ... Signed as free agent by Phoenix Coyotes (November 7, 2002).

Season Team	League	Gms.	G	A	Pts.	PIM	+/-	PP	SH	Gms.	G	A	Pts.	PIM
		REGULAR SEASON								**PLAYOFFS**				
92-93—Saskatoon	WHL	71	29	33	62	55	...	...	...	9	2	7	9	8
93-94—Saskatoon	WHL	65	28	39	67	99	...	...	...	16	8	11	19	36
94-95—Saskatoon	WHL	70	50	39	89	63	...	...	...	8	2	6	8	12
95-96—Saskatoon	WHL	72	*83	69	152	116	...	...	...	4	6	0	6	2
—Baltimore	AHL	9	1	4	5	0	...	...	...	7	1	1	2	2
96-97—Baltimore	AHL	21	11	13	24	4	...	...	...	—	—	—	—	—
—Anaheim	NHL	3	0	0	0	0	-2	0	0	—	—	—	—	—
97-98—Cincinnati	AHL	35	7	8	15	39	...	...	...	—	—	—	—	—
—Anaheim	NHL	21	9	2	11	12	-6	1	0	—	—	—	—	—
98-99—Cincinnati	AHL	66	22	27	49	20	...	...	...	3	0	1	1	0
99-00—Cincinnati	AHL	72	19	22	41	58	...	...	...	—	—	—	—	—
—Anaheim	NHL	3	0	0	0	2	0	0	0	—	—	—	—	—
00-01—Blues Espoo	Finland	56	24	27	51	70	...	...	...	—	—	—	—	—
01-02—Jokerit Helsinki	Finland	52	22	16	38	38	...	...	...	12	8	1	9	22
02-03—Springfield	AHL	62	23	17	40	36	...	...	...	—	—	—	—	—
—Phoenix	NHL	5	0	0	0	2	-1	0	0	—	—	—	—	—
NHL Totals (4 years)		32	9	2	11	16	-9	1	0	—	—	—	—	—

BARNABY, MATTHEW   LW   RANGERS

PERSONAL: Born May 4, 1973, in Ottawa ... 6-1/195. ... Shoots left.
TRANSACTIONS/CAREER NOTES: Selected by Buffalo Sabres in fourth round (fifth Sabres pick, 83rd overall) of NHL entry draft (June 20, 1992). ... Suffered back spasms (March 28, 1995); missed one game. ... Suspended one game by NHL for accumulating three game misconduct penalties (March 31, 1996). ... Injured groin (April 3, 1996); missed five games. ... Sprained knee ligament (April 2, 1997); missed final six games of regular season and four playoff games. ... Injured sternum (October 10, 1997); missed five games. ... Strained shoulder (February 2, 1998); missed one game. ... Suspended four games and fined $1,000 by NHL for striking another player in the head (November 5, 1998). ... Suffered back spasms (December 12, 1998); missed one game. ... Injured ankle (December 18, 1998); missed one game. ... Suffered from flu (January 11, 1999); missed one game. ... Traded by Sabres to Pittsburgh Penguins for C Stu Barnes (March 11, 1999). ... Strained knee (November 2, 1999); missed five games. ... Suffered concussion (December 15, 1999); missed seven games. ... Suffered concussion (January 13, 2000); missed one game. ... Suspended five games by NHL for fighting incident (February 13, 2000). ... Traded by Penguins to Tampa Bay Lightning for C Wayne Primeau (February 1, 2001). ... Injured elbow (October 14, 2001); missed one game. ... Traded by Lightning to New York Rangers for LW Zdeno Ciger (December 12, 2001).

Season Team	League	Gms.	G	A	Pts.	PIM	+/-	PP	SH	Gms.	G	A	Pts.	PIM
		REGULAR SEASON								**PLAYOFFS**				
90-91—Beauport	QMJHL	52	9	5	14	262	...	...	...	—	—	—	—	—
91-92—Beauport	QMJHL	63	29	37	66	*476	...	...	...	—	—	—	—	—
92-93—Victoriaville	QMJHL	65	44	67	111	*448	...	...	...	6	2	4	6	44
—Buffalo	NHL	2	1	0	1	10	0	1	0	1	0	1	1	4
93-94—Buffalo	NHL	35	2	4	6	106	-7	1	0	3	0	0	0	17
—Rochester	AHL	42	10	32	42	153	...	...	...	—	—	—	—	—
94-95—Rochester	AHL	56	21	29	50	274	...	...	...	—	—	—	—	—
—Buffalo	NHL	23	1	1	2	116	-2	0	0	—	—	—	—	—
95-96—Buffalo	NHL	73	15	16	31	*335	-2	0	0	—	—	—	—	—

Season Team	League	REGULAR SEASON								PLAYOFFS				
		Gms.	G	A	Pts.	PIM	+/-	PP	SH	Gms.	G	A	Pts.	PIM
96-97—Buffalo	NHL	68	19	24	43	249	16	2	0	8	0	4	4	36
97-98—Buffalo	NHL	72	5	20	25	289	8	0	0	15	7	6	13	22
98-99—Buffalo	NHL	44	4	14	18	143	-2	0	0	—	—	—	—	—
—Pittsburgh	NHL	18	2	2	4	34	-10	1	0	13	0	0	0	35
99-00—Pittsburgh	NHL	64	12	12	24	197	3	0	0	11	0	2	2	29
00-01—Pittsburgh	NHL	47	1	4	5	168	-7	0	0	—	—	—	—	—
—Tampa Bay	NHL	29	4	4	8	97	-3	1	0	—	—	—	—	—
01-02—Tampa Bay	NHL	29	0	0	0	70	-7	0	0	—	—	—	—	—
—New York Rangers	NHL	48	8	13	21	144	-3	0	0	—	—	—	—	—
02-03—New York Rangers	NHL	79	14	22	36	142	9	1	0	—	—	—	—	—
NHL Totals (11 years)		631	88	136	224	2100	-7	7	0	51	7	13	20	143

B BARNES, RYAN LW RED WINGS

PERSONAL: Born January 30, 1980, in Dunnville, Ont. ... 6-1/201. ... Shoots left.
TRANSACTIONS/CAREER NOTES: Selected by Detroit Red Wings in second round (second Red Wings pick, 55th overall) of NHL entry draft (June 27, 1998).

Season Team	League	REGULAR SEASON								PLAYOFFS				
		Gms.	G	A	Pts.	PIM	+/-	PP	SH	Gms.	G	A	Pts.	PIM
96-97—Quinte	Tier II Jr. A	46	15	19	34	245	...	...	...	—	—	—	—	—
97-98—Sudbury	OHL	46	13	18	31	111	...	...	...	10	0	2	2	24
98-99—Sudbury	OHL	8	2	0	2	23	...	...	...	—	—	—	—	—
—Toronto St. Michael's..	OHL	31	11	14	25	215	...	...	...	—	—	—	—	—
—Barrie	OHL	24	16	14	30	161	...	...	...	12	2	4	6	40
99-00—Barrie	OHL	31	17	12	29	98	...	...	...	25	7	7	14	49
00-01—Cincinnati	AHL	1	0	0	0	7	...	...	...	—	—	—	—	—
—Toledo	ECHL	16	2	4	6	31	...	...	...	—	—	—	—	—
01-02—Cincinnati	AHL	46	2	3	5	152	...	...	...	—	—	—	—	—
—Toledo	ECHL	1	1	0	1	0	...	...	...	—	—	—	—	—
02-03—Grand Rapids	AHL	73	5	6	11	151	...	...	...	—	—	—	—	—

BARNES, STU C STARS

PERSONAL: Born December 25, 1970, in Spruce Grove, Alta. ... 5-11/180. ... Shoots right. ... Full Name: Stu D. Barnes.
TRANSACTIONS/CAREER NOTES: Selected by Winnipeg Jets in first round (first Jets pick, fourth overall) of NHL entry draft (June 17, 1989). ... Traded by Jets to Florida Panthers for C Randy Gilhen (November 26, 1993). ... Strained left calf (January 1, 1994); missed one game. ... Suffered lacerations and bruises in and around left eye (February 15, 1995); missed seven games. ... Sprained left knee (March 10, 1996); missed 10 games. ... Traded by Panthers with D Jason Woolley to Pittsburgh Penguins for C Chris Wells (November 19, 1996). ... Injured hip (April 11, 1997); missed one game. ... Suffered back spasms (October 9, 1997); missed one game. ... Strained hip flexor (April 16, 1998); missed one game. ... Traded by Penguins to Buffalo Sabres for RW Matthew Barnaby (March 11, 1999). ... Injured groin (November 3, 2000); missed seven games. ... Suffered concussion (March 17, 2002); missed remainder of season. ... Traded by Sabres to Dallas Stars for C Mike Ryan and second-round pick in 2003 draft (March 10, 2003).
STATISTICAL PLATEAUS: Three-goal games: 1991-92 (1), 1997-98 (1), 1998-99 (1). Total: 3.

Season Team	League	REGULAR SEASON								PLAYOFFS				
		Gms.	G	A	Pts.	PIM	+/-	PP	SH	Gms.	G	A	Pts.	PIM
86-87—St. Albert	AJHL	57	43	32	75	80	...	...	...	—	—	—	—	—
87-88—New Westminster	WHL	71	37	64	101	88	...	...	...	5	2	3	5	6
88-89—Tri-City	WHL	70	59	82	141	117	...	...	...	7	6	5	11	10
89-90—Tri-City	WHL	63	52	92	144	165	...	...	...	7	1	5	6	26
90-91—Canadian nat'l team	Int'l	53	22	27	49	68	...	...	...	—	—	—	—	—
91-92—Winnipeg	NHL	46	8	9	17	26	-2	4	0	—	—	—	—	—
—Moncton	AHL	30	13	19	32	10	...	...	...	11	3	9	12	6
92-93—Moncton	AHL	42	23	31	54	58	...	...	...	—	—	—	—	—
—Winnipeg	NHL	38	12	10	22	10	-3	3	0	6	1	3	4	2
93-94—Winnipeg	NHL	18	5	4	9	8	-1	2	0	—	—	—	—	—
—Florida	NHL	59	18	20	38	30	5	6	1	—	—	—	—	—
94-95—Florida	NHL	41	10	19	29	8	7	1	0	—	—	—	—	—
95-96—Florida	NHL	72	19	25	44	46	-12	8	0	22	6	10	16	4
96-97—Florida	NHL	19	2	8	10	10	-3	1	0	—	—	—	—	—
—Pittsburgh	NHL	62	17	22	39	16	-20	4	0	5	0	1	1	0
97-98—Pittsburgh	NHL	78	30	35	65	30	15	15	1	6	3	3	6	2
98-99—Pittsburgh	NHL	64	20	12	32	20	-12	13	0	—	—	—	—	—
—Buffalo	NHL	17	0	4	4	10	1	0	0	21	7	3	10	6
99-00—Buffalo	NHL	82	20	25	45	16	-3	8	2	5	3	0	3	2
00-01—Buffalo	NHL	75	19	24	43	26	-2	3	2	13	4	4	8	2
01-02—Buffalo	NHL	68	17	31	48	26	6	5	0	—	—	—	—	—
02-03—Buffalo	NHL	68	11	21	32	20	-13	2	1	—	—	—	—	—
—Dallas	NHL	13	2	5	7	8	2	2	0	12	2	3	5	0
NHL Totals (12 years)		820	210	274	484	310	-35	77	7	90	26	27	53	18

BARNEY, SCOTT C KINGS

PERSONAL: Born March 27, 1979, in Oshawa, Ont. ... 6-4/198. ... Shoots right.
TRANSACTIONS/CAREER NOTES: Selected by Los Angeles Kings in second round (third Kings pick, 29th overall) of NHL entry draft (June 21, 1997).

		REGULAR SEASON								PLAYOFFS				
Season Team	League	Gms.	G	A	Pts.	PIM	+/-	PP	SH	Gms.	G	A	Pts.	PIM
94-95—North York	MTHL	41	16	19	35	88	...	...	...	—	—	—	—	—
95-96—Peterborough	OHL	60	22	24	46	52	...	...	...	24	6	8	14	38
96-97—Peterborough	OHL	64	21	33	54	110	...	...	...	9	0	3	3	16
97-98—Peterborough	OHL	62	44	32	76	60	...	...	...	4	1	0	1	6
98-99—Peterborough	OHL	44	41	26	67	80	...	...	...	5	4	1	5	4
—Springfield	AHL	5	0	0	0	2	...	...	...	1	0	0	0	2
99-00—					Did not play.									
00-01—					Did not play.									
01-02—					Did not play.									
02-03—Manchester	AHL	57	13	5	18	74	...	...	...	—	—	—	—	—
—Los Angeles	NHL	5	0	0	0	0	-1	0	0	—	—	—	—	—
NHL Totals (1 year)		5	0	0	0	0	-1	0	0					

BARON, MURRAY   D   B

PERSONAL: Born June 1, 1967, in Prince George, B.C. ... 6-3/235. ... Shoots left. ... Full Name: Murray D. Baron.

TRANSACTIONS/CAREER NOTES: Selected by Philadelphia Flyers in eighth round (seventh Flyers pick, 167th overall) of NHL entry draft (June 21, 1986). ... Separated left shoulder (October 5, 1989). ... Underwent surgery to have bone spur removed from foot (April 1990). ... Traded by Flyers with C Ron Sutter to St. Louis Blues for C Rod Brind'Amour and C Dan Quinn (September 22, 1991). ... Injured shoulder (December 3, 1991); missed seven games. ... Fractured foot (March 22, 1993); missed remainder of regular season. ... Injured groin (December 1, 1993); missed three games. ... Injured groin (December 11, 1993); missed three games. ... Injured knee (March 7, 1994); missed one game. ... Injured knee (April 18, 1995); missed last nine games of regular season. ... Traded by Blues with LW Shayne Corson and fifth-round pick (D Gennady Razin) in 1997 draft to Montreal Canadiens for C Pierre Turgeon, C Craig Conroy and D Rory Fitzpatrick (October 29, 1996). ... Bruised eye (November 21, 1996); missed one game. ... Traded by Canadiens with RW Chris Murray to Phoenix Coyotes for D Dave Manson (March 18, 1997). ... Fractured foot (April 6, 1997); missed remainder of regular season. ... Tore triceps muscle (November 17, 1997); missed 37 games. ... Signed as free agent by Vancouver Canucks (July 14, 1998). ... Fractured ankle (October 4, 2001); missed first 11 games of season. ... Suffered from the flu (November 23, 2001); missed one game. ... Suffered facial laceration (December 6, 2001); missed one game. ... Injured knee (December 22, 2001); missed three games. ... Injured hand (January 28, 2002); missed five games.

		REGULAR SEASON								PLAYOFFS				
Season Team	League	Gms.	G	A	Pts.	PIM	+/-	PP	SH	Gms.	G	A	Pts.	PIM
84-85—Vernon	BCJHL	37	5	9	14	93	...	...	...	—	—	—	—	—
85-86—Vernon	BCJHL	49	15	32	47	176	...	...	...	7	1	2	3	13
86-87—Univ. of North Dakota .	WCHA	41	4	10	14	62	...	...	...	—	—	—	—	—
87-88—Univ. of North Dakota .	WCHA	41	1	10	11	95	...	...	...	—	—	—	—	—
88-89—Univ. of North Dakota .	WCHA	40	2	6	8	92	...	...	...	—	—	—	—	—
—Hershey	AHL	9	0	3	3	8	...	...	...	—	—	—	—	—
89-90—Hershey	AHL	50	0	10	10	101	...	...	...	—	—	—	—	—
—Philadelphia	NHL	16	2	2	4	12	-1	0	0	—	—	—	—	—
90-91—Hershey	AHL	6	2	3	5	0	...	...	...	—	—	—	—	—
—Philadelphia	NHL	67	8	8	16	74	-3	3	0	—	—	—	—	—
91-92—St. Louis	NHL	67	3	8	11	94	-3	0	0	2	0	0	0	2
92-93—St. Louis	NHL	53	2	2	4	59	-5	0	0	11	0	0	0	12
93-94—St. Louis	NHL	77	5	9	14	123	-14	0	0	4	0	0	0	10
94-95—St. Louis	NHL	39	0	5	5	93	9	0	0	7	1	1	2	2
95-96—St. Louis	NHL	82	2	9	11	190	3	0	0	13	1	0	1	20
96-97—St. Louis	NHL	11	0	2	2	11	-4	0	0	—	—	—	—	—
—Montreal	NHL	60	1	5	6	107	-16	0	0	—	—	—	—	—
—Phoenix	NHL	8	0	0	0	4	0	0	0	1	0	0	0	0
97-98—Phoenix	NHL	45	1	5	6	106	-10	0	0	6	0	2	2	6
98-99—Vancouver	NHL	81	2	6	8	115	-23	0	0	—	—	—	—	—
99-00—Vancouver	NHL	81	2	10	12	67	8	0	0	—	—	—	—	—
00-01—Vancouver	NHL	82	3	8	11	63	-13	0	0	4	0	0	0	0
01-02—Vancouver	NHL	61	1	6	7	68	8	0	0	6	0	1	1	10
02-03—Vancouver	NHL	78	2	4	6	62	13	0	0	14	0	4	4	10
NHL Totals (14 years)		908	34	89	123	1248	-51	3	0	68	2	8	10	72

BARRASSO, TOM   G

PERSONAL: Born March 31, 1965, in Boston ... 6-3/210. ... Catches right. ... Full Name: Thomas Barrasso. ... Name pronounced buh-RAH-soh.

TRANSACTIONS/CAREER NOTES: Selected by Buffalo Sabres in first round (first Sabres pick, fifth overall) of NHL entry draft (June 8, 1983). ... Suffered chip fracture of ankle (November 1987). ... Pulled groin (April 9, 1988). ... Traded by Sabres with third-round pick in 1990 draft (RW Joe Dziedzic) to Pittsburgh Penguins for D Doug Bodger and LW Darrin Shannon (November 12, 1988). ... Pulled groin muscle (January 17, 1989). ... Injured shoulder (March 1989). ... Underwent surgery to right wrist (October 30, 1989); missed 21 games. ... Pulled groin (February 1990). ... Granted leave of absence to be with daughter as she underwent cancer treatment in Los Angeles (February 9, 1990). ... Rejoined the Penguins (March 19, 1990). ... Bruised right hand (October 29, 1991); missed two games. ... Bruised right ankle (December 26, 1991); missed three games. ... Suffered back spasms (March 1992); missed three games. ... Suffered from chicken pox (January 14, 1993); missed nine games. ... Strained groin (October 7, 1993); missed four games. ... Injured hip (November 18, 1993); missed 12 games. ... Underwent surgery on right wrist (January 20, 1995); missed first 43 games of season. ... Suffered sore wrist (May 3, 1995); missed one game. ... Pulled groin (December 7, 1995); missed eight games. ... Pulled groin and injured shoulder (February 6, 1996); missed four games. ... Suffered recurring shoulder problem (October 25, 1996); missed remainder of season. ... Strained leg muscle (November 5, 1997); missed one game. ... Strained quadriceps (December 29, 1997); missed five games. ... Hyperextended elbow (March 5, 1998); missed three games. ... Suffered from the flu (March 26, 1998); missed three games. ... Bruised knee (April 7, 1998); missed one game. ... Bruised finger (April 16, 1998); missed one game. ... Strained groin (October 17, 1998); missed six games. ... Strained hip (December 21, 1998); missed two games. ... Strained neck (January 26, 1999); missed three games. ... Strained hip flexor (February 11, 1999); missed two games. ... Fractured hand (March 3, 1999); missed 18 games. ... Sprained knee (October 7, 1999); missed 16 games. ... Suspended four games by NHL for slashing incident (December 6, 1999). ... Injured back (December 18, 1999); missed 12 games. ... Traded by Penguins to Ottawa Senators for G Ron Tugnutt and D Janne Laukkanen (March 14, 2000). ... Bruised finger (April 4, 2000); missed final three games of season. ... Signed as free agent by Carolina Hurricanes (July 17, 2001). ... Traded by Hurricanes to Toronto Maple Leafs for fourth-round pick in 2003 draft (March 15, 2002). ... Strained hamstring (March 30, 2002); missed four games. ... Signed as free agent by St. Louis Blues (November 4, 2002). ... Released by Blues (December 28, 2002). ... Announced retirement (June 18, 2003).

Season Team	League	REGULAR SEASON									PLAYOFFS							
		Gms.	Min	W	L	T	GA	SO	Avg.	SV%	Gms.	Min.	W	L	GA	SO	Avg.	SV%
81-82—Acton-Boxborough HS..	Mass. H.S.	23	1035	...	...	...	32	7	1.86	—	—	—	—	—	—	—	—	—
82-83—Acton-Boxborough HS..	Mass. H.S.	23	1035	...	...	...	17	10	.99	—	—	—	—	—	—	—	—	—
83-84—Buffalo	NHL	42	2475	26	12	3	117	2	2.84	.893	3	139	0	2	8	0	3.45	.864
84-85—Rochester	AHL	5	267	3	1	1	6	1	1.35	—	—	—	—	—	—	—	—	—
—Buffalo	NHL	54	3248	25	18	10	144	*5	*2.66	.887	5	300	2	3	22	0	4.40	.854
85-86—Buffalo	NHL	60	*3561	29	24	5	214	2	3.61	.880	—	—	—	—	—	—	—	—
86-87—Buffalo	NHL	46	2501	17	23	2	152	2	3.65	.874	—	—	—	—	—	—	—	—
87-88—Buffalo	NHL	54	3133	25	18	8	173	2	3.31	.896	4	224	1	3	16	0	4.29	.867
88-89—Buffalo	NHL	10	545	2	7	0	45	0	4.95	.842	—	—	—	—	—	—	—	—
—Pittsburgh	NHL	44	2406	18	15	7	162	0	4.04	.888	11	631	7	4	40	0	3.80	.897
89-90—Pittsburgh	NHL	24	1294	7	12	3	101	0	4.68	.865	—	—	—	—	—	—	—	—
90-91—Pittsburgh	NHL	48	2754	27	16	3	165	1	3.59	.896	20	1175	12	7	51	†1	*2.60	.919
91-92—Pittsburgh	NHL	57	3329	25	22	9	196	1	3.53	.885	*21	*1233	*16	5	*58	1	2.82	.907
92-93—Pittsburgh	NHL	63	3702	*43	14	5	186	4	3.01	.901	12	722	7	5	35	2	2.91	.905
93-94—Pittsburgh	NHL	44	2482	22	15	5	139	2	3.36	.893	6	356	2	4	17	0	2.87	.895
94-95—Pittsburgh	NHL	2	125	0	1	1	8	0	3.84	.893	2	80	0	1	8	0	6.00	.805
95-96—Pittsburgh	NHL	49	2799	29	16	2	160	2	3.43	.902	10	558	4	5	26	1	2.80	.923
96-97—Pittsburgh	NHL	5	270	0	5	0	26	0	5.78	.860	—	—	—	—	—	—	—	—
97-98—Pittsburgh	NHL	63	3542	31	14	13	122	7	2.07	.922	6	376	2	4	17	0	2.71	.901
98-99—Pittsburgh	NHL	43	2306	19	16	3	98	4	2.55	.901	13	787	6	7	35	1	2.67	.900
99-00—Pittsburgh	NHL	18	870	5	7	2	46	1	3.17	.881	—	—	—	—	—	—	—	—
—Ottawa	NHL	7	418	3	4	0	22	0	3.16	.879	6	372	2	4	16	0	2.58	.905
00-01 —									Did not play.									
01-02—Carolina	NHL	34	1908	13	12	5	83	2	2.61	.906	—	—	—	—	—	—	—	—
—U.S. Olympic team	Int'l	1	60	1	0	0	1	0	1.00	—	—	—	—	—	—	—	—	—
—Toronto	NHL	4	219	2	2	0	10	0	2.74	.909	—	—	—	—	—	—	—	—
02-03—St. Louis	NHL	6	293	1	4	0	16	1	3.28	.879	—	—	—	—	—	—	—	—
NHL Totals (20 years)		777	44180	369	277	86	2385	38	3.24	.892	119	6953	61	54	349	6	3.01	.902

BARTECKO, LUBOS   RW

PERSONAL: Born July 14, 1976, in Kezmarok, Czechoslovakia ... 6-0/210. ... Shoots left.
TRANSACTIONS/CAREER NOTES: Signed as non-drafted free agent by St. Louis Blues (October 3, 1997). ... Sprained ankle (December 2, 2000); missed 17 games. ... Reinjured ankle (January 15, 2001); missed nine games. ... Traded by Blues to Atlanta Thrashers for fourth-round pick (C Igor Valeev) in 2001 draft (June 24, 2001). ... Suffered concussion (September 24, 2001); missed first two games of season. ... Sprained medical collateral ligament in knee (November 7, 2001); missed one game. ... Bruised heel (March 4, 2002); missed two games.

Season Team	League	REGULAR SEASON							PLAYOFFS				
		Gms.	G	A	Pts.	PIM	+/-	PP	SH	Gms.	G	A	Pts.	PIM
95-96—Chicoutimi	QMJHL	70	32	41	73	50	...	...	...	17	8	15	23	10
96-97—Drummondville	QMJHL	58	40	51	91	49	...	...	...	8	1	8	9	4
97-98—Worcester	AHL	34	10	12	22	24	...	...	...	10	4	2	6	2
98-99—Poprad	Slovakia	1	1	0	1	0	...	...	...	—	—	—	—	—
—St. Louis	NHL	32	5	11	16	6	4	0	0	5	0	0	0	2
—Worcester	AHL	49	14	24	38	22	...	...	...	—	—	—	—	—
99-00—Worcester	AHL	12	4	7	11	4	...	...	...	—	—	—	—	—
—St. Louis	NHL	67	16	23	39	51	25	3	0	7	1	1	2	0
00-01—St. Louis	NHL	50	5	8	13	12	-1	0	0	—	—	—	—	—
01-02—Atlanta	NHL	71	13	14	27	30	-15	1	0	—	—	—	—	—
—Slovakian Oly. team	Int'l	4	0	1	1	0	...	...	...	—	—	—	—	—
02-03—Atlanta	NHL	37	7	9	16	8	3	0	0	—	—	—	—	—
NHL Totals (5 years)		257	46	65	111	107	16	4	0	12	1	1	2	2

BARTOVIC, MILAN   RW   SABRES

PERSONAL: Born August 9, 1981, in Trencin, Czechoslovakia ... 5-11/194. ... Shoots left.
TRANSACTIONS/CAREER NOTES: Selected by Buffalo Sabres in second round (second Sabres pick, 35th overall) of NHL entry draft (June 26, 1999).

Season Team	League	REGULAR SEASON							PLAYOFFS				
		Gms.	G	A	Pts.	PIM	+/-	PP	SH	Gms.	G	A	Pts.	PIM
97-98—Dukla Trencin	Slovakia Jrs.	26	2	6	8	15	...	...	...	—	—	—	—	—
98-99—Dukla Trencin	Slovakia Jrs.	46	36	35	71	62	...	...	...	6	9	3	12	10
99-00—Tri-City	WHL	18	8	9	17	12	...	...	...	—	—	—	—	—
—Brandon	WHL	38	18	22	40	28	...	...	...	—	—	—	—	—
00-01—Brandon	WHL	34	15	25	40	40	...	...	...	6	1	2	3	8
—Rochester	AHL	2	1	1	2	0	...	...	...	4	0	1	1	2
01-02—Rochester	AHL	73	15	11	26	56	...	...	...	2	0	0	0	0
02-03—Rochester	AHL	74	18	10	28	84	...	...	...	—	—	—	—	—
—Buffalo	NHL	3	1	0	1	0	0	0	0	—	—	—	—	—
NHL Totals (1 year)		3	1	0	1	0	0	0	0	—	—	—	—	—

BATEMAN, JEFF   C   STARS

PERSONAL: Born August 29, 1981, in Belleville, Ont. ... 5-11/165. ... Shoots left.
TRANSACTIONS/CAREER NOTES: Selected by Dallas Stars in fourth round (fourth Stars pick, 126th overall) of NHL entry draft (June 26, 1999).

Season Team	League	Gms.	G	A	Pts.	PIM	+/-	PP	SH	Gms.	G	A	Pts.	PIM
					REGULAR SEASON							PLAYOFFS		
98-99—Brampton..................	OHL	68	23	35	58	27	...	...	...	—	—	—	—	—
99-00—Brampton..................	OHL	64	23	41	64	62	...	...	...	6	2	1	3	4
00-01—Brampton..................	OHL	53	15	44	59	81	...	...	...	9	5	7	12	18
01-02—Utah........................	AHL	35	1	6	7	26	...	...	...	4	0	2	2	2
02-03—Utah........................	AHL	60	8	8	16	60	...	...	...	—	—	—	—	—
—Lexington...................	ECHL	2	1	1	2	8	...	...	...	—	—	—	—	—

BATES, SHAWN   C   ISLANDERS

PERSONAL: Born April 3, 1975, in Melrose, Mass. ... 6-0/208. ... Shoots right.
TRANSACTIONS/CAREER NOTES: Selected by Boston Bruins in fourth round (fourth Bruins pick, 103rd overall) of NHL entry draft (June 26, 1993). ... Involved in car accident (November 8, 1997); missed one game. ... Suffered from the flu (December 1, 1998); missed one game. ... Injured hamstring (April 15, 1999); missed two games. ... Injured shoulder (October 30, 1999); missed four games. ... Sprained wrist (December 9, 1999); missed 25 games. ... Sprained wrist (March 25, 2000); missed seven games. ... Strained groin (December 16, 2000); missed three games. ... Reinjured groin (January 10, 2001); missed 16 games. ... Signed as free agent by New York Islanders (July 8, 2001). ... Injured groin (November 23, 2001); missed 10 games. ... Strained groin (March 28, 2002); missed one game.

Season Team	League	Gms.	G	A	Pts.	PIM	+/-	PP	SH	Gms.	G	A	Pts.	PIM
					REGULAR SEASON							PLAYOFFS		
90-91—Medford H.S.	Mass. H.S.	22	18	43	61	6	...	...	...	—	—	—	—	—
91-92—Medford H.S.	Mass. H.S.	22	38	41	79	10	...	...	...	—	—	—	—	—
92-93—Medford H.S.	Mass. H.S.	25	49	46	95	20	...	...	...	—	—	—	—	—
93-94—Boston University	Hockey East	41	10	19	29	24	...	...	...	—	—	—	—	—
94-95—Boston University	Hockey East	38	18	12	30	48	...	...	...	—	—	—	—	—
95-96—Boston University	Hockey East	40	28	22	50	54	...	...	...	—	—	—	—	—
96-97—Boston University	Hockey East	41	17	18	35	64	...	...	...	—	—	—	—	—
97-98—Boston	NHL	13	2	0	2	2	-3	0	0	—	—	—	—	—
—Providence................	AHL	50	15	19	34	22	...	...	...	—	—	—	—	—
98-99—Providence................	AHL	37	25	21	46	39	...	...	...	—	—	—	—	—
—Boston	NHL	33	5	4	9	2	-3	0	0	12	0	0	0	4
99-00—Boston	NHL	44	5	7	12	14	-17	0	0	—	—	—	—	—
00-01—Boston	NHL	45	2	3	5	26	-12	0	0	—	—	—	—	—
—Providence................	AHL	11	5	8	13	12	...	...	...	8	2	6	8	8
01-02—New York Islanders.....	NHL	71	17	35	52	30	18	1	4	7	2	4	6	11
02-03—New York Islanders.....	NHL	74	13	29	42	52	-9	1	*6	5	1	0	1	0
NHL Totals (6 years)...........		**280**	**44**	**78**	**122**	**126**	**-20**	**2**	**10**	**24**	**3**	**4**	**7**	**15**

BATTAGLIA, BATES   LW   AVALANCHE

PERSONAL: Born December 13, 1975, in Chicago ... 6-2/205. ... Shoots left. ... Full Name: Jon Battaglia. ... Name pronounced buh-TAG-lee-uh.
TRANSACTIONS/CAREER NOTES: Selected by Mighty Ducks of Anaheim in sixth round (sixth Mighty Ducks pick, 132nd overall) of NHL entry draft (June 29, 1994). ... Traded by Mighty Ducks with fourth-round pick (C Josef Vasicek) in 1998 draft to Hartford Whalers for C Mark Janssens (March 18, 1997). ... Whalers franchise moved to North Carolina and renamed Carolina Hurricanes for 1997-98 season; NHL approved move on June 25, 1977. ... Injured shoulder (January 20, 2000); missed three games. ... Traded by Hurricanes to Colorado Avalanche for RW Radim Vrbata (March 11, 2003). ... Signed by Avalanche (July 15, 2003).
STATISTICAL PLATEAUS: Three-goal games: 1999-00 (1).

Season Team	League	Gms.	G	A	Pts.	PIM	+/-	PP	SH	Gms.	G	A	Pts.	PIM
					REGULAR SEASON							PLAYOFFS		
93-94—Caledon......................	Jr. A	44	15	33	48	104	...	...	...	—	—	—	—	—
94-95—Lake Superior State	CCHA	38	6	15	21	34	...	...	...	—	—	—	—	—
95-96—Lake Superior State	CCHA	40	13	22	35	48	...	...	...	—	—	—	—	—
96-97—Lake Superior State	CCHA	38	12	27	39	80	...	...	...	—	—	—	—	—
97-98—New Haven	AHL	48	15	21	36	48	...	...	...	1	0	0	0	0
—Carolina	NHL	33	2	4	6	10	-1	0	0	—	—	—	—	—
98-99—Carolina	NHL	60	7	11	18	22	7	0	0	6	0	3	3	8
99-00—Carolina	NHL	77	16	18	34	39	20	3	0	—	—	—	—	—
00-01—Carolina	NHL	80	12	15	27	76	-14	2	0	6	0	2	2	2
01-02—Carolina	NHL	82	21	25	46	44	-6	5	1	23	5	9	14	14
02-03—Carolina	NHL	70	5	14	19	90	-17	0	1	—	—	—	—	—
—Colorado	NHL	13	1	5	6	10	-2	1	0	7	0	2	2	4
NHL Totals (6 years)...........		**415**	**64**	**92**	**156**	**291**	**-13**	**11**	**2**	**42**	**5**	**16**	**21**	**28**

BAUMGARTNER, NOLAN   D   CANUCKS

PERSONAL: Born March 23, 1976, in Calgary ... 6-2/205. ... Shoots right.
TRANSACTIONS/CAREER NOTES: Selected by Washington Capitals in first round (first Capitals pick, 10th overall) of NHL entry draft (June 28, 1994). ... Traded by Capitals to Chicago Blackhawks for D Remi Royer (July 21, 2000). ... Signed as free agent by Vancouver Canucks (July 11, 2002).

B

Season Team	League	REGULAR SEASON								PLAYOFFS				
		Gms.	G	A	Pts.	PIM	+/-	PP	SH	Gms.	G	A	Pts.	PIM
92-93—Kamloops	WHL	43	0	5	5	30	...	...	...	11	1	1	2	0
93-94—Kamloops	WHL	69	13	42	55	109	...	...	...	19	3	14	17	33
94-95—Kamloops	WHL	62	8	36	44	71	...	...	...	21	4	13	17	16
95-96—Washington	NHL	1	0	0	0	0	-1	0	0	1	0	0	0	10
—Kamloops	WHL	28	13	15	28	45	...	...	...	16	1	9	10	26
96-97—Portland	AHL	8	2	2	4	4	...	...	...	—	—	—	—	—
97-98—Portland	AHL	70	2	24	26	70	...	...	...	10	1	4	5	10
—Washington	NHL	4	0	1	1	0	0	0	0	—	—	—	—	—
98-99—Portland	AHL	38	5	14	19	62	...	...	...	—	—	—	—	—
—Washington	NHL	5	0	0	0	0	-3	0	0	—	—	—	—	—
99-00—Portland	AHL	71	5	18	23	56	...	...	...	4	1	2	3	10
—Washington	NHL	8	0	1	1	2	1	0	0	—	—	—	—	—
00-01—Norfolk	AHL	63	5	28	33	75	...	...	...	9	2	3	5	11
—Chicago	NHL	8	0	0	0	6	-4	0	0	—	—	—	—	—
01-02—Norfolk	AHL	76	10	24	34	72	...	...	...	4	0	1	1	2
02-03—Manitoba	AHL	59	8	31	39	82	...	...	...	—	—	—	—	—
—Vancouver	NHL	8	1	2	3	4	4	1	0	2	0	0	0	0
NHL Totals (6 years)		34	1	4	5	12	-3	1	0	3	0	0	0	10

BAYDA, RYAN — LW — HURRICANES

PERSONAL: Born December 9, 1980, in Saskatoon, Sask. ... 5-11/185. ... Shoots left.

TRANSACTIONS/CAREER NOTES: Selected by Carolina Hurricanes in third round (second Hurricanes pick, 80th overall) of NHL entry draft (June 24, 2000).

Season Team	League	REGULAR SEASON								PLAYOFFS				
		Gms.	G	A	Pts.	PIM	+/-	PP	SH	Gms.	G	A	Pts.	PIM
98-99—Vernon	BCJHL	45	24	58	82	15	...	...	...	—	—	—	—	—
99-00—Univ. of North Dakota	WCHA	36	14	14	28	32	...	...	...	—	—	—	—	—
00-01—Univ. of North Dakota	WCHA	46	25	34	59	48	...	...	...	—	—	—	—	—
01-02—Univ. of North Dakota	WCHA	37	19	28	47	52	...	...	...	—	—	—	—	—
—Lowell	AHL	3	1	1	2	0	...	...	...	5	3	0	3	0
02-03—Lowell	AHL	53	11	32	43	32	...	...	...	—	—	—	—	—
—Carolina	NHL	25	4	10	14	16	-5	0	0	—	—	—	—	—
NHL Totals (1 year)		25	4	10	14	16	-5	0	0					

BEAUCHEMIN, FRANCOIS — D — CANADIENS

PERSONAL: Born June 4, 1980, in Sorel, Que. ... 6-0/214. ... Shoots left.

TRANSACTIONS/CAREER NOTES: Selected by Montreal Canadiens in third round (third Canadiens pick, 75th overall) of NHL entry draft (June 27, 1998). ... Re-signed by Canadiens (June 17, 2003).

Season Team	League	REGULAR SEASON								PLAYOFFS				
		Gms.	G	A	Pts.	PIM	+/-	PP	SH	Gms.	G	A	Pts.	PIM
96-97—Laval	QMJHL	66	7	20	27	112	...	...	...	3	0	0	0	2
97-98—Laval	QMJHL	70	12	35	47	132	...	...	...	16	1	3	4	23
98-99—Acadie-Bathurst	QMJHL	31	4	17	21	53	...	...	...	23	2	16	18	55
99-00—Acadie-Bathurst	QMJHL	38	11	36	47	64	...	...	...	—	—	—	—	—
—Moncton	QMJHL	33	8	31	39	35	...	...	...	16	2	11	13	14
00-01—Quebec	AHL	56	3	6	9	44	...	...	...	—	—	—	—	—
01-02—Quebec	AHL	56	8	11	19	88	...	...	...	3	0	1	1	0
—Mississippi	ECHL	7	1	3	4	2	...	...	...	—	—	—	—	—
02-03—Hamilton	AHL	75	7	21	28	92	...	...	...	—	—	—	—	—
—Montreal	NHL	1	0	0	0	0	-1	0	0	—	—	—	—	—
NHL Totals (1 year)		1	0	0	0	0	-1	0	0					

BEAUDOIN, ERIC — LW — PANTHERS

PERSONAL: Born May 3, 1980, in Ottawa ... 6-5/230. ... Shoots left. ... Name pronounced boh-DWEH.

TRANSACTIONS/CAREER NOTES: Selected by Tampa Bay Lightning in fourth round (fourth Lightning pick, 92nd overall) of NHL entry draft (June 27, 1998). ... Traded by Lightning to Florida Panthers for seventh-round pick (D Marek Priechodsky) in 2000 draft (June 2, 2000).

Season Team	League	REGULAR SEASON								PLAYOFFS				
		Gms.	G	A	Pts.	PIM	+/-	PP	SH	Gms.	G	A	Pts.	PIM
96-97—Ottawa	Tier II Jr. A	54	12	19	31	55	...	...	...	—	—	—	—	—
97-98—Guelph	OHL	62	9	13	22	43	...	...	...	12	3	2	5	4
98-99—Guelph	OHL	66	28	43	71	79	...	...	...	11	5	3	8	12
99-00—Guelph	OHL	68	38	34	72	126	...	...	...	6	3	0	3	2
00-01—Louisville	AHL	71	15	10	25	78	...	...	...	—	—	—	—	—
01-02—Utah	AHL	44	5	16	21	83	...	...	...	—	—	—	—	—
—Florida	NHL	8	1	3	4	4	-2	0	0	—	—	—	—	—
02-03—San Antonio	AHL	41	14	23	37	36	...	...	...	—	—	—	—	—
—Florida	NHL	15	0	1	1	25	-7	0	0	—	—	—	—	—
NHL Totals (2 years)		23	1	4	5	29	-9	0	0					

BEDNAR, JAROSLAV　　　　　　　　LW　　　　　　　　PANTHERS

PERSONAL: Born November 9, 1976, in Prague, Czechoslovakia ... 6-0/198. ... Shoots right. ... Name pronounced bed-NASH.
TRANSACTIONS/CAREER NOTES: Selected by Los Angeles Kings in second round (third Kings pick, 51st overall) of NHL entry draft (June 23, 2001). ... Traded by Kings with D Andreas Lilja to Florida Panthers for D Dmitry Yushkevich and fifth-round pick in 2003 draft (November 26, 2002). ... Re-signed by Panthers (July 30, 2003).

				REGULAR SEASON							PLAYOFFS			
Season Team	League	Gms.	G	A	Pts.	PIM	+/-	PP	SH	Gms.	G	A	Pts.	PIM
94-95—Slavia Praha	Czech Rep.	20	6	7	13	4	...	...	...	3	0	0	0	0
95-96—Slavia Praha	Czech Rep.	20	3	1	4	6	...	...	...	3	0	0	0	0
96-97—Slavia Praha	Czech Rep.	45	18	12	30	18	...	...	...	—	—	—	—	—
97-98—Slavia Praha	Czech Rep.	14	2	5	7	6	...	...	...	—	—	—	—	—
—HC Keramika Plzen	Czech Rep.	34	26	15	41	16	...	...	...	5	2	4	6	4
98-99—Sparta Praha	Czech Rep.	52	23	14	37	30	...	...	...	8	5	2	7	0
99-00—JyP Jyvaskyla	Finland	53	34	28	62	56	...	...	...	—	—	—	—	—
00-01—HIFK Helsinki	Finland	56	*32	28	60	51	...	...	...	5	3	1	4	0
01-02—Los Angeles	NHL	22	4	2	6	8	-4	1	0	3	0	0	0	0
—Manchester	AHL	48	16	21	37	16	...	...	...	—	—	—	—	—
02-03—Los Angeles	NHL	15	0	9	9	4	3	0	0	—	—	—	—	—
—Florida	NHL	52	5	13	18	14	-2	2	0	—	—	—	—	—
NHL Totals (2 years)		89	9	24	33	26	-3	3	0	3	0	0	0	0

BEECH, KRIS　　　　　　　　C　　　　　　　　PENGUINS

PERSONAL: Born February 5, 1981, in Salmon Arm, B.C. ... 6-2/199. ... Shoots left.
TRANSACTIONS/CAREER NOTES: Selected by Washington Capitals in first round (first Capitals pick, seventh overall) of NHL entry draft (June 26, 1999). ... Traded by Capitals with C Michal Sivek, D Ross Lupaschuk and future considerations to Pittsburgh Penguins for RW Jaromir Jagr and D Frantisek Kucera (July 11, 2001).

				REGULAR SEASON							PLAYOFFS			
Season Team	League	Gms.	G	A	Pts.	PIM	+/-	PP	SH	Gms.	G	A	Pts.	PIM
96-97—Sicamous	Jr. A	49	34	36	70	80	...	...	...	—	—	—	—	—
—Calgary	WHL	8	1	1	2	0	...	...	...	—	—	—	—	—
97-98—Calgary	WHL	68	26	41	67	103	...	...	...	—	—	—	—	—
98-99—Calgary	WHL	58	10	25	35	24	...	...	...	—	—	—	—	—
99-00—Calgary	WHL	66	32	54	86	99	...	...	...	5	3	5	8	16
00-01—Washington	NHL	4	0	0	0	2	-2	0	0	—	—	—	—	—
—Calgary	WHL	40	22	44	66	103	...	...	...	10	2	8	10	26
01-02—Pittsburgh	NHL	79	10	15	25	45	-25	2	0	—	—	—	—	—
02-03—Wilkes-Barre/Scranton	AHL	50	19	24	43	76	...	...	...	—	—	—	—	—
—Pittsburgh	NHL	12	0	1	1	6	-3	0	0	—	—	—	—	—
NHL Totals (3 years)		95	10	16	26	53	-30	2	0					

BEGIN, STEVE　　　　　　　　C　　　　　　　　SABRES

PERSONAL: Born June 14, 1978, in Trois-Rivieres, Que. ... 5-11/190. ... Shoots left. ... Name pronounced BAY-zhin.
TRANSACTIONS/CAREER NOTES: Selected by Calgary Flames in second round (third Flames pick, 40th overall) of NHL entry draft (June 22, 1996). ... Injured shoulder (October 10, 1997); missed six games. ... Dislocated fibula (March 18, 2000); missed final 10 games of season. ... Injured shoulder (January 17, 2002); missed nine games. ... Injured head (April 2, 2002); missed remainder of season. ... Traded by Flames to Buffalo Sabres with Chris Drury for Rhett Warrener and Steve Reinprecht (July 2, 2003).

				REGULAR SEASON							PLAYOFFS			
Season Team	League	Gms.	G	A	Pts.	PIM	+/-	PP	SH	Gms.	G	A	Pts.	PIM
95-96—Val-d'Or	QMJHL	64	13	23	36	218	...	...	...	13	1	3	4	33
96-97—Val-d'Or	QMJHL	58	13	33	46	207	...	...	...	10	0	3	3	8
—Saint John	AHL	—	—	—	—	—	—	—	—	4	0	2	2	6
97-98—Calgary	NHL	5	0	0	0	23	0	0	0	—	—	—	—	—
—Val-d'Or	QMJHL	35	18	17	35	73	...	...	...	15	2	12	14	34
98-99—Saint John	AHL	73	11	9	20	156	...	...	...	7	2	0	2	18
99-00—Calgary	NHL	13	1	1	2	18	-3	0	0	—	—	—	—	—
—Saint John	AHL	47	13	12	25	99	...	...	...	—	—	—	—	—
00-01—Saint John	AHL	58	14	14	28	109	...	...	...	19	10	7	17	18
—Calgary	NHL	4	0	0	0	21	0	0	0	—	—	—	—	—
01-02—Calgary	NHL	51	7	5	12	79	-3	1	0	—	—	—	—	—
02-03—Calgary	NHL	50	3	1	4	51	-7	0	0	—	—	—	—	—
NHL Totals (5 years)		123	11	7	18	192	-13	1	0					

BEKAR, DEREK　　　　　　　　C

PERSONAL: Born September 15, 1975, in Burnaby, B.C. ... 6-2/200. ... Shoots left.
TRANSACTIONS/CAREER NOTES: Selected by St. Louis Blues in eighth round (seventh Blues pick, 205th overall) of NHL entry draft (July 8, 1995). ... Traded by Blues to Washington Capitals for C Mike Peluso (November 29, 2000). ... Signed as free agent by Los Angeles Kings (September 25, 2001).

			REGULAR SEASON								PLAYOFFS				
Season Team	League	Gms.	G	A	Pts.	PIM	+/-	PP	SH		Gms.	G	A	Pts.	PIM
94-95—Powell River	BCJHL	46	33	29	62	35	...	...	...		—	—	—	—	—
95-96—Univ. of New Hamp.....	Hockey East	34	15	18	33	4	...	...	...		—	—	—	—	—
96-97—Univ. of New Hamp.....	Hockey East	39	18	21	39	34	...	...	...		—	—	—	—	—
97-98—Univ. of New Hamp.....	Hockey East	35	32	28	60	46	...	...	...		—	—	—	—	—
98-99—Worcester	AHL	51	16	20	36	6	...	...	...		4	0	0	0	0
99-00—Worcester	AHL	71	21	19	40	26	...	...	...		7	0	3	3	2
—St. Louis	NHL	1	0	0	0	0	0	0	0		—	—	—	—	—
00-01—Worcester	AHL	18	5	2	7	10	...	...	...		—	—	—	—	—
—Portland	AHL	58	19	16	35	49	...	...	...		3	0	0	0	0
01-02—Manchester	AHL	74	27	20	47	42	...	...	...		5	1	4	5	2
02-03—Manchester	AHL	51	19	19	38	49	...	...	...		—	—	—	—	—
—Los Angeles................	NHL	6	0	0	0	4	-1	0	0		—	—	—	—	—
NHL Totals (2 years)...........		7	0	0	0	4	-1	0	0		—	—	—	—	—

BELAK, WADE   D   MAPLE LEAFS

PERSONAL: Born July 3, 1976, in Saskatoon, Sask. ... 6-5/221. ... Shoots right. ... Brother of Graham Belak, defenseman, Colorado Avalanche organization (1997-98 and 1998-99). ... Name pronounced BEE-lak.

TRANSACTIONS/CAREER NOTES: Selected by Quebec Nordiques in first round (first Nordiques pick, 12th overall) of NHL entry draft (June 28, 1994). ... Nordiques franchise moved to Colorado and renamed Avalanche for 1995-96 season (June 21, 1995). ... Pulled abdominal muscle (March 5, 1998); missed six games. ... Strained groin (October 9, 1998); missed first two games of season. ... Strained groin (October 26, 1998); missed one game. ... Reinjured groin (November 2, 1998); missed 10 games. ... Traded by Avalanche with LW Rene Corbet and future considerations to Calgary Flames for RW Theo Fleury and LW Chris Dingman (February 28, 1999); Flames acquired D Robyn Regehr to complete deal (March 27, 1999). ... Suffered concussion (November 10, 1999); missed one game. ... Injured shoulder (February 10, 2000); missed 18 games. ... Injured groin (March 22, 2000); missed three games. ... Claimed on waivers by Toronto Maple Leafs (February 16, 2001). ... Suffered injury (March 29, 2001); missed final four games of regular season. ... Suffered from the flu (March 2, 2002); missed three games. ... Suspended two games by NHL for elbowing incident (November 27, 2002). ... Re-signed by Maple Leafs (July 16, 2003).

			REGULAR SEASON								PLAYOFFS				
Season Team	League	Gms.	G	A	Pts.	PIM	+/-	PP	SH		Gms.	G	A	Pts.	PIM
91-92—North Battleford	SJHL	57	6	20	26	186	...	...	...		—	—	—	—	—
92-93—North Battleford	SJHL	32	3	13	16	142	...	...	...		—	—	—	—	—
93-94—Saskatoon..................	WHL	69	4	13	17	226	...	...	...		16	2	2	4	43
94-95—Saskatoon..................	WHL	72	4	14	18	290	...	...	...		9	0	0	0	36
—Cornwall	AHL	—	—	—	—	—	—	—	—		11	1	2	3	40
95-96—Saskatoon..................	WHL	63	3	15	18	207	...	...	...		4	0	0	0	9
—Cornwall	AHL	5	0	0	0	18	...	...	...		2	0	0	0	2
96-97—Colorado	NHL	5	0	0	0	11	-1	0	0		—	—	—	—	—
—Hershey	AHL	65	1	7	8	320	...	...	...		16	0	1	1	61
97-98—Colorado	NHL	8	1	1	2	27	-3	0	0		—	—	—	—	—
—Hershey	AHL	11	0	0	0	30	...	...	...		—	—	—	—	—
98-99—Colorado	NHL	22	0	0	0	71	-2	0	0		—	—	—	—	—
—Hershey	AHL	17	0	1	1	49	...	...	...		—	—	—	—	—
—Saint John	AHL	12	0	2	2	43	...	...	...		6	0	1	1	23
—Calgary	NHL	9	0	1	1	23	3	0	0		—	—	—	—	—
99-00—Calgary	NHL	40	0	2	2	122	-4	0	0		—	—	—	—	—
00-01—Calgary	NHL	23	0	0	0	79	-2	0	0		—	—	—	—	—
—Toronto	NHL	16	1	1	2	31	-4	0	0		—	—	—	—	—
01-02—Toronto	NHL	63	1	3	4	142	2	0	0		16	1	0	1	18
02-03—Toronto	NHL	55	3	6	9	196	-2	0	0		2	0	0	0	4
NHL Totals (7 years)...........		241	6	14	20	702	-13	0	0		18	1	0	1	22

BELANGER, ERIC   C   KINGS

PERSONAL: Born December 16, 1977, in Sherbrooke, Que. ... 6-0/185. ... Shoots left. ... Name pronounced buh-LAH-zhay.

TRANSACTIONS/CAREER NOTES: Selected by Los Angeles Kings in fourth round (fifth Kings pick, 96th overall) of NHL entry draft (June 22, 1996). ... Suffered back spasms (February 25, 2001); missed two games. ... Underwent surgery on left wrist (January 15, 2002); missed 29 games.

STATISTICAL PLATEAUS: Three-goal games: 2002-03 (1).

			REGULAR SEASON								PLAYOFFS				
Season Team	League	Gms.	G	A	Pts.	PIM	+/-	PP	SH		Gms.	G	A	Pts.	PIM
94-95—Beauport....................	QMJHL	71	12	28	40	24	...	...	...		—	—	—	—	—
95-96—Beauport....................	QMJHL	59	35	48	83	18	...	...	...		20	13	14	27	6
96-97—Beauport....................	QMJHL	31	13	37	50	30	...	...	...		—	—	—	—	—
—Rimouski	QMJHL	31	26	41	67	36	...	...	...		4	2	3	5	10
97-98—Fredericton	AHL	56	17	34	51	28	...	...	...		4	2	1	3	2
98-99—Springfield	AHL	33	8	18	26	10	...	...	...		3	0	1	1	2
—Long Beach................	IHL	1	0	0	0	0	...	...	...		—	—	—	—	—
99-00—Lowell	AHL	65	15	25	40	20	...	...	...		7	3	3	6	2
00-01—Los Angeles	NHL	62	9	12	21	16	14	1	2		13	1	4	5	2
—Lowell	AHL	13	8	10	18	4	...	...	...		—	—	—	—	—
01-02—Los Angeles	NHL	53	8	16	24	21	2	2	1		7	0	0	0	4
02-03—Los Angeles	NHL	62	16	19	35	26	-5	0	3		—	—	—	—	—
NHL Totals (3 years)...........		177	33	47	80	63	11	3	6		20	1	4	5	6

BELANGER, KEN — LW

PERSONAL: Born May 14, 1974, in Sault Ste. Marie, Ont. ... 6-4/235. ... Shoots left. ... Name pronounced buh-LAH-zhay.

TRANSACTIONS/CAREER NOTES: Selected by Hartford Whalers in seventh round (seventh Whalers pick, 153rd overall) of NHL entry draft (June 20, 1992). ... Traded by Whalers to Toronto Maple Leafs for ninth-round pick (RW Matt Ball) in 1994 draft (March 18, 1994). ... Traded by Maple Leafs with G Damian Rhodes to New York Islanders for C Kirk Muller (January 23, 1996). ... Suffered concussion (February 6, 1996); missed two games. ... Suffered concussion (February 12, 1996); missed remainder of season. ... Suffered concussion (October 13, 1997); missed four games. ... Injured hand (November 15, 1997); missed three games. ... Suffered from the flu (November 26, 1997); missed three games. ... Reinjured hand (January 8, 1998); missed two games. ... Underwent thumb surgery (January 14, 1998); missed 22 games. ... Traded by Islanders to Boston Bruins for LW Ted Donato (November 7, 1998). ... Suffered facial laceration (November 8, 1998); missed two games. ... Suffered concussion (December 28, 1998); missed two games. ... Injured hand (April 3, 1999); missed one game. ... Suffered concussion (November 10, 1999); missed 34 games. ... Suffered groin injury (March 29, 2000); missed final six games of season. ... Strained hip (December 8, 2000); missed three games. ... Reinjured hip (January 10, 2001) and underwent surgery; missed 18 games. ... Signed as free agent by Los Angeles Kings (July 2, 2001). ... Fractured thumb (January 2, 2002); missed 20 games.

Season Team	League	REGULAR SEASON								PLAYOFFS				
		Gms.	G	A	Pts.	PIM	+/-	PP	SH	Gms.	G	A	Pts.	PIM
91-92—Ottawa	OHL	51	4	4	8	174	...	...	...	11	0	0	0	24
92-93—Ottawa	OHL	34	6	12	18	139	...	...	...	—	—	—	—	—
—Guelph	OHL	29	10	14	24	86	...	...	...	5	2	1	3	14
93-94—Guelph	OHL	55	11	22	33	185	...	...	...	9	2	3	5	30
94-95—St. John's	AHL	47	5	5	10	246	...	...	...	4	0	0	0	30
—Toronto	NHL	3	0	0	0	9	0	0	0	—	—	—	—	—
95-96—St. John's	AHL	40	16	14	30	222	...	...	...	—	—	—	—	—
—New York Islanders	NHL	7	0	0	0	27	-2	0	0	—	—	—	—	—
96-97—Kentucky	AHL	38	10	12	22	164	...	...	...	4	0	1	1	27
—New York Islanders	NHL	18	0	2	2	102	-1	0	0	—	—	—	—	—
97-98—New York Islanders	NHL	37	3	1	4	101	1	0	0	—	—	—	—	—
98-99—New York Islanders	NHL	9	1	1	2	30	1	0	0	—	—	—	—	—
—Boston	NHL	45	1	4	5	152	-2	0	0	12	1	0	1	16
99-00—Boston	NHL	37	2	2	4	44	-4	0	0	—	—	—	—	—
00-01—Boston	NHL	40	2	2	4	121	-6	0	0	—	—	—	—	—
—Providence	AHL	10	1	4	5	47	...	...	...	2	0	0	0	4
01-02—Los Angeles	NHL	43	2	0	2	85	-5	0	0	—	—	—	—	—
02-03—Los Angeles	NHL	4	0	0	0	17	0	0	0	—	—	—	—	—
NHL Totals (9 years)		243	11	12	23	688	-18	0	0	12	1	0	1	16

BELFOUR, ED — G — MAPLE LEAFS

PERSONAL: Born April 21, 1965, in Carman, Man. ... 5-11/202. ... Catches left. ... Full Name: Edward Belfour.

TRANSACTIONS/CAREER NOTES: Signed as non-drafted free agent by Chicago Blackhawks (June 18, 1987). ... Strained hip muscle (1993-94 season); missed four games. ... Sprained knee (January 31, 1996); missed one game. ... Injured back (February 19, 1996); missed three games. ... Traded by Blackhawks to San Jose Sharks for G Chris Terreri, D Michal Sykora and RW Ulf Dahlen (January 25, 1997). ... Injured knee ligament (February 1, 1997); missed 13 games. ... Suffered bulging disc in back (March 1, 1997); missed seven games. ... Signed as free agent by Dallas Stars (July 2, 1997). ... Strained lower back (February 2, 1998); missed three games. ... Strained groin (November 10, 1999); missed one game. ... Injured back (March 23, 2001); missed one game. ... Injured back (March 29, 2002); missed two games. ... Traded by Stars with RW Cameron Mann to Nashville Predators for C David Gosselin and fifth-round pick in 2003 draft (June 29, 2002). ... Signed as free agent by Toronto Maple Leafs (July 2, 2002).

Season Team	League	REGULAR SEASON									PLAYOFFS							
		Gms.	Min	W	L	T	GA	SO	Avg.	SV%	Gms.	Min.	W	L	GA	SO	Avg.	SV%
85-86—Winkler	MJHL	48	2880	...	...	...	124	1	2.58	—	—	—	—	—	—	—	—	—
86-87—Univ. of North Dakota	WCHA	34	2049	29	4	0	81	3	2.37	—	—	—	—	—	—	—	—	—
87-88—Saginaw	IHL	61	*3446	32	25	‡0	183	3	3.19	—	9	561	4	5	33	0	3.53	—
88-89—Chicago	NHL	23	1148	4	12	3	74	0	3.87	.878	—	—	—	—	—	—	—	—
—Saginaw	IHL	29	1760	12	10	‡0	92	0	3.14	—	5	298	2	3	14	0	2.82	—
89-90—Canadian nat'l team	Int'l	33	1808	...	...	...	93	...	3.09	—	—	—	—	—	—	—	—	—
—Chicago	NHL	—	—	—	—	—	—	—	—	—	9	409	4	2	17	0	2.49	.915
90-91—Chicago	NHL	*74	*4127	*43	19	7	170	4	*2.47	.910	6	295	2	4	20	0	4.07	.891
91-92—Chicago	NHL	52	2928	21	18	10	132	†5	2.70	.894	18	949	12	4	39	1	*2.47	.902
92-93—Chicago	NHL	*71	*4106	41	18	11	177	*7	2.59	.906	4	249	0	4	13	0	3.13	.866
93-94—Chicago	NHL	70	3998	37	24	6	178	†7	2.67	.906	6	360	2	4	15	0	2.50	.921
94-95—Chicago	NHL	42	2450	22	15	3	93	†5	2.28	.906	16	1014	9	†7	37	1	2.19	.923
95-96—Chicago	NHL	50	2956	22	17	10	135	1	2.74	.902	9	666	6	3	23	1	*2.07	.929
96-97—Chicago	NHL	33	1966	11	15	6	88	1	2.69	.907	—	—	—	—	—	—	—	—
—San Jose	NHL	13	757	3	9	0	43	1	3.41	.884	—	—	—	—	—	—	—	—
97-98—Dallas	NHL	61	3581	37	12	10	112	9	*1.88	.916	17	1039	10	7	31	1	1.79	.922
98-99—Dallas	NHL	61	3536	35	15	9	117	5	1.99	.915	*23	*1544	*16	7	43	*3	*1.67	.930
99-00—Dallas	NHL	62	3620	32	21	7	127	4	2.10	.919	†23	1443	14	*9	*45	*4	1.87	.931
00-01—Dallas	NHL	63	3687	35	20	7	144	8	2.34	.905	10	671	4	6	25	0	2.24	.910
01-02—Dallas	NHL	60	3467	21	27	†11	153	1	2.65	.895	—	—	—	—	—	—	—	—
—Can. Olympic team	Int'l								Did not play.									
02-03—Toronto	NHL	62	3738	37	20	5	141	7	2.26	.922	7	532	3	4	24	0	2.71	.915
NHL Totals (15 years)		797	46065	401	262	105	1884	65	2.45	.907	148	9171	82	61	332	11	2.17	.919

BELL, BRENDAN — D — MAPLE LEAFS

PERSONAL: Born March 31, 1983, in Ottawa. ... 6-1/198. ... Shoots left.

TRANSACTIONS/CAREER NOTES: Selected by Toronto Maple Leafs in third round (third Maple Leafs pick, 65th overall) of NHL entry draft (June 23, 2001).

Season Team	League	REGULAR SEASON								PLAYOFFS				
		Gms.	G	A	Pts.	PIM	+/-	PP	SH	Gms.	G	A	Pts.	PIM
99-00—Ottawa	OHL	48	1	32	33	34	...	...	...	5	0	1	1	4
00-01—Ottawa	OHL	68	7	32	39	59	...	...	...	20	1	11	12	22
01-02—Ottawa	OHL	67	10	36	46	56	...	...	...	13	2	5	7	25
02-03—Ottawa	OHL	55	14	39	53	46	...	...	...	—	—	—	—	—

BELL, MARK   LW   BLACKHAWKS

PERSONAL: Born August 5, 1980, in St. Paul's, Ont. ... 6-3/205. ... Shoots left.
TRANSACTIONS/CAREER NOTES: Selected by Chicago Blackhawks in first round (first Blackhawks pick, eighth overall) of NHL entry draft (June 27, 1998). ... Bruised hip (March 18, 2002); missed two games. ... Re-signed by Blackhawks (July 29, 2003).

Season Team	League	REGULAR SEASON								PLAYOFFS				
		Gms.	G	A	Pts.	PIM	+/-	PP	SH	Gms.	G	A	Pts.	PIM
95-96—Stratford Jr. B	OHA	47	8	15	23	32	...	...	...	—	—	—	—	—
96-97—Ottawa	OHL	65	8	12	20	40	...	...	...	24	4	7	11	13
97-98—Ottawa	OHL	55	34	26	60	87	...	...	...	13	6	5	11	14
98-99—Ottawa	OHL	44	29	26	55	69	...	...	...	9	6	5	11	8
99-00—Ottawa	OHL	48	34	38	72	95	...	...	...	2	0	1	1	0
00-01—Norfolk	AHL	61	15	27	42	126	...	...	...	9	4	3	7	10
—Chicago	NHL	13	0	1	1	4	0	0	0	—	—	—	—	—
01-02—Chicago	NHL	80	12	16	28	124	-6	1	0	5	0	0	0	8
02-03—Chicago	NHL	82	14	15	29	113	0	0	2	—	—	—	—	—
NHL Totals (3 years)		175	26	32	58	241	-6	1	2	5	0	0	0	8

BELLEFEUILLE, BLAKE   C

PERSONAL: Born December 27, 1977, in Framingham, Mass. ... 5-10/212. ... Shoots right. ... Name pronounced BELL-fay.
TRANSACTIONS/CAREER NOTES: Signed as non-drafted free agent by Columbus Blue Jackets (May 31, 2000).

Season Team	League	REGULAR SEASON								PLAYOFFS				
		Gms.	G	A	Pts.	PIM	+/-	PP	SH	Gms.	G	A	Pts.	PIM
94-95—Framingham	USHS (East)	20	42	50	92	...	...	...	...	—	—	—	—	—
95-96—Framingham	USHS (East)	20	31	60	91	...	...	...	...	—	—	—	—	—
96-97—Boston College	Hockey East	34	16	19	35	20	...	...	...	—	—	—	—	—
97-98—Boston College	Hockey East	41	19	20	39	35	...	...	...	—	—	—	—	—
98-99—Boston College	Hockey East	43	24	25	49	80	...	...	...	—	—	—	—	—
99-00—Boston College	Hockey East	41	19	32	51	28	...	...	...	—	—	—	—	—
00-01—Syracuse	AHL	50	5	5	10	18	...	...	...	5	0	0	0	0
01-02—Syracuse	AHL	75	11	19	30	33	...	...	...	4	2	0	2	0
—Columbus	NHL	2	0	1	1	0	1	0	0	—	—	—	—	—
02-03—Syracuse	AHL	63	12	19	31	44	...	...	...	—	—	—	—	—
—Columbus	NHL	3	0	0	0	0	0	0	0	—	—	—	—	—
NHL Totals (2 years)		5	0	1	1	0	1	0	0					

BEMBRIDGE, GARRETT   RW   FLAMES

PERSONAL: Born July 6, 1981, in Melfort, Sask. ... 6-0/164. ... Shoots right.
TRANSACTIONS/CAREER NOTES: Selected by New York Rangers in fifth round (sixth Rangers pick, 137th overall) of NHL entry draft (June 26, 1999). ... Returned to draft pool by Rangers and selected by Calgary Flames in seventh round (eighth Flames pick, 207th overall) of NHL entry draft (June 23, 2001).

Season Team	League	REGULAR SEASON								PLAYOFFS				
		Gms.	G	A	Pts.	PIM	+/-	PP	SH	Gms.	G	A	Pts.	PIM
97-98—Saskatoon	WHL	6	1	1	2	0	...	...	...	1	0	0	0	0
98-99—Saskatoon	WHL	68	23	27	50	30	...	...	...	—	—	—	—	—
99-00—Saskatoon	WHL	72	27	31	58	41	...	...	...	11	5	5	10	2
00-01—Saskatoon	WHL	72	38	40	78	40	...	...	...	—	—	—	—	—
—Hartford	AHL	7	1	0	1	0	...	...	...	—	—	—	—	—
01-02—Saint John	AHL	66	9	12	21	22	...	...	...	—	—	—	—	—
02-03—Saint John	AHL	64	9	10	19	33	...	...	...	—	—	—	—	—

BENDERA, SHANE   G   BLUE JACKETS

PERSONAL: Born July 13, 1982, in St. Albert, Alta. ... 5-10/170. ... Catches left.
TRANSACTIONS/CAREER NOTES: Selected by Columbus Blue Jackets in sixth round (sixth Blue Jackets pick, 169th overall) of NHL entry draft (June 24, 2000).

Season Team	League	REGULAR SEASON									PLAYOFFS							
		Gms.	Min	W	L	T	GA	SO	Avg.	SV%	Gms.	Min.	W	L	GA	SO	Avg.	SV%
97-98—Red Deer	WHL	1	9	0	0	0	0	0	...	—	—	—	—	—	—	—	—	—
98-99—Red Deer	WHL	2	72	0	1	0	7	0	5.83	—	—	—	—	—	—	—	—	—
99-00—Red Deer	WHL	*69	*4006	31	27	*9	202	0	3.03	—	3	76	0	2	15	0	11.84	—
00-01—Red Deer	WHL	45	2603	32	8	2	108	†5	*2.49	—	*22	*1404	*16	6	43	*4	1.84	—
01-02—Red Deer	WHL	20	1211	11	6	3	46	1	2.28	—	—	—	—	—	—	—	—	—
—Kelowna	WHL	30	1816	13	9	8	79	0	2.61	—	15	918	9	6	29	†2	1.90	—
02-03—Dayton	ECHL	39	2242	13	19	5	106	1	2.84	—	—	—	—	—	—	—	—	—

BENYSEK, LADISLAV   D

PERSONAL: Born March 24, 1975, in Olomouc, Czechoslovakia ... 6-2/190. ... Shoots left. ... Name pronounced BEHN-ih-sikh.
TRANSACTIONS/CAREER NOTES: Selected by Edmonton Oilers in 11th round (16th Oilers pick, 266th overall) of NHL entry draft (June 29, 1994). ... Claimed by Mighty Ducks of Anaheim from Oilers in NHL waiver draft (September 27, 1999). ... Selected by Minnesota Wild in NHL expansion draft (June 23, 2000). ... Fractured finger (February 7, 2001); missed one game. ... Bruised shoulder (March 4, 2001); missed one game. ... Bruised knee (December 5, 2001); missed two games.

Season Team	League	REGULAR SEASON								PLAYOFFS				
		Gms.	G	A	Pts.	PIM	+/-	PP	SH	Gms.	G	A	Pts.	PIM
93-94—HC Olomouc	Czech Rep.							Statistics unavailable.						
94-95—Cape Breton	AHL	58	2	7	9	54	...	...	...	—	—	—	—	—
95-96—HC Olomouc	Czech Rep.	33	1	4	5	...	...	...	...	—	—	—	—	—
96-97—HC Olomouc	Czech Rep.	14	0	1	1	8	...	...	...	—	—	—	—	—
—Sparta Praha	Czech Rep.	36	5	5	10	28	...	...	...	—	—	—	—	—
97-98—Edmonton	NHL	2	0	0	0	0	-2	0	0	—	—	—	—	—
—Hamilton	AHL	53	2	14	16	29	...	...	...	9	1	1	2	2
98-99—Sparta Praha	Czech Rep.	52	8	11	19	47	...	...	...	8	0	1	1	—
99-00—Sparta Praha	Czech Rep.	51	1	5	6	45	...	...	...	9	0	0	0	4
00-01—Minnesota	NHL	71	2	5	7	38	-11	1	0	—	—	—	—	—
01-02—Minnesota	NHL	74	1	7	8	28	-12	0	0	—	—	—	—	—
02-03—Houston	AHL	39	0	4	4	23	...	...	...	—	—	—	—	—
—Minnesota	NHL	14	0	0	0	8	-3	0	0	—	—	—	—	—
NHL Totals (4 years)		161	3	12	15	74	-28	1	0					

BERARD, BRYAN   D   BRUINS

PERSONAL: Born March 5, 1977, in Woonsocket, R.I. ... 6-2/218. ... Shoots left. ... Name pronounced buh-RAHRD.
TRANSACTIONS/CAREER NOTES: Selected by Ottawa Senators in first round (first Senators pick, first overall) of NHL entry draft (July 8, 1995). ... Traded by Senators with C Martin Straka to New York Islanders for D Wade Redden and G Damian Rhodes (January 23, 1996). ... Strained groin (October 16, 1997); missed one game. ... Reinjured groin (November 10, 1997); missed two games. ... Reinjured groin (November 15, 1997); missed three games. ... Bruised elbow (March 24, 1998); missed one game. ... Strained groin (December 18, 1998); missed nine games. ... Traded by Islanders with sixth-round pick (RW Jan Sochor) in 1999 draft to Toronto Maple Leafs for G Felix Potvin and sixth-round pick (C Fedor Fedorov) in 1999 draft (January 9, 1999). ... Strained groin (January 7, 1999); missed three games. ... Suffered from the flu (March 28, 1999); missed two games. ... Suspended two games by NHL for illegal check (October 19, 1999). ... Suffered injury (November 23, 1999); missed three games. ... Suffered eye injury (March 11, 2000); missed remainder of season. ... Missed entire 2000-01 season due to eye injury. ... Signed as free agent by New York Rangers (October 4, 2001). ... Signed as free agent by Boston Bruins (August 13, 2002).

Season Team	League	REGULAR SEASON								PLAYOFFS				
		Gms.	G	A	Pts.	PIM	+/-	PP	SH	Gms.	G	A	Pts.	PIM
91-92—Mt. St. Charles H.S.	R.I.H.S.	32	3	15	18	10	...	...	...	—	—	—	—	—
92-93—Mt. St. Charles H.S.	R.I.H.S.	32	8	12	20	18	...	...	...	—	—	—	—	—
93-94—Mt. St. Charles H.S.	R.I.H.S.	32	11	36	47	5	...	...	...	—	—	—	—	—
94-95—Det. Jr. Red Wings	OHL	58	20	55	75	97	...	...	...	21	4	20	24	38
95-96—Det. Jr. Red Wings	OHL	56	31	58	89	116	...	...	...	17	7	18	25	41
96-97—New York Islanders	NHL	82	8	40	48	86	1	3	0	—	—	—	—	—
97-98—New York Islanders	NHL	75	14	32	46	59	-32	8	1	—	—	—	—	—
—U.S. Olympic team	Int'l	2	0	0	0	0	...	...	...	—	—	—	—	—
98-99—New York Islanders	NHL	31	4	11	15	26	-6	2	0	—	—	—	—	—
—Toronto	NHL	38	5	14	19	22	7	2	0	17	1	8	9	8
99-00—Toronto	NHL	64	3	27	30	42	11	1	0	—	—	—	—	—
00-01—							Did not play.							
01-02—New York Rangers	NHL	82	2	21	23	60	-1	0	0	—	—	—	—	—
02-03—Boston	NHL	80	10	28	38	64	-4	4	0	3	1	0	1	2
NHL Totals (7 years)		452	46	173	219	359	-24	20	1	20	2	8	10	10

BEREHOWSKY, DRAKE   D   COYOTES

PERSONAL: Born January 3, 1972, in Toronto ... 6-2/217. ... Shoots right. ... Name pronounced BAIR-ih-HOW-skee.
TRANSACTIONS/CAREER NOTES: Selected by Toronto Maple Leafs in first round (first Maple Leafs pick, 10th overall) of NHL entry draft (June 16, 1990). ... Sprained knee (April 15, 1993); missed remainder of season. ... Underwent knee surgery prior to 1994-95 season; missed first four games of season. ... Traded by Maple Leafs to Pittsburgh Penguins for D Grant Jennings (April 7, 1995). ... Signed as free agent by Edmonton Oilers (September 29, 1997). ... Traded by Oilers with G Eric Fichaud and D Greg de Vries to Nashville Predators for F Jim Dowd and G Mikhail Shtalenkov (October 1, 1998). ... Sprained knee (February 4, 1999); missed two games. ... Injured neck (October 2, 1999); missed first game of season. ... Strained elbow (November 26, 2000); missed two games. ... Suspended one game by NHL for receiving match penalty (December 29, 2000). ... Traded by Predators to Vancouver Canucks for second-round pick (RW Timofei Shiskanov) in 2001 draft (March 9, 2001). ... Traded by Canucks with C Denis Pederson to Phoenix Coyotes for LW Todd Warriner, C Trevor Letowski, RW Tyler Bouck and third-round pick in 2003 draft (December 28, 2001).

Season Team	League	REGULAR SEASON								PLAYOFFS				
		Gms.	G	A	Pts.	PIM	+/-	PP	SH	Gms.	G	A	Pts.	PIM
87-88—Barrie Jr. B	OHA	40	10	36	46	81	...	...	...	—	—	—	—	—
88-89—Kingston	OHL	63	7	39	46	85	...	...	...	—	—	—	—	—
89-90—Kingston	OHL	9	3	11	14	28	...	...	...	—	—	—	—	—
90-91—Toronto	NHL	8	0	1	1	25	-6	0	0	—	—	—	—	—
—Kingston	OHL	13	5	13	18	28	...	...	...	—	—	—	—	—
—North Bay	OHL	26	7	23	30	51	...	...	...	10	2	7	9	21
91-92—North Bay	OHL	62	19	63	82	147	...	...	...	21	7	24	31	22
—Toronto	NHL	1	0	0	0	0	0	0	0	—	—	—	—	—
—St. John's	AHL	—	—	—	—	—	...	...	...	6	0	5	5	21

Season Team	League	REGULAR SEASON								PLAYOFFS				
		Gms.	G	A	Pts.	PIM	+/-	PP	SH	Gms.	G	A	Pts.	PIM
92-93—Toronto	NHL	41	4	15	19	61	1	1	0	—	—	—	—	—
—St. John's	AHL	28	10	17	27	38	...	...	...	—	—	—	—	—
93-94—Toronto	NHL	49	2	8	10	63	-3	2	0	—	—	—	—	—
—St. John's	AHL	18	3	12	15	40	...	...	...	—	—	—	—	—
94-95—Toronto	NHL	25	0	2	2	15	-10	0	0	—	—	—	—	—
—Pittsburgh	NHL	4	0	0	0	13	1	0	0	1	0	0	0	0
95-96—Cleveland	IHL	74	6	28	34	141	...	...	...	3	0	3	3	6
—Pittsburgh	NHL	1	0	0	0	0	1	0	0	—	—	—	—	—
96-97—San Antonio	IHL	16	3	4	7	36	...	...	...	—	—	—	—	—
—Carolina	AHL	49	2	15	17	55	...	...	...	—	—	—	—	—
97-98—Edmonton	NHL	67	1	6	7	169	1	1	0	12	1	2	3	14
—Hamilton	AHL	8	2	0	2	21	...	...	...	—	—	—	—	—
98-99—Nashville	NHL	74	2	15	17	140	-9	0	0	—	—	—	—	—
99-00—Nashville	NHL	79	12	20	32	87	-4	5	0	—	—	—	—	—
00-01—Nashville	NHL	66	6	18	24	100	-9	3	0	—	—	—	—	—
—Vancouver	NHL	14	1	1	2	21	0	1	0	4	0	0	0	12
01-02—Vancouver	NHL	25	1	2	3	18	-5	0	0	—	—	—	—	—
—Phoenix	NHL	32	1	4	5	42	5	0	0	5	0	1	1	4
02-03—Springfield	AHL	2	0	0	0	0	...	...	...	—	—	—	—	—
—Phoenix	NHL	7	1	2	3	27	0	0	0	—	—	—	—	—
NHL Totals (12 years)		493	31	94	125	781	-37	13	0	22	1	3	4	30

BERENZWEIG, BUBBA   D   STARS

PERSONAL: Born August 8, 1977, in Arlington Heights, Ill. ... 6-1/217. ... Shoots left. ... Full Name: Andrew Berenzweig.
TRANSACTIONS/CAREER NOTES: Selected by New York Islanders in fifth round (fifth Islanders pick, 109th overall) of NHL entry draft (June 22, 1996). ... Traded by Islanders to Nashville Predators for fourth-round pick (D Johan Halvardsson) in 1999 draft (April 19, 1999). ... Sprained ankle (January 8, 2002); missed 13 games. ... Traded by Predators with conditional pick in draft to Dallas Stars for LW Jon Sim (February 17, 2003). ... Re-signed by Stars (July 17, 2003).

Season Team	League	REGULAR SEASON								PLAYOFFS				
		Gms.	G	A	Pts.	PIM	+/-	PP	SH	Gms.	G	A	Pts.	PIM
92-93—Loomis-Chaffee	Conn. H.S.	22	5	13	18	...	...	...	...	—	—	—	—	—
93-94—Loomis-Chaffee	Conn. H.S.	22	12	27	39	...	...	...	...	—	—	—	—	—
94-95—Loomis-Chaffee	Conn. H.S.	23	19	23	42	24	...	...	...	—	—	—	—	—
95-96—Univ. of Michigan	CCHA	42	4	8	12	4	...	...	...	—	—	—	—	—
96-97—Univ. of Michigan	CCHA	38	7	12	19	49	...	...	...	—	—	—	—	—
97-98—Univ. of Michigan	CCHA	43	6	10	16	28	...	...	...	—	—	—	—	—
98-99—Univ. of Michigan	CCHA	42	7	24	31	38	...	...	...	—	—	—	—	—
99-00—Milwaukee	IHL	79	4	23	27	48	...	...	...	3	1	2	3	0
—Nashville	NHL	2	0	0	0	0	-1	0	0	—	—	—	—	—
00-01—Milwaukee	IHL	72	10	26	36	38	...	...	...	5	0	4	4	4
—Nashville	NHL	5	0	0	0	0	0	0	0	—	—	—	—	—
01-02—Milwaukee	AHL	23	2	5	7	23	...	...	...	—	—	—	—	—
—Nashville	NHL	26	3	7	10	14	-3	0	0	—	—	—	—	—
02-03—Milwaukee	AHL	48	6	11	17	26	...	...	...	—	—	—	—	—
—Nashville	NHL	4	0	0	0	0	0	0	0	—	—	—	—	—
—Utah	AHL	26	6	11	17	4	...	...	...	—	—	—	—	—
NHL Totals (4 years)		37	3	7	10	14	-4	0	0	—	—	—	—	—

BEREZIN, SERGEI   LW

PERSONAL: Born November 5, 1971, in Voskresensk, U.S.S.R. ... 5-10/196. ... Shoots right. ... Name pronounced BAIR-ih-zihn.
TRANSACTIONS/CAREER NOTES: Selected by Toronto Maple Leafs in 10th round (eighth Maple Leafs pick, 256th overall) of NHL entry draft (June 29, 1994). ... Injured hand (November 19, 1996); missed one game. ... Underwent hand surgery (December 3, 1996); missed six games. ... Strained knee (December 23, 1996); missed two games. ... Suffered hip pointer (October 30, 1998); missed four games. ... Bruised foot (November 12, 1998); missed two games. ... Suffered injury (January 8, 2000); missed five games. ... Injured hamstring (January 27, 2000); missed 14 games. ... Suffered injury (April 5, 2000); missed one game. ... Suffered injury (January 10, 2001); missed one game. ... Traded by Maple Leafs to Phoenix Coyotes for RW Mikael Renberg (June 22, 2001). ... Sprained knee (September 15, 2001); missed first seven games of season. ... Traded by Coyotes to Montreal Canadiens for RW Brian Savage, third-round pick (D Matt Jones) in 2002 draft and future considerations (January 25, 2002). ... Traded by Canadiens to Chicago Blackhawks for fourth-round pick in 2004 draft (June 30, 2002). ... Traded by Blackhawks to Washington Capitals for fourth-round pick in 2004 draft (March 11, 2003).
STATISTICAL PLATEAUS: Three-goal games: 1998-99 (2).

Season Team	League	REGULAR SEASON								PLAYOFFS				
		Gms.	G	A	Pts.	PIM	+/-	PP	SH	Gms.	G	A	Pts.	PIM
90-91—Khimik Voskresensk	USSR	30	6	2	8	4	...	...	...	—	—	—	—	—
91-92—Khimik Voskresensk	CIS	36	7	5	12	10	...	...	...	—	—	—	—	—
92-93—Khimik Voskresensk	CIS	38	9	3	12	12	...	...	...	2	1	0	1	0
93-94—Khimik Voskresensk	CIS	40	31	10	41	16	...	...	...	—	—	—	—	—
—Russian nat'l team	Int'l	6	2	1	3	2	...	...	...	—	—	—	—	—
—Russian Oly. team	Int'l	8	3	2	5	2	...	...	...	—	—	—	—	—
94-95—Koln	Germany	43	38	19	57	8	...	...	...	18	17	8	25	18
—Russian nat'l team	Int'l	6	7	1	8	4	...	...	...	—	—	—	—	—
95-96—Koln	Germany	45	49	31	80	8	...	...	...	14	13	9	22	4
—Russian nat'l team	Int'l	8	4	5	9	2	...	...	...	—	—	—	—	—
96-97—Toronto	NHL	73	25	16	41	2	-3	7	0	—	—	—	—	—
97-98—Toronto	NHL	68	16	15	31	10	-3	3	0	—	—	—	—	—
98-99—Toronto	NHL	76	37	22	59	12	16	9	1	17	6	6	12	4

Season Team	League	REGULAR SEASON								PLAYOFFS				
		Gms.	G	A	Pts.	PIM	+/-	PP	SH	Gms.	G	A	Pts.	PIM
99-00—Toronto	NHL	61	26	13	39	2	8	5	0	12	4	4	8	0
00-01—Toronto	NHL	79	22	28	50	8	2	10	0	11	2	5	7	2
01-02—Phoenix	NHL	41	7	9	16	4	-1	1	0	—	—	—	—	—
—Montreal	NHL	29	4	6	10	4	3	3	0	6	1	1	2	0
02-03—Chicago	NHL	66	18	13	31	8	-3	5	0	—	—	—	—	—
—Washington	NHL	9	5	4	9	4	10	0	0	6	0	1	1	0
NHL Totals (7 years)		502	160	126	286	54	29	43	1	52	13	17	30	6

BERG, AKI — D — MAPLE LEAFS

PERSONAL: Born July 28, 1977, in Turku, Finland ... 6-3/213. ... Shoots left. ... Full Name: Aki-Petteri Berg. ... Name pronounced AH-kee BUHRG.

TRANSACTIONS/CAREER NOTES: Selected by Los Angeles Kings in first round (first Kings pick, third overall) of NHL entry draft (July 8, 1995). ... Suffered charley horse (January 25, 1997); missed one game. ... Suffered concussion (February 3, 1997); missed two games. ... Sprained left ankle (April 9, 1997); missed final two games of regular season. ... Bruised right foot (December 4, 1997); missed one game. ... Sprained right wrist (March 10, 1998); missed two games. ... Suffered concussion (December 23, 1999); missed two games. ... Suffered concussion (March 13, 2000); missed two games. ... Suffered injury (January 4, 2001); missed three games. ... Traded by Kings to Toronto Maple Leafs for C Adam Mair and second-round pick (C Mike Cammalleri) in 2001 draft (March 13, 2001). ... Suffered injury (March 16, 2002); missed one game.

Season Team	League	REGULAR SEASON								PLAYOFFS				
		Gms.	G	A	Pts.	PIM	+/-	PP	SH	Gms.	G	A	Pts.	PIM
92-93—TPS Turku	Finland Jr.	39	18	24	42	59	...	...	...	—	—	—	—	—
93-94—TPS Turku	Finland Jr.	21	3	11	14	24	...	...	...	7	0	0	0	10
—TPS Turku	Finland	6	0	3	3	4	...	...	...	—	—	—	—	—
94-95—Kiekko-67	Finland Div. 2	20	3	9	12	34	...	...	...	—	—	—	—	—
—TPS Turku	Finland Jr.	8	1	0	1	30	...	...	...	—	—	—	—	—
—TPS Turku	Finland	5	0	0	0	4	...	...	...	—	—	—	—	—
95-96—Los Angeles	NHL	51	0	7	7	29	-13	0	0	—	—	—	—	—
—Phoenix	IHL	20	0	3	3	18	...	...	...	2	0	0	0	4
96-97—Los Angeles	NHL	41	2	6	8	24	-9	2	0	—	—	—	—	—
—Phoenix	IHL	23	1	3	4	21	...	...	...	—	—	—	—	—
97-98—Los Angeles	NHL	72	0	8	8	61	3	0	0	4	0	3	3	0
—Fin. Olympic team	Int'l	6	0	0	0	6	...	...	...	—	—	—	—	—
98-99—TPS Turku	Finland	48	8	7	15	137	...	...	...	9	1	1	2	45
99-00—Los Angeles	NHL	70	3	13	16	45	-1	0	0	2	0	0	0	2
00-01—Los Angeles	NHL	47	0	4	4	43	3	0	0	—	—	—	—	—
—Toronto	NHL	12	3	0	3	2	-6	3	0	11	0	2	2	4
01-02—Toronto	NHL	81	1	10	11	46	14	0	0	20	0	1	1	37
—Fin. Olympic team	Int'l	4	1	0	1	2	...	...	...	—	—	—	—	—
02-03—Toronto	NHL	78	4	7	11	28	3	0	0	7	1	1	2	2
NHL Totals (7 years)		452	13	55	68	278	-6	5	0	44	1	7	8	45

BERGENHEIM, SEAN — RW/LW — ISLANDERS

PERSONAL: Born February 8, 1981, in Helsinki, Finland. ... 5-11/194. ... Shoots left.
TRANSACTIONS/CAREER NOTES: Selected by New York Islanders in first round (first Islanders pick, 22nd overall) of NHL entry draft (June 22, 2002). ... Re-signed by Islanders (July 23, 2003).

Season Team	League	REGULAR SEASON								PLAYOFFS				
		Gms.	G	A	Pts.	PIM	+/-	PP	SH	Gms.	G	A	Pts.	PIM
01-02—Jokerit Helsinki	Finland	28	2	2	4	4	...	...	...	—	—	—	—	—
02-03—Jokerit Helsinki	Finland	38	3	3	6	4	...	...	...	—	—	—	—	—

BERGERON, MARC-ANDRE — D — OILERS

PERSONAL: Born October 13, 1980, in St-Louis-de-France, Que. ... 5-10/190. ... Shoots left.
TRANSACTIONS/CAREER NOTES: Signed as non-drafted free agent by Edmonton Oilers (July 20, 2001).

Season Team	League	REGULAR SEASON								PLAYOFFS				
		Gms.	G	A	Pts.	PIM	+/-	PP	SH	Gms.	G	A	Pts.	PIM
01-02—Hamilton	AHL	50	2	13	15	61	...	...	...	9	1	4	5	8
02-03—Hamilton	AHL	66	8	31	39	73	...	...	...	—	—	—	—	—
—Edmonton	NHL	5	1	1	2	9	2	0	0	1	0	1	1	0
NHL Totals (1 year)		5	1	1	2	9	2	0	0	1	0	1	1	0

BERGEVIN, MARC — D — PENGUINS

PERSONAL: Born August 11, 1965, in Montreal ... 6-1/214. ... Shoots left. ... Name pronounced BUHR-jih-vihn.
TRANSACTIONS/CAREER NOTES: Selected by Chicago Blackhawks in third round (third Blackhawks pick, 59th overall) of NHL entry draft (June 8, 1983). ... Sprained neck (March 18, 1987). ... Traded by Blackhawks with D Gary Nylund to New York Islanders for D Steve Konroyd and C Bob Bassen (November 25, 1988). ... Bruised ribs (November 25, 1989). ... Broke hand (May 1990). ... Traded by Islanders to Hartford Whalers for future considerations; Islanders later received fifth-round pick in 1992 draft (C Ryan Duthie) to complete deal (October 31, 1990). ... Signed as free agent by Tampa Bay Lightning (July 9, 1992). ... Injured foot (March 18, 1993); missed one game. ... Bruised back (November 19, 1993); missed one game. ... Injured elbow (March 10, 1995); missed one game. ... Suffered from sore neck (April 22, 1995); missed three games. ... Traded by Lightning with RW Ben Hankinson to Detroit Red Wings for LW Shawn Burr and third-round pick (traded to Boston) in 1996 draft (August 17, 1995). ... Suffered from the flu (November 1, 1995); missed one game. ... Injured groin (April 7, 1996); missed three games. ... Signed as free agent by St. Louis Blues (July 9, 1996). ... Injured ankle (December 13, 1997); missed one game. ... Strained abdominal muscle (January 9, 1999); missed 20 games. ... Reinjured abdominal muscle (April 3, 1999) and underwent surgery; missed remainder

of season. ... Fractured thumb (September 12, 2000); missed first 18 games of season. ... Traded by Blues to Pittsburgh Penguins for D Dan Trebil (December 28, 2000). ... Strained knee (February 21, 2001); missed seven games. ... Signed as free agent by Blues (November 6, 2001). ... Signed as free agent by Penguins (July 18, 2002). ... Traded by Penguins to Lightning for C Brian Holzinger (March 11, 2003).

				REGULAR SEASON						PLAYOFFS				
Season Team	League	Gms.	G	A	Pts.	PIM	+/-	PP	SH	Gms.	G	A	Pts.	PIM
82-83—Chicoutimi	QMJHL	64	3	27	30	113	...	...	...	—	—	—	—	—
83-84—Chicoutimi	QMJHL	70	10	35	45	125	...	...	...	—	—	—	—	—
—Springfield	AHL	7	0	1	1	2	...	...	...	—	—	—	—	—
84-85—Chicago	NHL	60	0	6	6	54	-9	0	0	6	0	3	3	2
—Springfield	AHL	—	—	—	—	—	—	—	—	4	0	0	0	0
85-86—Chicago	NHL	71	7	7	14	60	0	0	0	3	0	0	0	0
86-87—Chicago	NHL	66	4	10	14	66	4	0	0	3	1	0	1	2
87-88—Chicago	NHL	58	1	6	7	85	-19	0	0	—	—	—	—	—
—Saginaw	IHL	10	2	7	9	20	...	...	...	—	—	—	—	—
88-89—Chicago	NHL	11	0	0	0	18	-3	0	0	—	—	—	—	—
—New York Islanders	NHL	58	2	13	15	62	2	1	0	—	—	—	—	—
89-90—New York Islanders	NHL	18	0	4	4	30	-8	0	0	1	0	0	0	2
—Springfield	AHL	47	7	16	23	66	...	...	...	17	2	11	13	16
90-91—Hartford	NHL	4	0	0	0	4	-3	0	0	—	—	—	—	—
—Capital District	AHL	7	0	5	5	6	...	...	...	—	—	—	—	—
—Springfield	AHL	58	4	23	27	85	...	...	...	18	0	7	7	26
91-92—Hartford	NHL	75	7	17	24	64	-13	4	1	5	0	0	0	2
92-93—Tampa Bay	NHL	78	2	12	14	66	-16	0	0	—	—	—	—	—
93-94—Tampa Bay	NHL	83	1	15	16	87	-5	0	0	—	—	—	—	—
94-95—Tampa Bay	NHL	44	2	4	6	51	-6	0	1	—	—	—	—	—
95-96—Detroit	NHL	70	1	9	10	33	7	0	0	17	1	0	1	14
96-97—St. Louis	NHL	82	0	4	4	53	-9	0	0	6	1	0	1	8
97-98—St. Louis	NHL	81	3	7	10	90	-2	0	0	10	0	1	1	8
98-99—St. Louis	NHL	52	1	1	2	99	-14	0	0	—	—	—	—	—
99-00—St. Louis	NHL	81	1	8	9	75	27	0	0	7	0	1	1	6
00-01—St. Louis	NHL	2	0	0	0	0	1	0	0	—	—	—	—	—
—Pittsburgh	NHL	36	1	4	5	26	5	0	0	12	0	1	1	2
01-02—Worcester	AHL	2	0	0	0	0	...	...	...	—	—	—	—	—
—St. Louis	NHL	30	0	3	3	2	6	0	0	7	0	0	0	4
02-03—Pittsburgh	NHL	69	2	5	7	36	-9	0	0	—	—	—	—	—
—Tampa Bay	NHL	1	0	0	0	0	-2	0	0	—	—	—	—	—
NHL Totals (19 years)		1130	35	135	170	1061	-66	5	2	77	3	6	9	50

BERGLUND, CHRISTIAN — LW — DEVILS

PERSONAL: Born March 12, 1980, in Orebro, Sweden ... 5-11/190. ... Shoots left.
TRANSACTIONS/CAREER NOTES: Selected by New Jersey Devils in second round (third Devils pick, 37th overall) of NHL entry draft (June 27, 1998).

				REGULAR SEASON						PLAYOFFS				
Season Team	League	Gms.	G	A	Pts.	PIM	+/-	PP	SH	Gms.	G	A	Pts.	PIM
94-95—Karlskoga	Sweden Dv. 4	20	14	13	27		...	...	...	—	—	—	—	—
95-96—Kristinehamn	Sweden Dv. 3	23	8	8	16	12	...	...	...	—	—	—	—	—
96-97—Farjestad Karlstad	Sweden Jr.	21	2	3	5	24	...	...	...	—	—	—	—	—
97-98—Farjestad Karlstad	Sweden Jr.	29	23	19	42	88	...	...	...	2	0	0	0	0
—Farjestad Karlstad	Sweden	1	0	0	0	0	...	...	...	—	—	—	—	—
98-99—Farjestad Karlstad	Sweden Jr.	5	3	4	7	22	...	...	...	—	—	—	—	—
—Farjestad Karlstad	Sweden	37	2	4	6	37	...	...	...	4	1	0	1	4
99-00—Farjestad Karlstad	Sweden	43	8	6	14	44	...	...	...	7	2	1	3	10
—Bofors	Sweden Dv. 2	6	2	0	2	12	...	...	...	—	—	—	—	—
00-01—Farjestad Karlstad	Sweden	49	17	20	37	142	...	...	...	16	7	7	14	22
01-02—Albany	AHL	60	21	26	47	69	...	...	...	—	—	—	—	—
—New Jersey	NHL	15	2	7	9	8	-3	0	0	3	0	0	0	2
02-03—Albany	AHL	26	6	14	20	57	...	...	...	—	—	—	—	—
—New Jersey	NHL	38	4	5	9	20	3	0	0	—	—	—	—	—
NHL Totals (2 years)		53	6	12	18	28	0	0	0	3	0	0	0	2

BERRY, RICK — D — CAPITALS

PERSONAL: Born November 4, 1978, in Brandon, Man. ... 6-2/200. ... Shoots left.
TRANSACTIONS/CAREER NOTES: Selected by Colorado Avalanche in third round (third Avalanche pick, 55th overall) of NHL entry draft (June 21, 1997). ... Traded by Avalanche with LW Ville Nieminen to Pittsburgh Penguins for D Darius Kasparitis (March 19, 2002). ... Claimed by Washington Capitals from Penguins in NHL waiver draft (October 4, 2002). ... Re-signed by Capitals (July 27, 2003).

				REGULAR SEASON						PLAYOFFS				
Season Team	League	Gms.	G	A	Pts.	PIM	+/-	PP	SH	Gms.	G	A	Pts.	PIM
95-96—Seattle	WHL	59	4	9	13	103	...	...	...	1	0	0	0	0
96-97—Seattle	WHL	72	12	21	33	125	...	...	...	15	3	7	10	23
97-98—Spokane	WHL	59	9	21	30	131	...	...	...	17	1	4	5	26
—Seattle	WHL	37	5	12	17	100	...	...	...	—	—	—	—	—
98-99—Hershey	AHL	62	2	6	8	153	...	...	...	—	—	—	—	—
99-00—Hershey	AHL	64	9	16	25	148	...	...	...	13	2	3	5	24
00-01—Hershey	AHL	48	6	17	23	87	...	...	...	12	2	2	4	18
—Colorado	NHL	19	0	4	4	38	5	0	0	—	—	—	—	—
01-02—Colorado	NHL	57	0	0	0	60	1	0	0	—	—	—	—	—
—Pittsburgh	NHL	13	0	2	2	21	-4	0	0	—	—	—	—	—
02-03—Washington	NHL	43	2	1	3	87	-3	0	0	—	—	—	—	—
NHL Totals (3 years)		132	2	7	9	206	-1	0	0					

BERTRAND, ERIC   LW

PERSONAL: Born April 16, 1975, in St. Ephrem, Que. ... 6-1/205. ... Shoots left.
TRANSACTIONS/CAREER NOTES: Selected by New Jersey Devils in eighth round (ninth Devils pick, 207th overall) of NHL entry draft (June 29, 1994). ... Traded by Devils to with RW Wes Mason and seventh-round pick (LW Ken Magowan) in 2000 draft to Atlanta Thrashers for LW Jeff Williams and C Sylvain Cloutier (November 1, 1999). ... Traded by Thrashers to Philadelphia Flyers for RW Brian Wesenberg (December 9, 1999). ... Traded by Flyers to Nashville Predators for future consideration (February 14, 2000). ... Signed as free agent by Montreal Canadiens (July 7, 2000).

Season Team	League	REGULAR SEASON Gms.	G	A	Pts.	PIM	+/-	PP	SH	PLAYOFFS Gms.	G	A	Pts.	PIM
92-93—Granby	QMJHL	64	10	15	25	82	...	...	...	—	—	—	—	—
93-94—Granby	QMJHL	60	11	15	26	151	...	...	...	6	1	0	1	18
94-95—Granby	QMJHL	56	14	26	40	268	...	...	...	13	3	8	11	50
95-96—Albany	AHL	70	16	13	29	199	...	...	...	4	0	0	0	6
96-97—Albany	AHL	77	16	27	43	204	...	...	...	8	3	3	6	15
97-98—Albany	AHL	76	20	29	49	256	...	...	...	13	5	5	10	4
98-99—Albany	AHL	78	34	31	65	160	...	...	...	5	4	2	6	0
99-00—New Jersey	NHL	4	0	0	0	0	-1	0	0	—	—	—	—	—
—Atlanta	NHL	8	0	0	0	4	-5	0	0	—	—	—	—	—
—Philadelphia	AHL	15	3	6	9	67	...	...	...	—	—	—	—	—
—Milwaukee	IHL	27	7	9	16	56	...	...	...	3	0	0	0	2
00-01—Quebec	AHL	66	21	21	42	113	...	...	...	9	4	2	6	12
—Montreal	NHL	3	0	0	0	0	0	0	0	—	—	—	—	—
01-02—Kolner Haie	Germany	27	5	6	11	34	...	...	...	12	1	1	2	42
02-03—Hershey	AHL	67	19	40	59	87	...	...	...	—	—	—	—	—
NHL Totals (2 years)		15	0	0	0	4	-6	0	0					

BERTUZZI, TODD   RW   CANUCKS

PERSONAL: Born February 2, 1975, in Sudbury, Ont. ... 6-3/245. ... Shoots left. ... Name pronounced buhr-TOO-zee.
TRANSACTIONS/CAREER NOTES: Selected by New York Islanders in first round (first Islanders pick, 23rd overall) of NHL entry draft (June 26, 1993). ... Injured eye (February 22, 1996); missed two games. ... Suspended three games by NHL for attempting to break free of a lines-man (April 2, 1996). ... Suffered from bone chips in elbow (November 23, 1996); missed one game. ... Traded by Islanders with D Bryan McCabe and third-round pick (LW Jarkko Ruutu) in 1998 draft to Vancouver Canucks for C Trevor Linden (February 6, 1998). ... Bruised thigh (March 17, 1998); missed four games. ... Fractured tibia (November 1, 1998); missed 31 games. ... Tore anterior cruciate ligament in knee (March 5, 1999); missed remainder of season. ... Suffered concussion (October 20, 1999); missed one game. ... Injured thumb (February 23, 2000); missed one game. ... Bruised shoulder (January 28, 2001); missed three games. ... Suspended 10 games by NHL for elbowing incident (October 15, 2001).
STATISTICAL PLATEAUS: Three-goal games: 2000-01 (1), 2001-02 (1), 2002-03 (1). Total: 3.

Season Team	League	REGULAR SEASON Gms.	G	A	Pts.	PIM	+/-	PP	SH	PLAYOFFS Gms.	G	A	Pts.	PIM
91-92—Guelph	OHL	47	7	14	21	145	...	...	...	—	—	—	—	—
92-93—Guelph	OHL	59	27	32	59	164	...	...	...	5	2	2	4	6
93-94—Guelph	OHL	61	28	54	82	165	...	...	...	9	2	6	8	30
94-95—Guelph	OHL	62	54	65	119	58	...	...	...	14	*15	18	33	41
95-96—New York Islanders	NHL	76	18	21	39	83	-14	4	0	—	—	—	—	—
96-97—New York Islanders	NHL	64	10	13	23	68	-3	3	0	—	—	—	—	—
—Utah	IHL	13	5	5	10	16	...	...	...	—	—	—	—	—
97-98—New York Islanders	NHL	52	7	11	18	58	-19	1	0	—	—	—	—	—
—Vancouver	NHL	22	6	9	15	63	2	1	1	—	—	—	—	—
98-99—Vancouver	NHL	32	8	8	16	44	-6	1	0	—	—	—	—	—
99-00—Vancouver	NHL	80	25	25	50	126	-2	4	0	—	—	—	—	—
00-01—Vancouver	NHL	79	25	30	55	93	-18	14	0	4	2	2	4	8
01-02—Vancouver	NHL	72	36	49	85	110	21	14	0	6	2	2	4	14
02-03—Vancouver	NHL	82	46	51	97	144	2	*25	0	14	2	4	6	*60
NHL Totals (8 years)		559	181	217	398	789	-37	67	1	24	6	8	14	82

BERUBE, CRAIG   LW

PERSONAL: Born December 17, 1965, in Calahoo, Alta. ... 6-2/210. ... Shoots left. ... Name pronounced buh-ROO-bee.
TRANSACTIONS/CAREER NOTES: Signed as non-drafted free agent by Philadelphia Flyers (March 19, 1986). ... Sprained left knee (March 1988). ... Traded by Flyers with RW Scott Mellanby and C Craig Fisher to Edmonton Oilers for RW Dave Brown, D Corey Foster and the NHL rights to RW Jari Kurri (May 30, 1991). ... Traded by Oilers with G Grant Fuhr and RW/LW Glenn Anderson to Toronto Maple Leafs for LW Vincent Damphousse, D Luke Richardson, G Peter Ing, C Scott Thornton and future considerations (September 19, 1991). ... Traded by Maple Leafs with D Alexander Godynyuk, RW Gary Leeman, D Michel Petit and G Jeff Reese to Calgary Flames for C Doug Gilmour, D Jamie Macoun, LW Kent Manderville, D Ric Nattress and G Rick Wamsley (January 2, 1992). ... Traded by Flames to Washington Capitals for fifth-round pick (C Darryl LaFrance) in 1993 draft (June 26, 1993). ... Suffered from the flu (March 31, 1995); missed three games. ... Fractured jaw (September 14, 1995); missed seven games. ... Suffered mild concussion (November 10, 1995); missed four games. ... Suspended 10 games by NHL for coming off bench to fight (December 22, 1995). ... Injured right knee (March 22, 1996); missed 11 games. ... Suspended two games and fined $1,000 by NHL for slashing incident (January 19, 1997). ... Injured hip (October 15, 1997); missed seven games. ... Suspended one game by NHL for directing a racial slur at another player (November 25, 1997). ... Traded by Capitals for Philadelphia Flyers for future considerations (March 23, 1999). ... Suffered from the flu (January 11, 2000); missed one game. ... Signed as free agent by Capitals (July 7, 2000). ... Traded by Capitals to New York Islanders for ninth-round pick (F Robert Muller) in 2001 draft (January 11, 2001). ... Signed as free agent by Calgary Flames (September 18, 2001). ... Suspended three games by NHL for unsportsmanlike conduct (December 10, 2001). ... Suspended five games by NHL for cross-checking incident (December 18, 2001).

Season Team	League	REGULAR SEASON								PLAYOFFS				
		Gms.	G	A	Pts.	PIM	+/-	PP	SH	Gms.	G	A	Pts.	PIM
82-83—Williams Lake	PCJHL	33	9	24	33	99	...	...	...	—	—	—	—	—
—Kamloops	WHL	4	0	0	0	0	...	...	...	—	—	—	—	—
83-84—New Westminster	WHL	70	11	20	31	104	...	...	...	8	1	2	3	5
84-85—New Westminster	WHL	70	25	44	69	191	...	...	...	10	3	2	5	4
85-86—Kamloops	WHL	32	17	14	31	119	...	...	...	—	—	—	—	—
—Medicine Hat	WHL	34	14	16	30	95	...	...	...	25	7	8	15	102
86-87—Hershey	AHL	63	7	17	24	325	...	...	...	—	—	—	—	—
—Philadelphia	NHL	7	0	0	0	57	2	0	0	5	0	0	0	17
87-88—Hershey	AHL	31	5	9	14	119	...	...	...	—	—	—	—	—
—Philadelphia	NHL	27	3	2	5	108	1	0	0	—	—	—	—	—
88-89—Hershey	AHL	7	0	2	2	19	...	...	...	—	—	—	—	—
—Philadelphia	NHL	53	1	1	2	199	-15	0	0	16	0	0	0	56
89-90—Philadelphia	NHL	74	4	14	18	291	-7	0	0	—	—	—	—	—
90-91—Philadelphia	NHL	74	8	9	17	293	-6	0	0	—	—	—	—	—
91-92—Toronto	NHL	40	5	7	12	109	-2	1	0	—	—	—	—	—
—Calgary	NHL	36	1	4	5	155	-3	0	0	—	—	—	—	—
92-93—Calgary	NHL	77	4	8	12	209	-6	0	0	6	0	1	1	21
93-94—Washington	NHL	84	7	7	14	305	-4	0	0	8	0	0	0	21
94-95—Washington	NHL	43	2	4	6	173	-5	0	0	7	0	0	0	29
95-96—Washington	NHL	50	2	10	12	151	1	1	0	2	0	0	0	19
96-97—Washington	NHL	80	4	3	7	218	-11	0	0	—	—	—	—	—
97-98—Washington	NHL	74	6	9	15	189	-3	0	0	21	1	0	1	21
98-99—Washington	NHL	66	5	4	9	166	-7	0	0	—	—	—	—	—
—Philadelphia	NHL	11	0	0	0	28	-3	0	0	6	1	0	1	4
99-00—Philadelphia	NHL	77	4	8	12	162	3	0	0	18	1	0	1	23
00-01—Washington	NHL	22	0	1	1	18	-3	0	0	—	—	—	—	—
—New York Islanders	NHL	38	0	2	2	54	-5	0	0	—	—	—	—	—
01-02—Calgary	NHL	66	3	1	4	164	-2	1	0	—	—	—	—	—
02-03—Calgary	NHL	55	2	4	6	100	-6	0	0	—	—	—	—	—
NHL Totals (17 years)		1054	61	98	159	3149	-81	3	0	89	3	1	4	211

BETTS, BLAIR   C   FLAMES

PERSONAL: Born February 16, 1980, in Edmonton ... 6-3/200. ... Shoots left.

TRANSACTIONS/CAREER NOTES: Selected by Calgary Flames in second round (second Flames pick, 33rd overall) of NHL entry draft (June 27, 1998). ... Re-signed by Calgary (June 10, 2003).

Season Team	League	REGULAR SEASON								PLAYOFFS				
		Gms.	G	A	Pts.	PIM	+/-	PP	SH	Gms.	G	A	Pts.	PIM
96-97—Prince George	WHL	58	12	18	30	19	...	...	...	15	2	2	4	6
97-98—Prince George	WHL	71	35	41	76	38	...	...	...	11	4	6	10	8
98-99—Prince George	WHL	42	20	22	42	39	...	...	...	7	3	2	5	8
99-00—Prince George	WHL	44	24	35	59	38	...	...	...	13	11	11	22	6
00-01—Saint John	AHL	75	13	15	28	28	...	...	...	19	2	3	5	4
01-02—Saint John	AHL	67	20	29	49	10	...	...	...	—	—	—	—	—
—Calgary	NHL	6	1	0	1	2	-1	0	0	—	—	—	—	—
02-03—Saint John	AHL	19	6	7	13	6	...	...	...	—	—	—	—	—
—Calgary	NHL	9	1	3	4	0	3	0	0	—	—	—	—	—
NHL Totals (2 years)		15	2	3	5	2	2	0	0					

BEZINA, GORAN   D   COYOTES

PERSONAL: Born March 21, 1980, in Split, Yugoslavia. ... 6-3/203. ... Shoots left.

TRANSACTIONS/CAREER NOTES: Selected by Phoenix Coyotes in eighth round (eighth Coyotes pick, 234th overall) of NHL entry draft (June 27, 1999).

Season Team	League	REGULAR SEASON								PLAYOFFS				
		Gms.	G	A	Pts.	PIM	+/-	PP	SH	Gms.	G	A	Pts.	PIM
98-99—Fribourg-Gotteron	Switzerland Jr.	22	11	6	17	64	...	...	...	—	—	—	—	—
—Fribourg-Gotteron	Switzerland	38	0	0	0	14	...	...	...	4	0	0	0	2
99-00—Fribourg-Gotteron	Switzerland Jr.	2	0	1	1	16	...	...	...	2	1	1	2	8
—Fribourg-Gotteron	Switzerland	44	3	6	9	10	...	...	...	4	0	0	0	6
00-01—Fribourg-Gotteron	Switzerland	44	10	10	20	44	...	...	...	5	1	1	2	12
01-02—Springfield	AHL	66	2	11	13	50	...	...	...	—	—	—	—	—
02-03—Springfield	AHL	64	3	4	7	27	...	...	...					

BICANEK, RADIM   D

PERSONAL: Born January 18, 1975, in Uherske Hradiste, Czechoslovakia. ... 6-1/195. ... Shoots left. ... Name pronounced RA-deem bih-CHAN-ihk.

TRANSACTIONS/CAREER NOTES: Selected by Ottawa Senators in second round (second Senators pick, 27th overall) of NHL entry draft (June 26, 1993). ... Traded by Senators to Chicago Blackhawks for sixth-round pick (G Martin Prusek) in 1999 draft (March 12, 1999). ... Selected by Columbus Blue Jackets in NHL expansion draft (June 23, 2000).

Season Team	League	REGULAR SEASON								PLAYOFFS				
		Gms.	G	A	Pts.	PIM	+/-	PP	SH	Gms.	G	A	Pts.	PIM
92-93—Jihlava	Czech	43	2	3	5	...	...	...	...	—	—	—	—	—
93-94—Belleville	OHL	63	16	27	43	49	...	...	...	12	2	8	10	21
94-95—Belleville	OHL	49	13	26	39	61	...	...	...	16	6	5	11	30
—Ottawa	NHL	6	0	0	0	0	3	0	0	—	—	—	—	—
—Prin. Edward Island	AHL	—	—	—	—	—	—	—	—	3	0	1	1	0
95-96—Prin. Edward Island	AHL	74	7	19	26	87	...	...	...	5	0	2	2	6
96-97—Worcester	AHL	44	1	15	16	22	...	...	...	—	—	—	—	—
—Ottawa	NHL	21	0	1	1	8	-4	0	0	7	0	0	0	8
97-98—Ottawa	NHL	1	0	0	0	0	0	0	0	—	—	—	—	—
—Detroit	IHL	9	1	3	4	16	...	...	...	—	—	—	—	—
—Manitoba	IHL	42	1	7	8	52	...	...	...	—	—	—	—	—
98-99—Ottawa	NHL	7	0	0	0	4	-1	0	0	—	—	—	—	—
—Grand Rapids	IHL	46	8	17	25	48	...	...	...	—	—	—	—	—
—Chicago	NHL	7	0	0	0	6	-3	0	0	—	—	—	—	—
99-00—Cleveland	IHL	70	5	27	32	125	...	...	...	9	2	2	4	8
—Chicago	NHL	11	0	3	3	4	7	0	0	—	—	—	—	—
00-01—Syracuse	AHL	68	22	43	65	124	...	...	...	5	4	2	6	2
—Columbus	NHL	9	0	2	2	6	1	0	0	—	—	—	—	—
01-02—Columbus	NHL	60	1	5	6	34	-15	0	0	—	—	—	—	—
02-03—Syracuse	AHL	56	6	17	23	111	...	...	...	—	—	—	—	—
—Binghamton	AHL	21	3	10	13	42	...	...	...	—	—	—	—	—
NHL Totals (7 years)		122	1	11	12	62	-12	0	0	7	0	0	0	8

BICEK, JIRI   LW   DEVILS

PERSONAL: Born December 3, 1978, in Kosice, Czechoslovakia ... 5-10/195. ... Shoots left.
TRANSACTIONS/CAREER NOTES: Selected by New Jersey Devils in fifth round (fourth Devils pick, 131st overall) of NHL entry draft (June 21, 1997).

Season Team	League	REGULAR SEASON								PLAYOFFS				
		Gms.	G	A	Pts.	PIM	+/-	PP	SH	Gms.	G	A	Pts.	PIM
94-95—HC Kosice	Slovakia Jrs.	42	38	36	74	18	...	...	...	—	—	—	—	—
95-96—HC Kosice	Slovakia	30	10	15	25	16	...	...	...	9	2	4	6	0
96-97—HC Kosice	Slovakia	44	11	14	25	20	...	...	...	7	1	3	4	...
97-98—Albany	AHL	50	10	10	20	22	...	...	...	13	1	6	7	4
98-99—Albany	AHL	79	15	45	60	102	...	...	...	5	2	2	4	2
99-00—Albany	AHL	80	7	36	43	51	...	...	...	4	0	2	2	0
00-01—Albany	AHL	73	12	29	41	73	...	...	...	—	—	—	—	—
—New Jersey	NHL	5	1	0	1	4	0	0	0	—	—	—	—	—
01-02—Albany	AHL	62	15	19	34	45	...	...	...	—	—	—	—	—
—New Jersey	NHL	1	0	0	0	0	-1	0	0	—	—	—	—	—
02-03—Albany	AHL	24	4	10	14	28	...	...	...	—	—	—	—	—
—New Jersey	NHL	44	5	6	11	25	7	1	0	5	0	0	0	0
NHL Totals (3 years)		50	6	6	12	29	6	1	0	5	0	0	0	0

BIERK, ZAC   G   COYOTES

PERSONAL: Born September 17, 1976, in Peterborough, Ont. ... 6-4/205. ... Catches left. ... Name pronounced BUHRK.
TRANSACTIONS/CAREER NOTES: Selected by Tampa Bay Lightning in ninth round (eighth Lightning pick, 212th overall) of NHL entry draft (July 8, 1995). ... Injured neck (April 6, 2000); missed final two games of season. ... Selected by Minnesota Wild in NHL expansion draft (June 23, 2000). ... Signed as free agent by Phoenix Coyotes (August 30, 2001). ... Re-signed by Coyotes (July 28, 2003).

Season Team	League	REGULAR SEASON								PLAYOFFS							
		Gms.	Min	W	L	T	GA	SO	Avg.	SV%	Gms.	Min.	W	L	GA	SO	Avg.	SV%
93-94—Peterborough	Tier II Jr. A	4	205	...	...	...	17	0	4.98	—	—	—	—	—	—	—	—	—
—Peterborough	OHL	9	423	0	4	2	37	0	5.25	—	1	33	0	0	7	0	12.73	—
94-95—Peterborough	OHL	35	1798	12	15	5	118	0	3.94	—	6	301	2	3	24	0	4.78	—
95-96—Peterborough	OHL	58	3292	31	16	6	174	2	3.17	—	*22	*1383	*14	†7	*83	0	3.60	—
96-97—Peterborough	OHL	49	2744	*28	16	0	151	2	3.30	—	11	666	6	5	35	0	3.15	—
97-98—Adirondack	AHL	12	558	1	6	1	36	0	3.87	—	—	—	—	—	—	—	—	—
—Tampa Bay	NHL	13	433	1	4	1	30	0	4.16	.857	—	—	—	—	—	—	—	—
98-99—Cleveland	IHL	27	1556	11	12	‡4	79	0	3.05	—	—	—	—	—	—	—	—	—
—Tampa Bay	NHL	1	59	0	1	0	2	0	2.03	.905	—	—	—	—	—	—	—	—
99-00—Detroit	IHL	15	846	6	8	2	46	1	3.26	—	—	—	—	—	—	—	—	—
—Tampa Bay	NHL	12	509	4	4	1	31	0	3.65	.899	—	—	—	—	—	—	—	—
00-01—Cleveland	IHL	49	2785	24	18	‡5	134	6	2.89	—	4	182	0	3	10	0	3.30	—
—Minnesota	NHL	1	60	0	1	0	6	0	6.00	.778	—	—	—	—	—	—	—	—
01-02—Springfield	AHL	1	20	0	1	0	4	0	12.00	—	—	—	—	—	—	—	—	—
—Augusta	ECHL	30	1747	16	9	3	66	3	2.34	—	—	—	—	—	—	—	—	—
02-03—Springfield	AHL	13	685	6	4	1	33	0	2.89	—	—	—	—	—	—	—	—	—
—Phoenix	NHL	16	884	4	9	1	32	1	2.17	.932	—	—	—	—	—	—	—	—
NHL Totals (5 years)		43	1945	9	19	3	101	1	3.12	.903								

BILLINGTON, CRAIG   G   CAPITALS

PERSONAL: Born September 11, 1966, in London, Ont. ... 5-10/168. ... Catches left.
TRANSACTIONS/CAREER NOTES: Selected by New Jersey Devils in second round (second Devils pick, 23rd overall) of NHL entry draft (June 9, 1984). ... Injured hamstring (February 15, 1992); missed two games. ... Strained knee (March 11, 1992); missed six games. ... Underwent

knee surgery (April 13, 1992). ... Suffered from sore throat (March 27, 1993); missed one game. ... Traded by Devils with C/LW Troy Mallette and fourth-round pick (C Cosmo Dupaul) in 1993 draft to Ottawa Senators for G Peter Sidorkiewicz and future considerations (June 20, 1993). Senators sent LW Mike Peluso to Devils to complete deal (June 26, 1993). ... Injured knee (January 27, 1995); missed 17 games. ... Traded by Senators to Boston Bruins for eighth-round pick (D Ray Schultz) in 1995 draft (April 7, 1995). ... Signed as free agent by Florida Panthers (September 4, 1996). ... Selected by Colorado Avalanche in NHL waiver draft for cash (September 30, 1996). ... Sprained knee ligament (November 19, 1996); missed seven games. ... Traded by Avalanche to Washington Capitals for future considerations (July 16, 1999). ... Bruised hand (March 2, 2001); missed six games.

Season Team	League	REGULAR SEASON									PLAYOFFS							
		Gms.	Min	W	L	T	GA	SO	Avg.	SV%	Gms.	Min.	W	L	GA	SO	Avg.	SV%
82-83 —London Diamonds	OPJHL	23	1338	...	...	...	76	0	3.41	—	—	—	—	—	—	—	—	—
83-84 —Belleville......................	OHL	44	2335	20	19	0	162	1	4.16	—	1	30	0	0	3	0	6.00	—
84-85 —Belleville......................	OHL	47	2544	26	19	0	180	1	4.25	—	14	761	7	5	47	†1	3.71	—
85-86 —Belleville......................	OHL	3	180	2	1	0	11	0	3.67	—	†20	1133	9	6	*68	0	3.60	—
—New Jersey	NHL	18	901	4	9	1	77	0	5.13	.840	—	—	—	—	—	—	—	—
86-87 —Maine	AHL	20	1151	9	8	2	70	0	3.65	—	—	—	—	—	—	—	—	—
—New Jersey	NHL	22	1114	4	13	2	89	0	4.79	.844	—	—	—	—	—	—	—	—
87-88 —Utica..........................	AHL	*59	*3404	22	27	8	*208	1	3.67	—	—	—	—	—	—	—	—	—
88-89 —New Jersey	NHL	3	140	1	1	0	11	0	4.71	.831	—	—	—	—	—	—	—	—
—Utica..........................	AHL	41	2432	17	18	6	150	2	3.70	—	4	219	1	3	18	0	4.93	—
89-90 —Utica..........................	AHL	38	2087	20	13	1	138	2	3.97	—	—	—	—	—	—	—	—	—
90-91 —Canadian nat'l team	Int'l	34	1879	17	14	2	110	2	3.51	—	—	—	—	—	—	—	—	—
91-92 —New Jersey	NHL	26	1363	13	7	1	69	2	3.04	.892	—	—	—	—	—	—	—	—
92-93 —New Jersey	NHL	42	2389	21	16	4	146	2	3.67	.876	2	78	0	1	5	0	3.85	.872
93-94 —Ottawa.......................	NHL	63	3319	11	*41	4	*254	0	4.59	.859	—	—	—	—	—	—	—	—
94-95 —Boston	NHL	8	373	5	1	0	19	0	3.06	.864	1	25	0	0	1	0	2.40	.900
—Ottawa.......................	NHL	9	472	0	6	2	32	0	4.07	.867	—	—	—	—	—	—	—	—
95-96 —Boston	NHL	27	1380	10	13	3	79	1	3.43	.867	1	60	0	1	6	0	6.00	.786
96-97 —Colorado	NHL	23	1200	11	8	2	53	1	2.65	.909	1	20	0	1	1	0	3.00	.923
97-98 —Colorado	NHL	23	1162	8	7	4	45	1	2.32	.923	1	1	0	0	0	0	—	—
98-99 —Colorado	NHL	21	1086	11	8	1	52	0	2.87	.894	1	9	0	0	1	0	6.67	.833
99-00 —Washington..................	NHL	13	611	3	6	1	28	2	2.75	.910	1	20	0	0	1	0	3.00	.833
00-01 —Washington..................	NHL	12	660	3	5	2	27	0	2.45	.915	—	—	—	—	—	—	—	—
01-02 —Washington..................	NHL	17	710	4	5	3	36	0	3.04	.878	—	—	—	—	—	—	—	—
02-03 —Washington..................	NHL	5	217	1	3	1	17	0	4.70	.823	—	—	—	—	—	—	—	—
NHL Totals (15 years)...........		332	17097	110	149	31	1034	9	3.63	.877	8	213	0	2	15	0	4.23	.853

BIRBRAER, MAX — LW — PANTHERS

PERSONAL: Born December 15, 1980, in Ust-Kamenogorsk, U.S.S.R. ... 6-2/185. ... Shoots left.
TRANSACTIONS/CAREER NOTES: Selected by New Jersey Devils in third round (sixth Devils pick, 67th overall) of NHL entry draft (June 24, 2000). ... Signed by Florida Panthers (July 10, 2003).

Season Team	League	REGULAR SEASON								PLAYOFFS				
		Gms.	G	A	Pts.	PIM	+/-	PP	SH	Gms.	G	A	Pts.	PIM
97-98 —Shelburne	Jr. A	12	7	11	18	8	...	...	...	—	—	—	—	—
98-99 —Shelburne	Jr. A	35	20	22	42	25	...	...	...	—	—	—	—	—
99-00 —Newmarket	OPJA	47	50	32	82	52	...	...	...	—	—	—	—	—
00-01 —Albany......................	AHL	50	7	6	13	24	...	...	...	—	—	—	—	—
01-02 —Albany......................	AHL	40	6	7	13	22	...	...	...	—	—	—	—	—
02-03 —Albany......................	AHL	57	6	6	12	42	...	...	...	—	—	—	—	—

BIRON, MARTIN — G — SABRES

PERSONAL: Born August 15, 1977, in Lac St. Charles, Que. ... 6-2/168. ... Catches left. ... Brother of Mathieu Biron, defenseman, Tampa Bay Lightning.
TRANSACTIONS/CAREER NOTES: Selected by Buffalo Sabres in first round (second Sabres pick, 16th overall) of NHL entry draft (July 8, 1995). ... Missed first 12 games of 2000-01 season due to contract dispute.

Season Team	League	REGULAR SEASON									PLAYOFFS							
		Gms.	Min	W	L	T	GA	SO	Avg.	SV%	Gms.	Min.	W	L	GA	SO	Avg.	SV%
94-95 —Beauport	QMJHL	56	3193	29	16	9	132	3	2.48	—	16	902	8	7	37	4	2.46	—
95-96 —Beauport	QMJHL	55	3207	29	17	7	152	1	2.84	—	*19	1132	*12	†8	64	0	3.39	—
—Buffalo	NHL	3	119	0	2	0	10	0	5.04	.844	—	—	—	—	—	—	—	—
96-97 —Beauport	QMJHL	18	935	6	10	1	62	1	3.98	—	—	—	—	—	—	—	—	—
—Hull	QMJHL	16	972	11	4	1	43	2	2.65	—	6	326	3	1	19	0	3.50	—
97-98 —Rochester	AHL	41	2312	14	18	6	113	*5	2.93	—	4	239	1	3	16	0	4.02	—
—South Carolina	ECHL	2	86	0	1	1	3	0	2.09	—	—	—	—	—	—	—	—	—
98-99 —Rochester	AHL	52	3129	36	13	3	108	*6	*2.07	—	*20	1167	12	*8	42	†1	*2.16	—
—Buffalo	NHL	6	281	1	2	1	10	0	2.14	.917	—	—	—	—	—	—	—	—
99-00 —Rochester	AHL	6	344	6	0	0	12	1	2.09	—	—	—	—	—	—	—	—	—
—Buffalo	NHL	41	2229	19	18	2	90	5	2.42	.909	—	—	—	—	—	—	—	—
00-01 —Rochester	AHL	4	239	3	1	0	4	1	1.00	—	—	—	—	—	—	—	—	—
—Buffalo	NHL	18	918	7	7	1	39	2	2.55	.909	—	—	—	—	—	—	—	—
01-02 —Buffalo	NHL	72	4085	31	28	10	151	4	2.22	.915	—	—	—	—	—	—	—	—
02-03 —Buffalo	NHL	54	3170	17	28	6	135	4	2.56	.908	—	—	—	—	—	—	—	—
NHL Totals (6 years)............		194	10802	75	85	20	435	15	2.42	.910								

B

BIRON, MATHIEU　　　　　D　　　　　PANTHERS

PERSONAL: Born April 29, 1980, in Lac St. Charles, Que. ... 6-6/229. ... Shoots right. ... Brother of Martin Biron, goaltender, Buffalo Sabres.
TRANSACTIONS/CAREER NOTES: Selected by Los Angeles Kings in first round (first Kings pick, 21st overall) of NHL entry draft (June 27, 1998). ... Traded by Kings with C Olli Jokinen, LW Josh Green and first-round pick (LW Taylor Pyatt) in 1999 draft to New York Islanders for RW Zigmund Palffy, C Bryan Smolinski, G Marcel Cousineau and fourth-round pick (C Daniel Johansson) in 1999 draft (June 20, 1999). ... Traded by Islanders with second-round pick (traded to Washington) in 2002 draft to Tampa Bay Lightning for RW Alexander Kharitonov and D Adrian Aucoin (June 22, 2001). ... Claimed by Columbus Blue Jackets from Lightning in NHL waiver draft (October 4, 2002). ... Traded by Blue Jackets to Florida Panthers for RW Petr Tenkrat (October 4, 2002). ... Re-signed by Panthers (June 15, 2003).

					REGULAR SEASON							PLAYOFFS			
Season Team	League	Gms.	G	A	Pts.	PIM	+/-	PP	SH		Gms.	G	A	Pts.	PIM
97-98—Shawinigan	QMJHL	59	8	28	36	60	...	...	...		6	0	1	1	10
98-99—Shawinigan	QMJHL	69	13	32	45	116	...	...	...		6	0	2	2	6
99-00—New York Islanders	NHL	60	4	4	8	38	-13	2	0		—	—	—	—	—
00-01—Lowell	AHL	22	1	3	4	17	...	...	...		—	—	—	—	—
—New York Islanders	NHL	14	0	1	1	12	2	0	0		—	—	—	—	—
—Springfield	AHL	34	0	6	6	18	...	...	...		—	—	—	—	—
01-02—Springfield	AHL	35	4	9	13	16	...	...	...		—	—	—	—	—
—Tampa Bay	NHL	36	0	0	0	12	-16	0	0		—	—	—	—	—
02-03—San Antonio	AHL	43	3	8	11	58	...	...	...		—	—	—	—	—
—Florida	NHL	34	1	8	9	14	-18	0	1		—	—	—	—	—
NHL Totals (4 years)		144	5	13	18	76	-45	2	1		—	—	—	—	—

BLACKBURN, DAN　　　　　G　　　　　RANGERS

PERSONAL: Born May 20, 1983, in Montreal ... 6-1/180. ... Catches left.
TRANSACTIONS/CAREER NOTES: Selected by New York Rangers in first round (first Rangers pick, 10th overall) of NHL entry draft (June 23, 2001).

						REGULAR SEASON									PLAYOFFS				
Season Team	League	Gms.	Min	W	L	T	GA	SO	Avg.	SV%		Gms.	Min.	W	L	GA	SO	Avg.	SV%
99-00—Kootenay	WHL	51	3004	34	8	7	126	3	2.52	—		*21	*1272	*16	5	*43	2	2.03	—
00-01—Kootenay	WHL	50	2922	†33	14	2	135	1	2.77	—		11	706	7	4	23	1	1.95	—
01-02—New York Rangers	NHL	31	1737	12	16	0	95	0	3.28	.898		—	—	—	—	—	—	—	—
—Hartford	AHL	4	243	2	1	1	11	0	2.72	—		—	—	—	—	—	—	—	—
02-03—New York Rangers	NHL	32	1762	8	16	4	93	1	3.17	.890		—	—	—	—	—	—	—	—
NHL Totals (2 years)		63	3499	20	32	4	188	1	3.22	.894									

BLAKE, JASON　　　　　RW　　　　　ISLANDERS

PERSONAL: Born September 2, 1973, in Moorhead, Minn. ... 5-10/180. ... Shoots left.
TRANSACTIONS/CAREER NOTES: Signed as non-drafted free agent by Los Angeles Kings (April 17, 1999). ... Suffered concussion (December 19, 1999); missed four games. ... Traded by Kings to New York Islanders for fifth-round pick (D Joel Andersen) in 2002 draft (January 3, 2001). ... Suffered concussion (February 9, 2001); missed one game. ... Granted personal leave for final 13 games of season.
STATISTICAL PLATEAUS: Three-goal games: 2002-03 (1).

					REGULAR SEASON							PLAYOFFS			
Season Team	League	Gms.	G	A	Pts.	PIM	+/-	PP	SH		Gms.	G	A	Pts.	PIM
94-95—Ferris State	CCHA	36	16	16	32	46	...	...	...		—	—	—	—	—
96-97—Univ. of North Dakota	WCHA	43	19	32	51	44	...	...	...		—	—	—	—	—
97-98—Univ. of North Dakota	WCHA	38	24	27	51	62	...	...	...		—	—	—	—	—
98-99—Univ. of North Dakota	WCHA	38	*28	†41	*69	49	...	...	...		—	—	—	—	—
—Orlando	IHL	5	3	5	8	6	...	...	...		13	3	4	7	20
—Los Angeles	NHL	1	1	0	1	0	1	0	0		—	—	—	—	—
99-00—Los Angeles	NHL	64	5	18	23	26	4	0	0		3	0	0	0	0
—Long Beach	IHL	7	3	6	9	2	...	...	...		—	—	—	—	—
00-01—Los Angeles	NHL	17	1	3	4	10	-8	0	0		—	—	—	—	—
—Lowell	AHL	2	0	1	1	2	...	...	...		—	—	—	—	—
—New York Islanders	NHL	30	4	8	12	24	-12	1	1		—	—	—	—	—
01-02—New York Islanders	NHL	82	8	10	18	36	-11	0	0		7	0	1	1	13
02-03—New York Islanders	NHL	81	25	30	55	58	16	3	1		5	0	1	1	2
NHL Totals (5 years)		275	44	69	113	154	-10	4	2		15	0	2	2	15

BLAKE, ROB　　　　　D　　　　　AVALANCHE

PERSONAL: Born December 10, 1969, in Simcoe, Ont. ... 6-4/225. ... Shoots right. ... Full Name: Robert Bowlby Blake.
TRANSACTIONS/CAREER NOTES: Selected by Los Angeles Kings in fourth round (fourth Kings pick, 70th overall) of NHL entry draft (June 11, 1988). ... Sprained knee (April 1990). ... Injured knee (February 12, 1991); missed two games. ... Injured shoulder (October 8, 1991); missed 11 games. ... Sprained knee ligaments (November 28, 1991); missed six games. ... Suffered from the flu (January 21, 1992); missed one game. ... Suffered from the flu (February 13, 1992); missed one game. ... Strained shoulder (March 14, 1992); missed four games. ... Fractured rib (December 19, 1992); missed three games. ... Bruised lower back (April 3, 1993); missed final five games of regular season and one playoff game. ... Strained groin (January 23, 1995); missed 11 games. ... Strained groin (March 11, 1995); missed 12 games. ... Strained groin (April 7, 1995); missed one game. ... Suffered partial tear of left knee ligaments (October 20, 1995); missed 76 games. ... Fractured hand (December 26, 1996); missed 11 games. ... Suspended two games and fined $1,000 by NHL for high-sticking incident (February 5, 1997). ... Suffered tendinitis in left knee (February 22, 1997); missed seven games. ... Fractured right foot (November 6, 1998); missed 15 games. ... Suspended three games and fined $1,000 by NHL for slashing incident (December 14, 1998). ... Suspended two games by NHL for cross-checking incident (April 9, 1999). ... Strained groin (December 8, 1999); missed two games. ... Bruised knee (April 1, 2000); missed three games. ... Suffered hairline fracture of lumbar vertebrae (October 13, 2000); missed three games. ... Bruised shoulder (February 21, 2001); missed two games. ... Traded by Kings with C Steve Reinprecht to Colorado Avalanche for RW Adam Deadmarsh, D Aaron Miller, first-round pick (C David Steckel) in 2001 draft, a player to be named later and future first-round pick in 2003 draft (February 21, 2001); Kings acquired

C Jared Aulin to complete deal (March 22, 2001). ... Sprained knee (March 20, 2001); missed eight games. ... Injured groin (November 27, 2001); missed three games. ... Suffered from the flu (February 13, 2002); missed one game. ... Bruised knee (February 11, 2002); missed one game. ... Reinjured knee (February 26, 2002); missed two games.

STATISTICAL PLATEAUS: Three-goal games: 2000-01 (1).

			REGULAR SEASON								PLAYOFFS				
Season Team	League	Gms.	G	A	Pts.	PIM	+/-	PP	SH		Gms.	G	A	Pts.	PIM
86-87—Stratford Jr. B............	OHA	31	11	20	31	115	...	...	...		—	—	—	—	—
87-88—Bowling Green	CCHA	36	5	8	13	72	...	...	...		—	—	—	—	—
88-89—Bowling Green	CCHA	46	11	21	32	140	...	...	...		—	—	—	—	—
89-90—Bowling Green	CCHA	42	23	36	59	140	...	...	...		—	—	—	—	—
—Los Angeles.................	NHL	4	0	0	0	4	0	0	0		8	1	3	4	4
90-91—Los Angeles...............	NHL	75	12	34	46	125	3	9	0		12	1	4	5	26
91-92—Los Angeles...............	NHL	57	7	13	20	102	-5	5	0		6	2	1	3	12
92-93—Los Angeles...............	NHL	76	16	43	59	152	18	10	0		23	4	6	10	46
93-94—Los Angeles...............	NHL	84	20	48	68	137	-7	7	0		—	—	—	—	—
94-95—Los Angeles...............	NHL	24	4	7	11	38	-16	4	0		—	—	—	—	—
95-96—Los Angeles...............	NHL	6	1	2	3	8	0	0	0		—	—	—	—	—
96-97—Los Angeles...............	NHL	62	8	23	31	82	-28	4	0		—	—	—	—	—
97-98—Los Angeles...............	NHL	81	23	27	50	94	-3	11	0		4	0	0	0	6
—Can. Olympic team	Int'l	6	1	1	2	2	...	...	...		—	—	—	—	—
98-99—Los Angeles...............	NHL	62	12	23	35	128	-7	5	1		—	—	—	—	—
99-00—Los Angeles...............	NHL	77	18	39	57	112	10	12	0		4	0	2	2	4
00-01—Los Angeles...............	NHL	54	17	32	49	69	-8	9	0		—	—	—	—	—
—Colorado.................	NHL	13	2	8	10	8	11	1	0		23	6	13	19	16
01-02—Colorado.................	NHL	75	16	40	56	58	16	10	0		20	6	6	12	16
—Can. Olympic team	Int'l	6	1	2	3	2	...	...	...		—	—	—	—	—
02-03—Colorado.................	NHL	79	17	28	45	57	20	8	2		7	1	2	3	8
NHL Totals (14 years).........		829	173	367	540	1174	4	95	3		107	21	37	58	138

BLATNY, ZDENEK   LW   THRASHERS

PERSONAL: Born January 14, 1981, in Brno, Czechoslovakia ... 6-1/190. ... Shoots left.
TRANSACTIONS/CAREER NOTES: Selected by Atlanta Thrashers in third round (third Thrashers pick, 68th overall) of NHL entry draft (June 26, 1999).

			REGULAR SEASON								PLAYOFFS				
Season Team	League	Gms.	G	A	Pts.	PIM	+/-	PP	SH		Gms.	G	A	Pts.	PIM
97-98—Kometa Brno..............	Czech. Jrs.	42	22	21	43	40	...	...	...		—	—	—	—	—
98-99—Seattle.....................	WHL	44	18	15	33	25	...	...	...		11	4	0	4	24
99-00—Seattle.....................	WHL	7	4	5	9	12	...	...	...		—	—	—	—	—
—Kootenay.................	WHL	61	43	39	82	119	...	...	...		21	10	*17	27	46
00-01—Kootenay.................	WHL	58	37	48	85	120	...	...	...		11	8	10	18	24
01-02—Chicago...................	AHL	41	4	3	7	30	...	...	...		3	2	0	2	0
—Greenville.................	ECHL	12	5	5	10	17	...	...	...		9	2	8	10	14
02-03—Chicago...................	AHL	72	12	9	21	62	...	...	...		—	—	—	—	—
—Atlanta.....................	NHL	4	0	0	0	0	-1	0	0		—	—	—	—	—
NHL Totals (1 year)............		4	0	0	0	0	-1	0	0						

BLOUIN, SYLVAIN   LW   CANADIENS

PERSONAL: Born May 21, 1974, in Montreal ... 6-2/207. ... Shoots left. ... Name pronounced bloo-AN.
TRANSACTIONS/CAREER NOTES: Selected by New York Rangers in fourth round (fifth Rangers pick, 104th overall) of NHL entry draft (June 29, 1994). ... Bruised hand (February 19, 1997); missed two games. ... Suspended two games and fined $1,000 by NHL for illegal check (October 1, 1998). ... Suffered from the flu (March 11, 1999); missed two games. ... Traded by Rangers with sixth-round pick (traded to Phoenix) in 1999 draft to Montreal Canadiens for D Peter Popovic (June 30, 1999). ... Signed as free agent by St. Louis Blues (August 25, 1999). ... Signed as free agent by Canadiens (July 7, 2000). ... Claimed by Minnesota Wild from Canadiens in NHL waiver draft (September 29, 2000). ... Bruised shoulder (December 7, 2000); missed 14 games. ... Strained groin (October 5, 2001); missed first five games of season. ... Fractured right thumb (January 30, 2002); missed four games. ... Traded by Wild to Canadiens for seventh-round pick in 2003 draft (October 31, 2002).

			REGULAR SEASON								PLAYOFFS				
Season Team	League	Gms.	G	A	Pts.	PIM	+/-	PP	SH		Gms.	G	A	Pts.	PIM
91-92—Laval......................	QMJHL	28	0	0	0	23	...	...	...		9	0	0	0	35
92-93—Laval......................	QMJHL	68	0	10	10	373	...	...	...		13	1	0	1	*66
93-94—Laval......................	QMJHL	62	18	22	40	*492	...	...	...		21	4	13	17	*177
94-95—Binghamton	AHL	10	1	0	1	46	...	...	...		2	0	0	0	24
—Chicago...................	IHL	1	0	0	0	2	...	...	...		—	—	—	—	—
—Charlotte..................	ECHL	50	5	7	12	280	...	...	...		3	0	0	0	6
95-96—Binghamton	AHL	71	5	8	13	*352	...	...	...		4	0	3	3	4
96-97—Binghamton	AHL	62	13	17	30	301	...	...	...		4	2	1	3	16
—New York Rangers......	NHL	6	0	0	0	18	-1	0	0		—	—	—	—	—
97-98—Hartford	AHL	53	8	9	17	286	...	...	...		9	0	1	1	63
—New York Rangers......	NHL	1	0	0	0	5	0	0	0		—	—	—	—	—
98-99—Fredericton	AHL	67	6	10	16	333	...	...	...		15	2	0	2	*87
—Montreal...................	NHL	5	0	0	0	19	0	0	0		—	—	—	—	—
99-00—Worcester	AHL	70	16	18	34	337	...	...	...		8	3	5	8	30
00-01—Minnesota	NHL	41	3	2	5	117	-5	0	0		—	—	—	—	—
01-02—Minnesota	NHL	43	0	2	2	130	-11	0	0		—	—	—	—	—
02-03—Hamilton	AHL	19	2	4	6	39	...	...	...		—	—	—	—	—
—Minnesota	NHL	2	0	0	0	4	0	0	0		—	—	—	—	—
—Montreal	NHL	17	0	0	0	43	-3	0	0		—	—	—	—	—
NHL Totals (6 years)...........		115	3	4	7	336	-20	0	0						

BOGUNIECKI, ERIC   RW   BLUES

PERSONAL: Born May 6, 1975, in New Haven, Conn. ... 5-8/194. ... Shoots right.
TRANSACTIONS/CAREER NOTES: Selected by St. Louis Blues in eighth round (sixth Blues pick, 193rd overall) of NHL entry draft (June 29, 1993). ... Signed as free agent by Florida Panthers (July 20, 1999). ... Traded by Panthers to Blues for C Andrei Podkonicky (December 18, 2000).

Season Team	League	Gms.	G	A	Pts.	PIM	+/-	PP	SH	Gms.	G	A	Pts.	PIM
92-93—Westminster School ...	Conn. H.S.	24	30	24	54	55	...	...	...	—	—	—	—	—
93-94—Univ. of New Hamp.....	Hockey East	40	17	16	33	66	...	...	...	—	—	—	—	—
94-95—Univ. of New Hamp.....	Hockey East	34	12	19	31	62	...	...	...	—	—	—	—	—
95-96—Univ. of New Hamp.....	Hockey East	32	23	28	51	46	...	...	...	—	—	—	—	—
96-97—Univ. of New Hamp.....	Hockey East	36	26	31	57	58	...	...	...	—	—	—	—	—
97-98—Dayton	ECHL	26	19	18	37	36	...	...	...	—	—	—	—	—
—Fort Wayne	IHL	35	4	8	12	29	...	...	...	4	1	2	3	10
98-99—Fort Wayne	IHL	72	32	34	66	100	...	...	...	2	0	1	1	2
99-00—Louisville	AHL	57	33	42	75	148	...	...	...	4	3	2	5	20
—Florida	NHL	4	0	0	0	2	-1	0	0	—	—	—	—	—
00-01—Louisville	AHL	28	13	12	25	56	...	...	...	—	—	—	—	—
—Worcester	AHL	45	17	28	45	100	...	...	...	9	3	2	5	10
—St. Louis	NHL	1	0	0	0	0	-1	0	0	—	—	—	—	—
01-02—Worcester	AHL	63	†38	46	84	181	...	...	...	3	2	0	2	4
—St. Louis	NHL	8	0	1	1	4	-2	0	0	1	0	1	1	0
02-03—St. Louis	NHL	80	22	27	49	38	22	3	1	7	1	2	3	2
NHL Totals (4 years)		93	22	28	50	44	18	3	1	8	1	3	4	2

BOILEAU, PATRICK   D

PERSONAL: Born February 22, 1975, in Montreal ... 6-0/202. ... Shoots right. ... Name pronounced BOY-loh.
TRANSACTIONS/CAREER NOTES: Selected by Washington Capitals in third round (third Capitals pick, 69th overall) of NHL entry draft (June 26, 1993). ... Signed as free agent by Detroit Red Wings (August 5, 2002).

Season Team	League	Gms.	G	A	Pts.	PIM	+/-	PP	SH	Gms.	G	A	Pts.	PIM
92-93—Laval	QMJHL	69	4	19	23	73	...	...	...	13	1	2	3	10
93-94—Laval	QMJHL	64	13	57	70	56	...	...	...	21	1	7	8	24
94-95—Laval	QMJHL	38	8	25	33	46	...	...	...	20	4	16	20	24
95-96—Portland	AHL	78	10	28	38	41	...	...	...	19	1	3	4	12
96-97—Portland	AHL	67	16	28	44	63	...	...	...	5	1	1	2	4
—Washington	NHL	1	0	0	0	0	0	0	0	—	—	—	—	—
97-98—Portland	AHL	47	6	21	27	53	...	...	...	10	0	1	1	8
98-99—Portland	AHL	52	6	18	24	52	...	...	...	—	—	—	—	—
—Indianapolis	IHL	29	8	13	21	27	...	...	...	4	0	1	1	2
—Washington	NHL	4	0	1	1	2	-4	0	0	—	—	—	—	—
99-00—Portland	AHL	63	2	15	17	61	...	...	...	4	0	0	0	4
00-01—Portland	AHL	77	6	14	20	50	...	...	...	3	0	0	0	8
01-02—Portland	AHL	75	17	19	36	43	...	...	...	—	—	—	—	—
—Washington	NHL	2	0	0	0	2	-1	0	0	—	—	—	—	—
02-03—Grand Rapids	AHL	23	2	11	13	39	...	...	...	—	—	—	—	—
—Detroit	NHL	25	2	6	8	14	8	0	0	—	—	—	—	—
NHL Totals (4 years)		32	2	7	9	18	3	0	0					

BOMBARDIR, BRAD   D   WILD

PERSONAL: Born May 5, 1972, in Powell River, B.C. ... 6-1/205. ... Shoots left. ... Full Name: Luke Bradley Bombardir. ... Name pronounced BAHM-bahr-deer.
TRANSACTIONS/CAREER NOTES: Selected by New Jersey Devils in third round (fifth Devils pick, 56th overall) of NHL entry draft (June 16, 1990). ... Bruised left knee (November 29, 1997); missed six games. ... Suffered from the flu (April 14, 1999); missed three games. ... Suffered throat injury (October 27, 1999); missed four games. ... Bruised left hand (December 9, 1999); missed six games. ... Traded by Devils to Minnesota Wild for G Chris Terreri (June 23, 2000). ... Strained groin (October 20, 2000); missed six games. ... Suffered back spasms (March 19, 2001); missed two games. ... Fractured right ankle (October 14, 2001); missed 29 games. ... Bruised right ankle (December 26, 2001); missed one game. ... Reinjured ankle (January 9, 2002); missed 11 games. ... Reinjured ankle (February 10, 2002); missed two games. ... Reinjured ankle (March 10, 2002); missed four games. ... Reinjured ankle (April 5, 2002); missed remainder of season.

Season Team	League	Gms.	G	A	Pts.	PIM	+/-	PP	SH	Gms.	G	A	Pts.	PIM
88-89—Powell River	BCJHL	30	6	5	11	24	...	...	...	6	0	0	0	0
89-90—Powell River	BCJHL	60	10	35	45	93	...	...	...	8	2	3	5	4
90-91—Univ. of North Dakota	WCHA	33	3	6	9	18	...	...	...	—	—	—	—	—
91-92—Univ. of North Dakota	WCHA	35	3	14	17	54	...	...	...	—	—	—	—	—
92-93—Univ. of North Dakota	WCHA	38	8	15	23	34	...	...	...	—	—	—	—	—
93-94—Univ. of North Dakota	WCHA	38	5	17	22	38	...	...	...	—	—	—	—	—
94-95—Albany	AHL	77	5	22	27	22	...	...	...	14	0	3	3	6
95-96—Albany	AHL	80	6	25	31	63	...	...	...	3	0	1	1	4
96-97—Albany	AHL	32	0	8	8	6	...	...	...	16	1	3	4	8
97-98—New Jersey	NHL	43	1	5	6	8	11	0	0	—	—	—	—	—
—Albany	AHL	5	0	0	0	0	...	...	...	—	—	—	—	—
98-99—New Jersey	NHL	56	1	7	8	16	-4	0	0	5	0	0	0	0
99-00—New Jersey	NHL	32	3	1	4	6	-6	0	0	1	0	0	0	0
00-01—Minnesota	NHL	70	0	15	15	42	-6	0	0	—	—	—	—	—
01-02—Minnesota	NHL	28	1	2	3	14	-6	1	0	—	—	—	—	—
02-03—Minnesota	NHL	58	1	14	15	16	15	1	0	4	0	0	0	0
NHL Totals (6 years)		287	7	44	51	102	4	2	0	10	0	0	0	0

BONDRA, PETER — RW — CAPITALS

PERSONAL: Born February 7, 1968, in Luck, U.S.S.R. ... 6-1/202. ... Shoots left. ... Name pronounced BAHN-druh.
TRANSACTIONS/CAREER NOTES: Selected by Washington Capitals in eighth round (ninth Capitals pick, 156th overall) of NHL entry draft (June 16, 1990). ... Dislocated left shoulder (January 17, 1991). ... Suffered recurring shoulder problems (February 13, 1991); missed 13 games. ... Injured throat (April 4, 1993); missed one game. ... Fractured left hand (November 26, 1993); missed 12 games. ... Played in Europe during 1994-95 NHL lockout. ... Suffered from the flu (April 8, 1995); missed one game. ... Signed by Detroit Vipers of IHL during contract holdout (September 28, 1995); re-signed by Capitals (October 20, 1995). ... Separated shoulder (November 11, 1995); missed six games. ... Pulled groin (February 24, 1996); missed four games. ... Strained groin (December 4, 1996); missed three games. ... Suspended one game and fined $1,000 by NHL for kneeing incident (February 4, 1997). ... Suffered back spasms (April 1, 1997); missed one game. ... Injured foot (November 29, 1997); missed three games. ... Injured knee (April 8, 1998); missed two games. ... Injured hip (November 28, 1998); missed one game. ... Fractured hand (March 15, 1999); missed remainder of season. ... Underwent knee surgery (December 5, 1999); missed eight games. ... Injured knee (January 4, 2000); missed seven games. ... Injured shoulder (March 30, 1999); missed five games. ... Suffered from the flu (January 1, 2002); missed three games. ... Suffered from the flu (February 26, 2002); missed one game. ... Suffered from the flu (March 2, 2002); missed one game.
STATISTICAL PLATEAUS: Three-goal games: 1990-91 (1), 1994-95 (1), 1995-96 (2), 1996-97 (1), 1997-98 (1), 1998-99 (2), 1999-00 (1), 2000-01 (2), 2001-02 (1). Total: 12. ... Four-goal games: 1995-96 (2), 1996-97 (1), 1998-99 (1), 2000-01 (1). Total: 5. ... Five goal games: 1993-94 (1). ... Total hat tricks: 18.

Season Team	League	REGULAR SEASON								PLAYOFFS				
		Gms.	G	A	Pts.	PIM	+/-	PP	SH	Gms.	G	A	Pts.	PIM
86-87—Kosice	Czech.	32	4	5	9	24	...	...	...	—	—	—	—	—
87-88—Kosice	Czech.	45	27	11	38	20	...	...	...	—	—	—	—	—
88-89—Kosice	Czech.	40	30	10	40	20	...	...	...	—	—	—	—	—
89-90—Kosice	Czech.	42	29	17	46	...	...	...	...	—	—	—	—	—
90-91—Washington	NHL	54	12	16	28	47	-10	4	0	4	0	1	1	2
91-92—Washington	NHL	71	28	28	56	42	16	4	0	7	6	2	8	4
92-93—Washington	NHL	83	37	48	85	70	8	10	0	6	0	6	6	0
93-94—Washington	NHL	69	24	19	43	40	22	4	0	9	2	4	6	4
94-95—HC Kosice	Slovakia	2	1	0	1	0	...	...	...	—	—	—	—	—
—Washington	NHL	47	*34	9	43	24	9	12	*6	7	5	3	8	10
95-96—Detroit	IHL	7	8	1	9	0	...	...	...	—	—	—	—	—
—Washington	NHL	67	52	28	80	40	18	11	4	6	3	2	5	8
96-97—Washington	NHL	77	46	31	77	72	7	10	4	—	—	—	—	—
97-98—Washington	NHL	76	†52	26	78	44	14	11	5	17	7	5	12	12
—Slovakian Oly. team	Int'l	2	1	0	1	25	...	...	...	—	—	—	—	—
98-99—Washington	NHL	66	31	24	55	56	-1	6	3	—	—	—	—	—
99-00—Washington	NHL	62	21	17	38	30	5	5	3	5	1	1	2	4
00-01—Washington	NHL	82	45	36	81	60	8	*22	4	6	2	0	2	6
01-02—Washington	NHL	77	39	31	70	80	-2	*17	1	—	—	—	—	—
02-03—Washington	NHL	76	30	26	56	52	-3	9	2	6	4	2	6	8
NHL Totals (13 years)		907	451	339	790	657	91	125	32	73	30	26	56	54

BONK, RADEK — LW — SENATORS

PERSONAL: Born January 9, 1976, in Krnov, Czechoslovakia. ... 6-2/217. ... Shoots left. ... Name pronounced BAHNK.
TRANSACTIONS/CAREER NOTES: Selected by Ottawa Senators in first round (first Senators pick, third overall) of NHL entry draft (June 28, 1994). ... Injured ankle (April 26, 1995); missed last five games of season. ... Injured hand (1995-96 season); missed one game. ... Suffered abdominal strain (November 8, 1996); missed six games. ... Fractured left wrist (November 23, 1996); missed 23 games. ... Suffered knee (March 5, 1998); missed one game. ... Injured hip flexor (November 7, 1998); missed one game. ... Suffered from the flu (January 4, 2000); missed two games. ... Suffered from the flu (February 19, 2001); missed one game. ... Fractured left thumb (March 24, 2001); missed final seven games of regular season and two playoff games.
STATISTICAL PLATEAUS: Three-goal games: 2000-01 (1).

Season Team	League	REGULAR SEASON								PLAYOFFS				
		Gms.	G	A	Pts.	PIM	+/-	PP	SH	Gms.	G	A	Pts.	PIM
90-91—Opava	Czech.	35	47	42	89	25	...	...	...	—	—	—	—	—
91-92—ZPS Zlin	Czech Dv.II	45	47	36	83	30	...	...	...	—	—	—	—	—
92-93—ZPS Zlin	Czech.	30	5	5	10	10	...	...	...	—	—	—	—	—
93-94—Las Vegas	IHL	76	42	45	87	208	...	...	...	5	1	2	3	10
94-95—Las Vegas	IHL	33	7	13	20	62	...	...	...	—	—	—	—	—
—Ottawa	NHL	42	3	8	11	28	-5	1	0	—	—	—	—	—
—Prin. Edward Island	AHL	—	—	—	—	—	...	...	—	1	0	0	0	0
95-96—Ottawa	NHL	76	16	19	35	36	-5	5	0	—	—	—	—	—
96-97—Ottawa	NHL	53	5	13	18	14	-4	0	1	7	0	1	1	4
97-98—Ottawa	NHL	65	7	9	16	16	-13	1	0	5	0	0	0	2
98-99—Ottawa	NHL	81	16	16	32	48	15	0	1	4	0	0	0	6
99-00—HC Pardubice	Czech Rep.	3	1	0	1	4	...	...	...	—	—	—	—	—
—Ottawa	NHL	80	23	37	60	53	-2	10	0	6	0	0	0	8
00-01—Ottawa	NHL	74	23	36	59	52	27	5	2	2	0	0	0	2
01-02—Ottawa	NHL	82	25	45	70	52	3	6	2	12	3	7	10	6
02-03—Ottawa	NHL	70	22	32	54	36	6	11	0	18	6	5	11	10
NHL Totals (9 years)		623	140	215	355	335	22	39	6	54	9	13	22	38

BONNI, RYAN — D

PERSONAL: Born February 18, 1979, in Winnipeg. ... 6-4/190. ... Shoots left. ... Name pronounced BAH-nee.
TRANSACTIONS/CAREER NOTES: Selected by Vancouver Canucks in second round (second Canucks pick, 34th overall) of NHL entry draft (June 21, 1997). ... Traded by Canucks to Toronto Maple Leafs for future considerations (June 25, 2002).

Season Team	League	REGULAR SEASON								PLAYOFFS				
		Gms.	G	A	Pts.	PIM	+/-	PP	SH	Gms.	G	A	Pts.	PIM
95-96—Saskatoon	WHL	63	1	7	8	78	...	...	...	3	0	0	0	0
96-97—Saskatoon	WHL	69	11	19	30	219	...	...	...	—	—	—	—	—
97-98—Saskatoon	WHL	42	5	14	19	100	...	...	...	—	—	—	—	—
98-99—Saskatoon	WHL	51	6	26	32	211	...	...	...	—	—	—	—	—
—Red Deer	WHL	20	3	10	13	41	...	...	...	9	0	4	4	25
99-00—Syracuse	AHL	71	5	13	18	125	...	...	...	2	0	1	1	2
—Vancouver	NHL	3	0	0	0	0	-1	0	0	—	—	—	—	—
00-01—Kansas City	IHL	80	2	9	11	127	...	...	...	—	—	—	—	—
01-02—Manitoba	AHL	11	0	1	1	33	...	...	...	2	0	0	0	2
—Columbia	ECHL	46	3	18	21	128	...	...	...	4	0	4	4	10
02-03—St. John's	AHL	61	1	8	9	86	...	...	...	—	—	—	—	—
NHL Totals (1 year)		3	0	0	0	0	-1	0	0	—	—	—	—	—

BONVIE, DENNIS — RW

B

PERSONAL: Born July 23, 1973, in Antigonish, Nova Scotia ... 5-11/221. ... Shoots right. ... Name pronounced BAHN-vee.

TRANSACTIONS/CAREER NOTES: Signed as non-drafted free agent by Edmonton Oilers (August 26, 1994). ... Selected by Chicago Blackhawks from Oilers in NHL waiver draft (October 5, 1998). ... Traded by Blackhawks to Philadelphia Flyers for D Frank Bialowas (January 8, 1999). ... Signed as free agent by Pittsburgh Penguins (September 20, 1999). ... Signed as free agent by Boston Bruins (October 5, 2001). ... Strained muscle in abdomen (April 2, 2002); missed two games. ... Signed as free agent by Ottawa Senators (August 26, 2002).

Season Team	League	REGULAR SEASON								PLAYOFFS				
		Gms.	G	A	Pts.	PIM	+/-	PP	SH	Gms.	G	A	Pts.	PIM
90-91—Antigonish	N.S.Jr.A					Statistics unavailable.								
91-92—Kitchener	OHL	7	1	1	2	23	...	...	...	—	—	—	—	—
—North Bay	OHL	49	0	12	12	261	...	...	...	21	0	1	1	91
92-93—North Bay	OHL	64	3	21	24	316	...	...	...	5	0	0	0	34
93-94—Cape Breton	AHL	63	1	10	11	278	...	...	...	4	0	0	0	11
94-95—Cape Breton	AHL	74	5	15	20	422	...	...	...	—	—	—	—	—
—Edmonton	NHL	2	0	0	0	0	0	0	0	—	—	—	—	—
95-96—Edmonton	NHL	8	0	0	0	47	-3	0	0	—	—	—	—	—
—Cape Breton	AHL	38	13	14	27	269	...	...	...	—	—	—	—	—
96-97—Hamilton	AHL	73	9	20	29	*522	...	...	...	22	3	11	14	*91
97-98—Edmonton	NHL	4	0	0	0	27	0	0	0	—	—	—	—	—
—Hamilton	AHL	57	11	19	30	295	...	...	...	9	0	5	5	18
98-99—Chicago	NHL	11	0	0	0	44	-4	0	0	—	—	—	—	—
—Portland	AHL	3	1	0	1	16	...	...	...	—	—	—	—	—
—Philadelphia	AHL	37	4	10	14	158	...	...	...	14	3	3	6	26
99-00—Wilkes-Barre/Scranton	AHL	42	5	26	31	243	...	...	...	—	—	—	—	—
—Pittsburgh	NHL	28	0	0	0	80	-2	0	0	—	—	—	—	—
00-01—Pittsburgh	NHL	3	0	0	0	0	-1	0	0	—	—	—	—	—
—Wilkes-Barre/Scranton	AHL	65	5	18	23	221	...	...	...	21	0	4	4	35
01-02—Providence	AHL	55	8	8	16	290	...	...	...	—	—	—	—	—
—Boston	NHL	23	1	2	3	84	3	0	0	1	0	0	0	0
02-03—Binghamton	AHL	51	7	3	10	311	...	...	...	—	—	—	—	—
—Ottawa	NHL	12	0	0	0	29	-1	0	0	—	—	—	—	—
NHL Totals (8 years)		91	1	2	3	311	-8	0	0	1	0	0	0	0

BOTTERILL, JASON — LW

PERSONAL: Born May 19, 1976, in Edmonton ... 6-4/220. ... Shoots left. ... Name pronounced BAH-tuh-rihl.

TRANSACTIONS/CAREER NOTES: Selected by Dallas Stars in first round (first Stars pick, 20th overall) of NHL entry draft (June 28, 1994). ... Traded by Stars to Atlanta Thrashers for D Jamie Pushor (July 15, 1999). ... Traded by Thrashers with D Darryl Shannon to Calgary Flames for C Hnat Domenichelli and LW Dmitri Vlasenkov (February 11, 2000). ... Signed as free agent by Buffalo Sabres (August 12, 2002).

Season Team	League	REGULAR SEASON								PLAYOFFS				
		Gms.	G	A	Pts.	PIM	+/-	PP	SH	Gms.	G	A	Pts.	PIM
92-93—St. Paul's	USHL	22	22	26	48	...	...	...	...	—	—	—	—	—
93-94—Univ. of Michigan	CCHA	37	21	19	40	94	...	...	...	—	—	—	—	—
94-95—Univ. of Michigan	CCHA	34	14	14	28	117	...	...	...	—	—	—	—	—
95-96—Univ. of Michigan	CCHA	37	32	25	57	143	...	...	...	—	—	—	—	—
96-97—Univ. of Michigan	CCHA	42	37	24	61	129	...	...	...	—	—	—	—	—
97-98—Michigan	IHL	50	11	11	22	82	...	...	...	4	0	0	0	5
—Dallas	NHL	4	0	0	0	19	-1	0	0	—	—	—	—	—
98-99—Michigan	IHL	56	13	25	38	106	...	...	...	5	2	1	3	4
—Dallas	NHL	17	0	0	0	23	-2	0	0	—	—	—	—	—
99-00—Orlando	IHL	17	7	8	15	27	...	...	...	—	—	—	—	—
—Atlanta	NHL	25	1	4	5	17	-7	0	0	—	—	—	—	—
—Calgary	NHL	2	0	0	0	0	-4	0	0	—	—	—	—	—
—Saint John	AHL	21	3	4	7	39	...	...	...	3	0	0	0	19
00-01—Saint John	AHL	60	13	20	33	101	...	...	...	19	2	7	9	30
01-02—Saint John	AHL	71	21	21	42	121	...	...	...	—	—	—	—	—
—Calgary	NHL	4	1	0	1	2	-3	1	0	—	—	—	—	—
02-03—Rochester	AHL	64	37	22	59	105	...	...	...	—	—	—	—	—
—Buffalo	NHL	17	1	4	5	14	1	1	0	—	—	—	—	—
NHL Totals (5 years)		69	3	8	11	75	-16	2	0	—	—	—	—	—

BOUCHARD, JOEL — D — SABRES

PERSONAL: Born January 23, 1974, in Montreal ... 6-1/200. ... Shoots left.
TRANSACTIONS/CAREER NOTES: Selected by Calgary Flames in sixth round (sixth Flames pick, 129th overall) of NHL entry draft (June 20, 1992). ... Strained abdominal muscle (September 30, 1997); missed one game. ... Suffered concussion (January 24, 1998); missed six games. ... Selected by Nashville Predators in NHL expansion draft (June 26, 1998). ... Sprained ankle (October 27, 1998); missed 11 games. ... Sprained ankle (December 19, 1998); missed seven games. ... Suffered concussion (December 15, 1999); missed nine games. ... Claimed on waivers by Dallas Stars (March 14, 2000). ... Signed as free agent by Phoenix Coyotes (August 31, 2000). ... Suffered back spasms (December 30, 2000); missed two games. ... Signed as free agent by New Jersey Devils (October 25, 2001). ... Signed as free agent by New York Rangers (August 7, 2002). ... Traded by Rangers with RW Rico Fata, RW Mikael Samuelsson, D Richard Lintner and cash to Pittsburgh Penguins for RW Alexei Kovalev, LW Dan LaCouture, D Janne Laukkanen and D Mike Wilson (February 10, 2003). ... Signed by Buffalo Sabres (July 14, 2003).

| | | | | REGULAR SEASON | | | | | | | PLAYOFFS | | | | |
Season Team	League	Gms.	G	A	Pts.	PIM	+/-	PP	SH		Gms.	G	A	Pts.	PIM
90-91—Longueuil	QMJHL	53	3	19	22	34	...	...	...		8	0	1	1	11
91-92—Verdun	QMJHL	70	9	37	46	55	...	...	...		19	1	7	8	20
92-93—Verdun	QMJHL	60	10	49	59	126	...	...	...		4	0	2	2	4
93-94—Verdun	QMJHL	60	15	55	70	62	...	...	...		4	1	0	1	6
—Saint John	AHL	1	0	0	0	0	...	...	...		2	0	0	0	0
94-95—Saint John	AHL	77	6	25	31	63	...	...	...		5	1	0	1	4
—Calgary	NHL	2	0	0	0	0	0	0	0		—	—	—	—	—
95-96—Saint John	AHL	74	8	25	33	104	...	...	...		16	1	4	5	10
—Calgary	NHL	4	0	0	0	4	0	0	0		—	—	—	—	—
96-97—Calgary	NHL	76	4	5	9	49	-23	0	1		—	—	—	—	—
97-98—Calgary	NHL	44	5	7	12	57	0	0	1		—	—	—	—	—
—Saint John	AHL	3	2	1	3	6	...	...	...		—	—	—	—	—
98-99—Nashville	NHL	64	4	11	15	60	-10	0	0		—	—	—	—	—
99-00—Nashville	NHL	52	1	4	5	23	-11	0	0		—	—	—	—	—
—Dallas	NHL	2	0	0	0	2	1	0	0		—	—	—	—	—
00-01—Grand Rapids	IHL	19	3	9	12	8	...	...	...		—	—	—	—	—
—Phoenix	NHL	32	1	2	3	22	-8	0	0		—	—	—	—	—
01-02—Albany	AHL	70	9	22	31	28	...	...	...		—	—	—	—	—
—New Jersey	NHL	1	0	1	1	0	1	0	0		—	—	—	—	—
02-03—Hartford	AHL	22	6	14	20	22	...	...	...		—	—	—	—	—
—New York Rangers	NHL	27	5	7	12	14	6	1	0		—	—	—	—	—
—Pittsburgh	NHL	7	0	1	1	0	-6	0	0		—	—	—	—	—
NHL Totals (9 years)		311	20	38	58	231	-50	1	2						

BOUCHARD, PIERRE-MARC — C — WILD

PERSONAL: Born April 27, 1984, in Sherbrooke, Que. ... 5-10/162. ... Shoots left.
TRANSACTIONS/CAREER NOTES: Selected by Minnesota Wild in first round (first Wild pick, eighth overall) of NHL entry draft (June 22, 2002).

| | | | | REGULAR SEASON | | | | | | | PLAYOFFS | | | | |
Season Team	League	Gms.	G	A	Pts.	PIM	+/-	PP	SH		Gms.	G	A	Pts.	PIM
00-01—Chicoutimi	QMJHL	67	38	57	95	20	...	...	...		6	5	8	13	0
01-02—Chicoutimi	QMJHL	69	46	*94	*140	54	...	...	...		4	2	3	5	4
02-03—Minnesota	NHL	50	7	13	20	18	1	5	0		5	0	1	1	2
NHL Totals (1 year)		50	7	13	20	18	1	5	0		5	0	1	1	2

BOUCHER, BRIAN — G — COYOTES

PERSONAL: Born January 2, 1977, in Woonsocket, R.I. ... 6-2/190. ... Catches left. ... Name pronounced boo-SHAY.
TRANSACTIONS/CAREER NOTES: Selected by Philadelphia Flyers in first round (first Flyers pick, 22nd overall) of NHL entry draft (July 8, 1995). ... Suffered from throat infection (January 16, 2001); missed one game. ... Strained left hamstring (November 15, 2001); missed nine games. ... Traded by Flyers with third-round pick (D Joe Callahan) in 2002 draft to Phoenix Coyotes for G Robert Esche and C Michal Handzus (June 12, 2002).

| | | | REGULAR SEASON | | | | | | | | PLAYOFFS | | | | | | |
Season Team	League	Gms.	Min	W	L	T	GA	SO	Avg.	SV%		Gms.	Min.	W	L	GA	SO	Avg.	SV%
93-94—Mt. St. Charles H.S.	R.I.H.S.	23	1170	...	...	...	23	12	1.18	—		—	—	—	—	—	—	—	—
94-95—Wexford	Tier II Jr. A	8	425	...	...	...	23	0	3.25	—		—	—	—	—	—	—	—	—
—Tri-City	WHL	35	1969	17	11	2	108	1	3.29	—		13	795	6	5	50	0	3.77	—
95-96—Tri-City	WHL	55	3183	33	19	2	181	1	3.41	—		11	653	6	5	37	†2	3.40	—
96-97—Tri-City	WHL	41	2458	10	24	†6	149	1	3.64	—		—	—	—	—	—	—	—	—
97-98—Philadelphia	AHL	34	1901	16	12	3	101	0	3.19	—		2	31	0	0	1	0	1.94	—
98-99—Philadelphia	AHL	36	2061	20	8	5	89	2	2.59	—		16	947	9	7	45	0	2.85	—
99-00—Philadelphia	NHL	35	2038	20	10	3	65	4	*1.91	.918		18	1183	11	7	40	1	2.03	.917
—Philadelphia	AHL	1	65	0	0	1	3	0	2.77	—		—	—	—	—	—	—	—	—
00-01—Philadelphia	NHL	27	1470	8	12	5	80	1	3.27	.876		1	37	0	0	3	0	4.86	.824
01-02—Philadelphia	NHL	41	2295	18	16	4	92	2	2.41	.905		2	88	0	1	2	0	1.36	.939
02-03—Phoenix	NHL	45	2544	15	20	8	128	0	3.02	.894		—	—	—	—	—	—	—	—
NHL Totals (4 years)		148	8347	61	58	20	365	7	2.62	.899		21	1308	11	8	45	1	2.06	.916

BOUCHER, NICK — G — PENGUINS

PERSONAL: Born December 29, 1980, in Ostrava, Czechoslovakia. ... 5-11/175. ... Catches left.
COLLEGE: Dartmouth.
TRANSACTIONS/CAREER NOTES: Selected by Pittsburgh Penguins in ninth round (10th Penguins pick, 280th overall) of NHL entry draft (June 24, 2000).

Season Team	League	REGULAR SEASON									PLAYOFFS							
		Gms.	Min	W	L	T	GA	SO	Avg.	SV%	Gms.	Min.	W	L	GA	SO	Avg.	SV%
99-00—Dartmouth College	ECAC	24	1378	8	12	†3	66	1	2.87	—	—	—	—	—	—	—	—	—
00-01—Dartmouth College	ECAC	†33	*1966	†16	12	†4	84	1	2.56	—	—	—	—	—	—	—	—	—
01-02—Dartmouth College	ECAC	21	1187	9	7	4	57	1	2.88	—	—	—	—	—	—	—	—	—
02-03—Dartmouth College	ECAC	27	1602	17	9	0	80	0	3.00	—	—	—	—	—	—	—	—	—

BOUCHER, PHILIPPE D STARS

PERSONAL: Born March 24, 1973, in St. Apollinaire, Que. ... 6-3/221. ... Shoots right. ... Name pronounced fih-LEEP boo-SHAY.

TRANSACTIONS/CAREER NOTES: Selected by Buffalo Sabres in first round (first Sabres pick, 13th overall) of NHL entry draft (June 22, 1991). ... Traded by Sabres with G Grant Fuhr and D Denis Tsygurov to Los Angeles Kings for D Alexei Zhitnik, D Charlie Huddy, G Robb Stauber and fifth-round pick (D Marian Menhart) in 1995 draft (February 14, 1995). ... Sprained wrist (February 25, 1995); missed final 31 games of season. ... Suffered tendinitis in right wrist (October 6, 1995); missed first 25 games of season. ... Injured left hand (February 19, 1996); missed four games. ... Sprained right shoulder (October 4, 1996); missed 10 games. ... Suffered from the flu (December 18, 1997); missed two games. ... Suffered illness (January 10, 1998); missed 12 games. ... Suffered from the flu (March 3, 1999); missed two games. ... Underwent foot surgery (April 27, 1999); missed first 71 games of 1999-2000 season. ... Suffered from the flu (December 16, 2001); missed one game. ... Suffered concussion (January 17, 2002); missed one game. ... Signed as free agent by Dallas Stars (July 2, 2002).

Season Team	League	REGULAR SEASON							PLAYOFFS				
		Gms.	G	A	Pts.	PIM	+/-	PP	SH	Gms.	G	A	Pts.	PIM
90-91—Granby	QMJHL	69	21	46	67	92	...	...	...	—	—	—	—	—
91-92—Granby	QMJHL	49	22	37	59	47	...	...	...	—	—	—	—	—
—Laval	QMJHL	16	7	11	18	36	...	...	...	10	5	6	11	8
92-93—Laval	QMJHL	16	12	15	27	37	...	...	...	13	6	15	21	12
—Rochester	AHL	5	4	3	7	8	...	...	...	3	0	1	1	2
—Buffalo	NHL	18	0	4	4	14	1	0	0	—	—	—	—	—
93-94—Buffalo	NHL	38	6	8	14	29	-1	4	0	7	1	1	2	2
—Rochester	AHL	31	10	22	32	51	...	...	...	—	—	—	—	—
94-95—Rochester	AHL	43	14	27	41	26	...	...	...	—	—	—	—	—
—Buffalo	NHL	9	1	4	5	0	6	0	0	—	—	—	—	—
—Los Angeles	NHL	6	1	0	1	4	-3	0	0	—	—	—	—	—
95-96—Los Angeles	NHL	53	7	16	23	31	-26	5	0	—	—	—	—	—
—Phoenix	IHL	10	4	3	7	4	...	...	...	—	—	—	—	—
96-97—Los Angeles	NHL	60	7	18	25	25	0	2	0	—	—	—	—	—
97-98—Los Angeles	NHL	45	6	10	16	49	6	1	0	—	—	—	—	—
—Long Beach	IHL	2	0	1	1	4	...	...	...	—	—	—	—	—
98-99—Los Angeles	NHL	45	2	6	8	32	-12	1	0	—	—	—	—	—
99-00—Long Beach	IHL	14	4	11	15	8	...	...	...	6	0	9	9	8
—Los Angeles	NHL	1	0	0	0	0	0	0	0	—	—	—	—	—
00-01—Manitoba	IHL	45	10	22	32	99	...	...	...	—	—	—	—	—
—Los Angeles	NHL	22	2	4	6	20	4	2	0	13	0	1	1	2
01-02—Los Angeles	NHL	80	7	23	30	94	0	4	0	5	0	1	1	2
02-03—Dallas	NHL	80	7	20	27	94	28	1	1	11	1	2	3	11
NHL Totals (11 years)		457	46	113	159	392	3	20	1	36	2	5	7	17

BOUCK, TYLER RW CANUCKS

PERSONAL: Born January 13, 1980, in Camrose, Alta. ... 6-0/185. ... Shoots left.

TRANSACTIONS/CAREER NOTES: Selected by Dallas Stars in second round (second Stars pick, 57th overall) of NHL entry draft (June 27, 1998). ... Traded by Stars to Phoenix Coyotes for D Jyrki Lumme (January 29, 2001). ... Traded by Coyotes with LW Todd Warriner, C Trevor Letowski and third-round pick in 2003 draft to Vancouver Canucks for C Denis Pederson and D Drake Berehowsky (December 28, 2001).

Season Team	League	REGULAR SEASON							PLAYOFFS				
		Gms.	G	A	Pts.	PIM	+/-	PP	SH	Gms.	G	A	Pts.	PIM
96-97—Prince George	WHL	12	0	2	2	11	...	...	...	—	—	—	—	—
97-98—Prince George	WHL	65	11	26	37	90	...	...	...	11	1	0	1	21
98-99—Prince George	WHL	56	22	25	47	178	...	...	...	2	0	2	2	10
99-00—Prince George	WHL	57	30	33	63	183	...	...	...	13	6	13	19	36
00-01—Dallas	NHL	48	2	5	7	29	-3	0	0	1	0	0	0	0
—Utah	IHL	24	2	6	8	39*	...	...	...	—	—	—	—	—
01-02—Phoenix	NHL	7	0	0	0	4	-1	0	0	—	—	—	—	—
—Springfield	AHL	21	1	2	3	33	...	...	...	—	—	—	—	—
—Manitoba	AHL	41	5	6	11	58	...	...	...	—	—	—	—	—
02-03—Manitoba	AHL	76	10	28	38	103	...	...	...	—	—	—	—	—
NHL Totals (2 years)		55	2	5	7	33	-4	0	0	1	0	0	0	0

BOUGHNER, BOB D HURRICANES

PERSONAL: Born March 8, 1971, in Windsor, Ont. ... 6-0/203. ... Shoots right. ... Name pronounced BOOG-nuhr.

TRANSACTIONS/CAREER NOTES: Selected by Detroit Red Wings in second round (second Red Wings pick, 32nd overall) of NHL entry draft (June 17, 1989). ... Signed as free agent by Florida Panthers (August 10, 1994). ... Traded by Panthers to Buffalo Sabres for third-round pick (D Chris Allen) in 1996 draft (February 1, 1996). ... Bruised left thigh (February 28, 1996); missed one game. ... Bruised shoulder (February 7, 1998); missed two games. ... Injured wrist (March 12, 1998); missed three games. ... Bruised foot (April 29, 1998); missed one game. ... Selected by Nashville Predators in NHL expansion draft (June 26, 1998). ... Suffered from the flu (October 27, 1998); missed one game. ... Suffered from the flu (January 14, 1999); missed two games. ... Suffered from the flu (November, 1999); missed two games. ... Sprained ankle (December, 1999); missed two games. ... Fractured finger (February 2, 2000); missed three games. ... Traded by Predators to Pittsburgh Penguins for D Pavel Skrbek (March 13, 2000). ... Fractured wrist (November 11, 2000); missed 23 games. ... Bruised chest (March 2, 2001); missed one game. ... Signed as free agent by Calgary Flames (July 2, 2001). ... Suffered injury (November 10, 2001); missed one game. ... Suffered injury (March 9, 2002); missed one game. ... Suffered injury (March 16, 2002); missed one game. ... Traded by Calgary Flames to Carolina Hurricanes for 2004 second-draft pick and future considerations (July 16, 2003).

Season Team	League	REGULAR SEASON								PLAYOFFS				
		Gms.	G	A	Pts.	PIM	+/-	PP	SH	Gms.	G	A	Pts.	PIM
87-88—St. Mary's Jr. B	OHA	36	4	18	22	177	...	...	...	—	—	—	—	—
88-89—Sault Ste. Marie	OHL	64	6	15	21	182	...	...	...	—	—	—	—	—
89-90—Sault Ste. Marie	OHL	49	7	23	30	122	...	...	...	—	—	—	—	—
90-91—Sault Ste. Marie	OHL	64	13	33	46	156	...	...	...	14	2	9	11	35
91-92—Adirondack	AHL	1	0	0	0	7	...	...	...	—	—	—	—	—
—Toledo	ECHL	28	3	10	13	79	...	...	...	5	2	0	2	15
92-93—Adirondack	AHL	69	1	16	17	190	...	...	...	—	—	—	—	—
93-94—Adirondack	AHL	72	8	14	22	292	...	...	...	10	1	1	2	18
94-95—Cincinnati	IHL	81	2	14	16	192	...	...	...	10	0	0	0	18
95-96—Carolina	AHL	46	2	15	17	127	...	...	...	—	—	—	—	—
—Buffalo	NHL	31	0	1	1	104	3	0	0	—	—	—	—	—
96-97—Buffalo	NHL	77	1	7	8	225	12	0	0	11	0	1	1	9
97-98—Buffalo	NHL	69	1	3	4	165	5	0	0	14	0	4	4	15
98-99—Nashville	NHL	79	3	10	13	137	-6	0	0	—	—	—	—	—
99-00—Nashville	NHL	62	2	4	6	97	-13	0	0	—	—	—	—	—
—Pittsburgh	NHL	11	1	0	1	69	2	1	0	11	0	2	2	15
00-01—Pittsburgh	NHL	58	1	3	4	147	18	0	0	18	0	1	1	22
01-02—Calgary	NHL	79	2	4	6	170	9	0	0	—	—	—	—	—
02-03—Calgary	NHL	69	3	14	17	126	5	0	0	—	—	—	—	—
NHL Totals (8 years)		535	14	46	60	1240	35	1	0	54	0	8	8	61

BOUILLON, FRANCIS D CANADIENS

PERSONAL: Born October 17, 1975, in New York ... 5-8/194. ... Shoots left.

TRANSACTIONS/CAREER NOTES: Signed as non-drafted free agent by Montreal Canadiens (August 18, 1998). ... Fractured hand (November 14, 2000); missed 13 games. ... Sprained ankle (December 30, 2000); missed 23 games. ... Claimed by Nashville Predators from Canadiens in NHL waiver draft (October 4, 2002). ... Signed by Montreal Canadiens (May 30, 2003).

Season Team	League	REGULAR SEASON								PLAYOFFS				
		Gms.	G	A	Pts.	PIM	+/-	PP	SH	Gms.	G	A	Pts.	PIM
92-93—Laval	QMJHL	46	0	7	7	45	...	...	...	—	—	—	—	—
93-94—Laval	QMJHL	68	3	15	18	129	...	...	...	19	2	9	11	48
94-95—Laval	QMJHL	72	8	25	33	115	...	...	...	20	3	11	14	21
95-96—Granby	QMJHL	68	11	35	46	156	...	...	...	21	2	12	14	30
96-97—Wheeling	ECHL	69	10	32	42	77	...	...	...	3	0	2	2	10
97-98—Quebec	IHL	71	8	27	35	76	...	...	...	—	—	—	—	—
98-99—Fredericton	AHL	79	19	36	55	174	...	...	...	5	2	1	3	0
99-00—Montreal	NHL	74	3	13	16	38	-7	2	0	—	—	—	—	—
00-01—Montreal	NHL	29	0	6	6	26	3	0	0	—	—	—	—	—
—Quebec	AHL	4	0	0	0	0	...	...	...	—	—	—	—	—
01-02—Quebec	AHL	38	8	14	22	30	...	...	...	—	—	—	—	—
—Montreal	NHL	28	0	5	5	33	-5	0	0	—	—	—	—	—
02-03—Hamilton	AHL	29	1	12	13	31	...	...	...	—	—	—	—	—
—Nashville	NHL	4	0	0	0	2	-1	0	0	—	—	—	—	—
—Montreal	NHL	20	3	1	4	2	-1	0	1	—	—	—	—	—
NHL Totals (4 years)		155	6	25	31	101	-11	2	1					

BOULERICE, JESSE RW HURRICANES

PERSONAL: Born August 10, 1978, in Plattsburgh, N.Y. ... 6-2/203. ... Shoots right.

TRANSACTIONS/CAREER NOTES: Selected by Philadelphia Flyers in fifth round (fourth Flyers pick, 133rd overall) of NHL entry draft (June 22, 1996). ... Traded by Flyers to Carolina Hurricanes for C Greg Koehler (February 13, 2002).

Season Team	League	REGULAR SEASON								PLAYOFFS				
		Gms.	G	A	Pts.	PIM	+/-	PP	SH	Gms.	G	A	Pts.	PIM
95-96—Det. Jr. Red Wings	OHL	64	2	5	7	150	...	...	...	16	0	0	0	12
96-97—Detroit	OHL	33	10	14	24	209	...	...	...	—	—	—	—	—
97-98—Plymouth	OHL	53	20	23	43	170	...	...	...	13	2	4	6	35
98-99—Philadelphia	AHL	24	1	2	3	82	...	...	...	—	—	—	—	—
—New Orleans	ECHL	12	0	1	1	38	...	...	...	—	—	—	—	—
99-00—Philadelphia	AHL	40	3	4	7	85	...	...	...	4	0	2	2	4
—Trenton	ECHL	25	8	8	16	90	...	...	...	—	—	—	—	—
00-01—Philadelphia	AHL	60	3	4	7	256	...	...	...	10	1	1	2	28
01-02—Philadelphia	NHL	3	0	0	0	5	-1	0	0	—	—	—	—	—
—Philadelphia	AHL	41	2	5	7	204	...	...	...	—	—	—	—	—
—Lowell	AHL	56	4	9	13	284	...	...	...	5	0	2	2	6
02-03—Carolina	NHL	48	2	1	3	108	-2	0	0	—	—	—	—	—
NHL Totals (2 years)		51	2	1	3	113	-3	0	0					

BOULTON, ERIC LW SABRES

PERSONAL: Born August 17, 1976, in Halifax, Nova Scotia ... 6-0/226. ... Shoots left.

TRANSACTIONS/CAREER NOTES: Selected by New York Rangers in ninth round (12th Rangers pick, 234th overall) of NHL entry draft (June 29, 1994). ... Signed as free agent by Buffalo Sabres (August 20, 1999).

		REGULAR SEASON								PLAYOFFS				
Season Team	League	Gms.	G	A	Pts.	PIM	+/-	PP	SH	Gms.	G	A	Pts.	PIM
93-94—Cole Harbour	NSJHL					Statistics unavailable.								
—Oshawa	OHL	45	4	3	7	149	...	...	...	5	0	0	0	16
94-95—Oshawa	OHL	27	7	5	12	125	...	...	...	—	—	—	—	—
—Sarnia	OHL	24	3	7	10	134	...	...	...	4	0	1	1	10
95-96—Sarnia	OHL	66	14	29	43	243	...	...	...	9	0	3	3	29
96-97—Binghamton	AHL	23	2	3	5	67	...	...	...	3	0	0	0	4
—Charlotte	ECHL	44	14	11	25	325	...	...	...	3	0	1	1	6
97-98—Charlotte	ECHL	53	11	16	27	202	...	...	...	4	1	0	1	0
—Fort Wayne	IHL	8	0	2	2	42	...	...	...	—	—	—	—	—
98-99—Houston	IHL	7	1	0	1	41	...	...	...	—	—	—	—	—
—Florida	ECHL	26	9	13	22	143	...	...	...	—	—	—	—	—
—Kentucky	AHL	34	3	3	6	154	...	...	...	10	0	1	1	36
99-00—Rochester	AHL	76	2	2	4	276	...	...	...	18	2	1	3	53
00-01—Buffalo	NHL	35	1	2	3	94	-1	0	0	—	—	—	—	—
01-02—Buffalo	NHL	35	2	3	5	129	-1	0	0	—	—	—	—	—
02-03—Buffalo	NHL	58	1	5	6	178	1	0	0	—	—	—	—	—
NHL Totals (3 years)		128	4	10	14	401	-1	0	0	—	—	—	—	—

BOUMEDIENNE, JOSEF — D — CAPITALS

PERSONAL: Born January 12, 1978, in Stockholm, Sweden ... 6-1/200. ... Shoots left.

TRANSACTIONS/CAREER NOTES: Selected by New Jersey Devils in fourth round (seventh Devils pick, 91st overall) of NHL entry draft (June 22, 1996). ... Traded by Devils with D Sasha Goc and LW Anton But to Tampa Bay Lightning for D Andrei Zyuzin (November 9, 2001). ... Traded by Lightning to Ottawa Senators for seventh-round pick (G Fredrik Morrena) in 2002 draft (June 23, 2002). ... Traded by Senators to Washington Capitals for D Dean Melanson (December 16, 2002).

		REGULAR SEASON								PLAYOFFS				
Season Team	League	Gms.	G	A	Pts.	PIM	+/-	PP	SH	Gms.	G	A	Pts.	PIM
95-96—Huddinge	Sweden Jr.	25	2	4	6	66	...	...	...	—	—	—	—	—
—Huddinge	Sweden Dv. 2	7	0	0	0	14	...	...	...	—	—	—	—	—
96-97—Sodertalje SK	Sweden	32	1	1	2	32	...	...	...	—	—	—	—	—
97-98—Sodertalje SK	Sweden	26	3	3	6	28	...	...	...	—	—	—	—	—
98-99—Tappara Tampere	Finland	51	6	8	14	119	...	...	...	—	—	—	—	—
99-00—Tappara Tampere	Finland	50	8	24	32	160	...	...	...	4	1	2	3	10
00-01—Albany	AHL	79	8	29	37	117	...	...	...	—	—	—	—	—
01-02—New Jersey	NHL	1	0	1	1	2	-1	0	0	—	—	—	—	—
—Albany	AHL	9	0	3	3	10	...	...	...	—	—	—	—	—
—Springfield	AHL	62	7	28	35	67	...	...	...	—	—	—	—	—
—Tampa Bay	NHL	3	0	0	0	4	-1	0	0	—	—	—	—	—
02-03—Binghamton	AHL	26	2	15	17	62	...	...	...	—	—	—	—	—
—Washington	NHL	6	1	0	1	0	-1	0	0	—	—	—	—	—
—Portland	AHL	44	8	22	30	77	...	...	...	—	—	—	—	—
NHL Totals (2 years)		10	2	0	2	6	-3	0	0	—	—	—	—	—

BOUWMEESTER, JAY — D — PANTHERS

PERSONAL: Born September 27, 1983, in Edmonton, Alta. ... 6-4/210. ... Shoots left. ... Name pronounced boh-MEES-tuhr.

TRANSACTIONS/CAREER NOTES: Selected by Florida Panthers in first round (first Panthers pick, third overall) of NHL entry draft (June 22, 2002).

		REGULAR SEASON								PLAYOFFS				
Season Team	League	Gms.	G	A	Pts.	PIM	+/-	PP	SH	Gms.	G	A	Pts.	PIM
98-99—Medicine Hat	WHL	8	2	1	3	2	...	...	...	—	—	—	—	—
99-00—Medicine Hat	WHL	34	13	21	34	26	...	...	...	—	—	—	—	—
00-01—Medicine Hat	WHL	61	14	39	53	44	...	...	...	—	—	—	—	—
01-02—Medicine Hat	WHL	61	12	49	61	42	...	...	...	—	—	—	—	—
02-03—Florida	NHL	82	4	12	16	14	-29	2	0	—	—	—	—	—
NHL Totals (1 year)		82	4	12	16	14	-29	2	0	—	—	—	—	—

BOYCHUK, JOHNNY — D — AVALANCHE

PERSONAL: Born January 19, 1984, in Edmonton. ... 6-2/209. ... Shoots right.

TRANSACTIONS/CAREER NOTES: Selected by Colorado Avalanche in second round (second Avalanche pick, 61st overall) of NHL entry draft (June 22, 2002).

		REGULAR SEASON								PLAYOFFS				
Season Team	League	Gms.	G	A	Pts.	PIM	+/-	PP	SH	Gms.	G	A	Pts.	PIM
00-01—Calgary	WHL	66	4	8	12	61	...	...	...	12	1	1	2	17
01-02—Calgary	WHL	70	8	32	40	85	...	...	...	7	1	1	2	6
02-03—Moose Jaw	WHL	67	13	35	48	90	...	...	...	13	2	6	8	29

BOYES, BRAD — C — SHARKS

PERSONAL: Born April 17, 1982, in Mississauga, Ont. ... 6-0/181. ... Shoots right.

TRANSACTIONS/CAREER NOTES: Selected by Toronto Maple Leafs in first round (first Maple Leafs pick, 24th overall) of NHL entry draft (June 24, 2000). ... Traded by Maple Leafs with C Alyn McCauley and first-round pick in 2003 draft to San Jose Sharks for RW Owen Nolan (March 5, 2003).

B

Season Team	League	REGULAR SEASON								PLAYOFFS				
		Gms.	G	A	Pts.	PIM	+/-	PP	SH	Gms.	G	A	Pts.	PIM
98-99—Erie	OHL	59	24	36	60	30	...	...	...	5	1	2	3	10
99-00—Erie	OHL	68	36	46	82	38	...	...	...	13	6	8	14	10
00-01—Erie	OHL	59	45	45	90	42	...	...	...	15	10	13	23	8
01-02—Erie	OHL	47	36	41	77	42	...	...	...	21	22	*19	41	27
02-03—St. John's	AHL	65	23	28	51	45	...	...	...	—	—	—	—	—
—Cleveland	AHL	15	7	6	13	21	...	...	...	—	—	—	—	—

BOYLE, DAN — D — LIGHTNING

PERSONAL: Born July 12, 1976, in Ottawa ... 5-11/187. ... Shoots right.
TRANSACTIONS/CAREER NOTES: Signed as non-drafted free agent by Florida Panthers (March 30, 1998). ... Traded by Panthers to Tampa Bay Lightning for fifth-round pick in 2003 draft (January 7, 2002).

Season Team	League	REGULAR SEASON								PLAYOFFS				
		Gms.	G	A	Pts.	PIM	+/-	PP	SH	Gms.	G	A	Pts.	PIM
94-95—Miami of Ohio	CCHA	35	8	18	26	24	...	...	...	—	—	—	—	—
95-96—Miami of Ohio	CCHA	36	7	20	27	70	...	...	...	—	—	—	—	—
96-97—Miami of Ohio	CCHA	40	11	43	54	52	...	...	...	—	—	—	—	—
97-98—Miami of Ohio	CCHA	37	14	26	40	58	...	...	...	—	—	—	—	—
—Cincinnati	IHL	8	0	3	3	20	...	...	...	5	0	1	1	4
98-99—Kentucky	AHL	53	8	34	42	87	...	...	...	12	3	5	8	16
—Florida	NHL	22	3	5	8	6	0	1	0	—	—	—	—	—
99-00—Louisville	AHL	58	14	38	52	75	...	...	...	4	0	2	2	8
—Florida	NHL	13	0	3	3	4	-2	0	0	—	—	—	—	—
00-01—Florida	NHL	69	4	18	22	28	-14	1	0	—	—	—	—	—
—Louisville	AHL	6	0	5	5	12	...	...	...	—	—	—	—	—
01-02—Florida	NHL	25	3	3	6	12	-1	1	0	—	—	—	—	—
—Tampa Bay	NHL	41	5	15	20	27	-15	2	0	—	—	—	—	—
02-03—Tampa Bay	NHL	77	13	40	53	44	9	8	0	11	0	7	7	6
NHL Totals (5 years)		247	28	84	112	121	-23	13	0	11	0	7	7	6

BOYNTON, NICK — D — BRUINS

PERSONAL: Born January 14, 1979, in Etobicoke, Ont. ... 6-2/210. ... Shoots right. ... Full Name: Nicholas Boynton.
TRANSACTIONS/CAREER NOTES: Selected by Washington Capitals in first round (first Capitals pick, ninth overall) of NHL entry draft (June 21, 1997). ... Returned to draft pool by Capitals and selected by Boston Bruins in first round (first Bruins pick, 21st overall) of NHL entry draft (June 26, 1999). ... Suffered food poisoning (December 12, 2001); missed two games.

Season Team	League	REGULAR SEASON								PLAYOFFS				
		Gms.	G	A	Pts.	PIM	+/-	PP	SH	Gms.	G	A	Pts.	PIM
94-95—Caledon	Jr. A	44	10	35	45	139	...	...	...	—	—	—	—	—
95-96—Ottawa	OHL	64	10	14	24	90	...	...	...	4	0	3	3	10
96-97—Ottawa	OHL	63	13	51	64	143	...	...	...	24	4	24	28	38
97-98—Ottawa	OHL	40	7	31	38	94	...	...	...	13	0	4	4	24
98-99—Ottawa	OHL	51	11	48	59	83	...	...	...	9	1	9	10	18
99-00—Providence	AHL	53	5	14	19	66	...	...	...	12	1	0	1	6
—Boston	NHL	5	0	0	0	0	-5	0	0	—	—	—	—	—
00-01—Providence	AHL	78	6	27	33	105	...	...	...	17	0	2	2	35
—Boston	NHL	1	0	0	0	0	-1	0	0	—	—	—	—	—
01-02—Boston	NHL	80	4	14	18	107	18	0	0	6	1	2	3	8
02-03—Boston	NHL	78	7	17	24	99	8	0	1	5	0	1	1	4
NHL Totals (4 years)		164	11	31	42	206	20	0	1	11	1	3	4	12

BRADLEY, MATT — RW — PENGUINS

PERSONAL: Born June 13, 1978, in Stittsville, Ont. ... 6-2/195. ... Shoots right.
TRANSACTIONS/CAREER NOTES: Selected by San Jose Sharks in fourth round (fourth Sharks pick, 102nd overall) of NHL entry draft (June 22, 1996). ... Injured shoulder (February 14, 2001); missed seven games. ... Injured back (March 3, 2002); missed one game. ... Injured wrist (April 10, 2002); missed final two games of season. ... Traded by Sharks to Pittsburgh Penguins for C Wayne Primeau (March 11, 2003).

Season Team	League	REGULAR SEASON								PLAYOFFS				
		Gms.	G	A	Pts.	PIM	+/-	PP	SH	Gms.	G	A	Pts.	PIM
94-95—Cumberland	CJHL	49	13	20	33	18	...	...	...	—	—	—	—	—
95-96—Kingston	OHL	55	10	14	24	17	...	...	...	6	0	1	1	6
96-97—Kingston	OHL	65	24	24	48	41	...	...	...	5	0	4	4	2
—Kentucky	AHL	1	0	1	1	0	...	...	...	—	—	—	—	—
97-98—Kingston	OHL	55	33	50	83	24	...	...	...	8	3	4	7	7
—Kentucky	AHL	1	0	1	1	0	...	...	...	—	—	—	—	—
98-99—Kentucky	AHL	79	23	20	43	57	...	...	...	10	1	4	5	4
99-00—Kentucky	AHL	80	22	19	41	81	...	...	...	9	6	3	9	9
00-01—Kentucky	AHL	22	5	8	13	16	...	...	...	1	1	0	1	5
—San Jose	NHL	21	1	1	2	19	0	0	0	—	—	—	—	—
01-02—San Jose	NHL	54	9	13	22	43	22	0	0	10	0	0	0	0
02-03—San Jose	NHL	46	2	3	5	37	-1	0	0	—	—	—	—	—
NHL Totals (3 years)		121	12	17	29	99	21	0	0	10	0	0	0	0

BRANDNER, CHRISTOPH — LW — WILD

PERSONAL: Born May 7, 1975, in Bruck Mur, Austria. ... 6-4/225. ... Shoots left.
TRANSACTIONS/CAREER NOTES: Selected by Minnesota Wild in eighth round (eight Wild pick, 237th overall) of NHL entry draft (June 23, 2002). ... Signed by Wild (July 15, 2003).

Season Team	League	REGULAR SEASON								PLAYOFFS				
		Gms.	G	A	Pts.	PIM	+/-	PP	SH	Gms.	G	A	Pts.	PIM
01-02—Krefeld Pinguine	Germany	50	30	25	55	20	...	...	...	3	1	0	1	4
02-03—Krefeld Pinguine	Germany	49	28	17	45	26	...	...	...	14	9	9	18	8

BRASHEAR, DONALD — LW — FLYERS

B

PERSONAL: Born January 7, 1972, in Bedford, Ind. ... 6-2/235. ... Shoots left. ... Name pronounced brah-SHEER.
TRANSACTIONS/CAREER NOTES: Signed non-drafted as free agent by Montreal Canadiens (July 28, 1992). ... Bruised knee (November 23, 1993); missed one game. ... Injured shoulder (February 27, 1995); missed one game. ... Bruised hand (March 20, 1995); missed one game. ... Suffered cut to right thigh (December 30, 1995); missed seven games. ... Traded by Canadiens to Vancouver Canucks for D Jassen Cullimore (November 13, 1996). ... Strained back (February 8, 1997); missed three games. ... Suspended four games and fined $1,000 by NHL for fighting (February 25, 1997). ... Injured shoulder (March 11, 1998); missed two games. ... Suspended two games by NHL for illegal check (October 24, 1999). ... Suffered concussion (February 21, 2000); missed 20 games. ... Strained knee (October 18, 2000); missed one game. ... Strained back (November 21, 2000); missed two games. ... Injured leg (November 11, 2001); missed five games. ... Traded by Canucks with sixth-round pick (traded to Colorado) in 2002 draft to Philadelphia Flyers for LW Jan Hlavac and third-round pick (traded to Washington) in 2002 (December 17, 2001).

Season Team	League	REGULAR SEASON								PLAYOFFS				
		Gms.	G	A	Pts.	PIM	+/-	PP	SH	Gms.	G	A	Pts.	PIM
89-90—Longueuil	QMJHL	64	12	14	26	169	...	...	...	7	0	0	0	11
90-91—Longueuil	QMJHL	68	12	26	38	195	...	...	...	8	0	3	3	33
91-92—Verdun	QMJHL	65	18	24	42	283	...	...	...	18	4	2	6	98
92-93—Fredericton	AHL	76	11	3	14	261	...	...	...	5	0	0	0	8
93-94—Fredericton	AHL	62	38	28	66	250	...	...	...	—	—	—	—	—
—Montreal	NHL	14	2	2	4	34	0	0	0	2	0	0	0	0
94-95—Montreal	NHL	20	1	1	2	63	-5	0	0	—	—	—	—	—
—Fredericton	AHL	29	10	9	19	182	...	...	...	17	7	5	12	77
95-96—Montreal	NHL	67	0	4	4	223	-10	0	0	6	0	0	0	2
96-97—Montreal	NHL	10	0	0	0	38	-2	0	0	—	—	—	—	—
—Vancouver	NHL	59	8	5	13	207	-6	0	0	—	—	—	—	—
97-98—Vancouver	NHL	77	9	9	18	*372	-9	0	0	—	—	—	—	—
98-99—Vancouver	NHL	82	8	10	18	209	-25	2	0	—	—	—	—	—
99-00—Vancouver	NHL	60	11	2	13	136	-9	1	0	—	—	—	—	—
00-01—Vancouver	NHL	79	9	19	28	145	0	0	0	4	0	0	0	0
01-02—Vancouver	NHL	31	5	8	13	90	-8	1	0	—	—	—	—	—
—Philadelphia	NHL	50	4	15	19	109	0	0	0	5	0	0	0	19
02-03—Philadelphia	NHL	80	8	17	25	161	5	0	0	13	1	2	3	21
NHL Totals (10 years)		629	65	92	157	1787	-69	4	0	30	1	2	3	42

BRATHWAITE, FRED — G — BLUE JACKETS

PERSONAL: Born November 24, 1972, in Ottawa ... 5-8/194. ... Catches left. ... Name pronounced BRATH-wayt.
TRANSACTIONS/CAREER NOTES: Signed as non-drafted free agent by Edmonton Oilers (October 6, 1993). ... Signed as free agent by Calgary Flames (January 7, 1999). ... Injured groin (November 7, 2000); missed two games. ... Traded by Flames with C Daniel Tkaczuk, RW Sergei Varlamov and ninth-round pick (C Grant Jacobsen) in 2001 draft to St. Louis Blues for G Roman Turek and fourth-round pick (LW Egor Shastin) in 2001 draft (June 23, 2001). ... Suffered mouth injury (March 7, 2002); missed one game. ... Released by Blues (March 18, 2003). ... Signed by Columbus Blue Jackets (June 3, 2003).

Season Team	League	REGULAR SEASON									PLAYOFFS							
		Gms.	Min	W	L	T	GA	SO	Avg.	SV%	Gms.	Min.	W	L	GA	SO	Avg.	SV%
89-90—Oshawa	OHL	20	901	11	2	1	45	1	3.00	—	10	451	4	2	22	0	*2.93	—
90-91—Oshawa	OHL	39	1986	25	6	3	112	1	3.38	—	13	677	*9	2	43	0	3.81	—
91-92—Oshawa	OHL	24	1248	12	7	2	81	0	3.89	—	—	—	—	—	—	—	—	—
—London	OHL	23	1325	23	10	4	61	4	2.76	—	10	615	5	5	36	0	3.51	—
92-93—Det. Jr. Red Wings	OHL	37	2192	23	10	4	134	0	3.67	—	15	858	9	6	48	1	3.36	—
93-94—Cape Breton	AHL	2	119	1	1	0	6	0	3.03	—	—	—	—	—	—	—	—	—
—Edmonton	NHL	19	982	3	10	3	58	0	3.54	.889	—	—	—	—	—	—	—	—
94-95—Edmonton	NHL	14	601	2	5	1	40	0	3.99	.863	—	—	—	—	—	—	—	—
95-96—Cape Breton	AHL	31	1699	12	16	0	110	1	3.88	—	—	—	—	—	—	—	—	—
—Edmonton	NHL	7	293	0	2	0	12	0	2.46	.914	—	—	—	—	—	—	—	—
96-97—Manitoba	IHL	58	2945	22	22	5	167	1	3.40	—	—	—	—	—	—	—	—	—
97-98—Manitoba	IHL	51	2737	23	18	4	138	1	3.03	—	2	73	0	1	4	0	3.29	—
98-99—Canadian nat'l team	Int'l	24	989	6	8	3	47	...	2.85	—	—	—	—	—	—	—	—	—
—Calgary	NHL	28	1663	11	9	7	68	1	2.45	.915	—	—	—	—	—	—	—	—
99-00—Calgary	NHL	61	3448	25	25	7	158	5	2.75	.905	—	—	—	—	—	—	—	—
—Saint John	AHL	2	120	2	0	0	4	0	2.00	—	—	—	—	—	—	—	—	—
00-01—Calgary	NHL	49	2742	15	17	10	106	5	2.32	.910	—	—	—	—	—	—	—	—
01-02—St. Louis	NHL	25	1446	9	11	4	54	2	2.24	.901	1	1	0	0	0	0	0.00	—
02-03—St. Louis	NHL	30	1615	12	9	4	74	2	2.75	.883	—	—	—	—	—	—	—	—
NHL Totals (8 years)		233	12790	77	88	36	570	15	2.67	.901	1	1	0	0	0	0	0.00	—

BRENDL, PAVEL — RW — HURRICANES

PERSONAL: Born March 23, 1981, in Opocno, Czechoslovakia ... 6-1/206. ... Shoots right.

TRANSACTIONS/CAREER NOTES: Selected by New York Rangers in first round (first Rangers pick, fourth overall) of NHL entry draft (June 26, 1999). ... Traded by Rangers with LW Jan Hlavac, D Kim Johnsson and third-round pick in 2003 draft to Philadelphia Flyers for rights to C Eric Lindros and conditional first-round pick (August 20, 2001). ... Sprained right ankle (October 4, 2001); missed first seven games of season. ... Traded by Flyers with D Bruno St. Jacques to Carolina Hurricanes for RW Sami Kapanen and D Ryan Bast (February 7, 2003).

Season Team	League	REGULAR SEASON								PLAYOFFS				
		Gms.	G	A	Pts.	PIM	+/-	PP	SH	Gms.	G	A	Pts.	PIM
96-97—Olomouc	Czech. Jrs.	40	35	17	52	...	...	...	...	—	—	—	—	—
97-98—Olomouc	Czech. Jrs.	38	29	23	52	...	...	...	...	—	—	—	—	—
—Olomouc	Czech Dv.II	12	1	1	2	...	...	...	...	—	—	—	—	—
98-99—Calgary	WHL	68	*73	61	*134	40	...	...	...	20	*21	†25	*46	18
99-00—Calgary	WHL	61	*59	52	111	94	...	...	...	10	7	12	19	8
—Hartford	AHL	—	—	—	—	—	—	—	—	2	0	0	0	0
00-01—Calgary	WHL	49	40	35	75	66	...	...	...	10	7	6	13	6
01-02—Philadelphia	NHL	8	1	0	1	2	-1	0	0	2	0	0	0	0
—Philadelphia	AHL	64	15	22	37	22	...	...	...	5	4	1	5	0
02-03—Philadelphia	NHL	42	5	7	12	4	8	1	0	—	—	—	—	—
—Carolina	NHL	8	0	1	1	2	-3	0	0	—	—	—	—	—
NHL Totals (2 years)		58	6	8	14	8	4	1	0	2	0	0	0	0

BRENNAN, KIP — D — KINGS

PERSONAL: Born August 27, 1980, in Kingston, Ont. ... 6-4/228. ... Shoots left.

TRANSACTIONS/CAREER NOTES: Selected by Los Angeles Kings in fourth round (fourth Kings pick, 103rd overall) of NHL entry draft (June 27, 1998). ... Re-signed by Kings (July 31, 2003).

Season Team	League	REGULAR SEASON								PLAYOFFS				
		Gms.	G	A	Pts.	PIM	+/-	PP	SH	Gms.	G	A	Pts.	PIM
96-97—Windsor	OHL	42	0	10	10	156	...	...	...	5	0	1	1	16
97-98—Windsor	OHL	24	0	7	7	103	...	...	...	—	—	—	—	—
—Sudbury	OHL	24	0	3	3	85	...	...	...	—	—	—	—	—
98-99—Sudbury	OHL	38	9	12	21	160	...	...	...	—	—	—	—	—
99-00—Sudbury	OHL	55	16	16	32	228	...	...	...	12	3	3	6	67
00-01—Lowell	AHL	23	2	3	5	117	...	...	...	—	—	—	—	—
—Sudbury	OHL	27	7	14	21	94	...	...	...	12	5	6	11	*92
01-02—Manchester	AHL	44	4	1	5	269	...	...	...	4	0	1	1	26
—Los Angeles	NHL	4	0	0	0	22	1	0	0	—	—	—	—	—
02-03—Manchester	AHL	35	3	2	5	195	...	...	...	—	—	—	—	—
—Los Angeles	NHL	19	0	0	0	57	0	0	0	—	—	—	—	—
NHL Totals (2 years)		23	0	0	0	79	1	0	0					

BRENNAN, RICH — D — BRUINS

PERSONAL: Born November 26, 1972, in Schenectady, N.Y. ... 6-2/200. ... Shoots right.

TRANSACTIONS/CAREER NOTES: Selected by Quebec Nordiques in third round (third Nordiques pick, 56th overall) of NHL entry draft (June 22, 1991). ... Nordiques franchise moved to Colorado and renamed Avalanche for 1995-96 season (June 21, 1995). ... Signed as free agent by San Jose Sharks (July 9, 1997). ... Traded by Sharks to New York Rangers for G Jason Muzzatti (March 24, 1998). ... Signed as free agent by Nashville Predators (September 1999). ... Claimed by Los Angeles Kings from Predators in NHL waiver draft (September 27, 1999). ... Signed as free agent by Predators (August 8, 2001). ... Traded by Predators to Kings for D Brett Hauer (December 18, 2001). ... Signed as free agent by Boston Bruins (July 18, 2002).

Season Team	League	REGULAR SEASON								PLAYOFFS				
		Gms.	G	A	Pts.	PIM	+/-	PP	SH	Gms.	G	A	Pts.	PIM
88-89—Albany Academy	N.Y. H.S.	25	17	30	47	57	...	...	...	—	—	—	—	—
89-90—Tabor Academy	Mass. H.S.	33	12	14	26	68	...	...	...	—	—	—	—	—
90-91—Tabor Academy	Mass. H.S.	34	13	37	50	91	...	...	...	—	—	—	—	—
91-92—Boston University	Hockey East	31	4	13	17	54	...	...	...	—	—	—	—	—
92-93—Boston University	Hockey East	40	9	11	20	68	...	...	...	—	—	—	—	—
93-94—Boston University	Hockey East	41	8	27	35	82	...	...	...	—	—	—	—	—
94-95—Boston University	Hockey East	31	5	23	28	56	...	...	...	—	—	—	—	—
95-96—Brantford	Col.HL	5	1	2	3	2	...	...	...	—	—	—	—	—
96-97—Hershey	AHL	74	11	45	56	88	...	...	...	23	2	†16	18	22
—Colorado	NHL	2	0	0	0	0	0	0	0	—	—	—	—	—
97-98—Kentucky	AHL	42	11	17	28	71	...	...	...	—	—	—	—	—
—San Jose	NHL	11	1	2	3	2	-4	1	0	—	—	—	—	—
—Hartford	AHL	9	2	4	6	12	...	...	...	—	—	—	—	—
98-99—Hartford	AHL	47	4	24	28	42	...	...	...	—	—	—	—	—
—New York Rangers	NHL	24	1	3	4	23	-4	0	0	—	—	—	—	—
99-00—Lowell	AHL	67	15	30	45	110	...	...	...	7	1	5	6	0
00-01—Lowell	AHL	69	10	31	41	146	...	...	...	—	—	—	—	—
—Los Angeles	NHL	2	0	0	0	0	-3	0	0	—	—	—	—	—
01-02—Milwaukee	AHL	23	4	8	12	27	...	...	...	—	—	—	—	—
—Nashville	NHL	4	0	0	0	2	0	0	0	—	—	—	—	—
—Manchester	AHL	39	6	13	19	33	...	...	...	5	1	1	2	16
02-03—Providence	AHL	41	3	29	32	51	...	...	...	—	—	—	—	—
—Boston	NHL	7	0	1	1	6	3	0	0	—	—	—	—	—
NHL Totals (6 years)		50	2	6	8	33	-8	1	0					

BREWER, ERIC — D — OILERS

PERSONAL: Born April 17, 1979, in Vernon, B.C. ... 6-3/220. ... Shoots left.

TRANSACTIONS/CAREER NOTES: Selected by New York Islanders in first round (second Islanders pick, fifth overall) of NHL entry draft (June 21, 1997). ... Strained Achilles' tendon (April 8, 1999); missed four games. ... Injured toe (November 19, 1999); missed six games. ... Traded by Islanders with LW Josh Green and second-round pick (LW Brad Winchester) in 2000 draft to Edmonton Oilers for D Roman Hamrlik (June 24, 2000). ... Strained buttocks (October 6, 2000); missed four games. ... Sprained left shoulder (January 21, 2002); missed one game.

Season Team	League	Gms.	G	A	Pts.	PIM	+/-	PP	SH	Gms.	G	A	Pts.	PIM
95-96—Prince George	WHL	63	4	10	14	25	...	...	...	—	—	—	—	—
96-97—Prince George	WHL	71	5	24	29	81	...	...	...	15	2	4	6	16
97-98—Prince George	WHL	34	5	28	33	45	...	...	...	11	4	2	6	19
98-99—New York Islanders	NHL	63	5	6	11	32	-14	2	0	—	—	—	—	—
99-00—New York Islanders	NHL	26	0	2	2	20	-11	0	0	—	—	—	—	—
—Lowell	AHL	25	2	2	4	26	...	...	...	7	0	0	0	0
00-01—Edmonton	NHL	77	7	14	21	53	15	2	0	6	1	5	6	2
01-02—Edmonton	NHL	81	7	18	25	45	-5	6	0	—	—	—	—	—
—Can. Olympic team	Int'l	6	2	0	2	0	...	...	...	—	—	—	—	—
02-03—Edmonton	NHL	80	8	21	29	45	-11	1	0	6	1	3	4	6
NHL Totals (5 years)		327	27	61	88	195	-26	11	0	12	2	8	10	8

BRIERE, DANIEL — C — SABRES

PERSONAL: Born October 6, 1977, in Gatineau, Que. ... 5-10/178. ... Shoots right.

TRANSACTIONS/CAREER NOTES: Selected by Phoenix Coyotes in first round (second Coyotes pick, 24th overall) of NHL entry draft (June 22, 1996). ... Separated shoulder (March 21, 1998); missed five games. ... Suffered concussion (October 6, 1998); missed first two games of season. ... Strained groin (September 25, 2000); missed first game of season. ... Strained groin (October 6, 2001); missed one game. ... Traded by Coyotes with third-round pick in 2004 draft to Buffalo Sabres for C Chris Gratton and fourth-round pick in 2004 draft (March 10, 2003).

Season Team	League	Gms.	G	A	Pts.	PIM	+/-	PP	SH	Gms.	G	A	Pts.	PIM
94-95—Drummondville	QMJHL	72	51	72	123	54	...	...	...	—	—	—	—	—
95-96—Drummondville	QMJHL	67	*67	*96	*163	84	...	...	...	6	6	12	18	8
96-97—Drummondville	QMJHL	59	52	78	130	86	...	...	...	8	7	7	14	14
97-98—Springfield	AHL	68	36	56	92	42	...	...	...	4	1	2	3	4
—Phoenix	NHL	5	1	0	1	2	1	0	0	—	—	—	—	—
98-99—Las Vegas	IHL	1	1	1	2	0	...	...	...	—	—	—	—	—
—Phoenix	NHL	64	8	14	22	30	-3	2	0	—	—	—	—	—
—Springfield	AHL	13	2	6	8	20	...	...	...	3	0	1	1	2
99-00—Springfield	AHL	58	29	42	71	56	...	...	...	—	—	—	—	—
—Phoenix	NHL	13	1	1	2	0	0	0	0	1	0	0	0	0
00-01—Phoenix	NHL	30	11	4	15	12	-2	9	0	—	—	—	—	—
—Springfield	AHL	30	21	25	46	30	...	...	...	—	—	—	—	—
01-02—Phoenix	NHL	78	32	28	60	52	6	12	0	5	2	1	3	2
02-03—Phoenix	NHL	68	17	29	46	50	-21	4	0	—	—	—	—	—
—Buffalo	NHL	14	7	5	12	12	1	5	0	—	—	—	—	—
NHL Totals (6 years)		272	77	81	158	158	-18	32	0	6	2	1	3	2

BRIGLEY, TRAVIS — RW — AVALANCHE

PERSONAL: Born June 16, 1977, in Coronation, Alta. ... 6-1/200. ... Shoots left.

TRANSACTIONS/CAREER NOTES: Selected by Calgary Flames in second round (second Flames pick, 39th overall) of NHL entry draft (June 22, 1996). ... Traded by Flames with sixth-round pick (C Andrei Razin) in 2001 draft to Philadelphia Flyers for C/RW Marc Bureau (March 6, 2000). ... Signed as free agent by Mighty Ducks of Anaheim (June 11, 2002). ... Traded by Mighty Ducks to Colorado Avalanche for future considerations (August 13, 2003).

Season Team	League	Gms.	G	A	Pts.	PIM	+/-	PP	SH	Gms.	G	A	Pts.	PIM
93-94—Lethbridge	WHL	1	0	0	0	0	...	...	...	—	—	—	—	—
94-95—Lethbridge	WHL	64	14	18	32	14	...	...	...	—	—	—	—	—
95-96—Lethbridge	WHL	69	34	43	77	94	...	...	...	4	2	3	5	8
96-97—Lethbridge	WHL	71	43	47	90	56	...	...	...	†19	9	9	18	31
97-98—Saint John	AHL	79	17	15	32	28	...	...	...	8	0	0	0	0
—Calgary	NHL	2	0	0	0	2	0	0	0	—	—	—	—	—
98-99—Saint John	AHL	74	15	35	50	47	...	...	...	7	3	1	4	2
99-00—Calgary	NHL	17	0	2	2	4	-6	0	0	—	—	—	—	—
—Saint John	AHL	9	3	1	4	4	...	...	...	—	—	—	—	—
—Detroit	IHL	29	6	10	16	24	...	...	...	—	—	—	—	—
—Philadelphia	AHL	15	2	2	4	15	...	...	...	5	1	0	1	4
00-01—Louisville	AHL	49	14	21	35	34	...	...	...	—	—	—	—	—
01-02—Cincinnati	AHL	70	22	21	43	40	...	...	...	3	2	0	2	0
—Macon	ECHL	8	4	3	7	2	...	...	...	—	—	—	—	—
02-03—Cincinnati	AHL	64	18	27	45	58	...	...	...	—	—	—	—	—
—Hershey	AHL	13	3	5	8	4	...	...	...	—	—	—	—	—
NHL Totals (2 years)		19	0	2	2	6	-6	0	0					

B

BRIMANIS, ARIS   D   BLUES

PERSONAL: Born March 14, 1972, in Cleveland. ... 6-3/195. ... Shoots right. ... Full Name: Aris Aldis Brimanis. ... Name pronounced AIR-ihz brih-MAN-ihz.

TRANSACTIONS/CAREER NOTES: Selected by Philadelphia Flyers in fourth round (third Flyers pick, 86th overall) of NHL entry draft (June 22, 1991). ... Signed as free agent by New York Islanders (August 12, 1999). ... Signed as free agent by Mighty Ducks of Anaheim (August 1, 2001). ... Signed as free agent by St. Louis Blues (August 9, 2002).

		REGULAR SEASON								PLAYOFFS			
Season Team	League	Gms.	G	A	Pts.	PIM	+/-	PP	SH	Gms.	G	A	Pts.	PIM
88-89—Culver Military	Indiana H.S.	38	10	13	23	24	...	...	...	—	—	—	—	—
89-90—Culver Military	Indiana H.S.	37	15	10	25	52	...	...	...	—	—	—	—	—
90-91—Bowling Green	CCHA	38	3	6	9	42	...	...	...	—	—	—	—	—
91-92—Bowling Green	CCHA	32	2	9	11	38	...	...	...	—	—	—	—	—
92-93—Brandon	WHL	71	8	50	58	110	...	...	...	4	2	1	3	12
93-94—Philadelphia	NHL	1	0	0	0	0	-1	0	0	—	—	—	—	—
—Hershey	AHL	75	8	15	23	65	...	...	...	11	2	3	5	12
94-95—Hershey	AHL	76	8	17	25	68	...	...	...	6	1	1	2	14
95-96—Hershey	AHL	54	9	22	31	64	...	...	...	5	1	2	3	4
—Philadelphia	NHL	17	0	2	2	12	-1	0	0	—	—	—	—	—
96-97—Philadelphia	AHL	65	14	18	32	69	...	...	...	10	2	2	4	13
—Philadelphia	NHL	3	0	1	1	0	0	0	0	—	—	—	—	—
97-98—Philadelphia	AHL	30	1	11	12	26	...	...	...	—	—	—	—	—
—Michigan	IHL	35	3	9	12	24	...	...	...	4	1	0	1	4
98-99—Grand Rapids	IHL	66	16	21	37	70	...	...	...	—	—	—	—	—
—Fredericton	AHL	8	2	4	6	6	...	...	...	15	3	10	13	18
99-00—Kansas City	IHL	46	5	17	22	28	...	...	...	—	—	—	—	—
—New York Islanders	NHL	18	2	1	3	6	-5	2	0	—	—	—	—	—
00-01—Chicago	IHL	20	2	2	4	14	...	...	...	16	3	1	4	8
—New York Islanders	NHL	56	0	8	8	26	-12	0	0	—	—	—	—	—
01-02—Cincinnati	AHL	72	2	9	11	44	...	...	...	3	1	0	1	0
—Anaheim	NHL	5	0	0	0	9	-1	0	0	—	—	—	—	—
02-03—Worcester	AHL	38	8	13	21	51	...	...	...	—	—	—	—	—
NHL Totals (6 years)		100	2	12	14	53	-20	2	0					

BRIND'AMOUR, ROD   C   HURRICANES

PERSONAL: Born August 9, 1970, in Ottawa, Ont. ... 6-1/200. ... Shoots left. ... Full Name: Rod Jean Brind'Amour. ... Name pronounced BRIHN-duh-MOHR.

TRANSACTIONS/CAREER NOTES: Selected by St. Louis Blues in first round (first Blues pick, ninth overall) of NHL entry draft (June 11, 1988). ... Traded by Blues with C Dan Quinn to Philadelphia Flyers for C Ron Sutter and D Murray Baron (September 22, 1991). ... Lacerated elbow (November 19, 1992); missed two games. ... Bruised right hand (February 20, 1993); missed one game. ... Fractured foot (September 25, 1999) and underwent surgery; missed first 34 games of season. ... Traded by Flyers with G Jean-Marc Pelletier and second-round pick (traded to Colorado) in 2000 draft to Carolina Hurricanes for rights to C Keith Primeau and fifth-round pick (traded to New York Islanders) in 2000 draft (January 23, 2000). ... Suffered concussion (April 3, 2000); missed one game. ... Injured groin (December 27, 2000); missed three games. ... Suffered eye injury (February 8, 2002); missed one game.

STATISTICAL PLATEAUS: Three-goal games: 1992-93 (1), 2000-01 (1). Total: 2.

		REGULAR SEASON								PLAYOFFS			
Season Team	League	Gms.	G	A	Pts.	PIM	+/-	PP	SH	Gms.	G	A	Pts.	PIM
87-88—Notre Dame	SJHL	56	46	61	107	136	...	...	...	—	—	—	—	—
88-89—Michigan State	CCHA	42	27	32	59	63	...	...	...	—	—	—	—	—
—St. Louis	NHL	—	—	—	—	—				5	2	0	2	4
89-90—St. Louis	NHL	79	26	35	61	46	23	10	0	12	5	8	13	6
90-91—St. Louis	NHL	78	17	32	49	93	2	4	0	13	2	5	7	10
91-92—Philadelphia	NHL	80	33	44	77	100	-3	8	4	—	—	—	—	—
92-93—Philadelphia	NHL	81	37	49	86	89	-8	13	4	—	—	—	—	—
93-94—Philadelphia	NHL	84	35	62	97	85	-9	14	1	—	—	—	—	—
94-95—Philadelphia	NHL	48	12	27	39	33	-4	4	1	15	6	9	15	8
95-96—Philadelphia	NHL	82	26	61	87	110	20	4	4	12	2	5	7	6
96-97—Philadelphia	NHL	82	27	32	59	41	2	8	2	19	13	8	21	10
97-98—Philadelphia	NHL	82	36	38	74	54	-2	10	2	5	2	2	4	7
—Can. Olympic team	Int'l	6	1	2	3	0	...	...	...	—	—	—	—	—
98-99—Philadelphia	NHL	82	24	50	74	47	3	10	0	6	1	3	4	0
99-00—Philadelphia	NHL	12	5	3	8	4	-1	4	0	—	—	—	—	—
—Carolina	NHL	33	4	10	14	22	-12	0	1	—	—	—	—	—
00-01—Carolina	NHL	79	20	36	56	47	-7	5	1	6	1	3	4	6
01-02—Carolina	NHL	81	23	32	55	40	3	5	2	23	4	8	12	16
02-03—Carolina	NHL	48	14	23	37	37	-9	7	1	—	—	—	—	—
NHL Totals (15 years)		1031	339	534	873	848	-2	106	23	116	38	51	89	73

BRISEBOIS, PATRICE   D   CANADIENS

PERSONAL: Born January 27, 1971, in Montreal ... 6-2/203. ... Shoots right. ... Name pronounced pa-TREEZ BREES-bwah.

TRANSACTIONS/CAREER NOTES: Selected by Montreal Canadiens in second round (second Canadiens pick, 30th overall) of NHL entry draft (June 17, 1989). ... Sprained right ankle (October 10, 1992); missed two games. ... Suffered charley horse (December 16, 1992); missed two games. ... Injured knee (October 30, 1993); missed 10 games. ... Suffered hairline fracture of ankle (December 1, 1993); missed 14 games. ... Sprained ankle (February 21, 1994); missed seven games. ... Suffered acute herniated disc (April 3, 1995); missed 12 games. ... Injured rib cage (November 1, 1995). ... Sprained back (February 17, 1996); missed four games. ... Suffered mild disc irritation (March 25, 1996); missed last nine games of regular season. ... Separated shoulder (January 4, 1997); missed 27 games. ... Strained shoulder (March 22, 1997); missed four games. ... Injured rib (April 10, 1997); missed remainder of regular season and two playoff games. ... Sprained knee (April 15, 1998); missed three games. ... Injured back (October 2, 1998); missed first six games of season. ... Separated shoulder (December 23, 1998); missed nine games. ... Sprained knee (February 20, 1999); missed one game. ... Injured shoulder (March 11, 1999); missed 12 games. ... Injured back proir to start of 1999-2000 season; missed first 27 games of season. ... Injured back (January 28, 2001); missed five games. ... Fractured ankle (January 17, 2002); missed 10 games.

Season Team	League	REGULAR SEASON								PLAYOFFS				
		Gms.	G	A	Pts.	PIM	+/-	PP	SH	Gms.	G	A	Pts.	PIM
87-88—Laval	QMJHL	48	10	34	44	95	...	...	...	6	0	2	2	2
88-89—Laval	QMJHL	50	20	45	65	95	...	...	...	17	8	14	22	45
89-90—Laval	QMJHL	56	18	70	88	108	...	...	...	13	7	9	16	26
90-91—Montreal	NHL	10	0	2	2	4	1	0	0	—	—	—	—	—
—Drummondville	QMJHL	54	17	44	61	72	...	...	...	14	6	18	24	49
91-92—Fredericton	AHL	53	12	27	39	51	...	...	...	—	—	—	—	—
—Montreal	NHL	26	2	8	10	20	9	0	0	11	2	4	6	6
92-93—Montreal	NHL	70	10	21	31	79	6	4	0	20	0	4	4	18
93-94—Montreal	NHL	53	2	21	23	63	5	1	0	7	0	4	4	6
94-95—Montreal	NHL	35	4	8	12	26	-2	0	0	—	—	—	—	—
95-96—Montreal	NHL	69	9	27	36	65	10	3	0	6	1	2	3	6
96-97—Montreal	NHL	49	2	13	15	24	-7	0	0	3	1	1	2	24
97-98—Montreal	NHL	79	10	27	37	67	16	5	0	10	1	0	1	0
98-99—Montreal	NHL	54	3	9	12	28	-8	1	0	—	—	—	—	—
99-00—Montreal	NHL	54	10	25	35	18	-1	5	0	—	—	—	—	—
00-01—Montreal	NHL	77	15	21	36	28	-31	11	0	—	—	—	—	—
01-02—Montreal	NHL	71	4	29	33	25	9	2	1	10	1	1	2	2
02-03—Montreal	NHL	73	4	25	29	32	-14	1	0	—	—	—	—	—
NHL Totals (13 years)		720	75	236	311	479	-7	33	1	67	6	16	22	62

BRODEUR, MARTIN   G   DEVILS

PERSONAL: Born May 6, 1972, in Montreal ... 6-2/210. ... Catches left. ... Son of Denis Brodeur, goaltender with bronze medal-winning Canadian Olympic team (1956). ... Name pronounced MAHR-tan broh-DOOR.
TRANSACTIONS/CAREER NOTES: Selected by New Jersey Devils in first round (first Devils pick, 20th overall) of NHL entry draft (June 16, 1990). ... Suffered from the flu (December 30, 1997); missed two games.

Season Team	League	REGULAR SEASON									PLAYOFFS							
		Gms.	Min	W	L	T	GA	SO	Avg.	SV%	Gms.	Min.	W	L	GA	SO	Avg.	SV%
89-90—St. Hyacinthe	QMJHL	42	2333	23	13	2	156	0	4.01	—	12	678	5	7	46	0	4.07	—
90-91—St. Hyacinthe	QMJHL	52	2946	22	24	4	162	2	3.30	—	4	232	0	4	16	0	4.14	—
91-92—St. Hyacinthe	QMJHL	48	2846	27	16	4	161	2	3.39	—	5	317	2	3	14	0	2.65	—
—New Jersey	NHL	4	179	2	1	0	10	0	3.35	.882	1	32	0	1	3	0	5.63	.800
92-93—Utica	AHL	32	1952	14	13	5	131	0	4.03	—	4	258	1	3	18	0	4.19	—
93-94—New Jersey	NHL	47	2625	27	11	8	105	3	2.40	.915	17	1171	8	†9	38	1	1.95	.928
94-95—New Jersey	NHL	40	2184	19	11	6	89	3	2.45	.902	*20	*1222	*16	4	34	*3	*1.67	.927
95-96—New Jersey	NHL	77	*4433	34	†30	12	173	6	2.34	.911	—	—	—	—	—	—	—	—
96-97—New Jersey	NHL	67	3838	37	14	13	120	*10	*1.88	.927	10	659	5	5	19	2	1.73	.929
97-98—New Jersey	NHL	70	4128	*43	17	8	130	10	1.89	.917	6	366	2	4	12	0	1.97	.922
98-99—New Jersey	NHL	*70	*4239	*39	21	10	162	4	2.29	.906	7	425	3	4	20	0	2.82	.856
99-00—New Jersey	NHL	72	4312	*43	20	8	161	6	2.24	.910	†23	*1450	*16	7	39	2	*1.61	.927
00-01—New Jersey	NHL	72	4297	*42	17	11	166	9	2.32	.906	25	1505	15	10	52	4	2.07	.897
01-02—New Jersey	NHL	*73	*4347	38	26	9	156	4	2.15	.906	6	381	2	4	9	1	1.42	.938
—Can. Olympic team	Int'l	5	300	4	0	1	9	0	1.80	—	—	—	—	—	—	—	—	—
02-03—New Jersey	NHL	73	4374	*41	23	9	147	*9	2.02	.914	24	1491	*16	*8	41	*7	1.65	.934
NHL Totals (11 years)		665	38956	365	191	94	1419	64	2.19	.912	139	8702	83	56	267	20	1.84	.921

BROOKBANK, WADE   D   SENATORS

PERSONAL: Born September 29, 1977, in Lanigan, Sask. ... 6-4/219. ... Shoots left.
TRANSACTIONS/CAREER NOTES: Signed by Ottawa Senators (July 24, 2003).

Season Team	League	REGULAR SEASON								PLAYOFFS				
		Gms.	G	A	Pts.	PIM	+/-	PP	SH	Gms.	G	A	Pts.	PIM
01-02—Grand Rapids	AHL	73	1	6	7	337	...	...	...	3	0	1	1	14
02-03—Binghamton	AHL	8	0	0	0	28	...	...	...	—	—	—	—	—

BROWN, BRAD   D   WILD

PERSONAL: Born December 27, 1975, in Baie Verte, Nfld. ... 6-4/220. ... Shoots right.
TRANSACTIONS/CAREER NOTES: Selected by Montreal Canadiens in first round (first Canadiens pick, 18th overall) of NHL entry draft (June 28, 1994). ... Suffered back spasms (October 17, 1998); missed three games. ... Traded by Canadiens with G Jocelyn Thibault and D Dave Manson to Chicago Blackhawks for G Jeff Hackett, D Eric Weinrich, D Alain Nasreddine and fourth-round pick (D Chris Dyment) in 1999 draft (November 16, 1998). ... Suffered sore back (December 17, 1998); missed two games. ... Bruised foot (March 12, 1999); missed two games. ... Bruised wrist (October 4, 1999); missed three games. ... Lacerated hand (December 17, 1999); missed two games. ... Injured hand (December 26, 1999); missed 10 games. ... Injured left hand (March 15, 2000); missed four games. ... Traded by Blackhawks with LW Michal Grosek to New York Rangers for future considerations (October 5, 2000). ... Injured shoulder (January 4, 2001); missed 10 games. ... Fractured right foot (February 23, 2001); missed remainder of season. ... Signed as free agent by Minnesota Wild (July 31, 2001). ... Bruised kidney (November 25, 2001); missed four games. ... Bruised left ankle (December 22, 2001); missed one game. ... Fractured left ankle (December 26, 2001); missed 12 games. ... Sprained right knee (January 24, 2002); missed six games. ... Bruised left foot (April 5, 2002); missed two games.

Season Team	League	REGULAR SEASON								PLAYOFFS				
		Gms.	G	A	Pts.	PIM	+/-	PP	SH	Gms.	G	A	Pts.	PIM
91-92—North Bay	OHL	49	2	9	11	170	...	...	...	18	0	6	6	43
92-93—North Bay	OHL	61	4	9	13	228	...	...	...	2	0	2	2	13
93-94—North Bay	OHL	66	8	24	32	196	...	...	...	18	3	12	15	33
94-95—North Bay	OHL	64	8	38	46	172	...	...	...	6	1	4	5	8
95-96—Barrie	OHL	27	3	13	16	82	...	...	...	—	—	—	—	—
—Fredericton	AHL	38	0	3	3	148	...	...	...	10	2	1	3	6
96-97—Fredericton	AHL	64	3	7	10	368	...	...	...	—	—	—	—	—
—Montreal	NHL	8	0	0	0	22	-1	0	0	—	—	—	—	—
97-98—Fredericton	AHL	64	1	8	9	297	...	...	...	4	0	0	0	29
98-99—Montreal	NHL	5	0	0	0	21	0	0	0	—	—	—	—	—
—Chicago	NHL	61	1	7	8	184	-4	0	0	—	—	—	—	—
99-00—Chicago	NHL	57	0	9	9	134	-1	0	0	—	—	—	—	—
00-01—New York Rangers	NHL	48	1	3	4	107	0	0	0	—	—	—	—	—
01-02—Minnesota	NHL	51	0	4	4	123	-11	0	0	—	—	—	—	—
02-03—Minnesota	NHL	57	0	1	1	90	-1	0	0	11	0	0	0	16
NHL Totals (6 years)		287	2	24	26	681	-18	0	0	11	0	0	0	16

BROWN, CURTIS   C   SABRES

PERSONAL: Born February 12, 1976, in Unity, Sask. ... 6-0/196. ... Shoots left.
TRANSACTIONS/CAREER NOTES: Selected by Buffalo Sabres in second round (second Sabres pick, 43rd overall) of NHL entry draft (June 28, 1994). ... Injured ankle prior to 1995-96 season; missed two games. ... Bruised knee (February 11, 1999); missed two games. ... Bruised knee (March 27, 1999); missed one game. ... Missed first game of 1999-2000 season due to contract dispute. ... Suffered concussion (October 22, 1999); missed one game. ... Suffered from the flu (February 10, 2000); missed five games. ... Injured knee (December 23, 2000); missed eight games. ... Suffered back spasms (January 30, 2001); missed four games.
STATISTICAL PLATEAUS: Three-goal games: 2002-03 (1).

Season Team	League	REGULAR SEASON								PLAYOFFS				
		Gms.	G	A	Pts.	PIM	+/-	PP	SH	Gms.	G	A	Pts.	PIM
92-93—Moose Jaw	WHL	71	13	16	29	30	...	...	...	—	—	—	—	—
93-94—Moose Jaw	WHL	72	27	38	65	82	...	...	...	—	—	—	—	—
94-95—Moose Jaw	WHL	70	51	53	104	63	...	...	...	10	8	7	15	20
—Buffalo	NHL	1	1	1	2	2	2	0	0	—	—	—	—	—
95-96—Buffalo	NHL	4	0	0	0	0	0	0	0	—	—	—	—	—
—Moose Jaw	WHL	25	20	18	38	30	...			—	—	—	—	—
—Prince Albert	WHL	19	12	21	33	8	...			18	10	15	25	18
—Rochester	AHL	—	—	—	—	—				12	0	1	1	2
96-97—Buffalo	NHL	28	4	3	7	18	4	0	0	—	—	—	—	—
—Rochester	AHL	51	22	21	43	30				10	4	6	10	4
97-98—Buffalo	NHL	63	12	12	24	34	11	1	1	13	1	2	3	10
98-99—Buffalo	NHL	78	16	31	47	56	23	5	1	21	7	6	13	10
99-00—Buffalo	NHL	74	22	29	51	42	19	5	0	5	1	3	4	6
00-01—Buffalo	NHL	70	10	22	32	34	15	2	1	13	5	0	5	8
01-02—Buffalo	NHL	82	20	17	37	32	-4	4	1	—	—	—	—	—
02-03—Buffalo	NHL	74	15	16	31	40	4	3	4	—	—	—	—	—
NHL Totals (9 years)		474	100	131	231	258	74	20	8	52	14	11	25	34

BROWN, MIKE   LW

PERSONAL: Born April 27, 1979, in Surrey, B.C. ... 6-4/225. ... Shoots left.
TRANSACTIONS/CAREER NOTES: Selected by Florida Panthers in first round (first Panthers pick, 20th overall) of NHL entry draft (June 21, 1997). ... Traded by Panthers with D Ed Jovanovski, G Kevin Weekes, C Dave Gagner and first-round pick in 2000 (C Nathan Smith) draft to Vancouver Canucks for RW Pavel Bure, D Bret Hedican, D Brad Ference and third-round pick (RW Robert Fried) in 2000 draft (January 17, 1999). ... Claimed on waivers by Mighty Ducks of Anaheim (October 11, 2002).

Season Team	League	REGULAR SEASON								PLAYOFFS				
		Gms.	G	A	Pts.	PIM	+/-	PP	SH	Gms.	G	A	Pts.	PIM
94-95—Merritt	BCJHL	45	3	4	7	128	...	...	...	—	—	—	—	—
95-96—Red Deer	WHL	62	4	5	9	125	...	...	...	10	0	0	0	18
96-97—Red Deer	WHL	70	19	13	32	243	...	...	...	16	1	2	3	47
97-98—Kamloops	WHL	72	23	33	56	305	...	...	...	7	2	1	3	22
98-99—Kamloops	WHL	69	28	16	44	*285	...	...	...	15	3	7	10	68
99-00—Syracuse	AHL	71	13	18	31	284	...	...	...	4	0	0	0	0
00-01—Kansas City	IHL	78	14	13	27	214	...	...	...	—	—	—	—	—
—Vancouver	NHL	1	0	0	0	5	0	0	0	—	—	—	—	—
01-02—Manitoba	AHL	31	7	9	16	155	...	...	...	6	0	1	1	16
—Vancouver	NHL	15	0	0	0	72	1	0	0	—	—	—	—	—
02-03—Anaheim	NHL	16	1	1	2	44	0	0	0	—	—	—	—	—
—Cincinnati	AHL	27	3	3	6	85	...			—	—	—	—	—
NHL Totals (3 years)		32	1	1	2	121	1	0	0					

BROWN, SEAN   D   DEVILS

PERSONAL: Born November 5, 1976, in Oshawa, Ont. ... 6-3/205. ... Shoots left.
TRANSACTIONS/CAREER NOTES: Selected by Boston Bruins in first round (second Bruins pick, 21st overall) of NHL entry draft (July 8, 1995). ... Traded by Boston Bruins with RW Mariusz Czerkawski and first-round pick (D Mattieu Descoteaux) in 1996 draft to Edmonton Oilers for G Bill Ranford (January 11, 1996). ... Suspended three games by NHL for high-sticking incident (November 13, 1998). ... Traded by Oilers to Bruins for D Bobby Allen (March 19, 2002). ... Suspended one game by NHL for cross-checking incident (November 11, 2002). ... Signed by New Jersey Devils (July 24, 2003).

Season Team	League	REGULAR SEASON								PLAYOFFS				
		Gms.	G	A	Pts.	PIM	+/-	PP	SH	Gms.	G	A	Pts.	PIM
92-93—Oshawa	Tier II Jr. A	15	0	1	1	9	...	...	...	—	—	—	—	—
93-94—Wellington	OJHL	32	5	14	19	165	...	...	...	—	—	—	—	—
—Belleville	OHL	28	1	2	3	53	...	...	...	8	0	0	0	17
94-95—Belleville	OHL	58	2	16	18	200	...	...	...	16	4	2	6	67
95-96—Belleville	OHL	37	10	23	33	150	...	...	...	—	—	—	—	—
—Sarnia	OHL	26	8	17	25	112	...	...	...	10	1	0	1	38
96-97—Hamilton	AHL	61	1	7	8	238	...	...	...	19	1	0	1	47
—Edmonton	NHL	5	0	0	0	4	-1	0	0	—	—	—	—	—
97-98—Edmonton	NHL	18	0	1	1	43	-1	0	0	—	—	—	—	—
—Hamilton	AHL	43	4	6	10	166	...	...	...	6	0	2	2	38
98-99—Edmonton	NHL	51	0	7	7	188	1	0	0	1	0	0	0	10
99-00—Edmonton	NHL	72	4	8	12	192	1	0	0	3	0	0	0	23
00-01—Edmonton	NHL	62	2	3	5	110	2	0	0	—	—	—	—	—
01-02—Edmonton	NHL	61	6	4	10	127	8	3	0	—	—	—	—	—
—Boston	NHL	12	0	1	1	47	-1	0	0	4	0	0	0	2
02-03—Boston	NHL	69	1	5	6	117	-6	0	0	—	—	—	—	—
NHL Totals (7 years)		350	13	29	42	828	3	3	0	8	0	0	0	35

BRULE, STEVE   C

PERSONAL: Born January 15, 1975, in Montreal ... 6-0/200. ... Shoots right. ... Name pronounced broo-LAY.
TRANSACTIONS/CAREER NOTES: Selected by New Jersey Devils in sixth round (sixth Devils pick, 143rd overall) of NHL entry draft (June 26, 1993). ... Signed as free agent by Detroit Red Wings (July 20, 2000). ... Signed as free agent by Colorado Avalanche (July 22, 2002).

Season Team	League	REGULAR SEASON								PLAYOFFS				
		Gms.	G	A	Pts.	PIM	+/-	PP	SH	Gms.	G	A	Pts.	PIM
92-93—St. Jean	QMJHL	70	33	47	80	46	...	...	...	4	0	0	0	9
93-94—St. Jean	QMJHL	66	41	64	105	46	...	...	...	5	2	1	3	0
94-95—St. Jean	QMJHL	69	44	64	108	42	...	...	...	7	3	4	7	8
—Albany	AHL	3	1	4	5	0	...	...	...	14	9	5	14	4
95-96—Albany	AHL	80	30	21	51	37	...	...	...	4	0	0	0	17
96-97—Albany	AHL	79	28	48	76	27	...	...	...	16	7	7	14	12
97-98—Albany	AHL	80	34	43	77	34	...	...	...	13	8	3	11	4
98-99—Albany	AHL	78	32	52	84	35	...	...	...	5	3	1	4	4
99-00—Albany	AHL	75	30	46	76	18	...	...	...	5	1	2	3	0
—New Jersey	NHL	—	—	—	—	—	—	—	—	1	0	0	0	0
00-01—Manitoba	IHL	78	21	48	69	22	...	...	...	13	3	10	13	12
01-02—Cincinnati	AHL	77	21	42	63	50	...	...	...	3	0	1	1	0
02-03—Hershey	AHL	49	18	19	37	30	...	...	...	—	—	—	—	—
—Colorado	NHL	2	0	0	0	0	0	0	0	—	—	—	—	—
NHL Totals (2 years)		2	0	0	0	0	0	0	0	1	0	0	0	0

BRUNETTE, ANDREW   LW   WILD

PERSONAL: Born August 24, 1973, in Sudbury, Ont. ... 6-1/210. ... Shoots left. ... Name pronounced broo-NEHT.
TRANSACTIONS/CAREER NOTES: Selected by Washington Capitals in sixth round (sixth Capitals pick, 174th overall) of NHL entry draft (June 26, 1993). ... Selected by Nashville Predators in NHL expansion draft (June 26, 1998). ... Traded by Predators to Atlanta Thrashers for fifth-round pick (C Matt Hendricks) in 2000 draft (June 21, 1999). ... Suffered concussion (January 13, 2001); missed four games. ... Bruised thigh (February 15, 2001); missed one game. ... Signed as free agent by Minnesota Wild (July 6, 2001). ... Bruised shoulder (December 29, 2001); missed one game.

Season Team	League	REGULAR SEASON								PLAYOFFS				
		Gms.	G	A	Pts.	PIM	+/-	PP	SH	Gms.	G	A	Pts.	PIM
90-91—Owen Sound	OHL	63	15	20	35	15	...	...	...	—	—	—	—	—
91-92—Owen Sound	OHL	66	51	47	98	42	...	...	...	5	5	0	5	8
92-93—Owen Sound	OHL	66	*62	*100	*162	91	...	...	...	8	8	6	14	16
93-94—Portland	AHL	23	9	11	20	10	...	...	...	2	0	1	1	0
—Hampton	ECHL	20	12	18	30	32	...	...	...	7	7	6	13	18
—Providence	AHL	3	0	0	0	0	...	...	...	—	—	—	—	—
94-95—Portland	AHL	79	30	50	80	53	...	...	...	7	3	3	6	10
95-96—Portland	AHL	69	28	66	94	125	...	...	...	20	11	18	29	15
—Washington	NHL	11	3	3	6	0	5	0	0	6	1	3	4	0
96-97—Portland	AHL	50	22	51	73	48	...	...	...	5	1	2	3	0
—Washington	NHL	23	4	7	11	12	-3	2	0	—	—	—	—	—
97-98—Portland	AHL	43	21	46	67	64	...	...	...	10	1	11	12	12
—Washington	NHL	28	11	12	23	12	2	4	0	—	—	—	—	—
98-99—Nashville	NHL	77	11	20	31	26	-10	7	0	—	—	—	—	—
99-00—Atlanta	NHL	81	23	27	50	30	-32	9	0	—	—	—	—	—
00-01—Atlanta	NHL	77	15	44	59	26	-5	6	0	—	—	—	—	—
01-02—Minnesota	NHL	81	21	48	69	18	-4	10	0	—	—	—	—	—
02-03—Minnesota	NHL	82	18	28	46	30	-10	9	0	18	7	6	13	4
NHL Totals (8 years)		460	106	189	295	154	-57	47	0	24	8	9	17	4

BRYLIN, SERGEI   C   DEVILS

PERSONAL: Born January 13, 1974, in Moscow, U.S.S.R. ... 5-10/190. ... Shoots left. ... Name pronounced BREE-lihn.
TRANSACTIONS/CAREER NOTES: Selected by New Jersey Devils in second round (second Devils pick, 42nd overall) of NHL entry draft (June 20, 1992). ... Suffered from tonsillitis (May 3, 1995); missed last game of season. ... Fractured hand (November 16, 1995); missed 13 games. ... Injured knee (September 19, 1997); missed 19 games. ... Injured knee (November 28, 2000); missed one game. ... Injured knee (February 22, 2001); missed five games. ... Bruised knee (November 13, 2001); missed five games.

Season Team	League	REGULAR SEASON								PLAYOFFS				
		Gms.	G	A	Pts.	PIM	+/-	PP	SH	Gms.	G	A	Pts.	PIM
90-91—CSKA Moscow	USSR					Statistics unavailable.								
91-92—CSKA Moscow	CIS	44	1	6	7	4	...	...	...	—	—	—	—	—
92-93—CSKA Moscow	CIS	42	5	4	9	36	...	...	...	—	—	—	—	—
93-94—CSKA Moscow	CIS	39	4	6	10	36	...	...	...	3	0	1	1	0
—Russian Penguins	IHL	13	4	5	9	18	...	...	...	—	—	—	—	—
94-95—Albany	AHL	63	19	35	54	78	...	...	...	—	—	—	—	—
—New Jersey	NHL	26	6	8	14	8	12	0	0	12	1	2	3	4
95-96—New Jersey	NHL	50	4	5	9	26	-2	0	0	—	—	—	—	—
96-97—New Jersey	NHL	29	2	2	4	20	-13	0	0	—	—	—	—	—
—Albany	AHL	43	17	24	41	38	...	...	...	16	4	8	12	12
97-98—New Jersey	NHL	18	2	3	5	0	4	0	0	—	—	—	—	—
—Albany	AHL	44	21	22	43	60	...	...	...	—	—	—	—	—
98-99—New Jersey	NHL	47	5	10	15	28	8	3	0	5	3	1	4	4
99-00—New Jersey	NHL	64	9	11	20	20	0	1	0	17	3	5	8	0
00-01—New Jersey	NHL	75	23	29	52	24	25	3	1	20	3	4	7	6
01-02—New Jersey	NHL	76	16	28	44	10	21	5	0	6	0	2	2	2
02-03—New Jersey	NHL	52	11	8	19	16	-2	3	1	19	1	3	4	8
NHL Totals (9 years)		437	78	104	182	152	53	15	2	79	11	17	28	24

BRYZGALOV, ILJA G MIGHTY DUCKS

PERSONAL: Born June 22, 1980, in Togliatti, U.S.S.R. ... 6-3/196. ... Catches left.
TRANSACTIONS/CAREER NOTES: Selected by Mighty Ducks of Anaheim in second round (second Mighty Ducks pick, 44th overall) of NHL entry draft (June 24, 2000).

Season Team	League	REGULAR SEASON								PLAYOFFS						
		Gms.	Min	W	L	T	GA	SO	Avg.	SV%	Gms.	Min.	W	L	GA	SO	Avg.	SV%
97-98—Lada-2 Togliatti	Rus. Div. III	8	480	...	...	...	28	...	3.50	—	—	—	—	—	—	—	—	—
98-99—Lada-2 Togliatti	Rus.-4	20	1200	...	...	...	43	...	2.15	—	—	—	—	—	—	—	—	—
99-00—Spartak Moscow	Russian	9	500	...	...	...	21	...	2.52	—	—	—	—	—	—	—	—	—
—Lada Togliatti	Russian	14	796	...	...	...	18	3	1.36	—	7	407	...	...	10	1	1.47	—
00-01—Lada Togliatti	Russian	34	1992	...	...	...	61	*8	1.84	—	5	249	...	...	8	0	1.93	—
01-02—Cincinnati	AHL	45	2398	20	16	4	99	4	2.48	—	—	—	—	—	—	—	—	—
—Anaheim	NHL	1	32	0	0	0	1	0	1.88	.917	—	—	—	—	—	—	—	—
02-03—Cincinnati	AHL	54	3019	12	26	9	142	1	2.82	—	—	—	—	—	—	—	—	—
NHL Totals (1 year)		1	32	0	0	0	1	0	1.88	.917								

BUCHBERGER, KELLY RW PENGUINS

PERSONAL: Born December 2, 1966, in Langenburg, Sask. ... 6-2/200. ... Shoots left. ... Full Name: Kelly Michael Buchberger. ... Name pronounced BUK-buhr-guhr.
TRANSACTIONS/CAREER NOTES: Selected by Edmonton Oilers in ninth round (eighth Oilers pick, 188th overall) of NHL entry draft (June 15, 1985). ... Suspended six games by AHL for leaving bench to fight (March 30, 1988). ... Fractured right ankle (March 1989). ... Dislocated left shoulder (March 13, 1990). ... Reinjured shoulder (May 4, 1990). ... Strained shoulder (April 7, 1993); missed one game. ... Fractured right forearm (January 5, 1999); missed 30 games. ... Selected by Atlanta Thrashers in NHL expansion draft (June 25, 1999). ... Traded by Thrashers with RW Nelson Emerson to Los Angeles Kings for RW Donald Audette and D Frantisek Kaberle (March 13, 2000). ... Sprained right ankle (March 9, 2002); missed seven games. ... Signed as free agent by Phoenix Coyotes (July 7, 2002). ... Signed by Pittsburgh Penguins (July 31, 2003).
STATISTICAL PLATEAUS: Three-goal games: 1992-93 (1).

Season Team	League	REGULAR SEASON								PLAYOFFS				
		Gms.	G	A	Pts.	PIM	+/-	PP	SH	Gms.	G	A	Pts.	PIM
83-84—Melville	SAJHL	60	14	11	25	139	...	...	...	—	—	—	—	—
84-85—Moose Jaw	WHL	51	12	17	29	114	...	...	...	—	—	—	—	—
85-86—Moose Jaw	WHL	72	14	22	36	206	...	...	...	13	11	4	15	37
86-87—Nova Scotia	AHL	70	12	20	32	257	...	...	...	5	0	1	1	23
—Edmonton	NHL	—	—	—	—	—	—	—	—	3	0	1	1	5
87-88—Edmonton	NHL	19	1	0	1	81	-1	0	0	—	—	—	—	—
—Nova Scotia	AHL	49	21	23	44	206	...	...	...	2	0	0	0	11
88-89—Edmonton	NHL	66	5	9	14	234	-14	1	0	—	—	—	—	—
89-90—Edmonton	NHL	55	2	6	8	168	-8	0	0	19	0	5	5	13
90-91—Edmonton	NHL	64	3	1	4	160	-6	0	0	12	2	1	3	25
91-92—Edmonton	NHL	79	20	24	44	157	9	0	4	16	1	4	5	32
92-93—Edmonton	NHL	83	12	18	30	133	-27	1	2	—	—	—	—	—
93-94—Edmonton	NHL	84	3	18	21	199	-20	0	0	—	—	—	—	—
94-95—Edmonton	NHL	48	7	17	24	82	0	2	1	—	—	—	—	—
95-96—Edmonton	NHL	82	11	14	25	184	-20	0	2	—	—	—	—	—
96-97—Edmonton	NHL	81	8	30	38	159	4	0	0	12	5	2	7	16
97-98—Edmonton	NHL	82	6	17	23	122	-10	1	1	12	1	2	3	25
98-99—Edmonton	NHL	52	4	4	8	68	-6	0	2	4	0	0	0	0
99-00—Atlanta	NHL	68	5	12	17	139	-34	0	0	—	—	—	—	—
—Los Angeles	NHL	13	2	1	3	13	-2	0	0	4	0	0	0	4
00-01—Los Angeles	NHL	82	6	14	20	75	-10	0	0	8	1	0	1	2
01-02—Los Angeles	NHL	74	6	7	13	105	-13	0	0	7	0	0	0	7
02-03—Phoenix	NHL	79	3	9	12	109	0	0	1	—	—	—	—	—
NHL Totals (17 years)		1111	104	201	305	2188	-158	5	13	97	10	15	25	129

BUCKLEY, BRENDAN   D   PENGUINS

PERSONAL: Born February 26, 1977, in Boston. ... 6-2/196. ... Shoots right.
TRANSACTIONS/CAREER NOTES: Selected by Mighty Ducks of Anaheim in fifth round (third Mighty Ducks pick, 117th overall) of NHL entry draft (June 22, 1996). ... Signed as free agent by Pittsburgh Penguins (August 29, 2001).

Season Team	League	REGULAR SEASON								PLAYOFFS				
		Gms.	G	A	Pts.	PIM	+/-	PP	SH	Gms.	G	A	Pts.	PIM
94-95—Jr. Bruins	Jr. A	48	22	43	65	164	...	...	...	—	—	—	—	—
95-96—Boston College	Hockey East	36	0	4	4	72	...	...	...	—	—	—	—	—
96-97—Boston College	Hockey East	38	2	6	8	90	...	...	...	—	—	—	—	—
97-98—Boston College	Hockey East	41	1	12	13	69	...	...	...	—	—	—	—	—
98-99—Boston College	Hockey East	43	1	13	14	75	...	...	...	—	—	—	—	—
99-00—Quad City	UHL	61	1	10	11	73	...	...	...	9	1	0	1	10
—Cincinnati	AHL	4	0	0	0	6	...	...	...	—	—	—	—	—
00-01—Wilkes-Barre/Scranton	AHL	63	2	8	10	62	...	...	...	21	0	2	2	33
01-02—Wilkes-Barre/Scranton	AHL	80	1	19	20	116	...	...	...	—	—	—	—	—
02-03—Wilkes-Barre/Scranton	AHL	80	2	6	8	99	...	...	...	—	—	—	—	—

BULIS, JAN   LW   CANADIENS

PERSONAL: Born March 18, 1978, in Pardubice, Czechoslovakia ... 6-2/201. ... Shoots left. ... Name pronounced YAHN BOO-lihsh.
TRANSACTIONS/CAREER NOTES: Selected by Washington Capitals in second round (third Capitals pick, 43rd overall) of NHL entry draft (June 22, 1996). ... Suffered concussion (November 11, 1997); missed one game. ... Sprained ankle prior to 1998-99 season; missed first 13 games of season. ... Sprained ankle (November 21, 1998); missed 15 games. ... Suffered back spasms (November 11, 1999); missed one game. ... Bruised ribs (November 20, 1999); missed two games. ... Injured groin (December 15, 1999); missed three games. ... Separated shoulder (February 26, 2000); missed remainder of season. ... Fractured right thumb (November 22, 2000); missed 18 games. ... Traded by Capitals with RW Richard Zednik and first-round pick (C Alexander Perezhogin) in 2001 draft to Montreal Canadiens for C Trevor Linden, RW Dainius Zubrus and second-round pick (traded to Tampa Bay) in 2001 draft (March 13, 2001). ... Sprained knee (December 1, 2001); missed 20 games.

Season Team	League	REGULAR SEASON								PLAYOFFS				
		Gms.	G	A	Pts.	PIM	+/-	PP	SH	Gms.	G	A	Pts.	PIM
94-95—Kelowna	BCJHL	51	23	25	48	36	...	...	...	17	7	9	16	...
95-96—Barrie	OHL	59	29	30	59	22	...	...	...	7	2	3	5	2
96-97—Barrie	OHL	64	42	61	103	42	...	...	...	9	3	7	10	10
97-98—Washington	NHL	48	5	11	16	18	-5	0	0	—	—	—	—	—
—Portland	AHL	3	1	4	5	12	...	...	...	—	—	—	—	—
—Kingston	OHL	2	0	1	1	0	...	...	...	12	8	10	18	12
98-99—Washington	NHL	38	7	16	23	6	3	3	0	—	—	—	—	—
—Cincinnati	IHL	10	2	2	4	14	...	...	...	—	—	—	—	—
99-00—Washington	NHL	56	9	22	31	30	7	0	0	—	—	—	—	—
00-01—Washington	NHL	39	5	13	18	26	0	1	0	—	—	—	—	—
—Portland	AHL	4	0	2	2	0	...	...	...	—	—	—	—	—
—Montreal	NHL	12	0	5	5	0	-1	0	0	—	—	—	—	—
01-02—Montreal	NHL	53	9	10	19	8	-2	1	0	6	0	0	0	6
02-03—Montreal	NHL	82	16	24	40	30	9	0	0	—	—	—	—	—
NHL Totals (6 years)		328	51	101	152	118	11	5	0	6	0	0	0	6

BURE, PAVEL   RW   RANGERS

PERSONAL: Born March 31, 1971, in Moscow, U.S.S.R. ... 5-11/191. ... Shoots left. ... Brother of Valeri Bure, right winger, Florida Panthers. ... Name pronounced PA-vihl BOOR-ay. ... Nickname: The Russian Rocket.
TRANSACTIONS/CAREER NOTES: Selected by Vancouver Canucks in sixth round (fourth Canucks pick, 113th overall) of NHL entry draft (June 17, 1989). ... Strained groin (October 24, 1993); missed eight games. ... Played in Europe during 1994-95 NHL lockout. ... Suffered injury (March 17, 1995); missed two games. ... Tore knee ligament (November 9, 1995); missed remainder of season. ... Suspended one game and fined $1,000 by NHL for forearm blow (December 6, 1996). ... Suffered whiplash (March 3, 1997); missed remainder of season. ... Missed first 43 games of 1998-99 season due to contract dispute. ... Traded by Canucks with D Bret Hedican, D Brad Ference and third-round pick (Robert Fried) in 2000 draft to Florida Panthers for D Ed Jovanovski, G Kevin Weekes, C Dave Gagner, C Mike Brown and first-round pick (C Nathan Smith) in 2000 draft (January 17, 1999). ... Strained right knee (February 5, 1999); missed eight games. ... Reinjured knee (March 3, 1999); missed final 21 games of season. ... Strained groin (October 12, 1999); missed five games. ... Fractured finger (November 3, 1999); missed three games. ... Fractured left hand (January 9, 2002); missed five games. ... Traded by Panthers with second-round pick (C Lee Falardeau) in 2002 draft to New York Rangers for D Igor Ulanov, D Filip Novak, first-(traded to Calgary) and second-round (C/RW Rob Globke) picks in 2002 draft and fourth-round pick in 2003 draft (March 18, 2002).
STATISTICAL PLATEAUS: Three-goal games: 1992-93 (1), 1993-94 (1), 1994-95 (1), 1997-98 (3), 1998-99 (2), 1999-00 (3), 2000-01 (3), 2002-03 (1). Total: 17. ... Four-goal games: 1992-93 (1), 1999-00 (1), 2000-01 (1). Total: 3. ... Total hat tricks: 20.

Season Team	League	REGULAR SEASON								PLAYOFFS				
		Gms.	G	A	Pts.	PIM	+/-	PP	SH	Gms.	G	A	Pts.	PIM
87-88—CSKA Moscow	USSR	5	1	1	2	0	...	...	...	—	—	—	—	—
88-89—CSKA Moscow	USSR	32	17	9	26	8	...	...	...	—	—	—	—	—
89-90—CSKA Moscow	USSR	46	14	11	25	22	...	...	...	—	—	—	—	—
90-91—CSKA Moscow	USSR	46	35	12	47	24	...	...	...	—	—	—	—	—
91-92—Vancouver	NHL	65	34	26	60	30	0	7	3	13	6	4	10	14
92-93—Vancouver	NHL	83	60	50	110	69	35	13	†7	12	5	7	12	8
93-94—Vancouver	NHL	76	*60	47	107	86	1	†25	4	24	*16	15	31	40
94-95—Landshut	Germany	1	3	0	3	2	...	...	...	—	—	—	—	—
—Spartak Moscow	Russian	1	2	0	2	2	...	...	...	—	—	—	—	—
—Vancouver	NHL	44	20	23	43	47	-8	6	2	11	7	6	13	10
95-96—Vancouver	NHL	15	6	7	13	8	-2	1	1	—	—	—	—	—
96-97—Vancouver	NHL	63	23	32	55	40	-14	4	1	—	—	—	—	—

			REGULAR SEASON								PLAYOFFS				
Season Team	League	Gms.	G	A	Pts.	PIM	+/-	PP	SH		Gms.	G	A	Pts.	PIM
97-98—Vancouver...................	NHL	82	51	39	90	48	5	13	†6		—	—	—	—	—
—Russian Oly. team......	Int'l	6	9	0	9	2	...	...	...		—	—	—	—	—
98-99—Florida........................	NHL	11	13	3	16	4	3	5	1		—	—	—	—	—
99-00—Florida........................	NHL	74	*58	36	94	16	25	11	2		4	1	3	4	2
00-01—Florida........................	NHL	82	*59	33	92	58	-2	19	5		—	—	—	—	—
01-02—Florida........................	NHL	56	22	27	49	56	-14	9	1		—	—	—	—	—
—Russian Oly. team......	Int'l	6	2	1	3	8	...	...	...		—	—	—	—	—
—New York Rangers......	NHL	12	12	8	20	6	9	3	0		—	—	—	—	—
02-03—New York Rangers......	NHL	39	19	11	30	16	4	5	1		—	—	—	—	—
NHL Totals (12 years).........		702	437	342	779	484	42	121	34		64	35	35	70	74

BURE, VALERI — RW — PANTHERS

PERSONAL: Born June 13, 1974, in Moscow, U.S.S.R. ... 5-10/185. ... Shoots right. ... Brother of Pavel Bure, right winger, Florida Panthers. ... Name pronounced BOOR-ay.

TRANSACTIONS/CAREER NOTES: Selected by Montreal Canadiens in second round (second Canadiens pick, 33rd overall) of NHL entry draft (June 20, 1992). ... Bruised forearm (April 3, 1995); missed two games. ... Bruised kidney (October 19, 1996); missed 11 games. ... Bruised wrist (December 28, 1996); missed two games. ... Suffered concussion (January 4, 1997); missed five games. ... Bruised cheekbone (January 8, 1998); missed three games. ... Traded by Canadiens to Calgary Flames with fourth-round pick (C Shaun Sutter) in 1998 draft for D Zarley Zalapski and RW Jonas Hoglund (February 1, 1998). ... Suffered concussion (March 3, 1998); missed five games. ... Hyperextended shoulder (April 5, 1998); missed final seven games of season. ... Suffered concussion (January 10, 1999); missed two games. ... Traded by Flames with C Jason Wiemer to Florida Panthers for Rob Niedermayer and second-round pick (G Andrei Medvedev) in 2001 draft (June 23, 2001). ... Injured right knee (October 16, 2001); missed 37 games. ... Suffered knee injury (March 17, 2002); missed remainder of season. ... Traded by Panthers with conditional fifth-round pick in 2004 draft to St. Louis Blues for D Mike Van Ryn (March 11, 2003). ... Claimed by Panthers off waivers (June 24, 2003).

STATISTICAL PLATEAUS: Three-goal games: 1997-98 (1).

			REGULAR SEASON								PLAYOFFS				
Season Team	League	Gms.	G	A	Pts.	PIM	+/-	PP	SH		Gms.	G	A	Pts.	PIM
90-91—CSKA Moscow............	USSR	3	0	0	0	0	...	...	...		—	—	—	—	—
91-92—Spokane......................	WHL	53	27	22	49	78	...	...	...		10	11	6	17	10
92-93—Spokane......................	WHL	66	68	79	147	49	...	...	...		9	6	11	17	14
93-94—Spokane......................	WHL	59	40	62	102	48	...	...	...		3	5	3	8	2
94-95—Fredericton	AHL	45	23	25	48	32	...	...	...		—	—	—	—	—
—Montreal	NHL	24	3	1	4	6	-1	0	0		—	—	—	—	—
95-96—Montreal......................	NHL	77	22	20	42	28	10	5	0		6	0	1	1	6
96-97—Montreal......................	NHL	64	14	21	35	6	4	4	0		5	0	1	1	2
97-98—Montreal......................	NHL	50	7	22	29	33	-5	2	0		—	—	—	—	—
—Calgary	NHL	16	5	4	9	2	0	0	0		—	—	—	—	—
—Russian Oly. team......	Int'l	6	1	0	1	0	...	...	...		—	—	—	—	—
98-99—Calgary	NHL	80	26	27	53	22	0	7	0		—	—	—	—	—
99-00—Calgary	NHL	82	35	40	75	50	-7	13	0		—	—	—	—	—
00-01—Calgary	NHL	78	27	28	55	26	-21	16	0		—	—	—	—	—
01-02—Florida........................	NHL	31	8	10	18	12	-3	2	0		—	—	—	—	—
—Russian Oly. team......	Int'l	6	1	0	1	2	...	...	...		—	—	—	—	—
02-03—Florida........................	NHL	46	5	21	26	10	-11	3	0		—	—	—	—	—
—St. Louis	NHL	5	0	2	2	0	-2	0	0		6	0	2	2	8
NHL Totals (9 years)............		553	152	196	348	195	-36	52	0		17	0	4	4	16

BURKE, SEAN — G — COYOTES

PERSONAL: Born January 29, 1967, in Windsor, Ont. ... 6-4/208. ... Catches left. ... Name pronounced BUHRK.

TRANSACTIONS/CAREER NOTES: Selected by New Jersey Devils in second round (second Devils pick, 24th overall) of NHL entry draft (June 15, 1985). ... Injured groin (December 1988). ... Underwent arthroscopic surgery to right knee (September 5, 1989). ... Traded by Devils with D Eric Weinrich to Hartford Whalers for RW Bobby Holik, second-round pick (LW Jay Pandolfo) in 1993 draft and future considerations (August 28, 1992). ... Sprained ankle (December 27, 1992); missed seven games. ... Suffered back spasms (March 13, 1993); missed remainder of season. ... Pulled hamstring (September 29, 1993); missed seven games. ... Reinjured hamstring (October 27, 1993); missed 14 games. ... Suffered back spasms (December 23, 1993); missed one game. ... Strained groin (February 28, 1995); missed two games. ... Suffered back spasms (November 19, 1995); missed two games. ... Suffered back spasms (February 7, 1996); missed three games. ... Dislocated thumb (November 30, 1996); missed 19 games. ... Strained hip flexor (February 26, 1997); missed one game. ... Whalers franchise moved to North Carolina and renamed Carolina Hurricanes for 1997-98 season; NHL approved move on June 25, 1997. ... Traded by Hurricanes with LW Geoff Sanderson and D Enrico Ciccone to Vancouver Canucks for LW Martin Gelinas and G Kirk McLean (January 3, 1998). ... Traded by Canucks to Philadelphia Flyers for G Garth Snow (March 4, 1998). ... Suffered lower back spasms (March 8, 1998); missed six games. ... Signed as free agent by Florida Panthers (September 11, 1998). ... Strained hip flexor (April 10, 1999); missed final three games of season. ... Traded by Panthers with first-round pick (D Nate Kiser) in 2000 draft to Phoenix Coyotes for G Mikhail Shtalenkov and fourth-round pick (D Chris Eade) in 2000 draft (November 19, 1999). ... Suffered partially torn thumb ligament (November 26, 1999); missed 16 games. ... Strained hip flexor (January 12, 2000); missed one game. ... Injured groin (February 1, 2000); missed one game. ... Strained groin (March 1, 2000); missed one game. ... Injured elbow (November 30, 2000); missed one game. ... Bruised knee (February 11, 2001); missed two games. ... Strained groin (March 2, 2001); missed four games. ... Strained groin (November 17, 2001); missed three games. ... Strained groin (January 9, 2002); missed seven games. ... Suffered from the flu (March 17, 2002); missed one game.

			REGULAR SEASON								PLAYOFFS						
Season Team	League	Gms.	Min	W	L	T	GA	SO	Avg.	SV%		Gms.	Min.	W	L	GA SO	Avg.	SV%
83-84—St. Michael's H.S...........	MTHL	25	1482	...	...	...	120	0	4.86	—		—	—	—	—	— —	—	—
84-85—Toronto	OHL	49	2987	25	21	3	211	0	4.24	—		5	266	1	3	25 0	5.64	—
85-86—Toronto	OHL	47	2840	16	27	3	†233	0	4.92	—		4	238	0	4	24 0	6.05	—
—Canadian nat'l team	Int'l	5	284	...	...	...	22	0	4.65	—		—	—	—	—	— —	—	—
86-87—Canadian nat'l team	Int'l	42	2550	27	13	2	130	0	3.06	—		—	—	—	—	— —	—	—

		REGULAR SEASON									PLAYOFFS							
Season Team	League	Gms.	Min	W	L	T	GA	SO	Avg.	SV%	Gms.	Min.	W	L	GA	SO	Avg.	SV%
87-88—Canadian nat'l team	Int'l	37	1962	19	9	2	92	1	2.81	—	—	—	—	—	—	—	—	—
—Can. Olympic team	Int'l	4	238	1	2	1	12	0	3.03	—	—	—	—	—	—	—	—	—
—New Jersey	NHL	13	689	10	1	0	35	1	3.05	.883	17	1001	9	8	*57	†1	3.42	.889
88-89—New Jersey	NHL	62	3590	22	31	9	†230	3	3.84	.874	—	—	—	—	—	—	—	—
89-90—New Jersey	NHL	52	2914	22	22	6	175	0	3.60	.880	2	125	0	2	8	0	3.84	.860
90-91—New Jersey	NHL	35	1870	8	12	8	112	0	3.59	.872	—	—	—	—	—	—	—	—
91-92—Canadian nat'l team	Int'l	31	1721	18	6	4	75	1	2.61	—	—	—	—	—	—	—	—	—
—Can. Olympic team	Int'l	7	429	5	2	0	17	0	2.38	—	—	—	—	—	—	—	—	—
—San Diego	IHL	7	424	4	2	‡1	17	0	2.41	—	3	160	0	3	13	0	4.88	—
92-93—Hartford	NHL	50	2656	16	27	3	184	0	4.16	.876	—	—	—	—	—	—	—	—
93-94—Hartford	NHL	47	2750	17	24	5	137	2	2.99	.906	—	—	—	—	—	—	—	—
94-95—Hartford	NHL	42	2418	17	19	4	108	0	2.68	.912	—	—	—	—	—	—	—	—
95-96—Hartford	NHL	66	3669	28	28	6	190	4	3.11	.907	—	—	—	—	—	—	—	—
96-97—Hartford	NHL	51	2985	22	22	6	134	4	2.69	.914	—	—	—	—	—	—	—	—
97-98—Carolina	NHL	25	1415	7	11	5	66	1	2.80	.899	—	—	—	—	—	—	—	—
—Vancouver	NHL	16	838	2	9	4	49	0	3.51	.876	—	—	—	—	—	—	—	—
—Philadelphia	NHL	11	632	7	3	0	27	1	2.56	.913	5	283	1	4	17	0	3.60	.860
98-99—Florida	NHL	59	3402	21	24	14	151	3	2.66	.907	—	—	—	—	—	—	—	—
99-00—Florida	NHL	7	418	2	5	0	18	0	2.58	.913	—	—	—	—	—	—	—	—
—Phoenix	NHL	35	2074	17	14	3	88	3	2.55	.914	5	296	1	4	16	0	3.24	.904
00-01—Phoenix	NHL	62	3644	25	22	*13	138	4	2.27	.922	—	—	—	—	—	—	—	—
01-02—Phoenix	NHL	60	3587	33	21	6	137	5	2.29	.920	5	297	1	4	13	0	2.63	.902
02-03—Phoenix	NHL	22	1248	12	6	2	44	2	2.12	.930	—	—	—	—	—	—	—	—
NHL Totals (15 years)		715	40799	288	301	94	2023	33	2.98	.902	34	2002	12	22	111	1	3.33	.888

BURNETT, GARRETT   LW   MIGHTY DUCKS

PERSONAL: Born September 23, 1975, in Coquitlim, B.C. ... 6-3/230. ... Shoots left.
TRANSACTIONS/CAREER NOTES: Signed as free agent by San Jose Sharks (July 22, 1998).

		REGULAR SEASON								PLAYOFFS				
Season Team	League	Gms.	G	A	Pts.	PIM	+/-	PP	SH	Gms.	G	A	Pts.	PIM
94-95—S.S. Marie	OHL	14	0	1	1	78	...	...	...	—	—	—	—	—
—Kitchener	OHL	22	0	1	1	74	...	...	...	—	—	—	—	—
95-96—Utica	Col.HL	15	0	1	1	85	...	...	...	—	—	—	—	—
—Nashville	ECHL	3	0	0	0	22	...	...	...	—	—	—	—	—
—Oklahoma City	CHL	3	0	0	0	20	...	...	...	—	—	—	—	—
—Tulsa	CHL	6	1	0	1	94	...	...	...	—	—	—	—	—
—Jacksonville	ECHL	3	0	1	1	38	...	...	...	1	0	0	0	0
96-97—Knoxville	ECHL	50	5	11	16	321	...	...	...	—	—	—	—	—
97-98—Johnstown	ECHL	12	1	1	2	2	...	...	...	—	—	—	—	—
—Philadelphia	AHL	14	1	2	3	129	...	...	...	—	—	—	—	—
98-99—Kentucky	AHL	31	1	0	1	186	...	...	...	—	—	—	—	—
99-00—Kentucky	AHL	58	3	3	6	*506	...	...	...	4	0	0	0	31
00-01—Cleveland	IHL	54	2	4	6	250	...	...	...	—	—	—	—	—
01-02—Cincinnati	AHL	32	1	0	1	175	...	...	...	—	—	—	—	—
02-03—Hartford	AHL	62	6	1	7	346	...	...	...	—	—	—	—	—

BUT, ANTON   RW   LIGHTNING

PERSONAL: Born July 3, 1980, in Kharkov, U.S.S.R. ... 6-1/190. ... Shoots left.
TRANSACTIONS/CAREER NOTES: Selected by New Jersey Devils in fifth round (seventh Devils pick, 119th overall) of NHL entry draft (June 27, 1998). ... Traded by Devils with D Josef Boumedienne and D Sasha Goc to Tampa Bay Lightning for D Andrei Zyuzin (November 9, 2001).

		REGULAR SEASON								PLAYOFFS				
Season Team	League	Gms.	G	A	Pts.	PIM	+/-	PP	SH	Gms.	G	A	Pts.	PIM
95-96—Torpedo Yaroslavl	CIS Div. II	60	30	12	42	10	...	...	...	—	—	—	—	—
96-97—Torpedo Yaroslavl	Rus. Div. III	70	30	20	50	20	...	...	...	—	—	—	—	—
97-98—Torpedo Yaroslavl	Rus. Div. II	48	12	5	17	28	...	...	...	—	—	—	—	—
98-99—Torpedo Yaroslavl	Russian	5	0	0	0	0	...	...	...	—	—	—	—	—
99-00—Torpedo Yaroslavl	Russian	26	2	5	7	16	...	...	...	8	2	1	3	0
00-01—Lokomotiv Yaroslavl	Russian	42	14	6	20	14	...	...	...	11	1	3	4	8
01-02—Lokomotiv Yaroslavl	Russian	48	14	11	25	14	...	...	...	6	0	1	1	2
02-03—Lokomotiv Yaroslavl	Russian	44	16	13	29	16	...	...	...	—	—	—	—	—

BUTENSCHON, SVEN   D   ISLANDERS

PERSONAL: Born March 22, 1976, in Itzehoe, West Germany ... 6-4/215. ... Shoots left. ... Name pronounced BOO-tihn-SHAHN.
TRANSACTIONS/CAREER NOTES: Selected by Pittsburgh Penguins in third round (third Penguins pick, 57th overall) of NHL entry draft (June 29, 1994). ... Suffered from the flu (November 7, 1997); missed two games. ... Injured shoulder (March 3, 2001); missed four games. ... Traded by Penguins to Edmonton Oilers for LW Dan LaCouture (March 13, 2001). ... Signed as free agent by Florida Panthers (July 9, 2002). ... Traded by Panthers to New York Islanders for RW Juraj Kolnik and ninth-round pick in 2003 draft (October 11, 2002).

		REGULAR SEASON								PLAYOFFS				
Season Team	League	Gms.	G	A	Pts.	PIM	+/-	PP	SH	Gms.	G	A	Pts.	PIM
93-94—Brandon	WHL	70	3	19	22	51	...	...	...	4	0	0	0	6
94-95—Brandon	WHL	21	1	5	6	44	...	...	...	18	1	2	3	11
95-96—Brandon	WHL	70	4	37	41	99	...	...	...	19	1	12	13	18
96-97—Cleveland	IHL	75	3	12	15	68	...	...	...	10	0	1	1	4
97-98—Syracuse	AHL	65	14	23	37	66	...	...	...	5	1	2	3	0
—Pittsburgh	NHL	8	0	0	0	6	-1	0	0	—	—	—	—	—
98-99—Houston	IHL	57	1	4	5	81	...	...	...	—	—	—	—	—
—Pittsburgh	NHL	17	0	0	0	6	-7	0	0	—	—	—	—	—
99-00—Wilkes-Barre/Scranton	AHL	75	19	21	40	101	...	...	...	—	—	—	—	—
—Pittsburgh	NHL	3	0	0	0	0	3	0	0	—	—	—	—	—
00-01—Wilkes-Barre/Scranton	AHL	55	7	28	35	85	...	...	...	—	—	—	—	—
—Pittsburgh	NHL	5	0	1	1	2	1	0	0	—	—	—	—	—
—Edmonton	NHL	7	1	1	2	2	2	0	0	—	—	—	—	—
01-02—Hamilton	AHL	61	9	35	44	88	...	...	...	—	—	—	—	—
—Edmonton	NHL	14	0	0	0	4	0	0	0	—	—	—	—	—
02-03—Bridgeport	AHL	36	3	13	16	58	...	...	...	—	—	—	—	—
—New York Islanders	NHL	37	0	4	4	26	-6	0	0	—	—	—	—	—
NHL Totals (6 years)		91	1	6	7	46	-8	0	0					

B

BUTSAYEV, YURI   C   THRASHERS

PERSONAL: Born October 11, 1978, in Togliatti, U.S.S.R. ... 6-1/195. ... Shoots left. ... Brother of Slava Butsayev, center with six NHL teams (1992-93 through 1999-2000).

TRANSACTIONS/CAREER NOTES: Selected by Detroit Red Wings in second round (first Red Wings pick, 49th overall) of NHL entry draft (June 21, 1997). ... Traded by Red Wings with third-round pick (traded to Buffalo) in 2002 draft to Atlanta Thrashers for D Jiri Slegr (March 19, 2002).

		REGULAR SEASON								PLAYOFFS				
Season Team	League	Gms.	G	A	Pts.	PIM	+/-	PP	SH	Gms.	G	A	Pts.	PIM
95-96—Lada Togliatti	CIS	1	0	0	0	0	...	...	...	—	—	—	—	—
—Lada-2 Togliatti	CIS Div. II	35	19	7	26	...	...	...	...	—	—	—	—	—
96-97—Lada Togliatti	Russian	42	13	11	24	38	...	...	...	11	2	2	4	8
97-98—Lada Togliatti	Russian	44	8	9	17	63	...	...	...	—	—	—	—	—
98-99—Lada Togliatti	Russian	39	10	7	17	55	...	...	...	7	1	2	3	14
—Dynamo Moscow	Russian	1	0	1	1	0	...	...	...	—	—	—	—	—
99-00—Detroit	NHL	57	5	3	8	12	-6	0	0	—	—	—	—	—
—Cincinnati	AHL	9	0	1	1	0	...	...	...	—	—	—	—	—
00-01—Detroit	NHL	15	1	1	2	4	-2	0	0	—	—	—	—	—
—Cincinnati	AHL	54	29	17	46	26	...	...	...	4	0	2	2	2
01-02—Cincinnati	AHL	61	21	23	44	44	...	...	...	—	—	—	—	—
—Detroit	NHL	3	0	0	0	0	-1	0	0	—	—	—	—	—
—Chicago	AHL	4	1	1	2	0	...	...	...	22	7	4	11	20
—Atlanta	NHL	8	2	0	2	4	1	0	0	—	—	—	—	—
02-03—Chicago	AHL	7	6	3	9	0	...	...	...	—	—	—	—	—
—Atlanta	NHL	16	2	0	2	8	-5	0	0	—	—	—	—	—
NHL Totals (4 years)		99	10	4	14	28	-13	0	0					

BUZEK, PETR   D   FLAMES

PERSONAL: Born April 26, 1977, in Jihlava, Czechoslovakia ... 6-1/220. ... Shoots left. ... Name pronounced BOO-zihk.

TRANSACTIONS/CAREER NOTES: Selected by Dallas Stars in third round (third Stars pick, 63rd overall) of NHL entry draft (July 8, 1995). ... Selected by Atlanta Thrashers in NHL expansion draft (June 25, 1999). ... Suffered from dehydration (October 26, 1999); missed two games. ... Suffered concussion (November 13, 1999); missed six games. ... Sprained shoulder (December 17, 1999); missed one game. ... Strained groin (January 21, 2000); missed four games. ... Sprained neck (October 11, 2000); missed 76 games. ... Strained groin (November 8, 2001); missed five games. ... Traded by Thrashers with conditional draft pick to Calgary Flames for LW Jeff Cowan and D Kurtis Foster (December 18, 2001).

		REGULAR SEASON								PLAYOFFS				
Season Team	League	Gms.	G	A	Pts.	PIM	+/-	PP	SH	Gms.	G	A	Pts.	PIM
93-94—Jihlava	Czech Rep.	29	6	16	22	...	...	...	...	—	—	—	—	—
—Dukla Jihlava	Czech Rep.	3	0	0	0	...	...	...	...	—	—	—	—	—
94-95—Dukla Jihlava	Czech Rep.	43	2	5	7	...	...	...	...	2	0	0	0	...
95-96—Jihlava	Czech Rep.					Did not play.								
96-97—Michigan	IHL	67	4	6	10	48	...	...	...	—	—	—	—	—
97-98—Michigan	IHL	60	10	15	25	58	...	...	...	2	0	1	1	17
—Dallas	NHL	2	0	0	0	2	1	0	0	—	—	—	—	—
98-99—Michigan	IHL	74	5	14	19	68	...	...	...	5	0	0	0	10
—Dallas	NHL	2	0	0	0	2	0	0	0	—	—	—	—	—
99-00—Atlanta	NHL	63	5	14	19	41	-22	3	0	—	—	—	—	—
00-01—Atlanta	NHL	5	0	0	0	8	2	0	0	—	—	—	—	—
01-02—Atlanta	NHL	9	0	0	0	13	-4	0	0	—	—	—	—	—
—Chicago	AHL	4	0	1	1	2	...	...	...	—	—	—	—	—
—Calgary	NHL	32	1	3	4	14	4	0	0	—	—	—	—	—
02-03—Calgary	NHL	44	3	5	8	14	-6	3	0	—	—	—	—	—
NHL Totals (6 years)		157	9	22	31	94	-25	6	0					

BYFUGLIEN, DERRICK   D   SENATORS

PERSONAL: Born December 23, 1980, in Roseau, Minn. ... 6-1/202. ... Shoots left.
COLLEGE: North Dakota.
TRANSACTIONS/CAREER NOTES: Selected by Ottawa Senators in fourth round (fifth Senators pick, 122nd overall) of NHL entry draft (June 24, 2000).

		REGULAR SEASON								PLAYOFFS				
Season Team	League	Gms.	G	A	Pts.	PIM	+/-	PP	SH	Gms.	G	A	Pts.	PIM
98-99—Roseau H.S.	Minn. H.S.					Statistics unavailable.								
99-00—Fargo	USHL	50	5	11	16	106	...	...	...	—	—	—	—	—
00-01—Univ. of North Dakota	WCHA	6	0	1	1	2	...	...	...	—	—	—	—	—
—Erie	OHL	31	1	4	5	37	...	...	...	15	3	1	4	29
01-02—Florida	ECHL	43	2	4	6	81	...	...	...	—	—	—	—	—
—Roanoke	ECHL	21	3	2	5	39	...	...	...	4	0	1	1	6
02-03—Mississippi	ECHL	49	2	12	14	58	...	...	...	—	—	—	—	—
—Greensboro	ECHL	14	0	1	1	10	...	...	...	—	—	—	—	—

BYKOV, DMITRI   D   RED WINGS

PERSONAL: Born May 5, 1977, in Izhevsk, U.S.S.R. ... 5-10/169. ... Shoots left.
TRANSACTIONS/CAREER NOTES: Selected by Detroit Red Wings in eighth round (sixth Red Wings pick, 258th overall) of NHL entry draft (June 24, 2001).

		REGULAR SEASON								PLAYOFFS				
Season Team	League	Gms.	G	A	Pts.	PIM	+/-	PP	SH	Gms.	G	A	Pts.	PIM
95-96—CSK VVS Samara	CIS	50	1	2	3	39	...	...	...	—	—	—	—	—
96-97—CSK VVS Samara	Russian	44	1	6	7	20	...	...	...	2	0	0	0	2
97-98—Lada Togliatti	Russian	9	0	1	1	4	...	...	...	—	—	—	—	—
—CSK VVS Samara	Russian	27	0	5	5	14	...	...	...	—	—	—	—	—
—Yaroslavl	Russian	10	1	2	3	6	...	...	...	7	0	1	1	10
98-99—Lada Togliatti	Russian	39	0	6	6	24	...	...	...	7	1	0	1	8
—CSK VVS Samara	Russian	2	0	0	0	0	...	...	...	—	—	—	—	—
99-00—Ak Bars Kazan	Russian	35	3	8	11	18	...	...	...	18	0	2	2	8
00-01—Ak Bars Kazan	Russian	39	3	8	11	28	...	...	...	4	0	1	1	4
01-02—Ak Bars Kazan	Russian	44	1	1	2	38	...	...	...	11	0	0	0	4
02-03—Detroit	NHL	71	2	10	12	43	1	1	0	4	0	0	0	0
NHL Totals (1 year)		71	2	10	12	43	1	1	0	4	0	0	0	0

BYLSMA, DAN   RW   MIGHTY DUCKS

PERSONAL: Born September 19, 1970, in Grand Haven, Mich. ... 6-2/212. ... Shoots left. ... Full Name: Daniel Brian Bylsma. ... Name pronounced BIGHLS-muh.
TRANSACTIONS/CAREER NOTES: Selected by Winnipeg Jets in fourth round (sixth Jets pick, 69th overall) of NHL entry draft (June 17, 1989). ... Signed as free agent by Los Angeles Kings (July 14, 1994). ... Injured knee (March 19, 1997); missed one game. ... Strained groin (April 3, 1997); missed one game. ... Signed as free agent by Mighty Ducks of Anaheim (July 13, 2000).

		REGULAR SEASON								PLAYOFFS				
Season Team	League	Gms.	G	A	Pts.	PIM	+/-	PP	SH	Gms.	G	A	Pts.	PIM
87-88—St. Mary's Jr. B	OHA	40	30	39	69	33	...	...	...	—	—	—	—	—
88-89—Bowling Green	CCHA	39	4	7	11	16	...	...	...	—	—	—	—	—
89-90—Bowling Green	CCHA	44	13	17	30	32	...	...	...	—	—	—	—	—
90-91—Bowling Green	CCHA	40	9	12	21	48	...	...	...	—	—	—	—	—
91-92—Bowling Green	CCHA	34	11	14	25	24	...	...	...	—	—	—	—	—
92-93—Rochester	AHL	2	0	1	1	0	...	...	...	—	—	—	—	—
—Greensboro	ECHL	60	25	35	60	66	...	...	...	1	0	1	1	10
93-94—Albany	AHL	3	0	1	1	2	...	...	...	—	—	—	—	—
—Moncton	AHL	50	12	16	28	25	...	...	...	21	3	4	7	31
—Greensboro	ECHL	25	14	16	30	52	...	...	...	—	—	—	—	—
94-95—Phoenix	IHL	81	19	23	42	41	...	...	...	—	—	—	—	—
95-96—Phoenix	IHL	78	22	20	42	48	...	...	...	4	1	0	1	2
—Los Angeles	NHL	4	0	0	0	0	0	0	0	—	—	—	—	—
96-97—Los Angeles	NHL	79	3	6	9	32	-15	0	0	—	—	—	—	—
97-98—Long Beach	IHL	8	2	3	5	0	...	...	...	—	—	—	—	—
—Los Angeles	NHL	65	3	9	12	33	9	0	0	2	0	0	0	0
98-99—Long Beach	IHL	58	10	8	18	53	...	...	...	4	0	0	0	8
—Los Angeles	NHL	8	0	0	0	2	-1	0	0	—	—	—	—	—
—Springfield	AHL	2	0	2	2	2	...	...	...	—	—	—	—	—
99-00—Los Angeles	NHL	64	3	6	9	55	-2	0	1	3	0	0	0	0
—Long Beach	IHL	6	0	3	3	2	...	...	...	—	—	—	—	—
—Lowell	AHL	2	1	1	2	2	...	...	...	—	—	—	—	—
00-01—Anaheim	NHL	82	1	9	10	22	-12	0	0	—	—	—	—	—
01-02—Anaheim	NHL	77	8	9	17	28	5	0	1	—	—	—	—	—
02-03—Anaheim	NHL	39	1	4	5	12	-1	0	0	11	0	1	1	2
NHL Totals (8 years)		418	19	43	62	184	-17	0	2	16	0	1	1	2

BYRNE, TREVOR   D   BLUES

PERSONAL: Born May 7, 1980, in Hingham, Mass. ... 6-3/200. ... Shoots left.
HIGH SCHOOL: Deerfield (Mass.) Academy.
COLLEGE: Dartmouth.
TRANSACTIONS/CAREER NOTES: Selected by St. Louis Blues in fifth round (fourth Blues pick, 143rd overall) of NHL entry draft (June 26, 1999).

| Season Team | League | REGULAR SEASON | | | | | | | | PLAYOFFS | | | | |
		Gms.	G	A	Pts.	PIM	+/-	PP	SH	Gms.	G	A	Pts.	PIM
97-98—Deerfield Academy......	USHS (East)	25	5	14	19	16	...	...	...	—	—	—	—	—
98-99—Deerfield Academy......	USHS (East)	25	9	19	28	22	...	...	...	—	—	—	—	—
99-00—Dartmouth College......	ECAC	30	3	9	12	40	...	...	...	—	—	—	—	—
00-01—Dartmouth College......	ECAC	34	5	21	26	52	...	...	...	—	—	—	—	—
01-02—Dartmouth College......	ECAC	32	5	16	21	38	...	...	...	—	—	—	—	—
02-03—Dartmouth College......	ECAC	34	8	16	24	28	...	...	...	—	—	—	—	—

CAIRNS, ERIC — D — ISLANDERS

PERSONAL: Born June 27, 1974, in Oakville, Ont. ... 6-6/232. ... Shoots left. ... Name pronounced KAIR-ihns.

TRANSACTIONS/CAREER NOTES: Selected by New York Rangers in third round (third Rangers pick, 72nd overall) of NHL entry draft (June 20, 1992). ... Claimed on waivers by New York Islanders (December 22, 1998). ... Strained back (January 6, 2000); missed one game. ... Suspended four games by NHL for fighting incident (February 13, 2000). ... Fractured thumb (October 1, 2000); missed first 18 games of season. ... Underwent hand surgery (December 8, 2000); missed 17 games. ... Sprained left wrist (February 18, 2001); missed two games. ... Strained oblique muscle (December 2, 2001); missed five games. ... Bruised ribs (January 24, 2002); missed one game. ... Suspended two games by NHL for unsportsmanlike conduct (March 28, 2002).

| Season Team | League | REGULAR SEASON | | | | | | | | PLAYOFFS | | | | |
		Gms.	G	A	Pts.	PIM	+/-	PP	SH	Gms.	G	A	Pts.	PIM
90-91—Burlington Jr. B..........	OHA	37	5	16	21	120	...	...	...	—	—	—	—	—
91-92—Det. Jr. Red Wings......	OHL	64	1	11	12	237	...	...	...	7	0	0	0	31
92-93—Det. Jr. Red Wings......	OHL	64	3	13	16	194	...	...	...	15	0	3	3	24
93-94—Det. Jr. Red Wings......	OHL	59	7	35	42	204	...	...	...	17	0	4	4	46
94-95—Birmingham...............	ECHL	11	1	3	4	49	...	...	...	—	—	—	—	—
—Binghamton...............	AHL	27	0	3	3	134	...	...	...	9	1	1	2	28
95-96—Binghamton...............	AHL	46	1	13	14	192	...	...	...	4	0	0	0	37
—Charlotte....................	ECHL	6	0	1	1	34	...	...	...	—	—	—	—	—
96-97—New York Rangers......	NHL	40	0	1	1	147	-7	0	0	3	0	0	0	0
—Binghamton...............	AHL	10	1	1	2	96	...	...	...	—	—	—	—	—
97-98—New York Rangers......	NHL	39	0	3	3	92	-3	0	0	—	—	—	—	—
—Hartford....................	AHL	7	1	2	3	43	...	...	...	—	—	—	—	—
98-99—Hartford....................	AHL	11	0	2	2	49	...	...	...	—	—	—	—	—
—Lowell......................	AHL	24	0	0	0	91	...	...	...	3	1	0	1	32
—New York Islanders.....	NHL	9	0	3	3	23	1	0	0	—	—	—	—	—
99-00—Providence...............	AHL	4	1	1	2	14	...	...	...	—	—	—	—	—
—New York Islanders.....	NHL	67	2	7	9	196	-5	0	0	—	—	—	—	—
00-01—New York Islanders.....	NHL	45	2	2	4	106	-18	0	0	—	—	—	—	—
01-02—New York Islanders.....	NHL	74	2	5	7	176	-2	0	0	7	0	0	0	15
02-03—New York Islanders.....	NHL	60	1	4	5	124	-7	0	0	5	0	0	0	13
NHL Totals (7 years)...........		334	7	25	32	864	-41	0	0	15	0	0	0	28

CAJANEK, PETR — C/LW — BLUES

PERSONAL: Born August 18, 1975, in Zlin, Czechoslovakia ... 5-11/194. ... Shoots left.

TRANSACTIONS/CAREER NOTES: Selected by St. Louis Blues in eighth round (sixth Blues pick, 253rd overall) of NHL entry draft (June 23, 2001).

| Season Team | League | REGULAR SEASON | | | | | | | | PLAYOFFS | | | | |
		Gms.	G	A	Pts.	PIM	+/-	PP	SH	Gms.	G	A	Pts.	PIM
97-98—HC Continental Zlin.....	Czech Rep.	46	19	27	46	125	...	...	...	—	—	—	—	—
98-99—HC Continental Zlin.....	Czech Rep.	49	15	33	48	131	...	...	...	11	5	7	12	—
99-00—HC Continental Zlin.....	Czech Rep.	50	23	34	57	64	...	...	...	4	1	0	1	0
00-01—HC Continental Zlin.....	Czech Rep.	52	18	31	49	105	...	...	...	6	0	4	4	22
01-02—HC Continental Zlin.....	Czech Rep.	49	20	44	64	64	...	...	...	11	5	7	12	10
—Czech Rep. Oly. team...	Int'l	4	0	0	0	0	...	...	...	—	—	—	—	—
02-03—St. Louis	NHL	51	9	29	38	20	16	2	2	2	0	0	0	2
NHL Totals (1 year).............		51	9	29	38	20	16	2	2	2	0	0	0	2

CALDER, KYLE — LW — BLACKHAWKS

PERSONAL: Born January 5, 1979, in Mannville, Alta. ... 5-11/172. ... Shoots left.

TRANSACTIONS/CAREER NOTES: Selected by Chicago Blackhawks in fifth round (seventh Blackhawks pick, 130th overall) of NHL entry draft (June 21, 1997). ... Suffered concussion (January 9, 2002); missed one game.

| Season Team | League | REGULAR SEASON | | | | | | | | PLAYOFFS | | | | |
		Gms.	G	A	Pts.	PIM	+/-	PP	SH	Gms.	G	A	Pts.	PIM
95-96—Regina	WHL	27	1	8	9	10	...	...	...	11	0	0	0	0
96-97—Regina	WHL	62	25	34	59	17	...	...	...	5	3	0	3	6
97-98—Regina	WHL	62	27	50	77	58	...	...	...	2	0	1	1	0
98-99—Regina	WHL	34	23	28	51	29	...	...	...	—	—	—	—	—
—Kamloops	WHL	27	19	18	37	30	...	...	...	15	6	10	16	6
99-00—Cleveland	IHL	74	14	22	36	43	...	...	...	9	2	2	4	14
—Chicago....................	NHL	8	1	1	2	2	-3	0	0	—	—	—	—	—
00-01—Norfolk.....................	AHL	37	12	15	27	21	...	...	...	9	2	6	8	2
—Chicago....................	NHL	43	5	10	15	14	-4	0	0	—	—	—	—	—
01-02—Chicago.....................	NHL	81	17	36	53	47	8	6	0	5	2	0	2	2
02-03—Chicago.....................	NHL	82	15	27	42	40	-6	7	0	—	—	—	—	—
NHL Totals (4 years)...........		214	38	74	112	103	-5	13	0	5	2	0	2	2

CAMERON, SCOTT   LW   DEVILS

PERSONAL: Born April 11, 1981, in Sudbury, Ont. ... 6-0/180. ... Shoots left.
TRANSACTIONS/CAREER NOTES: Selected by New Jersey Devils in sixth round (sixth Devils pick, 185th overall) of NHL entry draft (June 26, 1999).

		REGULAR SEASON							PLAYOFFS				
Season Team	League	Gms.	G	A	Pts.	PIM	+/-	PP	SH	Gms.	G	A	Pts.	PIM
97-98—Port Colborne	Jr. B	48	16	35	51	73	...	...	...	—	—	—	—	—
98-99—Barrie	OHL	66	10	32	42	14	...	...	...	12	2	2	4	2
99-00—Barrie	OHL	21	2	4	6	19	...	...	...	—	—	—	—	—
—North Bay	OHL	49	26	28	54	13	...	...	...	6	3	0	3	4
—Albany	AHL	3	1	0	1	0	...	...	...	1	0	0	0	0
00-01—North Bay	OHL	68	37	43	80	45	...	...	...	4	0	1	1	2
01-02—Albany	AHL	54	3	6	9	12	...	...	...	—	—	—	—	—
02-03—Albany	AHL	80	9	19	28	17	...	...	...	—	—	—	—	—

CAMMALLERI, MICHAEL   C   KINGS

PERSONAL: Born June 8, 1982, in Richmond Hill, Ont. ... 5-9/180. ... Shoots left. ... Full Name: Mike Cammalleri.
TRANSACTIONS/CAREER NOTES: Selected by Los Angeles Kings in second round (third Kings pick, 49th overall) of NHL entry draft (June 23, 2001).

		REGULAR SEASON							PLAYOFFS				
Season Team	League	Gms.	G	A	Pts.	PIM	+/-	PP	SH	Gms.	G	A	Pts.	PIM
99-00—Univ. of Michigan	CCHA	39	13	13	26	32	...	...	...	—	—	—	—	—
00-01—Univ. of Michigan	CCHA	42	*29	32	61	24	...	...	...	—	—	—	—	—
01-02—Univ. of Michigan	CCHA	28	23	20	43	24	...	...	...	—	—	—	—	—
02-03—Manchester	AHL	13	5	15	20	12	...	...	...	—	—	—	—	—
—Los Angeles	NHL	28	5	3	8	22	-4	2	0	—	—	—	—	—
NHL Totals (1 year)		28	5	3	8	22	-4	2	0					

CAMPBELL, BRIAN   D   SABRES

PERSONAL: Born May 23, 1979, in Strathroy, Ont. ... 6-0/190. ... Shoots left.
TRANSACTIONS/CAREER NOTES: Selected by Buffalo Sabres in sixth round (seventh Sabres pick, 156th overall) of NHL entry draft (June 21, 1997). ... Separated shoulder (April 1, 2002); missed remainder of season.

		REGULAR SEASON							PLAYOFFS				
Season Team	League	Gms.	G	A	Pts.	PIM	+/-	PP	SH	Gms.	G	A	Pts.	PIM
94-95—Petrolia	Jr. B	50	1	2	3		...	...	...	—	—	—	—	—
95-96—Ottawa	OHL	66	5	22	27	23	...	...	...	4	0	1	1	2
96-97—Ottawa	OHL	66	7	36	43	12	...	...	...	24	2	11	13	8
97-98—Ottawa	OHL	66	14	39	53	31	...	...	...	13	1	14	15	0
98-99—Ottawa	OHL	62	12	75	87	27	...	...	...	9	2	10	12	6
—Rochester	AHL	—	—	—	—	—	...	...	...	2	0	0	0	0
99-00—Buffalo	NHL	12	1	4	5	4	-2	0	0	—	—	—	—	—
—Rochester	AHL	67	2	24	26	22	...	...	...	21	0	3	3	0
00-01—Rochester	AHL	65	7	25	32	24	...	...	...	4	0	1	1	0
—Buffalo	NHL	8	0	0	0	2	-2	0	0	—	—	—	—	—
01-02—Rochester	AHL	45	2	35	37	13	...	...	...	—	—	—	—	—
—Buffalo	NHL	29	3	3	6	12	0	0	0	—	—	—	—	—
02-03—Buffalo	NHL	65	2	17	19	20	-8	0	0	—	—	—	—	—
NHL Totals (4 years)		114	6	24	30	38	-12	0	0					

CAMPBELL, ED   D   BRUINS

PERSONAL: Born November 26, 1974, in Worcester, Mass. ... 6-2/200. ... Shoots left. ... Full Name: Edward Brien Campbell.
HIGH SCHOOL: Northwood School (Lake Placid, N.Y.) and Millard North (Omaha, Neb.).
TRANSACTIONS/CAREER NOTES: Selected by New York Rangers in eighth round (ninth Rangers pick, 190th overall) of NHL entry draft (June 26, 1993). ... Signed as free agent by Detroit Red Wings (August 5, 2002). ... Signed by Boston Bruins (July 31, 2003).

		REGULAR SEASON							PLAYOFFS				
Season Team	League	Gms.	G	A	Pts.	PIM	+/-	PP	SH	Gms.	G	A	Pts.	PIM
92-93—Omaha	Jr. A	42	9	19	28	160	...	...	...	—	—	—	—	—
93-94—Mass.-Lowell	Hockey East	40	8	16	24	114	...	...	...	—	—	—	—	—
94-95—Mass.-Lowell	Hockey East	34	6	23	29	105	...	...	...	—	—	—	—	—
95-96—Mass.-Lowell	Hockey East	39	6	33	39	107	...	...	...	—	—	—	—	—
96-97—Binghamton	AHL	74	5	17	22	108	...	...	...	4	0	0	0	2
97-98—Hartford	AHL	9	0	1	1	9	...	...	...	14	0	2	2	33
—Fort Wayne	IHL	50	10	5	15	147	...	...	...	—	—	—	—	—
98-99—Hartford	AHL	18	0	3	3	24	...	...	...	7	0	3	3	14
—Fort Wayne	IHL	46	1	16	17	137	...	...	...	—	—	—	—	—
99-00—Orlando	IHL	81	2	7	9	217	...	...	...	3	0	0	0	6
00-01—Worcester	AHL	78	5	27	32	207	...	...	...	10	1	0	1	10
01-02—Worcester	AHL	70	3	15	18	172	...	...	...	3	0	0	0	5
02-03—Grand Rapids	AHL	80	0	12	12	140	...	...	...	—	—	—	—	—

CAMPBELL, GREGORY   C   PANTHERS

PERSONAL: Born December 17, 1983, in Tillsonburg, Ont. ... 5-11/167. ... Shoots left. ... Son of Colin Campbell, Director of Hockey Operations for NHL.

TRANSACTIONS/CAREER NOTES: Selected by Florida Panthers in third round (fourth Panthers pick, 67th overall) of NHL entry draft (June 22, 2002).

		REGULAR SEASON								PLAYOFFS				
Season Team	League	Gms.	G	A	Pts.	PIM	+/-	PP	SH	Gms.	G	A	Pts.	PIM
00-01—Plymouth	OHL	65	2	12	14	40	...	...	...	21	15	4	19	34
01-02—Plymouth	OHL	65	17	36	53	105	...	...	...	6	0	2	2	13
02-03—Kitchener	OHL	55	23	33	56	116	...	...	...	—	—	—	—	—

CAMPBELL, JIM   RW

PERSONAL: Born April 3, 1973, in Worcester, Mass. ... 6-2/205. ... Shoots right. ... Full Name: James Tower Campbell.

TRANSACTIONS/CAREER NOTES: Selected by Montreal Canadiens in second round (second Canadiens pick, 28th overall) of NHL entry draft (June 22, 1991). ... Traded by Canadiens to Mighty Ducks of Anaheim for D Robert Dirk (January 21, 1996). ... Signed as free agent by St. Louis Blues (July 3, 1996). ... Strained thumb (February 25, 1997); missed 10 games. ... Reinjured thumb (April 6, 1997); missed remainder of regular season. ... Strained groin (December 6, 1997); missed one game. ... Injured left heel (January 20, 1998); missed five games. ... Bruised right shoulder (October 23, 1998); missed two games. ... Injured groin (February 9, 1999); missed three games. ... Injured abdominal muscle (March 18, 1999) and underwent surgery; missed remainder of season. ... Signed as free agent by Canadiens (August 22, 2000). ... Suffered concussion (October 17, 2000); missed one game. ... Strained groin (November 14, 2000); missed nine games. ... Signed as free agent by Chicago Blackhawks (November 19, 2001). ... Signed as free agent by Florida Panthers (July 19, 2002).

		REGULAR SEASON								PLAYOFFS				
Season Team	League	Gms.	G	A	Pts.	PIM	+/-	PP	SH	Gms.	G	A	Pts.	PIM
88-89—Northwood School	N.Y. H.S.	12	12	8	20	6	...	...	...	—	—	—	—	—
89-90—Northwood School	N.Y. H.S.	8	14	7	21	8	...	...	...	—	—	—	—	—
90-91—Northwood School	N.Y. H.S.	26	36	47	83	36	...	...	...	—	—	—	—	—
91-92—Hull	QMJHL	64	41	44	85	51	...	...	...	6	7	3	10	8
92-93—Hull	QMJHL	50	42	29	71	66	...	...	...	8	11	4	15	43
93-94—U.S. national team	Int'l	56	24	33	57	59	...	...	...	—	—	—	—	—
—U.S. Olympic team	Int'l	8	0	0	0	6	...	...	...	—	—	—	—	—
—Fredericton	AHL	19	6	17	23	6	...	...	...	—	—	—	—	—
94-95—Fredericton	AHL	77	27	24	51	103	...	...	...	12	0	7	7	8
95-96—Fredericton	AHL	44	28	23	51	24	...	...	...	—	—	—	—	—
—Baltimore	AHL	16	13	7	20	8	...	...	...	12	7	5	12	10
—Anaheim	NHL	16	2	3	5	36	0	1	0	—	—	—	—	—
96-97—St. Louis	NHL	68	23	20	43	68	3	5	0	4	1	0	1	6
97-98—St. Louis	NHL	76	22	19	41	55	0	7	0	10	7	3	10	12
98-99—St. Louis	NHL	55	4	21	25	41	-8	1	0	—	—	—	—	—
99-00—Manitoba	IHL	10	1	3	4	10	...	...	...	—	—	—	—	—
—Worcester	AHL	66	31	34	65	88	...	...	...	9	1	2	3	6
—St. Louis	NHL	2	0	0	0	9	0	0	0	—	—	—	—	—
00-01—Montreal	NHL	57	9	11	20	53	-3	6	0	—	—	—	—	—
—Quebec	AHL	3	5	0	5	6	...	...	...	—	—	—	—	—
01-02—Norfolk	AHL	44	11	14	25	26	...	...	...	4	3	1	4	2
—Chicago	NHL	9	1	1	2	4	-3	0	0	—	—	—	—	—
02-03—San Antonio	AHL	64	16	37	53	55	...	...	...	—	—	—	—	—
—Florida	NHL	1	0	0	0	0	0	0	0	—	—	—	—	—
NHL Totals (8 years)		284	61	75	136	266	-11	20	0	14	8	3	11	18

CARKNER, MATT   D   SHARKS

PERSONAL: Born November 3, 1980, in Winchester, Ont. ... 6-4/222. ... Shoots right.

TRANSACTIONS/CAREER NOTES: Selected by Montreal Canadiens in second round (second Canadiens pick, 58th overall) of NHL entry draft (June 26, 1999). ... Signed as free agent by San Jose Sharks (June 12, 2001).

		REGULAR SEASON								PLAYOFFS				
Season Team	League	Gms.	G	A	Pts.	PIM	+/-	PP	SH	Gms.	G	A	Pts.	PIM
96-97—Winchester	Jr. B	29	1	18	19	...	...	...	...	—	—	—	—	—
97-98—Peterborough	OHL	57	0	6	6	121	...	...	...	4	0	0	0	2
98-99—Peterborough	OHL	60	2	16	18	173	...	...	...	5	0	0	0	20
99-00—Peterborough	OHL	62	3	13	16	177	...	...	...	5	0	1	1	6
00-01—Peterborough	OHL	53	8	8	16	128	...	...	...	7	0	3	3	25
01-02—Cleveland	AHL	74	0	3	3	335	...	...	...	—	—	—	—	—
02-03—Cleveland	AHL	39	1	4	5	104	...	...	...	—	—	—	—	—

CARNEY, KEITH   D   MIGHTY DUCKS

PERSONAL: Born February 3, 1970, in Providence, R.I. ... 6-1/217. ... Shoots left. ... Full Name: Keith Edward Carney.

TRANSACTIONS/CAREER NOTES: Selected by Buffalo Sabres in fourth round (third Sabres pick, 76th overall) of NHL entry draft (June 11, 1988). ... Traded by Sabres to Chicago Blackhawks for D Craig Muni (October 27, 1993). ... Traded by Blackhawks with RW Jim Cummins to Phoenix Coyotes for C Chad Kilger and D Jayson More (March 4, 1998). ... Traded by Coyotes to Mighty Ducks of Anaheim for second-round pick (traded to New Jersey) in 2001 draft (June 19, 2001). ... Fractured bone in right hand (November 7, 2001); missed 17 games. ... Suffered hip pointer and lacerated right elbow (March 30, 2002); missed one game. ... Reinjured elbow (April 3, 2002); missed four games.

Season Team	League	Gms.	G	A	Pts.	PIM	+/-	PP	SH	Gms.	G	A	Pts.	PIM
88-89—Univ. of Maine	Hockey East	40	4	22	26	24	...	...	...	—	—	—	—	—
89-90—Univ. of Maine	Hockey East	41	3	41	44	43	...	...	...	—	—	—	—	—
90-91—Univ. of Maine	Hockey East	40	7	49	56	38	...	...	...	—	—	—	—	—
91-92—U.S. national team	Int'l	49	2	17	19	16	...	...	...	—	—	—	—	—
—Rochester	AHL	24	1	10	11	2	...	...	...	2	0	2	2	0
—Buffalo	NHL	14	1	2	3	18	-3	1	0	7	0	3	3	0
92-93—Buffalo	NHL	30	2	4	6	55	3	0	0	8	0	3	3	6
—Rochester	AHL	41	5	21	26	32	...	...	...	—	—	—	—	—
93-94—Louisville	ECHL	15	1	4	5	14	...	...	...	—	—	—	—	—
—Buffalo	NHL	7	1	3	4	4	-1	0	0	—	—	—	—	—
—Indianapolis	IHL	28	0	14	14	20	...	...	...	—	—	—	—	—
—Chicago	NHL	30	3	5	8	35	15	0	0	6	0	1	1	4
94-95—Chicago	NHL	18	1	0	1	11	-1	0	0	4	0	1	1	0
95-96—Chicago	NHL	82	5	14	19	94	31	1	0	10	0	3	3	4
96-97—Chicago	NHL	81	3	15	18	62	26	0	0	6	1	1	2	2
97-98—Chicago	NHL	60	2	13	15	73	-7	0	1	—	—	—	—	—
—U.S. Olympic team	Int'l	4	0	0	0	2	...	...	...	—	—	—	—	—
—Phoenix	NHL	20	1	6	7	18	5	1	0	6	0	0	0	4
98-99—Phoenix	NHL	82	2	14	16	62	15	0	2	7	1	2	3	10
99-00—Phoenix	NHL	82	4	20	24	87	11	0	0	5	0	0	0	17
00-01—Phoenix	NHL	82	2	14	16	86	15	0	0	—	—	—	—	—
01-02—Anaheim	NHL	60	5	9	14	30	14	0	0	—	—	—	—	—
02-03—Anaheim	NHL	81	4	18	22	65	8	0	0	21	0	4	4	16
NHL Totals (12 years)		729	36	137	173	700	131	3	3	80	2	18	20	63

CARON, SEBASTIEN   G   PENGUINS

PERSONAL: Born June 25, 1980, in Amqui, Que. ... 6-1/160. ... Catches left.

TRANSACTIONS/CAREER NOTES: Selected by Pittsburgh Penguins in third round (fourth Penguins pick, 86th overall) of NHL entry draft (June 26, 1999).

Season Team	League	Gms.	Min	W	L	T	GA	SO	Avg.	SV%	Gms.	Min.	W	L	GA	SO	Avg.	SV%
98-99—Rimouski	QMJHL	30	1570	13	10	3	85	0	3.25	—	2	68	1	0	0	0	...	—
99-00—Rimouski	QMJHL	54	3040	*38	11	3	179	1	3.53	—	14	828	*12	2	50	0	3.62	—
00-01—Wilkes-Barre/Scranton	AHL	30	1746	12	14	3	103	4	3.54	—	—	—	—	—	—	—	—	—
01-02—Wilkes-Barre/Scranton	AHL	46	2670	14	22	8	139	1	3.12	—	—	—	—	—	—	—	—	—
02-03—Wilkes-Barre/Scranton	AHL	27	1560	12	14	1	81	1	3.12	—	—	—	—	—	—	—	—	—
—Pittsburgh	NHL	24	1408	7	14	2	62	2	2.64	.916	—	—	—	—	—	—	—	—
NHL Totals (1 year)		24	1408	7	14	2	62	2	2.64	.916								

CARTER, ANSON   RW   RANGERS

PERSONAL: Born June 6, 1974, in Toronto ... 6-1/200. ... Shoots right.

TRANSACTIONS/CAREER NOTES: Selected by Quebec Nordiques in 10th round (10th Nordiques pick, 220th overall) of NHL entry draft (June 20, 1992). ... Nordiques franchise moved to Colorado and renamed Avalanche for 1995-96 season (June 21, 1995). ... Traded by Avalanche to Washington Capitals for first-round pick (D Ben Storey) in 1996 entry draft (April 3, 1996). ... Sprained thumb (February 7, 1997); missed five games. ... Traded by Capitals with G Jim Carey, C Jason Allison and third-round pick (RW Lee Goren) in 1997 draft to Boston Bruins for C Adam Oates, RW Rick Tocchet and G Bill Ranford (March 1, 1997). ... Strained hip flexor (October 7, 1997); missed two games. ... Suffered from upper respiratory infection (November 22, 1997); missed two games. ... Missed first 12 games of 1998-99 season due to contract dispute; played with Utah of IHL. ... Sprained ankle (January 2, 1999); missed 15 games. ... Bruised shoulder (February 21, 2000); missed eight games. ... Underwent wrist surgery (March 10, 2000); missed final 15 games of season. ... Traded by Bruins with second-round pick (D Doug Lynch) in 2001 draft and swap of first-round picks in 2001 to Edmonton Oilers for RW Bill Guerin (November 15, 2000). ... Traded by Oilers with D Ales Pisa to New York Rangers for RW Radek Dvorak and D Cory Cross (March 11, 2003).

STATISTICAL PLATEAUS: Three-goal games: 1998-99 (1).

Season Team	League	Gms.	G	A	Pts.	PIM	+/-	PP	SH	Gms.	G	A	Pts.	PIM
91-92—Wexford	OHA Jr. A	42	18	22	40	24	...	...	...	—	—	—	—	—
92-93—Michigan State	CCHA	36	19	11	30	20	...	...	...	—	—	—	—	—
93-94—Michigan State	CCHA	39	30	24	54	36	...	...	...	—	—	—	—	—
94-95—Michigan State	CCHA	39	34	17	51	40	...	...	...	—	—	—	—	—
95-96—Michigan State	CCHA	42	23	20	43	36	...	...	...	—	—	—	—	—
96-97—Washington	NHL	19	3	2	5	7	0	1	0	—	—	—	—	—
—Portland	AHL	27	19	19	38	11	...	...	...	—	—	—	—	—
—Boston	NHL	19	8	5	13	2	-7	1	1	—	—	—	—	—
97-98—Boston	NHL	78	16	27	43	31	7	6	0	6	1	1	2	0
98-99—Utah	IHL	6	1	1	2	0	...	...	...	—	—	—	—	—
—Boston	NHL	55	24	16	40	22	7	6	0	12	4	3	7	0
99-00—Boston	NHL	59	22	25	47	14	8	4	0	—	—	—	—	—
00-01—Edmonton	NHL	61	16	26	42	23	1	7	1	6	3	1	4	4
01-02—Edmonton	NHL	82	28	32	60	25	3	12	0	—	—	—	—	—
02-03—Edmonton	NHL	68	25	30	55	20	-11	10	0	—	—	—	—	—
—New York Rangers	NHL	11	1	4	5	6	0	0	0	—	—	—	—	—
NHL Totals (7 years)		452	143	167	310	150	8	47	2	24	8	5	13	4

CASSELS, ANDREW　　　　　　　　C　　　　　　　　BLUE JACKETS

PERSONAL: Born July 23, 1969, in Bramalea, Ont. ... 6-1/185. ... Shoots left. ... Name pronounced KAS-uhls.
TRANSACTIONS/CAREER NOTES: Selected by Montreal Canadiens in first round (first Canadiens pick, 17th overall) of NHL entry draft (June 13, 1987). ... Separated right shoulder (November 22, 1989); missed 10 games. ... Traded by Canadiens to Hartford Whalers for second-round pick (RW Valeri Bure) in 1992 draft (September 17, 1991). ... Bruised kneecap (December 4, 1993); missed one game. ... Suffered facial injury (March 13, 1994); missed four games. ... Bruised forearm (December 2, 1995); missed one game. ... Suffered charley horse (March 6, 1997); missed one game. ... Whalers franchise moved to North Carolina and renamed Carolina Hurricanes for 1997-98 season; NHL approved move on June 25, 1997. ... Traded by Hurricanes with G Jean-Sebastien Giguere to Calgary Flames for LW Gary Roberts and G Trevor Kidd (August 25, 1997). ... Strained rib cage (October 9, 1997); missed one game. ... Injured groin (February 1, 1999); missed 12 games. ... Signed as free agent by Vancouver Canucks (July 13, 1999). ... Sprained thumb (October 19, 1999); missed three games. ... Fractured toe (January 20, 2001); missed 10 games. ... Sprained ankle (March 25, 2001); missed remainder of season. ... Sprained medial collateral ligament in knee (October 23, 2001); missed 20 games. ... Suffered concussion (March 9, 2002); missed eight games. ... Signed as free agent by Columbus Blue Jackets (August 15, 2002). ... Re-signed by Blue Jackets (June 30, 2003).
STATISTICAL PLATEAUS: Three-goal games: 2000-01 (1).

			REGULAR SEASON								PLAYOFFS				
Season Team	League	Gms.	G	A	Pts.	PIM	+/-	PP	SH		Gms.	G	A	Pts.	PIM
85-86—Bramalea Jr. B	OHA	33	18	25	43	26	...	...	...		—	—	—	—	—
86-87—Ottawa	OHL	66	26	66	92	28	...	...	...		11	5	9	14	7
87-88—Ottawa	OHL	61	48	*103	*151	39	...	...	...		16	8	*24	†32	13
88-89—Ottawa	OHL	56	37	97	134	66	...	...	...		12	5	10	15	10
89-90—Sherbrooke	AHL	55	22	45	67	25	...	...	...		12	2	11	13	6
—Montreal	NHL	6	2	0	2	2	1	0	0		—	—	—	—	—
90-91—Montreal	NHL	54	6	19	25	20	2	1	0		8	0	2	2	2
91-92—Hartford	NHL	67	11	30	41	18	3	2	2		7	2	4	6	6
92-93—Hartford	NHL	84	21	64	85	62	-11	8	3		—	—	—	—	—
93-94—Hartford	NHL	79	16	42	58	37	-21	8	1		—	—	—	—	—
94-95—Hartford	NHL	46	7	30	37	18	-3	1	0		—	—	—	—	—
95-96—Hartford	NHL	81	20	43	63	39	8	6	0		—	—	—	—	—
96-97—Hartford	NHL	81	22	44	66	46	-16	8	0		—	—	—	—	—
97-98—Calgary	NHL	81	17	27	44	32	-7	6	1		—	—	—	—	—
98-99—Calgary	NHL	70	12	25	37	18	-12	4	1		—	—	—	—	—
99-00—Vancouver..................	NHL	79	17	45	62	16	8	6	0		—	—	—	—	—
00-01—Vancouver..................	NHL	66	12	44	56	10	1	2	0		—	—	—	—	—
01-02—Vancouver..................	NHL	53	11	39	50	22	5	7	0		6	2	1	3	0
02-03—Columbus	NHL	79	20	48	68	30	-4	9	1		—	—	—	—	—
NHL Totals (14 years).........		926	194	500	694	370	-46	68	9		21	4	7	11	8

CASSIVI, FREDERIC　　　　　　　G　　　　　　　　THRASHERS

PERSONAL: Born June 12, 1975, in Sorel, Que. ... 6-4/215. ... Catches left. ... Name pronounced kuh-SIH-vee.
TRANSACTIONS/CAREER NOTES: Selected by Ottawa Senators in ninth round (seventh Senators pick, 210th overall) of NHL entry draft (June 29, 1994). ... Signed as free agent by Colorado Avalanche (August 3, 1999). ... Traded by Avalanche to Atlanta Thrashers for D Brett Clark (January 24, 2002).

				REGULAR SEASON								PLAYOFFS					
Season Team	League	Gms.	Min	W	L	T	GA	SO	Avg.	SV%		Gms.	Min.	W	L	GA	SO	Avg.	SV%
93-94—St. Hyacinthe................	QMJHL	35	1751	15	13	3	127	1	4.35	—		0	0	0	0	0	0	—	—
94-95—Halifax..........................	QMJHL	24	1362	9	12	1	105	0	4.63	—		—	—	—	—	—	—	—	—
—St. Jean.........................	QMJHL	19	1021	12	6	0	55	1	3.23	—		5	258	2	3	18	0	4.19	—
95-96—Prin. Edward Island.......	AHL	41	2346	20	14	3	128	1	3.27	—		5	317	2	3	24	0	4.54	—
—Thunder Bay..................	Col.HL	12	714	6	4	2	51	0	4.29	—		—	—	—	—	—	—	—	—
96-97—Syracuse	AHL	55	3069	23	22	8	164	2	3.21	—		1	60	0	1	3	0	3.00	—
97-98—Worcester	AHL	45	2594	20	22	2	140	1	3.24	—		6	326	3	3	18	0	3.31	—
98-99—Cincinnati	IHL	44	2418	21	17	‡2	123	1	3.05	—		3	139	1	2	6	0	2.59	—
99-00—Hershey	AHL	31	1554	14	9	3	78	1	3.01	—		2	63	0	1	5	0	4.76	—
00-01—Hershey	AHL	49	2620	17	24	3	124	2	2.84	—		9	564	7	2	14	1	*1.49	—
01-02—Hershey	AHL	21	1201	6	10	4	50	0	2.50	—		—	—	—	—	—	—	—	—
—Chicago........................	AHL	12	624	6	2	1	26	0	2.50	—		5	264	2	2	11	0	2.50	—
—Atlanta..........................	NHL	6	307	2	3	0	17	0	3.32	.918		—	—	—	—	—	—	—	—
02-03—Chicago........................	AHL	21	1170	10	8	1	62	0	3.18	—		2	90	0	2	3	0	2.00	—
—Atlanta..........................	NHL	2	123	1	1	0	11	0	5.37	.810		—	—	—	—	—	—	—	—
NHL Totals (2 years).............		8	430	3	4	0	28	0	3.91	.894									

CAVANAUGH, DAN　　　　　　　C　　　　　　　　WILD

PERSONAL: Born March 3, 1980, in Springfield, Mass. ... 6-1/190. ... Shoots right.
COLLEGE: Boston University.
TRANSACTIONS/CAREER NOTES: Selected by Calgary Flames in second round (second Flames pick, 38th overall) of NHL entry draft (June 26, 1999). ... Rights traded by Flames with eighth-round pick (LW Jake Riddle) in 2001 draft to Minnesota Wild for G Mike Vernon (June 23, 2000).

			REGULAR SEASON								PLAYOFFS				
Season Team	League	Gms.	G	A	Pts.	PIM	+/-	PP	SH		Gms.	G	A	Pts.	PIM
97-98—New England...............	EJHL	51	39	59	98	58	...	...	...		—	—	—	—	—
98-99—Boston University	Hockey East	36	6	8	14	54	...	...	...		—	—	—	—	—
99-00—Boston University	Hockey East	40	9	25	34	62	...	...	...		—	—	—	—	—
00-01—Boston University	Hockey East	35	7	21	28	41	...	...	...		—	—	—	—	—
01-02—Houston......................	AHL	70	3	16	19	41	...	...	...		5	0	0	0	0
02-03—Houston......................	AHL	77	13	13	26	126	...	...	...		—	—	—	—	—

CAVOSIE, MARC — C/LW — WILD

PERSONAL: Born August 6, 1981, in Cohoes, N.Y. ... 6-0/180. ... Shoots left. ... Full Name: Marc Christian Cavosie. ... Name pronounced ca-VO-see.
HIGH SCHOOL: Albany (N.Y.) Academy.
COLLEGE: Rensselaer Polytechnic Institute (N.Y.).
TRANSACTIONS/CAREER NOTES: Selected by Minnesota Wild in fourth round (third Wild pick, 99th overall) of NHL entry draft (June 24, 2000).

Season Team	League	REGULAR SEASON Gms.	G	A	Pts.	PIM	+/-	PP	SH	PLAYOFFS Gms.	G	A	Pts.	PIM
98-99—Albany Academy	N.Y. H.S.	28	23	20	43	32	...	...	...	—	—	—	—	—
99-00—Rensselaer Poly. Inst..	ECAC	29	11	27	38	20	...	...	...	—	—	—	—	—
00-01—Rensselaer Poly. Inst..	ECAC	28	13	16	29	47	...	...	...	—	—	—	—	—
01-02—Rensselaer Poly. Inst..	ECAC	36	23	*27	*50	44	...	...	...	—	—	—	—	—
02-03—Houston	AHL	54	5	14	19	24	...	...	...	—	—	—	—	—

CECHMANEK, ROMAN — G — KINGS

PERSONAL: Born March 2, 1971, in Gottwaldov, Czechoslovakia ... 6-3/187. ... Catches left.
TRANSACTIONS/CAREER NOTES: Selected by Philadelphia Flyers in sixth round (third Flyers pick, 171st overall) of NHL entry draft (June 24, 2000). ... Suffered sinus infection (January 26, 2002); missed one game. ... Sprained right ankle (March 2, 2002); missed 13 games. ... Traded by Philadelphia to Los Angeles Kings for second-round pick in 2004 draft (May 28, 2003).

Season Team	League	REGULAR SEASON Gms.	Min	W	L	T	GA	SO	Avg.	SV%	PLAYOFFS Gms.	Min.	W	L	GA	SO	Avg.	SV%
94-95—HC Vsetin	Czech Rep.	52	3046	...	...	...	121	5	2.38	—	11	619	...	...	23	2	2.23	—
95-96—HC Vsetin	Czech Rep.	49	2925	...	...	...	94	4	1.93	—	13	783	...	...	17	2	1.30	—
96-97—HC Vsetin	Czech Rep.	58	3364	...	...	...	109	3	1.94	—	10	602	...	...	11	2	1.10	—
97-98—HC Vsetin	Czech Rep.	51	2906	...	...	...	92	...	1.90	—	10	600	...	...	16	1	1.60	—
98-99—HC Vsetin	Czech Rep.	46	2875	...	...	...	97	...	2.02	—	12	747	...	...	23	1	1.85	—
99-00—HC Vsetin	Czech Rep.	46	2875	...	...	...	97	...	2.02	—	9	545	...	...	15	...	1.65	—
00-01—Philadelphia	AHL	3	160	1	1	0	3	0	1.13	—	—	—	—	—	—	—	—	—
—Philadelphia	NHL	59	3431	35	15	6	115	10	2.01	.921	6	347	2	4	18	0	3.11	.891
01-02—Philadelphia	NHL	46	2603	24	13	6	89	4	2.05	.921	4	227	1	3	7	1	1.85	.936
02-03—Philadelphia	NHL	58	3350	33	15	10	102	6	1.83	.925	13	867	6	7	31	2	2.15	.909
NHL Totals (3 years)		163	9384	92	43	22	306	20	1.96	.923	23	1441	9	14	56	3	2.33	.909

CENTOMO, SEBASTIEN — G — MAPLE LEAFS

PERSONAL: Born March 26, 1981, in Montreal. ... 6-1/193. ... Catches right.
TRANSACTIONS/CAREER NOTES: Signed as non-drafted free agent by Toronto Maple Leafs (September 10, 1999).

Season Team	League	REGULAR SEASON Gms.	Min	W	L	T	GA	SO	Avg.	SV%	PLAYOFFS Gms.	Min.	W	L	GA	SO	Avg.	SV%
98-99—Rouyn-Noranda	QMJHL	32	1658	14	9	4	104	1	3.76	—	2	28	0	1	5	0	10.71	—
99-00—Rouyn-Noranda	QMJHL	50	2758	24	17	3	160	1	3.48	—	11	695	6	5	41	0	3.54	—
00-01—Rouyn-Noranda	QMJHL	46	2599	25	14	4	158	3	3.65	—	1	60	0	1	4	0	4.00	—
01-02—St. John's	AHL	25	1429	12	7	4	60	2	2.52	—	11	690	4	6	29	2	2.52	—
—Toronto	NHL	1	40	0	0	0	3	0	4.50	.750	—	—	—	—	—	—	—	—
02-03—St. John's	AHL	19	1045	7	10	1	68	0	3.90	—	—	—	—	—	—	—	—	—
—Greensboro	ECHL	10	564	3	3	3	24	1	2.55	—	—	—	—	—	—	—	—	—
NHL Totals (1 year)		1	40	0	0	0	3	0	4.50	.750	—	—	—	—	—	—	—	—

CEREDA, LUCA — C — MAPLE LEAFS

PERSONAL: Born September 7, 1981, in Lugano, Switzerland. ... 6-2/203. ... Shoots left.
TRANSACTIONS/CAREER NOTES: Selected by Toronto Maple Leafs in first round (first Maple Leafs pick, 24th overall) of NHL entry draft (June 26, 1999). ... Missed entire 2000-01 season due to heart surgery.

Season Team	League	REGULAR SEASON Gms.	G	A	Pts.	PIM	+/-	PP	SH	PLAYOFFS Gms.	G	A	Pts.	PIM
96-97—Ambri-Piotta	Switzerland Jr.	35	13	8	21	21	...	...	...	—	—	—	—	—
97-98—Ambri-Piotta	Switzerland Jr.	28	17	27	44	24	...	...	...	—	—	—	—	—
98-99—Ambri-Piotta	Switzerland	38	6	10	16	8	...	...	...	15	0	6	6	4
99-00—Ambri-Piotta	Switzerland	44	1	5	6	14	...	...	...	9	0	1	1	2
00-01—						Did not play.								
01-02—St. John's	AHL	71	5	8	13	23	...	...	...	11	2	1	3	10
02-03—St. John's	AHL	68	7	18	25	26	...	...	...	—	—	—	—	—

CHARA, ZDENO — D — SENATORS

PERSONAL: Born March 18, 1977, in Trencin, Czechoslovakia ... 6-9/260. ... Shoots left. ... Name pronounced zuh-DAY-noh CHAH-ruh.
TRANSACTIONS/CAREER NOTES: Selected by New York Islanders in third round (third Islanders pick, 56th overall) of NHL entry draft (June 22, 1996). ... Injured left shoulder (January 10, 2000); missed 16 games. ... Suffered from the flu (April 9, 2000); missed one game. ... Traded by Islanders with RW Bill Muckalt and first-round pick (C Jason Spezza) in 2001 draft to Ottawa Senators for C Alexei Yashin (June 23, 2001). ... Injured left shoulder (January 12, 2002); missed three games. ... Suffered from the flu (March 23, 2002); missed four games.

Season Team	League	REGULAR SEASON Gms.	G	A	Pts.	PIM	+/-	PP	SH	PLAYOFFS Gms.	G	A	Pts.	PIM
94-95—Dukla Trencin.............	Slovakia Jrs.	2	0	0	0	2	...	...	...	—	—	—	—	—
95-96—Dukla Trencin.............	Slovakia Jrs.	22	1	13	14	80	...	...	...	—	—	—	—	—
—HC Piestany................	Slov. Div. II	10	1	3	4	10	...	...	...	—	—	—	—	—
—Sparta Praha Jrs........	Czech Rep.	15	1	2	3	42	...	...	...	—	—	—	—	—
—Sparta Praha...........	Czech Rep.	1	0	0	0	0	...	...	...	—	—	—	—	—
96-97—Prince George..........	WHL	49	3	19	22	120	...	...	...	15	1	7	8	45
97-98—Kentucky....................	AHL	48	4	9	13	125	...	...	...	1	0	0	0	4
—New York Islanders.....	NHL	25	0	1	1	50	1	0	0	—	—	—	—	—
98-99—Lowell......................	AHL	23	2	2	4	47	...	...	...	—	—	—	—	—
—New York Islanders.....	NHL	59	2	6	8	83	-8	0	1	—	—	—	—	—
99-00—New York Islanders.....	NHL	65	2	9	11	57	-27	0	0	—	—	—	—	—
00-01—New York Islanders.....	NHL	82	2	7	9	157	-27	0	1	—	—	—	—	—
01-02—Dukla Trencin.............	Slovakia	8	2	2	4	32	...	...	...	—	—	—	—	—
—Ottawa	NHL	75	10	13	23	156	30	4	1	10	0	1	1	12
02-03—Ottawa	NHL	74	9	30	39	116	29	3	0	18	1	6	7	14
NHL Totals (6 years)...........		**380**	**25**	**66**	**91**	**619**	**-2**	**7**	**3**	**28**	**1**	**7**	**8**	**26**

CHARPENTIER, SEBASTIEN   G   CAPITALS

PERSONAL: Born April 18, 1977, in Drummondville, Que. ... 5-9/189. ... Catches left. ... Name pronounced SHAHR-pihnt-yay.
TRANSACTIONS/CAREER NOTES: Selected by Washington Capitals in fourth round (fourth Capitals pick, 93rd overall) of NHL entry draft (July 8, 1995).

Season Team	League	REGULAR SEASON Gms.	Min	W	L	T	GA	SO	Avg.	SV%	PLAYOFFS Gms.	Min.	W	L	GA	SO	Avg.	SV%
94-95—Laval	QMJHL	41	2152	25	12	1	99	2	2.76	—	16	886	9	4	45	0	3.05	—
95-96—Laval	QMJHL	18	938	4	10	0	97	0	6.20	—	—	—	—	—	—	—	—	—
—Val-d'Or.........................	QMJHL	33	1906	21	9	1	87	1	2.74	—	13	778	7	5	47	0	3.62	—
96-97—Shawinigan............	QMJHL	*62	*3474	*37	17	4	176	1	3.04	—	4	195	2	1	13	0	4.00	—
97-98—Hampton Roads...........	ECHL	43	2388	20	16	6	114	0	2.86	—	18	*1183	*14	4	38	1	*1.93	—
—Portland	AHL	4	230	1	3	0	10	0	2.61	—	—	—	—	—	—	—	—	—
98-99—Portland	AHL	3	180	0	3	0	10	0	3.33	—	—	—	—	—	—	—	—	—
—Quad City	UHL	6	4	0	0	0	0	0	...	—	—	—	—	—	—	—	—	—
99-00—Portland	AHL	18	1041	10	4	3	48	0	2.77	—	3	183	1	1	9	0	2.95	—
00-01—Portland	AHL	34	1978	16	16	1	113	1	3.43	—	1	102	0	1	3	0	1.76	—
01-02—Portland	AHL	49	2941	20	18	10	131	3	2.67	—	—	—	—	—	—	—	—	—
—Washington..................	NHL	2	122	1	1	0	5	0	2.46	.936	—	—	—	—	—	—	—	—
02-03—Portland	AHL	12	727	3	7	2	28	2	2.31	—	—	—	—	—	—	—	—	—
—Washington..................	NHL	17	859	5	7	1	40	0	2.79	.906	—	—	—	—	—	—	—	—
NHL Totals (2 years)............		**19**	**981**	**6**	**8**	**1**	**45**	**0**	**2.75**	**.911**								

CHARTIER, CHRISTIAN   D   MAPLE LEAFS

PERSONAL: Born October 29, 1980, in Russel, Man. ... 6-0/219. ... Shoots left.
TRANSACTIONS/CAREER NOTES: Selected by Edmonton Oilers in seventh round (eighth Oilers pick, 199th overall) of NHL entry draft (June 26, 1999). ... Signed as free agent by Toronto Maple Leafs (June 6, 2001).

Season Team	League	REGULAR SEASON Gms.	G	A	Pts.	PIM	+/-	PP	SH	PLAYOFFS Gms.	G	A	Pts.	PIM
96-97—Saskatoon..................	WHL	64	2	23	25	32	...	...	...	—	—	—	—	—
97-98—Saskatoon..................	WHL	68	8	33	41	43	...	...	...	6	0	3	3	12
98-99—Saskatoon..................	WHL	62	2	14	16	71	...	...	...	—	—	—	—	—
99-00—Saskatoon..................	WHL	11	2	2	4	4	...	...	...	—	—	—	—	—
—Prince George..............	WHL	51	16	29	45	24	...	...	...	13	4	9	13	12
00-01—Prince George...........	WHL	63	12	56	68	99	...	...	...	6	1	4	5	6
01-02—St. John's..................	AHL	65	5	10	15	18	...	...	...	11	0	4	4	4
02-03—St. John's..................	AHL	67	4	22	26	48	...	...	...	—	—	—	—	—

CHARTRAND, BRAD   C   KINGS

PERSONAL: Born December 14, 1974, in Winnipeg ... 5-11/185. ... Shoots left.
TRANSACTIONS/CAREER NOTES: Signed as non-drafted free agent by Los Angeles Kings (July 21, 1999). ... Strained muscle in abdomen (December 8, 2001); missed nine games.

Season Team	League	REGULAR SEASON Gms.	G	A	Pts.	PIM	+/-	PP	SH	PLAYOFFS Gms.	G	A	Pts.	PIM
88-89—Winnipeg	MAHA	24	30	50	80	40	...	...	...	—	—	—	—	—
89-90—Winnipeg	MAHA	24	26	55	81	40	...	...	...	—	—	—	—	—
90-91—Winnipeg	MAHA	34	26	45	71	40	...	...	...	—	—	—	—	—
91-92—St. James	MJHL						Statistics unavailable.							
92-93—Cornell University	ECAC	26	10	6	16	16	...	...	...	—	—	—	—	—
93-94—Cornell University	ECAC	30	4	14	18	48	...	...	...	—	—	—	—	—
94-95—Cornell University	ECAC	28	9	9	18	10	...	...	...	—	—	—	—	—
95-96—Cornell University	ECAC	34	24	19	43	16	...	...	...	—	—	—	—	—
96-97—Canadian nat'l team	Int'l	54	10	14	24	42	...	...	...	—	—	—	—	—
97-98—Canadian nat'l team	Int'l	60	24	30	54	47	...	...	...	—	—	—	—	—
—Rapperswil..................	Switzerland	8	2	3	5	4	...	...	...	—	—	—	—	—
98-99—St. John's..................	AHL	64	16	14	30	48	...	...	...	5	0	2	2	2

Season Team	League	REGULAR SEASON								PLAYOFFS				
		Gms.	G	A	Pts.	PIM	+/-	PP	SH	Gms.	G	A	Pts.	PIM
99-00—Los Angeles	NHL	50	6	6	12	17	4	0	1	4	0	0	0	6
—Long Beach	IHL	1	0	0	0	0	...	...	...	3	0	0	0	0
—Lowell	AHL	16	5	10	15	8	...	...	...	—	—	—	—	—
00-01—Lowell	AHL	72	17	34	51	44	...	...	...	4	0	1	1	8
—Los Angeles	NHL	4	1	0	1	2	-2	0	0	—	—	—	—	—
01-02—Manchester	AHL	22	10	12	22	31	...	...	...	—	—	—	—	—
—Los Angeles	NHL	46	7	9	16	40	5	0	0	7	1	1	2	2
02-03—Los Angeles	NHL	62	8	6	14	33	-10	0	1	—	—	—	—	—
NHL Totals (4 years)		162	22	21	43	92	-3	0	2	11	1	1	2	8

CHEBATURKIN, VLADIMIR — D — C

PERSONAL: Born April 23, 1975, in Tyumen, U.S.S.R. ... 6-2/212. ... Shoots left. ... Name pronounced VLAD-ih-meer chuh-buh-TUHR-kihn.
TRANSACTIONS/CAREER NOTES: Selected by New York Islanders in third round (third Islanders pick, 66th overall) of NHL entry draft (June 26, 1993). ... Signed as free agent by St. Louis Blues (June 12, 2000). ... Injured groin (September 27, 2000); missed first four games of season. ... Signed as free agent by Chicago Blackhawks (September 5, 2001). ... Signed as free agent by New York Rangers (July 18, 2002).

Season Team	League	REGULAR SEASON								PLAYOFFS				
		Gms.	G	A	Pts.	PIM	+/-	PP	SH	Gms.	G	A	Pts.	PIM
92-93—Kristall Elektrostal	CIS Div. II					Statistics unavailable.								
93-94—Kristall Elektrostal	CIS Div. II	42	4	4	8	38	...	...	...	—	—	—	—	—
94-95—Kristall Elektrostal	CIS	52	2	6	8	90	...	...	...	—	—	—	—	—
95-96—Kristall Elektrostal	CIS	44	1	6	7	30	...	...	...	1	0	0	0	0
96-97—Utah	IHL	68	0	4	4	34	...	...	...	—	—	—	—	—
97-98—Kentucky	AHL	54	6	8	14	52	...	...	...	2	0	0	0	4
—New York Islanders	NHL	2	0	2	2	0	-1	0	0	—	—	—	—	—
98-99—Lowell	AHL	69	2	12	14	85	...	...	...	3	0	0	0	0
—New York Islanders	NHL	8	0	0	0	12	6	0	0	—	—	—	—	—
99-00—Lowell	AHL	63	1	8	9	118	...	...	...	7	0	4	4	11
—New York Islanders	NHL	17	1	1	2	8	-3	0	0	—	—	—	—	—
00-01—St. Louis	NHL	22	1	2	3	26	5	0	0	—	—	—	—	—
—Worcester	AHL	33	0	7	7	73	...	...	...	10	1	0	1	10
01-02—Norfolk	AHL	57	2	8	10	78	...	...	...	—	—	—	—	—
—Chicago	NHL	13	0	2	2	6	0	0	0	3	0	0	0	2
02-03—Hartford	AHL	53	4	3	7	88	...	...	...	—	—	—	—	—
NHL Totals (5 years)		62	2	7	9	52	7	0	0	3	0	0	0	2

CHEECHOO, JONATHAN — RW — SHARKS

PERSONAL: Born July 15, 1980, in Moose Factory, Ont. ... 6-1/195. ... Shoots right.
TRANSACTIONS/CAREER NOTES: Selected by San Jose Sharks in second round (second Sharks pick, 29th overall) of NHL entry draft (June 27, 1998). ... Re-signed by Sharks (July 27, 2003).

Season Team	League	REGULAR SEASON								PLAYOFFS				
		Gms.	G	A	Pts.	PIM	+/-	PP	SH	Gms.	G	A	Pts.	PIM
96-97—Kitchener Jr. B	OHA	43	35	41	76	33	...	...	...	—	—	—	—	—
97-98—Belleville	OHL	64	31	45	76	62	...	...	...	10	4	2	6	10
98-99—Belleville	OHL	63	35	47	82	74	...	...	...	21	15	15	30	27
99-00—Belleville	OHL	66	45	46	91	102	...	...	...	16	5	12	17	16
00-01—Kentucky	AHL	75	32	34	66	63	...	...	...	3	0	0	0	0
01-02—Cleveland	AHL	53	21	25	46	54	...	...	...	—	—	—	—	—
02-03—Cleveland	AHL	9	3	4	7	16	...	...	...	—	—	—	—	—
—San Jose	NHL	66	9	7	16	39	-5	0	0	—	—	—	—	—
NHL Totals (1 year)		66	9	7	16	39	-5	0	0					

CHELIOS, CHRIS — D — RED WINGS

PERSONAL: Born January 25, 1962, in Chicago ... 6-1/190. ... Shoots right. ... Full Name: Christos K. Chelios. ... Cousin of Nikos Tselios, defenseman, Carolina Hurricanes organization. ... Name pronounced CHEH-lee-ohz.
TRANSACTIONS/CAREER NOTES: Selected by Montreal Canadiens in second round (fifth Canadiens pick, 40th overall) of NHL entry draft (June 10, 1981). ... Sprained right ankle (January 1985). ... Injured left knee (April 1985). ... Sprained knee (December 19, 1985). ... Reinjured knee (January 20, 1986). ... Suffered back spasms (October 1986). ... Fractured finger on left hand (December 1987). ... Bruised tailbone (February 7, 1988). ... Strained left knee ligaments (February 1990). ... Underwent surgery to repair torn abdominal muscle (April 30, 1990). ... Traded by Canadiens with second-round pick (C Michael Pomichter) in 1991 draft to Chicago Blackhawks for C Denis Savard (June 29, 1990). ... Lacerated left temple (February 9, 1991). ... Suspended four games by NHL (October 15, 1993). ... Suspended four games without pay and fined $500 by NHL for eye-scratching incident (February 5, 1994). ... Played in Europe during 1994-95 NHL lockout. ... Sprained knee (March 1, 1997); missed eight games. ... Suffered sore back (April 6, 1997); missed one game. ... Strained groin (November 12, 1998); missed five games. ... Traded by Blackhawks to Detroit Red Wings for D Anders Eriksson, first-round pick (D Steve McCarthy) in 1999 draft and first-round pick (G Adam Munro) in 2001 draft (March 23, 1999). ... Strained groin (April 7, 1999); missed two games. ... Suffered injury (April 7, 2000); missed one game. ... Injured knee and underwent surgery (October 18, 2000); missed five games. ... Underwent knee surgery (November 20, 2000); missed 44 games. ... Fractured thumb (March 17, 2001); missed final seven games of regular season.

Season Team	League	REGULAR SEASON Gms.	G	A	Pts.	PIM	+/-	PP	SH	PLAYOFFS Gms.	G	A	Pts.	PIM
79-80—Moose Jaw	SJHL	53	12	31	43	118	...	...	...	—	—	—	—	—
80-81—Moose Jaw	SJHL	54	23	64	87	175	...	...	...	—	—	—	—	—
81-82—Univ. of Wisconsin	WCHA	43	6	43	49	50	...	...	...	—	—	—	—	—
82-83—Univ. of Wisconsin	WCHA	45	16	32	48	62	...	...	...	—	—	—	—	—
83-84—U.S. national team	Int'l	60	14	35	49	58	...	...	...	—	—	—	—	—
—U.S. Olympic team	Int'l	6	0	3	3	8	...	...	...	—	—	—	—	—
—Montreal	NHL	12	0	2	2	12	-5	0	0	15	1	9	10	17
84-85—Montreal	NHL	74	9	55	64	87	11	2	1	9	2	8	10	17
85-86—Montreal	NHL	41	8	26	34	67	4	2	0	20	2	9	11	49
86-87—Montreal	NHL	71	11	33	44	124	-5	6	0	17	4	9	13	38
87-88—Montreal	NHL	71	20	41	61	172	14	10	1	11	3	1	4	29
88-89—Montreal	NHL	80	15	58	73	185	35	8	0	21	4	15	19	28
89-90—Montreal	NHL	53	9	22	31	136	20	1	2	5	0	1	1	8
90-91—Chicago	NHL	77	12	52	64	192	23	5	2	6	1	7	8	46
91-92—Chicago	NHL	80	9	47	56	245	24	2	2	18	6	15	21	37
92-93—Chicago	NHL	84	15	58	73	282	14	8	0	4	0	2	2	14
93-94—Chicago	NHL	76	16	44	60	212	12	7	1	6	1	1	2	8
94-95—Biel-Bienne	Switzerland	3	0	3	3	4	...	...	...	—	—	—	—	—
—Chicago	NHL	48	5	33	38	72	17	3	1	16	4	7	11	12
95-96—Chicago	NHL	81	14	58	72	140	25	7	0	9	0	3	3	8
96-97—Chicago	NHL	72	10	38	48	112	16	2	0	6	0	1	1	8
97-98—Chicago	NHL	81	3	39	42	151	-7	1	0	—	—	—	—	—
—U.S. Olympic team	Int'l	4	2	0	2	2	...	...	...	—	—	—	—	—
98-99—Chicago	NHL	65	8	26	34	89	-4	2	1	—	—	—	—	—
—Detroit	NHL	10	1	1	2	4	5	1	0	10	0	4	4	14
99-00—Detroit	NHL	81	3	31	34	103	48	0	0	9	0	1	1	8
00-01—Detroit	NHL	24	0	3	3	45	4	0	0	5	1	0	1	2
01-02—Detroit	NHL	79	6	33	39	126	*40	1	0	23	1	13	14	44
—U.S. Olympic team	Int'l	6	1	0	1	4	...	...	...	—	—	—	—	—
02-03—Detroit	NHL	66	2	17	19	78	4	0	1	4	0	0	0	2
NHL Totals (20 years)		1326	176	717	893	2634	295	68	12	214	30	106	136	389

CHIMERA, JASON — LW/LW — OILERS

PERSONAL: Born May 2, 1979, in Edmonton ... 6-0/215. ... Shoots left. ... Name pronounced chih-MAIR-uh.

TRANSACTIONS/CAREER NOTES: Selected by Edmonton Oilers in fifth round (fifth Oilers pick, 121st overall) of NHL entry draft (June 21, 1997).

Season Team	League	REGULAR SEASON Gms.	G	A	Pts.	PIM	+/-	PP	SH	PLAYOFFS Gms.	G	A	Pts.	PIM
96-97—Medicine Hat	WHL	71	16	23	39	64	...	...	...	4	0	1	1	4
97-98—Medicine Hat	WHL	72	34	32	66	93	...	...	...	—	—	—	—	—
—Hamilton	AHL	4	0	0	0	8	...	...	...	—	—	—	—	—
98-99—Medicine Hat	WHL	37	18	22	40	84	...	...	...	—	—	—	—	—
—Brandon	WHL	21	14	12	26	32	...	...	...	5	4	1	5	8
99-00—Hamilton	AHL	78	15	13	28	77	...	...	...	10	0	2	2	12
00-01—Hamilton	AHL	78	29	25	54	93	...	...	...	—	—	—	—	—
—Edmonton	NHL	1	0	0	0	0	0	0	0	—	—	—	—	—
01-02—Hamilton	AHL	77	26	51	77	158	...	...	...	15	4	6	10	10
—Edmonton	NHL	3	1	0	1	0	-3	0	0	—	—	—	—	—
02-03—Edmonton	NHL	66	14	9	23	36	-2	0	1	2	0	2	2	0
NHL Totals (3 years)		70	15	9	24	36	-5	0	1	2	0	2	2	0

CHISTOV, STANISLAV — LW — MIGHTY DUCKS

PERSONAL: Born April 17, 1983, in Chelyabinsk, U.S.S.R. ... 5-10/195. ... Shoots right.

TRANSACTIONS/CAREER NOTES: Selected by Mighty Ducks of Anaheim in first round (first Mighty Ducks pick, fifth overall) of NHL entry draft (June 23, 2001).

Season Team	League	REGULAR SEASON Gms.	G	A	Pts.	PIM	+/-	PP	SH	PLAYOFFS Gms.	G	A	Pts.	PIM
99-00—Avangard Omsk	Russian	3	1	0	1	2	...	...	...	—	—	—	—	—
00-01—Avangard Omsk	Russian	24	4	8	12	12	...	...	...	5	0	0	0	2
01-02—Avangard Omsk	Russian	9	0	0	0	4	...	...	...	—	—	—	—	—
02-03—Anaheim	NHL	79	12	18	30	54	4	3	0	21	4	2	6	8
NHL Totals (1 year)		79	12	18	30	54	4	3	0	21	4	2	6	8

CHOUINARD, ERIC — C — FLYERS

PERSONAL: Born July 8, 1980, in Atlanta ... 6-3/214. ... Shoots left. ... Son of Guy Chouinard, center with Atlanta/Calgary Flames (1974-75 through 1982-83) and St. Louis Blues (1983-84); and cousin of Marc Chouinard, center, Mighty Ducks of Anaheim. ... Name pronounced Shwee-NAHRD.

TRANSACTIONS/CAREER NOTES: Selected by Montreal Canadiens in first round (first Canadiens pick, 16th overall) of NHL entry draft (June 27, 1998). ... Traded by Canadiens to Philadelphia Flyers for second-round pick in 2003 draft (January 29, 2003). ... Re-signed by Philadelphia (June 10, 2003).

Season Team	League	Gms.	G	A	Pts.	PIM	+/-	PP	SH	Gms.	G	A	Pts.	PIM
97-98—Quebec	QMJHL	68	41	42	83	18	...	...	...	14	7	10	17	6
98-99—Quebec	QMJHL	62	50	59	109	56	...	...	...	13	8	10	18	8
99-00—Quebec	QMJHL	50	57	47	104	105	...	...	...	11	14	4	18	8
—Fredericton	AHL	—	—	—	—	—	—	—	—	6	3	2	5	0
00-01—Quebec	AHL	48	12	21	33	6	...	...	...	9	2	0	2	2
—Montreal	NHL	13	1	3	4	0	0	1	0	—	—	—	—	—
01-02—Quebec	AHL	65	19	23	42	18	...	...	...	2	0	0	0	0
02-03—Utah	AHL	32	12	12	24	16	...	...	...	—	—	—	—	—
—Philadelphia	NHL	28	4	4	8	8	2	1	0	—	—	—	—	—
NHL Totals (2 years)		41	5	7	12	8	2	2	0					

CHOUINARD, MARC — C — WILD

PERSONAL: Born May 6, 1977, in Charlesbourg, Que. ... 6-5/218. ... Shoots right. ... Cousin of Eric Chouinard, center, Montreal Canadiens organization; and nephew of Guy Chouinard, center with Atlanta/Calgary Flames (1974-75 through 1982-83) and St. Louis Blues (1983-84). ... Name pronounced shwee-NAHRD.

TRANSACTIONS/CAREER NOTES: Selected by Winnipeg Jets in second round (second Jets pick, 32nd overall) of NHL entry draft (July 8, 1995). ... Traded by Jets with RW Teemu Selanne and fourth-round pick (traded to Toronto) in 1996 draft to Mighty Ducks of Anaheim for C Chad Kilger, D Oleg Tverdovsky and third-round pick (D Per-Anton Lundstrom) in 1996 draft (February 7, 1996). ... Tore Achilles' tendon (October 31, 1997); missed remainder of season. ... Suffered injury (October 8, 2001); missed one game. ... Bruised right knee (October 14, 2001); missed one game. ... Strained left shoulder (February 27, 2002); missed remainder of season. ... Signed by Minnesota Wild (July 28, 2003).

Season Team	League	Gms.	G	A	Pts.	PIM	+/-	PP	SH	Gms.	G	A	Pts.	PIM
93-94—Beauport	QMJHL	62	11	19	30	23	...	...	...	13	2	5	7	2
94-95—Beauport	QMJHL	68	24	40	64	32	...	...	...	18	1	6	7	4
95-96—Beauport	QMJHL	30	14	21	35	19	...	...	...	—	—	—	—	—
—Halifax	QMJHL	24	6	12	18	17	...	...	...	6	2	1	3	2
96-97—Halifax	QMJHL	63	24	49	73	52	...	...	...	18	10	16	26	12
97-98—Cincinnati	AHL	8	1	2	3	4	...	...	...	—	—	—	—	—
98-99—Cincinnati	AHL	69	7	8	15	20	...	...	...	3	0	0	0	4
99-00—Cincinnati	AHL	70	17	16	33	29	...	...	...	—	—	—	—	—
00-01—Cincinnati	AHL	32	10	9	19	4	...	...	...					
—Anaheim	NHL	44	3	4	7	12	-5	0	0	—	—	—	—	—
01-02—Anaheim	NHL	45	4	5	9	10	2	0	0	—	—	—	—	—
02-03—Anaheim	NHL	70	3	4	7	40	-9	0	1	15	1	0	1	0
NHL Totals (3 years)		159	10	13	23	62	-12	0	1	15	1	0	1	0

CHRISTIE, RYAN — LW

PERSONAL: Born July 3, 1978, in Beamsville, Ont. ... 6-3/200. ... Shoots left.
TRANSACTIONS/CAREER NOTES: Selected by Dallas Stars in fifth round (third Stars pick, 112th overall) of NHL entry draft (June 22, 1996). ... Signed as free agent by Calgary Flames (August 2, 2001).

Season Team	League	Gms.	G	A	Pts.	PIM	+/-	PP	SH	Gms.	G	A	Pts.	PIM
95-96—Owen Sound	OHL	66	29	17	46	93	...	...	...	6	1	1	2	0
96-97—Owen Sound	OHL	66	23	29	52	136	...	...	...	4	1	1	2	8
97-98—Owen Sound	OHL	66	39	41	80	208	...	...	...	11	3	5	8	13
98-99—Michigan	IHL	48	4	5	9	74	...	...	...	3	1	1	2	2
99-00—Michigan	IHL	76	24	25	49	140	...	...	...	—	—	—	—	—
—Dallas	NHL	5	0	0	0	0	-1	0	0	—	—	—	—	—
00-01—Utah	IHL	69	22	16	38	88	...	...	...	—	—	—	—	—
01-02—Saint John	AHL	77	21	18	39	61	...	...	...	—	—	—	—	—
—Calgary	NHL	2	0	0	0	0	-1	0	0	—	—	—	—	—
02-03—Saint John	AHL	67	10	14	24	84	...	...	...	—	—	—	—	—
NHL Totals (2 years)		7	0	0	0	0	-2	0	0					

CHUBAROV, ARTEM — C — CANUCKS

PERSONAL: Born December 12, 1979, in Gorky, U.S.S.R. ... 6-1/205. ... Shoots left.
TRANSACTIONS/CAREER NOTES: Selected by Vancouver Canucks in second round (second Canucks pick, 31st overall) of NHL entry draft (June 27, 1998). ... Injured hip (February 19, 2000); missed nine games. ... Injured hand (February 28, 2002); missed two games.

Season Team	League	Gms.	G	A	Pts.	PIM	+/-	PP	SH	Gms.	G	A	Pts.	PIM
94-95—Tor. Nizhny Nov.	CIS Jr.	60	20	30	50	20	...	...	...	—	—	—	—	—
95-96—Tor. Nizhny Nov.	CIS Jr.	60	22	25	47	20	...	...	...	—	—	—	—	—
96-97—Tor. Nizhny Nov.	Rus. Div. III	40	24	5	29	16	...	...	...	—	—	—	—	—
—Tor. Nizhny Nov.	Rus. Div. II	15	1	1	2	8	...	...	...	—	—	—	—	—
97-98—Dynamo Moscow	Russian	30	1	4	5	4	...	...	...	—	—	—	—	—
98-99—Dynamo Moscow	Russian	34	8	2	10	10	...	...	...	12	0	0	0	4
99-00—Vancouver	NHL	49	1	8	9	10	-4	0	0	—	—	—	—	—
—Syracuse	AHL	14	7	6	13	4	...	...	...	1	0	0	0	0
00-01—Vancouver	NHL	1	0	0	0	0	-1	0	0	—	—	—	—	—
—Kansas City	IHL	10	7	4	11	12	...	...	...	—	—	—	—	—
01-02—Manitoba	AHL	19	7	12	19	4	...	...	...	—	—	—	—	—
—Vancouver	NHL	51	5	5	10	10	-3	0	0	6	0	1	1	0
02-03—Vancouver	NHL	62	7	13	20	6	4	1	0	14	0	2	2	4
NHL Totals (4 years)		163	13	26	39	26	-4	1	0	20	0	3	3	4

CIBAK, MARTIN   C   LIGHTNING

PERSONAL: Born May 17, 1980, in Liptovmikulas, Czechoslovakia. ... 6-1/195. ... Shoots left. ... Name pronounced SEE-back.
TRANSACTIONS/CAREER NOTES: Selected by Tampa Bay Lightning in eighth round (11th Lightning pick, 252nd overall) of NHL entry draft (June 28, 1998). ... Re-signed by Lightning (July 29, 2003).

		REGULAR SEASON								PLAYOFFS				
Season Team	League	Gms.	G	A	Pts.	PIM	+/-	PP	SH	Gms.	G	A	Pts.	PIM
95-96—Liptovsky Mikulas.......	Slovakia Jrs.	48	38	35	73	...	...	...	...	—	—	—	—	—
96-97—Liptovsky Mikulas.......	Slovakia Jrs.	45	22	18	40	...	...	...	...	—	—	—	—	—
97-98—Liptovsky Mikulas.......	Slovakia Jrs.	42	31	21	52	...	...	...	...	—	—	—	—	—
—HK 32 Lip. Mikulas	Slovakia	28	1	3	4	10	...	...	...	—	—	—	—	—
98-99—Medicine Hat..............	WHL	66	21	26	47	72	...	...	...	—	—	—	—	—
99-00—Medicine Hat..............	WHL	58	16	29	45	77	...	...	...	—	—	—	—	—
00-01—Detroit......................	IHL	79	10	28	38	88	...	...	...	—	—	—	—	—
01-02—Springfield	AHL	52	5	9	14	44	...	...	...	—	—	—	—	—
—Tampa Bay	NHL	26	1	5	6	8	-6	0	0	—	—	—	—	—
02-03—Springfield	AHL	62	5	15	20	78	...	...	...	—	—	—	—	—
NHL Totals (1 year)............		26	1	5	6	8	-6	0	0	—	—	—	—	—

CIERNIK, IVAN   LW

PERSONAL: Born October 30, 1977, in Levice, Czechoslovakia ... 6-0/218. ... Shoots left. ... Name pronounced SEER-nihk.
TRANSACTIONS/CAREER NOTES: Selected by Ottawa Senators in ninth round (sixth Senators pick, 216th overall) of NHL entry draft (June 22, 1996). ... Injured shoulder (January 29, 2001); missed four games. ... Injured right ankle (January 2, 2002); missed six games. ... Claimed on waivers by Washington Capitals (January 19, 2002).

		REGULAR SEASON								PLAYOFFS				
Season Team	League	Gms.	G	A	Pts.	PIM	+/-	PP	SH	Gms.	G	A	Pts.	PIM
94-95—HC Nitra	Slovakia Jrs.	30	22	15	37	36	...	...	...	—	—	—	—	—
—HC Nitra	Slovakia	7	1	0	1	2	...	...	...	—	—	—	—	—
95-96—HC Nitra	Slovakia	35	9	7	16	36	...	...	...	—	—	—	—	—
96-97—HC Nitra	Slovakia	41	11	19	30	...	...	...	...	—	—	—	—	—
97-98—Worcester	AHL	53	9	12	21	38	...	...	...	1	0	0	0	2
—Ottawa	NHL	2	0	0	0	0	0	0	0	—	—	—	—	—
98-99—Adirondack	AHL	21	1	4	5	4	...	...	...	—	—	—	—	—
—Cincinnati	AHL	32	10	3	13	10	...	...	...	2	0	0	0	2
99-00—Grand Rapids.............	IHL	66	13	12	25	64	...	...	...	6	0	6	6	2
00-01—Grand Rapids.............	IHL	66	27	38	65	53	...	...	...	—	—	—	—	—
—Ottawa	NHL	4	2	0	2	2	2	0	0	—	—	—	—	—
01-02—Ottawa	NHL	23	1	2	3	4	0	0	0	—	—	—	—	—
—Grand Rapids.............	AHL	2	2	1	3	0	...	...	...	—	—	—	—	—
—Washington	NHL	6	0	1	1	2	0	0	0	—	—	—	—	—
—Portland	AHL	26	10	5	15	28	...	...	...	—	—	—	—	—
02-03—Portland	AHL	13	4	6	10	6	...	...	...	—	—	—	—	—
—Washington	NHL	47	8	10	18	24	6	0	0	2	0	1	1	6
NHL Totals (4 years)...........		82	11	13	24	32	8	0	0	2	0	1	1	6

CLARK, BRETT   D   AVALANCHE

PERSONAL: Born December 23, 1976, in Wapella, Sask. ... 6-1/185. ... Shoots left.
TRANSACTIONS/CAREER NOTES: Selected by Montreal Canadiens in sixth round (seventh Canadiens pick, 154th overall) of NHL entry draft (June 22, 1996). ... Suffered concussion (November 19, 1998); missed four games. ... Selected by Atlanta Thrashers in NHL expansion draft (June 25, 1999). ... Traded by Thrashers to Colorado Avalanche for G Frederic Cassivi (January 24, 2002).

		REGULAR SEASON								PLAYOFFS				
Season Team	League	Gms.	G	A	Pts.	PIM	+/-	PP	SH	Gms.	G	A	Pts.	PIM
94-95—Melville	SJHL	62	19	32	51	77	...	...	...	—	—	—	—	—
95-96—Univ. of Maine	Hockey East	39	7	31	38	22	...	...	...	—	—	—	—	—
96-97—Canadian nat'l team	Int'l	60	12	20	32	87	...	...	...	—	—	—	—	—
97-98—Montreal	NHL	41	1	0	1	20	-3	0	0	—	—	—	—	—
—Fredericton	AHL	20	0	6	6	6	...	...	...	4	0	1	1	17
98-99—Montreal	NHL	61	2	2	4	16	-3	0	0	—	—	—	—	—
—Fredericton	AHL	3	1	0	1	0	...	...	...	—	—	—	—	—
99-00—Orlando......................	IHL	63	9	17	26	31	...	...	...	6	0	1	1	0
—Atlanta	NHL	14	0	1	1	4	-12	0	0	—	—	—	—	—
00-01—Atlanta	NHL	28	1	2	3	14	-12	0	0	—	—	—	—	—
—Orlando.....................	IHL	43	2	9	11	32	...	...	...	15	1	6	7	2
01-02—Chicago.....................	AHL	42	3	17	20	18	...	...	...	—	—	—	—	—
—Atlanta	NHL	2	0	0	0	0	-3	0	0	—	—	—	—	—
—Hershey	AHL	32	7	9	16	12	...	...	...	8	0	2	2	6
02-03—Hershey	AHL	80	8	27	35	26	...	...	...	—	—	—	—	—
NHL Totals (5 years)...........		146	4	5	9	54	-33	0	0					

CLARK, CHRIS   RW   FLAMES

PERSONAL: Born March 8, 1976, in South Windsor, Conn. ... 6-0/200. ... Shoots right.
TRANSACTIONS/CAREER NOTES: Selected by Calgary Flames in third round (third Flames pick, 77th overall) of NHL entry draft (June 29, 1994). ... Injured shoulder (January 15, 2000); missed one game. ... Suffered injury (March 31, 2000); missed remainder of season. ... Injured hip (November 7, 2001); missed two games. ... Suffered injury (December 6, 2001); missed one game. ... Bruised thigh (December 19, 2001); missed two games. ... Injured knee (January 19, 2002); missed 10 games. ... Re-signed by Calgary (May 28, 2003).

Season Team	League	Gms.	G	A	Pts.	PIM	+/-	PP	SH	Gms.	G	A	Pts.	PIM
93-94—Springfield Jr. B	NEJHL	35	31	26	57	185	...	...	...	—	—	—	—	—
94-95—Clarkson	ECAC	32	12	11	23	92	...	...	...	—	—	—	—	—
95-96—Clarkson	ECAC	38	10	8	18	108	...	...	...	—	—	—	—	—
96-97—Clarkson	ECAC	37	23	25	48	86	...	...	...	—	—	—	—	—
97-98—Clarkson	ECAC	35	18	21	39	*106	...	...	...	—	—	—	—	—
98-99—Saint John	AHL	73	13	27	40	123	...	...	...	7	2	4	6	15
99-00—Saint John	AHL	48	16	17	33	134	...	...	...	—	—	—	—	—
—Calgary	NHL	22	0	1	1	14	-3	0	0	—	—	—	—	—
00-01—Saint John	AHL	48	18	17	35	131	...	...	...	18	4	10	14	49
—Calgary	NHL	29	5	1	6	38	0	1	0	—	—	—	—	—
01-02—Calgary	NHL	64	10	7	17	79	-12	2	1	—	—	—	—	—
02-03—Calgary	NHL	81	10	12	22	126	-11	2	0	—	—	—	—	—
NHL Totals (4 years)		196	25	21	46	257	-26	5	1					

CLARKE, DALE — D

PERSONAL: Born March 23, 1978, in Belleville, Ont. ... 6-1/193. ... Shoots right.
TRANSACTIONS/CAREER NOTES: Signed as non-drafted free agent by St. Louis Blues (May 15, 2000). ... Traded by Blues to Colorado Avalanche for conditional draft pick (December 5, 2002).

Season Team	League	Gms.	G	A	Pts.	PIM	+/-	PP	SH	Gms.	G	A	Pts.	PIM
96-97—St. Lawrence	WCHA	34	1	6	7	20	...	...	...	—	—	—	—	—
97-98—St. Lawrence	WCHA	33	1	6	7	66	...	...	...	—	—	—	—	—
98-99—St. Lawrence	WCHA	39	3	13	16	44	...	...	...	—	—	—	—	—
99-00—St. Lawrence	WCHA	36	6	17	23	24	...	...	...	—	—	—	—	—
—Worcester	AHL	2	0	0	0	0	...	...	...	—	—	—	—	—
00-01—Worcester	AHL	67	7	25	32	26	...	...	...	1	0	0	0	0
—Peoria	ECHL	2	1	0	1	0	...	...	...	—	—	—	—	—
—St. Louis	NHL	3	0	0	0	0	1	0	0	—	—	—	—	—
01-02—Worcester	AHL	72	2	10	12	32	...	...	...	—	—	—	—	—
02-03—Hershey	AHL	33	1	5	6	12	...	...	...	—	—	—	—	—
—Cincinnati	AHL	13	1	6	7	6	...	...	...	—	—	—	—	—
NHL Totals (1 year)		3	0	0	0	0	1	0	0					

CLASSEN, GREG — C — PREDATORS

PERSONAL: Born August 24, 1977, in Aylshem, Sask. ... 6-1/200. ... Shoots left.
TRANSACTIONS/CAREER NOTES: Signed as non-drafted free agent by Nashville Predators (March 27, 2000). ... Sprained knee (November 28, 2000); missed 14 games. ... Suffered concussion (February 21, 2001); missed two games. ... Suffered concussion (March 9, 2002); missed nine games.

Season Team	League	Gms.	G	A	Pts.	PIM	+/-	PP	SH	Gms.	G	A	Pts.	PIM
98-99—Merrimack College	Hockey East	36	14	11	25	28	...	...	...	—	—	—	—	—
99-00—Merrimack College	Hockey East	36	14	16	30	16	...	...	...	—	—	—	—	—
—Milwaukee	IHL	9	1	0	1	2	...	...	...	2	0	0	0	2
00-01—Nashville	NHL	27	2	4	6	14	-4	1	0	—	—	—	—	—
—Milwaukee	IHL	23	5	10	15	31	...	...	...	5	0	0	0	0
01-02—Milwaukee	AHL	8	2	4	6	12	...	...	...	—	—	—	—	—
—Nashville	NHL	55	5	6	11	30	1	0	1	—	—	—	—	—
02-03—Milwaukee	AHL	72	20	28	48	61	...	...	...	—	—	—	—	—
—Nashville	NHL	8	0	0	0	4	-3	0	0	—	—	—	—	—
NHL Totals (3 years)		90	7	10	17	48	-6	1	1					

CLEARY, DAN — RW — COYOTES

PERSONAL: Born December 18, 1978, in Carbonear, Nfld. ... 6-0/203. ... Shoots left. ... Full Name: Daniel Cleary.
TRANSACTIONS/CAREER NOTES: Selected by Chicago Blackhawks in first round (first Blackhawks pick, 13th overall) of NHL entry draft (June 21, 1997). ... Traded by Blackhawks with C Chad Kilger, LW Ethan Moreau and D Christian Laflamme to Edmonton Oilers for D Boris Mironov, LW Dean McAmmond and D Jonas Elofsson (March 20, 1999). ... Underwent surgery on left knee (December 8, 2001); missed 14 games. ... Signed by Phoenix Coyotes (July 15, 2003).

Season Team	League	Gms.	G	A	Pts.	PIM	+/-	PP	SH	Gms.	G	A	Pts.	PIM
93-94—Kingston	Tier II Jr. A	41	18	28	46	33	...	...	...	—	—	—	—	—
94-95—Belleville	OHL	62	26	55	81	62	...	...	...	16	7	10	17	23
95-96—Belleville	OHL	64	53	62	115	74	...	...	...	14	10	17	27	40
96-97—Belleville	OHL	64	32	48	80	88	...	...	...	6	3	4	7	6
97-98—Chicago	NHL	6	0	0	0	0	-2	0	0	—	—	—	—	—
—Indianapolis	IHL	4	2	1	3	6	...	...	...	—	—	—	—	—
—Belleville	OHL	30	16	31	47	14	...	...	...	10	6	*17	*23	10
98-99—Chicago	NHL	35	4	5	9	24	-1	0	0	—	—	—	—	—
—Portland	AHL	30	9	17	26	74	...	...	...	—	—	—	—	—
—Hamilton	AHL	9	0	1	1	7	...	...	...	3	0	0	0	0
99-00—Hamilton	AHL	58	22	52	74	108	...	...	...	5	2	3	5	18
—Edmonton	NHL	17	3	2	5	8	-1	0	0	4	0	1	1	2
00-01—Edmonton	NHL	81	14	21	35	37	5	2	0	6	1	1	2	8
01-02—Edmonton	NHL	65	10	19	29	51	-1	2	1	—	—	—	—	—
02-03—Edmonton	NHL	57	4	13	17	31	5	0	0	—	—	—	—	—
NHL Totals (6 years)		261	35	60	95	151	5	4	1	10	1	2	3	10

CLEMMENSEN, SCOTT — G — DEVILS

PERSONAL: Born July 23, 1977, in Des Moines, Iowa. ... 6-2/185. ... Catches left.
COLLEGE: Boston College.
TRANSACTIONS/CAREER NOTES: Selected by New Jersey Devils in eighth round (seventh Devils pick, 215th overall) of NHL entry draft (June 21, 1997).

Season Team	League			REGULAR SEASON										PLAYOFFS				
		Gms.	Min	W	L	T	GA	SO	Avg.	SV%	Gms.	Min.	W	L	GA	SO	Avg.	SV%
96-97—Des Moines	USHL	36	2042	...	...	...	111	1	3.26	—	—	—	—	—	—	—	—	—
97-98—Boston College	Hockey East	37	2205	24	9	†4	102	*4	2.78	—	—	—	—	—	—	—	—	—
98-99—Boston College	Hockey East	*42	*2507	26	12	*4	*120	1	2.87	—	—	—	—	—	—	—	—	—
99-00—Boston College	Hockey East	29	1610	19	7	0	59	†3	2.20	—	—	—	—	—	—	—	—	—
00-01—Boston College	Hockey East	*39	*2312	*30	7	2	*82	3	2.13	—	—	—	—	—	—	—	—	—
01-02—New Jersey	NHL	2	20	0	0	0	1	0	3.00	.800	—	—	—	—	—	—	—	—
—Albany	AHL	29	1676	5	19	4	92	0	3.29	—	—	—	—	—	—	—	—	—
02-03—Albany	AHL	47	2694	12	24	8	119	1	2.65	—	—	—	—	—	—	—	—	—
NHL Totals (1 year)		2	20	0	0	0	1	0	3.00	.800								

CLOUTHIER, BRETT — LW — DEVILS

PERSONAL: Born June 9, 1981, in Ottawa. ... 6-4/220. ... Shoots left.
TRANSACTIONS/CAREER NOTES: Selected by New Jersey Devils in second round (third Devils pick, 50th overall) of NHL entry draft (June 26, 1999).

Season Team	League		REGULAR SEASON							PLAYOFFS				
		Gms.	G	A	Pts.	PIM	+/-	PP	SH	Gms.	G	A	Pts.	PIM
97-98—Kanata	OJHL	50	12	10	22	135	...	...	...	—	—	—	—	—
98-99—Kingston	OHL	64	8	14	22	227	...	...	...	5	1	1	2	4
99-00—Kingston	OHL	65	13	26	39	*266	...	...	...	5	2	0	2	17
00-01—Kingston	OHL	68	28	29	57	165	...	...	...	4	1	0	1	10
01-02—Albany	AHL	62	4	0	4	109	...	...	...	—	—	—	—	—
02-03—Albany	AHL	74	6	7	13	220	...	...	...	—	—	—	—	—

CLOUTIER, DAN — G — CANUCKS

PERSONAL: Born April 22, 1976, in Mont-Laurier, Que. ... 6-1/195. ... Catches left. ... Brother of Sylvain Cloutier, center, New Jersey Devils organization. ... Name pronounced KLOO-tee-yay.
TRANSACTIONS/CAREER NOTES: Selected by New York Rangers in first round (first Rangers pick, 26th overall) of NHL entry draft (June 28, 1994). ... Traded by Rangers with LW Niklas Sundstrom and first-(RW Nikita Alexeev) and third-round (traded to San Jose) picks in 2000 draft to Tampa Bay Lightning for first-round pick (RW Pavel Brendl) in 1999 draft (June 26, 1999). ... Strained groin (November 18, 1999); missed two games. ... Suspended four games by NHL for kicking incident (January 14, 2000). ... Strained groin (February 21, 2000); missed three games. ... Injured neck (March 14, 2000); missed four games. ... Strained medial collateral ligament in knee (March 28, 2000); missed five games. ... Strained biceps (October 22, 2000); missed nine games. ... Suffered from the flu (December 8, 2000); missed one game. ... Traded by Lightning to Vancouver Canucks for D Adrian Aucoin and second-round pick (C/LW Alexander Polushin) in 2001 draft (February 7, 2001). ... Injured ankle (January 23, 2002); missed nine games. ... Re-signed by Canucks (July 15, 2003).

Season Team	League			REGULAR SEASON										PLAYOFFS				
		Gms.	Min	W	L	T	GA	SO	Avg.	SV%	Gms.	Min.	W	L	GA	SO	Avg.	SV%
91-92—St. Thomas	Jr. B	14	823	...	...	...	80	...	5.83	—	—	—	—	—	—	—	—	—
92-93—Sault Ste. Marie	OHL	12	572	4	6	0	44	0	4.62	—	4	231	1	2	12	0	3.12	—
93-94—Sault Ste. Marie	OHL	55	2934	28	14	6	174	†2	3.56	—	14	833	†10	4	52	0	3.75	—
94-95—Sault Ste. Marie	OHL	45	2517	15	25	2	184	1	4.39	—	—	—	—	—	—	—	—	—
95-96—Sault Ste. Marie	OHL	13	641	9	3	0	43	0	4.02	—	—	—	—	—	—	—	—	—
—Guelph	OHL	17	1004	12	2	2	35	2	2.09	—	16	993	11	5	52	*2	3.14	—
96-97—Binghamton	AHL	60	3367	23	†28	8	199	3	3.55	—	4	236	1	3	13	0	3.31	—
97-98—Hartford	AHL	24	1417	12	8	3	62	0	2.63	—	8	479	5	3	24	0	3.01	—
—New York Rangers	NHL	12	551	4	5	1	23	0	2.50	.907	—	—	—	—	—	—	—	—
98-99—New York Rangers	NHL	22	1097	6	8	3	49	0	2.68	.914	—	—	—	—	—	—	—	—
99-00—Tampa Bay	NHL	52	2492	9	30	3	145	0	3.49	.885	—	—	—	—	—	—	—	—
00-01—Detroit	IHL	1	59	0	1	‡0	3	0	3.05	—	—	—	—	—	—	—	—	—
—Tampa Bay	NHL	24	1005	3	13	3	59	1	3.52	.891	—	—	—	—	—	—	—	—
—Vancouver	NHL	16	914	4	6	5	37	0	2.43	.894	2	117	0	2	9	0	4.62	.842
01-02—Vancouver	NHL	62	3502	31	22	5	142	7	2.43	.901	6	273	2	3	16	0	3.52	.870
02-03—Vancouver	NHL	57	3376	33	16	7	136	2	2.42	.908	14	833	7	7	*45	0	3.24	.868
NHL Totals (6 years)		245	12937	90	100	27	591	10	2.74	.900	22	1223	9	12	70	0	3.43	.866

CLOUTIER, FREDERIC — G — WILD

PERSONAL: Born May 14, 1981, in St. Honore, Que. ... 6-0/165. ... Catches right.
TRANSACTIONS/CAREER NOTES: Signed as non-drafted free agent by Minnesota Wild (November 23, 2001).

Season Team	League			REGULAR SEASON										PLAYOFFS				
		Gms.	Min	W	L	T	GA	SO	Avg.	SV%	Gms.	Min.	W	L	GA	SO	Avg.	SV%
99-00—Acadie-Bathurst	QMJHL	58	3262	16	†34	*6	208	3	3.83	—	1	60	0	1	5	0	5.00	—
00-01—Shawinigan	QMJHL	58	3270	*42	8	2	136	*6	2.50	—	9	467	5	2	24	1	3.08	—
01-02—Louisiana	ECHL	36	2154	28	5	2	66	*7	*1.84	—	1	115	0	1	5	0	2.61	—
02-03—Houston	AHL	12	586	4	3	2	24	0	2.46	—	—	—	—	—	—	—	—	—
—Louisiana	ECHL	26	1577	16	6	4	80	1	3.04	—	—	—	—	—	—	—	—	—

CLYMER, BEN   RW   LIGHTNING

PERSONAL: Born April 11, 1978, in Edina, Minn. ... 6-1/198. ... Shoots right.
TRANSACTIONS/CAREER NOTES: Selected by Boston Bruins in second round (third Bruins pick, 27th overall) of NHL entry draft (June 21, 1997). ... Signed as free agent by Tampa Bay Lightning (October 2, 1999). ... Re-signed by Lightning (July 22, 2003).

Season Team	League	REGULAR SEASON								PLAYOFFS				
		Gms.	G	A	Pts.	PIM	+/-	PP	SH	Gms.	G	A	Pts.	PIM
93-94—Thomas Jefferson......	Minn. H.S.	23	3	7	10	6	...	...	...	—	—	—	—	—
94-95—Thomas Jefferson......	Minn. H.S.	28	6	20	26	26	...	...	...	—	—	—	—	—
95-96—Thomas Jefferson......	Minn. H.S.	19	12	28	40	38	...	...	...	—	—	—	—	—
96-97—Univ. of Minnesota.....	WCHA	29	7	13	20	64	...	...	...	—	—	—	—	—
97-98—Univ. of Minnesota.....	WCHA	1	0	0	0	2	...	...	...	—	—	—	—	—
98-99—Seattle.....................	WHL	70	12	44	56	93	...	...	...	11	1	5	6	12
99-00—Detroit......................	IHL	19	1	9	10	30	...	...	...	—	—	—	—	—
—Tampa Bay	NHL	60	2	6	8	87	-26	2	0	—	—	—	—	—
00-01—Detroit......................	IHL	53	5	8	13	88	...	...	...	—	—	—	—	—
—Tampa Bay	NHL	23	5	1	6	21	-7	3	0	—	—	—	—	—
01-02—Tampa Bay	NHL	81	14	20	34	36	-10	4	0	—	—	—	—	—
02-03—Tampa Bay	NHL	65	6	12	18	57	-2	1	0	11	0	2	2	6
NHL Totals (4 years)...........		**229**	**27**	**39**	**66**	**201**	**-45**	**10**	**0**	**11**	**0**	**2**	**2**	**6**

COLAIACOVO, CARLO   D   MAPLE LEAFS

PERSONAL: Born January 27, 1983, in Toronto ... 6-1/188. ... Shoots left. ... Name pronounced KOH-lee-ah-kovo.
TRANSACTIONS/CAREER NOTES: Selected by Toronto Maple Leafs in first round (first Maple Leafs pick, 17th overall) of NHL entry draft (June 23, 2001).

Season Team	League	REGULAR SEASON								PLAYOFFS				
		Gms.	G	A	Pts.	PIM	+/-	PP	SH	Gms.	G	A	Pts.	PIM
99-00—Erie	OHL	52	4	18	22	12	...	...	...	13	2	4	6	9
00-01—Erie	OHL	62	12	27	39	59	...	...	...	14	4	7	11	16
01-02—Erie	OHL	60	13	27	40	49	...	...	...	21	7	10	17	20
02-03—Toronto	NHL	2	0	1	1	0	0	0	0	—	—	—	—	—
—Erie	OHL	35	14	21	35	12	...	...	...	—	—	—	—	—
NHL Totals (1 year).............		**2**	**0**	**1**	**1**	**0**	**0**	**0**	**0**					

COLE, ERIK   LW   HURRICANES

PERSONAL: Born November 6, 1978, in Oswego, N.Y. ... 6-2/200. ... Shoots left.
TRANSACTIONS/CAREER NOTES: Selected by Carolina Hurricanes in third round (third Hurricanes pick, 71st overall) of NHL entry draft (June 27, 1998). ... Suffered from the flu (November 8, 2001); missed one game.
STATISTICAL PLATEAUS: Three-goal games: 2001-02 (1), 2002-03 (1). Total: 2.

Season Team	League	REGULAR SEASON								PLAYOFFS				
		Gms.	G	A	Pts.	PIM	+/-	PP	SH	Gms.	G	A	Pts.	PIM
96-97—Des Moines.................	USHL	48	30	34	64	185	...	...	...	—	—	—	—	—
97-98—Clarkson	ECAC	34	11	20	31	55	...	...	...	—	—	—	—	—
98-99—Clarkson	ECAC	36	†22	20	42	50	...	...	...	—	—	—	—	—
99-00—Clarkson	ECAC	33	19	11	30	46	...	...	...	—	—	—	—	—
—Cincinnati.....................	IHL	9	4	3	7	2	...	...	...	7	1	1	2	2
00-01—Cincinnati.....................	IHL	69	23	20	43	28	...	...	...	5	1	0	1	2
01-02—Carolina	NHL	81	16	24	40	107	-10	3	0	23	6	3	9	30
02-03—Carolina	NHL	53	14	13	27	72	1	6	2	—	—	—	—	—
NHL Totals (2 years)...........		**134**	**30**	**37**	**67**	**107**	**-9**	**9**	**2**	**23**	**6**	**3**	**9**	**30**

COLLYMORE, SHAWN   RW   RANGERS

PERSONAL: Born May 2, 1983, in Lasalle, Que. ... 5-11/180. ... Shoots right.
TRANSACTIONS/CAREER NOTES: Selected by New York Rangers in fifth round (fifth Rangers pick, 139th overall) of NHL entry draft (June 23, 2001).

Season Team	League	REGULAR SEASON								PLAYOFFS				
		Gms.	G	A	Pts.	PIM	+/-	PP	SH	Gms.	G	A	Pts.	PIM
99-00—Quebec	QMJHL	64	8	16	24	22	...	...	...	11	0	2	2	0
00-01—Quebec	QMJHL	71	24	43	67	32	...	...	...	4	0	3	3	0
01-02—Quebec	QMJHL	52	23	34	57	37	...	...	...	9	2	4	6	0
02-03—Val-d'Or	QMJHL	34	18	16	34	34	...	...	...	—	—	—	—	—
—Quebec	QMJHL	35	15	16	31	11	...	...	...	—	—	—	—	—

COMMODORE, MIKE   D   FLAMES

PERSONAL: Born November 7, 1979, in Fort Sask., Alta. ... 6-4/230. ... Shoots right.
TRANSACTIONS/CAREER NOTES: Selected by New Jersey Devils in second round (second Devils pick, 42nd overall) of NHL entry draft (June 26, 1999). ... Suffered from the flu (March 20, 2002); missed two games. ... Traded by Devils with RW Petr Sykora, C Igor Pohanka and G J.F. Damphousse to Mighty Ducks of Anaheim for D Oleg Tverdovsky, LW Jeff Friesen and RW Maxin Balmochnykh (July 7, 2002). ... Traded by Mighty Ducks with G J.F. Damphousse to Calgary Flames for C Rob Niedermayer (March 11, 2003).

C

Season Team	League	Gms.	G	A	Pts.	PIM	+/-	PP	SH	Gms.	G	A	Pts.	PIM
96-97—Fort Saskatchewan	Tier II Jr. A	51	3	8	11	244	...	...	...	—	—	—	—	—
97-98—Univ. of North Dakota .	WCHA	29	0	5	5	74	...	...	...	—	—	—	—	—
98-99—Univ. of North Dakota .	WCHA	39	5	8	13	*154	...	...	...	—	—	—	—	—
99-00—Univ. of North Dakota .	WCHA	38	5	7	12	*154	...	...	...	—	—	—	—	—
00-01—Albany.......................	AHL	41	2	5	7	59	...	...	...	—	—	—	—	—
—New Jersey.................	NHL	20	1	4	5	14	5	0	0	—	—	—	—	—
01-02—Albany.......................	AHL	14	0	3	3	31	...	...	...	—	—	—	—	—
—New Jersey.................	NHL	37	0	1	1	30	-12	0	0	—	—	—	—	—
02-03—Cincinnati...................	AHL	61	2	9	11	210	...	...	...	—	—	—	—	—
—Calgary	NHL	6	0	1	1	19	2	0	0	—	—	—	—	—
—Saint John	AHL	7	0	3	3	18	...	...	...	—	—	—	—	—
NHL Totals (3 years)...........		63	1	6	7	63	-5	0	0					

COMRIE, MIKE — C — OILERS

PERSONAL: Born September 11, 1980, in Edmonton ... 5-9/175. ... Shoots left. ... Brother of Paul Comrie, center, Edmonton Oilers organization.
TRANSACTIONS/CAREER NOTES: Selected by Edmonton Oilers in third round (fifth Oilers pick, 91st overall) of NHL entry draft (June 26, 1999).

		REGULAR SEASON								PLAYOFFS				
Season Team	League	Gms.	G	A	Pts.	PIM	+/-	PP	SH	Gms.	G	A	Pts.	PIM
96-97—St. Albert	Jr. A	63	37	41	78	44	...	...	...	—	—	—	—	—
97-98—St. Albert	Jr. A	58	60	78	138	134	...	...	...	—	—	—	—	—
98-99—Univ. of Michigan........	CCHA	42	19	25	44	38	...	...	...	—	—	—	—	—
99-00—Univ. of Michigan........	CCHA	38	21	34	55	93	...	...	...	—	—	—	—	—
00-01—Kootenay	WHL	37	39	40	79	79	...	...	...	—	—	—	—	—
—Edmonton.................	NHL	41	8	14	22	14	6	3	0	6	1	2	3	0
01-02—Edmonton.................	NHL	82	33	27	60	45	16	8	0	—	—	—	—	—
02-03—Edmonton.................	NHL	69	20	31	51	90	-18	8	0	6	1	0	1	10
NHL Totals (3 years)...........		192	61	72	133	149	4	19	0	12	2	2	4	10

CONKLIN, TY — G — OILERS

PERSONAL: Born March 30, 1976, in Anchorage, Alaska. ... 6-0/180. ... Catches left.
TRANSACTIONS/CAREER NOTES: Signed as non-drafted free agent by Edmonton Oilers (April 18, 2000).

		REGULAR SEASON								PLAYOFFS							
Season Team	League	Gms.	Min	W	L	T	GA	SO	Avg.	SV%	Gms.	Min.	W	L	GA	SO	Avg.	SV%
98-99—Univ. of New Hamp......	Hockey East	22	1338	18	3	1	41	0	*1.84	—	—	—	—	—	—	—	—	—
99-00—Univ. of New Hamp......	Hockey East	*37	*2194	*22	8	*6	*91	1	2.49	—	—	—	—	—	—	—	—	—
00-01—Univ. of New Hamp......	Hockey East	34	2048	17	12	*5	70	*4	*2.05	—	—	—	—	—	—	—	—	—
01-02—Hamilton	AHL	37	2043	13	12	8	89	1	2.61	—	7	416	4	2	18	0	2.60	—
—Edmonton	NHL	4	148	2	0	0	4	0	1.62	.939	—	—	—	—	—	—	—	—
02-03—Hamilton	AHL	38	2140	19	13	3	91	1	2.55	—								
NHL Totals (1 year)...............		4	148	2	0	0	4	0	1.62	.939								

CONNOLLY, TIM — C — SABRES

PERSONAL: Born May 7, 1981, in Syracuse, N.Y. ... 6-1/186. ... Shoots right.
TRANSACTIONS/CAREER NOTES: Selected by New York Islanders in first round (first Islanders pick, fifth overall) of NHL entry draft (June 26, 1999). ... Traded by Islanders with LW Taylor Pyatt to Buffalo Sabres for C Michael Peca (June 24, 2001). ... Suspended four games by NHL for high-sticking incident (April 3, 2003).

		REGULAR SEASON								PLAYOFFS				
Season Team	League	Gms.	G	A	Pts.	PIM	+/-	PP	SH	Gms.	G	A	Pts.	PIM
96-97—Syracuse....................	Jr. A	50	42	62	104	34	...	...	...	—	—	—	—	—
97-98—Erie	OHL	59	30	32	62	32	...	...	...	7	1	6	7	6
98-99—Erie	OHL	46	34	34	68	50	...	...	...	—	—	—	—	—
99-00—New York Islanders.....	NHL	81	14	20	34	44	-25	2	1	—	—	—	—	—
00-01—New York Islanders.....	NHL	82	10	31	41	42	-14	5	0	—	—	—	—	—
01-02—Buffalo	NHL	82	10	35	45	34	4	3	0	—	—	—	—	—
02-03—Buffalo	NHL	80	12	13	25	32	-28	6	0	—	—	—	—	—
NHL Totals (4 years)...........		325	46	99	145	152	-63	16	1					

CONROY, CRAIG — C — FLAMES

PERSONAL: Born September 4, 1971, in Potsdam, N.Y. ... 6-2/197. ... Shoots right. ... Full Name: Craig Michael Conroy.
TRANSACTIONS/CAREER NOTES: Selected by Montreal Canadiens in sixth round (seventh Canadiens pick, 123rd overall) of NHL entry draft (June 16, 1990). ... Traded by Canadiens with C Pierre Turgeon and D Rory Fitzpatrick to St. Louis Blues for LW Shayne Corson, D Murray Baron and fifth-round pick (D Gennady Razin) in 1997 draft (October 29, 1996). ... Sprained ankle (March 12, 1999); missed 11 games. ... Reinjured ankle (April 7, 1999); missed two games. ... Suffered from the flu (October 2, 1999); missed one game. ... Traded by Blues with seventh-round pick (LW David Moss) in 2001 draft to Calgary Flames for LW Cory Stillman (March 13, 2001). ... Suffered injury (November 20, 2001); missed one game.
STATISTICAL PLATEAUS: Three-goal games: 1998-99 (1).

Season Team	League	REGULAR SEASON								PLAYOFFS				
		Gms.	G	A	Pts.	PIM	+/-	PP	SH	Gms.	G	A	Pts.	PIM
89-90—Northwood School......	N.Y. H.S.	31	33	43	76	...	...	...	...	—	—	—	—	—
90-91—Clarkson	ECAC	40	8	21	29	24	...	...	...	—	—	—	—	—
91-92—Clarkson	ECAC	31	19	17	36	36	...	...	...	—	—	—	—	—
92-93—Clarkson	ECAC	35	10	23	33	26	...	...	...	—	—	—	—	—
93-94—Clarkson	ECAC	34	26	40	66	66	...	...	...	—	—	—	—	—
94-95—Fredericton	AHL	55	26	18	44	29	...	...	...	11	7	3	10	6
—Montreal	NHL	6	1	0	1	0	-1	0	0	—	—	—	—	—
95-96—Fredericton	AHL	67	31	38	69	65	...	...	...	10	5	7	12	6
—Montreal	NHL	7	0	0	0	2	-4	0	0	—	—	—	—	—
96-97—Fredericton	AHL	9	10	6	16	10	...	...	...	—	—	—	—	—
—St. Louis	NHL	61	6	11	17	43	0	0	0	6	0	0	0	8
—Worcester	AHL	5	5	6	11	2	...	...	...	—	—	—	—	—
97-98—St. Louis	NHL	81	14	29	43	46	20	0	3	10	1	2	3	8
98-99—St. Louis	NHL	69	14	25	39	38	14	0	1	13	2	1	3	6
99-00—St. Louis	NHL	79	12	15	27	36	5	1	2	7	0	2	2	2
00-01—St. Louis	NHL	69	11	14	25	46	2	0	3	—	—	—	—	—
—Calgary	NHL	14	3	4	7	14	0	0	1	—	—	—	—	—
01-02—Calgary	NHL	81	27	48	75	32	24	7	2	—	—	—	—	—
02-03—Calgary	NHL	79	22	37	59	36	-4	5	0	—	—	—	—	—
NHL Totals (9 years)...........		546	110	183	293	293	56	13	12	36	3	5	8	24

COOKE, MATT   C   CANUCKS   C

PERSONAL: Born September 7, 1978, in Belleville, Ont. ... 5-11/205. ... Shoots left.
TRANSACTIONS/CAREER NOTES: Selected by Vancouver Canucks in sixth round (eighth Canucks pick, 144th overall) of NHL entry draft (June 21, 1997). ... Suspended two games by AHL for attempting to injure an opponent (February 24, 1999). ... Injured knee (March 2, 2001); missed one game.

Season Team	League	REGULAR SEASON								PLAYOFFS				
		Gms.	G	A	Pts.	PIM	+/-	PP	SH	Gms.	G	A	Pts.	PIM
95-96—Windsor	OHL	61	8	11	19	102	...	...	...	7	1	3	4	6
96-97—Windsor	OHL	65	45	50	95	146	...	...	...	5	5	5	10	4
97-98—Windsor	OHL	23	14	19	33	50	...	...	...	—	—	—	—	—
—Kingston	OHL	25	8	13	21	49	...	...	...	12	8	8	16	20
98-99—Vancouver.................	NHL	30	0	2	2	27	-12	0	0	—	—	—	—	—
—Syracuse	AHL	37	15	18	33	119	...	...	...	—	—	—	—	—
99-00—Syracuse	AHL	18	5	8	13	27	...	...	...	—	—	—	—	—
—Vancouver.................	NHL	51	5	7	12	39	3	0	1	—	—	—	—	—
00-01—Vancouver.................	NHL	81	14	13	27	94	5	0	2	4	0	0	0	4
01-02—Vancouver.................	NHL	82	13	20	33	111	4	1	0	6	3	2	5	0
02-03—Vancouver.................	NHL	82	15	27	42	82	21	1	4	14	2	1	3	12
NHL Totals (5 years)...........		326	47	69	116	353	21	2	7	24	5	3	8	16

CORAZZINI, CARL   LW   BRUINS

PERSONAL: Born April 21, 1979, in Framingham, Mass. ... 5-9/170. ... Shoots left.
TRANSACTIONS/CAREER NOTES: Signed as non-drafted free agent by Boston Bruins (August 8, 2001).

Season Team	League	REGULAR SEASON								PLAYOFFS				
		Gms.	G	A	Pts.	PIM	+/-	PP	SH	Gms.	G	A	Pts.	PIM
01-02—Providence.................	AHL	61	7	8	15	10	...	...	...	—	—	—	—	—
02-03—Providence.................	AHL	33	7	6	13	4	...	...	...	—	—	—	—	—
—Atlantic City	ECHL	27	13	8	21	14	...	...	...	—	—	—	—	—

CORBEIL, NICOLAS   C   MAPLE LEAFS

PERSONAL: Born March 30, 1983, in Laval, Que. ... 5-10/177. ... Shoots right.
TRANSACTIONS/CAREER NOTES: Selected by Toronto Maple Leafs in third round (fifth Maple Leafs pick, 88th overall) of NHL entry draft (June 23, 2001).

Season Team	League	REGULAR SEASON								PLAYOFFS				
		Gms.	G	A	Pts.	PIM	+/-	PP	SH	Gms.	G	A	Pts.	PIM
99-00—Sherbrooke.................	QMJHL	64	9	12	21	28	...	...	...	—	—	—	—	—
00-01—Sherbrooke.................	QMJHL	68	33	51	84	159	...	...	...	3	1	3	4	4
01-02—Sherbrooke.................	QMJHL	62	41	52	93	99	...	...	...	—	—	—	—	—
02-03—Sherbrooke.................	QMJHL	68	31	63	94	85	...	...	...	—	—	—	—	—

CORRINET, CHRIS   RW   CAPITALS

PERSONAL: Born October 29, 1978, in Derby, Conn. ... 6-3/220. ... Shoots right.
TRANSACTIONS/CAREER NOTES: Selected by Washington Capitals in fourth round (fourth Capitals pick, 107th overall) of NHL entry draft (June 27, 1998).

Season Team	League	REGULAR SEASON								PLAYOFFS				
		Gms.	G	A	Pts.	PIM	+/-	PP	SH	Gms.	G	A	Pts.	PIM
96-97—Deerfield Academy	USHS (East)	16	6	15	21	10	...	...	...	—	—	—	—	—
97-98—Princeton University	ECAC	31	3	6	9	22	...	...	...	—	—	—	—	—
98-99—Princeton University	ECAC	32	10	6	16	38	...	...	...	—	—	—	—	—
99-00—Princeton University	ECAC	30	10	14	24	41	...	...	...	—	—	—	—	—
00-01—Princeton University	ECAC	31	13	12	25	30	...	...	...	—	—	—	—	—
—Portland	AHL	6	0	1	1	4	...	...	...	2	1	0	1	0
01-02—Portland	AHL	51	15	18	33	64	...	...	...	—	—	—	—	—
—Washington	NHL	8	0	1	1	6	-4	0	0	—	—	—	—	—
02-03—Portland	AHL	33	0	3	3	23	...	...	...	—	—	—	—	—
—Worcester	AHL	8	6	12	18	27	...	...	...	—	—	—	—	—
—Philadelphia	AHL	1	0	0	0	0	...	...	...	—	—	—	—	—
NHL Totals (1 year)		8	0	1	1	6	-4	0	0					

CORSO, DANIEL   C

PERSONAL: Born April 3, 1978, in Montreal ... 5-10/191. ... Shoots left.

TRANSACTIONS/CAREER NOTES: Selected by St. Louis Blues in seventh round (fifth Blues pick, 169th overall) of NHL entry draft (June 22, 1996). ... Suffered from the flu (November 29, 2001); missed one game. ... Dislocated shoulder (March 2, 2002); missed five games.

Season Team	League	REGULAR SEASON								PLAYOFFS				
		Gms.	G	A	Pts.	PIM	+/-	PP	SH	Gms.	G	A	Pts.	PIM
94-95—Victoriaville	QMJHL	65	27	26	53	6	...	...	...	4	2	5	7	2
95-96—Victoriaville	QMJHL	65	49	65	114	77	...	...	...	12	6	7	13	4
96-97—Victoriaville	QMJHL	54	51	68	119	50	...	...	...	—	—	—	—	—
97-98—Victoriaville	QMJHL	35	24	51	75	20	...	...	...	3	1	1	2	2
98-99—Worcester	AHL	63	14	14	28	26	...	...	...	—	—	—	—	—
99-00—Worcester	AHL	71	21	34	55	19	...	...	...	9	2	3	5	10
00-01—Worcester	AHL	52	19	37	56	47	...	...	...	—	—	—	—	—
—St. Louis	NHL	28	10	3	13	14	0	5	0	12	0	1	1	0
01-02—St. Louis	NHL	41	4	7	11	6	3	1	0	2	0	0	0	0
02-03—Worcester	AHL	1	0	0	0	0	...	...	...	—	—	—	—	—
—St. Louis	NHL	1	0	0	0	0	-1	0	0	—	—	—	—	—
NHL Totals (3 years)		70	14	10	24	20	2	6	0	14	0	1	1	0

CORSON, SHAYNE   LW   MAPLE LEAFS

PERSONAL: Born August 13, 1966, in Barrie, Ont. ... 6-1/207. ... Shoots left.

TRANSACTIONS/CAREER NOTES: Selected by Montreal Canadiens in first round (second Canadiens pick, eighth overall) of NHL entry draft (June 9, 1984). ... Fractured jaw (January 24, 1987). ... Strained ligament in right knee (September 1987). ... Injured groin (March 1988). ... Injured knee (April 1988). ... Injured knee (April 1989). ... Bruised left shoulder (October 29, 1989). ... Fractured toe on right foot (December 1989). ... Suffered hip pointer (November 10, 1990); missed seven games. ... Pulled groin (February 11, 1991). ... Traded by Canadiens with LW Vladimir Vujtek and C Brent Gilchrist to Edmonton Oilers for LW Vincent Damphousse and fourth-round pick (D Adam Wiesel) in 1993 draft (August 27, 1992). ... Fractured fibula (February 18, 1994); missed 12 games. ... Injured leg (March 23, 1994); missed remainder of season. ... Signed by St. Louis Blues to an offer sheet (July 28, 1995); Oilers received Blues first-round picks in 1996 and 1997 drafts as compensation; Oilers then traded picks to Blues for rights to G Curtis Joseph and RW Michael Grier (August 4, 1995). ... Fractured jaw (March 26, 1996); missed five games. ... Traded by Blues with D Murray Baron and fifth-round pick (D Gennady Razin) in 1997 draft to Canadiens for C Pierre Turgeon, C Craig Conroy and D Rory Fitzpatrick (October 29, 1996). ... Injured knee (November 25, 1996) and underwent surgery; missed 10 games. ... Sprained ankle (December 26, 1996); missed 10 games. ... Strained hip flexor (February 3, 1997); missed five games. ... Strained hip flexor (January 21, 1998); missed six games. ... Strained abdominal muscle and groin (February 25, 1998); missed 13 games. ... Suffered charley horse (April 18, 1998); missed one game. ... Injured ribs (October 16, 1998); missed six games. ... Suffered nerve irritation in neck (November 19, 1998); missed four games. ... Sprained ankle (March 8, 1999); missed three games. ... Suspended six games by NHL for high-sticking incident (April 1, 1999). ... Suffered colitis (October 6, 1999); missed 10 games. ... Suffered eye injury (March 16, 2000); missed two games. ... Signed as free agent by Toronto Maple Leafs (July 4, 2000). ... Suffered injury (February 15, 2000); missed one game. ... Suffered injury (March 21, 2001); missed two games. ... Sprained shoulder (December 29, 2001); missed five games. ... Injured knee (April 1, 2002); missed three games. ... Suspended one playoff game by NHL for kicking incident (April 29, 2002).

STATISTICAL PLATEAUS: Three-goal games: 1988-89 (2), 1993-94 (1). Total: 3.

Season Team	League	REGULAR SEASON								PLAYOFFS				
		Gms.	G	A	Pts.	PIM	+/-	PP	SH	Gms.	G	A	Pts.	PIM
82-83—Barrie	COJHL	23	13	29	42	87	...	...	...	—	—	—	—	—
83-84—Brantford	OHL	66	25	46	71	165	...	...	...	6	4	1	5	26
84-85—Hamilton	OHL	54	27	63	90	154	...	...	...	11	3	7	10	19
85-86—Hamilton	OHL	47	41	57	98	153	...	...	...	—	—	—	—	—
—Montreal	NHL	3	0	0	0	2	-3	0	0	—	—	—	—	—
86-87—Montreal	NHL	55	12	11	23	144	10	0	1	17	6	5	11	30
87-88—Montreal	NHL	71	12	27	39	152	22	2	0	3	1	0	1	12
88-89—Montreal	NHL	80	26	24	50	193	-1	10	0	21	4	5	9	65
89-90—Montreal	NHL	76	31	44	75	144	33	7	0	11	2	8	10	20
90-91—Montreal	NHL	71	23	24	47	138	9	7	0	13	9	6	15	36
91-92—Montreal	NHL	64	17	36	53	118	15	3	0	10	2	5	7	15
92-93—Edmonton	NHL	80	16	31	47	209	-19	9	2	—	—	—	—	—
93-94—Edmonton	NHL	64	25	29	54	118	-8	11	0	—	—	—	—	—
94-95—Edmonton	NHL	48	12	24	36	86	-17	2	0	—	—	—	—	—
95-96—St. Louis	NHL	77	18	28	46	192	3	13	0	13	8	6	14	22
96-97—St. Louis	NHL	11	2	1	3	24	-4	1	0	—	—	—	—	—
—Montreal	NHL	47	6	15	21	80	-5	2	0	5	1	0	1	4
97-98—Montreal	NHL	62	21	34	55	108	2	14	1	10	3	6	9	26
—Can. Olympic team	Int'l	6	1	1	2	2	...	...	...	—	—	—	—	—
98-99—Montreal	NHL	63	12	20	32	147	-10	7	0	—	—	—	—	—
99-00—Montreal	NHL	70	8	20	28	115	-2	2	0	—	—	—	—	—
00-01—Toronto	NHL	77	8	18	26	189	1	0	0	11	1	1	2	14
01-02—Toronto	NHL	74	12	21	33	120	11	0	1	19	1	6	7	33
02-03—Toronto	NHL	46	7	8	15	49	-5	0	0	2	0	0	0	2
NHL Totals (18 years)		1139	268	415	683	2328	32	90	5	135	38	48	86	279

CORVO, JOE   D   KINGS

PERSONAL: Born June 20, 1977, in Oak Park, Ill. ... 6-1/205. ... Shoots right. ... Full Name: Joseph Corvo.
TRANSACTIONS/CAREER NOTES: Selected by Los Angeles Kings in fourth round (fourth Kings pick, 83rd overall) of NHL entry draft (June 21, 1997). ... Missed entire 1999-2000 season due to contract dispute.

Season Team	League	Gms.	G	A	Pts.	PIM	+/-	PP	SH	Gms.	G	A	Pts.	PIM
							REGULAR SEASON					PLAYOFFS		
95-96—Western Michigan	CCHA	41	5	25	30	38	...	...	...	—	—	—	—	—
96-97—Western Michigan	CCHA	32	12	21	33	85	...	...	...	—	—	—	—	—
97-98—Western Michigan	CCHA	32	5	12	17	93	...	...	...	—	—	—	—	—
98-99—Springfield	AHL	50	5	15	20	32	...	...	...	—	—	—	—	—
—Hampton Roads	ECHL	5	0	0	0	15	...	...	...	4	0	1	1	0
99-00—							Did not play.							
00-01—Lowell	AHL	77	10	23	33	31	...	...	...	4	3	1	4	0
01-02—Manchester	AHL	80	13	37	50	30	...	...	...	5	0	5	5	0
02-03—Manchester	AHL	26	8	18	26	8	...	...	...	—	—	—	—	—
—Los Angeles	NHL	50	5	7	12	14	2	2	0	—	—	—	—	—
NHL Totals (2 years)		50	5	7	12	14	2	2	0					

COTE, SYLVAIN   D   CAPITALS

PERSONAL: Born January 19, 1966, in Quebec City ... 5-11/195. ... Shoots right. ... Brother of Alain Cote, defenseman with five NHL teams (1985-86 through 1993-94). ... Name pronounced KOH-tay.
TRANSACTIONS/CAREER NOTES: Selected by Hartford Whalers in first round (first Whalers pick, 11th overall) of NHL entry draft (June 9, 1984). ... Fractured toe on left foot (October 28, 1989). ... Sprained left knee (December 1989). ... Fractured right foot (January 22, 1990). ... Traded by Whalers to Washington Capitals for second-round pick (LW Andrei Nikolishin) in 1992 draft (September 8, 1991). ... Fractured wrist (September 25, 1992); missed six games. ... Suffered hip pointer (January 7, 1993); missed one game. ... Injured ankle (January 16, 1996); missed one game. ... Tore medial collateral ligament in right knee (October 18, 1996); missed 19 games. ... Strained knee (December 6, 1996); missed five games. ... Traded by Capitals to Toronto Maple Leafs for D Jeff Brown (March 24, 1998). ... Sprained shoulder (March 27, 1999); missed three games. ... Traded by Maple Leafs to Chicago Blackhawks for second-round pick (D Karel Pilar) in 2001 draft and conditional pick in 2001 draft (October 8, 1999). ... Strained hamstring (December 6, 1999); missed four games. ... Traded by Blackhawks with D Dave Manson to Dallas Stars for C Derek Plante, D Kevin Dean and second-round pick (RW Matt Keith) in 2001 draft (February 8, 2000). ... Signed as free agent by Dallas (July 6, 2000). ... Injured back (March 16, 2002); missed five games.

Season Team	League	Gms.	G	A	Pts.	PIM	+/-	PP	SH	Gms.	G	A	Pts.	PIM
							REGULAR SEASON					PLAYOFFS		
82-83—Quebec	QMJHL	66	10	24	34	50	...	...	...	—	—	—	—	—
83-84—Quebec	QMJHL	66	15	50	65	89	...	...	...	5	1	1	2	0
84-85—Hartford	NHL	67	3	9	12	17	-30	1	0	—	—	—	—	—
85-86—Hartford	NHL	2	0	0	0	0	1	0	0	—	—	—	—	—
—Hull	QMJHL	26	10	33	43	14	...	...	...	13	6	*28	34	22
—Binghamton	AHL	12	2	6	8	0	...	...	...	—	—	—	—	—
86-87—Hartford	NHL	67	2	8	10	20	11	0	0	2	0	2	2	0
87-88—Hartford	NHL	67	7	21	28	30	-8	0	1	6	1	1	2	4
88-89—Hartford	NHL	78	8	9	17	49	-7	1	0	3	0	1	1	4
89-90—Hartford	NHL	28	4	2	6	14	2	1	0	5	0	0	0	2
90-91—Hartford	NHL	73	7	12	19	17	-17	1	0	6	0	2	2	2
91-92—Washington	NHL	78	11	29	40	31	7	6	0	7	1	2	3	4
92-93—Washington	NHL	77	21	29	50	34	28	8	2	6	1	1	2	4
93-94—Washington	NHL	84	16	35	51	66	30	3	2	9	1	8	9	6
94-95—Washington	NHL	47	5	14	19	53	2	1	0	7	1	3	4	2
95-96—Washington	NHL	81	5	33	38	40	5	3	0	6	2	0	2	12
96-97—Washington	NHL	57	6	18	24	28	11	2	0	—	—	—	—	—
97-98—Washington	NHL	59	1	15	16	36	-5	0	0	—	—	—	—	—
—Toronto	NHL	12	3	6	9	6	2	1	0	—	—	—	—	—
98-99—Toronto	NHL	79	5	24	29	28	22	0	0	17	2	1	3	10
99-00—Toronto	NHL	3	0	1	1	0	1	0	0	—	—	—	—	—
—Chicago	NHL	45	6	18	24	14	-4	5	0	—	—	—	—	—
—Dallas	NHL	28	2	8	10	14	6	0	0	23	2	1	3	8
00-01—Washington	NHL	68	7	11	18	18	-3	1	1	5	0	0	0	2
01-02—Washington	NHL	70	3	11	14	26	-15	1	0	—	—	—	—	—
02-03—Washington	NHL	1	0	0	0	4	0	0	0	—	—	—	—	—
NHL Totals (19 years)		1171	122	313	435	545	39	35	6	102	11	22	33	62

COWAN, JEFF   LW   THRASHERS

PERSONAL: Born September 27, 1976, in Scarborough, Ont. ... 6-2/210. ... Shoots left. ... Name pronounced KOW-ihn.
TRANSACTIONS/CAREER NOTES: Signed as non-drafted free agent by Calgary Flames (October 2, 1995). ... Suffered injury (March 3, 2000); missed one game. ... Suffered illness (March 25, 2000); missed final six games of season. ... Injured knee (February 10, 2001); missed 19 games. ... Reinjured knee (March 28, 2001); missed three games. ... Traded by Flames with D Kurtis Foster to Atlanta Thrashers for D Petr Buzek and conditional draft pick (December 18, 2001). ... Fractured hand (January 19, 2002); missed 10 games.

Season Team	League	Gms.	G	A	Pts.	PIM	+/-	PP	SH	Gms.	G	A	Pts.	PIM
							REGULAR SEASON					PLAYOFFS		
92-93—Guelph	Jr. B	45	8	8	16	22	...	...	...	—	—	—	—	—
93-94—Guelph	Jr. B	43	30	26	56	96	...	...	...	—	—	—	—	—
—Guelph	OHL	17	1	0	1	5	...	...	...	0	0	0	0	0
94-95—Guelph	OHL	51	10	7	17	14	...	...	...	14	1	1	2	0
95-96—Barrie	OHL	66	38	14	52	29	...	...	...	5	1	2	3	6

Season Team	League	REGULAR SEASON								PLAYOFFS				
		Gms.	G	A	Pts.	PIM	+/-	PP	SH	Gms.	G	A	Pts.	PIM
96-97—Saint John	AHL	22	5	5	10	8	...	...	...	—	—	—	—	—
—Roanoke	ECHL	47	21	13	34	42	...	...	...	—	—	—	—	—
97-98—Saint John	AHL	69	15	13	28	23	...	...	...	13	4	1	5	14
98-99—Saint John	AHL	71	7	12	19	117	...	...	...	4	0	1	1	10
99-00—Saint John	AHL	47	15	10	25	77	...	...	...	—	—	—	—	—
—Calgary	NHL	13	4	1	5	16	2	0	0	—	—	—	—	—
00-01—Calgary	NHL	51	9	4	13	74	-8	2	0	—	—	—	—	—
01-02—Calgary	NHL	19	1	0	1	40	-3	0	0	—	—	—	—	—
—Atlanta	NHL	38	4	1	5	50	-11	0	0	—	—	—	—	—
02-03—Atlanta	NHL	66	3	5	8	115	-15	0	0	—	—	—	—	—
NHL Totals (4 years)		187	21	11	32	295	-35	2	0					

COX, JUSTIN · RW · STARS

PERSONAL: Born March 13, 1981, in Merritt, B.C. ... 6-0/160. ... Shoots right.
TRANSACTIONS/CAREER NOTES: Selected by Dallas Stars in sixth round (sixth Stars pick, 184th overall) of NHL entry draft (June 26, 1999).

Season Team	League	REGULAR SEASON								PLAYOFFS				
		Gms.	G	A	Pts.	PIM	+/-	PP	SH	Gms.	G	A	Pts.	PIM
97-98—Prince George	WHL	40	1	4	5	15	...	...	...	2	0	0	0	0
98-99—Prince George	WHL	72	9	13	22	51	...	...	...	7	1	0	1	13
99-00—Prince George	WHL	71	33	38	71	74	...	...	...	13	2	4	6	16
00-01—Prince George	WHL	71	30	38	68	91	...	...	...	6	3	4	7	20
01-02—Utah	AHL	74	10	7	17	53	...	...	...	5	0	1	1	0
02-03—Utah	AHL	53	3	12	15	22	...	...	...	—	—	—	—	—

CROSS, CORY · D · OILERS

PERSONAL: Born January 3, 1971, in Lloydminster, Alta. ... 6-5/220. ... Shoots left. ... Full Name: Cory James Cross.
TRANSACTIONS/CAREER NOTES: Selected by Tampa Bay Lightning in NHL supplemental draft (June 19, 1992). ... Injured foot (November 3, 1995); missed one game. ... Bruised right foot (November 10, 1996); missed five games. ... Suffered from the flu (March 28, 1998); missed one game. ... Injured ankle (January 4, 1999); missed two games. ... Suffered hip pointer (January 30, 1999); missed one game. ... Traded by Lightning with seventh-round pick (F Ivan Kolozvary) in 2001 draft to Toronto Maple Leafs for RW Fredrik Modin (October 1, 1999). ... Suffered injury (November 15, 1999); missed two games. ... Suffered injury (March 29, 2000); missed two games. ... Suffered injury (November 10, 2000); missed five games. ... Injured hip (November 29, 2000); missed 14 games. ... Injured foot (February 10, 2001); missed 12 games. ... Suffered injury (March 20, 2001); missed five games. ... Injured groin (December 29, 2001); missed 19 games. ... Suffered injury (March 12, 2002); missed one game. ... Signed as free agent by New York Rangers (December 17, 2002). ... Traded by Rangers with RW Radek Dvorak to Edmonton Oilers for RW Anson Carter and D Ales Pisa (March 11, 2003). ... Re-signed by Oilers (June 22, 2003).

Season Team	League	REGULAR SEASON								PLAYOFFS				
		Gms.	G	A	Pts.	PIM	+/-	PP	SH	Gms.	G	A	Pts.	PIM
90-91—Univ. of Alberta	CWUAA	20	2	5	7	16	...	...	...	—	—	—	—	—
91-92—Univ. of Alberta	CWUAA	39	3	10	13	76	...	...	...	—	—	—	—	—
92-93—Univ. of Alberta	CWUAA	43	11	28	39	105	...	...	...	—	—	—	—	—
—Atlanta	IHL	7	0	1	1	2	...	...	...	4	0	0	0	6
93-94—Atlanta	IHL	70	4	14	18	72	...	...	...	9	1	2	3	14
—Tampa Bay	NHL	5	0	0	0	6	-3	0	0	—	—	—	—	—
94-95—Atlanta	IHL	41	5	10	15	67	...	...	...	—	—	—	—	—
—Tampa Bay	NHL	43	1	5	6	41	-6	0	0	—	—	—	—	—
95-96—Tampa Bay	NHL	75	2	14	16	66	4	0	0	6	0	0	0	22
96-97—Tampa Bay	NHL	72	4	5	9	95	6	0	0	—	—	—	—	—
97-98—Tampa Bay	NHL	74	3	6	9	77	-24	0	1	—	—	—	—	—
98-99—Tampa Bay	NHL	67	2	16	18	92	-25	0	0	—	—	—	—	—
99-00—Toronto	NHL	71	4	11	15	64	13	0	0	12	0	2	2	2
00-01—Toronto	NHL	41	3	5	8	50	7	1	0	11	2	1	3	10
01-02—Toronto	NHL	50	3	9	12	54	11	0	0	12	0	0	0	8
02-03—Hartford	AHL	2	0	0	0	2	...	...	...	—	—	—	—	—
—New York Rangers	NHL	26	0	4	4	16	13	0	0	—	—	—	—	—
—Edmonton	NHL	11	2	3	5	8	3	1	0	6	0	1	1	20
NHL Totals (10 years)		535	24	78	102	569	-1	2	1	47	2	4	6	62

CULLEN, MARK · C · WILD

PERSONAL: Born October 28, 1978, in Moorhead, Minn. ... 5-11/175. ... Shoots right.
TRANSACTIONS/CAREER NOTES: Signed as non-drafted free agent by Minnesota Wild (April 2002).

Season Team	League	REGULAR SEASON								PLAYOFFS				
		Gms.	G	A	Pts.	PIM	+/-	PP	SH	Gms.	G	A	Pts.	PIM
01-02—Colorado College	WCHA	43	14	36	50	14	...	...	...	—	—	—	—	—
02-03—Houston	AHL	72	22	25	47	20	...	...	...	—	—	—	—	—

CULLEN, MATT · C · PANTHERS

PERSONAL: Born November 2, 1976, in Virginia, Minn. ... 6-2/199. ... Shoots left.
TRANSACTIONS/CAREER NOTES: Selected by Mighty Ducks of Anaheim in second round (second Mighty Ducks pick, 35th overall) of NHL entry draft (June 22, 1996). ... Sprained ankle (December 16, 1998); missed one game. ... Traded by Mighty Ducks with D Pavel Trnka and fourth-round pick in 2003 draft to Florida Panthers for D Sandis Ozolinsh and D Lance Ward (January 30, 2003).

Season Team	League	REGULAR SEASON								PLAYOFFS				
		Gms.	G	A	Pts.	PIM	+/-	PP	SH	Gms.	G	A	Pts.	PIM
94-95—Moorhead Senior	Minn. H.S.	28	47	42	89	78	...	...	...	—	—	—	—	—
95-96—St. Cloud State	WCHA	39	12	29	41	28	...	...	...	—	—	—	—	—
96-97—St. Cloud State	WCHA	36	15	30	45	70	...	...	...	—	—	—	—	—
—Baltimore	AHL	6	3	3	6	7	...	...	...	3	0	2	2	0
97-98—Anaheim	NHL	61	6	21	27	23	-4	2	0	—	—	—	—	—
—Cincinnati	AHL	18	15	12	27	2	...	...	...	—	—	—	—	—
98-99—Anaheim	NHL	75	11	14	25	47	-12	5	1	4	0	0	0	0
—Cincinnati	AHL	3	1	2	3	8	...	...	...	—	—	—	—	—
99-00—Anaheim	NHL	80	13	26	39	24	5	1	0	—	—	—	—	—
00-01—Anaheim	NHL	82	10	30	40	38	-23	4	0	—	—	—	—	—
01-02—Anaheim	NHL	79	18	30	48	24	-1	3	1	—	—	—	—	—
02-03—Anaheim	NHL	50	7	14	21	12	-4	1	0	—	—	—	—	—
—Florida	NHL	30	6	6	12	22	-4	2	1	—	—	—	—	—
NHL Totals (6 years)		457	71	141	212	190	-43	18	3	4	0	0	0	0

CULLIMORE, JASSEN   D   LIGHTNING

PERSONAL: Born December 4, 1972, in Simcoe, Ont. ... 6-5/239. ... Shoots left. ... Name pronounced KUHL-ih-MOHR.

TRANSACTIONS/CAREER NOTES: Selected by Vancouver Canucks in second round (second Canucks pick, 29th overall) of NHL entry draft (June 22, 1991). ... Suffered knee injury (March 31, 1995); missed three games. ... Traded by Canucks to Montreal Canadiens for LW Donald Brashear (November 13, 1996). ... Bruised eye (March 1, 1997); missed one game. ... Claimed on waivers by Tampa Bay Lightning (January 22, 1998). ... Sprained knee (April 4, 1998); missed final seven games of season. ... Injured neck (October 14, 1998); missed two games. ... Injured wrist (December 11, 1998); missed one game. ... Injured knee (April 2, 2000); missed final four games of season. ... Bruised hand (November 27, 2000); missed one game. ... Injured knee (January 10, 2001); missed one game. ... Injured shin (February 10, 2001); missed one game. ... Strained muscle in abdomen (March 8, 2001); missed two games. ... Sprained left ankle (October 30, 2001); missed two games. ... Bruised right thigh (February 9, 2002); missed one game.

Season Team	League	REGULAR SEASON								PLAYOFFS				
		Gms.	G	A	Pts.	PIM	+/-	PP	SH	Gms.	G	A	Pts.	PIM
88-89—Peterborough	OHL	20	2	1	3	6	...	...	...	—	—	—	—	—
—Peterborough	Jr. B	29	11	17	28	88	...	...	...	—	—	—	—	—
89-90—Peterborough	OHL	59	2	6	8	61	...	...	...	11	0	2	2	8
90-91—Peterborough	OHL	62	8	16	24	74	...	...	...	4	1	0	1	7
91-92—Peterborough	OHL	54	9	37	46	65	...	...	...	10	3	6	9	8
92-93—Hamilton	AHL	56	5	7	12	60	...	...	...	—	—	—	—	—
93-94—Hamilton	AHL	71	8	20	28	86	...	...	...	3	0	1	1	2
94-95—Syracuse	AHL	33	2	7	9	66	...	...	...	—	—	—	—	—
—Vancouver	NHL	34	1	2	3	39	-2	0	0	11	0	0	0	12
95-96—Vancouver	NHL	27	1	1	2	21	4	0	0	—	—	—	—	—
96-97—Vancouver	NHL	3	0	0	0	2	-2	0	0	—	—	—	—	—
—Montreal	NHL	49	2	6	8	42	4	0	1	2	0	0	0	2
97-98—Montreal	NHL	3	0	0	0	4	0	0	0	—	—	—	—	—
—Fredericton	AHL	5	1	0	1	8	...	...	...	—	—	—	—	—
—Tampa Bay	NHL	25	1	2	3	22	-4	1	0	—	—	—	—	—
98-99—Tampa Bay	NHL	78	5	12	17	81	-22	1	1	—	—	—	—	—
99-00—Providence	AHL	16	5	10	15	31	...	...	...	—	—	—	—	—
—Tampa Bay	NHL	46	1	1	2	66	-12	0	0	—	—	—	—	—
00-01—Tampa Bay	NHL	74	1	6	7	80	-6	0	0	—	—	—	—	—
01-02—Tampa Bay	NHL	78	4	9	13	58	-1	0	0	—	—	—	—	—
02-03—Tampa Bay	NHL	28	1	3	4	31	3	0	0	11	1	1	2	4
NHL Totals (9 years)		445	17	42	59	446	-38	2	2	24	1	1	2	18

CUTTA, JAKUB   D   CAPITALS

PERSONAL: Born December 29, 1981, in Jablonec nad Nisou, Czechoslovakia. ... 6-3/217. ... Shoots left.

TRANSACTIONS/CAREER NOTES: Selected by Washington Capitals in second round (third Capitals pick, 61st overall) of NHL entry draft (June 24, 2000).

Season Team	League	REGULAR SEASON								PLAYOFFS				
		Gms.	G	A	Pts.	PIM	+/-	PP	SH	Gms.	G	A	Pts.	PIM
98-99—Swift Current	WHL	59	3	3	6	63	...	...	...	—	—	—	—	—
99-00—Swift Current	WHL	71	2	12	14	114	...	...	...	12	0	2	2	24
00-01—Washington	NHL	3	0	0	0	0	-1	0	0	—	—	—	—	—
—Swift Current	WHL	47	5	8	13	102	...	...	...	16	1	3	4	32
01-02—Portland	AHL	56	1	3	4	69	...	...	...	—	—	—	—	—
—Washington	NHL	2	0	0	0	0	-3	0	0	—	—	—	—	—
02-03—Portland	AHL	66	3	12	15	106	...	...	...	—	—	—	—	—
NHL Totals (2 years)		5	0	0	0	0	-4	0	0					

CZERKAWSKI, MARIUSZ   RW   ISLANDERS

PERSONAL: Born April 13, 1972, in Radomsko, Poland ... 6-1/200. ... Shoots right. ... Name pronounced MAIR-ee-uhz chuhr-KAW-skee.

TRANSACTIONS/CAREER NOTES: Selected by Boston Bruins (fifth Bruins pick, 106th overall) of NHL entry draft (June 22, 1991). ... Played in Europe during 1994-95 NHL lockout. ... Traded by Bruins with D Sean Brown and first-round pick (D Mathieu Descoteaux) in 1996 draft to Edmonton Oilers for G Bill Ranford (January 11, 1996). ... Injured finger (March 23, 1996); missed two games. ... Suffered hip pointer (January 11, 1997); missed two games. ... Traded by Oilers to New York Islanders for LW Dan Lacouture (August 25, 1997). ... Strained muscle in rib cage (December 15, 1999); missed three games. ... Traded by Islanders to Montreal Canadiens for RW/C Aaron Asham and fifth-round pick (F Markus Pahlsson) in 2002 draft (June 22, 2002). ... Signed by New York Islanders (July 17, 2003).

STATISTICAL PLATEAUS: Three-goal games: 1996-97 (2), 1999-00 (1), 2001-02 (1). Total: 4.

C

Season Team	League	REGULAR SEASON Gms.	G	A	Pts.	PIM	+/-	PP	SH	PLAYOFFS Gms.	G	A	Pts.	PIM
90-91—GKS Tychy	Poland	24	25	15	40	...	...	...	—	—	—	—	—	—
91-92—Djurgarden Stockholm	Sweden	39	8	5	13	4	...	...	3	0	0	0	2
—Polish Olympic Team..	Int'l	5	0	1	1	4	...	...	—	—	—	—	—
92-93—Hammarby	Sweden Dv. 2	32	39	30	69	74	...	...	—	—	—	—	—
93-94—Djurgarden Stockholm	Sweden	39	13	21	34	20	...	...	—	—	—	—	—
—Boston	NHL	4	2	1	3	0	-2	1	0	13	3	3	6	4
94-95—Kiekko-Espoo	Finland	7	9	3	12	10	...	...	—	—	—	—	—
—Boston	NHL	47	12	14	26	31	4	1	0	5	1	0	1	0
95-96—Boston	NHL	33	5	6	11	10	-11	1	0	—	—	—	—	—
—Edmonton	NHL	37	12	17	29	8	7	2	0	—	—	—	—	—
96-97—Edmonton	NHL	76	26	21	47	16	0	4	0	12	2	1	3	10
97-98—New York Islanders	NHL	68	12	13	25	23	11	2	0	—	—	—	—	—
98-99—New York Islanders	NHL	78	21	17	38	14	-10	4	0	—	—	—	—	—
99-00—New York Islanders	NHL	79	35	35	70	34	-16	16	0	—	—	—	—	—
00-01—New York Islanders	NHL	82	30	32	62	48	-24	10	1	—	—	—	—	—
01-02—New York Islanders	NHL	82	22	29	51	48	-8	6	0	7	2	2	4	4
02-03—Hamilton	AHL	20	8	12	20	12	...	...	—	—	—	—	—
—Montreal	NHL	43	5	9	14	16	-7	1	0	—	—	—	—	—
NHL Totals (10 years)		629	182	194	376	248	-56	48	1	37	8	6	14	18

DACKELL, ANDREAS — RW — CANADIENS

PERSONAL: Born December 29, 1972, in Gavle, Sweden ... 5-11/194. ... Shoots right. ... Name pronounced AHN-dray-uhz DA-kuhl.
TRANSACTIONS/CAREER NOTES: Selected by Ottawa Senators in sixth round (third Senators pick, 136th overall) of NHL entry draft (June 22, 1996). ... Suffered concussion (October 29, 1998); missed four games. ... Injured knee (January 14, 1999); missed one game. ... Suffered from the flu (November 18, 2000); missed one game. ... Traded by Senators to Montreal Canadiens for eighth-round pick (D Neil Petruic) in 2001 draft (June 24, 2001). ... Suffered illness (January 4, 2002); missed one game.
STATISTICAL PLATEAUS: Three-goal games: 2000-01 (1).

Season Team	League	REGULAR SEASON Gms.	G	A	Pts.	PIM	+/-	PP	SH	PLAYOFFS Gms.	G	A	Pts.	PIM
90-91—Brynas Gavle	Sweden	3	0	1	1	2	...	...	—	—	—	—	—
91-92—Brynas Gavle	Sweden	4	0	0	0	2	...	...	2	0	1	1	4
92-93—Brynas Gavle	Sweden	40	12	15	27	12	...	...	10	4	5	9	2
93-94—Brynas Gavle	Sweden	38	12	17	29	47	...	...	7	2	2	4	8
94-95—Brynas Gavle	Sweden	39	17	16	33	34	...	...	14	3	3	6	14
95-96—Brynas Gavle	Sweden	22	6	6	12	8	...	...	—	—	—	—	—
96-97—Ottawa	NHL	79	12	19	31	8	-6	2	0	7	1	0	1	0
97-98—Ottawa	NHL	82	15	18	33	24	-11	3	2	11	1	1	2	2
98-99—Ottawa	NHL	77	15	35	50	30	9	6	0	4	0	1	1	0
99-00—Ottawa	NHL	82	10	25	35	18	5	0	0	6	2	1	3	2
00-01—Ottawa	NHL	81	13	18	31	24	7	1	0	4	0	0	0	0
01-02—Montreal	NHL	79	15	18	33	24	-3	2	3	12	1	2	3	6
02-03—Montreal	NHL	73	7	18	25	24	-5	0	0	—	—	—	—	—
NHL Totals (7 years)		553	87	151	238	152	-4	14	5	44	5	5	10	10

DAFOE, BYRON — G — THRASHERS

PERSONAL: Born February 25, 1971, in Sussex, England ... 5-11/200. ... Catches left. ... Full Name: Byron Jaromir Dafoe.
TRANSACTIONS/CAREER NOTES: Selected by Washington Capitals in second round (second Capitals pick, 35th overall) of NHL entry draft (June 17, 1989). ... Traded by Capitals with RW Dimitri Khristich to Los Angeles Kings for first-(C Alexander Volchkov) and fourth-round (RW Justin Davis) picks in 1996 draft (July 8, 1995). ... Strained thumb (February 1, 1997); missed two games. ... Traded by Kings with RW Dimitri Khristich to Boston Bruins for C Jozef Stumpel, RW Sandy Moger and fourth-round pick (traded to New Jersey) in 1998 draft (August 29, 1997). ... Injured knee (February 21, 2000) and underwent surgery; missed remainder of season. ... Injured hamstring (October 13, 2000); missed 11 games. ... Injured knee (November 22, 2000); missed 11 games. ... Strained hamstring (February 10, 2001); missed 13 games.

Season Team	League	REGULAR SEASON Gms.	Min	W	L	T	GA	SO	Avg.	SV%	PLAYOFFS Gms.	Min.	W	L	GA	SO	Avg.	SV%
87-88—Juan de Fuca	BCJHL	32	1716	...	...	...	129	0	4.51	—	—	—	—	—	—	—	—	—
88-89—Portland	WHL	59	3279	29	24	3	*291	1	5.32	—	*18	*1091	10	8	*81	*1	4.45	—
89-90—Portland	WHL	40	2265	14	21	3	193	0	5.11	—	—	—	—	—	—	—	—	—
90-91—Portland	WHL	8	414	1	5	1	41	0	5.94	—	—	—	—	—	—	—	—	—
—Prince Albert	WHL	32	1839	13	12	4	124	0	4.05	—	—	—	—	—	—	—	—	—
91-92—New Haven	AHL	7	364	3	2	1	22	0	3.63	—	—	—	—	—	—	—	—	—
—Baltimore	AHL	33	1847	12	16	4	119	0	3.87	—	—	—	—	—	—	—	—	—
—Hampton Roads	ECHL	10	562	6	4	‡0	26	1	2.78	—	—	—	—	—	—	—	—	—
92-93—Baltimore	AHL	48	2617	16	*20	7	191	1	4.38	—	5	241	2	3	22	0	5.48	—
—Washington	NHL	1	1	0	0	0	0	0	0.00	—	—	—	—	—	—	—	—	—
93-94—Portland	AHL	47	2662	24	16	4	148	1	3.34	—	1	9	0	0	1	0	6.67	—
—Washington	NHL	5	230	2	2	0	13	0	3.39	.871	2	118	0	2	5	0	2.54	.872
94-95—Portland	AHL	6	330	5	0	0	16	0	2.91	—	7	417	3	4	29	0	4.17	—
—Phoenix	IHL	49	2744	25	16	‡6	169	2	3.70	—	—	—	—	—	—	—	—	—
—Washington	NHL	4	187	1	1	1	11	0	3.53	.863	1	20	0	0	1	0	3.00	.667
95-96—Los Angeles	NHL	47	2666	14	24	8	172	1	3.87	.888	—	—	—	—	—	—	—	—
96-97—Los Angeles	NHL	40	2162	13	17	5	112	6	3.11	.905	—	—	—	—	—	—	—	—
97-98—Boston	NHL	65	3693	30	25	9	138	6	2.24	.914	6	422	2	4	14	1	1.99	.912
98-99—Boston	NHL	68	4001	32	23	11	133	*10	1.99	.926	12	768	6	6	26	2	2.03	.921
99-00—Boston	NHL	41	2307	13	16	10	114	3	2.96	.889	—	—	—	—	—	—	—	—
00-01—Boston	NHL	45	2536	22	14	7	101	2	2.39	.906	—	—	—	—	—	—	—	—
01-02—Boston	NHL	64	3827	35	26	3	141	4	2.21	.907	6	358	2	4	19	0	3.18	.865
02-03—Atlanta	NHL	17	895	5	11	1	65	0	4.36	.862	—	—	—	—	—	—	—	—
NHL Totals (11 years)		397	22505	167	159	55	1000	26	2.67	.904	27	1686	10	16	65	3	2.31	.903

DAGENAIS, PIERRE   LW   CANADIENS

PERSONAL: Born March 4, 1978, in Blainville, Que. ... 6-5/215. ... Shoots left. ... Name pronounced da-zhih-NAY.
TRANSACTIONS/CAREER NOTES: Selected by New Jersey Devils in second round (fourth Devils pick, 47th overall) of NHL entry draft (June 22, 1996). ... Returned to draft pool by Devils and selected by Devils in fourth round (sixth Devils pick, 105th overall) of NHL entry draft (June 27, 1998). ... Claimed on waivers by Florida Panthers (January 12, 2002). ... Injured ankle (April 10, 2002); missed remainder of season. ... Signed by Montreal Canadiens (July 3, 2003).

Season Team	League	Gms.	G	A	Pts.	PIM	+/-	PP	SH	Gms.	G	A	Pts.	PIM
				REGULAR SEASON								PLAYOFFS		
95-96—Moncton	QMJHL	67	43	25	68	59	...	...	...	—	—	—	—	—
96-97—Moncton	QMJHL	6	4	2	6	0	...	...	...	—	—	—	—	—
—Laval	QMJHL	37	16	14	30	40	...	...	...	—	—	—	—	—
—Rouyn-Noranda	QMJHL	27	21	8	29	22	...	...	...	—	—	—	—	—
97-98—Rouyn-Noranda	QMJHL	60	*66	67	133	50	...	...	...	6	6	2	8	2
98-99—Albany	AHL	69	17	13	30	37	...	...	...	4	0	0	0	0
99-00—Albany	AHL	80	35	30	65	47	...	...	...	5	1	0	1	14
00-01—Albany	AHL	69	34	28	62	52	...	...	...	—	—	—	—	—
—New Jersey	NHL	9	3	2	5	6	1	1	0	—	—	—	—	—
01-02—New Jersey	NHL	16	3	3	6	4	-5	1	0	—	—	—	—	—
—Albany	AHL	6	0	2	2	2	...	...	...	—	—	—	—	—
—Florida	NHL	26	7	1	8	4	-5	2	0	—	—	—	—	—
—Utah	AHL	4	1	1	2	2	...	...	...	—	—	—	—	—
02-03—San Antonio	AHL	49	21	14	35	28	...	...	...	—	—	—	—	—
—Florida	NHL	9	0	0	0	4	-1	0	0	—	—	—	—	—
NHL Totals (3 years)		60	13	6	19	18	-10	4	0					

DAHLEN, ULF   RW

PERSONAL: Born January 12, 1967, in Ostersund, Sweden ... 6-3/204. ... Shoots left. ... Name pronounced DAH-lihn.
TRANSACTIONS/CAREER NOTES: Selected by New York Rangers in first round (first Rangers pick, seventh overall) of NHL entry draft (June 15, 1985). ... Bruised shin (November 1987). ... Bruised left shoulder (November 1988). ... Separated right shoulder (January 1989). ... Traded by Rangers with fourth-round pick (C Cal McGowan) in 1990 draft and future considerations to Minnesota North Stars for RW Mike Gartner (March 6, 1990). ... North Stars franchise moved from Minnesota to Dallas and renamed Stars for 1993-94 season. ... Traded by Stars with future considerations to San Jose Sharks for D Mike Lalor and D Doug Zmolek (March 19, 1994). ... Suffered from the flu (February 20, 1995); missed two games. ... Injured groin (October 28, 1995); missed three games. ... Fractured toe (January 11, 1996); missed 20 games. ... Traded by Sharks with G Chris Terreri and D Michal Sykora to Chicago Blackhawks for G Ed Belfour (January 25, 1997). ... Suffered back spasms (March 26, 1997); missed one game. ... Signed as free agent by Washington Capitals (July 21, 1999). ... Injured neck (March 15, 2000); missed one game. ... Injured back (December 14, 2000); missed four games. ... Suffered from the flu (February 7, 2001); missed one game. ... Injured neck (March 1, 2001); missed one game. ... Reinjured neck (March 6, 2001); missed two games. ... Bruised foot (March 30, 2001); missed one game. ... Bruised foot (December 21, 2001); missed four games. ... Reinjured foot (December 30, 2001); missed nine games. ... Signed as free agent by Stars (August 13, 2002).
STATISTICAL PLATEAUS: Three-goal games: 1987-88 (1), 1990-91 (1), 1992-93 (1), 1993-94 (1). Total: 4.

Season Team	League	Gms.	G	A	Pts.	PIM	+/-	PP	SH	Gms.	G	A	Pts.	PIM
				REGULAR SEASON								PLAYOFFS		
83-84—Ostersund	Sweden	36	15	11	26	10	...	...	...	—	—	—	—	—
84-85—Ostersund	Sweden	36	33	26	59	20	...	...	...	—	—	—	—	—
85-86—Bjorkloven	Sweden	22	4	3	7	8	...	...	...	—	—	—	—	—
86-87—Bjorkloven	Sweden	31	9	12	21	20	...	...	...	6	6	2	8	4
87-88—New York Rangers	NHL	70	29	23	52	26	5	11	0	—	—	—	—	—
—Colorado	IHL	2	2	2	4	0	...	...	...	—	—	—	—	—
88-89—New York Rangers	NHL	56	24	19	43	50	-6	8	0	4	0	0	0	0
89-90—New York Rangers	NHL	63	18	18	36	30	-4	13	0	—	—	—	—	—
—Minnesota	NHL	13	2	4	6	0	1	0	0	7	1	4	5	2
90-91—Minnesota	NHL	66	21	18	39	6	7	4	0	15	2	6	8	4
91-92—Minnesota	NHL	79	36	30	66	10	-5	16	1	7	0	3	3	2
92-93—Minnesota	NHL	83	35	39	74	6	-20	13	0	—	—	—	—	—
93-94—Dallas	NHL	65	19	38	57	10	-1	12	0	—	—	—	—	—
—San Jose	NHL	13	6	6	12	0	0	3	0	14	6	2	8	0
94-95—San Jose	NHL	46	11	23	34	11	-2	4	1	11	5	4	9	0
95-96—San Jose	NHL	59	16	12	28	27	-21	5	0	—	—	—	—	—
96-97—San Jose	NHL	43	8	11	19	8	-11	3	0	—	—	—	—	—
—Chicago	NHL	30	6	8	14	10	9	1	0	5	0	1	1	0
97-98—HV 71 Jonkoping	Sweden	29	9	22	31	16	...	...	...	—	—	—	—	—
—Swedish Oly. team	Int'l	4	1	0	1	2	...	...	...	—	—	—	—	—
98-99—HV 71 Jonkoping	Sweden	25	14	15	29	4	...	...	...	—	—	—	—	—
99-00—Washington	NHL	75	15	23	38	8	11	5	0	5	0	1	1	2
00-01—Washington	NHL	73	15	33	48	6	11	6	0	6	0	1	1	2
01-02—Washington	NHL	69	23	29	52	8	-5	7	0	—	—	—	—	—
—Swedish Oly. team	Int'l	4	1	2	3	0	...	...	...	—	—	—	—	—
02-03—Dallas	NHL	63	17	20	37	14	11	9	0	11	1	3	4	0
NHL Totals (14 years)		966	301	354	655	230	-20	120	2	85	15	25	40	12

DAHLMAN, TONI   RW

PERSONAL: Born September 3, 1979, in Helsinki, Finland ... 6-0/198. ... Shoots right.
TRANSACTIONS/CAREER NOTES: Selected by Ottawa Senators in ninth round (12th Senators pick, 286th overall) of NHL entry draft (June 23, 2001).

Season Team	League	REGULAR SEASON								PLAYOFFS				
		Gms.	G	A	Pts.	PIM	+/-	PP	SH	Gms.	G	A	Pts.	PIM
96-97—Karhu-Kissat	Finland Jr.	24	22	18	40	6	...	...	...	—	—	—	—	—
97-98—Jokerit Helsinki	Finland Jr.	21	13	11	24	14	...	...	...	7	2	2	4	0
98-99—Jokerit Helsinki	Finland Jr.	33	10	22	32	6	...	...	...	9	4	3	7	2
—Jokerit Helsinki	Finland	5	0	0	0	0	...	...	...	3	0	1	1	0
99-00—Jokerit Helsinki	Finland Jr.	12	6	8	14	4	...	...	...	12	7	7	14	4
—Hermes Kokkola	Finland Div. 2	23	6	3	9	4	...	...	...	—	—	—	—	—
—Jokerit Helsinki	Finland	1	0	0	0	0	...	...	...	—	—	—	—	—
00-01—Ilves Tampere	Finland	56	10	18	28	16	...	...	...	9	3	2	5	2
01-02—Grand Rapids	AHL	50	6	8	14	25	...	...	...	4	0	0	0	0
—Ottawa	NHL	10	0	1	1	0	-1	0	0	—	—	—	—	—
02-03—Binghamton	AHL	59	6	18	24	14	...	...	...	—	—	—	—	—
—Ottawa	NHL	12	1	0	1	0	-1	0	0	—	—	—	—	—
NHL Totals (2 years)		22	1	1	2	0	-2	0	0					

DAIGLE, ALEXANDRE   RW

PERSONAL: Born February 7, 1975, in Montreal ... 6-0/203. ... Shoots left. ... Name pronounced DAYG.
TRANSACTIONS/CAREER NOTES: Selected by Ottawa Senators in first round (first Senators pick, first overall) of NHL entry draft (June 26, 1993). ... Fractured left forearm (February 3, 1996); missed remainder of season. ... Traded by Senators to Flyers for C Vaclav Prospal, RW Pat Falloon and second round pick (LW Chris Bala) in 1998 draft (January 17, 1998). ... Suffered from concussion (October 29, 1998); missed two games. ... Strained left groin (November 14, 1998); missed one game. ... Traded by Flyers to Edmonton Oilers for RW Andrei Kovalenko (January 29, 1999). ... Traded by Oilers to Tampa Bay Lightning for RW Alexander Selivanov (January 29, 1999). ... Injured wrist (March 19, 1999); missed one game. ... Reinjured wrist (March 31, 1999); missed one game. ... Traded by Lightning to New York Rangers for future considerations (October 3, 1999). ... Signed as free agent by Pittsburgh Penguins (October 4, 2002).
STATISTICAL PLATEAUS: Three-goal games: 1994-95 (1), 1997-98 (1). Total: 2.

Season Team	League	REGULAR SEASON								PLAYOFFS				
		Gms.	G	A	Pts.	PIM	+/-	PP	SH	Gms.	G	A	Pts.	PIM
91-92—Victoriaville	QMJHL	66	35	75	110	63	...	...	...	—	—	—	—	—
92-93—Victoriaville	QMJHL	53	45	92	137	85	...	...	...	6	5	6	11	4
93-94—Ottawa	NHL	84	20	31	51	40	-45	4	0	—	—	—	—	—
94-95—Victoriaville	QMJHL	18	14	20	34	16	...	...	...	—	—	—	—	—
—Ottawa	NHL	47	16	21	37	14	-22	4	1	—	—	—	—	—
95-96—Ottawa	NHL	50	5	12	17	24	-30	1	0	—	—	—	—	—
96-97—Ottawa	NHL	82	26	25	51	33	-33	4	0	7	0	0	0	2
97-98—Ottawa	NHL	38	7	9	16	8	-7	4	0	—	—	—	—	—
—Philadelphia	NHL	37	9	17	26	6	-1	4	0	5	0	2	2	0
98-99—Philadelphia	NHL	31	3	2	5	2	-1	1	0	—	—	—	—	—
—Tampa Bay	NHL	32	6	6	12	2	-12	3	0	—	—	—	—	—
99-00—Hartford	AHL	16	6	13	19	4	...	...	...	—	—	—	—	—
—New York Rangers	NHL	58	8	18	26	23	-5	1	0	—	—	—	—	—
00-01—							Did not play.							
01-02—							Did not play.							
02-03—Wilkes-Barre/Scranton	AHL	40	9	29	38	18	...	...	...	—	—	—	—	—
—Pittsburgh	NHL	33	4	3	7	8	-10	1	0	—	—	—	—	—
NHL Totals (8 years)		492	104	144	248	160	-166	27	1	12	0	2	2	2

DAIGNEAULT, MAXIME   G   CAPITALS

PERSONAL: Born January 23, 1984, in St-Jacques-Le-Mineur, Que. ... 6-1/194. ... Catches left.
TRANSACTIONS/CAREER NOTES: Selected by Washington Capitals in second round (fourth Capitals pick, 59th overall) of NHL entry draft (June 22, 2002).

Season Team	League	REGULAR SEASON								PLAYOFFS							
		Gms.	Min	W	L	T	GA	SO	Avg.	SV%	Gms.	Min.	W	L	GA	SO	Avg.	SV%
01-02—Val-d'Or	QMJHL	61	3270	25	27	5	184	3	3.38	—	7	431	3	4	23	0	3.20	—
02-03—Val-d'Or	QMJHL	67	2694	23	18	3	138	2	3.07	—	—	—	—	—	—	—	—	—

DALEY, TREVOR   D   STARS

PERSONAL: Born October 9, 1983, in Toronto. ... 5-10/207. ... Shoots left.
TRANSACTIONS/CAREER NOTES: Selected by Dallas Stars in second round (fifth Stars pick, 43rd overall) of NHL entry draft (June 22, 2002).

Season Team	League	REGULAR SEASON								PLAYOFFS				
		Gms.	G	A	Pts.	PIM	+/-	PP	SH	Gms.	G	A	Pts.	PIM
99-00—Sault Ste. Marie	OHL	54	16	30	46	77	...	...	...	15	3	7	10	12
00-01—Sault Ste. Marie	OHL	58	14	27	41	105	...	...	...	—	—	—	—	—
01-02—Sault Ste. Marie	OHL	47	9	39	48	38	...	...	...	6	2	2	4	4
02-03—Sault Ste. Marie	OHL	57	20	33	53	128	...	...	...	—	—	—	—	—

DAMPHOUSSE, J.F.   G   CANADIENS

PERSONAL: Born July 21, 1979, in St. Alexis-des-Monts, Que. ... 6-0/175. ... Catches left. ... Full Name: Jean-Francois Damphousse. ... Name pronounced dahm-FOOZ.
TRANSACTIONS/CAREER NOTES: Selected by New Jersey Devils in first round (first Devils pick, 24th overall) of NHL entry draft (June 21, 1997). ... Traded by Devils with RW Petr Sykora, C Igor Pohanka and D Mike Commodore to Mighty Ducks of Anaheim for D Oleg Tverdovsky, LW Jeff Friesen and RW Maxin Balmochnykh (July 7, 2002). ... Traded by Mighty Ducks with D Mike Commodore to Calgary Flames for C Rob Niedermayer (March 11, 2003). ... Signed by Montreal Canadiens (July 3, 2003).

Season Team	League	REGULAR SEASON									PLAYOFFS							
		Gms.	Min	W	L	T	GA	SO	Avg.	SV%	Gms.	Min.	W	L	GA	SO	Avg.	SV%
96-97—Moncton	QMJHL	39	2063	6	25	2	190	0	5.53	—	—	—	—	—	—	—	—	—
97-98—Moncton	QMJHL	59	3400	24	26	*6	174	1	3.07	—	10	595	5	5	28	0	2.82	—
98-99—Moncton	QMJHL	40	2163	19	17	2	121	1	3.36	—	4	200	0	4	12	0	3.60	—
—Albany	AHL	1	59	0	1	0	3	0	3.05	—	—	—	—	—	—	—	—	—
99-00—Albany	AHL	26	1326	9	11	2	62	0	2.81	—	2	62	0	1	4	0	3.87	—
—Augusta	ECHL	14	676	6	7	0	49	0	4.35	—	—	—	—	—	—	—	—	—
00-01—Albany	AHL	55	2963	24	23	3	141	1	2.86	—	—	—	—	—	—	—	—	—
01-02—Albany	AHL	18	1000	3	11	2	57	0	3.42	—	—	—	—	—	—	—	—	—
—New Jersey	NHL	6	294	1	3	0	12	0	2.45	.896	—	—	—	—	—	—	—	—
02-03—Cincinnati	AHL	31	1668	12	14	4	87	0	3.13	—	—	—	—	—	—	—	—	—
—Saint John	AHL	10	591	5	5	0	23	0	2.34	—	—	—	—	—	—	—	—	—
NHL Totals (1 year)		6	294	1	3	0	12	0	2.45	.896								

DAMPHOUSSE, VINCENT   C   SHARKS

PERSONAL: Born December 17, 1967, in Montreal ... 6-1/205. ... Shoots left. ... Name pronounced dahm-FOOZ.

TRANSACTIONS/CAREER NOTES: Selected by Toronto Maple Leafs in first round (first Maple Leafs pick, sixth overall) of NHL entry draft (June 21, 1986). ... Traded by Maple Leafs with D Luke Richardson, G Peter Ing, C Scott Thornton and future considerations to Edmonton Oilers for G Grant Fuhr, LW//RW Glenn Anderson and LW Craig Berube (September 19, 1991). ... Traded by Oilers with fourth-round pick (D Adam Wiesel) in 1993 draft to Montreal Canadiens for LW Shayne Corson, LW Vladimir Vujtek and C Brent Gilchrist (August 27, 1992). ... Played in Europe during 1994-95 NHL lockout. ... Suspended two games and fined $1,000 by NHL for cross-checking incident (March 30, 1996). ... Partially dislocated left shoulder (March 11, 1998); missed six games. ... Suffered back spasms (November 27, 1998); missed five games. ... Traded by Canadiens to San Jose Sharks for fifth-round pick (RW Marc-Andre Thinel) in 1999 draft and first-round pick (C Marcel Hossa) in 2000 draft (March 23, 1999). ... Injured shoulder (January 15, 2001); missed 36 games.

STATISTICAL PLATEAUS: Three-goal games: 1988-89 (1), 1989-90 (2), 1992-93 (2), 1993-94 (2), 1996-97 (1), 1997-98 (2), 1998-99 (1). Total: 11. ... Four-goal games: 1991-92 (1). ... Total hat tricks: 12.

Season Team	League	REGULAR SEASON							PLAYOFFS				
		Gms.	G	A	Pts.	PIM	+/-	PP	SH	Gms.	G	A	Pts.	PIM
83-84—Laval	QMJHL	66	29	36	65	25	...	...	...	—	—	—	—	—
84-85—Laval	QMJHL	68	35	68	103	62	...	...	...	—	—	—	—	—
85-86—Laval	QMJHL	69	45	110	155	70	...	...	...	14	9	27	36	12
86-87—Toronto	NHL	80	21	25	46	26	-6	4	0	12	1	5	6	8
87-88—Toronto	NHL	75	12	36	48	40	2	1	0	6	0	1	1	10
88-89—Toronto	NHL	80	26	42	68	75	-8	6	0	—	—	—	—	—
89-90—Toronto	NHL	80	33	61	94	56	2	9	0	5	0	2	2	2
90-91—Toronto	NHL	79	26	47	73	65	-31	10	1	—	—	—	—	—
91-92—Edmonton	NHL	80	38	51	89	53	10	12	1	16	6	8	14	8
92-93—Montreal	NHL	84	39	58	97	98	5	9	3	20	11	12	23	16
93-94—Montreal	NHL	84	40	51	91	75	0	13	0	7	1	2	3	8
94-95—Ratingen	Germany	11	5	6	11	24	...	...	...	—	—	—	—	—
—Montreal	NHL	48	10	30	40	42	15	4	0	—	—	—	—	—
95-96—Montreal	NHL	80	38	56	94	158	5	11	4	6	4	4	8	0
96-97—Montreal	NHL	82	27	54	81	82	-6	7	2	5	0	0	0	2
97-98—Montreal	NHL	76	18	41	59	58	14	2	1	10	3	6	9	22
98-99—Montreal	NHL	65	12	24	36	46	-7	3	2	—	—	—	—	—
—San Jose	NHL	12	7	6	13	4	3	3	0	6	3	2	5	6
99-00—San Jose	NHL	82	21	49	70	58	4	3	1	12	1	7	8	16
00-01—San Jose	NHL	45	9	37	46	62	17	4	0	6	2	1	3	14
01-02—San Jose	NHL	82	20	38	58	60	8	7	2	12	2	6	8	12
02-03—San Jose	NHL	82	23	38	61	66	-13	15	0	—	—	—	—	—
NHL Totals (17 years)		1296	420	744	1164	1124	14	123	17	123	34	56	90	124

DANDENAULT, MATHIEU   D   RED WINGS

PERSONAL: Born February 3, 1976, in Sherbrooke, Que. ... 6-1/200. ... Shoots right. ... Cousin of Eric Dandenault, defenseman with Philadelphia Flyers organization (1991-92 through 1993-94). ... Name pronounced DAN-dih-noh.

TRANSACTIONS/CAREER NOTES: Selected by Detroit Red Wings in second round (second Red Wings pick, 49th overall) of NHL entry draft (June 28, 1994). ... Suffered from the flu (November 11, 1995); missed one game. ... Bruised ribs (March 10, 1997); missed four games. ... Re-signed by Red Wings (July 15, 2003).

Season Team	League	REGULAR SEASON							PLAYOFFS				
		Gms.	G	A	Pts.	PIM	+/-	PP	SH	Gms.	G	A	Pts.	PIM
91-92—Gloucester	OPJHL	6	3	4	7	0	...	...	...	—	—	—	—	—
92-93—Gloucester	OPJHL	55	11	26	37	64	...	...	...	—	—	—	—	—
93-94—Sherbrooke	QMJHL	67	17	36	53	67	...	...	...	12	4	10	14	12
94-95—Sherbrooke	QMJHL	67	37	70	107	76	...	...	...	7	1	7	8	10
95-96—Detroit	NHL	34	5	7	12	6	6	1	0	—	—	—	—	—
—Adirondack	AHL	4	0	0	0	0	...	...	...	—	—	—	—	—
96-97—Detroit	NHL	65	3	9	12	28	-10	0	0	—	—	—	—	—
97-98—Detroit	NHL	68	5	12	17	43	5	0	0	3	1	0	1	0
98-99—Detroit	NHL	75	4	10	14	59	17	0	0	10	0	1	1	0
99-00—Detroit	NHL	81	6	12	18	20	-12	0	0	6	0	0	0	2
00-01—Detroit	NHL	73	10	15	25	38	11	2	0	6	0	1	1	0
01-02—Detroit	NHL	81	8	12	20	44	-5	2	0	23	1	2	3	8
02-03—Detroit	NHL	74	4	15	19	64	25	1	0	4	0	0	0	2
NHL Totals (8 years)		551	45	92	137	302	37	6	0	52	2	4	6	12

DANEYKO, KEN   D

PERSONAL: Born April 17, 1964, in Windsor, Ont. ... 6-1/215. ... Shoots left. ... Full Name: Kenneth Daneyko. ... Name pronounced DAN-ih-koh.
TRANSACTIONS/CAREER NOTES: Selected by New Jersey Devils in first round (second Devils pick, 18th overall) of NHL entry draft (June 1982). ... Fractured right fibula (November 2, 1983). ... Suspended one game and fined $500 by NHL for playing in West Germany without permission (October 1985). ... Injured wrist (February 25, 1987). ... Fractured nose (February 24, 1988). ... Injured shoulder (March 29, 1994); missed six games. ... Injured knee (March 8, 1995); missed 23 games. ... Suffered from the flu (March 9, 1996); missed two games. ... Injured hip (October 12, 1996); missed one game. ... Suffered from the flu (January 31, 1997); missed one game. ... Voluntarily entered NHL/NHLPA substance abuse and behavioral health program (November 6, 1997); missed 45 games. ... Suffered injury (October 16, 1999); missed one game. ... Injured shoulder (December 10, 2001); missed seven games. ... Retired (July 10, 2003).

		REGULAR SEASON								PLAYOFFS				
Season Team	League	Gms.	G	A	Pts.	PIM	+/-	PP	SH	Gms.	G	A	Pts.	PIM
80-81—Spokane..................	WHL	62	6	13	19	140	...	...	...	4	0	0	0	6
—St. Albert	AJHL	1	0	0	0	4	...	...	...	—	—	—	—	—
81-82—Spokane..................	WHL	26	1	11	12	147	...	...	...	—	—	—	—	—
—Seattle..................	WHL	38	1	22	23	151	...	...	...	14	1	9	10	49
82-83—Seattle..................	WHL	69	17	43	60	150	...	...	...	4	1	3	4	14
83-84—Kamloops..............	WHL	19	6	28	34	52	...	...	...	17	4	9	13	28
—New Jersey..............	NHL	11	1	4	5	17	-1	0	0	—	—	—	—	—
84-85—New Jersey..............	NHL	1	0	0	0	10	-1	0	0	—	—	—	—	—
—Maine..................	AHL	80	4	9	13	206	...	...	...	11	1	3	4	36
85-86—Maine..................	AHL	21	3	2	5	75	...	...	...	—	—	—	—	—
—New Jersey..............	NHL	44	0	10	10	100	0	0	0	—	—	—	—	—
86-87—New Jersey..............	NHL	79	2	12	14	183	-13	0	0	—	—	—	—	—
87-88—New Jersey..............	NHL	80	5	7	12	239	-3	1	0	20	1	6	7	83
88-89—New Jersey..............	NHL	80	5	5	10	283	-22	1	0	—	—	—	—	—
89-90—New Jersey..............	NHL	74	6	15	21	219	15	0	1	6	2	0	2	21
90-91—New Jersey..............	NHL	80	4	16	20	249	-10	1	2	7	0	1	1	10
91-92—New Jersey..............	NHL	80	1	7	8	170	7	0	0	7	0	3	3	16
92-93—New Jersey..............	NHL	84	2	11	13	236	4	0	0	5	0	0	0	8
93-94—New Jersey..............	NHL	78	1	9	10	176	27	0	0	20	0	1	1	45
94-95—New Jersey..............	NHL	25	1	2	3	54	4	0	0	20	1	0	1	22
95-96—New Jersey..............	NHL	80	2	4	6	115	-10	0	0	—	—	—	—	—
96-97—New Jersey..............	NHL	77	2	7	9	70	24	0	0	10	0	0	0	28
97-98—New Jersey..............	NHL	37	0	1	1	57	3	0	0	6	0	1	1	10
98-99—New Jersey..............	NHL	82	2	9	11	63	27	0	0	7	0	0	0	8
99-00—New Jersey..............	NHL	78	0	6	6	98	13	0	0	23	1	2	3	14
00-01—New Jersey..............	NHL	77	0	4	4	87	8	0	0	25	0	3	3	21
01-02—New Jersey..............	NHL	67	0	6	6	60	2	0	0	6	0	0	0	8
02-03—New Jersey..............	NHL	69	2	7	9	33	6	0	0	13	0	0	0	2
NHL Totals (20 years).........		1283	36	142	178	2519	80	3	3	175	5	17	22	296

DANIELS, JEFF   LW   HURRICANES

PERSONAL: Born June 24, 1968, in Oshawa, Ont. ... 6-1/200. ... Shoots left.
TRANSACTIONS/CAREER NOTES: Selected by Pittsburgh Penguins in sixth round (sixth Penguins pick, 109th overall) of NHL entry draft (June 21, 1986). ... Traded by Penguins to Florida Panthers for D Greg Hawgood (March 19, 1994). ... Signed as free agent by Hartford Whalers (July 18, 1995). ... Tore knee ligament (December 20, 1996); missed 25 games. ... Whalers franchise moved to North Carolina and renamed Carolina Hurricanes for 1997-98 season; NHL approved move on June 25, 1997. ... Selected by Nashville Predators in NHL expansion draft (June 26, 1998). ... Signed as free agent by Carolina Hurricanes (August 31, 1999). ... Injured hip (October 29, 2000); missed one game. ... Suffered concussion (January 14, 2000); missed two games. ... Injured foot (March 11, 2001); missed one game. ... Strained groin (September 11, 2001); missed first three games of season. ... Injured groin (January 2, 2002); missed two games. ... Suffered concussion (March 26, 2002); missed four games.

		REGULAR SEASON								PLAYOFFS				
Season Team	League	Gms.	G	A	Pts.	PIM	+/-	PP	SH	Gms.	G	A	Pts.	PIM
84-85—Oshawa..................	OHL	59	7	11	18	16	...	...	...	—	—	—	—	—
85-86—Oshawa..................	OHL	62	13	19	32	23	...	...	...	6	0	1	1	0
86-87—Oshawa..................	OHL	54	14	9	23	22	...	...	...	15	3	2	5	5
87-88—Oshawa..................	OHL	64	29	39	68	59	...	...	...	4	2	3	5	0
88-89—Muskegon..............	IHL	58	21	21	42	58	...	...	...	11	3	5	8	11
89-90—Muskegon..............	IHL	80	30	47	77	39	...	...	...	6	1	1	2	7
90-91—Pittsburgh..............	NHL	11	0	2	2	2	0	0	0	—	—	—	—	—
—Muskegon..............	IHL	62	23	29	52	18	...	...	...	5	1	3	4	2
91-92—Pittsburgh..............	NHL	2	0	0	0	0	0	0	0	—	—	—	—	—
—Muskegon..............	IHL	44	19	16	35	38	...	...	...	10	5	4	9	9
92-93—Pittsburgh..............	NHL	58	5	4	9	14	-5	0	0	12	3	2	5	0
—Cleveland..................	IHL	3	2	1	3	0	...	...	...	—	—	—	—	—
93-94—Pittsburgh..............	NHL	63	3	5	8	20	-1	0	0	—	—	—	—	—
—Florida..................	NHL	7	0	0	0	0	0	0	0	—	—	—	—	—
94-95—Florida..................	NHL	3	0	0	0	0	0	0	0	—	—	—	—	—
—Detroit..................	IHL	25	8	12	20	6	...	...	...	5	1	0	1	0
95-96—Springfield..............	AHL	72	22	20	42	32	...	...	...	10	3	0	3	2
96-97—Springfield..............	AHL	38	18	14	32	19	...	...	...	16	7	3	10	4
—Hartford..................	NHL	10	0	2	2	0	2	0	0	—	—	—	—	—
97-98—New Haven..............	AHL	71	24	27	51	34	...	...	...	3	0	1	1	0
—Carolina..................	NHL	2	0	0	0	0	0	0	0	—	—	—	—	—
98-99—Milwaukee..............	IHL	62	12	31	43	19	...	...	...	2	1	1	2	0
—Nashville..................	NHL	9	1	3	4	2	-1	0	0	—	—	—	—	—
99-00—Carolina..................	NHL	69	3	4	7	10	-8	0	0	—	—	—	—	—
00-01—Carolina..................	NHL	67	1	1	2	15	-3	0	0	6	0	2	2	2
01-02—Carolina..................	NHL	65	4	1	5	12	-6	0	1	23	0	1	1	0
02-03—Carolina..................	NHL	59	0	4	4	8	-9	0	0	—	—	—	—	—
NHL Totals (12 years).........		425	17	26	43	83	-31	0	1	41	3	5	8	2

DANTON, MIKE   C   BLUES

PERSONAL: Born October 21, 1980, in Brampton, Ont. ... 5-9/185. ... Shoots right.
TRANSACTIONS/CAREER NOTES: Selected by New Jersey Devils in fifth round (ninth Devils pick, 135th overall) of NHL entry draft (June 24, 2000). ... Traded by Devils to St. Louis Blues (June 21, 2003). ... Signed by Blues (Juy 16, 2003).

Season Team	League	Gms.	G	A	Pts.	PIM	+/-	PP	SH	Gms.	G	A	Pts.	PIM
96-97—Quinte	Tier II Jr. A	35	10	18	28	281	...	...	...	—	—	—	—	—
97-98—Toronto	OHL	18	4	6	10	77	...	...	...	—	—	—	—	—
—Sarnia	OHL	12	6	1	7	37	...	...	...	—	—	—	—	—
98-99—Toronto	OHL	27	18	22	40	116	...	...	...	—	—	—	—	—
—Barrie	OHL	26	15	20	35	62	...	...	...	9	6	5	11	38
99-00—Barrie	OHL	58	34	53	87	203	...	...	...	25	7	16	23	*34
00-01—Albany	AHL	69	19	15	34	195	...	...	...	—	—	—	—	—
—New Jersey	NHL	2	0	0	0	6	0	0	0	—	—	—	—	—
01-02—					Did not play.									
02-03—New Jersey	NHL	17	2	0	2	35	0	0	0	—	—	—	—	—
NHL Totals (2 years)		19	2	0	2	41	0	0	0					

DARBY, CRAIG   C   DEVILS

PERSONAL: Born September 26, 1972, in Oneida, N.Y. ... 6-4/205. ... Shoots right.
TRANSACTIONS/CAREER NOTES: Selected by Montreal Canadiens in second round (third Canadiens pick, 43rd overall) of NHL entry draft (June 22, 1991). ... Traded by Canadiens with LW Kirk Muller and D Mathieu Schneider to New York Islanders for D Vladimir Malakhov and C Pierre Turgeon (April 5, 1995). ... Claimed on waivers by Philadelphia Flyers (June 4, 1996). ... Selected by Nashville Predators in NHL expansion draft (June 26, 1998). ... Signed as free agent by Canadiens (July 9, 1999). ... Separated shoulder (January 10, 2001); missed four games. ... Signed as free agent by New Jersey Devils (July 12, 2002).

Season Team	League	Gms.	G	A	Pts.	PIM	+/-	PP	SH	Gms.	G	A	Pts.	PIM
89-90—Albany Academy	N.Y. H.S.	29	32	53	85	...	...	...	...	—	—	—	—	—
90-91—Albany Academy	N.Y. H.S.	27	33	61	94	53	...	...	...	—	—	—	—	—
91-92—Providence College	Hockey East	35	17	24	41	47	...	...	...	—	—	—	—	—
92-93—Providence College	Hockey East	35	11	21	32	62	...	...	...	—	—	—	—	—
93-94—Fredericton	AHL	66	23	33	56	51	...	...	...	—	—	—	—	—
94-95—Fredericton	AHL	64	21	47	68	82	...	...	...	—	—	—	—	—
—Montreal	NHL	10	0	2	2	0	-5	0	0	—	—	—	—	—
—New York Islanders	NHL	3	0	0	0	0	-1	0	0	—	—	—	—	—
95-96—Worcester	AHL	68	22	28	50	47	...	...	...	4	1	1	2	2
—New York Islanders	NHL	10	0	2	2	0	-1	0	0	—	—	—	—	—
96-97—Philadelphia	AHL	59	26	33	59	24	...	...	...	10	3	6	9	0
—Philadelphia	NHL	9	1	4	5	2	2	0	1	—	—	—	—	—
97-98—Philadelphia	NHL	3	1	0	1	0	0	0	0	—	—	—	—	—
—Philadelphia	AHL	77	†42	45	87	34	...	...	...	20	5	9	14	4
98-99—Milwaukee	IHL	81	32	22	54	33	...	...	...	2	3	0	3	0
99-00—Montreal	NHL	76	7	10	17	14	-14	0	1	—	—	—	—	—
00-01—Montreal	NHL	78	12	16	28	16	-17	0	1	—	—	—	—	—
01-02—Quebec	AHL	66	16	55	71	18	...	...	...	3	2	1	3	0
—Montreal	NHL	2	0	0	0	0	0	0	0	—	—	—	—	—
02-03—Albany	AHL	76	23	51	74	42	...	...	...	—	—	—	—	—
—New Jersey	NHL	3	0	1	1	0	-1	0	0	—	—	—	—	—
NHL Totals (8 years)		194	21	35	56	32	-37	0	3					

DARBY, REGAN   D

PERSONAL: Born July 17, 1980, in Estevan, Sask. ... 6-2/200. ... Shoots left.
TRANSACTIONS/CAREER NOTES: Selected by Vancouver Canucks in fourth round (fifth Canucks pick, 90th overall) of NHL entry draft (June 27, 1998).

Season Team	League	Gms.	G	A	Pts.	PIM	+/-	PP	SH	Gms.	G	A	Pts.	PIM
97-98—Spokane	WHL	7	0	1	1	28	...	...	...	—	—	—	—	—
—Tri-City	WHL	32	1	2	3	125	...	...	...	—	—	—	—	—
98-99—Tri-City	WHL	38	2	4	6	152	...	...	...	—	—	—	—	—
—Red Deer	WHL	19	1	6	7	90	...	...	...	9	0	1	1	18
99-00—Red Deer	WHL	18	3	6	9	79	...	...	...	—	—	—	—	—
—Prince Albert	WHL	44	1	9	10	143	...	...	...	6	0	1	1	23
00-01—Kansas City	IHL	55	1	5	6	164	...	...	...	—	—	—	—	—
01-02—Manitoba	AHL	39	0	1	1	196	...	...	...	—	—	—	—	—
—Columbia	ECHL	7	0	2	2	14	...	...	...	3	0	0	0	0
02-03—Manitoba	AHL	10	0	0	0	30	...	...	...	—	—	—	—	—
—Columbia	ECHL	48	1	7	8	170	...	...	...	—	—	—	—	—

DARCHE, MATHIEU   LW

PERSONAL: Born November 26, 1976, in St. Laurent, Que. ... 6-1/211. ... Shoots left. ... Brother of Jean-Phillipe Darche, tight end, Seattle Seahawks.
TRANSACTIONS/CAREER NOTES: Signed as non-drafted free agent by Columbus Blue Jackets (May 8, 2000).

Season Team	League	Gms.	G	A	Pts.	PIM	+/-	PP	SH	Gms.	G	A	Pts.	PIM
96-97—McGill University	CIAU	23	1	2	3	27	...	...	...	—	—	—	—	—
97-98—McGill University	CIAU	40	28	17	45	69	...	...	...	—	—	—	—	—
98-99—McGill University	CIAU	32	16	24	40	60	...	...	...	—	—	—	—	—
99-00—McGill University	CIAU	38	33	49	82	54	...	...	...	—	—	—	—	—
00-01—Syracuse..................	AHL	66	16	24	40	21	...	...	...	5	0	1	1	4
—Columbus	NHL	9	0	0	0	0	-4	0	0	—	—	—	—	—
01-02—Syracuse..................	AHL	63	22	23	45	26	...	...	...	10	2	5	7	2
—Columbus	NHL	14	1	1	2	6	-5	0	0	—	—	—	—	—
02-03—Syracuse..................	AHL	76	32	32	64	38	...	...	...	—	—	—	—	—
—Columbus	NHL	1	0	0	0	0	-1	0	0	—	—	—	—	—
NHL Totals (3 years)............		24	1	1	2	6	-10	0	0					

DATSYUK, PAVEL   C   RED WINGS

PERSONAL: Born July 20, 1978, in Sverdolvsk, U.S.S.R. ... 5-11/185. ... Shoots left.
TRANSACTIONS/CAREER NOTES: Selected by Detroit Red Wings in sixth round (eighth Red Wings pick, 171st overall) of NHL entry draft (June 27, 1998). ... Suffered from the flu (February 26, 2002); missed one game. ... Re-signed by Red Wings (June 26, 2003).

Season Team	League	Gms.	G	A	Pts.	PIM	+/-	PP	SH	Gms.	G	A	Pts.	PIM
96-97—Spartak Yekaterinburg	Russian	18	2	2	4	4	...	...	...	—	—	—	—	—
—Spartak Yekaterinburg	Rus. Div. II	36	12	10	22	12	...	...	...	—	—	—	—	—
97-98—Dynamo-Energiya	Russian	24	3	5	8	4	...	...	...	—	—	—	—	—
—Dynamo-Energiya	Rus. Div. II	22	7	8	15	4	...	...	...	—	—	—	—	—
99-00—Dyn.-Energiya Yek.	Russian	15	1	3	4	4	...	...	...	—	—	—	—	—
00-01—Ak Bars Kazan............	Russian	42	9	18	27	10	...	...	...	4	0	1	1	2
01-02—Detroit......................	NHL	70	11	24	35	4	4	2	0	21	3	3	6	2
—Russian Oly. team.......	Int'l	6	1	2	3	0	...	...	...	—	—	—	—	—
02-03—Detroit......................	NHL	64	12	39	51	16	20	1	0	4	0	0	0	0
NHL Totals (2 years)............		134	23	63	86	20	24	3	0	25	3	3	6	2

D

DAVIDSON, MATT   RW   FLAMES

PERSONAL: Born August 9, 1977, in Flin Flon, Man. ... 6-3/196. ... Shoots right.
TRANSACTIONS/CAREER NOTES: Selected by Buffalo Sabres in fourth round (fifth Sabres pick, 94th overall) of NHL entry draft (July 8, 1995). ... Traded by Sabres with D Jean-Luc Grand-Pierre, fifth-round pick (C Tyler Kolarik) in 2000 draft and fifth-round pick (traded to Detroit) in 2001 draft to Columbus Blue Jackets for future considerations (June 23, 2000). ... Signed by Calgary Flames (July 15, 2003).

Season Team	League	Gms.	G	A	Pts.	PIM	+/-	PP	SH	Gms.	G	A	Pts.	PIM
93-94—Portland	WHL	59	4	12	16	18	...	...	...	10	0	0	0	4
94-95—Portland	WHL	72	17	20	37	51	...	...	...	9	1	3	4	0
95-96—Portland	WHL	70	24	26	50	96	...	...	...	7	2	2	4	2
96-97—Portland	WHL	72	44	27	71	47	...	...	...	6	0	1	1	2
97-98—Rochester	AHL	72	15	12	27	12	...	...	...	3	1	0	1	2
98-99—Rochester	AHL	80	26	15	41	42	...	...	...	18	2	1	3	6
99-00—Rochester	AHL	80	12	20	32	30	...	...	...	19	4	2	6	8
00-01—Syracuse....................	AHL	72	14	11	25	24	...	...	...	5	1	2	3	2
—Columbus	NHL	5	0	0	0	0	2	0	0	—	—	—	—	—
01-02—Syracuse....................	AHL	47	9	11	20	64	...	...	...	8	1	3	4	4
—Columbus	NHL	17	1	2	3	10	-11	0	0	—	—	—	—	—
02-03—Syracuse....................	AHL	48	18	16	34	26	...	...	...	—	—	—	—	—
—Columbus	NHL	34	4	5	9	18	-12	0	0	—	—	—	—	—
NHL Totals (3 years)............		56	5	7	12	28	-21	0	0					

DAVISON, ROB   D   SHARKS

PERSONAL: Born May 1, 1980, in St. Catherines, Ont. ... 6-2/225. ... Shoots left.
TRANSACTIONS/CAREER NOTES: Selected by San Jose Sharks in fourth round (fourth Sharks pick, 98th overall) of NHL entry draft (June 27, 1998). ... Re-signed by Sharks (July 10, 2003).

Season Team	League	Gms.	G	A	Pts.	PIM	+/-	PP	SH	Gms.	G	A	Pts.	PIM
96-97—St. Michael's	Tier II Jr. A	45	2	6	8	93	...	...	...	—	—	—	—	—
97-98—North Bay	OHL	59	0	11	11	200	...	...	...	—	—	—	—	—
98-99—North Bay	OHL	59	2	17	19	150	...	...	...	4	0	1	1	12
99-00—North Bay	OHL	67	4	6	10	194	...	...	...	6	0	1	1	8
00-01—Kentucky....................	AHL	72	0	4	4	230	...	...	...	3	0	0	0	0
01-02—Cleveland	AHL	70	1	3	4	206	...	...	...	—	—	—	—	—
02-03—Cleveland	AHL	42	1	3	4	82	...	...	...	—	—	—	—	—
—San Jose...................	NHL	15	1	2	3	22	4	0	0	—	—	—	—	—
NHL Totals (1 year)..............		15	1	2	3	22	4	0	0					

DAW, JEFF   C   MAPLE LEAFS

PERSONAL: Born February 28, 1972, in Carlisle, Ont. ... 6-3/190. ... Shoots right.
TRANSACTIONS/CAREER NOTES: Signed as non-drafted free agent by Edmonton Oilers (June 12, 1996). ... Signed as free agent by Chicago Blackhawks (July 22, 1999). ... Selected by Minnesota Wild in NHL expansion draft (June 23, 2000). ... Signed as free agent by Colorado Avalanche (July 23, 2001). ... Traded by Avalanche to Toronto Maple Leafs for future considerations (May 29, 2003).

Season Team	League	REGULAR SEASON								PLAYOFFS				
		Gms.	G	A	Pts.	PIM	+/-	PP	SH	Gms.	G	A	Pts.	PIM
92-93—Mass.-Lowell	Hockey East	37	12	18	30	14	...	...	...	—	—	—	—	—
93-94—Mass.-Lowell	Hockey East	40	6	12	18	12	...	...	...	—	—	—	—	—
94-95—Mass.-Lowell	Hockey East	40	27	15	42	24	...	...	...	—	—	—	—	—
95-96—Mass.-Lowell	Hockey East	40	23	28	51	10	...	...	...	—	—	—	—	—
96-97—Wheeling	ECHL	13	3	8	11	26	...	...	...	—	—	—	—	—
—Hamilton	AHL	56	11	8	19	39	...	...	...	19	4	5	9	0
97-98—Hamilton	AHL	79	28	35	63	20	...	...	...	9	6	3	9	0
98-99—Hamilton	AHL	66	18	29	47	10	...	...	...	11	0	3	3	4
99-00—Cleveland	IHL	9	4	1	5	2	...	...	...	—	—	—	—	—
—Houston	IHL	44	9	8	17	12	...	...	...	—	—	—	—	—
—Lowell	AHL	10	0	5	5	4	...	...	...	7	1	2	3	6
00-01—Cleveland	IHL	8	2	3	5	2	...	...	...	—	—	—	—	—
—Lowell	AHL	65	28	28	56	33	...	...	...	3	0	1	1	2
01-02—Hershey	AHL	79	26	25	51	22	...	...	...	8	1	1	2	4
—Colorado	NHL	1	0	1	1	0	0	0	0	—	—	—	—	—
02-03—Lowell	AHL	51	14	16	30	18	...	...	...	—	—	—	—	—
—Springfield	AHL	12	2	4	6	2	...	...	...	—	—	—	—	—
NHL Totals (1 year)		1	0	1	1	0	0	0	0					

DAWE, JASON — LW

PERSONAL: Born May 29, 1973, in North York, Ont. ... 5-10/190. ... Shoots left. ... Name pronounced DAW.

TRANSACTIONS/CAREER NOTES: Selected by Buffalo Sabres in second round (second Sabres pick, 35th overall) of NHL entry draft (June 22, 1991). ... Sprained knee (February 11, 1995); missed three games. ... Fractured ribs (February 21, 1996); missed six games. ... Traded by Sabres to New York Islanders for LW Paul Kruse and LW Jason Holland (March 24, 1998). ... Claimed on waivers by Montreal Canadiens (December 15, 1998). ... Suffered concussion (February 17, 1999); missed two games. ... Signed as free agent by Nashville Predators (October 2, 1999). ... Traded by Predators to New York Rangers for D John Namestnikov (February 2, 2000). ... Signed as free agent by St. Louis Blues (July 23, 2002).

STATISTICAL PLATEAUS: Three-goal games: 1995-96 (1), 1997-98 (1). Total: 2.

Season Team	League	REGULAR SEASON								PLAYOFFS				
		Gms.	G	A	Pts.	PIM	+/-	PP	SH	Gms.	G	A	Pts.	PIM
89-90—Peterborough	OHL	50	15	18	33	19	...	...	...	12	4	7	11	4
90-91—Peterborough	OHL	66	43	27	70	43	...	...	...	4	3	1	4	0
91-92—Peterborough	OHL	66	53	55	108	55	...	...	...	4	5	0	5	0
92-93—Peterborough	OHL	59	58	68	126	80	...	...	...	21	18	33	51	18
—Rochester	AHL	0	0	0	0	0	—	—	—	3	1	0	1	0
93-94—Rochester	AHL	48	22	14	36	44	...	...	...	—	—	—	—	—
—Buffalo	NHL	32	6	7	13	12	1	3	0	6	0	1	1	6
94-95—Rochester	AHL	44	27	19	46	24	...	...	...	—	—	—	—	—
—Buffalo	NHL	42	7	4	11	19	-6	0	1	5	2	1	3	6
95-96—Buffalo	NHL	67	25	25	50	33	-8	8	1	—	—	—	—	—
—Rochester	AHL	7	5	4	9	2	...	...	...	—	—	—	—	—
96-97—Buffalo	NHL	81	22	26	48	32	14	4	1	11	2	1	3	6
97-98—Buffalo	NHL	68	19	17	36	36	10	4	1	—	—	—	—	—
—New York Islanders	NHL	13	1	2	3	6	-2	0	0	—	—	—	—	—
98-99—New York Islanders	NHL	22	2	3	5	8	0	0	0	—	—	—	—	—
—Montreal	NHL	37	4	5	9	14	0	1	0	—	—	—	—	—
99-00—Milwaukee	IHL	41	11	13	24	24	...	...	...	—	—	—	—	—
—Hartford	AHL	27	9	9	18	24	...	...	...	21	10	7	17	37
—New York Rangers	NHL	3	0	1	1	2	0	0	0	—	—	—	—	—
00-01—Hartford	AHL	4	2	0	2	2	...	...	...	—	—	—	—	—
01-02—Hartford	AHL	79	28	37	65	46	...	...	...	9	4	0	4	15
—New York Rangers	NHL	1	0	0	0	0	-1	0	0	—	—	—	—	—
02-03—Worcester	AHL	71	17	28	45	47	...	...	...	—	—	—	—	—
NHL Totals (8 years)		366	86	90	176	162	8	20	4	22	4	3	7	18

DAZE, ERIC — LW — BLACKHAWKS

PERSONAL: Born July 2, 1975, in Montreal ... 6-6/228. ... Shoots left. ... Name pronounced dah-ZAY.

TRANSACTIONS/CAREER NOTES: Selected by Chicago Blackhawks in fourth round (fifth Blackhawks pick, 90th overall) of NHL entry draft (June 26, 1993). ... Sprained left ankle prior to 1996-97 season; missed eight games. ... Suffered from the flu (January 20, 1997); missed one game. ... Injured back (March 27, 1998); missed two games. ... Bruised ankle (October 22, 1998); missed three games. ... Suffered back spasms (October 27, 1999); missed three games. ... Suffered from the flu (January 2, 2000); missed one game. ... Suffered from migraine headache (February 16, 2000); missed one game. ... Suffered back spasms (March 3, 2000) and underwent surgery; missed final 18 games of season.

STATISTICAL PLATEAUS: Three-goal games: 1996-97 (1), 2001-02 (2), 2002-03 (2). Total: 5. ... Four-goal games: 1997-98 (1). ... Total hat tricks: 6.

Season Team	League	REGULAR SEASON								PLAYOFFS				
		Gms.	G	A	Pts.	PIM	+/-	PP	SH	Gms.	G	A	Pts.	PIM
92-93—Beauport	QMJHL	68	19	36	55	24	...	...	...	—	—	—	—	—
93-94—Beauport	QMJHL	66	59	48	107	31	...	...	...	15	16	8	24	2
94-95—Beauport	QMJHL	57	54	45	99	20	...	...	...	16	9	12	21	23
—Chicago	NHL	4	1	1	2	2	2	0	0	16	0	1	1	4
95-96—Chicago	NHL	80	30	23	53	18	16	2	0	10	3	5	8	0
96-97—Chicago	NHL	71	22	19	41	16	-4	11	0	6	2	1	3	2
97-98—Chicago	NHL	80	31	11	42	22	4	10	0	—	—	—	—	—
98-99—Chicago	NHL	72	22	20	42	22	-13	8	0	—	—	—	—	—
99-00—Chicago	NHL	59	23	13	36	28	-16	6	0	—	—	—	—	—
00-01—Chicago	NHL	79	33	24	57	16	1	9	1	—	—	—	—	—
01-02—Chicago	NHL	82	38	32	70	36	17	12	0	5	0	0	0	2
02-03—Chicago	NHL	54	22	22	44	14	10	3	0	—	—	—	—	—
NHL Totals (9 years)		581	222	165	387	174	17	61	1	37	5	7	12	8

DE VRIES, GREG   D   RANGERS

PERSONAL: Born January 4, 1973, in Sundridge, Ont. ... 6-2/214. ... Shoots left. ... Name pronounced duh-VREES.
TRANSACTIONS/CAREER NOTES: Signed as non-drafted free agent by Edmonton Oilers (March 28, 1994). ... Sprained ankle (January 26, 1997); missed four games. ... Traded by Oilers with G Eric Fichaud and D Drake Berehowsky to Nashville Predators for C Jim Dowd and G Mikhail Shtalenkov (October 1, 1998). ... Traded by Predators to Colorado Avalanche for third-round pick (RW Branko Radivojevic) in 1999 draft (October 25, 1998). ... Suffered from the flu (December 27, 1999); missed two games. ... Separated shoulder (February 19, 2001); missed three games. ... Signed by New York Rangers (July 14, 2003).

		REGULAR SEASON								PLAYOFFS				
Season Team	League	Gms.	G	A	Pts.	PIM	+/-	PP	SH	Gms.	G	A	Pts.	PIM
91-92—Bowling Green	CCHA	24	0	3	3	20	...	...	...	—	—	—	—	—
92-93—Niagara Falls	OHL	62	3	23	26	86	...	...	...	4	0	1	1	6
93-94—Niagara Falls	OHL	64	5	40	45	135	...	...	...	—	—	—	—	—
—Cape Breton	AHL	9	0	0	0	11	...	...	...	1	0	0	0	0
94-95—Cape Breton	AHL	77	5	19	24	68	...	...	...	—	—	—	—	—
95-96—Edmonton	NHL	13	1	1	2	12	-2	0	0	—	—	—	—	—
—Cape Breton	AHL	58	9	30	39	174	...	...	...	—	—	—	—	—
96-97—Hamilton	AHL	34	4	14	18	26	...	...	...	—	—	—	—	—
—Edmonton	NHL	37	0	4	4	52	-2	0	0	12	0	1	1	8
97-98—Edmonton	NHL	65	7	4	11	80	-17	1	0	7	0	0	0	21
98-99—Nashville	NHL	6	0	0	0	4	-4	0	0	—	—	—	—	—
—Colorado	NHL	67	1	3	4	60	-3	0	0	19	0	2	2	22
99-00—Colorado	NHL	69	2	7	9	73	-7	0	0	5	0	0	0	4
00-01—Colorado	NHL	79	5	12	17	51	23	0	0	23	0	1	1	20
01-02—Colorado	NHL	82	8	12	20	57	18	1	1	21	4	9	13	2
02-03—Colorado	NHL	82	6	26	32	70	15	0	0	7	2	0	2	0
NHL Totals (8 years)		**500**	**30**	**69**	**99**	**459**	**21**	**2**	**1**	**94**	**6**	**13**	**19**	**77**

DEADMARSH, ADAM   RW   KINGS

D

PERSONAL: Born May 10, 1975, in Trail, B.C. ... 6-0/210. ... Shoots right. ... Cousin of Butch Deadmarsh, left winger with three NHL teams (1970-71 through 1974-75); and brother of Jake Deadmarsh, left winger with San Jose Sharks organization (1996-97 and 1997-98).
TRANSACTIONS/CAREER NOTES: Selected by Quebec Nordiques in first round (second Nordiques pick, 14th overall) of NHL entry draft (June 26, 1993). ... Nordiques franchise moved to Colorado and renamed Avalanche for 1995-96 season (June 21, 1995). ... Strained groin (April 3, 1996); missed four games. ... Strained shoulder (December 13, 1997); missed one game. ... Suffered from the flu (January 14, 1998); missed one game. ... Strained hip flexor (March 19, 1998); missed one game. ... Injured shoulder (April 1, 1998); missed two games. ... Bruised thigh (April 11, 1998); missed two games. ... Bruised ribs (October 9, 1998); missed first two games of season. ... Suffered infected left elbow (October 24, 1998); missed three games. ... Suffered back spasms (March 16, 1999); missed five games. ... Injured eye (April 3, 1999); missed final six games of regular season. ... Suffered hip pointer prior to start of 1999-2000 regular season; missed first two games of season. ... Bruised toe (December 12, 1999); missed one game. ... Sprained knee (January 13, 2000); missed three games. ... Injured rib (February 15, 2000); missed five games. ... Injured eye (October 18, 2000); missed one game. ... Suffered concussion (November 1, 2000); missed 14 games. ... Injured knee (January 18, 2001); missed five games. ... Traded by Avalanche with D Aaron Miller, first-round pick (C David Steckel) in 2001 draft, a player to be named later and future considerations to Los Angeles Kings for C Steve Reinprecht and D Rob Blake (February 21, 2001); Kings acquired C Jared Aulin to complete deal (March 22, 2001). ... Bruised hand (March 5, 2001); missed three games. ... Strained groin (October 2, 2001); missed first game of season. ... Suffered injury (October 28, 2001); missed one game. ... Suffered injury (November 17, 2001); missed four games.
STATISTICAL PLATEAUS: Three-goal games: 1999-00 (1), 2002-03 (1). Total: 2.

		REGULAR SEASON								PLAYOFFS				
Season Team	League	Gms.	G	A	Pts.	PIM	+/-	PP	SH	Gms.	G	A	Pts.	PIM
91-92—Portland	WHL	68	30	30	60	81	...	...	...	6	3	3	6	13
92-93—Portland	WHL	58	33	36	69	126	...	...	...	16	7	8	15	29
93-94—Portland	WHL	65	43	56	99	212	...	...	...	10	9	8	17	33
94-95—Portland	WHL	29	28	20	48	129	...	...	...	—	—	—	—	—
—Quebec	NHL	48	9	8	17	56	16	0	0	6	0	1	1	0
95-96—Colorado	NHL	78	21	27	48	142	20	3	0	22	5	12	17	25
96-97—Colorado	NHL	78	33	27	60	136	8	10	3	17	3	6	9	24
97-98—Colorado	NHL	73	22	21	43	125	0	10	0	7	2	0	2	4
—U.S. Olympic team	Int'l	4	1	0	1	2	...	...	...	—	—	—	—	—
98-99—Colorado	NHL	66	22	27	49	99	-2	10	0	19	8	4	12	20
99-00—Colorado	NHL	71	18	27	45	106	-10	5	0	17	4	11	15	21
00-01—Colorado	NHL	39	13	13	26	59	-2	7	0	—	—	—	—	—
—Los Angeles	NHL	18	4	2	6	4	3	0	0	13	3	3	6	4
01-02—Los Angeles	NHL	76	29	33	62	71	8	12	0	4	1	3	4	2
—U.S. Olympic team	Int'l	6	1	1	2	2	...	...	...	—	—	—	—	—
02-03—Los Angeles	NHL	20	13	4	17	21	2	4	0	—	—	—	—	—
NHL Totals (9 years)		**567**	**184**	**189**	**373**	**819**	**43**	**61**	**3**	**105**	**26**	**40**	**66**	**100**

DEBRUSK, LOUIE   LW

PERSONAL: Born March 19, 1971, in Cambridge, Ont. ... 6-2/227. ... Shoots left. ... Full Name: Dennis Louis DeBrusk. ... Name pronounced dee-BRUHSK.
TRANSACTIONS/CAREER NOTES: Traded by Rangers with C Bernie Nicholls, RW Steven Rice and future considerations to Edmonton Oilers for C Mark Messier and future considerations (October 4, 1991); Rangers traded D David Shaw to Oilers for D Jeff Beukeboom to complete deal (November 12, 1991). ... Separated shoulder (January 28, 1992); missed four games. ... Strained groin (January 1993); missed five games. ... Strained abdominal muscle (January 1993); missed 11 games. ... Underwent blood tests (April 17, 1995); missed one game. ... Suspended two games by NHL for headbutting an opponent (October 6, 1995). ... Injured elbow (November 26, 1995); missed 14 games. ...

Suspended four games and fined $1,000 by NHL for slashing (October 9, 1996). ... Signed as free agent by Tampa Bay Lightning (August 26, 1997). ... Traded by Lightning with fifth-round pick (D Jay Leach) in 1998 draft to Phoenix Coyotes for C Craig Janney (June 11, 1998). ... Suffered from the flu (April 17, 1999); missed final game of regular season. ... Strained groin (December 5, 2000); missed two games. ... Signed by Edmonton Oilers (February 16, 2002). ... Signed by Chicago Blackhawks (August 30, 2002).

			REGULAR SEASON								PLAYOFFS			
Season Team	League	Gms.	G	A	Pts.	PIM	+/-	PP	SH	Gms.	G	A	Pts.	PIM
87-88—Stratford Jr. B	OHA	43	13	14	27	205	...	...	...	—	—	—	—	—
88-89—London	OHL	59	11	11	22	149	...	...	...	19	1	1	2	43
89-90—London	OHL	61	21	19	40	198	...	...	...	6	2	2	4	24
90-91—London	OHL	61	31	33	64	*223	...	...	...	7	2	2	4	14
—Binghamton	AHL	2	0	0	0	7	...	...	...	2	0	0	0	9
91-92—Edmonton	NHL	25	2	1	3	124	4	0	0	—	—	—	—	—
—Cape Breton	AHL	28	2	2	4	73	...	...	...	—	—	—	—	—
92-93—Edmonton	NHL	51	8	2	10	205	-16	0	0	—	—	—	—	—
93-94—Edmonton	NHL	48	4	6	10	185	-9	0	0	—	—	—	—	—
—Cape Breton	AHL	5	3	1	4	58	...	...	...	—	—	—	—	—
94-95—Edmonton	NHL	34	2	0	2	93	-4	0	0	—	—	—	—	—
95-96—Edmonton	NHL	38	1	3	4	96	-7	0	0	—	—	—	—	—
96-97—Edmonton	NHL	32	2	0	2	94	-6	0	0	6	0	0	0	4
97-98—Tampa Bay	NHL	54	1	2	3	166	-2	0	0	—	—	—	—	—
—San Antonio	IHL	17	7	4	11	130	...	...	...	—	—	—	—	—
98-99—Las Vegas	IHL	26	3	6	9	160	...	...	...	—	—	—	—	—
—Phoenix	NHL	15	0	0	0	34	-2	0	0	6	2	0	2	6
—Springfield	AHL	3	1	0	1	0	...	...	...	—	—	—	—	—
—Long Beach	IHL	24	5	5	10	134	...	...	...	—	—	—	—	—
99-00—Phoenix	NHL	61	4	3	7	78	1	0	0	3	0	0	0	0
00-01—Phoenix	NHL	39	0	0	0	79	-5	0	0	—	—	—	—	—
01-02—Quebec	AHL	9	0	0	0	44	...	...	...	—	—	—	—	—
—Hamilton	AHL	20	3	5	8	42	...	...	...	13	1	0	1	30
02-03—Norfolk	AHL	20	1	0	1	10	...	...	...	—	—	—	—	—
—Chicago	NHL	4	0	0	0	7	0	0	0	—	—	—	—	—
NHL Totals (11 years)		401	24	17	41	1161	-46	0	0	15	2	0	2	10

DEFAUW, BRAD — LW — HURRICANES

PERSONAL: Born November 11, 1977, in Edina, Minn. ... 6-2/220. ... Shoots left.
TRANSACTIONS/CAREER NOTES: Selected by Carolina Hurricanes in second round (second Hurricanes pick, 28th overall) of NHL entry draft (June 21, 1997).

			REGULAR SEASON								PLAYOFFS			
Season Team	League	Gms.	G	A	Pts.	PIM	+/-	PP	SH	Gms.	G	A	Pts.	PIM
95-96—Apple Valley	Minn. H.S.	28	21	34	55	14	...	...	...	—	—	—	—	—
96-97—Univ. of North Dakota	WCHA	37	7	6	13	39	...	...	...	—	—	—	—	—
97-98—Univ. of North Dakota	WCHA	36	9	11	20	34	...	...	...	—	—	—	—	—
98-99—Univ. of North Dakota	WCHA	34	11	12	23	64	...	...	...	—	—	—	—	—
99-00—Univ. of North Dakota	WCHA	43	13	9	22	52	...	...	...	—	—	—	—	—
00-01—Cincinnati	IHL	82	20	31	51	39	...	...	...	4	2	0	2	8
01-02—Lowell	AHL	63	17	21	38	29	...	...	...	5	2	1	3	6
02-03—Lowell	AHL	61	11	12	23	48	...	...	...	—	—	—	—	—
—Carolina	NHL	9	3	0	3	2	-2	1	0	—	—	—	—	—
NHL Totals (1 year)		9	3	0	3	2	-2	1	0					

DELMORE, ANDY — D — SABRES

PERSONAL: Born December 26, 1976, in LaSalle, Ont. ... 6-1/200. ... Shoots right.
TRANSACTIONS/CAREER NOTES: Signed as non-drafted free agent by Philadelphia Flyers (July 9, 1997). ... Sprained right knee (March 5, 2000); missed nine games. ... Traded by Flyers to Nashville Predators for third-round pick (traded to Phoenix) in 2002 draft (July 31, 2001). ... Strained hamstring (December 17, 2001); missed one game. ... Reinjured hamstring (December 23, 2001); missed eight games. ... Traded by Predators to Buffalo Sabres for third-round pick in 2004 draft (June 29, 2003).

			REGULAR SEASON								PLAYOFFS			
Season Team	League	Gms.	G	A	Pts.	PIM	+/-	PP	SH	Gms.	G	A	Pts.	PIM
92-93—Chatham Jr. B	OHA	47	4	21	25	38	...	...	...	—	—	—	—	—
93-94—North Bay	OHL	45	2	7	9	33	...	...	...	17	0	0	0	2
94-95—North Bay	OHL	40	2	14	16	21	...	...	...	—	—	—	—	—
—Sarnia	OHL	27	5	13	18	27	...	...	...	3	0	0	0	2
95-96—Sarnia	OHL	64	21	38	59	45	...	...	...	10	3	7	10	2
96-97—Sarnia	OHL	63	18	60	78	39	...	...	...	12	2	10	12	10
—Fredericton	AHL	4	0	1	1	0	...	...	...	—	—	—	—	—
97-98—Philadelphia	AHL	73	9	30	39	46	...	...	...	18	4	4	8	21
98-99—Philadelphia	AHL	70	5	18	23	51	...	...	...	15	1	4	5	6
—Philadelphia	NHL	2	0	1	1	0	-1	0	0	—	—	—	—	—
99-00—Philadelphia	AHL	39	12	14	26	31	...	...	...	—	—	—	—	—
—Philadelphia	NHL	27	2	5	7	8	-1	0	0	18	5	2	7	14
00-01—Philadelphia	NHL	66	5	9	14	16	2	2	0	2	1	0	1	2
01-02—Nashville	NHL	73	16	22	38	22	-13	11	0	—	—	—	—	—
02-03—Nashville	NHL	71	18	16	34	28	-17	14	0	—	—	—	—	—
NHL Totals (5 years)		239	41	53	94	74	-30	27	0	20	6	2	8	16

DEMARCHI, MATT — D — DEVILS

PERSONAL: Born May 4, 1981, in Bemidji, Minn. ... 6-3/180.
COLLEGE: Minnesota.
TRANSACTIONS/CAREER NOTES: Selected by New Jersey Devils in second round (fourth Devils pick, 57th overall) of NHL entry draft (June 24, 2000). ... Signed by Devils (July 15, 2003).

		REGULAR SEASON								PLAYOFFS				
Season Team	League	Gms.	G	A	Pts.	PIM	+/-	PP	SH	Gms.	G	A	Pts.	PIM
97-98—North Iowa	USHL	34	1	2	3	66	...	...	...	10	0	1	1	19
98-99—North Iowa	USHL	53	4	14	18	131	...	...	...	—	—	—	—	—
99-00—Univ. of Minnesota	WCHA	34	0	4	4	72	...	...	...	—	—	—	—	—
00-01—Univ. of Minnesota	WCHA	39	4	9	13	*149	...	...	...	—	—	—	—	—
01-02—Univ. of Minnesota	WCHA	36	3	8	11	*112	...	...	...	—	—	—	—	—
02-03—Univ. of Minnesota	WCHA	44	8	9	17	130	...	...	...	—	—	—	—	—

DEMITRA, PAVOL — C — BLUES

PERSONAL: Born November 29, 1974, in Dubnica, Czechoslovakia ... 6-0/206. ... Shoots left. ... Name pronounced PA-vuhl dih-MEE-truh.
TRANSACTIONS/CAREER NOTES: Selected by Ottawa Senators in ninth round (ninth Senators pick, 227th overall) of NHL entry draft (June 26, 1993). ... Fractured ankle (October 14, 1993); missed 23 games. ... Traded by Senators to St. Louis Blues for D Christer Olsson (November 27, 1996). ... Suffered back spasms and bruised tailbone (December 8, 1997); missed 10 games. ... Fractured jaw (March 7, 1998); missed 11 games. ... Injured triceps (December 26, 1999); missed three games. ... Suffered concussion (March 24, 2000); missed remainder of season. ... Suffered eye injury (December 30, 2000); missed 17 games. ... Injured hamstring (February 10, 2001); missed 14 games. ... Reinjured hamstring (March 14, 2001); missed seven games.
STATISTICAL PLATEAUS: Three-goal games: 1999-00 (1), 2000-01 (1), 2002-03 (1). Total: 3.

		REGULAR SEASON								PLAYOFFS				
Season Team	League	Gms.	G	A	Pts.	PIM	+/-	PP	SH	Gms.	G	A	Pts.	PIM
91-92—Sparta Dubnica	Czech Dv.II	28	13	10	23	12	...	...	...	—	—	—	—	—
92-93—Dukla Trencin	Czech.	46	11	17	28	0	...	...	...	—	—	—	—	—
—CAPEH Dubnica	Czech Dv.II	4	3	0	3	...	...	...	...	—	—	—	—	—
93-94—Ottawa	NHL	12	1	1	2	4	-7	1	0	—	—	—	—	—
—Prin. Edward Island	AHL	41	18	23	41	8	...	...	...	—	—	—	—	—
94-95—Prin. Edward Island	AHL	61	26	48	74	23	...	...	...	5	0	7	7	0
—Ottawa	NHL	16	4	3	7	0	-4	1	0	—	—	—	—	—
95-96—Prin. Edward Island	AHL	48	28	53	81	44	...	...	...	—	—	—	—	—
—Ottawa	NHL	31	7	10	17	6	-3	2	0	—	—	—	—	—
96-97—Las Vegas	IHL	22	8	13	21	10	...	...	...	—	—	—	—	—
—Grand Rapids	IHL	42	20	30	50	24	...	...	...	—	—	—	—	—
—Dukla Trencin	Slovakia	1	1	1	2	...	...	...	...	—	—	—	—	—
—St. Louis	NHL	8	3	0	3	2	0	2	0	6	1	3	4	6
97-98—St. Louis	NHL	61	22	30	52	22	11	4	4	10	3	3	6	2
98-99—St. Louis	NHL	82	37	52	89	16	13	14	0	13	5	4	9	4
99-00—St. Louis	NHL	71	28	47	75	8	34	8	0	—	—	—	—	—
00-01—St. Louis	NHL	44	20	25	45	16	27	5	0	15	2	4	6	2
01-02—St. Louis	NHL	82	35	43	78	46	13	11	0	10	4	7	11	6
—Slovakian Oly. team	Int'l	2	1	2	3	2	...	...	...	—	—	—	—	—
02-03—St. Louis	NHL	78	36	57	93	32	0	11	0	7	2	4	6	2
NHL Totals (10 years)		485	193	268	461	152	84	59	4	61	17	25	42	22

DEMPSEY, NATHAN — D — BLACKHAWKS

PERSONAL: Born July 14, 1974, in Spruce Grove, Alta. ... 6-0/191. ... Shoots left.
TRANSACTIONS/CAREER NOTES: Selected by Toronto Maple Leafs in 11th round (11th Leafs pick, 245th overall) of NHL entry draft (June 20, 1992). ... Signed as free agent by Chicago Blackhawks (July 12, 2002).

		REGULAR SEASON								PLAYOFFS				
Season Team	League	Gms.	G	A	Pts.	PIM	+/-	PP	SH	Gms.	G	A	Pts.	PIM
91-92—Regina	WHL	70	4	22	26	72	...	...	...	—	—	—	—	—
92-93—Regina	WHL	72	12	29	41	95	...	...	...	13	3	8	11	14
—St. John's	AHL	0	0	0	0	0	—	—	—	2	0	0	0	0
93-94—Regina	WHL	56	14	36	50	100	...	...	...	4	0	0	0	4
94-95—St. John's	AHL	74	7	30	37	91	...	...	...	5	1	0	1	11
95-96—St. John's	AHL	73	5	15	20	103	...	...	...	4	1	0	1	9
96-97—St. John's	AHL	52	8	18	26	108	...	...	...	6	1	0	1	4
—Toronto	NHL	14	1	1	2	2	-2	0	0	—	—	—	—	—
97-98—St. John's	AHL	68	12	16	28	85	...	...	...	4	0	0	0	0
98-99—St. John's	AHL	67	2	29	31	70	...	...	...	5	0	1	1	2
99-00—St. John's	AHL	44	15	12	27	40	...	...	...	—	—	—	—	—
—Toronto	NHL	6	0	2	2	2	2	0	0	—	—	—	—	—
00-01—St. John's	AHL	55	11	28	39	60	...	...	...	4	0	4	4	8
—Toronto	NHL	25	1	9	10	4	13	1	0	—	—	—	—	—
01-02—St. John's	AHL	75	13	48	61	66	...	...	...	11	1	5	6	8
—Toronto	NHL	3	0	0	0	0	1	0	0	6	0	2	2	0
02-03—Chicago	NHL	67	5	23	28	26	-7	1	0	—	—	—	—	—
NHL Totals (5 years)		115	7	35	42	34	7	2	0	6	0	2	2	0

DENIS, MARC   G   BLUE JACKETS

PERSONAL: Born August 1, 1977, in Montreal ... 6-1/193. ... Catches left. ... Name pronounced deh-NEE.
TRANSACTIONS/CAREER NOTES: Selected by Colorado Avalanche in first round (first Avalanche pick, 25th overall) of NHL entry draft (July 8, 1995). ... Traded by Avalanche to Columbus Blue Jackets for second-round pick (traded to Carolina) in 2000 draft (June 7, 2000). ... Strained groin (March 6, 2002); missed four games.

Season Team	League	Gms.	Min	W	L	T	GA	SO	Avg.	SV%	Gms.	Min.	W	L	GA	SO	Avg.	SV%
					REGULAR SEASON									PLAYOFFS				
94-95—Chicoutimi	QMJHL	32	1688	17	9	1	98	0	3.48	—	6	374	4	2	19	1	3.05	—
95-96—Chicoutimi	QMJHL	51	2895	23	21	4	157	2	3.25	—	16	917	8	†8	66	0	4.32	—
96-97—Chicoutimi	QMJHL	41	2317	22	15	2	104	4	*2.69	—	*21	*1226	*11	*10	*70	*1	3.43	—
—Colorado	NHL	1	60	0	1	0	3	0	3.00	.885	—	—	—	—	—	—	—	—
—Hershey	AHL	—	—	—	—	—	—	—	—	—	4	56	1	0	1	0	*1.07	—
97-98—Hershey	AHL	47	2589	17	23	4	125	1	2.90	—	6	347	3	3	15	0	2.59	—
98-99—Hershey	AHL	52	2908	20	23	5	137	4	2.83	—	3	143	1	1	7	0	2.94	—
—Colorado	NHL	4	217	1	1	1	9	0	2.49	.918	—	—	—	—	—	—	—	—
99-00—Colorado	NHL	23	1203	9	8	3	51	3	2.54	.917	—	—	—	—	—	—	—	—
00-01—Columbus	NHL	32	1830	6	20	4	99	0	3.25	.895	—	—	—	—	—	—	—	—
01-02—Columbus	NHL	42	2335	9	24	5	121	1	3.11	.899	—	—	—	—	—	—	—	—
02-03—Columbus	NHL	*77	*4511	27	*41	8	*232	5	3.09	.903	—	—	—	—	—	—	—	—
NHL Totals (6 years)		179	10156	52	95	21	515	9	3.04	.903								

DESJARDINS, ERIC   D   FLYERS

PERSONAL: Born June 14, 1969, in Rouyn, Que. ... 6-1/205. ... Shoots right. ... Name pronounced day-zhar-DAN.
TRANSACTIONS/CAREER NOTES: Selected by Montreal Canadiens in second round (third Canadiens pick, 38th overall) of NHL entry draft (June 13, 1987). ... Suffered from the flu (January 1989). ... Pulled groin (November 2, 1989); missed seven games. ... Sprained left ankle (January 26, 1991); missed 16 games. ... Fractured right thumb (December 8, 1991); missed two games. ... Traded by Canadiens with LW Gilbert Dionne and C John LeClair to Philadelphia Flyers for RW Mark Recchi and third-round pick (C Martin Hohenberger) in 1995 draft (February 9, 1995). ... Slightly strained groin (March 28, 1995); missed one game. ... Reinjured groin (April 1, 1995); missed three games. ... Suffered from the flu (December 26, 1995); missed one game. ... Suffered inflamed pelvic bone (October 1, 1997); missed five games. ... Strained groin (October 27, 1998); missed four games. ... Suffered from stomach virus (March 6, 1999); missed three games. ... Sprained left knee (March 21, 1999); missed seven games. ... Suffered head injury prior to start of 1999-2000 season; missed first game of season. ... Suffered from stromach virus (December 21, 2000); missed one game. ... Suffered concussion (March 8, 2001); missed two games. ... Strained lower back and injured left elbow (October 27, 2001); missed three games. ... Fractured finger (December 10, 2001); missed 12 games. ... Strained lower back (April 4, 2002); missed two games. ... Re-signed by Flyers (June 29, 2003).

Season Team	League	Gms.	G	A	Pts.	PIM	+/-	PP	SH	Gms.	G	A	Pts.	PIM
				REGULAR SEASON								PLAYOFFS		
86-87—Granby	QMJHL	66	14	24	38	75	...	...	...	8	3	2	5	10
87-88—Granby	QMJHL	62	18	49	67	138	...	...	...	5	0	3	3	10
—Sherbrooke	AHL	3	0	0	0	6	...	...	...	4	0	2	2	2
88-89—Montreal	NHL	36	2	12	14	26	9	1	0	14	1	1	2	6
89-90—Montreal	NHL	55	3	13	16	51	1	1	0	6	0	0	0	10
90-91—Montreal	NHL	62	7	18	25	27	7	0	0	13	1	4	5	8
91-92—Montreal	NHL	77	6	32	38	50	17	4	0	11	3	3	6	4
92-93—Montreal	NHL	82	13	32	45	98	20	7	0	20	4	10	14	23
93-94—Montreal	NHL	84	12	23	35	97	-1	6	1	7	0	2	2	4
94-95—Montreal	NHL	9	0	6	6	2	2	0	0	—	—	—	—	—
—Philadelphia	NHL	34	5	18	23	12	10	1	0	15	4	4	8	10
95-96—Philadelphia	NHL	80	7	40	47	45	19	5	0	12	0	6	6	2
96-97—Philadelphia	NHL	82	12	34	46	50	25	5	1	19	2	8	10	12
97-98—Philadelphia	NHL	77	6	27	33	36	11	2	1	5	0	1	1	0
—Can. Olympic team	Int'l	6	0	0	0	2	...	...	...	—	—	—	—	—
98-99—Philadelphia	NHL	68	15	36	51	38	18	6	0	6	2	2	4	4
99-00—Philadelphia	NHL	81	14	41	55	32	20	8	0	18	2	10	12	2
00-01—Philadelphia	NHL	79	15	33	48	50	-3	6	1	6	1	1	2	0
01-02—Philadelphia	NHL	65	6	19	25	24	-1	2	1	5	0	1	1	2
02-03—Philadelphia	NHL	79	8	24	32	35	30	1	0	5	2	1	3	0
NHL Totals (15 years)		1050	131	408	539	673	184	55	5	162	22	54	76	87

DESROCHERS, PATRICK   G   HURRICANES

PERSONAL: Born October 27, 1979, in Penetanguishene, Ont. ... 6-4/205. ... Catches left.
TRANSACTIONS/CAREER NOTES: Selected by Phoenix Coyotes in first round (first Coyotes pick, 14th overall) of NHL entry draft (June 27, 1998). ... Traded by Coyotes to Carolina Hurricanes for G Jean-Marc Pelletier and conditional draft pick (December 31, 2002).

Season Team	League	Gms.	Min	W	L	T	GA	SO	Avg.	SV%	Gms.	Min.	W	L	GA	SO	Avg.	SV%
					REGULAR SEASON									PLAYOFFS				
95-96—Sarnia	OHL	29	1265	12	6	2	96	0	4.55	—	3	71	0	1	5	0	4.23	—
96-97—Sarnia	OHL	50	2667	22	17	4	154	4	3.46	—	11	576	6	5	42	0	4.38	—
97-98—Sarnia	OHL	56	3205	26	17	11	179	1	3.35	—	4	160	1	2	12	0	4.50	—
98-99—Sarnia	OHL	8	425	3	5	0	26	0	3.67	—	—	—	—	—	—	—	—	—
—Kingston	OHL	44	2389	14	22	3	177	1	4.45	—	5	323	1	4	21	0	3.90	—
—Canadian nat'l team	Int'l	6	60	1	0	0	4	0	4.00	—	—	—	—	—	—	—	—	—
99-00—Springfield	AHL	52	2710	21	17	†7	137	1	3.03	—	2	120	1	1	7	1	3.50	—
00-01—Springfield	AHL	50	2807	17	24	5	156	0	3.33	—	—	—	—	—	—	—	—	—
01-02—Springfield	AHL	34	1864	12	18	1	94	2	3.03	—	—	—	—	—	—	—	—	—
—Phoenix	NHL	5	243	1	2	1	15	0	3.70	.848	—	—	—	—	—	—	—	—
02-03—Springfield	AHL	8	454	2	4	1	20	0	2.64	—	—	—	—	—	—	—	—	—
—Phoenix	NHL	4	175	0	3	0	11	0	3.77	.875	—	—	—	—	—	—	—	—
—Carolina	NHL	2	122	1	1	0	7	0	3.44	.901	—	—	—	—	—	—	—	—
—Lowell	AHL	17	1029	4	12	1	48	0	2.80	—	—	—	—	—	—	—	—	—
NHL Totals (2 years)		11	540	2	6	1	33	0	3.67	.872								

D

DESSNER, JEFF — D — THRASHERS

PERSONAL: Born April 16, 1977, in Glenview, Ill.. ... Shoots left. ... Full Name: Jeffrey Marc Dessner.
TRANSACTIONS/CAREER NOTES: Selected by New York Rangers in seventh round (sixth Rangers pick, 185th overall) of NHL entry draft (June 22, 1996). ... Traded by Rangers to Atlanta Thrashers for eighth-round pick (D Leonid Zhvachin) in 2001 draft (June 24, 2001).

Season Team	League	REGULAR SEASON								PLAYOFFS				
		Gms.	G	A	Pts.	PIM	+/-	PP	SH	Gms.	G	A	Pts.	PIM
97-98—Univ. of Wisconsin	WCHA	19	1	3	4	43	...	...	...	—	—	—	—	—
98-99—Univ. of Wisconsin	WCHA	37	7	14	21	46	...	...	...	—	—	—	—	—
99-00—Univ. of Wisconsin	WCHA	40	11	16	27	61	...	...	...	—	—	—	—	—
00-01—Univ. of Wisconsin	WCHA	39	7	12	19	58	...	...	...	—	—	—	—	—
01-02—Chicago	AHL	40	1	11	12	80	...	...	...	—	—	—	—	—
—Greenville	ECHL	5	1	2	3	8	...	...	...	13	3	5	8	10
02-03—Iserlohn	Germany	35	8	12	20	82	...	...	...	—	—	—	—	—

DEVEREAUX, BOYD — C — RED WINGS

PERSONAL: Born April 16, 1978, in Seaforth, Ont. ... 6-2/195. ... Shoots left. ... Name pronounced DEH-vuh-roh.
TRANSACTIONS/CAREER NOTES: Selected by Edmonton Oilers in first round (first Oilers pick, sixth overall) of NHL entry draft (June 22, 1996). ... Suffered concussion (April 1, 2000); missed remainder of season. ... Signed as free agent by Detroit Red Wings (August 23, 2000).
STATISTICAL PLATEAUS: Three-goal games: 1999-00 (1).

Season Team	League	REGULAR SEASON								PLAYOFFS				
		Gms.	G	A	Pts.	PIM	+/-	PP	SH	Gms.	G	A	Pts.	PIM
93-94—Stratford	OPJHL	46	12	27	39	8	...	...	...	—	—	—	—	—
94-95—Stratford	OPJHL	45	31	74	105	21	...	...	...	—	—	—	—	—
95-96—Kitchener	OHL	66	20	38	58	35	...	...	...	12	3	7	10	4
96-97—Kitchener	OHL	54	28	41	69	37	...	...	...	13	4	11	15	8
—Hamilton	AHL	—	—	—	—	—	—	—	—	1	0	1	1	0
97-98—Edmonton	NHL	38	1	4	5	6	-5	0	0	—	—	—	—	—
—Hamilton	AHL	14	5	6	11	6	...	...	...	9	1	1	2	8
98-99—Edmonton	NHL	61	6	8	14	23	2	0	1	1	0	0	0	0
—Hamilton	AHL	7	4	6	10	2	...	...	...	8	0	3	3	4
99-00—Edmonton	NHL	76	8	19	27	20	7	0	1	—	—	—	—	—
00-01—Detroit	NHL	55	5	6	11	14	1	0	0	2	0	0	0	0
01-02—Detroit	NHL	79	9	16	25	24	9	0	0	21	2	4	6	4
02-03—Detroit	NHL	61	3	9	12	16	4	0	0	—	—	—	—	—
NHL Totals (6 years)		370	32	62	94	103	18	0	2	24	2	4	6	4

DIMAIO, ROB — RW — STARS

PERSONAL: Born February 19, 1968, in Calgary ... 5-10/190. ... Shoots right. ... Full Name: Robert DiMaio. ... Name pronounced duh-MIGH-oh.
TRANSACTIONS/CAREER NOTES: Selected by New York Islanders in sixth round (sixth Islanders pick, 118th overall) of NHL entry draft (June 13, 1987). ... Bruised left hand (February 1989). ... Sprained clavicle (November 1989). ... Sprained wrist (February 20, 1992); missed four games. ... Reinjured wrist (February 29, 1992); missed remainder of season. ... Selected by Tampa Bay Lightning in NHL expansion draft (June 18, 1992). ... Bruised wrist (November 28, 1992); missed four games. ... Sprained ankle (February 14, 1993); missed nine games. ... Reinjured right ankle (March 20, 1993). ... Reinjured right ankle (April 1, 1993); missed remainder of season. ... Fractured left leg (October 16, 1993); missed 27 games. ... Traded by Lightning to Philadelphia Flyers for RW Jim Cummins and fourth-round pick in 1995 draft (March 18, 1994). ... Bruised foot (February 28, 1995); missed two games. ... Suffered from the flu (April 16, 1995); missed one game. ... Suffered bone bruise in left leg (December 15, 1995); missed 14 games. ... Sprained right knee (March 29, 1996); missed final eight games of regular season. ... Selected by San Jose Sharks from Flyers in NHL waiver draft for cash (September 30, 1996). ... Traded by Sharks to Boston Bruins for fifth-round pick (RW Adam Nittel) in 1997 draft (September 30, 1996). ... Strained knee (November 6, 1996); missed five games. ... Suffered from the flu (December 17, 1996); missed one game. ... Sprained knee (March 8, 1997); missed two games. ... Injured hip (April 5, 1997); missed two games. ... Strained groin (January 12, 1998); missed one game. ... Suffered concussion (February 26, 1998); missed one game. ... Injured ankle (November 3, 1998); missed one game. ... Suffered viral meningitis (December 26, 1998); missed five games. ... Strained elbow (April 1, 1999); missed one game. ... Reinjured elbow (April 7, 1999); missed two games. ... Injured hip (October 20, 1999); missed one game. ... Bruised foot (November 10, 1999); missed two games. ... Fractured foot (November 17, 1999); missed eight games. ... Injured wrist (February 25, 2000); missed seven games. ... Traded by Bruins to New York Rangers for RW Mike Knuble (March 10, 2000). ... Suffered concussion (March 19, 2000); missed one game. ... Traded by Rangers with LW Darren Langdon to Carolina Hurricanes for RW Sandy McCarthy and fourth-round (D Bryce Lampman) in 2001 draft (August 4, 2000). ... Suffered back spasms (November 4, 2000); missed three games. ... Strained shoulder (March 21, 2001); missed two games. ... Bruised sternum (March 30, 2001); missed three games. ... Signed as free agent by Dallas Stars (July 1, 2001).

Season Team	League	REGULAR SEASON								PLAYOFFS				
		Gms.	G	A	Pts.	PIM	+/-	PP	SH	Gms.	G	A	Pts.	PIM
84-85—Kamloops	WHL	55	9	18	27	29	...	...	...	—	—	—	—	—
85-86—Kamloops	WHL	6	1	0	1	0	...	...	...	—	—	—	—	—
—Medicine Hat	WHL	55	20	30	50	82	...	...	...	—	—	—	—	—
86-87—Medicine Hat	WHL	70	27	43	70	130	...	...	...	20	7	11	18	46
87-88—Medicine Hat	WHL	54	47	43	90	120	...	...	...	14	12	19	†31	59
88-89—New York Islanders	NHL	16	1	0	1	30	-6	0	0	—	—	—	—	—
—Springfield	AHL	40	13	18	31	67	...	...	...	—	—	—	—	—
89-90—New York Islanders	NHL	7	0	0	0	2	0	0	0	1	1	0	1	4
—Springfield	AHL	54	25	27	52	69	...	...	...	16	4	7	11	45
90-91—New York Islanders	NHL	1	0	0	0	0	0	0	0	—	—	—	—	—
—Capital District	AHL	12	3	4	7	22	...	...	...	—	—	—	—	—
91-92—New York Islanders	NHL	50	5	2	7	43	-23	0	2	—	—	—	—	—
92-93—Tampa Bay	NHL	54	9	15	24	62	0	2	0	—	—	—	—	—
93-94—Tampa Bay	NHL	39	8	7	15	40	-5	2	0	—	—	—	—	—
—Philadelphia	NHL	14	3	5	8	6	1	0	0	—	—	—	—	—

Season Team	League	REGULAR SEASON								PLAYOFFS				
		Gms.	G	A	Pts.	PIM	+/-	PP	SH	Gms.	G	A	Pts.	PIM
94-95—Philadelphia	NHL	36	3	1	4	53	8	0	0	15	2	4	6	4
95-96—Philadelphia	NHL	59	6	15	21	58	0	1	1	3	0	0	0	0
96-97—Boston	NHL	72	13	15	28	82	-21	0	3	—	—	—	—	—
97-98—Boston	NHL	79	10	17	27	82	-13	0	0	6	1	0	1	8
98-99—Boston	NHL	71	7	14	21	95	-14	1	0	12	2	0	2	8
99-00—Boston	NHL	50	5	16	21	42	-1	0	0	—	—	—	—	—
—New York Rangers......	NHL	12	1	3	4	8	-8	0	0	—	—	—	—	—
00-01—Carolina	NHL	74	6	18	24	54	-14	0	2	6	0	0	0	4
01-02—Dallas	NHL	61	6	6	12	25	-2	0	2	—	—	—	—	—
—Utah..........................	AHL	3	1	1	2	0	...	...	...	—	—	—	—	—
02-03—Dallas	NHL	69	10	9	19	76	18	0	0	12	1	4	5	10
NHL Totals (15 years).........		764	93	143	236	758	-80	6	10	55	7	8	15	38

DIMITRAKOS, NIKO   RW   SHARKS

PERSONAL: Born May 21, 1979, in Somersville, Mass. ... 5-11/190. ... Shoots right. ... Full Name: Nicholas Dimitrakos.
HIGH SCHOOL: Matignon (Cambridge, Mass.).
COLLEGE: Maine.
TRANSACTIONS/CAREER NOTES: Selected by San Jose Sharks in fifth round (fourth Sharks pick, 155th overall) of NHL entry draft (June 26, 1999).

Season Team	League	REGULAR SEASON								PLAYOFFS				
		Gms.	G	A	Pts.	PIM	+/-	PP	SH	Gms.	G	A	Pts.	PIM
98-99—Univ. of Maine	Hockey East	35	8	19	27	33	...	...	...	—	—	—	—	—
99-00—Univ. of Maine	Hockey East	32	11	16	27	16	...	...	...	—	—	—	—	—
00-01—Univ. of Maine	Hockey East	29	11	14	25	43	...	...	...	—	—	—	—	—
01-02—Univ. of Maine	Hockey East	43	20	31	51	44	...	...	...	—	—	—	—	—
02-03—Cleveland	AHL	55	15	29	44	30	...	...	...	—	—	—	—	—
—San Jose....................	NHL	21	6	7	13	8	-7	3	0	—	—	—	—	—
NHL Totals (1 year).............		21	6	7	13	8	-7	3	0	—	—	—	—	—

DINEEN, KEVIN   RW   **D**

PERSONAL: Born October 28, 1963, in Quebe City ... 5-11/190. ... Shoots right. ... Full Name: Kevin W. Dineen. ... Son of Bill Dineen, right winger with Detroit Red Wings (1953-54 through 1957-58) and Chicago Blackhawks (1957-58) and head coach with Philadelphia Flyers (1992-93); brother of Gord Dineen, defenseman with four NHL teams (1982-83 through 1994-95); and brother of Peter Dineen, defenseman with Los Angeles Kings (1986-87) and Red Wings (1989-90).
TRANSACTIONS/CAREER NOTES: Selected by Hartford Whalers in third round (third Whalers pick, 56th overall) of NHL entry draft (June 9, 1982). ... Sprained left shoulder (October 24, 1985); missed nine games. ... Fractured knuckle (January 12, 1986); missed seven games. ... Sprained knee (February 14, 1986). ... Suffered shoulder tendinitis (September 1988). ... Underwent surgery to right knee cartilage (August 1, 1990). ... Suffered hip pointer (November 28, 1990). ... Hospitalized due to complications caused by Crohn's disease (January 1, 1991); missed eight games. ... Injured groin (March 1991). ... Traded by Whalers to Philadelphia Flyers for LW Murray Craven and fourth-round pick (LW Kevin Smyth) in 1992 draft (November 13, 1991). ... Sprained wrist (February 4, 1992); missed one game. ... Strained right rotator cuff (December 3, 1992); missed one game. ... Suffered injury (October 9, 1993); missed one game. ... Bruised right shoulder (November 13, 1993); missed two games. ... Suffered recurrence of Crohn's disease (February 10, 1994); missed five games. ... Separated shoulder (March 8, 1994); missed three games. ... Strained left shoulder (January 31, 1995); missed three games. ... Reinjured left shoulder (February 11, 1995); missed three games. ... Traded by Flyers to Whalers for third-round pick (D Kris Mallette) in 1997 draft (December 28, 1995). ... Fractured bone in wrist (February 9, 1996); missed 27 games. ... Strained abdominal muscle (March 13, 1997); missed one game. ... Whalers franchise moved to North Carolina and renamed Carolina Hurricanes for 1997-98 season; NHL approved move on June 25, 1997. ... Strained hamstring (October 4, 1997); missed five games. ... Reinjured hamstring (November 21, 1997); missed six games. ... Reinjured hamstring (December 26, 1997); missed seven games. ... Reinjured hamstring (January 10, 1998); missed two games. ... Suffered charley horse (February 7, 1998); missed one game. ... Injured groin (March 23, 1998); missed four games. ... Reinjured groin (April 8, 1998); missed one game. ... Strained groin (November 4, 1998); missed four games. ... Suffered back spasms (February 20, 1999); missed five games. ... Injured groin (March 6, 1999); missed six games. ... Signed as free agent by Ottawa Senators (September 2, 1999). ... Suspended one game by NHL for elbowing incident (November 1, 1999). ... Strained groin (December 11, 1999); missed three games. ... Reinjured groin (January 16, 2000); missed two games. ... Strained groin (March 25, 2000); missed three games. ... Separated left shoulder (April 6, 2000); missed final two games of season. ... Selected by Columbus Blue Jackets in NHL expansion draft (June 23, 2000). ... Strained groin (October 14, 2000); missed one game. ... Strained groin (December 13, 2000); missed one game. ... Strained groin (January 6, 2001); missed one game. ... Sprained knee (January 15, 2001); missed six games. ... Tore anterior cruciate ligament and medial collateral ligament in knee (April 5, 2001); missed remainder of season. ... Strained groin (December 8, 2001); missed five games. ... Strained groin (January 16, 2002); missed two games. ... Separated rib (March 28, 2002); missed six games. ... Announced retirement (November 5, 2002).
STATISTICAL PLATEAUS: Three-goal games: 1985-86 (1), 1986-87 (1), 1988-89 (1), 1989-90 (2), 1992-93 (3), 1993-94 (1). Total: 9. ... Four-goal games: 1993-94 (1). ... Total hat tricks: 10.

Season Team	League	REGULAR SEASON								PLAYOFFS				
		Gms.	G	A	Pts.	PIM	+/-	PP	SH	Gms.	G	A	Pts.	PIM
80-81—St. Michael's Jr. B.......	ODHA	40	15	28	43	167	...	...	...	—	—	—	—	—
81-82—Univ. of Denver..........	WCHA	38	12	22	34	105	...	...	...	—	—	—	—	—
82-83—Univ. of Denver..........	WCHA	36	16	13	29	108	...	...	...	—	—	—	—	—
83-84—Canadian nat'l team	Int'l	52	5	11	16	2	...	...	...	—	—	—	—	—
—Can. Olympic team	Int'l	7	0	0	0	0	...	...	...	—	—	—	—	—
84-85—Binghamton	AHL	25	15	8	23	41	...	...	...	—	—	—	—	—
—Hartford	NHL	57	25	16	41	120	-6	8	4	—	—	—	—	—
85-86—Hartford	NHL	57	33	35	68	124	16	6	0	10	6	7	13	18
86-87—Hartford	NHL	78	40	39	79	110	7	11	0	6	2	1	3	31
87-88—Hartford	NHL	74	25	25	50	217	-14	5	0	6	4	4	8	8
88-89—Hartford	NHL	79	45	44	89	167	-6	20	1	4	1	0	1	10
89-90—Hartford	NHL	67	25	41	66	164	7	8	2	6	3	2	5	18
90-91—Hartford	NHL	61	17	30	47	104	-15	4	0	6	1	0	1	16

| | | REGULAR SEASON | | | | | | | | PLAYOFFS | | | | |
Season Team	League	Gms.	G	A	Pts.	PIM	+/-	PP	SH	Gms.	G	A	Pts.	PIM
91-92—Hartford	NHL	16	4	2	6	23	-6	1	0	—	—	—	—	—
—Philadelphia	NHL	64	26	30	56	130	1	5	3	—	—	—	—	—
92-93—Philadelphia	NHL	83	35	28	63	201	14	6	3	—	—	—	—	—
93-94—Philadelphia	NHL	71	19	23	42	113	-9	5	1	—	—	—	—	—
94-95—Houston	IHL	17	6	4	10	42	...	...	...	—	—	—	—	—
—Philadelphia	NHL	40	8	5	13	39	-1	4	0	15	6	4	10	18
95-96—Philadelphia	NHL	26	0	2	2	50	-8	0	0	—	—	—	—	—
—Hartford	NHL	20	2	7	9	67	7	0	0	—	—	—	—	—
96-97—Hartford	NHL	78	19	29	48	141	-6	8	0	—	—	—	—	—
97-98—Carolina	NHL	54	7	16	23	105	-7	0	0	—	—	—	—	—
98-99—Carolina	NHL	67	8	10	18	97	5	0	0	6	0	0	0	8
99-00—Ottawa	NHL	67	4	8	12	57	2	0	0	—	—	—	—	—
00-01—Columbus	NHL	66	8	7	15	126	2	0	0	—	—	—	—	—
01-02—Columbus	NHL	59	5	8	13	62	-6	0	0	—	—	—	—	—
02-03—Columbus	NHL	4	0	0	0	12	0	0	0	—	—	—	—	—
NHL Totals (19 years).........		1188	355	405	760	2229	-23	91	14	59	23	18	41	127

DINGMAN, CHRIS — LW — LIGHTNING

PERSONAL: Born July 6, 1976, in Edmonton ... 6-4/235. ... Shoots left.
TRANSACTIONS/CAREER NOTES: Selected by Calgary Flames in first round (first Flames pick, 19th overall) of NHL entry draft (June 28, 1994). ... Traded by Flames with RW Theo Fleury to Colorado Avalanche for LW Rene Corbet, D Wade Belak and future considerations (February 28, 1999); Flames acquired D Robyn Regehr to complete deal (March 27, 1999). ... Partially dislocated right shoulder (November 15, 1999); missed six games. ... Sprained knee (November 13, 2000); missed 13 games. ... Traded by Avalanche to Carolina Hurricanes for fifth-round pick (D Mikko Viitanen) in 2001 draft (June 24, 2001). ... Strained groin (September 26, 2001); missed first eight games of season. ... Injured groin (November 9, 2001); missed two games. ... Injured knee (December 12, 2001); missed 16 games. ... Traded by Hurricanes with RW Shane Willis to Tampa Bay Lightning for G Kevin Weekes (March 5, 2002). ... Suffered back spasms (March 30, 2002); missed five games. ... Suspended two games by NHL for high-sticking incident (October 16, 2002).

| | | REGULAR SEASON | | | | | | | | PLAYOFFS | | | | |
Season Team	League	Gms.	G	A	Pts.	PIM	+/-	PP	SH	Gms.	G	A	Pts.	PIM
92-93—Brandon....................	WHL	50	10	17	27	64	...	...	...	4	0	0	0	0
93-94—Brandon....................	WHL	45	21	20	41	77	...	...	...	13	1	7	8	39
94-95—Brandon....................	WHL	66	40	43	83	201	...	...	...	3	1	0	1	9
95-96—Brandon....................	WHL	40	16	29	45	109	...	...	...	19	12	11	23	60
—Saint John	AHL	—	—	—	—	—	...	...	...	1	0	0	0	0
96-97—Saint John	AHL	71	5	6	11	195	...	...	...	—	—	—	—	—
97-98—Calgary	NHL	70	3	3	6	149	-11	1	0	—	—	—	—	—
98-99—Saint John	AHL	50	5	7	12	140	...	...	...	—	—	—	—	—
—Calgary	NHL	2	0	0	0	17	-2	0	0	—	—	—	—	—
—Hershey	AHL	17	1	3	4	102	...	...	...	5	0	2	2	6
—Colorado..................	NHL	1	0	0	0	7	0	0	0	—	—	—	—	—
99-00—Colorado..................	NHL	68	8	3	11	132	-2	2	0	—	—	—	—	—
00-01—Colorado..................	NHL	41	1	1	2	108	-3	0	0	16	0	4	4	14
01-02—Carolina	NHL	30	0	1	1	77	-2	0	0	—	—	—	—	—
—Tampa Bay	NHL	14	0	4	4	26	-8	0	0	—	—	—	—	—
02-03—Tampa Bay	NHL	51	2	1	3	91	-11	0	0	10	1	0	1	4
NHL Totals (6 years)...........		277	14	13	27	607	-39	3	0	26	1	4	5	18

DIPENTA, JOEY — D — THRASHERS

PERSONAL: Born February 25, 1979, in Barrie, Ont. ... 6-4/215. ... Shoots right. ... Full Name: Joe DiPenta.
TRANSACTIONS/CAREER NOTES: Selected by Florida Panthers in third round (second Panthers pick, 61st overall) of NHL entry draft (June 27, 1998). ... Signed as free agent by Philadelphia Flyers (August 1, 2000). ... Traded by Flyers to Atlanta Thrashers for C Jarrod Skalde (March 4, 2002).

| | | REGULAR SEASON | | | | | | | | PLAYOFFS | | | | |
Season Team	League	Gms.	G	A	Pts.	PIM	+/-	PP	SH	Gms.	G	A	Pts.	PIM
96-97—Smith Falls................	OJHL	54	13	22	35	92	...	...	...	—	—	—	—	—
97-98—Boston University	Hockey East	38	2	16	18	50	...	...	...	—	—	—	—	—
98-99—Boston University	Hockey East	36	2	15	17	72	...	...	...	—	—	—	—	—
99-00—Halifax....................	QMJHL	63	13	43	56	83	...	...	...	10	3	4	7	26
00-01—Philadelphia	AHL	71	3	5	8	65	...	...	...	10	1	2	3	15
01-02—Philadelphia	AHL	61	2	4	6	71	...	...	...	—	—	—	—	—
—Chicago...................	AHL	15	0	2	2	15	...	...	...	25	1	3	4	22
02-03—Chicago...................	AHL	76	2	17	19	107	...	...	...	—	—	—	—	—
—Atlanta	NHL	3	1	1	2	0	3	0	0	—	—	—	—	—
NHL Totals (1 year)............		3	1	1	2	0	3	0	0	—	—	—	—	—

DIPIETRO, RICK — G — ISLANDERS

PERSONAL: Born September 19, 1981, in Winthrop, Mass. ... 5-11/190. ... Catches right.
TRANSACTIONS/CAREER NOTES: Selected by New York Islanders in first round (first Islanders pick, first overall) of NHL entry draft (June 24, 2000). ... Re-signed by Islanders (July 22, 2003).

Season Team	League	REGULAR SEASON									PLAYOFFS							
		Gms.	Min	W	L	T	GA	SO	Avg.	SV%	Gms.	Min.	W	L	GA	SO	Avg.	SV%
97-98—U.S. Jr. national team....	Int'l	46	2526	21	19	0	131	2	3.11	—	—	—	—	—	—	—	—	—
98-99—U.S. Jr. national team....	Int'l	30	1733	22	6	2	67	3	2.32	—	—	—	—	—	—	—	—	—
99-00—Boston University.........	Hockey East	30	1791	18	5	5	73	2	2.45	—	—	—	—	—	—	—	—	—
00-01—Chicago..................	IHL	14	778	4	5	‡2	44	0	3.39	—	—	—	—	—	—	—	—	—
—New York Islanders.......	NHL	20	1083	3	15	1	63	0	3.49	.878	—	—	—	—	—	—	—	—
01-02—Bridgeport..................	AHL	59	3471	*30	22	7	134	4	2.32	—	20	*1270	12	*8	*45	*3	2.13	—
02-03—Bridgeport..................	AHL	34	2044	16	10	8	73	3	2.14	—	—	—	—	—	—	—	—	—
—New York Islanders.......	NHL	10	585	2	5	2	29	0	2.97	.894	1	15	0	0	0	0	0.00	1.000
NHL Totals (2 years)............		30	1668	5	20	3	92	0	3.31	.883	1	15	0	0	0	0	0.00	1.000

DIVIS, REINHARD — G — BLUES

PERSONAL: Born July 4, 1975, in Vienna, Austria ... 5-11/196. ... Catches left.

TRANSACTIONS/CAREER NOTES: Selected by St. Louis Blues in eighth round (eighth Blues pick, 261st overall) of NHL entry draft (June 25, 2000).

Season Team	League	REGULAR SEASON									PLAYOFFS							
		Gms.	Min	W	L	T	GA	SO	Avg.	SV%	Gms.	Min.	W	L	GA	SO	Avg.	SV%
95-96—VEU Feldkirch..............	Austria	37	2200	...	...	...	85	0	2.32	—	—	—	—	—	—	—	—	—
96-97—VEU Feldkirch..............	Alpenliga	45	2792	...	...	...	105	0	2.26	—	—	—	—	—	—	—	—	—
—VEU Feldkirch..............	Austria	—	—	—	—	—	27	0	—	—	11	620	...	...	...	...		
97-98—VEU Feldkirch..............	Austria	13	779	...	...	...	22	0	1.69	—	—	—	—	—	—	—	—	—
—VEU Feldkirch..............	Alpenliga	27	1620	...	...	...	55	0	2.04	—	—	—	—	—	—	—	—	—
98-99—VEU Feldkirch..............	Austria	15	900	...	...	...	58	0	3.87	—	—	—	—	—	—	—	—	—
99-00—Leksand	Sweden Dv. 2	48	2839	...	...	...	160	3	3.38	—	—	—	—	—	—	—	—	—
00-01—Leksand	Sweden Dv. 2	41	2451	...	...	...	141	3	3.45	—	—	—	—	—	—	—	—	—
01-02—Worcester	AHL	55	3173	28	20	5	137	3	2.59	—	3	204	1	2	8	0	2.35	—
—Austrian Olympic team..	Int'l	4	238	1	3	0	12	0	3.03	—	—	—	—	—	—	—	—	—
—St. Louis	NHL	1	25	0	0	0	0	0	...	1.000	—	—	—	—	—	—	—	—
02-03—Worcester	AHL	9	452	6	1	0	17	0	2.26	—	—	—	—	—	—	—	—	—
—St. Louis	NHL	2	83	2	0	0	1	0	.72	.971	—	—	—	—	—	—	—	—
NHL Totals (2 years)............		3	108	2	0	0	1	0	.56	.974	—	—	—	—	—	—	—	—

DOAN, SHANE — C — COYOTES

PERSONAL: Born October 10, 1976, in Halkirk, Alta. ... 6-2/216. ... Shoots right. ... Name pronounced DOHN.

TRANSACTIONS/CAREER NOTES: Selected by Winnipeg Jets in first round (first Jets pick, seventh overall) of NHL entry draft (July 8, 1995). ... Suffered from the flu (January 8, 1996); missed one game. ... Bruised ribs (January 14, 1996); missed two games. ... Strained back (February 23, 1996); missed two games. ... Jets franchise moved to Phoenix and renamed Coyotes for 1996-97 season; NHL approved move on January 18, 1996. ... Sprained ankle (October 14, 1996); missed two games. ... Strained ligament in foot (November 8, 1996); missed eight games. ... Bruised hand (February 22, 1997); missed four games. ... Injured eye (February 20, 1999); missed one game. ... Injured forearm (March 15, 1999); missed one game. ... Injured knee (December 10, 2000); missed one game. ... Strained muscle in abdomen (January 24, 2001); missed five games. ... Sprained ankle (March 17, 2002); missed one game.

Season Team	League	REGULAR SEASON								PLAYOFFS				
		Gms.	G	A	Pts.	PIM	+/-	PP	SH	Gms.	G	A	Pts.	PIM
92-93—Kamloops	WHL	51	7	12	19	55	...	...	...	13	0	1	1	8
93-94—Kamloops	WHL	52	24	24	48	88	...	...	...	—	—	—	—	—
94-95—Kamloops	WHL	71	37	57	94	106	...	...	...	21	6	10	16	16
95-96—Winnipeg	NHL	74	7	10	17	101	-9	1	0	6	0	0	0	6
96-97—Phoenix...................	NHL	63	4	8	12	49	-3	0	0	4	0	0	0	2
97-98—Phoenix...................	NHL	33	5	6	11	35	-3	0	0	6	1	0	1	6
—Springfield	AHL	39	21	21	42	64	...	...	...	—	—	—	—	—
98-99—Phoenix...................	NHL	79	6	16	22	54	-5	0	0	7	2	2	4	6
99-00—Phoenix...................	NHL	81	26	25	51	66	6	1	1	4	1	2	3	8
00-01—Phoenix...................	NHL	76	26	37	63	89	0	6	1	—	—	—	—	—
01-02—Phoenix...................	NHL	81	20	29	49	61	11	6	0	5	2	2	4	6
02-03—Phoenix...................	NHL	82	21	37	58	86	3	7	0	—	—	—	—	—
NHL Totals (8 years)............		569	115	168	283	541	0	21	2	32	6	6	12	34

DOIG, JASON — D — CAPITALS

PERSONAL: Born January 29, 1977, in Montreal ... 6-3/223. ... Shoots right. ... Name pronounced DOYG.

TRANSACTIONS/CAREER NOTES: Selected by Winnipeg Jets in second round (third Jets pick, 34th overall) of NHL entry draft (July 8, 1995). ... Suffered irregular heart beat (November 17, 1995); missed four games. ... Jets franchise moved to Phoenix and renamed Coyotes for 1996-97 season; NHL approved move on January 18, 1996. ... Hyperextended elbow prior to 1996-97 season; missed first five games of season. ... Sprained knee (November 20, 1997); missed 26 games. ... Suffered torn pectoral muscle prior to the 1998-99 regular season; missed first 18 games of season. ... Traded by Coyotes with sixth-round pick (C Jay Dardis) in 1999 draft to New York Rangers for D Stan Neckar (March 23, 1999). ... Sprained knee (February 8, 2000); missed five games. ... Traded by Rangers with RW Jeff Ulmer to Ottawa Senators for D Sean Gagnon (June 29, 2001). ... Signed as free agent by Washington Capitals (September 13, 2002). ... Re-signed by Capitals (July 20, 2003).

Season Team	League	REGULAR SEASON								PLAYOFFS				
		Gms.	G	A	Pts.	PIM	+/-	PP	SH	Gms.	G	A	Pts.	PIM
93-94—St. Jean	QMJHL	63	8	17	25	65	...	...	...	5	0	2	2	2
94-95—Laval	QMJHL	55	13	42	55	259	...	...	...	20	4	13	17	39
95-96—Winnipeg	NHL	15	1	1	2	28	-2	0	0	—	—	—	—	—
—Springfield	AHL	5	0	0	0	28	...	...	...	—	—	—	—	—
—Laval	QMJHL	2	1	1	2	6	...	...	...	—	—	—	—	—
—Granby	QMJHL	27	6	35	41	*105	...	...	...	20	10	22	32	110
96-97—Las Vegas	IHL	6	0	1	1	19	...	...	...	—	—	—	—	—
—Granby	QMJHL	39	14	33	47	197	...	...	...	5	0	4	4	27
—Springfield	AHL	5	0	3	3	2	...	...	...	17	1	4	5	37
97-98—Springfield	AHL	46	2	25	27	153	...	...	...	3	0	0	0	2
—Phoenix	NHL	4	0	1	1	12	-4	0	0	—	—	—	—	—
98-99—Phoenix	NHL	9	0	1	1	10	2	0	0	—	—	—	—	—
—Springfield	AHL	32	3	5	8	67	...	...	...	—	—	—	—	—
—Hartford	AHL	8	1	4	5	40	...	...	...	7	1	1	2	39
99-00—New York Rangers	NHL	7	0	1	1	22	-2	0	0	—	—	—	—	—
—Hartford	AHL	27	3	11	14	70	...	...	...	21	1	5	6	20
00-01—New York Rangers	NHL	3	0	0	0	0	0	0	0	—	—	—	—	—
—Hartford	AHL	52	4	20	24	178	...	...	...	5	0	1	1	4
01-02—Grand Rapids	AHL	57	1	17	18	103	...	...	...	5	0	0	0	18
02-03—Portland	AHL	21	1	4	5	66	...	...	...	—	—	—	—	—
—Washington	NHL	55	3	5	8	108	-3	0	0	6	0	1	1	6
NHL Totals (6 years)		93	4	9	13	180	-9	0	0	6	0	1	1	6

DOME, ROBERT   C/LW   FLAMES

PERSONAL: Born January 29, 1979, in Skalica, Czechoslovakia ... 6-0/217. ... Shoots left. ... Name pronounced DEH-may.
TRANSACTIONS/CAREER NOTES: Selected by Pittsburgh Penguins in first round (first Penguins pick, 17th overall) of NHL entry draft (June 21, 1997). ... Signed as free agent by Calgary Flames (July 17, 2002).

Season Team	League	REGULAR SEASON								PLAYOFFS				
		Gms.	G	A	Pts.	PIM	+/-	PP	SH	Gms.	G	A	Pts.	PIM
94-95—Dukla Jrs.	Slov. Jr.	36	36	43	79	39	...	...	...	—	—	—	—	—
95-96—Utah	IHL	56	10	9	19	28	...	...	...	—	—	—	—	—
96-97—Long Beach	IHL	13	4	6	10	14	...	...	...	—	—	—	—	—
—Las Vegas	IHL	43	10	7	17	22	...	...	...	—	—	—	—	—
97-98—Pittsburgh	NHL	30	5	2	7	12	-1	1	0	—	—	—	—	—
—Syracuse	AHL	36	21	25	46	77	...	...	...	—	—	—	—	—
98-99—Syracuse	AHL	48	18	17	35	70	...	...	...	—	—	—	—	—
—Houston	IHL	20	2	4	6	24	...	...	...	—	—	—	—	—
99-00—Wilkes-Barre/Scranton	AHL	51	12	26	38	83	...	...	...	—	—	—	—	—
—Pittsburgh	NHL	22	2	5	7	0	1	0	0	—	—	—	—	—
00-01—HC Kladno	Czech Rep.	29	9	12	21	57	...	...	...	—	—	—	—	—
—HC Zelezarny Trinec	Czech Rep.	5	0	3	3	4	...	...	...	—	—	—	—	—
01-02—Wilkes-Barre/Scranton	AHL	39	9	8	17	53	...	...	...	—	—	—	—	—
02-03—Saint John	AHL	56	27	29	56	41	...	...	...	—	—	—	—	—
—Calgary	NHL	1	0	0	0	0	0	0	0	—	—	—	—	—
NHL Totals (3 years)		53	7	7	14	12	0	1	0					

DOMENICHELLI, HNAT   LW

PERSONAL: Born February 17, 1976, in Edmonton ... 6-0/195. ... Shoots left. ... Name pronounced NAT dah-mih-nuh-KEHL-ee.
TRANSACTIONS/CAREER NOTES: Selected by Hartford Whalers in fourth round (second Whalers pick, 83rd overall) of NHL entry draft (June 29, 1994). ... Traded by Whalers with D Glen Featherstone, second-round pick (D Dimitri Kokorev) in 1997 draft and third-round pick (D Paul Manning) in 1998 draft to Calgary Flames for D Steve Chiasson and third-round pick (D Francis Lessard) in 1997 draft (March 5, 1997). ... Traded by Flames with LW Dmitri Vlasenkov to Atlanta Thrashers for D Darryl Shannon and LW Jason Botterill (February 11, 2000). ... Sprained ankle (September 5, 2000); missed first three games of season. ... Strained groin (January 5, 2001); missed four games. ... Reinjured groin (January 18, 2001); missed 11 games. ... Traded by Thrashers to Minnesota Wild for D Andy Sutton (January 22, 2002).

Season Team	League	REGULAR SEASON								PLAYOFFS				
		Gms.	G	A	Pts.	PIM	+/-	PP	SH	Gms.	G	A	Pts.	PIM
92-93—Kamloops	WHL	45	12	8	20	15	...	...	...	11	1	1	2	2
93-94—Kamloops	WHL	69	27	40	67	31	...	...	...	19	10	12	22	0
94-95—Kamloops	WHL	72	52	62	114	34	...	...	...	19	9	9	18	9
95-96—Kamloops	WHL	62	59	89	148	37	...	...	...	16	7	9	16	29
96-97—Hartford	NHL	13	2	1	3	7	-4	1	0	—	—	—	—	—
—Springfield	AHL	39	24	24	48	12	...	...	...	—	—	—	—	—
—Calgary	NHL	10	1	2	3	2	1	0	0	—	—	—	—	—
—Saint John	AHL	1	1	1	2	0	...	...	...	5	5	0	5	2
97-98—Saint John	AHL	48	33	13	46	24	...	...	...	19	7	8	15	14
—Calgary	NHL	31	9	7	16	6	4	1	0	—	—	—	—	—
98-99—Saint John	AHL	51	25	21	46	26	...	...	...	7	4	4	8	2
—Calgary	NHL	23	5	5	10	11	-4	3	0	—	—	—	—	—
99-00—Saint John	AHL	12	6	7	13	8	...	...	...	—	—	—	—	—
—Calgary	NHL	32	5	9	14	12	0	1	0	—	—	—	—	—
—Atlanta	NHL	27	6	9	15	4	-21	0	0	—	—	—	—	—
00-01—Atlanta	NHL	63	15	12	27	18	-9	4	0	—	—	—	—	—
01-02—Atlanta	NHL	40	8	11	19	34	-18	1	0	—	—	—	—	—
—Minnesota	NHL	27	1	5	6	10	-5	0	0	—	—	—	—	—
02-03—Houston	AHL	62	29	34	63	58	...	...	...	—	—	—	—	—
—Minnesota	NHL	1	0	0	0	0	0	0	0	—	—	—	—	—
NHL Totals (7 years)		267	52	61	113	104	-56	11	0					

PERSONAL: Born November 1, 1969, in Windsor, Ont. ... 5-10/213. ... Shoots right. ... Full Name: Tahir Domi. ... Name pronounced TIGH DOH-mee. ... Nickname: The Albanian Agressor.

TRANSACTIONS/CAREER NOTES: Selected by Toronto Maple Leafs in second round (second Maple Leafs pick, 27th overall) of NHL entry draft (June 11, 1988). ... Traded by Maple Leafs with G Mark Laforest to New York Rangers for RW Greg Johnston (June 28, 1990). ... Suspended six games by AHL for pre-game fighting (November 25, 1990). ... Sprained right knee (March 11, 1992); missed eight games. ... Traded by Rangers with LW Kris King to Winnipeg Jets for C Ed Olczyk (December 28, 1992). ... Fined $500 by NHL for premeditated fight (January 4, 1993). ... Sprained knee (January 25, 1994); missed three games. ... Traded by Jets to Maple Leafs for C Mike Eastwood and third-round pick (RW Brad Isbister) in 1995 draft (April 7, 1995). ... Strained groin (April 8, 1995); missed two games. ... Suffered from the flu (April 19, 1995); missed one game. ... Suspended eight games by NHL for fighting (October 17, 1995). ... Sprained knee (December 2, 1995); missed two games. ... Fined $1,000 by NHL for fighting (November 13, 1996). ... Sprained ankle (April 2, 1997); missed two games. ... Strained abdominal muscle (October 25, 1997); missed two games. ... Sprained knee (January 7, 1999); missed 10 games. ... Suffered injury (October 30, 1999); missed five games. ... Suffered injury (January 14, 2000); missed seven games. ... Suspended remainder of playoffs and first eight games of 2001-02 regular season game by NHL for elbowing incident (May 4, 2001). ... Traded by Maple Leafs to Nashville Predators for eighth-round pick in 2003 draft (June 30, 2002). ... Signed as free agent by Maple Leafs (July 12, 2002). ... Suspended three games by NHL for unsportsmanlike conduct (March 5, 2003).

Season Team	League	REGULAR SEASON								PLAYOFFS				
		Gms.	G	A	Pts.	PIM	+/-	PP	SH	Gms.	G	A	Pts.	PIM
85-86—Windsor Jr. B.	OHA	32	8	17	25	346	...	...	...	—	—	—	—	—
86-87—Peterborough	OHL	18	1	1	2	79	...	...	...	—	—	—	—	—
87-88—Peterborough	OHL	60	22	21	43	*292	...	...	...	12	3	9	12	24
88-89—Peterborough	OHL	43	14	16	30	175	...	...	...	17	10	9	19	*70
89-90—Newmarket	AHL	57	14	11	25	285	...	...	...	—	—	—	—	—
—Toronto	NHL	2	0	0	0	42	0	0	0	—	—	—	—	—
90-91—New York Rangers	NHL	28	1	0	1	185	-5	0	0	—	—	—	—	—
—Binghamton	AHL	25	11	6	17	219	...	...	...	7	3	2	5	16
91-92—New York Rangers	NHL	42	2	4	6	246	-4	0	0	6	1	1	2	32
92-93—New York Rangers	NHL	12	2	0	2	95	-1	0	0	—	—	—	—	—
—Winnipeg	NHL	49	3	10	13	249	2	0	0	6	1	0	1	23
93-94—Winnipeg	NHL	81	8	11	19	*347	-8	0	0	—	—	—	—	—
94-95—Winnipeg	NHL	31	4	4	8	128	-6	0	0	—	—	—	—	—
—Toronto	NHL	9	0	1	1	31	1	0	0	7	1	0	1	0
95-96—Toronto	NHL	72	7	6	13	297	-3	0	0	6	0	2	2	4
96-97—Toronto	NHL	80	11	17	28	275	-17	2	0	—	—	—	—	—
97-98—Toronto	NHL	80	4	10	14	365	-5	0	0	—	—	—	—	—
98-99—Toronto	NHL	72	8	14	22	198	5	0	0	14	0	2	2	24
99-00—Toronto	NHL	70	5	9	14	198	-5	0	0	12	0	1	1	20
00-01—Toronto	NHL	82	13	7	20	214	2	1	0	8	0	1	1	20
01-02—Toronto	NHL	74	9	10	19	157	3	0	0	19	1	3	4	*61
02-03—Toronto	NHL	79	15	14	29	171	-1	4	0	7	1	0	1	13
NHL Totals (14 years)		863	92	117	209	3198	-42	7	0	85	5	10	15	197

PERSONAL: Born April 28, 1969, in Boston ... 5-10/186. ... Shoots left. ... Full Name: Edward Paul Donato. ... Brother of Dan Donato, infielder, Tampa Bay Devil Rays organization. ... Name pronounced duh-NAH-toh.

TRANSACTIONS/CAREER NOTES: Selected by Boston Bruins in sixth round (sixth Bruins pick, 98th overall) of NHL entry draft (June 13, 1987). ... Played in Europe during 1994-95 NHL lockout. ... Injured groin (November 21, 1996); missed two games. ... Fractured finger (March 9, 1997); missed 13 games. ... Suspended three games by NHL and fined $1,000 for high-sticking (December 22, 1997). ... Traded by Bruins to New York Islanders for LW Ken Belanger (November 7, 1998). ... Traded by Islanders to Ottawa Senators for fourth-round pick (traded to Phoenix) in 1999 draft (March 20, 1999). ... Traded by Senators with D Antti-Jussi Niemi to Mighty Ducks of Anaheim for G Patrick Lalime (June 18, 1999). ... Signed as free agent by Dallas Stars (August 17, 2000). ... Signed as free agent by Islanders (January 16, 2002). ... Claimed on waivers by Los Angeles Kings (January 30, 2002). ... Claimed on waivers by St. Louis Blues (March 6, 2002). ... Claimed on waivers by Kings (March 19, 2002). ... Signed as free agent by New York Rangers (July 8, 2002). ... Signed by Boston Bruins (July 22, 2003).

Season Team	League	REGULAR SEASON								PLAYOFFS				
		Gms.	G	A	Pts.	PIM	+/-	PP	SH	Gms.	G	A	Pts.	PIM
86-87—Catholic Memorial	Mass. H.S.	22	29	34	63	30	...	...	...	—	—	—	—	—
87-88—Harvard University	ECAC	28	12	14	26	24	...	...	...	—	—	—	—	—
88-89—Harvard University	ECAC	34	14	37	51	30	...	...	...	—	—	—	—	—
89-90—Harvard University	ECAC	16	5	6	11	34	...	...	...	—	—	—	—	—
90-91—Harvard University	ECAC	28	19	37	56	26	...	...	...	—	—	—	—	—
91-92—U.S. national team	Int'l	52	11	22	33	24	...	...	...	—	—	—	—	—
—U.S. Olympic team	Int'l	8	4	3	7	8	...	...	...	—	—	—	—	—
—Boston	NHL	10	1	2	3	8	-1	0	0	15	3	4	7	4
92-93—Boston	NHL	82	15	20	35	61	2	3	2	4	0	1	1	0
93-94—Boston	NHL	84	22	32	54	59	0	9	2	13	4	2	6	10
94-95—TuTu Turku	Finland	14	5	5	10	47	...	...	...	—	—	—	—	—
—Boston	NHL	47	10	10	20	10	3	1	0	5	0	0	0	4
95-96—Boston	NHL	82	23	26	49	46	6	7	0	5	1	2	3	2
96-97—Boston	NHL	67	25	26	51	37	-9	6	2	—	—	—	—	—
97-98—Boston	NHL	79	16	23	39	54	6	3	0	5	0	0	0	2
98-99—Boston	NHL	14	1	3	4	4	0	0	0	—	—	—	—	—
—New York Islanders	NHL	55	7	11	18	27	-10	2	0	—	—	—	—	—
—Ottawa	NHL	13	3	2	5	10	2	1	0	1	0	0	0	0
99-00—Anaheim	NHL	81	11	19	30	26	-3	2	0	—	—	—	—	—
00-01—Dallas	NHL	65	8	17	25	26	6	1	0	8	0	1	1	0
01-02—New York Islanders	NHL	1	0	0	0	0	-1	0	0	—	—	—	—	—
—Bridgeport	AHL	1	0	0	0	0	...	...	...	—	—	—	—	—
—Manchester	AHL	36	18	25	43	19	...	...	...	5	1	3	4	0
—Los Angeles	NHL	2	0	0	0	2	-2	0	0	—	—	—	—	—
—St. Louis	NHL	2	0	0	0	2	-2	0	0	—	—	—	—	—
02-03—Hartford	AHL	18	8	12	20	14	...	...	...	—	—	—	—	—
—New York Rangers	NHL	49	2	1	3	6	-1	0	0	—	—	—	—	—
NHL Totals (12 years)		733	144	192	336	378	-4	35	6	56	8	10	18	22

PERSONAL: Born January 22, 1975, in Timmins, Ont. ... 6-2/200. ... Shoots right. ... Name pronounced SHAWN DAHN-ih-vihn.

TRANSACTIONS/CAREER NOTES: Selected by San Jose Sharks in second round (second Sharks pick, 28th overall) of NHL entry draft (June 26, 1993). ... Suffered concussion (October 5, 1996); missed two games. ... Injured knee (December 21, 1996); missed two games. ... Traded by Sharks with first-round pick (C Alex Tanguay) in 1998 draft to Colorado Avalanche for C Mike Ricci and second-round pick (RW Jonathan Cheechoo) in 1998 draft (November 20, 1997). ... Bruised knee (January 3, 1998); missed one game. ... Bruised knee (January 21, 1998); missed three games. ... Suffered concussion (October 24, 1998); missed one game. ... Injured shoulder and jaw (February 5, 1999); missed one game. ... Injured hip (March 20, 1999); missed two games. ... Traded by Avalanche to Atlanta Thrashers for G Rick Tabaracci (December 8, 1999). ... Strained muscle in abdomen (January 1, 2000); missed three games. ... Fractured right foot (January 27, 2000); missed 20 games. ... Sprained medial collateral ligament in knee (December 9, 2000); missed 13 games. ... Bruised heel (January 22, 2002); missed one game. ... Claimed on waivers by Pittsburgh Penguins (March 15, 2002). ... Lacerated elbow (April 8, 2002); missed two games. ... Traded by Penguins to Calgary Flames for D Micki Dupont and C Mathias Johansson (March 11, 2003). ... Signed by Calgary (May 28, 2003).

STATISTICAL PLATEAUS: Three-goal games: 2000-01 (1).

Season Team	League	REGULAR SEASON								PLAYOFFS				
		Gms.	G	A	Pts.	PIM	+/-	PP	SH	Gms.	G	A	Pts.	PIM
91-92—Ottawa	OHL	58	11	8	19	14	...	...	...	11	1	0	1	5
92-93—Ottawa	OHL	66	29	23	52	33	...	...	...	—	—	—	—	—
93-94—Ottawa	OHL	62	35	49	84	63	...	...	...	17	10	11	21	14
94-95—Ottawa	OHL	29	22	19	41	41	...	...	...	—	—	—	—	—
—San Jose	NHL	14	0	0	0	6	-6	0	0	7	0	1	1	6
—Kansas City	IHL	5	0	2	2	7	...	...	...	14	5	3	8	23
95-96—Kansas City	IHL	4	0	0	0	8	...	...	...	5	0	0	0	8
—San Jose	NHL	74	13	8	21	39	-17	0	1	—	—	—	—	—
96-97—San Jose	NHL	73	9	6	15	42	-18	0	1	—	—	—	—	—
—Kentucky	AHL	3	1	3	4	18	...	...	...	—	—	—	—	—
—Canadian nat'l team	Int'l	10	0	1	1	31	...	...	...	—	—	—	—	—
97-98—San Jose	NHL	20	3	3	6	22	3	0	0	—	—	—	—	—
—Colorado	NHL	47	5	7	12	48	3	0	0	—	—	—	—	—
98-99—Colorado	NHL	68	7	12	19	37	4	1	0	5	0	0	0	2
99-00—Colorado	NHL	18	1	0	1	8	-4	0	0	—	—	—	—	—
—Atlanta	NHL	33	4	7	11	18	-13	1	0	—	—	—	—	—
00-01—Atlanta	NHL	63	12	11	23	47	-14	1	3	—	—	—	—	—
01-02—Atlanta	NHL	48	6	6	12	40	-16	1	0	—	—	—	—	—
—Pittsburgh	NHL	13	2	1	3	4	-5	0	0	—	—	—	—	—
02-03—Pittsburgh	NHL	52	4	5	9	30	-6	0	1	—	—	—	—	—
—Calgary	NHL	13	1	2	3	7	-2	0	0	—	—	—	—	—
NHL Totals (9 years)		536	67	68	135	348	-91	4	6	12	0	1	1	8

PERSONAL: Born December 2, 1968, in Sumperk, Czechoslovakia ... 6-4/210. ... Shoots left.

TRANSACTIONS/CAREER NOTES: Selected by Boston Bruins in sixth round (fourth Bruins pick, 133rd overall) of NHL entry draft (June 20, 1992). ... Returned to draft pool by Bruins and selected by New York Islanders in fifth round (fourth Islanders pick, 123rd overall) of NHL entry draft (June 27, 1998). ... Rights traded by Islanders to Florida Panthers for fifth-round pick (D Adam Johnson) in 1999 draft (June 26, 1999). ... Rights traded by Panthers to Philadelphia Flyers for second-round pick (traded to Calgary) in 2001 draft (June 23, 2001). ... Sprained medial collateral ligament in left knee (October 4, 2001); missed 15 games. ... Strained neck (January 26, 2002); missed five games. ... Suffered inflammation of right knee (March 23, 2002); missed six games. ... Reinjured knee (April 6, 2002) and underwent surgery; missed final four games of season. ... Traded by Flyers to Edmonton Oilers for third-round pick in 2003 draft and conditional fifth-round pick in 2004 draft (June 18, 2002). ... Released by Oilers (December 28, 2002).

STATISTICAL PLATEAUS: Four-goal games: 2001-02 (1).

Season Team	League	REGULAR SEASON								PLAYOFFS				
		Gms.	G	A	Pts.	PIM	+/-	PP	SH	Gms.	G	A	Pts.	PIM
88-89—DS Olomouc	Czech Dv.II					Statistics unavailable.								
89-90—Dukla Jihlava	Czech.	5	1	2	3	...	...	...	...	—	—	—	—	—
90-91—DS Olomouc	Czech.	42	11	13	24	...	...	...	...	—	—	—	—	—
91-92—DS Olomouc	Czech.	38	23	20	43	...	...	...	...	—	—	—	—	—
92-93—DS Olomouc	Czech.	28	12	17	29	...	...	...	...	—	—	—	—	—
—Eisbaren Berlin	Germany	11	7	8	15	49	...	...	...	4	3	5	8	5
94-95—Eisbaren Berlin	Germany	42	28	40	68	55	...	...	...	—	—	—	—	—
95-96—Petra Vsetin	Czech Rep.	38	19	20	39	20	...	...	...	13	9	11	20	10
96-97—Petra Vsetin	Czech Rep.	52	30	31	61	55	...	...	...	10	7	4	11	22
97-98—Petra Vsetin	Czech Rep.	50	21	34	55	64	...	...	...	10	*12	6	18	4
—Czech Rep. Oly. team	Int'l	6	1	2	3	0	...	...	...	—	—	—	—	—
98-99—HC Vsetin	Czech Rep.	50	19	32	51	43	...	...	...	12	1	6	7	...
99-00—HC Vsetin	Czech Rep.	49	*30	29	59	83	...	...	...	9	0	4	4	6
00-01—HC Vsetin	Czech Rep.	46	19	31	50	53	...	...	...	14	8	*13	*21	18
01-02—Philadelphia	NHL	52	11	16	27	8	9	3	0	—	—	—	—	—
—Czech Rep. Oly. team	Int'l	4	2	2	4	2	...	...	...	—	—	—	—	—
02-03—Edmonton	NHL	21	1	5	6	11	-4	0	0	—	—	—	—	—
NHL Totals (2 years)		73	12	21	33	19	5	3	0					

PERSONAL: Born December 25, 1968, in Brick, N.J. ... 6-1/190. ... Shoots right. ... Full Name: James Thomas Dowd Jr.

TRANSACTIONS/CAREER NOTES: Selected by New Jersey Devils in eighth round (seventh Devils pick, 149th overall) of NHL entry draft (June 13, 1987). ... Injured shoulder (February 2, 1995) and underwent shoulder surgery; missed 35 games. ... Traded by Devils with second-round pick (traded to Calgary) in 1997 draft to Hartford Whalers for RW Jocelyn Lemieux and second-round pick (traded to Dallas) in 1998 draft

(December 19, 1995). ... Traded by Whalers with D Frantisek Kucera and second-round pick (D Ryan Bonni) in 1997 draft to Vancouver Canucks for D Jeff Brown and fifth-round pick (traded to Dallas) in 1998 draft (December 19, 1995). ... Selected by New York Islanders from Canucks in waiver draft for cash (September 30, 1996). ... Signed as free agent by Calgary Flames (July 10, 1997). ... Traded by Flames to Nashville Predators for future considerations (June 27, 1998). ... Traded by Predators with G Mikhail Shtalenkov to Edmonton Oilers for G Eric Fichaud, D Drake Berehowsky and D Greg de Vries (October 1, 1998). ... Selected by Minnesota Wild in NHL expansion draft (June 23, 2000). ... Injured ribs (January 6, 2001); missed 10 games. ... Strained neck (March 31, 2001); missed four games.

		REGULAR SEASON								PLAYOFFS				
Season Team	League	Gms.	G	A	Pts.	PIM	+/-	PP	SH	Gms.	G	A	Pts.	PIM
83-84—Brick Township	N.J. H.S.	—	19	30	49	—	—	—	—	—	—	—	—	—
84-85—Brick Township	N.J. H.S.	—	58	55	113	—	—	—	—	—	—	—	—	—
85-86—Brick Township	N.J. H.S.	—	47	51	98	—	—	—	—	—	—	—	—	—
86-87—Brick Township	N.J. H.S.	24	22	33	55	...	—	—	—	—	—	—	—	—
87-88—Lake Superior State	CCHA	45	18	27	45	16	...	...	...	—	—	—	—	—
88-89—Lake Superior State	CCHA	46	24	35	59	40	...	...	...	—	—	—	—	—
89-90—Lake Superior State	CCHA	46	25	67	92	30	...	...	...	—	—	—	—	—
90-91—Lake Superior State	CCHA	44	24	54	78	53	...	...	...	—	—	—	—	—
91-92—Utica	AHL	78	17	42	59	47	...	...	...	4	2	2	4	4
—New Jersey	NHL	1	0	0	0	0	0	0	0	—	—	—	—	—
92-93—Utica	AHL	78	27	45	72	62	...	...	...	5	1	7	8	10
—New Jersey	NHL	1	0	0	0	0	-1	0	0	—	—	—	—	—
93-94—Albany......................	AHL	58	26	37	63	76	...	...	...	—	—	—	—	—
—New Jersey	NHL	15	5	10	15	0	8	2	0	19	2	6	8	8
94-95—New Jersey	NHL	10	1	4	5	0	-5	1	0	11	2	1	3	8
95-96—New Jersey	NHL	28	4	9	13	17	-1	0	0	—	—	—	—	—
—Vancouver..................	NHL	38	1	6	7	6	-8	0	0	1	0	0	0	0
96-97—New York Islanders.....	NHL	3	0	0	0	0	-1	0	0	—	—	—	—	—
—Utah	IHL	48	10	21	31	27	...	...	...	—	—	—	—	—
—Saint John	AHL	24	5	11	16	18	...	...	...	5	1	2	3	0
97-98—Saint John	AHL	35	8	30	38	20	...	...	...	19	3	13	16	10
—Calgary.......................	NHL	48	6	8	14	12	10	0	1	—	—	—	—	—
98-99—Hamilton	AHL	51	15	29	44	82	...	...	...	11	3	6	9	8
—Edmonton...................	NHL	1	0	0	0	0	0	0	0	—	—	—	—	—
99-00—Edmonton...................	NHL	69	5	18	23	45	10	2	0	5	2	1	3	4
00-01—Minnesota..................	NHL	68	7	22	29	80	-6	0	0	—	—	—	—	—
01-02—Minnesota..................	NHL	82	13	30	43	54	-14	5	0	—	—	—	—	—
02-03—Minnesota..................	NHL	78	8	17	25	31	-1	3	1	15	0	2	2	0
NHL Totals (12 years).........		442	50	124	174	245	-9	13	2	51	6	10	16	20

DOWNEY, AARON RW STARS

PERSONAL: Born August 27, 1974, in Shelburne, Ont. ... 6-1/216. ... Shoots right. ... Full Name: Aaron Douglas Downey.
TRANSACTIONS/CAREER NOTES: Signed as non-drafted free agent by Boston Bruins (January 20, 1998). ... Signed as free agent by Chicago Blackhawks (August 8, 2000). ... Signed as free agent by Dallas Stars (July 3, 2002).

		REGULAR SEASON								PLAYOFFS				
Season Team	League	Gms.	G	A	Pts.	PIM	+/-	PP	SH	Gms.	G	A	Pts.	PIM
92-93—Guelph	OHL	53	3	3	6	88	...	...	...	5	1	0	1	0
93-94—Cole Harbor	MWJHL	35	8	20	28	210	...	...	...	—	—	—	—	—
94-95—Cole Harbor	MWJHL	40	10	31	41	320	...	...	...	—	—	—	—	—
95-96—Hampton	ECHL	65	12	11	23	354	...	...	...	—	—	—	—	—
96-97—Hampton	ECHL	64	8	8	16	338	...	...	...	9	0	3	3	26
—Portland......................	AHL	3	0	0	0	19	...	...	...	—	—	—	—	—
—Manitoba.....................	IHL	2	0	0	0	17	...	...	...	—	—	—	—	—
97-98—Providence.................	AHL	78	5	10	15	*407	...	...	...	—	—	—	—	—
98-99—Providence.................	AHL	75	10	12	22	*401	...	...	...	19	1	1	2	46
99-00—Providence.................	AHL	47	6	4	10	221	...	...	...	14	1	0	1	24
—Boston	NHL	1	0	0	0	0	0	0	0	—	—	—	—	—
00-01—Norfolk.......................	AHL	67	6	15	21	234	...	...	...	9	0	0	0	4
—Chicago.......................	NHL	3	0	0	0	6	-1	0	0	—	—	—	—	—
01-02—Chicago......................	NHL	36	1	0	1	76	-2	0	0	4	0	0	0	8
—Norfolk.........................	AHL	12	0	2	2	21	...	...	...	—	—	—	—	—
02-03—Dallas........................	NHL	43	1	1	2	69	1	0	0	—	—	—	—	—
NHL Totals (4 years)...........		83	2	1	3	151	-2	0	0	4	0	0	0	8

DRAKE, DALLAS RW BLUES

PERSONAL: Born February 4, 1969, in Trail, B.C. ... 6-1/190. ... Shoots left. ... Full Name: Dallas James Drake.
TRANSACTIONS/CAREER NOTES: Selected by Detroit Red Wings in sixth round (sixth Red Wings pick, 116th overall) of NHL entry draft (June 17, 1989). ... Bruised left leg (November 27, 1992); missed three games. ... Suffered back spasms (December 28, 1992); missed one game. ... Bruised kneecap (January 23, 1993); missed three games. ... Suffered concussion (February 13, 1993); missed one game. ... Injured right wrist (October 16, 1993); missed three games. ... Injured tendon in right hand (December 14, 1993); missed 16 games. ... Traded by Detroit Red Wings with G Tim Cheveldae to Winnipeg Jets for G Bob Essensa and D Sergei Bautin (March 8, 1994). ... Suffered back spasms (March 17, 1995); missed four games. ... Bruised right shoulder (October 22, 1995); missed seven games. ... Suffered ear infection (November 21, 1995); missed two games. ... Strained Achilles' tendon (December 28, 1995); missed two games. ... Jets franchise moved to Phoenix and renamed Coyotes for 1996-97 season; NHL approved move on January 18, 1996. ... Sprained ankle (November 16, 1996); missed eight games. ... Sprained knee (January 29, 1997); missed 10 games. ... Suffered from the flu (October 19, 1997); missed one game. ... Injured knee (December 3, 1997); missed 12 games. ... Bruised knee (March 2, 1998); missed one game. ... Injured wrist (March 18, 1998); missed five games. ... Bruised ankle (October 21, 1998); missed one game. ... Suffered concussion (November 6, 1998); missed two games. ... Bruised elbow (December 28, 1998); missed one game. ... Suspended four games by NHL for illegal hit (December 29, 1998). ... Separated shoulder (January 29, 1999); missed 13 games. ... Strained shoulder (March 15, 1999); missed two games. ... Bruised shoulder (March 23, 1999); missed five games. ... Sprained shoulder (October 30, 1999); missed three games. ... Selected by Columbus Blue Jackets in NHL expansion draft (June 23, 2000). ... Signed as free agent by St. Louis Blues (July 1, 2000). ... Injured knee (Novmeber 6, 2001); missed one game.

Season Team	League	REGULAR SEASON								PLAYOFFS				
		Gms.	G	A	Pts.	PIM	+/-	PP	SH	Gms.	G	A	Pts.	PIM
84-85—Rossland	KIJHL	30	13	37	50	...	...	...	...	—	—	—	—	—
85-86—Rossland	KIJHL	41	53	73	126	...	...	...	...	—	—	—	—	—
86-87—Rossland	KIJHL	40	55	80	135	...	...	...	...	—	—	—	—	—
87-88—Vernon	BCJHL	47	39	85	124	50	...	...	...	11	9	17	26	30
88-89—N. Michigan Univ.	WCHA	45	18	24	42	26	...	...	...	—	—	—	—	—
89-90—N. Michigan Univ.	WCHA	36	13	24	37	42	...	...	...	—	—	—	—	—
90-91—N. Michigan Univ.	WCHA	44	22	36	58	89	...	...	...	—	—	—	—	—
91-92—N. Michigan Univ.	WCHA	40	*39	44	83	58	...	...	...	—	—	—	—	—
92-93—Detroit	NHL	72	18	26	44	93	15	3	2	7	3	3	6	6
93-94—Detroit	NHL	47	10	22	32	37	5	0	1	—	—	—	—	—
—Adirondack	AHL	1	2	0	2	0	...	...	...	—	—	—	—	—
—Winnipeg	NHL	15	3	5	8	12	-6	1	1	—	—	—	—	—
94-95—Winnipeg	NHL	43	8	18	26	30	-6	0	0	—	—	—	—	—
95-96—Winnipeg	NHL	69	19	20	39	36	-7	4	4	3	0	0	0	0
96-97—Phoenix	NHL	63	17	19	36	52	-11	5	1	7	0	1	1	2
97-98—Phoenix	NHL	60	11	29	40	71	17	3	0	4	0	1	1	2
98-99—Phoenix	NHL	53	9	22	31	65	17	0	0	7	4	3	7	4
99-00—Phoenix	NHL	79	15	30	45	62	11	0	2	5	0	1	1	4
00-01—St. Louis	NHL	82	12	29	41	71	18	2	0	15	4	2	6	16
01-02—St. Louis	NHL	80	11	15	26	87	8	1	3	8	0	0	0	8
02-03—St. Louis	NHL	80	20	10	30	66	-7	4	1	7	1	4	5	23
NHL Totals (11 years)		743	153	245	398	682	54	23	15	63	12	15	27	65

DRAPER, KRIS   C   RED WINGS

PERSONAL: Born May 24, 1971, in Toronto ... 5-11/190. ... Shoots left. ... Full Name: Kris Bruce Draper. ... Related to Kevin Grimes, defenseman, Ottawa Senators organization.

TRANSACTIONS/CAREER NOTES: Selected by Winnipeg Jets in third round (fourth Jets pick, 62nd overall) of NHL entry draft (June 17, 1989). ... Traded by Jets to Detroit Red Wings for future considerations (June 30, 1993). ... Sprained right knee ligament (February 4, 1995); missed eight games. ... Suffered from the flu (January 5, 1996); missed one game. ... Injured right knee (February 15, 1996); missed 12 games. ... Reinjured right knee (March 25, 1996); missed three games. ... Dislocated thumb (December 17, 1997) and underwent surgery; missed 18 games. ... Suspended two games by NHL for slashing incident (January 29, 1999). ... Suffered facial lacerations (November 15, 1999); missed three games. ... Fractured wrist (November 24, 1999); missed 25 games.

Season Team	League	REGULAR SEASON								PLAYOFFS				
		Gms.	G	A	Pts.	PIM	+/-	PP	SH	Gms.	G	A	Pts.	PIM
88-89—Canadian nat'l team	Int'l	60	11	15	26	16	...	...	...	—	—	—	—	—
89-90—Canadian nat'l team	Int'l	61	12	22	34	44	...	...	...	—	—	—	—	—
90-91—Winnipeg	NHL	3	1	0	1	5	0	0	0	—	—	—	—	—
—Moncton	AHL	7	2	1	3	2	...	...	...	—	—	—	—	—
—Ottawa	OHL	39	19	42	61	35	...	...	...	17	8	11	19	20
91-92—Moncton	AHL	61	11	18	29	113	...	...	...	4	0	1	1	6
—Winnipeg	NHL	10	2	0	2	2	0	0	0	2	0	0	0	0
92-93—Winnipeg	NHL	7	0	0	0	2	-6	0	0	—	—	—	—	—
—Moncton	AHL	67	12	23	35	40	...	...	...	5	2	2	4	18
93-94—Adirondack	AHL	46	20	23	43	49	...	...	...	—	—	—	—	—
—Detroit	NHL	39	5	8	13	31	11	0	1	7	2	2	4	4
94-95—Detroit	NHL	36	2	6	8	22	1	0	0	18	4	1	5	12
95-96—Detroit	NHL	52	7	9	16	32	2	0	1	18	4	2	6	18
96-97—Detroit	NHL	76	8	5	13	73	-11	1	0	20	2	4	6	12
97-98—Detroit	NHL	64	13	10	23	45	5	1	0	19	1	3	4	12
98-99—Detroit	NHL	80	4	14	18	79	2	0	1	10	0	1	1	6
99-00—Detroit	NHL	51	5	7	12	28	3	0	0	9	2	0	2	6
00-01—Detroit	NHL	75	8	17	25	38	17	0	1	6	0	1	1	2
01-02—Detroit	NHL	82	15	15	30	56	26	0	2	23	2	3	5	20
02-03—Detroit	NHL	82	14	21	35	82	6	0	1	4	0	0	0	4
NHL Totals (13 years)		657	84	112	196	495	56	2	7	136	17	17	34	96

DROZDETSKY, ALEXANDER   RW   FLYERS

PERSONAL: Born November 10, 1981, in Moscow, U.S.S.R. ... 6-0/174. ... Shoots left.

TRANSACTIONS/CAREER NOTES: Selected by Philadelphia Flyers in third round (second Flyers pick, 94th overall) of NHL entry draft (June 24, 2000).

Season Team	League	REGULAR SEASON								PLAYOFFS				
		Gms.	G	A	Pts.	PIM	+/-	PP	SH	Gms.	G	A	Pts.	PIM
99-00—SKA St. Petersburg	Russian	32	2	0	2	10	...	...	...	4	0	0	0	0
01-02—CSKA Moscow	Russian	49	11	6	17	26	...	...	...	—	—	—	—	—
—SKA St. Petersburg	Russian	42	6	7	13	74	...	...	...	—	—	—	—	—
02-03—CSKA Moscow	Russian	46	14	13	27	30	...	...	...	—	—	—	—	—

DRUKEN, HAROLD   C   MAPLE LEAFS

PERSONAL: Born January 26, 1979, in St. John's, Nfld. ... 6-0/200. ... Shoots left. ... Name pronounced DROO-kihn.

TRANSACTIONS/CAREER NOTES: Selected by Vancouver Canucks in second round (third Canucks pick, 36th overall) of NHL entry draft (June 21, 1997). ... Sprained ankle (November 30, 2001); missed 11 games. ... Traded by Canucks with LW Jan Hlavac to Carolina Hurricanes for D Marek Malik and LW Darren Langdon (November 1, 2002). ... Claimed on waivers by Toronto Maple Leafs (December 11, 2002). ... Claimed on waivers by Hurricanes (January 17, 2003). ... Traded by Carolina to Toronto Maple Leafs for D Allan Rourke (May 30, 2003). ... Re-signed by Maple Leafs (July 24, 2003).

STATISTICAL PLATEAUS: Three-goal games: 2000-01 (1).

Season Team	League	REGULAR SEASON								PLAYOFFS				
		Gms.	G	A	Pts.	PIM	+/-	PP	SH	Gms.	G	A	Pts.	PIM
95-96—Noble & Greenough....	Mass. H.S.	30	37	28	65	28	...	...	...	—	—	—	—	—
96-97—Detroit......................	OHL	63	27	31	58	14	...	...	...	5	3	2	5	0
97-98—Plymouth	OHL	64	38	44	82	12	...	...	...	15	9	11	20	4
98-99—Plymouth	OHL	60	*58	45	103	34	...	...	...	11	9	12	21	14
99-00—Syracuse	AHL	47	20	25	45	32	...	...	...	4	1	2	3	6
—Vancouver.................	NHL	33	7	9	16	10	14	2	0	—	—	—	—	—
00-01—Kansas City.............	IHL	15	5	9	14	20	...	...	...	—	—	—	—	—
—Vancouver.................	NHL	55	15	15	30	14	2	6	0	4	0	1	1	0
01-02—Vancouver.................	NHL	27	4	4	8	6	-1	1	0	—	—	—	—	—
—Manitoba....................	AHL	11	2	9	11	4	...	...	...	—	—	—	—	—
02-03—St. John's...................	AHL	6	0	3	3	2	...	...	...	—	—	—	—	—
—Vancouver.................	NHL	3	1	1	2	0	-1	0	0	—	—	—	—	—
—Carolina	NHL	14	0	1	1	2	-1	0	0	—	—	—	—	—
—Toronto	NHL	5	0	2	2	2	1	0	0	—	—	—	—	—
—Lowell........................	AHL	24	8	10	18	8	...	...	...	—	—	—	—	—
NHL Totals (4 years)...........		137	27	32	59	34	14	9	0	4	0	1	1	0

DRURY, CHRIS — LW — SABRES

PERSONAL: Born August 20, 1976, in Trumbull, Conn. ... 5-10/195. ... Shoots right. ... Brother of Ted Drury, center, Columbus Blue Jackets.
TRANSACTIONS/CAREER NOTES: Selected by Quebec Nordiques in third round (fifth Nordiques pick, 72nd overall) of NHL entry draft (June 29, 1994). ... Nordiques franchise moved to Colorado and renamed Avalanche for 1995-96 season (June 21, 1995). ... Suffered hip pointer (October 29, 1998); missed 11 games. ... Sprained knee (November 1, 2000); missed 11 games. ... Traded by Avalanche with C Stephane Yelle to Calgary Flames for D Derek Morris, LW Deam McAmmond and C Jeff Shantz (October 1, 2002). ... Traded by Flames to Buffalo Sabres with Steve Begin for Rhett Warrener and Steve Reinprecht (July 2, 2003).

Season Team	League	REGULAR SEASON								PLAYOFFS				
		Gms.	G	A	Pts.	PIM	+/-	PP	SH	Gms.	G	A	Pts.	PIM
92-93—Fairfield College Prep..	Conn. H.S.	24	25	32	57	15	...	...	...	—	—	—	—	—
93-94—Fairfield College Prep..	Conn. H.S.	24	37	18	55	...	...	...	...	—	—	—	—	—
94-95—Boston University	Hockey East	39	12	15	27	38	...	...	...	—	—	—	—	—
95-96—Boston University	Hockey East	37	35	33	68	46	...	...	...	—	—	—	—	—
96-97—Boston University	Hockey East	41	38	24	62	64	...	...	...	—	—	—	—	—
97-98—Boston University	Hockey East	38	28	29	57	88	...	...	...	—	—	—	—	—
98-99—Colorado	NHL	79	20	24	44	62	9	6	0	19	6	2	8	4
99-00—Colorado	NHL	82	20	47	67	42	8	7	0	17	4	10	14	4
00-01—Colorado	NHL	71	24	41	65	47	6	11	0	23	11	5	16	4
01-02—Colorado	NHL	82	21	25	46	38	1	5	0	21	5	7	12	10
02-03—Calgary	NHL	80	23	30	53	33	-9	5	1	—	—	—	—	—
NHL Totals (5 years)...........		394	108	167	275	222	15	34	1	80	26	24	50	22

DUBINSKY, STEVE — C

PERSONAL: Born July 9, 1970, in Montreal ... 6-0/190. ... Shoots left. ... Name pronounced doo-BIHN-skee.
TRANSACTIONS/CAREER NOTES: Selected by Chicago Blackhawks in 11th round (11th Blackhawks pick, 226th overall) of NHL entry draft (June 16, 1990). ... Traded by Blackhawks with C Jeff Shantz to Calgary Flames for D Jamie Allison, C/LW Marty McInnis and RW Erik Andersson (October 27, 1998). ... Injured knee (March 13, 1999); missed eight games. ... Injured knee (December 12, 1999); missed final 52 games of season. ... Signed as free agent by Blackhawks (August 25, 2000). ... Traded by Blackhawks to Nashville Predators for future considerations (February 6, 2002). ... Suffered hip pointer (April 11, 2002); missed remainder of season. ... Signed as free agent by St. Louis Blues (July 16, 2002).

Season Team	League	REGULAR SEASON								PLAYOFFS				
		Gms.	G	A	Pts.	PIM	+/-	PP	SH	Gms.	G	A	Pts.	PIM
89-90—Clarkson	ECAC	35	7	10	17	24	...	...	...	—	—	—	—	—
90-91—Clarkson	ECAC	38	15	23	38	26	...	...	...	—	—	—	—	—
91-92—Clarkson	ECAC	33	21	34	55	40	...	...	...	—	—	—	—	—
92-93—Clarkson	ECAC	35	18	26	44	58	...	...	...	—	—	—	—	—
93-94—Chicago......................	NHL	27	2	6	8	16	1	0	0	6	0	0	0	10
—Indianapolis...............	IHL	54	15	25	40	63	...	...	...	—	—	—	—	—
94-95—Indianapolis	IHL	62	16	11	27	29	...	...	...	—	—	—	—	—
—Chicago....................	NHL	16	0	0	0	8	-5	0	0	—	—	—	—	—
95-96—Indianapolis	IHL	16	8	8	16	10	...	...	...	—	—	—	—	—
—Chicago....................	NHL	43	2	3	5	14	3	0	0	—	—	—	—	—
96-97—Indianapolis	IHL	77	32	40	72	53	...	...	...	1	3	1	4	0
—Chicago....................	NHL	5	0	0	0	0	2	0	0	4	1	0	1	4
97-98—Chicago......................	NHL	82	5	13	18	57	-6	0	1	—	—	—	—	—
98-99—Chicago......................	NHL	1	0	0	0	0	0	0	0	—	—	—	—	—
—Calgary	NHL	61	4	10	14	14	-7	0	2	—	—	—	—	—
99-00—Calgary	NHL	23	0	1	1	4	-12	0	0	—	—	—	—	—
00-01—Norfolk......................	AHL	14	6	5	11	4	...	...	...	—	—	—	—	—
—Chicago....................	NHL	60	6	4	10	33	-4	0	1	—	—	—	—	—
01-02—Chicago......................	NHL	3	1	0	1	4	1	0	0	—	—	—	—	—
—Norfolk.....................	AHL	16	7	3	10	6	...	...	...	—	—	—	—	—
—Milwaukee	AHL	36	13	13	26	16	...	...	...	—	—	—	—	—
—Nashville	NHL	26	5	2	7	10	-2	0	0	—	—	—	—	—
02-03—Worcester	AHL	6	1	5	6	4	...	...	...	—	—	—	—	—
—St. Louis	NHL	28	0	6	6	4	3	0	0	—	—	—	—	—
NHL Totals (10 years).........		375	25	45	70	164	-26	0	4	10	1	0	1	14

D

PERSONAL: Born April 1, 1978, in Montreal ... 6-1/203. ... Shoots left. ... Full Name: Jean-Pierre Dumont.

TRANSACTIONS/CAREER NOTES: Selected by New York Islanders in first round (first Islanders pick, third overall) of NHL entry draft (June 22, 1996). ... Traded by Islanders with fifth-round pick (traded to Philadelphia) in 1998 draft to Chicago Blackhawks for C/LW Dmitri Nabokov (May 30, 1998). ... Injured back (April 8, 1999); missed two games. ... Traded by Blackhawks with C Doug Gilmour to Buffalo Sabres for LW Michal Grosek (March 10, 2000). ... Suffered rib injury (February 13, 2001); missed two games. ... Injured shoulder (April 1, 2002); missed remainder of season.

STATISTICAL PLATEAUS: Three-goal games: 1998-99 (1), 2000-01 (1), 2001-02 (1). Total: 3.

		REGULAR SEASON								PLAYOFFS				
Season Team	League	Gms.	G	A	Pts.	PIM	+/-	PP	SH	Gms.	G	A	Pts.	PIM
93-94—Val-d'Or	QMJHL	25	9	11	20	10	...	...	...	—	—	—	—	—
94-95—Val-d'Or	QMJHL	48	5	14	19	24	...	...	...	—	—	—	—	—
95-96—Val-d'Or	QMJHL	66	48	57	105	109	...	...	...	13	12	8	20	22
96-97—Val-d'Or	QMJHL	62	44	64	108	88	...	...	...	13	9	7	16	12
97-98—Val-d'Or	QMJHL	55	57	42	99	63	...	...	...	19	*31	15	*46	18
98-99—Portland	AHL	50	32	14	46	39	...	...	...	—	—	—	—	—
—Chicago	NHL	25	9	6	15	10	7	0	0	—	—	—	—	—
99-00—Chicago	NHL	47	10	8	18	18	-6	0	0	—	—	—	—	—
—Cleveland	IHL	7	5	2	7	8	...	...	...	—	—	—	—	—
—Rochester	AHL	13	7	10	17	18	...	...	...	21	*14	7	21	32
00-01—Buffalo	NHL	79	23	28	51	54	1	9	0	13	4	3	7	8
01-02—Buffalo	NHL	76	23	21	44	42	-10	7	0	—	—	—	—	—
02-03—Buffalo	NHL	76	14	21	35	44	-14	2	0	—	—	—	—	—
NHL Totals (5 years)		303	79	84	163	168	-22	18	0	13	4	3	7	8

PERSONAL: Born June 1, 1972, in Johnson City, N.Y. ... 6-3/200. ... Catches left. ... Full Name: Michael Francis Dunham.

TRANSACTIONS/CAREER NOTES: Selected by New Jersey Devils in third round (fourth Devils pick, 53rd overall) of NHL entry draft (June 16, 1990). ... Injured hand (January 1, 1998); missed three games. ... Injured knee and underwent surgery (March 5, 1998); missed 18 games. ... Selected by Nashville Predators in NHL expansion draft (June 26, 1998). ... Strained right groin (November 29, 1998); missed seven games. ... Reinjured groin (December 19, 1998); missed 13 games. ... Strained groin (March 27, 1999); missed six games. ... Suffered from the flu (December 26, 1999); missed one game. ... Sprained right thumb (February 3, 2000); missed four games. ... Sprained left knee (October 27, 2000); missed 15 games. ... Injured knee (December 4, 2000); missed two games. ... Strained neck (February 20, 2001); missed one game. ... Suffered concussion (April 6, 2002); missed remainder of season. ... Traded by Predators to New York Rangers for LW Rem Murray, D Tomas Kloucek and D Marek Zidlicky (December 12, 2002).

		REGULAR SEASON									PLAYOFFS							
Season Team	League	Gms.	Min	W	L	T	GA	SO	Avg.	SV%	Gms.	Min.	W	L	GA	SO	Avg.	SV%
87-88—Canterbury School	Conn. H.S.	29	1740	...	...	...	69	4	2.38	—	—	—	—	—	—	—	—	—
88-89—Canterbury School	Conn. H.S.	25	1500	...	...	...	63	2	2.52	—	—	—	—	—	—	—	—	—
89-90—Canterbury School	Conn. H.S.	32	1558	...	...	...	55	3	2.12	—	—	—	—	—	—	—	—	—
90-91—Univ. of Maine	Hockey East	23	1275	14	5	2	63	2	*2.96	—	—	—	—	—	—	—	—	—
91-92—Univ. of Maine	Hockey East	7	382	6	0	0	14	1	2.20	—	—	—	—	—	—	—	—	—
—U.S. national team	Int'l	3	157	0	1	1	10	0	3.82	—	—	—	—	—	—	—	—	—
92-93—Univ. of Maine	Hockey East	25	1429	21	1	1	63	0	2.65	—	—	—	—	—	—	—	—	—
—U.S. national team	Int'l	1	60	0	0	1	1	0	1.00	—	—	—	—	—	—	—	—	—
93-94—U.S. national team	Int'l	33	1983	22	9	2	125	2	3.78	—	—	—	—	—	—	—	—	—
—U.S. Olympic team	Int'l	3	180	0	1	2	15	0	5.00	—	—	—	—	—	—	—	—	—
—Albany	AHL	5	305	2	2	1	26	0	5.11	—	—	—	—	—	—	—	—	—
94-95—Albany	AHL	35	2120	20	7	8	99	1	2.80	—	7	420	6	1	20	1	2.86	—
95-96—Albany	AHL	44	2591	30	10	2	109	1	2.52	—	3	181	1	2	5	1	1.66	—
96-97—Albany	AHL	3	184	1	1	1	12	0	3.91	—	—	—	—	—	—	—	—	—
—New Jersey	NHL	26	1013	8	7	1	43	2	2.55	.906	—	—	—	—	—	—	—	—
97-98—New Jersey	NHL	15	773	5	5	3	29	1	2.25	.913	—	—	—	—	—	—	—	—
98-99—Nashville	NHL	44	2472	16	23	3	127	1	3.08	.908	—	—	—	—	—	—	—	—
99-00—Milwaukee	IHL	1	60	2	0	0	1	0	1.00	—	—	—	—	—	—	—	—	—
—Nashville	NHL	52	3077	19	27	4	146	0	2.85	.908	—	—	—	—	—	—	—	—
00-01—Nashville	NHL	48	2810	21	21	4	107	4	2.28	.923	—	—	—	—	—	—	—	—
01-02—Nashville	NHL	58	3316	23	24	9	144	3	2.61	.906	—	—	—	—	—	—	—	—
—U.S. Olympic team	Int'l	1	60	1	0	0	0	1	...	—	—	—	—	—	—	—	—	—
02-03—Nashville	NHL	15	819	2	9	2	43	0	3.15	.892	—	—	—	—	—	—	—	—
—New York Rangers	NHL	43	2467	19	17	5	94	5	2.29	.924	—	—	—	—	—	—	—	—
NHL Totals (7 years)		301	16747	113	133	33	733	16	2.63	.912	—	—	—	—	—	—	—	—

PERSONAL: Born April 15, 1980, in Calgary ... 5-10/186. ... Shoots right.

TRANSACTIONS/CAREER NOTES: Selected by Calgary Flames in ninth round (ninth Flames pick, 270th overall) of NHL entry draft (June 24, 2000). ... Traded by Flames with C Mathias Johansson to Pittsburgh Penguins for RW Shean Donovan (March 11, 2003).

Season Team	League	REGULAR SEASON								PLAYOFFS				
		Gms.	G	A	Pts.	PIM	+/-	PP	SH	Gms.	G	A	Pts.	PIM
96-97—Kamloops	WHL	59	8	27	35	...	...	...	...	5	0	4	4	8
97-98—Kamloops	WHL	71	13	41	54	93	...	...	...	7	0	1	1	10
98-99—Kamloops	WHL	59	8	27	35	110	...	...	...	15	2	8	10	22
99-00—Kamloops	WHL	70	26	62	88	159	...	...	...	4	0	2	2	17
—Long Beach	IHL	1	0	0	0	0	...	...	...	—	—	—	—	—
—San Diego	WCHL	—	—	—	—	—	—	—	—	7	2	2	4	0
00-01—Saint John	AHL	67	8	21	29	28	...	...	...	19	1	9	10	14
01-02—Saint John	AHL	77	7	33	40	77	...	...	...	—	—	—	—	—
—Calgary	NHL	2	0	0	0	2	0	0	0	—	—	—	—	—
02-03—Saint John	AHL	44	12	21	33	73	...	...	...	—	—	—	—	—
—Calgary	NHL	16	1	2	3	4	-5	0	0	—	—	—	—	—
—Wilkes-Barre/Scranton	AHL	14	1	4	5	16	...	...	...	—	—	—	—	—
NHL Totals (2 years)		18	1	2	3	6	-5	0	0					

DUPUIS, PASCAL — LW — WILD

PERSONAL: Born April 7, 1979, in Laval, Que. ... 6-0/196. ... Shoots left.
TRANSACTIONS/CAREER NOTES: Signed as non-drafted free agent by Minnesota Wild (September 18, 2000).

Season Team	League	REGULAR SEASON								PLAYOFFS				
		Gms.	G	A	Pts.	PIM	+/-	PP	SH	Gms.	G	A	Pts.	PIM
96-97—Rouyn-Noranda	QMJHL	44	9	15	24	20	...	...	...	—	—	—	—	—
97-98—Rouyn-Noranda	QMJHL	39	9	17	26	36	...	...	...	—	—	—	—	—
—Shawinigan	QMJHL	28	7	13	20	10	...	...	...	6	2	0	2	4
98-99—Shawinigan	QMJHL	57	30	42	72	118	...	...	...	6	1	8	9	18
99-00—Shawinigan	QMJHL	61	50	55	105	164	...	...	...	13	†15	7	22	4
00-01—Cleveland	IHL	70	19	24	43	37	...	...	...	4	0	0	0	0
—Minnesota	NHL	4	1	0	1	4	0	1	0	—	—	—	—	—
01-02—Minnesota	NHL	76	15	12	27	16	-10	3	2	—	—	—	—	—
02-03—Minnesota	NHL	80	20	28	48	44	17	6	0	16	4	4	8	8
NHL Totals (3 years)		160	36	40	76	64	7	10	2	16	4	4	8	8

DVORAK, RADEK — RW — OILERS

D

PERSONAL: Born March 9, 1977, in Tabor, Czechoslovakia. ... 6-2/202. ... Shoots right. ... Name pronounced RA-dihk duh-VOHR-ak.
TRANSACTIONS/CAREER NOTES: Selected by Florida Panthers in first round (first Panthers pick, 10th overall) of NHL entry draft (July 8, 1995). ... Fractured left wrist (October 30, 1997); missed 15 games. ... Traded by Panthers to San Jose Sharks for G Mike Vernon and third-round pick (RW Sean O'Connor) in 2000 draft (December 30, 1999). ... Traded by Sharks to New York Rangers for RW Todd Harvey and fourth-round pick (G Dimitri Patzold) in 2001 draft (December 30, 1999). ... Sprained left knee (November 23, 2001); missed three games. ... Tore anterior cruciate ligament in right knee (March 13, 2002); missed remainder of season. ... Traded by Rangers with D Cory Cross to Edmonton Oilers for RW Anson Carter and D Ales Pisa (March 11, 2003).
STATISTICAL PLATEAUS: Three-goal games: 1999-00 (1). ... Four-goal games: 2000-01 (1). ... Total hat tricks: 2.

Season Team	League	REGULAR SEASON								PLAYOFFS				
		Gms.	G	A	Pts.	PIM	+/-	PP	SH	Gms.	G	A	Pts.	PIM
92-93—Motor-Ceske Bude.	Czech.	35	44	46	90	...	...	...	...	—	—	—	—	—
93-94—HC Ceske Budejovice	Czech Rep.	8	0	0	0	...	...	...	...	—	—	—	—	—
—Motor-Ceske Bude.	Czech Rep.	20	17	18	35	...	...	...	...	—	—	—	—	—
94-95—HC Ceske Budejovice	Czech Rep.	10	3	5	8	...	...	...	...	9	5	1	6	...
95-96—Florida	NHL	77	13	14	27	20	5	0	0	16	1	3	4	0
96-97—Florida	NHL	78	18	21	39	30	-2	2	0	3	0	0	0	0
97-98—Florida	NHL	64	12	24	36	33	-1	2	3	—	—	—	—	—
98-99—Florida	NHL	82	19	24	43	29	7	0	4	—	—	—	—	—
99-00—Florida	NHL	35	7	10	17	6	5	0	0	—	—	—	—	—
—New York Rangers	NHL	46	11	22	33	10	0	2	1	—	—	—	—	—
00-01—New York Rangers	NHL	82	31	36	67	20	9	5	2	—	—	—	—	—
01-02—New York Rangers	NHL	65	17	20	37	14	-20	3	3	—	—	—	—	—
—Czech Rep. Oly. team	Int'l	4	0	0	0	0	...	...	...	—	—	—	—	—
02-03—New York Rangers	NHL	63	6	21	27	16	-3	2	0	—	—	—	—	—
—Edmonton	NHL	12	4	4	8	14	-3	1	0	4	1	0	1	0
NHL Totals (8 years)		604	138	196	334	192	-3	17	13	23	2	3	5	0

DWYER, GORDIE — LW — CANADIENS

PERSONAL: Born January 25, 1978, in Dalhousie, N.B. ... 6-3/206. ... Shoots left.
TRANSACTIONS/CAREER NOTES: Selected by St. Louis Blues in third round (second Blues pick, 67th overall) of NHL entry draft (June 22, 1996). ... Returned to draft pool by Blues and selected by Montreal Canadiens in sixth round (fifth Canadiens pick, 152nd overall) of NHL entry draft (June 27, 1998). ... Traded by Canadiens to Tampa Bay Lightning for D Mike McBain (November 26, 1999). ... Injured finger (April 8, 2000); missed final game of season. ... Suspended 23 games by NHL for abuse of an official (September 28, 2000). ... Underwent shoulder surgery (February 26, 2002); missed remainder of season. ... Traded by Lightning to New York Rangers for LW Boyd Kane (October 10, 2002).

Season Team	League	REGULAR SEASON								PLAYOFFS				
		Gms.	G	A	Pts.	PIM	+/-	PP	SH	Gms.	G	A	Pts.	PIM
94-95—Hull	QMJHL	57	3	7	10	204	...	...	...	17	1	3	4	54
95-96—Hull	QMJHL	25	5	9	14	199	...	...	...	—	—	—	—	—
—Laval	QMJHL	22	5	17	22	72	...	...	...	—	—	—	—	—
—Beauport	QMJHL	22	4	9	13	87	...	...	...	20	3	5	8	104
96-97—Drummondville	QMJHL	66	21	48	69	391	...	...	...	8	6	1	7	39

Season Team	League	REGULAR SEASON								PLAYOFFS				
		Gms.	G	A	Pts.	PIM	+/-	PP	SH	Gms.	G	A	Pts.	PIM
97-98—Quebec	QMJHL	59	18	27	45	365	...	...	...	14	4	9	13	67
98-99—Fredericton	AHL	14	0	0	0	46	...	...	...	—	—	—	—	—
—New Orleans	ECHL	36	1	3	4	163	...	...	...	11	0	0	0	27
99-00—Quebec	AHL	7	0	0	0	37	...	...	...	—	—	—	—	—
—Detroit	IHL	27	0	2	2	147	...	...	...	—	—	—	—	—
—Tampa Bay	NHL	24	0	1	1	135	-6	0	0	—	—	—	—	—
00-01—Tampa Bay	NHL	28	0	1	1	96	-7	0	0	—	—	—	—	—
—Detroit	IHL	24	2	3	5	169	...	...	...	—	—	—	—	—
01-02—Springfield	AHL	17	1	3	4	80	...	...	...	—	—	—	—	—
—Tampa Bay	NHL	26	0	2	2	60	-4	0	0	—	—	—	—	—
02-03—Hartford	AHL	15	3	2	5	117	...	...	...	—	—	—	—	—
—New York Rangers	NHL	17	0	1	1	50	-1	0	0	—	—	—	—	—
—Montreal	NHL	11	0	0	0	46	-2	0	0	—	—	—	—	—
NHL Totals (4 years)		106	0	5	5	387	-20	0	0					

DYKHUIS, KARL — D — CANADIENS

PERSONAL: Born July 8, 1972, in Sept-Iles, Que. ... 6-3/214. ... Shoots left. ... Name pronounced DIGH-kowz.

TRANSACTIONS/CAREER NOTES: Selected by Chicago Blackhawks in first round (first Blackhawks pick, 16th overall) of NHL entry draft (June 16, 1990). ... Traded by Blackhawks to Philadelphia Flyers for D Bob Wilkie (February 16, 1995). ... Sprained knee (November 26, 1996); missed two games. ... Suffered facial lacerations (December 31, 1996); missed two games. ... Dislocated shoulder (January 28, 1997); missed 13 games. ... Traded by Flyers with RW Mikael Renberg to Tampa Bay Lightning for C Chris Gratton (August 20, 1997). ... Suffered from the flu (November 14, 1997); missed one game. ... Suffered from the flu (January 31, 1998); missed one game. ... Traded by Lightning to Flyers for D Petr Svoboda (December 28, 1998). ... Fractured cheekbone (December 29, 1998); missed one game. ... Traded by Flyers to Montreal Canadiens for future considerations (October 20, 1999). ... Injured knee (March 6, 2000); missed one game. ... Injured groin (March 18, 2000); missed five games. ... Underwent off-season abdominal surgery (October 6, 2000); missed first 11 games of season.

Season Team	League	REGULAR SEASON								PLAYOFFS				
		Gms.	G	A	Pts.	PIM	+/-	PP	SH	Gms.	G	A	Pts.	PIM
88-89—Hull	QMJHL	63	2	29	31	59	...	...	...	9	1	9	10	6
89-90—Hull	QMJHL	69	10	45	55	119	...	...	...	11	2	5	7	2
90-91—Longueuil	QMJHL	3	1	4	5	6	...	...	...	—	—	—	—	—
—Canadian nat'l team	Int'l	37	2	9	11	16	...	...	...	—	—	—	—	—
91-92—Longueuil	QMJHL	29	5	19	24	55	...	...	...	17	0	12	12	14
—Chicago	NHL	6	1	3	4	4	-1	1	0	—	—	—	—	—
92-93—Indianapolis	IHL	59	5	18	23	76	...	...	...	5	1	1	2	8
—Chicago	NHL	12	0	5	5	0	2	0	0	—	—	—	—	—
93-94—Indianapolis	IHL	73	7	25	32	132	...	...	...	—	—	—	—	—
94-95—Indianapolis	IHL	52	2	21	23	63	...	...	...	—	—	—	—	—
—Hershey	AHL	1	0	0	0	0	...	...	...	—	—	—	—	—
—Philadelphia	NHL	33	2	6	8	37	7	1	0	15	4	4	8	14
95-96—Philadelphia	NHL	82	5	15	20	101	12	1	0	12	2	2	4	22
96-97—Philadelphia	NHL	62	4	15	19	35	6	2	0	18	0	3	3	2
97-98—Tampa Bay	NHL	78	5	9	14	110	-8	0	1	—	—	—	—	—
98-99—Tampa Bay	NHL	33	2	1	3	18	-21	0	0	—	—	—	—	—
—Philadelphia	NHL	45	2	4	6	32	-2	1	0	5	1	0	1	4
99-00—Philadelphia	NHL	5	0	1	1	6	-2	0	0	—	—	—	—	—
—Montreal	NHL	67	7	12	19	40	-3	3	1	—	—	—	—	—
00-01—Montreal	NHL	67	8	9	17	44	9	2	0	—	—	—	—	—
01-02—Montreal	NHL	80	5	7	12	32	16	0	0	12	1	1	2	8
02-03—Montreal	NHL	65	1	4	5	34	-5	0	0	—	—	—	—	—
NHL Totals (11 years)		635	42	91	133	493	10	11	2	62	8	10	18	50

DYMENT, CHRIS — D — WILD

PERSONAL: Born October 24, 1979, in Stoneham, Mass. ... 6-3/201. ... Shoots right.

TRANSACTIONS/CAREER NOTES: Selected by Montreal Canadiens in fourth round (third Canadiens pick, 97th overall) of NHL entry draft (June 26, 1999). ... Traded by Canadiens to Minnesota Wild for fifth-round pick in 2002 draft (May 24, 2002).

Season Team	League	REGULAR SEASON								PLAYOFFS				
		Gms.	G	A	Pts.	PIM	+/-	PP	SH	Gms.	G	A	Pts.	PIM
97-98—Reading H.S.	Mass. H.S.	22	22	22	44	15	...	...	...	—	—	—	—	—
98-99—Boston University	Hockey East	25	1	5	6	18	...	...	...	—	—	—	—	—
99-00—Boston University	Hockey East	42	11	20	31	42	...	...	...	—	—	—	—	—
00-01—Boston University	Hockey East	37	1	10	11	38	...	...	...	—	—	—	—	—
01-02—Boston University	Hockey East	38	7	17	24	24	...	...	...	—	—	—	—	—
02-03—Houston	AHL	40	2	3	5	64	...	...	...	—	—	—	—	—

EAGER, BEN — LW — COYOTES

PERSONAL: Born January 22, 1984, in Ottawa. ... 6-2/210. ... Shoots left.

TRANSACTIONS/CAREER NOTES: Selected by Phoenix Coyotes in first round (second Coyotes pick, 23rd overall) of NHL entry draft (June 22, 2002).

Season Team	League	REGULAR SEASON								PLAYOFFS				
		Gms.	G	A	Pts.	PIM	+/-	PP	SH	Gms.	G	A	Pts.	PIM
00-01—Oshawa	OHL	61	4	6	10	120	...	...	...	—	—	—	—	—
01-02—Oshawa	OHL	63	14	23	37	255	...	...	...	5	0	1	1	13
02-03—Oshawa	OHL	58	16	24	40	216	...	...	...	—	—	—	—	—

PERSONAL: Born February 27, 1967, in Dade City, Fla. ... 6-1/198. ... Shoots left. ... Name pronounced AY-kihns.

TRANSACTIONS/CAREER NOTES: Selected by Washington Capitals in 10th round (11th Capitals pick, 208th overall) of NHL entry draft (June 15, 1985). ... Injured back (October 1988). ... Signed as free agent by Winnipeg Jets (September 1989). ... Signed as free agent by Florida Panthers (July 14, 1993). ... Traded by Panthers to St. Louis Blues for fourth-round draft pick (RW Ivan Novoseltsev) in 1997 draft (September 28, 1995). ... Fractured wrist (December 8, 1995); missed 29 games. ... Claimed on waivers by Jets (March 20, 1996). ... Jets franchise moved to Phoenix and renamed Coyotes for 1996-97 season; NHL approved move on January 18, 1996. ... Suffered back spasms (November 26, 1996); missed three games. ... Traded by Coyotes with C Mike Eastwood to New York Rangers for D Jay More (February 6, 1997). ... Signed as free agent by Florida Panthers (July 7, 1997). ... Sprained left knee prior to 1997-98 season; missed first 11 games of season. ... Signed as free agent by Toronto Maple Leafs (July 14, 1998). ... Sprained shoulder (November 14, 1998); missed three games. ... Signed as free agent by New York Islanders (August 12, 1999). ... Traded by Islanders to Chicago Blackhawks for future considerations (March 3, 2000). ... Signed as free agent by Calgary Flames (July 27, 2000). ... Signed as free agent by Atlanta Thrashers (July 23, 2002).

Season Team	League	REGULAR SEASON								PLAYOFFS				
		Gms.	G	A	Pts.	PIM	+/-	PP	SH	Gms.	G	A	Pts.	PIM
84-85—Peterborough	OHL	48	0	8	8	96	...	...	...	7	0	0	0	18
85-86—Peterborough	OHL	60	6	16	22	134	...	...	...	16	0	1	1	30
86-87—Peterborough	OHL	54	3	11	14	145	...	...	...	12	1	4	5	37
87-88—Peterborough	OHL	64	11	27	38	129	...	...	...	12	3	12	15	16
88-89—Baltimore	AHL	62	0	10	10	139	...	...	...	—	—	—	—	—
89-90—Moncton	AHL	75	2	11	13	189	...	...	...	—	—	—	—	—
90-91—Moncton	AHL	75	1	12	13	132	...	...	...	9	0	1	1	44
91-92—Moncton	AHL	67	3	13	16	136	...	...	...	11	2	1	3	16
92-93—Moncton	AHL	55	4	6	10	132	...	...	...	—	—	—	—	—
—Winnipeg	NHL	14	0	2	2	38	2	0	0	—	—	—	—	—
93-94—Cincinnati	IHL	80	1	18	19	143	...	...	...	8	0	1	1	41
—Florida	NHL	1	0	0	0	0	0	0	0	—	—	—	—	—
94-95—Cincinnati	IHL	59	6	12	18	69	...	...	...	—	—	—	—	—
—Florida	NHL	17	0	1	1	35	2	0	0	—	—	—	—	—
95-96—St. Louis	NHL	16	0	1	1	34	-2	0	0	—	—	—	—	—
—Worcester	AHL	4	0	0	0	12	...	...	...	—	—	—	—	—
—Winnipeg	NHL	2	0	0	0	0	1	0	0	—	—	—	—	—
96-97—Springfield	AHL	38	6	7	13	63	...	...	...	—	—	—	—	—
—Phoenix	NHL	4	0	0	0	10	-3	0	0	—	—	—	—	—
—Binghamton	AHL	19	1	7	8	15	...	...	...	—	—	—	—	—
—New York Rangers	NHL	3	0	0	0	6	-1	0	0	4	0	0	0	4
97-98—Florida	NHL	23	0	1	1	44	1	0	0	—	—	—	—	—
—New Haven	AHL	4	0	1	1	7	...	...	...	—	—	—	—	—
98-99—Chicago	IHL	2	0	0	0	0	...	...	...	—	—	—	—	—
—Toronto	NHL	18	0	2	2	24	3	0	0	1	0	0	0	0
—St. John's	AHL	20	3	7	10	16	...	...	...	5	0	1	1	6
99-00—Chicago	IHL	68	5	26	31	99	...	...	...	16	1	4	5	16
—New York Islanders	NHL	2	0	1	1	2	3	0	0	—	—	—	—	—
00-01—Chicago	IHL	64	3	16	19	49	...	...	...	14	0	0	0	24
—Calgary	NHL	17	0	1	1	11	-1	0	0	—	—	—	—	—
01-02—Chicago	AHL	54	2	15	17	58	...	...	...	25	0	6	6	*53
—Calgary	NHL	3	0	0	0	4	1	0	0	—	—	—	—	—
02-03—Chicago	AHL	72	4	11	15	84	...	...	...	5	0	0	0	4
NHL Totals (10 years)		120	0	9	9	208	6	0	0	5	0	0	0	4

PERSONAL: Born July 1, 1967, in Ottawa, Ont. ... 6-3/216. ... Shoots right. ... Full Name: Michael Barry Eastwood.

TRANSACTIONS/CAREER NOTES: Selected by Toronto Maple Leafs in fifth round (fifth Maple Leafs pick, 91st overall) of NHL entry draft (June 13, 1987). ... Traded by Maple Leafs with third-round pick (RW Brad Isbister) in 1995 draft to Winnipeg Jets for RW Tie Domi (April 7, 1995). ... Jets franchise moved to Phoenix and renamed Coyotes for 1996-97 season; NHL approved move on January 18, 1996. ... Fractured wrist (October 28, 1996); missed eight games. ... Traded by Coyotes with D Dallas Eakins to New York Rangers for D Jay More (February 6, 1997). ... Traded by Rangers to St. Louis Blues for C Harry York (March 24, 1998). ... Suffered sore wrist (April 18, 1998); missed two games. ... Sprained ankle (October 8, 2000); missed three games. ... Suffered from the flu (March 10, 2001); missed one game. ... Claimed on waivers by Chicago Blackhawks (December 11, 2002). ... Signed by Pittsburgh Penguins (July 31, 2003).

STATISTICAL PLATEAUS: Three-goal games: 1999-00 (1).

Season Team	League	REGULAR SEASON								PLAYOFFS				
		Gms.	G	A	Pts.	PIM	+/-	PP	SH	Gms.	G	A	Pts.	PIM
86-87—Pembroke	COJHL					Statistics unavailable.								
87-88—Western Michigan	CCHA	42	5	8	13	14	...	...	...	—	—	—	—	—
88-89—Western Michigan	CCHA	40	10	13	23	87	...	...	...	—	—	—	—	—
89-90—Western Michigan	CCHA	40	25	27	52	36	...	...	...	—	—	—	—	—
90-91—Western Michigan	CCHA	42	29	32	61	84	...	...	...	—	—	—	—	—
91-92—St. John's	AHL	61	18	25	43	28	...	...	...	16	9	10	19	16
—Toronto	NHL	9	0	2	2	4	-4	0	0	—	—	—	—	—
92-93—St. John's	AHL	60	24	35	59	32	...	...	...	—	—	—	—	—
—Toronto	NHL	12	1	6	7	21	-2	0	0	10	1	2	3	8
93-94—Toronto	NHL	54	8	10	18	28	2	1	0	18	3	2	5	12
94-95—Toronto	NHL	36	5	5	10	32	-12	0	0	—	—	—	—	—
—Winnipeg	NHL	13	3	6	9	4	3	0	0	—	—	—	—	—
95-96—Winnipeg	NHL	80	14	14	28	20	-14	2	0	6	0	1	1	2
96-97—Phoenix	NHL	33	1	3	4	4	-3	0	0	—	—	—	—	—
—New York Rangers	NHL	27	1	7	8	10	2	0	0	15	1	2	3	22
97-98—New York Rangers	NHL	48	5	5	10	16	-2	0	0	—	—	—	—	—
—St. Louis	NHL	10	1	0	1	6	0	0	0	3	1	0	1	0

Season Team	League	REGULAR SEASON								PLAYOFFS				
		Gms.	G	A	Pts.	PIM	+/-	PP	SH	Gms.	G	A	Pts.	PIM
98-99—St. Louis	NHL	82	9	21	30	36	6	0	0	13	1	1	2	6
99-00—St. Louis	NHL	79	19	15	34	32	5	1	3	7	1	1	2	6
00-01—St. Louis	NHL	77	6	17	23	28	4	0	2	15	0	2	2	2
01-02—St. Louis	NHL	71	7	10	17	41	-2	0	0	10	0	0	0	6
02-03—St. Louis	NHL	17	1	3	4	8	1	1	0	—	—	—	—	—
—Chicago	NHL	53	2	10	12	24	-6	0	0	—	—	—	—	—
NHL Totals (12 years)		701	83	134	217	314	-22	5	5	97	8	11	19	64

EATON, MARK — D — PREDATORS

PERSONAL: Born May 6, 1977, in Wilmington, Del. ... 6-2/205. ... Shoots left. ... Full Name: Mark Andrew Eaton.

TRANSACTIONS/CAREER NOTES: Signed as non-drafted free agent by Philadelphia Flyers (July 28, 1998). ... Suffered from stomach virus (March 26, 2000); missed one game. ... Traded by Flyers to Nashville Predators for third-round pick (C Patrick Sharp) in 2001 draft (September 29, 2000). ... Strained back (October 18, 2001); missed seven games. ... Separated shoulder (December 20, 2001); missed two games. ... Re-signed by Predators (June 24, 2003).

Season Team	League	REGULAR SEASON								PLAYOFFS				
		Gms.	G	A	Pts.	PIM	+/-	PP	SH	Gms.	G	A	Pts.	PIM
97-98—Notre Dame	CCHA	41	12	17	29	32	...	...	...	—	—	—	—	—
98-99—Philadelphia	AHL	74	9	27	36	38	...	...	...	16	4	8	12	0
99-00—Philadelphia	NHL	27	1	1	2	8	1	0	0	7	0	0	0	0
—Philadelphia	AHL	47	9	17	26	6	...	...	...	—	—	—	—	—
00-01—Milwaukee	IHL	34	3	12	15	27	...	...	...	—	—	—	—	—
—Nashville	NHL	34	3	8	11	14	7	1	0	—	—	—	—	—
01-02—Nashville	NHL	58	3	5	8	24	-12	0	0	—	—	—	—	—
02-03—Milwaukee	AHL	3	1	0	1	2	...	...	...	—	—	—	—	—
—Nashville	NHL	50	2	7	9	22	1	0	0	—	—	—	—	—
NHL Totals (4 years)		169	9	21	30	68	-3	1	0	7	0	0	0	0

EHRHOFF, CHRISTIAN — D — SHARKS

PERSONAL: Born July 6, 1982, in Moers, West Germany. ... 6-2/183. ... Shoots left.

TRANSACTIONS/CAREER NOTES: Selected by San Jose Sharks in fourth round (second Sharks pick, 106th overall) of NHL entry draft (June 23, 2001). ... Re-signed by Sharks (June 22, 2003).

Season Team	League	REGULAR SEASON								PLAYOFFS				
		Gms.	G	A	Pts.	PIM	+/-	PP	SH	Gms.	G	A	Pts.	PIM
00-01—Krefeld Pinguine	Germany	58	3	11	14	73	...	...	...	—	—	—	—	—
01-02—Krefeld Pinguine	Germany	46	7	17	24	81	...	...	...	3	0	0	0	2
—German Oly. team	Int'l	7	0	0	0	8	...	...	...	—	—	—	—	—
02-03—Krefeld Pinguine	Germany	48	10	17	27	54	...	...	...	14	3	6	9	24

EKMAN, NILS — LW — RANGERS

PERSONAL: Born March 11, 1976, in Stockholm, Sweden. ... 5-11/182. ... Shoots left.

TRANSACTIONS/CAREER NOTES: Selected by Calgary Flames in fifth round (sixth Flames pick, 107th overall) of NHL entry draft (June 29, 1994). ... Rights traded by Flames with fourth-round pick (traded to New York Islanders) in 2000 draft to Tampa Bay Lightning for C/LW Andreas Johansson (November 20, 1999). ... Injured hip (January 20, 2000); missed one game. ... Traded by Lightning with LW Kyle Freadrich to New York Rangers for C Tim Taylor (July 1, 2001).

Season Team	League	REGULAR SEASON								PLAYOFFS				
		Gms.	G	A	Pts.	PIM	+/-	PP	SH	Gms.	G	A	Pts.	PIM
93-94—Hammarby	Sweden Dv. 2	18	7	2	9	4	...	...	...	—	—	—	—	—
94-95—Hammarby	Sweden Dv. 2	29	10	7	17	18	...	...	...	—	—	—	—	—
95-96—Hammarby	Sweden Dv. 2	22	9	7	16	20	...	...	...	—	—	—	—	—
96-97—Kiekko-Espoo	Finland	50	24	19	43	60	...	...	...	4	2	0	2	4
97-98—Kiekko-Espoo	Finland	43	14	14	28	86	...	...	...	7	2	2	4	27
—Saint John	AHL	—	—	—	—	—	—	—	—	1	0	0	0	2
98-99—Blues Espoo	Finland	52	20	14	34	96	...	...	...	3	1	1	2	6
99-00—Tampa Bay	NHL	28	2	2	4	36	-8	1	0	—	—	—	—	—
—Detroit	IHL	10	7	2	9	8	...	...	...	—	—	—	—	—
—Long Beach	IHL	27	11	12	23	26	...	...	...	5	3	3	6	4
00-01—Detroit	IHL	33	22	14	36	63	...	...	...	—	—	—	—	—
—Tampa Bay	NHL	43	9	11	20	40	-15	2	1	—	—	—	—	—
01-02—Djurgarden Stockholm	Sweden	38	16	15	31	57	...	...	...	4	1	0	1	32
02-03—Hartford	AHL	57	30	36	66	73	...	...	...	—	—	—	—	—
NHL Totals (2 years)		71	11	13	24	76	-23	3	1					

ELIAS, PATRIK — C — DEVILS

PERSONAL: Born April 13, 1976, in Trebic, Czechoslovakia ... 6-1/195. ... Shoots left. ... Name pronounced EH-lee-ahsh.

TRANSACTIONS/CAREER NOTES: Selected by New Jersey Devils in second round (second Devils pick, 51st overall) of NHL entry draft (June 28, 1994). ... Suffered from the flu (January 14, 1999); missed five games. ... Missed first nine games of 1999-2000 season due to contract dispute. ... Suffered finger infection (January 3, 2002); missed five games. ... Suffered from the flu (March 20, 2002); missed two games.

STATISTICAL PLATEAUS: Three-goal games: 2000-01 (3), 2001-02 (2). Total: 5. ... Four-goal games: 2002-03 (1). ... Total hat tricks: 6.

Season Team	League	REGULAR SEASON								PLAYOFFS				
		Gms.	G	A	Pts.	PIM	+/-	PP	SH	Gms.	G	A	Pts.	PIM
92-93—HC Kladno..................	Czech.	2	0	0	0	0	...	...	...	—	—	—	—	—
93-94—HC Kladno..................	Czech Rep.	15	1	2	3	...	...	...	...	11	2	2	4	...
—Czech Rep. Oly. team..	Int'l	5	2	5	7	...	...	...	...	—	—	—	—	—
94-95—HC Kladno..................	Czech Rep.	28	4	3	7	...	...	...	...	7	1	2	3	...
95-96—Albany..................	AHL	74	27	36	63	83	...	...	...	4	1	1	2	2
—New Jersey..................	NHL	1	0	0	0	0	-1	0	0	—	—	—	—	—
96-97—Albany..................	AHL	57	24	43	67	76	...	...	...	6	1	2	3	8
—New Jersey..................	NHL	17	2	3	5	2	-4	0	0	8	2	3	5	4
97-98—New Jersey..................	NHL	74	18	19	37	28	18	5	0	4	0	1	1	0
—Albany..................	AHL	3	3	0	3	2	...	...	...	—	—	—	—	—
98-99—New Jersey..................	NHL	74	17	33	50	34	19	3	0	7	0	5	5	6
99-00—SK Trebic..................	Czech Dv.II	2	2	1	3	2	...	...	...	—	—	—	—	—
—HC Pardubice.............	Czech Rep.	5	1	4	5	6	...	...	...	—	—	—	—	—
—New Jersey..................	NHL	72	35	37	72	58	16	9	0	23	7	†13	20	9
00-01—New Jersey..................	NHL	82	40	56	96	51	†45	8	3	25	9	14	23	10
01-02—New Jersey..................	NHL	75	29	32	61	36	4	8	1	6	2	4	6	6
—Czech Rep. Oly. team..	Int'l	4	1	1	2	0	...	...	...	—	—	—	—	—
02-03—New Jersey..................	NHL	81	28	29	57	22	17	6	0	24	5	8	13	26
NHL Totals (8 years)...........		476	169	209	378	231	114	39	4	97	25	48	73	61

ELICH, MATT   RW

PERSONAL: Born September 22, 1979, in Detroit. ... 6-3/196. ... Shoots right. ... Name pronounced EE-lihch.
TRANSACTIONS/CAREER NOTES: Selected by Tampa Bay Lightning in third round (third Lightning pick, 61st overall) of NHL entry draft (June 21, 1997).

Season Team	League	REGULAR SEASON								PLAYOFFS				
		Gms.	G	A	Pts.	PIM	+/-	PP	SH	Gms.	G	A	Pts.	PIM
95-96—Windsor.....................	OHL	52	10	2	12	17	...	...	...	5	1	0	1	2
96-97—Windsor.....................	OHL	58	15	13	28	19	...	...	...	5	0	1	1	6
97-98—Windsor.....................	OHL	20	9	12	21	8	...	...	...	—	—	—	—	—
—Kingston	OHL	34	14	4	18	2	...	...	...	12	2	4	6	2
98-99—Kingston	OHL	67	44	30	74	32	...	...	...	5	3	5	8	0
99-00—Detroit.....................	IHL	48	12	4	16	12	...	...	...	—	—	—	—	—
—Tampa Bay	NHL	8	1	1	2	0	-1	0	0	—	—	—	—	—
00-01—Detroit.....................	IHL	60	12	16	28	12	...	...	...	—	—	—	—	—
—Tampa Bay	NHL	8	0	0	0	0	-5	0	0	—	—	—	—	—
01-02—Springfield	AHL	22	2	2	4	4	...	...	...	—	—	—	—	—
02-03—Pensacola	ECHL	12	4	4	8	6	...	...	...	—	—	—	—	—
—Wheeling	ECHL	25	3	6	9	32	...	...	...	—	—	—	—	—
NHL Totals (2 years)...........		16	1	1	2	0	-6	0	0	—	—	—	—	—

ELLIS, DAN   G   STARS

PERSONAL: Born June 19, 1980, in Saskatoon, Sask. ... 6-0/180. ... Catches left.
COLLEGE: Nebraska-Omaha.
TRANSACTIONS/CAREER NOTES: Selected by Dallas Stars in second round (second Stars pick, 60th overall) of NHL entry draft (June 24, 2000).

Season Team	League	REGULAR SEASON									PLAYOFFS							
		Gms.	Min	W	L	T	GA	SO	Avg.	SV%	Gms.	Min.	W	L	GA	SO	Avg.	SV%
98-99—Newmarket..................	OPJHL	30	...	...	...	...	...	3	—		—	—	—	—	—	—	—	—
99-00—Omaha	USHL	55	...	34	16	4	...	11	—		—	—	—	—	—	—	—	—
00-01—Nebraska-Omaha	NCAA	40	2285	21	14	3	95	1	2.49	—	—	—	—	—	—	—	—	—
01-02—Nebraska-Omaha	NCAA	40	2405	20	15	4	97	3	2.42	—	—	—	—	—	—	—	—	—
02-03—Nebraska-Omaha	NCAA	39	2210	12	21	5	117	0	3.12	—	—	—	—	—	—	—	—	—

ELORANTA, MIKKO   LW

PERSONAL: Born August 24, 1972, in Turku, Finland ... 6-0/190. ... Shoots left.
TRANSACTIONS/CAREER NOTES: Selected by Boston Bruins in ninth round (ninth Bruins pick, 247th overall) of NHL entry draft (June 26, 1999). ... Fractured ankle (December 10, 1999); missed 26 games. ... Suffered from the flu (December 27, 2000); missed one game. ... Injured elbow (October 6, 2001); missed three games. ... Traded by Bruins with C Jason Allison to Los Angeles Kings for C Jozef Stumpel and RW Glen Murray (October 24, 2001).

Season Team	League	REGULAR SEASON								PLAYOFFS				
		Gms.	G	A	Pts.	PIM	+/-	PP	SH	Gms.	G	A	Pts.	PIM
95-96—Ilves Tampere	Finland	43	18	15	33	86	...	...	...	3	0	2	2	2
96-97—TPS Turku	Finland	31	6	15	21	52	...	...	...	10	5	2	7	6
97-98—TPS Turku	Finland	46	23	14	37	82	...	...	...	2	0	0	0	8
98-99—TPS Turku	Finland	52	19	21	40	103	...	...	...	10	1	6	7	26
99-00—Boston	NHL	50	6	12	18	36	-10	1	0	—	—	—	—	—
00-01—Boston	NHL	62	12	11	23	38	2	1	1	—	—	—	—	—
01-02—Boston	NHL	6	0	0	0	2	-1	0	0	—	—	—	—	—
—Los Angeles	NHL	71	9	9	18	54	0	1	0	7	1	1	2	2
—Fin. Olympic team.......	Int'l	4	2	0	2	2	...	...	...	—	—	—	—	—
02-03—Los Angeles...............	NHL	75	5	12	17	56	-15	1	0	—	—	—	—	—
NHL Totals (4 years)...........		264	32	44	76	186	-24	4	1	7	1	1	2	2

E

EMERY, RAY — G — SENATORS

PERSONAL: Born September 28, 1982, in Cayuga, Ont. ... 6-1/204. ... Catches left.
TRANSACTIONS/CAREER NOTES: Selected by Ottawa Senators in fourth round (fourth Senators pick, 99th overall) of NHL entry draft (June 23, 2001).

		REGULAR SEASON								PLAYOFFS						
Season Team	League	Gms.	Min	W	L	T	GA	SO	Avg.	SV%	Gms.	Min.	W	L	GA	SO	Avg.	SV%
99-00—Sault Ste. Marie	OHL	16	716	9	3	0	36	1	3.02	—	15	883	8	7	33	*3	*2.24	—
00-01—Sault Ste. Marie	OHL	52	2938	18	29	2	174	1	3.55	—	—	—	—	—	—	—	—	—
01-02—Sault Ste. Marie	OHL	*59	*3477	*33	17	*9	158	4	2.73	—	6	360	2	4	19	†1	3.17	—
02-03—Binghamton	AHL	50	2923	27	17	6	118	7	2.42	—	—	—	—	—	—	—	—	—
—Ottawa	NHL	3	85	1	0	0	2	0	1.41	.923	—	—	—	—	—	—	—	—
NHL Totals (1 year)		3	85	1	0	0	2	0	1.41	.923								

EMINGER, STEVE — D — CAPITALS

PERSONAL: Born October 31, 1983, in Woodbridge, Ont. ... 6-1/197. ... Shoots right.
TRANSACTIONS/CAREER NOTES: Selected by Washington Capitals in first round (first Capitals pick, 12th overall) of NHL entry draft (June 22, 2002).

		REGULAR SEASON							PLAYOFFS				
Season Team	League	Gms.	G	A	Pts.	PIM	+/-	PP	SH	Gms.	G	A	Pts.	PIM
99-00—Kitchener	OHL	50	2	14	16	74	...	...	...	5	0	0	0	0
00-01—Kitchener	OHL	54	6	26	32	66	...	...	...	—	—	—	—	—
01-02—Kitchener	OHL	64	19	39	58	93	...	...	...	4	0	2	2	10
02-03—Kitchener	OHL	23	2	27	29	40	...	...	...	—	—	—	—	—
—Washington	NHL	17	0	2	2	24	-3	0	0	—	—	—	—	—
NHL Totals (1 year)		17	0	2	2	24	-3	0	0					

ENDICOTT, SHANE — C — PENGUINS

PERSONAL: Born December 21, 1981, in Saskatoon, Sask. ... 6-4/200. ... Shoots left.
TRANSACTIONS/CAREER NOTES: Selected by Pittsburgh Penguins in second round (second Penguins pick, 52nd overall) of NHL entry draft (June 24, 2000).

		REGULAR SEASON							PLAYOFFS				
Season Team	League	Gms.	G	A	Pts.	PIM	+/-	PP	SH	Gms.	G	A	Pts.	PIM
97-98—Seattle	WHL	5	0	0	0	0	...	...	...	5	0	0	0	0
98-99—Seattle	WHL	72	13	26	39	27	...	...	...	11	0	1	1	0
99-00—Seattle	WHL	70	23	32	55	62	...	...	...	7	1	6	7	6
00-01—Seattle	WHL	72	36	43	79	86	...	...	...	9	4	5	9	12
01-02—Wilkes-Barre/Scranton	AHL	63	19	20	39	46	...	...	...	—	—	—	—	—
—Pittsburgh	NHL	4	0	1	1	4	-1	0	0	—	—	—	—	—
02-03—Wilkes-Barre/Scranton	AHL	74	13	26	39	68	...	...	...	—	—	—	—	—
NHL Totals (1 year)		4	0	1	1	4	-1	0	0					

ERAT, MARTIN — LW — PREDATORS

PERSONAL: Born August 28, 1981, in Trebic, Czechoslovakia ... 6-0/195. ... Shoots left.
TRANSACTIONS/CAREER NOTES: Selected by Nashville Predators in seventh round (12th Predators pick, 191st overall) of NHL entry draft (June 26, 1999).

		REGULAR SEASON							PLAYOFFS				
Season Team	League	Gms.	G	A	Pts.	PIM	+/-	PP	SH	Gms.	G	A	Pts.	PIM
97-98—ZPS Zlin	Czech. Jrs.	46	35	30	65	...	...	...	...	—	—	—	—	—
98-99—ZPS Zlin	Czech. Jrs.	35	21	23	44	...	...	...	...	—	—	—	—	—
—ZPS Zlin	Czech.	5	0	0	0	2	...	...	...	—	—	—	—	—
99-00—Saskatoon	WHL	66	27	26	53	82	...	...	...	11	4	8	12	16
00-01—Saskatoon	WHL	31	19	35	54	48	...	...	...	—	—	—	—	—
—Red Deer	WHL	17	4	24	28	24	...	...	...	22	*15	*21	*36	32
01-02—Nashville	NHL	80	9	24	33	32	-11	2	0	—	—	—	—	—
02-03—Milwaukee	AHL	45	10	22	32	41	...	...	...	—	—	—	—	—
—Nashville	NHL	27	1	7	8	14	-9	1	0	—	—	—	—	—
NHL Totals (2 years)		107	10	31	41	46	-20	3	0					

ERIKSSON, ANDERS — D — MAPLE LEAFS

PERSONAL: Born January 9, 1975, in Bollnas, Sweden ... 6-3/215. ... Shoots left.
TRANSACTIONS/CAREER NOTES: Selected by Detroit Red Wings in first round (first Red Wings pick, 22nd overall) of NHL entry draft (June 26, 1993). ... Traded by Red Wings with first-round pick (D Steve McCarthy) in 1999 draft and first-round pick (G Adam Munro) in 2001 draft to Chicago Blackhawks for D Chris Chelios (March 23, 1999). ... Traded by Blackhawks to Florida Panthers for D Jaroslav Spacek (November 6, 2000). ... Injured knee (November 10, 2000); missed one game. ... Sprained knee (February 22, 2001); missed nine games. ... Signed as free agent by Toronto Maple Leafs (July 4, 2001).

Season Team	League	REGULAR SEASON								PLAYOFFS				
		Gms.	G	A	Pts.	PIM	+/-	PP	SH	Gms.	G	A	Pts.	PIM
92-93—MoDo Ornskoldsvik....	Sweden	20	0	2	2	2	...	...	...	—	—	—	—	—
93-94—MoDo Ornskoldsvik....	Sweden	38	2	8	10	42	...	...	...	11	0	0	0	8
94-95—MoDo Ornskoldsvik....	Sweden	39	3	6	9	54	...	...	...	—	—	—	—	—
95-96—Adirondack	AHL	75	6	36	42	64	...	...	...	3	0	0	0	0
—Detroit	NHL	1	0	0	0	2	1	0	0	3	0	0	0	0
96-97—Detroit	NHL	23	0	6	6	10	5	0	0	—	—	—	—	—
—Adirondack	AHL	44	3	25	28	36	...	...	...	4	0	1	1	4
97-98—Detroit	NHL	66	7	14	21	32	21	1	0	18	0	5	5	16
98-99—Detroit	NHL	61	2	10	12	34	5	0	0	—	—	—	—	—
—Chicago	NHL	11	0	8	8	0	6	0	0	—	—	—	—	—
99-00—Chicago	NHL	73	3	25	28	20	4	0	0	—	—	—	—	—
00-01—Chicago	NHL	13	2	3	5	2	-4	1	0	—	—	—	—	—
—Florida	NHL	60	0	21	21	28	2	0	0	—	—	—	—	—
01-02—Toronto	NHL	34	0	2	2	12	-1	0	0	10	0	0	0	0
—St. John's	AHL	25	4	6	10	14	...	...	...	11	0	5	5	6
02-03—St. John's	AHL	72	5	34	39	133	...	...	...	—	—	—	—	—
—Toronto	NHL	4	0	0	0	0	1	0	0	—	—	—	—	—
NHL Totals (8 years)..........		346	14	89	103	140	40	2	0	31	0	5	5	16

ERSKINE, JOHN   D   STARS

PERSONAL: Born June 26, 1980, in Kingston, Ont. ... 6-4/215. ... Shoots left.
TRANSACTIONS/CAREER NOTES: Selected by Dallas Stars in second round (first Stars pick, 39th overall) of NHL entry draft (June 27, 1998). ... Fractured foot (March 8, 2002); missed 13 games. ... Re-signed by Stars (July 30, 2003).

Season Team	League	REGULAR SEASON								PLAYOFFS				
		Gms.	G	A	Pts.	PIM	+/-	PP	SH	Gms.	G	A	Pts.	PIM
96-97—Quinte	Tier II Jr. A	48	4	16	20	241	...	...	...	—	—	—	—	—
97-98—London	OHL	55	0	9	9	205	...	...	...	16	0	5	5	25
98-99—London	OHL	57	8	12	20	208	...	...	...	25	5	10	15	38
99-00—London	OHL	58	12	31	43	177	...	...	...	—	—	—	—	—
00-01—Utah	IHL	77	1	8	9	284	...	...	...	—	—	—	—	—
01-02—Utah	AHL	39	2	6	8	118	...	...	...	3	0	0	0	10
—Dallas	NHL	33	0	1	1	62	-8	0	0	—	—	—	—	—
02-03—Utah	AHL	52	2	8	10	274	...	...	...	—	—	—	—	—
—Dallas	NHL	16	2	0	2	29	1	0	0	—	—	—	—	—
NHL Totals (2 years)..........		49	2	1	3	91	-7	0	0					

ESCHE, ROBERT   G   FLYERS

PERSONAL: Born January 22, 1978, in Whitesboro, N.Y. ... 6-1/212. ... Catches left. ... Name pronounced EHSH.
TRANSACTIONS/CAREER NOTES: Selected by Phoenix Coyotes in sixth round (fifth Coyotes pick, 139th overall) of NHL entry draft (June 22, 1996). ... Strained hamstring (April 12, 2002); missed final game of season. ... Traded by Coyotes with C Michal Handzus to Philadelphia Flyers for G Brian Boucher and third-round pick (D Joe Callahan) in 2002 draft (June 12, 2002).

Season Team	League	REGULAR SEASON									PLAYOFFS							
		Gms.	Min	W	L	T	GA	SO	Avg.	SV%	Gms.	Min.	W	L	GA	SO	Avg.	SV%
95-96—Det. Jr. Red Wings.......	OHL	23	1219	13	6	4	76	1	3.74	—	3	105	0	2	4	0	2.29	—
96-97—Det. Jr. Red Wings.......	OHL	58	3241	24	28	2	206	2	3.81	—	5	317	1	4	19	0	3.60	—
97-98—Plymouth	OHL	48	2810	29	13	4	135	3	2.88	—	15	869	8	†7	45	0	3.11	—
98-99—Springfield	AHL	55	2957	24	20	6	138	1	2.80	—	1	60	0	1	4	0	4.00	—
—Phoenix	NHL	3	130	0	1	0	7	0	3.23	.860	—	—	—	—	—	—	—	—
99-00—Houston	IHL	7	419	4	2	1	16	2	2.29	—	—	—	—	—	—	—	—	—
—Phoenix	NHL	8	408	2	5	0	23	0	3.38	.893	—	—	—	—	—	—	—	—
—Springfield	AHL	21	1207	9	9	2	61	2	3.03	—	3	180	1	2	12	0	4.00	—
00-01—Phoenix	NHL	25	1350	10	8	4	68	2	3.02	.896	—	—	—	—	—	—	—	—
01-02—Phoenix	NHL	22	1145	6	10	2	52	1	2.72	.902	—	—	—	—	—	—	—	—
—Springfield	AHL	1	60	1	0	0	1	0	1	—	—	—	—	—	—	—	—	—
02-03—Philadelphia	NHL	30	1638	12	9	3	60	2	2.20	.907	1	30	0	0	1	0	2.00	.929
NHL Totals (5 years)..........		88	4671	30	33	9	210	5	2.70	.900	1	30	0	0	1	0	2.00	.929

EXELBY, GARNET   D   THRASHERS

PERSONAL: Born August 16, 1981, in Craik, Sask. ... 6-1/210. ... Shoots left.

Season Team	League	REGULAR SEASON								PLAYOFFS				
		Gms.	G	A	Pts.	PIM	+/-	PP	SH	Gms.	G	A	Pts.	PIM
01-02—Chicago......................	AHL	75	3	4	7	257	...	...	...	25	0	4	4	49
02-03—Chicago......................	AHL	53	3	6	9	140	...	...	...	—	—	—	—	—
—Atlanta	NHL	15	0	2	2	41	0	0	0	—	—	—	—	—
NHL Totals (1 year).............		15	0	2	2	41	0	0	0					

FAHEY, JIM   D   SHARKS

PERSONAL: Born May 11, 1979, in Boston ... 6-0/205. ... Shoots right.
COLLEGE: Northeastern.
TRANSACTIONS/CAREER NOTES: Selected by San Jose Sharks in eighth round (ninth Sharks pick, 212th overall) of NHL entry draft (June 27, 1998).

Season Team	League	REGULAR SEASON								PLAYOFFS				
		Gms.	G	A	Pts.	PIM	+/-	PP	SH	Gms.	G	A	Pts.	PIM
97-98—Catholic Memorial.......	Mass. H.S.	24	12	12	24	28	...	...	...	—	—	—	—	—
98-99—Northeastern Univ.......	Hockey East	32	5	13	18	34	...	...	...	—	—	—	—	—
99-00—Northeastern Univ.......	Hockey East	36	3	17	20	62	...	...	...	—	—	—	—	—
00-01—Northeastern Univ.......	Hockey East	36	4	23	27	48	...	...	...	—	—	—	—	—
01-02—Northeastern Univ.......	Hockey East	39	14	32	46	50	...	...	...	—	—	—	—	—
02-03—Cleveland	AHL	25	3	14	17	42	...	...	...	—	—	—	—	—
—San Jose	NHL	43	1	19	20	33	-3	0	0	—	—	—	—	—
NHL Totals (1 year).............		43	1	19	20	33	-3	0	0					

FALARDEAU, LEE   C   RANGERS

PERSONAL: Born July 22, 1983, in Midland, Mich. ... 6-4/196. ... Shoots left.

TRANSACTIONS/CAREER NOTES: Selected by New York Rangers in second round (first Rangers pick, 33rd overall) of NHL entry draft (June 22, 2002).

Season Team	League	REGULAR SEASON								PLAYOFFS				
		Gms.	G	A	Pts.	PIM	+/-	PP	SH	Gms.	G	A	Pts.	PIM
99-00—U.S. National..............	USHL	5	0	0	0	4	...	...	...	—	—	—	—	—
00-01—U.S. National..............	USHL	61	10	21	31	26	...	...	...	—	—	—	—	—
01-02—Michigan State...........	CCHA	29	4	9	13	22	...	...	...	—	—	—	—	—
02-03—Michigan State...........	CCHA	39	9	9	18	39	...	...	...	—	—	—	—	—

FARKAS, JEFF   C

PERSONAL: Born January 24, 1978, in Amherst, N.Y. ... 6-1/190. ... Shoots left.

TRANSACTIONS/CAREER NOTES: Selected by Toronto Maple Leafs in third round (first Maple Leafs pick, 57th overall) of NHL entry draft (June 21, 1997). ... Traded by Maple Leafs to Vancouver Canucks for C Josh Holden (June 22, 2002). ... Traded by Canucks to Atlanta Thrashers for LW Chris Herperger and RW Chris Nielsen (January 20, 2003).

Season Team	League	REGULAR SEASON								PLAYOFFS				
		Gms.	G	A	Pts.	PIM	+/-	PP	SH	Gms.	G	A	Pts.	PIM
94-95—Niagara	NAJHL	53	54	58	112	34	...	...	...	—	—	—	—	—
95-96—Niagara	NAJHL	74	64	107	171	95	...	...	...	—	—	—	—	—
96-97—Boston College	Hockey East	35	13	23	36	34	...	...	...	—	—	—	—	—
97-98—Boston College	Hockey East	40	11	28	39	42	...	...	...	—	—	—	—	—
98-99—Boston College	Hockey East	43	32	25	57	56	...	...	...	—	—	—	—	—
99-00—Boston College	Hockey East	41	32	26	*58	59	...	...	...	—	—	—	—	—
—Toronto	NHL	—	—	—	—	—	—	—	—	3	1	0	1	0
00-01—St. John's...................	AHL	77	28	40	68	62	...	...	...	4	1	2	3	4
—Toronto	NHL	2	0	0	0	2	-1	0	0	—	—	—	—	—
01-02—St. John's...................	AHL	71	16	34	50	49	...	...	...	4	0	0	0	0
—Toronto	NHL	6	0	2	2	4	1	0	0	2	0	0	0	0
02-03—Manitoba....................	AHL	39	11	14	25	28	...	...	...	—	—	—	—	—
—Atlanta	NHL	3	0	0	0	0	-1	0	0	—	—	—	—	—
—Chicago......................	AHL	24	5	12	17	14	...	...	...	—	—	—	—	—
NHL Totals (4 years)............		11	0	2	2	6	-1	0	0	5	1	0	1	0

FARRELL, MIKE   D   PREDATORS

PERSONAL: Born October 20, 1978, in Edina, Minn. ... 6-0/220. ... Shoots right. ... Full Name: Michael Farrell.

TRANSACTIONS/CAREER NOTES: Selected by Washington Capitals in eighth round (ninth Capitals pick, 220th overall) of NHL entry draft (June 27, 1998). ... Traded by Capitals to Nashville Predators for D Alexa Riazantsev (June 14, 2003). ... Re-signed by Predators (July 27, 2003).

Season Team	League	REGULAR SEASON								PLAYOFFS				
		Gms.	G	A	Pts.	PIM	+/-	PP	SH	Gms.	G	A	Pts.	PIM
97-98—Providence College.....	Hockey East	33	5	8	13	32	...	...	...	—	—	—	—	—
98-99—Providence College.....	Hockey East	29	3	12	15	51	...	...	...	—	—	—	—	—
99-00—Providence College.....	Hockey East	36	3	6	9	71	...	...	...	—	—	—	—	—
—Portland......................	AHL	7	2	0	2	0	...	...	...	4	0	1	1	0
00-01—Portland......................	AHL	79	6	18	24	61	...	...	...	3	0	2	2	2
01-02—Portland......................	AHL	61	12	15	27	62	...	...	...	—	—	—	—	—
—Washington	NHL	8	0	0	0	0	-1	0	0	—	—	—	—	—
02-03—Portland......................	AHL	68	12	12	24	107	...	...	...	—	—	—	—	—
—Washington	NHL	4	0	0	0	2	1	0	0	—	—	—	—	—
NHL Totals (2 years)............		12	0	0	0	2	0	0	0					

FATA, DREW   D   PENGUINS

PERSONAL: Born July 28, 1983, in Sault Ste. Marie, Ont. ... 6-1/211. ... Shoots left. ... Brother of Rico Fata, right winger, New York Rangers.

TRANSACTIONS/CAREER NOTES: Selected by Pittsburgh Penguins in third round (third Penguins pick, 86th overall) of NHL entry draft (June 23, 2001). ... Re-signed by Penguins (June 1, 2003).

Season Team	League	REGULAR SEASON								PLAYOFFS				
		Gms.	G	A	Pts.	PIM	+/-	PP	SH	Gms.	G	A	Pts.	PIM
00-01—Toronto St. Michael's..	OHL	58	5	15	20	134	...	...	...	18	1	3	4	26
01-02—Toronto St. Michael's..	OHL	67	7	21	28	175	...	...	...	15	1	9	10	38
02-03—Kingston	OHL	69	8	30	38	130	...	...	...	—	—	—	—	—

FATA, RICO   RW   PENGUINS

PERSONAL: Born February 12, 1980, in Sault Ste. Marie, Ont. ... 6-0/210. ... Shoots left. ... Brother of Drew Fata, defenseman, Pittsburgh Penguins organization.

TRANSACTIONS/CAREER NOTES: Selected by Calgary Flames in first round (first Flames pick, sixth overall) of NHL entry draft (June 27, 1998). ... Claimed on waivers by New York Rangers (October 3, 2001). ... Traded by Rangers with RW Mikael Samuelsson, D Joel Bouchard, D Richard Lintner and cash to Pittsburgh Penguins for RW Alexei Kovalev, LW Dan LaCouture, D Janne Laukkanen and D Mike Wilson (February 10, 2003).

		REGULAR SEASON								PLAYOFFS				
Season Team	League	Gms.	G	A	Pts.	PIM	+/-	PP	SH	Gms.	G	A	Pts.	PIM
95-96—Sault Ste. Marie	OMJHL	62	11	15	26	52	...	...	...	—	—	—	—	—
96-97—London	OHL	59	19	34	53	76	...	...	...	—	—	—	—	—
97-98—London	OHL	64	43	33	76	110	...	...	...	16	9	5	14	*49
98-99—Calgary	NHL	20	0	1	1	4	0	0	0	—	—	—	—	—
—London	OHL	23	15	18	33	41	...	...	...	25	10	12	22	42
99-00—Calgary	NHL	2	0	0	0	0	-1	0	0	—	—	—	—	—
—Saint John	AHL	76	29	29	58	65	...	...	...	3	0	0	0	4
00-01—Saint John	AHL	70	23	29	52	129	...	...	...	19	2	3	5	22
—Calgary	NHL	5	0	0	0	6	-3	0	0	—	—	—	—	—
01-02—New York Rangers	NHL	10	0	0	0	0	-2	0	0	—	—	—	—	—
—Hartford	AHL	61	35	36	71	36	...	...	...	10	2	5	7	4
02-03—Hartford	AHL	9	8	6	14	6	...	...	...	—	—	—	—	—
—New York Rangers	NHL	36	2	4	6	6	-1	0	0	—	—	—	—	—
—Pittsburgh	NHL	27	5	8	13	10	-6	0	0	—	—	—	—	—
NHL Totals (5 years)		100	7	13	20	26	-13	0	0					

FEDOROV, FEDOR   LW   CANUCKS

PERSONAL: Born June 11, 1981, in Moscow, U.S.S.R. ... 6-3/230. ... Shoots left. ... Brother of Sergei Fedorov, center, Detroit Red Wings. ... Name pronounced FEH-duh FEH-duhr-rahf.

TRANSACTIONS/CAREER NOTES: Selected by Tampa Bay Lightning in sixth round (seventh Lightning pick, 182nd overall) of NHL entry draft (June 26, 1999). ... Returned to draft pool by Lightning and selected by Vancouver Canucks in third round (second Canucks pick, 66th overall) of NHL entry draft (June 23, 2001).

		REGULAR SEASON								PLAYOFFS				
Season Team	League	Gms.	G	A	Pts.	PIM	+/-	PP	SH	Gms.	G	A	Pts.	PIM
97-98—Detroit Little Caesars	MNHL	13	3	7	10	18	...	...	...	—	—	—	—	—
98-99—Port Huron	UHL	42	2	5	7	20	...	...	...	—	—	—	—	—
99-00—Windsor	OHL	60	7	10	17	115	...	...	...	12	1	0	1	4
00-01—Sudbury	OHL	37	33	45	78	88	...	...	...	12	4	6	10	36
01-02—Manitoba	AHL	8	2	1	3	6	...	...	...	—	—	—	—	—
—Columbia	ECHL	2	0	2	2	0	...	...	...	—	—	—	—	—
02-03—Manitoba	AHL	50	10	13	23	61	...	...	...	—	—	—	—	—
—Vancouver	NHL	7	0	1	1	4	0	0	0	—	—	—	—	—
NHL Totals (1 year)		7	0	1	1	4	0	0	0					

FEDOROV, SERGEI   C   MIGHTY DUCKS

PERSONAL: Born December 13, 1969, in Pskov, U.S.S.R. ... 6-2/200. ... Shoots left. ... Brother of Fedor Fedorov, center, Vancouver Canucks organization. ... Name pronounced SAIR-gay FEH-duh-rahf.

TRANSACTIONS/CAREER NOTES: Selected by Detroit Red Wings in fourth round (fourth Red Wings pick, 74th overall) of NHL entry draft (June 17, 1989). ... Bruised left shoulder (October 1990). ... Reinjured left shoulder (January 16, 1991). ... Sprained left shoulder (November 27, 1992); missed seven games. ... Suffered from the flu (January 30, 1993); missed two games. ... Suffered charley horse (February 11, 1993); missed one game. ... Suffered concussion (April 5, 1994); missed two games. ... Suspended four games without pay and fined $500 by NHL for high-sticking incident in playoff game (May 17, 1994); suspension reduced to three games due to abbreviated 1994-95 season. ... Suffered from the flu (February 7, 1995); missed one game. ... Bruised right hamstring (April 9, 1995); missed one game. ... Suffered from tonsillitis (October 6, 1995); missed three games. ... Sprained left wrist (December 15, 1995); missed one game. ... Strained groin (January 9, 1997); missed two games. ... Reinjured groin (January 20, 1997); missed six games. ... Missed first 59 games of 1997-98 season due to contract dispute. ... Tendered offer sheet by Carolina Hurricanes (February 19, 1998). ... Offer matched by Red Wings (February 26, 1998). ... Suspended two games and fined $1,000 by NHL for illegal check (March 31, 1998). ... Suspended five games by NHL for slashing incident (March 3, 1999). ... Suffered head injury (November 20, 1999); missed six games. ... Injured neck (January 16, 2000); missed three games. ... Injured wrist (February 18, 2000); missed five games. ... Fractured nose (February 23, 2001); missed six games. ... Signed by Anaheim Mighty Ducks (July 20, 2003).

STATISTICAL PLATEAUS: Three-goal games: 1993-94 (1), 2000-01 (1), 2002-03 (2). Total: 4. ... Four-goal games: 1994-95 (1). ... Five-goal games: 1996-97 (1). ... Total hat tricks: 6.

		REGULAR SEASON								PLAYOFFS				
Season Team	League	Gms.	G	A	Pts.	PIM	+/-	PP	SH	Gms.	G	A	Pts.	PIM
85-86—Dynamo Minsk	USSR	15	6	1	7	10	...	...	...	—	—	—	—	—
86-87—CSKA Moscow	USSR	29	6	6	12	12	...	...	...	—	—	—	—	—
87-88—CSKA Moscow	USSR	48	7	9	16	20	...	...	...	—	—	—	—	—
88-89—CSKA Moscow	USSR	44	9	8	17	35	...	...	...	—	—	—	—	—
89-90—CSKA Moscow	USSR	48	19	10	29	20	...	...	...	—	—	—	—	—
90-91—Detroit	NHL	77	31	48	79	66	11	11	3	7	1	5	6	4
91-92—Detroit	NHL	80	32	54	86	72	26	7	2	11	5	5	10	8
92-93—Detroit	NHL	73	34	53	87	72	33	13	4	7	3	6	9	23
93-94—Detroit	NHL	82	56	64	120	34	48	13	4	7	1	7	8	6
94-95—Detroit	NHL	42	20	30	50	24	6	7	3	17	7	*17	*24	6
95-96—Detroit	NHL	78	39	68	107	48	49	11	3	19	2	*18	20	10
96-97—Detroit	NHL	74	30	33	63	30	29	9	2	20	8	12	20	12

F

Season Team	League	REGULAR SEASON								PLAYOFFS				
		Gms.	G	A	Pts.	PIM	+/-	PP	SH	Gms.	G	A	Pts.	PIM
97-98—Russian Oly. team.......	Int'l	6	1	5	6	8	...	...	...	—	—	—	—	—
—Detroit....................	NHL	21	6	11	17	25	10	2	0	22	10	10	20	12
98-99—Detroit...................	NHL	77	26	37	63	66	9	6	2	10	1	8	9	8
99-00—Detroit...................	NHL	68	27	35	62	22	8	4	4	9	4	4	8	4
00-01—Detroit...................	NHL	75	32	37	69	40	12	14	2	6	2	5	7	0
01-02—Detroit...................	NHL	81	31	37	68	36	20	10	0	23	5	14	19	20
—Russian Oly. team.......	Int'l	6	2	2	4	4	...	...	...	—	—	—	—	—
02-03—Detroit...................	NHL	80	36	47	83	52	15	10	2	4	1	2	3	0
NHL Totals (13 years).........		908	400	554	954	587	276	117	31	162	50	113	163	113

FEDORUK, TODD — LW — FLYERS

PERSONAL: Born February 13, 1979, in Redwater, Alta. ... 6-2/235. ... Shoots left.
TRANSACTIONS/CAREER NOTES: Selected by Philadelphia Flyers in seventh round (sixth Flyers pick, 16th overall) of NHL entry draft (June 21, 1997). ... Strained elbow (January 13, 2001); missed two games. ... Lacerated eyelid (January 31, 2001); missed one game.

Season Team	League	REGULAR SEASON								PLAYOFFS				
		Gms.	G	A	Pts.	PIM	+/-	PP	SH	Gms.	G	A	Pts.	PIM
96-97—Kelowna......................	WHL	31	1	5	6	87	...	...	...	6	0	0	0	13
97-98—Kelowna......................	WHL	31	3	5	8	120	...	...	...	—	—	—	—	—
—Regina	WHL	21	4	3	7	80	...	...	...	9	1	2	3	23
98-99—Regina	WHL	39	12	12	24	107	...	...	...	—	—	—	—	—
—Prince Albert................	WHL	28	6	4	10	75	...	...	...	—	—	—	—	—
99-00—Philadelphia	AHL	19	1	2	3	40	...	...	...	5	0	1	1	2
—Trenton	ECHL	18	2	5	7	118	...	...	...	—	—	—	—	—
00-01—Philadelphia	AHL	14	0	1	1	49	...	...	...	—	—	—	—	—
—Philadelphia	NHL	53	5	5	10	109	0	0	0	2	0	0	0	20
01-02—Philadelphia	NHL	55	3	4	7	141	-2	0	0	3	0	0	0	0
—Philadelphia	AHL	7	0	1	1	54	...	...	...	—	—	—	—	—
02-03—Philadelphia	NHL	63	1	5	6	105	1	0	0	1	0	0	0	0
NHL Totals (3 years)...........		171	9	14	23	355	-1	0	0	6	0	0	0	20

FEDOTENKO, RUSLAN — RW — LIGHTNING

PERSONAL: Born January 18, 1979, in Kiev, U.S.S.R. ... 6-2/195. ... Shoots left.
TRANSACTIONS/CAREER NOTES: Signed as non-drafted free agent by Philadelphia Flyers (August 3, 1999). ... Sprained right knee (February 27, 2002); missed four games. ... Traded by Flyers with two second-round picks (traded to Ottawa and traded to Phoenix) in 2002 draft to Tampa Bay Lightning for first-round pick (D Joni Pitkanen) in 2002 draft (June 21, 2002).

Season Team	League	REGULAR SEASON								PLAYOFFS				
		Gms.	G	A	Pts.	PIM	+/-	PP	SH	Gms.	G	A	Pts.	PIM
97-98—Melfort......................	SJHL	68	35	31	66	...	...	...	...	—	—	—	—	—
98-99—Sioux City	USHL	55	43	34	77	139	...	...	...	5	5	1	6	9
99-00—Philadelphia	AHL	67	16	34	50	42	...	...	...	2	0	0	0	0
—Trenton	ECHL	8	5	3	8	9	...	...	...	—	—	—	—	—
00-01—Philadelphia	AHL	8	1	0	1	8	...	...	...	—	—	—	—	—
—Philadelphia	NHL	74	16	20	36	72	8	3	0	6	0	1	1	4
01-02—Philadelphia	NHL	78	17	9	26	43	15	0	1	5	1	0	1	2
—Ukranian Oly. team	Int'l	1	1	0	1	4	...	...	...	—	—	—	—	—
02-03—Tampa Bay	NHL	76	19	13	32	44	-7	6	0	11	0	1	1	2
NHL Totals (3 years)...........		228	52	42	94	159	16	9	1	22	1	2	3	8

FERENCE, ANDREW — D — FLAMES

PERSONAL: Born March 17, 1979, in Edmonton ... 5-10/196. ... Shoots left.
TRANSACTIONS/CAREER NOTES: Selected by Pittsburgh Penguins in eighth round (eighth Penguins pick, 208th overall) of 1997 NHL entry draft. ... Suffered from the flu (December 9, 1999); missed two games. ... Suffered from the flu (December 26, 2001); missed one game. ... Traded by Penguins to Calgary Flames for conditional pick in 2003 or 2004 draft (February 10, 2003). ... Re-signed by Calgary (June 10, 2003).

Season Team	League	REGULAR SEASON								PLAYOFFS				
		Gms.	G	A	Pts.	PIM	+/-	PP	SH	Gms.	G	A	Pts.	PIM
95-96—Portland	WHL	72	9	31	40	159	...	...	...	7	1	3	4	12
96-97—Portland	WHL	72	12	32	44	163	...	...	...	—	—	—	—	—
97-98—Portland	WHL	72	11	57	68	142	...	...	...	16	2	18	20	28
98-99—Portland	WHL	40	11	21	32	104	...	...	...	4	1	4	5	10
—Kansas City................	IHL	5	1	2	3	4	...	...	...	3	0	0	0	9
99-00—Pittsburgh..................	NHL	30	2	4	6	20	3	0	0	—	—	—	—	—
—Wilkes-Barre/Scranton	AHL	44	8	20	28	58	...	...	...	—	—	—	—	—
00-01—Wilkes-Barre/Scranton	AHL	43	6	18	24	95	...	...	...	3	1	0	1	12
—Pittsburgh..................	NHL	36	4	11	15	28	6	1	0	18	3	7	10	16
01-02—Pittsburgh..................	NHL	75	4	7	11	73	-12	1	0	—	—	—	—	—
02-03—Wilkes-Barre/Scranton	AHL	1	0	0	0	2	...	...	...	—	—	—	—	—
—Pittsburgh..................	NHL	22	1	3	4	36	-16	1	0	—	—	—	—	—
—Calgary	NHL	16	0	4	4	6	1	0	0	—	—	—	—	—
NHL Totals (4 years)...........		179	11	29	40	163	-18	3	0	18	3	7	10	16

FERENCE, BRAD   D   COYOTES

PERSONAL: Born April 2, 1979, in Calgary ... 6-3/210. ... Shoots right.
TRANSACTIONS/CAREER NOTES: Selected by Vancouver Canucks in first round (first Canucks pick, 10th overall) of NHL entry draft (June 21, 1997). ... Traded by Canucks with RW Pavel Bure, D Bret Hedican and third-round pick (RW Robert Fried) in 2000 draft to Florida Panthers for D Ed Jovanovski, G Kevin Weekes, C Dave Gagner, C Mike Brown and first-round pick (C Nathan Smith) in 2000 draft (January 17, 1999). ... Fractured jaw (September 4, 2000); missed first nine games of season. ... Suspended two games for receiving three instigator penalties in one season (April 1, 2002). ... Traded by Panthers to Phoenix Coyotes for LW Darcy Hordichuk and second-round pick in 2003 draft (March 9, 2003).

Season Team	League	REGULAR SEASON								PLAYOFFS				
		Gms.	G	A	Pts.	PIM	+/-	PP	SH	Gms.	G	A	Pts.	PIM
95-96—Spokane	WHL	5	0	2	2	18	...	...	...	—	—	—	—	—
96-97—Spokane	WHL	67	6	20	26	324	...	...	...	9	0	4	4	21
97-98—Spokane	WHL	54	9	29	38	213	...	...	...	18	0	7	7	59
98-99—Spokane	WHL	31	3	22	25	125	...	...	...	—	—	—	—	—
—Tri-City	WHL	20	6	15	21	116	...	...	...	12	1	9	10	63
99-00—Louisville	AHL	58	2	7	9	231	...	...	...	2	0	0	0	2
—Florida	NHL	13	0	2	2	46	2	0	0	—	—	—	—	—
00-01—Florida	NHL	14	0	1	1	14	-10	0	0	—	—	—	—	—
—Louisville	AHL	52	3	21	24	200	...	...	...	—	—	—	—	—
01-02—Florida	NHL	80	2	15	17	254	-13	0	0	—	—	—	—	—
02-03—Florida	NHL	60	2	6	8	118	2	0	0	—	—	—	—	—
—Phoenix	NHL	15	0	1	1	28	-5	0	0	—	—	—	—	—
NHL Totals (4 years)		182	4	25	29	460	-24	0	0					

FERGUSON, SCOTT   D   OILERS

PERSONAL: Born January 6, 1973, in Camrose, Alta. ... 6-1/195. ... Shoots left.
TRANSACTIONS/CAREER NOTES: Signed as non-drafted free agent by Edmonton Oilers (June 2, 1994). ... Traded by Oilers to Ottawa Senators for D Frank Musil (March 9, 1998). ... Signed as free agent by Mighty Ducks of Anaheim (July 22, 1998). ... Signed as free agent by Oilers (July 5, 2000).

Season Team	League	REGULAR SEASON								PLAYOFFS				
		Gms.	G	A	Pts.	PIM	+/-	PP	SH	Gms.	G	A	Pts.	PIM
90-91—Kamloops	WHL	4	0	0	0	0	...	...	...	—	—	—	—	—
91-92—Kamloops	WHL	62	4	10	14	148	...	...	...	12	0	2	2	21
92-93—Kamloops	WHL	71	4	19	23	206	...	...	...	13	0	2	2	24
93-94—Kamloops	WHL	68	5	49	54	180	...	...	...	19	5	11	16	48
94-95—Wheeling	ECHL	5	1	5	6	16	...	...	...	—	—	—	—	—
—Cape Breton	AHL	58	4	6	10	103	...	...	...	—	—	—	—	—
95-96—Cape Breton	AHL	80	5	16	21	196	...	...	...	—	—	—	—	—
96-97—Hamilton	AHL	74	6	14	20	115	...	...	...	21	5	7	12	59
97-98—Hamilton	AHL	77	7	17	24	150	...	...	...	9	0	3	3	16
—Edmonton	NHL	1	0	0	0	0	1	0	0	—	—	—	—	—
98-99—Cincinnati	AHL	78	4	31	35	144	...	...	...	3	0	0	0	4
—Anaheim	NHL	2	0	1	1	0	0	0	0	—	—	—	—	—
99-00—Cincinnati	AHL	77	7	25	32	166	...	...	...	—	—	—	—	—
00-01—Hamilton	AHL	42	3	18	21	79	...	...	...	—	—	—	—	—
—Edmonton	NHL	20	0	1	1	13	2	0	0	6	0	0	0	0
01-02—Edmonton	NHL	50	3	2	5	75	11	0	0	—	—	—	—	—
02-03—Edmonton	NHL	78	3	5	8	120	11	0	0	5	0	0	0	8
NHL Totals (5 years)		151	6	9	15	208	25	0	0	11	0	0	0	8

FERNANDEZ, MANNY   G   WILD

PERSONAL: Born August 27, 1974, in Etobicoke, Ont. ... 6-0/185. ... Catches left. ... Full Name: Emmanuel Fernandez. ... Nephew of Jacques Lemaire, head coach, Minnesota Wild; and Hall of Fame center with Montreal Canadiens (1967-68 through 1978-79).
TRANSACTIONS/CAREER NOTES: Selected by Quebec Nordiques in third round (fourth Nordiques pick, 52nd overall) of NHL entry draft (June 20, 1992). ... Traded by Nordiques to Dallas Stars for D Tommy Sjodin and third-round pick (C Chris Drury) in 1994 draft (February 13, 1994). ... Traded by Stars with D Brad Lukowich to Minnesota Wild for third-round pick (C Joel Lundqvist) in 2000 draft and fourth-round pick (traded back to Minnesota) in 2002 draft (June 12, 2000). ... Injured right ankle (October 14, 2000); missed five games. ... Injured right knee (March 6, 2001); missed two games. ... Sprained left ankle (March 15, 2001); missed remainder of season. ... Sprained ankle (April 10, 2002); missed remainder of season. ... Re-signed by Wild (July 30, 2003).

Season Team	League	REGULAR SEASON									PLAYOFFS							
		Gms.	Min	W	L	T	GA	SO	Avg.	SV%	Gms.	Min.	W	L	GA	SO	Avg.	SV%
91-92—Laval	QMJHL	31	1593	14	13	2	99	1	3.73	—	9	468	3	5	†39	0	5.00	—
92-93—Laval	QMJHL	43	2348	26	14	2	141	1	3.60	—	13	818	12	1	42	0	3.08	—
93-94—Laval	QMJHL	51	2776	29	14	1	143	*5	3.09	—	19	1116	14	5	49	†1	*2.63	—
94-95—Kalamazoo	IHL	46	2470	21	10	†9	115	2	2.79	—	12	655	9	1	‡30	1	2.75	—
—Dallas	NHL	1	59	0	1	0	3	0	3.05	.889	—	—	—	—	—	—	—	—
95-96—Michigan	IHL	47	2663	22	15	‡9	133	†4	3.00	—	6	372	5	1	14	0	*2.26	—
—Dallas	NHL	5	249	0	1	1	19	0	4.58	.843	—	—	—	—	—	—	—	—
96-97—Michigan	IHL	48	2721	20	24	‡2	142	2	3.13	—	4	277	1	3	15	0	3.25	—
97-98—Michigan	IHL	55	3023	27	17	5	139	5	2.76	—	2	89	0	2	7	0	4.72	—
—Dallas	NHL	2	69	1	0	0	2	0	1.74	.943	1	2	0	0	0	0	...	—
98-99—Houston	IHL	50	2949	34	6	‡9	116	2	2.36	—	*19	*1126	*11	*8	49	1	2.61	—
—Dallas	NHL	1	60	0	1	0	2	0	2.00	.931	—	—	—	—	—	—	—	—
99-00—Dallas	NHL	24	1353	11	8	3	48	1	2.13	.920	1	17	0	0	1	0	3.53	.875
00-01—Minnesota	NHL	42	2461	19	17	4	92	4	2.24	.920	—	—	—	—	—	—	—	—
01-02—Minnesota	NHL	44	2463	12	24	5	125	1	3.05	.892	—	—	—	—	—	—	—	—
02-03—Minnesota	NHL	35	1979	19	13	2	74	2	2.24	.924	9	552	3	4	18	0	1.96	.929
NHL Totals (8 years)		154	8693	62	65	15	365	8	2.52	.911	11	571	3	4	19	0	2.00	.927

F

FERRARO, CHRIS   C   COYOTES

PERSONAL: Born January 24, 1973, in Port Jefferson, N.Y. ... 5-10/185. ... Shoots right. ... Twin brother of Peter Ferraro, center, Boston Bruins. ... Name pronounced fuh-RAH-roh.

COLLEGE: Maine.

TRANSACTIONS/CAREER NOTES: Selected by New York Rangers in fourth round (fourth Rangers pick, 85th overall) of NHL entry draft (June 20, 1992). ... Claimed on waivers by Pittsburgh Penguins (October 1, 1997). ... Signed as free agent by Edmonton Oilers (August 13, 1998). ... Signed as free agent by New York Islanders (July 7, 1999). ... Suffered concussion (March 21, 2000); missed eight games. ... Traded by Devils to Washington Capitals for future considerations (August 22, 2001). ... Signed by Phoenix Coyotes (July 17, 2003).

		REGULAR SEASON								PLAYOFFS				
Season Team	League	Gms.	G	A	Pts.	PIM	+/-	PP	SH	Gms.	G	A	Pts.	PIM
90-91—Dubuque	USHL	45	53	44	97	...	...	...	...	—	—	—	—	—
91-92—Waterloo	USHL	38	49	50	99	106	...	...	...	—	—	—	—	—
92-93—Univ. of Maine	Hockey East	39	25	26	51	46	...	...	...	—	—	—	—	—
93-94—U.S. national team	Int'l	48	8	34	42	58	...	...	...	—	—	—	—	—
—Univ. of Maine	Hockey East	4	0	1	1	8	...	...	...	—	—	—	—	—
94-95—Atlanta	IHL	54	13	14	27	72	...	...	...	—	—	—	—	—
—Binghamton	AHL	13	6	4	10	38	...	...	...	10	2	3	5	16
95-96—Binghamton	AHL	77	32	67	99	208	...	...	...	4	4	2	6	13
—New York Rangers	NHL	2	1	0	1	0	-3	1	0	—	—	—	—	—
96-97—Binghamton	AHL	53	29	34	63	94	...	...	...	—	—	—	—	—
—New York Rangers	NHL	12	1	1	2	6	1	0	0	—	—	—	—	—
97-98—Pittsburgh	NHL	46	3	4	7	43	-2	0	0	—	—	—	—	—
98-99—Hamilton	AHL	72	35	41	76	104	...	...	...	11	8	5	13	20
—Edmonton	NHL	2	1	0	1	0	1	0	0	—	—	—	—	—
99-00—New York Islanders	NHL	11	1	3	4	8	1	0	0	—	—	—	—	—
—Providence	AHL	21	9	9	18	32	...	...	...	—	—	—	—	—
00-01—Albany	AHL	74	24	42	66	111	...	...	...	—	—	—	—	—
01-02—Portland	AHL	2	1	1	2	6	...	...	...	—	—	—	—	—
—Washington	NHL	1	0	1	1	0	0	0	0	—	—	—	—	—
02-03—Portland	AHL	57	19	32	51	121	...	...	...	—	—	—	—	—
NHL Totals (6 years)		74	7	9	16	57	-2	1	0					

FERRARO, PETER   LW   COYOTES

PERSONAL: Born January 24, 1973, in Port Jefferson, N.Y. ... 5-9/180. ... Shoots right. ... Twin brother of Chris Ferraro, right wing/center, New York Islanders. ... Name pronounced fuh-RAH-roh.

COLLEGE: Maine.

TRANSACTIONS/CAREER NOTES: Selected by New York Rangers in first round (first Rangers pick, 24th overall) of NHL entry draft (June 20, 1992). ... Claimed on waivers by Pittsburgh Penguins (October 1, 1997). ... Claimed on waivers by Rangers (January 14, 1998). ... Signed as free agent by Boston Bruins (July 21, 1998). ... Sprained muscle in chest (November 27, 1998); missed nine games. ... Suffered concussion (January 4, 1999); missed three games. ... Injured foot (February 9, 1999); missed one game. ... Selected by Atlanta Thrashers in NHL expansion draft (June 25, 1999). ... Traded by Thrashers to Bruins for C Randy Robitaille (June 25, 1999). ... Signed as free agent by Washington Capitals (August 1, 2001). ... Signed by Phoenix Coyotes (July 17, 2003).

		REGULAR SEASON								PLAYOFFS				
Season Team	League	Gms.	G	A	Pts.	PIM	+/-	PP	SH	Gms.	G	A	Pts.	PIM
90-91—Dubuque	USHL	29	21	31	52	83	...	...	...	—	—	—	—	—
91-92—Waterloo	USHL	42	48	53	101	168	...	...	...	—	—	—	—	—
92-93—Univ. of Maine	Hockey East	36	18	32	50	106	...	...	...	—	—	—	—	—
93-94—U.S. national team	Int'l	59	28	39	67	48	...	...	...	—	—	—	—	—
—U.S. Olympic team	Int'l	8	6	0	6	6	...	...	...	—	—	—	—	—
—Univ. of Maine	Hockey East	4	3	6	9	16	...	...	...	—	—	—	—	—
94-95—Atlanta	IHL	61	15	24	39	118	...	...	...	—	—	—	—	—
—Binghamton	AHL	12	2	6	8	67	...	...	...	11	4	3	7	51
95-96—Binghamton	AHL	68	48	53	101	157	...	...	...	4	1	6	7	22
—New York Rangers	NHL	5	0	1	1	0	-5	0	0	—	—	—	—	—
96-97—Binghamton	AHL	75	38	39	77	171	...	...	...	4	3	1	4	18
—New York Rangers	NHL	2	0	0	0	0	0	0	0	2	0	0	0	0
97-98—Pittsburgh	NHL	29	3	4	7	12	-2	0	0	—	—	—	—	—
—Hartford	AHL	36	17	23	40	54	...	...	...	15	8	6	14	59
—New York Rangers	NHL	1	0	0	0	2	-2	0	0	—	—	—	—	—
98-99—Boston	NHL	46	6	8	14	44	10	1	0	—	—	—	—	—
—Providence	AHL	16	15	10	25	14	...	...	...	19	9	12	21	38
99-00—Providence	AHL	48	21	25	46	98	...	...	...	13	5	7	12	14
—Boston	NHL	5	0	1	1	0	-1	0	0	—	—	—	—	—
00-01—Providence	AHL	78	26	45	71	109	...	...	...	17	4	5	9	34
01-02—Portland	AHL	67	21	37	58	119	...	...	...	—	—	—	—	—
—Washington	NHL	4	0	1	1	0	-1	0	0	—	—	—	—	—
02-03—Portland	AHL	59	22	41	63	123	...	...	...	—	—	—	—	—
NHL Totals (6 years)		92	9	15	24	58	-1	1	0	2	0	0	0	0

FIBIGER, JESSE   D   SHARKS

PERSONAL: Born April 4, 1978, in Clearwater, B.C. ... 6-3/220. ... Shoots left.

TRANSACTIONS/CAREER NOTES: Signed as free agent by San Jose Sharks (August 15, 2001).

F

Season Team	League	REGULAR SEASON								PLAYOFFS				
		Gms.	G	A	Pts.	PIM	+/-	PP	SH	Gms.	G	A	Pts.	PIM
96-97—Victoria	BCJHL	53	6	18	24	...	...	...	...	—	—	—	—	—
97-98—Minnesota-Duluth	WCHA	40	3	6	9	82	...	...	...	—	—	—	—	—
98-99—Minnesota-Duluth	WCHA	36	4	16	20	61	...	...	...	—	—	—	—	—
99-00—Minnesota-Duluth	WCHA	37	4	6	10	83	...	...	...	—	—	—	—	—
00-01—Minnesota-Duluth	WCHA	37	0	8	8	56	...	...	...	—	—	—	—	—
01-02—Cleveland	AHL	79	6	12	18	94	...	...	...	—	—	—	—	—
02-03—Cleveland	AHL	59	3	11	14	63	...	...	...	—	—	—	—	—
—San Jose	NHL	16	0	0	0	2	-5	0	0	—	—	—	—	—
NHL Totals (1 year)		16	0	0	0	2	-5	0	0					

FICHAUD, ERIC   G   CANADIENS

PERSONAL: Born November 4, 1975, in Anjou, Que. ... 5-11/171. ... Catches left. ... Name pronounced FEE-shoh.
TRANSACTIONS/CAREER NOTES: Selected by Toronto Maple Leafs in first round (first Maple Leafs pick, 16th overall) of NHL entry draft (June 28, 1994). ... Traded by Maple Leafs to New York Islanders for C Benoit Hogue, third-round pick (RW Ryan Pepperall) in 1995 draft and fifth-round pick (D Brandon Sugden) in 1996 draft (April 6, 1995). ... Strained abdominal muscle (October 12, 1996); missed two games. ... Partially dislocated left shoulder (December 2, 1997); missed seven games. ... Underwent shoulder surgery while assigned to Utah Grizzlies of IHL (January 20, 1998); missed remainder of season. ... Traded by Islanders to Edmonton Oilers for LW Mike Watt (June 18, 1998). ... Traded by Oilers with D Drake Berehowsky and D Greg de Vries to Nashville Predators for F Jim Dowd and G Mikhail Shtalenkov (October 1, 1998). ... Partially dislocated left shoulder (December 8, 1998); missed five games. ... Reinjured shoulder (January 4, 1999) and underwent surgery; missed remainder of season. ... Traded by Predators to Carolina Hurricanes for fourth-round pick (C/RW Yevgeny Pavlov) in 1999 draft and future considerations (June 26, 1999). ... Claimed on waivers by Montreal Canadiens (February 11, 2000). ... Injured shoulder (February 11, 2000); missed 14 games. ... Announced retirement (October 28, 2001). ... Signed as free agent by Canadiens (September 10, 2002).

Season Team	League	REGULAR SEASON									PLAYOFFS							
		Gms.	Min	W	L	T	GA	SO	Avg.	SV%	Gms.	Min.	W	L	GA	SO	Avg.	SV%
92-93—Chicoutimi	QMJHL	43	2040	18	13	1	149	0	4.38	—	—	—	—	—	—	—	—	—
93-94—Chicoutimi	QMJHL	63	3493	37	21	3	192	4	3.30	—	26	1560	16	10	86	†1	3.31	—
94-95—Chicoutimi	QMJHL	46	2637	21	19	4	151	4	3.44	—	7	430	2	5	20	0	2.79	—
95-96—Worcester	AHL	34	1988	13	15	6	97	1	2.93	—	2	127	1	1	7	0	3.31	—
—New York Islanders	NHL	24	1234	7	12	2	68	1	3.31	.897	—	—	—	—	—	—	—	—
96-97—New York Islanders	NHL	34	1759	9	14	4	91	0	3.10	.899	—	—	—	—	—	—	—	—
97-98—New York Islanders	NHL	17	807	3	8	3	40	0	2.97	.905	—	—	—	—	—	—	—	—
—Utah	IHL	1	40	0	0	0	3	0	4.50	—	—	—	—	—	—	—	—	—
98-99—Milwaukee	IHL	8	480	5	2	‡1	25	0	3.13	—	—	—	—	—	—	—	—	—
—Nashville	NHL	9	447	0	6	0	24	0	3.22	.895	—	—	—	—	—	—	—	—
99-00—Carolina	NHL	9	490	3	5	1	24	1	2.94	.883	—	—	—	—	—	—	—	—
—Quebec	AHL	6	368	4	1	1	17	0	2.77	—	3	177	0	3	10	0	3.39	—
00-01—Quebec	AHL	42	2441	19	19	2	127	1	3.12	—	2	98	0	1	3	0	1.84	—
—Montreal	NHL	2	62	0	2	0	4	0	3.87	.875	—	—	—	—	—	—	—	—
01-02—Manitoba	AHL	5	278	2	3	0	13	1	2.81	—	—	—	—	—	—	—	—	—
—Krefeld Pinguine	Germany	9	401	...	...	...	11	0	1.65	—	3	197	...	...	8	0	2.44	—
02-03—Hamilton	AHL	27	1446	14	7	3	55	4	2.28	—	—	—	—	—	—	—	—	—
NHL Totals (6 years)		95	4799	22	47	10	251	2	3.14	.897								

FIDDLER, VERNON   C   PREDATORS

PERSONAL: Born May 9, 1980, in Edmonton ... 5-11/195. ... Shoots left.

Season Team	League	REGULAR SEASON								PLAYOFFS				
		Gms.	G	A	Pts.	PIM	+/-	PP	SH	Gms.	G	A	Pts.	PIM
97-98—Kelowna	WHL	65	10	11	21	31	...	...	...	7	0	1	1	4
98-99—Kelowna	WHL	68	22	21	43	82	...	...	...	6	2	0	2	8
99-00—Kelowna	WHL	64	20	28	48	60	...	...	...	5	1	3	4	4
00-01—Arkansas	ECHL	3	0	1	1	2	...	...	...	5	3	0	3	5
—Kelowna	WHL	3	0	2	2	0	...	...	...	—	—	—	—	—
—Medicine Hat	WHL	67	33	38	71	100	...	...	...	—	—	—	—	—
01-02—Norfolk	AHL	38	8	5	13	28	...	...	...	4	1	3	4	2
—Roanoke	ECHL	44	27	28	55	71	...	...	...	—	—	—	—	—
02-03—Milwaukee	AHL	54	8	16	24	70	...	...	...	—	—	—	—	—
—Nashville	NHL	19	4	2	6	14	2	0	0	—	—	—	—	—
NHL Totals (1 year)		19	4	2	6	14	2	0	0					

FIEDLER, JONAS   RW   SHARKS

PERSONAL: Born May 29, 1984, in Jihlava, Czechoslovakia. ... 6-2/173. ... Shoots right.
TRANSACTIONS/CAREER NOTES: Selected by San Jose Sharks in third round (third Sharks pick, 86th overall) of NHL entry draft (June 22, 2002).

Season Team	League	REGULAR SEASON								PLAYOFFS				
		Gms.	G	A	Pts.	PIM	+/-	PP	SH	Gms.	G	A	Pts.	PIM
01-02—Plymouth	OHL	68	8	12	20	27	...	...	...	6	0	1	1	4
02-03—Plymouth	OHL	63	7	21	28	59	...	...	...	—	—	—	—	—

FINLEY, BRIAN — G — PREDATORS

PERSONAL: Born July 3, 1981, in Sault Ste. Marie, Ont. ... 6-3/205. ... Catches right.

TRANSACTIONS/CAREER NOTES: Selected by Nashville Predators in first round (first Predators pick, sixth overall) of NHL entry draft (June 26, 1999).

Season Team	League	Gms.	Min	W	L	T	GA	SO	Avg.	SV%	Gms.	Min.	W	L	GA	SO	Avg.	SV%
97-98—Barrie	OHL	41	2154	23	14	1	105	3	2.92	—	5	260	1	3	13	0	3.00	—
98-99—Barrie	OHL	52	3063	*36	10	4	136	3	2.66	—	5	323	4	1	15	0	2.79	—
99-00—Barrie	OHL	47	2540	24	12	6	130	2	3.07	—	*23	1353	14	†8	*58	1	2.57	—
00-01—Barrie	OHL	16	818	5	8	0	42	0	3.08	—	—	—	—	—	—	—	—	—
—Brampton	OHL	11	631	7	3	1	31	0	2.95	—	9	503	5	4	26	1	3.10	—
02-03—Milwaukee	AHL	22	1207	7	11	2	59	2	2.93	—	—	—	—	—	—	—	—	—
—Toledo	ECHL	7	305	4	2	0	12	0	2.36	—	—	—	—	—	—	—	—	—
—Nashville	NHL	1	47	0	0	0	3	0	3.83	.769	—	—	—	—	—	—	—	—
NHL Totals (1 year)		1	47	0	0	0	3	0	3.83	.769								

FINLEY, JEFF — D — BLUES

PERSONAL: Born April 14, 1967, in Edmonton ... 6-2/203. ... Shoots left. ... Full Name: John Jeffrey Finley.

TRANSACTIONS/CAREER NOTES: Selected by New York Islanders in third round (fourth Islanders pick, 55th overall) of NHL entry draft (June 15, 1985). ... Suffered swollen left knee (September 1988). ... Traded by Islanders to Ottawa Senators for D Chris Luongo (June 30, 1993). ... Signed as free agent by Philadelphia Flyers (August 2, 1993). ... Traded to Flyers to Winnipeg Jets for LW Russ Romaniuk (June 26, 1995). ... Separated shoulder (December 10, 1995); missed one game. ... Jets franchise moved to Phoenix and renamed Coyotes for 1996-97 season; NHL approved move on January 18, 1996. ... Suffered from the flu (December 7, 1996); missed two games. ... Strained hip flexor (December 30, 1996); missed one game. ... Sprained ankle (March 27, 1997); missed remainder of regular season and first six games of playoffs. ... Signed as free agent by New York Rangers (July 16, 1997). ... Traded by Rangers with D Geoff Smith to St. Louis Blues for future consider-ations (February 13, 1999); Rangers acquired RW Chris Kenady to complete deal (February 22, 1999). ... Injured back (December 21, 1999); missed two games. ... Injured groin (March 12, 2000); missed one game. ... Suffered back spasms (March 30, 2000); missed final five games of regular season. ... Suffered from the flu (November 16, 2000); missed one game. ... Suffered concussion (March 25, 2001); missed final six games of regular season. ... Sprained hip (October 20, 2001); missed three games. ... Bruised hip (March 2, 2002); missed one game. ... Suspended four games by NHL for leaving penalty box to fight (March 24, 2003).

Season Team	League	Gms.	G	A	Pts.	PIM	+/-	PP	SH	Gms.	G	A	Pts.	PIM
83-84—Portland	WHL	5	0	0	0	0	...	...	...	5	0	1	1	4
—Summerland	BCJHL	49	0	21	21	14	...	...	...	—	—	—	—	—
84-85—Portland	WHL	69	6	44	50	57	...	...	...	6	1	2	3	2
85-86—Portland	WHL	70	11	59	70	83	...	...	...	15	1	7	8	16
86-87—Portland	WHL	72	13	53	66	113	...	...	...	20	1	†21	22	27
87-88—Springfield	AHL	52	5	18	23	50	...	...	...	—	—	—	—	—
—New York Islanders	NHL	10	0	5	5	15	5	0	0	1	0	0	0	2
88-89—New York Islanders	NHL	4	0	0	0	6	1	0	0	—	—	—	—	—
—Springfield	AHL	65	3	16	19	55	...	...	...	—	—	—	—	—
89-90—New York Islanders	NHL	11	0	1	1	0	0	0	0	5	0	2	2	2
—Springfield	AHL	57	1	15	16	41	...	...	...	13	1	4	5	23
90-91—Capital District	AHL	67	10	34	44	34	...	...	...	—	—	—	—	—
—New York Islanders	NHL	11	0	0	0	4	-1	0	0	—	—	—	—	—
91-92—Capital District	AHL	20	1	9	10	6	...	...	...	—	—	—	—	—
—New York Islanders	NHL	51	1	10	11	26	-6	0	0	—	—	—	—	—
92-93—Capital District	AHL	61	6	29	35	34	...	...	...	4	0	1	1	0
93-94—Philadelphia	NHL	55	1	8	9	24	16	0	0	—	—	—	—	—
94-95—Hershey	AHL	36	2	9	11	33	...	...	...	6	0	1	1	8
95-96—Springfield	AHL	14	3	12	15	22	...	...	...	—	—	—	—	—
—Winnipeg	NHL	65	1	5	6	81	-2	0	0	6	0	0	0	4
96-97—Phoenix	NHL	65	3	7	10	40	-8	1	0	1	0	0	0	2
97-98—New York Rangers	NHL	63	1	6	7	55	-3	0	0	—	—	—	—	—
98-99—Hartford	AHL	42	2	10	12	28	...	...	...	—	—	—	—	—
—New York Rangers	NHL	2	0	0	0	0	-1	0	0	—	—	—	—	—
—St. Louis	NHL	30	1	2	3	20	12	0	0	13	1	2	3	8
99-00—St. Louis	NHL	74	2	8	10	38	26	0	0	7	0	2	2	4
00-01—St. Louis	NHL	72	2	8	10	38	7	0	0	2	0	0	0	0
01-02—St. Louis	NHL	78	0	6	6	30	12	0	0	10	0	0	0	8
02-03—St. Louis	NHL	64	1	3	4	46	-2	0	0	6	0	0	0	6
NHL Totals (14 years)		655	13	69	82	423	56	1	0	51	1	6	7	36

FISCHER, JIRI — D — RED WINGS

PERSONAL: Born July 31, 1980, in Horovice, Czechoslovakia ... 6-5/225. ... Shoots left.

TRANSACTIONS/CAREER NOTES: Selected by Detroit Red Wings in first round (first Red Wings pick, 25th overall) of NHL entry draft (June 27, 1998). ... Sprained ankle (December 2, 2000); missed eight games. ... Suspended one playoff game by NHL for cross-checking incident (June 11, 2002).

F

Season Team	League	REGULAR SEASON Gms.	G	A	Pts.	PIM	+/-	PP	SH	PLAYOFFS Gms.	G	A	Pts.	PIM
95-96—Poldi Kladno	Czech Rep.	39	6	10	16	...	...	...	...	—	—	—	—	—
96-97—Poldi Kladno	Czech Rep.	38	11	16	27	...	...	...	...	—	—	—	—	—
97-98—Hull	QMJHL	70	3	19	22	112	...	...	...	11	1	4	5	16
98-99—Hull	QMJHL	65	22	56	78	141	...	...	...	23	6	17	23	44
99-00—Detroit	NHL	52	0	8	8	45	1	0	0	—	—	—	—	—
—Cincinnati	AHL	7	0	2	2	10	...	...	...	—	—	—	—	—
00-01—Detroit	NHL	55	1	8	9	59	3	0	0	5	0	0	0	9
—Cincinnati	AHL	18	2	6	8	22	...	...	...	—	—	—	—	—
01-02—Detroit	NHL	80	2	8	10	67	17	0	0	22	3	3	6	30
02-03—Detroit	NHL	15	1	5	6	16	0	0	0	—	—	—	—	—
NHL Totals (4 years)		202	4	29	33	187	21	0	0	27	3	3	6	39

FISHER, MIKE — C — SENATORS

PERSONAL: Born June 5, 1980, in Peterborough, Ont. ... 6-1/200. ... Shoots right.

TRANSACTIONS/CAREER NOTES: Selected by Ottawa Senators in second round (second Senators pick, 44th overall) of NHL entry draft (June 27, 1998). ... Suffered hip pointer (October 5, 1999); missed three games. ... Tore anterior cruciate ligament in right knee (December 30, 1999); missed remainder of season. ... Injured left shoulder (Novmeber 2, 2000); missed 22 games. ... Injured left shoulder (February 8, 2002); missed five games. ... Injured right shoulder (March 7, 2002); missed final 19 games of season.

Season Team	League	REGULAR SEASON Gms.	G	A	Pts.	PIM	+/-	PP	SH	PLAYOFFS Gms.	G	A	Pts.	PIM
96-97—Peterborough	Tier II Jr. A	51	26	30	56	33	...	...	...	—	—	—	—	—
97-98—Sudbury	OHL	66	24	25	49	65	...	...	...	9	2	2	4	13
98-99—Sudbury	OHL	68	41	65	106	55	...	...	...	4	2	1	3	4
99-00—Ottawa	NHL	32	4	5	9	15	-6	0	0	—	—	—	—	—
00-01—Ottawa	NHL	60	7	12	19	46	-1	0	0	4	0	1	1	4
01-02—Ottawa	NHL	58	15	9	24	55	8	0	3	10	2	1	3	0
02-03—Ottawa	NHL	74	18	20	38	54	13	5	1	18	2	2	4	16
NHL Totals (4 years)		224	44	46	90	170	14	5	4	32	4	4	8	20

FITZGERALD, TOM — RW — MAPLE LEAFS

PERSONAL: Born August 28, 1968, in Billerica, Mass. ... 6-0/190. ... Shoots right. ... Full Name: Thomas James Fitzgerald. ... Cousin of Keith Tkachuk, left winger, St. Louis Blues.

TRANSACTIONS/CAREER NOTES: Selected by New York Islanders in first round (first Islanders pick, 17th overall) of NHL entry draft (June 21, 1986). ... Bruised left knee (November 7, 1990). ... Strained abdominal muscle (October 22, 1991); missed 16 games. ... Tore rib cage muscle (October 24, 1992); missed four games. ... Selected by Florida Panthers in NHL expansion draft (June 24, 1993). ... Suffered sore hip (March 18, 1994); missed one game. ... Bruised eye (November 13, 1996); missed one game. ... Suffered from the flu (December 29, 1996); missed one game. ... Strained abdominal muscle (January 25, 1997); missed three games. ... Reinjured abdominal muscle (February 22, 1997); missed five games. ... Traded by Panthers to Colorado Avalanche for rights to LW Mark Parrish and third-round pick (D Lance Ward) in 1998 draft (March 24, 1998). ... Signed as free agent by Nashville Predators (July 6, 1998). ... Strained neck (December 8, 1998); missed one game. ... Injured ribs (December 15, 2001); missed three games. ... Traded by Predators to Chicago Blackhawks for fourth-round pick in 2003 draft (March 13, 2002). ... Signed as free agent by Toronto Maple Leafs (July 17, 2002).

Season Team	League	REGULAR SEASON Gms.	G	A	Pts.	PIM	+/-	PP	SH	PLAYOFFS Gms.	G	A	Pts.	PIM
84-85—Austin Prep	Mass. H.S.	18	20	21	41	...	...	...	...	—	—	—	—	—
85-86—Austin Prep	Mass. H.S.	24	35	38	73	...	...	...	...	—	—	—	—	—
86-87—Providence College	Hockey East	27	8	14	22	22	...	...	...	—	—	—	—	—
87-88—Providence College	Hockey East	36	19	15	34	50	...	...	...	—	—	—	—	—
88-89—Springfield	AHL	61	24	18	42	43	...	...	...	—	—	—	—	—
—New York Islanders	NHL	23	3	5	8	10	1	0	0	—	—	—	—	—
89-90—Springfield	AHL	53	30	23	53	32	...	...	...	14	2	9	11	13
—New York Islanders	NHL	19	2	5	7	4	-3	0	0	4	1	0	1	4
90-91—New York Islanders	NHL	41	5	5	10	24	-9	0	0	—	—	—	—	—
—Capital District	AHL	27	7	7	14	50	...	...	...	—	—	•	—	—
91-92—New York Islanders	NHL	45	6	11	17	28	-3	0	2	—	—	—	—	—
—Capital District	AHL	4	1	1	2	4	...	...	...	—	—	—	—	—
92-93—New York Islanders	NHL	77	9	18	27	34	-2	0	3	18	2	5	7	18
93-94—Florida	NHL	83	18	14	32	54	-3	0	3	—	—	—	—	—
94-95—Florida	NHL	48	3	13	16	31	-3	0	0	—	—	—	—	—
95-96—Florida	NHL	82	13	21	34	75	-3	1	6	22	4	4	8	34
96-97—Florida	NHL	71	10	14	24	64	7	0	2	5	0	1	1	0
97-98—Florida	NHL	69	10	5	15	57	-4	0	1	—	—	—	—	—
—Colorado	NHL	11	2	1	3	22	0	0	1	7	0	1	1	20
98-99—Nashville	NHL	80	13	19	32	48	-18	0	0	—	—	—	—	—
99-00—Nashville	NHL	82	13	9	22	66	-18	0	3	—	—	—	—	—
00-01—Nashville	NHL	82	9	9	18	71	-5	0	2	—	—	—	—	—
01-02—Nashville	NHL	63	7	9	16	33	-4	0	1	—	—	—	—	—
—Chicago	NHL	15	1	3	4	6	-3	0	1	5	0	0	0	4
02-03—Toronto	NHL	66	4	13	17	57	10	0	0	7	0	1	1	4
NHL Totals (15 years)		957	128	174	302	684	-60	1	25	68	7	12	19	84

F

FITZPATRICK, RORY — D — SABRES

PERSONAL: Born January 11, 1975, in Rochester, N.Y. ... 6-2/210. ... Shoots right.

TRANSACTIONS/CAREER NOTES: Selected by Montreal Canadiens in second round (second Canadiens pick, 47th overall) of NHL entry draft (June 26, 1993). ... Traded by Canadiens with C Pierre Turgeon and C Craig Conroy to St. Louis Blues for LW Shayne Corson, D Murray Baron and fifth-round pick (D Gennady Razin) in 1997 draft (October 29, 1996). ... Selected by Boston Bruins from Blues in NHL waiver draft (October 5, 1998). ... Claimed on waivers by Blues (October 7, 1998). ... Traded by Blues to Nashville Predators for D Dan Keczmer (February 9, 2000). ... Traded by Predators to Edmonton Oilers for future considerations (January 12, 2001). ... Signed as free agent by Buffalo Sabres (August 14, 2001).

Season Team	League	REGULAR SEASON								PLAYOFFS				
		Gms.	G	A	Pts.	PIM	+/-	PP	SH	Gms.	G	A	Pts.	PIM
90-91—Rochester Jr. B	OHA	40	0	5	5	...	...	...	...	—	—	—	—	—
91-92—Rochester Jr. B	OHA	28	8	28	36	141	...	...	...	—	—	—	—	—
92-93—Sudbury	OHL	58	4	20	24	68	...	...	...	14	0	0	0	17
93-94—Sudbury	OHL	65	12	34	46	112	...	...	...	10	2	5	7	10
94-95—Sudbury	OHL	56	12	36	48	72	...	...	...	18	3	15	18	21
—Fredericton	AHL	—	—	—	—	—	—	—	—	10	1	2	3	5
95-96—Fredericton	AHL	18	4	6	10	36	...	...	...	—	—	—	—	—
—Montreal	NHL	42	0	2	2	18	-7	0	0	6	1	1	2	0
96-97—Montreal	NHL	6	0	1	1	6	-2	0	0	—	—	—	—	—
—Worcester	AHL	49	4	13	17	78	...	...	...	5	1	2	3	0
—St. Louis	NHL	2	0	0	0	2	-2	0	0	—	—	—	—	—
97-98—Worcester	AHL	62	8	22	30	111	...	...	...	11	0	3	3	26
98-99—Worcester	AHL	53	5	16	21	82	...	...	...	4	0	1	1	17
—St. Louis	NHL	1	0	0	0	2	-3	0	0	—	—	—	—	—
99-00—Worcester	AHL	28	0	5	5	48	...	...	...	—	—	—	—	—
—Milwaukee	IHL	27	2	1	3	27	...	...	...	3	0	2	2	2
00-01—Hamilton	AHL	34	3	17	20	29	...	...	...	—	—	—	—	—
—Nashville	NHL	2	0	0	0	2	-2	0	0	—	—	—	—	—
—Milwaukee	IHL	22	0	2	2	32	...	...	...	—	—	—	—	—
01-02—Rochester	AHL	60	4	8	12	83	...	...	...	2	0	1	1	0
—Buffalo	NHL	5	0	0	0	4	-2	0	0	—	—	—	—	—
02-03—Rochester	AHL	41	5	11	16	65	...	...	...	—	—	—	—	—
—Buffalo	NHL	36	1	3	4	16	-7	0	0	—	—	—	—	—
NHL Totals (6 years)		94	1	6	7	50	-25	0	0	6	1	1	2	0

FLAHERTY, WADE   G   PREDATORS

PERSONAL: Born January 11, 1968, in Terrace, B.C. ... 6-0/170. ... Catches left.
TRANSACTIONS/CAREER NOTES: Selected by Buffalo Sabres in ninth round (10th Sabres pick, 181st overall) of NHL entry draft (June 11, 1988). ... Signed as free agent by San Jose Sharks (September 3, 1991). ... Injured ribs (February 28, 1995); missed three games. ... Strained groin (February 1, 1996); missed two games. ... Suffered back spasms (March 8, 1996); missed six games. ... Suffered back spasms (March 31, 1996); missed seven games. ... Fractured collarbone (September 12, 1996); missed 23 games. ... Signed as free agent by New York Islanders (July 1, 1997). ... Sprained shoulder (November 21, 1999) and underwent surgery; missed remainder of season. ... Traded by Islanders to Tampa Bay Lightning for conditional ninth-round pick (February 16, 2001). ... Signed as free agent by Florida Panthers (August 2, 2001). ... Traded by Panthers to Nashville Predators for D Pascal Trepanier (March 9, 2003). ... Re-signed by Predators (July 17, 2003).

Season Team	League	REGULAR SEASON									PLAYOFFS							
		Gms.	Min	W	L	T	GA	SO	Avg.	SV%	Gms.	Min.	W	L	GA	SO	Avg.	SV%
84-85—Kelowna	WHL	1	55	0	0	0	5	0	5.45	—	—	—	—	—	—	—	—	—
85-86—Seattle	WHL	9	271	1	3	0	36	0	7.97	—	—	—	—	—	—	—	—	—
—Spokane	WHL	5	161	0	3	0	21	0	7.83	—	—	—	—	—	—	—	—	—
86-87—Nanaimo	BCJHL	15	830	...	...	...	53	0	3.83	—	—	—	—	—	—	—	—	—
—Victoria	WHL	3	127	0	2	0	16	0	7.56	—	—	—	—	—	—	—	—	—
87-88—Victoria	WHL	36	2052	20	15	0	135	0	3.95	—	5	300	2	3	18	0	3.60	—
88-89—Victoria	WHL	42	2408	21	19	0	180	0	4.49	—	8	480	3	5	35	0	4.38	—
89-90—Kalamazoo	IHL	1	13	0	0	‡0	0	0	—	—	—	—	—	—	—	—	—	—
—Greensboro	ECHL	27	1308	12	10	‡0	96	...	4.40	—	†9	567	*8	1	21	0	*2.22	—
90-91—Kansas City	IHL	†56	2990	16	31	‡4	*224	0	4.49	—	—	—	—	—	—	—	—	—
91-92—Kansas City	IHL	43	2603	26	14	‡3	140	1	3.23	—	1	1	0	0	0	0	...	—
—San Jose	NHL	3	178	0	3	0	13	0	4.38	.892	—	—	—	—	—	—	—	—
92-93—Kansas City	IHL	61	*3642	*34	19	‡0	*195	2	3.21	—	12	*733	6	*5	†34	*1	2.78	—
—San Jose	NHL	1	60	0	1	0	5	0	5.00	.891	—	—	—	—	—	—	—	—
93-94—Kansas City	IHL	60	*3564	32	19	‡9	202	0	3.40	—	—	—	—	—	—	—	—	—
94-95—San Jose	NHL	18	852	5	6	1	44	1	3.10	.903	7	377	2	3	31	0	4.93	.860
95-96—San Jose	NHL	24	1137	3	12	1	92	0	4.85	.866	—	—	—	—	—	—	—	—
96-97—Kentucky	AHL	19	1032	8	6	2	54	1	3.14	—	3	200	1	2	11	0	3.30	—
—San Jose	NHL	7	359	2	4	0	31	0	5.18	.847	—	—	—	—	—	—	—	—
97-98—Utah	IHL	24	1341	16	5	3	40	3	1.79	—	—	—	—	—	—	—	—	—
—New York Islanders	NHL	16	694	4	4	3	23	3	1.99	.926	—	—	—	—	—	—	—	—
98-99—New York Islanders	NHL	20	1048	5	11	2	53	0	3.03	.892	—	—	—	—	—	—	—	—
—Lowell	AHL	5	305	1	3	1	16	0	3.15	—	—	—	—	—	—	—	—	—
99-00—New York Islanders	NHL	4	182	0	1	1	7	0	2.31	.914	—	—	—	—	—	—	—	—
00-01—New York Islanders	NHL	20	1017	6	10	0	56	1	3.30	.881	—	—	—	—	—	—	—	—
—Tampa Bay	NHL	2	118	0	2	0	8	0	4.07	.855	—	—	—	—	—	—	—	—
01-02—Utah	AHL	45	2351	22	13	5	92	2	2.35	—	5	311	2	3	11	0	2.12	—
—Florida	NHL	4	245	2	1	1	12	0	2.94	.919	—	—	—	—	—	—	—	—
02-03—San Antonio	AHL	30	1791	11	13	5	86	1	2.88	—	—	—	—	—	—	—	—	—
—Florida	NHL	0	—	—	—	—	—	—	—	—	—	—	—	—	—	—	—	—
—Nashville	NHL	1	51	0	1	0	4	0	4.71	.852	—	—	—	—	—	—	—	—
NHL Totals (11 years)		120	5941	27	56	9	348	5	3.51	.887	7	377	2	3	31	0	4.93	.860

FLEISCHMANN, TOMAS   LW   RED WINGS

PERSONAL: Born May 16, 1984, in Koprivnice, Czechoslovakia. ... 6-1/172. ... Shoots left.
TRANSACTIONS/CAREER NOTES: Selected by Detroit Red Wings in second round (second Red Wings pick, 63rd overall) of NHL entry draft (June 22, 2002).

Season Team	League	REGULAR SEASON								PLAYOFFS				
		Gms.	G	A	Pts.	PIM	+/-	PP	SH	Gms.	G	A	Pts.	PIM
01-02—HC Vitkovice	Czech. Jrs.	34	21	17	38	14	...	...	...	—	—	—	—	—
02-03—Moose Jaw	WHL	65	21	50	71	36	...	...	...	—	—	—	—	—

FLEURY, THEO   RW   BLACKHAWKS

PERSONAL: Born June 29, 1968, in Oxbow, Sask. ... 5-6/182. ... Shoots right. ... Full Name: Theoren Fleury. ... Name pronounced THAIR-ihn FLUH-ree.

TRANSACTIONS/CAREER NOTES: Selected by Calgary Flames in eighth round (ninth Flames pick, 166th overall) of NHL entry draft (June 13, 1987). ... Played in Europe during 1994-95 NHL lockout. ... Injured eye (April 6, 1996); missed two games. ... Injured knee (April 6, 1997); missed one game. ... Traded by Flames with LW Chris Dingman to Colorado Avalanche for LW Rene Corbet, D Wade Belak and future considerations (February 28, 1999); Flames acquired D Robyn Regehr to complete deal (March 27, 1999). ... Sprained knee (March 1, 1999); missed seven games. ... Signed as free agent by New York Rangers (July 8, 1999). ... Suffered back spasms (February 8, 2000); missed one game. ... Strained right knee (April 8, 2000); missed final game of season. ... Missed final 20 games of 2000-01 season due to personal problems. ... Traded by Rangers to San Jose Sharks for sixth-round pick (C Kim Hirschovits) in 2002 draft (June 26, 2002). ... Signed as free agent by Chicago Blackhawks (August 15, 2002). ... Suspended indefinitely by NHL for violating league substance abuse policy (October 8-December 5, 2002). ... Suspended indefinitely by NHL for violating league substance abuse policy (April 11, 2003-present).

STATISTICAL PLATEAUS: Three-goal games: 1990-91 (5), 1992-93 (1), 1993-94 (1), 1995-96 (3), 1996-97 (1), 1998-99 (3), 2000-01 (1). Total: 15.

Season Team	League	REGULAR SEASON								PLAYOFFS				
		Gms.	G	A	Pts.	PIM	+/-	PP	SH	Gms.	G	A	Pts.	PIM
84-85—Moose Jaw	WHL	71	29	46	75	82	...	...	...	—	—	—	—	—
85-86—Moose Jaw	WHL	72	43	65	108	124	...	...	...	—	—	—	—	—
86-87—Moose Jaw	WHL	66	61	68	129	110	...	...	...	9	7	9	16	34
87-88—Moose Jaw	WHL	65	68	92	†160	235	...	...	...	—	—	—	—	—
—Salt Lake City.............	IHL	2	3	4	7	7	...	...	...	8	11	5	16	16
88-89—Salt Lake City.............	IHL	40	37	37	74	81	...	...	...	—	—	—	—	—
—Calgary	NHL	36	14	20	34	46	5	5	0	22	5	6	11	24
89-90—Calgary	NHL	80	31	35	66	157	22	9	3	6	2	3	5	10
90-91—Calgary	NHL	79	51	53	104	136	†48	9	7	7	2	5	7	14
91-92—Calgary	NHL	80	33	40	73	133	0	11	1	—	—	—	—	—
92-93—Calgary	NHL	83	34	66	100	88	14	12	2	6	5	7	12	27
93-94—Calgary	NHL	83	40	45	85	186	30	16	1	7	6	4	10	5
94-95—Tappara	Finland	10	8	9	17	22	...	...	...	—	—	—	—	—
—Calgary	NHL	47	29	29	58	112	6	9	2	7	7	7	14	2
95-96—Calgary	NHL	80	46	50	96	112	17	17	5	4	2	1	3	14
96-97—Calgary	NHL	81	29	38	67	104	-12	9	2	—	—	—	—	—
97-98—Calgary	NHL	82	27	51	78	197	0	3	2	—	—	—	—	—
—Can. Olympic team	Int'l	6	1	3	4	2	...	...	...	—	—	—	—	—
98-99—Calgary	NHL	60	30	39	69	68	18	7	3	—	—	—	—	—
—Colorado	NHL	15	10	14	24	18	8	1	0	18	5	12	17	20
99-00—New York Rangers	NHL	80	15	49	64	68	-4	1	0	—	—	—	—	—
00-01—New York Rangers	NHL	62	30	44	74	122	0	8	7	—	—	—	—	—
01-02—New York Rangers	NHL	82	24	39	63	216	0	7	0	—	—	—	—	—
—Can. Olympic team	Int'l	6	0	2	2	6	...	...	...	—	—	—	—	—
02-03—Chicago......................	NHL	54	12	21	33	77	-7	1	0	—	—	—	—	—
NHL Totals (15 years).........		1084	455	633	1088	1840	145	125	35	77	34	45	79	116

FLINN, RYAN   LW   KINGS

PERSONAL: Born April 20, 1980, in Halifax, Nova Scotia ... 6-5/248. ... Shoots left.

TRANSACTIONS/CAREER NOTES: Selected by New Jersey Devils in fifth round (eighth Devils pick, 143rd overall) of NHL entry draft (June 27, 1998). ... Signed as free agent by Los Angeles Kings (January 9, 2002).

F

Season Team	League	REGULAR SEASON								PLAYOFFS				
		Gms.	G	A	Pts.	PIM	+/-	PP	SH	Gms.	G	A	Pts.	PIM
96-97—Laval	QMJHL	23	3	2	5	66	...	...	...	2	0	0	0	0
97-98—Laval	QMJHL	59	4	12	16	217	...	...	...	15	1	0	1	63
98-99—Acadie-Bathurst	QMJHL	44	3	4	7	195	...	...	...	23	2	0	2	37
99-00—Halifax........................	QMJHL	67	14	19	33	365	...	...	...	—	—	—	—	—
00-01—Cape Breton................	QMJHL	57	16	17	33	280	...	...	...	9	1	1	2	43
01-02—Reading	ECHL	20	1	3	4	130	...	...	...	—	—	—	—	—
—Manchester................	AHL	37	0	1	1	113	...	...	...	1	0	0	0	0
—Los Angeles...............	NHL	10	0	0	0	51	0	0	0	—	—	—	—	—
02-03—Manchester................	AHL	27	2	2	4	95	...	...	...	—	—	—	—	—
—Los Angeles...............	NHL	19	1	0	1	28	0	0	0	—	—	—	—	—
NHL Totals (2 years)...........		29	1	0	1	79	0	0	0					

FOCHT, DAN   D   PENGUINS

PERSONAL: Born December 31, 1977, in Regina, Sask. ... 6-6/234. ... Shoots left. ... Name pronounced FOHKT.

TRANSACTIONS/CAREER NOTES: Selected by Phoenix Coyotes in first round (first Coyotes pick, 11th overall) of NHL entry draft (June 22, 1996). ... Traded by Coyotes with LW Ramzi Abid and LW Guillaume Lefebvre to Pittsburgh Penguins for C Jan Hrdina and D Francois Leroux (March 11, 2003).

Season Team	League	REGULAR SEASON								PLAYOFFS				
		Gms.	G	A	Pts.	PIM	+/-	PP	SH	Gms.	G	A	Pts.	PIM
95-96—Tri-City	WHL	63	6	12	18	161	...	...	...	11	1	1	2	23
96-97—Tri-City	WHL	28	0	5	5	92	...	...	...	—	—	—	—	—
—Regina	WHL	22	2	2	4	59	...	...	...	5	0	2	2	8
—Springfield	AHL	1	0	0	0	2	...	...	...	—	—	—	—	—
97-98—Springfield	AHL	61	2	5	7	125	...	...	...	3	0	0	0	4
98-99—Springfield	AHL	30	0	2	2	58	...	...	...	3	1	0	1	10
—Mississippi	ECHL	2	0	0	0	6	...	...	...	—	—	—	—	—
99-00—Jokerit Helsinki	Finland	2	0	0	0	0	...	...	...	—	—	—	—	—
—Springfield	AHL	44	2	9	11	86	...	...	...	5	0	1	1	2
—Mississippi	ECHL	4	0	1	1	0	...	...	...	—	—	—	—	—
00-01—Springfield	AHL	69	0	6	6	156	...	...	...	—	—	—	—	—
01-02—Springfield	AHL	56	2	8	10	134	...	...	...	—	—	—	—	—
—Phoenix	NHL	8	0	0	0	11	0	0	0	1	0	1	1	0
02-03—Springfield	AHL	37	2	7	9	80	...	...	...	—	—	—	—	—
—Phoenix	NHL	10	0	0	0	10	-2	0	0	—	—	—	—	—
—Pittsburgh	NHL	12	0	3	3	19	-7	0	0	—	—	—	—	—
NHL Totals (2 years)		30	0	3	3	40	-9	0	0	1	0	1	1	0

FOOTE, ADAM — D — AVALANCHE

PERSONAL: Born July 10, 1971, in Toronto ... 6-2/215. ... Shoots right. ... Full Name: Adam David Vernon Foote.

TRANSACTIONS/CAREER NOTES: Selected by Quebec Nordiques in second round (second Nordiques pick, 22nd overall) of NHL entry draft (June 17, 1989). ... Fractured right thumb (February 1992); missed remainder of season. ... Injured knee (October 21, 1992); missed one game. ... Suffered from the flu (January 28, 1993); missed two games. ... Injured groin (January 18, 1994); missed eight games. ... Suffered herniated disc (February 11, 1994) and underwent surgery; missed remainder of season. ... Injured back (February 9, 1995); missed two games. ... Injured groin (February 28, 1995); missed two games. ... Injured groin (March 26, 1995); missed four games. ... Reinjured groin (April 6, 1995); missed five games. ... Nordiques franchise moved to Colorado and renamed Avalanche for 1995-96 season (June 21, 1995). ... Fractured wrist prior to 1995-96 season; missed first two games of season. ... Separated left shoulder (January 6, 1996); missed five games. ... Bruised left knee (February 8, 1997); missed two games. ... Bruised knee (January 2, 1998); missed one game. ... Bruised knee (January 10, 1998); missed three games. ... Injured elbow (October 24, 1998); missed 15 games. ... Suffered concussion (December 4, 1998); missed three games. ... Injured shoulder (October 10, 1999); missed one game. ... Reinjured shoulder (October 21, 1999); missed six games. ... Reinjured shoulder (November 17, 1999); missed eight games. ... Injured groin (January 9, 2000); missed one game. ... Injured groin (February 10, 2000); missed six games. ... Suffered stress fracture in heel (November 9, 2000); missed 12 games. ... Separated right shoulder (January 4, 2001); missed 35 games. ... Underwent shoulder surgery prior to start of 2000-01 season; missed first 16 games of season. ... Injured knee (December 27, 2001); missed six games. ... Injured finger (March 14, 2002); missed two games. ... Suspended two games by NHL for cross-checking incident (April 1, 2002). ... Injured groin (April 12, 2002); missed final game of season.

Season Team	League	REGULAR SEASON								PLAYOFFS				
		Gms.	G	A	Pts.	PIM	+/-	PP	SH	Gms.	G	A	Pts.	PIM
88-89—Sault Ste. Marie	OHL	66	7	32	39	120	...	...	...	—	—	—	—	—
89-90—Sault Ste. Marie	OHL	61	12	43	55	199	...	...	...	—	—	—	—	—
90-91—Sault Ste. Marie	OHL	59	18	51	69	93	...	...	...	14	5	12	17	28
91-92—Quebec	NHL	46	2	5	7	44	-4	0	0	—	—	—	—	—
—Halifax	AHL	6	0	1	1	2	...	...	...	—	—	—	—	—
92-93—Quebec	NHL	81	4	12	16	168	6	0	1	6	0	1	1	2
93-94—Quebec	NHL	45	2	6	8	67	3	0	0	—	—	—	—	—
94-95—Quebec	NHL	35	0	7	7	52	17	0	0	6	0	1	1	14
95-96—Colorado	NHL	73	5	11	16	88	27	1	0	22	1	3	4	36
96-97—Colorado	NHL	78	2	19	21	135	16	0	0	17	0	4	4	62
97-98—Colorado	NHL	77	3	14	17	124	-3	0	0	7	0	0	0	23
—Can. Olympic team	Int'l	6	0	1	1	4	...	...	...	—	—	—	—	—
98-99—Colorado	NHL	64	5	16	21	92	20	3	0	19	2	3	5	24
99-00—Colorado	NHL	59	5	13	18	98	5	1	0	16	0	7	7	28
00-01—Colorado	NHL	35	3	12	15	42	6	1	1	23	3	4	7	47
01-02—Colorado	NHL	55	5	22	27	55	7	1	1	21	1	6	7	28
—Can. Olympic team	Int'l	6	1	0	1	2	...	...	...	—	—	—	—	—
02-03—Colorado	NHL	78	11	20	31	88	30	3	0	6	0	1	1	8
NHL Totals (12 years)		726	47	157	204	1053	130	10	3	143	7	30	37	272

FORBES, COLIN — C

PERSONAL: Born February 16, 1976, in New Westminster, B.C. ... 6-3/220. ... Shoots left.

TRANSACTIONS/CAREER NOTES: Selected by Philadelphia Flyers in seventh round (fifth Flyers pick, 166th overall) of NHL entry draft (June 29, 1994). ... Bruised thumb (November 7, 1998); missed one game. ... Suffered from stomach virus (January 7, 1999); missed one game. ... Traded by Flyers with fifth-round pick (G Michal Lanicek) in 1999 draft to Tampa Bay Lightning for RW Mikael Andersson and RW Sandy McCarthy (March 20, 1999). ... Traded by Lightning to Ottawa Senators for C Bruce Gardiner (November 11, 1999). ... Traded by Senators to New York Rangers for LW Eric Lacroix (March 1, 2001). ... Signed as free agent by Washington Capitals (January 8, 2002).

Season Team	League	REGULAR SEASON								PLAYOFFS				
		Gms.	G	A	Pts.	PIM	+/-	PP	SH	Gms.	G	A	Pts.	PIM
93-94—Sherwood Park	AJHL	47	18	22	40	76	...	...	...	—	—	—	—	—
94-95—Portland	WHL	72	24	31	55	108	...	...	...	9	1	3	4	10
95-96—Portland	WHL	72	33	44	77	137	...	...	...	7	2	5	7	14
—Hershey	AHL	2	1	0	1	2	...	...	...	4	0	2	2	2
96-97—Philadelphia	AHL	74	21	28	49	108	...	...	...	10	5	5	10	33
—Philadelphia	NHL	3	1	0	1	0	0	0	0	3	0	0	0	0
97-98—Philadelphia	AHL	13	7	4	11	22	...	...	...	—	—	—	—	—
—Philadelphia	NHL	63	12	7	19	59	2	2	0	5	0	0	0	2

Season Team	League	REGULAR SEASON								PLAYOFFS				
		Gms.	G	A	Pts.	PIM	+/-	PP	SH	Gms.	G	A	Pts.	PIM
98-99—Philadelphia	NHL	66	9	7	16	51	0	0	0	—	—	—	—	—
—Tampa Bay	NHL	14	3	1	4	10	-5	0	1	—	—	—	—	—
99-00—Tampa Bay	NHL	8	0	0	0	18	-4	0	0	—	—	—	—	—
—Ottawa	NHL	45	2	5	7	12	-1	0	0	5	1	0	1	14
00-01—Ottawa	NHL	39	0	1	1	31	-3	0	0	—	—	—	—	—
—New York Rangers	NHL	19	1	4	5	15	-3	0	0	—	—	—	—	—
01-02—Utah	AHL	4	0	0	0	21	...	...	...	—	—	—	—	—
—Portland	AHL	14	4	5	9	18	...	...	...	—	—	—	—	—
—Washington	NHL	38	5	3	8	15	-2	0	1	—	—	—	—	—
02-03—Portland	AHL	69	22	38	60	73	...	...	...	—	—	—	—	—
—Washington	NHL	5	0	0	0	0	-2	0	0	—	—	—	—	—
NHL Totals (7 years)...........		300	33	28	61	211	-18	2	2	13	1	0	1	16

FORBES, IAN — D — FLYERS

PERSONAL: Born August 2, 1980, in Brampton, Ont. ... 6-6/180. ... Shoots left.
TRANSACTIONS/CAREER NOTES: Selected by Philadelphia Flyers in second round (third Flyers pick, 51st overall) of NHL entry draft (June 27, 1998).

Season Team	League	REGULAR SEASON								PLAYOFFS				
		Gms.	G	A	Pts.	PIM	+/-	PP	SH	Gms.	G	A	Pts.	PIM
96-97—Mississauga...............	OHL	39	10	32	42	178	...	...	...	—	—	—	—	—
97-98—Guelph	OHL	61	2	3	5	164	...	...	...	12	0	0	0	16
98-99—Guelph	OHL	60	1	8	9	182	...	...	...	5	0	1	1	8
99-00—Guelph	OHL	62	2	7	9	143	...	...	...	6	0	0	0	11
00-01—Trenton	ECHL	33	0	2	2	133	...	...	...	—	—	—	—	—
01-02—Trenton	ECHL	42	0	5	5	204	...	...	...	—	—	—	—	—
—Philadelphia	AHL	18	1	0	1	50	...	...	...	2	0	0	0	0
02-03—Philadelphia	AHL	20	1	1	2	38	...	...	...	—	—	—	—	—
—Trenton	ECHL	32	0	2	2	122	...	...	...	—	—	—	—	—

FORSBERG, PETER — LW — AVALANCHE

PERSONAL: Born July 20, 1973, in Ornskoldsvik, Sweden ... 6-1/205. ... Shoots left. ... Son of Kent Forsberg, head coach Swedish Olympic team and Swedish National team (1995-98).
TRANSACTIONS/CAREER NOTES: Selected by Philadelphia Flyers in first round (first Flyers pick, sixth overall) of NHL entry draft (June 22, 1991). ... Traded by Flyers with G Ron Hextall, C Mike Ricci, D Steve Duchesne, D Kerry Huffman, first-round pick (G Jocelyn Thibault) in 1993 draft, cash and future considerations to Quebec Nordiques for C Eric Lindros (June 20, 1992); Nordiques acquired LW Chris Simon and first-round pick (traded to Toronto) in 1994 draft to complete deal (July 21, 1992). ... Played in Europe during 1994-95 NHL lockout. ... Suffered from the flu (March 1, 1995); missed one game. ... Nordiques franchise moved to Colorado and renamed Avalanche for 1995-96 season (June 21, 1995). ... Bruised thigh (December 14, 1996); missed 17 games. ... Bruised shoulder (November 8, 1997); missed three games. ... Pulled groin (March 26, 1998); missed seven games. ... Suffered concussion (May 7, 1998); missed two playoff games. ... Suffered charley horse (May 22, 1998); missed one playoff game. ... Injured groin (December 14, 1998); missed one game. ... Injured elbow (March 4, 1999); missed three games. ... Underwent shoulder surgery prior to start of 1999-2000 season; missed first 23 games of season. ... Suffered hip pointer (November 30, 1999); missed two games. ... Suffered concussion (February 1, 2000); missed five games. ... Bruised shoulder (March 26, 2000); missed two games. ... Separated shoulder (April 7, 2000); missed final game of season. ... Injured ribs (November 11, 2000); missed eight games. ... Missed entire 2001-02 regular season due to shoulder and ankle surgery. ... Re-signed by Avalanche (June 24, 2003).
STATISTICAL PLATEAUS: Three-goal games: 1995-96 (2), 1996-97 (1), 1998-99 (1), 2002-03 (2). Total: 6.

Season Team	League	REGULAR SEASON								PLAYOFFS				
		Gms.	G	A	Pts.	PIM	+/-	PP	SH	Gms.	G	A	Pts.	PIM
89-90—MoDo Hockey	Sweden Jr.	30	15	12	27	42	...	...	...	—	—	—	—	—
90-91—MoDo Ornskoldsvik	Sweden	23	7	10	17	22	...	...	...	—	—	—	—	—
91-92—MoDo Ornskoldsvik	Sweden	39	9	19	28	78	...	...	...	—	—	—	—	—
92-93—MoDo Ornskoldsvik	Sweden	39	23	24	47	92	...	...	...	3	4	1	5	...
93-94—MoDo Ornskoldsvik	Sweden	39	18	26	44	82	...	...	...	11	9	7	16	14
—Swedish Oly. team	Int'l	8	2	6	8	6	...	...	...	—	—	—	—	—
94-95—Swedish National team	Sweden	11	5	9	14	20	...	...	...	—	—	—	—	—
—Quebec	NHL	47	15	35	50	16	17	3	0	6	2	4	6	4
95-96—Colorado	NHL	82	30	86	116	47	26	7	3	22	10	11	21	18
96-97—Colorado	NHL	65	28	58	86	73	31	5	4	14	5	12	17	10
97-98—Colorado	NHL	72	25	66	91	94	6	7	3	7	6	5	11	12
—Swedish Oly. team	Int'l	4	1	4	5	6	...	...	...	—	—	—	—	—
98-99—Colorado	NHL	78	30	67	97	108	27	9	2	19	8	16	*24	31
99-00—Colorado	NHL	49	14	37	51	52	9	3	0	16	7	8	15	12
00-01—Colorado	NHL	73	27	62	89	54	23	12	2	11	4	10	14	6
01-02—Colorado	NHL	—	—	—	—	—	—	—	—	20	9	*18	*27	20
02-03—Colorado	NHL	75	29	*77	*106	70	†52	8	0	7	2	6	8	6
NHL Totals (9 years)...........		541	198	488	686	514	191	54	14	122	53	90	143	119

FORTIN, JEAN-FRANCOIS — D — CAPITALS

PERSONAL: Born March 15, 1979, in Laval, Que. ... 6-3/214. ... Shoots right.
TRANSACTIONS/CAREER NOTES: Selected by Washington Capitals in second round (second Capitals pick, 35th overall) of NHL entry draft (June 21, 1997). ... Injured leg (January 22, 2002); missed two games. ... Re-signed by Capitals (July 15, 2003).

F

Season Team	League	REGULAR SEASON								PLAYOFFS				
		Gms.	G	A	Pts.	PIM	+/-	PP	SH	Gms.	G	A	Pts.	PIM
95-96—Sherbrooke	QMJHL	69	7	15	22	40	...	...	...	7	2	6	8	2
96-97—Sherbrooke	QMJHL	59	7	30	37	89	...	...	...	2	0	1	1	14
97-98—Sherbrooke	QMJHL	55	12	25	37	37	...	...	...	—	—	—	—	—
98-99—Sherbrooke	QMJHL	64	17	33	50	78	...	...	...	12	5	13	18	20
99-00—Portland	AHL	43	3	5	8	44	...	...	...	2	0	0	0	0
—Hampton Roads	ECHL	7	0	2	2	0	...	...	...	—	—	—	—	—
00-01—Portland	AHL	32	1	7	8	22	...	...	...	1	0	0	0	0
—Richmond	ECHL	15	0	4	4	2	...	...	...	—	—	—	—	—
01-02—Portland	AHL	44	4	9	13	20	...	...	...	—	—	—	—	—
—Washington	NHL	36	1	3	4	20	-1	0	0	—	—	—	—	—
02-03—Portland	AHL	10	2	1	3	17	...	...	...	—	—	—	—	—
—Washington	NHL	33	0	1	1	22	-3	0	0	—	—	—	—	—
NHL Totals (2 years)		69	1	4	5	42	-4	0	0					

FOSTER, KURTIS   D   THRASHERS

PERSONAL: Born November 24, 1981, in Carp, Ont. ... 6-5/230. ... Shoots right.
TRANSACTIONS/CAREER NOTES: Selected by Calgary Flames in second round (second Flames pick, 40th overall) of NHL entry draft (June 24, 2000). ... Traded by Flames with LW Jeff Cowan to Atlanta Thrashers for D Petr Buzek and conditional draft pick (December 18, 2001).

Season Team	League	REGULAR SEASON								PLAYOFFS				
		Gms.	G	A	Pts.	PIM	+/-	PP	SH	Gms.	G	A	Pts.	PIM
97-98—Peterborough	OHL	39	1	1	2	45	...	...	...	4	0	0	0	2
98-99—Peterborough	OHL	54	2	13	15	59	...	...	...	5	0	0	0	6
99-00—Peterborough	OHL	68	6	18	24	116	...	...	...	5	1	2	3	4
00-01—Peterborough	OHL	62	17	24	41	78	...	...	...	7	1	1	2	10
01-02—Peterborough	OHL	33	10	4	14	58	...	...	...	—	—	—	—	—
—Chicago	AHL	39	6	9	15	59	...	...	...	14	1	1	2	21
02-03—Chicago	AHL	75	15	27	42	159	...	...	...	—	—	—	—	—
—Atlanta	NHL	2	0	0	0	0	-2	0	0	—	—	—	—	—
NHL Totals (1 year)		2	0	0	0	0	-2	0	0					

FRANCIS, RON   C   HURRICANES

PERSONAL: Born March 1, 1963, in Sault Ste. Marie, Ont. ... 6-3/200. ... Shoots left. ... Full Name: Ronald Francis. ... Cousin of Mike Liut, goaltender with three NHL teams (1979-80 through 1991-92) and Cincinnati Stingers of WHA (1977-78 and 1978-79).
TRANSACTIONS/CAREER NOTES: Selected by Hartford Whalers in first round (first Whalers pick, fourth overall) of NHL entry draft (June 10, 1981). ... Injured eye (January 27, 1982); missed three weeks. ... Strained ligaments in right knee (November 30, 1983). ... Fractured left ankle (January 18, 1986); missed 27 games. ... Fractured left index finger (January 28, 1989); missed 11 games. ... Fractured nose (November 24, 1990). ... Traded by Whalers with D Ulf Samuelsson and D Grant Jennings to Pittsburgh Penguins for C John Cullen, D Zarley Zalapski and RW Jeff Parker (March 4, 1991). ... Suffered from the flu (February 19, 1995); missed one game. ... Suffered back spasms (February 21, 1995); missed three games. ... Strained hip flexor (January 5, 1996); missed two games. ... Suspended two games and fined $1000 by NHL for checking player from behind (February 27, 1996). ... Fractured left foot (May 11, 1996); missed remainder of playoffs. ... Injured groin (February 22, 1997); missed one game. ... Pulled hamstring (April 16, 1998); missed one game. ... Signed as free agent by Carolina Hurricanes (July 13, 1998). ... Suffered from vertigo (November 26, 1999); missed two games. ... Injured back (January 27, 2000); missed two games.
STATISTICAL PLATEAUS: Three-goal games: 1982-83 (1), 1984-85 (1), 1985-86 (2), 1987-88 (1), 1988-89 (1), 1989-90 (1), 1990-91 (1), 1995-96 (1), 1997-98 (1). Total: 10. ... Four-goal games: 1983-84 (1). ... Total hat tricks: 11.

Season Team	League	REGULAR SEASON								PLAYOFFS				
		Gms.	G	A	Pts.	PIM	+/-	PP	SH	Gms.	G	A	Pts.	PIM
80-81—Sault Ste. Marie	OMJHL	64	26	43	69	33	...	...	...	19	7	8	15	34
81-82—Sault Ste. Marie	OHL	25	18	30	48	46	...	...	...	—	—	—	—	—
—Hartford	NHL	59	25	43	68	51	-13	12	0	—	—	—	—	—
82-83—Hartford	NHL	79	31	59	90	60	-25	4	2	—	—	—	—	—
83-84—Hartford	NHL	72	23	60	83	45	-10	5	0	—	—	—	—	—
84-85—Hartford	NHL	80	24	57	81	66	-23	4	0	—	—	—	—	—
85-86—Hartford	NHL	53	24	53	77	24	8	7	1	10	1	2	3	4
86-87—Hartford	NHL	75	30	63	93	45	10	7	0	6	2	2	4	6
87-88—Hartford	NHL	80	25	50	75	87	-8	11	1	6	2	5	7	2
88-89—Hartford	NHL	69	29	48	77	36	4	8	0	4	0	2	2	0
89-90—Hartford	NHL	80	32	69	101	73	13	15	1	7	3	3	6	8
90-91—Hartford	NHL	67	21	55	76	51	-2	10	1	—	—	—	—	—
—Pittsburgh	NHL	14	2	9	11	21	0	0	0	24	7	10	17	24
91-92—Pittsburgh	NHL	70	21	33	54	30	-7	5	1	21	8	*19	27	6
92-93—Pittsburgh	NHL	84	24	76	100	68	6	9	2	12	6	11	17	19
93-94—Pittsburgh	NHL	82	27	66	93	62	-3	8	0	6	0	2	2	6
94-95—Pittsburgh	NHL	44	11	*48	59	18	*30	3	0	12	6	13	19	4
95-96—Pittsburgh	NHL	77	27	92	119	56	25	12	1	11	3	6	9	4
96-97—Pittsburgh	NHL	81	27	63	90	20	7	10	1	5	1	2	3	2
97-98—Pittsburgh	NHL	81	25	62	87	20	12	7	0	6	1	5	6	2
98-99—Carolina	NHL	82	21	31	52	34	-2	8	0	3	0	1	1	0
99-00—Carolina	NHL	78	23	50	73	18	10	7	0	—	—	—	—	—
00-01—Carolina	NHL	82	15	50	65	32	-15	7	0	3	0	0	0	0
01-02—Carolina	NHL	80	27	50	77	18	4	14	0	23	6	10	16	6
02-03—Carolina	NHL	82	22	35	57	30	-22	8	1	—	—	—	—	—
NHL Totals (22 years)		1651	536	1222	1758	965	-1	181	12	159	46	93	139	93

FRIESEN, JEFF   LW   DEVILS

PERSONAL: Born August 5, 1976, in Meadow Lake, Sask. ... 6-0/215. ... Shoots left. ... Name pronounced FREE-sihn.
TRANSACTIONS/CAREER NOTES: Selected by San Jose Sharks in first round (first Sharks pick, 11th overall) of NHL entry draft (June 28, 1994). ... Injured hand (October 18, 1996); missed two games. ... Missed first two games of 1997-98 season due to contract dispute. ... Injured shoulder (December 26, 1998); missed two games. ... Traded by Sharks with G Steve Shields and conditional pick in draft to Mighty Ducks of Anaheim for RW Teemu Selanne (March 5, 2001). ... Sprained left ankle (January 12, 2002); missed one game. ... Traded by Mighty Ducks with D Oleg Tverdovsky and RW Maxim Balmochnykh to New Jersey Devils for RW Petr Sykora, C Igor Pohanka, D Mike Commodore and G J.F. Damphousse (July 7, 2002).
STATISTICAL PLATEAUS: Three-goal games: 1995-96 (1), 1999-00 (1). Total: 2.

					REGULAR SEASON					PLAYOFFS				
Season Team	League	Gms.	G	A	Pts.	PIM	+/-	PP	SH	Gms.	G	A	Pts.	PIM
91-92—Regina	WHL	4	3	1	4	2	...	...	...	—	—	—	—	—
92-93—Regina	WHL	70	45	38	83	23	...	...	...	13	7	10	17	8
93-94—Regina	WHL	66	51	67	118	48	...	...	...	4	3	2	5	2
94-95—Regina	WHL	25	21	23	44	22	...	...	...	—	—	—	—	—
—San Jose	NHL	48	15	10	25	14	-8	5	1	11	1	5	6	4
95-96—San Jose	NHL	79	15	31	46	42	-19	2	0	—	—	—	—	—
96-97—San Jose	NHL	82	28	34	62	75	-8	6	2	—	—	—	—	—
97-98—San Jose	NHL	79	31	32	63	40	8	7	†6	6	0	1	1	2
98-99—San Jose	NHL	78	22	35	57	42	3	10	1	6	2	2	4	14
99-00—San Jose	NHL	82	26	35	61	47	-2	11	3	11	2	2	4	10
00-01—San Jose	NHL	64	12	24	36	56	7	2	0	—	—	—	—	—
—Anaheim	NHL	15	2	10	12	10	-2	2	0	—	—	—	—	—
01-02—Anaheim	NHL	81	17	26	43	44	-1	1	1	—	—	—	—	—
02-03—New Jersey	NHL	81	23	28	51	26	23	3	0	24	10	4	14	6
NHL Totals (9 years)		689	191	265	456	396	1	49	14	58	15	14	29	36

FROLOV, ALEXANDER   LW   KINGS

PERSONAL: Born July 26, 1982, in Moscow, U.S.S.R. ... 6-3/195. ... Shoots right.
TRANSACTIONS/CAREER NOTES: Selected by Los Angeles Kings in first round (first Kings pick, 20th overall) of NHL entry draft (June 24, 2000).

					REGULAR SEASON					PLAYOFFS				
Season Team	League	Gms.	G	A	Pts.	PIM	+/-	PP	SH	Gms.	G	A	Pts.	PIM
98-99—Torpedo Yaroslavl	Rus. Div. II						Statistics unavailable.							
99-00—Torpedo Yaroslavl	Rus. Div. II	36	27	13	40	30	...	...	...	—	—	—	—	—
00-01—Krylja Sovetov	Rus. Div. II	44	20	19	39	8	...	...	...	—	—	—	—	—
01-02—Kryla Sov. Moscow	Russian	43	18	12	30	16	...	...	...	3	1	0	1	0
02-03—Los Angeles	NHL	79	14	17	31	34	12	1	0	—	—	—	—	—
NHL Totals (1 year)		79	14	17	31	34	12	1	0					

FUSSEY, OWEN   RW   CAPITALS

PERSONAL: Born April 2, 1983, in Winnipeg. ... 6-0/185. ... Shoots left.
TRANSACTIONS/CAREER NOTES: Selected by Washington Capitals in third round (second Capitals pick, 90th overall) of NHL entry draft (June 23, 2001).

					REGULAR SEASON					PLAYOFFS				
Season Team	League	Gms.	G	A	Pts.	PIM	+/-	PP	SH	Gms.	G	A	Pts.	PIM
99-00—Calgary	WHL	51	7	6	13	35	...	...	...	12	3	4	7	2
00-01—Calgary	WHL	48	15	10	25	33	...	...	...	12	2	1	3	6
01-02—Calgary	WHL	72	43	27	70	61	...	...	...	7	3	1	4	4
02-03—Moose Jaw	WHL	66	41	30	71	51	...	...	...	—	—	—	—	—

GABORIK, MARIAN   RW   WILD

PERSONAL: Born February 14, 1982, in Trencin, Czechoslovakia ... 6-1/183. ... Shoots left.
TRANSACTIONS/CAREER NOTES: Selected by Minnesota Wild in first round (first Wild pick, third overall) of NHL entry draft (June 24, 2000). ... Bruised leg (November 15, 2000); missed six games. ... Strained muscle in abdomen (March 31, 2001); missed four games. ... Underwent hernia surgery prior to 2001-02 season; missed first game of season. ... Strained right quadriceps (December 20, 2001); missed three games.
STATISTICAL PLATEAUS: Three-goal games: 2001-02 (2), 2002-03 (3). Total: 5.

					REGULAR SEASON					PLAYOFFS				
Season Team	League	Gms.	G	A	Pts.	PIM	+/-	PP	SH	Gms.	G	A	Pts.	PIM
98-99—Dukla Trencin	Slovakia	33	11	9	20	6	...	...	...	3	1	0	1	2
99-00—Dukla Trencin	Slovakia	50	25	21	46	34	...	...	...	5	1	2	3	2
00-01—Minnesota	NHL	71	18	18	36	32	-6	6	0	—	—	—	—	—
01-02—Minnesota	NHL	78	30	37	67	34	0	10	0	—	—	—	—	—
02-03—Minnesota	NHL	81	30	35	65	46	12	5	1	18	9	8	17	6
NHL Totals (3 years)		230	78	90	168	112	6	21	1	18	9	8	17	6

F
G

GAGNE, SIMON   LW   FLYERS

PERSONAL: Born February 29, 1980, in Ste-Foy, Que. ... 6-0/190. ... Shoots left. ... Name pronounced see-MONE gahn-YAY.
TRANSACTIONS/CAREER NOTES: Selected by Philadelphia Flyers in first round (first Flyers pick, 22nd overall) of NHL entry draft (June 27, 1998). ... Suffered from the flu (January 2, 2000); missed one game. ... Suffered from the flu (March 23, 2000); missed one game. ... Strained

lower back (February 19, 2001); missed one game. ... Separated shoulder (February 24, 2001); missed 12 games. ... Bruised left shoulder (December 31, 2001); missed two games. ... Suffered injury (April 13, 2002); missed final game of season.

STATISTICAL PLATEAUS: Three-goal games: 2001-02 (1).

		REGULAR SEASON								PLAYOFFS				
Season Team	League	Gms.	G	A	Pts.	PIM	+/-	PP	SH	Gms.	G	A	Pts.	PIM
96-97—Beauport	QMJHL	51	9	22	31	39	...	...	...	—	—	—	—	—
97-98—Quebec	QMJHL	53	30	39	69	26	...	...	...	12	11	5	16	23
98-99—Quebec	QMJHL	61	50	70	120	42	...	...	...	13	9	8	17	4
99-00—Philadelphia	NHL	80	20	28	48	22	11	8	1	17	5	5	10	2
00-01—Philadelphia	NHL	69	27	32	59	18	24	6	0	6	3	0	3	0
01-02—Philadelphia	NHL	79	33	33	66	32	31	4	1	5	0	0	0	2
—Can. Olympic team	Int'l	6	1	3	4	0	...	...	...	—	—	—	—	—
02-03—Philadelphia	NHL	46	9	18	27	16	20	1	1	13	4	1	5	6
NHL Totals (4 years)		274	89	111	200	88	86	19	3	41	12	6	18	10

GAINEY, STEVE   LW   STARS

PERSONAL: Born January 26, 1979, in Montreal. ... 6-0/180. ... Shoots left. ... Son of Bob Gainey, coach of Minnesota/Dallas Stars (1990-91 through January 8, 1996), general manager of Stars (1992-93 through January 25, 2002) and Hall of Fame center with Montreal Canadiens (1973-74 through 1988-89).

TRANSACTIONS/CAREER NOTES: Selected by Dallas Stars in third round (third Stars pick, 77th overall) of NHL entry draft (June 21, 1997).

		REGULAR SEASON								PLAYOFFS				
Season Team	League	Gms.	G	A	Pts.	PIM	+/-	PP	SH	Gms.	G	A	Pts.	PIM
95-96—Kamloops	WHL	49	1	4	5	40	...	...	...	3	0	0	0	0
96-97—Kamloops	WHL	60	9	18	27	60	...	...	...	2	0	0	0	9
97-98—Kamloops	WHL	68	21	34	55	93	...	...	...	7	1	7	8	15
98-99—Kamloops	WHL	68	30	34	64	155	...	...	...	15	5	4	9	38
99-00—Michigan	IHL	58	8	10	18	41	...	...	...	—	—	—	—	—
—Fort Wayne	UHL	1	0	0	0	0	...	...	...	—	—	—	—	—
00-01—Utah	IHL	61	7	7	14	167	...	...	...	—	—	—	—	—
—Dallas	NHL	1	0	0	0	0	0	0	0	—	—	—	—	—
01-02—Utah	AHL	58	16	18	34	87	...	...	...	—	—	—	—	—
—Dallas	NHL	5	0	1	1	7	-1	0	0	—	—	—	—	—
02-03—Utah	AHL	68	9	17	26	106	...	...	...	—	—	—	—	—
NHL Totals (2 years)		6	0	1	1	7	-1	0	0					

GAMACHE, SIMON   LW   THRASHERS

PERSONAL: Born January 3, 1981, in Thetford Mines, Que. ... 5-9/185. ... Shoots left.

TRANSACTIONS/CAREER NOTES: Selected by Atlanta Thrashers in ninth round (14th Thrashers pick, 290th overall) of NHL entry draft (June 25, 2000).

		REGULAR SEASON								PLAYOFFS				
Season Team	League	Gms.	G	A	Pts.	PIM	+/-	PP	SH	Gms.	G	A	Pts.	PIM
98-99—Val-d'Or	QMJHL	70	19	43	62	54	...	...	...	—	—	—	—	—
99-00—Val-d'Or	QMJHL	72	64	79	143	74	...	...	...	—	—	—	—	—
00-01—Val-d'Or	QMJHL	72	*74	*110	*184	70	...	...	...	21	*22	*35	*57	18
01-02—Chicago	AHL	26	2	4	6	11	...	...	...	—	—	—	—	—
—Greenville	ECHL	31	19	19	38	35	...	...	...	17	*15	9	*24	22
02-03—Chicago	AHL	76	35	42	77	37	...	...	...	—	—	—	—	—
—Atlanta	NHL	2	0	0	0	2	-1	0	0	—	—	—	—	—
NHL Totals (1 year)		2	0	0	0	2	-1	0	0					

GARON, MATHIEU   G   CANADIENS

PERSONAL: Born January 9, 1978, in Chandler, Que. ... 6-2/199. ... Catches right.

TRANSACTIONS/CAREER NOTES: Selected by Montreal Canadiens in second round (second Canadiens pick, 44th overall) of NHL entry draft (June 22, 1996).

		REGULAR SEASON									PLAYOFFS						
Season Team	League	Gms.	Min	W	L	T	GA	SO	Avg.	SV%	Gms.	Min.	W	L	GA	SO	Avg.	SV%
95-96—Victoriaville	QMJHL	51	2709	18	27	0	189	1	4.19	—	12	676	7	4	38	1	3.37	—
96-97—Victoriaville	QMJHL	53	3026	29	18	3	148	*6	2.93	—	6	330	2	4	23	0	4.18	—
97-98—Victoriaville	QMJHL	47	2802	27	18	2	125	5	2.68	—	6	345	2	4	22	0	3.83	—
98-99—Fredericton	AHL	40	2222	14	22	2	114	3	3.08	—	6	208	1	1	12	0	3.46	—
99-00—Quebec	AHL	53	2884	17	28	3	149	2	3.10	—	1	20	0	0	3	0	9.00	—
00-01—Montreal	NHL	11	589	4	5	1	24	2	2.44	.897	—	—	—	—	—	—	—	—
—Quebec	AHL	31	1768	16	13	1	86	1	2.92	—	8	459	4	4	22	1	2.88	—
01-02—Quebec	AHL	50	2987	21	15	†12	136	2	2.73	—	3	198	0	3	12	0	3.64	—
—Montreal	NHL	5	261	1	4	0	19	0	4.37	.871	—	—	—	—	—	—	—	—
02-03—Hamilton	AHL	20	1150	15	2	2	34	4	1.77	—	—	—	—	—	—	—	—	—
—Montreal	NHL	8	482	3	5	0	16	2	1.99	.940	—	—	—	—	—	—	—	—
NHL Totals (3 years)		24	1332	8	14	1	59	4	2.66	.909								

G

GAUSTAD, PAUL — C — SABRES

PERSONAL: Born February 3, 1982, in Fargo, N.D. ... 6-4/225. ... Shoots left.

Season Team	League	Gms.	G	A	Pts.	PIM	+/-	PP	SH	Gms.	G	A	Pts.	PIM
99-00—Portland	WHL	56	6	8	14	110	...	...	...	—	—	—	—	—
00-01—Portland	WHL	70	11	30	41	168	...	...	...	—	—	—	—	—
01-02—Portland	WHL	72	36	44	80	202	...	...	...	—	—	—	—	—
02-03—Rochester	AHL	80	14	39	53	137	...	...	...	—	—	—	—	—
—Buffalo	NHL	1	0	0	0	0	0	0	0	—	—	—	—	—
NHL Totals (1 year)		1	0	0	0	0	0	0	0					

GAUTHIER, DENIS — D — FLAMES

PERSONAL: Born October 1, 1976, in Montreal ... 6-2/224. ... Shoots left. ... Full Name: Denis Gauthier Jr. ... Name pronounced GO-tee-ay.
TRANSACTIONS/CAREER NOTES: Selected by Calgary Flames in first round (first Flames pick, 20th overall) of NHL entry draft (July 8, 1995). ... Suffered concussion (September 27, 1997); missed two games. ... Suffered concussion (January 10, 1999); missed two games. ... Injured groin (March 25, 1999); missed two games. ... Injured shoulder (October 26, 1999); missed 11 games. ... Suspended two games by NHL for elbowing incident (December 7, 1999). ... Suffered hip pointer (February 1, 2000); missed remainder of season. ... Injured wrist (October 15, 2000); missed 17 games. ... Injured shoulder (March 16, 2001); missed two games. ... Strained oblique muscle (October 22, 2001); missed five games. ... Suffered facial injury (December 31, 2001); missed two games. ... Injured shoulder (April 2, 2002); missed remainder of season.

Season Team	League	Gms.	G	A	Pts.	PIM	+/-	PP	SH	Gms.	G	A	Pts.	PIM
92-93—Drummondville	QMJHL	61	1	7	8	136	...	...	...	10	0	5	5	40
93-94—Drummondville	QMJHL	60	0	7	7	176	...	...	...	9	2	0	2	41
94-95—Drummondville	QMJHL	64	9	31	40	190	...	...	...	4	0	5	5	12
95-96—Drummondville	QMJHL	53	25	49	74	140	...	...	...	6	4	4	8	32
—Saint John	AHL	5	2	0	2	8	...	...	...	16	1	6	7	20
96-97—Saint John	AHL	73	3	28	31	74	...	...	...	5	0	0	0	6
97-98—Calgary	NHL	10	0	0	0	16	-5	0	0	—	—	—	—	—
—Saint John	AHL	68	4	20	24	154	...	...	...	21	0	4	4	83
98-99—Saint John	AHL	16	0	3	3	31	...	...	...	—	—	—	—	—
—Calgary	NHL	55	3	4	7	68	3	0	0	—	—	—	—	—
99-00—Calgary	NHL	39	1	1	2	50	-4	0	0	—	—	—	—	—
00-01—Calgary	NHL	62	2	6	8	78	3	0	0	—	—	—	—	—
01-02—Calgary	NHL	66	5	8	13	91	9	0	1	—	—	—	—	—
02-03—Calgary	NHL	72	1	11	12	99	5	0	0	—	—	—	—	—
NHL Totals (6 years)		304	12	30	42	402	11	0	1					

GAVEY, AARON — C — MAPLE LEAFS

PERSONAL: Born February 22, 1974, in Sudbury, Ont. ... 6-2/189. ... Shoots left. ... Name pronounced GAY-vee.
TRANSACTIONS/CAREER NOTES: Selected by Tampa Bay Lightning in fourth round (fourth Lightning pick, 74th overall) of NHL entry draft (June 20, 1992). ... Suffered facial laceration (February 4, 1996); missed eight games. ... Traded by Lightning to Calgary Flames for G Rick Tabaracci (November 19, 1996). ... Strained neck (February 28, 1997); missed 14 games. ... Strained abdominal muscle (January 11, 1997); missed 37 games. ... Sprained thumb (April 15, 1998); missed two games. ... Traded by Flames to Dallas Stars for C Bob Bassen (July 14, 1998). ... Fractured hand (September 22, 1998); missed first three games of 1998-99 season. ... Sprained knee (February 2, 2000); missed one game. ... Traded by Stars with C Pavel Patera, eighth-round pick (C Eric Johansson) in 2000 draft and fourth-round pick (traded to Los Angeles) in 2002 draft to Minnesota Wild for D Brad Lukowich, third-(C Yared Hagos) and ninth-round (RW Dale Sullivan) picks in 2001 draft (June 25, 2000). ... Bruised foot (November 14, 2000); missed three games. ... Lacerated face (October 27, 2001); missed three games. ... Suffered from the flu (March 18, 2002); missed two games. ... Fractured left foot (April 10, 2002); missed remainder of season. ... Signed as free agent by Toronto Maple Leafs (July 24, 2002).

Season Team	League	Gms.	G	A	Pts.	PIM	+/-	PP	SH	Gms.	G	A	Pts.	PIM
90-91—Peterborough Jr. B	OHA	42	26	30	56	68	...	...	...	—	—	—	—	—
91-92—Sault Ste. Marie	OHL	48	7	11	18	27	...	...	...	19	5	1	6	10
92-93—Sault Ste. Marie	OHL	62	45	39	84	114	...	...	...	18	5	9	14	36
93-94—Sault Ste. Marie	OHL	60	42	60	102	116	...	...	...	14	11	10	21	22
94-95—Atlanta	IHL	66	18	17	35	85	...	...	...	5	0	1	1	9
95-96—Tampa Bay	NHL	73	8	4	12	56	-6	1	1	6	0	0	0	4
96-97—Tampa Bay	NHL	16	1	2	3	12	-1	0	0	—	—	—	—	—
—Calgary	NHL	41	7	9	16	34	-11	3	0	—	—	—	—	—
97-98—Calgary	NHL	26	2	3	5	24	-5	0	0	—	—	—	—	—
—Saint John	AHL	8	4	3	7	28	...	...	...	—	—	—	—	—
98-99—Dallas	NHL	7	0	0	0	10	-1	0	0	—	—	—	—	—
—Michigan	IHL	67	24	33	57	128	...	...	...	5	2	3	5	4
99-00—Michigan	IHL	28	14	15	29	73	...	...	...	—	—	—	—	—
—Dallas	NHL	41	7	6	13	44	0	1	0	13	1	2	3	10
00-01—Minnesota	NHL	75	10	14	24	52	-8	1	0	—	—	—	—	—
01-02—Minnesota	NHL	71	6	11	17	38	-21	1	0	—	—	—	—	—
02-03—St. John's	AHL	70	14	29	43	83	...	...	...	—	—	—	—	—
—Toronto	NHL	5	0	1	1	0	1	0	0	—	—	—	—	—
NHL Totals (8 years)		355	41	50	91	270	-52	7	1	19	1	2	3	14

G

GELINAS, MARTIN   LW   FLAMES

PERSONAL: Born June 5, 1970, in Shawinigan, Que. ... 5-11/195. ... Shoots left. ... Name pronounced MAHR-tahn ZHEHL-ih-nuh.
TRANSACTIONS/CAREER NOTES: Selected by Los Angeles Kings in first round (first Kings pick, seventh overall) of NHL entry draft (June 11, 1988). ... Traded by Kings with C Jimmy Carson, first-round picks in 1989 (traded to New Jersey), 1991 (LW Martin Rucinsky) and 1993 (D Nick Stajduhar) drafts and cash to Edmonton Oilers for C Wayne Gretzky, RW//D Marty McSorley and LW/C Mike Krushelnyski (August 9, 1988). ... Suspended five games by NHL (March 9, 1990). ... Underwent shoulder surgery (June 1990). ... Traded by Oilers with sixth-round pick (C Nicholas Checco) in 1993 draft to Quebec Nordiques for LW Scott Pearson (June 20, 1993). ... Injured thigh (October 20, 1993); missed one game. ... Separated left shoulder (November 25, 1993); missed 10 games. ... Claimed on waivers by Vancouver Canucks (January 15, 1994). ... Suffered charley horse (March 27, 1994); missed six games. ... Injured knee (April 30, 1995); missed last game of season and eight playoff games. ... Fractured rib (November 2, 1996); missed eight games. ... Sprained knee (October 13, 1997); missed 16 games. ... Traded by Canucks with G Kirk McLean to Carolina Hurricanes for LW Geoff Sanderson, D Enrico Ciccone and G Sean Burke (January 3, 1998). ... Strained quadriceps (October 27, 1998); missed two games. ... Bruised thigh (April 3, 1999); missed four games. ... Injured knee (February 8, 2001); missed three games. ... Injured ankle (October 11, 2001); missed three games. ... Suffered concussion (January 25, 2002); missed seven games. ... Signed as free agent by Calgary Flames (July 2, 2002).
STATISTICAL PLATEAUS: Three-goal games: 1989-90 (1), 1996-97 (1). Total: 2. ... Four-goal games: 1996-97 (1). ... Total hat tricks: 3.

Season Team	League	REGULAR SEASON								PLAYOFFS				
		Gms.	G	A	Pts.	PIM	+/-	PP	SH	Gms.	G	A	Pts.	PIM
87-88—Hull	QMJHL	65	63	68	131	74	...	...	...	17	15	18	33	32
88-89—Edmonton	NHL	6	1	2	3	0	-1	0	0	—				
—Hull	QMJHL	41	38	39	77	31	...	...	...	9	5	4	9	14
89-90—Edmonton	NHL	46	17	8	25	30	0	5	0	20	2	3	5	6
90-91—Edmonton	NHL	73	20	20	40	34	-7	4	0	18	3	6	9	25
91-92—Edmonton	NHL	68	11	18	29	62	14	1	0	15	1	3	4	10
92-93—Edmonton	NHL	65	11	12	23	30	3	0	0	—				
93-94—Quebec	NHL	31	6	6	12	8	-2	0	0	—				
—Vancouver	NHL	33	8	8	16	26	-6	3	0	24	5	4	9	14
94-95—Vancouver	NHL	46	13	10	23	36	8	1	0	3	0	1	1	0
95-96—Vancouver	NHL	81	30	26	56	59	8	3	4	6	1	1	2	12
96-97—Vancouver	NHL	74	35	33	68	42	6	6	1	—				
97-98—Vancouver	NHL	24	4	4	8	10	-6	1	1	—				
—Carolina	NHL	40	12	14	26	30	1	2	1	—				
98-99—Carolina	NHL	76	13	15	28	67	3	0	0	6	0	3	3	2
99-00—Carolina	NHL	81	14	16	30	40	-10	3	0	—				
00-01—Carolina	NHL	79	23	29	52	59	-4	6	1	6	0	1	1	6
01-02—Carolina	NHL	72	13	16	29	30	-1	3	0	23	3	4	7	10
02-03—Calgary	NHL	81	21	31	52	51	-3	6	0	—				
NHL Totals (15 years)		976	252	268	520	614	3	44	8	121	15	26	41	85

GERBER, MARTIN   G   MIGHTY DUCKS

PERSONAL: Born September 3, 1974, in Burgdorf, Switzerland ... 5-11/195. ... Catches left.

Season Team	League	REGULAR SEASON									PLAYOFFS							
		Gms.	Min	W	L	T	GA	SO	Avg.	SV%	Gms.	Min.	W	L	GA	SO	Avg.	SV%
01-02—Farjestad Karlstad	Sweden	44	2664	...	...	...	87	*4	*1.96	—	†10	*657	...	...	18	†2	*1.64	—
02-03—Cincinnati	AHL	1	60	1	0	0	2	0	2.00	—	—							
—Anaheim	NHL	22	1203	6	11	3	39	1	1.95	.929	2	20	0	0	1	0	3.00	.833
NHL Totals (1 year)		22	1203	6	11	3	39	1	1.95	.929	2	20	0	0	1	0	3.00	.833

GERNANDER, KEN   C/LW   RANGERS

PERSONAL: Born June 30, 1969, in Grand Rapids, Minn. ... 5-10/175. ... Shoots left. ... Full Name: Kenneth Robert Gernander. ... Name pronounced juhr-NAN-duhr.
HIGH SCHOOL: Greenway (Coleraine, Minn.).
COLLEGE: Minnesota.
TRANSACTIONS/CAREER NOTES: Selected by Winnipeg Jets in fifth round (fourth Jets pick, 96th overall) of NHL entry draft (June 13, 1987). ... Signed as free agent by New York Rangers (September 9, 1994).

Season Team	League	REGULAR SEASON								PLAYOFFS				
		Gms.	G	A	Pts.	PIM	+/-	PP	SH	Gms.	G	A	Pts.	PIM
85-86—Greenway H.S.	USHS (West)	23	14	23	37	...	...	...	...	—				
86-87—Greenway H.S.	USHS (West)	26	35	34	69	...	...	...	...	—				
87-88—Univ. of Minnesota	WCHA	44	14	14	28	14	...	...	...	—				
88-89—Univ. of Minnesota	WCHA	44	9	11	20	2	...	...	...	—				
89-90—Univ. of Minnesota	WCHA	44	32	17	49	24	...	...	...	—				
90-91—Univ. of Minnesota	WCHA	44	23	20	43	24	...	...	...	—				
91-92—Moncton	AHL	43	8	18	26	9	...	...	...	8	1	1	2	2
—Fort Wayne	IHL	13	7	6	13	2	...	...	...	—				
92-93—Moncton	AHL	71	18	29	47	20	...	...	...	5	1	4	5	0
93-94—Moncton	AHL	71	22	25	47	12	...	...	...	19	6	1	7	0
94-95—Binghamton	AHL	80	28	25	53	24	...	...	...	11	2	2	4	6
95-96—Binghamton	AHL	63	44	29	73	38	...	...	...	—				
—New York Rangers	NHL	10	2	3	5	4	-3	2	0	6	0	0	0	0
96-97—Binghamton	AHL	46	13	18	31	30	...	...	...	2	0	1	1	0
—New York Rangers	NHL	—								9	0	0	0	0
97-98—Hartford	AHL	80	35	28	63	26	...	...	...	12	5	6	11	4
98-99—Hartford	AHL	70	23	26	49	32	...	...	...	7	1	2	3	2
—U.S. national team	Int'l	3	0	1	1	0	...	...	...	—				
99-00—Hartford	AHL	79	28	29	57	24	...	...	...	23	5	5	10	0
00-01—Hartford	AHL	80	22	27	49	39	...	...	...	2	0	0	0	0
01-02—Hartford	AHL	75	18	31	49	19	...	...	...	10	1	3	4	4
02-03—Hartford	AHL	72	17	19	36	22	...	...	...	—				
NHL Totals (2 years)		10	2	3	5	4	-3	2	0	15	0	0	0	0

G

GIGUERE, JEAN-SEBASTIEN   G   MIGHTY DUCKS

PERSONAL: Born May 16, 1977, in Montreal ... 6-1/200. ... Catches left. ... Name pronounced zhee-GAIR.

TRANSACTIONS/CAREER NOTES: Selected by Hartford Whalers in first round (first Whalers pick, 13th overall) of NHL entry draft (July 8, 1995). ... Whalers franchise moved to North Carolina and renamed Carolina Hurricanes for 1997-98 season; NHL approved move on June 25, 1997. ... Traded by Hurricanes with C Andrew Cassels to Calgary Flames for LW Gary Roberts and G Trevor Kidd (August 25, 1997). ... Strained hamstring (December 27, 1998); missed seven games. ... Traded by Flames to Mighty Ducks of Anaheim for second-round pick (traded to Washington) in 2000 draft (June 10, 2000). ... Strained groin prior to start of 2001-02 season; missed first five games of season.

Season Team	League	Gms.	Min	W	L	T	GA	SO	Avg.	SV%	Gms.	Min.	W	L	GA	SO	Avg.	SV%
			REGULAR SEASON									PLAYOFFS						
93-94—Verdun	QMJHL	25	1234	13	5	2	66	0	3.21	—	—	—	—	—	—	—	—	—
94-95—Halifax	QMJHL	47	2755	14	27	5	181	2	3.94	—	7	417	3	4	17	1	2.45	—
95-96—Verdun	QMJHL	55	3228	26	23	2	185	1	3.44	—	6	356	1	5	24	0	4.04	—
96-97—Halifax	QMJHL	50	3009	28	19	3	169	2	3.37	—	16	954	9	7	58	0	3.65	—
—Hartford	NHL	8	394	1	4	0	24	0	3.65	.881	—	—	—	—	—	—	—	—
97-98—Saint John	AHL	31	1758	16	10	3	72	2	2.46	—	10	537	5	3	27	0	3.02	—
98-99—Saint John	AHL	39	2145	18	16	3	123	3	3.44	—	7	304	3	2	21	0	4.14	—
—Calgary	NHL	15	860	6	7	1	46	0	3.21	.897	—	—	—	—	—	—	—	—
99-00—Saint John	AHL	41	2243	17	17	3	114	0	3.05	—	3	178	0	3	9	0	3.03	—
—Calgary	NHL	7	330	1	3	1	15	0	2.73	.914	—	—	—	—	—	—	—	—
00-01—Cincinnati	AHL	23	1306	12	7	2	53	0	2.43	—	—	—	—	—	—	—	—	—
—Anaheim	NHL	34	2031	11	17	5	87	4	2.57	.911	—	—	—	—	—	—	—	—
01-02—Anaheim	NHL	53	3127	20	25	6	111	4	2.13	.920	—	—	—	—	—	—	—	—
02-03—Anaheim	NHL	65	3775	34	22	6	145	2	2.30	.920	21	1407	15	6	38	5	*1.62	*.945
NHL Totals (6 years)		182	10517	73	78	19	428	16	2.44	.914	21	1407	15	6	38	5	1.62	.945

GILCHRIST, BRENT   LW

PERSONAL: Born April 3, 1967, in Moose Jaw, Sask. ... 5-11/180. ... Shoots left.

TRANSACTIONS/CAREER NOTES: Selected by Montreal Canadiens in sixth round (sixth Canadiens pick, 79th overall) of NHL entry draft (June 15, 1985). ... Injured knee (January 1987). ... Fractured right index finger (November 17, 1990); missed 19 games. ... Separated left shoulder (February 6, 1991); missed two games. ... Reinjured left shoulder (February 13, 1991); missed five games. ... Traded by Canadiens with LW Shayne Corson and LW Vladimir Vujtek to Edmonton Oilers for LW Vincent Damphousse and fourth-round pick (D Adam Wiesel) in 1993 draft (August 27, 1992). ... Suffered concussion (October 1992); missed two games. ... Fractured nose (December 21, 1992); missed two games. ... Traded by Oilers to Minnesota North Stars for C Todd Elik (March 5, 1993). ... Separated shoulder (March 18, 1993); missed remainder of season. ... North Stars franchise moved from Minnesota to Dallas and renamed Stars for 1993-94 season. ... Strained shoulder (October 27, 1993); missed four games. ... Pulled groin (November 21, 1993); missed four games. ... Strained groin (February 20, 1995); missed two games. ... Strained groin and sprained wrist (February 26, 1995); missed 13 games. ... Suffered from sore wrist (April 11, 1995); missed one game. ... Injured groin (October 14, 1995); missed four games. ... Strained hip flexor (November 6, 1996); missed two games. ... Strained groin (December 21, 1996); missed three games. ... Strained groin (March 5, 1997); missed two games. ... Strained groin (March 16, 1997); missed seven games. ... Signed as free agent by Detroit Red Wings (July 8, 1997). ... Injured groin (March 4, 1998); missed 20 games. ... Selected by Tampa Bay Lightning from Red Wings in NHL waiver draft (October 5, 1998). ... Traded by Lightning to Red Wings for sixth-round pick (traded back to Detroit) in 1999 draft (October 5, 1998). ... Underwent surgery for hernia (September 21, 1998); missed first 68 games of season. ... Strained lower abdominal muscle (March 21, 1999); missed eight games. ... Suffered hernia prior to start of 1999-2000 season; missed first 56 games of season. ... Injured groin (November 17, 2000); missed four games. ... Suffered eye injury (November 7, 2001); missed three games. ... Claimed on waivers by Stars (February 13, 2002). ... Signed as free agent by Nashville Predators (July 11, 2002).

STATISTICAL PLATEAUS: Three-goal games: 1991-92 (1).

Season Team	League	Gms.	G	A	Pts.	PIM	+/-	PP	SH	Gms.	G	A	Pts.	PIM
			REGULAR SEASON								PLAYOFFS			
83-84—Kelowna	WHL	69	16	11	27	16	...	...	...	—	—	—	—	—
84-85—Kelowna	WHL	51	35	38	73	58	...	...	...	6	5	2	7	8
85-86—Spokane	WHL	52	45	45	90	57	...	...	...	9	6	7	13	19
86-87—Spokane	WHL	46	45	55	100	71	...	...	...	5	2	7	9	6
—Sherbrooke	AHL	—	—	—	—	—	—	—	—	10	2	7	9	2
87-88—Sherbrooke	AHL	77	26	48	74	83	...	...	...	6	1	3	4	6
88-89—Montreal	NHL	49	8	16	24	16	9	0	0	9	1	1	2	10
—Sherbrooke	AHL	7	6	5	11	7	...	...	...	—	—	—	—	—
89-90—Montreal	NHL	57	9	15	24	28	3	1	0	8	2	0	2	2
90-91—Montreal	NHL	51	6	9	15	10	-3	1	0	13	5	3	8	6
91-92—Montreal	NHL	79	23	27	50	57	29	2	0	11	2	4	6	6
92-93—Edmonton	NHL	60	10	10	20	47	-10	2	0	—	—	—	—	—
—Minnesota	NHL	8	0	1	1	2	-2	0	0	—	—	—	—	—
93-94—Dallas	NHL	76	17	14	31	31	0	3	1	9	3	1	4	2
94-95—Dallas	NHL	32	9	4	13	16	-3	1	3	5	0	1	1	2
95-96—Dallas	NHL	77	20	22	42	36	-11	6	1	—	—	—	—	—
96-97—Dallas	NHL	67	10	20	30	24	6	2	0	6	2	2	4	2
97-98—Detroit	NHL	61	13	14	27	40	4	5	0	15	2	1	3	12
98-99—Detroit	NHL	5	1	0	1	0	-1	0	0	3	0	0	0	0
99-00—Detroit	NHL	24	4	2	6	24	1	0	0	6	0	0	0	6
00-01—Detroit	NHL	60	1	8	9	41	-8	0	0	5	0	1	1	0
01-02—Detroit	NHL	19	1	1	2	8	-3	0	0	—	—	—	—	—
—Dallas	NHL	26	2	5	7	6	-6	0	0	—	—	—	—	—
02-03—Nashville	NHL	41	1	2	3	14	-11	0	0	—	—	—	—	—
NHL Totals (15 years)		792	135	170	305	400	-6	23	5	90	17	14	31	48

G

PERSONAL: Born April 6, 1975, in Concord, Mass. ... 6-7/230. ... Shoots left.
TRANSACTIONS/CAREER NOTES: Selected by Boston Bruins in eighth round (eighth Bruins pick, 207th overall) of NHL entry draft (June 26, 1993). ... Suffered from the flu (January 21, 1998); missed one game. ... Strained hip flexor (April 7, 1999); missed two games. ... Suffered from the flu (January 11, 2000); missed one game. ... Suffered tendinitis in shoulder (December 4, 2001); missed two games. ... Bruised foot (April 6, 2002); missed one game.

				REGULAR SEASON						PLAYOFFS				
Season Team	League	Gms.	G	A	Pts.	PIM	+/-	PP	SH	Gms.	G	A	Pts.	PIM
93-94—Providence College	Hockey East	31	1	2	3	26	...	...	...	—	—	—	—	—
94-95—Providence College	Hockey East	26	1	3	4	22	...	...	...	—	—	—	—	—
95-96—Providence College	Hockey East	39	5	12	17	54	...	...	...	—	—	—	—	—
96-97—Providence College	Hockey East	35	5	16	21	52	...	...	...	—	—	—	—	—
97-98—Boston	NHL	68	2	4	6	47	4	0	0	6	0	0	0	4
—Providence	AHL	4	1	0	1	23	...	...	...	—	—	—	—	—
98-99—Boston	NHL	80	3	7	10	63	-10	0	0	12	0	0	0	14
99-00—Boston	NHL	81	3	9	12	51	0	0	0	—	—	—	—	—
00-01—Boston	NHL	80	1	10	11	71	-2	0	0	—	—	—	—	—
01-02—Boston	NHL	79	4	18	22	77	16	0	0	6	0	1	1	2
02-03—Boston	NHL	76	4	13	17	56	21	0	0	5	0	0	0	4
NHL Totals (6 years)		464	17	61	78	365	29	0	0	29	0	1	1	24

PERSONAL: Born November 9, 1965, in Cardinal, Ont. ... 6-0/180. ... Shoots left.
TRANSACTIONS/CAREER NOTES: Selected by Toronto Maple Leafs in second round (second Maple Leafs pick, 25th overall) of NHL entry draft (June 9, 1984). ... Fractured right foot (October 1987). ... Bruised shoulder (March 1989). ... Fractured finger (October 15, 1991); missed three games. ... Strained back (February 8, 1992); missed three games. ... Injured back prior to 1992-93 season; missed first two games of season. ... Bruised foot (November 14, 1992); missed 11 games. ... Strained groin (November 1, 1993); missed 26 games. ... Suffered back spasms (February 24, 1994); missed 13 games. ... Injured shoulder (March 17, 1995); missed one game. ... Pulled hamstring (November 10, 1995); missed four games. ... Suffered back spasms (February 7, 1996); missed four games. ... Traded by Maple Leafs to San Jose Sharks for C Jamie Baker and fifth-round pick (C Peter Cava) in 1996 draft (June 14, 1996). ... Suffered sore knee (April 9, 1997); missed three games. ... Traded by Sharks to St. Louis Blues for RW Joe Murphy (March 24, 1998). ... Bruised foot (November 23, 1998); missed three games. ... Claimed on waivers by Detroit Red Wings (December 30, 1998). ... Fractured forearm (February 1, 1999); missed 24 games. ... Signed as free agent by Phoenix Coyotes (July 15, 1999). ... Strained muscle in abdomen (November 23, 1999); missed seven games. ... Lacerated face (December 22, 1999); missed one game. ... Strained muscle in abdomen (January 8, 2000); missed 13 games. ... Traded by Coyotes to Red Wings for LW Philippe Audet (March 13, 2000). ... Signed as free agent by Colorado Avalanche (July 24, 2001). ... Underwent shoulder surgery (November 12, 2001); missed seven games. ... Released by Avalanche (February 11, 2002). ... Signed by Chicago Blackhawks (March 5, 2003).

				REGULAR SEASON						PLAYOFFS				
Season Team	League	Gms.	G	A	Pts.	PIM	+/-	PP	SH	Gms.	G	A	Pts.	PIM
81-82—Brockville	OJHL	48	5	16	21	169	...	...	...	—	—	—	—	—
82-83—Windsor	OHL	70	12	24	36	108	...	...	...	3	0	0	0	11
83-84—Windsor	OHL	68	9	48	57	184	...	...	...	3	1	1	2	10
84-85—Toronto	NHL	10	1	0	1	13	-1	0	0	—	—	—	—	—
—Windsor	OHL	53	17	40	57	148	...	...	...	4	0	1	1	14
85-86—St. Catharines	AHL	58	8	25	33	90	...	...	...	10	1	6	7	17
—Toronto	NHL	15	1	2	3	28	0	0	0	1	0	0	0	0
86-87—Newmarket	AHL	11	1	8	9	33	...	...	...	—	—	—	—	—
—Toronto	NHL	61	4	27	31	92	-3	1	0	13	2	2	4	42
87-88—Newmarket	AHL	2	0	1	1	2	...	...	...	—	—	—	—	—
—Toronto	NHL	65	8	17	25	131	-20	1	0	6	1	3	4	20
88-89—Toronto	NHL	59	11	14	25	72	-3	0	0	—	—	—	—	—
89-90—Toronto	NHL	48	1	14	15	92	-8	0	0	5	0	3	3	16
90-91—Toronto	NHL	72	2	22	24	113	-4	0	0	—	—	—	—	—
91-92—Toronto	NHL	74	2	15	17	91	-22	1	0	—	—	—	—	—
92-93—Toronto	NHL	69	11	32	43	66	4	5	0	21	1	10	11	26
93-94—Toronto	NHL	45	4	24	28	44	8	2	0	18	1	5	6	37
94-95—Toronto	NHL	47	7	25	32	64	-8	3	1	7	0	3	3	6
95-96—Toronto	NHL	74	7	18	25	116	-15	1	0	6	0	0	0	24
96-97—San Jose	NHL	79	0	21	21	101	-20	0	0	—	—	—	—	—
97-98—San Jose	NHL	64	8	13	21	31	-13	4	0	—	—	—	—	—
—St. Louis	NHL	11	5	4	9	10	2	3	0	10	2	2	4	10
98-99—St. Louis	NHL	28	2	3	5	16	-6	1	0	—	—	—	—	—
—Detroit	NHL	23	2	2	4	11	-4	0	0	2	0	1	1	0
99-00—Phoenix	NHL	41	1	6	7	30	-10	0	0	—	—	—	—	—
—Detroit	NHL	13	2	0	2	15	2	0	0	9	0	1	1	4
00-01—Cincinnati	AHL	2	0	1	1	2	...	...	...	—	—	—	—	—
—Detroit	NHL	68	3	8	11	53	17	0	1	5	0	0	0	8
01-02—Colorado	NHL	36	0	4	4	25	3	0	0	—	—	—	—	—
02-03—Springfield	AHL	15	1	5	6	20	...	...	...	—	—	—	—	—
—Chicago	NHL	5	0	1	1	0	3	0	0	—	—	—	—	—
—Norfolk	AHL	9	0	3	3	10	...	...	...	—	—	—	—	—
NHL Totals (19 years)		1007	82	272	354	1214	-98	22	2	103	7	30	37	193

PERSONAL: Born June 25, 1963, in Kingston, Ont. ... 5-11/177. ... Shoots left. ... Full Name: Douglas Gilmour.
TRANSACTIONS/CAREER NOTES: Selected by St. Louis Blues in seventh round (fourth Blues pick, 134th overall) of NHL entry draft (June 9, 1982). ... Sprained ankle (October 7, 1985); missed four games. ... Suffered concussion (January 1988). ... Bruised shoulder (March 1988). ... Traded by Blues with RW Mark Hunter, LW Steve Bozek and D/RW Michael Dark to Calgary Flames for C Mike Bullard, C Craig Coxe and D Tim Corkery (September 5, 1988). ... Suffered abscessed jaw (March 1989); missed six games. ... Fractured bone in right foot (August 12, 1989). ... Traded by Flames with D Ric Nattress, D Jamie Macoun, LW Kent Manderville and G Rick Wamsley to Toronto Maple Leafs for LW

G

Craig Berube, D Alexander Godynyuk, LW Gary Leeman, D Michel Petit and G Jeff Reese (January 2, 1992). ... Suspended eight off-days and fined $500 by NHL for slashing (November 27, 1992). ... Suspended one preseason game and fined $500 by NHL for headbutting (September 26, 1993). ... Played in Europe during 1994-95 NHL lockout. ... Suffered pinched nerve in neck (February 8, 1995); missed one game. ... Fractured nose (April 7, 1995); missed three games. ... Bruised ribs (March 19, 1996); missed one game. ... Traded by Maple Leafs with D Dave Ellett and third-round pick (D Andre Lakos) in 1999 draft to New Jersey Devils for D Jason Smith, C Steve Sullivan and C Alyn McCauley (February 25, 1997). ... Bruised eye (March 5, 1997); missed three games. ... Injured knee (March 5, 1998) and underwent surgery; missed 18 games. ... Signed as free agent by Chicago Blackhawks (July 3, 1998). ... Injured back (March 27, 1999) and underwent surgery; missed final 10 games of season. ... Bruised ribs (March 1, 2000); missed five games. ... Traded by Blackhawks with RW Jean-Pierre Dumont to Buffalo Sabres for LW Michal Grosek (March 10, 2000). ... Suffered from the flu (April 7, 2000); missed final two games of season. ... Injured hip (November 22, 2000); missed 10 games. ... Signed as free agent by Montreal Canadiens (October 6, 2001). ... Suspended one game by NHL for unsportsmanlike conduct (October 27, 2001). ... Injured back (December 22, 2001); missed three games. ... Traded by Canadiens to Maple Leafs for sixth-round pick in 2003 draft (March 11, 2003).

STATISTICAL PLATEAUS: Three-goal games: 1985-86 (1), 1987-88 (1), 1993-94 (1). Total: 3.

			REGULAR SEASON								PLAYOFFS			
Season Team	League	Gms.	G	A	Pts.	PIM	+/-	PP	SH		Gms.	G	A	Pts.	PIM
80-81—Cornwall	QMJHL	51	12	23	35	35	...	...	...		—	—	—	—	—
81-82—Cornwall	OHL	67	46	73	119	42	...	...	...		5	6	9	15	2
82-83—Cornwall	OHL	68	*70	*107	*177	62	...	...	...		8	8	10	18	16
83-84—St. Louis	NHL	80	25	28	53	57	6	3	1		11	2	9	11	10
84-85—St. Louis	NHL	78	21	36	57	49	3	3	1		3	1	1	2	2
85-86—St. Louis	NHL	74	25	28	53	41	-3	2	1		19	9	12	†21	25
86-87—St. Louis	NHL	80	42	63	105	58	-2	17	1		6	2	2	4	16
87-88—St. Louis	NHL	72	36	50	86	59	-13	19	2		10	3	14	17	18
88-89—Calgary	NHL	72	26	59	85	44	45	11	0		22	11	11	22	20
89-90—Calgary	NHL	78	24	67	91	54	20	12	1		6	3	1	4	8
90-91—Calgary	NHL	78	20	61	81	144	27	2	2		7	1	1	2	0
91-92—Calgary	NHL	38	11	27	38	46	12	4	1		—	—	—	—	—
—Toronto	NHL	40	15	34	49	32	13	6	0		—	—	—	—	—
92-93—Toronto	NHL	83	32	95	127	100	32	15	3		21	10	†25	35	30
93-94—Toronto	NHL	83	27	84	111	105	25	10	1		18	6	22	28	42
94-95—Rapperswil	Switzerland	9	2	13	15	16	...	...	...		—	—	—	—	—
—Toronto	NHL	44	10	23	33	26	-5	3	0		7	0	6	6	6
95-96—Toronto	NHL	81	32	40	72	77	-5	10	2		6	1	7	8	12
96-97—Toronto	NHL	61	15	45	60	46	-5	2	1		—	—	—	—	—
—New Jersey	NHL	20	7	15	22	22	7	2	0		10	0	4	4	14
97-98—New Jersey	NHL	63	13	40	53	68	10	3	0		6	5	2	7	4
98-99—Chicago	NHL	72	16	40	56	56	-16	7	1		—	—	—	—	—
99-00—Chicago	NHL	63	22	34	56	51	-12	8	0		—	—	—	—	—
—Buffalo	NHL	11	3	14	17	12	3	2	0		5	0	1	1	0
00-01—Buffalo	NHL	71	7	31	38	70	3	4	0		13	2	4	6	12
01-02—Montreal	NHL	70	10	31	41	48	-7	5	0		12	4	6	10	16
02-03—Montreal	NHL	61	11	19	30	36	-6	3	0		—	—	—	—	—
—Toronto	NHL	1	0	0	0	0	0	0	0		—	—	—	—	—
NHL Totals (20 years)		1474	450	964	1414	1301	132	153	18		182	60	128	188	235

GIONTA, BRIAN   RW   DEVILS

PERSONAL: Born January 18, 1979, in Rochester, N.Y. ... 5-7/175. ... Shoots right.
TRANSACTIONS/CAREER NOTES: Selected by New Jersey Devils in third round (fourth Devils pick, 82nd overall) of NHL entry draft (June 27, 1998).

			REGULAR SEASON								PLAYOFFS			
Season Team	League	Gms.	G	A	Pts.	PIM	+/-	PP	SH		Gms.	G	A	Pts.	PIM
97-98—Boston College	Hockey East	40	30	32	62	44	...	...	...		—	—	—	—	—
98-99—Boston College	Hockey East	39	27	33	60	46	...	...	...		—	—	—	—	—
99-00—Boston College	Hockey East	42	*33	23	56	66	...	...	...		—	—	—	—	—
00-01—Boston College	Hockey East	43	*33	21	*54	47	...	...	...		—	—	—	—	—
01-02—Albany	AHL	37	9	16	25	18	...	...	...		—	—	—	—	—
—New Jersey	NHL	33	4	7	11	8	10	0	0		6	2	2	4	0
02-03—New Jersey	NHL	58	12	13	25	23	5	2	0		24	1	8	9	6
NHL Totals (2 years)		91	16	20	36	31	15	2	0		30	3	10	13	6

GIRARD, JONATHAN   D   BRUINS

PERSONAL: Born May 27, 1980, in Joliette, Que. ... 5-11/192. ... Shoots right.
TRANSACTIONS/CAREER NOTES: Selected by Boston Bruins in second round (first Bruins pick, 48th overall) of NHL entry draft (June 27, 1998). ... Re-signed by Bruins (July 15, 2003).

			REGULAR SEASON								PLAYOFFS			
Season Team	League	Gms.	G	A	Pts.	PIM	+/-	PP	SH		Gms.	G	A	Pts.	PIM
96-97—Laval	QMJHL	38	11	21	32	23	...	...	...		3	0	3	3	0
97-98—Laval	QMJHL	64	20	47	67	44	...	...	...		16	2	16	18	13
98-99—Acadie-Bathurst	QMJHL	50	9	58	67	60	...	...	...		23	13	18	31	22
—Boston	NHL	3	0	0	0	0	1	0	0		—	—	—	—	—
99-00—Boston	NHL	23	1	2	3	2	-1	0	0		—	—	—	—	—
—Providence	AHL	5	0	1	1	0	...	...	...		—	—	—	—	—
—Moncton	QMJHL	26	10	25	35	36	...	...	...		16	3	15	18	36
00-01—Boston	NHL	31	3	13	16	14	2	2	0		—	—	—	—	—
—Providence	AHL	39	3	21	24	6	...	...	...		17	0	5	5	4
01-02—Providence	AHL	59	6	31	37	36	...	...	...		—	—	—	—	—
—Boston	NHL	20	0	3	3	9	0	0	0		1	0	0	0	2
02-03—Boston	NHL	73	6	16	22	21	4	2	0		2	0	1	1	0
NHL Totals (5 years)		150	10	34	44	46	6	4	0		3	0	1	1	2

G

GIROUX, ALEXANDRE   C   SENATORS

PERSONAL: Born June 16, 1981, in Quebec. ... 6-2/165. ... Shoots left.
TRANSACTIONS/CAREER NOTES: Selected by Ottawa Senators in seventh round (ninth Senators pick, 213th overall) of NHL entry draft (June 26, 1999).

			REGULAR SEASON							PLAYOFFS				
Season Team	League	Gms.	G	A	Pts.	PIM	+/-	PP	SH	Gms.	G	A	Pts.	PIM
98-99—Hull	QMJHL	67	15	22	37	124	...	...	...	22	2	2	4	8
99-00—Hull	QMJHL	72	52	47	99	117	...	...	...	15	12	6	18	30
00-01—Hull	QMJHL	38	31	32	63	62	...	...	...	—	—	—	—	—
—Rouyn-Noranda	QMJHL	25	13	14	27	56	...	...	...	9	2	6	8	22
01-02—Grand Rapids	AHL	70	11	16	27	74	...	...	...	—	—	—	—	—
02-03—Binghamton	AHL	67	19	16	35	101	...	...	...	—	—	—	—	—

GIROUX, RAY   D   DEVILS

PERSONAL: Born July 20, 1976, in North Bay, Ont. ... 6-1/190. ... Shoots left. ... Full Name: Raymond Giroux.
COLLEGE: Yale.
TRANSACTIONS/CAREER NOTES: Selected by Philadelphia Flyers in eighth round (seventh Flyers pick, 202nd overall) of NHL entry draft (June 29, 1994). ... Rights traded by Flyers to New York Islanders for sixth-round pick (traded to Montreal) in 2000 draft (August 25, 1998). ... Fractured finger (February 10, 2000); missed 12 games. ... Signed as free agent by New Jersey Devils (July 12, 2002).

			REGULAR SEASON							PLAYOFFS				
Season Team	League	Gms.	G	A	Pts.	PIM	+/-	PP	SH	Gms.	G	A	Pts.	PIM
93-94—Powasson	Jr. A	36	10	40	50	42	...	...	...	—	—	—	—	—
94-95—Yale University	ECAC	31	1	9	10	20	...	...	...	—	—	—	—	—
95-96—Yale University	ECAC	30	3	17	20	36	...	...	...	—	—	—	—	—
96-97—Yale University	ECAC	32	9	12	21	38	...	...	...	—	—	—	—	—
97-98—Yale University	ECAC	35	9	30	39	62	...	...	...	—	—	—	—	—
98-99—Lowell	AHL	59	13	19	32	92	...	...	...	3	1	1	2	0
99-00—Lowell	AHL	49	12	21	33	34	...	...	...	7	0	0	0	2
—New York Islanders	NHL	14	0	9	9	10	0	0	0	—	—	—	—	—
00-01—AIK Solna	Sweden	9	0	1	1	16	...	...	...	—	—	—	—	—
—HIFK Helsinki	Finland	22	3	9	12	34	...	...	...	—	—	—	—	—
—Jokerit Helsinki	Finland	24	4	9	13	16	...	...	...	5	0	0	0	0
01-02—Bridgeport	AHL	79	13	40	53	73	...	...	...	19	1	7	8	20
—New York Islanders	NHL	2	0	0	0	2	-1	0	0	—	—	—	—	—
02-03—Albany	AHL	67	11	38	49	49	...	...	...	—	—	—	—	—
—New Jersey	NHL	11	0	1	1	6	-2	0	0	—	—	—	—	—
NHL Totals (3 years)		27	0	10	10	18	-3	0	0					

GLEASON, TIM   D   KINGS

PERSONAL: Born January 29, 1983, in Southfield, Mich. ... 6-0/199. ... Shoots left.
TRANSACTIONS/CAREER NOTES: Selected by Ottawa Senators in first round (second Senators pick, 23rd overall) of NHL entry draft (June 23, 2001). ... Traded by Senators to Los Angeles Kings for C Bryan Smolinski (March 11, 2003). ... Re-signed by Kings (June 1, 2003).

			REGULAR SEASON							PLAYOFFS				
Season Team	League	Gms.	G	A	Pts.	PIM	+/-	PP	SH	Gms.	G	A	Pts.	PIM
99-00—Windsor	OHL	55	5	13	18	101	...	...	...	12	2	4	6	14
00-01—Windsor	OHL	47	8	26	34	124	...	...	...	9	1	2	3	23
01-02—Windsor	OHL	67	17	42	59	109	...	...	...	16	7	13	20	40
02-03—Windsor	OHL	45	7	31	38	75	...	...	...	—	—	—	—	—

GLOBKE, ROB   C/RW   PANTHERS

PERSONAL: Born October 24, 1982, in Farmington, Mich. ... 6-2/200. ... Shoots right. ... Full Name: Rob ` Globke.
TRANSACTIONS/CAREER NOTES: Selected by Florida Panthers in second round (third Panthers pick, 40th overall) of NHL entry draft (June 22, 2002).

			REGULAR SEASON							PLAYOFFS				
Season Team	League	Gms.	G	A	Pts.	PIM	+/-	PP	SH	Gms.	G	A	Pts.	PIM
00-01—Univ. of Notre Dame	CCHA	33	17	9	26	74	...	...	...	—	—	—	—	—
01-02—Univ. of Notre Dame	CCHA	29	11	11	22	73	...	...	...	—	—	—	—	—
02-03—Univ. of Notre Dame	CCHA	40	21	15	36	44	...	...	...	—	—	—	—	—

GOC, MARCEL   C   SHARKS

PERSONAL: Born August 24, 1983, in Calw, West Germany. ... 6-1/187. ... Shoots left. ... Brother of Sasha Goc, defenseman, Tampa Bay Lightning.
TRANSACTIONS/CAREER NOTES: Selected by San Jose Sharks in first round (first Sharks pick, 20th overall) of NHL entry draft (June 23, 2001). ... Signed by Sharks (July 10, 2003).

			REGULAR SEASON							PLAYOFFS				
Season Team	League	Gms.	G	A	Pts.	PIM	+/-	PP	SH	Gms.	G	A	Pts.	PIM
99-00—Schwenningen	Germany	62	1	4	5	6	...	...	...	—	—	—	—	—
00-01—Schwenningen	Germany	58	13	28	41	12	...	...	...	—	—	—	—	—
01-02—Schwenningen	Germany	45	8	9	17	24	...	...	...	—	—	—	—	—
—Mannheim	Germany	8	0	2	2	0	...	...	...	—	—	—	—	—
02-03—Mannheim	Germany	36	6	14	20	16	...	...	...	8	1	2	3	0

G

GODARD, ERIC   RW   ISLANDERS

PERSONAL: Born March 7, 1980, in Vernon, B.C. ... 6-4/227. ... Shoots right.
TRANSACTIONS/CAREER NOTES: Signed as non-drafted free agent by Florida Panthers (September 24, 1999). ... Traded by Panthers to New York Islanders for third-round pick (C/LW Gregory Campbell) in 2002 draft (June 22, 2002). ... Suspended one playoff game by NHL for high-sticking incident (April 10, 2003). ... Re-signed by Islanders (June 24, 2003).

		REGULAR SEASON								PLAYOFFS				
Season Team	League	Gms.	G	A	Pts.	PIM	+/-	PP	SH	Gms.	G	A	Pts.	PIM
97-98—Lethbridge	WHL	7	0	0	0	26	...	...	...	2	0	0	0	0
98-99—Lethbridge	WHL	66	2	5	7	213	...	...	...	4	0	0	0	14
99-00—Lethbridge	WHL	60	3	5	8	*310	...	...	...	—	—	—	—	—
—Louisville	AHL	4	0	1	1	16	...	...	...	—	—	—	—	—
00-01—Louisville	AHL	45	0	0	0	132	...	...	...	—	—	—	—	—
01-02—Bridgeport	AHL	67	1	4	5	198	...	...	...	20	0	4	4	30
02-03—Bridgeport	AHL	46	2	2	4	199	...	...	...	—	—	—	—	—
—New York Islanders	NHL	19	0	0	0	48	-3	0	0	2	0	1	1	4
NHL Totals (1 year)		19	0	0	0	48	-3	0	0	2	0	1	1	4

GOEHRING, KARL   G   BLUE JACKETS

PERSONAL: Born August 23, 1978, in Apple Valley, Minn. ... 5-8/160. ... Catches left.
COLLEGE: North Dakota.
TRANSACTIONS/CAREER NOTES: Signed as non-drafted free agent by Columbus Blue Jackets (May 7, 2001).

		REGULAR SEASON								PLAYOFFS							
Season Team	League	Gms.	Min	W	L	T	GA	SO	Avg.	SV%	Gms.	Min.	W	L	GA	SO	Avg.	SV%
97-98—Univ. of North Dakota	WCHA	27	1504	23	3	1	57	1	2.27	—	—	—	—	—	—	—	—	—
98-99—Univ. of North Dakota	WCHA	31	1774	22	5	2	71	3	2.40	—	—	—	—	—	—	—	—	—
99-00—Univ. of North Dakota	WCHA	30	1747	19	6	†4	55	8	*1.89	—	—	—	—	—	—	—	—	—
00-01—Univ. of North Dakota	WCHA	30	1661	16	6	*6	66	†3	2.38	—	—	—	—	—	—	—	—	—
01-02—Syracuse	AHL	15	890	5	6	3	37	1	2.49	—	—	—	—	—	—	—	—	—
—Dayton	ECHL	23	1393	11	9	3	52	2	2.24	—	†14	*865	9	†5	*35	1	2.43	—
02-03—Syracuse	AHL	49	2608	18	21	4	116	4	2.67	—	—	—	—	—	—	—	—	—

GOMEZ, SCOTT   C   DEVILS

PERSONAL: Born December 23, 1979, in Anchorage, Ala. ... 5-11/200. ... Shoots left.
TRANSACTIONS/CAREER NOTES: Selected by New Jersey Devils in first round (second Devils pick, 27th overall) of NHL entry draft (June 27, 1998). ... Injured back (February 17, 2001); missed six games. ... Fractured left hand (April 1, 2002); missed remainder of season.
STATISTICAL PLATEAUS: Three-goal games: 1999-00 (1).

		REGULAR SEASON								PLAYOFFS				
Season Team	League	Gms.	G	A	Pts.	PIM	+/-	PP	SH	Gms.	G	A	Pts.	PIM
96-97—Surrey Jr. A	BCJHL	56	48	76	124	94	...	...	...	—	—	—	—	—
97-98—Tri-City	WHL	45	12	37	49	57	...	...	...	—	—	—	—	—
98-99—Tri-City	WHL	58	30	*78	108	55	...	...	...	10	6	13	19	31
99-00—New Jersey	NHL	82	19	51	70	78	14	7	0	23	4	6	10	4
00-01—New Jersey	NHL	76	14	49	63	46	-1	2	0	25	5	9	14	24
01-02—New Jersey	NHL	76	10	38	48	36	-4	1	0	—	—	—	—	—
02-03—New Jersey	NHL	80	13	42	55	48	17	2	0	24	3	9	12	2
NHL Totals (4 years)		314	56	180	236	208	26	12	0	72	12	24	36	30

GONCHAR, SERGEI   D   CAPITALS

PERSONAL: Born April 13, 1974, in Chelyabinsk, U.S.S.R. ... 6-1/212. ... Shoots left. ... Name pronounced GAHN-shahr.
TRANSACTIONS/CAREER NOTES: Selected by Washington Capitals in first round (first Capitals pick, 14th overall) of NHL entry draft (June 20, 1992). ... Injured groin (November 30, 1995); missed two games. ... Suffered from the flu (December 13, 1995); missed one game. ... Suffered from the flu (November 7, 1996); missed one game. ... Hyperextended elbow (November 18, 1996); missed one game. ... Suffered back spasms (December 28, 1996); missed eight games. ... Bruised knee (January 29, 1997); missed two games. ... Sprained knee (February 26, 1997); missed 12 games. ... Sprained knee (October 23, 1998); missed 10 games. ... Strained groin (January 1, 1999); missed one game. ... Sprained wrist (January 30, 1999); missed eight games. ... Sprained ankle (March 13, 1999); missed two games. ... Reinjured ankle (April 7, 1999); missed remainder of season. ... Suffered injury (November 11, 1999); missed five games. ... Injured neck (February 28, 2000); missed two games. ... Reinjured neck (March 5, 2000); missed two games. ... Missed first two games of 2000-01 season due to contract dispute. ... Injured neck (December 21, 2000); missed one game. ... Bruised shoulder (January 18, 2001); missed three games. ... Suffered injury (November 27, 2001); missed one game. ... Suffered concussion (March 21, 2002); missed five games.
STATISTICAL PLATEAUS: Three-goal games: 1999-00 (1).

		REGULAR SEASON								PLAYOFFS				
Season Team	League	Gms.	G	A	Pts.	PIM	+/-	PP	SH	Gms.	G	A	Pts.	PIM
90-91—Mechel Chelyabinsk	USSR	2	0	0	0	0	...	...	...	—	—	—	—	—
91-92—Traktor Chelyabinsk	CIS	31	1	0	1	6	...	...	...	—	—	—	—	—
92-93—Dynamo Moscow	CIS	31	1	3	4	70	...	...	...	10	0	0	0	12
93-94—Dynamo Moscow	CIS	44	4	5	9	36	...	...	...	10	0	3	3	14
—Portland	AHL	—	—	—	—	—	...	...	...	2	0	0	0	0
94-95—Portland	AHL	61	10	32	42	67	...	...	...	—	—	—	—	—
—Washington	NHL	31	2	5	7	22	4	0	0	7	2	2	4	2
95-96—Washington	NHL	78	15	26	41	60	25	4	0	6	2	4	6	4
96-97—Washington	NHL	57	13	17	30	36	-11	3	0	—	—	—	—	—

G

Season Team	League	REGULAR SEASON								PLAYOFFS				
		Gms.	G	A	Pts.	PIM	+/-	PP	SH	Gms.	G	A	Pts	PIM
97-98—Washington	NHL	72	5	16	21	66	2	2	0	21	7	4	11	30
—Russian Oly. team......	Int'l	6	0	2	2	0	...	...	...	—	—	—	—	—
98-99—Washington	NHL	53	21	10	31	57	1	13	1	—	—	—	—	—
99-00—Washington	NHL	73	18	36	54	52	26	5	0	5	1	0	1	6
00-01—Washington	NHL	76	19	38	57	70	12	8	0	6	1	3	4	2
01-02—Washington	NHL	76	26	33	59	58	-1	7	0	—	—	—	—	—
—Russian Oly. team......	Int'l	6	0	0	0	2	...	...	...	—	—	—	—	—
02-03—Washington	NHL	82	18	49	67	52	13	7	0	6	0	5	5	4
NHL Totals (9 years)............		598	137	230	367	473	71	49	1	51	13	18	31	48

GORDON, BOYD   RW   CAPITALS

PERSONAL: Born October 19, 1983, in Unity, Sask. ... 6-0/192. ... Shoots right.
TRANSACTIONS/CAREER NOTES: Selected by Washington Capitals in first round (third Capitals pick, 17th overall) of NHL entry draft (June 22, 2002).

Season Team	League	REGULAR SEASON								PLAYOFFS				
		Gms.	G	A	Pts.	PIM	+/-	PP	SH	Gms.	G	A	Pts.	PIM
99-00—Red Deer..................	WHL	66	10	26	36	24	...	...	...	4	0	1	1	2
00-01—Red Deer..................	WHL	72	12	27	39	39	...	...	...	22	3	6	9	2
01-02—Red Deer..................	WHL	66	22	29	51	19	...	...	...	23	10	12	22	8
02-03—Red Deer..................	WHL	56	33	48	81	28	...	...	...	—	—	—	—	—

GOREN, LEE   RW   PANTHERS

PERSONAL: Born December 26, 1977, in Winnipeg, Man. ... 6-3/207. ... Shoots right.
TRANSACTIONS/CAREER NOTES: Selected by Boston Bruins in third round (fifth Bruins pick, 63rd overall) of NHL entry draft (June 21, 1997). ... Signed by Florida Panthers (July 24, 2003).

Season Team	League	REGULAR SEASON								PLAYOFFS				
		Gms.	G	A	Pts.	PIM	+/-	PP	SH	Gms.	G	A	Pts.	PIM
95-96—Minote	Jr. A	64	31	55	86	...				—	—	—	—	—
96-97—Univ. of North Dakota.	WCHA						Did not play.							
97-98—Univ. of North Dakota.	WCHA	29	3	13	16	26	...	...	...	—	—	—	—	—
98-99—Univ. of North Dakota.	WCHA	38	26	19	45	20	...	...	...	—	—	—	—	—
99-00—Univ. of North Dakota.	WCHA	44	*34	29	63	42	...	...	...	—	—	—	—	—
00-01—Providence................	AHL	54	15	18	33	72	...	...	...	17	5	2	7	11
—Boston	NHL	21	2	0	2	7	-3	1	0	—	—	—	—	—
01-02—Providence................	AHL	71	11	26	37	121	...	...	...	—	—	—	—	—
02-03—Providence................	AHL	65	32	37	69	106	...	...	...	—	—	—	—	—
—Boston	NHL	14	2	1	3	7	-2	2	0	5	0	0	0	5
NHL Totals (2 years)............		35	4	1	5	14	-5	3	0	5	0	0	0	5

GRAHAME, JOHN   G   LIGHTNING

PERSONAL: Born August 31, 1975, in Denver ... 6-2/215. ... Catches left. ... Full Name: John Gillies Mark Grahame. ... Son of Ron Grahame, goaltender with three NHL teams (1977-78 through 1980-81). ... Name pronounced GRAY-ihm.
TRANSACTIONS/CAREER NOTES: Selected by Boston Bruins in ninth round (seventh Bruins pick, 229th overall) of NHL entry draft (June 29, 1994). ... Injured ankle (December 19, 2000) and underwent surgery; missed seven games. ... Traded by Bruins to Tampa Bay Lightning for fourth-round pick in 2004 draft (January 13, 2003). ... Re-signed by Lightning (July 20, 2003).

Season Team	League	REGULAR SEASON								PLAYOFFS							
		Gms.	Min	W	L	T	GA	SO	Avg.	SV%	Gms.	Min.	W	L	GA SO	Avg.	SV%
93-94—Sioux City..................	USHL	20	1136	...	...	...	72	0	3.80	—	—	—	—	—	— —	—	—
94-95—Lake Superior State	CCHA	28	1616	16	7	3	75	1	2.78	—	—	—	—	—	— —	—	—
95-96—Lake Superior State	CCHA	29	1658	21	4	2	67	2	2.42	—	—	—	—	—	— —	—	—
96-97—Lake Superior State	CCHA	37	2197	19	13	4	134	3	3.66	—	—	—	—	—	— —	—	—
97-98—Providence..................	AHL	55	3054	15	*31	4	164	3	3.22	—	—	—	—	—	— —	—	—
98-99—Providence..................	AHL	48	2771	*37	9	1	134	3	2.90	—	19	*1209	*15	4	*48 †1	2.38	—
99-00—Boston	NHL	24	1344	7	10	5	55	2	2.46	.910	—	—	—	—	— —	—	—
—Providence..................	AHL	27	1528	11	13	2	86	1	3.38	—	13	839	10	3	35 0	2.50	—
00-01—Boston	NHL	10	471	3	4	0	28	0	3.57	.867	—	—	—	—	— —	—	—
—Providence..................	AHL	16	893	4	7	3	47	0	3.16	—	17	1043	8	*9	46 2	2.65	—
01-02—Boston	NHL	19	1079	8	7	2	52	1	2.89	.897	—	—	—	—	— —	—	—
02-03—Boston	NHL	23	1352	11	9	2	61	1	2.71	.902	1	111	0	1	2 0	1.08	.958
—Tampa Bay	NHL	17	914	6	5	4	34	2	2.23	.920	—	—	—	—	— —	—	—
NHL Totals (4 years)............		93	5160	35	35	13	230	6	2.67	.903	1	111	0	1	2 0	1.08	.958

GRAND-PIERRE, JEAN-LUC   D   BLUE JACKETS

PERSONAL: Born February 2, 1977, in Montreal ... 6-3/223. ... Shoots right. ... Name pronounced zhah-LOOK GRAHN-pee-AIR.
TRANSACTIONS/CAREER NOTES: Selected by St. Louis Blues in seventh round (sixth Blues pick, 179th overall) of NHL entry draft (July 8, 1995). ... Traded by Blues with second-round pick (D Cory Sarich) in 1996 draft and third-round pick (RW Maxim Afinogenov) in 1997 draft to Buffalo Sabres for LW Yuri Khmylev and eighth-round pick (C Andrei Podkonicky) in 1996 draft (March 20, 1996). ... Suspended one game by NHL for tripping incident (April 10, 1999). ... Suffered from the flu (March 12, 2000); missed one game. ... Traded by Sabres with RW Matt Davidson, fifth-round pick (C Tyler Kolarik) in 2000 draft and fifth-round pick (traded to Detroit) in 2001 draft to Columbus Blue Jackets for future considerations (June 23, 2000). ... Bruised foot (October 21, 2000); missed two games. ... Suffered concussion (December 26, 2000); missed three games. ... Bruised foot (March 7, 2001); missed six games.

G

Season Team	League	REGULAR SEASON								PLAYOFFS				
		Gms.	G	A	Pts.	PIM	+/-	PP	SH	Gms.	G	A	Pts.	PIM
93-94—Beauport	QMJHL	46	1	4	5	27	...	...	...	1	0	0	0	0
94-95—Val-d'Or	QMJHL	59	10	13	23	126	...	...	...	—	—	—	—	—
95-96—Val-d'Or	QMJHL	67	13	21	34	209	...	...	...	13	1	4	5	47
96-97—Val-d'Or	QMJHL	58	9	24	33	196	...	...	...	13	5	8	13	46
97-98—Rochester	AHL	75	4	6	10	211	...	...	...	4	0	0	0	2
98-99—Rochester	AHL	56	5	4	9	90	...	...	...	—	—	—	—	—
—Buffalo	NHL	16	0	1	1	17	0	0	0	—	—	—	—	—
99-00—Buffalo	NHL	11	0	0	0	15	-1	0	0	4	0	0	0	4
—Rochester	AHL	62	5	8	13	124	...	...	...	17	0	1	1	40
00-01—Columbus	NHL	64	1	4	5	73	-6	0	0	—	—	—	—	—
01-02—Columbus	NHL	81	2	6	8	90	-28	0	0	—	—	—	—	—
02-03—Columbus	NHL	41	1	0	1	64	-6	0	0	—	—	—	—	—
NHL Totals (5 years)		213	4	11	15	259	-41	0	0	4	0	0	0	4

GRATTON, BENOIT   LW   CANADIENS

PERSONAL: Born December 28, 1976, in Montreal. ... 5-11/194. ... Shoots left. ... Name pronounced gruh-TAHN.
TRANSACTIONS/CAREER NOTES: Selected by Washington Capitals in fifth round (sixth Capitals pick, 105th overall) of NHL entry draft (July 8, 1995). ... Injured groin (December 20, 1997); missed one game. ... Traded by Capitals to Calgary Flames for D Steve Shirreffs (August 18, 1999). ... Suffered head injury (February 13, 2001). ... Claimed on waivers by Montreal Canadiens (April 11, 2001). ... Sprained ankle (January 5, 2002); missed 26 games.

Season Team	League	REGULAR SEASON								PLAYOFFS				
		Gms.	G	A	Pts.	PIM	+/-	PP	SH	Gms.	G	A	Pts.	PIM
93-94—Laval	QMJHL	51	9	14	23	70	...	...	...	20	2	1	3	19
94-95—Laval	QMJHL	71	30	58	88	199	...	...	...	20	8	21	29	42
95-96—Laval	QMJHL	38	21	39	60	130	...	...	...	—	—	—	—	—
—Granby	QMJHL	27	12	46	58	97	...	...	...	21	13	26	39	68
96-97—Portland	AHL	76	6	40	46	140	...	...	...	5	2	1	3	14
97-98—Portland	AHL	58	19	31	50	137	...	...	...	8	4	2	6	24
—Washington	NHL	6	0	1	1	6	1	0	0	—	—	—	—	—
98-99—Portland	AHL	64	18	42	60	135	...	...	...	—	—	—	—	—
—Washington	NHL	16	4	3	7	16	-1	0	0	—	—	—	—	—
99-00—Saint John	AHL	65	17	49	66	137	...	...	...	3	0	1	1	4
—Calgary	NHL	10	0	2	2	10	1	0	0	—	—	—	—	—
00-01—Saint John	AHL	53	10	36	46	153	...	...	...	—	—	—	—	—
—Calgary	NHL	14	1	3	4	14	0	0	0	—	—	—	—	—
01-02—Quebec	AHL	35	10	19	29	70	...	...	...	3	2	3	5	10
—Montreal	NHL	8	1	0	1	8	-1	0	0	—	—	—	—	—
02-03—Hamilton	AHL	43	21	39	60	78	...	...	...	—	—	—	—	—
NHL Totals (5 years)		54	6	9	15	54	0	0	0					

GRATTON, CHRIS   C   COYOTES

PERSONAL: Born July 5, 1975, in Brantford, Ont. ... 6-4/225. ... Shoots left. ... Name pronounced GRA-tuhn.
TRANSACTIONS/CAREER NOTES: Selected by Tampa Bay Lightning in first round (first Lightning pick, third overall) of NHL entry draft (June 26, 1993). ... Bruised shoulder (April 2, 1995); missed two games. ... Traded by Lightning to Philadelphia Flyers for RW Mikael Renberg and D Karl Dykhuis (August 20, 1997). ... Traded by Flyers with C/RW Mike Sillinger to Lightning for RW Mikael Renberg and C Daymond Langkow (December 12, 1998). ... Suspended three games by NHL for spitting at referee (December 25, 1998). ... Bruised right foot (February 17, 2000); missed seven games. ... Traded by Lightning with second-round pick (C Derek Roy) in 2001 draft to Buffalo Sabres for C/RW Brian Holzinger, C Wayne Primeau, D Cory Sarich and third-round pick (RW Alexandre Kharitonov) in 2000 draft (March 9, 2000). ... Traded by Sabres with fourth-round pick in 2004 draft to Phoenix Coyotes for C Daniel Briere and third-round pick in 2004 draft (March 10, 2003).
STATISTICAL PLATEAUS: Three-goal games: 1996-97 (1).

Season Team	League	REGULAR SEASON								PLAYOFFS				
		Gms.	G	A	Pts.	PIM	+/-	PP	SH	Gms.	G	A	Pts.	PIM
90-91—Brantford Jr. B	OHA	31	30	30	60	28	...	...	...	—	—	—	—	—
91-92—Kingston	OHL	62	27	39	66	35	...	...	...	—	—	—	—	—
92-93—Kingston	OHL	58	55	54	109	125	...	...	...	16	11	18	29	42
93-94—Tampa Bay	NHL	84	13	29	42	123	-25	5	1	—	—	—	—	—
94-95—Tampa Bay	NHL	46	7	20	27	89	-2	2	0	—	—	—	—	—
95-96—Tampa Bay	NHL	82	17	21	38	105	-13	7	0	6	0	2	2	27
96-97—Tampa Bay	NHL	82	30	32	62	201	-28	9	0	—	—	—	—	—
97-98—Philadelphia	NHL	82	22	40	62	159	11	5	0	5	2	0	2	10
98-99—Philadelphia	NHL	26	1	7	8	41	-8	0	0	—	—	—	—	—
—Tampa Bay	NHL	52	7	19	26	102	-20	1	0	—	—	—	—	—
99-00—Tampa Bay	NHL	58	14	27	41	121	-24	4	0	—	—	—	—	—
—Buffalo	NHL	14	1	7	8	15	1	0	0	5	0	1	1	4
00-01—Buffalo	NHL	82	19	21	40	102	0	5	0	13	6	4	10	14
01-02—Buffalo	NHL	82	15	24	39	75	0	1	0	—	—	—	—	—
02-03—Buffalo	NHL	66	15	29	44	86	-5	0	0	—	—	—	—	—
—Phoenix	NHL	14	0	1	1	21	-11	0	0	—	—	—	—	—
NHL Totals (10 years)		770	161	277	438	1240	-124	43	1	29	8	7	15	55

G

GRAVES, ADAM   LW

PERSONAL: Born April 12, 1968, in Toronto. ... 6-0/205. ... Shoots left.
TRANSACTIONS/CAREER NOTES: Selected by Detroit Red Wings in second round (second Red Wings pick, 22nd overall) of NHL entry draft (June 21, 1986). ... Traded by Red Wings with C/RW Joe Murphy, LW Petr Klima and D Jeff Sharples to Edmonton Oilers for C Jimmy Carson, C Kevin McClelland and fifth-round pick (traded to Montreal) in 1991 draft (November 2, 1989). ... Signed as free agent by New York Rangers (September 2, 1991); Oilers received C/LW Troy Mallette as compensation (September 9, 1991). ... Suffered from infected elbow (February

11, 1995); missed one game. ... Sprained right knee (October 26, 1997); missed 10 games. ... Traded by Rangers with D Rich Pilon and future considerations to San Jose Sharks for C Mikael Samuelsson and D Christian Gosselin (June 24, 2001). ... Injured back (December 21, 2001); missed one game.

STATISTICAL PLATEAUS: Three-goal games: 1989-90 (1), 1991-92 (1), 1992-93 (1), 1993-94 (1), 1994-95 (1), 1996-97 (1). Total: 6.

			REGULAR SEASON							PLAYOFFS				
Season Team	League	Gms.	G	A	Pts.	PIM	+/-	PP	SH	Gms.	G	A	Pts.	PIM
84-85—King City Jr. B.	OHA	25	23	33	56	29	...	...	...	—	—	—	—	—
85-86—Windsor	OHL	62	27	37	64	35	...	...	...	16	5	11	16	10
86-87—Windsor	OHL	66	45	55	100	70	...	...	...	14	9	8	17	32
—Adirondack	AHL	—	—	—	—	—	...	...	...	5	0	1	1	0
87-88—Detroit	NHL	9	0	1	1	8	-2	0	0	—	—	—	—	—
—Windsor	OHL	37	28	32	60	107	...	...	...	12	14	18	†32	16
88-89—Detroit	NHL	56	7	5	12	60	-5	0	0	5	0	0	0	4
—Adirondack	AHL	14	10	11	21	28	...	...	...	14	11	7	18	17
89-90—Detroit	NHL	13	0	1	1	13	-5	0	0	—	—	—	—	—
—Edmonton	NHL	63	9	12	21	123	5	1	0	22	5	6	11	17
90-91—Edmonton	NHL	76	7	18	25	127	-21	2	0	18	2	4	6	22
91-92—New York Rangers	NHL	80	26	33	59	139	19	4	4	10	5	3	8	22
92-93—New York Rangers	NHL	84	36	29	65	148	-4	12	1	—	—	—	—	—
93-94—New York Rangers	NHL	84	52	27	79	127	27	20	4	23	10	7	17	24
94-95—New York Rangers	NHL	47	17	14	31	51	9	9	0	10	4	4	8	8
95-96—New York Rangers	NHL	82	22	36	58	100	18	9	1	10	7	1	8	4
96-97—New York Rangers	NHL	82	33	28	61	66	10	10	4	15	2	1	3	12
97-98—New York Rangers	NHL	72	23	12	35	41	-30	10	0	—	—	—	—	—
98-99—New York Rangers	NHL	82	38	15	53	47	-12	14	2	—	—	—	—	—
99-00—New York Rangers	NHL	77	23	17	40	14	-15	11	0	—	—	—	—	—
00-01—New York Rangers	NHL	82	10	16	26	77	-16	1	0	—	—	—	—	—
01-02—San Jose	NHL	81	17	14	31	51	11	1	3	12	3	1	4	6
02-03—San Jose	NHL	82	9	9	18	32	-14	1	0	—	—	—	—	—
NHL Totals (16 years)		1152	329	287	616	1224	-25	105	19	125	38	27	65	119

GREEN, JOSH LW FLAMES

PERSONAL: Born November 16, 1977, in Camrose, Alta. ... 6-4/212. ... Shoots left.
TRANSACTIONS/CAREER NOTES: Selected by Los Angeles Kings in second round (first Kings pick, 30th overall) of NHL entry draft (June 22, 1996). ... Strained shoulder (October 18, 1998); missed three games. ... Traded by Kings with C Olli Jokinen, D Mathieu Biron and first-round pick (LW Taylor Pyatt) in 1999 draft to New York Islanders for RW Zigmund Palffy, C Bryan Smolinski, G Marcel Cousineau and fourth-round pick (C Daniel Johansson) in 1999 draft (June 20, 1999). ... Injured shoulder (March 21, 2000); missed remainder of season. ... Traded by Islanders with D Eric Brewer and second-round pick (LW Brad Winchester) in 2000 draft to Edmonton Oilers for D Roman Hamrlik (June 24, 2000). ... Dislocated shoulder (September 11, 2000); missed first 39 games of season. ... Reinjured shoulder (December 30, 2000); missed final 42 games of season. ... Bruised right hand (January 21, 2002); missed one game. ... Traded by Oilers to New York Rangers for conditional pick in 2004 draft (December 12, 2002). ... Claimed on waivers by Washington Capitals (January 15, 2003). ... Signed by Calgary Flames (July 17, 2003).

			REGULAR SEASON							PLAYOFFS				
Season Team	League	Gms.	G	A	Pts.	PIM	+/-	PP	SH	Gms.	G	A	Pts.	PIM
93-94—Medicine Hat	WHL	63	22	22	44	43	...	...	...	3	0	0	0	4
94-95—Medicine Hat	WHL	68	32	23	55	64	...	...	...	5	5	1	6	2
95-96—Medicine Hat	WHL	46	18	25	43	55	...	...	...	5	2	2	4	4
96-97—Medicine Hat	WHL	51	25	32	57	61	...	...	...	—	—	—	—	—
—Swift Current	WHL	23	10	15	25	33	...	...	...	10	9	7	16	19
97-98—Swift Current	WHL	5	9	1	10	9	...	...	...	—	—	—	—	—
—Portland	WHL	31	35	19	54	36	...	...	...	—	—	—	—	—
—Fredericton	AHL	43	16	15	31	14	...	...	...	4	1	3	4	6
98-99—Los Angeles	NHL	27	1	3	4	8	-5	1	0	—	—	—	—	—
—Springfield	AHL	41	15	15	30	29	...	...	...	—	—	—	—	—
99-00—Lowell	AHL	17	6	2	8	19	...	...	...	—	—	—	—	—
—New York Islanders	NHL	49	12	14	26	41	-7	2	0	—	—	—	—	—
00-01—Hamilton	AHL	2	2	0	2	2	...	...	...	—	—	—	—	—
—Edmonton	NHL	—	—	—	—	—	...	...	...	3	0	0	0	0
01-02—Edmonton	NHL	61	10	5	15	52	9	1	0	—	—	—	—	—
02-03—Edmonton	NHL	20	0	2	2	12	-3	0	0	—	—	—	—	—
—New York Rangers	NHL	4	0	0	0	2	-1	0	0	—	—	—	—	—
—Washington	NHL	21	1	2	3	7	1	0	0	—	—	—	—	—
NHL Totals (5 years)		182	24	26	50	122	-6	4	0	3	0	0	0	0

GREEN, MIKE C PANTHERS

PERSONAL: Born August 23, 1979, in Victoria, B.C. ... 5-11/192. ... Shoots right.
TRANSACTIONS/CAREER NOTES: Signed as non-drafted free agent by Florida Panthers (March 29, 2000).

			REGULAR SEASON							PLAYOFFS				
Season Team	League	Gms.	G	A	Pts.	PIM	+/-	PP	SH	Gms.	G	A	Pts.	PIM
96-97—Edmonton	WHL	7	0	2	2	0	...	...	...	—	—	—	—	—
97-98—Edmonton	WHL	71	15	26	41	16	...	...	...	—	—	—	—	—
98-99—Kootenay	WHL	73	35	45	80	37	...	...	...	7	2	2	4	4
99-00—Kootenay	WHL	69	42	48	90	63	...	...	...	21	9	16	25	20
00-01—Saskatoon	WHL	7	0	2	2	0	...	...	...	—	—	—	—	—
—Port Huron	UHL	11	1	5	6	6	...	...	...	—	—	—	—	—
—Louisville	AHL	24	2	1	3	4	...	...	...	—	—	—	—	—
—Knoxville	UHL	48	18	24	42	35	...	...	...	1	0	0	0	0
01-02—Macon	ECHL	54	27	35	62	18	...	...	...	—	—	—	—	—
—Cincinnati	AHL	22	2	9	11	4	...	...	...	3	0	0	0	0
02-03—San Antonio	AHL	80	26	34	60	25	...	...	...	—	—	—	—	—

G

GREEN, TRAVIS — C — MAPLE LEAFS

PERSONAL: Born December 20, 1970, in Castlegar, B.C. ... 6-2/200. ... Shoots right.
TRANSACTIONS/CAREER NOTES: Selected by New York Islanders in second round (second Islanders pick, 23rd overall) of NHL entry draft (June 17, 1989). ... Suffered sore groin (November 30, 1995); missed four games. ... Sprained knee (February 8, 1996); missed nine games. ... Traded by Islanders with D Doug Houda and RW Tony Tuzzolino to Mighty Ducks of Anaheim for D J.J. Daigneault, C Mark Janssens and RW Joe Sacco (February 6, 1998). ... Strained groin (February 7, 1998); missed five games. ... Sprained right knee (November 20, 1998); missed three games. ... Traded by Mighty Ducks with first-round pick (C Scott Kelman) in 1999 draft to Phoenix Coyotes for D Oleg Tverdovsky (June 26, 1999). ... Suffered knee infection (November 25, 1999); missed three games. ... Suffered concussion (March 21, 2000); missed one game. ... Bruised knee (March 4, 2001); missed three games. ... Traded by Coyotes with C Robert Reichel and RW Craig Mills to Toronto Maple Leafs for D Danny Markov (June 12, 2001).
STATISTICAL PLATEAUS: Three-goal games: 1993-94 (1).

Season Team	League	Gms.	G	A	Pts.	PIM	+/-	PP	SH	Gms.	G	A	Pts.	PIM
						REGULAR SEASON						PLAYOFFS		
85-86—Castlegar	KIJHL	35	30	40	70	41	...	...	...	—	—	—	—	—
86-87—Spokane	WHL	64	8	17	25	27	...	...	...	3	0	0	0	0
87-88—Spokane	WHL	72	33	53	86	42	...	...	...	15	10	10	20	13
88-89—Spokane	WHL	72	51	51	102	79	...	...	...	—	—	—	—	—
89-90—Spokane	WHL	50	45	44	89	80	...	...	...	—	—	—	—	—
—Medicine Hat	WHL	25	15	24	39	19	...	...	...	3	0	0	0	2
90-91—Capital District	AHL	73	21	34	55	26	...	...	...	—	—	—	—	—
91-92—Capital District	AHL	71	23	27	50	10	...	...	...	7	0	4	4	21
92-93—Capital District	AHL	20	12	11	23	39	...	...	...	—	—	—	—	—
—New York Islanders	NHL	61	7	18	25	43	4	1	0	12	3	1	4	6
93-94—New York Islanders	NHL	83	18	22	40	44	16	1	0	4	0	0	0	2
94-95—New York Islanders	NHL	42	5	7	12	25	-10	0	0	—	—	—	—	—
95-96—New York Islanders	NHL	69	25	45	70	42	-20	14	1	—	—	—	—	—
96-97—New York Islanders	NHL	79	23	41	64	38	-5	10	0	—	—	—	—	—
97-98—New York Islanders	NHL	54	14	12	26	66	-19	8	0	—	—	—	—	—
—Anaheim	NHL	22	5	11	16	16	-10	1	0	—	—	—	—	—
98-99—Anaheim	NHL	79	13	17	30	81	-7	3	1	4	0	1	1	4
99-00—Phoenix	NHL	78	25	21	46	45	-4	6	0	5	2	1	3	2
00-01—Phoenix	NHL	69	13	15	28	63	-11	3	0	—	—	—	—	—
01-02—Toronto	NHL	82	11	23	34	61	13	3	0	20	3	6	9	34
02-03—Toronto	NHL	75	12	12	24	67	2	2	1	4	2	1	3	4
NHL Totals (11 years)		793	171	244	415	591	-51	52	3	49	10	10	20	52

GREENE, MATT — D — OILERS

PERSONAL: Born May 13, 1983, in Grand Ledge. Mich. ... 6-2/210. ... Shoots right.
TRANSACTIONS/CAREER NOTES: Selected by Edmonton Oilers in second round (fourth Oilers pick, 44th overall) of NHL entry draft (June 22, 2002).

Season Team	League	Gms.	G	A	Pts.	PIM	+/-	PP	SH	Gms.	G	A	Pts.	PIM
						REGULAR SEASON						PLAYOFFS		
00-01—U.S. National	USHL	54	0	10	10	109	...	...	...	—	—	—	—	—
01-02—Green Bay	USHL	47	3	16	19	134	...	...	...	—	—	—	—	—
02-03—Univ. of North Dakota	WCHA	39	0	4	4	135	...	...	...	—	—	—	—	—

GREIG, MARK — RW

PERSONAL: Born January 25, 1970, in High River, Alta. ... 5-11/196. ... Shoots right. ... Brother of Bruce Greig, left winger with California Golden Seals (1973-74 and 1974-75). ... Name pronounced GRAYG.
TRANSACTIONS/CAREER NOTES: Selected by Hartford Whalers in first round (first Whalers pick, 15th overall) of NHL entry draft (June 16, 1990). ... Injured right knee (April 11, 1993); missed final three games of regular season. ... Traded by Whalers with sixth-round pick (G Doug Bonner) in 1995 draft to Toronto Maple Leafs for D Ted Crowley (January 25, 1994). ... Strained hip flexor (February 21, 1994); missed one game. ... Signed as free agent by Calgary Flames (August 9, 1994). ... Signed as free agent by Philadelphia Flyers (August 4, 1998).

Season Team	League	Gms.	G	A	Pts.	PIM	+/-	PP	SH	Gms.	G	A	Pts.	PIM
						REGULAR SEASON						PLAYOFFS		
86-87—Calgary	WHL	5	0	0	0	0	...	...	...	—	—	—	—	—
87-88—Lethbridge	WHL	65	9	18	27	38	...	...	...	—	—	—	—	—
88-89—Lethbridge	WHL	71	36	72	108	113	...	...	...	8	5	5	10	16
89-90—Lethbridge	WHL	65	55	80	135	149	...	...	...	18	11	21	32	35
90-91—Hartford	NHL	4	0	0	0	0	-1	0	0	—	—	—	—	—
—Springfield	AHL	73	32	55	87	73	...	...	...	17	2	6	8	22
91-92—Hartford	NHL	17	0	5	5	6	7	0	0	—	—	—	—	—
—Springfield	AHL	50	20	27	47	38	...	...	...	9	1	1	2	20
92-93—Hartford	NHL	22	1	7	8	27	-11	0	0	—	—	—	—	—
—Springfield	AHL	55	20	38	58	86	...	...	...	—	—	—	—	—
93-94—Hartford	NHL	31	4	5	9	31	-6	0	0	—	—	—	—	—
—Springfield	AHL	4	0	4	4	21	...	...	...	—	—	—	—	—
—Toronto	NHL	13	2	2	4	10	1	0	0	—	—	—	—	—
—St. John's	AHL	9	4	6	10	0	...	...	...	11	4	2	6	26
94-95—Saint John	AHL	67	31	50	81	82	...	...	...	2	0	1	1	0
—Calgary	NHL	8	1	1	2	2	1	0	0	—	—	—	—	—
95-96—Atlanta	IHL	71	25	48	73	104	...	...	...	3	2	1	3	4
96-97—Quebec	IHL	5	1	2	3	0	...	...	...	—	—	—	—	—
—Houston	IHL	59	12	30	42	59	...	...	...	13	5	8	13	2
97-98—Grand Rapids	IHL	69	26	36	62	103	...	...	...	3	0	4	4	4

G

Season Team	League	REGULAR SEASON								PLAYOFFS				
		Gms.	G	A	Pts.	PIM	+/-	PP	SH	Gms.	G	A	Pts.	PIM
98-99—Philadelphia	AHL	67	23	46	69	102	...	...	...	7	1	5	6	14
—Philadelphia	NHL	7	1	3	4	2	1	0	0	2	0	1	1	0
99-00—Philadelphia	AHL	68	34	48	82	116	...	...	...	5	3	2	5	6
—Philadelphia	NHL	11	3	2	5	6	0	0	0	3	0	0	0	0
00-01—Philadelphia	AHL	74	31	57	88	98	...	...	...	10	6	5	11	4
—Philadelphia	NHL	7	1	1	2	4	-2	0	0	—	—	—	—	—
01-02—Philadelphia	AHL	66	22	37	59	105	...	...	...	5	0	4	4	6
02-03—Philadelphia	AHL	73	30	44	74	127	...	...	...	—	—	—	—	—
—Philadelphia	NHL	5	0	1	1	2	1	0	0	—	—	—	—	—
NHL Totals (9 years)		125	13	27	40	90	-9	0	0	5	0	1	1	0

GRENIER, MARTIN   D   CANUCKS

PERSONAL: Born November 2, 1980, in Laval, Que. ... 6-5/244. ... Shoots left.

TRANSACTIONS/CAREER NOTES: Selected by Colorado Avalanche in second round (second Avalanche pick, 45th overall) of NHL entry draft (June 26, 1999). ... Traded by Avalanche with LW Brian Rolston, C Samual Pahlsson and first-round pick (Martin Samuelsson) in 2000 draft to Boston Bruins for D Ray Bourque and LW Dave Andreychuk (March 6, 2000). ... Signed as free agent by Phoenix Coyotes (June 5, 2001). ... Traded by Coyotes to Vancouver Canucks for D Bryan Helmer (July 27, 2003).

Season Team	League	REGULAR SEASON								PLAYOFFS				
		Gms.	G	A	Pts.	PIM	+/-	PP	SH	Gms.	G	A	Pts.	PIM
97-98—Quebec	QMJHL	61	4	11	15	202	...	...	...	14	0	2	2	36
98-99—Quebec	QMJHL	60	7	18	25	*479	...	...	...	13	0	4	4	29
99-00—Quebec	QMJHL	67	11	35	46	302	...	...	...	7	1	4	5	27
00-01—Quebec	QMJHL	26	5	16	21	82	...	...	...	—	—	—	—	—
—Victoriaville	QMJHL	28	9	19	28	108	...	...	...	13	2	8	10	51
01-02—Phoenix	NHL	5	0	0	0	5	0	0	0	—	—	—	—	—
—Springfield	AHL	69	2	6	8	241	...	...	...	—	—	—	—	—
02-03—Springfield	AHL	73	2	10	12	232	...	...	...	—	—	—	—	—
—Phoenix	NHL	3	0	0	0	0	-1	0	0	—	—	—	—	—
NHL Totals (2 years)		8	0	0	0	5	-1	0	0	—	—	—	—	—

GRIER, MIKE   RW   CAPITALS

PERSONAL: Born January 5, 1975, in Detroit ... 6-1/227. ... Shoots right.

TRANSACTIONS/CAREER NOTES: Selected by St. Louis Blues in ninth round (seventh Blues pick, 219th overall) of NHL entry draft (June 26, 1993). ... Rights traded by Blues with rights to G Curtis Joseph to Edmonton Oilers for first-round picks in 1996 (C Marty Reasoner) and 1997 (traded to Los Angeles) drafts (August 4, 1995); picks had been awarded earlier to Oilers as compensation for Blues signing free agent LW Shayne Corson (July 28, 1995). ... Strained medial collateral ligament in left knee (November 19, 1997); missed 14 games. ... Fractured clavicle (November 24, 1999); missed four games. ... Suffered torn triceps (March 13, 2000) and underwent surgery; missed remainder of season. ... Dislocated right shoulder (December 3, 2000); missed eight games. ... Traded by Oilers to Washington Capitals for second- and third-round picks in 2003 draft (October 7, 2002). ... Re-signed by Capitals (July 24, 2003).

STATISTICAL PLATEAUS: Three-goal games: 1998-99 (1).

Season Team	League	REGULAR SEASON								PLAYOFFS				
		Gms.	G	A	Pts.	PIM	+/-	PP	SH	Gms.	G	A	Pts.	PIM
92-93—St. Sebastian's	USHS (East)	22	16	27	43	32	...	...	...	—	—	—	—	—
93-94—Boston University	Hockey East	39	9	9	18	56	...	...	...	—	—	—	—	—
94-95—Boston University	Hockey East	37	29	26	55	85	...	...	...	—	—	—	—	—
95-96—Boston University	Hockey East	38	21	25	46	82	...	...	...	—	—	—	—	—
96-97—Edmonton	NHL	79	15	17	32	45	7	4	0	12	3	1	4	4
97-98—Edmonton	NHL	66	9	6	15	73	-3	1	0	12	2	2	4	13
98-99—Edmonton	NHL	82	20	24	44	54	5	3	2	4	1	1	2	6
99-00—Edmonton	NHL	65	9	22	31	68	9	0	3	—	—	—	—	—
00-01—Edmonton	NHL	74	20	16	36	20	11	2	3	6	0	0	0	8
01-02—Edmonton	NHL	82	8	17	25	32	1	0	2	—	—	—	—	—
02-03—Washington	NHL	82	15	17	32	36	-14	2	2	6	1	1	2	2
NHL Totals (7 years)		530	96	119	215	328	16	12	12	40	7	5	12	33

G GRIGORENKO, IGOR   LW   RED WINGS

PERSONAL: Born April 9, 1983, in Samara, U.S.S.R. ... 5-11/183. ... Shoots right.

TRANSACTIONS/CAREER NOTES: Selected by Detroit Red Wings in second round (first Red Wings pick, 62nd overall) of NHL entry draft (June 23, 2001).

Season Team	League	REGULAR SEASON								PLAYOFFS				
		Gms.	G	A	Pts.	PIM	+/-	PP	SH	Gms.	G	A	Pts.	PIM
98-99—Lada-2 Togliatti	Rus.-4	19	3	3	6	2	...	...	...	—	—	—	—	—
99-00—Lada-2 Togliatti	Rus. Div. III	38	17	18	35	36	...	...	...	—	—	—	—	—
00-01—Lada-2 Togliatti	Rus. Div. III	6	5	4	9		...	...	...	—	—	—	—	—
—CSK Samara	Rus. Div. II	39	10	10	20		...	...	...	—	—	—	—	—
—Lada Togliatti	Russian	—	—	—	—	—	...	...	...	5	1	0	1	4
01-02—Lada Togliatti	Russian	41	8	9	17	58	...	...	...	4	1	0	1	8
02-03—Lada Togliatti	Russian	47	19	11	30	82	...	...	...	—	—	—	—	—

GRON, STANISLAV C DEVILS

PERSONAL: Born October 28, 1978, in Bratislava, Czechoslovakia. ... 6-2/210. ... Shoots left.
TRANSACTIONS/CAREER NOTES: Selected by New Jersey Devils in second round (second Devils pick, 38th overall) of NHL entry draft (June 21, 1997).

		REGULAR SEASON								PLAYOFFS				
Season Team	League	Gms.	G	A	Pts.	PIM	+/-	PP	SH	Gms.	G	A	Pts.	PIM
94-95—Slov. Bratislava	Slovakia Jrs.	40	49	26	75	20	...	...	...	—	—	—	—	—
95-96—Slov. Bratislava	Slovakia Jrs.	43	33	25	58	14	...	...	...	—	—	—	—	—
—Slovan Bratislava	Slovakia	—	—	—	—	—	—	—	—	1	0	0	0	0
96-97—Slov. Bratislava	Slovakia Jrs.	22	20	16	36	...	...	...	...	—	—	—	—	—
—Slovan Bratislava	Slovakia	7	0	0	0	0	...	...	...	—	—	—	—	—
97-98—Seattle......................	WHL	61	9	29	38	21	...	...	...	5	1	5	6	0
98-99—Kootenay..................	WHL	49	28	18	46	18	...	...	...	7	3	8	11	12
—Utah	IHL	4	0	3	3	0	...	...	...	—	—	—	—	—
99-00—Albany......................	AHL	65	19	10	29	17	...	...	...	5	1	1	2	2
00-01—Albany......................	AHL	61	16	9	25	19	...	...	...	—	—	—	—	—
—New Jersey	NHL	1	0	0	0	0	1	0	0	—	—	—	—	—
01-02—Albany......................	AHL	76	13	15	28	34	...	...	...	—	—	—	—	—
02-03—HC Vitkovice	Czech.	49	8	12	20	45	...	...	...	—	—	—	—	—
NHL Totals (1 year)............		1	0	0	0	0	1	0	0					

GROSEK, MICHAL LW BRUINS

PERSONAL: Born June 1, 1975, in Vyskov, Czechoslovakia ... 6-2/207. ... Shoots right. ... Name pronounced GROH-shehk.
TRANSACTIONS/CAREER NOTES: Selected by Winnipeg Jets in sixth round (seventh Jets pick, 145th overall) of NHL entry draft (June 26, 1993). ... Sprained knee ligaments (February 15, 1995); missed four games. ... Fractured foot (April 5, 1995); missed remainder of season. ... Traded by Jets with D Darryl Shannon to Buffalo Sabres for D Craig Muni (February 15, 1996). ... Suffered back spasms (April 9, 1999); missed five games. ... Traded by Sabres to Chicago Blackhawks for C Doug Gilmour and RW Jean-Pierre Dumont (March 10, 2000). ... Traded by Blackhawks with D Brad Brown to New York Rangers for future considerations (October 5, 2000). ... Suffered from the flu (December 20, 2000); missed one game. ... Injured jaw and suffered from the flu (March 7, 2002); missed three games. ... Signed as free agent by Boston Bruins (July 16, 2002). ... Re-signed by Bruins (July 15, 2003).
STATISTICAL PLATEAUS: Three-goal games: 1996-97 (1).

		REGULAR SEASON								PLAYOFFS				
Season Team	League	Gms.	G	A	Pts.	PIM	+/-	PP	SH	Gms.	G	A	Pts.	PIM
92-93—ZPS Zlin.....................	Czech.	17	1	3	4	0	...	...	...	—	—	—	—	—
93-94—Moncton	AHL	20	1	2	3	47	...	...	...	2	0	0	0	0
—Tacoma	WHL	30	25	20	45	106	...	...	...	7	2	2	4	30
—Winnipeg	NHL	3	1	0	1	0	-1	0	0	—	—	—	—	—
94-95—Springfield	AHL	45	10	22	32	98	...	...	...	—	—	—	—	—
—Winnipeg	NHL	24	2	2	4	21	-3	0	0	—	—	—	—	—
95-96—Springfield	AHL	39	16	19	35	68	...	...	...	—	—	—	—	—
—Winnipeg	NHL	1	0	0	0	0	-1	0	0	—	—	—	—	—
—Buffalo	NHL	22	6	4	10	31	0	2	0	—	—	—	—	—
96-97—Buffalo	NHL	82	15	21	36	71	25	1	0	12	3	3	6	8
97-98—Buffalo	NHL	67	10	20	30	60	9	2	0	15	6	4	10	28
98-99—Buffalo	NHL	76	20	30	50	102	21	4	0	13	0	4	4	28
99-00—Buffalo	NHL	61	11	23	34	35	12	2	0	—	—	—	—	—
—Chicago...................	NHL	14	2	4	6	12	-1	1	0	—	—	—	—	—
00-01—New York Rangers......	NHL	65	9	11	20	61	-10	2	0	—	—	—	—	—
—Hartford	AHL	12	8	7	15	12	...	...	...	—	—	—	—	—
01-02—New York Rangers......	NHL	15	3	2	5	12	-3	0	0	—	—	—	—	—
—Hartford	AHL	48	14	30	44	167	...	...	...	—	—	—	—	—
02-03—Boston	NHL	63	2	18	20	71	2	0	0	5	0	0	0	13
NHL Totals (10 years).........		493	81	135	216	476	50	14	0	45	9	11	20	77

GUERIN, BILL RW STARS

G

PERSONAL: Born November 9, 1970, in Worcester, Mass. ... 6-2/210. ... Shoots right. ... Full Name: William Robert Guerin. ... Name pronounced GAIR-ihn.
TRANSACTIONS/CAREER NOTES: Selected by New Jersey Devils in first round (first Devils pick, fifth overall) of NHL entry draft (June 17, 1989). ... Suffered from the flu (February 1992); missed three games. ... Suffered from sore leg (March 19, 1994); missed two games. ... Suffered from the flu (December 6, 1995); missed two games. ... Missed first 21 games of 1997-98 season due to contract dispute. ... Traded by Devils with RW Valeri Zelepukin to Edmonton Oilers for C Jason Arnott and D Bryan Muir (January 4, 1998). ... Sprained medial collateral ligament in left knee (April 12, 1999); missed final two games of regular season and one playoff game. ... Suffered from the flu (December 9, 1999); missed one game. ... Traded by Oilers to Boston Bruins for C Anson Carter, second-round pick (D Doug Lynch) in 2001 draft and swap of first-round picks in 2001 (November 15, 2000). ... Suspended three games by NHL for high-sticking incident (October 8, 2001). ... Suffered charleyhorse (December 13, 2001); missed one game. ... Signed as free agent by Dallas Stars (July 3, 2002).
STATISTICAL PLATEAUS: Three-goal games: 1996-97 (1), 2001-02 (2). Total: 3.

		REGULAR SEASON								PLAYOFFS				
Season Team	League	Gms.	G	A	Pts.	PIM	+/-	PP	SH	Gms.	G	A	Pts.	PIM
85-86—Springfield Jr. B..........	NEJHL	48	26	19	45	71	...	...	...	—	—	—	—	—
86-87—Springfield Jr. B..........	NEJHL	32	34	20	54	40	...	...	...	—	—	—	—	—
87-88—Springfield Jr. B..........	NEJHL	38	31	44	75	146	...	...	...	—	—	—	—	—
88-89—Springfield Jr. B..........	NEJHL	31	32	37	69	90	...	...	...	—	—	—	—	—
89-90—Boston College	Hockey East	39	14	11	25	64	...	...	...	—	—	—	—	—
90-91—Boston College	Hockey East	38	26	19	45	102	...	...	...	—	—	—	—	—

Season Team	League	REGULAR SEASON Gms.	G	A	Pts.	PIM	+/-	PP	SH	PLAYOFFS Gms.	G	A	Pts.	PIM
91-92—U.S. national team	Int'l	46	12	15	27	67	...	...	...					
—Utica	AHL	22	13	10	23	6	...	...	...	4	1	3	4	14
—New Jersey	NHL	5	0	1	1	9	1	0	0	6	3	0	3	4
92-93—New Jersey	NHL	65	14	20	34	63	14	0	0	5	1	1	2	4
—Utica	AHL	18	10	7	17	47	...	...	...	—	—	—	—	—
93-94—New Jersey	NHL	81	25	19	44	101	14	2	0	17	2	1	3	35
94-95—New Jersey	NHL	48	12	13	25	72	6	4	0	20	3	8	11	30
95-96—New Jersey	NHL	80	23	30	53	116	7	8	0	—	—	—	—	—
96-97—New Jersey	NHL	82	29	18	47	95	-2	7	0	8	2	1	3	18
97-98—New Jersey	NHL	19	5	5	10	13	0	1	0	—	—	—	—	—
—Edmonton	NHL	40	13	16	29	80	1	8	0	12	7	1	8	17
—U.S. Olympic team	Int'l	4	0	3	3	2	...	...	...	—	—	—	—	—
98-99—Edmonton	NHL	80	30	34	64	133	7	13	0	3	0	2	2	2
99-00—Edmonton	NHL	70	24	22	46	123	4	11	0	5	3	2	5	9
00-01—Edmonton	NHL	21	12	10	22	18	11	4	0	—	—	—	—	—
—Boston	NHL	64	28	35	63	122	-4	7	1	—	—	—	—	—
01-02—Boston	NHL	78	41	25	66	91	-1	10	1	6	4	2	6	6
—U.S. Olympic team	Int'l	6	4	0	4	4	...	...	...	—	—	—	—	—
02-03—Dallas	NHL	64	25	25	50	113	5	11	0	4	0	0	0	4
NHL Totals (12 years)		797	281	273	554	1149	63	86	2	86	25	18	43	129

GUOLLA, STEPHEN   C   DEVILS

PERSONAL: Born March 15, 1973, in Scarborough, Ont. ... 6-0/190. ... Shoots left. ... Name pronounced GWAH-luh.
TRANSACTIONS/CAREER NOTES: Selected by Ottawa Senators (first Senators pick, third overall) in NHL supplemental draft (June 28, 1994). ... Signed as free agent by San Jose Sharks (August 26, 1996). ... Traded by Sharks with D Andrei Zyuzin, D Bill Houlder and LW Shawn Burr to Tampa Bay Lightning for LW Niklas Sundstrom and third-round pick (traded to Chicago) in 2000 draft (August 4, 1999). ... Injured ankle (October 23, 1999); missed four games. ... Strained groin (January 7, 2000); missed four games. ... Claimed on waivers by Atlanta Thrashers (March 1, 2000). ... Strained buttocks (January 29, 2001); missed three games. ... Signed as free agent by New Jersey Devils (October 20, 2001).

Season Team	League	REGULAR SEASON Gms.	G	A	Pts.	PIM	+/-	PP	SH	PLAYOFFS Gms.	G	A	Pts.	PIM
90-91—Wexford Jr. B	MTHL	—	37	42	79	—	—	—	—	—	—	—	—	—
91-92—Michigan State	CCHA	33	4	9	13	8	...	...	...	—	—	—	—	—
92-93—Michigan State	CCHA	39	19	35	54	6	...	...	...	—	—	—	—	—
93-94—Michigan State	CCHA	41	23	46	69	16	...	...	...	—	—	—	—	—
94-95—Michigan State	CCHA	40	16	35	51	16	...	...	...	—	—	—	—	—
95-96—Prin. Edward Island	AHL	72	32	48	80	28	...	...	...	3	0	0	0	0
96-97—Kentucky	AHL	34	22	22	44	10	...	...	...	4	2	1	3	0
—San Jose	NHL	43	13	8	21	14	-10	2	0	—	—	—	—	—
97-98—Kentucky	AHL	69	37	63	100	45	...	...	...	3	0	0	0	0
—San Jose	NHL	7	1	1	2	0	-2	0	0	—	—	—	—	—
98-99—Kentucky	AHL	53	29	47	76	33	...	...	...	—	—	—	—	—
—San Jose	NHL	14	2	2	4	6	3	0	0	—	—	—	—	—
99-00—Tampa Bay	NHL	46	6	10	16	11	2	2	0	—	—	—	—	—
—Atlanta	NHL	20	4	9	13	4	-13	2	0	—	—	—	—	—
00-01—Atlanta	NHL	63	12	16	28	23	-6	2	0	—	—	—	—	—
01-02—Albany	AHL	68	25	35	60	27	...	...	...	—	—	—	—	—
02-03—Albany	AHL	22	11	17	28	4	...	...	...	—	—	—	—	—
—New Jersey	NHL	12	2	0	2	2	1	0	0	—	—	—	—	—
NHL Totals (6 years)		205	40	46	86	60	-25	8	0	—	—	—	—	—

GUSTAFSON, DEREK   G

PERSONAL: Born June 21, 1979, in Gresham, Ore. ... 5-11/210. ... Catches left.
TRANSACTIONS/CAREER NOTES: Signed as non-drafted free agent by Minnesota Wild (June 9, 2000).

Season Team	League	REGULAR SEASON Gms.	Min	W	L	T	GA	SO	Avg.	SV%	PLAYOFFS Gms.	Min.	W	L	GA	SO	Avg.	SV%
96-97—Vernon	BCJHL	23	1241	...	...	...	70	0	3.38	—	—	—	—	—	—	—	—	—
97-98—Vernon	BCJHL	42	2270	27	13	2	144	1	3.81	—	6	257	2	1	13	0	3.04	—
98-99—Vernon	BCJHL	42	2505	39	3	0	94	—	2.25	—	—	—	—	—	—	—	—	—
99-00—St. Lawrence Univ.	ECAC	24	1475	17	4	2	51	2	2.07	—	—	—	—	—	—	—	—	—
00-01—Jackson	ECHL	7	404	4	3	0	15	1	2.23	—	—	—	—	—	—	—	—	—
—Cleveland	IHL	24	1293	14	7	‡1	59	2	2.74	—	2	53	0	1	5	0	5.66	—
—Minnesota	NHL	4	239	1	3	0	10	0	2.51	.897	—	—	—	—	—	—	—	—
01-02—Houston	AHL	38	2015	14	13	6	92	4	2.74	—	2	25	0	0	1	0	2.40	—
—Minnesota	NHL	1	26	0	0	0	0	0	...	1.000	—	—	—	—	—	—	—	—
02-03—Houston	AHL	41	2300	23	14	2	108	2	2.82	—	—	—	—	—	—	—	—	—
—Louisiana	ECHL	2	118	1	1	0	8	0	4.07	—	—	—	—	—	—	—	—	—
NHL Totals (2 years)		5	265	1	3	0	10	0	2.26	.904								

G
H

HAAKANA, KARI   D   OILERS

PERSONAL: Born November 8, 1973, in Outokumpu, Finland ... 6-1/222. ... Shoots left.
TRANSACTIONS/CAREER NOTES: Selected by Edmonton Oilers in eighth round (ninth Oilers pick, 248th overall) of NHL entry draft (June 24, 2001).

Season Team	League	REGULAR SEASON								PLAYOFFS				
		Gms.	G	A	Pts.	PIM	+/-	PP	SH	Gms.	G	A	Pts.	PIM
90-91—Kiekko Espoo	Finland-2	4	0	1	1	0	...	...	...	—	—	—	—	—
92-93—Lukko Rauma	Finland	4	0	0	0	0	...	...	...	—	—	—	—	—
93-94—Kiekko Espoo	Finland	47	3	2	5	40	...	...	...	—	—	—	—	—
94-95—Kiekko Espoo	Finland	48	4	3	7	54	...	...	...	4	0	0	0	0
95-96—Kiekko Espoo	Finland	45	1	7	8	48	...	...	...	—	—	—	—	—
96-97—Kiekko Espoo	Finland	48	0	12	12	69	...	...	...	—	—	—	—	—
97-98—Kiekko Espoo	Finland	47	4	1	5	59	...	...	...	8	0	1	1	6
98-99—Rosenheim	Germany	51	1	9	10	58	...	...	...	—	—	—	—	—
99-00—Rosenheim	Germany	51	3	5	8	46	...	...	...	10	1	4	5	28
00-01—Jokerit Helsinki	Finland	52	2	8	10	98	...	...	...	5	0	0	0	2
01-02—Jokerit Helsinki	Finland	36	0	3	3	40	...	...	...	12	2	2	4	2
—Hamilton	AHL	6	0	2	2	25	...	...	...	—	—	—	—	—
02-03—Hamilton	AHL	12	0	4	4	12	...	...	...	—	—	—	—	—
—Edmonton	NHL	13	0	0	0	4	-2	0	0	—	—	—	—	—
NHL Totals (1 year)		13	0	0	0	4	-2	0	0					

HACKETT, JEFF　　　　G　　　　FLYERS

PERSONAL: Born June 1, 1968, in London, Ont. ... 6-1/198. ... Catches left.

TRANSACTIONS/CAREER NOTES: Selected by New York Islanders in second round (second Islanders pick, 34th overall) of NHL entry draft (June 13, 1987). ... Strained groin (May 13, 1990). ... Selected by San Jose Sharks in NHL expansion draft (May 30, 1991). ... Injured groin and hamstring (December 3, 1991); missed nine games. ... Injured knee (March 23, 1992). ... Suffered from the flu (February 20, 1993); missed five games. ... Traded by Sharks to Chicago Blackhawks for third-round pick (C Alexei Yegorov) in 1994 draft (July 13, 1993). ... Pulled groin (October 17, 1995); missed three games. ... Fractured finger (March 22, 1996); missed three games. ... Fractured finger (October 6, 1996); missed 12 games. ... Pulled groin (March 18, 1997); missed two games. ... Sprained ankle (October 9, 1997); missed 11 games. ... Traded by Blackhawks with D Eric Weinrich, D Alain Nasreddine and fourth-round pick (D Chris Dyment) in 1999 draft to Montreal Canadiens for G Jocelyn Thibault, D Dave Manson and D Brad Brown (November 16, 1998). ... Injured knee (March 27, 1999); missed one game. ... Injured hip flexor (April 1, 1999); missed five games. ... Suffered back spasms and bruised shoulder (October 18, 1999); missed one game. ... Fractured right hand (October 24, 2000); missed 21 games. ... Reinjured hand (December 31, 2000); missed 15 games. ... Reinjured hand (February 24, 2001); missed remainder of season. ... Dislocated shoulder (October 20, 2001); missed 20 games. ... Dislocated left shoulder (March 6, 2002); missed remainder of season. ... Traded by Canadiens to Boston Bruins as part of three-team trade in which San Jose Sharks acquired D Kyle McLaren and fourth-round pick in 2004 draft, Canadiens acquired LW Niklas Sundstrom and third-round pick in 2004 draft and Bruins acquired D Jeff Jillson (January 23, 2003). ... Signed as free agent by Philadelphia Flyers (June 1, 2003).

Season Team	League	REGULAR SEASON								PLAYOFFS						
		Gms.	Min	W	L	T	GA	SO	Avg.	SV%	Gms.	Min.	W	L	GA SO	Avg.	SV%
84-85—London Jr. B	OHA	18	1078	...	...	...	73	1	4.06	—	—	—	—	—	— —	—	—
85-86—London Jr. B	OHA	19	1150	...	...	...	66	0	3.44	—	—	—	—	—	— —	—	—
86-87—Oshawa	OHL	31	1672	18	9	2	85	2	3.05	—	15	895	8	7	40 0	2.68	—
87-88—Oshawa	OHL	53	3165	30	21	2	205	0	3.89	—	7	438	3	4	31 0	4.25	—
88-89—New York Islanders	NHL	13	662	4	7	0	39	0	3.53	.881	—	—	—	—	— —	—	—
—Springfield	AHL	29	1677	12	14	2	116	0	4.15	—	—	—	—	—	— —	—	—
89-90—Springfield	AHL	54	3045	24	25	3	187	1	3.68	—	†17	934	10	5	*60 0	3.85	—
90-91—New York Islanders	NHL	30	1508	5	18	1	91	0	3.62	.877	—	—	—	—	— —	—	—
91-92—San Jose	NHL	42	2314	11	27	1	148	0	3.84	.892	—	—	—	—	— —	—	—
92-93—San Jose	NHL	36	2000	2	30	1	176	0	5.28	.856	—	—	—	—	— —	—	—
93-94—Chicago	NHL	22	1084	2	12	3	62	0	3.43	.890	—	—	—	—	— —	—	—
94-95—Chicago	NHL	7	328	1	3	2	13	0	2.38	.913	2	26	0	0	1 0	2.31	.909
95-96—Chicago	NHL	35	2000	18	11	4	80	4	2.40	.916	1	60	0	1	5 0	5.00	.844
96-97—Chicago	NHL	41	2473	19	18	4	89	2	2.16	.927	6	345	2	4	25 0	4.35	.868
97-98—Chicago	NHL	58	3441	21	25	11	126	8	2.20	.917	—	—	—	—	— —	—	—
98-99—Chicago	NHL	10	524	2	6	1	33	0	3.78	.871	—	—	—	—	— —	—	—
—Montreal	NHL	53	3091	24	20	9	117	5	2.27	.914	—	—	—	—	— —	—	—
99-00—Montreal	NHL	56	3301	23	25	7	132	3	2.40	.914	—	—	—	—	— —	—	—
00-01—Montreal	NHL	19	998	4	10	2	54	0	3.25	.887	—	—	—	—	— —	—	—
01-02—Montreal	NHL	15	717	5	5	2	38	0	3.18	.904	—	—	—	—	— —	—	—
02-03—Montreal	NHL	18	1063	7	8	2	45	0	2.54	.926	—	—	—	—	— —	—	—
—Boston	NHL	18	991	8	9	0	53	1	3.21	.894	3	179	1	2	5 0	1.68	.934
NHL Totals (14 years)		473	26495	156	234	50	1296	23	2.93	.902	12	610	3	7	36 0	3.54	.883

HAGMAN, NIKLAS　　　　LW　　　　PANTHERS

PERSONAL: Born December 5, 1979, in Espoo, Finland ... 6-0/205. ... Shoots left.

TRANSACTIONS/CAREER NOTES: Selected by Florida Panthers in third round (third Panthers pick, 70th overall) of NHL entry draft (June 26, 1999).

Season Team	League	REGULAR SEASON								PLAYOFFS				
		Gms.	G	A	Pts.	PIM	+/-	PP	SH	Gms.	G	A	Pts.	PIM
96-97—HIFK Helsinki	Finland Jr.	30	13	12	25	30	...	...	...	4	1	1	2	0
97-98—HIFK Helsinki	Finland	8	1	0	1	0	...	...	...	—	—	—	—	—
—HIFK Helsinki	Finland Jr.	26	9	5	14	16	...	...	...	—	—	—	—	—
98-99—HIFK Helsinki	Finland	17	1	1	2	14	...	...	...	—	—	—	—	—
—HIFK Helsinki	Finland Jr.	14	4	9	13	43	...	...	...	—	—	—	—	—
99-00—Espoo	Finland	14	1	1	2	2	...	...	...	—	—	—	—	—
—Karpat Oulu	Finland	41	17	18	35	12	...	...	...	7	4	2	6	...
00-01—Karpat Oulu	Finland	56	28	18	46	32	...	...	...	8	3	1	4	0
01-02—Florida	NHL	78	10	18	28	8	-6	0	1	—	—	—	—	—
—Fin. Olympic team	Int'l	4	1	2	3	0	...	...	...	—	—	—	—	—
02-03—Florida	NHL	80	8	15	23	20	-8	2	0	—	—	—	—	—
NHL Totals (2 years)		158	18	33	51	28	-14	2	1					

H

HAHL, RIKU   C   AVALANCHE

PERSONAL: Born November 1, 1980, in Hameenlinna, Finland ... 6-1/205. ... Shoots left.
TRANSACTIONS/CAREER NOTES: Selected by Colorado Avalanche in sixth round (eighth Avalanche pick, 183rd overall) of NHL entry draft (June 26, 1999).

		REGULAR SEASON								PLAYOFFS				
Season Team	League	Gms.	G	A	Pts.	PIM	+/-	PP	SH	Gms.	G	A	Pts.	PIM
97-98—HPK Hameenlinna......	Finland Jr.	35	13	6	19	12	...	...	...	—	—	—	—	—
98-99—HPK Hameenlinna......	Finland Jr.	6	0	2	2	6	...	...	...	—	—	—	—	—
—HPK Hameenlinna......	Finland	28	0	1	1	0	...	...	...	8	0	0	0	2
99-00—HPK Hameenlinna......	Finland	50	4	3	7	18	...	...	...	8	0	0	0	2
00-01—HPK Hameenlinna......	Finland	55	3	9	12	32	...	...	...	—	—	—	—	—
01-02—Hershey	AHL	52	6	17	23	16	...	...	...	—	—	—	—	—
—Colorado....................	NHL	22	2	3	5	14	1	0	0	21	1	2	3	0
02-03—Hershey	AHL	28	7	7	14	17	...	...	...	—	—	—	—	—
—Colorado....................	NHL	42	3	4	7	12	3	0	0	6	0	2	2	2
NHL Totals (2 years)...........		64	5	7	12	26	4	0	0	27	1	4	5	2

HAINSEY, RON   D   CANADIENS

PERSONAL: Born March 24, 1981, in Bolton, Conn. ... 6-3/211. ... Shoots left.
TRANSACTIONS/CAREER NOTES: Selected by Montreal Canadiens in first round (first Canadiens pick, 13th overall) of NHL entry draft (June 24, 2000).

		REGULAR SEASON								PLAYOFFS				
Season Team	League	Gms.	G	A	Pts.	PIM	+/-	PP	SH	Gms.	G	A	Pts.	PIM
98-99—U.S. National..............	USHL	48	5	12	17	45	...	...	...	—	—	—	—	—
99-00—Mass.-Lowell	Hockey East	30	3	8	11	20	...	...	...	—	—	—	—	—
00-01—Mass.-Lowell	Hockey East	33	10	26	36	51	...	...	...	—	—	—	—	—
—Quebec	AHL	4	1	0	1	0	...	...	...	1	0	0	0	0
01-02—Quebec	AHL	63	7	24	31	26	...	...	...	3	0	0	0	0
02-03—Hamilton	AHL	33	2	11	13	26	...	...	...	—	—	—	—	—
—Montreal	NHL	21	0	0	0	2	-1	0	0	—	—	—	—	—
NHL Totals (1 year).............		21	0	0	0	2	-1	0	0					

HAJT, CHRIS   D   CAPITALS

PERSONAL: Born July 5, 1978, in Saskatoon, Sask. ... 6-3/206. ... Shoots left. ... Son of Bill Hajt, defenseman with Buffalo Sabres (1973-74 through 1986-87). ... Name pronounced HIGHT.
TRANSACTIONS/CAREER NOTES: Selected by Edmonton Oilers in second round (third Oilers pick, 32nd overall) of NHL entry draft (June 22, 1996). ... Signed as free agent by Washington Capitals (July 23, 2002). ... Re-signed by Capitals (July 15, 2003).

		REGULAR SEASON								PLAYOFFS				
Season Team	League	Gms.	G	A	Pts.	PIM	+/-	PP	SH	Gms.	G	A	Pts.	PIM
94-95—Guelph	OHL	57	1	7	8	35	...	...	...	14	0	2	2	9
95-96—Guelph	OHL	63	8	27	35	69	...	...	...	16	0	6	6	13
96-97—Guelph	OHL	58	11	15	26	62	...	...	...	18	0	8	8	25
97-98—Guelph	OHL	44	2	21	23	42	...	...	...	12	1	5	6	11
98-99—Hamilton	AHL	64	0	4	4	36	...	...	...	—	—	—	—	—
99-00—Hamilton	AHL	54	0	8	8	30	...	...	...	10	0	2	2	0
00-01—Hamilton	AHL	70	0	10	10	48	...	...	...	—	—	—	—	—
—Edmonton..................	NHL	1	0	0	0	0	-1	0	0	—	—	—	—	—
01-02—Hamilton	AHL	39	2	3	5	34	...	...	...	15	1	2	3	8
02-03—Portland	AHL	71	11	15	26	61	...	...	...	—	—	—	—	—
NHL Totals (1 year).............		1	0	0	0	0	-1	0	0					

HALE, DAVID   D   DEVILS

PERSONAL: Born June 18, 1981, in Colorado Springs, Colo. ... 6-2/204. ... Shoots left.
COLLEGE: North Dakota.
TRANSACTIONS/CAREER NOTES: Selected by New Jersey Devils in first round (first Devils pick, 22nd overall) of NHL entry draft (June 24, 2000).

		REGULAR SEASON								PLAYOFFS				
Season Team	League	Gms.	G	A	Pts.	PIM	+/-	PP	SH	Gms.	G	A	Pts.	PIM
98-99—Sioux City	USHL	56	3	15	18	127	...	...	...	—	—	—	—	—
99-00—Sioux City	USHL	54	6	18	24	187	...	...	...	—	—	—	—	—
00-01—Univ. of North Dakota .	WCHA	44	4	5	9	79	...	...	...	—	—	—	—	—
01-02—Univ. of North Dakota .	WCHA	34	4	5	9	63	...	...	...	—	—	—	—	—
02-03—Univ. of North Dakota .	WCHA	26	2	6	8	49	...	...	...	—	—	—	—	—

HALKO, STEVE   D

H

PERSONAL: Born March 8, 1974, in Etobicoke, Ont. ... 6-1/200. ... Shoots right. ... Full Name: Steven Halko. ... Name pronounced HAHL-koh.
TRANSACTIONS/CAREER NOTES: Selected by Hartford Whalers in 10th round (10th Whalers pick, 225th overall) of NHL entry draft (June 20, 1992). ... Whalers franchise moved to North Carolina and renamed Carolina Hurricanes for 1997-98 season; NHL approved move on June 25, 1997. ... Traded by Hurricanes with fourth-round pick (traded to Atlanta) in 2002 to St. Louis Blues for D Sean Hill (December 5, 2001). ... Signed as free agent by Hurricanes (August 5, 2002).

Season Team	League	REGULAR SEASON								PLAYOFFS				
		Gms.	G	A	Pts.	PIM	+/-	PP	SH	Gms.	G	A	Pts.	PIM
91-92—Thornhill	OHA Jr. A	44	15	46	61	43	...	...	...	—	—	—	—	—
92-93—Univ. of Michigan.......	CCHA	39	1	12	13	12	...	...	...	—	—	—	—	—
93-94—Univ. of Michigan.......	CCHA	41	2	13	15	32	...	...	...	—	—	—	—	—
94-95—Univ. of Michigan.......	CCHA	39	2	14	16	20	...	...	...	—	—	—	—	—
95-96—Univ. of Michigan.......	CCHA	43	4	16	20	32	...	...	...	—	—	—	—	—
96-97—Springfield	AHL	70	1	5	6	37	...	...	...	11	0	2	2	8
97-98—Carolina	NHL	18	0	2	2	10	-1	0	0	—	—	—	—	—
—New Haven	AHL	65	1	19	20	44	...	...	...	1	0	0	0	0
98-99—New Haven	AHL	42	2	7	9	58	...	...	...	—	—	—	—	—
—Carolina	NHL	20	0	3	3	24	5	0	0	4	0	0	0	2
99-00—Carolina	NHL	58	0	8	8	25	0	0	0	—	—	—	—	—
00-01—Carolina	NHL	48	0	1	1	6	-10	0	0	—	—	—	—	—
01-02—Carolina	NHL	5	0	1	1	6	3	0	0	—	—	—	—	—
—Worcester	AHL	43	3	5	8	15	...	...	...	3	0	1	1	0
02-03—Lowell	AHL	71	4	22	26 ·	34	...	...	...	—	—	—	—	—
—Carolina	NHL	6	0	0	0	0	1	0	0	—	—	—	—	—
NHL Totals (6 years)...........		155	0	15	15	71	-2	0	0	4	0	0	0	2

HALL, ADAM — RW — PREDATORS

PERSONAL: Born August 14, 1980, in Kalamazoo, Mich. ... 6-3/205. ... Shoots right.
TRANSACTIONS/CAREER NOTES: Selected by Nashville Predators in second round (third Predators pick, 52nd overall) of NHL entry draft (June 26, 1999).

Season Team	League	REGULAR SEASON								PLAYOFFS				
		Gms.	G	A	Pts.	PIM	+/-	PP	SH	Gms.	G	A	Pts.	PIM
97-98—U.S. National..............	NAHL	72	43	23	66	63	...	...	...	—	—	—	—	—
98-99—Michigan State...........	CCHA	36	16	7	23	74	...	...	...	—	—	—	—	—
99-00—Michigan State...........	CCHA	39	*25	13	38	36	...	...	...	—	—	—	—	—
00-01—Michigan State...........	CCHA	42	18	12	30	42	...	...	...	—	—	—	—	—
01-02—Michigan State...........	CCHA	41	19	15	34	36	...	...	...	—	—	—	—	—
—Milwaukee..................	AHL	6	2	2	4	4	...	...	...	—	—	—	—	—
—Nashville...................	NHL	1	0	1	1	0	0	0	0	—	—	—	—	—
02-03—Milwaukee..................	AHL	1	0	0	0	2	...	...	...	—	—	—	—	—
—Nashville...................	NHL	79	16	12	28	31	-8	8	0	—	—	—	—	—
NHL Totals (2 years)...........		80	16	13	29	31	-8	8	0	—	—	—	—	—

HALPERN, JEFF — C — CAPITALS

PERSONAL: Born May 3, 1976, in Potomac, Md. ... 6-0/202. ... Shoots right.
TRANSACTIONS/CAREER NOTES: Signed as non-drafted free agent by Washington Capitals (March 29, 1999). ... Suffered back spasms (February 19, 2000); missed three games. ... Strained groin (January 8, 2001); missed two games. ... Tore anterior cruciate ligament in left knee (January 18, 2002); missed remainder of season.

Season Team	League	REGULAR SEASON								PLAYOFFS				
		Gms.	G	A	Pts.	PIM	+/-	PP	SH	Gms.	G	A	Pts.	PIM
95-96—Princeton University ...	ECAC	29	3	11	14	30	...	...	...	—	—	—	—	—
96-97—Princeton University ...	ECAC	33	7	24	31	35	...	...	...	—	—	—	—	—
97-98—Princeton University ...	ECAC	36	*28	25	*53	46	...	...	...	—	—	—	—	—
98-99—Princeton University ...	ECAC	33	†22	22	44	32	...	...	...	—	—	—	—	—
—Portland......................	AHL	6	2	1	3	4	...	...	...	—	—	—	—	—
99-00—Washington	NHL	79	18	11	29	39	21	4	4	5	2	1	3	0
00-01—Washington	NHL	80	21	21	42	60	13	2	1	6	2	3	5	17
01-02—Washington	NHL	48	5	14	19	29	-9	0	0	—	—	—	—	—
02-03—Washington	NHL	82	13	21	34	88	6	1	2	6	0	1	1	2
NHL Totals (4 years)...........		289	57	67	124	216	31	7	7	17	4	5	9	19

HAMEL, DENIS — RW — SENATORS

PERSONAL: Born May 10, 1977, in Lachute, Que. ... 6-1/203. ... Shoots left. ... Name pronounced uh-MEHL.
TRANSACTIONS/CAREER NOTES: Selected by St. Louis Blues in sixth round (fifth Blues pick, 153rd overall) of NHL entry draft (July 8, 1995). ... Traded by Blues to Buffalo Sabres for D Charlie Huddy and seventh-round pick (C Daniel Corso) in 1996 draft (March 19, 1996). ... Tore anterior cruciate ligament in knee (January 27, 2001); missed remainder of season. ... Signed by Ottawa Senators (July 6, 2003).

Season Team	League	REGULAR SEASON								PLAYOFFS				
		Gms.	G	A	Pts.	PIM	+/-	PP	SH	Gms.	G	A	Pts.	PIM
94-95—Chicoutimi	QMJHL	66	15	12	27	155	...	...	...	13	2	0	2	29
95-96—Chicoutimi	QMJHL	65	40	49	89	199	...	...	...	17	10	14	24	64
96-97—Chicoutimi	QMJHL	70	50	50	100	339	...	...	...	20	15	10	25	65
97-98—Rochester	AHL	74	10	15	25	98	...	...	...	4	1	2	3	0
98-99—Rochester	AHL	74	16	17	33	121	...	...	...	20	3	4	7	10
99-00—Rochester	AHL	76	34	24	58	122	...	...	...	21	6	7	13	49
—Buffalo	NHL	3	1	0	1	0	-1	0	0	—	—	—	—	—
00-01—Buffalo	NHL	41	8	3	11	22	-2	1	1	—	—	—	—	—
01-02—Buffalo	NHL	61	2	6	8	28	-1	0	0	—	—	—	—	—
02-03—Rochester	AHL	48	27	20	47	64	...	...	...	—	—	—	—	—
—Buffalo	NHL	25	2	0	2	17	-4	0	0	—	—	—	—	—
NHL Totals (4 years)...........		130	13	9	22	67	-8	1	1					

H

HAMHUIS, DAN — D — PREDATORS

PERSONAL: Born December 13, 1982, in Smithers, B.C. ... 6-0/195. ... Shoots left. ... Name pronounced HAM-hoos.
TRANSACTIONS/CAREER NOTES: Selected by Nashville Predators in first round (first Predators pick, 12th overall) of NHL entry draft (June 23, 2001).

Season Team	League	Gms.	G	A	Pts.	PIM	+/-	PP	SH	Gms.	G	A	Pts.	PIM
		REGULAR SEASON								PLAYOFFS				
98-99—Prince George	WHL	56	1	3	4	45	...	...	...	7	1	2	3	8
99-00—Prince George	WHL	70	10	23	33	140	...	...	...	13	2	3	5	35
00-01—Prince George	WHL	62	13	46	59	125	...	...	...	6	2	3	5	15
01-02—Prince George	WHL	72	10	50	60	135	...	...	...	7	0	5	5	16
02-03—Milwaukee	AHL	68	6	21	27	81	...	...	...	—	—	—	—	—

HAMRLIK, ROMAN — D — ISLANDERS

PERSONAL: Born April 12, 1974, in Zlin, Czechoslovakia ... 6-2/206. ... Shoots left. ... Brother of Martin Hamrlik, defenseman with Hartford Whalers (1991-92 through 1993-94) and St. Louis Blues (1993-94 and 1994-95) organizations. ... Name pronounced ROH-muhn HAM-uhr-lihk.
TRANSACTIONS/CAREER NOTES: Selected by Tampa Bay Lightning in first round (first Lightning pick, first overall) of NHL entry draft (June 20, 1992). ... Bruised shoulder (November 3, 1993); missed six games. ... Bruised shoulder (March 1, 1994); missed seven games. ... Played in Europe during 1994-95 NHL lockout. ... Suffered back spasms (January 9, 1997); missed two games. ... Traded by Lightning with C Paul Comrie to Edmonton Oilers for C Steve Kelly, D Bryan Marchment and C Jason Bonsignore (December 30, 1997). ... Fractured toe (January 5, 1999); missed six games. ... Bruised finger (December 1, 1999); missed two games. ... Traded by Oilers to Islanders for D Eric Brewer, LW Josh Green and second-round pick (LW Brad Winchester) in 2000 draft (June 24, 2000). ... Strained groin (December 21, 2000); missed five games. ... Strained hip flexor (January 31, 2001); missed one game. ... Sprained knee (November 27, 2001); missed one game. ... Injured right knee (December 29, 2001); missed 11 games.

Season Team	League	Gms.	G	A	Pts.	PIM	+/-	PP	SH	Gms.	G	A	Pts.	PIM
		REGULAR SEASON								PLAYOFFS				
90-91—TJ Zlin	Czech.	14	2	2	4	18	...	...	...	—	—	—	—	—
91-92—ZPS Zlin	Czech.	34	5	5	10	34	...	...	...	—	—	—	—	—
92-93—Tampa Bay	NHL	67	6	15	21	71	-21	1	0	—	—	—	—	—
—Atlanta	IHL	2	1	1	2	2	...	...	...	—	—	—	—	—
93-94—Tampa Bay	NHL	64	3	18	21	135	-14	0	0	—	—	—	—	—
94-95—ZPS Zlin	Czech Rep.	2	1	0	1	10	...	...	...	—	—	—	—	—
—Tampa Bay	NHL	48	12	11	23	86	-18	7	1	—	—	—	—	—
95-96—Tampa Bay	NHL	82	16	49	65	103	-24	12	0	5	0	1	1	4
96-97—Tampa Bay	NHL	79	12	28	40	57	-29	6	0	—	—	—	—	—
97-98—Tampa Bay	NHL	37	3	12	15	22	-18	1	0	—	—	—	—	—
—Edmonton	NHL	41	6	20	26	48	3	4	1	12	0	6	6	12
—Czech Rep. Oly. team..	Int'l	6	1	0	1	2	...	...	...	—	—	—	—	—
98-99—Edmonton	NHL	75	8	24	32	70	9	3	0	3	0	0	0	2
99-00—Edmonton	NHL	80	8	37	45	68	1	5	0	5	0	1	1	4
00-01—New York Islanders	NHL	76	16	30	46	92	-20	5	1	—	—	—	—	—
01-02—New York Islanders	NHL	70	11	26	37	78	7	4	1	7	1	6	7	6
—Czech Rep. Oly. team..	Int'l	4	0	1	1	2	...	...	...	—	—	—	—	—
02-03—New York Islanders	NHL	73	9	32	41	87	21	3	0	5	0	2	2	2
NHL Totals (11 years)		792	110	302	412	917	-103	51	4	37	1	16	17	30

HANDZUS, MICHAL — C — FLYERS

PERSONAL: Born March 11, 1977, in Banska Bystrica, Czechoslovakia ... 6-5/217. ... Shoots left. ... Name pronounced han-ZOOZ.
TRANSACTIONS/CAREER NOTES: Selected by St. Louis Blues in fourth round (third Blues pick, 101st overall) of NHL entry draft (July 8, 1995). ... Bruised shoulder (February 26, 1999); missed five games. ... Bruised shoulder (March 25, 1999); missed final 11 games of regular season and two playoffs games. ... Injured groin (October 1, 2000); missed first five games of season. ... Strained muscle in abdomen (January 11, 2001) and underwent surgery; missed 33 games. ... Traded by Blues with RW Ladislav Nagy, C Jeff Taffe and first-round pick (LW Ben Eager) in 2002 draft to Phoenix Coyotes for LW Keith Tkachuk (March 13, 2001). ... Strained groin (January 17, 2002); missed three games. ... Traded by Coyotes with G Robert Esche to Philadelphia Flyers for G Brian Boucher and third-round pick (D Joe Callahan) in 2002 draft (June 12, 2002).
STATISTICAL PLATEAUS: Three-goal games: 2000-01 (1).

Season Team	League	Gms.	G	A	Pts.	PIM	+/-	PP	SH	Gms.	G	A	Pts.	PIM
		REGULAR SEASON								PLAYOFFS				
93-94—IS Banska Byst.	Slovakia Jrs.	40	23	36	59	...	...	...	...	—	—	—	—	—
94-95—IS Banska Bystrica	Slov. Div. II	22	15	14	29	10	...	...	...	—	—	—	—	—
95-96—IS Banska Bystrica	Slov. Div. II	19	3	1	4	8	...	...	...	—	—	—	—	—
96-97—Poprad	Slovakia	44	15	18	33	...	...	...	...	—	—	—	—	—
97-98—Worcester	AHL	69	27	36	63	54	...	...	...	11	2	6	8	10
98-99—St. Louis	NHL	66	4	12	16	30	-9	0	0	11	0	2	2	8
99-00—St. Louis	NHL	81	25	28	53	44	19	3	4	7	0	3	3	6
00-01—St. Louis	NHL	36	10	14	24	12	11	3	2	—	—	—	—	—
—Phoenix	NHL	10	4	4	8	21	5	0	1	—	—	—	—	—
01-02—Phoenix	NHL	79	15	30	45	34	-8	3	1	5	0	0	0	2
—Slovakian Oly. team	Int'l	2	1	0	1	6	...	...	...	—	—	—	—	—
02-03—Philadelphia	NHL	82	23	21	44	46	13	1	1	13	2	6	8	6
NHL Totals (5 years)		354	81	109	190	187	31	10	9	36	2	11	13	22

H

HANKINSON, CASEY   LW   MIGHTY DUCKS

PERSONAL: Born May 8, 1976, in Edina, Minn. ... 6-1/187. ... Shoots left. ... Brother of Ben Hankinson, right winger with New Jersey Devils (1992-93 through 1994-95) and Tampa Bay Lightning (1994-95); and brother of Peter Hankinson, center with Winnipeg Jets organization (1989-90 through 1991-92).

TRANSACTIONS/CAREER NOTES: Selected by Chicago Blackhawks in eighth round (ninth Blackhawks pick, 201st overall) of NHL entry draft (July 8, 1995). ... Signed as free agent by Anaheim Mighty Ducks (July 25, 2003).

		REGULAR SEASON								PLAYOFFS				
Season Team	League	Gms.	G	A	Pts.	PIM	+/-	PP	SH	Gms.	G	A	Pts.	PIM
92-93—Edina High School	Minn. H.S.	25	20	26	46	...	...	...	...	—	—	—	—	—
93-94—Edina High School	Minn. H.S.	24	21	20	41	50	...	...	...	—	—	—	—	—
94-95—Univ. of Minnesota......	WCHA	33	7	1	8	86	...	...	...	—	—	—	—	—
95-96—Univ. of Minnesota......	WCHA	39	16	19	35	101	...	...	...	—	—	—	—	—
96-97—Univ. of Minnesota......	WCHA	42	17	24	41	79	...	...	...	—	—	—	—	—
97-98—Univ. of Minnesota......	WCHA	35	10	12	22	81	...	...	...	—	—	—	—	—
98-99—Portland	AHL	72	10	13	23	106	...	...	...	—	—	—	—	—
99-00—Cleveland	IHL	82	7	22	29	140	...	...	...	2	0	0	0	2
00-01—Norfolk.......................	AHL	69	30	21	51	74	...	...	...	9	5	4	9	2
—Chicago......................	NHL	11	0	1	1	9	-3	0	0	—	—	—	—	—
01-02—Norfolk.......................	AHL	72	19	30	49	85	...	...	...	4	1	2	3	0
—Chicago......................	NHL	3	0	0	0	0	-2	0	0	—	—	—	—	—
02-03—Norfolk.......................	AHL	78	27	28	55	59	...	...	...	—	—	—	—	—
NHL Totals (2 years)...........		14	0	1	1	9	-5	0	0					

HANNAN, SCOTT   D   SHARKS

PERSONAL: Born January 23, 1979, in Richmond, B.C. ... 6-2/220. ... Shoots left.

TRANSACTIONS/CAREER NOTES: Selected by San Jose Sharks in first round (second Sharks pick, 23rd overall) of NHL entry draft (June 21, 1997). ... Injured ankle (October 24, 2000); missed three games. ... Injured knee (March 3, 2002); missed six games.

		REGULAR SEASON								PLAYOFFS				
Season Team	League	Gms.	G	A	Pts.	PIM	+/-	PP	SH	Gms.	G	A	Pts.	PIM
94-95—Tacoma	WHL	2	0	0	0	0	...	...	...	—	—	—	—	—
95-96—Kelowna.....................	WHL	69	4	5	9	76	...	...	...	6	0	1	1	4
96-97—Kelowna.....................	WHL	70	17	26	43	101	...	...	...	6	0	0	0	8
97-98—Kelowna.....................	WHL	47	10	30	40	70	...	...	...	—	—	—	—	—
98-99—San Jose....................	NHL	5	0	2	2	6	0	0	0	—	—	—	—	—
—Kelowna.....................	WHL	47	15	30	45	92	...	...	...	6	1	2	3	14
—Kentucky....................	AHL	2	0	0	0	2	...	...	...	12	0	2	2	10
99-00—Kentucky....................	AHL	41	5	12	17	40	...	...	...	—	—	—	—	—
—San Jose....................	NHL	30	1	2	3	10	7	0	0	1	0	1	1	0
00-01—San Jose....................	NHL	75	3	14	17	51	10	0	0	6	0	1	1	6
01-02—San Jose....................	NHL	75	2	12	14	57	10	0	0	12	0	2	2	12
02-03—San Jose....................	NHL	81	3	19	22	61	0	1	0	—	—	—	—	—
NHL Totals (5 years)...........		266	9	49	58	185	27	1	0	19	0	4	4	18

HARDING, JOSH   G   WILD

PERSONAL: Born June 18, 1984, in Regina, Sask. ... 6-1/168. ... Catches right.

TRANSACTIONS/CAREER NOTES: Selected by Minnesota Wild in second round (second Wild pick, 38th overall) of NHL entry draft (June 22, 2002).

		REGULAR SEASON								PLAYOFFS							
Season Team	League	Gms.	Min	W	L	T	GA	SO	Avg.	SV%	Gms.	Min.	W	L	GA	SO	Avg.	SV%
01-02—Regina........................	WHL	42	2389	27	13	1	95	†4	2.39	—	6	325	2	4	16	0	2.95	—
02-03—Regina........................	WHL	57	3385	18	24	13	155	3	2.75	—	—	—	—	—	—	—	—	—

HARLOCK, DAVID   D

PERSONAL: Born March 16, 1971, in Toronto. ... 6-2/220. ... Shoots left. ... Full Name: David Alan Harlock.

TRANSACTIONS/CAREER NOTES: Selected by New Jersey Devils in second round (second Devils pick, 24th overall) of NHL entry draft (June 16, 1990). ... Signed as free agent by Toronto Maple Leafs (August 20, 1993). ... Loaned by Maple Leafs to Canadian national team (October 3, 1993). ... Signed as free agent by Washington Capitals (August 31, 1997). ... Signed as free agent by New York Islanders (August 19, 1998). ... Bruised foot (October 29, 1998); missed one game. ... Selected by Atlanta Thrashers in NHL expansion draft (June 25, 1999). ... Strained shoulder (December 23, 1999) and underwent surgery; missed 36 games. ... Injured neck (December 1, 2000); missed six games. ... Suffered lacerated ear (December 21, 2001); missed two games. ... Traded by Thrashers with third- and seventh-round picks in 2003 draft to Philadelphia Flyers for D Francis Lessard (March 15, 2002).

		REGULAR SEASON								PLAYOFFS				
Season Team	League	Gms.	G	A	Pts.	PIM	+/-	PP	SH	Gms.	G	A	Pts.	PIM
86-87—Toronto Red Wings.....	MTHL	86	17	55	72	60	...	...	...	—	—	—	—	—
87-88—Toronto Red Wings.....	MTHL	70	16	56	72	100	...	...	...	—	—	—	—	—
88-89—St. Michael's Jr. B.......	ODHA	25	4	15	19	34	...	...	...	—	—	—	—	—
89-90—Univ. of Michigan........	CCHA	42	2	13	15	44	...	...	...	—	—	—	—	—
90-91—Univ. of Michigan........	CCHA	39	2	8	10	70	...	...	...	—	—	—	—	—
91-92—Univ. of Michigan........	CCHA	44	1	6	7	80	...	...	...	—	—	—	—	—
92-93—Univ. of Michigan........	CCHA	38	3	9	12	58	...	...	...	—	—	—	—	—
—Canadian nat'l team	Int'l	4	0	0	0	2	...	...	...	—	—	—	—	—

H

Season Team	League	REGULAR SEASON								PLAYOFFS				
		Gms.	G	A	Pts.	PIM	+/-	PP	SH	Gms.	G	A	Pts.	PIM
93-94—Canadian nat'l team	Int'l	41	0	3	3	28	...	...	...	—	—	—	—	—
—Can. Olympic team	Int'l	8	0	0	0	8	...	...	...	—	—	—	—	—
—Toronto	NHL	6	0	0	0	0	-2	0	0	—	—	—	—	—
—St. John's..................	AHL	10	0	3	3	2	...	...	...	9	0	0	0	6
94-95—St. John's..................	AHL	58	0	6	6	44	...	...	...	5	0	0	0	0
—Toronto	NHL	1	0	0	0	0	-1	0	0	—	—	—	—	—
95-96—St. John's..................	AHL	77	0	12	12	92	...	...	...	4	0	1	1	2
—Toronto	NHL	1	0	0	0	0	0	0	0	—	—	—	—	—
—Portland	AHL	1	0	0	0	0	...	...	...	—	—	—	—	—
96-97—San Antonio...............	IHL	69	3	10	13	82	...	...	...	9	0	0	0	10
97-98—Portland	AHL	71	3	15	18	66	...	...	...	10	2	2	4	6
—Washington	NHL	6	0	0	0	4	2	0	0	—	—	—	—	—
98-99—New York Islanders.....	NHL	70	2	6	8	68	-16	0	0	—	—	—	—	—
99-00—Atlanta	NHL	44	0	6	6	36	-8	0	0	—	—	—	—	—
00-01—Atlanta	NHL	65	0	1	1	62	-28	0	0	—	—	—	—	—
01-02—Atlanta	NHL	19	0	1	1	18	-2	0	0	—	—	—	—	—
—Chicago	AHL	24	2	9	11	28	...	...	...	—	—	—	—	—
—Philadelphia	AHL	11	0	4	4	14	...	...	...	5	0	1	1	4
02-03—Philadelphia	AHL	59	2	18	20	83	...	...	...	—	—	—	—	—
NHL Totals (8 years)...........		212	2	14	16	188	-55	0	0					

HARRISON, JAY   D   MAPLE LEAFS

PERSONAL: Born November 3, 1982, in Oshawa, Ont. ... 6-3/200. ... Shoots left.
TRANSACTIONS/CAREER NOTES: Selected by Toronto Maple Leafs in third round (fourth Maple Leafs pick, 82nd overall) of NHL entry draft (June 23, 2001).

Season Team	League	REGULAR SEASON								PLAYOFFS				
		Gms.	G	A	Pts.	PIM	+/-	PP	SH	Gms.	G	A	Pts.	PIM
98-99—Brampton...................	OHL	63	1	14	15	108	...	...	...	—	—	—	—	—
99-00—Brampton...................	OHL	68	2	18	20	139	...	...	...	6	0	2	2	15
00-01—Brampton...................	OHL	53	4	15	19	112	...	...	...	9	1	1	2	17
01-02—Brampton...................	OHL	61	12	31	43	116	...	...	...	—	—	—	—	—
—St. John's..................	AHL	7	0	1	1	2	...	...	...	10	0	0	0	4
02-03—St. John's..................	AHL	72	2	8	10	72	...	...	...	—	—	—	—	—

HARTIGAN, MARK   C   BLUE JACKETS

PERSONAL: Born October 15, 1977, in Fort St. John, B.C. ... 6-0/205.
TRANSACTIONS/CAREER NOTES: Signed as non-drafted free agent by Atlanta Thrashers (March 27, 2002). ... Tore hamstring (April 3, 2002); missed remainder of season. ... Signed by Columbus Blue Jackets (July 15, 2003).

Season Team	League	REGULAR SEASON								PLAYOFFS				
		Gms.	G	A	Pts.	PIM	+/-	PP	SH	Gms.	G	A	Pts.	PIM
99-00—St. Cloud State...........	WCHA	37	22	20	42	24	...	...	...	—	—	—	—	—
00-01—St. Cloud State...........	WCHA	40	27	21	48	20	...	...	...	—	—	—	—	—
01-02—St. Cloud State...........	WCHA	42	*37	38	75	42	...	...	...	—	—	—	—	—
—Atlanta	NHL	2	0	0	0	2	-2	0	0	—	—	—	—	—
02-03—Chicago	AHL	55	15	31	46	43	...	...	...	—	—	—	—	—
—Atlanta	NHL	23	5	2	7	6	-8	1	0	—	—	—	—	—
NHL Totals (2 years)...........		25	5	2	7	8	-10	1	0					

HARTNELL, SCOTT   LW   PREDATORS

PERSONAL: Born April 18, 1982, in Regina, Sask. ... 6-2/208. ... Shoots left. ... Cousin of Mark Deyell, center, Toronto Maple Leafs organization.
TRANSACTIONS/CAREER NOTES: Selected by Nashville Predators in first round (first Predators pick, sixth overall) of NHL entry draft (June 24, 2000). ... Suffered concussion (November 26, 2000); missed six games. ... Bruised left eye (October 27, 2001); missed five games. ... Suffered concussion (April 9, 2002); missed remainder of season. ... Re-signed by Predators (July 9, 2003).

Season Team	League	REGULAR SEASON								PLAYOFFS				
		Gms.	G	A	Pts.	PIM	+/-	PP	SH	Gms.	G	A	Pts.	PIM
97-98—Lloydminster...............	Jr. A	56	9	16	25	82	...	...	...	4	2	1	3	8
—Prince Albert..............	WHL	1	0	1	1	2	...	...	...	—	—	—	—	—
98-99—Prince Albert.............	WHL	65	10	34	44	104	...	...	...	14	0	5	5	22
99-00—Prince Albert.............	WHL	62	27	55	82	124	...	...	...	6	3	2	5	6
00-01—Nashville	NHL	75	2	14	16	48	-8	0	0	—	—	—	—	—
01-02—Nashville	NHL	75	14	27	41	111	5	3	0	—	—	—	—	—
02-03—Nashville	NHL	82	12	22	34	101	-3	2	0	—	—	—	—	—
NHL Totals (3 years)...........		232	28	63	91	260	-6	5	0					

H HARVEY, TODD   RW   SHARKS

PERSONAL: Born February 17, 1975, in Hamilton, Ont. ... 6-0/205. ... Shoots right.
TRANSACTIONS/CAREER NOTES: Selected by Dallas Stars in first round (first Stars pick, ninth overall) of NHL entry draft (June 26, 1993). ... Strained back (March 13, 1995); missed one game. ... Sprained knee (October 30, 1995); missed two games. ... Strained groin (November 3, 1996); missed one game. ... Sprained knee (November 19, 1996); missed five games. ... Suffered from the flu (December 29, 1996); missed

one game. ... Suspended two games and fined $1,000 by NHL for elbowing incident (February 2, 1997). ... Bruised hand (April 4, 1997); missed one game. ... Suffered concussion (November 16, 1997); missed one game. ... Strained hip flexor (December 20, 1997); missed one game. ... Sprained knee (January 7, 1998); missed five games. ... Injured hand (February 4, 1998); missed one game. ... Strained lower back (March 13, 1998); missed one game. ... Underwent right knee surgery (March 22, 1998); missed 12 games. ... Traded by Stars with LW Bob Errey and fourth-round pick (LW Boyd Kane) in 1998 draft to New York Rangers for RW Mike Keane, C Brian Skrudland and sixth-round pick (RW Pavel Patera) in 1998 draft (March 24, 1998). ... Strained hip flexor (October 9, 1998); missed first two games of season. ... Suspended one game and fined $1,000 by NHL for roughing incident (December 13, 1998). ... Bruised right thumb (December 11, 1998); missed two games. ... Suffered medial collateral ligament (January 13, 1999); missed 10 games. ... Fractured thumb (February 17, 1999); missed final 27 games of season. ... Sprained knee (November 18, 1999); missed three games. ... Traded by Rangers with fourth-round pick (G Dimitri Patzold) in 2001 draft to San Jose Sharks for RW Radek Dvorak (December 30, 1999). ... Suffered concussion and whiplash (January 1, 2001); missed 10 games. ... Injured knee (November 27, 2001); missed three games. ... Injured shoulder (March 10, 2002); missed 10 games.

STATISTICAL PLATEAUS: Three-goal games: 1994-95 (1), 2000-01 (1). Total: 2.

| | | REGULAR SEASON | | | | | | | | PLAYOFFS | | | | |
Season Team	League	Gms.	G	A	Pts.	PIM	+/-	PP	SH	Gms.	G	A	Pts.	PIM
89-90—Cambridge Jr. B	OHA	41	35	27	62	213	...	...	...	—	—	—	—	—
90-91—Cambridge Jr. B	OHA	35	32	39	71	174	...	...	...	—	—	—	—	—
91-92—Det. Jr. Red Wings	OHL	58	21	43	64	141	...	...	...	7	3	5	8	32
92-93—Det. Jr. Red Wings	OHL	55	50	50	100	83	...	...	...	15	9	12	21	39
93-94—Det. Jr. Red Wings	OHL	49	34	51	85	75	...	...	...	17	10	12	22	26
94-95—Det. Jr. Red Wings	OHL	11	8	14	22	12	...	...	...	—	—	—	—	—
—Dallas	NHL	40	11	9	20	67	-3	2	0	5	0	0	0	8
95-96—Dallas	NHL	69	9	20	29	136	-13	3	0	—	—	—	—	—
—Michigan	IHL	5	1	3	4	8	...	...	...	—	—	—	—	—
96-97—Dallas	NHL	71	9	22	31	142	19	1	0	7	0	1	1	10
97-98—Dallas	NHL	59	9	10	19	104	5	0	0	—	—	—	—	—
98-99—New York Rangers	NHL	37	11	17	28	72	-1	6	0	—	—	—	—	—
99-00—New York Rangers	NHL	31	3	3	6	62	-9	0	0	—	—	—	—	—
—San Jose	NHL	40	8	4	12	78	-2	2	0	12	1	0	1	8
00-01—San Jose	NHL	69	10	11	21	72	6	1	0	6	0	0	0	8
01-02—San Jose	NHL	69	9	13	22	73	16	0	0	12	0	2	2	12
02-03—San Jose	NHL	76	3	16	19	74	5	0	0	—	—	—	—	—
NHL Totals (9 years)		561	82	125	207	880	23	15	0	42	1	3	4	46

HASEK, DOMINIK   G   RED WINGS

PERSONAL: Born January 29, 1965, in Pardubice, Czechoslovakia. ... 5-11/168. ... Catches left. ... Name pronounced HA-shehk.

TRANSACTIONS/CAREER NOTES: Selected by Chicago Blackhawks in 10th round (11th Blackhawks pick, 199th overall) of NHL entry draft (June 8, 1983). ... Traded by Blackhawks to Buffalo Sabres for G Stephane Beauregard and fourth-round pick (LW Eric Daze) in 1993 draft (August 7, 1992). ... Injured groin (November 25, 1992); missed three games. ... Strained abdominal muscle (January 6, 1993); missed six games. ... Played in Europe during 1994-95 NHL lockout. ... Strained rotator cuff (March 16, 1995); missed three games. ... Injured abdominal muscle (December 15, 1995); missed 10 games. ... Sprained left knee (April 6, 1996); missed last two games of season. ... Fractured rib (March 19, 1997); missed five games. ... Sprained knee ligament (April 21, 1997); missed six playoff games. ... Suspended three playoff games and fined $10,000 by NHL for grabbing a reporter who had written a critical column (May 1, 1997). ... Suffered ear infection (April 15, 1998); missed one game. ... Strained groin (February 17, 1999); missed 12 games. ... Strained back (March 23, 1999); missed one game. ... Tore groin muscle (October 29, 1999); missed 40 games. ... Injured knee (October 5, 2000); missed one game. ... Traded by Sabres to Detroit Red Wings for LW Slava Kozlov, first-round pick (traded to Columbus) in 2002 draft and future considerations (July 1, 2001). ... Announced retirement (June 25, 2002). ... Announced return from retirement (July 8, 2003).

| | | REGULAR SEASON | | | | | | | | | PLAYOFFS | | | | | | | |
Season Team	League	Gms.	Min	W	L	T	GA	SO	Avg.	SV%	Gms.	Min.	W	L	GA	SO	Avg.	SV%
81-82—Pardubice	Czech Rep.	12	661	...	...	...	34	...	3.09	—	—	—	—	—	—	—	—	—
82-83—Pardubice	Czech Rep.	42	2358	...	...	...	105	...	2.67	—	—	—	—	—	—	—	—	—
83-84—Pardubice	Czech Rep.	40	2304	...	...	...	108	...	2.81	—	—	—	—	—	—	—	—	—
84-85—Pardubice	Czech Rep.	42	2419	...	...	...	131	...	3.25	—	—	—	—	—	—	—	—	—
85-86—Pardubice	Czech Rep.	45	2689	...	...	...	138	...	3.08	—	—	—	—	—	—	—	—	—
86-87—Pardubice	Czech Rep.	23	2515	...	...	...	103	...	2.46	—	—	—	—	—	—	—	—	—
87-88—Pardubice	Czech Rep.	31	1862	...	...	...	93	...	3.00	—	—	—	—	—	—	—	—	—
—Czech. Olympic Team	Int'l	5	217	3	2	0	18	1	4.98	—	—	—	—	—	—	—	—	—
88-89—Pardubice	Czech Rep.	42	2507	...	...	...	114	...	2.73	—	—	—	—	—	—	—	—	—
89-90—Dukla Jihlava	Czech.	40	2251	...	...	...	80	...	2.13	—	—	—	—	—	—	—	—	—
90-91—Chicago	NHL	5	195	3	0	1	8	0	2.46	.914	3	69	0	0	3	0	2.61	.923
—Indianapolis	IHL	33	1903	20	11	‡4	80	*5	*2.52	—	1	60	1	0	3	0	3.00	—
91-92—Indianapolis	IHL	20	1162	7	10	‡3	69	1	3.56	—	—	—	—	—	—	—	—	—
—Chicago	NHL	20	1014	10	4	1	44	1	2.60	.893	3	158	0	2	8	0	3.04	.886
92-93—Buffalo	NHL	28	1429	11	10	4	75	0	3.15	.896	1	45	1	0	1	0	1.33	.958
93-94—Buffalo	NHL	58	3358	30	20	6	109	†7	*1.95	.930	7	484	3	4	13	2	*1.61	.950
94-95—HC Pardubice	Czech Rep.	2	125	...	...	...	6	...	2.88	—	—	—	—	—	—	—	—	—
—Buffalo	NHL	41	2416	19	14	7	85	†5	*2.11	.930	5	309	1	4	18	0	3.50	.863
95-96—Buffalo	NHL	59	3417	22	†30	6	161	2	2.83	.920	—	—	—	—	—	—	—	—
96-97—Buffalo	NHL	67	4037	37	20	10	153	5	2.27	.930	3	153	1	1	5	0	1.96	.926
97-98—Buffalo	NHL	*72	*4220	33	23	13	147	*13	2.09	.932	15	948	10	5	32	1	2.03	.938
—Czech Rep. Oly. team	Int'l	6	*369	*5	1	0	*6	*2	*0.97	—	—	—	—	—	—	—	—	—
98-99—Buffalo	NHL	64	3817	30	18	14	119	9	1.87	.937	19	1217	13	6	36	2	1.77	.939
99-00—Buffalo	NHL	35	2066	15	11	6	76	3	2.21	.919	5	301	1	4	12	0	2.39	.918
00-01—Buffalo	NHL	67	3904	37	24	4	137	*11	2.11	.921	13	833	7	6	29	1	2.09	.916
01-02—Detroit	NHL	65	3872	*41	15	8	140	5	2.17	.915	*23	*1455	*16	7	45	*6	1.86	.920
—Czech Rep. Oly. team	Int'l	4	239	1	2	1	8	0	2.01	—	—	—	—	—	—	—	—	—
02-03—							Did not play.											
NHL Totals (12 years)		581	33745	288	189	80	1254	61	2.23	.924	97	5972	53	39	202	12	2.03	.927

H

HATCHER, DERIAN   D   RED WINGS

PERSONAL: Born June 4, 1972, in Sterling Heights, Mich. ... 6-5/235. ... Shoots left. ... Brother of Kevin Hatcher, defenseman with five NHL teams (1984-85 through 2000-01).

TRANSACTIONS/CAREER NOTES: Selected by Minnesota North Stars in first round (first North Stars pick, eighth overall) of NHL entry draft (June 16, 1990). ... Suspended 10 games by NHL (December 1991). ... Fractured ankle in off-ice incident (January 19, 1992); missed 21 games. ... Sprained knee (January 6, 1993); missed 14 games. ... Suspended one game by NHL for game misconduct penalties (March 9, 1993). ... North Stars franchise moved from Minnesota to Dallas and renamed Stars for 1993-94 season. ... Sprained ankle (February 2, 1995); missed one game. ... Suffered staph infection on little finger (February 14, 1995); missed four games. ... Injured right knee ligament (May 1, 1995); missed entire playoffs. ... Injured shoulder (November 14, 1995); missed three games. ... Strained knee (December 8, 1996); missed 14 games. ... Underwent knee surgery (March 19, 1997); missed five games. ... Injured knee (March 8, 1998); missed seven games. ... Suspended four pre-season games and fined $1,000 by NHL for injuring another player (September 23, 1998). ... Suspended seven games by NHL for illegal check (April 17, 1999); missed final two games of regular season and first five playoff games. ... Suffered lacerated calf (December 17, 1999); missed 24 games. ... Strained Achilles' tendon (March 8, 2000); missed one game. ... Suspended two games by NHL for elbowing incident (March 27, 2001). ... Strained hamstring (November 21, 2001); missed two games. ... Suspended one playoff game by NHL for receiving second game misconduct during the playoffs (April 12, 2003). ... Signed by Detroit Red Wings (July 2, 2003).

Season Team	League	REGULAR SEASON Gms.	G	A	Pts.	PIM	+/-	PP	SH	PLAYOFFS Gms.	G	A	Pts.	PIM
88-89—Detroit G.P.D.	MNHL	51	19	35	54	100	...	...	...	—	—	—	—	—
89-90—North Bay	OHL	64	14	38	52	81	...	...	...	5	2	3	5	8
90-91—North Bay	OHL	64	13	50	63	163	...	...	...	10	2	10	12	28
91-92—Minnesota	NHL	43	8	4	12	88	7	0	0	5	0	2	2	8
92-93—Minnesota	NHL	67	4	15	19	178	-27	0	0	—	—	—	—	—
—Kalamazoo	IHL	2	1	2	3	21	...	...	...	—	—	—	—	—
93-94—Dallas	NHL	83	12	19	31	211	19	2	1	9	0	2	2	14
94-95—Dallas	NHL	43	5	11	16	105	3	2	0	—	—	—	—	—
95-96—Dallas	NHL	79	8	23	31	129	-12	2	0	—	—	—	—	—
96-97—Dallas	NHL	63	3	19	22	97	8	0	0	7	0	2	2	20
97-98—Dallas	NHL	70	6	25	31	132	9	3	0	17	3	3	6	39
—U.S. Olympic team	Int'l	4	0	0	0	0	...	...	...	—	—	—	—	—
98-99—Dallas	NHL	80	9	21	30	102	21	3	0	18	1	6	7	24
99-00—Dallas	NHL	57	2	22	24	68	6	0	0	23	1	3	4	29
00-01—Dallas	NHL	80	2	21	23	77	5	1	0	10	0	1	1	16
01-02—Dallas	NHL	80	4	21	25	87	12	1	0	—	—	—	—	—
02-03—Dallas	NHL	82	8	22	30	106	37	1	1	11	1	2	3	33
NHL Totals (12 years)		827	71	223	294	1380	88	15	2	100	6	21	27	183

HAVELID, NICLAS   D   MIGHTY DUCKS

PERSONAL: Born April 12, 1973, in Stockholm, Sweden ... 5-11/197. ... Shoots left.

TRANSACTIONS/CAREER NOTES: Selected by Mighty Ducks of Anaheim in third round (second Mighty Ducks pick, 83rd overall) of NHL entry draft (June 26, 1999). ... Fractured finger (January 15, 2000); missed 23 games. ... Tore anterior cruciate ligament in knee (January 15, 2001); missed remainder of season.

Season Team	League	REGULAR SEASON Gms.	G	A	Pts.	PIM	+/-	PP	SH	PLAYOFFS Gms.	G	A	Pts.	PIM
91-92—AIK Solna	Sweden	10	0	0	0	2	...	...	...	—	—	—	—	—
92-93—AIK Solna	Sweden	22	1	0	1	16	...	...	...	—	—	—	—	—
93-94—AIK Solna	Sweden Dv. 2			Statistics unavailable.						—	—	—	—	—
94-95—AIK Solna	Sweden	40	3	7	10	38	...	...	...	—	—	—	—	—
95-96—AIK Solna	Sweden	40	5	6	11	30	...	...	...	—	—	—	—	—
96-97—AIK Solna	Sweden	49	3	6	9	42	...	...	...	7	1	2	3	8
97-98—AIK Solna	Sweden	43	8	4	12	42	...	...	...	—	—	—	—	—
98-99—Malmo	Sweden	50	10	12	22	42	...	...	...	8	0	4	4	10
99-00—Anaheim	NHL	50	2	7	9	20	0	0	0	—	—	—	—	—
—Cincinnati	AHL	2	0	0	0	0	...	...	...	—	—	—	—	—
00-01—Anaheim	NHL	47	4	10	14	34	-6	2	0	—	—	—	—	—
01-02—Anaheim	NHL	52	1	2	3	40	-13	0	0	—	—	—	—	—
02-03—Anaheim	NHL	82	11	22	33	30	5	4	0	21	0	4	4	2
NHL Totals (4 years)		231	18	41	59	124	-14	6	0	21	0	4	4	2

HAVLAT, MARTIN   LW   SENATORS

PERSONAL: Born April 19, 1981, in Mlada Boleslav, Czechoslovakia ... 6-1/194. ... Shoots left.

TRANSACTIONS/CAREER NOTES: Selected by Ottawa Senators in first round (first Senators pick, 26th pick overall) of NHL entry draft (June 26, 1999). ... Injured shoulder (November 23, 2000); missed eight games. ... Strained groin (April 6, 2001); missed final game of regular season. ... Injured groin (January 30, 2002); missed one game. ... Strained groin (March 17, 2002); missed two games. ... Reinjured groin (March 28, 2002); missed final seven games of regular season.

STATISTICAL PLATEAUS: Three-goal games: 2000-01 (1), 2001-02 (1), 2002-03 (1). Total: 3.

Season Team	League	REGULAR SEASON Gms.	G	A	Pts.	PIM	+/-	PP	SH	PLAYOFFS Gms.	G	A	Pts.	PIM
96-97—Ytong Brno	Czech. Jrs.	34	43	27	70	...	...	...	...	—	—	—	—	—
97-98—Ytong Brno	Czech. Jrs.	32	38	29	67	...	...	...	...	—	—	—	—	—
98-99—Zelezarny Trinec	Czech. Jrs.	31	28	23	51	...	...	...	...	—	—	—	—	—
—Zelezarny Trinec	Czech Rep.	24	2	3	5	4	...	...	...	8	0	0	0	...
99-00—Zelezarny Trinec	Czech Rep.	46	13	29	42	42	...	...	...	4	0	2	2	8
00-01—Ottawa	NHL	73	19	23	42	20	8	7	0	4	0	0	0	2
01-02—Ottawa	NHL	72	22	28	50	66	-7	9	0	12	2	5	7	14
—Czech Rep. Oly. team	Int'l	4	3	1	4	27	...	...	...	—	—	—	—	—
02-03—Ottawa	NHL	67	24	35	59	30	20	9	0	18	5	6	11	14
NHL Totals (3 years)		212	65	86	151	116	21	25	0	34	7	11	18	30

H

HAWGOOD, GREG　　　　D

PERSONAL: Born August 10, 1968, in Edmonton. ... 5-10/190. ... Shoots left. ... Full Name: Gregory William Hawgood.
TRANSACTIONS/CAREER NOTES: Selected by Boston Bruins in 10th round (ninth Bruins pick, 202nd overall) of NHL entry draft (June 21, 1986). ... Announced that he would play in Italy for 1990-91 season (July 1990). ... Traded by Bruins to Edmonton Oilers for C Vladimir Ruzicka (October 22, 1990). ... Traded by Oilers with C Josef Beranek to Philadelphia Flyers for D Brian Benning (January 16, 1993). ... Traded by Flyers to Florida Panthers for future considerations (November 28, 1993). ... Bruised left thumb (January 13, 1994); missed seven games. ... Traded by Panthers to Pittsburgh Penguins for LW Jeff Daniels (March 19, 1994). ... Dislocated left shoulder (February 14, 1995); missed eight games. ... Signed as free agent by San Jose Sharks (September 8, 1996). ... Suspended two games and fined $1,000 by NHL for slashing incident (December 31, 1996). ... Signed as free agent by Vancouver Canucks (September 30, 1999). ... Sprained knee (November 15, 1999); missed one game. ... Signed as free agent by Dallas Stars (July 17, 2001).

		REGULAR SEASON								PLAYOFFS				
Season Team	League	Gms.	G	A	Pts.	PIM	+/-	PP	SH	Gms.	G	A	Pts.	PIM
83-84—Kamloops	WHL	49	10	23	33	39	...	...	...	—	—	—	—	—
84-85—Kamloops	WHL	66	25	40	65	72	...	...	...	—	—	—	—	—
85-86—Kamloops	WHL	71	34	85	119	86	...	...	...	16	9	22	31	16
86-87—Kamloops	WHL	61	30	93	123	139	...	...	...	—	—	—	—	—
87-88—Boston	NHL	1	0	0	0	0	-1	0	0	3	1	0	1	0
—Kamloops	WHL	63	48	85	133	142	...	...	...	16	10	16	26	33
88-89—Boston	NHL	56	16	24	40	84	4	5	0	10	0	2	2	2
—Maine	AHL	21	2	9	11	41	...	...	...	—	—	—	—	—
89-90—Boston	NHL	77	11	27	38	76	12	2	0	15	1	3	4	12
90-91—Asiago	Italy	2	3	0	3	9	...	...	...	—	—	—	—	—
—Maine	AHL	5	0	1	1	13	...	...	...	—	—	—	—	—
—Cape Breton	AHL	55	10	32	42	73	...	...	...	4	0	3	3	23
—Edmonton	NHL	6	0	1	1	6	-2	0	0	—	—	—	—	—
91-92—Cape Breton	AHL	56	20	55	75	26	...	...	...	3	2	2	4	0
—Edmonton	NHL	20	2	11	13	22	19	0	0	13	0	3	3	23
92-93—Edmonton	NHL	29	5	13	18	35	-1	2	0	—	—	—	—	—
—Philadelphia	NHL	40	6	22	28	39	-7	5	0	—	—	—	—	—
93-94—Philadelphia	NHL	19	3	12	15	19	2	3	0	—	—	—	—	—
—Florida	NHL	33	2	14	16	9	8	0	0	—	—	—	—	—
—Pittsburgh	NHL	12	1	2	3	8	-1	1	0	1	0	0	0	0
94-95—Cleveland	IHL	—	—	—	—	—	—	—	—	3	1	0	1	4
—Pittsburgh	NHL	21	1	4	5	25	2	1	0	—	—	—	—	—
95-96—Las Vegas	IHL	78	20	65	85	101	...	...	...	15	5	11	16	24
96-97—San Jose	NHL	63	6	12	18	69	-22	3	0	—	—	—	—	—
97-98—Houston	IHL	81	19	52	71	75	...	...	...	4	0	4	4	0
98-99—Houston	IHL	76	17	57	74	90	...	...	...	19	4	8	12	24
99-00—Vancouver	NHL	79	5	17	22	26	5	2	0	—	—	—	—	—
00-01—Vancouver	NHL	16	2	5	7	6	8	1	0	—	—	—	—	—
—Kansas City	IHL	46	6	16	22	21	...	...	...	—	—	—	—	—
01-02—Utah	AHL	67	18	43	61	83	...	...	...	5	0	2	2	2
—Dallas	NHL	2	0	0	0	2	0	0	0	—	—	—	—	—
02-03—Utah	AHL	70	15	42	57	76	...	...	...	—	—	—	—	—
NHL Totals (12 years)		474	60	164	224	426	26	25	0	42	2	8	10	37

HAY, DARRELL　　　　D

PERSONAL: Born April 2, 1980, in Kamloops, B.C. ... 6-0/190. ... Shoots right.

		REGULAR SEASON								PLAYOFFS				
Season Team	League	Gms.	G	A	Pts.	PIM	+/-	PP	SH	Gms.	G	A	Pts.	PIM
97-98—Tri-City	WHL	71	5	33	38	90	...	...	...	—	—	—	—	—
98-99—Tri-City	WHL	72	13	49	62	87	...	...	...	12	2	10	12	22
99-00—Tri-City	WHL	64	15	36	51	85	...	...	...	4	0	1	1	8
00-01—Kansas City	IHL	9	0	0	0	19	...	...	...	—	—	—	—	—
—Florida	ECHL	40	5	4	9	26	...	...	...	5	2	1	3	0
01-02—Manitoba	AHL	53	5	8	13	29	...	...	...	7	1	1	2	2
—Columbia	ECHL	15	0	13	13	15	...	...	...	—	—	—	—	—
02-03—Manitoba	AHL	43	3	10	13	29	...	...	...	—	—	—	—	—
—Columbia	ECHL	12	2	3	5	13	...	...	...	—	—	—	—	—

HAYDAR, DARREN　　　　RW　　　　PREDATORS

PERSONAL: Born October 22, 1979, in Toronto ... 5-9/170. ... Shoots left.
TRANSACTIONS/CAREER NOTES: Selected by Nashville Predators in ninth round (15th Predators pick, 248th overall) of NHL entry draft (June 26, 1999).

		REGULAR SEASON								PLAYOFFS				
Season Team	League	Gms.	G	A	Pts.	PIM	+/-	PP	SH	Gms.	G	A	Pts.	PIM
98-99—Univ. of New Hamp.	Hockey East	41	31	30	61	34	...	...	...	—	—	—	—	—
99-00—Univ. of New Hamp.	Hockey East	38	22	19	41	42	...	...	...	—	—	—	—	—
00-01—Univ. of New Hamp.	Hockey East	39	18	23	41	38	...	...	...	—	—	—	—	—
01-02—Univ. of New Hamp.	Hockey East	40	31	*45	*76	28	...	...	...	—	—	—	—	—
02-03—Milwaukee	AHL	75	29	46	75	36	...	...	...	—	—	—	—	—
—Nashville	NHL	2	0	0	0	0	-1	0	0	—	—	—	—	—
NHL Totals (1 year)		2	0	0	0	0	-1	0	0					

H

PERSONAL: Born March 20, 1975, in Edmonton ... 6-2/200. ... Shoots right.

TRANSACTIONS/CAREER NOTES: Selected by Philadelphia Flyers in eighth round (seventh Flyers pick, 192nd overall) of NHL entry draft (June 26, 1993). ... Traded by Flyers to Nashville Predators for RW Matt Henderson (September 27, 1999). ... Signed as free agent by Edmonton Oilers (August 31, 2000). ... Signed as free agent by Toronto Maple Leafs (July 24, 2001). ... Signed as free agent by New York Rangers (July 28, 2003).

Season Team	League	REGULAR SEASON Gms.	G	A	Pts.	PIM	+/-	PP	SH	PLAYOFFS Gms.	G	A	Pts.	PIM
92-93—Prince Albert	WHL	72	12	20	32	66	...	...	...	—	—	—	—	—
93-94—Prince Albert	WHL	63	23	26	49	70	...	...	...	—	—	—	—	—
94-95—Prince Albert	WHL	71	43	50	93	67	...	...	...	12	3	4	7	2
95-96—Hershey	AHL	61	7	15	22	35	...	...	...	—	—	—	—	—
96-97—Philadelphia	AHL	64	21	19	40	56	...	...	...	10	4	1	5	10
—Philadelphia	NHL	2	0	0	0	0	0	0	0	—	—	—	—	—
97-98—Philadelphia	AHL	71	34	18	52	48	...	...	...	20	6	2	8	4
—Philadelphia	NHL	4	0	0	0	12	0	0	0	—	—	—	—	—
98-99—Philadelphia	AHL	72	26	20	46	39	...	...	...	15	4	6	10	11
99-00—Milwaukee	IHL	76	21	18	39	28	...	...	...	3	1	2	3	0
00-01—Hamilton	AHL	79	39	32	71	34	...	...	...	—	—	—	—	—
01-02—St. John's	AHL	58	27	29	56	30	...	...	...	2	1	1	2	8
—Toronto	NHL	21	3	7	10	2	7	0	0	18	0	1	1	2
02-03—St. John's	AHL	17	6	10	16	12	...	...	...	—	—	—	—	—
—Toronto	NHL	44	3	7	10	16	8	1	0	4	0	1	1	2
NHL Totals (4 years)		71	6	14	20	30	15	1	0	22	0	2	2	4

PERSONAL: Born January 21, 1981, in Freiburg, West Germany ... 6-3/215. ... Shoots left. ... Full Name: Daniel James Heatley.

TRANSACTIONS/CAREER NOTES: Selected by Atlanta Thrashers in first round (first Thrashers pick, second overall) of NHL entry draft (June 24, 2000).

STATISTICAL PLATEAUS: Three-goal games: 2002-03 (2).

Season Team	League	REGULAR SEASON Gms.	G	A	Pts.	PIM	+/-	PP	SH	PLAYOFFS Gms.	G	A	Pts.	PIM
98-99—Calgary Royals	AJHL	60	*70	56	*126	91	...	...	...	13	*22	13	*35	6
99-00—Univ. of Wisconsin	WCHA	38	28	28	56	32	...	...	...	—	—	—	—	—
00-01—Univ. of Wisconsin	WCHA	39	24	33	57	74	...	...	...	—	—	—	—	—
01-02—Atlanta	NHL	82	26	41	67	56	-19	7	0	—	—	—	—	—
02-03—Atlanta	NHL	77	41	48	89	58	-8	19	1	—	—	—	—	—
NHL Totals (2 years)		159	67	89	156	114	-27	26	1					

PERSONAL: Born June 21, 1977, in Mannheim, West Germany ... 6-1/199. ... Shoots left. ... Full Name: Jochen Thomas Hecht.

TRANSACTIONS/CAREER NOTES: Selected by St. Louis Blues in second round (first Blues pick, 49th overall) of NHL entry draft (July 8, 1995). ... Sprained ankle (January 13, 2000); missed 13 games. ... Reinjured ankle (February 23, 2000); missed six games. ... Strained oblique muscle (January 27, 2001); missed one game. ... Strained oblique muscle (February 1, 2001); missed two games. ... Strained oblique muscle (March 24, 2001); missed seven games. ... Traded by Blues with C Marty Reasoner and D Jan Horacek to Edmonton Oilers for C Doug Weight and LW Michel Riesen (July 1, 2001). ... Traded by Oilers to Buffalo Sabres for two second-round (G Jeff Deslauriers and C Jarrett Stoll) picks in 2002 draft (June 22, 2002).

Season Team	League	REGULAR SEASON Gms.	G	A	Pts.	PIM	+/-	PP	SH	PLAYOFFS Gms.	G	A	Pts.	PIM
94-95—Mannheim	Germany	43	11	12	23	68	...	...	...	10	5	4	9	12
95-96—Mannheim	Germany	44	12	16	28	68	...	...	...	8	3	2	5	6
96-97—Mannheim	Germany	46	21	21	42	36	...	...	...	—	—	—	—	—
97-98—Mannheim	Germany	44	7	19	26	42	...	...	...	10	1	1	2	14
—German Oly. team	Int'l	4	1	0	1	6	...	...	...	—	—	—	—	—
98-99—Worcester	AHL	74	21	35	56	48	...	...	...	4	1	1	2	2
—St. Louis	NHL	3	0	0	0	0	-2	0	0	5	2	0	2	0
99-00—St. Louis	NHL	63	13	21	34	28	20	5	0	7	4	6	10	2
00-01—St. Louis	NHL	72	19	25	44	48	11	8	3	15	2	4	6	4
01-02—Edmonton	NHL	82	16	24	40	60	4	5	0	—	—	—	—	—
—German Oly. team	Int'l	4	1	1	2	2	...	...	...	—	—	—	—	—
02-03—Buffalo	NHL	49	10	16	26	30	4	2	0	—	—	—	—	—
NHL Totals (5 years)		269	58	86	144	166	37	20	3	27	8	10	18	6

PERSONAL: Born October 11, 1974, in Partizanske, Czechoslovakia ... 6-3/202. ... Shoots left.

Season Team	League	REGULAR SEASON Gms.	G	A	Pts.	PIM	+/-	PP	SH	PLAYOFFS Gms.	G	A	Pts.	PIM
96-97—Bratislava	Slovakia	36	1	5	6	...	...	...	...	—	—	—	—	—
97-98—Bratislava	Slovakia	6	2	1	3	6	...	...	...	—	—	—	—	—
98-99—Bratislava	Slovakia	40	5	10	15	...	...	...	...	—	—	—	—	—
99-00—Bratislava	Slovakia	41	2	7	9	61	...	...	...	—	—	—	—	—
00-01—Bratislava	Slovakia	25	2	5	7	8	...	...	...	—	—	—	—	—
01-02—Bratislava	Slovakia	50	7	13	20	22	...	...	...	—	—	—	—	—
02-03—Rochester	AHL	58	6	14	20	41	...	...	...	—	—	—	—	—
—Buffalo	NHL	14	0	0	0	2	0	0	0	—	—	—	—	—
NHL Totals (1 year)		14	0	0	0	2	0	0	0					

H

PERSONAL: Born May 3, 1973, in Leksand, Sweden ... 6-0/185. ... Catches left.

TRANSACTIONS/CAREER NOTES: Selected by Philadelphia Flyers in ninth round (eighth Flyers pick, 218th overall) of NHL entry draft (June 29, 1994). ... Traded by Flyers to San Jose Sharks for seventh-round pick (C Pavel Kasparik) in 1999 draft (July 6, 1998). ... Traded by Sharks with D Bobby Dollas to Pittsburgh Penguins for D Jeff Norton (March 12, 2001).

Season Team	League	Gms.	Min	W	L	T	GA	SO	Avg.	SV%	Gms.	Min.	W	L	GA	SO	Avg.	SV%
92-93—Leksand	Sweden Dv. 2	10	600	...	...	...	24		2.40	—	—	—	—	—	—	—	—	—
93-94—Leksand	Sweden Dv. 2	17	1020	...	...	...	48	0	2.82	—	—	—	—	—	—	—	—	—
94-95—Leksand	Sweden Dv. 2	17	986	...	...	...	58	1	3.53	—	—	—	—	—	—	—	—	—
95-96—Leksand	Sweden Dv. 2	34	2013	...	...	...	95		2.83	—	4	240	...	...	13		3.25	—
96-97—Leksand	Sweden Dv. 2	38	2260	...	...	...	95	3	2.52	—	4	581	...	...	18	1	1.86	—
97-98—Baton Rouge	ECHL	2	100	1	1	0	7	0	4.20	—	—	—	—	—	—	—	—	—
—Detroit	IHL	16	726	7	2	‡2	32	1	2.64	—	—	—	—	—	—	—	—	—
—Manitoba	IHL	14	745	8	4	‡1	32	1	2.58	—	2	106	0	2	6	0	3.40	—
98-99—Leksand	Sweden Dv. 2	48	2940	...	...	...	140	0	2.86	—	4	255	...	...	15	0	3.53	—
99-00—Kentucky	AHL	33	1973	18	9	5	88	3	2.68	—	5	311	3	2	10	1	1.93	—
00-01—Manitoba	IHL	46	2697	23	13	‡7	115	1	2.56	—	—	—	—	—	—	—	—	—
—Pittsburgh	NHL	9	545	7	1	1	24	0	2.64	.905	18	1123	9	9	43	2	2.30	.911
01-02—Pittsburgh	NHL	66	3877	25	*34	7	178	6	2.75	.904	—	—	—	—	—	—	—	—
—Swedish Oly. team	Int'l	1	60	1	0	0	1	0	1.00	—	—	—	—	—	—	—	—	—
02-03—Pittsburgh	NHL	41	2410	14	22	4	126	1	3.14	.895	—	—	—	—	—	—	—	—
NHL Totals (3 years)		116	6832	46	57	12	328	7	2.88	.901	18	1123	9	9	43	2	2.30	.911

HEDICAN, BRET   D   HURRICANES

PERSONAL: Born August 10, 1970, in St. Paul, Minn. ... 6-2/205. ... Shoots left. ... Full Name: Bret Michael Hedican. ... Name pronounced HEHD-ih-kihn.

TRANSACTIONS/CAREER NOTES: Selected by St. Louis Blues in 10th round (10th Blues pick, 198th overall) of NHL entry draft (June 11, 1988). ... Strained knee ligaments (September 27, 1992); missed first 15 games of season. ... Injured shoulder (October 24, 1993); missed three games. ... Injured groin (January 18, 1994); missed six games. ... Traded by Blues with D Jeff Brown and C Nathan LaFayette to Vancouver Canucks for C Craig Janney (March 21, 1994). ... Strained groin (March 27, 1994); missed three games. ... Injured back (February 1, 1996); missed three games. ... Strained back (October 5, 1996); missed six games. ... Strained groin (December 4, 1996); missed five games. ... Strained groin (December 26, 1996); missed four games. ... Missed one game for personal reasons (December 13, 1997). ... Strained back (January 21, 1998); missed one game. ... Strained abdominal muscle (February 17, 1998); missed six games. ... Sprained ankle (September 23, 1998); missed first game of season. ... Traded by Canucks with RW Pavel Bure, D Brad Ference and third-round pick (RW Robert Fried) in 2000 draft to Florida Panthers for D Ed Jovanovski, G Kevin Weekes, C Dave Gagner, C Mike Brown and first-round pick (C Nathan Smith) in 2000 draft (January 17, 1999). ... Injured eye (February 11, 1999); missed eight games. ... Strained groin (March 31, 1999); missed eight games. ... Suspended three games by NHL for slashing incident (November 3, 1999). ... Strained groin (October 22, 1999); missed two games. ... Strained groin (February 26, 2000); missed one game. ... Suffered concussion (December 4, 2000); missed three games. ... Sprained left ankle (December 29, 2000); missed nine games. ... Fractured jaw (September 29, 2001); missed first 14 games of season. ... Traded by Panthers with C Kevyn Adams, D Tomas Malec and conditional second-round draft pick in 2003 to Carolina Hurricanes for D Sandis Ozolinsh and C Byron Ritchie (January 16, 2002). ... Strained back (January 25, 2002); missed seven games.

Season Team	League	Gms.	G	A	Pts.	PIM	+/-	PP	SH	Gms.	G	A	Pts.	PIM
88-89—St. Cloud State	WCHA	28	5	3	8	28	...	...	...	—	—	—	—	—
89-90—St. Cloud State	WCHA	36	4	17	21	37	...	...	...	—	—	—	—	—
90-91—St. Cloud State	WCHA	41	18	30	48	52	...	...	...	—	—	—	—	—
91-92—U.S. national team	Int'l	54	1	8	9	59	...	...	...	—	—	—	—	—
—U.S. Olympic team	Int'l	8	0	0	0	4	...	...	...	—	—	—	—	—
—St. Louis	NHL	4	1	0	1	0	1	0	0	5	0	0	0	0
92-93—Peoria	IHL	19	0	8	8	10				—	—	—	—	—
—St. Louis	NHL	42	0	8	8	30	-2	0	0	10	0	0	0	14
93-94—St. Louis	NHL	61	0	11	11	64	-8	0	0	—	—	—	—	—
—Vancouver	NHL	8	0	1	1	0	1	0	0	24	1	6	7	16
94-95—Vancouver	NHL	45	2	11	13	34	-3	0	0	11	0	2	2	6
95-96—Vancouver	NHL	77	6	23	29	83	8	1	0	6	0	1	1	10
96-97—Vancouver	NHL	67	4	15	19	51	-3	2	0	—	—	—	—	—
97-98—Vancouver	NHL	71	3	24	27	79	3	1	0	—	—	—	—	—
98-99—Vancouver	NHL	42	2	11	13	34	7	0	2	—	—	—	—	—
—Florida	NHL	25	3	7	10	17	-2	0	0	—	—	—	—	—
99-00—Florida	NHL	76	6	19	25	68	4	2	0	4	0	0	0	0
00-01—Florida	NHL	70	5	15	20	72	-7	4	0	—	—	—	—	—
01-02—Florida	NHL	31	3	7	10	12	-4	0	0	—	—	—	—	—
—Carolina	NHL	26	2	4	6	10	3	0	0	23	1	4	5	20
02-03—Carolina	NHL	72	3	14	17	75	-24	1	0	—	—	—	—	—
NHL Totals (12 years)		717	40	170	210	629	-26	11	2	83	2	13	15	66

HEDSTROM, JONATHAN   RW   MIGHTY DUCKS

PERSONAL: Born December 27, 1977, in Skelleftea, Sweden ... 5-11/201. ... Shoots left. ... Full Name: Jonathon Hedstrom.

TRANSACTIONS/CAREER NOTES: Selected by Toronto Maple Leafs in ninth round (eighth Maple Leafs pick, 239th overall) of NHL entry draft (June 21, 1997). ... Rights traded by Maple Leafs to Mighty Ducks of Anaheim for sixth-(C Vadim Sozinov) and seventh-round (D Markus Seikola) picks in 2000 draft (June 25, 2000).

H

Season Team	League	REGULAR SEASON								PLAYOFFS				
		Gms.	G	A	Pts.	PIM	+/-	PP	SH	Gms.	G	A	Pts.	PIM
95-96—Skelleftea	Sweden Dv. 2	7	0	0	0	0	...	...	...	—	—	—	—	—
96-97—Skelleftea	Sweden Dv. 2	12	1	1	2	10	...	...	...	6	0	0	0	2
—Skelleftea	Sweden Jr.	9	4	4	8	...	...	...	...	—	—	—	—	—
97-98—Skelleftea	Sweden Dv. 2	16	2	3	5	...	...	...	...	—	—	—	—	—
—Skelleftea	Sweden Jr.	1	0	0	0	2	...	...	...	—	—	—	—	—
98-99—Skelleftea	Sweden Dv. 2	36	15	28	43	74	...	...	...	—	—	—	—	—
99-00—Lulea	Sweden	48	9	17	26	46	...	...	...	9	2	1	3	12
00-01—Lulea	Sweden	46	9	19	28	68	...	...	...	12	1	6	7	16
01-02—Lulea	Sweden	47	11	7	18	38	...	...	...	4	2	1	3	6
02-03—Cincinnati	AHL	50	14	21	35	62	...	...	...	—	—	—	—	—
—Anaheim	NHL	4	0	0	0	0	-1	0	0	—	—	—	—	—
NHL Totals (1 year).............		4	0	0	0	0	-1	0	0					

HEEREMA, JEFF · RW · HURRICANES

PERSONAL: Born January 17, 1980, in Thunder Bay, Ont. ... 6-1/190. ... Shoots right.
TRANSACTIONS/CAREER NOTES: Selected by Carolina Hurricanes in first round (first Hurricanes pick, 11th overall) of NHL entry draft (June 27, 1998). ... Signed by Hurricanes (July 15, 2003).

Season Team	League	REGULAR SEASON								PLAYOFFS				
		Gms.	G	A	Pts.	PIM	+/-	PP	SH	Gms.	G	A	Pts.	PIM
97-98—Sarnia	OHL	63	32	40	72	88	...	...	...	5	4	1	5	10
98-99—Sarnia	OHL	62	31	39	70	113	...	...	...	6	5	1	6	0
99-00—Sarnia	OHL	67	36	41	77	62	...	...	...	7	4	2	6	10
00-01—Cincinnati	IHL	73	17	16	33	42	...	...	...	4	0	0	0	0
01-02—Lowell	AHL	76	33	37	70	90	...	...	...	5	2	3	5	2
02-03—Lowell	AHL	36	15	17	32	25	...	...	...	—	—	—	—	—
—Carolina	NHL	10	3	0	3	2	-2	1	0	—	—	—	—	—
NHL Totals (1 year).............		10	3	0	3	2	-2	1	0					

HEFFERNAN, SCOTT · D · BLUE JACKETS

PERSONAL: Born March 9, 1982, in Montreal. ... 6-5/187. ... Shoots left.
TRANSACTIONS/CAREER NOTES: Selected by Columbus Blue Jackets in fifth round (fourth Blue Jackets pick, 138th overall) of NHL entry draft (June 24, 2000).

Season Team	League	REGULAR SEASON								PLAYOFFS				
		Gms.	G	A	Pts.	PIM	+/-	PP	SH	Gms.	G	A	Pts.	PIM
98-99—Pembrooke	BCJHL	43	3	5	8	51	...	...	...	—	—	—	—	—
99-00—Sarnia	OHL	55	5	10	15	24	...	...	...	—	—	—	—	—
00-01—Sarnia	OHL	51	2	20	22	30	...	...	...	4	0	1	1	0
01-02—Sarnia	OHL	10	0	9	9	16	...	...	...	—	—	—	—	—
—Toronto St. Michael's..	OHL	58	4	17	21	77	...	...	...	9	1	2	3	4
02-03—Dayton	ECHL	6	1	0	1	7	...	...	...	—	—	—	—	—

HEID, CHRIS · D · WILD

PERSONAL: Born March 14, 1983, in Langley, B.C. ... 6-1/205. ... Shoots left.
TRANSACTIONS/CAREER NOTES: Selected by Minnesota Wild in third round (third Wild pick, 74th overall) of NHL entry draft (June 23, 2001).

Season Team	League	REGULAR SEASON								PLAYOFFS				
		Gms.	G	A	Pts.	PIM	+/-	PP	SH	Gms.	G	A	Pts.	PIM
00-01—Spokane.....................	WHL	51	2	15	17	76	...	...	...	12	0	4	4	12
01-02—Spokane.....................	WHL	69	7	28	35	56	...	...	...	11	1	4	5	8
02-03—Spokane.....................	WHL	60	9	36	45	66	...	...	...	—	—	—	—	—

HEINS, SHAWN · D

PERSONAL: Born December 24, 1973, in Eganville, Ont. ... 6-3/210. ... Shoots left.
TRANSACTIONS/CAREER NOTES: Signed as non-drafted free agent by San Jose Sharks (January 5, 1998). ... Injured finger (February 29, 2000); missed five games. ... Injured knee (November 24, 2001); missed 18 games. ... Injured jaw (January 17, 2002); missed 14 games. ... Traded by Sharks to Pittsburgh Penguins for conditional pick in draft (February 8, 2003).

Season Team	League	REGULAR SEASON								PLAYOFFS				
		Gms.	G	A	Pts.	PIM	+/-	PP	SH	Gms.	G	A	Pts.	PIM
91-92—Peterborough..............	OHL	49	1	1	2	73	...	...	...	—	—	—	—	—
92-93—Peterborough..............	OHL	5	0	0	0	10	...	...	...	—	—	—	—	—
—Windsor.....................	OHL	53	7	10	17	107	...	...	...	—	—	—	—	—
93-94—Renfrew	EOGHL	32	16	34	50	250	...	...	...	—	—	—	—	—
94-95—Renfrew	EOGHL	49	40	90	130	175	...	...	...	—	—	—	—	—
95-96—Cape Breton..............	AHL	1	0	0	0	0	...	...	...	—	—	—	—	—
—Mobile........................	ECHL	62	7	20	27	152	...	...	...	—	—	—	—	—
96-97—Mobile.......................	ECHL	56	6	17	23	253	...	...	...	3	0	2	2	2
—Kansas City................	IHL	6	0	0	0	9	...	...	...	—	—	—	—	—
97-98—Kansas City................	IHL	82	22	28	50	303	...	...	...	11	1	0	1	49
98-99—Canadian nat'l team ...	Int'l	36	5	16	21	66	...	...	...	—	—	—	—	—
—San Jose....................	NHL	5	0	0	0	13	0	0	0	—	—	—	—	—
—Kentucky....................	AHL	18	2	2	4	108	...	...	...	12	2	7	9	10

H

Season Team	League	REGULAR SEASON								PLAYOFFS				
		Gms.	G	A	Pts.	PIM	+/-	PP	SH	Gms.	G	A	Pts.	PIM
99-00—Kentucky.................	AHL	69	11	52	63	238	...	...	...	9	3	3	6	44
—San Jose...................	NHL	1	0	0	0	2	-1	0	0	—	—	—	—	—
00-01—San Jose.................	NHL	38	3	4	7	57	2	2	0	2	0	0	0	0
01-02—San Jose.................	NHL	17	0	2	2	24	1	0	0	—	—	—	—	—
02-03—San Jose.................	NHL	20	0	1	1	9	-2	0	0	—	—	—	—	—
—Pittsburgh..................	NHL	27	1	1	2	33	-2	0	0	—	—	—	—	—
NHL Totals (5 years)...........		108	4	8	12	138	-2	2	0	2	0	0	0	0

HEINZE, STEVE   RW   KINGS

PERSONAL: Born January 30, 1970, in Lawrence, Mass. ... 5-11/202. ... Shoots right. ... Full Name: Stephen Herbert Heinze. ... Name pronounced HIGHNS.

TRANSACTIONS/CAREER NOTES: Selected by Boston Bruins in second round (second Bruins pick, 60th overall) of NHL entry draft (June 11, 1988). ... Injured shoulder (May 1, 1992). ... Injured shoulder (March 20, 1993); missed 11 games. ... Injured knee (February 18, 1994); missed five games. ... Reinjured knee (March 26, 1994); missed two games. ... Strained abdominal muscle (December 5, 1996); missed one game. ... Strained hip and groin and tore knee ligament (December 17, 1996); missed remainder of season. ... Sprained ankle (October 7, 1997); missed seven games. ... Fractured foot (October 23, 1997); missed 14 games. ... Injured finger (October 24, 1998); missed one game. ... Strained hip flexor (February 9, 1999); missed five games. ... Suffered from the flu (March 1, 1999); missed three games. ... Suffered from the flu (February 3, 2000); missed one game. ... Strained muscle in ribs (March 10, 2000); missed six games. ... Selected by Columbus Blue Jackets in NHL expansion draft (June 23, 2000). ... Suffered concussion (November 24, 2000); missed three games. ... Traded by Blue Jackets to Buffalo Sabres for third-round pick (C/RW Per Mars) in 2001 draft (March 13, 2001). ... Signed as free agent by Los Angeles Kings (July 3, 2001).

STATISTICAL PLATEAUS: Three-goal games: 1992-93 (1), 1995-96 (1), 1997-98 (2), 2000-01 (1). Total: 5.

Season Team	League	REGULAR SEASON								PLAYOFFS				
		Gms.	G	A	Pts.	PIM	+/-	PP	SH	Gms.	G	A	Pts.	PIM
86-87—Lawrence Academy.....	Mass. H.S.	23	26	24	50	...	...	...	...	—	—	—	—	—
87-88—Lawrence Academy.....	Mass. H.S.	23	30	25	55	...	...	...	...	—	—	—	—	—
88-89—Boston College	Hockey East	36	26	23	49	26	...	...	...	—	—	—	—	—
89-90—Boston College	Hockey East	40	27	36	63	41	...	...	...	—	—	—	—	—
90-91—Boston College	Hockey East	35	21	26	47	35	...	...	...	—	—	—	—	—
91-92—U.S. national team	Int'l	49	18	15	33	38	...	...	...	—	—	—	—	—
—U.S. Olympic team......	Int'l	8	1	3	4	8	...	...	...	—	—	—	—	—
—Boston	NHL	14	3	4	7	6	-1	0	0	7	0	3	3	17
92-93—Boston	NHL	73	18	13	31	24	20	0	2	4	1	1	2	2
93-94—Boston	NHL	77	10	11	21	32	-2	0	2	13	2	3	5	7
94-95—Boston	NHL	36	7	9	16	23	0	0	1	5	0	0	0	0
95-96—Boston	NHL	76	16	12	28	43	-3	0	1	5	1	1	2	4
96-97—Boston	NHL	30	17	8	25	27	-8	4	2	—	—	—	—	—
97-98—Boston	NHL	61	26	20	46	54	8	9	0	6	0	0	0	6
98-99—Boston	NHL	73	22	18	40	30	7	9	0	12	4	3	7	0
99-00—Boston	NHL	75	12	13	25	36	-8	2	0	—	—	—	—	—
00-01—Columbus	NHL	65	22	20	42	38	-19	14	0	—	—	—	—	—
—Buffalo	NHL	14	5	7	12	8	6	1	0	13	3	4	7	10
01-02—Los Angeles...............	NHL	73	15	16	31	46	-15	8	0	4	0	0	0	2
02-03—Manchester...............	AHL	18	8	9	17	12	...	...	...	—	—	—	—	—
—Los Angeles................	NHL	27	5	7	12	12	-5	1	0	—	—	—	—	—
NHL Totals (12 years).........		694	178	158	336	379	-20	48	8	69	11	15	26	48

HEISTEN, BARRETT   LW   STARS

PERSONAL: Born March 19, 1980, in Anchorage, Alaska. ... 6-1/189. ... Shoots left.

TRANSACTIONS/CAREER NOTES: Selected by Buffalo Sabres in first round (first Sabres pick, 20th overall) of NHL entry draft (June 26, 1999). ... Signed as free agent by New York Rangers (June 12, 2001). ... Traded by Rangers with C Manny Malhotra to Dallas Stars C Roman Lyashenko and LW Martin Rucinsky (March 12, 2002).

Season Team	League	REGULAR SEASON								PLAYOFFS				
		Gms.	G	A	Pts.	PIM	+/-	PP	SH	Gms.	G	A	Pts.	PIM
97-98—U.S. National.............	NAHL	50	11	26	37	245	...	...	...	—	—	—	—	—
98-99—Univ. of Maine	Hockey East	34	12	16	28	72	...	...	...	—	—	—	—	—
99-00—Univ. of Maine	Hockey East	37	13	24	37	86	...	...	...	—	—	—	—	—
00-01—Seattle..................	WHL	58	20	57	77	61	...	...	...	9	2	6	8	20
01-02—New York Rangers......	NHL	10	0	0	0	2	-4	0	0	—	—	—	—	—
—Hartford	AHL	49	9	9	18	60	...	...	...	—	—	—	—	—
—Utah.........................	AHL	12	5	1	6	14	...	...	...	5	1	0	1	4
02-03—Utah.....................	AHL	58	10	10	20	47	...	...	...	—	—	—	—	—
NHL Totals (1 year)...........		10	0	0	0	2	-4	0	0					

HEJDUK, MILAN   RW   AVALANCHE

PERSONAL: Born February 14, 1976, in Usti-nad-Labem, Czechoslovakia ... 6-0/190. ... Shoots right.

TRANSACTIONS/CAREER NOTES: Selected by Quebec Nordiques in fourth round (sixth Nordiques pick, 72nd overall) of NHL entry draft (June 29, 1994). ... Nordiques franchise moved to Colorado and renamed Avalanche for 1995-96 season (June 21, 1995). ... Strained back (January 7, 2000); missed one game. ... Strained muscle in abdomen (February 28, 2002); missed final 20 games of season.

STATISTICAL PLATEAUS: Three-goal games: 2002-03 (1).

H

Season Team	League	REGULAR SEASON								PLAYOFFS				
		Gms.	G	A	Pts.	PIM	+/-	PP	SH	Gms.	G	A	Pts.	PIM
93-94—HC Pardubice	Czech Rep.	22	6	3	9	...	...	...	...	10	5	1	6	...
94-95—HC Pardubice	Czech Rep.					Did not play.								
95-96—HC Pardubice	Czech Rep.	37	13	7	20	...	...	...	...	—	—	—	—	—
96-97—HC Pardubice	Czech Rep.	51	27	11	38	10	...	...	...	10	6	0	6	27
97-98—Pojistovna Pardubice..	Czech Rep.	48	26	19	45	20	...	...	...	3	0	0	0	2
—Czech Rep. Oly. team..	Int'l	4	0	0	0	2	...	...	...	—	—	—	—	—
98-99—Colorado	NHL	82	14	34	48	26	8	4	0	16	6	6	12	4
99-00—Colorado	NHL	82	36	36	72	16	14	13	0	17	5	4	9	6
00-01—Colorado	NHL	80	41	38	79	36	32	12	1	23	7	*16	23	6
01-02—Colorado	NHL	62	21	23	44	24	0	7	1	16	3	3	6	4
—Czech Rep. Oly. team..	Int'l	4	1	0	1	0	...	...	...	—	—	—	—	—
02-03—Colorado	NHL	82	*50	48	98	32	†52	18	0	7	2	2	4	2
NHL Totals (5 years)		388	162	179	341	134	106	54	2	79	23	31	54	22

HELBLING, TIMO   D   PREDATORS

PERSONAL: Born July 21, 1981, in Basel, Switzerland. ... 6-2/183. ... Shoots right.

TRANSACTIONS/CAREER NOTES: Selected by Nashville Predators in sixth round (12th Predators pick, 162nd overall) of NHL entry draft (June 26, 1999).

Season Team	League	REGULAR SEASON								PLAYOFFS				
		Gms.	G	A	Pts.	PIM	+/-	PP	SH	Gms.	G	A	Pts.	PIM
97-98—Davos	Switzerland Jr.	40	6	7	13	48	...	...	...	—	—	—	—	—
98-99—Davos	Switzerland Jr.	22	8	10	18	108	...	...	...	—	—	—	—	—
—Davos	Switzerland	25	0	1	1	12	...	...	...	4	0	0	0	0
99-00—Davos HC	Switzerland	44	0	0	0	49	...	...	...	5	0	0	0	0
00-01—Windsor	OHL	54	7	14	21	90	...	...	...	7	0	2	2	11
—Milwaukee	IHL	—	—	—	—	—	...	...	...	1	0	0	0	0
01-02—Milwaukee	AHL	67	2	6	8	59	...	...	...	—	—	—	—	—
02-03—Milwaukee	AHL	23	0	1	1	37	...	...	...	—	—	—	—	—
—Toledo	ECHL	35	3	8	11	75	...	...	...	—	—	—	—	—

HELENIUS, SAMI   D

PERSONAL: Born January 22, 1974, in Helsinki, Finland ... 6-6/230. ... Shoots left. ... Name pronounced huh-LEH-nuhz.

TRANSACTIONS/CAREER NOTES: Selected by Calgary Flames in fifth round (fifth Flames pick, 102nd overall) of NHL entry draft (June 20, 1992). ... Traded by Flames to Tampa Bay Lightning for future considerations (January 29, 1999). ... Traded by Lightning to Colorado Avalanche for future considerations (March 23, 1999). ... Signed as free agent by Dallas Stars (July 12, 2000). ... Traded by Stars with conditional pick in draft to Chicago Blackhawks for D Lyle Odelein (March 10, 2003).

Season Team	League	REGULAR SEASON								PLAYOFFS				
		Gms.	G	A	Pts.	PIM	+/-	PP	SH	Gms.	G	A	Pts.	PIM
91-92—Jokerit Helsinki	Finland Jr.					Statistics unavailable.								
92-93—Vantaa HT	Finland Div. 2	21	3	2	5	60	...	...	...	—	—	—	—	—
—Jokerit Helsinki	Finland Jr.	1	0	0	0	0	...	...	...	—	—	—	—	—
93-94—Reipas Lahti	Finland	37	2	3	5	46	...	...	...	—	—	—	—	—
94-95—Saint John	AHL	69	2	5	7	217	...	...	...	—	—	—	—	—
95-96—Saint John	AHL	68	0	3	3	231	...	...	...	10	0	0	0	9
96-97—Saint John	AHL	72	5	10	15	218	...	...	...	2	0	0	0	0
—Calgary	NHL	3	0	1	1	0	1	0	0	—	—	—	—	—
97-98—Saint John	AHL	63	1	2	3	185	...	...	...	—	—	—	—	—
—Las Vegas	IHL	10	0	1	1	19	...	...	...	4	0	0	0	25
98-99—Calgary	NHL	4	0	0	0	8	-2	0	0	—	—	—	—	—
—Chicago	IHL	4	0	0	0	11	...	...	...	—	—	—	—	—
—Tampa Bay	NHL	4	1	0	1	15	-3	0	1	—	—	—	—	—
—Las Vegas	IHL	42	2	3	5	193	...	...	...	5	0	0	0	16
—Hershey	AHL	8	0	0	0	29	...	...	...	—	—	—	—	—
99-00—Colorado	NHL	33	0	0	0	46	-5	0	0	—	—	—	—	—
—Hershey	AHL	12	0	1	1	31	...	...	...	9	0	0	0	40
00-01—Dallas	NHL	57	1	2	3	99	1	0	0	1	0	0	0	0
01-02—Dallas	NHL	39	0	0	0	58	-4	0	0	—	—	—	—	—
02-03—Utah	AHL	4	0	0	0	14	...	...	...	—	—	—	—	—
—Dallas	NHL	5	0	0	0	6	1	0	0	—	—	—	—	—
—Chicago	NHL	10	0	1	1	28	3	0	0	—	—	—	—	—
NHL Totals (6 years)		155	2	4	6	260	-8	0	1	1	0	0	0	0

H   HELMER, BRYAN   D   COYOTES

PERSONAL: Born July 15, 1972, in Sault Ste. Marie, Ont. ... 6-1/208. ... Shoots right.

TRANSACTIONS/CAREER NOTES: Signed as non-drafted free agent by New Jersey Devils (October 1, 1993). ... Signed as free agent by Phoenix Coyotes (July 22, 1998). ... Claimed on waivers by St. Louis Blues (December 19, 1998). ... Signed as free agent by Vancouver Canucks (August 21, 2000). ... Traded by Canucks to Phoenix Coyotes for D Martin Grenier (July 27, 2003).

Season Team	League	Gms.	G	A	Pts.	PIM	+/-	PP	SH	Gms.	G	A	Pts.	PIM
					REGULAR SEASON							PLAYOFFS		
89-90—Wellington	OJHL	51	6	22	28	204	...	...	...	—	—	—	—	—
—Belleville	OHL	6	0	1	1	0	...	...	...	—	—	—	—	—
90-91—Wellington	OJHL	50	11	14	25	109	...	...	...	—	—	—	—	—
91-92—Wellington	OJHL	45	19	32	51	66	...	...	...	—	—	—	—	—
92-93—Wellington	OJHL	57	25	62	87	62	...	...	...	—	—	—	—	—
93-94—Albany	AHL	65	4	19	23	79	...	...	...	5	0	0	0	9
94-95—Albany	AHL	77	7	36	43	101	...	...	...	7	1	0	1	0
95-96—Albany	AHL	80	14	30	44	107	...	...	...	4	2	0	2	6
96-97—Albany	AHL	77	12	27	39	113	...	...	...	16	1	7	8	10
97-98—Albany	AHL	80	14	49	63	101	...	...	...	13	4	9	13	18
98-99—Phoenix	NHL	11	0	0	0	23	2	0	0	—	—	—	—	—
—Las Vegas	IHL	8	1	3	4	28	...	...	...	—	—	—	—	—
—St. Louis	NHL	29	0	4	4	19	3	0	0	—	—	—	—	—
—Worcester	AHL	16	7	8	15	18	...	...	...	4	0	0	0	12
99-00—Worcester	AHL	54	10	25	35	124	...	...	...	9	1	4	5	10
—St. Louis	NHL	15	1	1	2	10	-3	1	0	—	—	—	—	—
00-01—Kansas City	IHL	42	4	15	19	76	...	...	...	—	—	—	—	—
—Vancouver	NHL	20	2	4	6	18	0	0	0	—	—	—	—	—
01-02—Manitoba	AHL	34	6	18	24	69	...	...	...	—	—	—	—	—
—Vancouver	NHL	40	5	5	10	53	10	2	0	6	0	0	0	0
02-03—Manitoba	AHL	60	7	24	31	82	...	...	...	—	—	—	—	—
—Vancouver	NHL	2	0	0	0	0	1	0	0	—	—	—	—	—
NHL Totals (5 years)		117	8	14	22	123	13	3	0	6	0	0	0	0

HEMSKY, ALES   RW   OILERS

PERSONAL: Born August 13, 1983, in Pardubice, Czechoslovakia ... 6-0/170. ... Shoots right.
TRANSACTIONS/CAREER NOTES: Selected by Edmonton Oilers in first round (first Oilers pick, 13th overall) of NHL entry draft (June 23, 2001).

Season Team	League	Gms.	G	A	Pts.	PIM	+/-	PP	SH	Gms.	G	A	Pts.	PIM
					REGULAR SEASON							PLAYOFFS		
99-00—Pardubice	Czech. Jrs.	52	24	50	74	90	...	...	...	—	—	—	—	—
—HC Pardubice	Czech Rep.	4	0	1	1	0	...	...	...	—	—	—	—	—
00-01—Hull	QMJHL	68	36	64	100	67	...	...	...	5	2	3	5	2
01-02—Hull	QMJHL	53	27	70	97	86	...	...	...	10	6	10	16	6
02-03—Edmonton	NHL	59	6	24	30	14	5	0	0	6	0	0	0	0
NHL Totals (1 year)		59	6	24	30	14	5	0	0	6	0	0	0	0

HENDERSON, JAY   LW

PERSONAL: Born September 17, 1978, in Edmonton. ... 5-11/188. ... Shoots left. ... Full Name: Jay Elliot Henderson.
TRANSACTIONS/CAREER NOTES: Selected by Boston Bruins in 12th round (12th Bruins pick, 246th overall) of NHL entry draft (June 21, 1997). ... Injured knee (April 4, 2000); missed final three games of season. ... Suffered concussion (September 21, 2000); missed first five games of season. ... Traded by Bruins to New York Rangers for ninth-round pick in 2004 draft (January 17, 2003). ... Traded by Rangers to Minnesota Wild for C Cory Larose (February 20, 2003).

Season Team	League	Gms.	G	A	Pts.	PIM	+/-	PP	SH	Gms.	G	A	Pts.	PIM
					REGULAR SEASON							PLAYOFFS		
94-95—Red Deer	WHL	54	3	9	12	80	...	...	...	—	—	—	—	—
95-96—Red Deer	WHL	71	15	13	28	139	...	...	...	10	1	1	2	11
96-97—Edmonton	WHL	66	28	32	60	127	...	...	...	—	—	—	—	—
97-98—Edmonton	WHL	72	49	45	94	132	...	...	...	—	—	—	—	—
—Providence	AHL	11	3	1	4	11	...	...	...	—	—	—	—	—
98-99—Providence	AHL	55	7	9	16	172	...	...	...	2	0	0	0	2
—Boston	NHL	4	0	0	0	2	-1	0	0	—	—	—	—	—
99-00—Providence	AHL	60	18	27	45	200	...	...	...	14	1	2	3	16
—Boston	NHL	16	1	3	4	9	1	0	0	—	—	—	—	—
00-01—Boston	NHL	13	0	0	0	26	-1	0	0	—	—	—	—	—
—Providence	AHL	41	9	7	16	121	...	...	...	1	0	0	0	2
01-02—Boston	NHL						Did not play.							
02-03—Providence	AHL	39	7	13	20	152	...	...	...	—	—	—	—	—
—Hartford	AHL	14	3	4	7	27	...	...	...	—	—	—	—	—
—Houston	AHL	22	7	4	11	65	...	...	...	—	—	—	—	—
NHL Totals (4 years)		33	1	3	4	37	-1	0	0	—	—	—	—	—

HENDERSON, MATT   RW

PERSONAL: Born March 1, 1974, in White Bear Lake, Minn. ... 6-1/205. ... Shoots left.
TRANSACTIONS/CAREER NOTES: Signed as non-drafted free agent by Nashville Predators (July 13, 1998). ... Traded by Predators to Philadelphia Flyers for RW Paul Healey (September 27, 1999). ... Signed as free agent by Chicago Blackhawks (September 5, 2001).

H

Season Team	League	Gms.	G	A	Pts.	PIM	+/-	PP	SH	Gms.	G	A	Pts.	PIM
		REGULAR SEASON								PLAYOFFS				
94-95—Univ. of North Dakota.	WCHA	19	1	3	4	16	...	...	...	—	—	—	—	—
95-96—Univ. of North Dakota.	WCHA	36	9	10	19	34	...	...	...	—	—	—	—	—
96-97—Univ. of North Dakota.	WCHA	42	14	17	31	71	...	...	...	—	—	—	—	—
97-98—Univ. of North Dakota.	WCHA	38	24	14	38	74	...	...	...	—	—	—	—	—
98-99—Milwaukee	IHL	77	19	19	38	117	...	...	...	2	0	0	0	0
—Nashville	NHL	2	0	0	0	2	-1	0	0	—	—	—	—	—
99-00—Trenton	ECHL	16	2	4	6	47	...	...	...	—	—	—	—	—
—Philadelphia	AHL	51	4	8	12	37	...	...	...	5	0	0	0	4
00-01—Norfolk	AHL	78	14	24	38	80	...	...	...	9	1	1	2	16
01-02—Norfolk	AHL	74	21	28	49	90	...	...	...	4	0	0	0	6
—Chicago	NHL	4	0	1	1	0	-1	0	0	—	—	—	—	—
02-03—Norfolk	AHL	77	18	29	47	95	...	...	...	—	—	—	—	—
NHL Totals (2 years)		6	0	1	1	2	-2	0	0					

HENDRICKS, MATT   C   PREDATORS

PERSONAL: Born June 19, 1981, in Minn. ... 5-11/190. ... Shoots left.
COLLEGE: St. Cloud State.
TRANSACTIONS/CAREER NOTES: Selected by Nashville Predators in fifth round (fifth Predators pick, 131st overall) of NHL entry draft (June 24, 2000).

Season Team	League	Gms.	G	A	Pts.	PIM	+/-	PP	SH	Gms.	G	A	Pts.	PIM
		REGULAR SEASON								PLAYOFFS				
98-99—Blaine	USHS (West)	22	23	34	57	42	...	...	...	—	—	—	—	—
99-00—Blaine	USHS (West)	21	23	30	53	28	...	...	...	—	—	—	—	—
00-01—St. Cloud State	WCHA	36	3	9	12	23	...	...	...	—	—	—	—	—
01-02—St. Cloud State	WCHA	42	19	20	39	74	...	...	...	—	—	—	—	—
02-03—St. Cloud State	WCHA	37	18	18	36	64	...	...	...	—	—	—	—	—

HENDRICKSON, DARBY   C   WILD

PERSONAL: Born August 28, 1972, in Richfield, Minn. ... 6-1/195. ... Shoots left.
TRANSACTIONS/CAREER NOTES: Selected by Toronto Maple Leafs in fourth round (third Maple Leafs pick, 73rd overall) of NHL entry draft (June 16, 1990). ... Suspended three games by NHL for kneeing incident (October 26, 1995). ... Suffered from the flu (December 30, 1995); missed one game. ... Traded by Maple Leafs with LW Sean Haggerty, D Kenny Jonsson and first-round pick (G Roberto Luongo) in 1997 draft to New York Islanders for LW Wendel Clark, D Mathieu Schneider and D D.J. Smith (March 13, 1996). ... Traded by Islanders to Maple Leafs for fifth-round pick (C Jiri Dopita) in 1998 draft (October 11, 1996). ... Strained back (January 27, 1997); missed five games. ... Suffered back spasms (November 4, 1997); missed two games. ... Suffered back spasms (November 3, 1998); missed six games. ... Traded by Maple Leafs to Vancouver Canucks for D/LW Chris McAllister (February 16, 1999). ... Injured ankle (September 11, 1999); missed four games. ... Selected by Minnesota Wild in NHL expansion draft (June 23, 2000). ... Suffered concussion (November 22, 2000); missed six games. ... Suffered head injury (February 14, 2001); missed three games. ... Strained groin (October 16, 2001); missed one game. ... Suffered back spasms (November 8, 2001); missed four games. ... Suffered sinus infection (November 24, 2001); missed three games. ... Injured left eye (April 2, 2002); missed remainder of season.

Season Team	League	Gms.	G	A	Pts.	PIM	+/-	PP	SH	Gms.	G	A	Pts.	PIM
		REGULAR SEASON								PLAYOFFS				
87-88—Richfield H.S.	Minn. H.S.	22	12	9	21	10	...	...	...	—	—	—	—	—
88-89—Richfield H.S.	Minn. H.S.	22	22	20	42	12	...	...	...	—	—	—	—	—
89-90—Richfield H.S.	Minn. H.S.	24	23	27	50	49	...	...	...	—	—	—	—	—
90-91—Richfield H.S.	Minn. H.S.	27	32	29	61	...	...	...	...	—	—	—	—	—
91-92—Univ. of Minnesota	WCHA	41	25	28	53	61	...	...	...	—	—	—	—	—
92-93—Univ. of Minnesota	WCHA	31	12	15	27	35	...	...	...	—	—	—	—	—
93-94—U.S. national team	Int'l	59	12	16	28	30	...	...	...	—	—	—	—	—
—U.S. Olympic team	Int'l	8	0	0	0	6	...	...	...	—	—	—	—	—
—St. John's	AHL	6	4	1	5	4	...	...	...	3	1	1	2	0
—Toronto	NHL	—	—	—	—	—	...	...	...	2	0	0	0	0
94-95—St. John's	AHL	59	16	20	36	48	...	...	...	—	—	—	—	—
—Toronto	NHL	8	0	1	1	4	0	0	0	—	—	—	—	—
95-96—Toronto	NHL	46	6	6	12	47	-2	0	0	—	—	—	—	—
—New York Islanders	NHL	16	1	4	5	33	-6	0	0	—	—	—	—	—
96-97—St. John's	AHL	12	5	4	9	21	...	...	...	—	—	—	—	—
—Toronto	NHL	64	11	6	17	47	-20	0	1	—	—	—	—	—
—U.S. national team	Int'l	8	0	1	1	8	...	...	...	—	—	—	—	—
97-98—Toronto	NHL	80	8	4	12	67	-20	0	0	—	—	—	—	—
98-99—Toronto	NHL	35	2	3	5	30	-4	0	0	—	—	—	—	—
—Vancouver	NHL	27	2	2	4	22	-15	1	0	—	—	—	—	—
99-00—Vancouver	NHL	40	5	4	9	14	-3	0	1	—	—	—	—	—
—Syracuse	AHL	20	5	8	13	16	...	...	...	—	—	—	—	—
00-01—Minnesota	NHL	72	18	11	29	36	1	3	1	—	—	—	—	—
01-02—Minnesota	NHL	68	9	15	24	50	-22	2	2	—	—	—	—	—
02-03—Minnesota	NHL	28	1	5	6	8	-3	0	0	17	2	3	5	4
NHL Totals (10 years)		484	63	61	124	358	-94	6	5	19	2	3	5	4

H   HENRICH, ADAM   LW   LIGHTNING

PERSONAL: Born January 19, 1984, in Toronto. ... 6-4/216. ... Shoots left. ... Brother of Michael Henrich, right winger, Edmonton Oilers organization.
TRANSACTIONS/CAREER NOTES: Selected by Tampa Bay Lightning in second round (first Lightning pick, 60th overall) of NHL entry draft (June 22, 2002).

Season Team	League	REGULAR SEASON								PLAYOFFS				
		Gms.	G	A	Pts.	PIM	+/-	PP	SH	Gms.	G	A	Pts.	PIM
00-01—Brampton..................	OHL	48	5	4	9	27	...	...	...	9	0	0	0	6
01-02—Brampton..................	OHL	66	33	30	63	92	...	...	...	—	—	—	—	—
02-03—Brampton..................	OHL	63	31	33	64	84	...	...	...	—	—	—	—	—

HENRY, ALEX D CAPITALS

PERSONAL: Born October 18, 1979, in Elliot Lake, Ont. ... 6-5/220. ... Shoots left.
TRANSACTIONS/CAREER NOTES: Selected by Edmonton Oilers in third round (second Oilers pick, 67th overall) of NHL entry draft (June 27, 1998). ... Claimed on waivers by Washington Capitals (October 24, 2002). ... Re-signed by Capitals (July 31, 2003).

Season Team	League	REGULAR SEASON								PLAYOFFS				
		Gms.	G	A	Pts.	PIM	+/-	PP	SH	Gms.	G	A	Pts.	PIM
96-97—London	OHL	61	1	10	11	65	...	...	...	—	—	—	—	—
97-98—London	OHL	62	5	9	14	97	...	...	...	16	0	3	3	14
98-99—London	OHL	68	5	23	28	105	...	...	...	25	3	10	13	22
99-00—Hamilton	AHL	60	1	0	1	69	...	...	...	—	—	—	—	—
00-01—Hamilton	AHL	56	2	3	5	87	...	...	...	—	—	—	—	—
01-02—Hamilton	AHL	69	4	8	12	143	...	...	...	15	1	2	3	16
02-03—Portland	AHL	3	0	1	1	0	...	...	...	—	—	—	—	—
—Edmonton	NHL	3	0	0	0	0	-1	0	0	—	—	—	—	—
—Washington	NHL	38	0	0	0	80	-4	0	0	—	—	—	—	—
NHL Totals (1 year)..............		41	0	0	0	80	-5	0	0					

HENRY, BURKE D BLACKHAWKS

PERSONAL: Born January 21, 1979, in Ste. Rose, Man. ... 6-3/195. ... Shoots left. ... Full Name: Larry Henry.
TRANSACTIONS/CAREER NOTES: Selected by New York Rangers in third round (third Rangers pick, 73rd overall) of NHL entry draft (June 21, 1997). ... Traded by Rangers to Calgary Flames for D Chris St. Croix (June 24, 2001). ... Signed as free agent by Chicago Blackhawks (December 11, 2002).

Season Team	League	REGULAR SEASON								PLAYOFFS				
		Gms.	G	A	Pts.	PIM	+/-	PP	SH	Gms.	G	A	Pts.	PIM
95-96—Brandon	WHL	50	6	11	17	58	...	...	...	19	0	4	4	19
96-97—Brandon	WHL	55	6	25	31	81	...	...	...	6	1	3	4	4
97-98—Brandon	WHL	72	18	65	83	153	...	...	...	18	3	16	19	37
98-99—Brandon	WHL	68	18	58	76	151	...	...	...	5	1	6	7	9
99-00—Hartford	AHL	64	3	12	15	47	...	...	...	5	0	0	0	2
00-01—Hartford	AHL	80	8	30	38	133	...	...	...	5	0	0	0	2
01-02—Saint John	AHL	58	0	17	17	92	...	...	...	—	—	—	—	—
02-03—Norfolk	AHL	60	6	22	28	121	...	...	...	—	—	—	—	—
—Chicago.....................	NHL	16	2	0	2	9	-13	0	0	—	—	—	—	—
NHL Totals (1 year)..............		16	2	0	2	9	-13	0	0					

HENTUNEN, JUKKA LW PREDATORS

PERSONAL: Born May 3, 1974, in Finland. ... 5-10/187. ... Shoots right.
TRANSACTIONS/CAREER NOTES: Selected by Calgary Flames in sixth round (seventh Flames pick, 176th overall) of NHL entry draft (June 24, 2000). ... Injured knee (December 27, 2001; missed 10 games. ... Injured knee (February 26, 2002). ... Traded by Flames to Nashville Predators for conditional pick in 2003 draft (March 17, 2002). ... Injured left knee (March 17, 2002); missed two games.

Season Team	League	REGULAR SEASON								PLAYOFFS				
		Gms.	G	A	Pts.	PIM	+/-	PP	SH	Gms.	G	A	Pts.	PIM
93-94—Kiekko Warkaus	Finland Dv.3	24	11	7	18	12	...			—	—	—	—	—
94-95—Kiekko Warkaus	Finland Dv.3	29	23	23	46	28	...			—	—	—	—	—
95-96—Diskos.......................	Finland Div. 2	53	28	24	52	18	...			—	—	—	—	—
96-97—Hermes Kokkola	Finland Div. 2	35	10	13	23	43	...			3	1	0	1	0
97-98—Hermes Kokkola	Finland Div. 2	49	19	16	35	36	...			3	3	3	6	0
98-99—Hermes Kokkola	Finland Div. 2	1	0	0	0	0	...			—	—	—	—	—
—HPK Hameenlinna.......	Finland	41	13	21	34	32	...			8	4	2	6	12
99-00—HPK Hameenlinna	Finland	53	17	28	45	76	...			—	—	—	—	—
00-01—Jokerit Helsinki	Finland	56	27	28	55	24	...			5	1	0	1	4
01-02—Calgary	NHL	28	2	3	5	4	-9	1	0	—	—	—	—	—
—Saint John	AHL	9	3	3	6	0	...			—	—	—	—	—
—Nashville	NHL	10	2	2	4	0	0	0	0	—	—	—	—	—
02-03—Jokerit Helsinki	Finland	48	11	28	39	...	...			—	—	—	—	—
NHL Totals (1 year)..............		38	4	5	9	4	-9	1	0					

HERPERGER, CHRIS LW

PERSONAL: Born February 24, 1974, in Esterhazy, Sask. ... 6-0/205. ... Shoots left. ... Name pronounced HUHR-puhr-guhr.
TRANSACTIONS/CAREER NOTES: Signed by Philadelphia Flyers in 10th round (10th Flyers pick, 223rd overall) of NHL entry draft (June 20, 1992). ... Traded by Flyers with seventh-round pick (LW Tony Mohagen) in 1997 draft to Mighty Ducks of Anaheim for C Bob Corkum (February 6, 1996). ... Signed as free agent by Chicago Blackhawks (September 2, 1998). ... Suffered concussion (January 21, 2001); missed three games. ... Bruised ribs (February 7, 2001); missed two games. ... Signed as free agent by Ottawa Senators (July 13, 2001). ... Suffered ankle infection (October 3, 2001); missed first five games of season. ... Injured groin (October 16, 2001); missed four games. ... Bruised right knee (January 9, 2002); missed one game. ... Signed as free agent by Atlanta Thrashers (August 1, 2002). ... Traded by Thrashers with RW Chris Nielsen to Vancouver Canucks for C Jeff Farkas (January 20, 2003).

H

Season Team	League	REGULAR SEASON Gms.	G	A	Pts.	PIM	+/-	PP	SH	PLAYOFFS Gms.	G	A	Pts.	PIM
90-91—Swift Current	WHL	10	0	1	1	5	...	...	...	—	—	—	—	—
91-92—Swift Current	WHL	72	14	19	33	44	...	...	...	8	0	1	1	9
92-93—Swift Current	WHL	20	9	7	16	31	...	...	...	—	—	—	—	—
—Seattle	WHL	66	29	18	47	61	...	...	...	5	1	1	2	6
93-94—Seattle	WHL	71	44	51	95	110	...	...	...	9	12	10	22	12
94-95—Seattle	WHL	59	49	52	101	106	...	...	...	4	4	0	4	6
—Hershey	AHL	4	0	0	0	0	...	...	...	—	—	—	—	—
95-96—Hershey	AHL	46	8	12	20	36	...	...	...	—	—	—	—	—
—Baltimore	AHL	21	2	3	5	17	...	...	...	9	2	3	5	6
96-97—Baltimore	AHL	67	19	22	41	88	...	...	...	3	0	0	0	0
97-98—Canadian nat'l team	Int'l	62	20	30	50	102	...	...	...	—	—	—	—	—
98-99—Indianapolis	IHL	79	19	29	48	81	...	...	...	7	0	4	4	4
99-00—Chicago	NHL	9	0	0	0	5	-2	0	0	—	—	—	—	—
—Cleveland	IHL	73	22	26	48	122	...	...	...	9	3	3	6	8
00-01—Norfolk	AHL	9	1	4	5	9	...	...	...	—	—	—	—	—
—Chicago	NHL	61	10	15	25	20	0	0	1	—	—	—	—	—
01-02—Ottawa	NHL	72	4	9	13	43	4	0	0	—	—	—	—	—
02-03—Chicago	AHL	7	1	1	2	14	...	...	...	—	—	—	—	—
—Atlanta	NHL	27	4	1	5	7	-11	0	0	—	—	—	—	—
—Manitoba	AHL	15	6	6	12	12	...	...	...	—	—	—	—	—
NHL Totals (4 years)		169	18	25	43	75	-9	0	1					

HERR, MATT — C — BRUINS

PERSONAL: Born May 26, 1976, in Hackensack, N.J. ... 6-2/204. ... Shoots left. ... Full Name: Matthew Herr.

TRANSACTIONS/CAREER NOTES: Selected by Washington Capitals in fourth round (fourth Capitals pick, 93rd overall) of NHL entry draft (June 29, 1994). ... Traded by Capitals to Philadelphia Flyers for D Dean Melanson (March 13, 2001). ... Signed as free agent by Florida Panthers (August 20, 2001). ... Signed as free agent by Boston Bruins (July 18, 2002).

Season Team	League	REGULAR SEASON Gms.	G	A	Pts.	PIM	+/-	PP	SH	PLAYOFFS Gms.	G	A	Pts.	PIM
90-91—Hotchkiss	Conn. H.S.	26	9	5	14		...	...	...	—	—	—	—	—
91-92—Hotchkiss	Conn. H.S.	25	17	16	33		...	...	...	—	—	—	—	—
92-93—Hotchkiss	Conn. H.S.	24	48	30	78		...	...	...	—	—	—	—	—
93-94—Hotchkiss	Conn. H.S.	20	28	19	47		...	...	...	—	—	—	—	—
94-95—Univ. of Michigan	CCHA	37	11	8	19	51	...	...	...	—	—	—	—	—
95-96—Univ. of Michigan	CCHA	40	18	13	31	55	...	...	...	—	—	—	—	—
96-97—Univ. of Michigan	CCHA	43	29	23	52	67	...	...	...	—	—	—	—	—
97-98—Univ. of Michigan	CCHA	29	13	17	30	60	...	...	...	—	—	—	—	—
98-99—Washington	NHL	30	2	2	4	8	-7	1	0	—	—	—	—	—
—Portland	AHL	46	15	14	29	29	...	...	...	—	—	—	—	—
99-00—Portland	AHL	77	22	21	43	51	...	...	...	4	1	1	2	4
00-01—Portland	AHL	40	21	13	34	58	...	...	...	—	—	—	—	—
—Washington	NHL	22	2	3	5	17	3	0	0	—	—	—	—	—
—Philadelphia	AHL	11	2	4	6	18	...	...	...	9	2	1	3	8
01-02—Hershey	AHL	61	18	16	34	68	...	...	...	7	1	2	3	15
—Florida	NHL	3	0	0	0	0	-2	0	0	—	—	—	—	—
02-03—Providence	AHL	77	34	38	72	146	...	...	...	—	—	—	—	—
—Boston	NHL	3	0	0	0	0	0	0	0	—	—	—	—	—
NHL Totals (4 years)		58	4	5	9	25	-6	1	0					

HIGGINS, CHRIS — C — CANADIENS

PERSONAL: Born June 2, 1983, in Smithtown, N.Y. ... 5-11/192. ... Shoots left.

TRANSACTIONS/CAREER NOTES: Selected by Montreal Canadiens in first round (first Canadiens pick, 14th overall) of NHL entry draft (June 22, 2002).

Season Team	League	REGULAR SEASON Gms.	G	A	Pts.	PIM	+/-	PP	SH	PLAYOFFS Gms.	G	A	Pts.	PIM
00-01—Avon Old Farms	USHS (East)	—	18	20	38	—	—	—	—	—	—	—	—	—
01-02—Yale University	ECAC	25	13	16	29	32	...	...	...	—	—	—	—	—
02-03—Yale University	ECAC	28	20	21	41	41	...	...	...	—	—	—	—	—

HIGGINS, MATT — C — ISLANDERS

PERSONAL: Born October 29, 1977, in Calgary. ... 6-2/190. ... Shoots left.

TRANSACTIONS/CAREER NOTES: Selected by Montreal Canadiens in first round (first Canadiens pick, 18th overall) of NHL entry draft (June 22, 1996). ... Suffered concussion (November 21, 1998); missed three games.

Season Team	League	REGULAR SEASON Gms.	G	A	Pts.	PIM	+/-	PP	SH	PLAYOFFS Gms.	G	A	Pts.	PIM
93-94—Moose Jaw	WHL	64	6	10	16	10	...	...	...	—	—	—	—	—
94-95—Moose Jaw	WHL	72	36	34	70	26	...	...	...	10	1	2	3	2
95-96—Moose Jaw	WHL	67	30	33	63	43	...	...	...	—	—	—	—	—
96-97—Moose Jaw	WHL	71	33	57	90	51	...	...	...	12	3	5	8	2
97-98—Fredericton	AHL	50	5	22	27	12	...	...	...	4	1	2	3	2
—Montreal	NHL	1	0	0	0	0	-1	0	0	—	—	—	—	—

H

Season Team	League	Gms.	G	A	Pts.	PIM	+/-	PP	SH		Gms.	G	A	Pts.	PIM
98-99—Montreal	NHL	25	1	0	1	0	-2	0	0		—	—	—	—	—
—Fredericton	AHL	11	3	4	7	6	...	...	...		5	0	2	2	0
99-00—Montreal	NHL	25	0	2	2	4	-6	0	0		—	—	—	—	—
—Quebec	AHL	29	1	15	16	21	...	...	...		—	—	—	—	—
00-01—Quebec	AHL	66	10	18	28	18	...	...	...		8	0	1	1	4
—Montreal	NHL	6	0	0	0	2	-2	0	0		—	—	—	—	—
01-02—Bridgeport	AHL	43	13	19	32	24	...	...	...		15	1	0	1	6
02-03—Bridgeport	AHL	45	11	12	23	30	...	...	...		—	—	—	—	—
NHL Totals (4 years)		57	1	2	3	6	-11	0	0						

HILBERT, ANDY   C/LW   BRUINS

PERSONAL: Born February 6, 1981, in Howell, Mich. ... 5-11/194. ... Shoots left.
TRANSACTIONS/CAREER NOTES: Selected by Boston Bruins in second round (third Bruins pick, 37th overall) of NHL entry draft (June 24, 2000).

		REGULAR SEASON									PLAYOFFS				
Season Team	League	Gms.	G	A	Pts.	PIM	+/-	PP	SH		Gms.	G	A	Pts.	PIM
98-99—U.S. National	USHL	46	23	35	58	140	...	...	...		—	—	—	—	—
99-00—Univ. of Michigan	CCHA	35	17	15	32	39	...	...	...		—	—	—	—	—
00-01—Univ. of Michigan	CCHA	42	26	38	64	72	...	...	...		—	—	—	—	—
01-02—Providence	AHL	72	26	27	53	74	...	...	...		—	—	—	—	—
—Boston	NHL	6	1	0	1	2	-2	0	0		—	—	—	—	—
02-03—Providence	AHL	64	35	35	70	119	...	...	...		—	—	—	—	—
—Boston	NHL	14	0	3	3	7	-1	0	0		—	—	—	—	—
NHL Totals (2 years)		20	1	3	4	9	-3	0	0						

HILL, SEAN   D   HURRICANES

PERSONAL: Born February 14, 1970, in Duluth, Minn. ... 6-0/205. ... Shoots right. ... Full Name: Sean Ronald Hill.
TRANSACTIONS/CAREER NOTES: Selected by Montreal Canadiens in eighth round (ninth Canadiens pick, 167th overall) of NHL entry draft (June 11, 1988). ... Strained abdominal muscle (October 13, 1992); missed 14 games. ... Selected by Mighty Ducks of Anaheim in NHL expansion draft (June 24, 1993). ... Sprained shoulder (January 6, 1994); missed nine games. ... Traded by Mighty Ducks with ninth-round pick (G Frederic Cassivi) in 1994 draft to Ottawa Senators for third-round pick (traded to Tampa Bay) in 1994 draft (June 29, 1994). ... Strained abdominal muscle during 1995-96 season; missed two games. ... Tore left knee ligament (October 18, 1996); missed remainder of season. ... Traded by Senators to Carolina Hurricanes for RW Chris Murray (November 18, 1997). ... Strained hip flexor (December 1, 1997); missed three games. ... Fractured fibula (March 26, 1998); missed final 11 games of season. ... Fractured ankle and strained abdominal muscle (December 21, 1998); missed 20 games. ... Strained abdominal muscle (February 13, 1999); missed one game. ... Sprained ankle (March 21, 1999); missed four games. ... Fractured cheekbone (April 14, 1999); missed final two games of season. ... Strained groin (December 22, 1999); missed 18 games. ... Reinjured groin (April 3, 2000); missed final two games of season. ... Signed as free agent by St. Louis Blues (July 1, 2000). ... Strained muscle in abdomen (November 29, 2000); missed 32 games. ... Strained groin (October 31, 2001); missed two games. ... Traded by Blues to Hurricanes for D Steve Halko and fourth-round pick (traded to Atlanta) in 2002 (December 5, 2001).

		REGULAR SEASON									PLAYOFFS				
Season Team	League	Gms.	G	A	Pts.	PIM	+/-	PP	SH		Gms.	G	A	Pts.	PIM
88-89—Univ. of Wisconsin	WCHA	45	2	23	25	69	...	...	...		—	—	—	—	—
89-90—Univ. of Wisconsin	WCHA	42	14	39	53	78	...	...	...		—	—	—	—	—
90-91—Univ. of Wisconsin	WCHA	37	19	32	51	122	...	...	...		—	—	—	—	—
—Fredericton	AHL	—	—	—	—	—	—	—	—		3	0	2	2	2
—Montreal	NHL	—	—	—	—	—	—	—	—		1	0	0	0	0
91-92—Fredericton	AHL	42	7	20	27	65	...	...	...		7	1	3	4	6
—U.S. national team	Int'l	12	4	3	7	16	...	...	...		—	—	—	—	—
—U.S. Olympic team	Int'l	8	2	0	2	6	...	...	...		—	—	—	—	—
—Montreal	NHL	—	—	—	—	—	—	—	—		4	1	0	1	2
92-93—Montreal	NHL	31	2	6	8	54	-5	1	0		3	0	0	0	4
—Fredericton	AHL	6	1	3	4	10	...	...	...		—	—	—	—	—
93-94—Anaheim	NHL	68	7	20	27	78	-12	2	1		—	—	—	—	—
94-95—Ottawa	NHL	45	1	14	15	30	-11	0	0		—	—	—	—	—
95-96—Ottawa	NHL	80	7	14	21	94	-26	2	0		—	—	—	—	—
96-97—Ottawa	NHL	5	0	0	0	4	1	0	0		—	—	—	—	—
97-98—Ottawa	NHL	13	1	1	2	6	-3	0	0		—	—	—	—	—
—Carolina	NHL	42	0	5	5	48	-2	0	0		—	—	—	—	—
98-99—Carolina	NHL	54	0	10	10	48	9	0	0		—	—	—	—	—
99-00—Carolina	NHL	62	13	31	44	59	3	8	0		—	—	—	—	—
00-01—St. Louis	NHL	48	1	10	11	51	5	0	0		15	0	1	1	12
01-02—St. Louis	NHL	23	0	3	3	28	1	0	0		—	—	—	—	—
—Carolina	NHL	49	7	23	30	61	-1	4	0		23	4	4	8	20
02-03—Carolina	NHL	82	5	24	29	141	4	1	0		—	—	—	—	—
NHL Totals (13 years)		602	44	161	205	702	-37	18	1		46	5	5	10	38

HINOTE, DAN   RW   AVALANCHE

PERSONAL: Born January 30, 1977, in Leesburg, Fla. ... 6-0/195. ... Shoots right.
TRANSACTIONS/CAREER NOTES: Selected by Colorado Avalanche in seventh round (ninth Avalanche pick, 167th overall) of NHL entry draft (June 22, 1996). ... Sprained knee (February 19, 2001); missed one game. ... Injured finger (November 10, 2001); missed one game. ... Injured knee (December 12, 2001); missed one game. ... Injured heel (January 5, 2002); missed 11 games. ... Injured shoulder (March 6, 2002); missed 11 games.

H

Season Team	League	REGULAR SEASON								PLAYOFFS				
		Gms.	G	A	Pts.	PIM	+/-	PP	SH	Gms.	G	A	Pts.	PIM
95-96—Army	Indep.	33	20	24	44	20	...	...	...	—	—	—	—	—
96-97—Oshawa	OHL	60	15	13	28	58	...	...	...	18	4	5	9	8
97-98—Hershey	AHL	24	1	4	5	25	...	...	...	—	—	—	—	—
—Oshawa	OHL	35	12	15	27	39	...	...	...	5	2	2	4	7
98-99—Hershey	AHL	65	4	16	20	95	...	...	...	5	3	1	4	6
99-00—Colorado	NHL	27	1	3	4	10	0	0	0	—	—	—	—	—
—Hershey	AHL	55	28	31	59	96	...	...	...	14	4	5	9	19
00-01—Colorado	NHL	76	5	10	15	51	1	1	0	23	2	4	6	21
01-02—Colorado	NHL	58	6	6	12	39	8	0	1	19	1	2	3	9
02-03—Colorado	NHL	60	6	4	10	49	4	0	0	7	1	2	3	2
NHL Totals (4 years)		221	18	23	41	149	13	1	1	49	4	8	12	32

HINZ, CHAD   RW   OILERS

PERSONAL: Born March 21, 1979, in Saskatoon, Sask. ... 5-10/190. ... Shoots right.
TRANSACTIONS/CAREER NOTES: Selected by Edmonton Oilers in seventh round (eighth Oilers pick, 187th overall) of NHL entry draft (June 21, 1997). ... Re-signed by Oilers (July 28, 2003).

Season Team	League	REGULAR SEASON								PLAYOFFS				
		Gms.	G	A	Pts.	PIM	+/-	PP	SH	Gms.	G	A	Pts.	PIM
95-96—Moose Jaw	WHL	70	22	32	54	65	...	...	...	—	—	—	—	—
96-97—Moose Jaw	WHL	72	37	47	84	47	...	...	...	12	4	1	5	11
97-98—Moose Jaw	WHL	72	20	57	77	45	...	...	...	4	1	2	3	2
98-99—Moose Jaw	WHL	71	42	75	117	40	...	...	...	11	4	12	16	12
—Hamilton	AHL	3	0	0	0	2	...	...	...	—	—	—	—	—
99-00—Hamilton	AHL	18	1	4	5	2	...	...	...	5	1	0	1	0
—Tallahassee	ECHL	49	15	25	40	35	...	...	...	—	—	—	—	—
00-01—Hamilton	AHL	78	13	22	35	30	...	...	...	—	—	—	—	—
01-02—Hamilton	AHL	71	6	13	19	27	...	...	...	15	2	8	10	8
02-03—Hamilton	AHL	65	12	12	24	36	...	...	...	—	—	—	—	—

HIRSCH, COREY   G

PERSONAL: Born August 10, 1972, in Medicine Hat, Alta. ... 5-10/160. ... Catches left.
TRANSACTIONS/CAREER NOTES: Selected by New York Rangers in eighth round (seventh Rangers pick, 169th overall) of NHL entry draft (June 22, 1991). ... Loaned by Rangers to Canadian national team (October 1, 1993). ... Returned to Rangers (March 8, 1994). ... Traded by Rangers to Vancouver Canucks for C Nathan LaFayette (April 7, 1995). ... Bruised ribs (October 6, 1996); missed five games. ... Signed as free agent by Nashville Predators (August 10, 1999). ... Traded by Predators to Mighty Ducks of Anaheim for future considerations (March 14, 2000). ... Signed as free agent by Washington Capitals (November 1, 2000). ... Signed as free agent by Dallas Stars (August 14, 2002).

Season Team	League	REGULAR SEASON									PLAYOFFS							
		Gms.	Min	W	L	T	GA	SO	Avg.	SV%	Gms.	Min.	W	L	GA	SO	Avg.	SV%
88-89—Kamloops	WHL	32	1516	11	12	2	106	2	4.20	—	5	245	3	2	19	0	4.65	—
89-90—Kamloops	WHL	63	3608	48	13	0	230	3	3.82	—	17	1043	14	3	60	0	3.45	—
90-91—Kamloops	WHL	38	1970	26	7	1	100	3	3.05	—	11	623	5	6	42	0	4.04	—
91-92—Kamloops	WHL	48	2732	35	10	2	124	*5	*2.72	—	*16	*954	*11	5	35	*2	*2.20	—
92-93—Binghamton	AHL	46	2692	*35	4	5	125	1	*2.79	—	14	831	7	7	46	0	3.32	—
—New York Rangers	NHL	4	224	1	2	1	14	0	3.75	.879	—	—	—	—	—	—	—	—
93-94—Canadian nat'l team	Int'l	37	2158	19	15	2	107	0	2.97	—	—	—	—	—	—	—	—	—
—Can. Olympic team	Int'l	8	495	5	2	1	17	0	2.06	—	—	—	—	—	—	—	—	—
—Binghamton	AHL	10	611	5	4	1	38	0	3.73	—	—	—	—	—	—	—	—	—
94-95—Binghamton	AHL	57	3371	31	20	5	175	0	3.11	—	—	—	—	—	—	—	—	—
95-96—Vancouver	NHL	41	2338	17	14	6	114	1	2.93	.903	6	338	2	3	21	0	3.73	.873
96-97—Vancouver	NHL	39	2127	12	20	4	116	2	3.27	.894	—	—	—	—	—	—	—	—
97-98—Vancouver	NHL	1	50	0	0	0	5	0	6.00	.853	—	—	—	—	—	—	—	—
—Syracuse	AHL	60	3513	30	22	6	187	1	3.19	—	5	297	2	3	10	1	2.02	—
98-99—Vancouver	NHL	20	919	3	8	3	48	1	3.13	.890	—	—	—	—	—	—	—	—
—Syracuse	AHL	5	300	2	3	0	14	0	2.80	—	—	—	—	—	—	—	—	—
99-00—Milwaukee	IHL	19	1098	11	8	1	49	0	2.68	—	—	—	—	—	—	—	—	—
—Utah	IHL	17	937	9	5	1	42	3	2.69	—	2	121	0	2	4	0	1.98	—
00-01—Washington	NHL	1	20	1	0	0	0	0	1.000	—	—	—	—	—	—	—	—	—
—Cincinnati	IHL	13	783	11	2	‡0	28	1	2.15	—	—	—	—	—	—	—	—	—
—Albany	AHL	4	199	0	4	0	19	0	5.73	—	—	—	—	—	—	—	—	—
—Portland	AHL	36	2142	17	17	2	104	1	2.91	—	2	118	0	2	7	0	3.56	—
01-02—Portland	AHL	23	1395	6	12	5	62	1	2.67	—	—	—	—	—	—	—	—	—
—Philadelphia	AHL	5	299	2	3	0	14	1	2.81	—	—	—	—	—	—	—	—	—
02-03—Utah	AHL	35	1953	14	16	2	86	0	2.64	—	—	—	—	—	—	—	—	—
—Dallas	NHL	2	97	0	1	0	4	0	2.47	.897	—	—	—	—	—	—	—	—
NHL Totals (7 years)		108	5775	34	45	14	301	4	3.13	.896	6	338	2	3	21	0	3.73	.873

H

HLAVAC, JAN   LW

PERSONAL: Born September 20, 1976, in Prague, Czechoslovakia. ... 6-0/200. ... Shoots left. ... Name pronounced YAHN luh-VAHCH.
TRANSACTIONS/CAREER NOTES: Selected by New York Islanders in second round (second Islanders pick, 28th overall) of NHL entry draft (July 8, 1995). ... Traded by Islanders to Calgary Flames for LW Jorgen Jonsson (July 14, 1998). ... Traded by Flames with first- (C Jamie Lundmark) and third-round (D Pat Aufiero) picks in 1999 draft to New York Rangers for C Marc Savard and first-round pick (C/LW Oleg

Saprykin) in 1999 draft (June 26, 1999). ... Strained hip flexor (March 15, 2000); missed two games. ... Bruised foot (April 4, 2000); missed one game. ... Injured shoulder (January 14, 2001); missed one game. ... Injured left knee (April 4, 2001); missed final two games of season. ... Traded by Rangers with D Kim Johnsson, RW Pavel Brendl and third-round pick in 2003 draft to Philadelphia Flyers for rights to C Eric Lindros and conditional first-round pick (August 20, 2001). ... Traded by Flyers with third-round pick (traded to Washington) in 2002 draft to Vancouver Canucks for LW Donald Brashear and sixth-round pick (traded to Colorado) in 2002 draft (December 17, 2001). ... Traded by Canucks with C Harold Druken to Carolina Hurricanes for D Marek Malik and LW Darren Langdon (November 1, 2002).

STATISTICAL PLATEAUS: Three-goal games: 1999-00 (1), 2000-01 (1), 2002-03 (1). Total: 3.

			REGULAR SEASON								PLAYOFFS				
Season Team	League	Gms.	G	A	Pts.	PIM	+/-	PP	SH		Gms.	G	A	Pts.	PIM
93-94—Sparta Prague............	Czech. Jrs.	27	12	15	27	...	...	...	...		—	—	—	—	—
—Sparta Prague............	Czech Rep.	9	1	1	2	...	...	...	...		—	—	—	—	—
94-95—Sparta Prague............	Czech Rep.	38	7	6	13	...	...	...	...		5	0	2	2	...
95-96—Sparta Prague............	Czech Rep.	34	8	5	13	...	...	...	...		12	1	2	3	...
96-97—Sparta Praha............	Czech Rep.	38	8	13	21	24	...	...	...		10	5	2	7	2
97-98—Sparta Praha............	Czech Rep.	48	17	30	47	40	...	...	...		5	1	0	1	2
98-99—Sparta Praha............	Czech Rep.	49	*33	20	53	52	...	...	...		6	1	3	4	...
99-00—New York Rangers......	NHL	67	19	23	42	16	3	6	0		—	—	—	—	—
—Hartford......................	AHL	3	1	0	1	0	...	...	...		—	—	—	—	—
00-01—New York Rangers......	NHL	79	28	36	64	20	3	5	0		—	—	—	—	—
01-02—Philadelphia...............	NHL	31	7	3	10	8	5	0	0		—	—	—	—	—
—Vancouver.................	NHL	46	9	12	21	10	4	1	0		5	0	1	1	0
02-03—Vancouver.................	NHL	9	1	1	2	6	-1	0	0		—	—	—	—	—
—Carolina	NHL	52	9	15	24	22	-9	6	0		—	—	—	—	—
NHL Totals (4 years)...........		284	73	90	163	82	5	18	0		5	0	1	1	0

HNIDY, SHANE — D — SENATORS

PERSONAL: Born November 8, 1975, in Neepawa, Man. ... 6-2/204. ... Shoots right. ... Name pronounced NIGH-dee.
TRANSACTIONS/CAREER NOTES: Selected by Buffalo Sabres in seventh round (Sabres seventh pick, 173rd overall) of NHL entry draft (June 28, 1994). ... Signed as free agent by Detroit Red Wings (August 6, 1998). ... Traded by Red Wings to Ottawa Senators for eighth-round pick (RW Todd Jackson) in 2000 draft (June 25, 2000). ... Bruised left foot (December 14, 2000); missed four games. ... Strained groin (March 26, 2001); missed final six game of regular season. ... Injured left ankle (December 23, 2001); missed 11 games. ... Re-signed by Senators (June 12, 2003).

			REGULAR SEASON								PLAYOFFS				
Season Team	League	Gms.	G	A	Pts.	PIM	+/-	PP	SH		Gms.	G	A	Pts.	PIM
91-92—Swift Current	WHL	56	1	3	4	11	...	...	...		—	—	—	—	—
92-93—Swift Current	WHL	72	7	22	29	105	...	...	...		—	—	—	—	—
93-94—Prince Albert...............	WHL	69	7	26	33	113	...	...	...		—	—	—	—	—
94-95—Prince Albert...............	WHL	72	5	29	34	169	...	...	...		15	4	7	11	29
95-96—Prince Albert...............	WHL	58	11	42	53	100	...	...	...		18	4	11	15	34
96-97—Baton Rouge...............	ECHL	21	3	10	13	50	...	...	...		—	—	—	—	—
—Saint John	AHL	44	2	12	14	112	...	...	...		—	—	—	—	—
97-98—Grand Rapids.............	IHL	77	6	12	18	210	...	...	...		3	0	2	2	23
98-99—Adirondack.................	AHL	68	9	20	29	121	...	...	...		3	0	1	1	0
99-00—Cincinnati....................	AHL	68	9	19	28	153	...	...	...		—	—	—	—	—
00-01—Ottawa	NHL	52	3	2	5	84	8	0	0		1	0	0	0	0
—Grand Rapids.............	IHL	2	0	0	0	2	...	...	...		—	—	—	—	—
01-02—Ottawa	NHL	33	1	1	2	57	-10	0	0		12	1	1	2	12
02-03—Ottawa	NHL	67	0	8	8	130	-1	0	0		1	0	0	0	0
NHL Totals (3 years)...........		152	4	11	15	271	-3	0	0		14	1	1	2	12

HNILICKA, MILAN — G — THRASHERS

PERSONAL: Born June 24, 1973, in Kladno, Czechoslovakia ... 6-1/190. ... Catches left. ... Name pronounced MEE-lahn nun-LEECH-kuh.
TRANSACTIONS/CAREER NOTES: Selected by New York Islanders in fourth round (fourth Islanders pick, 70th overall) of NHL entry draft (June 22, 1991). ... Signed as free agent by New York Rangers (July 22, 1999). ... Signed as free agent by Atlanta Thrashers (July 28, 2000).

			REGULAR SEASON									PLAYOFFS						
Season Team	League	Gms.	Min	W	L	T	GA	SO	Avg.	SV%		Gms.	Min.	W	L	GA	SO	Avg.	SV%
89-90—Poldi Kladno.................	Czech Rep.	24	1113	...	...	...	70	...	3.77	—		—	—	—	—	—	—	—	—
90-91—Poldi Kladno.................	Czech Rep.	35	2122	...	...	...	98	...	2.77	—		—	—	—	—	—	—	—	—
91-92—Poldi Kladno.................	Czech Rep.	30	1788	...	...	...	107	...	3.59	—		—	—	—	—	—	—	—	—
92-93—Swift Current...............	WHL	65	3679	*46	12	2	206	2	3.36	—		17	1017	12	5	54	*2	3.19	—
93-94—Salt Lake City..............	IHL	9	381	5	1	0	25	0	3.94	—		—	—	—	—	—	—	—	—
—Richmond....................	ECHL	43	2299	18	16	‡5	155	0	4.05	—		—	—	—	—	—	—	—	—
94-95—Denver	IHL	15	798	9	4	‡1	47	1	3.53	—		—	—	—	—	—	—	—	—
95-96—Poldi Kladno.................	Czech Rep.	33	1959	...	...	...	93	1	2.85	—		8	493	...	...	24	...	2.92	—
96-97—Poldi Kladno.................	Czech Rep.	48	2736	...	...	...	120	4	2.63	—		3	151	...	...	14	0	5.56	—
97-98—Sparta Praha	Czech Rep.	49	2847	...	...	...	99	...	2.09	—		11	632	...	...	31	...	2.94	—
98-99—Sparta Praha	Czech Rep.	50	2877	...	...	...	109	...	2.27	—		8	507	...	...	13	...	1.54	—
99-00—New York Rangers	NHL	2	86	0	1	0	5	0	3.49	.886		—	—	—	—	—	—	—	—
—Hartford	AHL	36	1979	22	11	0	71	5	2.15	—		3	99	0	1	6	0	3.64	—
00-01—Atlanta	NHL	36	1879	12	19	2	105	2	3.35	.890		—	—	—	—	—	—	—	—
01-02—Atlanta	NHL	60	3367	13	33	10	179	3	3.19	.908		—	—	—	—	—	—	—	—
02-03—Chicago	AHL	15	838	11	2	1	33	1	2.36	—		—	—	—	—	—	—	—	—
—Atlanta........................	NHL	21	1097	4	13	1	65	0	3.56	.893		—	—	—	—	—	—	—	—
NHL Totals (4 years)...........		119	6429	29	66	13	354	5	3.30	.900		—	—	—	—	—	—	—	—

H

HODSON, JAMIE   G   MAPLE LEAFS

PERSONAL: Born April 8, 1980, in Brandon, Man. ... 6-2/192. ... Catches left.
TRANSACTIONS/CAREER NOTES: Selected by Toronto Maple Leafs in third round (third Maple Leafs pick, 69th overall) of NHL entry draft (June 27, 1998). ... Re-signed by Maple Leafs (July 16, 2003).

			REGULAR SEASON									**PLAYOFFS**						
Season Team	League	Gms.	Min	W	L	T	GA	SO	Avg.	SV%	Gms.	Min.	W	L	GA	SO	Avg.	SV%
97-98—Brandon	WHL	20	964	12	2	2	52	2	3.24	—	6	337	5	0	16	0	2.85	—
98-99—Brandon	WHL	43	2295	23	12	3	123	4	3.22	—	5	275	1	4	26	0	5.67	—
99-00—Brandon	WHL	39	2321	13	22	3	130	2	3.36	—	—	—	—	—	—	—	—	—
00-01—Brandon	WHL	29	1587	9	17	1	92	0	3.48	—	1	59	0	1	3	0	3.05	—
—St. John's	AHL	4	137	0	2	0	13	0	5.69	—	—	—	—	—	—	—	—	—
01-02—South Carolina	ECHL	36	1996	20	9	3	100	1	3.01	—	1	59	0	1	3	0	3.05	—
02-03—St. John's	AHL	22	1136	8	7	2	64	1	3.38	—	—	—	—	—	—	—	—	—
—Greensboro	ECHL	14	816	9	4	1	33	0	2.43	—	—	—	—	—	—	—	—	—

HODSON, KEVIN   G

PERSONAL: Born March 27, 1972, in Winnipeg ... 6-0/180. ... Catches left.
TRANSACTIONS/CAREER NOTES: Signed as non-drafted free agent by Chicago Blackhawks (August 27, 1992). ... Signed as free agent by Detroit Red Wings (May 3, 1993). ... Strained hip flexor (October 10, 1998); missed two games. ... Reinjured hip (March 17, 1998); missed one game. ... Traded by Red Wings with second-round pick (RW Sheldon Keefe) in 1999 draft to Tampa Bay Lightning for LW Wendel Clark, G Bill Ranford and sixth-round pick (RW Kent McDonell) in 1999 draft (March 23, 1999). ... Injured groin (April 8, 1999); missed final five games of season. ... Traded by Lightning to Montreal Canadiens for seventh-round pick (traded to Philadelphia) in 2000 draft (June 2, 2000). ... Signed as free agent by Lightning (May 29, 2002). ... Announced retirement (January 16, 2003).

			REGULAR SEASON									**PLAYOFFS**						
Season Team	League	Gms.	Min	W	L	T	GA	SO	Avg.	SV%	Gms.	Min.	W	L	GA	SO	Avg.	SV%
90-91—S.S. Marie	OHL	30	1638	18	11	0	88	2	*3.22	—	10	600	*9	1	28	0	2.80	—
91-92—S.S. Marie	OHL	50	2722	28	12	4	151	0	3.33	—	18	1116	12	6	59	1	3.17	—
92-93—S.S. Marie	OHL	26	1470	18	5	2	76	1	*3.10	—	8	448	8	0	17	0	2.28	—
—Indianapolis	IHL	14	777	5	9	‡0	53	0	4.09	—	—	—	—	—	—	—	—	—
93-94—Adirondack..........	AHL	37	2083	20	10	5	102	2	2.94	—	3	89	0	2	10	0	6.74	—
94-95—Adirondack..........	AHL	51	2731	19	22	8	161	1	3.54	—	4	238	0	4	14	0	3.53	—
95-96—Adirondack..........	AHL	32	1654	13	13	2	87	0	3.16	—	3	149	0	2	8	0	3.22	—
—Detroit..........	NHL	4	163	2	0	0	3	1	1.10	.955	—	—	—	—	—	—	—	—
96-97—Detroit..........	NHL	6	294	2	2	1	8	1	1.63	.930	—	—	—	—	—	—	—	—
—Quebec..........	IHL	2	118	1	1	‡0	7	0	3.56	—	—	—	—	—	—	—	—	—
97-98—Detroit..........	NHL	21	988	9	3	3	44	2	2.67	.901	1	0	0	0	0	0	...	...
98-99—Detroit..........	NHL	4	175	0	2	0	9	0	3.09	.886	—	—	—	—	—	—	—	—
—Adirondack..........	AHL	6	349	1	3	2	19	0	3.27	—	—	—	—	—	—	—	—	—
—Tampa Bay	NHL	5	238	2	1	1	11	0	2.77	.907	—	—	—	—	—	—	—	—
99-00—Tampa Bay	NHL	24	769	2	7	4	47	0	3.67	.856	—	—	—	—	—	—	—	—
—Detroit..........	IHL	9	505	4	6	0	22	0	2.61	—	—	—	—	—	—	—	—	—
02-03—Tampa Bay	NHL	7	283	0	3	1	12	0	2.54	.881	—	—	—	—	—	—	—	—
NHL Totals (6 years)..........		71	2910	17	18	10	134	4	2.76	.893	1	0	0	0	0	0	...	...

HOGLUND, JONAS   LW

PERSONAL: Born August 29, 1972, in Hammaro, Sweden ... 6-4/214. ... Shoots right. ... Name pronounced YOH-nuhz HOHG-luhnd.
TRANSACTIONS/CAREER NOTES: Selected by Calgary Flames in 10th round (11th Flames pick, 222nd overall) of NHL entry draft (June 20, 1992). ... Traded by Flames with D Zarley Zalapski to Montreal Canadiens for RW Valeri Bure and fourth-round pick (C Shaun Sutter) in 1998 draft (February 1, 1998). ... Signed as free agent by Toronto Maple Leafs (July 7, 1999).
STATISTICAL PLATEAUS: Three-goal games: 2000-01 (1).

			REGULAR SEASON							**PLAYOFFS**				
Season Team	League	Gms.	G	A	Pts.	PIM	+/-	PP	SH	Gms.	G	A	Pts.	PIM
88-89—Farjestad Karlstad	Sweden	1	0	0	0	0	...	...	...	—	—	—	—	—
89-90—Farjestad Karlstad	Sweden	1	0	0	0	0	...	...	...	—	—	—	—	—
90-91—Farjestad Karlstad	Sweden	40	5	5	10	4	...	...	...	8	1	0	1	0
91-92—Farjestad Karlstad	Sweden	40	14	11	25	6	...	...	...	6	2	4	6	2
92-93—Farjestad Karlstad	Sweden	40	13	13	26	14	...	...	...	3	1	0	1	0
93-94—Farjestad Karlstad	Sweden	22	7	2	9	10	...	...	...	—	—	—	—	—
94-95—Farjestad Karlstad	Sweden	40	14	12	26	16	...	...	...	4	3	2	5	0
95-96—Farjestad Karlstad	Sweden	40	32	11	43	18	...	...	...	8	2	1	3	6
96-97—Calgary	NHL	68	19	16	35	12	-4	3	0	—	—	—	—	—
97-98—Calgary	NHL	50	6	8	14	16	-9	0	0	—	—	—	—	—
—Montreal	NHL	28	6	5	11	6	2	4	0	10	2	0	2	0
98-99—Montreal	NHL	74	8	10	18	16	-5	1	0	—	—	—	—	—
99-00—Toronto	NHL	82	29	27	56	10	-2	9	1	12	2	4	6	2
00-01—Toronto	NHL	82	23	26	49	14	1	5	0	10	0	0	0	4
01-02—Toronto	NHL	82	13	34	47	26	11	1	1	20	4	6	10	2
02-03—Toronto	NHL	79	13	19	32	12	2	2	0	7	0	1	1	0
NHL Totals (7 years)..........		545	117	145	262	112	-4	25	2	59	8	11	19	8

H

HOLDEN, JOSH   C   MAPLE LEAFS

PERSONAL: Born January 18, 1978, in Calgary ... 6-0/189. ... Shoots left.
TRANSACTIONS/CAREER NOTES: Selected by Vancouver Canucks in first round (first Canucks pick, 12th overall) of NHL entry draft (June 22, 1996). ... Suffered hernia prior to start of 1999-2000 season; missed first 22 games of season. ... Claimed by Carolina Hurricanes from Canucks in NHL waiver draft (September 28, 2001). ... Claimed on waivers by Canucks (October 25, 2001). ... Traded by Canucks to Toronto Maple Leafs for C Jeff Farkas (June 22, 2002). ... Re-signed by Maple Leafs (July 28, 2003).

Season Team	League	Gms.	G	A	Pts.	PIM	+/-	PP	SH	Gms.	G	A	Pts.	PIM
94-95—Regina	WHL	62	20	23	43	45	...	...	...	4	3	1	4	0
95-96—Regina	WHL	70	57	55	112	105	...	...	...	11	4	5	9	23
96-97—Regina	WHL	58	49	49	98	148	...	...	...	5	3	2	5	10
97-98—Regina	WHL	56	41	58	99	134	...	...	...	2	2	2	4	10
98-99—Syracuse	AHL	38	14	15	29	48	...	...	...	—	—	—	—	—
—Vancouver	NHL	30	2	4	6	10	-10	1	0	—	—	—	—	—
99-00—Syracuse	AHL	45	19	32	51	113	...	...	...	4	1	0	1	10
—Vancouver	NHL	6	1	5	6	2	2	0	0	—	—	—	—	—
00-01—Kansas City	IHL	60	27	26	53	136	...	...	...	—	—	—	—	—
—Vancouver	NHL	10	1	0	1	0	0	0	0	—	—	—	—	—
01-02—Carolina	NHL	8	0	0	0	2	0	0	0	—	—	—	—	—
—Manitoba	AHL	68	16	17	33	187	...	...	...	7	1	1	2	4
02-03—St. John's	AHL	65	24	29	53	123	...	...	...	—	—	—	—	—
—Toronto	NHL	5	1	0	1	2	-2	0	0	—	—	—	—	—
NHL Totals (5 years)		59	5	9	14	16	-10	1	0					

HOLIK, BOBBY   C   RANGERS

PERSONAL: Born January 1, 1971, in Jihlava, Czechoslovakia ... 6-4/235. ... Shoots right. ... Full Name: Robert Holik. ... Name pronounced hoh-LEEK.
TRANSACTIONS/CAREER NOTES: Selected by Hartford Whalers in first round (first Whalers pick, 10th overall) of NHL entry draft (June 17, 1989). ... Traded by Whalers with second-round pick (LW Jay Pandolfo) in 1993 draft and future considerations to New Jersey Devils for G Sean Burke and D Eric Weinrich (August 28, 1992). ... Bruised left shoulder (December 8, 1993); missed 11 games. ... Fractured left index finger (October 7, 1995); missed 13 games. ... Sprained left ankle (February 28, 1996); missed six games. ... Suspended two games and fined $1,000 by NHL for tripping incident (November 8, 1998). ... Suspended two games by NHL for slashing incident (March 23, 1999). ... Suspended three games by NHL for slashing incident (November 25, 1999). ... Injured knee (February 15, 2001); missed two games. ... Suspended one game by NHL for high-sticking incident (March 24, 2002). ... Signed as free agent by New York Rangers (July 1, 2002).
STATISTICAL PLATEAUS: Three-goal games: 1992-93 (2), 1998-99 (1). Total: 3.

Season Team	League	Gms.	G	A	Pts.	PIM	+/-	PP	SH	Gms.	G	A	Pts.	PIM
87-88—Dukla Jihlava	Czech.	31	5	9	14	...	...	...	...	—	—	—	—	—
88-89—Dukla Jihlava	Czech.	24	7	10	17	...	...	...	...	—	—	—	—	—
89-90—Dukla Jihlava	Czech.	42	15	26	41	...	...	...	...	—	—	—	—	—
—Czech. national team	Int'l	10	1	5	6	0	...	...	...	—	—	—	—	—
90-91—Hartford	NHL	78	21	22	43	113	-3	8	0	6	0	0	0	7
91-92—Hartford	NHL	76	21	24	45	44	4	1	0	7	0	1	1	6
92-93—Utica	AHL	1	0	0	0	2	...	...	...	—	—	—	—	—
—New Jersey	NHL	61	20	19	39	76	-6	7	0	5	1	1	2	6
93-94—New Jersey	NHL	70	13	20	33	72	28	2	0	20	0	3	3	6
94-95—New Jersey	NHL	48	10	10	20	18	9	0	0	20	4	4	8	22
95-96—New Jersey	NHL	63	13	17	30	58	9	1	0	—	—	—	—	—
96-97—New Jersey	NHL	82	23	39	62	54	24	5	0	10	2	3	5	4
97-98—New Jersey	NHL	82	29	36	65	100	23	8	0	5	0	0	0	8
98-99—New Jersey	NHL	78	27	37	64	119	16	5	0	7	0	7	7	6
99-00—New Jersey	NHL	79	23	23	46	106	7	7	0	23	3	7	10	14
00-01—New Jersey	NHL	80	15	35	50	97	19	3	0	25	6	10	16	37
01-02—New Jersey	NHL	81	25	29	54	97	7	6	0	6	4	1	5	2
02-03—New York Rangers	NHL	64	16	19	35	50	-1	3	0	—	—	—	—	—
NHL Totals (13 years)		942	256	330	586	1004	136	56	0	134	20	37	57	118

HOLLAND, JASON   D   KINGS

PERSONAL: Born April 30, 1976, in Morinville, Alta. ... 6-3/219. ... Shoots right.
TRANSACTIONS/CAREER NOTES: Selected by New York Islanders in second round (second Islanders pick, 38th overall) of NHL entry draft (June 28, 1994). ... Traded by Islanders with LW Paul Kruse to Buffalo Sabres for RW Jason Dawe (March 24, 1998). ... Injured shoulder (October 2, 1999); missed two games. ... Signed as free agent by Los Angeles Kings (August 23, 2001).

Season Team	League	Gms.	G	A	Pts.	PIM	+/-	PP	SH	Gms.	G	A	Pts.	PIM
92-93—Kamloops	WHL	4	0	0	0	2	...	...	...	—	—	—	—	—
93-94—Kamloops	WHL	59	14	15	29	80	...	...	...	18	2	3	5	4
94-95—Kamloops	WHL	71	9	32	41	65	...	...	...	21	2	7	9	9
95-96—Kamloops	WHL	63	24	33	57	98	...	...	...	16	4	9	13	22
96-97—Kentucky	AHL	72	14	25	39	46	...	...	...	4	0	2	2	0
—New York Islanders	NHL	4	1	0	1	0	1	0	0	—	—	—	—	—
97-98—Kentucky	AHL	50	10	16	26	29	...	...	...	—	—	—	—	—
—New York Islanders	NHL	8	0	0	0	4	-4	0	0	—	—	—	—	—
—Rochester	AHL	9	0	4	4	10	...	...	...	4	0	3	3	4
98-99—Buffalo	NHL	3	0	0	0	8	-1	0	0	—	—	—	—	—
—Rochester	AHL	74	4	25	29	36	...	...	...	20	2	5	7	8

H

Season Team	League	REGULAR SEASON								PLAYOFFS				
		Gms.	G	A	Pts.	PIM	+/-	PP	SH	Gms.	G	A	Pts.	PIM
99-00—Buffalo	NHL	9	0	1	1	0	0	0	0	1	0	0	0	0
—Rochester	AHL	54	3	15	18	24	...	...	...	12	1	0	1	2
00-01—Rochester	AHL	63	4	19	23	45	...	...	...	4	1	0	1	0
01-02—Manchester	AHL	65	9	18	27	39	...	...	...	5	1	0	1	5
—Los Angeles	NHL	3	0	0	0	0	-1	0	0	—	—	—	—	—
02-03—Manchester	AHL	67	4	27	31	53	...	...	...	—	—	—	—	—
—Los Angeles	NHL	2	0	1	1	0	1	0	0	—	—	—	—	—
NHL Totals (6 years)		29	1	2	3	12	-4	0	0	1	0	0	0	0

HOLMQVIST, ANDREAS   D   LIGHTNING

PERSONAL: Born July 23, 1981, in Stockholm, Sweden. ... 6-3/187. ... Shoots right.
TRANSACTIONS/CAREER NOTES: Selected by Tampa Bay Lightning in second round (third Lightning pick, 61st overall) of NHL entry draft (June 23, 2001).

Season Team	League	REGULAR SEASON								PLAYOFFS				
		Gms.	G	A	Pts.	PIM	+/-	PP	SH	Gms.	G	A	Pts.	PIM
99-00—Hammarby	Sweden Jr.	38	8	12	20	16	...	...	...	6	1	2	3	4
00-01—Hammarby	Sweden Jr.	47	6	15	21	40	...	...	...	—	—	—	—	—
02-03—Linkopings	Sweden	43	4	9	13	...	...	...	...	—	—	—	—	—
—Hammarby	Sweden 2	42	11	13	24	97	...	...	...	—	—	—	—	—

HOLMQVIST, JOHAN   G   WILD

PERSONAL: Born May 24, 1978, in Tolfta, Sweden ... 6-3/195. ... Catches left.
TRANSACTIONS/CAREER NOTES: Selected by New York Rangers in seventh round (ninth Rangers pick, 182nd overall) of NHL entry draft (June 21, 1997). ... Traded by Rangers to Minnesota Wild for D Lawrence Nycholat (March 11, 2003). ... Re-signed by Wild (July 8, 2003).

Season Team	League	REGULAR SEASON									PLAYOFFS						
		Gms.	Min	W	L	T	GA	SO	Avg.	SV%	Gms.	Min.	W	L	GA	SO	Avg.	SV%
96-97—Brynas Gavle	Sweden	2	80	0	0	0	4	...	3.00	—	—	—	—	—	—	...	—	—
97-98—Brynas Gavle	Sweden	33	1897	...	...	...	82	...	2.59	—	3	180	0	3	14	...	4.67	—
98-99—Brynas Gavle	Sweden	41	2383	...	...	...	111	4	2.79	—	14	855	9	5	34	0	2.39	—
99-00—Brynas Gavle	Sweden	41	2402	...	...	...	104	4	2.60	—	11	671	...	...	30	1	2.68	—
00-01—Hartford	AHL	43	2305	19	14	4	111	2	2.89	—	5	314	2	3	13	0	2.48	—
—New York Rangers	NHL	2	119	0	2	0	10	0	5.04	.859	—	—	—	—	—	—	—	—
01-02—Hartford	AHL	48	2733	26	12	6	140	1	3.07	—	4	163	1	2	12	0	4.42	—
—New York Rangers	NHL	1	9	0	0	0	0	0	0	1.000	—	—	—	—	—	—	—	—
02-03—Charlotte	ECHL	1	60	1	0	0	2	0	2.00	—	—	—	—	—	—	—	—	—
—Hartford	AHL	35	1904	14	13	5	84	2	2.65	—	—	—	—	—	—	—	—	—
—New York Rangers	NHL	1	39	0	1	0	2	0	3.08	.889	—	—	—	—	—	—	—	—
—Houston	AHL	8	479	5	3	0	23	1	2.88	—	—	—	—	—	—	—	—	—
NHL Totals (3 years)		4	167	0	3	0	12	0	4.31	.868	—	—	—	—	—	—	—	—

HOLMSTROM, TOMAS   LW   RED WINGS

PERSONAL: Born January 23, 1973, in Pieta, Sweden ... 6-0/200. ... Shoots left.
TRANSACTIONS/CAREER NOTES: Selected by Detroit Red Wings in 10th round (ninth Red Wings pick, 257th overall) of NHL entry draft (June 29, 1994). ... Sprained knee (October 30, 1996); missed seven games. ... Bruised shoulder (March 28, 1997); missed one game. ... Sprained knee (November 17, 1999); missed five games. ... Suffered injury (March 3, 2000); missed one game. ... Suffered facial lacerations (March 29, 2000); missed two games. ... Suffered charley horse (November 12, 2000); missed one game. ... Suffered back spasms (December 31, 2000); missed three games. ... Suffered injury (October 16, 2001); missed two games. ... Injured wrist (November 2, 2001); missed five games. ... Suffered from the flu (January 4, 2002); missed three games.
STATISTICAL PLATEAUS: Three-goal games: 2000-01 (1).

Season Team	League	REGULAR SEASON								PLAYOFFS				
		Gms.	G	A	Pts.	PIM	+/-	PP	SH	Gms.	G	A	Pts.	PIM
94-95—Lulea	Sweden	40	14	14	28	56	...	...	...	8	1	2	3	20
95-96—Lulea	Sweden	34	12	11	23	78	...	...	...	11	6	2	8	22
96-97—Detroit	NHL	47	6	3	9	33	-10	3	0	1	0	0	0	0
—Adirondack	AHL	6	3	1	4	7	...	...	...	—	—	—	—	—
97-98—Detroit	NHL	57	5	17	22	44	6	1	0	22	7	12	19	16
98-99—Detroit	NHL	82	13	21	34	69	-11	5	0	10	4	3	7	4
99-00—Detroit	NHL	72	13	22	35	43	4	4	0	9	3	1	4	16
00-01—Detroit	NHL	73	16	24	40	40	-12	9	0	6	1	3	4	8
01-02—Detroit	NHL	69	8	18	26	58	-12	6	0	23	8	3	11	8
—Swedish Oly. team	Int'l	4	1	0	1	2	...	...	...	—	—	—	—	—
02-03—Detroit	NHL	74	20	20	40	62	11	12	0	4	1	1	2	4
NHL Totals (7 years)		474	81	125	206	349	-24	40	0	75	24	23	47	56

HOLZINGER, BRIAN   C   PENGUINS

PERSONAL: Born October 10, 1972, in Parma, Ohio ... 5-11/186. ... Shoots right. ... Full Name: Brian Alan Holzinger. ... Name pronounced HOHL-zihng-uhr.
TRANSACTIONS/CAREER NOTES: Selected by Buffalo Sabres in sixth round (seventh Sabres pick, 124th overall) of NHL entry draft (June 22, 1991). ... Bruised heel (November 10, 1997); missed three games. ... Sprained ankle (March 1, 1998); missed seven games. ... Suffered from

the flu (January 7, 1999); missed one game. ... Injured shoulder (October 17, 1999); missed three games. ... Injured shoulder (January 6, 2000); missed three games. ... Traded by Sabres with C Wayne Primeau, D Cory Sarich and third-round pick (RW Alexandre Kharitonov) in 2000 draft to Tampa Bay Lightning for C Chris Gratton and second-round pick (C Derek Roy) in 2001 draft (March 9, 2000). ... Strained muscle in abdomen (March 12, 2000); missed three games. ... Fractured finger (December 2, 2000); missed five games. ... Injured foot (March 24, 2001); missed two games. ... Fractured right ankle (April 1, 2001); missed final two games of season. ... Injured left shoulder (November 25, 2001); missed three games. ... Reinjured shoulder (December 6, 2001); missed 10 games. ... Injured left shoulder (January 4, 2002); missed remainder of season. ... Traded by Lightning to Pittsburgh Penguins for D Marc Bergevin (March 11, 2003).

Season Team	League	REGULAR SEASON								PLAYOFFS				
		Gms.	G	A	Pts.	PIM	+/-	PP	SH	Gms.	G	A	Pts.	PIM
90-91—Det. Jr. Red Wings......	NAJHL	37	45	41	86	16	...	...	...	—	—	—	—	—
91-92—Bowling Green............	CCHA	30	14	8	22	36	...	...	...	—	—	—	—	—
92-93—Bowling Green............	CCHA	41	31	26	57	44	...	...	...	—	—	—	—	—
93-94—Bowling Green............	CCHA	38	22	15	37	24	...	...	...	—	—	—	—	—
94-95—Bowling Green............	CCHA	38	35	34	69	42	...	...	...	—	—	—	—	—
—Buffalo	NHL	4	0	3	3	0	2	0	0	4	2	1	3	2
95-96—Buffalo	NHL	58	10	10	20	37	-21	5	0	—	—	—	—	—
—Rochester	AHL	17	10	11	21	14	...	...	...	19	10	14	24	10
96-97—Buffalo	NHL	81	22	29	51	54	9	2	2	12	2	5	7	8
97-98—Buffalo	NHL	69	14	21	35	36	-2	4	2	15	4	7	11	18
98-99—Buffalo	NHL	81	17	17	34	45	2	5	0	21	3	5	8	33
99-00—Buffalo	NHL	59	7	17	24	30	4	0	1	—	—	—	—	—
—Tampa Bay	NHL	14	3	3	6	21	-7	1	1	—	—	—	—	—
00-01—Tampa Bay	NHL	70	11	25	36	64	-9	3	0	—	—	—	—	—
01-02—Tampa Bay	NHL	23	1	2	3	4	-4	0	0	—	—	—	—	—
02-03—Springfield	AHL	28	6	20	26	16	...	...	...	—	—	—	—	—
—Tampa Bay	NHL	5	0	1	1	2	1	0	0	—	—	—	—	—
—Pittsburgh..................	NHL	9	1	2	3	6	-6	0	0	—	—	—	—	—
NHL Totals (9 years)...........		473	86	130	216	299	-31	20	6	52	11	18	29	61

HORACEK, JAN — D — OILERS

PERSONAL: Born May 22, 1979, in Benesov, Czechoslovakia. ... 6-4/206. ... Shoots right. ... Name pronounced HOHR-ih-chehk.
TRANSACTIONS/CAREER NOTES: Selected by St. Louis Blues in fourth round (third Blues pick, 98th overall) of NHL entry draft (June 21, 1997). ... Traded by Blues with C Jochen Hecht and C Marty Reasoner to Edmonton Oilers for C Doug Weight and LW Michel Riesen (July 1, 2001).

Season Team	League	REGULAR SEASON								PLAYOFFS				
		Gms.	G	A	Pts.	PIM	+/-	PP	SH	Gms.	G	A	Pts.	PIM
95-96—Slavia Praha..............	Czech Rep.	8	0	1	1	4	...	...	...	—	—	—	—	—
—Slavia Praha..............	Czech. Jrs.	18	1	5	6	...	...	...	...	—	—	—	—	—
—HC Kralupy	Czech II	11	0	0	0	...	...	...	...	—	—	—	—	—
96-97—Slavia Praha..............	Czech. Jrs.	25	4	14	18	...	...	...	...	—	—	—	—	—
—Slavia Praha..............	Czech Rep.	9	0	0	0	6	...	...	...	3	0	0	0	...
—HC Beroun	Czech II	2	0	0	0	...	...	...	...	—	—	—	—	—
97-98—Moncton	QMJHL	54	3	18	21	146	...	...	...	10	1	5	6	20
98-99—Slavia Praha..............	Czech Rep.	1	0	0	0	2	...	...	...	—	—	—	—	—
—Worcester	AHL	53	1	13	14	119	...	...	...	4	0	0	0	6
99-00—Worcester	AHL	68	1	8	9	145	...	...	...	9	0	0	0	2
00-01—Worcester	AHL	11	0	1	1	20	...	...	...	2	0	0	0	2
—Peoria	ECHL	6	0	3	3	8	...	...	...	—	—	—	—	—
01-02—Hamilton	AHL	44	0	5	5	99	...	...	...	13	0	1	1	10
02-03—Havirov	Czech Rep.	39	1	5	6	114	...	...	...	—	—	—	—	—

HORCOFF, SHAWN — C — OILERS

PERSONAL: Born September 17, 1978, in Trail, B.C. ... 6-1/202. ... Shoots left.
TRANSACTIONS/CAREER NOTES: Selected by Edmonton Oilers in fourth round (third Oilers pick, 99th overall) of NHL entry draft (June 27, 1998).

Season Team	League	REGULAR SEASON								PLAYOFFS				
		Gms.	G	A	Pts.	PIM	+/-	PP	SH	Gms.	G	A	Pts.	PIM
95-96—Chilliwack	BCJHL	58	49	96	*145	44	...	...	...	—	—	—	—	—
96-97—Michigan State...........	CCHA	40	10	13	23	20	...	...	...	—	—	—	—	—
97-98—Michigan State...........	CCHA	34	14	13	27	50	...	...	...	—	—	—	—	—
98-99—Michigan State...........	CCHA	39	12	25	37	70	...	...	...	—	—	—	—	—
99-00—Michigan State...........	CCHA	41	14	*48	*62	46	...	...	...	—	—	—	—	—
00-01—Hamilton	AHL	24	10	18	28	19	...	...	...	—	—	—	—	—
—Edmonton	NHL	49	9	7	16	10	8	0	0	5	0	0	0	0
01-02—Edmonton	NHL	61	8	14	22	18	3	0	0	—	—	—	—	—
—Hamilton	AHL	2	1	2	3	6	...	...	...	—	—	—	—	—
02-03—Edmonton	NHL	78	12	21	33	55	10	2	0	6	3	1	4	6
NHL Totals (3 years)...........		188	29	42	71	83	21	2	0	11	3	1	4	6

HORDICHUK, DARCY — LW — PANTHERS

PERSONAL: Born August 10, 1980, in Kamsack, Sask. ... 6-1/215. ... Shoots left.
TRANSACTIONS/CAREER NOTES: Selected by Atlanta Thrashers in sixth round (eighth Thrashers pick, 180th overall) of NHL entry draft (June 24, 2000). ... Traded by Thrashers with fourth-(RW Lance Monych) and fifth-round (RW John Zeiler) picks in 2002 draft to Phoenix Coyotes for D Kirill Safronov, RW Ruslan Zainullin and fourth-round pick (RW Patrick Dwyer) in 2002 draft (March 19, 2002). ... Suspended 10 games by NHL for abuse of an official (November 1, 2002). ... Traded by Coyotes with second-round pick in 2003 draft to Florida Panthers for D Brad Ference (March 9, 2003). ... Re-signed by Panthers (July 24, 2003).

H

Season Team	League	REGULAR SEASON								PLAYOFFS				
		Gms.	G	A	Pts.	PIM	+/-	PP	SH	Gms.	G	A	Pts.	PIM
96-97—Calgary	WHL	3	0	0	0	2	...	...	...	—	—	—	—	—
98-99—Saskatoon	WHL	66	3	2	5	246	...	...	...	—	—	—	—	—
99-00—Saskatoon	WHL	63	6	8	14	269	...	...	...	—	—	—	—	—
00-01—Orlando	IHL	69	7	3	10	*369	...	...	...	16	3	3	6	*41
—Atlanta	NHL	11	0	0	0	38	-3	0	0	—	—	—	—	—
01-02—Chicago	AHL	34	5	4	9	127	...	...	...	—	—	—	—	—
—Atlanta	NHL	33	1	1	2	127	-5	0	0	—	—	—	—	—
—Phoenix	NHL	1	0	0	0	14	0	0	0	—	—	—	—	—
02-03—Springfield	AHL	22	1	3	4	38	...	...	...	—	—	—	—	—
—Phoenix	NHL	25	0	0	0	82	-1	0	0	—	—	—	—	—
—Florida	NHL	3	0	0	0	15	-1	0	0	—	—	—	—	—
NHL Totals (3 years)		73	1	1	2	276	-10	0	0					

HOSSA, MARCEL — LW — CANADIENS

PERSONAL: Born December 10, 1981, in Ilava, Czechoslovakia ... 6-2/212. ... Shoots left. ... Brother of Marian Hossa, left winger, Ottawa Senators. ... Name pronounced HOH-suh.

TRANSACTIONS/CAREER NOTES: Selected by Montreal Canadiens in first round (second Canadiens pick, 16th overall) of NHL entry draft (June 24, 2000). ... Injured wrist (January 14, 2002); missed two games. ... Reinjured wrist (January 19, 2002); missed five games.

Season Team	League	REGULAR SEASON								PLAYOFFS				
		Gms.	G	A	Pts.	PIM	+/-	PP	SH	Gms.	G	A	Pts.	PIM
96-97—Dukla Trencin	Slovakia Jrs.	45	30	21	51	30	...	...	...	—	—	—	—	—
97-98—Dukla Trencin	Slovakia Jrs.	39	11	38	49	44	...	...	...	—	—	—	—	—
98-99—Portland	WHL	70	7	14	21	66	...	...	...	2	0	0	0	0
99-00—Portland	WHL	60	24	29	53	58	...	...	...	—	—	—	—	—
00-01—Portland	WHL	58	34	56	90	58	...	...	...	16	5	7	12	14
01-02—Quebec	AHL	50	17	15	32	24	...	...	...	3	0	0	0	4
—Montreal	NHL	10	3	1	4	2	2	0	0	—	—	—	—	—
02-03—Hamilton	AHL	37	19	13	32	18	...	...	...	—	—	—	—	—
—Montreal	NHL	34	6	7	13	14	3	2	0	—	—	—	—	—
NHL Totals (2 years)		44	9	8	17	16	5	2	0					

HOSSA, MARIAN — RW — SENATORS

PERSONAL: Born January 12, 1979, in Stara Lubovna, Czechoslovakia ... 6-1/208. ... Shoots left. ... Brother of Marcel Hossa, center, Montreal Canadiens organization. ... Name pronounced HOH-suh.

TRANSACTIONS/CAREER NOTES: Selected by Ottawa Senators in first round (first Senators pick, 12th overall) of NHL entry draft (June 21, 1997). ... Tore anterior cruciate and medial collateral ligaments in knee (May 21, 1998); missed first 22 games of season. ... Suffered concussion (November 18, 1999); missed one game. ... Bruised left wrist (January 6, 2000); missed two games. ... Suffered illness (February 1, 2000); missed one game. ... Bruised calf (February 18, 2001); missed one game. ... Injured left knee (February 4, 2002); missed one game. ... Suffered from the flu (April 13, 2002); missed one game.

STATISTICAL PLATEAUS: Three-goal games: 2000-01 (1), 2002-03 (1). Total: 2. ... Four-goal games: 2002-03 (1). ... Total hat tricks: 3.

Season Team	League	REGULAR SEASON								PLAYOFFS				
		Gms.	G	A	Pts.	PIM	+/-	PP	SH	Gms.	G	A	Pts.	PIM
95-96—Dukla Trencin	Slovakia Jrs.	53	42	49	91	26	...	...	...	—	—	—	—	—
96-97—Dukla Trencin	Slovakia	46	25	19	44	33	...	...	...	7	5	5	10	...
97-98—Ottawa	NHL	7	0	1	1	0	-1	0	0	—	—	—	—	—
—Portland	WHL	53	45	40	85	50	...	...	...	16	13	6	19	6
98-99—Ottawa	NHL	60	15	15	30	37	18	1	0	4	0	2	2	4
99-00—Ottawa	NHL	78	29	27	56	32	5	5	0	6	0	0	0	2
00-01—Ottawa	NHL	81	32	43	75	44	19	11	2	4	1	1	2	4
01-02—Dukla Trencin	Slovakia	8	3	4	7	16	...	...	...	—	—	—	—	—
—Ottawa	NHL	80	31	35	66	50	11	9	1	12	4	6	10	2
—Slovakian Oly. team	Int'l	2	4	2	6	0	...	...	...	—	—	—	—	—
02-03—Ottawa	NHL	80	45	35	80	34	8	14	0	18	5	11	16	6
NHL Totals (6 years)		386	152	156	308	197	60	40	3	44	10	20	30	18

HOUDA, DOUG — D

PERSONAL: Born June 3, 1966, in Blairmore, Alta. ... 6-2/210. ... Shoots right. ... Name pronounced HOO-duh.

TRANSACTIONS/CAREER NOTES: Selected by Detroit Red Wings as underage junior in second round (second Red Wings pick, 28th overall) of NHL entry draft (June 9, 1984). ... Fractured left cheekbone (September 23, 1988). ... Injured knee and underwent surgery (November 21, 1989). ... Traded by Red Wings to Hartford Whalers for D Doug Crossman (February 20, 1991). ... Separated shoulder (February 28, 1994); missed three games. ... Strained shoulder (March 15, 1994); missed two games. ... Traded by Whalers to Los Angeles Kings for RW Marc Potvin (November 3, 1993). ... Traded by Kings to Buffalo Sabres for D Sean O'Donnell (July 26, 1994). ... Severed tendon in hand (February 11, 1995); missed 12 games. ... Signed as free agent by New York Islanders (October 23, 1996). ... Traded by Islanders with C Travis Green and RW Tony Tuzzolino to Mighty Ducks of Anaheim for D J.J. Daigneault, C Mark Janssens and RW Joe Sacco (February 6, 1998). ... Traded by Mighty Ducks to Red Wings for future considerations (October 8, 1998). ... Signed as free agent by Sabres (July 13, 1999).

H

		REGULAR SEASON								PLAYOFFS				
Season Team	League	Gms.	G	A	Pts.	PIM	+/-	PP	SH	Gms.	G	A	Pts.	PIM
81-82—Calgary	WHL	3	0	0	0	0	...	...	...	—	—	—	—	—
82-83—Calgary	WHL	71	5	23	28	99	...	...	...	16	1	3	4	44
83-84—Calgary	WHL	69	6	30	36	195	...	...	...	4	0	0	0	7
84-85—Calgary	WHL	65	20	54	74	182	...	...	...	8	3	4	7	29
—Kalamazoo	IHL	—	—	—	—	—	—	—	—	7	0	2	2	10
85-86—Calgary	WHL	16	4	10	14	60	...	...	...	—	—	—	—	—
—Medicine Hat	WHL	35	9	23	32	80	...	...	...	25	4	19	23	64
—Detroit	NHL	6	0	0	0	4	-7	0	0	—	—	—	—	—
86-87—Adirondack	AHL	77	6	23	29	142	...	...	...	11	1	8	9	50
87-88—Detroit	NHL	11	1	1	2	10	0	0	0	—	—	—	—	—
—Adirondack	AHL	71	10	32	42	169	...	...	...	11	0	3	3	44
88-89—Adirondack	AHL	7	0	3	3	8	...	...	...	—	—	—	—	—
—Detroit	NHL	57	2	11	13	67	17	0	0	6	0	1	1	0
89-90—Detroit	NHL	73	2	9	11	127	-5	0	0	—	—	—	—	—
90-91—Adirondack	AHL	38	9	17	26	67	...	...	...	—	—	—	—	—
—Detroit	NHL	22	0	4	4	43	-2	0	0	—	—	—	—	—
—Hartford	NHL	19	1	2	3	41	-3	0	0	6	0	0	0	8
91-92—Hartford	NHL	56	3	6	9	125	-2	1	0	6	0	2	2	13
92-93—Hartford	NHL	60	2	6	8	167	-19	0	0	—	—	—	—	—
93-94—Hartford	NHL	7	0	0	0	23	-4	0	0	—	—	—	—	—
—Los Angeles	NHL	54	2	6	8	165	-15	0	0	—	—	—	—	—
94-95—Buffalo	NHL	28	1	2	3	68	1	0	0	—	—	—	—	—
95-96—Buffalo	NHL	38	1	3	4	52	3	0	0	—	—	—	—	—
—Rochester	AHL	21	1	6	7	41	...	...	...	19	3	5	8	30
96-97—Utah	IHL	3	0	0	0	7	...	...	...	—	—	—	—	—
—New York Islanders	NHL	70	2	8	10	99	1	0	0	—	—	—	—	—
97-98—New York Islanders	NHL	31	1	2	3	47	-6	0	0	—	—	—	—	—
—Anaheim	NHL	24	1	2	3	52	-5	0	1	—	—	—	—	—
98-99—Adirondack	AHL	73	7	21	28	122	...	...	...	3	0	1	1	4
—Detroit	NHL	3	0	1	1	0	-2	0	0	—	—	—	—	—
99-00—Rochester	AHL	79	7	17	24	175	...	...	...	21	1	8	9	39
—Buffalo	NHL	1	0	0	0	12	0	0	0	—	—	—	—	—
00-01—Rochester	AHL	43	6	20	26	106	...	...	...	4	0	0	0	4
01-02—Rochester	AHL	64	6	22	28	170	...	...	...	2	0	0	0	4
02-03—Rochester	AHL	77	3	22	25	191	...	...	...	—	—	—	—	—
—Buffalo	NHL	1	0	0	0	2	-2	0	0	—	—	—	—	—
NHL Totals (15 years)		561	19	63	82	1104	-50	1	1	18	0	3	3	21

HOULDER, BILL   D

PERSONAL: Born March 11, 1967, in Thunder Bay, Ont. ... 6-2/217. ... Shoots left. ... Full Name: William Houlder.
TRANSACTIONS/CAREER NOTES: Selected by Washington Capitals in fourth round (fourth Capitals pick, 82nd overall) of NHL entry draft (June 15, 1985). ... Pulled groin (January 1989). ... Traded by Capitals to Buffalo Sabres for D Shawn Anderson (September 30, 1990). ... Selected by Mighty Ducks of Anaheim in NHL expansion draft (June 24, 1993). ... Traded by Mighty Ducks to St. Louis Blues for D Jason Marshall (August 29, 1994). ... Signed as free agent by Tampa Bay Lightning (August 1, 1995). ... Strained groin (October 7, 1995); missed two games. ... Injured ribs (November 8, 1995); missed four games. ... Strained groin (February 3, 1996); missed three games. ... Reinjured groin (March 5, 1996); missed six games ... Reinjured groin (March 26, 1996); missed five games. ... Bruised wrist (November 4, 1996); missed three games. ... Signed as free agent by San Jose Sharks (July 9, 1997). ... Injured knee (March 6, 1999); missed five games. ... Traded by Sharks with D Andrei Zyuzin, LW Shawn Burr and C Steve Guolla to Lightning for LW Niklas Sundstrom and third-round pick (traded to Chicago) in 2000 draft (August 4, 1999). ... Claimed on waivers by Nashville Predators (November 10, 1999). ... Suffered concussion (November 11, 1999); missed 11 games. ... Suffered from the flu (October 6, 2000); missed first game of season.

		REGULAR SEASON								PLAYOFFS				
Season Team	League	Gms.	G	A	Pts.	PIM	+/-	PP	SH	Gms.	G	A	Pts.	PIM
83-84—Thunder Bay Beavers	TBAHA	23	4	18	22	37	...	...	...	—	—	—	—	—
84-85—North Bay	OHL	66	4	20	24	37	...	...	...	8	0	0	0	2
85-86—North Bay	OHL	59	5	30	35	97	...	...	...	10	1	6	7	12
86-87—North Bay	OHL	62	17	51	68	68	...	...	...	22	4	19	23	20
87-88—Washington	NHL	30	1	2	3	10	-2	0	0	—	—	—	—	—
—Fort Wayne	IHL	43	10	14	24	32	...	...	...	—	—	—	—	—
88-89—Baltimore	AHL	65	10	36	46	50	...	...	...	—	—	—	—	—
—Washington	NHL	8	0	3	3	4	7	0	0	—	—	—	—	—
89-90—Baltimore	AHL	26	3	7	10	12	...	...	...	7	0	2	2	2
—Washington	NHL	41	1	11	12	28	8	0	0	—	—	—	—	—
90-91—Rochester	AHL	69	13	53	66	28	...	...	...	15	5	13	18	4
—Buffalo	NHL	7	0	2	2	4	-2	0	0	—	—	—	—	—
91-92—Rochester	AHL	42	8	26	34	16	...	...	...	16	5	6	11	4
—Buffalo	NHL	10	1	0	1	8	-2	0	0	—	—	—	—	—
92-93—San Diego	IHL	64	24	48	72	39	...	...	...	—	—	—	—	—
—Buffalo	NHL	15	3	5	8	6	5	0	0	8	0	2	2	4
93-94—Anaheim	NHL	80	14	25	39	40	-18	3	0	—	—	—	—	—
94-95—St. Louis	NHL	41	5	13	18	20	16	1	0	4	1	1	2	0
95-96—Tampa Bay	NHL	61	5	23	28	22	1	3	0	6	0	1	1	4
96-97—Tampa Bay	NHL	79	4	21	25	30	16	0	0	—	—	—	—	—
97-98—San Jose	NHL	82	7	25	32	48	13	4	0	6	1	2	3	2
98-99—San Jose	NHL	76	9	23	32	40	8	7	0	6	3	0	3	4
99-00—Tampa Bay	NHL	14	1	2	3	2	-3	1	0	—	—	—	—	—
—Nashville	NHL	57	2	12	14	24	-6	1	0	—	—	—	—	—
00-01—Nashville	NHL	81	4	12	16	40	-7	0	1	—	—	—	—	—
01-02—Nashville	NHL	82	0	8	8	40	-1	0	0	—	—	—	—	—
02-03—Nashville	NHL	82	2	4	6	46	-2	0	0	—	—	—	—	—
NHL Totals (16 years)		846	59	191	250	412	31	20	1	30	5	6	11	14

H

PERSONAL: Born March 9, 1964, in St. Paul, Minn. ... 5-10/188. ... Shoots left. ... Full Name: Phil F. Housley.

TRANSACTIONS/CAREER NOTES: Selected by Buffalo Sabres in first round (first Sabres pick, sixth overall) of NHL entry draft (June 9, 1982). ... Bruised shoulder (January 1984). ... Suspended three games by NHL (October 1984). ... Injured back (November 1987). ... Bruised back (January 12, 1989). ... Suffered hip pointer and bruised back (March 18, 1989). ... Pulled shoulder ligaments while playing at World Cup Tournament (April 1989). ... Traded by Sabres with LW Scott Arniel, RW Jeff Parker and first-round pick (C Keith Tkachuk) in 1990 draft to Winnipeg Jets for C Dale Hawerchuk and first-round pick (LW Brad May) in 1990 draft (June 16, 1990). ... Strained abdominal muscle (February 26, 1992); missed two games. ... Strained groin (October 31, 1992); missed two games. ... Sprained wrist (January 19, 1993); missed two games. ... Traded by Jets to St. Louis Blues for RW Nelson Emerson and D Stephane Quintal (September 24, 1993). ... Suffered back spasms (October 26, 1993); missed five games. ... Suffered sore back (November 18, 1993). ... Underwent back surgery (January 4, 1994); missed 53 games. ... Traded by Blues with second-round picks in 1996 (C Steve Begin) and 1997 (RW John Tripp) drafts to Calgary Flames for free-agent rights to D Al MacInnis and fourth-round pick (D Didier Tremblay) in 1997 draft (July 4, 1994). ... Played in Europe during 1994-95 NHL lockout. ... Injured right pinky (February 9, 1995); missed five games. ... Suffered from the flu (January 10, 1996); missed two games. ... Suffered from the flu (January 17, 1996); missed one game. ... Traded by Flames with D Dan Keczmer to New Jersey Devils for D Tommy Albelin, D Cale Hulse and LW Jocelyn Lemieux (February 26, 1996). ... Signed as free agent by Washington Capitals (July 22, 1996). ... Strained groin (March 16, 1997); missed five games. ... Fractured finger (March 7, 1998); missed 10 games. ... Claimed on waivers by Flames (July 21, 1998). ... Injured abdomen (February 19, 1999); missed one game. ... Injured foot (November 12, 2000); missed one game. ... Suffered concussion (November 18, 2000); missed three games. ... Suffered concussion (December 13, 2000); missed nine games. ... Claimed by Chicago Blackhawks from Flames in NHL waiver draft (September 28, 2001). ... Suffered concussion (October 25, 2001); missed two games. ... Traded by Blackhawks to Toronto Maple Leafs for fourth-round pick in 2003 draft and ninth-round pick in 2004 draft (March 11, 2003).

STATISTICAL PLATEAUS: Three-goal games: 1982-83 (1), 1987-88 (1). Total: 2.

Season Team	League	REGULAR SEASON								PLAYOFFS				
		Gms.	G	A	Pts.	PIM	+/-	PP	SH	Gms.	G	A	Pts.	PIM
80-81—St. Paul's	USHL	6	7	7	14	6	...	...	...	—	—	—	—	—
81-82—South St. Paul H.S.	Minn. H.S.	22	31	34	65	18	...	...	...	—	—	—	—	—
82-83—Buffalo	NHL	77	19	47	66	39	-4	11	0	10	3	4	7	2
83-84—Buffalo	NHL	75	31	46	77	33	3	13	2	3	0	0	0	6
84-85—Buffalo	NHL	73	16	53	69	28	15	3	0	5	3	2	5	2
85-86—Buffalo	NHL	79	15	47	62	54	-9	7	0	—	—	—	—	—
86-87—Buffalo	NHL	78	21	46	67	57	-2	8	1	—	—	—	—	—
87-88—Buffalo	NHL	74	29	37	66	96	-17	6	0	6	2	4	6	6
88-89—Buffalo	NHL	72	26	44	70	47	6	5	0	5	1	3	4	2
89-90—Buffalo	NHL	80	21	60	81	32	11	8	1	6	1	4	5	4
90-91—Winnipeg	NHL	78	23	53	76	24	-13	12	1	—	—	—	—	—
91-92—Winnipeg	NHL	74	23	63	86	92	-5	11	0	7	1	4	5	0
92-93—Winnipeg	NHL	80	18	79	97	52	-14	6	0	6	0	7	7	2
93-94—St. Louis	NHL	26	7	15	22	12	-5	4	0	4	2	1	3	4
94-95—Grasshoppers	Switz. Div. 2	10	6	8	14	34	...	...	...	—	—	—	—	—
—Calgary	NHL	43	8	35	43	18	17	3	0	7	0	9	9	0
95-96—Calgary	NHL	59	16	36	52	22	-2	6	0	—	—	—	—	—
—New Jersey	NHL	22	1	15	16	8	-4	0	0	—	—	—	—	—
96-97—Washington	NHL	77	11	29	40	24	-10	3	1	—	—	—	—	—
97-98—Washington	NHL	64	6	25	31	24	-10	4	1	18	0	4	4	4
98-99—Calgary	NHL	79	11	43	54	52	14	4	0	—	—	—	—	—
99-00—Calgary	NHL	78	11	44	55	24	-12	5	0	—	—	—	—	—
00-01—Calgary	NHL	69	4	30	34	24	-15	0	0	—	—	—	—	—
01-02—Chicago	NHL	80	15	24	39	34	-3	8	0	5	0	1	1	4
—U.S. Olympic team	Int'l	6	1	4	5	0	...	...	...	—	—	—	—	—
02-03—Chicago	NHL	57	6	23	29	24	7	2	0	—	—	—	—	—
—Toronto	NHL	1	0	0	0	2	-1	0	0	3	0	0	0	0
NHL Totals (21 years)		1495	338	894	1232	822	-53	129	7	85	13	43	56	36

PERSONAL: Born February 5, 1976, in Hradec Kralove, Czechoslovakia. ... 6-0/206. ... Shoots right. ... Name pronounced YAHN huhr-DEE-nuh.

TRANSACTIONS/CAREER NOTES: Selected by Pittsburgh Penguins in fifth round (fourth Penguins pick, 128th overall) of NHL entry draft (July 8, 1995). ... Sprained ankle (October 14, 1999); missed 12 games. ... Strained groin (December 5, 2000); missed three games. ... Suffered hip (January 12, 2001); missed one game. ... Strained back (January 23, 2002); missed two games. ... Suffered from the flu (April 3, 2002); missed one game. ... Traded by Penguins with D Francois Leroux to Phoenix Coyotes for LW Ramzi Abid, D Dan Focht and LW Guillaume Lefebvre (March 11, 2003).

Season Team	League	REGULAR SEASON								PLAYOFFS				
		Gms.	G	A	Pts.	PIM	+/-	PP	SH	Gms.	G	A	Pts.	PIM
93-94—Std.Hradec Kralove	Czech Rep.	21	1	5	6	...	...	...	...	—	—	—	—	—
94-95—Seattle	WHL	69	41	59	100	79	...	...	...	4	0	1	1	8
95-96—Seattle	WHL	30	19	28	47	37	...	...	...	—	—	—	—	—
—Spokane	WHL	18	10	16	26	25	...	...	...	18	5	14	19	49
96-97—Cleveland	IHL	68	23	31	54	82	...	...	...	13	1	2	3	8
97-98—Syracuse	AHL	72	20	24	44	82	...	...	...	5	1	3	4	10
98-99—Pittsburgh	NHL	82	13	29	42	40	-2	3	0	13	4	1	5	12
99-00—Pittsburgh	NHL	70	13	33	46	43	13	3	0	9	4	8	12	2
00-01—Pittsburgh	NHL	78	15	28	43	48	19	3	0	18	2	5	7	8
01-02—Pittsburgh	NHL	79	24	33	57	50	-7	6	0	—	—	—	—	—
—Czech Rep. Oly. team	Int'l	4	0	0	0	0	...	...	...	—	—	—	—	—
02-03—Pittsburgh	NHL	57	14	25	39	34	1	11	0	—	—	—	—	—
—Phoenix	NHL	4	0	4	4	8	3	0	0	—	—	—	—	—
NHL Totals (5 years)		370	79	152	231	223	27	26	0	40	10	14	24	22

H

HRKAC, TONY   C

PERSONAL: Born July 7, 1966, in Thunder Bay, Ont. ... 5-11/190. ... Shoots left. ... Full Name: Anthony J. Hrkac. ... Name pronounced HUHR-kuhz.

TRANSACTIONS/CAREER NOTES: Selected by St. Louis Blues in second round (second Blues pick, 32nd overall) of NHL entry draft (June 9, 1984). ... Bruised left leg (January 1987). ... Sprained shoulder (January 12, 1988). ... Lacerated ankle (March 1988). ... Bruised left shoulder (November 28, 1989). ... Traded by Blues with G Greg Millen to Quebec Nordiques for D Jeff Brown (December 13, 1989). ... Traded by Nordiques to San Jose Sharks for RW Greg Paslawski (May 30, 1991). ... Injured wrist during preseason (September 1991); missed first 27 games of season. ... Traded by Sharks to Chicago Blackhawks for future considerations (February 7, 1992). ... Signed as free agent by Blues (July 30, 1993). ... Signed as free agent by Dallas Stars (July 25, 1997). ... Claimed on waivers by Edmonton Oilers (January 6, 1998). ... Traded by Oilers with D Bobby Dollas to Pittsburgh Penguins for LW Josef Beranek (June 16, 1998). ... Selected by Nashville Predators in NHL expansion draft (June 26, 1998). ... Traded by Predators to Stars for future considerations (July 9, 1998). ... Signed as free agent by New York Islanders (July 29, 1999). ... Traded by Islanders with D Dean Malkoc to Mighty Ducks of Anaheim for C/LW Ted Drury (October 29, 1999). ... Signed as free agent by Atlanta Thrashers (July 16, 2001).

Season Team	League	REGULAR SEASON Gms.	G	A	Pts.	PIM	+/-	PP	SH	PLAYOFFS Gms.	G	A	Pts.	PIM
83-84—Orillia	OHA	42	*52	54	*106	20	...	...	...	—	—	—	—	—
84-85—Univ. of North Dakota	WCHA	36	18	36	54	16	...	...	...	—	—	—	—	—
85-86—Canadian nat'l team	Int'l	62	19	30	49	36	...	...	...	—	—	—	—	—
86-87—Univ. of North Dakota	WCHA	48	46	*70	*116	48	...	...	...	—	—	—	—	—
—St. Louis	NHL	—	—	—	—	—	—	—	—	3	0	0	0	0
87-88—St. Louis	NHL	67	11	37	48	22	5	2	1	10	6	1	7	4
88-89—St. Louis	NHL	70	17	28	45	8	-10	5	0	4	1	1	2	0
89-90—St. Louis	NHL	28	5	12	17	8	1	1	0	—	—	—	—	—
—Quebec	NHL	22	4	8	12	2	-5	2	0	—	—	—	—	—
—Halifax	AHL	20	12	21	33	4	...	...	...	6	5	9	14	4
90-91—Halifax	AHL	3	4	1	5	2	...	...	...	—	—	—	—	—
—Quebec	NHL	70	16	32	48	16	-22	6	0	—	—	—	—	—
91-92—San Jose	NHL	22	2	10	12	4	-2	0	0	—	—	—	—	—
—Chicago	NHL	18	1	2	3	6	4	0	0	3	0	0	0	2
92-93—Indianapolis	IHL	80	45	*87	*132	70	...	...	...	5	0	2	2	2
93-94—St. Louis	NHL	36	6	5	11	8	-11	1	1	4	0	0	0	0
—Peoria	IHL	45	30	51	81	25	...	...	...	1	1	2	3	0
94-95—Milwaukee	IHL	71	24	67	91	26	...	...	...	15	4	9	13	16
95-96—Milwaukee	IHL	43	14	28	42	18	...	...	...	5	1	3	4	4
96-97—Milwaukee	IHL	81	27	61	88	20	...	...	...	3	1	1	2	2
97-98—Michigan	IHL	20	7	15	22	6	...	...	...	—	—	—	—	—
—Dallas	NHL	13	5	3	8	0	0	3	0	—	—	—	—	—
—Edmonton	NHL	36	8	11	19	10	3	4	0	12	0	3	3	2
98-99—Dallas	NHL	69	13	14	27	26	2	2	0	5	0	2	2	4
99-00—New York Islanders	NHL	7	0	2	2	0	-1	0	0	—	—	—	—	—
—Anaheim	NHL	60	4	7	11	8	-2	1	0	—	—	—	—	—
00-01—Anaheim	NHL	80	13	25	38	29	0	0	0	—	—	—	—	—
01-02—Atlanta	NHL	80	18	26	44	12	-12	5	1	—	—	—	—	—
02-03—Atlanta	NHL	80	9	17	26	14	-16	2	0	—	—	—	—	—
NHL Totals (13 years)		758	132	239	371	173	-66	34	3	41	7	7	14	12

HUBACEK, PETR   C   PREDATORS

PERSONAL: Born September 2, 1979, in Brno, Czechoslovakia. ... 6-2/183. ... Shoots right.

TRANSACTIONS/CAREER NOTES: Selected by Philadelphia Flyers in ninth round (11th Flyers pick, 243rd overall) of NHL entry draft (June 27, 1998). ... Traded by Flyers with D Jason Beckett to Nashville Predators for LW Yves Sarault and pick in 2003 draft (January 11, 2002).

Season Team	League	REGULAR SEASON Gms.	G	A	Pts.	PIM	+/-	PP	SH	PLAYOFFS Gms.	G	A	Pts.	PIM
97-98—Brno	Czech. Jrs.	17	9	5	14	...	...	...	...	—	—	—	—	—
—Zetor Brno	Czech. Jrs.	48	6	10	16	...	...	...	...	—	—	—	—	—
98-99—Vitkovice	Czech. Jrs.	25	0	4	4	2	...	...	...	4	0	0	0	...
99-00—Vitkovice	Czech. Jrs.	48	11	12	23	81	...	...	...	—	—	—	—	—
00-01—Philadelphia	AHL	62	3	9	12	29	...	...	...	9	0	1	1	6
—Philadelphia	NHL	6	1	0	1	2	-1	0	0	—	—	—	—	—
01-02—Philadelphia	AHL	22	1	6	7	8	...	...	...	—	—	—	—	—
—Milwaukee	AHL	14	2	0	2	0	...	...	...	—	—	—	—	—
02-03—Vitkovice	Czech Rep.	51	5	19	24	24	...	...	...	—	—	—	—	—
NHL Totals (1 year)		6	1	0	1	2	-1	0	0					

HUDLER, JIRI   C   RED WINGS

PERSONAL: Born January 4, 1984, in Olomouc, Czechoslovakia. ... 5-9/176. ... Shoots left.

TRANSACTIONS/CAREER NOTES: Selected by Detroit Red Wings in second round (first Red Wings pick, 58th overall) of NHL entry draft (June 22, 2002). ... Re-signed by Red Wings (July 7, 2003).

Season Team	League	REGULAR SEASON Gms.	G	A	Pts.	PIM	+/-	PP	SH	PLAYOFFS Gms.	G	A	Pts.	PIM
01-02—HC Vsetin	Czech Rep.	46	15	31	46	54	...	...	...	—	—	—	—	—
02-03—Kazan	Rus. Div. III	11	1	5	6	12	...	...	...	—	—	—	—	—

H

HUET, CRISTOBAL   G   KINGS

PERSONAL: Born September 3, 1975, in St. Martin D'Heres, France ... 6-0/194. ... Catches left.
TRANSACTIONS/CAREER NOTES: Selected by Los Angeles Kings in seventh round (ninth Kings pick, 214th overall) of NHL entry draft (June 24, 2001).

Season Team	League		REGULAR SEASON									PLAYOFFS					
		Gms.	Min	W	L	T	GA	SO	Avg.	SV%	Gms.	Min.	W	L	GA	SO	Avg.	SV%
00-01—Lugano	Swiss	39	2365	...	...	...	77	6	1.95	...	—	—	—	—	—	—	—	—
01-02—Lugano	Swiss	39	2313	...	...	...	107	0	2.78	...	—	—	—	—	—	—	—	—
02-03—Los Angeles	NHL	12	541	4	4	1	21	1	2.33	.913	—	—	—	—	—	—	—	—
NHL Totals (1 year)		12	541	4	4	1	21	1	2.33	.913	—	—	—	—	—	—	—	—

HULL, BRETT   RW   RED WINGS

PERSONAL: Born August 9, 1964, in Belleville, Ont. ... 5-11/200. ... Shoots right. ... Full Name: Brett A. Hull. ... Son of Bobby Hull, Hall of Fame left winger with three NHL teams (1957-58 through 1971-72 and 1979-80) and Winnipeg Jets of WHA (1972-73 through 1978-79); and nephew of Dennis Hull, left winger with Chicago Blackhawks (1964-65 through 1976-77) and Detroit Red Wings (1977-78).
TRANSACTIONS/CAREER NOTES: Selected by Calgary Flames in sixth round (sixth Flames pick, 117th overall) of NHL entry draft (June 9, 1984). ... Traded by Flames with LW Steve Bozek to St. Louis Blues for D Rob Ramage and G Rick Wamsley (March 7, 1988). ... Sprained left ankle (January 15, 1991); missed two regular-season games and All-Star Game. ... Suffered back spasms (March 12, 1992); missed seven games. ... Suffered sore wrist (March 20, 1993); missed four games. ... Injured abdominal muscle (October 7, 1993); missed three games. ... Strained groin (November 1, 1995); missed two games. ... Reinjured groin (November 10, 1995); missed five games. ... Injured hamstring (March 28, 1996); missed four games. ... Strained groin (March 30, 1997); missed four games. ... Strained buttocks (December 8, 1997); missed two games. ... Fractured left hand (December 27, 1997); missed 13 games. ... Signed as free agent by Dallas Stars (July 3, 1998). ... Bruised kidney (November 20, 1998); missed two games. ... Strained groin (November 25, 1998); missed one game. ... Reinjured groin (December 2, 1998); missed six games. ... Strained back (January 10, 1999); missed one game. ... Strained hamstring (February 24, 1999); missed 11 games. ... Injured groin (January 12, 2000); missed one game. ... Fractured nose (February 9, 2000); missed one game. ... Strained hip flexor (March 8, 2000); missed one game. ... Strained lower back (December 23, 2000); missed three games. ... Signed as free agent by Detroit Red Wings (August 22, 2001).
STATISTICAL PLATEAUS: Three-goal games: 1987-88 (1), 1989-90 (5), 1990-91 (4), 1991-92 (8), 1993-94 (3), 1994-95 (1), 1995-96 (1), 1996-97 (2), 1997-98 (1), 2000-01 (1), 2001-02 (1), 2002-03 (2). Total: 30. ... Four-goal games: 1994-95 (1), 1995-96 (1), 2000-01 (1). Total: 3. ... Total hat tricks: 33.

Season Team	League		REGULAR SEASON								PLAYOFFS			
		Gms.	G	A	Pts.	PIM	+/-	PP	SH	Gms.	G	A	Pts.	PIM
82-83—Penticton	BCJHL	50	48	56	104	27	...	...	...	—	—	—	—	—
83-84—Penticton	BCJHL	56	*105	83	*188	20	...	...	...	—	—	—	—	—
84-85—Minnesota-Duluth	WCHA	48	32	28	60	24	...	...	...	—	—	—	—	—
85-86—Minnesota-Duluth	WCHA	42	*52	32	84	46	...	...	...	—	—	—	—	—
—Calgary	NHL	—	—	—	—	—	—	—	—	2	0	0	0	0
86-87—Moncton	AHL	67	50	42	92	16	...	...	...	3	2	2	4	2
—Calgary	NHL	5	1	0	1	0	-1	0	0	4	2	1	3	0
87-88—Calgary	NHL	52	26	24	50	12	10	4	0	—	—	—	—	—
—St. Louis	NHL	13	6	8	14	4	4	2	0	10	7	2	9	4
88-89—St. Louis	NHL	78	41	43	84	33	-17	16	0	10	5	5	10	6
89-90—St. Louis	NHL	80	*72	41	113	24	-1	*27	0	12	13	8	21	17
90-91—St. Louis	NHL	78	*86	45	131	22	23	*29	0	13	11	8	19	4
91-92—St. Louis	NHL	73	*70	39	109	48	-2	20	5	6	4	4	8	4
92-93—St. Louis	NHL	80	54	47	101	41	-27	29	0	11	8	5	13	2
93-94—St. Louis	NHL	81	57	40	97	38	-3	†25	3	4	2	1	3	0
94-95—St. Louis	NHL	48	29	21	50	10	13	9	3	7	6	2	8	0
95-96—St. Louis	NHL	70	43	40	83	30	4	16	5	13	6	5	11	10
96-97—St. Louis	NHL	77	42	40	82	10	-9	12	2	6	2	7	9	2
97-98—St. Louis	NHL	66	27	45	72	26	-1	10	0	10	3	3	6	2
—U.S. Olympic team	Int'l	4	2	1	3	0	...	...	...	—	—	—	—	—
98-99—Dallas	NHL	60	32	26	58	30	19	15	0	22	8	7	15	4
99-00—Dallas	NHL	79	24	35	59	43	-21	11	0	23	*11	†13	*24	4
00-01—Dallas	NHL	79	39	40	79	18	10	11	0	10	2	5	7	6
01-02—Detroit	NHL	82	30	33	63	35	18	7	1	23	*10	8	18	4
—U.S. Olympic team	Int'l	6	3	5	8	6	...	...	...	—	—	—	—	—
02-03—Detroit	NHL	82	37	39	76	22	11	12	1	4	0	1	1	0
NHL Totals (18 years)		1183	716	606	1322	446	30	255	20	190	100	85	185	69

HULL, JODY   RW   SENATORS

PERSONAL: Born February 2, 1969, in Petrolia, Ont. ... 6-1/195. ... Shoots right.
TRANSACTIONS/CAREER NOTES: Selected by Hartford Whalers in first round (first Whalers pick, 18th overall) of NHL entry draft (June 13, 1987). ... Injured hamstring (March 1989). ... Traded by Whalers to New York Rangers for C Carey Wilson and third-round pick (C Mikael Nylander) in 1991 draft (July 9, 1990). ... Sprained muscle in right hand (October 6, 1990). ... Bruised left big toe (November 19, 1990); missed six games. ... Injured knee (March 13, 1991). ... Traded by Rangers to Ottawa Senators for future considerations (July 28, 1992). ... Injured groin (December 7, 1992); missed three games. ... Suffered concussion (January 10, 1993); missed one game. ... Sprained ankle (January 19, 1993); missed eight games. ... Sprained left ankle (April 1, 1993); missed two games. ... Signed as free agent by Florida Panthers (August 10, 1993). ... Bruised right shoulder (February 1, 1994); missed one game. ... Separated right shoulder (March 4, 1994); missed three games. ... Separated right shoulder (March 18, 1994); missed six games. ... Suffered viral illness (February 1, 1995); missed two games. ... Fractured rib (October 28, 1995); missed four games. ... Suffered back spasms (May 5, 1996); missed four playoff games. ... Fractured left wrist (December 20, 1997); missed 13 games. ... Traded by Panthers with G Mark Fitzpatrick to Tampa Bay Lightning for RW Dino Ciccarelli and D Jeff Norton (January 15, 1998). ... Injured ankle (February 2, 1998); missed two games. ... Injured knee (April 2, 1998); missed three games. ... Signed as free agent by Philadelphia Flyers (October 7, 1998). ... Strained groin (October 31, 1998); missed two games. ... Suffered concussion (December 20, 1998); missed one game. ... Suffered post-concussion syndrome (December 26, 1998); missed four games. ...

H

Sprained left knee (April 8, 1999); missed two games. ... Selected by Atlanta Thrashers in NHL expansion draft (June 25, 1999). ... Traded by Thrashers to Flyers for future considerations (October 15, 1999). ... Sprained medial collateral ligament in left knee (January 27, 2000); missed 10 games. ... Sprained shoulder (September 27, 2000); missed first eight games of season. ... Bruised left foot (November 9, 2000); missed two games. ... Signed as free agent by Ottawa Senators (January 24, 2002). ... Injured right shoulder (March 23, 2002); missed five games. ... Re-signed by Senators (July 2, 2003).

STATISTICAL PLATEAUS: Three-goal games: 1988-89 (1).

			REGULAR SEASON							PLAYOFFS				
Season Team	League	Gms.	G	A	Pts.	PIM	+/-	PP	SH	Gms.	G	A	Pts.	PIM
84-85—Cambridge Jr. B.........	OHA	38	13	17	30	39	...	...	...	—	—	—	—	—
85-86—Peterborough..............	OHL	61	20	22	42	29	...	...	...	16	1	5	6	4
86-87—Peterborough..............	OHL	49	18	34	52	22	...	...	...	12	4	9	13	14
87-88—Peterborough..............	OHL	60	50	44	94	33	...	...	...	12	10	8	18	8
88-89—Hartford.....................	NHL	60	16	18	34	10	6	6	0	1	0	0	0	2
89-90—Binghamton	AHL	21	7	10	17	6	...	...	...	—	—	—	—	—
—Hartford.....................	NHL	38	7	10	17	21	-6	2	0	5	0	1	1	2
90-91—New York Rangers......	NHL	47	5	8	13	10	2	0	0	—	—	—	—	—
91-92—New York Rangers......	NHL	3	0	0	0	2	-4	0	0	—	—	—	—	—
—Binghamton	AHL	69	34	31	65	28	...	...	...	11	5	2	7	4
92-93—Ottawa......................	NHL	69	13	21	34	14	-24	5	1	—	—	—	—	—
93-94—Florida......................	NHL	69	13	13	26	8	6	0	1	—	—	—	—	—
94-95—Florida......................	NHL	46	11	8	19	8	-1	0	0	—	—	—	—	—
95-96—Florida......................	NHL	78	20	17	37	25	5	2	0	14	3	2	5	0
96-97—Florida......................	NHL	67	10	6	16	4	1	0	1	5	0	0	0	0
97-98—Florida......................	NHL	21	2	0	2	4	1	0	1	—	—	—	—	—
—Tampa Bay..................	NHL	28	2	4	6	4	2	0	0	—	—	—	—	—
98-99—Philadelphia..............	NHL	72	3	11	14	12	-2	0	0	6	0	0	0	4
99-00—Orlando.....................	IHL	1	0	0	0	0	...	...	...	—	—	—	—	—
—Philadelphia..............	NHL	67	10	3	13	4	8	0	2	18	0	1	1	0
00-01—Philadelphia..............	NHL	71	7	8	15	10	-1	0	2	6	0	0	0	4
01-02—Grand Rapids.............	AHL	3	2	1	3	2	...	...	...	—	—	—	—	—
—Ottawa	NHL	24	2	2	4	6	0	0	0	12	1	1	2	2
02-03—Ottawa	NHL	70	3	8	11	14	-3	0	0	2	0	0	0	0
NHL Totals (15 years).........		830	124	137	261	156	-10	15	8	69	4	5	9	14

HULSE, CALE   D   COYOTES

PERSONAL: Born November 10, 1973, in Edmonton ... 6-3/220. ... Shoots right. ... Name pronounced HUHLZ.

TRANSACTIONS/CAREER NOTES: Selected by New Jersey Devils in third round (third Devils pick, 66th overall) of NHL entry draft (June 20, 1992). ... Traded by Devils with D Tommy Albelin and RW Jocelyn Lemieux to Calgary Flames for D Phil Housley and D Dan Keczmer (February 26, 1996). ... Bruised ankle (February 28, 1997); missed four games. ... Reinjured ankle (March 7, 1997); missed one game. ... Reinjured ankle (March 21, 1997); missed one game. ... Suffered bruised ribs (April 1, 1999); missed six games. ... Fractured hand (September 18, 1999); missed first four games of season. ... Sprained ankle (February 23, 2000); missed nine games. ... Traded by Flames with third-round pick (C/LW Denis Platonov) in 2001 draft to Nashville Predators for RW Sergei Krivokrasov (March 14, 2000); missed Predators final 12 games due to sprained ankle. ... Fractured right hand (September 29, 2001); missed first 18 games of season. ... Strained right knee (March 10, 2002); missed one game. ... Suspended one game by NHL for cross-checking incident (February 23, 2003). ... Signed by Coyotes (July 9, 2003).

			REGULAR SEASON							PLAYOFFS				
Season Team	League	Gms.	G	A	Pts.	PIM	+/-	PP	SH	Gms.	G	A	Pts.	PIM
90-91—Calgary Royals...........	AJHL	49	3	23	26	220	...	...	...	—	—	—	—	—
91-92—Portland	WHL	70	4	18	22	250	...	...	...	6	0	2	2	27
92-93—Portland	WHL	72	10	26	36	284	...	...	...	16	4	4	8	*65
93-94—Albany.......................	AHL	79	7	14	21	186	...	...	...	5	0	3	3	11
94-95—Albany.......................	AHL	77	5	13	18	215	...	...	...	12	1	1	2	17
95-96—Albany.......................	AHL	42	4	23	27	107	...	...	...	—	—	—	—	—
—New Jersey................	NHL	8	0	0	0	15	-2	0	0	—	—	—	—	—
—Saint John	AHL	13	2	7	9	39	...	...	...	—	—	—	—	—
—Calgary	NHL	3	0	0	0	5	3	0	0	1	0	0	0	0
96-97—Calgary	NHL	63	1	6	7	91	-2	0	1	—	—	—	—	—
97-98—Calgary	NHL	79	5	22	27	169	1	1	1	—	—	—	—	—
98-99—Calgary	NHL	73	3	9	12	117	-8	0	0	—	—	—	—	—
99-00—Calgary	NHL	47	1	6	7	47	-11	0	0	—	—	—	—	—
00-01—Nashville	NHL	82	1	7	8	128	-5	0	0	—	—	—	—	—
01-02—Nashville	NHL	63	0	2	2	121	-18	0	0	—	—	—	—	—
02-03—Nashville	NHL	80	2	6	8	121	-11	0	0	—	—	—	—	—
NHL Totals (8 years)...........		498	13	58	71	814	-53	1	2	1	0	0	0	0

HUML, IVAN   LW   BRUINS

PERSONAL: Born September 6, 1981, in Kladno, Czechoslovakia ... 6-2/194. ... Shoots left.

TRANSACTIONS/CAREER NOTES: Selected by Boston Bruins in second round (fourth Bruins pick, 59th overall) of NHL entry draft (June 24, 2000).

			REGULAR SEASON							PLAYOFFS				
Season Team	League	Gms.	G	A	Pts.	PIM	+/-	PP	SH	Gms.	G	A	Pts.	PIM
98-99—Langley	BCHL	33	23	17	40	41	...	...	...	—	—	—	—	—
99-00—Langley	BCHL	49	53	51	104	72	...	...	...	—	—	—	—	—
00-01—Providence..................	AHL	79	13	6	19	28	...	...	...	17	0	0	0	2
01-02—Providence..................	AHL	76	28	19	47	75	...	...	...	—	—	—	—	—
—Boston	NHL	1	0	1	1	0	2	0	0	—	—	—	—	—
02-03—Providence..................	AHL	30	10	16	26	42	...	...	...	—	—	—	—	—
—Boston	NHL	41	6	11	17	30	3	0	0	—	—	—	—	—
NHL Totals (2 years)...........		42	6	12	18	30	5	0	0					

H

HUNTER, TRENT — RW — ISLANDERS

PERSONAL: Born July 5, 1980, in Red Deer, Alta. ... 6-3/210. ... Shoots right.

TRANSACTIONS/CAREER NOTES: Selected by Mighty Ducks of Anaheim in sixth round (fourth Mighty Ducks pick, 150th overall) of NHL entry draft (June 27, 1998). ... Traded by Mighty Ducks to New York Islanders for fourth-round pick (RW/LW Jonas Ronnqvist) in 2000 draft (May 23, 2000). ... Re-signed by Islanders (July 21, 2003).

		REGULAR SEASON								PLAYOFFS				
Season Team	League	Gms.	G	A	Pts.	PIM	+/-	PP	SH	Gms.	G	A	Pts.	PIM
96-97—Red Deer	AMHL	42	30	25	55	50	...	...	...	—	—	—	—	—
97-98—Prince George	WHL	60	13	14	27	34	...	...	...	8	1	0	1	4
98-99—Prince George	WHL	50	18	20	38	34	...	...	...	7	2	5	7	2
99-00—Prince George	WHL	67	46	49	95	47	...	...	...	13	7	15	22	6
00-01—Springfield	AHL	57	18	17	35	14	...	...	...	—	—	—	—	—
01-02—Bridgeport	AHL	80	30	35	65	30	...	...	...	17	8	11	19	6
—New York Islanders	NHL	—	—	—	—	—	...	...	...	4	1	1	2	2
02-03—Bridgeport	AHL	70	30	41	71	39	...	...	...	—	—	—	—	—
—New York Islanders	NHL	8	0	4	4	4	5	0	0	—	—	—	—	—
NHL Totals (2 years)		8	0	4	4	4	5	0	0	4	1	1	2	2

HURME, JANI — G — PANTHERS

PERSONAL: Born January 7, 1975, in Turku, Finland ... 6-0/197. ... Catches left. ... Name pronounced hoor-MAY.

TRANSACTIONS/CAREER NOTES: Selected by Ottawa Senators in third round (second Senators pick, 58th overall) of NHL entry draft (June 21, 1997). ... Injured right knee (February 27, 2001); missed six games. ... Strained groin (March 4, 2002); missed three games. ... Suffered from the flu (March 23, 2002); missed two games. ... Traded by Senators to Florida Panthers for C Greg Watson and G Billy Thompson (October 1, 2002).

		REGULAR SEASON									PLAYOFFS							
Season Team	League	Gms.	Min	W	L	T	GA	SO	Avg.	SV%	Gms.	Min.	W	L	GA	SO	Avg.	SV%
92-93—TPS Turku	Finland Jr.	12	669	...	...	...	47	0	4.22	—	1	60	...	...	...	1	...	—
93-94—TPS Turku	Finland	1	2	...	...	...	0	0	0	—	—	—	—	—	—	—	—	—
—Kiekko-67 Turku	Fin. Div. 2	3	190	...	...	...	7	0	2.21	—	—	—	—	—	—	—	—	—
—Kiekko-67 Turku	Finland Jr.	18	...	...	...	...	...	...	...	—	—	—	—	—	—	—	—	—
94-95—Kiekko-67 Turku	Fin. Div. 2	19	1049	...	...	...	53	...	3.03	—	3	180	...	...	6	...	2.00	—
—TPS Turku	Finland Jr.	2	125	...	...	...	5	0	2.40	—	—	—	—	—	—	—	—	—
—Kiekko-67 Turku	Finland Jr.	9	540	...	...	...	47	...	5.22	—	—	—	—	—	—	—	—	—
95-96—TPS Turku	Finland	16	945	...	...	...	34	2	2.16	—	10	545	...	...	22	2	2.42	—
—Kiekko-67 Turku	Fin. Div. 2	16	968	...	...	...	39	1	2.42	—	—	—	—	—	—	—	—	—
—TPS Turku	Finland Jr.	13	777	...	...	...	34	1	2.63	—	—	—	—	—	—	—	—	—
96-97—TPS Turku	Finland	48	2917	31	11	6	101	6	2.08	—	12	722	...	...	39	0	3.24	—
97-98—Detroit	IHL	6	290	2	2	‡2	20	0	4.14	—	—	—	—	—	—	—	—	—
—Indianapolis	IHL	29	1506	11	11	‡3	83	...	3.31	—	3	130	1	0	10	0	4.62	—
98-99—Detroit	IHL	12	643	7	3	‡1	26	1	2.43	—	—	—	—	—	—	—	—	—
—Cincinnati	IHL	26	1428	14	9	‡2	81	0	3.40	—	—	—	—	—	—	—	—	—
99-00—Grand Rapids	IHL	52	2948	35	15	‡4	107	4	2.18	—	*17	*1028	*10	*7	*37	1	2.16	—
—Ottawa	NHL	1	60	1	0	0	2	0	2.00	.895	—	—	—	—	—	—	—	—
00-01—Ottawa	NHL	22	1296	12	5	4	54	2	2.50	.904	—	—	—	—	—	—	—	—
01-02—Ottawa	NHL	25	1309	12	9	1	54	3	2.48	.907	—	—	—	—	—	—	—	—
—Fin. Olympic team	Int'l	3	119	1	2	0	9	0	3.02	—	—	—	—	—	—	—	—	—
02-03—Florida	NHL	28	1376	4	11	6	66	1	2.88	.907	—	—	—	—	—	—	—	—
NHL Totals (4 years)		76	4041	29	25	11	176	6	2.61	.906								

HUSELIUS, KRISTIAN — LW — PANTHERS

PERSONAL: Born October 10, 1978, in Stockholm, Sweden ... 6-1/190. ... Shoots left. ... Name pronounced hoo-say-LE-US.

TRANSACTIONS/CAREER NOTES: Selected by Florida Panthers in second round (second Panthers pick, 47th overall) of NHL entry draft (June 21, 1997). ... Suffered intestinal infection (December 15, 2001); missed three games.

		REGULAR SEASON								PLAYOFFS				
Season Team	League	Gms.	G	A	Pts.	PIM	+/-	PP	SH	Gms.	G	A	Pts.	PIM
94-95—Hammarby	Sweden Jr.	17	6	2	8	2	...	...	...	—	—	—	—	—
95-96—Hammarby	Sweden Jr.	25	13	8	21	14	...	...	...	—	—	—	—	—
—Hammarby	Sweden Dv. 2	6	1	0	1	0	...	...	...	—	—	—	—	—
96-97—Farjestad Karlstad	Sweden	13	2	0	2	4	...	...	...	5	1	0	1	0
97-98—Farjestad Karlstad	Sweden	34	2	1	3	2	...	...	...	11	0	0	0	0
98-99—Farjestad Karlstad	Sweden	28	4	4	8	4	...	...	...	—	—	—	—	—
—Vastra Frolunda	Sweden	20	2	2	4	2	...	...	...	4	1	0	1	0
99-00—Vastra Frolunda	Sweden	50	21	23	44	20	...	...	...	5	2	2	4	8
00-01—Vastra Frolunda	Sweden	49	*32	*35	*67	26	...	...	...	5	4	5	9	14
01-02—Florida	NHL	79	23	22	45	14	-4	6	1	—	—	—	—	—
02-03—Florida	NHL	78	20	23	43	20	-6	3	0	—	—	—	—	—
NHL Totals (2 years)		157	43	45	88	34	-10	9	1					

H — HUSKINS, KENT — D — BLACKHAWKS

PERSONAL: Born May 4, 1979, in Ottawa. ... 6-2/190. ... Shoots left.

COLLEGE: Clarkson (N.Y.).

TRANSACTIONS/CAREER NOTES: Selected by Chicago Blackhawks in sixth round (third Blackhawks pick, 156th overall) of NHL entry draft (June 27, 1998).

Season Team	League	REGULAR SEASON Gms.	G	A	Pts.	PIM	+/-	PP	SH	PLAYOFFS Gms.	G	A	Pts.	PIM
97-98—Clarkson	ECAC	35	2	8	10	46	...	...	...	—	—	—	—	—
98-99—Clarkson	ECAC	37	5	11	16	28	...	...	...	—	—	—	—	—
99-00—Clarkson	ECAC	28	2	16	18	30	...	...	...	—	—	—	—	—
00-01—Clarkson	ECAC	35	6	28	34	22	...	...	...	—	—	—	—	—
01-02—Norfolk	AHL	65	4	11	15	44	...	...	...	4	0	1	1	0
02-03—Norfolk	AHL	80	5	22	27	48	...	...	...	—	—	—	—	—

HUTCHINSON, ANDREW — D — PREDATORS

PERSONAL: Born March 24, 1980, in Evanston, Ill. ... 6-2/186. ... Shoots right.
COLLEGE: Michigan State.
TRANSACTIONS/CAREER NOTES: Selected by Nashville Predators in second round (fourth Predators pick, 54th overall) of NHL entry draft (June 26, 1999).

Season Team	League	REGULAR SEASON Gms.	G	A	Pts.	PIM	+/-	PP	SH	PLAYOFFS Gms.	G	A	Pts.	PIM
97-98—U.S. National	NAHL	60	7	22	29	63	...	...	...	—	—	—	—	—
98-99—Michigan State	CCHA	37	3	12	15	26	...	...	...	—	—	—	—	—
99-00—Michigan State	CCHA	41	4	11	15	62	...	...	...	—	—	—	—	—
00-01—Michigan State	CCHA	42	5	19	24	46	...	...	...	—	—	—	—	—
01-02—Michigan State	CCHA	39	6	16	22	24	...	...	...	—	—	—	—	—
—Milwaukee	AHL	5	0	1	1	0	...	...	...	—	—	—	—	—
02-03—Milwaukee	AHL	63	9	17	26	40	...	...	...	—	—	—	—	—
—Toledo	ECHL	10	2	5	7	4	...	...	...	—	—	—	—	—

HYMOVITZ, DAVE — LW

PERSONAL: Born May 30, 1974, in Boston. ... 5-11/188. ... Shoots left. ... Full Name: David Michael Hymovitz.
HIGH SCHOOL: Thayer Academy (Braintree, Mass.).
COLLEGE: Boston College.
TRANSACTIONS/CAREER NOTES: Selected by Chicago Blackhawks in ninth round (ninth Blackhawks pick, 209th overall) of NHL entry draft (June 20, 1992). ... Signed as free agent by Los Angeles Kings (June 1, 1999). ... Signed as free agent by Ottawa Senators (July 13, 2001).
STATISTICAL PLATEAUS: Three-goal games: 1994-95 (1).

Season Team	League	REGULAR SEASON Gms.	G	A	Pts.	PIM	+/-	PP	SH	PLAYOFFS Gms.	G	A	Pts.	PIM
91-92—Thayer Academy	Mass. H.S.	26	28	21	49	22	...	...	...	—	—	—	—	—
92-93—Boston College	Hockey East	37	7	6	13	6	...	...	...	—	—	—	—	—
93-94—Boston College	Hockey East	36	18	14	32	18	...	...	...	—	—	—	—	—
94-95—Boston College	Hockey East	35	21	19	40	22	...	...	...	—	—	—	—	—
95-96—Boston College	Hockey East	35	26	18	44	32	...	...	...	—	—	—	—	—
96-97—Indianapolis	IHL	6	0	1	1	0	...	...	...	1	0	0	0	0
97-98—Indianapolis	IHL	63	11	15	26	20	...	...	...	5	1	1	2	6
98-99—Indianapolis	IHL	78	46	30	76	42	...	...	...	5	2	3	5	2
99-00—Lowell	AHL	67	19	17	36	30	...	...	...	—	—	—	—	—
—Houston	IHL	18	10	3	13	16	...	...	...	11	3	4	7	8
00-01—Lowell	AHL	60	14	15	29	52	...	...	...	4	2	1	3	17
01-02—Grand Rapids	AHL	80	15	33	48	22	...	...	...	5	1	2	3	0
02-03—Binghamton	AHL	76	15	19	34	46	...	...	...	—	—	—	—	—

HYVONEN, HANNES — RW — BLUE JACKETS

PERSONAL: Born August 29, 1975, in Oulu, Finland ... 6-2/210. ... Shoots right. ... Name pronounced HAH-nuhs HOO-voh-nuhn.
TRANSACTIONS/CAREER NOTES: Selected by San Jose Sharks in ninth round (seventh Sharks pick, 257th overall) of NHL entry draft (June 26, 1999). ... Traded by Sharks to Florida Panthers for future considerations (July 16, 2002). ... Claimed on waivers by Columbus Blue Jackets (October 6, 2002).

Season Team	League	REGULAR SEASON Gms.	G	A	Pts.	PIM	+/-	PP	SH	PLAYOFFS Gms.	G	A	Pts.	PIM
93-94—Karpat Oulu	Finland Jr.	35	15	13	28	26	...	...	...	3	0	0	0	0
—Karpat Oulu	Finland Div. 2	3	3	1	4	2	...	...	...	—	—	—	—	—
94-95—TPS Turku	Finland Jr.	10	8	2	10	64	...	...	...	—	—	—	—	—
—Kiekko-67 Turku	Finland Jr.	1	1	0	1	0	...	...	...	—	—	—	—	—
—Kiekko-67 Turku	Finland Div. 2	16	4	2	6	10	...	...	...	—	—	—	—	—
—TPS Turku	Finland	9	4	3	7	16	...	...	...	5	0	0	0	7
95-96—Kiekko-67 Turku	Finland Div. 2	2	1	0	1	8	...	...	...	—	—	—	—	—
—TPS Turku	Finland	30	11	5	16	49	...	...	...	7	0	1	1	28
96-97—TPS Turku	Finland	41	10	5	15	48	...	...	...	10	4	2	6	14
97-98—TPS Turku	Finland	29	2	6	8	71	...	...	...	2	0	0	0	0
98-99—Blues Espoo	Finland	52	23	18	41	74	...	...	...	4	2	1	3	2
99-00—Blues Espoo	Finland	18	5	2	7	89	...	...	...	—	—	—	—	—
—HIFK Helsinki	Finland	22	2	2	4	100	...	...	...	9	4	0	4	8
00-01—HIFK Helsinki	Finland	56	14	12	26	34	...	...	...	5	0	0	0	8
01-02—Cleveland	AHL	67	24	18	42	136	...	...	...	—	—	—	—	—
—San Jose	NHL	6	0	0	0	0	-2	0	0	—	—	—	—	—
02-03—Columbus	NHL	36	4	5	9	22	-11	0	0	—	—	—	—	—
NHL Totals (2 years)		42	4	5	9	22	-13	0	0					

IGINLA, JAROME   RW   FLAMES

PERSONAL: Born July 1, 1977, in Edmonton ... 6-1/207. ... Shoots right. ... Name pronounced ih-GIHN-luh.
TRANSACTIONS/CAREER NOTES: Selected by Dallas Stars in first round (first Stars pick, 11th overall) of NHL entry draft (July 8, 1995). ... Traded by Stars with C Corey Millen to Calgary Flames for C Joe Nieuwendyk (December 19, 1995). ... Fractured bone in right hand (January 21, 1998); missed 10 games. ... Missed first three games of 1999-2000 season due to contract dispute. ... Bruised knee (March 22, 2000); missed two games. ... Injured knee (December 13, 2000); missed one game. ... Fractured wrist (March 31, 2001); missed remainder of season.
STATISTICAL PLATEAUS: Three-goal games: 2001-02 (1), 2002-03 (1). Total: 2. ... Four-goal games: 2002-03 (1). ... Total hat tricks: 3.

		REGULAR SEASON								PLAYOFFS				
Season Team	League	Gms.	G	A	Pts.	PIM	+/-	PP	SH	Gms.	G	A	Pts.	PIM
93-94—Kamloops	WHL	48	6	23	29	33	...	...	...	19	3	6	9	10
94-95—Kamloops	WHL	72	33	38	71	111	...	...	...	21	7	11	18	34
95-96—Kamloops	WHL	63	63	73	136	120	...	...	...	16	16	13	29	44
—Calgary	NHL	—	—	—	—	—	...	...	...	2	1	1	2	0
96-97—Calgary	NHL	82	21	29	50	37	-4	8	1	—	—	—	—	—
97-98—Calgary	NHL	70	13	19	32	29	-10	0	2	—	—	—	—	—
98-99—Calgary	NHL	82	28	23	51	58	1	7	0	—	—	—	—	—
99-00—Calgary	NHL	77	29	34	63	26	0	12	0	—	—	—	—	—
00-01—Calgary	NHL	77	31	40	71	62	-2	10	0	—	—	—	—	—
01-02—Calgary	NHL	82	*52	44	*96	77	27	16	1	—	—	—	—	—
—Can. Olympic team	Int'l	6	3	1	4	0	...	...	...					
02-03—Calgary	NHL	75	35	32	67	49	-10	11	3	—	—	—	—	—
NHL Totals (8 years)...........		545	209	221	430	338	2	64	7	2	1	1	2	0

INMAN, DAVID   C   RANGERS

PERSONAL: Born June 13, 1980, in New York. ... 6-1/205. ... Shoots left. ... Full Name: David Stanley Inman.
HIGH SCHOOL: North Toronto Collegiate Institute.
COLLEGE: Notre Dame.
TRANSACTIONS/CAREER NOTES: Selected by New York Rangers in second round (third Rangers pick, 59th overall) of NHL entry draft (June 26, 1999).

		REGULAR SEASON								PLAYOFFS				
Season Team	League	Gms.	G	A	Pts.	PIM	+/-	PP	SH	Gms.	G	A	Pts.	PIM
96-97—Wexford	OHA Jr. A	43	32	56	88	—	...	...	...	—	—	—	—	—
97-98—Wexford	OHA Jr. A	53	51	69	120	82	...	...	...	—	—	—	—	—
98-99—Notre Dame	CCHA	38	10	10	20	74	...	...	...	—	—	—	—	—
99-00—Univ. of Notre Dame ...	CCHA	32	13	7	20	12	...	...	...	—	—	—	—	—
00-01—Univ. of Notre Dame ...	CCHA	37	11	6	17	10	...	...	...	—	—	—	—	—
01-02—Univ. of Notre Dame ...	CCHA	38	19	18	37	24	...	...	...	—	—	—	—	—
02-03—Hartford	AHL	17	1	6	7	8	...	...	...	—	—	—	—	—
—Charlotte....................	ECHL	45	19	22	41	26	...	...	...	—	—	—	—	—

IRBE, ARTURS   G   HURRICANES

PERSONAL: Born February 2, 1967, in Riga, U.S.S.R. ... 5-8/190. ... Catches left. ... Name pronounced AHR-tuhrs UHR-bay.
TRANSACTIONS/CAREER NOTES: Selected by Minnesota North Stars in 10th round (11th North Stars pick, 196th overall) of NHL entry draft (June 17, 1989). ... Selected by San Jose Sharks in NHL dispersal draft (May 30, 1991). ... Sprained knee (November 27, 1992); missed 19 games. ... Injured foot (February 15, 1995); missed one game. ... Injured knee (January 17, 1996); remainder of season. ... Signed as free agent by Dallas Stars (July 22, 1996). ... Strained groin (November 8, 1996); missed six games. ... Signed as free agent by Vancouver Canucks (August 5, 1997). ... Signed as free agent by Carolina Hurricanes (September 10, 1998).

		REGULAR SEASON									PLAYOFFS							
Season Team	League	Gms.	Min	W	L	T	GA	SO	Avg.	SV%	Gms.	Min.	W	L	GA	SO	Avg.	SV%
86-87—Dynamo Riga	USSR	2	27	...	...	...	1	0	2.22	—	—	—	—	—	—	—	—	—
87-88—Dynamo Riga	USSR	34	1870	...	...	...	84	0	2.70	—	—	—	—	—	—	—	—	—
88-89—Dynamo Riga	USSR	41	2460	...	...	...	117	0	2.85	—	—	—	—	—	—	—	—	—
89-90—Dynamo Riga	USSR	48	2880	...	...	...	116	0	2.42	—	—	—	—	—	—	—	—	—
90-91—Dynamo Riga	USSR	46	2713	...	...	...	133	0	2.94	—	—	—	—	—	—	—	—	—
91-92—Kansas City	IHL	32	1955	24	7	‡1	80	0	*2.46	—	15	914	12	3	44	0	2.89	—
—San Jose	NHL	13	645	2	6	3	48	0	4.47	.868	—	—	—	—	—	—	—	—
92-93—Kansas City	IHL	6	364	3	3	0	20	0	3.30	—	—	—	—	—	—	—	—	—
—San Jose	NHL	36	2074	7	26	0	142	1	4.11	.886	—	—	—	—	—	—	—	—
93-94—San Jose	NHL	*74	*4412	30	28	*16	209	3	2.84	.899	14	806	7	7	50	0	3.72	.875
94-95—San Jose	NHL	38	2043	14	19	3	111	4	3.26	.895	6	316	2	4	27	0	5.13	.853
95-96—San Jose	NHL	22	1112	4	12	4	85	0	4.59	.860	—	—	—	—	—	—	—	—
—Kansas City	IHL	4	226	1	2	1	16	0	4.25	—	—	—	—	—	—	—	—	—
96-97—Dallas	NHL	35	1965	17	12	3	88	3	2.69	.893	1	13	0	0	0	0	...	1.000
97-98—Vancouver	NHL	41	1999	14	11	6	91	2	2.73	.907	—	—	—	—	—	—	—	—
98-99—Carolina	NHL	62	3643	27	20	12	135	6	2.22	.923	6	408	2	4	15	0	2.21	.917
99-00—Carolina	NHL	*75	4345	34	28	9	*175	5	2.42	.906	—	—	—	—	—	—	—	—
00-01—Carolina	NHL	*77	*4406	37	29	9	†180	6	2.45	.908	6	360	2	4	20	0	3.33	.900
01-02—Carolina	NHL	51	2974	20	19	†11	126	3	2.54	.902	18	1078	10	8	30	1	1.67	.938
—Latvian Olympic team ...	Int'l	1	60	0	1	0	4	0	4.00	—								
02-03—Lowell	AHL	7	426	3	3	1	21	0	2.96	—	—	—	—	—	—	—	—	—
—Carolina	NHL	34	1884	7	24	2	100	0	3.18	.877	—	—	—	—	—	—	—	—
NHL Totals (12 years)............		558	31502	213	234	78	1490	33	2.84	.899	51	2981	23	27	142	1	2.86	.902

ISBISTER, BRAD   LW   OILERS

PERSONAL: Born May 7, 1977, in Edmonton ... 6-4/220. ... Shoots right. ... Name pronounced ihs-BIH-stuhr.

TRANSACTIONS/CAREER NOTES: Selected by Winnipeg Jets in third round (fourth Jets pick, 67th overall) of NHL entry draft (July 8, 1995). ... Jets franchise moved to Phoenix and renamed Coyotes for 1996-97 season; NHL approved move on January 18, 1996. ... Strained muscle in abdomen (November 22, 1997); missed six games. ... Strained groin (January 8, 1999); missed six games. ... Suffered from hernia (January 27, 1999); missed 19 games. ... Strained groin (March 11, 1999); missed remainder of season. ... Traded by Coyotes with third-round pick (C Brian Collins) in 1999 draft to New York Islanders for C Robert Reichel and third- (C/LW Jason Jaspers) and fourth-round (C Preston Mizzi) picks in 1999 draft (March 20, 1999). ... Sprained ankle (January 26, 2000); missed 18 games. ... Fractured jaw (December 12, 2000); missed 15 games. ... Suffered from the flu (February 1, 2001); missed one game. ... Sprained medial collateral ligament in right knee (March 3, 2001); missed remainder of season. ... Injured back (February 26, 2002); missed three games. ... Traded by Islanders with LW Raffi Torres to Edmonton Oilers for D Janne Niinimaa and second-round pick in 2003 draft (March 11, 2003). ... Re-signed by Oilers (July 29, 2003).

		REGULAR SEASON								PLAYOFFS				
Season Team	League	Gms.	G	A	Pts.	PIM	+/-	PP	SH	Gms.	G	A	Pts.	PIM
93-94—Portland	WHL	64	7	10	17	45	...	...	...	10	0	2	2	0
94-95—Portland	WHL	67	16	20	36	123	...	...	...	—	—	—	—	—
95-96—Portland	WHL	71	45	44	89	184	...	...	...	7	2	4	6	20
96-97—Springfield	AHL	7	3	1	4	14	...	...	...	9	1	2	3	10
—Portland	WHL	24	15	18	33	45	...	...	...	6	2	1	3	16
97-98—Phoenix	NHL	66	9	8	17	102	4	1	0	5	0	0	0	2
—Springfield	AHL	9	8	2	10	36	...	...	...	—	—	—	—	—
98-99—Las Vegas	IHL	2	0	0	0	9	...	...	...	—	—	—	—	—
—Springfield	AHL	4	1	1	2	12	...	...	...	—	—	—	—	—
—Phoenix	NHL	32	4	4	8	46	1	0	0	—	—	—	—	—
99-00—New York Islanders	NHL	64	22	20	42	100	-18	9	0	—	—	—	—	—
00-01—New York Islanders	NHL	51	18	14	32	59	-19	7	1	—	—	—	—	—
01-02—New York Islanders	NHL	79	17	21	38	113	1	4	0	3	1	1	2	17
02-03—New York Islanders	NHL	53	10	13	23	34	-9	2	0	—	—	—	—	—
—Edmonton	NHL	13	3	2	5	9	0	0	0	6	0	1	1	12
NHL Totals (6 years)		358	83	82	165	463	-40	23	1	14	1	2	3	31

JACKMAN, BARRET   D   BLUES

PERSONAL: Born March 5, 1981, in Trail, B.C. ... 6-0/197. ... Shoots left.

TRANSACTIONS/CAREER NOTES: Selected by St. Louis Blues in first round (first Blues pick, 17th overall) of NHL entry draft (June 26, 1999).

		REGULAR SEASON								PLAYOFFS				
Season Team	League	Gms.	G	A	Pts.	PIM	+/-	PP	SH	Gms.	G	A	Pts.	PIM
97-98—Regina	WHL	68	2	11	13	224	...	...	...	9	0	3	3	32
98-99—Regina	WHL	70	8	36	44	259	...	...	...	—	—	—	—	—
99-00—Regina	WHL	53	9	37	46	175	...	...	...	6	1	1	2	19
—Worcester	AHL	—	—	—	—	—	...	...	...	2	0	0	0	13
00-01—Regina	WHL	43	9	27	36	138	...	...	...	6	0	3	3	8
01-02—Worcester	AHL	75	2	12	14	266	...	...	...	3	0	1	1	4
—St. Louis	NHL	1	0	0	0	0	0	0	0	1	0	0	0	2
02-03—St. Louis	NHL	82	3	16	19	190	23	0	0	7	0	0	0	14
NHL Totals (2 years)		83	3	16	19	190	23	0	0	8	0	0	0	16

JACKMAN, RIC   D   MAPLE LEAFS

PERSONAL: Born June 28, 1978, in Toronto ... 6-2/197. ... Shoots right. ... Full Name: Richard Jackman.

TRANSACTIONS/CAREER NOTES: Selected by Dallas Stars in first round (first Stars pick, fifth overall) of NHL entry draft (June 22, 1996). ... Traded by Stars to Boston Bruins for RW Cameron Mann (June 24, 2001). ... Separated shoulder (September 20, 2001); missed first four games of season. ... Traded by Bruins to Toronto Maple Leafs for C Kris Vernarsky (May 13, 2002). ... Re-signed by Maple Leafs (July 15, 2003).

		REGULAR SEASON								PLAYOFFS				
Season Team	League	Gms.	G	A	Pts.	PIM	+/-	PP	SH	Gms.	G	A	Pts.	PIM
95-96—Sault Ste. Marie	OHL	66	13	29	42	97	...	...	...	4	1	0	1	15
96-97—Sault Ste. Marie	OHL	53	13	34	47	116	...	...	...	10	2	6	8	24
97-98—Sault Ste. Marie	OHL	60	33	40	73	111	...	...	...	—	—	—	—	—
—Michigan	IHL	14	1	5	6	10	...	...	...	4	0	0	0	10
98-99—Michigan	IHL	71	13	17	30	106	...	...	...	5	0	4	4	6
99-00—Michigan	IHL	50	3	16	19	51	...	...	...	—	—	—	—	—
—Dallas	NHL	22	1	2	3	6	-1	1	0	—	—	—	—	—
00-01—Dallas	NHL	16	0	0	0	18	-6	0	0	—	—	—	—	—
—Utah	IHL	57	9	19	28	24	...	...	...	—	—	—	—	—
01-02—Boston	NHL	2	0	0	0	2	-1	0	0	—	—	—	—	—
—Providence	AHL	9	0	1	1	8	...	...	...	—	—	—	—	—
02-03—St. John's	AHL	8	2	6	8	24	...	...	...	—	—	—	—	—
—Toronto	NHL	42	0	2	2	41	-10	0	0	—	—	—	—	—
NHL Totals (4 years)		82	1	4	5	67	-18	1	0					

JACKMAN, TIM   RW   BLUE JACKETS

PERSONAL: Born November 14, 1981, in Minot, N.D. ... 6-2/190. ... Shoots right.

TRANSACTIONS/CAREER NOTES: Selected by Columbus Blue Jackets in second round (second Blue Jackets pick, 38th overall) of NHL entry draft (June 23, 2001).

Season Team	League	Gms.	G	A	Pts.	PIM	+/-	PP	SH	Gms.	G	A	Pts.	PIM
99-00—Park Center	USHS (West)	19	34	22	56	...	...	...	...	—	—	—	—	—
00-01—Minnesota-Mankato	WCHA	35	11	14	25	82	...	...	...	—	—	—	—	—
01-02—Minnesota-Mankato	WCHA	36	14	14	28	86	...	...	...	—	—	—	—	—
02-03—Syracuse	AHL	77	9	7	16	48	...	...	...	—	—	—	—	—

JAGR, JAROMIR   RW   CAPITALS

PERSONAL: Born February 15, 1972, in Kladno, Czechoslovakia ... 6-2/233. ... Shoots left. ... Name pronounced YAHR-oh-meer YAH-gihr.

TRANSACTIONS/CAREER NOTES: Selected by Pittsburgh Penguins in first round (first Penguins pick, fifth overall) of NHL entry draft (June 16, 1990). ... Separated shoulder (February 23, 1993); missed three games. ... Strained groin (January 21, 1994); missed four games. ... Played in Europe during 1994-95 NHL lockout. ... Suffered from the flu (January 11, 1997); missed one game. ... Strained groin (February 16, 1997); missed three games. ... Pulled groin (February 27, 1997); missed 13 games. ... Strained groin (April 10, 1997); missed two games. ... Strained hip flexor and groin (November 14, 1997); missed four games. ... Injured groin (April 16, 1998); missed one game. ... Injured groin (April 5, 1999); missed one game. ... Bruised thigh (November 18, 1999); missed one game. ... Strained muscle in abdomen (January 15, 2000); missed four games. ... Injured hamstring (February 21, 2000); missed 12 games. ... Bruised upper back (March 26, 2000); missed two games. ... Bruised finger (April 7, 2001); missed one game. ... Traded by Penguins with D Frantisek Kucera to Washington Capitals for C Kris Beech, C Michal Sivek, D Ross Lupaschuk and future considerations (July 11, 2001). ... Injured knee (October 10, 2001); missed three games. ... Strained knee (November 2, 2001); missed four games. ... Strained groin (January 11, 2002); missed six games.

STATISTICAL PLATEAUS: Three-goal games: 1990-91 (1), 1994-95 (1), 1996-97 (2), 1999-00 (2), 2000-01 (2), 2002-03 (2). Total: 10. ... Four-goal games: 2000-01 (1). ... Total hat tricks: 11.

Season Team	League	Gms.	G	A	Pts.	PIM	+/-	PP	SH	Gms.	G	A	Pts.	PIM
88-89—Poldi Kladno	Czech.	39	8	10	18	...	...	...	...	—	—	—	—	—
89-90—Poldi Kladno	Czech.	51	30	30	60	...	...	...	...	—	—	—	—	—
90-91—Pittsburgh	NHL	80	27	30	57	42	-4	7	0	24	3	10	13	6
91-92—Pittsburgh	NHL	70	32	37	69	34	12	4	0	†21	11	13	24	6
92-93—Pittsburgh	NHL	81	34	60	94	61	30	10	1	12	5	4	9	23
93-94—Pittsburgh	NHL	80	32	67	99	61	15	9	0	6	2	4	6	16
94-95—HC Kladno	Czech Rep.	11	8	14	22	10	...	...	...	—	—	—	—	—
—HC Bolzano	Euro	5	8	8	16	4	...	...	...	—	—	—	—	—
—HC Bolzano	Italy	1	0	0	0	0	...	...	...	—	—	—	—	—
—Schalker Haie	Ger. Div. II	1	1	10	11	0	...	...	...	—	—	—	—	—
—Pittsburgh	NHL	48	32	38	†70	37	23	8	3	12	10	5	15	6
95-96—Pittsburgh	NHL	82	62	87	149	96	31	20	1	18	11	12	23	18
96-97—Pittsburgh	NHL	63	47	48	95	40	22	11	2	5	4	4	8	4
97-98—Pittsburgh	NHL	77	35	†67	102	64	17	7	0	6	4	5	9	2
—Czech Rep. Oly. team..	Int'l	6	1	4	5	2	...	...	...	—	—	—	—	—
98-99—Pittsburgh	NHL	81	44	*83	*127	66	17	10	1	9	5	7	12	16
99-00—Pittsburgh	NHL	63	42	54	*96	50	25	10	0	11	8	8	16	6
00-01—Pittsburgh	NHL	81	52	†69	*121	42	19	14	1	16	2	10	12	18
01-02—Washington	NHL	69	31	48	79	30	0	10	0	—	—	—	—	—
—Czech Rep. Oly. team..	Int'l	4	2	3	5	4	...	...	...	—	—	—	—	—
02-03—Washington	NHL	75	36	41	77	38	5	13	2	6	2	5	7	2
NHL Totals (13 years)		950	506	729	1235	661	212	133	11	146	67	87	154	123

JAKES, JIRI   RW   BRUINS

PERSONAL: Born October 4, 1982, in Prague, Czechoslovakia. ... 6-4/225. ... Shoots left.

TRANSACTIONS/CAREER NOTES: Selected by Boston Bruins in fifth round (fourth Bruins pick, 147th overall) of NHL entry draft (June 23, 2001).

Season Team	League	Gms.	G	A	Pts.	PIM	+/-	PP	SH	Gms.	G	A	Pts.	PIM
00-01—Brandon	WHL	64	22	16	38	73	...	...	...	6	1	1	2	4
01-02—Brandon	WHL	56	16	18	34	73	...	...	...	19	3	3	6	30
02-03—Anchorage	WCHL	21	4	8	12	4	...	...	...	—	—	—	—	—
—Vancouver	WHL	41	18	21	39	72	...	...	...	—	—	—	—	—

JAKOPIN, JOHN   D

PERSONAL: Born May 16, 1975, in Toronto ... 6-6/245. ... Shoots right. ... Name pronounced JAK-oh-pihn.

TRANSACTIONS/CAREER NOTES: Selected by Detroit Red Wings in fourth round (fourth Red Wings pick, 97th overall) of NHL entry draft (June 26, 1993). ... Signed as free agent by Florida Panthers (June 4, 1997). ... Strained neck (November 5, 1999); missed five games. ... Injured groin (February 1, 2000); missed remainder of season. ... Claimed on waivers by Pittsburgh Penguins (October 2, 2001). ... Signed as free agent by San Jose Sharks (September 5, 2002).

Season Team	League	Gms.	G	A	Pts.	PIM	+/-	PP	SH	Gms.	G	A	Pts.	PIM
92-93—St. Michael's	Tier II Jr. A	45	9	21	30	42	...	...	...	—	—	—	—	—
93-94—Merrimack College	Hockey East	36	2	8	10	64	...	...	...	—	—	—	—	—
94-95—Merrimack College	Hockey East	37	4	10	14	42	...	...	...	—	—	—	—	—
95-96—Merrimack College	Hockey East	32	10	15	25	68	...	...	...	—	—	—	—	—
96-97—Merrimack College	Hockey East	31	4	12	16	68	...	...	...	—	—	—	—	—
—Adirondack	AHL	3	0	0	0	9	...	...	...	—	—	—	—	—
97-98—New Haven	AHL	60	2	18	20	151	...	...	...	3	0	0	0	0
—Florida	NHL	2	0	0	0	4	-3	0	0	—	—	—	—	—
98-99—New Haven	AHL	60	2	7	9	154	...	...	...	—	—	—	—	—
—Florida	NHL	3	0	0	0	0	-1	0	0	—	—	—	—	—

Season Team	League	Gms.	G	A	Pts.	PIM	+/-	PP	SH	Gms.	G	A	Pts.	PIM
99-00—Florida	NHL	17	0	0	0	26	-2	0	0	—	—	—	—	—
—Louisville	AHL	23	4	6	10	47	...	...	...	—	—	—	—	—
00-01—Louisville	AHL	8	0	1	1	21	...	...	...	—	—	—	—	—
—Florida	NHL	60	1	2	3	62	-4	0	0	—	—	—	—	—
01-02—Pittsburgh	NHL	19	0	4	4	42	2	0	0	—	—	—	—	—
—Wilkes-Barre/Scranton	AHL	30	3	5	8	90	...	...	...	—	—	—	—	—
02-03—Cleveland	AHL	18	0	4	4	27	...	...	...	—	—	—	—	—
—San Jose	NHL	12	0	0	0	11	0	0	0	—	—	—	—	—
NHL Totals (6 years)		113	1	6	7	145	-8	0	0					

JANCEVSKI, DAN D STARS

PERSONAL: Born June 15, 1981, in Windsor, Ont. ... 6-3/208. ... Shoots left.
TRANSACTIONS/CAREER NOTES: Selected by Dallas Stars in second round (second Stars pick, 66th overall) of NHL entry draft (June 22, 1999).

Season Team	League	Gms.	G	A	Pts.	PIM	+/-	PP	SH	Gms.	G	A	Pts.	PIM
97-98—Tecumseh	Jr. B	49	3	11	14	145	...	...	...	—	—	—	—	—
98-99—London	OHL	68	2	12	14	115	...	...	...	25	1	7	8	24
99-00—London	OHL	59	8	15	23	138	...	...	...	—	—	—	—	—
00-01—London	OHL	39	4	23	27	95	...	...	...	—	—	—	—	—
—Sudbury	OHL	31	3	14	17	42	...	...	...	12	0	9	9	17
01-02—Utah	AHL	77	0	13	13	147	...	...	...	5	0	0	0	4
02-03—Utah	AHL	76	1	10	11	172	...	...	...	—	—	—	—	—

JANIK, DOUG D SABRES

PERSONAL: Born March 26, 1980, in Agawam, Mass. ... 6-2/212. ... Shoots left.
TRANSACTIONS/CAREER NOTES: Selected by Buffalo Sabres in second round (third Sabres pick, 55th overall) of NHL entry draft (June 26, 1999).

Season Team	League	Gms.	G	A	Pts.	PIM	+/-	PP	SH	Gms.	G	A	Pts.	PIM
97-98—U.S. National	NAHL	65	8	26	34	105	...	...	...	—	—	—	—	—
98-99—Univ. of Maine	Hockey East	35	3	13	16	44	...	...	...	—	—	—	—	—
99-00—Univ. of Maine	Hockey East	36	6	13	19	54	...	...	...	—	—	—	—	—
00-01—Univ. of Maine	Hockey East	39	3	15	18	52	...	...	...	—	—	—	—	—
01-02—Rochester	AHL	80	6	17	23	100	...	...	...	2	0	0	0	0
02-03—Rochester	AHL	75	3	13	16	120	...	...	...	—	—	—	—	—
—Buffalo	NHL	6	0	0	0	2	1	0	0	—	—	—	—	—
NHL Totals (1 year)		6	0	0	0	2	1	0	0					

JARDINE, RYAN LW PANTHERS

PERSONAL: Born March 15, 1980, in Ottawa. ... 6-0/210. ... Shoots left.
TRANSACTIONS/CAREER NOTES: Selected by Florida Panthers in fourth round (fourth Panthers pick, 89th overall) of NHL entry draft (June 27, 1998).

Season Team	League	Gms.	G	A	Pts.	PIM	+/-	PP	SH	Gms.	G	A	Pts.	PIM
96-97—Kanata Valley	Tier II Jr. A	52	30	27	57	70	...	...	...	—	—	—	—	—
97-98—Sault Ste. Marie	OHL	65	28	32	60	16	...	...	...	—	—	—	—	—
98-99—Sault Ste. Marie	OHL	68	27	34	61	56	...	...	...	5	0	1	1	6
99-00—Sault Ste. Marie	OHL	65	43	34	77	58	...	...	...	17	11	8	19	16
00-01—Louisville	AHL	77	12	14	26	38	...	...	...	—	—	—	—	—
01-02—Utah	AHL	64	16	16	32	56	...	...	...	4	1	1	2	0
—Florida	NHL	8	0	2	2	2	0	0	0	—	—	—	—	—
02-03—San Antonio	AHL	64	14	17	31	37	...	...	...	—	—	—	—	—
NHL Totals (1 year)		8	0	2	2	2	0	0	0					

JASPERS, JASON C COYOTES

PERSONAL: Born April 8, 1981, in Thunder Bay, Ont. ... 5-11/197. ... Shoots left.
TRANSACTIONS/CAREER NOTES: Selected by Phoenix Coyotes in third round (fourth Coyotes pick, 71st overall) of NHL entry draft (June 26, 1999).

Season Team	League	Gms.	G	A	Pts.	PIM	+/-	PP	SH	Gms.	G	A	Pts.	PIM
97-98—Thunder Bay	NOHA	72	45	75	120	90	...	...	...	—	—	—	—	—
98-99—Sudbury	OHL	68	28	33	61	81	...	...	...	4	2	1	3	13
99-00—Sudbury	OHL	68	46	61	107	107	...	...	...	12	4	6	10	27
00-01—Sudbury	OHL	63	42	42	84	77	...	...	...	12	3	16	19	18
01-02—Springfield	AHL	71	25	23	48	55	...	...	...	—	—	—	—	—
—Phoenix	NHL	4	0	1	1	4	-1	0	0	—	—	—	—	—
02-03—Springfield	AHL	63	4	15	19	57	...	...	...	—	—	—	—	—
—Phoenix	NHL	2	0	0	0	0	-1	0	0	—	—	—	—	—
NHL Totals (2 years)		6	0	1	1	4	-2	0	0					

JILLSON, JEFF   D   BRUINS

PERSONAL: Born July 24, 1980, in North Smithfield, R.I. ... 6-3/220. ... Shoots right.
TRANSACTIONS/CAREER NOTES: Selected by San Jose Sharks in first round (first Sharks pick, 14th overall) of NHL entry draft (June 26, 1999). ... Traded by Sharks to Boston Bruins as part of three-team trade in which Montreal Canadiens acquired LW Niklas Sundstrom and third-round pick in 2004 draft, Bruins acquired G Jeff Hackett and Sharks acquired D Kyle McLaren and fourth-round pick in 2004 draft (January 23, 2003).

		REGULAR SEASON								PLAYOFFS				
Season Team	League	Gms.	G	A	Pts.	PIM	+/-	PP	SH	Gms.	G	A	Pts.	PIM
96-97—Mount St. Charles	USHS (East)	15	16	14	30	20	...	...	...	—	—	—	—	—
97-98—Mount St. Charles	USHS (East)	15	10	13	23	32	...	...	...	—	—	—	—	—
98-99—Univ. of Michigan	CCHA	38	5	19	24	71	...	...	...	—	—	—	—	—
99-00—Univ. of Michigan	CCHA	36	8	26	34	111	...	...	...	—	—	—	—	—
00-01—Univ. of Michigan	CCHA	43	10	20	30	74	...	...	...	—	—	—	—	—
01-02—San Jose	NHL	48	5	13	18	29	2	3	0	4	0	0	0	0
—Cleveland	AHL	27	2	13	15	45	...	...	...	—	—	—	—	—
02-03—Cleveland	AHL	19	3	5	8	12	...	...	...	—	—	—	—	—
—San Jose	NHL	26	0	6	6	9	-7	0	0	—	—	—	—	—
—Providence	AHL	30	4	11	15	26	...	...	...	—	—	—	—	—
NHL Totals (2 years)		74	5	19	24	38	-5	3	0	4	0	0	0	0

JOHANSSON, ANDREAS   LW/LW   PREDATORS

PERSONAL: Born May 19, 1973, in Hofors, Sweden ... 6-0/205. ... Shoots left. ... Name pronounced yoh-HAN-suhn.
TRANSACTIONS/CAREER NOTES: Selected by New York Islanders in seventh round (seventh Islanders pick, 136th overall) of NHL entry draft (June 22, 1991). ... Injured back (April 5, 1996); missed three games. ... Traded by Islanders with D Darius Kasparaitis to Pittsburgh Penguins for C Bryan Smolinski (November 17, 1996). ... Bruised shoulder (December 10, 1996); missed 12 games. ... Suffered from the flu (January 26, 1997); missed one game. ... Suffered back spasms (February 15, 1997); missed one game. ... Bruised ribs (November 15, 1997); missed six games. ... Sprained medial collateral ligament in knee (March 8, 1998); missed 10 games. ... Signed as free agent by Ottawa Senators (September 29, 1998). ... Injured left knee (January 18, 1999); missed two games. ... Reinjured left knee (February 25, 1999); missed three games. ... Strained hamstring (March 8, 1999); missed two games. ... Injured knee (April 5, 1999); missed two games. ... Suffered back spasms (April 15, 1999); missed one game. ... Traded by Senators to Tampa Bay Lightning for LW Rob Zamuner and second-round pick in 2000, 2001 or 2002 draft to complete deal that allowed Tampa Bay to sign general manager Rick Dudley (June 30, 1999). ... Suffered concussion (October 7, 1999); missed one game. ... Bruised foot (November 2, 1999); missed four games. ... Traded by Lightning to Calgary Flames for rights to LW Nils Ekman and fourth-round pick (traded to New York Islanders) in 2000 draft (November 20, 1999). ... Suffered injury (December 21, 1999); missed three games. ... Suffered from the flu (January 5, 2000); missed three games. ... Suffered back spasms (January 12, 2000); missed 15 games. ... Injured back (March 11, 2000); missed remainder of season. ... Claimed by New York Rangers from Flames in NHL waiver draft (September 29, 2000). ... Fractured left wrist (January 14, 2002); missed 11 games. ... Suffered from the flu (March 16, 2002); missed one game. ... Signed as free agent by Nashville Predators (September 6, 2002). ... Re-signed by Predators (June 29, 2003).
STATISTICAL PLATEAUS: Three-goal games: 2002-03 (1).

		REGULAR SEASON								PLAYOFFS				
Season Team	League	Gms.	G	A	Pts.	PIM	+/-	PP	SH	Gms.	G	A	Pts.	PIM
90-91—Falun	Sweden	31	12	10	22	38	...	...	...	—	—	—	—	—
91-92—Farjestad Karlstad	Sweden	30	3	1	4	4	...	...	...	6	0	0	0	4
92-93—Farjestad Karlstad	Sweden	38	4	7	11	38	...	...	...	2	0	0	0	0
93-94—Farjestad Karlstad	Sweden	20	3	6	9	6	...	...	...	—	—	—	—	—
94-95—Farjestad Karlstad	Sweden	36	9	10	19	42	...	...	...	4	0	0	0	10
95-96—Worcester	AHL	29	5	5	10	32	...	...	...	—	—	—	—	—
—Utah	IHL	22	4	13	17	28	...	...	...	12	0	5	5	6
—New York Islanders	NHL	3	0	1	1	0	1	0	0	—	—	—	—	—
96-97—New York Islanders	NHL	15	2	2	4	0	-6	1	0	—	—	—	—	—
—Pittsburgh	NHL	27	2	7	9	20	-6	0	0	—	—	—	—	—
—Cleveland	IHL	10	2	4	6	42	...	...	...	11	1	5	6	8
97-98—Pittsburgh	NHL	50	5	10	15	20	4	0	1	1	0	0	0	0
—Swedish Oly. team	Int'l	3	0	0	0	2	...	...	...	—	—	—	—	—
98-99—Ottawa	NHL	69	21	16	37	34	1	7	0	2	0	0	0	0
99-00—Tampa Bay	NHL	12	2	3	5	8	1	0	0	—	—	—	—	—
—Calgary	NHL	28	3	7	10	14	-3	1	0	—	—	—	—	—
00-01—Bern	Switzerland	40	15	29	44	94	...	...	...	7	5	4	9	0
01-02—New York Rangers	NHL	70	14	10	24	46	6	3	0	—	—	—	—	—
02-03—Nashville	NHL	56	20	17	37	22	-4	10	0	—	—	—	—	—
NHL Totals (7 years)		330	69	73	142	164	-6	22	1	3	0	0	0	0

JOHANSSON, CALLE   D   CAPITALS

PERSONAL: Born February 14, 1967, in Goteborg, Sweden ... 5-11/203. ... Shoots left. ... Name pronounced KAL-ee yoh-HAHN-suhn.
TRANSACTIONS/CAREER NOTES: Selected by Buffalo Sabres in first round (first Sabres pick, 14th overall) of NHL entry draft (June 15, 1985). ... Dislocated thumb (October 9, 1988). ... Traded by Sabres with second-round pick (G Byron Dafoe) in 1989 draft to Washington Capitals for D Grant Ledyard, G Clint Malarchuk and sixth-round pick (C Brian Holzinger) in 1991 draft (March 6, 1989). ... Injured back (October 7, 1989); missed 10 games. ... Bruised ribs (January 9, 1993); missed seven games. ... Played in Europe during 1994-95 NHL lockout. ... Suffered from the flu (March 25, 1995); missed two games. ... Fractured hand (April 4, 1996); missed remainder of season. ... Fractured jaw (November 12, 1996); missed 16 games. ... Bruised foot (February 14, 1997); missed one game. ... Sprained knee (January 13, 1998); missed nine games. ... Sprained knee (March 15, 1999); missed remainder of season. ... Suffered sore back (November 2, 2000); missed five games. ... Suffered injury (October 8, 2001); missed one game. ... Suffered injury (October 19, 2001); missed four games. ... Underwent shoulder surgery (November 10, 2001); missed remainder of season.

Season Team	League	REGULAR SEASON Gms.	G	A	Pts.	PIM	+/-	PP	SH	PLAYOFFS Gms.	G	A	Pts.	PIM
83-84—Vastra Frolunda	Sweden	34	5	10	15	20	...	...	...	—	—	—	—	—
84-85—Vastra Frolunda	Sweden	36	14	15	29	20	...	...	...	6	1	2	3	4
85-86—Bjorkloven.................	Sweden	17	1	1	2	14	...	...	...	—	—	—	—	—
86-87—Bjorkloven.................	Sweden	30	2	13	15	18	...	...	...	6	1	3	4	6
87-88—Buffalo	NHL	71	4	38	42	37	12	2	0	6	0	1	1	0
88-89—Buffalo	NHL	47	2	11	13	33	-7	0	0	—	—	—	—	—
—Washington	NHL	12	1	7	8	4	1	1	0	6	1	2	3	0
89-90—Washington	NHL	70	8	31	39	25	7	4	0	15	1	6	7	4
90-91—Washington	NHL	80	11	41	52	23	-2	2	1	10	2	7	9	8
91-92—Washington	NHL	80	14	42	56	49	2	5	2	7	0	5	5	4
92-93—Washington	NHL	77	7	38	45	56	3	6	0	6	0	5	5	4
93-94—Washington	NHL	84	9	33	42	59	3	4	0	6	1	3	4	4
94-95—Kloten	Switzerland	5	1	2	3	8	...	...	...	—	—	—	—	—
—Washington	NHL	46	5	26	31	35	-6	4	0	7	3	1	4	0
95-96—Washington	NHL	78	10	25	35	50	13	4	0	—	—	—	—	—
96-97—Washington	NHL	65	6	11	17	16	-2	2	0	—	—	—	—	—
97-98—Washington	NHL	73	15	20	35	30	-11	10	1	21	2	8	10	16
—Swedish Oly. team	Int'l	4	0	0	0	2	...	...	...	—	—	—	—	—
98-99—Washington	NHL	67	8	21	29	22	10	2	0	—	—	—	—	—
99-00—Washington	NHL	82	7	25	32	24	13	1	0	5	1	2	3	0
00-01—Washington	NHL	76	7	29	36	26	11	5	0	6	1	2	3	2
01-02—Washington	NHL	11	2	0	2	8	-4	0	0	—	—	—	—	—
02-03—Washington	NHL	82	3	12	15	22	9	1	0	6	0	1	1	0
NHL Totals (16 years).........		1101	119	410	529	519	52	53	4	101	12	43	55	42

JOHANSSON, JONAS   RW/LW   AVALANCHE

PERSONAL: Born March 18, 1984, in Jonkoping, Sweden. ... 6-1/180. ... Shoots right.
TRANSACTIONS/CAREER NOTES: Selected by Colorado Avalanche in first round (first Avalanche pick, 28th overall) of NHL entry draft (June 22, 2002).

Season Team	League	REGULAR SEASON Gms.	G	A	Pts.	PIM	+/-	PP	SH	PLAYOFFS Gms.	G	A	Pts.	PIM
01-02—HV 71 Jonkoping........	Sweden Jr.	26	15	19	34	20	...	...	...	—	—	—	—	—
—HV 71 Jonkoping........	Sweden	5	0	0	0	0	...	...	...	2	0	0	0	0
02-03—Kamloops	WCHL	26	10	25	35	35	...	...	...	—	—	—	—	—

JOHANSSON, MATHIAS   C

PERSONAL: Born February 22, 1974, in Farjestad, Sweden ... 6-2/201. ... Shoots left.
TRANSACTIONS/CAREER NOTES: Selected by Calgary Flames in third round (third Flames pick, 54th overall) of NHL entry draft (June 20, 1992). ... Traded by Flames with D Micki Dupont to Pittsburgh Penguins for RW Shean Donovan (March 11, 2003).

Season Team	League	REGULAR SEASON Gms.	G	A	Pts.	PIM	+/-	PP	SH	PLAYOFFS Gms.	G	A	Pts.	PIM
90-91—Farjestad Karlstad	Sweden	3	0	0	0	0	...	...	...	—	—	—	—	—
91-92—Farjestad Karlstad	Sweden	16	0	0	0	2	...	...	...	—	—	—	—	—
92-93—Farjestad Karlstad	Sweden	11	2	1	3	4	...	...	...	—	—	—	—	—
93-94—Farjestad Karlstad	Sweden	16	2	1	3	4	...	...	...	—	—	—	—	—
94-95—Farjestad Karlstad	Sweden	40	7	8	15	30	...	...	...	4	4	3	7	2
95-96—Farjestad Karlstad	Sweden	40	8	21	29	16	...	...	...	8	2	1	3	4
96-97—Farjestad Karlstad	Sweden	48	12	15	27	14	...	...	...	14	4	4	8	12
97-98—Farjestad Karlstad	Sweden	46	8	21	29	36	...	...	...	12	2	1	3	10
98-99—Farjestad Karlstad	Sweden	50	9	15	24	14	...	...	...	3	0	1	1	4
99-00—Farjestad Karlstad	Sweden	49	20	19	39	40	...	...	...	7	2	1	3	4
00-01—Farjestad Karlstad	Sweden	49	15	20	35	42	...	...	...	16	4	9	13	18
01-02—Farjestad Karlstad	Sweden	50	4	11	15	22	...	...	...	10	6	1	7	8
—Swedish Oly. team	Int'l	4	1	0	1	0	...	...	...	—	—	—	—	—
02-03—Calgary	NHL	46	4	5	9	12	-15	1	0	—	—	—	—	—
—Pittsburgh..................	NHL	12	1	5	6	4	1	1	0	—	—	—	—	—
NHL Totals (1 year)............		58	5	10	15	16	-14	2	0					

JOHNSON, BRENT   G   BLUES

PERSONAL: Born March 12, 1977, in Farmington, Mich. ... 6-2/199. ... Catches left. ... Full Name: Brent Spencer Johnson. ... Son of Bob Johnson, goalie with St. Louis Blues (1972-73) and Pittsburgh Penguins (1974-75).
TRANSACTIONS/CAREER NOTES: Selected by Colorado Avalanche in fifth round (fifth Avalanche pick, 129th overall) of NHL entry draft (July 8, 1995). ... Traded by Avalanche to St. Louis Blues for third-round pick (RW Ville Nieminen) in 1997 draft and conditional third-round pick in 2000 draft (May 30, 1997). ... Injured knee (January 23, 2001); missed three games. ... Suffered from the flu (November 23, 2001); missed one game. ... Strained hip flexor (April 7, 2002); missed one game. ... Re-signed by Blues (July 17, 2003).

Season Team	League	REGULAR SEASON Gms.	Min.	W	L	T	GA	SO	Avg.	SV%	PLAYOFFS Gms.	Min.	W	L	GA	SO	Avg.	SV%
94-95—Owen Sound	OHL	18	904	3	9	1	75	0	4.98	—	4	253	0	4	24	0	5.69	—
95-96—Owen Sound	OHL	58	3211	24	28	1	243	1	4.54	—	6	371	2	4	29	0	4.69	—
96-97—Owen Sound	OHL	50	2798	20	28	1	201	1	4.31	—	4	253	0	4	24	0	5.69	—
97-98—Worcester	AHL	42	2241	14	15	7	119	0	3.19	—	6	332	3	2	19	0	3.43	—
98-99—Worcester	AHL	49	2925	22	22	4	146	2	2.99	—	4	238	1	3	12	0	3.03	—
—St. Louis	NHL	6	286	3	2	0	10	0	2.10	.921	—	—	—	—	—	—	—	—

Season Team	League	REGULAR SEASON									PLAYOFFS							
		Gms.	Min	W	L	T	GA	SO	Avg.	SV%	Gms.	Min.	W	L	GA	SO	Avg.	SV%
99-00—Worcester	AHL	58	3319	24	27	5	161	3	2.91	—	9	561	4	5	23	1	2.46	—
00-01—St. Louis	NHL	31	1744	19	9	2	63	4	2.17	.907	2	62	0	1	2	0	1.94	.944
01-02—St. Louis	NHL	58	3491	34	20	4	127	5	2.18	.902	10	590	5	5	18	3	1.83	.929
02-03—Worcester	AHL	2	125	0	1	1	8	0	3.84	—	—	—	—	—	—	—	—	—
—St. Louis	NHL	38	2042	16	13	5	84	2	2.47	.900	—	—	—	—	—	—	—	—
NHL Totals (4 years)		133	7563	72	44	11	284	11	2.25	.903	12	652	5	6	20	3	1.84	.931

JOHNSON, CRAIG LW

PERSONAL: Born March 8, 1972, in St. Paul, Minn. ... 6-2/200. ... Shoots left.

TRANSACTIONS/CAREER NOTES: Selected by St. Louis Blues in second round (first Blues pick, 33rd overall) of NHL entry draft (June 16, 1990). ... Traded by Blues with C Patrice Tardiff, C Roman Vopat, fifth-round pick (D Peter Hogan) in 1996 draft and first-round pick (LW Matt Zultek) in 1997 draft to Los Angeles Kings for C Wayne Gretzky (February 27, 1996). ... Sprained left shoulder (March 13, 1996); missed seven games. ... Strained abdominal muscle prior to 1996-97 season; missed first seven games of season. ... Strained groin (November 2, 1996); missed one game. ... Strained abdominal muscle (November 30, 1996); missed 36 games. ... Strained groin (March 29, 1997); missed six games. ... Suffered from the flu (December 18, 1997); missed two games. ... Bruised abdomen (February 2, 1998); missed three games. ... Injured ribs (January 14, 1999); missed four games. ... Lacerated finger (February 16, 2000); missed three games. ... Lacerated tendon in right leg (December 26, 2000); missed remainder of season. ... Suffered eye injury (January 21, 2002); missed two games. ... Underwent eye surgery (March 19, 2002); missed eight games.

Season Team	League	REGULAR SEASON								PLAYOFFS				
		Gms.	G	A	Pts.	PIM	+/-	PP	SH	Gms.	G	A	Pts.	PIM
87-88—Hill-Murray H.S.	Minn. H.S.	28	14	20	34	4	...	...	...	—	—	—	—	—
88-89—Hill-Murray H.S.	Minn. H.S.	24	22	30	52	10	...	...	...	—	—	—	—	—
89-90—Hill-Murray H.S.	Minn. H.S.	23	15	36	51	...	...	...	...	—	—	—	—	—
90-91—Univ. of Minnesota	WCHA	33	13	18	31	34	...	...	...	—	—	—	—	—
91-92—Univ. of Minnesota	WCHA	44	19	39	58	70	...	...	...	—	—	—	—	—
92-93—Univ. of Minnesota	WCHA	42	22	24	46	70	...	...	...	—	—	—	—	—
93-94—U.S. national team	Int'l	54	25	26	51	64	...	...	...	—	—	—	—	—
—U.S. Olympic team	Int'l	8	0	4	4	4	...	...	...	—	—	—	—	—
94-95—Peoria	IHL	16	2	6	8	25	...	...	...	9	0	4	4	10
—St. Louis	NHL	15	3	3	6	6	4	0	0	1	0	0	0	2
95-96—Worcester	AHL	5	3	0	3	2	...	...	...	—	—	—	—	—
—St. Louis	NHL	49	8	7	15	30	-4	1	0	—	—	—	—	—
—Los Angeles	NHL	11	5	4	9	6.	-4	3	0	—	—	—	—	—
96-97—Mobile	ECHL	4	0	0	0	74	...	...	...	—	—	—	—	—
—Los Angeles	NHL	31	4	3	7	26	-7	1	0	—	—	—	—	—
—Oklahoma City	CHL	36	6	11	17	134	...	...	...	—	—	—	—	—
—Michigan	IHL	2	0	0	0	2	...	...	...	—	—	—	—	—
—Manitoba	IHL	16	2	2	4	38	...	...	...	—	—	—	—	—
97-98—Los Angeles	NHL	74	17	21	38	42	9	6	0	4	1	0	1	4
98-99—Los Angeles	NHL	69	7	12	19	32	-12	2	0	—	—	—	—	—
—Houston	IHL	1	0	0	0	0	...	...	...	—	—	—	—	—
99-00—Los Angeles	NHL	76	9	14	23	28	-10	1	0	4	1	0	1	2
00-01—Los Angeles	NHL	26	4	5	9	16	0	0	0	—	—	—	—	—
01-02—Los Angeles	NHL	72	13	14	27	24	14	4	1	7	1	2	3	2
02-03—Los Angeles	NHL	70	3	6	9	22	-13	0	0	—	—	—	—	—
NHL Totals (9 years)		493	73	89	162	232	-23	18	1	16	3	2	5	10

JOHNSON, GREG C PREDATORS

PERSONAL: Born March 16, 1971, in Thunder Bay, Ont. ... 5-11/202. ... Shoots left. ... Full Name: Gregory Johnson. ... Brother of Ryan Johnson, center, Florida Panthers.

TRANSACTIONS/CAREER NOTES: Selected by Philadelphia Flyers in second round (first Flyers pick, 33rd overall) of NHL entry draft (June 17, 1989). ... Separated right shoulder (November 24, 1990). ... Rights traded by Flyers with fifth-round pick (G Frederic Deschenes) in 1994 draft to Detroit Red Wings for RW Jim Cummins and fourth-round pick (traded to Boston) in 1993 draft (June 20, 1993). ... Loaned to Canadian Olympic Team (January 19, 1994). ... Returned to Red Wings (March 1, 1994). ... Sprained left ankle (April 14, 1995); missed final nine games of season. ... Injured left hand (October 8, 1995); missed two games. ... Injured knee (March 19, 1996); missed 12 games. ... Traded by Red Wings to Pittsburgh Penguins for RW Tomas Sandstrom (January 27, 1997). ... Bruised shoulder (April 3, 1997); missed one game. ... Strained groin (October 3, 1997); missed five games. ... Traded by Penguins to Chicago Blackhawks for D Tuomas Gronman (October 27, 1997). ... Strained groin (October 31, 1997); missed three games. ... Selected by Nashville Predators in NHL expansion draft (June 26, 1998). ... Suffered concussion (December 10, 1998); missed four games. ... Strained groin (February 20, 1999); missed three games. ... Suffered stress fracture in ankle (April 7, 1999); missed final five games of season.

Season Team	League	REGULAR SEASON								PLAYOFFS				
		Gms.	G	A	Pts.	PIM	+/-	PP	SH	Gms.	G	A	Pts.	PIM
88-89—Thunder Bay Jrs.	USHL	47	32	64	96	4	...	...	...	12	5	13	18	...
89-90—Univ. of North Dakota	WCHA	44	17	38	55	11	...	...	...	—	—	—	—	—
90-91—Univ. of North Dakota	WCHA	38	18	*61	79	6	...	...	...	—	—	—	—	—
91-92—Univ. of North Dakota	WCHA	39	20	54	74	8	...	...	...	—	—	—	—	—
92-93—Canadian nat'l team	Int'l	23	6	14	20	2	...	...	...	—	—	—	—	—
—Univ. of North Dakota	WCHA	34	19	45	64	18	...	...	...	—	—	—	—	—
93-94—Detroit	NHL	52	6	11	17	22	-7	1	1	7	2	2	4	2
—Canadian nat'l team	Int'l	6	2	6	8	4	...	...	...	—	—	—	—	—
—Can. Olympic team	Int'l	8	0	3	3	0	...	...	...	—	—	—	—	—
—Adirondack	AHL	3	2	4	6	0	...	...	...	4	0	4	4	2
94-95—Detroit	NHL	22	3	5	8	14	1	2	0	1	0	0	0	0
95-96—Detroit	NHL	60	18	22	40	30	6	5	0	13	3	1	4	8

Season Team	League	REGULAR SEASON								PLAYOFFS				
		Gms.	G	A	Pts.	PIM	+/-	PP	SH	Gms.	G	A	Pts.	PIM
96-97—Detroit	NHL	43	6	10	16	12	-5	0	0	—	—	—	—	—
—Pittsburgh	NHL	32	7	9	16	14	-13	1	0	5	1	0	1	2
97-98—Pittsburgh	NHL	5	1	0	1	2	0	0	0	—	—	—	—	—
—Chicago	NHL	69	11	22	33	38	-2	4	0	—	—	—	—	—
98-99—Nashville	NHL	68	16	34	50	24	-8	2	3	—	—	—	—	—
99-00—Nashville	NHL	82	11	33	44	40	-15	2	0	—	—	—	—	—
00-01—Nashville	NHL	82	15	17	32	46	-6	1	0	—	—	—	—	—
01-02—Nashville	NHL	82	18	26	44	38	-14	3	0	—	—	—	—	—
02-03—Nashville	NHL	38	8	9	17	22	7	0	0	—	—	—	—	—
NHL Totals (10 years)		635	120	198	318	302	-56	21	4	26	6	3	9	12

JOHNSON, MATT   LW   WILD

PERSONAL: Born November 23, 1975, in Welland, Ont. ... 6-5/235. ... Shoots left.

TRANSACTIONS/CAREER NOTES: Selected by Los Angeles Kings in second round (second Kings pick, 33rd overall) of NHL entry draft (June 28, 1994). ... Suffered from the flu (February 25, 1995); missed one game. ... Bruised right hand (April 3, 1995); missed four games. ... Strained shoulder (December 18, 1996); missed six games. ... Suffered concussion (February 1, 1997); missed one game. ... Suspended four games and fined $1,000 by NHL for elbowing incident (February 5, 1997). ... Strained back (March 10, 1997); missed final 13 games of season. ... Suspended four games and fined $1,000 by NHL for slashing incident (September 29, 1997). ... Strained groin (December 23, 1997); missed one game. ... Strained left biceps (March 21, 1998); missed three games. ... Suspended 12 games by NHL for deliberately injuring another player (November 23, 1998). ... Selected by Atlanta Thrashers in NHL expansion draft (June 25, 1999). ... Injured groin (October 7, 1999); missed two games. ... Strained hip flexor (November 25, 1999); missed two games. ... Suffered eye injury (December 13, 1999); missed nine games. ... Sprained medial collateral ligament in knee (March 28, 2000); missed two games. ... Traded by Thrashers to Minnesota Wild for third-round pick (traded to Pittsburgh) in 2001 draft (September 29, 2000). ... Sprained finger (November 7, 2000); missed four games. ... Suffered concussion (November 26, 2000); missed eight games. ... Suffered concussion and bruised hand (January 14, 2001); missed seven games. ... Suffered from dizziness (March 1, 2001); missed 10 games. ... Bruised right foot (February 8, 2002); missed three games. ... Suspended five games by NHL for unsportsmanlike conduct (March 10, 2002).

Season Team	League	REGULAR SEASON								PLAYOFFS				
		Gms.	G	A	Pts.	PIM	+/-	PP	SH	Gms.	G	A	Pts.	PIM
91-92—Welland	Jr. B	38	6	19	25	214	...	...	...	—	—	—	—	—
92-93—Peterborough	OHL	66	8	17	25	211	...	...	...	16	1	1	2	54
93-94—Peterborough	OHL	50	13	24	37	233	...	...	...	—	—	—	—	—
94-95—Peterborough	OHL	14	1	2	3	43	...	...	...	—	—	—	—	—
—Los Angeles	NHL	14	1	0	1	102	0	0	0	—	—	—	—	—
95-96—Los Angeles	NHL	1	0	0	0	5	0	0	0	—	—	—	—	—
—Phoenix	IHL	29	4	4	8	87	...			—	—	—	—	—
96-97—Los Angeles	NHL	52	1	3	4	194	-4	0	0	—	—	—	—	—
97-98—Los Angeles	NHL	66	2	4	6	249	-8	0	0	4	0	0	0	6
98-99—Los Angeles	NHL	49	2	1	3	131	-5	0	0	—	—	—	—	—
99-00—Atlanta	NHL	64	2	5	7	144	-11	0	0	—	—	—	—	—
00-01—Minnesota	NHL	50	1	1	2	137	-6	0	0	—	—	—	—	—
01-02—Minnesota	NHL	60	4	0	4	183	-13	0	0	—	—	—	—	—
02-03—Minnesota	NHL	60	3	5	8	201	-8	0	0	12	0	0	0	25
NHL Totals (9 years)		416	16	19	35	1346	-55	0	0	16	0	0	0	31

JOHNSON, MIKE   RW   COYOTES

PERSONAL: Born October 3, 1974, in Scarborough, Ont. ... 6-2/201. ... Shoots right. ... Full Name: Michael Johnson.

TRANSACTIONS/CAREER NOTES: Signed as non-drafted free agent by Toronto Maple Leafs (March 16, 1997). ... Suspended two games by NHL for elbowing incident (April 8, 1999). ... Traded by Maple Leafs with D Marek Posmyk and fifth-(F Pavel Sedov) and sixth-round (D Aaron Gionet) picks in 2000 draft to Tampa Bay Lightning for C Darcy Tucker and fourth-round pick (RW Miguel Delisle) in 2000 draft (February 9, 2000). ... Suffered injury (November 27, 1999); missed two games. ... Suffered facial fracture (March 17, 2000); missed one game. ... Injured ribs (December 2, 2000); missed two games. ... Traded by Lightning with D Paul Mara, RW Ruslan Zainullin and second-round pick (D Matthew Spiller) in 2001 draft to Phoenix Coyotes for G Nikolai Khabibulin and D Stan Neckar (March 5, 2001). ... Injured shoulder (March 8, 2001); missed four games. ... Injured neck (November 20, 2001); missed one game. ... Sprained knee (November 29, 2001); missed 11 games. ... Reinjured knee (December 28, 2001); missed 11 games.

Season Team	League	REGULAR SEASON								PLAYOFFS				
		Gms.	G	A	Pts.	PIM	+/-	PP	SH	Gms.	G	A	Pts.	PIM
92-93—Aurora	OPJHL	48	25	40	65	18	...	...	...	—	—	—	—	—
93-94—Bowling Green	CCHA	38	6	14	20	18	...	...	...	—	—	—	—	—
94-95—Bowling Green	CCHA	37	16	33	49	35	...	...	...	—	—	—	—	—
95-96—Bowling Green	CCHA	30	12	19	31	22	...	...	...	—	—	—	—	—
96-97—Bowling Green	CCHA	38	30	32	62	46	...	...	...	—	—	—	—	—
—Toronto	NHL	13	2	2	4	4	-2	0	1	—	—	—	—	—
97-98—Toronto	NHL	82	15	32	47	24	-4	5	0	—	—	—	—	—
98-99—Toronto	NHL	79	20	24	44	35	13	5	3	17	3	2	5	4
99-00—Toronto	NHL	52	11	14	25	23	8	2	1	—	—	—	—	—
—Tampa Bay	NHL	28	10	12	22	4	-2	4	0	—	—	—	—	—
00-01—Tampa Bay	NHL	64	11	27	38	38	-10	3	1	—	—	—	—	—
—Phoenix	NHL	12	2	3	5	4	0	1	0	—	—	—	—	—
01-02—Phoenix	NHL	57	5	22	27	28	14	1	2	5	1	1	2	6
02-03—Phoenix	NHL	82	23	40	63	47	9	8	0	—	—	—	—	—
NHL Totals (7 years)		469	99	176	275	207	26	29	8	22	4	3	7	10

JOHNSON, RYAN   C   BLUES

PERSONAL: Born June 14, 1976, in Thunder Bay, Ont. ... 6-1/205. ... Shoots left. ... Brother of Greg Johnson, center, Nashville Predators.
TRANSACTIONS/CAREER NOTES: Selected by Florida Panthers in second round (fourth Panthers pick, 36th overall) of NHL entry draft (June 28, 1994). ... Loaned to Canadian national team prior to 1995-96 season. ... Bruised left ankle (October 16, 1999); missed two games. ... Suffered from the flu (January 6, 2000); missed one game. ... Traded by Panthers with LW Dwayne Hay to Tampa Bay Lightning for C/RW Mike Sillinger (March 14, 2000). ... Suffered from virus (December 2, 2000); missed two games. ... Traded by Lightning with sixth-round pick in 2003 draft to Florida Panthers for C Vaclav Prospal (July 10, 2001). ... Fractured left foot (November 24, 2001); missed five games. ... Suffered concussion (December 22, 2001); missed remainder of season. ... Claimed on waivers by St. Louis Blues (February 19, 2003). ... Re-signed by Blues (July 16, 2003).

Season Team	League	REGULAR SEASON								PLAYOFFS				
		Gms.	G	A	Pts.	PIM	+/-	PP	SH	Gms.	G	A	Pts.	PIM
93-94—Thunder Bay Jrs.	USHL	48	14	36	50	28	...	...	...	—	—	—	—	—
94-95—Univ. of North Dakota	WCHA	38	6	22	28	39	...	...	...	—	—	—	—	—
95-96—Canadian nat'l team	Int'l	28	5	12	17	14	...	...	...	—	—	—	—	—
—Univ. of North Dakota	WCHA	21	2	17	19	14	...	...	...	—	—	—	—	—
96-97—Carolina	AHL	79	18	24	42	28	...	...	...	—	—	—	—	—
97-98—New Haven	AHL	64	19	48	67	12	...	...	...	3	0	1	1	0
—Florida	NHL	10	0	2	2	0	-4	0	0	—	—	—	—	—
98-99—New Haven	AHL	37	8	19	27	18	...	...	...	—	—	—	—	—
—Florida	NHL	1	1	0	1	0	0	0	0	—	—	—	—	—
99-00—Florida	NHL	66	4	12	16	14	1	0	0	—	—	—	—	—
—Tampa Bay	NHL	14	0	2	2	2	-9	0	0	—	—	—	—	—
00-01—Tampa Bay	NHL	80	7	14	21	44	-20	1	0	—	—	—	—	—
01-02—Florida	NHL	29	1	3	4	10	-5	0	0	—	—	—	—	—
02-03—Florida	NHL	58	2	5	7	26	-13	0	0	—	—	—	—	—
—St. Louis	NHL	17	0	0	0	12	0	0	0	6	0	2	2	6
NHL Totals (6 years)		275	15	38	53	108	-50	1	0	6	0	2	2	6

JOHNSSON, KIM   D   FLYERS

PERSONAL: Born March 16, 1976, in Malmo, Sweden ... 6-1/205. ... Shoots left. ... Full Name: Kimmo Johnsson.
TRANSACTIONS/CAREER NOTES: Selected by New York Rangers in 11th round (15th Rangers pick, 286th overall) of NHL entry draft (June 29, 1994). ... Suffered eye injury (February 8, 2000); missed one game. ... Fractured hand (November 2, 2000); missed five games. ... Traded by Rangers with LW Jan Hlavac, RW Pavel Brendl and third-round pick in 2003 draft to Philadelphia Flyers for rights to C Eric Lindros and conditional first-round pick (August 20, 2001).

Season Team	League	REGULAR SEASON								PLAYOFFS				
		Gms.	G	A	Pts.	PIM	+/-	PP	SH	Gms.	G	A	Pts.	PIM
93-94—Malmo	Sweden					Statistics unavailable.								
94-95—Malmo	Sweden	13	0	0	0	4	...	...	...	1	0	0	0	0
95-96—Malmo	Sweden	38	2	0	2	30	...	...	...	4	0	1	1	8
96-97—Malmo	Sweden	49	4	9	13	42	...	...	...	4	0	0	0	2
97-98—Malmo	Sweden	45	5	9	14	29	...	...	...	—	—	—	—	—
98-99—Malmo	Sweden	49	9	8	17	76	...	...	...	8	2	3	5	12
99-00—New York Rangers	NHL	76	6	15	21	46	-13	1	0	—	—	—	—	—
00-01—New York Rangers	NHL	75	5	21	26	40	-3	4	0	—	—	—	—	—
01-02—Philadelphia	NHL	82	11	30	41	42	12	5	0	5	0	0	0	2
—Swedish Oly. team	Int'l	4	1	1	2	0	...	...	...	—	—	—	—	—
02-03—Philadelphia	NHL	82	10	29	39	38	11	5	0	13	0	3	3	8
NHL Totals (4 years)		315	32	95	127	166	7	15	0	18	0	3	3	10

JOKELA, MIKKO   D   CANUCKS

PERSONAL: Born March 4, 1980, in Lappeenranta, Finland ... 6-1/215. ... Shoots right.
TRANSACTIONS/CAREER NOTES: Selected by New Jersey Devils in fourth round (fifth Devils pick, 96th overall) of NHL entry draft (June 27, 1998). ... Traded by Devils to Vancouver Canucks for LW Steve Kariya (January 24, 2003).

Season Team	League	REGULAR SEASON								PLAYOFFS				
		Gms.	G	A	Pts.	PIM	+/-	PP	SH	Gms.	G	A	Pts.	PIM
95-96—KalPa Kuopio	Finland Jr.	11	2	1	3	20	...	...	...	—	—	—	—	—
96-97—KalPa Kuopio	Finland Jr.	45	5	7	12	26	...	...	...	5	1	1	2	4
97-98—Helsinki IFK	Finland	16	0	0	0	0	...	...	...	—	—	—	—	—
—Helsinki IFK	Finland Jr.	22	2	5	7	14	...	...	...	—	—	—	—	—
98-99—HIFK Helsinki	Finland	3	0	0	0	2	...	...	...	—	—	—	—	—
—KalPa Kuopio	Finland	45	1	2	3	18	...	...	...	—	—	—	—	—
99-00—SaiPa	Finland	48	0	5	5	50	...	...	...	—	—	—	—	—
00-01—SaiPa	Finland	50	1	0	1	24	...	...	...	—	—	—	—	—
01-02—Albany	AHL	56	5	13	18	28	...	...	...	—	—	—	—	—
02-03—Albany	AHL	44	8	11	19	35	...	...	...	—	—	—	—	—
—Vancouver	NHL	1	0	0	0	0	0	0	0	—	—	—	—	—
—Manitoba	AHL	32	3	7	10	17	...	...	...	—	—	—	—	—
NHL Totals (1 year)		1	0	0	0	0	0	0	0	—	—	—	—	—

JOKINEN, OLLI   C   PANTHERS

PERSONAL: Born December 5, 1978, in Kuopio, Finland ... 6-3/210. ... Shoots left. ... Name pronounced OH-lee YOH-kih-nehn.
TRANSACTIONS/CAREER NOTES: Selected by Los Angeles Kings in first round (first Kings pick, third overall) of NHL entry draft (June 21, 1997). ... Traded by Kings with LW Josh Green, D Mathieu Biron and first-round pick (LW Taylor Pyatt) in 1999 draft to New York Islanders for RW Zigmund Palffy, C Bryan Smolinski, G Marcel Cousineau and fourth-round pick (C Daniel Johansson) in 1999 draft (June 20, 1999). ... Traded by Islanders with G Roberto Luongo to Florida Panthers for RW Mark Parrish and LW Oleg Kvasha (June 24, 2000). ... Re-signed by Panthers (July 16, 2003).

Season Team	League	REGULAR SEASON								PLAYOFFS				
		Gms.	G	A	Pts.	PIM	+/-	PP	SH	Gms.	G	A	Pts.	PIM
94-95—KalPa Kuopio	Finland Jr.	6	0	1	1	6	...	...	...	—	—	—	—	—
95-96—KalPa Kuopio	Finland Jr.	15	1	1	2	2	...	...	...	—	—	—	—	—
—KalPa Kuopio	Finland	15	1	1	2	2	...	...	...	—	—	—	—	—
96-97—HIFK Helsinki	Finland	50	14	27	41	88	...	...	...	—	—	—	—	—
97-98—Los Angeles	NHL	8	0	0	0	6	-5	0	0	—	—	—	—	—
—HIFK Helsinki	Finland	30	11	28	39	8	...	...	...	9	7	2	9	2
98-99—Springfield	AHL	9	3	6	9	6	...	...	...	—	—	—	—	—
—Los Angeles	NHL	66	9	12	21	44	-10	3	1	—	—	—	—	—
99-00—New York Islanders	NHL	82	11	10	21	80	0	1	2	—	—	—	—	—
00-01—Florida.......................	NHL	78	6	10	16	106	-22	0	0	—	—	—	—	—
01-02—Florida.......................	NHL	80	9	20	29	98	-16	3	1	—	—	—	—	—
—Fin. Olympic team.......	Int'l	4	2	1	3	0	...	...	...	—	—	—	—	—
02-03—Florida.......................	NHL	81	36	29	65	79	-17	13	3	—	—	—	—	—
NHL Totals (6 years)...........		395	71	81	152	413	-70	20	7	—	—	—	—	—

JONSSON, HANS   D

PERSONAL: Born August 2, 1973, in Jarved, Sweden ... 6-1/205. ... Shoots left. ... Name pronounced YAHN-suhn.

TRANSACTIONS/CAREER NOTES: Selected by Pittsburgh Penguins in 11th round (11th Penguins pick, 286th overall) of NHL entry draft (June 29, 1993). ... Bruised hip (February 1, 2000); missed two games. ... Suffered lacerated elbow (March 19, 2000); missed one game. ... Bruised foot (September 21, 2000); missed first two games of season. ... Suffered concussion (October 13, 2000); missed four games. ... Bruised hip (January 27, 2001); missed five games. ... Strained shoulder (February 21, 2001); missed seven games. ... Suffered infected elbow (March 29, 2001); missed final five games of season. ... Fractured foot (September 27, 2001); missed first 14 games of season. ... Fractured finger (January 24, 2002); missed eight games.

Season Team	League	REGULAR SEASON								PLAYOFFS				
		Gms.	G	A	Pts.	PIM	+/-	PP	SH	Gms.	G	A	Pts.	PIM
91-92—MoDo Ornskoldsvik	Sweden	6	0	1	1	4	...	...	...	—	—	—	—	—
92-93—MoDo Ornskoldsvik	Sweden	40	2	2	4	24	...	...	...	3	0	1	1	2
93-94—MoDo Ornskoldsvik	Sweden	23	4	1	5	18	...	...	...	10	0	1	1	12
94-95—MoDo Ornskoldsvik	Sweden	39	4	6	10	30	...	...	...	—	—	—	—	—
95-96—MoDo Ornskoldsvik	Sweden	36	10	6	16	30	...	...	...	8	2	1	3	24
96-97—MoDo Ornskoldsvik	Sweden	27	7	5	12	18	...	...	...	—	—	—	—	—
97-98—MoDo Ornskoldsvik	Sweden	40	8	6	14	40	...	...	...	8	1	1	2	12
98-99—MoDo Ornskoldsvik	Sweden	41	3	4	7	40	...	...	...	13	2	4	6	22
99-00—Pittsburgh..................	NHL	68	3	11	14	12	-5	0	1	11	0	1	1	6
00-01—Pittsburgh..................	NHL	58	4	18	22	22	11	2	0	16	0	0	0	8
01-02—Pittsburgh..................	NHL	53	2	5	7	22	-12	2	0	—	—	—	—	—
02-03—Pittsburgh..................	NHL	63	1	4	5	36	-23	0	0	—	—	—	—	—
NHL Totals (4 years)...........		242	10	38	48	92	-29	4	1	27	0	1	1	14

JONSSON, KENNY   D   ISLANDERS

PERSONAL: Born October 6, 1974, in Angelholm, Sweden ... 6-3/215. ... Shoots left. ... Brother of Jorgen Jonsson, left winger with New York Islanders (1999-2000) and Mighty Ducks of Anaheim (1999-2000). ... Name pronounced YAHN-suhn.

TRANSACTIONS/CAREER NOTES: Selected by Toronto Maple Leafs in first round (first Maple Leafs pick, 12th overall) of NHL entry draft (June 26, 1993). ... Played in Europe during 1994-95 NHL lockout. ... Suffered from the flu (February 13, 1995); missed two games. ... Strained hip flexor (February 27, 1995); missed one game. ... Suffered hip pointer (April 7, 1995); missed one game. ... Suffered from the flu (April 19, 1995); missed one game. ... Strained back (December 9, 1995); missed one game. ... Separated shoulder (January 30, 1996); missed 17 games. ... Traded by Maple Leafs with C Darby Hendrickson, LW Sean Haggerty and first-round pick (G Robert Luongo) in 1997 draft to New York Islanders for LW Wendel Clark, D Mathieu Schneider and D D.J. Smith (March 13, 1996). ... Suffered from the flu (December 23, 1996); missed one game. ... Sprained knee (February 4, 1998); missed one game. ... Suffered concussion (November 17, 1998); missed eight games. ... Sprained knee (January 16, 1999); missed nine games. ... Fractured finger (April 17, 1999); missed final game of season. ... Suffered illness (December 30, 1999); missed four games. ... Suffered concussion (January 19, 2000); missed 11 games. ... Sprained left wrist (March 26, 2000); missed one game. ... Suffered headaches (April 1, 2000); missed final five games of regular season. ... Injured neck (December 3, 2000); missed one game. ... Sprained medial collateral ligament in left knee (December 19, 2000); missed 13 games. ... Injured knee (January 23, 2001); missed one game. ... Suffered concussion (December 22, 2001); missed two games. ... Suffered from the flu (January 23, 2002); missed two games. ... Strained neck (January 30, 2002); missed one game. ... Injured quadricep (April 15, 2002); missed final game of season. ... Re-signed by Islanders (July 9, 2003).

Season Team	League	REGULAR SEASON								PLAYOFFS				
		Gms.	G	A	Pts.	PIM	+/-	PP	SH	Gms.	G	A	Pts.	PIM
91-92—Rogle Angelholm	Sweden	30	4	11	15	24	...	...	...	—	—	—	—	—
92-93—Rogle Angelholm	Sweden	39	3	10	13	42	...	...	...	—	—	—	—	—
93-94—Rogle Angelholm	Sweden	36	4	13	17	40	...	...	...	3	1	1	2	...
—Swedish Oly. team	Int'l	3	1	0	1	0	...	...	...	—	—	—	—	—
94-95—Rogle Angelholm	Sweden	8	3	1	4	20	...	...	...	—	—	—	—	—
—St. John's...................	AHL	10	2	5	7	2	...	...	...	—	—	—	—	—
—Toronto	NHL	39	2	7	9	16	-8	0	0	4	0	0	0	0
95-96—Toronto	NHL	50	4	22	26	22	12	3	0	—	—	—	—	—
—New York Islanders	NHL	16	0	4	4	10	-5	0	0	—	—	—	—	—
96-97—New York Islanders	NHL	81	3	18	21	24	10	1	0	—	—	—	—	—
97-98—New York Islanders	NHL	81	14	26	40	58	-2	6	0	—	—	—	—	—
98-99—New York Islanders	NHL	63	8	18	26	34	-18	6	0	—	—	—	—	—
99-00—New York Islanders	NHL	65	1	24	25	32	-15	1	0	—	—	—	—	—
00-01—New York Islanders	NHL	65	8	21	29	30	-22	5	0	—	—	—	—	—
01-02—New York Islanders	NHL	76	10	22	32	26	15	2	1	5	1	2	3	4
—Swedish Oly. team	Int'l	3	1	0	1	2	...	...	...	—	—	—	—	—
02-03—New York Islanders	NHL	71	8	18	26	24	-8	3	1	5	0	1	1	0
NHL Totals (9 years)...........		607	58	180	238	276	-41	27	2	14	1	3	4	4

JOSEPH, CURTIS G RED WINGS

PERSONAL: Born April 29, 1967, in Keswick, Ont. ... 5-11/190. ... Catches left. ... Full Name: Curtis Shayne Joseph. ... Nickname: Cujo.
TRANSACTIONS/CAREER NOTES: Signed as non-drafted free agent by St. Louis Blues (June 16, 1989). ... Dislocated left shoulder (April 11, 1990). ... Underwent surgery to left shoulder (May 10, 1990). ... Sprained right knee (February 26, 1991); missed remainder of season. ... Injured ankle (March 12, 1992); missed seven games. ... Suffered sore knee (January 2, 1993); missed three games. ... Suffered from the flu (February 9, 1993); missed one game. ... Slightly strained groin (January 26, 1995); missed three games. ... Pulled hamstring (April 16, 1995); missed four games. ... Traded by Blues with rights to RW Michael Grier to Edmonton Oilers for first-round picks in 1996 (C Marty Reasoner) and 1997 (traded to Los Angeles) drafts (August 4, 1995); picks had been awarded to Oilers as compensation for Blues signing free agent LW Shayne Corson (July 28, 1995). ... Injured right knee (March 30, 1996); missed three games. ... Strained groin (December 18, 1996); missed seven games. ... Signed as free agent by Toronto Maple Leafs (July 15, 1998). ... Strained groin (January 21, 1999); missed one game. ... Fractured hand (February 26, 2002); missed 20 games. ... Traded by Maple Leafs to Calgary Flames for conditional eighth-round pick in 2004 draft (June 30, 2002). ... Signed as free agent by Detroit Red Wings (July 2, 2002).

Season Team	League	Gms.	Min	W	L	T	GA	SO	Avg.	SV%	Gms.	Min.	W	L	GA	SO	Avg.	SV%
86-87—Richmond Hill	OHA								Statistics unavailable.									
87-88—Notre Dame	SCMHL	36	2174	25	4	7	94	1	2.59	—	—	—	—	—	—	—	—	—
88-89—Univ. of Wisconsin	WCHA	38	2267	21	11	5	94	1	2.49	—	—	—	—	—	—	—	—	—
89-90—Peoria	IHL	23	1241	10	8	‡2	80	0	3.87	—	—	—	—	—	—	—	—	—
—St. Louis	NHL	15	852	9	5	1	48	0	3.38	.890	6	327	4	1	18	0	3.30	.892
90-91—St. Louis	NHL	30	1710	16	10	2	89	0	3.12	.898	—	—	—	—	—	—	—	—
91-92—St. Louis	NHL	60	3494	27	20	10	175	2	3.01	.910	6	379	2	4	23	0	3.64	.894
92-93—St. Louis	NHL	68	3890	29	28	9	196	1	3.02	.911	11	715	7	4	27	2	2.27	.938
93-94—St. Louis	NHL	71	4127	36	23	11	213	1	3.10	.911	4	246	0	4	15	0	3.66	.905
94-95—St. Louis	NHL	36	1914	20	10	1	89	1	2.79	.902	7	392	3	3	24	0	3.67	.865
95-96—Las Vegas	IHL	15	873	12	2	1	29	1	1.99	—	—	—	—	—	—	—	—	—
—Edmonton	NHL	34	1936	15	16	2	111	0	3.44	.886	—	—	—	—	—	—	—	—
96-97—Edmonton	NHL	72	4100	32	29	9	200	6	2.93	.907	12	767	5	7	36	2	2.82	.911
97-98—Edmonton	NHL	71	4132	29	31	9	181	8	2.63	.905	12	716	5	7	23	3	1.93	.928
98-99—Toronto	NHL	67	4001	35	24	7	†171	3	2.56	.910	17	1011	9	†8	41	1	2.43	.907
99-00—Toronto	NHL	63	3801	36	20	7	158	4	2.49	.915	12	729	6	6	25	1	2.06	.932
00-01—Toronto	NHL	68	4100	33	27	8	163	6	2.39	.915	11	685	7	4	24	3	2.10	.927
01-02—Toronto	NHL	51	3065	29	17	5	114	4	2.23	.906	20	1253	10	†10	48	3	2.30	.914
—Can. Olympic team	Int'l	1	60	0	1	0	5	0	5.00	—	—	—	—	—	—	—	—	—
02-03—Detroit	NHL	61	3566	34	19	6	148	5	2.49	.912	4	289	0	4	10	0	2.08	.917
NHL Totals (14 years)		767	44688	380	279	87	2056	41	2.76	.908	122	7509	58	62	314	15	2.51	.915

JOVANOVSKI, ED D CANUCKS

PERSONAL: Born June 26, 1976, in Windsor, Ont. ... 6-2/210. ... Shoots left. ... Name pronounced joh-vuh-NAHV-skee.
TRANSACTIONS/CAREER NOTES: Selected by Florida Panthers in first round (first Panthers pick, first overall) of NHL entry draft (June 28, 1994). ... Fractured right index finger (September 29, 1995); missed first 11 games of season. ... Sprained knee (January 15, 1997); missed 16 games. ... Traded by Panthers with G Kevin Weekes, C Dave Gagner, C Mike Brown and first-round pick (C Nathan Smith) in 2000 draft to Vancouver Canucks for RW Pavel Bure, D Bret Hedican, D Brad Ference and third-round pick (RW Robert Fried) in 2000 draft (January 17, 1999). ... Fractured foot (February 9, 1999); missed eight games. ... Injured groin (January 12, 2000); missed six games. ... Injured hip (March 13, 2000); missed one game. ... Strained oblique muscle (March 27, 2000); missed one game.

Season Team	League	Gms.	G	A	Pts.	PIM	+/-	PP	SH	Gms.	G	A	Pts.	PIM
92-93—Windsor	OHL Jr. B	48	7	46	53	88	...	...	...	—	—	—	—	—
93-94—Windsor	OHL	62	15	35	50	221	...	...	...	4	0	0	0	15
94-95—Windsor	OHL	50	23	42	65	198	...	...	...	9	2	7	9	39
95-96—Florida	NHL	70	10	11	21	137	-3	2	0	22	1	8	9	52
96-97—Florida	NHL	61	7	16	23	172	-1	3	0	5	0	0	0	4
97-98—Florida	NHL	81	9	14	23	158	-12	2	1	—	—	—	—	—
98-99—Florida	NHL	41	3	13	16	82	-4	1	0	—	—	—	—	—
—Vancouver	NHL	31	2	9	11	44	-5	0	0	—	—	—	—	—
99-00—Vancouver	NHL	75	5	21	26	54	-3	1	0	—	—	—	—	—
00-01—Vancouver	NHL	79	12	35	47	102	-1	4	0	4	1	1	2	0
01-02—Vancouver	NHL	82	17	31	48	101	-7	7	1	6	1	4	5	8
—Can. Olympic team	Int'l	6	0	3	3	4	...	...	...	—	—	—	—	—
02-03—Vancouver	NHL	67	6	40	46	113	19	2	0	14	7	1	8	22
NHL Totals (8 years)		587	71	190	261	963	-17	22	2	51	10	14	24	86

JUNEAU, JOE C CANADIENS

PERSONAL: Born January 5, 1968, in Pont-Rouge, Que. ... 6-0/190. ... Shoots left. ... Name pronounced zhoh-AY ZHOO-noh.
TRANSACTIONS/CAREER NOTES: Selected by Boston Bruins in fourth round (third Bruins pick, 81st overall) of NHL entry draft (June 11, 1988). ... Fractured jaw (November 7, 1993); missed seven games. ... Reinjured jaw (February 18, 1994); missed two games. ... Traded by Bruins to Washington Capitals for D Al Iafrate (March 21, 1994). ... Strained hip flexor (January 29, 1995); missed one game. ... Strained back (February 15, 1995); missed one game. ... Bruised arm (April 11, 1995); missed one game. ... Injured leg (April 30, 1995); missed one game. ... Suffered from the flu (January 17, 1996); missed two games. ... Pulled hamstring (November 19, 1996); missed eight games. ... Bruised back and shoulder (January 1, 1997); missed two games. ... Sprained shoulder (February 7, 1997); missed four games. ... Sprained shoulder (February 18, 1997); missed five games. ... Strained hip (March 26, 1997); missed four games. ... Strained hip (April 12, 1997); missed one game. ... Strained groin (October 29, 1997); missed eight games. ... Strained posterior cruciate ligament in knee (December 13, 1997); missed 16 games. ... Suffered from the flu (December 17, 1998); missed one game. ... Bruised foot (February 28, 1999); missed one game. ... Suffered from headaches (March 9, 1999); missed five games. ... Traded by Capitals with third-round pick (LW Tim Preston) in 1999 draft to Buffalo Sabres for D Alexei Tezikov and future considerations (March 23, 1999). ... Suffered from the flu (March 27, 1999); missed two games. ...

Suffered concussion (April 13, 1999); missed final three games of regular season. ... Signed as free agent by Ottawa Senators (October 25, 1999). ... Strained hip flexor (February 19, 2000); missed five games. ... Strained hip flexor (April 4, 2000); missed two games. ... Selected by Minnesota Wild in NHL expansion draft (June 23, 2000). ... Traded by Wild to Phoenix Coyotes for C Rickard Wallin (June 23, 2000). ... Strained shoulder (October 27, 2000); missed 10 games. ... Suffered concussion (February 14, 2001); missed two games. ... Suffered eye contusion (April 6, 2001); missed one game. ... Traded by Coyotes to Montreal Canadiens for future considerations (June 15, 2001). ... Injured knee (November 29, 2001); missed eight games. ... Suffered illness (January 4, 2002); missed one game. ... Injured back (February 27, 2002); missed one game. ... Injured back (March 22, 2002); missed one game.

STATISTICAL PLATEAUS: Three-goal games: 1992-93 (1), 1996-97 (1). Total: 2.

Season Team	League	REGULAR SEASON								PLAYOFFS				
		Gms.	G	A	Pts.	PIM	+/-	PP	SH	Gms.	G	A	Pts.	PIM
87-88—R.P.I.	ECAC	31	16	29	45	18	...	...	...	—	—	—	—	—
88-89—R.P.I.	ECAC	30	12	23	35	40	...	...	...	—	—	—	—	—
89-90—R.P.I.	ECAC	34	18	*52	*70	31	...	...	...	—	—	—	—	—
—Canadian nat'l team	Int'l	3	0	2	2	4	...	...	...	—	—	—	—	—
90-91—R.P.I.	ECAC	29	23	40	63	70	...	...	...	—	—	—	—	—
—Canadian nat'l team	Int'l	7	2	3	5	0	...	...	...	—	—	—	—	—
91-92—Canadian nat'l team	Int'l	60	20	49	69	35	...	...	...	—	—	—	—	—
—Can. Olympic team	Int'l	8	6	9	15	4	...	...	...	—	—	—	—	—
—Boston	NHL	14	5	14	19	4	6	2	0	15	4	8	12	21
92-93—Boston	NHL	84	32	70	102	33	23	9	0	4	2	4	6	6
93-94—Boston	NHL	63	14	58	72	35	11	4	0	—	—	—	—	—
—Washington	NHL	11	5	8	13	6	0	2	0	11	4	5	9	6
94-95—Washington	NHL	44	5	38	43	8	-1	3	0	7	2	6	8	2
95-96—Washington	NHL	80	14	50	64	30	-3	7	2	5	0	7	7	6
96-97—Washington	NHL	58	15	27	42	8	-11	9	1	—	—	—	—	—
97-98—Washington	NHL	56	9	22	31	26	-8	4	1	21	7	10	17	8
98-99—Washington	NHL	63	14	27	41	20	-3	2	1	—	—	—	—	—
—Buffalo	NHL	9	1	1	2	2	-1	0	0	20	3	8	11	10
99-00—Ottawa	NHL	65	13	24	37	22	3	2	0	6	2	1	3	0
00-01—Phoenix	NHL	69	10	23	33	28	-2	5	0	—	—	—	—	—
01-02—Montreal	NHL	70	8	28	36	10	-3	1	0	12	1	4	5	6
02-03—Montreal	NHL	72	6	16	22	20	-10	0	0	—	—	—	—	—
NHL Totals (12 years)		758	151	406	557	252	1	50	5	101	25	53	78	65

JUNTUNEN, HENRIK   RW   KINGS

PERSONAL: Born April 24, 1983, in Goteburg, Sweden. ... 6-2/185. ... Shoots right.
TRANSACTIONS/CAREER NOTES: Selected by Los Angeles Kings in third round (fourth Kings pick, 83rd overall) of NHL entry draft (June 23, 2001).

Season Team	League	REGULAR SEASON								PLAYOFFS				
		Gms.	G	A	Pts.	PIM	+/-	PP	SH	Gms.	G	A	Pts.	PIM
00-01—Karpat Oulu	Finland Jr.	17	4	4	8	12	...	...	...	—	—	—	—	—
—Karpat Oulu	Finland	—	—	—	—	—	...	...	...	2	0	0	0	0
01-02—Karpat Oulu	Finland	13	0	0	0	2	...	...	...	—	—	—	—	—
02-03—Karpat Oulu	Finland	50	5	4	9	30	...	...	...	—	—	—	—	—

JURCINA, MILAN   D   BRUINS

PERSONAL: Born June 7, 1983, in Liptovsky Mikulas, Czechoslovakia. ... 6-4/198. ... Shoots right.
TRANSACTIONS/CAREER NOTES: Signed by Boston Bruins (May 30, 2003).

Season Team	League	REGULAR SEASON								PLAYOFFS				
		Gms.	G	A	Pts.	PIM	+/-	PP	SH	Gms.	G	A	Pts.	PIM
00-01—Halifax	QMJHL	68	0	5	5	56	...	...	...	6	0	2	2	12
01-02—Halifax	QMJHL	61	4	16	20	58	...	...	...	13	5	3	8	10
02-03—Halifax	QMJHL	51	15	13	28	102	...	...	...	—	—	—	—	—

KABERLE, FRANTISEK   D   THRASHERS

PERSONAL: Born November 8, 1973, in Kladno, Czechoslovakia ... 6-1/190. ... Shoots left. ... Brother of Tomas Kaberle, defenseman, Toronto Maple Leafs.
TRANSACTIONS/CAREER NOTES: Selected by Los Angeles Kings in third round (third Kings pick, 76th overall) of NHL entry draft (June 26, 1999). ... Traded by Kings with RW Donald Audette to Atlanta Thrashers for RW Kelly Buchberger and RW Nelson Emerson (March 13, 2000). ... Bruised foot (October 15, 2000); missed one game. ... Suffered from the flu (January 25, 2001); missed one game. ... Fractured foot (February 1, 2001); missed 25 games. ... Strained groin (April 1, 2001); missed final three games of season. ... Strained right shoulder (November 23, 2001); missed four games. ... Strained groin and hamstring (March 1, 2002); missed 17 games.

Season Team	League	REGULAR SEASON								PLAYOFFS				
		Gms.	G	A	Pts.	PIM	+/-	PP	SH	Gms.	G	A	Pts.	PIM
91-92—Poldi Kladno	Czech.	37	1	4	5	8	...	...	...	8	0	1	1	0
92-93—Poldi Kladno	Czech.	49	6	9	15		...	...	...	—	—	—	—	—
93-94—HC Kladno	Czech Rep.	40	4	15	19		...	...	...	9	1	2	3	...
94-95—HC Kladno	Czech Rep.	40	7	17	24		...	...	...	8	0	3	3	...
95-96—MoDo Ornskoldsvik	Sweden	40	5	7	12	34	...	...	...	8	0	1	1	0
96-97—MoDo Ornskoldsvik	Sweden	50	3	11	14	28	...	...	...	—	—	—	—	—
97-98—MoDo Ornskoldsvik	Sweden	46	5	4	9	22	...	...	...	9	1	1	2	4
98-99—MoDo Ornskoldsvik	Sweden	45	15	18	33	4	...	...	...	13	2	5	7	8

Season Team	League	REGULAR SEASON								PLAYOFFS				
		Gms.	G	A	Pts.	PIM	+/-	PP	SH	Gms.	G	A	Pts.	PIM
99-00—Los Angeles	NHL	37	0	9	9	4	3	0	0	—	—	—	—	—
—Long Beach	IHL	18	2	8	10	8	...	...	...	—	—	—	—	—
—Lowell	AHL	4	0	2	2	0	...	...	...	—	—	—	—	—
—Atlanta	NHL	14	1	6	7	6	-13	0	1	—	—	—	—	—
00-01—Atlanta	NHL	51	4	11	15	18	11	1	0	—	—	—	—	—
01-02—Atlanta	NHL	61	5	20	25	24	-11	1	0	—	—	—	—	—
02-03—Atlanta	NHL	79	7	19	26	32	-19	3	1	—	—	—	—	—
NHL Totals (4 years)		242	17	65	82	84	-29	5	2					

KABERLE, TOMAS   D   MAPLE LEAFS

PERSONAL: Born March 2, 1978, in Rakovnik, Czechoslovakia ... 6-1/198. ... Shoots left. ... Brother of Frantisek Kaberle, defenseman, Atlanta Thrashers.

TRANSACTIONS/CAREER NOTES: Selected by Toronto Maple Leafs in eighth round (13th Maple Leafs pick, 204th overall) of NHL entry draft (June 22, 1996). ... Missed first 12 games of 2001-02 season due to contract dispute; played in Europe.

Season Team	League	REGULAR SEASON								PLAYOFFS				
		Gms.	G	A	Pts.	PIM	+/-	PP	SH	Gms.	G	A	Pts.	PIM
94-95—Kladno	Czech. Jrs.	38	7	10	17	...	...	...	...	—	—	—	—	—
—Poldi Kladno	Czech Rep.	1	0	1	1	0	...	...	...	3	0	0	0	2
95-96—Poldi Kladno	Czech. Jrs.	23	6	13	19	19	...	...	...	—	—	—	—	—
—Poldi Kladno	Czech Rep.	23	0	1	1	2	...	...	...	2	0	0	0	0
96-97—Poldi Kladno	Czech Rep.	49	0	5	5	26	...	...	...	3	0	0	0	0
97-98—Poldi Kladno	Czech Rep.	47	4	19	23	12	...	...	...	—	—	—	—	—
—St. John's	AHL	2	0	0	0	0	...	...	...	—	—	—	—	—
98-99—Toronto	NHL	57	4	18	22	12	3	0	0	14	0	3	3	2
99-00—Toronto	NHL	82	7	33	40	24	3	2	0	12	1	4	5	0
00-01—Toronto	NHL	82	6	39	45	24	10	0	0	11	1	3	4	0
01-02—HC Kladno	Czech Rep.	9	1	7	8	4	...	...	...	—	—	—	—	—
—Toronto	NHL	69	10	29	39	2	5	5	0	20	2	8	10	16
—Czech Rep. Oly. team..	Int'l	4	0	1	1	2	...	...	...	—	—	—	—	—
02-03—Toronto	NHL	82	11	36	47	30	20	4	1	7	2	1	3	0
NHL Totals (5 years)		372	38	155	193	92	41	11	1	64	6	19	25	18

KADEYKIN, ANTON   D   DEVILS

PERSONAL: Born April 17, 1984, in Elektrostal, U.S.S.R. ... 6-2/180.

TRANSACTIONS/CAREER NOTES: Selected by New Jersey Devils in second round (first Devils pick, 51st overall) of NHL entry draft (June 22, 2002).

Season Team	League	REGULAR SEASON								PLAYOFFS				
		Gms.	G	A	Pts.	PIM	+/-	PP	SH	Gms.	G	A	Pts.	PIM
01-02—Elektrostal	Russian Div. 1	20	0	0	0	...	...	...	...	—	—	—	—	—
02-03—Sarnia	OHL	55	2	8	10	34	...	...	...	—	—	—	—	—

KALININ, DMITRI   D   SABRES

PERSONAL: Born July 22, 1980, in Cheljabinsk, U.S.S.R. ... 6-3/210. ... Shoots left.

TRANSACTIONS/CAREER NOTES: Selected by Buffalo Sabres in first round (first Sabres pick, 18th overall) of NHL entry draft (June 27, 1998). ... Fractured thumb (October 26, 2001); missed 18 games. ... Suffered from the flu (April 5, 2002); missed one game.

Season Team	League	REGULAR SEASON								PLAYOFFS				
		Gms.	G	A	Pts.	PIM	+/-	PP	SH	Gms.	G	A	Pts.	PIM
95-96—Traktor Chelyabinsk	CIS Jr.	30	10	10	20	60	...	...	...	—	—	—	—	—
—Nadezhda Chelyabinsk	CIS Div. II	20	0	3	3	10	...	...	...	—	—	—	—	—
96-97—Traktor Chelyabinsk	Russian	2	0	0	0	0	...	...	...	0	—	—	—	—
—Traktor-2 Chelyabinsk .	Rus. Div. III	20	0	0	0	10	...	...	...	—	—	—	—	—
97-98—Traktor Chelyabinsk	Russian	26	0	2	2	24	...	...	...	—	—	—	—	—
98-99—Moncton	QMJHL	39	7	18	25	44	...	...	...	4	1	1	2	0
—Rochester	AHL	3	0	1	1	14	...	...	...	7	0	0	0	6
99-00—Rochester	AHL	75	2	19	21	52	...	...	...	21	2	9	11	8
—Buffalo	NHL	4	0	0	0	4	0	0	0	—	—	—	—	—
00-01—Buffalo	NHL	79	4	18	22	38	-2	2	0	13	0	2	2	4
01-02—Buffalo	NHL	58	2	11	13	26	-6	0	0	—	—	—	—	—
02-03—Rochester	AHL	1	0	0	0	0	...	...	...	—	—	—	—	—
—Buffalo	NHL	65	8	13	21	57	-7	3	1	—	—	—	—	—
NHL Totals (4 years)		206	14	42	56	125	-15	5	1	13	0	2	2	4

KALLIO, TOMI   RW   FLYERS

PERSONAL: Born January 27, 1977, in Turku, Finland ... 6-0/195. ... Shoots left.

TRANSACTIONS/CAREER NOTES: Selected by Colorado Avalanche in fourth round (fourth Avalanche pick, 81st overall) of NHL entry draft (July 8, 1995). ... Selected by Atlanta Thrashers in NHL expansion draft (June 25, 1999). ... Strained groin (October 20, 2000); missed three games. ... Fractured shoulder (December 15, 2000); missed 23 games. ... Suffered concussion (October 26, 2001); missed five games. ... Suffered concussion (December 1, 2001); missed six games. ... Suffered from the flu (December 26, 2001); missed one game. ... Strained groin (January 2, 2002); missed one game. ... Traded by Thrashers with D Pauli Levokari to Columbus Blue Jackets for RW Chris Nielsen and D Petteri Nummelin (December 2, 2002). ... Claimed on waivers by Philadelphia Flyers (January 1, 2003).

STATISTICAL PLATEAUS: Three-goal games: 2000-01 (1).

K

Season Team	League	REGULAR SEASON								PLAYOFFS				
		Gms.	G	A	Pts.	PIM	+/-	PP	SH	Gms.	G	A	Pts.	PIM
93-94—TPS Turku	Finland Jr.	33	9	7	16	16	...	...	...	6	0	1	1	2
94-95—Kiekko-67	Finland Div. 2	25	8	5	13	16	...	...	...	7	3	1	4	6
—TPS Turku	Finland Jr.	14	5	12	17	24	...	...	...	—	—	—	—	—
95-96—Kiekko-67	Finland Div. 2	29	10	11	21	28	...	...	...	—	—	—	—	—
—TPS Turku	Finland	8	2	3	5	10	...	...	...	4	0	0	0	2
—TPS Turku	Finland Jr.	8	8	3	11	14	...	...	...	—	—	—	—	—
96-97—TPS Turku	Finland	47	9	10	19	18	...	...	...	8	2	0	2	2
97-98—TPS Turku	Finland	47	10	10	20	8	...	...	...	4	0	2	2	0
98-99—TPS Turku	Finland	54	15	21	36	20	...	...	...	10	3	4	7	6
99-00—TPS Turku	Finland	50	26	27	53	40	...	...	...	11	4	†9	13	4
00-01—Atlanta	NHL	56	14	13	27	22	-3	2	0	—	—	—	—	—
01-02—Atlanta	NHL	60	8	14	22	12	-8	1	0	—	—	—	—	—
—Fin. Olympic team	Int'l	4	1	2	3	2	...	...	...	—	—	—	—	—
02-03—Atlanta	NHL	5	0	2	2	4	-2	0	0	—	—	—	—	—
—Columbus	NHL	12	1	2	3	8	-7	0	0	—	—	—	—	—
—Philadelphia	NHL	7	1	0	1	2	-1	0	0	—	—	—	—	—
NHL Totals (3 years)		140	24	31	55	48	-21	3	0	—	—	—	—	—

KANE, BOYD — LW — FLYERS

PERSONAL: Born April 18, 1978, in Swift Current, Sask. ... 6-2/218. ... Shoots left.
TRANSACTIONS/CAREER NOTES: Selected by Pittsburgh Penguins in third round (third Penguins pick, 72nd overall) of NHL entry draft (June 22, 1996). ... Returned to draft pool by Penguins and selected by New York Rangers in fourth round (fourth Rangers pick, 114th overall) of NHL entry draft (June 27, 1998). ... Traded by Rangers to Tampa Bay Lightning for LW Gordie Dwyer (October 10, 2002). ... Signed by Philadelphia Flyers (July 14, 2003).

Season Team	League	REGULAR SEASON								PLAYOFFS				
		Gms.	G	A	Pts.	PIM	+/-	PP	SH	Gms.	G	A	Pts.	PIM
94-95—Regina	WHL	25	6	5	11	6	...	...	...	4	0	0	0	0
95-96—Regina	WHL	72	21	42	63	155	...	...	...	11	5	7	12	12
96-97—Regina	WHL	66	25	50	75	154	...	...	...	5	1	1	2	15
97-98—Regina	WHL	68	48	45	93	133	...	...	...	9	5	7	12	29
98-99—Hartford	AHL	56	3	5	8	23	...	...	...	—	—	—	—	—
—Charlotte	ECHL	12	5	6	11	14	...	...	...	—	—	—	—	—
99-00—Hartford	AHL	8	0	0	0	9	...	...	...	—	—	—	—	—
—B.C.	UHL	3	0	2	2	4	...	...	...	—	—	—	—	—
—Charlotte	ECHL	47	10	19	29	110	...	...	...	—	—	—	—	—
00-01—Hartford	AHL	56	11	17	28	81	...	...	...	5	2	0	2	2
—Charlotte	ECHL	12	9	8	17	6	...	...	...	—	—	—	—	—
01-02—Hartford	AHL	78	17	22	39	193	...	...	...	10	1	2	3	50
02-03—Springfield	AHL	72	15	22	37	121	...	...	...	—	—	—	—	—

KAPANEN, NIKO — C — STARS

PERSONAL: Born April 29, 1978, in Hattula, Finland ... 5-9/180. ... Shoots left.
TRANSACTIONS/CAREER NOTES: Selected by Dallas Stars in sixth round (fifth Stars pick, 173rd overall) of NHL entry draft (June 27, 1998).

Season Team	League	REGULAR SEASON								PLAYOFFS				
		Gms.	G	A	Pts.	PIM	+/-	PP	SH	Gms.	G	A	Pts.	PIM
93-94—HPK Hameenlinna	Finland Jr.	31	17	33	50	34	...	...	...	—	—	—	—	—
94-95—HPK Hameenlinna	Finland Jr.	37	19	44	63	40	...	...	...	—	—	—	—	—
95-96—HPK Hameenlinna	Finland Jr.	26	15	22	37	34	...	...	...	—	—	—	—	—
—HPK Hameenlinna	Finland	7	1	0	1	0	...	...	...	—	—	—	—	—
96-97—HPK Hameenlinna	Finland	41	6	9	15	12	...	...	...	10	4	5	9	2
—HPK Hameenlinna	Finland Jr.	5	1	7	8	2	...	...	...	2	0	1	1	2
97-98—HPK Hameenlinna	Finland	48	8	18	26	44	...	...	...	—	—	—	—	—
—HPK Hameenlinna	Finland Jr.	2	1	1	2	0	...	...	...	—	—	—	—	—
98-99—HPK Hameenlinna	Finland	53	14	29	43	49	...	...	...	8	3	4	7	4
99-00—HPK Hameenlinna	Finland	53	20	28	48	40	...	...	...	8	1	†9	10	4
00-01—TPS Turku	Finland	56	11	21	32	20	...	...	...	10	2	1	3	4
01-02—Dallas	NHL	9	0	1	1	2	-1	0	0	—	—	—	—	—
—Utah	AHL	59	13	28	41	40	...	...	...	5	2	1	3	0
02-03—Dallas	NHL	82	5	29	34	44	25	0	1	12	4	3	7	12
NHL Totals (2 years)		91	5	30	35	46	24	0	1	12	4	3	7	12

KAPANEN, SAMI — LW — FLYERS

PERSONAL: Born June 14, 1973, in Vantae, Finland ... 5-10/180. ... Shoots left. ... Name pronounced KAP-ih-nehn.
TRANSACTIONS/CAREER NOTES: Selected by Hartford Whalers in fourth round (fourth Whalers pick, 87th overall) of NHL entry draft (July 8, 1995). ... Suffered from the flu (October 20, 1996); missed two games. ... Sprained knee (November 30, 1996); missed 16 games. ... Sprained knee (January 10, 1997); missed nine games. ... Sprained knee (February 26, 1997); missed three games. ... Sprained knee (March 15, 1997); missed six games. ... Suffered from the flu (April 5, 1997); missed one game. ... Whalers franchise moved to North Carolina and renamed Carolina Hurricanes for 1997-98 season; NHL approved move on June 25, 1997. ... Suffered from the flu (March 12, 1998); missed one game. ... Bruised knee (October 24, 1998); missed one game. ... Bruised shoulder (February 19, 2000); missed two games. ... Suffered concussion (March 29, 2000); missed four games. ... Injured back (October 18, 2001); missed two games. ... Lacerated hand (February 8, 2002); missed one game. ... Traded by Hurricanes with D Ryan Bast to Philadelphia Flyers for RW Pavel Brendl and D Bruno St. Jacques (February 7, 2003). ... Re-signed by Flyers (June 10, 2003).
STATISTICAL PLATEAUS: Three-goal games: 1997-98 (2), 2001-02 (1). Total: 3.

Season Team	League	REGULAR SEASON								PLAYOFFS				
		Gms.	G	A	Pts.	PIM	+/-	PP	SH	Gms.	G	A	Pts.	PIM
90-91—KalPa Kuopio	Finland	14	1	2	3	2	...	...	...	8	2	1	3	2
91-92—KalPa Kuopio	Finland	42	15	10	25	8	...	...	...	—	—	—	—	—
92-93—KalPa Kuopio	Finland	37	4	17	21	12	...	...	...	—	—	—	—	—
93-94—KalPa Kuopio	Finland	48	23	32	55	16	...	...	...	—	—	—	—	—
94-95—HIFK Helsinki	Finland	49	14	28	42	42	...	...	...	3	0	0	0	0
95-96—Springfield	AHL	28	14	17	31	4	...	...	...	3	1	2	3	0
—Hartford	NHL	35	5	4	9	6	0	0	0	—	—	—	—	—
96-97—Hartford	NHL	45	13	12	25	2	6	3	0	—	—	—	—	—
97-98—Carolina	NHL	81	26	37	63	16	9	4	0	—	—	—	—	—
—Fin. Olympic team	Int'l	6	0	1	1	0	...	...	...	—	—	—	—	—
98-99—Carolina	NHL	81	24	35	59	10	-1	5	0	5	1	1	2	0
99-00—Carolina	NHL	76	24	24	48	12	10	7	0	—	—	—	—	—
00-01—Carolina	NHL	82	20	37	57	24	-12	7	0	6	2	3	5	0
01-02—Carolina	NHL	77	27	42	69	23	9	11	0	23	1	8	9	6
—Fin. Olympic team	Int'l	4	1	2	3	4	...	...	...	—	—	—	—	—
02-03—Carolina	NHL	43	6	12	18	12	-17	3	0	—	—	—	—	—
—Philadelphia	NHL	28	4	9	13	6	-1	2	0	13	4	3	7	6
NHL Totals (8 years)		548	149	212	361	111	3	42	0	47	8	15	23	12

KARIYA, PAUL — LW — AVALANCHE

PERSONAL: Born October 16, 1974, in Vancouver ... 5-10/182. ... Shoots left. ... Brother of Steve Kariya, left winger, Vancouver Canucks. ... Name pronounced kuh-REE-uh.

TRANSACTIONS/CAREER NOTES: Selected by Mighty Ducks of Anaheim in first round (first Mighty Ducks pick, fourth overall) of NHL entry draft (June 26, 1993). ... Suffered lower back spasms (February 12, 1995); missed one game. ... Strained abdominal muscle prior to 1996-97 season; missed first 11 games of season. ... Suffered mild concussion (November 13, 1996); missed two games. ... Missed first 32 games of 1997-98 season due to contract dispute. ... Suffered concussion (February 1, 1998); missed remainder of season. ... Injured hip prior to start of 1999-2000 season; missed first game of season. ... Fractured right foot (February 18, 2000); missed seven games. ... Fractured right foot (December 20, 2000); missed 16 games. ... Signed by Colorado Avalance (July 2, 2003).

STATISTICAL PLATEAUS: Three-goal games: 1996-97 (2), 1997-98 (1), 2000-01 (2), 2001-02 (2), 2002-03 (1). Total: 8.

Season Team	League	REGULAR SEASON								PLAYOFFS				
		Gms.	G	A	Pts.	PIM	+/-	PP	SH	Gms.	G	A	Pts.	PIM
90-91—Penticton	BCJHL	54	45	67	112	8	...	...	...	—	—	—	—	—
91-92—Penticton	BCJHL	40	46	86	132	16	...	...	...	—	—	—	—	—
92-93—Univ. of Maine	Hockey East	39	25	*75	*100	12	...	...	...	—	—	—	—	—
93-94—Canadian nat'l team	Int'l	23	7	34	41	2	...	...	...	—	—	—	—	—
—Can. Olympic team	Int'l	8	3	4	7	2	...	...	...	—	—	—	—	—
—Univ. of Maine	Hockey East	12	8	16	24	4	...	...	...	—	—	—	—	—
94-95—Anaheim	NHL	47	18	21	39	4	-17	7	1	—	—	—	—	—
95-96—Anaheim	NHL	82	50	58	108	20	9	20	3	—	—	—	—	—
96-97—Anaheim	NHL	69	44	55	99	6	36	15	3	11	7	6	13	4
97-98—Anaheim	NHL	22	17	14	31	23	12	3	0	—	—	—	—	—
98-99—Anaheim	NHL	82	39	62	101	40	17	11	2	3	1	3	4	0
99-00—Anaheim	NHL	74	42	44	86	24	22	11	3	—	—	—	—	—
00-01—Anaheim	NHL	66	33	34	67	20	-9	18	3	—	—	—	—	—
01-02—Anaheim	NHL	82	32	25	57	28	-15	11	0	—	—	—	—	—
—Can. Olympic team	Int'l	6	3	1	4	0	...	...	...	—	—	—	—	—
02-03—Anaheim	NHL	82	25	56	81	48	-3	11	1	21	6	6	12	6
NHL Totals (9 years)		606	300	369	669	213	52	107	16	35	14	15	29	10

KARIYA, STEVE — LW — DEVILS

PERSONAL: Born December 22, 1977, in Vancouver. ... 5-7/170. ... Shoots right. ... Brother of Paul Kariya, left winger, Mighty Ducks of Anaheim. ... Name pronounced kuh-REE-uh.

TRANSACTIONS/CAREER NOTES: Signed as non-drafted free agent by Vancouver Canucks (April 16, 1999). ... Traded by Canucks to New Jersey Devils for D Mikko Jokela (January 24, 2003).

Season Team	League	REGULAR SEASON								PLAYOFFS				
		Gms.	G	A	Pts.	PIM	+/-	PP	SH	Gms.	G	A	Pts.	PIM
94-95—Nanaimo	BCJHL	60	39	60	99	...	...	...	...	—	—	—	—	—
95-96—Univ. of Maine	Hockey East	39	7	15	22	38	...	...	...	—	—	—	—	—
96-97—Univ. of Maine	Hockey East	35	19	31	50	10	...	...	...	—	—	—	—	—
97-98—Univ. of Maine	Hockey East	35	25	25	50	22	...	...	...	—	—	—	—	—
98-99—Univ. of Maine	Hockey East	41	27	38	65	24	...	...	...	—	—	—	—	—
99-00—Vancouver	NHL	45	8	11	19	22	9	0	0	—	—	—	—	—
—Syracuse	AHL	29	18	23	41	22	...	...	...	4	2	1	3	0
00-01—Vancouver	NHL	17	1	6	7	8	-1	1	0	—	—	—	—	—
—Kansas City	IHL	43	15	29	44	51	...	...	...	—	—	—	—	—
01-02—Manitoba	AHL	67	25	37	62	48	...	...	...	7	1	2	3	2
—Vancouver	NHL	3	0	1	1	2	-2	0	0	—	—	—	—	—
02-03—Manitoba	AHL	38	14	14	28	18	...	...	...	—	—	—	—	—
—Albany	AHL	31	12	19	31	20	...	...	...	—	—	—	—	—
NHL Totals (3 years)		65	9	18	27	32	6	1	0					

KARLSSON, ANDREAS — C

PERSONAL: Born August 19, 1975, in Ludvika, Sweden. ... 6-3/195. ... Shoots left.

TRANSACTIONS/CAREER NOTES: Selected by Calgary Flames in sixth round (eighth Flames pick, 148th overall) of NHL entry draft (June 26, 1993). ... Traded by Flames to Atlanta Thrashers for future considerations (June 25, 1999). ... Strained shoulder (February 3, 2000); missed 11 games. ... Strained hip flexor (January 14, 2001); missed 15 games. ... Strained hip flexor (November 13, 2001); missed nine games.

Season Team	League	REGULAR SEASON								PLAYOFFS				
		Gms.	G	A	Pts.	PIM	+/-	PP	SH	Gms.	G	A	Pts.	PIM
92-93—Leksand	Sweden Dv. 2	13	0	0	0	6	...	...	...	—	—	—	—	—
93-94—Leksand	Sweden Dv. 2	21	0	0	0	10	...	...	...	—	—	—	—	—
94-95—Leksand	Sweden Dv. 2	24	7	8	15	4	...	...	...	4	0	1	1	0
95-96—Leksand	Sweden Dv. 2	40	10	13	23	10	...	...	...	5	2	1	3	4
96-97—Leksand	Sweden Dv. 2	49	13	11	24	39	...	...	...	9	2	0	2	2
97-98—Leksand	Sweden Dv. 2	33	9	14	23	20	...	...	...	4	1	0	1	0
98-99—Leksand	Sweden Dv. 2	49	18	15	33	18	...	...	...	4	1	0	1	6
99-00—Orlando	IHL	18	5	5	10	6	...	...	...	—	—	—	—	—
—Atlanta	NHL	51	5	9	14	14	-17	1	0	—	—	—	—	—
00-01—Atlanta	NHL	60	5	11	16	16	-2	0	1	—	—	—	—	—
01-02—Atlanta	NHL	42	1	7	8	20	-8	0	0	—	—	—	—	—
—Chicago	AHL	16	6	14	20	11	...	...	...	23	7	14	21	6
02-03—Chicago	AHL	41	12	20	32	16	...	...	...	—	—	—	—	—
NHL Totals (3 years)		153	11	27	38	50	-27	1	1					

KARLSSON, JENS   RW   KINGS

PERSONAL: Born November 7, 1982, in Goteburg, Sweden. ... 6-3/200. ... Shoots right.
TRANSACTIONS/CAREER NOTES: Selected by Los Angeles Kings in first round (first Kings pick, 18th overall) of NHL entry draft (June 23, 2001).

Season Team	League	REGULAR SEASON								PLAYOFFS				
		Gms.	G	A	Pts.	PIM	+/-	PP	SH	Gms.	G	A	Pts.	PIM
97-98—Vastra Frolunda	Sweden Jr.	17	2	3	5	4	...	...	...	—	—	—	—	—
98-99—Vastra Frolunda	Sweden Jr.	32	27	17	44	110	...	...	...	4	2	2	4	0
99-00—Vastra Frolunda	Sweden Jr.	33	25	14	39	100	...	...	...	4	2	2	4	0
00-01—Vastra Frolunda	Sweden Jr.	15	8	7	15	97	...	...	...	1	0	1	1	2
—Molndal	Sweden Dv. 2	5	1	1	2	35	...	...	...	—	—	—	—	—
—Vastra Frolunda	Sweden	19	2	0	2	4	...	...	...	5	1	3	4	50
01-02—Vastra Frolunda	Sweden	46	6	9	15	44	...	...	...	10	1	0	1	18
02-03—Vastra Frolunda	Sweden	45	5	6	11	101	...	...	...	11	3	2	5	41

KARPA, DAVID   D

PERSONAL: Born May 7, 1971, in Regina, Sask. ... 6-1/204. ... Shoots right. ... Full Name: David James Karpa.
TRANSACTIONS/CAREER NOTES: Selected by Quebec Nordiques in fourth round (fourth Nordiques pick, 68th overall) of NHL entry draft (June 22, 1991). ... Fractured right wrist (January 26, 1994); missed 18 games. ... Traded by Nordiques to Los Angeles Kings for fourth-round pick in 1995 or 1996 draft (February 28, 1995); trade invalidated by NHL because Karpa failed his physical examination (March 3, 1995). ... Traded by Nordiques to Mighty Ducks of Anaheim for fourth-round pick (traded to St. Louis) in 1997 draft (March 8, 1995). ... Underwent right wrist surgery (May 9, 1995). ... Bruised right knee (November 24, 1995); missed eight games. ... Fractured right hand (February 4, 1997); missed 13 games. ... Traded by Mighty Ducks with fourth-round pick (traded to Atlanta) in 2000 draft to Carolina Hurricanes for LW Stu Grimson and D Kevin Haller (August 11, 1998). ... Injured hamstring (December 6, 1997); missed two games. ... Suffered torn anterior cruciate ligament and medial collateral ligament in knee (November 22, 1998); missed 41 games. ... Bruised shoulder (March 10, 1999); missed five games. ... Reinjured shoulder (March 26, 1999); missed three games. ... Injured foot (March 29, 2000); missed final five games of season. ... Bruised ribs (February 27, 2001); missed two games. ... Signed as free agent by New York Rangers (July 1, 2001). ... Separated left shoulder (October 22, 2001); missed six games. ... Injured wrist (January 12, 2002); missed one game.

Season Team	League	REGULAR SEASON								PLAYOFFS				
		Gms.	G	A	Pts.	PIM	+/-	PP	SH	Gms.	G	A	Pts.	PIM
88-89—Notre Dame	SCMHL	—	16	37	53	—	—	...	...	—	—	—	—	—
89-90—Notre Dame	SCMHL	43	9	19	28	271	...	...	...	—	—	—	—	—
90-91—Ferris State	CCHA	41	6	19	25	109	...	...	...	—	—	—	—	—
91-92—Ferris State	CCHA	34	7	12	19	124	...	...	...	—	—	—	—	—
—Halifax	AHL	2	0	0	0	4	...	...	...	—	—	—	—	—
—Quebec	NHL	4	0	0	0	14	2	0	0	—	—	—	—	—
92-93—Halifax	AHL	71	4	27	31	167	...	...	...	—	—	—	—	—
—Quebec	NHL	12	0	1	1	13	-6	0	0	3	0	0	0	0
93-94—Quebec	NHL	60	5	12	17	148	0	2	0	—	—	—	—	—
—Cornwall	AHL	1	0	0	0	0	...	...	...	12	2	2	4	27
94-95—Cornwall	AHL	6	0	2	2	19	...	...	...	—	—	—	—	—
—Quebec	NHL	2	0	0	0	0	-1	0	0	—	—	—	—	—
—Anaheim	NHL	26	1	5	6	91	0	0	0	—	—	—	—	—
95-96—Anaheim	NHL	72	3	16	19	270	-3	0	1	—	—	—	—	—
96-97—Anaheim	NHL	69	2	11	13	210	11	0	0	8	1	1	2	20
97-98—Anaheim	NHL	78	1	11	12	217	-3	0	0	—	—	—	—	—
98-99—Carolina	NHL	33	0	2	2	55	1	0	0	2	0	0	0	2
99-00—Cincinnati	IHL	39	1	8	9	147	...	...	...	—	—	—	—	—
—Carolina	NHL	27	1	4	5	52	9	0	0	—	—	—	—	—
00-01—Carolina	NHL	80	4	6	10	159	-19	2	0	6	0	0	0	17
01-02—New York Rangers	NHL	75	1	10	11	131	-9	0	0	—	—	—	—	—
02-03—Hartford	AHL	34	0	7	7	70	...	...	...	—	—	—	—	—
—New York Rangers	NHL	19	0	2	2	14	-1	0	0	—	—	—	—	—
NHL Totals (12 years)		557	18	80	98	1374	-19	4	1	19	1	1	2	39

KARPOVTSEV, ALEXANDER   D   BLACKHAWKS

PERSONAL: Born April 7, 1970, in Moscow, U.S.S.R. ... 6-3/221. ... Shoots right. ... Name pronounced KAHR-puht-sehf.
TRANSACTIONS/CAREER NOTES: Selected by Quebec Nordiques in seventh round (seventh Nordiques pick, 158th overall) of NHL entry draft (June 16, 1990). ... Traded by Nordiques to New York Rangers for D Mike Hurlbut (September 9, 1993). ... Bruised buttocks (October 9, 1993); missed one game. ... Bruised hip (November 3, 1993); missed six games. ... Reinjured hip (November 23, 1993); missed one game. ... Injured

face (February 28, 1994); missed two games. ... Suffered injury (March 14, 1994); missed two games. ... Played in Europe during 1994-95 NHL lockout. ... Suffered sore ankle (April 14, 1995); missed one game. ... Hyperextended elbow (October 29, 1995); missed one game. ... Suffered back spasms (February 10, 1996); missed one game. ... Suffered back spasms (February 18, 1996); missed two games. ... Bruised thumb (March 13, 1996); missed two games. ... Suffered back spasms (March 27, 1996); missed six games. ... Bruised toe (April 3, 1997); missed one game. ... Hyperextended elbow (April 10, 1997); missed one game. ... Suffered throat infection (October 10, 1997); missed one game. ... Sprained right wrist (January 19, 1998); missed one game. ... Underwent wrist surgery (February 2, 1998); missed 28 games. ... Bruised knee (October 13, 1998); missed two games. ... Traded by Rangers with fourth-round pick (LW Mirko Murovic) in 1999 draft to Toronto Maple Leafs for D Mathieu Schneider (October 14, 1998). ... Fractured thumb (November 14, 1998); missed 12 games. ... Sprained wrist (January 2, 1999); missed three games. ... Strained wrist (February 2, 1999); missed three games. ... Fractured finger (March 17, 1999); missed three games. ... Strained shoulder (April 26, 1999); missed three playoff games. ... Suffered injury (November 5, 1999); missed one game. ... Sprained shoulder (November 26, 1999); missed five games. ... Fractured hand (January 11, 2000); missed four games. ... Suffered injury (March 16, 2000); missed one game. ... Suffered injury (March 23, 2000); missed one game. ... Traded by Maple Leafs with fourth-round pick (D Vladimir Gusev) in 2001 draft to Chicago Blackhawks for D Bryan McCabe (October 2, 2000). ... Bruised ankle (November 2, 2000); missed one game. ... Reinjured ankle (November 5, 2000); missed two games. ... Injured knee (December 3, 2000); missed one game. ... Underwent knee surgery (December 10, 2000); missed 11 games. ... Lacerated arm (January 7, 2001); missed one game. ... Suspended two games by NHL elbowing incident (February 10, 2001). ... Bruised knee (February 27, 2001); missed three games. ... Injured elbow (March 24, 2001); missed remainder of season. ... Sprained ankle (October 23, 2001); missed one game. ... Sprained knee (November 9, 2001); missed two games. ... Strained groin (November 19, 2001); missed three games. ... Bruised ribs (Janaury 10, 2002); missed three games. ... Underwent knee surgery (March 3, 2002); missed final seven games of season.

| | | REGULAR SEASON | | | | | | | | PLAYOFFS | | | | |
Season Team	League	Gms.	G	A	Pts.	PIM	+/-	PP	SH	Gms.	G	A	Pts.	PIM
89-90—Dynamo Moscow	USSR	35	1	1	2	27	...	...	...	—	—	—	—	—
90-91—Dynamo Moscow	USSR	40	0	5	5	15	...	...	...	—	—	—	—	—
91-92—Dynamo Moscow	CIS	28	3	2	5	22	...	...	...	—	—	—	—	—
92-93—Dynamo Moscow	CIS	40	3	11	14	100	...	...	...	—	—	—	—	—
93-94—New York Rangers	NHL	67	3	15	18	58	12	1	0	17	0	4	4	12
94-95—Dynamo Moscow	CIS	13	0	2	2	10	...	...	...	—	—	—	—	—
—New York Rangers	NHL	47	4	8	12	30	-4	1	0	8	1	0	1	0
95-96—New York Rangers	NHL	40	2	16	18	26	12	1	0	6	0	1	1	4
96-97—New York Rangers	NHL	77	9	29	38	59	1	6	1	13	1	3	4	20
97-98—New York Rangers	NHL	47	3	7	10	38	-1	1	0	—	—	—	—	—
98-99—New York Rangers	NHL	2	1	0	1	0	1	0	0	—	—	—	—	—
—Toronto	NHL	56	2	25	27	52	38	1	0	14	1	3	4	12
99-00—Toronto	NHL	69	3	14	17	54	9	3	0	11	0	3	3	4
00-01—Dynamo Moscow	Russian	5	0	1	1	0	...	...	...	—	—	—	—	—
—Chicago	NHL	53	2	13	15	39	-4	1	0	—	—	—	—	—
01-02—Chicago	NHL	65	1	9	10	40	10	0	1	5	1	0	1	0
02-03—Chicago	NHL	40	4	10	14	12	-8	3	0	—	—	—	—	—
NHL Totals (10 years)		563	34	146	180	408	66	18	2	74	4	14	18	52

K

KASPARAITIS, DARIUS   D   RANGERS

PERSONAL: Born October 16, 1972, in Elektrenai, U.S.S.R. ... 6-0/215. ... Shoots left. ... Name pronounced kas-puhr-IGH-tihz.

TRANSACTIONS/CAREER NOTES: Selected by New York Islanders in first round (first Islanders pick, fifth overall) of NHL entry draft (June 20, 1992). ... Suffered back spasms (February 12, 1993); missed two games. ... Strained back (April 15, 1993); missed one game. ... Strained lower back (November 10, 1993); missed two games. ... Jammed wrist (March 5, 1994); missed four games. ... Tore knee ligament (February 20, 1995); missed remainder of season and first 15 games of 1995-96 season. ... Suffered from the flu (December 2, 1995); missed two games. ... Severed two tendons in right hand (December 9, 1995); missed 16 games. ... Injured groin (February 8, 1996); missed two games. ... Traded by Islanders with C Andreas Johansson to Pittsburgh Penguins for C Bryan Smolinski (November 17, 1996). ... Suffered concussion (December 23, 1996); missed two games. ... Suffered facial laceration (January 2, 1997); missed one game. ... Twisted ankle (January 23, 1997); missed one game. ... Suffered concussion (March 18, 1997); missed three games. ... Suffered from the flu (March 29, 1998); missed one game. ... Injured knee (September 20, 1998); missed first eight games of season. ... Strained knee (December 21, 1998); missed one game. ... Strained groin (February 24, 1999); missed two games. ... Strained knee (March 5, 1999) and underwent surgery; missed remainder of season. ... Injured knee prior to start of 1999-2000 season; missed first four games of season. ... Suspended two games by NHL for elbowing incident (October 20, 1999). ... Suffered from headaches (December 30, 1999); missed two games. ... Suspended one game by NHL for second major penalty and game misconduct in season (January 19, 2000); missed three games. ... Bruised foot (December 16, 2000); missed three games. ... Suffered injury (April 4, 2001); missed final two games of season. ... Traded by Penguins to Colorado Avalanche for LW Ville Nieminen and D Rick Berry (March 19, 2002). ... Signed as free agent by New York Rangers (July 2, 2002).

| | | REGULAR SEASON | | | | | | | | PLAYOFFS | | | | |
Season Team	League	Gms.	G	A	Pts.	PIM	+/-	PP	SH	Gms.	G	A	Pts.	PIM
88-89—Dynamo Moscow	USSR	3	0	0	0	0	...	...	...	—	—	—	—	—
89-90—Dynamo Moscow	USSR	1	0	0	0	0	...	...	...	—	—	—	—	—
90-91—Dynamo Moscow	USSR	17	0	1	1	10	...	...	...	—	—	—	—	—
91-92—Dynamo Moscow	CIS	31	2	10	12	14	...	...	...	—	—	—	—	—
—Unif. Olympic team	Int'l	8	0	2	2	2	...	...	...	—	—	—	—	—
92-93—Dynamo Moscow	CIS	7	1	3	4	8	...	...	...	—	—	—	—	—
—New York Islanders	NHL	79	4	17	21	166	15	0	0	18	0	5	5	31
93-94—New York Islanders	NHL	76	1	10	11	142	-6	0	0	4	0	0	0	8
94-95—New York Islanders	NHL	13	0	1	1	22	-11	0	0	—	—	—	—	—
95-96—New York Islanders	NHL	46	1	7	8	93	-12	0	0	—	—	—	—	—
96-97—New York Islanders	NHL	18	0	5	5	16	-7	0	0	—	—	—	—	—
—Pittsburgh	NHL	57	2	16	18	84	24	0	0	5	0	0	0	6
97-98—Pittsburgh	NHL	81	4	8	12	127	3	0	2	5	0	0	0	8
—Russian Oly. team	Int'l	6	0	2	2	6	...	...	...	—	—	—	—	—
98-99—Pittsburgh	NHL	48	1	4	5	70	12	0	0	—	—	—	—	—
99-00—Pittsburgh	NHL	73	3	12	15	146	-12	1	0	11	1	1	2	10
00-01—Pittsburgh	NHL	77	3	16	19	111	11	1	0	17	1	1	2	26
01-02—Pittsburgh	NHL	69	2	12	14	123	-1	0	0	—	—	—	—	—
—Russian Oly. team	Int'l	6	1	0	1	4	...	...	...	—	—	—	—	—
—Colorado	NHL	11	0	0	0	19	1	0	0	21	0	3	3	18
02-03—New York Rangers	NHL	80	3	11	14	85	5	0	0	—	—	—	—	—
NHL Totals (11 years)		728	24	119	143	1204	22	2	2	81	2	10	12	107

KAVANAGH, PAT   RW   CANUCKS

PERSONAL: Born March 14, 1979, in Ottawa ... 6-3/205. ... Shoots right.
TRANSACTIONS/CAREER NOTES: Selected by Philadelphia Flyers in second round (second Flyers pick, 50th overall) of NHL entry draft (June 21, 1997). ... Traded by Flyers to Vancouver Canucks for sixth-round pick (F Konstantin Rudenko) in 1999 draft (June 1, 1999).

				REGULAR SEASON						PLAYOFFS				
Season Team	League	Gms.	G	A	Pts.	PIM	+/-	PP	SH	Gms.	G	A	Pts.	PIM
96-97—Peterborough	OHL	43	6	8	14	53	...	...	...	11	1	1	2	12
97-98—Peterborough	OHL	66	10	16	26	85	...	...	...	4	1	0	1	6
98-99—Peterborough	OHL	68	26	43	69	118	...	...	...	5	0	5	5	10
99-00—Syracuse	AHL	68	12	8	20	56	...	...	...	4	0	0	0	0
00-01—Kansas City	IHL	78	26	15	41	86	...	...	...	—	—	—	—	—
—Vancouver	NHL	—	—	—	—	—	—	—	—	3	0	0	0	2
01-02—Manitoba	AHL	70	13	19	32	100	...	...	...	7	1	0	1	6
02-03—Manitoba	AHL	63	15	15	30	96	...	...	...	—	—	—	—	—
—Vancouver	NHL	3	1	0	1	2	2	0	0	—	—	—	—	—
NHL Totals (2 years)		3	1	0	1	2	2	0	0	3	0	0	0	2

KEANE, MIKE   LW   AVALANCHE

PERSONAL: Born May 29, 1967, in Winnipeg ... 5-10/190. ... Shoots right. ... Name pronounced KEEN.
TRANSACTIONS/CAREER NOTES: Signed as non-drafted free agent by Montreal Canadiens (September 25, 1985). ... Separated right shoulder (December 21, 1988). ... Lacerated left kneecap (October 31, 1990); missed seven games. ... Injured neck (March 1991). ... Sprained ankle (January 16, 1992); missed four games. ... Reinjured ankle (February 1, 1992); missed 10 games. ... Bruised ankle (March 11, 1992); missed one game. ... Suspended four off-days and fined $500 by NHL for swinging stick in preseason game (October 13, 1992). ... Suffered wrist tendinitis (January 26, 1993); missed three games. ... Suffered back spasms (February 12, 1993); missed two games. ... Fractured toe (February 27, 1993); missed two games. ... Suffered back spasms (October 16, 1993); missed one game. ... Suffered back spasms (January 12, 1994); missed three games. ... Injured groin (November 1, 1995); missed one game. ... Injured neck (November 18, 1995); missed three games. ... Injured groin (November 25, 1995); missed two games. ... Traded by Canadiens with G Patrick Roy to Colorado Avalanche for G Jocelyn Thibault, LW Martin Rucinsky and RW Andrei Kovalenko (December 6, 1995). ... Signed as free agent by New York Rangers (July 7, 1997). ... Traded by Rangers with C Brian Skrudland and sixth-round pick (RW Pavel Patera) in 1998 draft to Dallas Stars for LW Bob Errey, RW Todd Harvey and fourth-round pick (LW Boyd Kane) in 1998 draft (March 24, 1998). ... Strained back (March 5, 2000); missed one game. ... Injured groin (December 13, 2000); missed five games. ... Bruised ankle (January 17, 2001); missed two games. ... Fractured ankle (January 22, 2001); missed six games. ... Bruised chest muscle (April 2, 2001); missed final two games of regular season. ... Signed as free agent by St. Louis Blues (July 5, 2001). ... Traded by Blues to Avalanche for LW Shjon Podein (February 11, 2002). ... Suffered back spasms (April 1, 2002); missed one game.

				REGULAR SEASON						PLAYOFFS				
Season Team	League	Gms.	G	A	Pts.	PIM	+/-	PP	SH	Gms.	G	A	Pts.	PIM
83-84—Winnipeg	WHL	1	0	0	0	0	...	...	...	—	—	—	—	—
84-85—Moose Jaw	WHL	65	17	26	43	141	...	...	...	—	—	—	—	—
85-86—Moose Jaw	WHL	67	34	49	83	162	...	...	...	13	6	8	14	9
86-87—Moose Jaw	WHL	53	25	45	70	107	...	...	...	9	3	9	12	11
—Sherbrooke	AHL	—	—	—	—	—	...	...	...	9	2	2	4	16
87-88—Sherbrooke	AHL	78	25	43	68	70	...	...	...	6	1	1	2	18
88-89—Montreal	NHL	69	16	19	35	69	9	5	0	21	4	3	7	17
89-90—Montreal	NHL	74	9	15	24	78	0	1	0	11	0	1	1	8
90-91—Montreal	NHL	73	13	23	36	50	6	2	1	12	3	2	5	6
91-92—Montreal	NHL	67	11	30	41	64	16	2	0	8	1	1	2	16
92-93—Montreal	NHL	77	15	45	60	95	29	0	0	19	2	13	15	6
93-94—Montreal	NHL	80	16	30	46	119	6	6	2	6	3	1	4	4
94-95—Montreal	NHL	48	10	10	20	15	5	1	0	—	—	—	—	—
95-96—Montreal	NHL	18	0	7	7	6	-6	0	0	—	—	—	—	—
—Colorado	NHL	55	10	10	20	40	1	0	2	22	3	2	5	16
96-97—Colorado	NHL	81	10	17	27	63	2	0	1	17	3	1	4	24
97-98—New York Rangers	NHL	70	8	10	18	47	-12	2	0	—	—	—	—	—
—Dallas	NHL	13	2	3	5	5	0	0	0	17	4	4	8	0
98-99—Dallas	NHL	81	6	23	29	62	-2	1	1	23	5	2	7	6
99-00—Dallas	NHL	81	13	21	34	41	9	0	4	23	2	4	6	14
00-01—Dallas	NHL	67	10	14	24	35	4	1	0	10	3	2	5	4
01-02—St. Louis	NHL	56	4	6	10	22	-2	1	0	—	—	—	—	—
—Colorado	NHL	22	2	5	7	16	-2	0	0	18	1	4	5	8
02-03—Colorado	NHL	65	5	5	10	34	0	0	1	6	0	0	0	2
NHL Totals (15 years)		1097	160	293	453	861	63	22	12	213	34	40	74	131

KEEFE, SHELDON   RW   LIGHTNING

PERSONAL: Born September 17, 1980, in Brampton, Ont. ... 5-11/184. ... Shoots right.
TRANSACTIONS/CAREER NOTES: Selected by Tampa Bay Lightning in second round (first Lightning pick, 47th overall) of NHL entry draft (June 26, 1999). ... Sprained medial collateral ligament in right knee (January 13, 2002); missed 14 games. ... Re-signed by Lightning (July 30, 2003).

				REGULAR SEASON						PLAYOFFS				
Season Team	League	Gms.	G	A	Pts.	PIM	+/-	PP	SH	Gms.	G	A	Pts.	PIM
96-97—Quinte	Tier II Jr. A	44	21	23	44	...	...	...	...	—	—	—	—	—
97-98—Caledon	Jr. A	51	52	51	103	117	...	...	...	—	—	—	—	—
98-99—Toronto St. Michael's	OHL	38	37	37	74	80	...	...	...	—	—	—	—	—
—Barrie	OHL	28	14	28	42	60	...	...	...	10	5	5	10	31
99-00—Barrie	OHL	66	48	*73	*121	95	...	...	...	25	10	13	23	41
00-01—Detroit	IHL	13	7	5	12	23	...	...	...	—	—	—	—	—
—Tampa Bay	NHL	49	4	0	4	38	-13	0	0	—	—	—	—	—
01-02—Springfield	AHL	24	9	9	18	26	...	...	...	—	—	—	—	—
—Tampa Bay	NHL	39	6	7	13	16	-11	0	0	—	—	—	—	—
02-03—Springfield	AHL	33	16	15	31	28	...	...	...	—	—	—	—	—
—Tampa Bay	NHL	37	2	5	7	24	-1	0	0	—	—	—	—	—
NHL Totals (3 years)		125	12	12	24	78	-25	0	0					

KELLEHER, CHRIS   D

PERSONAL: Born March 23, 1975, in Cambridge, Mass. ... 6-1/210. ... Shoots left.
TRANSACTIONS/CAREER NOTES: Selected by Pittsburgh Penguins in fifth round (fifth Penguins pick, 130th overall) of NHL entry draft (June 26, 1993). ... Signed as free agent by Boston Bruins (July 23, 2001).

		REGULAR SEASON								PLAYOFFS				
Season Team	League	Gms.	G	A	Pts.	PIM	+/-	PP	SH	Gms.	G	A	Pts.	PIM
90-91—Belmont Hill	Mass. H.S.	20	4	23	27	14	...	...	...	—	—	—	—	—
91-92—St. Sebastian's	USHS (East)	28	7	27	34	12	...	...	...	—	—	—	—	—
92-93—St. Sebastian's	USHS (East)	25	8	30	38	16	...	...	...	—	—	—	—	—
93-94—St. Sebastian's	USHS (East)	24	10	21	31	...	...	...	...	—	—	—	—	—
94-95—Boston University	Hockey East	35	3	17	20	62	...	...	...	—	—	—	—	—
95-96—Boston University	Hockey East	37	7	18	25	43	...	...	...	—	—	—	—	—
96-97—Boston University	Hockey East	39	10	24	34	54	...	...	...	—	—	—	—	—
97-98—Boston University	Hockey East	37	4	26	30	40	...	...	...	—	—	—	—	—
98-99—Syracuse	AHL	45	1	4	5	43	...	...	...	—	—	—	—	—
99-00—Wilkes-Barre/Scranton	AHL	67	0	12	12	40	...	...	...	—	—	—	—	—
00-01—Wilkes-Barre/Scranton	AHL	66	6	13	19	37	...	...	...	21	7	18	*25	4
01-02—Providence	AHL	31	6	13	19	14	...	...	...	—	—	—	—	—
—Boston	NHL	1	0	0	0	0	0	0	0	—	—	—	—	—
02-03—Providence	AHL	72	8	27	35	50	...	...	...	—	—	—	—	—
NHL Totals (1 year)		1	0	0	0	0	0	0	0					

K

KELLY, CHRIS   LW   SENATORS

PERSONAL: Born November 11, 1980, in Toronto. ... 6-0/179. ... Shoots left.
TRANSACTIONS/CAREER NOTES: Selected by Ottawa Senators in third round (fourth Senators pick, 94th overall) of NHL entry draft (June 26, 1999).

		REGULAR SEASON								PLAYOFFS				
Season Team	League	Gms.	G	A	Pts.	PIM	+/-	PP	SH	Gms.	G	A	Pts.	PIM
96-97—Aurora	OPJHL	49	14	20	34	11	...	...	...	—	—	—	—	—
97-98—London	OHL	54	15	14	29	4	...	...	...	16	4	5	9	12
98-99—London	OHL	68	36	41	77	60	...	...	...	25	9	17	26	22
99-00—London	OHL	63	29	43	72	57	...	...	...	—	—	—	—	—
00-01—London	OHL	31	21	34	55	46	...	...	...	—	—	—	—	—
—Sudbury	OHL	19	5	16	21	17	...	...	...	12	11	5	16	14
01-02—Grand Rapids	AHL	31	3	3	6	20	...	...	...	5	1	1	2	5
02-03—Binghamton	AHL	77	17	14	31	73	...	...	...	—	—	—	—	—

KELLY, REGAN   D   MAPLE LEAFS

PERSONAL: Born March 9, 1981, in Watrous, Sask. ... 6-2/185. ... Shoots left.
TRANSACTIONS/CAREER NOTES: Selected by Philadelphia Flyers in eighth round (sixth Flyers pick, 259th overall) of 2001 NHL draft. ... Rights traded by Flyers to Toronto Maple Leafs for D Chris McAllister (September 26, 2000).

		REGULAR SEASON								PLAYOFFS				
Season Team	League	Gms.	G	A	Pts.	PIM	+/-	PP	SH	Gms.	G	A	Pts.	PIM
00-01—Providence College	Hockey East	36	4	21	25	58	...	...	...	—	—	—	—	—
01-02—Providence College	Hockey East	38	6	10	16	48	...	...	...	—	—	—	—	—
02-03—St. John's	AHL	71	3	15	18	36	...	...	...	—	—	—	—	—

KELLY, STEVE   C   KINGS

PERSONAL: Born October 26, 1976, in Vancouver ... 6-2/205. ... Shoots left.
TRANSACTIONS/CAREER NOTES: Selected by Edmonton Oilers in first round (first Oilers pick, sixth overall) of NHL entry draft (July 8, 1995). ... Traded by Oilers to Tampa Bay Lightning with C Jason Bonsignore and D Bryan Marchment for D Roman Hamrlik and C Paul Comrie (December 30, 1997). ... Suffered from the flu (January 21, 1998); missed two games. ... Suffered from the flu (January 31, 1998); missed one game. ... Suffered concussion (October 10, 1998); missed eight games. ... Traded by Lightning to New Jersey Devils for seventh-round pick (G Brian Eklund) in 2000 draft (October 7, 1999). ... Traded by Devils to Los Angeles Kings for future considerations (February 27, 2001). ... Strained lower back (March 19, 2001); missed two games. ... Underwent abdominal surgery (September 18, 2001); missed first 16 games of season. ... Re-signed by Kings (July 27, 2003).

		REGULAR SEASON								PLAYOFFS				
Season Team	League	Gms.	G	A	Pts.	PIM	+/-	PP	SH	Gms.	G	A	Pts.	PIM
92-93—Prince Albert	WHL	65	11	9	20	75	...	...	...	—	—	—	—	—
93-94—Prince Albert	WHL	65	19	42	61	106	...	...	...	—	—	—	—	—
94-95—Prince Albert	WHL	68	31	41	72	153	...	...	...	15	7	9	16	35
95-96—Prince Albert	WHL	70	27	74	101	203	...	...	...	18	13	18	31	47
96-97—Hamilton	AHL	48	9	29	38	111	...	...	...	11	3	3	6	24
—Edmonton	NHL	8	1	0	1	6	-1	0	0	6	0	0	0	2
97-98—Edmonton	NHL	19	0	2	2	8	-4	0	0	—	—	—	—	—
—Hamilton	AHL	11	2	8	10	18	...	...	...	—	—	—	—	—
—Tampa Bay	NHL	24	2	1	3	15	-9	1	0	—	—	—	—	—
—Milwaukee	IHL	5	0	1	1	19	...	...	...	—	—	—	—	—
—Cleveland	IHL	5	1	1	2	29	...	...	...	1	0	1	1	0
98-99—Tampa Bay	NHL	34	1	3	4	27	-15	0	0	—	—	—	—	—
—Cleveland	IHL	18	6	7	13	36	...	...	...	—	—	—	—	—

Season Team	League	REGULAR SEASON								PLAYOFFS				
		Gms.	G	A	Pts.	PIM	+/-	PP	SH	Gms.	G	A	Pts.	PIM
99-00—Detroit.........................	IHL	1	0	0	0	4	...	...	...	—	—	—	—	—
—Albany............................	AHL	76	21	36	57	131	...	...	...	3	1	1	2	2
—New Jersey.................	NHL	1	0	0	0	0	0	0	0	10	0	0	0	4
00-01—New Jersey.................	NHL	24	2	2	4	21	0	0	0	—	—	—	—	—
—Los Angeles................	NHL	11	1	0	1	4	0	0	0	8	0	0	0	2
01-02—Manchester.................	AHL	49	10	21	31	88	...	...	...	5	1	8	9	4
—Los Angeles................	NHL	8	0	1	1	2	-1	0	0	1	0	0	0	0
02-03—Manchester.................	AHL	54	19	44	63	144	...	...	...	—	—	—	—	—
—Los Angeles................	NHL	15	2	3	5	0	-6	0	0	—	—	—	—	—
NHL Totals (7 years)..........		144	9	12	21	83	-36	1	0	25	0	0	0	8

KESA, TEEMU D DEVILS

PERSONAL: Born June 7, 1981, in Nurmijarvi, Finland. ... 6-0/185. ... Shoots left.
TRANSACTIONS/CAREER NOTES: Selected by New Jersey Devils in fourth round (fifth Devils pick, 100th overall) of NHL entry draft (June 26, 1999).

Season Team	League	REGULAR SEASON								PLAYOFFS				
		Gms.	G	A	Pts.	PIM	+/-	PP	SH	Gms.	G	A	Pts.	PIM
97-98—Ilves Tampere	Finland Jr.	33	8	1	9	78	...	...	...	—	—	—	—	—
98-99—Ilves Tampere	Finland Jr.	25	4	4	8	129	...	...	...	—	—	—	—	—
99-00—Ilves Tampere	Finland	5	0	0	0	8	...	...	...	—	—	—	—	—
01-02—Lukko Rauma	Finland	34	2	0	2	32	...	...	...	—	—	—	—	—
02-03—Lukko Rauma	Finland	37	1	0	1	22	...	...	...	—	—	—	—	—

K

KHABIBULIN, NIKOLAI G LIGHTNING

PERSONAL: Born January 13, 1973, in Sverdlovsk, U.S.S.R. ... 6-1/196. ... Catches left. ... Name pronounced hah-bee-BOO-lihn.
TRANSACTIONS/CAREER NOTES: Selected by Winnipeg Jets in ninth round (eighth Jets pick, 204th overall) of NHL entry draft (June 20, 1992). ... Sprained knee (November 30, 1995); missed 20 games. ... Jets franchise moved to Phoenix and renamed Coyotes for 1996-97 season; NHL approved move on January 18, 1996. ... Bruised hand (November 6, 1998); missed two games. ... Strained groin (March 2, 1999); missed one game. ... Traded by Coyotes with D Stan Neckar to Tampa Bay Lightning for D Paul Mara, RW Mike Johnson, RW Ruslan Zainullin and second-round pick (D Matthew Spiller) in 2001 (March 5, 2001).

Season Team	League	REGULAR SEASON									PLAYOFFS						
		Gms.	Min	W	L	T	GA	SO	Avg.	SV%	Gms.	Min.	W	L	GA	SO	Avg.	SV%
88-89—Avtomo. Sverdlovsk......	USSR	1	3	0	0	0	0	0	...	—	—							
89-90—Avtomo. Sverd. Jr.	USSR Jr.					Statistics unavailable.					—							
90-91—Sputnik Nizhny Tagil	USSR Dv.III					Statistics unavailable.					—							
91-92—CSKA Moscow	CIS	2	34	...	...	...	2	...	3.53	—	—							
92-93—CSKA Moscow	CIS	13	491	...	...	...	27	...	3.30	—	—							
93-94—Russian Penguins	IHL	12	639	2	7	‡2	47	0	4.41	—	—							
—CSKA Moscow	CIS	46	2625	...	...	...	116	5	2.65	—	3	193	1	2	11	0	3.42	—
94-95—Springfield	AHL	23	1240	9	9	3	80	0	3.87	—	—							
—Winnipeg......................	NHL	26	1339	8	9	4	76	0	3.41	.895	—							
95-96—Winnipeg......................	NHL	53	2914	26	20	3	152	2	3.13	.908	6	359	2	4	19	0	3.18	.911
96-97—Phoenix......................	NHL	72	4091	30	33	6	193	7	2.83	.908	7	426	3	4	15	1	2.11	.932
97-98—Phoenix......................	NHL	70	4026	30	28	10	†184	4	2.74	.900	4	185	2	1	13	0	4.22	.877
98-99—Phoenix......................	NHL	63	3657	32	23	7	130	8	2.13	.923	7	449	3	4	18	0	2.41	.924
99-00—Long Beach	IHL	33	1936	26	11	1	59	5	*1.83	—	5	321	2	3	15	0	2.80	—
00-01—Tampa Bay	NHL	2	123	1	1	0	6	0	2.93	.913	—							
01-02—Tampa Bay	NHL	70	3896	24	32	10	153	7	2.36	.920	—							
—Russian Oly. team........	Int'l	6	359	3	2	1	14	1	2.34	—	—							
02-03—Tampa Bay	NHL	65	3787	30	22	11	156	4	2.47	.911	10	644	5	5	26	0	2.42	.913
NHL Totals (8 years)..........		421	23833	181	168	51	1050	32	2.64	.911	34	2063	15	18	91	1	2.65	.916

KHAVANOV, ALEXANDER D BLUES

PERSONAL: Born January 30, 1972, in Moscow, U.S.S.R. ... 6-1/197. ... Full Name: Alexander P. Khavanov.
TRANSACTIONS/CAREER NOTES: Selected by St. Louis Blues in eighth round (eighth Blues pick, 232nd overall) of NHL entry draft (June 24, 2000).

Season Team	League	REGULAR SEASON								PLAYOFFS				
		Gms.	G	A	Pts.	PIM	+/-	PP	SH	Gms.	G	A	Pts.	PIM
92-93—Birmingham.................	ECHL	19	0	3	3	14	...	...	...	—	—	—	—	—
—Raleigh	ECHL	17	0	6	6	8	...	...	...	—	—	—	—	—
93-94—St. Petersburg	CIS	41	1	2	3	24	...	...	...	—	—	—	—	—
94-95—St. Petersburg	CIS	49	7	0	7	32	...	...	...	3	0	0	0	0
95-96—St. Petersburg	CIS	32	1	5	6	41	...	...	...	—	—	—	—	—
—HPK Hameenlinna.......	Finland	16	0	2	2	4	...	...	...	9	0	0	0	0
96-97—Cherepovets.................	Russian	39	3	8	11	56	...	...	...	3	1	0	1	4
97-98—Cherepovets.................	Russian	44	3	5	8	46	...	...	...	—	—	—	—	—
98-99—Dynamo	Russian	40	2	7	9	14	...	...	...	16	1	5	6	35
99-00—Dynamo	Russian	38	5	12	17	49	...	...	...	17	0	3	3	4
00-01—St. Louis	NHL	74	7	16	23	52	16	2	0	15	3	2	5	14
01-02—St. Louis	NHL	81	3	21	24	55	9	0	0	4	0	0	0	2
02-03—St. Louis	NHL	81	8	25	33	48	-1	2	1	7	2	3	5	2
NHL Totals (3 years)..........		236	18	62	80	155	24	4	1	26	5	5	10	18

KIDD, TREVOR — G — MAPLE LEAFS

PERSONAL: Born March 26, 1972, in Dugald, Man. ... 6-2/213. ... Catches left.

TRANSACTIONS/CAREER NOTES: Selected by Calgary Flames in first round (first Flames pick, 11th overall) of NHL entry draft (June 16, 1990). ... Sprained left ankle (October 18, 1993); missed one game. ... Traded by Flames with LW Gary Roberts to Carolina Hurricanes for G Jean-Sebastien Giguere and C Andrew Cassels (August 25, 1997). ... Strained groin (November 9, 1997); missed seven games. ... Fractured finger on right hand (December 20, 1997); missed seven games. ... Injured groin (April 16, 1998); missed three games. ... Selected by Atlanta Thrashers in NHL expansion draft (June 25, 1999). ... Traded by Thrashers to Florida Panthers for D Gord Murphy, C Herbert Vasiljevs, D Daniel Tjarnqvist and sixth-round pick (traded to Dallas) in 1999 draft (June 25, 1999). ... Separated shoulder (December 13, 1999); missed 29 games. ... Released by Panthers (August 23, 2002). ... Signed as free agent by Toronto Maple Leafs (August 26, 2002).

		REGULAR SEASON									PLAYOFFS							
Season Team	League	Gms.	Min	W	L	T	GA	SO	Avg.	SV%	Gms.	Min.	W	L	GA	SO	Avg.	SV%
88-89—Brandon	WHL	32	1509	11	13	1	102	0	4.06	—	—	—	—	—	—	—	—	—
89-90—Brandon	WHL	*63	*3676	24	32	2	254	2	4.15	—	—	—	—	—	—	—	—	—
90-91—Brandon	WHL	30	1730	10	19	1	117	0	4.06	—	—	—	—	—	—	—	—	—
—Spokane	WHL	14	749	8	3	0	44	0	3.52	—	15	926	*14	1	32	*2	*2.07	—
91-92—Canadian nat'l team	Int'l	28	1349	18	4	4	79	2	3.51	—	—	—	—	—	—	—	—	—
—Can. Olympic team	Int'l	1	60	1	0	0	0	1	...	—	—	—	—	—	—	—	—	—
—Calgary	NHL	2	120	1	1	0	8	0	4.00	.857	—	—	—	—	—	—	—	—
92-93—Salt Lake City	IHL	30	1696	10	16	‡0	111	1	3.93	—	—	—	—	—	—	—	—	—
93-94—Calgary	NHL	31	1614	13	7	6	85	0	3.16	.887	—	—	—	—	—	—	—	—
94-95—Calgary	NHL	‡43	2463	22	14	6	107	3	2.61	.909	7	434	3	4	26	1	3.59	.856
95-96—Calgary	NHL	47	2570	15	21	8	119	3	2.78	.895	2	83	0	1	9	0	6.51	.775
96-97—Calgary	NHL	55	2979	21	23	6	141	4	2.84	.900	—	—	—	—	—	—	—	—
97-98—Carolina	NHL	47	2685	21	21	3	97	3	2.17	.922	—	—	—	—	—	—	—	—
98-99—Carolina	NHL	25	1358	7	10	6	61	2	2.70	.905	—	—	—	—	—	—	—	—
99-00—Florida	NHL	28	1574	14	11	2	69	1	2.63	.915	—	—	—	—	—	—	—	—
—Louisville	AHL	1	60	0	1	0	5	0	5.00	—	—	—	—	—	—	—	—	—
00-01—Florida	NHL	42	2354	10	23	6	130	1	3.31	.893	—	—	—	—	—	—	—	—
01-02—Florida	NHL	33	1683	4	16	5	90	1	3.21	.895	—	—	—	—	—	—	—	—
02-03—Toronto	NHL	19	1143	6	10	2	59	0	3.10	.896	—	—	—	—	—	—	—	—
NHL Totals (11 years)		372	20543	134	157	50	966	18	2.82	.902	9	517	3	5	35	1	4.06	.842

KILGER, CHAD — LW — CANADIENS

PERSONAL: Born November 27, 1976, in Cornwall, Ont. ... 6-4/224. ... Shoots left. ... Son of Bob Kilger, former NHL referee (1970-71 through 1979-80).

TRANSACTIONS/CAREER NOTES: Selected by Mighty Ducks of Anaheim in first round (first Mighty Ducks pick, fourth overall) of NHL entry draft (July 8, 1995). ... Traded by Mighty Ducks with D Oleg Tverdovsky and third-round pick (D Per-Anton Lundstrom) in 1996 draft to Winnipeg Jets for C Marc Chouinard, RW Teemu Selanne and fourth-round pick (traded to Toronto) in 1996 draft (February 7, 1996). ... Suffered from the flu (February 21, 1996); missed one game. ... Jets franchise moved to Phoenix and renamed Coyotes for 1996-97 season; NHL approved move on January 18, 1996. ... Bruised thigh (October 7, 1996); missed one game. ... Traded by Coyotes with D Jayson More to Chicago Blackhawks for D Keith Carney and RW Jim Cummins (March 4, 1998). ... Suffered concussion (February 19, 1999); missed three games. ... Traded by Blackhawks with LW Daniel Cleary, LW Ethan Moreau and D Christian Laflamme to Edmonton Oilers for D Boris Mironov, LW Dean McAmmond and D Jonas Elofsson (March 20, 1999). ... Suffered hip pointer (December 30, 1999); missed five games. ... Suffered hip pointer (February 23, 2000); missed two games. ... Traded by Oilers to Montreal Canadiens for C Sergei Zholtok (December 18, 2000). ... Suffered concussion (March 3, 2001); missed five games. ... Strained groin (April 2, 2001); missed one game. ... Strained neck (January 8, 2002); missed seven games. ... Re-signed by Canadiens (June 30, 2003).

		REGULAR SEASON							PLAYOFFS				
Season Team	League	Gms.	G	A	Pts.	PIM	+/-	PP	SH	Gms.	G	A	Pts.	PIM
92-93—Cornwall	CJHL	55	30	36	66	26	...	...	...	6	0	0	0	0
93-94—Kingston	OHL	66	17	35	52	23	...	...	...	6	7	2	9	8
94-95—Kingston	OHL	65	42	53	95	95	...	...	...	6	5	2	7	10
95-96—Anaheim	NHL	45	5	7	12	22	-2	0	0	—	—	—	—	—
—Winnipeg	NHL	29	2	3	5	12	-2	0	0	4	1	0	1	0
96-97—Phoenix	NHL	24	4	3	7	13	-5	1	0	—	—	—	—	—
—Springfield	AHL	52	17	28	45	36	...	...	...	16	5	7	12	56
97-98—Springfield	AHL	35	14	14	28	33	...	...	...	—	—	—	—	—
—Phoenix	NHL	10	0	1	1	4	-2	0	0	—	—	—	—	—
—Chicago	NHL	22	3	8	11	6	2	2	0	—	—	—	—	—
98-99—Chicago	NHL	64	14	11	25	30	-1	2	1	—	—	—	—	—
—Edmonton	NHL	13	1	1	2	4	-3	0	0	4	0	0	0	4
99-00—Edmonton	NHL	40	3	2	5	18	-6	0	0	3	0	0	0	0
—Hamilton	AHL	3	3	3	6	0	...	...	...	—	—	—	—	—
00-01—Edmonton	NHL	34	5	2	7	17	-7	1	0	—	—	—	—	—
—Montreal	NHL	43	9	16	25	34	-1	1	1	—	—	—	—	—
01-02—Montreal	NHL	75	8	15	23	27	-7	0	1	12	0	1	1	9
02-03—Montreal	NHL	60	9	7	16	21	-4	0	0	—	—	—	—	—
NHL Totals (8 years)		459	63	76	139	208	-38	7	3	23	1	1	2	13

KING, DEREK — LW

PERSONAL: Born February 11, 1967, in Hamilton, Ont. ... 5-11/212. ... Shoots left.

TRANSACTIONS/CAREER NOTES: Selected by New York Islanders in first round (second Islanders pick, 13th overall) of NHL entry draft (June 15, 1985). ... Fractured left wrist (December 12, 1987). ... Separated shoulder (November 23, 1988). ... Suffered concussion (November 2, 1990). ... Separated right shoulder (February 14, 1991). ... Bruised hip (November 27, 1992); missed two games. ... Suffered hip pointer (December 26, 1992); missed four games. ... Fractured finger on left hand (April 3, 1993); missed one game. ... Suffered hip pointer (January

8, 1994); missed two games. ... Injured knee (March 9, 1995); missed one game. ... Injured elbow (April 28, 1995); missed two games. ... Injured foot (November 24, 1995); missed one game. ... Fractured jaw and suffered concussion (March 3, 1996); missed remainder of season. ... Traded by Islanders to Hartford Whalers for fifth-round pick (C Adam Edinger) in 1997 draft (March 18, 1997). ... Signed as free agent by Toronto Maple Leafs (July 3, 1997). ... Sprained ankle (October 7, 1997); missed five games. ... Traded by Maple Leafs with conditional eighth-round pick in 2000 draft to St. Louis Blues for D Tyler Harlton and conditional eighth-round pick in 2000 draft (October 20, 1999). ... Signed as free agent by Ottawa Senators (August 10, 2000). ... Signed as free agent by Detroit Red Wings (July 24, 2002).

STATISTICAL PLATEAUS: Three-goal games: 1989-90 (1), 1991-92 (2), 1993-94 (1), 1996-97 (1), 1997-98 (1). Total: 6. ... Four-goal games: 1990-91 (1). ... Total hat tricks: 7.

		REGULAR SEASON								PLAYOFFS				
Season Team	League	Gms.	G	A	Pts.	PIM	+/-	PP	SH	Gms.	G	A	Pts.	PIM
83-84—Hamilton Jr. A.	OHA	37	10	14	24	142	...	...	...	—	—	—	—	—
84-85—Sault Ste. Marie	OHL	63	35	38	73	106	...	...	...	16	3	13	16	11
85-86—Sault Ste. Marie	OHL	25	12	17	29	33	...	...	...	—	—	—	—	—
—Oshawa	OHL	19	8	13	21	15	...	...	...	6	3	2	5	13
86-87—Oshawa	OHL	57	53	53	106	74	...	...	...	17	14	10	24	40
—New York Islanders	NHL	2	0	0	0	0	0	0	0	—	—	—	—	—
87-88—New York Islanders	NHL	55	12	24	36	30	7	1	0	5	0	2	2	2
—Springfield	AHL	10	7	6	13	6	...	...	...	—	—	—	—	—
88-89—Springfield	AHL	4	4	0	4	0	...	...	...	—	—	—	—	—
—New York Islanders	NHL	60	14	29	43	14	10	4	0	—	—	—	—	—
89-90—Springfield	AHL	21	11	12	23	33	...	...	...	—	—	—	—	—
—New York Islanders	NHL	46	13	27	40	20	2	5	0	4	0	0	0	4
90-91—New York Islanders	NHL	66	19	26	45	44	1	2	0	—	—	—	—	—
91-92—New York Islanders	NHL	80	40	38	78	46	-10	21	0	—	—	—	—	—
92-93—New York Islanders	NHL	77	38	38	76	47	-4	21	0	18	3	11	14	14
93-94—New York Islanders	NHL	78	30	40	70	59	18	10	0	4	0	1	1	0
94-95—New York Islanders	NHL	43	10	16	26	41	-5	7	0	—	—	—	—	—
95-96—New York Islanders	NHL	61	12	20	32	23	-10	5	1	—	—	—	—	—
96-97—New York Islanders	NHL	70	23	30	53	20	-6	5	0	—	—	—	—	—
—Hartford	NHL	12	3	3	6	2	0	1	0	—	—	—	—	—
97-98—Toronto	NHL	77	21	25	46	43	-7	4	0	—	—	—	—	—
98-99—Toronto	NHL	81	24	28	52	20	15	8	0	16	1	3	4	4
99-00—Toronto	NHL	3	0	0	0	2	-2	0	0	—	—	—	—	—
—St. Louis	NHL	19	2	7	9	6	0	1	0	—	—	—	—	—
—Grand Rapids	IHL	52	19	30	49	25	...	...	...	17	7	8	15	8
00-01—Grand Rapids	IHL	76	32	51	†83	19	...	...	...	10	5	5	10	4
01-02—Munich	Germany	60	19	26	45	22	...	...	...	9	2	4	6	4
02-03—Grand Rapids	AHL	59	13	28	41	20	...	...	...	—	—	—	—	—
NHL Totals (14 years)		830	261	351	612	417	9	95	1	47	4	17	21	24

KING, JASON   RW   CANUCKS

PERSONAL: Born September 14, 1981, in Corner Brook, Nfld. ... 6-1/195. ... Shoots left.

		REGULAR SEASON								PLAYOFFS				
Season Team	League	Gms.	G	A	Pts.	PIM	+/-	PP	SH	Gms.	G	A	Pts.	PIM
99-00—Halifax	QMJHL	53	3	7	10	8	...	...	...	10	0	0	0	2
00-01—Halifax	QMJHL	72	48	41	89	78	...	...	...	6	3	2	5	16
01-02—Halifax	QMJHL	61	63	36	99	39	...	...	...	13	9	8	17	13
02-03—Manitoba	AHL	67	20	20	40	15	...	...	...	—	—	—	—	—
—Vancouver	NHL	8	0	2	2	0	0	0	0	—	—	—	—	—
NHL Totals (1 year)		8	0	2	2	0	0	0	0					

KIPRUSOFF, MIIKKA   G   SHARKS

PERSONAL: Born October 26, 1976, in Turku, Finland ... 6-2/190. ... Catches left. ... Brother of Marko Kiprusoff, defenseman with Montreal Canadiens (1995-96) and New York Islanders (2001-02).

TRANSACTIONS/CAREER NOTES: Selected by San Jose Sharks in fifth round (fifth Sharks pick, 115th overall) of NHL entry draft (July 8, 1995). ... Signed by Sharks (July 15, 2003).

		REGULAR SEASON								PLAYOFFS						
Season Team	League	Gms.	Min	W	L	T	GA	SO	Avg.	SV%	Gms.	Min.	W	L	GA SO	Avg.	SV%
93-94—TPS Turku	Finland Jr.	35	...	...	...	...	...	...	...	—	6	...	...	...	...	...	—
94-95—TPS Turku	Finland Jr.	31	1880	...	...	...	93	...	2.97	—	—	—	—	—	—	—	—
—TPS Turku	Finland	4	240	...	...	...	12	0	3.00	—	2	120	...	...	7 ...	3.50	—
95-96—TPS Turku	Finland	12	550	...	...	...	38	...	4.15	—	—	—	—	—	—	—	—
—Kiekko	Finland	5	300	...	...	...	7	...	1.40	—	—	—	—	—	—	—	—
96-97—AIK	Sweden	42	2466	...	...	...	104	3	2.53	—	7	420	...	...	23 0	3.29	—
97-98—AIK Solna	Sweden	42	2457	...	...	...	110	...	2.69	—	—	—	—	—	—	—	—
98-99—TPS Turku	Finland	39	2259	*26	6	6	70	4	1.86	—	10	580	*9	1	15 *3	*1.55	—
99-00—Kentucky	AHL	47	2759	23	19	4	114	3	2.48	—	5	239	1	3	13 0	3.26	—
00-01—Kentucky	AHL	36	2038	19	9	6	76	2	2.24	—	—	—	—	—	—	—	—
—San Jose	NHL	5	154	2	1	0	5	0	1.95	.902	3	149	1	1	5 0	2.01	.937
01-02—San Jose	NHL	20	1037	7	6	3	43	2	2.49	.915	1	8	0	0	0 0	...	1.000
—Cleveland	AHL	4	242	4	0	0	7	0	1.74	—	—	—	—	—	—	—	—
02-03—San Jose	NHL	22	1199	5	14	0	65	1	3.25	.879	—	—	—	—	—	—	—
NHL Totals (3 years)		47	2390	14	21	3	113	3	2.84	.897	4	157	1	1	5 0	1.91	.938

KJELLBERG, PATRIC   RW

PERSONAL: Born June 17, 1969, in Trelleborg, Sweden ... 6-3/218. ... Shoots left.
TRANSACTIONS/CAREER NOTES: Selected by Montreal Canadiens in fourth round (fourth Canadiens pick, 83rd overall) of NHL entry draft (June 11, 1988). ... Signed as free agent by Nashville Predators (June 26, 1998). ... Bruised hip (March 28, 1999); missed final nine games of season. ... Suffered back spasms (January 17, 2001); missed one game. ... Traded by Predators to Anaheim Mighty Ducks for RW Petr Tenkrat (November 1, 2001). ... Suffered sore neck (March 17, 2002); missed five games.

		REGULAR SEASON								PLAYOFFS				
Season Team	League	Gms.	G	A	Pts.	PIM	+/-	PP	SH	Gms.	G	A	Pts.	PIM
86-87—Falun	Sweden	27	11	13	24	14	...	...	...	—	—	—	—	—
87-88—Falun	Sweden	29	15	10	25	18	...	...	...	—	—	—	—	—
88-89—AIK Solna	Sweden	25	7	9	16	8	...	...	...	—	—	—	—	—
89-90—AIK Solna	Sweden	33	8	16	24	6	...	...	...	3	1	0	1	0
90-91—AIK Solna	Sweden	38	4	11	15	18	...	...	...	—	—	—	—	—
91-92—AIK Solna	Sweden	40	20	13	33	16	...	...	...	—	—	—	—	—
—Swedish Oly. team	Int'l	8	1	3	4	0	...	...	...	—	—	—	—	—
92-93—Montreal	NHL	7	0	0	0	2	-3	0	0	—	—	—	—	—
—Fredericton	AHL	41	10	27	37	14	...	...	...	5	2	2	4	0
93-94—HV 71 Jonkoping	Sweden	40	11	17	28	18	...	...	...	—	—	—	—	—
—Swedish Oly. team	Int'l	8	0	1	1	2	...	...	...	—	—	—	—	—
94-95—HV 71 Jonkoping	Sweden	29	5	15	20	12	...	...	...	—	—	—	—	—
95-96—Djurgarden Stockholm	Sweden	40	9	7	16	10	...	...	...	4	0	2	2	2
96-97—Djurgarden Stockholm	Sweden	49	29	11	40	18	...	...	...	4	2	3	5	2
97-98—Swedish Oly. team	Int'l	4	1	0	1	0	...	...	...	—	—	—	—	—
—Djurgarden Stockholm	Sweden	46	30	18	48	16	...	...	...	15	7	3	10	12
98-99—Nashville	NHL	71	11	20	31	24	-13	2	0	—	—	—	—	—
99-00—Nashville	NHL	82	23	23	46	14	-11	9	0	—	—	—	—	—
00-01—Nashville	NHL	81	14	31	45	12	-2	5	0	—	—	—	—	—
01-02—Nashville	NHL	12	1	3	4	6	-3	0	0	—	—	—	—	—
—Anaheim	NHL	65	7	8	15	10	-9	4	0	—	—	—	—	—
02-03—Anaheim	NHL	76	8	11	19	16	-9	2	1	10	0	0	0	0
NHL Totals (6 years)		394	64	96	160	84	-50	22	1	10	0	0	0	0

KLATT, TRENT   RW   CANUCKS

PERSONAL: Born January 30, 1971, in Robbinsdale, Minn. ... 6-1/225. ... Shoots right. ... Full Name: Trent Thomas Klatt.
TRANSACTIONS/CAREER NOTES: Selected by Washington Capitals in fourth round (fifth Capitals pick, 82nd overall) of NHL entry draft (June 17, 1989). ... Rights traded by Capitals with LW Steve Maltais to Minnesota North Stars for D Sean Chambers (June 21, 1991). ... Injured finger (January 7, 1993); missed three games. ... North Stars franchise moved from Minnesota to Dallas and renamed Stars for 1993-94 season. ... Strained back (November 7, 1993); missed one game. ... Sprained knee (November 11, 1993); missed two games. ... Sprained knee (February 6, 1994); missed three games. ... Traded by Stars to Philadelphia Flyers for LW Brent Fedyk (December 13, 1995). ... Suffered concussion (March 9, 1997); missed two games. ... Traded by Flyers to Vancouver Canucks for sixth-round pick (traded to Atlanta) in 2000 draft (October 19, 1998). ... Suffered skin rash (February 14, 2001); missed five games. ... Strained muscle in abdomen (November 20, 2001); missed 25 games. ... Strained muscle in abdomen (February 12, 2002); missed remainder of season. ... Re-signed by Canucks (July 7, 2003).
STATISTICAL PLATEAUS: Three-goal games: 1996-97 (1).

		REGULAR SEASON								PLAYOFFS				
Season Team	League	Gms.	G	A	Pts.	PIM	+/-	PP	SH	Gms.	G	A	Pts.	PIM
87-88—Osseo H.S.	Minn. H.S.	22	19	17	36	...	...	...	...	—	—	—	—	—
88-89—Osseo H.S.	Minn. H.S.	22	24	39	63	...	...	...	...	—	—	—	—	—
89-90—Univ. of Minnesota	WCHA	38	22	14	36	16	...	...	...	—	—	—	—	—
90-91—Univ. of Minnesota	WCHA	39	16	28	44	58	...	...	...	—	—	—	—	—
91-92—Univ. of Minnesota	WCHA	44	30	36	66	78	...	...	...	—	—	—	—	—
—Minnesota	NHL	1	0	0	0	0	0	0	0	6	0	0	0	2
92-93—Kalamazoo	IHL	31	8	11	19	18	...	...	...	—	—	—	—	—
—Minnesota	NHL	47	4	19	23	38	2	1	0	—	—	—	—	—
93-94—Dallas	NHL	61	14	24	38	30	13	3	0	9	2	1	3	4
—Kalamazoo	IHL	6	3	2	5	4	...	...	...	—	—	—	—	—
94-95—Dallas	NHL	47	12	10	22	26	-2	5	0	5	1	0	1	0
95-96—Dallas	NHL	22	4	4	8	23	0	0	0	—	—	—	—	—
—Michigan	IHL	2	1	2	3	5	...	...	...	—	—	—	—	—
—Philadelphia	NHL	49	3	8	11	21	2	0	0	12	4	1	5	0
96-97—Philadelphia	NHL	76	24	21	45	20	9	5	5	19	4	3	7	12
97-98—Philadelphia	NHL	82	14	28	42	16	2	5	0	5	0	0	0	0
98-99—Philadelphia	NHL	2	0	0	0	0	0	0	0	—	—	—	—	—
—Vancouver	NHL	73	4	10	14	12	-3	0	0	—	—	—	—	—
99-00—Syracuse	AHL	24	13	10	23	6	...	...	...	—	—	—	—	—
—Vancouver	NHL	47	10	10	20	26	-8	8	0	—	—	—	—	—
00-01—Vancouver	NHL	77	13	20	33	31	8	3	0	4	3	0	3	0
01-02—Vancouver	NHL	34	8	7	15	10	9	2	1	—	—	—	—	—
02-03—Vancouver	NHL	82	16	13	29	8	10	3	0	14	2	4	6	2
NHL Totals (12 years)		700	126	174	300	261	42	35	6	74	16	9	25	20

KLEE, KEN   D

PERSONAL: Born April 24, 1971, in Indianapolis ... 6-0/214. ... Shoots right. ... Full Name: Kenneth William Klee.
TRANSACTIONS/CAREER NOTES: Selected by Washington Capitals in ninth round (11th Capitals pick, 177th overall) of NHL entry draft (June 16, 1990). ... Injured foot (January 27, 1995); missed six games. ... Pulled groin (March 12, 1996); missed 13 games. ... Sprained knee (April 10, 1996); missed two games. ... Fractured facial bone (March 28, 1998); missed eight games. ... Bruised foot (February 12, 2000); missed one game. ... Injured wrist (October 19, 2000); missed six games. ... Strained left knee (December 12, 2000); missed one game. ... Strained back (February 13, 2001); missed six games. ... Suffered concussion (March 7, 2001); missed two games. ... Injured ribs (November 8, 2001); missed three games. ... Injured groin (January 18, 2002); missed four games. ... Injured foot (March 29, 2002); missed five games.

K

Season Team	League	REGULAR SEASON								PLAYOFFS				
		Gms.	G	A	Pts.	PIM	+/-	PP	SH	Gms.	G	A	Pts.	PIM
89-90—Bowling Green	CCHA	39	0	5	5	52	...	...	...	—	—	—	—	—
90-91—Bowling Green	CCHA	37	7	28	35	50	...	...	...	—	—	—	—	—
91-92—Bowling Green	CCHA	10	0	1	1	14	...	...	...	—	—	—	—	—
92-93—Baltimore	AHL	77	4	14	18	68	...	...	...	7	0	1	1	15
93-94—Portland	AHL	65	2	9	11	87	...	...	...	17	1	2	3	14
94-95—Portland	AHL	49	5	7	12	89	...	...	...	—	—	—	—	—
—Washington	NHL	23	3	1	4	41	2	0	0	7	0	0	0	4
95-96—Washington	NHL	66	8	3	11	60	-1	0	1	1	0	0	0	0
96-97—Washington	NHL	80	3	8	11	115	-5	0	0	—	—	—	—	—
97-98—Washington	NHL	51	4	2	6	46	-3	0	0	9	1	0	1	10
98-99—Washington	NHL	78	7	13	20	80	-9	0	0	—	—	—	—	—
99-00—Washington	NHL	80	7	13	20	79	8	0	0	5	0	1	1	10
00-01—Washington	NHL	54	2	4	6	60	-5	0	0	6	0	1	1	8
01-02—Washington	NHL	68	8	8	16	38	4	2	0	—	—	—	—	—
02-03—Washington	NHL	70	1	16	17	89	22	0	0	6	0	0	0	6
NHL Totals (9 years)		570	43	68	111	608	13	2	1	34	1	2	3	38

KLEMM, JON   D   BLACKHAWKS

K

PERSONAL: Born January 8, 1970, in Cranbrook, B.C. ... 6-2/200. ... Shoots right. ... Full Name: Jonathan Darryl Klemm.
TRANSACTIONS/CAREER NOTES: Signed as non-drafted free agent by Quebec Nordiques (May 14, 1991). ... Injured abdomen (March 28, 1995); missed five games. ... Reinjured abdomen (April 8, 1995); missed remainder of season. ... Nordiques franchise moved to Colorado and renamed Avalanche for 1995-96 season (June 21, 1995). ... Injured groin (January 27, 1996); missed one game. ... Sprained left thumb (October 30, 1997) and underwent surgery; missed 11 games. ... Strained groin (December 27, 1997); missed one game. ... Tore patella tendon in knee (November 15, 1998); missed 29 games. ... Suffered from appendicitis (March 25, 1999); missed six games. ... Injured groin (October 20, 1999); missed seven games. ... Suffered back spasms (February 25, 2000); missed one game. ... Injured hamstring (December 5, 2000); missed three games. ... Signed as free agent by Chicago Blackhawks (July 1, 2001).

Season Team	League	REGULAR SEASON								PLAYOFFS				
		Gms.	G	A	Pts.	PIM	+/-	PP	SH	Gms.	G	A	Pts.	PIM
87-88—Seattle......................	WHL	68	6	7	13	24	...	...	...	—	—	—	—	—
88-89—Seattle......................	WHL	2	1	1	2	0	...	...	...	—	—	—	—	—
—Spokane....................	WHL	66	6	34	40	42	...	...	...	—	—	—	—	—
89-90—Spokane....................	WHL	66	3	28	31	100	...	...	...	6	1	1	2	5
90-91—Spokane....................	WHL	72	7	58	65	65	...	...	...	15	3	6	9	8
91-92—Halifax.....................	AHL	70	6	13	19	40	...	...	...	—	—	—	—	—
—Quebec....................	NHL	4	0	1	1	0	2	0	0	—	—	—	—	—
92-93—Halifax.....................	AHL	80	3	20	23	32	...	...	...	—	—	—	—	—
93-94—Cornwall...................	AHL	66	4	26	30	78	...	...	...	13	1	2	3	6
—Quebec....................	NHL	7	0	0	0	4	-1	0	0	—	—	—	—	—
94-95—Cornwall...................	AHL	65	6	13	19	84	...	...	...	—	—	—	—	—
—Quebec....................	NHL	4	1	0	1	2	3	0	0	—	—	—	—	—
95-96—Colorado..................	NHL	56	3	12	15	20	12	0	1	15	2	1	3	0
96-97—Colorado..................	NHL	80	9	15	24	37	12	1	2	17	1	1	2	6
97-98—Colorado..................	NHL	67	6	8	14	30	-3	0	0	4	0	0	0	0
98-99—Colorado..................	NHL	39	1	2	3	31	4	0	0	19	0	1	1	10
99-00—Colorado..................	NHL	73	5	7	12	34	26	0	0	17	2	1	3	9
00-01—Colorado..................	NHL	78	4	11	15	54	22	2	0	22	1	2	3	16
01-02—Chicago....................	NHL	82	4	16	20	42	-3	2	0	5	0	1	1	4
02-03—Chicago....................	NHL	70	2	14	16	44	-9	1	0	—	—	—	—	—
NHL Totals (11 years)		560	35	86	121	298	65	6	3	99	6	7	13	45

KLEPIS, JAKUB   C   SABRES

PERSONAL: Born June 5, 1984, in Prague, Czechoslovakia. ... 6-0/200. ... Shoots right.
TRANSACTIONS/CAREER NOTES: Selected by Ottawa Senators in first round (first Senators pick, 16th pick overall) of NHL entry draft (June 22, 2002). ... Traded by Senators to Buffalo Sabres for RW Vaclav Varada and fifth-round pick in 2003 draft (February 25, 2003).

Season Team	League	REGULAR SEASON								PLAYOFFS				
		Gms.	G	A	Pts.	PIM	+/-	PP	SH	Gms.	G	A	Pts.	PIM
01-02—Portland	WHL	70	14	50	64	111	...	...	...	7	0	3	3	22
02-03—Slavia Praha...............	Czech. Jrs.	38	2	6	8	22	...	...	...	—	—	—	—	—

KLESLA, ROSTISLAV   D   BLUE JACKETS

PERSONAL: Born March 21, 1982, in Novy Jicin, Czechoslovakia ... 6-3/208. ... Shoots left.
TRANSACTIONS/CAREER NOTES: Selected by Columbus Blue Jackets in first round (first Blue Jackets pick, fourth overall) of NHL entry draft (June 24, 2000). ... Strained shoulder (January 24, 2002); missed seven games.

Season Team	League	REGULAR SEASON								PLAYOFFS				
		Gms.	G	A	Pts.	PIM	+/-	PP	SH	Gms.	G	A	Pts.	PIM
97-98—Opava	Czech. Jrs.	40	11	16	27	...	...	...	...	—	—	—	—	—
98-99—Sioux City	USHL	54	4	12	16	100	...	...	...	—	—	—	—	—
99-00—Brampton....................	OHL	67	16	29	45	174	...	...	...	6	1	1	2	21
00-01—Columbus	NHL	8	2	0	2	6	-1	0	0	—	—	—	—	—
—Brampton....................	OHL	45	18	36	54	59	...	...	...	9	2	9	11	26
01-02—Columbus	NHL	75	8	8	16	74	-6	1	0	—	—	—	—	—
02-03—Columbus	NHL	72	2	14	16	71	-22	0	0	—	—	—	—	—
NHL Totals (3 years)		155	12	22	34	151	-29	1	0	—	—	—	—	—

KLOUCEK, TOMAS — D — PREDATORS

PERSONAL: Born March 7, 1980, in Prague, Czechoslovakia ... 6-3/225. ... Shoots left.
TRANSACTIONS/CAREER NOTES: Selected by New York Rangers in fifth round (sixth Rangers pick, 131st overall) of NHL entry draft (June 27, 1998). ... Bruised ankle (February 19, 2001); missed one game. ... Bruised shoulder (March 10, 2001): mised two games. ... Bruised heel (March 25, 2001); missed two games. ... Injured knee (April 1, 2001); missed final three games of season. ... Underwent knee surgery prior to start of 2001-02 season; missed first five games of season. ... Reinjured knee (October 19, 2001); missed one game. ... Suffered back spasms (November 18, 2001); missed two games. ... Traded by Rangers with LW Rem Murray and D Marek Zidlicky to Nashville Predators for G Mike Dunham (December 12, 2002).

Season Team	League	Gms.	G	A	Pts.	PIM	+/-	PP	SH	Gms.	G	A	Pts.	PIM
95-96—Slavia Praha	Czech. Jrs.	40	2	8	10	...	...	...	...	—	—	—	—	—
96-97—Slavia Praha	Czech. Jrs.	43	4	14	18	44	...	...	...	—	—	—	—	—
97-98—Slavia Praha	Czech. Jrs.	43	1	9	10	...	...	...	...	—	—	—	—	—
98-99—Cape Breton	QMJHL	59	4	17	21	162	...	...	...	2	0	0	0	4
99-00—Hartford	AHL	73	2	8	10	113	...	...	...	23	0	4	4	18
00-01—Hartford	AHL	21	0	2	2	44	...	...	...	—	—	—	—	—
—New York Rangers	NHL	43	1	4	5	74	-3	0	0	—	—	—	—	—
01-02—New York Rangers	NHL	52	1	3	4	137	-2	0	0	—	—	—	—	—
—Hartford	AHL	9	0	2	2	27	...	...	...	10	1	1	2	8
02-03—Hartford	AHL	20	3	4	7	102	...	...	...	—	—	—	—	—
—Nashville	NHL	3	0	0	0	2	1	0	0	—	—	—	—	—
—Milwaukee	AHL	34	0	6	6	80	...	...	...	—	—	—	—	—
NHL Totals (3 years)		98	2	7	9	213	-4	0	0					

KNOPP, BEN — LW — BLUE JACKETS

PERSONAL: Born April 8, 1982, in Calgary. ... 6-0/185. ... Shoots right.
TRANSACTIONS/CAREER NOTES: Selected by Columbus Blue Jackets in third round (second Blue Jackets pick, 69th overall) of NHL entry draft (June 24, 2000).

Season Team	League	Gms.	G	A	Pts.	PIM	+/-	PP	SH	Gms.	G	A	Pts.	PIM
98-99—Calgary	Tier II Jr. A	55	37	45	82	161	...	...	...	—	—	—	—	—
99-00—Moose Jaw	WHL	72	30	30	60	101	...	...	...	—	—	—	—	—
00-01—Moose Jaw	WHL	58	22	34	56	105	...	...	...	4	0	0	0	11
01-02—Moose Jaw	WHL	37	18	14	32	56	...	...	...	—	—	—	—	—
—Kamloops	WHL	41	26	25	51	63	...	...	...	4	0	1	1	4
02-03—Syracuse	AHL	12	1	1	2	2	...	...	...	—	—	—	—	—
—Dayton	ECHL	53	7	13	20	83	...	...	...	—	—	—	—	—

KNUBLE, MIKE — LW — BRUINS

PERSONAL: Born July 4, 1972, in Toronto ... 6-3/225. ... Shoots right. ... Full Name: Michael Knuble. ... Name pronounced kuh-NOO-buhl.
TRANSACTIONS/CAREER NOTES: Selected by Detroit Red Wings in fourth round (fourth Red Wings pick, 76th overall) of NHL entry draft (June 22, 1991). ... Traded by Red Wings to New York Rangers for third-round pick (traded back to New York Rangers) in 2000 draft (October 1, 1998). ... Traded by Rangers to Boston Bruins for LW Rob DiMaio (March 10, 2000). ... Fractured vetebra (November 20, 2001); missed nine games. ... Injured back (March 1, 2002); missed four games.

Season Team	League	Gms.	G	A	Pts.	PIM	+/-	PP	SH	Gms.	G	A	Pts.	PIM
88-89—East Kentwood H.S.	Mich. H.S.	28	52	37	89	60	...	...	...	—	—	—	—	—
89-90—East Kentwood H.S.	Mich. H.S.	29	63	40	103	40	...	...	...	—	—	—	—	—
90-91—Kalamazoo	NAJHL	36	18	24	42	30	...	...	...	—	—	—	—	—
91-92—Univ. of Michigan	CCHA	43	7	8	15	48	...	...	...	—	—	—	—	—
92-93—Univ. of Michigan	CCHA	39	26	16	42	57	...	...	...	—	—	—	—	—
93-94—Univ. of Michigan	CCHA	41	32	26	58	71	...	...	...	—	—	—	—	—
94-95—Univ. of Michigan	CCHA	34	38	22	60	62	...	...	...	—	—	—	—	—
95-96—Adirondack	AHL	80	22	23	45	59	...	...	...	3	1	0	1	0
96-97—Adirondack	AHL	68	28	35	63	54	...	...	...	—	—	—	—	—
—Detroit	NHL	9	1	0	1	0	-1	0	0	—	—	—	—	—
97-98—Detroit	NHL	53	7	6	13	16	2	0	0	3	0	1	1	0
98-99—New York Rangers	NHL	82	15	20	35	26	-7	3	0	—	—	—	—	—
99-00—New York Rangers	NHL	59	9	5	14	18	-5	1	0	—	—	—	—	—
—Boston	NHL	14	3	3	6	8	-2	1	0	—	—	—	—	—
00-01—Boston	NHL	82	7	13	20	37	0	0	1	—	—	—	—	—
01-02—Boston	NHL	54	8	6	14	42	9	0	0	2	0	0	0	0
02-03—Boston	NHL	75	30	29	59	45	18	9	0	5	0	2	2	2
NHL Totals (7 years)		428	80	82	162	192	14	14	1	10	0	3	3	2

KNUTSEN, ESPEN — C — BLUE JACKETS

PERSONAL: Born January 12, 1972, in Oslo, Norway ... 5-11/190. ... Shoots left. ... Name pronounced kuh-NOOT-sihn.
TRANSACTIONS/CAREER NOTES: Selected by Hartford Whalers in 10th round (ninth Whalers pick, 204th overall) of NHL entry draft (June 16, 1990). ... Traded by Whalers to Mighty Ducks of Anaheim for RW Kevin Brown (October 1, 1996). ... Traded by Mighty Ducks to Columbus Blue Jackets for fourth-round pick (D Vladimir Korsunov) in 2001 draft (May 25, 2000). ... Fractured finger (September 20, 2000); missed first eight games of season. ... Suffered from the flu (December 10, 2000); missed one game. ... Suffered from the flu (January 15, 2001); missed one game. ... Strained neck (March 26, 2001); missed six games. ... Suffered hip pointer (November 6, 2001); missed three games. ... Suffered from the flu (February 4, 2002); missed one game. ... Bruised knee (March 25, 2002); missed one game.
STATISTICAL PLATEAUS: Three-goal games: 2001-02 (1).

Season Team	League	REGULAR SEASON								PLAYOFFS				
		Gms.	G	A	Pts.	PIM	+/-	PP	SH	Gms.	G	A	Pts.	PIM
88-89—Valerengen Jr.	Norway	36	14	7	21	18	...	...	...	—	—	—	—	—
89-90—Valerengen	Norway	34	22	26	48	...	...	...	...	—	—	—	—	—
90-91—Valerengen	Norway	31	30	24	54	42	...	...	...	5	3	4	7	...
91-92—Valerengen	Norway	30	28	26	54	37	...	...	...	8	7	8	15	15
92-93—Valerengen	Norway	13	11	13	24	4	...	...	...	—	—	—	—	—
93-94—Valerengen	Norway	38	32	26	58	20	...	...	...	—	—	—	—	—
94-95—Djurgarden Stockholm	Sweden	30	6	14	20	18	...	...	...	3	0	1	1	0
95-96—Djurgarden Stockholm	Sweden	32	10	23	33	50	...	...	...	4	1	0	1	2
96-97—Djurgarden Stockholm	Sweden	39	16	33	49	20	...	...	...	4	2	4	6	6
97-98—Anaheim	NHL	19	3	0	3	6	-10	1	0	—	—	—	—	—
—Cincinnati	AHL	41	4	13	17	18	...	...	...	—	—	—	—	—
98-99—Djurgarden Stockholm	Sweden	39	18	24	42	32	...	...	...	4	0	1	1	2
99-00—Djurgarden Stockholm	Sweden	48	18	35	53	65	...	...	...	13	5	*16	*21	2
00-01—Columbus	NHL	66	11	42	53	30	-3	2	0	—	—	—	—	—
01-02—Columbus	NHL	77	11	31	42	47	-28	5	2	—	—	—	—	—
02-03—Columbus	NHL	31	5	4	9	20	-15	3	0	—	—	—	—	—
NHL Totals (4 years)		193	30	77	107	103	-56	11	2					

KNYAZEV, IGOR — D — COYOTES

PERSONAL: Born January 27, 1983, in Elektrosal, U.S.S.R. ... 6-0/183. ... Shoots left.
TRANSACTIONS/CAREER NOTES: Selected by Carolina Hurricanes in first round (first Hurricanes pick, 15th overall) of NHL entry draft (June 23, 2001). ... Traded by Hurricanes to Phoenix Coyotes with Danny Terube for D Danny Markov and fourth-round draft pick in 2004 (June 22, 2003).

Season Team	League	REGULAR SEASON								PLAYOFFS				
		Gms.	G	A	Pts.	PIM	+/-	PP	SH	Gms.	G	A	Pts.	PIM
00-01—Spartak	Russian Div. 1	43	6	3	9	66	...	...	...	—	—	—	—	—
01-02—Spartak Moscow	Russian	3	0	0	0	8	...	...	...	—	—	—	—	—
—Ak Bars Kazan	Russian	14	0	1	1	4	...	...	...	3	0	0	0	0
02-03—Lowell	AHL	68	2	5	7	68	...	...	...	—	—	—	—	—

KOBASEW, CHUCK — RW — FLAMES

PERSONAL: Born April 17, 1982, in Osoyoos, B.C. ... 6-1/190. ... Shoots right.
TRANSACTIONS/CAREER NOTES: Selected by Calgary Flames in first round (first Flames pick, 14th overall) of NHL entry draft (June 23, 2001).

Season Team	League	REGULAR SEASON								PLAYOFFS				
		Gms.	G	A	Pts.	PIM	+/-	PP	SH	Gms.	G	A	Pts.	PIM
98-99—Penticton	BCHL	30	11	17	28	18	...	...	...	—	—	—	—	—
99-00—Penticton	BCHL	58	54	52	106	...	...	...	...	—	—	—	—	—
00-01—Boston College	Hockey East	43	27	22	49	38	...	...	...	—	—	—	—	—
01-02—Kelowna	WHL	55	41	21	62	114	...	...	...	15	10	5	15	22
02-03—Saint John	AHL	48	21	12	33	61	...	...	...	—	—	—	—	—
—Calgary	NHL	23	4	2	6	8	-3	1	0	—	—	—	—	—
NHL Totals (1 year)		23	4	2	6	8	-3	1	0					

KOCHAN, DIETER — G

PERSONAL: Born November 5, 1974, in Saskatoon, Sask. ... 6-1/180. ... Catches left.
TRANSACTIONS/CAREER NOTES: Selected by Vancouver Canucks in fourth round (third Canucks pick, 98th overall) of NHL entry draft (June 26, 1993). ... Signed as free agent by Tampa Bay Lightning (March 27, 2000). ... Signed as free agent by Minnesota Wild (August 5, 2002).

Season Team	League	REGULAR SEASON									PLAYOFFS							
		Gms.	Min	W	L	T	GA	SO	Avg.	SV%	Gms.	Min.	W	L	GA	SO	Avg.	SV%
91-92—Sioux City	USHL	23	1131	7	10	0	100	...	5.31	—	—	—	—	—	—	—	—	—
92-93—Kelowna	BCJHL	44	2582	34	8	0	137	1	*3.18	—	—	—	—	—	—	—	—	—
93-94—N. Michigan U.	WCHA	16	984	9	7	0	57	2	3.48	—	—	—	—	—	—	—	—	—
94-95—N. Michigan U.	WCHA	29	1512	8	17	3	107	0	4.25	—	—	—	—	—	—	—	—	—
95-96—N. Michigan U.	WCHA	31	1627	7	21	2	123	0	4.54	—	—	—	—	—	—	—	—	—
96-97—N. Michigan U.	WCHA	26	1528	8	15	2	99	0	3.89	—	—	—	—	—	—	—	—	—
97-98—Louisville Riverfrogs	ECHL	18	980	7	9	2	61	1	3.73	—	—	—	—	—	—	—	—	—
98-99—Binghamton	UHL	40	2321	18	16	5	115	2	2.97	4	207	1	2	9	0	2.61	—
99-00—Binghamton	UHL	43	2544	29	11	3	110	4	2.59	—	—	—	—	—	—	—	—
—Orlando	IHL	4	240	4	0	0	4	1	1.00	—	—	—	—	—	—	—	—
—Grand Rapids	IHL	2	93	1	0	1	1	0	.65	—	—	—	—	—	—	—	—
—Springfield	AHL	2	120	1	1	0	5	1	2.50	—	—	—	—	—	—	—	—
—Tampa Bay	NHL	5	238	1	4	0	17	0	4.29	.847	—	—	—	—	—	—	—
00-01—Detroit	IHL	49	2606	13	*28	3	*154	0	3.55	—	—	—	—	—	—	—	—
—Tampa Bay	NHL	10	314	0	3	0	18	0	3.44	.870	—	—	—	—	—	—	—
01-02—Springfield	AHL	45	2518	21	20	1	112	2	2.67	—	—	—	—	—	—	—	—
—Tampa Bay	NHL	5	237	0	3	1	16	0	4.05	.876	—	—	—	—	—	—	—
02-03—Houston	AHL	25	1446	15	6	3	61	1	2.53	—	—	—	—	—	—	—	—
—Minnesota	NHL	1	60	0	1	0	5	0	5.00	.821	—	—	—	—	—	—	—
NHL Totals (4 years)		21	849	1	11	1	56	0	3.96	.862								

K

KOCI, DAVID   D   PENGUINS

PERSONAL: Born May 12, 1981, in Prague, Czechoslovakia. ... 6-6/216. ... Shoots left.
TRANSACTIONS/CAREER NOTES: Selected by Pittsburgh Penguins in fifth round (fifth Penguins pick, 146th overall) of NHL entry draft (June 24, 2000).

		REGULAR SEASON								PLAYOFFS				
Season Team	League	Gms.	G	A	Pts.	PIM	+/-	PP	SH	Gms.	G	A	Pts.	PIM
99-00—Sparta Praha..............	Czech. Jrs.	47	0	7	7	124	...	...	...	—	—	—	—	—
00-01—Prince George............	WHL	70	2	7	9	155	...	...	...	6	0	0	0	20
01-02—Wilkes-Barre/Scranton	AHL	26	1	3	4	98	...	...	...	—	—	—	—	—
—Wheeling...................	ECHL	33	2	4	6	105	...	...	...	—	—	—	—	—
02-03—Wilkes-Barre/Scranton	AHL	9	0	0	0	4	...	...	...	—	—	—	—	—
—Wheeling...................	ECHL	48	0	1	1	103	...	...	...	—	—	—	—	—

KOEHLER, GREG   C

PERSONAL: Born February 27, 1975, in Scarborough, Ont. ... 6-2/195. ... Shoots left.
TRANSACTIONS/CAREER NOTES: Signed as non-drafted free agent by Carolina Hurricanes (March 31, 1998). ... Traded by Hurricanes to Philadelphia Flyers for LW Jesse Boulerice (February 13, 2002). ... Signed as free agent by Nashville Predators (July 15, 2002). ... Traded by Predators to Los Angeles Kings for future considerations (February 4, 2003).

		REGULAR SEASON								PLAYOFFS				
Season Team	League	Gms.	G	A	Pts.	PIM	+/-	PP	SH	Gms.	G	A	Pts.	PIM
96-97—Mass.-Lowell	Hockey East	37	16	20	36	49	...	...	...	—	—	—	—	—
97-98—Mass.-Lowell	Hockey East	33	20	17	37	62	...	...	...	—	—	—	—	—
—New Haven	AHL	3	0	0	0	2	...	...	...	—	—	—	—	—
98-99—Florida...................	ECHL	29	13	14	27	62	...	...	...	6	2	3	5	12
—New Haven	AHL	26	4	0	4	29	...	...	...	—	—	—	—	—
99-00—Cincinnati..................	IHL	74	12	13	25	157	...	...	...	8	0	3	3	14
00-01—Cincinnati..................	IHL	80	35	36	71	122	...	...	...	5	2	2	4	6
—Carolina	NHL	1	0	0	0	0	0	0	0	—	—	—	—	—
01-02—Lowell	AHL	56	18	18	36	58	...	...	...	—	—	—	—	—
—Philadelphia	AHL	22	8	4	12	34	...	...	...	5	1	2	3	6
02-03—Milwaukee	AHL	43	16	10	26	51	...	...	...	—	—	—	—	—
—Manchester.................	AHL	13	1	13	14	26	...	...	...	—	—	—	—	—
NHL Totals (1 year)............		**1**	**0**	**0**	**0**	**0**	**0**	**0**	**0**					

KOHN, LADISLAV   RW

PERSONAL: Born March 4, 1975, in Uherske Hradiste, Czechoslovakia ... 5-11/194. ... Shoots left. ... Name pronounced KOHN.
TRANSACTIONS/CAREER NOTES: Selected by Calgary Flames in seventh round (ninth Flames pick, 175th overall) in NHL entry draft (June 29, 1994). ... Suffered concussion (November 26, 1997); missed 12 games. ... Traded by Flames to Toronto Maple Leafs for D David Cooper (July 2, 1998). ... Claimed by Atlanta Thrashers from Maple Leafs in NHL waiver draft (September 27, 1999). ... Traded by Thrashers to Mighty Ducks of Anaheim for eighth-round pick (D Evan Nielsen) in 2000 draft (September 27, 1999). ... Strained groin (November 26, 1999); missed five games. ... Traded by Mighty Ducks to Thrashers for D Sergei Vyshedkevich and G Scott Langkow (February 9, 2001). ... Signed as free agent by Detroit Red Wings (October 10, 2001). ... Traded by Red Wings to Calgary Flames for future considerations (September 11, 2002).

		REGULAR SEASON								PLAYOFFS				
Season Team	League	Gms.	G	A	Pts.	PIM	+/-	PP	SH	Gms.	G	A	Pts.	PIM
93-94—Brandon	WHL	2	0	0	0	0	...	...	...	—	—	—	—	—
—Swift Current	WHL	69	33	35	68	68	...	...	...	7	5	4	9	8
94-95—Swift Current	WHL	65	32	60	92	122	...	...	...	6	2	6	8	14
—Saint John	AHL	1	0	0	0	0	...	...	...	—	—	—	—	—
95-96—Saint John	AHL	73	28	45	73	97	...	...	...	16	6	5	11	12
—Calgary	NHL	5	1	0	1	2	-1	0	0	—	—	—	—	—
96-97—Saint John	AHL	76	28	29	57	81	...	...	...	5	0	0	0	0
97-98—Saint John	AHL	65	25	31	56	90	...	...	...	21	*14	6	20	20
—Calgary	NHL	4	0	1	1	0	2	0	0	—	—	—	—	—
98-99—St. John's...................	AHL	61	27	42	69	90	...	...	...	—	—	—	—	—
—Toronto	NHL	16	1	3	4	4	1	0	0	2	0	0	0	5
99-00—Anaheim	NHL	77	5	16	21	27	-17	1	0	—	—	—	—	—
00-01—Anaheim	NHL	51	4	3	7	42	-15	0	1	—	—	—	—	—
—Atlanta	NHL	26	3	4	7	44	-12	0	1	—	—	—	—	—
01-02—Cincinnati	AHL	4	0	0	0	9	...	...	...	—	—	—	—	—
—Blues Espoo...............	Finland	40	22	13	35	103	...	...	...	3	0	0	0	14
—Detroit.......................	NHL	4	0	0	0	4	0	0	0	—	—	—	—	—
02-03—Saint John	AHL	35	8	19	27	30	...	...	...	—	—	—	—	—
—Calgary	NHL	3	0	1	1	2	1	0	0	—	—	—	—	—
—Philadelphia	AHL	15	4	7	11	2	...	...	...	—	—	—	—	—
NHL Totals (7 years)...........		**186**	**14**	**28**	**42**	**125**	**-41**	**1**	**2**	**2**	**0**	**0**	**0**	**5**

KOIVISTO, TOMAS   D   BLUES

PERSONAL: Born June 4, 1974, in Turku, Finland ... 5-10/195. ... Shoots right. ... Full Name: Tom Koivisto.
TRANSACTIONS/CAREER NOTES: Signed by St. Louis Blues (July 17, 2003).

		REGULAR SEASON								PLAYOFFS				
Season Team	League	Gms.	G	A	Pts.	PIM	+/-	PP	SH	Gms.	G	A	Pts.	PIM
01-02—Jokerit Helsinki	Finland	43	8	14	22	30	...	...	...	12	3	8	11	2
02-03—Worcester	AHL	47	4	13	17	32	...	...	...	—	—	—	—	—
—St. Louis	NHL	22	2	4	6	10	1	0	0	—	—	—	—	—
NHL Totals (1 year).............		**22**	**2**	**4**	**6**	**10**	**1**	**0**	**0**					

KOIVU, MIKKO   C   WILD

PERSONAL: Born March 12, 1983, in Turku, Finland. ... 6-2/183. ... Shoots left. ... Brother of Saku Koivu, center, Montreal Canadiens.
TRANSACTIONS/CAREER NOTES: Selected by Minnesota Wild in first round (first Wild pick, sixth overall) of NHL entry draft (June 23, 2001). ... Re-signed by Wild (July 17, 2003).

| Season Team | League | REGULAR SEASON | | | | | | | | PLAYOFFS | | | | |
		Gms.	G	A	Pts.	PIM	+/-	PP	SH	Gms.	G	A	Pts.	PIM
99-00—TPS Turku	Finland Jr.	30	4	8	12	22	...	...	...	—	—	—	—	—
00-01—TPS Turku	Finland Jr.	30	11	38	49	34	...	...	...	—	—	—	—	—
—TPS Turku	Finland	21	0	1	1	2	...	...	...	—	—	—	—	—
01-02—TPS Turku	Finland	48	4	3	7	34	...	...	...	8	0	3	3	4
02-03—TPS Turku	Finland	37	7	13	20	20	...	...	...	—	—	—	—	—

KOIVU, SAKU   C   CANADIENS

PERSONAL: Born November 23, 1974, in Turku, Finland ... 5-10/181. ... Shoots left. ... Brother of Mikko Koivu, center, Minnesota Wild organization. ... Name pronounced SAK-oo KOY-voo.
TRANSACTIONS/CAREER NOTES: Selected by Montreal Canadiens in first round (first Canadiens pick, 21st overall) of NHL entry draft (June 26, 1993). ... Tore knee ligament (December 7, 1996); missed 26 games. ... Sprained shoulder (March 10, 1997); missed five games. ... Suffered from tonsillitis (March 29, 1997); missed one game. ... Strained ribcage (January 8, 1998); missed seven games. ... Fractured hand (April 7, 1998); missed six games. ... Strained abdominal muscle (October 24, 1998); missed 12 games. ... Suffered from elbow infection (January 18, 1999); missed three games. ... Injured knee (March 24, 1999); missed two games. ... Suffered injury (October 30, 1999); missed five games. ... Separated shoulder (November 2, 1999); missed 40 games. ... Tore medial collateral ligament in knee (March 11, 2000); missed remainder of season. ... Tore medial collateral ligament in left knee (October 11, 2000) and underwent surgery; missed 28 games. ... Diagnosed with non-Hodgkin's intra-abdominal lymphoma prior to start of 2001-02 season; missed first 79 games of season.
STATISTICAL PLATEAUS: Three-goal games: 2002-03 (1).

| Season Team | League | REGULAR SEASON | | | | | | | | PLAYOFFS | | | | |
		Gms.	G	A	Pts.	PIM	+/-	PP	SH	Gms.	G	A	Pts.	PIM
90-91—TPS Turku	Finland Jr.	24	20	28	48	26	...	...	...	—	—	—	—	—
91-92—TPS Turku	Finland Jr.	42	30	37	67	63	...	...	...	—	—	—	—	—
92-93—TPS Turku	Finland	46	3	7	10	28	...	...	...	—	—	—	—	—
93-94—TPS Turku	Finland	47	23	30	53	42	...	...	...	11	4	8	12	16
—Fin. Olympic team	Int'l	8	4	3	7	12	...	...	...	—	—	—	—	—
94-95—TPS Turku	Finland	45	27	47	74	73	...	...	...	13	7	10	17	16
95-96—Montreal	NHL	82	20	25	45	40	-7	8	3	6	3	1	4	8
96-97—Montreal	NHL	50	17	39	56	38	7	5	0	5	1	3	4	10
97-98—Montreal	NHL	69	14	43	57	48	8	2	2	6	2	3	5	2
—Fin. Olympic team	Int'l	6	2	8	10	4	...	...	...	—	—	—	—	—
98-99—Montreal	NHL	65	14	30	44	38	-7	4	2	—	—	—	—	—
99-00—Montreal	NHL	24	3	18	21	14	7	1	0	—	—	—	—	—
00-01—Montreal	NHL	54	17	30	47	40	2	7	0	—	—	—	—	—
01-02—Montreal	NHL	3	0	2	2	0	0	0	0	12	4	6	10	4
02-03—Montreal	NHL	82	21	50	71	72	5	5	1	—	—	—	—	—
NHL Totals (8 years)		429	106	237	343	290	15	32	8	29	10	13	23	24

KOLANOS, KRYSTOFER   C   COYOTES

PERSONAL: Born July 27, 1981, in Calgary ... 6-3/203. ... Shoots right.
TRANSACTIONS/CAREER NOTES: Selected by Phoenix Coyotes in first round (first Coyotes pick, 19th overall) of NHL entry draft (June 24, 2000). ... Suffered concussion (January 19, 2002); missed 22 games.

| Season Team | League | REGULAR SEASON | | | | | | | | PLAYOFFS | | | | |
		Gms.	G	A	Pts.	PIM	+/-	PP	SH	Gms.	G	A	Pts.	PIM
98-99—Calgary Royals	AJHL	58	43	67	110	98	...	...	...	—	—	—	—	—
99-00—Boston College	Hockey East	34	14	13	27	44	...	...	...	—	—	—	—	—
00-01—Boston College	Hockey East	41	25	25	50	54	...	...	...	—	—	—	—	—
01-02—Phoenix	NHL	57	11	11	22	48	6	0	0	2	0	0	0	6
02-03—Phoenix	NHL	2	0	0	0	0	0	0	0	—	—	—	—	—
NHL Totals (2 years)		59	11	11	22	48	6	0	0	2	0	0	0	6

KOLNIK, JURAJ   RW   PANTHERS

PERSONAL: Born November 13, 1980, in Nitra, Czechoslovakia ... 5-11/190. ... Shoots right.
TRANSACTIONS/CAREER NOTES: Selected by New York Islanders in fourth round (seventh Islanders pick, 101st overall) of NHL entry draft (June 26, 1999). ... Traded by Islanders with ninth-round pick in 2003 draft to Florida Panthers for D Sven Butenschon (October 11, 2002).

| Season Team | League | REGULAR SEASON | | | | | | | | PLAYOFFS | | | | |
		Gms.	G	A	Pts.	PIM	+/-	PP	SH	Gms.	G	A	Pts.	PIM
97-98—Plastika Nitra	Slovakia	28	1	3	4	6	...	...	...	—	—	—	—	—
98-99—Quebec	QMJHL	12	6	5	11	6	...	...	...	—	—	—	—	—
—Rimouski	QMJHL	50	36	37	73	34	...	...	...	11	9	6	15	6
99-00—Rimouski	QMJHL	47	53	53	106	53	...	...	...	14	10	17	27	16
00-01—Lowell	AHL	25	2	6	8	18	...	...	...	—	—	—	—	—
—Springfield	AHL	29	15	20	35	20	...	...	...	—	—	—	—	—
—New York Islanders	NHL	29	4	3	7	12	-8	0	0	—	—	—	—	—
01-02—Bridgeport	AHL	67	18	30	48	40	...	...	...	20	7	14	21	17
—New York Islanders	NHL	7	2	0	2	0	-2	1	0	—	—	—	—	—
02-03—San Antonio	AHL	65	25	15	40	36	...	...	...	—	—	—	—	—
—Florida	NHL	10	0	1	1	0	1	0	0	—	—	—	—	—
NHL Totals (3 years)		46	6	4	10	12	-9	1	0					

K

KOLTSOV, KIRILL — D — CANUCKS

PERSONAL: Born February 1, 1983, in Chelyabinsk, U.S.S.R. ... 5-11/183. ... Shoots left.
TRANSACTIONS/CAREER NOTES: Selected by Vancouver Canucks in second round (first Canucks pick, 49th overall) of NHL entry draft (June 22, 2002).

Season Team	League	REGULAR SEASON								PLAYOFFS				
		Gms.	G	A	Pts.	PIM	+/-	PP	SH	Gms.	G	A	Pts.	PIM
00-01—Avangard Omsk	Russian	39	0	1	1	20	...	...	...	16	1	3	4	12
01-02—Avangard Omsk	Russian	41	1	5	6	34	...	...	...	11	1	0	1	18
02-03—Avangard Omsk	Russian	45	4	8	12	54	...	...	...	—	—	—	—	—

KOLTSOV, KONSTANTIN — LW — PENGUINS

PERSONAL: Born April 17, 1981, in Minsk, U.S.S.R. ... 6-0/190. ... Shoots left.
TRANSACTIONS/CAREER NOTES: Selected by Pittsburgh Penguins in first round (first Penguins pick, 18th overall) of NHL entry draft (June 26, 1999).

Season Team	League	REGULAR SEASON								PLAYOFFS				
		Gms.	G	A	Pts.	PIM	+/-	PP	SH	Gms.	G	A	Pts.	PIM
97-98—Minsk	Russian Div. 1	52	15	18	33	60	...	...	...	—	—	—	—	—
—Severstal Cherepovets	Russian	2	0	0	0	2	...	...	...	—	—	—	—	—
—Severstal-2 Cherepov..	Rus. Div. III	44	11	12	23	16	...	...	...	—	—	—	—	—
98-99—Severstal Cherepovets	Russian	33	3	0	3	8	...	...	...	1	0	0	0	2
99-00—Metallurg Nov.	Russian	30	3	4	7	28	...	...	...	14	1	1	2	8
00-01—Ak Bars Kazan	Russian	24	7	8	15	10	...	...	...	2	0	0	0	4
01-02—Ak Bars Kazan	Russian	10	1	2	3	2	...	...	...	—	—	—	—	—
—Spartak Moscow	Russian	23	1	0	1	12	...	...	...	—	—	—	—	—
—Belarus Oly. team	Int'l	2	0	0	0	0	...	...	...	—	—	—	—	—
02-03—Wilkes-Barre/Scranton	AHL	65	9	21	30	41	...	...	...	6	2	4	6	4
—Pittsburgh	NHL	2	0	0	0	0	-2	0	0	—	—	—	—	—
NHL Totals (1 year)		2	0	0	0	0	-2	0	0					

KOLZIG, OLAF — G — CAPITALS

PERSONAL: Born April 9, 1970, in Johannesburg, South Africa ... 6-3/225. ... Catches left. ... Name pronounced OH-lahf KOHL-zihg.
TRANSACTIONS/CAREER NOTES: Selected by Washington Capitals in first round (first Capitals pick, 19th overall) of NHL entry draft (June 17, 1989). ... Dislocated kneecap (October 13, 1993); missed 14 games. ... Suffered from mononucleosis (October 8, 1996); missed three games. ... Underwent knee surgery (September 26, 2000); missed first two games of regular season. ... Sprained ankle (December 14, 2001); missed one game. ... Injured knee (February 8, 2002); missed two games.

Season Team	League	REGULAR SEASON									PLAYOFFS							
		Gms.	Min	W	L	T	GA	SO	Avg.	SV%	Gms.	Min.	W	L	GA	SO	Avg.	SV%
87-88—New Westminster	WHL	15	650	6	5	0	48	1	4.43	—	3	149	0	0	11	0	4.43	—
88-89—Tri-City	WHL	30	1671	16	10	2	97	1	*3.48	—	—	—	—	—	—	—	—	—
89-90—Washington	NHL	2	120	0	2	0	12	0	6.00	.810	—	—	—	—	—	—	—	—
—Tri-City	WHL	48	2504	27	27	3	187	1	4.48	—	6	318	4	0	27	0	5.09	—
90-91—Baltimore	AHL	26	1367	10	12	1	72	0	3.16	—	—	—	—	—	—	—	—	—
—Hampton Roads	ECHL	21	1248	11	9	‡1	71	2	3.41	—	3	180	1	2	14	0	4.67	—
91-92—Baltimore	AHL	28	1503	5	17	2	105	1	4.19	—	—	—	—	—	—	—	—	—
—Hampton Roads	ECHL	14	847	11	3	0	41	0	2.90	—	—	—	—	—	—	—	—	—
92-93—Rochester	AHL	49	2737	25	16	4	168	0	3.68	—	17	*1040	9	*8	61	0	3.52	—
—Washington	NHL	1	20	0	0	0	2	0	6.00	.714	—	—	—	—	—	—	—	—
93-94—Portland	AHL	29	1726	16	8	5	88	3	3.06	—	17	1035	†12	5	44	0	*2.55	—
—Washington	NHL	7	224	0	3	0	20	0	5.36	.844	—	—	—	—	—	—	—	—
94-95—Washington	NHL	14	724	2	8	2	30	0	2.49	.902	2	44	1	0	1	0	1.36	.952
—Portland	AHL	2	125	1	0	1	3	0	1.44	—	—	—	—	—	—	—	—	—
95-96—Washington	NHL	18	897	4	8	2	46	0	3.08	.887	5	341	2	3	11	0	1.94	.934
—Portland	AHL	5	300	5	0	0	7	1	1.40	—	—	—	—	—	—	—	—	—
96-97—Washington	NHL	29	1645	8	15	4	71	2	2.59	.906	—	—	—	—	—	—	—	—
97-98—Washington	NHL	64	3788	33	18	10	139	5	2.20	.920	21	1351	12	9	44	*4	1.95	.941
—German Oly. team	Int'l	2	120	2	0	0	2	1	1.00	—	—	—	—	—	—	—	—	—
98-99—Washington	NHL	64	3586	26	†31	3	154	4	2.58	.900	—	—	—	—	—	—	—	—
99-00—Washington	NHL	73	*4371	41	20	11	163	5	2.24	.917	5	284	1	4	16	0	3.38	.845
00-01—Washington	NHL	72	4279	37	26	8	177	5	2.48	.909	6	375	2	4	14	1	2.24	.908
01-02—Washington	NHL	71	4131	31	29	8	*192	6	2.79	.903	—	—	—	—	—	—	—	—
02-03—Washington	NHL	66	3894	33	25	6	156	4	2.40	.919	6	404	2	4	14	1	2.08	.927
NHL Totals (12 years)		481	27679	215	185	54	1162	31	2.52	.909	45	2799	20	24	100	6	2.14	.927

KOMADOSKI, NEIL — D — SENATORS

PERSONAL: Born February 10, 1982, in St. Louis. ... 6-1/212. ... Shoots left. ... Full Name: Neil Komadoski Jr. ... Son of Neil Komadoski Sr., defenseman with Los Angeles Kings (1972-73 through 1977-78) and St. Louis Blues (1977-78 through 1979-80).
TRANSACTIONS/CAREER NOTES: Selected by Ottawa Senators in third round (third Senators pick, 81st overall) of NHL entry draft (June 23, 2001).

Season Team	League	REGULAR SEASON								PLAYOFFS				
		Gms.	G	A	Pts.	PIM	+/-	PP	SH	Gms.	G	A	Pts.	PIM
00-01—Univ. of Notre Dame	CCHA	30	2	5	7	106	...	...	...	—	—	—	—	—
01-02—Univ. of Notre Dame	CCHA	37	2	9	11	100	...	...	...	—	—	—	—	—
02-03—Univ. of Notre Dame	CCHA	40	1	23	24	46	...	...	...	—	—	—	—	—

K

KOMARNISKI, ZENITH D CANUCKS

PERSONAL: Born August 13, 1978, in Vegreville, Alta. ... 6-0/200. ... Shoots left. ... Name pronounced ZEH-nihth koh-mahr-NIH-skee.
TRANSACTIONS/CAREER NOTES: Selected by Vancouver Canucks in third round (second Canucks pick, 75th overall) of NHL entry draft (June 22, 1996). ... Injured shoulder (November 26, 1999); missed four games.

		REGULAR SEASON								PLAYOFFS				
Season Team	League	Gms.	G	A	Pts.	PIM	+/-	PP	SH	Gms.	G	A	Pts.	PIM
94-95—Tri-City	WHL	66	5	19	24	110	...	...	...	17	1	2	3	47
95-96—Tri-City	WHL	42	5	21	26	85	...	...	...	—	—	—	—	—
96-97—Tri-City	WHL	58	12	44	56	112	...	...	...	—	—	—	—	—
97-98—Tri-City	WHL	3	0	4	4	18	...	...	...	—	—	—	—	—
—Spokane	WHL	43	7	20	27	90	...	...	...	18	4	6	10	49
98-99—Syracuse	AHL	58	9	19	28	89	...	...	...	—	—	—	—	—
99-00—Syracuse	AHL	42	4	12	16	130	...	...	...	4	2	0	2	6
—Vancouver	NHL	18	1	1	2	8	-1	0	0	—	—	—	—	—
00-01—Kansas City	IHL	70	7	22	29	191	...	...	...	—	—	—	—	—
01-02—Manitoba	AHL	77	5	20	25	153	...	...	...	7	0	2	2	13
02-03—Manitoba	AHL	53	15	8	23	94	...	...	...	—	—	—	—	—
—Vancouver	NHL	1	0	0	0	2	0	0	0	—	—	—	—	—
NHL Totals (2 years)		19	1	1	2	10	-1	0	0					

KOMISAREK, MIKE D CANADIENS

PERSONAL: Born January 19, 1982, in West Islip, N.Y. ... 6-4/240. ... Shoots right.
TRANSACTIONS/CAREER NOTES: Selected by Montreal Canadiens in first round (first Canadiens pick, seventh overall) of NHL entry draft (June 23, 2001).

		REGULAR SEASON								PLAYOFFS				
Season Team	League	Gms.	G	A	Pts.	PIM	+/-	PP	SH	Gms.	G	A	Pts.	PIM
99-00—U.S. National	USHL	51	5	8	13	124	...	...	...	—	—	—	—	—
00-01—Univ. of Michigan	CCHA	41	4	12	16	77	...	...	...	—	—	—	—	—
01-02—Univ. of Michigan	CCHA	39	11	19	30	68	...	...	...	—	—	—	—	—
02-03—Hamilton	AHL	56	5	25	30	79	...	...	...	—	—	—	—	—
—Montreal	NHL	21	0	1	1	28	-6	0	0	—	—	—	—	—
NHL Totals (1 year)		21	0	1	1	28	-6	0	0					

KONOWALCHUK, STEVE LW CAPITALS

PERSONAL: Born November 11, 1972, in Salt Lake City, Utah ... 6-2/204. ... Shoots left. ... Full Name: Steven Reed Konowalchuk. ... Name pronounced kah-nah-WAHL-chuhk.
TRANSACTIONS/CAREER NOTES: Selected by Washington Capitals in third round (fifth Capitals pick, 58th overall) of NHL entry draft (June 22, 1991). ... Separated shoulder (October 13, 1995); missed four games. ... Injured left hand (March 26, 1996); missed eight games. ... Separated rib cartilage prior to 1996-97 season; missed four games. ... Strained groin (January 28, 1998); missed two games. ... Sprained ankle (October 10, 1998); missed 15 games. ... Suffered concussion (March 2, 1999); missed remainder of season. ... Injured shoulder (October 13, 2001) and underwent surgery; missed 54 games.
STATISTICAL PLATEAUS: Three-goal games: 1995-96 (2), 2000-01 (1). Total: 3.

		REGULAR SEASON								PLAYOFFS				
Season Team	League	Gms.	G	A	Pts.	PIM	+/-	PP	SH	Gms.	G	A	Pts.	PIM
90-91—Portland	WHL	72	43	49	92	78	...	...	...	—	—	—	—	—
91-92—Portland	WHL	64	51	53	104	95	...	...	...	6	3	6	9	12
—Baltimore	AHL	3	1	1	2	0	...	...	...	—	—	—	—	—
—Washington	NHL	1	0	0	0	0	0	0	0	—	—	—	—	—
92-93—Baltimore	AHL	37	18	28	46	74	...	...	...	—	—	—	—	—
—Washington	NHL	36	4	7	11	16	4	1	0	2	0	1	1	0
93-94—Portland	AHL	8	11	4	15	4	...	...	...	—	—	—	—	—
—Washington	NHL	62	12	14	26	33	9	0	0	11	0	1	1	10
94-95—Washington	NHL	46	11	14	25	44	7	3	3	7	2	5	7	12
95-96—Washington	NHL	70	23	22	45	92	13	7	1	2	0	2	2	0
96-97—Washington	NHL	78	17	25	42	67	-3	2	1	—	—	—	—	—
97-98—Washington	NHL	80	10	24	34	80	9	2	0	—	—	—	—	—
98-99—Washington	NHL	45	12	12	24	26	0	4	1	—	—	—	—	—
99-00—Washington	NHL	82	16	27	43	80	19	3	0	5	1	0	1	2
00-01—Washington	NHL	82	24	23	47	87	8	6	0	6	2	3	5	14
01-02—Washington	NHL	28	2	12	14	23	-2	0	0	—	—	—	—	—
02-03—Washington	NHL	77	15	15	30	71	3	2	0	6	0	0	0	6
NHL Totals (12 years)		687	146	195	341	619	67	30	6	39	5	12	17	44

KONSTANTINOV, EVGENY G LIGHTNING

PERSONAL: Born March 29, 1981, in Kazan, U.S.S.R. ... 6-0/180. ... Catches left. ... Name pronounced ev-GEHN-ee kohn-stahn-TEE-nanf.
TRANSACTIONS/CAREER NOTES: Selected by Tampa Bay Lightning in third round (second Lightning pick, 67th overall) of NHL entry draft (June 26, 1999).

		REGULAR SEASON									PLAYOFFS							
Season Team	League	Gms.	Min	W	L	T	GA	SO	Avg.	SV%	Gms.	Min.	W	L	GA	SO	Avg.	SV%
97-98—Ak Bars-2 Kazan............	Rus. Div. III	34	2040	...	...	...	129	...	3.79	—	—	—	—	—	—	—	—	—
98-99—Ak Bars-2 Kazan............	Rus. Div. III	17	1020	...	...	...	38	...	2.24	—	—	—	—	—	—	—	—	—
99-00—Ak Bars Kazan..............	Russian	2	59	...	...	...	5	0	5.08	—	—	—	—	—	—	—	—	—
00-01—Detroit.........................	IHL	27	1197	4	15	‡2	85	0	4.26	—	—	—	—	—	—	—	—	—
—Tampa Bay...................	NHL	1	1	0	0	0	0	0	0.00	—	—	—	—	—	—	—	—	—
—Louisiana	ECHL	8	458	4	4	0	21	0	2.75	—	12	637	5	6	32	0	3.01	—
01-02—Pensacola....................	ECHL	24	1228	10	10	0	71	0	3.47	—	—	—	—	—	—	—	—	—
—Springfield	AHL	3	177	1	2	0	5	0	1.69	—	—	—	—	—	—	—	—	—
02-03—Springfield	AHL	39	2188	13	23	1	118	1	3.24	—	—	—	—	—	—	—	—	—
—Tampa Bay	NHL	1	20	0	0	0	1	0	3.00	.833	—	—	—	—	—	—	—	—
NHL Totals (2 years)............		2	21	0	0	0	1	0	2.86	.833								

KOPECKY, TOMAS — C — RED WINGS

PERSONAL: Born February 2, 1982, in Ilava, Czechoslovakia. ... 6-3/187. ... Shoots left.
TRANSACTIONS/CAREER NOTES: Selected by Detroit Red Wings in second round (second Red Wings pick, 38th overall) of NHL entry draft (June 24, 2000).

		REGULAR SEASON								PLAYOFFS				
Season Team	League	Gms.	G	A	Pts.	PIM	+/-	PP	SH	Gms.	G	A	Pts.	PIM
98-99—Dukla Trencin..............	Slovakia Jrs.	44	13	16	29	...	...	...	...	—	—	—	—	—
99-00—Dukla Trencin..............	Slovakia	52	3	4	7	24	...	...	...	5	0	0	0	0
—Dukla Trencin..............	Slovakia Jrs.	12	11	13	24	10	...	...	...	—	—	—	—	—
00-01—Lethbridge	WHL	49	22	28	50	52	...	...	...	5	1	1	2	6
—Cincinnati...................	AHL	1	0	0	0	0	...	...	...	—	—	—	—	—
01-02—Lethbridge	WHL	60	34	42	76	94	...	...	...	4	2	1	3	15
—Cincinnati...................	AHL	2	1	1	2	6	...	...	...	2	0	0	0	0
02-03—Grand Rapids..............	AHL	70	17	21	38	32	...	...	...	—	—	—	—	—

KOROLEV, EVGENY — D — ISLANDERS

PERSONAL: Born July 24, 1978, in Moscow, U.S.S.R. ... 6-1/214. ... Shoots left.
TRANSACTIONS/CAREER NOTES: Selected by New York Islanders in sixth round (seventh Islanders pick, 138th overall) of NHL entry draft (June 22, 1996).

		REGULAR SEASON								PLAYOFFS				
Season Team	League	Gms.	G	A	Pts.	PIM	+/-	PP	SH	Gms.	G	A	Pts.	PIM
95-96—Peterborough..............	OHL	60	2	12	14	60	...	...	...	6	0	0	0	2
96-97—Peterborough..............	OHL	64	5	17	22	60	...	...	...	11	1	1	2	8
97-98—Peterborough..............	OHL	37	5	21	26	39	...	...	...	—	—	—	—	—
—London	OHL	27	4	10	14	36	...	...	...	15	2	7	9	29
98-99—Lowell	AHL	54	2	6	8	48	...	...	...	2	0	1	1	0
—Roanoke	ECHL	2	0	1	1	0	...	...	...	—	—	—	—	—
99-00—Lowell	AHL	57	1	10	11	61	...	...	...	6	0	0	0	4
—New York Islanders.....	NHL	17	1	2	3	8	-10	0	0	—	—	—	—	—
00-01—New York Islanders.....	NHL	8	0	0	0	6	0	0	0	—	—	—	—	—
—Louisville	AHL	36	2	14	16	68	...	...	...	—	—	—	—	—
01-02—Bridgeport..................	AHL	53	5	8	13	30	...	...	...	—	—	—	—	—
—New York Islanders.....	NHL	17	0	2	2	6	0	0	0	2	0	0	0	0
02-03—Lokomotiv Yaroslavl ...	Russian	16	1	1	2	22	...	...	...	—	—	—	—	—
NHL Totals (3 years)............		42	1	4	5	20	-10	0	0	2	0	0	0	0

KOROLEV, IGOR — C — BLACKHAWKS

PERSONAL: Born September 6, 1970, in Moscow, U.S.S.R. ... 6-1/196. ... Shoots left. ... Name pronounced EE-gohr KOHR-ih-lehv.
TRANSACTIONS/CAREER NOTES: Selected by St. Louis Blues in second round (first Blues pick, 38th overall) of NHL entry draft (June 20, 1992). ... Suffered from the flu (March 3, 1994); missed one game. ... Injured hip (March 12, 1994); missed three games. ... Selected by Winnipeg Jets from Blues in NHL waiver draft for cash (January 18, 1995). ... Played in Europe during 1994-95 NHL lockout. ... Fractured wrist (December 10, 1995); missed two games. ... Suffered hip pointer (February 1, 1996); missed three games. ... Jets franchise moved to Phoenix and renamed Coyotes for 1996-97 season; NHL approved move on January 18, 1996. ... Signed as free agent by Toronto Maple Leafs (September 28, 1997). ... Sprained shoulder (October 28, 1997); missed one game. ... Strained back (January 6, 1998); missed one game. ... Suffered back spasms (January 9, 1999); missed three games. ... Fractured finger (March 20, 1999); missed 13 games. ... Fractured fibula (April 22, 1999); missed remainder of playoffs. ... Suffered injury (October 13, 1999); missed two games. ... Suffered injury (February 8, 2001); missed five games. ... Traded by Maple Leafs to Chicago Blackhawks for third-round pick (C Nicolas Corbeil) in 2001 draft (June 23, 2001).
STATISTICAL PLATEAUS: Three-goal games: 1995-96 (1).

		REGULAR SEASON								PLAYOFFS				
Season Team	League	Gms.	G	A	Pts.	PIM	+/-	PP	SH	Gms.	G	A	Pts.	PIM
88-89—Dynamo Moscow........	USSR	1	0	0	0	2	...	...	...	—	—	—	—	—
89-90—Dynamo Moscow........	USSR	17	3	2	5	2	...	...	...	—	—	—	—	—
90-91—Dynamo Moscow........	USSR	38	12	4	16	12	...	...	...	—	—	—	—	—
91-92—Dynamo Moscow........	CIS	39	15	12	27	16	...	...	...	—	—	—	—	—
92-93—Dynamo Moscow........	CIS	5	1	2	3	4	...	...	...	—	—	—	—	—
—St. Louis	NHL	74	4	23	27	20	-1	2	0	3	0	0	0	0
93-94—St. Louis	NHL	73	6	10	16	40	-12	0	0	2	0	0	0	0
94-95—Dynamo Moscow........	CIS	13	4	6	10	18	...	...	...	—	—	—	—	—
—Winnipeg	NHL	45	8	22	30	10	1	1	0	—	—	—	—	—

Season Team	League	REGULAR SEASON Gms.	G	A	Pts.	PIM	+/-	PP	SH	PLAYOFFS Gms.	G	A	Pts.	PIM
95-96—Winnipeg	NHL	73	22	29	51	42	1	8	0	6	0	3	3	0
96-97—Michigan	IHL	4	2	2	4	0	...	...	...	—	—	—	—	—
—Phoenix	IHL	4	2	6	8	4	...	...	...	—	—	—	—	—
—Phoenix	NHL	41	3	7	10	28	-5	2	0	1	0	0	0	0
97-98—Toronto	NHL	78	17	22	39	22	-18	6	3	—	—	—	—	—
98-99—Toronto	NHL	66	13	34	47	46	11	1	0	1	0	0	0	0
99-00—Toronto	NHL	80	20	26	46	22	12	5	3	12	0	4	4	6
00-01—Toronto	NHL	73	10	19	29	28	3	2	0	11	0	0	0	0
01-02—Chicago	NHL	82	9	20	29	20	-5	0	1	5	0	1	1	0
02-03—Norfolk	AHL	14	4	3	7	0	...	...	...	—	—	—	—	—
—Chicago	NHL	48	4	5	9	30	-1	1	0	—	—	—	—	—
NHL Totals (11 years)		733	116	217	333	308	-14	28	7	41	0	8	8	6

KOROLYUK, ALEX   RW   SHARKS

PERSONAL: Born January 15, 1976, in Moscow, U.S.S.R. ... 5-9/195. ... Shoots left. ... Full Name: Alexander Korolyuk. ... Name pronounced KOH-rohl-yook.

TRANSACTIONS/CAREER NOTES: Selected by San Jose Sharks in sixth round (sixth Sharks pick, 141st overall) of NHL entry draft (June 29, 1994). ... Suffered eye injury (December 2, 1999); missed three games. ... Injured back (January 19, 2000); missed eight games. ... Reinjured back (February 11, 2000); missed four games. ... Re-signed by Sharks (June 22, 2003).

Season Team	League	REGULAR SEASON Gms.	G	A	Pts.	PIM	+/-	PP	SH	PLAYOFFS Gms.	G	A	Pts.	PIM
93-94—Soviet Wings	CIS	22	4	4	8	20	...	...	...	3	1	0	1	4
94-95—Soviet Wings	CIS	52	16	13	29	62	...	...	...	4	1	2	3	4
95-96—Soviet Wings	CIS	50	30	19	49	77	...	...	...	—	—	—	—	—
96-97—Soviet Wings	CIS	17	8	5	13	46	...	...	...	—	—	—	—	—
—Manitoba	IHL	42	20	16	36	71	...	...	...	—	—	—	—	—
97-98—San Jose	NHL	19	2	3	5	6	-5	1	0	—	—	—	—	—
—Kentucky	AHL	44	16	23	39	96	...	...	...	3	0	0	0	0
98-99—Kentucky	AHL	23	9	13	22	16	...	...	...	—	—	—	—	—
—San Jose	NHL	55	12	18	30	26	3	2	0	6	1	3	4	2
99-00—San Jose	NHL	57	14	21	35	35	4	3	0	9	0	3	3	6
00-01—Ak Bars Kazan	Russian	6	0	5	5	4	...	...	...	—	—	—	—	—
—San Jose	NHL	70	12	13	25	41	2	3	0	2	0	0	0	0
01-02—San Jose	NHL	32	3	7	10	14	2	0	0	—	—	—	—	—
02-03—Kazan	Rus. Div. III	46	14	17	31	122	...	...	...	17	1	6	7	8
NHL Totals (5 years)		233	43	62	105	122	6	9	0	17	1	6	7	8

KOSTOPOULOS, TOM   RW   PENGUINS

PERSONAL: Born January 24, 1979, in Mississauga, Ont. ... 6-0/200. ... Shoots right.
TRANSACTIONS/CAREER NOTES: Selected by Pittsburgh Penguins in ninth round (ninth Penguins pick, 204th overall) of NHL entry draft (June 26, 1999).

Season Team	League	REGULAR SEASON Gms.	G	A	Pts.	PIM	+/-	PP	SH	PLAYOFFS Gms.	G	A	Pts.	PIM
96-97—London	OHL	64	13	12	25	67	...	...	...	—	—	—	—	—
97-98—London	OHL	66	24	26	50	108	...	...	...	16	6	4	10	26
98-99—London	OHL	66	27	60	87	114	...	...	...	25	19	16	35	32
99-00—Wilkes-Barre/Scranton	AHL	76	26	32	58	121	...	...	...	—	—	—	—	—
00-01—Wilkes-Barre/Scranton	AHL	80	16	36	52	120	...	...	...	21	3	9	12	6
01-02—Wilkes-Barre/Scranton	AHL	70	27	26	53	112	...	...	...	—	—	—	—	—
—Pittsburgh	NHL	11	1	2	3	9	-1	0	0	—	—	—	—	—
02-03—Wilkes-Barre/Scranton	AHL	71	21	42	63	131	...	...	...	—	—	—	—	—
—Pittsburgh	NHL	8	0	1	1	0	-4	0	0	—	—	—	—	—
NHL Totals (2 years)		19	1	3	4	9	-5	0	0					

KOTALIK, ALES   RW   SABRES

PERSONAL: Born December 23, 1978, in Jindrichuv Hradec, Czechoslovakia ... 6-1/222. ... Shoots right.
TRANSACTIONS/CAREER NOTES: Selected by Buffalo Sabres in sixth round (seventh Sabres pick, 164th overall) of NHL entry draft (June 27, 1998).

Season Team	League	REGULAR SEASON Gms.	G	A	Pts.	PIM	+/-	PP	SH	PLAYOFFS Gms.	G	A	Pts.	PIM
93-94—HC Ceske Budejovice	Czech. Jrs.	28	12	12	24	...	...	...	...	—	—	—	—	—
94-95—HC Ceske Budejovice	Czech. Jrs.	36	26	17	43	...	...	...	...	—	—	—	—	—
95-96—HC Ceske Budejovice	Czech. Jrs.	28	6	7	13	...	...	...	...	—	—	—	—	—
96-97—HC Ceske Budejovice	Czech. Jrs.	36	15	16	31	24	...	...	...	—	—	—	—	—
97-98—ZPS Zlin	Czech.	47	9	7	16	14	...	...	...	—	—	—	—	—
98-99—HC Ceske Budejovice	Czech Rep.	41	8	13	21	16	...	...	...	3	0	0	0	0
99-00—HC Ceske Budejovice	Czech Rep.	43	7	12	19	34	...	...	...	3	0	1	1	6
00-01—HC Ceske Budejovice	Czech Rep.	52	19	29	48	54	...	...	...	—	—	—	—	—
01-02—Rochester	AHL	68	18	25	43	55	...	...	...	1	0	0	0	0
—Buffalo	NHL	13	1	3	4	2	-1	0	0	—	—	—	—	—
02-03—Rochester	AHL	8	0	2	2	4	...	...	...	—	—	—	—	—
—Buffalo	NHL	68	21	14	35	30	-2	4	0	—	—	—	—	—
NHL Totals (2 years)		81	22	17	39	32	-3	4	0					

K

KOVALCHUK, ILYA   LW   THRASHERS

PERSONAL: Born April 15, 1983, in Tver, U.S.S.R. ... 6-2/235. ... Shoots right.
TRANSACTIONS/CAREER NOTES: Selected by Atlanta Thrashers in first round (first Thrashers pick, first overall) of NHL entry draft (June 23, 2001). ... Injured shoulder (March 10, 2002); missed remainder of season.
STATISTICAL PLATEAUS: Three-goal games: 2002-03 (1).

		REGULAR SEASON								PLAYOFFS				
Season Team	League	Gms.	G	A	Pts.	PIM	+/-	PP	SH	Gms.	G	A	Pts.	PIM
00-01—Spartak	Russian Div. 1	40	28	18	46	78	...	...	...	—	—	—	—	—
01-02—Atlanta	NHL	65	29	22	51	28	-19	7	0	—	—	—	—	—
—Russian Oly. team	Int'l	6	1	2	3	14	...	...	...	—	—	—	—	—
02-03—Atlanta	NHL	81	38	29	67	57	-24	9	0	—	—	—	—	—
NHL Totals (2 years)		146	67	51	118	85	-43	16	0					

KOVALEV, ALEXEI   RW   ○ RANGERS

PERSONAL: Born February 24, 1973, in Togliatti, U.S.S.R. ... 6-1/220. ... Shoots left. ... Name pronounced KOH-vuh-lahf.
TRANSACTIONS/CAREER NOTES: Selected by New York Rangers in first round (first Rangers pick, 15th overall) of NHL entry draft (June 22, 1991). ... Suffered back spasms (January 16, 1993); missed one game. ... Suspended one game by NHL (November 10, 1993). ... Suspended five games by NHL for tripping (November 30, 1993). ... Suspended two games by NHL (February 12, 1994). ... Played in Europe during 1994-95 NHL lockout. ... Suffered from the flu (December 2, 1995); missed one game. ... Tore knee ligament (January 8, 1997); missed remainder of season. ... Sprained knee and underwent athroscopic surgery (January 22, 1998); missed eight games. ... Separated shoulder (October 27, 1998); missed five games. ... Bruised shoulder (November 21, 1998); missed one game. ... Traded by Rangers with C Harry York and future considerations to Pittsburgh Penguins for C Petr Nedved, D Janne Laukkanen and D Chris Tamer (November 25, 1998). ... Bruised shoulder (November 21, 1998); missed one game. ... Suspended three games by NHL for unsportsmanline conduct (March 24, 2001). ... Underwent knee surgery (October 16, 2001); missed 13 games. ... Injured hip (April 6, 2002); missed one game. ... Reinjured hip (April 12, 2002); missed remainder of season. ... Traded by Penguins with LW Dan LaCouture, D Janne Laukkanen and D Mike Wilson to Rangers for RW Rico Fata, RW Mikael Samuelsson, D Joel Bouchard, D Richard Lintner and cash (February 10, 2003).
STATISTICAL PLATEAUS: Three-goal games: 1992-93 (1), 1996-97 (1), 2000-01 (4), 2001-02 (3), 2002-03 (1). Total: 10.

		REGULAR SEASON								PLAYOFFS				
Season Team	League	Gms.	G	A	Pts.	PIM	+/-	PP	SH	Gms.	G	A	Pts.	PIM
89-90—Dynamo Moscow	USSR	1	0	0	0	0	...	...	...	—	—	—	—	—
90-91—Dynamo Moscow	USSR	18	1	2	3	4	...	...	...	—	—	—	—	—
91-92—Dynamo Moscow	CIS	33	16	9	25	20	...	...	...	—	—	—	—	—
—Unif. Olympic team	Int'l	8	1	2	3	14	...	...	...	—	—	—	—	—
92-93—New York Rangers	NHL	65	20	18	38	79	-10	3	0	—	—	—	—	—
—Binghamton	AHL	13	13	11	24	35	...	...	...	9	3	5	8	14
93-94—New York Rangers	NHL	76	23	33	56	154	18	7	0	23	9	12	21	18
94-95—Lada Togliatti	CIS	12	8	8	16	49	...	...	...	—	—	—	—	—
—New York Rangers	NHL	48	13	15	28	30	-6	1	1	10	4	7	11	10
95-96—New York Rangers	NHL	81	24	34	58	98	5	8	1	11	3	4	7	14
96-97—New York Rangers	NHL	45	13	22	35	42	11	1	0	—	—	—	—	—
97-98—New York Rangers	NHL	73	23	30	53	44	-22	8	0	—	—	—	—	—
98-99—New York Rangers	NHL	14	3	4	7	12	-6	1	0	—	—	—	—	—
—Pittsburgh	NHL	63	20	26	46	37	8	5	1	10	5	7	12	14
99-00—Pittsburgh	NHL	82	26	40	66	94	-3	9	2	11	1	5	6	10
00-01—Pittsburgh	NHL	79	44	51	95	96	12	12	2	18	5	5	10	16
01-02—Pittsburgh	NHL	67	32	44	76	80	2	8	1	—	—	—	—	—
—Russian Oly. team	Int'l	6	3	1	4	4	...	...	...	—	—	—	—	—
02-03—Pittsburgh	NHL	54	27	37	64	50	-11	8	0	—	—	—	—	—
—New York Rangers	NHL	24	10	3	13	20	2	3	0	—	—	—	—	—
NHL Totals (11 years)		771	278	357	635	836	0	74	8	83	27	40	67	82

KOZLOV, SLAVA   RW   THRASHERS

PERSONAL: Born May 3, 1972, in Voskresensk, U.S.S.R. ... 5-10/185. ... Shoots left. ... Full Name: Vyacheslav Kozlov. ... Name pronounced VYACH-ih-slav KAHS-lahf.
TRANSACTIONS/CAREER NOTES: Selected by Detroit Red Wings in third round (second Red Wings pick, 45th overall) of NHL entry draft (June 16, 1990). ... Played in Europe during 1994-95 NHL lockout. ... Bruised left foot (April 16, 1995); missed one game. ... Sprained knee (April 15, 1998); missed two games. ... Suspended three games by NHL for elbowing incident (December 18, 1998). ... Injured ankle (December 22, 1999); missed three games. ... Reinjured ankle (January 4, 2000); missed four games. ... Suffered concussion (March 29, 2000); missed two games. ... Traded by Red Wings with first-round pick (traded to Columbus) in 2002 draft and future considerations to Buffalo Sabres for G Dominik Hasek (July 1, 2001). ... Injured Achilles' tendon (December 29, 2001); missed remainder of season. ... Traded by Sabres with second-round pick (traded to Columbus) in 2002 draft to Atlanta Thrashers for second-(traded to Edmonton) and third-round (traded to Columbus) picks in 2002 draft (June 22, 2002). ... Suspended three games by NHL for abuse of an official (January 3, 2003). ... Re-signed by Thrashers (July 26, 2003).
STATISTICAL PLATEAUS: Three-goal games: 1993-94 (1), 1998-99 (1). Total: 2. ... Four-goal games: 1995-96 (1). ... Total hat tricks: 3.

		REGULAR SEASON								PLAYOFFS				
Season Team	League	Gms.	G	A	Pts.	PIM	+/-	PP	SH	Gms.	G	A	Pts.	PIM
87-88—Khimik	USSR	2	0	1	1	0	...	...	...	—	—	—	—	—
88-89—Khimik	USSR	13	0	1	1	2	...	...	...	—	—	—	—	—
89-90—Khimik	USSR	45	14	12	26	38	...	...	...	—	—	—	—	—
90-91—Khimik	USSR	45	11	13	24	46	...	...	...	—	—	—	—	—
91-92—Khimik	USSR	11	6	5	11	12	...	...	...	—	—	—	—	—
—Detroit	NHL	7	0	2	2	2	-2	0	0	—	—	—	—	—
92-93—Detroit	NHL	17	4	1	5	14	-1	0	0	4	0	2	2	2
—Adirondack	AHL	45	23	36	59	54	...	...	...	4	1	1	2	4

Season Team	League	REGULAR SEASON								PLAYOFFS				
		Gms.	G	A	Pts.	PIM	+/-	PP	SH	Gms.	G	A	Pts.	PIM
93-94—Detroit	NHL	77	34	39	73	50	27	8	2	7	2	5	7	12
—Adirondack	AHL	3	0	1	1	15	...	...	...	—	—	—	—	—
94-95—CSKA Moscow	CIS	10	3	4	7	14	...	...	...	—	—	—	—	—
—Detroit	NHL	46	13	20	33	45	12	5	0	18	9	7	16	10
95-96—Detroit	NHL	82	36	37	73	70	33	9	0	19	5	7	12	10
96-97—Detroit	NHL	75	23	22	45	46	21	3	0	20	8	5	13	14
97-98—Detroit	NHL	80	25	27	52	46	14	6	0	22	6	8	14	10
98-99—Detroit	NHL	79	29	29	58	45	10	6	1	10	6	1	7	4
99-00—Detroit	NHL	72	18	18	36	28	11	4	0	8	2	1	3	12
00-01—Detroit	NHL	72	20	18	38	30	9	4	0	6	4	1	5	2
01-02—Buffalo	NHL	38	9	13	22	16	0	3	0	—	—	—	—	—
02-03—Atlanta	NHL	79	21	49	70	66	-10	9	1	—	—	—	—	—
NHL Totals (12 years)		724	232	275	507	458	124	57	4	114	42	37	79	76

KOZLOV, VIKTOR   RW   PANTHERS

K

PERSONAL: Born February 14, 1975, in Togliatti, U.S.S.R. ... 6-5/225. ... Shoots right. ... Name pronounced KAHZ-lahf.

TRANSACTIONS/CAREER NOTES: Selected by San Jose Sharks in first round (first Sharks pick, sixth overall) of NHL entry draft (June 26, 1993). ... Suffered displaced ankle fracture (November 27, 1994); missed 13 games. ... Played in Europe during 1994-95 NHL lockout. ... Bruised ankle (March 26, 1997); missed four games. ... Traded by Sharks with fifth-round pick (D Jaroslav Spacek) in 1998 draft to Florida Panthers for LW Dave Lowry and first-round pick (traded to Tampa Bay) in 1998 draft (November 13, 1997). ... Separated right shoulder (November 18, 1997); missed 16 games. ... Suffered concussion (April 1, 1998); missed three games. ... Separated shoulder (October 30, 1998); missed six games. ... Reinjured shoulder (January 8, 1999); missed one game. ... Strained shoulder (January 20, 1999); missed three games. ... Fractured finger (April 3, 1999); missed final seven games of season. ... Sprained shoulder (March 8, 2000); missed two games. ... Injured shoulder (October 25, 2000); missed six games. ... Injured left shoulder (December 13, 2000); missed nine games. ... Injured groin (March 14, 2001); missed five games. ... Reinjured groin (March 28, 2001); missed final five games of season. ... Injured groin and hip (December 6, 2001); missed seven games. ... Strained muscle in abdomen (February 9, 2002); missed remainder of season. ... Re-signed by Panthers (July 16, 2003).

STATISTICAL PLATEAUS: Three-goal games: 1999-00 (1).

Season Team	League	REGULAR SEASON								PLAYOFFS				
		Gms.	G	A	Pts.	PIM	+/-	PP	SH	Gms.	G	A	Pts.	PIM
90-91—Lada Togliatti	USSR Div. II	2	2	0	2	0	...	...	...	—	—	—	—	—
91-92—Lada Togliatti	CIS	3	0	0	0	0	...	...	...	—	—	—	—	—
92-93—Dynamo Moscow	CIS	30	6	5	11	4	...	...	...	10	3	0	3	0
93-94—Dynamo Moscow	CIS	42	16	9	25	14	...	...	...	7	3	2	5	0
94-95—Dynamo Moscow	CIS	3	1	1	2	2	...	...	...	—	—	—	—	—
—San Jose	NHL	16	2	0	2	2	-5	0	0	—	—	—	—	—
—Kansas City	IHL	—	—	—	—	—	—	—	—	13	4	5	9	12
95-96—Kansas City	IHL	15	4	7	11	12	...	...	...	—	—	—	—	—
—San Jose	NHL	62	6	13	19	6	-15	1	0	—	—	—	—	—
96-97—San Jose	NHL	78	16	25	41	40	-16	4	0	—	—	—	—	—
97-98—San Jose	NHL	18	5	2	7	2	-2	2	0	—	—	—	—	—
—Florida	NHL	46	12	11	23	14	-1	3	2	—	—	—	—	—
98-99—Florida	NHL	65	16	35	51	24	13	5	1	—	—	—	—	—
99-00—Florida	NHL	80	17	53	70	16	24	6	0	4	0	1	1	0
00-01—Florida	NHL	51	14	23	37	10	-4	6	0	—	—	—	—	—
01-02—Florida	NHL	50	9	18	27	20	-16	6	0	—	—	—	—	—
02-03—Florida	NHL	74	22	34	56	18	-8	7	1	— *	—	—	—	—
NHL Totals (9 years)		540	119	214	333	152	-30	40	4	4	0	1	1	0

KRAFT, MILAN   C   PENGUINS

PERSONAL: Born January 17, 1980, in Plzen, Czechoslovakia ... 6-3/211. ... Shoots right.

TRANSACTIONS/CAREER NOTES: Selected by Pittsburgh Penguins in first round (first Penguins pick, 23rd overall) of NHL entry draft (June 27, 1998).

Season Team	League	REGULAR SEASON								PLAYOFFS				
		Gms.	G	A	Pts.	PIM	+/-	PP	SH	Gms.	G	A	Pts.	PIM
96-97—Plzen	Czech. Jrs.	36	26	17	43	...	...	...	...	—	—	—	—	—
—ZKZ Plzen	Czech Rep.	9	0	1	1	2	...	...	...	—	—	—	—	—
97-98—Plzen	Czech. Jrs.	24	22	23	45	12	...	...	...	—	—	—	—	—
—ZKZ Plzen	Czech Rep.	16	0	5	5	0	...	...	...	—	—	—	—	—
98-99—Prince Albert	WHL	68	40	46	86	32	...	...	...	14	7	13	20	6
99-00—Prince Albert	WHL	56	34	35	69	42	...	...	...	6	4	1	5	4
00-01—Pittsburgh	NHL	42	7	7	14	8	-6	1	1	8	0	0	0	2
—Wilkes-Barre/Scranton	AHL	40	21	23	44	27	...	...	...	14	12	7	19	6
01-02—Pittsburgh	NHL	68	8	8	16	16	-9	1	0	—	—	—	—	—
—Wilkes-Barre/Scranton	AHL	8	4	4	8	10	...	...	...	—	—	—	—	—
02-03—Wilkes-Barre/Scranton	AHL	40	13	24	37	28	...	...	...	—	—	—	—	—
—Pittsburgh	NHL	31	7	5	12	10	-8	0	0	—	—	—	—	—
NHL Totals (3 years)		141	22	20	42	34	-23	2	1	8	0	0	0	2

KRAFT, RYAN   C

PERSONAL: Born November 7, 1975, in Bottineau, N.D. ... 5-9/185.

TRANSACTIONS/CAREER NOTES: Selected by San Jose Sharks in eighth round (11th Sharks pick, 194th overall) of NHL entry draft (July 8, 1995).

Season Team	League	REGULAR SEASON								PLAYOFFS				
		Gms.	G	A	Pts.	PIM	+/-	PP	SH	Gms.	G	A	Pts.	PIM
93-94—Moorhead Senior	Minn. H.S.	27	44	40	84	40	...	...	...	—	—	—	—	—
94-95—Univ. of Minnesota	WCHA	44	13	33	46	40	...	...	...	—	—	—	—	—
95-96—Univ. of Minnesota	WCHA	41	13	24	37	24	...	...	...	—	—	—	—	—
96-97—Univ. of Minnesota	WCHA	42	25	21	46	37	...	...	...	—	—	—	—	—
97-98—Univ. of Minnesota	WCHA	32	11	26	37	16	...	...	...	—	—	—	—	—
98-99—Richmond	ECHL	63	28	36	64	35	...	...	...	18	10	10	20	4
99-00—Richmond	ECHL	44	32	35	67	32	...	...	...	—	—	—	—	—
—Kentucky	AHL	15	7	6	13	2	...	...	...	5	3	1	4	0
—Cleveland	IHL	1	0	1	1	0	...	...	...	—	—	—	—	—
00-01—Kentucky	AHL	77	38	50	88	36	...	...	...	3	2	0	2	0
01-02—Cleveland	AHL	63	19	41	60	42	...	...	...	—	—	—	—	—
02-03—Cleveland	AHL	53	14	27	41	12	...	...	...	—	—	—	—	—
—San Jose	NHL	7	0	1	1	0	2	0	0	—	—	—	—	—
NHL Totals (1 year)		7	0	1	1	0	2	0	0					

KRAVCHUK, IGOR D

PERSONAL: Born September 13, 1966, in Ufa, U.S.S.R. ... 6-1/218. ... Shoots left. ... Name pronounced EE-gohr KRAV-chuhk.
TRANSACTIONS/CAREER NOTES: Selected by Chicago Blackhawks in fourth round (fifth Blackhawks pick, 71st overall) of NHL entry draft (June 22, 1991). ... Sprained knee (October 25, 1992); missed four games. ... Sprained left ankle (December 29, 1992); missed 18 games. ... Traded by Blackhawks with C Dean McAmmond to Edmonton Oilers for RW Joe Murphy (February 25, 1993). ... Sprained left knee (April 6, 1993); missed remainder of season. ... Strained groin (November 15, 1993); missed three games. ... Injured left knee (January 30, 1995) and underwent surgery (February 6, 1995); missed 12 games. ... Suffered deep bone bruise to left leg (October 21, 1995); missed six games. ... Injured knee (November 20, 1995); missed four games. ... Traded by Oilers with D Ken Sutton to St. Louis Blues for D Donald Dufresne and D Jeff Norton (January 4, 1996). ... Traded by Blues to Ottawa Senators for D Steve Duchesne (August 25, 1997). ... Bruised hip (March 20, 1998); missed one game. ... Strained hip flexor (November 26, 1998); missed one game. ... Suffered from the flu (March 30, 1999); missed one game. ... Bruised leg (April 10, 1999); missed one game. ... Suffered partially torn medial collateral ligament in left knee (October 30, 1999); missed 15 games. ... Sprained left knee (December 11, 1999); missed one game. ... Bruised right foot (January 11, 2000); missed one game. ... Claimed on waivers by Calgary Flames (November 10, 2000). ... Injured knee (Feburary 16, 2001); missed two games. ... Injured knee (February 24, 2001); missed remainder of season. ... Injured groin (November 17, 2001); missed four games. ... Signed as free agent by Florida Panthers (March 11, 2003).

Season Team	League	REGULAR SEASON								PLAYOFFS				
		Gms.	G	A	Pts.	PIM	+/-	PP	SH	Gms.	G	A	Pts.	PIM
87-88—CSKA Moscow	USSR	47	1	8	9	12	...	...	...	—	—	—	—	—
—Unif. Olympic team	Int'l	6	1	0	1	0	...	...	...	—	—	—	—	—
88-89—CSKA Moscow	USSR	27	3	4	7	2	...	...	...	—	—	—	—	—
89-90—CSKA Moscow	USSR	48	1	3	4	16	...	...	...	—	—	—	—	—
90-91—CSKA Moscow	USSR	41	6	5	11	16	...	...	...	—	—	—	—	—
91-92—CSKA Moscow	CIS	30	3	7	10	2	...	...	...	—	—	—	—	—
—Unif. Olympic team	Int'l	8	3	2	5	6	...	...	...	—	—	—	—	—
—Chicago	NHL	18	1	8	9	4	-3	0	0	18	2	6	8	8
92-93—Chicago	NHL	38	6	9	15	30	11	3	0	—	—	—	—	—
—Edmonton	NHL	17	4	8	12	2	-8	1	0	—	—	—	—	—
93-94—Edmonton	NHL	81	12	38	50	16	-12	5	0	—	—	—	—	—
94-95—Edmonton	NHL	36	7	11	18	29	-15	3	1	—	—	—	—	—
95-96—Edmonton	NHL	26	4	4	8	10	-13	3	0	—	—	—	—	—
—St. Louis	NHL	40	3	12	15	24	-6	0	0	10	1	5	6	4
96-97—St. Louis	NHL	82	4	24	28	35	7	1	0	2	0	0	0	2
97-98—Ottawa	NHL	81	8	27	35	8	-19	3	1	11	2	3	5	4
—Russian Oly. team	Int'l	6	0	2	2	2	...	...	...	—	—	—	—	—
98-99—Ottawa	NHL	79	4	21	25	32	14	3	0	4	0	0	0	0
99-00—Ottawa	NHL	64	6	12	18	20	-5	5	0	6	1	1	2	0
00-01—Ottawa	NHL	15	1	5	6	14	4	0	0	—	—	—	—	—
—Calgary	NHL	37	0	8	8	4	-12	0	0	—	—	—	—	—
01-02—Calgary	NHL	78	4	22	26	19	3	1	0	—	—	—	—	—
—Russian Oly. team	Int'l	6	0	2	2	0	...	...	...	—	—	—	—	—
02-03—Florida	NHL	7	0	1	1	4	-3	0	0	—	—	—	—	—
NHL Totals (12 years)		699	64	210	274	251	-57	28	2	51	6	15	21	18

KRESTANOVICH, JORDAN LW AVALANCHE

PERSONAL: Born June 14, 1981, in Langley, B.C. ... 6-0/170. ... Shoots left.
TRANSACTIONS/CAREER NOTES: Selected by Colorado Avalanche in fifth round (sixth Avalanche pick, 152nd overall) of NHL entry draft (June 26, 1999).

Season Team	League	REGULAR SEASON								PLAYOFFS				
		Gms.	G	A	Pts.	PIM	+/-	PP	SH	Gms.	G	A	Pts.	PIM
97-98—Calgary	WHL	22	1	0	1	0	...	...	...	13	0	0	0	0
98-99—Calgary	WHL	62	6	13	19	10	...	...	...	20	3	8	11	4
99-00—Calgary	WHL	72	19	24	43	22	...	...	...	13	7	7	14	4
—Hershey	AHL	—	—	—	—	—	...	...	...	1	0	0	0	0
00-01—Calgary	WHL	70	40	60	100	32	...	...	...	12	8	4	12	8
—Hershey	AHL	—	—	—	—	—	...	...	...	2	0	0	0	0
01-02—Hershey	AHL	68	12	22	34	18	...	...	...	8	1	0	1	0
—Colorado	NHL	8	0	2	2	0	1	0	0	—	—	—	—	—
02-03—Hershey	AHL	70	13	21	34	24	...	...	...	—	—	—	—	—
NHL Totals (1 year)		8	0	2	2	0	1	0	0					

KRISTEK, JAROSLAV   RW   •   SABRES

PERSONAL: Born March 16, 1980, in Zlin, Czechoslovakia ... 6-1/185. ... Shoots left. ... Full Name: Jaroslov Kristek.
TRANSACTIONS/CAREER NOTES: Selected by Buffalo Sabres in second round (fourth Sabres pick, 50th overall) of NHL entry draft (June 27, 1998).

Season Team	League	Gms.	G	A	Pts.	PIM	+/-	PP	SH	Gms.	G	A	Pts.	PIM
95-96—ZPS Zlin	Czech. Jrs.	34	33	20	53	...	...	...	...	—	—	—	—	—
96-97—ZPS Zlin	Czech. Jrs.	44	28	27	55	...	...	...	...	—	—	—	—	—
97-98—ZPS Zlin	Czech. Jrs.	7	8	5	13	...	...	...	...	—	—	—	—	—
—ZPS Zlin	Czech Rep.	37	2	8	10	20	...	...	...	—	—	—	—	—
—Prostejov	Czech Rp. Dv.2	4	0	0	0	0	...	...	...	—	—	—	—	—
98-99—Tri-City	WHL	70	38	48	86	55	...	...	...	12	4	3	7	2
99-00—Tri-City	WHL	45	26	25	51	16	...	...	...	2	0	0	0	0
00-01—Rochester	AHL	35	5	3	8	20	...	...	...	—	—	—	—	—
01-02—Rochester	AHL	43	3	6	9	20	...	...	...	1	0	0	0	0
02-03—Rochester	AHL	47	15	17	32	24	...	...	...	—	—	—	—	—
—Buffalo	NHL	6	0	0	0	4	-2	0	0	—	—	—	—	—
NHL Totals (1 year)		**6**	**0**	**0**	**0**	**4**	**-2**	**0**	**0**					

KRISTOFFERSON, MARCUS   RW   STARS

PERSONAL: Born January 22, 1979, in Ostersund, Sweden. ... 6-3/200. ... Shoots left.
TRANSACTIONS/CAREER NOTES: Selected by Dallas Stars in fourth round (fourth Stars pick, 105th overall) of NHL entry draft (June 21, 1997).

Season Team	League	Gms.	G	A	Pts.	PIM	+/-	PP	SH	Gms.	G	A	Pts.	PIM
95-96—Mora Jrs.	Sweden	16	2	2	4	28	...	...	...	—	—	—	—	—
—Mora	Sweden Dv. 1	26	1	0	1	20	...	...	...	5	0	0	0	2
96-97—Mora	Sweden Dv. 1	33	1	5	6	26	...	...	...	—	—	—	—	—
97-98—Mora	Sweden Dv. 1	13	5	3	8	16	...	...	...	—	—	—	—	—
98-99—HV 71 Jonkoping	Sweden	34	0	1	1	65	...	...	...	—	—	—	—	—
99-00—HV 71 Jonkoping	Sweden	10	0	0	0	0	...	...	...	—	—	—	—	—
—Blues Espoo	Finland	29	7	4	11	42	...	...	...	1	1	0	1	0
00-01—Assat Pori	Finland	9	1	0	1	16	...	...	...	—	—	—	—	—
—Djurgarden Stockholm	Sweden	29	4	2	6	72	...	...	...	12	2	2	4	45
01-02—Utah	AHL	50	6	10	16	42	...	...	...	—	—	—	—	—
02-03—Utah	AHL	62	10	9	19	58	...	...	...	—	—	—	—	—

KROG, JASON   LW   MIGHTY DUCKS

PERSONAL: Born October 9, 1975, in Fernie, B.C. ... 5-11/189. ... Shoots right.
TRANSACTIONS/CAREER NOTES: Signed as non-drafted free agent by New York Islanders (April 10, 1999). ... Sprained right ankle (March 27, 2000); missed final six games of season. ... Dislocated left shoulder (December 15, 2000); missed 20 games.

Season Team	League	Gms.	G	A	Pts.	PIM	+/-	PP	SH	Gms.	G	A	Pts.	PIM
95-96—Univ. of New Hamp.	Hockey East	34	4	16	20	20	...	...	...	—	—	—	—	—
96-97—Univ. of New Hamp.	Hockey East	39	23	44	67	28	...	...	...	—	—	—	—	—
97-98—Univ. of New Hamp.	Hockey East	38	†33	33	66	44	...	...	...	—	—	—	—	—
98-99—Univ. of New Hamp.	Hockey East	41	*34	*51	*85	38	...	...	...	—	—	—	—	—
99-00—Lowell	AHL	45	6	21	27	22	...	...	...	—	—	—	—	—
—New York Islanders	NHL	17	2	4	6	6	-1	1	0	—	—	—	—	—
—Providence	AHL	11	9	8	17	4	...	...	...	6	2	2	4	0
00-01—Lowell	AHL	26	11	16	27	6	...	...	...	—	—	—	—	—
—Springfield	AHL	24	7	23	30	4	...	...	...	—	—	—	—	—
—New York Islanders	NHL	9	0	3	3	0	4	0	0	—	—	—	—	—
01-02—Bridgeport	AHL	64	26	36	62	13	...	...	...	20	10	13	23	8
—New York Islanders	NHL	2	0	0	0	0	0	0	0	—	—	—	—	—
02-03—Cincinnati	AHL	9	3	4	7	6	...	...	...	—	—	—	—	—
—Anaheim	NHL	67	10	15	25	12	1	0	1	21	3	1	4	4
NHL Totals (4 years)		**95**	**12**	**22**	**34**	**18**	**4**	**1**	**1**	**21**	**3**	**1**	**4**	**4**

KRON, ROBERT   C   BLUE JACKETS

PERSONAL: Born February 27, 1967, in Brno, Czechoslovakia. ... 5-11/182. ... Shoots left. ... Name pronounced KRAHN.
TRANSACTIONS/CAREER NOTES: Selected by Vancouver Canucks in fourth round (fifth Canucks pick, 88th overall) of NHL entry draft (June 15, 1985). ... Underwent surgery to repair torn knee ligaments and wrist fracture (March 22, 1991). ... Fractured ankle (January 28, 1992); missed 22 games. ... Traded by Canucks with third-round pick (D Marek Malik) in 1993 draft and future considerations to Hartford Whalers for C/LW Murray Craven and fifth-round pick (D Scott Walker) in 1993 draft (March 22, 1993); Whalers aquired RW Jim Sandlak to complete deal (May 17, 1993). ... Sprained shoulder (February 26, 1994); missed seven games. ... Fractured thumb (March 29, 1995); missed 11 games. ... Injured groin (March 27, 1996); missed one game. ... Strained abdominal muscle (April 8, 1996); missed three games. ... Sprained knee (January 25, 1997); missed 12 games. ... Whalers franchise moved to North Carolina and renamed Carolina Hurricanes for 1997-98 season; NHL approved move on June 25, 1997. ... Strained groin (November 11, 1998); missed one game. ... Strained groin (February 26, 1999); missed five games. ... Selected by Columbus Blue Jackets in NHL expansion draft (June 23, 2000). ... Strained muscle in abdomen (December 10, 2000); missed 15 games. ... Fractured ankle (March 24, 2001); missed remainder of season. ... Strained knee (December 12, 2001); missed five games. ... Bruised ankle (March 3, 2002); missed two games. ... Fractured foot (March 25, 2002); missed remainder of season.

Season Team	League	REGULAR SEASON								PLAYOFFS				
		Gms.	G	A	Pts.	PIM	+/-	PP	SH	Gms.	G	A	Pts.	PIM
84-85—Zetor Brno	Czech.	40	6	8	14	6	...	...	...	—	—	—	—	—
85-86—Zetor Brno	Czech.	44	5	6	11	...	...	...	...	—	—	—	—	—
86-87—Zetor Brno	Czech.	28	14	11	25	...	▪	...	...	—	—	—	—	—
87-88—Zetor Brno	Czech.	32	12	6	18	...	...	...	...	—	—	—	—	—
88-89—Dukla Trencin	Czech.	43	28	19	47	26	...	...	...	—	—	—	—	—
89-90—Dukla Trencin	Czech.	39	22	22	44	...	...	...	...	—	—	—	—	—
90-91—Vancouver	NHL	76	12	20	32	21	-11	2	3	—	—	—	—	—
91-92—Vancouver	NHL	36	2	2	4	2	-9	0	0	11	1	2	3	2
92-93—Vancouver	NHL	32	10	11	21	14	10	2	2	—	—	—	—	—
—Hartford	NHL	13	4	2	6	4	-5	2	0	—	—	—	—	—
93-94—Hartford	NHL	77	24	26	50	8	0	2	1	—	—	—	—	—
94-95—Hartford	NHL	37	10	8	18	10	-3	3	1	—	—	—	—	—
95-96—Hartford	NHL	77	22	28	50	6	-1	8	1	—	—	—	—	—
96-97—Hartford	NHL	68	10	12	22	10	-18	2	0	—	—	—	—	—
97-98—Carolina	NHL	81	16	20	36	12	-8	4	0	—	—	—	—	—
98-99—Carolina	NHL	75	9	16	25	10	-13	3	1	5	2	0	2	0
99-00—Carolina	NHL	81	13	27	40	8	-4	2	1	—	—	—	—	—
00-01—Columbus	NHL	59	8	11	19	10	4	0	1	—	—	—	—	—
01-02—Columbus	NHL	59	4	11	15	4	-14	1	0	—	—	—	—	—
—Syracuse	AHL	6	2	4	6	5	...	...	...	—	—	—	—	—
02-03—Lukko	Finland	23	4	8	12	6	...	...	...	—	—	—	—	—
NHL Totals (12 years)		771	144	194	338	119	-72	31	11	16	3	2	5	2

K KRONWALL, NIKLAS — D — RED WINGS

PERSONAL: Born January 12, 1981, in Stockholm, Sweden. ... 5-11/165. ... Shoots left.
TRANSACTIONS/CAREER NOTES: Selected by Detroit Red Wings in first round (first Red Wings pick, 29th overall) of NHL entry draft (June 24, 2000). ... Signed by Red Wings (July 15, 2003).

Season Team	League	REGULAR SEASON								PLAYOFFS				
		Gms.	G	A	Pts.	PIM	+/-	PP	SH	Gms.	G	A	Pts.	PIM
98-99—Huddinge	Sweden	14	0	1	1	10	...	...	...	—	—	—	—	—
99-00—Djurgarden Stockholm	Sweden	37	1	4	5	16	...	...	...	8	0	0	0	8
00-01—Djurgarden Stockholm	Sweden	31	1	9	10	32	...	...	...	15	0	1	1	8
01-02—Djurgarden Stockholm	Sweden	48	5	7	12	34	...	...	...	5	0	0	0	0
02-03—Djurgarden Stockholm	Sweden	50	5	13	18	46	...	...	...	12	3	2	5	18

KRUPP, UWE — D

PERSONAL: Born June 24, 1965, in Cologne, West Germany ... 6-6/233. ... Shoots right. ... Name pronounced YOO-ee KROOP.
TRANSACTIONS/CAREER NOTES: Selected by Buffalo Sabres in 11th round (13th Sabres pick, 214th overall) of NHL entry draft (June 8, 1983). ... Bruised hip (November 1987). ... Injured head (April 1988). ... Broke rib (January 6, 1989). ... Banned from international competition for 18 months by IIHF after failing random substance test (April 20, 1990). ... Suffered from cyst on foot (January 2, 1991). ... Traded by Sabres with C Pierre Turgeon, RW Benoit Hogue and C Dave McLlwain to New York Islanders for C Pat LaFontaine, LW Randy Wood, D Randy Hillier and future considerations; Sabres received fourth-round pick (D Dean Melanson) in 1992 draft to complete deal (October 25, 1991). ... Sprained left knee (December 28, 1991); missed five games. ... Bruised thigh (February 7, 1992). ... Suffered from the flu (March 2, 1993); missed one game. ... Suffered sore shoulder (April 10, 1993); missed three games. ... Broke toe (October 10, 1993); missed three games. ... Fractured sinus bone (October 26, 1993); missed 17 games. ... Suffered severely sprained hamstring (December 19, 1993); missed nine games. ... Suffered from the flu, bruised jaw and sprained wrist (February 27, 1994); missed four games. ... Sprained wrist (March 5, 1994); missed nine games. ... Traded by Islanders with first-round pick (D Wade Belak) in 1994 draft to Quebec Nordiques for C Ron Sutter and first-round pick (RW Brett Lindros) in 1994 draft (June 28, 1994). ... Played in Europe during 1994-95 NHL lockout. ... Injured hip (February 23, 1995); missed two games. ... Injured hip flexor (April 18, 1995); missed two games. ... Nordiques franchise moved to Colorado and renamed Avalanche for 1995-96 season (June 21, 1995). ... Tore knee ligaments (October 6, 1995); missed first 76 games of season. ... Separated shoulder (November 8, 1996); missed five games. ... Suffered tendinitis in elbow (February 18, 1997); missed eight games. ... Suffered sore back (March 26, 1997); missed five games. ... Injured back (January 21, 1998); missed two games. ... Suffered sore back (March 11, 1998); missed one game. ... Selected by Nashville Predators in NHL expansion draft (June 26, 1998). ... Signed as free agent by Detroit Red Wings (July 6, 1998). ... Bruised knee (October 16, 1998); missed one game. ... Injured hamstring (October 23, 1998); missed seven games. ... Injured back (December 22, 1998); missed remainder of season. ... Missed entire 1999-2000 and 2000-01 seasons due to contract dispute. ... Injured shoulder (October 4, 2001); missed first seven games of season. ... Reinjured shoulder (October 26, 2001) and underwent surgery; missed 64 games. ... Signed as free agent by Atlanta Thrashers (July 19, 2002).
STATISTICAL PLATEAUS: Three-goal games: 1994-95 (1).

Season Team	League	REGULAR SEASON								PLAYOFFS				
		Gms.	G	A	Pts.	PIM	+/-	PP	SH	Gms.	G	A	Pts.	PIM
82-83—Koln	Germany	68	8	15	23	209	...	...	...	—	—	—	—	—
83-84—KEC	W. Germ.	40	0	4	4	22	...	...	...	—	—	—	—	—
84-85—KEC	W. Germ.	39	11	8	19	36	...	...	...	—	—	—	—	—
85-86—KEC	W. Germ.	45	10	21	31	83	...	...	...	—	—	—	—	—
86-87—Rochester	AHL	42	3	19	22	50	...	...	...	17	1	11	12	16
—Buffalo	NHL	26	1	4	5	23	-9	0	0	—	—	—	—	—
87-88—Buffalo	NHL	75	2	9	11	151	-1	0	0	6	0	0	0	15
88-89—Buffalo	NHL	70	5	13	18	55	0	0	1	5	0	1	1	4
89-90—Buffalo	NHL	74	3	20	23	85	15	0	1	6	0	0	0	4
90-91—Buffalo	NHL	74	12	32	44	66	14	6	0	6	1	1	2	6
91-92—Buffalo	NHL	8	2	0	2	6	0	0	0	—	—	—	—	—
—New York Islanders	NHL	59	6	29	35	43	13	2	0	—	—	—	—	—
92-93—New York Islanders	NHL	80	9	29	38	67	6	2	0	18	1	5	6	12
93-94—New York Islanders	NHL	41	7	14	21	30	11	3	0	4	0	1	1	4
94-95—Landshut	Germany	5	1	2	3	6	...	...	...	—	—	—	—	—
—Quebec	NHL	44	6	17	23	20	14	3	0	5	0	2	2	2

Season Team	League	REGULAR SEASON Gms.	G	A	Pts.	PIM	+/-	PP	SH	PLAYOFFS Gms.	G	A	Pts.	PIM
95-96—Colorado	NHL	6	0	3	3	4	4	0	0	22	4	12	16	33
96-97—Colorado	NHL	60	4	17	21	48	12	2	0	—	—	—	—	—
97-98—Colorado	NHL	78	9	22	31	38	21	5	0	7	0	1	1	4
—German Oly. team	Int'l	2	0	2	2	4	...	...	...	—	—	—	—	—
98-99—Detroit	NHL	22	3	2	5	6	0	0	0	—	—	—	—	—
99-00—							Did not play.							
00-01—							Did not play.							
01-02—Detroit	NHL	8	0	1	1	8	-1	0	0	2	0	0	0	2
02-03—Atlanta	NHL	4	0	0	0	10	-2	0	0	—	—	—	—	—
NHL Totals (17 years)		729	69	212	281	660	97	23	2	81	6	23	29	86

KUBA, FILIP — D — WILD

PERSONAL: Born December 29, 1976, in Ostrava, Czechoslovakia ... 6-3/205. ... Shoots left. ... Name pronounced KOO-buh.

TRANSACTIONS/CAREER NOTES: Selected by Florida Panthers in eighth round (eighth Panthers pick, 192nd overall) of NHL entry draft (July 8, 1995). ... Traded by Panthers to Calgary Flames for RW Rocky Thompson (March 16, 2000). ... Selected by Minnesota Wild in NHL expansion draft (June 23, 2000). ... Bruised ribs (November 15, 2000); missed five games. ... Bruised knee (January 19, 2001); missed one game. ... Fractured right hand (February 10, 2002); missed 20 games.

Season Team	League	REGULAR SEASON Gms.	G	A	Pts.	PIM	+/-	PP	SH	PLAYOFFS Gms.	G	A	Pts.	PIM
94-95—Vitkovice	Czech. Jrs.	35	10	15	25	...	...	...	...	—	—	—	—	—
—Vitkovice	Czech Rep.	—	—	—	—	...	...	...	...	4	0	0	0	2
95-96—Vitkovice	Czech Rep.	19	0	1	1	...	...	...	...	—	—	—	—	—
96-97—Carolina	AHL	51	0	12	12	38	...	...	...	—	—	—	—	—
97-98—New Haven	AHL	77	4	13	17	58	...	...	...	3	1	1	2	0
98-99—Kentucky	AHL	45	2	8	10	33	...	...	...	10	0	1	1	4
—Florida	NHL	5	0	1	1	0	2	0	0	—	—	—	—	—
99-00—Florida	NHL	13	1	5	6	2	-3	1	0	—	—	—	—	—
—Houston	IHL	27	3	6	9	13	...	...	...	11	1	2	3	4
00-01—Minnesota	NHL	75	9	21	30	28	-6	4	0	—	—	—	—	—
01-02—Minnesota	NHL	62	5	19	24	32	-6	3	0	—	—	—	—	—
02-03—Minnesota	NHL	78	8	21	29	29	0	4	2	18	3	5	8	24
NHL Totals (5 years)		233	23	67	90	91	-13	12	2	18	3	5	8	24

KUBINA, PAVEL — D — LIGHTNING

PERSONAL: Born April 15, 1977, in Caledna, Czechoslovakia ... 6-4/236. ... Shoots right. ... Name pronounced koo-BEE-nuh.

TRANSACTIONS/CAREER NOTES: Selected by Tampa Bay Lightning in seventh round (sixth Lightning pick, 179th overall) of NHL entry draft (June 22, 1996). ... Injured knee (November 8, 1998); missed two games. ... Injured shoulder (November 29, 1998); missed three games. ... Bruised rib (January 5, 2000); missed two games. ... Bruised hand (March 1, 2000); missed one game. ... Injured ankle (March 21, 2000); missed final nine games of season. ... Suffered concussion (November 3, 2000); missed two games. ... Lacerated finger (December 30, 2000); missed two games. ... Injured leg (Feburary 24, 2001); missed eight games.

Season Team	League	REGULAR SEASON Gms.	G	A	Pts.	PIM	+/-	PP	SH	PLAYOFFS Gms.	G	A	Pts.	PIM
93-94—HC Vitkovice	Czech Rep.	1	0	0	0	0	...	...	...	—	—	—	—	—
94-95—HC Vitkovice	Czech Rep.	8	2	0	2	0	...	...	...	4	0	0	0	0
95-96—HC Vitkovice	Czech Rep.	32	3	4	7	0	...	...	...	4	0	0	0	0
96-97—Moose Jaw	WHL	61	12	32	44	116	...	...	...	11	2	5	7	27
—HC Vitkovice	Czech Rep.	1	0	0	0	0	...	...	...	—	—	—	—	—
97-98—Adirondack	AHL	55	4	8	12	86	...	...	...	1	1	0	1	14
—Tampa Bay	NHL	10	1	2	3	22	-1	0	0	—	—	—	—	—
98-99—Tampa Bay	NHL	68	9	12	21	80	-33	3	1	—	—	—	—	—
—Cleveland	IHL	6	2	2	4	16	...	...	...	—	—	—	—	—
99-00—Tampa Bay	NHL	69	8	18	26	93	-19	6	0	—	—	—	—	—
00-01—Tampa Bay	NHL	70	11	19	30	103	-14	6	1	—	—	—	—	—
01-02—Tampa Bay	NHL	82	11	23	34	106	-22	5	2	—	—	—	—	—
—Czech Rep. Oly. team	Int'l	4	0	1	1	0	...	...	...	—	—	—	—	—
02-03—Tampa Bay	NHL	75	3	19	22	78	-7	0	0	11	0	0	0	12
NHL Totals (6 years)		374	43	93	136	482	-96	20	4	11	0	0	0	12

KUDROC, KRISTIAN — D — PANTHERS

PERSONAL: Born May 21, 1981, in Michalovce, Czechoslovakia. ... 6-6/229. ... Shoots right.

TRANSACTIONS/CAREER NOTES: Selected by New York Islanders in first round (fourth Islanders pick, 28th overall) of NHL entry draft (June 26, 1999). ... Traded by Islanders with G Kevin Weekes and second-round pick (traded to Phoenix) in 2001 draft to Tampa Bay Lightning for first-(LW Raffi Torres), fourth-(RW/LW Vladimir Gorbunov) and seventh-round (D Ryan Caldwell) picks in 2000 draft (June 24, 2000). ... Signed by Florida Panthers (July 2, 2003).

Season Team	League	REGULAR SEASON Gms.	G	A	Pts.	PIM	+/-	PP	SH	PLAYOFFS Gms.	G	A	Pts.	PIM
97-98—Michalovce	Slovakia Jrs.	47	7	4	11	...	...	...	...	—	—	—	—	—
—HK Michalovce	Slov. Div. II	4	0	0	0	0	...	...	...	—	—	—	—	—
98-99—Michalovce	Slovakia	17	0	3	3	12	...	...	...	—	—	—	—	—
99-00—Quebec	QMJHL	57	9	22	31	172	...	...	...	11	2	5	7	29
00-01—Detroit	IHL	44	4	3	7	80	...	...	...	—	—	—	—	—
—Tampa Bay	NHL	22	2	2	4	36	0	0	0	—	—	—	—	—
01-02—Tampa Bay	NHL	2	0	0	0	0	0	0	0	—	—	—	—	—
—Springfield	AHL	55	0	8	8	126	...	...	...	—	—	—	—	—
—Philadelphia	AHL	10	0	3	3	14	...	...	...	5	1	1	2	21
02-03—Springfield	AHL	35	0	4	4	58	...	...	...	—	—	—	—	—
NHL Totals (2 years)		24	2	2	4	36	0	0	0	—	—	—	—	—

KULESHOV, MIKHAIL — LW — AVALANCHE

PERSONAL: Born January 7, 1981, in Perm, U.S.S.R. ... 6-2/200. ... Shoots right.
TRANSACTIONS/CAREER NOTES: Selected by Colorado Avalanche in first round (first Avalanche pick, 25th overall) of NHL entry draft (June 26, 1999).

Season Team	League	REGULAR SEASON								PLAYOFFS				
		Gms.	G	A	Pts.	PIM	+/-	PP	SH	Gms.	G	A	Pts.	PIM
97-98—Avangard Omsk	Russian	4	1	0	1	4	...	...	...	—	—	—	—	—
—Avangard-VDV Omsk..	Rus. Div. III	12	12	3	15	12	...	...	...	—	—	—	—	—
98-99—Severstal Cherepovets	Russian	15	2	0	2	8	...	...	...	3	0	0	0	4
99-00—Severstal Cherepovets	Russian	8	0	0	0	4	...	...	...	3	0	0	0	2
00-01—SKA St. Petersburg	Russian	7	0	0	0	8	...	...	...	—	—	—	—	—
—Hershey	AHL	3	0	0	0	4	...	...	...	11	1	0	1	0
01-02—Hershey	AHL	60	8	11	19	43	...	...	...	7	0	1	1	4
02-03—Hershey	AHL	77	7	13	20	76	...	...	...	—	—	—	—	—

KULTANEN, JARNO — D — BRUINS

PERSONAL: Born January 8, 1973, in Luumaki, Finland ... 6-2/198. ... Shoots left.
TRANSACTIONS/CAREER NOTES: Selected by Boston Bruins in sixth round (eighth Bruins pick, 174th overall) of NHL entry draft (June 24, 2000). ... Sprained ankle (January 1, 2001); missed nine games. ... Suffered from the flu (February 1, 2001); missed nine games. ... Sprained knee (November 6, 2001); missed 12 games. ... Underwent surgery on right knee (March 15, 2002); missed 14 games.

Season Team	League	REGULAR SEASON								PLAYOFFS				
		Gms.	G	A	Pts.	PIM	+/-	PP	SH	Gms.	G	A	Pts.	PIM
91-92—KooKoo Kouvola	Finland Jr.	22	7	17	24	28	...	...	...	—	—	—	—	—
—KooKoo Kouvola	Finland Div. 2	1	0	0	0	0	...	...	...	—	—	—	—	—
92-93—KooKoo Kouvola	Finland Jr.	11	6	5	11	8	...	...	...	—	—	—	—	—
—KooKoo Kouvola	Finland Div. 2	27	1	1	2	33	...	...	...	—	—	—	—	—
—Centers Pietrassari	Finland Div. 2	1	1	0	1	0	...	...	...	—	—	—	—	—
93-94—KooKoo Kouvola	Finland Jr.	3	1	0	1	2	...	...	...	—	—	—	—	—
—KooKoo Kouvola	Finland Div. 2	45	7	10	17	17	...	...	...	—	—	—	—	—
94-95—KalPa Kuopio	Finland	47	5	12	17	26	...	...	...	3	0	0	0	8
95-96—KalPa Kuopio	Finland	49	4	10	14	42	...	...	...	—	—	—	—	—
96-97—Helsinki IFK	Finland	24	1	3	4	6	...	...	...	—	—	—	—	—
97-98—Helsinki IFK	Finland	25	0	1	1	37	...	...	...	—	—	—	—	—
98-99—Helsinki IFK	Finland	51	6	6	12	53	...	...	...	—	—	—	—	—
99-00—HIFK Helsinki	Finland	46	6	8	14	51	...	...	...	—	—	—	—	—
00-01—Boston	NHL	62	2	8	10	26	-3	0	0	—	—	—	—	—
01-02—Boston	NHL	38	0	3	3	33	-1	0	0	—	—	—	—	—
02-03—Providence	AHL	59	9	25	34	35	...	...	...	—	—	—	—	—
—Boston	NHL	2	0	0	0	0	1	0	0	—	—	—	—	—
NHL Totals (3 years)		102	2	11	13	59	-3	0	0					

KURKA, TOMAS — LW — HURRICANES

PERSONAL: Born December 14, 1981, in Most, Czechoslovakia ... 5-11/190. ... Shoots left.
TRANSACTIONS/CAREER NOTES: Selected by Carolina Hurricanes in second round (first Hurricanes pick, 32nd overall) of NHL entry draft (June 24, 2000).

Season Team	League	REGULAR SEASON								PLAYOFFS				
		Gms.	G	A	Pts.	PIM	+/-	PP	SH	Gms.	G	A	Pts.	PIM
97-98—Litvinov	Czech. Jrs.	44	38	23	61		...	...	...	—	—	—	—	—
98-99—Litvinov	Czech. Jrs.	48	60	42	102	38	...	...	...	—	—	—	—	—
—Litvinov	Czech.	6	0	0	0	0	...	...	...	—	—	—	—	—
99-00—Plymouth	OHL	64	36	28	64	37	...	...	...	17	7	6	13	6
00-01—Plymouth	OHL	47	15	29	44	20	...	...	...	16	8	13	21	13
01-02—Lowell	AHL	71	13	15	28	24	...	...	...	5	1	1	2	2
02-03—Lowell	AHL	61	17	12	29	10	...	...	...	—	—	—	—	—
—Carolina	NHL	14	3	2	5	2	1	0	0	—	—	—	—	—
NHL Totals (1 year)		14	3	2	5	2	1	0	0					

KURTZ, JUSTIN — D — CANUCKS

PERSONAL: Born January 14, 1977, in Winnipeg. ... 6-0/200. ... Shoots left.
TRANSACTIONS/CAREER NOTES: Selected by Winnipeg Jets in fourth round (fifth Jets pick, 84th overall) of NHL entry draft (July 8, 1995). ... Jets franchise moved to Phoenix and renamed Coyotes for 1996-97 season; NHL approved move on January 18, 1996. ... Signed as free agent by Vancouver Canucks (October 2001).

Season Team	League	REGULAR SEASON								PLAYOFFS				
		Gms.	G	A	Pts.	PIM	+/-	PP	SH	Gms.	G	A	Pts.	PIM
93-94—Brandon	WHL	63	3	13	16	37	...	...	...	14	1	3	4	24
94-95—Brandon	WHL	65	8	34	42	75	...	...	...	18	2	2	4	26
95-96—Brandon	WHL	53	19	55	74	107	...	...	...	18	4	6	10	37
96-97—Brandon	WHL	59	24	44	68	85	...	...	...	6	3	2	5	4
97-98—Las Vegas	IHL	63	11	11	22	62	...	...	...	—	—	—	—	—
—Saint John	AHL	4	0	0	0	6	...	...	...	6	0	0	0	0
98-99—Louisiana	ECHL	6	1	4	5	6	...	...	...	—	—	—	—	—
—Manitoba	IHL	38	4	6	10	40	...	...	...	5	0	0	0	4
99-00—Manitoba	IHL	66	3	15	18	94	...	...	...	2	0	0	0	0
00-01—Manitoba	IHL	69	8	22	30	62	...	...	...	13	2	3	5	4
01-02—Manitoba	AHL	52	10	29	39	64	...	...	...	7	0	4	4	4
—Vancouver	NHL	27	3	5	8	14	-4	2	0	—	—	—	—	—
02-03—Manitoba	AHL	71	11	29	40	65	...	...	...	—	—	—	—	—
NHL Totals (1 year)		27	3	5	8	14	-4	2	0					

KUTLAK, ZDENEK   D   BRUINS

PERSONAL: Born February 13, 1980, in Ceske Budejovice, Czechoslovakia ... 6-3/221. ... Shoots left.
TRANSACTIONS/CAREER NOTES: Selected by Boston Bruins in eighth round (10th Bruins pick, 237th overall) of NHL entry draft (June 24, 2000). ... Re-signed by Bruins (July 31, 2003).

				REGULAR SEASON							PLAYOFFS			
Season Team	League	Gms.	G	A	Pts.	PIM	+/-	PP	SH	Gms.	G	A	Pts.	PIM
98-99—HC Ceske Budejovice..	Czech. Jrs.	2	1	3	4	4	...	...	...	3	0	0	0	0
99-00—HC Ceske Budejovice..	Czech. Jrs.	28	1	0	1	2	...	...	...	1	0	0	0	0
00-01—Providence................	AHL	62	4	5	9	16	...	...	...	—	—	—	—	—
—Boston	NHL	10	0	2	2	4	-3	0	0	—	—	—	—	—
01-02—Providence................	AHL	80	5	15	20	73	...	...	...	—	—	—	—	—
02-03—Providence................	AHL	68	4	12	16	52	...	...	...	—	—	—	—	—
—Boston	NHL	4	1	0	1	0	0	0	0	—	—	—	—	—
NHL Totals (2 years)...........		14	1	2	3	4	-3	0	0					

KUZNETSOV, MAXIM   D   KINGS

PERSONAL: Born March 24, 1977, in Pavlodar, U.S.S.R. ... 6-5/235. ... Shoots left. ... Name pronounced koos-NEHT-sahf.
TRANSACTIONS/CAREER NOTES: Selected by Detroit Red Wings in first round (first Red Wings pick, 26th overall) of NHL entry draft (July 8, 1995). ... Sprained medial collateral ligament in knee (November 22, 2000); missed nine games. ... Strained rib muscle (December 22, 2000); missed 18 games. ... Injured back (March 11, 2001); missed one game. ... Strained hip flexor (November 7, 2001); missed nine games. ... Traded by Red Wings with C Sean Avery, first-round pick in 2003 draft and second-round pick in 2004 to Los Angeles Kings for D Mathieu Schneider (March 11, 2003). ... Re-signed by Kings (July 28, 2003).

				REGULAR SEASON							PLAYOFFS			
Season Team	League	Gms.	G	A	Pts.	PIM	+/-	PP	SH	Gms.	G	A	Pts.	PIM
94-95—Dynamo Moscow.......	CIS	11	0	0	0	8	...	...	...	—	—	—	—	—
95-96—Dynamo Moscow.......	CIS	9	1	1	2	22	...	...	...	4	0	0	0	0
96-97—Dynamo Moscow.......	CIS	23	0	2	2	16	...	...	...	—	—	—	—	—
—Adirondack	AHL	2	0	1	1	6	...	...	...	2	0	0	0	0
97-98—Adirondack	AHL	51	5	5	10	43	...	...	...	3	0	1	1	4
98-99—Adirondack	AHL	60	0	4	4	30	...	...	...	3	0	0	0	0
99-00—Cincinnati...................	AHL	47	2	9	11	36	...	...	...	—	—	—	—	—
00-01—Detroit........................	NHL	25	1	2	3	23	-1	0	0	—	—	—	—	—
01-02—Detroit........................	NHL	39	1	2	3	40	0	0	0	—	—	—	—	—
—Cincinnati...................	AHL	7	1	0	1	4	...	...	...	—	—	—	—	—
02-03—Detroit........................	NHL	53	0	3	3	54	0	0	0	—	—	—	—	—
—Los Angeles...............	NHL	3	0	0	0	0	1	0	0	—	—	—	—	—
NHL Totals (3 years)...........		120	2	7	9	117	0	0	0					

KVASHA, OLEG   LW   ISLANDERS

PERSONAL: Born July 26, 1978, in Moscow, U.S.S.R. ... 6-5/230. ... Shoots right. ... Name pronounced kuh-VA-shuh.
TRANSACTIONS/CAREER NOTES: Selected by Florida Panthers in third round (third Panthers pick, 65th overall) of NHL entry draft (June 22, 1996). ... Bruised right ankle (December 16, 1998); missed one game. ... Bruised shoulder (February 27, 1999); missed one game. ... Separated left shoulder (March 31, 1999); missed final nine games of season. ... Sprained knee (March 7, 2000); missed two games. ... Traded by Panthers with RW Mark Parrish to New York Islanders for C Olli Jokinen and G Roberto Luongo (June 24, 2000). ... Strained back (December 6, 2000); missed two games. ... Sprained medial collateral ligament in right knee (January 12, 2001); missed 10 games. ... Injured left knee (February 10, 2001); missed eight games. ... Injured shoulder (November 21, 2001); missed two games. ... Suffered from the flu (December 18, 2001); missed one game. ... Injured knee and underwent surgery (February 28, 2002); missed five games.

				REGULAR SEASON							PLAYOFFS			
Season Team	League	Gms.	G	A	Pts.	PIM	+/-	PP	SH	Gms.	G	A	Pts.	PIM
94-95—CSKA	CIS Jr.				Statistics unavailable.									
95-96—CSKA Moscow...........	CIS	38	2	3	5	14	...	...	...	2	0	0	0	0
96-97—CSKA Moscow...........	USSR	44	20	22	42	115	...	...	...	—	—	—	—	—
97-98—New Haven	AHL	57	13	16	29	46	...	...	...	3	2	1	3	0
98-99—Florida.......................	NHL	68	12	13	25	45	5	4	0	—	—	—	—	—
99-00—Florida.......................	NHL	78	5	20	25	34	3	2	0	4	0	0	0	0
00-01—New York Islanders.....	NHL	62	11	9	20	46	-15	0	0	—	—	—	—	—
01-02—New York Islanders.....	NHL	71	13	25	38	80	-4	2	0	7	0	1	1	6
—Russian Oly. team.......	Int'l	5	0	0	0	0	...	...	...	—	—	—	—	—
02-03—New York Islanders.....	NHL	69	12	14	26	44	4	0	1	5	0	1	1	2
NHL Totals (5 years)...........		348	53	81	134	249	-7	8	1	16	0	2	2	8

KWIATKOWSKI, JOEL   D

PERSONAL: Born March 22, 1977, in Kindersley, Sask. ... 5-11/201. ... Shoots left. ... Name pronounced kwee-iht-KOW-skee.
TRANSACTIONS/CAREER NOTES: Signed as non-drafted free agent by Mighty Ducks of Anaheim (June 18, 1998). ... Traded by Mighty Ducks to Ottawa Senators for D Patrick Traverse (June 12, 2000). ... Traded by Senators to Washington Capitals for 2003 ninth-round draft pick (January 15, 2003).

Season Team	League	REGULAR SEASON Gms.	G	A	Pts.	PIM	+/-	PP	SH	PLAYOFFS Gms.	G	A	Pts.	PIM
94-95—Tacoma	WHL	70	4	13	17	66	...	...	...	4	0	0	0	2
95-96—Prince George	WHL	72	12	28	40	133	...	...	...	—	—	—	—	—
96-97—Prince George	WHL	72	16	36	52	94	...	...	...	4	4	2	6	24
97-98—Prince George	WHL	62	21	43	64	65	...	...	...	11	3	6	9	6
98-99—Cincinnati	AHL	80	12	21	33	48	...	...	...	3	2	0	2	0
99-00—Cincinnati	AHL	70	4	22	26	28	...	...	...	—	—	—	—	—
00-01—Grand Rapids	IHL	77	4	17	21	58	...	...	...	10	1	0	1	4
—Ottawa	NHL	4	1	0	1	0	1	0	0	—	—	—	—	—
01-02—Grand Rapids	AHL	65	8	21	29	94	...	...	...	5	1	2	3	12
—Ottawa	NHL	11	0	0	0	12	5	0	0	—	—	—	—	—
02-03—Binghamton	AHL	1	0	0	0	2	...	...	...	—	—	—	—	—
—Ottawa	NHL	20	0	2	2	6	2	0	0	—	—	—	—	—
—Washington	NHL	34	0	3	3	12	1	0	0	6	0	0	0	2
NHL Totals (3 years)		69	1	5	6	30	9	0	0	6	0	0	0	2

LAAKSONEN, ANTTI   LW   WILD

PERSONAL: Born October 3, 1973, in Tammela, Finland ... 6-0/180. ... Shoots left. ... Full Name: Antti Akseli Laaksonen.
TRANSACTIONS/CAREER NOTES: Selected by Boston Bruins in eighth round (10th Bruins pick, 191st overall) of NHL entry draft (July 21, 1997). ... Signed as free agent by Minnesota Wild (July 20, 2000). ... Re-signed by Wild (July 23, 2003).
STATISTICAL PLATEAUS: Three-goal games: 2000-01 (1).

Season Team	League	REGULAR SEASON Gms.	G	A	Pts.	PIM	+/-	PP	SH	PLAYOFFS Gms.	G	A	Pts.	PIM
92-93—HPK Hameenlinna	Finland	2	0	0	0	0	...	...	...	—	—	—	—	—
93-94—Univ. of Denver	WCHA	36	12	9	21	38	...	...	...	—	—	—	—	—
94-95—Univ. of Denver	WCHA	40	17	18	35	42	...	...	...	—	—	—	—	—
95-96—Univ. of Denver	WCHA	39	25	28	53	71	...	...	...	—	—	—	—	—
96-97—Univ. of Denver	WCHA	39	21	17	38	63	...	...	...	—	—	—	—	—
97-98—Providence	AHL	38	3	2	5	14	...	...	...	—	—	—	—	—
—Charlotte	ECHL	15	4	3	7	12	...	...	...	6	0	3	3	0
98-99—Boston	NHL	11	1	2	3	2	-1	0	0	—	—	—	—	—
—Providence	AHL	66	25	33	58	52	...	...	...	19	7	2	9	28
99-00—Providence	AHL	40	10	12	22	57	...	...	...	14	5	4	9	4
—Boston	NHL	27	6	3	9	2	3	0	0	—	—	—	—	—
00-01—Minnesota	NHL	82	12	16	28	24	-7	0	2	—	—	—	—	—
01-02—Minnesota	NHL	82	16	17	33	22	-5	0	0	—	—	—	—	—
02-03—Minnesota	NHL	82	15	16	31	26	4	1	2	16	1	3	4	4
NHL Totals (5 years)		284	50	54	104	76	-6	1	4	16	1	3	4	4

LABARBERA, JASON   G   RANGERS

PERSONAL: Born January 18, 1980, in Burnaby, B.C. ... 6-2/205. ... Catches left.
TRANSACTIONS/CAREER NOTES: Selected by New York Rangers in third round (third Rangers pick, 66th overall) of NHL entry draft (June 27, 1998).

Season Team	League	REGULAR SEASON Gms.	Min	W	L	T	GA	SO	Avg.	SV%	PLAYOFFS Gms.	Min.	W	L	GA	SO	Avg.	SV%
96-97—Tri-City	WHL	2	...	1	0	0	...	...	...	—	—	—	—	—	—	—	—	—
—Portland	WHL	9	443	5	1	1	18	0	2.44	—	—	—	—	—	—	—	—	—
97-98—Portland	WHL	23	1305	18	4	0	72	1	3.31	—	—	—	—	—	—	—	—	—
98-99—Portland	WHL	51	2991	18	23	9	170	4	3.41	—	4	252	0	4	19	0	4.52	—
99-00—Portland	WHL	34	2005	8	24	2	123	1	3.68	—	—	—	—	—	—	—	—	—
—Spokane	WHL	21	1146	12	6	2	50	0	2.62	—	9	435	6	1	18	1	2.48	—
00-01—Hartford	AHL	4	156	1	1	0	12	0	4.62	—	—	—	—	—	—	—	—	—
—New York Rangers	NHL	1	10	0	0	0	0	0	...	1.000	—	—	—	—	—	—	—	—
—Charlotte	ECHL	35	2100	18	10	7	112	1	3.20	—	2	143	1	1	5	0	2.10	—
01-02—Hartford	AHL	20	1057	7	11	1	55	0	3.12	—	—	—	—	—	—	—	—	—
—Charlotte	ECHL	13	743	9	3	1	29	0	2.34	—	4	212	2	2	12	0	3.40	—
02-03—Hartford	AHL	46	2451	18	17	6	105	2	2.57	—	—	—	—	—	—	—	—	—
NHL Totals (1 year)		1	10	0	0	0	0	0	...	1.000								

LABBE, JEAN-FRANCOIS   G

PERSONAL: Born June 15, 1972, in Sherbrooke, Que. ... 5-10/170. ... Catches left. ... Name pronounced lah-BAY.
TRANSACTIONS/CAREER NOTES: Signed as non-drafted free agent by Ottawa Senators (May 12, 1994). ... Traded by Senators to Colorado Avalanche for conditional draft pick (September 20, 1995). ... Signed as free agent by Edmonton Oilers (August 8, 1997). ... Signed as free agent by New York Rangers (July 16, 1998). ... Traded by Rangers to Columbus Blue Jackets for D Bert Robertsson (November 9, 2000).

Season Team	League	REGULAR SEASON Gms.	Min	W	L	T	GA	SO	Avg.	SV%	PLAYOFFS Gms.	Min.	W	L	GA	SO	Avg.	SV%
89-90—Trois-Rivieres	QMJHL	28	1499	13	10	0	106	1	4.24	—	3	132	1	1	8	0	3.64	—
90-91—Trois-Rivieres	QMJHL	54	2870	35	14	0	158	5	3.30	—	5	230	1	4	19	0	4.96	—
91-92—Trois-Rivieres	QMJHL	48	2749	31	13	3	142	3	*3.10	—	15	791	10	3	33	†1	*2.50	—
92-93—Hull	QMJHL	46	2701	25	16	2	155	2	3.44	—	10	518	6	3	24	†1	*2.78	—
93-94—Prin. Edward Island	AHL	7	390	4	3	0	22	0	3.38	—	—	—	—	—	—	—	—	—
—Thunder Bay	Col.HL	52	*2900	*35	11	4	150	*2	*3.10	—	8	493	7	1	18	*2	*2.19	—

			REGULAR SEASON								PLAYOFFS							
Season Team	League	Gms.	Min	W	L	T	GA	SO	Avg.	SV%	Gms.	Min.	W	L	GA	SO	Avg.	SV%
94-95—Prin. Edward Island.......	AHL	32	1817	13	14	3	94	2	3.10	—	—	—	—	—	—	—	—	—
—Thunder Bay................	Col.HL	2	...	2	0	0	...	...	...	—	—	—	—	—	—	—	—	—
95-96—Cornwall......................	AHL	55	2971	25	21	5	144	3	2.91	—	8	470	3	5	21	1	2.68	—
96-97—Hershey......................	AHL	66	3811	†34	22	9	160	*6	*2.52	—	*23	*1364	*14	8	59	1	2.60	—
97-98—Hamilton	AHL	52	3139	24	17	11	149	2	2.85	—	7	414	3	4	20	0	2.90	—
98-99—Hartford	AHL	*59	*3392	28	26	3	*182	2	3.22	—	7	447	3	4	22	0	2.95	—
99-00—Hartford	AHL	49	2853	27	13	†7	120	1	2.52	—	*22	*1320	*15	7	*48	3	2.18	—
—New York Rangers	NHL	1	60	0	1	0	3	0	3.00	.864	—	—	—	—	—	—	—	—
00-01—Hartford	AHL	8	394	4	2	1	20	0	3.05	—	—	—	—	—	—	—	—	—
—Syracuse	AHL	37	2201	15	15	5	105	2	2.86	—	5	323	2	3	18	0	3.34	—
01-02—Syracuse	AHL	51	2993	27	16	7	109	*9	2.19	—	10	596	6	4	19	2	*1.91	—
—Columbus......................	NHL	3	117	1	1	0	6	0	3.08	.912	—	—	—	—	—	—	—	—
02-03—Syracuse	AHL	4	246	1	2	1	11	0	2.68	—	—	—	—	—	—	—	—	—
—Columbus......................	NHL	11	451	2	4	0	27	0	3.59	.884	—	—	—	—	—	—	—	—
NHL Totals (3 years)............		15	628	3	6	0	36	0	3.44	.889								

LACHANCE, SCOTT   D   BLUE JACKETS

PERSONAL: Born October 22, 1972, in Charlottesville, Va. ... 6-2/215. ... Shoots left. ... Full Name: Scott Joseph Lachance. ... Brother of Bob Lachance, right winger with St. Louis Blues organization (1992-93 through 1997-98) and Atlanta Thrashers organization (1999-2000).

TRANSACTIONS/CAREER NOTES: Selected by New York Islanders in first round (first Islanders pick, fourth overall) of NHL entry draft (June 22, 1991). ... Sprained wrist (April 13, 1993); missed remainder of season. ... Underwent wrist surgery (April 30, 1993). ... Suffered mild separation of right shoulder (October 8, 1993); missed four games. ... Fractured ankle (February 25, 1995); missed 22 games. ... Injured groin (October 31, 1995); missed 27 games. ... Suffered broken finger (November 1, 1997); missed two games. ... Strained abdominal muscle (March 14, 1998); missed five games. ... Reinjured abdomen (March 28, 1998); missed 11 games. ... Suffered charley horse (November 21, 1998); missed one game. ... Suffered from the flu (December 22, 1998); missed one game. ... Sprained knee (January 5, 1999); missed one game. ... Traded by Islanders to Montreal Canadiens for third-round pick (RW Mattias Weinhandl) in 1999 draft (March 9, 1999). ... Injured back (November 23, 1999); missed 12 games. ... Signed as free agent by Vancouver Canucks (August 14, 2000). ... Suffered from the flu (December 8, 2000); missed one game. ... Sprained knee (January 28, 2001); missed five games. ... Injured knee (December 22, 2001); missed one game. ... Signed as free agent by Columbus Blue Jackets (July 4, 2002).

			REGULAR SEASON							PLAYOFFS			
Season Team	League	Gms.	G	A	Pts.	PIM	+/-	PP	SH	Gms.	G	A	Pts.	PIM
88-89—Springfield Jr. B.........	NEJHL	36	8	28	36	20	...	...	...	—	—	—	—	—
89-90—Springfield Jr. B.........	NEJHL	34	25	41	66	62	...	...	...	—	—	—	—	—
90-91—Boston University	Hockey East	31	5	19	24	48	...	...	...	—	—	—	—	—
91-92—U.S. national team	Int'l	36	1	10	11	34	...	...	...	—	—	—	—	—
—U.S. Olympic team......	Int'l	8	0	1	1	6	...	...	...	—	—	—	—	—
—New York Islanders.....	NHL	17	1	4	5	9	13	0	0	—	—	—	—	—
92-93—New York Islanders.....	NHL	75	7	17	24	67	-1	0	1	—	—	—	—	—
93-94—New York Islanders.....	NHL	74	3	11	14	70	-5	0	0	3	0	0	0	0
94-95—New York Islanders.....	NHL	26	6	7	13	26	2	3	0	—	—	—	—	—
95-96—New York Islanders.....	NHL	55	3	10	13	54	-19	1	0	—	—	—	—	—
96-97—New York Islanders.....	NHL	81	3	11	14	47	-7	1	0	—	—	—	—	—
97-98—New York Islanders.....	NHL	63	2	11	13	45	-11	1	0	—	—	—	—	—
98-99—New York Islanders.....	NHL	59	1	8	9	30	-19	1	0	—	—	—	—	—
—Montreal	NHL	17	1	1	2	11	-2	0	0	—	—	—	—	—
99-00—Montreal	NHL	57	0	6	6	22	-4	0	0	—	—	—	—	—
00-01—Vancouver...................	NHL	76	3	11	14	46	5	0	0	2	0	1	1	2
01-02—Vancouver...................	NHL	81	1	10	11	50	15	0	0	6	1	1	2	4
02-03—Columbus	NHL	61	0	1	1	46	-20	0	0	—	—	—	—	—
NHL Totals (12 years).........		742	31	108	139	523	-53	7	1	11	1	2	3	6

LACOUTURE, DAN   LW   RANGERS

PERSONAL: Born April 18, 1977, in Hyannis, Mass. ... 6-2/208. ... Shoots left. ... Name pronounced LA-kuh-toor.

TRANSACTIONS/CAREER NOTES: Selected by New York Islanders in second round (second Islanders pick, 29th overall) of NHL entry draft (June 22, 1996). ... Traded by Islanders to Edmonton Oilers for RW Mariusz Czerkawski (August 25, 1997). ... Traded by Oilers to Pittsburgh Penguins for D Steve Butenschon (March 13, 2001). ... Traded by Penguins with RW Alexei Kovalev, D Janne Laukkanen and D Mike Wilson to New York Rangers for RW Rico Fata, RW Mikael Samuelsson, D Joel Bouchard, D Richard Lintner and cash (February 10, 2003). ... Re-signed by Rangers (June 22, 2003).

			REGULAR SEASON							PLAYOFFS			
Season Team	League	Gms.	G	A	Pts.	PIM	+/-	PP	SH	Gms.	G	A	Pts.	PIM
94-95—Springfield Jr. B.........	EJHL	49	37	39	76	100	...	...	...	—	—	—	—	—
95-96—Jr. Whalers	EJHL	42	36	48	84	102	...	...	...	—	—	—	—	—
96-97—Boston University	Hockey East	31	13	12	25	18	...	...	...	—	—	—	—	—
97-98—Hamilton	AHL	77	15	10	25	31	...	...	...	5	1	0	1	0
98-99—Hamilton	AHL	72	17	14	31	73	...	...	...	9	2	1	3	2
—Edmonton..................	NHL	3	0	0	0	0	1	0	0	—	—	—	—	—
99-00—Hamilton	AHL	70	23	17	40	85	...	...	...	6	2	1	3	0
—Edmonton..................	NHL	5	0	0	0	10	0	0	0	1	0	0	0	0
00-01—Edmonton..................	NHL	37	2	4	6	29	-2	0	0	—	—	—	—	—
—Pittsburgh..................	NHL	11	0	0	0	14	0	0	0	5	0	0	0	2
01-02—Pittsburgh..................	NHL	82	6	11	17	71	-19	0	1	—	—	—	—	—
02-03—Pittsburgh..................	NHL	44	2	2	4	72	-8	0	0	—	—	—	—	—
—New York Rangers......	NHL	24	1	4	5	0	4	0	0	—	—	—	—	—
NHL Totals (5 years)..........		206	11	21	32	196	-24	0	1	6	0	0	0	2

LAFLAMME, CHRISTIAN   D   BLUES

PERSONAL: Born November 24, 1976, in St. Charles, Que. ... 6-1/206. ... Shoots right. ... Name pronounced lah-FLAHM.
TRANSACTIONS/CAREER NOTES: Selected by Chicago Blackhawks in second round (second Blackhawks pick, 45th overall) of NHL entry draft (July 8, 1995). ... Fractured left foot (October 1, 1997); missed six games. ... Fractured right cheekbone (January 24, 1998); missed four games. ... Traded by Blackhawks with C Chad Kilger, LW Daniel Cleary and LW Ethan Moreau to Edmonton Oilers for D Boris Mironov, LW Dean McAmmond and D Jonas Elofsson (March 20, 1999). ... Suffered concussion (March 28, 1999); missed one game. ... Bruised shoulder (January 11, 2000); missed one game. ... Traded by Oilers with D Mathieu Descoteaux to Montreal Canadiens for D Igor Ulanov and D Alain Nasreddine (March 9, 2000). ... Suffered concussion (October 24, 2000); missed six games. ... Strained groin (December 11, 2000); missed 10 games. ... Signed as free agent by St. Louis Blues (August 21, 2001). ... Re-signed by Blues (July 16, 2003).

| | | | REGULAR SEASON | | | | | | | | PLAYOFFS | | | | |
Season Team	League	Gms.	G	A	Pts.	PIM	+/-	PP	SH		Gms.	G	A	Pts.	PIM
92-93—Verdun	QMJHL	69	2	17	19	70	...	...	...		3	0	2	2	6
93-94—Verdun	QMJHL	72	4	34	38	85	...	...	...		4	0	3	3	4
94-95—Beauport	QMJHL	67	6	41	47	82	...	...	...		8	1	4	5	6
95-96—Beauport	QMJHL	41	13	23	36	63	...	...	...		20	7	17	24	32
96-97—Indianapolis	IHL	62	5	15	20	60	...	...	...		4	1	1	2	16
—Chicago	NHL	4	0	1	1	2	3	0	0		—	—	—	—	—
97-98—Chicago	NHL	72	0	11	11	59	14	0	0		—	—	—	—	—
98-99—Chicago	NHL	62	2	11	13	70	0	0	0		—	—	—	—	—
—Portland	AHL	2	0	1	1	2	...	...	...		—	—	—	—	—
—Edmonton	NHL	11	0	1	1	0	-3	0	0		4	0	1	1	2
99-00—Edmonton	NHL	50	0	5	5	32	-4	0	0		—	—	—	—	—
—Montreal	NHL	15	0	2	2	8	-5	0	0		—	—	—	—	—
00-01—Montreal	NHL	39	0	3	3	42	-11	0	0		—	—	—	—	—
01-02—Worcester	AHL	62	2	17	19	52	...	...	...		—	—	—	—	—
—St. Louis	NHL	8	0	1	1	4	3	0	0		—	—	—	—	—
02-03—Worcester	AHL	8	0	4	4	6	...	...	...		—	—	—	—	—
—St. Louis	NHL	47	0	9	9	45	1	0	0		5	0	0	0	4
NHL Totals (7 years)		308	2	44	46	262	-2	0	0		9	0	1	1	6

LAINE, TEEMU   RW   DEVILS

PERSONAL: Born August 9, 1982, in Helsinki, Finland. ... 6-0/194. ... Shoots left.
TRANSACTIONS/CAREER NOTES: Selected by New Jersey Devils in second round (second Devils pick, 39th overall) of NHL entry draft (June 24, 2000).

| | | | REGULAR SEASON | | | | | | | | PLAYOFFS | | | | |
Season Team	League	Gms.	G	A	Pts.	PIM	+/-	PP	SH		Gms.	G	A	Pts.	PIM
98-99—Jokerit Helsinki	Finland Jr. B	34	20	19	39	87	...	...	...		—	—	—	—	—
99-00—Jokerit Helsinki	Finland	14	1	1	2	8	...	...	...		—	—	—	—	—
—Jokerit Helsinki	Finland Jr.	23	5	9	14	14	...	...	...		—	—	—	—	—
00-01—Jokerit Helsinki	Finland	25	3	2	5	10	...	...	...		5	1	0	1	2
01-02—Jokerit Helsinki	Finland	38	0	1	1	45	...	...	...		7	0	0	0	2
02-03—Jokerit Helsinki	Finland	53	7	5	12	52	...	...	...		—	—	—	—	—

LALIME, PATRICK   G   SENATORS

PERSONAL: Born July 7, 1974, in St. Bonaventure, Que. ... 6-3/192. ... Catches left. ... Name pronounced luh-LEEM.
TRANSACTIONS/CAREER NOTES: Selected by Pittsburgh Penguins in sixth round (sixth Penguins pick, 156th overall) of NHL entry draft (June 26, 1993). ... Rights traded by Penguins to Mighty Ducks of Anaheim for C Sean Pronger (March 24, 1998). ... Traded by Mighty Ducks to Ottawa Senators for LW Ted Donato and D Antti-Jussi Niemi (June 18, 1999). ... Suffered from the flu (February 1, 2000); missed one game. ... Sprained ligament in left knee (October 14, 2000); missed 10 games.

| | | | REGULAR SEASON | | | | | | | | PLAYOFFS | | | | | | |
Season Team	League	Gms.	Min	W	L	T	GA	SO	Avg.	SV%	Gms.	Min.	W	L	GA	SO	Avg.	SV%
92-93—Shawinigan	QMJHL	44	2467	10	24	4	192	0	4.67	—	—	—	—	—	—	—	—	—
93-94—Shawinigan	QMJHL	48	2733	22	20	2	192	1	4.22	—	5	223	1	3	25	0	6.73	—
94-95—Hampton Roads	ECHL	26	1471	15	7	‡3	82	2	3.34	—	—	—	—	—	—	—	—	—
—Cleveland	IHL	23	1230	7	10	‡4	91	0	4.44	—	—	—	—	—	—	—	—	—
95-96—Cleveland	IHL	41	2314	20	12	‡7	149	0	3.86	—	—	—	—	—	—	—	—	—
96-97—Cleveland	IHL	14	834	6	6	‡2	45	1	3.24	—	—	—	—	—	—	—	—	—
—Pittsburgh	NHL	39	2058	21	12	2	101	3	2.94	.913	—	—	—	—	—	—	—	—
97-98—Grand Rapids	IHL	31	1749	10	10	‡9	76	2	2.61	—	1	77	0	1	4	0	3.12	—
98-99—Kansas City	IHL	*66	*3789	*39	20	‡4	*190	2	3.01	—	3	179	1	2	6	1	2.01	—
99-00—Ottawa	NHL	38	2038	19	14	3	79	3	2.33	.905	—	—	—	—	—	—	—	—
00-01—Ottawa	NHL	60	3607	36	19	5	141	7	2.35	.914	4	251	0	4	10	0	2.39	.899
01-02—Ottawa	NHL	61	3583	27	24	8	148	7	2.48	.903	12	778	7	5	18	4	*1.39	*.946
02-03—Ottawa	NHL	67	3943	39	20	7	142	8	2.16	.911	18	1122	11	7	34	1	1.82	.924
NHL Totals (5 years)		265	15229	142	89	25	611	28	2.41	.910	34	2151	18	16	62	5	1.73	.930

LAMBERT, DENNY   RW   MIGHTY DUCKS

PERSONAL: Born January 7, 1970, in Wawa, Ont. ... 5-10/215. ... Shoots left. ... Name pronounced lam-BAIR.
TRANSACTIONS/CAREER NOTES: Signed as non-drafted free agent by Mighty Ducks of Anaheim (August 16, 1993). ... Signed as free agent by Ottawa Senators (July 8, 1996). ... Selected by Nashville Predators in NHL expansion draft (June 26, 1998). ... Suspended four games and fined $1,000 by NHL for slashing incident (October 23, 1998). ... Suffered illness (February 4, 1999); missed two games. ... Traded by Predators to Atlanta Thrashers for C Randy Robitaille (August 16, 1999). ... Injured thumb (March 31, 2000); missed four games. ... Separated shoulder (January 10, 2001); missed three games. ... Strained shoulder (February 25, 2001); missed three games. ... Bruised thumb (March 27, 2001); missed two games. ... Traded by Thrashers to Mighty Ducks for future considerations (July 2, 2001).

Season Team	League	REGULAR SEASON								PLAYOFFS				
		Gms.	G	A	Pts.	PIM	+/-	PP	SH	Gms.	G	A	Pts.	PIM
88-89—Sault Ste. Marie	OHL	61	14	15	29	203	...	...	...	—	—	—	—	—
89-90—Sault Ste. Marie	OHL	61	23	29	52	*276	...	...	...	—	—	—	—	—
90-91—Sault Ste. Marie	OHL	59	28	39	67	169	...	...	...	14	7	9	16	48
91-92—San Diego	IHL	71	17	14	31	229	...	...	...	3	0	0	0	10
92-93—St. Thomas	Col.HL	5	2	6	8	9	...	...	...	—	—	—	—	—
—San Diego	IHL	56	18	12	30	277	...	...	...	14	1	1	2	44
93-94—San Diego	IHL	79	13	14	27	314	...	...	...	6	1	0	1	45
94-95—San Diego	IHL	75	25	35	60	222	...	...	...	—	—	—	—	—
—Anaheim	NHL	13	1	3	4	4	3	0	0	—	—	—	—	—
95-96—Anaheim	NHL	33	0	8	8	55	-2	0	0	—	—	—	—	—
—Baltimore	AHL	44	14	28	42	126	...	...	...	12	3	9	12	39
96-97—Ottawa	NHL	80	4	16	20	217	-4	0	0	6	0	1	1	9
97-98—Ottawa	NHL	72	9	10	19	250	4	0	0	11	0	0	0	19
98-99—Nashville	NHL	76	5	11	16	218	-3	1	0	—	—	—	—	—
99-00—Atlanta	NHL	73	5	6	11	*219	-17	2	0	—	—	—	—	—
00-01—Atlanta	NHL	67	1	7	8	215	-5	0	0	—	—	—	—	—
01-02—Anaheim	NHL	73	2	5	7	213	1	0	0	—	—	—	—	—
02-03—Milwaukee.................	AHL	39	12	12	24	132	...	...	...	—	—	—	—	—
NHL Totals (8 years)..........		487	27	66	93	1391	-23	3	0	17	0	1	1	28

LAMOTHE, MARC   G

PERSONAL: Born February 27, 1974, in New Liskeard, Ont. ... 6-2/210. ... Catches left. ... Name pronounced luh-MAHTH.
TRANSACTIONS/CAREER NOTES: Selected by Montreal Canadiens in fourth round (sixth Canadiens pick, 92nd overall) of NHL entry draft (June 20, 1992). ... Signed as free agent by Chicago Blackhawks (August 21, 1996). ... Signed as free agent by Detroit Red Wings (August 5, 2002).

Season Team	League	REGULAR SEASON									PLAYOFFS							
		Gms.	Min	W	L	T	GA	SO	Avg.	SV%	Gms.	Min.	W	L	GA	SO	Avg.	SV%
90-91—Ottawa..........................	OHA Mj. Jr.	25	1220	...	...	...	82	1	4.03	—	—	—	—	—	—	—	—	—
91-92—Kingston	OHL	42	2378	10	25	2	189	1	4.77	—	—	—	—	—	—	—	—	—
92-93—Kingston	OHL	45	2489	23	12	6	162	†1	3.91	—	15	733	8	5	46	†1	3.77	—
93-94—Kingston	OHL	48	2828	23	20	5	177	†2	3.76	—	6	224	2	2	12	0	3.21	—
94-95—Fredericton	AHL	9	428	2	5	0	32	0	4.49	—	—	—	—	—	—	—	—	—
—Wheeling	ECHL	13	737	9	2	‡1	38	0	3.09	—	—	—	—	—	—	—	—	—
95-96—Fredericton	AHL	23	1165	5	9	3	73	1	3.76	—	3	160	1	2	9	0	3.38	—
96-97—Indianapolis	IHL	38	2271	20	14	‡4	100	1	2.64	—	1	20	0	1	0	0	3.00	—
97-98—Indianapolis	IHL	31	1773	18	10	2	72	3	2.44	—	4	178	1	3	10	0	3.37	—
98-99—Indianapolis	IHL	32	1823	9	16	‡6	115	1	3.78	—	6	338	3	3	10	*2	1.78	—
—Detroit	IHL	—	—	—	—	—	—	—	—	—	1	80	0	1	5	0	3.75	—
99-00—Cleveland	IHL	44	2455	23	18	4	112	2	2.74	—	4	325	2	2	12	0	2.22	—
—Chicago	NHL	2	116	1	1	0	10	0	5.17	.800	—	—	—	—	—	—	—	—
00-01—Syracuse	AHL	42	2323	17	15	*7	112	2	2.89	—	—	—	—	—	—	—	—	—
01-02—Hamilton	AHL	45	2569	22	19	2	102	3	2.38	—	9	550	6	3	18	0	1.96	—
02-03—Grand Rapids	AHL	60	3438	33	18	8	122	6	2.13	—	—	—	—	—	—	—	—	—
NHL Totals (1 year)..............		2	116	1	1	0	10	0	5.17	.800								

LAMPMAN, BRYCE   D   RANGERS

PERSONAL: Born August 31, 1982, in Rochester, Minn. ... 6-1/193. ... Shoots left.
TRANSACTIONS/CAREER NOTES: Selected by New York Rangers in fourth round (fourth Rangers pick, 113th overall) of NHL entry draft (June 23, 2001).

Season Team	League	REGULAR SEASON								PLAYOFFS				
		Gms.	G	A	Pts.	PIM	+/-	PP	SH	Gms.	G	A	Pts.	PIM
00-01—Omaha..........................	USHL	55	10	11	21	77	...	...	...	—	—	—	—	—
01-02—Nebraska-Omaha	CCHA	26	0	4	4	28	...	...	...	—	—	—	—	—
02-03—Hartford	AHL	45	0	6	6	32	...	...	...	—	—	—	—	—

LANDRY, ERIC   C

PERSONAL: Born January 20, 1975, in Gatineau, Que. ... 5-11/185. ... Shoots left.
TRANSACTIONS/CAREER NOTES: Selected by San Jose Sharks in eighth round (eighth Sharks pick, 193rd overall) of NHL entry draft (June 29, 1994). ... Signed as free agent by Calgary Flames (August 6, 1997). ... Suffered concussion (November 22, 1997); missed one game. ... Traded by Flames to Sharks for D Fredrik Oduya (July 12, 1999). ... Signed as free agent by Montreal Canadiens (July 7, 2000).

Season Team	League	REGULAR SEASON								PLAYOFFS				
		Gms.	G	A	Pts.	PIM	+/-	PP	SH	Gms.	G	A	Pts.	PIM
93-94—St. Hyacinthe	QMJHL	69	42	34	76	128	...	...	...	7	4	2	6	13
94-95—St. Hyacinthe	QMJHL	68	38	36	74	249	...	...	...	5	2	1	3	10
95-96—Cape Breton	AHL	74	19	33	52	187	...	...	...	—	—	—	—	—
96-97—Hamilton	AHL	74	15	17	32	139	...	...	...	22	6	7	13	43
97-98—St. John's.................	AHL	61	17	21	38	194	...	...	...	20	4	6	10	58
—Calgary	NHL	12	1	0	1	4	-2	0	0	—	—	—	—	—
98-99—St. John's.................	AHL	56	19	22	41	158	...	...	...	7	2	5	7	12
—Calgary	NHL	3	0	1	1	0	1	0	0	—	—	—	—	—
99-00—Kentucky	AHL	79	35	31	66	170	...	...	...	9	3	6	9	2
00-01—Quebec	AHL	27	14	18	32	90	...	...	...	9	4	4	8	35
—Montreal	NHL	51	4	7	11	43	-9	2	0	—	—	—	—	—
01-02—Quebec	AHL	63	32	43	75	125	...	...	...	3	1	1	2	16
—Montreal	NHL	2	0	1	1	0	2	0	0	—	—	—	—	—
02-03—Utah..........................	AHL	73	26	36	62	119	...	...	...	—	—	—	—	—
NHL Totals (4 years)..........		68	5	9	14	47	-8	2	0					

LANG, ROBERT C CAPITALS

PERSONAL: Born December 19, 1970, in Teplice, Czechoslovakia ... 6-2/217. ... Shoots right.

TRANSACTIONS/CAREER NOTES: Selected by Los Angeles Kings in seventh round (sixth Kings pick, 133rd overall) of NHL entry draft (June 16, 1990). ... Dislocated shoulder (April 3, 1994); missed remainder of season. ... Played in Europe during 1994-95 NHL lockout. ... Strained left shoulder (March 26, 1995); missed one game. ... Strained back (November 20, 1995); missed seven games. ... Signed as free agent by Edmonton Oilers (October 19, 1996). ... Loaned by Oilers to Sparta Praha of Czech Republic League (October 19, 1996). ... Signed as free agent by Pittsburgh Penguins (September 2, 1997). ... Claimed by Boston Bruins from Penguins in NHL waiver draft (September 28, 1997). ... Claimed on waivers by Penguins (October 25, 1997). ... Fractured thumb (March 21, 1998); missed nine games. ... Bruised ankle (March 23, 1999); missed 10 games. ... Suffered back spasms (October 16, 1999); missed one game. ... Injured thumb (December 14, 1999); missed one game. ... Suffered facial injury (March 9, 2000); missed two games. ... Underwent oral surgery (January 26, 2002); missed two games. ... Fractured hand (March 5, 2002); missed seven games. ... Reinjured hand (March 23, 2002); missed remainder of season. ... Signed as free agent by Washington Capitals (July 1, 2002).

Season Team	League	REGULAR SEASON								PLAYOFFS				
		Gms.	G	A	Pts.	PIM	+/-	PP	SH	Gms.	G	A	Pts.	PIM
88-89—Litvinov	Czech.	7	3	2	5	0	...	...	...	—	—	—	—	—
89-90—Litvinov	Czech.	39	11	10	21	20	...	...	...	—	—	—	—	—
90-91—Litvinov	Czech.	56	26	26	52	38	...	...	...	—	—	—	—	—
91-92—Litvinov	Czech.	43	12	31	43	34	...	...	...	—	—	—	—	—
—Czech. national team ..	Int'l	8	5	8	13	8	...	...	...	—	—	—	—	—
—Czech. Olympic Team .	Int'l	8	5	8	13	8	...	...	...	—	—	—	—	—
92-93—Los Angeles	NHL	11	0	5	5	2	-3	0	0	—	—	—	—	—
—Phoenix	IHL	38	9	21	30	20	...	...	...	—	—	—	—	—
93-94—Phoenix	IHL	44	11	24	35	34	...	...	...	—	—	—	—	—
—Los Angeles	NHL	32	9	10	19	10	7	0	0	—	—	—	—	—
94-95—Chem. Litvinov	Czech Rep.	16	4	19	23	28	...	...	...	—	—	—	—	—
—Los Angeles	NHL	36	4	8	12	4	-7	0	0	—	—	—	—	—
95-96—Los Angeles	NHL	68	6	16	22	10	-15	0	2	—	—	—	—	—
96-97—Sparta Praha	Czech Rep.	38	14	27	41	30	...	...	...	5	1	2	3	4
97-98—Boston	NHL	3	0	0	0	2	1	0	0	—	—	—	—	—
—Houston	IHL	9	1	7	8	4	...	...	...	—	—	—	—	—
—Pittsburgh	NHL	51	9	13	22	14	6	1	1	6	0	3	3	2
—Czech Rep. Oly. team..	Int'l	6	0	3	3	0	...	...	...	—	—	—	—	—
98-99—Pittsburgh	NHL	72	21	23	44	24	-10	7	0	12	0	2	2	0
99-00—Pittsburgh	NHL	78	23	42	65	14	-9	13	0	11	3	3	6	0
00-01—Pittsburgh	NHL	82	32	48	80	28	20	10	0	16	4	4	8	4
01-02—Pittsburgh	NHL	62	18	32	50	16	9	5	1	—	—	—	—	—
—Czech Rep. Oly. team..	Int'l	4	1	2	3	2	...	...	...	—	—	—	—	—
02-03—Washington	NHL	82	22	47	69	22	12	10	0	6	2	1	3	2
NHL Totals (10 years)		577	144	244	388	146	11	46	4	51	9	13	22	8

LANGDON, DARREN LW CANUCKS

PERSONAL: Born January 8, 1971, in Deer Lake, Nfld. ... 6-1/205. ... Shoots left.

TRANSACTIONS/CAREER NOTES: Signed as non-drafted free agent by New York Rangers (August 16, 1993). ... Suspended three games by NHL for abuse of an official in preseason game (September 23, 1995). ... Sprained right knee (December 13, 1996); missed 13 games. ... Suspended two games by NHL for initiating an altercation (March 7, 1997). ... Sprained knee (November 21, 1997); missed six games. ... Bruised sternum (March 4, 1998); missed three games. ... Strained groin (January 2, 2000); missed remainder of season. ... Traded by Rangers with RW Rob DiMaio to Carolina Hurricanes for RW Sandy McCarthy and fourth-round pick (D Bryce Lampman) in 2001 draft (August 4, 2000). ... Injured groin (February 7, 2001); missed nine games. ... Injured shoulder (March 26, 2002); missed four games. ... Traded by Hurricanes with D Marek Malik to Vancouver Canucks for LW Jan Hlavac and C Harold Druken (November 1, 2002).

Season Team	League	REGULAR SEASON								PLAYOFFS				
		Gms.	G	A	Pts.	PIM	+/-	PP	SH	Gms.	G	A	Pts.	PIM
91-92—Summerside	MJHL	44	34	49	83	441	...	...	...	—	—	—	—	—
92-93—Binghamton	AHL	18	3	4	7	115	...	...	...	8	0	1	1	14
—Dayton	ECHL	54	23	22	45	429	...	...	...	3	0	1	1	40
93-94—Binghamton	AHL	54	2	7	9	327	...	...	...	—	—	—	—	—
94-95—Binghamton	AHL	55	6	14	20	296	...	...	...	11	1	3	4	84
—New York Rangers	NHL	18	1	1	2	62	0	0	0	—	—	—	—	—
95-96—New York Rangers	NHL	64	7	4	11	175	2	0	0	2	0	0	0	0
—Binghamton	AHL	1	0	0	0	12	...	...	...	—	—	—	—	—
96-97—New York Rangers	NHL	60	3	6	9	195	-1	0	0	10	0	0	0	2
97-98—New York Rangers	NHL	70	3	3	6	197	0	0	0	—	—	—	—	—
98-99—New York Rangers	NHL	44	0	0	0	80	-3	0	0	—	—	—	—	—
99-00—New York Rangers	NHL	21	0	1	1	26	-2	0	0	—	—	—	—	—
00-01—Carolina	NHL	54	0	2	2	94	-4	0	0	4	0	0	0	12
01-02—Carolina	NHL	58	2	1	3	106	2	0	0	—	—	—	—	—
02-03—Carolina	NHL	9	0	0	0	16	0	0	0	—	—	—	—	—
—Vancouver	NHL	45	0	1	1	143	-2	0	0	—	—	—	—	—
NHL Totals (9 years)		443	16	19	35	1094	-8	0	0	16	0	0	0	14

LANGENBRUNNER, JAMIE RW DEVILS

PERSONAL: Born July 24, 1975, in Duluth, Minn. ... 6-1/200. ... Shoots right. ... Name pronounced LANG-ihn-BRUH-nuhr.

TRANSACTIONS/CAREER NOTES: Selected by Dallas Stars in second round (second Stars pick, 35th overall) of NHL entry draft (June 26, 1993). ... Suffered back spasms (February 21, 1997); missed one game. ... Suffered whiplash (January 12, 1998); missed one game. ... Injured shoulder (January 6, 1999); missed five games. ... Strained abdominal muscle (March 26, 1999); missed one game. ... Suffered concussion (November 30, 1999); missed one game. ... Sprained shoulder (December 17, 1999); missed one game. ... Suffered pinched nerve in neck (January 7, 2000); missed one game. ... Strained neck (February 16, 2000); missed three games. ... Stained muscle in abdomen (December 20, 2000); missed 22 games. ... Reinjured abdominal muscle (March 4, 2001); missed five games. ... Strained back (March 31, 2001); missed one game. ... Traded by Stars with C Joe Nieuwendyk to New Jersey Devils for C Jason Arnott, RW Randy McKay and first-round pick (traded to Columbus) in 2002 draft (March 19, 2002).

				REGULAR SEASON							PLAYOFFS			
Season Team	League	Gms.	G	A	Pts.	PIM	+/-	PP	SH	Gms.	G	A	Pts.	PIM
90-91—Cloquet H.S.	Minn. H.S.	20	6	16	22	8	...	...	...	—	—	—	—	—
91-92—Cloquet H.S.	Minn. H.S.	23	16	23	39	24	...	...	...	—	—	—	—	—
92-93—Cloquet H.S.	Minn. H.S.	27	27	62	89	18	...	...	...	—	—	—	—	—
93-94—Peterborough.............	OHL	62	33	58	91	53	...	...	...	7	4	6	10	2
94-95—Peterborough.............	OHL	62	42	57	99	84	...	...	...	11	8	14	22	12
—Dallas........................	NHL	2	0	0	0	2	0	0	0	—	—	—	—	—
—Kalamazoo	IHL	—	—	—	—	—				11	1	3	4	2
95-96—Michigan....................	IHL	59	25	40	65	129	...	...	...	10	3	10	13	8
—Dallas........................	NHL	12	2	2	4	6	-2	1	0	—	—	—	—	—
96-97—Dallas........................	NHL	76	13	26	39	51	-2	3	0	5	1	1	2	14
97-98—Dallas........................	NHL	81	23	29	52	61	9	8	0	16	1	4	5	14
—U.S. Olympic team......	Int'l	3	0	0	0	4	...	...	...	—	—	—	—	—
98-99—Dallas........................	NHL	75	12	33	45	62	10	4	0	23	10	7	17	16
99-00—Dallas........................	NHL	65	18	21	39	68	16	4	2	15	1	7	8	18
00-01—Dallas........................	NHL	53	12	18	30	57	4	3	2	10	2	2	4	6
01-02—Dallas........................	NHL	68	10	16	26	54	-11	0	1	—	—	—	—	—
—New Jersey	NHL	14	3	3	6	23	2	0	0	5	0	1	1	8
02-03—New Jersey	NHL	78	22	33	55	65	17	5	1	24	*11	7	†18	16
NHL Totals (9 years)...........		524	115	181	296	449	43	28	6	98	26	29	55	92

LANGFELD, JOSH RW SENATORS

PERSONAL: Born July 17, 1977, in Fridley, Minn. ... 6-3/216. ... Shoots right.
TRANSACTIONS/CAREER NOTES: Selected by Ottawa Senators in third round (third Senators pick, 66th overall) of NHL entry draft (June 21, 1997). ... Suffered concussion (March 30, 2002); missed two games. ... Re-signed by Senators (July 24, 2003).

				REGULAR SEASON							PLAYOFFS			
Season Team	League	Gms.	G	A	Pts.	PIM	+/-	PP	SH	Gms.	G	A	Pts.	PIM
96-97—Lincoln......................	Jr. A	38	35	23	58	100	...	...	...	—	—	—	—	—
97-98—Univ. of Michigan.......	CCHA	46	19	17	36	66	...	...	...	—	—	—	—	—
98-99—Univ. of Michigan.......	CCHA	41	21	14	35	84	...	...	...	—	—	—	—	—
99-00—Univ. of Michigan.......	CCHA	37	9	20	29	56	...	...	...	—	—	—	—	—
00-01—Univ. of Michigan.......	CCHA	42	16	12	28	44	...	...	...	—	—	—	—	—
01-02—Grand Rapids..............	AHL	68	21	16	37	29	...	...	...	5	2	0	2	0
—Ottawa	NHL	1	0	0	0	2	0	0	0	—	—	—	—	—
02-03—Binghamton	AHL	59	14	21	35	38	...	...	...	—	—	—	—	—
—Ottawa	NHL	12	0	1	1	4	2	0	0	—	—	—	—	—
NHL Totals (2 years)...........		13	0	1	1	6	2	0	0					

LANGKOW, DAYMOND C COYOTES

PERSONAL: Born September 27, 1976, in Edmonton ... 5-11/192. ... Shoots left. ... Brother of Scott Langkow, goaltender with Winnipeg Jets (1995-96), Phoenix Coyotes (1997-98 and 1998-99) and Atlanta Thrashers (1999-2000).
TRANSACTIONS/CAREER NOTES: Selected by Tampa Bay Lightning in first round (first Lightning pick, fifth overall) of NHL entry draft (July 8, 1995). ... Suffered from the flu (October 1, 1997); missed one game. ... Suffered from concussion (January 7, 1998); missed two games. ... Suffered from the flu (January 31, 1998); missed three games. ... Traded by Lightning with RW Mikael Renberg to Philadelphia Flyers for C Chris Gratton and C/RW Mike Sillinger (December 12, 1998). ... Fractured right foot (February 25, 2001); missed 11 games. ... Traded by Flyers to Phoenix Coyotes for second-round pick (traded to Tampa Bay) in 2002 draft and first-round pick in 2003 draft (July 2, 2001). ... Fractured toe (January 3, 2002); missed two games.
STATISTICAL PLATEAUS: Three-goal games: 2001-02 (1), 2002-03 (1). Total: 2.

				REGULAR SEASON							PLAYOFFS			
Season Team	League	Gms.	G	A	Pts.	PIM	+/-	PP	SH	Gms.	G	A	Pts.	PIM
91-92—Tri-City	WHL	1	0	0	0	0	...	...	...	4	2	2	4	15
92-93—Tri-City	WHL	65	22	42	64	96	...	...	...	4	1	0	1	4
93-94—Tri-City	WHL	61	40	43	83	174	...	...	...	4	2	2	4	15
94-95—Tri-City	WHL	72	67	73	140	142	...	...	...	17	12	15	27	52
95-96—Tampa Bay	NHL	4	0	1	1	0	-1	0	0	—	—	—	—	—
—Tri-City	WHL	48	30	61	91	103	...	...	...	11	14	13	27	20
96-97—Adirondack	AHL	2	1	1	2	0	...	...	...	—	—	—	—	—
—Tampa Bay	NHL	79	15	13	28	35	1	3	1	—	—	—	—	—
97-98—Tampa Bay	NHL	68	8	14	22	62	-9	2	0	—	—	—	—	—
98-99—Cleveland	IHL	4	1	1	2	18	...	...	...	—	—	—	—	—
—Tampa Bay	NHL	22	4	6	10	15	0	1	0	—	—	—	—	—
—Philadelphia	NHL	56	10	13	23	24	-8	3	1	6	0	2	2	2
99-00—Philadelphia	NHL	82	18	32	50	56	1	5	0	16	5	5	10	23
00-01—Philadelphia	NHL	71	13	41	54	50	12	3	0	6	2	4	6	2
01-02—Phoenix......................	NHL	80	27	35	62	36	18	6	3	5	1	0	1	0
02-03—Phoenix......................	NHL	82	20	32	52	56	20	4	2	—	—	—	—	—
NHL Totals (8 years)...........		544	115	187	302	334	34	27	7	33	8	11	19	27

PERSONAL: Born January 19, 1974, in Montreal ... 6-1/208. ... Shoots right. ... Name pronounced EE-ihn luh-PAIR-ee-AIR.

TRANSACTIONS/CAREER NOTES: Selected by St. Louis Blues in seventh round (sixth Blues pick, 158th overall) of NHL entry draft (June 20, 1992). ... Suffered concussion (March 26, 1995); missed three games. ... Traded by Blues to New York Rangers for LW Stephane Matteau (December 28, 1995). ... Traded by Rangers with C Ray Ferraro, C Nathan Lafayette, D Matis Norstrom and fourth-round pick (D Sean Blanchard) in 1997 draft to Los Angeles Kings for RW Shane Churla, LW Jari Kurri and D/RW Marty McSorley (March 14, 1996). ... Sprained left shoulder (March 16, 1996); missed two games. ... Strained shoulder (October 29, 1996); missed three games. ... Strained hip flexor (February 1, 1997); missed three games. ... Suffered concussion (February 25, 1997); missed two games. ... Underwent shoulder surgery (March 17, 1997); missed final 11 games of regular season. ... Suffered blurred vision (December 31, 1997); missed three games. ... Suffered partial tear of anterior cruciate ligament in knee (October 12, 1998); missed nine games. ... Suffered inflammation of left knee (January 2, 1999); missed one game. ... Sprained knee (December 30, 1999); missed three games. ... Strained hip flexor (October 15, 2000); missed one game. ... Suffered concussion (April 3, 2001); missed two games.

STATISTICAL PLATEAUS: Three-goal games: 2000-01 (1).

Season Team	League	REGULAR SEASON								PLAYOFFS				
		Gms.	G	A	Pts.	PIM	+/-	PP	SH	Gms.	G	A	Pts.	PIM
90-91—Drummondville	QMJHL	65	19	29	48	117	...	...	...	—	—	—	—	—
91-92—Drummondville	QMJHL	70	28	49	77	160	...	...	...	—	—	—	—	—
92-93—Drummondville	QMJHL	60	44	†96	140	188	...	...	...	10	6	13	19	20
93-94—Drummondville	QMJHL	62	41	72	113	150	...	...	...	9	4	6	10	35
—St. Louis	NHL	1	0	0	0	0	0	0	0	—	—	—	—	—
—Peoria	IHL	—	—	—	—	—	—	—	—	5	1	3	4	2
94-95—Peoria	IHL	51	16	32	48	111	...	...	...	—	—	—	—	—
—St. Louis	NHL	37	13	14	27	85	12	1	0	7	0	4	4	21
95-96—St. Louis	NHL	33	3	6	9	87	-4	1	0	—	—	—	—	—
—Worcester	AHL	3	2	1	3	22	...	...	...	—	—	—	—	—
—New York Rangers	NHL	28	1	2	3	53	-5	0	0	—	—	—	—	—
—Los Angeles	NHL	10	2	3	5	15	-2	0	0	—	—	—	—	—
96-97—Los Angeles	NHL	62	8	15	23	102	-25	0	1	—	—	—	—	—
97-98—Los Angeles	NHL	77	6	15	21	131	0	0	1	4	1	0	1	6
98-99—Los Angeles	NHL	72	3	10	13	138	-5	0	0	—	—	—	—	—
99-00—Los Angeles	NHL	79	9	13	22	185	-14	0	0	4	0	0	0	2
00-01—Los Angeles	NHL	79	8	10	18	141	5	0	0	13	1	2	3	12
01-02—Los Angeles	NHL	81	8	14	22	125	5	0	0	7	0	1	1	9
02-03—Los Angeles	NHL	73	7	12	19	122	-9	1	1	—	—	—	—	—
NHL Totals (10 years)		632	68	114	182	1184	-42	3	3	35	2	7	9	50

PERSONAL: Born December 1, 1979, in St. Maurice, Que. ... 6-0/185. ... Shoots left.

TRANSACTIONS/CAREER NOTES: Selected by San Jose Sharks in third round (third Sharks pick, 65th overall) of NHL entry draft (June 27, 1998).

Season Team	League	REGULAR SEASON								PLAYOFFS				
		Gms.	G	A	Pts.	PIM	+/-	PP	SH	Gms.	G	A	Pts.	PIM
96-97—Halifax	QMJHL	68	20	30	50	253	...	...	...	18	3	10	13	28
97-98—Halifax	QMJHL	40	19	22	41	193	...	...	...	—	—	—	—	—
98-99—Drummondville	QMJHL	42	14	25	39	258	...	...	...	—	—	—	—	—
—Quebec	QMJHL	23	4	17	21	58	...	...	...	13	8	7	15	45
99-00—Quebec	QMJHL	47	24	35	59	234	...	...	...	10	3	5	8	*83
00-01—Kentucky	AHL	62	5	8	13	181	...	...	...	3	0	0	0	6
01-02—Cleveland	AHL	78	7	14	21	326	...	...	...	—	—	—	—	—
02-03—Cleveland	AHL	76	8	10	18	240	...	...	...	—	—	—	—	—

PERSONAL: Born October 11, 1968, in Lachine, Que. ... 5-9/188. ... Shoots left. ... Name pronounced KLOHD luh-pwah.

TRANSACTIONS/CAREER NOTES: Selected by Quebec Nordiques in 12th round (12th Nordiques pick, 234th overall) of NHL entry draft (June 11, 1988). ... Tore groin muscle (February 9, 1991). ... Injured groin (October 23, 1991); missed one game. ... Injured back in training camp (September 1992); missed first five games of season. ... Bruised hip (April 6, 1993); missed two games. ... Sprained left knee (October 18, 1993); missed 13 games. ... Sprained back (February 1, 1994); missed nine games. ... Injured back (March 19, 1994); missed three games. ... Suffered lower back pain (January 21, 1995); missed 16 games. ... Suffered from the flu (April 16, 1995); missed one game. ... Injured hip (April 30, 1995); missed one game. ... Nordiques franchise moved to Colorado and renamed Avalanche for 1995-96 season (June 21, 1995). ... Traded by Avalanche to Calgary Flames for seventh-round pick (C Samuel Pahlsson) in 1996 draft (November 1, 1995). ... Injured groin (December 20, 1995); missed one game. ... Reinjured groin (December 27, 1995); missed three games. ... Reinjured groin (January 5, 1996); missed three games. ... Injured hip (January 26, 1996); missed 17 games. ... Signed as free agent by New York Islanders (August 22, 1996). ... Hyperextended ankle (January 2, 1997); missed one game. ... Suffered sore ankle (January 25, 1997); missed one game. ... Bruised foot (January 22, 1998); missed one game. ... Fractured toe (February 1, 1998); missed three games. ... Injured foot (October 16, 1999); missed one game. ... Sprained medial collateral ligament in knee (October 30, 1999); missed two games. ... Suffered facial lacerations (December 29, 1999); missed one game. ... Suffered from the flu (April 6, 2000); missed two games. ... Injured toe (February 25, 2001); missed one game. ... Bruised foot (March 28, 2001); missed one game. ... Suffered from the flu (December 12, 2001); missed one game. ... Suffered from the flu (January 3, 2002); missed one game. ... Traded by Islanders to Philadelphia Flyers for fifth-round pick in 2003 draft (March 9, 2003). ... Re-signed by Flyers (June 29, 2003).

Season Team	League	REGULAR SEASON									PLAYOFFS				
		Gms.	G	A	Pts.	PIM	+/-	PP	SH		Gms.	G	A	Pts.	PIM
85-86—Trois-Rivieres	QMJHL	72	19	38	57	74	...	...	...		—	—	—	—	—
86-87—Trois-Rivieres	QMJHL	70	47	57	104	123	...	...	...		—	—	—	—	—
87-88—Laval	QMJHL	69	37	83	120	143	...	...	...		13	2	17	19	53
88-89—Laval	QMJHL	63	32	72	104	158	...	...	...		17	5	14	19	66
89-90—Halifax	AHL	63	18	19	37	51	...	...	...		6	1	1	2	34
90-91—Quebec	NHL	13	2	2	4	4	3	0	0		—	—	—	—	—
—Halifax	AHL	43	17	17	34	46	...	...	...		—	—	—	—	—
91-92—Quebec	NHL	78	13	20	33	86	-8	0	2		—	—	—	—	—
92-93—Quebec	NHL	74	10	26	36	98	5	0	0		6	2	4	6	8
93-94—Quebec	NHL	59	11	17	28	70	2	1	1		—	—	—	—	—
94-95—Quebec	NHL	29	4	8	12	41	5	0	0		5	0	0	0	8
95-96—Colorado	NHL	3	0	0	0	0	-1	0	0		—	—	—	—	—
—Calgary	NHL	32	4	5	9	20	2	0	2		2	0	0	0	0
—Saint John	AHL	12	5	3	8	10	...	...	...		—	—	—	—	—
96-97—Utah	IHL	9	7	6	13	14	...	...	...		—	—	—	—	—
—New York Islanders	NHL	73	13	5	18	49	-12	0	3		—	—	—	—	—
97-98—New York Islanders	NHL	78	10	10	20	47	-9	0	1		—	—	—	—	—
98-99—New York Islanders	NHL	82	14	23	37	62	-19	2	2		—	—	—	—	—
99-00—New York Islanders	NHL	76	15	16	31	60	-22	0	1		—	—	—	—	—
00-01—New York Islanders	NHL	80	9	23	32	56	-2	1	1		—	—	—	—	—
01-02—New York Islanders	NHL	80	9	12	21	60	-9	0	3		7	0	0	0	14
02-03—New York Islanders	NHL	66	6	6	12	20	-3	0	0		—	—	—	—	—
—Philadelphia	NHL	14	2	2	4	16	5	0	0		13	2	3	5	14
NHL Totals (13 years)		837	122	175	297	689	-63	6	16		33	4	7	11	44

LAPOINTE, MARTIN   RW   BRUINS

PERSONAL: Born September 12, 1973, in Ville Ste-Pierre, Que. ... 5-11/200. ... Shoots right. ... Name pronounced MAHR-tahn luh-POYNT.

TRANSACTIONS/CAREER NOTES: Selected by Detroit Red Wings in first round (first Red Wings pick, 10th overall) of NHL entry draft (June 22, 1991). ... Fractured wrist (October 9, 1991); missed 22 games. ... Injured left knee (February 29, 1996); missed eight games. ... Injured leg (April 10, 1996); missed two games. ... Fractured finger (December 1, 1996); missed four games. ... Strained hamstring (February 25, 1998); missed one game. ... Suspended two games and fined $1,000 by NHL for cross-checking incident (March 18, 1998). ... Suffered back spasms (December 22, 1998); missed one game. ... Bruised knee (February 12, 1999); missed three games. ... Signed as free agent by Boston Bruins (July 2, 2001). ... Strained hamstring (January 30, 2002); missed seven games. ... Reinjured hamstring (March 6, 2002); missed five games.

STATISTICAL PLATEAUS: Three-goal games: 1999-00 (1), 2002-03 (1). Total: 2.

Season Team	League	REGULAR SEASON									PLAYOFFS				
		Gms.	G	A	Pts.	PIM	+/-	PP	SH		Gms.	G	A	Pts.	PIM
89-90—Laval	QMJHL	65	42	54	96	77	...	...	...		14	8	17	25	54
90-91—Laval	QMJHL	64	44	54	98	66	...	...	...		13	7	14	21	26
91-92—Detroit	NHL	4	0	1	1	5	2	0	0		3	0	1	1	4
—Laval	QMJHL	31	25	30	55	84	...	...	...		10	4	10	14	32
—Adirondack	AHL	—									8	2	2	4	4
92-93—Adirondack	AHL	8	1	2	3	9	...	...	...		—	—	—	—	—
—Detroit	NHL	3	0	0	0	0	-2	0	0		—	—	—	—	—
—Laval	QMJHL	35	38	51	89	41	...	...	...		13	*13	*17	*30	22
93-94—Adirondack	AHL	28	25	21	46	47	...	...	...		4	1	1	2	8
—Detroit	NHL	50	8	8	16	55	7	2	0		4	0	0	0	6
94-95—Adirondack	AHL	39	29	16	45	80	...	...	...		—	—	—	—	—
—Detroit	NHL	39	4	6	10	73	1	0	0		2	0	1	1	8
95-96—Detroit	NHL	58	6	3	9	93	0	1	0		11	1	2	3	12
96-97—Detroit	NHL	78	16	17	33	167	-14	5	1		20	4	8	12	60
97-98—Detroit	NHL	79	15	19	34	106	0	4	0		21	9	6	15	20
98-99—Detroit	NHL	77	16	13	29	141	7	7	1		10	0	2	2	20
99-00—Detroit	NHL	82	16	25	41	121	17	1	0		9	3	1	4	20
00-01—Detroit	NHL	82	27	30	57	127	3	13	0		6	0	1	1	8
01-02—Boston	NHL	68	17	23	40	101	12	4	0		6	1	2	3	12
02-03—Boston	NHL	59	8	10	18	87	-19	1	0		5	1	0	1	14
NHL Totals (12 years)		679	133	155	288	1076	14	38	3		97	19	24	43	184

LARAQUE, GEORGES   RW   OILERS

PERSONAL: Born December 7, 1976, in Montreal. ... 6-3/245. ... Shoots right. ... Name pronounced la-RAHK.

TRANSACTIONS/CAREER NOTES: Selected by Edmonton Oilers in second round (second Oilers pick, 31st overall) of NHL entry draft (July 8, 1995). ... Fractured left foot (November 17, 1997); missed five games. ... Tore cartilage in right knee (December 5, 1997); missed seven games. ... Suspended two games by AHL for checking from behind (October 21, 1998). ... Bruised sternum (January 17, 1999); missed two games. ... Sprained ankle (March 24, 1999); missed three games. ... Suffered concussion (April 1, 1999); missed three games. ... Suffered eye injury (December 19, 1999); missed two games. ... Sprained knee (March 27, 2000); missed one game. ... Suffered tendinitis in right forearm (January 18, 2002); missed two games.

STATISTICAL PLATEAUS: Three-goal games: 1999-00 (1).

Season Team	League	REGULAR SEASON									PLAYOFFS				
		Gms.	G	A	Pts.	PIM	+/-	PP	SH		Gms.	G	A	Pts.	PIM
93-94—St. Jean	QMJHL	70	11	11	22	142	...	...	...		4	0	0	0	7
94-95—St. Jean	QMJHL	62	19	22	41	259	...	...	...		7	1	1	2	42
95-96—Laval	QMJHL	11	8	13	21	76	...	...	...		—	—	—	—	—
—St. Hyacinthe	QMJHL	8	3	4	7	59	...	...	...		—	—	—	—	—
—Granby	QMJHL	22	9	7	16	125	...	...	...		18	7	6	13	104

Season Team	League	REGULAR SEASON								PLAYOFFS				
		Gms.	G	A	Pts.	PIM	+/-	PP	SH	Gms.	G	A	Pts.	PIM
96-97—Hamilton	AHL	73	14	20	34	179	...	...	...	15	1	3	4	12
97-98—Hamilton	AHL	46	10	20	30	154	...	...	...	3	0	0	0	11
—Edmonton	NHL	11	0	0	0	59	-4	0	0	—	—	—	—	—
98-99—Hamilton	AHL	25	6	8	14	93	...	...	...	—	—	—	—	—
—Edmonton	NHL	39	3	2	5	57	-1	0	0	4	0	0	0	2
99-00—Edmonton	NHL	76	8	8	16	123	5	0	0	5	0	1	1	6
00-01—Edmonton	NHL	82	13	16	29	148	5	1	0	6	1	1	2	8
01-02—Edmonton	NHL	80	5	14	19	157	6	1	0	—	—	—	—	—
02-03—Edmonton	NHL	64	6	7	13	110	-4	0	0	6	1	3	4	4
NHL Totals (6 years)		352	35	47	82	654	7	2	0	21	2	5	7	20

LARIONOV, IGOR   C

PERSONAL: Born December 3, 1960, in Voskresensk, U.S.S.R. ... 5-11/170. ... Shoots left. ... Name pronounced EE-gohr LAIR-ee-AH-nahf.
TRANSACTIONS/CAREER NOTES: Selected by Vancouver Canucks in 11th round (11th Canucks pick, 214th overall) of NHL entry draft (June 15, 1985). ... Injured groin (October 25, 1990); missed four games. ... Sprained ankle (January 8, 1991). ... Reinjured ankle (January 30, 1991); missed seven games. ... Signed to play with Lugano of Switzerland (July 14, 1992). ... Selected by San Jose Sharks in NHL waiver draft (October 4, 1992). ... Injured shoulder (September 30, 1993); missed four games. ... Reinjured shoulder (October 16, 1993); missed four games. ... Suffered from the flu (November 7, 1993); missed two games. ... Sprained knee (December 12, 1993); missed 10 games. ... Suffered from respiratory infection (February 11, 1994); missed one game. ... Suffered from the flu (February 26, 1994); missed two games. ... Injured groin (February 15, 1995); missed three games. ... Injured foot (February 26, 1995); missed 12 games. ... Traded by Sharks with second-round pick (traded to St. Louis) in 1998 draft to Detroit Red Wings for RW Ray Sheppard (October 25, 1995). ... Suffered from the flu (December 29, 1995); missed two games. ... Pulled groin (October 15, 1996); missed four games. ... Bruised wrist (October 30, 1996); missed seven games. ... Suffered from the flu (March 21, 1997); missed one game. ... Bruised back (April 8, 1997); missed three games. ... Injured groin (December 5, 1997); missed two games. ... Strained groin (December 26, 1997); missed one game. ... Reinjured groin (December 29, 1997); missed one game. ... Strained groin (March 18, 1998); missed two games. ... Reinjured groin (March 26, 1998); missed three games. ... Injured elbow (April 9, 1998); missed four games. ... Injured groin (March 17, 1999); missed three games. ... Signed as free agent by Florida Panthers (July 1, 2000). ... Strained hip flexor (November 4, 2000); missed nine games. ... Traded by Panthers to Red Wings for D Yan Golubovsky (December 28, 2000). ... Suffered from the flu (October 30, 2001); missed two games. ... Injured groin (December 10, 2001); missed one game. ... Injured knee (February 27, 2002); missed two games.
STATISTICAL PLATEAUS: Three-goal games: 1991-92 (2), 1993-94 (2). Total: 4.

Season Team	League	REGULAR SEASON								PLAYOFFS				
		Gms.	G	A	Pts.	PIM	+/-	PP	SH	Gms.	G	A	Pts.	PIM
77-78—Khimik Voskresensk	USSR	6	3	0	3	4	...	...	...	—	—	—	—	—
78-79—Khimik Voskresensk	USSR	25	3	4	7	12	...	...	...	—	—	—	—	—
79-80—Khimik Voskresensk	USSR	42	11	7	18	24	...	...	...	—	—	—	—	—
80-81—Khimik Voskresensk	USSR	56	22	23	45	36	...	...	...	—	—	—	—	—
81-82—CSKA Moscow	USSR	46	31	22	53	6	...	...	...	—	—	—	—	—
82-83—CSKA Moscow	USSR	44	20	19	39	20	...	...	...	—	—	—	—	—
83-84—CSKA Moscow	USSR	43	15	26	41	30	...	...	...	—	—	—	—	—
—Soviet Olympic Team	Int'l	7	1	4	5	6	...	...	...	—	—	—	—	—
84-85—CSKA Moscow	USSR	40	18	28	46	20	...	...	...	—	—	—	—	—
85-86—CSKA Moscow	USSR	40	21	31	52	33	...	...	...	—	—	—	—	—
86-87—CSKA Moscow	USSR	39	20	26	46	34	...	...	...	—	—	—	—	—
87-88—CSKA Moscow	USSR	51	25	32	57	54	...	...	...	—	—	—	—	—
—Soviet Olympic Team	Int'l	8	4	9	13	4	...	...	...	—	—	—	—	—
88-89—CSKA Moscow	USSR	31	15	12	27	22	...	...	...	—	—	—	—	—
89-90—Vancouver	NHL	74	17	27	44	20	-5	8	0	—	—	—	—	—
90-91—Vancouver	NHL	64	13	21	34	14	-3	1	1	6	1	0	1	6
91-92—Vancouver	NHL	72	21	44	65	54	7	10	3	13	3	7	10	4
92-93—Lugano	Switzerland	24	10	19	29	44	...	...	...	—	—	—	—	—
93-94—San Jose	NHL	60	18	38	56	40	20	3	2	14	5	13	18	10
94-95—San Jose	NHL	33	4	20	24	14	-3	0	0	11	1	8	9	2
95-96—San Jose	NHL	4	1	1	2	0	-6	1	0	—	—	—	—	—
—Detroit	NHL	69	21	50	71	34	37	9	1	19	6	7	13	6
96-97—Detroit	NHL	64	12	42	54	26	31	2	1	20	4	8	12	8
97-98—Detroit	NHL	69	8	39	47	40	14	3	0	22	3	10	13	12
98-99—Detroit	NHL	75	14	49	63	48	13	4	2	7	0	2	2	0
99-00—Detroit	NHL	79	9	38	47	28	13	3	0	9	1	2	3	6
00-01—Florida	NHL	26	5	6	11	10	-11	2	0	—	—	—	—	—
—Detroit	NHL	39	4	25	29	28	6	2	0	6	1	3	4	2
01-02—Detroit	NHL	70	11	32	43	50	-5	4	0	18	5	6	11	4
—Russian Oly. team	Int'l	6	0	3	3	4	...	...	...	—	—	—	—	—
02-03—Detroit	NHL	74	10	33	43	48	-7	5	0	4	0	1	1	0
NHL Totals (13 years)		872	168	465	633	454	101	57	10	149	30	67	97	60

LAROSE, CORY   C   RANGERS

PERSONAL: Born May 14, 1975, in Campellton, N.B. ... 6-0/188. ... Shoots left.
TRANSACTIONS/CAREER NOTES: Signed as non-drafted free agent by Minnesota Wild. ... Traded by Wild to New York Rangers for LW Jay Henderson (February 20, 2003).

Season Team	League	REGULAR SEASON								PLAYOFFS				
		Gms.	G	A	Pts.	PIM	+/-	PP	SH	Gms.	G	A	Pts.	PIM
96-97—Univ. of Maine	Hockey East	35	10	27	37	32	...	...	...	—	—	—	—	—
97-98—Univ. of Maine	Hockey East	34	15	25	40	22	...	...	...	—	—	—	—	—
98-99—Univ. of Maine	Hockey East	38	21	31	52	34	...	...	...	—	—	—	—	—
99-00—Univ. of Maine	Hockey East	39	15	36	51	45	...	...	...	—	—	—	—	—
00-01—Cleveland	IHL	4	1	1	2	6	...	...	...	—	—	—	—	—
—Jackson	ECHL	63	21	32	53	73	...	...	...	5	2	2	4	12
01-02—Houston	AHL	78	32	32	64	73	...	...	...	14	6	8	14	15
02-03—Houston	AHL	58	18	38	56	57	...	...	...	—	—	—	—	—
—Hartford	AHL	24	9	10	19	20	...	...	...	—	—	—	—	—

LARRIVEE, CHRISTIAN C CANADIENS

PERSONAL: Born August 25, 1982, in Gaspe, Que. ... 6-2/185. ... Shoots left.
TRANSACTIONS/CAREER NOTES: Selected by Montreal Canadiens in fourth round (sixth Canadiens pick, 114th overall) of NHL entry draft (June 24, 2000).

		REGULAR SEASON								PLAYOFFS				
Season Team	League	Gms.	G	A	Pts.	PIM	+/-	PP	SH	Gms.	G	A	Pts.	PIM
99-00—Chicoutimi	QMJHL	69	8	15	23	18	...	...	...	—	—	—	—	—
00-01—Chicoutimi	QMJHL	72	32	48	80	46	...	...	...	7	3	1	4	4
01-02—Chicoutimi	QMJHL	72	48	52	100	60	...	...	...	4	2	5	7	0
02-03—Chicoutimi	QMJHL	50	18	40	58	49	...	...	...	—	—	—	—	—

LARSEN, BRAD LW AVALANCHE

PERSONAL: Born June 28, 1977, in Nakusp, B.C. ... 6-1/200. ... Shoots left.
TRANSACTIONS/CAREER NOTES: Selected by Ottawa Senators in third round (third Senators pick, 53rd overall) of NHL entry draft (July 8, 1995). ... Rights traded by Senators to Colorado Avalanche for D Janne Laukkanen (January 25, 1996); did not sign. ... Returned to draft pool by Avalanche and selected by Avalanche in fourth round (fifth Avalanche pick, 87th overall) of NHL entry draft (June 21, 1997). ... Injured ribs (December 27, 2001); missed 11 games. ... Strained back (April 1, 2002); missed four games.

		REGULAR SEASON								PLAYOFFS				
Season Team	League	Gms.	G	A	Pts.	PIM	+/-	PP	SH	Gms.	G	A	Pts.	PIM
92-93—Nelson	Tier II Jr. A	42	31	37	68	164	...	...	...	—	—	—	—	—
93-94—Swift Current	WHL	64	15	18	33	37	...	...	...	7	1	2	3	4
94-95—Swift Current	WHL	62	24	33	57	73	...	...	...	6	0	1	1	2
95-96—Swift Current	WHL	51	30	47	77	67	...	...	...	6	3	2	5	13
96-97—Swift Current	WHL	61	36	46	82	61	...	...	...	—	—	—	—	—
97-98—Hershey	AHL	65	12	10	22	80	...	...	...	7	3	2	5	2
—Colorado	NHL	1	0	0	0	0	0	0	0	—	—	—	—	—
98-99—Hershey	AHL	18	3	4	7	11	...	...	...	5	1	0	1	6
99-00—Hershey	AHL	52	13	26	39	66	...	...	...	14	5	2	7	29
00-01—Hershey	AHL	67	21	25	46	93	...	...	...	10	1	3	4	6
—Colorado	NHL	9	0	0	0	0	1	0	0	—	—	—	—	—
01-02—Colorado	NHL	50	2	7	9	47	4	1	0	21	1	1	2	13
02-03—Hershey	AHL	25	3	6	9	25	...	...	...	—	—	—	—	—
—Colorado	NHL	6	0	3	3	2	3	0	0	—	—	—	—	—
NHL Totals (4 years)		66	2	10	12	49	8	1	0	21	1	1	2	13

LASAK, JAN G PREDATORS

PERSONAL: Born April 10, 1979, in Zvolen, Czechoslovakia ... 6-1/204. ... Catches left.
TRANSACTIONS/CAREER NOTES: Selected by Nashville Predators in second round (sixth Predators pick, 65th overall) of NHL entry draft (June 26, 1999).

		REGULAR SEASON									PLAYOFFS							
Season Team	League	Gms.	Min	W	L	T	GA	SO	Avg.	SV%	Gms.	Min.	W	L	GA	SO	Avg.	SV%
96-97—HKM Zvolen	Slovakia Jrs.	49	2940	...	...	...	111	...	2.27	—	—	—	—	—	—	—	—	—
97-98—HKM Zvolen	Slovakia Jrs.	48	2881	...	...	...	119	...	2.48	—	—	—	—	—	—	—	—	—
98-99—Zvolen	Slovakia	8	387	...	...	...	29	...	4.50	—	—	—	—	—	—	—	—	—
—HKM Zvolen	Slovakia Jrs.	43	2580	...	...	...	91	...	2.12	—	—	—	—	—	—	—	—	—
99-00—Hampton Roads	ECHL	†59	*3409	*43	17	4	145	0	2.55	—	10	610	5	5	28	1	2.75	—
00-01—Milwaukee	IHL	43	2439	23	17	‡2	106	1	2.61	—	3	60	0	1	5	0	5.00	—
01-02—Milwaukee	AHL	34	1980	12	18	3	79	2	2.39	—	—	—	—	—	—	—	—	—
—Slovakian Oly. team	Int'l	2	94	0	1	1	6	0	3.83	—	—	—	—	—	—	—	—	—
—Nashville	NHL	3	177	0	3	0	13	0	4.41	.875	—	—	—	—	—	—	—	—
02-03—Milwaukee	AHL	40	2377	18	14	7	113	1	2.85	—	—	—	—	—	—	—	—	—
—Nashville	NHL	3	90	0	1	0	5	0	3.33	.872	—	—	—	—	—	—	—	—
NHL Totals (2 years)		6	267	0	4	0	18	0	4.04	.874	—	—	—	—	—	—	—	—

LAUKKANEN, JANNE D LIGHTNING

PERSONAL: Born March 19, 1970, in Lahti, Finland ... 6-1/196. ... Shoots left. ... Name pronounced YAH-nee LOW-kih-nihn.
TRANSACTIONS/CAREER NOTES: Selected by Quebec Nordiques in eighth round (eighth Nordiques pick, 156th overall) of NHL entry draft (June 22, 1991). ... Injured groin (April 14, 1995); missed four games. ... Reinjured groin (April 30, 1995); missed last game of season. ... Nordiques franchise moved to Colorado and renamed Avalanche for 1995-96 season (June 21, 1995). ... Traded by Avalanche to Ottawa Senators for LW Brad Larsen (January 25, 1996). ... Suffered hip flexor during 1995-96 season; missed five games. ... Sprained left knee (March 25, 1996); missed two games. ... Bruised finger (November 15, 1996); missed one game. ... Suffered from the flu (December 10, 1996); missed two games. ... Suffered from the flu (March 17, 1997); missed one game. ... Injured knee (March 25, 1997); missed two games. ... Suffered concussion (October 19, 1997); missed two games. ... Strained groin (November 20, 1997); missed five games. ... Suffered from the flu (February 2, 1998); missed one game. ... Bruised foot (March 1, 1998); missed one game. ... Strained groin (March 13, 1998); missed five games. ... Reinjured groin (March 25, 1998); missed eight games. ... Underwent offseason abdominal surgery; missed first 19 games of 1998-99 season. ... Injured groin (November 23, 1998); missed four games. ... Suffered back spasms (January 26, 1999); missed three games. ... Strained back (April 3, 1999); missed one game. ... Suffered concussion (April 7, 1999); missed five games. ... Injured left shoulder (November 30, 1999); missed three games. ... Injured right ankle (December 29, 1999); missed one game. ... Suffered from the flu (January 20, 2000); missed one game. ... Suffered illness (January 26, 2000); missed three games. ... Traded by Senators with G Ron Tugnutt to Pittsburgh Penguins for G Tom Barrasso (March 14, 2000). ... Bruised ribs (March 24, 2000); missed one game. ... Reinjured ribs (April 5, 2000); missed one game. ... Bruised knee (October 13, 2000); missed three games. ... Sprained knee (November 13, 2000); missed 18 games.

... Suffered from the flu (February 16, 2001); missed one game. ... Injured groin (February 23, 2001); missed one game. ... Sprained knee (March 10, 2001); missed six games. ... Reinjured knee (March 29, 2001); missed three games. ... Underwent knee surgery prior to start of 2001-02 season; missed first 21 games of season. ... Traded by Penguins with RW Alexei Kovalev, LW Dan LaCouture and D Mike Wilson to New York Rangers for RW Rico Fata, RW Mikael Samuelsson, D Joel Bouchard, D Richard Lintner and cash (February 10, 2003). ... Claimed on waivers by Tampa Bay Lightning (March 11, 2003).

		REGULAR SEASON								PLAYOFFS				
Season Team	League	Gms.	G	A	Pts.	PIM	+/-	PP	SH	Gms.	G	A	Pts.	PIM
89-90—Ilves Tampere	Finland	39	5	6	11	10	...	...	...	—	—	—	—	—
90-91—Reipas Lahti...............	Finland	44	8	14	22	56	...	...	...	—	—	—	—	—
91-92—Helsinki HPK..............	Finland	43	5	14	19	62	...	...	...	—	—	—	—	—
—Fin. Olympic team.......	Int'l	8	0	1	1	6	...	...	...	—	—	—	—	—
92-93—HPK Hameenlinna......	Finland	47	8	21	29	76	...	...	...	12	1	4	5	10
93-94—HPK Hameenlinna......	Finland	48	5	24	29	46	...	...	...	—	—	—	—	—
—Fin. Olympic team.......	Int'l	8	0	2	2	12	...	...	...	—	—	—	—	—
94-95—Cornwall	AHL	55	8	26	34	41	...	...	...	—	—	—	—	—
—Québec	NHL	11	0	3	3	4	3	0	0	6	1	0	1	2
95-96—Cornwall	AHL	35	7	20	27	60	...	...	...	—	—	—	—	—
—Colorado	NHL	3	1	0	1	0	-1	1	0	—	—	—	—	—
—Ottawa	NHL	20	0	2	2	14	0	0	0	—	—	—	—	—
96-97—Ottawa	NHL	76	3	18	21	76	-14	2	0	7	0	1	1	6
97-98—Ottawa	NHL	60	4	17	21	64	-15	2	0	11	2	2	4	8
—Fin. Olympic team.......	Int'l	6	0	0	0	4	...	...	...	—	—	—	—	—
98-99—Ottawa	NHL	50	1	11	12	40	18	0	0	4	0	0	0	4
99-00—Ottawa	NHL	60	1	11	12	55	14	0	0	—	—	—	—	—
—Pittsburgh.................	NHL	11	1	7	8	12	3	1	0	11	2	4	6	10
00-01—Pittsburgh.................	NHL	50	3	17	20	34	9	0	0	18	2	2	4	14
01-02—Pittsburgh.................	NHL	47	6	7	13	28	-18	3	0	—	—	—	—	—
02-03—Hartford...................	AHL	5	0	3	3	2	...	...	...	—	—	—	—	—
—Pittsburgh.................	NHL	17	1	6	7	8	-3	0	0	—	—	—	—	—
—Tampa Bay	NHL	2	1	0	1	0	1	0	0	2	0	0	0	2
NHL Totals (9 years)............		407	22	99	121	335	-3	9	0	59	7	9	16	46

LAW, KIRBY   RW   FLYERS

PERSONAL: Born March 11, 1977, in McCreary, Man. ... 6-1/190. ... Shoots right.
TRANSACTIONS/CAREER NOTES: Signed as non-drafted free agent by Atlanta Thrashers (July 6, 1999). ... Traded by Thrashers to Philadelphia Flyers for sixth-round pick (D Jeff Dwyer) in 2000 draft and conditional sixth-round pick (G Pasi Nurminen) in 2001 draft (March 14, 2000).

		REGULAR SEASON								PLAYOFFS				
Season Team	League	Gms.	G	A	Pts.	PIM	+/-	PP	SH	Gms.	G	A	Pts.	PIM
93-94—Saskatoon...................	WHL	66	9	11	20	39	...	...	...	16	0	0	0	6
94-95—Saskatoon...................	WHL	46	10	15	25	44	...	...	...	—	—	—	—	—
—Lethbridge	WHL	24	4	10	14	38	...	...	...	—	—	—	—	—
95-96—Lethbridge	WHL	71	17	45	62	133	...	...	...	4	0	0	0	12
96-97—Lethbridge	WHL	72	39	52	91	200	...	...	...	†19	4	14	18	60
98-99—Orlando......................	IHL	67	18	13	31	136	...	...	...	—	—	—	—	—
—Adirondack	AHL	11	2	3	5	40	...	...	...	3	1	0	1	2
99-00—Orlando......................	IHL	1	1	0	1	0	...	...	...	—	—	—	—	—
—Louisville	AHL	66	31	21	52	173	...	...	...	—	—	—	—	—
—Philadelphia	AHL	12	1	4	5	6	...	...	...	5	2	0	2	2
00-01—Philadelphia	AHL	78	27	34	61	150	...	...	...	10	1	6	7	16
—Philadelphia	NHL	1	0	0	0	0	-1	0	0	—	—	—	—	—
01-02—Philadelphia	AHL	71	18	24	42	102	...	...	...	5	0	0	0	0
02-03—Philadelphia	AHL	74	22	19	41	166	...	...	...	—	—	—	—	—
—Philadelphia	NHL	2	0	0	0	2	0	0	0	—	—	—	—	—
NHL Totals (2 years)............		3	0	0	0	2	-1	0	0	—	—	—	—	—

LECAVALIER, VINCENT   C   LIGHTNING

PERSONAL: Born April 21, 1980, in Ile-Bizard, Que. ... 6-4/207. ... Shoots left.
TRANSACTIONS/CAREER NOTES: Selected by Tampa Bay Lightning in first round (first Lightning pick, first overall) of NHL entry draft (June 27, 1998). ... Injured ankle (April 6, 2000); missed final two games of season. ... Fractured left foot (January 12, 2001); missed 14 games. ... Fractured left ankle (February 9, 2002); missed four games.
STATISTICAL PLATEAUS: Three-goal games: 2002-03 (2).

		REGULAR SEASON								PLAYOFFS				
Season Team	League	Gms.	G	A	Pts.	PIM	+/-	PP	SH	Gms.	G	A	Pts.	PIM
95-96—Notre Dame	SJHL	22	52	52	104	...	...	...	...	—	—	—	—	—
96-97—Rimouski	QMJHL	64	42	60	102	36	...	...	...	4	4	3	7	2
97-98—Rimouski	QMJHL	58	44	71	115	117	...	...	...	18	15	†26	41	46
98-99—Tampa Bay	NHL	82	13	15	28	23	-19	2	0	—	—	—	—	—
99-00—Tampa Bay	NHL	80	25	42	67	43	-25	6	0	—	—	—	—	—
00-01—Tampa Bay	NHL	68	23	28	51	66	-26	7	0	—	—	—	—	—
01-02—Tampa Bay	NHL	76	20	17	37	61	-18	5	0	—	—	—	—	—
02-03—Tampa Bay	NHL	80	33	45	78	39	0	11	2	11	3	3	6	22
NHL Totals (5 years)............		386	114	147	261	232	-88	31	2	11	3	3	6	22

LECLAIR, JOHN — LW — FLYERS

PERSONAL: Born July 5, 1969, in St. Albans, Vt. ... 6-3/225. ... Shoots left. ... Full Name: John Clark LeClair.

TRANSACTIONS/CAREER NOTES: Selected by Montreal Canadiens in second round (second Canadiens pick, 33rd overall) of NHL entry draft (June 13, 1987). ... Injured shoulder (January 15, 1992); missed four games. ... Suffered charley horse (January 20, 1993); missed four games. ... Sprained knee (October 2, 1993); missed eight games. ... Bruised sternum (March 28, 1994); missed two games. ... Traded by Canadiens with LW Gilbert Dionne and D Eric Desjardins to Philadelphia Flyers for RW Mark Recchi and third-round pick (C Martin Hohenberger) in 1995 draft (February 9, 1995). ... Strained right hip (April 18, 1995); missed one playoff game. ... Strained hip flexor (March 9, 1999); missed two games. ... Suffered back spasms (April 1, 1999); missed two games. ... Injured back (October 9, 2000); missed 20 games. ... Strained lower back (December 9, 2000); missed 46 games.

STATISTICAL PLATEAUS: Three-goal games: 1994-95 (2), 1995-96 (2), 1996-97 (1), 1997-98 (1), 1998-99 (1), 2000-01 (1). Total: 8. ... Four-goal games: 1996-97 (1), 1998-99 (1), 2002-03 (1). Total: 3. ... Total hat tricks: 11.

		REGULAR SEASON							PLAYOFFS				
Season Team	League	Gms.	G	A	Pts.	PIM	+/-	PP	SH	Gms.	G	A	Pts.	PIM
85-86—Bellows Free Acad.	VT. H.S.	22	41	28	69	14	...	...	...	—	—	—	—	—
86-87—Bellows Free Acad.	VT. H.S.	23	44	40	84	25	...	...	...	—	—	—	—	—
87-88—Univ. of Vermont	ECAC	31	12	22	34	62	...	...	...	—	—	—	—	—
88-89—Univ. of Vermont	ECAC	19	9	12	21	40	...	...	...	—	—	—	—	—
89-90—Univ. of Vermont	ECAC	10	10	6	16	38	...	...	...	—	—	—	—	—
90-91—Univ. of Vermont	ECAC	33	25	20	45	58	...	...	...	—	—	—	—	—
—Montreal	NHL	10	2	5	7	2	1	0	0	3	0	0	0	0
91-92—Montreal	NHL	59	8	11	19	14	5	3	0	8	1	1	2	4
—Fredericton	AHL	8	7	7	14	10	...	...	...	2	0	0	0	4
92-93—Montreal	NHL	72	19	25	44	33	11	2	0	20	4	6	10	14
93-94—Montreal	NHL	74	19	24	43	32	17	1	0	7	2	1	3	8
94-95—Montreal	NHL	9	1	4	5	10	-1	1	0	—	—	—	—	—
—Philadelphia	NHL	37	25	24	49	20	21	5	0	15	5	7	12	4
95-96—Philadelphia	NHL	82	51	46	97	64	21	19	0	11	6	5	11	6
96-97—Philadelphia	NHL	82	50	47	97	58	*44	10	0	19	9	12	21	10
97-98—Philadelphia	NHL	82	51	36	87	32	30	16	0	5	1	1	2	8
—U.S. Olympic team	Int'l	4	0	1	1	0	...	...	...	—	—	—	—	—
98-99—Philadelphia	NHL	76	43	47	90	30	36	16	0	6	3	0	3	12
99-00—Philadelphia	NHL	82	40	37	77	36	8	13	0	18	6	7	13	6
00-01—Philadelphia	NHL	16	7	5	12	0	2	3	0	6	1	2	3	2
01-02—Philadelphia	NHL	82	25	26	51	30	5	4	0	5	0	0	0	2
—U.S. Olympic team	Int'l	6	6	1	7	2	...	...	...	—	—	—	—	—
02-03—Philadelphia	NHL	35	18	10	28	16	10	8	0	13	2	3	5	10
NHL Totals (13 years)		798	359	347	706	377	210	101	0	136	40	45	85	86

LECLERC, MIKE — LW — MIGHTY DUCKS

PERSONAL: Born November 10, 1976, in Winnipeg ... 6-2/215. ... Shoots left. ... Name pronounced luh-KLAIR.

TRANSACTIONS/CAREER NOTES: Selected by Mighty Ducks of Anaheim in third round (third Mighty Ducks pick, 55th overall) of NHL entry draft (July 8, 1995). ... Underwent elbow surgery (October 29, 1999); missed 11 games. ... Injured elbow (December 17, 1999); missed two games. ... Injured knee (December 28, 2000); missed 15 games. ... Strained muscle in abdomen (March 11, 2001); missed remainder of season. ... Re-signed by Anaheim (July 15, 2003).

		REGULAR SEASON							PLAYOFFS				
Season Team	League	Gms.	G	A	Pts.	PIM	+/-	PP	SH	Gms.	G	A	Pts.	PIM
91-92—St. Boniface	Tier II Jr. A	43	16	12	28	25	...	...	...	—	—	—	—	—
—Victoria	WHL	2	0	0	0	0	...	...	...	—	—	—	—	—
92-93—Victoria	WHL	70	4	11	15	118	...	...	...	—	—	—	—	—
93-94—Victoria	WHL	68	29	11	40	112	...	...	...	—	—	—	—	—
94-95—Prince George	WHL	43	20	36	56	78	...	...	...	—	—	—	—	—
—Brandon	WHL	23	5	8	13	50	...	...	...	18	10	6	16	33
95-96—Brandon	WHL	71	58	53	111	161	...	...	...	19	6	19	25	25
96-97—Baltimore	AHL	71	29	27	56	134	...	...	...	—	—	—	—	—
—Anaheim	NHL	5	1	1	2	0	2	0	0	1	0	0	0	0
97-98—Cincinnati	AHL	48	18	22	40	83	...	...	...	—	—	—	—	—
—Anaheim	NHL	7	0	0	0	6	-6	0	0	—	—	—	—	—
98-99—Cincinnati	AHL	65	25	28	53	153	...	...	...	3	0	1	1	19
—Anaheim	NHL	7	0	0	0	4	-2	0	0	1	0	0	0	0
99-00—Anaheim	NHL	69	8	11	19	70	-15	0	0	—	—	—	—	—
00-01—Anaheim	NHL	54	15	20	35	26	-1	3	0	—	—	—	—	—
01-02—Anaheim	NHL	82	20	24	44	107	12	8	0	—	—	—	—	—
02-03—Anaheim	NHL	57	9	19	28	34	-8	1	0	21	2	9	11	12
NHL Totals (7 years)		281	53	75	128	247	-42	12	0	23	2	9	11	12

LEEB, BRAD — LW — MAPLE LEAFS

PERSONAL: Born August 27, 1979, in Red Deer, Alta. ... 5-11/180. ... Shoots right.

TRANSACTIONS/CAREER NOTES: Signed as non-drafted free agent by Vancouver Canucks (October 8, 1999). ... Traded by Canucks to Toronto Maple Leafs for D Tomas Mojzis (September 4, 2002).

		REGULAR SEASON							PLAYOFFS				
Season Team	League	Gms.	G	A	Pts.	PIM	+/-	PP	SH	Gms.	G	A	Pts.	PIM
94-95—Red Deer	WHL	3	0	0	0	4	...	...	...	—	—	—	—	—
95-96—Red Deer	WHL	38	3	6	9	30	...	...	...	10	2	0	2	11
96-97—Red Deer	WHL	70	15	20	35	76	...	...	...	16	3	3	6	6
97-98—Red Deer	WHL	63	23	23	46	88	...	...	...	3	2	0	2	2
98-99—Red Deer	WHL	64	32	47	79	84	...	...	...	9	5	9	14	10

Season Team	League	REGULAR SEASON								PLAYOFFS				
		Gms.	G	A	Pts.	PIM	+/-	PP	SH	Gms.	G	A	Pts.	PIM
99-00—Syracuse....................	AHL	61	19	18	37	50	...	...	...	4	0	0	0	6
—Vancouver....................	NHL	2	0	0	0	2	-2	0	0	—	—	—	—	—
00-01—Kansas City................	IHL	53	18	16	34	53	...	...	...	—	—	—	—	—
01-02—Manitoba..................	AHL	·60	17	15	32	45	...	...	...	—	—	—	—	—
—Vancouver....................	NHL	2	0	0	0	0	1	0	0	—	—	—	—	—
02-03—St. John's................	AHL	79	35	26	61	78	...	...	...	—	—	—	—	—
NHL Totals (2 years)..........		4	0	0	0	2	-1	0	0					

LEETCH, BRIAN D RANGERS

PERSONAL: Born March 3, 1968, in Corpus Christi, Texas ... 6-0/185. ... Shoots left. ... Full Name: Brian Joseph Leetch.

TRANSACTIONS/CAREER NOTES: Selected by New York Rangers in first round (first Rangers pick, ninth overall) of NHL entry draft (June 21, 1986). ... Fractured bone in left foot (December 1988). ... Suffered hip pointer (March 15, 1989). ... Fractured left ankle (March 14, 1990). ... Injured ankle (November 21, 1992); missed one game. ... Suffered stretched nerve in neck (December 17, 1992); missed 34 games. ... Fractured ankle (March 19, 1993) and underwent ankle surgery; missed remainder of season. ... Suffered nerve compression in right leg (January 4, 1998); missed two games. ... Suffered head injury (April 5, 1998); missed four games. ... Fractured arm (November 24, 1999); missed 32 games. ... Re-signed by Rangers (July 30, 2003).

Season Team	League	REGULAR SEASON								PLAYOFFS				
		Gms.	G	A	Pts.	PIM	+/-	PP	SH	Gms.	G	A	Pts.	PIM
84-85—Avon Old Farms H.S. ..	Conn. H.S.	26	30	46	76	15	...	...	...	—	—	—	—	—
85-86—Avon Old Farms H.S. ..	Conn. H.S.	28	40	44	84	18	...	...	...	—	—	—	—	—
86-87—Boston College	Hockey East	37	9	38	47	10	...	...	...	—	—	—	—	—
87-88—U.S. national team	Int'l	60	13	61	74	38	...	...	...	—	—	—	—	—
—U.S. Olympic team......	Int'l	6	1	5	6	4	...	...	...	—	—	—	—	—
—New York Rangers......	NHL	17	2	12	14	0	5	1	0	—	—	—	—	—
88-89—New York Rangers......	NHL	68	23	48	71	50	8	8	3	4	3	2	5	2
89-90—New York Rangers......	NHL	72	11	45	56	26	-18	5	0	—	—	—	—	—
90-91—New York Rangers......	NHL	80	16	72	88	42	2	6	0	6	1	3	4	0
91-92—New York Rangers......	NHL	80	22	80	102	26	25	10	1	13	4	11	15	4
92-93—New York Rangers......	NHL	36	6	30	36	26	2	2	1	—	—	—	—	—
93-94—New York Rangers......	NHL	84	23	56	79	67	28	17	1	23	11	*23	*34	6
94-95—New York Rangers......	NHL	48	9	32	41	18	0	3	0	10	6	8	14	8
95-96—New York Rangers......	NHL	82	15	70	85	30	12	7	0	11	1	6	7	4
96-97—New York Rangers......	NHL	82	20	58	78	40	31	9	0	15	2	8	10	6
97-98—New York Rangers......	NHL	76	17	33	50	32	-36	11	0	—	—	—	—	—
—U.S. Olympic team......	Int'l	4	1	1	2	0	...	...	...	—	—	—	—	—
98-99—New York Rangers......	NHL	82	13	42	55	42	-7	4	0	—	—	—	—	—
99-00—New York Rangers......	NHL	50	7	19	26	20	-16	3	0	—	—	—	—	—
00-01—New York Rangers......	NHL	82	21	58	79	34	-18	10	1	—	—	—	—	—
01-02—New York Rangers......	NHL	82	10	45	55	28	14	1	0	—	—	—	—	—
—U.S. Olympic team......	Int'l	6	0	5	5	0	...	...	...	—	—	—	—	—
02-03—New York Rangers......	NHL	51	12	18	30	20	-3	5	0	—	—	—	—	—
NHL Totals (16 years).........		1072	227	718	945	501	29	102	7	82	28	61	89	30

LEFEBVRE, GUILLAUME LW PENGUINS

PERSONAL: Born May 7, 1981, in Amos, Que. ... 6-1/200. ... Shoots left.

TRANSACTIONS/CAREER NOTES: Selected by Philadelphia Flyers in eighth round (sixth Flyers pick, 227th overall) of NHL entry draft (June 25, 2000). ... Traded by Flyers with third-round pick in 2003 draft and second-round pick in 2004 draft to Phoenix Coyotes for RW Tony Amonte (March 10, 2003). ... Traded by Coyotes with LW Ramzi Abid and D Dan Focht to Pittsburgh Penguins for C Jan Hrdina and D Francois Leroux (March 11, 2003).

Season Team	League	REGULAR SEASON								PLAYOFFS				
		Gms.	G	A	Pts.	PIM	+/-	PP	SH	Gms.	G	A	Pts.	PIM
98-99—Shawinigan.................	QMJHL	40	3	1	4	49	...	...	...	—	—	—	—	—
—Cape Breton...............	QMJHL	24	2	7	9	13	...	...	...	5	0	1	1	0
99-00—Cape Breton...............	QMJHL	44	26	28	54	82	...	...	...	—	—	—	—	—
—Quebec....................	QMJHL	2	3	1	4	0	...	...	...	—	—	—	—	—
—Rouyn-Noranda...........	QMJHL	25	4	11	15	39	...	...	...	11	4	0	4	25
00-01—Rouyn-Noranda...........	QMJHL	61	24	43	67	160	...	...	...	9	3	1	4	22
01-02—Philadelphia...............	AHL	78	19	15	34	111	...	...	...	5	0	0	0	4
—Philadelphia...............	NHL	3	0	0	0	0	-1	0	0	—	—	—	—	—
02-03—Philadelphia...............	AHL	47	7	6	13	113	...	...	...	—	—	—	—	—
—Philadelphia...............	NHL	14	0	0	0	4	1	0	0	—	—	—	—	—
—Pittsburgh..................	NHL	12	2	4	6	0	1	0	0	—	—	—	—	—
—Wilkes-Barre/Scranton	AHL	1	1	0	1	0	...	...	...	—	—	—	—	—
NHL Totals (2 years)..........		29	2	4	6	4	1	0	0					

LEFEBVRE, SYLVAIN D

PERSONAL: Born October 14, 1967, in Richmond, Que. ... 6-2/207. ... Shoots left. ... Name pronounced luh-FAYV.

TRANSACTIONS/CAREER NOTES: Signed as non-drafted free agent by Montreal Canadiens (September 24, 1986). ... Traded by Canadiens to Toronto Maple Leafs for third-round pick (D Martin Belanger) in 1994 draft (August 20, 1992). ... Traded by Maple Leafs with LW Wendel Clark, RW Landon Wilson and first-round pick (D Jeffrey Kealty) in 1994 draft to Quebec Nordiques for C Mats Sundin, D Garth Butcher, LW Todd Warriner and first-round pick (traded to Washington) in 1994 draft (June 28, 1994). ... Nordiques franchise moved to Colorado and renamed Avalanche for 1995-96 season (June 21, 1995). ... Sprained right ankle (November 29, 1995); missed six games. ... Fractured forearm

(December 18, 1996); missed 10 games. ... Suffered sore hip (December 12, 1997); missed one game. ... Injured eye (November 8, 1998); missed six games. ... Signed as free agent by New York Rangers (July 16, 1999). ... Sprained shoulder (March 25, 2001); missed final seven games of season. ... Underwent shoulder surgery prior to start of 2000-01 season; missed first 16 games of season. ... Injured left knee (March 27, 2002); missed remainder of season.

			REGULAR SEASON								PLAYOFFS				
Season Team	League	Gms.	G	A	Pts.	PIM	+/-	PP	SH		Gms.	G	A	Pts.	PIM
84-85—Laval	QMJHL	66	7	5	12	31	...	...	...		—	—	—	—	—
85-86—Laval	QMJHL	71	8	17	25	48	...	...	...		14	1	0	1	25
86-87—Laval	QMJHL	70	10	36	46	44	...	...	...		15	1	6	7	12
87-88—Sherbrooke	AHL	79	3	24	27	73	...	...	...		6	2	3	5	4
88-89—Sherbrooke	AHL	77	15	32	47	119	...	...	...		6	1	3	4	4
89-90—Montreal	NHL	68	3	10	13	61	18	0	0		6	0	0	0	2
90-91—Montreal	NHL	63	5	18	23	30	-11	1	0		11	1	0	1	6
91-92—Montreal	NHL	69	3	14	17	91	9	0	0		2	0	0	0	2
92-93—Toronto	NHL	81	2	12	14	90	8	0	0		21	3	3	6	20
93-94—Toronto	NHL	84	2	9	11	79	33	0	0		18	0	3	3	16
94-95—Quebec	NHL	48	2	11	13	17	13	0	0		6	0	2	2	2
95-96—Colorado	NHL	75	5	11	16	49	26	2	0		22	0	5	5	12
96-97—Colorado	NHL	71	2	11	13	30	12	1	0		17	0	0	0	25
97-98—Colorado	NHL	81	0	10	10	48	2	0	0		7	0	0	0	4
98-99—Colorado	NHL	76	2	18	20	48	18	0	0		19	0	1	1	12
99-00—New York Rangers	NHL	82	2	10	12	43	-13	0	0		—	—	—	—	—
00-01—New York Rangers	NHL	71	2	13	15	55	3	0	0		—	—	—	—	—
01-02—Hartford	AHL	15	0	5	5	11	...	...	...		—	—	—	—	—
—New York Rangers	NHL	41	0	5	5	23	-3	0	0		—	—	—	—	—
02-03—New York Rangers	NHL	35	0	2	2	10	-7	0	0		—	—	—	—	—
NHL Totals (14 years)		945	30	154	184	674	108	4	0		129	4	14	18	101

LEGACE, MANNY — G — RED WINGS

PERSONAL: Born February 4, 1973, in Toronto ... 5-9/162. ... Catches left. ... Name pronounced LEH-guh-see.
TRANSACTIONS/CAREER NOTES: Selected by Hartford Whalers in eighth round (fifth Whalers pick, 188th overall) of NHL entry draft (June 26, 1993). ... Whalers franchise moved to North Carolina and renamed Carolina Hurricanes for 1997-98 season; NHL approved move on June 25, 1997. ... Traded by Hurricanes to Los Angeles Kings for conditional pick in 1999 draft (July 31, 1998); Legace did not meet conditions for the pick and the draft choice was forfeited. ... Signed as free agent by Detroit Red Wings (July 15, 1999). ... Claimed on waivers by Vancouver Canucks (September 30, 1999). ... Claimed on waivers by Detroit Red Wings (October 13, 1999). ... Suffered injury (November 27, 2000); missed two games. ... Injured elbow (March 31, 2001); missed one game. ... Strained hip flexor (February 11, 2002); missed one game.

			REGULAR SEASON								PLAYOFFS						
Season Team	League	Gms.	Min	W	L	T	GA	SO	Avg.	SV%	Gms.	Min.	W	L	GA	SO	Avg.	SV%
89-90—Vaughan-Thornhill Jr. B	OHA	29	1660	...	...	...	119	1	4.30	—	—	—	—	—	—	—	—	—
90-91—Niagara Falls	OHL	30	1515	13	11	2	107	0	4.24	—	4	119	...	...	10	0	5.04	—
91-92—Niagara Falls	OHL	43	2384	21	16	3	143	0	3.60	—	14	791	...	...	56	0	4.25	—
92-93—Niagara Falls	OHL	†48	*2630	22	19	3	*170	0	3.88	—	4	240	0	4	18	0	4.50	—
93-94—Canadian nat'l team	Int'l	16	859	8	6	0	36	2	2.51	—	—	—	—	—	—	—	—	—
94-95—Springfield	AHL	39	2169	12	17	6	128	2	3.54	—	—	—	—	—	—	—	—	—
95-96—Springfield	AHL	37	2196	20	12	4	83	*5	*2.27	—	4	220	1	3	18	0	4.91	—
96-97—Springfield	AHL	36	2119	17	14	5	107	1	3.03	—	12	746	9	3	25	†2	2.01	—
—Richmond	ECHL	3	157	2	1	0	8	0	3.06	—	—	—	—	—	—	—	—	—
97-98—Las Vegas	IHL	41	2107	18	16	4	111	1	3.16	—	4	237	1	3	16	0	4.05	—
—Springfield	AHL	6	345	4	2	0	16	0	2.78	—	—	—	—	—	—	—	—	—
98-99—Long Beach	IHL	33	1796	22	8	‡1	67	2	2.24	—	6	338	4	2	9	0	1.60	—
—Los Angeles	NHL	17	899	2	9	2	39	0	2.60	.911	—	—	—	—	—	—	—	—
99-00—Manitoba	IHL	42	2409	20	18	5	104	2	2.59	—	2	141	0	2	7	0	2.98	—
—Detroit	NHL	4	240	4	0	0	11	0	2.75	.906	—	—	—	—	—	—	—	—
00-01—Detroit	NHL	39	2136	24	5	5	73	2	2.05	.920	—	—	—	—	—	—	—	—
01-02—Detroit	NHL	20	1117	10	6	2	45	1	2.42	.911	1	11	0	0	1	0	5.45	.500
02-03—Detroit	NHL	25	1406	14	5	4	51	0	2.18	.925	—	—	—	—	—	—	—	—
NHL Totals (5 years)		105	5798	54	25	13	219	3	2.27	.917	1	11	0	0	1	0	5.45	.500

LEGWAND, DAVID — C — PREDATORS

PERSONAL: Born August 17, 1980, in Detroit ... 6-2/190. ... Shoots left.
TRANSACTIONS/CAREER NOTES: Selected by Nashville Predators in first round (first Predators pick, second overall) of NHL entry draft (June 27, 1998). ... Fractured left foot (January 13, 2000); missed 11 games. ... Injured back (January 30, 2002); missed 12 games. ... Strained back (March 30, 2002); missed remainder of season.

			REGULAR SEASON								PLAYOFFS				
Season Team	League	Gms.	G	A	Pts.	PIM	+/-	PP	SH		Gms.	G	A	Pts.	PIM
96-97—Detroit	Jr. A	44	21	41	62	58	...	...	...		—	—	—	—	—
97-98—Plymouth	OHL	59	54	51	105	56	...	...	...		15	8	12	20	24
98-99—Plymouth	OHL	55	31	49	80	65	...	...	...		11	3	8	11	8
—Nashville	NHL	1	0	0	0	0	0	0	0		—	—	—	—	—
99-00—Nashville	NHL	71	13	15	28	30	-6	4	0		—	—	—	—	—
00-01—Nashville	NHL	81	13	28	41	38	1	3	0		—	—	—	—	—
01-02—Nashville	NHL	63	11	19	30	54	1	1	1		—	—	—	—	—
02-03—Nashville	NHL	64	17	31	48	34	-2	3	1		—	—	—	—	—
NHL Totals (5 years)		280	54	93	147	156	-6	11	2						

LEHTINEN, JERE   RW   STARS

PERSONAL: Born June 24, 1973, in Espoo, Finland ... 6-0/200. ... Shoots right. ... Name pronounced YAIR-ee LEH-tih-nehn.

TRANSACTIONS/CAREER NOTES: Selected by Minnesota North Stars in fourth round (third North Stars pick, 88th overall) of NHL entry draft (June 20, 1992). ... North Stars franchise moved from Minnesota to Dallas and renamed Stars for 1993-94 season. ... Strained groin (December 21, 1995); missed six games. ... Reinjured groin (January 10, 1996); missed one game. ... Sprained ankle (March 20, 1996); missed remainder of season. ... Sprained knee (January 31, 1997); missed 13 games. ... Sprained knee (March 5, 1997); missed five games. ... Separated shoulder (October 19, 1997); missed 10 games. ... Fractured thumb (November 14, 1998); missed five games. ... Sprained ankle (March 25, 1999); missed two games. ... Fractured ankle (October 16, 1999); missed 30 games. ... Injured ankle (January 19, 2000); missed 35 games. ... Suffered from the flu (November 14, 2000); missed one game. ... Sprained ankle (December 6, 2000); missed five games. ... Suffered from hip flexor (February 15, 2001); missed two games. ... Injured knee (January 29, 2002) and underwent surgery; missed one game. ... Bruised ankle (March 20, 2002); missed eight games.

STATISTICAL PLATEAUS: Three-goal games: 2000-01 (1), 2002-03 (1). Total: 2.

Season Team	League	REGULAR SEASON Gms.	G	A	Pts.	PIM	+/-	PP	SH	PLAYOFFS Gms.	G	A	Pts.	PIM
90-91—Kiekko-Espoo	Finland	32	15	9	24	12	...	...	...	—	—	—	—	—
91-92—Kiekko-Espoo	Finland	43	32	17	49	6	...	...	...	—	—	—	—	—
92-93—Kiekko-Espoo	Finland	45	13	14	27	6	...	...	...	—	—	—	—	—
93-94—TPS Turku	Finland	42	19	20	39	6	...	...	...	11	11	2	13	2
—Fin. Olympic team	Int'l	8	3	0	3	11	...	...	...	—	—	—	—	—
94-95—TPS Turku	Finland	39	19	23	42	33	...	...	...	13	8	6	14	4
95-96—Dallas	NHL	57	6	22	28	16	5	0	0	—	—	—	—	—
—Michigan	IHL	1	1	0	1	0	...	...	...	—	—	—	—	—
96-97—Dallas	NHL	63	16	27	43	2	26	3	1	7	2	2	4	0
97-98—Dallas	NHL	72	23	19	42	20	19	7	2	12	3	5	8	2
—Fin. Olympic team	Int'l	6	4	2	6	2	...	...	...	—	—	—	—	—
98-99—Dallas	NHL	74	20	32	52	18	29	7	1	23	10	3	13	2
99-00—Dallas	NHL	17	3	5	8	0	1	0	0	13	1	5	6	2
00-01—Dallas	NHL	74	20	25	45	24	14	7	0	10	1	0	1	2
01-02—Dallas	NHL	73	25	24	49	14	27	7	1	—	—	—	—	—
—Fin. Olympic team	Int'l	4	1	2	3	2	...	...	...	—	—	—	—	—
02-03—Dallas	NHL	80	31	17	48	20	39	5	0	12	3	2	5	0
NHL Totals (8 years)		510	144	171	315	114	160	36	5	77	20	17	37	8

LEHTONEN, KARI   G   THRASHERS

PERSONAL: Born November 16, 1983, in Helsinki, Finland. ... 6-3/189. ... Catches left.

TRANSACTIONS/CAREER NOTES: Selected by Atlanta Thrashers in first round (first Thrashers pick, second overall) of NHL entry draft (June 22, 2002). ... Re-signed by Thrashers (June 4, 2003).

Season Team	League	REGULAR SEASON Gms.	Min.	W	L	T	GA	SO	Avg.	SV%	PLAYOFFS Gms.	Min.	W	L	GA	SO	Avg.	SV%
99-00—Jokerit Helsinki	Finland	2	...	...	...	...	...	...	...	—	—	—	—	—	—	—	—	—
00-01—Jokerit Helsinki	Finland	4	189	3	0	0	6	0	1.90	—	—	—	—	—	—	—	—	—
01-02—Jokerit Helsinki	Finland	23	1242	13	5	3	37	4	1.79	—	*11	*623	*8	†3	†18	*3	1.73	—
02-03—Jokerit Helsinki	Finland	49	...	...	...	...	...	...	...	—	—	—	—	—	—	—	—	—

LEIGHTON, MICHAEL   G   BLACKHAWKS

PERSONAL: Born May 19, 1981, in Petrolia, Ont. ... 6-2/186. ... Catches left.

TRANSACTIONS/CAREER NOTES: Selected by Chicago Blackhawks in sixth round (fifth Blackhawks pick, 165th overall) of NHL entry draft (June 26, 1999).

Season Team	League	REGULAR SEASON Gms.	Min.	W	L	T	GA	SO	Avg.	SV%	PLAYOFFS Gms.	Min.	W	L	GA	SO	Avg.	SV%
97-98—Petrolia	Jr. B	30	...	...	...	...	...	...	...	—	—	—	—	—	—	—	—	—
98-99—Windsor	OHL	28	1389	4	17	2	112	0	4.84	—	3	80	0	1	10	0	7.50	—
99-00—Windsor	OHL	42	2272	17	17	2	118	1	3.12	—	12	616	5	6	32	0	3.12	—
00-01—Windsor	OHL	54	3035	32	13	5	138	2	2.73	—	—	—	—	—	—	—	—	—
01-02—Norfolk	AHL	52	3114	27	16	8	111	6	2.14	—	4	237	1	2	8	0	2.03	—
02-03—Norfolk	AHL	36	2183	18	13	5	91	4	2.50	—	—	—	—	—	—	—	—	—
—Chicago	NHL	8	447	2	3	2	21	1	2.82	.913	—	—	—	—	—	—	—	—
NHL Totals (1 year)		8	447	2	3	2	21	1	2.82	.913								

LEMIEUX, CLAUDE   RW   STARS

PERSONAL: Born July 16, 1965, in Buckingham, Que. ... 6-1/227. ... Shoots right. ... Brother of Jocelyn Lemieux, right winger with seven NHL teams (1986-87 through 1997-98). ... Name pronounced luh-MYOO.

TRANSACTIONS/CAREER NOTES: Selected by Montreal Canadiens in second round (second Canadiens pick, 26th overall) of NHL entry draft (June 8, 1983). ... Tore ankle ligaments (October 1987). ... Fractured orbital bone above right eye (January 14, 1989). ... Pulled groin (March 1989). ... Underwent surgery to repair torn stomach muscle (November 1, 1989); missed 41 games. ... Traded by Canadiens to New Jersey Devils for LW Sylvain Turgeon (September 4, 1990). ... Bruised right eye retina (February 25, 1991). ... Suffered sore back (November 27, 1991); missed four games. ... Injured ankle (March 11, 1992); missed two games. ... Suffered back spasms (October 24, 1992); missed three games. ... Injured right elbow (March 21, 1993); missed one game. ... Suspended three games and fined $500 by NHL for altercation with opponent's bench (March 28, 1995). ... Traded by Devils to New York Islanders for RW Steve Thomas (October 3, 1995). ... Traded by Islanders to Colorado Avalanche for LW Wendel Clark (October 3, 1995). ... Fractured finger (December 3, 1995); missed one playoff game and fined $1,000 by NHL for punching another player (May 24, 1996). ... Suspended two games in Stanley Cup finals and fined $1,000 by NHL for checking from behind (June 2, 1996). ... Tore abdominal muscle (October 5, 1996); missed 37 games. ... Injured back (March 2, 1998); missed two games. ... Traded by Avalanche with second-round pick (D Matt DeMarchi) in 2000 draft and swap of first-round picks in 2000 draft to Devils for LW Brian Rolston and a conditional third-round pick in the 2001 draft (November 3, 1999). ... Signed as free agent by Phoenix Coyotes (December 2, 2000). ... Sprained ankle (March 4, 2001); missed eight games. ... Traded by Coyotes to Dallas Stars for LW Scott Pellerin and conditional pick in 2004 draft (January 16, 2003).

STATISTICAL PLATEAUS: Three-goal games: 1988-89 (1), 1990-91 (2), 1992-93 (1), 1995-96 (2), 1997-98 (1). Total: 7.

Season Team	League			REGULAR SEASON								PLAYOFFS		
		Gms.	G	A	Pts.	PIM	+/-	PP	SH	Gms.	G	A	Pts.	PIM
82-83—Trois-Rivieres..............	QMJHL	62	28	38	66	187	...	...	...	4	1	0	1	30
83-84—Verdun......................	QMJHL	51	41	45	86	225	...	...	...	9	8	12	20	63
—Montreal	NHL	8	1	1	2	12	-2	0	0	—	—	—	—	—
—Nova Scotia	AHL	—	—	—	—	—				2	1	0	1	0
84-85—Verdun	QMJHL	52	58	66	124	152	...	...	...	14	*23	17	*40	38
—Montreal	NHL	1	0	1	1	7	1	0	0	—	—	—	—	—
85-86—Sherbrooke.................	AHL	58	21	32	53	145				—	—	—	—	—
—Montreal	NHL	10	1	2	3	22	-6	1	0	20	10	6	16	68
86-87—Montreal	NHL	76	27	26	53	156	0	5	0	17	4	9	13	41
87-88—Montreal	NHL	78	31	30	61	137	16	6	0	11	3	2	5	20
88-89—Montreal	NHL	69	29	22	51	136	14	7	0	18	4	3	7	58
89-90—Montreal	NHL	39	8	10	18	106	-8	3	0	11	1	3	4	38
90-91—New Jersey	NHL	78	30	17	47	105	-8	10	0	7	4	0	4	34
91-92—New Jersey	NHL	74	41	27	68	109	9	13	1	7	4	3	7	26
92-93—New Jersey	NHL	77	30	51	81	155	3	13	0	5	2	0	2	19
93-94—New Jersey	NHL	79	18	26	44	86	13	5	0	20	7	11	18	44
94-95—New Jersey	NHL	45	6	13	19	86	2	1	0	20	*13	3	16	20
95-96—Colorado	NHL	79	39	32	71	117	14	9	2	19	5	7	12	55
96-97—Colorado	NHL	45	11	17	28	43	-4	5	0	17	13	10	23	32
97-98—Colorado	NHL	78	26	27	53	115	-7	11	1	7	3	3	6	8
98-99—Colorado	NHL	82	27	24	51	102	0	11	0	19	3	11	14	26
99-00—Colorado	NHL	13	3	6	9	4	0	0	0	—	—	—	—	—
—New Jersey	NHL	70	17	21	38	86	-3	7	0	23	4	6	10	28
00-01—Phoenix....................	NHL	46	10	16	26	58	1	2	0	—	—	—	—	—
01-02—Phoenix....................	NHL	82	16	25	41	70	-5	4	1	5	0	0	0	2
02-03—Phoenix....................	NHL	36	6	8	14	30	-3	1	1	—	—	—	—	—
—Dallas....................	NHL	32	2	4	6	14	-9	0	0	7	0	1	1	10
NHL Totals (20 years).........		1197	379	406	785	1756	18	114	6	233	80	78	158	529

LEMIEUX, MARIO   C   PENGUINS

L

PERSONAL: Born October 5, 1965, in Montreal ... 6-4/230. ... Shoots right. ... Brother of Alain Lemieux, center for three NHL teams (1981-82 through 1986-87). ... Name pronounced luh-MYOO.

TRANSACTIONS/CAREER NOTES: Selected by Pittsburgh Penguins in first round (first Penguins pick, first overall) of NHL entry draft (June 9, 1984). ... Sprained left knee (September 1984). ... Reinjured knee (December 2, 1984). ... Sprained right knee (December 20, 1986). ... Bruised right shoulder (November 1987). ... Sprained right wrist (November 3, 1988). ... Suffered herniated disk (February 14, 1990); missed 21 games. ... Underwent surgery to remove part of herniated disk (July 11, 1990); missed first 50 games of season. ... Suffered back spasms (October 1991); missed three games. ... Suffered back spasms (January 4, 1992); missed three games. ... Injured back (January 29, 1992); missed six games. ... Suffered from the flu (February 1992); missed one game. ... Fractured bone in hand (May 5, 1992). ... Injured heel (December 1992); missed one game. ... Injured back (January 5, 1993); missed three games. ... Diagnosed with Hodgkin's Disease (January 12, 1993) and underwent radiation treatment (February 1-March 2); missed 20 games. ... Injured back prior to 1993-94 season; missed first 10 games of season. ... Injured back (October 28, 1993); missed one game. ... Injured back (November 2, 1993); missed one game. ... Suffered from the flu (November 9, 1993); missed one game. ... Injured back (November 11, 1993); missed 38 games. ... Injured back (February 13, 1994); missed two games. ... Injured back (February 19, 1994); missed two games. ... Injured back (March 12, 1994); missed four games. ... Fined $500 by NHL for charging at a referee (April 6, 1994). ... On medical leave of absence during entire 1994-95 season. ... Suffered back spasms (November 9, 1996); missed one game. ... Suffered back spasms (January 21, 1997); missed one game. ... Suffered back spasms (February 4, 1997); missed one game. ... Strained hip flexor (March 4, 1997); missed one game. ... Strained hip flexor (March 14, 1997); missed two games. ... Strained hip flexor (October 3, 2001); missed two games. ... Underwent hip surgery (October 28, 2001); missed six games. ... Injured hip (November 17, 2001); missed 23 games. ... Reinjured hip (February 27, 2002); missed remainder of season.

STATISTICAL PLATEAUS: Three-goal games: 1986-87 (5), 1987-88 (3), 1988-89 (7), 1989-90 (3), 1990-91 (1), 1991-92 (1), 1992-93 (1), 1995-96 (4), 1996-97 (1), 2000-01 (1). Total: 27. ... Four-goal games: 1985-86 (1), 1986-87 (1), 1987-88 (2), 1988-89 (1), 1989-90 (1), 1992-93 (2), 1995-96 (1). Total: 10. ... Five-goal games: 1988-89 (1), 1992-93 (1), 1995-96 (1). Total: 3. ... Total hat tricks: 40.

Season Team	League			REGULAR SEASON								PLAYOFFS		
		Gms.	G	A	Pts.	PIM	+/-	PP	SH	Gms.	G	A	Pts.	PIM
81-82—Laval	QMJHL	64	30	66	96	22	...	...	...	18	5	9	14	31
82-83—Laval	QMJHL	66	84	100	184	76	...	...	...	12	†14	18	32	18
83-84—Laval	QMJHL	70	*133	*149	*282	92	...	...	...	14	*29	*23	*52	29
84-85—Pittsburgh	NHL	73	43	57	100	54	-35	11	0	—	—	—	—	—
85-86—Pittsburgh	NHL	79	48	93	141	43	-6	17	0	—	—	—	—	—
86-87—Pittsburgh	NHL	63	54	53	107	57	13	19	0	—	—	—	—	—
87-88—Pittsburgh	NHL	77	*70	98	*168	92	23	22	*10	—	—	—	—	—
88-89—Pittsburgh	NHL	76	*85	†114	*199	100	41	*31	*13	11	12	7	19	16
89-90—Pittsburgh	NHL	59	45	78	123	78	-18	14	3	—	—	—	—	—
90-91—Pittsburgh	NHL	26	19	26	45	30	8	6	1	23	16	*28	*44	16
91-92—Pittsburgh	NHL	64	44	87	*131	94	27	12	4	15	*16	18	*34	2
92-93—Pittsburgh	NHL	60	69	91	*160	38	*55	16	6	11	8	10	18	10
93-94—Pittsburgh	NHL	22	17	20	37	32	-2	7	0	6	4	3	7	2
94-95—Pittsburgh	NHL				Did not play.									
95-96—Pittsburgh	NHL	70	*69	†92	*161	54	10	*31	*8	18	11	16	27	33
96-97—Pittsburgh	NHL	76	50	†72	*122	65	27	15	3	5	3	3	6	4
97-98—					Did not play.									
98-99—					Did not play.									
99-00—					Did not play.									
00-01—Pittsburgh	NHL	43	35	41	76	18	15	16	1	18	6	11	17	4
01-02—Pittsburgh	NHL	24	6	25	31	14	0	2	0	—	—	—	—	—
—Can. Olympic team	Int'l	5	2	4	6	0	...	...	...	—	—	—	—	—
02-03—Pittsburgh	NHL	67	28	63	91	43	-25	14	0	—	—	—	—	—
NHL Totals (19 years).........		879	682	1010	1692	812	133	233	49	107	76	96	172	87

LEOPOLD, JORDAN   D   FLAMES

PERSONAL: Born August 3, 1980, in Golden Valley, Minn. ... 6-0/210. ... Shoots left.

TRANSACTIONS/CAREER NOTES: Selected by Mighty Ducks of Anaheim in second round (first Mighty Ducks pick, 44th overall) of NHL entry draft (June 26, 1999). ... Traded by Mighty Ducks to Calgary Flames for LW Andrei Nazarov and second-round pick (traded back to Calgary) in 2001 draft (September 26, 2000).

		REGULAR SEASON								PLAYOFFS				
Season Team	League	Gms.	G	A	Pts.	PIM	+/-	PP	SH	Gms.	G	A	Pts.	PIM
97-98—U.S. National	NAHL	60	11	12	23	16	...	...	...	—	—	—	—	—
98-99—Univ. of Minnesota	WCHA	39	7	16	23	20	...	...	...	—	—	—	—	—
99-00—Univ. of Minnesota	WCHA	39	6	18	24	20	...	...	...	—	—	—	—	—
00-01—Univ. of Minnesota	WCHA	42	12	37	49	38	...	...	...	—	—	—	—	—
01-02—Univ. of Minnesota	WCHA	44	20	28	48	28	...	...	...	—	—	—	—	—
02-03—Saint John	AHL	3	1	2	3	0	...	...	...	—	—	—	—	—
—Calgary	NHL	58	4	10	14	12	-15	3	0	—	—	—	—	—
NHL Totals (1 year)		58	4	10	14	12	-15	3	0	—	—	—	—	—

LESCHYSHYN, CURTIS   D   SENATORS

PERSONAL: Born September 21, 1969, in Thompson, Man. ... 6-1/207. ... Shoots left. ... Full Name: Curtis Michael Leschyshyn. ... Name pronounced luh-SIH-shihn.

TRANSACTIONS/CAREER NOTES: Selected by Quebec Nordiques in first round (first Nordiques pick, third overall) of NHL entry draft (June 11, 1988). ... Separated shoulder (January 10, 1989). ... Sprained left knee (November 1989). ... Damaged knee ligaments (February 18, 1991) and underwent surgery; missed final 19 games of 1990-91 season and first 30 games of 1991-92 season. ... Strained back (October 13, 1992); missed two games. ... Injured right collarbone (December 30, 1994); missed two games. ... Pulled thigh muscle (March 19, 1994); missed two games. ... Injured groin (March 31, 1994); missed remainder of season. ... Lacerated groin (April 22, 1995); missed last four games of season. ... Nordiques franchise moved to Colorado and renamed Avalanche for 1995-96 season (June 21, 1995). ... Injured hip flexor (January 17, 1996); missed three games. ... Traded by Avalanche with LW Chris Simon to Washington Capitals for RW Keith Jones and first- (D Scott Parker) and fourth-round (traded back to Washington) picks in 1998 draft (November 2, 1996). ... Traded by Capitals to Hartford Whalers for C Andrei Nikolishin (November 9, 1996). ... Injured abdominal muscle (March 7, 1997); missed five games. ... Whalers franchise moved to North Carolina and renamed Carolina Hurricanes for 1997-98 season; NHL approved move on June 25, 1997. ... Strained groin (September 25, 1997); missed four games. ... Strained groin (November 13, 1997); missed one game. ... Suffered back spasms (February 28, 1998); missed one game. ... Suffered back spasms (December 5, 1998); missed three games. ... Bruised sternum (December 19, 1998); missed one game. ... Strained groin (January 4, 1999); missed six games. ... Strained groin (March 24, 1999); missed six games. ... Strained groin (January 27, 2000); missed 20 games. ... Reinjured groin (March 17, 2000); missed nine games. ... Selected by Minnesota Wild in NHL expansion draft (June 23, 2000). ... Strained groin (October 20, 2000); missed one game. ... Reinjured groin (November 3, 2000); missed three games. ... Reinjured groin (November 28, 2000); missed 10 games. ... Traded by Wild to Ottawa Senators for third-round pick (C Stephane Veilleux) in 2001 draft and future considerations (March 13, 2001). ... Suffered concussion (April 3, 2001); missed final two games of regular season. ... Injured back (December 1, 2001); missed one game. ... Suffered from the flu (February 6, 2002); missed two games.

		REGULAR SEASON								PLAYOFFS				
Season Team	League	Gms.	G	A	Pts.	PIM	+/-	PP	SH	Gms.	G	A	Pts.	PIM
85-86—Saskatoon	WHL	1	0	0	0	0	...	...	...	—	—	—	—	—
86-87—Saskatoon	WHL	70	14	26	40	107	...	...	...	11	1	5	6	14
87-88—Saskatoon	WHL	56	14	41	55	86	...	...	...	10	2	5	7	16
88-89—Quebec	NHL	71	4	9	13	71	-32	1	1	—	—	—	—	—
89-90—Quebec	NHL	68	2	6	8	44	-41	1	0	—	—	—	—	—
90-91—Quebec	NHL	55	3	7	10	49	-19	2	0	—	—	—	—	—
91-92—Quebec	NHL	42	5	12	17	42	-28	3	0	—	—	—	—	—
—Halifax	AHL	6	0	2	2	4	...	...	...	—	—	—	—	—
92-93—Quebec	NHL	82	9	23	32	61	25	4	0	6	1	1	2	6
93-94—Quebec	NHL	72	5	17	22	65	-2	3	0	—	—	—	—	—
94-95—Quebec	NHL	44	2	13	15	20	29	0	0	3	0	1	1	4
95-96—Colorado	NHL	77	4	15	19	73	32	0	0	17	1	2	3	8
96-97—Colorado	NHL	11	0	5	5	6	1	0	0	—	—	—	—	—
—Washington	NHL	2	0	0	0	2	0	0	0	—	—	—	—	—
—Hartford	NHL	64	4	13	17	30	-19	1	1	—	—	—	—	—
97-98—Carolina	NHL	73	2	10	12	45	-2	1	0	—	—	—	—	—
98-99—Carolina	NHL	65	2	7	9	50	-1	0	0	6	0	0	0	6
99-00—Carolina	NHL	53	0	2	2	14	-19	0	0	—	—	—	—	—
00-01—Minnesota	NHL	54	2	3	5	19	-2	1	0	—	—	—	—	—
—Ottawa	NHL	11	0	4	4	0	7	0	0	4	0	0	0	0
01-02—Ottawa	NHL	79	1	9	10	44	-5	0	0	12	0	1	1	0
02-03—Ottawa	NHL	54	1	6	7	18	11	0	0	18	0	1	1	10
NHL Totals (15 years)		977	46	161	207	653	-65	17	2	66	2	6	8	34

LESSARD, FRANCIS   D   THRASHERS

PERSONAL: Born May 30, 1979, in Montreal ... 6-3/225. ... Shoots right. ... Name pronounced luh-SAHRD.

TRANSACTIONS/CAREER NOTES: Selected by Carolina Hurricanes in third round (third Hurricanes pick, 80th overall) of NHL entry draft (June 21, 1997). ... Traded by Hurricanes to Philadelphia Flyers for eighth-round pick (G Antti Jokela) in 1999 draft (May 25, 1999). ... Traded by Flyers to Atlanta Thrashers for D David Harlock, third- and seventh-round picks in 2003 draft (March 15, 2002).

Season Team	League	REGULAR SEASON								PLAYOFFS				
		Gms.	G	A	Pts.	PIM	+/-	PP	SH	Gms.	G	A	Pts.	PIM
96-97—Val-d'Or	QMJHL	66	1	9	10	287	...			—	—	—	—	—
97-98—Val-d'Or	QMJHL	63	3	20	23	338	...			19	1	6	7	*101
98-99—Drummondville	QMJHL	53	12	36	48	295	...			—	—	—	—	—
99-00—Philadelphia	AHL	78	4	8	12	416	...			5	0	1	1	7
00-01—Philadelphia	AHL	64	3	7	10	330	...			10	0	0	0	33
01-02—Philadelphia	AHL	60	0	6	6	251	...			—	—	—	—	—
—Chicago	AHL	7	2	1	3	34	...			15	0	1	1	40
—Atlanta	NHL	5	0	0	0	26	0	0	0	—	—	—	—	—
02-03—Chicago	AHL	50	2	5	7	194	...			—	—	—	—	—
—Atlanta	NHL	18	0	2	2	61	1	0	0	—	—	—	—	—
NHL Totals (2 years)		23	0	2	2	87	1	0	0					

LETANG, ALAN — D — ISLANDERS

PERSONAL: Born September 4, 1975, in Renfrew, Ont. ... 6-1/202. ... Shoots left. ... Name pronounced luh-TANG.
TRANSACTIONS/CAREER NOTES: Signed as non-drafted free agent by Dallas Stars (March 22, 1999). ... Separated shoulder (November 17, 1999); missed five games. ... Signed as free agent by Calgary Flames (August 22, 2001). ... Signed as free agent by New York Islanders (July 19, 2002).

Season Team	League	REGULAR SEASON								PLAYOFFS				
		Gms.	G	A	Pts.	PIM	+/-	PP	SH	Gms.	G	A	Pts.	PIM
91-92—Cornwall	OHL	47	1	4	5	45	...			6	0	0	0	2
92-93—Newmarket	OHL	66	1	25	26	14	...			6	0	3	3	2
93-94—Newmarket	OHL	58	3	21	24	30	...			—	—	—	—	—
94-95—Sarnia	OHL	62	5	36	41	35	...			4	2	2	4	6
95-96—Fredericton	AHL	71	0	26	26	40	...			10	0	3	3	4
96-97—Fredericton	AHL	60	2	9	11	8	...			—	—	—	—	—
97-98—Kaufbeuren	Germany	15	1	5	6	8	...			—	—	—	—	—
—SC Langnau	Switzerland	11	4	3	7	6	...			—	—	—	—	—
—Augsburger Panther	Germany	17	0	1	1	4	...			—	—	—	—	—
98-99—Canadian nat'l team	Int'l	42	3	9	12	20	...			—	—	—	—	—
—Michigan	IHL	12	3	3	6	0	...			5	0	2	2	0
99-00—Dallas	NHL	8	0	0	0	2	-5	0	0	—	—	—	—	—
—Michigan	IHL	51	1	12	13	30	...			—	—	—	—	—
00-01—Utah	IHL	79	6	24	30	26	...			—	—	—	—	—
01-02—Saint John	AHL	61	4	24	28	33	...			—	—	—	—	—
—Calgary	NHL	2	0	0	0	0	-2	0	0	—	—	—	—	—
02-03—Bridgeport	AHL	70	3	21	24	21	...			—	—	—	—	—
—New York Islanders	NHL	4	0	0	0	0	-1	0	0	—	—	—	—	—
NHL Totals (3 years)		14	0	0	0	2	-8	0	0					

LETOWSKI, TREVOR — C — BLUE JACKETS

PERSONAL: Born April 5, 1977, in Thunder Bay, Ont. ... 5-10/178. ... Shoots right.
TRANSACTIONS/CAREER NOTES: Selected by Phoenix Coyotes in seventh round (sixth Coyotes pick, 174th overall) of NHL entry draft (June 22, 1996). ... Traded by Coyotes with LW Todd Warriner, RW Tyler Bouck and third-round pick in 2003 draft to Vancouver Canucks for C Denis Pederson and D Drake Berehowsky (December 28, 2001). ... Signed by Columbus Blue Jackets (July 3, 2003).

Season Team	League	REGULAR SEASON								PLAYOFFS				
		Gms.	G	A	Pts.	PIM	+/-	PP	SH	Gms.	G	A	Pts.	PIM
94-95—Sarnia	OHL	66	22	19	41	33	...			4	0	1	1	9
95-96—Sarnia	OHL	66	36	63	99	66	...			10	9	5	14	10
96-97—Sarnia	OHL	55	35	73	108	51	...			12	9	12	21	20
97-98—Springfield	AHL	75	11	20	31	26	...			4	1	2	3	18
98-99—Springfield	AHL	67	32	35	67	46	...			3	1	0	1	2
—Phoenix	NHL	14	2	2	4	2	1	0	0	—	—	—	—	—
99-00—Phoenix	NHL	82	19	20	39	20	2	3	4	5	1	1	2	4
00-01—Phoenix	NHL	77	7	15	22	32	-2	0	1	—	—	—	—	—
01-02—Phoenix	NHL	33	2	6	8	4	2	0	0	—	—	—	—	—
—Vancouver	NHL	42	7	10	17	15	2	1	0	6	0	1	1	8
02-03—Vancouver	NHL	78	11	14	25	36	8	1	1	6	0	1	1	0
NHL Totals (5 years)		326	48	67	115	109	13	5	6	17	1	3	4	12

LIDSTROM, NICKLAS — D — RED WINGS

PERSONAL: Born April 28, 1970, in Vasteras, Sweden ... 6-2/190. ... Shoots left. ... Name pronounced NIHK-luhs LIHD-struhm.
TRANSACTIONS/CAREER NOTES: Selected by Detroit Red Wings in third round (third Red Wings pick, 53rd overall) of NHL entry draft (June 17, 1989). ... Played in Europe during 1994-95 NHL lockout. ... Suffered back spasms (April 9, 1995); missed five games. ... Suffered from the flu (April 14, 1996); missed one game. ... Suffered from the flu (January 20, 1997); missed one game.

Season Team	League	REGULAR SEASON								PLAYOFFS				
		Gms.	G	A	Pts.	PIM	+/-	PP	SH	Gms.	G	A	Pts.	PIM
87-88—Vasteras	Sweden	3	0	0	0	0	...			—	—	—	—	—
88-89—Vasteras	Sweden	19	0	2	2	4	...			—	—	—	—	—
89-90—Vasteras	Sweden	39	8	8	16	14	...			—	—	—	—	—
90-91—Vasteras	Sweden	20	2	12	14	14	...			—	—	—	—	—
91-92—Detroit	NHL	80	11	49	60	22	36	5	0	11	1	2	3	0
92-93—Detroit	NHL	84	7	34	41	28	7	3	0	7	1	0	1	0

L

Season Team	League	REGULAR SEASON								PLAYOFFS				
		Gms.	G	A	Pts.	PIM	+/-	PP	SH	Gms.	G	A	Pts.	PIM
93-94—Detroit	NHL	84	10	46	56	26	43	4	0	7	3	2	5	0
94-95—Vasteras	Sweden	13	2	10	12	4	...	...	...	—	—	—	—	—
—Detroit	NHL	43	10	16	26	6	15	7	0	18	4	12	16	8
95-96—Vasteras	Sweden	13	2	10	12	4	...	...	...	—	—	—	—	—
—Detroit	NHL	81	17	50	67	20	29	8	1	19	5	9	14	10
96-97—Detroit	NHL	79	15	42	57	30	11	8	0	20	2	6	8	2
97-98—Detroit	NHL	80	17	42	59	18	22	7	1	22	6	13	19	8
—Swedish Oly. team	Int'l	4	1	1	2	2	...	...	...	—	—	—	—	—
98-99—Detroit	NHL	81	14	43	57	14	14	6	2	10	2	9	11	4
99-00—Detroit	NHL	81	20	53	73	18	19	9	4	9	2	4	6	4
00-01—Detroit	NHL	82	15	56	71	18	9	8	0	6	1	7	8	0
01-02—Detroit	NHL	78	9	50	59	20	13	6	0	23	5	11	16	2
—Swedish Oly. team	Int'l	4	1	5	6	0	...	...	...	—	—	—	—	—
02-03—Detroit	NHL	82	18	44	62	38	40	8	1	4	0	2	2	0
NHL Totals (12 years)		935	163	525	688	258	258	79	9	156	32	77	109	38

LILJA, ANDREAS   D   PANTHERS

PERSONAL: Born July 13, 1975, in Landskrona, Sweden ... 6-3/228. ... Shoots left.

TRANSACTIONS/CAREER NOTES: Selected by Los Angeles Kings in second round (second Kings pick, 54th overall) of NHL entry draft (June 24, 2000). ... Sprained left knee (October 13, 2001); missed 19 games. ... Traded by Kings with RW Jaroslav Bednar to Florida Panthers for D Dmitry Yushkevich and fifth-round pick in 2003 draft (November 26, 2002).

Season Team	League	REGULAR SEASON								PLAYOFFS				
		Gms.	G	A	Pts.	PIM	+/-	PP	SH	Gms.	G	A	Pts.	PIM
95-96—Malmo	Sweden	40	1	5	6	63	...	...	...	5	0	1	1	2
96-97—Malmo	Sweden	47	1	0	1	22	...	...	...	4	0	0	0	10
97-98—Malmo	Sweden	10	0	0	0	0	...	...	...	—	—	—	—	—
98-99—Malmo	Sweden	41	0	3	3	14	...	...	...	1	0	0	0	4
99-00—Malmo	Sweden	49	8	11	19	88	...	...	...	6	0	0	0	8
00-01—Lowell	AHL	61	7	29	36	149	...	...	...	4	0	6	6	6
—Los Angeles	NHL	2	0	0	0	4	-2	0	0	1	0	0	0	0
01-02—Los Angeles	NHL	26	1	4	5	22	3	1	0	5	0	0	0	6
—Manchester	AHL	4	0	1	1	4	...	...	...	—	—	—	—	—
02-03—Los Angeles	NHL	17	0	3	3	14	5	0	0	—	—	—	—	—
—Florida	NHL	56	4	8	12	56	8	0	0	—	—	—	—	—
NHL Totals (3 years)		101	5	15	20	96	14	1	0	6	0	0	0	6

LINDEN, TREVOR   RW   CANUCKS

PERSONAL: Born April 11, 1970, in Medicine Hat, Alta. ... 6-4/220. ... Shoots right. ... Brother of Jamie Linden, right winger with Florida Panthers organization (1993-94 through 1996-97).

TRANSACTIONS/CAREER NOTES: Selected by Vancouver Canucks in first round (first Canucks pick, second overall) of NHL entry draft (June 11, 1988). ... Hyperextended elbow (October 1989). ... Separated shoulder (March 17, 1990). ... Sprained knee ligament (December 1, 1996); missed 24 games. ... Bruised ribs (March 8, 1997); missed eight games. ... Injured knee (April 5, 1997); missed one game. ... Strained groin (November 16, 1997); missed eight games. ... Sprained medial collateral ligament in knee (January 26, 1998); missed six games. ... Traded by Canucks to New York Islanders for D Bryan McCabe, LW Todd Bertuzzi and third-round pick (LW Jarkko Ruutu) in 1998 draft (February 6, 1998). ... Traded by Islanders to Montreal Canadiens for first-round pick (D Branislav Mezei) in 1999 draft (May 29, 1999). ... Sprained ankle (December 1, 1999); missed 14 games. ... Reinjured ankle (January 6, 2000); missed six games. ... Fractured ribs (March 14, 2000); missed final 12 games of regular season. ... Bruised foot (December 8, 2000); missed one game. ... Bruised foot (December 30, 2000); missed 12 games. ... Traded by Canadiens with RW Dainius Zubrus and second-round pick (traded to Tampa Bay) in 2001 draft to Washington Capitals for F Jan Bulis, F Richard Zednik and first-round pick (C Alexander Perezhogin) in 2001 draft (March 13, 2001). ... Traded by Capitals with second-round pick in 2003 draft to Canucks for first-round pick (RW Boyd Gordon) in 2002 draft and third-round pick in 2003 draft (November 10, 2001).

STATISTICAL PLATEAUS: Three-goal games: 1988-89 (2), 1990-91 (1), 1995-96 (1), 1999-00 (1). Total: 5.

Season Team	League	REGULAR SEASON								PLAYOFFS				
		Gms.	G	A	Pts.	PIM	+/-	PP	SH	Gms.	G	A	Pts.	PIM
85-86—Medicine Hat	WHL	5	2	0	2	0	...	...	...	—	—	—	—	—
86-87—Medicine Hat	WHL	72	14	22	36	59	...	...	...	20	5	4	9	17
87-88—Medicine Hat	WHL	67	46	64	110	76	...	...	...	16	†13	12	25	19
88-89—Vancouver	NHL	80	30	29	59	41	-10	10	1	7	3	4	7	8
89-90—Vancouver	NHL	73	21	30	51	43	-17	6	2	—	—	—	—	—
90-91—Vancouver	NHL	80	33	37	70	65	-25	16	2	6	0	7	7	2
91-92—Vancouver	NHL	80	31	44	75	101	3	6	1	13	4	8	12	6
92-93—Vancouver	NHL	84	33	39	72	64	19	8	0	12	5	8	13	16
93-94—Vancouver	NHL	84	32	29	61	73	6	10	2	24	12	13	25	18
94-95—Vancouver	NHL	48	18	22	40	40	-5	9	0	11	2	6	8	12
95-96—Vancouver	NHL	82	33	47	80	42	6	12	1	6	4	4	8	6
96-97—Vancouver	NHL	49	9	31	40	27	5	2	2	—	—	—	—	—
97-98—Vancouver	NHL	42	7	14	21	49	-13	2	0	—	—	—	—	—
—New York Islanders	NHL	25	10	7	17	33	-1	3	2	—	—	—	—	—
—Can. Olympic team	Int'l	6	0	1	1	10	...	...	...	—	—	—	—	—
98-99—New York Islanders	NHL	82	18	29	47	32	-14	8	1	—	—	—	—	—
99-00—Montreal	NHL	50	13	17	30	34	-3	4	0	—	—	—	—	—
00-01—Montreal	NHL	57	12	21	33	52	-2	6	0	—	—	—	—	—
—Washington	NHL	12	3	1	4	8	2	0	0	6	0	4	4	14
01-02—Washington	NHL	16	1	2	3	6	-2	1	0	—	—	—	—	—
—Vancouver	NHL	64	12	22	34	65	-3	2	0	6	1	4	5	0
02-03—Vancouver	NHL	71	19	22	41	30	-1	4	1	14	1	2	3	10
NHL Totals (15 years)		1079	335	443	778	805	-55	109	15	105	32	60	92	92

LINDGREN, MATS　　　　　C　　　　　CANUCKS

PERSONAL: Born October 1, 1974, in Skelleftea, Sweden ... 6-2/205. ... Shoots left.
TRANSACTIONS/CAREER NOTES: Selected by Winnipeg Jets in first round (first Jets pick, 15th overall) of NHL entry draft (June 26, 1993). ... Traded by Jets with D Boris Mironov and first-(C Jason Bonsignore) and fourth-round (RW Adam Copeland) picks in 1994 draft to Edmonton Oilers for D Dave Manson and sixth-round pick (traded to New Jersey) in 1994 draft (March 15, 1994). ... Strained lower back (March 17, 1995); missed 23 games. ... Suffered dislocated shoulder (September 23, 1998); missed first seven games of season. ... Suffered from the flu (November 14, 1998); missed one game. ... Traded by Oilers with eighth-round pick (F Radek Martinek) in 1999 draft to New York Islanders for G Tommy Salo (March 20, 1999). ... Injured shoulder (January 17, 2000) and underwent surgery; missed remainder of season. ... Dislocated left shoulder (November 24, 2000) and underwent surgery; missed remainder of season. ... Suffered back spasms (October 11, 2001); missed one game. ... Signed as free agent by Vancouver Canucks (November 3, 2002). ... Re-signed by Canucks (July 17, 2003).

Season Team	League	REGULAR SEASON								PLAYOFFS				
		Gms.	G	A	Pts.	PIM	+/-	PP	SH	Gms.	G	A	Pts.	PIM
90-91—Skelleftea	Sweden Dv. 2	1	0	0	0	0	...	...	...	—	—	—	—	—
91-92—Skelleftea	Sweden Dv. 2	29	14	8	22	14	...	...	...	—	—	—	—	—
92-93—Skelleftea	Sweden Dv. 2	32	20	14	34	18	...	...	...	—	—	—	—	—
93-94—Farjestad Karlstad	Sweden	22	11	6	17	26	...	...	...	—	—	—	—	—
94-95—Farjestad Karlstad	Sweden	37	17	15	32	20	...	...	...	3	0	0	0	4
95-96—Cape Breton	AHL	13	7	5	12	6	...	...	...	—	—	—	—	—
96-97—Hamilton	AHL	9	6	7	13	6	...	...	...	—	—	—	—	—
—Edmonton	NHL	69	11	14	25	12	-7	2	3	12	0	4	4	0
97-98—Edmonton	NHL	82	13	13	26	42	0	1	3	12	1	1	2	10
—Swedish Oly. team	Int'l	4	0	0	0	2	...	...	...	—	—	—	—	—
98-99—Edmonton	NHL	48	5	12	17	22	4	0	1	—	—	—	—	—
—New York Islanders	NHL	12	5	3	8	2	2	3	0	—	—	—	—	—
99-00—New York Islanders	NHL	43	9	7	16	24	0	1	0	—	—	—	—	—
00-01—New York Islanders	NHL	20	3	4	7	10	4	0	2	—	—	—	—	—
01-02—New York Islanders	NHL	59	3	12	15	16	0	0	0	—	—	—	—	—
02-03—Manitoba	AHL	4	0	1	1	6	...	...	...	—	—	—	—	—
—Vancouver	NHL	54	5	9	14	18	-2	0	2	—	—	—	—	—
NHL Totals (7 years)		387	54	74	128	146	1	7	11	24	1	5	6	10

LINDROS, ERIC　　　　RW　　　　RANGERS

PERSONAL: Born February 28, 1973, in Toronto ... 6-5/240. ... Shoots right. ... Brother of Brett Lindros, right winger with New York Islanders (1994-95 and 1995-96). ... Name pronounced LIHND-rahz.
TRANSACTIONS/CAREER NOTES: Selected by Quebec Nordiques in first round (first Nordiques pick, first overall) of NHL entry draft (June 22, 1991); refused to report. ... Traded by Nordiques to Philadelphia Flyers for G Ron Hextall, C Mike Ricci, C Peter Forsberg, D Steve Duchesne, D Kerry Huffman, first-round pick (G Jocelyn Thibault) in 1993 draft, cash and future considerations (June 20, 1992); Nordiques aquired LW Chris Simon and first-round pick (traded to Toronto Maple Leafs) in 1994 draft to complete deal (July 21, 1992). ... Sprained knee ligament (November 22, 1992); missed nine games. ... Injured knee (December 29, 1992); missed two games. ... Reinjured knee (January 10, 1993); missed 12 games. ... Tore ligament in right knee (November 12, 1993); missed 14 games. ... Suffered back spasms (March 6, 1994); missed one game. ... Sprained shoulder (April 4, 1994); missed remainder of season. ... Suffered from the flu (January 29, 1995); missed one game. ... Bruised eye (April 30, 1995); missed last game of season and first three playoff games. ... Bruised left knee (November 2, 1995); missed seven games. ... Injured knee (April 5, 1996); missed two games. ... Pulled right groin (October 1, 1996); missed 23 games. ... Bruised bone in back (February 13, 1997); missed two games. ... Suffered charley horse (March 2, 1997); missed one game. ... Bruised calf (March 22, 1997); missed two games. ... Suspended two games and fined $2,000 by NHL for two high-sticking incidents (April 9, 1997). ... Bruised ribs (November 6, 1997); missed one game. ... Suffered concussion (March 8, 1998); missed 18 games. ... Fined $1,000 by NHL for slashing incident (December 5, 1998). ... Suffered concussion (December 29, 1998); missed two games. ... Suspended two games by NHL for high-sticking incident (March 28, 1999). ... Suffered collapsed lung (April 1, 1999); missed remainder of season. ... Suffered illness (October 28, 1999); missed two games. ... Bruised left hand (December 11, 1999); missed two games. ... Suffered concussion (January 14, 2000); missed four games. ... Suffered back spasms (February 20, 2000); missed five games. ... Suffered concussion (March 13, 2000); missed final 14 games of regular season and missed 16 playoff games. ... Missed entire 2000-01 season due to contract dispute. ... Rights traded by Flyers with conditional first-round pick to New York Rangers for LW Jan Hlavac, D Kim Johnsson, RW Pavel Brendl and third-round pick in 2003 draft (August 20, 2001). ... Sprained right knee (December 12, 2001); missed three games. ... Suffered concussion (December 28, 2001); missed four games. ... Sprained right knee (January 28, 2002); missed one game. ... Bruised foot (March 9, 2002); missed two games. ... Suspended one game by NHL for high-sticking incident (October 12, 2002).
STATISTICAL PLATEAUS: Three-goal games: 1992-93 (3), 1993-94 (1), 1994-95 (3), 1995-96 (1), 1997-98 (1), 1999-00 (1), 2001-02 (2). Total: 12. ... Four-goal games: 1996-97 (1). ... Total hat tricks: 13.

Season Team	League	REGULAR SEASON								PLAYOFFS				
		Gms.	G	A	Pts.	PIM	+/-	PP	SH	Gms.	G	A	Pts.	PIM
88-89—St. Michaels	MTHL	37	24	43	67	193	...	...	...	—	—	—	—	—
89-90—Detroit	NAJHL	14	23	29	52	123	...	...	...	—	—	—	—	—
—Oshawa	OHL	25	17	19	36	61	...	...	...	17	*18	18	36	*76
90-91—Oshawa	OHL	57	*71	78	*149	189	...	...	...	16	*18	20	*38	*93
91-92—Oshawa	OHL	13	9	22	31	54	...	...	...	—	—	—	—	—
—Canadian nat'l team	Int'l	24	19	16	35	34	...	...	...	—	—	—	—	—
—Can. Olympic team	Int'l	8	5	6	11	6	...	...	...	—	—	—	—	—
92-93—Philadelphia	NHL	61	41	34	75	147	28	8	1	—	—	—	—	—
93-94—Philadelphia	NHL	65	44	53	97	103	16	13	2	—	—	—	—	—
94-95—Philadelphia	NHL	46	29	41	†70	60	27	7	0	12	4	11	15	18
95-96—Philadelphia	NHL	73	47	68	115	163	26	15	0	12	6	6	12	43
96-97—Philadelphia	NHL	52	32	47	79	136	31	9	0	19	12	14	26	40
97-98—Philadelphia	NHL	63	30	41	71	134	14	10	1	5	1	2	3	17
—Can. Olympic team	Int'l	6	2	3	5	2	...	...	...	—	—	—	—	—
98-99—Philadelphia	NHL	71	40	53	93	120	35	10	1	—	—	—	—	—
99-00—Philadelphia	NHL	55	27	32	59	83	11	10	1	2	1	0	1	0
00-01—							Did not play.							
01-02—New York Rangers	NHL	72	37	36	73	138	19	12	1	—	—	—	—	—
—Can. Olympic team	Int'l	6	1	0	1	8	...	...	...	—	—	—	—	—
02-03—New York Rangers	NHL	81	19	34	53	141	5	9	0	—	—	—	—	—
NHL Totals (11 years)		639	346	439	785	1225	212	103	7	50	24	33	57	118

L

LINDSAY, BILL — LW

PERSONAL: Born May 17, 1971, in Fernie, B.C. ... 6-3/224. ... Shoots left. ... Full Name: William Hamilton Lindsay.

TRANSACTIONS/CAREER NOTES: Selected by Quebec Nordiques in fifth round (sixth Nordiques pick, 103rd overall) of NHL entry draft (June 22, 1991). ... Separated right shoulder (December 26, 1992); missed four games. ... Selected by Florida Panthers in NHL expansion draft (June 24, 1993). ... Lacerated left hand (February 22, 1996); missed seven games. ... Strained hip flexor (April 1, 1996); missed three games. ... Sprained knee (March 26, 1999); missed one game. ... Reinjured knee (April 7, 1999); missed final six games of season. ... Traded by Panthers to Calgary Flames for D Todd Simpson (September 30, 1999). ... Suffered injury (March 7, 2000); missed one game. ... Suffered injury (March 15, 2000); missed one game. ... Suspended two games by NHL for elbowing incident (December 14, 2000). ... Traded by Flames to San Jose Sharks for eighth-round pick (D Joe Campbell) in 2001 draft (March 6, 2001). ... Signed as free agent by Panthers (August 23, 2001). ... Claimed on waivers by Montreal Canadiens (March 19, 2002).

Season Team	League	REGULAR SEASON								PLAYOFFS				
		Gms.	G	A	Pts.	PIM	+/-	PP	SH	Gms.	G	A	Pts.	PIM
88-89—Vernon	BCJHL	56	24	29	53	166	...	...	...	—	—	—	—	—
89-90—Tri-City	WHL	72	40	45	85	84	...	...	...	—	—	—	—	—
90-91—Tri-City	WHL	63	46	47	93	151	...	...	...	—	—	—	—	—
91-92—Tri-City	WHL	42	34	59	93	111	...	...	...	3	2	3	5	16
—Quebec	NHL	23	2	4	6	14	-6	0	0	—	—	—	—	—
92-93—Quebec	NHL	44	4	9	13	16	0	0	0	—	—	—	—	—
—Halifax	AHL	20	11	13	24	18	...	...	...	—	—	—	—	—
93-94—Florida	NHL	84	6	6	12	97	-2	0	0	—	—	—	—	—
94-95—Florida	NHL	48	10	9	19	46	1	0	1	—	—	—	—	—
95-96—Florida	NHL	73	12	22	34	57	13	0	3	22	5	5	10	18
96-97—Florida	NHL	81	11	23	34	120	1	0	1	3	0	1	1	8
97-98—Florida	NHL	82	12	16	28	80	-2	0	2	—	—	—	—	—
98-99—Florida	NHL	75	12	15	27	92	-1	0	1	—	—	—	—	—
99-00—Calgary	NHL	80	8	12	20	86	-7	0	0	—	—	—	—	—
00-01—Calgary	NHL	52	1	9	10	97	-8	0	0	—	—	—	—	—
—San Jose	NHL	16	0	4	4	29	2	0	0	6	0	0	0	16
01-02—Florida	NHL	63	4	7	11	117	-11	0	0	—	—	—	—	—
—Montreal	NHL	13	1	3	4	23	0	0	0	11	2	2	4	2
02-03—Hamilton	AHL	28	6	12	18	89	...	...	...	—	—	—	—	—
—Montreal	NHL	19	0	2	2	23	-1	0	0	—	—	—	—	—
NHL Totals (12 years)		**753**	**83**	**141**	**224**	**897**	**-21**	**0**	**8**	**42**	**7**	**8**	**15**	**44**

LING, DAVID — RW — BLUE JACKETS

PERSONAL: Born January 9, 1975, in Halifax, Nova Scotia ... 5-10/204. ... Shoots right.

TRANSACTIONS/CAREER NOTES: Selected by Quebec Nordiques in seventh round (ninth Nordiques pick, 179th overall) of NHL entry draft (June 29, 1993). ... Nordiques franchise moved to Colorado and renamed Avalanche for 1995-96 season (June 21, 1995). ... Traded by Avalanche with ninth-round pick (D Steve Shirreffs) to Calgary Flames for ninth-round pick (RW Chris George) in 1995 draft (July 7, 1995). ... Traded by Flames with sixth-round pick (LW Gordie Dwyer) in 1998 draft to Montreal Canadiens for C Scott Fraser (October 24, 1996). ... Traded by Canadiens to Chicago Blackhawks for F Martin Gendron (March 14, 1998). ... Traded by Blackhawks to Dallas Stars for future considerations (August 11, 2000). ... Signed as free agent by Columbus Blue Jackets (July 10, 2001). ... Re-signed by Blue Jackets (July 24, 2003).

Season Team	League	REGULAR SEASON								PLAYOFFS				
		Gms.	G	A	Pts.	PIM	+/-	PP	SH	Gms.	G	A	Pts.	PIM
92-93—Kingston	OHL	64	17	46	63	275	...	...	...	16	3	12	15	72
93-94—Kingston	OHL	61	37	40	77	254	...	...	...	6	4	2	6	16
94-95—Kingston	OHL	62	*61	74	135	136	...	...	...	6	7	8	15	12
95-96—Saint John	AHL	75	24	32	56	179	...	...	...	9	0	5	5	12
96-97—Fredericton	AHL	48	22	36	58	229	...	...	...	—	—	—	—	—
—Montreal	NHL	2	0	0	0	0	0	0	0	—	—	—	—	—
—Saint John	AHL	5	0	2	2	19	...	...	...	—	—	—	—	—
97-98—Fredericton	AHL	67	25	41	66	148	...	...	...	—	—	—	—	—
—Montreal	NHL	1	0	0	0	0	-1	0	0	—	—	—	—	—
—Indianapolis	IHL	12	8	6	14	30	...	...	...	5	4	1	5	31
98-99—Kansas City	IHL	82	30	42	72	112	...	...	...	3	1	0	1	20
99-00—Kansas City	IHL	82	35	48	83	210	...	...	...	—	—	—	—	—
00-01—Utah	IHL	79	15	28	43	202	...	...	...	—	—	—	—	—
01-02—Syracuse	AHL	71	19	41	60	240	...	...	...	10	5	5	10	16
—Columbus	NHL	5	0	0	0	7	-1	0	0	—	—	—	—	—
02-03—Syracuse	AHL	46	7	34	41	129	...	...	...	—	—	—	—	—
—Columbus	NHL	35	3	2	5	86	-6	0	0	—	—	—	—	—
NHL Totals (4 years)		**43**	**3**	**2**	**5**	**93**	**-8**	**0**	**0**					

LINTNER, RICHARD — D — PENGUINS

PERSONAL: Born November 15, 1977, in Trencin, Czechoslovakia ... 6-4/213. ... Shoots right.

TRANSACTIONS/CAREER NOTES: Selected by Phoenix Coyotes in fifth round (fourth Coyotes pick, 119th overall) of NHL entry draft (June 22, 1996). ... Traded by Coyotes with C Cliff Ronning to Nashville Predators for future considerations (October 31, 1998). ... Injured shoulder (April 3, 2000); missed final two games of season. ... Strained groin (October 7, 2000); missed four games. ... Strained groin (November 28, 2000); missed seven games. ... Suffered concussion (December 20, 2000); missed one game. ... Traded by Predators to New York Rangers for D Peter Smrek (March 19, 2002). ... Traded by Rangers with RW Rico Fata, RW Mikael Samuelsson, D Joel Bouchard and cash to Pittsburgh Penguins for RW Alexei Kovalev, LW Dan LaCouture, D Janne Laukkanen and D Mike Wilson (February 10, 2003).

Season Team	League	Gms.	G	A	Pts.	PIM	+/-	PP	SH		Gms.	G	A	Pts.	PIM
94-95—Dukla Trencin	Slovakia Jrs.	42	12	13	25	25	...	...	...		—	—	—	—	—
95-96—Dukla Trencin	Slovakia Jrs.	30	15	17	32	210	...	...	...		—	—	—	—	—
—Dukla Trencin	Slovakia	2	0	0	0	0	...	...	...		—	—	—	—	—
96-97—Spisska Nova Ves	Slovakia	35	2	1	3	...					—	—	—	—	—
97-98—Springfield	AHL	71	6	9	15	61	...	...	...		3	1	1	2	4
98-99—Springfield	AHL	8	0	1	1	16	...	...	...		—	—	—	—	—
—Milwaukee	IHL	66	9	16	25	75	...	...	...		—	—	—	—	—
99-00—Nashville	NHL	33	1	5	6	22	-6	0	0		—	—	—	—	—
—Milwaukee	IHL	31	13	8	21	37	...	...	...		—	—	—	—	—
00-01—Nashville	NHL	50	3	5	8	22	2	1	0		—	—	—	—	—
01-02—Dukla Trencin	Slovakia	6	2	0	2	0	...	...	...		—	—	—	—	—
—MoDo Ornskoldsvik	Sweden	28	12	9	21	85	...	...	...		14	3	0	3	8
—Slovakian Oly. team	Int'l	4	1	1	2	0	...	...	...		—	—	—	—	—
02-03—Hartford	AHL	26	6	15	21	30	...	...	...		—	—	—	—	—
—New York Rangers	NHL	10	1	0	1	0	-5	1	0		—	—	—	—	—
—Pittsburgh	NHL	19	3	2	5	10	-9	1	0		—	—	—	—	—
—Wilkes-Barre/Scranton	AHL	6	1	4	5	2	...	...	...		—	—	—	—	—
NHL Totals (3 years)		112	8	12	20	54	-18	3	0						

LITTLE, NEIL   G   FLYERS

PERSONAL: Born December 18, 1971, in Medicine Hat, Alta. ... 6-1/193. ... Catches left.
TRANSACTIONS/CAREER NOTES: Selected by Philadelphia Flyers in 11th round (10th Flyers pick, 226th overall) of NHL entry draft (June 22, 1991).

Season Team	League	Gms.	Min	W	L	T	GA	SO	Avg.	SV%		Gms.	Min.	W	L	GA	SO	Avg.	SV%
89-90—Estevan	SJHL	46	2707	21	19	4	150	1	3.32	—		—	—	—	—	—	—	—	—
90-91—Rensselaer Poly. Inst.	ECAC	18	1032	9	8	0	71	0	4.13	—		—	—	—	—	—	—	—	—
91-92—Rensselaer Poly. Inst.	ECAC	28	1532	11	11	3	96	0	3.76	—		—	—	—	—	—	—	—	—
92-93—Rensselaer Poly. Inst.	ECAC	31	1801	19	9	3	88	0	2.93	—		—	—	—	—	—	—	—	—
93-94—Rensselaer Poly. Inst.	ECAC	27	1570	16	7	4	88	0	3.36	—		—	—	—	—	—	—	—	—
—Hershey	AHL	1	18	0	0	0	1	0	3.33	—		—	—	—	—	—	—	—	—
94-95—Hershey	AHL	19	919	5	7	3	60	0	3.92	—		—	—	—	—	—	—	—	—
—Johnstown	ECHL	16	897	7	6	‡1	55	0	3.68	—		3	145	0	2	11	0	4.55	—
95-96—Hershey	AHL	48	2679	21	18	6	149	0	3.34	—		1	59	0	1	4	0	4.07	—
96-97—Philadelphia	AHL	54	3007	31	12	7	145	0	2.89	—		10	620	6	4	20	1	1.94	—
97-98—Philadelphia	AHL	51	2961	*31	11	7	145	0	2.94	—		*20	*1193	*15	†5	*48	*3	2.41	—
98-99—Grand Rapids	IHL	50	2740	18	21	‡5	144	3	3.15	—		—	—	—	—	—	—	—	—
99-00—Philadelphia	AHL	51	2830	26	18	2	143	1	3.03	—		5	298	2	3	15	0	3.02	—
00-01—Philadelphia	AHL	*58	*3117	22	27	4	148	2	2.85	—		10	631	5	5	23	1	2.19	—
01-02—Philadelphia	AHL	35	2078	13	15	7	70	2	2.02	—		5	298	2	3	13	0	2.62	—
—Philadelphia	NHL	1	60	0	1	0	4	0	4.00	.862		—	—	—	—	—	—	—	—
02-03—Philadelphia	AHL	42	2478	18	19	4	103	4	2.49	—									
NHL Totals (1 year)		1	60	0	1	0	4	0	4.00	.862									

LIV, STEFAN   G   RED WINGS

PERSONAL: Born December 21, 1980, in Sweden. ... 6-0/172. ... Catches left.
TRANSACTIONS/CAREER NOTES: Selected by Detroit Red Wings in fourth round (third Red Wings pick, 102nd overall) of NHL entry draft (June 24, 2000).

Season Team	League	Gms.	Min	W	L	T	GA	SO	Avg.	SV%		Gms.	Min.	W	L	GA	SO	Avg.	SV%
99-00—HV 71 Jonkoping	Sweden Jr.	12	...	...	...	...	...	...	...	—		—	—	—	—	—	—	—	—
00-01—HV 71 Jonkoping	Sweden	*46	*2752	...	...	...	*127	4	2.77	—		—	—	—	—	—	—	—	—
01-02—HV 71 Jonkoping	Sweden	38	2184	...	...	...	95	4	2.61	—		8	517	...	...	27	0	3.13	—
02-03—HV 71 Jonkoping	Sweden	50	...	...	...	...	...	...	...	—		7	...	...	...	...	...	...	—

LOW, REED   RW   BLUES

PERSONAL: Born June 21, 1976, in Moose Jaw, Sask. ... 6-4/219. ... Shoots right. ... Full Name: Reed David Low.
TRANSACTIONS/CAREER NOTES: Selected by St. Louis Blues in seventh round (seventh Blues pick, 177th overall) of NHL entry draft (June 22, 1996). ... Injured thumb (January 29, 2001); missed three games. ... Injured knee (October 22, 2001); missed two games. ... Suspended two games by NHL for receiving third instigator penalty in one season (March 24, 2003). ... Re-signed by Blues (July 27, 2003).

Season Team	League	Gms.	G	A	Pts.	PIM	+/-	PP	SH		Gms.	G	A	Pts.	PIM
94-95—Regina	WHL	2	0	0	0	5	...	...	...		—	—	—	—	—
95-96—Moose Jaw	WHL	61	12	7	19	221	...	...	...		—	—	—	—	—
96-97—Moose Jaw	WHL	62	16	11	27	228	...	...	...		12	2	1	3	50
97-98—Baton Rouge	ECHL	39	4	2	6	145	...	...	...		—	—	—	—	—
—Worcester	AHL	17	1	1	2	75	...	...	...		3	0	0	0	0
98-99—Worcester	AHL	77	5	6	11	239	...	...	...		4	0	0	0	2
99-00—Worcester	AHL	80	12	16	28	203	...	...	...		9	1	3	4	16
00-01—St. Louis	NHL	56	1	5	6	159	4	0	0		—	—	—	—	—
01-02—St. Louis	NHL	58	0	5	5	160	-3	0	0		—	—	—	—	—
02-03—St. Louis	NHL	79	2	4	6	234	3	0	0		—	—	—	—	—
NHL Totals (3 years)		193	3	14	17	553	4	0	0						

LOWRY, DAVE — LW

PERSONAL: Born February 14, 1965, in Sudbury, Ont. ... 6-1/195. ... Shoots left. ... Name pronounced LOW-ree.
TRANSACTIONS/CAREER NOTES: Selected by Vancouver Canucks in sixth round (fourth Canucks pick, 110th overall) of NHL entry draft (June 8, 1983). ... Traded by Canucks to St. Louis Blues for C Ernie Vargas (September 29, 1988). ... Injured groin (March 1990). ... Sprained shoulder (October 1991); missed two games. ... Injured knee (October 26, 1992); missed 26 games. ... Selected by Florida Panthers in NHL expansion draft (June 24, 1993). ... Fractured cheekbone (November 26, 1993); missed three games. ... Injured knee (December 12, 1993); missed one game. ... Suffered abrasion to right cornea (April 28, 1995); missed three games. ... Sprained left knee (October 24, 1995); missed 18 games. ... Sprained knee ligament (February 9, 1997); missed three games. ... Traded by Panthers with first-round pick (traded to Tampa Bay) in 1998 draft to San Jose Sharks for LW Viktor Kozlov and fifth-round pick (D Jaroslav Spacek) in 1998 draft (November 13, 1997). ... Signed as free agent by San Jose Sharks (October 5, 1998). ... Injured shoulder (October 24, 1999); missed five games. ... Reinjured shoulder (November 27, 1999); missed 12 games. ... Injured back (January 29, 2000); missed six games. ... Signed as free agent by Calgary Flames (July 25, 2000). ... Injured hip (March 14, 2001); missed three games. ... Injured shoulder (March 4, 2002); missed remainder of season.

Season Team	League	Gms.	G	A	Pts.	PIM	+/-	PP	SH	Gms.	G	A	Pts.	PIM
82-83—London	OHL	42	11	16	27	48	...	...	...	3	0	0	0	14
83-84—London	OHL	66	29	47	76	125	...	...	...	8	6	6	12	41
84-85—London	OHL	61	60	60	120	94	...	...	...	8	6	5	11	10
85-86—Vancouver	NHL	73	10	8	18	143	-21	1	0	3	0	0	0	0
86-87—Vancouver	NHL	70	8	10	18	176	-23	0	0	—	—	—	—	—
87-88—Fredericton	AHL	46	18	27	45	59				14	7	3	10	72
—Vancouver	NHL	22	1	3	4	38	-2	0	0	—	—	—	—	—
88-89—Peoria	IHL	58	31	35	66	45				—	—	—	—	—
—St. Louis	NHL	21	3	3	6	11	1	0	1	10	0	5	5	4
89-90—St. Louis	NHL	78	19	6	25	75	1	0	2	12	2	1	3	39
90-91—St. Louis	NHL	79	19	21	40	168	19	0	2	13	1	4	5	35
91-92—St. Louis	NHL	75	7	13	20	77	-11	0	0	6	0	1	1	20
92-93—St. Louis	NHL	58	5	8	13	101	-18	0	0	11	2	0	2	14
93-94—Florida	NHL	80	15	22	37	64	-4	3	0	—	—	—	—	—
94-95—Florida	NHL	45	10	10	20	25	-3	2	0	—	—	—	—	—
95-96—Florida	NHL	63	10	14	24	36	-2	0	0	22	10	7	17	39
96-97—Florida	NHL	77	15	14	29	51	2	2	0	5	0	0	0	0
97-98—Florida	NHL	7	0	0	0	2	-1	0	0	—	—	—	—	—
—San Jose	NHL	50	4	4	8	51	0	0	0	6	0	0	0	18
98-99—San Jose	NHL	61	6	9	15	24	-5	2	0	1	0	0	0	0
99-00—San Jose	NHL	32	1	4	5	18	1	0	0	12	1	2	3	6
00-01—Calgary	NHL	79	18	17	35	47	-2	5	0	—	—	—	—	—
01-02—Calgary	NHL	62	7	6	13	51	-20	2	1	—	—	—	—	—
02-03—Saint John	AHL	22	3	6	9	16				—	—	—	—	—
—Calgary	NHL	34	5	14	19	22	4	1	0	—	—	—	—	—
NHL Totals (18 years)		1066	163	186	349	1180	-84	18	6	101	16	20	36	175

LOYNS, LYNN — C — SHARKS

PERSONAL: Born February 22, 1981, in Naicam, Sask. ... 5-11/200.
TRANSACTIONS/CAREER NOTES: Signed as un-drafted free agent by San Jose Sharks (October 3, 2001).

Season Team	League	Gms.	G	A	Pts.	PIM	+/-	PP	SH	Gms.	G	A	Pts.	PIM
97-98—Spokane	WHL	49	1	12	13	8	...	...	...	13	1	4	5	2
98-99—Spokane	WHL	72	20	30	50	43	...	...	...	—	—	—	—	—
99-00—Spokane	WHL	71	20	29	49	47	...	...	...	14	3	2	5	12
00-01—Spokane	WHL	66	31	42	73	81	...	...	...	—	—	—	—	—
01-02—Cleveland	AHL	76	9	9	18	81	...	...	...	—	—	—	—	—
02-03—Cleveland	AHL	36	7	8	15	39	...	...	...	—	—	—	—	—
—San Jose	NHL	19	3	0	3	19	-4	0	0	—	—	—	—	—
NHL Totals (1 year)		19	3	0	3	19	-4	0	0					

LUKOWICH, BRAD — D — LIGHTNING

PERSONAL: Born August 12, 1976, in Cranbrook, B.C. ... 6-1/205. ... Shoots left. ... Name pronounced LOO-kih-wihch.
TRANSACTIONS/CAREER NOTES: Selected by New York Islanders in fourth round (fourth Islanders pick, 90th overall) of NHL entry draft (June 29, 1994). ... Traded by Islanders to Dallas Stars for third-round pick (D Robert Schnabel) in 1997 draft (June 1, 1996). ... Suffered back spasms (December 6, 1999); missed one game. ... Traded by Stars with G Manny Fernandez to Minnesota Wild for third-round pick (C Joel Lundqvist) in 2000 draft and fourth-round pick (traded back to Minnesota) in 2002 draft (June 12, 2000). ... Traded by Wild with third-(C Yared Hagos) and ninth-round (RW Dale Sullivan) picks in 2001 draft to Stars for C Aaron Gavey, C Pavel Patera, eighth-round pick (C Eric Johansson) in 2000 draft and fourth-round pick (traded to Los Angeles) in 2002 draft (June 25, 2000). ... Fractured finger (January 2, 2002); missed five games. ... Traded by Stars with seventh-round pick in 2003 draft to Tampa Bay Lightning for second-round pick (G Tobias Stephan) in 2002 draft (June 22, 2002). ... Re-signed by Lightning (July 15, 2003).

Season Team	League	Gms.	G	A	Pts.	PIM	+/-	PP	SH	Gms.	G	A	Pts.	PIM
92-93—Cranbook	Tier II Jr. A	54	21	41	62	162	...	...	...	—	—	—	—	—
—Kamloops	WHL	1	0	0	0	0	...	...	...	—	—	—	—	—
93-94—Kamloops	WHL	42	5	11	16	166	...	...	...	16	0	1	1	35
94-95—Kamloops	WHL	63	10	35	45	125	...	...	...	18	0	7	7	21
95-96—Kamloops	WHL	65	14	55	69	114	...	...	...	13	2	10	12	29
96-97—Michigan	IHL	69	2	6	8	77	...	...	...	4	0	1	1	2
97-98—Michigan	IHL	60	6	27	33	104	...	...	...	4	0	4	4	14
—Dallas	NHL	4	0	1	1	2	-2	0	0	—	—	—	—	—

Season Team	League	REGULAR SEASON								PLAYOFFS				
		Gms.	G	A	Pts.	PIM	+/-	PP	SH	Gms.	G	A	Pts.	PIM
98-99—Michigan	IHL	67	8	21	29	95	...	...	...	—	—	—	—	—
—Dallas	NHL	14	1	2	3	19	3	0	0	8	0	1	1	4
99-00—Dallas	NHL	60	3	1	4	50	-14	0	0	—	—	—	—	—
00-01—Dallas	NHL	80	4	10	14	76	28	0	0	10	1	0	1	4
01-02—Dallas	NHL	66	1	6	7	40	-1	0	0	—	—	—	—	—
02-03—Tampa Bay	NHL	70	1	14	15	46	4	0	0	9	0	1	1	2
NHL Totals (6 years)		294	10	34	44	233	18	0	0	27	1	2	3	10

LUMME, JYRKI   D   MAPLE LEAFS

PERSONAL: Born July 16, 1966, in Tampere, Finland ... 6-1/209. ... Shoots left. ... Name pronounced YUHR-kee LOO-mee.

TRANSACTIONS/CAREER NOTES: Selected by Montreal Canadiens in third round (third Canadiens pick, 57th overall) of NHL entry draft (June 21, 1986). ... Strained left knee ligaments (December 1988). ... Stretched knee ligaments (February 21, 1989). ... Bruised right foot (November 1989). ... Traded by Canadiens to Vancouver Canucks for second-round pick (C Craig Darby) in 1991 draft (March 6, 1990). ... Cut eye (November 19, 1991); missed three games. ... Sprained knee (January 19, 1993); missed nine games. ... Played in Europe during 1994-95 NHL lockout. ... Injured knee (February 15, 1995); missed six games. ... Bruised ribs (March 1, 1995); missed five games. ... Sprained ankle (November 13, 1996); missed two games. ... Strained shoulder (December 23, 1996); missed 11 games. ... Suffered charley horse (March 13, 1997); missed three games. ... Injured groin (October 11, 1997); missed two games. ... Strained groin (October 26, 1997); missed five games. ... Signed as free agent by Phoenix Coyotes (July 3, 1998). ... Strained groin (February 8, 1999); missed four games. ... Strained shoulder (March 2, 1999); missed 16 games. ... Suffered sore shoulder (April 14, 1999); missed two games. ... Bruised shoulder (November 14, 1999); missed three games. ... Bruised hand (March 5, 2000); missed four games. ... Suffered back spasms (December 26, 2000); missed 19 games. ... Strained shoulder (February 28, 2001); missed five games. ... Traded by Coyotes to Dallas Stars for RW Tyler Bouck (June 23, 2001). ... Traded by Stars to Toronto Maple Leafs for D Dave Manson (November 21, 2001). ... Suffered injury (December 11, 2001); missed three games. ... Suspended two games by NHL for cross-checking incident (March 5, 2002). ... Strained shoulder (March 28, 2002); missed four games.

Season Team	League	REGULAR SEASON								PLAYOFFS				
		Gms.	G	A	Pts.	PIM	+/-	PP	SH	Gms.	G	A	Pts.	PIM
84-85—Koo Vee	Finland	30	6	4	10	44	...	...	...	—	—	—	—	—
85-86—Ilves Tampere	Finland	31	1	5	6	4	...	...	...	—	—	—	—	—
86-87—Ilves Tampere	Finland	43	12	12	24	52	...	...	...	4	0	1	1	0
87-88—Ilves Tampere	Finland	43	8	22	30	75	...	...	...	—	—	—	—	—
—Fin. Olympic team	Int'l	6	0	1	1	2	...	...	...	—	—	—	—	—
88-89—Montreal	NHL	21	1	3	4	10	3	1	0	—	—	—	—	—
—Sherbrooke	AHL	26	4	11	15	10	...	...	...	6	1	3	4	4
89-90—Montreal	NHL	54	1	19	20	41	17	0	0	—	—	—	—	—
—Vancouver	NHL	11	3	7	10	8	0	0	0	—	—	—	—	—
90-91—Vancouver	NHL	80	5	27	32	59	-15	1	0	6	2	3	5	0
91-92—Vancouver	NHL	75	12	32	44	65	25	3	1	13	2	3	5	4
92-93—Vancouver	NHL	74	8	36	44	55	30	3	2	12	0	5	5	6
93-94—Vancouver	NHL	83	13	42	55	50	3	1	3	24	2	11	13	16
94-95—Ilves Tampere	Finland	12	4	4	8	24	...	...	...	—	—	—	—	—
—Vancouver	NHL	36	5	12	17	26	4	3	0	11	2	6	8	8
95-96—Vancouver	NHL	80	17	37	54	50	-9	8	0	6	1	3	4	2
96-97—Vancouver	NHL	66	11	24	35	32	8	5	0	—	—	—	—	—
97-98—Vancouver	NHL	74	9	21	30	34	-25	4	0	—	—	—	—	—
—Fin. Olympic team	Int'l	6	1	0	1	16	...	...	...	—	—	—	—	—
98-99—Phoenix	NHL	60	7	21	28	34	5	1	0	7	0	1	1	6
99-00—Phoenix	NHL	74	8	32	40	44	9	4	0	5	0	1	1	2
00-01—Phoenix	NHL	58	4	21	25	44	3	0	0	—	—	—	—	—
01-02—Dallas	NHL	15	0	1	1	4	-5	0	0	—	—	—	—	—
—Toronto	NHL	51	4	8	12	18	13	1	2	14	0	0	0	4
—Fin. Olympic team	Int'l	4	0	1	1	0	...	...	...	—	—	—	—	—
02-03—Toronto	NHL	73	6	11	17	46	10	1	0	7	0	2	2	4
NHL Totals (15 years)		985	114	354	468	620	76	36	8	105	9	35	44	52

LUNDMARK, JAMIE   C   RANGERS

PERSONAL: Born January 16, 1981, in Edmonton ... 6-0/195. ... Shoots right.

TRANSACTIONS/CAREER NOTES: Selected by New York Rangers in first round (second Rangers pick, ninth overall) of NHL entry draft (June 26, 1999).

Season Team	League	REGULAR SEASON								PLAYOFFS				
		Gms.	G	A	Pts.	PIM	+/-	PP	SH	Gms.	G	A	Pts.	PIM
97-98—St. Albert	Jr. A	53	33	58	91	176	...	...	...	—	—	—	—	—
98-99—Moose Jaw	WHL	70	40	51	91	121	...	...	...	11	5	4	9	24
99-00—Moose Jaw	WHL	37	21	27	48	33	...	...	...	—	—	—	—	—
00-01—Seattle	WHL	52	35	42	77	49	...	...	...	9	4	4	8	16
01-02—Hartford	AHL	79	27	32	59	56	...	...	...	10	3	4	7	16
02-03—Hartford	AHL	22	9	9	18	18	...	...	...	—	—	—	—	—
—New York Rangers	NHL	55	8	11	19	16	-3	0	0	—	—	—	—	—
NHL Totals (1 year)		55	8	11	19	16	-3	0	0					

LUNDQVIST, JOEL   C   STARS

PERSONAL: Born March 2, 1982, in Are, Sweden ... 6-0/183. ... Shoots left.

TRANSACTIONS/CAREER NOTES: Selected by Dallas Stars in third round (third Stars pick, 68th overall) of NHL entry draft (June 24, 2000).

Season Team	League	REGULAR SEASON								PLAYOFFS				
		Gms.	G	A	Pts.	PIM	+/-	PP	SH	Gms.	G	A	Pts.	PIM
99-00—Vastra Frolunda	Sweden Jr.	25	7	12	19	2	...	...	...	—	—	—	—	—
00-01—Vastra Frolunda	Sweden Jr.	9	0	0	0	0	...	...	...	—	—	—	—	—
01-02—Vastra Frolunda	Sweden	46	12	14	26	28	...	...	...	10	1	3	4	8
02-03—Vastra Frolunda	Sweden	50	17	20	37	113	...	...	...	16	6	3	9	12

LUONGO, ROBERTO　　　　　　G　　　　　　PANTHERS

PERSONAL: Born April 4, 1979, in Montreal ... 6-3/205. ... Catches left. ... Name pronounced luh-WAHN-goh.
TRANSACTIONS/CAREER NOTES: Selected by New York Islanders in first round (first Islanders pick, fourth overall) of NHL entry draft (June 21, 1997). ... Traded by Islanders with C Olli Jokinen to Florida Panthers for RW Mark Parrish and LW Oleg Kvasha (June 24, 2000). ... Lacerated forearm (October 10, 2001); missed four games. ... Sprained right ankle (March 20, 2002); missed remainder of season.

Season Team	League	REGULAR SEASON									PLAYOFFS							
		Gms.	Min	W	L	T	GA	SO	Avg.	SV%	Gms.	Min.	W	L	GA	SO	Avg.	SV%
95-96—Val-d'Or	QMJHL	23	1199	6	11	4	74	0	3.70	—	3	68	0	1	5	0	4.41	—
96-97—Val-d'Or	QMJHL	60	3305	32	21	2	171	2	3.10	—	13	777	8	5	44	0	3.40	—
97-98—Val-d'Or	QMJHL	54	3046	27	20	5	157	*7	3.09	—	*17	*1019	*14	3	37	*2	*2.18	—
98-99—Val-d'Or	QMJHL	21	1177	6	10	2	77	1	3.93	—	—	—	—	—	—	—	—	—
—Acadie-Bathurst	QMJHL	22	1341	14	7	1	74	0	3.31	—	*23	*1400	*16	6	64	0	2.74	—
99-00—Lowell	AHL	26	1517	10	12	4	74	1	2.93	—	6	359	3	3	18	0	3.01	—
—New York Islanders	NHL	24	1292	7	14	1	70	1	3.25	.904	—	—	—	—	—	—	—	—
00-01—Florida	NHL	47	2628	12	24	7	107	5	2.44	.920	—	—	—	—	—	—	—	—
—Louisville	AHL	3	178	1	2	0	10	0	3.37	—	—	—	—	—	—	—	—	—
01-02—Florida	NHL	58	3030	16	33	4	140	4	2.77	.915	—	—	—	—	—	—	—	—
02-03—Florida	NHL	65	3627	20	34	7	164	6	2.71	.918	—	—	—	—	—	—	—	—
NHL Totals (4 years)		194	10577	55	105	19	481	16	2.73	.916								

LUPASCHUK, ROSS　　　　　　D　　　　　　PENGUINS

PERSONAL: Born January 19, 1981, in Edmonton ... 6-1/211. ... Shoots right.
TRANSACTIONS/CAREER NOTES: Selected by Washington Capitals in second round (fourth Capitals pick, 34th overall) of NHL entry draft (June 26, 1999). ... Traded by Capitals with C Michal Sivek, C Kris Beech and future considerations to Pittsburgh Penguins for RW Jaromir Jagr and D Frantisek Kucera (July 11, 2001).

Season Team	League	REGULAR SEASON								PLAYOFFS				
		Gms.	G	A	Pts.	PIM	+/-	PP	SH	Gms.	G	A	Pts.	PIM
97-98—Prince Albert	WHL	67	6	12	18	170	...	...	...	—	—	—	—	—
98-99—Prince Albert	WHL	67	8	19	27	127	...	...	...	14	4	9	13	16
99-00—Prince Albert	WHL	22	8	8	16	42	...	...	...	—	—	—	—	—
—Red Deer	WHL	46	13	27	40	116	...	...	...	4	0	1	1	10
00-01—Red Deer	WHL	65	28	37	65	135	...	...	...	22	5	10	15	54
01-02—Wilkes-Barre/Scranton	AHL	72	9	20	29	91	...	...	...	—	—	—	—	—
02-03—Wilkes-Barre/Scranton	AHL	74	18	18	36	101	...	...	...	—	—	—	—	—
—Pittsburgh	NHL	3	0	0	0	4	-3	0	0	—	—	—	—	—
NHL Totals (1 year)		3	0	0	0	4	-3	0	0					

LUPUL, JOFFREY　　　　　　RW　　　　　　MIGHTY DUCKS

PERSONAL: Born September 23, 1983, in Edmonton ... 6-1/194. ... Shoots right.
TRANSACTIONS/CAREER NOTES: Selected by Mighty Ducks of Anaheim in first round (first Mighty Ducks pick, seventh overall) of NHL entry draft (June 22, 2002).

Season Team	League	REGULAR SEASON								PLAYOFFS				
		Gms.	G	A	Pts.	PIM	+/-	PP	SH	Gms.	G	A	Pts.	PIM
00-01—Medicine Hat	WHL	69	30	26	56	39	...	...	...	—	—	—	—	—
01-02—Medicine Hat	WHL	72	*56	50	106	95	...	...	...	—	—	—	—	—
02-03—Medicine Hat	WHL	50	41	37	78	82	...	...	...	—	—	—	—	—

IN MEMORIAM — ROMAN LYASHENKO

PERSONAL: Born May 2, 1979, in Murmansk, U.S.S.R. ... Died July 6, 2003. ... 6-0/196. ... Shot right.
TRANSACTIONS/CAREER NOTES: Selected by Dallas Stars in second round (second Stars pick, 52nd overall) of NHL entry draft (June 21, 1997). ... Separated shoulder (November 17, 1999); missed five games. ... Sprained shoulder (December 21, 1999); missed one game. ... Sprained shoulder (December 31, 1999); missed two games. ... Traded by Stars with LW Martin Rucinsky to New York Rangers for C Manny Malhotra and LW Barrett Heisten (March 12, 2002).

Season Team	League	REGULAR SEASON								PLAYOFFS				
		Gms.	G	A	Pts.	PIM	+/-	PP	SH	Gms.	G	A	Pts.	PIM
95-96—Torpedo Yaroslavl	CIS Div. II	60	7	10	17	12	...	...	...	—	—	—	—	—
96-97—Torpedo Yaroslavl	Russian	42	5	7	12	16	...	...	...	9	3	0	3	6
—Torpedo Yaroslavl	Rus. Div. III	2	1	1	2	8	...	...	...	—	—	—	—	—
97-98—Torpedo Yaroslavl	Russian	46	7	6	13	28	...	...	...	—	—	—	—	—
98-99—Torpedo Yaroslavl	Russian	42	10	9	19	51	...	...	...	9	0	4	4	8
99-00—Michigan	IHL	9	3	2	5	8	...	...	...	—	—	—	—	—
—Dallas	NHL	58	6	6	12	10	-2	0	0	16	2	1	3	0
00-01—Dallas	NHL	60	6	3	9	45	-1	0	0	1	0	0	0	0
—Utah	IHL	6	0	1	1	2	...	...	...	—	—	—	—	—

Season Team	League	Gms.	G	A	Pts.	PIM	+/-	PP	SH	Gms.	G	A	Pts.	PIM
01-02—Utah	AHL	58	11	25	36	37	...			—	—	—	—	—
—Dallas	NHL	4	0	0	0	0	-2	0	0	—	—	—	—	—
—New York Rangers	NHL	15	2	0	2	0	0	0	0	—	—	—	—	—
02-03—Hartford	AHL	71	23	35	58	44	...			—	—	—	—	—
—New York Rangers	NHL	2	0	0	0	0	-2	0	0	—	—	—	—	—
NHL Totals (4 years)		139	14	9	23	55	-7	0	0	17	2	1	3	0

LYDMAN, TONI   D   FLAMES

PERSONAL: Born September 25, 1977, in Lahti, Finland ... 6-1/202. ... Shoots left.
TRANSACTIONS/CAREER NOTES: Selected by Calgary Flames in fourth round (fifth Flames pick, 89th overall) of NHL entry draft (June 22, 1996). ... Suffered concussion (January 5, 2001); missed 12 games. ... Suffered illness (December 26, 2001); missed two games. ... Suffered illness (March 28, 2002); missed one game.

Season Team	League	Gms.	G	A	Pts.	PIM	+/-	PP	SH	Gms.	G	A	Pts.	PIM
93-94—Reipas Lahti	Finland Jr.	1	0	0	0	0	...			—	—	—	—	—
94-95—Reipas Lahti	Finland Jr.	26	6	4	10	10	...			—	—	—	—	—
95-96—Reipas Lahti	Finland Jr.	1	0	0	0	0	...			—	—	—	—	—
—Reipas Lahti	Finland	39	5	2	7	30	...			—	—	—	—	—
96-97—Tappara	Finland	49	1	2	3	65	...			3	0	0	0	6
97-98—Tappara Tampere	Finland	48	4	10	14	48	...			4	0	2	2	0
98-99—HIFK Helsinki	Finland	42	4	7	11	36	...			11	0	3	3	2
99-00—HIFK Helsinki	Finland	46	4	18	22	36	...			9	0	4	4	6
00-01—Calgary	NHL	62	3	16	19	30	-7	1	0	—	—	—	—	—
01-02—Calgary	NHL	79	6	22	28	52	-8	1	0	—	—	—	—	—
02-03—Calgary	NHL	81	6	20	26	28	-7	3	0	—	—	—	—	—
NHL Totals (3 years)		222	15	58	73	110	-22	5	0					

LYSAK, BRETT   C   HURRICANES

PERSONAL: Born December 30, 1980, in Edmonton. ... 6-0/190. ... Shoots left.
TRANSACTIONS/CAREER NOTES: Selected by Carolina Hurricanes in second round (second Hurricanes pick, 49th overall) of NHL entry draft (June 26, 1999).

Season Team	League	Gms.	G	A	Pts.	PIM	+/-	PP	SH	Gms.	G	A	Pts.	PIM
96-97—Regina	WHL	66	11	14	25	41	...			5	0	1	1	5
97-98—Regina	WHL	70	22	38	60	82	...			9	6	2	8	8
98-99—Regina	WHL	61	39	49	88	84	...			—	—	—	—	—
99-00—Regina	WHL	70	38	40	78	24	...			7	5	4	9	2
00-01—Regina	WHL	64	35	48	83	44	...			6	5	1	6	4
01-02—Lowell	AHL	53	6	8	14	26	...			3	0	0	0	0
—Florida	ECHL	16	2	7	9	14	...			6	3	1	4	6
02-03—Lowell	AHL	49	6	9	15	59	...			—	—	—	—	—

MAATTA, TERO   D   SHARKS

PERSONAL: Born January 2, 1982, in Vantaa, Finland. ... 6-1/205. ... Shoots left.
TRANSACTIONS/CAREER NOTES: Selected by San Jose Sharks in second round (first Sharks pick, 41st overall) of NHL entry draft (June 24, 2000).

Season Team	League	Gms.	G	A	Pts.	PIM	+/-	PP	SH	Gms.	G	A	Pts.	PIM
98-99—Jokerit Helsinki	Finland Jr.	20	0	0	0	30	...			—	—	—	—	—
—Jokerit Helsinki	Finland Jr. B	33	5	11	16	53	...			—	—	—	—	—
99-00—Jokerit Helsinki	Finland Jr.	31	4	4	8	53	...			—	—	—	—	—
00-01—Blues Espoo	Finland	44	4	4	8	24	...			—	—	—	—	—
01-02—Blues Espoo	Finland	51	4	6	10	65	...			3	0	0	0	0
02-03—Blues Espoo	Finland	50	0	3	3	85	...			—	—	—	—	—

MacDONALD, CRAIG   C   HURRICANES

PERSONAL: Born April 7, 1977, in Antigonish, Nova Scotia ... 6-1/195. ... Shoots left.
TRANSACTIONS/CAREER NOTES: Selected by Hartford Whalers in fourth round (third Whalers pick, 88th overall) of NHL entry draft (June 22, 1996). ... Whalers franchise moved to North Carolina and renamed Carolina Hurricanes for 1997-98 season; NHL approved move on June 25, 1997.

Season Team	League	Gms.	G	A	Pts.	PIM	+/-	PP	SH	Gms.	G	A	Pts.	PIM
94-95—Lawrence Academy	Mass. H.S.	30	25	52	77	10	...			—	—	—	—	—
95-96—Harvard University	ECAC	34	7	10	17	10	...			—	—	—	—	—
96-97—Harvard University	ECAC	32	6	10	16	20	...			—	—	—	—	—
97-98—Canadian nat'l team	Int'l	51	15	20	35	133	...			—	—	—	—	—
98-99—New Haven	AHL	62	17	31	48	77	...			—	—	—	—	—
—Carolina	NHL	11	0	0	0	0	0	0	0	1	0	0	0	0
99-00—Cincinnati	IHL	78	12	24	36	76	...			11	4	1	5	8
00-01—Cincinnati	IHL	82	20	28	48	104	...			5	0	1	1	6
01-02—Lowell	AHL	64	19	22	41	61	...			—	—	—	—	—
—Carolina	NHL	12	1	1	2	0	-1	0	0	4	0	0	0	2
02-03—Lowell	AHL	27	7	20	27	38	...			—	—	—	—	—
—Carolina	NHL	35	1	3	4	20	-3	0	0	—	—	—	—	—
NHL Totals (3 years)		58	2	4	6	20	-4	0	0	5	0	0	0	2

L
M

PERSONAL: Born July 11, 1963, in Inverness, Nova Scotia ... 6-2/204. ... Shoots right. ... Full Name: Allan MacInnis. ... Name pronounced muh-KIHN-ihz.

TRANSACTIONS/CAREER NOTES: Selected by Calgary Flames in first round (first Flames pick, 15th overall) of NHL entry draft (June 10, 1981). ... Twisted knee (February 1985). ... Lacerated hand (March 23, 1986). ... Stretched ligaments of knee (April 8, 1990). ... Separated shoulder (November 22, 1991); missed eight games. ... Dislocated left hip (November 12, 1992); missed 34 games. ... Strained shoulder (December 22, 1993); missed one game. ... Strained shoulder (January 2, 1994); missed four games. ... Bruised knee (February 24, 1994); missed four games. ... Traded by Flames with fourth-round pick (D Didier Tremblay) in 1997 draft to St. Louis Blues for D Phil Housley and second-round pick in 1996 (C Steve Begin) and 1997 (RW John Tripp) drafts (July 4, 1994). ... Injured shoulder (January 31, 1995); missed eight games. ... Suffered from the flu (April 9, 1995); missed three games. ... Injured shoulder (April 25, 1995); missed final five games of season. ... Dislocated shoulder (February 4, 1997); missed nine games. ... Dislocated shoulder (December 13, 1997); missed nine games. ... Suffered laceration around left eye (April 12, 1998); missed one game. ... Fractured fibula (October 9, 1999); missed 11 games. ... Suffered rib injury (January 14, 2000); missed one game. ... Suffered collapsed lung (January 21, 2000); missed five games. ... Suffered back spasms (February 10, 2000); missed three games. ... Suffered eye injury (January 29, 2001); missed 23 games. ... Bruised ankle (November 17, 2001); missed four games. ... Suffered back spasms (January 5, 2002); missed three games. ... Bruised foot (January 28, 2002); missed three games.

STATISTICAL PLATEAUS: Three-goal games: 1991-92 (1), 1996-97 (1), 1998-99 (1). Total: 3.

Season Team	League	REGULAR SEASON								PLAYOFFS				
		Gms.	G	A	Pts.	PIM	+/-	PP	SH	Gms.	G	A	Pts.	PIM
79-80—Regina Blues	SJHL	59	20	28	48	110	...	...	...	—	—	—	—	—
80-81—Kitchener	OMJHL	47	11	28	39	59	...	...	...	18	4	12	16	20
81-82—Kitchener	OHL	59	25	50	75	145	...	...	...	15	5	10	15	44
—Calgary	NHL	2	0	0	0	0	0	0	0	—	—	—	—	—
82-83—Kitchener	OHL	51	38	46	84	67	...	...	...	8	3	8	11	9
—Calgary	NHL	14	1	3	4	9	0	0	0	—	—	—	—	—
83-84—Colorado	CHL	19	5	14	19	22	...	...	...	—	—	—	—	—
—Calgary	NHL	51	11	34	45	42	0	7	0	11	2	12	14	13
84-85—Calgary	NHL	67	14	52	66	75	7	8	0	4	1	2	3	8
85-86—Calgary	NHL	77	11	57	68	76	38	4	0	21	4	*15	19	30
86-87—Calgary	NHL	79	20	56	76	97	20	7	0	4	1	0	1	0
87-88—Calgary	NHL	80	25	58	83	114	13	7	2	7	3	6	9	18
88-89—Calgary	NHL	79	16	58	74	126	38	8	0	22	7	*24	*31	46
89-90—Calgary	NHL	79	28	62	90	82	20	14	1	6	2	3	5	8
90-91—Calgary	NHL	78	28	75	103	90	42	17	0	7	2	3	5	8
91-92—Calgary	NHL	72	20	57	77	83	13	11	0	—	—	—	—	—
92-93—Calgary	NHL	50	11	43	54	61	15	7	0	6	1	6	7	10
93-94—Calgary	NHL	75	28	54	82	95	35	12	1	7	2	6	8	12
94-95—St. Louis	NHL	32	8	20	28	43	19	2	0	7	1	5	6	10
95-96—St. Louis	NHL	82	17	44	61	88	5	9	1	13	3	4	7	20
96-97—St. Louis	NHL	72	13	30	43	65	2	6	1	6	1	2	3	4
97-98—St. Louis	NHL	71	19	30	49	80	6	9	1	8	2	6	8	12
—Can. Olympic team	Int'l	6	2	0	2	2	...			—	—	—	—	—
98-99—St. Louis	NHL	82	20	42	62	70	33	11	1	13	4	8	12	20
99-00—St. Louis	NHL	61	11	28	39	34	20	6	0	7	1	3	4	14
00-01—St. Louis	NHL	59	12	42	54	52	23	6	1	15	2	8	10	18
01-02—Can. Olympic team	Int'l	6	0	0	0	8	...			—	—	—	—	—
—St. Louis	NHL	71	11	35	46	52	3	6	0	10	0	7	7	4
02-03—St. Louis	NHL	80	16	52	68	61	22	9	1	3	0	1	1	0
NHL Totals (22 years)		1413	340	932	1272	1495	374	166	10	177	39	121	160	255

PERSONAL: Born June 11, 1981, in Sudbury, Ont. ... 5-11/169. ... Shoots left.

TRANSACTIONS/CAREER NOTES: Selected by Atlanta Thrashers in fifth round (sixth Thrashers pick, 128th overall) of NHL entry draft (June 20, 1999).

Season Team	League	REGULAR SEASON								PLAYOFFS				
		Gms.	G	A	Pts.	PIM	+/-	PP	SH	Gms.	G	A	Pts.	PIM
97-98—Sudbury	OHL	59	9	11	20	26	...	...	...	10	0	1	1	6
98-99—Sudbury	OHL	68	22	65	87	74	...	...	...	4	2	4	6	2
99-00—Sudbury	OHL	68	24	33	57	110	...	...	...	12	5	9	14	16
00-01—Sudbury	OHL	62	40	49	89	89	...	...	...	12	6	8	14	16
01-02—Chicago	AHL	68	13	12	25	80	...	...	...	25	4	2	6	20
—Atlanta	NHL	1	0	0	0	2	-1	0	0	—	—	—	—	—
02-03—Chicago	AHL	80	14	18	32	97	...	...	...	—	—	—	—	—
NHL Totals (1 year)		1	0	0	0	2	-1	0	0					

PERSONAL: Born January 14, 1977, in Sydney, Nova Scotia. ... 6-2/199. ... Shoots left. ... Full Name: Donald MacLean.

TRANSACTIONS/CAREER NOTES: Selected by Los Angeles Kings in second round (second Kings pick, 33rd overall) of NHL entry draft (July 8, 1995). ... Traded by Kings to Toronto Maple Leafs for C Craig Charron (February 23, 2000). ... Signed as free agent by Columbus Blue Jackets (July 17, 2002). ... Re-signed by Blue Jackets (June 12, 2003).

Season Team	League	REGULAR SEASON								PLAYOFFS				
		Gms.	G	A	Pts.	PIM	+/-	PP	SH	Gms.	G	A	Pts.	PIM
94-95—Beauport	QMJHL	64	15	27	42	37	...	...	...	17	4	4	8	6
95-96—Beauport	QMJHL	1	0	1	1	0	...	...	...	—	—	—	—	—
—Laval	QMJHL	21	17	11	28	29	...	...	...	—	—	—	—	—
—Hull	QMJHL	39	26	34	60	44	...	...	...	17	6	7	13	14
96-97—Hull	QMJHL	69	34	47	81	67	...	...	...	14	11	10	21	29
97-98—Los Angeles	NHL	22	5	2	7	4	-1	2	0	—	—	—	—	—
—Fredericton	AHL	39	9	5	14	32	...	...	...	4	1	3	4	2
98-99—Springfield	AHL	41	5	14	19	31	...	...	...	—	—	—	—	—
—Grand Rapids	IHL	28	6	13	19	8	...	...	...	—	—	—	—	—
99-00—Lowell	AHL	40	11	17	28	18	...	...	...	—	—	—	—	—
—St. John's	AHL	21	14	12	26	8	...	...	...	—	—	—	—	—
00-01—Toronto	NHL	3	0	1	1	2	-2	0	0	—	—	—	—	—
—St. John's	AHL	61	26	34	60	48	...	...	...	4	2	1	3	2
01-02—St. John's	AHL	75	33	†54	*87	49	...	...	...	9	5	5	10	6
—Toronto	NHL	—	—	—	—	—	—	—	—	3	0	0	0	0
02-03—Syracuse	AHL	17	9	9	18	6	...	...	...	—	—	—	—	—
NHL Totals (3 years)		25	5	3	8	6	-3	2	0	3	0	0	0	0

MacMILLAN, JEFF   D   STARS

PERSONAL: Born March 30, 1979, in Durham, Ontario. ... 6-3/202. ... Shoots left.
TRANSACTIONS/CAREER NOTES: Selected by Dallas Stars in seventh round (eighth Star pick, 215th overall) of NHL entry draft (June 26, 1999). ... Re-signed by Stars (July 17, 2003).

Season Team	League	REGULAR SEASON								PLAYOFFS				
		Gms.	G	A	Pts.	PIM	+/-	PP	SH	Gms.	G	A	Pts.	PIM
95-96—Hanover	OJHL	29	7	13	20	26	...	...	...	—	—	—	—	—
96-97—Oshawa	OHL	39	0	4	4	15	...	...	...	15	0	0	0	4
97-98—Oshawa	OHL	64	3	12	15	72	...	...	...	7	0	3	3	11
98-99—Oshawa	OHL	65	3	18	21	109	...	...	...	15	3	6	9	28
99-00—Michigan	IHL	53	0	3	3	54	...	...	...	—	—	—	—	—
—Fort Wayne	UHL	7	1	1	2	25	...	...	...	9	0	2	2	10
00-01—Utah	IHL	81	5	15	20	105	...	...	...	—	—	—	—	—
01-02—Utah	AHL	77	6	9	15	146	...	...	...	5	1	0	1	17
02-03—Utah	AHL	78	8	7	15	132	...	...	...	—	—	—	—	—

MacNEIL, IAN   C   FLYERS

PERSONAL: Born April 27, 1977, in Halifax, Nova Scotia ... 6-2/190. ... Shoots left.
TRANSACTIONS/CAREER NOTES: Selected by Hartford Whalers in fourth round (third Whalers pick, 85th overall) of NHL entry draft (July 8, 1995). ... Whalers franchise moved to North Carolina and renamed Carolina Hurricanes for 1997-98 season; NHL approved move on June 25, 1997. ... Signed as free agent by Philadelphia Flyers (July 2, 2002).

Season Team	League	REGULAR SEASON								PLAYOFFS				
		Gms.	G	A	Pts.	PIM	+/-	PP	SH	Gms.	G	A	Pts.	PIM
94-95—Oshawa	OHL	60	7	21	28	57	...	...	...	7	0	2	2	0
95-96—Oshawa	OHL	49	15	17	32	54	...	...	...	5	1	2	3	8
96-97—Oshawa	OHL	64	23	20	43	96	...	...	...	18	2	3	5	37
97-98—New Haven	AHL	68	12	21	33	67	...	...	...	3	1	0	1	10
98-99—New Haven	AHL	47	6	4	10	62	...	...	...	—	—	—	—	—
99-00—Cincinnati	IHL	81	19	18	37	100	...	...	...	11	3	2	5	25
00-01—Cincinnati	IHL	82	17	22	39	139	...	...	...	5	0	1	1	4
01-02—Lowell	AHL	79	14	20	34	128	...	...	...	2	0	1	1	4
02-03—Philadelphia	AHL	71	10	13	23	132	...	...	...	—	—	—	—	—
—Philadelphia	NHL	2	0	0	0	0	1	0	0	—	—	—	—	—
NHL Totals (1 year)		2	0	0	0	0	1	0	0					

MADDEN, JOHN   C   DEVILS

PERSONAL: Born May 4, 1975, in Barrie, Ont. ... 5-11/190. ... Shoots left.
TRANSACTIONS/CAREER NOTES: Signed as non-drafted free agent by New Jersey Devils (June 26, 1997). ... Injured toe (January 20, 2001); missed one game.
STATISTICAL PLATEAUS: Three-goal games: 2002-03 (1). ... Four-goal games: 2000-01 (1). ... Total hat tricks: 2.

Season Team	League	REGULAR SEASON								PLAYOFFS				
		Gms.	G	A	Pts.	PIM	+/-	PP	SH	Gms.	G	A	Pts.	PIM
92-93—Barrie	COJHL	43	49	75	124	62	...	...	...	—	—	—	—	—
93-94—Univ. of Michigan	CCHA	36	6	11	17	14	...	...	...	—	—	—	—	—
94-95—Univ. of Michigan	CCHA	39	21	22	43	8	...	...	...	—	—	—	—	—
95-96—Univ. of Michigan	CCHA	43	27	30	57	45	...	...	...	—	—	—	—	—
96-97—Univ. of Michigan	CCHA	42	26	37	63	56	...	...	...	—	—	—	—	—
97-98—Albany	AHL	74	20	36	56	40	...	...	...	13	3	13	16	14
98-99—Albany	AHL	75	38	60	98	44	...	...	...	5	2	2	4	6
—New Jersey	NHL	4	0	1	1	0	-2	0	0	—	—	—	—	—
99-00—New Jersey	NHL	74	16	9	25	6	7	0	*6	20	3	4	7	0
00-01—New Jersey	NHL	80	23	15	38	12	24	0	3	25	4	3	7	6
01-02—New Jersey	NHL	82	15	8	23	25	6	0	0	6	0	0	0	0
02-03—New Jersey	NHL	80	19	22	41	26	13	2	2	24	6	10	16	2
NHL Totals (5 years)		320	73	55	128	69	48	2	11	75	13	17	30	8

MAIR, ADAM   C   SABRES

PERSONAL: Born February 15, 1979, in Hamilton, Ont. ... 6-1/205. ... Shoots right.
TRANSACTIONS/CAREER NOTES: Selected by Toronto Maple Leafs in fourth round (second Maple Leafs pick, 84th overall) of NHL entry draft (June 21, 1997). ... Traded by Maple Leafs with second-round pick (C Mike Cammaleri) in 2001 draft to Los Angeles Kings for D Aki Berg (March 13, 2001). ... Suspended 10 games by NHL for leaving bench to fight (December 21, 2001). ... Traded by Kings with fifth-round pick in 2003 draft to Buffalo Sabres for LW Erik Rasmussen (July 24, 2002). ... Re-signed by Sabres (July 31, 2003).

Season Team	League	Gms.	G	A	Pts.	PIM	+/-	PP	SH	Gms.	G	A	Pts.	PIM
											REGULAR SEASON → PLAYOFFS			
94-95—Ohsweken	Jr. B	39	21	23	44	91	...	...	...	—	—	—	—	—
95-96—Owen Sound	OHL	62	12	15	27	63	...	...	...	6	0	0	0	2
96-97—Owen Sound	OHL	65	16	35	51	113	...	...	...	4	1	0	1	2
97-98—Owen Sound	OHL	56	25	27	52	179	...	...	...	11	6	3	9	31'
98-99—Owen Sound	OHL	43	23	41	64	109	...	...	...	16	10	10	20	47
—Saint John	AHL	24	5	12	17	31	...	...	...	3	1	0	1	6
—Toronto	NHL	—	—	—	—	—	—	—	—	5	1	0	1	14
99-00—St. John's	AHL	66	22	27	49	124	...	...	...	—	—	—	—	—
—Toronto	NHL	8	1	0	1	6	-1	0	0	5	0	0	0	8
00-01—St. John's	AHL	47	18	27	45	69	...	...	...	—	—	—	—	—
—Toronto	NHL	16	0	2	2	14	3	0	0	—	—	—	—	—
—Los Angeles	NHL	10	0	0	0	6	-3	0	0	—	—	—	—	—
01-02—Manchester	AHL	27	10	9	19	48	...	...	...	5	5	1	6	10
—Los Angeles	NHL	18	1	1	2	57	1	0	0	—	—	—	—	—
02-03—Buffalo	NHL	79	6	11	17	146	-4	0	1	—	—	—	—	—
NHL Totals (5 years)		131	8	14	22	229	-4	0	1	10	1	0	1	22

MAJESKY, IVAN   D   THRASHERS

PERSONAL: Born September 2, 1976, in Bystrica, Czechoslovakia ... 6-5/225.
TRANSACTIONS/CAREER NOTES: Selected by Florida Panthers in ninth round (12th Panthers pick, 267th overall) of NHL entry draft (June 24, 2001). ... Traded by Panthers to Atlanta Thrashers for second-round pick (C Kamil Kreps) in 2003 (June 20, 2003). ... Signed by Atlanta Thrashers (July 17, 2003).

Season Team	League	Gms.	G	A	Pts.	PIM	+/-	PP	SH	Gms.	G	A	Pts.	PIM
95-96—Banska Bystrica	Slovakia	17	0	0	0	18	...	...	...	—	—	—	—	—
96-97—Banska Bystrica	Slovakia	49	2	4	6	...	...	...	...	—	—	—	—	—
97-98—Banska Bystrica	Slov. Div. II	—	—	—	—	—	...	...	...	—	—	—	—	—
98-99—Banska Bystrica	Slovakia	48	7	7	14	68	...	...	...	—	—	—	—	—
—Hkm Zvolen	Slovakia	—	—	—	—	—	...	...	...	6	0	2	2	2
99-00—Hkm Zvolen	Slovakia	51	7	9	16	68	...	...	...	10	0	4	4	2
00-01—Ilves Tampere	Finland	54	2	14	16	99	...	...	...	9	0	1	1	6
01-02—Slovakian Oly. team	Int'l	2	0	1	1	2	...	...	...	—	—	—	—	—
—Ilves Tampere	Finland	44	6	6	12	84	...	...	...	—	—	—	—	—
02-03—Florida	NHL	82	4	8	12	92	-18	0	0	—	—	—	—	—
NHL Totals (1 year)		82	4	8	12	92	-18	0	0	—	—	—	—	—

MAKELA, TUUKKA   D   BRUINS

PERSONAL: Born May 24, 1982, in Helsinki, Finland. ... 6-3/202. ... Shoots left.
TRANSACTIONS/CAREER NOTES: Selected by Boston Bruins in third round (fourth Bruins pick, 59th overall) of NHL entry draft (June 24, 2000).

Season Team	League	Gms.	G	A	Pts.	PIM	+/-	PP	SH	Gms.	G	A	Pts.	PIM
98-99—Helsinki IFK	Finland	35	1	2	3	10	...	...	...	—	—	—	—	—
99-00—HIFK Helsinki	Finland Jr.	36	2	5	7	22	...	...	...	—	—	—	—	—
00-01—Montreal	QMJHL	9	2	1	3	14	...	...	...	—	—	—	—	—
01-02—HPK Hameenlinna	Finland	49	2	3	5	44	...	...	...	8	0	0	0	10
02-03—HPK Hameenlinna	Finland	52	1	5	6	86	...	...	...	—	—	—	—	—

MAKI, TOMI   RW   FLAMES

PERSONAL: Born August 19, 1983, in Helsinki, Finland. ... 5-11/172. ... Shoots left.
TRANSACTIONS/CAREER NOTES: Selected by Calgary Flames in fourth round (fourth Flames pick, 108th overall) of NHL entry draft (June 23, 2001).

Season Team	League	Gms.	G	A	Pts.	PIM	+/-	PP	SH	Gms.	G	A	Pts.	PIM
00-01—Jokerit Helsinki	Finland Jr.	41	7	8	15	12	...	...	...	—	—	—	—	—
01-02—Jokerit Helsinki	Finland	8	0	1	1	2	...	...	...	—	—	—	—	—
02-03—Jokerit Helsinki	Finland	18	2	2	4	4	...	...	...	—	—	—	—	—

MALAKHOV, VLADIMIR   D   RANGERS

PERSONAL: Born August 30, 1968, in Ekaterinburg, U.S.S.R. ... 6-5/230. ... Shoots left. ... Name pronounced MAL-uh-kahf.
TRANSACTIONS/CAREER NOTES: Selected by New York Islanders in 10th round (12th Islanders pick, 191st overall) of NHL entry draft (June

17, 1989). ... Suffered sore groin prior to 1992-93 season; missed first two games of season. ... Injured right shoulder (January 16, 1993); missed eight games. ... Sprained shoulder (March 14, 1993); missed five games. ... Suffered concussion (December 7, 1993); missed one game. ... Strained lower back (December 28, 1993); missed six games. ... Strained hip flexor (February 9, 1995); missed five games. ... Suffered charley horse (March 14, 1995); missed two games. ... Traded by Islanders with C Pierre Turgeon to Montreal Canadiens for LW Kirk Muller, D Mathieu Schneider and C Craig Darby (April 5, 1995). ... Strained hip flexor (April 24, 1995); missed one game. ... Suffered from stomach flu (October 25, 1995); missed two games. ... Bruised right leg (December 12, 1995); missed two games. ... Bruised ribs (October 24, 1996); missed one game. ... Fractured thumb (December 23, 1996); missed 16 games. ... Bruised lower back (October 29, 1997); missed one game. ... Sprained knee (December 10, 1997); missed four games. ... Suffered shoulder tendinitis (February 28, 1998); missed three games. ... Suffered back spasms (November 9, 1998); missed two games. ... Suffered back spasms (December 5, 1998); missed six games. ... Suffered back spasms (January 31, 1999); missed two games. ... Sprained knee (March 28, 1999); missed six games. ... Reinjured knee (April 10, 1999); missed final three games of season. ... Torn anterior cruciate ligament in knee (September 17, 1999); missed first 53 games of 1999-2000 season. ... Injured knee (February 14, 2000); missed two games. ... Traded by Canadiens to New Jersey Devils for D Sheldon Souray, D Josh DeWolf and second-round draft pick (traded to Washington) in 2001 draft (March 1, 2000). ... Signed as free agent by New York Rangers (July 10, 2000). ... Sprained anterior cruciate ligament in knee (October 7, 2000); missed 14 games. ... Reinjured knee (November 15, 2000); missed remainder of season. ... Suffered from the flu (February 6, 2002); missed one game.

STATISTICAL PLATEAUS: Three-goal games: 1997-98 (1).

		REGULAR SEASON								PLAYOFFS				
Season Team	League	Gms.	G	A	Pts.	PIM	+/-	PP	SH	Gms.	G	A	Pts.	PIM
86-87—Spartak Moscow	USSR	22	0	1	1	12	...	...	...	—	—	—	—	—
87-88—Spartak Moscow	USSR	28	2	2	4	26	...	...	...	—	—	—	—	—
88-89—CSKA Moscow	USSR	34	6	2	8	16	...	...	...	—	—	—	—	—
89-90—CSKA Moscow	USSR	48	2	10	12	34	...	...	...	—	—	—	—	—
90-91—CSKA Moscow	USSR	46	5	13	18	22	...	...	...	—	—	—	—	—
91-92—CSKA Moscow	CIS	40	1	9	10	12	...	...	...	—	—	—	—	—
—Unif. Olympic team	Int'l	8	3	0	3	4	...			—	—	—	—	—
92-93—Capital District	AHL	3	2	1	3	11	...			—	—	—	—	—
—New York Islanders	NHL	64	14	38	52	59	14	7	0	17	3	6	9	12
93-94—New York Islanders	NHL	76	10	47	57	80	29	4	0	4	0	0	0	6
94-95—New York Islanders	NHL	26	3	13	16	32	-1	1	0	—	—	—	—	—
—Montreal	NHL	14	1	4	5	14	-2	0	0	—	—	—	—	—
95-96—Montreal	NHL	61	5	23	28	79	7	2	0	—	—	—	—	—
96-97—Montreal	NHL	65	10	20	30	43	3	5	0	5	0	0	0	6
97-98—Montreal	NHL	74	13	31	44	70	16	8	0	9	3	4	7	10
98-99—Montreal	NHL	62	13	21	34	77	-7	8	0	—	—	—	—	—
99-00—Montreal	NHL	7	0	0	0	4	0	0	0	—	—	—	—	—
—New Jersey	NHL	17	1	4	5	19	1	1	0	23	1	4	5	18
00-01—New York Rangers	NHL	3	0	2	2	4	0	0	0	—	—	—	—	—
01-02—New York Rangers	NHL	81	6	22	28	83	10	1	0	—	—	—	—	—
—Russian Oly. team	Int'l	6	1	3	4	4	...	...	...	—	—	—	—	—
02-03—New York Rangers	NHL	71	3	14	17	52	-7	1	0	—	—	—	—	—
NHL Totals (11 years)		621	79	239	318	616	63	38	0	58	7	14	21	52

MALEC, TOMAS   D   HURRICANES

PERSONAL: Born May 13, 1982, in Skalica, Czechoslovakia ... 6-2/193. ... Shoots left.
TRANSACTIONS/CAREER NOTES: Selected by Florida Panthers in third round (fourth Panthers pick, 64th overall) of NHL entry draft (June 23, 2001). ... Traded by Panthers with D, Bret Hedican, C Kevyn Adams and conditional second-round draft pick in 2003 to Carolina Hurricanes for D Sandis Ozolinsh and C Byron Ritchie (January 16, 2002).

		REGULAR SEASON								PLAYOFFS				
Season Team	League	Gms.	G	A	Pts.	PIM	+/-	PP	SH	Gms.	G	A	Pts.	PIM
00-01—Rimouski	QMJHL	64	13	50	63	198	...	...	...	11	0	11	11	26
01-02—Rimouski	QMJHL	51	14	32	46	164	...	...	...	7	3	1	4	10
—Lowell	AHL	—	—	—	—	—	—	—	—	4	0	0	0	4
02-03—Lowell	AHL	30	0	4	4	50	...	...	...	—	—	—	—	—
—Carolina	NHL	41	0	2	2	43	-5	0	0	—	—	—	—	—
NHL Totals (1 year)		41	0	2	2	43	-5	0	0					

MALHOTRA, MANNY   LW   STARS

PERSONAL: Born May 18, 1980, in Mississauga, Ont. ... 6-2/215. ... Shoots left.
TRANSACTIONS/CAREER NOTES: Selected by New York Rangers in first round (first Rangers pick, seventh overall) of NHL entry draft (June 27, 1998). ... Sprained ankle (November 18, 1999); missed four games. ... Sprained ankle (November 6, 2001); missed three games. ... Traded by Rangers with LW Barrett Heisten to Dallas Stars for C Roman Lyashenko and LW Martin Rucinsky (March 12, 2002). ... Suffered from the flu (April 14, 2002); missed one game.

		REGULAR SEASON								PLAYOFFS				
Season Team	League	Gms.	G	A	Pts.	PIM	+/-	PP	SH	Gms.	G	A	Pts.	PIM
96-97—Guelph	OHL	61	16	28	44	26	...	...	...	18	7	7	14	11
97-98—Guelph	OHL	57	16	35	51	29	...	...	...	12	7	6	13	8
98-99—New York Rangers	NHL	73	8	8	16	13	-2	1	0	—	—	—	—	—
99-00—New York Rangers	NHL	27	0	0	0	4	-6	0	0	—	—	—	—	—
—Hartford	AHL	12	1	5	6	2	...			23	1	2	3	10
—Guelph	OHL	5	2	2	4	4	...			6	0	2	2	4
00-01—Hartford	AHL	28	5	6	11	69	...	...	...	5	0	0	0	0
—New York Rangers	NHL	50	4	8	12	31	-10	0	0	—	—	—	—	—
01-02—New York Rangers	NHL	56	7	6	13	42	-1	0	1	—	—	—	—	—
—Dallas	NHL	16	1	0	1	5	-3	0	0	—	—	—	—	—
02-03—Dallas	NHL	59	3	7	10	42	-2	0	0	5	1	0	1	0
NHL Totals (5 years)		281	23	29	52	137	-24	1	1	5	1	0	1	0

MALIK, MAREK — D — CANUCKS

PERSONAL: Born June 24, 1975, in Ostrava, Czechoslovakia ... 6-5/235. ... Shoots left. ... Name pronounced muh-REHK muh-LEEK.
TRANSACTIONS/CAREER NOTES: Selected by Hartford Whalers in third round (second Whalers pick, 72nd overall) of NHL entry draft (June 26, 1993). ... Suffered from the flu (January 20, 1997); missed three games. ... Bruised shin (March 20, 1997); missed four games. ... Whalers franchise moved to North Carolina and renamed Carolina Hurricanes for 1997-98 season; NHL approved move on June 25, 1997. ... Injured knee (April 7, 1999); missed one game. ... Suffered from whiplash (September 30, 2000); missed first six games of season. ... Traded by Hurricanes with LW Darren Langdon to Vancouver Canucks for LW Jan Hlavac and C Harold Druken (November 1, 2002). ... Re-signed by Canucks (July 15, 2003).

		REGULAR SEASON								PLAYOFFS				
Season Team	League	Gms.	G	A	Pts.	PIM	+/-	PP	SH	Gms.	G	A	Pts.	PIM
91-92—TJ Vitkovice	Czech. Jrs.						Statistics unavailable.							
92-93—TJ Vitkovice	Czech.	20	5	10	15	16	...	...	...	—	—	—	—	—
93-94—HC Vitkovice	Czech Rep.	38	3	3	6	...	...	...	...	3	0	1	1	...
94-95—Springfield	AHL	58	11	30	41	91	...	...	...	—	—	—	—	—
—Hartford	NHL	1	0	1	1	0	1	0	0	—	—	—	—	—
95-96—Springfield	AHL	68	8	14	22	135	...	...	...	8	1	3	4	20
—Hartford	NHL	7	0	0	0	4	-3	0	0	—	—	—	—	—
96-97—Springfield	AHL	3	0	3	3	4	...	...	...	—	—	—	—	—
—Hartford	NHL	47	1	5	6	50	5	0	0	—	—	—	—	—
97-98—Malmoif	Sweden	37	1	5	6	21	...	...	...	—	—	—	—	—
98-99—HC Vitkovice	Czech Rep.	1	1	0	1	6	...	...	...	—	—	—	—	—
—New Haven	AHL	21	2	8	10	28	...	...	...	—	—	—	—	—
—Carolina	NHL	52	2	9	11	36	-6	1	0	4	0	0	0	4
99-00—Carolina	NHL	57	4	10	14	63	13	0	0	—	—	—	—	—
00-01—Carolina	NHL	61	6	14	20	34	-4	1	0	3	0	0	0	6
01-02—Carolina	NHL	82	4	19	23	88	8	0	0	23	0	3	3	18
02-03—Carolina	NHL	10	0	2	2	16	-3	0	0	—	—	—	—	—
—Vancouver	NHL	69	7	11	18	52	23	1	1	14	1	1	2	10
NHL Totals (8 years)		**386**	**24**	**71**	**95**	**343**	**34**	**3**	**1**	**44**	**1**	**4**	**5**	**38**

MALTBY, KIRK — LW — RED WINGS

PERSONAL: Born December 22, 1972, in Guelph, Ont. ... 6-0/190. ... Shoots right.
TRANSACTIONS/CAREER NOTES: Selected by Edmonton Oilers in third round (fourth Oilers pick, 65th overall) of NHL entry draft (June 20, 1992). ... Suffered chip fracture of ankle bone (February 2, 1994); missed 13 games. ... Lacerated right eye (March 1, 1995); missed last game of season. ... Scratched left cornea (February 1, 1996); missed 16 games. ... Traded by Oilers to Detroit Red Wings for D Dan McGillis (March 20, 1996). ... Separated shoulder (September 24, 1997); missed 16 games. ... Suffered from lower abdminal pain (November 14, 1998); missed 19 games. ... Sprained knee (December 31, 1998); missed five games. ... Injured ankle (March 31, 1999); missed one game. ... Suspended four games by NHL for slashing incident (March 17, 1999). ... Suffered hernia (October 5, 1999); missed 41 games.
STATISTICAL PLATEAUS: Three-goal games: 1997-98 (1).

		REGULAR SEASON								PLAYOFFS				
Season Team	League	Gms.	G	A	Pts.	PIM	+/-	PP	SH	Gms.	G	A	Pts.	PIM
88-89—Cambridge Jr. B	OHA	48	28	18	46	138	...	...	...	—	—	—	—	—
89-90—Owen Sound	OHL	61	12	15	27	90	...	...	...	12	1	6	7	15
90-91—Owen Sound	OHL	66	34	32	66	100	...	...	...	—	—	—	—	—
91-92—Owen Sound	OHL	64	50	41	91	99	...	...	...	5	3	3	6	18
92-93—Cape Breton	AHL	73	22	23	45	130	...	...	...	16	3	3	6	45
93-94—Edmonton	NHL	68	11	8	19	74	-2	0	1	—	—	—	—	—
94-95—Edmonton	NHL	47	8	3	11	49	-11	0	2	—	—	—	—	—
95-96—Edmonton	NHL	49	2	6	8	61	-16	0	0	—	—	—	—	—
—Cape Breton	AHL	4	1	2	3	6	...	...	...	—	—	—	—	—
—Detroit	NHL	6	1	0	1	6	0	0	0	8	0	1	1	4
96-97—Detroit	NHL	66	3	5	8	75	3	0	0	20	5	2	7	24
97-98—Detroit	NHL	65	14	9	23	89	11	2	1	22	3	1	4	30
98-99—Detroit	NHL	53	8	6	14	34	-6	0	1	10	1	0	1	8
99-00—Detroit	NHL	41	6	8	14	24	1	0	2	8	0	1	1	4
00-01—Detroit	NHL	79	12	7	19	22	16	1	3	6	0	0	0	6
01-02—Detroit	NHL	82	9	15	24	40	15	0	1	23	3	3	6	32
02-03—Detroit	NHL	82	14	23	37	91	17	0	4	4	0	0	0	4
NHL Totals (10 years)		**638**	**88**	**90**	**178**	**565**	**28**	**3**	**15**	**101**	**12**	**8**	**20**	**112**

MANDERVILLE, KENT — C

PERSONAL: Born April 12, 1971, in Edmonton ... 6-3/200. ... Shoots left. ... Full Name: Kent Stephen Manderville.
TRANSACTIONS/CAREER NOTES: Selected by Calgary Flames in first round (first Flames pick, 24th overall) of NHL entry draft (June 17, 1989). ... Traded by Flames with C Doug Gilmour, D Jamie Macoun, D Ric Nattress and G Rick Wamsley to Toronto Maple Leafs for LW Craig Berube, D Alexander Godynyuk, RW Gary Leeman, D Michel Petit and G Jeff Reese (January 2, 1992). ... Bruised hand (October 5, 1993); missed one game. ... Suffered from the flu (December 17, 1993); missed two games. ... Sprained ankle (January 30, 1995); missed one game. ... Traded by Maple Leafs to Edmonton Oilers for C Peter White and fourth-round pick (RW Jason Sessa) in 1996 draft (December 4, 1995). ... Sprained left wrist (February 18, 1996); missed nine games. ... Signed as free agent by Hartford Whalers (October 1, 1996). ... Whalers franchise moved to North Carolina and renamed Carolina Hurricanes for 1997-98 season; NHL approved move on June 25, 1997. ... Strained abdominal muscle (March 12, 1998); missed four games. ... Suffered concussion (December 15, 1999); missed 10 games. ... Traded by Hurricanes to Philadelphia Flyers for RW Sandy McCarthy (March 14, 2000). ... Sprained right ankle (October 25, 2001). ... Traded by Flyers to Pittsburgh Penguins for RW Billy Tibbetts (March 17, 2002). ... Injured ankle (March 23, 2002); missed four games. ... Reinjured ankle (April 4, 2002); missed remainder of season.
STATISTICAL PLATEAUS: Three-goal games: 1996-97 (1).

Season Team	League	REGULAR SEASON								PLAYOFFS				
		Gms.	G	A	Pts.	PIM	+/-	PP	SH	Gms.	G	A	Pts.	PIM
88-89—Notre Dame	SJHL	58	39	36	75	165	...	...	...	—	—	—	—	—
89-90—Cornell University	ECAC	26	11	15	26	28	...	...	...	—	—	—	—	—
90-91—Cornell University	ECAC	28	17	14	31	60	...	...	...	—	—	—	—	—
—Canadian nat'l team	Int'l	3	1	2	3	0	...	...	...	—	—	—	—	—
91-92—Canadian nat'l team	Int'l	63	16	23	39	75	...	...	...	—	—	—	—	—
—Can. Olympic team	Int'l	8	1	2	3	0	...	...	...	—	—	—	—	—
—Toronto	NHL	15	0	4	4	0	1	0	0	—	—	—	—	—
—St. John's	AHL	—	—	—	—	—	...	...	...	12	5	9	14	14
92-93—Toronto	NHL	18	1	1	2	17	-9	0	0	18	1	0	1	8
—St. John's	AHL	56	19	28	47	86	...	...	...	2	0	2	2	0
93-94—Toronto	NHL	67	7	9	16	63	5	0	0	12	1	0	1	4
94-95—Toronto	NHL	36	0	1	1	22	-2	0	0	7	0	0	0	6
95-96—St. John's	AHL	27	16	12	28	26	...	...	...	—	—	—	—	—
—Edmonton	NHL	37	3	5	8	38	-5	0	2	—	—	—	—	—
96-97—Springfield	AHL	23	5	20	25	18	...	...	...	—	—	—	—	—
—Hartford	NHL	44	6	5	11	18	3	0	0	—	—	—	—	—
97-98—Carolina	NHL	77	4	4	8	31	-6	0	0	—	—	—	—	—
98-99—Carolina	NHL	81	5	11	16	38	9	0	0	6	0	0	0	2
99-00—Carolina	NHL	56	1	4	5	12	-8	0	0	—	—	—	—	—
—Philadelphia	NHL	13	0	3	3	4	2	0	0	18	0	1	1	22
00-01—Philadelphia	NHL	82	5	10	15	47	-2	0	3	6	1	2	3	2
01-02—Philadelphia	NHL	34	2	5	7	8	2	0	0	—	—	—	—	—
—Pittsburgh	NHL	4	1	0	1	4	1	0	0	—	—	—	—	—
02-03—Pittsburgh	NHL	82	2	5	7	46	-22	0	0	—	—	—	—	—
NHL Totals (12 years)		646	37	67	104	348	-31	0	5	67	3	3	6	44

MANLOW, ERIC　　　　　C　　　　　ISLANDERS

PERSONAL: Born April 7, 1975, in Belleville, Ont. ... 6-0/205. ... Shoots left.
TRANSACTIONS/CAREER NOTES: Selected by Chicago Blackhawks in second round (second Blackhawks pick, 50th overall) of NHL entry draft (June 26, 1993). ... Released by Blackhawks (June 18, 1998). ... Signed as free agent by Boston Bruins (July 11, 2000). ... Signed as free agent by New York Islanders (July 19, 2002).

Season Team	League	REGULAR SEASON								PLAYOFFS				
		Gms.	G	A	Pts.	PIM	+/-	PP	SH	Gms.	G	A	Pts.	PIM
91-92—Kitchener	OHL	59	12	20	32	17	...	...	...	14	2	5	7	8
92-93—Kitchener	OHL	53	26	21	47	31	...	...	...	4	0	1	1	2
93-94—Kitchener	OHL	49	28	32	60	25	...	...	...	3	0	1	1	4
94-95—Kitchener	OHL	44	25	29	54	26	...	...	...	—	—	—	—	—
—Det. Jr. Red Wings	OHL	16	4	16	20	11	...	...	...	21	11	10	21	18
95-96—Indianapolis	IHL	75	6	11	17	32	...	...	...	4	0	1	1	4
96-97—Columbus	ECHL	32	18	18	36	20	...	...	...	—	—	—	—	—
—Baltimore	AHL	36	6	6	12	13	...	...	...	3	0	0	0	0
97-98—Indianapolis	IHL	60	8	11	19	25	...	...	...	3	1	0	1	0
98-99—Florida	ECHL	18	8	15	23	11	...	...	...	—	—	—	—	—
—Long Beach	IHL	51	9	19	28	30	...	...	...	8	0	0	0	8
99-00—Florida	ECHL	26	14	24	38	24	...	...	...	—	—	—	—	—
—Providence	AHL	46	17	16	33	14	...	...	...	14	6	8	14	8
00-01—Providence	AHL	60	16	51	67	18	...	...	...	17	6	7	13	6
—Boston	NHL	8	0	1	1	2	0	0	0	—	—	—	—	—
01-02—Providence	AHL	70	13	35	48	30	...	...	...	—	—	—	—	—
—Boston	NHL	3	0	0	0	0	0	0	0	—	—	—	—	—
02-03—Bridgeport	AHL	62	19	40	59	58	...	...	...	—	—	—	—	—
—New York Islanders	NHL	8	2	1	3	4	2	1	0	—	—	—	—	—
NHL Totals (3 years)		19	2	2	4	6	2	1	0	—	—	—	—	—

MANN, CAMERON　　　　　RW

PERSONAL: Born April 20, 1977, in Thompson, Man. ... 6-0/195. ... Shoots right.
TRANSACTIONS/CAREER NOTES: Selected by Boston Bruins in fourth round (fifth Bruins pick, 99th overall) of NHL entry draft (July 8, 1995). ... Suffered from the flu (March 21, 1999); missed one game. ... Traded by Bruins to Dallas Stars for D Richard Jackman (June 24, 2001). ... Traded by Stars with G Ed Belfour to Nashville Predators for C David Gosselin and fifth-round pick in 2003 draft (June 29, 2002).

Season Team	League	REGULAR SEASON								PLAYOFFS				
		Gms.	G	A	Pts.	PIM	+/-	PP	SH	Gms.	G	A	Pts.	PIM
93-94—Peterborough	Tier II Jr. A	16	3	14	17	23	...	...	...	—	—	—	—	—
—Peterborough	OHL	49	8	17	25	18	...	...	...	7	1	1	2	2
94-95—Peterborough	OHL	64	18	25	43	40	...	...	...	11	3	8	11	4
95-96—Peterborough	OHL	66	42	60	102	108	...	...	...	24	*27	16	*43	33
96-97—Peterborough	OHL	51	33	50	83	91	...	...	...	11	10	18	28	16
97-98—Providence	AHL	71	21	26	47	99	...	...	...	—	—	—	—	—
—Boston	NHL	9	0	1	1	4	1	0	0	—	—	—	—	—
98-99—Providence	AHL	43	21	25	46	65	...	...	...	11	7	7	14	4
—Boston	NHL	33	5	2	7	17	0	1	0	1	0	0	0	0
99-00—Boston	NHL	32	8	4	12	13	-6	1	0	—	—	—	—	—
—Providence	AHL	29	7	12	19	45	...	...	...	11	6	7	13	0
00-01—Boston	NHL	15	1	3	4	6	0	0	0	—	—	—	—	—
—Providence	AHL	39	24	23	47	59	...	...	...	—	—	—	—	—
01-02—Utah	AHL	61	19	32	51	83	...	...	...	5	0	0	0	6
02-03—Milwaukee	AHL	59	26	31	57	75	...	...	...	—	—	—	—	—
—Nashville	NHL	4	0	0	0	0	-2	0	0	—	—	—	—	—
NHL Totals (5 years)		93	14	10	24	40	-7	2	0	1	0	0	0	0

M

MANNING, PAUL D BLUE JACKETS

PERSONAL: Born April 15, 1979, in Red Deer, Alta. ... 6-4/208. ... Shoots left.
COLLEGE: Colorado College.
TRANSACTIONS/CAREER NOTES: Selected by Calgary Flames in third round (third Flames pick, 62nd overall) of NHL entry draft (June 27, 1998). ... Traded by Flames to Columbus Blue Jackets for fifth-round pick (traded to Detroit) in 2001 draft (June 24, 2001).

		REGULAR SEASON								PLAYOFFS				
Season Team	League	Gms.	G	A	Pts.	PIM	+/-	PP	SH	Gms.	G	A	Pts.	PIM
97-98—Colorado College	WCHA	26	1	5	6	16	...	...	...	—	—	—	—	—
98-99—Colorado College	WCHA	41	3	10	13	75	...	...	...	—	—	—	—	—
99-00—Colorado College	WCHA	39	6	17	23	26	...	...	...	—	—	—	—	—
00-01—Colorado College	WCHA	34	2	28	30	48	...	...	...	—	—	—	—	—
01-02—Syracuse....................	AHL	35	1	4	5	16	...	...	...	—	—	—	—	—
02-03—Syracuse....................	AHL	52	2	5	7	37	...	...	...	—	—	—	—	—
—Columbus....................	NHL	8	0	0	0	2	0	0	0	—	—	—	—	—
NHL Totals (1 year).............		8	0	0	0	2	0	0	0					

MAPLETOFT, JUSTIN C ISLANDERS

PERSONAL: Born January 11, 1981, in Lloydminster, Sask. ... 6-1/198. ... Shoots left.
TRANSACTIONS/CAREER NOTES: Selected by New York Islanders in fifth round (ninth Islanders pick, 130th overall) of NHL entry draft (June 26, 1999).

		REGULAR SEASON								PLAYOFFS				
Season Team	League	Gms.	G	A	Pts.	PIM	+/-	PP	SH	Gms.	G	A	Pts.	PIM
97-98—Red Deer....................	WHL	65	9	4	13	41	...	...	...	5	1	0	1	0
98-99—Red Deer....................	WHL	72	24	22	46	81	...	...	...	9	2	3	5	12
99-00—Red Deer....................	WHL	72	39	57	96	135	...	...	...	4	2	1	3	28
00-01—Red Deer....................	WHL	70	43	†77	*120	111	...	...	...	22	13	21	34	59
01-02—Bridgeport..................	AHL	80	13	20	33	60	...	...	...	20	7	10	17	23
02-03—Bridgeport..................	AHL	63	13	26	39	47	...	...	...	—	—	—	—	—
—New York Islanders.....	NHL	11	2	2	4	2	-1	1	0	2	0	0	0	0
NHL Totals (1 year).............		11	2	2	4	2	-1	1	0	2	0	0	0	0

MARA, PAUL D COYOTES

PERSONAL: Born September 7, 1979, in Ridgewood, N.J. ... 6-4/218. ... Shoots left.
TRANSACTIONS/CAREER NOTES: Selected by Tampa Bay Lightning in first round (first Lightning pick, seventh overall) of NHL entry draft (June 21, 1997). ... Fractured jaw (November 9, 1999); missed 13 games. ... Strained hip flexor (November 14, 2000); missed six games. ... Strained muscle in abdomen (December 2, 2000); missed four games. ... Traded by Lightning with RW Mike Johnson, RW Ruslan Zainullin and second-round pick (D Matthew Spiller) in 2001 draft to Phoenix Coyotes for G Nikolai Khabibulin and D Stan Neckar (March 5, 2001). ... Bruised wrist (October 30, 2001); missed two games. ... Bruised foot (March 3, 2002); missed five games.

		REGULAR SEASON								PLAYOFFS				
Season Team	League	Gms.	G	A	Pts.	PIM	+/-	PP	SH	Gms.	G	A	Pts.	PIM
94-95—Belmont Hill...............	Mass. H.S.	29	19	24	43	24	...	...	...	—	—	—	—	—
95-96—Belmont Hill...............	Mass. H.S.	28	18	20	38	40	...	...	...	—	—	—	—	—
96-97—Sudbury.....................	OHL	44	9	34	43	61	...	...	...	—	—	—	—	—
97-98—Sudbury.....................	OHL	25	8	18	26	79	...	...	...	—	—	—	—	—
—Plymouth	OHL	25	8	15	23	30	...	...	...	15	3	14	17	30
98-99—Plymouth	OHL	52	13	41	54	95	...	...	...	11	5	7	12	28
—Tampa Bay...................	NHL	1	1	1	2	0	-3	1	0	—	—	—	—	—
99-00—Detroit.......................	IHL	15	3	5	8	22	...	...	...	—	—	—	—	—
—Tampa Bay...................	NHL	54	7	11	18	73	-27	4	0	—	—	—	—	—
00-01—Tampa Bay...................	NHL	46	6	10	16	40	-17	2	0	—	—	—	—	—
—Detroit.......................	IHL	10	3	3	6	22	...	...	...	—	—	—	—	—
—Phoenix.....................	NHL	16	0	4	4	14	1	0	0	—	—	—	—	—
01-02—Phoenix.....................	NHL	75	7	17	24	58	-6	2	0	5	0	0	0	4
02-03—Phoenix.....................	NHL	73	10	15	25	78	-7	1	0	—	—	—	—	—
NHL Totals (5 years)...........		265	31	58	89	263	-59	10	0	5	0	0	0	4

MARACLE, NORM G

PERSONAL: Born October 2, 1974, in Belleville, Ont. ... 5-9/195. ... Catches left. ... Name pronounced MAIR-ih-kuhl.
TRANSACTIONS/CAREER NOTES: Selected by Detroit Red Wings in fifth round (sixth Red Wings pick, 126th overall) of NHL entry draft (June 26, 1993). ... Selected by Atlanta Thrashers in NHL expansion draft (June 25, 1999). ... Sprained ankle (November 1, 1999); missed 12 games.

		REGULAR SEASON								PLAYOFFS						
Season Team	League	Gms.	Min	W	L	T	GA	SO	Avg.	SV%	Gms.	Min.	W	L	GA SO	Avg.	SV%
91-92—Saskatoon	WHL	29	1529	13	6	3	87	1	3.41	—	15	860	9	5	37 0	2.58	—
92-93—Saskatoon	WHL	53	2939	27	18	3	160	1	3.27	—	9	569	4	5	33 0	3.48	—
93-94—Saskatoon	WHL	56	3219	*41	13	1	148	2	2.76	—	16	939	†11	5	48 †1	3.07	—
94-95—Adirondack	AHL	39	1997	12	15	2	119	0	3.58	—	—	—	—	—	— —	—	—
95-96—Adirondack	AHL	54	2949	27	18	6	135	2	2.75	—	1	29	0	1	4 0	8.28	—
96-97—Adirondack	AHL	*68	*3843	†34	22	9	*173	5	2.70	—	4	192	1	3	10 1	3.13	—
97-98—Adirondack	AHL	*66	*3710	27	29	8	*190	1	3.07	—	3	180	0	3	10 0	3.33	—
—Detroit..........................	NHL	4	178	2	0	1	6	0	2.02	.905	—	—	—	—	— —	—	—

			REGULAR SEASON								PLAYOFFS						
Season Team	League	Gms.	Min	W	L	T	GA	SO	Avg.	SV%	Gms.	Min.	W	L	GA SO	Avg.	SV%
98-99 —Adirondack.................	AHL	6	359	3	3	0	18	0	3.01	—	—	—	—	—	— —	—	—
—Detroit......................	NHL	16	821	6	5	2	31	0	2.27	.918	2	58	0	0	3 0	3.10	.864
99-00 —Atlanta......................	NHL	32	1618	4	19	2	94	1	3.49	.890	—	—	—	—	— —	—	—
00-01 —Atlanta......................	NHL	13	753	2	8	3	43	0	3.43	.894	—	—	—	—	— —	—	—
—Orlando......................	IHL	51	2963	33	13	3	100	*8	*2.02	—	*16	*1003	*12	4	*37 1	2.21	—
01-02 —Chicago....................	AHL	51	2918	21	25	4	141	3	2.90	—	2	55	0	1	4 0	4.36	—
—Atlanta......................	NHL	1	60	0	1	0	3	0	3.00	.850	—	—	—	—	— —	—	—
02-03 —Chicago....................	AHL	49	2794	22	18	6	134	2	2.88	—	—	—	—	—	— —	—	—
NHL Totals (5 years).............		66	3430	14	33	8	177	1	3.10	.897	2	58	0	0	3 0	3.10	.864

MARCHANT, TODD   C   BLUE JACKETS

PERSONAL: Born August 12, 1973, in Buffalo ... 5-10/178. ... Shoots left. ... Brother of Terry Marchant, left winger with Edmonton Oilers organization (1994-95 through 1998-99). ... Name pronounced MAHR-shahnt.
TRANSACTIONS/CAREER NOTES: Selected by New York Rangers in seventh round (eighth Rangers pick, 164th overall) of NHL entry draft (June 26, 1993). ... Traded by Rangers to Edmonton Oilers for C Craig MacTavish (March 21, 1994). ... Suffered concussion (March 9, 1997); missed three games. ... Strained groin (November 10, 1997); missed four games. ... Scratched left eye (February 4, 1998); missed two games. ... Separated left shoulder (January 10, 2001); missed 10 games. ... Sprained right knee (February 12, 2001); missed one game. ... Signed by Columbus Blue Jackets (July 2, 2003).

			REGULAR SEASON							PLAYOFFS				
Season Team	League	Gms.	G	A	Pts.	PIM	+/-	PP	SH	Gms.	G	A	Pts.	PIM
91-92 —Clarkson	ECAC	33	20	12	32	32	...	...	...	—	—	—	—	—
92-93 —Clarkson	ECAC	33	18	28	46	38	...	...	...	—	—	—	—	—
93-94 —U.S. national team	Int'l	59	28	39	67	48	...	...	...	—	—	—	—	—
—U.S. Olympic team.......	Int'l	8	1	1	2	6	...	...	...	—	—	—	—	—
—Binghamton	AHL	8	2	7	9	6	...	...	...	—	—	—	—	—
—New York Rangers	NHL	1	0	0	0	0	-1	0	0	—	—	—	—	—
—Edmonton	NHL	3	0	1	1	2	-1	0	0	—	—	—	—	—
—Cape Breton	AHL	3	1	4	5	2	...	...	...	5	1	1	2	0
94-95 —Cape Breton	AHL	38	22	25	47	25	...	...	...	—	—	—	—	—
—Edmonton	NHL	45	13	14	27	32	-3	3	2	—	—	—	—	—
95-96 —Edmonton	NHL	81	19	19	38	66	-19	2	3	—	—	—	—	—
96-97 —Edmonton	NHL	79	14	19	33	44	11	0	4	12	4	2	6	12
97-98 —Edmonton	NHL	76	14	21	35	71	9	2	1	12	1	1	2	10
98-99 —Edmonton	NHL	82	14	22	36	65	3	3	1	4	1	1	2	12
99-00 —Edmonton	NHL	82	17	23	40	70	7	0	1	3	1	0	1	2
00-01 —Edmonton	NHL	71	13	26	39	51	1	0	4	6	0	0	0	4
01-02 —Edmonton	NHL	82	12	22	34	41	7	0	3	—	—	—	—	—
02-03 —Edmonton	NHL	77	20	40	60	48	13	7	1	6	0	2	2	2
NHL Totals (10 years).........		679	136	207	343	490	27	17	20	43	7	6	13	42

MARCHMENT, BRYAN   D   MAPLE LEAFS   M

PERSONAL: Born May 1, 1969, in Scarborough, Ont. ... 6-1/200. ... Shoots left.
TRANSACTIONS/CAREER NOTES: Selected by Winnipeg Jets in first round (first Jets pick, 16th overall) of NHL entry draft (June 13, 1987). ... Sprained shoulder (March 1990). ... Suffered back spasms (March 13, 1991). ... Traded by Jets with D Chris Norton to Chicago Blackhawks for C Troy Murray and LW Warren Rychel (July 22, 1991). ... Fractured cheekbone (December 12, 1991); missed 12 games. ... Suspended one preseason game and fined $500 by NHL for headbutting (September 30, 1993). ... Traded by Blackhawks with RW Steve Larmer to Hartford Whalers for LW Patrick Poulin and D Eric Weinrich (November 2, 1993). ... Suspended two games and fined $500 by NHL for illegal check (December 21, 1993). ... Sprained ankle (January 14, 1994); missed three games. ... Sprained ankle (February 19, 1994); missed remainder of season. ... Awarded to Edmonton Oilers as compensation when Whalers signing free agent RW Steven Rice (August 30, 1994). ... Suspended one game by NHL for game misconduct penalties (March 22, 1995). ... Suspended two games by NHL for game misconduct penalties (March 27, 1995). ... Strained lower back (April 15, 1995); missed two games. ... Suspended three games and fined $500 by NHL for leaving bench to fight (April 29, 1995). ... Suspended five games by NHL for kneeing player in preseason game (September 25, 1995). ... Injured ribs (October 22, 1996); missed two games. ... Suffered from the flu (January 28, 1997); missed one game. ... Cracked ribs (February 13, 1997); missed eight games. ... Suffered concussion (April 18, 1997); missed remainder of season. ... Suspended three games and fined $1,000 by NHL for hitting another player (December 5, 1997). ... Traded by Oilers to Tampa Bay Lightning with C Steve Kelly and C Jason Bonsignore for D Roman Hamrlik and C Paul Comrie (December 30, 1997). ... Suspended three games by NHL for kneeing incident (February 6, 1998). ... Suspended eight games and fined $1,000 by NHL for kneeing incident (February 25, 1998). ... Traded by Lightning with D David Shaw and first-round pick (traded to Nashville) in 1998 draft to San Jose Sharks for LW Andrei Nazarov, first-round pick (C Vincent Lecavalier) in 1998 draft and future considerations (March 24, 1998). ... Injured shoulder (January 7, 1999); missed 20 games. ... Suspended one game by NHL for unsportsmanlike conduct (April 6, 1999). ... Injured knee (October 2, 1999); missed nine games. ... Suffered from the flu (December 8, 1999); missed one game. ... Injured ankle (January 5, 2000); missed 14 games. ... Injured groin (March 2, 2000); missed five games. ... Suspended three games by NHL for spearing incident (March 19, 2000). ... Injured neck (April 3, 2000); missed one game. ... Suspended three games by NHL for kneeing incident (March 13, 2001). ... Suspended six games by NHL for elbowing incident (Novmeber 10, 2001). ... Injured back (April 6, 2002); missed final four games of season. ... Traded by Sharks to Colorado Avalanche for third- and fifth-round picks in 2003 draft (March 9, 2003). ... Signed by Toronto Maple Leafs (July 10, 2003).

			REGULAR SEASON							PLAYOFFS				
Season Team	League	Gms.	G	A	Pts.	PIM	+/-	PP	SH	Gms.	G	A	Pts.	PIM
84-85 —Toronto Nationals	MTHL	—	14	35	49	229	—	—	—	—	—	—	—	—
85-86 —Belleville	OHL	57	5	15	20	225	...	...	...	21	0	7	7	*83
86-87 —Belleville	OHL	52	6	38	44	238	...	...	...	6	0	4	4	17
87-88 —Belleville	OHL	56	7	51	58	200	...	...	...	6	1	3	4	19
88-89 —Belleville	OHL	43	14	36	50	198	...	...	...	5	0	1	1	12
—Winnipeg	NHL	2	0	0	0	2	0	0	0	—	—	—	—	—
89-90 —Winnipeg	NHL	7	0	2	2	28	0	0	0	—	—	—	—	—
—Moncton	AHL	56	4	19	23	217	...	...	...	—	—	—	—	—

Season Team	League	REGULAR SEASON								PLAYOFFS				
		Gms.	G	A	Pts.	PIM	+/-	PP	SH	Gms.	G	A	Pts.	PIM
90-91—Winnipeg	NHL	28	2	2	4	91	-5	0	0	—	—	—	—	—
—Moncton	AHL	33	2	11	13	101	...	...	...	—	—	—	—	—
91-92—Chicago	NHL	58	5	10	15	168	-4	2	0	16	1	0	1	36
92-93—Chicago	NHL	78	5	15	20	313	15	1	0	4	0	0	0	12
93-94—Chicago	NHL	13	1	4	5	42	-2	0	0	—	—	—	—	—
—Hartford	NHL	42	3	7	10	124	-12	0	1	—	—	—	—	—
94-95—Edmonton	NHL	40	1	5	6	184	-11	0	0	—	—	—	—	—
95-96—Edmonton	NHL	78	3	15	18	202	-7	0	0	—	—	—	—	—
96-97—Edmonton	NHL	71	3	13	16	132	13	1	0	3	0	0	0	4
97-98—Edmonton	NHL	27	0	4	4	58	-2	0	0	—	—	—	—	—
—Tampa Bay	NHL	22	2	4	6	43	-3	0	0	—	—	—	—	—
—San Jose	NHL	12	0	3	3	43	2	0	0	6	0	0	0	10
98-99—San Jose	NHL	59	2	6	8	101	-7	0	0	6	0	0	0	4
99-00—San Jose	NHL	49	0	4	4	72	3	0	0	11	2	1	3	12
00-01—San Jose	NHL	75	7	11	18	204	15	0	1	5	0	1	1	2
01-02—San Jose	NHL	72	2	20	22	178	22	0	0	12	1	1	2	10
02-03—San Jose	NHL	67	2	9	11	108	-2	0	0	—	—	—	—	—
—Colorado	NHL	14	0	3	3	33	4	0	0	7	0	0	0	4
NHL Totals (15 years)		814	38	137	175	2126	19	4	2	70	4	3	7	94

MARKKANEN, JUSSI — G — RANGERS

PERSONAL: Born May 8, 1975, in Imatra, Finland ... 5-11/183. ... Catches left.
TRANSACTIONS/CAREER NOTES: Selected by Edmonton Oilers in fifth round (fifth Oilers pick, 133rd overall) of NHL entry draft (June 23, 2001). ... Traded by Oilers with fourth-round pick in 2004 to New York Rangers for D Brian Leetch (June 30, 2003).

Season Team	League	REGULAR SEASON									PLAYOFFS							
		Gms.	Min	W	L	T	GA	SO	Avg.	SV%	Gms.	Min.	W	L	GA	SO	Avg.	SV%
91-92—SaiPa	Finland Jr.	2	120	...	...	...	11	0	5.50	—	—	—	—	—	—	—	—	—
92-93—SaiPa	Finland Jr.	7	367	...	...	...	28	...	4.58	—	—	—	—	—	—	—	—	—
—SaiPa	Fin. Div. 2	16	798	...	...	...	60	...	4.51	—	—	—	—	—	—	—	—	—
93-94—SaiPa	Fin. Div. 2	30	1726	...	...	...	97	...	3.37	—	—	—	—	—	—	—	—	—
94-95—SaiPa	Fin. Div. 2	43	2493	...	...	...	122	...	2.94	—	3	179	...	...	5	...	1.68	—
95-96—Tappara Tampere	Finland Jr.	5	298	...	...	...	21	...	4.23	—	—	—	—	—	—	—	—	—
—Tappara Tampere	Finland	23	1238	11	8	2	59	1	2.86	—	—	—	—	—	—	—	—	—
96-97—SaiPa	Finland	41	2340	9	24	7	132	0	3.38	—	—	—	—	—	—	—	—	—
97-98—SaiPa	Finland	48	2870	21	20	5	138	4	2.89	—	3	164	0	3	11	0	4.02	—
98-99—SaiPa	Finland	45	2633	21	19	4	105	4	2.39	—	7	366	3	3	21	0	3.44	—
99-00—SaiPa	Finland	48	2794	4	23	9	150	2	3.22	—	—	—	—	—	—	—	—	—
00-01—Tappara Tampere	Finland	52	3076	*30	17	5	107	*9	2.09	—	†10	*608	7	3	18	1	1.78	—
01-02—Edmonton	NHL	14	784	6	4	2	24	2	1.84	.929	—	—	—	—	—	—	—	—
—Hamilton	AHL	4	239	2	2	0	9	0	2.26	—	—	—	—	—	—	—	—	—
02-03—Edmonton	NHL	22	1180	7	8	3	51	3	2.59	.904	1	14	0	0	1	0	4.29	.917
NHL Totals (2 years)		36	1964	13	12	5	75	5	2.29	.914	1	14	0	0	1	0	4.29	.917

MARKOV, ANDREI — D — CANADIENS

PERSONAL: Born December 20, 1978, in Voskresensk, U.S.S.R. ... 6-0/198. ... Shoots left.
TRANSACTIONS/CAREER NOTES: Selected by Montreal Canadiens in sixth round (sixth Canadiens pick, 162nd overall) of NHL entry draft (June 27, 1998).

Season Team	League	REGULAR SEASON								PLAYOFFS				
		Gms.	G	A	Pts.	PIM	+/-	PP	SH	Gms.	G	A	Pts.	PIM
95-96—Khimik Voskresensk	CIS	36	0	0	0	14	...	...	...	—	—	—	—	—
96-97—Khimik Voskresensk	Russian	43	8	4	12	32	...	...	...	2	1	1	2	0
97-98—Khimik Voskresensk	Russian	43	10	5	15	83	...	...	...	—	—	—	—	—
98-99—Dynamo Moscow	Russian	38	10	11	21	32	...	...	...	16	3	6	9	6
99-00—Dynamo Moscow	Russian	29	11	12	23	28	...	...	...	17	4	3	7	8
00-01—Montreal	NHL	63	6	17	23	18	-6	2	0	—	—	—	—	—
—Quebec	AHL	14	0	5	5	4	...	...	...	7	1	1	2	2
01-02—Quebec	AHL	12	4	6	10	7	...	...	...	—	—	—	—	—
—Montreal	NHL	56	5	19	24	24	-1	2	0	12	1	3	4	8
02-03—Montreal	NHL	79	13	24	37	34	13	3	0	—	—	—	—	—
NHL Totals (3 years)		198	24	60	84	76	6	7	0	12	1	3	4	8

MARKOV, DANNY — D — HURRICANES

PERSONAL: Born July 30, 1976, in Moscow, U.S.S.R. ... 6-1/190. ... Shoots left. ... Full Name: Daniil Markov.
TRANSACTIONS/CAREER NOTES: Selected by Toronto Maple Leafs in ninth round (seventh Maple Leafs pick, 223rd overall) of NHL entry draft (July 8, 1995). ... Suffered concussion (October 16, 1998); missed one game. ... Fractured foot (November 11, 1998); missed two games. ... Suffered throat injury (November 23, 1998); missed two games. ... Suffered back spasms (December 7, 1998); missed two games. ... Separated shoulder (December 16, 1998); missed 11 games. ... Suffered injury (December 15, 1999); missed three games. ... Injured ankle (January 5, 2000); missed 10 games. ... Suffered injury (March 15, 2000); missed one game. ... Injured foot (March 23, 2000); missed final eight games of season. ... Suffered injury (January 6, 2001); missed one game. ... Injured back (January 31, 2001); missed 22 games. ... Traded by Maple Leafs to Phoenix Coyotes for C Robert Reichel, C Travis Green and RW Craig Mills (June 12, 2001). ... Fractured foot (March 24, 2002); missed remainder of season. ... Traded by Coyotes with fourth-round draft pick in 2004 to Carolina Hurricanes for D DavidTanabe and D Igor Knyazev (June 22, 2003).

Season Team	League	REGULAR SEASON								PLAYOFFS				
		Gms.	G	A	Pts.	PIM	+/-	PP	SH	Gms.	G	A	Pts.	PIM
93-94—Spartak Moscow........	Russian	13	1	0	1	6	...	...	...	1	0	0	0	0
94-95—Spartak Moscow........	Russian	39	0	1	1	36	...	...	...	—	—	—	—	—
95-96—Spartak Moscow........	Russian	38	2	0	2	12	...	...	...	2	0	0	0	2
96-97—Spartak Moscow........	Russian	36	3	6	9	41	...	...	...	—	—	—	—	—
—St. John's..................	AHL	10	2	4	6	18	...	...	...	11	2	6	8	14
97-98—St. John's..................	AHL	52	3	23	26	124	...	...	...	2	0	1	1	0
—Toronto	NHL	25	2	5	7	28	0	1	0	—	—	—	—	—
98-99—Toronto	NHL	57	4	8	12	47	5	0	0	17	0	6	6	18
99-00—Toronto	NHL	59	0	10	10	28	13	0	0	12	0	3	3	10
00-01—Toronto	NHL	59	3	13	16	34	6	1	0	11	1	1	2	12
01-02—Phoenix	NHL	72	6	30	36	67	-7	4	0	—	—	—	—	—
—Russian Oly. team.......	Int'l	5	0	1	1	0	...	...	...	—	—	—	—	—
02-03—Phoenix...................	NHL	64	4	16	20	36	2	2	0	—	—	—	—	—
NHL Totals (6 years)...........		336	19	82	101	240	19	8	0	40	1	10	11	40

MARLEAU, PATRICK   C   SHARKS

PERSONAL: Born September 15, 1979, in Aneroid, Sask. ... 6-2/210. ... Shoots left. ... Name pronounced MAHR-loh.
TRANSACTIONS/CAREER NOTES: Selected by San Jose Sharks in first round (first Sharks pick, second overall) of NHL entry draft (June 21, 1997). ... Re-signed by Sharks (July 10, 2003).
STATISTICAL PLATEAUS: Three-goal games: 2001-02 (1).

Season Team	League	REGULAR SEASON								PLAYOFFS				
		Gms.	G	A	Pts.	PIM	+/-	PP	SH	Gms.	G	A	Pts.	PIM
93-94—Swift Current	Jr. A	53	72	95	167	...	...	...	...	—	—	—	—	—
94-95—Swift Current	Jr. A	30	30	22	52	20	...	...	...	—	—	—	—	—
95-96—Seattle.......................	WHL	72	32	42	74	22	...	...	...	5	3	4	7	4
96-97—Seattle.......................	WHL	71	51	74	125	37	...	...	...	15	7	16	23	12
97-98—San Jose....................	NHL	74	13	19	32	14	5	1	0	5	0	1	1	0
98-99—San Jose....................	NHL	81	21	24	45	24	10	4	0	6	2	1	3	4
99-00—San Jose....................	NHL	81	17	23	40	36	-9	3	0	5	1	1	2	2
00-01—San Jose....................	NHL	81	25	27	52	22	7	5	0	6	2	0	2	4
01-02—San Jose....................	NHL	79	21	23	44	40	9	3	0	12	6	5	11	6
02-03—San Jose....................	NHL	82	28	29	57	33	-10	8	1	—	—	—	—	—
NHL Totals (6 years)...........		478	125	145	270	169	12	24	1	34	11	8	19	16

MARSHALL, GRANT   RW   DEVILS

PERSONAL: Born June 9, 1973, in Mississauga, Ont. ... 6-1/196. ... Shoots right.
TRANSACTIONS/CAREER NOTES: Selected by Toronto Maple Leafs in first round (second Maple Leafs pick, 23rd overall) of NHL entry draft (June 20, 1992). ... Awarded to Dallas Stars with C Peter Zezel as compensation for Maple Leafs signing free-agent RW Mike Craig (August 10, 1994). ... Strained muscle (November 15, 1996); missed four games. ... Sprained shoulder (December 8, 1996); missed four games. ... Suffered concussion (January 4, 1997); missed two games. ... Strained groin (November 21, 1997); missed five games. ... Strained groin (April 16, 1998); missed one game. ... Fined $1,000 by NHL for elbowing incident (May 8, 1998). ... Injured groin prior to start of 1999-2000 season; missed first four games of season. ... Reinjured groin (October 13, 1999); missed 22 games. ... Reinjured groin (December 15, 1999); missed two games. ... Reinjured groin (December 27, 1999); missed five games. ... Reinjured groin (March 13, 2000); missed three games. ... Strained thigh muscle (December 17, 2000); missed five games. ... Traded by Stars to Columbus Blue Jackets for second-round pick in 2003 draft (August 29, 2001). ... Traded by Blue Jackets to New Jersey Devils for conditional fourth- or fifth-round pick in 2004 draft (March 10, 2003).

Season Team	League	REGULAR SEASON								PLAYOFFS				
		Gms.	G	A	Pts.	PIM	+/-	PP	SH	Gms.	G	A	Pts.	PIM
90-91—Ottawa	OHL	26	6	11	17	25	...	...	...	1	0	0	0	0
91-92—Ottawa	OHL	61	32	51	83	132	...	...	...	11	6	11	17	11
92-93—Newmarket	OHL	31	12	25	37	85	...	...	...	7	4	7	11	20
—Ottawa	OHL	30	14	28	42	83	...	...	...	—	—	—	—	—
—St. John's..................	AHL	2	0	0	0	0	...	...	...	2	0	0	0	2
93-94—St. John's..................	AHL	67	11	29	40	155	...	...	...	11	1	5	6	17
94-95—Kalamazoo	IHL	61	17	29	46	96	...	...	...	16	9	3	12	27
—Dallas........................	NHL	2	0	1	1	0	1	0	0	—	—	—	—	—
95-96—Dallas........................	NHL	70	9	19	28	111	0	0	0	—	—	—	—	—
96-97—Dallas........................	NHL	56	6	4	10	98	5	0	0	5	0	2	2	8
97-98—Dallas........................	NHL	72	9	10	19	96	-2	3	0	17	0	2	2	47
98-99—Dallas........................	NHL	82	13	18	31	85	1	2	0	14	0	3	3	20
99-00—Dallas........................	NHL	45	2	6	8	38	-5	1	0	14	0	1	1	4
00-01—Dallas........................	NHL	75	13	24	37	64	1	4	0	9	0	0	0	0
01-02—Columbus	NHL	81	15	18	33	86	-20	6	0	—	—	—	—	—
02-03—Columbus	NHL	66	8	20	28	71	-8	3	0	—	—	—	—	—
—New Jersey	NHL	10	1	3	4	7	-3	0	0	24	6	2	8	8
NHL Totals (9 years)...........		559	76	123	199	656	-30	19	0	83	6	10	16	87

MARSHALL, JASON   LW   WILD

PERSONAL: Born February 22, 1971, in Cranbrook, B.C. ... 6-2/196. ... Shoots right.
TRANSACTIONS/CAREER NOTES: Selected by St. Louis Blues in first round (first Blues pick, ninth overall) of NHL entry draft (June 17, 1989). ... Traded by Blues to Mighty Ducks of Anaheim for D Bill Houlder (August 29, 1994). ... Lacerated finger (November 24, 1996); missed two games. ... Bruised hand (March 19, 1997); missed five games. ... Separated right shoulder (December 19, 1997); missed eight games. ... Strained left hamstring (December 18, 1998); missed six games. ... Suffered illness (March 17, 1999); missed one game. ... Traded by Mighty Ducks to Washington Capitals for D Alexei Tezikov and fourth-round pick (D Brandon Rogers) in 2001 draft (March 13, 2001). ... Signed as free agent by Minnesota Wild (July 2, 2001).

M

Season Team	League	REGULAR SEASON								PLAYOFFS				
		Gms.	G	A	Pts.	PIM	+/-	PP	SH	Gms.	G	A	Pts.	PIM
87-88—Columbia Valley	KIJHL	40	4	28	32	150	...	...	...	—	—	—	—	—
88-89—Vernon	BCJHL	48	10	30	40	197	...	...	...	31	6	6	12	141
—Canadian nat'l team	Int'l	2	0	1	1	0	...	...	...	—	—	—	—	—
89-90—Canadian nat'l team	Int'l	72	1	11	12	57	...	...	...	—	—	—	—	—
90-91—Tri-City	WHL	59	10	34	44	236	...	...	...	7	1	2	3	20
—Peoria	IHL	—	—	—	—	—	—	—	—	18	0	1	1	48
91-92—Peoria	IHL	78	4	18	22	178	...	...	...	10	0	1	1	16
—St. Louis	NHL	2	1	0	1	4	0	0	0	—	—	—	—	—
92-93—Peoria	IHL	77	4	16	20	229	...	...	...	4	0	0	0	20
93-94—Peoria	IHL	20	1	1	2	72	...	...	...	3	2	0	2	2
—Canadian nat'l team	Int'l	41	3	10	13	60	...	...	...	—	—	—	—	—
94-95—San Diego	IHL	80	7	18	25	218	...	...	...	5	0	1	1	8
—Anaheim	NHL	1	0	0	0	0	-2	0	0	—	—	—	—	—
95-96—Baltimore	AHL	57	1	13	14	150	...	...	...	—	—	—	—	—
—Anaheim	NHL	24	0	1	1	42	3	0	0	—	—	—	—	—
96-97—Anaheim	NHL	73	1	9	10	140	6	0	0	7	0	1	1	4
97-98—Anaheim	NHL	72	3	6	9	189	-8	1	0	—	—	—	—	—
98-99—Anaheim	NHL	72	1	7	8	142	-5	0	0	4	1	0	1	10
99-00—Anaheim	NHL	55	0	3	3	88	-10	0	0	—	—	—	—	—
00-01—Anaheim	NHL	50	3	4	7	105	-12	2	1	—	—	—	—	—
—Washington	NHL	5	0	0	0	17	-1	0	0	—	—	—	—	—
01-02—Minnesota.................	NHL	80	5	6	11	148	-8	1	0	—	—	—	—	—
02-03—Minnesota.................	NHL	45	1	5	6	69	4	0	0	15	1	1	2	16
NHL Totals (10 years).........		479	15	41	56	944	-33	4	1	26	2	2	4	30

MARTIN, PAUL   D   DEVILS

PERSONAL: Born March 5, 1981, in Minneapolis. ... 6-1/170. ... Shoots left.
HIGH SCHOOL: Elk River (Minn.).
COLLEGE: Minnesota.
TRANSACTIONS/CAREER NOTES: Selected by New Jersey Devils in second round (fifth Devils pick, 62nd overall) of NHL entry draft (June 24, 2000).

Season Team	League	REGULAR SEASON								PLAYOFFS				
		Gms.	G	A	Pts.	PIM	+/-	PP	SH	Gms.	G	A	Pts.	PIM
98-99—Elk River	USHS (West)	25	9	21	30	28	...	...	...	—	—	—	—	—
99-00—Elk River	USHS (West)	24	15	35	50	26	...	...	...	—	—	—	—	—
00-01—Univ. of Minnesota......	WCHA	38	3	17	20	8	...	...	...	—	—	—	—	—
01-02—Univ. of Minnesota......	WCHA	44	8	30	38	22	...	...	...	—	—	—	—	—
02-03—Univ. of Minnesota......	WCHA	45	9	30	39	32	...	...	...	—	—	—	—	—

M

MARTINEK, RADEK   D   ISLANDERS

PERSONAL: Born August 31, 1976, in Havlicko, Czechoslovakia ... 6-1/203. ... Shoots left.
TRANSACTIONS/CAREER NOTES: Selected by New York Islanders in eighth round (12th Islanders pick, 228th overall) of NHL entry draft (June 27, 1999). ... Sprained knee (November 8, 2001); missed seven games. ... Reinjured knee (December 11, 2001); missed remainder of season. ... Re-signed by Islanders (July 14, 2003).

Season Team	League	REGULAR SEASON								PLAYOFFS				
		Gms.	G	A	Pts.	PIM	+/-	PP	SH	Gms.	G	A	Pts.	PIM
96-97—HC Ceske Budejovice ..	Czech Rep.	52	3	5	8	40	...	...	...	5	0	1	1	2
97-98—HC Ceske Budejovice ..	Czech Rep.	42	2	7	9	36	...	...	...	—	—	—	—	—
98-99—HC Ceske Budejovice ..	Czech Rep.	52	12	13	25	50	...	...	...	3	0	2	2	...
99-00—HC Ceske Budejovice ..	Czech Rep.	45	5	18	23	24	...	...	...	3	0	0	0	6
00-01—HC Ceske Budejovice ..	Czech.	44	8	10	18	45	...	...	...	—	—	—	—	—
01-02—New York Islanders.....	NHL	23	1	4	5	16	5	0	0	—	—	—	—	—
02-03—Bridgeport.................	AHL	3	0	3	3	2	...	...	...	—	—	—	—	—
—New York Islanders.....	NHL	66	2	11	13	26	15	0	0	4	0	0	0	4
NHL Totals (2 years)...........		89	3	15	18	42	20	0	0	4	0	0	0	4

MARTINS, STEVE   C   BLUES

PERSONAL: Born April 13, 1972, in Gatineau, Que. ... 5-9/185. ... Shoots left.
TRANSACTIONS/CAREER NOTES: Selected by Hartford Whalers in first round (first Whalers pick, fifth overall) of NHL supplemental draft (June 24, 1994). ... Whalers franchise moved to North Carolina and renamed Carolina Hurricanes for 1997-98 season; NHL approved move on June 25, 1997. ... Signed as free agent by Ottawa Senators (July 22, 1998). ... Suffered back spasms (December 4, 1998); missed four games. ... Injured hip flexor (February 13, 1999); missed three games. ... Reinjured hip flexor (February 23, 1999); missed four games. ... Suffered from the flu (March 24, 1999); missed four games. ... Claimed on waivers by Tampa Bay Lightning (October 29, 1999). ... Strained groin (November 13, 1999); missed one game. ... Sprained ankle (December 4, 1999); missed 12 games. ... Strained groin (November 14, 2000); missed three games. ... Traded by Lightning to New York Islanders for conditional pick in 2001 draft (January 4, 2001). ... Sprained muscle in chest (January 16, 2001); missed one game. ... Signed as free agent by Senators (August 30, 2001). ... Injured right knee (March 2, 2002); missed final 21 games of regular season. ... Claimed on waivers by St. Louis Blues (January 15, 2003). ... Re-signed by Blues (July 16, 2003).

Season Team	League	REGULAR SEASON								PLAYOFFS				
		Gms.	G	A	Pts.	PIM	+/-	PP	SH	Gms.	G	A	Pts.	PIM
91-92—Harvard University	ECAC	20	13	14	27	26	...	...	...	—	—	—	—	—
92-93—Harvard University	ECAC	18	6	8	14	40	...	...	...	—	—	—	—	—
93-94—Harvard University	ECAC	32	25	35	60	93	...	...	...	—	—	—	—	—
94-95—Harvard University	ECAC	28	15	23	38	93	...	...	...	—	—	—	—	—
95-96—Springfield	AHL	30	9	20	29	10	...	...	...	—	—	—	—	—
—Hartford	NHL	23	1	3	4	8	-3	0	0	—	—	—	—	—
96-97—Springfield	AHL	63	12	31	43	78	...	...	...	17	1	3	4	26
—Hartford	NHL	2	0	1	1	0	0	0	0	—	—	—	—	—
97-98—Chicago	IHL	78	20	41	61	122	...	...	...	21	6	14	20	28
—Carolina	NHL	3	0	0	0	0	0	0	0	—	—	—	—	—
98-99—Detroit	IHL	4	1	6	7	16	...	...	...	—	—	—	—	—
—Ottawa	NHL	36	4	3	7	10	4	1	0	—	—	—	—	—
99-00—Ottawa	NHL	2	1	0	1	0	-1	0	0	—	—	—	—	—
—Tampa Bay	NHL	57	5	7	12	37	-11	0	1	—	—	—	—	—
00-01—Tampa Bay	NHL	20	1	1	2	13	-9	0	0	—	—	—	—	—
—Detroit	IHL	8	5	4	9	4	...	...	...	—	—	—	—	—
—New York Islanders	NHL	39	1	3	4	20	-7	0	1	—	—	—	—	—
—Chicago	IHL	5	1	2	3	0	...	...	...	16	1	6	7	22
01-02—Ottawa	NHL	14	1	0	1	4	1	0	0	2	0	0	0	0
—Grand Rapids	AHL	51	10	21	31	66	...	...	...	3	0	0	0	0
02-03—Binghamton	AHL	26	5	11	16	31	...	...	...	—	—	—	—	—
—Ottawa	NHL	14	2	3	5	10	3	0	0	—	—	—	—	—
—St. Louis	NHL	28	3	3	6	18	-8	0	1	2	0	1	1	0
NHL Totals (8 years)		238	19	24	43	120	-31	1	3	4	0	1	1	0

MASON, CHRIS G PANTHERS

PERSONAL: Born April 20, 1976, in Red Deer, Alta. ... 6-0/189. ... Catches left.

TRANSACTIONS/CAREER NOTES: Selected by New Jersey Devils in fifth round (seventh Devils pick, 122nd overall) of NHL entry draft (July 8, 1995). ... Signed as free agent by Mighty Ducks of Anaheim (May 31, 1996). ... Traded by Mighty Ducks with D Marc Moro to Nashville Predators for G Dominic Roussel (October 5, 1998). ... Re-signed by Panthers (July 2, 2003).

Season Team	League	REGULAR SEASON									PLAYOFFS							
		Gms.	Min	W	L	T	GA	SO	Avg.	SV%	Gms.	Min.	W	L	GA	SO	Avg.	SV%
93-94—Victoria	WHL	3	129	0	3	0	16		7.44	—	—	—	—	—	—		—	—
94-95—Prince George	WHL	44	2288	8	30	1	192	1	5.03	—	—	—	—	—	—		—	—
95-96—Prince George	WHL	59	3289	16	37	1	236	1	4.31	—	—	—	—	—	—		—	—
96-97—Prince George	WHL	50	2851	19	24	4	172	2	3.62	—	15	938	9	6	44	†1	2.81	—
97-98—Cincinnati	AHL	47	2368	13	19	7	136	0	3.45	—	—	—	—	—	—		—	—
98-99—Milwaukee	IHL	34	1901	15	12	‡6	92	1	2.90	—	—	—	—	—	—		—	—
—Nashville	NHL	3	69	0	0	0	6	0	5.22	.864	—	—	—	—	—		—	—
99-00—Milwaukee	IHL	53	2952	27	21	8	137	2	2.78	—	3	252	1	2	11	0	2.62	—
00-01—Nashville	NHL	1	59	0	1	0	2	0	2.03	.900	—	—	—	—	—		—	—
—Milwaukee	IHL	37	2226	17	14	‡5	87	5	2.35	—	4	239	1	3	12	0	3.01	—
01-02—Milwaukee	AHL	48	2755	17	21	7	116	2	2.53	—	—	—	—	—	—		—	—
02-03—San Antonio	AHL	50	2914	25	18	6	122	1	2.51	—	—	—	—	—	—		—	—
NHL Totals (2 years)		4	128	0	1	0	8	0	3.75	.875								

MATTEAU, STEPHANE LW

PERSONAL: Born September 2, 1969, in Rouyn-Noranda, Que. ... 6-4/220. ... Shoots left. ... Name pronounced muh-TOH.

TRANSACTIONS/CAREER NOTES: Selected by Calgary Flames in second round (second Flames pick, 25th overall) of NHL entry draft (June 13, 1987). ... Bruised thigh (October 10, 1991); missed 43 games. ... Traded by Flames to Chicago Blackhawks for D Trent Yawney (December 16, 1991). ... Fractured left foot (January 27, 1992); missed 12 games. ... Suffered tonsillitis (September 1992); missed first three games of 1992-93 season. ... Pulled groin (December 17, 1993); missed three games. ... Traded by Blackhawks with RW Brian Noonan to New York Rangers for RW Tony Amonte and rights to LW Matt Oates (March 21, 1994). ... Suffered from the flu (February 1, 1995); missed one game. ... Suffered back spasms (April 24, 1995); missed two games. ... Fractured hand (September 24, 1995); missed six games. ... Traded by Rangers to St. Louis Blues for C Ian Laperriere (December 28, 1995). ... Traded by Blues to San Jose Sharks for C Darren Turcotte (July 25, 1997). ... Injured back (October 9, 1997); missed three games. ... Injured back (December 16, 1997); missed two games. ... Injured hand (March 12, 1998); missed four games. ... Injured back (October 9, 1998); missed first game of season. ... Injured neck (November 7, 1998); missed two games. ... Injured thumb (November 27, 1998); missed three games. ... Injured back (January 5, 1999); missed three games. ... Injured back (March 9, 1999); missed three games. ... Reinjured back (April 8, 1999); missed one game. ... Injured back (March 6, 2000); missed four games. ... Suffered injury (March 18, 2002); missed 12 games. ... Signed as free agent by Florida Panthers (August 2, 2002).

Season Team	League	REGULAR SEASON								PLAYOFFS				
		Gms.	G	A	Pts.	PIM	+/-	PP	SH	Gms.	G	A	Pts.	PIM
85-86—Hull	QMJHL	60	6	8	14	19	...	...	...	4	0	0	0	0
86-87—Hull	QMJHL	69	27	48	75	113	...	...	...	8	3	7	10	8
87-88—Hull	QMJHL	57	17	40	57	179	...	...	...	18	5	14	19	84
88-89—Hull	QMJHL	59	44	45	89	202	...	...	...	9	8	6	14	30
—Salt Lake City	IHL	—	—	—	—	—	—	—	—	9	0	4	4	13
89-90—Salt Lake City	IHL	81	23	35	58	130	...	...	...	10	6	3	9	38
90-91—Calgary	NHL	78	15	19	34	93	17	0	1	5	0	1	1	0
91-92—Calgary	NHL	4	1	0	1	19	2	0	0	—	—	—	—	—
—Chicago	NHL	20	5	8	13	45	3	1	0	18	4	6	10	24
92-93—Chicago	NHL	79	15	18	33	98	6	2	0	3	0	1	1	2
93-94—Chicago	NHL	65	15	16	31	55	10	2	0	—	—	—	—	—
—New York Rangers	NHL	12	4	3	7	2	5	1	0	23	6	3	9	20
94-95—New York Rangers	NHL	41	3	5	8	25	-8	0	0	9	0	1	1	10

Season Team	League	REGULAR SEASON Gms	G	A	Pts.	PIM	+/-	PP	SH	PLAYOFFS Gms	G	A	Pts.	PIM
95-96—New York Rangers	NHL	32	4	2	6	22	-4	1	0	—	—	—	—	—
—St. Louis	NHL	46	7	13	20	65	-4	3	0	11	0	2	2	8
96-97—St. Louis	NHL	74	16	20	36	50	11	1	2	5	0	0	0	0
97-98—San Jose	NHL	73	15	14	29	60	4	1	0	4	0	1	1	0
98-99—San Jose	NHL	68	8	15	23	73	2	0	0	5	0	0	0	6
99-00—San Jose	NHL	69	12	12	24	61	-3	0	0	10	0	2	2	8
00-01—San Jose	NHL	80	13	19	32	32	5	1	0	6	1	3	4	0
01-02—San Jose	NHL	55	7	4	11	15	4	1	1	10	1	2	3	2
02-03—San Antonio	AHL	3	0	0	0	4	...	...	...	—	—	—	—	—
—Florida	NHL	52	4	4	8	27	-9	0	0	—	—	—	—	—
NHL Totals (13 years)		848	144	172	316	742	41	14	4	109	12	22	34	80

MATTEUCCI, MIKE — D — DEVILS

PERSONAL: Born December 12, 1971, in Trail, B.C. ... 6-3/225. ... Shoots left.
TRANSACTIONS/CAREER NOTES: Signed as non-drafted free agent by Edmonton Oilers (September 10, 1998). ... Traded by Oilers to Boston Bruins for G Kay Whitmore (December 29, 1999). ... Signed as free agent by Minnesota Wild (July 20, 2000). ... Signed as free agent by New Jersey Devils (July 12, 2002).

Season Team	League	REGULAR SEASON Gms	G	A	Pts.	PIM	+/-	PP	SH	PLAYOFFS Gms	G	A	Pts.	PIM
92-93—Lake Superior State	CCHA	19	1	3	4	16	...	...	...	—	—	—	—	—
93-94—Lake Superior State	CCHA	45	6	11	17	64	...	...	...	—	—	—	—	—
94-95—Lake Superior State	CCHA	38	3	11	14	52	...	...	...	—	—	—	—	—
95-96—Lake Superior State	CCHA	40	3	13	16	82	...	...	...	—	—	—	—	—
—Los Angeles	IHL	4	0	0	0	7	...	...	...	—	—	—	—	—
96-97—Long Beach	IHL	81	4	4	8	254	...	...	...	18	0	1	1	42
97-98—Long Beach	IHL	79	1	7	8	258	...	...	...	17	0	2	2	57
98-99—Long Beach	IHL	79	3	9	12	253	...	...	...	8	0	1	1	12
99-00—Long Beach	IHL	64	0	4	4	170	...	...	...	6	0	0	0	16
00-01—Cleveland	IHL	69	0	7	7	189	...	...	...	4	0	0	0	15
—Minnesota	NHL	3	0	0	0	2	-2	0	0	—	—	—	—	—
01-02—Houston	AHL	69	3	10	13	128	...	...	...	14	1	1	2	33
—Minnesota	NHL	3	0	0	0	2	1	0	0	—	—	—	—	—
02-03—Albany	AHL	68	1	3	4	133	...	...	...	—	—	—	—	—
NHL Totals (2 years)		6	0	0	0	4	-1	0	0	—	—	—	—	—

MATVICHUK, RICHARD — D — STARS

PERSONAL: Born February 5, 1973, in Edmonton ... 6-2/215. ... Shoots left. ... Name pronounced MAT-vih-chuhk.
TRANSACTIONS/CAREER NOTES: Selected by Minnesota North Stars in first round (first North Stars pick, eighth overall) of 1991 NHL entry draft (June 22, 1991). ... Strained lower back (November 9, 1992); missed two games. ... Sprained ankle (December 27, 1992); missed 10 games. ... North Stars franchise moved from Minnesota to Dallas and renamed Stars for 1993-94 season. ... Bruised shoulder (April 5, 1994); missed one game. ... Tore knee ligaments (September 20, 1994) and underwent surgery; missed first 16 games of season. ... Suffered concussion (March 13, 1996); missed five games. ... Bruised shoulder (October 26, 1996); missed two games. ... Strained groin (February 18, 1997); missed 19 games. ... Tore anterior cruciate ligament in knee (January 21, 1998); missed eight games. ... Bruised thigh (December 31, 1998); missed one game. ... Suffered from headaches (January 8, 1999); missed one game. ... Strained groin (March 14, 1999); missed two games. ... Reinjured groin (March 19, 1999); missed final 14 games of regular season and one playoff game. ... Injured knee (October 16, 1999); missed three games. ... Injured knee (November 10, 1999); missed three games. ... Suffered from the flu (January 23, 2000); missed one game. ... Sprained thumb (February 2, 2000); missed one game. ... Sprained knee (March 1, 2000); missed one game. ... Fractured jaw (January 24, 2001); missed four games.

Season Team	League	REGULAR SEASON Gms	G	A	Pts.	PIM	+/-	PP	SH	PLAYOFFS Gms	G	A	Pts.	PIM
88-89—Fort Saskatchewan	AJHL	58	7	36	43	147	...	...	...	—	—	—	—	—
89-90—Saskatoon	WHL	56	8	24	32	126	...	...	...	10	2	8	10	16
90-91—Saskatoon	WHL	68	13	36	49	117	...	...	...	—	—	—	—	—
91-92—Saskatoon	WHL	58	14	40	54	126	...	...	...	22	1	9	10	61
92-93—Minnesota	NHL	53	2	3	5	26	-8	1	0	—	—	—	—	—
—Kalamazoo	IHL	3	0	1	1	6	...	...	...	—	—	—	—	—
93-94—Kalamazoo	IHL	43	8	17	25	84	...	...	...	—	—	—	—	—
—Dallas	NHL	25	0	3	3	22	1	0	0	7	1	1	2	12
94-95—Dallas	NHL	14	0	2	2	14	-7	0	0	5	0	2	2	4
—Kalamazoo	IHL	17	0	6	6	16	...	...	...	—	—	—	—	—
95-96—Dallas	NHL	73	6	16	22	71	4	0	0	—	—	—	—	—
96-97—Dallas	NHL	57	5	7	12	87	1	0	2	7	0	1	1	20
97-98—Dallas	NHL	74	3	15	18	63	7	0	0	16	1	1	2	14
98-99—Dallas	NHL	64	3	9	12	51	23	1	0	22	1	5	6	20
99-00—Dallas	NHL	70	4	21	25	42	7	0	0	23	2	5	7	14
00-01—Dallas	NHL	78	4	16	20	62	5	2	0	10	0	0	0	14
01-02—Dallas	NHL	82	9	12	21	52	11	4	0	—	—	—	—	—
02-03—Dallas	NHL	68	1	5	6	58	1	0	0	12	0	3	3	8
NHL Totals (11 years)		658	37	109	146	548	45	8	2	102	5	18	23	106

MAY, BRAD — LW — CANUCKS

PERSONAL: Born November 29, 1971, in Toronto ... 6-1/213. ... Shoots left.
TRANSACTIONS/CAREER NOTES: Selected by Buffalo Sabres in first round (first Sabres pick, 14th overall) of NHL entry draft (June 16, 1990). ... Fractured bone in hand (March 11, 1995); missed 15 games. ... Injured left arm (March 3, 1996); missed one game. ... Suspended one game for accumulating three game misconduct penalties (March 31, 1996). ... Underwent right shoulder surgery (October 14, 1996); missed 27 games. ... Broken right hand (December 20, 1996); missed nine games. ... Fractured thumb (March 1, 1997); missed four games. ... Strained shoulder (September 27, 1997); missed first six games of season. ... Sprained knee (December 29, 1997); missed 11 games. ... Traded by Sabres with third-round pick (traded to Tampa Bay) in 1999 draft to Vancouver Canucks for LW Geoff Sanderson (February 4, 1998).

M

... Strained groin (October 30, 1998); missed five games. ... Fractured hand (March 26, 1999); missed final 10 games of season. ... Sprained medial collateral ligament in knee (December 10, 1999); missed 13 games. ... Traded by Canucks to Phoenix Coyotes for future considerations (June 25, 2000). ... Suspended 20 games by NHL for slashing incident (November 15, 2000). ... Fractured rib (January 3, 2002); missed 10 games. ... Traded by Coyotes to Canucks for second- or third-round pick in 2003 draft (March 11, 2003). ... Re-signed by Canucks (July 10, 2003).

			REGULAR SEASON							PLAYOFFS				
Season Team	League	Gms.	G	A	Pts.	PIM	+/-	PP	SH	Gms.	G	A	Pts.	PIM
87-88—Markham Jr. B	OHA	6	1	1	2	21	...	...	...	—	—	—	—	—
88-89—Niagara Falls	OHL	65	8	14	22	304	...	...	...	17	0	1	1	55
89-90—Niagara Falls	OHL	61	33	58	91	223	...	...	...	16	9	13	22	64
90-91—Niagara Falls	OHL	34	37	32	69	93	...	...	...	14	11	14	25	53
91-92—Buffalo	NHL	69	11	6	17	309	-12	1	0	7	1	4	5	2
92-93—Buffalo	NHL	82	13	13	26	242	3	0	0	8	1	1	2	14
93-94—Buffalo	NHL	84	18	27	45	171	-6	3	0	7	0	2	2	9
94-95—Buffalo	NHL	33	3	3	6	87	5	1	0	4	0	0	0	2
95-96—Buffalo	NHL	79	15	29	44	295	6	3	0	—	—	—	—	—
96-97—Buffalo	NHL	42	3	4	7	106	-8	1	0	10	1	1	2	32
97-98—Buffalo	NHL	36	4	7	11	113	2	0	0	—	—	—	—	—
—Vancouver	NHL	27	9	3	12	41	0	4	0	—	—	—	—	—
98-99—Vancouver	NHL	66	6	11	17	102	-14	1	0	—	—	—	—	—
99-00—Vancouver	NHL	59	9	7	16	90	-2	0	0	—	—	—	—	—
00-01—Phoenix	NHL	62	11	14	25	107	10	0	0	—	—	—	—	—
01-02—Phoenix	NHL	72	10	12	22	95	11	1	0	5	0	0	0	0
02-03—Phoenix	NHL	20	3	4	7	32	3	0	0	—	—	—	—	—
—Vancouver	NHL	3	0	0	0	10	1	0	0	14	0	0	0	15
NHL Totals (12 years)		734	115	140	255	1800	-1	15	0	55	3	8	11	74

MAYERS, JAMAL　　　　RW　　　　BLUES

PERSONAL: Born October 24, 1974, in Toronto ... 6-1/217. ... Shoots right. ... Full Name: Jamal David Mayers.
TRANSACTIONS/CAREER NOTES: Selected by St. Louis Blues in fourth round (third Blues pick, 89th overall) of NHL entry draft (June 26, 1993). ... Suspended one playoff game by NHL for slashing incident (May 7, 1999). ... Suffered from the flu (March 24, 2001); missed one game. ... Strained groin (October 3, 2001); missed first four games of season. ... Bruised left foot (January 17, 2002); missed one game.

			REGULAR SEASON							PLAYOFFS				
Season Team	League	Gms.	G	A	Pts.	PIM	+/-	PP	SH	Gms.	G	A	Pts.	PIM
90-91—Thornhill	Jr. A	44	12	24	36	78	...	...	...	—	—	—	—	—
91-92—Thornhill	Jr. A	56	38	69	107	36	...	...	...	—	—	—	—	—
92-93—Western Michigan	CCHA	38	8	17	25	26	...	...	...	—	—	—	—	—
93-94—Western Michigan	CCHA	40	17	32	49	40	...	...	...	—	—	—	—	—
94-95—Western Michigan	CCHA	39	13	33	46	40	...	...	...	—	—	—	—	—
95-96—Western Michigan	CCHA	38	17	22	39	75	...	...	...	—	—	—	—	—
96-97—Worcester	AHL	62	12	14	26	104	...	...	...	5	4	4	8	4
—St. Louis	NHL	6	0	1	1	2	-3	0	0	—	—	—	—	—
97-98—Worcester	AHL	61	19	24	43	117	...	...	...	11	3	4	7	10
98-99—Worcester	AHL	20	9	7	16	34	...	...	...	—	—	—	—	—
—St. Louis	NHL	34	4	5	9	40	-3	0	0	11	0	1	1	8
99-00—St. Louis	NHL	79	7	10	17	90	0	0	0	7	0	4	4	2
00-01—St. Louis	NHL	77	8	13	21	117	-3	0	0	15	2	3	5	8
01-02—St. Louis	NHL	77	9	8	17	99	9	0	1	10	3	0	3	2
02-03—St. Louis	NHL	15	2	5	7	8	1	0	0	—	—	—	—	—
NHL Totals (6 years)		288	30	42	72	356	1	0	1	43	5	8	13	20

McALLISTER, CHRIS　　　　D　　　　AVALANCHE

PERSONAL: Born June 16, 1975, in Saskatoon, Sask. ... 6-8/240. ... Shoots left.
TRANSACTIONS/CAREER NOTES: Selected by Vancouver Canucks in second round (first Canucks pick, 40th overall) of NHL entry draft (July 8, 1995). ... Suffered from heel spur (December 13, 1997); missed three games. ... Traded by Canucks to Toronto Maple Leafs for C Darby Hendrickson (February 16, 1999). ... Suspended two games by NHL for leaving the bench during an altercation (February 26, 1999). ... Suffered injury (October 20, 1999); missed six games. ... Suffered injury (January 22, 2000); missed one game. ... Injured foot (March 30, 2000); missed final five games of season. ... Traded by Maple Leafs to Philadelphia Flyers for D Regan Kelly (September 26, 2000). ... Sprained wrist (December 21, 2000); missed two games. ... Reinjured wrist (December 30, 2000); missed five games. ... Fractured left wrist (April 6, 2002); missed remainder of season. ... Traded by Flyers to Colorado Avalanche for sixth-round pick in 2003 draft (February 5, 2003).

			REGULAR SEASON							PLAYOFFS				
Season Team	League	Gms.	G	A	Pts.	PIM	+/-	PP	SH	Gms.	G	A	Pts.	PIM
93-94—Humboldt	SJHL	50	3	5	8	150	...	...	...	—	—	—	—	—
—Saskatoon	WHL	2	0	0	0	5	...	...	...	—	—	—	—	—
94-95—Saskatoon	WHL	65	2	8	10	134	...	...	...	10	0	0	0	28
95-96—Syracuse	AHL	68	0	2	2	142	...	...	...	16	0	0	0	34
96-97—Syracuse	AHL	43	3	1	4	108	...	...	...	3	0	0	0	6
97-98—Syracuse	AHL	23	0	1	1	71	...	...	...	5	0	0	0	21
—Vancouver	NHL	36	1	2	3	106	-12	0	0	—	—	—	—	—
98-99—Vancouver	NHL	28	1	1	2	63	-7	0	0	—	—	—	—	—
—Syracuse	AHL	5	0	0	0	24	...	...	...	—	—	—	—	—
—Toronto	NHL	20	0	2	2	39	4	0	0	6	0	1	1	4
99-00—Toronto	NHL	36	0	3	3	68	-4	0	0	—	—	—	—	—
00-01—Philadelphia	NHL	60	2	2	4	124	1	0	0	2	0	0	0	0
01-02—Philadelphia	NHL	42	0	5	5	113	-7	0	0	—	—	—	—	—
02-03—Philadelphia	AHL	4	0	0	0	12	...	...	...	—	—	—	—	—
—Philadelphia	NHL	19	0	0	0	21	-2	0	0	—	—	—	—	—
—Colorado	NHL	14	0	1	1	26	6	0	0	1	0	0	0	0
NHL Totals (6 years)		255	4	16	20	560	-21	0	0	9	0	1	1	4

M

McALPINE, CHRIS   D

PERSONAL: Born December 1, 1971, in Roseville, Minn. ... 6-1/215. ... Shoots right. ... Full Name: Christopher McAlpine. ... Name pronounced muh-KAL-pighn.

TRANSACTIONS/CAREER NOTES: Selected by New Jersey Devils in seventh round (seventh Devils pick, 137th overall) of NHL entry draft (June 16, 1990). ... Injured thumb (March 26, 1995); missed four games. ... Traded by Devils with ninth-round pick (C James Desmarais) in 1999 draft to St. Louis Blues for C Peter Zezel (February 11, 1997). ... Suffered from the flu (March 14, 1998); missed one game. ... Bruised thigh (December 17, 1998); missed nine games. ... Traded by Blues with G Rich Parent to Tampa Bay Lightning for RW Stephane Richer (January 13, 2000). ... Suffered concussion (January 29, 2000); missed two games. ... Traded by Lightning to Atlanta Thrashers for D Mikko Kuparinen (March 11, 2000). ... Strained groin (March 23, 2000); missed six games. ... Signed as free agent by Chicago Blackhawks (July 27, 2000). ... Separated shoulder (December 21, 2000); missed five games. ... Lacerated elbow (January 5, 2002); missed 10 games. ... Signed as free agent by Los Angeles Kings (August 27, 2002).

				REGULAR SEASON									PLAYOFFS			
Season Team	League	Gms.	G	A	Pts.	PIM	+/-	PP	SH		Gms.	G	A	Pts.	PIM
89-90—Roseville H.S.	Minn. H.S.	25	15	13	28	...	...	...	...		—	—	—	—	—
90-91—Univ. of Minnesota......	WCHA	38	7	9	16	112	...	...	...		—	—	—	—	—
91-92—Univ. of Minnesota......	WCHA	39	3	9	12	126	...	...	...		—	—	—	—	—
92-93—Univ. of Minnesota......	WCHA	41	14	9	23	82	...	...	...		—	—	—	—	—
93-94—Univ. of Minnesota......	WCHA	36	12	18	30	121	...	...	...		—	—	—	—	—
94-95—Albany......................	AHL	48	4	18	22	49	...	...	...		—	—	—	—	—
—New Jersey	NHL	24	0	3	3	17	4	0	0		—	—	—	—	—
95-96—Albany......................	AHL	57	5	14	19	72	...	...	...		4	0	0	0	13
96-97—Albany......................	AHL	44	1	9	10	48	...	...	...		—	—	—	—	—
—St. Louis	NHL	15	0	0	0	24	-2	0	0		4	0	1	1	0
97-98—St. Louis	NHL	54	3	7	10	36	14	0	0		10	0	0	0	16
98-99—St. Louis	NHL	51	1	1	2	50	-10	0	0		13	0	0	0	2
99-00—St. Louis	NHL	21	1	1	2	14	1	0	0		—	—	—	—	—
—Worcester.................	AHL	10	1	4	5	4	...	...	...		—	—	—	—	—
—Tampa Bay.................	NHL	10	1	1	2	10	-5	0	0		—	—	—	—	—
—Detroit......................	IHL	8	0	0	0	6	...	...	...		—	—	—	—	—
—Atlanta.....................	NHL	3	0	0	0	2	-4	0	0		—	—	—	—	—
00-01—Norfolk....................	AHL	13	4	7	11	6	...	...	...		—	—	—	—	—
—Chicago...................	NHL	50	0	6	6	32	5	0	0		—	—	—	—	—
01-02—Norfolk....................	AHL	8	0	4	4	4	...	...	...		—	—	—	—	—
—Chicago...................	NHL	40	0	3	3	36	8	0	0		1	0	0	0	0
02-03—Manchester................	AHL	3	0	0	0	0	...	...	...		—	—	—	—	—
—Los Angeles................	NHL	21	0	2	2	24	-4	0	0		—	—	—	—	—
NHL Totals (8 years)..........		**289**	**6**	**24**	**30**	**245**	**7**	**0**	**0**		**28**	**0**	**1**	**1**	**18**

McAMMOND, DEAN   LW   FLAMES

M

PERSONAL: Born June 15, 1973, in Grand Cache, Alta. ... 5-11/193. ... Shoots left.

TRANSACTIONS/CAREER NOTES: Selected by Chicago Blackhawks in first round (first Blackhawks pick, 22nd overall) of NHL entry draft (June 22, 1991). ... Traded by Blackhawks with D Igor Kravchuk to Edmonton Oilers for RW Joe Murphy (February 25, 1993). ... Severed left Achilles' tendon (February 1, 1995); missed final 41 games of season. ... Fractured nose (November 11, 1996); missed two games. ... Suffered from the flu (January 21, 1997); missed two games. ... Suffered back spasms (March 1, 1997); missed remainder of season. ... Traded by Oilers with D Boris Mironov and D Jonas Elofsson to Blackhawks for C Chad Kilger, LW Daniel Cleary, LW Ethan Moreau and D Christian Laflamme (March 20, 1999). ... Bruised ribs (October 4, 1999); missed five games. ... Suffered sore wrist (December 9, 1999); missed one game. ... Traded by Blackhawks to Philadelphia Flyers for third-round pick (traded to Toronto) in 2001 draft (March 13, 2001). ... Traded by Flyers to Calgary Flames for fourth-round pick (D Rosario Ruggeri) in 2002 draft (June 24, 2001). ... Injured back (January 19, 2002); missed one game. ... Injured ribs (January 24, 2002); missed eight games. ... Traded by Flames with D Derek Morris and C Jeff Shantz to Colorado Avalanche for LW Chris Drury and C Stephane Yelle (October 1, 2002). ... Traded by Avalanche to Flames for fifth-round pick in 2003 draft (March 11, 2003).

				REGULAR SEASON									PLAYOFFS			
Season Team	League	Gms.	G	A	Pts.	PIM	+/-	PP	SH		Gms.	G	A	Pts.	PIM
89-90—Prince Albert..............	WHL	53	11	11	22	49	...	...	...		14	2	3	5	18
90-91—Prince Albert..............	WHL	71	33	35	68	108	...	...	...		2	0	1	1	6
91-92—Prince Albert..............	WHL	63	37	54	91	189	...	...	...		10	12	11	23	26
—Chicago...................	NHL	5	0	2	2	0	-2	0	0		3	0	0	0	2
92-93—Prince Albert..............	WHL	30	19	29	48	44	...	...	...		—	—	—	—	—
—Swift Current	WHL	18	10	13	23	29	...	...	...		17	*16	19	35	20
93-94—Edmonton	NHL	45	6	21	27	16	12	2	0		—	—	—	—	—
—Cape Breton.............	AHL	28	9	12	21	38	...	...	...		—	—	—	—	—
94-95—Edmonton	NHL	6	0	0	0	0	-1	0	0		—	—	—	—	—
95-96—Edmonton	NHL	53	15	15	30	23	6	4	0		—	—	—	—	—
—Cape Breton.............	AHL	22	9	15	24	55	...	...	...		—	—	—	—	—
96-97—Edmonton	NHL	57	12	17	29	28	-15	4	0		—	—	—	—	—
97-98—Edmonton	NHL	77	19	31	50	46	9	8	0		12	1	4	5	12
98-99—Edmonton	NHL	65	9	16	25	36	5	1	0		—	—	—	—	—
—Chicago...................	NHL	12	1	4	5	2	3	0	0		—	—	—	—	—
99-00—Chicago...................	NHL	76	14	18	32	72	11	1	0		—	—	—	—	—
00-01—Chicago...................	NHL	61	10	16	26	43	4	1	0		—	—	—	—	—
—Philadelphia	NHL	10	1	1	2	0	-1	1	0		4	0	0	0	2
01-02—Calgary	NHL	73	21	30	51	60	2	7	0		—	—	—	—	—
02-03—Colorado	NHL	41	10	8	18	10	1	2	0		—	—	—	—	—
NHL Totals (11 years).........		**581**	**118**	**179**	**297**	**336**	**34**	**31**	**0**		**19**	**1**	**4**	**5**	**16**

McCABE, BRYAN D MAPLE LEAFS

PERSONAL: Born June 8, 1975, in St. Catharines, Ont. ... 6-2/220. ... Shoots left.
TRANSACTIONS/CAREER NOTES: Selected by New York Islanders in second round (second Islanders pick, 40th overall) of NHL entry draft (June 26, 1993). ... Traded by Islanders with LW Todd Bertuzzi and third-round pick (LW Jarkko Ruutu) in 1998 draft to Vancouver Canucks for C Trevor Linden (February 6, 1998). ... Missed first 13 games of 1998-99 season due to contract dispute. ... Traded by Canucks with first-round pick (RW Pavel Vorobiev) in 2000 draft to Chicago Blackhawks for first-round pick (traded to Tampa Bay) in 1999 draft (June 26, 1999). ... Fractured orbital bone (March 11, 2000); missed two games. ... Traded by Blackhawks to Toronto Maple Leafs for D Alexander Karpovtsev and fourth-round pick (D Vladimir Gusev) in 2001 draft (October 2, 2000).

		REGULAR SEASON								PLAYOFFS				
Season Team	League	Gms.	G	A	Pts.	PIM	+/-	PP	SH	Gms.	G	A	Pts.	PIM
91-92—Medicine Hat............	WHL	68	6	24	30	157	...	...	...	4	0	0	0	6
92-93—Medicine Hat............	WHL	14	0	13	13	83	...	...	...	—	—	—	—	—
—Spokane..................	WHL	46	3	44	47	134	...	...	...	10	1	5	6	28
93-94—Spokane..................	WHL	64	22	62	84	218	...	...	...	3	0	4	4	4
94-95—Spokane..................	WHL	42	14	39	53	115	...	...	...	—	—	—	—	—
—Brandon.................	WHL	20	6	10	16	38	...	...	...	18	4	13	17	59
95-96—New York Islanders.....	NHL	82	7	16	23	156	-24	3	0	—	—	—	—	—
96-97—New York Islanders.....	NHL	82	8	20	28	165	-2	2	1	—	—	—	—	—
97-98—New York Islanders.....	NHL	56	3	9	12	145	9	1	0	—	—	—	—	—
—Vancouver..............	NHL	26	1	11	12	64	10	0	1	—	—	—	—	—
98-99—Vancouver..............	NHL	69	7	14	21	120	-11	1	2	—	—	—	—	—
99-00—Chicago.................	NHL	79	6	19	25	139	-8	2	0	—	—	—	—	—
00-01—Toronto	NHL	82	5	24	29	123	16	3	0	11	2	3	5	16
01-02—Toronto	NHL	82	17	26	43	129	16	8	0	20	5	5	10	30
02-03—Toronto	NHL	75	6	18	24	135	9	3	0	7	0	3	3	10
NHL Totals (8 years)............		633	60	157	217	1176	15	23	4	38	7	11	18	56

McCARTHY, SANDY RW RANGERS

PERSONAL: Born June 15, 1972, in Toronto ... 6-3/222. ... Shoots right.
TRANSACTIONS/CAREER NOTES: Selected by Calgary Flames in third round (third Flames pick, 52nd overall) of NHL entry draft (June 22, 1991). ... Strained right shoulder (December 18, 1993); missed two games. ... Strained shoulder (December 27, 1993); missed one game. ... Strained right knee (January 20, 1995); missed five games. ... Suffered hernia (February 3, 1995); missed six games. ... Injured ribs (December 16, 1995); missed seven games. ... Fractured ankle (October 9, 1996); missed 25 games. ... Reinjured left ankle (January 9, 1997) and underwent surgery; missed 23 games. ... Bruised shoulder (November 13, 1997); missed six games. ... Injured groin (December 9, 1997); missed two games. ... Suffered hip pointer (December 22, 1997); missed four games. ... Suffered charley horse (January 24, 1998); missed one game. ... Traded by Flames with third- (LW Brad Richards) and fifth-round (D Curtis Rich) picks in 1998 draft to Tampa Bay Lightning for C Jason Wiemer (March 24, 1998). ... Traded by Lightning with RW Mikael Andersson to Philadelphia Flyers for LW Colin Forbes and fifth-round pick (G Michal Lanicek) in 1999 draft (March 20, 1999). ... Sprained right knee (November 5, 1999); missed one game. ... Injured groin (February 19, 2000); missed four games. ... Traded by Flyers to Carolina Hurricanes for C Kent Manderville (March 14, 2000). ... Traded by Hurricanes with fourth-round pick (D Bryce Lampman) in 2001 draft to New York Rangers for RW Rob DiMaio and LW Darren Langdon (August 4, 2000).

		REGULAR SEASON								PLAYOFFS				
Season Team	League	Gms.	G	A	Pts.	PIM	+/-	PP	SH	Gms.	G	A	Pts.	PIM
89-90—Laval	QMJHL	65	10	11	21	269	...	...	...	—	—	—	—	—
90-91—Laval	QMJHL	68	21	19	40	297	...	...	...	—	—	—	—	—
91-92—Laval	QMJHL	62	39	51	90	326	...	...	...	8	4	5	9	81
92-93—Salt Lake City............	IHL	77	18	20	38	220	...	...	...	—	—	—	—	—
93-94—Calgary	NHL	79	5	5	10	173	-3	0	0	7	0	0	0	34
94-95—Calgary	NHL	37	5	3	8	101	1	0	0	6	0	1	1	17
95-96—Calgary	NHL	75	9	7	16	173	-8	3	0	4	0	0	0	10
96-97—Calgary	NHL	33	3	5	8	113	-8	1	0	—	—	—	—	—
97-98—Calgary	NHL	52	8	5	13	170	-18	1	0	—	—	—	—	—
—Tampa Bay	NHL	14	0	5	5	71	-1	0	0	—	—	—	—	—
98-99—Tampa Bay	NHL	67	5	7	12	145	-22	1	0	—	—	—	—	—
—Philadelphia	NHL	13	0	1	1	25	-2	0	0	6	0	1	1	0
99-00—Philadelphia	NHL	58	6	5	11	111	-5	1	0	—	—	—	—	—
—Carolina	NHL	13	0	0	0	9	2	0	0	—	—	—	—	—
00-01—New York Rangers	NHL	81	11	10	21	171	3	0	0	—	—	—	—	—
01-02—New York Rangers	NHL	82	10	13	23	171	-8	1	0	—	—	—	—	—
02-03—New York Rangers	NHL	82	6	9	15	81	-4	0	0	—	—	—	—	—
NHL Totals (10 years)..........		686	68	75	143	1504	-73	8	0	23	0	2	2	61

McCARTHY, STEVE D BLACKHAWKS

PERSONAL: Born February 3, 1981, in Trail, B.C. ... 6-1/198. ... Shoots left.
TRANSACTIONS/CAREER NOTES: Selected by Chicago Blackhawks in first round (first Blackhawks pick, 23rd overall) of NHL entry draft (June 26, 1999).

		REGULAR SEASON								PLAYOFFS				
Season Team	League	Gms.	G	A	Pts.	PIM	+/-	PP	SH	Gms.	G	A	Pts.	PIM
96-97—Edmonton	WHL	2	0	0	0	0	...	...	...	—	—	—	—	—
97-98—Edmonton	WHL	58	11	29	40	59	...	...	...	—	—	—	—	—
98-99—Kootenay	WHL	57	19	33	52	79	...	...	...	6	0	5	5	8
99-00—Chicago	NHL	5	1	1	2	4	0	1	0	—	—	—	—	—
—Kootenay	WHL	37	13	23	36	36	...	...	...	—	—	—	—	—
00-01—Chicago	NHL	44	0	5	5	8	-7	0	0	—	—	—	—	—
—Norfolk	AHL	7	0	4	4	2	...	...	...	—	—	—	—	—
01-02—Chicago	NHL	3	0	0	0	2	-1	0	0	—	—	—	—	—
—Norfolk	AHL	77	7	21	28	37	...	...	...	2	0	3	3	2
02-03—Norfolk	AHL	19	1	6	7	14	...	...	...	—	—	—	—	—
—Chicago	NHL	57	1	4	5	23	-1	0	0	—	—	—	—	—
NHL Totals (4 years)............		109	2	10	12	37	-9	1	0					

M

McCARTY, DARREN — RW — RED WINGS

PERSONAL: Born April 1, 1972, in Burnaby, B.C. ... 6-1/215. ... Shoots right.

TRANSACTIONS/CAREER NOTES: Selected by Detroit Red Wings in second round (second Red Wings pick, 46th overall) of NHL entry draft (June 20, 1992). ... Injured groin (January 29, 1994); missed five games. ... Injured shoulder (March 23, 1994); missed five games. ... Separated right shoulder (February 7, 1995); missed eight games. ... Injured right hand (March 30, 1995); missed two games. ... Injured left knee (April 9, 1995); missed five games. ... Injured right heel (November 7, 1995); missed one game ... Separated shoulder (December 2, 1995); missed six games. ... Lacerated right forearm (January 12, 1996); missed three games. ... Injured left hand (February 15, 1996); missed seven games. ... Injured hand (January 3, 1997); missed seven games. ... Bruised thigh (January 29, 1997); missed four games. ... Injured groin (April 5, 1997); missed two games. ... Fractured foot (January 11, 1998); missed eight games. ... Suffered from vertigo (April 4, 1998); missed three games. ... Strained groin (March 12, 1999); missed 10 games. ... Reinjured groin (April 5, 1999); missed three games. ... Strained groin (November 12, 1999); missed 39 games. ... Injured leg (March 5, 2000); missed final 17 games of regular season. ... Suffered back spasms (December 1, 2000); missed one game. ... Sprained ankle (March 18, 2001); missed remainder of regular season. ... Injured shoulder (September 21, 2001); missed first two games of season. ... Sprained knee (October 13, 2001); missed 11 games. ... Suffered infected finger (March 2, 2002); missed six games. ... Re-signed by Red Wings (June 30, 2003).

			REGULAR SEASON								PLAYOFFS				
Season Team	League	Gms.	G	A	Pts.	PIM	+/-	PP	SH		Gms.	G	A	Pts.	PIM
88-89—Peterborough Jr. B	OHA	34	18	17	35	135	...	...	...		—	—	—	—	—
89-90—Belleville	OHL	63	12	15	27	142	...	...	...		11	1	1	2	21
90-91—Belleville	OHL	60	30	37	67	151	...	...	...		6	2	2	4	13
91-92—Belleville	OHL	65	*55	72	127	177	...	...	...		5	1	4	5	13
92-93—Adirondack	AHL	73	17	19	36	278	...	...	...		11	0	1	1	33
.93-94—Detroit	NHL	67	9	17	26	181	12	0	0		7	2	2	4	8
94-95—Detroit	NHL	31	5	8	13	88	5	1	0		18	3	2	5	14
95-96—Detroit	NHL	63	15	14	29	158	14	8	0		19	3	2	5	20
96-97—Detroit	NHL	68	19	30	49	126	14	5	0		20	3	4	7	34
97-98—Detroit	NHL	71	15	22	37	157	0	5	1		22	3	8	11	34
98-99—Detroit	NHL	69	14	26	40	108	10	6	0		10	1	1	2	23
99-00—Detroit	NHL	24	6	6	12	48	1	0	0		9	0	1	1	12
00-01—Detroit	NHL	72	12	10	22	123	-5	1	1		6	1	0	1	2
01-02—Detroit	NHL	62	5	7	12	98	2	0	0		23	4	4	8	34
02-03—Detroit	NHL	73	13	9	22	138	10	1	0		4	0	0	0	6
NHL Totals (10 years)		600	113	149	262	1225	63	27	2		138	20	24	44	187

McCAULEY, ALYN — C — SHARKS

PERSONAL: Born May 29, 1977, in Brockville, Ont. ... 6-0/192. ... Shoots left.

TRANSACTIONS/CAREER NOTES: Selected by New Jersey Devils in fourth round (fifth Devils pick, 79th overall) of NHL entry draft (July 8, 1995). ... Traded by Devils with D Jason Smith and C Steve Sullivan to Toronto Maple Leafs for C Doug Gilmour, D Dave Ellett and third-round pick (D Andre Lakos) in 1999 draft (February 25, 1997). ... Fractured ankle (December 31, 1997); missed 17 games. ... Strained shoulder (February 26, 1998); missed three games. ... Sprained left knee (December 30, 1998); missed 22 games. ... Suffered concussion (March 3, 1999); missed remainder of season. ... Suffered injury (October 9, 1999); missed one game. ... Suffered from flu (December 4, 1999); missed six games. ... Suffered illness (January 11, 2000); missed one game. ... Sprained wrist (October 11, 2000); missed four games. ... Traded by Maple Leafs with C Brad Boyes and first-round pick in 2003 draft to San Jose Sharks for RW Owen Nolan (March 5, 2003). ... Signed by Sharks (July 15, 2003).

			REGULAR SEASON								PLAYOFFS				
Season Team	League	Gms.	G	A	Pts.	PIM	+/-	PP	SH		Gms.	G	A	Pts.	PIM
92-93—Kingston Jr. A	MTHL	38	31	29	60	18	...	...	...		—	—	—	—	—
93-94—Ottawa	OHL	38	13	23	36	10	...	...	...		13	5	14	19	4
94-95—Ottawa	OHL	65	16	38	54	20	...	...	...		—	—	—	—	—
95-96—Ottawa	OHL	55	34	48	82	24	...	...	...		2	0	0	0	0
96-97—Ottawa	OHL	50	†56	56	112	16	...	...	...		22	14	22	36	14
—St. John's	AHL	—	—	—	—	—	—	—	—		3	0	1	1	0
97-98—Toronto	NHL	60	6	10	16	6	-7	0	0		—	—	—	—	—
98-99—Toronto	NHL	39	9	15	24	2	7	1	0		—	—	—	—	—
99-00—Toronto	NHL	45	5	5	10	10	-6	1	0		5	0	0	0	6
—St. John's	AHL	5	1	1	2	0	...	...	...		—	—	—	—	—
00-01—Toronto	NHL	14	1	0	1	0	0	0	0		10	0	0	0	2
—St. John's	AHL	47	16	28	44	12	...	...	...		—	—	—	—	—
01-02—Toronto	NHL	82	6	10	16	18	10	0	1		20	5	10	15	4
02-03—Toronto	NHL	64	6	9	15	16	3	0	0		—	—	—	—	—
—San Jose	NHL	16	3	7	10	4	-2	3	0		—	—	—	—	—
NHL Totals (6 years)		320	36	56	92	56	5	5	1		35	5	10	15	12

McCONNELL, BRIAN — C — FLAMES

PERSONAL: Born February 1, 1983, in Boston. ... 6-2/190. ... Shoots left.

TRANSACTIONS/CAREER NOTES: Selected by Calgary Flames in second round (second Flames pick, 39th overall) of NHL entry draft (June 22, 2002).

			REGULAR SEASON								PLAYOFFS				
Season Team	League	Gms.	G	A	Pts.	PIM	+/-	PP	SH		Gms.	G	A	Pts.	PIM
00-01—U.S. National	USHL	62	19	25	44	143	...	...	...		—	—	—	—	—
01-02—Boston University	Hockey East	34	11	14	25	58	...	...	...		—	—	—	—	—
02-03—Boston University	Hockey East	34	11	14	25	70	...	...	...		—	—	—	—	—

M

McCORMICK, CODY　　　　　C/RW　　　　AVALANCHE

PERSONAL: Born April 18, 1983, in London, Ont. ... 6-2/200. ... Shoots right.
TRANSACTIONS/CAREER NOTES: Selected by Colorado Avalanche in fifth round (fourth Avalanche pick, 144th overall) of NHL entry draft (June 23, 2001). ... Re-signed by Avalanche (June 4, 2003).

Season Team	League		REGULAR SEASON								PLAYOFFS			
		Gms.	G	A	Pts.	PIM	+/-	PP	SH	Gms.	G	A	Pts.	PIM
00-01—Belleville	OHL	66	7	16	23	135	...	...	...	10	1	1	2	23
01-02—Belleville	OHL	63	10	17	27	118	...	...	...	11	2	4	6	24
02-03—Belleville	OHL	61	36	33	69	166	...	...	...	—	—	—	—	—

McDONALD, ANDY　　　　　C　　　　MIGHTY DUCKS

PERSONAL: Born August 25, 1977, in Strathroy, Ont. ... 5-10/186. ... Shoots left.
TRANSACTIONS/CAREER NOTES: Signed as non-drafted free agent by Mighty Ducks of Anaheim (April 3, 2000). ... Suffered concussion (January 12, 2001); missed seven games. ... Suffered concussion (February 27, 2002); missed three games.

Season Team	League		REGULAR SEASON								PLAYOFFS			
		Gms.	G	A	Pts.	PIM	+/-	PP	SH	Gms.	G	A	Pts.	PIM
96-97—Colgate University	ECAC	33	9	10	19	19	...	...	...	—	—	—	—	—
97-98—Colgate University	ECAC	35	13	19	32	26	...	...	...	—	—	—	—	—
98-99—Colgate University	ECAC	35	20	26	46	42	...	...	...	—	—	—	—	—
99-00—Colgate University	ECAC	34	25	*33	*58	49	...	...	...	—	—	—	—	—
00-01—Cincinnati	AHL	46	15	25	40	21	...	...	...	3	0	1	1	2
—Anaheim	NHL	16	1	0	1	6	0	0	0	—	—	—	—	—
01-02—Cincinnati	AHL	21	7	25	32	6	...	...	...	—	—	—	—	—
—Anaheim	NHL	53	7	21	28	10	2	2	0	—	—	—	—	—
02-03—Anaheim	NHL	46	10	11	21	14	-1	3	0	—	—	—	—	—
NHL Totals (3 years)		115	18	32	50	30	1	5	0					

McDONELL, KENT　　　　　RW　　　　BLUE JACKETS

PERSONAL: Born March 1, 1979, in Williamstown, Ont. ... 6-2/200. ... Shoots right.
TRANSACTIONS/CAREER NOTES: Selected by Carolina Hurricanes in ninth round (ninth Hurricanes pick, 225th overall) of NHL entry draft (June 21, 1997). ... Returned to draft pool by Hurricanes and selected by Detroit Red Wings in sixth round (third Red Wings pick, 181st overall) of NHL entry draft (June 26, 1999). ... Traded by Red Wings to Columbus Blue Jackets for sixth-round pick in 2003 draft (August 17, 2000).

Season Team	League		REGULAR SEASON								PLAYOFFS			
		Gms.	G	A	Pts.	PIM	+/-	PP	SH	Gms.	G	A	Pts.	PIM
96-97—Guelph	OHL	56	7	5	12	57	...	...	...	16	0	2	2	4
97-98—Guelph	OHL	57	28	23	51	76	...	...	...	12	7	4	11	18
98-99—Guelph	OHL	60	31	38	69	110	...	...	...	11	4	3	7	36
99-00—Guelph	OHL	56	35	35	70	100	...	...	...	6	1	4	5	6
00-01—Syracuse	AHL	32	3	3	6	36	...	...	...	3	1	0	1	0
—Dayton	ECHL	28	16	9	25	94	...	...	...	3	0	0	0	4
01-02—Syracuse	AHL	72	18	13	31	122	...	...	...	3	0	2	2	0
02-03—Syracuse	AHL	72	14	24	38	93	...	...	...	—	—	—	—	—
—Columbus	NHL	3	0	0	0	0	-1	0	0	—	—	—	—	—
NHL Totals (1 year)		3	0	0	0	0	-1	0	0					

M

McEACHERN, SHAWN　　　　　LW　　　　THRASHERS

PERSONAL: Born February 28, 1969, in Waltham, Mass. ... 5-11/200. ... Shoots left. ... Full Name: Shawn K. McEachern. ... Name pronounced muh-KEH-kuhrn.
TRANSACTIONS/CAREER NOTES: Selected by Pittsburgh Penguins in sixth round (sixth Penguins pick, 110th overall) of NHL entry draft (June 13, 1987). ... Traded by Penguins to Los Angeles Kings for D Marty McSorley (August 27, 1993). ... Traded by Kings to Penguins for D Marty McSorley and D Jim Paek (February 15, 1994). ... Played in Europe during 1994-95 NHL lockout. ... Suspended for first three games of 1994-95 season and fined $500 by NHL for slashing incident (September 21, 1994); suspension reduced to two games due to abbreviated 1994-95 season. ... Traded by Penguins with LW Kevin Stevens to Boston Bruins for C Bryan Smolinski and RW Glen Murray (August 2, 1995). ... Traded by Bruins to Ottawa Senators for RW Trent McCleary and third-round pick (LW Eric Naud) in 1996 draft (June 22, 1996). ... Fractured jaw (December 6, 1996); missed 17 games. ... Suffered back spasms (February 7, 1998); missed one game. ... Injured wrist (April 3, 1999); missed one game. ... Injured groin (April 8, 1999); missed four games. ... Suffered illness (February 1, 2000); missed one game. ... Bruised shoulder (February 26, 2000); missed four games. ... Fractured left thumb (March 25, 2000); missed final eight games of season. ... Injured groin (April 9, 2002); missed final two games of regular season. ... Traded by Senators with sixth-round pick in 2004 draft to Atlanta Thrashers for D Brian Pothier (June 30, 2002).
STATISTICAL PLATEAUS: Three-goal games: 1997-98 (1), 2002-03 (1). Total: 2.

Season Team	League		REGULAR SEASON								PLAYOFFS			
		Gms.	G	A	Pts.	PIM	+/-	PP	SH	Gms.	G	A	Pts.	PIM
85-86—Matignon	Mass. H.S.	20	32	20	52	...	...	...	...	—	—	—	—	—
86-87—Matignon	Mass. H.S.	16	29	28	57	...	...	...	...	—	—	—	—	—
87-88—Matignon	Mass. H.S.	22	52	40	92	...	...	...	...	—	—	—	—	—
88-89—Boston University	Hockey East	36	20	28	48	32	...	...	...	—	—	—	—	—
89-90—Boston University	Hockey East	43	25	31	56	78	...	...	...	—	—	—	—	—
90-91—Boston University	Hockey East	41	34	48	82	43	...	...	...	—	—	—	—	—
91-92—U.S. national team	Int'l	57	26	23	49	38	...	...	...	—	—	—	—	—
—U.S. Olympic team	Int'l	8	1	0	1	10	...	...	...	—	—	—	—	—
—Pittsburgh	NHL	15	0	4	4	0	1	0	0	19	2	7	9	4

			REGULAR SEASON								PLAYOFFS				
Season Team	League	Gms.	G	A	Pts.	PIM	+/-	PP	SH	Gms.	G	A	Pts.	PIM
92-93—Pittsburgh	NHL	84	28	33	61	46	21	7	0	12	3	2	5	10
93-94—Los Angeles	NHL	49	8	13	21	24	1	0	3	—	—	—	—	—
—Pittsburgh	NHL	27	12	9	21	10	13	0	2	6	1	0	1	2
94-95—Kiekko-Espoo	Finland	8	1	3	4	6	...	...	...	—	—	—	—	—
—Pittsburgh	NHL	44	13	13	26	22	4	1	2	11	0	2	2	8
95-96—Boston	NHL	82	24	29	53	34	-5	3	2	5	2	1	3	8
96-97—Ottawa	NHL	65	11	20	31	18	-5	0	1	7	2	0	2	8
97-98—Ottawa	NHL	81	24	24	48	42	1	8	2	11	0	4	4	8
98-99—Ottawa	NHL	77	31	25	56	46	8	7	0	4	2	0	2	6
99-00—Ottawa	NHL	69	29	22	51	24	2	10	0	6	0	3	3	4
00-01—Ottawa	NHL	82	32	40	72	62	10	9	0	4	0	2	2	2
01-02—Ottawa	NHL	80	15	31	46	52	9	5	0	12	0	4	4	2
02-03—Atlanta	NHL	46	10	16	26	28	-27	4	1	—	—	—	—	—
NHL Totals (12 years)		801	237	279	516	408	33	54	13	97	12	25	37	62

McGILLIS, DAN   D   BRUINS

PERSONAL: Born July 1, 1972, in Hawkesbury, Ont. ... 6-2/230. ... Shoots left. ... Full Name: Daniel McGillis.
TRANSACTIONS/CAREER NOTES: Selected by Detroit Red Wings in 10th round (10th Red Wings pick, 238th overall) of NHL entry draft (June 20, 1992). ... Signed as free agent by Edmonton Oilers (September 6, 1996). ... Traded by Oilers with second-round pick (D Jason Beckett) in 1998 draft to Philadelphia Flyers for D Janne Niinimaa (March 24, 1998). ... Suffered neck spasms (February 21, 1999); missed two games. ... Injured left knee (March 30, 1999); missed one game. ... Fractured right foot (November 28, 1999); missed four games. ... Strained groin (February 22, 2000); missed 10 games. ... Strained groin (November 3, 2001); missed one game. ... Strained lower back (January 19, 2002); missed six games. ... Traded by Flyers to San Jose Sharks for D Marcus Ragnarsson (December 6, 2002). ... Traded by Sharks to Boston Bruins for second-round pick in 2003 draft (March 11, 2003).

			REGULAR SEASON								PLAYOFFS				
Season Team	League	Gms.	G	A	Pts.	PIM	+/-	PP	SH	Gms.	G	A	Pts.	PIM
91-92—Hawkesbury	Tier II Jr. A	36	5	19	24	106	...	...	...	—	—	—	—	—
92-93—Northeastern Univ.	Hockey East	35	5	12	17	42	...	...	...	—	—	—	—	—
93-94—Northeastern Univ.	Hockey East	38	4	25	29	82	...	...	...	—	—	—	—	—
94-95—Northeastern Univ.	Hockey East	34	9	22	31	70	...	...	...	—	—	—	—	—
95-96—Northeastern Univ.	Hockey East	34	12	24	36	50	...	...	...	—	—	—	—	—
96-97—Edmonton	NHL	73	6	16	22	52	2	2	1	12	0	5	5	24
97-98—Edmonton	NHL	67	10	15	25	74	-17	5	0	—	—	—	—	—
—Philadelphia	NHL	13	1	5	6	35	-4	1	0	5	1	2	3	10
98-99—Philadelphia	NHL	78	8	37	45	61	16	6	0	6	0	1	1	12
99-00—Philadelphia	NHL	68	4	14	18	55	16	3	0	18	2	6	8	12
00-01—Philadelphia	NHL	82	14	35	49	86	13	4	0	6	1	0	1	6
01-02—Philadelphia	NHL	75	5	14	19	46	17	2	0	5	1	0	1	8
02-03—Philadelphia	NHL	24	0	3	3	20	7	0	0	—	—	—	—	—
—San Jose	NHL	37	3	13	16	30	-6	2	0	—	—	—	—	—
—Boston	NHL	10	0	1	1	10	2	0	0	5	3	0	3	2
NHL Totals (7 years)		527	51	153	204	469	46	25	1	57	8	14	22	74

M

McGRATTAN, BRIAN   RW   SENATORS

PERSONAL: Born September 2, 1981, in Hamilton, Ont. ... 6-3/210. ... Shoots right.
TRANSACTIONS/CAREER NOTES: Selected by Los Angeles Kings in fourth round (fifth Kings pick, 104th overall) of NHL entry draft (June 26, 1999). ... Signed by Ottawa Senators (June 3, 2003).

			REGULAR SEASON								PLAYOFFS				
Season Team	League	Gms.	G	A	Pts.	PIM	+/-	PP	SH	Gms.	G	A	Pts.	PIM
97-98—Guelph	OHL	25	3	2	5	11	...	...	...	—	—	—	—	—
98-99—Guelph	OHL	6	1	3	4	15	...	...	...	—	—	—	—	—
—Sudbury	OHL	53	7	10	17	153	...	...	...	4	0	0	0	8
99-00—Sudbury	OHL	25	2	8	10	79	...	...	...	—	—	—	—	—
—Mississauga	OHL	42	9	13	22	166	...	...	...	—	—	—	—	—
00-01—Mississauga	OHL	31	20	9	29	83	...	...	...	—	—	—	—	—
01-02—Mississauga	OHL	7	2	3	5	16	...	...	...	—	—	—	—	—
—Owen Sound	OHL	2	0	0	0	0	...	...	...	—	—	—	—	—
—Oshawa	OHL	25	10	5	15	72	...	...	...	—	—	—	—	—
—Sault Ste. Marie	OHL	26	8	7	15	71	...	...	...	6	2	0	2	20
02-03—Binghamton	AHL	59	9	10	19	173	...	...	...	—	—	—	—	—

McINNIS, MARTY   RW   BRUINS

PERSONAL: Born June 2, 1970, in Hingham, Mass. ... 5-11/184. ... Shoots right. ... Full Name: Martin Edward McInnis. ... Name pronounced muh-KIH-nihz.
TRANSACTIONS/CAREER NOTES: Selected by New York Islanders in eighth round (10th Islanders pick, 163rd overall) of NHL entry draft (June 11, 1988). ... Injured eye (March 9, 1993); missed two games. ... Fractured patella (March 27, 1993); missed remainder of regular season and 14 playoff games. ... Sprained wrist (April 18, 1995); missed one game. ... Injured ribs (March 7, 1996); missed one game. ... Injured ribs (March 16, 1996); missed six games. ... Traded by Islanders with G Tyrone Garner and sixth-round pick (D Ilja Demidov) in 1997 draft to Calgary Flames for C Robert Reichel (March 18, 1997). ... Injured shoulder (December 23, 1997); missed six games. ... Traded by Flames with D Jamie Allison and RW Erik Andersson to Chicago Blackhawks for C Jeff Shantz and C/LW Steve Dubinsky (October 27, 1998). ... Traded by Blackhawks with Mighty Ducks of Anaheim for fourth-round pick (traded to Washington) in 2000 draft (October 27, 1998). ... Strained groin (January 28, 2000); missed 11 games. ... Reinjured groin (March 8, 2000); missed nine games. ... Sprained neck (October 29, 2000); missed three games. ... Strained groin (January 21, 2001); missed three games. ... Sprained right wrist (November 2, 2001); missed two games. ... Traded by Mighty Ducks to Boston Bruins for third-round pick (traded to Nashville) in 2002 draft (March 5, 2002).
STATISTICAL PLATEAUS: Three-goal games: 1997-98 (1), 2000-01 (1), 2002-03 (1). Total: 3.

Season Team	League	REGULAR SEASON Gms.	G	A	Pts.	PIM	+/-	PP	SH	PLAYOFFS Gms.	G	A	Pts.	PIM
86-87—Milton Academy	Mass. H.S.	—	21	19	40	—	—	—	—	—	—	—	—	—
87-88—Milton Academy	Mass. H.S.	25	26	25	51	...	...	...	...	—	—	—	—	—
88-89—Boston College	Hockey East	39	13	19	32	8	...	...	...	—	—	—	—	—
89-90—Boston College	Hockey East	41	24	29	53	43	...	...	...	—	—	—	—	—
90-91—Boston College	Hockey East	38	21	36	57	40	...	...	...	—	—	—	—	—
91-92—U.S. national team	Int'l	54	15	19	34	20	...	...	...	—	—	—	—	—
—U.S. Olympic team	Int'l	8	5	2	7	4	...	...	...	—	—	—	—	—
—New York Islanders	NHL	15	3	5	8	0	6	0	0	—	—	—	—	—
92-93—New York Islanders	NHL	56	10	20	30	24	7	0	1	3	0	1	1	0
—Capital District	AHL	10	4	12	16	2	...	...	...	—	—	—	—	—
93-94—New York Islanders	NHL	81	25	31	56	24	31	3	5	4	0	0	0	0
94-95—New York Islanders	NHL	41	9	7	16	8	-1	0	0	—	—	—	—	—
95-96—New York Islanders	NHL	74	12	34	46	39	-11	2	0	—	—	—	—	—
96-97—New York Islanders	NHL	70	20	22	42	20	-7	4	1	—	—	—	—	—
—Calgary	NHL	10	3	4	7	2	-1	1	0	—	—	—	—	—
97-98—Calgary	NHL	75	19	25	44	34	1	5	4	—	—	—	—	—
98-99—Calgary	NHL	6	1	1	2	6	-1	0	0	—	—	—	—	—
—Anaheim	NHL	75	18	34	52	36	-14	11	1	4	2	0	2	2
99-00—Anaheim	NHL	62	10	18	28	26	-4	2	1	—	—	—	—	—
00-01—Anaheim	NHL	75	20	22	42	40	-21	10	0	—	—	—	—	—
01-02—Anaheim	NHL	60	9	14	23	25	-14	2	0	—	—	—	—	—
—Boston	NHL	19	2	3	5	8	-1	0	0	6	0	1	1	0
02-03—Boston	NHL	77	9	10	19	38	-11	0	0	5	1	0	1	2
NHL Totals (12 years)		796	170	250	420	330	-41	40	13	22	3	2	5	4

McKAY, RANDY RW

PERSONAL: Born January 25, 1967, in Montreal ... 6-2/210. ... Shoots right. ... Full Name: Hugh Randall McKay.

TRANSACTIONS/CAREER NOTES: Selected by Detroit Red Wings in sixth round (sixth Red Wings pick, 113th overall) of NHL entry draft (June 15, 1985). ... Injured knee (February 1989). ... Lacerated forearm (February 23, 1991). ... Sent by Red Wings with C Dave Barr to New Jersey Devils as compensation for Red Wings signing free agent RW Troy Crowder (September 9, 1991). ... Sprained knee (January 16, 1993); missed nine games. ... Bruised shoulder (November 3, 1993); missed three games. ... Bruised shoulder (January 24, 1994); missed three games. ... Injured groin (February 24, 1995); missed nine games. ... Reinjured groin (March 18, 1995); missed six games. ... Suffered charley horse (May 26, 1995); missed one playoff game. ... Suffered concussion (December 31, 1995); missed five games. ... Bruised eye (February 27, 1997); missed five games. ... Sprained left knee (March 26, 1998); missed eight games. ... Strained groin (September 23, 1998); missed first four games of season. ... Suffered infected elbow (December 19, 1998); missed one game. ... Suffered from the flu (December 26, 1998); missed four games. ... Suffered sore back (January 20, 1999); missed one game. ... Bruised knee (April 3, 1999); missed one game. ... Suspended three games by NHL for slashing incident (November 1, 1999). ... Suffered injury (January 3, 2000); missed one game. ... Strained hip flexor (January 17, 2000); missed two games. ... Suffered injury (January 29, 2000); missed one game. ... Suffered injury (February 3, 2000); missed one game. ... Injured ankle (March 2, 2000); missed seven games. ... Bruised tailbone (February 27, 2001); missed three games. ... Injured ribs (October 2, 2001); missed first game of season. ... Injured hip (January 10, 2002); missed 10 games. ... Traded by Devils with C Jason Arnott and first-round pick (traded to Columbus) in 2002 draft to Dallas Stars for C Joe Nieuwendyk and RW Jamie Langenbrunner (March 19, 2002). ... Signed as free agent by Montreal Canadiens (July 4, 2002).

STATISTICAL PLATEAUS: Three-goal games: 1996-97 (1), 1997-98 (1). Total: 2. ... Four-goal games: 2000-01 (1). ... Total hat tricks: 3.

Season Team	League	REGULAR SEASON Gms.	G	A	Pts.	PIM	+/-	PP	SH	PLAYOFFS Gms.	G	A	Pts.	PIM
84-85—Michigan Tech	WCHA	25	4	5	9	32	...	...	...	—	—	—	—	—
85-86—Michigan Tech	WCHA	40	12	22	34	46	...	...	...	—	—	—	—	—
86-87—Michigan Tech	WCHA	39	5	11	16	46	...	...	...	—	—	—	—	—
87-88—Michigan Tech	WCHA	41	17	24	41	70	...	...	...	—	—	—	—	—
—Adirondack	AHL	10	0	3	3	12	...	...	...	6	0	4	4	0
88-89—Adirondack	AHL	58	29	34	63	170	...	...	...	14	4	7	11	60
—Detroit	NHL	3	0	0	0	0	-1	0	0	2	0	0	0	2
89-90—Detroit	NHL	33	3	6	9	51	1	0	0	—	—	—	—	—
—Adirondack	AHL	36	16	23	39	99	...	...	...	6	3	0	3	35
90-91—Detroit	NHL	47	1	7	8	183	-15	0	0	5	0	1	1	41
91-92—New Jersey	NHL	80	17	16	33	246	6	2	0	7	1	3	4	10
92-93—New Jersey	NHL	73	11	11	22	206	0	1	0	5	0	0	0	16
93-94—New Jersey	NHL	78	12	15	27	244	24	0	0	20	1	2	3	24
94-95—New Jersey	NHL	33	5	7	12	44	10	0	0	19	8	4	12	11
95-96—New Jersey	NHL	76	11	10	21	145	7	3	0	—	—	—	—	—
96-97—New Jersey	NHL	77	9	18	27	109	15	0	0	10	1	1	2	0
97-98—New Jersey	NHL	74	24	24	48	86	30	8	0	6	0	1	1	0
98-99—New Jersey	NHL	70	17	20	37	143	10	3	0	7	3	2	5	2
99-00—New Jersey	NHL	67	16	23	39	80	8	3	0	23	0	6	6	9
00-01—New Jersey	NHL	77	23	20	43	50	3	12	0	19	6	3	9	8
01-02—New Jersey	NHL	55	6	7	13	65	2	3	0	—	—	—	—	—
—Dallas	NHL	14	1	4	5	7	2	0	0	—	—	—	—	—
02-03—Montreal	NHL	75	6	13	19	72	-14	2	0	—	—	—	—	—
NHL Totals (15 years)		932	162	201	363	1731	88	37	0	123	20	23	43	123

McKEE, JAY D SABRES

PERSONAL: Born September 8, 1977, in Kingston, Ont. ... 6-3/214. ... Shoots left.

TRANSACTIONS/CAREER NOTES: Selected by Buffalo Sabres in first round (first Sabres pick, 14th overall) of NHL entry draft (July 8, 1995). ... Bruised stomach (March 29, 1998); missed two games. ... Bruised hand (October 30, 1998); missed one game. ... Bruised foot (February 13, 1999); missed six games. ... Suffered from the flu (March 13, 1999); missed two games. ... Suffered injury (November 25, 2000); missed five games. ... Injured hand (March 16, 2001); missed three games. ... Suffered from the flu (January 23, 2002); missed one game.

M

Season Team	League	REGULAR SEASON Gms.	G	A	Pts.	PIM	+/-	PP	SH	PLAYOFFS Gms.	G	A	Pts.	PIM
92-93—Ernestown..................	Jr. C	36	0	17	17	37	...	...	...	—	—	—	—	—
93-94—Sudbury.....................	OHL	51	0	1	1	51	...	...	...	3	0	0	0	0
94-95—Sudbury.....................	OHL	39	6	6	12	91	...	...	...	—	—	—	—	—
—Niagara Falls..............	OHL	26	3	13	16	60	...	...	...	6	2	3	5	10
95-96—Niagara Falls..............	OHL	64	5	41	46	129	...	...	...	10	1	5	6	16
—Rochester	AHL	4	0	1	1	15	...	...	...	—	—	—	—	—
—Buffalo	NHL	1	0	1	1	2	1	0	0	—	—	—	—	—
96-97—Buffalo	NHL	43	1	9	10	35	3	0	0	3	0	0	0	0
—Rochester	AHL	7	2	5	7	4	...	...	...	—	—	—	—	—
97-98—Buffalo	NHL	56	1	13	14	42	-1	0	0	1	0	0	0	0
—Rochester	AHL	13	1	7	8	11	...	...	...	—	—	—	—	—
98-99—Buffalo	NHL	72	0	6	6	75	20	0	0	21	0	3	3	24
99-00—Buffalo	NHL	78	5	12	17	50	5	1	0	1	0	0	0	0
00-01—Buffalo	NHL	74	1	10	11	76	9	0	0	8	1	0	1	6
01-02—Buffalo	NHL	81	2	11	13	43	18	0	0	—	—	—	—	—
02-03—Buffalo	NHL	59	0	5	5	49	-16	0	0	—	—	—	—	—
NHL Totals (8 years)...........		464	10	67	77	372	39	1	0	34	1	3	4	30

McKENNA, STEVE — LW — PENGUINS

PERSONAL: Born August 21, 1973, in Toronto ... 6-8/255. ... Shoots left.

TRANSACTIONS/CAREER NOTES: Signed as non-drafted free agent by Los Angeles Kings (May 17, 1996). ... Strained abdominal muscle (November 9, 1998); missed 14 games. ... Reinjured abdominal muscle (December 9, 1998); missed 42 games. ... Lacerated eye (October 4, 1999); missed six games. ... Selected by Minnesota Wild in NHL expansion draft (June 23, 2000). ... Suffered back spasms (September 8, 2000); missed 12 games. ... Traded by Wild to Pittsburgh Penguins for C Roman Simicek (January 13, 2001). ... Signed as free agent by New York Rangers (August 28, 2001). ... Signed as free agent by Penguins (July 12, 2002).

Season Team	League	REGULAR SEASON Gms.	G	A	Pts.	PIM	+/-	PP	SH	PLAYOFFS Gms.	G	A	Pts.	PIM
93-94—Merrimack College......	Hockey East	37	1	2	3	74	...	...	...	—	—	—	—	—
94-95—Merrimack College......	Hockey East	37	1	9	10	74	...	...	...	—	—	—	—	—
95-96—Merrimack College......	Hockey East	33	3	11	14	67	...	...	...	—	—	—	—	—
96-97—Phoenix.....................	IHL	66	6	5	11	187	...	...	...	—	—	—	—	—
—Los Angeles................	NHL	9	0	0	0	37	1	0	0	—	—	—	—	—
97-98—Fredericton	AHL	6	2	1	3	48	...	...	...	—	—	—	—	—
—Los Angeles................	NHL	62	4	4	8	150	-9	1	0	3	0	1	1	8
98-99—Los Angeles...............	NHL	20	1	0	1	36	-3	0	0	—	—	—	—	—
99-00—Los Angeles...............	NHL	46	0	5	5	125	3	0	0	—	—	—	—	—
00-01—Minnesota.................	NHL	20	1	1	2	19	0	0	0	—	—	—	—	—
—Pittsburgh..................	NHL	34	0	0	0	100	-4	0	0	—	—	—	—	—
01-02—New York Rangers......	NHL	54	2	1	3	144	0	1	0	—	—	—	—	—
—Hartford	AHL	3	0	0	0	11	...	...	...	—	—	—	—	—
02-03—Pittsburgh.................	NHL	79	9	1	10	128	-18	5	0	—	—	—	—	—
NHL Totals (7 years)...........		324	17	12	29	739	-30	7	0	3	0	1	1	8

McKENZIE, JIM — LW — PREDATORS

PERSONAL: Born November 3, 1969, in Gull Lake, Sask. ... 6-5/225. ... Shoots left.

TRANSACTIONS/CAREER NOTES: Selected by Hartford Whalers in fourth round (third Whalers pick, 73rd overall) of NHL entry draft (June 17, 1989). ... Injured elbow (January 31, 1992); missed two games. ... Suffered hip flexor (November 11, 1992); missed three games. ... Suffered hip flexor (December 5, 1992); missed four games. ... Suffered back spasms (January 24, 1993); missed three games. ... Suspended two games by NHL for game misconduct penalties (April 3, 1993). ... Suspended three games by NHL for game misconduct penalties (April 10, 1993). ... Traded by Whalers to Florida Panthers for D Alexander Godynyuk (December 16, 1993). ... Traded by Panthers to Dallas Stars for fourth-round pick (LW Jamie Wright) in 1994 draft (December 16, 1993). ... Traded by Stars to Pittsburgh Penguins for RW Mike Needham (March 21, 1994). ... Fractured toe (November 24, 1993); missed four games. ... Bruised hand (March 11, 1995); missed one game. ... Sprained wrist (April 5, 1995); missed seven games. ... Signed as free agent by New York Islanders (July 31, 1995). ... Claimed by Winnipeg Jets in NHL waiver draft (October 2, 1995). ... Jets franchise moved to Phoenix and renamed Coyotes for 1996-97 season; NHL approved move on January 18, 1996. ... Fractured leg (November 8, 1996); missed five games. ... Suffered from the flu (January 27, 1997); missed one game. ... Fractured leg (December 23, 1997); missed 11 games. ... Traded by Coyotes to Mighty Ducks of Anaheim for C J.F. Jomphe (June 18, 1998). ... Suffered laceration below right eye (January 10, 1999); missed five games. ... Injured ankle (February 3, 1999); missed two games. ... Suspended four games by NHL for fighting incident (October 5, 1999). ... Fractured right hand (November 9, 1999); missed 10 games. ... Claimed on waivers by Washington Capitals (January 18, 2000). ... Signed as free agent by New Jersey Devils (July 3, 2000). ... Suffered from the flu (March 2, 2002); missed one game. ... Signed by Nashville Predators (July 22, 2003).

STATISTICAL PLATEAUS: Three-goal games: 1996-97 (1).

Season Team	League	REGULAR SEASON Gms.	G	A	Pts.	PIM	+/-	PP	SH	PLAYOFFS Gms.	G	A	Pts.	PIM
85-86—Moose Jaw	WHL	3	0	2	2	0	...	...	...	—	—	—	—	—
86-87—Moose Jaw	WHL	65	5	3	8	125	...	...	...	9	0	0	0	7
87-88—Moose Jaw	WHL	62	1	17	18	134	...	...	...	—	—	—	—	—
88-89—Victoria	WHL	67	15	27	42	176	...	...	...	8	1	4	5	30
89-90—Binghamton	AHL	56	4	12	16	149	...	...	...	—	—	—	—	—
—Hartford	NHL	5	0	0	0	4	0	0	0	—	—	—	—	—
90-91—Springfield	AHL	24	3	4	7	102	...	...	...	—	—	—	—	—
—Hartford	NHL	41	4	3	7	108	-7	0	0	6	0	0	0	8
91-92—Hartford	NHL	67	5	1	6	87	-6	0	0	—	—	—	—	—
92-93—Hartford	NHL	64	3	6	9	202	-10	0	0	—	—	—	—	—
93-94—Hartford	NHL	26	1	2	3	67	-6	0	0	—	—	—	—	—
—Dallas.......................	NHL	34	2	3	5	63	4	0	0	—	—	—	—	—
—Pittsburgh..................	NHL	11	0	0	0	16	-5	0	0	3	0	0	0	0

Season Team	League	REGULAR SEASON								PLAYOFFS				
		Gms.	G	A	Pts.	PIM	+/-	PP	SH	Gms.	G	A	Pts.	PIM
94-95—Pittsburgh	NHL	39	2	1	3	63	-7	0	0	5	0	0	0	4
95-96—Winnipeg	NHL	73	4	2	6	202	-4	0	0	1	0	0	0	2
96-97—Phoenix	NHL	65	5	3	8	200	-5	0	0	7	0	0	0	2
97-98—Phoenix	NHL	64	3	4	7	146	-7	0	0	1	0	0	0	0
98-99—Anaheim	NHL	73	5	4	9	99	-18	1	0	4	0	0	0	4
99-00—Anaheim	NHL	31	3	3	6	48	-5	0	0	—	—	—	—	—
—Washington	NHL	30	1	2	3	16	0	0	0	1	0	0	0	0
00-01—New Jersey	NHL	53	2	2	4	119	0	0	0	3	0	0	0	2
01-02—New Jersey	NHL	67	3	5	8	123	0	1	0	6	0	0	0	2
02-03—New Jersey	NHL	76	4	8	12	88	3	0	0	13	0	0	0	14
NHL Totals (14 years)		819	47	49	96	1651	-73	2	0	50	0	0	0	38

McLACHLAN, DARREN   LW   COYOTES

PERSONAL: Born February 16, 1983, in Penticton, B.C. ... 6-1/230. ... Shoots left.

TRANSACTIONS/CAREER NOTES: Selected by Boston Bruins in third round (second Bruins pick, 77th overall) of NHL entry draft (June 23, 2001). ... Traded by Bruins with fifth-round draft pick in 2004 to Phoenix Coyotes (June 1, 2003). ... Signed by Coyotes (June 1, 2003).

Season Team	League	REGULAR SEASON								PLAYOFFS				
		Gms.	G	A	Pts.	PIM	+/-	PP	SH	Gms.	G	A	Pts.	PIM
00-01—Seattle	WHL	42	10	9	19	161	...	...	...	9	1	3	4	18
01-02—Seattle	WHL	51	15	16	31	153	...	...	...	10	1	0	1	20
02-03—Seattle	WHL	66	17	43	60	195	...	...	...	—	—	—	—	—

McLAREN, KYLE   D   SHARKS

PERSONAL: Born June 18, 1977, in Humboldt, Sask. ... 6-4/225. ... Shoots left.

TRANSACTIONS/CAREER NOTES: Selected by Boston Bruins in first round (first Bruins pick, ninth overall) of NHL entry draft (July 8, 1995). ... Injured back (November 21, 1995); missed one game. ... Injured knee (November 25, 1995); missed five games. ... Suffered from the flu (January 3, 1996); missed one game. ... Suffered concussion (March 10, 1996); missed one game. ... Suffered charley horse (October 26, 1996); missed two games. ... Strained shoulder (February 2, 1997); missed 13 games. ... Injured foot (March 15, 1997); missed one game. ... Sprained thumb (March 27, 1997); missed remainder of season. ... Suffered hip pointer (November 1, 1997); missed five games. ... Injured knee (December 17, 1997); missed one game. ... Fractured foot (March 19, 1998); missed seven games. ... Strained groin (April 7, 1998); missed three games. ... Missed first 15 games of 1998-99 season due to contract dispute. ... Separated shoulder (January 15, 1999); missed 14 games. ... Injured foot (April 10, 1999); missed one game. ... Strained thumb (November 18, 1999); missed seven games. ... Tore knee cartilage (April 1, 2000); missed final four games of season. ... Injured knee (October 20, 2000); missed 24 games. ... Sprained chest muscle (October 8, 2001); missed 12 games. ... Bruised right knee (November 17, 2001); missed one game. ... Tore ligament in right wrist (December 22, 2001) and underwent surgery; missed 31 games. ... Suspended three playoff games by NHL for elbowing incident (April 26, 2002). ... Traded by Bruins with fourth-round pick in 2004 draft to San Jose Sharks as part of three-team trade in which Bruins acquired G Jeff Hackett and D Jeff Jillson and Montreal Canadiens acquired LW Niklas Sundstrom and third-round pick in 2004 draft (January 23, 2003).

Season Team	League	REGULAR SEASON								PLAYOFFS				
		Gms.	G	A	Pts.	PIM	+/-	PP	SH	Gms.	G	A	Pts.	PIM
93-94—Tacoma	WHL	62	1	9	10	53	...	...	...	6	1	4	5	6
94-95—Tacoma	WHL	47	13	19	32	68	...	...	...	4	1	1	2	4
95-96—Boston	NHL	74	5	12	17	73	16	0	0	5	0	0	0	14
96-97—Boston	NHL	58	5	9	14	54	-9	0	0	—	—	—	—	—
97-98—Boston	NHL	66	5	20	25	56	13	2	0	6	1	0	1	4
98-99—Boston	NHL	52	6	18	24	48	1	3	0	12	0	3	3	10
99-00—Boston	NHL	71	8	11	19	67	-4	2	0	—	—	—	—	—
00-01—Boston	NHL	58	5	12	17	53	-5	2	0	—	—	—	—	—
01-02—Boston	NHL	38	0	8	8	19	-4	0	0	4	0	0	0	20
02-03—San Jose	NHL	33	0	8	8	30	-10	0	0	—	—	—	—	—
NHL Totals (8 years)		450	34	98	132	400	-2	9	0	27	1	3	4	48

McLEAN, BRETT   C   BLACKHAWKS

PERSONAL: Born August 14, 1978, in Comox, B.C. ... 5-11/185. ... Shoots left.

TRANSACTIONS/CAREER NOTES: Signed as free agent by Chicago Blackhawks (July 23, 2002).

Season Team	League	REGULAR SEASON								PLAYOFFS				
		Gms.	G	A	Pts.	PIM	+/-	PP	SH	Gms.	G	A	Pts.	PIM
94-95—Tacoma	WHL	67	11	23	34	33	...	...	...	4	0	1	1	0
95-96—Kelowna	WHL	71	37	42	79	60	...	...	...	6	2	2	4	6
96-97—Kelowna	WHL	72	44	60	104	96	...	...	...	4	4	2	6	12
97-98—Kelowna	WHL	54	42	46	88	91	...	...	...	7	4	5	9	17
98-99—Kelowna	WHL	44	32	38	70	46	...	...	...	—	—	—	—	—
—Brandon	WHL	21	15	16	31	20	...	...	...	5	1	6	7	8
—Cincinnati	AHL	7	0	3	3	6	...	...	...	—	—	—	—	—
99-00—Saint John	AHL	72	15	23	38	115	...	...	...	3	0	1	1	2
—Johnstown	ECHL	8	4	7	11	6	...	...	...	—	—	—	—	—
00-01—Cleveland	IHL	74	20	24	44	54	...	...	...	4	0	0	0	18
01-02—Houston	AHL	78	24	21	45	71	...	...	...	14	1	6	7	12
02-03—Norfolk	AHL	77	23	38	61	60	...	...	...	—	—	—	—	—
—Chicago	NHL	2	0	0	0	0	-1	0	0	—	—	—	—	—
NHL Totals (1 year)		2	0	0	0	0	-1	0	0					

McLENNAN, JAMIE G FLAMES

PERSONAL: Born June 30, 1971, in Edmonton ... 6-0/190. ... Catches left.
TRANSACTIONS/CAREER NOTES: Selected by New York Islanders in third round (third Islanders pick, 48th overall) of NHL entry draft (June 22, 1991). ... Signed as free agent by St. Louis Blues (July 3, 1996). ... Strained groin (October 29, 1997); missed two games. ... Strained groin (March 22, 1998); missed one game. ... Strained hip flexor (January 19, 1999); missed one game. ... Suffered from the flu (March 11, 1999); missed two games. ... Selected by Minnesota Wild in NHL expansion draft (June 23, 2000). ... Bruised forearm (November 11, 2000); missed one game. ... Suffered illness (March 5, 2001); missed four games. ... Traded by Wild to Calgary Flames for ninth-round pick (F Mika Hannula) in 2002 draft (June 22, 2002).

Season Team	League	Gms.	Min	W	L	T	GA	SO	Avg.	SV%	Gms.	Min.	W	L	GA	SO	Avg.	SV%
88-89 —Spokane	WHL	11	578	...	...	...	63	0	6.54	—	—	—	—	—	—	—	—	—
—Lethbridge	WHL	7	368	...	...	...	22	0	3.59	—	—	—	—	—	—	—	—	—
89-90 —Lethbridge	WHL	34	1690	20	4	2	110	1	3.91	—	13	677	6	5	44	0	3.90	—
90-91 —Lethbridge	WHL	56	3230	32	18	4	205	0	3.81	—	*16	*970	8	8	*56	0	3.46	—
91-92 —Capital District	AHL	18	952	4	10	2	60	1	3.78	—	—	—	—	—	—	—	—	—
—Richmond	ECHL	32	1837	16	12	‡2	114	0	3.72	—	—	—	—	—	—	—	—	—
92-93 —Capital District	AHL	38	2171	17	14	6	117	1	3.23	—	1	20	0	1	5	0	15.00	—
93-94 —Salt Lake City	IHL	24	1320	8	12	‡2	80	0	3.64	—	—	—	—	—	—	—	—	—
—New York Islanders	NHL	22	1287	8	7	6	61	0	2.84	.905	2	82	0	1	6	0	4.39	.872
94-95 —New York Islanders	NHL	21	1185	6	11	2	67	0	3.39	.876	—	—	—	—	—	—	—	—
—Denver	IHL	4	240	3	0	‡1	12	0	3.00	—	11	641	8	2	23	1	*2.15	—
95-96 —Utah	IHL	14	728	9	2	2	29	0	2.39	—	—	—	—	—	—	—	—	—
—New York Islanders	NHL	13	636	3	9	1	39	0	3.68	.886	—	—	—	—	—	—	—	—
—Worcester	AHL	22	1215	14	7	1	57	0	2.81	—	2	118	0	2	8	0	4.07	—
96-97 —Worcester	AHL	39	2152	18	13	4	100	2	2.79	—	4	262	2	2	16	0	3.66	—
97-98 —St. Louis	NHL	30	1658	16	8	2	60	2	2.17	.903	1	14	0	0	1	0	4.29	.750
98-99 —St. Louis	NHL	33	1763	13	14	4	70	3	2.38	.891	1	37	0	1	0	0	...	1.000
99-00 —St. Louis	NHL	19	1009	9	5	2	33	2	1.96	.903	—	—	—	—	—	—	—	—
00-01 —Minnesota	NHL	38	2230	5	23	9	98	2	2.64	.905	—	—	—	—	—	—	—	—
01-02 —Houston	AHL	51	2851	25	18	4	130	3	2.74	—	14	879	8	6	31	2	2.12	—
02-03 —Calgary	NHL	22	1165	2	11	4	58	0	2.99	.892	—	—	—	—	—	—	—	—
NHL Totals (8 years)		198	10933	62	88	30	486	9	2.67	.896	4	133	0	2	7	0	3.16	.879

McLEOD, KIEL C COYOTES

PERSONAL: Born December 30, 1982, in Fort Saskatchewan, Alta. ... 6-5/211. ... Shoots right. ... Brother of Gavin McLeod, defenseman, Ottawa Senators organization.
TRANSACTIONS/CAREER NOTES: Selected by Columbus Blue Jackets in second round (third Blue Jackets pick, 53rd overall) of NHL entry draft (June 23, 2001). ... Signed by Phoenix Coyotes (June 9, 2003).

Season Team	League	Gms.	G	A	Pts.	PIM	+/-	PP	SH	Gms.	G	A	Pts.	PIM
98-99 —Kelowna	WHL	55	12	15	27	48	...	...	...	6	0	1	1	2
99-00 —Kelowna	WHL	59	17	13	30	100	...	...	...	5	2	1	3	2
00-01 —Kelowna	WHL	65	38	28	66	94	...	...	...	4	4	1	5	8
01-02 —Kelowna	WHL	41	17	31	48	62	...	...	...	15	3	10	13	14
02-03 —Kelowna	WHL	68	39	51	90	163	...	...	...	—	—	—	—	—

McMORROW, SEAN RW SABRES

PERSONAL: Born January 19, 1982, in Vancouver ... 6-4/220. ... Shoots right.
TRANSACTIONS/CAREER NOTES: Selected by Buffalo Sabres in eigth round (seventh Sabres pick, 258th overall) of NHL entry draft (June 25, 2002).

Season Team	League	Gms.	G	A	Pts.	PIM	+/-	PP	SH	Gms.	G	A	Pts.	PIM
99-00 —Kitchener	OHL	31	0	1	1	67	...	...	...	—	—	—	—	—
—Sarnia	OHL	31	0	1	1	75	...	...	...	—	—	—	—	—
00-01 —London	OHL	29	0	3	3	75	...	...	...	—	—	—	—	—
—Kingston	OHL	7	0	1	1	22	...	...	...	—	—	—	—	—
—Mississauga	OHL	13	0	0	0	34	...	...	...	—	—	—	—	—
01-02 —Oshawa	OHL	27	6	1	7	63	...	...	...	—	—	—	—	—
—London	OHL	38	0	1	1	107	...	...	...	—	—	—	—	—
02-03 —Rochester	AHL	64	0	1	1	315	...	...	...	—	—	—	—	—
—Buffalo	NHL	1	0	0	0	0	0	0	0	—	—	—	—	—
NHL Totals (1 year)		1	0	0	0	0	0	0	0					

McNEILL, GRANT D PANTHERS

PERSONAL: Born June 8, 1983, in Vermilion, Alta. ... 6-2/196. ... Shoots left.
TRANSACTIONS/CAREER NOTES: Selected by Florida Panthers in third round (fifth Panthers pick, 68th overall) of NHL entry draft (June 23, 2001).

Season Team	League	Gms.	G	A	Pts.	PIM	+/-	PP	SH	Gms.	G	A	Pts.	PIM
99-00 —Prince Albert	WHL	58	1	1	2	43	...	...	...	6	0	1	1	0
00-01 —Prince Albert	WHL	61	2	6	8	280	...	...	...	—	—	—	—	—
01-02 —Prince Albert	WHL	70	7	6	13	*326	...	...	...	—	—	—	—	—
02-03 —Prince Albert	WHL	71	1	8	9	280	...	...	...	—	—	—	—	—

MELANSON, DEAN — D

PERSONAL: Born November 19, 1973, in Antigonish, Nova Scotia ... 5-11/196. ... Shoots right. ... Name pronounced muh-LAHN-suhn.
TRANSACTIONS/CAREER NOTES: Selected by Buffalo Sabres in fourth round (fourth Sabres pick, 80th overall) of NHL entry draft (June 20, 1992). ... Signed as free agent by Philadelphia Flyers (July 13, 1999). ... Traded by Flyers to Washington Capitals for C Matthew Herr (March 13, 2001). ... Traded by Capitals to Ottawa Senators for D Josef Boumedienne (December 16, 2002).

Season Team	League	REGULAR SEASON								PLAYOFFS				
		Gms.	G	A	Pts.	PIM	+/-	PP	SH	Gms.	G	A	Pts.	PIM
90-91—St. Hyacinthe	QMJHL	69	10	17	27	110	...	...	...	4	0	1	1	2
91-92—St. Hyacinthe	QMJHL	42	8	19	27	158	...	...	...	6	1	2	3	25
92-93—St. Hyacinthe	QMJHL	57	13	29	42	253	...	...	...	—	—	—	—	—
—Rochester	AHL	8	0	1	1	6	...	...	...	14	1	6	7	18
93-94—Rochester	AHL	80	1	21	22	138	...	...	...	4	0	1	1	2
94-95—Rochester	AHL	43	4	7	11	84	...	...	...	—	—	—	—	—
—Buffalo	NHL	5	0	0	0	4	-1	0	0	—	—	—	—	—
95-96—Rochester	AHL	70	3	13	16	204	...	...	...	14	3	3	6	22
96-97—Quebec	IHL	72	3	21	24	95	...	...	...	7	0	2	2	12
97-98—Rochester	AHL	73	7	9	16	228	...	...	...	4	0	2	2	0
98-99—Rochester	AHL	79	7	27	34	192	...	...	...	17	3	2	5	32
99-00—Philadelphia	AHL	58	11	25	36	178	...	...	...	4	2	3	5	10
00-01—Philadelphia	AHL	15	1	4	5	48	...	...	...	—	—	—	—	—
—Portland	AHL	13	1	4	5	14	...	...	...	2	0	0	0	10
—Chicago	IHL	42	1	7	8	80	...	...	...	—	—	—	—	—
01-02—Portland	AHL	70	2	14	16	140	...	...	...	—	—	—	—	—
—Washington	NHL	4	0	0	0	4	1	0	0	—	—	—	—	—
02-03—Portland	AHL	23	1	4	5	40	...	...	...	—	—	—	—	—
—Binghamton	AHL	35	4	3	7	93	...	...	...	—	—	—	—	—
NHL Totals (2 years)		9	0	0	0	8	0	0	0					

MELICHAR, JOSEF — D — PENGUINS

PERSONAL: Born January 20, 1979, in Ceske Budejovice, Czechoslovakia ... 6-2/221. ... Shoots left.
TRANSACTIONS/CAREER NOTES: Selected by Pittsburgh Penguins in third round (third Penguins pick, 71st overall) of NHL entry draft (June 21, 1997). ... Bruised hip (December 6, 2001); missed one game. ... Dislocated shoulder (February 12, 2002); missed 15 games. ... Reinjured shoulder (April 4, 2002); missed remainder of season.

Season Team	League	REGULAR SEASON								PLAYOFFS				
		Gms.	G	A	Pts.	PIM	+/-	PP	SH	Gms.	G	A	Pts.	PIM
95-96—HC Ceske Budejovice	Czech. Jrs.	38	3	4	7	...	...	...	...	—	—	—	—	—
96-97—HC Ceske Budejovice	Czech. Jrs.	41	2	3	5	10	...	...	...	—	—	—	—	—
97-98—Tri-City	WHL	67	9	24	33	152	...	...	...	—	—	—	—	—
98-99—Tri-City	WHL	65	8	28	36	125	...	...	...	11	1	0	1	15
99-00—Wilkes-Barre/Scranton	AHL	80	3	9	12	126	...	...	...	—	—	—	—	—
00-01—Wilkes-Barre/Scranton	AHL	46	2	5	7	69	...	...	...	21	0	5	5	6
—Pittsburgh	NHL	18	0	2	2	21	-5	0	0	—	—	—	—	—
01-02—Pittsburgh	NHL	60	0	3	3	68	-1	0	0	—	—	—	—	—
02-03—Pittsburgh	NHL	8	0	0	0	2	-2	0	0	—	—	—	—	—
NHL Totals (3 years)		86	0	5	5	91	-8	0	0					

MELLANBY, SCOTT — RW — BLUES

PERSONAL: Born June 11, 1966, in Montreal ... 6-1/203. ... Shoots right. ... Full Name: Scott Edgar Mellanby.
TRANSACTIONS/CAREER NOTES: Selected by Philadelphia Flyers in second round (first Flyers pick, 27th overall) of NHL entry draft (June 9, 1984). ... Lacerated right index finger (October 1987). ... Severed nerve and damaged tendon in left forearm (August 1989); missed first 20 games of season. ... Suffered viral infection (November 1989). ... Traded by Flyers with LW Craig Berube and C Craig Fisher to Edmonton Oilers for RW Dave Brown, D Corey Foster and rights to RW Jari Kurri (May 30, 1991). ... Injured shoulder (February 14, 1993); missed 15 games. ... Selected by Florida Panthers in NHL expansion draft (June 24, 1993). ... Fractured nose and lacerated face (February 1, 1994); missed four games. ... Fractured finger (March 7, 1996); missed three games. ... Sprained left knee (January 9, 1998); missed three games. ... Strained groin (September 29, 1998); missed first nine games of season. ... Injured neck (January 16, 1999); missed one game. ... Reinjured neck (January 21, 1999); missed three games. ... Suspended one game by NHL for cross-checking incident (March 21, 1999). ... Suffered slight concussion (April 5, 1999); missed one game. ... Suffered concussion (October 12, 1999); missed three games. ... Suffered from the flu (March 3, 2000); missed one game. ... Strained neck (October 28, 2000). ... Strained back (November 13, 2000); missed 12 games. ... Traded by Panthers to St. Louis Blues for RW David Morisset and fifth-round pick (C Vince Bellissimo) in 2002 draft (February 9, 2001). ... Fractured jaw (September 28, 2001); missed first 12 games of season.
STATISTICAL PLATEAUS: Four-goal games: 2002-03 (1).

Season Team	League	REGULAR SEASON								PLAYOFFS				
		Gms.	G	A	Pts.	PIM	+/-	PP	SH	Gms.	G	A	Pts.	PIM
83-84—Henry Carr H.S.	MTHL	39	37	37	74	97	...	...	...	—	—	—	—	—
84-85—Univ. of Wisconsin	WCHA	40	14	24	38	60	...	...	...	—	—	—	—	—
85-86—Univ. of Wisconsin	WCHA	32	21	23	44	89	...	...	...	—	—	—	—	—
—Philadelphia	NHL	2	0	0	0	0	-1	0	0	—	—	—	—	—
86-87—Philadelphia	NHL	71	11	21	32	94	8	1	0	24	5	5	10	46
87-88—Philadelphia	NHL	75	25	26	51	185	-7	7	0	7	0	1	1	16
88-89—Philadelphia	NHL	76	21	29	50	183	-13	11	0	19	4	5	9	28
89-90—Philadelphia	NHL	57	6	17	23	77	-4	0	0	—	—	—	—	—
90-91—Philadelphia	NHL	74	20	21	41	155	8	5	0	—	—	—	—	—
91-92—Edmonton	NHL	80	23	27	50	197	5	7	0	16	2	1	3	29
92-93—Edmonton	NHL	69	15	17	32	147	-4	6	0	—	—	—	—	—
93-94—Florida	NHL	80	30	30	60	149	0	17	0	—	—	—	—	—

Season Team	League	REGULAR SEASON								PLAYOFFS				
		Gms.	G	A	Pts.	PIM	+/-	PP	SH	Gms.	G	A	Pts.	PIM
94-95—Florida	NHL	48	13	12	25	90	-16	4	0	—	—	—	—	—
95-96—Florida	NHL	79	32	38	70	160	4	19	0	22	3	6	9	44
96-97—Florida	NHL	82	27	29	56	170	7	9	1	5	0	2	2	4
97-98—Florida	NHL	79	15	24	39	127	-14	6	0	—	—	—	—	—
98-99—Florida	NHL	67	18	27	45	85	5	4	0	—	—	—	—	—
99-00—Florida	NHL	77	18	28	46	126	14	6	0	4	0	1	1	2
00-01—Florida	NHL	40	4	9	13	46	-13	1	0	—	—	—	—	—
—St. Louis	NHL	23	7	1	8	25	0	2	0	15	3	3	6	17
01-02—St. Louis	NHL	64	15	26	41	93	-5	8	0	10	7	3	10	18
02-03—St. Louis	NHL	80	26	31	57	176	1	13	0	6	0	1	1	10
NHL Totals (18 years)		1223	326	413	739	2285	-25	126	1	128	24	28	52	214

MELOCHE, ERIC　　　　　RW　　　　　PENGUINS

PERSONAL: Born May 1, 1976, in Montreal ... 5-10/195. ... Shoots right.
TRANSACTIONS/CAREER NOTES: Selected by Pittsburgh Penguins in seventh round (seventh Penguins pick, 186th overall) of NHL entry draft (June 22, 1996).

Season Team	League	REGULAR SEASON								PLAYOFFS				
		Gms.	G	A	Pts.	PIM	+/-	PP	SH	Gms.	G	A	Pts.	PIM
95-96—Cornwall	Tier II	64	68	53	121	162	...	...	...	—	—	—	—	—
96-97—Ohio State	CCHA	39	12	11	23	78	...	...	...	—	—	—	—	—
97-98—Ohio State	CCHA	42	26	22	48	86	...	...	...	—	—	—	—	—
98-99—Ohio State	CCHA	35	11	16	27	87	...	...	...	—	—	—	—	—
99-00—Ohio State	CCHA	35	20	11	31	*136	...	...	...	—	—	—	—	—
00-01—Wilkes-Barre/Scranton	AHL	79	20	20	40	72	...	...	...	21	6	10	16	17
01-02—Wilkes-Barre/Scranton	AHL	55	13	14	27	91	...	...	...	—	—	—	—	—
—Pittsburgh	NHL	23	0	1	1	8	-7	0	0	—	—	—	—	—
02-03—Wilkes-Barre/Scranton	AHL	59	12	17	29	95	...	...	...	—	—	—	—	—
—Pittsburgh	NHL	13	5	1	6	4	-2	2	0	—	—	—	—	—
NHL Totals (2 years)		36	5	2	7	12	-9	2	0					

MESSIER, ERIC　　　　　LW　　　　　PANTHERS

PERSONAL: Born October 29, 1973, in Drummondville, Que. ... 6-2/195. ... Shoots left. ... Name pronounced MEHZ-yay.
TRANSACTIONS/CAREER NOTES: Signed as non-drafted free agent by Colorado Avalanche (June 14, 1995). ... Sprained ankle (October 28, 1997); missed three games. ... Fractured left elbow (October 10, 1998); missed 27 games. ... Injured eye (December 19, 1998); missed two games. ... Suffered injury (November 26, 1999); missed one game. ... Fractured lower leg (February 19, 2001); missed 17 games. ... Injured knee (January 15, 2002); missed eight games. ... Traded by Colorado Avalanche to Florida Panthers with C Vaclav Nedorost for F Peter Worrell and 2004 second-round draft pick (July 20, 2003).

M

Season Team	League	REGULAR SEASON								PLAYOFFS				
		Gms.	G	A	Pts.	PIM	+/-	PP	SH	Gms.	G	A	Pts.	PIM
91-92—Trois-Rivieres	QMJHL	58	2	10	12	28	...	...	...	15	2	2	4	13
92-93—Sherbrooke	QMJHL	51	4	17	21	82	...	...	...	15	0	4	4	18
93-94—Sherbrooke	QMJHL	67	4	24	28	69	...	...	...	12	1	7	8	14
94-95—Univ. of Quebec	OUAA	13	8	5	13	20	...	...	...	4	0	3	3	8
95-96—Cornwall	AHL	72	5	9	14	111	...	...	...	8	1	1	2	20
96-97—Hershey	AHL	55	16	26	42	69	...	...	...	9	3	8	11	14
—Colorado	NHL	21	0	0	0	4	7	0	0	6	0	0	0	4
97-98—Colorado	NHL	62	4	12	16	20	4	0	0	—	—	—	—	—
98-99—Colorado	NHL	31	4	2	6	14	0	1	0	3	0	0	0	0
—Hershey	AHL	6	1	3	4	4	...	...	...	—	—	—	—	—
99-00—Colorado	NHL	61	3	6	9	24	0	1	0	14	0	1	1	4
00-01—Colorado	NHL	64	5	7	12	26	-3	0	0	23	2	2	4	14
01-02—Colorado	NHL	74	5	10	15	26	-5	0	0	21	1	2	3	0
02-03—Colorado	NHL	72	4	10	14	16	-2	0	1	5	0	0	0	0
NHL Totals (7 years)		385	25	47	72	130	1	2	1	72	3	5	8	22

MESSIER, MARK　　　　　C

PERSONAL: Born January 18, 1961, in Edmonton ... 6-1/213. ... Shoots left. ... Full Name: Mark Douglas Messier. ... Brother of Paul Messier, center with Colorado Rockies (1978-79); cousin of Mitch Messier, center/right winger with Minnesota North Stars (1987-88 through 1990-91); cousin of Joby Messier, defenseman with New York Rangers (1992-93 through 1994-95); and brother-in-law of John Blum, defenseman with four NHL teams (1982-83 through 1989-90). ... Name pronounced MEHZ-yay.
TRANSACTIONS/CAREER NOTES: Signed as non-drafted free agent to 10-game trial by Indianapolis Racers (November 5, 1978). ... Signed as free agent by Cincinnati Stingers of WHA (December 1978). ... Selected by Edmonton Oilers in third round (second Oilers pick, 48th overall) of NHL entry draft (August 9, 1979). ... Injured ankle (November 7, 1981). ... Fractured wrist (March 1983). ... Suspended six games by NHL for hitting another player with stick (January 18, 1984). ... Sprained knee ligaments (November 1984). ... Suspended 10 games by NHL for injuring another player (December 26, 1984). ... Bruised left foot (December 3, 1985); missed 17 games. ... Suspended six games by NHL for injuring another player with his stick (October 23, 1988). ... Twisted left knee (January 28, 1989). ... Strained right knee (February 3, 1989). ... Bruised left knee (February 12, 1989). ... Sprained left knee ligaments (October 16, 1990); missed 10 games. ... Reinjured left knee (December 12, 1990); missed three games. ... Reinjured knee (December 22, 1990); missed nine games. ... Fractured left thumb (February 11, 1991); missed eight games. ... Missed one game due to contract dispute (October 1991). ... Traded by Oilers with future considerations to New York Rangers for C Bernie Nicholls, LW Louie DeBrusk, RW Steven Rice and future considerations (October 4, 1991); Oilers traded D Jeff Beukeboom to Rangers for D David Shaw to complete deal (November 12, 1991). ... Sprained ligament in wrist (January 19, 1993); missed six games. ... Strained rib cage muscle (February 27, 1993); missed two games. ... Strained rib cage muscle (March 11, 1993); missed one game. ... Suspended three off-days and fined $500 by NHL for stick-swinging incident (March 18, 1993). ... Sprained wrist (December

22, 1993); missed six games. ... Bruised thigh (March 16, 1994); missed two games. ... Suffered back spasms (April 30, 1995); missed two games. ... Bruised shoulder (February 27, 1996); missed two games. ... Bruised ribs (April 4, 1996); missed six games. ... Suspended two games and fined $1,000 by NHL for checking opponent from behind (October 8, 1996). ... Hyperextended elbow (December 7, 1996); missed four games. ... Suffered back spasms (February 23, 1997); missed two games. ... Suffered charley horse (March 27, 1997); missed two games. ... Signed as free agent by Vancouver Canucks (July 28, 1997). ... Suffered concussion (December 22, 1998); missed one game. ... Sprained medial collateral ligament in knee (February 11, 1999); missed 18 games. ... Injured groin (March 31, 1999); missed four games. ... Sprained medial collateral ligament in knee (November 9, 1999); missed 15 games. ... Injured knee (December 29, 2000); missed one game. ... Signed as free agent by Rangers (July 13, 2000). ... Strained muscle in ribs (October 13, 2001); missed two games. ... Suffered back spasms and strained shoulder (December 6, 2001); missed one game. ... Suffered back spasms and reinjured shoulder (December 17, 2001); missed four games. ... Reinjured shoulder (January 2, 2002); missed 11 games. ... Reinjured shoulder (February 13, 2002); missed remainder of season.

STATISTICAL PLATEAUS: Three-goal games: 1980-81 (1), 1981-82 (2), 1982-83 (1), 1983-84 (2), 1985-86 (1), 1987-88 (1), 1989-90 (2), 1991-92 (2), 1995-96 (1), 1996-97 (2). Total: 15. ... Four-goal games: 1982-83 (1), 1988-89 (1), 1989-90 (1), 1991-92 (1). Total: 4. ... Total hat tricks: 19.

			REGULAR SEASON							PLAYOFFS				
Season Team	League	Gms.	G	A	Pts.	PIM	+/-	PP	SH	Gms.	G	A	Pts.	PIM
76-77—Spruce Grove.............	AJHL	57	27	39	66	91				—	—	—	—	—
77-78—St. Albert	AJHL						Statistics unavailable.							
—Portland	WHL	—	—	—	—	—	—	—	—	7	4	1	5	2
78-79—Indianapolis	WHA	5	0	0	0	0	...	...	...	—	—	—	—	—
—Cincinnati..................	WHA	47	1	10	11	58	...	...	...	—	—	—	—	—
79-80—Houston	CHL	4	0	3	3	4	...	...	...	—	—	—	—	—
—Edmonton	NHL	75	12	21	33	120	-10	1	1	3	1	2	3	2
80-81—Edmonton	NHL	72	23	40	63	102	-12	4	0	9	2	5	7	13
81-82—Edmonton	NHL	78	50	38	88	119	21	10	0	5	1	2	3	8
82-83—Edmonton	NHL	77	48	58	106	72	19	12	1	15	15	6	21	14
83-84—Edmonton	NHL	73	37	64	101	165	40	7	4	19	8	18	26	19
84-85—Edmonton	NHL	55	23	31	54	57	8	4	5	18	12	13	25	12
85-86—Edmonton	NHL	63	35	49	84	68	36	10	5	10	4	6	10	18
86-87—Edmonton	NHL	77	37	70	107	73	21	7	4	21	12	16	28	16
87-88—Edmonton	NHL	77	37	74	111	103	21	12	3	19	11	23	34	29
88-89—Edmonton	NHL	72	33	61	94	130	-5	6	6	7	1	11	12	8
89-90—Edmonton	NHL	79	45	84	129	79	19	13	6	22	9	*22	†31	20
90-91—Edmonton	NHL	53	12	52	64	34	15	3	1	18	4	11	15	16
91-92—New York Rangers......	NHL	79	35	72	107	76	31	12	4	11	7	7	14	6
92-93—New York Rangers......	NHL	75	25	66	91	72	-6	7	2	—	—	—	—	—
93-94—New York Rangers......	NHL	76	26	58	84	76	25	6	2	23	12	18	30	33
94-95—New York Rangers......	NHL	46	14	39	53	40	8	3	3	10	3	10	13	8
95-96—New York Rangers......	NHL	74	47	52	99	122	29	14	1	11	4	7	11	16
96-97—New York Rangers......	NHL	71	36	48	84	88	12	7	5	15	3	9	12	6
97-98—Vancouver	NHL	82	22	38	60	58	-10	8	2	—	—	—	—	—
98-99—Vancouver	NHL	59	13	35	48	33	-12	4	2	—	—	—	—	—
99-00—Vancouver	NHL	66	17	37	54	30	-15	6	0	—	—	—	—	—
00-01—New York Rangers......	NHL	82	24	43	67	89	-25	12	3	—	—	—	—	—
01-02—New York Rangers......	NHL	41	7	16	23	32	-1	2	0	—	—	—	—	—
02-03—New York Rangers......	NHL	78	18	22	40	30	-2	8	1	—	—	—	—	—
WHA Totals (1 year)		52	1	10	11	58	...	...	...					
NHL Totals (24 years).........		1680	676	1168	1844	1868	207	178	61	236	109	186	295	244

METHOT, FRANCOIS   C   SABRES

PERSONAL: Born April 26, 1978, in Montreal. ... 6-0/175. ... Shoots right. ... Name pronounced meh-TOH.
TRANSACTIONS/CAREER NOTES: Selected by Buffalo Sabres in third round (fourth Sabres pick, 54th overall) of NHL entry draft (June 22, 1996).

			REGULAR SEASON							PLAYOFFS				
Season Team	League	Gms.	G	A	Pts.	PIM	+/-	PP	SH	Gms.	G	A	Pts.	PIM
94-95—St. Hyacinthe	QMJHL	60	14	38	52	22	...	...	...	5	0	1	1	0
95-96—St. Hyacinthe	QMJHL	68	32	62	94	22	...	...	...	12	6	6	12	4
96-97—Rouyn-Noranda	QMJHL	47	21	30	51	22	...	...	...	—	—	—	—	—
—Shawinigan.................	QMJHL	18	9	17	26	2	...	...	...	7	2	6	8	2
97-98—Shawinigan.................	QMJHL	36	23	42	65	10	...	...	...	6	1	3	4	5
98-99—Rochester	AHL	58	5	3	8	8	...	...	...	9	0	1	1	0
99-00—Rochester	AHL	80	14	18	32	20	...	...	...	21	2	4	6	16
00-01—Rochester	AHL	79	22	33	55	35	...	...	...	4	1	3	4	0
01-02—Rochester	AHL	59	17	17	34	28	...	...	...	2	1	0	1	0
02-03—Rochester	AHL	58	19	34	53	22	...	...	...	—	—	—	—	—

METROPOLIT, GLEN   C   CAPITALS

PERSONAL: Born June 25, 1974, in Toronto ... 5-10/193. ... Shoots right.
TRANSACTIONS/CAREER NOTES: Signed as non-drafted free agent by Washington Capitals (July 20, 1999). ... Claimed by Tampa Bay Lightning from Capitals in NHL waiver draft (September 28, 2001). ... Claimed on waivers by Capitals (October 20, 2001).

			REGULAR SEASON							PLAYOFFS				
Season Team	League	Gms.	G	A	Pts.	PIM	+/-	PP	SH	Gms.	G	A	Pts.	PIM
92-93—Richmond Hill.............	OJHL	43	27	36	63	36	...	...	...	—	—	—	—	—
93-94—Richmond Hill.............	OJHL	49	38	62	100	83	...	...	...	—	—	—	—	—
94-95—Vernon	BCJHL	60	43	74	117	92	...	...	...	—	—	—	—	—
95-96—Nashville	ECHL	58	30	31	61	62	...	...	...	5	3	8	11	2
—Atlanta	IHL	1	0	0	0	0	...	...	...	—	—	—	—	—

Season Team	League	REGULAR SEASON								PLAYOFFS				
		Gms.	G	A	Pts.	PIM	+/-	PP	SH	Gms.	G	A	Pts.	PIM
96-97—Pensacola	ECHL	54	35	47	82	45	...	...	...	12	9	16	25	28
—Quebec	IHL	22	5	4	9	14	...	...	...	5	0	0	0	2
97-98—Grand Rapids	IHL	79	20	35	55	90	...	...	...	3	1	1	2	0
98-99—Grand Rapids	IHL	77	28	53	81	92	...	...	...	—	—	—	—	—
99-00—Washington	NHL	30	6	13	19	4	5	1	0	2	0	0	0	2
—Portland	AHL	48	18	42	60	73	...	...	...	1	1	0	1	0
00-01—Washington	NHL	15	1	5	6	10	-2	0	0	1	0	0	0	0
—Portland	AHL	51	25	42	67	59	...	...	...	—	—	—	—	—
01-02—Tampa Bay	NHL	2	0	0	0	0	-2	0	0	—	—	—	—	—
—Portland	AHL	32	17	22	39	20	...	...	...	—	—	—	—	—
—Washington	NHL	33	1	16	17	6	3	0	0	—	—	—	—	—
02-03—Portland	AHL	33	7	23	30	23	...	...	...	—	—	—	—	—
—Washington	NHL	23	2	3	5	6	4	0	0	—	—	—	—	—
NHL Totals (4 years)		103	10	37	47	26	8	1	0	3	0	0	0	2

MEZEI, BRANISLAV — D — PANTHERS

PERSONAL: Born October 8, 1980, in Nitra, Czechoslovakia ... 6-5/236. ... Shoots left. ... Name pronounced MEE-zy.
TRANSACTIONS/CAREER NOTES: Selected by New York Islanders in first round (third Islanders pick, 10th overall) of NHL entry draft (June 26, 1999). ... Separated left shoulder (January 16, 2001); missed 13 games. ... Traded by Islanders to Florida Panthers for C Jason Wiemer (July 3, 2002). ... Re-signed by Florida (June 12, 2003).

Season Team	League	REGULAR SEASON								PLAYOFFS				
		Gms.	G	A	Pts.	PIM	+/-	PP	SH	Gms.	G	A	Pts.	PIM
96-97—Plastika Nitra	Slovakia Jrs.	40	8	17	25	42	...	...	...	—	—	—	—	—
97-98—Belleville	OHL	53	3	5	8	58	...	...	...	8	0	2	2	8
98-99—Belleville	OHL	60	5	18	23	90	...	...	...	18	0	4	4	29
99-00—Belleville	OHL	58	7	21	28	99	...	...	...	6	0	3	3	10
00-01—Lowell	AHL	20	0	3	3	28	...	...	...	—	—	—	—	—
—New York Islanders	NHL	42	1	4	5	53	-5	0	0	—	—	—	—	—
01-02—Bridgeport	AHL	59	1	9	10	137	...	...	...	20	0	3	3	48
—New York Islanders	NHL	24	0	2	2	12	2	0	0	—	—	—	—	—
02-03—San Antonio	AHL	1	0	0	0	0	...	...	...	—	—	—	—	—
—Florida	NHL	11	2	0	2	10	-2	0	0	—	—	—	—	—
NHL Totals (3 years)		77	3	6	9	75	-5	0	0					

MICHAUD, OLIVIER — G — CANADIENS

PERSONAL: Born September 14, 1983, in Beloeil, Que. ... 5-11/160. ... Catches left.
TRANSACTIONS/CAREER NOTES: Signed as non-drafted free agent by Montreal Canadiens (September 18, 2001).

Season Team	League	REGULAR SEASON									PLAYOFFS							
		Gms.	Min.	W	L	T	GA	SO	Avg.	SV%	Gms.	Min.	W	L	GA	SO	Avg.	SV%
99-00—Shawinigan	QMJHL	1	49	0	1	0	2	0	2.45	—	—	—	—	—	—	—	—	—
00-01—Shawinigan	QMJHL	21	1096	12	4	4	54	1	2.96	—	3	150	1	2	6	0	2.40	—
01-02—Shawinigan	QMJHL	46	2650	29	11	3	108	3	*2.45	—	12	744	7	5	36	0	2.90	—
—Montreal	NHL	1	18	0	0	0	0	0	...	1.000	—	—	—	—	—	—	—	—
02-03—Baie-Comeau	QMJHL	71	1775	23	5	2	90	3	3.04	—	—	—	—	—	—	—	—	—
NHL Totals (1 year)		1	18	0	0	0	0	0	...	1.000								

MILLER, AARON — D — KINGS

PERSONAL: Born August 11, 1971, in Buffalo ... 6-4/218. ... Shoots right. ... Full Name: Aaron Michael Miller.
TRANSACTIONS/CAREER NOTES: Selected by New York Rangers in fifth round (sixth Rangers pick, 88th overall) of NHL entry draft (June 17, 1989). ... Traded by Rangers with fifth-round pick (LW Bill Lindsay) in 1991 draft to Quebec Nordiques for D Joe Cirella (January 17, 1991). ... Nordiques franchise moved to Colorado and renamed Avalanche for 1995-96 season (June 21, 1995). ... Suffered concussion (October 24, 1998); missed one game. ... Bruised knee (November 8, 1998); missed one game. ... Suffered back spasms (March 17, 1999); missed three games. ... Bruised sternum (November 17, 1999); missed 27 games. ... Bruised right hand (November 22, 2000); missed five games. ... Traded by Avalanche with RW Adam Deadmarsh, first-round pick (C David Steckel) in 2001 draft, a player to be named later and first-round pick in 2003 draft to Los Angeles Kings for C Steve Reinprecht and D Rob Blake (February 21, 2001); Kings acquired C Jared Aulin to complete deal (March 22, 2001). ... Sprained wrist (March 19, 2001); missed final nine games of season. ... Suffered back spasms (October 20, 2001); missed eight games.

Season Team	League	REGULAR SEASON								PLAYOFFS				
		Gms.	G	A	Pts.	PIM	+/-	PP	SH	Gms.	G	A	Pts.	PIM
87-88—Niagara	NAJHL	30	4	9	13	2	...	...	...	—	—	—	—	—
88-89—Niagara	NAJHL	59	24	38	62	60	...	...	...	—	—	—	—	—
89-90—Univ. of Vermont	ECAC	31	1	15	16	24	...	...	...	—	—	—	—	—
90-91—Univ. of Vermont	ECAC	30	3	7	10	22	...	...	...	—	—	—	—	—
91-92—Univ. of Vermont	ECAC	31	3	16	19	36	...	...	...	—	—	—	—	—
92-93—Univ. of Vermont	ECAC	30	4	13	17	16	...	...	...	—	—	—	—	—
93-94—Cornwall	AHL	64	4	10	14	49	...	...	...	13	0	2	2	10
—Quebec	NHL	1	0	0	0	0	-1	0	0	—	—	—	—	—
94-95—Cornwall	AHL	76	4	18	22	69	...	...	...	—	—	—	—	—
—Quebec	NHL	9	0	3	3	6	2	0	0	—	—	—	—	—
95-96—Cornwall	AHL	62	4	23	27	77	...	...	...	8	0	1	1	6
—Colorado	NHL	5	0	0	0	0	0	0	0	—	—	—	—	—
96-97—Colorado	NHL	56	5	12	17	15	15	0	0	17	1	2	3	10

Season Team	League	REGULAR SEASON								PLAYOFFS				
		Gms.	G	A	Pts.	PIM	+/-	PP	SH	Gms.	G	A	Pts.	PIM
97-98—Colorado	NHL	55	2	2	4	51	0	0	0	7	0	0	0	8
98-99—Colorado	NHL	76	5	13	18	42	3	1	0	19	1	5	6	10
99-00—Colorado	NHL	53	1	7	8	36	3	0	0	17	1	1	2	6
00-01—Colorado	NHL	56	4	9	13	29	19	0	0	—	—	—	—	—
—Los Angeles	NHL	13	0	5	5	14	3	0	0	13	0	1	1	6
01-02—U.S. Olympic team	Int'l	6	0	0	0	4	...			—	—	—	—	—
—Los Angeles	NHL	74	5	12	17	54	14	0	1	7	0	0	0	0
02-03—Los Angeles	NHL	49	1	5	6	24	-7	0	0	—	—	—	—	—
NHL Totals (10 years)		447	23	68	91	271	51	1	1	80	3	9	12	40

MILLER, KIP — LW — CAPITALS

PERSONAL: Born June 11, 1969, in Lansing, Mich. ... 5-10/188. ... Shoots left. ... Full Name: Kip Charles Miller. ... Brother of Kelly Miller, right winger with New York Rangers (1984-85 through 1986-87) and Washington Capitals (1986-87 through 1998-99); and brother of Kevin Miller, left winger with nine NHL teams (1988-89 through 1999-2000).

TRANSACTIONS/CAREER NOTES: Selected by Quebec Nordiques in fourth round (fourth Nordiques pick, 72nd overall) of NHL entry draft (June 13, 1987). ... Traded by Nordiques to Minnesota North Stars for LW Steve Maltais (March 8, 1992). ... North Stars franchise moved from Minnesota to Dallas and renamed Stars for 1993-94 season. ... Signed as free agent by San Jose Sharks (August 10, 1993). ... Signed as free agent by New York Islanders (August 2, 1994). ... Signed as free agent by Chicago Blackhawks (August 10, 1995). ... Signed as free agent by Islanders (November 26, 1997). ... Selected by Pittsburgh Penguins from Islanders in NHL waiver draft (October 5, 1998). ... Injured eye (March 20, 1999); missed one game. ... Sprained knee (October 30, 1999); missed one game. ... Traded by Penguins to Mighty Ducks of Anaheim for future considerations (January 30, 2000). ... Signed as free agent by Penguins (September 24, 2000). ... Strained groin (November 28, 2000); missed four games. ... Signed as free agent by Islanders (January 17, 2002). ... Signed as free agent by Washington Capitals (July 9, 2002).

Season Team	League	REGULAR SEASON								PLAYOFFS				
		Gms.	G	A	Pts.	PIM	+/-	PP	SH	Gms.	G	A	Pts.	PIM
86-87—Michigan State	CCHA	41	20	19	39	92	...	...	...	—	—	—	—	—
87-88—Michigan State	CCHA	39	16	25	41	51	...	...	...	—	—	—	—	—
88-89—Michigan State	CCHA	47	32	45	77	94	...	...	...	—	—	—	—	—
89-90—Michigan State	CCHA	45	*48	53	*101	60	...	...	...	—	—	—	—	—
90-91—Quebec	NHL	13	4	3	7	7	-1	0	0	—	—	—	—	—
—Halifax	AHL	66	36	33	69	40	...			—	—	—	—	—
91-92—Quebec	NHL	36	5	10	15	12	-21	1	0	—	—	—	—	—
—Halifax	AHL	24	9	17	26	8	...			—	—	—	—	—
—Minnesota	NHL	3	1	2	3	2	-1	1	0	—	—	—	—	—
—Kalamazoo	IHL	6	1	8	9	4	...			12	3	9	12	12
92-93—Kalamazoo	IHL	61	17	39	56	59	...			—	—	—	—	—
93-94—San Jose	NHL	11	2	2	4	6	-1	0	0	—	—	—	—	—
—Kansas City	IHL	71	38	54	92	51	...			—	—	—	—	—
94-95—Denver	IHL	71	46	60	106	54	...			17	*15	14	29	8
—New York Islanders	NHL	8	0	1	1	0	1	0	0	—	—	—	—	—
95-96—Indianapolis	IHL	73	32	59	91	46	...			5	2	6	8	2
—Chicago	NHL	10	1	4	5	2	1	0	0	—	—	—	—	—
96-97—Chicago	IHL	43	11	41	52	32	...			—	—	—	—	—
—Indianapolis	IHL	37	17	24	41	18	...			4	2	2	4	2
97-98—Utah	IHL	72	38	59	97	30	...			4	3	2	5	10
—New York Islanders	NHL	9	1	3	4	2	-2	0	0	—	—	—	—	—
98-99—Pittsburgh	NHL	77	19	23	42	22	1	1	0	13	2	7	9	19
99-00—Pittsburgh	NHL	44	4	15	19	10	-1	0	0	—	—	—	—	—
—Anaheim	NHL	30	6	17	23	4	1	2	0	—	—	—	—	—
00-01—Pittsburgh	NHL	33	3	8	11	6	0	1	0	—	—	—	—	—
—Grand Rapids	IHL	34	16	19	35	12	...			10	5	8	13	2
01-02—Grand Rapids	AHL	41	21	35	56	27	...			—	—	—	—	—
—New York Islanders	NHL	37	7	17	24	6	2	2	0	7	4	2	6	2
02-03—Washington	NHL	72	12	38	50	18	-1	3	0	5	0	2	2	2
NHL Totals (11 years)		383	65	143	208	97	-22	11	0	25	6	11	17	23

MILLER, RYAN — G — SABRES

PERSONAL: Born July 17, 1980, in East Lansing, Mich. ... 6-2/166. ... Catches left.
TRANSACTIONS/CAREER NOTES: Selected by Buffalo Sabres in fifth round (seventh Sabres pick, 138th overall) of NHL entry draft (June 26, 1999).

Season Team	League	REGULAR SEASON									PLAYOFFS							
		Gms.	Min	W	L	T	GA	SO	Avg.	SV%	Gms.	Min.	W	L	GA	SO	Avg.	SV%
98-99—Soo	NAHL	47	2711	31	14	1	104	8	2.30	—	4	218	2	2	10	1	2.75	—
99-00—Michigan State	CCHA	26	1525	16	4	3	39	*8	*1.53	—	—	—	—	—	—	—	—	—
00-01—Michigan State	CCHA	40	2447	*31	5	4	54	*10	*1.32	—	—	—	—	—	—	—	—	—
01-02—Michigan State	CCHA	40	2411	26	9	†5	71	*8	*1.77	—	—	—	—	—	—	—	—	—
02-03—Rochester	AHL	47	2816	23	18	5	110	2	2.34	—	—	—	—	—	—	—	—	—
—Buffalo	NHL	15	912	6	8	1	40	1	2.63	.902	—	—	—	—	—	—	—	—
NHL Totals (1 year)		15	912	6	8	1	40	1	2.63	.902								

MILLEY, NORM — RW — SABRES

PERSONAL: Born February 14, 1980, in Toronto ... 6-0/205. ... Shoots right. ... Full Name: Norman Milley.
TRANSACTIONS/CAREER NOTES: Selected by Buffalo Sabres in second round (third Sabres pick, 47th overall) of NHL entry draft (June 27, 1998).

M

Season Team	League	REGULAR SEASON								PLAYOFFS				
		Gms.	G	A	Pts.	PIM	+/-	PP	SH	Gms.	G	A	Pts.	PIM
95-96—Toronto Red Wings.....	MTHL	42	42	36	78	109	...	...	...	—	—	—	—	—
96-97—Sudbury	OHL	61	30	32	62	15	...	...	...	—	—	—	—	—
97-98—Sudbury	OHL	62	33	41	74	48	...	...	...	10	0	1	1	4
98-99—Sudbury	OHL	68	52	68	120	47	...	...	...	4	2	3	5	4
99-00—Sudbury	OHL	68	*52	60	112	47	...	...	...	12	8	11	19	6
00-01—Rochester	AHL	77	20	27	47	56	...	...	...	4	0	0	0	2
01-02—Rochester	AHL	74	20	18	38	20	...	...	...	2	0	3	3	6
—Buffalo	NHL	5	0	1	1	0	0	0	0	—	—	—	—	—
02-03—Rochester	AHL	67	16	32	48	39	...	...	...	—	—	—	—	—
—Buffalo	NHL	8	0	2	2	6	-2	0	0	—	—	—	—	—
NHL Totals (2 years)		13	0	3	3	6	-2	0	0					

MILLS, CRAIG   RW

PERSONAL: Born August 27, 1976, in Toronto. ... 6-0/195. ... Shoots right.

TRANSACTIONS/CAREER NOTES: Selected by Winnipeg Jets in fifth round (fifth Jets pick, 108th overall) of NHL entry draft (June 29, 1994). ... Jets franchise moved to Phoenix and renamed Coyotes for 1996-97 season; NHL approved move on January 18, 1996. ... Traded by Coyotes with C Alexei Zhamnov and first-round pick (RW Ty Jones) in 1997 draft to Chicago Blackhawks for C Jeremy Roenick (August 16, 1996). ... Traded by Blackhawks to Coyotes for future considerations (September 11, 1999). ... Traded by Coyotes with C Robert Reichel and C Travis Green to Toronto Maple Leafs for D Danny Markov (June 12, 2001).

Season Team	League	REGULAR SEASON								PLAYOFFS				
		Gms.	G	A	Pts.	PIM	+/-	PP	SH	Gms.	G	A	Pts.	PIM
92-93—St. Michael's	Tier II Jr. A	44	8	12	20	51	...	...	...	—	—	—	—	—
93-94—Belleville	OHL	63	15	18	33	88	...	...	...	12	2	1	3	11
94-95—Belleville	OHL	62	39	41	80	104	...	...	...	13	7	9	16	8
95-96—Belleville	OHL	48	10	19	29	113	...	...	...	14	4	5	9	32
—Winnipeg	NHL	4	0	2	2	0	0	0	0	1	0	0	0	0
—Springfield	AHL	—	—	—	—	—				2	0	0	0	0
96-97—Indianapolis	IHL	80	12	7	19	199	...	...	...	4	0	0	0	4
97-98—Chicago	NHL	20	0	3	3	34	1	0	0	—	—	—	—	—
—Indianapolis	IHL	42	8	11	19	119	...	...	...	5	0	0	0	27
98-99—Chicago	NHL	7	0	0	0	2	-2	0	0	—	—	—	—	—
—Chicago	IHL	5	0	0	0	14	...	...	...	—	—	—	—	—
—Indianapolis	IHL	12	2	3	5	14	...	...	...	6	1	0	1	5
99-00—Springfield	AHL	78	10	13	23	151	...	...	...	5	2	1	3	6
00-01—Springfield	AHL	64	8	5	13	131	...	...	...	—	—	—	—	—
01-02—St. John's	AHL	74	10	21	31	137	...	...	...	11	3	3	6	22
02-03—St. John's	AHL	65	10	16	26	121	...	...	...	—	—	—	—	—
NHL Totals (3 years)		31	0	5	5	36	-1	0	0	1	0	0	0	0

MILROY, DUNCAN   RW   CANADIENS

PERSONAL: Born February 8, 1983, in Edmonton. ... 6-0/180. ... Shoots right.

TRANSACTIONS/CAREER NOTES: Selected by Montreal Canadiens in second round (third Canadiens pick, 37th overall) of NHL entry draft (June 23, 2001). ... Signed by Montreal (May 30, 2003).

Season Team	League	REGULAR SEASON								PLAYOFFS				
		Gms.	G	A	Pts.	PIM	+/-	PP	SH	Gms.	G	A	Pts.	PIM
98-99—Swift Current	WHL	3	0	0	0	0	...	...	...	—	—	—	—	—
99-00—Swift Current	WHL	68	15	15	30	20	...	...	...	12	3	5	8	12
00-01—Swift Current	WHL	68	38	54	92	51	...	...	...	19	9	12	21	6
01-02—Swift Current	WHL	26	20	11	31	20	...	...	...	—	—	—	—	—
—Kootenay	WHL	38	25	31	56	24	...	...	...	22	*17	*20	*37	26
02-03—Kootenay	WHL	61	34	44	78	40	...	...	...	—	—	—	—	—

MIRONOV, BORIS   D

PERSONAL: Born March 21, 1972, in Moscow, U.S.S.R. ... 6-3/225. ... Shoots right. ... Brother of Dmitri Mironov, defenseman with five NHL teams (1991-92 through 2000-01). ... Name pronounced MIHR-ih-nahf.

TRANSACTIONS/CAREER NOTES: Selected by Winnipeg Jets in second round (second Jets pick, 27th overall) of NHL entry draft (June 20, 1992). ... Traded by Jets with C Mats Lindgren and first- (C Jason Bonsignore) and fourth-round (RW Adam Copeland) picks in 1994 draft to Edmonton Oilers for D Dave Manson and sixth-round pick (D Chris Kibermanis) in 1994 draft (March 15, 1994). ... Bruised ankle (April 3, 1995); missed one game. ... Strained lower back (April 13, 1995); missed 10 games. ... Strained abdominal muscle (January 21, 1997); missed 12 games. ... Strained groin (February 19, 1997); missed five games. ... Strained groin (March 7, 1997); missed five games. ... Bruised right shoulder (February 3, 1999); missed two games. ... Traded by Oilers with LW Dean McAmmond and D Jonas Elofsson to Chicago Blackhawks for C Chad Kilger, LW Daniel Cleary, LW Ethan Moreau and D Christian Laflamme (March 20, 1999). ... Suffered charley horse (March 25, 1999); missed one game. ... Suffered hip pointer (December 4, 1999); missed one game. ... Sprained knee (March 26, 2000); missed final seven games of season. ... Tore ligament in wrist (January 25, 2001); missed 15 games. ... Strained side muscle (December 31, 2001); missed three games. ... Dislocated shoulder (March 11, 2002); missed nine games. ... Strained groin (April 3, 2002); missed final five games of season. ... Traded by Blackhawks to New York Rangers for fourth-round pick in 2004 draft (January 8, 2003).

Season Team	League	REGULAR SEASON								PLAYOFFS				
		Gms.	G	A	Pts.	PIM	+/-	PP	SH	Gms.	G	A	Pts.	PIM
88-89—CSKA Moscow	USSR	1	0	0	0	0	...	...	...	—	—	—	—	—
89-90—CSKA Moscow	USSR	7	0	0	0	0	...	...	...	—	—	—	—	—
90-91—CSKA Moscow	USSR	36	1	5	6	16	...	...	...	—	—	—	—	—
91-92—CSKA Moscow	CIS	36	2	1	3	22	...	...	...	—	—	—	—	—
92-93—CSKA Moscow	CIS	19	0	5	5	20	...	...	...	—	—	—	—	—
93-94—Winnipeg	NHL	65	7	22	29	96	-29	5	0	—	—	—	—	—
—Edmonton	NHL	14	0	2	2	14	-4	0	0	—	—	—	—	—
94-95—Cape Breton	AHL	4	2	5	7	23	...	...	...	—	—	—	—	—
—Edmonton	NHL	29	1	7	8	40	-9	0	0	—	—	—	—	—
95-96—Edmonton	NHL	78	8	24	32	101	-23	7	0	—	—	—	—	—
96-97—Edmonton	NHL	55	6	26	32	85	2	2	0	12	2	8	10	16
97-98—Edmonton	NHL	81	16	30	46	100	-8	10	1	12	3	3	6	27
—Russian Oly. team	Int'l	6	0	2	2	2	...	...	...	—	—	—	—	—
98-99—Edmonton	NHL	63	11	29	40	104	6	5	0	—	—	—	—	—
—Chicago	NHL	12	0	9	9	27	7	0	0	—	—	—	—	—
99-00—Chicago	NHL	58	9	28	37	72	-3	4	2	—	—	—	—	—
00-01—Chicago	NHL	66	5	17	22	42	-14	3	0	—	—	—	—	—
01-02—Chicago	NHL	64	4	14	18	68	15	0	0	1	0	0	0	2
—Russian Oly. team	Int'l	6	1	0	1	2	...	...	...	—	—	—	—	—
02-03—Chicago	NHL	20	3	1	4	22	-1	1	0	—	—	—	—	—
—New York Rangers	NHL	36	3	9	12	34	3	1	0	—	—	—	—	—
NHL Totals (10 years)		641	73	218	291	805	-58	38	3	25	5	11	16	45

MITCHELL, WILLIE   D   WILD

PERSONAL: Born April 23, 1977, in Port McNeill, B.C. ... 6-3/205. ... Shoots left. ... Full Name: Willis Mitchell.
TRANSACTIONS/CAREER NOTES: Selected by New Jersey Devils in eighth round (12th Devils pick, 199th overall) of NHL entry draft (June 22, 1996). ... Traded by Devils with future considerations to Minnesota Wild for D Sean O'Donnell (March 4, 2001). ... Bruised right shoulder (October 16, 2001); missed five games. ... Strained groin (December 10, 2001); missed three games. ... Bruised left wrist (January 19, 2002); missed five games.

Season Team	League	REGULAR SEASON								PLAYOFFS				
		Gms.	G	A	Pts.	PIM	+/-	PP	SH	Gms.	G	A	Pts.	PIM
95-96—Melfort	Jr. A	19	2	6	8	0	...	...	...	14	0	2	2	12
96-97—Melfort	Jr. A	64	14	42	56	227	...	...	...	4	0	1	1	23
97-98—Clarkson	ECAC	34	9	17	26	105	...	...	...	—	—	—	—	—
98-99—Clarkson	ECAC	34	10	19	29	40	...	...	...	—	—	—	—	—
—Albany	AHL	6	1	3	4	29	...	...	...	—	—	—	—	—
99-00—Albany	AHL	63	5	14	19	71	...	...	...	5	1	2	3	4
—New Jersey	NHL	2	0	0	0	0	1	0	0	—	—	—	—	—
00-01—Albany	AHL	41	3	13	16	94	...	...	...	—	—	—	—	—
—New Jersey	NHL	16	0	2	2	29	0	0	0	—	—	—	—	—
—Minnesota	NHL	17	1	7	8	11	4	0	0	—	—	—	—	—
01-02—Minnesota	NHL	68	3	10	13	68	-16	0	0	—	—	—	—	—
02-03—Minnesota	NHL	69	2	12	14	84	13	0	1	18	1	3	4	14
NHL Totals (4 years)		172	6	31	37	192	2	0	1	18	1	3	4	14

MODANO, MIKE   C   STARS

PERSONAL: Born June 7, 1970, in Livonia, Mich. ... 6-3/205. ... Shoots left. ... Full Name: Michael Modano. ... Name pronounced muh-DAH-noh.
TRANSACTIONS/CAREER NOTES: Selected by Minnesota North Stars in first round (first North Stars pick, first overall) of NHL entry draft (June 11, 1988). ... Fractured nose (March 4, 1990). ... Pulled groin (November 30, 1992); missed two games. ... North Stars franchise moved from Minnesota to Dallas and renamed Stars for 1993-94 season. ... Strained medial collateral ligament in knee (January 6, 1994); missed six games. ... Suffered concussion (February 26, 1994); missed two games. ... Bruised ankle (March 12, 1995); missed four games. ... Ruptured tendons in ankle (April 4, 1995) and underwent surgery; missed remainder of season. ... Injured stomach muscle (November 9, 1995); missed four games. ... Suffered from the flu (February 9, 1997); missed one game. ... Bruised ankle (November 12, 1997); missed one game. ... Tore medial collateral ligament in knee (December 5, 1997); missed 10 games. ... Reinjured knee (January 2, 1998); missed two games. ... Separated shoulder (March 13, 1998); missed seven games. ... Strained groin (March 31, 1999); missed four games. ... Strained ligaments in neck, suffered concussion and fractured nose (October 2, 1999); missed three games. ... Suffered concussion (January 12, 2000); missed one game. ... Strained hip flexor (March 28, 2000); missed one game. ... Strained back (October 10, 2000); missed one game. ... Bruised thigh (October 20, 2001); missed one game. ... Strained lower back (November 7, 2001); missed two games.
STATISTICAL PLATEAUS: Three-goal games: 1989-90 (1), 1993-94 (1), 1997-98 (1), 1998-99 (3). Total: 6. ... Four-goal games: 1995-96 (1). ... Total hat tricks: 7.

Season Team	League	REGULAR SEASON								PLAYOFFS				
		Gms.	G	A	Pts.	PIM	+/-	PP	SH	Gms.	G	A	Pts.	PIM
86-87—Prince Albert	WHL	70	32	30	62	96	...	...	...	8	1	4	5	4
87-88—Prince Albert	WHL	65	47	80	127	80	...	...	...	9	7	11	18	18
88-89—Prince Albert	WHL	41	39	66	105	74	...	...	...	—	—	—	—	—
—Minnesota	NHL	—	—	—	—	—				2	0	0	0	0
89-90—Minnesota	NHL	80	29	46	75	63	-7	12	0	7	1	1	2	12
90-91—Minnesota	NHL	79	28	36	64	65	2	9	0	23	8	12	20	16
91-92—Minnesota	NHL	76	33	44	77	46	-9	5	0	7	3	2	5	4
92-93—Minnesota	NHL	82	33	60	93	83	-7	9	0	—	—	—	—	—
93-94—Dallas	NHL	76	50	43	93	54	-8	18	0	9	7	3	10	16
94-95—Dallas	NHL	30	12	17	29	8	7	4	1	—	—	—	—	—
95-96—Dallas	NHL	78	36	45	81	63	-12	8	4	—	—	—	—	—
96-97—Dallas	NHL	80	35	48	83	42	43	9	5	7	4	1	5	0

Season Team	League	REGULAR SEASON								PLAYOFFS				
		Gms.	G	A	Pts.	PIM	+/-	PP	SH	Gms.	G	A	Pts.	PIM
97-98—Dallas...............	NHL	52	21	38	59	32	25	7	5	17	4	10	14	12
—U.S. Olympic team......	Int'l	4	2	0	2	0	...	...	...	—	—	—	—	—
98-99—Dallas...............	NHL	77	34	47	81	44	29	6	4	23	5	*18	23	16
99-00—Dallas...............	NHL	77	38	43	81	48	0	11	1	23	10	†13	23	10
00-01—Dallas...............	NHL	81	33	51	84	52	26	8	3	9	3	4	7	0
01-02—Dallas...............	NHL	78	34	43	77	38	14	6	2	—	—	—	—	—
—U.S. Olympic team.....	Int'l	6	0	6	6	4	...	...	...	—	—	—	—	—
02-03—Dallas...............	NHL	79	28	57	85	30	34	5	2	12	5	10	15	4
NHL Totals (15 years).........		1025	444	618	1062	668	137	117	27	139	50	74	124	90

MODIN, FREDRIK   LW   LIGHTNING

PERSONAL: Born October 8, 1974, in Sundsvall, Sweden ... 6-4/220. ... Shoots left. ... Name pronounced moh-DEEN.
TRANSACTIONS/CAREER NOTES: Selected by Toronto Maple Leafs in third round (third Maple Leafs pick, 64th overall) of NHL entry draft (June 29, 1994). ... Suffered concussion (October 22, 1996); missed three games. ... Suffered from the flu (March 10, 1997); missed one game. ... Strained groin (December 2, 1997); missed two games. ... Fractured collar bone (February 13, 1999); missed 15 games. ... Traded by Maple Leafs to Tampa Bay Lightning for D Cory Cross and seventh-round pick (F Ivan Kolozvary) in 2001 draft (October 1, 1999). ... Bruised thigh (December 8, 2000); missed one game. ... Suffered from the flu (January 4, 2001); missed one game. ... Bruised hip (March 4, 2001); missed two games. ... Suffered charley horse (November 29, 2001); missed two games. ... Injured right wrist (January 26, 2002); missed 26 games. ... Re-signed by Lightning (July 17, 2003).
STATISTICAL PLATEAUS: Three-goal games: 2000-01 (1).

Season Team	League	REGULAR SEASON								PLAYOFFS				
		Gms.	G	A	Pts.	PIM	+/-	PP	SH	Gms.	G	A	Pts.	PIM
91-92—Sundsvall Timra.........	Sweden Dv. 2	11	1	0	1	0	...	...	...	—	—	—	—	—
92-93—Sundsvall Timra.........	Sweden Dv. 2	30	5	7	12	12	...	...	...	—	—	—	—	—
93-94—Sundsvall Timra.........	Sweden Dv. 2	30	16	15	31	36	...	...	...	—	—	—	—	—
94-95—Brynas Gavle	Sweden	38	9	10	19	33	...	...	...	14	4	4	8	6
95-96—Brynas Gavle	Sweden	22	4	8	12	22	...	...	...	—	—	—	—	—
96-97—Toronto	NHL	76	6	7	13	24	-14	0	0	—	—	—	—	—
97-98—Toronto	NHL	74	16	16	32	32	-5	1	0	—	—	—	—	—
98-99—Toronto	NHL	67	16	15	31	35	14	1	0	8	0	0	0	6
99-00—Tampa Bay	NHL	80	22	26	48	18	-26	3	0	—	—	—	—	—
00-01—Tampa Bay	NHL	76	32	24	56	48	-1	8	0	—	—	—	—	—
01-02—Tampa Bay	NHL	54	14	17	31	27	0	2	0	—	—	—	—	—
02-03—Tampa Bay	NHL	76	17	23	40	43	7	2	1	11	2	0	2	18
NHL Totals (7 years)............		503	123	128	251	227	-25	17	1	19	2	0	2	24

MODRY, JAROSLAV   D   KINGS

M

PERSONAL: Born February 27, 1971, in Ceske Budejovice, Czechoslovakia ... 6-2/226. ... Shoots left. ... Name pronounced MOH-dree.
TRANSACTIONS/CAREER NOTES: Selected by New Jersey Devils in ninth round (10th Devils pick, 179th overall) of NHL entry draft (June 16, 1990). ... Played in Europe during 1994-95 NHL lockout. ... Injured ankle (January 31, 1995); missed two games. ... Reinjured ankle (February 18, 1995); missed three games. ... Traded by Devils to Ottawa Senators for fourth-round pick (C Alyn McCauley) in 1995 draft (July 8, 1995). ... Ruptured eardrum (December 27, 1995). ... Traded by Senators to Los Angeles Kings for RW Kevin Brown (March 20, 1996). ... Sprained left knee (January 14, 1997); missed one game. ... Strained hip flexor (January 5, 2002); missed one game. ... Suffered from the flu (April 14, 2002); missed one game.

Season Team	League	REGULAR SEASON								PLAYOFFS				
		Gms.	G	A	Pts.	PIM	+/-	PP	SH	Gms.	G	A	Pts.	PIM
88-89—Budejovice	Czech.	28	0	1	1	...	...	...	...	—	—	—	—	—
89-90—Budejovice	Czech.	41	2	2	4	...	...	...	...	—	—	—	—	—
90-91—Dukla Trencin............	Czech.	33	1	9	10	6	...	...	...	—	—	—	—	—
91-92—Dukla Trencin............	Czech.	18	0	4	4	...	...	...	...	—	—	—	—	—
—Budejovice	Czech Dv.II	14	4	10	14	...	...	...	...	—	—	—	—	—
92-93—Utica	AHL	80	7	35	42	62	...	...	...	5	0	2	2	2
93-94—New Jersey	NHL	41	2	15	17	18	10	2	0	—	—	—	—	—
—Albany	AHL	19	1	5	6	25	...	...	...	—	—	—	—	—
94-95—HC Ceske Budejovice ..	Czech Rep.	19	1	3	4	30	...	...	...	—	—	—	—	—
—New Jersey	NHL	11	0	0	0	0	-1	0	0	—	—	—	—	—
—Albany	AHL	18	5	6	11	14	...	...	...	14	3	3	6	4
95-96—Ottawa	NHL	64	4	14	18	38	-17	1	0	—	—	—	—	—
—Los Angeles................	NHL	9	0	3	3	6	-4	0	0	—	—	—	—	—
96-97—Los Angeles................	NHL	30	3	3	6	25	-13	1	1	—	—	—	—	—
—Phoenix.....................	IHL	23	3	12	15	17	...	...	...	—	—	—	—	—
—Utah..........................	IHL	11	1	4	5	20	...	...	...	7	0	1	1	6
97-98—Utah..........................	IHL	74	12	21	33	72	...	...	...	4	0	2	2	6
98-99—Long Beach	IHL	64	6	29	35	44	...	...	...	8	4	2	6	4
—Los Angeles................	NHL	5	0	1	1	0	1	0	0	—	—	—	—	—
99-00—Los Angeles................	NHL	26	5	4	9	18	-2	5	0	2	0	0	0	2
—Long Beach	IHL	11	2	4	6	8	...	...	...	—	—	—	—	—
00-01—Los Angeles................	NHL	63	4	15	19	48	16	0	0	10	1	0	1	4
01-02—Los Angeles................	NHL	80	4	38	42	65	-4	4	0	7	0	2	2	0
02-03—Los Angeles................	NHL	82	13	25	38	68	-13	8	0	—	—	—	—	—
NHL Totals (9 years)............		411	35	118	153	286	-27	21	1	19	1	2	3	6

MOEN, TRAVIS   LW   BLACKHAWKS

PERSONAL: Born April 6, 1982, in Swift Current, Sask. ... 6-2/198. ... Shoots left.
TRANSACTIONS/CAREER NOTES: Selected by Calgary Flames in fifth round (sixth Flames pick, 141st overall) of NHL entry draft (June 24, 2000). ... Signed as free agent by Chicago Blackhawks (October 21, 2002).

Season Team	League	Gms.	G	A	Pts.	PIM	+/-	PP	SH	Gms.	G	A	Pts.	PIM
						REGULAR SEASON						PLAYOFFS		
99-00—Kelowna	WHL	66	9	6	15	96	...	...	...	—	—	—	—	—
00-01—Kelowna	WHL	40	8	8	16	106	...	...	...	—	—	—	—	—
01-02—Kelowna	WHL	71	10	17	27	197	...	...	...	13	1	0	1	28
02-03—Norfolk	AHL	42	1	2	3	62	...	...	...	—	—	—	—	—

MOGILNY, ALEXANDER   RW   MAPLE LEAFS

PERSONAL: Born February 18, 1969, in Khabarovsk, U.S.S.R. ... 6-0/209. ... Shoots left. ... Name pronounced moh-GIHL-nee.
TRANSACTIONS/CAREER NOTES: Selected by Buffalo Sabres in fifth round (fourth Sabres pick, 89th overall) of NHL entry draft (June 11, 1988). ... Suffered from the flu (November 26, 1989). ... Missed games due to fear of flying (January 22, 1990); spent remainder of season traveling on ground. ... Separated shoulder (February 8, 1991); missed six games. ... Suffered from the flu (November 1991); missed two games. ... Suffered from the flu (December 18, 1991); missed one game. ... Bruised shoulder (October 10, 1992); missed six games. ... Fractured fibula and tore ankle ligaments (May 6, 1993); missed remainder of 1992-93 playoffs and first nine games of 1993-94 season. ... Suffered sore ankle (February 2, 1994); missed four games. ... Suffered inflamed tendon in ankle (February 15, 1994); missed four games. ... Played in Europe during 1994-95 NHL lockout. ... Pinched nerve in neck (April 9, 1995); missed three games. ... Traded by Sabres with fifth-round pick (LW Todd Norman) in 1995 draft to Vancouver Canucks for RW Mike Peca, D Mike Wilson and first-round pick (D Jay McKee) in 1995 draft (July 8, 1995). ... Pulled hamstring (October 28, 1995); missed three games. ... Suffered from the flu (December 3, 1996); missed two games. ... Strained groin (April 4, 1997); missed remainder of season. ... Missed first 16 games of 1997-98 season due to contract dispute. ... Injured groin (December 15, 1997); missed 11 games. ... Strained back (February 24, 1998); missed four games. ... Sprained medial collateral ligament in knee (November 21, 1998); missed 17 games. ... Bruised kidney (January 4, 1999); missed two games. ... Strained abdominal muscle (February 20, 1999); missed four games. ... Injured back (November 26, 1999); missed eight games. ... Injured hip (January 12, 2000); missed seven games. ... Injured shoulder (February 12, 2000); missed eight games. ... Traded by Canucks to New Jersey Devils for C Brendan Morrison and C Denis Pederson (March 14, 2000). ... Injured neck (February 10, 2000); missed four games. ... Bruised abdomen (February 14, 2001); missed four games. ... Strained groin (April 4, 2001); missed one game. ... Signed as free agent by Toronto Maple Leafs (July 3, 2001). ... Suffered back spasms (January 12, 2002); missed three games. ... Injured back (January 29, 2002); missed 13 games.
STATISTICAL PLATEAUS: Three-goal games: 1990-91 (1), 1991-92 (1), 1992-93 (5), 1993-94 (1), 1995-96 (3), 1996-97 (1), 2000-01 (1), 2002-03 (2). Total: 15. ... Four-goal games: 1992-93 (2). ... Total hat tricks: 17.

Season Team	League	Gms.	G	A	Pts.	PIM	+/-	PP	SH	Gms.	G	A	Pts.	PIM
						REGULAR SEASON						PLAYOFFS		
86-87—CSKA Moscow	USSR	28	15	1	16	4	...	...	...	—	—	—	—	—
87-88—CSKA Moscow	USSR	39	12	8	20	20	...	...	...	—	—	—	—	—
88-89—CSKA Moscow	USSR	31	11	11	22	24	...	...	...	—	—	—	—	—
89-90—Buffalo	NHL	65	15	28	43	16	8	4	0	4	0	1	1	2
90-91—Buffalo	NHL	62	30	34	64	16	14	3	3	6	0	6	6	2
91-92—Buffalo	NHL	67	39	45	84	73	7	15	0	2	0	2	2	0
92-93—Buffalo	NHL	77	†76	51	127	40	7	27	0	7	7	3	10	6
93-94—Buffalo	NHL	66	32	47	79	22	8	17	0	7	4	2	6	6
94-95—Spartak Moscow	Russian	1	0	1	1	0	...	...	...	—	—	—	—	—
—Buffalo	NHL	44	19	28	47	36	0	12	0	5	3	2	5	2
95-96—Vancouver	NHL	79	55	52	107	16	14	10	5	6	1	8	9	8
96-97—Vancouver	NHL	76	31	42	73	18	9	7	1	—	—	—	—	—
97-98—Vancouver	NHL	51	18	27	45	36	-6	5	4	—	—	—	—	—
98-99—Vancouver	NHL	59	14	31	45	58	0	3	2	—	—	—	—	—
99-00—Vancouver	NHL	47	21	17	38	16	7	3	1	—	—	—	—	—
—New Jersey	NHL	12	3	3	6	4	-4	2	0	23	4	3	7	4
00-01—New Jersey	NHL	75	43	40	83	43	10	12	0	25	5	11	16	8
01-02—Toronto	NHL	66	24	33	57	8	1	5	0	20	8	3	11	8
02-03—Toronto	NHL	73	33	46	79	12	4	5	3	6	5	2	7	4
NHL Totals (14 years)		919	453	524	977	414	79	130	19	111	37	43	80	50

MONTADOR, STEVE   D   FLAMES

PERSONAL: Born December 21, 1979, in Vancouver ... 6-0/210. ... Shoots right.
TRANSACTIONS/CAREER NOTES: Signed as non-drafted free agent by Calgary Flames (September 5, 2000). ... Re-signed by Flames (June 25, 2003).

Season Team	League	Gms.	G	A	Pts.	PIM	+/-	PP	SH	Gms.	G	A	Pts.	PIM
						REGULAR SEASON						PLAYOFFS		
96-97—North Bay	OHL	63	7	28	35	129	...	...	...	—	—	—	—	—
97-98—North Bay	OHL	37	5	16	21	54	...	...	...	—	—	—	—	—
—Erie	OHL	26	3	17	20	35	...	...	...	7	1	1	2	8
98-99—Erie	OHL	61	9	33	42	114	...	...	...	5	0	2	2	9
99-00—Peterborough	OHL	64	14	42	56	97	...	...	...	5	0	2	2	4
00-01—Saint John	AHL	58	1	6	7	95	...	...	...	19	0	8	8	13
01-02—Saint John	AHL	67	9	16	25	107	...	...	...	—	—	—	—	—
—Calgary	NHL	11	1	2	3	26	-2	0	0	—	—	—	—	—
02-03—Saint John	AHL	11	1	7	8	20	...	...	...	—	—	—	—	—
—Calgary	NHL	50	1	1	2	114	-9	0	0	—	—	—	—	—
NHL Totals (2 years)		61	2	3	5	140	-11	0	0					

M

MONTGOMERY, JIM   C

PERSONAL: Born June 30, 1969, in Montreal ... 5-10/180. ... Shoots right.
TRANSACTIONS/CAREER NOTES: Signed as non-drafted free agent by St. Louis Blues (June 2, 1993). ... Suspended four games and fined $500 by NHL for high-sticking incident (October 4, 1993). ... Traded by Blues to Montreal Canadiens for C Guy Carbonneau (August 19, 1994). ... Claimed on waivers by Philadelphia Flyers (February 10, 1995). ... Signed as free agent by San Jose Sharks (August 15, 2000). ... Signed as free agent by Dallas Stars (July 10, 2001).

Season Team	League	Gms.	G	A	Pts.	PIM	+/-	PP	SH	Gms.	G	A	Pts.	PIM
89-90—Univ. of Maine	Hockey East	45	26	34	60	35	...	...	...	—	—	—	—	—
90-91—Univ. of Maine	Hockey East	43	24	57	81	44	...	...	...	—	—	—	—	—
91-92—Univ. of Maine	Hockey East	37	21	44	65	46	...	...	...	—	—	—	—	—
92-93—Univ. of Maine	Hockey East	45	32	63	95	40	...	...	...	—	—	—	—	—
93-94—St. Louis	NHL	67	6	14	20	44	-1	0	0	—	—	—	—	—
—Peoria	IHL	12	7	8	15	10	...	...	...	—	—	—	—	—
94-95—Montreal	NHL	5	0	0	0	2	-2	0	0	—	—	—	—	—
—Philadelphia	NHL	8	1	1	2	6	-2	0	0	7	1	0	1	2
—Hershey	AHL	16	8	6	14	14	...	...	...	6	3	2	5	25
95-96—Hershey	AHL	78	34	†71	105	95	...	...	...	4	3	2	5	6
—Philadelphia	NHL	5	1	2	3	9	1	0	0	1	0	0	0	0
96-97—Kolner Haie	Germany	50	12	35	47	11	...	...	...	—	—	—	—	—
97-98—Philadelphia	AHL	68	19	43	62	75	...	...	...	20	13	16	29	55
98-99—Philadelphia	AHL	78	29	58	87	89	...	...	...	16	4	11	15	20
99-00—Philadelphia	AHL	13	3	9	12	22	...	...	...	—	—	—	—	—
—Manitoba	IHL	67	18	28	46	11	...	...	...	—	—	—	—	—
00-01—Kentucky	AHL	55	22	52	74	44	...	...	...	3	1	2	3	5
—San Jose	NHL	28	1	6	7	19	-1	1	0	—	—	—	—	—
01-02—Utah	AHL	71	28	43	71	90	...	...	...	5	0	1	1	23
—Dallas	NHL	8	0	2	2	0	-1	0	0	—	—	—	—	—
02-03—Utah	AHL	72	22	46	68	109	...	...	...	—	—	—	—	—
—Dallas	NHL	1	0	0	0	0	0	0	0	—	—	—	—	—
NHL Totals (6 years)		122	9	25	34	80	-6	1	0	8	1	0	1	2

MOORE, DOMINIC   C   RANGERS

PERSONAL: Born August 3, 1980, in Ont. ... 6-0/180. ... Shoots left. ... Brother of Steve Moore, center, Colorado Avalanche organization; and brother of Mark Moore, defenseman, Pittsburgh Penguins organization.
TRANSACTIONS/CAREER NOTES: Selected by New York Rangers in third round (second Rangers pick, 95th overall) of NHL entry draft (June 24, 2000).

M

Season Team	League	Gms.	G	A	Pts.	PIM	+/-	PP	SH	Gms.	G	A	Pts.	PIM
98-99—Aurora	OPJHL	51	34	53	87	70	...	...	...	—	—	—	—	—
99-00—Harvard University	ECAC	28	12	8	20	28	...	...	...	—	—	—	—	—
00-01—Harvard University	ECAC	32	15	28	43	40	...	...	...	—	—	—	—	—
01-02—Harvard University	ECAC	32	13	16	29	37	...	...	...	—	—	—	—	—
02-03—Harvard University	ECAC	34	24	27	51	30	...	...	...	—	—	—	—	—

MOORE, STEVE   C   AVALANCHE

PERSONAL: Born September 22, 1978, in Windsor, Ont. ... 6-2/205. ... Shoots right. ... Brother of Dominic Moore, center, New York Rangers organization; and brother of Mark Moore, defenseman, Pittsburgh Penguins organization.
TRANSACTIONS/CAREER NOTES: Selected by Colorado Avalanche in second round (seventh Avalanche pick, 53rd overall) of NHL entry draft (June 27, 1998).

Season Team	League	Gms.	G	A	Pts.	PIM	+/-	PP	SH	Gms.	G	A	Pts.	PIM
95-96—Thornhill	OHA Jr. A	77	30	43	73	90	...	...	...	—	—	—	—	—
96-97—Thornhill	OHA Jr. A	50	34	52	86	52	...	...	...	—	—	—	—	—
97-98—Harvard University	ECAC	33	10	23	33	46	...	...	...	—	—	—	—	—
98-99—Harvard University	ECAC	30	18	13	31	34	...	...	...	—	—	—	—	—
99-00—Harvard University	ECAC	27	10	16	26	53	...	...	...	—	—	—	—	—
—Kansas City	IHL	1	0	0	0	2	...	...	...	—	—	—	—	—
00-01—Kansas City	IHL	32	7	26	33	43	...	...	...	—	—	—	—	—
01-02—Hershey	AHL	68	10	17	27	31	...	...	...	8	0	1	1	6
—Colorado	NHL	8	0	0	0	4	-4	0	0	—	—	—	—	—
02-03—Hershey	AHL	58	10	13	23	41	...	...	...	—	—	—	—	—
—Colorado	NHL	4	0	0	0	0	0	0	0	—	—	—	—	—
NHL Totals (2 years)		12	0	0	0	4	-4	0	0					

MORAN, BRAD   C   BLUE JACKETS

PERSONAL: Born March 20, 1979, in Abbotsford, B.C. ... 5-11/180. ... Shoots left.
TRANSACTIONS/CAREER NOTES: Selected by Buffalo Sabres in seventh round (eighth Sabres pick, 191st pick overall) of NHL entry draft (June 27, 1998). ... Signed as free agent by Columbus Blue Jackets (June 5, 2000). ... Re-signed by Blue Jackets (July 24, 2003).

Season Team	League	REGULAR SEASON Gms.	G	A	Pts.	PIM	+/-	PP	SH	PLAYOFFS Gms.	G	A	Pts.	PIM
95-96—Calgary	WHL	70	13	31	44	28	...	...	...	—	—	—	—	—
96-97—Calgary	WHL	72	30	36	66	61	...	...	...	—	—	—	—	—
97-98—Calgary	WHL	72	53	49	102	64	...	...	...	18	10	8	18	20
98-99—Calgary	WHL	71	60	58	118	96	...	...	...	21	17	†25	42	26
99-00—Calgary	WHL	72	48	*72	*120	84	...	...	...	13	7	15	22	18
00-01—Syracuse	AHL	71	11	19	30	30	...	...	...	5	3	4	7	3
01-02—Syracuse	AHL	64	25	24	49	51	...	...	...	10	5	8	13	2
—Columbus	NHL	3	0	0	0	0	0	0	0	—	—	—	—	—
02-03—Syracuse	AHL	47	12	19	31	22	...	...	...	—	—	—	—	—
NHL Totals (1 year)		3	0	0	0	0	0	0	0					

MORAN, IAN — D — BRUINS

PERSONAL: Born August 24, 1972, in Cleveland ... 6-0/200. ... Shoots right. ... Name pronounced muh-RAN.

TRANSACTIONS/CAREER NOTES: Selected by Pittsburgh Penguins in sixth round (fifth Penguins pick, 107th overall) of NHL entry draft (June 16, 1990). ... Bruised shoulder (November 22, 1995); missed nine games. ... Injured shoulder (February 21, 1996); missed one game. ... Underwent shoulder surgery (March 21, 1996); missed remainder of season. ... Injured back and neck (April 10, 1997); missed two games. ... Bruised kneecap and underwent surgery (September 30, 1997); missed 34 games. ... Suffered concussion (February 2, 1998); missed four games. ... Injured knee (March 21, 1998); missed five games. ... Injured ankle (October 26, 1998); missed five games. ... Reinjured ankle (November 7, 1998); missed nine games. ... Bruised ankle (January 5, 1999); missed two games. ... Bruised right testicle (February 5, 1999); missed three games. ... Injured ankle (April 3, 1999); missed one game. ... Fractured foot (December 2, 1999); missed two games. ... Suffered from the flu (January 2, 2000); missed one game. ... Bruised ankle (April 7, 2000); missed final game of season. ... Injured knee (October 18, 2000); missed seven games. ... Fractured hand (November 10, 2000); missed 15 games. ... Suffered from the flu (February 16, 2001); missed one game. ... Fractured thumb (February 19, 2001); missed 18 games. ... Fractured foot (December 8, 2001); missed 12 games. ... Injured hip (April 3, 2002); missed remainder of season. ... Traded by Penguins to Boston Bruins for fourth-round pick in 2003 draft (March 11, 2003). ... Re-signed by Bruins (July 28, 2003).

Season Team	League	REGULAR SEASON Gms.	G	A	Pts.	PIM	+/-	PP	SH	PLAYOFFS Gms.	G	A	Pts.	PIM
87-88—Belmont Hill	Mass. H.S.	25	3	13	16	15	...	...	...	—	—	—	—	—
88-89—Belmont Hill	Mass. H.S.	23	7	25	32	8	...	...	...	—	—	—	—	—
89-90—Belmont Hill	Mass. H.S.	—	10	36	46	0	—	—	—	—	—	—	—	—
90-91—Belmont Hill	Mass. H.S.	23	7	44	51	12	...	...	...	—	—	—	—	—
91-92—Boston College	Hockey East	30	2	16	18	44	...	...	...	—	—	—	—	—
92-93—Boston College	Hockey East	31	8	12	20	32	...	...	...	—	—	—	—	—
93-94—U.S. national team	Int'l	50	8	15	23	69	...	...	...	—	—	—	—	—
—Cleveland	IHL	33	5	13	18	39	...	...	...	—	—	—	—	—
94-95—Cleveland	IHL	64	7	31	38	94	...	...	...	4	0	1	1	2
—Pittsburgh	NHL	—	—	—	—	—	—	—	—	8	0	0	0	0
95-96—Pittsburgh	NHL	51	1	1	2	47	-1	0	0	—	—	—	—	—
96-97—Cleveland	IHL	36	6	23	29	26	...	...	...	—	—	—	—	—
—Pittsburgh	NHL	36	4	5	9	22	-11	0	0	5	1	2	3	4
97-98—Pittsburgh	NHL	37	1	6	7	19	0	0	0	6	0	0	0	2
98-99—Pittsburgh	NHL	62	4	5	9	37	1	0	1	13	0	2	2	8
99-00—Pittsburgh	NHL	73	4	8	12	28	-10	0	0	11	0	1	1	4
00-01—Pittsburgh	NHL	40	3	4	7	28	5	0	0	18	0	1	1	4
01-02—Pittsburgh	NHL	64	2	8	10	54	-11	0	0	—	—	—	—	—
02-03—Pittsburgh	NHL	70	0	7	7	46	-17	0	0	—	—	—	—	—
—Boston	NHL	8	0	1	1	2	-1	0	0	5	0	1	1	4
NHL Totals (9 years)		441	19	45	64	283	-45	0	1	66	1	7	8	24

M

MOREAU, ETHAN — LW — OILERS

PERSONAL: Born September 22, 1975, in Huntsville, Ont. ... 6-2/211. ... Shoots left. ... Name pronounced MOHR-oh.

TRANSACTIONS/CAREER NOTES: Selected by Chicago Blackhawks in first round (first Blackhawks pick, 14th overall) of NHL entry draft (June 28, 1994). ... Fractured knuckle (November 16, 1997); missed seven games. ... Fractured ankle (December 14, 1997); missed 20 games. ... Traded by Blackhawks with LW Daniel Cleary, C Chad Kilger and D Christian Laflamme to Edmonton Oilers for D Boris Mironov, LW Dean McAmmond and D Jonas Elofsson (March 20, 1999). ... Injured ribs (November 24, 1999); missed eight games. ... Suffered from the flu (December 27, 1999); missed one game. ... Underwent shoulder surgery (May 24, 2000); missed first 14 games of season. ... Bruised ankle (December 16, 2001); missed one game.

Season Team	League	REGULAR SEASON Gms.	G	A	Pts.	PIM	+/-	PP	SH	PLAYOFFS Gms.	G	A	Pts.	PIM
90-91—Orillia	OHA	42	17	22	39	26	...	...	...	—	—	—	—	—
91-92—Niagara Falls	OHL	62	20	35	55	39	...	...	...	17	4	6	10	4
92-93—Niagara Falls	OHL	65	32	41	73	69	...	...	...	4	0	3	3	4
93-94—Niagara Falls	OHL	59	44	54	98	100	...	...	...	—	—	—	—	—
94-95—Niagara Falls	OHL	39	25	41	66	69	...	...	...	—	—	—	—	—
—Sudbury	OHL	23	13	17	30	22	...	...	...	18	6	12	18	26
95-96—Indianapolis	IHL	71	21	20	41	126	...	...	...	5	4	0	4	8
—Chicago	NHL	8	0	1	1	4	1	0	0	—	—	—	—	—
96-97—Chicago	NHL	82	15	16	31	123	13	0	0	6	1	0	1	9
97-98—Chicago	NHL	54	9	9	18	73	0	2	0	—	—	—	—	—
98-99—Chicago	NHL	66	9	6	15	84	-5	0	0	—	—	—	—	—
—Edmonton	NHL	14	1	5	6	8	2	0	0	4	0	3	3	6
99-00—Edmonton	NHL	73	17	10	27	62	8	1	0	5	0	1	1	0
00-01—Edmonton	NHL	68	9	10	19	90	-6	0	1	4	0	0	0	2
01-02—Edmonton	NHL	80	11	5	16	81	4	0	2	—	—	—	—	—
02-03—Edmonton	NHL	78	14	17	31	112	-7	2	3	6	0	1	1	16
NHL Totals (8 years)		523	85	79	164	637	10	5	6	25	1	5	6	33

MORGAN, JASON   C   FLAMES

PERSONAL: Born October 9, 1976, in Kitchener, Ont. ... 6-1/200. ... Shoots left.
HIGH SCHOOL: Loyalist C & VI (Kingston, Ont.).
TRANSACTIONS/CAREER NOTES: Selected by Los Angeles Kings in fifth round (fifth Kings pick, 118th overall) of NHL entry draft (July 8, 1995). ... Signed as free agent by Calgary Flames (July 11, 2002).

				REGULAR SEASON								PLAYOFFS			
Season Team	League	Gms.	G	A	Pts.	PIM	+/-	PP	SH		Gms.	G	A	Pts.	PIM
93-94—Kitchener	OHL	65	6	15	21	16	...	...	...		5	1	0	1	0
94-95—Kitchener	OHL	35	3	15	18	25	...	...	...		—	—	—	—	—
—Kingston	OHL	20	0	3	3	14	...	...	...		6	0	2	2	0
95-96—Kingston	OHL	66	16	38	54	50	...	...	...		6	1	2	3	0
96-97—Phoenix	IHL	57	3	6	9	29	...	...	...		—	—	—	—	—
—Mississippi	ECHL	6	3	0	3	0	...	...	...		3	1	1	2	6
—Los Angeles	NHL	3	0	0	0	0	-3	0	0		—	—	—	—	—
97-98—Springfield	AHL	58	13	22	35	66	...	...	...		3	1	0	1	18
—Los Angeles	NHL	11	1	0	1	4	-7	0	0		—	—	—	—	—
98-99—Long Beach	IHL	13	4	6	10	18	...	...	...		—	—	—	—	—
—Springfield	AHL	46	6	16	22	51	...	...	...		3	0	0	0	6
99-00—Florida	ECHL	48	14	25	39	79	...	...	...		5	2	2	4	16
—Cincinnati	IHL	15	1	3	4	14	...	...	...		—	—	—	—	—
00-01—Hamilton	AHL	11	2	0	2	10	...	...	...		—	—	—	—	—
—Springfield	AHL	16	1	4	5	19	...	...	...		6	0	1	1	2
—Florida	ECHL	37	15	22	37	41	...	...	...		5	2	3	5	17
01-02—Saint John	AHL	76	17	20	37	69	...	...	...		—	—	—	—	—
02-03—Saint John	AHL	80	13	40	53	63	...	...	...		—	—	—	—	—
NHL Totals (2 years)		14	1	0	1	4	-10	0	0						

MORISSET, DAVID   RW   PANTHERS

PERSONAL: Born April 6, 1981, in Langley, B.C. ... 6-2/195. ... Shoots right.
TRANSACTIONS/CAREER NOTES: Selected by St. Louis Blues in second round (second Blues pick, 65th overall) of NHL entry draft (June 24, 2000). ... Traded by Blues with fifth-round pick (C Vince Bellissimo) in 2002 draft to Florida Panthers for RW Scott Mellanby (February 9, 2001).

				REGULAR SEASON								PLAYOFFS			
Season Team	League	Gms.	G	A	Pts.	PIM	+/-	PP	SH		Gms.	G	A	Pts.	PIM
97-98—Seattle	WHL	58	6	2	8	104	...	...	...		5	1	0	1	6
98-99—Seattle	WHL	17	4	0	4	31	...	...	...		11	1	1	2	22
99-00—Seattle	WHL	60	23	34	57	71	...	...	...		7	3	4	7	12
00-01—Seattle	WHL	61	32	36	68	95	...	...	...		9	4	2	6	12
01-02—Bridgeport	AHL	62	9	10	19	46	...	...	...		19	0	1	1	13
—Florida	NHL	4	0	0	0	5	-7	0	0		—	—	—	—	—
02-03—San Antonio	AHL	30	3	3	6	13	...	...	...		—	—	—	—	—
NHL Totals (1 year)		4	0	0	0	5	-7	0	0						

MORO, MARC   D   MAPLE LEAFS

PERSONAL: Born July 17, 1977, in Toronto. ... 6-1/220. ... Shoots left. ... Name pronounced muh-ROH.
TRANSACTIONS/CAREER NOTES: Selected by Ottawa Senators in second round (second Senators pick, 27th overall) of NHL entry draft (July 8, 1995). ... Rights traded by Senators with C Ted Drury to Mighty Ducks of Anaheim for C Shaun Van Allen and D Jason York (October 1, 1996). ... Traded by Mighty Ducks with G Chris Mason to Nashville Predators for G Dominic Roussel (October 5, 1998). ... Suffered injury (March 29, 2000); missed final four games of season. ... Traded by Predators to Toronto Maple Leafs for D D.J. Smith and D Marty Wilford (March 1, 2003).

				REGULAR SEASON								PLAYOFFS			
Season Team	League	Gms.	G	A	Pts.	PIM	+/-	PP	SH		Gms.	G	A	Pts.	PIM
92-93—Mississauga	MTHL	42	9	18	27	56	...	...	...		—	—	—	—	—
—Mississauga	Jr. A	2	0	0	0	0	...	...	...		—	—	—	—	—
93-94—Kingston	Tier II Jr. A	12	0	2	2	20	...	...	...		—	—	—	—	—
—Kingston	OHL	43	0	3	3	81	...	...	...		—	—	—	—	—
94-95—Kingston	OHL	64	4	12	16	255	...	...	...		6	0	0	0	23
95-96—Kingston	OHL	66	4	17	21	261	...	...	...		6	0	0	0	12
—Prin. Edward Island	AHL	2	0	0	0	7	...	...	...		2	0	0	0	4
96-97—Kingston	OHL	37	4	8	12	97	...	...	...		—	—	—	—	—
—Sault Ste. Marie	OHL	63	4	13	17	171	...	...	...		11	1	6	7	38
97-98—Cincinnati	AHL	74	1	6	7	181	...	...	...		—	—	—	—	—
—Anaheim	NHL	1	0	0	0	0	0	0	0		—	—	—	—	—
98-99—Milwaukee	IHL	80	0	5	5	264	...	...	...		2	0	0	0	4
99-00—Milwaukee	IHL	64	5	5	10	203	...	...	...		—	—	—	—	—
—Nashville	NHL	8	0	0	0	40	-3	0	0		—	—	—	—	—
00-01—Milwaukee	IHL	68	2	9	11	190	...	...	...		5	1	0	1	10
—Nashville	NHL	6	0	0	0	12	1	0	0		—	—	—	—	—
01-02—Nashville	NHL	13	0	0	0	23	-3	0	0		—	—	—	—	—
—Milwaukee	AHL	41	1	8	9	81	...	...	...		—	—	—	—	—
—St. John's	AHL	7	1	0	1	21	...	...	...		—	—	—	—	—
—Toronto	NHL	2	0	0	0	2	0	0	0		—	—	—	—	—
02-03—St. John's	AHL	68	3	8	11	128	...	...	...		—	—	—	—	—
NHL Totals (4 years)		30	0	0	0	77	-5	0	0						

MOROZOV, ALEKSEY   LW   PENGUINS

PERSONAL: Born February 16, 1977, in Moscow, U.S.S.R. ... 6-1/202. ... Shoots left. ... Name pronounced muh-ROH-sahf.
TRANSACTIONS/CAREER NOTES: Selected by Pittsburgh Penguins in first round (first Penguins pick, 24th overall) of NHL entry draft (July 8, 1995). ... Fractured toe (December 27, 1997); missed one game. ... Suffered concussion (November 14, 1998); missed three games. ... Suffered concussion (December 21, 1998); missed 12 games. ... Suffered charley horse (October 30, 1999); missed eight games. ... Bruised back (January 25, 2000); missed two games. ... Suffered charley horse (March 16, 2000); missed four games. ... Bruised shoulder (December 12, 2001); missed five games. ... Injured shoulder (January 3, 2002); missed four games.
STATISTICAL PLATEAUS: Three-goal games: 1999-00 (1), 2001-02 (1). Total: 2.

Season Team	League	Gms.	G	A	Pts.	PIM	+/-	PP	SH	Gms.	G	A	Pts.	PIM
93-94—Soviet Wings	CIS	7	0	0	0	0	...	...	...	3	0	0	0	2
94-95—Soviet Wings	CIS	48	15	12	27	53	...	...	...	4	0	3	3	0
95-96—Soviet Wings	CIS	47	12	9	21	26	...	...	...	—	—	—	—	—
96-97—Kryla Sov. Moscow	Russian	44	21	11	32	32	...	...	...	2	0	1	1	2
97-98—Pittsburgh	NHL	76	13	13	26	8	-4	2	0	6	0	1	1	2
—Russian Oly. team	Int'l	6	2	2	4	0	...	...	...	—	—	—	—	—
98-99—Pittsburgh	NHL	67	9	10	19	14	5	0	0	10	1	1	2	0
99-00—Pittsburgh	NHL	68	12	19	31	14	12	0	1	5	0	0	0	0
00-01—Pittsburgh	NHL	66	5	14	19	6	-8	0	0	18	3	3	6	6
01-02—Pittsburgh	NHL	72	20	29	49	16	-7	7	0	—	—	—	—	—
02-03—Pittsburgh	NHL	27	9	16	25	16	-3	6	0	—	—	—	—	—
NHL Totals (6 years)		376	68	101	169	74	-5	15	1	39	4	5	9	8

MORRIS, DEREK   D   AVALANCHE

PERSONAL: Born August 24, 1978, in Edmonton ... 6-0/210. ... Shoots right.
TRANSACTIONS/CAREER NOTES: Selected by Calgary Flames in first round (first Flames pick, 13th overall) of NHL entry draft (June 22, 1996). ... Separated shoulder (February 22, 1999); missed 10 games. ... Suffered concussion (December 14, 1999); missed three games. ... Missed first 27 games of 2000-01 season due to contract dispute. ... Suffered injury (November 8, 2001); missed one game. ... Injured wrist (November 29, 2001); missed 20 games. ... Traded by Flames with LW Dean McAmmond and C Jeff Shantz to Colorado Avalanche for LW Chris Drury and C Stephane Yelle (October 1, 2002).

Season Team	League	Gms.	G	A	Pts.	PIM	+/-	PP	SH	Gms.	G	A	Pts.	PIM
95-96—Regina	WHL	67	8	44	52	70	...	...	...	11	1	7	8	26
96-97—Regina	WHL	67	18	57	75	180	...	...	...	5	0	3	3	9
—Saint John	AHL	7	0	3	3	7	...	...	...	5	0	3	3	7
97-98—Calgary	NHL	82	9	20	29	88	1	5	1	—	—	—	—	—
98-99—Calgary	NHL	71	7	27	34	73	4	3	0	—	—	—	—	—
99-00—Calgary	NHL	78	9	29	38	80	2	3	0	—	—	—	—	—
00-01—Saint John	AHL	3	1	2	3	2	...	...	...	—	—	—	—	—
—Calgary	NHL	51	5	23	28	56	-15	3	1	—	—	—	—	—
01-02—Calgary	NHL	61	4	30	34	88	-4	2	0	—	—	—	—	—
02-03—Colorado	NHL	75	11	37	48	68	16	9	0	7	0	3	3	6
NHL Totals (6 years)		418	45	166	211	453	4	25	2	7	0	3	3	6

MORRIS, MIKE   RW   SHARKS

PERSONAL: Born July 14, 1983, in Dorchester, Mass. ... 6-0/182. ... Shoots right.
TRANSACTIONS/CAREER NOTES: Selected by San Jose Sharks in first round (first Sharks pick, 27th overall) of NHL entry draft (June 22, 2002).

Season Team	League	Gms.	G	A	Pts.	PIM	+/-	PP	SH	Gms.	G	A	Pts.	PIM
00-01—St. Sebastian's	USHS (East)	28	20	28	48	18	...	...	...	—	—	—	—	—
01-02—St. Sebastian's	USHS (East)	31	29	29	58	26	...	...	...	—	—	—	—	—
02-03—Northeastern	ECAC	26	9	12	21	16	...	...	...	—	—	—	—	—

MORRISON, BRENDAN   C   CANUCKS

PERSONAL: Born August 15, 1975, in Pitt Meadows, B.C. ... 5-11/185. ... Shoots left.
TRANSACTIONS/CAREER NOTES: Selected by New Jersey Devils in second round (third Devils pick, 39th overall) of NHL entry draft (June 26, 1993). ... Missed first nine games of 1999-2000 season due to contract dispute. ... Suffered injury (October 29, 1999); missed two games. ... Traded by Devils with C Denis Pederson to Vancouver Canucks for RW Alexander Mogilny (March 14, 2000).

Season Team	League	Gms.	G	A	Pts.	PIM	+/-	PP	SH	Gms.	G	A	Pts.	PIM
92-93—Penticton	BCJHL	56	35	59	94	45	...	...	...	—	—	—	—	—
93-94—Univ. of Michigan	CCHA	38	20	28	48	24	...	...	...	—	—	—	—	—
94-95—Univ. of Michigan	CCHA	39	23	53	76	42	...	...	...	—	—	—	—	—
95-96—Univ. of Michigan	CCHA	35	28	44	72	41	...	...	...	—	—	—	—	—
96-97—Univ. of Michigan	CCHA	43	31	57	88	52	...	...	...	—	—	—	—	—
97-98—Albany	AHL	72	35	49	84	44	...	...	...	8	3	4	7	19
—New Jersey	NHL	11	5	4	9	0	3	0	0	3	0	1	1	0
98-99—New Jersey	NHL	76	13	33	46	18	-4	5	0	7	0	2	2	0
99-00—HC Pardubice	Czech Rep.	6	5	2	7	2	...	...	...	—	—	—	—	—
—New Jersey	NHL	44	5	21	26	8	8	2	0	—	—	—	—	—
—Vancouver	NHL	12	2	7	9	10	4	0	0	—	—	—	—	—
00-01—Vancouver	NHL	82	16	38	54	42	2	3	2	4	1	2	3	0
01-02—Vancouver	NHL	82	23	44	67	26	18	6	0	6	0	2	2	6
02-03—Vancouver	NHL	82	25	46	71	36	18	6	2	14	4	7	11	18
NHL Totals (6 years)		389	89	193	282	140	49	22	4	34	5	14	19	24

M

MORRISON, JUSTIN　　　　RW　　　　CANUCKS

PERSONAL: Born August 10, 1979, in Los Angeles. ... 6-3/200. ... Shoots right.
COLLEGE: Colorado College.
TRANSACTIONS/CAREER NOTES: Selected by Vancouver Canucks in third round (fourth Canucks pick, 81st overall) of NHL entry draft (June 27, 1998).

			REGULAR SEASON							PLAYOFFS				
Season Team	League	Gms.	G	A	Pts.	PIM	+/-	PP	SH	Gms.	G	A	Pts.	PIM
96-97—Omaha	USHL	62	12	24	36	44	...	...	...	—	—	—	—	—
97-98—Colorado College	WCHA	42	4	9	13	8	...	...	...	—	—	—	—	—
98-99—Colorado College	WCHA	38	13	15	28	33	...	...	...	—	—	—	—	—
99-00—Colorado College	WCHA	38	7	19	26	28	...	...	...	—	—	—	—	—
00-01—Colorado College	WCHA	41	21	14	35	42	...	...	...	—	—	—	—	—
02-03—Manitoba	AHL	30	10	6	16	13	...	...	...	—	—	—	—	—
—Columbia	ECHL	40	20	35	55	39	...	...	...	—	—	—	—	—

MORRISONN, SHAONE　　　　D　　　　BRUINS

PERSONAL: Born December 23, 1982, in Vancouver ... 6-3/205. ... Shoots left. ... Name pronounced Shane.
TRANSACTIONS/CAREER NOTES: Selected by Boston Bruins in first round (first Bruins pick, 19th overall) of NHL entry draft (June 23, 2001).

			REGULAR SEASON							PLAYOFFS				
Season Team	League	Gms.	G	A	Pts.	PIM	+/-	PP	SH	Gms.	G	A	Pts.	PIM
99-00—Kamloops	WHL	57	1	6	7	80	...	...	...	4	0	0	0	6
00-01—Kamloops	WHL	61	13	25	38	132	...	...	...	4	0	0	0	6
01-02—Kamloops	WHL	61	11	26	37	106	...	...	...	4	0	2	2	2
02-03—Providence	AHL	60	5	16	21	103	...	...	...	—	—	—	—	—
—Boston	NHL	11	0	0	0	8	0	0	0	—	—	—	—	—
NHL Totals (1 year)		11	0	0	0	8	0	0	0					

MORROW, BRENDEN　　　　LW　　　　STARS

PERSONAL: Born January 16, 1979, in Carlyle, Sask. ... 5-11/210. ... Shoots left.
TRANSACTIONS/CAREER NOTES: Selected by Dallas Stars in first round (first Stars pick, 25th overall) of NHL entry draft (June 21, 1997). ... Injured medial collateral ligament in knee (December 1, 2001); missed 10 games.

			REGULAR SEASON							PLAYOFFS				
Season Team	League	Gms.	G	A	Pts.	PIM	+/-	PP	SH	Gms.	G	A	Pts.	PIM
95-96—Portland	WHL	65	13	12	25	61	...	...	...	7	0	0	0	8
96-97—Portland	WHL	71	39	49	88	178	...	...	...	6	2	1	3	4
97-98—Portland	WHL	68	34	52	86	184	...	...	...	16	10	8	18	65
98-99—Portland	WHL	61	41	44	85	248	...	...	...	4	0	4	4	18
99-00—Michigan	IHL	9	2	0	2	18	...	...	...	—	—	—	—	—
—Dallas	NHL	64	14	19	33	81	8	3	0	21	2	4	6	22
00-01—Dallas	NHL	82	20	24	44	128	18	7	0	10	0	3	3	12
01-02—Dallas	NHL	72	17	18	35	109	12	4	0	—	—	—	—	—
02-03—Dallas	NHL	71	21	22	43	134	20	2	3	12	3	5	8	16
NHL Totals (4 years)		289	72	83	155	452	58	16	3	43	5	12	17	50

MOSS, TYLER　　　　G　　　　CANUCKS

PERSONAL: Born June 29, 1975, in Ottawa ... 6-0/185. ... Catches right.
TRANSACTIONS/CAREER NOTES: Selected by Tampa Bay Lightning in second round (second Lightning pick, 29th overall) of NHL entry draft (June 26, 1993). ... Traded by Lightning to Calgary Flames for D Jamie Huscroft (March 18, 1997). ... Injured groin (December 12, 1998); missed 18 games. ... Traded by Flames with LW Rene Corbet to Pittsburgh Penguins for D Brad Werenka (March 14, 2000). ... Signed as free agent by Carolina Hurricanes (August 9, 2000). ... Signed as free agent by Vancouver Canucks (July 5, 2002).

			REGULAR SEASON								PLAYOFFS							
Season Team	League	Gms.	Min	W	L	T	GA	SO	Avg.	SV%	Gms.	Min.	W	L	GA	SO	Avg.	SV%
91-92—Nepean	COJHL	26	1335	7	12	1	109	0	4.90	—	—	—	—	—	—	—	—	—
92-93—Kingston	OHL	31	1537	13	7	5	97	0	3.79	—	6	228	1	2	19	0	5.00	—
93-94—Kingston	OHL	13	795	6	4	3	42	1	3.17	—	3	136	0	2	8	0	3.53	—
94-95—Kingston	OHL	57	3249	33	17	5	164	1	3.03	—	6	333	4	2	27	0	4.86	—
95-96—Atlanta	IHL	40	2030	11	19	‡4	138	1	4.08	—	3	213	0	3	11	0	3.10	—
96-97—Adirondack	AHL	11	507	1	5	2	42	1	4.97	—	—	—	—	—	—	—	—	—
—Grand Rapids	IHL	15	715	5	6	‡1	35	0	2.94	—	—	—	—	—	—	—	—	—
—Saint John	AHL	9	534	6	1	1	17	0	1.91	—	5	242	2	3	15	0	3.72	—
—Muskegon	Col.HL	2	119	1	1	0	5	0	2.52	—	—	—	—	—	—	—	—	—
97-98—Saint John	AHL	39	2194	19	10	7	91	0	2.49	—	15	762	8	†5	37	0	2.91	—
—Calgary	NHL	6	367	2	3	1	20	0	3.27	.892	—	—	—	—	—	—	—	—
98-99—Calgary	NHL	11	550	3	7	0	23	0	2.51	.922	—	—	—	—	—	—	—	—
—Saint John	AHL	9	475	2	5	1	25	0	3.16	—	—	—	—	—	—	—	—	—
—Orlando	IHL	9	515	6	2	1	21	1	2.45	—	17	1017	10	7	*53	0	3.13	—
99-00—Kansas City	IHL	36	2116	21	12	5	105	3	2.98	—	—	—	—	—	—	—	—	—
—Wilkes-Barre/Scranton	AHL	4	188	1	1	1	11	0	3.51	—	—	—	—	—	—	—	—	—
00-01—Carolina	NHL	12	557	1	6	0	37	0	3.99	.853	—	—	—	—	—	—	—	—
—Cincinnati	IHL	9	506	5	3	‡1	24	2	2.85	—	—	—	—	—	—	—	—	—
01-02—Lowell	AHL	43	2571	20	16	7	106	1	2.47	—	—	—	—	—	—	—	—	—
02-03—Manitoba	AHL	42	2502	21	15	5	117	3	2.81	—	—	—	—	—	—	—	—	—
—Vancouver	NHL	1	22	0	0	0	1	0	2.73	.929	—	—	—	—	—	—	—	—
NHL Totals (4 years)		30	1496	6	16	1	81	0	3.25	.891								

MOTTAU, MIKE   D   MIGHTY DUCKS

PERSONAL: Born March 19, 1978, in Quincy, Mass. ... 6-0/193. ... Shoots left.
TRANSACTIONS/CAREER NOTES: Selected by New York Rangers in seventh round (10th pick, 182nd overall) of 1997 NHL entry draft. ... Traded by Rangers to Calgary Flames for sixth-round pick in 2003 or 2004 draft (January 22, 2003). ... Signed as free agent by Anaheim Mighty Ducks (July 25, 2003).

Season Team	League	REGULAR SEASON								PLAYOFFS				
		Gms.	G	A	Pts.	PIM	+/-	PP	SH	Gms.	G	A	Pts.	PIM
96-97—Boston College	Hockey East	38	5	18	23	77	...	...	...	—	—	—	—	—
97-98—Boston College	Hockey East	40	13	36	49	50	...	...	...	—	—	—	—	—
98-99—Boston College	Hockey East	43	3	39	42	44	...	...	...	—	—	—	—	—
99-00—Boston College	Hockey East	42	6	*37	43	57	...	...	...	—	—	—	—	—
00-01—Hartford	AHL	61	10	33	43	45	...	...	...	5	0	1	1	19
—New York Rangers	NHL	18	0	3	3	13	-6	0	0	—	—	—	—	—
01-02—Hartford	AHL	80	9	42	51	56	...	...	...	10	0	5	5	4
—New York Rangers	NHL	1	0	0	0	0	0	0	0	—	—	—	—	—
02-03—Hartford	AHL	29	1	18	19	24	...	...	...	—	—	—	—	—
—Calgary	NHL	4	0	0	0	0	-1	0	0	—	—	—	—	—
—Saint John	AHL	32	5	12	17	14	...	...	...	—	—	—	—	—
NHL Totals (3 years)		23	0	3	3	13	-7	0	0					

MOWERS, MARK   C   RED WINGS

PERSONAL: Born February 16, 1974, in Whitesboro, N.Y. ... 5-11/184. ... Shoots right.
TRANSACTIONS/CAREER NOTES: Signed as non-drafted free agent by Nashville Predators (June 11, 1998). ... Injured knee (March 19, 2000); missed final nine games of season. ... Signed as free agent by Detroit Red Wings (August 5, 2002). ... Re-signed by Red Wings (July 16, 2003).

Season Team	League	REGULAR SEASON								PLAYOFFS				
		Gms.	G	A	Pts.	PIM	+/-	PP	SH	Gms.	G	A	Pts.	PIM
94-95—Univ. of New Hamp.	Hockey East	36	13	23	36	16	...	...	...	—	—	—	—	—
95-96—Univ. of New Hamp.	Hockey East	34	21	26	47	18	...	...	...	—	—	—	—	—
96-97—Univ. of New Hamp.	Hockey East	39	26	32	58	52	...	...	...	—	—	—	—	—
97-98—Univ. of New Hamp.	Hockey East	35	25	31	56	32	...	...	...	—	—	—	—	—
98-99—Milwaukee	IHL	51	14	22	36	24	...	...	...	1	0	0	0	0
—Nashville	NHL	30	0	6	6	4	-4	0	0	—	—	—	—	—
99-00—Milwaukee	IHL	23	11	15	26	34	...	...	...	—	—	—	—	—
—Nashville	NHL	41	4	5	9	10	0	0	0	—	—	—	—	—
00-01—Milwaukee	IHL	63	25	25	50	54	...	...	...	58	1	2	3	2
01-02—Milwaukee	AHL	45	19	20	39	34	...	...	...	—	—	—	—	—
—Nashville	NHL	14	1	2	3	2	-2	0	0	—	—	—	—	—
02-03—Grand Rapids	AHL	78	34	47	81	47	...	...	...	—	—	—	—	—
NHL Totals (3 years)		85	5	13	18	16	-6	0	0					

MROZIK, RICK   D

PERSONAL: Born January 2, 1975, in Duluth, Minn. ... 6-2/214. ... Shoots left. ... Full Name: Richard Donald Mrozik. ... Name pronounced MROH-zihk.
HIGH SCHOOL: Cloquet (Minn.).
COLLEGE: Minnesota-Duluth.
TRANSACTIONS/CAREER NOTES: Selected by Dallas Stars in sixth round (fourth Stars pick, 136th overall) of NHL entry draft (June 26, 1993). ... Rights traded by Stars with D Mark Tinordi to Washington Capitals for D Kevin Hatcher (January 18, 1995). ... Signed as free agent by Calgary Flames (August 6, 2001).

Season Team	League	REGULAR SEASON								PLAYOFFS				
		Gms.	G	A	Pts.	PIM	+/-	PP	SH	Gms.	G	A	Pts.	PIM
92-93—Cloquet H.S.	Minn. H.S.	28	9	38	47	12	...	...	...	—	—	—	—	—
93-94—Minnesota-Duluth	WCHA	38	2	9	11	38	...	...	...	—	—	—	—	—
94-95—Minnesota-Duluth	WCHA	3	0	0	0	2	...	...	...	—	—	—	—	—
95-96—Minnesota-Duluth	WCHA	33	3	19	22	63	...	...	...	—	—	—	—	—
96-97—Minnesota-Duluth	WCHA	38	11	23	34	56	...	...	...	—	—	—	—	—
97-98—Portland	AHL	75	2	15	17	52	...	...	...	10	1	3	4	2
98-99—Portland	AHL	70	4	8	12	63	...	...	...	—	—	—	—	—
99-00—Worcester	AHL	3	0	0	0	0	...	...	...	—	—	—	—	—
—Pee Dee	ECHL	60	9	19	28	44	...	...	...	5	2	0	2	6
—Syracuse	AHL	1	0	0	0	0	...	...	...	—	—	—	—	—
00-01—Saint John	AHL	76	5	11	16	26	...	...	...	19	1	1	2	6
01-02—Saint John	AHL	55	2	5	7	27	...	...	...	—	—	—	—	—
02-03—Saint John	AHL	68	2	10	12	46	...	...	...	—	—	—	—	—
—Calgary	NHL	2	0	0	0	0	0	0	0	—	—	—	—	—
NHL Totals (1 year)		2	0	0	0	0	0	0	0					

M

MUCKALT, BILL   RW   WILD

PERSONAL: Born July 15, 1974, in Surrey, B.C. ... 6-2/200. ... Shoots right.
TRANSACTIONS/CAREER NOTES: Selected by Vancouver Canucks in ninth round (seventh Canucks pick, 221st overall) of NHL entry draft (June 29, 1994). ... Sprained ankle (March 27, 1999); missed final nine games of season. ... Traded by Canucks with G Kevin Weekes and C Dave Scatchard to New York Islanders for G Felix Potvin, second-(traded to Atlanta) and third-round (C Thatcher Bell) picks in 2000 draft

(December 19, 1999). ... Separated left shoulder (January 13, 2000) and underwent surgery; missed remainder of season. ... Separated right shoulder (October 17, 2000); missed 21 games. ... Traded by Islanders with D Zdeno Chara and first-round pick (C Jason Spezza) in 2001 draft to Ottawa Senators for C Alexei Yashin (June 23, 2001). ... Injured right leg (December 27, 2001); missed nine games. ... Signed as free agent by Minnesota Wild (July 3, 2002).

| | | REGULAR SEASON | | | | | | | | PLAYOFFS | | | | |
Season Team	League	Gms.	G	A	Pts.	PIM	+/-	PP	SH	Gms.	G	A	Pts.	PIM
91-92—Merritt........................	BCJHL	55	14	11	25	75	...	...	...	—	—	—	—	—
92-93—Merritt........................	BCJHL	59	31	43	74	80	...	...	...	5	5	2	7	11
93-94—Merritt........................	BCJHL	43	58	51	109	99	...	...	...	—	—	—	—	—
—Kelowna........................	BCJHL	15	12	10	22	20	...	...	...	28	19	19	38	25
94-95—Univ. of Michigan........	CCHA	39	19	18	37	42	...	...	...	—	—	—	—	—
95-96—Univ. of Michigan........	CCHA	41	28	30	58	34	...	...	...	—	—	—	—	—
96-97—Univ. of Michigan........	CCHA	36	26	38	64	69	...	...	...	—	—	—	—	—
97-98—Univ. of Michigan........	CCHA	44	32	*33	*65	94	...	...	...	—	—	—	—	—
98-99—Vancouver...................	NHL	73	16	20	36	98	-9	4	2	—	—	—	—	—
99-00—Vancouver...................	NHL	33	4	8	12	17	6	1	0	—	—	—	—	—
—New York Islanders........	NHL	12	4	3	7	4	5	0	0	—	—	—	—	—
00-01—New York Islanders.....	NHL	60	11	15	26	33	-4	1	0	—	—	—	—	—
01-02—Ottawa........................	NHL	70	0	8	8	46	-3	0	0	—	—	—	—	—
02-03—Minnesota....................	NHL	8	5	3	8	6	5	0	0	5	0	0	0	0
NHL Totals (5 years)............		256	40	57	97	204	0	6	2	5	0	0	0	0

MUIR, BRYAN — D — AVALANCHE

PERSONAL: Born June 8, 1973, in Winnipeg ... 6-4/215. ... Shoots left. ... Name pronounced MYOOR.
TRANSACTIONS/CAREER NOTES: Signed as non-drafted free agent by Edmonton Oilers (April 30, 1996). ... Traded by Oilers with C Jason Arnott to New Jersey Devils for RW Bill Guerin and RW Valeri Zelepukin (January 4, 1998). ... Traded by Devils to Chicago Blackhawks for future considerations (November 13, 1998). ... Injured back (April 5, 1999); missed three games. ... Traded by Blackhawks with LW Reid Simpson to Tampa Bay Lightning for C Michael Nylander (November 12, 1999). ... Fractured ankle (November 17, 1999); missed 18 games. ... Injured ankle (March 12, 2000); missed 11 games. ... Traded by Lightning to Colorado Avalanche for eighth-round pick (LW Dimitri Bezrukov) in 2001 draft (January 23, 2001).

| | | REGULAR SEASON | | | | | | | | PLAYOFFS | | | | |
Season Team	League	Gms.	G	A	Pts.	PIM	+/-	PP	SH	Gms.	G	A	Pts.	PIM
91-92—Wexford......................	OJHL	50	11	35	46	...	...	...	...	—	—	—	—	—
92-93—Univ. of New Hamp.....	Hockey East	26	1	2	3	24	...	...	...	—	—	—	—	—
93-94—Univ. of New Hamp.....	Hockey East	36	0	4	4	48	...	...	...	—	—	—	—	—
94-95—Univ. of New Hamp.....	Hockey East	28	9	9	18	48	...	...	...	—	—	—	—	—
95-96—Canadian nat'l team	Int'l	42	6	12	18	36	...	...	...	—	—	—	—	—
—Edmonton...................	NHL	5	0	0	0	6	-4	0	0	—	—	—	—	—
96-97—Hamilton.....................	AHL	75	8	16	24	80	...	...	...	14	0	5	5	12
—Edmonton...................	NHL	—	—	—	—	—	—	—	—	5	0	0	0	4
97-98—Hamilton.....................	AHL	28	3	10	13	62	...	...	...	—	—	—	—	—
—Edmonton...................	NHL	7	0	0	0	17	0	0	0	—	—	—	—	—
—Albany........................	AHL	41	3	10	13	67	...	...	...	13	3	0	3	12
98-99—New Jersey.................	NHL	1	0	0	0	0	0	0	0	—	—	—	—	—
—Albany........................	AHL	10	0	0	0	29	...	...	...	—	—	—	—	—
—Chicago......................	NHL	53	1	4	5	50	1	0	0	—	—	—	—	—
—Portland......................	AHL	2	1	1	2	2	...	...	...	—	—	—	—	—
99-00—Chicago......................	NHL	11	2	3	5	13	-1	0	1	—	—	—	—	—
—Tampa Bay..................	NHL	30	1	1	2	32	-8	0	0	—	—	—	—	—
00-01—Tampa Bay..................	NHL	10	0	3	3	15	-7	0	0	—	—	—	—	—
—Detroit........................	IHL	21	5	7	12	36	...	...	...	—	—	—	—	—
—Hershey......................	AHL	26	5	8	13	50	...	...	...	—	—	—	—	—
—Colorado	NHL	8	0	0	0	4	0	0	0	3	0	0	0	0
01-02—Hershey	AHL	59	10	16	26	133	...	...	...	—	—	—	—	—
—Colorado....................	NHL	22	1	1	2	9	1	0	0	21	0	0	0	2
02-03—Hershey......................	AHL	36	9	12	21	75	...	...	...	—	—	—	—	—
—Colorado....................	NHL	32	0	2	2	19	3	0	0	—	—	—	—	—
NHL Totals (8 years)............		179	5	14	19	165	-15	0	1	29	0	0	0	6

MULLER, KIRK — C

PERSONAL: Born February 8, 1966, in Kingston, Ont. ... 6-0/205. ... Shoots left. ... Name pronounced MUH-luhr.
TRANSACTIONS/CAREER NOTES: Selected by New Jersey Devils in first round (first Devils pick, second overall) of NHL entry draft (June 9, 1984). ... Strained knee (January 13, 1986). ... Fractured ribs (April 1986). ... Traded by Devils with G Roland Melanson to Montreal Canadiens for RW Stephane Richer and RW Tom Chorske (September 1991). ... Injured eye (January 21, 1992); missed one game. ... Bruised ribs (November 7, 1992); missed one game. ... Sprained wrist (March 6, 1993); missed two games. ... Injured shoulder (October 11, 1993); missed eight games. ... Traded by Canadiens with D Mathieu Schneider and C Craig Darby to New York Islanders for C Pierre Turgeon and D Vladimir Malakhov (April 5, 1995). ... Traded by Islanders to Toronto Maple Leafs for LW Ken Belanger and G Damian Rhodes (January 23, 1996). ... Separated shoulder (January 3, 1997); missed two games. ... Bruised ankle (March 8, 1997); missed two games. ... Traded by Maple Leafs to Florida Panthers for RW Jason Podollan (March 18, 1997). ... Suspended two games and fined $1,000 by NHL for high-sticking incident (December 1, 1997). ... Sprained left knee (December 20, 1997); missed eight games. ... Signed as free agent by Dallas Stars (December 15, 1999). ... Suffered back spasms (March 28, 2000); missed one game. ... Bruised chest (December 27, 2000); missed 24 games. ... Injured knee (March 31, 2001); missed one game. ... Claimed by Columbus Blue Jackets from Stars in NHL waiver draft (September 28, 2001). ... Traded by Blue Jackets to Stars for D Evgeny Patrochinin (September 28, 2001). ... Suffered injury (October 9, 2001); missed one game. ... Sprained shoulder (October 13, 2001); missed three games.
STATISTICAL PLATEAUS: Three-goal games: 1986-87 (1), 1987-88 (3), 1991-92 (2), 1995-96 (1). Total: 7.

Season Team	League	Gms.	G	A	Pts.	PIM	+/-	PP	SH	Gms.	G	A	Pts.	PIM
				REGULAR SEASON								PLAYOFFS		
80-81—Kingston	OMJHL	2	0	0	0	0	...	...	...	—	—	—	—	—
81-82—Kingston	OHL	67	12	39	51	27	...	...	...	4	5	1	6	4
82-83—Guelph	OHL	66	52	60	112	41	...	...	...	—	—	—	—	—
83-84—Can. Olympic team	Int'l	15	2	2	4	6	...	...	...	—	—	—	—	—
—Canadian nat'l team	Int'l	15	2	2	4	6	...	...	...	—	—	—	—	—
—Guelph	OHL	49	31	63	94	27	...	...	...	—	—	—	—	—
84-85—New Jersey	NHL	80	17	37	54	69	-31	9	1	—	—	—	—	—
85-86—New Jersey	NHL	77	25	41	66	45	-20	5	1	—	—	—	—	—
86-87—New Jersey	NHL	79	26	50	76	75	-7	10	1	—	—	—	—	—
87-88—New Jersey	NHL	80	37	57	94	114	19	17	2	20	4	8	12	37
88-89—New Jersey	NHL	80	31	43	74	119	-23	12	1	—	—	—	—	—
89-90—New Jersey	NHL	80	30	56	86	74	-1	9	0	6	1	3	4	11
90-91—New Jersey	NHL	80	19	51	70	76	1	7	0	7	0	2	2	10
91-92—Montreal	NHL	78	36	41	77	86	15	15	1	11	4	3	7	31
92-93—Montreal	NHL	80	37	57	94	77	8	12	0	20	10	7	17	18
93-94—Montreal	NHL	76	23	34	57	96	-1	9	2	7	6	2	8	4
94-95—Montreal	NHL	33	8	11	19	33	-21	3	0	—	—	—	—	—
—New York Islanders	NHL	12	3	5	8	14	3	1	1	—	—	—	—	—
95-96—New York Islanders	NHL	15	4	3	7	15	-10	0	0	—	—	—	—	—
—Toronto	NHL	36	9	16	25	42	-3	7	0	6	3	2	5	0
96-97—Toronto	NHL	66	20	17	37	85	-23	9	1	—	—	—	—	—
—Florida	NHL	10	1	2	3	4	-2	1	0	5	1	2	3	4
97-98—Florida	NHL	70	8	21	29	54	-14	1	0	—	—	—	—	—
98-99—Florida	NHL	82	4	11	15	49	-11	0	0	—	—	—	—	—
99-00—Dallas	NHL	47	7	15	22	24	-3	3	0	23	2	3	5	18
00-01—Dallas	NHL	55	1	9	10	26	-4	0	0	10	1	3	4	12
01-02—Dallas	NHL	78	10	20	30	28	-12	4	0	—	—	—	—	—
02-03—Dallas	NHL	55	1	5	6	18	-6	0	0	12	1	1	2	8
NHL Totals (19 years)		1349	357	602	959	1223	-146	134	11	127	33	36	69	153

MURLEY, MATT — LW — PENGUINS

PERSONAL: Born December 17, 1979, in Troy, N.Y. ... 6-1/192. ... Shoots left. ... Full Name: Matthew Thomas Murley.
TRANSACTIONS/CAREER NOTES: Selected by Pittsburgh Penguins in second round (second Penguins pick, 51st overall) of NHL entry draft (June 26, 1999).

Season Team	League	Gms.	G	A	Pts.	PIM	+/-	PP	SH	Gms.	G	A	Pts.	PIM
				REGULAR SEASON								PLAYOFFS		
97-98—Syracuse	Jr. A	49	56	70	126	203	...	...	...	—	—	—	—	—
98-99—Rensselaer Poly. Inst.	ECAC	36	17	32	49	32	...	...	...	—	—	—	—	—
99-00—Rensselaer Poly. Inst.	ECAC	35	9	29	38	42	...	...	...	—	—	—	—	—
00-01—Rensselaer Poly. Inst.	ECAC	34	*24	18	42	34	...	...	...	—	—	—	—	—
01-02—Rensselaer Poly. Inst.	ECAC	32	*24	22	46	26	...	...	...	—	—	—	—	—
02-03—Wilkes-Barre/Scranton	AHL	73	21	37	58	45	...	...	...	—	—	—	—	—

MURPHY, CURTIS — D — PREDATORS

PERSONAL: Born December 3, 1975, in Kerrobert, Sask. ... 5-8/185. ... Shoots right.
HIGH SCHOOL: Kerrobert composite School (Sask.).
COLLEGE: North Dakota.
TRANSACTIONS/CAREER NOTES: Signed as non-drafted free agent by Minnesota Wild (June 19, 2001). ... Traded by Wild to Nashville Predators (June 26, 2003). ... Signed by Predators (July 8, 2003).

Season Team	League	Gms.	G	A	Pts.	PIM	+/-	PP	SH	Gms.	G	A	Pts.	PIM
				REGULAR SEASON								PLAYOFFS		
94-95—Univ. of North Dakota	WCHA	33	6	10	16	28	...	...	...	3	1	0	1	4
95-96—Univ. of North Dakota	WCHA	38	6	12	18	58	...	...	...	2	0	1	1	2
96-97—Univ. of North Dakota	WCHA	43	12	30	42	36	...	...	...	—	—	—	—	—
97-98—Univ. of North Dakota	WCHA	39	8	34	42	78	...	...	...	—	—	—	—	—
98-99—Orlando	IHL	80	22	35	57	60	...	...	...	17	4	5	9	16
99-00—Orlando	IHL	81	8	43	51	59	...	...	...	6	0	2	2	6
00-01—Orlando	IHL	51	19	30	49	55	...	...	...	16	3	11	14	18
01-02—Houston	AHL	80	12	35	47	75	...	...	...	14	2	4	6	10
02-03—Houston	AHL	80	23	31	54	63	...	...	...	—	—	—	—	—
—Minnesota	NHL	1	0	0	0	0	0	0	0	—	—	—	—	—
NHL Totals (1 year)		1	0	0	0	0	0	0	0					

MURPHY, JOE — LW — SENATORS

PERSONAL: Born January 21, 1975, in Didsbury, Alta. ... 6-0/194. ... Shoots right.
TRANSACTIONS/CAREER NOTES: Signed as non-drafted free agent by Buffalo Sabres (July 28, 1998). ... Signed as free agent by Ottawa Senators (July 13, 2001).

| | | | REGULAR SEASON | | | | | | | | PLAYOFFS | | | | |
Season Team	League	Gms.	G	A	Pts.	PIM	+/-	PP	SH		Gms.	G	A	Pts.	PIM
93-94—Olds	AJHL	52	34	38	72	121	...	...	...		—	—	—	—	—
94-95—Olds	AJHL	52	30	29	59	65	...	...	...		—	—	—	—	—
95-96—Univ. of Denver........	WCHA	29	1	6	7	16	...	...	...		—	—	—	—	—
96-97—Univ. of Denver........	WCHA	36	8	14	22	40	...	...	...		—	—	—	—	—
97-98—Univ. of Denver........	WCHA	38	7	14	21	60	...	...	...		—	—	—	—	—
98-99—Univ. of Denver........	WCHA	33	3	13	16	25	...	...	...		—	—	—	—	—
—Huntsville....................	CHL	—	—	—	—	—	—	—	—		13	1	5	6	20
99-00—Roanoke	ECHL	34	12	19	31	34	...	...	...		—	—	—	—	—
—Rochester	AHL	32	0	6	6	8	...	...	...		21	4	2	6	27
00-01—Rochester	AHL	74	20	15	35	43	...	...	...		4	0	1	1	4
01-02—Grand Rapids............	AHL	57	8	14	22	24	...	...	...		5	1	0	1	0
02-03—Binghamton	AHL	73	22	24	46	27	...	...	...		—	—	—	—	—

MURPHY, MARK — LW — FLYERS

PERSONAL: Born August 6, 1976, in Stoughton, Mass. ... 5-11/202. ... Shoots left.

TRANSACTIONS/CAREER NOTES: Signed as non-drafted free agent by Washington Capitals (July 13, 2000). ... Signed by Philadelphia Flyers (July 24, 2003).

| | | | REGULAR SEASON | | | | | | | | PLAYOFFS | | | | |
Season Team	League	Gms.	G	A	Pts.	PIM	+/-	PP	SH		Gms.	G	A	Pts.	PIM
01-02—Portland....................	AHL	77	20	37	57	56	...	...	...		—	—	—	—	—
02-03—Portland....................	AHL	55	18	24	42	84	...	...	...		—	—	—	—	—

MURRAY, GARTH — LW — RANGERS

PERSONAL: Born September 17, 1982, in Regina, Sask. ... 6-1/205. ... Shoots left.

TRANSACTIONS/CAREER NOTES: Selected by New York Rangers in third round (third Rangers pick, 79th overall) of NHL entry draft (June 23, 2001).

| | | | REGULAR SEASON | | | | | | | | PLAYOFFS | | | | |
Season Team	League	Gms.	G	A	Pts.	PIM	+/-	PP	SH		Gms.	G	A	Pts.	PIM
97-98—Regina	WHL	4	0	0	0	2	...	...	...		2	0	0	0	0
98-99—Regina	WHL	60	3	5	8	101	...	...	...		—	—	—	—	—
99-00—Regina	WHL	68	14	26	40	155	...	...	...		7	1	1	2	7
00-01—Regina	WHL	72	28	16	44	183	...	...	...		6	1	1	2	10
01-02—Regina	WHL	62	33	30	63	154	...	...	...		6	2	3	5	9
—Hartford.....................	AHL	4	0	0	0	0	...	...	...		9	1	3	4	6
02-03—Hartford.....................	AHL	64	10	14	24	121	...	...	...		—	—	—	—	—

M

MURRAY, GLEN — RW — BRUINS

PERSONAL: Born November 1, 1972, in Halifax, Nova Scotia ... 6-3/225. ... Shoots right.

TRANSACTIONS/CAREER NOTES: Selected by Boston Bruins in first round (first Bruins pick, 18th overall) of NHL entry draft (June 22, 1991). ... Injured elbow (December 15, 1993); missed two games. ... Traded by Bruins with C Bryan Smolinski to Pittsburgh Penguins for LW Kevin Stevens and LW Shawn McEachern (August 2, 1995). ... Separated shoulder (January 1, 1996); missed 10 games. ... Suffered concussion (April 11, 1996); missed one game. ... Traded by Penguins to Los Angeles Kings for C Ed Olczyk (March 18, 1997). ... Suffered from the flu (November 13, 1997); missed one game. ... Tore medial collateral ligament in right knee (January 2, 1999); missed 19 games. ... Strained groin (March 28, 1999); missed two games. ... Bruised chest (January 13, 2000); missed three games. ... Strained quadriceps (November 18, 2000); missed six games. ... Traded by Kings with C Jozef Stumpel to Bruins for C Jason Allison and C/LW Mikko Eloranta (October 24, 2001).

STATISTICAL PLATEAUS: Three-goal games: 1997-98 (1), 1999-00 (1), 2001-02 (1), 2002-03 (1). Total: 4.

| | | | REGULAR SEASON | | | | | | | | PLAYOFFS | | | | |
Season Team	League	Gms.	G	A	Pts.	PIM	+/-	PP	SH		Gms.	G	A	Pts.	PIM
89-90—Sudbury.....................	OHL	62	8	28	36	17	...	...	...		7	0	0	0	4
90-91—Sudbury.....................	OHL	66	27	38	65	82	...	...	...		5	8	4	12	10
91-92—Sudbury.....................	OHL	54	37	47	84	93	...	...	...		11	7	4	11	18
—Boston......................	NHL	5	3	1	4	0	2	1	0		15	4	2	6	10
92-93—Providence................	AHL	48	30	26	56	42	...	...	...		6	1	4	5	4
—Boston......................	NHL	27	3	4	7	8	-6	2	0		—	—	—	—	—
93-94—Boston......................	NHL	81	18	13	31	48	-1	0	0		13	4	5	9	14
94-95—Boston......................	NHL	35	5	2	7	46	-11	0	0		2	0	0	0	2
95-96—Pittsburgh.................	NHL	69	14	15	29	57	4	0	0		18	2	6	8	10
96-97—Pittsburgh.................	NHL	66	11	11	22	24	-19	3	0		—	—	—	—	—
—Los Angeles..............	NHL	11	5	3	8	8	-2	0	0		—	—	—	—	—
97-98—Los Angeles..............	NHL	81	29	31	60	54	6	7	3		4	2	0	2	6
98-99—Los Angeles..............	NHL	61	16	15	31	36	-14	3	3		—	—	—	—	—
99-00—Los Angeles..............	NHL	78	29	33	62	60	13	10	1		4	0	0	0	2
00-01—Los Angeles..............	NHL	64	18	21	39	32	9	3	1		13	4	3	7	4
01-02—Los Angeles..............	NHL	9	6	5	11	0	5	4	0		—	—	—	—	—
—Boston......................	NHL	73	35	25	60	40	26	5	0		6	1	4	5	4
02-03—Boston	NHL	82	44	48	92	64	9	12	0		5	1	1	2	4
NHL Totals (12 years).........		742	236	227	463	477	21	50	8		80	18	21	39	56

MURRAY, MARTY   C   HURRICANES

PERSONAL: Born February 16, 1975, in Deloraine, Man. ... 5-9/180. ... Shoots left.
TRANSACTIONS/CAREER NOTES: Selected by Calgary Flames in fourth round (fifth Flames pick, 96th overall) of NHL entry draft (June 26, 1993). ... Bruised foot (April 8, 1996); missed three games. ... Strained hip flexor (October 12, 2000); missed nine games. ... Signed as free agent by Philadelphia Flyers (July 9, 2001). ... Strained muscle in rib cage (March 28, 2002); missed five games. ... Traded by Flyers for sixth-round draft pick in 2004 to Carolina Hurricanes (June 22, 2003).

Season Team	League	Gms.	G	A	Pts.	PIM	+/-	PP	SH		Gms.	G	A	Pts.	PIM
91-92—Brandon	WHL	68	20	36	56	12	...	...	...		—	—	—	—	—
92-93—Brandon	WHL	67	29	65	94	50	...	...	...		4	1	3	4	0
93-94—Brandon	WHL	64	43	71	114	33	...	...	...		14	6	14	20	14
94-95—Brandon	WHL	65	40	88	128	53	...	...	...		18	9	20	29	16
95-96—Calgary	NHL	15	3	3	6	0	-4	2	0		—	—	—	—	—
—Saint John	AHL	58	25	31	56	20	...	...	...		14	2	4	6	4
96-97—Saint John	AHL	67	19	39	58	40	...	...	...		5	2	3	5	4
—Calgary	NHL	2	0	0	0	4	0	0	0		—	—	—	—	—
97-98—Calgary	NHL	2	0	0	0	2	1	0	0		—	—	—	—	—
—Saint John	AHL	41	10	30	40	16	...	...	...		21	10	10	20	12
99-00—Kolner Haie	Germany	56	12	47	59	28	...	...	...		10	4	3	7	2
00-01—Calgary	NHL	7	0	0	0	0	-2	0	0		—	—	—	—	—
—Saint John	AHL	56	24	52	76	36	...	...	...		19	4	16	20	18
01-02—Philadelphia	AHL	3	0	3	3	2	...	...	...		—	—	—	—	—
—Philadelphia	NHL	74	12	15	27	10	10	1	1		5	0	1	1	0
02-03—Philadelphia	NHL	76	11	15	26	13	-1	1	1		4	0	0	0	4
NHL Totals (6 years)		176	26	33	59	29	4	4	2		9	0	1	1	4

MURRAY, REM   C   PREDATORS

PERSONAL: Born October 9, 1972, in Stratford, Ont. ... 6-2/196. ... Shoots left. ... Full Name: Raymond Murray.
TRANSACTIONS/CAREER NOTES: Selected by Los Angeles Kings in sixth round (fifth Kings pick, 135th overall) of NHL entry draft (June 20, 1992). ... Signed as free agent by Edmonton Oilers (August 17, 1995). ... Missed first five games of 1997-98 season recovering from wrist injury and off-season appendectomy. ... Strained neck (March 17, 1998); missed one game. ... Suffered from the flu (April 6, 1998); missed three games. ... Separated shoulder (October 7, 1999); missed seven games. ... Sprained medial collateral ligament in knee (November 3, 1999); missed 28 games. ... Traded by Oilers with D Tom Poti to New York Rangers for C Mike York and fourth-round pick (D Ivan Koltsov) in 2002 draft (March 19, 2002). ... Traded by Rangers with D Tomas Kloucek and D Marek Zidlicky to Nashville Predators for G Mike Dunham (December 12, 2002). ... Re-signed by Predators (June 30, 2003).
STATISTICAL PLATEAUS: Three-goal games: 1996-97 (1).

Season Team	League	Gms.	G	A	Pts.	PIM	+/-	PP	SH		Gms.	G	A	Pts.	PIM
90-91—Stratford Jr. B	OHA	48	39	59	98	22	...	...	...		—	—	—	—	—
91-92—Michigan State	CCHA	44	12	36	48	16	...	...	...		—	—	—	—	—
92-93—Michigan State	CCHA	40	22	35	57	24	...	...	...		—	—	—	—	—
93-94—Michigan State	CCHA	41	16	38	54	18	...	...	...		—	—	—	—	—
94-95—Michigan State	CCHA	40	20	36	56	21	...	...	...		—	—	—	—	—
95-96—Cape Breton	AHL	79	31	59	90	40	...	...	...		—	—	—	—	—
96-97—Edmonton	NHL	82	11	20	31	16	9	1	0		12	1	2	3	4
97-98—Edmonton	NHL	61	9	9	18	39	-9	2	2		11	1	4	5	2
98-99—Edmonton	NHL	78	21	18	39	20	4	4	1		4	1	1	2	2
99-00—Edmonton	NHL	44	9	5	14	8	-2	2	0		5	0	1	1	2
00-01—Edmonton	NHL	82	15	21	36	24	5	1	3		6	2	0	2	6
01-02—Edmonton	NHL	69	7	17	24	14	5	0	2		—	—	—	—	—
—New York Rangers	NHL	11	1	2	3	4	-9	0	0		—	—	—	—	—
02-03—New York Rangers	NHL	§32	6	6	12	4	-3	1	1		—	—	—	—	—
—Nashville	NHL	§53	6	13	19	18	1	1	0		—	—	—	—	—
NHL Totals (7 years)		512	85	111	196	147	1	12	9		38	5	8	13	16

MYHRES, BRANTT   RW

PERSONAL: Born March 18, 1974, in Edmonton ... 6-4/220. ... Shoots right. ... Name pronounced MIGH-urhs.
TRANSACTIONS/CAREER NOTES: Selected by Tampa Bay Lightning in fifth round (fifth Lightning pick, 97th overall) of NHL entry draft (June 20, 1992). ... Injured shoulder (April 11, 1995); missed one game. ... Injured hip (February 1, 1997); missed one game. ... Sprained ankle (February 23, 1997); missed three games. ... Suffered from the flu (April 4, 1997); missed three games. ... Traded by Lightning with third-round pick (D Alex Henry) in 1998 draft to Edmonton Oilers for C Vladimir Vujtek (July 16, 1997). ... Traded by Oilers to Philadelphia Flyers for F Jason Bowen (October 15, 1997). ... Bruised left hand (November 26, 1997); missed two games. ... Signed as free agent by San Jose Sharks (September 11, 1998). ... Suspended 12 games by NHL for leaving the bench to start a fight (February 12, 1999). ... Injured hand (October 28, 1999); missed seven games. ... Injured back (February 15, 2000); missed eight games. ... Signed as free agent by Nashville Predators (August 15, 2000). ... Traded by Predators to Washington Capitals for future considerations (February 1, 2001).

Season Team	League	Gms.	G	A	Pts.	PIM	+/-	PP	SH		Gms.	G	A	Pts.	PIM
90-91—Portland	WHL	59	2	7	9	125	...	...	...		—	—	—	—	—
91-92—Portland	WHL	4	0	2	2	22	...	...	...		—	—	—	—	—
—Lethbridge	WHL	53	4	11	15	359	...	...	...		5	0	0	0	36
92-93—Lethbridge	WHL	64	13	35	48	277	...	...	...		3	0	0	0	11
93-94—Atlanta	IHL	2	0	0	0	17	...	...	...		—	—	—	—	—
—Lethbridge	WHL	34	10	21	31	103	...	...	...		—	—	—	—	—
—Spokane	WHL	27	10	22	32	139	...	...	...		3	1	4	5	7
94-95—Atlanta	IHL	40	5	5	10	213	...	...	...		—	—	—	—	—
—Tampa Bay	NHL	15	2	0	2	81	-2	0	0		—	—	—	—	—
95-96—Atlanta	IHL	12	0	2	2	58	...	...	...		—	—	—	—	—

M

Season Team	League	REGULAR SEASON								PLAYOFFS				
		Gms.	G	A	Pts.	PIM	+/-	PP	SH	Gms.	G	A	Pts.	PIM
96-97—San Antonio	IHL	12	0	0	0	98	...	...	...	—	—	—	—	—
—Tampa Bay	NHL	47	3	1	4	136	1	0	0	—	—	—	—	—
97-98—Philadelphia	AHL	18	4	4	8	67	...	...	...	—	—	—	—	—
—Philadelphia	NHL	23	0	0	0	169	-1	0	0	—	—	—	—	—
98-99—San Jose	NHL	30	1	0	1	116	-2	0	0	—	—	—	—	—
—Kentucky	AHL	4	0	0	0	16	...	...	...	—	—	—	—	—
99-00—San Jose	NHL	13	0	1	1	97	0	0	0	—	—	—	—	—
—Kentucky	AHL	10	1	5	6	18	...	...	...	7	0	1	1	21
00-01—Nashville	NHL	20	0	0	0	28	-5	0	0	—	—	—	—	—
—Milwaukee	IHL	6	0	1	1	10	...	...	...	—	—	—	—	—
—Portland	AHL	9	1	0	1	53	...	...	...	—	—	—	—	—
—Washington	NHL	5	0	0	0	29	0	0	0	—	—	—	—	—
02-03—Providence	AHL	63	3	10	13	185	0	0	0	—	—	—	—	—
—Boston	NHL	1	0	0	0	31	0	0	0	—	—	—	—	—
NHL Totals (7 years)		154	6	2	8	687	-9	0	0					

NABOKOV, EVGENI G SHARKS

PERSONAL: Born July 25, 1975, in Kamenogorsk, U.S.S.R. ... 6-0/200. ... Catches left. ... Name pronounced nuh-BAH-kahf.
TRANSACTIONS/CAREER NOTES: Selected by San Jose Sharks in ninth round (ninth Sharks pick, 219th overall) of NHL entry draft (June 29, 1994).

Season Team	League	REGULAR SEASON									PLAYOFFS							
		Gms.	Min	W	L	T	GA	SO	Avg.	SV%	Gms.	Min.	W	L	GA	SO	Avg.	SV%
92-93—Torpedo Ust-Kam.	CIS	4	109	...	...	...	5	...	2.75	—	—	—	—	—	—	—	—	—
93-94—Torpedo Ust-Kam.	CIS	11	539	...	...	...	29	0	3.23	—	—	—	—	—	—	—	—	—
94-95—Dynamo Moscow	CIS	37	2075	...	...	...	70	...	2.02	—	—	—	—	—	—	—	—	—
95-96—Dynamo Moscow	CIS	37	1948	...	...	...	70	...	2.16	—	6	298	...	...	7	...	1.41	—
96-97—Dynamo Moscow	Russian	27	1588	...	...	...	56	2	2.12	—	4	255	...	...	12	0	2.82	—
97-98—Kentucky	AHL	33	1867	10	21	2	122	0	3.92	—	1	23	0	0	1	0	2.61	—
98-99—Kentucky	AHL	43	2429	26	14	1	106	5	2.62	—	11	599	6	5	30	2	3.01	—
99-00—Cleveland	IHL	20	1164	16	4	3	52	0	2.68	—								
—San Jose	NHL	11	414	2	2	1	15	1	2.17	.910	1	20	0	0	0	0	...	1.000
—Kentucky	AHL	2	120	1	1	0	3	1	1.50	—								
00-01—San Jose	NHL	66	3700	32	21	7	135	6	2.19	.915	4	218	1	3	10	1	2.75	.903
01-02—San Jose	NHL	67	3901	37	24	5	149	7	2.29	.918	12	712	7	5	31	0	2.61	.904
02-03—San Jose	NHL	55	3227	19	28	8	146	3	2.71	.906	—	—	—	—	—	—	—	—
NHL Totals (4 years)		199	11242	90	75	21	445	17	2.38	.913	17	950	8	8	41	1	2.59	.906

NAGY, LADISLAV LW COYOTES

PERSONAL: Born June 1, 1979, in Saca, Czechoslovakia ... 5-11/186. ... Shoots left.
TRANSACTIONS/CAREER NOTES: Selected by St. Louis Blues in seventh round (sixth Blues pick, 177th overall) of NHL entry draft (June 21, 1997). ... Traded by Blues with C Michal Handzus, C Jeff Taffe and first-round pick (LW Ben Eager) in 2002 draft to Phoenix Coyotes for LW Keith Tkachuk (March 13, 2001). ... Bruised knee (October 24, 2001); missed seven games. ... Bruised shoulder (November 10, 2001); missed one game.

Season Team	League	REGULAR SEASON								PLAYOFFS				
		Gms.	G	A	Pts.	PIM	+/-	PP	SH	Gms.	G	A	Pts.	PIM
96-97—Dragon Presov	Slov. Div. II	11	6	5	11	...	...	...	...	—	—	—	—	—
97-98—HC Kosice	Slovakia	29	19	15	34	41	...	...	...	—	—	—	—	—
98-99—Halifax	QMJHL	63	*71	55	126	148	...	...	...	5	3	3	6	18
—Worcester	AHL	—	—	—	—	—				3	2	2	4	0
99-00—Worcester	AHL	69	23	28	51	67	...	...	...	2	1	0	1	0
—St. Louis	NHL	11	2	4	6	2	2	1	0	6	1	1	2	0
00-01—St. Louis	NHL	40	8	8	16	20	-2	2	0	—	—	—	—	—
—Worcester	AHL	20	6	14	20	36	...	...	...	—	—	—	—	—
—Phoenix	NHL	6	0	1	1	2	0	0	0	—	—	—	—	—
01-02—Phoenix	NHL	74	23	19	42	50	6	5	0	5	0	0	0	21
02-03—Phoenix	NHL	80	22	35	57	92	17	8	0	—	—	—	—	—
NHL Totals (4 years)		211	55	67	122	166	23	16	0	11	1	1	2	21

NASH, RICK LW BLUE JACKETS

PERSONAL: Born June 16, 1984, in Brampton, Ont. ... 6-4/195. ... Shoots left.
TRANSACTIONS/CAREER NOTES: Selected by Columbus Blue Jackets in first round (first Blue Jackets pick, first overall) of NHL entry draft (June 22, 2002).

Season Team	League	REGULAR SEASON								PLAYOFFS				
		Gms.	G	A	Pts.	PIM	+/-	PP	SH	Gms.	G	A	Pts.	PIM
00-01—London	OHL	58	31	35	66	56	...	...	...	4	3	3	6	8
01-02—London	OHL	54	32	40	72	88	...	...	...	12	10	9	19	21
02-03—Columbus	NHL	74	17	22	39	78	-27	6	0	—	—	—	—	—
NHL Totals (1 year)		74	17	22	39	78	-27	6	0					

PERSONAL: Born March 11, 1975, in Edmonton ... 5-11/194. ... Shoots left. ... Full Name: Tyson Scott Nash.

TRANSACTIONS/CAREER NOTES: Selected by Vancouver Canucks in 10th round (eighth Canucks pick, 247th overall) of NHL entry draft (June 29, 1994). ... Signed as free agent by St. Louis Blues (July 24, 1998). ... Suffered concussion (December 5, 1999); missed three games. ... Injured shoulder (March 11, 2000); missed final 13 games of regular season. ... Injured shoulder (December 5, 2000); missed one game. ... Torn anterior cruciate ligament in knee (February 11, 2001); missed 16 games. ... Reinjured knee (March 22, 2001); missed remainder of season. ... Underwent knee and abdominal surgery prior to start of 2001-02 season; missed first four games of season. ... Injured elbow (November 13, 2001); missed two games. ... Suffered hip pointer (December 28, 2001); missed six games. ... Fractured nose (January 26, 2002); missed one game. ... Traded by Blues for fifth-round draft pick in 2003 to Phoenix Coyotes (June 22, 2003). ... Re-signed by Coyotes (July 20, 2003).

			REGULAR SEASON								PLAYOFFS				
Season Team	League	Gms.	G	A	Pts.	PIM	+/-	PP	SH		Gms.	G	A	Pts.	PIM
90-91—Kamloops	WHL	3	0	0	0	0	...	...	...		—	—	—	—	—
91-92—Kamloops	WHL	33	1	6	7	32	...	...	...		4	0	0	0	0
92-93—Kamloops	WHL	61	10	16	26	78	...	...	...		13	3	2	5	32
93-94—Kamloops	WHL	65	20	36	56	137	...	...	...		16	3	3	6	12
94-95—Kamloops	WHL	63	34	41	75	70	...	...	...		21	10	7	17	30
95-96—Syracuse	AHL	50	4	7	11	58	...	...	...		4	0	0	0	11
—Raleigh	ECHL	6	1	1	2	8	...	...	...		—	—	—	—	—
96-97—Syracuse	AHL	77	17	17	34	105	...	...	...		3	0	2	2	0
97-98—Syracuse	AHL	74	20	20	40	184	...	...	...		5	0	2	2	28
98-99—Worcester	AHL	55	14	22	36	143	...	...	...		4	4	1	5	27
—St. Louis	NHL	2	0	0	0	5	-1	0	0		1	0	0	0	2
99-00—St. Louis	NHL	66	4	9	13	150	6	0	1		6	1	0	1	24
00-01—St. Louis	NHL	57	8	7	15	110	8	0	1		—	—	—	—	—
01-02—St. Louis	NHL	64	6	7	13	100	2	0	0		9	0	1	1	20
02-03—St. Louis	NHL	66	6	3	9	114	0	1	0		7	2	1	3	6
NHL Totals (5 years)		255	24	26	50	479	15	1	2		23	3	2	5	52

PERSONAL: Born July 30, 1973, in Ornskoldsvik, Sweden ... 6-0/195. ... Shoots left. ... Name pronounced NAZ-luhnd.

TRANSACTIONS/CAREER NOTES: Selected by Pittsburgh Penguins in first round (first Penguins pick, 16th overall) of NHL entry draft (June 22, 1991). ... Traded by Penguins to Vancouver Canucks for LW Alex Stojanov (March 20, 1996). ... Suffered from flu (November 26, 1996); missed one game. ... Fractured leg (March 16, 2001); missed remainder of season.

STATISTICAL PLATEAUS: Three-goal games: 1995-96 (1), 1995-96 (1), 1998-99 (1), 2000-01 (1), 2001-02 (3), 2002-03 (1). Total: 8. ... Four-goal games: 2002-03 (1). ... Total hat tricks: 9.

			REGULAR SEASON								PLAYOFFS				
Season Team	League	Gms.	G	A	Pts.	PIM	+/-	PP	SH		Gms.	G	A	Pts.	PIM
89-90—MoDo Hockey	Sweden Jr.	33	43	35	78	20	...	...	...		—	—	—	—	—
90-91—MoDo Ornskoldsvik	Sweden	32	10	9	19	14	...	...	...		—	—	—	—	—
91-92—MoDo Ornskoldsvik	Sweden	39	22	18	40	54	...	...	...		—	—	—	—	—
92-93—MoDo Ornskoldsvik	Sweden	39	22	17	39	67	...	...	...		3	3	2	5	...
93-94—Pittsburgh	NHL	71	4	7	11	27	-3	1	0		—	—	—	—	—
—Cleveland	IHL	5	1	6	7	4	...	...	...		—	—	—	—	—
94-95—Pittsburgh	NHL	14	2	2	4	2	0	0	0		—	—	—	—	—
—Cleveland	IHL	7	3	4	7	6	...	...	...		4	1	3	4	8
95-96—Pittsburgh	NHL	66	19	33	52	36	17	3	0		—	—	—	—	—
—Vancouver	NHL	10	3	0	3	6	3	1	0		6	1	2	3	8
96-97—Vancouver	NHL	78	21	20	41	30	-15	4	0		—	—	—	—	—
97-98—Vancouver	NHL	76	14	20	34	56	5	2	1		—	—	—	—	—
98-99—Vancouver	NHL	80	36	30	66	74	-13	15	2		—	—	—	—	—
99-00—Vancouver	NHL	82	27	38	65	64	-5	6	2		—	—	—	—	—
00-01—Vancouver	NHL	72	41	34	75	58	-2	18	1		—	—	—	—	—
01-02—Vancouver	NHL	81	40	50	90	50	22	8	0		6	1	1	2	2
—Swedish Oly. team	Int'l	4	2	1	3	0	...	...	...		—	—	—	—	—
02-03—Vancouver	NHL	82	48	56	104	52	6	24	0		14	5	9	14	18
NHL Totals (10 years)		712	255	290	545	455	15	82	6		26	7	12	19	28

PERSONAL: Born July 10, 1975, in Montreal ... 6-1/201. ... Shoots left. ... Name pronounced AL-ai NAS-rih-DEEN.

TRANSACTIONS/CAREER NOTES: Selected by Florida Panthers in sixth round (eighth Panthers pick, 135th overall) of NHL entry draft (June 26, 1993). ... Traded by Panthers with conditional pick in 1999 draft to Chicago Blackhawks for D Ivan Droppa (December 8, 1996). ... Traded by Blackhawks with G Jeff Hackett, D Eric Weinrich and fourth-round pick (D Chris Dyment) in 1999 draft to Montreal Canadiens for G Jocelyn Thibault, D Dave Manson and D Brad Brown (November 16, 1998). ... Suspended two games and fined $1,000 by NHL for physically demeaning a linesman (December 11, 1998). ... Traded by Canadiens with D Igor Ulanov to Edmonton Oilers for D Christian LaFlamme and D Mathieu Descoteaux (March 9, 2000).

			REGULAR SEASON								PLAYOFFS				
Season Team	League	Gms.	G	A	Pts.	PIM	+/-	PP	SH		Gms.	G	A	Pts.	PIM
91-92—Drummondville	QMJHL	61	1	9	10	78	...	...	...		4	0	0	0	17
92-93—Drummondville	QMJHL	64	0	14	14	137	...	...	...		10	0	1	1	36
93-94—Chicoutimi	QMJHL	60	3	24	27	218	...	...	...		26	2	10	12	118
94-95—Chicoutimi	QMJHL	67	8	31	39	342	...	...	...		13	3	5	8	40
95-96—Carolina	AHL	63	0	5	5	245	...	...	...		—	—	—	—	—
96-97—Carolina	AHL	26	0	4	4	109	...	...	...		—	—	—	—	—
—Indianapolis	IHL	49	0	2	2	248	...	...	...		4	1	1	2	27

N

Season Team	League	REGULAR SEASON								PLAYOFFS				
		Gms.	G	A	Pts.	PIM	+/-	PP	SH	Gms.	G	A	Pts.	PIM
97-98—Indianapolis	IHL	75	1	12	13	258	...	...	...	5	0	2	2	12
98-99—Chicago	NHL	7	0	0	0	19	-2	0	0	—	—	—	—	—
—Portland	AHL	7	0	1	1	36	...	...	...	—	—	—	—	—
—Fredericton	AHL	38	0	10	10	108	...	...	...	15	0	3	3	39
—Montreal	NHL	8	0	0	0	33	1	0	0	—	—	—	—	—
99-00—Quebec	AHL	59	1	6	7	178	...	...	...	—	—	—	—	—
—Hamilton	AHL	11	0	0	0	12	...	...	...	10	1	1	2	14
00-01—Hamilton	AHL	74	4	14	18	164	...	...	...	—	—	—	—	—
01-02—Hamilton	AHL	79	7	10	17	154	...	...	...	12	1	3	4	22
02-03—Bridgeport	AHL	67	3	9	12	114	...	...	...	—	—	—	—	—
—New York Islanders	NHL	3	0	0	0	2	0	0	0	—	—	—	—	—
NHL Totals (2 years)		18	0	0	0	54	-1	0	0	—	—	—	—	—

NAZAROV, ANDREI   LW   COYOTES

PERSONAL: Born May 22, 1974, in Chelyabinsk, U.S.S.R. ... 6-5/240. ... Shoots right. ... Name pronounced nuh-ZAH-rahf.

TRANSACTIONS/CAREER NOTES: Selected by San Jose Sharks in first round (second Sharks pick, 10th overall) of NHL entry draft (June 20, 1992). ... Suspended four games and fined $500 by NHL for head-butting (March 8, 1995). ... Suffered facial fracture (February 5, 1997); missed 14 games. ... Suspended 13 games by NHL for physical abuse of officials (March 25, 1997). ... Injured knee (October 13, 1997); missed seven games. ... Traded by Sharks with first-round pick (C Vincent Lecavalier) in 1998 draft and future considerations to Tampa Bay Lightning for D Bryan Marchment, D David Shaw and first-round pick (traded to Nashville) in 1998 draft (March 24, 1998). ... Injured finger (November 8, 1998); missed one game. ... Suspended seven games and fined $1,000 by NHL for cross-checking incident (November 19, 1998). ... Traded by Lightning to Calgary Flames for C Michael Nylander (January 19, 1999). ... Traded by Flames with second-round pick (traded back to Calgary) in 2001 draft to Mighty Ducks of Anaheim for D Jordan Leopold (September 26, 2000). ... Traded by Mighty Ducks with D Patrick Traverse to Boston Bruins for C Samuel Pahlsson (November 18, 2000). ... Traded by Bruins to Phoenix Coyotes for fifth-round pick (G Peter Hamerlik) in 2002 draft (January 25, 2002). ... Suspended four games by NHL for receiving match penalty in game (March 10, 2003).

Season Team	League	REGULAR SEASON								PLAYOFFS				
		Gms.	G	A	Pts.	PIM	+/-	PP	SH	Gms.	G	A	Pts.	PIM
90-91—Mechel Chelyabinsk	USSR	2	0	0	0	0	...	...	...	—	—	—	—	—
91-92—Dynamo Moscow	CIS	2	1	0	1	2	...	...	...	—	—	—	—	—
92-93—Dynamo Moscow	CIS	42	8	2	10	79	...	...	...	10	1	1	2	8
93-94—Kansas City	IHL	71	15	18	33	64	...	...	...	—	—	—	—	—
—San Jose	NHL	1	0	0	0	0	0	0	0	—	—	—	—	—
94-95—Kansas City	IHL	43	15	10	25	55	...	...	...	—	—	—	—	—
—San Jose	NHL	26	3	5	8	94	-1	0	0	6	0	0	0	9
95-96—San Jose	NHL	42	7	7	14	62	-15	2	0	—	—	—	—	—
—Kansas City	IHL	27	4	6	10	118	...	...	...	2	0	0	0	2
96-97—San Jose	NHL	60	12	15	27	222	-4	1	0	—	—	—	—	—
—Kentucky	AHL	3	1	2	3	4	...	...	...	—	—	—	—	—
97-98—San Jose	NHL	40	1	1	2	112	-4	0	0	—	—	—	—	—
—Tampa Bay	NHL	14	1	1	2	58	-9	0	0	—	—	—	—	—
98-99—Tampa Bay	NHL	26	2	0	2	43	-5	0	0	—	—	—	—	—
—Calgary	NHL	36	5	9	14	30	1	0	0	—	—	—	—	—
99-00—Calgary	NHL	76	10	22	32	78	3	1	0	—	—	—	—	—
00-01—Anaheim	NHL	16	1	0	1	29	-9	0	0	—	—	—	—	—
—Boston	NHL	63	1	4	5	200	-14	0	0	—	—	—	—	—
01-02—Boston	NHL	47	0	2	2	164	-2	0	0	—	—	—	—	—
—Phoenix	NHL	30	6	3	9	51	7	0	0	3	0	0	0	2
02-03—Phoenix	NHL	59	3	0	3	135	-9	2	0	—	—	—	—	—
NHL Totals (10 years)		536	52	69	121	1278	-61	6	0	9	0	0	0	11

N   NECKAR, STAN   D

PERSONAL: Born December 22, 1975, in Ceske Budejovice, Czechoslovakia ... 6-1/209. ... Shoots left. ... Full Name: Stanislav Neckar. ... Name pronounced NEHTS-kash.

TRANSACTIONS/CAREER NOTES: Selected by Ottawa Senators in second round (second Senators pick, 29th overall) of NHL entry draft (June 28, 1994). ... Suffered partially torn knee ligament (October 18, 1996); missed remainder of the season. ... Injured right knee (January 24, 1998); missed two games. ... Reinjured knee (April 3, 1998) and underwent surgery; missed final nine games of season. ... Fractured right foot (October 22, 1998); missed 16 games. ... Traded by Senators to New York Rangers for LW Bill Berg and second-round pick (traded to Anaheim) in 1999 draft (November 27, 1998). ... Traded by Rangers to Phoenix Coyotes for D Jason Doig and sixth-round pick (C Jay Dardis) in 1999 draft (March 23, 1999). ... Strained knee (October 18, 1999); missed 13 games. ... Injured ankle (November 21, 2000); missed 12 games. ... Traded by Coyotes with G Nikolai Khabibulin to Tampa Bay Lightning for D Paul Mara, RW Mike Johnson, RW Ruslan Zainullin and second-round pick (D Matthew Spiller) in 2001 (March 5, 2001).

Season Team	League	REGULAR SEASON								PLAYOFFS				
		Gms.	G	A	Pts.	PIM	+/-	PP	SH	Gms.	G	A	Pts.	PIM
91-92—Budejovice	Czech Dv.II	18	1	3	4	...	...	...	...	—	—	—	—	—
92-93—Motor-Ceske Bude.	Czech.	42	2	9	11	12	...	...	...	—	—	—	—	—
93-94—HC Ceske Budejovice	Czech Rep.	12	3	2	5	2	...	...	...	3	0	0	0	0
94-95—Detroit	IHL	15	2	2	4	15	...	...	...	—	—	—	—	—
—Ottawa	NHL	48	1	3	4	37	-20	0	0	—	—	—	—	—
95-96—Ottawa	NHL	82	3	9	12	54	-16	1	0	—	—	—	—	—
96-97—Ottawa	NHL	5	0	0	0	2	2	0	0	—	—	—	—	—
97-98—Ottawa	NHL	60	2	2	4	31	-14	0	0	9	0	0	0	2
98-99—Ottawa	NHL	3	0	2	2	0	-1	0	0	—	—	—	—	—
—New York Rangers	NHL	18	0	0	0	8	-1	0	0	—	—	—	—	—
—Phoenix	NHL	11	0	1	1	10	3	0	0	6	0	1	1	4

Season Team	League	REGULAR SEASON								PLAYOFFS				
		Gms.	G	A	Pts.	PIM	+/-	PP	SH	Gms.	G	A	Pts.	PIM
99-00—Phoenix......................	NHL	66	2	8	10	36	1	0	0	5	0	0	0	0
00-01—Phoenix......................	NHL	53	2	2	4	63	-2	0	0	—	—	—	—	—
—Tampa Bay................	NHL	16	0	2	2	8	-1	0	0	—	—	—	—	—
01-02—Tampa Bay................	NHL	77	1	7	8	24	-18	0	1	—	—	—	—	—
02-03—Tampa Bay................	NHL	70	1	4	5	43	-6	0	0	7	0	2	2	2
NHL Totals (9 years)...........		509	12	40	52	316	-73	1	1	27	0	3	3	8

NEDOROST, ANDREJ   C   BLUE JACKETS

PERSONAL: Born April 30, 1980, in Trencin, Czechoslovakia ... 6-1/190. ... Shoots left.
TRANSACTIONS/CAREER NOTES: Selected by Columbus Blue Jackets in ninth round (10th Blue Jackets pick, 286th overall) of NHL entry draft (June 24, 2000).

Season Team	League	REGULAR SEASON								PLAYOFFS				
		Gms.	G	A	Pts.	PIM	+/-	PP	SH	Gms.	G	A	Pts.	PIM
95-96—Dukla Trencin.............	Slovakia Jrs.	40	50	35	85	...	...	...	...	—	—	—	—	—
96-97—Dukla Trencin.............	Slovakia Jrs.	45	15	16	31	...	...	...	...	—	—	—	—	—
97-98—Dukla Trencin.............	Slovakia Jrs.	45	27	22	49	61	...	...	...	—	—	—	—	—
—Dukla Trencin.............	Slovakia	1	0	0	0	0	...	...	...	—	—	—	—	—
98-99—Essen........................	Germany	30	3	5	8	22	...	...	...	—	—	—	—	—
99-00—Essen........................	Germany	66	7	5	12	44	...	...	...	—	—	—	—	—
00-01—HC Keramika Plzen	Czech Rep.	33	10	29	39	22	...	...	...	—	—	—	—	—
01-02—Syracuse...................	AHL	37	5	13	18	28	...	...	...	10	1	3	4	4
—Columbus	NHL	7	0	2	2	2	-3	0	0	—	—	—	—	—
02-03—Syracuse...................	AHL	63	14	19	33	85	...	...	...	—	—	—	—	—
—Columbus	NHL	12	0	1	1	4	-6	0	0	—	—	—	—	—
NHL Totals (2 years)..........		19	0	3	3	6	-9	0	0					

NEDOROST, VACLAV   C   PANTHERS

PERSONAL: Born March 16, 1982, in Ceske Budejovice, Czechoslovakia ... 6-1/185. ... Shoots left.
TRANSACTIONS/CAREER NOTES: Selected by Colorado Avalanche in first round (first Avalanche pick, 14th overall) of NHL entry draft (June 24, 2000). ... Suffered hip pointer (November 18, 2001); missed two games. ... Traded by Colorado Avalanche to Florida Panthers with F/D Eric Messier for F Peter Worrell and 2004 second-round draft pick (July 20, 2003).

Season Team	League	REGULAR SEASON								PLAYOFFS				
		Gms.	G	A	Pts.	PIM	+/-	PP	SH	Gms.	G	A	Pts.	PIM
98-99—Budejovice	Czech. Jrs.	35	5	13	18	10	...	...	...	—	—	—	—	—
99-00—Budejovice	Czech Rep.	38	8	6	14	6	...	...	...	3	0	0	0	0
—Budejovice	Czech. Jrs.	7	2	5	7	6	...	...	...	—	—	—	—	—
00-01—HC Ceske Budejovice..	Czech Rep.	36	3	12	15	22	...	...	...	—	—	—	—	—
01-02—Colorado	NHL	25	2	2	4	2	-4	1	0	—	—	—	—	—
—Hershey	AHL	49	12	22	34	16	...	...	·	7	2	3	5	2
02-03—Hershey	AHL	5	3	2	5	0	...	...	...	—	—	—	—	—
—Colorado	NHL	42	4	5	9	20	8	1	0	—	—	—	—	—
NHL Totals (2 years)..........		67	6	7	13	22	4	2	0					

NEDVED, PETR   LW   RANGERS

PERSONAL: Born December 9, 1971, in Liberec, Czechoslovakia ... 6-3/197. ... Shoots left. ... Name pronounced NEHD-VEHD.
TRANSACTIONS/CAREER NOTES: Selected by Vancouver Canucks in first round (first Canucks pick, second overall) of NHL entry draft (June 16, 1990). ... Signed to offer sheet by St. Louis Blues (March 4, 1994); C Craig Janney and second-round pick (C Dave Scatchard) in 1994 draft awarded to Canucks as compensation (March 14, 1994). ... Traded by Blues to New York Rangers for LW Esa Tikkanen and D Doug Lidster (July 24, 1994); trade arranged as compensation for Blues signing coach Mike Keenan. ... Strained abdomen (February 27, 1995); missed two games. ... Traded by Rangers with D Sergei Zubov to Pittsburgh Penguins for LW Luc Robitaille and D Ulf Samuelsson (August 31, 1995). ... Bruised thigh (November 18, 1995); missed two games. ... Bruised tailbone (December 19, 1996); missed two games. ... Sprained wrist (January 14, 1997); missed two games. ... Suffered charley horse (February 8, 1997); missed one game. ... Sprained wrist (March 20, 1997); missed three games. ... Missed all of 1997-98 season and first 18 games of 1998-99 season due to contract dispute; played for Las Vegas of IHL. ... Traded by Penguins with C Sean Pronger and D Chris Tamer to Rangers for RW Alexei Kovalev, C Harry York and future considerations (November 25, 1998). ... Strained muscle in ribcage (April 2, 1999); missed final seven games of season. ... Strained groin (December 2, 1999); missed four games. ... Bruised ribs (March 15, 2000); missed two games. ... Suspended three games by NHL for high-sticking incident (December 12, 2000). ... Suffered concussion (October 31, 2001); missed four games.
STATISTICAL PLATEAUS: Three-goal games: 1998-99 (1), 1999-00 (3), 2000-01 (1), 2002-03 (1). Total: 6. ... Four-goal games: 1995-96 (1). ... Total hat tricks: 7.

Season Team	League	REGULAR SEASON								PLAYOFFS				
		Gms.	G	A	Pts.	PIM	+/-	PP	SH	Gms.	G	A	Pts.	PIM
88-89—Litvinov......................	Czech. Jrs.	20	32	19	51	12	...	...	...	—	—	—	—	—
89-90—Seattle.......................	WHL	71	65	80	145	80	...	...	...	11	4	9	13	2
90-91—Vancouver..................	NHL	61	10	6	16	20	-21	1	0	6	0	1	1	0
91-92—Vancouver..................	NHL	77	15	22	37	36	-3	5	0	10	1	4	5	16
92-93—Vancouver..................	NHL	84	38	33	71	96	20	2	1	12	2	3	5	2
93-94—Canadian nat'l team	Int'l	17	19	12	31	16	...	...	...	—	—	—	—	—
—Can. Olympic team	Int'l	8	5	1	6	6	...	...	...	—	—	—	—	—
—St. Louis	NHL	19	6	14	20	8	2	2	0	4	0	1	1	4
94-95—New York Rangers......	NHL	46	11	12	23	26	-1	1	0	10	3	2	5	6
95-96—Pittsburgh..................	NHL	80	45	54	99	68	37	8	1	18	10	10	20	16
96-97—Pittsburgh..................	NHL	74	33	38	71	66	-2	12	3	5	1	2	3	12

N

Season Team	League	REGULAR SEASON Gms.	G	A	Pts.	PIM	+/-	PP	SH	PLAYOFFS Gms.	G	A	Pts.	PIM
97-98—Sparta Praha	Czech Rep.	5	2	3	5	8	...	...	...	6	0	2	2	52
—Las Vegas	IHL	3	3	3	6	4	...	...	...	—	—	—	—	—
98-99—Las Vegas	IHL	13	8	10	18	32	...	...	...	—	—	—	—	—
—New York Rangers	NHL	56	20	27	47	50	-6	9	1	—	—	—	—	—
99-00—New York Rangers	NHL	76	24	44	68	40	2	6	2	—	—	—	—	—
00-01—New York Rangers	NHL	79	32	46	78	54	10	9	1	—	—	—	—	—
01-02—New York Rangers	NHL	78	21	25	46	36	-8	6	1	—	—	—	—	—
02-03—New York Rangers	NHL	78	27	31	58	64	-4	8	3	—	—	—	—	—
NHL Totals (12 years)		808	282	352	634	564	26	69	13	65	17	23	40	56

NEIL, CHRIS — RW — SENATORS

PERSONAL: Born June 18, 1979, in Markdale, Ont. ... 6-0/216. ... Shoots right. ... Full Name: Christopher Neil.

TRANSACTIONS/CAREER NOTES: Selected by Ottawa Senators in sixth round (seventh Senators pick, 161st overall) of NHL entry draft (June 27, 1998). ... Injured hip (March 19, 2002); missed one game. ... Reinjured hip (March 24, 2002); missed three games.

Season Team	League	REGULAR SEASON Gms.	G	A	Pts.	PIM	+/-	PP	SH	PLAYOFFS Gms.	G	A	Pts.	PIM
96-97—North Bay	OHL	65	13	16	29	150	...	...	...	—	—	—	—	—
97-98—North Bay	OHL	59	26	29	55	231	...	...	...	—	—	—	—	—
98-99—North Bay	OHL	66	26	46	72	215	...	...	...	4	1	0	1	15
99-00—Grand Rapids	IHL	51	9	10	19	*301	...	...	...	8	0	2	2	24
—Mobile	ECHL	4	0	2	2	39	...	...	...	—	—	—	—	—
00-01—Grand Rapids	IHL	78	15	21	36	354	...	...	...	10	2	2	4	22
01-02—Ottawa	NHL	72	10	7	17	231	5	1	0	12	0	0	0	12
02-03—Ottawa	NHL	68	6	4	10	147	8	0	0	15	1	0	1	24
NHL Totals (2 years)		140	16	11	27	378	13	1	0	27	1	0	1	36

NEWBURY, KRIS — C — SHARKS

PERSONAL: Born February 19, 1982, in Brampton, Ont. ... 5-10/197. ... Shoots left.

TRANSACTIONS/CAREER NOTES: Selected by San Jose Sharks in fifth round (fourth Sharks pick, 139th overall) of NHL entry draft (June 23, 2002).

Season Team	League	REGULAR SEASON Gms.	G	A	Pts.	PIM	+/-	PP	SH	PLAYOFFS Gms.	G	A	Pts.	PIM
01-02—Sarnia	OHL	66	42	62	104	141	...	...	...	5	1	3	4	15
02-03—Sarnia	OHL	64	34	58	92	149	...	...	...	—	—	—	—	—

NEWMAN, JARED — D — HURRICANES

PERSONAL: Born March 7, 1982, in Detroit. ... 6-2/201. ... Shoots right.

TRANSACTIONS/CAREER NOTES: Selected by Carolina Hurricanes in fourth round (fourth Hurricanes pick, 110th overall) of NHL entry draft (June 24, 2000).

Season Team	League	REGULAR SEASON Gms.	G	A	Pts.	PIM	+/-	PP	SH	PLAYOFFS Gms.	G	A	Pts.	PIM
99-00—Plymouth	OHL	50	1	15	16	123	...	...	...	—	—	—	—	—
00-01—Plymouth	OHL	34	0	4	4	114	...	...	...	6	0	3	3	26
01-02—Plymouth	OHL	60	2	14	16	106	...	...	...	6	0	1	1	8
02-03—Florida	ECHL	29	1	1	2	82	...	...	...	—	—	—	—	—

NICHOL, SCOTT — C — BLACKHAWKS

PERSONAL: Born December 31, 1974, in Edmonton ... 5-8/173. ... Shoots right.

TRANSACTIONS/CAREER NOTES: Selected by Buffalo Sabres in 11th round (ninth Sabres pick, 272nd overall) of NHL entry draft (June 26, 1993). ... Signed as free agent by Calgary Flames (August 2, 2001). ... Injured hand (October 10, 2001); missed one game. ... Injured hip (October 25, 2001); missed one game. ... Suspended two games by NHL for unsportsmanlike conduct (December 10, 2001). ... Injured hip (January 5, 2002); missed three games. ... Injured knee (February 26, 2002); missed 14 games. ... Suspended five games by NHL for high-sticking incident (December 20, 2002). ... Signed as free agent by Chicago Blackhawks (July 1, 2003).

Season Team	League	REGULAR SEASON Gms.	G	A	Pts.	PIM	+/-	PP	SH	PLAYOFFS Gms.	G	A	Pts.	PIM
92-93—Portland	WHL	67	31	33	64	146	...	...	...	—	—	—	—	—
93-94—Portland	WHL	65	40	53	93	144	...	...	...	—	—	—	—	—
94-95—Rochester	AHL	71	11	16	27	136	...	...	...	5	0	3	3	14
95-96—Rochester	AHL	62	14	17	31	170	...	...	...	19	7	6	13	36
—Buffalo	NHL	2	0	0	0	10	0	0	0	—	—	—	—	—
96-97—Rochester	AHL	68	22	21	43	133	...	...	...	10	2	1	3	26
97-98—Rochester	AHL	35	13	7	20	113	...	...	...	—	—	—	—	—
—Buffalo	NHL	3	0	0	0	4	0	0	0	—	—	—	—	—
98-99—Rochester	AHL	53	13	20	33	120	...	...	...	—	—	—	—	—
99-00—Rochester	AHL	37	7	11	18	141	...	...	...	—	—	—	—	—
00-01—Detroit	IHL	67	7	24	31	198	...	...	...	—	—	—	—	—
01-02—Calgary	NHL	60	8	9	17	107	-9	2	1	—	—	—	—	—
02-03—Calgary	NHL	68	5	5	10	149	-7	0	1	—	—	—	—	—
NHL Totals (4 years)		133	13	14	27	270	-16	2	2					

PERSONAL: Born March 25, 1975, in Hyannis, Mass. ... 6-1/201. ... Shoots right.

TRANSACTIONS/CAREER NOTES: Selected by Boston Bruins in fourth round (third Bruins pick, 99th overall) of NHL entry draft (June 29, 1994). ... Suffered from charley horse (September 22, 2000); missed first three games of season. ... Bruised ribs (October 14, 2000); missed two games. ... Signed as free agent by St. Louis Blues (July 16, 2002).

STATISTICAL PLATEAUS: Three-goal games: 1996-97 (1).

					REGULAR SEASON						PLAYOFFS			
Season Team	League	Gms.	G	A	Pts.	PIM	+/-	PP	SH	Gms.	G	A	Pts.	PIM
91-92—Barnstable H.S..........	Mass. Jr. A	24	30	25	55	...				—	—	—	—	—
92-93—Tabor Academy.........	Mass. H.S.	28	25	25	50	...				—	—	—	—	—
93-94—Cushing Academy........	Mass. H.S.	25	46	36	82	...				—	—	—	—	—
94-95—Univ. of New Hamp.....	Hockey East	33	15	9	24	32	...			—	—	—	—	—
95-96—Univ. of New Hamp.....	Hockey East	34	26	12	38	66	...			—	—	—	—	—
96-97—Univ. of New Hamp.....	Hockey East	39	29	22	51	80	...			—	—	—	—	—
97-98—Orlando......................	IHL	76	22	9	31	77	...			6	0	0	0	10
98-99—Providence.................	AHL	75	31	27	58	83	...			18	8	12	20	33
—Boston	NHL	2	0	0	0	0	0	0	0	1	0	0	0	2
99-00—Providence.................	AHL	40	6	6	12	37	...			12	2	3	5	20
—Providence.................	NHL	20	5	6	11	12	-1	1	0	—	—	—	—	—
00-01—Boston	NHL	7	0	0	0	4	-2	0	0	—	—	—	—	—
—Providence.................	AHL	62	20	23	43	100	...			12	4	4	8	24
01-02—Worcester	AHL	54	11	25	36	48	...			3	0	1	1	2
02-03—Worcester	AHL	39	17	16	33	40	...			—	—	—	—	—
—St. Louis	NHL	8	0	1	1	6	-2	0	0	—	—	—	—	—
NHL Totals (4 years)..........		37	5	7	12	22	-5	1	0	1	0	0	0	2

PERSONAL: Born December 28, 1974, in Cassiar, B.C. ... 6-2/205. ... Shoots left. ... Brother of Scott Niedermayer, defenseman, New Jersey Devils. ... Name pronounced NEE-duhr-MIGH-uhr.

TRANSACTIONS/CAREER NOTES: Selected by Florida Panthers in first round (first Panthers pick, fifth overall) of NHL entry draft (June 26, 1993). ... Separated right shoulder (November 18, 1993); missed 17 games. ... Sprained knee ligament (November 22, 1996); missed 17 games. ... Strained groin (March 5, 1997); missed two games. ... Sprained wrist (March 20, 1997); missed three games. ... Suffered concussion (October 1, 1997); missed 10 games. ... Dislocated right thumb (November 18, 1997); missed 15 games. ... Underwent knee surgery during 1997-98 All-Star break; missed eight games. ... Suffered post-concussion syndrome (March 19, 1998); missed remainder of season. ... Suffered head injury (March 3, 2000); missed one game. ... Suffered concussion (February 21, 2001); missed 15 games. ... Traded by Panthers with second-round pick (G Andrei Medvedev) in 2001 draft to Calgary Flames for RW Valeri Bure and C Jason Wiemer (June 23, 2001). ... Bruised hip (October 13, 2001); missed four games. ... Suffered injury (November 17, 2001); missed one game. ... Sprained knee and ankle (January 8, 2002); missed 18 games. ... Suffered injury (March 6, 2002); missed two games. ... Traded by Flames to Mighty Ducks of Anaheim for D Mike Commodore and G J.F. Damphousse (March 11, 2003).

					REGULAR SEASON						PLAYOFFS			
Season Team	League	Gms.	G	A	Pts.	PIM	+/-	PP	SH	Gms.	G	A	Pts.	PIM
90-91—Medicine Hat..............	WHL	71	24	26	50	8	...			12	3	7	10	2
91-92—Medicine Hat..............	WHL	71	32	46	78	77	...			4	2	3	5	2
92-93—Medicine Hat..............	WHL	52	43	34	77	67	...			—	—	—	—	—
93-94—Florida.......................	NHL	65	9	17	26	51	-11	3	0	—	—	—	—	—
94-95—Medicine Hat..............	WHL	13	9	15	24	14	...			—	—	—	—	—
—Florida.........................	NHL	48	4	6	10	36	-13	1	0	—	—	—	—	—
95-96—Florida.......................	NHL	82	26	35	61	107	1	11	0	22	5	3	8	12
96-97—Florida.......................	NHL	60	14	24	38	54	4	3	0	5	2	1	3	6
97-98—Florida.......................	NHL	33	8	7	15	41	-9	5	0	—	—	—	—	—
98-99—Florida.......................	NHL	82	18	33	51	50	-13	6	1	—	—	—	—	—
99-00—Florida.......................	NHL	81	10	23	33	46	-5	1	0	4	1	0	1	6
00-01—Florida.......................	NHL	67	12	20	32	50	-12	3	1	—	—	—	—	—
01-02—Calgary	NHL	57	6	14	20	49	-15	1	2	—	—	—	—	—
02-03—Calgary	NHL	54	8	10	18	42	-13	2	0	—	—	—	—	—
—Anaheim	NHL	12	2	2	4	15	3	1	0	21	3	7	10	18
NHL Totals (10 years).........		641	117	191	308	541	-83	37	4	52	11	11	22	42

PERSONAL: Born August 31, 1973, in Edmonton ... 6-1/200. ... Shoots left. ... Brother of Rob Niedermayer, center, Mighty Ducks of Anaheim. ... Name pronounced NEE-duhr-MIGH-uhr.

TRANSACTIONS/CAREER NOTES: Selected by New Jersey Devils in first round (first Devils pick, third overall) of NHL entry draft (June 22, 1991). ... Suffered sore back (December 9, 1992); missed four games. ... Injured knee (December 19, 1995); missed three games. ... Strained groin (February 12, 1997); missed one game. ... Suffered from the flu (February 4, 1998); missed one game. ... Missed first nine games of 1998-99 season due to contact dispute; played for Utah of IHL. ... Strained hip flexor (January 15, 2000); missed one game. ... Suffered illness (January 26, 2000); missed one game. ... Suspended final nine games of regular season and one playoff game by NHL for high-sticking incident (March 21, 2000). ... Missed first 19 games of 2000-01 season due to contract dispute. ... Injured knee (January 20, 2001); missed one game. ... Injured knee (February 8, 2001); missed five games. ... Strained lower back (October 5, 2001); missed first two games of season. ... Suffered pinched nerve in neck (February 27, 2002); missed three games.

Season Team	League	REGULAR SEASON Gms.	G	A	Pts.	PIM	+/-	PP	SH	PLAYOFFS Gms.	G	A	Pts.	PIM
89-90—Kamloops	WHL	64	14	55	69	64	...	...	...	17	2	14	16	35
90-91—Kamloops	WHL	57	26	56	82	52	...	...	...	—	—	—	—	—
91-92—New Jersey	NHL	4	0	1	1	2	1	0	0	—	—	—	—	—
—Kamloops	WHL	35	7	32	39	61	...	...	...	17	9	14	23	28
92-93—New Jersey	NHL	80	11	29	40	47	8	5	0	5	0	3	3	2
93-94—New Jersey	NHL	81	10	36	46	42	34	5	0	20	2	2	4	8
94-95—New Jersey	NHL	48	4	15	19	18	19	4	0	20	4	7	11	10
95-96—New Jersey	NHL	79	8	25	33	46	5	6	0	—	—	—	—	—
96-97—New Jersey	NHL	81	5	30	35	64	-4	3	0	10	2	4	6	6
97-98—New Jersey	NHL	81	14	43	57	27	5	11	0	6	0	2	2	4
98-99—Utah	IHL	5	0	2	2	0	...	...	...	—	—	—	—	—
—New Jersey	NHL	72	11	35	46	26	16	1	1	7	1	3	4	18
99-00—New Jersey	NHL	71	7	31	38	48	19	1	0	22	5	2	7	10
00-01—New Jersey	NHL	57	6	29	35	22	14	1	0	21	0	6	6	14
01-02—New Jersey	NHL	76	11	22	33	30	12	2	0	6	0	2	2	6
—Can. Olympic team	Int'l	6	1	1	2	4	...	...	...	—	—	—	—	—
02-03—New Jersey	NHL	81	11	28	39	62	23	3	0	24	2	*16	†18	16
NHL Totals (12 years)		811	98	324	422	434	152	42	1	141	16	47	63	94

NIELSEN, CHRIS   RW   CANUCKS

PERSONAL: Born February 16, 1980, in Moshi, Tanzania. ... 6-1/190. ... Shoots right.

TRANSACTIONS/CAREER NOTES: Selected by New York Islanders in second round (second Islanders pick, 36th overall) of NHL entry draft (June 27, 1998). ... Traded by Islanders to Columbus Blue Jackets for fourth-(traded to Anaheim) and ninth-round (F Dmitri Altarev) picks in 2000 draft (May 11, 2000). ... Injured groin (October 8, 2001); missed 14 games. ... Traded by Blue Jackets with D Petteri Nummelin to Atlanta Thrashers for RW Tomi Kallio and D Pauli Levokari (December 2, 2002). ... Traded by Thrashers with LW Chris Herperger to Vancouver Canucks for C Jeff Farkas (January 20, 2003).

Season Team	League	REGULAR SEASON Gms.	G	A	Pts.	PIM	+/-	PP	SH	PLAYOFFS Gms.	G	A	Pts.	PIM
95-96—Calgary	WHL	6	0	0	0	0	...	...	...	—	—	—	—	—
—Southwest	MAHA	39	37	35	72	59	...	...	...	—	—	—	—	—
96-97—Calgary	WHL	62	11	19	30	39	...	...	...	18	2	4	6	10
97-98—Calgary	WHL	68	22	29	51	31	...	...	...	—	—	—	—	—
98-99—Calgary	WHL	70	22	24	46	45	...	...	...	21	11	5	16	28
99-00—Calgary	WHL	62	38	31	69	86	...	...	...	13	14	9	23	20
00-01—Syracuse	AHL	47	10	11	21	24	...	...	...	5	2	2	4	4
—Columbus	NHL	29	4	5	9	4	4	0	0	—	—	—	—	—
01-02—Columbus	NHL	23	2	3	5	4	-3	0	0	—	—	—	—	—
—Syracuse	AHL	47	12	12	24	18	...	...	...	10	2	2	4	2
02-03—Syracuse	AHL	19	1	3	4	8	...	...	...	—	—	—	—	—
—Chicago	AHL	18	3	4	7	4	...	...	...	—	—	—	—	—
—Manitoba	AHL	33	3	10	13	13	...	...	...	—	—	—	—	—
NHL Totals (2 years)		52	6	8	14	8	1	0	0					

NIEMINEN, VILLE   LW   BLACKHAWKS

PERSONAL: Born April 6, 1977, in Tampere, Finland. ... 6-0/200. ... Shoots left.

TRANSACTIONS/CAREER NOTES: Selected by Colorado Avalanche in third round (fourth Avalanche pick, 78th overall) of NHL entry draft (June 21, 1997). ... Suffered concussion (October 13, 2001); missed six games. ... Traded by Avalanche with D Rick Berry to Pittsburgh Penguins for D Darius Kasparitis (March 19, 2002). ... Signed by Chicago Blackhawks (July 29, 2003).

N

Season Team	League	REGULAR SEASON Gms.	G	A	Pts.	PIM	+/-	PP	SH	PLAYOFFS Gms.	G	A	Pts.	PIM
94-95—Tappara Tampere	Finland Jr.	16	11	21	32	47	...	...	...	—	—	—	—	—
—Tappara Tampere	Finland	16	0	0	0	0	...	...	...	—	—	—	—	—
95-96—Tappara Tampere	Finland Jr.	20	20	23	43	63	...	...	...	—	—	—	—	—
—Tappara Tampere	Finland	4	0	1	1	8	...	...	...	—	—	—	—	—
—KooVee Tampere	Finland	7	2	1	3	4	...	...	...	—	—	—	—	—
96-97—Tappara Tampere	Finland	49	10	13	23	120	...	...	...	3	1	0	1	8
97-98—Hershey	AHL	74	14	22	36	85	...	...	...	—	—	—	—	—
98-99—Hershey	AHL	67	24	19	43	127	...	...	...	3	0	1	1	0
99-00—Hershey	AHL	74	21	30	51	54	...	...	...	9	2	4	6	6
—Colorado	NHL	1	0	0	0	0	0	0	0	—	—	—	—	—
00-01—Hershey	AHL	28	10	11	21	48	...	...	...	—	—	—	—	—
—Colorado	NHL	50	14	8	22	38	8	2	0	23	4	6	10	20
01-02—Colorado	NHL	53	10	14	24	30	1	1	0	—	—	—	—	—
—Fin. Olympic team	Int'l	4	0	1	1	2	...	...	...	—	—	—	—	—
—Pittsburgh	NHL	13	1	2	3	8	-2	0	0	—	—	—	—	—
02-03—Pittsburgh	NHL	75	9	12	21	93	-25	0	2	—	—	—	—	—
NHL Totals (4 years)		192	34	36	70	169	-18	3	2	23	4	6	10	20

NIEUWENDYK, JOE   C

PERSONAL: Born September 10, 1966, in Oshawa, Ont. ... 6-2/205. ... Shoots left. ... Full Name: Joe T. Nieuwendyk. ... Nephew of Ed Kea, defenseman with Atlanta Flames (1973-74 through 1978-79) and St. Louis Blues (1979-80 through 1982-83); and cousin of Jeff Beukeboom, defenseman with Edmonton Oilers (1985-86 through 1991-92) and New York Rangers (1991-92 through 1998-99). ... Name pronounced NOO-ihn-dighk.

TRANSACTIONS/CAREER NOTES: Selected by Calgary Flames in second round (second Flames pick, 27th overall) of NHL entry draft (June

15, 1985). ... Suffered concussion (November 1987). ... Bruised ribs (May 25, 1989). ... Tore left knee ligament (April 17, 1990). ... Underwent arthroscopic knee surgery (September 28, 1991); missed 12 games. ... Suffered from the flu (November 19, 1992); missed one game. ... Strained right knee (March 26, 1993); missed four games. ... Suffered charley horse (November 13, 1993); missed three games. ... Strained right knee ligaments (February 24, 1994); missed 17 games. ... Strained back (April 29, 1995); missed two games. ... Traded by Flames to Dallas Stars for C Corey Millen and rights to C/RW Jarome Iginla (December 19, 1995). ... Bruised chest (October 5, 1996); missed 12 games. ... Sprained knee (December 18, 1997); missed eight games. ... Reinjured knee (January 9, 1998); missed one game. ... Suffered inflammed knee (January 10, 1999); missed five games. ... Sprained ankle (February 23, 1999); missed one game. ... Suffered back spasms (March 16, 1999); missed one game. ... Injured knee (March 31, 1999); missed one game. ... Suffered back spasms (October 20, 1999); missed three games. ... Bruised chest (December 17, 1999); missed 10 games. ... Separated shoulder (January 19, 2000); missed 21 games. ... Suffered from the flu (January 4, 2001); missed two games. ... Strained groin (February 28, 2001); missed 11 games. ... Suffered from the flu (February 10, 2002); missed one game. ... Traded by Stars with RW Jamie Langenbrunner to New Jersey Devils for C Jason Arnott, RW Randy McKay and first-round pick (traded to Columbus) in 2002 draft (March 19, 2002).

STATISTICAL PLATEAUS: Three-goal games: 1987-88 (2), 1988-89 (1), 1989-90 (1), 1992-93 (1), 1993-94 (1), 1994-95 (1), 1997-98 (1), 2000-01 (1). Total: 9. ... Four-goal games: 1987-88 (2), 1997-98 (1). Total: 3. ... Five-goal games: 1988-89 (1). ... Total hat tricks: 13.

			REGULAR SEASON							PLAYOFFS				
Season Team	League	Gms.	G	A	Pts.	PIM	+/-	PP	SH	Gms.	G	A	Pts.	PIM
83-84—Pickering Jr. B	MTHL	38	30	28	58	35	...	...	...	—	—	—	—	—
84-85—Cornell University	ECAC	23	18	21	39	20	...	...	...	—	—	—	—	—
85-86—Cornell University	ECAC	21	21	21	42	45	...	...	...	—	—	—	—	—
86-87—Cornell University	ECAC	23	26	26	52	26	...	...	...	—	—	—	—	—
—Canadian nat'l team	Int'l	5	2	0	2	0	...	...	...	—	—	—	—	—
—Calgary	NHL	9	5	1	6	0	0	2	0	6	2	2	4	0
87-88—Calgary	NHL	75	51	41	92	23	20	*31	3	8	3	4	7	2
88-89—Calgary	NHL	77	51	31	82	40	26	19	3	22	10	4	14	10
89-90—Calgary	NHL	79	45	50	95	40	32	18	0	6	4	6	10	4
90-91—Calgary	NHL	79	45	40	85	36	19	22	4	7	4	1	5	10
91-92—Calgary	NHL	69	22	34	56	55	-1	7	0	—	—	—	—	—
92-93—Calgary	NHL	79	38	37	75	52	9	14	0	6	3	6	9	10
93-94—Calgary	NHL	64	36	39	75	51	19	14	1	6	2	2	4	0
94-95—Calgary	NHL	46	21	29	50	33	11	3	0	5	4	3	7	0
95-96—Dallas	NHL	52	14	18	32	41	-17	8	0	—	—	—	—	—
96-97—Dallas	NHL	66	30	21	51	32	-5	8	0	7	2	2	4	6
97-98—Dallas	NHL	73	39	30	69	30	16	14	0	1	1	0	1	0
—Can. Olympic team	Int'l	6	2	3	5	2	...	...	...	—	—	—	—	—
98-99—Dallas	NHL	67	28	27	55	34	11	8	0	23	*11	10	21	19
99-00—Dallas	NHL	48	15	19	34	26	-1	7	0	23	7	3	10	18
00-01—Dallas	NHL	69	29	23	52	30	5	12	0	7	4	0	4	4
01-02—Dallas	NHL	67	23	24	47	18	-2	6	0	—	—	—	—	—
—Can. Olympic team	Int'l	6	1	1	2	0	...	...	...	—	—	—	—	—
—New Jersey	NHL	14	2	9	11	4	2	0	0	5	0	1	1	0
02-03—New Jersey	NHL	80	17	28	45	56	10	3	0	17	3	6	9	4
NHL Totals (17 years)		1113	511	501	1012	601	154	196	11	149	60	50	110	87

NIINIMAA, JANNE D ISLANDERS

PERSONAL: Born May 22, 1975, in Raahe, Finland ... 6-1/220. ... Shoots left. ... Name pronounced YAH-nee NEE-nuh-muh.
TRANSACTIONS/CAREER NOTES: Selected by Philadelphia Flyers in second round (first Flyers pick, 36th overall) of NHL entry draft (June 26, 1993). ... Traded by Flyers to Edmonton Oilers for D Dan McGillis and second-round pick (D Jason Beckett) in 1998 draft (March 24, 1998). ... Suffered back spasms (November 4, 1998); missed one game. ... Suffered back spasms (November 24, 1999); missed one game. ... Traded by Oilers with second-round pick in 2003 draft to New York Islanders for LW Brad Isbister and LW Raffi Torres (March 11, 2003).

			REGULAR SEASON							PLAYOFFS				
Season Team	League	Gms.	G	A	Pts.	PIM	+/-	PP	SH	Gms.	G	A	Pts.	PIM
91-92—Karpat Oulu	Finland Div. 2	41	2	11	13	49	...	...	...	—	—	—	—	—
92-93—Karpat Oulu	Finland Div. 2	29	2	3	5	14	...	...	...	—	—	—	—	—
—Karpat	Finland Jr.	10	3	9	12	16	...	...	...	—	—	—	—	—
93-94—Jokerit Helsinki	Finland	45	3	8	11	24	...	...	...	12	1	1	2	4
94-95—Jokerit Helsinki	Finland	42	7	10	17	36	...	...	...	10	1	4	5	35
95-96—Jokerit Helsinki	Finland	49	5	15	20	79	...	...	...	11	0	2	2	12
96-97—Philadelphia	NHL	77	4	40	44	58	12	1	0	19	1	12	13	16
97-98—Philadelphia	NHL	66	3	31	34	56	6	2	0	—	—	—	—	—
—Fin. Olympic team	Int'l	6	0	3	3	8	...	...	...	—	—	—	—	—
—Edmonton	NHL	11	1	8	9	6	7	1	0	11	1	1	2	12
98-99—Edmonton	NHL	81	4	24	28	88	7	2	0	4	0	0	0	2
99-00—Edmonton	NHL	81	8	25	33	89	14	2	2	5	0	2	2	2
00-01—Edmonton	NHL	82	12	34	46	90	6	8	0	6	0	2	2	6
01-02—Edmonton	NHL	81	5	39	44	80	13	1	0	—	—	—	—	—
—Fin. Olympic team	Int'l	4	0	3	3	2	...	...	...	—	—	—	—	—
02-03—Edmonton	NHL	63	4	24	28	66	-7	2	0	—	—	—	—	—
—New York Islanders	NHL	13	1	5	6	14	-2	1	0	5	0	1	1	12
NHL Totals (7 years)		555	42	230	272	547	56	20	2	50	2	18	20	50

NIINIMAKI, JESSE C OILERS

PERSONAL: Born August 19, 1983, in Tampere, Finland. ... 6-2/183. ... Shoots left.
TRANSACTIONS/CAREER NOTES: Selected by Edmonton Oilers in first round (first Oilers pick, 15th overall) of NHL entry draft (June 22, 2002).

			REGULAR SEASON							PLAYOFFS				
Season Team	League	Gms.	G	A	Pts.	PIM	+/-	PP	SH	Gms.	G	A	Pts.	PIM
01-02—Ilves Tampere	Finland	16	2	4	6	4	...	...	...	3	0	0	0	0
02-03—Ilves Tampere	Finland	41	4	13	17	12	...	...	...	—	—	—	—	—

PERSONAL: Born March 25, 1973, in Vorkuta, U.S.S.R. ... 6-0/213. ... Shoots left. ... Name pronounced nih-koh-LEE-shihn.
TRANSACTIONS/CAREER NOTES: Selected by Hartford Whalers in second round (second Whalers pick, 47th overall) of NHL entry draft (June 20, 1992). ... Played in Europe during 1994-95 NHL lockout. ... Sprained ankle (October 21, 1995); missed one game. ... Injured back (November 15, 1995); missed five games. ... Strained back (December 2, 1995); missed 15 games. ... Traded by Whalers to Washington Capitals for D Curtis Leschyshyn (November 9, 1996). ... Suffered bulging disc in back (February 2, 1997); missed eight games. ... Injured knee prior to 1997-98 season; missed first 42 games. ... Missed first nine games of 1998-99 season due to contract dispute; played in Russia. ... Strained abdominal muscle (March 28, 2000); missed four games. ... Bruised leg (December 11, 2001); missed two games. ... Traded by Capitals with LW Chris Simon to Chicago Blackhawks for C Michael Nylander and conditional third-round pick in 2004 (November 1, 2002). ... Traded by Blackhawks to Colorado Avalanche (June 22, 2003).

Season Team	League	REGULAR SEASON								PLAYOFFS				
		Gms.	G	A	Pts.	PIM	+/-	PP	SH	Gms.	G	A	Pts.	PIM
90-91—Dynamo Moscow	USSR	2	0	0	0	0	...	...	...	—	—	—	—	—
91-92—Dynamo Moscow	CIS	18	1	0	1	4	...	...	...	—	—	—	—	—
92-93—Dynamo Moscow	CIS	42	5	7	12	30	...	...	...	10	2	1	3	8
93-94—Dynamo Moscow	CIS	41	8	12	20	30	...	...	...	9	1	3	4	4
—Russian Oly. team	Int'l	8	2	5	7	6	...	...	...	—	—	—	—	—
94-95—Dynamo Moscow	CIS	12	7	2	9	6	...	...	...	—	—	—	—	—
—Hartford	NHL	39	8	10	18	10	7	1	1	—	—	—	—	—
95-96—Hartford	NHL	61	14	37	51	34	-2	4	1	—	—	—	—	—
96-97—Hartford	NHL	12	2	5	7	2	-2	0	0	—	—	—	—	—
—Washington	NHL	59	7	14	21	30	5	1	0	—	—	—	—	—
97-98—Portland	AHL	2	0	0	0	2	...	...	...	—	—	—	—	—
—Washington	NHL	38	6	10	16	14	1	1	0	21	1	13	14	12
98-99—Dynamo Moscow	Russian	4	0	0	0	0	...	...	...	—	—	—	—	—
—Washington	NHL	73	8	27	35	28	0	0	1	—	—	—	—	—
99-00—Washington	NHL	76	11	14	25	28	6	0	2	5	0	2	2	4
00-01—Washington	NHL	81	13	25	38	34	9	4	0	6	0	0	0	2
01-02—Washington	NHL	80	13	23	36	40	-1	1	0	—	—	—	—	—
—Russian Oly. team	Int'l	6	0	1	1	6	...	...	...	—	—	—	—	—
02-03—Chicago	NHL	60	6	15	21	26	-3	0	1	—	—	—	—	—
NHL Totals (9 years)		579	88	180	268	246	20	12	6	32	1	15	16	18

PERSONAL: Born March 1, 1978, in Balsta, Sweden ... 6-2/195. ... Shoots right.
TRANSACTIONS/CAREER NOTES: Selected by Florida Panthers in first round (first Panthers pick, 20th overall) of NHL entry draft (June 22, 1996). ... Suspended one game by NHL for slashing incident (March 16, 2002).

Season Team	League	REGULAR SEASON								PLAYOFFS				
		Gms.	G	A	Pts.	PIM	+/-	PP	SH	Gms.	G	A	Pts.	PIM
94-95—Djurgarden	Sweden Jr.	24	7	8	15	22	...	...	...	—	—	—	—	—
95-96—Djurgarden	Sweden Jr.	25	19	17	36	46	...	...	...	2	1	1	2	12
—Djurgarden Stockholm	Sweden	12	0	0	0	0	...	...	...	1	0	0	0	0
96-97—Djurgarden Stockholm	Sweden	37	0	3	3	33	...	...	...	4	0	0	0	0
97-98—Djurgarden Stockholm	Sweden	41	4	7	11	18	...	...	...	15	2	1	3	16
98-99—New Haven	AHL	69	8	25	33	10	...	...	...	—	—	—	—	—
—Florida	NHL	8	1	1	2	5	2	0	0	—	—	—	—	—
99-00—Louisville	AHL	64	9	23	32	52	...	...	...	4	0	0	0	2
—Florida	NHL	9	0	2	2	2	2	0	0	—	—	—	—	—
00-01—Florida	NHL	78	12	24	36	74	-3	0	0	—	—	—	—	—
01-02—Florida	NHL	81	14	19	33	55	-14	6	1	—	—	—	—	—
02-03—Florida	NHL	82	15	19	34	31	2	7	1	—	—	—	—	—
NHL Totals (5 years)		258	42	65	107	167	-11	13	2	—	—	—	—	—

PERSONAL: Born February 12, 1972, in Belfast, Northern Ireland ... 6-1/215. ... Shoots right.
TRANSACTIONS/CAREER NOTES: Selected by Quebec Nordiques in first round (first Nordiques pick, first overall) of NHL entry draft (June 16, 1990). ... Suffered concussion, sore knee and sore back (October 1990). ... Suspended four off-days by NHL for cross-checking incident (December 7, 1992). ... Bruised hand (March 2, 1993); missed three games. ... Bruised shoulder (March 15, 1993); eight games. ... Injured right shoulder (October 19, 1993); missed 11 games. ... Dislocated left shoulder (November 12, 1993); missed remainder of season. ... Bruised shoulder (April 16, 1995); missed two games. ... Nordiques franchise moved to Colorado and renamed Avalanche for 1995-96 season (June 21, 1995). ... Traded by Avalanche to San Jose Sharks for D Sandis Ozolinsh (October 26, 1995). ... Suffered from the flu (March 5, 1996); missed two games. ... Suffered from an illness (November 27, 1996); missed one game. ... Bruised shoulder (January 9, 1997); missed two games. ... Suffered sore ankle (March 20, 1997); missed four games. ... Strained groin (April 7, 1997); missed three games. ... Strained shoulder (March 26, 1998); missed six games. ... Missed first two games of 1998-99 season due to contract dispute. ... Injured back (January 26, 1999); missed one game. ... Reinjured back (February 4, 1999); missed one game. ... Injured shoulder (March 29, 2000); missed four games. ... Underwent hernia surgery (August 19, 2000); missed first four games of season. ... Strained muscle in abdomen (October 24, 2000); missed 10 games. ... Suspended 11 games by NHL for illegal check (February 2, 2001). ... Injured groin (November 3, 2001); missed one game. ... Injured back (December 26, 2001); missed one game. ... Injured back (January 21, 2002); missed three games. ... Injured leg (March 21, 2002); missed one game. ... Traded by Sharks to Toronto Maple Leafs for C Alyn McCauley, C Brad Boyes and first-round pick in 2003 draft (March 5, 2003).
STATISTICAL PLATEAUS: Three-goal games: 1991-92 (2), 1992-93 (2), 1994-95 (3), 1996-97 (1), 1999-00 (1). Total: 9. ... Four-goal games: 1995-96 (1). ... Total hat tricks: 10.

		REGULAR SEASON								PLAYOFFS				
Season Team	League	Gms.	G	A	Pts.	PIM	+/-	PP	SH	Gms.	G	A	Pts.	PIM
88-89—Cornwall	OHL	62	34	25	59	213	...	...	...	18	5	11	16	41
89-90—Cornwall	OHL	58	51	59	110	240	...	...	...	6	7	5	12	26
90-91—Quebec	NHL	59	3	10	13	109	-19	0	0	—	—	—	—	—
—Halifax	AHL	6	4	4	8	11	...	...	...	—	—	—	—	—
91-92—Quebec	NHL	75	42	31	73	183	-9	17	0	—	—	—	—	—
92-93—Quebec	NHL	73	36	41	77	185	-1	15	0	5	1	0	1	2
93-94—Quebec	NHL	6	2	2	4	8	2	0	0	—	—	—	—	—
94-95—Quebec	NHL	46	30	19	49	46	21	13	2	6	2	3	5	6
95-96—Colorado	NHL	9	4	4	8	9	-3	4	0	—	—	—	—	—
—San Jose	NHL	72	29	32	61	137	-30	12	1	—	—	—	—	—
96-97—San Jose	NHL	72	31	32	63	155	-19	10	0	—	—	—	—	—
97-98—San Jose	NHL	75	14	27	41	144	-2	3	1	6	2	2	4	26
98-99—San Jose	NHL	78	19	26	45	129	16	6	2	6	1	1	2	6
99-00—San Jose	NHL	78	44	40	84	110	-1	*18	4	10	8	2	10	6
00-01—San Jose	NHL	57	24	25	49	75	0	10	1	6	1	1	2	8
01-02—San Jose	NHL	75	23	43	66	93	7	8	2	12	3	6	9	8
—Can. Olympic team	Int'l	6	0	3	3	2	...	...	...	—	—	—	—	—
02-03—San Jose	NHL	61	22	20	42	91	-5	8	3	—	—	—	—	—
—Toronto	NHL	14	7	5	12	16	2	5	0	7	0	2	2	2
NHL Totals (13 years)		850	330	357	687	1490	-41	129	16	58	18	17	35	64

NORONEN, MIKA G SABRES

PERSONAL: Born June 17, 1979, in Tampere, Finland ... 6-2/199. ... Catches left.
TRANSACTIONS/CAREER NOTES: Selected by Buffalo Sabres in first round (first Sabres pick, 21st overall) of NHL entry draft (June 21, 1997).

		REGULAR SEASON								PLAYOFFS							
Season Team	League	Gms.	Min.	W	L	T	GA	SO	Avg.	SV%	Gms.	Min.	W	L	GA	SO	Avg.	SV%
95-96—Tappara Tampere	Finland Jr.	16	962	...	...	...	37	2	2.31	—	—	—	—	—	—	—	—	—
96-97—Tappara Tampere	Finland	5	215	...	...	...	17	0	4.74	—	—	—	—	—	—	—	—	—
97-98—Tappara Tampere	Finland	47	1703	14	12	3	83	1	2.92	—	4	196	1	2	12	0	3.67	—
98-99—Tappara Tampere	Finland	43	2494	18	20	5	*135	2	3.25	—	—	—	—	—	—	—	—	—
99-00—Rochester	AHL	54	3089	*33	13	4	112	†6	*2.18	—	21	1235	13	*8	37	*6	*1.80	—
00-01—Buffalo	NHL	2	108	2	0	0	5	0	2.78	.872	—	—	—	—	—	—	—	—
—Rochester	AHL	47	2753	26	15	5	100	4	2.18	—	4	250	1	3	11	0	2.64	—
01-02—Rochester	AHL	45	2763	16	17	†12	115	3	2.50	—	1	58	0	1	3	0	3.10	—
—Buffalo	NHL	10	518	4	3	1	23	0	2.66	.894	—	—	—	—	—	—	—	—
02-03—Rochester	AHL	19	1168	5	9	5	55	2	2.83	—	—	—	—	—	—	—	—	—
—Buffalo	NHL	16	891	4	9	3	36	1	2.42	.912	—	—	—	—	—	—	—	—
NHL Totals (3 years)		28	1517	10	12	4	64	1	2.53	.904								

NORSTROM, MATTIAS D KINGS

PERSONAL: Born January 2, 1972, in Stockholm, Sweden ... 6-1/222. ... Shoots left. ... Name pronounced muh-TEE-uhz NOHR-struhm.
TRANSACTIONS/CAREER NOTES: Selected by New York Rangers in second round (second Rangers pick, 48th overall) of NHL entry draft (June 20, 1992). ... Suffered from the flu (April 28, 1995); missed two games. ... Separated shoulder (December 30, 1995); missed six games. ... Traded by Rangers with C Ray Ferraro, C Ian Laperriere, C Nathan Lafayette and fourth-round pick (D Sean Blanchard) in 1997 draft to Los Angeles Kings for RW Shane Churla, LW Jari Kurri and D Marty McSorley (March 14, 1996). ... Bruised left wrist (November 7, 1996); missed one game. ... Suspended one game by NHL for illegal check (January 12, 1998). ... Bruised ribs (April 11, 1999); missed four games. ... Bruised ribs (October 13, 2001); missed three games.

		REGULAR SEASON								PLAYOFFS				
Season Team	League	Gms.	G	A	Pts.	PIM	+/-	PP	SH	Gms.	G	A	Pts.	PIM
91-92—AIK Solna	Sweden	39	4	4	8	28	...	...	...	—	—	—	—	—
92-93—AIK Solna	Sweden	22	0	1	1	16	...	...	...	—	—	—	—	—
93-94—New York Rangers	NHL	9	0	2	2	6	0	0	0	—	—	—	—	—
—Binghamton	AHL	55	1	9	10	70	...	...	...	—	—	—	—	—
94-95—Binghamton	AHL	63	9	10	19	91	...	...	...	—	—	—	—	—
—New York Rangers	NHL	9	0	3	3	2	2	0	0	3	0	0	0	0
95-96—New York Rangers	NHL	25	2	1	3	22	5	0	0	—	—	—	—	—
—Los Angeles	NHL	11	0	1	1	18	-8	0	0	—	—	—	—	—
96-97—Los Angeles	NHL	80	1	21	22	84	-4	0	0	—	—	—	—	—
97-98—Los Angeles	NHL	73	1	12	13	90	14	0	0	4	0	0	0	2
—Swedish Oly. team	Int'l	4	0	1	1	2	...	...	...	—	—	—	—	—
98-99—Los Angeles	NHL	78	2	5	7	36	-10	0	1	—	—	—	—	—
99-00—Los Angeles	NHL	82	1	13	14	66	22	0	0	4	0	0	0	6
00-01—Los Angeles	NHL	82	0	18	18	60	10	0	0	13	0	2	2	18
01-02—Los Angeles	NHL	79	2	9	11	38	-2	0	0	7	0	0	0	4
—Swedish Oly. team	Int'l	4	0	0	0	0	...	...	...	—	—	—	—	—
02-03—Los Angeles	NHL	82	0	6	6	49	0	0	0	—	—	—	—	—
NHL Totals (10 years)		610	9	91	100	471	29	0	1	31	0	2	2	30

N

NORTON, BRAD D KINGS

PERSONAL: Born February 13, 1975, in Cambridge, Mass. ... 6-4/225. ... Shoots left. ... Full Name: Brad Joseph Norton. ... Brother of Jeff Norton, defenseman with six NHL teams (1987-88 through 1999-2000).
TRANSACTIONS/CAREER NOTES: Selected by Edmonton Oilers in ninth round (ninth Oilers pick, 215th overall) of NHL entry draft (June 26, 1993). ... Suspended three games by NHL for unsportsmanlike conduct (October 4, 2000). ... Strained hip flexor (October 11, 2000); missed 10 games. ... Signed as free agent by Florida Panthers (July 27, 2001). ... Suffered illness (February 11, 2002); missed one game. ... Signed as free agent by Los Angeles Kings (October 8, 2002). ... Re-signed by Kings (July 28, 2003).

Season Team	League	REGULAR SEASON									PLAYOFFS				
		Gms.	G	A	Pts.	PIM	+/-	PP	SH		Gms.	G	A	Pts.	PIM
92-93—Cushing Academy......	Mass. H.S.	31	10	26	36	36					—	—	—	—	—
93-94 Cushing Academy......	Mass. H.S						Statistics unavailable.								
94-95—Univ. of Mass.............	Hockey East	30	0	6	6	89	...				—	—	—	—	—
95-96—Univ. of Mass.............	Hockey East	34	4	12	16	99	...				—	—	—	—	—
96-97—Univ. of Mass.............	Hockey East	35	2	16	18	88	...				—	—	—	—	—
97-98—Univ. of Mass.............	Hockey East	20	2	13	15	28	...				—	—	—	—	—
—Detroit......................	IHL	33	1	4	5	56	...				22	0	2	2	87
98-99—Hamilton..................	AHL	58	1	8	9	134					11	0	1	1	6
99-00—Hamilton..................	AHL	40	5	12	17	104					10	1	4	5	26
00-01—Hamilton..................	AHL	46	3	15	18	114					—	—	—	—	—
01-02—Hershey..................	AHL	40	0	10	10	62	...	...			2	0	0	0	6
—Florida......................	NHL	22	0	2	2	45	-2	0	0		—	—	—	—	—
02-03—Los Angeles...............	NHL	53	3	3	6	97	1	0	0		—	—	—	—	—
NHL Totals (2 years)...........		75	3	5	8	142	-1	0	0						

NOVAK, FILIP — D — PANTHERS

PERSONAL: Born May 7, 1982, in Ceske Budejovice, Czechoslovakia. ... 6-0/174. ... Shoots left.
TRANSACTIONS/CAREER NOTES: Selected by New York Rangers in second round (first Rangers pick, 64th overall) of NHL entry draft (June 24, 2000). ... Traded by Rangers with D Igor Ulanov, first- and second-round picks in 2002 draft and fourth-round pick in 2003 draft to Florida Panthers for RW Pavel Bure and second-round pick in 2003 draft (March 18, 2002).

Season Team	League	REGULAR SEASON									PLAYOFFS				
		Gms.	G	A	Pts.	PIM	+/-	PP	SH		Gms.	G	A	Pts.	PIM
98-99—Budejovice	Czech. Jrs.	68	8	10	18	34	...	...	...		—	—	—	—	—
99-00—Regina	WHL	47	7	32	39	70	...	...	...		7	1	4	5	5
00-01—Regina	WHL	64	17	50	67	75	...	...	...		6	1	4	5	6
01-02—Regina	WHL	60	12	46	58	125	...	...	...		6	2	2	4	19
02-03—San Antonio	AHL	57	10	17	27	79	...	...	...		—	—	—	—	—

NOVOSELTSEV, IVAN — RW — PANTHERS

PERSONAL: Born January 23, 1979, in Golitsino, U.S.S.R. ... 6-1/210. ... Shoots left. ... Name pronounced noh-vuh-SEHLT-sehf.
TRANSACTIONS/CAREER NOTES: Selected by Florida Panthers in fourth round (fifth Panthers pick, 95th overall) of NHL entry draft (June 21, 1997). ... Suffered back spasms (February 9, 2002); missed two games. ... Injured back (March 30, 2002); missed three games.

Season Team	League	REGULAR SEASON									PLAYOFFS				
		Gms.	G	A	Pts.	PIM	+/-	PP	SH		Gms.	G	A	Pts.	PIM
95-96—Krylja Sov. Moscow	CIS	1	0	0	0	0	...		...		—	—	—	—	—
96-97—Kryla Sov. Moscow	Russian	30	0	3	3	18	...	...	...		2	0	0	0	4
—Krylja Sov. Moscow	Rus. Div. III	19	5	3	8	39	...	...	...		—	—	—	—	—
97-98—Sarnia	OHL	53	26	22	48	41	...	...	...		5	1	1	2	8
98-99—Sarnia	OHL	68	57	39	96	45	...	...	...		5	2	4	6	6
99-00—Louisville	AHL	47	14	21	35	22	...	...	...		4	1	0	1	6
—Florida.......................	NHL	14	2	1	3	8	-3	2	0		—	—	—	—	—
00-01—Louisville	AHL	34	2	10	12	8	...	...	...		—	—	—	—	—
—Florida.......................	NHL	38	3	6	9	16	-5	0	0		—	—	—	—	—
01-02—Florida.......................	NHL	70	13	16	29	44	-10	1	1		—	—	—	—	—
02-03—Florida.......................	NHL	78	10	17	27	30	-16	1	0		—	—	—	—	—
NHL Totals (4 years)..........		200	28	40	68	98	-34	4	1						

N

NOVOTNY, JIRI — C — SABRES

PERSONAL: Born August 12, 1983, in Pelhrimov, Czechoslovakia. ... 6-2/187. ... Shoots right.
TRANSACTIONS/CAREER NOTES: Selected by Buffalo Sabres in first round (first Sabres pick, 22nd overall) of NHL entry draft (June 23, 2001).

Season Team	League	REGULAR SEASON									PLAYOFFS				
		Gms.	G	A	Pts.	PIM	+/-	PP	SH		Gms.	G	A	Pts.	PIM
99-00—Budejovice	Czech. Jrs.	39	11	12	23	14	...	...	...		—	—	—	—	—
00-01—Budejovice	Czech. Jrs.	33	10	10	20		...	...	...		—	—	—	—	—
—HC Ceske Budejovice..	Czech Rep.	19	0	4	4	2	...	...	...		—	—	—	—	—
01-02—HC Ceske Budejovice..	Czech Rep.	41	8	6	14	6	...	...	...		—	—	—	—	—
02-03—Rochester	AHL	43	2	9	11	14	...	...	...		—	—	—	—	—

NOWAK, BRETT — C/LW — BRUINS

PERSONAL: Born May 20, 1981, in New Haven, Connecticut. ... 6-2/192. ... Shoots left. ... Full Name: James Brett Nowak.
COLLEGE: Harvard.
TRANSACTIONS/CAREER NOTES: Selected by Boston Bruins in fourth round (seventh Bruins pick, 103rd overall) of NHL entry draft (June 24, 2000).

Season Team	League	REGULAR SEASON									PLAYOFFS				
		Gms.	G	A	Pts.	PIM	+/-	PP	SH		Gms.	G	A	Pts.	PIM
98-99—Hotchkiss...................	Conn. H.S.	21	24	42	66	42	...	...	...		—	—	—	—	—
99-00—Harvard University	ECAC	24	5	10	15	20	...	...	...		—	—	—	—	—
00-01—Harvard University	ECAC	33	7	14	21	8	...	...	...		—	—	—	—	—
01-02—Harvard University	ECAC	33	14	17	31	50	...	...	...		—	—	—	—	—
02-03—Harvard University	ECAC	33	12	29	41	57	...	...	...		—	—	—	—	—

NUMMINEN, TEPPO　　　　D　　　　STARS

PERSONAL: Born July 3, 1968, in Tampere, Finland ... 6-2/198. ... Shoots right. ... Full Name: Teppo Kalevi Numminen. ... Name pronounced TEH-poh NOO-mih-nehn.

TRANSACTIONS/CAREER NOTES: Selected by Winnipeg Jets in second round (second Jets pick, 29th overall) of NHL entry draft (June 21, 1986). ... Separated shoulder (March 5, 1989). ... Fractured thumb (April 14, 1990). ... Fractured foot (January 28, 1993); missed 17 games. ... Dislocated thumb (February 9, 1994); missed remainder of season. ... Played in Europe during 1994-95 NHL lockout. ... Suffered from stomach flu (January 23, 1995); missed one game. ... Suffered stress fracture in right knee (February 22, 1995); missed five games. ... Separated shoulder (November 28, 1995); missed eight games. ... Jets franchise moved to Phoenix and renamed Coyotes for 1996-97 season; NHL approved move on January 18, 1996. ... Strained hip flexor (March 1, 2000); missed two games. ... Sprained ankle (December 30, 2000); missed one game. ... Bruised foot (November 14, 2000); missed two games. ... Bruised foot (November 29, 2000); missed three games. ... Bruised foot (March 6, 2001); missed one game. ... Strained hip flexor (March 15, 2001); missed two games. ... Bruised foot (April 6, 2001); missed one game. ... Fractured bone in foot (November 4, 2001); missed six games. ... Re-signed by Coyotes (June 29, 2003). ... Traded by Coyotes to Dallas Stars for C Mike Sillinger (July 22, 2003).

Season Team	League	Gms.	G	A	Pts.	PIM	+/-	PP	SH	Gms.	G	A	Pts.	PIM
84-85—Tappara	Finland	30	14	17	31	10	...	...	...	—	—	—	—	—
85-86—Tappara	Finland	39	2	4	6	6	...	...	...	8	0	0	0	0
86-87—Tappara	Finland	44	9	9	18	16	...	...	...	9	4	1	5	4
87-88—Tappara	Finland	44	10	10	20	29	...	...	...	10	6	6	12	6
—Fin. Olympic team	Int'l	6	1	4	5	0	...	...	...	—	—	—	—	—
88-89—Winnipeg	NHL	69	1	14	15	36	-11	0	1	—	—	—	—	—
89-90—Winnipeg	NHL	79	11	32	43	20	-4	1	0	7	1	2	3	10
90-91—Winnipeg	NHL	80	8	25	33	28	-15	3	0	—	—	—	—	—
91-92—Winnipeg	NHL	80	5	34	39	32	15	4	0	7	0	0	0	0
92-93—Winnipeg	NHL	66	7	30	37	33	4	3	1	6	1	1	2	2
93-94—Winnipeg	NHL	57	5	18	23	28	-23	4	0	—	—	—	—	—
94-95—TuTu Turku	Finland	12	3	8	11	4	...	...	...	—	—	—	—	—
—Winnipeg	NHL	42	5	16	21	16	12	2	0	—	—	—	—	—
95-96—Winnipeg	NHL	74	11	43	54	22	-4	6	0	6	0	0	0	2
96-97—Phoenix	NHL	82	2	25	27	28	-3	0	0	7	3	3	6	0
97-98—Phoenix	NHL	82	11	40	51	30	25	6	0	1	0	0	0	0
—Fin. Olympic team	Int'l	6	1	1	2	2	...	...	...	—	—	—	—	—
98-99—Phoenix	NHL	82	10	30	40	30	3	1	0	7	2	1	3	4
99-00—Phoenix	NHL	79	8	34	42	16	21	2	0	5	1	1	2	0
00-01—Phoenix	NHL	72	5	26	31	36	9	1	0	—	—	—	—	—
01-02—Phoenix	NHL	76	13	35	48	20	13	4	0	4	0	0	0	2
—Fin. Olympic team	Int'l	4	0	1	1	0	...	...	...	—	—	—	—	—
02-03—Phoenix	NHL	78	6	24	30	30	0	2	0	—	—	—	—	—
NHL Totals (15 years)		1098	108	426	534	405	42	39	2	50	8	8	16	20

NURMINEN, PASI　　　　G　　　　THRASHERS

PERSONAL: Born December 17, 1975, in Lahti, Finland ... 5-10/210. ... Catches left.

TRANSACTIONS/CAREER NOTES: Selected by Atlanta Thrashers in sixth round (sixth Thrashers pick, 189th overall) of NHL entry draft (June 24, 2001). ... Injured knee (October 1, 2001); missed first 10 games of season.

Season Team	League	Gms.	Min	W	L	T	GA	SO	Avg.	SV%	Gms.	Min.	W	L	GA	SO	Avg.	SV%
93-94—Reipas Lahti	Finland Jr.	14	847	...	...	...	58	0	4.11	—	—	—	—	—	—	—	—	—
—Reipas Lahti	Finland	1	30	...	...	...	2	0	4.00	—	—	—	—	—	—	—	—	—
94-95—Reipas Lahti	Finland Jr.	9	542	...	...	...	22	0	2.44	—	—	—	—	—	—	—	—	—
—Reipas Lahti	Fin. Div. 2	9	423	...	...	...	44	0	6.24	—	—	—	—	—	—	—	—	—
95-96—Kettera Imatra	Fin. Div. 2	38	2204	...	...	...	146	0	3.97	—	—	—	—	—	—	—	—	—
96-97—Pelicans Lahti	Fin. Div. 2	30	1726	...	...	...	69	0	2.40	—	3	204	...	...	8	...	2.35	—
97-98—Pelicans Lahti	Fin. Div. 2	35	2044	...	...	...	59	0	1.73	—	3	180	...	...	4	...	1.33	—
98-99—HPK Hameenlinna	Finland	48	2810	24	17	6	127	2	2.71	—	7	425	3	4	24	1	3.39	—
99-00—Jokerit Helsinki	Finland	48	2770	24	15	8	104	6	2.25	—	11	719	7	4	22	2	1.84	—
00-01—Jokerit Helsinki	Finland	52	2971	30	13	7	107	5	2.16	—	5	308	2	3	11	1	2.14	—
01-02—Chicago	AHL	20	1165	9	9	1	57	2	2.94	—	*21	1267	*15	5	41	2	1.94	—
—Atlanta	NHL	9	465	2	5	0	28	0	3.61	.898	—	—	—	—	—	—	—	—
—Fin. Olympic team	Int'l	1	60	1	0	0	1	0	1.00	—	—	—	—	—	—	—	—	—
02-03—Atlanta	NHL	52	2856	21	19	5	137	2	2.88	.906	—	—	—	—	—	—	—	—
NHL Totals (2 years)		61	3321	23	24	5	165	2	2.98	.904	—	—	—	—	—	—	—	—

NYCHOLAT, LAWRENCE　　　　D　　　　RANGERS

PERSONAL:.

TRANSACTIONS/CAREER NOTES: Signed as non-drafted free agent by Minnesota Wild (August 31, 2000). ... Traded by Wild to New York Rangers for G Johan Holmqvist (March 11, 2003).

Season Team	League	Gms.	G	A	Pts.	PIM	+/-	PP	SH	Gms.	G	A	Pts.	PIM
00-01—Jackson	ECHL	5	1	2	3	5	...	...	...	—	—	—	—	—
—Cleveland	IHL	42	3	7	10	69	...	...	...	4	0	0	0	2
01-02—Houston	AHL	72	3	11	14	92	...	...	...	14	1	0	1	23
02-03—Houston	AHL	66	11	28	39	155	...	...	...	—	—	—	—	—
—Hartford	AHL	15	2	9	11	6	...	...	...	—	—	—	—	—

N

NYLANDER, MICHAEL — C — CAPITALS

PERSONAL: Born October 3, 1972, in Stockholm, Sweden ... 6-1/189. ... Shoots left. ... Full Name: Mikael Nylander. ... Name pronounced NEE-lan-duhr.

TRANSACTIONS/CAREER NOTES: Selected by Hartford Whalers in third round (fourth Whalers pick, 59th overall) of NHL entry draft (June 22, 1991). ... Fractured jaw (January 23, 1993); missed 15 games. ... Traded by Whalers with D Zarley Zalapski and D James Patrick to Calgary Flames for D Gary Suter, LW Paul Ranheim and C Ted Drury (March 10, 1994). ... Played in Europe during 1994-95 NHL lockout. ... Fractured left wrist and forearm (January 24, 1995); missed 42 games. ... Injured wrist (January 16, 1996); missed three games. ... Injured left knee (March 26, 1998); missed final 11 games of season and first 23 games of 1998-99 season. ... Traded by Flames to Tampa Bay Lightning for RW Andrei Nazarov (January 19, 1999). ... Suffered concussion (April 8, 1999); missed final five games of season. ... Traded by Lightning to Chicago Blackhawks for D Bryan Muir and LW Reid Simpson (November 12, 1999). ... Traded by Blackhawks with conditional third-round pick in 2004 to Washington Capitals for C Andrei Nikolishin and LW Chris Simon (November 1, 2002).

STATISTICAL PLATEAUS: Three-goal games: 1992-93 (1). ... Four-goal games: 1999-00 (1). ... Total hat tricks: 2.

			REGULAR SEASON								PLAYOFFS				
Season Team	League	Gms.	G	A	Pts.	PIM	+/-	PP	SH		Gms.	G	A	Pts.	PIM
89-90—Huddinge	Sweden	31	7	15	22	4	...	...	...		—	—	—	—	—
90-91—Huddinge	Sweden	33	14	20	34	10	...	...	...		—	—	—	—	—
91-92—AIK Solna	Sweden	40	11	17	28	30	...	...	...		—	—	—	—	—
—Swedish Oly. team	Int'l	6	0	1	1	0	...	...	...		—	—	—	—	—
92-93—Hartford	NHL	59	11	22	33	36	-7	3	0		—	—	—	—	—
—Springfield	AHL	59	11	22	33	36	...	...	...		—	—	—	—	—
93-94—Hartford	NHL	58	11	33	44	24	-2	4	0		—	—	—	—	—
—Springfield	AHL	4	0	9	9	0	...	...	...		—	—	—	—	—
—Calgary	NHL	15	2	9	11	6	10	0	0		3	0	0	0	0
94-95—JyP HT	Finland	16	11	19	30	63	...	...	...		—	—	—	—	—
—Calgary	NHL	6	0	1	1	2	1	0	0		6	0	6	6	2
95-96—Calgary	NHL	73	17	38	55	20	0	4	0		4	0	0	0	0
96-97—Lugano	Switzerland	36	12	43	55	...	...	...	...		—	—	—	—	—
97-98—Calgary	NHL	65	13	23	36	24	10	0	0		—	—	—	—	—
—Swedish Oly. team	Int'l	4	0	0	0	6	...	...	...		—	—	—	—	—
98-99—Calgary	NHL	9	2	3	5	2	1	1	0		—	—	—	—	—
—Tampa Bay	NHL	24	2	7	9	6	-10	0	0		—	—	—	—	—
99-00—Tampa Bay	NHL	11	1	2	3	4	-3	1	0		—	—	—	—	—
—Chicago	NHL	66	23	28	51	26	9	4	0		—	—	—	—	—
00-01—Chicago	NHL	82	25	39	64	32	7	4	0		—	—	—	—	—
01-02—Chicago	NHL	82	15	46	61	50	28	6	0		5	0	3	3	2
—Swedish Oly. team	Int'l	4	1	2	3	0	...	...	...		—	—	—	—	—
02-03—Chicago	NHL	9	0	4	4	4	0	0	0		—	—	—	—	—
—Washington	NHL	71	17	39	56	36	3	7	0		6	3	2	5	8
NHL Totals (10 years)		630	139	294	433	272	47	34	0		24	3	11	14	12

NYSTROM, ERIC — LW — FLAMES

PERSONAL: Born February 14, 1983, in Syosset, N.Y. ... 6-1/195. ... Shoots left. ... Son of Bobby Nystrom, right winger with New York Islanders (1972-73 through 1985-86).

TRANSACTIONS/CAREER NOTES: Selected by Calgary Flames in first round (first Flames pick, 10th overall) of NHL entry draft (June 22, 2002).

			REGULAR SEASON								PLAYOFFS				
Season Team	League	Gms.	G	A	Pts.	PIM	+/-	PP	SH		Gms.	G	A	Pts.	PIM
00-01—U.S. National	USHL	66	15	17	32	102	...	...	...		—	—	—	—	—
01-02—Univ. of Michigan	CCHA	32	15	9	24	32	...	...	...		—	—	—	—	—
02-03—Univ. of Michigan	CCHA	39	15	11	26	24	...	...	...		—	—	—	—	—

OATES, ADAM — C

PERSONAL: Born August 27, 1962, in Weston, Ont. ... 5-11/190. ... Shoots right. ... Full Name: Adam R. Oates. ... Name pronounced OHTS.

TRANSACTIONS/CAREER NOTES: Signed as non-drafted free agent by Detroit Red Wings (June 28, 1985). ... Pulled abdominal muscle (October 1987). ... Suffered from chicken pox (November 1988). ... Bruised thigh (December 1988). ... Traded by Red Wings with RW Paul MacLean to St. Louis Blues for LW Tony McKegney and C Bernie Federko (June 15, 1989). ... Tore rib and abdominal muscles (November 5, 1990); missed 18 games. ... Traded by Blues to Boston Bruins for C Craig Janney and D Stephane Quintal (February 7, 1992). ... Injured groin (January 6, 1994); missed seven games. ... Injured knee (October 28, 1995); missed 12 games. ... Traded by Bruins with RW Rick Tocchet and G Bill Ranford to Washington Capitals for G Jim Carey, C Jason Allison, C Anson Carter and third-round pick (RW Lee Goren) in 1997 draft (March 1, 1997). ... Injured back (April 10, 1997); missed two games. ... Strained groin (November 27, 1998); missed 23 games. ... Injured leg (October 30, 2001); missed three games. ... Traded by Capitals to Philadelphia Flyers for G Maxime Ouellet, first-(traded to Dallas), second-(G Maxime Daigneault) and third-round (C Derek Krestanovich) picks in 2002 draft (March 19, 2002). ... Signed as free agent by Mighty Ducks of Anaheim (July 1, 2002).

STATISTICAL PLATEAUS: Three-goal games: 1992-93 (3), 1993-94 (2), 1997-98 (1). Total: 6. ... Four-goal games: 1995-96 (1). ... Total hat tricks: 7.

			REGULAR SEASON								PLAYOFFS				
Season Team	League	Gms.	G	A	Pts.	PIM	+/-	PP	SH		Gms.	G	A	Pts.	PIM
82-83—R.P.I.	ECAC	22	9	33	42	8	...	...	...		—	—	—	—	—
83-84—R.P.I.	ECAC	38	26	57	83	15	...	...	...		—	—	—	—	—
84-85—R.P.I.	ECAC	38	31	60	91	29	...	...	...		—	—	—	—	—
85-86—Adirondack	AHL	34	18	28	46	4	...	...	...		17	7	14	21	4
—Detroit	NHL	38	9	11	20	10	-24	1	0		—	—	—	—	—
86-87—Detroit	NHL	76	15	32	47	21	0	4	0		16	4	7	11	6
87-88—Detroit	NHL	63	14	40	54	20	16	3	0		16	8	12	20	6
88-89—Detroit	NHL	69	16	62	78	14	-1	2	0		6	0	8	8	2

N
O

Season Team	League	REGULAR SEASON								PLAYOFFS				
		Gms.	G	A	Pts.	PIM	+/-	PP	SH	Gms.	G	A	Pts.	PIM
89-90—St. Louis	NHL	80	23	79	102	30	9	6	2	12	2	12	14	4
90-91—St. Louis	NHL	61	25	90	115	29	15	3	1	13	7	13	20	10
91-92—St. Louis	NHL	54	10	59	69	12	-4	3	0	—	—	—	—	—
—Boston	NHL	26	10	20	30	10	-5	3	0	15	5	14	19	4
92-93—Boston	NHL	84	45	*97	142	32	15	24	1	4	0	9	9	4
93-94—Boston	NHL	77	32	80	112	45	10	16	2	13	3	9	12	8
94-95—Boston	NHL	48	12	41	53	8	-11	4	1	5	1	0	1	2
95-96—Boston	NHL	70	25	67	92	18	16	7	1	5	2	5	7	2
96-97—Boston	NHL	63	18	52	70	10	-3	2	2	—	—	—	—	—
—Washington	NHL	17	4	8	12	4	-2	1	0	—	—	—	—	—
97-98—Washington	NHL	82	18	58	76	36	6	3	2	21	6	11	17	8
98-99—Washington	NHL	59	12	42	54	22	-1	3	0	—	—	—	—	—
99-00—Washington	NHL	82	15	56	71	14	13	5	0	5	0	3	3	4
00-01—Washington	NHL	81	13	†69	82	28	-9	5	0	6	0	0	0	0
01-02—Washington	NHL	66	11	§57	68	22	-2	3	0	—	—	—	—	—
—Philadelphia..............	NHL	14	3	§7	10	6	-2	0	0	5	0	2	2	0
02-03—Anaheim	NHL	67	9	36	45	16	-1	4	0	21	4	9	13	6
NHL Totals (18 years).........		1277	339	1063	1402	407	35	102	12	163	42	114	156	66

OBSUT, JAROSLAV D CANUCKS

PERSONAL: Born September 3, 1976, in Presov, Czechoslovakia. ... 6-1/185. ... Shoots left. ... Name pronounced ahb-SOOT.
TRANSACTIONS/CAREER NOTES: Selected by Winnipeg Jets in eighth round (ninth Jets pick, 188th overall) of NHL entry draft (July 8, 1995). ... Jets franchise moved to Phoenix and renamed Coyotes for 1996-97 season; NHL approved move on January 18, 1996. ... Signed as free agent by St. Louis Blues (May 25, 1999). ... Suffered from headaches (March 17, 2001); missed one game. ... Signed as free agent by Colorado Avalanche (August 9, 2001). ... Signed as free agent by Vancouver Canucks (July 10, 2002).

Season Team	League	REGULAR SEASON								PLAYOFFS				
		Gms.	G	A	Pts.	PIM	+/-	PP	SH	Gms.	G	A	Pts.	PIM
94-95—North Battleford	SJHL	55	21	30	51	126	...	...	...	—	—	—	—	—
95-96—Swift Current	WHL	72	10	11	21	57	...	...	...	6	0	0	0	2
96-97—Edmonton	WHL	13	2	9	11	4	...	...	...	—	—	—	—	—
—Medicine Hat..............	WHL	50	8	26	34	42	...	...	...	—	—	—	—	—
—Toledo	ECHL	3	1	0	1	0	...	...	...	5	0	1	1	6
97-98—Raleigh	ECHL	60	6	26	32	46	...	...	...	—	—	—	—	—
—Syracuse....................	AHL	4	0	1	1	4	...	...	...	—	—	—	—	—
98-99—Manitoba....................	IHL	2	0	0	0	0	...	...	...	—	—	—	—	—
—Augusta.....................	ECHL	41	11	25	36	42	...	...	...	—	—	—	—	—
—Worcester..................	AHL	31	2	8	10	14	...	...	...	4	0	1	1	2
99-00—Worcester	AHL	7	0	2	2	4	...	...	...	—	—	—	—	—
00-01—Peoria	ECHL	3	0	4	4	2	...	...	...	—	—	—	—	—
—Worcester..................	AHL	47	9	12	21	20	...	...	...	7	0	1	1	4
—St. Louis	NHL	4	0	0	0	2	1	0	0	—	—	—	—	—
01-02—Colorado	NHL	3	0	0	0	0	0	0	0	—	—	—	—	—
—Hershey	AHL	58	3	22	25	48	...	...	...	8	0	2	2	2
—Slovakian Oly. team	Int'l	4	0	0	0	2	...	...	...	—	—	—	—	—
02-03—Manitoba....................	AHL	60	6	13	19	59	...	...	...	—	—	—	—	—
NHL Totals (2 years)...........		7	0	0	0	2	1	0	0					

O'CONNOR, SEAN RW PANTHERS

PERSONAL: Born October 19, 1981, in Victoria, B.C. ... 6-2/211. ... Shoots right.
TRANSACTIONS/CAREER NOTES: Selected by Florida Panthers in third round (third Panthers pick, 82nd overall) of NHL entry draft (June 24, 2000).

Season Team	League	REGULAR SEASON								PLAYOFFS				
		Gms.	G	A	Pts.	PIM	+/-	PP	SH	Gms.	G	A	Pts.	PIM
97-98—Victoria	BCJHL	50	9	17	26	145	...	...	...	—	—	—	—	—
98-99—Victoria	BCJHL	53	17	18	35	197	...	...	...	—	—	—	—	—
99-00—Moose Jaw	WHL	51	5	8	13	166	...	...	...	—	—	—	—	—
00-01—Moose Jaw	WHL	71	34	15	49	192	...	...	...	4	0	1	1	15
01-02—Moose Jaw	WHL	62	15	19	34	135	...	...	...	12	0	3	3	4
02-03—San Antonio..............	AHL	8	0	0	0	4	...	...	...	—	—	—	—	—
—Jackson	ECHL	49	12	11	23	149	...	...	...	—	—	—	—	—

ODELEIN, LYLE D

PERSONAL: Born July 21, 1968, in Quill Lake, Sask. ... 6-0/206. ... Shoots right. ... Brother of Selmar Odelein, defenseman with Edmonton Oilers (1985-86 through 1988-89). ... Name pronounced OH-duh-lighn.
TRANSACTIONS/CAREER NOTES: Selected by Montreal Canadiens in seventh round (eighth Canadiens pick, 141st overall) of NHL entry draft (June 21, 1986). ... Bruised right ankle (January 22, 1991); missed five games. ... Twisted right ankle (February 9, 1991). ... Suspended one game by NHL for game misconduct penalties (March 1, 1993). ... Bruised shoulder (January 24, 1994); missed three games. ... Suspended two games without pay and fined $1,000 by NHL for shooting puck into the opposing team's bench (April 3, 1996). ... Traded by Canadiens to New Jersey Devils for RW Stephane Richer (August 22, 1996). ... Bruised knee (January 21, 1997); missed three games. ... Bruised shoulder (November 12, 1997); missed one game. ... Suffered from the flu (January 11, 1999); missed two games. ... Bruised right knee (March 22, 1999); missed nine games. ... Injured back (November 5, 1999); missed three games. ... Suffered from the flu (January 14, 2000); missed three games. ... Traded by Devils to Phoenix Coyotes for D Deron Quint and third-round pick (traded back to Phoenix) in 2001 draft (March 7, 2000). ... Selected by Columbus Blue Jackets in NHL expansion draft (June 23, 2000). ... Bruised knee (March 15, 2001); missed one game. ... Suffered back spasms (January 16, 2002); missed three games. ... Traded by Blue Jackets to Chicago Blackhawks for D Jaroslav Spacek and second-round pick in 2003 draft (March 19, 2002). ... Suspended one playoff game by NHL for cross-checking incident (April 22, 2002). ... Traded by Blackhawks to Dallas Stars for D Sami Helenius and conditional pick in draft (March 10, 2003).
STATISTICAL PLATEAUS: Three-goal games: 1993-94 (1).

Season Team	League	REGULAR SEASON								PLAYOFFS				
		Gms.	G	A	Pts.	PIM	+/-	PP	SH	Gms.	G	A	Pts.	PIM
85-86—Moose Jaw	WHL	67	9	37	46	117	...	...	...	13	1	6	-7	34
86-87—Moose Jaw	WHL	59	9	50	59	70	...	...	...	9	2	5	7	26
87-88—Moose Jaw	WHL	63	15	43	58	166	...	...	...	—	—	—	—	—
88-89—Sherbrooke	AHL	33	3	4	7	120	...	...	...	3	0	2	2	5
—Peoria	IHL	36	2	8	10	116	...	...	...	—	—	—	—	—
89-90—Sherbrooke	AHL	68	7	24	31	265	...	...	...	12	6	5	11	79
—Montreal	NHL	8	0	2	2	33	-1	0	0	—	—	—	—	—
90-91—Montreal	NHL	52	0	2	2	259	7	0	0	12	0	0	0	54
91-92—Montreal	NHL	71	1	7	8	212	15	0	0	7	0	0	0	11
92-93—Montreal	NHL	83	2	14	16	205	35	0	0	20	1	5	6	30
93-94—Montreal	NHL	79	11	29	40	276	8	6	0	7	0	0	0	17
94-95—Montreal	NHL	48	3	7	10	152	-13	0	0	—	—	—	—	—
95-96—Montreal	NHL	79	3	14	17	230	8	0	1	6	1	1	2	6
96-97—New Jersey	NHL	79	3	13	16	110	16	1	0	10	2	2	4	19
97-98—New Jersey	NHL	79	4	19	23	171	11	1	0	6	1	1	2	21
98-99—New Jersey	NHL	70	5	26	31	114	6	1	0	7	0	3	3	10
99-00—New Jersey	NHL	57	1	15	16	104	-10	0	0	—	—	—	—	—
—Phoenix	NHL	16	1	7	8	19	1	1	0	5	0	0	0	16
00-01—Columbus	NHL	81	3	14	17	118	-16	1	0	—	—	—	—	—
01-02—Columbus	NHL	65	2	14	16	89	-28	0	0	—	—	—	—	—
—Chicago	NHL	12	0	2	2	4	0	0	0	4	0	1	1	25
02-03—Chicago	NHL	65	7	4	11	76	7	0	0	—	—	—	—	—
—Dallas	NHL	3	0	0	0	6	0	0	0	2	0	0	0	0
NHL Totals (14 years)		947	46	189	235	2178	46	11	1	86	5	13	18	209

ODGERS, JEFF　　　RW

PERSONAL: Born May 31, 1969, in Spy Hill, Sask. ... 6-0/205. ... Shoots right. ... Name pronounced AH-juhrs.

TRANSACTIONS/CAREER NOTES: Signed as non-drafted free agent by San Jose Sharks (September 3, 1991). ... Injured hand (December 21, 1991); missed four games. ... Fractured hand (November 5, 1992); missed 15 games. ... Suspended one game by NHL for accumulating three game-misconduct penalties (January 29, 1993). ... Suspended two games by NHL for accumulating four game-misconduct penalties (February 19, 1993). ... Traded by Sharks with fifth-round pick (D Elias Abrahamsson) in 1996 draft to Boston Bruins for D Al Iafrate (June 21, 1996). ... Injured neck (January 9, 1997); missed one game. ... Signed as free agent by Colorado Avalanche (October 24, 1997). ... Suffered from the flu (January 26, 1998); missed one game. ... Suffered from appendicitis (January 31, 1999); missed seven games. ... Selected by Minnesota Wild in NHL expansion draft (June 23, 2000). ... Claimed by Atlanta Thrashers from Wild in NHL waiver draft (September 29, 2000). ... Fractured ankle (November 1, 2001); missed 36 games.

Season Team	League	REGULAR SEASON								PLAYOFFS				
		Gms.	G	A	Pts.	PIM	+/-	PP	SH	Gms.	G	A	Pts.	PIM
86-87—Brandon	WHL	70	7	14	21	150	...	...	...	—	—	—	—	—
87-88—Brandon	WHL	70	17	18	35	202	...	...	...	4	1	1	2	14
88-89—Brandon	WHL	71	31	29	60	277	...	...	...	—	—	—	—	—
89-90—Brandon	WHL	64	37	28	65	209	...	...	...	—	—	—	—	—
90-91—Kansas City	IHL	77	12	19	31	*318	...	...	...	—	—	—	—	—
91-92—Kansas City	IHL	12	2	2	4	56	...	...	...	9	3	0	3	13
—San Jose	NHL	61	7	4	11	217	-21	0	0	—	—	—	—	—
92-93—San Jose	NHL	66	12	15	27	253	-26	6	0	—	—	—	—	—
93-94—San Jose	NHL	81	13	8	21	222	-13	7	0	11	0	0	0	11
94-95—San Jose	NHL	48	4	3	7	117	-8	0	0	11	1	1	2	23
95-96—San Jose	NHL	78	12	4	16	192	-4	0	0	—	—	—	—	—
96-97—Boston	NHL	80	7	8	15	197	-15	1	0	—	—	—	—	—
97-98—Providence	AHL	4	0	0	0	31	...	...	...	—	—	—	—	—
—Colorado	NHL	68	5	8	13	213	5	0	0	6	0	0	0	25
98-99—Colorado	NHL	75	2	3	5	259	-3	1	0	15	1	0	1	14
99-00—Colorado	NHL	62	1	2	3	162	-7	0	0	4	0	0	0	0
00-01—Atlanta	NHL	82	6	7	13	226	-8	0	0	—	—	—	—	—
01-02—Atlanta	NHL	46	4	4	8	135	-3	0	0	—	—	—	—	—
02-03—Atlanta	NHL	74	2	4	6	171	-13	0	0	—	—	—	—	—
NHL Totals (12 years)		821	75	70	145	2364	-116	15	0	47	2	1	3	73

O'DONNELL, SEAN　　　D　　　BRUINS

PERSONAL: Born October 13, 1971, in Ottawa ... 6-3/230. ... Shoots left.

TRANSACTIONS/CAREER NOTES: Selected by Buffalo Sabres in sixth round (sixth Sabres pick, 123rd overall) of NHL entry draft (June 22, 1991). ... Traded by Sabres to Los Angeles Kings for D Doug Houda (July 26, 1994). ... Bruised sternum (February 4, 1995); missed two games. ... Sprained left wrist (January 27, 1996); missed eight games. ... Sprained wrist (December 26, 1996); missed nine games. ... Suspended one game by NHL for an altercation while on the bench (January 30, 1997). ... Strained back (March 1, 1997); missed two games. ... Suspended two games by NHL for cross-checking and spearing incidents (April 14, 1999). ... Selected by Minnesota Wild in NHL expansion draft (June 23, 2000). ... Suffered from the flu (February 11, 2001); missed one game. ... Traded by Wild to New Jersey Devils for D Willie Mitchell and future considerations (March 4, 2001). ... Signed as free agent by Boston Bruins (July 2, 2001). ... Suffered back spasms (March 21, 2002); missed two games.

Season Team	League	REGULAR SEASON								PLAYOFFS				
		Gms.	G	A	Pts.	PIM	+/-	PP	SH	Gms.	G	A	Pts.	PIM
88-89—Sudbury	OHL	56	1	9	10	49	...	...	...	—	—	—	—	—
89-90—Sudbury	OHL	64	7	19	26	84	...	...	...	—	—	—	—	—
90-91—Sudbury	OHL	66	8	23	31	114	...	...	...	5	1	4	5	10
91-92—Rochester	AHL	73	4	9	13	193	...	...	...	16	1	2	3	21
92-93—Rochester	AHL	74	3	18	21	203	...	...	...	17	1	6	7	38

Season Team	League	Gms.	G	A	Pts.	PIM	+/-	PP	SH	Gms.	G	A	Pts.	PIM
93-94—Rochester	AHL	64	2	10	12	242	...	...	...	4	0	1	1	21
94-95—Phoenix	IHL	61	2	18	20	132	...	...	...	9	0	1	1	21
—Los Angeles	NHL	15	0	2	2	49	-2	0	0	—	—	—	—	—
95-96—Los Angeles	NHL	71	2	5	7	127	3	0	0	—	—	—	—	—
96-97—Los Angeles	NHL	55	5	12	17	144	-13	2	0	—	—	—	—	—
97-98—Los Angeles	NHL	80	2	15	17	179	7	0	0	4	1	0	1	36
98-99—Los Angeles	NHL	80	1	13	14	186	1	0	0	—	—	—	—	—
99-00—Los Angeles	NHL	80	2	12	14	114	4	0	0	4	1	0	1	4
00-01—Minnesota	NHL	63	4	12	16	128	-2	1	0	—	—	—	—	—
—New Jersey	NHL	17	0	1	1	33	2	0	0	23	1	2	3	41
01-02—Boston	NHL	80	3	22	25	89	27	1	0	6	0	2	2	4
02-03—Boston	NHL	70	1	15	16	76	8	0	0	—	—	—	—	—
NHL Totals (9 years)		611	20	109	129	1125	35	4	0	37	3	4	7	85

OHLUND, MATTIAS　　　D　　　CANUCKS

PERSONAL: Born September 9, 1976, in Pitea, Sweden ... 6-3/220. ... Shoots left. ... Name pronounced muh-TEE-uhz OH-luhnd.

TRANSACTIONS/CAREER NOTES: Selected by Vancouver Canucks in first round (first Canucks pick, 13th overall) of NHL entry draft (June 28, 1994). ... Suffered concussion (March 26, 1998); missed four games. ... Sprained shoulder (February 23, 1999); missed three games. ... Suffered concussion (April 3, 1999); missed final five games of season. ... Injured eye (September 12, 1999); missed first 38 games of season. ... Injured groin (March 8, 2000); missed two games. ... Underwent eye surgery (October 20, 2000); missed 17 games. ... Suffered from the flu (October 6, 2001); missed one game.

Season Team	League	Gms.	G	A	Pts.	PIM	+/-	PP	SH	Gms.	G	A	Pts.	PIM
92-93—Pitea	Sweden Dv. 2	22	0	6	6	16	...	...	...	—	—	—	—	—
93-94—Pitea	Sweden Dv. 2	28	7	10	17	62	...	...	...	—	—	—	—	—
94-95—Lulea	Sweden	34	6	10	16	34	...	...	...	9	4	0	4	16
95-96—Lulea	Sweden	38	4	10	14	26	...	...	...	13	0	1	1	47
96-97—Lulea	Sweden	47	7	9	16	38	...	...	...	10	1	2	3	8
97-98—Vancouver	NHL	77	7	23	30	76	3	1	0	—	—	—	—	—
—Swedish Oly. team	Int'l	4	0	1	1	4	...	...	...	—	—	—	—	—
98-99—Vancouver	NHL	74	9	26	35	83	-19	2	1	—	—	—	—	—
99-00—Vancouver	NHL	42	4	16	20	24	6	2	1	—	—	—	—	—
00-01—Vancouver	NHL	65	8	20	28	46	-16	1	1	4	1	3	4	6
01-02—Vancouver	NHL	81	10	26	36	56	16	4	1	6	1	1	2	6
—Swedish Oly. team	Int'l	4	0	2	2	2	...	...	...	—	—	—	—	—
02-03—Vancouver	NHL	59	2	27	29	42	1	0	0	13	3	4	7	12
NHL Totals (6 years)		398	40	138	178	327	-9	10	4	23	5	8	13	24

OLAUSSON, FREDRIK　　　D

PERSONAL: Born October 5, 1966, in Dadsejo, Sweden ... 6-1/195. ... Shoots right. ... Name pronounced OHL-ih-suhn.

TRANSACTIONS/CAREER NOTES: Selected by Winnipeg Jets in fourth round (fourth Jets pick, 81st overall) of NHL entry draft (June 15, 1985). ... Dislocated shoulder (August 1987). ... Underwent shoulder surgery (November 1987). ... Signed five-year contract with Farjestad, Sweden (June 19, 1989); Farjestad agreed to allow Olausson to remain in Winnipeg. ... Sprained knee (January 22, 1993); missed 11 games. ... Lacerated ankle (November 8, 1993); missed two games. ... Suffered from the flu (January 18, 1993); missed one game. ... Sprained knee (January 23, 1993); missed 11 games. ... Suffered from the flu (March 4, 1993); missed one game. ... Traded by Jets with seventh-round pick (LW Curtis Sheptak) in 1994 draft to Edmonton Oilers for third-round pick (C Tavis Hansen) in 1994 draft (December 5, 1993). ... Strained knee (January 11, 1994). ... Played in Europe during 1994-95 NHL lockout. ... Suffered from the flu (February 17, 1995); missed one game. ... Suffered colitis (March 3, 1995); missed 10 games. ... Cracked ribs (November 4, 1995); missed 14 games. ... Suffered irregular heartbeat (December 6, 1995); missed five games. ... Claimed on waivers by Mighty Ducks of Anaheim (January 16, 1996) ... Traded by Mighty Ducks with C Alex Hicks to Pittsburgh Penguins for LW Shawn Antoski and D Dmitri Mironov (November 19, 1996). ... Fractured cheekbone (January 26, 1997); missed nine games. ... Strained groin (February 27, 1997); missed three games. ... Bruised foot (November 2, 1997); missed three games. ... Bruised wrist (December 9, 1997); missed two games. ... Signed as free agent by Mighty Ducks (August 29, 1998). ... Injured ribs (March 17, 1999); missed two games. ... Sprained ankle (October 15, 1999); missed two games. ... Suffered injury (November 13, 1999); missed one game. ... Suffered illness (December 15, 1999); missed two games. ... Suffered illness (April 3, 2000); missed one game. ... Announced retirement (April 10, 2000). ... Signed as free agent by Detroit Red Wings (May 24, 2001). ... Suffered upper respiratory infection (December 30, 2001); missed seven games. ... Suffered from the flu (March 6, 2002); missed three games. ... Injured ribs (March 17, 2002); missed eight games. ... Signed as free agent by Mighty Ducks (July 12, 2002).

Season Team	League	Gms.	G	A	Pts.	PIM	+/-	PP	SH	Gms.	G	A	Pts.	PIM
82-83—Nybro	Sweden	31	4	4	8	12	...	...	...	—	—	—	—	—
83-84—Nybro	Sweden	28	8	14	22	32	...	...	...	—	—	—	—	—
84-85—Farjestad Karlstad	Sweden	34	6	12	18	24	...	...	...	3	1	0	1	0
85-86—Farjestad Karlstad	Sweden	33	5	12	17	14	...	...	...	8	3	2	5	6
86-87—Winnipeg	NHL	72	7	29	36	24	-3	1	0	10	2	3	5	4
87-88—Winnipeg	NHL	38	5	10	15	18	3	2	0	5	1	1	2	0
88-89—Winnipeg	NHL	75	15	47	62	32	6	4	0	—	—	—	—	—
89-90—Winnipeg	NHL	77	9	46	55	32	-1	3	0	7	0	4	4	2
90-91—Winnipeg	NHL	71	12	29	41	24	-22	5	0	—	—	—	—	—
91-92—Winnipeg	NHL	77	20	42	62	34	-31	13	1	7	1	5	6	4
92-93—Winnipeg	NHL	68	16	41	57	22	-4	11	0	6	0	2	2	2
93-94—Winnipeg	NHL	18	2	5	7	10	-3	1	0	—	—	—	—	—
—Edmonton	NHL	55	9	19	28	20	-4	6	0	—	—	—	—	—
94-95—Ehrwald	Austria	10	4	3	7	8	...	...	...	—	—	—	—	—
—Edmonton	NHL	33	0	10	10	20	-4	0	0	—	—	—	—	—
95-96—Edmonton	NHL	20	0	6	6	14	-14	0	0	—	—	—	—	—
—Anaheim	NHL	36	2	16	18	24	7	1	0	—	—	—	—	—

Season Team	League	REGULAR SEASON								PLAYOFFS				
		Gms.	G	A	Pts.	PIM	+/-	PP	SH	Gms.	G	A	Pts.	PIM
96-97—Anaheim	NHL	20	2	9	11	8	-5	1	0	—	—	—	—	—
—Pittsburgh	NHL	51	7	20	27	24	21	2	0	4	0	1	1	0
97-98—Pittsburgh	NHL	76	6	27	33	42	13	2	0	6	0	3	3	2
98-99—Anaheim	NHL	74	16	40	56	30	17	10	0	4	0	2	2	4
99-00—Anaheim	NHL	70	15	19	34	28	-13	8	0	—	—	—	—	—
00-01—Bern	Switzerland	43	12	15	27	28	...	...	...	4	1	4	5	0
01-02—Detroit	NHL	47	2	13	15	22	9	0	1	21	2	4	6	10
—Swedish Oly. team	Int'l	4	0	0	0	2	...	...	...	—	—	—	—	—
02-03—Anaheim	NHL	44	2	6	8	22	0	2	0	1	0	0	0	0
NHL Totals (16 years)		1022	147	434	581	450	-28	72	2	71	6	23	29	28

OLIVER, DAVID · RW · STARS

PERSONAL: Born April 17, 1971, in Sechelt, B.C. ... 6-0/190. ... Shoots right.

TRANSACTIONS/CAREER NOTES: Selected by Edmonton Oilers in seventh round (seventh Oilers pick, 144th overall) of NHL entry draft (June 22, 1991). ... Suffered hip pointer (January 24, 1997); missed one game. ... Claimed on waivers by New York Rangers (February 22, 1997). ... Signed as free agent by Ottawa Senators (July 2, 1998). ... Signed as free agent by Phoenix Coyotes (July 16, 1999). ... Signed as free agent by Ottawa Senators (August 2, 2000). ... Suffered hip pointer (November 17, 2000); missed two games. ... Strained groin (November 19, 2000); missed five games. ... Signed as free agent by Dallas Stars (July 30, 2002). ... Re-signed by Stars (July 17, 2003).

STATISTICAL PLATEAUS: Three-goal games: 1994-95 (1).

Season Team	League	REGULAR SEASON								PLAYOFFS				
		Gms.	G	A	Pts.	PIM	+/-	PP	SH	Gms.	G	A	Pts.	PIM
90-91—Univ. of Michigan	CCHA	27	13	11	24	34	...	...	...	—	—	—	—	—
91-92—Univ. of Michigan	CCHA	44	31	27	58	32	...	...	...	—	—	—	—	—
92-93—Univ. of Michigan	CCHA	40	35	20	55	18	...	...	...	—	—	—	—	—
93-94—Univ. of Michigan	CCHA	41	28	40	68	16	...	...	...	—	—	—	—	—
94-95—Cape Breton	AHL	32	11	18	29	8	...	...	...	—	—	—	—	—
—Edmonton	NHL	44	16	14	30	20	-11	10	0	—	—	—	—	—
95-96—Edmonton	NHL	80	20	19	39	34	-22	14	0	—	—	—	—	—
96-97—Edmonton	NHL	17	1	2	3	4	-8	0	0	—	—	—	—	—
—New York Rangers	NHL	14	2	1	3	4	3	0	0	3	0	0	0	0
97-98—Houston	IHL	78	38	27	65	60	...	...	...	4	3	0	3	4
98-99—Ottawa	NHL	17	2	5	7	4	1	0	0	—	—	—	—	—
—Houston	IHL	37	18	17	35	30	...	...	...	19	10	6	16	22
99-00—Hartford	AHL	9	0	0	0	19	...	...	...	—	—	—	—	—
—Huntington	ECHL	26	6	9	15	151	...	...	...	5	0	1	1	17
—Phoenix	NHL	9	1	0	1	2	0	1	0	—	—	—	—	—
00-01—Grand Rapids	IHL	51	14	17	31	35	...	...	...	10	6	2	8	8
—Ottawa	NHL	7	0	0	0	2	0	0	0	—	—	—	—	—
01-02—Munich	Germany	59	20	14	34	30	...	...	...	9	2	2	4	6
02-03—Utah	AHL	37	11	14	25	14	...	...	...	—	—	—	—	—
—Bossier-Shreveport	CHL	42	14	21	35	61	...	...	...	—	—	—	—	—
—Pensacola	ECHL	16	1	2	3	70	...	...	...	—	—	—	—	—
—Dallas	NHL	6	0	3	3	2	1	0	0	6	0	0	0	2
NHL Totals (7 years)		194	42	44	86	72	-36	25	0	9	0	0	0	2

OLIWA, KRZYSZTOF · LW · FLAMES

PERSONAL: Born April 12, 1973, in Tychy, Poland ... 6-5/243. ... Shoots left. ... Name pronounced KRIH-stahf OH-lee-vuh.

TRANSACTIONS/CAREER NOTES: Selected by New Jersey Devils in third round (fourth Devils pick, 65th overall) of NHL entry draft (June 26, 1993). ... Injured foot (November 10, 1997); missed two games. ... Strained groin (November 28, 1998); missed one game. ... Sprained left knee (October 30, 1999); missed six games. ... Suffered from the flu (January 11, 2000); missed one game. ... Injured left knee (April 2, 2000); missed final three games of season. ... Traded by Devils to Columbus Blue Jackets for third-round pick (C/LW Brandon Nolan) in 2001 draft and future considerations (June 12, 2000); Devils acquired RW Turner Stevenson to complete deal (June 23, 2000). ... Fractured arm (October 28, 2000); missed 23 games. ... Traded by Blue Jackets to Pittsburgh Penguins for third-round pick (D Aaron Johnson) in 2001 draft (January 14, 2001). ... Injured hamstring (March 20, 2001); missed five games. ... Traded by Penguins to New York Rangers for future considerations (June 22, 2002). ... Suspended five games NHL for unsportsmanlike conduct (November 11, 2002). ... Traded by Rangers to Boston Bruins for ninth-round pick in 2004 draft (January 6, 2003). ... Signed by Calgary Flames (July 30, 2003).

Season Team	League	REGULAR SEASON								PLAYOFFS				
		Gms.	G	A	Pts.	PIM	+/-	PP	SH	Gms.	G	A	Pts.	PIM
90-91—GKS Katowice	Poland Jrs.	5	4	4	8	10	...	...	...	—	—	—	—	—
91-92—GKS Tychy	Poland	10	3	7	10	6	...	...	...	—	—	—	—	—
92-93—Welland Jr. B	OHA	30	13	21	34	127	...	...	...	—	—	—	—	—
93-94—Albany	AHL	33	2	4	6	151	...	...	...	—	—	—	—	—
—Raleigh	ECHL	15	0	2	2	65	...	...	...	9	0	0	0	35
94-95—Albany	AHL	20	1	1	2	77	...	...	...	—	—	—	—	—
—Detroit	IHL	4	0	1	1	24	...	...	...	—	—	—	—	—
—Saint John	AHL	14	1	4	5	79	...	...	...	—	—	—	—	—
—Raleigh	ECHL	5	0	2	2	32	...	...	...	—	—	—	—	—
95-96—Albany	AHL	51	5	11	16	217	...	...	...	—	—	—	—	—
—Raleigh	ECHL	9	1	0	1	53	...	...	...	—	—	—	—	—
96-97—Albany	AHL	60	13	14	27	322	...	...	...	15	7	1	8	49
—New Jersey	NHL	1	0	0	0	5	-1	0	0	—	—	—	—	—
97-98—New Jersey	NHL	73	2	3	5	295	3	0	0	6	0	0	0	23
98-99—New Jersey	NHL	64	5	7	12	240	4	0	0	1	0	0	0	2
99-00—New Jersey	NHL	69	6	10	16	184	-2	1	0	—	—	—	—	—
00-01—Columbus	NHL	10	0	2	2	34	1	0	0	—	—	—	—	—
—Pittsburgh	NHL	26	1	2	3	131	-4	0	0	5	0	0	0	16

O

Season Team	League	Gms.	G	A	Pts.	PIM	+/-	PP	SH	Gms.	G	A	Pts.	PIM
01-02—Pittsburgh	NHL	57	0	2	2	150	-5	0	0	—	—	—	—	—
02-03—Hartford	AHL	15	0	1	1	30	...	...	...	—	—	—	—	—
—New York Rangers	NHL	9	0	0	0	51	1	0	0	—	—	—	—	—
—Boston	NHL	33	0	0	0	110	-4	0	0	—	—	—	—	—
NHL Totals (7 years)		342	14	26	40	1200	-7	1	0	12	0	0	0	41

OLSON, JOSH　　　　LW　　　　PANTHERS

PERSONAL: Born July 13, 1981, in Grand Forks, N.D. ... 6-5/220. ... Shoots left.
TRANSACTIONS/CAREER NOTES: Selected by Florida Panthers in sixth round (sixth Panthers pick, 190th overall) of NHL entry draft (June 24, 2000).

			REGULAR SEASON							PLAYOFFS				
Season Team	League	Gms.	G	A	Pts.	PIM	+/-	PP	SH	Gms.	G	A	Pts.	PIM
99-00—Fargo	USHL	18	2	5	7	37	...	...	...	—	—	—	—	—
—Omaha	USHL	61	8	12	20	81	...	...	...	4	0	0	0	4
00-01—Portland	WHL	72	22	38	60	86	...	...	...	16	5	4	9	17
01-02—Portland	WHL	72	40	48	88	85	...	...	...	7	4	3	7	8
—Utah	AHL	1	0	0	0	0	...	...	...	1	0	0	0	0
02-03—San Antonio	AHL	23	0	1	1	14	...	...	...	—	—	—	—	—
—Jackson	ECHL	39	10	17	27	13	...	...	...	—	—	—	—	—

OLVESTAD, JIMMIE　　　　RW　　　　LIGHTNING

PERSONAL: Born February 16, 1980, in Stockholm, Sweden ... 6-1/194. ... Shoots left.
TRANSACTIONS/CAREER NOTES: Selected by Tampa Bay Lightning in third round (fourth Lightning pick, 88th overall) of NHL entry draft (June 26, 1999). ... Sprained right shoulder (October 30, 2001); missed three games. ... Suffered concussion (January 13, 2002); missed four games.

			REGULAR SEASON							PLAYOFFS				
Season Team	League	Gms.	G	A	Pts.	PIM	+/-	PP	SH	Gms.	G	A	Pts.	PIM
96-97—Huddinge	Sweden Jr.	40	15	16	31	...	...	...	...	—	—	—	—	—
97-98—Huddinge	Sweden Dv. 2	11	0	0	0	6	...	...	...	—	—	—	—	—
—Djurgarden Stockholm	Sweden Jr.	15	6	4	10	...	...	...	...	—	—	—	—	—
98-99—Djurgarden Stockholm	Sweden	44	2	4	6	18	...	...	...	4	0	0	0	8
99-00—Djurgarden Stockholm	Sweden	50	6	3	9	34	...	...	...	13	1	2	3	12
00-01—Djurgarden Stockholm	Sweden	50	7	8	15	79	...	...	...	16	7	2	9	14
01-02—Tampa Bay	NHL	74	3	11	14	24	3	0	0	—	—	—	—	—
02-03—Springfield	AHL	6	0	1	1	13	...	...	...	—	—	—	—	—
—Tampa Bay	NHL	37	0	3	3	16	-2	0	0	—	—	—	—	—
NHL Totals (2 years)		111	3	14	17	40	1	0	0					

O'NEILL, JEFF　　　　RW　　　　HURRICANES

PERSONAL: Born February 23, 1976, in Richmond Hill, Ont. ... 6-1/195. ... Shoots right.
TRANSACTIONS/CAREER NOTES: Selected by Hartford Whalers in first round (first Whalers pick, fifth overall) of NHL entry draft (June 28, 1994). ... Bruised foot (December 30, 1995); missed four games. ... Reinjured foot (January 10, 1996); missed four games. ... Injured shoulder (February 17, 1996); missed four games. ... Injured groin (January 2, 1997); missed one game. ... Sprained wrist (April 2, 1997); missed four games. ... Whalers franchise moved to North Carolina and renamed Carolina Hurricanes for 1997-98 season; NHL approved move on June 25, 1997. ... Suffered concussion (December 20, 1997); missed one game. ... Fractured kneecap (April 13, 1998); missed three games. ... Strained neck (February 3, 1999); missed seven games. ... Suffered back spasms (November 24, 1999); missed two games. ... Injured back (December 31, 2001); missed four games. ... Suspended one playoff game by NHL for checking from behind (May 4, 2002).
STATISTICAL PLATEAUS: Three-goal games: 1996-97 (1).

			REGULAR SEASON							PLAYOFFS				
Season Team	League	Gms.	G	A	Pts.	PIM	+/-	PP	SH	Gms.	G	A	Pts.	PIM
91-92—Thornhill	Tier II Jr. A	43	27	53	80	48	...	...	...	—	—	—	—	—
92-93—Guelph	OHL	65	32	47	79	88	...	...	...	5	2	2	4	6
93-94—Guelph	OHL	66	45	81	126	95	...	...	...	9	2	11	13	31
94-95—Guelph	OHL	57	43	81	124	56	...	...	...	14	8	18	26	34
95-96—Hartford	NHL	65	8	19	27	40	-3	1	0	—	—	—	—	—
96-97—Hartford	NHL	72	14	16	30	40	-24	2	1	—	—	—	—	—
—Springfield	AHL	1	0	0	0	0	...	...	...	—	—	—	—	—
97-98—Carolina	NHL	74	19	20	39	67	-8	7	1	—	—	—	—	—
98-99—Carolina	NHL	75	16	15	31	66	3	4	0	6	0	1	1	0
99-00—Carolina	NHL	80	25	38	63	72	-9	4	0	—	—	—	—	—
00-01—Carolina	NHL	82	41	26	67	106	-18	17	0	6	1	2	3	10
01-02—Carolina	NHL	76	31	33	64	63	-5	11	0	22	8	5	13	27
02-03—Carolina	NHL	82	30	31	61	38	-21	11	0	—	—	—	—	—
NHL Totals (8 years)		606	184	198	382	492	-85	57	2	34	9	8	17	37

ORPIK, BROOKS　　　　D　　　　PENGUINS

PERSONAL: Born September 26, 1980, in Amherst, N.Y. ... 6-3/217. ... Shoots left.
TRANSACTIONS/CAREER NOTES: Selected by Pittsburgh Penguins in first round (first Penguins pick, 18th overall) of NHL entry draft (June 24, 2000).

O

Season Team	League	REGULAR SEASON								PLAYOFFS				
		Gms.	G	A	Pts.	PIM	+/-	PP	SH	Gms.	G	A	Pts.	PIM
97-98—Thayer Academy........	Mass. H.S.	22	0	7	7	...	...	...	...	—	—	—	—	—
98-99—Boston College	Hockey East	41	1	10	11	96	...	...	...	—	—	—	—	—
99-00—Boston College	Hockey East	38	1	9	10	100	...	...	...	—	—	—	—	—
00-01—Boston College	Hockey East	40	0	20	20	*124	...	...	...	—	—	—	—	—
01-02—Wilkes-Barre/Scranton	AHL	78	2	18	20	99	...	...	...	—	—	—	—	—
02-03—Wilkes-Barre/Scranton	AHL	71	4	14	18	105	...	...	...	—	—	—	—	—
—Pittsburgh..................	NHL	6	0	0	0	2	-5	0	0	—	—	—	—	—
NHL Totals (1 year)............		6	0	0	0	2	-5	0	0	—	—	—	—	—

ORSZAGH, VLADIMIR   RW   PREDATORS

PERSONAL: Born May 24, 1977, in Banska Bystrica, Czechoslovakia ... 5-11/193. ... Shoots left. ... Name pronounced OHR-sahg.
TRANSACTIONS/CAREER NOTES: Selected by New York Islanders in fifth round (fourth Islanders pick, 106th overall) of NHL entry draft (July 8, 1995). ... Suffered tendinitis (December 14, 1999); missed one game. ... Signed as free agent by Nashville Predators (June 1, 2001). ... Suffered charley horse (March 2, 2002); missed two games.

Season Team	League	REGULAR SEASON								PLAYOFFS				
		Gms.	G	A	Pts.	PIM	+/-	PP	SH	Gms.	G	A	Pts.	PIM
93-94—IS Banska Byst.	Slovakia Jrs.	—	38	27	65	...	...	...	...	—	—	—	—	—
94-95—Banska Bystrica	Slov. Div. II	38	18	12	30	...	...	...	...	—	—	—	—	—
—Martimex ZTS Martin..	Slovakia	1	0	0	0	0	...	...	...	—	—	—	—	—
95-96—Banska Bystrica	Slovakia	31	9	5	14	22	...	...	...	—	—	—	—	—
96-97—Utah	IHL	68	12	15	27	30	...	...	...	3	0	1	1	4
97-98—Utah	IHL	62	13	10	23	60	...	...	...	4	2	0	2	0
—New York Islanders.....	NHL	11	0	1	1	2	-3	0	0	—	—	—	—	—
98-99—Lowell	AHL	68	18	23	41	57	...	...	...	3	2	2	4	2
—New York Islanders.....	NHL	12	1	0	1	6	2	0	0	—	—	—	—	—
99-00—Lowell	AHL	55	8	12	20	22	...	...	...	7	3	3	6	2
—New York Islanders.....	NHL	11	2	1	3	4	1	0	0	—	—	—	—	—
00-01—Djurgarden Stockholm	Sweden	50	23	13	36	62	...	...	...	16	7	3	10	20
01-02—Nashville	NHL	79	15	21	36	56	-15	5	0	—	—	—	—	—
02-03—Nashville	NHL	78	16	16	32	38	-1	3	0	—	—	—	—	—
NHL Totals (5 years)...........		191	34	39	73	106	-16	8	0					

OSGOOD, CHRIS   G   BLUES

PERSONAL: Born November 26, 1972, in Peace River, Alta. ... 5-11/179. ... Catches left.
TRANSACTIONS/CAREER NOTES: Selected by Detroit Red Wings in third round (third Red Wings pick, 54th overall) of NHL entry draft (June 22, 1991). ... Strained hamstring (January 14, 1997); missed five games. ... Strained groin (March 14, 1998); missed four games. ... Strained hip flexor (November 19, 1998); missed six games. ... Injured right knee (April 27, 1999); missed four playoff games. ... Injured hand (November 24, 1999); missed 15 games. ... Claimed by New York Islanders from Red Wings in NHL waiver draft (September 28, 2001). ... Suffered tendinitis in wrist (January 22, 2002); missed three games. ... Traded by Islanders with third-round pick in 2003 draft to St. Louis Blues for C Justin Papineau and second-round pick in 2003 draft (March 11, 2003). ... Re-signed by Blues (June 12, 2003).

Season Team	League	REGULAR SEASON								PLAYOFFS						
		Gms.	Min	W	L	T	GA	SO	Avg.	SV%	Gms.	Min.	W	L	GA SO	Avg.	SV%
89-90—Medicine Hat................	WHL	57	3094	24	28	2	228	0	4.42	—	3	173	3	4	17 0	5.90	—
90-91—Medicine Hat................	WHL	46	2630	23	18	3	173	2	3.95	—	12	714	7	5	42 0	3.53	—
91-92—Medicine Hat................	WHL	15	819	10	3	0	44	0	3.22	—	—	—	—	—	— —	—	—
—Brandon....................	WHL	16	890	3	10	1	60	1	4.04	—	—	—	—	—	— —	—	—
—Seattle......................	WHL	21	1217	12	7	1	65	1	3.20	—	15	904	9	6	51 0	3.38	—
92-93—Adirondack.................	AHL	45	2438	19	19	2	159	0	3.91	—	1	59	0	1	2 0	2.03	—
93-94—Adirondack.................	AHL	4	240	3	1	0	13	0	3.25	—	—	—	—	—	— —	—	—
—Detroit......................	NHL	41	2206	23	8	5	105	2	2.86	.895	6	307	3	2	12 1	2.35	.891
94-95—Adirondack.................	AHL	2	120	1	1	0	6	0	3.00	—	—	—	—	—	— —	—	—
—Detroit......................	NHL	19	1087	14	5	0	41	1	2.26	.917	2	68	0	2	2 0	1.76	.920
95-96—Detroit......................	NHL	50	2933	*39	6	5	106	5	2.17	.911	15	936	8	7	33 2	2.12	.898
96-97—Detroit......................	NHL	47	2769	23	13	9	106	6	2.30	.910	2	47	0	0	2 0	2.55	.905
97-98—Detroit......................	NHL	64	3807	33	20	11	140	6	2.21	.913	22	1361	*16	6	48 2	2.12	.918
98-99—Detroit......................	NHL	63	3691	34	25	4	149	3	2.42	.910	6	358	4	2	14 1	2.35	.919
99-00—Detroit......................	NHL	53	3148	30	14	8	126	6	2.40	.907	9	547	5	4	18 2	1.97	.924
00-01—Detroit......................	NHL	52	2834	25	19	4	127	1	2.69	.903	6	365	2	4	15 1	2.47	.905
01-02—New York Islanders.......	NHL	66	3743	32	25	6	156	4	2.50	.910	7	392	3	4	17 0	2.60	.912
02-03—New York Islanders.......	NHL	37	1993	17	14	4	97	2	2.92	.894	7	417	3	4	17 1	2.45	.907
—St. Louis	NHL	9	532	4	3	2	27	2	3.05	.888	—	—	—	—	— —	—	—
NHL Totals (10 years)...........		501	28743	274	152	58	1180	38	2.46	.907	82	4798	44	33	178 10	2.23	.911

O'SULLIVAN, CHRIS   D

PERSONAL: Born May 15, 1974, in Dorchester, Mass. ... 6-2/213. ... Shoots left.
TRANSACTIONS/CAREER NOTES: Selected by Calgary Flames in second round (second Flames pick, 30th overall) of NHL entry draft (June 20, 1992). ... Suffered concussion (December 20, 1997); missed three games. ... Traded by Flames to New York Rangers for D Lee Sorochan (March 23, 1999). ... Signed as free agent by Vancouver Canucks (August 11, 1999). ... Signed as free agent by Mighty Ducks of Anaheim (July 20, 2000).

Season Team	League	REGULAR SEASON								PLAYOFFS				
		Gms.	G	A	Pts.	PIM	+/-	PP	SH	Gms.	G	A	Pts.	PIM
91-92—Catholic Memorial......	Mass. H.S.	26	26	23	49	65	...	...	...	—	—	—	—	—
92-93—Boston University	Hockey East	5	0	2	2	4	...	...	...	—	—	—	—	—
93-94—Boston University	Hockey East	32	5	18	23	25	...	...	...	—	—	—	—	—
94-95—Boston University	Hockey East	40	23	33	56	48	...	...	...	—	—	—	—	—
95-96—Boston University	Hockey East	37	12	35	47	50	...	...	...	—	—	—	—	—
96-97—Calgary	NHL	27	2	8	10	2	0	1	0	—	—	—	—	—
—Saint John	AHL	29	3	8	11	17	...	...	...	5	0	4	4	0
97-98—Saint John	AHL	32	4	10	14	2	...	...	...	21	2	17	19	18
—Calgary	NHL	12	0	2	2	10	4	0	0	—	—	—	—	—
98-99—Saint John	AHL	41	7	29	36	24	...	...	...	—	—	—	—	—
—Calgary	NHL	10	0	1	1	2	-1	0	0	—	—	—	—	—
—Hartford	AHL	10	1	4	5	0	...	...	...	7	1	3	4	11
99-00—Syracuse	AHL	59	18	47	65	24	...	...	...	4	0	1	1	0
—Vancouver.................	NHL	11	0	5	5	2	2	0	0	—	—	—	—	—
00-01—Cincinnati..................	AHL	60	9	40	49	31	...	...	...	4	0	3	3	0
01-02—Kloten	Switzerland	39	7	16	23	34	...	...	...	6	1	2	3	12
02-03—Cincinnati..................	AHL	27	2	13	15	8	...	...	...	—	—	—	—	—
—Anaheim	NHL	2	0	1	1	0	0	0	0	—	—	—	—	—
NHL Totals (5 years)...........		62	2	17	19	16	5	1	0					

OTT, STEVE — C/LW — STARS

PERSONAL: Born August 19, 1982, in Summerside, Prince Edward Island ... 6-0/185. ... Shoots left.
TRANSACTIONS/CAREER NOTES: Selected by Dallas Stars in first round (first Stars pick, 25th overall) of NHL entry draft (June 24, 2000).

Season Team	League	REGULAR SEASON								PLAYOFFS				
		Gms.	G	A	Pts.	PIM	+/-	PP	SH	Gms.	G	A	Pts.	PIM
98-99—Leamington.................	Jr. B	48	14	30	44	110	...	...	...	—	—	—	—	—
99-00—Windsor	OHL	66	23	39	62	131	...	...	...	12	3	5	8	21
00-01—Windsor	OHL	55	50	37	87	164	...	...	...	9	3	8	11	27
01-02—Windsor	OHL	53	43	45	88	178	...	...	...	14	6	10	16	49
02-03—Utah	AHL	40	9	11	20	98	...	...	...	—	—	—	—	—
—Dallas........................	NHL	26	3	4	7	31	6	0	0	1	0	0	0	0
NHL Totals (1 year).............		26	3	4	7	31	6	0	0	1	0	0	0	0

OUELLET, MAXIME — G — CAPITALS

PERSONAL: Born June 17, 1981, in Beauport, Que. ... 6-0/180. ... Catches left.
TRANSACTIONS/CAREER NOTES: Selected by Philadelphia Flyers in first round (first Flyers pick, 22nd overall) of NHL entry draft (June 26, 1999). ... Traded by Flyers with first-(traded to Dallas), second-(G Maxime Daigneault) and third-round (C Derek Krestanovich) picks in 2002 draft to Washington Capitals for C Adam Oates (March 19, 2002).

Season Team	League	REGULAR SEASON									PLAYOFFS							
		Gms.	Min	W	L	T	GA	SO	Avg.	SV%	Gms.	Min.	W	L	GA	SO	Avg.	SV%
97-98—Quebec.........................	QMJHL	24	1199	12	7	1	66	0	3.30	—	7	305	3	1	16	0	3.15	—
98-99—Quebec.........................	QMJHL	*58	*3447	*40	12	*6	155	3	*2.70	—	13	803	6	7	41	†1	3.06	—
99-00—Quebec.........................	QMJHL	53	2984	31	16	4	133	2	2.67	—	11	638	7	4	28	*2	*2.63	—
00-01—Philadelphia	NHL	2	76	0	1	0	3	0	2.37	.889	—	—	—	—	—	—	—	—
—Philadelphia	AHL	2	86	1	0	0	4	0	2.79	—	—	—	—	—	—	—	—	—
—Rouyn-Noranda...........	QMJHL	25	1471	18	6	1	65	3	2.65	—	8	490	4	4	25	0	3.06	—
01-02—Philadelphia	AHL	41	2294	16	13	8	104	1	2.72	—	—	—	—	—	—	—	—	—
—Portland	AHL	6	358	3	3	0	17	0	2.85	—	—	—	—	—	—	—	—	—
02-03—Portland	AHL	48	2773	22	16	7	111	7	2.40	—	—	—	—	—	—	—	—	—
NHL Totals (1 year)..............		2	76	0	1	0	3	0	2.37	.889								

OUELLET, MICHEL — RW — PENGUINS

PERSONAL: Born March 5, 1982, in Rimouski, Que. ... 6-1/182. ... Shoots right.
TRANSACTIONS/CAREER NOTES: Selected by Pittsburgh Penguins in fourth round (fourth Penguins pick, 124th overall) of NHL entry draft (June 24, 2000).

Season Team	League	REGULAR SEASON								PLAYOFFS				
		Gms.	G	A	Pts.	PIM	+/-	PP	SH	Gms.	G	A	Pts.	PIM
98-99—Rimouski	QMJHL	28	7	13	20	10	...	...	...	—	—	—	—	—
99-00—Rimouski	QMJHL	72	36	53	89	38	...	...	...	—	—	—	—	—
00-01—Rimouski	QMJHL	63	42	50	92	50	...	...	...	11	6	7	13	8
01-02—Rimouski	QMJHL	61	40	58	98	66	...	...	...	7	3	6	9	4
02-03—Wilkes-Barre/Scranton	AHL	4	0	2	2	0	...	...	...	—	—	—	—	—
—Wheeling....................	ECHL	55	20	26	46	40	...	...	...	—	—	—	—	—

OZOLINSH, SANDIS — D — MIGHTY DUCKS

PERSONAL: Born August 3, 1972, in Riga, U.S.S.R. ... 6-3/215. ... Shoots left. ... Name pronounced SAN-diz OH-zoh-lihnsh.
TRANSACTIONS/CAREER NOTES: Selected by San Jose Sharks in second round (third Sharks pick, 30th overall) of NHL entry draft (June 22, 1991). ... Strained back (November 7, 1992); missed one game. ... Tore anterior cruciate ligament in knee (December 30, 1992); missed remainder of season. ... Injured knee (December 11, 1993); missed one game. ... Traded by Sharks to Colorado Avalanche for RW Owen Nolan

(October 26, 1995). ... Separated left shoulder (December 7, 1995); missed four games. ... Fractured finger (February 23, 1996); missed two games. ... Suffered back spasms (March 9, 1997); missed two games. ... Separated shoulder (October 7, 1997); missed two games. ... Injured knee (October 17, 1997) and underwent arthroscopic surgery; missed 13 games. ... Missed first 38 games of 1998-99 season due to contract dispute. ... Bruised sternum (February 9, 1999); missed two games. ... Traded by Avalanche with second-round pick (LW Tomas Kurka) in 2000 draft to Carolina Hurricanes for D Nolan Pratt, first-(C Vaclav Nedorost) and two second-round (C Jared Aulin and D Argis Saviels) picks in 2000 draft (June 24, 2000). ... Injured knee (December 29, 2000) and underwent surgery; missed 10 games. ... Sprained knee (October 18, 2001); missed three games. ... Traded by Hurricanes with C Byron Ritchie to Florida Panthers for D Bret Hedican, C Kevyn Adams, D Tomas Malec and conditional second-round draft pick in 2003 (January 16, 2002). ... Traded by Panthers with D Lance Ward to Mighty Ducks of Anaheim for C Matt Cullen, D Pavel Trnka and fourth-round pick in 2003 (January 30, 2003).
STATISTICAL PLATEAUS: Three-goal games: 1999-00 (1), 2000-01 (1). Total: 2.

			REGULAR SEASON							PLAYOFFS				
Season Team	League	Gms.	G	A	Pts.	PIM	+/-	PP	SH	Gms.	G	A	Pts.	PIM
90-91—Dynamo Riga	USSR	44	0	3	3	49	...	...	...	—				
91-92—HC Riga	CIS	30	5	0	5	42	...	...	...	—				
—Kansas City	IHL	34	6	9	15	20	...	...	...	15	2	5	7	22
92-93—San Jose	NHL	37	7	16	23	40	-9	2	0	—				
93-94—San Jose	NHL	81	26	38	64	24	16	4	0	14	0	10	10	8
94-95—San Jose	NHL	48	9	16	25	30	-6	3	1	11	3	2	5	6
95-96—San Francisco	IHL	2	1	0	1	0	...	...	...	—				
—San Jose	NHL	7	1	3	4	4	2	1	0	—				
—Colorado	NHL	66	13	37	50	50	0	7	1	22	5	14	19	16
96-97—Colorado	NHL	80	23	45	68	88	4	13	0	17	4	13	17	24
97-98—Colorado	NHL	66	13	38	51	65	-12	9	0	7	0	7	7	14
98-99—Colorado	NHL	39	7	25	32	22	10	4	0	19	4	8	12	22
99-00—Colorado	NHL	82	16	36	52	46	17	6	0	17	5	5	10	20
00-01—Carolina	NHL	72	12	32	44	71	-25	4	2	6	0	2	2	5
01-02—Carolina	NHL	§46	4	19	23	34	-4	1	0	—				
—Florida	NHL	§37	10	19	29	24	-3	2	0	—				
—Latvian Olympic team	Int'l	1	0	4	4	0	...	...	...	—				
02-03—Florida	NHL	51	7	19	26	40	-16	5	0	—				
—Anaheim	NHL	31	5	13	18	16	10	1	0	21	2	6	8	10
NHL Totals (11 years)		743	153	356	509	554	-16	62	4	134	23	67	90	125

PAETSCH, NATHAN   D   CAPITALS

PERSONAL: Born March 30, 1983, in Humboldt, Sask. ... 6-0/195. ... Shoots left.
TRANSACTIONS/CAREER NOTES: Selected by Washington Capitals in second round (first Capitals pick, 58th overall) of NHL entry draft (June 23, 2001).

			REGULAR SEASON							PLAYOFFS				
Season Team	League	Gms.	G	A	Pts.	PIM	+/-	PP	SH	Gms.	G	A	Pts.	PIM
98-99—Moose Jaw	WHL	2	0	0	0	0	...	...	...	—				
99-00—Moose Jaw	WHL	68	9	35	44	48	...	...	...	4	0	1	1	0
00-01—Moose Jaw	WHL	70	8	54	62	118	...	...	...	4	1	2	3	6
01-02—Moose Jaw	WHL	59	16	36	52	86	...	...	...	12	0	4	4	16
02-03—Moose Jaw	WHL	59	15	39	54	81	...	...	...	—				

PAHLSSON, SAMUEL   C   MIGHTY DUCKS

PERSONAL: Born December 17, 1977, in Ornskoldsvik, Sweden ... 6-0/208. ... Shoots left.
TRANSACTIONS/CAREER NOTES: Selected by Colorado Avalanche in seventh round (10th Avalanche pick, 176th overall) of NHL entry draft (June 22, 1996). ... Traded by Avalanche with LW Brian Rolston, D Martin Grenier and first-round pick (LW Martin Samuelsson) in 2000 draft to Boston Bruins for D Ray Bourque and LW Dave Andreychuk (March 6, 2000). ... Traded by Bruins to Mighty Ducks for Anaheim for LW Andrei Nazarov and D Patrick Traverse (November 18, 2000). ... Re-signed by Mighty Ducks (July 22, 2003).

			REGULAR SEASON							PLAYOFFS				
Season Team	League	Gms.	G	A	Pts.	PIM	+/-	PP	SH	Gms.	G	A	Pts.	PIM
94-95—MoDo Ornskoldsvik	Sweden Jr.	30	10	11	21	26	...	...	...	—				
—MoDo Ornskoldsvik	Sweden						...	...	...	—				
95-96—MoDo Ornskoldsvik	Sweden	36	1	3	4	8	...	...	...	—				
—MoDo Ornskoldsvik	Sweden Jr.	5	2	6	8	2	...	...	...	—				
96-97—MoDo Ornskoldsvik	Sweden	49	8	9	17	83	...	...	...	—				
97-98—MoDo Ornskoldsvik	Sweden	23	6	11	17	24	...	...	...	9	3	0	3	6
98-99—MoDo Ornskoldsvik	Sweden	50	17	17	34	44	...	...	...	13	3	3	6	10
99-00—MoDo Ornskoldsvik	Sweden	47	16	11	27	67	...	...	...	13	3	3	6	8
00-01—Boston	NHL	17	1	1	2	6	-5	0	0	—				
—Anaheim	NHL	59	3	4	7	14	-9	1	1	—				
01-02—Anaheim	NHL	80	6	14	20	26	-16	1	1	—				
02-03—Cincinnati	AHL	13	1	7	8	24	...	...	...	—				
—Anaheim	NHL	34	4	11	15	18	10	0	1	21	2	4	6	12
NHL Totals (3 years)		190	14	30	44	64	-20	2	3	21	2	4	6	12

PAILLE, DAN   LW   SABRES

PERSONAL: Born April 15, 1984, in Welland, Ont. ... 6-0/200. ... Shoots left.
TRANSACTIONS/CAREER NOTES: Selected by Buffalo Sabres in first round (second Sabres pick, 20th overall) of NHL entry draft (June 22, 2002).

			REGULAR SEASON							PLAYOFFS				
Season Team	League	Gms.	G	A	Pts.	PIM	+/-	PP	SH	Gms.	G	A	Pts.	PIM
00-01—Guelph	OHL	64	22	31	53	57	...	...	...	4	0	2	2	2
01-02—Guelph	OHL	62	27	30	57	54	...	...	...	9	5	2	7	9
02-03—Guelph	OHL	54	30	27	57	57	...	...	...	11	8	6	14	6

PALFFY, ZIGMUND   RW   KINGS

P

PERSONAL: Born May 5, 1972, in Skalica, Czechoslovakia ... 5-10/180. ... Shoots left. ... Name pronounced PAL-fee.
TRANSACTIONS/CAREER NOTES: Selected by New York Islanders in second round (second Islanders pick, 26th overall) of NHL entry draft (June 22, 1991). ... Suffered concussion (February 17, 1996); missed one game. ... Sprained shoulder (January 13, 1997); missed two games. ... Missed first 32 games of 1998-99 season due to contract dispute; played in Europe. ... Traded by Islanders with C Bryan Smolinski, G Marcel Cousineau and fourth-round pick (C Daniel Johansson) in 1999 draft to Los Angeles Kings for C Olli Jokinen, LW Josh Green, D Mathieu Biron and first-round pick (LW Taylor Pyatt) in 1999 draft (June 20, 1999). ... Suffered back spasms (December 4, 1999); missed four games. ... Suffered back spasms (January 4, 2000); missed one game. ... Strained right shoulder (March 15, 2000); missed final 12 games of regular season. ... Strained hamstring (December 16, 2000); missed eight games. ... Suffered from the flu (January 8, 2001); missed one game. ... Suffered back spasms (October 26, 2001); missed five games. ... Fractured rib (December 1, 2001); missed 14 games.
STATISTICAL PLATEAUS: Three-goal games: 1995-96 (2), 1996-97 (1), 1997-98 (2), 1998-99 (1), 2000-01 (1), 2001-02 (1). Total: 8.

				REGULAR SEASON							PLAYOFFS			
Season Team	League	Gms.	G	A	Pts.	PIM	+/-	PP	SH	Gms.	G	A	Pts.	PIM
90-91—Nitra............................	Czech.	50	34	16	50	...	...	...	...	—	—	—	—	—
91-92—Dukla Trencin..............	Czech.	32	23	25	*48	...	...	...	...	—	—	—	—	—
92-93—Dukla Trencin..............	Czech.	43	38	41	79	...	...	...	...	—	—	—	—	—
93-94—Salt Lake City..............	IHL	57	25	32	57	83	...	...	...	—	—	—	—	—
—Slovakian Oly. team	Int'l	8	3	7	10	8	...	...	...	—	—	—	—	—
—New York Islanders.....	NHL	5	0	0	0	0	-6	0	0	—	—	—	—	—
94-95—Denver	IHL	33	20	23	43	40	...	...	...	—	—	—	—	—
—New York Islanders.....	NHL	33	10	7	17	6	3	1	0	—	—	—	—	—
95-96—New York Islanders.....	NHL	81	43	44	87	56	-17	17	1	—	—	—	—	—
96-97—New York Islanders.....	NHL	80	48	42	90	43	21	6	4	—	—	—	—	—
97-98—New York Islanders.....	NHL	82	45	42	87	34	-2	*17	2	—	—	—	—	—
98-99—HK 36 Skalica	Slovakia	9	11	8	19	6	...	...	...	—	—	—	—	—
—New York Islanders.....	NHL	50	22	28	50	34	-6	5	2	—	—	—	—	—
99-00—Los Angeles...............	NHL	64	27	39	66	32	18	4	0	4	2	0	2	0
00-01—Los Angeles...............	NHL	73	38	51	89	20	22	12	4	13	3	5	8	8
01-02—Los Angeles...............	NHL	63	32	27	59	26	5	15	1	7	4	5	9	0
—Slovakian Oly. team	Int'l	1	0	0	0	0	...	...	...	—	—	—	—	—
02-03—Los Angeles...............	NHL	76	37	48	85	47	22	10	2	—	—	—	—	—
NHL Totals (10 years).........		607	302	328	630	298	60	87	16	24	9	10	19	8

PANDOLFO, JAY   LW   DEVILS

PERSONAL: Born December 27, 1974, in Winchester, Mass. ... 6-1/190. ... Shoots left.
TRANSACTIONS/CAREER NOTES: Selected by New Jersey Devils in second round (second Devils pick, 32nd overall) of NHL entry draft (June 26, 1993). ... Suffered from the flu (January 14, 1999); missed two games. ... Bruised shoulder (March 17, 1999); missed 10 games. ... Suffered facial lacerations (January 29, 2000); missed three games. ... Bruised shoulder (October 14, 2000); missed 13 games. ... Bruised ribs (December 19, 2001); missed six games. ... Bruised hip (January 21, 2002); missed 10 games.

				REGULAR SEASON							PLAYOFFS			
Season Team	League	Gms.	G	A	Pts.	PIM	+/-	PP	SH	Gms.	G	A	Pts.	PIM
89-90—Burlington H.S.	Mass. H.S.	23	33	30	63	18	...	...	...	—	—	—	—	—
90-91—Burlington H.S.	Mass. H.S.	20	19	27	46	10	...	...	...	—	—	—	—	—
91-92—Burlington H.S.	Mass. H.S.	20	35	34	69	14	...	...	...	—	—	—	—	—
92-93—Boston University	Hockey East	37	16	22	38	16	...	...	...	—	—	—	—	—
93-94—Boston University	Hockey East	37	17	25	42	27	...	...	...	—	—	—	—	—
94-95—Boston University	Hockey East	20	7	13	20	6	...	...	...	—	—	—	—	—
95-96—Boston University	Hockey East	39	38	29	67	6	...	...	...	—	—	—	—	—
—Albany......................	AHL	5	3	1	4	0	...	...	...	3	0	0	0	0
96-97—Albany......................	AHL	12	3	9	12	0	...	...	...	—	—	—	—	—
—New Jersey	NHL	46	6	8	14	6	-1	0	0	6	0	1	1	0
97-98—New Jersey	NHL	23	1	3	4	4	-4	0	0	3	0	2	2	0
—Albany......................	AHL	51	18	19	37	24	...	...	...	—	—	—	—	—
98-99—New Jersey	NHL	70	14	13	27	10	3	1	1	7	1	0	1	0
99-00—New Jersey	NHL	71	7	8	15	4	0	0	0	23	0	5	5	0
00-01—New Jersey	NHL	63	4	12	16	16	3	0	0	25	1	4	5	4
01-02—New Jersey	NHL	65	4	10	14	15	12	0	1	6	0	0	0	0
02-03—New Jersey	NHL	68	6	11	17	23	12	0	1	24	6	6	12	2
NHL Totals (7 years)..........		406	42	65	107	78	25	1	3	94	8	18	26	6

PANDOLFO, MIKE   LW   BLUE JACKETS

PERSONAL: Born September 15, 1979, in Winchester, Mass. ... 6-3/226. ... Shoots left.
TRANSACTIONS/CAREER NOTES: Selected by Buffalo Sabres in third round (fifth Sabres pick, 77th overall) of NHL entry draft (June 27, 1998). ... Traded by Sabres to with first-round pick (traded to Atlanta) in 2002 draft to Columbus Blue Jackets for first-round pick (LW Dan Paille) in 2002 draft (June 22, 2002).

				REGULAR SEASON							PLAYOFFS			
Season Team	League	Gms.	G	A	Pts.	PIM	+/-	PP	SH	Gms.	G	A	Pts.	PIM
96-97—St. Sebastian's...........	USHS (East)	32	27	28	55	30	...	...	...	—	—	—	—	—
97-98—St. Sebastian's...........	USHS (East)	28	29	23	52	18	...	...	...	—	—	—	—	—
98-99—Boston University	Hockey East	34	13	4	17	26	...	...	...	—	—	—	—	—
99-00—Boston University	Hockey East	41	13	10	23	37	...	...	...	—	—	—	—	—
00-01—Boston University	Hockey East	37	16	13	29	30	...	...	...	—	—	—	—	—
01-02—Boston University	Hockey East	38	22	18	40	22	...	...	...	—	—	—	—	—
02-03—Syracuse....................	AHL	74	9	9	18	31	...	...	...	—	—	—	—	—

PANZER, JEFF   C   BLUES

PERSONAL: Born April 7, 1978, in Grand Forks, N.D. ... 5-10/160. ... Shoots left.
TRANSACTIONS/CAREER NOTES: Signed as non-drafted free agent by St. Louis Blues (May 7, 2001).

Season Team	League	Gms.	G	A	Pts.	PIM	+/-	PP	SH	Gms.	G	A	Pts.	PIM
97-98—Univ. of North Dakota.	WCHA	37	14	23	37	18	...	...	...	—	—	—	—	—
98-99—Univ. of North Dakota.	WCHA	39	21	26	47	14	...	...	...	—	—	—	—	—
99-00—Univ. of North Dakota.	WCHA	44	19	*44	63	16	...	...	...	—	—	—	—	—
00-01—Univ. of North Dakota.	WCHA	46	26	*55	*81	28	...	...	...	—	—	—	—	—
—Worcester	AHL	—	—	—	—	—	—	—	—	5	1	2	3	0
01-02—Worcester	AHL	70	26	27	53	29	...	...	...	3	0	2	2	0
02-03—Worcester	AHL	80	22	32	54	36	...	...	...	—	—	—	—	—

PAPINEAU, JUSTIN   C   ISLANDERS

PERSONAL: Born January 15, 1980, in Ottawa ... 5-11/191. ... Shoots left.
TRANSACTIONS/CAREER NOTES: Selected by Los Angeles Kings in second round (second Kings pick, 46th overall) of NHL entry draft (June 27, 1998). ... Returned to draft pool by Kings and selected by St. Louis Blues in third round (third Blues pick, 75th overall) of NHL entry draft (June 24, 2000). ... Traded by Blues with second-round pick in 2003 draft to New York Islanders for G Chris Osgood and third-round pick in 2003 draft (March 11, 2003).

Season Team	League	Gms.	G	A	Pts.	PIM	+/-	PP	SH	Gms.	G	A	Pts.	PIM
95-96—Ottawa	OHA Jr. A	52	31	19	50	51	...	...	...	—	—	—	—	—
96-97—Belleville	OHL	40	10	32	42	32	...	...	...	—	—	—	—	—
97-98—Belleville	OHL	66	41	53	94	34	...	...	...	10	5	9	14	6
98-99—Belleville	OHL	68	52	47	99	28	...	...	...	21	*21	*30	*51	20
99-00—Belleville	OHL	60	40	36	76	52	...	...	...	16	4	12	16	16
00-01—Worcester	AHL	43	7	22	29	33	...	...	...	11	7	3	10	8
01-02—Worcester	AHL	75	†38	38	76	86	...	...	...	3	1	2	3	4
—St. Louis	NHL	1	0	0	0	0	-2	0	0	—	—	—	—	—
02-03—Worcester	AHL	44	21	17	38	42	...	...	...	—	—	—	—	—
—St. Louis	NHL	11	2	1	3	0	-1	0	0	—	—	—	—	—
—New York Islanders	NHL	5	1	2	3	4	1	0	0	1	0	0	0	0
—Bridgeport	AHL	5	7	1	8	4	...	...	...	—	—	—	—	—
NHL Totals (2 years)...........		17	3	3	6	4	-2	0	0	1	0	0	0	0

PARK, RICHARD   RW   WILD

PERSONAL: Born May 27, 1976, in Seoul, South Korea ... 5-11/190. ... Shoots right.
TRANSACTIONS/CAREER NOTES: Selected by Pittsburgh Penguins in second round (second Penguins pick, 50th overall) of NHL entry draft (June 28, 1994). ... Traded by Penguins to Mighty Ducks of Anaheim for RW Roman Oksiuta (March 18, 1997). ... Signed as free agent by Philadelphia Flyers (August 24, 1998). ... Signed as free agent by Minnesota Wild (June 2, 2000).

Season Team	League	Gms.	G	A	Pts.	PIM	+/-	PP	SH	Gms.	G	A	Pts.	PIM
91-92—Williams Lake	PCJHL	76	49	58	107	91	...	...	...	—	—	—	—	—
92-93—Belleville	OHL	66	23	38	61	38	...	...	...	5	0	0	0	14
93-94—Belleville	OHL	59	27	49	76	70	...	...	...	12	3	5	8	18
94-95—Belleville	OHL	45	28	51	79	35	...	...	...	16	9	18	27	12
—Pittsburgh...................	NHL	1	0	1	1	2	1	0	0	3	0	0	0	2
95-96—Belleville	OHL	6	7	6	13	2	...	...	...	14	18	12	30	10
—Pittsburgh...................	NHL	56	4	6	10	36	3	0	1	1	0	0	0	0
96-97—Cleveland	IHL	50	12	15	27	30	...	...	...	—	—	—	—	—
—Pittsburgh...................	NHL	1	0	0	0	0	-1	0	0	—	—	—	—	—
—Anaheim.....................	NHL	11	1	1	2	10	0	0	0	11	0	1	1	2
97-98—Cincinnati.................	AHL	56	17	26	43	36	...	...	...	—	—	—	—	—
—Anaheim.....................	NHL	15	0	2	2	8	-3	0	0	—	—	—	—	—
98-99—Philadelphia	AHL	75	41	42	83	33	...	...	...	16	9	6	15	4
—Philadelphia	NHL	7	0	0	0	0	-1	0	0	—	—	—	—	—
99-00—Utah......................	IHL	82	28	32	60	36	...	...	...	5	1	0	1	0
00-01—Cleveland	IHL	75	27	21	48	29	...	...	...	4	0	2	2	4
01-02—Houston	AHL	13	4	10	14	6	...	...	...	—	—	—	—	—
—Minnesota..................	NHL	63	10	15	25	10	-1	2	1	—	—	—	—	—
02-03—Minnesota..................	NHL	81	14	10	24	16	-3	2	2	18	3	3	6	4
NHL Totals (7 years)...........		235	29	35	64	82	-5	4	4	33	3	4	7	8

PARKER, SCOTT   RW   SHARKS

PERSONAL: Born January 29, 1978, in Hanford, Calif. ... 6-5/225. ... Shoots right.
TRANSACTIONS/CAREER NOTES: Selected by New Jersey Devils in third round (sixth Devils pick, 63rd overall) of NHL entry draft (June 22, 1996). ... Returned to draft pool by Devils and selected by Colorado Avalanche in first round (fourth Avalanche pick, 20th overall) of NHL entry draft (June 27, 1998). ... Bruised shoulder (December 11, 2000); missed four games. ... Bruised foot (February 17, 2001); missed three games. ... Suspended two games by NHL for unsportsmanlike conduct (October 15, 2001). ... Injured thumb and fractured nose (January 28, 2002); missed one game. ... Traded by Avalanche for fifth-round draft pick in 2003 to San Jose Sharks (June 22, 2003).

Season Team	League	REGULAR SEASON								PLAYOFFS				
		Gms.	G	A	Pts.	PIM	+/-	PP	SH	Gms.	G	A	Pts.	PIM
94-95—Spokane	KIJHL	43	7	21	28	128	...	...	...	—	—	—	—	—
95-96—Kelowna	WHL	64	3	4	7	159	...	...	...	6	0	0	0	12
96-97—Kelowna	WHL	68	18	8	26	*330	...	...	...	6	0	2	2	4
97-98—Kelowna	WHL	71	30	22	52	243	...	...	...	7	6	0	6	23
98-99—Hershey	AHL	32	4	3	7	143	...	...	...	4	0	0	0	6
—Colorado	NHL	27	0	0	0	71	-3	0	0	—	—	—	—	—
99-00—Hershey	AHL	68	12	7	19	206	...	...	...	11	1	1	2	56
00-01—Colorado	NHL	69	2	3	5	155	-2	0	0	4	0	0	0	2
01-02—Colorado	NHL	63	1	4	5	154	0	0	0	—	—	—	—	—
02-03—Colorado	NHL	43	1	3	4	82	6	0	0	1	0	0	0	2
NHL Totals (4 years)		202	4	10	14	462	1	0	0	5	0	0	0	4

PARRISH, MARK   RW   ISLANDERS

PERSONAL: Born February 2, 1977, in Edina, Minn. ... 5-11/194. ... Shoots right.

TRANSACTIONS/CAREER NOTES: Selected by Colorado Avalanche in third round (third Avalanche pick, 79th overall) of NHL entry draft (June 22, 1996). ... Rights traded by Avalanche with third-round pick (D Lance Ward) in 1998 draft to Florida Panthers for RW/C Tom Fitzgerald (March 24, 1998). ... Strained back (February 14, 2000); missed one game. ... Traded by Panthers with LW Oleg Kvasha to New York Islanders for C Olli Jokinen and G Roberto Luongo (June 24, 2000). ... Sprained medial collateral ligament in right knee (February 9, 2001); missed 12 games. ... Injured ribs (January 15, 2002); missed four games.

STATISTICAL PLATEAUS: Three-goal games: 2001-02 (2), 2002-03 (1). Total: 3. ... Four-goal games: 1998-99 (1). ... Total hat tricks: 4.

Season Team	League	REGULAR SEASON								PLAYOFFS				
		Gms.	G	A	Pts.	PIM	+/-	PP	SH	Gms.	G	A	Pts.	PIM
94-95—Thomas Jefferson	Minn. H.S.	27	40	20	60	42	...	...	...	—	—	—	—	—
95-96—St. Cloud State	WCHA	38	15	14	29	28	...	...	...	—	—	—	—	—
96-97—St. Cloud State	WCHA	35	27	15	42	60	...	...	...	—	—	—	—	—
97-98—Seattle	WHL	54	54	38	92	29	...	...	...	5	2	3	5	2
—New Haven	AHL	1	1	0	1	2	...	...	...	—	—	—	—	—
98-99—Florida	NHL	73	24	13	37	25	-6	5	0	—	—	—	—	—
—New Haven	AHL	2	1	0	1	0	...	...	...	—	—	—	—	—
99-00—Florida	NHL	81	26	18	44	39	1	6	0	4	0	1	1	0
00-01—New York Islanders	NHL	70	17	13	30	28	-27	6	0	—	—	—	—	—
01-02—New York Islanders	NHL	78	30	30	60	32	10	9	1	7	2	1	3	6
02-03—New York Islanders	NHL	81	23	25	48	28	-11	9	0	5	1	0	1	4
NHL Totals (5 years)		383	120	99	219	152	-33	35	1	16	3	2	5	10

PARSSINEN, TIMO   LW   MIGHTY DUCKS

PERSONAL: Born January 19, 1977, in Lohja, Finland. ... 5-10/176. ... Shoots left.

TRANSACTIONS/CAREER NOTES: Selected by Mighty Ducks of Anaheim in fourth round (fourth Mighty Ducks pick, 102nd overall) of NHL entry draft (June 23, 2001).

Season Team	League	REGULAR SEASON								PLAYOFFS				
		Gms.	G	A	Pts.	PIM	+/-	PP	SH	Gms.	G	A	Pts.	PIM
94-95—TuTu Turku	Finland Jr.	14	9	6	15	33	...	...	...	—	—	—	—	—
—TuTu Turku	Finland	1	1	0	1	0	...	...	...	—	—	—	—	—
95-96—TuTu Turku	Finland Jr.	14	18	15	33	12	...	...	...	11	12	6	18	36
—TuTu Turku	Finland	7	0	0	0	4	...	...	...	—	—	—	—	—
96-97—Tutu Turku	Finland Div. 2	39	21	29	50	30	...	...	...	—	—	—	—	—
—TuTu Turku	Finland Jr.	—	—	—	—	—	...	...	...	9	2	14	16	36
97-98—Hermes Kokkola	Finland Div. 2	46	29	39	68	66	...	...	...	3	1	0	1	4
98-99—HPK Hameenlinna	Finland	46	15	24	39	46	...	...	...	8	2	3	5	8
99-00—HPK Hameenlinna	Finland	53	25	27	52	60	...	...	...	8	5	5	10	8
00-01—HPK Hameenlinna	Finland	54	18	31	49	48	...	...	...	—	—	—	—	—
01-02—Anaheim	NHL	17	0	3	3	2	0	0	0	—	—	—	—	—
—Cincinnati	AHL	49	14	24	38	22	...	...	...	3	0	2	2	0
02-03—HIFK Helsinki	Finland	55	16	31	47	41	...	...	...	—	—	—	—	—
NHL Totals (1 year)		17	0	3	3	2	0	0	0					

PASSMORE, STEVE   G   BLACKHAWKS

PERSONAL: Born January 29, 1973, in Thunder Bay, Ont. ... 5-9/165. ... Catches left.

TRANSACTIONS/CAREER NOTES: Selected by Quebec Nordiques in ninth round (10th Nordiques pick, 196th overall) of NHL entry draft (June 20, 1992). ... Traded by Nordiques to Edmonton Oilers for D Brad Werenka (March 21, 1994). ... Signed as free agent by Chicago Blackhawks (July 7, 1999). ... Traded by Blackhawks to Los Angeles Kings for fourth-round pick (D Olli Malmivaara) in 2000 draft (May 1, 2000). ... Traded by Kings to Blackhawks for eighth-round pick (D Mike Gabinet) in 2001 draft (February 28, 2001). ... Sprained knee (November 2, 2001); missed two games.

Season Team	League	REGULAR SEASON									PLAYOFFS							
		Gms.	Min	W	L	T	GA	SO	Avg.	SV%	Gms.	Min.	W	L	GA	SO	Avg.	SV%
88-89—Tri-City	WHL	1	60	0	1	0	6	0	6.00	—	—	—	—	—	—	—	—	—
89-90—Tri-City	WHL	4	215	...	...	...	17	0	4.74	—	—	—	—	—	—	—	—	—
90-91—Victoria	WHL	35	1838	3	25	1	190	0	6.20	—	—	—	—	—	—	—	—	—
91-92—Victoria	WHL	*71	*4228	15	50	7	347	0	4.92	—	—	—	—	—	—	—	—	—
92-93—Victoria	WHL	43	2402	14	24	2	150	1	3.75	—	—	—	—	—	—	—	—	—
—Kamloops	WHL	25	1479	19	6	0	69	1	2.80	—	7	401	4	2	22	1	3.29	—
93-94—Kamloops	WHL	36	1927	22	9	2	88	1	*2.74	—	18	1099	†11	7	60	0	3.28	—

Season Team	League	REGULAR SEASON									PLAYOFFS							
		Gms.	Min	W	L	T	GA	SO	Avg.	SV%	Gms.	Min.	W	L	GA	SO	Avg.	SV%
94-95—Cape Breton	AHL	25	1455	8	13	3	93	0	3.84	—	—	—	—	—	—	—	—	—
95-96—Cape Breton	AHL	2	90	1	0	0	2	0	1.33	—	—	—	—	—	—	—	—	—
96-97—Raleigh	ECHL	2	118	1	1	‡0	13	0	6.61	—	—	—	—	—	—	—	—	—
—Hamilton	AHL	27	1568	12	12	3	70	1	2.68	—	22	1325	12	*10	*61	†2	2.76	—
97-98—Hamilton	AHL	27	1656	11	10	6	87	2	3.15	—	3	133	0	2	14	0	6.32	—
—San Antonio	IHL	14	737	3	8	2	56	0	4.56	—	—	—	—	—	—	—	—	—
98-99—Hamilton	AHL	54	3148	24	21	†7	117	4	2.23	—	11	680	5	6	31	0	2.74	—
—Edmonton	NHL	6	362	1	4	1	17	0	2.82	.907	—	—	—	—	—	—	—	—
99-00—Chicago	NHL	24	1388	7	12	3	63	1	2.72	.904	—	—	—	—	—	—	—	—
—Cleveland	IHL	2	120	1	0	1	3	1	1.50	—	—	—	—	—	—	—	—	—
00-01—Lowell	AHL	6	333	2	4	0	24	0	4.32	—	—	—	—	—	—	—	—	—
—Los Angeles	NHL	14	718	3	8	1	37	1	3.09	.881	—	—	—	—	—	—	—	—
—Chicago	IHL	6	340	2	2	‡2	22	0	3.88	—	—	—	—	—	—	—	—	—
—Chicago	NHL	6	340	0	4	1	14	0	2.47	.905	—	—	—	—	—	—	—	—
01-02—Chicago	NHL	23	1142	8	5	4	43	0	2.26	.904	3	138	0	2	6	0	2.61	.903
—Norfolk	AHL	2	120	2	0	0	6	0	3.00	—	—	—	—	—	—	—	—	—
02-03—Norfolk	AHL	14	831	4	7	2	33	2	2.38	—	—	—	—	—	—	—	—	—
—Chicago	NHL	11	617	2	5	2	38	0	3.70	.866	—	—	—	—	—	—	—	—
NHL Totals (5 years)		84	4567	21	38	12	212	2	2.79	.895	3	138	0	2	6	0	2.61	.903

PATRICK, JAMES — D — SABRES

PERSONAL: Born June 14, 1963, in Winnipeg ... 6-2/205. ... Shoots right. ... Full Name: James A. Patrick. ... Brother of Steve Patrick, right winger with three NHL teams (1980-81 through 1985-86).

TRANSACTIONS/CAREER NOTES: Selected by New York Rangers in first round (first Rangers pick, ninth overall) of NHL entry draft (June 10, 1981). ... Injured groin (October 1984). ... Pinched nerve (December 15, 1985). ... Strained left knee ligaments (March 1988). ... Bruised shoulder and chest (December 1988). ... Pulled groin (March 13, 1989). ... Sprained shoulder (November 4, 1992); missed three games. ... Bruised right shoulder (November 27, 1992); missed three games. ... Sprained left knee (January 27, 1993); missed four games. ... Suffered herniated disc (February 24, 1993); missed two games. ... Suffered herniated disc (March 28, 1993); missed remainder of season. ... Traded by Rangers with C Darren Turcotte to Hartford Whalers for RW Steve Larmer, LW Nick Kypreos and sixth-round pick (C Yuri Litvinov) in 1994 draft (November 2, 1993). ... Suffered herniated disc (December 7, 1993); missed five games. ... Traded by Whalers with C Michael Nylander and D Zarley Zalapski to Calgary Flames for D Gary Suter, LW Paul Ranheim and C Ted Drury (March 10, 1994). ... Strained left hip (March 10, 1995); missed five games. ... Suffered concussion (April 9, 1996); missed two games. ... Injured back (October 16, 1996); missed one game. ... Strained knee (October 24, 1996); missed five games. ... Suffered concussion (November 20, 1996); missed two games. ... Underwent knee surgery (December 12, 1996); missed remainder of season. ... Strained neck (October 22, 1997); missed six games. ... Reinjured neck (November 13, 1997); missed nine games. ... Suffered charley horse (January 5, 1998); missed one game. ... Signed as free agent by Buffalo Sabres (October 7, 1998). ... Suffered pinched nerve in neck (October 10, 1998); missed four games. ... Suffered concussion (February 24, 1999); missed one game. ... Suffered back spasms (February 17, 2000); missed two games. ... Injured shoulder (September 23, 2000); missed first five games of season. ... Suffered head injury (November 27, 2001); missed one game.

Season Team	League	REGULAR SEASON							PLAYOFFS				
		Gms.	G	A	Pts.	PIM	+/-	PP	SH	Gms.	G	A	Pts.	PIM
80-81—Prince Albert	SJHL	59	21	61	82	162	...	...	...	4	1	6	7	0
81-82—Univ. of North Dakota	WCHA	42	5	24	29	26	...	...	...	—	—	—	—	—
82-83—Univ. of North Dakota	WCHA	36	12	36	48	29	...	...	...	—	—	—	—	—
83-84—Can. Olympic team	Int'l	63	7	24	31	52	...	...	...	—	—	—	—	—
—New York Rangers	NHL	12	1	7	8	2	6	0	0	5	0	3	3	2
84-85—New York Rangers	NHL	75	8	28	36	71	-17	4	1	3	0	0	0	4
85-86—New York Rangers	NHL	75	14	29	43	88	14	2	1	16	1	5	6	34
86-87—New York Rangers	NHL	78	10	45	55	62	13	5	0	6	1	2	3	2
87-88—New York Rangers	NHL	70	17	45	62	52	16	9	0	—	—	—	—	—
88-89—New York Rangers	NHL	68	11	36	47	41	3	6	0	4	0	1	1	2
89-90—New York Rangers	NHL	73	14	43	57	50	4	9	0	10	3	8	11	0
90-91—New York Rangers	NHL	74	10	49	59	58	-5	6	0	6	0	0	0	6
91-92—New York Rangers	NHL	80	14	57	71	54	34	6	0	13	0	7	7	12
92-93—New York Rangers	NHL	60	5	21	26	61	1	3	0	—	—	—	—	—
93-94—New York Rangers	NHL	6	0	3	3	2	1	0	0	—	—	—	—	—
—Hartford	NHL	47	8	20	28	32	-12	4	1	—	—	—	—	—
—Calgary	NHL	15	2	2	4	6	6	1	0	7	0	1	1	6
94-95—Calgary	NHL	43	0	10	10	14	-3	0	0	5	0	1	1	4
95-96—Calgary	NHL	80	3	32	35	30	3	1	0	4	0	0	0	2
96-97—Calgary	NHL	19	3	1	4	6	2	1	0	—	—	—	—	—
97-98—Calgary	NHL	60	6	11	17	26	-2	1	0	—	—	—	—	—
98-99—Buffalo	NHL	45	1	7	8	16	12	0	0	20	0	1	1	12
99-00—Buffalo	NHL	66	5	8	13	22	8	0	0	5	0	1	1	2
00-01—Buffalo	NHL	54	4	9	13	12	9	1	0	13	1	2	3	2
01-02—Buffalo	NHL	56	5	8	13	16	3	1	0	—	—	—	—	—
02-03—Buffalo	NHL	69	4	12	16	26	-3	2	0	—	—	—	—	—
NHL Totals (20 years)		1225	145	483	628	747	93	62	3	117	6	32	38	86

PAUL, JEFF — D

PERSONAL: Born March 1, 1978, in London, Ont. ... 6-4/225. ... Shoots right.

TRANSACTIONS/CAREER NOTES: Selected by Chicago Blackhawks in second round (second Blackhawks pick, 42nd overall) of NHL entry draft (June 22, 1996).

Season Team	League	REGULAR SEASON								PLAYOFFS				
		Gms.	G	A	Pts.	PIM	+/-	PP	SH	Gms.	G	A	Pts.	PIM
94-95—Niagara Falls	OHL	57	3	10	13	64	...	...	...	6	0	2	2	0
95-96—Niagara Falls	OHL	48	1	7	8	81	...	...	...	10	0	4	4	37
96-97—Erie	OHL	60	4	23	27	152	...	...	...	5	2	0	2	12
97-98—Erie	OHL	48	3	17	20	108	...	...	...	7	0	2	2	13
98-99—Portland	AHL	6	0	0	0	4	...	...	...	—	—	—	—	—
—Indianapolis	IHL	55	0	7	7	120	...	...	...	7	0	2	2	12
99-00—Cleveland	IHL	69	6	6	12	210	...	...	...	9	1	0	1	12
00-01—Norfolk	AHL	59	5	6	11	171	...	...	...	9	0	2	2	12
01-02—Hershey	AHL	58	1	13	14	201	...	...	...	7	0	1	1	6
02-03—Hershey	AHL	50	2	3	5	123	...	...	...	—	—	—	—	—
—Colorado	NHL	2	0	0	0	7	0	0	0	—	—	—	—	—
NHL Totals (1 year)		2	0	0	0	7	0	0	0					

PAYER, SERGE   C   PANTHERS

PERSONAL: Born May 7, 1979, in Rockland, Ont. ... 5-11/175. ... Shoots left.
TRANSACTIONS/CAREER NOTES: Signed as non-drafted free agent by Florida Panthers (October 2, 1997).

Season Team	League	REGULAR SEASON								PLAYOFFS				
		Gms.	G	A	Pts.	PIM	+/-	PP	SH	Gms.	G	A	Pts.	PIM
95-96—Kitchener	OHL	66	8	16	24	18	...	...	...	12	0	2	2	2
96-97—Kitchener	OHL	63	7	16	23	27	...	...	...	13	1	3	4	2
97-98—Kitchener	OHL	44	20	21	41	51	...	...	...	6	3	0	3	7
98-99—Kitchener	OHL	40	18	19	37	22	...	...	...	—	—	—	—	—
99-00—Kitchener	OHL	44	10	26	36	53	...	...	...	5	0	3	3	6
00-01—Louisville	AHL	32	6	6	12	15	...	...	...	—	—	—	—	—
—Florida	NHL	43	5	1	6	21	0	0	1	—	—	—	—	—
01-02—Utah	AHL	20	6	2	8	9	...	...	...	—	—	—	—	—
02-03—San Antonio	AHL	78	10	31	41	30	...	...	...	—	—	—	—	—
NHL Totals (1 year)		43	5	1	6	21	0	0	1					

PEAT, STEPHEN   RW   CAPITALS

PERSONAL: Born March 10, 1980, in Princeton, B.C. ... 6-2/226. ... Shoots right.
TRANSACTIONS/CAREER NOTES: Selected by Mighty Ducks of Anaheim in second round (second Mighty Ducks pick, 32nd overall) of NHL entry draft (June 27, 1998). ... Traded by Mighty Ducks to Washington Capitals for fourth-round pick (RW Michel Ouellet) in 2000 draft (June 1, 2000). ... Strained groin (January 30, 2002); missed six games. ... Re-signed by Capitals (July 22, 2003).

Season Team	League	REGULAR SEASON								PLAYOFFS				
		Gms.	G	A	Pts.	PIM	+/-	PP	SH	Gms.	G	A	Pts.	PIM
95-96—Red Deer	WHL	1	0	0	0	0	...	...	...	—	—	—	—	—
96-97—Red Deer	WHL	68	3	14	17	161	...	...	...	16	0	2	2	22
97-98—Red Deer	WHL	63	6	12	18	189	...	...	...	5	0	0	0	8
98-99—Red Deer	WHL	31	2	6	8	98	...	...	...	—	—	—	—	—
—Tri-City	WHL	5	0	0	0	19	...	...	...	—	—	—	—	—
99-00—Tri-City	WHL	12	0	2	2	48	...	...	...	—	—	—	—	—
—Calgary	WHL	23	0	8	8	100	...	...	...	13	0	1	1	33
00-01—Portland	AHL	6	0	0	0	16	...	...	...	—	—	—	—	—
01-02—Washington	NHL	38	2	2	4	85	-1	0	0	—	—	—	—	—
—Portland	AHL	17	2	2	4	57	...	...	...	—	—	—	—	—
02-03—Portland	AHL	18	0	0	0	52	...	...	...	—	—	—	—	—
—Washington	NHL	27	1	0	1	57	-3	0	0	—	—	—	—	—
NHL Totals (2 years)		65	3	2	5	142	-4	0	0					

PECA, MICHAEL   C   ISLANDERS

PERSONAL: Born March 26, 1974, in Toronto ... 5-11/183. ... Shoots right. ... Name pronounced PEH-kuh.
TRANSACTIONS/CAREER NOTES: Selected by Vancouver Canucks in second round (second Canucks pick, 40th overall) of NHL entry draft (June 20, 1992). ... Fractured cheek bone (February 9, 1995); missed 12 games. ... Injured wrist (April 26, 1995); missed one game. ... Traded by Canucks with D Mike Wilson and first-round pick (D Jay McKee) in 1995 draft to Buffalo Sabres for RW Alexander Mogilny and fifth-round pick (LW Todd Norman) in 1995 draft (July 8, 1995). ... Strained back (October 29, 1995); missed six games. ... Bruised sternum (December 2, 1995); missed one game. ... Sprained right knee (March 18, 1996); missed seven games. ... Injured shoulder (November 27, 1996); missed three games. ... Missed first 11 games of 1997-98 season due to contract dispute. ... Injured hip (November 6, 1997); missed three games. ... Suspended three games and fined $1,000 by NHL for elbowing incident (March 27, 1998). ... Reinjured hip (April 8, 1998); missed two games. ... Sprained knee (April 15, 1998); missed final two games of regular season and two playoff games. ... Dislocated shoulder (March 5, 2000); missed seven games. ... Suspended two games by NHL for elbowing incident (March 25, 2000). ... Missed entire 2000-01 season due to contract dispute. ... Traded by Sabres to New York Islanders for C Tim Connolly and LW Taylor Pyatt (June 24, 2001). ... Suffered concussion (October 11, 2001); missed two games.
STATISTICAL PLATEAUS: Three-goal games: 1999-00 (1).

Season Team	League	REGULAR SEASON								PLAYOFFS				
		Gms.	G	A	Pts.	PIM	+/-	PP	SH	Gms.	G	A	Pts.	PIM
90-91—Sudbury	OHL	62	14	27	41	24	...	...	...	5	1	0	1	7
91-92—Sudbury	OHL	39	16	34	50	61	...	...	...	—	—	—	—	—
—Ottawa	OHL	27	8	17	25	32	...	...	...	11	6	10	16	6
92-93—Ottawa	OHL	55	38	64	102	80	...	...	...	—	—	—	—	—
—Hamilton	AHL	9	6	3	9	11	...	...	...	—	—	—	—	—
93-94—Ottawa	OHL	55	50	63	113	101	...	...	...	17	7	22	29	30
—Vancouver	NHL	4	0	0	0	2	-1	0	0	—	—	—	—	—

Season Team	League	REGULAR SEASON								PLAYOFFS				
		Gms.	G	A	Pts.	PIM	+/-	PP	SH	Gms.	G	A	Pts.	PIM
94-95—Syracuse	AHL	35	10	24	34	75	...							
—Vancouver	NHL	33	6	6	12	30	-6	2	0	5	0	1	1	8
95-96—Buffalo	NHL	68	11	20	31	67	-1	4	3	—	—	—	—	—
96-97—Buffalo	NHL	79	20	29	49	80	26	5	*6	10	0	2	2	8
97-98—Buffalo	NHL	61	18	22	40	57	12	6	5	13	3	2	5	8
98-99—Buffalo	NHL	82	27	29	56	81	7	10	0	21	5	8	13	18
99-00—Buffalo	NHL	73	20	21	41	67	6	2	0	5	0	1	1	4
00-01—Buffalo	NHL					Did not play.								
01-02—New York Islanders	NHL	80	25	35	60	62	19	3	6	5	1	0	1	2
—Can. Olympic team	Int'l	6	0	2	2	2				—	—	—	—	—
02-03—New York Islanders	NHL	66	13	29	42	43	-4	4	2	5	0	0	0	4
NHL Totals (10 years)		546	140	191	331	489	58	36	22	64	9	14	23	52

PECKER, CORY   C   MIGHTY DUCKS

PERSONAL: Born March 20, 1981, in Montreal. ... 6-0/190. ... Shoots right.
TRANSACTIONS/CAREER NOTES: Selected by Calgary Flames in sixth round (seventh Flames pick, 166th overall) of NHL entry draft (June 26, 1999). ... Signed as free agent by Mighty Ducks of Anaheim (July 8, 2002).

Season Team	League	REGULAR SEASON								PLAYOFFS				
		Gms.	G	A	Pts.	PIM	+/-	PP	SH	Gms.	G	A	Pts.	PIM
97-98—Sault Ste. Marie	OHL	29	3	4	7	15	...	...	...	—	—	—	—	—
98-99—Sault Ste. Marie	OHL	68	25	34	59	24	...	...	...	5	1	2	3	2
99-00—Sault Ste. Marie	OHL	65	33	36	69	38	...	...	...	12	6	8	14	8
00-01—Sault Ste. Marie	OHL	31	24	16	40	37	...	...	...	—	—	—	—	—
—Erie	OHL	30	17	22	39	32	...	...	...	15	*14	9	23	16
01-02—Erie	OHL	56	53	46	99	108	...	...	...	21	*25	17	*42	36
02-03—Cincinnati	AHL	77	20	13	33	66	...	...	...	—	—	—	—	—

PEDERSON, DENIS   C

PERSONAL: Born September 10, 1975, in Prince Albert, Sask. ... 6-2/205. ... Shoots right. ... Name pronounced PEE-duhr-suhn.
TRANSACTIONS/CAREER NOTES: Selected by New Jersey Devils in first round (first Devils pick, 13th overall) of NHL entry draft (June 26, 1993). ... Bruised thigh (December 31, 1996); missed one game. ... Suffered head injury (February 19, 1997); missed one game. ... Suffered from the flu (March 11, 1997); missed one game. ... Injured back (January 21, 1999); missed one game. ... Reinjured back (March 28, 1999); missed three games. ... Reinjured back (April 10, 1999); missed two games. ... Injured groin (October 5, 1999); missed eight games. ... Reinjured groin (November 6, 1999); missed 14 games. ... Suffered illness (March 10, 2000); missed two games. ... Traded by Devils with C Brendan Morrison to Vancouver Canucks for RW Alexander Mogilny (March 14, 2000). ... Injured hand (November 24, 2000); missed three games. ... Sprained wrist (December 23, 2000); missed 18 games. ... Traded by Canucks with D Drake Berehowsky to Phoenix Coyotes for LW Todd Warriner, C Trevor Letowski, RW Tyler Bouck and third-round pick in 2003 draft (December 28, 2001). ... Fractured sternum (February 8, 2002); missed 11 games. ... Suffered hip pointer (March 19, 2002); missed seven games. ... Signed as free agent by Nashville Predators (July 24, 2002).

Season Team	League	REGULAR SEASON								PLAYOFFS				
		Gms.	G	A	Pts.	PIM	+/-	PP	SH	Gms.	G	A	Pts.	PIM
91-92—Prince Albert	WHL	10	0	0	0	6	...	...	...	7	0	1	1	13
92-93—Prince Albert	WHL	72	33	40	73	134	...	...	...	—	—	—	—	—
93-94—Prince Albert	WHL	71	53	45	98	157	...	...	...	—	—	—	—	—
94-95—Prince Albert	WHL	63	30	38	68	122	...	...	...	15	11	14	25	14
—Albany	AHL	—								3	0	0	0	2
95-96—Albany	AHL	68	28	43	71	104	...	...	...	4	1	2	3	0
—New Jersey	NHL	10	3	1	4	0	-1	1	0	—	—	—	—	—
96-97—Albany	AHL	3	1	3	4	7				—	—	—	—	—
—New Jersey	NHL	70	12	20	32	62	7	3	0	9	0	0	0	2
97-98—New Jersey	NHL	80	15	13	28	97	-6	7	0	6	1	1	2	2
98-99—New Jersey	NHL	76	11	12	23	66	-10	3	0	3	0	1	1	0
99-00—New Jersey	NHL	35	3	3	6	16	-7	0	0	—	—	—	—	—
—Vancouver	NHL	12	3	2	5	2	1	0	0	—	—	—	—	—
00-01—Vancouver	NHL	61	4	8	12	65	0	0	1	4	0	1	1	4
01-02—Vancouver	NHL	29	1	5	6	31	-2	0	0	—	—	—	—	—
—Phoenix	NHL	19	1	1	2	20	-2	0	0	5	0	2	2	0
02-03—Nashville	NHL	43	4	6	10	39	2	0	0	—	—	—	—	—
NHL Totals (8 years)		435	57	71	128	398	-18	14	1	27	1	5	6	8

PELLERIN, SCOTT   LW

PERSONAL: Born January 9, 1970, in Shediac, N.B. ... 5-11/190. ... Shoots left. ... Full Name: Jaque-Frederick Scott Pellerin. ... Name pronounced PEHL-ih-rihn.
TRANSACTIONS/CAREER NOTES: Selected by New Jersey Devils in third round (fourth Devils pick, 47th overall) of NHL entry draft (June 17, 1989). ... Signed as free agent by St. Louis Blues (July 3, 1996). ... Suffered sore ankle (March 9, 1998); missed one game. ... Suffered concussion (November 28, 1998); missed one game. ... Suffered from the flu (February 3, 2000); missed one game. ... Selected by Minnesota Wild in NHL expansion draft (June 23, 2000). ... Bruised shoulder (November 10, 2000); missed three games. ... Suffered from the flu (January 14, 2001); missed one game. ... Traded by Wild to Carolina Hurricanes for LW Askhat Rakhmatullin, third-round pick (traded to New York Rangers) in 2001 draft and future considerations (March 1, 2001). ... Signed as free agent by Boston Bruins (July 26, 2001). ... Injured eye (November 15, 2001); missed four games. ... Traded by Bruins to Dallas Stars for C Benoit Hogue (January 13, 2002). ... Traded by Stars with conditional pick in 2004 draft to Phoenix Coyotes for RW Claude Lemieux (January 16, 2003).

Season Team	League	REGULAR SEASON Gms.	G	A	Pts.	PIM	+/-	PP	SH	PLAYOFFS Gms.	G	A	Pts.	PIM
86-87—Notre Dame H.S.	SASK. H.S.	72	62	68	130	98	...	...	...	—	—	—	—	—
87-88—Notre Dame	SJHL	57	37	49	86	139	...	...	...	—	—	—	—	—
88-89—Univ. of Maine	Hockey East	45	29	33	62	92	...	...	...	—	—	—	—	—
89-90—Univ. of Maine	Hockey East	42	22	34	56	68	...	...	...	—	—	—	—	—
90-91—Univ. of Maine	Hockey East	43	23	25	48	60	...	...	...	—	—	—	—	—
91-92—Univ. of Maine	Hockey East	37	32	25	57	54	...	...	...	—	—	—	—	—
—Utica	AHL	—	—	—	—	—				3	1	0	1	0
92-93—Utica	AHL	27	15	18	33	33	...	...	...	2	0	1	1	0
—New Jersey	NHL	45	10	11	21	41	-1	1	2	—	—	—	—	—
93-94—Albany	IHL	73	28	46	74	84	...	...	...	5	2	1	3	11
—New Jersey	NHL	1	0	0	0	2	0	0	0	—	—	—	—	—
94-95—Albany	AHL	74	23	33	56	95	...	...	...	14	6	4	10	8
95-96—Albany	AHL	75	35	47	82	142	...	...	...	4	0	3	3	10
—New Jersey	NHL	6	2	1	3	0	1	0	0	—	—	—	—	—
96-97—Worcester	AHL	24	10	16	26	37	...	...	...	—	—	—	—	—
—St. Louis	NHL	54	8	10	18	35	12	0	2	6	0	0	0	6
97-98—St. Louis	NHL	80	8	21	29	62	14	1	1	10	0	2	2	10
98-99—St. Louis	NHL	80	20	21	41	42	1	0	†5	8	1	0	1	4
99-00—St. Louis	NHL	80	8	15	23	48	8	0	2	7	0	0	0	2
00-01—Minnesota	NHL	58	11	28	39	45	6	2	2	—	—	—	—	—
—Carolina	NHL	19	0	5	5	6	-4	0	0	6	0	0	0	4
01-02—Boston	NHL	35	1	5	6	6	-6	0	0	—	—	—	—	—
—Dallas	NHL	33	3	5	8	15	-5	0	0	—	—	—	—	—
02-03—Dallas	NHL	20	1	3	4	8	-3	1	0	—	—	—	—	—
—Phoenix	NHL	23	0	1	1	8	-5	0	0	—	—	—	—	—
NHL Totals (10 years)		534	72	126	198	318	18	5	14	37	1	2	3	26

P

PELLETIER, JEAN-MARC   G   COYOTES

PERSONAL: Born March 4, 1978, in Atlanta ... 6-3/200. ... Catches left.
TRANSACTIONS/CAREER NOTES: Selected by Philadelphia Flyers in second round (first Flyers pick, 30th overall) of NHL entry draft (June 21, 1997). ... Traded by Flyers with C Rod Brind'Amour and second-round pick (traded to Colorado) in 2000 draft to Carolina Hurricanes for rights to C Keith Primeau and fifth-round pick (traded to New York Islanders) in 2000 draft (January 23, 2000). ... Traded by Hurricanes with conditional draft pick to Phoenix Coyotes for G Patrick DesRochers (December 31, 2002).

Season Team	League	REGULAR SEASON Gms.	Min	W	L	T	GA	SO	Avg.	SV%	PLAYOFFS Gms.	Min.	W	L	GA	SO	Avg.	SV%
95-96—Cornell University	ECAC	5	179	1	2	0	15	0	5.03	—	—	—	—	—	—	—	—	—
96-97—Cornell University	ECAC	11	678	5	2	3	28	1	2.48	—	—	—	—	—	—	—	—	—
97-98—Rimouski	QMJHL	34	1913	17	11	3	118	0	3.70	—	16	895	11	3	†51	1	3.42	—
98-99—Philadelphia	AHL	47	2636	25	16	4	122	2	2.78	—	1	27	0	0	0	0	...	—
—Philadelphia	NHL	1	60	0	1	0	5	0	5.00	.828	—	—	—	—	—	—	—	—
99-00—Philadelphia	AHL	24	1405	14	10	0	58	3	2.48	—	—	—	—	—	—	—	—	—
—Cincinnati	IHL	22	1278	16	4	‡2	52	2	2.44	—	3	160	1	1	8	1	3.00	—
00-01—Cincinnati	IHL	39	2261	18	14	‡5	119	2	3.16	—	5	518	1	3	15	0	1.74	—
01-02—Lowell	AHL	40	2284	21	12	4	98	2	2.57	—	5	298	2	3	13	0	2.62	—
02-03—Lowell	AHL	17	861	6	10	0	51	1	3.55	—	—	—	—	—	—	—	—	—
—Phoenix	NHL	2	119	0	2	0	6	0	3.03	.875	—	—	—	—	—	—	—	—
—Springfield	AHL	24	1390	12	7	4	55	2	2.37	—	—	—	—	—	—	—	—	—
NHL Totals (2 years)		3	179	0	3	0	11	0	3.69	.857								

PELUSO, MIKE   RW   BLACKHAWKS

PERSONAL: Born September 2, 1974, in Denver. ... 6-1/208. ... Shoots right. ... Full Name: Michael James Peluso. ... Cousin of Mike Peluso, left winger for six NHL teams (1989-90 through 1997-98).
TRANSACTIONS/CAREER NOTES: Selected by Calgary Flames in 10th round (11th Flames pick, 253rd overall) of NHL entry draft (June 29, 1994). ... Signed as free agent by Washington Capitals (February 10, 1999). ... Traded by Capitals to St. Louis Blues for LW/C Derek Bekar (November 29, 2000). ... Signed as free agent by Chicago Blackhawks (August 1, 2001).

Season Team	League	REGULAR SEASON Gms.	G	A	Pts.	PIM	+/-	PP	SH	PLAYOFFS Gms.	G	A	Pts.	PIM
91-92—Bismarck H.S.	N.D. H.S.	23	50	49	99	...	...	...	...	—	—	—	—	—
92-93—Omaha	USHL				Statistics unavailable.									
93-94—Omaha	USHL	48	36	29	65	77	...	...	...	—	—	—	—	—
94-95—Minnesota-Duluth	WCHA	38	11	23	34	38	...	...	...	—	—	—	—	—
95-96—Minnesota-Duluth	WCHA	38	25	19	44	64	...	...	...	—	—	—	—	—
96-97—Minnesota-Duluth	WCHA	37	20	20	40	53	...	...	...	—	—	—	—	—
97-98—Minnesota-Duluth	WCHA	40	24	21	45	100	...	...	...	—	—	—	—	—
98-99—Portland	AHL	26	7	6	13	6	...	...	...	—	—	—	—	—
99-00—Portland	AHL	71	25	29	54	86	...	...	...	4	2	0	2	0
00-01—Portland	AHL	19	12	10	22	17	...	...	...	—	—	—	—	—
—Worcester	AHL	44	17	23	40	22	...	...	...	11	3	3	6	4
01-02—Norfolk	AHL	29	18	9	27	4	...	...	...	4	1	0	1	0
—Chicago	NHL	37	4	2	6	19	-3	0	0	—	—	—	—	—
02-03—Norfolk	AHL	74	24	31	55	35	...	...	...	—	—	—	—	—
NHL Totals (1 year)		37	4	2	6	19	-3	0	0	—	—	—	—	—

PERREAULT, JOEL   C   MIGHTY DUCKS

PERSONAL: Born April 6, 1983, in Montreal. ... 6-2/165. ... Shoots right.
TRANSACTIONS/CAREER NOTES: Selected by Mighty Ducks of Anaheim in fifth round (seventh Mighty Ducks pick, 137th overall) of NHL entry draft (June 23, 2001).

		REGULAR SEASON								PLAYOFFS				
Season Team	League	Gms.	G	A	Pts.	PIM	+/-	PP	SH	Gms.	G	A	Pts.	PIM
00-01—Baie-Comeau	QMJHL	68	10	14	24	46	...	...	...	11	1	1	2	10
01-02—Baie-Comeau	QMJHL	57	18	44	62	96	...	...	...	5	2	0	2	6
02-03—Baie-Comeau	QMJHL	70	51	65	116	93	...	...	...	—	—	—	—	—

PERREAULT, YANIC   C   CANADIENS

PERSONAL: Born April 4, 1971, in Sherbrooke, Que. ... 5-11/185. ... Shoots left. ... Name pronounced YAH-nihk puh-ROH.
TRANSACTIONS/CAREER NOTES: Selected by Toronto Maple Leafs in third round (first Maple Leafs pick, 47th overall) of NHL entry draft (June 22, 1991). ... Signed as free agent by Los Angeles Kings (July 14, 1994). ... Strained abdominal muscle (December 13, 1996); missed 11 games. ... Underwent kidney surgery (February 3, 1997); missed remainder of season. ... Traded by Kings to Maple Leafs for C/RW Jason Podollan and third-round pick (G Cory Campbell) in 1999 draft (March 23, 1999). ... Fractured arm (December 4, 1999); missed 23 games. ... Signed as free agent by Montreal Canadiens (July 4, 2001).
STATISTICAL PLATEAUS: Three-goal games: 1997-98 (2), 2001-02 (1). Total: 3. ... Four-goal games: 1998-99 (1). ... Total hat tricks: 4.

		REGULAR SEASON								PLAYOFFS				
Season Team	League	Gms.	G	A	Pts.	PIM	+/-	PP	SH	Gms.	G	A	Pts.	PIM
88-89—Trois-Rivieres	QMJHL	70	53	55	108	48	...	...	...	—	—	—	—	—
89-90—Trois-Rivieres	QMJHL	63	51	63	114	75	...	...	...	7	6	5	11	19
90-91—Trois-Rivieres	QMJHL	67	*87	98	*185	103	...	...	...	6	4	7	11	6
91-92—St. John's	AHL	62	38	38	76	19	...	...	...	16	7	8	15	4
92-93—St. John's	AHL	79	49	46	95	56	...	...	...	9	4	5	9	2
93-94—St. John's	AHL	62	45	60	105	38	...	...	...	11	*12	6	18	14
—Toronto	NHL	13	3	3	6	0	1	2	0	—	—	—	—	—
94-95—Phoenix	IHL	68	51	48	99	52	...	...	...	—	—	—	—	—
—Los Angeles	NHL	26	2	5	7	20	3	0	0	—	—	—	—	—
95-96—Los Angeles	NHL	78	25	24	49	16	-11	8	3	—	—	—	—	—
96-97—Los Angeles	NHL	41	11	14	25	20	0	1	1	—	—	—	—	—
97-98—Los Angeles	NHL	79	28	20	48	32	6	3	2	4	1	2	3	6
98-99—Los Angeles	NHL	64	10	17	27	30	-3	2	2	—	—	—	—	—
—Toronto	NHL	12	7	8	15	12	10	2	1	17	3	6	9	6
99-00—Toronto	NHL	58	18	27	45	22	3	5	0	1	0	1	1	0
00-01—Toronto	NHL	76	24	28	52	52	0	5	0	11	2	3	5	4
01-02—Montreal	NHL	82	27	29	56	40	-3	6	0	11	3	5	8	0
02-03—Montreal	NHL	73	24	22	46	30	-11	7	0	—	—	—	—	—
NHL Totals (10 years)		602	179	197	376	274	-5	41	9	44	9	17	26	16

PERRIN, ERIC   C   LIGHTNING

PERSONAL: Born November 1, 1975, in Laval, Que. ... 5-9/175. ... Shoots right.
TRANSACTIONS/CAREER NOTES: Signed by Tampa Bay Lightning (June 19, 2003).

		REGULAR SEASON								PLAYOFFS				
Season Team	League	Gms.	G	A	Pts.	PIM	+/-	PP	SH	Gms.	G	A	Pts.	PIM
98-99—Kansas City	IHL	82	24	37	61	71	...	...	...	3	0	0	0	0
99-00—Kansas City	IHL	21	3	15	18	16	...	...	...	—	—	—	—	—
00-01—Jokerit Helsinki	Finland	6	1	1	2	2	...	...	...	—	—	—	—	—
—Assat Pori	Finland	43	15	23	38	70	...	...	...	—	—	—	—	—
01-02—Assat Pori	Finland	45	13	13	26	16	...	...	...	—	—	—	—	—
—HPK Hameenlinna	Finland	12	5	10	15	4	...	...	...	8	2	4	6	6
02-03—HPK Hameenlinna	Finland	56	18	28	46	36	...	...	...	—	—	—	—	—

PERROTT, NATHAN   RW   MAPLE LEAFS

PERSONAL: Born December 8, 1976, in Owen Sound, Ont. ... 6-0/225. ... Shoots right. ... Name pronounced PAIR-iht.
HIGH SCHOOL: Henry Street (Whitby, Ont.).
TRANSACTIONS/CAREER NOTES: Selected by New Jersey Devils in second round (second Devils pick, 44th overall) of NHL entry draft (July 8, 1995). ... Signed by Chicago Blackhawks (August 27, 1997). ... Traded by Blackhawks to Nashville Predators for pick in 2003 draft (October 9, 2001). ... Traded by Predators to Toronto Maple Leafs for C Bob Wren (December 31, 2002). ... Re-signed by Maple Leafs (July 14, 2003).

		REGULAR SEASON								PLAYOFFS				
Season Team	League	Gms.	G	A	Pts.	PIM	+/-	PP	SH	Gms.	G	A	Pts.	PIM
93-94—St. Mary's Jr. B	OHA	41	11	26	37	249	...	...	...	—	—	—	—	—
94-95—Oshawa	OHL	63	18	28	46	233	...	...	...	2	1	1	2	9
95-96—Oshawa	OHL	59	30	32	62	158	...	...	...	5	2	3	5	8
96-97—Sault Ste. Marie	OHL	42	19	23	42	137	...	...	...	11	5	5	10	*60
97-98—Indianapolis	IHL	31	4	3	7	76	...	...	...	—	—	—	—	—
—Jacksonville	ECHL	30	6	8	14	135	...	...	...	—	—	—	—	—
98-99—Indianapolis	IHL	72	14	11	25	307	...	...	...	7	3	1	4	45
99-00—Cleveland	IHL	65	12	9	21	248	...	...	...	9	2	1	3	19
00-01—Norfolk	AHL	73	11	17	28	268	...	...	...	9	2	0	2	18
01-02—Norfolk	AHL	2	0	0	0	5	...	...	...	—	—	—	—	—
—Milwaukee	AHL	56	6	10	16	190	...	...	...	—	—	—	—	—
—Nashville	NHL	22	1	2	3	74	-1	0	0	—	—	—	—	—
02-03—Milwaukee	AHL	27	1	2	3	106	...	...	...	—	—	—	—	—
—Nashville	NHL	1	0	0	0	5	0	0	0	—	—	—	—	—
—St. John's	AHL	36	7	8	15	97	...	...	...	—	—	—	—	—
NHL Totals (2 years)		23	1	2	3	79	-1	0	0					

PETERS, ANDREW   LW   SABRES

PERSONAL: Born May 5, 1980, in St. Catharines, Ont. ... 6-4/195. ... Shoots left.
TRANSACTIONS/CAREER NOTES: Selected by Buffalo Sabres in second round (second Sabres pick, 34th overall) of NHL entry draft (June 27, 1998).

		REGULAR SEASON								PLAYOFFS				
Season Team	League	Gms.	G	A	Pts.	PIM	+/-	PP	SH	Gms.	G	A	Pts.	PIM
96-97—Georgetown	Tier II Jr. A	46	11	16	27	105	...	...	...	—	—	—	—	—
97-98—Oshawa	OHL	60	11	7	18	220	...	...	...	7	2	0	2	19
98-99—Oshawa	OHL	54	14	10	24	137	...	...	...	15	2	7	9	36
99-00—Kitchener	OHL	42	6	13	19	95	...	...	...	4	0	1	1	14
00-01—Rochester	AHL	49	0	4	4	118	...	...	...	—	—	—	—	—
01-02—Rochester	AHL	67	4	1	5	*388	...	...	...	—	—	—	—	—
02-03—Rochester	AHL	57	3	0	3	223	...	...	...	—	—	—	—	—

PETERS, DAN   D

PERSONAL: Born November 24, 1977, in St. Paul, Minn. ... 5-10/185.
COLLEGE: Colorado College.
TRANSACTIONS/CAREER NOTES: Signed as non-drafted free agent by Philadelphia Flyers (June 6, 2000).

		REGULAR SEASON								PLAYOFFS				
Season Team	League	Gms.	G	A	Pts.	PIM	+/-	PP	SH	Gms.	G	A	Pts.	PIM
96-97—Colorado College	WCHA	36	4	12	16	62	...	...	...	—	—	—	—	—
97-98—Colorado College	WCHA	37	5	16	21	108	...	...	...	—	—	—	—	—
98-99—Colorado College	WCHA	36	8	21	29	82	...	...	...	—	—	—	—	—
99-00—Colorado College	WCHA	27	2	8	10	58	...	...	...	—	—	—	—	—
00-01—Philadelphia	AHL	73	2	14	16	71	...	...	...	6	1	4	5	8
01-02—Philadelphia	AHL	66	6	12	18	91	...	...	...	5	0	1	1	2
02-03—Philadelphia	AHL	41	1	4	5	48	...	...	...	—	—	—	—	—

PETERSEN, TOBY   LW   PENGUINS

PERSONAL: Born October 27, 1978, in Minneapolis. ... 5-10/196. ... Shoots left.
TRANSACTIONS/CAREER NOTES: Selected by Pittsburgh Penguins in ninth round (ninth Penguins pick, 244th overall) of NHL entry draft (June 27, 1998). ... Suffered dehydration (October 14, 2001); missed one game.
STATISTICAL PLATEAUS: Three-goal games: 2001-02 (1).

		REGULAR SEASON								PLAYOFFS				
Season Team	League	Gms.	G	A	Pts.	PIM	+/-	PP	SH	Gms.	G	A	Pts.	PIM
95-96—Thomas Jefferson	Minn. H.S.	25	29	30	59	...	...	...	...	—	—	—	—	—
96-97—Colorado College	WCHA	40	17	21	38	18	...	...	...	—	—	—	—	—
97-98—Colorado College	WCHA	34	13	15	28	30	...	...	...	—	—	—	—	—
98-99—Colorado College	WCHA	21	12	12	24	2	...	...	...	—	—	—	—	—
99-00—Colorado College	WCHA	37	14	19	33	8	...	...	...	—	—	—	—	—
00-01—Wilkes-Barre/Scranton	AHL	73	26	41	67	22	...	...	...	21	7	6	13	4
—Pittsburgh	NHL	12	2	6	8	4	3	0	0	—	—	—	—	—
01-02—Pittsburgh	NHL	79	8	10	18	4	-15	1	1	—	—	—	—	—
02-03—Wilkes-Barre/Scranton	AHL	80	31	35	66	24	...	...	...	—	—	—	—	—
NHL Totals (2 years)		91	10	16	26	8	-12	1	1					

PETROV, OLEG   RW

PERSONAL: Born April 18, 1971, in Moscow, U.S.S.R. ... 5-9/172. ... Shoots left.
TRANSACTIONS/CAREER NOTES: Selected by Montreal Canadiens in sixth round (ninth Canadiens pick, 127th overall) of NHL entry draft (June 22, 1991). ... Suffered injury (January 5, 1994); missed one game. ... Sprained ankle (April 6, 1994); missed three games. ... Torn medial collateral ligament in knee (December 11, 1999); missed 22 games. ... Injured right knee (April 5, 2001); missed final game of season. ... Bruised shoulder (October 19, 2001); missed six games. ... Traded by Canadiens to Nashville Predators for fourth-round pick in 2003 draft (March 3, 2003).
STATISTICAL PLATEAUS: Three-goal games: 1993-94 (1), 2001-02 (1). Total: 2.

		REGULAR SEASON								PLAYOFFS				
Season Team	League	Gms.	G	A	Pts.	PIM	+/-	PP	SH	Gms.	G	A	Pts.	PIM
89-90—CSKA Moscow	USSR	30	4	7	11	4	...	...	...	—	—	—	—	—
90-91—CSKA Moscow	USSR	43	7	4	11	8	...	...	...	—	—	—	—	—
91-92—CSKA Moscow	CIS	34	8	13	21	6	...	...	...	—	—	—	—	—
92-93—Montreal	NHL	9	2	1	3	10	2	0	0	1	0	0	0	0
—Fredericton	AHL	55	26	29	55	36	...	...	...	5	4	1	5	0
93-94—Fredericton	AHL	23	8	20	28	18	...	...	...	—	—	—	—	—
—Montreal	NHL	55	12	15	27	2	7	1	0	2	0	0	0	0
94-95—Montreal	NHL	12	2	3	5	4	-7	0	0	—	—	—	—	—
—Fredericton	AHL	17	7	11	18	12	...	...	...	17	5	6	11	10
95-96—Montreal	NHL	36	4	7	11	23	-9	0	0	5	0	1	1	0
—Fredericton	AHL	22	12	18	30	71	...	...	...	6	2	6	8	0
96-97—Ambri-Piotta	Switzerland	45	24	28	52	44	...	...	...	—	—	—	—	—
—HC Meran	Italy	12	5	12	17	4	...	...	...	—	—	—	—	—
97-98—Ambri-Piotta	Switzerland	40	30	*63	*93	60	...	...	...	14	11	11	22	40
98-99—Ambri-Piotta	Switzerland	45	35	52	87	52	...	...	...	15	9	11	20	32
99-00—Quebec	AHL	16	7	7	14	4	...	...	...	—	—	—	—	—
—Montreal	NHL	44	2	24	26	8	10	1	0	—	—	—	—	—
00-01—Montreal	NHL	81	17	30	47	24	-11	4	2	—	—	—	—	—
01-02—Montreal	NHL	75	24	17	41	12	-4	3	1	12	1	5	6	2
02-03—Montreal	NHL	53	7	16	23	16	-2	2	0	—	—	—	—	—
—Nashville	NHL	17	2	2	4	2	-4	0	0	—	—	—	—	—
NHL Totals (8 years)		382	72	115	187	101	-18	11	3	20	1	6	7	2

PETROVICKY, RONALD — LW/RW — RANGERS

PERSONAL: Born February 15, 1977, in Zilina, Czechoslovakia ... 6-0/190. ... Shoots right.
TRANSACTIONS/CAREER NOTES: Signed as non-drafted free agent by Calgary Flames (June 1, 1998). ... Injured wrist (October 5, 2000); missed 49 games. ... Claimed by New York Rangers from Flames in NHL waiver draft (October 4, 2002). ... Re-signed by Rangers (June 29, 2003).

Season Team	League	REGULAR SEASON								PLAYOFFS				
		Gms.	G	A	Pts.	PIM	+/-	PP	SH	Gms.	G	A	Pts.	PIM
93-94—Dukla Trencin	Slovakia	36	28	27	55	42	...	...	...	—	—	—	—	—
94-95—Tri-City	WHL	39	4	11	15	86	...	...	...	—	—	—	—	—
—Prince George	WHL	21	4	6	10	37	...	...	...	—	—	—	—	—
95-96—Prince George	WHL	39	19	21	40	61	...	...	...	—	—	—	—	—
96-97—Prince George	WHL	72	32	37	69	119	...	...	...	15	4	9	13	31
97-98—Regina	WHL	71	64	49	113	45	...	...	...	9	2	4	6	11
98-99—Saint John	AHL	78	12	21	33	114	...	...	...	7	1	2	3	19
99-00—Saint John	AHL	67	23	33	56	131	...	...	...	3	1	1	2	6
00-01—Calgary	NHL	30	4	5	9	54	0	1	0	—	—	—	—	—
01-02—Calgary	NHL	77	5	7	12	85	0	1	0	—	—	—	—	—
02-03—New York Rangers	NHL	66	5	9	14	77	-12	2	1	—	—	—	—	—
NHL Totals (3 years)		173	14	21	35	216	-12	4	1					

PETRUK, RANDY — G — HURRICANES

PERSONAL: Born April 23, 1978, in Cranbrook, B.C. ... 5-10/185. ... Catches right.
TRANSACTIONS/CAREER NOTES: Selected by Colorado Avalanche in fourth round (fifth Avalanche pick, 107th overall) of NHL entry draft (June 22, 1996). ... Rights traded by Avalanche to Carolina Hurricanes for fifth-round pick (D William Magnuson) in 1999 draft (June 1, 1998).

Season Team	League	REGULAR SEASON									PLAYOFFS						
		Gms.	Min	W	L	T	GA	SO	Avg.	SV%	Gms.	Min.	W	L	GA	SO	Avg.	SV%
94-95—Kamloops	WHL	27	1462	16	3	4	71	1	2.91	—	7	423	5	2	19	0	2.70	—
95-96—Kamloops	WHL	52	3071	34	15	1	181	1	3.54	—	16	990	9	‡6	58	0	3.52	—
96-97—Kamloops	WHL	*60	*3475	25	28	5	210	0	3.63	—	—	—	—	—	—	—	—	—
97-98—Kamloops	WHL	57	3097	31	21	1	157	3	3.04	—	7	425	3	4	21	0	2.96	—
98-99—New Haven	AHL	1	65	0	0	1	3	0	2.77	—	—	—	—	—	—	—	—	—
—Florida	ECHL	25	1441	13	10	‡2	66	1	2.75	—	1	60	0	1	5	0	5.00	—
99-00—Cincinnati	IHL	26	1436	18	9	3	84	2	3.51	—	9	...	...	...	...	...	...	—
—Florida	ECHL	6	339	7	0	1	19	0	3.36	—	—	—	—	—	—	—	—	—
00-01—Cincinnati	IHL	8	420	4	3	‡0	23	1	3.29	—	—	—	—	—	—	—	—	—
—Florida	ECHL	13	742	5	7	1	41	0	3.32	—	—	—	—	—	—	—	—	—
01-02—Florida	ECHL	51	3087	27	18	5	140	3	2.72	—	5	259	1	3	14	0	3.24	—
02-03—Lowell	AHL	30	1641	4	20	3	84	1	3.07	—	—	—	—	—	—	—	—	—
—Florida	ECHL	6	365	3	2	1	23	0	3.78	—	—	—	—	—	—	—	—	—

PETTINEN, TOMI — D — ISLANDERS

PERSONAL: Born June 17, 1977, in Ylojarvi, Finland ... 6-3/211. ... Shoots left.
TRANSACTIONS/CAREER NOTES: Selected by New York Islanders in ninth round (ninth Islanders choice, 267th overall) of NHL entry draft (June 25, 2000).

Season Team	League	REGULAR SEASON								PLAYOFFS				
		Gms.	G	A	Pts.	PIM	+/-	PP	SH	Gms.	G	A	Pts.	PIM
96-97—Ilves Tampere	Finland	16	1	0	1	12	...	...	...	—	—	—	—	—
97-98—Ilves Tampere	Finland	3	0	0	0	0	...	...	...	—	—	—	—	—
—Lukko Rauma	Finland-2	4	0	0	0	2	...	...	...	—	—	—	—	—
—Lukko Rauma	Finland	27	0	2	2	16	...	...	...	—	—	—	—	—
98-99—Hermes Kokkola	Finland-2	42	8	6	14	76	...	...	...	3	0	0	0	6
—HIFK Helsinki	Finland	4	0	0	0	2	...	...	...	—	—	—	—	—
99-00—Ilves Tampere	Finland	51	1	6	7	78	...	...	...	3	1	2	3	2
00-01—Ilves Tampere	Finland	56	2	2	4	86	...	...	...	9	0	0	0	4
01-02—Ilves Tampere	Finland	48	5	4	9	51	...	...	...	3	0	0	0	4
—Bridgeport	AHL	...	...	...	...	...	...	...	...	9	0	1	1	0
02-03—Bridgeport	AHL	75	1	8	9	56	...	...	...	—	—	—	—	—
—New York Islanders	NHL	2	0	0	0	0	1	0	0	—	—	—	—	—
NHL Totals (1 year)		2	0	0	0	0	1	0	0					

PETTINGER, MATT — LW — CAPITALS

PERSONAL: Born October 22, 1980, in Edmonton ... 6-1/210. ... Shoots left. ... Nephew of Gord Pettinger, center with three NHL teams (1932-33 through 1939-40).
TRANSACTIONS/CAREER NOTES: Selected by Washington Capitals in second round (second Capitals pick, 43rd overall) of NHL entry draft (June 24, 2000). ... Suffered from the flu (January 14, 2002); missed two games. ... Re-signed by Capitals (July 28, 2003).

Season Team	League	REGULAR SEASON								PLAYOFFS				
		Gms.	G	A	Pts.	PIM	+/-	PP	SH	Gms.	G	A	Pts.	PIM
98-99—Univ. of Denver	WCHA	38	14	6	20	52	...	...	...	—	—	—	—	—
99-00—Univ. of Denver	WCHA	19	2	6	8	...	...	...	...	—	—	—	—	—
—Calgary	WHL	27	14	6	20	41	...	...	...	11	2	6	8	30
00-01—Portland	AHL	64	19	17	36	92	...	...	...	2	0	0	0	4
—Washington	NHL	10	0	0	0	2	-1	0	0	—	—	—	—	—
01-02—Portland	AHL	9	3	3	6	24	...	...	...	—	—	—	—	—
—Washington	NHL	61	7	3	10	44	-8	1	0	—	—	—	—	—
02-03—Portland	AHL	69	14	13	27	72	...	...	...	—	—	—	—	—
—Washington	NHL	1	0	0	0	0	0	0	0	—	—	—	—	—
NHL Totals (3 years)		72	7	3	10	46	-9	1	0					

PHILLIPS, CHRIS — D — SENATORS

PERSONAL: Born March 9, 1978, in Fort McMurray, Alta. ... 6-3/215. ... Shoots left. ... Nephew of Rod Phillips, Edmonton Oilers play-by-play announcer.

TRANSACTIONS/CAREER NOTES: Selected by Ottawa Senators in first round (first Senators pick, first overall) of NHL entry draft (June 22, 1996). ... Bruised knee (November 13, 1997); missed two games. ... Bruised eye (February 25, 1998); missed five games. ... Suffered back spasms (November 18, 1998); missed three games. ... Sprained right ankle (January 1, 1999); missed 21 games. ... Reinjured right ankle (February 20, 1999); missed 23 games. ... Injured right ankle (December 9, 1999) and underwent surgery; missed 17 games. ... Suffered back spasms (November 2, 2000); missed three games. ... Suffered back spasms (December 2, 2000); missed two games. ... Injured left shoulder (April 1, 2001); missed final three games of regular season. ... Injured shoulder (September 19, 2001); missed first three games of season. ... Injured left elbow (December 18, 2001); missed 15 games.

Season Team	League	REGULAR SEASON								PLAYOFFS				
		Gms.	G	A	Pts.	PIM	+/-	PP	SH	Gms.	G	A	Pts.	PIM
93-94—Fort McMurray	AJHL	56	6	16	22	72	...	...	...	—	—	—	—	—
94-95—Fort McMurray	AJHL	48	16	32	48	127	...	...	...	—	—	—	—	—
95-96—Prince Albert	WHL	61	10	30	40	97	...	...	...	18	2	12	14	30
96-97—Prince Albert	WHL	32	3	23	26	58	...	...	...	—	—	—	—	—
—Lethbridge	WHL	26	4	18	22	28	...	...	...	19	4	*21	25	20
97-98—Ottawa	NHL	72	5	11	16	38	2	2	0	11	0	2	2	2
98-99—Ottawa	NHL	34	3	3	6	32	-5	2	0	3	0	0	0	0
99-00—Ottawa	NHL	65	5	14	19	39	12	0	0	6	0	1	1	4
00-01—Ottawa	NHL	73	2	12	14	31	8	2	0	1	1	0	1	0
01-02—Ottawa	NHL	63	6	16	22	29	5	1	0	12	0	0	0	12
02-03—Ottawa	NHL	78	3	16	19	71	7	2	0	18	2	4	6	12
NHL Totals (6 years)		385	24	72	96	240	29	9	0	51	3	7	10	30

PICARD, MICHEL — LW — RED WINGS

PERSONAL: Born November 7, 1969, in Beauport, Que. ... 5-11/202. ... Shoots left. ... Name pronounced pih-KAHRD.

TRANSACTIONS/CAREER NOTES: Selected by Hartford Whalers in ninth round (eighth Whalers pick, 178th overall) of NHL entry draft (June 17, 1989). ... Separated shoulder (November 14, 1991); missed seven games. ... Traded by Whalers to San Jose Sharks for future considerations (October 9, 1992); Whalers acquired LW Yvon Corriveau to complete deal (January 21, 1993). ... Signed as free agent by Ottawa Senators (June 23, 1994). ... Suspended two games and fined $1,000 by NHL for cross-checking (March 16, 1996). ... Traded by Senators to Washington Capitals for cash (May 21, 1996). ... Signed as free agent by St. Louis Blues (January 30, 1998). ... Signed as free agent by Edmonton Oilers (December 2, 1999). ... Signed as free agent by Philadelphia Flyers (August 14, 2000). ... Signed as free agent by Detroit Red Wings (July 24, 2002).

Season Team	League	REGULAR SEASON								PLAYOFFS				
		Gms.	G	A	Pts.	PIM	+/-	PP	SH	Gms.	G	A	Pts.	PIM
86-87—Trois-Rivieres	QMJHL	66	33	35	68	53	...	...	...	—	—	—	—	—
87-88—Trois-Rivieres	QMJHL	69	40	55	95	71	...	...	...	—	—	—	—	—
88-89—Trois-Rivieres	QMJHL	66	59	81	140	107	...	...	...	4	1	3	4	2
89-90—Binghamton	AHL	67	16	24	40	98	...	...	...	—	—	—	—	—
90-91—Hartford	NHL	5	1	0	1	2	-2	0	0	—	—	—	—	—
—Springfield	AHL	77	*56	40	96	61	...	...	...	18	8	13	21	18
91-92—Hartford	NHL	25	3	5	8	6	-2	1	0	—	—	—	—	—
—Springfield	AHL	40	21	17	38	44	...	...	...	11	2	0	2	34
92-93—Kansas City	IHL	33	7	10	17	51	...	...	...	12	3	2	5	20
—San Jose	NHL	25	4	0	4	24	-17	2	0	—	—	—	—	—
93-94—Portland	AHL	61	41	44	85	99	...	...	...	17	11	10	21	22
94-95—Prin. Edward Island	AHL	57	32	57	89	58	...	...	...	8	4	4	8	6
—Ottawa	NHL	24	5	8	13	14	-1	1	0	—	—	—	—	—
95-96—Prin. Edward Island	AHL	55	37	45	82	79	...	...	...	5	5	1	6	2
—Ottawa	NHL	17	2	6	8	10	-1	0	0	—	—	—	—	—
96-97—Grand Rapids	IHL	82	46	55	101	58	...	...	...	5	2	0	2	10
—Vastra Frolunda	Sweden	3	0	1	1	0	...	...	...	—	—	—	—	—
97-98—Grand Rapids	IHL	58	28	41	69	42	...	...	...	—	—	—	—	—
—St. Louis	NHL	16	1	8	9	29	3	0	0	—	—	—	—	—
98-99—St. Louis	NHL	45	11	11	22	16	5	0	0	5	0	0	0	2
—Grand Rapids	IHL	6	2	2	4	2	...	...	...	—	—	—	—	—
99-00—Edmonton	NHL	2	0	0	0	2	0	0	0	—	—	—	—	—
—Grand Rapids	IHL	65	33	35	68	50	...	...	...	17	8	10	†18	4
00-01—Philadelphia	AHL	72	31	39	70	22	...	...	...	10	4	5	9	4
—Philadelphia	NHL	7	1	4	5	0	6	1	0	—	—	—	—	—
01-02—Mannheim	Germany	60	24	28	52	30	...	...	...	12	7	6	13	4
02-03—Grand Rapids	AHL	78	32	52	84	34	...	...	...	—	—	—	—	—
NHL Totals (9 years)		166	28	42	70	103	-9	5	0	5	0	0	0	2

PILAR, KAREL — D — MAPLE LEAFS

PERSONAL: Born December 23, 1977, in Prague, Czechoslovakia ... 6-3/207. ... Shoots right. ... Name pronounced pee-LAHSH.

TRANSACTIONS/CAREER NOTES: Selected by Toronto Maple Leafs in second round (second Maple Leafs pick, 39th overall) of NHL entry draft (June 23, 2001).

Season Team	League	REGULAR SEASON								PLAYOFFS				
		Gms.	G	A	Pts.	PIM	+/-	PP	SH	Gms.	G	A	Pts.	PIM
99-00—Litvinov	Czech Rep.	49	2	12	14	53	...	...	...	7	0	0	0	4
00-01—Litvinov	Czech Rep.	52	12	26	38	52	...	...	...	4	1	1	2	25
01-02—St. John's	AHL	52	10	14	24	26	...	...	...	—	—	—	—	—
—Toronto	NHL	23	1	3	4	8	3	0	0	11	0	4	4	12
02-03—St. John's	AHL	7	2	5	7	28	...	...	...	—	—	—	—	—
—Toronto	NHL	17	3	4	7	12	-7	1	0	—	—	—	—	—
NHL Totals (2 years)		40	4	7	11	20	-4	1	0	11	0	4	4	12

PIRJETA, LASSE — LW — BLUE JACKETS

PERSONAL: Born April 4, 1974, in Oulu, Finland ... 6-4/225. ... Shoots left.
TRANSACTIONS/CAREER NOTES: Selected by Columbus Blue Jackets in fifth round (seventh Blue Jackets pick, 133rd overall) of NHL entry draft (June 23, 2002).

		REGULAR SEASON								PLAYOFFS				
Season Team	League	Gms.	G	A	Pts.	PIM	+/-	PP	SH	Gms.	G	A	Pts.	PIM
93-94—TPS Turku	Finland	43	9	9	18	14	...	...	...	11	4	0	4	2
94-95—TPS Turku	Finland	49	7	13	20	64	...	...	...	8	0	1	1	29
95-96—TPS Turku	Finland	45	13	14	27	34	...	...	...	11	6	3	9	4
96-97—Vastra Frolunda..........	Sweden	50	14	8	22	36	...	...	...	3	0	1	1	4
—Vastra Frolunda	EuroHL	5	2	6	8	4	...	...	...	—	—	—	—	—
97-98—Tappara Tampere........	Finland	48	24	22	46	20	...	...	...	4	1	1	2	2
98-99—Tappara Tampere........	Finland	54	22	19	41	32	...	...	...	—	—	—	—	—
99-00—HIFK Helsinki..............	Finland	54	18	25	43	24	...	...	...	9	2	3	5	10
—HIFK Helsinki	EuroHL	6	1	3	4	6	...	...	...	2	1	1	2	0
00-01—HIFK Helsinki..............	Finland	55	15	18	33	24	...	...	...	—	—	—	—	—
01-02—Karpat Oulu.................	Finland	55	15	26	41	24	...	...	...	4	2	2	4	4
02-03—Columbus	NHL	51	11	10	21	12	-4	2	0	—	—	—	—	—
NHL Totals (1 year)..............		51	11	10	21	12	-4	2	0	—	—	—	—	—

PIROS, KAMIL — C — THRASHERS

PERSONAL: Born November 20, 1978, in Most, Czechoslovakia ... 6-0/200. ... Shoots left. ... Name pronounced ca-MEEL PEE-rose.
TRANSACTIONS/CAREER NOTES: Selected by Buffalo Sabres in eighth round (ninth Sabres pick, 212th overall) of NHL entry draft (June 21, 1997). ... Traded by Sabres with fourth-round pick (traded to St. Louis) in 2001 draft to Atlanta Thrashers for RW Donald Audette (March 13, 2001). ... Bruised knee (March 23, 2002); missed three games. ... Re-signed by Thrashers (July 24, 2003).
STATISTICAL PLATEAUS: Three-goal games: 2002-03 (1).

		REGULAR SEASON								PLAYOFFS				
Season Team	League	Gms.	G	A	Pts.	PIM	+/-	PP	SH	Gms.	G	A	Pts.	PIM
93-94—Most Jrs.	Czech. Jrs.	16	12	10	22	...	...	...	...	—	—	—	—	—
—Chemopetrol Litvinov .	Czech. Jrs.	22	6	13	19	...	...	...	...	—	—	—	—	—
94-95—Chemopetrol Litvinov .	Czech. Jrs.	40	27	16	43	...	...	...	...	—	—	—	—	—
95-96—Chemopetrol Litvinov .	Czech. Jrs.	42	16	13	29	...	...	...	...	—	—	—	—	—
96-97—Litvinov......................	Czech Rep.	38	4	19	23	0	...	...	...	—	—	—	—	—
97-98—Chem. Litvinov............	Czech Rep.	14	0	1	1	2	...	...	...	—	—	—	—	—
—HC Vitkovice	Czech Rep.	26	2	9	11	14	...	...	...	—	—	—	—	—
98-99—Chem. Litvinov............	Czech Rep.	41	7	9	16	10	...	...	...	—	—	—	—	—
99-00—Chem. Litvinov............	Czech Rep.	40	8	8	16	18	...	...	...	7	0	3	3	2
00-01—Chem. Litvinov............	Czech Rep.	48	11	13	24	28	...	...	...	6	1	1	2	2
01-02—Atlanta	NHL	8	0	1	1	4	-2	0	0	—	—	—	—	—
—Chicago.....................	AHL	64	19	30	49	16	...	...	...	25	6	11	17	6
02-03—Chicago.....................	AHL	51	10	9	19	16	...	...	...	—	—	—	—	—
—Atlanta	NHL	3	3	2	5	2	4	0	0	—	—	—	—	—
NHL Totals (2 years)...........		11	3	3	6	6	2	0	0	—	—	—	—	—

PISA, ALES — D — RANGERS

PERSONAL: Born January 2, 1977, in Pardubice, Czechoslovakia ... 6-0/194. ... Shoots left.
TRANSACTIONS/CAREER NOTES: Selected by Edmonton Oilers in ninth round (10th Oilers pick, 272nd overall) of NHL entry draft (June 24, 2001). ... Traded by Oilers with RW Anson Carter to New York Rangers for RW Radek Dvorak and D Cory Cross (March 11, 2003).

		REGULAR SEASON								PLAYOFFS				
Season Team	League	Gms.	G	A	Pts.	PIM	+/-	PP	SH	Gms.	G	A	Pts.	PIM
93-94—HC Pardubice..............	Czech Rep.	2	0	0	0	0	...	...	...	—	—	—	—	—
94-95—HC Pardubice..............	Czech Rep.	22	0	0	0	18	...	...	...	2	0	0	0	0
95-96—HC Pardubice..............	Czech Rep.	33	0	4	4	82	...	...	...	—	—	—	—	—
96-97—HC Pardubice..............	Czech Rep.	41	4	2	6	70	...	...	...	6	0	2	2	6
97-98—HC Pardubice..............	Czech Rep.	50	4	9	13	107	...	...	...	3	0	0	0	4
98-99—HC Pardubice..............	Czech Rep.	48	7	12	19	74	...	...	...	3	0	1	1	...
99-00—HC Pardubice..............	Czech Rep.	51	5	11	16	58	...	...	...	1	0	0	0	4
00-01—HC Pardubice..............	Czech Rep.	47	10	13	23	75	...	...	...	7	2	2	4	4
01-02—Hamilton	AHL	52	6	12	18	62	...	...	...	14	1	4	5	8
—Edmonton	NHL	2	0	0	0	2	0	0	0	—	—	—	—	—
02-03—Hamilton	AHL	7	0	1	1	14	...	...	...	—	—	—	—	—
—Edmonton	NHL	48	1	3	4	24	11	1	0	—	—	—	—	—
—New York Rangers	NHL	3	0	0	0	0	1	0	0	—	—	—	—	—
NHL Totals (2 years)...........		53	1	3	4	26	12	1	0	—	—	—	—	—

PISANI, FERNANDO — RW — OILERS

PERSONAL: Born December 27, 1976, in Edmonton ... 6-1/185. ... Shoots left.
TRANSACTIONS/CAREER NOTES: Selected by Edmonton Oilers in eighth round (ninth Oilers pick, 195th overall) of NHL entry draft (June 22, 1996).
STATISTICAL PLATEAUS: Three-goal games: 2002-03 (1).

Season Team	League	Gms.	G	A	Pts.	PIM	+/-	PP	SH	Gms.	G	A	Pts.	PIM
		REGULAR SEASON								PLAYOFFS				
95-96—St. Albert	AJHL	58	40	63	103	134	...	...	...	18	7	22	29	28
96-97—Providence College	Hockey East	35	12	18	30	36	...	...	...	—	—	—	—	—
97-98—Providence College	Hockey East	36	16	18	34	20	...	...	...	—	—	—	—	—
98-99—Providence College	Hockey East	38	14	37	51	42	...	...	...	—	—	—	—	—
99-00—Providence College	Hockey East	38	14	24	38	56	...	...	...	—	—	—	—	—
00-01—Hamilton	AHL	52	12	13	25	28	...	...	...	—	—	—	—	—
01-02—Hamilton	AHL	79	26	34	60	60	...	...	...	15	4	6	10	4
02-03—Hamilton	AHL	41	17	15	32	24	...	...	...	—	—	—	—	—
—Edmonton	NHL	35	8	5	13	10	9	0	1	6	1	0	1	2
NHL Totals (1 year)		35	8	5	13	10	9	0	1	6	1	0	1	2

PITKANEN, JONI   D   FLYERS

PERSONAL: Born September 19, 1983, in Oulu, Finland. ... 6-3/202. ... Shoots left.
TRANSACTIONS/CAREER NOTES: Selected by Philadelphia Flyers in first round (first Flyers pick, fourth overall) of NHL entry draft (June 22, 2002). ... Signed by Flyers (July 15, 2003).

Season Team	League	Gms.	G	A	Pts.	PIM	+/-	PP	SH	Gms.	G	A	Pts.	PIM
		REGULAR SEASON								PLAYOFFS				
00-01—Karpat Oulu	Finland	21	0	0	0	10	...	...	...	2	0	0	0	2
01-02—Karpat Oulu	Finland	49	4	15	19	65	...	...	...	4	0	0	0	12
02-03—Karpat Oulu	Finland	35	5	15	20	38	...	...	...	—	—	—	—	—

PITTIS, DOMENIC   C

PERSONAL: Born October 1, 1974, in Calgary. ... 5-11/190. ... Shoots left. ... Name pronounced PIHT-ihz.
TRANSACTIONS/CAREER NOTES: Selected by Pittsburgh Penguins in second round (second Penguins pick, 52nd overall) of NHL entry draft (June 26, 1993). ... Signed as free agent by Buffalo Sabres (July 30, 1998). ... Suffered from the flu (October 27, 1999); missed one game. ... Injured ankle (November 9, 1999); missed three games. ... Signed as free agent by Edmonton Oilers (July 26, 2000). ... Strained groin (January 23, 2002); missed four games. ... Suffered concussion (February 22, 2002); missed 20 games. ... Signed as free agent by Nashville Predators (July 24, 2002).

Season Team	League	Gms.	G	A	Pts.	PIM	+/-	PP	SH	Gms.	G	A	Pts.	PIM
		REGULAR SEASON								PLAYOFFS				
91-92—Lethbridge	WHL	65	6	17	23	48	...	...	...	5	0	2	2	4
92-93—Lethbridge	WHL	66	46	73	119	69	...	...	...	4	3	3	6	8
93-94—Lethbridge	WHL	72	58	69	127	93	...	...	...	8	4	11	15	16
94-95—Cleveland	IHL	62	18	32	50	66	...	...	...	3	0	2	2	2
95-96—Cleveland	IHL	74	10	28	38	100	...	...	...	3	0	0	0	2
96-97—Pittsburgh	NHL	1	0	0	0	0	-1	0	0	—	—	—	—	—
—Long Beach	IHL	65	23	43	66	91	...	...	...	18	5	9	14	26
97-98—Syracuse	AHL	75	23	41	64	90	...	...	...	5	1	3	4	4
98-99—Rochester	AHL	76	38	66	*104	108	...	...	...	20	7	†14	*21	40
—Buffalo	NHL	3	0	0	0	2	0	0	0	—	—	—	—	—
99-00—Buffalo	NHL	7	1	0	1	6	1	0	0	—	—	—	—	—
—Rochester	AHL	53	17	48	65	85	...	...	...	21	4	*26	*30	28
00-01—Edmonton	NHL	47	4	5	9	49	-5	0	0	3	0	0	0	2
01-02—Edmonton	NHL	22	0	6	6	8	-2	0	0	—	—	—	—	—
02-03—Milwaukee	AHL	30	11	21	32	65	...	...	...	—	—	—	—	—
—Nashville	NHL	2	0	0	0	2	0	0	0	—	—	—	—	—
NHL Totals (6 years)		82	5	11	16	67	-7	0	0	3	0	0	0	2

PIVKO, LIBOR   LW   PREDATORS

PERSONAL: Born March 29, 1980, in Novy Vicin, Czechoslovakia. ... 6-3/192. ... Shoots left.
TRANSACTIONS/CAREER NOTES: Selected by Nashville Predators in third round (fourth Predators pick, 89th overall) of NHL entry draft (June 24, 2000).

Season Team	League	Gms.	G	A	Pts.	PIM	+/-	PP	SH	Gms.	G	A	Pts.	PIM
		REGULAR SEASON								PLAYOFFS				
98-99—Opava	Czech.	5	0	1	1	0	...	...	...	—	—	—	—	—
99-00—Havirov	Czech Rep.	40	11	11	22	41	...	...	...	—	—	—	—	—
00-01—Havirov	Czech Rep.	37	4	15	19	28	...	...	...	—	—	—	—	—
01-02—HC Continental Zlin	Czech Rep.	46	8	20	28	36	...	...	...	9	5	3	8	8
02-03—HC Continental Zlin	Czech Rep.	52	13	12	25	60	...	...	...	—	—	—	—	—

PLEKANEC, TOMAS   LW   CANADIENS

PERSONAL: Born October 31, 1982, in Kladno, Czechoslovakia. ... 5-10/189. ... Shoots left.
TRANSACTIONS/CAREER NOTES: Selected by Montreal Canadiens in third round (fourth Canadiens pick, 71st overall) of NHL entry draft (June 23, 2001).

Season Team	League	Gms.	G	A	Pts.	PIM	+/-	PP	SH	Gms.	G	A	Pts.	PIM
		REGULAR SEASON								PLAYOFFS				
00-01—HC Kladno	Czech Rep.	47	9	9	18	24	...	...	...	—	—	—	—	—
01-02—HC Kladno	Czech Rep.	48	7	16	23	28	...	...	...	—	—	—	—	—
02-03—Hamilton	AHL	77	19	27	46	74	...	...	...	—	—	—	—	—

PLIHAL, TOMAS — LW/RW — SHARKS

PERSONAL: Born March 28, 1983, in Frydlant, Czechoslovakia. ... 6-1/180. ... Shoots left.
TRANSACTIONS/CAREER NOTES: Selected by San Jose Sharks in fifth round (fourth Sharks pick, 140th overall) of NHL entry draft (June 23, 2001).

		REGULAR SEASON								PLAYOFFS				
Season Team	League	Gms.	G	A	Pts.	PIM	+/-	PP	SH	Gms.	G	A	Pts.	PIM
00-01—Liberic	Czech. Jrs.	33	16	12	28	0	...	...	...	—	—	—	—	—
01-02—Kootenay	WHL	72	32	54	86	28	...	...	...	22	4	10	14	14
02-03—Kootenay	WHL	67	35	42	77	113	...	...	...	—	—	—	—	—

POAPST, STEVE — D — BLACKHAWKS

PERSONAL: Born January 3, 1969, in Cornwall, Ont. ... 6-0/194. ... Shoots left. ... Name pronounced PAHPS.
TRANSACTIONS/CAREER NOTES: Signed as non-drafted free agent by Washington Capitals (February 4, 1995). ... Signed as free agent by Chicago Blackhawks (July 27, 2000). ... Strained groin (April 1, 2001); missed three games.

		REGULAR SEASON								PLAYOFFS				
Season Team	League	Gms.	G	A	Pts.	PIM	+/-	PP	SH	Gms.	G	A	Pts.	PIM
86-87—Smith Falls	OJHL	54	10	27	37	94	...	...	...	—	—	—	—	—
87-88—Colgate University	ECAC	32	3	13	16	22	...	...	...	—	—	—	—	—
88-89—Colgate University	ECAC	30	0	5	5	38	...	...	...	—	—	—	—	—
89-90—Colgate University	ECAC	38	4	15	19	54	...	...	...	—	—	—	—	—
90-91—Colgate University	ECAC	32	6	15	21	43	...	...	...	—	—	—	—	—
91-92—Hampton Roads	ECHL	55	8	20	28	29	...	...	...	14	1	4	5	12
92-93—Hampton Roads	ECHL	63	10	35	45	57	...	...	...	4	0	1	1	4
—Baltimore	AHL	7	0	1	1	4	...	...	...	7	0	3	3	6
93-94—Portland	AHL	78	14	21	35	47	...	...	...	12	0	3	3	8
94-95—Portland	AHL	71	8	22	30	60	...	...	...	7	0	1	1	16
95-96—Portland	AHL	70	10	24	34	79	...	...	...	20	2	6	8	16
—Washington	NHL	3	1	0	1	0	-1	0	0	6	0	0	0	0
96-97—Portland	AHL	47	1	20	21	34	...	...	...	5	0	1	1	6
97-98—Portland	AHL	76	8	29	37	46	...	...	...	10	2	3	5	8
98-99—Portland	AHL	54	3	21	24	36	...	...	...	—	—	—	—	—
—Washington	NHL	22	0	0	0	8	-8	0	0	—	—	—	—	—
99-00—Portland	AHL	56	0	14	14	20	...	...	...	3	1	0	1	2
00-01—Norfolk	AHL	37	1	8	9	14	...	...	...	—	—	—	—	—
—Chicago	NHL	36	2	3	5	12	3	0	0	—	—	—	—	—
01-02—Chicago	NHL	56	1	7	8	30	6	0	0	5	0	0	0	0
02-03—Chicago	NHL	75	2	11	13	50	14	0	0	—	—	—	—	—
NHL Totals (5 years)		192	6	21	27	100	14	0	0	11	0	0	0	0

PODEIN, SHJON — LW

PERSONAL: Born March 5, 1968, in Rochester, Minn. ... 6-2/200. ... Shoots left. ... Name pronounced SHAWN poh-DEEN.
TRANSACTIONS/CAREER NOTES: Selected by Edmonton Oilers in eighth round (ninth Oilers pick, 166th overall) of NHL entry draft (June 11, 1988). ... Injured knee (March 9, 1994); missed five games. ... Signed as free agent by Philadelphia Flyers (July 27, 1994). ... Bruised right foot (February 22, 1996); missed three games. ... Traded by Flyers to Colorado Avalanche for RW Keith Jones (November 12, 1998). ... Fractured lower right leg (December 4, 1998); missed 25 games. ... Bruised foot (March 30, 1999); missed one game. ... Injured knee prior to start of 1999-2000 season; missed first five games of season. ... Fractured foot (January 7, 2000); missed two games. ... Bruised knee (October 11, 2001); missed one game. ... Injured knee (December 27, 2001); missed eight games. ... Injured knee (January 24, 2002); missed nine games. ... Traded by Avalanche to St. Louis Blues for RW Mike Keane (February 11, 2002).
STATISTICAL PLATEAUS: Three-goal games: 1999-00 (1).

		REGULAR SEASON								PLAYOFFS				
Season Team	League	Gms.	G	A	Pts.	PIM	+/-	PP	SH	Gms.	G	A	Pts.	PIM
87-88—Minnesota-Duluth	WCHA	30	4	4	8	48	...	...	...	—	—	—	—	—
88-89—Minnesota-Duluth	WCHA	36	7	5	12	46	...	...	...	—	—	—	—	—
89-90—Minnesota-Duluth	WCHA	35	21	18	39	36	...	...	...	—	—	—	—	—
90-91—Cape Breton	AHL	63	14	15	29	65	...	...	...	4	0	0	0	5
91-92—Cape Breton	AHL	80	30	24	54	46	...	...	...	5	3	1	4	2
92-93—Cape Breton	AHL	38	18	21	39	32	...	...	...	9	2	2	4	29
—Edmonton	NHL	40	13	6	19	25	-2	2	1	—	—	—	—	—
93-94—Edmonton	NHL	28	3	5	8	8	3	0	0	—	—	—	—	—
—Cape Breton	AHL	5	4	4	8	4	...	...	...	—	—	—	—	—
94-95—Philadelphia	NHL	44	3	7	10	33	-2	0	0	15	1	3	4	10
95-96—Philadelphia	NHL	79	15	10	25	89	25	0	4	12	1	2	3	50
96-97—Philadelphia	NHL	82	14	18	32	41	7	0	0	19	4	3	7	16
97-98—Philadelphia	NHL	82	11	13	24	53	8	1	1	5	0	0	0	10
98-99—Philadelphia	NHL	14	1	0	1	0	-2	0	0	—	—	—	—	—
—Colorado	NHL	41	2	6	8	24	-3	0	0	19	1	1	2	12
99-00—Colorado	NHL	75	11	8	19	29	12	0	1	17	5	0	5	8
00-01—Colorado	NHL	82	15	17	32	68	7	0	0	23	2	3	5	14
01-02—Colorado	NHL	41	6	6	12	39	0	0	1	—	—	—	—	—
—St. Louis	NHL	23	2	4	6	2	2	0	0	10	0	0	0	6
02-03—St. Louis	NHL	68	4	6	10	28	7	1	0	7	0	1	1	6
NHL Totals (11 years)		699	100	106	206	439	62	4	8	127	14	13	27	132

PODHRADSKY, PETER   D

PERSONAL: Born December 10, 1979, in Bratislava, Czechoslovakia. ... 6-1/185. ... Shoots right.
TRANSACTIONS/CAREER NOTES: Selected by Mighty Ducks of Anaheim in fifth round (fourth Mighty Ducks pick, 134th overall) of NHL entry draft (June 24, 2000).

Season Team	League	Gms.	G	A	Pts.	PIM	+/-	PP	SH	Gms.	G	A	Pts.	PIM
					REGULAR SEASON							PLAYOFFS		
98-99—Bratislava	Slovakia	23	1	4	5	37	...	...	...	4	0	0	0	0
99-00—Bratislava	Slovakia	25	1	4	5	2	...	...	...	—	—	—	—	—
00-01—Cincinnati	AHL	59	4	5	9	27	...	...	...	2	0	0	0	0
01-02—Cincinnati	AHL	49	0	8	8	19	...	...	...	—	—	—	—	—
02-03—Cincinnati	AHL	78	9	8	17	85	...	...	...	—	—	—	—	—

POHANKA, IGOR   C   MIGHTY DUCKS

PERSONAL: Born July 5, 1983, in Plestany, Czechoslovakia. ... 6-3/185. ... Shoots left.
TRANSACTIONS/CAREER NOTES: Selected by New Jersey Devils in second round (second Devils pick, 44th overall) of NHL entry draft (June 23, 2001). ... Traded by Devils with RW Petr Sykora, D Mike Commodore and G J.F. Damphousse to Mighty Ducks of Anaheim for D Oleg Tverdovsky, LW Jeff Friesen and RW Maxin Balmochnykh (July 7, 2002).

Season Team	League	Gms.	G	A	Pts.	PIM	+/-	PP	SH	Gms.	G	A	Pts.	PIM
					REGULAR SEASON							PLAYOFFS		
99-00—Bratislava	Slov. Jr.	32	12	18	30	29	...	...	...	—	—	—	—	—
00-01—Prince Albert	WHL	70	16	33	49	24	...	...	...	—	—	—	—	—
01-02—Prince Albert	WHL	58	25	43	68	18	...	...	...	—	—	—	—	—
02-03—Prince Albert	WHL	56	25	31	56	28	...	...	...	—	—	—	—	—

POHL, JOHN   C   BLUES

PERSONAL: Born June 1, 1979, in Rochester, Minn. ... 6-1/186. ... Shoots right.
COLLEGE: Minnesota.
TRANSACTIONS/CAREER NOTES: Selected by St. Louis Blues in ninth round (eighth Blues pick, 255th overall) of NHL entry draft (June 27, 1998).

Season Team	League	Gms.	G	A	Pts.	PIM	+/-	PP	SH	Gms.	G	A	Pts.	PIM
					REGULAR SEASON							PLAYOFFS		
97-98—Red Wing H.S.	Minn. H.S.	28	30	77	107	18	...	...	...	—	—	—	—	—
—Twin Cities	USHL	10	5	3	8	10	...	...	...	—	—	—	—	—
98-99—Univ. of Minnesota	WCHA	42	7	10	17	18	...	...	...	—	—	—	—	—
99-00—Univ. of Minnesota	WCHA	41	18	49	67	26	...	...	...	—	—	—	—	—
00-01—Univ. of Minnesota	WCHA	38	19	26	45	24	...	...	...	—	—	—	—	—
01-02—Univ. of Minnesota	WCHA	44	27	*52	*79	26	...	...	...	—	—	—	—	—
02-03—Worcester	AHL	58	26	32	58	34	...	...	...	—	—	—	—	—

POLLOCK, JAME   RW   BLUES

PERSONAL: Born June 16, 1979, in Quebec City. ... 6-1/190. ... Shoots right.
TRANSACTIONS/CAREER NOTES: Selected by St. Louis Blues in fourth round (fourth Blues pick, 106th overall) of NHL entry draft (June 21, 1997).

Season Team	League	Gms.	G	A	Pts.	PIM	+/-	PP	SH	Gms.	G	A	Pts.	PIM
					REGULAR SEASON							PLAYOFFS		
95-96—Seattle	WHL	32	0	1	1	15	...	...	...	—	—	—	—	—
96-97—Seattle	WHL	66	15	19	34	94	...	...	...	15	3	5	8	16
97-98—Seattle	WHL	66	11	36	47	78	...	...	...	5	0	1	1	17
98-99—Seattle	WHL	59	10	32	42	78	...	...	...	11	3	4	7	8
99-00—Worcester	AHL	56	12	12	24	50	...	...	...	9	5	3	8	6
00-01—Worcester	AHL	55	15	8	23	36	...	...	...	11	1	7	8	10
01-02—Worcester	AHL	71	23	43	66	89	...	...	...	3	1	0	1	2
02-03—Worcester	AHL	44	5	17	22	50	...	...	...	—	—	—	—	—

POMINVILLE, JASON   RW   SABRES

PERSONAL: Born November 30, 1982, in Repentigny, Que. ... 5-11/174. ... Shoots right.
TRANSACTIONS/CAREER NOTES: Selected by Buffalo Sabres in second round (fourth Sabres pick, 55th overall) of NHL entry draft (June 23, 2001).

Season Team	League	Gms.	G	A	Pts.	PIM	+/-	PP	SH	Gms.	G	A	Pts.	PIM
					REGULAR SEASON							PLAYOFFS		
98-99—Shawinigan	QMJHL	2	0	0	0	0	...	...	...	—	—	—	—	—
99-00—Shawinigan	QMJHL	60	4	17	21	12	...	...	...	13	2	3	5	0
00-01—Shawinigan	QMJHL	71	46	61	107	24	...	...	...	10	6	6	12	0
01-02—Shawinigan	QMJHL	66	†57	64	121	32	...	...	...	2	0	0	0	0
02-03—Rochester	AHL	73	13	21	34	16	...	...	...	—	—	—	—	—

PONIKAROVSKY, ALEXEI   RW   MAPLE LEAFS

PERSONAL: Born April 9, 1980, in Kiev, U.S.S.R. ... 6-4/220. ... Shoots left.

TRANSACTIONS/CAREER NOTES: Selected by Toronto Maple Leafs in fourth round (fourth Maple Leafs pick, 87th overall) of NHL entry draft (June 27, 1998). ... Re-signed by Maple Leafs (July 20, 2003).

		REGULAR SEASON								PLAYOFFS				
Season Team	League	Gms.	G	A	Pts.	PIM	+/-	PP	SH	Gms.	G	A	Pts.	PIM
95-96—Dynamo Moscow........	CIS Jr.	70	14	10	24	20	...	...	...	—	—	—	—	—
96-97—Dynamo Moscow........	Russian Jr.	60	12	15	27	30	...	...	...	—	—	—	—	—
—Dynamo Moscow........	Rus. Div. III	2	0	0	0	2	...	...	...	—	—	—	—	—
97-98—Dynamo Moscow........	Rus. Div. II	24	1	2	3	30	...	...	...	—	—	—	—	—
98-99—Dynamo Moscow........	Russian	—	—	—	—	—	...	...	...	3	0	0	0	2
99-00—Dynamo Moscow........	Russian	19	1	0	1	8	...	...	...	1	0	0	0	0
00-01—St. John's.................	AHL	49	12	24	36	44	...	...	...	4	0	0	0	4
—Toronto	NHL	22	1	3	4	14	-1	0	0	—	—	—	—	—
01-02—St. John's.................	AHL	72	21	27	48	74	...	...	...	5	2	1	3	8
—Toronto	NHL	8	2	0	2	0	2	0	0	10	0	0	0	4
02-03—St. John's.................	AHL	63	24	22	46	68	...	...	...	—	—	—	—	—
—Toronto	NHL	13	0	3	3	11	4	0	0	—	—	—	—	—
NHL Totals (3 years)...........		**43**	**3**	**6**	**9**	**25**	**5**	**0**	**0**	**10**	**0**	**0**	**0**	**4**

POPOVIC, MARK   D   MIGHTY DUCKS

PERSONAL: Born October 11, 1982, in Stoney Creek, Ont. ... 6-1/194. ... Shoots left.

TRANSACTIONS/CAREER NOTES: Selected by Mighty Ducks of Anaheim in second round (second Mighty Ducks pick, 35th overall) of NHL entry draft (June 23, 2001).

		REGULAR SEASON								PLAYOFFS				
Season Team	League	Gms.	G	A	Pts.	PIM	+/-	PP	SH	Gms.	G	A	Pts.	PIM
98-99—Toronto St. Michael's..	OHL	60	6	26	32	46	...	...	...	—	—	—	—	—
99-00—Toronto St. Michael's..	OHL	68	11	29	40	68	...	...	...	—	—	—	—	—
00-01—Toronto St. Michael's..	OHL	61	7	35	42	54	...	...	...	18	3	5	8	22
01-02—Toronto St. Michael's..	OHL	58	12	29	41	42	...	...	...	15	1	11	12	10
02-03—Cincinnati...................	AHL	73	3	21	24	46	...	...	...	—	—	—	—	—

POTHIER, BRIAN   D   SENATORS

PERSONAL: Born April 15, 1977, in New Bedford, Mass. ... 6-0/198. ... Shoots right.

TRANSACTIONS/CAREER NOTES: Signed as non-drafted free agent by Atlanta Thrashers (April 8, 2000). ... Suffered concussion (March 22, 2002); missed remainder of season. ... Traded by Thrashers to Ottawa Senators for LW Shawn McEachern and sixth-round pick in 2004 draft (June 30, 2002).

		REGULAR SEASON								PLAYOFFS				
Season Team	League	Gms.	G	A	Pts.	PIM	+/-	PP	SH	Gms.	G	A	Pts.	PIM
96-97—R.P.I.	ECAC	34	1	11	12	42	...	...	...	—	—	—	—	—
97-98—R.P.I.	ECAC	35	2	9	11	28	...	...	...	—	—	—	—	—
98-99—R.P.I.	ECAC	37	5	13	18	36	...	...	...	—	—	—	—	—
99-00—R.P.I.	ECAC	36	9	24	33	44	...	...	...	—	—	—	—	—
00-01—Orlando	IHL	76	12	29	41	69	...	...	...	16	3	5	8	11
—Atlanta	NHL	3	0	0	0	2	4	0	0	—	—	—	—	—
01-02—Atlanta	NHL	33	3	6	9	22	-19	1	0	—	—	—	—	—
—Chicago......................	AHL	39	6	13	19	30	...	...	...	—	—	—	—	—
02-03—Binghamton	AHL	68	7	40	47	58	...	...	...	—	—	—	—	—
—Ottawa	NHL	14	2	4	6	6	11	0	0	1	0	0	0	2
NHL Totals (3 years)...........		**50**	**5**	**10**	**15**	**30**	**-4**	**1**	**0**	**1**	**0**	**0**	**0**	**2**

POTI, TOM   D   RANGERS

PERSONAL: Born March 22, 1977, in Worcester, Mass. ... 6-3/209. ... Shoots left.

TRANSACTIONS/CAREER NOTES: Selected by Edmonton Oilers in third round (fourth Oilers pick, 59th overall) of NHL entry draft (June 22, 1996). ... Bruised right knee (November 10, 1999); missed one game. ... Strained neck (December 4, 1999); missed two games. ... Bruised thumb (January 14, 2000); missed one game. ... Bruised ankle (February 13, 2000); missed one game. ... Reinjured ankle (February 29, 2000); missed one game. ... Fractured finger (December 21, 2001); missed seven games. ... Traded by Oilers with LW Rem Murray to New York Rangers for C Mike York and fourth-round pick (D Ivan Koltsov) in 2002 draft (March 19, 2002).

		REGULAR SEASON								PLAYOFFS				
Season Team	League	Gms.	G	A	Pts.	PIM	+/-	PP	SH	Gms.	G	A	Pts.	PIM
94-95—Cushing Academy.......	Mass. H.S.	36	16	47	63	35	...	...	...	—	—	—	—	—
95-96—Cushing Academy.......	Mass. H.S.	29	14	59	73	18	...	...	...	—	—	—	—	—
96-97—Boston University	Hockey East	38	4	17	21	54	...	...	...	—	—	—	—	—
97-98—Boston University	Hockey East	38	13	29	42	60	...	...	...	—	—	—	—	—
98-99—Edmonton	NHL	73	5	16	21	42	10	2	0	4	0	1	1	2
99-00—Edmonton	NHL	76	9	26	35	65	8	2	1	5	0	1	1	0
00-01—Edmonton	NHL	81	12	20	32	60	-4	6	0	6	0	2	2	2
01-02—Edmonton	NHL	55	1	16	17	42	-6	1	0	—	—	—	—	—
—U.S. Olympic team.....	Int'l	6	0	1	1	4	...	...	...	—	—	—	—	—
—New York Rangers......	NHL	11	1	7	8	2	-4	1	0	—	—	—	—	—
02-03—New York Rangers......	NHL	80	11	37	48	60	-6	3	0	—	—	—	—	—
NHL Totals (5 years)...........		**376**	**39**	**122**	**161**	**271**	**-2**	**15**	**1**	**15**	**0**	**4**	**4**	**4**

POTVIN, FELIX G

PERSONAL: Born June 23, 1971, in Anjou, Que. ... 6-1/190. ... Catches left. ... Name pronounced PAHT-vihn. ... Nickname: The Cat.

TRANSACTIONS/CAREER NOTES: Selected by Toronto Maple Leafs in second round (second Maple Leafs pick, 31st overall) of NHL entry draft (June 16, 1990). ... Traded by Maple Leafs with sixth-round pick (traded to Tampa Bay) in 1999 draft to New York Islanders for D Bryan Berard and sixth-round pick (RW Jan Sochor) in 1999 draft (January 9, 1999). ... Strained groin (February 13, 1999); missed 22 games. ... Traded by Islanders with second-(traded to Atlanta) and third-round (C Thatcher Bell) picks in 2000 draft to Vancouver Canucks for G Kevin Weekes, C Dave Scatchard and RW Bill Muckalt (December 19, 1999). ... Injured knee (January 23, 2000); missed five games. ... Traded by Canucks to Los Angeles Kings for future considerations (February 15, 2001).

			REGULAR SEASON									PLAYOFFS						
Season Team	League	Gms.	Min	W	L	T	GA	SO	Avg.	SV%	Gms.	Min.	W	L	GA	SO	Avg.	SV%
88-89—Chicoutimi	QMJHL	*65	*3489	25	31	1	*271	†2	4.66	—	—	—	—	—	—	—	—	—
89-90—Chicoutimi	QMJHL	*62	*3478	31	26	2	231	†2	3.99	—	—	—	—	—	—	—	—	—
90-91—Chicoutimi	QMJHL	54	3216	33	15	4	145	*6	†2.71	—	*16	*992	*11	5	46	0	*2.78	—
91-92—St. John's	AHL	35	2070	18	10	6	101	2	2.93	—	11	642	7	4	41	0	3.83	—
—Toronto	NHL	4	210	0	2	1	8	0	2.29	.933	—	—	—	—	—	—	—	—
92-93—Toronto	NHL	48	2781	25	15	7	116	2	*2.50	.910	21	1308	11	10	62	1	2.84	.903
—St. John's	AHL	5	309	3	0	2	18	0	3.50	—	—	—	—	—	—	—	—	—
93-94—Toronto	NHL	66	3883	34	22	9	187	3	2.89	.907	18	1124	9	†9	46	3	2.46	.912
94-95—Toronto	NHL	36	2144	15	13	7	104	0	2.91	.907	7	424	3	4	20	1	2.83	.921
95-96—Toronto	NHL	69	4009	30	26	11	192	2	2.87	.910	6	350	2	4	19	0	3.26	.904
96-97—Toronto	NHL	*74	*4271	27	*36	7	*224	0	3.15	.908	—	—	—	—	—	—	—	—
97-98—Toronto	NHL	67	3864	26	*33	7	176	5	2.73	.906	—	—	—	—	—	—	—	—
98-99—Toronto	NHL	5	299	3	2	0	19	0	3.81	.866	—	—	—	—	—	—	—	—
—New York Islanders	NHL	11	606	2	7	1	37	0	3.66	.893	—	—	—	—	—	—	—	—
99-00—New York Islanders	NHL	22	1273	5	14	3	68	1	3.21	.892	—	—	—	—	—	—	—	—
—Vancouver	NHL	34	1966	12	13	7	85	0	2.59	.906	—	—	—	—	—	—	—	—
00-01—Vancouver	NHL	35	2006	14	17	3	103	1	3.08	.887	—	—	—	—	—	—	—	—
—Los Angeles	NHL	23	1410	13	5	5	46	5	1.96	.919	13	812	7	6	33	2	2.44	.909
01-02—Los Angeles	NHL	71	4071	31	27	8	157	6	2.31	.907	7	417	3	4	15	1	2.16	.925
02-03—Los Angeles	NHL	42	2367	17	20	3	105	3	2.66	.894	—	—	—	—	—	—	—	—
NHL Totals (12 years)		607	35160	254	252	79	1627	28	2.78	.905	72	4435	35	37	195	8	2.64	.910

PRATT, NOLAN D LIGHTNING

PERSONAL: Born August 14, 1975, in Fort McMurray, Alta. ... 6-3/203. ... Shoots left. ... Brother of Harlan Pratt, defenseman, Carolina Hurricanes organization.

TRANSACTIONS/CAREER NOTES: Selected by Hartford Whalers in fifth round (fourth Whalers pick, 115th overall) of NHL entry draft (June 26, 1993). ... Whalers franchise moved to North Carolina and renamed Carolina Hurricanes for 1997-98 season; NHL approved move on June 25, 1997. ... Suffered back spasms (December 21, 1998); missed eight games. ... Injured hip (December 20, 1999); missed two games. ... Injured hand (April 3, 2000); missed final two games of season. ... Traded by Hurricanes with first-(C Vaclav Nedorost) and two second-round (C Jared Aulin and D Argis Saviels) picks in 2000 draft to Colorado Avalanche for D Sandis Ozolinsh and second-round pick (LW Tomas Kurka) in 2000 draft (June 24, 2000). ... Injured wrist (October 4, 2000); missed two games. ... Traded by Avalanche to Tampa Bay Lightning for sixth-round pick (RW Scott Horvath) in 2001 draft (June 24, 2001). ... Fractured foot (September 29, 2001); missed first 11 games of season. ... Fractured right leg (December 31, 2001); missed 25 games.

			REGULAR SEASON							PLAYOFFS				
Season Team	League	Gms.	G	A	Pts.	PIM	+/-	PP	SH	Gms.	G	A	Pts.	PIM
91-92—Portland	WHL	22	2	9	11	13	...	...	...	6	1	3	4	12
92-93—Portland	WHL	70	4	19	23	97	...	...	...	16	2	7	9	31
93-94—Portland	WHL	72	4	32	36	105	...	...	...	10	1	2	3	14
94-95—Portland	WHL	72	6	37	43	196	...	...	...	9	1	6	7	10
95-96—Richmond	ECHL	4	1	0	1	2	...	...	...	—	—	—	—	—
—Springfield	AHL	62	2	6	8	72	...	...	...	2	0	0	0	0
96-97—Hartford	NHL	9	0	2	2	6	0	0	0	—	—	—	—	—
—Springfield	AHL	66	1	18	19	127	...	...	...	17	0	3	3	18
97-98—New Haven	AHL	54	3	15	18	135	...	...	...	—	—	—	—	—
—Carolina	NHL	23	0	2	2	44	-2	0	0	—	—	—	—	—
98-99—Carolina	NHL	61	1	14	15	95	15	0	0	3	0	0	0	2
99-00—Carolina	NHL	64	3	1	4	90	-22	0	0	—	—	—	—	—
00-01—Colorado	NHL	46	1	2	3	40	2	0	0	—	—	—	—	—
01-02—Tampa Bay	NHL	46	0	3	3	51	4	0	0	—	—	—	—	—
02-03—Tampa Bay	NHL	67	1	7	8	35	-6	0	0	4	0	1	1	0
NHL Totals (7 years)		316	6	31	37	361	-17	0	0	7	0	1	1	2

PRIMEAU, KEITH C FLYERS

PERSONAL: Born November 24, 1971, in Toronto ... 6-5/220. ... Shoots left. ... Brother of Wayne Primeau, center, Pittsburgh Penguins. ... Name pronounced PREE-moh.

TRANSACTIONS/CAREER NOTES: Selected by Detroit Red Wings in first round (first Red Wings pick, third overall) of NHL entry draft (June 16, 1990). ... Suffered from the flu (January 13, 1993); missed two games. ... Sprained right shoulder (February 9, 1993); missed one game. ... Sprained right knee (March 2, 1993); missed two games. ... Sprained right knee (April 1, 1993); missed four games. ... Injured right thumb (February 10, 1995); missed one game. ... Suffered from the flu (February 25, 1995); missed one game. ... Reinjured thumb (March 2, 1995); missed one game. ... Injured ribs (November 1, 1995); missed eight games. ... Injured left knee (January 13, 1996); missed one game. ... Traded by Red Wings with D Paul Coffey and first-round pick (traded to San Jose) in 1997 draft to Hartford Whalers for LW Brendan Shanahan and D Brian Glynn (October 9, 1996). ... Suffered from the flu (December 3, 1996); missed one game. ... Suffered concussion (December 21, 1996); missed one game. ... Suspended two games by NHL for slashing incident (January 3, 1997). ... Suffered from asthma (February 12, 1997); missed one game. ... Whalers franchise moved to North Carolina and renamed Carolina Hurricanes for 1997-98 season; NHL approved move on June 25, 1997. ... Strained hip flexor (November 13, 1997); missed one game. ... Injured wrist (February 13, 1999); missed one game. ... Strained lower back (April 10, 1999); missed three games. ... Missed first 47 games of 1999-2000 season due to contract dispute. ... Rights traded to Hurricanes with fifth-round pick (traded to New York Islanders) in 2000 draft to Philadelphia Flyers for C Rod Brind'Amour, G Jean-Marc Pelletier and second-round pick (traded to Colorado) in 2000 draft (January 23, 2000). ... Fractured rib (February 12, 2000); missed nine games. ... Reinjured ribs (March 4, 2000); missed three games. ... Suffered headaches (October 29, 2000); missed two games. ... Bruised shoulder (December 27, 2000); missed three games. ... Sprained medial collateral ligament in left knee (March 26, 2001); missed final six games of regular season and two playoff games. ... Sprained right ankle (October 13, 2001); missed three games. ... Strained muscle in ribs (March 4, 2002); missed two games. ... Reinjured ribs (March 18, 2002); missed two games.

STATISTICAL PLATEAUS: Three-goal games: 2000-01 (1).

			REGULAR SEASON							PLAYOFFS				
Season Team	League	Gms.	G	A	Pts.	PIM	+/-	PP	SH	Gms.	G	A	Pts.	PIM
87-88—Hamilton	OHL	47	6	6	12	69	...	...	...	11	0	2	2	2
88-89—Niagara Falls	OHL	48	20	35	55	56	...	...	...	17	9	6	15	12
89-90—Niagara Falls	OHL	65	*57	70	*127	97	...	...	...	16	*16	17	*33	49
90-91—Detroit	NHL	58	3	12	15	106	-12	0	0	5	1	1	2	25
—Adirondack	AHL	6	3	5	8	8	...	...	...	—	—	—	—	—
91-92—Detroit	NHL	35	6	10	16	83	9	0	0	11	0	0	0	14
—Adirondack	AHL	42	21	24	45	89	...	...	...	9	1	7	8	27
92-93—Detroit	NHL	73	15	17	32	152	-6	4	1	7	0	2	2	26
93-94—Detroit	NHL	78	31	42	73	173	34	7	3	7	0	2	2	6
94-95—Detroit	NHL	45	15	27	42	99	17	1	0	17	4	5	9	45
95-96—Detroit	NHL	74	27	25	52	168	19	6	2	17	1	4	5	28
96-97—Hartford	NHL	75	26	25	51	161	-3	6	3	—	—	—	—	—
97-98—Carolina	NHL	81	26	37	63	110	19	7	3	—	—	—	—	—
—Can. Olympic team	Int'l	6	2	1	3	4	...	...	...	—	—	—	—	—
98-99—Carolina	NHL	78	30	32	62	75	8	9	1	6	0	3	3	6
99-00—Philadelphia	NHL	23	7	10	17	31	10	1	0	18	2	11	13	13
00-01—Philadelphia	NHL	71	34	39	73	76	17	11	0	4	0	3	3	8
01-02—Philadelphia	NHL	75	19	29	48	128	-3	5	0	5	0	0	0	6
02-03—Philadelphia	NHL	80	19	27	46	93	4	6	0	13	1	1	2	14
NHL Totals (13 years)		846	258	332	590	1455	113	63	13	110	9	32	41	191

PRIMEAU, WAYNE   C   SHARKS

PERSONAL: Born June 4, 1976, in Scarborough, Ont. ... 6-3/220. ... Shoots left. ... Brother of Keith Primeau, center, Philadelphia Flyers. ... Name pronounced PREE-moh.

TRANSACTIONS/CAREER NOTES: Selected by Buffalo Sabres in first round (first Sabres pick, 17th overall) of NHL entry draft (June 28, 1994). ... Bruised shoulder (November 4, 1998); missed four games. ... Reinjured shoulder (December 5, 1998); missed four games. ... Reinjured shoulder (January 11, 1999); missed one game. ... Strained groin (March 7, 1999); missed one game. ... Injured hip (January 1, 2000); missed 20 games. ... Traded by Sabres with C/RW Brian Holzinger, D Cory Sarich and third-round pick (RW Alexandre Kharitonov) in 2000 draft to Tampa Bay Lightning for C Chris Gratton and second-round pick (C Derek Roy) in 2001 draft (March 9, 2000). ... Suspended by NHL two games for slashing incident (January 23, 2001). ... Traded by Lightning to Pittsburgh Penguins for LW Matthew Barnaby (February 1, 2001). ... Injured neck (Feburary 14, 2001); missed one game. ... Suffered injury (March 14, 2001); missed one game. ... Injured heel prior to start of 2001-02 season; missed first eight games of season. ... Underwent knee surgery (January 6, 2002); missed remainder of season. ... Traded by Penguins to San Jose Sharks for RW Matt Bradley (March 11, 2003).

			REGULAR SEASON							PLAYOFFS				
Season Team	League	Gms.	G	A	Pts.	PIM	+/-	PP	SH	Gms.	G	A	Pts.	PIM
92-93—Owen Sound	OHL	66	10	27	37	110	...	...	...	8	1	4	5	0
93-94—Owen Sound	OHL	65	25	50	75	75	...	...	...	9	1	6	7	8
94-95—Owen Sound	OHL	66	34	62	96	84	...	...	...	10	4	9	13	15
—Buffalo	NHL	1	1	0	1	0	-2	0	0	—	—	—	—	—
95-96—Buffalo	NHL	2	0	0	0	0	0	0	0	—	—	—	—	—
—Owen Sound	OHL	28	15	29	44	52	...	...	...	—	—	—	—	—
—Oshawa	OHL	24	12	13	25	33	...	...	...	3	2	3	5	2
—Rochester	AHL	8	2	3	5	6	...	...	...	17	3	1	4	11
96-97—Rochester	AHL	24	9	5	14	27	...	...	...	1	0	0	0	0
—Buffalo	NHL	45	2	4	6	64	-2	1	0	9	0	0	0	6
97-98—Buffalo	NHL	69	6	6	12	87	9	2	0	14	1	3	4	6
98-99—Buffalo	NHL	67	5	8	13	38	-6	0	0	19	3	4	7	6
99-00—Buffalo	NHL	41	5	7	12	38	-8	2	0	—	—	—	—	—
—Tampa Bay	NHL	17	2	3	5	25	-4	0	0	—	—	—	—	—
00-01—Tampa Bay	NHL	47	2	13	15	77	-17	0	0	—	—	—	—	—
—Pittsburgh	NHL	28	1	6	7	54	0	0	0	18	1	3	4	2
01-02—Pittsburgh	NHL	33	3	7	10	18	-1	0	1	—	—	—	—	—
02-03—Pittsburgh	NHL	70	5	11	16	55	-30	1	0	—	—	—	—	—
—San Jose	NHL	7	1	1	2	0	2	0	0	—	—	—	—	—
NHL Totals (9 years)		427	33	66	99	456	-59	6	1	60	5	10	15	20

PRONGER, CHRIS   D   BLUES

PERSONAL: Born October 10, 1974, in Dryden, Ont. ... 6-6/206. ... Shoots left. ... Full Name: Christopher Robert Pronger. ... Brother of Sean Pronger, center, Columbus Blue Jackets.

TRANSACTIONS/CAREER NOTES: Selected by Hartford Whalers in first round (first Whalers pick, second overall) of NHL entry draft (June 26, 1993). ... Bruised left wrist (March 29, 1994); missed three games. ... Injured left shoulder (January 21, 1995); missed five games. ... Traded by Whalers to St. Louis Blues for LW Brendan Shanahan (July 27, 1995). ... Suspended four games by NHL for slashing incident (November 1, 1995). ... Injured hand (February 15, 1997); missed one game. ... Suspended four games by NHL for slashing incident (December 19, 1998). ... Bruised ankle (February 11, 1999); missed 11 games. ... Suffered back spasms (March 12, 2000); missed one game. ... Suspended one game by NHL for fighting incident (October 13, 2000). ... Underwent knee surgery (January 21, 2001); missed 15 games. ... Fractured forearm (February 26, 2001); missed 15 games. ... Injured wrist (November 13, 2001); missed one game. ... Suspended two games by NHL for cross-checking incident (April 4, 2002).

Season Team	League	REGULAR SEASON								PLAYOFFS				
		Gms.	G	A	Pts.	PIM	+/-	PP	SH	Gms.	G	A	Pts.	PIM
90-91—Stratford	OPJHL	48	15	37	52	132	...	...	...	—	—	—	—	—
91-92—Peterborough	OHL	63	17	45	62	90	...	...	...	10	1	8	9	28
92-93—Peterborough	OHL	61	15	62	77	108	...	...	...	21	15	25	40	51
93-94—Hartford	NHL	81	5	25	30	113	-3	2	0	—	—	—	—	—
94-95—Hartford	NHL	43	5	9	14	54	-12	3	0	—	—	—	—	—
95-96—St. Louis	NHL	78	7	18	25	110	-18	3	1	13	1	5	6	16
96-97—St. Louis	NHL	79	11	24	35	143	15	4	0	6	1	1	2	22
97-98—St. Louis	NHL	81	9	27	36	180	*47	1	0	10	1	9	10	26
—Can. Olympic team	Int'l	6	0	0	0	4	...	...	...	—	—	—	—	—
98-99—St. Louis	NHL	67	13	33	46	113	3	8	0	13	1	4	5	28
99-00—St. Louis	NHL	79	14	48	62	92	*52	8	0	7	3	4	7	32
00-01—St. Louis	NHL	51	8	39	47	75	21	4	0	15	1	7	8	32
01-02—St. Louis	NHL	78	7	40	47	120	23	4	1	9	1	7	8	24
—Can. Olympic team	Int'l	6	0	1	1	2	...	...	...	—	—	—	—	—
02-03—St. Louis	NHL	5	1	3	4	10	-2	0	0	7	1	3	4	14
NHL Totals (10 years)		642	80	266	346	1010	126	37	2	80	10	40	50	194

PRONGER, SEAN — C — BLUE JACKETS

PERSONAL: Born November 30, 1972, in Dryden, Ont. ... 6-3/209. ... Shoots left. ... Full Name: Sean James Pronger. ... Brother of Chris Pronger, defenseman, St. Louis Blues.

TRANSACTIONS/CAREER NOTES: Selected by Vancouver Canucks in third round (third Canucks pick, 51st overall) of NHL entry draft (June 22, 1991). ... Signed as free agent by Mighty Ducks of Anaheim (February 14, 1995). ... Strained abdominal muscle (February 17, 1997); missed two games. ... Traded by Mighty Ducks to Pittsburgh Penguins for rights to G Patrick Lalime (March 24, 1998). ... Fractured foot (April 4, 1998); missed seven games. ... Traded by Penguins with C Petr Nedved and D Chris Tamer to New York Rangers for RW Alexei Kovalev, C Harry York and future considerations (November 25, 1998). ... Traded by Rangers to Los Angeles Kings for LW Eric Lacroix (February 12, 1999). ... Tore medial collateral ligament in left knee (March 18, 1999); missed final 14 games of season. ... Signed as free agent by Boston Bruins (August 25, 1999). ... Claimed on waivers by Columbus Blue Jackets (May 18, 2001).

Season Team	League	REGULAR SEASON								PLAYOFFS				
		Gms.	G	A	Pts.	PIM	+/-	PP	SH	Gms.	G	A	Pts.	PIM
89-90—Thunder Bay Flyers	USHL	48	18	34	52	61	...	...	...	—	—	—	—	—
90-91—Bowling Green	CCHA	40	3	7	10	30	...	...	...	—	—	—	—	—
91-92—Bowling Green	CCHA	34	9	7	16	28	...	...	...	—	—	—	—	—
92-93—Bowling Green	CCHA	39	23	23	46	35	...	...	...	—	—	—	—	—
93-94—Bowling Green	CCHA	38	17	17	34	38	...	...	...	—	—	—	—	—
94-95—Knoxville	ECHL	34	18	23	41	55	...	...	...	—	—	—	—	—
—Greensboro	ECHL	2	0	2	2	0	...	...	...	—	—	—	—	—
—San Diego	IHL	8	0	0	0	2	...	...	...	—	—	—	—	—
95-96—Baltimore	AHL	72	16	17	33	61	...	...	...	12	3	7	10	16
—Anaheim	NHL	7	0	1	1	6	0	0	0	—	—	—	—	—
96-97—Baltimore	AHL	41	26	17	43	17	...	...	...	—	—	—	—	—
—Anaheim	NHL	39	7	7	14	20	6	1	0	9	0	2	2	4
97-98—Anaheim	NHL	62	5	15	20	30	-9	1	0	—	—	—	—	—
—Pittsburgh	NHL	5	1	0	1	2	-1	0	0	5	0	0	0	4
98-99—Houston	IHL	16	11	7	18	32	...	...	...	—	—	—	—	—
—Pittsburgh	NHL	2	0	0	0	0	0	0	0	—	—	—	—	—
—New York Rangers	NHL	14	0	3	3	4	-3	0	0	—	—	—	—	—
—Los Angeles	NHL	13	0	1	1	4	2	0	0	—	—	—	—	—
99-00—Providence	AHL	51	11	18	29	26	...	...	...	—	—	—	—	—
—Boston	NHL	11	0	1	1	13	-4	0	0	—	—	—	—	—
—Manitoba	IHL	14	3	5	8	21	...	...	...	2	0	1	1	2
00-01—Manitoba	IHL	82	18	21	39	85	...	...	...	13	3	6	9	2
01-02—Syracuse	AHL	54	23	26	49	53	...	...	...	8	4	1	5	10
—Columbus	NHL	26	3	1	4	4	-4	0	0	—	—	—	—	—
02-03—Columbus	NHL	78	7	6	13	72	-26	1	0	—	—	—	—	—
NHL Totals (7 years)		257	23	35	58	155	-39	3	0	14	0	2	2	8

PROSPAL, VACLAV — LW — MIGHTY DUCKS

PERSONAL: Born February 17, 1975, in Ceske-Budejovice, Czechoslovakia ... 6-2/194. ... Shoots left. ... Name pronounced PRAHS-puhl.

TRANSACTIONS/CAREER NOTES: Selected by Philadelphia Flyers in third round (second Flyers pick, 71st overall) of NHL entry draft (June 26, 1993). ... Fractured left fibula (January 3, 1998); missed 18 games. ... Traded by Flyers with RW Pat Falloon and second round draft pick (LW Chris Bala) in 1998 draft to Ottawa Senators for RW Alexandre Daigle (January 17, 1998). ... Bruised thumb (April 2, 1998); missed two games. ... Bruised mouth (April 7, 1998); missed four games. ... Suffered from the flu (November 29, 1998); missed one game. ... Traded by Senators to Florida Panthers for fourth-round pick (G Ray Emery) in 2001 draft and third-round pick (traded back to Ottawa) in 2002 draft (January 21, 2001). ... Traded by Panthers to Tampa Bay Lightning for C Ryan Johnson and sixth-round pick in 2003 draft (July 10, 2001). ... Suffered from the flu (December 26, 2001); missed one game. ... Suspended two games by NHL for cross-checking incident (January 21, 2003). ... Signed by Anaheim Mighty Ducks (July 17, 2003).

Season Team	League	REGULAR SEASON								PLAYOFFS				
		Gms.	G	A	Pts.	PIM	+/-	PP	SH	Gms.	G	A	Pts.	PIM
91-92—Motor-Ceske Bude.	Czech. Jrs.	36	16	16	32	12	...	...	...	—	—	—	—	—
92-93—Motor-Ceske Bude.	Czech. Jrs.	36	26	31	57	24	...	...	...	—	—	—	—	—
93-94—Hershey	AHL	55	14	21	35	38	...	...	...	2	0	0	0	2
94-95—Hershey	AHL	69	13	32	45	36	...	...	...	2	1	0	1	4
95-96—Hershey	AHL	68	15	36	51	59	...	...	...	5	2	4	6	2
96-97—Philadelphia	AHL	63	32	63	95	70	...	...	...	—	—	—	—	—
—Philadelphia	NHL	18	5	10	15	4	3	0	0	5	1	3	4	4

Season Team	League	REGULAR SEASON									PLAYOFFS				
		Gms.	G	A	Pts.	PIM	+/-	PP	SH		Gms.	G	A	Pts.	PIM
97-98—Philadelphia	NHL	41	5	13	18	17	-10	4	0		—	—	—	—	—
—Ottawa	NHL	15	1	6	7	4	-1	0	0		6	0	0	0	0
98-99—Ottawa	NHL	79	10	26	36	58	8	2	0		4	0	0	0	0
99-00—Ottawa	NHL	79	22	33	55	40	-2	5	0		6	0	4	4	4
00-01—Ottawa	NHL	40	1	12	13	12	1	0	0		—	—	—	—	—
—Florida......................	NHL	34	4	12	16	10	-2	1	0		—	—	—	—	—
01-02—Tampa Bay	NHL	81	18	37	55	38	-11	7	0		—	—	—	—	—
02-03—Tampa Bay	NHL	80	22	57	79	53	9	9	0		11	4	2	6	8
NHL Totals (7 years)..........		467	88	206	294	236	-5	28	0		32	5	9	14	16

PRUSEK, MARTIN   G   SENATORS

PERSONAL: Born December 11, 1975, in Ostrava, Czechoslovakia ... 6-1/186. ... Catches right.
TRANSACTIONS/CAREER NOTES: Selected by Ottawa Senators in sixth round (sixth Senators pick, 164th overall) of NHL entry draft (June 26, 1999). ... Signed by Senators (July 15, 2003).

Season Team	League	REGULAR SEASON									PLAYOFFS							
		Gms.	Min	W	L	T	GA	SO	Avg.	SV%		Gms.	Min.	W	L	GA	SO	Avg.	SV%
94-95—HC Vitkovice.................	Czech Rep.	4	232	...	...	...	18	...	4.66	—		—	—	...	...	—	—	—	—
95-96—HC Vitkovice.................	Czech Rep.	40	...	...	...	...	114	1	...	—		4	...	...	...	10	...	...	—
96-97—HC Vitkovice.................	Czech Rep.	49	...	...	...	...	109	8	...	—		9	...	...	...	19	1	...	—
97-98—HC Vitkovice.................	Czech Rep.	50	...	...	...	...	129	...	...	—		9	...	...	...	26	...	...	—
98-99—HC Vitkovice.................	Czech Rep.	37	1905	...	...	...	85	...	2.68	—		4	250	...	...	12	...	2.88	—
99-00—HC Vitkovice.................	Czech Rep.	50	2647	...	...	...	132	...	2.99	—		—	—	—	—	—	—	—	—
00-01—HC Vitkovice.................	Czech Rep.	30	1679	...	...	...	64	...	2.29	—		9	460	...	...	25	...	3.26	—
01-02—Grand Rapids................	AHL	33	1903	18	8	5	58	4	*1.83	—		5	277	2	3	10	0	2.17	—
—Ottawa......................	NHL	1	62	0	1	0	3	0	2.90	.800		—	—	—	—	—	—	—	—
02-03—Binghamton	AHL	4	242	1	2	1	7	1	1.74	—		—	—	—	—	—	—	—	—
—Ottawa......................	NHL	18	935	12	2	1	37	0	2.37	.911		—	—	—	—	—	—	—	—
NHL Totals (2 years).............		19	997	12	3	1	40	0	2.41	.907									

PUDLICK, MIKE   D

PERSONAL: Born February 24, 1978, in Fridley, Minn. ... 6-3/192. ... Shoots left.
COLLEGE: St. Cloud State.
TRANSACTIONS/CAREER NOTES: Signed as non-drafted free agent by Los Angeles Kings (April 1, 2000).

Season Team	League	REGULAR SEASON									PLAYOFFS				
		Gms.	G	A	Pts.	PIM	+/-	PP	SH		Gms.	G	A	Pts.	PIM
98-99—St. Cloud State............	WCHA	37	13	12	25	74	...	...	...		—	—	—	—	—
99-00—St. Cloud State............	WCHA	39	7	22	29	65	...	...	...		—	—	—	—	—
00-01—Lowell	AHL	57	7	13	20	39	...	...	...		4	0	1	1	2
01-02—Manchester.................	AHL	64	9	6	15	42	...	...	...		3	0	0	0	6
02-03—Manchester.................	AHL	68	7	17	24	52	...	...	...		—	—	—	—	—

PURINTON, DALE   D   RANGERS

PERSONAL: Born October 11, 1976, in Fort Wayne, Ind. ... 6-2/229. ... Shoots left.
TRANSACTIONS/CAREER NOTES: Selected by New York Rangers in fifth round (fourth Ranger pick, 117th overall) of NHL entry draft (July 8, 1995). ... Injured ribs (December 15, 2000); missed five games. ... Injured arm (January 16, 2001); missed four games. ... Suspended seven games by NHL for cross-checking incident (October 12, 2001). ... Bruised wrist (November 17, 2001); missed two games. ... Suspended three games by NHL for fighting incident (February 5, 2002). ... Strained muscle in ribs (January 3, 2002); missed two games.

Season Team	League	REGULAR SEASON									PLAYOFFS				
		Gms.	G	A	Pts.	PIM	+/-	PP	SH		Gms.	G	A	Pts.	PIM
93-94—Vernon	Tier II Jr. A	42	1	6	7	194	...	...	...		—	—	—	—	—
94-95—Tacoma	WHL	65	0	8	8	291	...	...	...		3	0	0	0	13
95-96—Kelowna	WHL	22	1	4	5	88	...	...	...		—	—	—	—	—
—Lethbridge	WHL	37	3	6	9	144	...	...	...		4	1	1	2	25
96-97—Lethbridge	WHL	51	6	26	32	254	...	...	...		18	3	5	8	*88
97-98—Charlotte	ECHL	34	3	5	8	186	...	...	...		—	—	—	—	—
—Hartford	AHL	17	0	0	0	95	...	...	...		—	—	—	—	—
98-99—Hartford	AHL	45	1	3	4	306	...	...	...		7	0	2	2	24
99-00—Hartford	AHL	62	4	4	8	415	...	...	...		23	0	3	3	*87
—New York Rangers......	NHL	1	0	0	0	7	-1	0	0		—	—	—	—	—
00-01—Hartford	AHL	11	0	1	1	75	...	...	...		—	—	—	—	—
—New York Rangers......	NHL	42	0	2	2	180	5	0	0		—	—	—	—	—
01-02—New York Rangers......	NHL	40	0	4	4	113	4	0	0		—	—	—	—	—
02-03—New York Rangers......	NHL	58	3	9	12	161	-2	0	0		—	—	—	—	—
NHL Totals (4 years)..........		141	3	15	18	461	6	0	0		—	—	—	—	—

PUSHOR, JAMIE   D

PERSONAL: Born February 11, 1973, in Lethbridge, Alta. ... 6-4/223. ... Shoots right. ... Full Name: James Pushor. ... Name pronounced PUSH-uhr.
TRANSACTIONS/CAREER NOTES: Selected by Detroit Red Wings in second round (second Wings pick, 32nd overall) of NHL entry draft (June 22, 1991). ... Strained groin (November 21, 1997); missed three games. ... Traded by Red Wings with fourth-round pick (C Viktor Wallin) in 1998 draft to Mighty Ducks of Anaheim for D Dmitri Mironov (March 24, 1998). ... Fractured right finger (April 15, 1998); missed remainder of season. ... Suffered eye injury (January 6, 1999); missed two games. ... Bruised left shoulder and chest (February 14, 1999); missed four

games. ... Selected by Atlanta Thrashers in NHL expansion draft (June 25, 1999). ... Traded by Thrashers to Dallas Stars for LW Jason Botterill (July 15, 1999). ... Selected by Columbus Blue Jackets in NHL expansion draft (June 23, 2000). ... Sprained knee (March 26, 2001); missed seven games. ... Traded by Blue Jackets to Pittsburgh Penguins for fourth-round pick in 2003 draft (March 15, 2002).

			REGULAR SEASON							PLAYOFFS				
Season Team	League	Gms.	G	A	Pts.	PIM	+/-	PP	SH	Gms.	G	A	Pts.	PIM
88-89—Lethbridge	WHL	2	0	0	0	0	...	...	...	—	—	—	—	—
89-90—Lethbridge	WHL	10	0	2	2	2	...	...	...	—	—	—	—	—
90-91—Lethbridge	WHL	71	1	13	14	193	...	...	...	—	—	—	—	—
91-92—Lethbridge	WHL	49	2	15	17	232	...	...	...	5	0	0	0	33
92-93—Lethbridge	WHL	72	6	22	28	200	...	...	...	4	0	1	1	9
93-94—Adirondack	AHL	73	1	17	18	124	...	...	...	12	0	0	0	22
94-95—Adirondack	AHL	58	2	11	13	129	...	...	...	4	0	1	1	0
95-96—Detroit	NHL	5	0	1	1	17	2	0	0	—	—	—	—	—
—Adirondack	AHL	65	2	16	18	126	...	...	...	3	0	0	0	5
96-97—Detroit	NHL	75	4	7	11	129	1	0	0	5	0	1	1	5
97-98—Detroit	NHL	54	2	5	7	71	2	0	0	—	—	—	—	—
—Anaheim	NHL	10	0	2	2	10	1	0	0	—	—	—	—	—
98-99—Anaheim	NHL	70	1	2	3	112	-20	0	0	4	0	0	0	6
99-00—Dallas	NHL	62	0	8	8	53	0	0	0	5	0	0	0	5
00-01—Columbus	NHL	75	3	10	13	94	7	0	1	—	—	—	—	—
01-02—Columbus	NHL	61	0	6	6	54	-10	0	0	—	—	—	—	—
—Pittsburgh	NHL	15	0	2	2	30	-3	0	0	—	—	—	—	—
02-03—Pittsburgh	NHL	76	3	1	4	76	-28	0	0	—	—	—	—	—
NHL Totals (8 years)		503	13	44	57	646	-48	0	1	14	0	1	1	16

PYATT, TAYLOR   LW   SABRES

PERSONAL: Born August 19, 1981, in Thunder Bay, Ont. ... 6-4/225. ... Shoots left. ... Son of Nelson Pyatt, center/left winger with three NHL teams (1973-74 through 1979-80).
TRANSACTIONS/CAREER NOTES: Selected by New York Islanders in first round (second Islanders pick, eighth overall) of NHL entry draft (June 26, 1999). ... Traded by Islanders with C Tim Connolly to Buffalo Sabres for C Michael Peca (June 24, 2001).
STATISTICAL PLATEAUS: Three-goal games: 2002-03 (1).

			REGULAR SEASON							PLAYOFFS				
Season Team	League	Gms.	G	A	Pts.	PIM	+/-	PP	SH	Gms.	G	A	Pts.	PIM
97-98—Sudbury	OHL	58	14	17	31	104	...	...	...	10	3	1	4	6
98-99—Sudbury	OHL	68	37	38	75	95	...	...	...	4	0	4	4	6
99-00—Sudbury	OHL	68	40	49	89	98	...	...	...	12	8	7	15	25
00-01—New York Islanders	NHL	78	4	14	18	39	-17	1	0	—	—	—	—	—
01-02—Rochester	AHL	27	6	4	10	36	...	...	...	—	—	—	—	—
—Buffalo	NHL	48	10	10	20	35	4	0	0	—	—	—	—	—
02-03—Buffalo	NHL	78	14	14	28	38	-8	2	0	—	—	—	—	—
NHL Totals (3 years)		204	28	38	66	112	-21	3	0					

QUINT, DERON   D   COYOTES

PERSONAL: Born March 12, 1976, in Durham, N.H. ... 6-2/209. ... Shoots left.
TRANSACTIONS/CAREER NOTES: Selected by Winnipeg Jets in second round (first Jets pick, 30th overall) of NHL entry draft (June 28, 1994). ... Suffered from the flu (January 29, 1996); missed two games. ... Jets franchise moved to Phoenix and renamed Coyotes for 1996-97 season; NHL approved move on January 18, 1996. ... Separated shoulder (November 27, 1997); missed six games. ... Suffered concussion (January 30, 1998); missed one game. ... Underwent hernia surgery (March 8, 1998); missed 11 games. ... Suffered concussion (October 6, 1998); missed first nine games of season. ... Separated shoulder (January 31, 1999); missed three games. ... Suffered concussion (March 30, 1999); missed final seven games of season. ... Traded by Coyotes with third-round pick (traded back to Phoenix) in 2001 draft to New Jersey Devils for D Lyle Odelein (March 7, 2000). ... Traded by Devils to Columbus Blue Jackets for past considerations (June 25, 2000). ... Suffered from the flu (January 3, 2001); missed one game. ... Bruised thigh (February 8, 2002); missed one game.
STATISTICAL PLATEAUS: Three-goal games: 2000-01 (1).

			REGULAR SEASON							PLAYOFFS				
Season Team	League	Gms.	G	A	Pts.	PIM	+/-	PP	SH	Gms.	G	A	Pts.	PIM
90-91—Cardigan Prep School.	USHS (East)	31	67	54	121		...	...	...	—	—	—	—	—
91-92—Cardigan Prep School.	USHS (East)	32	111	68	179		...	...	...	—	—	—	—	—
92-93—Tabor Academy	Mass. H.S.	28	15	26	41	30	...	...	...	1	0	2	2	0
93-94—Seattle	WHL	63	15	29	44	47	...	...	...	9	4	12	16	8
94-95—Seattle	WHL	65	29	60	89	82	...	...	...	3	1	2	3	6
95-96—Winnipeg	NHL	51	5	13	18	22	-2	2	0	—	—	—	—	—
—Springfield	AHL	11	2	3	5	4	...	...	...	10	2	3	5	6
—Seattle	WHL	—	—	—	—	—	...	...	...	5	4	1	5	6
96-97—Springfield	AHL	43	6	18	24	20	...	...	...	12	2	7	9	4
—Phoenix	NHL	27	3	11	14	4	-4	1	0	7	0	2	2	0
97-98—Phoenix	NHL	32	4	7	11	16	-6	1	0	—	—	—	—	—
—Springfield	AHL	8	1	7	8	10	...	...	...	1	0	0	0	0
98-99—Phoenix	NHL	60	5	8	13	20	-10	2	0	—	—	—	—	—
99-00—Phoenix	NHL	50	3	7	10	22	0	0	0	—	—	—	—	—
—New Jersey	NHL	4	1	0	1	2	-2	0	0	—	—	—	—	—
00-01—Syracuse	AHL	21	5	15	20	30	...	...	...	—	—	—	—	—
—Columbus	NHL	57	7	16	23	16	-19	3	0	—	—	—	—	—
01-02—Columbus	NHL	75	7	18	25	26	-34	3	0	—	—	—	—	—
02-03—Springfield	AHL	4	1	2	3	4	...	...	...	—	—	—	—	—
—Phoenix	NHL	51	7	10	17	20	-5	2	0	—	—	—	—	—
NHL Totals (8 years)		407	42	90	132	148	-82	14	0	7	0	2	2	0

P
Q

QUINTAL, STEPHANE   D   CANADIENS

PERSONAL: Born October 22, 1968, in Boucherville, Que. ... 6-3/231. ... Shoots right. ... Name pronounced steh-FAN kahn-TAHL.

TRANSACTIONS/CAREER NOTES: Selected by Boston Bruins in first round (second Bruins pick, 14th overall) of NHL entry draft (June 13, 1987). ... Fractured bone near eye (October 1988). ... Injured knee (January 1989). ... Sprained right knee (October 17, 1989); missed eight games. ... Fractured left ankle (April 9, 1991); missed remainder of playoffs. ... Traded by Bruins with C Craig Janney to St. Louis Blues for C Adam Oates (February 7, 1992). ... Traded by Blues with RW Nelson Emerson to Winnipeg Jets for D Phil Housley (September 24, 1993). ... Sprained wrist (January 16, 1994); missed two games. ... Sprained neck (April 6, 1994); missed one game. ... Sprained ankle (February 6, 1995); missed five games. ... Traded by Jets to Montreal Canadiens for second-round pick (D Jason Doig) in 1995 draft (July 8, 1995). ... Suffered concussion (November 11, 1995); missed one game. ... Sprained right Knee (February 7, 1996); missed seven games. ... Underwent knee surgery (March 19, 1996); missed five games. ... Bruised foot (December 21, 1996); missed two games. ... Injured collarbone (January 1, 1997); missed five games. ... Sprained left knee (February 6, 1997); missed seven games. ... Suffered concussion (November 8, 1997); missed one game. ... Strained hip flexor (February 7, 1998); missed one game. ... Sprained ankle (April 1, 1998); missed nine games. ... Signed as free agent by New York Rangers (July 6, 1999). ... Suffered concussion (November 24, 1999); missed one game. ... Suffered neck spasms (January 4, 2000); missed one game. ... Claimed on waivers by Chicago Blackhawks (October 5, 2000). ... Strained groin (January 21, 2001); missed two games. ... Suffered sinus infection (April 4, 2001); missed three games. ... Traded by Blackhawks to Canadiens for fourth-round pick (D Brent MacLellan) in 2001 draft (June 23, 2001). ... Separated shoulder (November 3, 2001); missed three games. ... Injured jaw (December 8, 2001); missed one game.

					REGULAR SEASON							PLAYOFFS			
Season Team	League	Gms.	G	A	Pts.	PIM	+/-	PP	SH		Gms.	G	A	Pts.	PIM
85-86—Granby	QMJHL	67	2	17	19	144	...	...	...		—	—	—	—	—
86-87—Granby	QMJHL	67	13	41	54	178	...	...	...		8	0	9	9	10
87-88—Hull	QMJHL	38	13	23	36	138	...	...	...		19	7	12	19	30
88-89—Maine	AHL	16	4	10	14	28	...	...	...		—	—	—	—	—
—Boston	NHL	26	0	1	1	29	-5	0	0		—	—	—	—	—
89-90—Boston	NHL	38	2	2	4	22	-11	0	0		—	—	—	—	—
—Maine	AHL	37	4	16	20	27	...				—	—	—	—	—
90-91—Maine	AHL	23	1	5	6	30	...				—	—	—	—	—
—Boston	NHL	45	2	6	8	89	2	1	0		3	0	1	1	7
91-92—Boston	NHL	49	4	10	14	77	-8	0	0		—	—	—	—	—
—St. Louis	NHL	26	0	6	6	32	-3	0	0		4	1	2	3	6
92-93—St. Louis	NHL	75	1	10	11	100	-6	0	1		9	0	0	0	8
93-94—Winnipeg	NHL	81	8	18	26	119	-25	1	1		—	—	—	—	—
94-95—Winnipeg	NHL	43	6	17	23	78	0	3	0		—	—	—	—	—
95-96—Montreal	NHL	68	2	14	16	117	-4	0	1		6	0	1	1	6
96-97—Montreal	NHL	71	7	15	22	100	1	1	0		5	0	1	1	6
97-98—Montreal	NHL	71	6	10	16	97	13	0	0		9	0	2	2	4
98-99—Montreal	NHL	82	8	19	27	84	-23	1	1		—	—	—	—	—
99-00—New York Rangers	NHL	75	2	14	16	77	-10	0	0		—	—	—	—	—
00-01—Chicago	NHL	72	1	18	19	60	-9	0	0		—	—	—	—	—
01-02—Montreal	NHL	75	6	10	16	87	-7	1	0		12	1	3	4	12
02-03—Montreal	NHL	67	5	5	10	70	-4	0	0		—	—	—	—	—
NHL Totals (15 years)		964	60	175	235	1238	-99	8	4		48	2	10	12	49

RACHUNEK, KAREL   D   SENATORS

PERSONAL: Born August 27, 1979, in Gottwaldov, Czechoslovakia ... 6-2/211. ... Shoots right.

TRANSACTIONS/CAREER NOTES: Selected by Ottawa Senators in ninth round (eighth Senators pick, 229th overall) of NHL entry draft (June 21, 1997). ... Suffered partially torn medial collateral ligament in right knee (November 17, 1999); missed 12 games. ... Sprained medial collateral ligament in left knee (November 25, 2000); missed seven games. ... Bruised left knee (April 1, 2001); missed one game. ... Injured back (October 3, 2001); missed first two games of season. ... Injured left shoulder (December 8, 2001); missed seven games. ... Underwent surgery on left shoulder (March 7, 2002); missed remainder of season.

					REGULAR SEASON							PLAYOFFS			
Season Team	League	Gms.	G	A	Pts.	PIM	+/-	PP	SH		Gms.	G	A	Pts.	PIM
95-96—ZPS Zlin	Czech. Jrs.	38	8	11	19	...	...	...	...		—	—	—	—	—
96-97—ZPS Zlin	Czech. Jrs.	27	2	11	13	...	...	...	...		—	—	—	—	—
97-98—ZPS Zlin	Czech. Rep.	27	1	2	3	16	...	...	...		—	—	—	—	—
98-99—ZPS Zlin	Czech. Rep.	39	3	9	12	88	...	...	...		6	0	0	0	...
99-00—Grand Rapids	IHL	62	6	20	26	64	...	...	...		9	0	5	5	6
—Ottawa	NHL	6	0	0	0	2	0	0	0		—	—	—	—	—
00-01—Ottawa	NHL	71	3	30	33	60	17	3	0		3	0	0	0	0
01-02—Ottawa	NHL	51	3	15	18	24	7	1	0		—	—	—	—	—
02-03—Binghamton	AHL	6	0	2	2	10	...	...	...		—	—	—	—	—
—Ottawa	NHL	58	4	25	29	30	23	3	0		17	1	3	4	14
NHL Totals (4 years)		186	10	70	80	116	47	7	0		20	1	3	4	14

RADIVOJEVIC, BRANKO   RW   COYOTES

PERSONAL: Born November 24, 1980, in Piestany, Czechoslovakia ... 6-1/206. ... Shoots right. ... Name pronounced rah-dih-VOI-uh-vich.

TRANSACTIONS/CAREER NOTES: Selected by Colorado Avalanche in third round (third Avalanche pick, 93rd overall) of NHL entry draft (June 26, 1999). ... Signed as free agent by Phoenix Coyotes (June 19, 2001).

					REGULAR SEASON							PLAYOFFS			
Season Team	League	Gms.	G	A	Pts.	PIM	+/-	PP	SH		Gms.	G	A	Pts.	PIM
97-98—Dukla Trencin	Slovakia Jrs.	52	30	33	63	50	...	...	...		—	—	—	—	—
98-99—Belleville	OHL	68	20	38	58	61	...	...	...		21	7	17	24	18
99-00—Belleville	OHL	59	23	49	72	86	...	...	...		16	5	8	13	32
00-01—Belleville	OHL	61	34	70	104	77	...	...	...		10	6	10	16	18
01-02—Springfield	AHL	62	18	21	39	64	...	...	...		—	—	—	—	—
—Phoenix	NHL	18	4	2	6	4	1	0	0		1	0	0	0	2
02-03—Phoenix	NHL	79	12	15	27	63	-2	1	0		—	—	—	—	—
NHL Totals (2 years)		97	16	17	33	67	-1	1	0		1	0	0	0	2

RADULOV, IGOR   LW   BLACKHAWKS

PERSONAL: Born August 23, 1982, in Nizhny Tagil, U.S.S.R. ... 6-1/186. ... Shoots left.
TRANSACTIONS/CAREER NOTES: Selected by Chicago Blackhawks in third round (fourth Blackhawks pick, 74th overall) of NHL entry draft (June 24, 2000).

		REGULAR SEASON							PLAYOFFS				
Season Team	League	Gms.	G	A	Pts.	PIM	+/-	PP	SH	Gms.	G	A	Pts.	PIM
99-00—Yaroslavl	CIS	45	20	7	27	36	...	...	...	—	—	—	—	—
00-01—SKA St. Petersburg	Russian	8	1	0	1	6	...	...	...	—	—	—	—	—
01-02—Mississauga	OHL	62	33	30	63	30	...	...	...	—	—	—	—	—
02-03—Norfolk	AHL	62	18	9	27	26	...	...	...	—	—	—	—	—
—Chicago	NHL	7	5	0	5	4	-3	3	0	—	—	—	—	—
NHL Totals (1 year)		7	5	0	5	4	-3	3	0					

RAFALSKI, BRIAN   D   DEVILS

PERSONAL: Born September 28, 1973, in Dearborn, Mich. ... 5-9/190. ... Shoots right.
TRANSACTIONS/CAREER NOTES: Signed as non-drafted free agent by New Jersey Devils (June 18, 1999). ... Suffered illness (January 3, 2000); missed one game. ... Bruised ribs (March 17, 2000); missed five games. ... Bruised left shoulder (February 8, 2001); missed three games. ... Sprained knee (January 24, 2002); missed four games.

		REGULAR SEASON							PLAYOFFS				
Season Team	League	Gms.	G	A	Pts.	PIM	+/-	PP	SH	Gms.	G	A	Pts.	PIM
91-92—Univ. of Wisconsin	WCHA	34	3	14	17	34	...	...	...	—	—	—	—	—
92-93—Univ. of Wisconsin	WCHA	32	0	13	13	10	...	...	...	—	—	—	—	—
93-94—Univ. of Wisconsin	WCHA	37	6	17	23	26	...	...	...	—	—	—	—	—
94-95—Univ. of Wisconsin	WCHA	43	11	34	45	48	...	...	...	—	—	—	—	—
95-96—Brynas Gavle	Sweden Dv. 2	18	3	6	9	12	...	...	...	9	0	1	1	2
—Brynas Gavle	Sweden	22	1	8	9	14	...	...	...	—	—	—	—	—
96-97—HPK Hameenlinna	Finland	49	11	24	35	26	...	...	...	10	6	5	11	4
97-98—HIFK Helsinki	Finland	40	13	10	23	24	...	...	...	9	5	6	11	0
98-99—HIFK Helsinki	Finland	53	19	34	53	18	...	...	...	11	5	†9	14	4
99-00—New Jersey	NHL	75	5	27	32	28	21	1	0	23	2	6	8	8
00-01—New Jersey	NHL	78	9	43	52	26	36	6	0	25	7	11	18	7
01-02—New Jersey	NHL	76	7	40	47	18	15	2	0	6	3	2	5	4
—U.S. Olympic team	Int'l	6	1	2	3	2	...	...	...	—	—	—	—	—
02-03—New Jersey	NHL	79	3	37	40	14	18	2	0	23	2	9	11	8
NHL Totals (4 years)		308	24	147	171	86	90	11	0	77	14	28	42	27

RAGNARSSON, MARCUS   D   FLYERS

PERSONAL: Born August 13, 1971, in Ostervala, Sweden ... 6-1/215. ... Shoots left. ... Name pronounced RAG-nuhr-suhn.
TRANSACTIONS/CAREER NOTES: Selected by San Jose Sharks in fifth round (fifth Sharks pick, 99th overall) of NHL entry draft (June 20, 1992). ... Injured foot (November 8, 1995); missed two games. ... Injured head (December 5, 1995); missed two games. ... Injured knee (January 10, 1996); missed one game. ... Suffered from the flu (January 16, 1996); missed one game. ... Injured hamstring (February 10, 1996); missed four games. ... Injured back (March 22, 1996); missed one game. ... Injured leg (November 1, 1996); missed two games. ... Fractured toe (December 9, 1996); missed two games. ... Suspended one game by NHL for high-sticking incident (November 3, 1997). ... Injured thumb (October 3, 1998); missed first eight games of season. ... Injured foot (October 19, 1999); missed 16 games. ... Suffered concussion (February 22, 2000); missed three games. ... Injured knee (November 1, 2000); missed seven games. ... Injured shoulder (February 16, 2001); missed five games. ... Injured finger (January 5, 2002); missed 12 games. ... Traded by Sharks to Philadelphia Flyers for D Dan McGillis (December 6, 2002).

		REGULAR SEASON							PLAYOFFS				
Season Team	League	Gms.	G	A	Pts.	PIM	+/-	PP	SH	Gms.	G	A	Pts.	PIM
89-90—Djurgarden Stockholm	Sweden	13	0	2	2	0	...	...	...	1	0	0	0	0
90-91—Djurgarden Stockholm	Sweden	35	4	1	5	12	...	...	...	7	0	0	0	6
91-92—Djurgarden Stockholm	Sweden	40	8	5	13	14	...	...	...	—	—	—	—	—
92-93—Djurgarden Stockholm	Sweden	35	3	3	6	53	...	...	...	6	0	2	2	...
93-94—Djurgarden Stockholm	Sweden	19	0	4	4	24	...	...	...	—	—	—	—	—
94-95—Djurgarden Stockholm	Sweden	38	7	9	16	20	...	...	...	3	0	0	0	4
95-96—San Jose	NHL	71	8	31	39	42	-24	4	0	—	—	—	—	—
96-97—San Jose	NHL	69	3	14	17	63	-18	2	0	—	—	—	—	—
97-98—San Jose	NHL	79	5	20	25	65	-11	3	0	6	0	0	0	4
—Swedish Oly. team	Int'l	3	0	1	1	0	...	...	...	—	—	—	—	—
98-99—San Jose	NHL	74	0	13	13	66	7	0	0	6	0	1	1	6
99-00—San Jose	NHL	63	3	13	16	38	13	0	0	12	0	3	3	10
00-01—San Jose	NHL	68	3	12	15	44	2	1	0	5	0	1	1	8
01-02—San Jose	NHL	70	5	15	20	44	4	2	0	12	1	3	4	12
—Swedish Oly. team	Int'l	4	0	2	2	2	...	...	...	—	—	—	—	—
02-03—San Jose	NHL	25	1	7	8	30	2	0	0	—	—	—	—	—
—Philadelphia	NHL	43	2	6	8	32	5	1	0	13	0	1	1	6
NHL Totals (8 years)		562	30	131	161	424	-20	13	0	54	1	9	10	46

RANHEIM, PAUL   LW

PERSONAL: Born January 25, 1966, in St. Louis ... 6-1/210. ... Shoots right. ... Full Name: Paul Stephen Ranheim. ... Name pronounced RAN-highm.
TRANSACTIONS/CAREER NOTES: Selected by Calgary Flames in second round (third Flames pick, 38th overall) of NHL entry draft (June 8, 1983). ... Fractured right ankle (December 11, 1990); missed 41 games. ... Traded by Flames with D Gary Suter and C Ted Drury to Hartford Whalers for C Michael Nylander, D Zarley Zalapski and D James Patrick (March 10, 1994). ... Suffered finger infection on left hand (November 28, 1995); missed six games. ... Suffered abdominal strain (October 27, 1996); missed five games. ... Suffered sore groin (November 11,

1996); missed one game. ... Whalers franchise moved to North Carolina and renamed Carolina Hurricanes for 1997-98 season; NHL approved move on June 25, 1997. ... Injured back (March 22, 2000); missed two games. ... Traded by Hurricanes to Philadelphia Flyers for eigth-round pick (traded to Tampa Bay) in 2002 draft (May 31, 2000). ... Bruised right ankle (March 27, 2002); missed one game. ... Traded by Flyers to Phoenix Coyotes for conditional pick in 2004 draft (December 19, 2002).

STATISTICAL PLATEAUS: Three-goal games: 1991-92 (1).

Season Team	League	REGULAR SEASON								PLAYOFFS				
		Gms.	G	A	Pts.	PIM	+/-	PP	SH	Gms.	G	A	Pts.	PIM
82-83—Edina High School	Minn. H.S.	26	12	25	37	4	...	...	...	—	—	—	—	—
83-84—Edina High School	Minn. H.S.	26	16	24	40	6	...	...	...	—	—	—	—	—
84-85—Univ. of Wisconsin......	WCHA	42	11	11	22	40	...	...	...	—	—	—	—	—
85-86—Univ. of Wisconsin......	WCHA	33	17	17	34	34	...	...	...	—	—	—	—	—
86-87—Univ. of Wisconsin......	WCHA	42	24	35	59	54	...	...	...	—	—	—	—	—
87-88—Univ. of Wisconsin......	WCHA	44	36	26	62	63	...	...	...	—	—	—	—	—
88-89—Calgary	NHL	5	0	0	0	0	-3	0	0	—	—	—	—	—
—Salt Lake City........	IHL	75	*68	29	97	16	...	...	...	14	5	5	10	8
89-90—Calgary	NHL	80	26	28	54	23	27	1	3	6	1	3	4	2
90-91—Calgary	NHL	39	14	16	30	4	20	2	0	7	2	2	4	0
91-92—Calgary	NHL	80	23	20	43	32	16	1	3	—	—	—	—	—
92-93—Calgary	NHL	83	21	22	43	26	-4	3	4	6	0	1	1	0
93-94—Calgary	NHL	67	10	14	24	20	-7	0	2	—	—	—	—	—
—Hartford	NHL	15	0	3	3	2	-11	0	0	—	—	—	—	—
94-95—Hartford	NHL	47	6	14	20	10	-3	0	0	—	—	—	—	—
95-96—Hartford	NHL	73	10	20	30	14	-2	0	1	—	—	—	—	—
96-97—Hartford	NHL	67	10	11	21	18	-13	0	3	—	—	—	—	—
97-98—Carolina	NHL	73	5	9	14	28	-11	0	1	—	—	—	—	—
98-99—Carolina	NHL	78	9	10	19	39	4	0	2	6	0	0	0	2
99-00—Carolina	NHL	79	9	13	22	6	-14	0	0	—	—	—	—	—
00-01—Philadelphia	NHL	80	10	7	17	14	2	0	2	6	0	2	2	2
01-02—Philadelphia	NHL	79	5	4	9	36	5	1	0	5	0	0	0	0
02-03—Philadelphia	NHL	28	0	4	4	6	-4	0	0	—	—	—	—	—
—Phoenix................	NHL	40	3	4	7	10	-4	0	0	—	—	—	—	—
NHL Totals (15 years).........		1013	161	199	360	288	-2	8	21	36	3	8	11	6

RASMUSSEN, ERIK   LW   DEVILS

PERSONAL: Born March 28, 1977, in Minneapolis ... 6-2/207. ... Shoots left. ... Name pronounced RAS-muh-suhn.
TRANSACTIONS/CAREER NOTES: Selected by Buffalo Sabres in first round (first Sabres pick, seventh overall) of NHL entry draft (June 22, 1996). ... Injured shoulder (October 26, 1997); missed one game. ... Injured foot (April 13, 1999); missed one game. ... Bruised hand (December 4, 1999); missed five games. ... Suffered back spasms (March 23, 2000); missed one game. ... Injured knee (October 6, 2001); missed one game. ... Bruised knee (December 12, 2001); missed seven games. ... Injured shoulder (January 23, 2002); missed three games. ... Traded by Sabres to Los Angeles Kings for C Adam Mair and fifth-round pick in 2003 draft (July 24, 2002). ... Signed by New Jersey Devils (July 27, 2003).

Season Team	League	REGULAR SEASON								PLAYOFFS				
		Gms.	G	A	Pts.	PIM	+/-	PP	SH	Gms.	G	A	Pts.	PIM
92-93—Saint Louis Park	Minn. H.S.	23	16	24	40	50	...	...	...	—	—	—	—	—
93-94—Saint Louis Park	Minn. H.S.	18	25	18	43	60	...	...	...	—	—	—	—	—
94-95—Saint Louis Park	Minn. H.S.	23	19	33	52	80	...	...	...	—	—	—	—	—
95-96—Univ. of Minnesota......	WCHA	40	16	32	48	55	...	...	...	—	—	—	—	—
96-97—Univ. of Minnesota......	WCHA	34	15	12	27	123	...	...	...	—	—	—	—	—
97-98—Buffalo	NHL	21	2	3	5	14	2	0	0	—	—	—	—	—
—Rochester	AHL	53	9	14	23	83	...	...	...	1	0	0	0	5
98-99—Rochester	AHL	37	12	14	26	47	...	...	...	—	—	—	—	—
—Buffalo	NHL	42	3	7	10	37	6	0	0	21	2	4	6	18
99-00—Buffalo	NHL	67	8	6	14	43	1	0	0	3	0	0	0	4
00-01—Buffalo	NHL	82	12	19	31	51	0	1	0	3	0	1	1	0
01-02—Buffalo	NHL	69	8	11	19	34	-1	0	0	—	—	—	—	—
02-03—Los Angeles................	NHL	57	4	12	16	28	-1	0	0	—	—	—	—	—
NHL Totals (6 years)..........		338	37	58	95	207	7	1	0	27	2	5	7	22

RATCHUK, PETER   D

PERSONAL: Born September 10, 1977, in Buffalo. ... 6-1/185. ... Shoots left.
TRANSACTIONS/CAREER NOTES: Selected by Colorado Avalanche in first round (first Avalanche pick, 25th overall) of NHL entry draft (June 22, 1996). ... Signed as free agent by Florida Panthers (June 17, 1998). ... Signed as free agent by Pittsburgh Penguins (August 14, 2001). ... Signed as free agent by Buffalo Sabres (August 7, 2002).

Season Team	League	REGULAR SEASON								PLAYOFFS				
		Gms.	G	A	Pts.	PIM	+/-	PP	SH	Gms.	G	A	Pts.	PIM
94-95—Lawrence Academy.....	Mass. H.S.	31	8	15	23	18	...	...	...	—	—	—	—	—
95-96—Shattuck-Saint Mary's	Minn. H.S.	32	16	27	43	30	...	...	...	—	—	—	—	—
96-97—Bowling Green	CCHA	35	9	12	21	14	...	...	...	—	—	—	—	—
97-98—Hull	QMJHL	60	23	31	54	34	...	...	...	11	3	6	9	8
98-99—New Haven	AHL	53	7	20	27	44	...	...	...	—	—	—	—	—
—Florida......................	NHL	24	1	1	2	10	-1	0	0	—	—	—	—	—
99-00—Louisville	AHL	76	9	17	26	64	...	...	...	4	1	2	3	0
00-01—Louisville	AHL	64	5	13	18	85	...	...	...	—	—	—	—	—
—Florida......................	NHL	8	0	0	0	0	-1	0	0	—	—	—	—	—
01-02—Wilkes-Barre/Scranton	AHL	75	16	23	39	55	...	...	...	—	—	—	—	—
02-03—Rochester	AHL	70	11	21	32	64	...	...	...	—	—	—	—	—
NHL Totals (2 years)..........		32	1	1	2	10	-2	0	0	—	—	—	—	—

PERSONAL: Born May 11, 1974, in Mannville, Alta. ... 6-5/240. ... Shoots left. ... Full Name: Michael Rathje. ... Name pronounced RATH-jee.

TRANSACTIONS/CAREER NOTES: Selected by San Jose Sharks in first round (first Sharks pick, third overall) of NHL entry draft (June 20, 1992). ... Strained abdominal muscle (February 19, 1994); missed three games. ... Sprained knee (February 26, 1994); missed four games. ... Sprained knee (February 2, 1995); missed three games. ... Injured foot (February 15, 1995); missed one game. ... Injured hip flexor (April 25, 1995); missed two games. ... Strained abdominal muscle (October 6, 1995); missed first two games of season. ... Injured shoulder (November 14, 1995); missed 12 games. ... Strained groin (November 8, 1996); missed 50 games. ... Injured groin (November 12, 1999); missed 16 games. ... Missed first 28 games of 2001-02 season due to contract dispute. ... Injured knee (January 23, 2002); missed two games.

| | | | REGULAR SEASON | | | | | | | | PLAYOFFS | | | |
Season Team	League	Gms.	G	A	Pts.	PIM	+/-	PP	SH	Gms.	G	A	Pts.	PIM
90-91—Medicine Hat	WHL	64	1	16	17	28	...	...	...	12	0	4	4	2
91-92—Medicine Hat	WHL	67	11	23	34	109	...	...	...	4	0	1	1	2
92-93—Medicine Hat	WHL	57	12	37	49	103	...	...	...	10	3	3	6	12
—Kansas City	IHL	—	—	—	—	—	—	—	—	5	0	0	0	12
93-94—San Jose	NHL	47	1	9	10	59	-9	1	0	1	0	0	0	0
—Kansas City	IHL	6	0	2	2	0	...	...	...	—	—	—	—	—
94-95—Kansas City	IHL	6	0	1	1	7	...	...	...	—	—	—	—	—
—San Jose	NHL	42	2	7	9	29	-1	0	0	11	5	2	7	4
95-96—Kansas City	IHL	36	6	11	17	34	...	...	...	—	—	—	—	—
—San Jose	NHL	27	0	7	7	14	-16	0	0	—	—	—	—	—
96-97—San Jose	NHL	31	0	8	8	21	-1	0	0	—	—	—	—	—
97-98—San Jose	NHL	81	3	12	15	59	-4	1	0	6	1	0	1	6
98-99—San Jose	NHL	82	5	9	14	36	15	2	0	6	0	0	0	4
99-00—San Jose	NHL	66	2	14	16	31	-2	0	0	12	1	3	4	8
00-01—San Jose	NHL	81	0	11	11	48	7	0	0	6	0	1	1	4
01-02—San Jose	NHL	52	5	12	17	48	23	4	0	12	1	3	4	6
02-03—San Jose	NHL	82	7	22	29	48	-19	3	0	—	—	—	—	—
NHL Totals (10 years)		591	25	111	136	393	-7	11	0	54	8	9	17	32

PERSONAL: Born June 8, 1968, in Stirling, Ont. ... 6-0/222. ... Shoots left.

TRANSACTIONS/CAREER NOTES: Selected by Buffalo Sabres in fifth round (fifth Sabres pick, 97th overall) of NHL entry draft (June 11, 1988). ... Tore right knee ligament (April 11, 1993); missed remainder of season. ... Suffered from the flu (March 11, 1995); missed one game. ... Fractured right cheekbone (November 27, 1995); missed eight games. ... Fractured thumb (November 22, 1997); missed 19 games. ... Suspended one playoff game by NHL for verbally abusing officials (April 26, 1998). ... Suspended four games by NHL for slew-footing incident (November 29, 1998). ... Bruised knee (February 6, 1999); missed one game. ... Injured shoulder (November 13, 2000); missed seven games. ... Suspended seven games by NHL for abusing an official (January 11, 2001). ... Suspended five games by NHL for delivering a blow to the head of opponent (April 1, 2002). ... Traded by Sabres to Ottawa Senators for future considerations (March 10, 2003).

| | | | REGULAR SEASON | | | | | | | | PLAYOFFS | | | |
Season Team	League	Gms.	G	A	Pts.	PIM	+/-	PP	SH	Gms.	G	A	Pts.	PIM
84-85—Whitby Lawmen	OPJHL	35	5	10	15	318	...	...	...	—	—	—	—	—
85-86—Cornwall	OHL	53	6	13	19	253	...	...	...	6	0	0	0	26
86-87—Cornwall	OHL	46	17	20	37	158	...	...	...	5	1	1	2	16
87-88—Cornwall	OHL	61	11	41	52	179	...	...	...	11	2	3	5	33
88-89—Rochester	AHL	74	11	18	29	*446	...	...	...	—	—	—	—	—
89-90—Buffalo	NHL	27	2	1	3	99	-2	0	0	—	—	—	—	—
—Rochester	AHL	43	2	13	15	335	...	...	...	17	1	3	4	*115
90-91—Rochester	AHL	8	1	1	2	15	...	...	...	—	—	—	—	—
—Buffalo	NHL	66	8	8	16	*350	-11	0	0	6	1	1	2	56
91-92—Buffalo	NHL	63	5	3	8	354	-9	0	0	7	0	0	0	2
92-93—Buffalo	NHL	68	3	2	5	211	-3	1	0	—	—	—	—	—
93-94—Buffalo	NHL	82	3	4	7	274	2	0	0	7	1	0	1	43
94-95—Buffalo	NHL	47	0	3	3	173	-4	0	0	5	0	0	0	14
95-96—Buffalo	NHL	71	3	6	9	287	-8	0	0	—	—	—	—	—
96-97—Buffalo	NHL	82	7	3	10	286	3	0	0	12	0	1	1	28
97-98—Buffalo	NHL	63	2	4	6	234	2	1	0	10	0	0	0	24
98-99—Buffalo	NHL	76	0	4	4	*261	-2	0	0	5	1	0	1	0
99-00—Buffalo	NHL	69	1	3	4	158	0	0	0	—	—	—	—	—
00-01—Buffalo	NHL	63	4	6	10	210	2	0	0	3	0	0	0	2
01-02—Buffalo	NHL	71	2	3	5	200	-3	0	0	—	—	—	—	—
02-03—Buffalo	NHL	41	0	0	0	92	-5	0	0	—	—	—	—	—
—Ottawa	NHL	5	0	0	0	4	0	0	0	—	—	—	—	—
NHL Totals (14 years)		894	40	50	90	3193	-38	2	0	55	3	2	5	169

PERSONAL: Born May 4, 1980, in Belleville, Ont. ... 6-0/171. ... Catches left.

TRANSACTIONS/CAREER NOTES: Selected by Boston Bruins in fifth round (fourth Bruins pick, 135th overall) of NHL entry draft (June 27, 1998). ... Re-signed by Bruins (July 31, 2003).

			REGULAR SEASON								PLAYOFFS							
Season Team	League	Gms.	Min	W	L	T	GA	SO	Avg.	SV%	Gms.	Min.	W	L	GA	SO	Avg.	SV%
96-97—Wellington	Tier II Jr. A	27	1402	...	...	...	92	0	3.94	—	—	—	—	—	—	—	—	—
97-98—Sudbury	OHL	33	1802	8	16	5	125	0	4.16	—	2	89	0	1	8	0	5.39	—
98-99—Sudbury	OHL	45	2528	17	22	†5	173	1	4.11	—	3	96	0	2	13	0	8.13	—
99-00—Kingston	OHL	*61	3340	33	20	5	191	0	3.43	—	5	300	1	4	21	0	4.20	—
00-01—Boston	NHL	15	649	4	6	0	32	0	2.96	.890	—	—	—	—	—	—	—	—
—Providence	AHL	26	1459	8	14	4	82	1	3.37	—	—	—	—	—	—	—	—	—
01-02—Providence	AHL	56	3317	25	24	6	142	4	2.57	—	—	—	—	—	—	—	—	—
—Boston	NHL	1	65	0	0	1	3	0	2.77	.897	—	—	—	—	—	—	—	—
02-03—Providence	AHL	39	2255	23	10	3	94	1	2.50	—	—	—	—	—	—	—	—	—
—Boston	NHL	5	300	2	3	0	12	0	2.40	.918	—	—	—	—	—	—	—	—
NHL Totals (3 years)		21	1014	6	9	1	47	0	2.78	.899								

READY, RYAN   LW   CANUCKS

PERSONAL: Born November 7, 1978, in Peterborough, Ont. ... 6-0/195. ... Shoots left.
TRANSACTIONS/CAREER NOTES: Selected by Calgary Flames in fourth round (eighth Flames pick, 100th overall) of NHL entry draft (June 21, 1997). ... Signed as free agent by Vancouver Canucks (June 16, 1999).

			REGULAR SEASON							PLAYOFFS			
Season Team	League	Gms.	G	A	Pts.	PIM	+/-	PP	SH	Gms.	G	A	Pts.	PIM
94-95—Trentway	Jr. A	48	20	33	53	56	...	...	...	—	—	—	—	—
95-96—Belleville	OHL	63	5	13	18	54	...	...	...	10	0	2	2	2
96-97—Belleville	OHL	66	23	24	47	102	...	...	...	6	1	3	4	4
97-98—Belleville	OHL	66	33	39	72	80	...	...	...	10	5	2	7	12
98-99—Belleville	OHL	63	33	59	92	73	...	...	...	21	10	28	38	22
99-00—Syracuse	AHL	70	4	12	16	59	...	...	...	2	0	0	0	0
00-01—Kansas City	IHL	67	10	15	25	75	...	...	...	—	—	—	—	—
01-02—Manitoba	AHL	72	23	32	55	73	...	...	...	7	5	1	6	4
02-03—Manitoba	AHL	68	24	26	50	52	...	...	...	—	—	—	—	—

REASONER, MARTY   C   OILERS

PERSONAL: Born February 26, 1977, in Rochester, N.Y. ... 6-1/190. ... Shoots left.
TRANSACTIONS/CAREER NOTES: Selected by St. Louis Blues in first round (first Blues pick, 14th overall) of NHL entry draft (June 22, 1996). ... Traded by Blues with C Jochen Hecht and D Jan Horacek to Edmonton Oilers for C Doug Weight and LW Michel Riesen (July 1, 2001). ... Sprained medial collateral ligament in left knee (January 23, 2002); missed four games.

			REGULAR SEASON							PLAYOFFS			
Season Team	League	Gms.	G	A	Pts.	PIM	+/-	PP	SH	Gms.	G	A	Pts.	PIM
93-94—Deerfield Academy	Mass. H.S.	22	27	24	51	...	...	...	...	—	—	—	—	—
94-95—Deerfield Academy	Mass. H.S.	26	25	32	57	14	...	...	...	—	—	—	—	—
95-96—Boston College	Hockey East	34	16	29	45	32	...	...	...	—	—	—	—	—
96-97—Boston College	Hockey East	35	20	24	44	31	...	...	...	—	—	—	—	—
97-98—Boston College	Hockey East	42	†33	40	*73	56	...	...	...	—	—	—	—	—
98-99—St. Louis	NHL	22	3	7	10	8	2	1	0	—	—	—	—	—
—Worcester	AHL	44	17	22	39	24	...	...	...	4	2	1	3	6
99-00—Worcester	AHL	44	23	28	51	39	...	...	...	—	—	—	—	—
—St. Louis	NHL	32	10	14	24	20	9	3	0	7	2	1	3	4
00-01—St. Louis	NHL	41	4	9	13	14	-5	0	0	10	3	1	4	0
—Worcester	AHL	34	17	18	35	25	...	...	...	—	—	—	—	—
01-02—Edmonton	NHL	52	6	5	11	41	0	3	0	—	—	—	—	—
02-03—Hamilton	AHL	2	0	2	2	2	...	...	...	—	—	—	—	—
—Edmonton	NHL	70	11	20	31	28	19	2	2	6	1	0	1	2
NHL Totals (5 years)		217	34	55	89	111	25	9	2	23	6	2	8	6

RECCHI, MARK   RW   FLYERS

PERSONAL: Born February 1, 1968, in Kamloops, B.C. ... 5-10/185. ... Shoots left. ... Name pronounced REH-kee.
TRANSACTIONS/CAREER NOTES: Selected by Pittsburgh Penguins in fourth round (fourth Penguins pick, 67th overall) of NHL entry draft (June 11, 1988). ... Injured left shoulder (December 23, 1990). ... Sprained right knee (March 30, 1991). ... Traded by Penguins with D Brian Benning and first-round pick (LW Jason Bowen) in 1992 draft to Philadelphia Flyers for RW Rick Tocchet, D Kjell Samuelsson, G Ken Wregget and third-round pick (C Dave Roche) in 1993 draft (February 19, 1992). ... Traded by Flyers with third-round pick (C Martin Hohenberger) in 1995 draft to Montreal Canadiens for D Eric Desjardins, LW Gilbert Dionne and LW John LeClair (February 9, 1995). ... Suffered from pneumonia (December 12, 1998); missed four games. ... Traded by Canadiens to Flyers for RW Dainius Zubrus and second-round pick (D Matt Carkner) in 1999 draft (March 10, 1999). ... Suffered concussion (March 22, 1999); missed three games. ... Suffered from headaches (April 1, 1999); missed two games. ... Suffered mild concussion (April 13, 1999); missed two games. ... Suffered from headaches (October 11, 2000); missed four games. ... Suffered from fatigue (October 24, 2000); missed nine games. ... Suspended two games by NHL for elbowing incident (March 8, 2002).
STATISTICAL PLATEAUS: Three-goal games: 1991-92 (1), 1996-97 (1), 1997-98 (1), 2001-02 (1), 2002-03 (1). Total: 5.

			REGULAR SEASON							PLAYOFFS			
Season Team	League	Gms.	G	A	Pts.	PIM	+/-	PP	SH	Gms.	G	A	Pts.	PIM
84-85—Langley Eagles	BCJHL	51	26	39	65	39	...	...	...	—	—	—	—	—
85-86—New Westminster	WHL	72	21	40	61	55	...	...	...	—	—	—	—	—
86-87—Kamloops	WHL	40	26	50	76	63	...	...	...	13	3	16	19	17
87-88—Kamloops	WHL	62	61	*93	154	75	...	...	...	17	10	*21	†31	18
88-89—Pittsburgh	NHL	15	1	1	2	0	-2	0	0	—	—	—	—	—
—Muskegon	IHL	63	50	49	99	86	...	...	...	14	7	*14	†21	28

Season Team	League	REGULAR SEASON								PLAYOFFS				
		Gms.	G	A	Pts.	PIM	+/-	PP	SH	Gms.	G	A	Pts.	PIM
89-90—Muskegon	IHL	4	7	4	11	2	...	...	...	—	—	—	—	—
—Pittsburgh	NHL	74	30	37	67	44	6	6	2	—	—	—	—	—
90-91—Pittsburgh	NHL	78	40	73	113	48	0	12	0	24	10	24	34	33
91-92—Pittsburgh	NHL	58	33	37	70	78	-16	16	1	—	—	—	—	—
—Philadelphia	NHL	22	10	17	27	18	-5	4	0	—	—	—	—	—
92-93—Philadelphia	NHL	84	53	70	123	95	1	15	4	—	—	—	—	—
93-94—Philadelphia	NHL	84	40	67	107	46	-2	11	0	—	—	—	—	—
94-95—Philadelphia	NHL	10	2	3	5	12	-6	1	0	—	—	—	—	—
—Montreal	NHL	39	14	29	43	16	-3	8	0	—	—	—	—	—
95-96—Montreal	NHL	82	28	50	78	69	20	11	2	6	3	3	6	0
96-97—Montreal	NHL	82	34	46	80	58	-1	7	2	5	4	2	6	2
97-98—Montreal	NHL	82	32	42	74	51	11	9	1	10	4	8	12	6
—Can. Olympic team	Int'l	5	0	2	2	0	...	...	...	—	—	—	—	—
98-99—Montreal	NHL	61	12	35	47	28	-4	3	0	—	—	—	—	—
—Philadelphia	NHL	10	4	2	6	6	-3	0	0	6	0	1	1	2
99-00—Philadelphia	NHL	82	28	*63	91	50	20	7	1	18	6	12	18	6
00-01—Philadelphia	NHL	69	27	50	77	33	15	7	1	6	2	2	4	2
01-02—Philadelphia	NHL	80	22	42	64	46	5	7	2	4	0	0	0	2
02-03—Philadelphia	NHL	79	20	32	52	35	0	8	1	13	7	3	10	2
NHL Totals (15 years)		1091	430	696	1126	733	36	132	17	92	36	55	91	55

REDDEN, WADE   D   SENATORS   R

PERSONAL: Born June 12, 1977, in Lloydminster, Sask. ... 6-2/208. ... Shoots left.
TRANSACTIONS/CAREER NOTES: Selected by New York Islanders in first round (first Islanders pick, second overall) of NHL entry draft (July 8, 1995). ... Traded by Islanders with G Damian Rhodes to Ottawa Senators for G Don Beaupre, D Bryan Berard and C Martin Straka (January 23, 1996). ... Bruised left foot (January 29, 1998); missed one game. ... Suffered back spasms (December 22, 1998); missed two games. ... Injured shoulder (March 4, 1999); missed eight games. ... Suffered illness (February 1, 2000); missed one game. ... Bruised hand (September 25, 2000); missed first four games of regular season. ... Suffered from the flu (April 8, 2002); missed final three games of regular season. ... Re-signed by Senators (July 16, 2003).

Season Team	League	REGULAR SEASON								PLAYOFFS				
		Gms.	G	A	Pts.	PIM	+/-	PP	SH	Gms.	G	A	Pts.	PIM
92-93—Lloydminster	SJHL	34	4	11	15	64	...	...	...	—	—	—	—	—
93-94—Brandon	WHL	64	4	35	39	98	...	...	...	14	2	4	6	10
94-95—Brandon	WHL	64	14	46	60	83	...	...	...	18	5	10	15	8
95-96—Brandon	WHL	51	9	45	54	55	...	...	...	19	5	10	15	19
96-97—Ottawa	NHL	82	6	24	30	41	1	2	0	7	1	3	4	2
97-98—Ottawa	NHL	80	8	14	22	27	17	3	0	9	0	2	2	2
98-99—Ottawa	NHL	72	8	21	29	54	7	3	0	4	1	2	3	2
99-00—Ottawa	NHL	81	10	26	36	49	-1	3	0	—	—	—	—	—
00-01—Ottawa	NHL	78	10	37	47	49	22	4	0	4	0	0	0	0
01-02—Ottawa	NHL	79	9	25	34	48	22	4	1	12	3	2	5	6
02-03—Ottawa	NHL	76	10	35	45	70	23	4	0	18	1	8	9	10
NHL Totals (7 years)		548	61	182	243	338	91	23	1	54	6	17	23	22

REGEHR, ROBYN   D   FLAMES

PERSONAL: Born April 19, 1980, in Recife, Brazil ... 6-3/226. ... Shoots left. ... Name pronounced ruh-ZHEER.
TRANSACTIONS/CAREER NOTES: Selected by Colorado Avalanche in first round (third Avalanche pick, 19th overall) of NHL entry draft (June 27, 1998). ... Traded by Avalanche to Calgary Flames (March 27, 1999); completing deal in which Flames traded RW Theo Fleury and LW Chris Dingman to Avalanche for LW Rene Corbet, D Wade Belak and future considerations (February 28, 1999). ... Fractured legs prior to start of 1999-2000 season; missed first five games of season. ... Suffered concussion (January 11, 2000); missed 11 games. ... Injured knee (November 4, 2000); missed six games. ... Injured knee (December 22, 2000); missed two games. ... Injured wrist (November 7, 2001); missed one game. ... Re-signed by Flames (June 5, 2003).

Season Team	League	REGULAR SEASON								PLAYOFFS				
		Gms.	G	A	Pts.	PIM	+/-	PP	SH	Gms.	G	A	Pts.	PIM
96-97—Kamloops	WHL	64	4	19	23	96	...	...	...	5	0	1	1	18
97-98—Kamloops	WHL	65	4	10	14	120	...	...	...	5	0	3	3	8
98-99—Kamloops	WHL	54	12	20	32	130	...	...	...	12	1	4	5	21
99-00—Saint John	AHL	5	0	0	0	0	...	...	...	—	—	—	—	—
—Calgary	NHL	57	5	7	12	46	-2	2	0	—	—	—	—	—
00-01—Calgary	NHL	71	1	3	4	70	-7	0	0	—	—	—	—	—
01-02—Calgary	NHL	77	2	6	8	93	-24	0	0	—	—	—	—	—
02-03—Calgary	NHL	76	0	12	12	87	-9	0	0	—	—	—	—	—
NHL Totals (4 years)		281	8	28	36	296	-42	2	0					

REICH, JEREMY   LW   BLUE JACKETS

PERSONAL: Born February 11, 1979, in Craik, Sask. ... 6-1/190. ... Shoots left. ... Nephew of Jim Archibald, right winger with Minnesota North Stars (1984-85 through 1986-87). ... Name pronounced REECH.
TRANSACTIONS/CAREER NOTES: Selected by Chicago Blackhawks in second round (third Blackhawks pick, 39th overall) of NHL entry draft (June 21, 1997). ... Signed as free agent by Columbus Blue Jackets (May 16, 2000).

Season Team	League	Gms.	G	A	Pts.	PIM	+/-	PP	SH	Gms.	G	A	Pts.	PIM
94-95—Saskatoon	SJHL	35	13	20	33	81	...	...	...	—	—	—	—	—
95-96—Seattle	WHL	65	11	11	22	88	...	...	...	5	0	1	1	10
96-97—Seattle	WHL	62	19	31	50	134	...	...	...	15	2	5	7	36
97-98—Seattle	WHL	43	24	23	47	121	...	...	...	—	—	—	—	—
—Swift Current	WHL	35	32	31	63	168	...	...	...	12	5	6	11	37
98-99—Swift Current	WHL	67	21	28	49	220	...	...	...	6	0	3	3	26
99-00—Swift Current	WHL	72	33	58	91	167	...	...	...	12	2	10	12	19
00-01—Syracuse	AHL	56	6	9	15	108	...	...	...	5	0	0	0	6
01-02—Syracuse	AHL	59	9	7	16	178	...	...	...	10	4	0	4	16
02-03—Syracuse	AHL	78	14	13	27	195	...	...	...	—	—	—	—	—

REICHEL, ROBERT   C   MAPLE LEAFS

PERSONAL: Born June 25, 1971, in Litvinov, Czechoslovakia ... 5-10/180. ... Shoots left. ... Brother of Martin Reichel, right winger, Edmonton Oilers organization. ... Name pronounced RIGH-kuhl.

TRANSACTIONS/CAREER NOTES: Selected by Calgary Flames in fourth round (fifth Flames pick, 70th overall) of NHL entry draft (June 17, 1989). ... Strained right knee (March 16, 1993); missed three games. ... Played in Europe during 1994-95 NHL lockout. ... Traded by Flames to New York Islanders for LW Marty McInnis, G Tyrone Garner and sixth-round pick (D Ilja Demidov) in 1997 draft (March 18, 1997). ... Traded by Islanders with third- (C/LW Jason Jaspers) and fourth-round pick (C Preston Mizzi) picks in 1999 draft to Phoenix Coyotes for RW Brad Isbister and third-round pick (C Brian Collins) in 1999 draft (March 20, 1999). ... Missed entire 1999-2000 and 2000-01 seasons due to contract dispute; played in Europe. ... Traded by Coyotes with C Travis Green and RW Craig Mills to Toronto Maple Leafs for D Danny Markov (June 12, 2001). ... Suffered injury (March 21, 2002); missed two games. ... Suffered injury (April 12, 2002); missed final two games of season.

STATISTICAL PLATEAUS: Three-goal games: 1992-93 (2), 1993-94 (2), 1997-98 (1). Total: 5.

Season Team	League	Gms.	G	A	Pts.	PIM	+/-	PP	SH	Gms.	G	A	Pts.	PIM
87-88—Litvinov	Czech.	36	17	10	27	8	...	...	...	—	—	—	—	—
88-89—Litvinov	Czech.	44	23	25	48	32	...	...	...	—	—	—	—	—
89-90—Litvinov	Czech.	52	49	34	83	...	...	...	...	—	—	—	—	—
90-91—Calgary	NHL	66	19	22	41	22	17	3	0	6	1	1	2	0
91-92—Calgary	NHL	77	20	34	54	32	1	8	0	—	—	—	—	—
92-93—Calgary	NHL	80	40	48	88	54	25	12	0	6	2	4	6	2
93-94—Calgary	NHL	84	40	53	93	58	20	14	0	7	0	5	5	0
94-95—Frankfurt	Germany	21	19	24	43	41	...	...	...	—	—	—	—	—
—Calgary	NHL	48	18	17	35	28	-2	5	0	7	2	4	6	4
95-96—Frankfurt	Germany	46	47	54	101	84	...	...	...	3	1	3	4	0
96-97—Calgary	NHL	70	16	27	43	22	-2	6	0	—	—	—	—	—
—New York Islanders	NHL	12	5	14	19	4	7	0	1	—	—	—	—	—
97-98—New York Islanders	NHL	82	25	40	65	32	-11	8	0	—	—	—	—	—
—Czech Rep. Oly. team	Int'l	6	3	0	3	0	...	...	...	—	—	—	—	—
98-99—New York Islanders	NHL	70	19	37	56	50	-15	5	1	—	—	—	—	—
—Phoenix	NHL	13	7	6	13	4	2	3	0	7	1	3	4	2
99-00—Litvinov	Czech Rep.	45	25	32	57	24	...	...	...	7	3	4	7	2
00-01—Litvinov	Czech Rep.	49	23	33	56	72	...	...	...	5	1	2	3	4
01-02—Toronto	NHL	78	20	31	51	26	7	1	0	18	0	3	3	4
—Czech Rep. Oly. team	Int'l	4	1	0	1	2	...	...	...	—	—	—	—	—
02-03—Toronto	NHL	81	12	30	42	26	7	1	1	7	2	1	3	0
NHL Totals (10 years)		**761**	**241**	**359**	**600**	**358**	**56**	**66**	**3**	**58**	**8**	**21**	**29**	**12**

REID, BRANDON   C   CANUCKS

PERSONAL: Born March 9, 1981, in Kirkland, Que. ... 5-9/180. ... Shoots right.

TRANSACTIONS/CAREER NOTES: Selected by Vancouver Canucks in seventh round (fifth Canucks pick, 208th overall) of NHL entry draft (June 24, 2000).

Season Team	League	Gms.	G	A	Pts.	PIM	+/-	PP	SH	Gms.	G	A	Pts.	PIM
98-99—Halifax	QMJHL	70	32	25	57	33	...	...	...	5	2	2	4	...
99-00—Halifax	QMJHL	62	44	80	124	10	...	...	...	10	7	11	18	...
00-01—Val-d'Or	QMJHL	57	45	81	126	18	...	...	...	21	13	29	42	14
01-02—Manitoba	AHL	60	18	19	37	6	...	...	...	7	0	3	3	0
02-03—Manitoba	AHL	73	18	36	54	18	...	...	...	—	—	—	—	—
—Vancouver	NHL	7	2	3	5	0	4	0	0	9	0	1	1	0
NHL Totals (1 year)		**7**	**2**	**3**	**5**	**0**	**4**	**0**	**0**	**9**	**0**	**1**	**1**	**0**

REINPRECHT, STEVE   C   FLAMES

PERSONAL: Born May 7, 1976, in Edmonton ... 6-0/190. ... Shoots left.

TRANSACTIONS/CAREER NOTES: Signed as non-drafted free agent by Los Angeles Kings (March 31, 2000). ... Traded by Kings with D Rob Blake to Colorado Avalanche for RW Adam Deadmarsh, D Aaron Miller, first-round pick (C David Steckel) in 2001 draft, a player to be named later and future considerations (February 21, 2001); Kings acquired C Jared Aulin to complete deal (March 22, 2001). ... Injured knee (January 15, 2002); missed 13 games. ... Injured foot (March 21, 2002); missed one game. ... Traded by Avalanche to Buffalo Sabres for D Keith Ballard (July 2, 2003). ... Traded by Sabres to Calgary Flames with D Rhett Warrener for C Steve Begin and LW Chris Drury (July 2, 2003). ... Re-signed by Flames (July 16, 2003).

STATISTICAL PLATEAUS: Three-goal games: 2001-02 (1), 2002-03 (1). Total: 2.

Season Team	League	REGULAR SEASON								PLAYOFFS				
		Gms.	G	A	Pts.	PIM	+/-	PP	SH	Gms.	G	A	Pts.	PIM
96-97—Univ. of Wisconsin......	WCHA	38	11	9	20	12	...	...	...	—	—	—	—	—
97-98—Univ. of Wisconsin......	WCHA	41	19	24	43	18	...	...	...	—	—	—	—	—
98-99—Univ. of Wisconsin......	WCHA	38	16	17	33	14	...	...	...	—	—	—	—	—
99-00—Univ. of Wisconsin......	WCHA	37	26	40	*66	14	...	...	...	—	—	—	—	—
—Los Angeles................	NHL	1	0	0	0	2	0	0	0	—	—	—	—	—
00-01—Los Angeles................	NHL	59	12	17	29	12	11	3	2	—	—	—	—	—
—Colorado....................	NHL	21	3	4	7	2	-1	0	0	22	2	3	5	2
01-02—Colorado....................	NHL	67	19	27	46	18	14	4	0	21	7	5	12	8
02-03—Colorado....................	NHL	77	18	33	51	18	-6	2	1	7	1	2	3	0
NHL Totals (4 years)..........		225	52	81	133	52	18	9	3	50	10	10	20	10

REIRDEN, TODD — D — MIGHTY DUCKS

PERSONAL: Born June 25, 1971, in Deerfield, Ill. ... 6-5/220. ... Shoots left. ... Full Name: Todd Raymond Reirden.
TRANSACTIONS/CAREER NOTES: Selected by New Jersey Devils in 12th round (14th Devils pick, 242nd overall) of NHL entry draft (June 16, 1990). ... Signed as free agent by Edmonton Oilers (May 31, 1998). ... Claimed on waivers by St. Louis Blues (September 30, 1999). ... Strained shoulder (December 4, 1999); missed three games. ... Fractured foot (January 28, 2000); missed 18 games. ... Underwent foot surgery (July 2000); missed first 25 games of season. ... Strained oblique muscle (January 23, 2001); missed one game. ... Signed as free agent by Atlanta Thrashers (July 16, 2001). ... Strained groin (September 25, 2001); missed first five games of season. ... Injured elbow (December 31, 2001); missed three games. ... Signed as free agent by Anaheim Mighty Ducks (July 17, 2002).

Season Team	League	REGULAR SEASON								PLAYOFFS				
		Gms.	G	A	Pts.	PIM	+/-	PP	SH	Gms.	G	A	Pts.	PIM
90-91—Bowling Green	CCHA	28	1	5	6	22	...	...	...	—	—	—	—	—
91-92—Bowling Green	CCHA	33	8	7	15	34	...	...	...	—	—	—	—	—
92-93—Bowling Green	CCHA	41	8	17	25	48	...	...	...	—	—	—	—	—
93-94—Bowling Green	CCHA	38	7	23	30	56	...	...	...	—	—	—	—	—
94-95—Albany........................	AHL	2	0	1	1	2	...	...	...	—	—	—	—	—
—Raleigh	ECHL	26	2	13	15	33	...	...	...	—	—	—	—	—
—Tallahassee	ECHL	43	5	25	30	61	...	...	...	13	2	5	7	10
95-96—Chicago....................	IHL	31	0	2	2	39	...	...	...	9	0	2	2	16
—Tallahassee	ECHL	7	1	3	4	10	...	...	...	—	—	—	—	—
—Jacksonville	ECHL	15	1	10	11	41	...	...	...	1	0	2	2	4
96-97—Chicago....................	IHL	57	3	10	13	108	...	...	...	—	—	—	—	—
—San Antonio..............	IHL	23	2	5	7	51	...	...	...	9	0	1	1	17
97-98—San Antonio..............	IHL	70	5	14	19	132	...	...	...	—	—	—	—	—
—Fort Wayne	IHL	11	2	2	4	16	...	...	...	4	0	2	2	4
98-99—Hamilton	AHL	58	9	25	34	84	...	...	...	11	0	5	5	6
—Edmonton	NHL	17	2	3	5	20	-1	0	0	—	—	—	—	—
99-00—St. Louis	NHL	56	4	21	25	32	18	0	0	4	0	1	1	0
00-01—Worcester	AHL	7	2	6	8	20	...	...	...	—	—	—	—	—
—St. Louis	NHL	38	2	4	6	43	-2	1	0	1	0	0	0	0
01-02—Atlanta	NHL	65	3	5	8	82	-25	1	0	—	—	—	—	—
02-03—Cincinnati..................	AHL	58	7	13	20	97	...	...	...	—	—	—	—	—
NHL Totals (4 years)..........		176	11	33	44	177	-10	2	0	5	0	1	1	0

REITZ, ERIC — D — WILD

PERSONAL: Born August 29, 1982, in Detroit. ... 6-0/192. ... Shoots right.
TRANSACTIONS/CAREER NOTES: Selected by Minnesota Wild in sixth round (fifth Wild pick, 170th overall) of NHL entry draft (June 24, 2000).

Season Team	League	REGULAR SEASON								PLAYOFFS				
		Gms.	G	A	Pts.	PIM	+/-	PP	SH	Gms.	G	A	Pts.	PIM
99-00—Barrie........................	OHL	63	2	10	12	85	...	...	...	—	—	—	—	—
00-01—Barrie........................	OHL	68	5	21	26	178	...	...	...	5	1	0	1	21
01-02—Barrie........................	OHL	61	13	27	40	153	...	...	...	20	4	16	20	40
02-03—Houston	AHL	62	6	13	19	112	...	...	...	—	—	—	—	—

RENBERG, MIKAEL — LW — MAPLE LEAFS

PERSONAL: Born May 5, 1972, in Pitea, Sweden ... 6-2/235. ... Shoots left.
TRANSACTIONS/CAREER NOTES: Selected by Philadelphia Flyers in second round (third Flyers pick, 40th overall) of NHL entry draft (June 16, 1990). ... Played in Europe during 1994-95 NHL lockout. ... Suffered sore shoulder (March 25, 1995); missed one game. ... Strained abdominal muscles (December 30, 1995); missed one game. ... Strained lower abdominal muscles (January 22, 1996); missed 17 games. ... Reinjured lower abdominal muscles (March 12, 1996); missed one game. ... Reinjured lower abdominal muscles (March 16, 1996); missed one game. ... Reinjured lower abdominal muscles (March 19, 1996); missed 11 games. ... Underwent abdominal surgery (May 1996). ... Strained groin (March 8, 1997); missed one game. ... Cut face (April 6, 1997); missed remainder of regular season. ... Traded by Flyers with D Karl Dykhuis to Tampa Bay Lightning for C Chris Gratton (August 20, 1997). ... Suffered from the flu (October 15, 1997); missed one game. ... Fractured wrist (December 13, 1997); missed 13 games. ... Fractured left thumb (November 10, 1998); missed seven games. ... Traded by Lightning with C Daymond Langkow to Flyers for C Chris Gratton and C/RW Mike Sillinger (December 12, 1998). ... Separated shoulder (December 23, 1998); missed nine games. ... Suffered from the flu (February 9, 2000); missed two games. ... Traded by Flyers to Phoenix Coyotes for RW Rick Tocchet (March 8, 2000). ... Strained hip flexor (March 15, 2000); missed six games. ... Suffered from the flu (February 9, 2000); missed two games. ... Signed by Lulea, Swedish Elite League (June 13, 2000). ... Traded by Coyotes to Toronto Maple Leafs for LW Sergei Berezin (June 22, 2001). ... Suffered injury (December 18, 2001); missed two games. ... Suffered injury (March 6, 2002); missed four games. ... Strained hamstring (March 23, 2002); missed four games.
STATISTICAL PLATEAUS: Three-goal games: 1993-94 (1), 1997-98 (1). Total: 2.

Season Team	League	Gms.	G	A	Pts.	PIM	+/-	PP	SH	Gms.	G	A	Pts.	PIM
88-89—Pitea	Sweden	12	6	3	9	...	...	...	...	—	—	—	—	—
89-90—Pitea	Sweden	29	15	19	34	...	...	...	...	—	—	—	—	—
90-91—Lulea	Sweden	29	11	6	17	12	...	...	...	5	1	1	2	4
91-92—Lulea	Sweden	38	8	15	23	20	...	...	...	2	0	0	0	0
92-93—Lulea	Sweden	39	19	13	32	61	...	...	...	11	4	4	8	...
93-94—Philadelphia	NHL	83	38	44	82	36	8	9	0	—	—	—	—	—
94-95—Lulea	Sweden	10	9	4	13	16	...	...	...	—	—	—	—	—
—Philadelphia	NHL	47	26	31	57	20	20	8	0	15	6	7	13	6
95-96—Philadelphia	NHL	51	23	20	43	45	8	9	0	11	3	6	9	14
96-97—Philadelphia	NHL	77	22	37	59	65	36	1	0	18	5	6	11	4
97-98—Tampa Bay	NHL	68	16	22	38	34	-37	6	3	—	—	—	—	—
—Swedish Oly. team	Int'l	4	1	2	3	4	...	...	...	—	—	—	—	—
98-99—Tampa Bay	NHL	20	4	8	12	4	-2	2	0	—	—	—	—	—
—Philadelphia	NHL	46	11	15	26	14	7	4	0	6	0	1	1	0
99-00—Philadelphia	NHL	62	8	21	29	30	-1	3	0	—	—	—	—	—
—Phoenix	NHL	10	2	4	6	2	0	0	0	5	1	2	3	4
00-01—Lulea	Sweden	48	22	32	54	36	...	...	...	11	6	5	11	35
01-02—Toronto	NHL	71	14	38	52	36	11	4	0	3	0	0	0	2
—Swedish Oly. team	Int'l	4	1	0	1	4	...	...	...	—	—	—	—	—
02-03—Toronto	NHL	67	14	21	35	36	5	7	0	7	1	0	1	8
NHL Totals (9 years)		602	178	261	439	322	55	53	3	65	16	22	38	38

R | REYNOLDS, PETER — D — HURRICANES

PERSONAL: Born April 27, 1981, in Waterloo, Ont. ... 6-3/190. ... Shoots right.
TRANSACTIONS/CAREER NOTES: Selected by Toronto Maple Leafs in second round (second Maple Leafs pick, 60th overall) of NHL entry draft (June 26, 1999). ... Returned to draft pool by Maple Leafs and selected by Carolina Hurricanes in ninth round (eighth Hurricanes pick, 274th overall) of NHL entry draft (June 23, 2001).

Season Team	League	Gms.	G	A	Pts.	PIM	+/-	PP	SH	Gms.	G	A	Pts.	PIM
97-98—London	OHL	55	0	8	8	30	...	...	...	16	0	0	0	10
98-99—London	OHL	59	2	25	27	55	...	...	...	23	2	3	5	24
99-00—North Bay	OHL	61	3	29	32	53	...	...	...	6	1	3	4	10
00-01—North Bay	OHL	58	2	27	29	85	...	...	...	4	0	1	1	7
—St. John's	AHL	2	0	0	0	0	...	...	...	1	0	0	0	0
01-02—Lowell	AHL	44	1	2	3	38	...	...	...	—	—	—	—	—
—Florida	ECHL	7	0	0	0	10	...	...	...	—	—	—	—	—
02-03—Florida	ECHL	66	1	9	10	111	...	...	...	—	—	—	—	—

RHEAUME, PASCAL — C — DEVILS

PERSONAL: Born June 21, 1973, in Quebec City ... 6-1/220. ... Shoots left. ... Name pronounced ray-OHM.
TRANSACTIONS/CAREER NOTES: Signed as non-drafted free agent by New Jersey Devils (October 1, 1992). ... Claimed by St. Louis Blues from Devils in NHL waiver draft (September 28, 1997). ... Suffered concussion (February 28, 1999); missed 10 games. ... Underwent shoulder surgery prior to 1999-2000 season; missed first 62 games of season. ... Signed as free agent by Chicago Blackhawks (July 31, 2001). ... Claimed on waivers by Atlanta Thrashers (November 14, 2001). ... Strained hamstring (December 3, 2001); missed 21 games. ... Suffered from pneumonia (April 7, 2002); missed two games. ... Traded by Thrashers to Devils for conditional pick in 2004 draft (February 24, 2003).
STATISTICAL PLATEAUS: Four-goal games: 2001-02 (1).

Season Team	League	Gms.	G	A	Pts.	PIM	+/-	PP	SH	Gms.	G	A	Pts.	PIM
91-92—Trois-Rivieres	QMJHL	65	17	20	37	84	...	...	...	14	5	4	9	23
92-93—Sherbrooke	QMJHL	65	28	34	62	88	...	...	...	14	6	5	11	31
93-94—Albany	AHL	55	17	18	35	43	...	...	...	5	0	1	1	0
94-95—Albany	AHL	78	19	25	44	46	...	...	...	14	3	6	9	19
95-96—Albany	AHL	68	26	42	68	50	...	...	...	4	1	2	3	2
96-97—Albany	AHL	51	22	23	45	40	...	...	...	16	2	8	10	16
—New Jersey	NHL	2	1	0	1	0	1	0	0	—	—	—	—	—
97-98—St. Louis	NHL	48	6	9	15	35	4	1	0	10	1	3	4	8
98-99—St. Louis	NHL	60	9	18	27	24	10	2	0	5	1	0	1	4
99-00—St. Louis	NHL	7	1	1	2	6	-2	0	0	—	—	—	—	—
—Worcester	AHL	7	1	1	2	4	...	...	...	—	—	—	—	—
00-01—Worcester	AHL	56	23	36	59	63	...	...	...	11	2	4	6	2
—St. Louis	NHL	8	2	0	2	5	-1	2	0	3	0	1	1	0
01-02—Chicago	NHL	19	0	2	2	4	-1	0	0	—	—	—	—	—
—Atlanta	NHL	42	11	9	20	25	-3	6	0	—	—	—	—	—
02-03—Atlanta	NHL	56	4	9	13	24	-8	0	2	—	—	—	—	—
—New Jersey	NHL	21	4	1	5	8	3	0	1	24	1	2	3	13
NHL Totals (7 years)		263	38	49	87	131	3	11	3	42	3	6	9	25

RHODES, DAMIAN — G

PERSONAL: Born May 28, 1969, in St. Paul, Minn. ... 6-0/180. ... Catches left. ... Full Name: Damian G. Rhodes.
TRANSACTIONS/CAREER NOTES: Selected by Toronto Maple Leafs in sixth round (sixth Maple Leafs pick, 112th overall) of NHL entry draft (June 13, 1987). ... Traded by Maple Leafs with LW Ken Belanger to New York Islanders for LW Kirk Muller (January 23, 1996). ... Traded by Islanders with D Wade Redden to Ottawa Senators for D Bryan Berard and C Martin Straka (January 23, 1996). ... Bruised calf (February 23, 1997); missed 10 games. ... Suffered from the flu (December 22, 1998); missed one game. ... Traded by Senators to Atlanta Thrashers for

future considerations (June 18, 1999). ... Sprained ankle (November 17, 1999); missed 49 games. ... Sprained knee (October 30, 2000); missed one game. ... Sprained right knee (November 4, 2000); missed 18 games. ... Strained groin (February 25, 2001); missed 16 games. ... Suffered sports hernia (January 9, 2002); missed remainder of season. ... Released by Thrashers (July 1, 2002).

			REGULAR SEASON								PLAYOFFS						
Season Team	League	Gms.	Min	W	L	T	GA	SO	Avg.	SV%	Gms.	Min.	W	L	GA	SO	Avg.	SV%
85-86 —Richfield H.S.	Minn. H.S.	16	720	...	...	...	56	0	4.67	—	—	—	—	—	—	—	—	—
86-87 —Richfield H.S.	Minn. H.S.	19	673	...	...	...	51	1	4.55	—	—	—	—	—	—	—	—	—
87-88 —Michigan Tech	WCHA	29	1623	16	10	1	114	0	4.21	—	—	—	—	—	—	—	—	—
88-89 —Michigan Tech	WCHA	37	2216	15	22	0	163	0	4.41	—	—	—	—	—	—	—	—	—
89-90 —Michigan Tech	WCHA	25	1358	6	17	0	119	0	5.26	—	—	—	—	—	—	—	—	—
90-91 —Toronto	NHL	1	60	1	0	0	1	0	1.00	—	—	—	—	—	—	—	—	—
—Newmarket	AHL	38	2154	8	24	3	144	1	4.01	—	—	—	—	—	—	—	—	—
91-92 —St. John's	AHL	43	2454	20	16	5	148	0	3.62	—	6	331	4	1	16	0	2.90	—
92-93 —St. John's	AHL	52	*3074	27	16	8	184	1	3.59	—	9	538	4	5	37	0	4.13	—
93-94 —Toronto	NHL	22	1213	9	7	3	53	0	2.62	.902	1	1	0	0	0	0	—	—
94-95 —Toronto	NHL	13	760	6	6	1	34	0	2.68	.916	—	—	—	—	—	—	—	—
95-96 —Toronto	NHL	11	624	4	5	1	29	0	2.79	.904	—	—	—	—	—	—	—	—
—Ottawa	NHL	36	2123	10	22	4	98	2	2.77	.906	—	—	—	—	—	—	—	—
96-97 —Ottawa	NHL	50	2934	14	20	*14	133	1	2.72	.890	—	—	—	—	—	—	—	—
97-98 —Ottawa	NHL	50	2743	19	19	7	107	5	2.34	.907	10	590	5	5	21	0	2.14	.911
98-99 —Ottawa	NHL	45	2480	22	13	7	101	3	2.44	.905	2	150	0	2	6	0	2.40	.908
99-00 —Atlanta	NHL	28	1561	5	19	3	101	1	3.88	.874	—	—	—	—	—	—	—	—
00-01 —Atlanta	NHL	38	2072	7	19	7	116	0	3.36	.897	—	—	—	—	—	—	—	—
01-02 —Atlanta	NHL	15	769	2	10	1	47	0	3.67	.893	—	—	—	—	—	—	—	—
02-03 —Lowell	AHL	7	379	1	4	0	26	0	4.12	—	—	—	—	—	—	—	—	—
—Greenville	ECHL	12	686	2	8	2	43	1	3.76	—	—	—	—	—	—	—	—	—
NHL Totals (10 years)		309	17339	99	140	48	820	12	2.84	.899	13	741	5	7	27	0	2.19	.910

RIAZANTSEV, ALEX — D — CAPITALS

PERSONAL: Born March 15, 1980, in Moscow, U.S.S.R. ... 5-11/200. ... Shoots right. ... Full Name: Alexander Riazantsev.
TRANSACTIONS/CAREER NOTES: Selected by Colorado Avalanche in sixth round (10th Avalanche pick, 167th overall) of NHL entry draft (June 27, 1998). ... Traded by Avalanche to Nashville Predators for seventh-round pick in 2003 draft (March 11, 2003). ... Traded by Predators to Washington Capitals for F Mike Farrell (July 14, 2003).

			REGULAR SEASON							PLAYOFFS				
Season Team	League	Gms.	G	A	Pts.	PIM	+/-	PP	SH	Gms.	G	A	Pts.	PIM
96-97 —Spartak Moscow	Russian	20	1	2	3	4	...	...	...	—	—	—	—	—
—SAK Moscow	Rus. Div. III	18	0	0	0	8	...	...	...	—	—	—	—	—
97-98 —Spartak-2 Moscow	Rus. Div. III	31	3	8	11	26	...	...	...	—	—	—	—	—
—Victoriaville	QMJHL	22	6	9	15	14	...	...	...	4	0	0	0	0
98-99 —Victoriaville	QMJHL	64	17	40	57	57	...	...	...	6	0	3	3	10
—Hershey	AHL	2	0	0	0	0	...	...	...	—	—	—	—	—
99-00 —Victoriaville	QMJHL	48	17	45	62	45	...	...	...	6	2	5	7	20
—Hershey	AHL	2	0	1	1	2	...	...	...	6	1	1	2	0
00-01 —Hershey	AHL	66	5	18	23	26	...	...	...	11	0	0	0	2
01-02 —Hershey	AHL	76	5	19	24	28	...	...	...	5	0	1	1	4
02-03 —Hershey	AHL	57	5	10	15	65	...	...	...	—	—	—	—	—
—Milwaukee	AHL	14	3	4	7	9	...	...	...	—	—	—	—	—

RIBEIRO, MIKE — C — CANADIENS

PERSONAL: Born February 10, 1980, in Montreal ... 6-1/176. ... Shoots left.
TRANSACTIONS/CAREER NOTES: Selected by Montreal Canadiens in second round (second Canadiens pick, 45th overall) of NHL entry draft (June 27, 1998). ... Re-signed by Canadiens (July 24, 2003).

			REGULAR SEASON							PLAYOFFS				
Season Team	League	Gms.	G	A	Pts.	PIM	+/-	PP	SH	Gms.	G	A	Pts.	PIM
97-98 —Rouyn-Noranda	QMJHL	67	40	85	125	55	...	...	...	—	—	—	—	—
98-99 —Rouyn-Noranda	QMJHL	69	67	*100	*167	137	...	...	...	11	5	11	16	12
—Fredericton	AHL	—	—	—	—	—	...	...	...	5	0	1	1	2
99-00 —Montreal	NHL	19	1	1	2	2	-6	1	0	—	—	—	—	—
—Quebec	AHL	3	0	0	0	2	...	...	...	—	—	—	—	—
—Rouyn-Noranda	QMJHL	2	1	3	4	0	...	...	...	—	—	—	—	—
—Quebec	QMJHL	21	17	28	45	30	...	...	...	11	3	20	23	38
00-01 —Quebec	AHL	74	26	40	66	44	...	...	...	9	1	5	6	23
—Montreal	NHL	2	0	0	0	2	0	0	0	—	—	—	—	—
01-02 —Montreal	NHL	43	8	10	18	12	-11	3	0	—	—	—	—	—
—Quebec	AHL	23	9	14	23	36	...	...	...	3	0	3	3	0
02-03 —Hamilton	AHL	3	0	1	1	0	...	...	...	—	—	—	—	—
—Montreal	NHL	52	5	12	17	6	-3	2	0	—	—	—	—	—
NHL Totals (4 years)		116	14	23	37	22	-20	6	0					

RICCI, MIKE — C — SHARKS

PERSONAL: Born October 27, 1971, in Scarborough, Ont. ... 6-0/190. ... Shoots left. ... Name pronounced REE-chee.
TRANSACTIONS/CAREER NOTES: Selected by Philadelphia Flyers in first round (first Flyers pick, fourth overall) of NHL entry draft (June 16, 1990). ... Fractured right index finger and thumb (October 4, 1990); missed nine games. ... Traded by Flyers with G Ron Hextall, C Peter

Forsberg, D Steve Duchesne, D Kerry Huffman, first-round pick (G Jocelyn Thibault) in 1993 draft, cash and future considerations to Quebec Nordiques for C Eric Lindros (June 20, 1992); Nordiques acquired LW Chris Simon and first-round pick (traded to Toronto) in 1994 draft to complete deal (July 21, 1992). ... Sprained left wrist (November 3, 1992); missed four games. ... Suffered from the flu (January 5, 1993); missed two games. ... Nordiques franchise moved to Colorado and renamed Avalanche for 1995-96 season (July 21, 1995). ... Underwent sinus surgery (October 15, 1995); missed one game. ... Injured ankle (November 5, 1995); missed one game. ... Sprained left ankle (December 11, 1995); missed two games. ... Suffered back spasms (January 4, 1996); missed 16 games. ... Strained shoulder (October 30, 1996); missed 11 games. ... Fractured thumb (January 6, 1997); missed four games. ... Underwent shoulder surgery prior to 1997-98 season; missed first 16 games of season. ... Traded by Avalanche with second-round pick (RW Jonathan Cheechoo) in 1998 draft to San Jose Sharks for RW Shean Donovan and first-round pick (C Alex Tanguay) in 1998 draft (November 20, 1997). ... Injured back (March 3, 2002); missed one game. ... Injured shoulder (March 10, 2002); missed two games.

STATISTICAL PLATEAUS: Three-goal games: 2000-01 (1). ... Five-goal games: 1993-94 (1). ... Total hat tricks: 2.

Season Team	League	REGULAR SEASON								PLAYOFFS				
		Gms.	G	A	Pts.	PIM	+/-	PP	SH	Gms.	G	A	Pts.	PIM
87-88—Peterborough	OHL	41	24	37	61	20	...	...	...	8	5	5	10	4
88-89—Peterborough	OHL	60	54	52	106	43	...	...	...	17	19	16	35	18
89-90—Peterborough	OHL	60	52	64	116	39	...	...	...	12	5	7	12	26
90-91—Philadelphia	NHL	68	21	20	41	64	-8	9	0	—				
91-92—Philadelphia	NHL	78	20	36	56	93	-10	11	2	—				
92-93—Quebec	NHL	77	27	51	78	123	8	12	1	6	0	6	6	8
93-94—Quebec	NHL	83	30	21	51	113	-9	13	3	—				
94-95—Quebec	NHL	48	15	21	36	40	5	9	0	6	1	3	4	8
95-96—Colorado	NHL	62	6	21	27	52	1	3	0	22	6	11	17	18
96-97—Colorado	NHL	63	13	19	32	59	-3	5	0	17	2	4	6	17
97-98—Colorado	NHL	6	0	4	4	2	0	0	0	—				
—San Jose	NHL	59	9	14	23	30	-4	5	0	6	1	3	4	6
98-99—San Jose	NHL	82	13	26	39	68	1	2	1	6	2	3	5	10
99-00—San Jose	NHL	82	20	24	44	60	14	10	0	12	5	1	6	2
00-01—San Jose	NHL	81	22	22	44	60	3	9	2	6	0	3	3	0
01-02—San Jose	NHL	79	19	34	53	44	9	5	2	12	4	6	10	4
02-03—San Jose	NHL	75	11	23	34	53	-12	5	1	—				
NHL Totals (13 years)		943	226	336	562	861	-5	98	12	93	21	40	61	73

RICHARDS, BRAD   C   LIGHTNING

PERSONAL: Born May 2, 1980, in Montague, Prince Edward Island ... 6-1/194. ... Shoots left.
TRANSACTIONS/CAREER NOTES: Selected by Tampa Bay Lightning in third round (second Lightning pick, 64th overall) of NHL entry draft (June 27, 1998).

Season Team	League	REGULAR SEASON								PLAYOFFS				
		Gms.	G	A	Pts.	PIM	+/-	PP	SH	Gms.	G	A	Pts.	PIM
96-97—Notre Dame	SJHL	63	39	48	87	73	...	...	...	—				
97-98—Rimouski	QMJHL	68	33	82	115	44	...	...	...	19	8	24	32	2
98-99—Rimouski	QMJHL	59	39	92	131	55	...	...	...	11	9	12	21	6
99-00—Rimouski	QMJHL	63	*71	*115	*186	69	...	...	...	12	13	*24	*37	16
00-01—Tampa Bay	NHL	82	21	41	62	14	-10	7	0	—				
01-02—Tampa Bay	NHL	82	20	42	62	13	-18	5	0	—				
02-03—Tampa Bay	NHL	80	17	57	74	24	3	4	0	11	0	5	5	12
NHL Totals (3 years)		244	58	140	198	51	-25	16	0	11	0	5	5	12

RICHARDSON, LUKE   D   BLUE JACKETS

PERSONAL: Born March 26, 1969, in Ottawa ... 6-4/215. ... Shoots left. ... Full Name: Luke Glen Richardson.
TRANSACTIONS/CAREER NOTES: Selected by Toronto Maple Leafs in first round (first Maple Leafs pick, seventh overall) of NHL entry draft (June 13, 1987). ... Traded by Maple Leafs with LW Vincent Damphousse, G Peter Ing, C Scott Thornton and future considerations to Edmonton Oilers for G Grant Fuhr, LW Glenn Anderson and LW Craig Berube (September 19, 1991). ... Strained clavicular joint (February 11, 1992); missed three games. ... Suffered from the flu (March 1993); missed one game. ... Fractured cheekbone (January 7, 1994); missed 15 games. ... Suffered from the flu (February 28, 1995); missed two games. ... Signed as free agent by Philadelphia Flyers (July 14, 1997). ... Suspended two games by NHL for fighting (January 30, 2000). ... Bruised shoulder (February 24, 2000); missed five games. ... Fractured right foot (November 10, 2001); missed 10 games. ... Signed as free agent by Columbus Blue Jackets (July 4, 2002).

Season Team	League	REGULAR SEASON								PLAYOFFS				
		Gms.	G	A	Pts.	PIM	+/-	PP	SH	Gms.	G	A	Pts.	PIM
84-85—Ottawa Jr. B	ODHA	35	5	26	31	72	...	...	...	—				
85-86—Peterborough	OHL	63	6	18	24	57	...	...	...	16	2	1	3	50
86-87—Peterborough	OHL	59	13	32	45	70	...	...	...	12	0	5	5	24
87-88—Toronto	NHL	78	4	6	10	90	-25	0	0	2	0	0	0	0
88-89—Toronto	NHL	55	2	7	9	106	-15	0	0	—				
89-90—Toronto	NHL	67	4	14	18	122	-1	0	0	5	0	0	0	22
90-91—Toronto	NHL	78	1	9	10	238	-28	0	0	—				
91-92—Edmonton	NHL	75	2	19	21	118	-9	0	0	16	0	5	5	45
92-93—Edmonton	NHL	82	3	10	13	142	-18	0	2	—				
93-94—Edmonton	NHL	69	2	6	8	131	-13	0	0	—				
94-95—Edmonton	NHL	46	3	10	13	40	-6	1	1	—				
95-96—Edmonton	NHL	82	2	9	11	108	-27	0	0	—				
96-97—Edmonton	NHL	82	1	11	12	91	9	0	0	12	0	2	2	14
97-98—Philadelphia	NHL	81	2	3	5	139	7	2	0	5	0	0	0	0
98-99—Philadelphia	NHL	78	0	6	6	106	-3	0	0	—				
99-00—Philadelphia	NHL	74	2	5	7	140	14	0	0	18	0	1	1	41
00-01—Philadelphia	NHL	82	2	6	8	131	23	0	1	6	0	0	0	4
01-02—Philadelphia	NHL	72	1	8	9	102	18	0	0	5	0	0	0	4
02-03—Columbus	NHL	82	0	13	13	73	-16	0	0	—				
NHL Totals (16 years)		1183	31	142	173	1877	-90	3	4	69	0	8	8	130

R

RICHTER, MIKE   G   RANGERS

PERSONAL: Born September 22, 1966, in Abington, Penn. ... 5-10/190. ... Catches left. ... Full Name: Michael Thomas Richter. ... Name pronounced RIHK-tuhr.

TRANSACTIONS/CAREER NOTES: Selected by New York Rangers in second round (second Rangers pick, 28th overall) of NHL entry draft (June 15, 1985). ... Bruised thigh (January 30, 1992); missed 12 games. ... Injured groin (December 30, 1995); missed 15 games. ... Reinjured groin (February 18, 1996); missed eight games. ... Separated left shoulder (January 19, 1997); missed two games. ... Selected by Nashville Predators in NHL expansion draft (June 26, 1998). ... Signed as free agent by Rangers (July 14, 1998). ... Injured back (October 2, 1999); missed five games. ... Sprained left knee (February 5, 2000); missed two games. ... Reinjured left knee (February 18, 2000); missed two games. ... Reinjured left knee (March 13, 2000); missed one game ... Reinjured left knee (March 27, 2000); missed four games. ... Underwent knee surgery (April 5, 2000); missed first five games of season. ... Tore anterior cruciate ligament in right knee (February 19, 2001); missed remainder of season. ... Suffered head injury (March 22, 2002); missed remainder of season. ... Traded by Rangers to Edmonton Oilers for future considerations (June 30, 2002). ... Signed as free agent by Rangers (July 4, 2002). ... Suffered head injury (November 5, 2002); missed remainder of season.

		REGULAR SEASON									PLAYOFFS							
Season Team	League	Gms.	Min	W	L	T	GA	SO	Avg.	SV%	Gms.	Min.	W	L	GA	SO	Avg.	SV%
84-85—Northwood School	N.Y. H.S.	24	1374	...	...	...	52	2	2.27	—	—	—	—	—	—	—	—	—
85-86—Univ. of Wisconsin	WCHA	24	1394	14	9	0	92	1	3.96	—	—	—	—	—	—	—	—	—
86-87—Univ. of Wisconsin	WCHA	36	2136	19	16	1	126	0	3.54	—	—	—	—	—	—	—	—	—
87-88—U.S. national team	Int'l	29	1559	17	7	2	86	0	3.31	—	—	—	—	—	—	—	—	—
—U.S. Olympic team	Int'l	4	230	2	2	0	15	0	3.91	—	—	—	—	—	—	—	—	—
—Colorado	IHL	22	1298	16	5	0	68	1	3.14	—	10	536	5	3	35	0	3.92	—
88-89—Denver	IHL	*57	3031	23	26	‡0	*217	1	4.30	—	4	210	0	4	21	0	6.00	—
—New York Rangers	NHL	—	—	—	—	—	—	—	—	—	1	58	0	1	4	0	4.14	—
89-90—New York Rangers	NHL	23	1320	12	5	5	66	0	3.00	.904	6	330	3	2	19	0	3.45	.896
—Flint	IHL	13	782	7	4	‡2	49	0	3.76	—	—	—	—	—	—	—	—	—
90-91—New York Rangers	NHL	45	2596	21	13	7	135	0	3.12	.903	6	313	2	4	14	†1	2.68	.923
91-92—New York Rangers	NHL	41	2298	23	12	2	119	3	3.11	.901	7	412	4	2	24	1	3.50	.894
92-93—New York Rangers	NHL	38	2105	13	19	3	134	1	3.82	.886	—	—	—	—	—	—	—	—
—Binghamton	AHL	5	305	4	0	1	6	0	1.18	—	—	—	—	—	—	—	—	—
93-94—New York Rangers	NHL	68	3710	*42	12	6	159	5	2.57	.910	23	1417	*16	7	49	†4	2.07	.921
94-95—New York Rangers	NHL	35	1993	14	17	2	97	2	2.92	.890	7	384	2	5	23	0	3.59	.878
95-96—New York Rangers	NHL	41	2396	24	13	3	107	3	2.68	.912	11	661	5	6	36	0	3.27	.883
96-97—New York Rangers	NHL	61	3598	33	22	6	161	4	2.68	.917	15	939	9	6	33	3	2.11	.932
97-98—New York Rangers	NHL	72	4143	21	31	*15	†184	0	2.66	.903	—	—	—	—	—	—	—	—
—U.S. Olympic team	Int'l	4	237	1	3	0	14	0	3.54	—	—	—	—	—	—	—	—	—
98-99—New York Rangers	NHL	68	3878	27	30	8	170	2	2.63	.910	—	—	—	—	—	—	—	—
99-00—New York Rangers	NHL	61	3622	22	†31	8	173	4	2.87	.905	—	—	—	—	—	—	—	—
00-01—New York Rangers	NHL	45	2635	20	21	3	144	0	3.28	.893	—	—	—	—	—	—	—	—
01-02—New York Rangers	NHL	55	3195	24	26	4	157	2	2.95	.906	—	—	—	—	—	—	—	—
—U.S. Olympic team	Int'l	4	240	2	1	1	9	1	2.25	—	—	—	—	—	—	—	—	—
02-03—New York Rangers	NHL	13	694	5	6	1	34	0	2.94	.897	—	—	—	—	—	—	—	—
NHL Totals (15 years)		666	38183	301	258	73	1840	24	2.89	.904	76	4514	41	33	202	9	2.68	.908

RITA, JANI   LW   OILERS

PERSONAL: Born July 25, 1981, in Helsinki, Finland ... 6-1/206. ... Shoots right. ... Name pronounced YAH-nee REE-tah.

TRANSACTIONS/CAREER NOTES: Selected by Edmonton Oilers in first round (first Oilers pick, 13th overall) of NHL entry draft (June 26, 1999). ... Injured shoulder (March 6, 2002); missed one game.

		REGULAR SEASON								PLAYOFFS				
Season Team	League	Gms.	G	A	Pts.	PIM	+/-	PP	SH	Gms.	G	A	Pts.	PIM
96-97—Jokerit Helsinki	Finland Jr.	3	0	0	0	0	...	...	...	—	—	—	—	—
97-98—Jokerit Helsinki	Finland Jr.	36	15	9	24	2	...	...	...	8	4	1	5	0
—Jokerit Helsinki	Finland	—	—	—	—	—	—	—	—	1	0	0	0	0
98-99—Jokerit Helsinki	Finland	41	3	2	5	39	...	...	...	—	—	—	—	—
—Jokerit Helsinki	Finland Jr.	20	9	13	22	8	...	...	...	—	—	—	—	—
99-00—Jokerit Helsinki	Finland	49	6	3	9	10	...	...	...	11	1	0	1	0
00-01—Jokerit Helsinki	Finland	50	5	10	15	18	...	...	...	5	0	0	0	2
01-02—Hamilton	AHL	76	25	17	42	32	...	...	...	15	8	4	12	0
—Edmonton	NHL	1	0	0	0	0	0	0	0	—	—	—	—	—
02-03—Hamilton	AHL	64	21	27	48	18	...	...	...	—	—	—	—	—
—Edmonton	NHL	12	3	1	4	0	2	0	0	—	—	—	—	—
NHL Totals (2 years)		13	3	1	4	0	2	0	0					

RITCHIE, BYRON   C   PANTHERS

PERSONAL: Born April 24, 1977, in Burnaby, B.C. ... 5-10/195. ... Shoots left.

TRANSACTIONS/CAREER NOTES: Selected by Hartford Whalers in seventh round (sixth Whalers pick, 165th overall) of NHL entry draft (July 8, 1995). ... Whalers franchise moved to North Carolina and renamed Carolina Hurricanes for 1997-98 season; NHL approved move on June 25, 1997. ... Traded by Hurricanes with D Sandis Ozolinsh to Florida Panthers for D Bret Hedican, C Kevyn Adams, D Tomas Malec and conditional second-round draft pick in 2003 (January 16, 2002).

Season Team	League	REGULAR SEASON								PLAYOFFS				
		Gms.	G	A	Pts.	PIM	+/-	PP	SH	Gms.	G	A	Pts.	PIM
93-94—Lethbridge	WHL	44	4	11	15	44	...	...	...	6	0	0	0	14
94-95—Lethbridge	WHL	58	22	28	50	132	...	...	...	—	—	—	—	—
95-96—Lethbridge	WHL	66	55	51	106	163	...	...	...	4	0	2	2	4
—Springfield	AHL	6	2	1	3	4	...	...	...	8	0	3	3	0
96-97—Lethbridge	WHL	63	50	76	126	115	...	...	...	18	16	12	*28	28
97-98—New Haven	AHL	65	13	18	31	97	...	...	...	—	—	—	—	—
98-99—New Haven	AHL	66	24	33	57	139	...	...	...	—	—	—	—	—
—Carolina	NHL	3	0	0	0	0	0	0	0	—	—	—	—	—
99-00—Carolina	NHL	26	0	2	2	17	-10	0	0	—	—	—	—	—
—Cincinnati	IHL	34	8	13	21	81	...	...	...	10	1	6	7	32
00-01—Cincinnati	IHL	77	31	35	66	166	...	...	...	5	3	2	5	10
01-02—Lowell	AHL	43	25	30	55	38	...	...	...	—	—	—	—	—
—Carolina	NHL	4	0	0	0	2	0	0	0	—	—	—	—	—
—Florida	NHL	31	5	6	11	34	-2	2	0	—	—	—	—	—
02-03—San Antonio	AHL	26	3	14	17	68	...	...	...	—	—	—	—	—
—Florida	NHL	30	0	3	3	19	-4	0	0	—	—	—	—	—
NHL Totals (4 years)		94	5	11	16	72	-16	2	0					

RIVERS, JAMIE   D   RED WINGS

PERSONAL: Born March 16, 1975, in Ottawa ... 6-1/210. ... Shoots left. ... Brother of Shawn Rivers, defenseman with Tampa Bay Lightning (1992-93).

TRANSACTIONS/CAREER NOTES: Selected by St. Louis Blues in third round (second Blues pick, 63rd overall) of NHL entry draft (June 26, 1993). ... Claimed by New York Islanders from Blues in NHL waiver draft (September 27, 1999). ... Bruised ankle (February 26, 2000); missed three games. ... Signed as free agent by Ottawa Senators (November 10, 2000). ... Claimed on waivers by Boston Bruins (October 13, 2001). ... Signed by Detroit Red Wings (July 29, 2003).

Season Team	League	REGULAR SEASON								PLAYOFFS				
		Gms.	G	A	Pts.	PIM	+/-	PP	SH	Gms.	G	A	Pts.	PIM
90-91—Ottawa	OHA Jr. A	55	4	30	34	74	...	...	...	—	—	—	—	—
91-92—Sudbury	OHL	55	3	13	16	20	...	...	...	8	0	0	0	0
92-93—Sudbury	OHL	62	12	43	55	20	...	...	...	14	7	19	26	4
93-94—Sudbury	OHL	65	32	*89	121	58	...	...	...	10	1	9	10	14
94-95—Sudbury	OHL	46	9	56	65	30	...	...	...	18	7	26	33	22
95-96—St. Louis	NHL	3	0	0	0	2	-1	0	0	—	—	—	—	—
—Worcester	AHL	75	7	45	52	130	...	...	...	4	0	1	1	4
96-97—Worcester	AHL	63	8	35	43	83	...	...	...	5	1	2	3	14
—St. Louis	NHL	15	2	5	7	6	-4	1	0	—	—	—	—	—
97-98—St. Louis	NHL	59	2	4	6	36	5	1	0	—	—	—	—	—
98-99—St. Louis	NHL	76	2	5	7	47	-3	1	0	9	1	1	2	2
99-00—New York Islanders	NHL	75	1	16	17	84	-4	1	0	—	—	—	—	—
00-01—Grand Rapids	IHL	2	0	0	0	2	...	...	...	—	—	—	—	—
—Ottawa	NHL	45	2	4	6	44	6	0	0	1	0	0	0	4
01-02—Ottawa	NHL	2	0	0	0	4	-3	0	0	—	—	—	—	—
—Boston	NHL	64	4	2	6	45	6	1	0	3	0	0	0	0
02-03—San Antonio	AHL	50	6	19	25	68	...	...	...	—	—	—	—	—
—Florida	NHL	1	0	0	0	2	-2	0	0	—	—	—	—	—
NHL Totals (8 years)		340	13	36	49	270	0	5	0	13	1	1	2	6

RIVET, CRAIG   D   CANADIENS

PERSONAL: Born September 13, 1974, in North Bay, Ont. ... 6-2/207. ... Shoots right. ... Name pronounced REE-vay.

TRANSACTIONS/CAREER NOTES: Selected by Montreal Canadiens in third round (fourth Canadiens pick, 68th overall) of NHL entry draft (June 20, 1992). ... Separated shoulder (January 20, 1997); missed six games. ... Bruised back (November 1, 1997); missed one game. ... Suffered concussion (December 19, 1997); missed seven games. ... Sprained shoulder (November 9, 1998); missed five games. ... Suffered back spasms and suffered from the flu (January 18, 1999); missed three games. ... Strained groin (March 13, 1999); missed three games. ... Reinjured groin (March 24, 1999); missed five games. ... Fractured cheekbone (October 8, 1999); missed nine games. ... Suffered illness (November 3, 1999); missed four games. ... Strained groin (January 4, 2000); missed eight games. ... Injured shoulder (November 29, 2000); missed five games. ... Reinjured shoulder (December 15, 2000) and underwent surgery; missed remainder of season.

Season Team	League	REGULAR SEASON								PLAYOFFS				
		Gms.	G	A	Pts.	PIM	+/-	PP	SH	Gms.	G	A	Pts.	PIM
90-91—Barrie Jr. B	OHA	42	9	17	26	55	...	...	...	—	—	—	—	—
91-92—Kingston	OHL	66	5	21	26	97	...	...	...	—	—	—	—	—
92-93—Kingston	OHL	64	19	55	74	117	...	...	...	16	5	7	12	39
93-94—Fredericton	AHL	4	0	2	2	2	...	...	...	—	—	—	—	—
—Kingston	OHL	61	12	52	64	100	...	...	...	6	0	3	3	6
94-95—Fredericton	AHL	78	5	27	32	126	...	...	...	12	0	4	4	17
—Montreal	NHL	5	0	1	1	5	2	0	0	—	—	—	—	—
95-96—Fredericton	AHL	49	5	18	23	189	...	...	...	6	0	0	0	12
—Montreal	NHL	19	1	4	5	54	4	0	0	—	—	—	—	—
96-97—Montreal	NHL	35	0	4	4	54	7	0	0	5	0	1	1	14
—Fredericton	AHL	23	3	12	15	99	...	...	...	—	—	—	—	—
97-98—Montreal	NHL	61	0	2	2	93	-3	0	0	5	0	0	0	2
98-99—Montreal	NHL	66	2	8	10	66	-3	0	0	—	—	—	—	—
99-00—Montreal	NHL	61	3	14	17	76	11	0	0	—	—	—	—	—
00-01—Montreal	NHL	26	1	2	3	36	-8	0	0	—	—	—	—	—
01-02—Montreal	NHL	82	8	17	25	76	1	0	0	12	0	3	3	4
02-03—Montreal	NHL	82	7	15	22	71	1	3	0	—	—	—	—	—
NHL Totals (9 years)		437	22	67	89	531	12	3	0	22	0	4	4	20

ROBERTS, GARY LW MAPLE LEAFS

PERSONAL: Born May 23, 1966, in North York, Ont. ... 6-2/215. ... Shoots left.

TRANSACTIONS/CAREER NOTES: Selected by Calgary Flames in first round (first Flames pick, 12th overall) of NHL entry draft (June 9, 1984). ... Injured back (January 1989). ... Suffered whiplash (November 9, 1991); missed one game. ... Suffered from the flu (January 19, 1993); missed one game. ... Suffered left quadricep hematoma (February 16, 1993); missed 25 games. ... Suspended one game by NHL for high-sticking (November 19, 1993). ... Suspended four games and fined $500 by NHL for two slashing incidents and fined $500 for high-sticking (January 7, 1994). ... Fractured thumb (March 20, 1994); missed one game. ... Fractured thumb (April 3, 1994); missed last five games of season. ... Suffered neck and spinal injury (February 4, 1995); underwent surgery and missed last 40 games of 1994-95 season and first 42 games of 1995-96 season. ... Injured neck (April 3, 1996); missed five games. ... Announced retirement (June 17, 1996); did not play during 1996-97 season. ... Traded by Flames with G Trevor Kidd to Carolina Hurricanes for G Jean-Sebastien Giguere and C Andrew Cassels (August 25, 1997). ... Strained abdominal muscle (November 12, 1997); missed six games. ... Strained rib muscle (January 11, 1998); missed 10 games. ... Suffered from the flu (March 31, 1998); missed one game. ... Injured groin (April 13, 1998); missed final three games of season. ... Sprained wrist (December 2, 1998); missed four games. ... Strained neck (April 14, 1999); missed one game. ... Strained shoulder (October 7, 1999); missed one game. ... Injured groin (October 23, 1999); missed four game. ... Suffered from the flu (January 18, 2000); missed one game. ... Injured groin (February 12, 2000); missed seven games. ... Signed as free agent by Toronto Maple Leafs (July 4, 2000). ... Suffered injury (January 11, 2002); missed one game. ... Suffered back spasms (January 24, 2002); missed two games. ... Strained rib muscle (March 25, 2002); missed final 10 games of season.

STATISTICAL PLATEAUS: Three-goal games: 1989-90 (1), 1991-92 (2), 1992-93 (2), 1993-94 (1), 1995-96 (3), 1997-98 (1), 2001-02 (1). Total: 11. ... Four-goal games: 1993-94 (1). ... Total hat tricks: 12.

			REGULAR SEASON							PLAYOFFS				
Season Team	League	Gms.	G	A	Pts.	PIM	+/-	PP	SH	Gms.	G	A	Pts.	PIM
82-83—Ottawa	OHL	53	12	8	20	83	...	...	...	5	1	0	1	19
83-84—Ottawa	OHL	48	27	30	57	144	...	...	...	13	10	7	17	*62
84-85—Ottawa	OHL	59	44	62	106	186	...	...	...	5	2	8	10	10
—Moncton	AHL	7	4	2	6	7	...	...	...	—	—	—	—	—
85-86—Ottawa	OHL	24	26	25	51	83	...	...	...	—	—	—	—	—
—Guelph	OHL	23	18	15	33	65	...	...	...	20	18	13	31	43
86-87—Moncton	AHL	38	20	18	38	72	...	...	...	—	—	—	—	—
—Calgary	NHL	32	5	10	15	85	6	0	0	2	0	0	0	4
87-88—Calgary	NHL	74	13	15	28	282	24	0	0	9	2	3	5	29
88-89—Calgary	NHL	71	22	16	38	250	32	0	1	22	5	7	12	57
89-90—Calgary	NHL	78	39	33	72	222	31	5	0	6	2	5	7	41
90-91—Calgary	NHL	80	22	31	53	252	15	0	0	7	1	3	4	18
91-92—Calgary	NHL	76	53	37	90	207	32	15	0	—	—	—	—	—
92-93—Calgary	NHL	58	38	41	79	172	32	8	3	5	1	6	7	43
93-94—Calgary	NHL	73	41	43	84	145	37	12	3	7	2	6	8	24
94-95—Calgary	NHL	8	2	2	4	43	1	2	0	—	—	—	—	—
95-96—Calgary	NHL	35	22	20	42	78	15	9	0	—	—	—	—	—
96-97—					Did not play.									
97-98—Carolina	NHL	61	20	29	49	103	3	4	0	—	—	—	—	—
98-99—Carolina	NHL	77	14	28	42	178	2	1	1	6	1	1	2	8
99-00—Carolina	NHL	69	23	30	53	62	-10	12	0	—	—	—	—	—
00-01—Toronto	NHL	82	29	24	53	109	16	8	2	11	2	9	11	0
01-02—Toronto	NHL	69	21	27	48	63	-4	6	2	19	7	12	19	*56
02-03—Toronto	NHL	14	5	3	8	10	-2	3	0	7	1	1	2	8
NHL Totals (17 years)		957	369	389	758	2261	230	85	12	101	24	53	77	288

ROBERTSSON, BERT D PENGUINS

PERSONAL: Born June 30, 1974, in Sodertalje, Sweden. ... 6-3/210. ... Shoots left. ... Name pronounced ROH-behrt-suhn.

TRANSACTIONS/CAREER NOTES: Selected by Vancouver Canucks in 10th round (eighth Canucks pick, 254th overall) of NHL entry draft (June 29, 1993). ... Injured groin (April 1, 1999); missed four games. ... Signed as free agent by Edmonton Oilers (August 19, 1999). ... Selected by Columbus Blue Jackets in NHL expansion draft (June 23, 2000). ... Traded by Blue Jackets to New York Rangers for G Jean-Francois Labbe (November 9, 2000). ... Traded by Rangers to Nashville Predators for LW Ryan Tobler (March 7, 2001). ... Traded by Predators to Mighty Ducks of Anaheim for LW Jay Legault (December 4, 2001). ... Traded by Mighty Ducks to Pittsburgh Penguins for D Mark Moore (March 8, 2002).

			REGULAR SEASON							PLAYOFFS				
Season Team	League	Gms.	G	A	Pts.	PIM	+/-	PP	SH	Gms.	G	A	Pts.	PIM
92-93—Sodertalje	Sweden Dv. 2	23	1	2	3	24	...	...	...	—	—	—	—	—
93-94—Sodertalje	Sweden Dv. 2	28	0	1	1	12	...	...	...	—	—	—	—	—
94-95—Sodertalje	Sweden Dv. 2	23	1	2	3	24	...	...	...	—	—	—	—	—
95-96—Syracuse	AHL	65	1	7	8	109	...	...	...	16	0	1	1	26
96-97—Syracuse	AHL	80	4	9	13	132	...	...	...	3	1	0	1	4
97-98—Syracuse	AHL	42	5	9	14	87	...	...	...	3	0	0	0	6
—Vancouver	NHL	30	2	4	6	24	2	0	0	—	—	—	—	—
98-99—Vancouver	NHL	39	2	2	4	13	-7	0	0	—	—	—	—	—
—Syracuse	AHL	8	1	0	1	21	...	...	...	—	—	—	—	—
99-00—Hamilton	AHL	6	0	3	3	12	...	...	...	—	—	—	—	—
—Edmonton	NHL	52	0	4	4	34	-3	0	0	5	0	0	0	0
00-01—Houston	IHL	14	0	0	0	26	...	...	...	—	—	—	—	—
—New York Rangers	NHL	2	0	0	0	4	-1	0	0	—	—	—	—	—
—Hartford	AHL	27	7	5	12	27	...	...	...	—	—	—	—	—
—Milwaukee	IHL	10	0	0	0	0	...	...	...	5	0	1	1	2
01-02—Milwaukee	AHL	14	0	1	1	18	...	...	...	—	—	—	—	—
—Cincinnati	AHL	16	0	2	2	39	...	...	...	—	—	—	—	—
—Wilkes-Barre/Scranton	AHL	13	0	0	0	15	...	...	...	—	—	—	—	—
02-03—Ilves Tampere	Finland	54	1	4	5	111	...	...	...	—	—	—	—	—
NHL Totals (4 years)		123	4	10	14	75	-9	0	0	5	0	0	0	0

ROBIDAS, STEPHANE   D   STARS

PERSONAL: Born March 3, 1977, in Sherbrooke, Que. ... 5-11/189. ... Shoots right.

TRANSACTIONS/CAREER NOTES: Selected by Montreal Canadiens in seventh round (seventh Canadiens pick, 164th overall) of NHL entry draft (June 26, 1995). ... Bruised shoulder (December 16, 2000); missed two games. ... Claimed by Atlanta Thrashers from Canadiens in NHL waiver draft (October 4, 2002). ... Traded by Thrashers to Dallas Stars for future considerations (October 4, 2002).

		REGULAR SEASON								PLAYOFFS			
Season Team	League	Gms.	G	A	Pts.	PIM	+/-	PP	SH	Gms.	G	A	Pts.	PIM
93-94—Shawinigan	QMJHL	67	3	18	21	33	...	...	...	1	0	0	0	0
94-95—Shawinigan	QMJHL	71	13	56	69	44	...	...	...	15	7	12	19	4
95-96—Shawinigan	QMJHL	67	23	56	79	53	...	...	...	6	1	5	6	10
96-97—Shawinigan	QMJHL	67	24	51	75	59	...	...	...	7	4	6	10	14
97-98—Fredericton	AHL	79	10	21	31	50	...	...	...	4	0	2	2	0
98-99—Fredericton	AHL	79	8	33	41	59	...	...	...	15	1	5	6	10
99-00—Quebec	AHL	76	14	31	45	36	...	...	...	3	0	1	1	0
—Montreal	NHL	1	0	0	0	0	0	0	0	—	—	—	—	—
00-01—Montreal	NHL	65	6	6	12	14	0	1	0	—	—	—	—	—
01-02—Montreal	NHL	56	1	10	11	14	-25	1	0	2	0	0	0	4
02-03—Dallas	NHL	76	3	7	10	35	15	0	0	12	0	1	1	20
NHL Totals (4 years)		198	10	23	33	63	-10	2	0	14	0	1	1	24

ROBITAILLE, LUC   LW   KINGS

R

PERSONAL: Born February 17, 1966, in Montreal ... 6-1/215. ... Shoots left. ... Name pronounced ROH-bih-tigh.

TRANSACTIONS/CAREER NOTES: Selected by Los Angeles Kings in ninth round (ninth Kings pick, 171st overall) of NHL entry draft (June 9, 1984). ... Suspended four games by NHL for crosschecking from behind (November 10, 1990). ... Underwent surgery to repair slight fracture of right ankle (June 15, 1994). ... Traded by Kings to Pittsburgh Penguins for RW Rick Tocchet and second-round pick (RW Pavel Rosa) in 1995 draft (July 29, 1994). ... Suspended by NHL for two games for high-sticking (February 7, 1995). ... Traded by Penguins with D Ulf Samuelsson to New York Rangers for D Sergei Zubov and C Petr Nedved (August 31, 1995). ... Suffered stress fracture in ankle (December 15, 1995); missed five games. ... Fractured foot (March 12, 1997); missed final 13 games of regular season. ... Traded by Rangers to Kings for LW Kevin Stevens (August 28, 1997). ... Injured right groin and abdomen (February 25, 1998) and underwent surgery; missed final 25 games of regular season. ... Fractured foot (November 3, 1999); missed 10 games. ... Signed as free agent by Detroit Red Wings (July 2, 2001). ... Signed by Los Angeles Kings (July 24, 2003).

STATISTICAL PLATEAUS: Three-goal games: 1986-87 (1), 1987-88 (3), 1988-89 (1), 1989-90 (2), 1992-93 (2), 1998-99 (1), 1999-00 (1). Total: 11. ... Four-goal games: 1991-92 (1), 1993-94 (1), 1994-95 (1). Total: 3. ... Total hat tricks: 14.

		REGULAR SEASON								PLAYOFFS			
Season Team	League	Gms.	G	A	Pts.	PIM	+/-	PP	SH	Gms.	G	A	Pts.	PIM
83-84—Hull	QMJHL	70	32	53	85	48	...	...	...	—	—	—	—	—
84-85—Hull	QMJHL	64	55	94	149	115	...	...	...	5	4	2	6	27
85-86—Hull	QMJHL	63	68	*123	†191	93	...	...	...	15	17	27	*44	28
86-87—Los Angeles	NHL	79	45	39	84	28	-18	18	0	5	1	4	5	2
87-88—Los Angeles	NHL	80	53	58	111	82	-9	17	0	5	2	5	7	18
88-89—Los Angeles	NHL	78	46	52	98	65	5	10	0	11	2	6	8	10
89-90—Los Angeles	NHL	80	52	49	101	38	8	20	0	10	5	5	10	12
90-91—Los Angeles	NHL	76	45	46	91	68	28	11	0	12	12	4	16	22
91-92—Los Angeles	NHL	80	44	63	107	95	-4	26	0	6	3	4	7	12
92-93—Los Angeles	NHL	84	63	62	125	100	18	24	2	24	9	13	22	28
93-94—Los Angeles	NHL	83	44	42	86	86	-20	24	0	—	—	—	—	—
94-95—Pittsburgh	NHL	46	23	19	42	37	10	5	0	12	7	4	11	26
95-96—New York Rangers	NHL	77	23	46	69	80	13	11	0	11	1	5	6	8
96-97—New York Rangers	NHL	69	24	24	48	48	16	5	0	15	4	7	11	4
97-98—Los Angeles	NHL	57	16	24	40	66	5	5	0	4	1	2	3	6
98-99—Los Angeles	NHL	82	39	35	74	54	-1	11	0	—	—	—	—	—
99-00—Los Angeles	NHL	71	36	38	74	68	11	13	0	4	2	2	4	6
00-01—Los Angeles	NHL	82	37	51	88	66	10	16	1	13	4	3	7	10
01-02—Detroit	NHL	81	30	20	50	38	-2	13	0	23	4	5	9	10
02-03—Detroit	NHL	81	11	20	31	50	4	3	0	4	1	0	1	0
NHL Totals (17 years)		1286	631	688	1319	1069	74	232	3	159	58	69	127	174

ROBITAILLE, RANDY   C   ISLANDERS

PERSONAL: Born October 12, 1975, in Ottawa ... 5-11/196. ... Shoots left. ... Name pronounced ROH-bih-tigh.

TRANSACTIONS/CAREER NOTES: Signed as non-drafted free agent by Boston Bruins (March 27, 1997). ... Injured shoulder (March 27, 1997); missed remainder of season. ... Traded by Bruins to Atlanta Thrashers for RW Peter Ferraro (June 25, 1999). ... Traded by Thrashers to Nashville Predators for LW Denny Lambert (August 16, 1999). ... Signed as free agent by Los Angeles Kings (July 6, 2001). ... Separated shoulder (December 3, 2001); missed 12 games. ... Claimed on waivers by Pittsburgh Penguins (January 4, 2002). ... Traded by Penguins to New York Islanders for fifth-round pick in 2003 draft (March 9, 2003).

		REGULAR SEASON								PLAYOFFS			
Season Team	League	Gms.	G	A	Pts.	PIM	+/-	PP	SH	Gms.	G	A	Pts.	PIM
94-95—Ottawa	CJHL	54	48	77	125	111	...	...	...	—	—	—	—	—
95-96—Miami of Ohio	CCHA	36	14	31	45	26	...	...	...	—	—	—	—	—
96-97—Miami of Ohio	CCHA	39	27	34	61	44	...	...	...	—	—	—	—	—
—Boston	NHL	1	0	0	0	0	0	0	0	—	—	—	—	—
97-98—Providence	AHL	48	15	29	44	16	...	...	...	—	—	—	—	—
—Boston	NHL	4	0	0	0	0	-2	0	0	—	—	—	—	—
98-99—Providence	AHL	74	28	*74	102	34	...	...	...	19	6	†14	20	20
—Boston	NHL	4	0	2	2	0	-1	0	0	1	0	0	0	0
99-00—Nashville	NHL	69	11	14	25	10	-13	2	0	—	—	—	—	—

Season Team	League	REGULAR SEASON								PLAYOFFS				
		Gms.	G	A	Pts.	PIM	+/-	PP	SH	Gms.	G	A	Pts.	PIM
00-01—Milwaukee..................	IHL	19	10	23	33	4	...	...	...	—	—	—	—	—
—Nashville...............	NHL	62	9	17	26	12	-11	5	0	—	—	—	—	—
01-02—Los Angeles................	NHL	18	4	3	7	17	-9	2	0	—	—	—	—	—
—Manchester................	AHL	6	7	3	10	0	...	...	...	—	—	—	—	—
—Pittsburgh.................	NHL	40	10	20	30	16	-14	3	0	—	—	—	—	—
02-03—Pittsburgh.................	NHL	41	5	12	17	8	5	1	0	—	—	—	—	—
—New York Islanders.....	NHL	10	1	2	3	2	0	1	0	5	1	1	2	0
NHL Totals (7 years)............		249	40	70	110	65	-45	14	0	6	1	1	2	0

ROCHE, DAVE — LW

PERSONAL: Born June 13, 1975, in Lindsay, Ont. ... 6-4/230. ... Shoots left. ... Brother of Scott Roche, goaltender with St. Louis Blues system (1995-96 through 1998-99). ... Name pronounced ROHCH.

TRANSACTIONS/CAREER NOTES: Selected by Pittsburgh Penguins in third round (third Penguins pick, 62nd overall) of NHL entry draft (June 26, 1993). ... Sprained ankle (November 21, 1995); missed three games. ... Injured shoulder (April 10, 1996); missed eight games. ... Suspended one playoff game and fined $1,000 by NHL for butt-ending opponent (May 26, 1996). ... Traded by Penguins with G Ken Wregget to Calgary Flames for C German Titov and C Todd Hlushko (June 17, 1998). ... Injured knee (January 2, 1999); missed 18 games. ... Traded by Islanders to Mighty Ducks of Anaheim for RW Jim Cummins (January 17, 2002). ... Traded by Mighty Ducks to Islanders for RW Ben Guite and RW Bjorn Melin (March 19, 2002). ... Signed as free agent by New Jersey Devils (August 26, 2002).

Season Team	League	REGULAR SEASON								PLAYOFFS				
		Gms.	G	A	Pts.	PIM	+/-	PP	SH	Gms.	G	A	Pts.	PIM
90-91—Peterborough Jr. B	OHA	40	22	17	39	85	...	...	...	—	—	—	—	—
91-92—Peterborough.............	OHL	62	10	17	27	105	...	...	...	10	0	0	0	34
92-93—Peterborough.............	OHL	56	40	60	100	105	...	...	...	21	14	15	29	42
93-94—Peterborough.............	OHL	34	15	22	37	127	...	...	...	—	—	—	—	—
—Windsor....................	OHL	29	14	20	34	73	...	...	...	4	1	1	2	15
94-95—Windsor....................	OHL	66	55	59	114	180	...	...	...	10	9	6	15	16
95-96—Pittsburgh.................	NHL	71	7	7	14	130	-5	0	0	16	2	7	9	26
96-97—Pittsburgh.................	NHL	61	5	5	10	155	-13	2	0	—	—	—	—	—
—Cleveland	IHL	18	5	5	10	25	...	...	...	13	6	3	9	*87
97-98—Syracuse....................	AHL	73	12	20	32	307	...	...	...	5	2	0	2	10
98-99—Calgary....................	NHL	36	3	3	6	44	-1	1	0	—	—	—	—	—
—Saint John	AHL	7	0	3	3	6	...	...	...	—	—	—	—	—
99-00—Saint John	AHL	67	22	21	43	130	...	...	...	3	0	1	1	8
—Calgary....................	NHL	2	0	0	0	5	-1	0	0	—	—	—	—	—
00-01—Saint John	AHL	79	32	26	58	179	...	...	...	19	3	6	9	43
01-02—Bridgeport.................	AHL	48	25	14	39	64	...	...	...	20	3	0	3	20
—New York Islanders.....	NHL	1	0	0	0	0	0	0	0	—	—	—	—	—
—Cincinnati..................	AHL	29	6	7	13	41	...	...	...	—	—	—	—	—
02-03—Albany......................	AHL	76	21	16	37	89	...	...	...	—	—	—	—	—
NHL Totals (5 years)............		171	15	15	30	334	-20	3	0	16	2	7	9	26

ROCHE, TRAVIS — D — WILD

PERSONAL: Born June 17, 1978, in Whitecourt, Alta. ... 6-1/190. ... Shoots right.
TRANSACTIONS/CAREER NOTES: Signed as non-drafted free agent by Minnesota Wild (April 8, 2001).

Season Team	League	REGULAR SEASON								PLAYOFFS				
		Gms.	G	A	Pts.	PIM	+/-	PP	SH	Gms.	G	A	Pts.	PIM
99-00—Univ. of North Dakota .	WCHA	42	6	22	28	60	...	...	...	—	—	—	—	—
00-01—Univ. of North Dakota .	WCHA	41	10	35	45	40	...	...	...	—	—	—	—	—
—Minnesota..................	NHL	1	0	0	0	0	0	0	0	—	—	—	—	—
01-02—Houston....................	AHL	60	13	21	34	107	...	...	...	12	2	3	5	6
—Minnesota..................	NHL	4	0	0	0	2	-1	0	0	—	—	—	—	—
02-03—Houston	AHL	65	14	34	48	42	...	...	...	—	—	—	—	—
NHL Totals (2 years)............		5	0	0	0	2	-1	0	0					

ROENICK, JEREMY — C — FLYERS

PERSONAL: Born January 17, 1970, in Boston ... 6-1/211. ... Shoots right. ... Brother of Trevor Roenick, center with Hartford Whalers/Carolina Hurricanes organization (1993-94 through 1996-97). ... Name pronounced ROH-nihk.

TRANSACTIONS/CAREER NOTES: Selected by Chicago Blackhawks in first round (first Blackhawks pick, eighth overall) of NHL entry draft (June 11, 1988). ... Sprained knee ligaments (January 9, 1989); missed one month. ... Played in Europe during 1994-95 NHL lockout. ... Sprained knee ligament (April 2, 1995); missed remainder of regular season and first eight games of playoffs. ... Pulled thigh muscle (March 4, 1996); missed three games. ... Sprained ankle (March 17, 1996); missed 12 games. ... Traded by Blackhawks to Phoenix Coyotes for C Alexei Zhamnov, RW Craig Mills and first-round pick (RW Ty Jones) in 1997 draft (August 16, 1996). ... Missed first four games of 1996-97 season due to contract dispute. ... Sprained knee (November 23, 1996); missed six games. ... Suffered mild concussion (December 5, 1997); missed one game. ... Suffered concussion (December 28, 1998); missed two games. ... Fractured jaw (April 14, 1999); missed final two games of regular season and six playoff games. ... Suspended five games by NHL for slashing incident (October 11, 1999). ... Suffered injury (March 3, 2000); missed one game. ... Suffered concussion (November 14, 2000); missed one game. ... Signed as free agent by Philadelphia Flyers (July 2, 2001). ... Sprained right knee (March 18, 2002); missed seven games. ... Suspended two games by NHL for checking from behind (December 18, 2002).

STATISTICAL PLATEAUS: Three-goal games: 1989-90 (1), 1990-91 (2), 1992-93 (1), 1999-00 (2), 2000-01 (1). Total: 7. ... Four-goal games: 1991-92 (1), 1993-94 (1). Total: 2. ... Total hat tricks: 9.

Season Team	League	REGULAR SEASON Gms.	G	A	Pts.	PIM	+/-	PP	SH	PLAYOFFS Gms.	G	A	Pts.	PIM
86-87—Thayer Academy	Mass. H.S.	24	31	34	65	...	...	...	...	—	—	—	—	—
87-88—Thayer Academy	Mass. H.S.	24	34	50	84	...	...	...	...	—	—	—	—	—
88-89—U.S. national team	Int'l	11	8	8	16	0	...	...	...	—	—	—	—	—
—Chicago	NHL	20	9	9	18	4	4	2	0	10	1	3	4	7
—Hull	QMJHL	28	34	36	70	14	...	...	...	—	—	—	—	—
89-90—Chicago	NHL	78	26	40	66	54	2	6	0	20	11	7	18	8
90-91—Chicago	NHL	79	41	53	94	80	38	15	4	6	3	5	8	4
91-92—Chicago	NHL	80	53	50	103	98	23	22	3	18	12	10	22	12
92-93—Chicago	NHL	84	50	57	107	86	15	22	3	4	1	2	3	2
93-94—Chicago	NHL	84	46	61	107	125	21	24	5	6	1	6	7	2
94-95—Koln	Germany	3	3	1	4	2	...	...	...	—	—	—	—	—
—Chicago	NHL	33	10	24	34	14	5	5	0	8	1	2	3	16
95-96—Chicago	NHL	66	32	35	67	109	9	12	4	10	5	7	12	2
96-97—Phoenix	NHL	72	29	40	69	115	-7	10	3	6	2	4	6	4
97-98—Phoenix	NHL	79	24	32	56	103	5	6	1	6	5	3	8	4
—U.S. Olympic team	Int'l	4	0	1	1	6	...	...	...	—	—	—	—	—
98-99—Phoenix	NHL	78	24	48	72	130	7	4	0	1	0	0	0	0
99-00—Phoenix	NHL	75	34	44	78	102	11	6	3	5	2	2	4	10
00-01—Phoenix	NHL	80	30	46	76	114	-1	13	0	—	—	—	—	—
01-02—Philadelphia	NHL	75	21	46	67	74	32	5	0	5	0	0	0	14
—U.S. Olympic team	Int'l	6	1	4	5	2	...	...	...	—	—	—	—	—
02-03—Philadelphia	NHL	79	27	32	59	75	20	8	1	13	3	5	8	8
NHL Totals (15 years)		1062	456	617	1073	1283	184	160	27	118	47	56	103	93

ROEST, STACY   RW   RED WINGS

PERSONAL: Born March 15, 1974, in Lethbridge, Alta. ... 5-9/185. ... Shoots right. ... Name pronounced ROHST.
TRANSACTIONS/CAREER NOTES: Signed as non-drafted free agent by Detroit Red Wings (June 9, 1997). ... Selected by Minnesota Wild in NHL expansion draft (June 23, 2000). ... Signed as free agent by Red Wings (August 27, 2002).

Season Team	League	REGULAR SEASON Gms.	G	A	Pts.	PIM	+/-	PP	SH	PLAYOFFS Gms.	G	A	Pts.	PIM
92-93—Medicine Hat	WHL	72	33	73	106	30	...	...	...	10	3	10	13	6
93-94—Medicine Hat	WHL	72	48	72	120	48	...	...	...	3	1	0	1	4
94-95—Medicine Hat	WHL	69	37	78	115	32	...	...	...	5	2	7	9	2
—Adirondack	AHL	3	0	0	0	0	...	...	...	—	—	—	—	—
95-96—Adirondack	AHL	76	16	39	55	40	...	...	...	3	0	0	0	0
96-97—Adirondack	AHL	78	25	41	66	30	...	...	...	4	1	1	2	0
97-98—Adirondack	AHL	80	34	58	92	30	...	...	...	3	2	1	3	6
98-99—Detroit	NHL	59	4	8	12	14	-7	0	0	—	—	—	—	—
—Adirondack	AHL	2	0	1	1	0	...	...	...	—	—	—	—	—
99-00—Detroit	NHL	49	7	9	16	12	-1	1	0	3	0	0	0	0
00-01—Minnesota	NHL	76	7	20	27	20	3	1	0	—	—	—	—	—
01-02—Minnesota	NHL	58	10	11	21	8	-3	1	4	—	—	—	—	—
02-03—Grand Rapids	AHL	70	24	48	72	28	...	...	...	—	—	—	—	—
—Detroit	NHL	2	0	0	0	0	0	0	0	—	—	—	—	—
NHL Totals (5 years)		244	28	48	76	54	-8	3	4	3	0	0	0	0

ROHLOFF, TODD   D

PERSONAL: Born January 16, 1974, in Grand Rapids, Minn. ... 6-3/213. ... Shoots left.
COLLEGE: Miami of Ohio.
TRANSACTIONS/CAREER NOTES: Signed as non-drafted free agent by Chicago Blackhawks (March 24, 1998). ... Signed as free agent by Washington Capitals (July 21, 2000).

Season Team	League	REGULAR SEASON Gms.	G	A	Pts.	PIM	+/-	PP	SH	PLAYOFFS Gms.	G	A	Pts.	PIM
94-95—Miami of Ohio	CCHA	38	1	6	7	22	...	...	...	—	—	—	—	—
95-96—Miami of Ohio	CCHA	23	2	4	6	24	...	...	...	—	—	—	—	—
96-97—Miami of Ohio	CCHA	38	2	12	14	48	...	...	...	—	—	—	—	—
97-98—Miami of Ohio	CCHA	17	2	5	7	38	...	...	...	—	—	—	—	—
—Indianapolis	IHL	5	0	1	1	6	...	...	...	—	—	—	—	—
98-99—Portland	AHL	58	1	6	7	59	...	...	...	—	—	—	—	—
—Indianapolis	IHL	12	2	0	2	8	...	...	...	5	1	1	2	6
99-00—Cleveland	IHL	77	1	13	14	88	...	...	...	9	0	0	0	6
00-01—Portland	AHL	58	3	8	11	59	...	...	...	3	0	0	0	2
01-02—Portland	AHL	17	1	3	4	22	...	...	...	—	—	—	—	—
—Washington	NHL	16	0	1	1	14	-2	0	0	—	—	—	—	—
02-03—Portland	AHL	64	2	10	12	65	...	...	...	—	—	—	—	—
NHL Totals (1 year)		16	0	1	1	14	-2	0	0	—	—	—	—	—

ROLOSON, DWAYNE   G   WILD

PERSONAL: Born October 12, 1969, in Simcoe, Ont. ... 6-1/178. ... Catches left. ... Full Name: Dwayne A. Roloson. ... Name pronounced ROH-luh-suhn.
TRANSACTIONS/CAREER NOTES: Signed as non-drafted free agent by Calgary Flames (July 4, 1994). ... Signed as free agent by Buffalo Sabres (July 9, 1998). ... Selected by Columbus Blue Jackets in NHL expansion draft (June 23, 2000). ... Signed as free agent by St. Louis Blues (July 14, 2000). ... Signed as free agent by Minnesota Wild (July 2, 2001).

			REGULAR SEASON								PLAYOFFS						
Season Team	League	Gms.	Min	W	L	T	GA	SO	Avg.	SV%	Gms.	Min.	W	L	GA	SO	Avg.	SV%
90-91 —Mass.-Lowell................	Hockey East	15	823	5	9	0	63	0	4.59	—	—	—	—	—	—	—	—	—
91-92 —Mass.-Lowell................	Hockey East	12	660	3	8	0	52	0	4.73	—	—	—	—	—	—	—	—	—
92-93 —Mass.-Lowell................	Hockey East	39	2342	20	17	2	150	0	3.84	—	—	—	—	—	—	—	—	—
93-94 —Mass.-Lowell................	Hockey East	40	2305	23	10	7	106	0	2.76	—	—	—	—	—	—	—	—	—
94-95 —Saint John....................	AHL	46	2734	16	21	8	156	1	3.42	—	5	299	1	4	13	0	2.61	—
95-96 —Saint John....................	AHL	67	4026	33	22	11	190	1	2.83	—	16	1027	10	6	49	1	2.86	—
96-97 —Calgary........................	NHL	31	1618	9	14	3	78	1	2.89	.897	—	—	—	—	—	—	—	—
—Saint John....................	AHL	8	481	6	2	0	22	1	2.74	—	—	—	—	—	—	—	—	—
97-98 —Saint John....................	AHL	4	245	3	0	1	8	0	1.96	—	—	—	—	—	—	—	—	—
—Calgary........................	NHL	39	2205	11	16	8	110	0	2.99	.890	—	—	—	—	—	—	—	—
98-99 —Buffalo.........................	NHL	18	911	6	8	2	42	1	2.77	.909	4	139	1	1	10	0	4.32	.851
—Rochester....................	AHL	2	120	2	0	0	4	0	2.00	—	—	—	—	—	—	—	—	—
99-00 —Buffalo.........................	NHL	14	677	1	7	3	32	0	2.84	.884	—	—	—	—	—	—	—	—
00-01 —Worcester	AHL	52	3127	*32	15	5	113	*6	*2.17	—	11	697	6	5	23	1	1.98	—
01-02 —Minnesota	NHL	45	2506	14	20	7	112	5	2.68	.901	—	—	—	—	—	—	—	—
02-03 —Minnesota	NHL	50	2945	23	16	8	98	4	2.00	.927	11	579	5	6	25	0	2.59	.903
NHL Totals (6 years).............		197	10862	64	81	31	472	11	2.61	.905	15	718	6	7	35	0	2.92	.892

ROLSTON, BRIAN   C   BRUINS

R

PERSONAL: Born February 21, 1973, in Flint, Mich. ... 6-2/205. ... Shoots left.

TRANSACTIONS/CAREER NOTES: Selected by New Jersey Devils in first round (second Devils pick, 11th overall) of NHL entry draft (June 22, 1991). ... Loaned by Devils to U.S. Olympic Team (November 2, 1993). ... Fractured foot (October 17, 1995); missed 11 games. ... Injured hamstring (January 12, 1998); missed one game. ... Suffered from the flu (January 28, 1998); missed one game. ... Traded by Devils with a conditional third-round pick in the 2001 draft to Colorado Avalanche for RW Claude Lemieux, second-round pick (D Matt DeMarchi) in 2000 draft and swap of first-round picks in 2000 draft (November 3, 1999). ... Bruised ankle (January 27, 2000); missed three games. ... Traded by Avalanche with D Martin Grenier, C Samual Pahlsson and first-round pick (LW Martin Samuelsson) in 2000 draft to Boston Bruins for D Ray Bourque and LW Dave Andreychuk (March 6, 2000). ... Injured ribs (October 28, 2000); missed five games.

STATISTICAL PLATEAUS: Three-goal games: 1996-97 (1).

			REGULAR SEASON							PLAYOFFS				
Season Team	League	Gms.	G	A	Pts.	PIM	+/-	PP	SH	Gms.	G	A	Pts.	PIM
89-90 —Detroit.........................	NAJHL	40	36	37	73	57	...	...	...	—	—	—	—	—
90-91 —Detroit.........................	NAJHL	36	49	46	95	14	...	...	...	—	—	—	—	—
91-92 —Lake Superior State	CCHA	41	18	28	46	16	...	...	...	—	—	—	—	—
92-93 —Lake Superior State	CCHA	39	33	31	64	20	...	...	...	—	—	—	—	—
—U.S. Jr. national team .	Int'l	7	6	2	8	2	...	...	...	—	—	—	—	—
93-94 —U.S. national team	Int'l	41	20	28	48	36	...	...	...	—	—	—	—	—
—U.S. Olympic team......	Int'l	8	7	0	7	8	...	...	...	—	—	—	—	—
—Albany.......................	AHL	17	5	5	10	8	...	...	...	5	1	2	3	0
94-95 —Albany.......................	AHL	18	9	11	20	10	...	...	...	—	—	—	—	—
—New Jersey	NHL	40	7	11	18	17	5	2	0	6	2	1	3	4
95-96 —New Jersey	NHL	58	13	11	24	8	9	3	1	—	—	—	—	—
96-97 —New Jersey	NHL	81	18	27	45	20	6	2	2	10	4	1	5	6
97-98 —New Jersey	NHL	76	16	14	30	16	7	0	2	6	1	0	1	2
98-99 —New Jersey	NHL	82	24	33	57	14	11	5	†5	7	1	0	1	2
99-00 —New Jersey	NHL	11	3	1	4	0	-2	1	0	—	—	—	—	—
—Colorado	NHL	50	8	10	18	12	-6	1	0	—	—	—	—	—
—Boston	NHL	16	5	4	9	6	-4	3	0	—	—	—	—	—
00-01 —Boston	NHL	77	19	39	58	28	6	5	0	—	—	—	—	—
01-02 —Boston	NHL	82	31	31	62	30	11	6	*9	6	4	1	5	0
—U.S. Olympic team......	Int'l	6	0	3	3	0	...	...	...	—	—	—	—	—
02-03 —Boston	NHL	81	27	32	59	32	1	6	5	5	0	2	2	0
NHL Totals (9 years)...........		654	171	213	384	183	44	34	24	40	12	5	17	14

RONNING, CLIFF   C

PERSONAL: Born October 1, 1965, in Burnaby, B.C. ... 5-8/165. ... Shoots left.

TRANSACTIONS/CAREER NOTES: Selected by St. Louis Blues in seventh round (ninth Blues pick, 134th overall) of NHL entry draft (June 9, 1984). ... Injured groin (November 1988). ... Agreed to play in Italy for 1989-90 season (August 1989). ... Fractured right index finger (November 12, 1990); missed 12 games. ... Traded by Blues with LW Geoff Courtnall, D Robert Dirk, LW Sergio Momesso and fifth-round pick (RW Brian Loney) in 1992 draft to Vancouver Canucks for C Dan Quinn and D Garth Butcher (March 5, 1991). ... Sprained hand (January 4, 1993); missed five games. ... Separated shoulder (January 8, 1994); missed eight games. ... Strained groin (February 9, 1995); missed four games. ... Injured groin (October 8, 1995); missed two games. ... Signed as free agent by Phoenix Coyotes (July 2, 1996). ... Fractured hand (October 10, 1996); missed 12 games. ... Suffered from the flu (December 17, 1996); missed one game. ... Traded by Coyotes with D Richard Lintner to Nashville Predators for future considerations (October 31, 1998). ... Bruised knee (April 14, 1999); missed one game. ... Injured hamstring (January 7, 2001); missed two games. ... Traded by Predators to Los Angeles Kings for D Jere Karalahti and conditional pick in 2003 draft (March 16, 2002). ... Traded by Kings to Minnesota Wild for fourth-round pick (D Aaron Rome) in 2002 draft (June 22, 2002).

STATISTICAL PLATEAUS: Three-goal games: 1986-87 (1), 1992-93 (1), 1995-96 (1). Total: 3.

			REGULAR SEASON							PLAYOFFS				
Season Team	League	Gms.	G	A	Pts.	PIM	+/-	PP	SH	Gms.	G	A	Pts.	PIM
82-83 —New Westminster	BCJHL	52	82	68	150	42	...	...	...	—	—	—	—	—
83-84 —New Westminster	WHL	71	69	67	136	10	...	...	...	9	8	13	21	10
84-85 —New Westminster	WHL	70	*89	108	*197	20	...	...	...	11	10	14	24	4
85-86 —Canadian nat'l team	Int'l	71	55	63	118	53	...	...	...	—	—	—	—	—
—St. Louis	NHL	—	—	—	—	—	—	—	—	5	1	1	2	2
86-87 —Canadian nat'l team	Int'l	26	16	16	32	12	...	...	...	—	—	—	—	—
—St. Louis	NHL	42	11	14	25	6	-1	2	0	4	0	1	1	0

Season Team	League	Gms.	G	A	Pts.	PIM	+/-	PP	SH	Gms.	G	A	Pts.	PIM
87-88—St. Louis	NHL	26	5	8	13	12	6	1	0	—	—	—	—	—
88-89—St. Louis	NHL	64	24	31	55	18	3	16	0	7	1	3	4	0
—Peoria	IHL	12	11	20	31	8	...	...	...	—	—	—	—	—
89-90—Asiago	Italy	42	76	60	136	30	...	...	...	6	7	12	19	4
90-91—St. Louis	NHL	48	14	18	32	10	2	5	0	—	—	—	—	—
—Vancouver	NHL	11	6	6	12	0	-2	2	0	6	6	3	9	12
91-92—Vancouver	NHL	80	24	47	71	42	18	6	0	13	8	5	13	6
92-93—Vancouver	NHL	79	29	56	85	30	19	10	0	12	2	9	11	6
93-94—Vancouver	NHL	76	25	43	68	42	7	10	0	24	5	10	15	16
94-95—Vancouver	NHL	41	6	19	25	27	-4	3	0	11	3	5	8	2
95-96—Vancouver	NHL	79	22	45	67	42	16	5	0	6	0	2	2	6
96-97—Phoenix	NHL	69	19	32	51	26	-9	8	0	7	0	7	7	12
97-98—Phoenix	NHL	80	11	44	55	36	5	3	0	6	1	3	4	4
98-99—Phoenix	NHL	7	2	5	7	2	3	2	0	—	—	—	—	—
—Nashville	NHL	72	18	35	53	40	-6	8	0	—	—	—	—	—
99-00—Nashville	NHL	82	26	36	62	34	-13	7	0	—	—	—	—	—
00-01—Nashville	NHL	80	19	43	62	28	4	6	0	—	—	—	—	—
01-02—Nashville	NHL	67	18	31	49	24	0	4	0	—	—	—	—	—
—Los Angeles	NHL	14	1	4	5	8	0	1	0	4	0	1	1	2
02-03—Minnesota	NHL	80	17	31	48	24	-6	8	0	17	2	7	9	4
NHL Totals (17 years)		1097	297	548	845	451	42	107	0	122	29	57	86	72

R — ROSA, PAVEL   RW   KINGS

PERSONAL: Born June 7, 1977, in Most, Czechoslovakia ... 5-11/188. ... Shoots right.
TRANSACTIONS/CAREER NOTES: Selected by Los Angeles Kings in second round (third Kings pick, 50th overall) of NHL entry draft (July 8, 1995).

Season Team	League	Gms.	G	A	Pts.	PIM	+/-	PP	SH	Gms.	G	A	Pts.	PIM
94-95—Chemopetrol Litvinov	Czech. Jrs.	40	56	42	98		...	...	...	—	—	—	—	—
—Chem. Litvinov	Czech Rep.	2	0	0	0	0	...	...	...	1	0	0	0	0
95-96—Hull	QMJHL	61	46	70	116	39	...	...	...	18	14	22	36	25
96-97—Hull	QMJHL	68	*63	*89	*152	56	...	...	...	14	18	13	31	16
97-98—Fredericton	AHL	1	0	0	0	0	...	...	...	—	—	—	—	—
—Long Beach	IHL	2	0	1	1	0	...	...	...	1	1	1	2	0
98-99—Long Beach	IHL	31	17	13	30	28	...	...	...	6	1	2	3	0
—Los Angeles	NHL	29	4	12	16	6	0	0	0	—	—	—	—	—
99-00—Long Beach	IHL	74	22	31	53	76	...	...	...	6	2	2	4	4
—Los Angeles	NHL	3	0	0	0	0	-1	0	0	—	—	—	—	—
00-01—HPK Hameenlinna	Finland	54	25	25	50	53	...	...	...	—	—	—	—	—
01-02—Jokerit Helsinki	Finland	46	21	22	43	37	...	...	...	12	3	5	8	18
02-03—Manchester	AHL	61	28	35	63	20	...	...	...	—	—	—	—	—
—Los Angeles	NHL	2	0	0	0	0	-1	0	0	—	—	—	—	—
NHL Totals (3 years)		34	4	12	16	6	-2	0	0					

ROSSITER, KYLE   D   PANTHERS

PERSONAL: Born June 9, 1980, in Edmonton ... 6-3/217. ... Shoots left.
TRANSACTIONS/CAREER NOTES: Selected by Florida Panthers in second round (first Panthers pick, 30th overall) of NHL entry draft (June 27, 1998).

Season Team	League	Gms.	G	A	Pts.	PIM	+/-	PP	SH	Gms.	G	A	Pts.	PIM
96-97—Spokane	WHL	50	0	2	2	65	...	...	...	9	0	0	0	6
97-98—Spokane	WHL	61	6	16	22	190	...	...	...	15	0	3	3	28
98-99—Spokane	WHL	71	4	17	21	206	...	...	...	—	—	—	—	—
99-00—Spokane	WHL	63	11	22	33	155	...	...	...	14	1	4	5	21
00-01—Louisville	AHL	78	2	5	7	110	...	...	...	—	—	—	—	—
01-02—Utah	AHL	74	3	7	10	88	...	...	...	5	0	1	1	0
—Florida	NHL	2	0	0	0	2	-1	0	0	—	—	—	—	—
02-03—San Antonio	AHL	67	0	7	7	107	...	...	...	—	—	—	—	—
—Florida	NHL	3	0	0	0	0	-2	0	0	—	—	—	—	—
NHL Totals (2 years)		5	0	0	0	2	-3	0	0					

ROULEAU, ALEXANDRE   D   PENGUINS

PERSONAL: Born July 29, 1983, in Mont-Laurier, Que. ... 6-1/180. ... Shoots left.
TRANSACTIONS/CAREER NOTES: Selected by Pittsburgh Penguins in third round (fourth Penguins pick, 96th overall) of NHL entry draft (June 23, 2001). ... Re-signed by Penguins (June 1, 2003).

Season Team	League	Gms.	G	A	Pts.	PIM	+/-	PP	SH	Gms.	G	A	Pts.	PIM
00-01—Val-d'Or	QMJHL	70	8	17	25	124	...	...	...	21	1	0	1	46
01-02—Val-d'Or	QMJHL	69	14	25	39	174	...	...	...	7	0	2	2	16
02-03—Val-d'Or	QMJHL	31	7	12	19	74	...	...	...	—	—	—	—	—
—Quebec	QMJHL	24	9	17	26	74	...	...	...	—	—	—	—	—

ROURKE, ALLAN   D   HURRICANES

PERSONAL: Born March 6, 1980, in Mississauga, Ont. ... 6-2/210. ... Shoots left.
TRANSACTIONS/CAREER NOTES: Selected by Toronto Maple Leafs in sixth round (sixth Maple Leafs pick, 154th overall) of NHL entry draft (June 27, 1998). ... Traded by Toronto to Carolina Hurricanes for C Harold Druken (May 30, 2003). ... Re-signed by Hurricanes (July 14, 2003).

Season Team	League	REGULAR SEASON								PLAYOFFS				
		Gms.	G	A	Pts.	PIM	+/-	PP	SH	Gms.	G	A	Pts.	PIM
96-97—Kitchener	OHL	25	1	1	2	12	...	...	...	6	0	0	0	0
97-98—Kitchener	OHL	48	5	17	22	59	...	...	...	6	1	1	2	6
98-99—Kitchener	OHL	66	11	28	39	79	...	...	...	1	0	0	0	2
99-00—Kitchener	OHL	67	31	43	74	57	...	...	...	5	0	6	6	13
00-01—St. John's	AHL	64	9	19	28	36	...	...	...	—	—	—	—	—
01-02—St. John's	AHL	62	2	9	11	48	...	...	...	10	0	2	2	6
02-03—St. John's	AHL	65	12	19	31	49	...	...	...	—	—	—	—	—

ROY, ANDRE   LW   LIGHTNING

PERSONAL: Born February 8, 1975, in Port Chester, N.Y. ... 6-4/213. ... Shoots left. ... Full Name: Andre Christopher Roy. ... Name pronounced WAH.
TRANSACTIONS/CAREER NOTES: Selected by Boston Bruins in sixth round (fifth Bruins pick, 151st overall) of NHL entry draft (June 29, 1994). ... Signed as free agent by Ottawa Senators (March 19, 1999). ... Injured right knee (November 18, 1999); missed one game. ... Suffered back spasms (November 6, 2000); missed two games. ... Suffered from the flu (January 13, 2001); missed two games. ... Suspended two games by NHL for unsportsmanlike conduct (February 26, 2001). ... Strained groin (March 30, 2001); missed one game. ... Injured left ankle (February 6, 2002); missed 11 games. ... Traded by Senators with sixth-round pick (D Paul Ranger) in 2002 draft to Tampa Bay Lightning for C Juha Ylonen (March 15, 2002). ... Suspended 13 games by NHL for leaving penalty box to fight (April 2, 2002). ... Suspended three games by NHL for abuse of official (February 13, 2003). ... Re-signed by Lightning (July 15, 2003).

Season Team	League	REGULAR SEASON								PLAYOFFS				
		Gms.	G	A	Pts.	PIM	+/-	PP	SH	Gms.	G	A	Pts.	PIM
93-94—Beauport	QMJHL	33	6	7	13	125	...	...	...	—	—	—	—	—
—Chicoutimi	QMJHL	32	4	14	18	152	...	...	...	25	3	6	9	94
94-95—Chicoutimi	QMJHL	20	15	8	23	90	...	...	...	—	—	—	—	—
—Drummondville	QMJHL	34	18	13	31	233	...	...	...	4	2	0	2	34
95-96—Providence	AHL	58	7	8	15	167	...	...	...	1	0	0	0	10
—Boston	NHL	3	0	0	0	0	0	0	0	—	—	—	—	—
96-97—Providence	AHL	50	17	11	28	234	...	...	...	—	—	—	—	—
—Boston	NHL	10	0	2	2	12	-5	0	0	—	—	—	—	—
97-98—Providence	AHL	36	3	11	14	154	...	...	...	—	—	—	—	—
—Charlotte	ECHL	27	10	8	18	132	...	...	...	7	2	3	5	34
98-99—Fort Wayne	IHL	65	15	6	21	395	...	...	...	2	0	0	0	11
99-00—Ottawa	NHL	73	4	3	7	145	3	0	0	5	0	0	0	2
00-01—Ottawa	NHL	64	3	5	8	169	1	0	0	2	0	0	0	16
01-02—Ottawa	NHL	56	6	8	14	148	3	0	0	—	—	—	—	—
—Tampa Bay	NHL	9	1	1	2	63	-5	0	0	—	—	—	—	—
02-03—Tampa Bay	NHL	62	10	7	17	119	0	0	0	5	0	1	1	2
NHL Totals (6 years)		277	24	26	50	656	-3	0	0	12	0	1	1	20

ROY, DEREK   C   SABRES

PERSONAL: Born May 4, 1983, in Ottawa. ... 5-8/187. ... Shoots left.
TRANSACTIONS/CAREER NOTES: Selected by Buffalo Sabres in second round (second Sabres pick, 32nd overall) of NHL entry draft (June 23, 2001). ... Signed by Buffalo (May 28, 2003).

Season Team	League	REGULAR SEASON								PLAYOFFS				
		Gms.	G	A	Pts.	PIM	+/-	PP	SH	Gms.	G	A	Pts.	PIM
99-00—Kitchener	OHL	66	34	53	87	44	...	...	...	5	4	1	5	6
00-01—Kitchener	OHL	65	42	39	81	114	...	...	...	—	—	—	—	—
01-02—Kitchener	OHL	62	43	46	89	92	...	...	...	4	1	2	3	2
02-03—Kitchener	OHL	49	28	50	78	73	...	...	...	—	—	—	—	—

ROY, PATRICK   G

PERSONAL: Born October 5, 1965, in Quebec City ... 6-2/190. ... Catches left. ... Name pronounced WAH.
TRANSACTIONS/CAREER NOTES: Announced retirement (May 28, 2003). ... Suspended eight games by NHL for slashing (October 19, 1987). ... Sprained left knee ligaments (December 12, 1990); missed nine games. ... Tore left ankle ligaments (January 27, 1991); missed 14 games. ... Reinjured left ankle (March 16, 1991). ... Strained hip flexor (March 6, 1993); missed two games. ... Suffered stiff neck (December 11, 1993); missed two games. ... Strained neck (December 22, 1993); missed four games. ... Traded by Canadiens with RW Mike Keane to Colorado Avalanche for G Jocelyn Thibault, LW Martin Rucinsky and RW Andrei Kovalenko (December 6, 1995). ... Sprained thumb (January 23, 1997); missed two games. ... Injured shoulder (March 26, 1997); missed two games. ... Partially dislocated shoulder (November 17, 1997); missed two games. ... Injured left knee (December 26, 1998); missed four games. ... Suffered back spasms (January 4, 1999); missed four games. ... Injured groin (February 21, 1999); missed two games. ... Injured neck (February 15, 2000); missed one game. ... Injured groin (February 18, 2000); missed two games. ... Suffered tendinitis in knee (March 20, 2001); missed one game. ... Injured hip (October 23, 2001); missed two games. ... Announced retirement (May 28, 2003).

		REGULAR SEASON									PLAYOFFS							
Season Team	League	Gms.	Min	W	L	T	GA	SO	Avg.	SV%	Gms.	Min.	W	L	GA SO	Avg.	SV%
82-83—Granby	QMJHL	54	2808	13	35	1	293	0	6.26	—	—	—	—	—	—	—	—
83-84—Granby	QMJHL	61	3585	29	29	1	265	0	4.44	—	4	244	0	4	22 0	5.41	—
84-85—Granby	QMJHL	44	2463	16	25	1	228	0	5.55	—	—	—	—	—	—	—	—
—Montreal	NHL	1	20	1	0	0	0	0	...	1.000	—	—	—	—	—	—	—
—Sherbrooke	AHL	1	60	1	0	0	4	0	4.00	—	*13	*769	10	3	37 0	*2.89	—
85-86—Montreal	NHL	47	2651	23	18	3	148	1	3.35	.875	20	1218	*15	5	39 †1	1.92	.923
86-87—Montreal	NHL	46	2686	22	16	6	131	1	2.93	.892	6	330	4	2	22 0	4.00	.873
87-88—Montreal	NHL	45	2586	23	12	9	125	3	2.90	.900	8	430	3	4	24 0	3.35	.890
88-89—Montreal	NHL	48	2744	33	5	6	113	4	*2.47	.908	19	1206	13	6	42 2	*2.09	.920
89-90—Montreal	NHL	54	3173	31	16	5	134	3	2.53	.912	11	641	5	6	26 1	2.43	.911
90-91—Montreal	NHL	48	2835	25	15	6	128	1	2.71	.906	13	785	7	5	40 0	3.06	.898
91-92—Montreal	NHL	67	3935	36	22	8	155	†5	*2.36	.914	11	686	4	7	30 1	2.62	.904
92-93—Montreal	NHL	62	3595	31	25	5	192	2	3.20	.894	20	1293	*16	4	46 0	*2.13	.929
93-94—Montreal	NHL	68	3867	35	17	11	161	†7	2.50	.918	6	375	3	3	16 0	2.56	.930
94-95—Montreal	NHL	†43	2566	17	20	6	127	1	2.97	.906	—	—	—	—	—	—	—
95-96—Montreal	NHL	22	1260	12	9	1	62	1	2.95	.907	—	—	—	—	—	—	—
—Colorado	NHL	39	2305	22	15	1	103	1	2.68	.909	22	*1454	*16	6	*51 *3	2.10	.921
96-97—Colorado	NHL	62	3698	*38	15	7	143	7	2.32	.923	17	1034	10	7	38 3	2.21	.932
97-98—Colorado	NHL	65	3835	31	19	13	153	4	2.39	.916	7	430	3	4	18 0	2.51	.906
—Can. Olympic team	Int'l	6	369	4	2	0	9	1	1.46	—	—	—	—	—	—	—	—
98-99—Colorado	NHL	61	3648	32	19	8	139	5	2.29	.917	19	1173	11	†8	*52 1	2.66	.920
99-00—Colorado	NHL	63	3704	32	21	8	141	2	2.28	.914	17	1039	11	6	31 3	1.79	.928
00-01—Colorado	NHL	62	3585	40	13	7	132	4	2.21	.913	23	1451	*16	7	41 †4	*1.70	.934
01-02—Colorado	NHL	63	3773	32	23	8	122	*9	*1.94	.925	21	1241	11	†10	*52 3	2.51	.909
02-03—Colorado	NHL	63	3769	35	15	13	137	5	2.18	.920	7	423	3	4	16 1	2.27	.910
NHL Totals (19 years)		1029	60235	551	315	131	2546	66	2.54	.910	247	15209	151	94	584 23	2.30	.918

ROYER, GAETAN — RW

PERSONAL: Born March 13, 1976, in Donnacona, Que. ... 6-3/193. ... Shoots right. ... Brother of Remi Royer, defenseman, Chicago Blackhawks system.

TRANSACTIONS/CAREER NOTES: Signed as non-drafted free agent by Calgary Flames (September 12, 2000). ... Signed as free agent by Tampa Bay Lightning (October 19, 2001).

		REGULAR SEASON								PLAYOFFS				
Season Team	League	Gms.	G	A	Pts.	PIM	+/-	PP	SH	Gms.	G	A	Pts.	PIM
94-95—Sherbrooke	QMJHL	65	11	25	36	194	...	...	...	7	0	2	2	6
95-96—Beauport	QMJHL	61	36	36	72	233	...	...	...	19	5	9	14	47
96-97—Indianapolis	IHL	29	2	4	6	60	...	...	...	—	—	—	—	—
—Jacksonville	ECHL	28	7	8	15	149	...	...	...	—	—	—	—	—
97-98—Canadian nat'l team	Int'l	55	10	17	27	101	...	...	...	—	—	—	—	—
98-99—Grand Rapids	IHL	52	12	6	18	177	...	...	...	—	—	—	—	—
—Saint John	AHL	15	1	0	1	36	...	...	...	7	0	1	1	8
99-00—Michigan	IHL	20	6	2	8	64	...	...	...	—	—	—	—	—
00-01—Saint John	AHL	58	8	4	12	134	...	...	...	14	0	0	0	16
01-02—Pensacola	ECHL	33	13	10	23	129	...	...	...	—	—	—	—	—
—Springfield	AHL	40	6	4	10	112	...	...	...	—	—	—	—	—
—Tampa Bay	NHL	3	0	0	0	2	-1	0	0	—	—	—	—	—
02-03—Springfield	AHL	33	2	5	7	50	...	...	...	—	—	—	—	—
—Jackson	ECHL	11	3	6	9	58	...	...	...	—	—	—	—	—
—Pensacola	ECHL	20	3	10	13	60	...	...	...	—	—	—	—	—
NHL Totals (1 year)		3	0	0	0	2	-1	0	0	—	—	—	—	—

ROZSIVAL, MICHAL — D — PENGUINS

PERSONAL: Born September 3, 1978, in Vlasim, Czechoslovakia ... 6-1/208. ... Shoots right. ... Name pronounced RAH-sih-vahl.

TRANSACTIONS/CAREER NOTES: Selected by Pittsburgh Penguins in fourth round (fifth Penguins pick, 105th overall) of NHL entry draft (June 22, 1996). ... Strained hip flexor (March 21, 2000); missed two games. ... Injured groin (April 4, 2002); missed two games.

		REGULAR SEASON								PLAYOFFS				
Season Team	League	Gms.	G	A	Pts.	PIM	+/-	PP	SH	Gms.	G	A	Pts.	PIM
94-95—Czech Rep.	Czech Rep.	31	8	13	21	...	...	...	...	—	—	—	—	—
95-96—Czech Rep.	Czech Rep.	36	3	4	7	...	...	...	...	—	—	—	—	—
96-97—Swift Current	WHL	63	8	31	39	80	...	...	...	10	0	6	6	15
97-98—Swift Current	WHL	71	14	55	69	122	...	...	...	12	0	5	5	33
98-99—Syracuse	AHL	49	3	22	25	72	...	...	...	—	—	—	—	—
99-00—Pittsburgh	NHL	75	4	17	21	48	11	1	0	2	0	0	0	4
00-01—Pittsburgh	NHL	30	1	4	5	26	3	0	0	—	—	—	—	—
—Wilkes-Barre/Scranton	AHL	29	8	8	16	32	...	...	...	21	3	*19	22	23
01-02—Pittsburgh	NHL	79	9	20	29	47	-6	4	0	—	—	—	—	—
02-03—Pittsburgh	NHL	53	4	6	10	40	-5	1	0	—	—	—	—	—
NHL Totals (4 years)		237	18	47	65	161	3	6	0	2	0	0	0	4

RUCCHIN, STEVE — C — MIGHTY DUCKS

PERSONAL: Born July 4, 1971, in Thunder Bay, Ont. ... 6-3/212. ... Shoots left. ... Full Name: Steven Andrew Rucchin. ... Name pronounced ROO-chihn.

TRANSACTIONS/CAREER NOTES: Selected by Mighty Ducks of Anaheim in first round (first Mighty Ducks pick, second overall) of NHL supplemental draft (June 28, 1994). ... Suffered from the flu (March 7, 1995); missed two games. ... Sprained left knee (November 27, 1995);

missed 18 games. ... Strained groin (October 3, 1997); missed eight games. ... Strained left knee (April 9, 1998); missed two games. ... Injured groin (March 18, 1999); missed three games. ... Reinjured groin (March 31, 1999); missed seven games. ... Suffered infected left ankle (December 28, 1999); missed 11 games. ... Fractured hand (September 22, 2000); missed six games. ... Fractured nose and cheek bone (November 15, 2000) and underwent surgery; missed 10 games. ... Suffered from concussion (December 13, 2001); missed remainder of season. ... Suffered stress fracture in leg (November 11, 2001); missed 44 games.

| | | | REGULAR SEASON | | | | | | | | PLAYOFFS | | | | |
Season Team	League	Gms.	G	A	Pts.	PIM	+/-	PP	SH		Gms.	G	A	Pts.	PIM
90-91—Univ. of W. Ontario	OUAA	34	13	16	29	14	...	...	...		—	—	—	—	—
91-92—Univ. of W. Ontario	OUAA	37	28	34	62	36	...	...	...		—	—	—	—	—
92-93—Univ. of W. Ontario	OUAA	34	22	26	48	16	...	...	...		—	—	—	—	—
93-94—Univ. of W. Ontario	OUAA	35	30	23	53	30	...	...	...		—	—	—	—	—
94-95—San Diego	IHL	41	11	15	26	14	...	...	...		—	—	—	—	—
—Anaheim	NHL	43	6	11	17	23	7	0	0		—	—	—	—	—
95-96—Anaheim	NHL	64	19	25	44	12	3	8	1		—	—	—	—	—
96-97—Anaheim	NHL	79	19	48	67	24	26	6	1		8	1	2	3	10
97-98—Anaheim	NHL	72	17	36	53	13	8	8	1		—	—	—	—	—
98-99—Anaheim	NHL	69	23	39	62	22	11	5	1		4	0	3	3	0
99-00—Anaheim	NHL	71	19	38	57	16	9	10	0		—	—	—	—	—
00-01—Anaheim	NHL	16	3	5	8	0	-5	2	0		—	—	—	—	—
01-02—Anaheim	NHL	38	7	16	23	6	-3	4	0		—	—	—	—	—
02-03—Anaheim	NHL	82	20	38	58	12	-14	6	1		21	7	3	10	2
NHL Totals (9 years)..........		534	133	256	389	128	42	49	5		33	8	8	16	12

RUCINSKY, MARTIN   LW

R

PERSONAL: Born March 11, 1971, in Most, Czechoslovakia ... 6-1/205. ... Shoots left. ... Name pronounced roo-SHIHN-skee.

TRANSACTIONS/CAREER NOTES: Selected by Edmonton Oilers in first round (second Oilers pick, 20th overall) of NHL entry draft (June 22, 1991). ... Traded by Oilers to Quebec Nordiques for G Ron Tugnutt and LW Brad Zavisha (March 10, 1992). ... Suffered from the flu (February 28, 1993); missed one game. ... Bruised buttocks (December 3, 1994); missed one game. ... Sprained right wrist (January 11, 1994); missed one game. ... Fractured left cheekbone (January 30, 1994); missed four games. ... Suffered hairline fracture of right wrist (March 7, 1994); missed one game. ... Reinjured right wrist (March 21, 1994); missed six games. ... Reinjured right wrist (April 5, 1994); missed one game. ... Played in Europe during 1994-95 NHL lockout. ... Separated shoulder (February 25, 1995); missed 17 games. ... Reinjured shoulder (April 6, 1995); missed remainder of season. ... Nordiques franchise moved to Colorado and renamed Avalanche for 1995-96 season (June 21, 1995). ... Injured groin (November 28, 1995); missed one game. ... Traded by Avalanche with G Jocelyn Thibault and RW Andrei Kovalenko to Montreal Canadiens for G Patrick Roy and RW Mike Keane (December 6, 1995). ... Sprained right knee (April 6, 1996); missed two games. ... Injured hand (October 19, 1996); missed one game. ... Strained knee (November 25, 1996); missed one game. ... Separated shoulder (December 28, 1996); missed 10 games. ... Bruised foot (October 17, 1997); missed one game. ... Sprained ankle (April 4, 1998); missed three games. ... Injured shoulder (March 6, 1999); missed three games. ... Suffered concussion (November 16, 1999); missed one game. ... Suffered back spasms (March 25, 2000); missed one game. ... Sprained medial collateral ligament in knee (December 18, 2000); missed 21 games. ... Bruised left thigh (March 12, 2001); missed four games. ... Suffered eye injury (November 3, 2001); missed two games. ... Traded by Canadiens with LW Benoit Brunet to Dallas Stars for RW Donald Audette and C Shaun Van Allen (November 21, 2001). ... Traded by Stars with C Roman Lyashenko to New York Rangers for C Manny Malhotra and LW Barrett Heisten (March 12, 2002). ... Signed as free agent by St. Louis Blues (October 24, 2002).

STATISTICAL PLATEAUS: Three-goal games: 1995-96 (1), 1996-97 (1). Total: 2.

| | | | REGULAR SEASON | | | | | | | | PLAYOFFS | | | | |
Season Team	League	Gms.	G	A	Pts.	PIM	+/-	PP	SH		Gms.	G	A	Pts.	PIM
88-89—CHZ Litvinov	Czech.	3	1	0	1	2	...	...	...		—	—	—	—	—
89-90—CHZ Litvinov	Czech.	47	12	6	18	...	...	...	...		—	—	—	—	—
90-91—CHZ Litvinov	Czech.	49	23	18	41	79	...	...	...		—	—	—	—	—
—Czechoslovakia Jr.	Czech.	7	9	5	14	2	...	...	...		—	—	—	—	—
91-92—Cape Breton	AHL	35	11	12	23	34	...	...	...		—	—	—	—	—
—Edmonton	NHL	2	0	0	0	0	-3	0	0		—	—	—	—	—
—Halifax........................	AHL	7	1	1	2	6	...	...	...		—	—	—	—	—
—Quebec	NHL	4	1	1	2	2	1	0	0		—	—	—	—	—
92-93—Quebec	NHL	77	18	30	48	51	16	4	0		6	1	1	2	4
93-94—Quebec	NHL	60	9	23	32	58	4	4	0		—	—	—	—	—
94-95—Chem. Litvinov............	Czech Rep.	13	12	10	22	34	...	...	...		—	—	—	—	—
—Quebec	NHL	20	3	6	9	14	5	0	0		—	—	—	—	—
95-96—HC Vsetin	Czech Rep.	1	1	1	2	0	...	...	...		—	—	—	—	—
—Colorado	NHL	22	4	11	15	14	10	0	0		—	—	—	—	—
—Montreal	NHL	56	25	35	60	54	8	9	2		—	—	—	—	—
96-97—Montreal	NHL	70	28	27	55	62	1	6	3		5	0	0	0	4
97-98—Montreal	NHL	78	21	32	53	84	13	5	3		10	3	0	3	4
—Czech Rep. Oly. team..	Int'l	6	3	1	4	4	...	...	...		—	—	—	—	—
98-99—Montreal	NHL	73	17	17	34	50	-25	5	0		—	—	—	—	—
99-00—Montreal	NHL	80	25	24	49	70	1	7	1		—	—	—	—	—
00-01—Montreal	NHL	57	16	22	38	66	-5	5	1		—	—	—	—	—
01-02—Montreal	NHL	18	2	6	8	12	-1	1	0		—	—	—	—	—
—Dallas........................	NHL	42	6	11	17	24	3	2	0		—	—	—	—	—
—Czech Rep. Oly. team..	Int'l	4	0	3	3	2	...	...	...		—	—	—	—	—
—New York Rangers	NHL	15	3	10	13	6	6	0	0		—	—	—	—	—
02-03—St. Louis	NHL	61	16	14	30	38	-1	4	4		7	4	2	6	4
NHL Totals (12 years).........		735	194	269	463	605	33	52	14		28	8	3	11	16

RUDKOWSKY, CODY　　　　　G　　　　　BLUES

PERSONAL: Born July 21, 1978, in Willingdon, Alta. ... 6-1/216. ... Catches left.
TRANSACTIONS/CAREER NOTES: Signed as non-drafted free agent by St. Louis Blues (March 25, 1999).

| | | REGULAR SEASON | | | | | | | | | PLAYOFFS | | | | | | |
Season Team	League	Gms.	Min	W	L	T	GA	SO	Avg.	SV%	Gms.	Min.	W	L	GA	SO	Avg.	SV%
95-96—Seattle	WHL	2	21	0	0	0	3	0	8.57	—	—	—	—	—	—	—	...	—
96-97—Seattle	WHL	40	2162	19	16	1	124	0	3.44	—	1	30	1	0	0	0	...	—
97-98—Seattle	WHL	53	2805	20	22	3	175	1	3.74	—	5	278	1	4	18	0	3.88	—
98-99—Seattle	WHL	64	3665	34	17	*10	177	*7	2.90	—	11	637	5	*6	31	1	2.92	—
99-00—Worcester	AHL	28	1405	9	7	6	75	0	3.20	—	—	—	—	—	—	—	—	—
—Peoria	ECHL	11	599	7	4	0	32	0	3.21	—	2	119	1	1	6	0	3.03	—
00-01—Worcester	AHL	25	1477	13	8	3	66	3	2.68	—	—	—	—	—	—	—	—	—
01-02—Worcester	AHL	21	1108	6	10	2	50	1	2.71	—	—	—	—	—	—	—	—	—
—Peoria	ECHL	12	709	5	2	4	24	3	2.03	—	2	77	0	1	4	0	3.12	—
02-03—Worcester	AHL	10	577	1	5	3	28	0	2.91	—	—	—	—	—	—	—	—	—
—Trenton	ECHL	31	1866	17	9	5	85	2	2.73	—	—	—	—	—	—	—	—	—
—St. Louis	NHL	1	30	1	0	0	0	0	0.00	1.000	—	—	—	—	—	—	—	—
NHL Totals (1 year)		1	30	1	0	0	0	0	0.00	1.000								

RULLIER, JOE　　　　　D　　　　　KINGS

PERSONAL: Born January 28, 1980, in Montreal. ... 6-3/198. ... Shoots right.
TRANSACTIONS/CAREER NOTES: Selected by Los Angeles Kings in fifth round (fifth Kings pick, 133rd overall) of NHL entry draft (June 27, 1998).

| | | REGULAR SEASON | | | | | | | | PLAYOFFS | | | | |
Season Team	League	Gms.	G	A	Pts.	PIM	+/-	PP	SH	Gms.	G	A	Pts.	PIM
96-97—Rimouski	QMJHL	23	0	3	3	77	...	...	...	4	0	0	0	11
97-98—Rimouski	QMJHL	55	1	10	11	176	...	...	...	16	1	4	5	34
98-99—Rimouski	QMJHL	54	7	32	39	202	...	...	...	11	2	3	5	26
99-00—Rimouski	QMJHL	49	3	32	35	161	...	...	...	14	1	8	9	34
00-01—Lowell	AHL	63	1	1*	2	162	...	...	...	4	0	1	1	2
01-02—Manchester	AHL	62	2	2	4	133	...	...	...	3	0	0	0	5
02-03—Manchester	AHL	62	3	6	9	166	...	...	...	—	—	—	—	—

RUMBLE, DARREN　　　　　D　　　　　LIGHTNING

PERSONAL: Born January 23, 1969, in Barrie, Ont. ... 6-1/200. ... Shoots left. ... Full Name: Darren William Rumble.
TRANSACTIONS/CAREER NOTES: Selected by Philadelphia Flyers in first round (first Flyers pick, 20th overall) of NHL entry draft (June 13, 1987). ... Stretched knee ligaments (November 27, 1988). ... Selected by Ottawa Senators in NHL expansion draft (June 18, 1992). ... Bruised thigh (November 29, 1993); missed four games. ... Injured thumb (March 5, 1994); missed one game. ... Signed as free agent by Flyers (July 31, 1995). ... Signed as free agent by St. Louis Blues (January 31, 2001). ... Injured hip (February 15, 2001); missed two games. ... Suspended two games by NHL for kneeing incident (February 28, 2001). ... Injured hip (March 10, 2001); missed one game. ... Signed as free agent by Tampa Bay Lightning (September 11, 2002). ... Re-signed by Lightning (July 15, 2003).

| | | REGULAR SEASON | | | | | | | | PLAYOFFS | | | | |
Season Team	League	Gms.	G	A	Pts.	PIM	+/-	PP	SH	Gms.	G	A	Pts.	PIM
85-86—Barrie Jr. B	OHA	46	14	32	46	91	...	...	...	—	—	—	—	—
86-87—Kitchener	OHL	64	11	32	43	44	...	...	...	4	0	1	1	9
87-88—Kitchener	OHL	55	15	50	65	64	...	...	...	—	—	—	—	—
88-89—Kitchener	OHL	46	11	28	39	25	...	...	...	5	1	0	1	2
89-90—Hershey	AHL	57	2	13	15	31	...	...	...	—	—	—	—	—
90-91—Philadelphia	NHL	3	1	0	1	0	1	0	0	—	—	—	—	—
—Hershey	AHL	73	6	35	41	48	...	...	...	3	0	5	5	2
91-92—Hershey	AHL	79	12	54	66	118	...	...	...	6	0	3	3	2
92-93—Ottawa	NHL	69	3	13	16	61	-24	0	0	—	—	—	—	—
—New Haven	AHL	2	1	0	1	0	...	...	...	—	—	—	—	—
93-94—Ottawa	NHL	70	6	9	15	116	-50	0	0	—	—	—	—	—
—Prin. Edward Island	AHL	3	2	0	2	0	...	...	...	—	—	—	—	—
94-95—Prin. Edward Island	AHL	70	7	46	53	77	...	...	...	11	0	6	6	4
95-96—Philadelphia	NHL	5	0	0	0	4	0	0	0	—	—	—	—	—
—Hershey	AHL	58	13	37	50	83	...	...	...	5	0	0	0	6
96-97—Philadelphia	AHL	72	18	44	62	83	...	...	...	7	0	3	3	19
—Philadelphia	NHL	10	0	0	0	0	-2	0	0	—	—	—	—	—
97-98—San Antonio	IHL	46	7	22	29	47	...	...	...	—	—	—	—	—
98-99—Grand Rapids	IHL	53	6	22	28	44	...	...	...	—	—	—	—	—
—Utah	IHL	10	1	4	5	10	...	...	...	—	—	—	—	—
99-00—Grand Rapids	IHL	29	3	10	13	20	...	...	...	—	—	—	—	—
—Worcester	AHL	39	0	17	17	31	...	...	...	9	0	2	2	6
00-01—Worcester	AHL	53	6	24	30	65	...	...	...	8	0	1	1	10
—St. Louis	NHL	12	0	4	4	27	7	0	0	—	—	—	—	—
01-02—Worcester	AHL	60	3	29	32	48	...	...	...	3	0	4	4	2
02-03—Springfield	AHL	33	5	17	22	18	...	...	...	—	—	—	—	—
—Tampa Bay	NHL	19	0	0	0	6	-2	0	0	—	—	—	—	—
NHL Totals (7 years)		188	10	26	36	214	-70	0	0					

RUPP, MICHAEL — RW — DEVILS

PERSONAL: Born January 13, 1980, in Cleveland ... 6-5/230. ... Shoots left.
TRANSACTIONS/CAREER NOTES: Selected by New York Islanders in first round (first Islanders pick, ninth overall) of NHL entry draft (June 27, 1998). ... Returned to draft pool by Islanders and selected by New Jersey Devils in third round (seventh Devils pick, 76th overall) of NHL entry draft (June 24, 2000).

Season Team	League	Gms.	G	A	Pts.	PIM	+/-	PP	SH	Gms.	G	A	Pts.	PIM
96-97—St. Edward's	USHS (East)	20	26	24	50	...	...	...	...	—	—	—	—	—
97-98—Windsor	OHL	38	9	8	17	60	...	...	...	—	—	—	—	—
—Erie	OHL	26	7	3	10	57	...	...	...	7	3	1	4	6
98-99—Erie	OHL	63	22	25	47	102	...	...	...	5	0	2	2	25
99-00—Erie	OHL	58	32	21	53	134	...	...	...	13	5	5	10	22
00-01—Albany	AHL	71	10	10	20	63	...	...	...	—	—	—	—	—
01-02—Albany	AHL	78	13	17	30	90	...	...	...	—	—	—	—	—
02-03—Albany	AHL	47	8	11	19	74	...	...	...	—	—	—	—	—
—New Jersey	NHL	26	5	3	8	21	0	2	0	4	1	3	4	0
NHL Totals (1 year)		26	5	3	8	21	0	2	0	4	1	3	4	0

RUUTU, JARKKO — LW — CANUCKS

PERSONAL: Born August 23, 1975, in Helsinki, Finland ... 6-2/200. ... Shoots left. ... Brother of Tuomo Ruutu, center/right wing, Chicago Blackhawks organization; brother of Mikko Ruutu, left wing, Ottawa Senators organization.
TRANSACTIONS/CAREER NOTES: Selected by Vancouver Canucks in third round (third Canucks pick, 68th overall) of NHL entry draft (June 27, 1998). ... Re-signed by Canucks (July 2, 2003).

Season Team	League	Gms.	G	A	Pts.	PIM	+/-	PP	SH	Gms.	G	A	Pts.	PIM
91-92—HIFK Helsinki	Finland Jr.	1	0	0	0	0	...	...	...	—	—	—	—	—
92-93—HIFK Helsinki	Finland Jr.	34	26	21	47	53	...	...	...	—	—	—	—	—
93-94—HIFK Helsinki	Finland Jr.	19	9	12	21	44	...	...	...	—	—	—	—	—
94-95—HIFK Helsinki	Finland Jr.	35	26	22	48	117	...	...	...	—	—	—	—	—
95-96—Michigan Tech	WCHA	39	12	10	22	96	...	...	...	—	—	—	—	—
96-97—HIFK Helsinki	Finland	48	11	10	21	155	...	...	...	—	—	—	—	—
97-98—HIFK Helsinki	Finland	37	10	10	20	87	...	...	...	8	7	4	11	10
98-99—HIFK Helsinki	Finland	25	10	4	14	136	...	...	...	9	0	2	2	43
99-00—Syracuse	AHL	65	26	32	58	164	...	...	...	4	3	1	4	8
—Vancouver	NHL	8	0	1	1	6	-1	0	0	—	—	—	—	—
00-01—Kansas City	IHL	46	11	18	29	111	...	...	...	—	—	—	—	—
—Vancouver	NHL	21	3	3	6	32	1	0	1	4	0	1	1	8
01-02—Vancouver	NHL	49	2	7	9	74	-1	0	0	1	0	0	0	0
—Fin. Olympic team	Int'l	4	0	0	0	4	...	...	...	—	—	—	—	—
02-03—Vancouver	NHL	36	2	2	4	66	-7	0	0	13	0	2	2	14
NHL Totals (4 years)		114	7	13	20	178	-8	0	1	18	0	3	3	22

RUUTU, TUOMO — C — BLACKHAWKS

PERSONAL: Born February 16, 1983, in Vantaa, Finland. ... 6-2/196. ... Shoots left. ... Brother of Jarkko Ruutu, right wing, Vancouver Canucks; brother of Mikko Ruutu, left wing, Ottawa Senators organization.
TRANSACTIONS/CAREER NOTES: Selected by Chicago Blackhawks in first round (first Blackhawks pick, ninth overall) of NHL entry draft (June 23, 2001).

Season Team	League	Gms.	G	A	Pts.	PIM	+/-	PP	SH	Gms.	G	A	Pts.	PIM
99-00—HIFK Helsinki	Finland Jr.	35	11	16	27	32	...	...	...	—	—	—	—	—
00-01—Jokerit Helsinki	Finland	47	11	11	22	86	...	...	...	5	0	0	0	4
01-02—Jokerit Helsinki	Finland	51	7	16	23	69	...	...	...	10	0	6	6	29
02-03—HIFK Helsinki	Finland	30	12	15	27	24	...	...	...	—	—	—	—	—

RYCROFT, MARK — RW — BLUES

PERSONAL: Born July 12, 1978, in Nanaimo, B.C. ... 5-11/197. ... Shoots right.
TRANSACTIONS/CAREER NOTES: Signed as non-drafted free agent by St. Louis Blues (May 15, 2000).

Season Team	League	Gms.	G	A	Pts.	PIM	+/-	PP	SH	Gms.	G	A	Pts.	PIM
97-98—Univ. of Denver	WCHA	35	15	17	32	28	...	...	...	—	—	—	—	—
98-99—Univ. of Denver	WCHA	41	19	18	37	36	...	...	...	—	—	—	—	—
99-00—Univ. of Denver	WCHA	41	17	17	34	87	...	...	...	—	—	—	—	—
00-01—Worcester	AHL	71	24	26	50	68	...	...	...	11	2	5	7	4
01-02—St. Louis	NHL	9	0	3	3	4	0	0	0	—	—	—	—	—
—Worcester	AHL	66	12	19	31	68	...	...	...	3	0	1	1	0
02-03—Worcester	AHL	45	8	18	26	35	...	...	...	—	—	—	—	—
NHL Totals (1 year)		9	0	3	3	4	0	0	0					

RYDER, MICHAEL   C   CANADIENS

PERSONAL: Born March 31, 1980, in St. John's, Nfld. ... 6-0/187. ... Shoots right.
TRANSACTIONS/CAREER NOTES: Selected by Montreal Canadiens in ninth round (ninth Canadiens pick, 216th overall) of NHL entry draft (June 27, 1998). ... Re-signed by Canadiens (July 22, 2003).

		REGULAR SEASON								PLAYOFFS				
Season Team	League	Gms.	G	A	Pts.	PIM	+/-	PP	SH	Gms.	G	A	Pts.	PIM
97-98—Hull	QMJHL	69	34	28	62	41	...	...	...	10	4	2	6	4
98-99—Hull	QMJHL	69	44	43	87	41	...	...	...	23	†20	16	36	39
99-00—Hull	QMJHL	63	50	58	108	50	...	...	...	15	11	17	28	28
00-01—Quebec	AHL	61	6	9	15	14	...	...	...	—	—	—	—	—
—Tallahassee	ECHL	5	4	5	9	6	...	...	...	—	—	—	—	—
01-02—Quebec	AHL	50	11	17	28	9	...	...	...	3	0	1	1	2
—Mississippi	ECHL	20	14	13	27	2	...	...	...	—	—	—	—	—
02-03—Hamilton	AHL	69	34	33	67	43	...	...	...	—	—	—	—	—

SABOURIN, DANY   G   FLAMES

PERSONAL: Born September 2, 1980, in Val d'Or, Que. ... 6-2/165. ... Catches left.
TRANSACTIONS/CAREER NOTES: Selected by Calgary Flames in fourth round (fifth Flames pick, 108th overall) of NHL entry draft (June 27, 1998). ... Re-signed by Flames (June 24, 2003).

		REGULAR SEASON								PLAYOFFS						
Season Team	League	Gms.	Min	W	L	T	GA	SO	Avg.	SV%	Gms.	Min.	W	L	GA	SO	Avg.	SV%
97-98—Sherbrooke	QMJHL	37	1906	15	15	2	128	1	4.03	—	—	—	—	—	—	—	—	—
98-99—Sherbrooke	QMJHL	30	1477	8	13	2	102	1	4.14	—	1	49	0	1	2	0	2.45	—
99-00—Sherbrooke	QMJHL	55	3066	25	22	5	181	1	3.54	—	5	324	1	4	18	0	3.33	—
00-01—Saint John	AHL	1	40	1	0	0	0	0	—	—	—	—	—	—	—	—	—	—
—Johnstown	ECHL	19	903	4	9	1	56	0	3.72	—	1	40	0	0	2	0	3.00	—
01-02—Johnstown	ECHL	27	1538	14	10	1	84	0	3.28	—	3	137	0	2	5	0	2.19	—
—Saint John	AHL	10	447	4	4	0	18	1	2.42	—	—	—	—	—	—	—	—	—
02-03—Saint John	AHL	41	2219	15	17	4	100	4	2.70	—	—	—	—	—	—	—	—	—

SACCO, JOE   RW

PERSONAL: Born February 4, 1969, in Medford, Mass. ... 6-0/194. ... Shoots left. ... Full Name: Joseph William Sacco. ... Brother of David Sacco, left winger with Toronto Maple Leafs (1993-94) and Mighty Ducks of Anaheim (1994-95 and 1995-96). ... Name pronounced SA-koh.
TRANSACTIONS/CAREER NOTES: Selected by Toronto Maple Leafs in fourth round (fourth Maple Leafs pick, 71st overall) of NHL entry draft (June 13, 1987). ... Selected by Mighty Ducks of Anaheim in NHL expansion draft (June 24, 1993). ... Bruised left thumb (February 5, 1995); missed seven games. ... Strained chest muscle (January 22, 1997); missed five games. ... Traded by Mighty Ducks with D J.J. Daigneault and C Mark Janssens to New York Islanders for C Travis Green, D Doug Houda and RW Tony Tuzzolino (February 6, 1998). ... Strained hip flexor (March 14, 1998); missed one game. ... Injured wrist (November 12, 1998); missed four games. ... Injured shoulder (April 10, 1999) and underwent surgery; missed final three games of season. ... Signed as free agent by Washington Capitals (July 27, 1999). ... Bruised leg (November 26, 1999); missed two games. ... Suffered from the flu (February 3, 2000); missed one game. ... Strained hip flexor (November 17, 2000); missed four games. ... Bruised shoulder (January 18, 2001); missed three games. ... Bruised shoulder (February 1, 2001); missed six games. ... Suffered from the flu (January 11, 2002); missed two games. ... Signed as free agent by Philadelphia Flyers (January 15, 2003).

		REGULAR SEASON								PLAYOFFS				
Season Team	League	Gms.	G	A	Pts.	PIM	+/-	PP	SH	Gms.	G	A	Pts.	PIM
85-86—Medford H.S.	Mass. H.S.	20	30	30	60	...	...	...	...	—	—	—	—	—
86-87—Medford H.S.	Mass. H.S.	21	22	32	54	...	...	...	...	—	—	—	—	—
87-88—Boston University	Hockey East	34	14	22	36	38	...	...	...	—	—	—	—	—
88-89—Boston University	Hockey East	33	21	19	40	66	...	...	...	—	—	—	—	—
89-90—Boston University	Hockey East	44	28	24	52	70	...	...	...	—	—	—	—	—
90-91—Newmarket	AHL	49	18	17	35	24	...	...	...	—	—	—	—	—
—Toronto	NHL	20	0	5	5	2	-5	0	0	—	—	—	—	—
91-92—U.S. national team	Int'l	50	11	26	37	51	...	...	...	—	—	—	—	—
—U.S. Olympic team	Int'l	8	0	2	2	0	...	...	...	—	—	—	—	—
—Toronto	NHL	17	7	4	11	4	8	0	0	—	—	—	—	—
—St. John's	AHL	—	—	—	—	—	—	—	—	1	1	1	2	0
92-93—Toronto	NHL	23	4	4	8	-4	0	0		—	—	—	—	—
—St. John's	AHL	37	14	16	30	45	...	...	...	7	6	4	10	2
93-94—Anaheim	NHL	84	19	18	37	61	-11	3	1	—	—	—	—	—
94-95—Anaheim	NHL	41	10	8	18	23	-8	2	0	—	—	—	—	—
95-96—Anaheim	NHL	76	13	14	27	40	1	1	2	—	—	—	—	—
96-97—Anaheim	NHL	77	12	17	29	35	1	1	1	11	2	0	2	2
97-98—Anaheim	NHL	55	8	11	19	24	-1	0	2	—	—	—	—	—
—New York Islanders	NHL	25	3	3	6	10	1	0	0	—	—	—	—	—
98-99—New York Islanders	NHL	73	3	0	3	45	-24	0	1	—	—	—	—	—
99-00—Washington	NHL	79	7	16	23	50	7	0	0	5	0	0	0	4
00-01—Washington	NHL	69	7	7	14	48	4	0	0	6	0	0	0	2
01-02—Washington	NHL	65	0	7	7	51	-13	0	0	—	—	—	—	—
02-03—Philadelphia	AHL	6	4	3	7	4	...	...	...	—	—	—	—	—
—Philadelphia	NHL	34	1	5	6	20	0	0	0	4	0	0	0	0
NHL Totals (13 years)		738	94	119	213	421	-44	7	7	26	2	0	2	8

SAFRONOV, KIRILL   D   THRASHERS

PERSONAL: Born February 26, 1981, in Leningrad, U.S.S.R. ... 6-2/215. ... Shoots left.

TRANSACTIONS/CAREER NOTES: Selected by Phoenix Coyotes in first round (second Coyotes pick, 19th overall) of NHL entry draft (June 26, 1999). ... Traded by Coyotes with RW Ruslan Zainullin and fourth-round pick (RW Patrick Dwyer) in 2002 draft to Atlanta Thrashers for LW Darcy Hordichuk, fourth-(RW Lance Monych) and fifth-round (RW Josh Zeiler) picks in 2002 draft (March 19, 2002).

		REGULAR SEASON								PLAYOFFS				
Season Team	League	Gms.	G	A	Pts.	PIM	+/-	PP	SH	Gms.	G	A	Pts.	PIM
96-97—SKA St. Petersburg.....	Russian	1	0	0	0	0	...	...	...	—	—	—	—	—
97-98—SKA St. Petersburg.....	Russian	9	0	1	1	4	...	...	...	—	—	—	—	—
—SKA-2 St. Petersburg .	Rus. Div. III	34	4	3	7	36	...	...	...	—	—	—	—	—
98-99—SKA St. Petersburg.....	Russian	35	1	1	2	26	...	...	...	—	—	—	—	—
99-00—Quebec	QMJHL	55	11	32	43	95	...	...	...	11	2	4	6	14
00-01—Springfield	AHL	66	5	13	18	77	...	...	...	—	—	—	—	—
01-02—Springfield	AHL	68	3	19	22	26	...	...	...	—	—	—	—	—
—Phoenix	NHL	1	0	0	0	0	-2	0	0	—	—	—	—	—
—Chicago	AHL	8	0	2	2	2	...	...	...	25	2	6	8	8
—Atlanta	NHL	2	0	0	0	2	-3	0	0	—	—	—	—	—
02-03—Chicago	AHL	44	4	15	19	29	...	...	...	—	—	—	—	—
—Atlanta	NHL	32	2	2	4	14	-10	0	0	—	—	—	—	—
NHL Totals (2 years)...........		35	2	2	4	16	-15	0	0					

SAKIC, JOE   C   AVALANCHE

PERSONAL: Born July 7, 1969, in Burnaby, B.C. ... 5-11/180. ... Shoots left. ... Full Name: Joseph Steve Sakic. ... Brother of Brian Sakic, left winger with Washington Capitals (1990-91 and 1991-92) and New York Rangers organizations (1992-93 through 1994-95). ... Name pronounced SAK-ihk.

TRANSACTIONS/CAREER NOTES: Selected by Quebec Nordiques in first round (second Nordiques pick, 15th overall) of NHL entry draft (June 13, 1987). ... Sprained right ankle (November 28, 1988). ... Developed bursitis in left ankle (January 21, 1992); missed three games. ... Suffered recurrence of bursitis in left ankle (January 30, 1992); missed eight games. ... Injured eye (January 2, 1993); missed six games. ... Nordiques franchise moved to Colorado and renamed Avalanche for 1995-96 season (June 21, 1995). ... Lacerated calf (January 4, 1997); missed 17 games. ... Injured knee (February 18, 1998); missed 18 games. ... Suspended one game and fined $1,000 by NHL for kneeing incident (April 21, 1998). ... Sprained right shoulder (December 17, 1998); missed seven games. ... Injured rib cartilage (November 8, 1999); missed six games. ... Reinjured rib cartilage (November 26, 1999); missed 13 games. ... Suffered from the flu (January 18, 2000); missed one game. ... Injured groin (January 25, 2000); missed two games.

STATISTICAL PLATEAUS: Three-goal games: 1988-89 (2), 1989-90 (1), 1990-91 (1), 1996-97 (1), 1998-99 (1), 1999-00 (2), 2000-01 (2), 2002-03 (1). Total: 11. ... Four-goal games: 1991-92 (1). ... Total hat tricks: 12.

		REGULAR SEASON								PLAYOFFS				
Season Team	League	Gms.	G	A	Pts.	PIM	+/-	PP	SH	Gms.	G	A	Pts.	PIM
86-87—Swift Current	WHL	72	60	73	133	31	...	...	...	4	0	1	1	0
87-88—Swift Current	WHL	64	†78	82	†160	64	...	...	...	10	11	13	24	12
88-89—Quebec	NHL	70	23	39	62	24	-36	10	0	—	—	—	—	—
89-90—Quebec	NHL	80	39	63	102	27	-40	8	1	—	—	—	—	—
90-91—Quebec	NHL	80	48	61	109	24	-26	12	3	—	—	—	—	—
91-92—Quebec	NHL	69	29	65	94	20	5	6	3	—	—	—	—	—
92-93—Quebec	NHL	78	48	57	105	40	-3	20	2	6	3	3	6	2
93-94—Quebec	NHL	84	28	64	92	18	-8	10	1	—	—	—	—	—
94-95—Quebec	NHL	47	19	43	62	30	7	3	2	6	4	1	5	0
95-96—Colorado	NHL	82	51	69	120	44	14	17	6	22	*18	16	*34	14
96-97—Colorado	NHL	65	22	52	74	34	-10	10	2	17	8	17	25	14
97-98—Colorado	NHL	64	27	36	63	50	0	12	1	6	2	3	5	6
—Can. Olympic team	Int'l	4	1	2	3	4	...	...	...	—	—	—	—	—
98-99—Colorado	NHL	73	41	55	96	29	23	12	†5	19	6	13	19	8
99-00—Colorado	NHL	60	28	53	81	28	30	5	1	17	2	7	9	8
00-01—Colorado	NHL	82	54	64	118	30	45	19	3	21	13	13	26	6
01-02—Colorado	NHL	82	26	53	79	18	12	9	1	21	9	10	19	4
—Can. Olympic team	Int'l	6	4	3	7	0	...	...	...	—	—	—	—	—
02-03—Colorado	NHL	58	26	32	58	24	4	8	0	7	6	3	9	2
NHL Totals (15 years).........		1074	509	806	1315	440	17	161	31	142	71	86	157	64

SALEI, RUSLAN   D   MIGHTY DUCKS

PERSONAL: Born November 2, 1974, in Minsk, U.S.S.R. ... 6-0/207. ... Shoots left. ... Name pronounced ROO-slahn suh-LAY.

TRANSACTIONS/CAREER NOTES: Selected by Mighty Ducks of Anaheim in first round (first Mighty Ducks pick, ninth overall) of NHL entry draft (June 22, 1996). ... Suffered charley horse (November 22, 1997); missed one game. ... Fractured bone in left foot (December 10, 1997); missed one game. ... Suspended two games and fined $1,000 by NHL for head-butting incident (February 4, 1998). ... Suspended five games and fined $1,000 by NHL for illegal hit in preseason game (October 9, 1998). ... Injured shoulder (March 17, 1999); missed two games. ... Suspended 10 games by NHL for checking from behind incident (October 5, 1999). ... Injured foot (October 20, 2000); missed two games. ... Reinjured foot (October 23, 2000); missed six games. ... Injured back (December 17, 2000); missed one game. ... Suffered from headaches (January 21, 2001); missed 23 games.

		REGULAR SEASON								PLAYOFFS				
Season Team	League	Gms.	G	A	Pts.	PIM	+/-	PP	SH	Gms.	G	A	Pts.	PIM
92-93—Tivali Minsk	CIS	9	1	0	1	10	...	...	...	—	—	—	—	—
93-94—Tivali Minsk	CIS	39	2	3	5	50	...	...	...	—	—	—	—	—
94-95—Tivali Minsk	CIS	51	4	2	6	44	...	...	...	—	—	—	—	—
95-96—Las Vegas	IHL	76	7	23	30	123	...	...	...	15	3	7	10	18
96-97—Anaheim	NHL	30	0	1	1	37	-8	0	0	—	—	—	—	—
—Baltimore	AHL	12	1	4	5	12	...	...	...	—	—	—	—	—
—Las Vegas	IHL	8	0	2	2	24	...	...	...	3	2	1	3	6

Season Team	League	REGULAR SEASON								PLAYOFFS				
		Gms.	G	A	Pts.	PIM	+/-	PP	SH	Gms.	G	A	Pts.	PIM
97-98—Anaheim	NHL	66	5	10	15	70	7	1	0	—	—	—	—	—
—Cincinnati...................	AHL	6	3	6	9	14	...	...	...	—	—	—	—	—
—Belarus Oly. team........	Int'l	7	1	0	1	4	...	...	...	—	—	—	—	—
98-99—Anaheim	NHL	74	2	14	16	65	1	1	0	3	0	0	0	4
99-00—Anaheim	NHL	71	5	5	10	94	3	1	0	—	—	—	—	—
00-01—Anaheim	NHL	50	1	5	6	70	-14	0	0	—	—	—	—	—
01-02—Anaheim	NHL	82	4	7	11	97	-10	0	0	—	—	—	—	—
—Belarus Oly. team.......	Int'l	6	2	1	3	4	...	...	...	—	—	—	—	—
02-03—Anaheim	NHL	61	4	8	12	78	2	0	0	21	2	3	5	26
NHL Totals (7 years)..........		434	21	50	71	511	-19	3	0	24	2	3	5	30

SALMELAINEN, TONY   LW   OILERS

PERSONAL: Born August 8, 1981, in Espoo, Finland. ... 5-9/176. ... Shoots right.

TRANSACTIONS/CAREER NOTES: Selected by Edmonton Oilers in second round (third Oilers pick, 41st overall) of NHL entry draft (June 26, 1999).

Season Team	League	REGULAR SEASON								PLAYOFFS				
		Gms.	G	A	Pts.	PIM	+/-	PP	SH	Gms.	G	A	Pts.	PIM
97-98—HIFK Helsinki	Finland Jr.	33	23	16	39	30	...	...	...	—	—	—	—	—
98-99—HIFK Helsinki	Finland Jr.	30	21	17	38	53	...	...	...	—	—	—	—	—
99-00—HIFK Helsinki	Finland Jr.	1	1	0	1	0	...	...	...	—	—	—	—	—
00-01—HIFK Helsinki	Finland	19	1	0	1	6	...	...	...	—	—	—	—	—
—Ilves Tampere	Finland	26	3	10	13	4	...	...	...	3	0	0	0	0
01-02—Ilves Tampere	Finland	49	10	9	19	30	...	...	...	3	0	0	0	2
02-03—Hamilton	AHL	67	14	19	33	14	...	...	...	—	—	—	—	—

SALO, SAMI   D   CANUCKS

PERSONAL: Born September 2, 1974, in Turku, Finland ... 6-3/212. ... Shoots right.

TRANSACTIONS/CAREER NOTES: Selected by Ottawa Senators in ninth round (seventh Senators pick, 239th overall) of NHL entry draft (June 22, 1996). ... Strained groin (October 17, 1998); missed five games. ... Strained groin (November 28, 1998); missed six games. ... Bruised thigh (February 18, 1999); missed one game. ... Strained shoulder (April 14, 1999); missed two games. ... Bruised chest (October 2, 1999); missed one game. ... Fractured left wrist (October 30, 1999); missed 23 games. ... Reinjured left wrist (December 29, 1999); missed 19 games. ... Sprained medial collateral ligament in right knee (February 29, 2000); missed one game. ... Suffered from the flu (September 30, 2000); missed first two games of season. ... Injured left shoulder (November 16, 2000); missed six games. ... Reinjured left shoulder (December 9, 2000) and underwent surgery; missed 38 games. ... Bruised right foot (March 21, 2001); missed one game. ... Suffered concussion (March 26, 2001); missed one game. ... Injured right knee (April 1, 2001); missed final three games of regular season. ... Injured groin (September 23, 2001); missed first three games of season. ... Suffered from the flu (October 18, 2001); missed one game. ... Injured right hand (December 27, 2001); missed six games. ... Suffered back spasms (March 9, 2002); missed five games. ... Injured back (March 23, 2002); missed one game. ... Traded by Senators to Vancouver Canucks for LW Peter Schaefer (September 21, 2002). ... Re-signed by Canucks (July 17, 2003).

STATISTICAL PLATEAUS: Three-goal games: 1998-99 (1).

Season Team	League	REGULAR SEASON								PLAYOFFS				
		Gms.	G	A	Pts.	PIM	+/-	PP	SH	Gms.	G	A	Pts.	PIM
94-95—TPS Turku	Finland	7	1	2	3	6	..	...	...	—	—	—	—	—
—Kiekko-67	Finland Div. 2	19	4	2	6	4	...	...	...	—	—	—	—	—
95-96—TPS Turku	Finland	47	7	14	21	32	...	...	...	11	1	3	4	8
96-97—TPS Turku	Finland	48	9	6	15	10	...	...	...	10	2	3	5	4
97-98—Jokerit Helsinki	Finland	35	3	5	8	10	...	...	...	8	0	1	1	2
98-99—Ottawa	NHL	61	7	12	19	24	20	2	0	4	0	0	0	0
—Detroit......................	IHL	5	0	2	2	0	...	...	...	—	—	—	—	—
99-00—Ottawa	NHL	37	6	8	14	2	6	3	0	6	1	1	2	0
00-01—Ottawa	NHL	31	2	16	18	10	9	1	0	4	0	0	0	0
01-02—Ottawa	NHL	66	4	14	18	14	1	1	1	12	2	1	3	4
—Fin. Olympic team.......	Int'l	4	0	0	0	0	...	...	...	—	—	—	—	—
02-03—Vancouver..................	NHL	79	9	21	30	10	9	4	0	12	1	3	4	0
NHL Totals (5 years)...........		274	28	71	99	60	45	11	1	38	4	5	9	4

SALO, TOMMY   G   OILERS

PERSONAL: Born February 1, 1971, in Surahammar, Sweden ... 5-11/173. ... Catches left. ... Name pronounced SAH-loh.

TRANSACTIONS/CAREER NOTES: Selected by New York Islanders in fifth round (fifth Islanders pick, 118th overall) of NHL entry draft (June 26, 1993). ... Suffered from tonsillitis (February 8, 1997); missed one game. ... Fractured finger (December 20, 1998); missed six games. ... Traded by Islanders to Edmonton Oilers for LW Mats Lindgren and eighth-round pick (F Radek Martinek) in 1999 draft (March 20, 1999).

Season Team	League	REGULAR SEASON								PLAYOFFS					
		Gms.	Min	W	L	T	GA	SO	Avg.	SV%	Gms.	Min.	W	L	GA SO	Avg. SV%
90-91 —Vasteras	Sweden	2	100	...	...	...	11	0	6.60	—	—	—	—	—	—	—	—
91-92 —Vasteras	Sweden							Did not play.							
92-93 —Vasteras	Sweden	24	1431	...	...	...	59	2	2.47	—	—	—	—	—	—	—	—
93-94 —Vasteras	Sweden	32	1896	...	...	...	106	...	3.35	—	—	—	—	—	—	—	—
—Swedish Oly. team	Int'l	6	370	...	...	...	13	1	2.11	—	—	—	—	—	—	—	—
94-95 —Denver	IHL	65	*3810	*45	14	‡4	165	†3	*2.60	—	8	390	7	0	20 0	3.08	—
—New York Islanders	NHL	6	358	1	5	0	18	0	3.02	.905	—	—	—	—	—	—	—
95-96 —New York Islanders	NHL	10	523	1	7	1	35	0	4.02	.860	—	—	—	—	—	—	—
—Utah	IHL	45	2695	28	15	‡2	119	†4	2.65	—	22	1341	*15	7	51 *3	2.28	—
96-97 —New York Islanders	NHL	58	3208	20	27	8	151	5	2.82	.904	—	—	—	—	—	—	—

Season Team	League	REGULAR SEASON									PLAYOFFS							
		Gms.	Min	W	L	T	GA	SO	Avg.	SV%	Gms.	Min.	W	L	GA	SO	Avg.	SV%
97-98—New York Islanders	NHL	62	3461	23	29	5	152	4	2.64	.906	—	—	—	—	—	—	—	—
—Swedish Oly. team	Int'l	4	238	2	2	0	9	0	2.27		—	—	—	—	—	—	—	—
98-99—New York Islanders	NHL	51	3018	17	26	7	132	5	2.62	.904	—	—	—	—	—	—	—	—
—Edmonton	NHL	13	700	8	2	2	27	0	2.31	.903	4	296	0	4	11	0	2.23	.926
99-00—Edmonton	NHL	70	4164	27	28	*13	162	2	2.33	.914	5	297	1	4	14	0	2.83	.895
00-01—Edmonton	NHL	73	4364	36	25	12	179	8	2.46	.904	6	406	2	4	15	0	2.22	.920
01-02—Edmonton	NHL	69	4035	30	28	10	149	6	2.22	.913	—	—	—	—	—	—	—	—
—Swedish Oly. team	Int'l	3	179	2	1	...	7	0	2.35		—	—	—	—	—	—	—	—
02-03—Edmonton	NHL	65	3814	29	27	8	172	4	2.71	.899	6	343	2	4	18	0	3.15	.888
NHL Totals (9 years)		477	27645	192	204	66	1177	34	2.55	.905	21	1342	5	16	58	0	2.59	.908

SALOMONSSON, ANDREAS   RW   CAPITALS

PERSONAL: Born December 19, 1973, in Ornskoldsvik, Sweden ... 6-1/200. ... Shoots left.
TRANSACTIONS/CAREER NOTES: Selected by New Jersey Devils in fourth round (eighth Devils pick, 163rd overall) of NHL entry draft (June 23, 2001). ... Injured hand (February 27, 2002). ... Claimed on waivers by Washington Capitals (October 15, 2002).

Season Team	League	REGULAR SEASON								PLAYOFFS				
		Gms.	G	A	Pts.	PIM	+/-	PP	SH	Gms.	G	A	Pts.	PIM
92-93—MoDo Ornskoldsvik	Sweden	33	1	1	2	0	...	...	...	—	—	—	—	—
93-94—MoDo Ornskoldsvik	Sweden	38	15	8	23	33	...	...	...	—	—	—	—	—
94-95—MoDo Ornskoldsvik	Sweden	40	5	9	14	34	...	...	...	—	—	—	—	—
95-96—MoDo Ornskoldsvik	Sweden	38	13	6	19	22	...	...	...	7	0	4	4	8
96-97—MoDo Ornskoldsvik	Sweden	23	6	6	12	22	...	...	...	—	—	—	—	—
97-98—MoDo Ornskoldsvik	Sweden	45	6	15	21	69	...	...	...	8	4	3	7	4
98-99—MoDo Ornskoldsvik	Sweden	46	13	13	26	60	...	...	...	13	4	5	9	12
99-00—MoDo Ornskoldsvik	Sweden	48	9	15	24	38	...	...	...	12	0	4	4	12
00-01—Djurgarden Stockholm	Sweden	48	10	12	22	46	...	...	...	13	3	4	7	31
01-02—Albany	AHL	19	3	10	13	6	...	...	...	—	—	—	—	—
—New Jersey	NHL	39	4	5	9	22	-12	1	0	4	0	1	1	0
02-03—Portland	AHL	31	7	17	24	23	...	...	...	—	—	—	—	—
—Washington	NHL	32	1	4	5	14	-1	0	0	—	—	—	—	—
NHL Totals (2 years)		71	5	9	14	36	-13	1	0	4	0	1	1	0

SALVADOR, BRYCE   D   BLUES   S

PERSONAL: Born February 11, 1976, in Brandon, Man. ... 6-2/215. ... Shoots left. ... Full Name: Bryce Chad Salvador.
TRANSACTIONS/CAREER NOTES: Selected by Tampa Bay Lightning in sixth round (sixth Lightning pick, 138th overall) of NHL entry draft (June 29, 1994). ... Signed as free agent by St. Louis Blues (December 16, 1996). ... Strained hamstring (February 8, 2001); missed four games. ... Injured foot (March 6, 2001); missed one game. ... Injured wrist (March 20, 2001); missed one game. ... Strained rib muscle (October 10, 2001); missed seven games. ... Injured chest (February 7, 2002); missed one game. ... Suffered concussion (March 28, 2002); missed eight games. ... Re-signed by Blues (July 17, 2003).

Season Team	League	REGULAR SEASON								PLAYOFFS				
		Gms.	G	A	Pts.	PIM	+/-	PP	SH	Gms.	G	A	Pts.	PIM
92-93—Lethbridge	WHL	64	1	4	5	29	...	...	...	4	0	0	0	0
93-94—Lethbridge	WHL	61	4	14	18	36	...	...	...	9	0	1	1	2
94-95—Lethbridge	WHL	67	1	9	10	88	...	...	...	—	—	—	—	—
95-96—Lethbridge	WHL	56	4	12	16	75	...	...	...	3	0	1	1	2
96-97—Lethbridge	WHL	63	8	32	40	81	...	...	...	19	0	7	7	14
97-98—Worcester	AHL	46	2	8	10	74	...	...	...	11	0	1	1	45
98-99—Worcester	AHL	69	5	13	18	129	...	...	...	4	0	1	1	2
99-00—Worcester	AHL	55	0	13	13	53	...	...	...	9	0	1	1	2
00-01—St. Louis	NHL	75	3	8	10	69	-4	0	0	14	2	0	2	18
01-02—St. Louis	NHL	66	5	7	12	78	3	1	0	10	0	1	1	4
02-03—St. Louis	NHL	71	2	8	10	95	7	1	0	7	0	0	0	2
NHL Totals (3 years)		212	9	23	32	242	6	2	0	31	2	1	3	24

SAMSONOV, SERGEI   LW   BRUINS

PERSONAL: Born October 27, 1978, in Moscow, U.S.S.R. ... 5-8/180. ... Shoots right. ... Name pronounced sam-SAH-nahf.
TRANSACTIONS/CAREER NOTES: Selected by Boston Bruins in first round (second Bruins pick, eighth overall) of NHL entry draft (June 21, 1997). ... Suffered from the flu (December 20, 1997); missed one game. ... Bruised thigh (February 12, 1998); missed one game. ... Suffered sinus infection (February 23, 1999); missed two games. ... Strained knee (January 4, 2000); missed five games. ... Sprained knee (December 4, 2001); missed six games. ... Suffered from the flu (December 28, 2001); missed two games.
STATISTICAL PLATEAUS: Three-goal games: 1997-98 (1).

Season Team	League	REGULAR SEASON								PLAYOFFS				
		Gms.	G	A	Pts.	PIM	+/-	PP	SH	Gms.	G	A	Pts.	PIM
94-95—CSKA Moscow	CIS	13	2	2	4	14	...	...	...	2	0	0	0	0
—CSKA Moscow Jrs.	CIS	50	110	72	182	...	...	...	...	—	—	—	—	—
95-96—CSKA Moscow	CIS	51	21	17	38	12	...	...	...	3	1	1	2	4
96-97—Detroit	IHL	73	29	35	64	18	...	...	...	19	8	4	12	12
97-98—Boston	NHL	81	22	25	47	8	9	7	0	6	2	5	7	0
98-99—Boston	NHL	79	25	26	51	18	-6	6	0	11	3	1	4	0
99-00—Boston	NHL	77	19	26	45	4	-6	6	0	—	—	—	—	—
00-01—Boston	NHL	82	29	46	75	18	6	3	0	—	—	—	—	—
01-02—Boston	NHL	74	29	41	70	27	21	3	0	6	2	2	4	0
—Russian Oly. team	Int'l	6	1	2	3	4	...	...	...	—	—	—	—	—
02-03—Boston	NHL	8	5	6	11	2	8	1	0	5	0	2	2	0
NHL Totals (6 years)		401	129	170	299	77	32	26	0	28	7	10	17	0

SAMUELSSON, MARTIN   LW   BRUINS

PERSONAL: Born January 25, 1982, in Upplands-Vasby, Sweden ... 6-2/189. ... Shoots left.
TRANSACTIONS/CAREER NOTES: Selected by Boston Bruins in first round (second Bruins pick, 27th overall) of NHL entry draft (June 24, 2000).

Season Team	League		REGULAR SEASON								PLAYOFFS				
		Gms.	G	A	Pts.	PIM	+/-	PP	SH		Gms.	G	A	Pts.	PIM
98-99—MoDo Ornskoldsvik....	Sweden Jr.					Statistics unavailable.									
99-00—MoDo Ornskoldsvik....	Sweden Jr.	19	9	8	17	18	...	...	...		2	1	0	1	2
00-01—Hammarby	Sweden Jr.	1	0	1	1	0	...	...	...		—	—	—	—	—
—Hammarby	Sweden Dv. 2	38	15	6	21	28	...	...	...		—	—	—	—	—
01-02—Hammarby	Sweden Dv. 2	30	7	6	13	18	...	...	...		—	—	—	—	—
02-03—Providence.................	AHL	64	24	15	39	34	...	...	...		—	—	—	—	—
—Boston	NHL	8	0	1	1	2	-1	0	0		—	—	—	—	—
NHL Totals (1 year)..............		8	0	1	1	2	-1	0	0						

SAMUELSSON, MIKAEL   RW   PANTHERS

PERSONAL: Born December 23, 1976, in Mariefred, Sweden ... 6-2/211. ... Shoots right.
TRANSACTIONS/CAREER NOTES: Selected by San Jose Sharks in fifth round (seventh Sharks pick, 145th overall) of NHL entry draft (June 27, 1998). ... Traded by Sharks with D Christian Gosselin to New York Rangers for LW Adam Graves (June 24, 2001). ... Traded by Rangers with RW Rico Fata, D Joel Bouchard, D Richard Lintner and cash to Pittsburgh Penguins for RW Alexei Kovalev, LW Dan LaCouture, D Janne Laukkanen and D Mike Wilson (February 10, 2003). ... Traded by Penguins to Florida Panthers for first-round pick in 2003 draft (June 22, 2003).

Season Team	League		REGULAR SEASON								PLAYOFFS				
		Gms.	G	A	Pts.	PIM	+/-	PP	SH		Gms.	G	A	Pts.	PIM
94-95—Sodertalje	Sweden Jr.	30	8	6	14	12	...	...	...		—	—	—	—	—
95-96—Sodertalje	Sweden Dv. 2	18	5	1	6	0	...	...	...		4	0	0	0	0
—Sodertalje	Sweden Jr.	22	13	12	25	20	...	...	...		—	—	—	—	—
96-97—Sodertalje	Sweden	29	3	2	5	10	...	...	...		—	—	—	—	—
—Sodertalje	Sweden Jr.	2	2	1	3	...	...	...	...		—	—	—	—	—
97-98—Sodertalje	Sweden	31	8	8	16	47	...	...	...		—	—	—	—	—
98-99—Sodertalje	Sweden	12	7	9	16	20	...	...	...		—	—	—	—	—
—Vastra Frolunda	Sweden	27	0	5	5	10	...	...	...		—	—	—	—	—
99-00—Brynas Gavle	Sweden	40	4	3	7	76	...	...	...		11	7	2	9	6
00-01—Kentucky	AHL	66	32	46	78	58	...	...	...		3	1	0	1	0
—San Jose....................	NHL	4	0	0	0	0	0	0	0		—	—	—	—	—
01-02—Hartford	AHL	8	3	6	9	12	...	...	...		—	—	—	—	—
—New York Rangers......	NHL	67	6	10	16	23	10	1	2		—	—	—	—	—
02-03—New York Rangers......	NHL	58	8	14	22	32	0	1	1		—	—	—	—	—
—Pittsburgh	NHL	22	2	0	2	8	-21	1	0		—	—	—	—	—
NHL Totals (3 years)............		151	16	24	40	63	-11	3	3						

SANDERSON, GEOFF   LW   BLUE JACKETS

PERSONAL: Born February 1, 1972, in Hay River, Northwest Territorie ... 6-0/185. ... Shoots left.
TRANSACTIONS/CAREER NOTES: Selected by Hartford Whalers in second round (second Whalers pick, 36th overall) of NHL entry draft (June 16, 1990). ... Bruised shoulder (October 14, 1991); missed one game. ... Injured groin (November 13, 1991); missed three games. ... Bruised knee (December 7, 1991); missed five games. ... Suffered from the flu (February 1, 1994). ... Played in Europe during 1994-95 NHL lockout. ... Whalers franchise moved to North Carolina and renamed Carolina Hurricanes for 1997-98 season; NHL approved move on June 25, 1997. ... Traded by Hurricanes to Vancouver Canucks with D Enrico Ciccone and G Sean Burke for LW Martin Gelinas and G Kirk McLean (January 3, 1998). ... Injured shoulder (January 21, 1998); missed eight games. ... Traded by Canucks to Buffalo Sabres for LW Brad May and third-round pick (traded to Tampa Bay) in 1999 draft (February 4, 1998). ... Bruised hip (April 13, 1998); missed one game. ... Injured back (January 18, 1999); missed one game. ... Injured hip (February 19, 1999); missed one game. ... Injured knee (March 1, 2000); missed five games. ... Selected by Columbus Blue Jackets in NHL expansion draft (June 23, 2000). ... Fractured finger (February 25, 2001); missed one game. ... Sprained knee (March 14, 2001); missed 13 games. ... Bruised back (November 1, 2001); missed 10 games. ... Suffered hernia (December 6, 2001) and underwent surgery; missed 24 games. ... Suffered concussion (April 1, 2002); missed remainder of season.
STATISTICAL PLATEAUS: Three-goal games: 1992-93 (2), 1994-95 (1), 1995-96 (2), 1998-99 (1), 2000-01 (1). Total: 7. ... Four-goal games: 2002-03 (1). :.. Total hat tricks: 8.

Season Team	League		REGULAR SEASON								PLAYOFFS				
		Gms.	G	A	Pts.	PIM	+/-	PP	SH		Gms.	G	A	Pts.	PIM
88-89—Swift Current	WHL	58	17	11	28	16	...	...	...		12	3	5	8	6
89-90—Swift Current	WHL	70	32	62	94	56	...	...	...		4	1	4	5	8
90-91—Swift Current	WHL	70	62	50	112	57	...	...	...		3	1	2	3	4
—Hartford	NHL	2	1	0	1	0	-2	0	0		3	0	0	0	0
—Springfield	AHL	—	—	—	—	—	—	—	—		1	0	0	0	2
91-92—Hartford	NHL	64	13	18	31	18	5	2	0		7	1	0	1	2
92-93—Hartford	NHL	82	46	43	89	28	-21	21	2		—	—	—	—	—
93-94—Hartford	NHL	82	41	26	67	42	-13	15	1		—	—	—	—	—
94-95—HPK Hameenlinna	Finland	12	6	4	10	24	...	...	...		—	—	—	—	—
—Hartford	NHL	46	18	14	32	24	-10	4	0		—	—	—	—	—
95-96—Hartford	NHL	81	34	31	65	40	0	6	0		—	—	—	—	—
96-97—Hartford	NHL	82	36	31	67	29	-9	12	1		—	—	—	—	—
97-98—Carolina	NHL	40	7	10	17	14	-4	2	0		—	—	—	—	—
—Vancouver	NHL	9	0	3	3	4	-1	0	0		—	—	—	—	—
—Buffalo	NHL	26	4	5	9	20	6	0	0		14	3	1	4	4
98-99—Buffalo	NHL	75	12	18	30	22	8	1	0		19	4	6	10	14
99-00—Buffalo	NHL	67	13	13	26	22	4	4	0		5	0	2	2	8
00-01—Columbus	NHL	68	30	26	56	46	4	9	0		—	—	—	—	—
01-02—Columbus	NHL	42	11	5	16	12	-15	5	0		—	—	—	—	—
02-03—Columbus	NHL	82	34	33	67	34	-4	15	2		—	—	—	—	—
NHL Totals (13 years).........		848	300	276	576	355	-52	96	6		48	8	9	17	28

SANFORD, CURTIS — G — BLUES

PERSONAL: Born October 5, 1979, in Owen Sound, Ont. ... 5-10/187. ... Catches left.

Season Team	League	REGULAR SEASON									PLAYOFFS							
		Gms.	Min	W	L	T	GA	SO	Avg.	SV%	Gms.	Min.	W	L	GA	SO	Avg.	SV%
01-02 —Peoria	ECHL	24	1418	13	8	2	58	1	2.45	—	—	—	—	—	—	—	—	—
—Worcester	AHL	9	537	5	4	0	22	0	2.46	—	—	—	—	—	—	—	—	—
02-03—Worcester	AHL	41	2316	18	14	8	93	3	2.41	—	3	179	0	3	8	0	2.68	—
—St. Louis	NHL	8	397	5	1	0	13	1	1.96	.912	—	—	—	—	—	—	—	—
NHL Totals (1 year)		8	397	5	1	0	13	1	1.96	.912	—	—	—	—	—	—	—	—

SAPRYKIN, OLEG — LW — FLAMES

PERSONAL: Born February 12, 1981, in Moscow, U.S.S.R. ... 6-1/195. ... Shoots left.
TRANSACTIONS/CAREER NOTES: Selected by Calgary Flames in first round (first Flames pick, 11th overall) of NHL entry draft (June 26, 1999). ... Suffered concussion (January 5, 2001); missed 11 games. ... Injured neck (September 16, 2001); missed first 12 games of season. ... Re-signed by Flames (June 25, 2003).

Season Team	League	REGULAR SEASON								PLAYOFFS				
		Gms.	G	A	Pts.	PIM	+/-	PP	SH	Gms.	G	A	Pts.	PIM
97-98—CSKA Moscow	Russian	20	0	2	2	8	...	...	...	—	—	—	—	—
—HC CSKA	Rus. Div. II	15	0	3	3	6	...	...	...	—	—	—	—	—
98-99—Seattle	WHL	66	47	46	93	107	...	...	...	11	5	11	16	36
99-00—Calgary	NHL	4	0	1	1	2	-4	0	0	—	—	—	—	—
—Seattle	WHL	48	30	36	66	89	...	...	...	6	3	3	6	37
00-01—Calgary	NHL	59	9	14	23	43	4	2	0	—	—	—	—	—
01-02—Calgary	NHL	3	0	0	0	0	-2	0	0	—	—	—	—	—
—Saint John	AHL	52	5	19	24	53	...	...	...	—	—	—	—	—
02-03—Saint John	AHL	21	12	9	21	22	...	...	...	—	—	—	—	—
—Calgary	NHL	52	8	15	23	46	5	1	0	—	—	—	—	—
NHL Totals (4 years)		118	17	30	47	91	3	3	0					

SARICH, CORY — D — LIGHTNING

PERSONAL: Born August 16, 1978, in Saskatoon, Sask. ... 6-4/203. ... Shoots right. ... Name pronounced SAIRCH.
TRANSACTIONS/CAREER NOTES: Selected by Buffalo Sabres in second round (second Sabres pick, 27th overall) of NHL entry draft (June 22, 1996). ... Traded by Sabres with C Wayne Primeau, C/RW Brian Holzinger and third-round pick (RW Alexandre Kharitonov) in 2000 draft to Tampa Bay Lightning for C Chris Gratton and second-round pick (C Derek Roy) in 2001 draft (March 9, 2000). ... Bruised right knee (October 13, 2001); missed two games. ... Suffered concussion (October 27, 2001); missed one game. ... Bruised right shoulder (November 6, 2001); missed four games.

Season Team	League	REGULAR SEASON								PLAYOFFS				
		Gms.	G	A	Pts.	PIM	+/-	PP	SH	Gms.	G	A	Pts.	PIM
94-95—Saskatoon	WHL	6	0	0	0	4	...	...	...	3	0	1	1	0
95-96—Saskatoon	WHL	59	5	18	23	54	...	...	...	3	0	0	0	4
96-97—Saskatoon	WHL	58	6	27	33	158	...	...	...	—	—	—	—	—
97-98—Seattle	WHL	46	8	40	48	137	...	...	...	—	—	—	—	—
98-99—Rochester	AHL	77	3	26	29	82	...	...	...	20	2	4	6	14
—Buffalo	NHL	4	0	0	0	0	3	0	0	—	—	—	—	—
99-00—Buffalo	NHL	42	0	4	4	35	2	0	0	—	—	—	—	—
—Rochester	AHL	15	0	6	6	44	...	...	...	—	—	—	—	—
—Tampa Bay	NHL	17	0	2	2	42	-8	0	0	—	—	—	—	—
00-01—Tampa Bay	NHL	73	1	8	9	106	-25	0	0	—	—	—	—	—
—Detroit	IHL	3	0	2	2	2	...	...	...	—	—	—	—	—
01-02—Tampa Bay	NHL	72	0	11	11	105	-4	0	0	—	—	—	—	—
—Springfield	AHL	2	0	0	0	0	...	...	...	—	—	—	—	—
02-03—Tampa Bay	NHL	82	5	9	14	63	-3	0	0	11	0	2	2	6
NHL Totals (5 years)		290	6	34	40	351	-35	0	0	11	0	2	2	6

SARNO, PETER — C — OILERS

PERSONAL: Born July 26, 1979, in Toronto. ... 5-11/185. ... Shoots left.
TRANSACTIONS/CAREER NOTES: Selected by Edmonton Oilers in sixth round (sixth Oilers pick, 141st overall) of NHL entry draft (June 21, 1997).

Season Team	League	REGULAR SEASON								PLAYOFFS				
		Gms.	G	A	Pts.	PIM	+/-	PP	SH	Gms.	G	A	Pts.	PIM
95-96—North York Flames	OPJHL	52	39	57	96	27	...	...	...	—	—	—	—	—
96-97—Windsor	OHL	66	20	63	83	59	...	...	...	5	0	3	3	6
97-98—Windsor	OHL	64	33	*88	*121	18	...	...	...	—	—	—	—	—
—Hamilton	AHL	8	1	1	2	2	...	...	...	—	—	—	—	—
98-99—Sarnia	OHL	68	37	*93	*130	49	...	...	...	6	1	7	8	2
99-00—Hamilton	AHL	67	10	36	46	31	...	...	...	—	—	—	—	—
00-01—Hamilton	AHL	79	19	46	65	64	...	...	...	—	—	—	—	—
01-02—Hamilton	AHL	76	12	40	52	38	...	...	...	15	6	7	13	4
02-03—Blues Espoo	Finland	45	17	23	40	34	...	...	...	—	—	—	—	—

SATAN, MIROSLAV   LW   SABRES

PERSONAL: Born October 22, 1974, in Topolcany, Czechoslovakia ... 6-3/191. ... Shoots left. ... Name pronounced shuh-TAN.
TRANSACTIONS/CAREER NOTES: Selected by Edmonton Oilers in fifth round (sixth Oilers pick, 111th overall) of NHL entry draft (June 26, 1993). ... Suffered collapsed lung (October 1, 1995); missed two games. ... Separated right shoulder (January 13, 1996); missed four games. ... Suffered from the flu (March 9, 1997); missed one game. ... Traded by Oilers to Buffalo Sabres for D Craig Millar and LW Barrie Moore (March 18, 1997). ... Suffered from the flu (November 28, 1998); missed one game. ... Injured foot (April 25, 1999); missed nine playoff games.
STATISTICAL PLATEAUS: Three-goal games: 1996-97 (1), 1997-98 (1), 1999-00 (1), 2002-03 (1). Total: 4.

		REGULAR SEASON								PLAYOFFS				
Season Team	League	Gms.	G	A	Pts.	PIM	+/-	PP	SH	Gms.	G	A	Pts.	PIM
91-92—VTJ Topolcany	Czech Dv.II	9	2	1	3	6	...	...	...	—	—	—	—	—
—VTJ Topolcany Jrs	Czech. Jrs.	31	30	22	52	...	...	...	...	—	—	—	—	—
92-93—Dukla Trencin..............	Czech.	38	11	6	17	...	...	...	...	—	—	—	—	—
93-94—Dukla Trencin..............	Slovakia	30	32	16	48	16	...	...	...	—	—	—	—	—
—Slovakian Oly. team	Int'l	8	9	0	9	0	...	...	...	—	—	—	—	—
94-95—Detroit...................	IHL	8	1	3	4	4	...	...	...	—	—	—	—	—
—San Diego..................	IHL	6	0	2	2	6	...	...	...	—	—	—	—	—
—Cape Breton................	AHL	25	24	16	40	15	...	...	...	—	—	—	—	—
95-96—Edmonton..................	NHL	62	18	17	35	22	0	6	0	—	—	—	—	—
96-97—Edmonton..................	NHL	64	17	11	28	22	-4	5	0	—	—	—	—	—
—Buffalo......................	NHL	12	8	2	10	4	1	2	0	7	0	0	0	0
97-98—Buffalo...................	NHL	79	22	24	46	34	2	9	0	14	5	4	9	4
98-99—Buffalo...................	NHL	81	40	26	66	44	24	13	3	12	3	5	8	2
99-00—Dukla Trencin..............	Slovakia	3	2	8	10	2	...	...	...	—	—	—	—	—
—Buffalo......................	NHL	81	33	34	67	32	16	5	3	5	3	2	5	0
00-01—Buffalo...................	NHL	82	29	33	62	36	5	8	2	13	3	10	13	8
01-02—Buffalo...................	NHL	82	37	36	73	33	14	15	5	—	—	—	—	—
—Slovakian Oly. team	Int'l	2	0	1	1	0	...	...	...	—	—	—	—	—
02-03—Buffalo...................	NHL	79	26	49	75	20	-3	11	1	—	—	—	—	—
NHL Totals (8 years)...........		622	230	232	462	247	55	74	14	51	14	21	35	14

SAUER, KURT   D   MIGHTY DUCKS

PERSONAL: Born January 16, 1981, in St. Cloud, Minn. ... 6-3/219. ... Shoots left.
TRANSACTIONS/CAREER NOTES: Selected by Colorado Avalanche in third round (fifth Avalanche pick, 88th overall) of NHL entry draft (June 24, 2000).

		REGULAR SEASON								PLAYOFFS				
Season Team	League	Gms.	G	A	Pts.	PIM	+/-	PP	SH	Gms.	G	A	Pts.	PIM
99-00—Spokane.....................	WHL	71	3	12	15	48	...	...	...	—	—	—	—	—
00-01—Spokane.....................	WHL	48	5	10	15	85	...	...	...	3	1	0	1	2
01-02—Spokane.....................	WHL	61	4	20	24	73	...	...	...	11	0	3	3	12
02-03—Anaheim....................	NHL	80	1	2	3	74	-23	0	0	21	1	1	2	6
NHL Totals (1 year)..............		80	1	2	3	74	-23	0	0	21	1	1	2	6

SAUVE, PHILIPPE   G   AVALANCHE

PERSONAL: Born February 27, 1980, in Buffalo. ... 6-0/175. ... Catches left.
TRANSACTIONS/CAREER NOTES: Selected by Colorado Avalanche in second round (sixth Avalanche pick, 38th overall) of NHL entry draft (June 27, 1998).

		REGULAR SEASON								PLAYOFFS						
Season Team	League	Gms.	Min	W	L	T	GA	SO	Avg.	SV%	Gms.	Min.	W	L	GA SO	Avg. SV%
96-97—Rimouski....................	QMJHL	26	1332	11	9	2	84	0	3.78	—	1	14	0	0	3 0	12.86 —
97-98—Rimouski....................	QMJHL	40	2326	23	16	0	131	1	3.38	—	7	262	0	5	33 0	7.56 —
98-99—Rimouski....................	QMJHL	44	2401	16	19	4	155	0	3.87	—	11	595	6	4	30 †1	3.03 —
99-00—Drummondville	QMJHL	28	1526	12	12	2	106	0	4.17	—	—	—	—	—	— —	— —
—Hull	QMJHL	17	992	9	7	1	57	0	3.45	—	12	735	6	6	47 0	3.84 —
00-01—Hershey....................	AHL	42	2182	17	18	1	100	3	2.75	—	3	218	0	3	10 0	2.75 —
01-02—Hershey....................	AHL	55	3129	25	20	6	111	6	2.13	—	8	486	3	5	21 0	2.59 —
02-03—Hershey....................	AHL	60	3394	26	20	12	134	5	2.37	—	—	—	—	—	— —	— —

SAVAGE, ANDRE   C   FLYERS

PERSONAL: Born May 27, 1975, in Ottawa, Ont. ... 6-0/186. ... Shoots right. ... Full Name: Andre Ronald Savage. ... Name pronounced suh-VAHJ.
TRANSACTIONS/CAREER NOTES: Signed as non-drafted free agent by Boston Bruins (June 12, 1998). ... Bruised sternum (March 8, 2000); missed two games. ... Strained trapezius muscle (April 1, 2000); missed final four games of season. ... Dislocated shoulder (September 21, 2000) and underwent surgery; missed first 39 games of season. ... Signed as free agent by Vancouver Canucks (August 2, 2001).

		REGULAR SEASON								PLAYOFFS				
Season Team	League	Gms.	G	A	Pts.	PIM	+/-	PP	SH	Gms.	G	A	Pts.	PIM
94-95—Michigan Tech	WCHA	39	7	17	24	56	...	...	...	—	—	—	—	—
95-96—Michigan Tech	WCHA	40	13	27	40	42	...	...	...	—	—	—	—	—
96-97—Michigan Tech	WCHA	37	18	20	38	34	...	...	...	—	—	—	—	—
97-98—Michigan Tech	WCHA	33	14	27	41	34	...	...	...	—	—	—	—	—

Season Team	League	REGULAR SEASON								PLAYOFFS				
		Gms.	G	A	Pts.	PIM	+/-	PP	SH	Gms.	G	A	Pts.	PIM
98-99—Providence	AHL	63	27	42	69	54	...	...	...	5	0	1	1	0
—Boston	NHL	6	1	0	1	0	2	0	0	—	—	—	—	—
99-00—Providence	AHL	30	15	17	32	22	...	...	...	14	6	7	13	22
—Boston	NHL	43	7	13	20	10	-8	2	0	—	—	—	—	—
00-01—Providence	AHL	35	13	15	28	47	...	...	...	17	3	4	7	18
—Boston	NHL	1	0	0	0	0	0	0	0	—	—	—	—	—
01-02—Manitoba	AHL	76	35	26	61	115	...	...	...	6	2	3	5	16
02-03—Philadelphia	AHL	64	11	31	42	66	...	...	...	—	—	—	—	—
—Philadelphia	NHL	16	2	1	3	4	2	0	0	—	—	—	—	—
NHL Totals (4 years)		66	10	14	24	14	-4	2	0					

SAVAGE, BRIAN   LW   COYOTES

PERSONAL: Born February 24, 1971, in Sudbury, Ont. ... 6-1/200. ... Shoots left.

TRANSACTIONS/CAREER NOTES: Selected by Montreal Canadiens in eighth round (11th Canadiens pick, 171st overall) of NHL entry draft (June 22, 1991). ... Bruised knee (February 4, 1995); missed 10 games. ... Suffered hip pointer (February 17, 1996); missed six games. ... Suffered from the flu (April 1, 1996); missed one game. ... Injured groin (October 26, 1996); missed one game. ... Fractured hand (October 1, 1997); missed seven games. ... Bruised thigh (November 26, 1997); missed one game. ... Fractured thumb (March 21, 1998); missed 10 games. ... Strained groin (November 4, 1998); missed one game. ... Reinjured groin (December 9, 1998); missed 11 games. ... Tore muscle in rib cage (January 21, 1999); missed 11 games. ... Fractured vertebrae in neck (November 20, 1999); missed 44 games. ... Fractured thumb (January 20, 2001); missed 20 games. ... Injured wrist (January 14, 2002); missed four games. ... Traded by Canadiens with third-round pick (D Matt Jones) in 2002 and future considerations to Phoenix Coyotes for LW Sergei Berezin (January 25, 2002). ... Strained hip flexor (April 10, 2002); missed final two games of season.

STATISTICAL PLATEAUS: Three-goal games: 1995-96 (1), 1996-97 (1), 1999-00 (2), 2000-01 (1), 2001-02 (1). Total: 6. ... Four-goal games: 1997-98 (1). ... Total hat tricks: 7.

Season Team	League	REGULAR SEASON								PLAYOFFS				
		Gms.	G	A	Pts.	PIM	+/-	PP	SH	Gms.	G	A	Pts.	PIM
89-90—Sudbury	OHA Mj. Jr.	32	45	40	85	61	...	...	...	—	—	—	—	—
90-91—Miami of Ohio	CCHA	28	5	6	11	26	...	...	...	—	—	—	—	—
91-92—Miami of Ohio	CCHA	40	24	16	40	43	...	...	...	—	—	—	—	—
92-93—Miami of Ohio	CCHA	38	37	21	58	44	...	...	...	—	—	—	—	—
—Canadian nat'l team	Int'l	9	3	0	3	12	...	...	...	—	—	—	—	—
93-94—Canadian nat'l team	Int'l	51	20	26	46	38	...	...	...	—	—	—	—	—
—Can. Olympic team	Int'l	8	2	2	4	6	...	...	...	—	—	—	—	—
—Fredericton	AHL	17	12	15	27	4	...	...	...	—	—	—	—	—
—Montreal	NHL	3	1	0	1	0	0	0	0	3	0	2	2	0
94-95—Montreal	NHL	37	12	7	19	27	5	0	0	—	—	—	—	—
95-96—Montreal	NHL	75	25	8	33	28	-8	4	0	6	0	2	2	2
96-97—Montreal	NHL	81	23	37	60	39	-14	5	0	5	1	1	2	0
97-98—Montreal	NHL	64	26	17	43	36	11	8	0	9	0	2	2	6
98-99—Montreal	NHL	54	16	10	26	20	-14	5	0	—	—	—	—	—
99-00—Montreal	NHL	38	17	12	29	19	-4	6	1	—	—	—	—	—
00-01—Montreal	NHL	62	21	24	45	26	-13	12	0	—	—	—	—	—
01-02—Montreal	NHL	47	14	15	29	30	-14	7	0	—	—	—	—	—
—Phoenix	NHL	30	6	6	12	8	1	2	0	5	0	0	0	0
02-03—Phoenix	NHL	43	6	10	16	22	-4	1	0	—	—	—	—	—
NHL Totals (10 years)		534	167	146	313	255	-54	50	1	28	1	7	8	8

SAVARD, MARC   C   THRASHERS

PERSONAL: Born July 17, 1977, in Ottawa, Ont. ... 5-10/188. ... Shoots left. ... Name pronounced suh-VAHRD.

TRANSACTIONS/CAREER NOTES: Selected by New York Rangers in fourth round (third Rangers pick, 91st overall) of NHL entry draft (July 8, 1995). ... Traded by Rangers with first-round pick (C/LW Oleg Saprykin) in 1999 draft to Calgary Flames for rights to LW Jan Hlavac and first- (C Jamie Lundmark) and third-round (D Pat Aufiero) picks in 1999 draft (June 26, 1999). ... Suffered concussion (January 8, 2000); missed two games. ... Missed first two games of 2000-01 season due to contract dispute. ... Suffered concussion (December 31, 2000); missed three games. ... Injured knee (October 10, 2001); missed 15 games. ... Injured head (March 23, 2002); missed remainder of season. ... Traded by Flames to Atlanta Thrashers for RW Ruslan Zainullan (November 15, 2002).

STATISTICAL PLATEAUS: Three-goal games: 2001-02 (1). ... Four-goal games: 1999-00 (1). ... Total hat tricks: 2.

Season Team	League	REGULAR SEASON								PLAYOFFS				
		Gms.	G	A	Pts.	PIM	+/-	PP	SH	Gms.	G	A	Pts.	PIM
92-93—Metcalfe	Jr. B	31	46	53	99	26	...	...	...	—	—	—	—	—
93-94—Oshawa	OHL	61	18	39	57	24	...	...	...	5	4	3	7	8
94-95—Oshawa	OHL	66	43	96	*139	78	...	...	...	7	5	6	11	8
95-96—Oshawa	OHL	48	28	59	87	77	...	...	...	5	4	5	9	6
96-97—Oshawa	OHL	64	43	*87	*130	94	...	...	...	18	13	†24	*37	20
97-98—New York Rangers	NHL	28	1	5	6	4	-4	0	0	—	—	—	—	—
—Hartford	AHL	58	21	53	74	66	...	...	...	15	8	19	27	24
98-99—Hartford	AHL	9	3	10	13	16	...	...	...	7	1	12	13	16
—New York Rangers	NHL	70	9	36	45	38	-7	4	0	—	—	—	—	—
99-00—Calgary	NHL	78	22	31	53	56	-2	4	0	—	—	—	—	—
00-01—Calgary	NHL	77	23	42	65	46	-12	10	1	—	—	—	—	—
01-02—Calgary	NHL	56	14	19	33	48	-18	7	0	—	—	—	—	—
02-03—Calgary	NHL	10	1	2	3	8	-3	0	0	—	—	—	—	—
—Atlanta	NHL	57	16	31	47	77	-11	6	0	—	—	—	—	—
NHL Totals (6 years)		376	86	166	252	277	-57	31	1					

SAWYER, KEVIN   LW

PERSONAL: Born February 21, 1974, in Christina Lake, B.C. ... 6-2/207. ... Shoots left.
TRANSACTIONS/CAREER NOTES: Signed as non-drafted free agent by St. Louis Blues (February 16, 1995). ... Traded by Blues with D Steve Staios to Boston Bruins for RW Steve Leach (March 8, 1996). ... Signed as free agent by Dallas Stars (July 25, 1997). ... Signed as free agent by Blues (September 4, 1998). ... Signed as free agent by Phoenix Coyotes (August 15, 1999). ... Signed as free agent by Mighty Ducks of Anaheim (July 13, 2000). ... Suspended five games by NHL for unsportsmanlike conduct (December 10, 2001). ... Suspended two games by NHL for charging a goaltender (January 23, 2002).

						REGULAR SEASON						PLAYOFFS			
Season Team	League	Gms.	G	A	Pts.	PIM	+/-	PP	SH	Gms.	G	A	Pts.	PIM
91-92—Kelowna	BCJHL	3	0	0	0	9	...	...	...	—	—	—	—	—
—Vernon	BCJHL	12	0	1	1	18	...	...	...	—	—	—	—	—
—Penticton	BCJHL	3	0	0	0	13	...	...	...	—	—	—	—	—
92-93—Spokane	WHL	62	4	3	7	274	...	...	...	—	—	—	—	—
93-94—Spokane	WHL	60	10	15	25	350	...	...	...	3	0	1	1	6
94-95—Spokane	WHL	54	7	9	16	365	...	...	...	11	2	0	2	58
—Peoria	IHL	—	—	—	—	—	—	—	—	2	0	0	0	12
95-96—Worcester	AHL	41	3	4	7	268	...	...	...	—	—	—	—	—
—St. Louis	NHL	6	0	0	0	23	-2	0	0	—	—	—	—	—
—Providence	AHL	4	0	0	0	29	...	...	...	4	0	1	1	9
—Boston	NHL	2	0	0	0	5	1	0	0	—	—	—	—	—
96-97—Providence	AHL	60	8	9	17	367	...	...	...	6	0	0	0	32
—Boston	NHL	2	0	0	0	0	0	0	0	—	—	—	—	—
97-98—Michigan	IHL	60	2	5	7	*398	...	...	...	3	0	0	0	23
98-99—Worcester	AHL	70	8	14	22	299	...	...	...	4	0	1	1	4
99-00—Phoenix	NHL	3	0	0	0	12	1	0	0	—	—	—	—	—
—Springfield	AHL	56	4	8	12	321	...	...	...	4	0	0	0	6
00-01—Cincinnati	AHL	41	2	12	14	211	...	...	...	—	—	—	—	—
—Anaheim	NHL	9	0	1	1	27	-1	0	0	—	—	—	—	—
01-02—Anaheim	NHL	57	1	1	2	221	-4	0	0	—	—	—	—	—
02-03—Anaheim	NHL	31	2	1	3	115	-2	0	0	—	—	—	—	—
NHL Totals (6 years)		110	3	3	6	403	-7	0	0					

SCATCHARD, DAVE   C   ISLANDERS

PERSONAL: Born February 20, 1976, in Hinton, Alta. ... 6-3/217. ... Shoots right. ... Name pronounced SKATCH-uhrd.
TRANSACTIONS/CAREER NOTES: Selected by Vancouver Canucks in second round (third Canucks pick, 42nd overall) of NHL entry draft (June 28, 1994). ... Suffered hip pointer (December 15, 1997); missed two games. ... Bruised ankle (October 13, 1999); missed five games. ... Traded by Canucks with G Kevin Weekes and RW Bill Muckalt to New York Islanders for G Felix Potvin, second-(traded to Atlanta) and third-round (C Thatcher Bell) picks in 2000 draft (December 19, 1999). ... Suffered concussion (March 22, 2000); missed final eight games of season. ... Strained neck (November 9, 2000); missed one game.
STATISTICAL PLATEAUS: Three-goal games: 2002-03 (2).

						REGULAR SEASON						PLAYOFFS			
Season Team	League	Gms.	G	A	Pts.	PIM	+/-	PP	SH	Gms.	G	A	Pts.	PIM
92-93—Kimberley	RMJHL	51	20	23	43	61	...	...	...	—	—	—	—	—
93-94—Portland	WHL	47	9	11	20	46	...	...	...	10	2	1	3	4
94-95—Portland	WHL	71	20	30	50	148	...	...	...	8	0	3	3	21
95-96—Portland	WHL	59	19	28	47	146	...	...	...	7	1	8	9	14
—Syracuse	AHL	1	0	0	0	0	...	...	...	15	2	5	7	29
96-97—Syracuse	AHL	26	8	7	15	65	...	...	...	—	—	—	—	—
97-98—Vancouver	NHL	76	13	11	24	165	-4	0	0	—	—	—	—	—
98-99—Vancouver	NHL	82	13	13	26	140	-12	0	2	—	—	—	—	—
99-00—Vancouver	NHL	21	0	4	4	24	-3	0	0	—	—	—	—	—
—New York Islanders	NHL	44	12	14	26	93	0	0	1	—	—	—	—	—
00-01—New York Islanders	NHL	81	21	24	45	114	-9	4	0	—	—	—	—	—
01-02—New York Islanders	NHL	80	12	15	27	111	-4	3	1	7	1	1	2	22
02-03—New York Islanders	NHL	81	27	18	45	108	9	5	0	5	1	0	1	6
NHL Totals (6 years)		465	98	99	197	755	-23	12	4	12	2	1	3	28

SCHAEFER, PETER   LW   SENATORS

PERSONAL: Born July 12, 1977, in Yellow Grass, Sask. ... 5-11/195. ... Shoots left.
TRANSACTIONS/CAREER NOTES: Selected by Vancouver Canucks in third round (third Canucks pick, 66th overall) of NHL entry draft (July 8, 1995). ... Sprained shoulder (April 2, 1999); missed final six games of season. ... Suffered illness (November 20, 1999); missed one game. ... Injured knee (February 14, 2000); missed three games. ... Reinjured knee (February 23, 2000); missed four games. ... Suffered from the flu (April 2, 2000); missed one game. ... Missed entire 2001-02 season due to contract dispute; played in Europe. ... Traded by Canucks to Ottawa Senators for D Sami Salo (September 21, 2002).

						REGULAR SEASON						PLAYOFFS			
Season Team	League	Gms.	G	A	Pts.	PIM	+/-	PP	SH	Gms.	G	A	Pts.	PIM
93-94—Brandon	WHL	2	1	0	1	0	...	...	...	—	—	—	—	—
94-95—Brandon	WHL	68	27	32	59	34	...	...	...	18	5	3	8	18
95-96—Brandon	WHL	69	47	61	108	53	...	...	...	19	10	13	23	5
96-97—Brandon	WHL	61	49	74	123	85	...	...	...	6	1	4	5	4
—Syracuse	AHL	5	0	3	3	0	...	...	...	3	1	3	4	14
97-98—Syracuse	AHL	73	19	44	63	41	...	...	...	5	2	1	3	2
98-99—Syracuse	AHL	41	10	19	29	66	...	...	...	—	—	—	—	—
—Vancouver	NHL	25	4	4	8	8	-1	1	0	—	—	—	—	—
99-00—Vancouver	NHL	71	16	15	31	20	0	2	2	—	—	—	—	—
—Syracuse	AHL	2	0	0	0	2	...	...	...	—	—	—	—	—
00-01—Vancouver	NHL	82	16	20	36	22	4	3	4	3	0	0	0	0
01-02—TPS Turku	Finland	33	16	15	31	93	...	...	...	8	1	2	3	2
02-03—Ottawa	NHL	75	6	17	23	32	11	0	0	16	2	3	5	6
NHL Totals (4 years)		253	42	56	98	82	14	6	6	19	2	3	5	6

SCHASTLIVY, PETR LW SENATORS

PERSONAL: Born April 18, 1979, in Angarsk, U.S.S.R. ... 6-1/204. ... Shoots left.
TRANSACTIONS/CAREER NOTES: Selected by Ottawa Senators in fourth round (fifth Senators pick, 101st overall) of NHL entry draft (June 27, 1998). ... Tore anterior cruciate ligament in right knee (December 29, 2001); missed remainder of season.

Season Team	League	Gms.	G	A	Pts.	PIM	+/-	PP	SH	Gms.	G	A	Pts.	PIM
					REGULAR SEASON							PLAYOFFS		
96-97—Yermak Angarsk	Rus. Div. III						Statistics unavailable.							
97-98—Torpedo Yaroslavl	Rus. Div. II	47	15	9	24	34	...	...	...	—	—	—	—	—
—Torpedo Yaroslavl	Russian	4	0	0	0	0	...	...	...	—	—	—	—	—
98-99—Torpedo Yaroslavl	Russian	40	6	1	7	28	...	...	...	6	0	0	0	2
99-00—Grand Rapids	IHL	46	16	12	28	10	...	...	...	17	8	7	15	6
—Ottawa	NHL	13	2	5	7	2	4	1	0	1	0	0	0	0
00-01—Grand Rapids	IHL	43	10	14	24	10	...	...	...	7	4	4	8	0
—Ottawa	NHL	17	3	2	5	6	-1	0	0	—	—	—	—	—
01-02—Grand Rapids	AHL	31	22	13	35	10	...	...	...	—	—	—	—	—
—Ottawa	NHL	1	0	1	1	0	1	0	0	—	—	—	—	—
02-03—Ottawa	NHL	33	9	10	19	4	3	5	0	—	—	—	—	—
NHL Totals (4 years)		64	14	18	32	12	7	6	0	1	0	0	0	0

SCHILL, JONATHAN LW

PERSONAL: Born June 28, 1979, in Kitchener, Ont. ... 6-1/201. ... Shoots left.
TRANSACTIONS/CAREER NOTES: Signed as non-drafted free agent by Columbus Blue Jackets (May 8, 2000).

Season Team	League	Gms.	G	A	Pts.	PIM	+/-	PP	SH	Gms.	G	A	Pts.	PIM
					REGULAR SEASON							PLAYOFFS		
96-97—Kingston	OHL	52	3	7	10	16	...	...	...	4	0	0	0	0
97-98—Kingston	OHL	67	14	17	31	34	...	...	...	12	1	1	2	4
98-99—Kingston	OHL	68	32	27	59	93	...	...	...	5	2	1	3	6
99-00—Kingston	OHL	65	39	48	87	79	...	...	...	3	1	1	2	6
00-01—Syracuse	AHL	4	0	1	1	8	...	...	...	—	—	—	—	—
—Dayton	ECHL	58	18	6	24	153	...	...	...	6	2	3	5	22
01-02—Syracuse	AHL	44	3	4	7	61	...	...	...	9	0	0	0	4
—Dayton	ECHL	5	0	1	1	15	...	...	...	—	—	—	—	—
02-03—Syracuse	AHL	31	0	1	1	22	...	...	...	—	—	—	—	—
—Dayton	ECHL	9	2	2	4	23	...	...	...	—	—	—	—	—

SCHMIDT, CHRIS C KINGS

PERSONAL: Born March 1, 1976, in Beaver Lodge, Alta. ... 6-3/212. ... Shoots left.
HIGH SCHOOL: Meadowdale (Lynwood, Wash.).
TRANSACTIONS/CAREER NOTES: Selected by Los Angeles Kings in fifth round (fourth Kings pick, 111th overall) of NHL entry draft (June 29, 1994). ... Signed by Kings (June 30, 2003).

Season Team	League	Gms.	G	A	Pts.	PIM	+/-	PP	SH	Gms.	G	A	Pts.	PIM
					REGULAR SEASON							PLAYOFFS		
92-93—Seattle	WHL	61	6	7	13	17	...	...	...	5	0	1	1	0
93-94—Seattle	WHL	68	7	17	24	26	...	...	...	9	3	1	4	2
94-95—Seattle	WHL	61	21	11	32	31	...	...	...	3	0	0	0	0
95-96—Seattle	WHL	61	39	23	62	135	...	...	...	5	1	5	6	9
96-97—Mississippi	ECHL	18	7	7	14	35	...	...	...	—	—	—	—	—
—Phoenix	IHL	37	3	6	9	60	...	...	...	—	—	—	—	—
97-98—Fredericton	AHL	69	8	5	13	67	...	...	...	4	0	0	0	2
98-99—Springfield	AHL	17	3	2	5	19	...	...	...	1	0	0	0	0
—Mississippi	ECHL	6	1	0	1	2	...	...	...	18	6	8	14	10
99-00—Lowell	AHL	38	8	10	18	38	...	...	...	7	2	1	3	8
00-01—Lowell	AHL	79	21	32	53	84	...	...	...	4	2	2	4	2
01-02—Manchester	AHL	62	9	12	21	43	...	...	...	5	0	2	2	0
02-03—Manchester	AHL	53	12	13	25	58	...			—	—	—	—	—
—Los Angeles	NHL	10	0	2	2	5	-1	0	0	—	—	—	—	—
NHL Totals (1 year)		10	0	2	2	5	-1	0	0					

SCHNABEL, ROBERT D PREDATORS

PERSONAL: Born November 10, 1978, in Prague, Czechoslovakia ... 6-5/230. ... Shoots left. ... Name pronounced SHNAY-buhl.
TRANSACTIONS/CAREER NOTES: Selected by New York Islanders in third round (fifth Islanders pick, 79th overall) of NHL entry draft (June 21, 1997). ... Returned to draft pool by Islanders and selected by Phoenix Coyotes in sixth round (seventh Coyotes pick, 129th overall) of NHL entry draft (June 27, 1998). ... Claimed on waivers by Atlanta Thrashers (January 2, 2001). ... Signed as free agent by Nashville Predators (July 13, 2001). ... Re-signed by Predators (July 17, 2003).

Season Team	League	Gms.	G	A	Pts.	PIM	+/-	PP	SH	Gms.	G	A	Pts.	PIM
					REGULAR SEASON							PLAYOFFS		
94-95—Slavia Praha	Czech. Jrs.	35	11	6	17	14	...	...	...	—	—	—	—	—
95-96—Slavia Praha	Czech. Jrs.	38	3	5	8	...	...	...	...	—	—	—	—	—
96-97—Slavia Praha	Czech. Jrs.	36	5	2	7	...	...	...	...	—	—	—	—	—
—Slavia Praha	Czech Rep.	4	0	0	0	4	...	...	...	1	0	0	0	0
97-98—Red Deer	WHL	61	1	22	23	143	...	...	...	5	0	0	0	16

Season Team	League	REGULAR SEASON								PLAYOFFS				
		Gms.	G	A	Pts.	PIM	+/-	PP	SH	Gms.	G	A	Pts.	PIM
98-99—Red Deer	WHL	1	0	0	0	2	...	...	...	—	—	—	—	—
—Springfield	AHL	77	1	7	8	155	...	...	...	3	1	0	1	4
99-00—Springfield	AHL	40	2	8	10	133	...	...	...	5	0	0	0	4
00-01—Timra	Sweden	16	0	2	2	72	...	...	...	—	—	—	—	—
—Springfield	AHL	22	1	2	3	38	...	...	...	—	—	—	—	—
01-02—Milwaukee	AHL	67	2	7	9	130	...	...	...	—	—	—	—	—
—Nashville	NHL	1	0	0	0	0	0	0	0	—	—	—	—	—
02-03—Milwaukee	AHL	62	3	6	9	178	...	...	...	—	—	—	—	—
—Nashville	NHL	1	0	0	0	0	0	0	0	—	—	—	—	—
NHL Totals (2 years)		2	0	0	0	0	0	0	0					

SCHNEIDER, MATHIEU — D — RED WINGS

PERSONAL: Born June 12, 1969, in New York ... 6-0/194. ... Shoots left.

TRANSACTIONS/CAREER NOTES: Selected by Montreal Canadiens in third round (fourth Canadiens pick, 44th overall) of NHL entry draft (June 13, 1987). ... Bruised left shoulder (February 1990). ... Sprained left ankle (January 26, 1991); missed nine games. ... Sprained ankle (January 27, 1993); missed 24 games. ... Separated shoulder (April 18, 1993); missed seven playoff games. ... Injured ankle (December 6, 1993); missed two games. ... Underwent elbow surgery (March 29, 1994); missed five games. ... Suffered illness (February 27, 1995); missed one game. ... Traded by Canadiens with LW Kirk Muller and C Craig Darby to New York Islanders for D Vladimir Malakhov and C Pierre Turgeon (April 5, 1995). ... Bruised ribs (October 28, 1995); missed one game. ... Traded by Islanders with LW Wendel Clark and D D.J. Smith to Toronto Maple Leafs for LW Sean Haggerty, C Darby Hendrickson, D Kenny Jonsson and first-round pick (G Roberto Luongo) in 1997 draft (March 13, 1996). ... Suspended three games by NHL for elbowing incident (November 14, 1996). ... Strained groin (December 12, 1996); missed 27 games. ... Reinjured groin (February 12, 1997) and underwent surgery; and missed final 26 games of season. ... Suffered concussion and facial lacerations (December 2, 1997); missed two games. ... Bruised shoulder (January 6, 1998); missed two games. ... Strained upper abdominal muscle (February 2, 1998); missed one game. ... Strained groin (April 6, 1998); missed one game. ... Traded by Maple Leafs to New York Rangers for D Alexander Karpovtsev and fourth-round pick (LW Mirko Murovic) in 1999 draft (October 14, 1998). ... Suffered from the flu (January 27, 2000); missed one game. ... Suffered from the flu (March 26, 2000); missed one game. ... Selected by Columbus Blue Jackets in NHL expansion draft (June 23, 2000). ... Signed as free agent by Los Angeles Kings (August 13, 2000). ... Strained back (November 16, 2000); missed one game. ... Strained groin (February 23, 2001); missed eight games. ... Suffered hernia (November 9, 2001); missed 23 games. ...ₓ Strained left shoulder (January 28, 2002); missed two games. ... Traded by Kings to Detroit Red Wings for C Sean Avery, D Maxim Kuznetsov, first-round pick in 2003 draft and second-round pick in 2004 draft (March 11, 2003).

Season Team	League	REGULAR SEASON								PLAYOFFS				
		Gms.	G	A	Pts.	PIM	+/-	PP	SH	Gms.	G	A	Pts.	PIM
85-86—Mt. St. Charles H.S.	R.I.H.S.	19	3	27	30	...	...	...	...	—	—	—	—	—
86-87—Cornwall	OHL	63	7	29	36	75	...	...	...	5	0	0	0	22
87-88—Montreal	NHL	4	0	0	0	2	-1	0	0	—	—	—	—	—
—Cornwall	OHL	48	21	40	61	85	...	...	...	11	2	6	8	14
—Sherbrooke	AHL	—	—	—	—	—	—	—	—	3	0	3	3	12
88-89—Cornwall	OHL	59	16	57	73	96	...	...	...	18	7	20	27	30
89-90—Sherbrooke	AHL	28	6	13	19	20	...	...	...	—	—	—	—	—
—Montreal	NHL	44	7	14	21	25	2	5	0	9	1	3	4	31
90-91—Montreal	NHL	69	10	20	30	63	7	5	0	13	2	7	9	18
91-92—Montreal	NHL	78	8	24	32	72	10	2	0	10	1	4	5	6
92-93—Montreal	NHL	60	13	31	44	91	8	3	0	11	1	2	3	16
93-94—Montreal	NHL	75	20	32	52	62	15	11	0	1	0	0	0	0
94-95—Montreal	NHL	30	5	15	20	49	-3	2	0	—	—	—	—	—
—New York Islanders	NHL	13	3	6	9	30	-5	1	0	—	—	—	—	—
95-96—New York Islanders	NHL	65	11	36	47	93	-18	7	0	—	—	—	—	—
—Toronto	NHL	13	2	5	7	10	-2	0	0	6	0	4	4	8
96-97—Toronto	NHL	26	5	7	12	20	3	1	0	—	—	—	—	—
97-98—Toronto	NHL	76	11	26	37	44	-12	4	1	—	—	—	—	—
—U.S. Olympic team	Int'l	4	0	0	0	6	...	...	...	—	—	—	—	—
98-99—New York Rangers	NHL	75	10	24	34	71	-19	5	0	—	—	—	—	—
99-00—New York Rangers	NHL	80	10	20	30	78	-6	3	0	—	—	—	—	—
00-01—Los Angeles	NHL	73	16	35	51	56	0	7	1	13	0	9	9	10
01-02—Los Angeles	NHL	55	7	23	30	68	3	4	0	7	0	1	1	18
02-03—Los Angeles	NHL	65	14	29	43	57	0	10	0	—	—	—	—	—
—Detroit	NHL	13	2	5	7	16	2	1	0	4	0	0	0	6
NHL Totals (15 years)		914	154	352	506	907	-16	71	2	74	5	30	35	113

SCHUBERT, CHRISTOPH — D — SENATORS

PERSONAL: Born February 5, 1982, in Germany. ... 6-1/186. ... Shoots left.

TRANSACTIONS/CAREER NOTES: Selected by Ottawa Senators in fourth round (fifth Senators pick, 127th overall) of NHL entry draft (June 23, 2001).

Season Team	League	REGULAR SEASON								PLAYOFFS				
		Gms.	G	A	Pts.	PIM	+/-	PP	SH	Gms.	G	A	Pts.	PIM
00-01—Munchen	Ger. Div. II	55	6	3	9	80	...	...	...	—	—	—	—	—
01-02—Munich	Germany	50	5	11	16	125	...	...	...	9	3	4	7	32
—German Oly. team	Int'l	7	0	1	1	6	...	...	...	—	—	—	—	—
02-03—Binghamton	AHL	70	2	8	10	102	...	...	...	—	—	—	—	—

SCHULTZ, NICK — D — WILD

PERSONAL: Born August 25, 1982, in Strasbourg, Sask. ... 6-0/187. ... Shoots left.

TRANSACTIONS/CAREER NOTES: Selected by Minnesota Wild in second round (second Wild pick, 33rd overall) of NHL entry draft (June 24, 2000). ... Bruised shoulder (February 6, 2002); missed one game.

Season Team	League	REGULAR SEASON								PLAYOFFS				
		Gms.	G	A	Pts.	PIM	+/-	PP	SH	Gms.	G	A	Pts.	PIM
98-99—Prince Albert	WHL	58	5	10	15	37	...	...	...	—	—	—	—	—
99-00—Prince Albert	WHL	72	11	33	44	38	...	...	...	6	0	3	3	2
00-01—Prince Albert	WHL	59	17	30	47	120	...	...	...	—	—	—	—	—
—Cleveland	IHL	4	1	1	2	2	...	...	...	3	0	1	1	0
01-02—Minnesota	NHL	52	4	6	10	14	0	1	0	—	—	—	—	—
—Houston	AHL	0	0	0	0	0	0	0	0	14	1	5	6	2
02-03—Minnesota	NHL	75	3	7	10	23	11	0	0	18	0	1	1	10
NHL Totals (2 years)		127	7	13	20	37	11	1	0	18	0	1	1	10

SCHULTZ, RAY   D   PREDATORS

PERSONAL: Born November 14, 1976, in Red Deer, Alta. ... 6-2/208. ... Shoots left. ... Cousin of Rene Chapdelaine, defenseman with Los Angeles Kings (1990-91 through 1992-93).

TRANSACTIONS/CAREER NOTES: Selected by Ottawa Senators in eighth round (eighth Senators pick, 184th overall) of NHL entry draft (July 8, 1995). ... Signed as free agent by New York Islanders (June 17, 1997). ... Signed by Nashville Predators (July 17, 2003).

Season Team	League	REGULAR SEASON								PLAYOFFS				
		Gms.	G	A	Pts.	PIM	+/-	PP	SH	Gms.	G	A	Pts.	PIM
93-94—Tri-City	WHL	3	0	0	0	11	...	...	...	—	—	—	—	—
94-95—Tri-City	WHL	63	1	8	9	209	...	...	...	11	0	0	0	16
95-96—Calgary	WHL	66	3	17	20	282	...	...	...	—	—	—	—	—
96-97—Calgary	WHL	32	3	17	20	141	...	...	...	—	—	—	—	—
—Kelowna	WHL	23	3	11	14	63	...	...	...	6	0	2	2	12
97-98—Kentucky	AHL	51	2	4	6	179	...	...	...	1	0	0	0	25
—New York Islanders	NHL	13	0	1	1	45	3	0	0	—	—	—	—	—
98-99—Lowell	AHL	54	0	3	3	184	...	...	...	1	0	0	0	4
—New York Islanders	NHL	4	0	0	0	7	-2	0	0	—	—	—	—	—
99-00—Kansas City	IHL	65	5	5	10	208	...	...	...	—	—	—	—	—
—New York Islanders	NHL	9	0	1	1	30	1	0	0	—	—	—	—	—
00-01—Lowell	AHL	13	0	1	1	33	...	...	...	—	—	—	—	—
—Cleveland	IHL	44	3	5	8	127	...	...	...	3	1	0	1	16
—New York Islanders	NHL	13	0	2	2	40	-1	0	0	—	—	—	—	—
01-02—Bridgeport	AHL	69	0	15	15	205	...	...	...	19	1	3	4	18
—New York Islanders	NHL	2	0	0	0	5	-1	0	0	2	0	0	0	2
02-03—Bridgeport	AHL	51	2	8	10	105	...	...	...	—	—	—	—	—
—New York Islanders	NHL	4	0	0	0	28	-1	0	0	—	—	—	—	—
NHL Totals (6 years)		45	0	4	4	155	-1	0	0	2	0	0	0	2

SCHWAB, COREY   G   DEVILS

PERSONAL: Born November 4, 1970, in North Battleford, Sask. ... 6-0/180. ... Catches left. ... Name pronounced SHWAHB.

TRANSACTIONS/CAREER NOTES: Selected by New Jersey Devils in 10th round (12th Devils pick, 200th overall) of NHL entry draft (June 16, 1990). ... Injured groin (October 12, 1995); missed six games. ... Traded by Devils to Tampa Bay Lightning for G Jeff Reese and second-(LW Pierre Dagenais) and eighth-(RW Jason Bertsch) round picks in 1996 draft (June 22, 1996). ... Injured groin (January 9, 1997); missed one game. ... Injured groin (December 23, 1997); missed one game. ... Injured ankle (December 31, 1997); missed remainder of season. ... Selected by Atlanta Thrashers in NHL expansion draft (June 25, 1999). ... Traded by Thrashers to Vancouver Canucks for conditional pick in 2000 draft (October 29, 1999). ... Signed as free agent by Toronto Maple Leafs (October 1, 2001). ... Signed as free agent by Devils (July 8, 2002).

Season Team	League	REGULAR SEASON									PLAYOFFS							
		Gms.	Min	W	L	T	GA	SO	Avg.	SV%	Gms.	Min.	W	L	GA	SO	Avg.	SV%
88-89—Seattle	WHL	10	386	2	2	0	31	0	4.82	—	—	—	—	—	—	—	—	—
89-90—Seattle	WHL	27	1150	15	2	1	69	0	3.60	—	3	49	0	0	2	0	2.45	—
90-91—Seattle	WHL	58	3289	32	18	3	224	1	4.09	—	6	382	1	5	25	0	3.93	—
91-92—Utica	AHL	24	1322	9	12	1	95	1	4.31	—	—	—	—	—	—	—	—	—
—Cincinnati	AHL	8	450	6	0	1	31	0	4.13	—	9	540	6	3	29	0	3.22	—
92-93—Cincinnati	IHL	3	185	1	2	‡0	17	0	5.51	—	—	—	—	—	—	—	—	—
—Utica	AHL	40	2387	18	16	5	169	2	4.25	—	1	59	0	1	6	0	6.10	—
93-94—Albany	AHL	51	3059	27	21	3	184	0	3.61	—	5	298	1	4	20	0	4.03	—
94-95—Albany	AHL	45	2711	25	10	9	117	3	*2.59	—	7	425	6	1	19	0	2.68	—
95-96—Albany	AHL	5	298	3	2	0	13	0	2.62	—	—	—	—	—	—	—	—	—
—New Jersey	NHL	10	331	0	3	0	12	0	2.18	.899	—	—	—	—	—	—	—	—
96-97—Tampa Bay	NHL	31	1462	11	12	1	74	2	3.04	.897	—	—	—	—	—	—	—	—
97-98—Tampa Bay	NHL	16	821	2	9	1	40	1	2.92	.892	—	—	—	—	—	—	—	—
98-99—Cleveland	IHL	8	477	1	6	‡1	31	0	3.90	—	—	—	—	—	—	—	—	—
—Tampa Bay	NHL	40	2146	8	25	3	126	0	3.52	.891	—	—	—	—	—	—	—	—
99-00—Orlando	IHL	16	868	13	4	2	31	1	2.14	—	—	—	—	—	—	—	—	—
—Vancouver	NHL	6	269	2	1	1	16	0	3.57	.861	—	—	—	—	—	—	—	—
—Syracuse	AHL	12	720	7	5	0	42	0	3.50	—	4	246	1	3	11	1	2.68	—
00-01—Kansas City	IHL	50	2866	22	24	‡1	150	2	3.14	—	—	—	—	—	—	—	—	—
01-02—Toronto	NHL	30	1646	12	10	5	75	1	2.73	.894	1	12	0	0	0	0	...	1.000
02-03—New Jersey	NHL	11	614	5	3	1	15	1	1.47	.933	2	28	0	0	0	0	...	1.000
NHL Totals (7 years)		144	7289	40	63	12	358	5	2.95	.895	3	40	0	0	0	0	...	1.000

SCOTT, RICHARD   LW   RANGERS

PERSONAL: Born August 1, 1978, in Orillia, Ont. ... 6-2/195. ... Shoots right.
TRANSACTIONS/CAREER NOTES: Signed as non-drafted free agent by New York Rangers (May 8, 2001).

Season Team	League	Gms.	G	A	Pts.	PIM	+/-	PP	SH	Gms.	G	A	Pts.	PIM
96-97—Orillia	OPJHL	10	0	0	0	23	...	...	...	—	—	—	—	—
97-98—Couchiching	OPJHL	45	13	19	32	166	...	...	...	—	—	—	—	—
98-99—Oshawa	OHL	54	12	12	24	193	...	...	...	—	—	—	—	—
99-00—Charlotte	ECHL	55	1	5	6	317	...	...	...	—	—	—	—	—
00-01—Hartford	AHL	64	2	5	7	320	...	...	...	1	0	0	0	0
—Charlotte	ECHL	4	1	1	2	22	...	...	...	—	—	—	—	—
01-02—Hartford	AHL	39	2	3	5	211	...	...	...	—	—	—	—	—
—New York Rangers	NHL	5	0	0	0	5	0	0	0	—	—	—	—	—
02-03—Hartford	AHL	32	0	5	5	150	...	...	...	—	—	—	—	—
—Charlotte	ECHL	3	0	1	1	4	...	...	...	—	—	—	—	—
NHL Totals (1 year)		5	0	0	0	5	0	0	0					

SCOTT, TRAVIS   G   KINGS

PERSONAL: Born September 14, 1975, in Kanata, Ont. ... 6-2/185. ... Catches left.
TRANSACTIONS/CAREER NOTES: Signed as non-drafted free agent by St. Louis Blues (December 30, 1996). ... Signed by Los Angeles Kings (February 18, 2000).

Season Team	League	Gms.	Min	W	L	T	GA	SO	Avg.	SV%	Gms.	Min.	W	L	GA	SO	Avg.	SV%
91-92—Smiths Falls-Nepean	Jr. A	22	1151	...	...	...	90	1	4.69	—	—	—	—	—	—	—	—	—
92-93—Nepean	COJHL	36	1968	...	...	...	133	0	4.05	—	—	—	—	—	—	—	—	—
93-94—Windsor	OHL	45	2312	20	18	0	158	1	4.10	—	4	240	0	4	16	0	4.00	—
94-95—Windsor	OHL	48	2644	26	14	3	147	*3	3.34	—	3	94	0	1	6	1	3.83	—
95-96—Oshawa	OHL	31	1763	15	9	4	78	†3	*2.65	—	5	315	1	4	23	0	4.38	—
96-97—Baton Rouge	ECHL	10	501	5	2	1	22	0	2.63	—	—	—	—	—	—	—	—	—
—Worcester	AHL	29	1482	14	10	1	75	1	3.04	—	—	—	—	—	—	—	—	—
97-98—Baton Rouge	ECHL	36	1949	14	11	6	96	1	2.96	—	—	—	—	—	—	—	—	—
98-99—Mississippi	ECHL	44	2337	22	12	‡5	112	1	2.88	—	†18	*1252	*14	4	42	3	2.01	—
99-00—Lowell	AHL	46	2595	15	23	3	126	3	2.91	—	1	60	0	1	2	0	2.00	—
00-01—Lowell	AHL	34	1977	16	15	1	83	2	2.52	—	4	209	1	2	7	1	2.01	—
—Los Angeles	NHL	1	25	0	0	0	3	0	7.20	.700	—	—	—	—	—	—	—	—
01-02—Manchester	AHL	39	2169	21	12	3	83	6	2.30	—	5	326	2	3	15	0	2.76	—
02-03—Manchester	AHL	50	2829	23	19	5	116	4	2.46	—	—	—	—	—	—	—	—	—
NHL Totals (1 year)		1	25	0	0	0	3	0	7.20	.700								

SCOVILLE, DARREL   D   BLUE JACKETS

PERSONAL: Born October 13, 1975, in Swift Current, Sask. ... 6-3/208. ... Shoots left.
TRANSACTIONS/CAREER NOTES: Signed as non-drafted free agent by Calgary Flames (June 12, 1998). ... Signed as free agent by Columbus Blue Jackets (July 10, 2001). ... Re-signed by Blue Jackets (July 20, 2003).

Season Team	League	Gms.	G	A	Pts.	PIM	+/-	PP	SH	Gms.	G	A	Pts.	PIM
95-96—Merrimack College	Hockey East	34	6	20	26	54	...	...	...	—	—	—	—	—
96-97—Merrimack College	Hockey East	35	7	16	23	71	...	...	...	—	—	—	—	—
97-98—Merrimack College	Hockey East	38	4	26	30	84	...	...	...	—	—	—	—	—
98-99—Saint John	AHL	61	1	7	8	66	...	...	...	7	1	2	3	13
99-00—Saint John	AHL	64	11	25	36	99	...	...	...	3	1	2	3	0
—Calgary	NHL	6	0	0	0	2	1	0	0	—	—	—	—	—
00-01—Saint John	AHL	76	17	32	49	125	...	...	...	19	3	7	10	12
01-02—Syracuse	AHL	51	5	16	21	60	...	...	...	10	0	0	0	6
02-03—Syracuse	AHL	24	4	9	13	26	...	...	...	—	—	—	—	—
—Columbus	NHL	2	0	0	0	4	0	0	0	—	—	—	—	—
NHL Totals (2 years)		8	0	0	0	6	1	0	0					

SCUDERI, ROBERT   D   PENGUINS

PERSONAL: Born December 30, 1978, in Syosset, N.Y. ... 6-1/194. ... Shoots left.
TRANSACTIONS/CAREER NOTES: Selected by Pittsburgh Penguins in fifth round (fifth Penguins pick, 134th overall) of NHL entry draft (June 27, 1998).

Season Team	League	Gms.	G	A	Pts.	PIM	+/-	PP	SH	Gms.	G	A	Pts.	PIM
96-97—NY AppleCore	Jr. B	80	42	70	112	52	...	...	...	—	—	—	—	—
97-98—Boston College	Hockey East	42	0	24	24	12	...	...	...	—	—	—	—	—
98-99—Boston College	Hockey East	41	2	8	10	20	...	...	...	—	—	—	—	—
99-00—Boston College	Hockey East	42	1	13	14	24	...	...	...	—	—	—	—	—
00-01—Boston College	Hockey East	43	4	19	23	42	...	...	...	—	—	—	—	—
01-02—Wilkes-Barre/Scranton	AHL	75	1	22	23	66	...	...	...	—	—	—	—	—
02-03—Wilkes-Barre/Scranton	AHL	74	4	17	21	44	...	...	...	—	—	—	—	—

SEDIN, DANIEL — LW — CANUCKS

PERSONAL: Born September 26, 1980, in Ornskoldsvik, Sweden ... 6-2/190. ... Shoots left. ... Twin brother of Henrik Sedin, center, Vancouver Canucks.

TRANSACTIONS/CAREER NOTES: Selected by Vancouver Canucks in first round (first Canucks pick, second overall) of NHL entry draft (June 26, 1999). ... Strained shoulder (November 30, 2000); missed four games. ... Injured back (March 25, 2001); missed two games. ... Reinjured back (April 2, 2001); missed one game. ... Sprained knee (December 19, 2001); missed two games. ... Re-signed by Canucks (July 28, 2003).

| | | | | REGULAR SEASON | | | | | | | | PLAYOFFS | | | |
Season Team	League	Gms.	G	A	Pts.	PIM	+/-	PP	SH	Gms.	G	A	Pts.	PIM
96-97—MoDo Ornskoldsvik....	Sweden Jr.	26	26	14	40	...	...	...	...	—	—	—	—	—
97-98—MoDo Ornskoldsvik....	Sweden	45	4	8	12	26	...	...	...	9	0	0	0	2
—MoDo Ornskoldsvik....	Sweden Jr.	4	3	3	6	4	...	...	...	—	—	—	—	—
98-99—MoDo Ornskoldsvik....	Sweden	50	21	21	42	20	...	...	...	13	4	8	12	14
99-00—MoDo Ornskoldsvik....	Sweden	50	19	26	45	28	...	...	...	13	†8	6	14	18
00-01—Vancouver..................	NHL	75	20	14	34	24	-3	10	0	4	1	2	3	0
01-02—Vancouver..................	NHL	79	9	23	32	32	1	4	0	6	0	1	1	0
02-03—Vancouver..................	NHL	79	14	17	31	34	8	4	0	14	1	5	6	8
NHL Totals (3 years)..........		**233**	**43**	**54**	**97**	**90**	**6**	**18**	**0**	**24**	**2**	**8**	**10**	**8**

SEDIN, HENRIK — C — CANUCKS

PERSONAL: Born September 26, 1980, in Ornskoldsvik, Sweden ... 6-2/192. ... Shoots left. ... Twin brother of Daniel Sedin, left winger, Vancouver Canucks.

TRANSACTIONS/CAREER NOTES: Selected by Vancouver Canucks in first round (second Canucks pick, third overall) of NHL entry draft (June 26, 1999). ... Re-signed by Canucks (July 28, 2003).

| | | | | REGULAR SEASON | | | | | | | | PLAYOFFS | | | |
Season Team	League	Gms.	G	A	Pts.	PIM	+/-	PP	SH	Gms.	G	A	Pts.	PIM
96-97—MoDo Ornskoldsvik....	Sweden Jr.	26	14	22	36	...	...	...	...	—	—	—	—	—
97-98—MoDo Ornskoldsvik....	Sweden	39	1	4	5	8	...	...	...	7	0	0	0	0
—MoDo Ornskoldsvik....	Sweden Jr.	8	4	7	11	6	...	...	...	—	—	—	—	—
98-99—MoDo Ornskoldsvik....	Sweden	49	12	22	34	32	...	...	...	13	2	8	10	6
99-00—MoDo Ornskoldsvik....	Sweden	50	9	38	47	22	...	...	...	13	5	9	14	2
00-01—Vancouver..................	NHL	82	9	20	29	38	-2	2	0	4	0	4	4	0
01-02—Vancouver..................	NHL	82	16	20	36	36	9	3	0	6	3	0	3	0
02-03—Vancouver..................	NHL	78	8	31	39	38	9	4	1	14	3	2	5	8
NHL Totals (3 years)..........		**242**	**33**	**71**	**104**	**112**	**16**	**9**	**1**	**24**	**6**	**6**	**12**	**8**

SEIDENBERG, DENNIS — D — FLYERS

PERSONAL: Born July 18, 1981, in Schwenningen, West Germany ... 6-0/180. ... Shoots left.

| | | | | REGULAR SEASON | | | | | | | | PLAYOFFS | | | |
Season Team	League	Gms.	G	A	Pts.	PIM	+/-	PP	SH	Gms.	G	A	Pts.	PIM
01-02—Mannheim..................	Germany	55	7	13	20	56	...	...	...	8	0	0	0	2
02-03—Philadelphia	AHL	19	5	6	11	17	...	...	...	—	—	—	—	—
—Philadelphia	NHL	58	4	9	13	20	8	1	0	—	—	—	—	—
NHL Totals (1 year)..............		**58**	**4**	**9**	**13**	**20**	**8**	**1**	**0**					

SEJNA, PETER — LW — BLUES

PERSONAL: Born October 5, 1979, in Liptovsky Mikulas, Czechoslovakia ... 5-11/200.

TRANSACTIONS/CAREER NOTES: Signed as non-drafted free agent by St. Louis Blues (April 6, 2003).

| | | | | REGULAR SEASON | | | | | | | | PLAYOFFS | | | |
Season Team	League	Gms.	G	A	Pts.	PIM	+/-	PP	SH	Gms.	G	A	Pts.	PIM
02-03—St. Louis	NHL	1	1	0	1	0	0	1	0	—	—	—	—	—
NHL Totals (1 year)..............		**1**	**1**	**0**	**1**	**0**	**0**	**1**	**0**					

SEKERAS, LUBOMIR — D

PERSONAL: Born November 18, 1968, in Trencin, Czechoslovakia ... 6-0/183. ... Shoots left. ... Name pronounced SEH-kuhr-ahsh.

TRANSACTIONS/CAREER NOTES: Selected by Minnesota Wild in eighth round (eighth Wild pick, 232nd overall) of NHL entry draft (June 24, 2000). ... Bruised foot (January 10, 2001); missed one game. ... Suffered from the flu (April 4, 2001); missed one game. ... Sprained right knee (October 30, 2001); missed seven games. ... Suffered from the flu (April 8, 2002); missed remainder of season.

| | | | | REGULAR SEASON | | | | | | | | PLAYOFFS | | | |
Season Team	League	Gms.	G	A	Pts.	PIM	+/-	PP	SH	Gms.	G	A	Pts.	PIM
88-89—Dukla Trencin..............	Czech.	16	2	5	7	22	...	...	...	11	0	4	4	0
89-90—Dukla Trencin..............	Czech.	44	6	8	14	...	...	...	...	9	0	2	2	...
90-91—Dukla Trencin..............	Czech.	52	6	16	22	...	...	...	...	6	0	1	1	...
91-92—Dukla Trencin..............	Czech.	30	2	6	8	32	...	...	...	13	1	1	2	0
92-93—Dukla Trencin..............	Czech.	40	5	19	24	48	...	...	...	11	4	9	13	0
93-94—Dukla Trencin..............	Slovakia	36	9	12	21	46	...	...	...	9	2	4	6	10
94-95—Dukla Trencin..............	Slovakia	36	11	11	22	24	...	...	...	9	2	7	9	8
95-96—Trinec......................	Czech	40	11	13	24	44	...	...	...	3	0	0	0	0
96-97—Trinec......................	Czech	52	14	21	35	56	...	...	...	4	1	0	1	2
97-98—Trinec......................	Czech	50	11	33	44	42	...	...	...	13	2	10	12	4
98-99—Trinec......................	Czech	50	8	15	23	38	...	...	...	10	2	6	8	...
99-00—Trinec......................	Czech	52	7	24	31	36	...	...	...	4	0	2	2	2
00-01—Minnesota..................	NHL	80	11	23	34	52	-8	4	0	—	—	—	—	—
01-02—Minnesota..................	NHL	69	4	20	24	38	-7	4	0	—	—	—	—	—
02-03—Minnesota..................	NHL	60	2	9	11	30	-12	1	0	15	1	1	2	6
NHL Totals (3 years)..........		**209**	**17**	**52**	**69**	**120**	**-27**	**9**	**0**	**15**	**1**	**1**	**2**	**6**

S

SELANNE, TEEMU — RW — AVALANCHE

PERSONAL: Born July 3, 1970, in Helsinki, Finland ... 6-0/204. ... Shoots right. ... Name pronounced TAY-moo suh-LAH-nay. ... Nickname: The Finnish Flash.

TRANSACTIONS/CAREER NOTES: Selected by Winnipeg Jets in first round (first Jets pick, 10th overall) of NHL entry draft (June 11, 1988). ... Severed Achilles' tendon (January 26, 1994); missed 33 games. ... Played in Europe during 1994-95 NHL lockout. ... Suffered from patella tendonitis (February 28, 1995); missed one game. ... Suspended two games and fined $500 by NHL (March 28, 1995). ... Traded by Jets with C Marc Chouinard and fourth-round pick (traded to Toronto) in 1996 draft to Mighty Ducks of Anaheim for C Chad Kilger, D Oleg Tverdovsky and third-round pick (D Per-Anton Lundstrom) in 1996 draft (Febraury 7, 1996). ... Strained abdominal muscle (March 23, 1997); missed four games. ... Strained abdominal muscle (February 7, 1998); missed five games. ... Strained groin (April 9, 1998); missed final four games of season. ... Strained thigh muscle (November 11,1998); missed six games. ... Reinjured thigh muscle (December 3, 1998); missed one game. ... Strained groin (November 14, 1999); missed three games. ... Strained groin (December 13, 2000); missed two games. ... Strained groin (December 22, 2000); missed two games. ... Injured knee (March 1, 2001) and underwent surgery; missed five games. ... Traded by Mighty Ducks to San Jose Sharks for LW Jeff Friesen, G Steve Shields and conditional pick in draft (March 5, 2001). ... Signed by Colorado Avalanche (July 2, 2003).

STATISTICAL PLATEAUS: Three-goal games: 1992-93 (4), 1993-94 (2), 1995-96 (2), 1996-97 (1), 1997-98 (3), 1998-99 (1), 1999-00 (1), 2000-01 (2). Total: 16. ... Four-goal games: 1992-93 (1), 1995-96 (1). Total: 2. ... Total hat tricks: 18.

Season Team	League	Gms.	G	A	Pts.	PIM	+/-	PP	SH	Gms.	G	A	Pts.	PIM
87-88—Jokerit Helsinki	Finland Jr.	33	43	23	66	18	...	...	...	5	4	3	7	2
—Jokerit Helsinki	Finland	5	1	1	2	0	...	...	...	—	—	—	—	—
88-89—Jokerit Helsinki	Finland	34	35	33	68	12	...	...	...	5	7	3	10	4
89-90—Jokerit Helsinki	Finland	11	4	8	12	0	...	...	...	—	—	—	—	—
90-91—Jokerit Helsinki	Finland	42	*33	25	58	12	...	...	...	—	—	—	—	—
91-92—Fin. Olympic team	Int'l	8	7	4	11	...	...	...	...	—	—	—	—	—
—Jokerit Helsinki	Finland	44	39	23	62	20	...	...	...	—	—	—	—	—
92-93—Winnipeg	NHL	84	†76	56	132	45	8	24	0	6	4	2	6	2
93-94—Winnipeg	NHL	51	25	29	54	22	-23	11	0	—	—	—	—	—
94-95—Jokerit Helsinki	Finland	20	7	12	19	6	...	...	...	—	—	—	—	—
—Winnipeg	NHL	45	22	26	48	2	1	8	2	—	—	—	—	—
95-96—Winnipeg	NHL	51	24	48	72	18	3	6	1	—	—	—	—	—
—Anaheim	NHL	28	16	20	36	4	2	3	0	—	—	—	—	—
96-97—Anaheim	NHL	78	51	58	109	34	28	11	1	11	7	3	10	4
97-98—Anaheim	NHL	73	†52	34	86	30	12	10	1	—	—	—	—	—
—Fin. Olympic team	Int'l	5	4	6	10	8	...	...	...	—	—	—	—	—
98-99—Anaheim	NHL	75	*47	60	107	30	18	*25	0	4	2	2	4	2
99-00—Anaheim	NHL	79	33	52	85	12	6	8	0	—	—	—	—	—
00-01—Anaheim	NHL	61	26	33	59	36	-8	10	0	—	—	—	—	—
—San Jose	NHL	12	7	6	13	0	1	2	0	6	0	2	2	2
01-02—San Jose	NHL	82	29	25	54	40	-11	9	1	12	5	3	8	2
—Fin. Olympic team	Int'l	4	3	0	3	2	...	...	...	—	—	—	—	—
02-03—San Jose	NHL	82	28	36	64	30	-6	7	0	—	—	—	—	—
NHL Totals (11 years)		801	436	483	919	303	31	134	6	39	18	12	30	12

SELIG, SCOTT — C/RW — CANADIENS

PERSONAL: Born March 2, 1981, in Philadelphia. ... 6-2/178. ... Shoots right.
COLLEGE: Northeastern.
TRANSACTIONS/CAREER NOTES: Selected by Montreal Canadiens in sixth round (eighth Canadiens pick, 172nd overall) of NHL entry draft (June 24, 2000).

Season Team	League	Gms.	G	A	Pts.	PIM	+/-	PP	SH	Gms.	G	A	Pts.	PIM
99-00—Thayer Academy	Mass. H.S.	28	32	25	57	25	...	...	...	—	—	—	—	—
00-01—Northeastern	ECAC	35	7	8	15	34	...	...	...	—	—	—	—	—
01-02—Northeastern	ECAC	26	3	1	4	28	...	...	...	—	—	—	—	—
02-03—Northeastern	ECAC	33	3	7	10	22	...	...	...	—	—	—	—	—

SELLARS, LUKE — D — THRASHERS

PERSONAL: Born May 21, 1981, in Toronto. ... 6-1/195. ... Shoots left.
TRANSACTIONS/CAREER NOTES: Selected by Atlanta Thrashers in second round (second Thrashers pick, 30th overall) of NHL entry draft (June 26, 1999).

Season Team	League	Gms.	G	A	Pts.	PIM	+/-	PP	SH	Gms.	G	A	Pts.	PIM
97-98—Wexford	OHA Jr. A	40	7	30	37	170	...	...	...	—	—	—	—	—
98-99—Ottawa	OHL	56	4	19	23	87	...	...	...	—	—	—	—	—
99-00—Ottawa	OHL	56	8	34	42	147	...	...	...	11	4	6	10	28
00-01—Ottawa	OHL	59	9	21	30	136	...	...	...	18	4	10	14	47
01-02—Chicago	AHL	31	2	4	6	87	...	...	...	—	—	—	—	—
—Greenville	ECHL	21	2	6	8	61	...	...	...	17	7	6	13	44
—Atlanta	NHL	1	0	0	0	2	0	0	0	—	—	—	—	—
02-03—Chicago	AHL	42	4	11	15	117	...	...	...	—	—	—	—	—
—Greenville	ECHL	4	2	2	4	6	...	...	...	—	—	—	—	—
NHL Totals (1 year)		1	0	0	0	2	0	0	0					

SEMENOV, ALEXEI   D   OILERS

PERSONAL: Born April 10, 1981, in Murmansk, U.S.S.R. ... 6-6/210. ... Shoots left.
TRANSACTIONS/CAREER NOTES: Selected by Edmonton Oilers in second round (second Oilers pick, 36th overall) of NHL entry draft (June 26, 1999).

Season Team	League	REGULAR SEASON								PLAYOFFS				
		Gms.	G	A	Pts.	PIM	+/-	PP	SH	Gms.	G	A	Pts.	PIM
97-98—Krylja Sovetov-2 Mos.	Rus. Div. III	52	1	2	3	48	...	...	...	—	—	—	—	—
98-99—Sudbury	OHL	28	0	3	3	28	...	...	...	2	0	0	0	4
99-00—Sudbury	OHL	65	9	35	44	135	...	...	...	12	1	3	4	23
—Hamilton	AHL	—	—	—	—	—	—	—	—	3	0	0	0	0
00-01—Sudbury	OHL	65	21	42	63	106	...	...	...	12	4	13	17	17
01-02—Hamilton	AHL	78	5	11	16	67	...	...	...	—	—	—	—	—
02-03—Hamilton	AHL	37	4	3	7	45	...	...	...	—	—	—	—	—
—Edmonton	NHL	46	1	6	7	58	-7	0	0	6	0	0	0	0
NHL Totals (1 year)		46	1	6	7	58	-7	0	0	6	0	0	0	0

SEVERSON, CAM   LW   MIGHTY DUCKS

PERSONAL: Born January 15, 1978, in Canora, Sask. ... 6-1/222. ... Shoots left.
TRANSACTIONS/CAREER NOTES: Signed by Anaheim Mighty Ducks (July 15, 2003).

Season Team	League	REGULAR SEASON								PLAYOFFS				
		Gms.	G	A	Pts.	PIM	+/-	PP	SH	Gms.	G	A	Pts.	PIM
98-99—Spokane	WHL	46	16	17	33	190	...	...	...	—	—	—	—	—
—Oklahoma City	CHL	5	6	3	9	4	...	...	...	10	4	0	4	26
99-00—Louisiana	ECHL	7	0	2	2	22	...	...	...	—	—	—	—	—
—Peoria	ECHL	56	19	8	27	138	...	...	...	18	3	4	7	41
00-01—Portland	AHL	8	0	0	0	11	...	...	...	—	—	—	—	—
—Cincinnati	AHL	20	4	7	11	60	...	...	...	3	1	1	2	0
01-02—Hartford	AHL	65	11	10	21	116	...	...	...	5	0	0	0	7
02-03—Cincinnati	AHL	71	12	9	21	156	...	...	...	—	—	—	—	—
—Anaheim	NHL	2	0	0	0	8	0	0	0	1	0	0	0	0
NHL Totals (1 year)		2	0	0	0	8	0	0	0	1	0	0	0	0

SHANAHAN, BRENDAN   LW   RED WINGS

PERSONAL: Born January 23, 1969, in Mimico, Ont. ... 6-3/215. ... Shoots right. ... Full Name: Brendan Frederick Shanahan.
TRANSACTIONS/CAREER NOTES: Selected by New Jersey Devils in first round (first Devils pick, second overall) of NHL entry draft (June 13, 1987). ... Fractured nose (December 1987). ... Suffered back spasms (March 1989). ... Suspended five games by NHL for stick-fighting (January 13, 1990). ... Suffered lower abdominal strain (February 1990). ... Suffered lacerations to lower right side of face and underwent surgery (January 8, 1991); missed five games. ... Signed as free agent by St. Louis Blues (July 25, 1991); D Scott Stevens awarded to Devils as compensation (September 3, 1991). ... Pulled groin (October 24, 1992); missed 12 games. ... Suspended six off-days and fined $500 by NHL for hitting another player in face with his stick (January 7, 1993). ... Suspended one game by NHL for high-sticking incident (February 23, 1993). ... Suffered viral infection (November 18, 1993); missed one game. ... Injured hamstring (March 22, 1994); missed two games. ... Played in Europe during 1994-95 NHL lockout. ... Suffered viral infection (January 20, 1995); missed three games. ... Fractured ankle (May 15, 1995); missed last two games of playoffs. ... Traded by Blues to Hartford Whalers for D Chris Pronger (July 27, 1995). ... Sprained wrist (November 11, 1995); missed eight games. ... Traded by Whalers with D Brian Glynn to Detroit Red Wings for C Keith Primeau, D Paul Coffey and first-round pick (traded to San Jose) in 1997 draft (October 9, 1996). ... Suspended one game and fined $1,000 by NHL for cross-checking incident (October 11, 1996). ... Strained groin (October 30, 1996); missed one game. ... Suffered stiff neck (October 12, 1997); missed four games. ... Suffered back spasms (April 15, 1998); missed final game of regular season and two playoff games. ... Suspended two games by NHL for stick-swinging incident (November 9, 1999).
STATISTICAL PLATEAUS: Three-goal games: 1988-89 (1), 1992-93 (1), 1993-94 (4), 1995-96 (1), 1996-97 (3), 1998-99 (2), 2001-02 (1), 2002-03 (1). Total: 14. ... Four-goal games: 2000-01 (1). ... Total hat tricks: 15.

Season Team	League	REGULAR SEASON								PLAYOFFS				
		Gms.	G	A	Pts.	PIM	+/-	PP	SH	Gms.	G	A	Pts.	PIM
84-85—Mississauga	MTHL	36	20	21	41	26	...	...	...	—	—	—	—	—
85-86—London	OHL	59	28	34	62	70	...	...	...	5	5	5	10	5
86-87—London	OHL	56	39	53	92	128	...	...	...	—	—	—	—	—
87-88—New Jersey	NHL	65	7	19	26	131	-20	2	0	12	2	1	3	44
88-89—New Jersey	NHL	68	22	28	50	115	2	9	0	—	—	—	—	—
89-90—New Jersey	NHL	73	30	42	72	137	15	8	0	6	3	3	6	20
90-91—New Jersey	NHL	75	29	37	66	141	4	7	0	7	3	5	8	12
91-92—St. Louis	NHL	80	33	36	69	171	-3	13	0	6	2	3	5	14
92-93—St. Louis	NHL	71	51	43	94	174	10	18	0	11	4	3	7	18
93-94—St. Louis	NHL	81	52	50	102	211	-9	15	*7	4	2	5	7	4
94-95—Dusseldorf	Germany	3	5	3	8	4	...	...	...	—	—	—	—	—
—St. Louis	NHL	45	20	21	41	136	7	6	2	5	4	5	9	14
95-96—Hartford	NHL	74	44	34	78	125	2	17	2	—	—	—	—	—
96-97—Hartford	NHL	2	1	0	1	0	1	0	1	—	—	—	—	—
—Detroit	NHL	79	46	41	87	131	31	†20	2	20	9	8	17	43
97-98—Detroit	NHL	75	28	29	57	154	6	15	1	20	5	4	9	22
—Can. Olympic team	Int'l	6	2	0	2	0	...	...	...	—	—	—	—	—
98-99—Detroit	NHL	81	31	27	58	123	2	5	0	10	3	7	10	6
99-00—Detroit	NHL	78	41	37	78	105	24	13	1	9	3	2	5	10
00-01—Detroit	NHL	81	31	45	76	81	9	15	1	2	2	2	4	0
01-02—Detroit	NHL	80	37	38	75	118	23	12	3	23	8	11	19	20
—Can. Olympic team	Int'l	6	0	1	1	0	...	...	...	—	—	—	—	—
02-03—Detroit	NHL	78	30	38	68	103	5	13	0	4	1	1	2	4
NHL Totals (16 years)		1186	533	565	1098	2156	109	188	20	139	51	60	111	231

S

– 363 –

SHANTZ, JEFF   C

PERSONAL: Born October 10, 1973, in Duchess, Alta. ... 6-0/200. ... Shoots right.
TRANSACTIONS/CAREER NOTES: Selected by Chicago Blackhawks in second round (second Blackhawks pick, 36th overall) of NHL entry draft (June 20, 1992). ... Bruised right shoulder (1993-94 season); missed six games. ... Suffered swollen eye (November 30, 1996); missed one game. ... Sprained knee (February 25, 1997); missed 10 games. ... Separated shoulder (January 4, 1998); missed six games. ... Tore anterior cruciate ligament in left knee (March 19, 1998); missed final 14 games of season. ... Traded by Blackhawks with C/LW Steve Dubinsky to Calgary Flames for D Jamie Allison, C/LW Marty McInnis and RW Erik Andersson (October 27, 1998). ... Suffered concussion (November 14, 1998); missed two games. ... Injured shoulder (March 25, 1999); missed four games. ... Bruised ribs (December 6, 1999); missed eight games. ... Injured knee (March 22, 2001); missed remainder of season. ... Injured knee (October 3, 2001). ... Traded by Flames with D Derek Morris and LW Dean McAmmond to Colorado Avalanche for LW Chris Drury and C Stephane Yelle (October 1, 2002).

		REGULAR SEASON								PLAYOFFS				
Season Team	League	Gms.	G	A	Pts.	PIM	+/-	PP	SH	Gms.	G	A	Pts.	PIM
89-90—Regina	WHL	1	0	0	0	0	...	...	...	—	—	—	—	—
—Medicine Hat..............	AMHL	36	18	31	49	30	...	...	...	—	—	—	—	—
90-91—Regina	WHL	69	16	21	37	22	...	...	...	8	2	2	4	2
91-92—Regina	WHL	72	39	50	89	75	...	...	...	—	—	—	—	—
92-93—Regina	WHL	64	29	54	83	75	...	...	...	13	2	12	14	14
93-94—Chicago...............	NHL	52	3	13	16	30	-14	0	0	6	0	0	0	6
—Indianapolis	IHL	19	5	9	14	20	...	...	...	—	—	—	—	—
94-95—Indianapolis	IHL	32	9	15	24	20	...	...	...	—	—	—	—	—
—Chicago...................	NHL	45	6	12	18	33	11	0	2	16	3	1	4	2
95-96—Chicago...............	NHL	78	6	14	20	24	12	1	2	10	2	3	5	6
96-97—Chicago...............	NHL	69	9	21	30	28	11	0	1	6	0	4	4	6
97-98—Chicago...............	NHL	61	11	20	31	36	0	1	2	—	—	—	—	—
98-99—Chicago...............	NHL	7	1	0	1	4	-1	0	0	—	—	—	—	—
—Calgary	NHL	69	12	17	29	40	15	1	1	—	—	—	—	—
99-00—Calgary	NHL	74	13	18	31	30	-13	6	0	—	—	—	—	—
00-01—Calgary	NHL	73	5	15	20	58	-7	0	0	—	—	—	—	—
01-02—Saint John	AHL	2	0	1	1	0	...	...	...	—	—	—	—	—
—Calgary	NHL	40	3	3	6	23	-3	2	0	—	—	—	—	—
02-03—Colorado..............	NHL	74	3	6	9	35	-12	0	0	6	0	0	0	4
NHL Totals (10 years).........		642	72	139	211	341	-1	11	8	44	5	8	13	24

SHARP, PATRICK   C   FLYERS

PERSONAL: Born December 27, 1981, in Thunder Bay, Ont. ... 6-0/188. ... Shoots right.
TRANSACTIONS/CAREER NOTES: Selected by Philadelphia Flyers in third round (second Flyers pick, 95th overall) of NHL entry draft (June 23, 2001).

		REGULAR SEASON								PLAYOFFS				
Season Team	League	Gms.	G	A	Pts.	PIM	+/-	PP	SH	Gms.	G	A	Pts.	PIM
98-99—Thunder Bay Flyers.....	USHL	55	19	24	43	48	...	...	...	3	1	1	2	0
99-00—Thunder Bay Flyers.....	USHL	56	20	35	55	41	...	...	...	—	—	—	—	—
00-01—Univ. of Vermont........	ECAC	30	11	13	24	34	...	...	...	—	—	—	—	—
01-02—Univ. of Vermont........	ECAC	31	13	13	26	50	...	...	...	—	—	—	—	—
02-03—Philadelphia	AHL	53	14	19	33	39	...	...	...	—	—	—	—	—
—Philadelphia	NHL	3	0	0	0	2	0	0	0	—	—	—	—	—
NHL Totals (1 year)............		3	0	0	0	2	0	0	0	—	—	—	—	—

SHASBY, MATT   D   CANADIENS

PERSONAL: Born July 2, 1980, in Sioux Falls, S.D. ... 6-3/188. ... Shoots left.
COLLEGE: Alaska-Anchorage.
TRANSACTIONS/CAREER NOTES: Selected by Montreal Canadiens in fifth round (seventh Canadiens pick, 150th overall) of NHL entry draft (June 26, 1999).

		REGULAR SEASON								PLAYOFFS				
Season Team	League	Gms.	G	A	Pts.	PIM	+/-	PP	SH	Gms.	G	A	Pts.	PIM
97-98—Lincoln....................	USHL	43	1	15	16	30	...	...	...	—	—	—	—	—
98-99—Des Moines	USHL	49	4	22	26	34	...	...	...	—	—	—	—	—
99-00—Alaska-Anchorage.......	WCHA	32	1	8	9	36	...	...	...	—	—	—	—	—
00-01—Alaska-Anchorage.......	WCHA	35	4	14	18	32	...	...	...	—	—	—	—	—
01-02—Alaska-Anchorage......	WCHA	35	7	20	27	72	...	...	...	—	—	—	—	—
02-03—Alaska-Anchorage.......	WCHA	25	0	11	11	18	...	...	...	—	—	—	—	—

SHELLEY, JODY   LW   BLUE JACKETS

PERSONAL: Born February 7, 1976, in Thompson, Man. ... 6-4/225. ... Shoots left.
TRANSACTIONS/CAREER NOTES: Signed as non-drafted free agent by Calgary Flames (September 1, 1998). ... Signed as free agent by Columbus Blue Jackets (February 1, 2001). ... Suspended one game by NHL for fighting incident (December 5, 2002).

		REGULAR SEASON								PLAYOFFS				
Season Team	League	Gms.	G	A	Pts.	PIM	+/-	PP	SH	Gms.	G	A	Pts.	PIM
94-95—Halifax....................	QMJHL	72	10	12	22	194	...	...	...	7	0	1	1	12
95-96—Halifax....................	QMJHL	50	13	19	32	319	...	...	...	6	0	2	2	36
96-97—Halifax....................	QMJHL	58	25	19	44	448	...	...	...	17	6	6	12	123
97-98—Dalhousie University....	AUAA	19	6	11	17	145	...	...	...	—	—	—	—	—
—Saint John	AHL	18	1	1	2	50	...	...	...	—	—	—	—	—

Season Team	League	REGULAR SEASON								PLAYOFFS				
		Gms.	G	A	Pts.	PIM	+/-	PP	SH	Gms.	G	A	Pts.	PIM
98-99—Saint John	AHL	8	0	0	0	46	...	...	...	—	—	—	—	—
—Johnstown	ECHL	52	12	17	29	†325	...	...	...	—	—	—	—	—
99-00—Johnstown	ECHL	36	9	17	26	256	...	...	...	—	—	—	—	—
—Saint John	AHL	22	1	4	5	93	...	...	...	3	0	0	0	2
00-01—Syracuse	AHL	69	1	7	8	*357	...	...	...	5	0	0	0	21
—Columbus	NHL	1	0	0	0	10	0	0	0	—	—	—	—	—
01-02—Columbus	NHL	52	3	3	6	206	1	0	0	—	—	—	—	—
—Syracuse	AHL	22	3	5	8	165	...	...	...	—	—	—	—	—
02-03—Columbus	NHL	68	1	4	5	*249	-5	0	0	—	—	—	—	—
NHL Totals (3 years)		121	4	7	11	465	-4	0	0					

SHIELDS, COLIN   RW   FLYERS

PERSONAL: Born January 27, 1980, in Glasgow, Scotland.. ... Shoots right.
TRANSACTIONS/CAREER NOTES: Selected by Philadelphia Flyers in sixth round (fourth Flyers pick, 195th overall) of NHL entry draft (June 24, 2000).

Season Team	League	REGULAR SEASON								PLAYOFFS				
		Gms.	G	A	Pts.	PIM	+/-	PP	SH	Gms.	G	A	Pts.	PIM
98-99—Cleveland	NAHL	55	30	30	60	44	...	...	...	—	—	—	—	—
99-00—Cleveland	NAHL				Statistics unavailable.									
01-02—Univ. of Maine	Hockey East	42	29	17	46	39	...	...	...	—	—	—	—	—
02-03—Univ. of Maine	Hockey East	34	14	13	27	18	...	...	...	—	—	—	—	—

SHIELDS, STEVE   G   BRUINS

PERSONAL: Born July 19, 1972, in Toronto ... 6-3/215. ... Catches left.
TRANSACTIONS/CAREER NOTES: Selected by Buffalo Sabres in fifth round (fifth Sabres pick, 101st overall) of NHL entry draft (June 22, 1991). ... Traded by Sabres with fourth-round pick (RW Miroslav Zalesak) in 1998 draft to San Jose Sharks for G Kay Whitmore, second-round pick (RW Jaroslav Kristek) in 1998 draft and fifth-round pick (traded to Columbus) in 2000 draft (June 18, 1998). ... Sprained ankle (October 12, 2000); missed eight games. ... Traded by Sharks with LW Jeff Friesen and conditional pick in draft to Mighty Ducks of Anaheim for RW Teemu Selanne (March 5, 2001). ... Injured ligaments in left shoulder and underwent surgery (March 7, 2001); missed remainder of season. ... Lacerated face and bruised jaw (April 3, 2002); missed remainder of season. ... Traded by Mighty Ducks to Boston Bruins for third-round pick in 2003 draft (June 25, 2002).

Season Team	League	REGULAR SEASON									PLAYOFFS							
		Gms.	Min	W	L	T	GA	SO	Avg.	SV%	Gms.	Min.	W	L	GA	SO	Avg.	SV%
90-91—Univ. of Michigan	CCHA	37	1963	26	6	3	106	0	3.24	—	—	—	—	—	—	—	—	—
91-92—Univ. of Michigan	CCHA	*37	*2091	*27	7	2	98	1	2.81	—	—	—	—	—	—	—	—	—
92-93—Univ. of Michigan	CCHA	*39	*2027	*30	6	2	75	2	2.22	—	—	—	—	—	—	—	—	—
93-94—Univ. of Michigan	CCHA	36	1961	*28	6	1	87	0	2.66	—	—	—	—	—	—	—	—	—
94-95—South Carolina	ECHL	21	1158	11	5	‡2	52	2	2.69	—	3	144	0	2	11	0	4.58	—
—Rochester	AHL	13	673	3	8	0	53	0	4.73	—	1	20	0	0	3	0	9.00	—
95-96—Rochester	AHL	43	2356	20	17	2	140	1	3.57	—	*19	*1126	*15	3	47	1	2.50	—
—Buffalo	NHL	2	75	1	0	0	4	0	3.20	.875	—	—	—	—	—	—	—	—
96-97—Rochester	AHL	23	1331	14	6	2	60	1	2.70	—	—	—	—	—	—	—	—	—
—Buffalo	NHL	13	789	3	8	2	39	0	2.97	.913	10	570	4	6	26	1	2.74	.922
97-98—Buffalo	NHL	16	785	3	6	4	37	0	2.83	.909	—	—	—	—	—	—	—	—
—Rochester	AHL	1	59	0	1	0	3	0	3.05	—	—	—	—	—	—	—	—	—
98-99—San Jose	NHL	37	2162	15	11	8	80	4	2.22	.921	1	60	0	1	6	0	6.00	.833
99-00—San Jose	NHL	67	3797	27	30	8	162	4	2.56	.911	12	696	5	7	36	0	3.10	.889
00-01—San Jose	NHL	21	1135	6	8	5	47	2	2.48	.911	—	—	—	—	—	—	—	—
01-02—Anaheim	NHL	33	1777	9	20	2	79	0	2.67	.907	—	—	—	—	—	—	—	—
02-03—Boston	NHL	36	2112	12	13	9	97	0	2.76	.896	2	119	0	2	6	0	3.03	.897
NHL Totals (8 years)		225	12632	76	96	38	545	10	2.59	.910	25	1445	9	16	74	1	3.07	.901

SHVIDKI, DENIS   RW   PANTHERS

PERSONAL: Born November 21, 1980, in Kharkov, U.S.S.R. ... 6-2/215. ... Shoots left.
TRANSACTIONS/CAREER NOTES: Selected by Florida Panthers in first round (first Panthers pick, 12th overall) of NHL entry draft (June 26, 1999). ... Strained tendon in foot (February 28, 2001); missed three games. ... Suffered concussion (September 12, 2001); missed first 24 games of season. ... Re-signed by Panthers (July 24, 2003).

Season Team	League	REGULAR SEASON								PLAYOFFS				
		Gms.	G	A	Pts.	PIM	+/-	PP	SH	Gms.	G	A	Pts.	PIM
96-97—Torpedo-Yaroslavl	Russian	17	3	2	5	6	...	...	...	—	—	—	—	—
97-98—Torpedo-Yaroslavl	Russian	15	1	1	2	2	...	...	...	—	—	—	—	—
—Torpedo Yaroslavl	Rus. Div. II	32	20	13	33	20	...	...	...	—	—	—	—	—
98-99—Barrie	OHL	61	35	59	94	8	...	...	...	12	7	9	16	2
99-00—Barrie	OHL	61	41	65	106	55	...	...	...	9	3	1	4	2
00-01—Florida	NHL	43	6	10	16	16	6	0	0	—	—	—	—	—
—Louisville	AHL	34	15	11	26	20	...	...	...	—	—	—	—	—
01-02—Florida	NHL	8	1	2	3	2	-4	0	0	—	—	—	—	—
—Utah	AHL	8	2	4	6	2	...	...	...	—	—	—	—	—
02-03—San Antonio	AHL	54	8	18	26	28	...	...	...	—	—	—	—	—
—Florida	NHL	23	4	2	6	12	-7	2	0	—	—	—	—	—
NHL Totals (3 years)		74	11	14	25	30	-5	2	0					

S

PERSONAL: Born December 18, 1979, in Meadow Lake, Sask. ... 6-5/225. ... Shoots right.

TRANSACTIONS/CAREER NOTES: Selected by Washington Capitals in fifth round (fifth Capitals pick, 118th overall) of NHL entry draft (June 27, 1998). ... Signed as free agent by Philadelphia Flyers (January 27, 2003). ... Re-signed by Flyers (July 14, 2003).

Season Team	League	REGULAR SEASON								PLAYOFFS				
		Gms.	G	A	Pts.	PIM	+/-	PP	SH	Gms.	G	A	Pts.	PIM
97-98—Olds	AJHL	54	10	17	27	120	...	...	...	—	—	—	—	—
—Seattle	WHL	1	0	0	0	0	...	...	...	5	0	0	0	6
98-99—Seattle	WHL	68	19	13	32	115	...	...	...	11	6	6	12	24
99-00—Portland	AHL	9	0	0	0	14	...	...	...	—	—	—	—	—
—Hampton Roads	ECHL	58	7	4	11	62	...	...	...	8	1	0	1	15
00-01—Portland	AHL	3	0	0	0	0	...	...	...	—	—	—	—	—
—Richmond	ECHL	65	19	18	37	117	...	...	...	4	0	0	0	34
01-02—Richmond	ECHL	55	13	21	34	111	...	...	...	—	—	—	—	—
—Portland	AHL	8	1	0	1	2	...	...	...	—	—	—	—	—
02-03—Philadelphia	AHL	64	6	6	12	169	...	...	...	—	—	—	—	—
—Philadelphia	NHL	1	0	0	0	0	0	0	0	—	—	—	—	—
NHL Totals (1 year)		1	0	0	0	0	0	0	0					

PERSONAL: Born June 29, 1971, in Regina, Sask. ... 5-11/199. ... Shoots right. ... Name pronounced SIHL-in-juhr.

TRANSACTIONS/CAREER NOTES: Selected by Detroit Red Wings in first round (first Red Wings pick, 11th overall) of NHL entry draft (June 17, 1989). ... Fractured rib in training camp (September 1990). ... Suffered from the flu (March 5, 1993); missed three games. ... Strained rotator cuff (October 9, 1993); missed four games. ... Played in Europe during 1994-95 NHL lockout. ... Injured eye (January 17, 1995); missed four games. ... Traded by Red Wings with D Jason York to Mighty Ducks of Anaheim for LW Stu Grimson, D Mark Ferner and sixth-round pick (LW Magnus Nilsson) in 1996 draft (April 4, 1995). ... Traded by Mighty Ducks to Vancouver Canucks for RW Roman Oksuita (March 15, 1996). ... Suffered concussion (March 26, 1997); missed two games. ... Traded by Canucks to Flyers for sixth-round pick (traded back to Philadelphia) in 1998 draft (February 5, 1998). ... Sprained left knee (October 22, 1998); missed one game. ... Traded by Flyers with C Chris Gratton to Tampa Bay Lightning for RW Mikael Renberg and C Daymond Langkow (December 12, 1998). ... Traded by Lightning to Florida Panthers for C Ryan Johnson and LW Dwayne Hay (March 14, 2000). ... Fractured foot (November 8, 2000); missed 12 games. ... Strained groin (January 24, 2001); missed three games. ... Traded by Panthers to Ottawa Senators for third-round pick (traded to New York Rangers) in 2002 draft and future considerations (March 13, 2001). ... Signed as free agent by Columbus Blue Jackets (July 5, 2001). ... Suffered concussion (November 1, 2001); missed one game. ... Sprained knee (December 31, 2001); missed one game. ... Traded by Blue Jackets to Dallas Stars with 2004 second-round draft pick for D Darryl Sydor. (July 22, 2003). ... Traded by Stars to Phoenix Coyotes for D Teppo Numminen (July 22, 2003).

Season Team	League	REGULAR SEASON								PLAYOFFS				
		Gms.	G	A	Pts.	PIM	+/-	PP	SH	Gms.	G	A	Pts.	PIM
87-88—Regina	WHL	67	18	25	43	17	...	...	...	4	2	2	4	0
88-89—Regina	WHL	72	53	78	131	52	...	...	...	—	—	—	—	—
89-90—Regina	WHL	70	57	72	129	41	...	...	...	11	12	10	22	2
—Adirondack	AHL	—	—	—	—	—	...	...	...	1	0	0	0	0
90-91—Regina	WHL	57	50	66	116	42	...	...	...	8	6	9	15	4
—Detroit	NHL	3	0	1	1	0	-2	0	0	3	0	1	1	0
91-92—Adirondack	AHL	64	25	41	66	26	...	...	...	15	9	*19	*28	12
—Detroit	NHL	—	—	—	—	—	...	...	...	8	2	2	4	2
92-93—Detroit	NHL	51	4	17	21	16	0	0	0	—	—	—	—	—
—Adirondack	AHL	15	10	20	30	31	...	...	...	11	5	13	18	10
93-94—Detroit	NHL	62	8	21	29	10	2	0	1	—	—	—	—	—
94-95—Wien	Austria	13	13	14	27	10	...	...	...	—	—	—	—	—
—Detroit	NHL	13	2	6	8	2	3	0	0	—	—	—	—	—
—Anaheim	NHL	15	2	5	7	6	1	2	0	—	—	—	—	—
95-96—Anaheim	NHL	62	13	21	34	32	-20	7	0	—	—	—	—	—
—Vancouver	NHL	12	1	3	4	6	2	0	1	6	0	0	0	2
96-97—Vancouver	NHL	78	17	20	37	25	-3	3	3	—	—	—	—	—
97-98—Vancouver	NHL	48	10	9	19	34	-14	1	2	—	—	—	—	—
—Philadelphia	NHL	27	11	11	22	16	3	1	2	3	1	0	1	0
98-99—Philadelphia	NHL	25	0	3	3	8	-9	0	0	—	—	—	—	—
—Tampa Bay	NHL	54	8	2	10	28	-20	0	2	—	—	—	—	—
99-00—Tampa Bay	NHL	67	19	25	44	86	-29	6	3	—	—	—	—	—
—Florida	NHL	13	4	4	8	16	-1	2	0	4	2	1	3	—
00-01—Florida	NHL	55	13	21	34	44	-12	1	0	—	—	—	—	—
—Ottawa	NHL	13	3	4	7	4	1	0	0	4	0	0	0	2
01-02—Columbus	NHL	80	20	23	43	54	-35	8	0	—	—	—	—	—
02-03—Columbus	NHL	75	18	25	43	52	-21	9	3	—	—	—	—	—
NHL Totals (13 years)		753	153	221	374	439	-154	40	17	28	5	4	9	8

PERSONAL: Born September 29, 1977, in New Glasgow, Nova Scotia ... 5-10/190. ... Shoots left. ... Full Name: Jonathan Sim.

TRANSACTIONS/CAREER NOTES: Selected by Dallas Stars in third round (second Stars pick, 70th overall) of NHL entry draft (June 22, 1996). ... Fractured shoulder blade (September 16, 2000); missed first six games of season. ... Traded by Stars to Nashville Predators for D Bubba Berenzweig and conditional pick in draft (February 17, 2003). ... Claimed on waivers by Los Angeles Kings (March 9, 2003).

Season Team	League	Gms.	G	A	Pts.	PIM	+/-	PP	SH	Gms.	G	A	Pts.	PIM
94-95—Laval	QMJHL	9	0	1	1	6	...	...	...	—	—	—	—	—
—Sarnia	OHL	25	9	12	21	19	...	...	...	4	3	2	5	2
95-96—Sarnia	OHL	63	56	46	102	130	...	...	...	10	8	7	15	26
96-97—Sarnia	OHL	64	†56	39	95	109	...	...	...	12	9	5	14	32
97-98—Sarnia	OHL	59	44	50	94	95	...	...	...	5	1	4	5	14
98-99—Michigan	IHL	68	24	27	51	91	...	...	...	5	3	1	4	18
—Dallas	NHL	7	1	0	1	12	1	0	0	4	0	0	0	0
99-00—Michigan	IHL	35	14	16	30	65	...	...	...	—	—	—	—	—
—Dallas	NHL	25	5	3	8	10	4	2	0	7	1	0	1	6
00-01—Dallas	NHL	15	0	3	3	6	-2	0	0	—	—	—	—	—
—Utah	IHL	39	16	13	29	44	...	...	...	—	—	—	—	—
01-02—Utah	AHL	31	21	6	27	63	...	...	...	—	—	—	—	—
—Dallas	NHL	26	3	0	3	10	-3	1	0	—	—	—	—	—
02-03—Utah	AHL	42	16	31	47	85	...	...	...	—	—	—	—	—
—Dallas	NHL	4	0	0	0	0	-1	0	0	—	—	—	—	—
—Nashville	NHL	4	1	0	1	0	0	0	0	—	—	—	—	—
—Los Angeles	NHL	14	0	2	2	19	-3	0	0	—	—	—	—	—
NHL Totals (5 years)		95	10	8	18	57	-4	3	0	11	1	0	1	6

SIMON, BEN   C   PREDATORS

PERSONAL: Born June 14, 1978, in Shaker Heights, Ohio ... 6-0/200. ... Shoots left. ... Full Name: Benjamin Clarke Simon.
TRANSACTIONS/CAREER NOTES: Selected by Chicago Blackhawks in fifth round (fifth Blackhawks pick, 110th overall) of NHL entry draft (June 21, 1997). ... Rights traded by Blackhawks to Atlanta Thrashers for ninth-round pick (C Peter Flache) in 2000 draft (June 25, 2000). ... Signed by Nashville Predators (July 14, 2003).

Season Team	League	Gms.	G	A	Pts.	PIM	+/-	PP	SH	Gms.	G	A	Pts.	PIM
92-93—Shaker Heights	Ohio H.S.	—	15	21	36	—	—	—	—	—	—	—	—	—
93-94—Shaker Heights	Ohio H.S.	—	45	41	86	—	—	—	—	—	—	—	—	—
94-95—Shaker Heights	Ohio H.S.	—	61	68	129	—	—	—	—	—	—	—	—	—
95-96—Cleveland	NAHL	50	45	46	91	...	...	...	...	—	—	—	—	—
96-97—Univ. of Notre Dame	CCHA	30	4	15	19	79	...	...	...	—	—	—	—	—
97-98—Univ. of Notre Dame	CCHA	37	9	28	37	91	...	...	...	—	—	—	—	—
98-99—Univ. of Notre Dame	CCHA	37	18	24	42	65	...	...	...	—	—	—	—	—
99-00—Univ. of Notre Dame	CCHA	40	13	19	32	53	...	...	...	—	—	—	—	—
00-01—Orlando	IHL	77	8	12	20	47	...	...	...	16	6	5	11	20
01-02—Chicago	AHL	74	11	23	34	56	...	...	...	25	2	3	5	24
—Atlanta	NHL	6	0	0	0	6	1	0	0	—	—	—	—	—
02-03—Chicago	AHL	69	15	17	32	78	...	...	...	—	—	—	—	—
—Atlanta	NHL	10	0	1	1	9	0	0	0	—	—	—	—	—
NHL Totals (2 years)		16	0	1	1	15	1	0	0	—	—	—	—	—

SIMON, CHRIS   LW   RANGERS

PERSONAL: Born January 30, 1972, in Wawa, Ont. ... 6-4/236. ... Shoots left.
TRANSACTIONS/CAREER NOTES: Selected by Philadelphia Flyers in second round (second Flyers pick, 25th overall) of NHL entry draft (June 16, 1990). ... Traded by Flyers with first-round pick (traded to Toronto) in 1994 draft to Quebec Nordiques (July 21, 1992) completing deal in which Flyers sent G Ron Hextall, C Mike Ricci, C Peter Forsberg, D Steve Duchesne, first-round pick (G Jocelyn Thibault) in 1993 draft and cash to Nordiques for C Eric Lindros (June 20, 1992). ... Suffered from the flu (March 13, 1993); missed one game. ... Injured back (December 1, 1993); missed 31 games. ... Injured back (February 16, 1994); missed one game. ... Injured back (March 6, 1994); missed one game. ... Injured back (March 18, 1994); missed remainder of season. ... Injured back (January 31, 1995); missed six games. ... Injured shoulder (March 22, 1995); missed 13 games. ... Nordiques franchise moved to Colorado and renamed Avalanche for 1995-96 season (June 21, 1995). ... Suffered back spasms (January 6, 1996); missed two games. ... Injured shoulder (February 5, 1996); missed four games. ... Traded by Avalanche with D Curtis Leschyshyn to Washington Capitals for RW Keith Jones and first- (D Scott Parker) and fourth-round (traded back to Washington) picks in 1998 draft (November 2, 1996). ... Injured arm (December 20, 1996); missed two games. ... Suffered back spasms (January 24, 1997); missed 17 games. ... Suffered back spasms (March 22, 1997); missed one game. ... Strained shoulder (March 29, 1997); missed six games. ... Suspended three games by NHL for alleged racial remarks (November 9, 1997). ... Bruised shoulder (October 25, 1997); missed five games. ... Reinjured shoulder (December 20, 1997) and underwent shoulder surgery; missed remainder of regular season. ... Strained shoulder (December 5, 1998) and underwent shoulder surgery; missed remainder of season. ... Strained neck (November 27, 1999); missed six games. ... Reinjured neck (December 21, 1999); missed one game. ... Suspended one playoff game by NHL for cross-checking incident (April 14, 2000). ... Missed first nine games of 2000-01 season due to contract dispute. ... Injured shoulder (March 1, 2001); missed five games. ... Reinjured shoulder (March 19, 2001); missed five games. ... Suspended two games by NHL for elbowing incident (April 6, 2001). ... Traded by Capitals with C Andrei Nikolishin to Chicago Blackhawks for C Michael Nylander and conditional third-round pick in 2004 draft (November 1, 2002). ... Signed by New York Rangers (July 27, 2003).

Season Team	League	Gms.	G	A	Pts.	PIM	+/-	PP	SH	Gms.	G	A	Pts.	PIM
87-88—Sault Ste. Marie	OHA	55	42	36	78	172	...	...	...	—	—	—	—	—
88-89—Ottawa	OHL	36	4	2	6	31	...	...	...	—	—	—	—	—
89-90—Ottawa	OHL	57	36	38	74	146	...	...	...	3	2	1	3	4
90-91—Ottawa	OHL	20	16	6	22	69	...	...	...	17	5	9	14	59
91-92—Ottawa	OHL	2	1	1	2	24	...	...	...	—	—	—	—	—
—Sault Ste. Marie	OHL	31	19	25	44	143	...	...	...	11	5	8	13	49
92-93—Halifax	AHL	36	12	6	18	131	...	...	...	—	—	—	—	—
—Quebec	NHL	16	1	1	2	67	-2	0	0	5	0	0	0	26
93-94—Quebec	NHL	37	4	4	8	132	-2	0	0	—	—	—	—	—
94-95—Quebec	NHL	29	3	9	12	106	14	0	0	6	1	1	2	19
95-96—Colorado	NHL	64	16	18	34	250	10	4	0	12	1	2	3	11

Season Team	League	REGULAR SEASON Gms.	G	A	Pts.	PIM	+/-	PP	SH	PLAYOFFS Gms.	G	A	Pts.	PIM
96-97—Washington	NHL	42	9	13	22	165	-1	3	0	—	—	—	—	—
97-98—Washington	NHL	28	7	10	17	38	-1	4	0	18	1	0	1	26
98-99—Washington	NHL	23	3	7	10	48	-4	0	0	—	—	—	—	—
99-00—Washington	NHL	75	29	20	49	146	11	7	0	4	2	0	2	24
00-01—Washington	NHL	60	10	10	20	109	-12	4	0	6	0	1	1	4
01-02—Washington	NHL	82	14	17	31	137	-8	1	0	—	—	—	—	—
02-03—Washington	NHL	10	0	2	2	23	-3	0	0	—	—	—	—	—
—Chicago	NHL	61	12	6	18	125	-4	2	0	—	—	—	—	—
NHL Totals (11 years)		**527**	**108**	**117**	**225**	**1346**	**-2**	**25**	**0**	**51**	**5**	**4**	**9**	**110**

SIMPSON, REID — LW

PERSONAL: Born May 21, 1969, in Flin Flon, Man. ... 6-2/217. ... Shoots left. ... Full Name: Reid Philip Simpson.

TRANSACTIONS/CAREER NOTES: Selected by Philadelphia Flyers in fourth round (third Flyers pick, 72nd overall) of NHL entry draft (June 17, 1989). ... Signed as free agent by Minnesota North Stars (December 13, 1992). ... North Stars franchise moved from Minnesota to Dallas and renamed Stars for 1993-94 season. ... Traded by Stars with D Roy Mitchell to New Jersey Devils for future considerations (March 21, 1994). ... Bruised right shoulder (November 27, 1995); missed six games. ... Strained groin (September 9, 1996); missed first two games of season. ... Reinjured groin (October 16, 1996); underwent groin surgery (November 22, 1996) and missed 38 games. ... Injured hamstring (November 8, 1997); missed 13 games. ... Traded by Devils to Chicago Blackhawks for fourth-round pick (D Mikko Jokela) in 1998 draft and future considerations (January 8, 1998). ... Strained hip flexor (March 12, 1998); missed two games. ... Fractured hand (September 20, 1998); missed first eight games of season. ... Suspended two games and fined $1,000 by NHL for actions toward a spectator (November 14, 1998). ... Traded by Blackhawks with D Bryan Muir to Tampa Bay Lightning for C Michael Nylander (November 12, 1999). ... Fractured jaw (January 13, 2000); missed final 40 games of regular season. ... Signed as free agent by St. Louis Blues (August 24, 2000). ... Injured groin (November 21, 2000); missed five games. ... Injured groin (February 1, 2001); missed seven games. ... Signed as free agent by Montreal Canadiens (September 10, 2001). ... Claimed on waivers by Nashville Predators (January 30, 2002).

Season Team	League	REGULAR SEASON Gms.	G	A	Pts.	PIM	+/-	PP	SH	PLAYOFFS Gms.	G	A	Pts.	PIM
85-86—Flin Flon	MJHL	40	20	21	41	200	...	...	...	—	—	—	—	—
—New Westminster	WHL	2	0	0	0	0	...	...	...	—	—	—	—	—
86-87—Prince Albert	WHL	47	3	8	11	105	...	...	...	—	—	—	—	—
87-88—Prince Albert	WHL	72	13	14	27	164	...	...	...	10	1	0	1	43
88-89—Prince Albert	WHL	59	26	29	55	264	...	...	...	4	2	1	3	30
89-90—Prince Albert	WHL	29	15	17	32	121	...	...	...	14	4	7	11	34
—Hershey	AHL	28	2	2	4	175	...	...	...	—	—	—	—	—
90-91—Hershey	AHL	54	9	15	24	183	...	...	...	1	0	0	0	0
91-92—Hershey	AHL	60	11	7	18	145	...	...	...	—	—	—	—	—
—Philadelphia	NHL	1	0	0	0	0	0	0	0	—	—	—	—	—
92-93—Kalamazoo	IHL	45	5	5	10	193	...	...	...	—	—	—	—	—
—Minnesota	NHL	1	0	0	0	5	0	0	0	—	—	—	—	—
93-94—Kalamazoo	IHL	5	0	0	0	16	...	...	...	—	—	—	—	—
—Albany	AHL	37	9	5	14	135	...	...	...	5	1	1	2	18
94-95—Albany	AHL	70	18	25	43	268	...	...	...	14	1	8	9	13
—New Jersey	NHL	9	0	0	0	27	-1	0	0	—	—	—	—	—
95-96—New Jersey	NHL	23	1	5	6	79	2	0	0	—	—	—	—	—
—Albany	AHL	6	1	3	4	17	...	...	...	—	—	—	—	—
96-97—Albany	AHL	3	0	0	0	10	...	...	...	—	—	—	—	—
—New Jersey	NHL	27	0	4	4	60	0	0	0	5	0	0	0	29
97-98—New Jersey	NHL	6	0	0	0	16	-2	0	0	—	—	—	—	—
—Chicago	NHL	38	3	2	5	102	-1	1	0	—	—	—	—	—
98-99—Chicago	NHL	53	5	4	9	145	2	1	0	—	—	—	—	—
99-00—Cleveland	IHL	12	2	2	4	56	...	...	...	—	—	—	—	—
—Tampa Bay	NHL	26	1	0	1	103	-3	0	0	—	—	—	—	—
00-01—St. Louis	NHL	38	2	1	3	96	-3	0	0	5	0	0	0	2
01-02—Montreal	NHL	25	1	1	2	63	0	0	0	—	—	—	—	—
—Milwaukee	AHL	2	1	0	1	37	...	...	...	—	—	—	—	—
—Nashville	NHL	26	5	0	5	69	-1	0	0	—	—	—	—	—
02-03—Milwaukee	AHL	17	6	6	12	40	...	...	...	—	—	—	—	—
—Nashville	NHL	26	0	1	1	56	-4	0	0	—	—	—	—	—
NHL Totals (11 years)		**299**	**18**	**18**	**36**	**821**	**-11**	**2**	**0**	**10**	**0**	**0**	**0**	**31**

SIMPSON, TODD — D — COYOTES

PERSONAL: Born May 28, 1973, in North Vancouver, B.C. ... 6-3/218. ... Shoots left.

TRANSACTIONS/CAREER NOTES: Signed as non-drafted free agent by Calgary Flames (July 6, 1994). ... Injured knee (October 1, 1997) and underwent surgery; missed 10 games. ... Injured shoulder (November 15, 1997); missed four games. ... Suffered concussion (March 19, 1998); missed final 15 games of season. ... Suffered facial injury (March 13, 1999); missed nine games. ... Traded by Flames to Florida Panthers for LW Bill Lindsay (September 30, 1999). ... Fractured toe (October 9, 2000); missed five games. ... Suffered concussion (December 4, 2000); missed 40 games. ... Traded by Panthers to Phoenix Coyotes for second-round draft pick (traded to New Jersey) in 2001 draft (March 13, 2001). ... Fractured foot (November 20, 2001); missed 15 games. ... Suspended three games by NHL for high-sticking incident (November 27, 2002). ... Suspended two games by NHL for high-sticking incident (December 28, 2002).

Season Team	League	REGULAR SEASON Gms.	G	A	Pts.	PIM	+/-	PP	SH	PLAYOFFS Gms.	G	A	Pts.	PIM
91-92—Brown University	ECAC	14	1	3	4	18	...	...	...	—	—	—	—	—
92-93—Tri-City	WHL	69	5	18	23	196	...	...	...	4	0	0	0	13
93-94—Tri-City	WHL	12	2	3	5	32	...	...	...	—	—	—	—	—
—Saskatoon	WHL	51	7	19	26	175	...	...	...	16	1	5	6	42
94-95—Saint John	AHL	80	3	10	13	321	...	...	...	5	0	0	0	4
95-96—Calgary	NHL	6	0	0	0	32	0	0	0	—	—	—	—	—
—Saint John	AHL	66	4	13	17	277	...	...	...	16	2	3	5	32

			REGULAR SEASON							PLAYOFFS				
Season Team	League	Gms.	G	A	Pts.	PIM	+/-	PP	SH	Gms.	G	A	Pts.	PIM
96-97—Calgary	NHL	82	1	13	14	208	-14	0	0	—	—	—	—	—
97-98—Calgary	NHL	53	1	5	6	109	-10	0	0	—	—	—	—	—
98-99—Calgary	NHL	73	2	8	10	151	18	0	0	—	—	—	—	—
99-00—Florida	NHL	82	1	6	7	202	5	0	0	4	0	0	0	4
00-01—Florida	NHL	25	1	3	4	74	0	0	0	—	—	—	—	—
—Phoenix	NHL	13	0	1	1	12	-4	0	0	—	—	—	—	—
01-02—Phoenix	NHL	67	2	13	15	152	20	0	0	5	0	2	2	6
02-03—Phoenix	NHL	66	2	7	9	135	7	0	0	—	—	—	—	—
NHL Totals (8 years)		467	10	56	66	1075	22	0	0	9	0	2	2	10

SIVEK, MICHAL — C — PENGUINS

PERSONAL: Born January 21, 1981, in Nachod, Czechoslovakia ... 6-3/209. ... Shoots left.
TRANSACTIONS/CAREER NOTES: Selected by Washington Capitals in second round (second Capitals pick, 29th overall) of NHL entry draft (June 26, 1999). ... Traded by Capitals with C Kris Beech, D Ross Lupaschuk and future considerations to Pittsburgh Penguins for RW Jaromir Jagr and D Frantisek Kucera (July 11, 2001).

			REGULAR SEASON							PLAYOFFS				
Season Team	League	Gms.	G	A	Pts.	PIM	+/-	PP	SH	Gms.	G	A	Pts.	PIM
96-97—Sparta Praha Jrs.	Czech Rep.	38	18	11	29	...	...	...	...	—	—	—	—	—
97-98—Sparta Praha	Czech Rep.	25	1	1	2	10	...	...	...	5	1	0	1	0
—Sparta Praha Jrs.	Czech Rep.	31	13	8	21	...	...	...	...	—	—	—	—	—
98-99—Sparta Praha	Czech Rep.	1	1	0	1	2	...	...	...	—	—	—	—	—
—Velvana Kladno	Czech Rep.	34	3	8	11	24	...	...	...	—	—	—	—	—
99-00—Prince Albert	WHL	53	23	37	60	65	...	...	...	6	1	4	5	10
00-01—Sparta Praha	Czech Rep.	32	6	7	13	28	...	...	...	13	4	2	6	8
01-02—Wilkes-Barre/Scranton	AHL	25	4	8	12	30	...	...	...	—	—	—	—	—
—Sparta Praha	Czech Rep.	17	5	3	8	20	...	...	...	12	0	1	1	10
02-03—Wilkes-Barre/Scranton	AHL	40	10	17	27	33	...	...	...	—	—	—	—	—
—Pittsburgh	NHL	38	3	3	6	14	-5	1	0	—	—	—	—	—
NHL Totals (1 year)		38	3	3	6	14	-5	1	0					

SKALDE, JARROD — C — STARS — S

PERSONAL: Born February 26, 1971, in Niagara Falls, Ont. ... 6-0/185. ... Shoots left. ... Name pronounced SKAHL-dee.
TRANSACTIONS/CAREER NOTES: Selected by New Jersey Devils in second round (third Devils pick, 26th overall) of NHL entry draft (June 17, 1989). ... Traded by Oshawa Generals to Belleville Bulls for RW Rob Pearson (November 18, 1990). ... Selected by Mighty Ducks of Anaheim in NHL expansion draft (June 24, 1993). ... Signed as free agent by Las Vegas Thunder (August 18, 1994). ... Signed as free agent by Mighty Ducks (May 31, 1995). ... Traded by Mighty Ducks to Calgary Flames for D Bobby Marshall (October 30, 1995). ... Signed as free agent by San Jose Sharks (August 13, 1997). ... Claimed on waivers by Dallas Stars (January 27, 1998). ... Claimed on waivers by Chicago Blackhawks (February 12, 1998). ... Claimed on waivers by Sharks (March 6, 1998). ... Signed as free agent by Atlanta Thrashers (July 21, 2000). ... Traded by Thrashers to Philadelphia Flyers for D Joe DiPenta (March 4, 2002). ... Signed by Dallas Stars (July 17, 2003).

			REGULAR SEASON							PLAYOFFS				
Season Team	League	Gms.	G	A	Pts.	PIM	+/-	PP	SH	Gms.	G	A	Pts.	PIM
86-87—Fort Erie Jr. B	OHA	41	27	34	61	36	...	...	...	—	—	—	—	—
87-88—Oshawa	OHL	60	12	16	28	24	...	...	...	7	2	1	3	2
88-89—Oshawa	OHL	65	38	38	76	36	...	...	...	6	1	5	6	2
89-90—Oshawa	OHL	62	40	52	92	66	...	...	...	17	10	7	17	6
90-91—New Jersey	NHL	1	0	1	1	0	0	0	0	—	—	—	—	—
—Utica	AHL	3	3	2	5	0	...	...	...	—	—	—	—	—
—Oshawa	OHL	15	8	14	22	14	...	...	...	—	—	—	—	—
—Belleville	OHL	40	30	52	82	21	...	...	...	6	9	6	15	10
91-92—Utica	AHL	62	20	20	40	56	...	...	...	4	3	1	4	8
—New Jersey	NHL	15	2	4	6	4	-1	0	0	—	—	—	—	—
92-93—Cincinnati	IHL	4	1	2	3	4	...	...	...	—	—	—	—	—
—Utica	AHL	59	21	39	60	76	...	...	...	5	0	2	2	19
—New Jersey	NHL	11	0	2	2	4	-3	0	0	—	—	—	—	—
93-94—San Diego	IHL	57	25	38	63	79	...	...	...	9	3	12	15	10
—Anaheim	NHL	20	5	4	9	10	-3	2	0	—	—	—	—	—
94-95—Las Vegas	IHL	74	34	41	75	103	...	...	...	9	2	4	6	8
95-96—Baltimore	AHL	11	2	6	8	55	...	...	...	—	—	—	—	—
—Saint John	AHL	68	27	40	67	98	...	...	...	16	4	9	13	6
—Calgary	NHL	1	0	0	0	0	0	0	0	—	—	—	—	—
96-97—Saint John	AHL	65	32	36	68	94	...	...	...	3	0	0	0	14
97-98—Kentucky	AHL	23	5	15	20	48	...	...	...	3	3	0	3	6
—San Jose	NHL	22	4	6	10	14	-2	0	0	—	—	—	—	—
—Chicago	NHL	7	0	1	1	4	0	0	0	—	—	—	—	—
—Indianapolis	IHL	2	0	2	2	0	...	...	...	—	—	—	—	—
—Dallas	NHL	1	0	0	0	0	0	0	0	—	—	—	—	—
98-99—San Jose	NHL	17	1	1	2	4	-6	0	0	—	—	—	—	—
—Kentucky	AHL	54	17	40	57	75	...	...	...	12	4	5	9	16
99-00—Utah	IHL	77	25	54	79	98	...	...	...	5	0	1	1	10
00-01—Atlanta	NHL	19	1	2	3	20	-8	0	0	—	—	—	—	—
—Orlando	IHL	60	14	40	54	56	...	...	...	15	3	6	9	20
01-02—Chicago	AHL	64	15	37	52	71	...	...	...	—	—	—	—	—
—Philadelphia	AHL	16	4	4	8	23	...	...	...	4	0	2	2	4
—Philadelphia	NHL	1	0	0	0	2	0	0	0	—	—	—	—	—
02-03—Lausanne HC	Switzerland	23	7	8	15	28	...	...	...	—	—	—	—	—
NHL Totals (9 years)		115	13	21	34	62	-23	2	0					

SKOULA, MARTIN　　　　D　　　　AVALANCHE

PERSONAL: Born October 28, 1979, in Litomerice, Czechoslovakia ... 6-3/220. ... Shoots left.
TRANSACTIONS/CAREER NOTES: Selected by Colorado Avalanche in first round (second Avalanche pick, 17th overall) of NHL entry draft (June 27, 1998). ... Injured shoulder (January 5, 2000); missed two games.

Season Team	League	Gms.	G	A	Pts.	PIM	+/-	PP	SH	Gms.	G	A	Pts.	PIM
						REGULAR SEASON						PLAYOFFS		
95-96—Litvinov	Czech. Jrs.	38	0	4	4	...	...	...	...	—	—	—	—	—
—Litvinov	Czech Rep.	—	—	—	—	—	—	—	—	1	0	0	0	0
96-97—Litvinov	Czech. Jrs.	38	2	9	11	...	...	...	...	—	—	—	—	—
—Litvinov	Czech Rep.	1	0	0	0	0	...	...	...	—	—	—	—	—
97-98—Barrie	COJHL	66	8	36	44	36	...	...	...	6	1	3	4	4
98-99—Barrie	OHL	67	13	46	59	46	...	...	...	12	3	10	13	13
—Hershey	AHL	—	—	—	—	—	—	—	—	1	0	0	0	0
99-00—Colorado	NHL	80	3	13	16	20	5	2	0	17	0	2	2	4
00-01—Colorado	NHL	82	8	17	25	38	8	3	0	23	1	4	5	8
01-02—Colorado	NHL	82	10	21	31	42	-3	5	0	21	0	6	6	2
—Czech Rep. Oly. team..	Int'l	4	0	0	0	0	...	...	...	—	—	—	—	—
02-03—Colorado	NHL	81	4	21	25	68	11	2	0	7	0	1	1	4
NHL Totals (4 years)		**325**	**25**	**72**	**97**	**168**	**21**	**12**	**0**	**68**	**1**	**13**	**14**	**18**

SKRASTINS, KARLIS　　　　D　　　　AVALANCHE

PERSONAL: Born July 9, 1974, in Riga, U.S.S.R. ... 6-1/212. ... Shoots left.
TRANSACTIONS/CAREER NOTES: Selected by Nashville Predators in ninth round (eighth Predators pick, 230th overall) of 1998 NHL entry draft (June 27, 1998). ... Traded by Predators to Colorado Avalanche for future considerations (June 30, 2003). ... Signed by Avalanche (July 15, 2003).

Season Team	League	Gms.	G	A	Pts.	PIM	+/-	PP	SH	Gms.	G	A	Pts.	PIM
						REGULAR SEASON						PLAYOFFS		
92-93—Riga Stars	CIS	40	3	5	8	16	...	...	...	2	0	0	0	0
93-94—Riga Stars	CIS	42	7	5	12	18	...	...	...	2	1	0	1	4
94-95—Riga Stars	CIS	52	4	14	18	69	...	...	...	—	—	—	—	—
95-96—TPS Turku	Finland	50	4	11	15	32	...	...	...	11	2	2	4	10
96-97—TPS Turku	Finland	50	2	8	10	20	...	...	...	—	—	—	—	—
97-98—TPS Turku	Finland	48	4	15	19	67	...	...	...	—	—	—	—	—
98-99—Milwaukee	IHL	75	8	36	44	47	...	...	...	2	0	1	1	2
—Nashville	NHL	2	0	1	1	0	0	0	0	—	—	—	—	—
99-00—Milwaukee	IHL	19	3	8	11	10	...	...	...	—	—	—	—	—
—Nashville	NHL	59	5	6	11	20	-7	1	0	—	—	—	—	—
00-01—Nashville	NHL	82	1	11	12	30	-12	0	0	—	—	—	—	—
01-02—Nashville	NHL	82	4	13	17	36	-12	0	0	—	—	—	—	—
—Latvian Olympic team .	Int'l	1	0	0	0	0	...	...	...	—	—	—	—	—
02-03—Nashville	NHL	82	3	10	13	44	-18	0	1	—	—	—	—	—
NHL Totals (5 years)		**307**	**13**	**41**	**54**	**130**	**-49**	**1**	**1**					

SKRBEK, PAVEL　　　　D　　　　PREDATORS

PERSONAL: Born August 9, 1978, in Kladno, Czechoslovakia. ... 6-3/213. ... Shoots left.
TRANSACTIONS/CAREER NOTES: Selected by Pittsburgh Penguins in second round (second Penguins pick, 28th overall) of NHL entry draft (June 22, 1996). ... Traded by Penguins to Nashville Predators for D Bob Boughner (March 13, 2000). ... Suffered concussion (March 17, 2001); missed six games. ... Suffered concussion prior to start of 2001-02 season; missed first two games of season.

Season Team	League	Gms.	G	A	Pts.	PIM	+/-	PP	SH	Gms.	G	A	Pts.	PIM
						REGULAR SEASON						PLAYOFFS		
94-95—Poldi Kladno	Czech Rep.	29	7	6	13	...	...	...	...	—	—	—	—	—
95-96—HC Kladno Jrs	Czech Rep.	29	10	12	22	...	...	...	...	—	—	—	—	—
—HC Kladno	Czech Rep.	13	0	1	1	...	...	...	...	5	0	0	0	...
96-97—Poldi Kladno	Czech Rep.	35	1	5	6	26	...	...	...	3	0	0	0	4
97-98—Poldi Kladno	Czech Rep.	47	4	10	14	126	...	...	...	—	—	—	—	—
98-99—Syracuse	AHL	64	6	16	22	38	...	...	...	—	—	—	—	—
—Pittsburgh	NHL	4	0	0	0	2	2	0	0	—	—	—	—	—
99-00—Wilkes-Barre/Scranton	AHL	51	7	16	23	50	...	...	...	—	—	—	—	—
—Milwaukee	IHL	6	0	0	0	0	...	...	...	—	—	—	—	—
00-01—Milwaukee	IHL	54	2	22	24	55	...	...	...	5	0	0	0	2
—Nashville	NHL	5	0	0	0	4	1	0	0	—	—	—	—	—
01-02—Nashville	NHL	3	0	0	0	2	-2	0	0	—	—	—	—	—
—HC Kladno	Czech Rep.	24	2	3	5	30	...	...	...	—	—	—	—	—
02-03—Lulea	Sweden	39	2	2	4	61	...	...	...	4	0	0	0	10
NHL Totals (3 years)		**12**	**0**	**0**	**0**	**8**	**1**	**0**	**0**					

SKUDRA, PETER　　　　G

PERSONAL: Born April 24, 1973, in Riga, U.S.S.R. ... 6-1/185. ... Catches left. ... Name pronounced SKOO-druh.
TRANSACTIONS/CAREER NOTES: Signed as non-drafted free agent by Pittsburgh Penguins (September 25, 1997). ... Separated shoulder (September 8, 1998); missed first two games of season. ... Bruised lower left leg (November 3, 1998); missed 14 games. ... Injured ankle (November 6, 1999); missed three games. ... Suffered concussion (December 26, 1999); missed two games. ... Suffered from the flu (February 11, 2000); missed two games. ... Signed as free agent by Boston Bruins (October 3, 2000). ... Claimed on waivers by Buffalo Sabres (October 6, 2000). ... Claimed on waivers by Bruins (November 14, 2000). ... Signed as free agent by Vancouver Canucks (November 7, 2001).

		REGULAR SEASON									PLAYOFFS							
Season Team	League	Gms.	Min	W	L	T	GA	SO	Avg.	SV%	Gms.	Min.	W	L	GA	SO	Avg.	SV%
92-93 —Pardaugava Riga	CIS	27	1498	...	...	...	74	...	2.96	—	1	60	...	...	5	0	5.00	—
93-94 —Pardaugava Riga	CIS	14	783	...	...	...	42	...	3.22	—	1	55	...	...	4	0	4.36	—
94-95 —Greensboro	ECHL	33	1612	13	9	5	113	0	4.21	—	6	341	2	2	28	0	4.93	—
95-96 —Erie	ECHL	12	681	3	8	1	47	0	4.14	—	—	—	—	—	—	—	—	—
—Johnstown	ECHL	30	1657	12	11	4	98	0	3.55	—	—	—	—	—	—	—	—	—
96-97 —Johnstown	ECHL	4	200	2	1	1	11	0	3.30	—	—	—	—	—	—	—	—	—
—Hamilton	AHL	32	1615	8	16	2	101	0	3.75	—	—	—	—	—	—	—	—	—
97-98 —Houston	IHL	9	499	5	3	1	23	0	2.77	—	—	—	—	—	—	—	—	—
—Pittsburgh	NHL	17	851	6	4	3	26	0	1.83	.924	—	—	—	—	—	—	—	—
—Kansas City	IHL	13	776	10	3	0	37	0	2.86	—	8	513	4	4	20	1	*2.34	—
98-99 —Pittsburgh	NHL	37	1914	15	11	5	89	3	2.79	.892	—	—	—	—	—	—	—	—
99-00 —Pittsburgh	NHL	20	922	5	7	3	48	1	3.12	.872	1	20	0	0	1	0	3.00	.909
00-01 —Buffalo	NHL	1	0	0	0	0	0	0	0	—	—	—	—	—	—	—	—	—
—Rochester	AHL	2	120	2	0	0	5	0	2.50	—	—	—	—	—	—	—	—	—
—Boston	NHL	25	1116	6	12	1	62	0	3.33	.879	—	—	—	—	—	—	—	—
—Providence	AHL	3	180	3	0	0	5	0	1.67	—	—	—	—	—	—	—	—	—
01-02 —Hartford	AHL	3	178	2	1	0	8	0	2.70	—	—	—	—	—	—	—	—	—
—Vancouver	NHL	23	1166	10	8	2	47	1	2.42	.907	2	96	0	1	5	0	3.13	.891
02-03 —Manitoba	AHL	1	60	1	0	0	3	0	3.00	—	—	—	—	—	—	—	—	—
—Vancouver	NHL	23	1192	9	5	6	54	1	2.72	.897	—	—	—	—	—	—	—	—
NHL Totals (6 years)		146	7161	51	47	20	326	6	2.73	.894	3	116	0	1	6	0	3.10	.895

SLANEY, JOHN D FLYERS

PERSONAL: Born February 7, 1972, in St. John's, Nfld. ... 6-0/185. ... Shoots left. ... Full Name: John G. Slaney.

TRANSACTIONS/CAREER NOTES: Selected by Washington Capitals in first round (first Capitals pick, ninth overall) of NHL entry draft (June 16, 1990). ... Sprained right ankle (March 9, 1994); missed six games. ... Traded by Capitals to Colorado Avalanche for third-round pick (C Shawn McNeil) in 1996 draft (July 12, 1995). ... Traded by Avalanche to Los Angeles Kings for sixth-round pick (RW Brian Willsie) in 1996 draft (December 28, 1995). ... Fractured right hand (March 6, 1996); missed 12 games. ... Suffered concussion (November 17, 1996); missed one game. ... Signed as free agent by Phoenix Coyotes (August 18, 1997). ... Bruised thigh (October 30, 1997); missed one game. ... Suffered from the flu (December 10, 1997); missed one game. ... Fractured thumb (January 24, 1998); missed seven games. ... Injured hamstring (April 18, 1998); missed one game. ... Selected by Nashville Predators in NHL expansion draft (June 26, 1998). ... Bruised thumb (January 28, 1999); missed two games. ... Sprained wrist (February 5, 1999); missed three games. ... Injured rib (March 28, 1999); missed final nine games of season. ... Signed as free agent by Pittsburgh Penguins (September 30, 1999). ... Traded by Penguins to Philadelphia Flyers for LW Kevin Stevens (January 14, 2001).

		REGULAR SEASON								PLAYOFFS				
Season Team	League	Gms.	G	A	Pts.	PIM	+/-	PP	SH	Gms.	G	A	Pts.	PIM
88-89 —Cornwall	OHL	66	16	43	59	23	...	...	...	18	8	16	24	10
89-90 —Cornwall	OHL	64	38	59	97	60	...	...	...	6	0	8	8	11
90-91 —Cornwall	OHL	34	21	25	46	28	...	...	...	—	—	—	—	—
91-92 —Cornwall	OHL	34	19	41	60	43	...	...	...	6	3	8	11	0
—Baltimore	AHL	6	2	4	6	0	...	...	...	—	—	—	—	—
92-93 —Baltimore	AHL	79	20	46	66	60	...	...	...	7	0	7	7	8
93-94 —Portland	AHL	29	14	13	27	17	...	...	...	—	—	—	—	—
—Washington	NHL	47	7	9	16	27	3	3	0	11	1	1	2	2
94-95 —Washington	NHL	16	0	3	3	6	-3	0	0	—	—	—	—	—
—Portland	AHL	8	3	10	13	4	...	...	...	7	1	3	4	4
95-96 —Colorado	NHL	7	0	3	3	4	2	0	0	—	—	—	—	—
—Cornwall	AHL	5	0	4	4	2	...	...	...	—	—	—	—	—
—Los Angeles	NHL	31	6	11	17	10	5	3	1	—	—	—	—	—
96-97 —Los Angeles	NHL	32	3	11	14	4	-10	1	0	—	—	—	—	—
—Phoenix	IHL	35	9	25	34	8	...	...	...	—	—	—	—	—
97-98 —Las Vegas	IHL	5	2	2	4	10	...	...	...	—	—	—	—	—
—Phoenix	NHL	55	3	14	17	24	-3	1	0	—	—	—	—	—
98-99 —Nashville	NHL	46	2	12	14	14	-12	0	0	—	—	—	—	—
—Milwaukee	IHL	7	0	1	1	0	...	...	...	—	—	—	—	—
99-00 —Pittsburgh	NHL	29	1	4	5	10	-10	1	0	2	1	0	1	2
—Wilkes-Barre/Scranton	AHL	49	30	30	60	25	...	...	...	—	—	—	—	—
00-01 —Wilkes-Barre/Scranton	AHL	40	12	38	50	4	...	...	...	—	—	—	—	—
—Philadelphia	AHL	25	6	11	17	10	...	...	...	10	2	6	8	6
01-02 —Philadelphia	AHL	64	20	39	59	26	...	...	...	5	2	1	3	0
—Philadelphia	NHL	1	0	0	0	0	2	0	0	1	0	0	0	0
02-03 —Philadelphia	AHL	55	9	33	42	36	...	...	...	—	—	—	—	—
NHL Totals (8 years)		264	22	67	89	99	-26	9	1	14	2	1	3	4

SLOAN, BLAKE RW

PERSONAL: Born July 27, 1975, in Park Ridge, Ill. ... 5-10/196. ... Shoots right.

TRANSACTIONS/CAREER NOTES: Signed as non-drafted free agent by Dallas Stars (March 10, 1999). ... Sprained ankle (February 21, 2000); missed 15 games. ... Claimed on waivers by Columbus Blue Jackets (March 13, 2001). ... Traded by Blue Jackets to Calgary Flames for D Jamie Allison (March 19, 2002).

Season Team	League	REGULAR SEASON								PLAYOFFS				
		Gms.	G	A	Pts.	PIM	+/-	PP	SH	Gms.	G	A	Pts.	PIM
93-94—Univ. of Michigan	CCHA	38	2	4	6	48	...	...	...	—	—	—	—	—
94-95—Univ. of Michigan	CCHA	39	2	15	17	60	...	...	...	—	—	—	—	—
95-96—Univ. of Michigan	CCHA	41	6	24	30	57	...	...	...	—	—	—	—	—
96-97—Univ. of Michigan	CCHA	41	2	15	17	52	...	...	...	—	—	—	—	—
97-98—Houston	IHL	70	2	13	15	86	...	...	...	2	0	0	0	0
98-99—Houston	IHL	62	8	10	18	76	...	...	...	—	—	—	—	—
—Dallas	NHL	14	0	0	0	10	-1	0	0	19	0	2	2	8
99-00—Dallas	NHL	67	4	13	17	50	11	0	0	16	0	0	0	12
00-01—Dallas	NHL	33	2	2	4	4	-2	0	0	—	—	—	—	—
—Houston	IHL	20	7	4	11	18	...	...	...	—	—	—	—	—
—Columbus	NHL	14	1	0	1	13	-2	0	0	—	—	—	—	—
01-02—Columbus	NHL	60	2	7	9	46	-18	0	0	—	—	—	—	—
—Calgary	NHL	7	0	2	2	4	1	0	0	—	—	—	—	—
02-03—Calgary	NHL	67	2	8	10	28	-5	0	0	—	—	—	—	—
NHL Totals (5 years)		262	11	32	43	155	-16	0	0	35	0	2	2	20

SLOVAK, TOMAS — D — AVALANCHE

PERSONAL: Born April 5, 1983, in Kosice, Czechoslovakia. ... 6-1/191. ... Shoots right.

TRANSACTIONS/CAREER NOTES: Selected by Nashville Predators in second round (third Predators pick, 42nd overall) of NHL entry draft (June 23, 2001). ... Traded by Predators for F Sergei Soin to Colorado Avalanche (June 22, 2003). ... Signed by Avalanche (July 15, 2003).

Season Team	League	REGULAR SEASON								PLAYOFFS				
		Gms.	G	A	Pts.	PIM	+/-	PP	SH	Gms.	G	A	Pts.	PIM
99-00—VSZ Kosice	Slovakia	2	0	0	0	0	...	...	...	—	—	—	—	—
00-01—HC Kosice	Slovakia	43	5	5	10	28	...	...	...	3	1	0	1	2
01-02—Kelowna	WHL	53	2	24	26	41	...	...	...	15	0	0	0	8
02-03—Kelowna	WHL	65	18	53	71	86	...	...	...	—	—	—	—	—

S — SMEHLIK, RICHARD — D

PERSONAL: Born January 23, 1970, in Ostrava, Czechoslovakia ... 6-3/230. ... Shoots left. ... Name pronounced SHMEHL-ihk.

TRANSACTIONS/CAREER NOTES: Selected by Buffalo Sabres in fifth round (third Sabres pick, 97th overall) of NHL entry draft (June 16, 1990). ... Injured hip (October 30, 1992); missed two games. ... Played in Europe during 1994-95 NHL lockout. ... Bruised shoulder (January 27, 1995); missed six games. ... Tore knee ligaments (August 10, 1995); missed entire 1995-96 season. ... Suffered tendonitis in knee (January 12, 1996); missed five games. ... Suffered sore knee (November 19, 1996); missed six games. ... Suffered sore knee (February 23, 1997); missed one game. ... Strained groin (March 30, 1997); missed three games. ... Injured wrist (February 4, 1998); missed two games. ... Bruised eye (February 25, 1998); missed seven games. ... Suspended one game and fined $1,000 by NHL for high-sticking incident (October 15, 1998). ... Bruised quadricep muscle (November 21, 1998); missed seven games. ... Injured rib (December 17, 1999); missed nine games. ... Suffered back spasms (February 17, 2000); missed three games. ... Strained groin (January 17, 2001); missed five games. ... Injured groin (February 22, 2001); missed eight games. ... Injured ribs (March 14, 2001); missed 11 games. ... Strained groin (October 22, 2001); missed three games. ... Injured shoulder (March 1, 2002); missed 15 games. ... Signed as free agent by Atlanta Thrashers (July 10, 2002). ... Traded by Thrashers to New Jersey Devils for fourth-round pick in 2003 draft and conditional pick in 2004 draft (March 10, 2003).

Season Team	League	REGULAR SEASON								PLAYOFFS				
		Gms.	G	A	Pts.	PIM	+/-	PP	SH	Gms.	G	A	Pts.	PIM
88-89—Vitkovice	Czech.	38	2	5	7	12	...	...	...	—	—	—	—	—
89-90—Vitkovice	Czech.	43	4	3	7		...	...	...	—	—	—	—	—
90-91—Dukla Jihlava	Czech.	51	4	2	6	22	...	...	...	—	—	—	—	—
91-92—Vitkovice	Czech.	47	9	10	19		...	...	...	—	—	—	—	—
—Czech. Olympic Team	Int'l	8	0	1	1	2	...	...	...	—	—	—	—	—
92-93—Buffalo	NHL	80	4	27	31	59	9	0	0	8	0	4	4	2
93-94—Buffalo	NHL	84	14	27	41	69	22	3	3	7	0	2	2	10
94-95—HC Vitkovice	Czech Rep.	13	5	2	7	12	...	...	...	—	—	—	—	—
—Buffalo	NHL	39	4	7	11	46	5	0	1	5	0	0	0	2
95-96—Buffalo	NHL						Did not play.							
96-97—Buffalo	NHL	62	11	19	30	43	19	2	0	12	0	2	2	4
97-98—Buffalo	NHL	72	3	17	20	62	11	0	1	15	0	2	2	6
—Czech Rep. Oly. team	Int'l	6	0	1	1	4	...	...	...	—	—	—	—	—
98-99—Buffalo	NHL	72	3	11	14	44	-9	0	0	21	0	3	3	10
99-00—Buffalo	NHL	64	2	9	11	50	13	0	0	5	1	0	1	0
00-01—Buffalo	NHL	56	3	12	15	4	6	0	0	10	0	1	1	4
01-02—Buffalo	NHL	60	3	6	9	22	-9	0	0	—	—	—	—	—
—Czech Rep. Oly. team	Int'l	4	0	0	0	4	...	...	...	—	—	—	—	—
02-03—Atlanta	NHL	43	2	9	11	16	-4	0	0	—	—	—	—	—
—New Jersey	NHL	12	0	2	2	0	-1	0	0	5	0	0	0	2
NHL Totals (11 years)		644	49	146	195	415	62	5	5	88	1	14	15	40

SMIRNOV, ALEXEI — LW — MIGHTY DUCKS

PERSONAL: Born January 28, 1982, in Tver, U.S.S.R. ... 6-4/218. ... Shoots left.

TRANSACTIONS/CAREER NOTES: Selected by Might Ducks of Anaheim in first round (first Mighty Ducks pick, 12th overall) of NHL entry draft (June 24, 2000).

Season Team	League	Gms.	G	A	Pts.	PIM	+/-	PP	SH	Gms.	G	A	Pts.	PIM
97-98—Dynamo Moscow	Rus. Div. II	11	1	1	2	4	...	...	...	—	—	—	—	—
98-99—Dynamo Moscow	Russian	1	0	0	0	0	...	...	...	—	—	—	—	—
—Dynamo Moscow	Rus. Div. II	27	9	3	12	24	...	...	...	—	—	—	—	—
99-00—Dynamo Moscow	Russian	1	0	0	0	0	...	...	...	—	—	—	—	—
—Dynamo Moscow	Rus. Div. III	12	5	3	8	34	...	...	...	—	—	—	—	—
—Tver	Russian	35	3	5	8	24	...	...	...	—	—	—	—	—
00-01—Dynamo Moscow	Russian	29	2	0	2	16	...	...	...	—	—	—	—	—
01-02—CSKA Moscow	Russian	51	5	11	16	42	...	...	...	—	—	—	—	—
02-03—Cincinnati	AHL	19	7	3	10	12	...	...	...	—	—	—	—	—
—Anaheim	NHL	44	3	2	5	18	-1	0	0	4	0	0	0	2
NHL Totals (1 year)		44	3	2	5	18	-1	0	0	4	0	0	0	2

SMITH, BRANDON — D — ISLANDERS

PERSONAL: Born February 25, 1973, in Hazelton, B.C. ... 6-1/196. ... Shoots left. ... Full Name: Brandon Stuart Smith.
TRANSACTIONS/CAREER NOTES: Signed as non-drafted free agent by Detroit Red Wings (July 28, 1997). ... Signed as free agent by Boston Bruins (July 22, 1998). ... Separated shoulder (January 10, 2001); missed nine games. ... Signed as free agent by San Jose Sharks (July 23, 2001). ... Signed as free agent by New York Islanders (August 3, 2002).

		REGULAR SEASON								PLAYOFFS				
Season Team	League	Gms.	G	A	Pts.	PIM	+/-	PP	SH	Gms.	G	A	Pts.	PIM
89-90—Portland	WHL	59	2	17	19	16	...	...	...	—	—	—	—	—
90-91—Portland	WHL	17	8	5	13	8	...	...	...	—	—	—	—	—
91-92—Portland	WHL	70	12	32	44	63	...	...	...	—	—	—	—	—
92-93—Portland	WHL	72	20	54	74	38	...	...	...	16	4	9	13	6
93-94—Portland	WHL	72	19	63	82	47	...	...	...	10	2	10	12	8
94-95—Dayton	ECHL	60	16	49	65	57	...	...	...	4	2	3	5	0
—Adirondack	AHL	14	1	2	3	7	...	...	...	3	0	0	0	2
95-96—Adirondack	AHL	48	4	13	17	22	...	...	...	3	0	1	1	2
96-97—Adirondack	AHL	80	8	26	34	30	...	...	...	4	0	0	0	0
97-98—Adirondack	AHL	64	9	27	36	26	...	...	...	1	0	1	1	0
98-99—Providence	AHL	72	16	46	62	32	...	...	...	19	1	9	10	12
—Boston	NHL	5	0	0	0	0	2	0	0	—	—	—	—	—
99-00—Providence	AHL	55	8	30	38	20	...	...	...	14	1	11	12	2
—Boston	NHL	22	2	4	6	10	-4	0	0	—	—	—	—	—
00-01—Providence	AHL	63	11	28	39	30	...	...	...	17	0	5	5	6
—Boston	NHL	3	1	0	1	0	-1	1	0	—	—	—	—	—
01-02—Cleveland	AHL	59	6	29	35	26	...	...	...	—	—	—	—	—
02-03—Bridgeport	AHL	63	9	32	41	37	...	...	...	—	—	—	—	—
—New York Islanders	NHL	3	0	0	0	0	-2	0	0	—	—	—	—	—
NHL Totals (4 years)		33	3	4	7	10	-5	1	0					

SMITH, D.J. — D — AVALANCHE

PERSONAL: Born May 13, 1977, in Windsor, Ont. ... 6-1/205. ... Shoots right. ... Full Name: Denis Smith.
TRANSACTIONS/CAREER NOTES: Selected by New York Islanders in second round (third Islanders pick, 41st overall) of NHL entry draft (July 8, 1995). ... Rights traded by Islanders with LW Wendel Clark and D Mathieu Schneider to Toronto Maple Leafs for LW Sean Haggerty, C Darby Hendrickson, D Kenny Jonsson and first-round pick (G Roberto Luongo) in 1997 draft (March 13, 1996). ... Traded by Maple Leafs with D Marty Wilford to Nashville Predators for D Marc Moro (March 1, 2002). ... Traded by Predators to Colorado Avalanche for conditional pick in 2002 draft (March 1, 2002).

		REGULAR SEASON								PLAYOFFS				
Season Team	League	Gms.	G	A	Pts.	PIM	+/-	PP	SH	Gms.	G	A	Pts.	PIM
92-93—Belle River	Jr. C	50	11	29	40	101	...	...	...	—	—	—	—	—
93-94—Windsor	Jr. B	51	8	34	42	267	...	...	...	—	—	—	—	—
94-95—Windsor	OHL	61	4	13	17	201	...	...	...	10	1	3	4	41
95-96—Windsor	OHL	64	14	45	59	260	...	...	...	7	1	7	8	23
96-97—Windsor	OHL	63	15	52	67	190	...	...	...	5	1	7	8	11
—Toronto	NHL	8	0	1	1	7	-5	0	0	—	—	—	—	—
—St. John's	AHL	...	...	...	...	...	...	...	...	1	0	0	0	0
97-98—St. John's	AHL	65	4	11	15	237	...	...	...	4	0	0	0	4
98-99—St. John's	AHL	79	7	28	35	216	...	...	...	5	0	1	1	0
99-00—St. John's	AHL	74	6	22	28	197	...	...	...	—	—	—	—	—
—Toronto	NHL	3	0	0	0	5	-1	0	0	—	—	—	—	—
00-01—St. John's	AHL	59	7	12	19	106	...	...	...	4	0	0	0	11
01-02—St. John's	AHL	59	6	10	16	152	...	...	...	—	—	—	—	—
—Hershey	AHL	14	0	3	3	33	...	...	...	8	1	0	1	33
02-03—Hershey	AHL	2	0	0	0	4	...	...	...	—	—	—	—	—
—Colorado	NHL	34	1	0	1	55	2	0	0	—	—	—	—	—
NHL Totals (3 years)		45	1	1	2	67	-4	0	0					

SMITH, JASON — D — OILERS

PERSONAL: Born November 2, 1973, in Calgary ... 6-3/210. ... Shoots right.
TRANSACTIONS/CAREER NOTES: Selected by New Jersey Devils in first round (first Devils pick, 18th overall) of NHL entry draft (June 20, 1992). ... Injured right knee (November 5, 1994); missed 37 games. ... Bruised hand (November 5, 1995); missed 15 games. ... Traded by Devils with C Steve Sullivan and C Alyn McCauley to Toronto Maple Leafs for C Doug Gilmour, D Dave Ellett and third-round pick (D Andre Lakos) in 1999 draft (February 25, 1997). ... Fractured toe (March 30, 1998); missed one game. ... Traded by Maple Leafs to Edmonton Oilers

for fourth-round pick (D Jonathan Zion) in 1999 draft and second-round pick (C Kris Vernarsky) in 2000 (March 23, 1999). ... Bruised shoulder (February 23, 2000); missed one game. ... Injured elbow (November 2, 2001); missed two games. ... Strained lower back (December 5, 2001); missed six games. ... Re-signed by Oilers (July 28, 2003).

			REGULAR SEASON								PLAYOFFS				
Season Team	League	Gms.	G	A	Pts.	PIM	+/-	PP	SH		Gms.	G	A	Pts.	PIM
90-91—Calgary Canucks	AJHL	45	3	15	18	69	...	...	...		—	—	—	—	—
—Regina	WHL	2	0	0	0	7	...	...	...		—	—	—	—	—
91-92—Regina	WHL	62	9	29	38	168	...	...	...		—	—	—	—	—
92-93—Regina	WHL	64	14	52	66	175	...	...	...		13	4	8	12	39
—Utica	AHL	—	—	—	—	—					1	0	0	0	2
93-94—New Jersey	NHL	41	0	5	5	43	7	0	0		6	0	0	0	7
—Albany	AHL	20	6	3	9	31	...				—	—	—	—	—
94-95—Albany	AHL	7	0	2	2	15	...				11	2	2	4	19
—New Jersey	NHL	2	0	0	0	0	-3	0	0		—	—	—	—	—
95-96—New Jersey	NHL	64	2	1	3	86	5	0	0		—	—	—	—	—
96-97—New Jersey	NHL	57	1	2	3	38	-8	0	0		—	—	—	—	—
—Toronto	NHL	21	0	5	5	16	-4	0	0		—	—	—	—	—
97-98—Toronto	NHL	81	3	13	16	100	-5	0	0		—	—	—	—	—
98-99—Toronto	NHL	60	2	11	13	40	-9	0	0		—	—	—	—	—
—Edmonton	NHL	12	1	1	2	11	0	0	0		4	0	1	1	4
99-00—Edmonton	NHL	80	3	11	14	60	16	0	0		5	0	1	1	4
00-01—Edmonton	NHL	82	5	15	20	120	14	1	1		6	0	2	2	6
01-02—Edmonton	NHL	74	5	13	18	103	14	0	1		—	—	—	—	—
02-03—Edmonton	NHL	68	4	8	12	64	5	0	0		6	0	0	0	19
NHL Totals (10 years)		642	26	85	111	681	32	1	2		27	0	4	4	40

SMITH, MARK C SHARKS

PERSONAL: Born October 24, 1977, in Edmonton ... 5-10/205. ... Shoots left.
TRANSACTIONS/CAREER NOTES: Selected by San Jose Sharks in ninth round (seventh Sharks pick, 219th overall) in NHL entry draft (June 21, 1997). ... Suffered concussion (November 5, 2000); missed seven games. ... Injured knee (February 26, 2001); missed three games. ... Suffered from the flu (April 13, 2002); missed one game. ... Re-signed by Sharks (July 15, 2003).

			REGULAR SEASON								PLAYOFFS				
Season Team	League	Gms.	G	A	Pts.	PIM	+/-	PP	SH		Gms.	G	A	Pts.	PIM
94-95—Lethbridge	WHL	49	3	4	7	25	...	...	...		—	—	—	—	—
95-96—Lethbridge	WHL	71	11	24	35	59	...	...	...		19	7	13	20	51
96-97—Lethbridge	WHL	62	19	38	57	125	...	...	...		19	7	13	20	51
97-98—Lethbridge	WHL	70	42	67	109	206	...	...	...		3	0	2	2	18
98-99—Kentucky	AHL	78	18	21	39	101	...	...	...		12	2	7	9	16
99-00—Kentucky	AHL	79	21	45	66	153	...	...	...		9	0	5	5	22
00-01—San Jose	NHL	42	2	2	4	51	2	0	0		—	—	—	—	—
—Kentucky	AHL	6	2	6	8	23	...				—	—	—	—	—
01-02—San Jose	NHL	49	3	3	6	72	-1	0	0		—	—	—	—	—
02-03—San Jose	NHL	75	4	11	15	64	1	0	0		—	—	—	—	—
NHL Totals (3 years)		166	9	16	25	187	2	0	0						

SMITH, MIKE G STARS

PERSONAL: Born March 22, 1982, in Kingston, Ont. ... 6-3/189. ... Catches left.
TRANSACTIONS/CAREER NOTES: Selected by Dallas Stars in fifth round (fifth Stars pick, 70th overall) of NHL entry draft (June 23, 2001).

			REGULAR SEASON								PLAYOFFS						
Season Team	League	Gms.	Min	W	L	T	GA	SO	Avg.	SV%	Gms.	Min.	W	L	GA	SO	Avg.	SV%
00-01—Sudbury	OHL	43	2571	22	13	7	108	3	2.52	—	12	735	7	5	26	2	*2.12	—
01-02—Sudbury	OHL	53	3082	19	†28	5	157	3	3.06	—	5	302	1	4	15	0	2.98	—
02-03—Utah	AHL	11	613	5	5	0	33	0	3.23	—	—	—	—	—	—	—	—	—

SMITH, NATHAN C CANUCKS

PERSONAL: Born February 9, 1982, in Strathcona, Alta. ... 6-1/192. ... Shoots left. ... Brother of Jarrett Smith, center, Mighty Ducks of Anaheim organization.
TRANSACTIONS/CAREER NOTES: Selected by Vancouver Canucks in first round (first Canucks pick, 23rd overall) of NHL entry draft (June 24, 2000).

			REGULAR SEASON								PLAYOFFS				
Season Team	League	Gms.	G	A	Pts.	PIM	+/-	PP	SH		Gms.	G	A	Pts.	PIM
98-99—Swift Current	WHL	47	5	8	13	26	...	...	...		—	—	—	—	—
99-00—Swift Current	WHL	70	21	28	49	72	...	...	...		12	1	6	7	4
00-01—Swift Current	WHL	67	28	62	90	78	...	...	...		19	4	3	7	20
01-02—Swift Current	WHL	47	22	38	60	52	...	...	...		12	3	6	9	18
02-03—Manitoba	AHL	53	9	8	17	30	...	...	...		—	—	—	—	—

SMITH, NICK C MIGHTY DUCKS

PERSONAL: Born March 23, 1979, in Hamilton, Ont. ... 6-2/196. ... Shoots left.
TRANSACTIONS/CAREER NOTES: Selected by Florida Panthers in third round (fourth Panthers pick, 74th overall) of NHL entry draft (June 21, 1997). ... Signed as free agent by Anaheim Mighty Ducks (August 22, 2002). ... Re-signed by Mighty Ducks (July 23, 2003).

Season Team	League	REGULAR SEASON								PLAYOFFS				
		Gms.	G	A	Pts.	PIM	+/-	PP	SH	Gms.	G	A	Pts.	PIM
95-96—Shelburne	Jr. A	42	13	18	31	12	...	...	...	—	—	—	—	—
96-97—Barrie	OHL	63	10	18	28	15	...	...	...	9	3	8	11	13
97-98—Barrie	OHL	63	13	21	34	21	...	...	...	6	1	2	3	4
98-99—Barrie	OHL	68	19	34	53	18	...	...	...	12	3	8	11	8
99-00—Louisville	AHL	53	8	4	12	8	...	...	...	4	0	0	0	0
—Port Huron	UHL	2	1	1	2	0	...	...	...	—	—	—	—	—
00-01—Louisville	AHL	23	1	2	3	25	...	...	...	—	—	—	—	—
01-02—Bridgeport	AHL	22	3	6	9	4	...	...	...	—	—	—	—	—
—Florida	NHL	15	0	0	0	0	-1	0	0	—	—	—	—	—
—Saint John	AHL	41	8	9	17	10	...	...	...	—	—	—	—	—
02-03—Cincinnati	AHL	79	12	26	38	28	...	...	...	—	—	—	—	—
NHL Totals (1 year)		15	0	0	0	0	-1	0	0					

SMITH, TIM   C   CANUCKS

PERSONAL: Born July 21, 1981, in Rochfort Bridge, Alta. ... 5-9/160. ... Shoots left.
TRANSACTIONS/CAREER NOTES: Selected by Vancouver Canucks in ninth round (seventh Canucks pick, 272nd overall) of NHL entry draft (June 24, 2000).

Season Team	League	REGULAR SEASON								PLAYOFFS				
		Gms.	G	A	Pts.	PIM	+/-	PP	SH	Gms.	G	A	Pts.	PIM
98-99—Spokane	WHL	57	5	20	25	21	...	...	...	—	—	—	—	—
99-00—Spokane	WHL	71	26	70	96	65	...	...	...	15	7	7	14	32
00-01—Spokane	WHL	38	19	37	56	65	...	...	...	—	—	—	—	—
—Swift Current	WHL	30	12	22	34	38	...	...	...	19	10	14	24	38
01-02—Swift Current	WHL	67	28	47	75	123	...	...	...	12	7	6	13	20
02-03—Manitoba	AHL	3	0	0	0	0	...	...	...	—	—	—	—	—
—Columbia	ECHL	68	22	37	59	44	...	...	...	—	—	—	—	—

SMITH, WYATT   C   PREDATORS

PERSONAL: Born February 13, 1977, in Thief River Falls, Minn. ... 5-11/208. ... Shoots left.
TRANSACTIONS/CAREER NOTES: Selected by Phoenix Coyotes in ninth round (sixth Coyotes pick, 233rd overall) of NHL entry draft (June 21, 1997). ... Signed as free agent by Nashville Predators (July 15, 2002).

Season Team	League	REGULAR SEASON								PLAYOFFS				
		Gms.	G	A	Pts.	PIM	+/-	PP	SH	Gms.	G	A	Pts.	PIM
95-96—Univ. of Minnesota	WCHA	32	4	5	9	32	...	...	...	—	—	—	—	—
96-97—Univ. of Minnesota	WCHA	39	24	23	47	62	...	...	...	—	—	—	—	—
97-98—Univ. of Minnesota	WCHA	39	24	23	47	62	...	...	...	—	—	—	—	—
98-99—Univ. of Minnesota	WCHA	43	23	20	43	37	...	...	...	—	—	—	—	—
99-00—Springfield	AHL	60	14	26	40	26	...	...	...	5	2	3	5	13
—Phoenix	NHL	2	0	0	0	0	-2	0	0	—	—	—	—	—
00-01—Phoenix	NHL	42	3	7	10	13	7	0	1	—	—	—	—	—
—Springfield	AHL	18	5	7	12	11	...	...	...	—	—	—	—	—
01-02—Springfield	AHL	69	23	32	55	69	...	...	...	—	—	—	—	—
—Phoenix	NHL	10	0	0	0	0	-5	0	0	—	—	—	—	—
02-03—Milwaukee	AHL	56	24	27	51	89	...	...	...	—	—	—	—	—
—Nashville	NHL	11	1	0	1	0	-1	0	0	—	—	—	—	—
NHL Totals (4 years)		65	4	7	11	13	-1	0	1					

SMITHSON, JERRED   C   KINGS

PERSONAL: Born February 4, 1979, in Vernon, B.C. ... 6-2/197. ... Shoots left.
TRANSACTIONS/CAREER NOTES: Signed by Los Angeles Kings (July 31, 2003).

Season Team	League	REGULAR SEASON								PLAYOFFS				
		Gms.	G	A	Pts.	PIM	+/-	PP	SH	Gms.	G	A	Pts.	PIM
00-01—Lowell	AHL	24	1	1	2	10	...	...	...	—	—	—	—	—
—Trenton	ECHL	3	0	1	1	2	...	...	...	—	—	—	—	—
01-02—Manchester	AHL	78	5	13	18	45	...	...	...	—	—	—	—	—
02-03—Manchester	AHL	38	4	21	25	60	...	...	...	—	—	—	—	—
—Los Angeles	NHL	22	0	2	2	21	-5	0	0	—	—	—	—	—
NHL Totals (1 year)		22	0	2	2	21	-5	0	0					

SMOLINSKI, BRYAN   C   SENATORS

PERSONAL: Born December 27, 1971, in Toledo, Ohio ... 6-1/208. ... Shoots right. ... Full Name: Bryan Anthony Smolinski.
TRANSACTIONS/CAREER NOTES: Selected by Boston Bruins in first round (first Bruins pick, 21st overall) of NHL entry draft (June 16, 1990). ... Injured knee (April 14, 1994); missed one game. ... Suffered charley horse (April 1995); missed four games. ... Traded by Bruins with RW Glen Murray to Pittsburgh Penguins for LW Kevin Stevens and C Shawn McEachern (August 2, 1995). ... Bruised knee (January 16, 1996); missed one game. ... Traded by Penguins to New York Islanders for D Darius Kasparaitis and C Andreas Johansson (November 17, 1996). ... Traded by Islanders with RW Zigmund Palffy, G Marcel Cousineau and fourth-round pick (C Daniel Johansson) in 1999 draft to Los Angeles Kings for C Olli Jokinen, LW Josh Green, D Mathieu Biron and first-round pick (LW Taylor Pyatt) in 1999 draft (June 20, 1999). ... Sprained knee (April 3, 1999); missed final three games of season. ... Suffered back spasms (April 3, 2001); missed final two games of season. ... Suffered back spasms (October 26, 2001); missed one game. ... Suffered from the flu (January 24, 2002); missed one game. ... Traded by Kings to Ottawa Senators for D Tim Gleason (March 11, 2003). ... Re-signed by Senators (June 22, 2003).
STATISTICAL PLATEAUS: Three-goal games: 1994-95 (1), 2000-01 (1), 2002-03 (1). Total: 3.

Season Team	League	REGULAR SEASON								PLAYOFFS				
		Gms.	G	A	Pts.	PIM	+/-	PP	SH	Gms.	G	A	Pts.	PIM
87-88—Detroit Little Caesars ..	MNHL	80	43	77	120	...	...	...	...	—	—	—	—	—
88-89—Stratford Jr. B	OHA	46	32	62	94	132	...	...	...	—	—	—	—	—
89-90—Michigan State	CCHA	39	10	17	27	45	...	...	...	—	—	—	—	—
90-91—Michigan State	CCHA	35	9	12	21	24	...	...	...	—	—	—	—	—
91-92—Michigan State	CCHA	44	30	35	65	59	...	...	...	—	—	—	—	—
92-93—Michigan State	CCHA	40	31	37	68	93	...	...	...	—	—	—	—	—
—Boston	NHL	9	1	3	4	0	3	0	0	4	1	0	1	2
93-94—Boston	NHL	83	31	20	51	82	4	4	3	13	5	4	9	4
94-95—Boston	NHL	44	18	13	31	31	-3	6	0	5	0	1	1	4
95-96—Pittsburgh	NHL	81	24	40	64	69	6	8	2	18	5	4	9	10
96-97—Detroit	IHL	6	5	7	12	10	...	...	...	—	—	—	—	—
—New York Islanders	NHL	64	28	28	56	25	9	9	0	—	—	—	—	—
97-98—New York Islanders	NHL	81	13	30	43	34	-16	3	0	—	—	—	—	—
98-99—New York Islanders	NHL	82	16	24	40	49	-7	7	0	—	—	—	—	—
99-00—Los Angeles	NHL	79	20	36	56	48	2	2	0	4	0	0	0	2
00-01—Los Angeles	NHL	78	27	32	59	40	10	5	3	13	1	5	6	14
01-02—Los Angeles	NHL	80	13	25	38	56	7	4	1	7	2	0	2	2
02-03—Los Angeles	NHL	58	18	20	38	18	-1	6	1	—	—	—	—	—
—Ottawa	NHL	10	3	5	8	2	1	0	0	18	2	7	9	6
NHL Totals (11 years)		749	212	276	488	454	15	54	10	82	16	21	37	44

SMREK, PETER   D   SENATORS

PERSONAL: Born February 16, 1979, in Martin, Czechoslovakia. ... 6-1/194. ... Shoots right. ... Name pronounced SMAIR-ehk.
TRANSACTIONS/CAREER NOTES: Selected by St. Louis Blues in third round (second Blues pick, 85th overall) of NHL entry draft (June 26, 1999). ... Traded by Blues to New York Rangers for D Alexei Gusarov (March 5, 2001). ... Bruised ribs (March 10, 2001); missed two games. ... Traded by Rangers to Nashville Predators for D Richard Lintner (March 19, 2002). ... Traded by Predators to Ottawa Senators (June 25, 2003).

Season Team	League	REGULAR SEASON								PLAYOFFS				
		Gms.	G	A	Pts.	PIM	+/-	PP	SH	Gms.	G	A	Pts.	PIM
97-98—Martimex Martin Jrs. ...	Slov. Jr.	23	0	5	5	24	...	...	...	—	—	—	—	—
98-99—Des Moines	USHL	52	6	26	32	59	...	...	...	—	—	—	—	—
99-00—Worcester	AHL	64	5	19	24	26	...	...	...	2	0	0	0	4
—Peoria	ECHL	4	1	1	2	2	...	...	...	—	—	—	—	—
00-01—Worcester	AHL	50	2	7	9	71	...	...	...	—	—	—	—	—
—St. Louis	NHL	6	2	0	2	2	1	0	0	—	—	—	—	—
—New York Rangers	NHL	14	0	3	3	12	1	0	0	—	—	—	—	—
—Hartford	AHL	—	—	—	—	—	...	...	...	5	0	2	2	2
01-02—New York Rangers	NHL	8	0	1	1	4	-7	0	0	—	—	—	—	—
—Hartford	AHL	50	2	5	7	36	...	...	...	—	—	—	—	—
—Slovakian Oly. team	Int'l	4	0	0	0	0	...	...	...	—	—	—	—	—
—Milwaukee	AHL	8	0	2	2	4	...	...	...	—	—	—	—	—
02-03—Milwaukee	AHL	68	3	20	23	70	...	...	...	—	—	—	—	—
NHL Totals (2 years)		28	2	4	6	18	-5	0	0					

SMYTH, BRAD   RW   SENATORS

PERSONAL: Born March 13, 1973, in Ottawa ... 6-1/200. ... Shoots right. ... Name pronounced SMIHTH.
TRANSACTIONS/CAREER NOTES: Signed as non-drafted free agent by Florida Panthers (October 4, 1993). ... Traded by Panthers to Los Angeles Kings for third-round pick (D Vratislav Cech) in 1997 draft (November 28, 1996). ... Traded by Kings to New York Rangers for conditional draft pick (November 14, 1997). ... Signed as free agent by Nashville Predators (July 16, 1998). ... Traded by Predators to New York Rangers for future considerations (May 3, 1999). ... Signed as free agent by Ottawa Senators (August 1, 2002).

Season Team	League	REGULAR SEASON								PLAYOFFS				
		Gms.	G	A	Pts.	PIM	+/-	PP	SH	Gms.	G	A	Pts.	PIM
90-91—London	OHL	29	2	6	8	22	...	...	...	—	—	—	—	—
91-92—London	OHL	58	17	18	35	93	...	...	...	10	2	0	2	8
92-93—London	OHL	66	54	55	109	118	...	...	...	12	7	8	15	25
93-94—Cincinnati	IHL	30	7	3	10	54	...	...	...	—	—	—	—	—
—Birmingham	ECHL	29	26	30	56	38	...	...	...	10	8	8	16	19
94-95—Cincinnati	IHL	26	2	11	13	34	...	...	...	1	0	0	0	2
—Birmingham	ECHL	36	33	35	68	52	...	...	...	3	5	2	7	0
—Springfield	AHL	3	0	0	0	7	...	...	...	—	—	—	—	—
95-96—Carolina	AHL	68	*68	58	*126	80	...	...	...	—	—	—	—	—
—Florida	NHL	7	1	1	2	4	-3	1	0	—	—	—	—	—
96-97—Florida	NHL	8	1	0	1	2	-3	0	0	—	—	—	—	—
—Los Angeles	NHL	44	8	8	16	74	-7	0	0	—	—	—	—	—
—Phoenix	IHL	3	5	2	7	0	...	...	...	—	—	—	—	—
97-98—Los Angeles	NHL	9	1	3	4	4	-1	0	0	—	—	—	—	—
—Hartford	AHL	57	29	33	62	79	...	...	...	15	12	8	20	11
—New York Rangers	NHL	1	0	0	0	0	0	0	0	—	—	—	—	—
98-99—Milwaukee	IHL	34	11	16	27	21	...	...	...	—	—	—	—	—
—Nashville	NHL	3	0	0	0	6	-1	0	0	—	—	—	—	—
—Hartford	AHL	36	25	19	44	48	...	...	...	7	6	0	6	14
99-00—Hartford	AHL	80	39	37	76	62	...	...	...	23	13	10	23	8
00-01—Hartford	AHL	77	*50	29	79	110	...	...	...	5	2	3	5	8
—New York Rangers	NHL	4	1	0	1	4	0	0	0	—	—	—	—	—
01-02—Hartford	AHL	79	34	48	82	90	...	...	...	10	3	8	11	14
02-03—Binghamton	AHL	69	24	32	56	77	...	...	...	—	—	—	—	—
—Ottawa	NHL	12	3	1	4	15	-2	2	0	—	—	—	—	—
NHL Totals (6 years)		88	15	13	28	109	-17	3	0					

SMYTH, RYAN   LW   OILERS

PERSONAL: Born February 21, 1976, in Banff, Alta. ... 6-1/195. ... Shoots left. ... Brother of Kevin Smyth, left winger with Hartford Whalers (1993-94 through 1995-96). ... Name pronounced SMIHTH.
TRANSACTIONS/CAREER NOTES: Selected by Edmonton Oilers in first round (second Oilers pick, sixth overall) of NHL entry draft (June 28, 1994). ... Tore medial collateral ligament in knee (January 20, 1998); missed 15 games. ... Bruised thigh (December 27, 1998); missed one game. ... Fractured jaw (March 10, 1999); missed seven games. ... Fractured right ankle (November 16, 2001); missed 21 games.
STATISTICAL PLATEAUS: Three-goal games: 1996-97 (1), 1999-00 (1), 2000-01 (2). Total: 4.

				REGULAR SEASON							PLAYOFFS			
Season Team	League	Gms.	G	A	Pts.	PIM	+/-	PP	SH	Gms.	G	A	Pts.	PIM
91-92—Moose Jaw	WHL	2	0	0	0	0	...	...	...	—	—	—	—	—
92-93—Moose Jaw	WHL	64	19	14	33	59	...	...	...	—	—	—	—	—
93-94—Moose Jaw	WHL	72	50	55	105	88	...	...	...	—	—	—	—	—
94-95—Moose Jaw	WHL	50	41	45	86	66	...	...	...	10	6	9	15	22
—Edmonton	NHL	3	0	0	0	0	-1	0	0	—	—	—	—	—
95-96—Edmonton	NHL	48	2	9	11	28	-10	1	0	—	—	—	—	—
—Cape Breton	AHL	9	6	5	11	4	...	...	...	—	—	—	—	—
96-97—Edmonton	NHL	82	39	22	61	76	-7	†20	0	12	5	5	10	12
97-98—Edmonton	NHL	65	20	13	33	44	-24	10	0	12	1	3	4	16
98-99—Edmonton	NHL	71	13	18	31	62	0	6	0	3	3	0	3	0
99-00—Edmonton	NHL	82	28	26	54	58	-2	11	0	5	1	0	1	6
00-01—Edmonton	NHL	82	31	39	70	58	10	11	0	6	3	4	7	4
01-02—Edmonton	NHL	61	15	35	50	48	7	7	1	—	—	—	—	—
—Can. Olympic team	Int'l	6	0	1	1	0	...	...	...	—	—	—	—	—
02-03—Edmonton	NHL	66	27	34	61	67	5	10	0	6	2	0	2	16
NHL Totals (9 years)		560	175	196	371	441	-22	76	1	44	15	12	27	54

SNOW, GARTH   G   ISLANDERS

PERSONAL: Born July 28, 1969, in Wrentham, Mass. ... 6-3/208. ... Catches left.
TRANSACTIONS/CAREER NOTES: Selected by Quebec Nordiques in sixth round (sixth Nordiques pick, 114th overall) of NHL entry draft (June 13, 1987). ... Nordiques franchise moved to Colorado and renamed Avalanche for 1995-96 season (June 21, 1995). ... Rights traded by Avalanche to Philadelphia Flyers for third-(traded to Washington) and sixth-(G Kai Fischer) round picks in 1996 draft (July 12, 1995). ... Pulled groin (March 27, 1997); missed three games. ... Traded by Flyers to Vancouver Canucks for G Sean Burke (March 4, 1998). ... Strained hip flexor (March 18, 1998); missed three games. ... Strained hip flexor (October 31, 1998); missed two games. ... Injured finger (September 21, 1999); missed two games. ... Fractured finger (October 13, 1999); missed 15 games. ... Signed as free agent by Pittsburgh Penguins (October 10, 2000). ... Suspended two games by NHL for fighting incident (December 16, 2000). ... Strained groin (February 7, 2001); missed 25 games. ... Signed as free agent by New York Islanders (July 1, 2001). ... Suspended two games by NHL for attempting to injure another player (November 22, 2002). ... Re-signed by Islanders (July 22, 2003).

					REGULAR SEASON						PLAYOFFS						
Season Team	League	Gms.	Min.	W	L	T	GA	SO	Avg.	SV%	Gms.	Min.	W	L	GA	SO	Avg.	SV%
88-89—Univ. of Maine	Hockey East	5	241	2	2	0	14	1	3.49	—	—	—	—	—	—	—	—	—
89-90—Univ. of Maine	Hockey East								Did not play.		—	—	—	—	—	—	—	—
90-91—Univ. of Maine	Hockey East	25	1290	18	4	0	64	0	2.98	—	—	—	—	—	—	—	—	—
91-92—Univ. of Maine	Hockey East	31	1792	25	4	2	73	2	2.44	—	—	—	—	—	—	—	—	—
92-93—Univ. of Maine	Hockey East	23	1210	21	0	1	42	1	2.08	—	—	—	—	—	—	—	—	—
93-94—U.S. national team	Int'l	23	1324	13	5	3	71	1	3.22	—	—	—	—	—	—	—	—	—
—Quebec	NHL	5	279	3	2	0	16	0	3.44	.874	—	—	—	—	—	—	—	—
—U.S. Olympic team	Int'l	5	299	1	2	2	17	0	3.41	—	—	—	—	—	—	—	—	—
—Cornwall	AHL	16	927	6	5	3	51	0	3.30	—	13	790	8	5	42	0	3.19	—
94-95—Cornwall	AHL	62	3558	*32	20	7	162	3	2.73	—	8	402	4	3	14	†2	*2.09	—
—Quebec	NHL	2	119	1	1	0	11	0	5.55	.825	1	9	0	1	1	0	6.67	.667
95-96—Philadelphia	NHL	26	1437	12	8	4	69	0	2.88	.894	1	1	0	0	0	0	...	—
96-97—Philadelphia	NHL	35	1884	14	8	8	79	2	2.52	.903	12	699	8	4	33	0	2.83	.892
97-98—Philadelphia	NHL	29	1651	14	9	4	67	1	2.43	.902	—	—	—	—	—	—	—	—
—Vancouver	NHL	12	504	3	6	0	26	0	3.10	.901	—	—	—	—	—	—	—	—
98-99—Vancouver	NHL	65	3501	20	†31	8	†171	6	2.93	.900	—	—	—	—	—	—	—	—
99-00—Vancouver	NHL	32	1712	10	15	3	76	1	2.66	.902	—	—	—	—	—	—	—	—
00-01—Wilkes-Barre/Scranton	AHL	3	178	2	1	0	7	0	2.36	—	—	—	—	—	—	—	—	—
—Pittsburgh	NHL	35	2032	14	15	4	101	3	2.98	.900	—	—	—	—	—	—	—	—
01-02—New York Islanders	NHL	25	1217	10	7	2	55	2	2.71	.900	1	26	0	0	2	0	4.62	.895
02-03—New York Islanders	NHL	43	2390	16	17	5	92	1	2.31	.918	5	305	1	4	12	1	2.36	.910
NHL Totals (10 years)		309	16726	117	119	38	763	15	2.74	.902	20	1040	9	8	48	1	2.77	.896

SNYDER, DAN   C   THRASHERS

PERSONAL: Born February 23, 1978, in Elmira, Ont. ... 6-0/190. ... Shoots left.
TRANSACTIONS/CAREER NOTES: Signed as non-drafted free agent by Atlanta Thrashers (June 28, 1999). ... Suspended three games by NHL for elbowing incident (March 25, 2002).

				REGULAR SEASON							PLAYOFFS			
Season Team	League	Gms.	G	A	Pts.	PIM	+/-	PP	SH	Gms.	G	A	Pts.	PIM
95-96—Owen Sound	OHL	63	8	17	25	78	...	...	...	—	—	—	—	—
96-97—Owen Sound	OHL	57	17	29	46	96	...	...	...	4	2	3	5	8
97-98—Owen Sound	OHL	46	23	33	56	74	...	...	...	—	—	—	—	—
98-99—Owen Sound	OHL	64	27	67	94	110	...	...	...	16	8	5	13	30
99-00—Orlando	IHL	68	12	13	25	121	...	...	...	6	1	2	3	4
00-01—Orlando	IHL	78	13	30	43	127	...	...	...	16	7	3	10	20
—Atlanta	NHL	2	0	0	0	0	0	0	0	—	—	—	—	—
01-02—Chicago	AHL	56	11	24	35	115	...	...	...	22	7	10	17	25
—Atlanta	NHL	11	1	1	2	30	-3	0	0	—	—	—	—	—
02-03—Chicago	AHL	35	11	12	23	39	...	...	...	—	—	—	—	—
—Atlanta	NHL	36	10	4	14	34	-4	0	1	—	—	—	—	—
NHL Totals (3 years)		49	11	5	16	64	-7	0	1					

S

SOIN, SERGEI — C/LW — PREDATORS

PERSONAL: Born March 31, 1982, in Moscow, U.S.S.R. ... 6-0/176. ... Shoots left.
TRANSACTIONS/CAREER NOTES: Selected by Colorado Avalanche in second round (third Avalanche pick, 50th overall) of NHL entry draft (June 24, 2000). ... Traded by Avalanche to Nashville Predators for D Tomas Slovak (June 22, 2003).

		REGULAR SEASON								PLAYOFFS				
Season Team	League	Gms.	G	A	Pts.	PIM	+/-	PP	SH	Gms.	G	A	Pts.	PIM
98-99—Kryla Sov. Moscow.....	Russian	20	1	2	3	4	...	...	...	—	—	—	—	—
99-00—Kryla Sov. Moscow.....	Russian					Statistics unavailable.				—	—	—	—	—
01-02—Kryla Sov. Moscow.....	Russian	41	5	7	12	8	...	...	...	—	—	—	—	—
02-03—Kryla Sov. Moscow.....	Russ9	8	6	14	40	...	...	...	—	—	—	—	—	—

SOMERVUORI, EERO — RW — LIGHTNING

PERSONAL: Born February 7, 1979, in Jarvenpaa, Finland ... 5-10/167. ... Shoots right. ... Name pronounced ai-AIR-oh soh-muhr-VOH-ree.
TRANSACTIONS/CAREER NOTES: Selected by Tampa Bay Lightning in seventh round (ninth Lightning pick, 170th overall) of NHL entry draft (June 21, 1997). ... Re-signed by Lightning (June 4, 2003).

		REGULAR SEASON								PLAYOFFS				
Season Team	League	Gms.	G	A	Pts.	PIM	+/-	PP	SH	Gms.	G	A	Pts.	PIM
94-95—Jokerit Helsinki	Finland Jr.	26	9	12	21	6	...	...	...	—	—	—	—	—
95-96—Jokerit Helsinki	Finland Jr.	28	14	12	26	10	...	...	...	9	4	1	5	4
—Jokerit Helsinki	Finland	6	1	2	3	0	...	...	...	—	—	—	—	—
—Jarvenpaa	Finland Div. 2	1	0	0	0	0	...	...	...	—	—	—	—	—
96-97—Jokerit Helsinki	Finland	35	1	1	2	2	...	...	...	5	0	0	0	0
—Jokerit Helsinki	Finland Jr.	28	20	19	39	30	...	...	...	5	3	0	3	4
97-98—Jokerit Helsinki	Finland	42	3	7	10	12	...	...	...	8	2	1	3	6
—Jokerit Helsinki	Finland Jr.	14	4	8	12	2	...	...	...	—	—	—	—	—
98-99—Jokerit Helsinki	Finland	50	7	8	15	24	...	...	...	3	1	0	1	6
—Jokerit Helsinki	Finland Jr.	4	1	1	2	2	...	...	...	—	—	—	—	—
99-00—Jokerit Helsinki	Finland	54	6	6	12	10	...	...	...	11	1	0	1	0
00-01—HPK Hameenlinna......	Finland	56	14	6	20	35	...	...	...	—	—	—	—	—
01-02—HPK Hameenlinna......	Finland	56	25	23	48	34	...	...	...	8	2	2	4	6
02-03—HPK Hameenlinna......	Finland	56	21	24	45	42	...	...	...	—	—	—	—	—

S

SOMIK, RADOVAN — RW — FLYERS

PERSONAL: Born May 5, 1977, in Martin, Czechoslovakia ... 6-2/194. ... Shoots right.
TRANSACTIONS/CAREER NOTES: Re-signed by Flyers (July 30, 2003).

		REGULAR SEASON								PLAYOFFS				
Season Team	League	Gms.	G	A	Pts.	PIM	+/-	PP	SH	Gms.	G	A	Pts.	PIM
93-94—Martimex ZTS Martin..	Slovakia	1	0	0	0	0	...	...	...	—	—	—	—	—
94-95—Martimex ZTS Martin..	Slovakia	28	4	0	4	31	...	...	...	3	1	0	1	2
95-96—Martimex ZTS Martin..	Slovakia	25	3	6	9	8	...	...	...	9	1	0	1	...
96-97—Martimex ZTS Martin..	Slovakia	35	3	5	8		...	...	...	3	0	0	0	...
97-98—Martimex ZTS Martin..	Slovakia	26	6	9	15	10	...	...	...	3	0	0	0	0
98-99—Dulka Trencin..............	Slovakia	26	1	4	5	6	...	...	...	—	—	—	—	—
99-00—Martimex ZTS Martin..	Slovakia	40	38	28	66	32	...	...	...	—	—	—	—	—
00-01—HC Continental Zlin.....	Czech Rep.	46	15	10	25	22	...	...	...	6	1	0	1	0
01-02—HC Continental Zlin.....	Czech Rep.	37	14	14	28	22	...	...	...	11	4	3	7	37
02-03—Philadelphia	NHL	60	8	10	18	10	9	0	1	5	1	1	2	6
NHL Totals (1 year)..............		60	8	10	18	10	9	0	1	5	1	1	2	6

SONNENBERG, MARTIN — LW — FLAMES

PERSONAL: Born January 23, 1978, in Wetaskiwin, Alta. ... 6-0/184. ... Shoots left.
TRANSACTIONS/CAREER NOTES: Signed as non-drafted free agent by Pittsburgh Penguins (October 9, 1998). ... Signed as free agent by Calgary Flames (July 9, 2002).

		REGULAR SEASON								PLAYOFFS				
Season Team	League	Gms.	G	A	Pts.	PIM	+/-	PP	SH	Gms.	G	A	Pts.	PIM
95-96—Saskatoon...................	WHL	58	8	7	15	24	...	...	...	3	0	0	0	2
96-97—Saskatoon...................	WHL	72	38	26	64	79	...	...	...	—	—	—	—	—
97-98—Saskatoon...................	WHL	72	40	52	92	87	...	...	...	6	1	3	4	9
98-99—Syracuse	AHL	37	16	9	25	31	...	...	...	—	—	—	—	—
—Pittsburgh...................	NHL	44	1	1	2	19	-2	0	0	7	0	0	0	0
99-00—Pittsburgh...................	NHL	14	1	2	3	0	0	1	0	—	—	—	—	—
—Wilkes-Barre/Scranton	AHL	62	20	33	53	109	...	...	...	—	—	—	—	—
00-01—Wilkes-Barre/Scranton	AHL	73	14	18	32	89	...	...	...	21	4	3	7	6
01-02—Wilkes-Barre/Scranton	AHL	78	20	30	50	127	...	...	...	—	—	—	—	—
02-03—Saint John	AHL	54	11	10	21	63	...	...	...	—	—	—	—	—
NHL Totals (2 years)...........		58	2	3	5	19	-2	1	0	7	0	0	0	0

SOPEL, BRENT — D — CANUCKS

PERSONAL: Born January 7, 1977, in Calgary ... 6-1/213. ... Shoots right. ... Name pronounced SOH-puhl.
TRANSACTIONS/CAREER NOTES: Selected by Vancouver Canucks in sixth round (sixth Canucks pick, 144th overall) of NHL entry draft (July 8, 1995).

Season Team	League	REGULAR SEASON								PLAYOFFS				
		Gms.	G	A	Pts.	PIM	+/-	PP	SH	Gms.	G	A	Pts.	PIM
93-94—Saskatoon..................	WHL	11	2	2	4	2	...	...	...	—	—	—	—	—
94-95—Saskatoon..................	WHL	22	1	10	11	31	...	...	...	—	—	—	—	—
—Swift Current	WHL	41	4	19	23	50	...	...	...	3	0	3	3	0
95-96—Swift Current	WHL	71	13	48	61	87	...	...	...	6	1	2	3	4
—Syracuse..................	AHL	1	0	0	0	0	...	...	...	—	—	—	—	—
96-97—Swift Current	WHL	62	15	41	56	109	...	...	...	10	5	11	16	32
—Syracuse..................	AHL	2	0	0	0	0	...	...	...	3	0	0	0	0
97-98—Syracuse..................	AHL	76	10	33	43	70	...	...	...	5	0	7	7	12
98-99—Syracuse..................	AHL	53	10	21	31	59	...	...	...	—	—	—	—	—
—Vancouver...............	NHL	5	1	0	1	4	-1	1	0	—	—	—	—	—
99-00—Syracuse..................	AHL	50	6	25	31	67	...	...	...	4	0	2	2	8
—Vancouver...............	NHL	18	2	4	6	12	9	0	0	—	—	—	—	—
00-01—Vancouver...............	NHL	52	4	10	14	10	4	0	0	4	0	0	0	2
—Kansas City...............	IHL	4	0	1	1	0	...	...	...	—	—	—	—	—
01-02—Vancouver...............	NHL	66	8	17	25	44	21	1	0	6	0	2	2	2
02-03—Vancouver..................	NHL	81	7	30	37	23	-15	6	0	14	2	6	8	4
NHL Totals (5 years)...........		222	22	61	83	93	18	8	0	24	2	8	10	8

SOUZA, MIKE   LW/C

PERSONAL: Born January 28, 1978, in Melrose, Mass. ... 6-1/190. ... Shoots left.
HIGH SCHOOL: Wakefield (Mass.).
COLLEGE: New Hampshire.
TRANSACTIONS/CAREER NOTES: Selected by Chicago Blackhawks in third round (fourth Blackhawks pick, 67th overall) of NHL entry draft (June 21, 1997).

Season Team	League	REGULAR SEASON								PLAYOFFS				
		Gms.	G	A	Pts.	PIM	+/-	PP	SH	Gms.	G	A	Pts.	PIM
95-96—Wakefield HS	Mass. H.S.	21	25	31	56	22	...	...	...	—	—	—	—	—
96-97—Univ. of New Hamp.....	Hockey East	33	14	10	24	14	...	...	...	—	—	—	—	—
97-98—Univ. of New Hamp.....	Hockey East	38	13	12	25	36	...	...	...	—	—	—	—	—
98-99—Univ. of New Hamp.....	Hockey East	41	23	42	65	38	...	...	...	—	—	—	—	—
99-00—Univ. of New Hamp.....	Hockey East	38	15	25	40	58	...	...	...	—	—	—	—	—
00-01—Norfolk......................	AHL	75	14	17	31	44	...	...	...	3	0	0	0	2
01-02—Norfolk......................	AHL	66	20	11	31	58	...	...	...	—	—	—	—	—
02-03—Norfolk......................	AHL	5	2	2	4	7	...	...	...	—	—	—	—	—
—Bridgeport..................	AHL	59	7	15	22	89	...	...	...	—	—	—	—	—

SPACEK, JAROSLAV   D   BLUE JACKETS

PERSONAL: Born February 11, 1974, in Rokycany, Czechoslovakia ... 5-11/204. ... Shoots left.
TRANSACTIONS/CAREER NOTES: Selected by Florida Panthers in fifth round (fifth Panthers pick, 117th overall) of NHL entry draft (June 27, 1998). ... Suffered from the flu (April 7, 1999); missed three games. ... Traded by Panthers to Chicago Blackhawks for D Anders Eriksson (November 6, 2000). ... Fractured left shoulder (January 14, 2001); missed 18 games. ... Suffered injury (November 13, 2001); missed two games. ... Fractured finger (November 25, 2001); missed eight games. ... Traded by Blackhawks with second-round pick in 2003 draft to Columbus Blue Jackets for D Lyle Odelein (March 19, 2002).

Season Team	League	REGULAR SEASON								PLAYOFFS				
		Gms.	G	A	Pts.	PIM	+/-	PP	SH	Gms.	G	A	Pts.	PIM
92-93—Skoda Plzen................	Czech.	16	1	3	4		...	...	...	—	—	—	—	—
93-94—Skoda Plzen................	Czech Rep.	34	2	10	12		...	...	...	—	—	—	—	—
94-95—Interconex Plzen	Czech Rep.	38	4	8	12	14	...	...	...	3	1	0	1	2
95-96—ZKZ Plzen	Czech Rep.	40	3	10	13	42	...	...	...	3	0	1	1	4
96-97—ZKZ Plzen	Czech Rep.	52	9	29	38	44	...	...	...	—	—	—	—	—
97-98—Farjestad Karlstad	Sweden	45	10	16	26	63	...	...	...	12	2	5	7	14
98-99—Florida......................	NHL	63	3	12	15	28	15	2	1	—	—	—	—	—
—New Haven	AHL	14	4	8	12	15	...	...	...	—	—	—	—	—
99-00—Florida......................	NHL	82	10	26	36	53	7	4	0	4	0	0	0	0
00-01—Florida......................	NHL	12	2	1	3	8	-4	1	0	—	—	—	—	—
—Chicago....................	NHL	50	5	18	23	20	7	2	0	—	—	—	—	—
01-02—Chicago....................	NHL	60	3	10	13	29	5	0	0	—	—	—	—	—
—Czech Rep. Oly. team..	Int'l	4	0	0	0	0	...	...	...	—	—	—	—	—
—Columbus	NHL	14	2	3	5	24	-9	1	1	—	—	—	—	—
02-03—Columbus	NHL	81	9	36	45	70	-23	5	0	—	—	—	—	—
NHL Totals (5 years)...........		362	34	106	140	232	-2	15	2	4	0	0	0	0

SPANG, DAN   D   SHARKS

PERSONAL: Born August 16, 1983, in Winchester, Mass. ... 6-0/200. ... Shoots left.
TRANSACTIONS/CAREER NOTES: Selected by San Jose Sharks in second round (second Sharks pick, 52nd overall) of NHL entry draft (June 22, 2002).

Season Team	League	REGULAR SEASON								PLAYOFFS				
		Gms.	G	A	Pts.	PIM	+/-	PP	SH	Gms.	G	A	Pts.	PIM
01-02—Winchester	USHS (East)	6	9	8	17	14	...	...	...	—	—	—	—	—
02-03—Boston University	ECAC	27	3	6	9	14	...	...	...	—	—	—	—	—

SPANHEL, MARTIN LW BLUE JACKETS

PERSONAL: Born July 1, 1977, in Zlin, Czechoslovakia. ... 6-2/202. ... Shoots left. ... Name pronounced spah-NEHL.
TRANSACTIONS/CAREER NOTES: Selected by Philadelphia Flyers in sixth round (fifth Flyers pick, 152nd overall) of NHL entry draft (July 8, 1995). ... Traded by Flyers with first (traded to Winnipeg)- and fourth-round (traded to Buffalo) picks in 1996 draft to San Jose Sharks for RW Pat Falloon (November 16, 1995). ... Signed as free agent by Columbus Blue Jackets (June 7, 2000).

		REGULAR SEASON								PLAYOFFS				
Season Team	League	Gms.	G	A	Pts.	PIM	+/-	PP	SH	Gms.	G	A	Pts.	PIM
94-95—ZPS Zlin	Czech. Jrs.	33	25	16	41	...	...	...	...	—	—	—	—	—
—ZPS Zlin	Czech. Jrs.	33	25	16	41	...	...	...	...	—	—	—	—	—
—ZPS Zlin	Czech Rep.	1	0	0	0	...	...	...	...	—	—	—	—	—
95-96—Moose Jaw	WHL	61	4	12	16	33	...	...	...	—	—	—	—	—
—Lethbridge	WHL	6	1	0	1	0	...	...	...	—	—	—	—	—
96-97—ZPS Zlin	Czech Rep.	22	3	6	9	20	...	...	...	—	—	—	—	—
—ZPS Zlin	Czech. Jrs.	6	6	3	9	2	...	...	...	—	—	—	—	—
—Karlovy Vary	Czech. D-II	7	4	3	7		...	...	...	—	—	—	—	—
97-98—ZPS Zlin	Czech Rep.	40	7	9	16	70	...	...	...	—	—	—	—	—
98-99—HC Keramika Plzen	Czech Rep.	49	13	13	26	60	...	...	...	5	2	1	3	...
99-00—HC Keramika Plzen	Czech Rep.	52	21	27	48	86	...	...	...	7	1	4	5	12
00-01—Syracuse	AHL	67	11	13	24	75	...	...	...	2	0	0	0	8
—Columbus	NHL	6	1	0	1	2	-1	0	0	—	—	—	—	—
01-02—Syracuse	AHL	50	7	12	19	43	...	...	...	—	—	—	—	—
—Columbus	NHL	4	1	0	1	2	-2	0	0	—	—	—	—	—
02-03—Sparta Praha	Czech Rep.	40	5	5	10	46	...	...	...	—	—	—	—	—
NHL Totals (2 years)		10	2	0	2	4	-3	0	0					

SPEZZA, JASON C SENATORS

PERSONAL: Born June 13, 1983, in Mississauga, Ont. ... 6-2/201. ... Shoots right. ... Name pronounced speh-ZUH.
TRANSACTIONS/CAREER NOTES: Selected by Ottawa Senators in first round (first Senators pick, second overall) of NHL entry draft (June 23, 2001).

		REGULAR SEASON								PLAYOFFS				
Season Team	League	Gms.	G	A	Pts.	PIM	+/-	PP	SH	Gms.	G	A	Pts.	PIM
98-99—Brampton	OHL	67	22	49	71	18	...	...	...	—	—	—	—	—
99-00—Mississauga	OHL	52	24	37	61	33	...	...	...	—	—	—	—	—
00-01—Mississauga	OHL	15	7	23	30	11	...	...	...	—	—	—	—	—
—Windsor	OHL	41	36	50	86	32	...	...	...	9	4	5	9	10
01-02—Windsor	OHL	27	19	26	45	16	...	...	...	—	—	—	—	—
—Belleville	OHL	26	23	37	60	26	...	...	...	11	5	6	11	18
—Grand Rapids	AHL	—	—	—	—	—	...	...	...	3	1	0	1	2
02-03—Binghamton	AHL	43	22	32	54	71	...	...	...	—	—	—	—	—
—Ottawa	NHL	33	7	14	21	8	-3	3	0	3	1	1	2	0
NHL Totals (1 year)		33	7	14	21	8	-3	3	0	3	1	1	2	0

SPILLER, MATTHEW D COYOTES

PERSONAL: Born February 7, 1983, in Daysland, Alta. ... 6-5/210. ... Shoots left.
TRANSACTIONS/CAREER NOTES: Selected by Phoenix Coyotes in second round (second Coyotes pick, 31st overall) of NHL entry draft (June 23, 2001). ... Re-signed by Coyotes (June 1, 2003).

		REGULAR SEASON								PLAYOFFS				
Season Team	League	Gms.	G	A	Pts.	PIM	+/-	PP	SH	Gms.	G	A	Pts.	PIM
99-00—Seattle	WHL	60	1	10	11	108	...	...	...	7	0	0	0	25
00-01—Seattle	WHL	71	4	7	11	174	...	...	...	9	1	0	1	22
01-02—Seattle	WHL	72	8	23	31	168	...	...	...	1	0	0	0	4
02-03—Seattle	WHL	68	11	24	35	198	...	...	...	—	—	—	—	—

ST. JACQUES, BRUNO D HURRICANES

PERSONAL: Born August 22, 1980, in Montreal ... 6-2/204. ... Shoots left.
TRANSACTIONS/CAREER NOTES: Selected by Philadelphia Flyers in ninth round (12th Flyers pick, 253rd overall) of NHL entry draft (June 27, 1998). ... Traded by Flyers with RW Pavel Brendl to Carolina Hurricanes for RW Sami Kapanen and D Ryan Bast (February 7, 2003). ... Re-signed by Hurricanes (July 9, 2003).

		REGULAR SEASON								PLAYOFFS				
Season Team	League	Gms.	G	A	Pts.	PIM	+/-	PP	SH	Gms.	G	A	Pts.	PIM
97-98—Baie-Comeau	QMJHL	63	13	29	42	253	...	...	...	—	—	—	—	—
98-99—Baie-Comeau	QMJHL	49	1	21	22	138	...	...	...	—	—	—	—	—
99-00—Baie-Comeau	QMJHL	60	8	28	36	120	...	...	...	—	—	—	—	—
—Philadelphia	AHL	3	0	1	1	0	...	...	...	1	0	0	0	0
00-01—Philadelphia	AHL	45	1	16	17	83	...	...	...	10	1	0	1	16
01-02—Philadelphia	AHL	55	3	11	14	59	...	...	...	4	0	0	0	0
—Philadelphia	NHL	7	0	0	0	2	4	0	0	—	—	—	—	—
02-03—Philadelphia	AHL	30	0	7	7	46	...	...	...	—	—	—	—	—
—Philadelphia	NHL	6	0	0	0	2	-1	0	0	—	—	—	—	—
—Carolina	NHL	18	2	5	7	12	-3	0	0	—	—	—	—	—
—Lowell	AHL	8	1	1	2	8	...	...	...	—	—	—	—	—
NHL Totals (2 years)		31	2	5	7	16	0	0	0					

ST. LOUIS, MARTIN   RW   LIGHTNING

PERSONAL: Born June 18, 1975, in Laval, Que. ... 5-9/181. ... Shoots left.

TRANSACTIONS/CAREER NOTES: Signed as non-drafted free agent by Calgary Flames (February 18, 1998). ... Suffered concussion (March 15, 2000); missed two games. ... Signed as free agent by Tampa Bay Lightning (July 31, 2000). ... Bruised heel (November 6, 2001); missed one game. ... Fractured right leg (January 23, 2002); missed 26 games.

STATISTICAL PLATEAUS: Three-goal games: 2002-03 (1).

Season Team	League	REGULAR SEASON								PLAYOFFS				
		Gms.	G	A	Pts.	PIM	+/-	PP	SH	Gms.	G	A	Pts.	PIM
93-94—Vermont	ECAC	33	15	36	51	24	...	...	...	—	—	—	—	—
94-95—Vermont	ECAC	35	23	48	71	36	...	...	...	—	—	—	—	—
95-96—Vermont	ECAC	35	29	56	85	36	...	...	...	—	—	—	—	—
96-97—Vermont	ECAC	35	24	26	50	65	...	...	...	—	—	—	—	—
97-98—Cleveland	IHL	56	16	34	50	24	...	...	...	—	—	—	—	—
—Saint John	AHL	25	15	11	26	20	...	...	...	20	5	15	20	16
98-99—Calgary	NHL	13	1	1	2	10	-2	0	0	—	—	—	—	—
—Saint John	AHL	53	28	34	62	30	...	...	...	7	4	4	8	2
99-00—Saint John	AHL	17	15	11	26	14	...	...	...	—	—	—	—	—
—Calgary	NHL	56	3	15	18	22	-5	0	0	—	—	—	—	—
00-01—Tampa Bay	NHL	78	18	22	40	12	-4	3	3	—	—	—	—	—
01-02—Tampa Bay	NHL	53	16	19	35	20	4	6	1	—	—	—	—	—
02-03—Tampa Bay	NHL	82	33	37	70	32	10	12	3	11	7	5	12	0
NHL Totals (5 years)		282	71	94	165	96	3	21	7	11	7	5	12	0

STAIOS, STEVE   D   OILERS

PERSONAL: Born July 28, 1973, in Hamilton, Ont. ... 6-1/200. ... Shoots right. ... Name pronounced STAY-ohz.

TRANSACTIONS/CAREER NOTES: Selected by St. Louis Blues in second round (first Blues pick, 27th overall) of NHL entry draft (June 22, 1991). ... Traded by Blues with LW Kevin Sawyer to Boston Bruins for RW Steve Leach (March 8, 1996). ... Strained groin (November 6, 1996); missed 13 games. ... Claimed on waivers by Vancouver Canucks (March 18, 1997). ... Injured knee (February 24, 1999); missed 16 games. ... Selected by Atlanta Thrashers in NHL expansion draft (June 25, 1999). ... Sprained medial collateral ligament in right knee (November 20, 1999); missed four games. ... Injured groin (December 30, 1999); missed 16 games. ... Reinjured groin (February 15, 2000); missed final 27 games of season. ... Traded by Thrashers to New Jersey Devils for ninth-round pick (C Simon Gamache) in 2000 draft (June 12, 2000). ... Traded by Devils to Thrashers for future considerations (July 10, 2000). ... Suffered concussion (November 27, 2000); missed five games. ... Bruised foot (December 22, 2000); missed two games. ... Strained hamstring (January 23, 2001); missed two games. ... Strained groin (February 7, 2001); missed three games. ... Signed as free agent by Edmonton Oilers (July 12, 2001). ... Bruised foot (October 20, 2001); missed one game. ... Strained groin (February 5, 2002); missed four games.

Season Team	League	REGULAR SEASON								PLAYOFFS				
		Gms.	G	A	Pts.	PIM	+/-	PP	SH	Gms.	G	A	Pts.	PIM
89-90—Hamilton Jr. B	OHA	40	9	27	36	66	...	...	...	—	—	—	—	—
90-91—Niagara Falls	OHL	66	17	29	46	115	...	...	...	12	2	3	5	10
91-92—Niagara Falls	OHL	65	11	42	53	122	...	...	...	17	7	8	15	27
92-93—Niagara Falls	OHL	12	4	14	18	30	...	...	...	—	—	—	—	—
—Sudbury	OHL	53	13	44	57	67	...	...	...	11	5	6	11	22
93-94—Peoria	IHL	38	3	9	12	42	...	...	...	—	—	—	—	—
94-95—Peoria	IHL	60	3	13	16	64	...	...	...	6	0	0	0	10
95-96—Peoria	IHL	6	0	1	1	14	...	...	...	—	—	—	—	—
—Worcester	AHL	57	1	11	12	114	...	...	...	—	—	—	—	—
—Providence	AHL	7	1	4	5	8	...	...	...	—	—	—	—	—
—Boston	NHL	12	0	0	0	4	-5	0	0	3	0	0	0	0
96-97—Boston	NHL	54	3	8	11	71	-26	0	0	—	—	—	—	—
—Vancouver	NHL	9	0	6	6	20	2	0	0	—	—	—	—	—
97-98—Vancouver	NHL	77	3	4	7	134	-3	0	0	—	—	—	—	—
98-99—Vancouver	NHL	57	0	2	2	54	-12	0	0	—	—	—	—	—
99-00—Atlanta	NHL	27	2	3	5	66	-5	0	0	—	—	—	—	—
00-01—Atlanta	NHL	70	9	13	22	137	-23	4	0	—	—	—	—	—
01-02—Edmonton	NHL	73	5	5	10	108	10	0	0	—	—	—	—	—
02-03—Edmonton	NHL	76	5	21	26	96	13	1	3	6	0	0	0	4
NHL Totals (8 years)		455	27	62	89	690	-49	5	3	9	0	0	0	4

STAJAN, MATT   C   MAPLE LEAFS

PERSONAL: Born December 19, 1983, in Mississauga, Ont. ... 6-1/178. ... Shoots left. ... Full Name: Matthew Stajan.

TRANSACTIONS/CAREER NOTES: Selected by Toronto Maple Leafs in second round (second Maple Leafs pick, 57th overall) of NHL entry draft (June 22, 2002).

Season Team	League	REGULAR SEASON								PLAYOFFS				
		Gms.	G	A	Pts.	PIM	+/-	PP	SH	Gms.	G	A	Pts.	PIM
00-01—Belleville	OHL	57	9	18	27	27	...	...	...	7	1	6	7	5
01-02—Belleville	OHL	68	33	52	85	50	...	...	...	11	3	8	11	14
02-03—Belleville	OHL	57	34	60	94	75	...	...	...	—	—	—	—	—
—St. John's	AHL	1	0	1	1	0	...	...	...	—	—	—	—	—
—Toronto	NHL	1	1	0	1	0	1	0	0	—	—	—	—	—
NHL Totals (1 year)		1	1	0	1	0	1	0	0					

STEEN, ALEXANDER   C   MAPLE LEAFS

PERSONAL: Born March 1, 1984, in Winnipeg. ... 6-1/183. ... Shoots left. ... Son of Thomas Steen, center with Winnipeg Jets (1981-82 through 1994-95).

TRANSACTIONS/CAREER NOTES: Selected by Toronto Maple Leafs in first round (first Maple Leafs pick, 24th overall) of NHL entry draft (June 22, 2002).

Season Team	League	REGULAR SEASON								PLAYOFFS				
		Gms.	G	A	Pts.	PIM	+/-	PP	SH	Gms.	G	A	Pts.	PIM
01-02—Vastra Frolunda	Sweden	26	0	3	3	14	...	...	...	10	1	2	3	0
02-03—Vastra Frolunda	Sweden	45	5	10	15	18	...	...	...	16	2	3	5	4

STEFAN, PATRIK   C   THRASHERS

PERSONAL: Born September 16, 1980, in Pribram, Czechoslovakia ... 6-2/210. ... Shoots left.

TRANSACTIONS/CAREER NOTES: Selected by Atlanta Thrashers in first round (first Thrashers pick, first overall) of NHL entry draft (June 26, 1999). ... Suffered concussion (November 19, 1999); missed two games. ... Suffered back spasms (February 29, 2000); missed three games. ... Suffered from the flu (March 22, 2000); missed two games. ... Injured groin (September 26, 2000); missed first five games of season. ... Suffered from the flu (November 17, 2000); missed one game. ... Suffered concussion (November 22, 2000); missed three games. ... Suffered head injury (Deceber 29, 2000); missed one game. ... Strained groin (January 29, 2001); missed one games. ... Strained groin (February 7, 2001); missed three games. ... Suffered from the flu (February 23, 2001); missed one game. ... Fractured jaw (October 6, 2001); missed eight games. ... Injured elbow (November 4, 2001); missed nine games.

Season Team	League	REGULAR SEASON								PLAYOFFS				
		Gms.	G	A	Pts.	PIM	+/-	PP	SH	Gms.	G	A	Pts.	PIM
96-97—Sparta Praha	Czech Rep.	5	0	1	1	2	...	...	...	7	1	0	1	0
97-98—Sparta Praha	Czech Rep.	27	2	6	8	16	...	...	...	—	—	—	—	—
—Long Beach	IHL	25	5	15	20	10	...	...	...	10	1	1	2	2
98-99—Long Beach	IHL	33	11	24	35	26	...	...	...	—	—	—	—	—
99-00—Atlanta	NHL	72	5	20	25	30	-20	1	0	—	—	—	—	—
00-01—Atlanta	NHL	66	10	21	31	22	-3	0	0	—	—	—	—	—
01-02—Atlanta	NHL	59	7	16	23	22	-4	0	1	—	—	—	—	—
—Chicago	AHL	5	3	0	3	0	...	...	...	—	—	—	—	—
02-03—Atlanta	NHL	71	13	21	34	12	-10	3	0	—	—	—	—	—
NHL Totals (4 years)		268	35	78	113	86	-37	4	1					

STEPHENS, CHARLIE   C/RW   AVALANCHE

PERSONAL: Born April 5, 1981, in London, Ont. ... 6-3/220. ... Shoots right.

TRANSACTIONS/CAREER NOTES: Selected by Washington Capitals in second round (third Capitals pick, 31st overall) of NHL entry draft (June 26, 1999). ... Returned to draft pool by Capitals and selected by Colorado Avalanche in sixth round (ninth Avalanche pick, 196th overall) of NHL entry draft (June 23, 2001).

Season Team	League	REGULAR SEASON								PLAYOFFS				
		Gms.	G	A	Pts.	PIM	+/-	PP	SH	Gms.	G	A	Pts.	PIM
97-98—Toronto St. Michael's	OHL	58	9	21	30	38	...	...	...	—	—	—	—	—
98-99—Toronto St. Michael's	OHL	7	2	4	6	8	...	...	...	—	—	—	—	—
—Guelph	OHL	61	24	28	52	72	...	...	...	11	3	5	8	19
99-00—Guelph	OHL	56	16	34	50	87	...	...	...	6	1	3	4	15
00-01—Guelph	OHL	67	38	38	76	53	...	...	...	4	0	2	2	2
01-02—Guelph	OHL	4	1	2	3	2	...	...	...	—	—	—	—	—
—London	OHL	56	23	33	56	55	...	...	...	12	6	10	16	18
—Hershey	AHL	—	—	—	—	—	—	—	—	1	0	0	0	0
02-03—Hershey	AHL	74	17	33	50	38	...	...	...	—	—	—	—	—
—Colorado	NHL	2	0	0	0	0	0	0	0	—	—	—	—	—
NHL Totals (1 year)		2	0	0	0	0	0	0	0					

STEPP, JOEL   C/LW   MIGHTY DUCKS

PERSONAL: Born February 11, 1983, in Estevan, Sask. ... 6-1/185. ... Shoots left.

TRANSACTIONS/CAREER NOTES: Selected by Mighty Ducks of Anaheim in third round (third Mighty Ducks pick, 69th overall) of NHL entry draft (June 23, 2001).

Season Team	League	REGULAR SEASON								PLAYOFFS				
		Gms.	G	A	Pts.	PIM	+/-	PP	SH	Gms.	G	A	Pts.	PIM
00-01—Red Deer	WHL	70	24	13	37	89	...	...	...	22	6	3	9	24
01-02—Red Deer	WHL	70	27	26	53	59	...	...	...	23	11	11	22	24
02-03—Red Deer	WHL	24	4	11	15	18	...	...	...	—	—	—	—	—

STEVENS, SCOTT   D   DEVILS

PERSONAL: Born April 1, 1964, in Kitchener, Ont. ... 6-2/215. ... Shoots left. ... Brother of Mike Stevens, center/left winger with four NHL teams (1984-85 and 1987-88 through 1989-90).

TRANSACTIONS/CAREER NOTES: Selected by Washington Capitals in first round (first Capitals pick, fifth overall) of NHL entry draft (June 9, 1982). ... Bruised right knee (November 6, 1985); missed seven games. ... Fractured right index finger (December 14, 1986). ... Bruised shoulder (April 1988). ... Suffered from poison oak (November 1988). ... Fractured left foot (December 29, 1989); missed 17 games. ... Suspended three games by NHL for scratching (February 27, 1990). ... Bruised left shoulder (March 27, 1990). ... Dislocated left shoulder (May 3, 1990). ... Signed as free agent by St. Louis Blues (July 9, 1990); Blues owed Capitals two first-round draft picks among the top seven over next two years and $100,000 cash; upon failing to get a pick in the top seven in 1991, Blues forfeited their first-round pick in 1991 (LW Trevor Halverson), 1992 (D Sergei Gonchar), 1993 (D Brendan Witt), 1994 (traded to Toronto) and 1995 (LW Miikka Elomo) drafts to Capitals (July 9, 1990). ... Awarded to New Jersey Devils as compensation for Blues signing free agent RW/LW Brendan Shanahan (September 3, 1991). ... Strained right knee (February 20, 1992); missed 12 games. ... Suffered concussion (December 27, 1992); missed three games. ... Strained knee (November 19, 1993); missed one game. ... Suspended one game by NHL for highsticking incident (October 7, 1996). ... Suffered from the flu (December 23, 1996); missed one game. ... Suffered hip pointer (February 28, 1998); missed one game. ... Suffered from the flu (December 8, 1998); missed one game. ... Suffered back spasms (December 19, 1998); missed one game. ... Strained groin (March 15, 1999); missed five games. ... Suffered from the flu (January 8, 2000); missed two games. ... Suffered from the flu (March 24, 2000); missed one game.

			REGULAR SEASON								PLAYOFFS				
Season Team	League	Gms.	G	A	Pts.	PIM	+/-	PP	SH	Gms.	G	A	Pts.	PIM
80-81—Kitchener Jr. B	OHA	39	7	33	40	82	...	...	...	—	—	—	—	—
—Kitchener	OHL	1	0	0	0	0	...	...	...	—	—	—	—	—
81-82—Kitchener	OHL	68	6	36	42	158	...	...	...	15	1	10	11	71
82-83—Washington	NHL	77	9	16	25	195	14	0	0	4	1	0	1	26
83-84—Washington	NHL	78	13	32	45	201	26	7	0	8	1	8	9	21
84-85—Washington	NHL	80	21	44	65	221	19	16	0	5	0	1	1	20
85-86—Washington	NHL	73	15	38	53	165	0	3	0	9	3	8	11	12
86-87—Washington	NHL	77	10	51	61	283	13	2	0	7	0	5	5	19
87-88—Washington	NHL	80	12	60	72	184	14	5	1	13	1	11	12	46
88-89—Washington	NHL	80	7	61	68	225	1	6	0	6	1	4	5	11
89-90—Washington	NHL	56	11	29	40	154	1	7	0	15	2	7	9	25
90-91—St. Louis	NHL	78	5	44	49	150	23	1	0	13	0	3	3	36
91-92—New Jersey	NHL	68	17	42	59	124	24	7	1	7	2	1	3	29
92-93—New Jersey	NHL	81	12	45	57	120	14	8	0	5	2	2	4	10
93-94—New Jersey	NHL	83	18	60	78	112	*53	5	1	20	2	9	11	42
94-95—New Jersey	NHL	48	2	20	22	56	4	1	0	20	1	7	8	24
95-96—New Jersey	NHL	82	5	23	28	100	7	2	1	—	—	—	—	—
96-97—New Jersey	NHL	79	5	19	24	70	26	0	0	10	0	4	4	2
97-98—New Jersey	NHL	80	4	22	26	80	19	1	0	6	1	0	1	8
—Can. Olympic team	Int'l	6	0	0	0	2	...	...	...	—	—	—	—	—
98-99—New Jersey	NHL	75	5	22	27	64	29	0	0	7	2	1	3	10
99-00—New Jersey	NHL	78	8	21	29	103	30	0	1	23	3	8	11	6
00-01—New Jersey	NHL	81	9	22	31	71	40	3	0	25	1	7	8	37
01-02—New Jersey	NHL	82	1	16	17	44	15	0	0	6	0	0	0	4
02-03—New Jersey	NHL	81	4	16	20	41	18	0	0	24	3	6	9	14
NHL Totals (21 years)		1597	193	703	896	2763	390	74	5	233	26	92	118	402

S

STEVENSON, JEREMY   LW   WILD

PERSONAL: Born July 28, 1974, in San Bernardino, Calif. ... 6-2/217. ... Shoots left. ... Full Name: Jeremy Joseph Stevenson.

TRANSACTIONS/CAREER NOTES: Selected by Winnipeg Jets in third round (third Jets pick, 60th overall) of NHL entry draft (June 20, 1992). ... Returned to draft pool by Jets and selected by Mighty Ducks of Anaheim in 11th round (10th Mighty Ducks pick, 262nd overall) of NHL entry draft (June 28, 1994). ... Fractured ankle (October 24, 1996); missed 33 games. ... Suffered concussion prior to 1997-98 season; missed first four games of season. ... Signed as free agent by Nashville Predators (September 25, 2000). ... Signed as free agent by Minnesota Wild (November 26, 2002).

			REGULAR SEASON								PLAYOFFS				
Season Team	League	Gms.	G	A	Pts.	PIM	+/-	PP	SH	Gms.	G	A	Pts.	PIM
90-91—Cornwall	OHL	58	13	20	33	124	...	...	...	—	—	—	—	—
91-92—Cornwall	OHL	63	15	23	38	176	...	...	...	6	3	1	4	4
92-93—Newmarket	OHL	54	28	28	56	144	...	...	...	5	5	1	6	28
93-94—Newmarket	OHL	9	2	4	6	27	...	...	...	—	—	—	—	—
—Sault Ste. Marie	OHL	48	18	19	37	183	...	...	...	14	1	1	2	23
94-95—Greensboro	ECHL	43	14	13	27	231	...	...	...	17	6	11	17	64
95-96—Baltimore	AHL	60	11	10	21	295	...	...	...	12	4	2	6	23
—Anaheim	NHL	3	0	1	1	12	1	0	0	—	—	—	—	—
96-97—Baltimore	AHL	25	8	8	16	125	...	...	...	3	0	0	0	8
—Anaheim	NHL	5	0	0	0	14	-1	0	0	—	—	—	—	—
97-98—Anaheim	NHL	45	3	5	8	101	-4	0	0	—	—	—	—	—
—Cincinnati	AHL	10	0	5	5	34	...	...	...	—	—	—	—	—
98-99—Cincinnati	AHL	22	4	4	8	83	...	...	...	3	1	0	1	2
99-00—Cincinnati	AHL	41	11	14	25	100	...	...	...	—	—	—	—	—
—Anaheim	NHL	3	0	0	0	7	-1	0	0	—	—	—	—	—
00-01—Milwaukee	IHL	60	16	13	29	262	...	...	...	5	2	1	3	12
—Nashville	NHL	8	1	0	1	39	-1	0	0	—	—	—	—	—
01-02—Milwaukee	AHL	53	12	7	19	192	...	...	...	—	—	—	—	—
—Nashville	NHL	4	0	0	0	9	0	0	0	—	—	—	—	—
02-03—Houston	AHL	18	6	7	13	77	...	...	...	—	—	—	—	—
—Minnesota	NHL	32	5	6	11	69	6	1	0	14	0	5	5	12
NHL Totals (7 years)		100	9	12	21	251	0	1	0	14	0	5	5	12

STEVENSON, TURNER   RW   DEVILS

PERSONAL: Born May 18, 1972, in Prince George, B.C. ... 6-3/220. ... Shoots right.

TRANSACTIONS/CAREER NOTES: Selected by Montreal Canadiens in first round (first Canadiens pick, 12th overall) of NHL entry draft (June 16, 1990). ... Suffered from the flu (October 21, 1995); missed two games. ... Sprained knee (October 7, 1996); missed five games. ... Sprained knee (October 26, 1996); missed four games. ... Sprained knee (November 11, 1996); missed seven games. ... Strained left shoulder (November 12, 1997); missed eight games. ... Tore cartilage in ribs (December 19, 1997); missed five games. ... Strained hamstring (April 15, 1998); missed three games. ... Suspended two games and fined $1,000 by NHL for elbowing incident (October 19, 1998). ... Suffered back spasms (December 29, 1998); missed one game. ... Sprained ankle (December 31, 1998); missed 10 games. ... Suffered back spasms (October 9, 1999); missed two games. ... Strained back (November 16, 1999); missed 13 games. ... Suffered from the flu (January 11, 2000); missed three games. ... Selected by Columbus Blue Jackets in NHL expansion draft (June 23, 2000). ... Traded by Blue Jackets to New Jersey Devils (June 23, 2000), completing deal in which Devils traded RW Krzysztof Oliwa to Blue Jackets for third-round pick (C/LW Brandon Nolan) in 2001 draft and future considerations (June 12, 2000). ... Sprained ankle (March 21, 2001); missed nine games. ... Injured right knee (October 17, 2001); missed 12 games. ... Reinjured knee (December 29, 2001); missed remainder of season.

			REGULAR SEASON								PLAYOFFS				
Season Team	League	Gms.	G	A	Pts.	PIM	+/-	PP	SH		Gms.	G	A	Pts.	PIM
88-89—Seattle................	WHL	69	15	12	27	84	...	...	...		—	—	—	—	—
89-90—Seattle................	WHL	62	29	32	61	276	...	...	...		13	3	2	5	35
90-91—Seattle................	WHL	57	36	27	63	222	...	...	...		6	1	5	6	15
—Fredericton	AHL	—	—	—	—	—					4	0	0	0	5
91-92—Seattle................	WHL	58	20	32	52	264	...	...	...		15	9	3	12	55
92-93—Fredericton	AHL	79	25	34	59	102	...	...	...		5	2	3	5	11
—Montreal	NHL	1	0	0	0	0	-1	0	0		—	—	—	—	—
93-94—Fredericton	AHL	66	19	28	47	155	...	...	...		—	—	—	—	—
—Montreal	NHL	2	0	0	0	2	-2	0	0		3	0	2	2	0
94-95—Fredericton	AHL	37	12	12	24	109	...	...	...		—	—	—	—	—
—Montreal	NHL	41	6	1	7	86	0	0	0		—	—	—	—	—
95-96—Montreal	NHL	80	9	16	25	167	-2	0	0		6	0	1	1	2
96-97—Montreal	NHL	65	8	13	21	97	-14	1	0		5	1	1	2	2
97-98—Montreal	NHL	63	4	6	10	110	-8	1	0		10	3	4	7	12
98-99—Montreal	NHL	69	10	17	27	88	6	0	0		—	—	—	—	—
99-00—Montreal	NHL	64	8	13	21	61	-1	0	0		—	—	—	—	—
00-01—New Jersey	NHL	69	8	18	26	97	11	2	0		23	1	3	4	20
01-02—New Jersey	NHL	21	0	2	2	25	-3	0	0		1	0	0	0	4
02-03—New Jersey	NHL	77	7	13	20	115	7	0	0		14	1	1	2	26
NHL Totals (11 years).........		552	60	99	159	848	-7	4	0		62	6	12	18	66

STILLMAN, CORY   LW   LIGHTNING

S

PERSONAL: Born December 20, 1973, in Peterborough, Ont. ... 6-0/197. ... Shoots left. ... Full Name: Cory Scott Stillman. ... Second cousin of Cory Stillman, center, New York Islanders organization.
TRANSACTIONS/CAREER NOTES: Selected by Calgary Flames in first round (first Flames pick, sixth overall) of NHL entry draft (June 20, 1992). ... Suspended four games by AHL for incident involving on-ice official (March 29, 1995). ... Suffered from the flu (October 8, 1995); missed one game. ... Bruised knee (January 14, 1996); missed two games. ... Injured shoulder (December 16, 1996); missed five games. ... Bruised ribs (October 11, 1997); missed six games. ... Strained knee (December 27, 1998); missed five games. ... Injured shoulder (December 27, 1999); missed final 45 games of season. ... Injured shoulder (October 30, 2000); missed one game. ... Traded by Flames to St. Louis Blues for C Craig Conroy and seventh-round pick (LW David Moss) in 2001 draft (March 13, 2001). ... Injured knee (November 8, 2001); missed two games. ... Traded by Blues to Tampa Bay Lightning for second-round draft pick in 2003 (June 22, 2003).
STATISTICAL PLATEAUS: Three-goal games: 1997-98 (1), 2000-01 (1), 2001-02 (1). Total: 3.

			REGULAR SEASON								PLAYOFFS				
Season Team	League	Gms.	G	A	Pts.	PIM	+/-	PP	SH		Gms.	G	A	Pts.	PIM
89-90—Peterborough Jr. B	OHA	41	30	54	84	76	...	...	...		—	—	—	—	—
90-91—Windsor....................	OHL	64	31	70	101	31	...	...	...		11	3	6	9	8
91-92—Windsor....................	OHL	53	29	61	90	59	...	...	...		7	2	4	6	8
92-93—Peterborough.............	OHL	61	25	55	80	55	...	...	...		18	3	8	11	18
—Canadian nat'l team	Int'l	1	0	0	0	0					—	—	—	—	—
93-94—Saint John	AHL	79	35	48	83	52	...	...	...		7	2	4	6	16
94-95—Saint John	AHL	63	28	53	81	70	...	...	...		5	0	2	2	2
—Calgary	NHL	10	0	2	2	2	1	0	0		—	—	—	—	—
95-96—Calgary	NHL	74	16	19	35	41	-5	4	1		2	1	1	2	0
96-97—Calgary	NHL	58	6	20	26	14	-6	2	0		—	—	—	—	—
97-98—Calgary	NHL	72	27	22	49	40	-9	9	4		—	—	—	—	—
98-99—Calgary	NHL	76	27	30	57	38	7	9	3		—	—	—	—	—
99-00—Calgary	NHL	37	12	9	21	12	-9	6	0		—	—	—	—	—
00-01—Calgary	NHL	66	21	24	45	45	-6	7	0		—	—	—	—	—
—St. Louis	NHL	12	3	4	7	6	-2	3	0		15	3	5	8	8
01-02—St. Louis	NHL	80	23	22	45	36	8	6	0		9	0	2	2	2
02-03—St. Louis	NHL	79	24	43	67	56	12	6	0		6	2	2	4	2
NHL Totals (9 years)...........		564	159	195	354	290	-9	52	8		32	6	10	16	12

STOCK, P.J.   C   BRUINS

PERSONAL: Born May 26, 1975, in Victoriaville, Que. ... 5-10/190. ... Shoots left.
TRANSACTIONS/CAREER NOTES: Signed as non-drafted free agent by New York Rangers (September 2, 1997). ... Signed as free agent by Montreal Canadiens (July 7, 2000). ... Traded by Canadiens with sixth-round pick (D Dennis Seidenberg) in 2001 draft to Philadelphia Flyers for LW Gino Odjick (December 7, 2000). ... Strained neck (April 7, 2001); missed final game of regular season. ... Signed as free agent by Rangers (August 23, 2001). ... Claimed by Boston Bruins from Rangers in NHL waiver draft (September 28, 2001). ... Sprained ankle (November 8, 2001); missed 12 games. ... Underwent facial surgery (February 5, 2002); missed six games. ... Re-signed by Bruins (June 22, 2003).

			REGULAR SEASON								PLAYOFFS				
Season Team	League	Gms.	G	A	Pts.	PIM	+/-	PP	SH		Gms.	G	A	Pts.	PIM
94-95—Victoriaville	QMJHL	70	9	46	55	386	...	...	...		4	0	0	0	60
95-96—Victoriaville	QMJHL	67	19	43	62	432	...	...	...		12	5	4	9	79
96-97—St. Francis Xavier........	CIAU	27	11	20	31	110	...	...	...		3	0	4	4	14
97-98—Hartford	AHL	41	8	8	16	202	...	...	...		11	1	3	4	79
—New York Rangers	NHL	38	2	3	5	114	4	0	0		—	—	—	—	—

Season Team	League	Gms.	G	A	Pts.	PIM	+/-	PP	SH	Gms.	G	A	Pts.	PIM
98-99—New York Rangers......	NHL	5	0	0	0	6	-1	0	0	—	—	—	—	—
—Hartford.....................	AHL	55	4	14	18	250	...	...	...	6	0	1	1	35
99-00—Hartford.....................	AHL	64	13	23	36	290	...	...	...	23	1	11	12	69
—New York Rangers......	NHL	11	0	1	1	11	1	0	0	—	—	—	—	—
00-01—Montreal....................	NHL	20	1	2	3	32	-1	0	0	—	—	—	—	—
—Philadelphia...............	NHL	31	1	3	4	78	-2	0	0	2	0	0	0	0
—Philadelphia...............	AHL	9	1	2	3	37	...	...	...	—	—	—	—	—
01-02—Boston......................	NHL	58	0	3	3	122	-2	0	0	6	1	0	1	19
02-03—Boston......................	NHL	71	1	9	10	160	-5	1	0	—	—	—	—	—
NHL Totals (6 years)...........		234	5	21	26	523	-6	1	0	8	1	0	1	19

STOLL, JARRET   C   OILERS

PERSONAL: Born June 24, 1982, in Melville, Sask. ... 6-1/199. ... Shoots right. ... Full Name: Jarrett Stoll.

TRANSACTIONS/CAREER NOTES: Selected by Calgary Flames in second round (third Flames pick, 46th overall) of NHL entry draft (June 24, 2000). ... Returned to draft pool and selected by Edmonton Oilers in second round (third Oilers pick, 36th overall) of NHL entry draft (June 22, 2002).

Season Team	League	Gms.	G	A	Pts.	PIM	+/-	PP	SH	Gms.	G	A	Pts.	PIM
98-99—Kootenay..................	WHL	57	13	21	34	40	...	...	...	4	0	0	0	2
99-00—Kootenay..................	WHL	71	37	38	75	64	...	...	...	20	7	9	16	24
00-01—Kootenay..................	WHL	62	40	66	106	105	...	...	...	11	5	9	14	22
01-02—Kootenay..................	WHL	47	32	34	66	64	...	...	...	22	6	13	19	35
02-03—Hamilton	AHL	76	21	33	54	86	...	...	...	23	5	8	13	25
—Edmonton..................	NHL	4	0	1	1	0	-3	0	0	—	—	—	—	—
NHL Totals (1 year).............		4	0	1	1	0	-3	0	0					

STORR, JAMIE   G

PERSONAL: Born December 28, 1975, in Brampton, Ont. ... 6-2/203. ... Catches left. ... Name pronounced STOHR.

TRANSACTIONS/CAREER NOTES: Selected by Los Angeles Kings in first round (first Kings pick, seventh overall) of NHL entry draft (June 28, 1994). ... Strained right groin (October 1, 1997); missed 12 games. ... Strained left groin (October 18, 1998); missed 16 games. ... Sprained ankle (April 2, 1999); missed final eight games of season. ... Strained right groin (November 23, 1999); missed one game. ... Suffered concussion (December 16, 1999); missed 10 games.

Season Team	League	Gms.	Min	W	L	T	GA	SO	Avg.	SV%	Gms.	Min.	W	L	GA	SO	Avg.	SV%
90-91—Brampton.....................	Jr. B	24	1145	...	...	...	91	0	4.77	—	—	—	—	—	—	—	—	—
91-92—Owen Sound	OHL	34	1733	11	16	1	128	0	4.43	—	5	299	1	4	28	0	5.62	—
92-93—Owen Sound	OHL	41	2362	20	17	3	180	0	4.57	—	8	454	4	4	35	0	4.63	—
93-94—Owen Sound	OHL	35	2004	21	11	1	120	1	3.59	—	9	547	4	5	44	0	4.83	—
94-95—Owen Sound	OHL	17	977	5	9	2	64	0	3.93	—								
—Los Angeles	NHL	5	263	1	3	1	17	0	3.88	.888	—	—	—	—	—	—	—	—
—Windsor	OHL	4	241	3	1	0	8	1	1.99	—	10	520	6	3	34	1	3.92	—
95-96—Los Angeles	NHL	5	262	3	1	0	12	0	2.75	.918	—	—	—	—	—	—	—	—
—Phoenix	IHL	48	2711	22	20	‡4	139	2	3.08	—	2	118	1	1	4	1	2.03	—
96-97—Phoenix	IHL	44	2441	16	22	‡4	147	0	3.61	—								
—Los Angeles	NHL	5	265	2	1	1	11	0	2.49	.925	—	—	—	—	—	—	—	—
97-98—Los Angeles	NHL	17	920	9	5	1	34	2	2.22	.929	3	145	0	2	9	0	3.72	.883
—Long Beach.................	IHL	11	629	7	2	1	31	0	2.96	—								
98-99—Los Angeles	NHL	28	1525	12	12	2	61	4	2.40	.916	—	—	—	—	—	—	—	—
99-00—Los Angeles	NHL	42	2206	18	15	5	93	4	2.53	.908	1	36	0	1	2	0	3.33	.920
00-01—Los Angeles	NHL	45	2498	19	18	6	114	4	2.74	.899	—	—	—	—	—	—	—	—
01-02—Los Angeles	NHL	19	886	9	4	3	28	2	1.90	.922	1	0	0	0	0	0	—	—
02-03—Los Angeles	NHL	39	2027	12	19	2	86	3	2.55	.905	—	—	—	—	—	—	—	—
NHL Totals (9 years)............		205	10852	85	78	21	456	16	2.52	.910	5	181	0	3	11	0	3.65	.892

STRAKA, MARTIN   LW   PENGUINS

PERSONAL: Born September 3, 1972, in Plzen, Czechoslovakia ... 5-9/178. ... Shoots left. ... Name pronounced STRAH-kuh.

TRANSACTIONS/CAREER NOTES: Selected by Pittsburgh Penguins in first round (first Penguins pick, 19th overall) of NHL entry draft (June 20, 1992). ... Played in Europe during 1994-95 NHL lockout. ... Suffered from the flu (February 14, 1995); missed four games. ... Traded by Penguins to Ottawa Senators for D Norm Maciver and C Troy Murray (April 7, 1995). ... Strained knee (April 19, 1995); missed remainder of season. ... Injured hamstring (November 11, 1995); missed one game. ... Traded by Senators with D Bryan Berard to New York Islanders for D Wade Redden and G Damian Rhodes (January 23, 1996). ... Claimed on waivers by Florida Panthers (March 15, 1996). ... Bruised buttocks (April 10, 1996); missed final two games of season. ... Strained groin (January 1, 1997); missed one game. ... Strained groin (January 8, 1997); missed two games. ... Strained groin (January 22, 1997); missed four games. ... Strained groin (March 5, 1997); missed nine games. ... Signed as free agent by Penguins (August 7, 1997). ... Fractured foot (December 29, 1997); missed seven games. ... Bruised shoulder (March 3, 1999); missed one game. ... Bruised shoulder (April 8, 1999); missed one game. ... Bruised knee (October 16, 1999); missed one game. ... Reinjured knee (October 27, 1999); missed two games. ... Bruised ribs (December 15, 1999); missed seven games. ... Bruised shin (April 5, 2000); missed one game. ... Fractured leg (October 28, 2001); missed 47 games. ... Fractured orbital and sinus bones (February 27, 2002); missed four games. ... Reinjured leg (March 7, 2002); missed remainder of season.

STATISTICAL PLATEAUS: Three-goal games: 1993-94 (1), 1997-98 (1), 1998-99 (1), 2000-01 (1). Total: 4.

Season Team	League	REGULAR SEASON								PLAYOFFS				
		Gms.	G	A	Pts.	PIM	+/-	PP	SH	Gms.	G	A	Pts.	PIM
89-90—Skoda Plzen	Czech.	1	0	3	3	...	...	...	...	—	—	—	—	—
90-91—Skoda Plzen	Czech.	47	7	24	31	6	...	...	...	—	—	—	—	—
91-92—Skoda Plzen	Czech.	50	27	28	55	20	...	...	...	—	—	—	—	—
92-93—Pittsburgh	NHL	42	3	13	16	29	2	0	0	11	2	1	3	2
—Cleveland	IHL	4	4	3	7	0	...	...	...	—	—	—	—	—
93-94—Pittsburgh	NHL	84	30	34	64	24	24	2	0	6	1	0	1	2
94-95—Interconex Plzen	Czech Rep.	19	10	11	21	18	...	...	...	—	—	—	—	—
—Pittsburgh	NHL	31	4	12	16	16	0	0	0	—	—	—	—	—
—Ottawa	NHL	6	1	1	2	0	-1	0	0	—	—	—	—	—
95-96—Ottawa	NHL	43	9	16	25	29	-14	5	0	—	—	—	—	—
—New York Islanders	NHL	22	2	10	12	6	-6	0	0	—	—	—	—	—
—Florida	NHL	12	2	4	6	6	1	1	0	13	2	2	4	2
96-97—Florida	NHL	55	7	22	29	12	9	2	0	4	0	0	0	0
97-98—Pittsburgh	NHL	75	19	23	42	28	-1	4	3	6	2	0	2	2
—Czech Rep. Oly. team	Int'l	6	1	2	3	0	...	...	...	—	—	—	—	—
98-99—Pittsburgh	NHL	80	35	48	83	26	12	5	4	13	6	9	15	6
99-00—Pittsburgh	NHL	71	20	39	59	26	24	3	1	11	3	9	12	10
00-01—Pittsburgh	NHL	82	27	68	95	38	19	7	1	18	5	8	13	8
01-02—Pittsburgh	NHL	13	5	4	9	0	3	1	0	—	—	—	—	—
02-03—Pittsburgh	NHL	60	18	28	46	12	-18	7	0	—	—	—	—	—
NHL Totals (11 years)		676	182	322	504	252	54	37	9	82	21	29	50	32

STRUDWICK, JASON　　　D　　　BLACKHAWKS

PERSONAL: Born July 17, 1975, in Edmonton ... 6-3/230. ... Shoots left. ... Name pronounced STRUHD-wihk.

TRANSACTIONS/CAREER NOTES: Selected by New York Islanders in third round (third Islanders pick, 63rd overall) of NHL entry draft (June 29, 1994). ... Traded by Islanders to Vancouver Canucks for LW Gino Odjick (March 23, 1998). ... Injured back (November 17, 1999); missed 10 games. ... Strained knee (February 24, 2001); missed 11 games. ... Signed as free agent by Chicago Blackhawks (July 15, 2002). ... Re-signed by Blackhawks (July 1, 2003).

Season Team	League	REGULAR SEASON								PLAYOFFS				
		Gms.	G	A	Pts.	PIM	+/-	PP	SH	Gms.	G	A	Pts.	PIM
93-94—Kamloops	WHL	61	6	8	14	118	...	...	...	19	0	4	4	24
94-95—Kamloops	WHL	72	3	11	14	183	...	...	...	21	1	1	2	39
95-96—Worcester	AHL	60	2	7	9	119	...	...	...	4	0	1	1	0
—New York Islanders	NHL	1	0	0	0	7	0	0	0	—	—	—	—	—
96-97—Kentucky	AHL	80	1	9	10	198	...	...	...	4	0	0	0	0
97-98—Kentucky	AHL	39	3	1	4	87	...	...	...	—	—	—	—	—
—New York Islanders	NHL	17	0	1	1	36	1	0	0	—	—	—	—	—
—Vancouver	NHL	11	0	1	1	29	-3	0	0	—	—	—	—	—
—Syracuse	AHL	—	—	—	—	—	—	—	—	3	0	0	0	6
98-99—Vancouver	NHL	65	0	3	3	114	-19	0	0	—	—	—	—	—
99-00—Vancouver	NHL	63	1	3	4	64	-13	0	0	—	—	—	—	—
00-01—Vancouver	NHL	60	1	4	5	64	16	0	0	2	0	0	0	0
01-02—Vancouver	NHL	44	2	4	6	96	4	0	0	—	—	—	—	—
02-03—Chicago	NHL	48	2	3	5	87	-4	0	0	—	—	—	—	—
NHL Totals (7 years)		309	6	19	25	497	-18	0	0	2	0	0	0	0

STUART, BRAD　　　D　　　SHARKS

PERSONAL: Born November 6, 1979, in Rocky Mountain House, Alta. ... 6-2/215. ... Shoots left.

TRANSACTIONS/CAREER NOTES: Selected by San Jose Sharks in first round (first Sharks pick, third overall) of NHL entry draft (June 27, 1998). ... Suspended two games by NHL for cross-checking incident (March 9, 2001).

Season Team	League	REGULAR SEASON								PLAYOFFS				
		Gms.	G	A	Pts.	PIM	+/-	PP	SH	Gms.	G	A	Pts.	PIM
96-97—Regina	WHL	57	7	36	43	58	...	...	...	5	0	4	4	14
97-98—Regina	WHL	72	20	45	65	82	...	...	...	9	3	4	7	10
98-99—Regina	WHL	29	10	19	29	43	...	...	...	—	—	—	—	—
—Calgary	WHL	30	11	22	33	26	...	...	...	21	8	15	23	59
99-00—San Jose	NHL	82	10	26	36	32	3	5	1	12	1	0	1	6
00-01—San Jose	NHL	77	5	18	23	56	10	1	0	5	1	0	1	0
01-02—San Jose	NHL	82	6	23	29	39	13	2	0	12	0	3	3	8
02-03—San Jose	NHL	36	4	10	14	46	-6	2	0	—	—	—	—	—
NHL Totals (4 years)		277	25	77	102	173	20	10	1	29	2	3	5	14

STUMPEL, JOZEF　　　C　　　KINGS

PERSONAL: Born July 20, 1972, in Nitra, Czechoslovakia ... 6-3/225. ... Shoots right. ... Name pronounced JOH-sehf STUHM-puhl.

TRANSACTIONS/CAREER NOTES: Selected by Boston Bruins in second round (second Bruins pick, 40th overall) of NHL entry draft (June 22, 1991). ... Injured shoulder (December 1992); missed nine games. ... Injured knee (March 17, 1994); missed nine games. ... Played in Europe during 1994-95 NHL lockout. ... Injured knee (April 1995). ... Fractured cheek bone (February 27, 1996); missed three games. ... Suffered back spasms (January 4, 1997); missed one game. ... Suffered back spasms (February 1, 1997); missed three games. ... Traded by Bruins with RW Sandy Moger and fourth-round pick (traded to New Jersey) in 1998 draft to Los Angeles Kings for LW Dimitri Khristich and G Byron Dafoe (August 29, 1997). ... Suffered from the flu (February 7, 1998); missed one game. ... Bruised kidney (March 5, 1998); missed four games. ... Strained hip flexor and strained abdominal muscle (October 18, 1998); missed 10 games. ... Sprained right ankle (November 16, 1998);

missed three games. ... Sprained right knee (April 8, 1999); missed final five games of season. ... Suffered hernia (November 3, 1999); missed 18 games. ... Bruised left knee (January 3, 2000); missed seven games. ... Missed first seven games of 2000-01 season due to contract dispute. ... Fractured toe (December 14, 2000); missed two games. ... Strained right hamstring (February 10, 2001); missed two games. ... Fractured rib (March 4, 2001); missed seven games. ... Traded by Kings with RW Glen Murray to Bruins for C Jason Allison and C/LW Mikko Eloranta (October 24, 2001). ... Strained groin (March 26, 2002); missed one game. ... Traded by Bruins with seventh-round draft pick in 2003 to Los Angeles Kings for fourth-round draft pick in 2003 and second-round draft pick in 2004 (June 22, 2003). ... Re-signed by Kings (July 31, 2003).

STATISTICAL PLATEAUS: Three-goal games: 1995-96 (1), 1997-98 (1). Total: 2.

			REGULAR SEASON								PLAYOFFS				
Season Team	League	Gms.	G	A	Pts.	PIM	+/-	PP	SH		Gms.	G	A	Pts.	PIM
89-90—Nitra	Czech.	38	12	11	23	0	...	...	...		—	—	—	—	—
90-91—Nitra	Czech.	49	23	22	45	14	...	...	...		—	—	—	—	—
91-92—Boston	NHL	4	1	0	1	0	1	0	0		—	—	—	—	—
—Koln	Germany	33	19	18	37	35	...	...	...		—	—	—	—	—
92-93—Providence	AHL	56	31	61	92	26	...	...	...		6	4	4	8	0
—Boston	NHL	13	1	3	4	4	-3	0	0		—	—	—	—	—
93-94—Boston	NHL	59	8	15	23	14	4	0	0		13	1	7	8	4
—Providence	AHL	17	5	12	17	4	...	...	...		—	—	—	—	—
94-95—Koln	Germany	25	16	23	39	18	...	...	...		—	—	—	—	—
—Boston	NHL	44	5	13	18	8	4	1	0		5	0	0	0	0
95-96—Boston	NHL	76	18	36	54	14	-8	5	0		5	1	2	3	0
96-97—Boston	NHL	78	21	55	76	14	-22	6	0		—	—	—	—	—
97-98—Los Angeles	NHL	77	21	58	79	53	17	4	0		4	1	2	3	2
98-99—Los Angeles	NHL	64	13	21	34	10	-18	1	0		—	—	—	—	—
99-00—Los Angeles	NHL	57	17	41	58	10	23	3	0		4	0	4	4	8
00-01—Slovan Bratislava	Slovakia	9	2	4	6	16	...	...	...		—	—	—	—	—
—Los Angeles	NHL	63	16	39	55	14	20	9	0		13	3	5	8	10
01-02—Los Angeles	NHL	9	1	3	4	4	1	0	0		—	—	—	—	—
—Boston	NHL	72	7	47	54	14	21	1	0		6	0	2	2	0
—Slovakian Oly. team	Int'l	2	1	3	0	...	...	...		—	—	—	—	—
02-03—Boston	NHL	78	14	37	51	12	0	4	0		5	0	2	2	0
NHL Totals (12 years)		694	143	368	511	171	40	34	0		55	6	24	30	24

STURM, MARCO   LW   SHARKS   S

PERSONAL: Born September 8, 1978, in Dingolfing, West Germany ... 6-0/195. ... Shoots left.
TRANSACTIONS/CAREER NOTES: Selected by San Jose Sharks in first round (second Sharks pick, 21st overall) of NHL entry draft (June 22, 1996). ... Sprained wrist (April 1, 1998); missed six games. ... Injured foot (March 3, 1999); missed two games. ... Suffered concussion (December 2, 1999); missed four games. ... Injured elbow (January 4, 2002); missed two games. ... Suffered from the flu (January 27, 2002); missed one game. ... Injured hand (March 20, 2002); missed two games. ... Re-signed by Sharks (July 15, 2003).
STATISTICAL PLATEAUS: Three-goal games: 1998-99 (1).

			REGULAR SEASON								PLAYOFFS				
Season Team	League	Gms.	G	A	Pts.	PIM	+/-	PP	SH		Gms.	G	A	Pts.	PIM
95-96—Landshut	Germany	47	12	20	32	50	...	...	...		—	—	—	—	—
96-97—Landshut	Germany	46	16	27	43	40	...	...	...		7	1	4	5	6
97-98—San Jose	NHL	74	10	20	30	40	-2	2	0		2	0	0	0	0
—German Oly. team	Int'l	2	0	0	0	0	...	...	...		—	—	—	—	—
98-99—San Jose	NHL	78	16	22	38	52	7	3	0		6	2	2	4	4
99-00—San Jose	NHL	74	12	15	27	22	4	2	4		12	1	3	4	6
00-01—San Jose	NHL	81	14	18	32	28	9	2	3		6	0	2	2	0
01-02—San Jose	NHL	77	21	20	41	32	23	4	3		12	3	2	5	2
—German Oly. team	Int'l	5	0	1	1	0	...	...	...		—	—	—	—	—
02-03—San Jose	NHL	82	28	20	48	16	9	6	0		—	—	—	—	—
NHL Totals (6 years)		466	101	115	216	190	50	19	12		38	6	9	15	12

SUCHY, RADOSLAV   D   COYOTES

PERSONAL: Born April 7, 1976, in Kezmarok, Czechoslovakia ... 6-2/204. ... Shoots left.
TRANSACTIONS/CAREER NOTES: Signed as non-drafted free agent by Phoenix Coyotes (September 25, 1997). ... Bruised finger (December 21, 2001); missed one game.

			REGULAR SEASON								PLAYOFFS				
Season Team	League	Gms.	G	A	Pts.	PIM	+/-	PP	SH		Gms.	G	A	Pts.	PIM
93-94—Poprad	Slovakia				Statistics unavailable.										
94-95—Sherbrooke	QMJHL	69	12	32	44	30	...	...	...		7	0	3	3	2
95-96—Sherbrooke	QMJHL	68	15	53	68	68	...	...	...		7	0	3	3	2
96-97—Sherbrooke	QMJHL	32	6	34	40	14	...	...	...		—	—	—	—	—
—Chicoutimi	QMJHL	28	5	24	29	24	...	...	...		19	6	15	21	12
97-98—Las Vegas	IHL	26	1	4	5	10	...	...	...		—	—	—	—	—
—Springfield	AHL	41	6	15	21	16	...	...	...		4	0	1	1	2
98-99—Springfield	AHL	69	4	32	36	10	...	...	...		3	0	1	1	0
99-00—Springfield	AHL	2	0	1	1	0	...	...	...		—	—	—	—	—
—Phoenix	NHL	60	0	6	6	16	2	0	0		5	0	1	1	0
00-01—Phoenix	NHL	72	0	10	10	22	1	0	0		—	—	—	—	—
01-02—Phoenix	NHL	81	4	13	17	10	25	1	0		5	1	0	1	0
02-03—Phoenix	NHL	77	1	8	9	18	2	1	0		—	—	—	—	—
NHL Totals (4 years)		290	5	37	42	66	30	2	0		10	1	1	2	0

SULLIVAN, STEVE　　　　RW　　　　BLACKHAWKS

PERSONAL: Born July 6, 1974, in Timmins, Ont. ... 5-9/155. ... Shoots right.

TRANSACTIONS/CAREER NOTES: Selected by New Jersey Devils in ninth round (10th Devils pick, 233rd overall) of NHL entry draft (June 29, 1994). ... Traded by Devils with D Jason Smith and C Alyn McCauley to Toronto Maple Leafs for C Doug Gilmour, D Dave Ellett and third-round pick (D Andre Lakos) in 1999 draft (February 25, 1997). ... Suffered from the flu (March 7, 1998); missed three games. ... Back spasms (May 11, 1999); missed one playoff game. ... Claimed on waivers by Chicago Blackhawks (October 23, 1999). ... Suffered from the flu (February 18, 2000); missed one game. ... Suffered from the flu (December 13, 2000); missed one game. ... Separated shoulder (March 20, 2002); missed four games.

STATISTICAL PLATEAUS: Three-goal games: 2000-01 (1), 2002-03 (1). Total: 2. ... Four-goal games: 1998-99 (1). ... Total hat tricks: 3.

			REGULAR SEASON								PLAYOFFS				
Season Team	League	Gms.	G	A	Pts.	PIM	+/-	PP	SH		Gms.	G	A	Pts.	PIM
91-92—Timmins	OJHL	47	66	55	121	141	...	...	...		—	—	—	—	—
92-93—Sault Ste. Marie	OHL	62	36	27	63	44	...	...	...		16	3	8	11	18
93-94—Sault Ste. Marie	OHL	63	51	62	113	82	...	...	...		14	9	16	25	22
94-95—Albany..........................	AHL	75	31	50	81	124	...	...	...		14	4	7	11	10
95-96—Albany..........................	AHL	53	33	42	75	127	...	...	...		4	3	0	3	6
—New Jersey	NHL	16	5	4	9	8	3	2	0		—	—	—	—	—
96-97—Albany..........................	AHL	15	8	7	15	16	...	...	...		—	—	—	—	—
—New Jersey	NHL	33	8	14	22	14	9	2	0		—	—	—	—	—
—Toronto	NHL	21	5	11	16	23	5	1	0		—	—	—	—	—
97-98—Toronto	NHL	63	10	18	28	40	-8	1	0		—	—	—	—	—
98-99—Toronto	NHL	63	20	20	40	28	12	4	0		13	3	3	6	14
99-00—Toronto	NHL	7	0	1	1	4	-1	0	0		—	—	—	—	—
—Chicago......................	NHL	73	22	42	64	52	20	2	1		—	—	—	—	—
00-01—Chicago.......................	NHL	81	34	41	75	54	3	6	*8		—	—	—	—	—
01-02—Chicago.......................	NHL	78	21	39	60	67	23	3	0		5	1	0	1	2
02-03—Chicago.......................	NHL	82	26	35	61	42	15	4	2		—	—	—	—	—
NHL Totals (8 years)..........		517	151	225	376	332	81	25	11		18	4	3	7	16

SUNDIN, MATS　　　　C　　　　MAPLE LEAFS

PERSONAL: Born February 13, 1971, in Bromma, Sweden ... 6-5/231. ... Shoots right. ... Full Name: Mats Johan Sundin. ... Name pronounced suhn-DEEN.

TRANSACTIONS/CAREER NOTES: Selected by Quebec Nordiques in first round (first Nordiques pick, first overall) of NHL entry draft (June 17, 1989). ... Separated right shoulder (January 2, 1993). ... Suspended one game by NHL for second stick-related infraction (March 2, 1993). ... Traded by Nordiques with D Garth Butcher, LW Todd Warriner and first-round pick (traded to Washington) in 1994 draft to Toronto Maple Leafs for LW Wendel Clark, D Sylvain Lefebvre, RW Landon Wilson and first-round pick (D Jeffrey Kealty) in 1994 draft (June 28, 1994). ... Played in Europe during 1994-95 NHL lockout. ... Sprained shoulder (March 25, 1995); missed one game. ... Suffered slight tear of knee cartilage (October 24, 1995); missed four games. ... Fractured ankle (October 9, 1999); missed nine games.

STATISTICAL PLATEAUS: Three-goal games: 1990-91 (2), 1992-93 (1), 1996-97 (1), 1998-99 (1). Total: 5. ... Five-goal games: 1991-92 (1). ... Total hat tricks: 6.

			REGULAR SEASON								PLAYOFFS				
Season Team	League	Gms.	G	A	Pts.	PIM	+/-	PP	SH		Gms.	G	A	Pts.	PIM
88-89—Nacka..........................	Sweden	25	10	8	18	18	...	...	...		—	—	—	—	—
89-90—Djurgarden Stockholm	Sweden	34	10	8	18	16	...	...	...		8	7	0	7	4
90-91—Quebec	NHL	80	23	36	59	58	-24	4	0		—	—	—	—	—
91-92—Quebec	NHL	80	33	43	76	103	-19	8	2		—	—	—	—	—
92-93—Quebec	NHL	80	47	67	114	96	21	13	4		6	3	1	4	6
93-94—Quebec	NHL	84	32	53	85	60	1	6	2		—	—	—	—	—
94-95—Djurgarden Stockholm	Sweden	12	7	2	9	14	...	...	...		—	—	—	—	—
—Toronto	NHL	47	23	24	47	14	-5	9	0		7	5	4	9	4
95-96—Toronto	NHL	76	33	50	83	46	8	7	6		6	3	1	4	4
96-97—Toronto	NHL	82	41	53	94	59	6	7	4		—	—	—	—	—
97-98—Toronto	NHL	82	33	41	74	49	-3	9	1		—	—	—	—	—
—Swedish Oly. team	Int'l	4	3	0	3	4	...	...	...		—	—	—	—	—
98-99—Toronto	NHL	82	31	52	83	58	22	4	0		17	8	8	16	16
99-00—Toronto	NHL	73	32	41	73	46	16	10	2		12	3	5	8	10
00-01—Toronto	NHL	82	28	46	74	76	15	9	0		11	6	7	13	14
01-02—Toronto	NHL	82	41	39	80	94	6	10	2		8	2	5	7	4
—Swedish Oly. team	Int'l	4	5	4	9	10	...	...	...		—	—	—	—	—
02-03—Toronto	NHL	75	37	35	72	58	1	16	3		7	1	3	4	6
NHL Totals (13 years)..........		1005	434	580	1014	817	45	112	26		74	31	34	65	64

SUNDSTROM, NIKLAS　　　　RW　　　　CANADIENS

PERSONAL: Born June 6, 1975, in Ornskoldsvik, Sweden ... 6-0/195. ... Shoots left.

TRANSACTIONS/CAREER NOTES: Selected by New York Rangers in first round (first Rangers pick, eighth overall) of NHL entry draft (June 26, 1993). ... Fractured finger and sprained knee (December 5, 1997); missed 10 games. ... Traded by Rangers with G Dan Cloutier and first-(RW Nikita Alexeev) and third-round (traded to San Jose) picks in 2000 draft to Tampa Bay Lightning for first-round pick (RW Pavel Brendl) in 1999 draft (June 26, 1999). ... Traded by Lightning with third-round pick (traded to Chicago) in 2000 draft to San Jose Sharks for D Andrei Zyuzin, D Bill Houlder, LW Shawn Burr and C Steve Guolla (August 4, 1999). ... Injured knee (November 29, 2001); missed one game. ... Injured knee (March 21, 2002); missed eight games. ... Traded by Sharks with third-round pick in 2004 draft to Montreal Canadiens as part of three-team trade in which Boston Bruins acquired G Jeff Hackett and D Jeff Jillson and Sharks acquired D Kyle McLaren and fourth-round pick in 2004 draft (January 23, 2003).

Season Team	League	REGULAR SEASON								PLAYOFFS				
		Gms.	G	A	Pts.	PIM	+/-	PP	SH	Gms.	G	A	Pts.	PIM
91-92—MoDo Ornskoldsvik....	Sweden	9	1	3	4	0	...	...	...	—	—	—	—	—
92-93—MoDo Ornskoldsvik....	Sweden	40	7	11	18	18	...	...	...	—	—	—	—	—
93-94—MoDo Ornskoldsvik....	Sweden	37	7	12	19	28	...	...	...	11	4	3	7	2
94-95—MoDo Ornskoldsvik....	Sweden	33	8	13	21	30	...	...	...	—	—	—	—	—
95-96—New York Rangers......	NHL	82	9	12	21	14	2	1	1	11	4	3	7	4
96-97—New York Rangers......	NHL	82	24	28	52	20	23	5	1	9	0	5	5	2
97-98—New York Rangers......	NHL	70	19	28	47	24	0	4	0	—	—	—	—	—
—Swedish Oly. team......	Int'l	4	1	1	2	2	...	...	...	—	—	—	—	—
98-99—New York Rangers......	NHL	81	13	30	43	20	-2	1	2	—	—	—	—	—
99-00—San Jose..................	NHL	79	12	25	37	22	9	2	1	12	0	2	2	2
00-01—San Jose..................	NHL	82	10	39	49	28	10	4	1	6	0	3	3	2
01-02—San Jose..................	NHL	73	9	30	39	50	7	0	1	12	1	6	7	6
—Swedish Oly. team......	Int'l	4	1	3	4	0	...	...	...	—	—	—	—	—
02-03—San Jose..................	NHL	47	2	10	12	22	-4	0	0	—	—	—	—	—
—Montreal	NHL	33	5	9	14	8	3	0	0	—	—	—	—	—
NHL Totals (8 years)...........		629	103	211	314	208	48	17	7	50	5	19	24	16

SURMA, DAMIAN — LW — HURRICANES

PERSONAL: Born January 22, 1981, in Lincoln Park, Mich. ... 5-10/200. ... Shoots left.
TRANSACTIONS/CAREER NOTES: Selected by Carolina Hurricanes in sixth round (fifth Hurricanes pick, 174th overall) of NHL entry draft (June 26, 1999).

Season Team	League	REGULAR SEASON								PLAYOFFS				
		Gms.	G	A	Pts.	PIM	+/-	PP	SH	Gms.	G	A	Pts.	PIM
98-99—Plymouth	OHL	65	17	15	32	62	...	...	...	11	3	6	9	15
99-00—Plymouth	OHL	66	34	44	78	114	...	...	...	20	9	8	17	10
00-01—Plymouth	OHL	55	26	34	60	62	...	...	...	19	8	9	17	25
01-02—Plymouth	OHL	55	28	27	55	68	...	...	...	6	3	0	3	10
—Lowell	AHL	1	0	0	0	0	...	...	...	4	0	0	0	0
02-03—Lowell	AHL	68	11	11	22	46	...	...	...	—	—	—	—	—
—Carolina	NHL	1	1	0	1	0	0	0	0	—	—	—	—	—
NHL Totals (1 year).............		1	1	0	1	0	0	0	0	—	—	—	—	—

SUROVY, TOMAS — LW/LW — PENGUINS

PERSONAL: Born September 24, 1981, in Banska Bystrica, Czechoslovakia ... 6-1/187. ... Shoots left.
TRANSACTIONS/CAREER NOTES: Selected by Pittsburgh Penguins in fourth round (fifth Penguins pick, 120th overall) of NHL entry draft (June 23, 2001).

Season Team	League	REGULAR SEASON								PLAYOFFS				
		Gms.	G	A	Pts.	PIM	+/-	PP	SH	Gms.	G	A	Pts.	PIM
00-01—HC SKP Poprad	Slovakia	53	22	28	50	30	...	...	...	6	2	1	3	14
01-02—Wilkes-Barre/Scranton	AHL	65	23	10	33	37	...	...	...	—	—	—	—	—
02-03—Wilkes-Barre/Scranton	AHL	39	19	20	39	18	...	...	...	—	—	—	—	—
—Pittsburgh..................	NHL	26	4	7	11	10	0	1	0	—	—	—	—	—
NHL Totals (1 year).............		26	4	7	11	10	0	1	0					

SUTHERBY, BRIAN — C — CAPITALS

PERSONAL: Born March 1, 1982, in Edmonton ... 6-3/205. ... Shoots left.
TRANSACTIONS/CAREER NOTES: Selected by Washington Capitals in first round (first Capitals pick, 26th overall) of NHL entry draft (June 24, 2000).

Season Team	League	REGULAR SEASON								PLAYOFFS				
		Gms.	G	A	Pts.	PIM	+/-	PP	SH	Gms.	G	A	Pts.	PIM
98-99—Moose Jaw	WHL	66	9	12	21	47	...	...	...	11	0	1	1	0
99-00—Moose Jaw	WHL	47	18	17	35	102	...	...	...	4	1	1	2	12
00-01—Moose Jaw	WHL	59	34	43	77	138	...	...	...	4	2	1	3	10
01-02—Washington	NHL	7	0	0	0	2	-3	0	0	—	—	—	—	—
—Moose Jaw	WHL	36	18	27	45	75	...	...	...	12	7	5	12	33
02-03—Portland....................	AHL	5	0	5	5	11	...	...	...	—	—	—	—	—
—Washington	NHL	72	2	9	11	93	7	0	0	5	0	0	0	10
NHL Totals (2 years)...........		79	2	9	11	95	4	0	0	5	0	0	0	10

SUTTON, ANDY — D — THRASHERS

PERSONAL: Born March 10, 1975, in Kingston, Ont. ... 6-6/245. ... Shoots left. ... Full Name: Andy Cameron Sutton.
TRANSACTIONS/CAREER NOTES: Signed as non-drafted free agent by San Jose Sharks (March 20, 1998). ... Injured wrist (November 27, 1999); missed three games. ... Reinjured wrist (December 8, 1999); missed three games. ... Reinjured wrist (December 20, 1999); missed seven games. ... Reinjured wrist (January 12, 2000); missed 10 games. ... Traded by Sharks with seventh-round pick (RW/LW Peter Bartos) in 2000 draft and third-round pick (traded to Atlanta) in 2001 draft to Minnesota Wild for eighth-round pick (traded to Calgary) in 2001 draft and future considerations (June 12, 2000). ... Bruised knee (November 8, 2000); missed two games. ... Dislocated shoulder (March 6, 2001); missed one game. ... Separated right shoulder (October 30, 2001); missed 12 games. ... Strained groin (January 9, 2002); missed four games. ... Traded by Wild to Atlanta Thrashers for LW Hnat Domenichelli (January 22, 2002). ... Suffered concussion (April 2, 2002); missed two games. ... Re-signed by Thrashers (July 17, 2003).

Season Team	League	REGULAR SEASON								PLAYOFFS				
		Gms.	G	A	Pts.	PIM	+/-	PP	SH	Gms.	G	A	Pts.	PIM
94-95—Michigan Tech	WCHA	19	2	1	3	42	...	...	...	—	—	—	—	—
95-96—Michigan Tech	WCHA	32	2	2	4	38	...	...	...	—	—	—	—	—
96-97—Michigan Tech	WCHA	32	2	7	9	73	...	...	...	—	—	—	—	—
97-98—Michigan Tech	WCHA	38	16	24	40	97	...	...	...	—	—	—	—	—
—Kentucky	AHL	7	0	0	0	33	...	...	...	—	—	—	—	—
98-99—San Jose	NHL	31	0	3	3	65	-4	0	0	—	—	—	—	—
—Kentucky	AHL	21	5	10	15	53	...	...	...	5	0	0	0	23
99-00—San Jose	NHL	40	1	1	2	80	-5	0	0	—	—	—	—	—
—Kentucky	AHL	3	0	1	1	0	...	...	...	—	—	—	—	—
00-01—Minnesota	NHL	69	3	4	7	131	-11	2	0	—	—	—	—	—
01-02—Minnesota	NHL	19	2	4	6	35	-4	1	0	—	—	—	—	—
—Atlanta	NHL	24	0	4	4	46	0	0	0	—	—	—	—	—
02-03—Atlanta	NHL	53	3	18	21	114	-8	1	1	—	—	—	—	—
NHL Totals (5 years)		236	9	34	43	471	-32	4	1					

SUTTON, KEN   D

PERSONAL: Born November 5, 1969, in Edmonton. ... 6-1/205. ... Shoots left. ... Full Name: Kenneth Sutton.

TRANSACTIONS/CAREER NOTES: Selected by Buffalo Sabres in fifth round (fourth Sabres pick, 98th overall) of NHL entry draft (June 17, 1989). ... Separated shoulder (March 3, 1992); missed six games. ... Fractured ankle (September 15, 1992); missed first 19 games of season. ... Fractured finger (February 15, 1995); missed 10 games. ... Traded by Sabres to Edmonton Oilers for LW Scott Pearson (April 7, 1995). ... Traded by Oilers with D Igor Kravchuk to St. Louis Blues for D Donald Dufresne and D Jeff Norton (January 4, 1996). ... Traded by Blues with second-round pick (LW Brett Clouthier) in 1999 draft to New Jersey Devils for LW Mike Peluso and D Ricard Persson (November 26, 1996). ... Traded by Devils with RW John MacLean to San Jose Sharks for D Doug Bodger and LW Dody Wood (December 7, 1997). ... Traded by Sharks to Devils for fifth-round pick (RW Nicholas Dimitrakos) in 1999 draft (August 26, 1998). ... Claimed by Washington Capitals from Devils in NHL waiver draft (September 27, 1999). ... Traded by Capitals to Devils for future considerations (October 5, 1999). ... Signed as free agent by New York Islanders (July 5, 2001). ... Signed as free agent by Devils (August 26, 2002).

Season Team	League	REGULAR SEASON								PLAYOFFS				
		Gms.	G	A	Pts.	PIM	+/-	PP	SH	Gms.	G	A	Pts.	PIM
87-88—Calgary Canucks	AJHL	53	13	43	56	228	...	...	...	—	—	—	—	—
88-89—Saskatoon	WHL	71	22	31	53	104	...	...	...	8	2	5	7	12
89-90—Rochester	AHL	57	5	14	19	83	...	...	...	11	1	6	7	15
90-91—Buffalo	NHL	15	3	6	9	13	2	2	0	6	0	1	1	2
—Rochester	AHL	62	7	24	31	65	...	...	...	3	1	1	2	14
91-92—Buffalo	NHL	64	2	18	20	71	5	0	0	7	0	2	2	4
92-93—Buffalo	NHL	63	8	14	22	30	-3	1	0	8	3	1	4	8
93-94—Buffalo	NHL	78	4	20	24	71	-6	1	0	4	0	0	0	2
94-95—Buffalo	NHL	12	1	2	3	30	-2	0	0	—	—	—	—	—
—Edmonton	NHL	12	3	1	4	12	-1	0	0	—	—	—	—	—
95-96—Edmonton	NHL	32	0	8	8	39	-12	0	0	—	—	—	—	—
—St. Louis	NHL	6	0	0	0	4	-1	0	0	1	0	0	0	0
—Worcester	AHL	32	4	16	20	60	...	...	...	4	0	2	2	21
96-97—Manitoba	IHL	20	3	10	13	48	...	...	...	—	—	—	—	—
—Albany	AHL	61	6	13	19	79	...	...	...	16	4	8	12	55
97-98—Albany	AHL	10	0	7	7	15	...	...	...	—	—	—	—	—
—New Jersey	NHL	13	0	0	0	6	1	0	0	—	—	—	—	—
—San Jose	NHL	8	0	0	0	15	-4	0	0	—	—	—	—	—
98-99—Albany	AHL	75	13	42	55	118	...	...	...	5	0	2	2	12
—New Jersey	NHL	5	1	0	1	0	1	0	0	—	—	—	—	—
99-00—New Jersey	NHL	6	0	2	2	2	2	0	0	—	—	—	—	—
—Albany	AHL	57	5	16	21	129	...	...	...	—	—	—	—	—
00-01—New Jersey	NHL	53	1	7	8	37	9	0	0	6	0	0	0	13
01-02—New York Islanders	NHL	21	0	2	2	8	-5	0	0	—	—	—	—	—
—Bridgeport	AHL	28	1	10	11	51	...	...	...	20	2	8	10	24
02-03—Albany	AHL	74	6	26	32	70	...	...	...	—	—	—	—	—
NHL Totals (11 years)		388	23	80	103	338	-14	4	0	32	3	4	7	29

SVARTVADET, PER   LW

PERSONAL: Born May 17, 1975, in Solleftea, Sweden ... 6-2/205. ... Shoots left. ... Name pronounced PAIR SVAHRT-vuh-deht.

TRANSACTIONS/CAREER NOTES: Selected by Dallas Stars in sixth round (fifth Stars pick, 139th overall) of NHL entry draft (June 26, 1993). ... Traded by Stars to Atlanta Thrashers for sixth-round pick (RW Justin Cox) in 1999 draft (June 26, 1999). ... Fractured finger (October 16, 1999); missed one game. ... Sprained ankle (January 13, 2001); missed nine games.

Season Team	League	REGULAR SEASON								PLAYOFFS				
		Gms.	G	A	Pts.	PIM	+/-	PP	SH	Gms.	G	A	Pts.	PIM
91-92—MoDo Hockey	Sweden Jr.	30	17	19	36	36	...	...	...	—	—	—	—	—
92-93—MoDo Ornskoldsvik	Sweden	2	0	0	0	0	...	...	...	—	—	—	—	—
—MoDo Hockey	Sweden Jr.	22	19	27	46	38	...	...	...	—	—	—	—	—
93-94—MoDo Ornskoldsvik	Sweden	36	2	1	3	4	...	...	...	11	0	0	0	6
94-95—MoDo Ornskoldsvik	Sweden	40	6	9	15	31	...	...	...	—	—	—	—	—
95-96—MoDo Ornskoldsvik	Sweden	40	9	14	23	26	...	...	...	8	2	3	5	0
96-97—MoDo Ornskoldsvik	Sweden	50	7	18	25	38	...	...	...	—	—	—	—	—
97-98—MoDo Ornskoldsvik	Sweden	46	6	12	18	28	...	...	...	7	3	2	5	2
98-99—MoDo Ornskoldsvik	Sweden	50	9	23	32	30	...	...	...	13	3	6	9	6
99-00—Atlanta	NHL	38	3	4	7	6	-8	0	0	—	—	—	—	—
—Orlando	IHL	27	4	6	10	10	...	...	...	5	0	1	1	0
00-01—Atlanta	NHL	69	10	11	21	20	-6	0	2	—	—	—	—	—
01-02—Atlanta	NHL	78	3	12	15	24	-12	0	0	—	—	—	—	—
02-03—Chicago	AHL	3	0	0	0	2	...	...	...	—	—	—	—	—
—Atlanta	NHL	62	1	7	8	8	-11	0	0	—	—	—	—	—
NHL Totals (4 years)		247	17	34	51	58	-37	0	2					

SVEHLA, ROBERT   D   MAPLE LEAFS

PERSONAL: Born January 2, 1969, in Martin, Czechoslovakia ... 6-0/209. ... Shoots right. ... Name pronounced SVAY-luh.
TRANSACTIONS/CAREER NOTES: Selected by Calgary Flames in fourth round (fourth Flames pick, 78th overall) of NHL entry draft (June 20, 1992). ... Traded by Flames with D Magnus Svensson to Florida Panthers for third-round pick (LW Dmitri Vlasenkov) in 1996 draft and fourth-round pick (LW Ryan Ready) in 1997 draft (September 29, 1994). ... Sprained left rotator cuff (April 22, 1995); missed two games. ... Reinjured left rotator cuff (April 28, 1995); missed one game. ... Suffered back spasms (March 4, 1998); missed three games. ... Traded by Panthers to Toronto Maple Leafs for D Dmitry Yushkevich (July 18, 2002).

					REGULAR SEASON						PLAYOFFS			
Season Team	League	Gms.	G	A	Pts.	PIM	+/-	PP	SH	Gms.	G	A	Pts.	PIM
89-90—Dukla Trencin..............	Czech.	29	4	3	7	...	...	...	...	—	—	—	—	—
90-91—Dukla Trencin..............	Czech.	58	16	9	25	...	...	...	...	—	—	—	—	—
91-92—Dukla Trencin..............	Czech.	51	23	28	51	0	...	...	...	—	—	—	—	—
—Czech. Olympic Team .	Int'l	8	2	1	3	...	...	...	...	—	—	—	—	—
92-93—Malmo	Sweden	40	19	10	29	86	...	...	...	6	0	1	1	14
93-94—Malmo	Sweden	37	14	25	39	*127	...	...	...	10	5	1	6	23
—Slovakian Oly. team	Int'l	8	2	4	6	26	...	...	...	—	—	—	—	—
94-95—Malmo	Sweden	32	11	13	24	83	...	...	...	9	2	3	5	6
—Florida......................	NHL	5	1	1	2	0	3	1	0	—	—	—	—	—
95-96—Florida......................	NHL	81	8	49	57	94	-3	7	0	22	0	6	6	32
96-97—Florida......................	NHL	82	13	32	45	86	2	5	0	5	1	4	5	4
97-98—Florida......................	NHL	79	9	34	43	113	-3	3	0	—	—	—	—	—
—Slovakian Oly. team	Int'l	2	0	1	1	0	...	...	...	—	—	—	—	—
98-99—Florida......................	NHL	80	8	29	37	83	-13	4	0	—	—	—	—	—
99-00—Florida......................	NHL	82	9	40	49	64	23	3	0	4	0	1	1	4
00-01—Florida......................	NHL	82	6	22	28	76	-8	0	0	—	—	—	—	—
01-02—Florida......................	NHL	82	7	22	29	87	-19	3	0	—	—	—	—	—
02-03—Toronto	NHL	82	7	38	45	46	13	2	0	7	0	3	3	2
NHL Totals (9 years)............		**655**	**68**	**267**	**335**	**649**	**-5**	**28**	**0**	**38**	**1**	**14**	**15**	**42**

SVITOV, ALEXANDER   C   LIGHTNING

PERSONAL: Born November 3, 1982, in Omsk, U.S.S.R. ... 6-3/217. ... Shoots left.
TRANSACTIONS/CAREER NOTES: Selected by Tampa Bay Lightning in first round (first Lightning pick, third overall) of NHL entry draft (June 23, 2001).

					REGULAR SEASON						PLAYOFFS			
Season Team	League	Gms.	G	A	Pts.	PIM	+/-	PP	SH	Gms.	G	A	Pts.	PIM
99-00—Avangard Omsk	Russian	18	3	3	6	45	...	...	...	6	1	0	1	16
00-01—Avangard Omsk	Russian	39	8	6	14	115	...	...	...	14	2	1	3	34
01-02—Avangard Omsk	Russian	2	0	1	1	2	...	...	...	—	—	—	—	—
02-03—Springfield	AHL	11	4	5	9	17	...	...	...	—	—	—	—	—
—Tampa Bay	NHL	63	4	4	8	58	-4	1	0	7	0	0	0	6
NHL Totals (1 year)............		**63**	**4**	**4**	**8**	**58**	**-4**	**1**	**0**	**7**	**0**	**0**	**0**	**6**

SVOBODA, JAROSLAV   RW   HURRICANES

PERSONAL: Born June 1, 1980, in Cervenka, Czechoslovakia ... 6-2/190.
TRANSACTIONS/CAREER NOTES: Selected by Carolina Hurricanes in eighth round (eighth Hurricanes pick, 208th overall) of NHL entry draft (June 21, 1997).

					REGULAR SEASON						PLAYOFFS			
Season Team	League	Gms.	G	A	Pts.	PIM	+/-	PP	SH	Gms.	G	A	Pts.	PIM
97-98—Olomouc	Czech. Jrs.	43	15	18	33	0	...	...	...	—	—	—	—	—
98-99—Kootenay....................	WHL	54	26	33	59	46	...	...	...	7	2	2	4	11
99-00—Kootenay....................	WHL	56	23	43	66	97	...	...	...	21	*15	13	*28	51
00-01—Cincinnati	IHL	52	4	10	14	25	...	...	...	—	—	—	—	—
01-02—Lowell	AHL	66	12	16	28	58	...	...	...	—	—	—	—	—
—Carolina	NHL	10	2	2	4	2	0	0	0	23	1	4	5	28
02-03—Lowell	AHL	9	1	1	2	10	...	...	...	—	—	—	—	—
—Carolina	NHL	48	3	11	14	32	-5	1	0	—	—	—	—	—
NHL Totals (2 years)............		**58**	**5**	**13**	**18**	**34**	**-5**	**1**	**0**	**23**	**1**	**4**	**5**	**28**

SWANSON, BRIAN   C   THRASHERS

PERSONAL: Born March 24, 1976, in Eagle River, Alaska ... 5-10/185. ... Shoots left.
TRANSACTIONS/CAREER NOTES: Selected by San Jose Sharks in fifth round (fifth Sharks pick, 115th overall) of NHL entry draft (June 29, 1994). ... Traded by Sharks with D Jayson More and fourth-round pick (D Tomi Kallarsson) in 1997 draft to New York Rangers for D Marty McSorley (August 20, 1996). ... Signed as free agent by Edmonton Oilers (August 20, 1999). ... Signed by Atlanta Thrashers (July 24, 2003).

					REGULAR SEASON						PLAYOFFS			
Season Team	League	Gms.	G	A	Pts.	PIM	+/-	PP	SH	Gms.	G	A	Pts.	PIM
93-94—Omaha	USHL	47	38	42	80	40	...	...	...	—	—	—	—	—
94-95—Portland	WHL	65	3	18	21	91	...	...	...	9	2	1	3	18
95-96—Colorado College	WCHA	40	26	33	59	24	...	...	...	—	—	—	—	—
96-97—Colorado College	WCHA	43	19	32	51	47	...	...	...	—	—	—	—	—
97-98—Colorado College	WCHA	42	18	*38	*56	26	...	...	...	—	—	—	—	—
98-99—Colorado College	WCHA	42	25	†41	66	28	...	...	...	—	—	—	—	—
—Hartford	AHL	4	0	0	0	4	...	...	...	—	—	—	—	—
99-00—Hamilton	AHL	69	19	40	59	18	...	...	...	10	2	5	7	6
00-01—Edmonton	NHL	16	1	1	2	6	-1	0	0	—	—	—	—	—
—Hamilton	AHL	49	18	29	47	20	...	...	...	—	—	—	—	—
01-02—Hamilton	AHL	65	34	39	73	26	...	...	...	15	7	6	13	6
—Edmonton	NHL	8	1	1	2	0	-1	0	0	—	—	—	—	—
02-03—Edmonton	NHL	44	2	10	12	10	-7	1	0	—	—	—	—	—
NHL Totals (3 years)............		**68**	**4**	**12**	**16**	**16**	**-9**	**1**	**0**	—	—	—	—	—

PERSONAL: Born August 17, 1966, in St. Stephen, N.B. ... 5-10/186. ... Shoots left. ... Full Name: Donald Clark Sweeney.

TRANSACTIONS/CAREER NOTES: Selected by Boston Bruins in eighth round (eighth Bruins pick, 166th overall) of NHL entry draft (June 9, 1984). ... Bruised left heel (February 22, 1990). ... Injured knee (October 12, 1991); missed four games. ... Sprained knee (October 5, 1993); missed six games. ... Injured ribs (December 15, 1993); missed three games. ... Injured shoulder (October 17, 1995); missed three games. ... Injured shoulder (October 31, 1995); missed two games. ... Fractured shoulder (March 1, 1998); missed remainder of season. ... Suffered from the flu (January 13, 2000); missed one game. ... Underwent knee surgery (December 13, 2000); missed eight games. ... Injured knee (January 27, 2001); missed two games. ... Suffered from the flu (January 12, 2002); missed one game. ... Signed by Dallas Stars (July 14, 2003).

Season Team	League	REGULAR SEASON								PLAYOFFS				
		Gms.	G	A	Pts.	PIM	+/-	PP	SH	Gms.	G	A	Pts.	PIM
83-84—St. Paul N.B. H.S.	N.B. H.S.	22	33	26	59	...	...	...	...	—	—	—	—	—
84-85—Harvard University	ECAC	29	3	7	10	30	...	...	...	—	—	—	—	—
85-86—Harvard University	ECAC	31	4	5	9	29	...	...	...	—	—	—	—	—
86-87—Harvard University	ECAC	34	7	14	21	22	...	...	...	—	—	—	—	—
87-88—Harvard University	ECAC	30	6	23	29	37	...	...	...	—	—	—	—	—
—Maine	AHL	—	—	—	—	—	—	—	—	6	1	3	4	0
88-89—Maine	AHL	42	8	17	25	24	...	...	...	—	—	—	—	—
—Boston	NHL	36	3	5	8	20	-6	0	0	—	—	—	—	—
89-90—Boston	NHL	58	3	5	8	58	11	0	0	21	1	5	6	18
—Maine	AHL	11	0	8	8	8	...	...	...	—	—	—	—	—
90-91—Boston	NHL	77	8	13	21	67	2	0	1	19	3	0	3	25
91-92—Boston	NHL	75	3	11	14	74	-9	0	0	15	0	0	0	10
92-93—Boston	NHL	84	7	27	34	68	34	0	1	4	0	0	0	4
93-94—Boston	NHL	75	6	15	21	50	29	1	2	12	2	1	3	4
94-95—Boston	NHL	47	3	19	22	24	6	1	0	5	0	0	0	4
95-96—Boston	NHL	77	4	24	28	42	-4	2	0	5	0	2	2	6
96-97—Boston	NHL	82	3	23	26	39	-5	0	0	—	—	—	—	—
97-98—Boston	NHL	59	1	15	16	24	12	0	0	—	—	—	—	—
98-99—Boston	NHL	81	2	10	12	64	14	0	0	11	3	0	3	6
99-00—Boston	NHL	81	1	13	14	48	-14	0	0	—	—	—	—	—
00-01—Boston	NHL	72	2	10	12	26	-1	1	0	—	—	—	—	—
01-02—Boston	NHL	81	3	15	18	35	22	1	0	6	0	1	1	2
02-03—Boston	NHL	67	3	5	8	24	-1	0	0	5	0	1	1	0
NHL Totals (15 years)		1052	52	210	262	663	90	6	4	103	9	10	19	79

PERSONAL: Born May 13, 1972, in Edmonton ... 6-1/205. ... Shoots left. ... Full Name: Darryl Marion Sydor. ... Name pronounced sih-DOHR.

TRANSACTIONS/CAREER NOTES: Selected by Los Angeles Kings in first round (first Kings pick, seventh overall) of NHL entry draft (June 16, 1990). ... Bruised hip (November 27, 1992); missed two games. ... Sprained right shoulder (March 15, 1993); missed two games. ... Traded by Kings with seventh-round pick (G Eoin McInerney) in 1996 draft to Dallas Stars for RW Shane Churla and D Doug Zmolek (February 17, 1996). ... Sprained knee (February 21, 1999); missed three games. ... Reinjured knee (March 7, 1999); missed five games. ... Fractured eye socket (October 2, 1999); missed three games. ... Injured groin (October 20, 1999); missed three games. ... Injured neck (March 26, 2000); missed two games. ... Suffered from the flu (December 31, 2000); missed one game. ... Injured ankle (November 17, 2001); missed one game. ... Suffered concussion (December 14, 2001); missed three games. ... Traded by Stars to Columbus Blue Jackets for C Mike Sillinger and 2004 second-round draft pick (July 22, 2003).

STATISTICAL PLATEAUS: Three-goal games: 1997-98 (1).

Season Team	League	REGULAR SEASON								PLAYOFFS				
		Gms.	G	A	Pts.	PIM	+/-	PP	SH	Gms.	G	A	Pts.	PIM
88-89—Kamloops	WHL	65	12	14	26	86	...	...	...	15	1	4	5	19
89-90—Kamloops	WHL	67	29	66	95	129	...	...	...	17	2	9	11	28
90-91—Kamloops	WHL	66	27	78	105	88	...	...	...	12	3	*22	25	10
91-92—Kamloops	WHL	29	9	39	48	43	...	...	...	17	3	15	18	18
—Los Angeles	NHL	18	1	5	6	22	-3	0	0	—	—	—	—	—
92-93—Los Angeles	NHL	80	6	23	29	63	-2	0	0	24	3	8	11	16
93-94—Los Angeles	NHL	84	8	27	35	94	-9	1	0	—	—	—	—	—
94-95—Los Angeles	NHL	48	4	19	23	36	-2	3	0	—	—	—	—	—
95-96—Los Angeles	NHL	58	1	11	12	34	-11	1	0	—	—	—	—	—
—Dallas	NHL	26	2	6	8	41	-1	1	0	—	—	—	—	—
96-97—Dallas	NHL	82	8	40	48	51	37	2	0	7	0	2	2	0
97-98—Dallas	NHL	79	11	35	46	51	17	4	1	17	0	5	5	14
98-99—Dallas	NHL	74	14	34	48	50	-1	9	0	23	3	9	12	16
99-00—Dallas	NHL	74	8	26	34	32	6	5	0	23	1	6	7	6
00-01—Dallas	NHL	81	10	37	47	34	5	8	0	10	1	3	4	0
01-02—Dallas	NHL	78	4	29	33	50	3	2	0	—	—	—	—	—
02-03—Dallas	NHL	81	5	31	36	40	22	2	0	12	0	6	6	6
NHL Totals (12 years)		863	82	323	405	598	61	38	1	116	8	39	47	58

PERSONAL: Born December 21, 1978, in Pardubice, Czechoslovakia. ... 6-2/180. ... Shoots right.

TRANSACTIONS/CAREER NOTES: Selected by Detroit Red Wings in third round (second Red Wings pick, 76th overall) of NHL entry draft (June 21, 1997). ... Traded by Red Wings with third-round pick (traded to Edmonton) in 1999 draft and future considerations to Nashville Predators for RW Doug Brown (July 14, 1998). ... Traded by Predators to Washington Capitals for conditional pick in 2003 draft (June 23, 2002).

Season Team	League	REGULAR SEASON								PLAYOFFS				
		Gms.	G	A	Pts.	PIM	+/-	PP	SH	Gms.	G	A	Pts.	PIM
94-95—HC Pardubice.............	Czech. Jrs.	38	35	33	68	...	...	...	...	—	—	—	—	—
95-96—HC Pardubice.............	Czech. Jrs.	26	13	9	22	...	...	...	...	—	—	—	—	—
96-97—Pojistovna Pardubice..	Czech Rep.	29	1	3	4	4	...	...	...	—	—	—	—	—
—Poji. Pardubice	Czech. Jrs.	12	14	4	18	...	...	...	...	—	—	—	—	—
97-98—Pojistovna Pardubice..	Czech Rep.	39	4	5	9	8	...	...	...	3	0	0	0	0
98-99—Milwaukee..................	IHL	73	14	15	29	50	...	...	...	2	1	1	2	0
—Nashville..................	NHL	2	0	0	0	0	-1	0	0	—	—	—	—	—
99-00—Milwaukee..................	IHL	3	0	1	1	2	...	...	...	—	—	—	—	—
—HC Pardubice.............	Czech Rep.	36	7	13	20	49	...	...	...	3	0	0	0	2
00-01—HC Pardubice.............	Czech Rep.	47	26	18	44	42	...	...	...	7	5	3	8	6
01-02—HC Pardubice.............	Czech Rep.	32	18	8	26	72	...	...	...	6	1	2	3	26
02-03—HC Pardubice.............	Czech Rep.	45	18	18	36	86	...	...	...	—	—	—	—	—
NHL Totals (1 year)............		**2**	**0**	**0**	**0**	**0**	**-1**	**0**	**0**					

SYKORA, PETR — RW — MIGHTY DUCKS

PERSONAL: Born November 19, 1976, in Plzen, Czechoslovakia ... 5-11/191. ... Shoots left. ... Name pronounced sih-KOHR-uh.
TRANSACTIONS/CAREER NOTES: Selected by New Jersey Devils in first round (first Devils pick, 18th overall) of NHL entry draft (July 8, 1995). ... Injured back (February 21, 1996); missed two games. ... Injured groin (October 5, 1996); missed two games. ... Reinjured groin (November 9, 1996); missed four games. ... Reinjured groin (November 30, 1996); missed three games. ... Bruised shoulder (November 5, 1997); missed two games. ... Sprained left ankle (November 29, 1997); missed 20 games. ... Suffered from food poisoning (January 2, 1999); missed two games ... Suffered from the flu (March 2, 2000); missed three games. ... Injured groin (October 26, 2000); missed three games. ... Reinjured groin (November 4, 2000); missed one game. ... Bruised shoulder (February 17, 2001); missed five games. ... Suffered illness (December 26, 2001); missed three games. ... Bruised ribs (February 9, 2002); missed one game. ... Suffered from the flu (March 20, 2002); missed five games. ... Traded by Devils with C Igor Pohanka, D Mike Commodore and G J.F. Damphousse to Mighty Ducks of Anaheim for D Oleg Tverdovsky, LW Jeff Friesen and RW Maxin Balmochnykh (July 7, 2002).

Season Team	League	REGULAR SEASON								PLAYOFFS				
		Gms.	G	A	Pts.	PIM	+/-	PP	SH	Gms.	G	A	Pts.	PIM
91-92—Skoda Plzen...............	Czech.	30	50	50	100	...	...	...	...	—	—	—	—	—
92-93—Skoda Plzen...............	Czech.	19	12	5	17	...	...	...	...	—	—	—	—	—
93-94—Skoda Plzen...............	Czech Rep.	37	10	16	26	...	...	...	...	4	0	1	1	...
—Cleveland	IHL	13	4	5	9	8	...	...	...	—	—	—	—	—
94-95—Detroit......................	IHL	29	12	17	29	16	...	...	...	—	—	—	—	—
95-96—Albany......................	AHL	5	4	1	5	0	...	...	...	—	—	—	—	—
—New Jersey	NHL	63	18	24	42	32	7	8	0	—	—	—	—	—
96-97—New Jersey	NHL	19	1	2	3	4	-8	0	0	2	0	0	0	2
—Albany......................	AHL	43	20	25	45	48	...	...	...	4	1	4	5	2
97-98—New Jersey	NHL	58	16	20	36	22	0	3	1	2	0	0	0	0
—Albany......................	AHL	2	4	1	5	0	...	...	...	—	—	—	—	—
98-99—New Jersey	NHL	80	29	43	72	22	16	15	0	7	3	3	6	4
99-00—New Jersey	NHL	79	25	43	68	26	24	5	1	23	9	8	17	10
00-01—New Jersey	NHL	73	35	46	81	32	36	9	2	25	10	12	22	12
01-02—New Jersey	NHL	73	21	27	48	44	12	4	0	4	0	1	1	0
—Czech Rep. Oly. team..	Int'l	4	1	0	1	0	...	...	...	—	—	—	—	—
02-03—Anaheim	NHL	82	34	25	59	24	-7	15	1	21	4	9	13	12
NHL Totals (8 years)...........		**527**	**179**	**230**	**409**	**206**	**80**	**59**	**5**	**84**	**26**	**33**	**59**	**40**

SZUPER, LAVENTE — G

PERSONAL: Born June 11, 1980, in Budapest, Hungary. ... 5-11/178. ... Catches left.
TRANSACTIONS/CAREER NOTES: Selected by Calgary Flames in fourth round (fourth Flames pick, 116th overall) of NHL entry draft (June 24, 2000).

Season Team	League	REGULAR SEASON									PLAYOFFS							
		Gms.	Min	W	L	T	GA	SO	Avg.	SV%	Gms.	Min.	W	L	GA	SO	Avg.	SV%
98-99—Ottawa........................	OHL	32	1800	22	6	3	70	4	2.33	—	4	241	2	2	11	*1	2.74	—
99-00—Ottawa........................	OHL	53	2862	31	15	2	122	5	2.56	—	11	680	6	5	35	1	3.09	—
00-01—Saint John....................	AHL	34	1750	16	10	2	73	2	2.50	—	1	36	1	0	0	0	...	—
01-02—Saint John....................	AHL	43	2428	15	18	5	98	5	2.42	—	—	—	—	—	—	—	—	—
02-03—Saint John....................	AHL	35	1903	12	18	2	82	1	2.59	—	—	—	—	—	—	—	—	—

TAFFE, JEFF — C — COYOTES

PERSONAL: Born February 19, 1981, in Hastings, Minn. ... 6-3/193. ... Shoots left. ... Name pronounced TAYFE.
HIGH SCHOOL: Hastings (Minn.).
COLLEGE: Minnesota.
TRANSACTIONS/CAREER NOTES: Selected by St. Louis Blues in first round (first Blues pick, 30th overall) of NHL entry draft (June 24, 2000). ... Traded by Blues with C Michal Handzus, RW Ladislav Nagy and first-round pick (LW Ben Eager) in 2002 draft to Phoenix Coyotes for LW Keith Tkachuk (March 13, 2001).

Season Team	League	REGULAR SEASON								PLAYOFFS				
		Gms.	G	A	Pts.	PIM	+/-	PP	SH	Gms.	G	A	Pts.	PIM
98-99—Hastings H.S..............	USHS (West)	25	38	48	86	26	...	...	...	—	—	—	—	—
99-00—Univ. of Minnesota......	WCHA	34	9	10	19	16	...	...	...	—	—	—	—	—
00-01—Univ. of Minnesota......	WCHA	38	12	23	35	56	...	...	...	—	—	—	—	—
01-02—Univ. of Minnesota......	WCHA	43	*34	24	58	86	...	...	...	—	—	—	—	—
02-03—Springfield	AHL	57	23	26	49	44	...	...	...	—	—	—	—	—
—Phoenix.....................	NHL	20	3	1	4	4	-4	1	0	—	—	—	—	—
NHL Totals (1 year)............		**20**	**3**	**1**	**4**	**4**	**-4**	**1**	**0**					

S

T

TALLAS, ROB   G

PERSONAL: Born March 20, 1973, in Edmonton. ... 6-0/163. ... Catches left. ... Name pronounced TAL-ihz.
TRANSACTIONS/CAREER NOTES: Signed as non-drafted free agent by Boston Bruins (September 13, 1995). ... Injured ankle (March 24, 1997); missed eight games. ... Strained hamstring (January 24, 1998); missed eight games. ... Lacerated finger (November 24, 1999); missed two games. ... Signed as free agent by Chicago Blackhawks (July 31, 2000). ... Signed as free agent by Pittsburgh Penguins (August 14, 2001).

			REGULAR SEASON									PLAYOFFS						
Season Team	League	Gms.	Min	W	L	T	GA	SO	Avg.	SV%	Gms.	Min.	W	L	GA	SO	Avg.	SV%
91-92—Seattle	WHL	14	708	4	7	0	52	0	4.41	—	—	—	—	—	—	—	—	—
92-93—Seattle	WHL	52	3151	24	23	3	194	2	3.69	—	5	333	1	4	18	0	3.24	—
93-94—Seattle	WHL	51	2849	23	21	3	188	0	3.96	—	9	567	5	4	40	0	4.23	—
94-95—Charlotte	ECHL	36	2011	21	9	‡3	114	0	3.40	—	—	—	—	—	—	—	—	—
—Providence	AHL	2	82	1	0	0	4	1	2.93	—	—	—	—	—	—	—	—	—
95-96—Boston	NHL	1	60	1	0	0	3	0	3.00	.897	—	—	—	—	—	—	—	—
—Providence	AHL	37	2136	12	16	7	117	1	3.29	—	2	135	0	2	9	0	4.00	—
96-97—Providence	AHL	24	1423	9	14	1	83	0	3.50	—	—	—	—	—	—	—	—	—
—Boston	NHL	28	1244	8	12	1	69	1	3.33	.882	—	—	—	—	—	—	—	—
97-98—Providence	AHL	10	575	1	8	1	39	0	4.07	—	—	—	—	—	—	—	—	—
—Boston	NHL	14	788	6	3	3	24	1	1.83	.926	—	—	—	—	—	—	—	—
98-99—Boston	NHL	17	987	7	7	2	43	1	2.61	.898	—	—	—	—	—	—	—	—
99-00—Boston	NHL	27	1363	4	13	4	72	0	3.17	.885	—	—	—	—	—	—	—	—
00-01—Chicago	NHL	12	627	2	7	0	35	0	3.35	.868	—	—	—	—	—	—	—	—
—Norfolk	AHL	6	333	2	2	2	12	0	2.16	—	—	—	—	—	—	—	—	—
—Chicago	IHL	3	87	0	1	‡0	6	0	4.14	—	—	—	—	—	—	—	—	—
01-02—Wilkes-Barre/Scranton	AHL	38	2183	6	25	5	126	0	3.46	—	—	—	—	—	—	—	—	—
02-03—Wilkes-Barre/Scranton	AHL	33	1762	14	11	3	99	0	3.37	—	—	—	—	—	—	—	—	—
NHL Totals (6 years)		99	5069	28	42	10	246	3	2.91	.891								

TALLINDER, HENRIK   D   SABRES

PERSONAL: Born January 10, 1979, in Stockholm, Sweden ... 6-3/217. ... Shoots left.
TRANSACTIONS/CAREER NOTES: Selected by Buffalo Sabres in second round (second Sabres pick, 48th overall) of NHL entry draft (June 21, 1997).

			REGULAR SEASON							PLAYOFFS			
Season Team	League	Gms.	G	A	Pts.	PIM	+/-	PP	SH	Gms.	G	A	Pts.	PIM
95-96—AIK Solna Jrs.	Sweden	40	4	13	17	55	...	...	...	—	—	—	—	—
96-97—AIK Solna Jrs.	Sweden					Statistics unavailable.								
—AIK Solna	Sweden	1	0	0	0	0	...	...	...	—	—	—	—	—
97-98—AIK Solna	Sweden	34	0	0	0	26	...	...	...	—	—	—	—	—
98-99—AIK Solna	Sweden	36	0	0	0	30	...	...	...	—	—	—	—	—
99-00—AIK Solna	Sweden	50	0	2	2	59	...	...	...	—	—	—	—	—
00-01—TPS Turku	Finland	56	5	9	14	62	...	...	...	10	2	1	3	8
01-02—Rochester	AHL	73	6	14	20	26	...	...	...	2	0	0	0	0
—Buffalo	NHL	2	0	0	0	0	-1	0	0	—	—	—	—	—
02-03—Buffalo	NHL	46	3	10	13	28	-3	1	0	—	—	—	—	—
NHL Totals (2 years)		48	3	10	13	28	-4	1	0					

TAMER, CHRIS   D   THRASHERS

PERSONAL: Born November 17, 1970, in Dearborn, Mich. ... 6-2/205. ... Shoots left. ... Full Name: Chris Thomas Tamer. ... Name pronounced TAY-muhr.
TRANSACTIONS/CAREER NOTES: Selected by Pittsburgh Penguins in fourth round (third Penguins pick, 68th overall) of NHL entry draft (June 16, 1990). ... Injured shoulder (March 27, 1994); missed four games. ... Fractured ankle (May 6, 1995); missed eight playoff games. ... Pulled abdominal muscle (December 17, 1995); missed five games. ... Sprained wrist (December 30, 1995); missed five games. ... Fractured jaw (January 17, 1996); missed two games. ... Pulled abdominal muscle (November 22, 1996); missed 20 games. ... Strained hip flexor (January 4, 1997); missed 13 games. ... Strained hip flexor (March 4, 1997); missed four games. ... Traded by Penguins with C Petr Nedved and C Sean Pronger to New York Rangers for RW Alexei Kovalev, C Harry York and future considerations (November 25, 1998). ... Selected by Atlanta Thrashers in NHL expansion draft (June 25, 1999). ... Sprained medial collateral ligament in knee (February 29, 2000); missed six games. ... Suspended two games by NHL for cross-checking incident (April 1, 2003).

			REGULAR SEASON							PLAYOFFS			
Season Team	League	Gms.	G	A	Pts.	PIM	+/-	PP	SH	Gms.	G	A	Pts.	PIM
87-88—Redford	NAJHL	40	10	20	30	217	...	...	...	—	—	—	—	—
88-89—Redford	NAJHL	31	6	13	19	79	...	...	...	—	—	—	—	—
89-90—Univ. of Michigan	CCHA	42	2	7	9	147	...	...	...	—	—	—	—	—
90-91—Univ. of Michigan	CCHA	45	8	19	27	130	...	...	...	—	—	—	—	—
91-92—Univ. of Michigan	CCHA	43	4	15	19	125	...	...	...	—	—	—	—	—
92-93—Univ. of Michigan	CCHA	39	5	18	23	113	...	...	...	—	—	—	—	—
93-94—Cleveland	IHL	53	1	2	3	160	...	...	...	—	—	—	—	—
—Pittsburgh	NHL	12	0	0	0	9	3	0	0	5	0	0	0	2
94-95—Cleveland	IHL	48	4	10	14	204	...	...	...	—	—	—	—	—
—Pittsburgh	NHL	36	2	0	2	82	0	0	0	4	0	0	0	18
95-96—Pittsburgh	NHL	70	4	10	14	153	20	0	0	18	0	7	7	24
96-97—Pittsburgh	NHL	45	2	4	6	131	-25	0	1	4	0	0	0	4
97-98—Pittsburgh	NHL	79	0	7	7	181	4	0	0	6	0	1	1	4
98-99—Pittsburgh	NHL	11	0	0	0	32	-2	0	0	—	—	—	—	—
—New York Rangers	NHL	52	1	5	6	92	-12	0	0	—	—	—	—	—
99-00—Atlanta	NHL	69	2	8	10	91	-32	0	0	—	—	—	—	—
00-01—Atlanta	NHL	82	4	13	17	128	-1	0	1	—	—	—	—	—
01-02—Atlanta	NHL	78	3	3	6	111	-11	0	1	—	—	—	—	—
02-03—Atlanta	NHL	72	1	9	10	118	-10	0	0	—	—	—	—	—
NHL Totals (10 years)		606	19	59	78	1128	-66	0	3	37	0	8	8	52

TANABE, DAVID — D — COYOTES

PERSONAL: Born July 19, 1980, in White Bear Lake, Minn. ... 6-1/195. ... Shoots right. ... Full Name: David Michael Tanabe. ... Name pronounced tuh-nah-BEE.
TRANSACTIONS/CAREER NOTES: Selected by Carolina Hurricanes in first round (first Hurricanes pick, 16th overall) of NHL entry draft (June 26, 1999). ... Suffered concussion (October 18, 2000); missed five games. ... Suffered hip pointer (March 2, 2001); missed three games. ... Suffered from the flu (October 13, 2001); missed one game. ... Traded by Carolina to Phoenix Coyotes with D Igor Knyazev for D Danny Markow and fourth-round draft pick in 2004.

		REGULAR SEASON								PLAYOFFS				
Season Team	League	Gms.	G	A	Pts.	PIM	+/-	PP	SH	Gms.	G	A	Pts.	PIM
97-98—U.S. National	NAHL	73	8	21	29	96	...	...	...	—	—	—	—	—
98-99—Univ. of Wisconsin	WCHA	35	10	12	22	44	...	...	...	—	—	—	—	—
99-00—Carolina	NHL	31	4	0	4	14	-4	3	0	—	—	—	—	—
—Cincinnati	IHL	32	0	13	13	14	...	...	...	11	1	4	5	6
00-01—Carolina	NHL	74	7	22	29	42	-9	5	0	6	2	0	2	12
01-02—Carolina	NHL	78	1	15	16	35	-13	0	0	1	0	1	1	0
02-03—Carolina	NHL	68	3	10	13	24	-27	2	0	—	—	—	—	—
NHL Totals (4 years)		251	15	47	62	115	-53	10	0	7	2	1	3	12

TANGUAY, ALEX — LW — AVALANCHE

PERSONAL: Born November 21, 1979, in Ste-Justine, Que. ... 6-1/190. ... Shoots left. ... Name pronounced tan-GAY.
TRANSACTIONS/CAREER NOTES: Selected by Colorado Avalanche in first round (first Avalanche pick, 12th overall) of NHL entry draft (June 27, 1998). ... Strained neck (March 14, 2000); missed six games. ... Suffered sinus infection (November 10, 2001); missed six games. ... Bruised ankle (December 23, 2001); missed one game. ... Reinjured ankle (December 27, 2001); missed three games. ... Bruised hip (January 29, 2002); missed two games.
STATISTICAL PLATEAUS: Three-goal games: 2002-03 (1).

		REGULAR SEASON								PLAYOFFS				
Season Team	League	Gms.	G	A	Pts.	PIM	+/-	PP	SH	Gms.	G	A	Pts.	PIM
96-97—Halifax	QMJHL	70	27	41	68	50	...	...	...	12	4	8	12	8
97-98—Halifax	QMJHL	51	47	38	85	32	...	...	...	5	7	6	13	4
98-99—Halifax	QMJHL	31	27	34	61	30	...	...	...	5	1	2	3	2
—Hershey	AHL	5	1	2	3	2	...	...	...	5	0	2	2	0
99-00—Colorado	NHL	76	17	34	51	22	6	5	0	17	2	1	3	2
00-01—Colorado	NHL	82	27	50	77	37	35	7	1	23	6	15	21	8
01-02—Colorado	NHL	70	13	35	48	36	8	7	0	19	5	8	13	0
02-03—Colorado	NHL	82	26	41	67	36	34	3	0	7	1	2	3	4
NHL Totals (4 years)		310	83	160	243	131	83	22	1	66	14	26	40	14

TAPPER, BRAD — RW — THRASHERS

PERSONAL: Born April 28, 1978, in Scarborough, Ont. ... 6-0/190. ... Shoots right.
TRANSACTIONS/CAREER NOTES: Signed as non-drafted free agent by Atlanta Thrashers (April 11, 2000).

		REGULAR SEASON								PLAYOFFS				
Season Team	League	Gms.	G	A	Pts.	PIM	+/-	PP	SH	Gms.	G	A	Pts.	PIM
97-98—Rensselaer Poly. Inst.	ECAC	34	14	11	25	62	...	...	...	—	—	—	—	—
98-99—Rensselaer Poly. Inst.	ECAC	35	20	20	40	60	...	...	...	—	—	—	—	—
99-00—Rensselaer Poly. Inst.	ECAC	37	*31	20	51	81	...	...	...	—	—	—	—	—
00-01—Atlanta	NHL	16	2	3	5	6	1	0	0	—	—	—	—	—
—Orlando	IHL	45	7	9	16	39	...	...	...	2	0	0	0	2
01-02—Atlanta	NHL	20	2	4	6	43	-3	0	0	—	—	—	—	—
—Chicago	AHL	50	14	12	26	62	...	...	...	19	3	4	7	42
02-03—Chicago	AHL	28	9	14	23	42	...	...	...	—	—	—	—	—
—Atlanta	NHL	35	10	4	14	23	2	1	0	—	—	—	—	—
NHL Totals (3 years)		71	14	11	25	72	0	1	0					

TARNSTROM, DICK — D — PENGUINS

PERSONAL: Born January 20, 1975, in Sundbyberg, Sweden. ... 6-2/200. ... Shoots left.
TRANSACTIONS/CAREER NOTES: Selected by New York Islanders in 11th round (12th Islanders pick, 272nd overall) of NHL entry draft (June 29, 1994). ... Injured wrist (March 27, 2002); missed seven games. ... Claimed on waivers by Pittsburgh Penguins (August 6, 2002).

		REGULAR SEASON								PLAYOFFS				
Season Team	League	Gms.	G	A	Pts.	PIM	+/-	PP	SH	Gms.	G	A	Pts.	PIM
92-93—AIK	Sweden	3	0	0	0	0	...	...	...	—	—	—	—	—
93-94—AIK	Sweden	33	1	4	5		...	...	...	—	—	—	—	—
94-95—AIK	Sweden	37	8	4	12	26	...	...	...	—	—	—	—	—
95-96—AIK	Sweden	40	0	5	5	32	...	...	...	—	—	—	—	—
96-97—AIK	Sweden	49	5	3	8	38	...	...	...	7	0	1	1	6
97-98—AIK Solna	Sweden	45	2	12	14	30	...	...	...	—	—	—	—	—
98-99—AIK Solna	Sweden	47	9	14	23	36	...	...	...	—	—	—	—	—
99-00—AIK Solna	Sweden	42	7	15	22	20	...	...	...	—	—	—	—	—
00-01—AIK Solna	Sweden	50	10	18	28	28	...	...	...	5	0	0	0	8
01-02—Bridgeport	AHL	9	0	2	2	2	...	...	...	—	—	—	—	—
—New York Islanders	NHL	62	3	16	19	38	-12	0	0	5	0	0	0	2
02-03—Pittsburgh	NHL	61	7	34	41	50	-11	3	0	—	—	—	—	—
NHL Totals (2 years)		123	10	50	60	88	-23	3	0	5	0	0	0	2

TAYLOR, CHRIS — C

PERSONAL: Born March 6, 1972, in Stratford, Ont. ... 6-2/196. ... Shoots left. ... Brother of Tim Taylor, center, Tampa Bay Lightning.
TRANSACTIONS/CAREER NOTES: Selected by New York Islanders in second round (second Islanders pick, 27th overall) of NHL entry draft (June 16, 1990). ... Signed as free agent by Los Angeles Kings (August 1, 1997). ... Signed as free agent by Boston Bruins (July 22, 1998). ... Signed as free agent by Buffalo Sabres (August 13, 1999).

		REGULAR SEASON								PLAYOFFS				
Season Team	League	Gms.	G	A	Pts.	PIM	+/-	PP	SH	Gms.	G	A	Pts.	PIM
88-89—London	OHL	62	7	16	23	52	...	...	...	15	0	2	2	15
89-90—London	OHL	66	45	60	105	60	...	...	...	6	3	2	5	6
90-91—London	OHL	65	50	78	128	50	...	...	...	7	4	8	12	6
91-92—London	OHL	66	48	74	122	57	...	...	...	10	8	16	24	9
92-93—Roanoke	ECHL	5	2	1	3	0	...	...	...	—	—	—	—	—
—Capital District	AHL	77	19	43	62	32	...	...	...	4	0	1	1	2
93-94—Raleigh	ECHL	2	0	0	0	0	...	...	...	—	—	—	—	—
—Salt Lake City	IHL	79	21	20	41	38	...	...	...	—	—	—	—	—
94-95—Denver	IHL	78	38	48	86	47	...	...	...	14	7	6	13	10
—Roanoke	ECHL	1	0	0	0	2	...	...	...	—	—	—	—	—
—New York Islanders	NHL	10	0	3	3	2	1	0	0	—	—	—	—	—
95-96—Utah	IHL	50	18	23	41	60	...	...	...	22	5	11	16	26
—New York Islanders	NHL	11	0	1	1	2	1	0	0	—	—	—	—	—
96-97—Utah	IHL	71	27	40	67	24	...	...	...	7	1	2	3	0
—New York Islanders	NHL	1	0	0	0	0	0	0	0	—	—	—	—	—
97-98—Utah	IHL	79	28	56	84	66	...	...	...	4	0	2	2	6
98-99—Boston	NHL	37	3	5	8	12	-3	0	1	—	—	—	—	—
—Providence	AHL	21	6	11	17	6	...	...	...	—	—	—	—	—
—Las Vegas	IHL	14	3	12	15	2	...	...	...	—	—	—	—	—
99-00—Rochester	AHL	49	21	28	49	21	...	...	...	—	—	—	—	—
—Buffalo	NHL	11	1	1	2	2	-2	0	0	2	0	0	0	2
00-01—Rochester	AHL	45	20	24	44	25	...	...	...	—	—	—	—	—
—Buffalo	NHL	14	0	2	2	6	1	0	0	—	—	—	—	—
01-02—Rochester	AHL	77	21	45	66	66	...	...	...	2	0	1	1	0
02-03—Rochester	AHL	61	12	55	67	44	...	...	...	—	—	—	—	—
—Buffalo	NHL	11	1	3	4	2	-1	0	0	—	—	—	—	—
NHL Totals (7 years)		95	5	15	20	26	-3	0	1	2	0	0	0	2

TAYLOR, TIM — C — LIGHTNING

PERSONAL: Born February 6, 1969, in Stratford, Ont. ... 6-1/188. ... Shoots left. ... Full Name: Tim Robertson Taylor. ... Brother of Chris Taylor, center, Buffalo Sabres organization.
TRANSACTIONS/CAREER NOTES: Selected by Washington Capitals in second round (second Capitals pick, 36th overall) of NHL entry draft (June 11, 1988). ... Traded by Capitals to Vancouver Canucks for C Eric Murano (January 29, 1993). ... Signed as free agent by Detroit Red Wings (July 28, 1993). ... Injured right shoulder (April 5, 1996); missed three games. ... Sprained shoulder (October 15, 1996); missed 16 games. ... Suffered from an illness (April 9, 1997); missed two games. ... Selected by Boston Bruins from Red Wings in NHL waiver draft (September 28, 1997). ... Injured ribs (March 21, 1998); missed one game. ... Injured hip (March 22, 1998); missed two games. ... Sprained ankle (October 14, 1998); missed 12 games. ... Reinjured ankle (November 13, 1998); missed six games. ... Reinjured ankle (December 10, 1998); missed 14 games. ... Strained groin (April 17, 1999); missed final game of season. ... Signed as free agent by New York Rangers (July 15, 1999). ... Suffered concussion (October 2, 1999); missed two games. ... Injured hand (October 20, 1999); missed one game. ... Injured rib (November 24, 1999); missed one game. ... Suffered from the flu (February 13, 2000); missed two games. ... Injured shoulder (November 28, 2000); missed one game. ... Suffered abdominal muscle tear (December 31, 2000); missed remainder of season. ... Traded by Rangers to Tampa Bay Lightning for LW Nils Ekman and LW Kyle Freadrich (July 1, 2001). ... Strained groin (January 3, 2002); missed four games. ... Reinjured groin (January 18, 2002); missed four games. ... Reinjured groin (February 4, 2002); missed four games. ... Reinjured groin (March 2, 2002); missed remainder of season.

		REGULAR SEASON								PLAYOFFS				
Season Team	League	Gms.	G	A	Pts.	PIM	+/-	PP	SH	Gms.	G	A	Pts.	PIM
86-87—London	OHL	34	7	9	16	11	...	...	...	—	—	—	—	—
87-88—London	OHL	64	46	50	96	66	...	...	...	12	9	9	18	26
88-89—London	OHL	61	34	80	114	93	...	...	...	21	*21	25	*46	58
89-90—Baltimore	AHL	74	22	21	43	63	...	...	...	9	2	2	4	13
90-91—Baltimore	AHL	79	25	42	67	75	...	...	...	5	0	1	1	4
91-92—Baltimore	AHL	65	9	18	27	131	...	...	...	—	—	—	—	—
92-93—Baltimore	AHL	41	15	16	31	49	...	...	...	—	—	—	—	—
—Hamilton	AHL	36	15	22	37	37	...	...	...	—	—	—	—	—
93-94—Adirondack	AHL	79	36	*81	117	86	...	...	...	12	2	10	12	12
—Detroit	NHL	1	1	0	1	0	-1	0	0	—	—	—	—	—
94-95—Detroit	NHL	22	0	4	4	16	3	0	0	6	0	1	1	12
95-96—Detroit	NHL	72	11	14	25	39	11	1	1	18	0	4	4	4
96-97—Detroit	NHL	44	3	4	7	52	-6	0	1	2	0	0	0	0
97-98—Boston	NHL	79	20	11	31	57	-16	1	3	6	0	0	0	10
98-99—Boston	NHL	49	4	7	11	55	-10	0	0	12	0	3	3	8
99-00—New York Rangers	NHL	76	9	11	20	72	-4	0	0	—	—	—	—	—
00-01—New York Rangers	NHL	38	2	5	7	16	-6	0	0	—	—	—	—	—
01-02—Tampa Bay	NHL	48	4	4	8	25	-2	0	1	—	—	—	—	—
02-03—Tampa Bay	NHL	82	4	8	12	38	-13	0	0	11	0	1	1	6
NHL Totals (10 years)		511	58	68	126	370	-44	2	6	55	0	9	9	40

TELLQVIST, MIKAEL   G   MAPLE LEAFS

PERSONAL: Born September 19, 1979, in Sundbyberg, Sweden ... 5-11/194.
TRANSACTIONS/CAREER NOTES: Selected by Toronto Maple Leafs in third round (third Maple Leafs pick, 70th overall) of NHL entry draft (June 24, 2000).

Season Team	League	Gms.	Min	W	L	T	GA	SO	Avg.	SV%	Gms.	Min.	W	L	GA	SO	Avg.	SV%
98-99—Djurgarden Stockholm..	Sweden	3	124	...	...	...	8	0	3.87	—	4	240	...	...	11	0	2.75	—
99-00—Djurgarden Stockholm..	Sweden	30	1909	...	...	...	66	2	2.07	—	13	814	...	...	21	3	1.55	—
00-01—Djurgarden Stockholm..	Sweden	43	2622	...	...	...	91	†5	*2.08	—	*16	*1006	...	...	*45	†1	2.68	—
01-02—St. John's	AHL	28	1521	8	11	6	79	0	3.12	—	1	14	1	0	0	0	...	—
02-03—St. John's	AHL	47	2651	17	25	3	148	1	3.35	—	—	—	—	—	—	—	—	—
—Toronto	NHL	3	86	1	1	0	4	0	2.79	.895	—	—	—	—	—	—	—	—
NHL Totals (1 year)		3	86	1	1	0	4	0	2.79	.895								

TENKRAT, PETR   RW   BLUE JACKETS

PERSONAL: Born May 31, 1977, in Kladno, Czechoslovakia. ... 6-1/185. ... Shoots right.
TRANSACTIONS/CAREER NOTES: Selected by Mighty Ducks of Anaheim in eighth round (sixth Mighty Ducks pick, 230th overall) of NHL entry draft (June 26, 1999). ... Traded by Mighty Ducks to Nashville Predators for RW Patric Kjellberg (November 1, 2001). ... Strained hip flexor (January 19, 2002); missed one game. ... Claimed by Florida Panthers from Predators in NHL waiver draft (October 4, 2002). ... Traded by Panthers to Columbus Blue Jackets for D Mathieu Biron (October 4, 2002).
STATISTICAL PLATEAUS: Three-goal games: 2001-02 (1).

Season Team	League	Gms.	G	A	Pts.	PIM	+/-	PP	SH	Gms.	G	A	Pts.	PIM
94-95—Poldi Kladno	Czech Rep.	—								1	0	0	0	...
95-96—Poldi Kladno	Czech Rep.	18	0	3	3	...	...	...	...	3	0	0	0	...
96-97—Poldi Kladno	Czech Rep.	43	5	9	14	6	...	...	...	3	0	1	1	0
97-98—Poldi Kladno	Czech Rep.	52	9	10	19	24	...	...	...	—	—	—	—	—
98-99—Velvana Kladno	Czech Rep.	50	21	14	35	32	...	...	...	—	—	—	—	—
99-00—Ilves Tampere	Finland	53	35	14	49	75	...	...	...	3	1	1	2	14
00-01—Cincinnati	AHL	25	9	9	18	24	...	...	...	4	3	2	5	0
—Anaheim	NHL	46	5	9	14	16	-11	0	0	—	—	—	—	—
01-02—Anaheim	NHL	9	0	0	0	6	-6	0	0	—	—	—	—	—
—Cincinnati	AHL	3	2	3	5	2	...	...	...	—	—	—	—	—
—Milwaukee	AHL	4	0	0	0	2	...	...	...	—	—	—	—	—
—Nashville	NHL	58	8	16	24	28	-4	0	1	—	—	—	—	—
02-03—Karpat Oulu	Finland	51	21	19	40	60	...	...	...	—	—	—	—	—
NHL Totals (2 years)		113	13	25	38	50	-21	0	1					

TETARENKO, JOEY   D   HURRICANES

PERSONAL: Born March 3, 1978, in Prince Albert, Sask. ... 6-2/210. ... Shoots right.
TRANSACTIONS/CAREER NOTES: Selected by Florida Panthers in fourth round (fourth Panthers pick, 82nd overall) of NHL entry draft (June 22, 1996). ... Scratched cornea (March 21, 2001); missed one game. ... Dislocated jaw and suffered concussion (October 31, 2001); missed 10 games. ... Suffered torn retina (February 13, 2002); missed one game. ... Suffered back injury (March 20, 2002); missed six games. ... Traded by Panthers to Ottawa Senators for G Simon Lajeunesse (March 4, 2003). ... Signed by Carolina Panthers (July 1, 2003).

Season Team	League	Gms.	G	A	Pts.	PIM	+/-	PP	SH	Gms.	G	A	Pts.	PIM
94-95—Portland	WHL	59	0	1	1	134	...	...	...	9	0	0	0	8
95-96—Portland	WHL	71	4	11	15	190	...	...	...	7	0	1	1	17
96-97—Portland	WHL	68	8	18	26	182	...	...	...	2	0	0	0	2
97-98—Portland	WHL	49	2	12	14	148	...	...	...	16	0	2	2	30
98-99—New Haven	AHL	65	4	10	14	154	...	...	...	—	—	—	—	—
99-00—Louisville	AHL	57	3	11	14	136	...	...	...	4	0	0	0	2
00-01—Florida	NHL	29	3	1	4	44	-1	0	0	—	—	—	—	—
01-02—Florida	NHL	38	1	0	1	123	-5	0	0	—	—	—	—	—
02-03—San Antonio	AHL	50	4	12	16	123	...	...	...	—	—	—	—	—
—Florida	NHL	2	0	0	0	4	-1	0	0	—	—	—	—	—
—Ottawa	NHL	2	0	0	0	5	0	0	0	—	—	—	—	—
—Binghamton	AHL	14	2	2	4	33	...	...	...	—	—	—	—	—
NHL Totals (3 years)		71	4	1	5	176	-7	0	0					

THEODORE, JOSE   G   CANADIENS

PERSONAL: Born September 13, 1976, in Laval, Que. ... 5-11/179. ... Catches right. ... Name pronounced JO-zhay THEE-uh-dohr.
TRANSACTIONS/CAREER NOTES: Selected by Montreal Canadiens in second round (second Canadiens pick, 44th overall) of NHL entry draft (June 28, 1994). ... Strained groin (March 29, 2000); missed three games. ... Suffered concussion (October 26, 2001); missed four games.

Season Team	League	Gms.	Min	W	L	T	GA	SO	Avg.	SV%	Gms.	Min.	W	L	GA	SO	Avg.	SV%
92-93—St. Jean	QMJHL	34	1776	12	16	2	112	0	3.78	—	3	175	0	2	11	0	3.77	—
93-94—St. Jean	QMJHL	57	3225	20	29	6	194	0	3.61	—	5	296	1	4	18	1	3.65	—
94-95—Hull	QMJHL	58	3348	32	22	2	193	5	3.46	—	21	1263	15	6	59	1	2.80	—
—Fredericton	AHL	—	—	—	—	—	—	—	—	1.000	1	60	0	1	3	0	3.00	—
95-96—Hull	QMJHL	48	2803	33	11	2	158	0	3.38	—	5	300	2	3	20	0	4.00	—
—Montreal	NHL	1	9	0	0	0	1	0	6.67	.500	—	—	—	—	—	—	—	—

Season Team	League	REGULAR SEASON									PLAYOFFS							
		Gms.	Min	W	L	T	GA	SO	Avg.	SV%	Gms.	Min.	W	L	GA	SO	Avg.	SV%
96-97 —Fredericton	AHL	26	1469	12	12	0	87	0	3.55	—								
—Montreal	NHL	16	821	5	6	2	53	0	3.87	.896	2	168	1	1	7	0	2.50	.935
97-98 —Fredericton	AHL	53	3053	20	23	8	145	2	2.85	—	4	237	1	3	13	0	3.29	—
—Montreal	NHL	—	—	—	—	—	—	—	—	—	3	120	0	1	1	0	.50	.971
98-99 —Montreal	NHL	18	913	4	12	0	50	1	3.29	.877								
—Fredericton	AHL	27	1609	12	13	2	77	2	2.87	—	13	694	8	5	35	†1	3.03	—
99-00 —Montreal	NHL	30	1655	12	13	2	58	5	2.10	.919	—							
00-01 —Quebec	AHL	3	180	3	0	0	9	0	3.00	—								
—Montreal	NHL	59	3298	20	29	5	141	2	2.57	.909	—							
01-02 —Montreal	NHL	67	3864	30	24	10	136	7	2.11	*.931	12	686	6	6	35	0	3.06	*.915
02-03 —Montreal	NHL	57	3419	20	31	6	165	2	2.90	.908	—							
NHL Totals (8 years)		248	13979	91	115	25	604	17	2.59	.913	17	974	7	8	43	0	2.65	.923

THERIEN, CHRIS — D — FLYERS

PERSONAL: Born December 14, 1971, in Ottawa ... 6-5/235. ... Shoots left. ... Name pronounced TAIR-ee-uhn.
TRANSACTIONS/CAREER NOTES: Selected by Philadelphia Flyers in third round (seventh Flyers pick, 47th overall) of NHL entry draft (June 16, 1990). ... Suffered from the flu (November 3, 1997); missed one game. ... Sprained left knee (April 8, 1998); missed three games. ... Strained shoulder (October 9, 1998); missed first three games of season. ... Bruised left thigh (December 13, 1998); missed three games. ... Injured back (September 14, 2000). ... Injured back (October 17, 2000); missed eight games. ... Suffered concussion (November 15, 2001); missed five games.

Season Team	League	REGULAR SEASON								PLAYOFFS				
		Gms.	G	A	Pts.	PIM	+/-	PP	SH	Gms.	G	A	Pts.	PIM
89-90 —Northwood School	N.Y. H.S.	31	35	37	72	54	...	...	...	—				
90-91 —Providence College	Hockey East	36	4	18	22	36	...	...	...	—				
91-92 —Providence College	Hockey East	36	16	25	41	38	...	...	...	—				
92-93 —Providence College	Hockey East	33	8	11	19	52	...	...	...	—				
—Canadian nat'l team	Int'l	8	1	4	5	8	...	...	...	—				
93-94 —Canadian nat'l team	Int'l	59	7	15	22	46	...	...	...	—				
—Can. Olympic team	Int'l	4	0	0	0	4	...	...	...	—				
—Hershey	AHL	6	0	0	0	2	...	...	...	—				
94-95 —Hershey	AHL	34	3	13	16	27	...	...	...	—				
—Philadelphia	NHL	48	3	10	13	38	8	1	0	15	0	0	0	10
95-96 —Philadelphia	NHL	82	6	17	23	89	16	3	0	12	0	0	0	18
96-97 —Philadelphia	NHL	71	2	22	24	64	27	0	0	19	1	6	7	6
97-98 —Philadelphia	NHL	78	3	16	19	80	5	1	0	5	0	1	1	4
98-99 —Philadelphia	NHL	74	3	15	18	48	16	1	0	6	0	0	0	6
99-00 —Philadelphia	NHL	80	4	9	13	66	11	1	0	18	0	1	1	12
00-01 —Philadelphia	NHL	73	2	12	14	48	22	1	0	6	1	0	1	8
01-02 —Philadelphia	NHL	77	4	10	14	30	16	0	2	5	0	0	0	2
02-03 —Philadelphia	NHL	67	1	6	7	36	10	0	0	13	0	2	2	2
NHL Totals (9 years)		650	28	117	145	499	131	8	2	99	2	10	12	68

THIBAULT, JOCELYN — G — BLACKHAWKS

PERSONAL: Born January 12, 1975, in Montreal ... 5-11/169. ... Catches left. ... Name pronounced TEE-boh.
TRANSACTIONS/CAREER NOTES: Selected by Quebec Nordiques in first round (first Nordiques pick, 10th overall) of NHL entry draft (June 26, 1993). ... Sprained shoulder (March 28, 1995); missed 10 games. ... Nordiques franchise moved to Colorado and renamed Avalanche for 1995-96 season (June 21, 1995). ... Traded by Avalanche with LW Martin Rucinsky and RW Andrei Kovalenko to Montreal Canadiens for G Patrick Roy and RW Mike Keane (December 6, 1995). ... Bruised right hand (February 21, 1996); missed two games. ... Fractured finger (October 24, 1996); missed nine games. ... Suffered from the flu (February 3, 1997); missed one game. ... Bruised collarbone (January 8, 1998); missed one game. ... Traded by Canadiens with D Dave Manson and D Brad Brown to Chicago Blackhawks for G Jeff Hackett, D Eric Weinrich, D Alain Nasreddine and fourth-round pick (D Chris Dyment) in 1999 draft (November 16, 1998). ... Fractured finger (November 27, 1999); missed six games. ... Suffered from the flu (December 10, 2000); missed one game.

Season Team	League	REGULAR SEASON									PLAYOFFS							
		Gms.	Min	W	L	T	GA	SO	Avg.	SV%	Gms.	Min.	W	L	GA	SO	Avg.	SV%
91-92 —Trois-Rivieres	QMJHL	30	1497	14	7	1	77	0	3.09	—	3	110	1	1	4	0	2.18	—
92-93 —Sherbrooke	QMJHL	56	3190	34	14	5	159	*3	*2.99	—	15	883	9	6	57	0	3.87	—
93-94 —Quebec	NHL	29	1504	8	13	3	83	0	3.31	.892	—							
—Cornwall	AHL	4	240	4	0	0	9	1	2.25	—								
94-95 —Sherbrooke	QMJHL	13	776	6	6	1	38	1	2.94	—								
—Quebec	NHL	18	898	12	2	2	35	1	2.34	.917	3	148	1	2	8	0	3.24	.895
95-96 —Colorado	NHL	10	558	3	4	2	28	0	3.01	.888								
—Montreal	NHL	40	2334	23	13	3	110	3	2.83	.913	6	311	2	4	18	0	3.47	.904
96-97 —Montreal	NHL	61	3397	22	24	11	164	1	2.90	.910	3	179	0	3	13	0	4.36	.871
97-98 —Montreal	NHL	47	2652	19	15	8	109	2	2.47	.902	2	43	0	0	4	0	5.58	.750
98-99 —Montreal	NHL	10	529	3	4	2	23	1	2.61	.908								
—Chicago	NHL	52	3014	21	26	5	136	4	2.71	.905								
99-00 —Chicago	NHL	60	3438	25	26	7	158	3	2.76	.906								
00-01 —Chicago	NHL	66	3844	27	32	7	†180	6	2.81	.895								
01-02 —Chicago	NHL	67	3838	33	23	9	159	6	2.49	.902	3	159	1	2	7	0	2.64	.909
02-03 —Chicago	NHL	62	3650	26	28	7	144	8	2.37	.915								
NHL Totals (10 years)		522	29656	222	210	66	1329	35	2.69	.905	17	840	4	11	50	0	3.57	.891

T

THOMAS, STEVE   RW

PERSONAL: Born July 15, 1963, in Stockport, England ... 5-10/188. ... Shoots left.
TRANSACTIONS/CAREER NOTES: Signed as non-drafted free agent by Toronto Maple Leafs (May 12, 1984). ... Fractured wrist during training camp (September 1984). ... Traded by Maple Leafs with RW Rick Vaive and D Bob McGill to Chicago Blackhawks for LW Al Secord and RW Ed Olczyk (September 3, 1987). ... Pulled stomach muscle (October 1987). ... Separated left shoulder (February 20, 1988) and underwent surgery. ... Pulled back muscle (October 18, 1988). ... Separated right shoulder (December 21, 1988). ... Underwent surgery to repair chronic shoulder separation problem (January 25, 1989). ... Strained knee ligaments during training camp (September 1990); missed first 11 games of season. ... Traded by Blackhawks with C Adam Creighton to New York Islanders for C Brent Sutter and RW Brad Lauer (October 25, 1991). ... Bruised ribs (March 10, 1992); missed one game. ... Bruised ribs (November 21, 1992); missed three games. ... Suffered neck muscle spasms (January 4, 1994); missed five games. ... Injured back and thumb (January 24, 1995); missed one game. ... Traded by Islanders to New Jersey Devils for RW Claude Lemieux (October 3, 1995). ... Injured head (February 1, 1996); missed one game. ... Suffered from the flu (October 24, 1996); missed two games. ... Strained ankle (November 30, 1996); missed 10 games. ... Strained knee (December 31, 1996); missed 12 games. ... Strained groin (October 23, 1997); missed 20 games. ... Bruised ribs (January 5, 1998); missed four games. ... Suffered back spasms (April 5, 1998); missed three games. ... Signed as free agent by Maple Leafs (July 12, 1998). ... Suffered back spasms (March 1, 1999); missed one game. ... Fractured toe (March 9, 1999); missed three games. ... Suffered injury (February 29, 2000); missed one game. ... Lacerated hand (October 21, 2000); missed three games. ... Injured knee (november 30, 2000); missed 22 games. ... Signed as free agent by Blackhawks (July 18, 2001). ... Fractured ankle (November 15, 2001); missed 17 games. ... Reinjured ankle and underwent surgery (December 23, 2001); missed 30 games. ... Suffered from the flu (March 31, 2002); missed one game. ... Traded by Blackhawks to Mighty Ducks of Anaheim for fifth-round pick in 2003 draft (March 11, 2003).
STATISTICAL PLATEAUS: Three-goal games: 1987-88 (1), 1989-90 (1), 1990-91 (1), 1993-94 (1). Total: 4. ... Four-goal games: 1989-90 (1), 1991-92 (1). Total: 2. ... Total hat tricks: 6.

		REGULAR SEASON								PLAYOFFS				
Season Team	League	Gms.	G	A	Pts.	PIM	+/-	PP	SH	Gms.	G	A	Pts.	PIM
81-82—Markham Tier II Jr. A..	OHA	48	68	57	125	113	...	...	...	—	—	—	—	—
82-83—Toronto	OHL	61	18	20	38	42	...	...	...	—	—	—	—	—
83-84—Toronto	OHL	70	51	54	105	77	...	...	...	—	—	—	—	—
84-85—Toronto	NHL	18	1	1	2	2	-13	0	0	—	—	—	—	—
—St. Catharines	AHL	64	42	48	90	56	...	...	...	—	—	—	—	—
85-86—St. Catharines	AHL	19	18	14	32	35	...	...	...	—	—	—	—	—
—Toronto	NHL	65	20	37	57	36	-15	5	0	10	6	8	14	9
86-87—Toronto	NHL	78	35	27	62	114	-3	3	0	13	2	3	5	13
87-88—Chicago	NHL	30	13	13	26	40	1	5	0	3	1	2	3	6
88-89—Chicago	NHL	45	21	19	40	69	-2	8	0	12	3	5	8	10
89-90—Chicago	NHL	76	40	30	70	91	-3	13	0	20	7	6	13	33
90-91—Chicago	NHL	69	19	35	54	129	8	2	0	6	1	2	3	15
91-92—Chicago	NHL	11	2	6	8	26	-3	0	0	—	—	—	—	—
—New York Islanders	NHL	71	28	42	70	71	11	3	0	—	—	—	—	—
92-93—New York Islanders	NHL	79	37	50	87	111	3	12	0	18	9	8	17	37
93-94—New York Islanders	NHL	78	42	33	75	139	-9	17	0	4	1	0	1	8
94-95—New York Islanders	NHL	47	11	15	26	60	-14	3	0	—	—	—	—	—
95-96—New Jersey	NHL	81	26	35	61	98	-2	6	0	—	—	—	—	—
96-97—New Jersey	NHL	57	15	19	34	46	9	1	0	10	1	1	2	18
97-98—New Jersey	NHL	55	14	10	24	32	4	3	0	6	0	3	3	2
98-99—Toronto	NHL	78	28	45	73	33	26	11	0	17	6	3	9	12
99-00—Toronto	NHL	81	26	37	63	68	1	9	0	12	6	3	9	10
00-01—Toronto	NHL	57	8	26	34	46	0	1	0	11	6	3	9	4
01-02—Chicago	NHL	34	11	4	15	17	0	3	0	5	1	1	2	0
02-03—Chicago	NHL	69	4	13	17	51	0	0	0	—	—	—	—	—
—Anaheim	NHL	12	10	3	13	2	10	1	0	21	4	4	8	8
NHL Totals (19 years)		1191	411	500	911	1281	9	106	0	168	54	52	106	185

THOMAS, TIM   G

PERSONAL: Born April 15, 1974, in Davison, Mich. ... 5-11/181. ... Catches left.
COLLEGE: Vermont.
TRANSACTIONS/CAREER NOTES: Selected by Quebec Nordiques in ninth round (11th Nordiques pick, 217th overall) of NHL entry draft (June 29, 1994). ... Nordiques franchise moved to Colorado and renamed Avalanche for 1995-96 season (June 21, 1995). ... Signed as free agent by Edmonton Oilers (June 4, 1998). ... Signed as free agent by Boston Bruins (September 13, 2001).

		REGULAR SEASON									PLAYOFFS							
Season Team	League	Gms.	Min	W	L	T	GA	SO	Avg.	SV%	Gms.	Min.	W	L	GA	SO	Avg.	SV%
92-93—Lakeland	Tier II	27	1580	...	...	...	87	...	3.30	—	—	—	—	—	—	—	—	—
93-94—Univ. of Vermont	ECAC	33	1863	15	11	6	95	1	3.06	—	—	—	—	—	—	—	—	—
94-95—Univ. of Vermont	ECAC	34	2011	18	14	2	90	3	2.69	—	—	—	—	—	—	—	—	—
95-96—Univ. of Vermont	ECAC	37	2254	26	7	4	88	3	2.34	—	—	—	—	—	—	—	—	—
96-97—Univ. of Vermont	ECAC	36	2158	22	11	3	101	2	2.81	—	—	—	—	—	—	—	—	—
97-98—Birmingham	ECHL	6	360	4	1	1	13	1	2.17	—	—	—	—	—	—	—	—	—
—Houston	IHL	1	60	0	1	0	4	0	4.00	—	—	—	—	—	—	—	—	—
—HIFK Helsinki	Finland	22	1035	22	4	1	28	2	1.62	—	9	551	9	0	14	3	1.52	—
98-99—Hamilton	AHL	15	837	6	8	0	45	0	3.23	—	—	—	—	—	—	—	—	—
—HIFK Helsinki	Finland	14	833	8	3	3	31	2	2.23	—	*11	*658	7	†4	*25	...	2.28	—
99-00—Detroit	IHL	36	2020	15	21	3	120	1	3.56	—	—	—	—	—	—	—	—	—
00-01—AIK Solna	Sweden	43	2542	...	...	...	105	3	2.48	—	5	299	...	...	20	0	4.01	—
01-02—Karpat Oulu	Finland	32	1937	15	12	5	79	...	2.45	—	3	180	1	2	12	0	4.00	—
02-03—Providence	AHL	35	2048	18	12	5	98	1	2.87	—	—	—	—	—	—	—	—	—
—Boston	NHL	4	220	3	1	0	11	0	3.00	.907	—	—	—	—	—	—	—	—
NHL Totals (1 year)		4	220	3	1	0	11	0	3.00	.907								

T

THOMPSON, BRENT   D

PERSONAL: Born January 9, 1971, in Calgary. ... 6-2/205. ... Shoots left. ... Full Name: Brenton Keith Thompson.

TRANSACTIONS/CAREER NOTES: Stretched knee ligaments and separated shoulder (September 1987). ... Selected by Los Angeles Kings in second round (first Kings pick, 39th overall) of NHL entry draft (June 17, 1989). ... Strained hip flexor prior to 1992-93 season; missed first six games of season. ... Strained abdominal muscles (January 23, 1992); missed 17 games. ... Traded by Kings to Winnipeg Jets for D Ruslan Batyrshin and second-round pick (RW Marian Cisar) in 1996 draft (August 8, 1994). ... Jets franchise moved to Phoenix and renamed Coyotes for 1996-97 season; NHL approved move on January 18, 1996. ... Signed as free agent by New York Rangers (August 26, 1997). ... Signed as free agent by Florida Panthers (July 21, 1999).

Season Team	League	REGULAR SEASON								PLAYOFFS				
		Gms.	G	A	Pts.	PIM	+/-	PP	SH	Gms.	G	A	Pts.	PIM
88-89—Medicine Hat	WHL	72	3	10	13	160	...	...	...	3	0	0	0	2
89-90—Medicine Hat	WHL	68	10	35	45	167	...	...	...	3	0	1	1	14
90-91—Medicine Hat	WHL	51	5	40	45	87	...	...	...	12	1	7	8	16
—Phoenix	IHL	—	—	—	—	—				4	0	1	1	6
91-92—Phoenix	IHL	42	4	13	17	139	...	...	...	—				
—Los Angeles	NHL	27	0	5	5	89	-7	0	0	4	0	0	0	4
92-93—Phoenix	IHL	22	0	5	5	112	...	...	...	—				
—Los Angeles	NHL	30	0	4	4	76	-4	0	0	—				
93-94—Phoenix	IHL	26	1	11	12	118	...	...	...	—				
—Los Angeles	NHL	24	1	0	1	81	-1	0	0	—				
94-95—Winnipeg	NHL	29	0	0	0	78	-17	0	0	—				
95-96—Winnipeg	NHL	10	0	1	1	21	-2	0	0	—				
—Springfield	AHL	58	2	10	12	203	...	...	...	10	1	4	5	*55
96-97—Phoenix	IHL	12	0	1	1	67	...	...	...	—				
—Springfield	AHL	64	2	15	17	215	...	...	...	17	0	2	2	31
—Phoenix	NHL	1	0	0	0	7	-1	0	0	—				
97-98—Hartford	AHL	77	4	15	19	308	...	...	...	15	0	4	4	25
98-99—Hartford	AHL	76	3	15	18	265	...	...	...	7	0	0	0	23
99-00—Louisville	AHL	67	4	22	26	311	...	...	...	3	0	0	0	11
00-01—Louisville	AHL	59	1	9	10	170	...	...	...	—				
—Hershey	AHL	15	0	1	1	44	...	...	...	12	0	0	0	10
01-02—Hershey	AHL	79	8	16	24	178	...	...	...	8	0	0	0	21
02-03—Hershey	AHL	61	2	17	19	134	...	...	...	—				
NHL Totals (6 years)		121	1	10	11	352	-32	0	0	4	0	0	0	4

THOMPSON, ROCKY   RW   OILERS

PERSONAL: Born August 8, 1977, in Calgary. ... 6-2/205. ... Shoots right.

TRANSACTIONS/CAREER NOTES: Selected by Calgary Flames in third round (third Flames pick, 72nd overall) of NHL entry draft (July 8, 1995). ... Injured neck (February 3, 1998); missed two games. ... Suffered concussion (January 16, 1999); missed final 38 games of season. ... Traded by Flames to Florida Panthers for D Filip Kuba (March 16, 2000). ... Injured Achilles' tendon (September 12, 2001); missed first 27 games of season. ... Signed by Edmonton Oilers (July 20, 2003).

Season Team	League	REGULAR SEASON								PLAYOFFS				
		Gms.	G	A	Pts.	PIM	+/-	PP	SH	Gms.	G	A	Pts.	PIM
93-94—Medicine Hat	WHL	68	1	4	5	166	...	...	...	3	0	0	0	2
94-95—Medicine Hat	WHL	63	1	6	7	220	...	...	...	5	0	0	0	17
95-96—Medicine Hat	WHL	71	9	20	29	260	...	...	...	5	2	3	5	26
—Saint John	AHL	4	0	0	0	33	...	...	...	—				
96-97—Medicine Hat	WHL	47	6	9	15	170	...	...	...	—				
—Swift Current	WHL	22	3	5	8	90	...	...	...	10	1	2	3	22
97-98—Saint John	AHL	51	3	0	3	187	...	...	...	18	1	1	2	47
—Calgary	NHL	12	0	0	0	61	0	0	0	—				
98-99—Saint John	AHL	27	2	2	4	108	...	...	...	—				
—Calgary	NHL	3	0	0	0	25	0	0	0	—				
99-00—Saint John	AHL	53	2	8	10	125	...	...	...	—				
—Louisville	AHL	3	0	1	1	54	...	...	...	4	0	0	0	4
00-01—Louisville	AHL	55	3	5	8	193	...	...	...	—				
—Florida	NHL	4	0	0	0	19	0	0	0	—				
01-02—Hershey	AHL	42	0	3	3	143	...	...	...	8	1	0	1	19
—Florida	NHL	6	0	0	0	12	0	0	0	—				
02-03—San Antonio	AHL	79	1	11	12	275	...	...	...	—				
NHL Totals (4 years)		25	0	0	0	117	0	0	0					

THORBURN, CHRIS   C   SABRES

PERSONAL: Born May 3, 1983, in Sault Ste. Marie, Ont. ... 6-2/190. ... Shoots right.

TRANSACTIONS/CAREER NOTES: Selected by Buffalo Sabres in second round (second Sabres pick, 50th overall) of NHL entry draft (June 23, 2001). ... Signed by Buffalo (May 28, 2003).

Season Team	League	REGULAR SEASON								PLAYOFFS				
		Gms.	G	A	Pts.	PIM	+/-	PP	SH	Gms.	G	A	Pts.	PIM
99-00—North Bay	OHL	56	12	8	20	33	...	...	...	6	0	2	2	0
00-01—North Bay	OHL	66	22	32	54	64	...	...	...	4	0	1	1	9
01-02—North Bay	OHL	67	15	43	58	112	...	...	...	5	1	2	3	8
02-03—Plymouth	OHL	64	30	41	71	124	...	...	...	—				

THORNTON, JOE   C   BRUINS

PERSONAL: Born July 2, 1979, in London, Ont. ... 6-4/220. ... Shoots left. ... Cousin of Scott Thornton, left winger, San Jose Sharks.

TRANSACTIONS/CAREER NOTES: Selected by Boston Bruins in first round (first Bruins pick, first overall) of NHL entry draft (June 21, 1997). ... Suffered broken forearm prior to 1997-98 season; missed first three games. ... Injured ankle (December 13, 1997); missed 10 games. ... Suffered from viral infection (March 28, 1998); missed six games. ... Suffered chest injury (April 17, 1999); missed final game of regular season and one playoff game. ... Bruised knee (November 20, 1999); missed one game. ... Suffered charley horse (November 24, 2000); missed six games. ... Suspended two games by NHL for cross-checking incident (December 18, 2000). ... Suspended two games by NHL for cross-checking incident (February 6, 2001). ... Suspended three games by NHL for cross-checking incident (March 1, 2002). ... Injured shoulder (March 7, 2002); missed 13 games.

STATISTICAL PLATEAUS: Three-goal games: 2000-01 (1), 2001-02 (1). Total: 2.

		REGULAR SEASON								PLAYOFFS				
Season Team	League	Gms.	G	A	Pts.	PIM	+/-	PP	SH	Gms.	G	A	Pts.	PIM
94-95—St. Thomas	Jr. B	50	40	64	104	53	...	...	...	—	—	—	—	—
95-96—Sault Ste. Marie	OHL	66	30	46	76	51	...	...	...	4	1	1	2	11
96-97—Sault Ste. Marie	OHL	59	41	81	122	123	...	...	...	11	11	8	19	24
97-98—Boston	NHL	55	3	4	7	19	-6	0	0	6	0	0	0	9
98-99—Boston	NHL	81	16	25	41	69	3	7	0	11	3	6	9	4
99-00—Boston	NHL	81	23	37	60	82	-5	5	0	—	—	—	—	—
00-01—Boston	NHL	72	37	34	71	107	-4	19	1	—	—	—	—	—
01-02—Boston	NHL	66	22	46	68	127	7	6	0	6	2	4	6	10
02-03—Boston	NHL	77	36	65	101	109	12	12	2	5	1	2	3	4
NHL Totals (6 years)		432	137	211	348	513	7	49	3	28	6	12	18	27

THORNTON, SCOTT   LW   SHARKS

PERSONAL: Born January 9, 1971, in London, Ont. ... 6-3/215. ... Shoots left. ... Full Name: Scott C. Thornton. ... Cousin of Joe Thornton, center, Boston Bruins.

TRANSACTIONS/CAREER NOTES: Selected by Toronto Maple Leafs in first round (first Maple Leafs pick, third overall) of NHL entry draft (June 17, 1989). ... Separated shoulder (January 24, 1991); missed eight games. ... Traded by Maple Leafs with LW Vincent Damphousse, D Luke Richardson, G Peter Ing and future considerations to Edmonton Oilers for G Grant Fuhr, RW//LW Glenn Anderson and LW Craig Berube (September 19, 1991). ... Suffered concussion (November 23, 1991); missed one game. ... Sprained ankle (October 6, 1993); missed 13 games. ... Suffered back spasms (November 21, 1993); missed one game. ... Suffered wrist contusion (April 14, 1994); missed one game. ... Suffered from Cytomegalo virus (January 9, 1996); missed three games. ... Traded by Oilers to Montreal Canadiens for RW Andrei Kovalenko (September 6, 1996). ... Bruised hand (December 28, 1996); missed three games. ... Suffered from the flu (February 10, 1997); missed one game. ... Underwent arthroscopic knee surgery (March 6, 1997); missed five games. ... Separated shoulder (January 3, 1998); missed two games. ... Injured neck (February 7, 1998); missed one game. ... Fractured rib (March 18, 1998); missed eight games. ... Injured shoulder (April 15, 1998); missed three games. ... Strained abdominal muscle (November 3, 1998) and underwent surgery; missed 31 games. ... Suffered from migraines (February 2, 1999); missed three games. ... Suffered back spasms (April 13, 1999); missed one game. ... Injured tricep (September 20, 1999); missed first two games of 1999-2000 season. ... Reinjured tricep (October 8, 1999); missed three games. ... Strained groin (December 12, 1999); missed one game. ... Traded by Canadiens to Dallas Stars for LW Juha Lind (January 22, 2000). ... Suffered from the flu (March 8, 2000); missed one game. ... Suspended for three games by NHL for high-sticking incident (March 22, 2000). ... Signed as free agent by San Jose Sharks (July 1, 2000). ... Injured neck (January 4, 2001); missed three games. ... Injured neck (January 30, 2001); missed five games. ... Injured wrist (March 10, 2002); missed one game.

STATISTICAL PLATEAUS: Three-goal games: 2000-01 (1).

		REGULAR SEASON								PLAYOFFS				
Season Team	League	Gms.	G	A	Pts.	PIM	+/-	PP	SH	Gms.	G	A	Pts.	PIM
86-87—London Diamonds	OPJHL	31	10	7	17	10	...	...	...	—	—	—	—	—
87-88—Belleville	OHL	62	11	19	30	54	...	...	...	6	0	1	1	2
88-89—Belleville	OHL	59	28	34	62	103	...	...	...	5	1	1	2	6
89-90—Belleville	OHL	47	21	28	49	91	...	...	...	11	2	10	12	15
90-91—Belleville	OHL	3	2	1	3	2	...	...	...	6	0	7	7	14
—Newmarket	AHL	5	1	0	1	4	...	...	...	—	—	—	—	—
—Toronto	NHL	33	1	3	4	30	-15	0	0	—	—	—	—	—
91-92—Edmonton	NHL	15	0	1	1	43	-6	0	0	1	0	0	0	0
—Cape Breton	AHL	49	9	14	23	40	...	...	...	5	1	0	1	8
92-93—Cape Breton	AHL	58	23	27	50	102	...	...	...	16	1	2	3	35
—Edmonton	NHL	9	0	1	1	0	-4	0	0	—	—	—	—	—
93-94—Edmonton	NHL	61	4	7	11	104	-15	0	0	—	—	—	—	—
—Cape Breton	AHL	2	1	1	2	31	...	...	...	—	—	—	—	—
94-95—Edmonton	NHL	47	10	12	22	89	-4	0	1	—	—	—	—	—
95-96—Edmonton	NHL	77	9	9	18	149	-25	0	2	—	—	—	—	—
96-97—Montreal	NHL	73	10	10	20	128	-19	1	1	5	1	0	1	2
97-98—Montreal	NHL	67	6	9	15	158	0	1	0	9	0	2	2	10
98-99—Montreal	NHL	47	7	4	11	87	-2	1	0	—	—	—	—	—
99-00—Montreal	NHL	35	2	3	5	70	-7	0	0	—	—	—	—	—
—Dallas	NHL	30	6	3	9	38	-5	1	0	†23	2	7	9	28
00-01—San Jose	NHL	73	19	17	36	114	4	4	0	6	3	0	3	8
01-02—San Jose	NHL	77	26	16	42	116	11	6	0	12	3	3	6	6
02-03—San Jose	NHL	41	9	12	21	41	-7	4	0	—	—	—	—	—
NHL Totals (13 years)		685	109	107	216	1167	-94	18	4	56	9	12	21	54

THORNTON, SHAWN   LW   BLACKHAWKS

PERSONAL: Born July 23, 1977, in Oshawa, Ont. ... 6-1/203. ... Shoots right.

TRANSACTIONS/CAREER NOTES: Selected by Toronto Maple Leafs in seventh round (sixth Maple Leafs pick, 190th overall) of NHL entry draft (June 21, 1997). ... Traded by Maple Leafs to Chicago Blackhawks for D Marty Wilford (September 30, 2001). ... Re-signed by Blackhawks (June 30, 2003).

Season Team	League	REGULAR SEASON Gms.	G	A	Pts.	PIM	+/-	PP	SH	PLAYOFFS Gms.	G	A	Pts.	PIM
95-96—Peterborough	OHL	63	4	10	14	192	...	...	...	24	3	0	3	25
96-97—Peterborough	OHL	61	19	10	29	204	...	...	...	11	2	4	6	20
97-98—St. John's	AHL	59	0	3	3	225				—	—	—	—	—
98-99—St. John's	AHL	78	8	11	19	354				*5	0	0	0	9
99-00—St. John's	AHL	60	4	12	16	316				—	—	—	—	—
00-01—St. John's	AHL	79	5	12	17	320				3	1	2	3	2
01-02—Norfolk	AHL	70	8	14	22	281				4	0	0	0	4
02-03—Norfolk	AHL	50	11	2	13	213				—	—	—	—	—
—Chicago	NHL	13	1	1	2	31	-4	0	0	—	—	—	—	—
NHL Totals (1 year)		13	1	1	2	31	-4	0	0					

TIBBETTS, BILLY   RW

PERSONAL: Born October 14, 1974, in Boston ... 6-0/206. ... Shoots right.

TRANSACTIONS/CAREER NOTES: Signed as non-drafted free agent by Pittsburgh Penguins (April 10, 2000). ... Suspended four games by NHL for fighting (January 29, 2001). ... Suspended one game by NHL for kneeing incident (February 21, 2001). ... Suffered from the flu (March 14, 2001); missed one game. ... Traded by Penguins to Philadelphia Flyers for C Kent Manderville (March 17, 2002). ... Signed as free agent by New York Rangers (December 16, 2002).

Season Team	League	REGULAR SEASON Gms.	G	A	Pts.	PIM	+/-	PP	SH	PLAYOFFS Gms.	G	A	Pts.	PIM
93-94—Tri-City	WHL	9	0	2	2	39	...	...	...	—	—	—	—	—
94-95—Birmingham	ECHL	2	0	1	1	18	...	...	...	—	—	—	—	—
95-96—Johnstown	ECHL	58	37	31	68	300	...	...	...	—	—	—	—	—
96-97—					Did not play.									
97-98—					Did not play.									
98-99—					Did not play.									
99-00—					Did not play.									
00-01—Wilkes-Barre/Scranton	AHL	38	14	24	38	185	...	...	...	12	4	6	10	55
—Pittsburgh	NHL	29	1	2	3	79	-2	0	0	—	—	—	—	—
01-02—Wilkes-Barre/Scranton	AHL	24	13	17	30	193	...	...	...	—	—	—	—	—
—Pittsburgh	NHL	33	1	5	6	109	-13	0	0	—	—	—	—	—
—Philadelphia	NHL	9	0	1	1	69	-3	0	0	—	—	—	—	—
02-03—Hartford	AHL	35	7	10	17	172	...	...	...	—	—	—	—	—
—New York Rangers	NHL	11	0	0	0	12	-2	0	0	—	—	—	—	—
NHL Totals (7 years)		82	2	8	10	269	-20	0	0					

TIMANDER, MATTIAS   D   ISLANDERS

PERSONAL: Born April 16, 1974, in Solleftea, Sweden ... 6-3/228. ... Shoots left. ... Name pronounced tih-MAN-duhr.

TRANSACTIONS/CAREER NOTES: Selected by Boston Bruins in second round (seventh Bruins pick, 208th overall) of NHL entry draft (June 21, 1992). ... Injured shoulder (November 26, 1996); missed four games. ... Injured finger (November 17, 1997); missed two games. ... Injured shoulder (March 2, 1999); missed two games. ... Reinjured shoulder (March 13, 1999); missed one game. ... Injured shoulder (November 22, 1999); missed 11 games. ... Selected by Columbus Blue Jackets in NHL expansion draft (June 23, 2000). ... Strained neck (December 16, 2000); missed five games. ... Suffered neck spasms (February 14, 2001); missed one game. ... Bruised hip (November 27, 2001); missed three games. ... Traded by Blue Jackets to New York Islanders for fourth-round pick (D Jekabs Redlihs) in 2002 draft (June 22, 2002).

Season Team	League	REGULAR SEASON Gms.	G	A	Pts.	PIM	+/-	PP	SH	PLAYOFFS Gms.	G	A	Pts.	PIM
92-93—MoDo Ornskoldsvik	Sweden	1	0	0	0	0	...	...	...	—	—	—	—	—
93-94—MoDo Ornskoldsvik	Sweden	23	2	2	4	6	...	...	...	11	2	0	2	10
94-95—MoDo Ornskoldsvik	Sweden	39	8	9	17	24	...	...	...	—	—	—	—	—
95-96—MoDo Ornskoldsvik	Sweden	37	4	10	14	34	...	...	...	7	1	1	2	8
96-97—Boston	NHL	41	1	8	9	14	-9	0	0	—	—	—	—	—
—Providence	AHL	32	3	11	14	20	...	...	...	10	1	1	2	12
97-98—Boston	NHL	23	1	1	2	6	-9	0	0	—	—	—	—	—
—Providence	AHL	31	3	7	10	25	...	...	...	—	—	—	—	—
98-99—Providence	AHL	43	2	22	24	24	...	...	...	—	—	—	—	—
—Boston	NHL	22	0	6	6	10	4	0	0	4	1	1	2	2
99-00—Boston	NHL	60	0	8	8	22	-11	0	0	—	—	—	—	—
—Hershey	AHL	1	0	0	0	2	...	...	...	—	—	—	—	—
00-01—Columbus	NHL	76	2	9	11	24	-8	0	0	—	—	—	—	—
01-02—Columbus	NHL	78	4	7	11	44	-34	1	0	—	—	—	—	—
02-03—New York Islanders	NHL	80	3	13	16	24	-2	0	0	1	0	0	0	0
NHL Totals (7 years)		380	11	52	63	144	-69	1	0	5	1	1	2	2

TIMONEN, KIMMO   D   PREDATORS

PERSONAL: Born March 18, 1975, in Kuopio, Finland ... 5-10/196. ... Shoots left. ... Brother of Jussi Timonen, defenseman, Philadelphia Flyers organization. ... Name pronounced KEE-moh TEE-muh-nehn.

TRANSACTIONS/CAREER NOTES: Selected by Los Angeles Kings in 10th round (11th Kings pick, 250th overall) of NHL entry draft (June 26, 1993). ... Rights traded by Kings with D Jan Vopat to Nashville Predators for future considerations (June 26, 1998). ... Lacerated lip (January 26, 1999); missed one game. ... Strained abdominal muscle (December 18, 1999); missed four games. ... Fractured wrist (January 11, 2000); missed 15 games. ... Fractured ankle (March 14, 2000); missed remainder of season.

Season Team	League	REGULAR SEASON								PLAYOFFS				
		Gms.	G	A	Pts.	PIM	+/-	PP	SH	Gms.	G	A	Pts.	PIM
91-92—KalPa Kuopio	Finland	5	0	0	0	0	...	...	...	—	—	—	—	—
92-93—KalPa Kuopio	Finland	33	0	2	2	4	...	...	...	—	—	—	—	—
93-94—KalPa Kuopio	Finland	46	6	7	13	55	...	...	...	—	—	—	—	—
94-95—TPS Turku	Finland	45	3	4	7	10	...	...	...	13	0	1	1	6
95-96—TPS Turku	Finland	48	3	21	24	22	...	...	...	9	1	2	3	12
96-97—TPS Turku	Finland	50	10	14	24	18	...	...	...	12	2	7	9	8
97-98—HIFK Helsinki	Finland	45	10	15	25	59	...	...	...	9	3	4	7	8
—Fin. Olympic team	Int'l	6	0	1	1	2	...	...	...	—	—	—	—	—
98-99—Milwaukee	IHL	29	2	13	15	22	...	...	...	—	—	—	—	—
—Nashville	NHL	50	4	8	12	30	-4	1	0	—	—	—	—	—
99-00—Nashville	NHL	51	8	25	33	26	-5	2	1	—	—	—	—	—
00-01—Nashville	NHL	82	12	13	25	50	-6	6	0	—	—	—	—	—
01-02—Nashville	NHL	82	13	29	42	28	2	9	0	—	—	—	—	—
—Fin. Olympic team	Int'l	4	0	1	1	2	...	...	...	—	—	—	—	—
02-03—Nashville	NHL	72	6	34	40	46	-3	4	0	—	—	—	—	—
NHL Totals (5 years)		337	43	109	152	180	-16	22	1					

TJARNQVIST, DANIEL   D   THRASHERS

PERSONAL: Born October 14, 1976, in Umea, Sweden ... 6-2/195. ... Shoots left. ... Brother of Mathias Tjarnqvist, center, Dallas Stars organization. ... Name pronounced TAHRN-kuh-vihst.

TRANSACTIONS/CAREER NOTES: Selected by Florida Panthers in fourth round (fifth Panthers pick, 88th overall) of NHL entry draft (July 8, 1995). ... Traded by Panthers with D Gord Murphy, C Herbert Vasiljevs and sixth-round pick (traded to Dallas) in 1999 draft to Atlanta Thrashers for G Trevor Kidd (June 25, 1999).

Season Team	League	REGULAR SEASON								PLAYOFFS				
		Gms.	G	A	Pts.	PIM	+/-	PP	SH	Gms.	G	A	Pts.	PIM
94-95—Rogle Angelholm	Sweden	33	2	4	6	2	...	...	...	—	—	—	—	—
95-96—Rogle Angelholm	Sweden	22	1	7	8	6	...	...	...	—	—	—	—	—
96-97—Jokerit Helsinki	Finland	44	3	8	11	4	...	...	...	9	0	3	3	4
97-98—Djurgarden Stockholm	Sweden	40	5	9	14	12	...	...	...	15	1	1	2	2
98-99—Djurgarden Stockholm	Sweden	40	4	3	7	16	...	...	...	4	0	0	0	2
99-00—Djurgarden Stockholm	Sweden	42	3	16	19	8	...	...	...	5	0	0	0	2
00-01—Djurgarden Stockholm	Sweden	45	9	17	26	26	...	...	...	16	6	5	11	2
01-02—Atlanta	NHL	75	2	16	18	14	-22	1	0	—	—	—	—	—
02-03—Atlanta	NHL	75	3	12	15	26	-20	1	0	—	—	—	—	—
NHL Totals (2 years)		150	5	28	33	40	-42	2	0					

TJARNQVIST, MATHIAS   C   STARS

PERSONAL: Born April 15, 1979, in Umea, Sweden. ... 6-1/183. ... Shoots left. ... Brother of Daniel Tjarnqvist, defenseman, Atlanta Thrashers system.

TRANSACTIONS/CAREER NOTES: Selected by Dallas Stars in third round (third Stars pick, 96th overall) of NHL entry draft (June 26, 1999). ... Signed by Stars (July 15, 2003).

Season Team	League	REGULAR SEASON								PLAYOFFS				
		Gms.	G	A	Pts.	PIM	+/-	PP	SH	Gms.	G	A	Pts.	PIM
98-99—Rogle	Sweden Dv. 2	—	—	—	—	—	—	—	—	—	—	—	—	—
99-00—Djurgarden Stockholm	Sweden	50	12	12	24	20	...	...	...	13	3	2	5	16
00-01—Djurgarden Stockholm	Sweden	47	11	8	19	53	...	...	...	16	1	2	3	6
01-02—Djurgarden Stockholm	Sweden	6	0	1	1	4	...	...	...	2	0	0	0	2
02-03—Djurgarden Stockholm	Sweden	38	11	13	24	30	...	...	...	9	4	1	5	12

TKACHUK, KEITH   LW   BLUES

PERSONAL: Born March 28, 1972, in Melrose, Mass. ... 6-2/227. ... Shoots left. ... Full Name: Keith Matthew Tkachuk. ... Cousin of Tom Fitzgerald, right winger, Toronto Maple Leafs. ... Name pronounced kuh-CHUHK.

TRANSACTIONS/CAREER NOTES: Selected by Winnipeg Jets in first round (first Jets pick, 19th overall) of NHL entry draft (June 16, 1990). ... Lacerated forearm (November 12, 1993); missed one game. ... Strained groin (October 9, 1995); missed three games. ... Suffered concussion (November 26, 1995); missed one game. ... Suspended two games and fined $1,000 by NHL for stick-swinging incident (March 16, 1996). ... Jets franchise moved to Phoenix and renamed Coyotes for 1996-97 season; NHL approved move on January 18, 1996. ... Suffered from the flu (March 5, 1997); missed one game. ... Injured groin (March 2, 1998); missed two games. ... Suffered hairline fracture of rib (March 12, 1998); missed seven games. ... Injured groin (December 14, 1998); missed two games. ... Fractured ribs (December 20, 1998); missed eight games. ... Strained lower back (February 2, 1999); missed two games. ... Injured neck (December 4, 1999); missed three games. ... Suffered back spasms (December 26, 1999); missed four games. ... Sprained ankle (January 31, 2000); missed one game. ... Sprained ankle (February 12, 2000); missed 16 games. ... Suspended two games by NHL for high-sticking incident (March 24, 2000). ... Sprained ankle (March 29, 2000); missed final six games of regular season. ... Strained groin (October 12, 2000); missed one game. ... Suffered injury (October 30, 2000); missed one game. ... Suffered concussion (January 26, 2001); missed two games. ... Suffered injury (February 9, 2001); missed one game. ... Traded by Coyotes to St. Louis Blues for C Michal Handzus, RW Ladislav Nagy, C Jeff Taffe and first-round pick (LW Ben Eager) in 2002 draft (March 13, 2001). ... Bruised thigh (February 16, 2002); missed eight games. ... Suspended one game by NHL for slashing incident (March 25, 2002). ... Suspended four games by NHL for cross-checking incident (February 25, 2003).

STATISTICAL PLATEAUS: Three-goal games: 1993-94 (1), 1996-97 (1), 1997-98 (3), 1998-99 (1), 2000-01 (1). Total: 7. ... Four-goal games: 1995-96 (1), 1996-97 (1). Total: 2. ... Total hat tricks: 9.

Season Team	League	REGULAR SEASON								PLAYOFFS				
		Gms.	G	A	Pts.	PIM	+/-	PP	SH	Gms.	G	A	Pts.	PIM
88-89—Malden Catholic H.S. ..	Mass. H.S.	21	30	16	46	...	...	...	...	—	—	—	—	—
89-90—Malden Catholic H.S. ..	Mass. H.S.	6	12	14	26	...	...	...	...	—	—	—	—	—
90-91—Boston University	Hockey East	36	17	23	40	70	...	...	...	—	—	—	—	—
91-92—U.S. national team	Int'l	45	10	10	20	141	...	...	...	—	—	—	—	—
—U.S. Olympic team	Int'l	8	1	1	2	12	...	...	...	—	—	—	—	—
—Winnipeg	NHL	17	3	5	8	28	0	2	0	7	3	0	3	30
92-93—Winnipeg	NHL	83	28	23	51	201	-13	12	0	6	4	0	4	14
93-94—Winnipeg	NHL	84	41	40	81	255	-12	22	3	—	—	—	—	—
94-95—Winnipeg	NHL	48	22	29	51	152	-4	7	2	—	—	—	—	—
95-96—Winnipeg	NHL	76	50	48	98	156	11	20	2	6	1	2	3	22
96-97—Phoenix......	NHL	81	*52	34	86	228	-1	9	2	7	6	0	6	7
97-98—Phoenix......	NHL	69	40	26	66	147	9	11	0	6	3	3	6	10
—U.S. Olympic team	Int'l	4	0	2	2	6	...	...	...	—	—	—	—	—
98-99—Phoenix......	NHL	68	36	32	68	151	22	11	2	7	1	3	4	13
99-00—Phoenix......	NHL	50	22	21	43	82	7	5	1	5	1	1	2	4
00-01—Phoenix......	NHL	64	29	42	71	108	6	15	0	—	—	—	—	—
—St. Louis	NHL	12	6	2	8	14	-3	2	0	15	2	7	9	20
01-02—St. Louis	NHL	73	38	37	75	117	21	13	0	10	5	5	10	18
—U.S. Olympic team	Int'l	5	2	0	2	2	...	...	...	—	—	—	—	—
02-03—St. Louis	NHL	56	31	24	55	139	1	14	0	7	1	3	4	14
NHL Totals (12 years).........		781	398	363	761	1778	44	143	12	76	27	24	51	152

TKACZUK, DANIEL   C   BLUES

PERSONAL: Born June 10, 1979, in Toronto. ... 6-1/197. ... Shoots left. ... Name pronounced kuh-CHOOK.
TRANSACTIONS/CAREER NOTES: Selected by Calgary Flames in first round (first Flames pick, sixth overall) of NHL entry draft (June 21, 1997). ... Suffered head injury (January 23, 2001); missed five games. ... Traded by Flames with G Fred Brathwaite, RW Sergei Varlamov and ninth-round pick (C Grant Jacobsen) in 2001 draft to St. Louis Blues for G Roman Turek and fourth-round pick (F Egor Shastin) in 2001 draft (June 23, 2001).

Season Team	League	REGULAR SEASON								PLAYOFFS				
		Gms.	G	A	Pts.	PIM	+/-	PP	SH	Gms.	G	A	Pts.	PIM
95-96—Barrie..........................	OHL	61	22	39	61	38	...	...	...	7	1	2	3	8
96-97—Barrie..........................	OHL	62	45	48	93	49	...	...	...	9	7	2	9	2
97-98—Barrie..........................	OHL	57	35	40	75	38	...	...	...	6	2	3	5	8
98-99—Barrie..........................	OHL	58	43	62	105	58	...	...	...	12	7	8	15	10
99-00—Saint John	AHL	80	25	41	66	56	...	...	...	3	0	0	0	0
00-01—Saint John	AHL	50	15	21	36	48	...	...	...	14	10	9	19	4
—Calgary	NHL	19	4	7	11	14	1	1	0	—	—	—	—	—
01-02—Worcester	AHL	75	10	27	37	37	...	...	...	3	1	1	2	2
02-03—Bridgeport..................	AHL	69	9	18	27	44	...	...	...	—	—	—	—	—
NHL Totals (1 year).............		19	4	7	11	14	1	1	0					

TOBLER, RYAN   LW

PERSONAL: Born May 13, 1976, in Calgary. ... 6-3/192. ... Shoots left.
TRANSACTIONS/CAREER NOTES: Signed as non-drafted free agent by Nashville Predators (May 1, 2000). ... Traded by Predators to New York Rangers for D Bert Robertsson (March 7, 2001). ... Signed as free agent by Tampa Bay Lightning (August 21, 2001).

Season Team	League	REGULAR SEASON								PLAYOFFS				
		Gms.	G	A	Pts.	PIM	+/-	PP	SH	Gms.	G	A	Pts.	PIM
93-94—Calgary	Tier II Jr. A	56	32	17	49	195	...	...	...	—	—	—	—	—
94-95—Saskatoon..................	WHL	61	11	19	30	81	...	...	...	10	1	2	3	8
95-96—Calgary	WHL	16	10	3	13	8	...	...	...	—	—	—	—	—
—Swift Current	WHL	25	17	11	28	31	...	...	...	6	1	1	2	2
96-97—Swift Current	WHL	39	10	17	27	40	...	...	...	—	—	—	—	—
—Moose Jaw	WHL	24	6	15	21	16	...	...	...	12	1	6	7	16
97-98—Lake Charles	WPHL	66	22	34	56	204	...	...	...	—	—	—	—	—
—Utah............................	IHL	3	1	0	1	2	...	...	...	—	—	—	—	—
98-99—Adirondack	AHL	64	9	18	27	157	...	...	...	3	0	0	0	2
99-00—Milwaukee.................	IHL	78	19	28	47	293	...	...	...	2	0	0	0	0
00-01—Milwaukee.................	IHL	49	7	9	16	196	...	...	...	—	—	—	—	—
—Hartford	AHL	13	1	5	6	71	...	...	...	5	0	0	0	2
01-02—Tampa Bay.................	NHL	4	0	0	0	5	-2	0	0	—	—	—	—	—
—Springfield..................	AHL	73	17	24	41	215	...	...	...	—	—	—	—	—
02-03—Springfield..................	AHL	11	0	2	2	44	...	...	...	—	—	—	—	—
—Chicago......................	AHL	58	13	18	31	143	...	...	...	—	—	—	—	—
NHL Totals (1 year).............		4	0	0	0	5	-2	0	0					

TOLKUNOV, DMITRI   D   PANTHERS

PERSONAL: Born May 5, 1979, in Kiev, U.S.S.R. ... 6-2/191. ... Shoots right.
TRANSACTIONS/CAREER NOTES: Signed as non-drafted free agent by Chicago Blackhawks (October 8, 1998). ... Traded to Florida Panthers for ninth pick in 2003 draft (June 22, 2003).

Season Team	League	Gms.	G	A	Pts.	PIM	+/-	PP	SH	Gms.	G	A	Pts.	PIM
				REGULAR SEASON								PLAYOFFS		
96-97—Hull	QMJHL	34	3	8	11	99	...	...	...	—	—	—	—	—
—Beauport	QMJHL	27	3	7	10	18	...	...	...	—	—	—	—	—
97-98—Quebec	QMJHL	66	10	25	35	81	...	...	...	—	—	—	—	—
98-99—Quebec	QMJHL	69	11	57	68	110	...	...	...	13	2	7	9	22
99-00—Cleveland	IHL	65	3	12	15	54	...	...	...	8	0	0	0	2
00-01—Norfolk	AHL	78	5	18	23	93	...	...	...	9	0	1	1	4
01-02—Norfolk	AHL	51	1	18	19	23	...	...	...	4	0	0	0	2
02-03—Norfolk	AHL	47	1	17	18	39	...	...	...	—	—	—	—	—

TOMS, JEFF   LW   PANTHERS

PERSONAL: Born June 4, 1974, in Swift Current, Sask. ... 6-5/210. ... Shoots left.
TRANSACTIONS/CAREER NOTES: Selected by New Jersey Devils in ninth round (10th Devils pick, 210th overall) of NHL entry draft (June 26, 1993). ... Traded by Devils to Tampa Bay Lightning for fourth-round pick (traded to Calgary) in 1994 draft (May 31, 1994). ... Claimed on waivers by Washington Capitals (November 19, 1997). ... Sprained knee (December 12, 1997); missed 11 games. ... Strained abdominal muscle (January 7, 1999); missed 30 games. ... Signed as free agent by New York Islanders (July 27, 2000). ... Claimed on waivers by New York Rangers (January 13, 2001). ... Lacerated finger (November 8, 2001); missed two games. ... Claimed on waivers by Pittsburgh Penguins (March 16, 2002). ... Signed as free agent by Florida Panthers (July 10, 2002).
STATISTICAL PLATEAUS: Three-goal games: 2001-02 (1).

Season Team	League	Gms.	G	A	Pts.	PIM	+/-	PP	SH	Gms.	G	A	Pts.	PIM
				REGULAR SEASON								PLAYOFFS		
91-92—Sault Ste. Marie	OHL	36	9	5	14	0	...	...	...	16	0	1	1	2
92-93—Sault Ste. Marie	OHL	59	16	23	39	20	...	...	...	16	4	4	8	7
93-94—Sault Ste. Marie	OHL	64	52	45	97	19	...	...	...	14	11	4	15	2
94-95—Atlanta	IHL	40	7	8	15	10	...	...	...	4	0	0	0	4
95-96—Atlanta	IHL	68	16	18	34	18	...	...	...	1	0	0	0	0
—Tampa Bay	NHL	1	0	0	0	0	0	0	0	—	—	—	—	—
96-97—Adirondack	AHL	37	11	16	27	8	...	...	...	4	1	2	3	0
—Tampa Bay	NHL	34	2	8	10	10	2	0	0	—	—	—	—	—
97-98—Tampa Bay	NHL	13	1	2	3	7	-6	0	0	—	—	—	—	—
—Washington	NHL	33	3	4	7	8	-11	0	0	1	0	0	0	0
98-99—Portland	AHL	20	3	7	10	8	...	...	...	—	—	—	—	—
—Washington	NHL	21	1	5	6	2	0	0	0	—	—	—	—	—
99-00—Washington	NHL	20	1	2	3	4	-1	0	0	—	—	—	—	—
—Portland	AHL	33	16	21	37	16	...	...	...	4	1	1	2	2
00-01—New York Islanders	NHL	39	2	4	6	10	-7	0	0	—	—	—	—	—
—Springfield	AHL	5	6	5	11	0	...	...	...	—	—	—	—	—
—New York Rangers	NHL	15	1	1	2	0	-3	0	0	—	—	—	—	—
—Hartford	AHL	12	4	9	13	2	...	...	...	5	6	0	6	2
01-02—Hartford	AHL	9	6	6	12	4	...	...	...	—	—	—	—	—
—New York Rangers	NHL	38	7	4	11	10	-4	2	0	—	—	—	—	—
—Pittsburgh	NHL	14	2	1	3	4	-5	0	0	—	—	—	—	—
02-03—San Antonio	AHL	64	30	33	63	28	...	...	...	—	—	—	—	—
—Florida	NHL	8	2	2	4	4	2	0	0	—	—	—	—	—
NHL Totals (8 years)		236	22	33	55	59	-33	2	0	1	0	0	0	0

TOOTOO, JORDAN   RW   PREDATORS

PERSONAL: Born February 2, 1983, in Churchill, Man. ... 5-8/185. ... Shoots right.
TRANSACTIONS/CAREER NOTES: Selected by Nashville Predators in fourth round (sixth Predators pick, 98th overall) of NHL entry draft (June 23, 2001). ... Signed by Nashville (May 30, 2003).

Season Team	League	Gms.	G	A	Pts.	PIM	+/-	PP	SH	Gms.	G	A	Pts.	PIM
				REGULAR SEASON								PLAYOFFS		
99-00—Brandon	WHL	45	6	10	16	214	...	...	...	—	—	—	—	—
00-01—Brandon	WHL	60	20	28	48	172	...	...	...	6	2	4	6	18
01-02—Brandon	WHL	64	32	39	71	272	...	...	...	16	4	3	7	*58
02-03—Brandon	WHL	51	35	39	74	216	...	...	...	—	—	—	—	—

TORRES, RAFFI   LW   OILERS

PERSONAL: Born October 8, 1981, in Toronto ... 6-0/210. ... Shoots left.
TRANSACTIONS/CAREER NOTES: Selected by New York Islanders in first round (second Islanders pick, fifth overall) of NHL entry draft (June 24, 2000). ... Traded by Islanders with LW Brad Isbister to Edmonton Oilers for D Janne Niinimaa and second-round pick in 2003 draft (March 11, 2003).

Season Team	League	Gms.	G	A	Pts.	PIM	+/-	PP	SH	Gms.	G	A	Pts.	PIM
				REGULAR SEASON								PLAYOFFS		
97-98—Thornhill	Jr. A	46	17	16	33	90	...	...	...	—	—	—	—	—
98-99—Brampton	OHL	62	35	27	62	32	...	...	...	—	—	—	—	—
99-00—Brampton	OHL	68	43	48	91	40	...	...	...	6	5	2	7	23
00-01—Brampton	OHL	55	33	37	70	76	...	...	...	8	7	4	11	19
01-02—Bridgeport	AHL	59	20	10	30	45	...	...	...	20	8	9	17	26
—New York Islanders	NHL	14	0	1	1	6	2	0	0	—	—	—	—	—
02-03—Bridgeport	AHL	49	17	15	32	54	...	...	...	—	—	—	—	—
—Hamilton	AHL	11	1	7	8	14	...	...	...	—	—	—	—	—
—New York Islanders	NHL	17	0	5	5	10	0	0	0	—	—	—	—	—
NHL Totals (2 years)		31	0	6	6	16	2	0	0					

TOSKALA, VESA — G — SHARKS

PERSONAL: Born May 20, 1977, in Tampere, Finland ... 5-10/195. ... Catches left.
TRANSACTIONS/CAREER NOTES: Selected by San Jose Sharks in fourth round (fourth Sharks pick, 90th overall) of NHL entry draft (July 8, 1995).

Season Team	League	Gms.	Min	W	L	T	GA	SO	Avg.	SV%	Gms.	Min.	W	L	GA	SO	Avg.	SV%
93-94—Ilves Jrs.	Finland	2	...	...	...	...	...	...	...	—	—	—	—	—	—	—	—	—
94-95—Ilves Jrs.	Finland	17	956	...	...	...	36	...	2.26	—	—	—	—	—	—	—	—	—
95-96—Ilves Tampere	Finland	37	2073	...	...	...	109	1	3.15	—	2	78	...	...	11	0	8.46	—
—Koo Vee	Finland	2	119	...	...	...	5	...	2.52	—	—	—	—	—	—	—	—	—
—Ilves Jrs.	Finland	3	180	...	...	...	3	...	1.00	—	—	—	—	—	—	—	—	—
96-97—Ilves Tampere	Finland	40	2270	22	12	5	108	0	2.85	—	8	479	3	5	29	0	3.63	—
97-98—Ilves Tampere	Finland	48	2555	26	13	3	118	1	2.77	—	9	519	6	3	18	1	2.08	—
98-99—Ilves Tampere	Finland	33	1966	21	12	0	70	†5	2.14	—	4	248	1	3	14	...	3.39	—
99-00—Farjestad Karlstad	Sweden	44	2652	...	...	...	118	3	2.67	—	7	439	...	...	19	0	2.60	—
00-01—Kentucky	AHL	44	2466	22	13	5	114	2	2.77	—	3	197	0	3	8	0	2.44	—
01-02—Cleveland	AHL	*62	*3574	19	*33	7	*178	3	2.99	—	—	—	—	—	—	—	—	—
—San Jose	NHL	1	10	0	0	0	0	0	...	1.000	—	—	—	—	—	—	—	—
02-03—Cleveland	AHL	49	2824	15	30	2	151	1	3.21	—	—	—	—	—	—	—	—	—
—San Jose	NHL	11	537	4	3	1	21	1	2.35	.927	—	—	—	—	—	—	—	—
NHL Totals (2 years)		12	547	4	3	1	21	1	2.30	.927	—	—	—	—	—	—	—	—

TRAVERSE, PATRICK — D — CANADIENS

PERSONAL: Born March 14, 1974, in Montreal ... 6-4/227. ... Shoots left.
TRANSACTIONS/CAREER NOTES: Selected by Ottawa Senators in third round (third Senators pick, 50th overall) of NHL entry draft (June 20, 1992). ... Suffered concussion (January 30, 1999); missed three games. ... Sprained shoulder (February 20, 1999); missed 13 games. ... Bruised right shoulder (February 17, 2000); missed seven games. ... Traded by Senators to Mighty Ducks of Anaheim for D Joel Kwiatkowski (June 12, 2000). ... Traded by Mighty Ducks with LW Andrei Nazarov to Boston Bruins for C Samuel Pahlsson (November 19, 2000). ... Traded by Bruins to Montreal Canadiens for D Eric Weinrich (February 21, 2001). ... Injured neck (April 5, 2001); missed final game of season. ... Sprained medial collateral ligament in knee (November 5, 2001); missed 12 games. ... Suffered concussion (January 10, 2002); missed 12 games.

Season Team	League	Gms.	G	A	Pts.	PIM	+/-	PP	SH	Gms.	G	A	Pts.	PIM
91-92—Shawinigan	QMJHL	59	3	11	14	12	...	...	...	10	0	0	0	4
92-93—Shawinigan	QMJHL	53	5	24	29	24	...	...	...	—	—	—	—	—
—New Haven	AHL	2	0	0	0	2	...	...	...	—	—	—	—	—
—St. Jean	QMJHL	15	1	6	7	0	...	...	...	4	0	1	1	2
93-94—Prin. Edward Island	AHL	3	0	1	1	2	...	...	...	—	—	—	—	—
—St. Jean	QMJHL	66	15	37	52	30	...	...	...	5	0	4	4	4
94-95—Prin. Edward Island	AHL	70	5	13	18	19	...	...	...	7	0	2	2	0
95-96—Prin. Edward Island	AHL	55	4	21	25	32	...	...	...	5	1	2	3	2
—Ottawa	NHL	5	0	0	0	2	-1	0	0	—	—	—	—	—
96-97—Worcester	AHL	24	0	4	4	23	...	...	...	—	—	—	—	—
—Grand Rapids	IHL	10	2	1	3	10	...	...	...	2	0	1	1	2
97-98—Hershey	AHL	71	14	15	29	67	...	...	...	7	1	3	4	4
98-99—Ottawa	NHL	46	1	9	10	22	12	0	0	—	—	—	—	—
99-00—Ottawa	NHL	66	6	17	23	21	17	1	0	6	0	0	0	2
00-01—Anaheim	NHL	15	1	0	1	6	-6	0	0	—	—	—	—	—
—Boston	NHL	37	2	6	8	14	4	1	0	—	—	—	—	—
—Montreal	NHL	19	2	3	5	10	-8	0	0	—	—	—	—	—
01-02—Montreal	NHL	25	2	3	5	14	-7	2	0	—	—	—	—	—
—Quebec	AHL	4	0	2	2	4	...	...	...	—	—	—	—	—
02-03—Montreal	NHL	65	0	13	13	24	-9	0	0	—	—	—	—	—
NHL Totals (6 years)		278	14	51	65	113	2	4	0	6	0	0	0	2

TREMBLAY, YANNICK — D — THRASHERS

PERSONAL: Born November 15, 1975, in Pointe-aux-Trembles, Que. ... 6-2/200. ... Shoots right.
TRANSACTIONS/CAREER NOTES: Selected by Toronto Maple Leafs in sixth round (fourth Maple Leafs pick, 145th overall) of NHL entry draft (July 8, 1995). ... Selected by Atlanta Thrashers in NHL expansion draft (June 25, 1999). ... Strained groin (October 23, 1999); missed one game. ... Injured hip (December 8, 1999); missed one game. ... Strained hip flexor (February 7, 2000); missed one game. ... Suffered from the flu (April 8, 2000); missed two games. ... Suffered from the flu (December 11, 2000). ... Injured leg (December 19, 2000); missed three games. ... Reinjured leg (December 28, 2000); missed five games. ... Injured shoulder (February 10, 2001); missed remainder of season. ... Dislocated right shoulder (November 4, 2001); missed 10 games. ... Injured groin (March 8, 2002); missed two games.

Season Team	League	Gms.	G	A	Pts.	PIM	+/-	PP	SH	Gms.	G	A	Pts.	PIM
93-94—St. Thomas Univ.	AUAA	25	2	3	5	10	...	...	...	—	—	—	—	—
94-95—Beauport	QMJHL	70	10	32	42	22	...	...	...	17	6	8	14	6
95-96—Beauport	QMJHL	61	12	33	45	42	...	...	...	20	3	16	19	18
—St. John's	AHL	3	0	1	1	0	...	...	...	—	—	—	—	—
96-97—Sherbrooke	QMJHL	42	21	25	46	212	...	...	...	—	—	—	—	—
—St. John's	AHL	67	7	25	32	34	...	...	...	11	2	9	11	0
—Toronto	NHL	5	0	0	0	0	-4	0	0	—	—	—	—	—
97-98—St. John's	AHL	17	3	6	9	4	...	...	...	4	0	1	1	5
—Toronto	NHL	38	2	4	6	6	-6	1	0	—	—	—	—	—

Season Team	League	REGULAR SEASON								PLAYOFFS				
		Gms.	G	A	Pts.	PIM	+/-	PP	SH	Gms.	G	A	Pts.	PIM
98-99—Toronto	NHL	35	2	7	9	16	0	0	0	—	—	—	—	—
99-00—Atlanta	NHL	75	10	21	31	22	-42	4	1	—	—	—	—	—
00-01—Atlanta	NHL	46	4	8	12	30	-6	1	0	—	—	—	—	—
01-02—Atlanta	NHL	66	9	15	24	47	-15	1	0	—	—	—	—	—
02-03—Atlanta	NHL	75	8	22	30	32	-27	5	0	—	—	—	—	—
NHL Totals (7 years)		340	35	77	112	153	-100	12	1					

TREPANIER, PASCAL   D   LIGHTNING

PERSONAL: Born September 4, 1973, in Gaspe, Que. ... 6-0/210. ... Shoots right. ... Name pronounced TREH-puhn-yeh.
TRANSACTIONS/CAREER NOTES: Signed as non-drafted free agent by Colorado Avalanche (August 30, 1996). ... Selected by Mighty Ducks of Anaheim from Avalanche in NHL waiver draft (October 5, 1998). ... Bruised left leg (March 3, 1999); missed one game. ... Injured anterior cruciate ligament and meniscus in right knee (April 6, 1999) and underwent knee surgery; missed remainder of season. ... Suspended five games by NHL for elbowing incident (October 5, 1999). ... Suffered head injury (December 17, 1999); missed six games. ... Bruised left ankle (March 3, 2000); missed nine games. ... Signed as free agent by Nashville Predators (July 16, 2002). ... Traded by Predators to Florida Panthers for G Wade Flaherty (March 9, 2003). ... Signed by Tampa Bay Lightning (July 23, 2003).

Season Team	League	REGULAR SEASON								PLAYOFFS				
		Gms.	G	A	Pts.	PIM	+/-	PP	SH	Gms.	G	A	Pts.	PIM
90-91—Hull	QMJHL	46	3	3	6	56	...	...	...	4	0	2	2	7
91-92—Trois-Rivieres	QMJHL	53	4	18	22	125	...	...	...	15	3	5	8	21
92-93—Sherbrooke	QMJHL	59	15	33	48	130	...	...	...	15	5	7	12	36
93-94—Sherbrooke	QMJHL	48	16	41	57	67	...	...	...	12	1	8	9	14
94-95—Cornwall	AHL	4	0	0	0	9	...	...	...	—	—	—	—	—
—Dayton	ECHL	36	16	28	44	113	...	...	...	—	—	—	—	—
—Kalamazoo	IHL	14	1	2	3	47	...	...	...	—	—	—	—	—
95-96—Cornwall	AHL	70	13	20	33	142	...	...	...	8	1	2	3	24
96-97—Hershey	AHL	73	14	39	53	151	...	...	...	23	6	13	19	59
97-98—Colorado	NHL	15	0	1	1	18	-2	0	0	—	—	—	—	—
—Hershey	AHL	43	13	18	31	105	...	...	...	7	4	2	6	8
98-99—Anaheim	NHL	45	2	4	6	48	0	0	0	—	—	—	—	—
99-00—Anaheim	NHL	37	0	4	4	54	2	0	0	—	—	—	—	—
00-01—Anaheim	NHL	57	6	4	10	73	-12	3	0	—	—	—	—	—
01-02—Colorado	NHL	74	4	9	13	59	4	2	0	2	0	0	0	0
02-03—Milwaukee	AHL	52	9	15	24	33	...	...	...	—	—	—	—	—
—Nashville	NHL	1	0	0	0	0	0	0	0	—	—	—	—	—
—San Antonio	AHL	12	4	6	10	10	...	...	...	—	—	—	—	—
NHL Totals (6 years)		229	12	22	34	252	-8	5	0	2	0	0	0	0

TRIPP, JOHN   RW   KINGS

PERSONAL: Born May 4, 1977, in Kingston, Ont. ... 6-3/223. ... Shoots right.
HIGH SCHOOL: Henry Street (Whitby, Ont.).
TRANSACTIONS/CAREER NOTES: Selected by Colorado Avalanche in third round (third Avalanche pick, 77th overall) of NHL entry draft (July 8, 1995). ... Returned to draft pool by Avalanche and selected by Calgary Flames in second round (third Flames pick, 42nd overall) of NHL entry draft (June 21, 1997). ... Signed by New York Rangers (September 3, 2002). ... Signed as free agent by Los Angeles Kings (August 6, 2003).

Season Team	League	REGULAR SEASON								PLAYOFFS				
		Gms.	G	A	Pts.	PIM	+/-	PP	SH	Gms.	G	A	Pts.	PIM
93-94—St. Mary's Jr. B	OHA	42	15	29	44	116	...	...	...	—	—	—	—	—
94-95—Oshawa	OHL	58	6	11	17	53	...	...	...	7	0	1	1	4
95-96—Oshawa	OHL	56	13	14	27	95	...	...	...	5	1	1	2	13
96-97—Oshawa	OHL	59	28	20	48	126	...	...	...	18	16	10	26	42
97-98—Roanoke	ECHL	9	0	2	2	22	...	...	...	—	—	—	—	—
—Saint John	AHL	61	1	11	12	66	...	...	...	2	0	1	1	0
98-99—Saint John	AHL	2	0	0	0	10	...	...	...	—	—	—	—	—
—Johnstown	ECHL	7	2	0	2	12	...	...	...	—	—	—	—	—
99-00—Johnstown	ECHL	38	13	11	24	64	...	...	...	—	—	—	—	—
—Saint John	AHL	29	8	7	15	38	...	...	...	3	0	0	0	2
00-01—Hershey	AHL	5	0	1	1	0	...	...	...	—	—	—	—	—
—Pensacola	ECHL	36	19	14	33	110	...	...	...	—	—	—	—	—
—Houston	IHL	15	0	6	6	14	...	...	...	—	—	—	—	—
—Milwaukee	IHL	12	0	1	1	31	...	...	...	—	—	—	—	—
01-02—Pensacola	ECHL	49	25	27	52	114	...	...	...	—	—	—	—	—
—Hartford	AHL	23	4	9	13	22	...	...	...	10	4	2	6	17
02-03—Hartford	AHL	57	29	21	50	68	...	...	...	—	—	—	—	—
—New York Rangers	NHL	9	1	2	3	2	1	0	0	—	—	—	—	—
NHL Totals (1 year)		9	1	2	3	2	1	0	0					

TRNKA, PAVEL   D   PANTHERS

PERSONAL: Born July 27, 1976, in Plzen, Czechoslovakia ... 6-2/206. ... Shoots left. ... Name pronounced TRIHN-kuh.
TRANSACTIONS/CAREER NOTES: Selected by Mighty Ducks of Anaheim in fifth round (fifth Mighty Ducks pick, 106th overall) of NHL entry draft (June 29, 1994). ... Suffered concussion (January 12, 1998); missed one game. ... Strained groin (December 8, 1999); missed five games. ... Sprained ankle (March 17, 2000); missed final nine games of season. ... Sprained ankle (October 8, 2000); missed 17 games. ... Traded by Mighty Ducks with C Matt Cullen and fourth-round pick in 2003 draft to Florida Panthers for D Sandis Ozolinsh and D Lance Ward (January 30, 2003).

Season Team	League	REGULAR SEASON								PLAYOFFS				
		Gms.	G	A	Pts.	PIM	+/-	PP	SH	Gms.	G	A	Pts.	PIM
92-93—Skoda Plzen Jrs.........	Czech.					Statistics unavailable.								
93-94—Skoda Plzen...............	Czech Rep.	12	0	1	1	...	...	...	...	—	—	—	—	—
94-95—HC Kladno..................	Czech Rep.	28	0	5	5	...	...	...	...	—	—	—	—	—
—Interconex Plzen.......	Czech Rep.	6	0	0	0	...	...	...	...	—	—	—	—	—
95-96—Baltimore	AHL	69	2	6	8	44	...	...	...	6	0	0	0	2
96-97—Baltimore	AHL	69	6	14	20	86	...	...	...	3	0	0	0	2
97-98—Cincinnati	AHL	23	3	5	8	28	...	...	...	—	—	—	—	—
—Anaheim	NHL	48	3	4	7	40	-4	1	0	—	—	—	—	—
98-99—Anaheim	NHL	63	0	4	4	60	-6	0	0	4	0	1	1	2
99-00—Anaheim	NHL	57	2	15	17	34	12	0	0	—	—	—	—	—
00-01—Anaheim	NHL	59	1	7	8	42	-12	0	0	—	—	—	—	—
01-02—Anaheim	NHL	71	2	11	13	66	-5	1	0	—	—	—	—	—
02-03—Anaheim	NHL	24	3	6	9	6	2	1	0	—	—	—	—	—
—Florida......................	NHL	22	0	3	3	24	-1	0	0	—	—	—	—	—
NHL Totals (6 years)...........		344	11	50	61	272	-14	3	0	4	0	1	1	2

TRUDEL, JEAN-GUY   LW

PERSONAL: Born October 18, 1975, in Sudbury, Ont. ... 5-11/202. ... Shoots right.

TRANSACTIONS/CAREER NOTES: Signed as non-drafted free agent by Phoenix Coyotes (July 16, 1999). ... Signed as free agent by Minnesota Wild (July 16, 2002).

Season Team	League	REGULAR SEASON								PLAYOFFS				
		Gms.	G	A	Pts.	PIM	+/-	PP	SH	Gms.	G	A	Pts.	PIM
94-95—Hull	QMJHL	54	29	42	71	76	...	...	...	19	4	13	17	25
95-96—Hull	QMJHL	70	50	71	121	96	...	...	...	17	11	18	29	8
96-97—Peoria	ECHL	37	25	29	54	47	...	...	...	9	9	10	19	22
—San Antonio...............	IHL	12	1	5	6	4	...	...	...	—	—	—	—	—
—Chicago.....................	IHL	6	1	2	3	2	...	...	...	—	—	—	—	—
97-98—Peoria	ECHL	62	39	74	113	147	...	...	...	3	0	0	0	2
98-99—Kansas City...............	IHL	76	24	25	49	66	...	...	...	3	1	0	1	0
99-00—Springfield	AHL	72	34	39	73	80	...	...	...	3	0	1	1	4
—Phoenix.....................	NHL	1	0	0	0	0	-1	0	0	—	—	—	—	—
00-01—Springfield	AHL	80	34	65	99	89	...	...	...	—	—	—	—	—
01-02—Springfield	AHL	76	22	48	70	83	...	...	...	—	—	—	—	—
—Phoenix.....................	NHL	3	0	0	0	2	0	0	0	—	—	—	—	—
02-03—Houston	AHL	79	31	54	85	85	...	...	...	—	—	—	—	—
—Minnesota..................	NHL	1	0	0	0	2	0	0	0	—	—	—	—	—
NHL Totals (3 years)...........		5	0	0	0	4	-1	0	0					

TSELIOS, NIKOS   D   COYOTES

PERSONAL: Born January 20, 1979, in Oak Park, Ill. ... 6-4/187. ... Shoots left. ... Cousin of Chris Chelios, defenseman, Detroit Red Wings. ... Name pronounced NEE-kohz CHEL-yoz.

TRANSACTIONS/CAREER NOTES: Selected by Carolina Hurricanes in first round (first Hurricanes pick, 22nd overall) of NHL entry draft (June 21, 1997). ... Signed by Phoenix Coyotes (July 21, 2003).

Season Team	League	REGULAR SEASON								PLAYOFFS				
		Gms.	G	A	Pts.	PIM	+/-	PP	SH	Gms.	G	A	Pts.	PIM
95-96—Chicago......................	MNHL	27	5	8	13	40	...	...	...	—	—	—	—	—
96-97—Belleville	OHL	64	9	37	46	61	...	...	...	—	—	—	—	—
97-98—Belleville	OHL	20	2	10	12	16	...	...	...	—	—	—	—	—
—Plymouth...................	OHL	41	8	20	28	27	...	...	...	15	1	8	9	27
98-99—Plymouth...................	OHL	60	21	39	60	60	...	...	...	11	4	10	14	8
99-00—Cincinnati..................	IHL	80	3	19	22	75	...	...	...	10	0	2	2	4
00-01—Cincinnati..................	IHL	79	7	18	25	98	...	...	...	5	0	3	3	0
01-02—Lowell	AHL	70	3	16	19	64	...	...	...	—	—	—	—	—
—Carolina....................	NHL	2	0	0	0	6	-2	0	0	—	—	—	—	—
02-03—Lowell	AHL	61	4	8	12	65	...	...	...	—	—	—	—	—
—Springfield	AHL	13	0	2	2	12	...	...	...	—	—	—	—	—
NHL Totals (1 year).............		2	0	0	0	6	-2	0	0					

TUCKER, DARCY   LW   MAPLE LEAFS

PERSONAL: Born March 15, 1975, in Castor, Alta. ... 5-10/178. ... Shoots left.

TRANSACTIONS/CAREER NOTES: Selected by Montreal Canadiens in sixth round (eighth Canadiens pick, 151st overall) of NHL entry draft (June 26, 1993). ... Bruised knee (December 16, 1996); missed one game. ... Traded by Canadiens with RW Stephane Richer and D David Wilkie to Tampa Bay Lightning for C Patrick Poulin, RW Mick Vukota and D Igor Ulanov (January 15, 1998). ... Suspended two games by NHL for spearing incident (December 28, 1999). ... Traded by Lightning with fourth-round pick (RW Miguel Delisle) in 2000 draft to Toronto Maple Leafs for RW Mike Johnson, D Marek Posmyk and fifth-(RW Pavel Sedov) and sixth-round (D Aaron Gionet) picks in 2000 draft (February 9, 2000). ... Suffered concussion (November 19, 2001); missed three games. ... Suspended five games by NHL for unsportsmanlike conduct (March 5, 2003).

Season Team	League	REGULAR SEASON Gms.	G	A	Pts.	PIM	+/-	PP	SH	PLAYOFFS Gms.	G	A	Pts.	PIM
91-92—Kamloops	WHL	26	3	10	13	42	...	...	...	9	0	1	1	16
92-93—Kamloops	WHL	67	31	58	89	155	...	...	...	13	7	6	13	34
93-94—Kamloops	WHL	66	52	88	140	143	...	...	...	19	9	*18	*27	43
94-95—Kamloops	WHL	64	64	73	137	94	...	...	...	21	16	15	31	19
95-96—Fredericton	AHL	74	29	64	93	174	...	...	...	7	7	3	10	14
—Montreal	NHL	3	0	0	0	0	-1	0	0	—	—	—	—	—
96-97—Montreal	NHL	73	7	13	20	110	-5	1	0	4	0	0	0	0
97-98—Montreal	NHL	39	1	5	6	57	-6	0	0	—	—	—	—	—
—Tampa Bay	NHL	35	6	8	14	89	-8	1	1	—	—	—	—	—
98-99—Tampa Bay	NHL	82	21	22	43	176	-34	8	2	—	—	—	—	—
99-00—Tampa Bay	NHL	50	14	20	34	108	-15	1	0	—	—	—	—	—
—Toronto	NHL	27	7	10	17	55	3	0	2	12	4	2	6	15
00-01—Toronto	NHL	82	16	21	37	141	6	2	0	11	0	2	2	6
01-02—Toronto	NHL	77	24	35	59	92	24	7	0	17	4	4	8	38
02-03—Toronto	NHL	77	10	26	36	119	-7	4	1	6	0	3	3	6
NHL Totals (8 years)		545	106	160	266	947	-43	24	6	50	8	11	19	65

TUGNUTT, RON   G   STARS

PERSONAL: Born October 22, 1967, in Scarborough, Ont. ... 5-11/165. ... Catches left. ... Full Name: Ronald Frederick Bradley Tugnutt.

TRANSACTIONS/CAREER NOTES: Selected by Quebec Nordiques in fourth round (fourth Nordiques pick, 81st overall) of NHL entry draft (June 21, 1986). ... Sprained ankle (March 1989). ... Sprained knee (January 13, 1990). ... Injured hamstring (January 29, 1991); missed 11 games. ... Traded by Nordiques with LW Brad Zavisha to Edmonton Oilers for LW Martin Rucinsky (March 10, 1992). ... Selected by Mighty Ducks of Anaheim in NHL expansion draft (June 24, 1993). ... Traded by Mighty Ducks to Montreal Canadiens for C Stephan Lebeau (February 20, 1994). ... Strained knee (January 28, 1995); missed five games. ... Signed as free agent by Washington Capitals (September 20, 1995). ... Signed as free agent by Ottawa Senators (July 17, 1996). ... Strained hip flexor (January 31, 1998); missed two games. ... Injured right knee (March 6, 1999); missed two games. ... Strained left knee prior to 1999-2000 season; missed two games. ... Reinjured left knee (November 28, 1999); missed three games. ... Suffered illness (January 28, 2000); missed three games. ... Traded by Senators with D Janne Laukkanen to Pittsburgh Penguins for G Tom Barrasso (March 14, 2000). ... Signed as free agent by Columbus Blue Jackets (July 4, 2000). ... Strained hip flexor (December 2, 2000); missed two games. ... Sprained thumb (December 29, 2000); missed five games. ... Traded by Blue Jackets with second-round pick (F Janos Vas) in 2002 draft to Dallas Stars for first-round pick (traded to Buffalo) in 2002 draft (June 18, 2002).

Season Team	League	REGULAR SEASON Gms.	Min	W	L	T	GA	SO	Avg.	SV%	PLAYOFFS Gms.	Min.	W	L	GA	SO	Avg.	SV%
84-85—Peterborough	OHL	18	938	7	4	2	59	0	3.77	—	—	—	—	—	—	—	—	—
85-86—Peterborough	OHL	26	1543	18	7	0	74	1	2.88	—	3	133	2	0	6	0	2.71	—
86-87—Peterborough	OHL	31	1891	21	7	2	88	2	*2.79	—	6	374	3	3	21	1	3.37	—
87-88—Quebec	NHL	6	284	2	3	0	16	0	3.38	.870	—	—	—	—	—	—	—	—
—Fredericton	AHL	34	1962	20	9	4	118	1	3.61	—	4	204	1	2	11	0	3.24	—
88-89—Quebec	NHL	26	1367	10	10	3	82	0	3.60	.892	—	—	—	—	—	—	—	—
—Halifax	AHL	24	1368	14	7	2	79	1	3.46	—	—	—	—	—	—	—	—	—
89-90—Quebec	NHL	35	1978	5	24	3	152	0	4.61	.859	—	—	—	—	—	—	—	—
—Halifax	AHL	6	366	1	5	0	23	0	3.77	—	—	—	—	—	—	—	—	—
90-91—Halifax	AHL	2	100	0	1	0	8	0	4.80	—	—	—	—	—	—	—	—	—
—Quebec	NHL	56	3144	12	†29	10	212	0	4.05	.885	—	—	—	—	—	—	—	—
91-92—Quebec	NHL	30	1583	6	17	3	106	1	4.02	.864	—	—	—	—	—	—	—	—
—Halifax	AHL	8	447	3	3	1	30	0	4.03	—	—	—	—	—	—	—	—	—
—Edmonton	NHL	3	124	1	1	0	10	0	4.84	.863	2	60	0	0	3	0	3.00	.912
92-93—Edmonton	NHL	26	1338	9	12	2	93	0	4.17	.879	—	—	—	—	—	—	—	—
93-94—Anaheim	NHL	28	1520	10	15	1	76	1	3.00	.908	—	—	—	—	—	—	—	—
—Montreal	NHL	8	378	2	3	1	24	0	3.81	.860	1	59	0	1	5	0	5.08	.800
94-95—Montreal	NHL	7	346	1	3	1	18	0	3.12	.895	—	—	—	—	—	—	—	—
95-96—Portland	AHL	58	3067	21	23	6	171	2	3.35	—	13	781	7	6	36	1	2.77	—
96-97—Ottawa	NHL	37	1991	17	15	1	93	3	2.80	.895	7	425	3	4	14	1	1.98	.917
97-98—Ottawa	NHL	42	2236	15	14	8	84	3	2.25	.905	2	74	0	1	6	0	4.86	.760
98-99—Ottawa	NHL	43	2508	22	10	8	75	3	*1.79	.925	2	118	0	2	6	0	3.05	.854
99-00—Ottawa	NHL	44	2435	18	12	8	103	4	2.54	.899	—	—	—	—	—	—	—	—
—Pittsburgh	NHL	7	374	4	2	0	15	0	2.41	.924	11	746	6	5	22	2	1.77	.945
00-01—Columbus	NHL	53	3129	22	25	5	127	4	2.44	.917	—	—	—	—	—	—	—	—
01-02—Columbus	NHL	44	2502	12	27	3	119	2	2.85	.900	—	—	—	—	—	—	—	—
02-03—Dallas	NHL	31	1701	15	10	5	70	0	2.47	.896	—	—	—	—	—	—	—	—
NHL Totals (15 years)		526	28938	183	232	62	1475	25	3.06	.895	25	1482	9	13	56	3	2.27	.919

TURCO, MARTY   G   STARS

PERSONAL: Born August 13, 1975, in Sault Ste. Marie, Ont. ... 5-11/183. ... Catches left.

TRANSACTIONS/CAREER NOTES: Selected by Dallas Stars in fifth round (fourth Stars pick, 124th overall) of NHL entry draft (June 29, 1994). ... Suspended one game by NHL for high-sticking incident (January 21, 2003).

Season Team	League	REGULAR SEASON Gms.	Min	W	L	T	GA	SO	Avg.	SV%	PLAYOFFS Gms.	Min.	W	L	GA	SO	Avg.	SV%
93-94—Cambridge Jr. B	OHA	34	1937	...	...	...	114	0	3.53	—	—	—	—	—	—	—	—	—
94-95—Univ. of Michigan	CCHA	37	2064	27	7	1	95	1	2.76	—	—	—	—	—	—	—	—	—
95-96—Univ. of Michigan	CCHA	42	2334	34	7	1	84	5	2.16	—	—	—	—	—	—	—	—	—
96-97—Univ. of Michigan	CCHA	41	2296	33	4	4	87	4	2.27	—	—	—	—	—	—	—	—	—
97-98—Univ. of Michigan	CCHA	*45	*2640	*33	10	1	95	3	2.16	—	—	—	—	—	—	—	—	—
98-99—Michigan	IHL	54	3127	24	17	‡10	136	1	2.61	—	5	300	2	3	14	0	2.80	—
99-00—Michigan	IHL	60	3399	28	*27	‡7	*139	*7	2.45	—	—	—	—	—	—	—	—	—
00-01—Dallas	NHL	26	1266	13	6	1	40	0	*1.90	.925	—	—	—	—	—	—	—	—
01-02—Dallas	NHL	31	1519	15	6	2	53	2	2.09	.921	—	—	—	—	—	—	—	—
02-03—Dallas	NHL	55	3203	31	10	10	92	7	*1.72	*.932	12	798	6	6	25	0	1.88	*.919
NHL Totals (3 years)		112	5988	59	22	13	185	12	1.85	.928	12	798	6	6	25	0	1.88	.919

PERSONAL: Born May 21, 1970, in Strakonice, Czechoslovakia ... 6-4/220. ... Catches right. ... Name pronounced ROH-mahn TOOR-ihk.

TRANSACTIONS/CAREER NOTES: Selected by Minnesota North Stars in sixth round (sixth North Stars pick, 113th overall) of NHL entry draft (June 16, 1990). ... North Stars franchise moved from Minnesota to Dallas and renamed Stars for 1993-94 season. ... Strained groin (January 8, 1997); missed three games. ... Injured knee (March 31, 1997); missed seven games. ... Strained groin (November 15, 1997); missed 12 games. ... Strained groin (December 10, 1998); missed three games. ... Sprained knee (April 14, 1999); missed final three games of season. ... Traded by Stars to St. Louis Blues for second-round pick (D Dan Jancevski) in 1999 draft (June 20, 1999). ... Injured elbow (February 6, 2001); missed one game. ... Traded by Blues with fourth-round pick (F Egor Shastin) in 2001 draft to Calgary Flames for G Fred Brathwaite, C Daniel Tkaczuk, RW Sergei Varlamov and ninth-round pick (C Grant Jacobsen) in 2001 draft (June 23, 2001). ... Suffered injury (December 6, 2001); missed two games.

Season Team	League	Gms.	Min	W	L	T	GA	SO	Avg.	SV%	Gms.	Min.	W	L	GA	SO	Avg.	SV%
								REGULAR SEASON							PLAYOFFS			
90-91—Budejovice	Czech.	26	1244	...	...	...	98	0	4.73	—	—	—	—	—	—	—	—	—
91-92—Budejovice	Czech Dv.II								Did not play.									
92-93—Budejovice	Czech.	43	2555	...	...	...	121	...	2.84	—	—	—	—	—	—	—	—	—
93-94—Budejovice	Czech Rep.	44	2584	...	...	...	111	...	2.58	—	3	180	...	...	12	...	4.00	—
—Czech Rep. Oly. team	Int'l	2	120	2	0	0	4	2	2.00	—	—	—	—	—	—	—	—	—
94-95—Budejovice	Czech Rep.	44	2587	...	...	...	119	...	2.76	—	9	498	...	...	25	...	3.01	—
95-96—Nurnberg	Germany	48	2787	...	...	...	154	...	3.32	—	5	338	...	...	14	...	2.49	—
96-97—Michigan	IHL	29	1555	8	13	‡4	77	0	2.97	—	—	—	—	—	—	—	—	—
—Dallas	NHL	6	263	3	1	0	9	0	2.05	.930	—	—	—	—	—	—	—	—
97-98—Dallas	NHL	23	1324	11	10	1	49	1	2.22	.901	—	—	—	—	—	—	—	—
—Michigan	IHL	2	119	1	1	0	5	0	2.52	—	—	—	—	—	—	—	—	—
98-99—Dallas	NHL	26	1382	16	3	3	48	1	2.08	.915	—	—	—	—	—	—	—	—
99-00—St. Louis	NHL	67	3960	42	15	9	129	*7	1.95	.912	7	415	3	4	19	0	2.75	.882
00-01—St. Louis	NHL	54	3232	24	18	10	123	6	2.28	.901	14	908	9	5	31	0	2.05	.919
01-02—Calgary	NHL	69	4081	30	28	†11	172	5	2.53	.906	—	—	—	—	—	—	—	—
02-03—Calgary	NHL	65	3822	27	29	9	164	4	2.57	.902	—	—	—	—	—	—	—	—
NHL Totals (7 years)		310	18064	153	104	43	694	24	2.31	.907	21	1323	12	9	50	0	2.27	.908

PERSONAL: Born August 28, 1969, in Rouyn, Que. ... 6-1/199. ... Shoots left. ... Brother of Sylvain Turgeon, left winger with four NHL teams (1983-84 through 1994-95). ... Name pronounced TUHR-zhaw.

TRANSACTIONS/CAREER NOTES: Selected by Buffalo Sabres in first round (first Sabres pick, first overall) of NHL entry draft (June 13, 1987). ... Traded by Sabres with RW Benoit Hogue, D Uwe Krupp and C Dave McLlwain to New York Islanders for C Pat LaFontaine, LW Randy Wood, D Randy Hillier and future considerations; Sabres later received fourth-round pick (D Dean Melanson) in 1992 draft to complete deal (October 25, 1991). ... Injured right knee (January 3, 1992); missed three games. ... Separated shoulder (April 28, 1993); missed six playoff games. ... Suffered from tendinitis in right wrist (October 5, 1993); missed one game. ... Suffered from the flu (December 29, 1993); missed one game. ... Fractured cheekbone (January 26, 1994); missed 12 games. ... Traded by Islanders with D Vladimir Malakhov to Montreal Canadiens for LW Kirk Muller, D Mathieu Schneider and C Craig Darby (April 5, 1995). ... Strained shoulder (November 8, 1995); missed two games. ... Bruised thigh (October 24, 1996); missed one game. ... Traded by Canadiens with C Craig Conroy and D Rory Fitzpatrick to St. Louis Blues for LW Shayne Corson, D Murray Baron and fifth-round pick (D Gennady Razin) in 1997 draft (October 29, 1996). ... Fractured right forearm (October 4, 1997); missed 22 games. ... Fractured hand (December 14, 1998); missed 14 games. ... Suffered back spasms (November 20, 1999); missed four games. ... Suffered from the flu (January 11, 2000); missed one game. ... Injured thumb (January 29, 2000); missed 24 games. ... Suffered concussion (January 11, 2001); missed three games. ... Signed as free agent by Dallas Stars (July 1, 2001). ... Sprained ankle (October 29, 2001); missed 12 games. ... Strained shoulder (March 12, 2002); missed four games.

STATISTICAL PLATEAUS: Three-goal games: 1989-90 (1), 1990-91 (1), 1991-92 (2), 1992-93 (4), 1993-94 (2), 1994-95 (1), 1995-96 (1), 1998-99 (1), 1999-00 (1), 2000-01 (1). Total: 15.

Season Team	League	Gms.	G	A	Pts.	PIM	+/-	PP	SH	Gms.	G	A	Pts.	PIM
					REGULAR SEASON							PLAYOFFS		
85-86—Granby	QMJHL	69	47	67	114	31	...	...	...	—	—	—	—	—
86-87—Granby	QMJHL	58	69	85	154	8	...	...	...	7	9	6	15	15
87-88—Buffalo	NHL	76	14	28	42	34	-8	8	0	6	4	3	7	4
88-89—Buffalo	NHL	80	34	54	88	26	-2	19	0	5	3	5	8	2
89-90—Buffalo	NHL	80	40	66	106	29	10	17	1	6	2	4	6	2
90-91—Buffalo	NHL	78	32	47	79	26	14	13	2	6	3	1	4	6
91-92—Buffalo	NHL	8	2	6	8	4	-1	0	0	—	—	—	—	—
—New York Islanders	NHL	69	38	49	87	16	8	13	0	—	—	—	—	—
92-93—New York Islanders	NHL	83	58	74	132	26	-1	24	0	11	6	7	13	0
93-94—New York Islanders	NHL	69	38	56	94	18	14	10	4	4	0	1	1	0
94-95—New York Islanders	NHL	34	13	14	27	10	-12	3	2	—	—	—	—	—
—Montreal	NHL	15	11	9	20	4	12	2	0	—	—	—	—	—
95-96—Montreal	NHL	80	38	58	96	44	19	17	1	6	2	4	6	2
96-97—Montreal	NHL	9	1	10	11	2	4	0	0	—	—	—	—	—
—St. Louis	NHL	69	25	49	74	12	4	5	0	5	1	1	2	2
97-98—St. Louis	NHL	60	22	46	68	24	13	6	0	10	4	4	8	2
98-99—St. Louis	NHL	67	31	34	65	36	4	10	0	13	4	9	13	6
99-00—St. Louis	NHL	52	26	40	66	8	30	8	0	7	0	7	7	0
00-01—St. Louis	NHL	79	30	52	82	37	14	11	0	15	5	10	15	2
01-02—Dallas	NHL	66	15	32	47	16	-4	7	0	—	—	—	—	—
02-03—Dallas	NHL	65	12	30	42	18	4	3	0	5	0	1	1	0
NHL Totals (16 years)		1139	480	754	1234	390	122	176	10	99	34	57	91	28

PERSONAL: Born October 9, 1975, in Buffalo. ... 6-2/202. ... Shoots right. ... Name pronounced TUZZ-oh-LEEN-oh.

TRANSACTIONS/CAREER NOTES: Selected by Quebec Nordiques in fifth round (seventh Nordiques pick, 113th overall) of NHL entry draft (June 29, 1994). ... Nordiques franchise moved to Colorado and renamed Avalanche for 1995-96 season (June 21, 1995). ... Signed as free agent by New York Islanders (April 23, 1997). ... Traded by Islanders with C Travis Green and D Doug Houda to Mighty Ducks of Anaheim for D J.J. Daigneault, C Mark Janssens and RW Joe Sacco (February 6, 1998). ... Signed as free agent by New York Rangers (October 5, 2000). ... Signed as free agent by Boston Bruins (July 23, 2001). ... Signed as free agent by Minnesota Wild (July 9, 2002).

Season Team	League	Gms.	G	A	Pts.	PIM	+/-	PP	SH	Gms.	G	A	Pts.	PIM
91-92—Niagara	NAJHL	45	19	27	46	82	...	...	...	—	—	—	—	—
92-93—Niagara	NAJHL	50	36	41	77	134	...	...	...	—	—	—	—	—
93-94—Michigan State	CCHA	38	4	3	7	50	...	...	...	—	—	—	—	—
94-95—Michigan State	CCHA	39	9	19	28	81	...	...	...	—	—	—	—	—
95-96—Michigan State	CCHA	41	12	17	29	120	...	...	...	—	—	—	—	—
96-97—Michigan State	CCHA	39	14	18	32	45	...	...	...	—	—	—	—	—
97-98—Kentucky	AHL	35	9	14	23	83	...	...	...	—	—	—	—	—
—Cincinnati	AHL	13	3	3	6	6	...	...	...	—	—	—	—	—
—Anaheim	NHL	1	0	0	0	2	-2	0	0	—	—	—	—	—
98-99—Cincinnati	AHL	50	4	10	14	55	...	...	...	—	—	—	—	—
—Cleveland	IHL	15	2	4	6	22	...	...	...	—	—	—	—	—
99-00—Cincinnati	AHL	15	0	3	3	8	...	...	...	—	—	—	—	—
—Huntington	ECHL	20	6	13	19	43	...	...	...	—	—	—	—	—
—Hartford	AHL	32	3	8	11	41	...	...	...	19	2	2	4	16
00-01—Hartford	AHL	47	12	23	35	136	...	...	...	5	0	2	2	6
—New York Rangers	NHL	6	0	0	0	5	-1	0	0	—	—	—	—	—
01-02—Providence	AHL	59	10	19	29	123	...	...	...	—	—	—	—	—
—Boston	NHL	2	0	0	0	0	-1	0	0	—	—	—	—	—
02-03—Houston	AHL	50	9	6	15	92	...	...	...	—	—	—	—	—
—Louisiana	ECHL	12	8	7	15	47	...	...	...	—	—	—	—	—
NHL Totals (3 years)		9	0	0	0	7	-4	0	0					

PERSONAL: Born May 18, 1976, in Donetsk, U.S.S.R. ... 6-1/205. ... Shoots left. ... Name pronounced OH-lehg teh-vuhr-DAHV-skee.

TRANSACTIONS/CAREER NOTES: Selected by Mighty Ducks of Anaheim in first round (first Mighty Ducks pick, second overall) of NHL entry draft (June 28, 1994). ... Suffered from pink eye (March 15, 1995); missed two games. ... Traded by Mighty Ducks with C Chad Kilger and third-round pick (D Per-Anton Lundstrom) in 1996 draft to Winnipeg Jets for C Marc Chouinard, RW Teemu Selanne and fourth-round pick (traded to Toronto) in 1996 draft (February 7, 1996). ... Jets franchise moved to Phoenix and renamed Coyotes for 1996-97 season; NHL approved move on January 18, 1996. ... Pulled rib muscle (December 23, 1997); missed one game. ... Traded by Coyotes to Mighty Ducks for C Travis Green and first-round pick (C Scott Kelman) in 1999 draft (June 26, 1999). ... Strained groin (March 24, 2002); missed remainder of season. ... Traded by Mighty Ducks with LW Jeff Friesen and RW Maxim Balmochnykh to New Jersey Devils for RW Petr Sykora, C Igor Pohanka, D Mike Commodore and G J.F. Damphousse (July 7, 2002).

Season Team	League	Gms.	G	A	Pts.	PIM	+/-	PP	SH	Gms.	G	A	Pts.	PIM
92-93—Soviet Wings	CIS	21	0	1	1	6	...	...	...	6	0	0	0	...
93-94—Soviet Wings	CIS	46	4	10	14	22	...	...	...	3	1	0	1	2
94-95—Brandon	WHL	7	1	4	5	4	...	...	...	—	—	—	—	—
—Anaheim	NHL	36	3	9	12	14	-6	1	1	—	—	—	—	—
95-96—Anaheim	NHL	51	7	15	22	35	0	2	0	—	—	—	—	—
—Winnipeg	NHL	31	0	8	8	6	-7	0	0	6	0	1	1	0
96-97—Phoenix	NHL	82	10	45	55	30	-5	3	1	7	0	1	1	0
97-98—Hamilton	AHL	9	8	6	14	2	...	...	...	—	—	—	—	—
—Phoenix	NHL	46	7	12	19	12	1	4	0	6	0	7	7	6
98-99—Phoenix	NHL	82	7	18	25	32	11	2	0	6	0	2	2	6
99-00—Anaheim	NHL	82	15	36	51	30	5	5	0	—	—	—	—	—
00-01—Anaheim	NHL	82	14	39	53	32	-11	8	0	—	—	—	—	—
01-02—Anaheim	NHL	73	6	26	32	31	0	2	0	—	—	—	—	—
—Russian Oly. team	Int'l	6	1	1	2	0	...	...	...	—	—	—	—	—
02-03—New Jersey	NHL	50	5	8	13	22	2	2	0	15	0	3	3	0
NHL Totals (9 years)		615	74	216	290	244	-10	29	2	40	0	14	14	6

T

PERSONAL: Born January 21, 1981, in Trencin, Czecholslovakia. ... 6-1/189. ... Shoots left.

TRANSACTIONS/CAREER NOTES: Selected by Washington Capitals in fifth round (sixth Capitals pick, 132nd overall) of NHL entry draft (June 26, 1999).

Season Team	League	Gms.	G	A	Pts.	PIM	+/-	PP	SH	Gms.	G	A	Pts.	PIM
97-98—Dukla Trencin	Slovakia Jrs.	48	4	12	16		...	...	...	—	—	—	—	—
98-99—Dukla Trencin	Slovakia Jrs.	49	23	23	46	20	...	...	...	6	4	4	8	4
99-00—Spokane	WHL	69	26	44	70	40	...	...	...	14	4	7	11	16
00-01—Spokane	WHL	62	28	34	62	55	...	...	...	12	5	11	16	0
01-02—Portland	AHL	49	5	9	14	22	...	...	...	—	—	—	—	—
02-03—Portland	AHL	35	5	4	9	17	...	...	...	—	—	—	—	—

UCHEVATOV, VICTOR　　　　D　　　　DEVILS

PERSONAL: Born February 10, 1983, in Angarsk, U.S.S.R. ... 6-4/205. ... Shoots left.
TRANSACTIONS/CAREER NOTES: Selected by New Jersey Devils in second round (fourth Devils pick, 60th overall) of NHL entry draft (June 23, 2001).

Season Team	League	Gms.	G	A	Pts.	PIM	+/-	PP	SH	Gms.	G	A	Pts.	PIM
						REGULAR SEASON						PLAYOFFS		
00-01—Torpedo Yaroslavl.......	Russian						Statistics unavailable.							
01-02—Albany........................	AHL	64	0	2	2	50	...	...	...	—	—	—	—	—
02-03—Albany........................	AHL	55	0	2	2	27	...	...	...	—	—	—	—	—

ULANOV, IGOR　　　　D　　　　PANTHERS

PERSONAL: Born October 1, 1969, in Krasnokamsk, U.S.S.R. ... 6-3/215. ... Shoots right. ... Name pronounced EE-gohr yoo-LAH-nahf.
TRANSACTIONS/CAREER NOTES: Selected by Winnipeg Jets in 10th round (eighth Jets pick, 203rd overall) of NHL entry draft (June 22, 1991). ... Suffered back spasms (March 7, 1992); missed five games. ... Fractured foot (March 16, 1995); missed 19 games. ... Traded by Jets with C Mike Eagles to Washington Capitals for third-round (traded to Dallas Stars) and fifth-round (G Brian Elder) picks in 1995 draft (April 7, 1995). ... Traded by Capitals to Chicago Blackhawks for third-round draft pick (G Dave Weninger) in 1996 draft (October 17, 1995). ... Traded by Blackhawks with LW Patrick Poulin and second-round pick (D Jeff Paul) in 1996 draft to Tampa Bay Lightning for D Enrico Ciccone (March 20, 1996). ... Injured ribs (October 5, 1996); missed three games. ... Strained groin (February 14, 1997); missed six games. ... Traded by Lightning with C Patrick Poulin and RW Mick Vukota to Montreal Canadiens for RW Stephane Richer, C Darcy Tucker and D David Wilkie (January 15, 1998). ... Tore ligaments in left knee (January 21, 1998); missed remainder of season. ... Fractured left foot (November 3, 1999); missed 13 games. ... Traded by Canadiens with D Alain Nasreddine to Edmonton Oilers for D Christian LaFlamme and D Mathieu Descoteaux (March 9, 2000). ... Bruised ankle (November 19, 2000); missed one game. ... Bruised right hand (December 2, 2000); missed two games. ... Suspended two games by NHL for cross-checking incident (December 14, 2000). ... Injured left eye (February 24, 2001); missed three games. ... Reinjured left eye (March 2, 2001); missed six games. ... Signed as free agent by New York Rangers (July 1, 2001). ... Suspended seven games by NHL for cross-checking incident (October 12, 2001). ... Traded by Rangers with D Filip Novak, first-(traded to Calgary) and second-round (C/RW Rob Globke) picks in 2002 draft and fourth-round pick in 2003 draft to Florida Panthers for RW Pavel Bure and second-round pick (C Lee Falardeau) in 2002 draft (March 18, 2002).

Season Team	League	Gms.	G	A	Pts.	PIM	+/-	PP	SH	Gms.	G	A	Pts.	PIM
						REGULAR SEASON						PLAYOFFS		
90-91—Khimik	USSR	41	2	2	4	52	...	...	...	—	—	—	—	—
91-92—Khimik	CIS	27	1	4	5	24	...	...	...	—	—	—	—	—
—Winnipeg	NHL	27	2	9	11	67	5	0	0	7	0	0	0	39
—Moncton	AHL	3	0	1	1	16	...	...	...	—	—	—	—	—
92-93—Moncton	AHL	9	1	3	4	26	...	...	...	—	—	—	—	—
—Fort Wayne	IHL	3	0	1	1	29	...	...	...	—	—	—	—	—
—Winnipeg	NHL	56	2	14	16	124	6	0	0	4	0	0	0	4
93-94—Winnipeg	NHL	74	0	17	17	165	-11	0	0	—	—	—	—	—
94-95—Winnipeg	NHL	19	1	3	4	27	-2	0	0	—	—	—	—	—
—Washington	NHL	3	0	1	1	2	3	0	0	2	0	0	0	4
95-96—Indianapolis	IHL	1	0	0	0	0	...	...	...	—	—	—	—	—
—Chicago	NHL	53	1	8	9	92	12	0	0	—	—	—	—	—
—Tampa Bay	NHL	11	2	1	3	24	-1	0	0	5	0	0	0	15
96-97—Tampa Bay	NHL	59	1	7	8	108	2	0	0	—	—	—	—	—
97-98—Tampa Bay	NHL	45	2	7	9	85	-5	1	0	—	—	—	—	—
—Montreal	NHL	4	0	1	1	12	-2	0	0	10	1	4	5	12
98-99—Montreal	NHL	76	3	9	12	109	-3	0	0	—	—	—	—	—
99-00—Montreal	NHL	43	1	5	6	76	-11	0	0	—	—	—	—	—
—Edmonton	NHL	14	0	3	3	10	-3	0	0	5	0	0	0	6
00-01—Edmonton	NHL	67	3	20	23	90	15	1	0	6	0	0	0	4
01-02—New York Rangers	NHL	39	0	6	6	53	-4	0	0	—	—	—	—	—
—Hartford	AHL	6	1	1	2	2	...	...	...	—	—	—	—	—
—Florida.......................	NHL	14	0	4	4	11	-3	0	0	—	—	—	—	—
02-03—San Antonio	AHL	5	1	0	1	4	...	...	...	—	—	—	—	—
—Florida.......................	NHL	56	1	1	2	39	7	0	0	—	—	—	—	—
NHL Totals (12 years).........		660	19	116	135	1094	5	2	0	39	1	4	5	84

ULMER, JEFF　　　　LW

PERSONAL: Born April 27, 1977, in Wilcox, Sask. ... 5-11/190. ... Shoots right.
TRANSACTIONS/CAREER NOTES: Signed as non-drafted free agent by New York Rangers (July 27, 2000). ... Traded by Rangers with D Jason Doig to Ottawa Senators for D Sean Gagnon (June 29, 2001).

Season Team	League	Gms.	G	A	Pts.	PIM	+/-	PP	SH	Gms.	G	A	Pts.	PIM
						REGULAR SEASON						PLAYOFFS		
95-96—Univ. of North Dakota .	WCHA	29	5	3	8	26	...	...	...	—	—	—	—	—
96-97—Univ. of North Dakota .	WCHA	26	6	11	17	16	...	...	...	—	—	—	—	—
97-98—Univ. of North Dakota .	WCHA	32	12	12	24	44	...	...	...	—	—	—	—	—
98-99—Univ. of North Dakota .	WCHA	38	16	20	36	46	...	...	...	—	—	—	—	—
99-00—Canadian nat'l team	Int'l	48	14	25	39	20	...	...	...	—	—	—	—	—
—Houston....................	IHL	5	1	0	1	0	...	...	...	11	2	4	6	6
00-01—Hartford	AHL	48	11	14	25	34	...	...	...	—	—	—	—	—
—New York Rangers	NHL	21	3	0	3	8	-6	0	0	—	—	—	—	—
01-02—Grand Rapids.............	AHL	73	9	17	26	65	...	...	...	5	0	1	1	11
02-03—Binghamton	AHL	57	8	12	20	40	...	...	...	—	—	—	—	—
NHL Totals (1 year).............		21	3	0	3	8	-6	0	0					

UMBERGER, R.J.   C   CANUCKS

PERSONAL: Born May 3, 1982, in Pittsburgh. ... 6-2/200. ... Shoots left.
TRANSACTIONS/CAREER NOTES: Selected by Vancouver Canucks in first round (first Canucks pick, 16th overall) of NHL entry draft (June 23, 2001).

Season Team	League	Gms.	G	A	Pts.	PIM	+/-	PP	SH	Gms.	G	A	Pts.	PIM
					REGULAR SEASON							PLAYOFFS		
99-00—U.S. National	USHL	57	33	35	68	20	...	...	...	—	—	—	—	—
00-01—Ohio State	CCHA	32	14	23	37	18	...	...	...	—	—	—	—	—
01-02—Ohio State	CCHA	37	18	21	39	31	...	...	...	—	—	—	—	—
02-03—Ohio State	CCHA	43	26	27	53	16	...	...	...	—	—	—	—	—

UPSHALL, SCOTTIE   RW   PREDATORS

PERSONAL: Born October 7, 1983, in Fort McMurray, Alta. ... 6-0/184. ... Shoots left.
TRANSACTIONS/CAREER NOTES: Selected by Nashville Predators in first round (first Predators pick, sixth overall) of NHL entry draft (June 22, 2002).

Season Team	League	Gms.	G	A	Pts.	PIM	+/-	PP	SH	Gms.	G	A	Pts.	PIM
					REGULAR SEASON							PLAYOFFS		
00-01—Kamloops	WHL	70	42	45	87	111	...	...	...	4	0	2	2	10
01-02—Kamloops	WHL	61	32	51	83	139	...	...	...	4	1	2	3	21
02-03—Kamloops	WHL	42	25	31	56	113	...	...	...	—	—	—	—	—
—Milwaukee	AHL	2	1	0	1	2	...	...	...	—	—	—	—	—
—Nashville	NHL	8	1	0	1	0	2	0	0	—	—	—	—	—
NHL Totals (1 year)		8	1	0	1	0	2	0	0					

USTRNUL, LIBOR   D   THRASHERS

PERSONAL: Born February 20, 1982, in Olomouc, Czechoslovakia. ... 6-5/228. ... Shoots left.
TRANSACTIONS/CAREER NOTES: Selected by Atlanta Thrashers in second round (third Thrashers pick, 42nd overall) of NHL entry draft (June 24, 2000).

Season Team	League	Gms.	G	A	Pts.	PIM	+/-	PP	SH	Gms.	G	A	Pts.	PIM
					REGULAR SEASON							PLAYOFFS		
98-99—Thunder Bay Flyers	USHL	52	2	5	7	65	...	...	...	—	—	—	—	—
99-00—Plymouth	OHL	68	0	15	15	208	...	...	...	23	0	3	3	29
00-01—Plymouth	OHL	35	3	13	16	66	...	...	...	19	1	4	5	19
01-02—Plymouth	OHL	43	1	8	9	84	...	...	...	2	0	0	0	6
—Chicago	AHL	1	0	0	0	0	...	...	...	1	0	0	0	5
02-03—Chicago	AHL	40	1	1	2	94	...	...	...	—	—	—	—	—

VAANANEN, OSSI   D   COYOTES

PERSONAL: Born August 18, 1980, in Vantaa, Finland ... 6-4/212. ... Shoots left.
TRANSACTIONS/CAREER NOTES: Selected by Phoenix Coyotes in second round (second Coyotes pick, 43rd overall) of NHL entry draft (June 27, 1998). ... Bruised shoulder (March 17, 2002); missed six games.

Season Team	League	Gms.	G	A	Pts.	PIM	+/-	PP	SH	Gms.	G	A	Pts.	PIM
					REGULAR SEASON							PLAYOFFS		
95-96—Jokerit Helsinki	Finland Jr. B	2	0	0	0	0	...	...	...	—	—	—	—	—
96-97—Jokerit Helsinki	Finland Jr. B	17	1	2	3	43	...	...	...	—	—	—	—	—
97-98—Jokerit Helsinki	Finland Jr.	31	0	6	6	24	...	...	...	—	—	—	—	—
98-99—Jokerit Helsinki	Finland	48	0	1	1	42	...	...	...	3	0	1	1	2
99-00—Jokerit Helsinki	Finland	49	1	6	7	46	...	...	...	11	1	1	2	2
00-01—Phoenix	NHL	81	4	12	16	90	9	0	0	—	—	—	—	—
01-02—Phoenix	NHL	76	2	12	14	74	6	0	1	5	0	0	0	6
—Fin. Olympic team	Int'l	2	0	1	1	0	...	...	...	—	—	—	—	—
02-03—Phoenix	NHL	67	2	7	9	82	1	0	0	—	—	—	—	—
NHL Totals (3 years)		224	8	31	39	246	16	0	1	5	0	0	0	6

VAGNER, MARTIN   D   STARS

PERSONAL: Born March 16, 1984, in Jaromer, Czechoslovakia. ... 6-1/214. ... Shoots left.
TRANSACTIONS/CAREER NOTES: Selected by Dallas Stars in first round (first Stars pick, 26th overall) of NHL entry draft (June 22, 2002).

Season Team	League	Gms.	G	A	Pts.	PIM	+/-	PP	SH	Gms.	G	A	Pts.	PIM
					REGULAR SEASON							PLAYOFFS		
01-02—Hull	QMJHL	64	6	28	34	81	...	...	...	8	0	1	1	10
02-03—Hull	QMJHL	53	1	12	13	98	...	...	...					

VALEEV, IGOR   RW   BLUES

PERSONAL: Born January 9, 1981, in Chelyabinsk, U.S.S.R. ... 5-11/203. ... Shoots left.
TRANSACTIONS/CAREER NOTES: Selected by St. Louis Blues in fourth round (third Blues pick, 122nd overall) of NHL entry draft (June 23, 2001).

U
V

Season Team	League	REGULAR SEASON Gms.	G	A	Pts.	PIM	+/-	PP	SH	PLAYOFFS Gms.	G	A	Pts.	PIM
98-99—Lethbridge	WHL	8	2	3	5	13	...	...	...	—	—	—	—	—
—Saskatoon	WHL	23	2	2	4	36	...	...	...	—	—	—	—	—
99-00—Swift Current	WHL	36	7	5	12	78	...	...	...	6	0	0	0	19
00-01—North Bay	OHL	62	17	61	78	175	...	...	...	4	0	1	1	22
01-02—Worcester	AHL	29	3	6	9	72	...	...	...	—	—	—	—	—
02-03—Worcester	AHL	72	6	12	18	153	...	...	...	—	—	—	—	—

VALICEVIC, ROB   RW

PERSONAL: Born January 6, 1971, in Detroit ... 6-2/208. ... Shoots right. ... Full Name: Robert Valicevic.
TRANSACTIONS/CAREER NOTES: Selected by New York Islanders in sixth round (sixth Islanders pick, 114th overall) of NHL entry draft (June 22, 1991). ... Signed as free agent by Nashville Predators (June 8, 1998). ... Suffered concussion (January 31, 2000); missed two games. ... Injured right knee (November 6, 2000); missed three games. ... Underwent knee surgery (November 16, 2000); missed eight games. ... Injured knee (December 4, 2000); missed two games. ... Suffered concussion (March 10, 2001); missed three games. ... Signed as free agent by Los Angeles Kings (August 16, 2001). ... Signed as free agent by Anaheim Mighty Ducks (July 24, 2002).
STATISTICAL PLATEAUS: Three-goal games: 1999-00 (1).

Season Team	League	REGULAR SEASON Gms.	G	A	Pts.	PIM	+/-	PP	SH	PLAYOFFS Gms.	G	A	Pts.	PIM
90-91—Detroit	USHL	39	31	44	75	54	...	...	...	—	—	—	—	—
91-92—Lake Superior State	CCHA	32	8	4	12	12	...	...	...	—	—	—	—	—
92-93—Lake Superior State	CCHA	43	21	20	41	28	...	...	...	—	—	—	—	—
93-94—Lake Superior State	CCHA	45	18	20	38	46	...	...	...	—	—	—	—	—
94-95—Lake Superior State	CCHA	37	10	22	32	40	...	...	...	—	—	—	—	—
95-96—Louisiana	ECHL	60	42	20	62	85	...	...	...	5	2	3	5	8
—Springfield	AHL	2	0	0	0	2	...	...	...	—	—	—	—	—
96-97—Houston	IHL	58	11	12	23	42	...	...	...	12	1	3	4	11
—Louisiana	ECHL	8	7	2	9	21	...	...	...	—	—	—	—	—
97-98—Houston	IHL	72	29	28	57	47	...	...	...	4	2	0	2	2
98-99—Houston	IHL	57	16	33	49	62	...	...	...	19	7	10	17	8
—Nashville	NHL	19	4	2	6	2	4	0	0	—	—	—	—	—
99-00—Nashville	NHL	80	14	11	25	21	-11	2	1	—	—	—	—	—
00-01—Nashville	NHL	60	8	6	14	26	-2	1	0	—	—	—	—	—
01-02—Manchester	AHL	59	11	23	34	25	...	...	...	5	1	0	1	4
—Los Angeles	NHL	17	1	1	2	8	-4	0	0	—	—	—	—	—
02-03—Cincinnati	AHL	69	17	26	43	38	...	...	...	—	—	—	—	—
—Anaheim	NHL	10	1	0	1	2	1	0	0	—	—	—	—	—
NHL Totals (5 years)		186	28	20	48	59	-12	3	1					

VALK, GARRY   RW   BLACKHAWKS

PERSONAL: Born November 27, 1967, in Edmonton ... 6-1/200. ... Shoots left. ... Full Name: Garry P. Valk. ... Name pronounced VAHLK.
TRANSACTIONS/CAREER NOTES: Selected by Vancouver Canucks in sixth round (fifth Canucks pick, 108th overall) of NHL entry draft (June 13, 1987). ... Sprained thumb (November 24, 1991); missed one game. ... Sprained shoulder (January 21, 1992); missed eight games. ... Sprained knee (February 26, 1993); missed 12 games. ... Selected by Mighty Ducks of Anaheim in NHL waiver draft (October 3, 1993). ... Suffered concussion (December 5, 1993); missed one game. ... Suffered post-concussion syndrome (December 5, 1993); missed four games. ... Sprained left knee (January 16, 1995); missed 10 games. ... Injured right eye (December 7, 1995); missed one game. ... Injured ear (December 22, 1995); missed one game. ... Traded by Mighty Ducks to Pittsburgh Penguins for D J.J. Daigneault (February 21, 1997). ... Bruised ribs (March 16, 1997); missed five games. ... Injured knee (April 11, 1997); missed one game. ... Suffered charley horse (October 1, 1997); missed two games. ... Injured groin (October 24, 1997); missed three games. ... Strained abdomen (March 5, 1998); missed 13 games. ... Signed as free agent by Toronto Maple Leafs (October 6, 1998). ... Strained neck (November 25, 1998); missed two games. ... Strained muscle in abdomen (January 20, 1999); missed two games. ... Strained back (February 6, 1999); missed one game. ... Suffered injury (November 9, 1999); missed two games. ... Suffered injury (March 18, 2000); missed one game. ... Suffered injury (March 25, 2000); missed five games. ... Suffered injury (December 4, 2000); missed two games. ... Suffered injury (March 24, 2001); missed final six games of regular season. ... Suffered injury (November 24, 2001); missed one game. ... Injured shoulder (January 7, 2002); missed seven games. ... Suffered injury (April 4, 2002); missed two games. ... Signed as free agent by Chicago Blackhawks (October 9, 2002).
STATISTICAL PLATEAUS: Three-goal games: 1995-96 (1).

Season Team	League	REGULAR SEASON Gms.	G	A	Pts.	PIM	+/-	PP	SH	PLAYOFFS Gms.	G	A	Pts.	PIM
85-86—Sherwood Park	AJHL	40	20	26	46	116	...	...	...	—	—	—	—	—
86-87—Sherwood Park	AJHL	59	42	44	86	204	...	...	...	—	—	—	—	—
87-88—Univ. of North Dakota	WCHA	38	23	12	35	64	...	...	...	—	—	—	—	—
88-89—Univ. of North Dakota	WCHA	40	14	17	31	71	...	...	...	—	—	—	—	—
89-90—Univ. of North Dakota	WCHA	43	22	17	39	92	...	...	...	—	—	—	—	—
90-91—Vancouver	NHL	59	10	11	21	67	-23	1	0	5	0	0	0	20
—Milwaukee	IHL	10	12	4	16	13	...	...	...	3	0	0	0	2
91-92—Vancouver	NHL	65	8	17	25	56	3	2	1	4	0	0	0	5
92-93—Vancouver	NHL	48	6	7	13	77	6	0	0	7	0	1	1	12
—Hamilton	AHL	7	3	6	9	6	...	...	...	—	—	—	—	—
93-94—Anaheim	NHL	78	18	27	45	100	8	4	1	—	—	—	—	—
94-95—Anaheim	NHL	36	3	6	9	34	-4	0	0	—	—	—	—	—
95-96—Anaheim	NHL	79	12	12	24	125	8	1	1	—	—	—	—	—
96-97—Anaheim	NHL	53	7	7	14	53	-2	0	0	—	—	—	—	—
—Pittsburgh	NHL	17	3	4	7	25	-6	0	0	—	—	—	—	—
97-98—Pittsburgh	NHL	39	2	1	3	33	-3	0	0	—	—	—	—	—
98-99—Toronto	NHL	77	8	21	29	53	8	1	0	17	3	4	7	22
99-00—Toronto	NHL	73	10	14	24	44	-2	0	1	12	1	2	3	14
00-01—Toronto	NHL	74	8	18	26	46	4	1	0	5	0	1	1	2
01-02—Toronto	NHL	63	5	10	15	28	2	0	0	11	1	0	1	4
02-03—Chicago	NHL	16	0	1	1	6	0	0	0	—	—	—	—	—
—Norfolk	AHL	22	6	5	11	16	...	...	...	—	—	—	—	—
NHL Totals (13 years)		777	100	156	256	747	-1	10	4	61	6	7	13	79

V

VAN ALLEN, SHAUN — C — SENATORS

PERSONAL: Born August 29, 1967, in Calgary ... 6-1/206. ... Shoots left. ... Full Name: Shaun Kelly Van Allen.

TRANSACTIONS/CAREER NOTES: Selected by Edmonton Oilers in fifth round (fifth Oilers pick, 105th overall) of NHL entry draft (June 13, 1987). ... Suffered concussion (January 9, 1993); missed 11 games. ... Signed as free agent by Mighty Ducks of Anaheim (July 22, 1993). ... Suffered back spasms (February 7, 1995); missed two games. ... Suffered from the flu (May 1, 1995); missed one game. ... Dislocated right thumb (November 15, 1995); missed 21 games. ... Suffered back spasms (February 7, 1996); missed four games. ... Traded by Mighty Ducks with D Jason York to Ottawa Senators for C Ted Drury and rights to D Marc Moro (October 1, 1996). ... Suffered back spasms (February 2, 1998); missed one game. ... Strained left knee (December 30, 1999); missed one game. ... Strained muscle in abdomen (January 12, 2000); missed five games. ... Signed as free agent by Dallas Stars (July 12, 2000). ... Suffered back spasms (October 10, 2000); missed five games. ... Injured shoulder (October 28, 2001); missed one game. ... Traded by Stars with RW Donald Audette to Montreal Canadiens for LW Martin Rucinsky and LW Benoit Brunet (November 21, 2001). ... Sprained wrist (November 19, 2001); missed four games. ... Signed as free agent by Senators (July 24, 2002).

Season Team	League		REGULAR SEASON								PLAYOFFS			
		Gms.	G	A	Pts.	PIM	+/-	PP	SH	Gms.	G	A	Pts.	PIM
84-85—Swift Current	SAJHL	61	12	20	32	136	...	...	...	—	—	—	—	—
85-86—Saskatoon	WHL	55	12	11	23	43	...	...	...	13	4	8	12	28
86-87—Saskatoon	WHL	72	38	59	97	116	...	...	...	11	4	6	10	24
87-88—Nova Scotia	AHL	19	4	10	14	17	...	...	...	4	1	1	2	4
—Milwaukee	IHL	40	14	28	42	34	...	...	...	—	—	—	—	—
88-89—Cape Breton	AHL	76	32	42	74	81	...	...	...	—	—	—	—	—
89-90—Cape Breton	AHL	61	25	44	69	83	...	...	...	4	0	2	2	8
90-91—Edmonton	NHL	2	0	0	0	0	0	0	0	—	—	—	—	—
—Cape Breton	AHL	76	25	75	100	182	...	...	...	4	0	1	1	8
91-92—Cape Breton	AHL	77	29	*84	*113	80	...	...	...	5	3	7	10	14
92-93—Cape Breton	AHL	43	14	62	76	68	...	...	...	15	8	9	17	18
—Edmonton	NHL	21	1	4	5	6	-2	0	0	—	—	—	—	—
93-94—Anaheim	NHL	80	8	25	33	64	0	2	2	—	—	—	—	—
94-95—Anaheim	NHL	45	8	21	29	32	-4	1	1	—	—	—	—	—
95-96—Anaheim	NHL	49	8	17	25	41	13	0	0	—	—	—	—	—
96-97—Ottawa	NHL	80	11	14	25	35	-8	1	1	7	0	1	1	4
97-98—Ottawa	NHL	80	4	15	19	48	4	0	0	11	0	1	1	10
98-99—Ottawa	NHL	79	6	11	17	30	3	0	1	4	0	0	0	0
99-00—Ottawa	NHL	75	9	19	28	37	20	0	2	6	0	1	1	9
00-01—Dallas	NHL	59	7	16	23	16	5	0	2	8	0	2	2	8
01-02—Dallas	NHL	19	2	4	6	6	-5	0	0	—	—	—	—	—
—Montreal	NHL	54	6	9	15	20	5	0	1	7	0	1	1	2
02-03—Ottawa	NHL	78	12	20	32	66	17	2	2	18	1	1	2	12
NHL Totals (12 years)		721	82	175	257	401	48	6	12	61	1	7	8	45

VAN BUSKIRK, RYAN — D — CAPITALS

PERSONAL: Born January 12, 1980, in Sault Ste. Marie, Mich. ... 6-2/207. ... Shoots left.

TRANSACTIONS/CAREER NOTES: Selected by Phoenix Coyotes in fourth round (fourth Coyotes pick, 100th overall) of NHL entry draft (June 27, 1998). ... Returned by Coyotes to draft pool and selected by Washington Capitals in fourth round (fourth Capitals pick, 121st pick overall) of NHL entry draft (June 24, 2000).

Season Team	League		REGULAR SEASON								PLAYOFFS			
		Gms.	G	A	Pts.	PIM	+/-	PP	SH	Gms.	G	A	Pts.	PIM
96-97—Petrolia	Jr. B	43	7	28	35	133	...	...	...	—	—	—	—	—
97-98—Sarnia	OHL	61	8	17	25	84	...	...	...	5	1	2	3	4
98-99—Sarnia	OHL	66	15	33	48	85	...	...	...	6	1	2	3	4
99-00—Sarnia	OHL	45	8	20	28	62	...	...	...	7	1	2	3	16
—Springfield	AHL	1	0	0	0	0	...	...	...	—	—	—	—	—
00-01—Portland	AHL	18	0	0	0	16	...	...	...	—	—	—	—	—
—Richmond	ECHL	15	0	2	2	16	...	...	...	3	0	0	0	0
01-02—Portland	AHL	42	2	3	5	62	...	...	...	—	—	—	—	—
02-03—Portland	AHL	1	0	0	0	0	...	...	...	—	—	—	—	—
—Richmond	ECHL	60	4	9	13	125	...	...	...	—	—	—	—	—

VAN DRUNEN, DAVID — D — SENATORS

PERSONAL: Born January 31, 1976, in Sherwood Park, Alta. ... 5-11/206. ... Shoots right. ... Name pronounced van DROO-nehn.

TRANSACTIONS/CAREER NOTES: Signed as non-drafted free agent by Ottawa Senators (May 2, 1997).

Season Team	League		REGULAR SEASON								PLAYOFFS			
		Gms.	G	A	Pts.	PIM	+/-	PP	SH	Gms.	G	A	Pts.	PIM
92-93—Sherwood Park	AJHL	32	3	16	19	114	...	...	...	—	—	—	—	—
93-94—Prince Albert	WHL	63	3	10	13	95	...	...	...	—	—	—	—	—
94-95—Prince Albert	WHL	71	2	14	16	132	...	...	...	15	3	4	7	36
95-96—Prince Albert	WHL	70	10	23	33	172	...	...	...	18	1	5	6	37
96-97—Prince Albert	WHL	72	18	47	65	216	...	...	...	0	0	4	4	24
97-98—Baton Rouge	ECHL	59	8	22	30	107	...	...	...	—	—	—	—	—
—Detroit	IHL	1	0	0	0	2	...	...	...	—	—	—	—	—
—Hershey	AHL	5	0	0	0	2	...	...	...	—	—	—	—	—
—Portland	AHL	4	0	0	0	2	...	...	...	—	—	—	—	—
98-99—UHL	UHL	63	5	17	22	126	...	...	...	—	—	—	—	—
—Cincinnati	IHL	1	0	0	0	0	...	...	...	—	—	—	—	—
—Dayton	ECHL	9	2	4	6	12	...	...	...	4	0	0	0	12

V

Season Team	League	Gms.	G	A	Pts.	PIM	+/-	PP	SH	Gms.	G	A	Pts.	PIM
99-00—Mobile	ECHL	29	1	9	10	78	...	...	...	5	1	1	2	14
—Grand Rapids	IHL	36	0	6	6	76	...	...	...	1	0	0	0	2
—Ottawa	NHL	1	0	0	0	0	0	0	0	—	—	—	—	—
00-01—Grand Rapids	IHL	36	2	5	7	24	...	...	...	10	0	1	1	22
—Mobile	ECHL	33	2	18	20	52	...	...	...	—	—	—	—	—
01-02—Grand Rapids	AHL	48	2	2	4	56	...	...	...	5	0	0	0	14
—Mobile	ECHL	3	1	3	4	10	...	...	...	—	—	—	—	—
02-03—Grand Rapids	AHL	80	3	10	13	106	...	...	...	—	—	—	—	—
NHL Totals (1 year)		1	0	0	0	0	0	0	0					

VAN HOOF, JEREMY — D — LIGHTNING

PERSONAL: Born August 12, 1981, in Lindsay, Ont. ... 6-3/200. ... Shoots left.
TRANSACTIONS/CAREER NOTES: Selected by Pittsburgh Penguins in second round (third Penguins pick, 57th overall) of NHL entry draft (June 26, 1999). ... Returned to draft pool by Penguins and selected by Tampa Bay Lightning in third round (ninth Lightning pick, 222nd overall) of NHL entry draft (June 23, 2001).

Season Team	League	Gms.	G	A	Pts.	PIM	+/-	PP	SH	Gms.	G	A	Pts.	PIM
97-98—Lindsay	OPJHL	50	2	8	10	40	...	...	...	—	—	—	—	—
98-99—Ottawa	OHL	54	0	13	13	46	...	...	...	5	1	0	1	2
99-00—Ottawa	OHL	66	4	14	18	71	...	...	...	11	1	0	1	12
00-01—Ottawa	OHL	65	1	14	15	49	...	...	...	20	3	4	7	27
01-02—Pensacola	ECHL	72	2	14	16	86	...	...	...	3	0	0	0	9
02-03—Springfield	AHL	4	0	0	0	6	...	...	...	—	—	—	—	—
—Pensacola	ECHL	66	4	5	9	51	...	...	...	—	—	—	—	—

VAN IMPE, DARREN — D

PERSONAL: Born May 18, 1973, in Saskatoon, Sask. ... 6-1/205. ... Shoots left. ... Name pronounced VAN-IHMP.
TRANSACTIONS/CAREER NOTES: Selected by New York Islanders in seventh round (seventh Islanders pick, 170th overall) of NHL entry draft (June 26, 1993). ... Traded by Islanders to Mighty Ducks of Anaheim for ninth-round pick (LW Mike Broda) in 1995 draft (September 2, 1994). ... Claimed on waivers by Boston Bruins (November 26, 1997). ... Strained shoulder (January 7, 1998); missed one game. ... Hyperextended elbow (November 29, 1998); missed two games. ... Separated shoulder (February 9, 1999); missed 12 games. ... Sprained ankle (March 25, 1999); missed four games. ... Suffered concussion (April 4, 2000); missed final three games of season. ... Strained shoulder (October 29, 2000); missed two games. ... Sprained knee (December 1, 2000); missed five games. ... Injured shoulder (December 23, 2000); missed one games. ... Underwent shoulder surgery (January 10, 2001); missed remainder of season. ... Claimed on waivers by New York Rangers (August 7, 2001). ... Claimed on waivers by Florida Panthers (December 18, 2001). ... Traded by Panthers to Islanders for fifth-round pick in 2003 draft (March 19, 2002). ... Signed as free agent by Columbus Blue Jackets (January 20, 2003).

Season Team	League	Gms.	G	A	Pts.	PIM	+/-	PP	SH	Gms.	G	A	Pts.	PIM
90-91—Prince Albert	WHL	70	15	45	60	57	...	...	...	3	1	1	2	2
91-92—Prince Albert	WHL	69	9	37	46	129	...	...	...	8	1	5	6	10
92-93—Red Deer	WHL	54	23	47	70	118	...	...	...	4	2	5	7	16
93-94—Red Deer	WHL	58	20	64	84	125	...	...	...	4	2	4	6	6
94-95—San Diego	IHL	76	6	17	23	74	...	...	...	5	0	0	0	0
—Anaheim	NHL	1	0	1	1	4	0	0	0	—	—	—	—	—
95-96—Baltimore	AHL	63	11	47	58	79	...	...	...	—	—	—	—	—
—Anaheim	NHL	16	1	2	3	14	8	0	0	—	—	—	—	—
96-97—Anaheim	NHL	74	4	19	23	90	3	2	0	9	0	2	2	16
97-98—Anaheim	NHL	19	1	3	4	4	-10	0	0	—	—	—	—	—
—Boston	NHL	50	2	8	10	36	4	2	0	6	2	1	3	0
98-99—Boston	NHL	60	5	15	20	66	-5	4	0	11	1	2	3	4
99-00—Boston	NHL	79	5	23	28	73	-19	4	0	—	—	—	—	—
00-01—Boston	NHL	31	3	10	13	41	-9	2	0	—	—	—	—	—
01-02—New York Rangers	NHL	17	1	0	1	12	3	1	0	—	—	—	—	—
—Florida	NHL	36	1	6	7	31	3	1	0	—	—	—	—	—
—New York Islanders	NHL	14	1	2	3	16	6	0	0	7	0	4	4	8
02-03—Syracuse	AHL	6	1	4	5	8	...	...	...	—	—	—	—	—
—Columbus	NHL	14	1	1	2	10	-6	0	1	—	—	—	—	—
NHL Totals (9 years)		411	25	90	115	397	-22	16	1	33	3	9	12	28

V

VAN OENE, DARREN — LW — BRUINS

PERSONAL: Born January 18, 1978, in Edmonton. ... 6-3/207. ... Shoots left. ... Name pronounced van OH-ihn.
TRANSACTIONS/CAREER NOTES: Selected by Buffalo Sabres in second round (third Sabres pick, 33rd overall) of NHL entry draft (June 22, 1996). ... Signed as free agent by Boston Bruins (July 29, 2002).

Season Team	League	Gms.	G	A	Pts.	PIM	+/-	PP	SH	Gms.	G	A	Pts.	PIM
94-95—Brandon	WHL	59	5	13	18	108	...	...	...	18	1	1	2	34
95-96—Brandon	WHL	47	10	18	28	126	...	...	...	18	1	6	7	*78
96-97—Brandon	WHL	56	21	27	48	139	...	...	...	6	2	3	5	19
97-98—Brandon	WHL	51	23	24	47	161	...	...	...	17	6	7	13	51
98-99—Rochester	AHL	73	11	20	31	143	...	...	...	12	2	4	6	8
99-00—Rochester	AHL	80	20	18	38	153	...	...	...	21	1	3	4	24
00-01—Rochester	AHL	64	10	12	22	147	...	...	...	4	1	0	1	4
01-02—Rochester	AHL	52	8	6	14	73	...	...	...	2	0	0	0	4
02-03—Providence	AHL	78	11	17	28	109	...	...	...	—	—	—	—	—

VAN RYN, MIKE D PANTHERS

PERSONAL: Born May 14, 1979, in London, Ont. ... 6-1/202. ... Shoots right.
TRANSACTIONS/CAREER NOTES: Selected by New Jersey Devils in first round (first Devils pick, 26th overall) of NHL entry draft (June 27, 1998). ... Signed as free agent by St. Louis Blues (June 30, 2000). ... Traded by Blues to Florida Panthers for RW Valeri Bure and conditional fifth-round pick in 2004 draft (March 11, 2003).

Season Team	League	REGULAR SEASON								PLAYOFFS				
		Gms.	G	A	Pts.	PIM	+/-	PP	SH	Gms.	G	A	Pts.	PIM
95-96—London Jr. B	OHA	44	9	14	23	24	...	...	...	—	—	—	—	—
96-97—London Jr. B	OHA	46	14	31	45	32	...	...	...	—	—	—	—	—
97-98—Univ. of Michigan	CCHA	25	4	14	18	36	...	...	...	—	—	—	—	—
98-99—Univ. of Michigan	CCHA	37	10	13	23	52	...	...	...	—	—	—	—	—
99-00—Sarnia	OHL	61	6	35	41	34	...	...	...	7	0	5	5	4
00-01—St. Louis	NHL	1	0	0	0	0	-2	0	0	—	—	—	—	—
—Worcester	AHL	37	3	10	13	12	...	...	...	7	1	1	2	2
01-02—Worcester	AHL	24	2	7	9	17	...	...	...	—	—	—	—	—
—St. Louis	NHL	48	2	8	10	18	10	0	0	9	0	0	0	0
02-03—Worcester	AHL	33	2	8	10	16	...	...	...	—	—	—	—	—
—St. Louis	NHL	20	0	3	3	8	3	0	0	—	—	—	—	—
—San Antonio	AHL	11	0	3	3	20	...	...	...	—	—	—	—	—
NHL Totals (3 years)		69	2	11	13	26	11	0	0	9	0	0	0	0

VANDENBUSSCHE, RYAN RW BLACKHAWKS

PERSONAL: Born February 28, 1973, in Simcoe, Ont. ... 6-0/200. ... Shoots right. ... Name pronounced VAN-dihn-bush.
TRANSACTIONS/CAREER NOTES: Selected by Toronto Maple Leafs in eighth round (173rd overall) of NHL entry draft (June 20, 1992). ... Signed as free agent by New York Rangers (August 22, 1995). ... Traded by Rangers to Chicago Blackhawks for D Ryan Risidore (March 24, 1998). ... Suspended one game by NHL for head-butting incident (March 28, 1999). ... Underwent elbow surgery prior to 1999-2000 season; missed first six games of season. ... Suffered sore back (December 3, 1999); missed five games. ... Lacerated left hand (March 3, 2000); missed 10 games.

Season Team	League	REGULAR SEASON								PLAYOFFS				
		Gms.	G	A	Pts.	PIM	+/-	PP	SH	Gms.	G	A	Pts.	PIM
90-91—Cornwall	OHL	49	3	8	11	139	...	...	...	—	—	—	—	—
91-92—Cornwall	OHL	61	13	15	28	232	...	...	...	6	0	2	2	9
92-93—Newmarket	OHL	30	15	12	27	161	...	...	...	—	—	—	—	—
—Guelph	OHL	29	3	14	17	99	...	...	...	5	1	3	4	13
—St. John's	AHL	1	0	0	0	0	...	...	...	—	—	—	—	—
93-94—St. John's	AHL	44	4	10	14	124	...	...	...	—	—	—	—	—
—Springfield	AHL	9	1	2	3	29	...	...	...	5	0	0	0	16
94-95—St. John's	AHL	53	2	13	15	239	...	...	...	—	—	—	—	—
95-96—Binghamton	AHL	68	3	17	20	240	...	...	...	4	0	0	0	9
96-97—Binghamton	AHL	38	8	11	19	133	...	...	...	—	—	—	—	—
—New York Rangers	NHL	11	1	0	1	30	-2	0	0	—	—	—	—	—
97-98—New York Rangers	NHL	16	1	0	1	38	-2	0	0	—	—	—	—	—
—Hartford	AHL	15	2	0	2	45	...	...	...	—	—	—	—	—
—Chicago	NHL	4	0	1	1	5	0	0	0	—	—	—	—	—
—Indianapolis	IHL	3	1	1	2	4	...	...	...	—	—	—	—	—
98-99—Indianapolis	IHL	34	3	10	13	130	...	...	...	—	—	—	—	—
—Portland	AHL	37	4	1	5	119	...	...	...	—	—	—	—	—
—Chicago	NHL	6	0	0	0	17	0	0	0	—	—	—	—	—
99-00—Chicago	NHL	52	0	1	1	143	-3	0	0	—	—	—	—	—
00-01—Chicago	NHL	64	2	5	7	146	-8	0	0	—	—	—	—	—
01-02—Chicago	NHL	50	1	2	3	103	-10	0	0	1	0	0	0	0
02-03—Norfolk	AHL	4	0	1	1	5	...	...	...	—	—	—	—	—
—Chicago	NHL	22	0	0	0	58	0	0	0	—	—	—	—	—
NHL Totals (7 years)		225	5	9	14	540	-25	0	0	1	0	0	0	0

VANDERMEER, JIM D FLYERS

PERSONAL: Born February 21, 1980, in Caroline, Alta. ... 6-1/210. ... Shoots left.
TRANSACTIONS/CAREER NOTES: Signed as undrafted free agent by Philadelphia Flyers (July 6, 2001). ... Re-signed by Philadelphia Flyers (July 14, 2003).

Season Team	League	REGULAR SEASON								PLAYOFFS				
		Gms.	G	A	Pts.	PIM	+/-	PP	SH	Gms.	G	A	Pts.	PIM
97-98—Red Deer	WHL	35	0	3	3	55	...	...	...	2	0	0	0	0
98-99—Red Deer	WHL	70	5	23	28	258	...	...	...	9	0	1	1	24
99-00—Red Deer	WHL	71	8	30	38	221	...	...	...	4	0	1	1	16
00-01—Red Deer	WHL	65	28	37	65	180	...	...	...	22	3	13	16	43
01-02—Philadelphia	AHL	74	1	13	14	88	...	...	...	5	0	2	2	14
02-03—Philadelphia	AHL	48	4	8	12	122	...	...	...	—	—	—	—	—
—Philadelphia	NHL	24	2	1	3	27	9	0	0	8	0	1	1	9
NHL Totals (1 year)		24	2	1	3	27	9	0	0	8	0	1	1	9

VARADA, VACLAV RW SENATORS

PERSONAL: Born April 26, 1976, in Vsetin, Czechoslovakia ... 6-0/208. ... Shoots left. ... Name pronounced vuh-RAH-duh.
TRANSACTIONS/CAREER NOTES: Selected by San Jose Sharks in fourth round (fourth Sharks pick, 89th overall) of NHL entry draft (June 29, 1994). ... Traded by Sharks with LW Martin Spahnel and fourth-round pick (D Mike Martone) in 1996 draft to Buffalo Sabres for D Doug Bodger

... (November 16, 1995). ... Fractured left hand (February 2, 1997); missed 15 games. ... Sprained ankle (February 9, 1999); missed 10 games. ... Suffered ear injury (January 18, 2000); missed three games. ... Suffered concussion (February 25, 2001); missed six games. ... Suspended one game by NHL for unsportsmanlike conduct (October 27, 2001). ... Suspended three games by NHL for hich-sticking incident (November 10, 2001). ... Suspended one game by NHL for checking from behind (January 20, 2002). ... Traded by Sabres with fifth-round pick in 2003 draft to Ottawa Senators for C Jakub Klepis (February 25, 2003).

		REGULAR SEASON								PLAYOFFS				
Season Team	League	Gms.	G	A	Pts.	PIM	+/-	PP	SH	Gms.	G	A	Pts.	PIM
92-93—TJ Vitkovice	Czech.	1	0	0	0	0	...	...	...	—	—	—	—	—
93-94—HC Vitkovice	Czech Rep.	24	6	7	13	...	...	...	...	5	1	1	2	...
94-95—Tacoma	WHL	68	50	38	88	108	...	...	...	4	4	3	7	11
—Czech. Jr. nat'l team ...	Int'l	7	6	4	10	25	...	...	...	—	—	—	—	—
95-96—Kelowna	WHL	59	39	46	85	100	...	...	...	6	3	3	6	16
—Rochester	AHL	5	3	0	3	4	...	...	...	—	—	—	—	—
—Buffalo	NHL	1	0	0	0	0	0	0	0	—	—	—	—	—
—Czech. Jr. nat'l team ...	Int'l	6	5	1	6	8	...	...	...	—	—	—	—	—
96-97—Rochester	AHL	53	23	25	48	81	...	...	...	10	1	6	7	27
—Buffalo	NHL	5	0	0	0	2	0	0	0	—	—	—	—	—
97-98—Rochester	AHL	45	30	26	56	74	...	...	...	—	—	—	—	—
—Buffalo	NHL	27	5	6	11	15	0	0	0	15	3	4	7	18
98-99—Buffalo	NHL	72	7	24	31	61	11	1	0	21	5	4	9	14
99-00—HC Vitkovice	Czech Rep.	5	2	3	5	12	...	...	...	—	—	—	—	—
—Buffalo	NHL	76	10	27	37	62	12	0	0	5	0	0	0	8
00-01—Buffalo	NHL	75	10	21	31	81	-2	2	0	13	0	4	4	8
01-02—Buffalo	NHL	76	7	16	23	82	-7	1	0	—	—	—	—	—
02-03—Buffalo	NHL	44	7	4	11	23	-2	1	0	—	—	—	—	—
—Ottawa	NHL	11	2	6	8	8	3	1	0	18	2	4	6	18
NHL Totals (8 years)		387	48	104	152	334	15	6	0	72	10	16	26	66

VARLAMOV, SERGEI   LW   BLUES

PERSONAL: Born July 21, 1978, in Kiev, U.S.S.R. ... 5-11/203. ... Shoots left. ... Name pronounced VAHR-luh-mahf.
TRANSACTIONS/CAREER NOTES: Signed as non-drafted free agent by Calgary Flames (September 18, 1996). ... Traded by Flames with G Fred Brathwaite, C Daniel Tkaczuk, and ninth-round pick (C Grant Jacobsen) in 2001 draft to St. Louis Blues for G Roman Turek and fourth-round pick (F Egor Shastin) in 2001 draft (June 23, 2001).

		REGULAR SEASON								PLAYOFFS				
Season Team	League	Gms.	G	A	Pts.	PIM	+/-	PP	SH	Gms.	G	A	Pts.	PIM
95-96—Swift Current	WHL	55	23	21	44	65	...	...	...	—	—	—	—	—
96-97—Swift Current	WHL	72	46	39	85	94	...	...	...	—	—	—	—	—
—Saint John	AHL	1	0	0	0	2	...	...	...	—	—	—	—	—
97-98—Swift Current	WHL	72	*66	53	*119	132	...	...	...	12	10	5	15	28
—Calgary	NHL	1	0	0	0	0	0	0	0	—	—	—	—	—
—Saint John	AHL	—	—	—	—	—	—	—	—	3	0	0	0	0
98-99—Saint John	AHL	76	24	33	57	66	...	...	...	7	0	4	4	8
99-00—Saint John	AHL	68	20	21	41	88	...	...	...	3	0	0	0	24
—Calgary	NHL	7	3	0	3	0	0	0	0	—	—	—	—	—
00-01—Saint John	AHL	55	21	30	51	56	...	...	...	19	*15	8	23	10
01-02—St. Louis	NHL	52	5	7	12	26	4	0	0	1	0	0	0	2
—Ukranian Oly. team ...	Int'l	2	1	0	1	14	...	...	...	—	—	—	—	—
02-03—Worcester	AHL	72	23	38	61	79	...	...	...	—	—	—	—	—
—St. Louis	NHL	3	0	0	0	0	1	0	0	—	—	—	—	—
NHL Totals (4 years)		63	8	7	15	26	5	0	0	1	0	0	0	2

VASICEK, JOSEF   C   HURRICANES

PERSONAL: Born September 12, 1980, in Havlickuv Brod, Czechoslovakia ... 6-4/200. ... Shoots left.
TRANSACTIONS/CAREER NOTES: Selected by Carolina Hurricanes in fourth round (fourth Hurricanes pick, 91st overall) of NHL entry draft (June 27, 1998). ... Injured knee (January 14, 2002); missed four games.

		REGULAR SEASON								PLAYOFFS				
Season Team	League	Gms.	G	A	Pts.	PIM	+/-	PP	SH	Gms.	G	A	Pts.	PIM
95-96—Havlickuv Brod	Czech. Jrs.	36	25	25	50		...	...	...	—	—	—	—	—
96-97—Slavia Praha	Czech. Jrs.	37	20	40	60	...	...	...	...	—	—	—	—	—
97-98—Slavia Praha	Czech. Jrs.	34	13	20	33	...	...	...	...	—	—	—	—	—
98-99—Sault Ste. Marie	OHL	66	21	35	56	30	...	...	...	5	3	0	3	10
99-00—Sault Ste. Marie	OHL	54	26	46	72	49	...	...	...	17	5	15	20	8
00-01—Carolina	NHL	76	8	13	21	53	-8	1	0	6	2	0	2	0
—Cincinnati	IHL	—	—	—	—	—	—	—	—	3	0	0	0	0
01-02—Carolina	NHL	78	14	17	31	53	-7	3	0	23	3	2	5	12
02-03—Carolina	NHL	57	10	10	20	33	-19	4	0	—	—	—	—	—
NHL Totals (3 years)		211	32	40	72	139	-34	8	0	29	5	2	7	12

VASILJEVS, HERBERT   C

PERSONAL: Born May 27, 1976, in Riga, U.S.S.R. ... 5-11/180. ... Shoots right.
TRANSACTIONS/CAREER NOTES: Signed as non-drafted free agent by Florida Panthers (October 3, 1997). ... Traded by Panthers with D Gord Murphy, D Daniel Tjarnqvist and sixth-round pick (traded to Dallas) in 1999 draft to Atlanta Thrashers for G Trevor Kidd (June 25, 1999). ... Signed as free agent by Vancouver Canucks (August 10, 2001).

V

Season Team	League	REGULAR SEASON								PLAYOFFS				
		Gms.	G	A	Pts.	PIM	+/-	PP	SH	Gms.	G	A	Pts.	PIM
94-95—Krefeld Pinguine	Germany	57	5	9	14	34	...	...	...	—	—	—	—	—
95-96—Guelph	OHL	65	34	33	67	63	...	...	...	16	6	13	19	6
96-97—Carolina	AHL	54	13	18	31	30	...	...	...	—	—	—	—	—
—Port Huron....................	Col.HL	3	3	2	5	4	...	...	...	—	—	—	—	—
—Knoxville......................	ECHL	3	1	1	2	0	...	...	...	—	—	—	—	—
97-98—New Haven	AHL	76	36	30	66	60	...	...	...	3	1	0	1	2
98-99—Kentucky.....................	AHL	76	28	48	76	66	...	...	...	12	2	1	3	4
—Florida.........................	NHL	5	0	0	0	2	-1	0	0	—	—	—	—	—
99-00—Orlando......................	IHL	73	25	35	60	60	...	...	...	6	2	2	4	6
—Atlanta.........................	NHL	7	1	0	1	4	-3	0	0	—	—	—	—	—
00-01—Orlando......................	IHL	58	22	26	48	32	...	...	...	12	8	3	11	14
—Atlanta.........................	NHL	21	4	5	9	14	-11	2	0	—	—	—	—	—
01-02—Vancouver..................	NHL	18	3	2	5	2	0	2	0	—	—	—	—	—
—Manitoba......................	AHL	31	12	14	26	10	...	...	...	—	—	—	—	—
02-03—Manitoba....................	AHL	69	10	29	39	30	...	...	...	—	—	—	—	—
NHL Totals (4 years)...........		51	8	7	15	22	-15	4	0					

VEILLEUX, STEPHANE   C   WILD

PERSONAL: Born November 16, 1981, in Beauceville, Que. ... 6-1/181. ... Shoots left.
TRANSACTIONS/CAREER NOTES: Selected by Minnesota Wild in third round (fourth Wild pick, 93rd overall) of NHL entry draft (June 23, 2001).

Season Team	League	REGULAR SEASON								PLAYOFFS				
		Gms.	G	A	Pts.	PIM	+/-	PP	SH	Gms.	G	A	Pts.	PIM
98-99—Victoriaville	QMJHL	65	6	13	19	35	...	...	...	6	1	3	4	2
99-00—Victoriaville	QMJHL	22	1	4	5	17	...	...	...	—	—	—	—	—
—Val-d'Or	QMJHL	50	14	28	42	100	...	...	...	—	—	—	—	—
00-01—Val-d'Or	QMJHL	68	48	67	115	90	...	...	...	21	15	18	33	42
01-02—Houston	AHL	77	13	22	35	113	...	...	...	14	2	4	6	20
02-03—Houston	AHL	29	8	4	12	43	...	...	...	—	—	—	—	—
—Minnesota..................	NHL	38	3	2	5	23	-6	1	0	—	—	—	—	—
NHL Totals (1 year).............		38	3	2	5	23	-6	1	0					

VERMETTE, ANTOINE   C   SENATORS

PERSONAL: Born July 20, 1982, in St-Agapit, Que. ... 6-0/184. ... Shoots left.
TRANSACTIONS/CAREER NOTES: Selected by Ottawa Senators in second round (third Senators pick, 55th overall) of NHL entry draft (June 24, 2000).

Season Team	League	REGULAR SEASON								PLAYOFFS				
		Gms.	G	A	Pts.	PIM	+/-	PP	SH	Gms.	G	A	Pts.	PIM
98-99—Quebec	QMJHL	57	9	17	26	32	...	...	...	13	0	0	0	2
99-00—Victoriaville	QMJHL	71	30	41	71	87	...	...	...	6	0	1	1	6
00-01—Victoriaville	QMJHL	71	57	62	119	102	...	...	...	9	4	6	10	14
01-02—Victoriaville	QMJHL	4	0	2	2	6	...	...	...	22	10	16	26	10
02-03—Binghamton	AHL	80	34	28	62	57	...	...	...	—	—	—	—	—

VERNARSKY, KRIS   C   BRUINS

PERSONAL: Born April 5, 1982, in Detroit ... 6-3/200. ... Shoots left. ... Full Name: Kristopher Vernarsky.
TRANSACTIONS/CAREER NOTES: Selected by Toronto Maple Leafs in second round (second Maple Leafs pick, 51st overall) of NHL entry draft (June 24, 2000). ... Traded by Maple Leafs to Boston Bruins for D Richard Jackman (May 13, 2002).

Season Team	League	REGULAR SEASON								PLAYOFFS				
		Gms.	G	A	Pts.	PIM	+/-	PP	SH	Gms.	G	A	Pts.	PIM
98-99—Plymouth	OHL	45	3	14	17	30	...	...	...	11	0	0	0	2
99-00—Plymouth	OHL	64	16	22	38	63	...	...	...	19	3	6	9	24
00-01—Plymouth	OHL	60	14	21	35	35	...	...	...	19	7	10	17	19
01-02—Plymouth	OHL	59	19	36	55	98	...	...	...	6	1	2	3	15
02-03—Providence.................	AHL	65	12	15	27	49	...	...	...	—	—	—	—	—
—Boston	NHL	14	1	0	1	2	-2	0	0	—	—	—	—	—
NHL Totals (1 year).............		14	1	0	1	2	-2	0	0					

VIGIER, J.P.   RW   THRASHERS

PERSONAL: Born September 11, 1976, in Notre Dame de Lourdes, Man. ... 6-0/205. ... Shoots right. ... Full Name: Jean-Pierre Vigier.
TRANSACTIONS/CAREER NOTES: Signed as non-drafted free agent by Atlanta Thrashers (March 24, 2000).

Season Team	League	REGULAR SEASON								PLAYOFFS				
		Gms.	G	A	Pts.	PIM	+/-	PP	SH	Gms.	G	A	Pts.	PIM
96-97—N. Michigan U............	CCHA	36	10	14	24	54	...	...	...	—	—	—	—	—
97-98—N. Michigan U............	CCHA	36	12	15	27	60	...	...	...	—	—	—	—	—
98-99—N. Michigan U............	CCHA	42	21	18	39	80	...	...	...	—	—	—	—	—
99-00—N. Michigan U............	CCHA	39	18	17	35	72	...	...	...	—	—	—	—	—
—Orlando.......................	IHL	1	0	0	0	0	...	...	...	—	—	—	—	—
00-01—Orlando......................	IHL	78	23	17	40	66	...	...	...	16	6	6	12	14
—Atlanta	NHL	2	0	0	0	0	-2	0	0	—	—	—	—	—
01-02—Chicago......................	AHL	62	25	16	41	26	...	...	...	21	7	7	14	20
—Atlanta	NHL	15	4	1	5	4	-5	0	0	—	—	—	—	—
02-03—Chicago......................	AHL	63	29	27	56	54	...	...	...	—	—	—	—	—
—Atlanta	NHL	13	0	0	0	4	-13	0	0	—	—	—	—	—
NHL Totals (3 years)...........		30	4	1	5	8	-20	0	0					

V

VIKINGSTAD, TORE   LW   BLUES

PERSONAL: Born October 8, 1975, in Oslo, Norway. ... 6-4/202. ... Shoots left.
TRANSACTIONS/CAREER NOTES: Selected by St. Louis Blues in sixth round (fifth Blues pick, 180th overall) of NHL entry draft (June 26, 1999).

Season Team	League	REGULAR SEASON								PLAYOFFS				
		Gms.	G	A	Pts.	PIM	+/-	PP	SH	Gms.	G	A	Pts.	PIM
97-98—Stjernen Fredrikstad ...	Norway	44	26	31	57	0	...	...	...	—	—	—	—	—
98-99—Farjestad Karlstad	Sweden	49	9	11	20	18	...	...	...	4	2	3	5	0
99-00—Farjestad Karlstad	Sweden	47	8	19	27	26	...	...	...	7	3	0	3	6
00-01—Leksand	Sweden Dv. 2	41	10	15	25	24	...	...	...	—	—	—	—	—
01-02—DEG Metro Stars........	Germany	58	18	30	48	6	...	...	...	—	—	—	—	—
02-03—DEG Metro Stars........	Germany	45	13	18	31	40	...	...	...	5	1	0	1	0

VIRTA, TONY   RW

PERSONAL: Born June 28, 1972, in Hameenlinna, Finland. ... 5-10/187. ... Shoots left.
TRANSACTIONS/CAREER NOTES: Selected by Minnesota Wild in fourth round (fifth Wild pick, 103rd overall) of NHL entry draft (June 23, 2001).

Season Team	League	REGULAR SEASON								PLAYOFFS				
		Gms.	G	A	Pts.	PIM	+/-	PP	SH	Gms.	G	A	Pts.	PIM
90-91—HPK Hameenlinna.......	Finland Jr.	28	17	34	51	42	...	...	...	—	—	—	—	—
91-92—HPK Hameenlinna.......	Finland Jr.	35	24	31	55	114	...	...	...	—	—	—	—	—
92-93—HPK Hameenlinna.......	Finland Jr.	2	1	2	3	2	...	...	...	—	—	—	—	—
—HPK Hameenlinna.......	Finland	48	9	8	17	35	...	...	...	12	1	0	1	0
93-94—HPK Hameenlinna.......	Finland	47	17	16	33	50	...	...	...	—	—	—	—	—
94-95—HPK Hameenlinna.......	Finland	43	9	24	33	75	...	...	...	—	—	—	—	—
95-96—HPK Hameenlinna.......	Finland	48	15	19	34	12	...	...	...	9	1	3	4	31
96-97—Frankfurt.................	Germany	48	13	13	26	40	...	...	...	8	1	2	3	56
97-98—TPS Turku	Finland	48	17	15	32	26	...	...	...	3	0	0	0	0
98-99—TPS Turku	Finland	54	16	27	43	32	...	...	...	10	6	6	12	8
99-00—TPS Turku	Finland	53	14	37	51	57	...	...	...	11	2	7	9	6
00-01—TPS Turku	Finland	56	27	33	60	24	...	...	...	10	2	5	7	6
01-02—Houston	AHL	67	25	33	58	29	...	...	...	14	1	9	10	10
—Minnesota............	NHL	8	2	3	5	0	0	0	0	—	—	—	—	—
02-03—Houston	AHL	39	6	12	18	14	...	...	...	—	—	—	—	—
NHL Totals (1 year)............		8	2	3	5	0	0	0	0					

VISHNEVSKI, VITALY   D   MIGHTY DUCKS

PERSONAL: Born March 18, 1980, in Kharkov, U.S.S.R. ... 6-2/203. ... Shoots left.
TRANSACTIONS/CAREER NOTES: Selected by Mighty Ducks of Anaheim in first round (first Mighty Ducks pick, fifth overall) of NHL entry draft (June 27, 1998). ... Suffered injury (April 5, 2000); missed final two games of season. ... Strained hip muscle (January 30, 2001); missed three games. ... Strained shoulder (March 16, 2001); missed three games. ... Suffered back spasms (December 23, 2001); missed one game. ... Sprained left wrist (December 26, 2001); missed five games. ... Suspended two games by NHL for elbowing incident (March 15, 2002). ... Re-signed by Mighty Ducks (July 23, 2003).

Season Team	League	REGULAR SEASON								PLAYOFFS				
		Gms.	G	A	Pts.	PIM	+/-	PP	SH	Gms.	G	A	Pts.	PIM
95-96—Torpedo Yaroslavl	CIS Div. II	40	4	4	8	20	...	...	...	—	—	—	—	—
96-97—Torpedo Yaroslavl	Rus. Div. III	45	0	2	2	30	...	...	...	—	—	—	—	—
97-98—Torpedo Yaroslavl	Rus. Div. II	47	8	9	17	164	...	...	...	—	—	—	—	—
98-99—Torpedo Yaroslavl	Russian	34	3	4	7	38	...	...	...	10	0	0	0	4
99-00—Cincinnati..................	AHL	35	1	3	4	45	...	...	...	—	—	—	—	—
—Anaheim	NHL	31	1	1	2	26	0	1	0	—	—	—	—	—
00-01—Anaheim	NHL	76	1	10	11	99	-1	0	0	—	—	—	—	—
01-02—Anaheim	NHL	74	0	3	3	60	-10	0	0	—	—	—	—	—
02-03—Anaheim	NHL	80	2	6	8	76	-8	0	1	21	0	1	1	6
NHL Totals (4 years)...........		261	4	20	24	261	-19	1	1	21	0	1	1	6

VISNOVSKY, LUBOMIR   D   KINGS

V

PERSONAL: Born August 11, 1976, in Topolcany, Czechoslovakia ... 5-10/188. ... Shoots left.
TRANSACTIONS/CAREER NOTES: Selected by Los Angeles Kings in fourth round (fourth Kings pick, 118th overall) of NHL entry draft (June 24, 2000). ... Suffered back spasms (December 3, 2000); missed one game.

Season Team	League	REGULAR SEASON								PLAYOFFS				
		Gms.	G	A	Pts.	PIM	+/-	PP	SH	Gms.	G	A	Pts.	PIM
94-95—Bratislava..................	Slovakia	36	11	12	23	10	...	...	...	9	1	3	4	2
95-96—Bratislava..................	Slovakia	35	8	6	14	22	...	...	...	13	1	5	6	2
96-97—Bratislava..................	Slovakia	44	11	12	23	...	...	...	...	2	0	1	1	...
97-98—Bratislava..................	Slovakia	36	7	9	16	16	...	...	...	11	2	4	6	8
98-99—Bratislava..................	Slovakia	40	9	10	19	31	...	...	...	10	5	5	10	0
99-00—Bratislava..................	Slovakia	52	21	24	45	38	...	...	...	8	5	3	8	16
00-01—Los Angeles	NHL	81	7	32	39	36	16	3	0	8	0	0	0	0
01-02—Los Angeles	NHL	72	4	17	21	14	-5	1	0	4	0	1	1	0
—Slovakian Oly. team	Int'l	3	1	2	3	0	...	...	...	—	—	—	—	—
02-03—Los Angeles	NHL	57	8	16	24	28	2	1	0	—	—	—	—	—
NHL Totals (3 years)...........		210	19	65	84	78	13	5	0	12	0	1	1	0

VOKOUN, TOMAS　　　　G　　　　PREDATORS

PERSONAL: Born July 2, 1976, in Karlovy Vary, Czechoslovakia ... 6-0/195. ... Catches right. ... Name pronounced TOH-mahz voh-KOON.
TRANSACTIONS/CAREER NOTES: Selected by Montreal Canadiens in ninth round (11th Canadiens pick, 226th overall) of NHL entry draft (June 29, 1994). ... Selected by Nashville Predators in NHL expansion draft (June 26, 1998). ... Strained neck (January 19, 1999); missed one game. ... Suffered injury (March 31, 2000); missed final four games of season. ... Bruised foot (October 16, 2000); missed three games. ... Sprained ankle (April 6, 2002); missed remainder of season.

			REGULAR SEASON									PLAYOFFS						
Season Team	League	Gms.	Min	W	L	T	GA	SO	Avg.	SV%	Gms.	Min.	W	L	GA	SO	Avg.	SV%
93-94—Poldi Kladno	Czech Rep.	1	20	...	...	...	2	0	6.00	—	—	—	—	—	—	—	—	—
94-95—Poldi Kladno	Czech Rep.	26	1368	...	...	...	70	...	3.07	—	5	240	...	...	19	...	4.75	—
95-96—Wheeling	ECHL	35	1911	20	10	‡2	117	0	3.67	—	7	436	4	3	19	0	2.61	—
—Fredericton	AHL	—	—	—	—	—	—	—	—	—	1	59	0	1	4	0	4.07	—
96-97—Fredericton	AHL	47	2645	12	26	7	154	2	3.49	—	—	—	—	—	—	—	—	—
—Montreal	NHL	1	20	0	0	0	4	0	12.00	.714	—	—	—	—	—	—	—	—
97-98—Fredericton	AHL	31	1735	13	13	2	90	0	3.11	—	—	—	—	—	—	—	—	—
98-99—Milwaukee	IHL	9	539	3	2	‡4	22	1	2.45	—	2	149	0	2	8	0	3.22	—
—Nashville	NHL	37	1954	12	18	4	96	1	2.95	.908	—	—	—	—	—	—	—	—
99-00—Nashville	NHL	33	1879	9	20	1	87	1	2.78	.904	—	—	—	—	—	—	—	—
—Milwaukee	IHL	7	364	6	2	0	17	0	2.80	—	—	—	—	—	—	—	—	—
00-01—Nashville	NHL	37	2088	13	17	5	85	2	2.44	.910	—	—	—	—	—	—	—	—
01-02—Nashville	NHL	29	1471	5	14	4	66	2	2.69	.903	—	—	—	—	—	—	—	—
02-03—Nashville	NHL	69	3974	25	31	11	146	3	2.20	.918	—	—	—	—	—	—	—	—
NHL Totals (6 years)		206	11386	64	100	25	484	9	2.55	.910								

VOLCHENKOV, ANTON　　　　D　　　　SENATORS

PERSONAL: Born February 25, 1982, in Moscow, U.S.S.R. ... 6-0/225. ... Shoots left.
TRANSACTIONS/CAREER NOTES: Selected by Ottawa Senators in first round (first Senators pick, 21st overall) of NHL entry draft (June 24, 2000).

		REGULAR SEASON							PLAYOFFS				
Season Team	League	Gms.	G	A	Pts.	PIM	+/-	PP	SH	Gms.	G	A	Pts.	PIM
99-00—CSKA	Rus. Div. II	30	2	9	11	36	...	...	...	—	—	—	—	—
00-01—Krylja Sovetov	Rus. Div. II	34	3	4	7	56	...	...	...	—	—	—	—	—
01-02—Kryla Sov. Moscow	Russian	47	4	16	20	50	...	...	...	3	0	0	0	29
02-03—Ottawa	NHL	57	3	13	16	40	-4	0	0	17	1	1	2	4
NHL Totals (1 year)		57	3	13	16	40	-4	0	0	17	1	1	2	4

VOROBIEV, PAVEL　　　　RW　　　　BLACKHAWKS

PERSONAL: Born May 5, 1982, in Karaganda, U.S.S.R. ... 6-0/183. ... Shoots left.
TRANSACTIONS/CAREER NOTES: Selected by Chicago Blackhawks in first round (second Blackhawks pick, 11th overall) of NHL entry draft (June 24, 2000). ... Signed by Blackhawks (June 3, 2003).

		REGULAR SEASON							PLAYOFFS				
Season Team	League	Gms.	G	A	Pts.	PIM	+/-	PP	SH	Gms.	G	A	Pts.	PIM
98-99—Torpedo Yaroslavl	Rus. Div. II	17	0	1	1	0	...	...	...	—	—	—	—	—
99-00—Torpedo Yaroslavl	Russian	8	2	0	2	4	...	...	...	—	—	—	—	—
—Torpedo Yaroslavl	Rus. Div. II	40	19	15	34	8	...	...	...	—	—	—	—	—
00-01—Lokomotiv Yaroslavl	Russian	36	8	8	16	28	...	...	...	10	4	1	5	8
01-02—Lokomotiv Yaroslavl	Russian	9	3	2	5	6	...	...	...	7	0	0	0	4
02-03—Lokomotiv Yaroslavl	Russian	44	10	18	28	10	...	...	...	—	—	—	—	—

VRBATA, RADIM　　　　RW　　　　HURRICANES

PERSONAL: Born June 13, 1981, in Mlada Boleslav, Czechoslovakia ... 6-1/190. ... Shoots right. ... Name pronounced ra-DEEM vuhr-BA-tuh.
TRANSACTIONS/CAREER NOTES: Selected by Colorado Avalanche in eighth round (10th Avalanche pick, 212th overall) of NHL entry draft (June 26, 1999). ... Injured ribs (December 21, 2001); missed eight games. ... Suffered from the flu (March 6, 2002); missed one game. ... Traded by Avalanche to Carolina Hurricanes for LW Bates Battaglia (March 11, 2003).
STATISTICAL PLATEAUS: Three-goal games: 2001-02 (1).

		REGULAR SEASON							PLAYOFFS				
Season Team	League	Gms.	G	A	Pts.	PIM	+/-	PP	SH	Gms.	G	A	Pts.	PIM
98-99—Hull	QMJHL	64	22	38	60	16	...	...	...	23	6	13	19	6
99-00—Hull	QMJHL	58	29	45	74	26	...	...	...	15	3	9	12	8
00-01—Shawinigan	QMJHL	55	56	64	120	67	...	...	...	10	4	7	11	4
—Hershey	AHL	—	—	—	—	—	—	—	—	1	0	1	1	2
01-02—Hershey	AHL	20	8	14	22	8	...	...	...	—	—	—	—	—
—Colorado	NHL	52	18	12	30	14	7	6	0	9	0	0	0	0
02-03—Colorado	NHL	66	11	19	30	16	0	3	0	—	—	—	—	—
—Carolina	NHL	10	5	0	5	2	-7	3	0	—	—	—	—	—
NHL Totals (2 years)		128	34	31	65	32	0	12	0	9	0	0	0	0

V

VUJTEK, VLADIMIR   C

PERSONAL: Born February 17, 1972, in Ostrava, Czechoslovakia ... 6-1/190. ... Shoots left. ... Name pronounced VWEE-tehk.
TRANSACTIONS/CAREER NOTES: Selected by Montreal Canadiens in fourth round (fifth Canadiens pick, 73rd overall) of NHL entry draft (June 22, 1991). ... Traded by Canadiens with LW Shayne Corson and C Brent Gilchrist to Edmonton Oilers for LW Vincent Damphousse and fourth-round pick (D Adam Wiesel) in 1993 draft (August 27, 1992). ... Suffered charley horse (October 6, 1992); missed eight games. ... Suspended by Oilers after failing to report to assigned team (January 4, 1993). ... Strained lower back (March 17, 1993); missed five games. ... Injured shoulder (January 11, 1994); missed seven games. ... Injured shoulder and underwent surgery (February 14, 1994); missed remainder of season. ... Played in Europe during 1994-95 NHL lockout. ... Traded by Oilers to Tampa Bay Lightning for RW Brantt Myhres and conditional draft pick (July 16, 1997). ... Suffered from the flu (October 3, 1997); missed one game. ... Suffered from chest virus (November 8, 1997); missed 42 games. ... Signed as free agent by Atlanta Thrashers (July 19, 1999). ... Lacerated face (September 18, 1999); missed first six games of 1999-2000 season. ... Signed as free agent by Pittsburgh Penguins (July 15, 2002).

Season Team	League	REGULAR SEASON								PLAYOFFS				
		Gms.	G	A	Pts.	PIM	+/-	PP	SH	Gms.	G	A	Pts.	PIM
89-90—Vitkovice	Czech.	29	3	4	7	...	...	...	...	—	—	—	—	—
90-91—Tri-City	WHL	37	26	18	44	25	...	...	...	—	—	—	—	—
—Vitkovice	Czech.	26	7	4	11	...	...	...	...	—	—	—	—	—
91-92—Tri-City	WHL	53	41	61	102	114	...	...	...	—	—	—	—	—
—Montreal	NHL	2	0	0	0	0	-1	0	0	—	—	—	—	—
92-93—Edmonton	NHL	30	1	10	11	8	-1	0	0	—	—	—	—	—
—Cape Breton	AHL	20	10	9	19	14	...	...	...	1	0	0	0	0
93-94—Edmonton	NHL	40	4	15	19	14	-7	1	0	—	—	—	—	—
94-95—HC Vitkovice	Czech Rep.	18	5	7	12	51	...	...	...	—	—	—	—	—
—Cape Breton	AHL	30	10	11	21	30	...	...	...	—	—	—	—	—
—Las Vegas	IHL	1	0	0	0	0	...	...	...	—	—	—	—	—
95-96—TJ Vitkovice	Czech Rep.	26	6	7	13	0	...	...	...	4	1	1	2	0
96-97—Assat Pori	Finland	50	27	31	58	48	...	...	...	4	1	2	3	2
97-98—Tampa Bay	NHL	30	2	4	6	16	-2	0	0	—	—	—	—	—
—Adirondack	AHL	2	1	2	3	0	...	...	...	—	—	—	—	—
98-99—HC Vitkovice	Czech Rep.	47	20	35	55	75	...	...	...	—	—	—	—	—
99-00—Atlanta	NHL	3	0	0	0	0	0	0	0	—	—	—	—	—
—Sparta Praha	Czech Rep.	21	12	19	31	10	...	...	...	8	2	3	5	10
00-01—Sparta Praha	Czech Rep.	38	11	18	29	28	...	...	...	13	3	6	9	4
01-02—HPK Hameenlinna	Finland	45	19	39	58	38	...	...	...	8	4	7	11	6
02-03—Pittsburgh	NHL	5	0	1	1	0	-4	0	0	—	—	—	—	—
NHL Totals (6 years)		110	7	30	37	38	-15	1	0					

VYBORNY, DAVID   RW   BLUE JACKETS

PERSONAL: Born June 2, 1975, in Jihlava, Czechoslovakia ... 5-10/183. ... Shoots right. ... Name pronounced vigh-BOHR-nee.
TRANSACTIONS/CAREER NOTES: Selected by Edmonton Oilers in second round (third Oilers pick, 33rd overall) of NHL entry draft (June 26, 1993). ... Signed as free agent by Columbus Blue Jackets (June 7, 2000). ... Strained hip flexor (February 20, 2001); missed one game. ... Strained groin (April 1, 2001); missed two games. ... Strained hip flexor (November 29, 2001); missed one game. ... Sprained knee (January 24, 2002); missed three games.

Season Team	League	REGULAR SEASON								PLAYOFFS				
		Gms.	G	A	Pts.	PIM	+/-	PP	SH	Gms.	G	A	Pts.	PIM
90-91—Sparta Prague	Czech.	3	0	0	0	0	...	...	...	—	—	—	—	—
91-92—Sparta Prague	Czech.	32	6	9	15	2	...	...	...	—	—	—	—	—
92-93—Sparta Prague	Czech.	52	20	24	44	...	...	...	...	—	—	—	—	—
93-94—Sparta Prague	Czech Rep.	44	15	20	35	...	...	...	...	6	4	7	11	...
94-95—Cape Breton	AHL	76	23	38	61	30	...	...	...	—	—	—	—	—
95-96—Sparta Praha	Czech Rep.	52	19	36	55	42	...	...	...	—	—	—	—	—
96-97—Sparta Praha	Czech Rep.	47	20	29	49	14	...	...	...	—	—	—	—	—
97-98—MoDo Ornskoldsvik	Sweden	45	16	21	37	34	...	...	...	—	—	—	—	—
98-99—Sparta Praha	Czech Rep.	52	24	†46	*70	22	...	...	...	8	1	3	4	...
99-00—Sparta Praha	Czech Rep.	50	25	38	63	30	...	...	...	9	3	8	*11	4
00-01—Columbus	NHL	79	13	19	32	22	-9	5	0	—	—	—	—	—
01-02—Columbus	NHL	75	13	18	31	6	-14	6	0	—	—	—	—	—
02-03—Columbus	NHL	79	20	26	46	16	12	4	1	—	—	—	—	—
NHL Totals (3 years)		233	46	63	109	44	-11	15	1					

VYDARENY, RENE   D   CANUCKS

PERSONAL: Born May 6, 1981, in Bratislava, Czechoslovakia. ... 6-1/198. ... Shoots left. ... Name pronounced VEE-duh-RE-nee.
TRANSACTIONS/CAREER NOTES: Selected by Vancouver Canucks in third round (third Canucks pick, 69th overall) of NHL entry draft (June 26, 1999).

Season Team	League	REGULAR SEASON								PLAYOFFS				
		Gms.	G	A	Pts.	PIM	+/-	PP	SH	Gms.	G	A	Pts.	PIM
97-98—Bratislava	Slov. Jr.	50	5	14	19	74	...	...	...	—	—	—	—	—
98-99—Bratislava	Slov. Jr.	42	4	7	11	65	...	...	...	2	0	0	0	2
99-00—Rimouski	QMJHL	51	7	23	30	41	...	...	...	14	2	2	4	20
00-01—Kansas City	IHL	39	0	1	1	25	...	...	...	—	—	—	—	—
01-02—Manitoba	AHL	61	3	11	14	15	...	...	...	7	0	2	2	4
—Columbia	ECHL	10	2	1	3	9	...	...	...	—	—	—	—	—
02-03—Manitoba	AHL	71	2	8	10	46	...	...	...	—	—	—	—	—

WALKER, MATT — D — BLUES

PERSONAL: Born April 7, 1980, in Beaverlodge, Alta. ... 6-3/236. ... Shoots right.
TRANSACTIONS/CAREER NOTES: Selected by St. Louis Blues in third round (third Blues pick, 83rd overall) of NHL entry draft (June 27, 1998). ... Re-signed by Blues (July 27, 2003).

		REGULAR SEASON								PLAYOFFS				
Season Team	League	Gms.	G	A	Pts.	PIM	+/-	PP	SH	Gms.	G	A	Pts.	PIM
97-98—Portland	WHL	64	2	13	15	124	...	...	...	16	0	0	0	21
98-99—Portland	WHL	64	1	10	11	151	...	...	...	—	—	—	—	—
99-00—Portland	WHL	38	2	7	9	97	...	...	...	—	—	—	—	—
—Kootenay	WHL	69	6	26	32	150	...	...	...	—	—	—	—	—
00-01—Worcester	AHL	61	4	8	12	131	...	...	...	11	0	0	0	6
—Peoria	ECHL	8	1	0	1	70	...	...	...	—	—	—	—	—
01-02—Worcester	AHL	49	2	11	13	164	...	...	...	3	0	0	0	8
02-03—Worcester	AHL	40	1	8	9	58	...	...	...	—	—	—	—	—
—St. Louis	NHL	16	0	1	1	38	0	0	0	—	—	—	—	—
NHL Totals (1 year)		16	0	1	1	38	0	0	0					

WALKER, SCOTT — RW — PREDATORS

PERSONAL: Born July 19, 1973, in Cambridge, Ont. ... 5-10/196. ... Shoots right.
TRANSACTIONS/CAREER NOTES: Selected by Vancouver Canucks in fifth round (fourth Canucks pick, 124th overall) of NHL entry draft (June 26, 1993). ... Strained abdominal muscle (October 12, 1996); missed eight games. ... Strained groin (December 13, 1996); missed six games. ... Fractured nasal bone (November 16, 1997); missed four games. ... Selected by Nashville Predators in NHL expansion draft (June 26, 1998). ... Separated shoulder (November 19, 1999); missed nine games. ... Suffered ear infection (January 26, 1999); missed two games. ... Suffered concussion (December 6, 1999); missed 10 games. ... Bruised foot (January 21, 2000); missed three games. ... Separated left shoulder (January 19, 2001); missed eight games. ... Suffered concussion (November 13, 2001); missed three games. ... Suffered concussion (December 1, 2001); missed 12 games. ... Suffered post-concussion syndrome (January 10, 2002); missed remainder of season.
STATISTICAL PLATEAUS: Three-goal games: 2000-01 (1).

		REGULAR SEASON								PLAYOFFS				
Season Team	League	Gms.	G	A	Pts.	PIM	+/-	PP	SH	Gms.	G	A	Pts.	PIM
89-90—Kitch.-Cambridge Jr.	OHA	33	7	27	34	91	...	...	...	—	—	—	—	—
90-91—Cambridge Jr. B	OHA	45	10	27	37	241	...	...	...	—	—	—	—	—
91-92—Owen Sound	OHL	53	7	31	38	128	...	...	...	5	0	7	7	8
92-93—Owen Sound	OHL	57	23	68	91	110	...	...	...	8	1	5	6	16
—Canadian nat'l team	Int'l	2	3	0	3	0	...	...	...	—	—	—	—	—
93-94—Hamilton	AHL	77	10	29	39	272	...	...	...	4	0	1	1	25
94-95—Syracuse	AHL	74	14	38	52	334	...	...	...	—	—	—	—	—
—Vancouver	NHL	11	0	1	1	33	0	0	0	—	—	—	—	—
95-96—Vancouver	NHL	63	4	8	12	137	-7	0	1	—	—	—	—	—
—Syracuse	AHL	15	3	12	15	52	...	...	...	16	9	8	17	39
96-97—Vancouver	NHL	64	3	15	18	132	2	0	0	—	—	—	—	—
97-98—Vancouver	NHL	59	3	10	13	164	-8	0	1	—	—	—	—	—
98-99—Nashville	NHL	71	15	25	40	103	0	0	1	—	—	—	—	—
99-00—Nashville	NHL	69	7	21	28	90	-16	0	1	—	—	—	—	—
00-01—Nashville	NHL	74	25	29	54	66	-2	9	3	—	—	—	—	—
01-02—Nashville	NHL	28	4	5	9	18	-13	1	0	—	—	—	—	—
02-03—Nashville	NHL	60	15	18	33	58	2	7	0	—	—	—	—	—
NHL Totals (9 years)		499	76	132	208	801	-42	17	7					

WALLIN, JESSE — D — FLAMES

PERSONAL: Born March 10, 1978, in Saskatoon, Sask. ... 6-2/190. ... Shoots left. ... Name pronounced WAH-lihn.
TRANSACTIONS/CAREER NOTES: Selected by Detroit Red Wings in first round (first Red Wings pick, 26th overall) of NHL entry draft (June 22, 1996). ... Injured groin (September 29, 2001); missed first 42 games of season. ... Signed by Calgary Flames (July 31, 2003).

		REGULAR SEASON								PLAYOFFS				
Season Team	League	Gms.	G	A	Pts.	PIM	+/-	PP	SH	Gms.	G	A	Pts.	PIM
94-95—Prince Albert	WHL	72	4	20	24	72	...	...	...	—	—	—	—	—
95-96—Red Deer	WHL	70	5	19	24	61	...	...	...	9	0	3	3	4
96-97—Red Deer	WHL	59	6	33	39	70	...	...	...	16	1	4	5	10
97-98—Red Deer	WHL	14	1	6	7	17	...	...	...	5	0	1	1	2
98-99—Adirondack	AHL	76	4	12	16	34	...	...	...	3	0	2	2	2
99-00—Cincinnati	AHL	75	3	14	17	61	...	...	...	—	—	—	—	—
—Detroit	NHL	1	0	0	0	0	-2	0	0	—	—	—	—	—
00-01—Cincinnati	AHL	76	2	15	17	50	...	...	...	4	0	1	1	4
—Detroit	NHL	1	0	0	0	2	0	0	0	—	—	—	—	—
01-02—Cincinnati	AHL	5	1	1	2	2	...	...	...	—	—	—	—	—
—Detroit	NHL	15	0	1	1	13	-1	0	0	—	—	—	—	—
02-03—Detroit	NHL	32	0	1	1	19	-2	0	0	—	—	—	—	—
NHL Totals (4 years)		49	0	2	2	34	-5	0	0					

WALLIN, NICLAS — D — HURRICANES

PERSONAL: Born February 20, 1975, in Boden, Sweden ... 6-3/220. ... Shoots left.
TRANSACTIONS/CAREER NOTES: Selected by Carolina Hurricanes in fourth round (third Hurricanes pick, 97th overall) of NHL entry draft (June 24, 2000). ... Fractured wrist (October 5, 2000); missed six games. ... Strained shoulder (January 29, 2001); missed five games.

W

Season Team	League	Gms.	G	A	Pts.	PIM	+/-	PP	SH	Gms.	G	A	Pts.	PIM
96-97—Brynas Gavle	Sweden	47	1	1	2	16	...		...	—	—	—	—	—
97-98—Brynas Gavle	Sweden	44	2	3	5	57	...		...	3	0	1	1	4
98-99—Brynas Gavle	Sweden	46	2	4	6	52	...		...	14	0	0	0	8
99-00—Brynas Gavle	Sweden	48	7	9	16	73	...		...	—	—	—	—	—
00-01—Carolina	NHL	37	2	3	5	21	-11	0	0	3	0	0	0	2
—Cincinnati..................	IHL	8	1	2	3	4	...			—	—	—	—	—
01-02—Carolina	NHL	52	1	2	3	36	1	0	0	23	2	1	3	12
02-03—Carolina	NHL	77	2	8	10	71	-19	0	0	—	—	—	—	—
NHL Totals (3 years)...........		166	5	13	18	128	-29	0	0	26	2	1	3	14

WALLIN, RICKARD   C   WILD

PERSONAL: Born April 19, 1980, in Stockholm, Sweden ... 6-2/185. ... Shoots left.

TRANSACTIONS/CAREER NOTES: Selected by Phoenix Coyotes in sixth round (eighth Coyotes pick, 160th overall) of NHL entry draft (June 27, 1998). ... Traded by Coyotes to Minnesota Wild for C Joe Juneau (June 23, 2000).

		REGULAR SEASON								PLAYOFFS				
Season Team	League	Gms.	G	A	Pts.	PIM	+/-	PP	SH	Gms.	G	A	Pts.	PIM
96-97—Vasteras.....................	Sweden Jr.	26	3	3	6	...	...	...	...	—	—	—	—	—
97-98—Farjestad Karlstad	Sweden Jr.	29	20	20	40	32	...	...	...	2	1	1	2	2
98-99—Farjestad Karlstad	Sweden Jr.	5	0	0	0	0	...	...	...	—	—	—	—	—
99-00—Troja-Ljungby.............	Sweden Dv. 2	46	15	22	37	54	...	...	...	—	—	—	—	—
00-01—Farjestad Karlstad	Sweden	47	9	22	31	24	...	...	...	16	*11	3	14	4
01-02—Farjestad Karlstad	Sweden	50	12	31	43	56	...	...	...	10	4	9	13	8
02-03—Houston.....................	AHL	52	13	22	35	70	...	...	...	—	—	—	—	—
—Minnesota..................	NHL	4	1	0	1	0	1	0	0	—	—	—	—	—
NHL Totals (1 year)............		4	1	0	1	0	1	0	0					

WALSER, DERRICK   D   BLUE JACKETS

PERSONAL: Born May 12, 1978, in New Glasgow, Nova Scotia ... 5-10/199. ... Shoots left.

TRANSACTIONS/CAREER NOTES: Signed as non-drafted free agent by Columbus Blue Jackets (September 17, 2001). ... Re-signed by Blue Jackets (July 20, 2003).

		REGULAR SEASON								PLAYOFFS				
Season Team	League	Gms.	G	A	Pts.	PIM	+/-	PP	SH	Gms.	G	A	Pts.	PIM
95-96—Beauport....................	QMJHL	69	9	31	40	56	...	...	...	2	2	11	13	16
96-97—Beauport....................	QMJHL	37	13	25	38	26	...	...	...	—	—	—	—	—
—Rimouski	QMJHL	31	15	30	45	44	...	...	...	4	2	2	4	6
97-98—Rimouski	QMJHL	70	41	69	110	135	...	...	...	18	10	26	36	49
98-99—Johnstown.................	ECHL	24	8	12	20	29	...	...	...	—	—	—	—	—
—Saint John	AHL	40	3	7	10	24	...	...	...	—	—	—	—	—
99-00—Saint John	AHL	14	2	3	5	10	...	...	...	—	—	—	—	—
—Johnstown.................	ECHL	54	17	26	43	104	...	...	...	7	3	3	6	8
00-01—Saint John	AHL	76	19	36	55	36	...	...	...	19	7	9	16	14
01-02—Syracuse	AHL	73	23	38	61	70	...	...	...	10	1	5	6	12
—Columbus	NHL	2	1	0	1	0	-2	0	0	—	—	—	—	—
02-03—Syracuse	AHL	28	7	14	21	30	...	...	...	—	—	—	—	—
—Columbus	NHL	53	4	13	17	34	-9	3	0	—	—	—	—	—
NHL Totals (2 years)...........		55	5	13	18	34	-11	3	0					

WALSH, TOM   D   SHARKS

PERSONAL: Born April 22, 1983, in Arlington, Mass. ... 6-0/190. ... Shoots left.

TRANSACTIONS/CAREER NOTES: Selected by San Jose Sharks in fifth round (fifth Sharks pick, 163rd overall) of NHL entry draft (June 23, 2002).

		REGULAR SEASON								PLAYOFFS				
Season Team	League	Gms.	G	A	Pts.	PIM	+/-	PP	SH	Gms.	G	A	Pts.	PIM
01-02—Deerfield Academy......	USHS (East)	21	3	18	21	8	...	...	...	—	—	—	—	—
02-03—Harvard University......	ECAC	32	1	6	7	30	...	...	...	—	—	—	—	—

WALZ, WES   C   WILD

PERSONAL: Born May 15, 1970, in Calgary ... 5-10/180. ... Shoots right.

TRANSACTIONS/CAREER NOTES: Selected by Boston Bruins in third round (third Bruins pick, 57th overall) of NHL entry draft (June 17, 1989). ... Traded by Bruins with D Garry Galley and future considerations to Philadelphia Flyers for D Gord Murphy, RW Brian Dobbin and third-round pick (LW Sergei Zholtok) in 1992 draft (January 2, 1992). ... Signed as free agent by Calgary Flames (August 31, 1993). ... Strained hip (February 26, 1995); missed one game. ... Signed as free agent by Detroit Red Wings (August 11, 1995). ... Signed as free agent by Minnesota Wild (June 28, 2000). ... Sprained ankle (October 7, 2001); missed eight games. ... Bruised left shoulder (February 25, 2002); missed 10 games.

W

Season Team	League	Gms.	G	A	Pts.	PIM	+/-	PP	SH	Gms.	G	A	Pts.	PIM
87-88—Prince Albert.............	WHL	1	1	1	2	0	...	...	...	—	—	—	—	—
88-89—Lethbridge	WHL	63	29	75	104	32	...	...	...	8	1	5	6	6
89-90—Boston	NHL	2	1	1	2	0	-1	1	0	—	—	—	—	—
—Lethbridge	WHL	56	54	86	140	69	...	...	...	19	13	*24	†37	33
90-91—Maine	AHL	20	8	12	20	19	...	...	...	2	0	0	0	21
—Boston	NHL	56	8	8	16	32	-14	1	0	2	0	0	0	0
91-92—Boston	NHL	15	0	3	3	12	-3	0	0	—	—	—	—	—
—Maine........................	AHL	21	13	11	24	38	...	...	...	—	—	—	—	—
—Hershey	AHL	41	13	28	41	37	...	...	...	6	1	2	3	0
—Philadelphia	NHL	2	1	0	1	0	1	0	0	—	—	—	—	—
92-93—Hershey	AHL	78	35	45	80	106	...	...	...	—	—	—	—	—
93-94—Calgary	NHL	53	11	27	38	16	20	1	0	6	3	0	3	2
—Saint John	AHL	15	6	6	12	14	...	...	...	—	—	—	—	—
94-95—Calgary	NHL	39	6	12	18	11	7	4	0	1	0	0	0	0
95-96—Adirondack	AHL	38	20	35	55	58	...	...	...	—	—	—	—	—
—Detroit.......................	NHL	2	0	0	0	0	0	0	0	—	—	—	—	—
96-97—Zug	Switzerland	41	24	22	46	67	...	...	...	—	—	—	—	—
97-98—Zug	Switzerland	38	18	34	52	32	...	...	...	20	16	12	28	18
98-99—Zug	Switzerland	42	22	27	49	75	...	...	...	10	3	9	12	2
99-00—Long Beach.................	IHL	6	4	3	7	8	...	...	...	—	—	—	—	—
—Lugano	Switzerland	13	7	11	18	14	...	...	...	5	3	4	7	4
00-01—Minnesota..................	NHL	82	18	12	30	37	-8	0	7	—	—	—	—	—
01-02—Minnesota..................	NHL	64	10	20	30	43	0	0	2	—	—	—	—	—
02-03—Minnesota..................	NHL	80	13	19	32	63	11	0	0	18	7	6	13	14
NHL Totals (9 years)...........		395	68	102	170	214	13	7	9	27	10	6	16	16

WANVIG, KYLE RW WILD

PERSONAL: Born January 29, 1981, in Calgary ... 6-2/219. ... Shoots right.
TRANSACTIONS/CAREER NOTES: Selected by Boston Bruins in third round (third Bruins pick, 89th overall) of NHL entry draft (June 26, 1999). ... Returned to draft pool by Bruins and selected by Minnesota Wild in second round (second Wild pick, 36th overall) of NHL entry draft (June 23, 2001).

		REGULAR SEASON								PLAYOFFS				
Season Team	League	Gms.	G	A	Pts.	PIM	+/-	PP	SH	Gms.	G	A	Pts.	PIM
97-98—Edmonton..................	WHL	62	17	12	29	69	...	...	...	—	—	—	—	—
98-99—Kootenay...................	WHL	71	12	20	32	119	...	...	...	7	1	3	4	18
99-00—Kootenay...................	WHL	6	2	2	4	12	...	...	...	—	—	—	—	—
—Red Deer...................	WHL	58	21	18	39	123	...	...	...	4	1	0	1	4
00-01—Red Deer...................	WHL	69	55	46	101	202	...	...	...	22	10	12	22	47
01-02—Houston	AHL	34	6	7	13	43	...	...	...	9	0	1	1	23
02-03—Houston	AHL	57	13	16	29	137	...	...	...	21	6	4	10	27
—Minnesota..................	NHL	7	1	0	1	13	0	0	0	—	—	—	—	—
NHL Totals (1 year).............		7	1	0	1	13	0	0	0					

WARD, AARON D HURRICANES

PERSONAL: Born January 17, 1973, in Windsor, Ont. ... 6-2/225. ... Shoots right. ... Full Name: Aaron Christian Ward.
TRANSACTIONS/CAREER NOTES: Selected by Winnipeg Jets in first round (first Jets pick, fifth overall) of NHL entry draft (June 22, 1991). ... Traded by Jets with fourth-round pick (D John Jakopin) in 1993 draft and future considerations to Detroit Red Wings for RW Paul Ysebaert (June 11, 1993); Red Wings acquired RW Alan Kerr to complete deal (June 18, 1993). ... Suffered bronchitis (December 22, 1996); missed three games. ... Suffered from the flu (October 26, 1997); missed two games. ... Bruised knee (November 26, 1997); missed one game. ... Fractured right foot (December 3, 1997); missed 19 games. ... Sprained shoulder (February 7, 1998); missed two games. ... Strained rotator cuff (November 21, 1998); missed two games. ... Injured ribs (October 22, 1999); missed seven games. ... Suffered injury (December 4, 1999); missed four games. ... Injured shoulder (January 22, 2000); missed final 35 games of regular season. ... Suffered from the flu (January 7, 2001); missed two games. ... Traded by Red Wings to Carolina Hurricanes for second-round pick (C Jiri Hudler) in 2002 draft (July 9, 2001). ... Suffered from the flu (December 12, 2001); missed one game. ... Injured arm (March 8, 2002); missed one game.

		REGULAR SEASON								PLAYOFFS				
Season Team	League	Gms.	G	A	Pts.	PIM	+/-	PP	SH	Gms.	G	A	Pts.	PIM
88-89—Nepean	COJHL	56	2	17	19	44	...	...	...	—	—	—	—	—
89-90—Nepean	COJHL	52	6	33	39	85	...	...	...	—	—	—	—	—
90-91—Univ. of Michigan.......	CCHA	46	8	11	19	126	...	...	...	—	—	—	—	—
91-92—Univ. of Michigan.......	CCHA	42	7	12	19	64	...	...	...	—	—	—	—	—
92-93—Univ. of Michigan.......	CCHA	30	5	8	13	73	...	...	...	—	—	—	—	—
—Canadian nat'l team	Int'l	4	0	0	0	8	...	...	...	—	—	—	—	—
93-94—Detroit	NHL	5	1	0	1	4	2	0	0	—	—	—	—	—
—Adirondack	AHL	58	4	12	16	87	...	...	...	9	2	6	8	6
94-95—Adirondack	AHL	76	11	24	35	87	...	...	...	4	0	1	1	0
—Detroit.......................	NHL	1	0	1	1	2	1	0	0	—	—	—	—	—
95-96—Adirondack	AHL	74	5	10	15	133	...	...	...	3	0	0	0	6
96-97—Detroit	NHL	49	2	5	7	52	-9	0	0	19	0	0	0	17
97-98—Detroit	NHL	52	5	5	10	47	-1	0	0	—	—	—	—	—
98-99—Detroit	NHL	60	3	8	11	52	-5	0	0	8	0	1	1	8
99-00—Detroit	NHL	36	1	3	4	24	-4	0	0	3	0	0	0	0
00-01—Detroit	NHL	73	4	5	9	57	-4	0	0	—	—	—	—	—
01-02—Carolina	NHL	79	3	11	14	74	0	0	0	23	1	1	2	22
02-03—Carolina	NHL	77	3	6	9	90	-23	0	0	—	—	—	—	—
NHL Totals (9 years)...........		432	22	44	66	402	-43	0	0	53	1	2	3	47

W

PERSONAL: Born February 29, 1984, in Sherwood Park, Alta. ... 6-0/176. ... Catches left.
TRANSACTIONS/CAREER NOTES: Selected by Carolina Hurricanes in first round (first Hurricanes pick, 25th overall) of NHL entry draft (June 22, 2002).

		REGULAR SEASON									PLAYOFFS						
Season Team	League	Gms.	Min	W	L	T	GA	SO	Avg.	SV%	Gms.	Min.	W	L	GA SO	Avg.	SV%
00-01—Red Deer	WHL	1	60	1	0	0	0	1	...	—	—	—	—	—	— —	—	—
01-02—Red Deer	WHL	46	2694	30	11	4	102	1	*2.27	—	*23	*1502	14	*9	*53 †2	2.12	—
02-03—Red Deer	WHL	57	3368	40	13	3	118	5	2.10	—	—	—	—	—	— —	—	—

PERSONAL: Born September 23, 1968, in Leduc, Alta. ... 6-0/200. ... Shoots right. ... Full Name: Dixon M. Ward Jr.
TRANSACTIONS/CAREER NOTES: Selected by Vancouver Canucks in seventh round (sixth Canucks pick, 128th overall) of NHL entry draft (June 11, 1988). ... Sprained ankle (March 14, 1993); missed four games. ... Suspended three games and fined $500 by NHL for checking from behind (October 15, 1993). ... Traded by Canucks to Los Angeles Kings for C Jimmy Carson (January 8, 1994). ... Traded by Kings with C Guy Leveque, RW Shayne Toporowski and C Kelly Fairchild to Toronto Maple Leafs for LW Eric Lacroix, D Chris Snell and fourth-round pick (C Eric Belanger) in 1996 draft (October 3, 1994). ... Signed as free agent by Buffalo Sabres (August 24, 1995). ... Bruised sternum (April 10, 1999); missed two games. ... Injured neck (November 4, 1999); missed three games. ... Signed as free agent by Boston Bruins (November 3, 2000). ... Fractured foot (December 30, 2000); missed six games. ... Signed as free agent by New York Rangers (October 1, 2002).
STATISTICAL PLATEAUS: Three-goal games: 1998-99 (1).

		REGULAR SEASON								PLAYOFFS				
Season Team	League	Gms.	G	A	Pts.	PIM	+/-	PP	SH	Gms.	G	A	Pts.	PIM
86-87—Red Deer	AJHL	59	46	40	86	153	...	...	...	—	—	—	—	—
87-88—Red Deer	AJHL	51	60	71	131	167	...	...	...	—	—	—	—	—
88-89—Univ. of North Dakota	WCHA	37	8	9	17	26	...	...	...	—	—	—	—	—
89-90—Univ. of North Dakota	WCHA	45	35	34	69	44	...	...	...	—	—	—	—	—
90-91—Univ. of North Dakota	WCHA	43	34	35	69	84	...	...	...	—	—	—	—	—
91-92—Univ. of North Dakota	WCHA	38	33	31	64	90	...	...	...	—	—	—	—	—
92-93—Vancouver	NHL	70	22	30	52	82	34	4	1	9	2	3	5	0
93-94—Vancouver	NHL	33	6	1	7	37	-14	2	0	—	—	—	—	—
—Los Angeles	NHL	34	6	2	8	45	-8	2	0	—	—	—	—	—
94-95—Toronto	NHL	22	0	3	3	31	-4	0	0	—	—	—	—	—
—St. John's	AHL	6	3	3	6	19	...	...	...	—	—	—	—	—
—Detroit	IHL	7	3	6	9	7	...	...	...	5	3	0	3	7
95-96—Rochester	AHL	71	38	56	94	74	...	...	...	19	11	*24	*35	8
—Buffalo	NHL	8	2	2	4	6	1	0	0	—	—	—	—	—
96-97—Buffalo	NHL	79	13	32	45	36	17	1	2	12	2	3	5	6
97-98—Buffalo	NHL	71	10	13	23	42	9	0	2	15	3	8	11	6
98-99—Buffalo	NHL	78	20	24	44	44	10	2	1	21	7	5	12	32
99-00—Buffalo	NHL	71	11	9	20	41	1	1	2	5	0	1	1	2
00-01—Boston	NHL	63	5	13	18	65	-1	0	0	—	—	—	—	—
01-02—SC Langnau	Switzerland	23	8	19	27	38	...	...	...	9	3	6	9	2
02-03—Hartford	AHL	67	23	41	64	108	...	...	...	—	—	—	—	—
—New York Rangers	NHL	8	0	0	0	2	-2	0	0	—	—	—	—	—
NHL Totals (10 years)		537	95	129	224	431	43	12	8	62	14	20	34	46

PERSONAL: Born January 16, 1979, in Chapleau, Ont. ... 6-3/197. ... Shoots right.
TRANSACTIONS/CAREER NOTES: Selected by Montreal Canadiens in first round (first Canadiens pick, 11th overall) of NHL entry draft (June 21, 1997). ... Fractured cheekbone (February 10, 2000); missed seven games. ... Injured knee (January 12, 2001); missed remainder of season.

		REGULAR SEASON								PLAYOFFS				
Season Team	League	Gms.	G	A	Pts.	PIM	+/-	PP	SH	Gms.	G	A	Pts.	PIM
94-95—Oshawa	Tier II Jr. A	47	30	31	61	75	...	...	...	—	—	—	—	—
95-96—Niagara Falls	OHL	64	15	35	50	139	...	...	...	10	6	4	10	23
96-97—Erie	OHL	58	25	39	64	137	...	...	...	5	1	2	3	2
97-98—Erie	OHL	21	7	9	16	42	...	...	...	—	—	—	—	—
—Windsor	OHL	26	19	27	46	34	...	...	...	—	—	—	—	—
—Fredericton	AHL	7	1	0	1	2	...	...	...	1	0	0	0	2
98-99—Windsor	OHL	12	8	11	19	25	...	...	...	—	—	—	—	—
—Plymouth	OHL	23	14	13	27	28	...	...	...	11	6	8	14	12
—Fredericton	AHL	—	—	—	—	—	...	...	...	10	4	2	6	22
99-00—Quebec	AHL	40	14	12	26	30	...	...	...	3	2	1	3	4
—Montreal	NHL	32	2	1	3	10	-1	1	0	—	—	—	—	—
00-01—Quebec	AHL	23	7	12	19	69	...	...	...	—	—	—	—	—
—Montreal	NHL	12	0	0	0	12	3	0	0	—	—	—	—	—
01-02—Quebec	AHL	78	24	33	57	128	...	...	...	3	0	0	0	2
02-03—Hamilton	AHL	69	31	41	72	78	...	...	...	—	—	—	—	—
—Montreal	NHL	8	3	2	5	0	3	0	0	—	—	—	—	—
NHL Totals (3 years)		52	5	3	8	22	5	1	0					

W

WARD, LANCE — D — MIGHTY DUCKS

PERSONAL: Born June 2, 1978, in Lloydminster, Alta. ... 6-3/210. ... Shoots left.

TRANSACTIONS/CAREER NOTES: Selected by New Jersey Devils in first round (first Devils pick, 10th overall) of NHL entry draft (June 22, 1996). ... Returned to draft pool by Devils and selected by Florida Panthers in third round (third Panthers pick, 63rd overall) of NHL entry draft (June 27, 1998). ... Injured back (February 28, 2001); missed 17 games. ... Suffered concussion (March 13, 2002); missed 13 games. ... Suspended one game by NHL for unsportsmanlike conduct (October 21, 2002). ... Traded by Panthers with D Sandis Ozolinsh to Mighty Ducks of Anaheim for C Matt Cullen, D Pavel Trnka and fourth-round pick in 2003 (January 30, 2003). ... Re-signed by Mighty Ducks (July 22, 2003).

		REGULAR SEASON								PLAYOFFS				
Season Team	League	Gms.	G	A	Pts.	PIM	+/-	PP	SH	Gms.	G	A	Pts.	PIM
93-94—Medicine Hat	WHL	68	1	4	5	166	...	...	...	3	0	0	0	2
94-95—Red Deer	WHL	28	0	0	0	57	...	...	...	—	—	—	—	—
95-96—Red Deer	WHL	72	4	13	17	127	...	...	...	10	0	4	4	10
96-97—Red Deer	WHL	70	5	34	39	229	...	...	...	16	0	3	3	36
97-98—Red Deer	WHL	71	8	25	33	233	...	...	...	5	0	0	0	16
98-99—Miami	ECHL	6	1	0	1	12	...	...	...	—	—	—	—	—
—Fort Wayne	IHL	13	0	2	2	28	...	...	...	—	—	—	—	—
—New Haven	AHL	43	2	5	7	51	...	...	...	—	—	—	—	—
99-00—Louisville	AHL	80	4	16	20	190	...	...	...	4	0	0	0	6
00-01—Louisville	AHL	35	3	2	5	78	...	...	...	—	—	—	—	—
—Florida	NHL	30	0	2	2	45	-3	0	0	—	—	—	—	—
01-02—Florida	NHL	68	1	4	5	131	-20	0	0	—	—	—	—	—
02-03—Florida	NHL	36	3	1	4	78	-4	0	0	—	—	—	—	—
—Anaheim	NHL	29	0	1	1	43	-2	0	0	—	—	—	—	—
NHL Totals (3 years)		163	4	8	12	297	-29	0	0					

WARRENER, RHETT — D — FLAMES

PERSONAL: Born January 27, 1976, in Shaunavon, Sask. ... 6-2/215. ... Shoots right. ... Name pronounced REHT WAHR-uh-nuhr.

TRANSACTIONS/CAREER NOTES: Selected by Florida Panthers in second round (second Panthers pick, 27th overall) of NHL entry draft (June 28, 1994). ... Strained groin (October 20, 1996); missed four games. ... Reinjured groin (November 11, 1996); missed two games. ... Reinjured groin (December 22, 1996); missed 10 games. ... Strained groin (November 2, 1998); missed 12 games. ... Traded by Panthers with fifth-round pick (G Ryan Miller) in 1999 draft to Buffalo Sabres for D Mike Wilson (March 23, 1999). ... Injured shoulder (October 30, 1999); missed two games. ... Strained hip muscle (January 1, 2000); missed four games. ... Injured groin (February 21, 2000); missed eight games. ... Suffered concussion (November 17, 2000); missed five games. ... Injured groin (October 26, 2001); missed 14 games. ... Injured wrist (January 8, 2002); missed one game. ... Suspended two games by NHL for receiving third instigator penalty in one season (March 29, 2002). ... Traded by Sabres to Calgary Flames with Steve Reinprecht for Steve Begin and Chris Drury (July 2, 2003).

		REGULAR SEASON								PLAYOFFS				
Season Team	League	Gms.	G	A	Pts.	PIM	+/-	PP	SH	Gms.	G	A	Pts.	PIM
91-92—Saskatoon	WHL	2	0	0	0	0	...	...	...	—	—	—	—	—
92-93—Saskatoon	WHL	68	2	17	19	100	...	...	...	9	0	0	0	14
93-94—Saskatoon	WHL	61	7	19	26	131	...	...	...	16	0	5	5	33
94-95—Saskatoon	WHL	66	13	26	39	137	...	...	...	10	0	3	3	6
95-96—Carolina	AHL	9	0	0	0	4	...	...	...	—	—	—	—	—
—Florida	NHL	28	0	3	3	46	4	0	0	21	0	3	3	10
96-97—Florida	NHL	62	4	9	13	88	20	1	0	5	0	0	0	0
97-98—Florida	NHL	79	0	4	4	99	-16	0	0	—	—	—	—	—
98-99—Florida	NHL	48	0	7	7	64	-1	0	0	—	—	—	—	—
—Buffalo	NHL	13	1	0	1	20	3	0	0	20	1	3	4	32
99-00—Buffalo	NHL	61	0	3	3	89	18	0	0	5	0	0	0	2
00-01—Buffalo	NHL	77	3	16	19	78	10	0	0	13	0	2	2	4
01-02—Buffalo	NHL	65	5	5	10	113	15	0	0	—	—	—	—	—
02-03—Buffalo	NHL	50	0	9	9	63	1	0	0	—	—	—	—	—
NHL Totals (8 years)		483	13	56	69	660	54	1	0	64	1	8	9	48

WARRINER, TODD — LW

PERSONAL: Born January 3, 1974, in Blenheim, Ont. ... 6-2/209. ... Shoots left. ... Name pronounced WAHR-ih-nuhr.

TRANSACTIONS/CAREER NOTES: Selected by Quebec Nordiques in first round (first Nordiques pick, fourth overall) of NHL entry draft (June 20, 1992). ... Traded by Nordiques with C Mats Sundin, D Garth Butcher and first-round pick (traded to Washington) in 1994 draft to Toronto Maple Leafs for LW Wendel Clark, D Sylvain Lefebvre, RW Landon Wilson and first-round pick (D Jeffrey Kealty) in 1994 draft (June 28, 1994). ... Suffered hip pointer (December 7, 1995); missed eight games. ... Injured hip flexor (October 3, 1996); missed one game. ... Injured hip flexor (November 19, 1996); missed four games. ... Suffered from the flu (April 2, 1997); missed one game. ... Sprained shoulder (October 15, 1997); missed three games. ... Bruised thigh (November 17, 1997); missed 27 games. ... Sprained knee (March 4, 1999); missed four games. ... Traded by Maple Leafs to Tampa Bay Lightning for third-round pick (G Mikael Tellqvist) in 2000 draft (November 29, 1999). ... Injured hip (January 15, 2000); missed two games. ... Strained groin (March 8, 2000); missed one game. ... Suffered from the flu (November 10, 2000); missed one game. ... Strained groin (March 4, 2000); missed two games. ... Strained medial collateral ligament in knee (March 8, 2001); missed final 14 games of season. ... Traded by Lightning to Phoenix Coyotes for C Yuha Ylonen (June 18, 2001). ... Sprained knee (October 11, 2001); missed five games. ... Traded by Coyotes with C Trevor Letowski, RW Tyler Bouck and third-round pick in 2003 draft to Vancouver Canucks for D Drake Berehowsky and C Denis Pederson (December 28, 2001). ... Traded by Canucks to Philadelphia Flyers for conditional pick in 2004 draft (February 5, 2003). ... Claimed on waivers by Nashville Predators (March 11, 2003).

W

Season Team	League	REGULAR SEASON								PLAYOFFS				
		Gms.	G	A	Pts.	PIM	+/-	PP	SH	Gms.	G	A	Pts.	PIM
88-89—Blenheim Jr. C	OHA	10	1	4	5	0	...	...	...	—	—	—	—	—
89-90—Chatham Jr. B	OHA	40	24	21	45	12	...	...	...	—	—	—	—	—
90-91—Windsor	OHL	57	36	28	64	26	...	...	...	11	5	6	11	12
91-92—Windsor	OHL	50	41	42	83	66	...	...	...	7	5	4	9	6
92-93—Windsor	OHL	23	13	21	34	29	...	...	...	—	—	—	—	—
—Kitchener	OHL	32	19	24	43	35	...	...	...	7	5	14	19	14
93-94—Canadian nat'l team	Int'l	50	11	20	31	33	...	...	...	—	—	—	—	—
—Can. Olympic team	Int'l	4	1	1	2	0	...	...	...	—	—	—	—	—
—Kitchener	OHL	—	—	—	—	—	—	—	—	1	0	1	1	0
—Cornwall	AHL	—	—	—	—	—	—	—	—	10	1	4	5	4
94-95—St. John's	AHL	46	8	10	18	22	...	...	...	4	1	0	1	2
—Toronto	NHL	5	0	0	0	0	-3	0	0	—	—	—	—	—
95-96—St. John's	AHL	11	5	6	11	16	...	...	...	—	—	—	—	—
—Toronto	NHL	57	7	8	15	26	-11	1	0	6	1	1	2	2
96-97—Toronto	NHL	75	12	21	33	41	-3	2	2	—	—	—	—	—
97-98—Toronto	NHL	45	5	8	13	20	5	0	0	—	—	—	—	—
98-99—Toronto	NHL	53	9	10	19	28	-6	1	0	9	0	0	0	0
99-00—Toronto	NHL	18	3	1	4	2	6	0	0	—	—	—	—	—
—Tampa Bay	NHL	55	11	13	24	34	-14	3	1	—	—	—	—	—
00-01—Tampa Bay	NHL	64	10	11	21	46	-13	3	2	—	—	—	—	—
01-02—Phoenix	NHL	18	0	3	3	8	-3	0	0	—	—	—	—	—
—Springfield	AHL	2	0	0	0	0	...	...	...	—	—	—	—	—
—Manitoba	AHL	30	7	13	20	32	...	...	...	—	—	—	—	—
—Vancouver	NHL	14	2	4	6	12	4	0	0	6	1	0	1	2
02-03—Vancouver	NHL	30	4	6	10	22	0	0	0	—	—	—	—	—
—Philadelphia	NHL	13	2	3	5	6	2	0	0	—	—	—	—	—
—Nashville	NHL	6	0	1	1	4	-1	0	0	—	—	—	—	—
NHL Totals (9 years)		453	65	89	154	249	-37	10	5	21	2	1	3	6

WATSON, DAN — D

PERSONAL: Born October 5, 1979, in Glencoe, Ont. ... 6-2/221. ... Shoots left.
TRANSACTIONS/CAREER NOTES: Signed as non-drafted free agent by Columbus Blue Jackets (May 16, 2000).

Season Team	League	REGULAR SEASON								PLAYOFFS				
		Gms.	G	A	Pts.	PIM	+/-	PP	SH	Gms.	G	A	Pts.	PIM
96-97—Sarnia	OHL	10	0	2	2	7	...	...	...	—	—	—	—	—
97-98—Sarnia	OHL	66	6	15	21	19	...	...	...	5	0	1	1	4
98-99—Sarnia	OHL	68	2	18	20	27	...	...	...	6	0	0	0	4
99-00—Sarnia	OHL	68	1	15	16	40	...	...	...	7	0	0	0	4
00-01—Syracuse	AHL	59	3	4	7	12	...	...	...	4	0	0	0	6
01-02—Syracuse	AHL	53	1	3	4	25	...	...	...	—	—	—	—	—
—Dayton	ECHL	4	0	0	0	6	...	...	...	—	—	—	—	—
02-03—Syracuse	AHL	50	2	7	9	36	...	...	...	—	—	—	—	—
—Cleveland	AHL	17	2	4	6	12	...	...	...	—	—	—	—	—

WATSON, GREG — C — SENATORS

PERSONAL: Born March 2, 1983, in Eastend, Sask. ... 6-1/177. ... Shoots left.
TRANSACTIONS/CAREER NOTES: Selected by Florida Panthers in second round (third Panthers pick, 34th overall) of NHL entry draft (June 23, 2001). ... Traded by Panthers with G Billy Thompson to Ottawa Senators for G Jani Hurme (October 1, 2002). ... Re-signed by Ottawa (June 3, 2003).

Season Team	League	REGULAR SEASON								PLAYOFFS				
		Gms.	G	A	Pts.	PIM	+/-	PP	SH	Gms.	G	A	Pts.	PIM
98-99—Prince Albert	WHL	2	0	0	0	5	...	...	...	—	—	—	—	—
99-00—Prince Albert	WHL	67	10	5	15	63	...	...	...	6	0	2	2	2
00-01—Prince Albert	WHL	71	22	28	50	72	...	...	...	—	—	—	—	—
01-02—Prince Albert	WHL	51	22	30	52	88	...	...	...	—	—	—	—	—
02-03—Brandon	WHL	69	17	29	46	95	...	...	...	—	—	—	—	—

WATT, MIKE — LW/C

PERSONAL: Born March 31, 1976, in Seaforth, Ont. ... 6-2/212. ... Shoots left.
TRANSACTIONS/CAREER NOTES: Selected by Edmonton Oilers in second round (third Oilers pick, 32nd overall) of NHL entry draft (June 28, 1994). ... Traded by Oilers to New York Islanders for G Eric Fichaud (June 18, 1998). ... Suffered charley horse (October 24, 1998); missed one game. ... Strained hand (November 6, 1999); missed three games. ... Claimed on waivers by Nashville Predators (May 23, 2000). ... Traded by Predators to Philadelphia Flyers for D Mikhail Chernov (May 24, 2001). ... Signed as free agent by Carolina Hurricanes (August 9, 2002).

Season Team	League	REGULAR SEASON								PLAYOFFS				
		Gms.	G	A	Pts.	PIM	+/-	PP	SH	Gms.	G	A	Pts.	PIM
91-92—Stratford Jr. B	OHA	46	5	26	31	...	...	...	...	—	—	—	—	—
92-93—Stratford Jr. B	OHA	45	20	35	55	100	...	...	...	—	—	—	—	—
93-94—Stratford Jr. B	OHA	48	34	34	68	165	...	...	...	—	—	—	—	—
94-95—Michigan State	CCHA	39	12	6	18	64	...	...	...	—	—	—	—	—
95-96—Michigan State	CCHA	37	17	22	39	60	...	...	...	—	—	—	—	—
96-97—Michigan State	CCHA	39	24	17	41	109	...	...	...	—	—	—	—	—
97-98—Hamilton	AHL	63	24	25	49	65	...	...	...	9	2	2	4	8
—Edmonton	NHL	14	1	2	3	4	-4	0	0	—	—	—	—	—

W

Season Team	League	REGULAR SEASON								PLAYOFFS				
		Gms.	G	A	Pts.	PIM	+/-	PP	SH	Gms.	G	A	Pts.	PIM
98-99—New York Islanders.....	NHL	75	8	17	25	12	-2	0	0	—	—	—	—	—
99-00—New York Islanders.....	NHL	45	5	6	11	17	-8	0	1	—	—	—	—	—
—Lowell	AHL	16	6	11	17	6	...	...	...	7	1	1	2	4
00-01—Milwaukee................	IHL	60	20	20	40	48	...	...	...	5	1	2	3	6
—Nashville	NHL	18	1	1	2	8	-2	0	0	—	—	—	—	—
01-02—Philadelphia	AHL	53	11	13	24	38	...	...	...	5	2	1	3	6
02-03—Lowell	AHL	61	9	14	23	35	...	...	...	—	—	—	—	—
—Carolina	NHL	5	0	0	0	0	-1	0	0	—	—	—	—	—
NHL Totals (5 years)...........		157	15	26	41	41	-17	0	1					

WEAVER, MIKE — D — THRASHERS

PERSONAL: Born May 2, 1978, in Bramalea, Ont. ... 5-9/185. ... Shoots right.
TRANSACTIONS/CAREER NOTES: Signed as non-drafted free agent by Atlanta Thrashers (June 15, 2000).

Season Team	League	REGULAR SEASON								PLAYOFFS				
		Gms.	G	A	Pts.	PIM	+/-	PP	SH	Gms.	G	A	Pts.	PIM
96-97—Michigan State...........	CCHA	39	0	7	7	46	...	...	...	—	—	—	—	—
97-98—Michigan State...........	CCHA	44	4	22	26	68	...	...	...	—	—	—	—	—
98-99—Michigan State...........	CCHA	42	1	6	7	54	...	...	...	—	—	—	—	—
99-00—Michigan State...........	CCHA	37	0	8	8	34	...	...	...	—	—	—	—	—
00-01—Orlando....................	IHL	68	0	8	8	34	...	...	...	16	0	2	2	8
01-02—Chicago...................	AHL	58	2	8	10	67	...	...	...	25	1	3	4	21
—Atlanta	NHL	16	0	1	1	10	0	0	0	—	—	—	—	—
02-03—Chicago...................	AHL	33	2	2	4	32	...	...	...	—	—	—	—	—
—Atlanta	NHL	40	0	5	5	20	-5	0	0	—	—	—	—	—
NHL Totals (2 years)...........		56	0	6	6	30	-5	0	0					

WEBB, STEVE — RW

PERSONAL: Born April 30, 1975, in Peterborough, Ont. ... 6-0/218. ... Shoots right.
TRANSACTIONS/CAREER NOTES: Selected by Buffalo Sabres in seventh round (eighth Sabres pick, 176th overall) of NHL entry draft (June 29, 1994). ... Signed as free agent by New York Islanders (October 14, 1996). ... Injured lower back (October 27, 1999); missed one game. ... Injured back (November 4, 1999); missed four games. ... Suffered from the flu (April 9, 2000); missed final game of season. ... Strained back (November 7, 2000); missed two games. ... Strained left knee (November 18, 2000); missed 11 games. ... Reinjured knee (December 12, 2000); missed 16 games. ... Reinjured knee (January 21, 2001); missed 22 games. ... Injured hip (October 30, 2001); missed one game. ... Injured hand (January 6, 2002); missed 17 games. ... Suffered concussion (March 27, 2002); missed one game.

Season Team	League	REGULAR SEASON								PLAYOFFS				
		Gms.	G	A	Pts.	PIM	+/-	PP	SH	Gms.	G	A	Pts.	PIM
91-92—Peterborough..............	Jr. B	37	9	9	18	195	...	...	...	—	—	—	—	—
92-93—Windsor....................	OHL	63	14	25	39	181	...	...	...	—	—	—	—	—
93-94—Windsor....................	OHL	33	6	15	21	117	...	...	...	—	—	—	—	—
—Peterborough..............	OHL	2	0	1	1	9	...	...	...	—	—	—	—	—
94-95—Peterborough..............	OHL	42	8	16	24	109	...	...	...	11	3	3	6	22
95-96—Muskegon..................	Col.HL	58	18	24	42	263	...	...	...	5	1	2	3	22
—Detroit....................	IHL	4	0	0	0	24	...	...	...	—	—	—	—	—
96-97—Kentucky..................	AHL	25	6	6	12	103	...	...	...	2	0	0	0	19
—New York Islanders.....	NHL	41	1	4	5	144	-10	1	0	—	—	—	—	—
97-98—Kentucky..................	AHL	37	5	13	18	139	...	...	...	3	0	1	1	10
—New York Islanders.....	NHL	20	0	0	0	35	-2	0	0	—	—	—	—	—
98-99—Lowell	AHL	23	2	4	6	80	...	...	...	—	—	—	—	—
—New York Islanders.....	NHL	45	0	0	0	32	-10	0	0	—	—	—	—	—
99-00—New York Islanders.....	NHL	65	1	3	4	103	-4	0	0	—	—	—	—	—
00-01—New York Islanders.....	NHL	31	0	2	2	35	1	0	0	—	—	—	—	—
01-02—New York Islanders.....	NHL	60	2	4	6	104	0	0	0	7	0	0	0	12
02-03—New York Islanders.....	NHL	49	1	0	1	75	-5	0	0	5	0	0	0	10
NHL Totals (7 years)..........		311	5	13	18	528	-30	1	0	12	0	0	0	22

WEEKES, KEVIN — G — HURRICANES

PERSONAL: Born April 4, 1975, in Toronto. ... 6-0/195. ... Catches right. ... Name pronounced WEEKS.
TRANSACTIONS/CAREER NOTES: Selected by Florida Panthers in second round (second Panthers pick, 41st overall) of NHL entry draft (June 26, 1993). ... Sprained right knee (March 19, 1998); missed remainder of season. ... Traded by Panthers with D Ed Jovanovski, C Dave Gagner, C Mike Brown and first-round pick (C Nathan Smith) in 2000 draft to Vancouver Canucks for RW Pavel Bure, D Bret Hedican, D Brad Ference and third-round pick (RW Robert Fried) in 2000 draft (January 17, 1999). ... Injured knee (October 28, 1999); missed three games. ... Traded by Canucks with C Dave Scatchard and RW Bill Muckalt to New York Islanders for G Felix Potvin, second-(traded to Atlanta) and third-round (C Thatcher Bell) picks in 2000 draft (December 19, 1999). ... Sore neck (April 9, 2000); missed final game of season. ... Traded by Islanders with D Kristian Kudroc and second-round pick (traded to Phoenix) in 2001 draft to Tampa Bay Lightning for first-(LW Raffi Torres), fourth-(RW/LW Vladimir Gorbunov) and seventh-round (D Ryan Caldwell) picks in 2000 draft (June 24, 2000). ... Injured knee (December 2, 2000); missed three games. ... Strained groin (January 7, 2001); missed three games. ... Strained groin (April 4, 2001); missed final three games of season. ... Traded by Lightning to Carolina Hurricanes for RW Shane Willis and LW Craig Dingman (March 5, 2002). ... Re-signed by Hurricanes (June 8, 2003).

W

Season Team	League	REGULAR SEASON									PLAYOFFS							
		Gms.	Min	W	L	T	GA	SO	Avg.	SV%	Gms.	Min.	W	L	GA	SO	Avg.	SV%
91-92—Toronto St. Mikes	OJHL	35	1575	...	...	...	68	4	2.59	—	—	—	—	—	—	—	—	—
—St. Michael's	Tier II Jr. A	2	127	...	...	...	11	0	5.20	—	—	—	—	—	—	—	—	—
92-93—Owen Sound	OHL	29	1645	9	12	5	143	0	5.22	—	1	26	0	0	5	0	11.54	—
93-94—Owen Sound	OHL	34	1974	13	19	1	158	0	4.80	—	—	—	—	—	—	—	—	—
94-95—Ottawa	OHL	41	2266	13	23	4	154	1	4.08	—	—	—	—	—	—	—	—	—
95-96—Carolina.......................	AHL	60	3403	24	25	8	229	2	4.04	—	—	—	—	—	—	—	—	—
96-97—Carolina.......................	AHL	51	2899	17	†28	4	172	1	3.56	—	—	—	—	—	—	—	—	—
97-98—Fort Wayne	IHL	12	719	9	2	‡1	34	1	2.84	—	—	—	—	—	—	—	—	—
—Florida..........................	NHL	11	485	0	5	1	32	0	3.96	.870	—	—	—	—	—	—	—	—
98-99—Detroit.........................	IHL	33	1857	19	5	‡7	64	*4	*2.07	—	—	—	—	—	—	—	—	—
—Vancouver	NHL	11	532	0	8	1	34	0	3.83	.868	—	—	—	—	—	—	—	—
99-00—Vancouver	NHL	20	987	6	7	4	47	1	2.86	.898	—	—	—	—	—	—	—	—
—New York Islanders	NHL	36	2026	10	20	4	115	1	3.41	.902	—	—	—	—	—	—	—	—
00-01—Tampa Bay	NHL	61	3378	20	*33	3	177	4	3.14	.898	—	—	—	—	—	—	—	—
01-02—Tampa Bay	NHL	19	830	3	9	0	40	2	2.89	.915	—	—	—	—	—	—	—	—
—Carolina.......................	NHL	2	120	2	0	0	3	0	1.50	.927	8	408	3	2	11	2	1.62	.939
02-03—Carolina.......................	NHL	51	2965	14	24	9	126	5	2.55	.912	—	—	—	—	—	—	—	—
NHL Totals (6 years).............		211	11323	55	106	22	574	13	3.04	.902	8	408	3	2	11	2	1.62	.939

WEIGHT, DOUG   C   BLUES

PERSONAL: Born January 21, 1971, in Warren, Mich. ... 5-11/198. ... Shoots left. ... Full Name: Douglas Daniel Weight. ... Name pronounced WAYT.

TRANSACTIONS/CAREER NOTES: Selected by New York Rangers in second round (second Rangers pick, 34th overall) of NHL entry draft (June 16, 1990). ... Sprained elbow (October 14, 1991); missed three games. ... Damaged ligaments (January 11, 1991). ... Suspended four off-days and fined $500 by NHL for cross-checking (November 5, 1992). ... Traded by Rangers to Edmonton Oilers for LW Esa Tikkanen (March 17, 1993). ... Played in Europe during 1994-95 NHL lockout. ... Sprained ankle (February 15, 1997); missed one game. ... Injured ankle (February 21, 1997); missed one game. ... Sprained left shoulder (March 15, 1998); missed two games. ... Tore medial collateral ligament in right knee (October 28, 1998); missed 34 games. ... Fractured ribs (December 14, 1999); missed five games. ... Traded by Oilers with LW Michel Riesen to St. Louis Blues for C Marty Reasoner, C Jochen Hecht and D Jan Horacek (July 1, 2001). ... Sprained medial collateral ligament in knee and injured hip (February 28, 2002); missed 20 games.

STATISTICAL PLATEAUS: Three-goal games: 1995-96 (1).

Season Team	League	REGULAR SEASON							PLAYOFFS				
		Gms.	G	A	Pts.	PIM	+/-	PP	SH	Gms.	G	A	Pts.	PIM
88-89—Bloomfield	NAJHL	34	26	53	79	105	...	...	...	—	—	—	—	—
89-90—Lake Superior State	CCHA	46	21	48	69	44	...	...	...	—	—	—	—	—
90-91—Lake Superior State	CCHA	42	29	46	75	86	...	...	...	—	—	—	—	—
—New York Rangers	NHL	—	—	—	—	—	—	—	—	1	0	0	0	0
91-92—New York Rangers......	NHL	53	8	22	30	23	-3	0	0	7	2	2	4	0
—Binghamton	AHL	9	3	14	17	2	...	...	...	4	1	4	5	6
92-93—New York Rangers......	NHL	65	15	25	40	55	4	3	0	—	—	—	—	—
—Edmonton	NHL	13	2	6	8	10	-2	0	0	—	—	—	—	—
93-94—Edmonton	NHL	84	24	50	74	47	-22	4	1	—	—	—	—	—
94-95—Rosenheim	Germany	8	2	3	5	18	...	...	...	—	—	—	—	—
—Edmonton	NHL	48	7	33	40	69	-17	1	0	—	—	—	—	—
95-96—Edmonton	NHL	82	25	79	104	95	-19	9	0	—	—	—	—	—
96-97—Edmonton	NHL	80	21	61	82	80	1	4	0	12	3	8	11	8
97-98—Edmonton	NHL	79	26	44	70	69	1	9	0	12	2	7	9	14
—U.S. Olympic team......	Int'l	4	0	2	2	2	...	...	...	—	—	—	—	—
98-99—Edmonton	NHL	43	6	31	37	12	-8	1	0	4	1	1	2	15
99-00—Edmonton	NHL	77	21	51	72	54	6	3	1	5	3	2	5	4
00-01—Edmonton	NHL	82	25	65	90	91	12	8	0	6	1	5	6	17
01-02—St. Louis	NHL	61	15	34	49	40	20	3	0	10	1	1	2	4
—U.S. Olympic team......	Int'l	6	0	3	3	4	...	...	...	—	—	—	—	—
02-03—St. Louis	NHL	70	15	52	67	52	-6	7	0	7	5	8	13	2
NHL Totals (13 years).........		837	210	553	763	697	-33	52	2	64	18	34	52	64

WEINHANDL, MATTIAS   RW   ISLANDERS

PERSONAL: Born June 1, 1980, in Ljungby, Sweden ... 6-0/190. ... Shoots right.
TRANSACTIONS/CAREER NOTES: Selected by New York Islanders in third round (fifth Islanders pick, 78th overall) of NHL entry draft (June 26, 1999).

Season Team	League	REGULAR SEASON							PLAYOFFS				
		Gms.	G	A	Pts.	PIM	+/-	PP	SH	Gms.	G	A	Pts.	PIM
97-98—Troja-Ljungby..............	Sweden Dv. 2	29	4	2	6	10	...	...	...	—	—	—	—	—
98-99—Troja-Ljungby..............	Sweden Dv. 2	38	20	20	40	30	...	...	...	—	—	—	—	—
99-00—MoDo Ornskoldsvik	Sweden	32	15	9	24	6	...	...	...	13	5	3	8	8
00-01—MoDo Ornskoldsvik	Sweden	48	16	16	32	14	...	...	...	6	1	3	4	6
01-02—MoDo Ornskoldsvik	Sweden	50	18	16	34	10	...	...	...	14	4	*11	*15	4
02-03—Bridgeport....................	AHL	23	9	12	21	14	...	...	...	—	—	—	—	—
—New York Islanders.....	NHL	47	6	17	23	10	-2	1	0	—	—	—	—	—
NHL Totals (1 year).............		47	6	17	23	10	-2	1	0	—	—	—	—	—

W

WEINRICH, ERIC   D   FLYERS

PERSONAL: Born December 19, 1966, in Roanoke, Va. ... 6-1/215. ... Shoots left. ... Full Name: Eric John Weinrich. ... Name pronounced WIGHN-rihch.

TRANSACTIONS/CAREER NOTES: Selected by New Jersey Devils in second round (third Devils pick, 32nd overall) of NHL entry draft (June 15, 1985). ... Traded by Devils with G Sean Burke to Hartford Whalers for RW Bobby Holik, second-round pick (LW Jay Pandolfo) in 1993 draft and future considerations (August 28, 1992). ... Suffered concussion (November 25, 1992); missed two games. ... Sprained knee (September 22, 1993); missed five games. ... Injured right knee (October 5, 1993); missed five games. ... Traded with LW Patrick Poulin by Whalers to the Chicago Blackhawks for RW Steve Larmer and D Bryan Marchment (November 2, 1993). ... Fractured jaw (February 24, 1994); missed 17 games. ... Cut eye (November 1, 1995); missed three games. ... Cut thigh (December 31, 1996); missed one game. ... Traded by Blackhawks with G Jeff Hackett, D Alain Nasreddine and fourth-round pick (D Chris Dyment) in 1999 draft to Montreal Canadiens for G Jocelyn Thibault, D Dave Manson and D Brad Brown (November 16, 1998). ... Fractured foot (March 22, 2000); missed five games. ... Traded by Canadiens to Boston Bruins for D Patrick Traverse (February 21, 2001). ... Signed as free agent by Philadelphia Flyers (July 5, 2001). ... Strained left shoulder (October 30, 2001); missed two games.

		REGULAR SEASON								PLAYOFFS				
Season Team	League	Gms.	G	A	Pts.	PIM	+/-	PP	SH	Gms.	G	A	Pts.	PIM
83-84—North Yarmouth Acad.	Maine H.S.	17	23	33	56	...	...	...	...	—	—	—	—	—
84-85—North Yarmouth Acad.	Maine H.S.	20	6	21	27	...	...	...	...	—	—	—	—	—
85-86—Univ. of Maine	Hockey East	34	0	15	15	26	...	...	...	—	—	—	—	—
86-87—Univ. of Maine	Hockey East	41	12	32	44	59	...	...	...	—	—	—	—	—
87-88—Univ. of Maine	Hockey East	8	4	7	11	22	...	...	...	—	—	—	—	—
—U.S. national team	Int'l	39	3	9	12	24	...	...	...	—	—	—	—	—
—U.S. Olympic team......	Int'l	3	0	0	0	24	...	...	...	—	—	—	—	—
88-89—Utica	AHL	80	17	27	44	70	...	...	...	5	0	1	1	8
—New Jersey................	NHL	2	0	0	0	0	-1	0	0	—	—	—	—	—
89-90—Utica	AHL	57	12	48	60	38	...	...	...	—	—	—	—	—
—New Jersey................	NHL	19	2	7	9	11	1	1	0	6	1	3	4	17
90-91—New Jersey.............	NHL	76	4	34	38	48	10	1	0	7	1	2	3	6
91-92—New Jersey.............	NHL	76	7	25	32	55	10	5	0	7	0	2	2	4
92-93—Hartford..................	NHL	79	7	29	36	76	-11	0	2	—	—	—	—	—
93-94—Hartford..................	NHL	8	1	1	2	2	-5	1	0	—	—	—	—	—
—Chicago.....................	NHL	54	3	23	26	31	6	1	0	6	0	2	2	6
94-95—Chicago..................	NHL	48	3	10	13	33	1	1	0	16	1	5	6	4
95-96—Chicago..................	NHL	77	5	10	15	65	14	0	0	10	1	4	5	10
96-97—Chicago..................	NHL	81	7	25	32	62	19	1	0	6	0	1	1	4
97-98—Chicago..................	NHL	82	2	21	23	106	10	0	0	—	—	—	—	—
98-99—Chicago..................	NHL	14	1	3	4	12	-13	0	0	—	—	—	—	—
—Montreal	NHL	66	6	12	18	77	-12	4	0	—	—	—	—	—
99-00—Montreal	NHL	77	4	25	29	39	4	2	0	—	—	—	—	—
00-01—Montreal	NHL	60	6	19	25	34	-1	2	0	—	—	—	—	—
—Boston	NHL	22	1	5	6	10	-8	1	0	—	—	—	—	—
01-02—Philadelphia	NHL	80	4	20	24	26	27	0	0	5	0	0	0	4
02-03—Philadelphia	NHL	81	2	18	20	40	16	1	1	13	2	3	5	12
NHL Totals (15 years).........		1002	65	287	352	727	67	21	3	76	6	22	28	67

WEISS, STEPHEN   C   PANTHERS

PERSONAL: Born April 3, 1983, in Toronto ... 6-0/183. ... Shoots left.
TRANSACTIONS/CAREER NOTES: Selected by Florida Panthers in first round (first Panthers pick, fourth overall) of NHL entry draft (June 23, 2001).

		REGULAR SEASON								PLAYOFFS				
Season Team	League	Gms.	G	A	Pts.	PIM	+/-	PP	SH	Gms.	G	A	Pts.	PIM
99-00—Plymouth	OHL	64	24	42	66	35	...	...	...	23	8	18	26	18
00-01—Plymouth	OHL	62	40	47	87	45	...	...	...	18	7	16	23	10
01-02—Plymouth	OHL	46	25	45	70	69	...	...	...	6	2	7	9	13
—Florida........................	NHL	7	1	1	2	0	0	1	0	—	—	—	—	—
02-03—Florida........................	NHL	77	6	15	21	17	-13	0	0	—	—	—	—	—
NHL Totals (2 years)...........		84	7	16	23	17	-13	1	0					

WELLWOOD, KYLE   C   MAPLE LEAFS

PERSONAL: Born May 16, 1983, in Windsor, Ont. ... 5-9/190. ... Shoots right.
TRANSACTIONS/CAREER NOTES: Selected by Toronto Maple Leafs in sixth round (sixth Maple Leafs pick, 134th overall) of NHL entry draft (June 23, 2001).

		REGULAR SEASON								PLAYOFFS				
Season Team	League	Gms.	G	A	Pts.	PIM	+/-	PP	SH	Gms.	G	A	Pts.	PIM
98-99—Tecumseh	Jr. B	51	22	41	63	12	...	...	...	—	—	—	—	—
99-00—Belleville	OHL	65	14	37	51	14	...	...	...	16	3	7	10	6
00-01—Belleville	OHL	68	35	*83	*118	24	...	...	...	10	3	16	19	4
01-02—Belleville	OHL	28	16	24	40	4	...	...	...	—	—	—	—	—
—Windsor......................	OHL	26	14	21	35	0	...	...	...	16	12	12	24	0
02-03—Windsor......................	OHL	57	41	59	100	0	...	...	...	—	—	—	—	—

WESLEY, GLEN　　　　D　　　　HURRICANES

PERSONAL: Born October 2, 1968, in Red Deer, Alta. ... 6-1/205. ... Shoots left. ... Brother of Blake Wesley, defenseman with four NHL teams (1979-80 through 1985-86).

TRANSACTIONS/CAREER NOTES: Selected by Boston Bruins in first round (first Bruins pick, third overall) of NHL entry draft (June 13, 1987). ... Sprained left knee (October 1988). ... Fractured foot (November 24, 1992); missed 14 games. ... Injured groin (February 1993); missed one game. ... Injured groin (March 1993); missed three games. ... Injured groin (April 1993); missed two games. ... Injured kidney (March 3, 1994); missed three games. ... Traded by Bruins to Hartford Whalers for first-round picks in 1995 (D Kyle McLaren), 1996 (D Johnathan Aitken) and 1997 (C Sergei Samsonov) drafts (August 26, 1994). ... Bruised shin (November 4, 1995); missed two games. ... Injured groin (December 28, 1995); missed three games. ... Sprained knee (January 6, 1996); missed three games. ... Injured groin (January 17, 1996); missed four games. ... Injured groin (January 25, 1996); missed three games. ... Strained hip flexor (November 4, 1996); missed one game. ... Fractured foot (November 16, 1996); missed 10 games. ... Suffered from the flu (February 5, 1997); missed one game. ... Whalers franchise moved to North Carolina and renamed Carolina Hurricanes for 1997-98 season; NHL approved move on June 25, 1997. ... Sprained ankle (March 24, 1999); missed eight games. ... Strained groin (November 22, 1999); missed two games. ... Suffered eye injury (February 17, 2000); missed two games. ... Fractured jaw (March 4, 2001); missed 11 games. ... Injured shoulder (April 3, 2002); missed final five games of season. ... Traded by Hurricanes to Toronto Maple Leafs for second-round pick in 2004 draft (March 9, 2003). ... Signed by Hurricanes (July 8, 2003).

STATISTICAL PLATEAUS: Three-goal games: 1993-94 (1).

Season Team	League	REGULAR SEASON								PLAYOFFS				
		Gms.	G	A	Pts.	PIM	+/-	PP	SH	Gms.	G	A	Pts.	PIM
83-84—Red Deer	AJHL	57	9	20	29	40	...	...	...	—	—	—	—	—
—Portland	WHL	3	1	2	3	0	...	...	...	—	—	—	—	—
84-85—Portland	WHL	67	16	52	68	76	...	...	...	6	1	6	7	8
85-86—Portland	WHL	69	16	75	91	96	...	...	...	15	3	11	14	29
86-87—Portland	WHL	63	16	46	62	72	...	...	...	20	8	18	26	27
87-88—Boston	NHL	79	7	30	37	69	21	1	2	23	6	8	14	22
88-89—Boston	NHL	77	19	35	54	61	23	8	1	10	0	2	2	4
89-90—Boston	NHL	78	9	27	36	48	6	5	0	21	2	6	8	36
90-91—Boston	NHL	80	11	32	43	78	0	5	1	19	2	9	11	19
91-92—Boston	NHL	78	9	37	46	54	-9	4	0	15	2	4	6	16
92-93—Boston	NHL	64	8	25	33	47	-2	4	1	4	0	0	0	0
93-94—Boston	NHL	81	14	44	58	64	1	6	1	13	3	3	6	12
94-95—Hartford	NHL	48	2	14	16	50	-6	1	0	—	—	—	—	—
95-96—Hartford	NHL	68	8	16	24	88	-9	6	0	—	—	—	—	—
96-97—Hartford	NHL	68	6	26	32	40	0	3	1	—	—	—	—	—
97-98—Carolina	NHL	82	6	19	25	36	7	1	0	—	—	—	—	—
98-99—Carolina	NHL	74	7	17	24	44	14	0	0	6	0	0	0	2
99-00—Carolina	NHL	78	7	15	22	38	-4	1	0	—	—	—	—	—
00-01—Carolina	NHL	71	5	16	21	42	-2	3	0	6	0	0	0	0
01-02—Carolina	NHL	77	5	13	18	56	-8	1	0	22	0	2	2	12
02-03—Carolina	NHL	63	1	7	8	40	-5	1	0	—	—	—	—	—
—Toronto	NHL	7	0	3	3	4	3	0	0	5	0	1	1	2
NHL Totals (16 years)		1173	124	376	500	859	30	50	7	144	15	35	50	125

WESTCOTT, DUVIE　　　　D　　　　BLUE JACKETS

PERSONAL: Born October 30, 1977, in Winnipeg ... 5-11/197. ... Shoots right.

TRANSACTIONS/CAREER NOTES: Signed as non-drafted free agent by Columbus Blue Jackets (May 10, 2001).

Season Team	League	REGULAR SEASON								PLAYOFFS				
		Gms.	G	A	Pts.	PIM	+/-	PP	SH	Gms.	G	A	Pts.	PIM
96-97—Winnipeg	MJHL	52	12	47	59	...	...	...	...	—	—	—	—	—
97-98—Alaska-Anchorage	WCHA	25	3	5	8	43	...	...	...	—	—	—	—	—
—Omaha	USHL	12	3	3	6	31	...	...	...	14	0	8	8	84
98-99—St. Cloud State	WCHA				Did not play—transfer student.									
99-00—St. Cloud State	WCHA	36	1	18	19	67	...	...	...	—	—	—	—	—
00-01—St. Cloud State	WCHA	38	10	24	34	116	...	...	...	—	—	—	—	—
01-02—Syracuse	AHL	68	4	29	33	99	...	...	...	10	0	1	1	12
—Columbus	NHL	4	0	0	0	2	-2	0	0	—	—	—	—	—
02-03—Syracuse	AHL	22	1	10	11	54	...	...	...	—	—	—	—	—
—Columbus	NHL	39	0	7	7	77	-3	0	0	—	—	—	—	—
NHL Totals (2 years)		43	0	7	7	79	-5	0	0	—	—	—	—	—

WESTLUND, TOMMY　　　　LW

PERSONAL: Born December 29, 1974, in Fors, Sweden ... 6-0/202. ... Shoots right.

TRANSACTIONS/CAREER NOTES: Selected by Carolina Hurricanes in fourth round (fifth Hurricanes pick, 93rd overall) of NHL entry draft (June 27, 1998). ... Injured wrist (October 20, 2001); missed three games. ... Suffered back spasms (November 19, 2001); missed two games. ... Strained back (January 24, 2002); missed 24 games.

Season Team	League	REGULAR SEASON								PLAYOFFS				
		Gms.	G	A	Pts.	PIM	+/-	PP	SH	Gms.	G	A	Pts.	PIM
91-92—Avesta	Sweden Dv. 3	27	11	9	20	8	...	...	...	—	—	—	—	—
92-93—Avesta	Sweden Dv. 2	32	9	5	14	32	...	...	...	—	—	—	—	—
93-94—Avesta	Sweden Dv. 2	31	20	11	31	34	...	...	...	—	—	—	—	—
94-95—Avesta	Sweden Dv. 2	32	17	13	30	22	...	...	...	—	—	—	—	—
95-96—Brynas Gavle	Sweden	18	2	1	3	2	...	...	...	—	—	—	—	—
—Brynas Gavle	Sweden Dv. 2	18	10	10	20	4	...	...	...	8	1	0	1	4
96-97—Brynas Gavle	Sweden	50	21	13	34	16	...	...	...	—	—	—	—	—
97-98—Brynas Gavle	Sweden	46	29	9	38	45	...	...	...	3	0	1	1	0
98-99—New Haven	AHL	50	8	18	26	31	...	...	...	—	—	—	—	—

Season Team	League	REGULAR SEASON									PLAYOFFS				
		Gms.	G	A	Pts.	PIM	+/-	PP	SH		Gms.	G	A	Pts.	PIM
99-00—Carolina	NHL	81	4	8	12	19	-10	0	1		—	—	—	—	—
00-01—Carolina	NHL	79	5	3	8	23	-9	0	0		6	0	0	0	17
01-02—Carolina	NHL	40	0	2	2	6	-8	0	0		19	1	0	1	0
02-03—Lowell	AHL	22	1	3	4	12	...	...	...		—	—	—	—	—
—Carolina	NHL	3	0	0	0	0	0	0	0		—	—	—	—	—
NHL Totals (4 years)		203	9	13	22	48	-27	0	1		25	1	0	1	17

WHITE, COLIN — D — DEVILS

PERSONAL: Born December 12, 1977, in New Glasgow, Nova Scotia ... 6-4/215. ... Shoots left. ... Full Name: John Colin White.

TRANSACTIONS/CAREER NOTES: Selected by New Jersey Devils in second round (fifth Devils pick, 49th overall) of NHL entry draft (June 22, 1996). ... Suffered injury (January 28. 2000); missed two games. ... Suffered stiff neck (March 10, 2000); missed three games. ... Injured neck (December 26, 2001); missed two games. ... Reinjured neck (January 3, 2002); missed two games. ... Strained neck (January 23, 2002); missed two games. ... Injured neck (April 1, 2002); missed one game.

Season Team	League	REGULAR SEASON									PLAYOFFS				
		Gms.	G	A	Pts.	PIM	+/-	PP	SH		Gms.	G	A	Pts.	PIM
94-95—Laval	QMJHL	7	0	1	1	32	...	...	...		—	—	—	—	—
—Hull	QMJHL	5	0	1	1	4	...	...	...		12	0	0	0	23
95-96—Hull	QMJHL	62	2	8	10	303	...	...	...		18	0	4	4	42
96-97—Hull	QMJHL	63	3	12	15	297	...	...	...		14	3	12	15	65
97-98—Albany	AHL	76	3	13	16	235	...	...	...		13	0	0	0	55
98-99—Albany	AHL	77	2	12	14	265	...	...	...		5	0	1	1	8
99-00—Albany	AHL	52	5	21	26	176	...	...	...		—	—	—	—	—
—New Jersey	NHL	21	2	1	3	40	3	0	0		23	1	5	6	18
00-01—New Jersey	NHL	82	1	19	20	155	32	0	0		25	0	3	3	42
01-02—New Jersey	NHL	73	2	3	5	133	6	0	0		6	0	0	0	2
02-03—New Jersey	NHL	72	5	8	13	98	19	0	0		24	0	5	5	29
NHL Totals (4 years)		248	10	31	41	426	60	0	0		78	1	13	14	91

WHITE, PETER — C — FLYERS

PERSONAL: Born March 15, 1969, in Montreal ... 5-11/201. ... Shoots left. ... Full Name: Peter Toby White.

TRANSACTIONS/CAREER NOTES: Selected by Edmonton Oilers in fifth round (fourth Oilers pick, 92nd overall) of NHL entry draft (June 17, 1989). ... Traded by Oilers with fourth-round pick (RW Jason Sessa) in 1996 draft to Toronto Maple Leafs for LW Kent Manderville (December 4, 1995). ... Signed as free agent by Philadelphia Flyers (July 17, 1996). ... Re-signed by Philadelphia Flyers (July 14, 2003). ... Traded by Blackhawks to Flyers for future considerations (March 11, 2003).

Season Team	League	REGULAR SEASON									PLAYOFFS				
		Gms.	G	A	Pts.	PIM	+/-	PP	SH		Gms.	G	A	Pts.	PIM
87-88—Pembroke	COJHL	56	90	136	226	32	...	...	...		—	—	—	—	—
88-89—Michigan State	CCHA	46	20	33	53	17	...	...	...		—	—	—	—	—
89-90—Michigan State	CCHA	45	22	40	62	6	...	...	...		—	—	—	—	—
90-91—Michigan State	CCHA	37	7	31	38	28	...	...	...		—	—	—	—	—
91-92—Michigan State	CCHA	44	26	51	77	32	...	...	...		—	—	—	—	—
92-93—Cape Breton	AHL	64	12	28	40	10	...	...	...		16	3	3	6	12
93-94—Cape Breton	AHL	45	21	49	70	12	...	...	...		5	2	3	5	2
—Edmonton	NHL	26	3	5	8	2	1	0	0		—	—	—	—	—
94-95—Cape Breton	AHL	65	36	†69	*105	30	...	...	...		—	—	—	—	—
—Edmonton	NHL	9	2	4	6	0	1	2	0		—	—	—	—	—
95-96—Edmonton	NHL	26	5	3	8	0	-14	1	0		—	—	—	—	—
—Toronto	NHL	1	0	0	0	0	0	0	0		—	—	—	—	—
—St. John's	AHL	17	6	7	13	6	...	...	...		—	—	—	—	—
—Atlanta	IHL	36	21	20	41	4	...	...	...		3	0	3	3	2
96-97—Philadelphia	AHL	80	*44	61	*105	28	...	...	...		10	6	8	14	6
97-98—Philadelphia	AHL	80	27	*78	*105	28	...	...	...		20	9	9	18	6
98-99—Philadelphia	AHL	77	31	59	90	20	...	...	...		16	4	13	17	12
—Philadelphia	NHL	3	0	0	0	0	0	0	0		—	—	—	—	—
99-00—Philadelphia	AHL	62	20	41	61	38	...	...	...		—	—	—	—	—
—Philadelphia	NHL	21	1	5	6	6	1	0	0		16	0	2	2	0
00-01—Philadelphia	NHL	77	9	16	25	16	1	1	0		3	0	0	0	0
01-02—Norfolk	AHL	24	4	19	23	18	...	...	...		4	0	1	1	0
—Chicago	NHL	48	3	3	6	10	-8	1	0		—	—	—	—	—
02-03—Norfolk	AHL	31	6	17	23	21	...	...	...		—	—	—	—	—
—Chicago	NHL	6	0	1	1	0	0	0	0		—	—	—	—	—
—Philadelphia	AHL	47	17	26	43	16	...	...	...		—	—	—	—	—
NHL Totals (8 years)		217	23	37	60	34	-18	5	0		19	0	2	2	0

WHITE, TODD — C — SENATORS

PERSONAL: Born May 21, 1975, in Kanata, Ont. ... 5-10/194. ... Shoots left.

TRANSACTIONS/CAREER NOTES: Signed as non-drafted free agent by Chicago Blackhawks (August 6, 1997). ... Suffered charley horse (October 4, 1997); missed one game. ... Bruised ribs prior to 1998-99 season; missed first six games of season. ... Traded by Blackhawks to Philadelphia Flyers for conditional pick in 2001 draft (January 26, 2000). ... Signed as free agent by Ottawa Senators (July 12, 2000). ... Suffered concussion (January 15, 2002); missed one game.

W

Season Team	League	Gms.	G	A	Pts.	PIM	+/-	PP	SH	Gms.	G	A	Pts.	PIM
93-94—Clarkson	ECAC	33	10	12	22	28	...	...	...	—	—	—	—	—
94-95—Clarkson	ECAC	34	13	16	29	44	...	...	...	—	—	—	—	—
95-96—Clarkson	ECAC	38	29	43	72	36	...	...	...	—	—	—	—	—
96-97—Clarkson	ECAC	37	38	36	74	22	...	...	...	—	—	—	—	—
97-98—Chicago	NHL	7	1	0	1	2	0	0	0	—	—	—	—	—
—Indianapolis	IHL	65	†46	36	82	28	...	...	...	5	2	3	5	4
98-99—Chicago	IHL	25	11	13	24	8	...	...	...	10	1	4	5	8
—Chicago	NHL	35	5	8	13	20	-1	2	0	—	—	—	—	—
99-00—Cleveland	IHL	42	21	30	51	32	...	...	...	—	—	—	—	—
—Chicago	NHL	1	0	0	0	0	0	0	0	—	—	—	—	—
—Philadelphia	AHL	32	19	24	43	12	...	...	...	5	2	1	3	8
—Philadelphia	NHL	3	1	0	1	0	-1	0	0	—	—	—	—	—
00-01—Grand Rapids	IHL	64	22	32	54	20	...	...	...	10	4	4	8	10
—Ottawa	NHL	16	4	1	5	4	5	0	0	2	0	0	0	0
01-02—Ottawa	NHL	81	20	30	50	24	12	4	0	12	2	2	4	6
02-03—Ottawa	NHL	80	25	35	60	28	19	8	1	18	5	1	6	6
NHL Totals (6 years)		223	56	74	130	78	34	14	1	32	7	3	10	12

WHITFIELD, TRENT   C   CAPITALS

PERSONAL: Born June 17, 1977, in Estevan, Sask. ... 5-11/205. ... Shoots left.
TRANSACTIONS/CAREER NOTES: Selected by Boston Bruins in fourth round (fifth Bruins pick, 100th overall) of NHL entry draft (June 22, 1996). ... Signed as free agent by Washington Capitals (September 1, 1998). ... Claimed on waivers by New York Rangers (January 16, 2002). ... Claimed on waivers by Capitals (February 1, 2002). ... Re-signed by Capitals (July 21, 2003).

Season Team	League	Gms.	G	A	Pts.	PIM	+/-	PP	SH	Gms.	G	A	Pts.	PIM
93-94—Spokane	WHL	5	1	1	2	0	...	...	...	—	—	—	—	—
94-95—Spokane	WHL	48	8	17	25	26	...	...	...	11	7	6	13	5
95-96—Spokane	WHL	72	33	51	84	75	...	...	...	18	8	10	18	10
96-97—Spokane	WHL	58	34	42	76	74	...	...	...	9	5	7	12	10
97-98—Spokane	WHL	65	38	44	82	97	...	...	...	18	9	10	19	15
98-99—Portland	AHL	50	10	8	18	20	...	...	...	—	—	—	—	—
—Hampton Roads	ECHL	19	13	12	25	12	...	...	...	4	2	0	2	14
99-00—Portland	AHL	79	18	35	53	52	...	...	...	3	1	1	2	2
—Washington	NHL	—	—	—	—	—	...	...	...	3	0	0	0	0
00-01—Portland	AHL	19	9	11	20	27	...	...	...	—	—	—	—	—
—Washington	NHL	61	2	4	6	35	3	0	0	5	0	0	0	2
01-02—Portland	AHL	45	14	20	34	24	...	...	...	—	—	—	—	—
—New York Rangers	NHL	1	0	0	0	0	1	0	0	—	—	—	—	—
—Washington	NHL	24	0	1	1	28	-3	0	0	—	—	—	—	—
02-03—Portland	AHL	64	27	34	61	42	...	...	...	—	—	—	—	—
—Washington	NHL	14	1	1	2	6	1	0	0	6	0	0	0	10
NHL Totals (4 years)		100	3	6	9	69	2	0	0	14	0	0	0	12

WHITNEY, RAY   LW   RED WINGS

PERSONAL: Born May 8, 1972, in Fort Sask., Alta. ... 5-10/178. ... Shoots right.
TRANSACTIONS/CAREER NOTES: Selected by San Jose Sharks in second round (second Sharks pick, 23rd overall) of NHL entry draft (June 22, 1991). ... Sprained knee (October 30, 1993); missed 18 games. ... Suffered from the flu (December 15, 1993); missed one game. ... Injured ankle (February 20, 1995) and suffered eye infection (February 28, 1995); missed seven games. ... Suffered eye infection (March 21, 1995); missed one game. ... Suffered from the flu (April 9, 1995); missed one game. ... Injured groin (December 15, 1995); missed three games. ... Injured wrist (February 18, 1996); missed 17 games. ... Signed as free agent by Edmonton Oilers (October 1, 1997). ... Claimed on waivers by Florida Panthers (November 6, 1997). ... Strained groin (October 22, 1999); missed one game. ... Injured groin (November 10, 2000). ... Strained back (January 17, 2001); missed six games. ... Strained back (February 9, 2001); missed 28 games. ... Traded by Panthers with future considerations to Columbus Blue Jackets for C Kevyn Adams and fourth-round pick (RW Michael Woodford) in 2001 draft (March 13, 2001). ... Strained chest muscle (October 12, 2001); missed 11 games. ... Suffered illness (December 8, 2001); missed one game. ... Strained lower back (March 25, 2002); missed one game. ... Signed by Detroit Red Wings (July 30, 2003).
STATISTICAL PLATEAUS: Three-goal games: 2002-03 (1).

Season Team	League	Gms.	G	A	Pts.	PIM	+/-	PP	SH	Gms.	G	A	Pts.	PIM
88-89—Spokane	WHL	71	17	33	50	16	...	...	...	—	—	—	—	—
89-90—Spokane	WHL	71	57	56	113	50	...	...	...	6	3	4	7	6
90-91—Spokane	WHL	72	67	118	*185	36	...	...	...	15	13	18	*31	12
91-92—San Diego	IHL	63	36	54	90	12	...	...	...	4	0	0	0	0
—San Jose	NHL	2	0	3	3	0	-1	0	0	—	—	—	—	—
—Koln	Germany	10	3	6	9	4	...	...	...	—	—	—	—	—
92-93—Kansas City	IHL	46	20	33	53	14	...	...	...	12	5	7	12	2
—San Jose	NHL	26	4	6	10	4	-14	1	0	—	—	—	—	—
93-94—San Jose	NHL	61	14	26	40	14	2	1	0	14	0	4	4	8
94-95—San Jose	NHL	39	13	12	25	14	-7	4	0	11	4	4	8	2
95-96—San Jose	NHL	60	17	24	41	16	-23	4	2	—	—	—	—	—
96-97—Kentucky	AHL	9	1	7	8	2	...	...	...	—	—	—	—	—
—Utah	IHL	43	13	35	48	34	...	...	...	7	3	1	4	6
—San Jose	NHL	12	0	2	2	4	-6	0	0	—	—	—	—	—
97-98—Edmonton	NHL	9	1	3	4	0	-1	0	0	—	—	—	—	—
—Florida	NHL	68	32	29	61	28	10	12	0	—	—	—	—	—
98-99—Florida	NHL	81	26	38	64	18	-3	7	0	—	—	—	—	—

W

Season Team	League	REGULAR SEASON								PLAYOFFS				
		Gms.	G	A	Pts.	PIM	+/-	PP	SH	Gms.	G	A	Pts.	PIM
99-00—Florida	NHL	81	29	42	71	35	16	5	0	4	1	0	1	4
00-01—Florida	NHL	43	10	21	31	28	-16	5	0	—	—	—	—	—
—Columbus	NHL	3	0	3	3	2	-1	0	0	—	—	—	—	—
01-02—Columbus	NHL	67	21	40	61	12	-22	6	0	—	—	—	—	—
02-03—Columbus	NHL	81	24	52	76	22	-26	8	2	—	—	—	—	—
NHL Totals (12 years)		633	191	301	492	197	-92	53	4	29	5	8	13	14

WIDING, DANIEL — RW — PREDATORS

PERSONAL: Born April 13, 1982, in Gavle, Sweden. ... 6-0/185. ... Shoots right.
TRANSACTIONS/CAREER NOTES: Selected by Nashville Predators in second round (second Predators pick, 36th overall) of NHL entry draft (June 24, 2000).

Season Team	League	REGULAR SEASON								PLAYOFFS				
		Gms.	G	A	Pts.	PIM	+/-	PP	SH	Gms.	G	A	Pts.	PIM
99-00—Leksand	Sweden Jr.	34	15	12	27	65	...	...	...	—	—	—	—	—
—Leksand	Sweden Dv. 2	3	0	0	0	2	...	...	...	—	—	—	—	—
00-01—Leksand	Sweden Dv. 2	40	6	5	11	18	...	...	...	—	—	—	—	—
02-03—Leksand	Sweden Dv. 2	47	2	2	4	8	...	...	...	5	0	0	0	2

WIEMER, JASON — C — ISLANDERS

PERSONAL: Born April 14, 1976, in Kimberley, B.C. ... 6-1/224. ... Shoots left. ... Name pronounced WEE-muhr.
TRANSACTIONS/CAREER NOTES: Selected by Tampa Bay Lightning in first round (first Lightning pick, eighth overall) of NHL entry draft (June 28, 1994). ... Suffered from the flu (March 2, 1995); missed one game. ... Injured jaw (November 3, 1995); missed one game. ... Injured back (April 12, 1996); missed one game. ... Broke bursa sac in elbow (November 30, 1996); missed 14 games. ... Traded by Lightning to Calgary Flames for RW Sandy McCarthy and third- (LW Brad Richards) and fifth-round (D Curtis Rich) picks in 1998 draft (March 24, 1998). ... Injured hand (March 30, 1999); missed three games. ... Injured knee prior to start of 1999-2000 season; missed first 10 games of season. ... Reinjured knee (October 28, 1999); missed three games. ... Suffered injury (March 31, 2000); missed final five games of season. ... Suffered concussion (December 31, 2000); missed 17 games. ... Traded by Flames with RW Valeri Bure to Florida Panthers for C Rob Niedermayer and second-round pick (G Andrei Medvedev) in 2001 draft (June 23, 2001). ... Suspended seven games by NHL for butt-ending opponent with stick (November 20, 2001). ... Suffered concussion (April 5, 2002); missed remainder of season. ... Traded by Panthers to New York Islanders for D Branislav Mezei (July 3, 2002). ... Re-signed by Islanders (July 20, 2003).
STATISTICAL PLATEAUS: Three-goal games: 1995-96 (1).

Season Team	League	REGULAR SEASON								PLAYOFFS				
		Gms.	G	A	Pts.	PIM	+/-	PP	SH	Gms.	G	A	Pts.	PIM
91-92—Kimberley	RMJHL	45	34	33	67	211	...	...	...	—	—	—	—	—
—Portland	WHL	2	0	1	1	0	...	...	...	—	—	—	—	—
92-93—Portland	WHL	68	18	34	52	159	...	...	...	16	7	3	10	27
93-94—Portland	WHL	72	45	51	96	236	...	...	...	10	4	4	8	32
94-95—Portland	WHL	16	10	14	24	63	...	...	...	—	—	—	—	—
—Tampa Bay	NHL	36	1	4	5	44	-2	0	0	—	—	—	—	—
95-96—Tampa Bay	NHL	66	9	9	18	81	-9	4	0	6	1	0	1	28
96-97—Tampa Bay	NHL	63	9	5	14	134	-13	2	0	—	—	—	—	—
—Adirondack	AHL	4	1	0	1	7	...	...	...	—	—	—	—	—
97-98—Tampa Bay	NHL	67	8	9	17	132	-9	2	0	—	—	—	—	—
—Calgary	NHL	12	4	1	5	28	-1	1	0	—	—	—	—	—
98-99—Calgary	NHL	78	8	13	21	177	-12	1	0	—	—	—	—	—
99-00—Calgary	NHL	64	11	11	22	120	-10	2	0	—	—	—	—	—
00-01—Calgary	NHL	65	10	5	15	177	-15	3	0	—	—	—	—	—
01-02—Florida	NHL	70	11	20	31	178	-4	5	1	—	—	—	—	—
02-03—New York Islanders	NHL	81	9	19	28	116	5	0	1	5	0	0	0	23
NHL Totals (9 years)		602	80	96	176	1187	-70	20	2	11	1	0	1	51

WILLIAMS, JASON — C — RED WINGS

PERSONAL: Born August 11, 1980, in London, Ont. ... 5-11/185. ... Shoots right.
TRANSACTIONS/CAREER NOTES: Signed as non-drafted free agent by Detroit Red Wings (September 22, 2000).

Season Team	League	REGULAR SEASON								PLAYOFFS				
		Gms.	G	A	Pts.	PIM	+/-	PP	SH	Gms.	G	A	Pts.	PIM
96-97—Peterborough	OHL	60	4	8	12	8	...	...	...	10	1	0	1	2
97-98—Peterborough	OHL	55	8	27	35	31	...	...	...	4	0	1	1	2
98-99—Peterborough	OHL	68	26	48	74	42	...	...	...	5	1	2	3	2
99-00—Peterborough	OHL	66	36	37	73	64	...	...	...	5	2	1	3	2
00-01—Cincinnati	AHL	76	24	45	69	48	...	...	...	1	0	0	0	2
—Detroit	NHL	5	0	3	3	2	1	0	0	2	0	0	0	0
01-02—Cincinnati	AHL	52	23	27	50	27	...	...	...	3	0	1	1	6
—Detroit	NHL	25	8	2	10	4	2	4	0	9	0	0	0	2
02-03—Grand Rapids	AHL	45	23	22	45	18	...	...	...	—	—	—	—	—
—Detroit	NHL	16	3	3	6	2	3	1	0	—	—	—	—	—
NHL Totals (3 years)		46	11	8	19	8	6	5	0	11	0	0	0	2

W

WILLIAMS, JUSTIN   RW   FLYERS

PERSONAL: Born October 4, 1981, in Cobourg, Ont. ... 6-1/190. ... Shoots right.

TRANSACTIONS/CAREER NOTES: Selected by Philadelphia Flyers in first round (first Flyers pick, 28th overall) of NHL entry draft (June 24, 2000). ... Fractured hand (February 19, 2001); missed 12 games. ... Suffered from the flu (November 10, 2001); missed one game. ... Strained right shoulder (December 8, 2001); missed two games. ... Re-signed by Flyers (July 30, 2003).

		REGULAR SEASON								PLAYOFFS				
Season Team	League	Gms.	G	A	Pts.	PIM	+/-	PP	SH	Gms.	G	A	Pts.	PIM
97-98—Colborne	Jr. C	36	32	35	67	26	...	...	...	—	—	—	—	—
—Cobourg	Tier II Jr. A	17	0	3	3	5	...	...	...	—	—	—	—	—
98-99—Plymouth	OHL	47	4	8	12	28	...	...	...	7	1	2	3	0
99-00—Plymouth	OHL	68	37	46	83	46	...	...	...	23	*14	16	*30	10
00-01—Philadelphia	NHL	63	12	13	25	22	6	0	0	—	—	—	—	—
01-02—Philadelphia	NHL	75	17	23	40	32	11	0	0	5	0	0	0	4
02-03—Philadelphia	NHL	41	8	16	24	22	15	0	0	12	1	5	6	8
NHL Totals (3 years)		179	37	52	89	76	32	0	0	17	1	5	6	12

WILLIS, SHANE   RW   LIGHTNING

PERSONAL: Born June 13, 1977, in Edmonton. ... 6-0/176. ... Shoots right.

TRANSACTIONS/CAREER NOTES: Selected by Tampa Bay Lightning in third round (third Lightning pick, 56th overall) of NHL entry draft (July 8, 1995). ... Returned to draft pool by Lightning and selected by Carolina Hurricanes in fourth round (fourth Hurricanes pick, 88th overall) of NHL entry draft (June 21, 1997). ... Suffered back spasms (December 23, 2000); missed five games. ... Sprained ankle (March 1, 2001); missed four games. ... Injured back (September 26, 2001); missed first three games of season. ... Traded by Hurricanes with LW Craig Dingman to Lightning for G Kevin Weekes (March 5, 2002). ... Re-signed by Lightning (July 30, 2003).

STATISTICAL PLATEAUS: Three-goal games: 2000-01 (1).

		REGULAR SEASON								PLAYOFFS				
Season Team	League	Gms.	G	A	Pts.	PIM	+/-	PP	SH	Gms.	G	A	Pts.	PIM
94-95—Prince Albert	WHL	65	24	19	43	38	...	...	...	13	3	4	7	6
95-96—Prince Albert	WHL	69	41	40	81	47	...	...	...	18	11	10	21	18
96-97—Prince Albert	WHL	41	34	22	56	63	...	...	...	—	—	—	—	—
—Lethbridge	WHL	26	22	17	39	24	...	...	...	19	13	11	24	20
97-98—New Haven	AHL	1	0	1	1	2	...	...	...	—	—	—	—	—
—Lethbridge	WHL	64	58	54	112	73	...	...	...	4	2	3	5	6
98-99—New Haven	AHL	73	31	50	81	49	...	...	...	—	—	—	—	—
—Carolina	NHL	7	0	0	0	0	-2	0	0	—	—	—	—	—
99-00—Cincinnati	IHL	80	35	25	60	64	...	...	...	11	5	3	8	8
—Carolina	NHL	2	0	0	0	0	-1	0	0	—	—	—	—	—
00-01—Carolina	NHL	73	20	24	44	45	-6	9	0	2	0	0	0	0
01-02—Carolina	NHL	59	7	10	17	24	-8	2	0	—	—	—	—	—
—Tampa Bay	NHL	21	4	3	7	6	0	0	0	—	—	—	—	—
02-03—Springfield	AHL	56	16	16	32	26	...	...	...	—	—	—	—	—
NHL Totals (4 years)		162	31	37	68	75	-17	11	0	2	0	0	0	0

WILLSIE, BRIAN   RW   AVALANCHE

PERSONAL: Born March 16, 1978, in London, Ont. ... 6-1/200. ... Shoots right.

TRANSACTIONS/CAREER NOTES: Selected by Colorado Avalanche in sixth round (seventh Avalanche pick, 146th overall) of NHL entry draft (June 22, 1996).

		REGULAR SEASON								PLAYOFFS				
Season Team	League	Gms.	G	A	Pts.	PIM	+/-	PP	SH	Gms.	G	A	Pts.	PIM
95-96—Guelph	OHL	65	13	21	34	18	...	...	...	16	4	2	6	6
96-97—Guelph	OHL	64	37	31	68	37	...	...	...	18	15	4	19	10
97-98—Guelph	OHL	57	45	31	76	41	...	...	...	12	9	5	14	18
98-99—Hershey	AHL	72	19	10	29	28	...	...	...	3	1	0	1	0
99-00—Hershey	AHL	78	20	39	59	44	...	...	...	12	2	6	8	8
—Colorado	NHL	1	0	0	0	0	0	0	0	—	—	—	—	—
00-01—Hershey	AHL	48	18	23	41	20	...	...	...	12	7	2	9	14
01-02—Colorado	NHL	56	7	7	14	14	4	2	0	4	0	1	1	2
02-03—Hershey	AHL	59	29	28	57	49	...	...	...	—	—	—	—	—
—Colorado	NHL	12	0	1	1	15	0	0	0	6	1	0	1	2
NHL Totals (3 years)		69	7	8	15	29	4	2	0	10	1	1	2	4

W   WILM, CLARKE   C

PERSONAL: Born October 24, 1976, in Central Butte, Sask. ... 6-0/202. ... Shoots left. ... Name pronounced WIHLM.

TRANSACTIONS/CAREER NOTES: Selected by Calgary Flames in sixth round (fifth Flames pick, 150th overall) of NHL entry draft (July 8, 1995). ... Suffered concussion (November 27, 1998); missed two games. ... Injured eye (January 26, 2002); missed two games. ... Suffered injury (March 9, 2001); missed two games. ... Injured ankle (March 18, 2002); missed remainder of season. ... Signed as free agent by Nashville Predators (July 11, 2002).

Season Team	League	REGULAR SEASON								PLAYOFFS				
		Gms.	G	A	Pts.	PIM	+/-	PP	SH	Gms.	G	A	Pts.	PIM
91-92—Saskatoon	WHL	—	—	—	—	—	...	...	...	1	0	0	0	0
92-93—Saskatoon	WHL	69	14	19	33	71	...	...	...	9	4	2	6	13
93-94—Saskatoon	WHL	70	18	32	50	181	...	...	...	16	0	9	9	19
94-95—Saskatoon	WHL	71	20	39	59	179	...	...	...	10	6	1	7	21
95-96—Saskatoon	WHL	72	49	61	110	83	...	...	...	4	1	1	2	4
96-97—Saint John	AHL	62	9	19	28	107	...	...	...	5	2	0	2	15
97-98—Saint John	AHL	68	13	26	39	112	...	...	...	21	5	9	14	8
98-99—Calgary	NHL	78	10	8	18	53	11	2	2	—	—	—	—	—
99-00—Calgary	NHL	78	10	12	22	67	-6	1	3	—	—	—	—	—
00-01—Calgary	NHL	81	7	8	15	69	-11	2	0	—	—	—	—	—
01-02—Calgary	NHL	66	4	14	18	61	-1	0	1	—	—	—	—	—
02-03—Nashville	NHL	82	5	11	16	36	-11	0	0	—	—	—	—	—
NHL Totals (5 years)		385	36	53	89	286	-18	5	6					

WILSON, LANDON   RW   COYOTES

PERSONAL: Born March 13, 1975, in St. Louis ... 6-3/226. ... Shoots right. ... Son of Rick Wilson, defenseman with three NHL teams (1973-74 through 1976-77).

TRANSACTIONS/CAREER NOTES: Selected by Toronto Maple Leafs in first round (second Maple Leafs pick, 19th overall) of NHL entry draft (June 26, 1993). ... Traded by Maple Leafs with LW Wendel Clark, D Sylvain Lefebvre and first-round pick (D Jeffrey Kealty) in 1994 draft to Quebec Nordiques for C Mats Sundin, D Garth Butcher, LW Todd Warriner and first-round pick (traded to Washington Capitals) in 1994 draft (June 28, 1994). ... Nordiques franchise moved to Colorado and renamed Avalanche for 1995-96 season (June 21, 1995). ... Traded by Avalanche with D Anders Myrvold to Boston Bruins for first-round pick (D Robyn Regehr) in 1998 draft (November 22, 1996). ... Sprained shoulder (December 12, 1996); missed 10 games. ... Suffered charley horse (January 7, 1997); missed 12 games. ... Suffered concussion (March 9, 1999); missed two games. ... Strained abdominal muscle (April 15, 1999); missed one game. ... Strained shoulder (April 28, 1999); missed remainder of playoffs. ... Injured shoulder (November 4, 1999); missed seven games. ... Signed as free agent by Phoenix Coyotes (July 7, 2000). ... Suffered back spasms (November 19, 2000); missed one game. ... Strained knee (January 1, 2001); missed six games. ... Strained calf (March 13, 2001); missed five games. ... Sprained ankle (September 5, 2001); missed first 24 games of season. ... Suffered eye injury (December 13, 2002); missed final 51 games of the season. ... Re-signed by Coyotes (July 7, 2003).

Season Team	League	REGULAR SEASON								PLAYOFFS				
		Gms.	G	A	Pts.	PIM	+/-	PP	SH	Gms.	G	A	Pts.	PIM
92-93—Dubuque	USHL	43	29	36	65	284	...	...	...	—	—	—	—	—
93-94—Univ. of North Dakota	WCHA	35	18	15	33	147	...	...	...	—	—	—	—	—
94-95—Univ. of North Dakota	WCHA	31	7	16	23	141	...	...	...	—	—	—	—	—
—Cornwall	AHL	8	4	4	8	25	...	...	...	13	3	4	7	68
95-96—Cornwall	AHL	53	21	13	34	154	...	...	...	8	1	3	4	22
—Colorado	NHL	7	1	0	1	6	3	0	0	—	—	—	—	—
96-97—Colorado	NHL	9	1	2	3	23	1	0	0	—	—	—	—	—
—Boston	NHL	40	7	10	17	49	-6	0	0	—	—	—	—	—
—Providence	AHL	2	2	1	3	2	...	...	...	10	3	4	7	16
97-98—Boston	NHL	28	1	5	6	7	3	0	0	1	0	0	0	0
—Providence	AHL	42	18	10	28	146	...	...	...	—	—	—	—	—
98-99—Providence	AHL	48	31	22	53	89	...	...	...	11	7	1	8	19
—Boston	NHL	22	3	3	6	17	0	0	0	8	1	1	2	8
99-00—Boston	NHL	40	1	3	4	18	-6	0	0	—	—	—	—	—
—Providence	AHL	17	5	5	10	45	...	...	...	9	2	3	5	38
00-01—Phoenix	NHL	70	18	13	31	92	3	2	0	—	—	—	—	—
01-02—Springfield	AHL	2	2	1	3	2	...	...	...	—	—	—	—	—
—Phoenix	NHL	47	7	12	19	46	4	1	0	4	0	0	0	12
02-03—Phoenix	NHL	31	6	8	14	26	1	0	0	—	—	—	—	—
NHL Totals (8 years)		294	45	56	101	284	3	3	0	13	1	1	2	20

WILSON, MIKE   D   RANGERS

PERSONAL: Born February 26, 1975, in Brampton, Ont. ... 6-6/229. ... Shoots left.

TRANSACTIONS/CAREER NOTES: Selected by Vancouver Canucks in first round (first Canucks pick, 20th overall) of NHL entry draft (June 26, 1993). ... Traded by Canucks with RW Michael Peca and first-round pick (D Jay McKee) in 1995 draft to Buffalo Sabres for RW Alexander Mogilny and fifth-round pick (LW Todd Norman) in 1995 draft (July 8, 1995). ... Suffered concussion (January 26, 1996); missed two games. ... Bruised chest (November 13, 1997); missed one game. ... Suffered mild concussion (January 8, 1998); missed two games. ... Missed first 19 games of 1998-99 season due to contract dispute; played with Las Vegas of IHL. ... Traded by Sabres to Florida Panthers for D Rhett Warrener and fifth-round pick (G Ryan Miller) in 1999 draft (March 23, 1999). ... Suffered concussion (March 31, 1999); missed final nine games of season. ... Injured shoulder (October 22, 2000); missed 61 games. ... Signed as free agent by Pittsburgh Penguins (July 5, 2001). ... Traded by Penguins with RW Alexei Kovalev, LW Dan LaCouture and D Janne Laukkanen to New York Rangers for RW Rico Fata, RW Mikael Samuelsson, D Joel Bouchard, D Richard Lintner and cash (February 10, 2003).

Season Team	League	REGULAR SEASON								PLAYOFFS				
		Gms.	G	A	Pts.	PIM	+/-	PP	SH	Gms.	G	A	Pts.	PIM
91-92—Georgetown Jr. B	OHA	41	9	13	22	65	...	...	...	—	—	—	—	—
92-93—Sudbury	OHL	53	6	7	13	58	...	...	...	14	1	1	2	21
93-94—Sudbury	OHL	60	4	22	26	62	...	...	...	9	1	3	4	8
94-95—Sudbury	OHL	64	13	34	47	46	...	...	...	18	1	8	9	10
95-96—Rochester	AHL	15	0	5	5	38	...	...	...	—	—	—	—	—
—Buffalo	NHL	58	4	8	12	41	13	1	0	—	—	—	—	—
96-97—Buffalo	NHL	77	2	9	11	51	13	0	0	10	0	1	1	2
97-98—Buffalo	NHL	66	4	4	8	48	13	0	0	15	0	1	1	13
98-99—Las Vegas	IHL	6	3	1	4	6	...	...	...	—	—	—	—	—
—Buffalo	NHL	30	1	2	3	47	10	0	0	—	—	—	—	—
—Florida	NHL	4	0	0	0	0	2	0	0	—	—	—	—	—

W

Season Team	League	REGULAR SEASON								PLAYOFFS				
		Gms.	G	A	Pts.	PIM	+/-	PP	SH	Gms.	G	A	Pts.	PIM
99-00—Florida	NHL	60	4	16	20	35	10	0	0	4	0	0	0	0
00-01—Florida	NHL	19	0	1	1	25	-7	0	0	—	—	—	—	—
—Louisville	AHL	4	0	2	2	5	...	...	...	—	—	—	—	—
01-02—Pittsburgh	NHL	21	1	1	2	17	-12	0	0	—	—	—	—	—
—Wilkes-Barre/Scranton	AHL	46	3	9	12	59	...	...	...	—	—	—	—	—
02-03—Wilkes-Barre/Scranton	AHL	45	4	5	9	89	...	...	...	—	—	—	—	—
—New York Rangers	NHL	1	0	0	0	0	1	0	0	—	—	—	—	—
—Hartford	AHL	5	1	2	3	5	...	...	...	—	—	—	—	—
NHL Totals (8 years)		336	16	41	57	264	43	1	0	29	0	2	2	15

WINCHESTER, BRAD   LW   OILERS

PERSONAL: Born March 1, 1981, in Madison, Wis. ... 6-5/208. ... Shoots left.
HIGH SCHOOL: Madison (Wis.) West, then Huron (Ann Arbor, Mich.).
COLLEGE: Wisconsin.
TRANSACTIONS/CAREER NOTES: Selected by Edmonton Oilers in second round (second Oilers pick, 35th overall) of NHL entry draft (June 24, 2000).

Season Team	League	REGULAR SEASON								PLAYOFFS				
		Gms.	G	A	Pts.	PIM	+/-	PP	SH	Gms.	G	A	Pts.	PIM
98-99—U.S. National	USHL	68	21	36	57	...	...	...	...	—	—	—	—	—
99-00—Univ. of Wisconsin	WCHA	29	8	8	16	48	...	...	...	—	—	—	—	—
00-01—Univ. of Wisconsin	WCHA	41	7	9	16	71	...	...	...	—	—	—	—	—
01-02—Univ. of Wisconsin	WCHA	38	14	20	34	38	...	...	...	—	—	—	—	—
02-03—Univ. of Wisconsin	WCHA	38	10	6	16	58	...	...	...	—	—	—	—	—

WISEMAN, CHAD   LW   SHARKS

PERSONAL: Born March 25, 1981, in Burlington, Ont. ... 6-0/205. ... Shoots left.
TRANSACTIONS/CAREER NOTES: Selected by San Jose Sharks in eighth round (eighth Sharks pick, 246th overall) in 2000 NHL entry draft (June 25, 2000).

Season Team	League	REGULAR SEASON								PLAYOFFS				
		Gms.	G	A	Pts.	PIM	+/-	PP	SH	Gms.	G	A	Pts.	PIM
97-98—Burlington	OPJHL	50	28	36	64	31	...	...	...	—	—	—	—	—
98-99—Mississauga	OHL	64	11	25	36	29	...	...	...	—	—	—	—	—
99-00—Mississauga	OHL	68	23	45	68	53	...	...	...	—	—	—	—	—
00-01—Mississauga	OHL	30	15	29	44	22	...	...	...	—	—	—	—	—
—Plymouth	OHL	32	11	16	27	12	...	...	...	19	12	8	20	22
01-02—Cleveland	AHL	76	21	29	50	61	...	...	...	—	—	—	—	—
02-03—Cleveland	AHL	77	17	35	52	44	...	...	...	—	—	—	—	—
—San Jose	NHL	4	0	0	0	4	-2	0	0	—	—	—	—	—
NHL Totals (1 year)		4	0	0	0	4	-2	0	0					

WITT, BRENDAN   D   CAPITALS

PERSONAL: Born February 20, 1975, in Humboldt, Sask. ... 6-2/231. ... Shoots left.
TRANSACTIONS/CAREER NOTES: Selected by Washington Capitals in first round (first Capitals pick, 11th overall) of NHL entry draft (June 26, 1993). ... Missed entire 1994-95 season due to contract dispute. ... Fractured wrist (January 28, 1996); missed 34 games. ... Suffered from the flu (November 15, 1996); missed five games. ... Bruised shoulder (November 27, 1997); missed seven games. ... Suffered illness (January 6, 1998); missed three games. ... Injured wrist (April 6, 1998); missed final six games of regular season and five playoff games. ... Sprained knee (October 18, 1998); missed one game. ... Strained hip flexor (October 28, 1998); missed five games. ... Missed game for personal reasons (January 26, 1999). ... Sprained wrist (February 3, 1999); missed 15 games. ... Sprained knee (October 16, 1999); missed two games. ... Strained back (November 26, 1999); missed one game. ... Strained groin (March 11, 2000); missed one game. ... Injured thigh (March 25, 2000); missed one game. ... Injured left arm (October 17, 2000); missed one game. ... Suffered from the flu (December 16, 2000); missed three games. ... Separated shoulder (December 29, 2000); missed five games. ... Injured leg (October 10, 2001); missed two games. ... Injured leg (November 6, 2001); missed five games. ... Sprained thumb (January 3, 2002); missed seven games.

Season Team	League	REGULAR SEASON								PLAYOFFS				
		Gms.	G	A	Pts.	PIM	+/-	PP	SH	Gms.	G	A	Pts.	PIM
90-91—Seattle	WHL	—	—	—	—	—	—	—	—	1	0	0	0	0
91-92—Seattle	WHL	67	3	9	12	212	...	...	...	15	1	1	2	84
92-93—Seattle	WHL	70	2	26	28	239	...	...	...	5	1	2	3	30
93-94—Seattle	WHL	56	8	31	39	235	...	...	...	9	3	8	11	23
94-95—							Did not play.							
95-96—Washington	NHL	48	2	3	5	85	-4	0	0	—	—	—	—	—
96-97—Washington	NHL	44	3	2	5	88	-20	0	0	—	—	—	—	—
—Portland	AHL	30	2	4	6	56	...	...	...	5	1	0	1	30
97-98—Washington	NHL	64	1	7	8	112	-11	0	0	16	1	0	1	14
98-99—Washington	NHL	54	2	5	7	87	-6	0	0	—	—	—	—	—
99-00—Washington	NHL	77	1	7	8	114	5	0	0	3	0	0	0	0
00-01—Washington	NHL	72	3	3	6	101	2	0	0	6	2	0	2	12
01-02—Washington	NHL	68	3	7	10	78	-1	0	0	—	—	—	—	—
02-03—Washington	NHL	69	2	9	11	106	12	0	0	6	1	0	1	0
NHL Totals (9 years)		496	17	43	60	771	-23	0	0	31	4	0	4	26

W

WOOLLEY, JASON   D   RED WINGS

PERSONAL: Born July 27, 1969, in Toronto ... 6-0/206. ... Shoots left. ... Full Name: Jason Douglas Woolley.

TRANSACTIONS/CAREER NOTES: Selected by Washington Capitals in third round (fourth Capitals pick, 61st overall) of NHL entry draft (June 17, 1989). ... Fractured wrist (October 12, 1992); missed 24 games. ... Tore abdominal muscle (January 2, 1994). ... Signed as free agent by Detroit Vipers (October 7, 1994). ... Contract sold by Vipers to Florida Panthers (February 14, 1995). ... Separated left shoulder (October 15, 1995); missed two games. ... Fractured left thumb (November 18, 1995); missed 13 games. ... Traded by Panthers with C Stu Barnes to Pittsburgh Penguins for C Chris Wells (November 19, 1996). ... Injured groin (November 22, 1996); missed one game. ... Strained groin (February 27, 1997); missed one game. ... Strained groin (March 4, 1997); missed two games. ... Bruised wrist (March 18, 1997); missed two games. ... Traded by Penguins to Buffalo Sabres for fifth-round pick (D Robert Scuderi) in 1998 draft (September 24, 1997). ... Fractured thumb (October 1, 1997); missed nine games. ... Suffered from the flu (February 15, 1999); missed one game. ... Strained groin (April 14, 1999); missed one game. ... Injured rib (November 12, 1999); missed four games. ... Suffered from the flu (March 4, 2000); missed two games. ... Injured groin (December 12, 2000); missed four games. ... Injured knee (February 25, 2001); missed two games. ... Suffered from the flu (November 11, 2001); missed three games. ... Traded by Sabres to Detroit Red Wings for conditional pick in 2003 draft (November 17, 2002). ... Re-signed by Red Wings (June 22, 2003).

				REGULAR SEASON							PLAYOFFS			
Season Team	League	Gms.	G	A	Pts.	PIM	+/-	PP	SH	Gms.	G	A	Pts.	PIM
87-88—St. Michael's Jr. B	ODHA	31	19	37	56	22	...	...	...	—	—	—	—	—
88-89—Michigan State	CCHA	47	12	25	37	26	...	...	...	—	—	—	—	—
89-90—Michigan State	CCHA	45	10	38	48	26	...	...	...	—	—	—	—	—
90-91—Michigan State	CCHA	40	15	44	59	24	...	...	...	—	—	—	—	—
91-92—Canadian nat'l team	Int'l	60	14	30	44	36	...	...	...	—	—	—	—	—
—Can. Olympic team	Int'l	8	0	5	5	4	...	...	...	—	—	—	—	—
—Baltimore	AHL	15	1	10	11	6	...	...	...	—	—	—	—	—
—Washington	NHL	1	0	0	0	0	1	0	0	—	—	—	—	—
92-93—Baltimore	AHL	29	14	27	41	22	...	...	...	1	0	2	2	0
—Washington	NHL	26	0	2	2	10	3	0	0	—	—	—	—	—
93-94—Portland	AHL	41	12	29	41	14	...	...	...	9	2	2	4	4
—Washington	NHL	10	1	2	3	4	2	0	0	4	1	0	1	4
94-95—Detroit	IHL	48	8	28	36	38	...	...	...	—	—	—	—	—
—Florida	NHL	34	4	9	13	18	-1	1	0	—	—	—	—	—
95-96—Florida	NHL	52	6	28	34	32	-9	3	0	13	2	6	8	14
96-97—Florida	NHL	3	0	0	0	2	1	0	0	—	—	—	—	—
—Pittsburgh	NHL	57	6	30	36	28	3	2	0	5	0	3	3	0
97-98—Buffalo	NHL	71	9	26	35	35	8	3	0	15	2	9	11	12
98-99—Buffalo	NHL	80	10	33	43	62	16	4	0	21	4	11	15	10
99-00—Buffalo	NHL	74	8	25	33	52	14	2	0	5	0	2	2	2
00-01—Buffalo	NHL	67	5	18	23	46	0	4	0	8	1	5	6	2
01-02—Buffalo	NHL	59	8	20	28	34	-6	6	0	—	—	—	—	—
02-03—Buffalo	NHL	14	0	3	3	29	-1	0	0	—	—	—	—	—
—Detroit	NHL	62	6	17	23	22	12	1	0	4	1	0	1	0
NHL Totals (12 years)		**610**	**63**	**213**	**276**	**374**	**43**	**26**	**0**	**75**	**11**	**36**	**47**	**44**

WORRELL, PETER   LW   AVALANCHE

PERSONAL: Born August 18, 1977, in Pierrefonds, Que. ... 6-6/235. ... Shoots left. ... Name pronounced wuh-REHL.

TRANSACTIONS/CAREER NOTES: Selected by Florida Panthers in seventh round (seventh Panthers pick, 166th overall) of NHL entry draft (July 8, 1995). ... Suspended three games and fined $1,000 by NHL for elbowing incident (November 18, 1998). ... Sprained knee (September 21, 1999); missed nine games. ... Partially tore anterior collateral ligament in right knee (October 29, 1999); missed 12 games. ... Sprained knee (January 14, 2000); missed six games. ... Suffered head injury (March 19, 2000); missed six games. ... Strained back (March 2, 2001; missed one game. ... Injured shoulder (March 16, 2001); missed final 10 games of the season. ... Strained groin (October 18, 2001); missed one game. ... Injured hand (November 19, 2001); missed one game. ... Injured back (November 29, 2001); missed one game. ... Traded by Florida Panthers to Colorado Avalanche with 2004 second-round draft pick for F/D Eric Messier and F Vaclav Nedorost (July 20, 2003).

				REGULAR SEASON							PLAYOFFS			
Season Team	League	Gms.	G	A	Pts.	PIM	+/-	PP	SH	Gms.	G	A	Pts.	PIM
94-95—Hull	QMJHL	56	1	8	9	243	...	...	...	21	0	1	1	91
95-96—Hull	QMJHL	63	23	36	59	464	...	...	...	18	11	8	19	81
96-97—Hull	QMJHL	62	18	45	63	*495	...	...	...	14	3	13	16	83
97-98—New Haven	AHL	50	15	12	27	309	...	...	...	1	0	1	1	6
—Florida	NHL	19	0	0	0	153	-4	0	0	—	—	—	—	—
98-99—Florida	NHL	62	4	5	9	258	0	0	0	—	—	—	—	—
—New Haven	AHL	10	3	1	4	65	...	...	...	—	—	—	—	—
99-00—Florida	NHL	48	3	6	9	169	-7	2	0	4	1	0	1	8
00-01—Florida	NHL	71	3	7	10	248	-10	0	0	—	—	—	—	—
01-02—Florida	NHL	79	4	5	9	*354	-15	0	0	—	—	—	—	—
02-03—Florida	NHL	63	2	3	5	193	-14	0	0	—	—	—	—	—
NHL Totals (6 years)		**342**	**16**	**26**	**42**	**1375**	**-50**	**2**	**0**	**4**	**1**	**0**	**1**	**8**

WOTTON, MARK   D   STARS   **W**

PERSONAL: Born November 16, 1973, in Foxwarren, Man. ... 6-1/195. ... Shoots left. ... Name pronounced WAH-tehn.

TRANSACTIONS/CAREER NOTES: Selected by Vancouver Canucks in 10th round (11th Canucks pick, 237th overall) of NHL entry draft (June 20, 1992). ... Suffered blood clot in eye (May 17, 1995); missed six playoff games. ... Signed as free agent by Dallas Stars (July 7, 1999).

Season Team	League	REGULAR SEASON								PLAYOFFS				
		Gms.	G	A	Pts.	PIM	+/-	PP	SH	Gms.	G	A	Pts.	PIM
89-90—Saskatoon	WHL	51	2	3	5	31	...	...	...	7	1	1	2	15
90-91—Saskatoon	WHL	45	4	11	15	37	...	...	...	—	—	—	—	—
91-92—Saskatoon	WHL	64	11	25	36	92	...	...	...	—	—	—	—	—
92-93—Saskatoon	WHL	71	15	51	66	90	...	...	...	9	6	5	11	18
93-94—Saskatoon	WHL	65	12	34	46	108	...	...	...	16	3	12	15	32
94-95—Syracuse	AHL	75	12	29	41	50	...	...	...	—	—	—	—	—
—Vancouver	NHL	1	0	0	0	0	1	0	0	5	0	0	0	4
95-96—Syracuse	AHL	80	10	35	45	96	...	...	...	15	1	12	13	20
96-97—Syracuse	AHL	27	2	8	10	25	...	...	...	2	0	0	0	4
—Vancouver	NHL	36	3	6	9	19	8	0	1	—	—	—	—	—
97-98—Vancouver	NHL	5	0	0	0	6	-2	0	0	—	—	—	—	—
—Syracuse	AHL	56	12	21	33	80	...	...	...	5	0	0	0	12
98-99—Syracuse	AHL	72	4	31	35	74	...	...	...	—	—	—	—	—
99-00—Michigan	IHL	70	3	7	10	72	...	...	...	—	—	—	—	—
00-01—Utah	IHL	63	2	2	4	64	...	...	...	—	—	—	—	—
—Dallas	NHL	1	0	0	0	0	0	0	0	—	—	—	—	—
01-02—Utah	AHL	57	9	18	27	68	...	...	...	4	0	1	1	6
02-03—Utah	AHL	69	8	26	34	68	...	...	...	—	—	—	—	—
NHL Totals (4 years)		43	3	6	9	25	7	0	1	5	0	0	0	4

WOYWITKA, JEFF — D — FLYERS

PERSONAL: Born September 1, 1983, in Vermillion, Alta. ... 6-2/197. ... Shoots left.

TRANSACTIONS/CAREER NOTES: Selected by Philadelphia Flyers in first round (first Flyers pick, 27th overall) of NHL entry draft (June 23, 2001).

Season Team	League	REGULAR SEASON								PLAYOFFS				
		Gms.	G	A	Pts.	PIM	+/-	PP	SH	Gms.	G	A	Pts.	PIM
99-00—Red Deer	WHL	67	4	12	16	40	...	...	...	4	0	3	3	2
00-01—Red Deer	WHL	72	7	28	35	113	...	...	...	22	2	8	10	25
01-02—Red Deer	WHL	72	14	23	37	109	...	...	...	23	2	10	12	22
02-03—Red Deer	WHL	57	16	36	52	65	...	...	...	—	—	—	—	—

WREN, BOB — C

PERSONAL: Born September 16, 1974, in Preston, Ont. ... 5-10/182. ... Shoots left.

TRANSACTIONS/CAREER NOTES: Selected by Los Angeles Kings in fourth round (third Kings pick, 94th overall) of NHL entry draft (June 26, 1993). ... Signed as free agent by Hartford Whalers (September 6, 1994). ... Signed as free agent by Mighty Ducks of Anaheim (October 17, 1996). ... Signed as free agent by Toronto Maple Leafs (July 24, 2001). ... Traded by Maple Leafs to Nashville Predators for RW Nathan Perrott (December 31, 2002). ... Traded by Predators to Ottawa Senators for future considerations (March 10, 2003).

Season Team	League	REGULAR SEASON								PLAYOFFS				
		Gms.	G	A	Pts.	PIM	+/-	PP	SH	Gms.	G	A	Pts.	PIM
89-90—Guelph	Jr. B	48	24	36	60	12	...	...	...	—	—	—	—	—
90-91—Kingston	Jr. B	32	27	28	55	85	...	...	...	—	—	—	—	—
91-92—Det. Jr. Red Wings	OHL	62	13	36	49	58	...	...	...	7	3	4	7	19
92-93—Det. Jr. Red Wings	OHL	63	57	88	145	91	...	...	...	15	4	11	15	20
93-94—Det. Jr. Red Wings	OHL	57	45	64	109	81	...	...	...	17	12	18	30	20
94-95—Springfield	AHL	61	16	15	31	118	...	...	...	—	—	—	—	—
—Richmond	ECHL	2	0	1	1	0	...	...	...	—	—	—	—	—
95-96—Detroit	IHL	1	0	0	0	0	...	...	...	—	—	—	—	—
—Knoxville	ECHL	50	21	35	56	257	...	...	...	8	4	11	15	32
96-97—Baltimore	AHL	72	23	36	59	97	...	...	...	3	1	1	2	0
97-98—Cincinnati	AHL	77	†42	58	100	151	...	...	...	—	—	—	—	—
—Anaheim	NHL	3	0	0	0	0	0	0	0	—	—	—	—	—
98-99—Cincinnati	AHL	73	27	43	70	102	...	...	...	3	1	2	3	8
99-00—Cincinnati	AHL	57	24	38	62	61	...	...	...	—	—	—	—	—
00-01—Cincinnati	AHL	70	20	47	67	103	...	...	...	4	4	2	6	2
—Anaheim	NHL	1	0	0	0	0	-1	0	0	—	—	—	—	—
01-02—St. John's	AHL	69	24	49	73	83	...	...	...	11	5	7	12	6
—Toronto	NHL	1	0	0	0	0	1	0	0	1	0	0	0	0
02-03—St. John's	AHL	27	8	11	19	25	...	...	...	—	—	—	—	—
—Milwaukee	AHL	16	1	6	7	17	...	...	...	—	—	—	—	—
—Binghamton	AHL	14	2	12	14	23	...	...	...	—	—	—	—	—
NHL Totals (3 years)		5	0	0	0	0	0	0	0	1	0	0	0	0

W

WRIGHT, JAMIE — LW

PERSONAL: Born May 13, 1976, in Kitchener, Ont. ... 6-0/194. ... Shoots left.

TRANSACTIONS/CAREER NOTES: Selected by Dallas Stars in fourth round (third Stars pick, 98th overall) of NHL entry draft (June 29, 1994). ... Signed as free agent by Calgary Flames (August 2, 2001). ... Traded by Flames to Philadelphia Flyers for future considerations (January 22, 2003).

Season Team	League	REGULAR SEASON								PLAYOFFS				
		Gms.	G	A	Pts.	PIM	+/-	PP	SH	Gms.	G	A	Pts.	PIM
91-92—Elmira Jr. B	OHA	44	17	11	28	46	...	...	...	—	—	—	—	—
92-93—Elmira Jr. B	OHA	47	22	32	54	52	...	...	...	—	—	—	—	—
93-94—Guelph	OHL	65	17	15	32	34	...	...	...	8	2	1	3	10
94-95—Guelph	OHL	65	43	39	82	36	...	...	...	14	6	8	14	6
95-96—Guelph	OHL	55	30	36	66	45	...	...	...	16	10	12	22	35
96-97—Michigan	IHL	60	6	8	14	34	...	...	...	1	0	0	0	0
97-98—Michigan	IHL	53	15	11	26	31	...	...	...	—	—	—	—	—
—Dallas	NHL	21	4	2	6	2	8	0	0	5	0	0	0	0
98-99—Dallas	NHL	11	0	0	0	0	-3	0	0	—	—	—	—	—
—Michigan	IHL	64	16	15	31	92	...	...	...	2	0	0	0	2
99-00—Michigan	IHL	49	12	4	16	64	...	...	...	—	—	—	—	—
—Dallas	NHL	23	1	4	5	16	4	0	0	—	—	—	—	—
00-01—Utah	IHL	74	25	27	52	126	...	...	...	—	—	—	—	—
—Dallas	NHL	2	1	0	1	0	-3	0	0	—	—	—	—	—
01-02—Saint John	AHL	34	11	13	24	34	...	...	...	—	—	—	—	—
—Calgary	NHL	44	4	12	16	20	6	0	0	—	—	—	—	—
02-03—Saint John	AHL	3	2	1	3	0	...	...	...	—	—	—	—	—
—Calgary	NHL	19	2	2	4	12	1	0	0	—	—	—	—	—
—Philadelphia	NHL	4	0	0	0	4	-1	0	0	—	—	—	—	—
—Philadelphia	AHL	33	10	14	24	31	...	...	...	—	—	—	—	—
NHL Totals (6 years)		124	12	20	32	54	12	0	0	5	0	0	0	0

W
Y

WRIGHT, TYLER — C — BLUE JACKETS

PERSONAL: Born April 6, 1973, in Kamsack, Sask. ... 6-0/190. ... Shoots right.
TRANSACTIONS/CAREER NOTES: Selected by Edmonton Oilers in first round (first Oilers pick, 12th overall) of NHL entry draft (June 22, 1991). ... Traded by Oilers to Pittsburgh Penguins for seventh-round pick (RW Brandon LaFrance) in 1996 draft (June 22, 1996). ... Bruised ribs (December 13, 1996); missed one game. ... Suffered back spasms (January 18, 2000); missed two games. ... Strained knee (April 3, 2000); missed two games. ... Selected by Columbus Blue Jackets in NHL expansion draft (June 23, 2000). ... Bruised ribs (December 23, 2000); missed five games. ... Suffered from the flu (February 21, 2001); missed one game. ... Suffered concussion (November 1, 2001); missed five games.
STATISTICAL PLATEAUS: Three-goal games: 2000-01 (1), 2002-03 (2). Total: 3.

Season Team	League	REGULAR SEASON								PLAYOFFS				
		Gms.	G	A	Pts.	PIM	+/-	PP	SH	Gms.	G	A	Pts.	PIM
89-90—Swift Current	WHL	67	14	18	32	119	...	...	...	4	0	0	0	12
90-91—Swift Current	WHL	66	41	51	92	157	...	...	...	3	0	0	0	6
91-92—Swift Current	WHL	63	36	46	82	295	...	...	...	8	2	5	7	16
92-93—Swift Current	WHL	37	24	41	65	76	...	...	...	17	9	17	26	49
—Edmonton	NHL	7	1	1	2	19	-4	0	0	—	—	—	—	—
93-94—Cape Breton	AHL	65	14	27	41	160	...	...	...	5	2	0	2	11
—Edmonton	NHL	5	0	0	0	4	-3	0	0	—	—	—	—	—
94-95—Cape Breton	AHL	70	16	15	31	184	...	...	...	—	—	—	—	—
—Edmonton	NHL	6	1	0	1	14	1	0	0	—	—	—	—	—
95-96—Edmonton	NHL	23	1	0	1	33	-7	0	0	—	—	—	—	—
—Cape Breton	AHL	31	6	12	18	158	...	...	...	—	—	—	—	—
96-97—Pittsburgh	NHL	45	2	2	4	70	-7	0	0	—	—	—	—	—
—Cleveland	IHL	10	4	3	7	34	...	...	...	14	4	2	6	44
97-98—Pittsburgh	NHL	82	3	4	7	112	-3	1	0	6	0	1	1	4
98-99—Pittsburgh	NHL	61	0	0	0	90	-2	0	0	13	0	0	0	19
99-00—Wilkes-Barre/Scranton	AHL	25	5	15	20	86	...	...	...	—	—	—	—	—
—Pittsburgh	NHL	50	12	10	22	45	4	0	0	11	3	1	4	17
00-01—Columbus	NHL	76	16	16	32	140	-9	4	1	—	—	—	—	—
01-02—Columbus	NHL	77	13	11	24	100	-40	4	0	—	—	—	—	—
02-03—Columbus	NHL	70	19	11	30	113	-25	3	2	—	—	—	—	—
NHL Totals (11 years)		502	68	55	123	740	-95	12	3	30	3	2	5	40

YACHMENEV, VITALI — LW

PERSONAL: Born January 8, 1975, in Chelyabinsk, U.S.S.R. ... 5-11/200. ... Shoots left. ... Name pronounced vee-TAL-ee YAHCH-mih-nehf.
TRANSACTIONS/CAREER NOTES: Selected by Los Angeles Kings in third round (third Kings pick, 59th overall) of NHL entry draft (June 29, 1994). ... Sprained left shoulder (October 4, 1996); missed eight games. ... Sprained ankle (December 27, 1996); missed seven games. ... Suffered from the flu (February 11, 1997); missed one game. ... Traded by Kings to Nashville Predators for future considerations (July 7, 1998). ... Partially dislocated shoulder (February 4, 1999); missed 10 games. ... Sprained wrist (November 3, 1999); missed three games. ... Reinjured wrist (November 13, 1999); missed seven games. ... Suffered concussion (March 12, 2000); missed four games. ... Strained back joint (December 17, 2000); missed four games. ... Bruised right foot (November 23, 2001); missed four games. ... Strained back (March 17, 2002); missed three games.
STATISTICAL PLATEAUS: Three-goal games: 1995-96 (1).

Season Team	League	REGULAR SEASON								PLAYOFFS				
		Gms.	G	A	Pts.	PIM	+/-	PP	SH	Gms.	G	A	Pts.	PIM
90-91—Traktor Chelyabinsk	USSR	80	88	60	148	72	...	...	...	—	—	—	—	—
91-92—Traktor Chelyabinsk	CIS	80	82	70	152	20	...	...	...	—	—	—	—	—
92-93—Mechel Chelyabinsk	CIS Div. II	51	23	20	43	12	...	...	...	—	—	—	—	—
93-94—North Bay	OHL	66	*61	52	113	18	...	...	...	18	13	19	32	12
94-95—North Bay	OHL	59	53	52	105	8	...	...	...	6	1	8	9	2
—Phoenix	IHL	—	—	—	—	—	—	—	—	4	1	0	1	0
95-96—Los Angeles	NHL	80	19	34	53	16	-3	6	1	—	—	—	—	—
96-97—Los Angeles	NHL	65	10	22	32	10	-9	2	0	—	—	—	—	—

			REGULAR SEASON								PLAYOFFS				
Season Team	League	Gms.	G	A	Pts.	PIM	+/-	PP	SH	Gms.	G	A	Pts.	PIM
97-98—Los Angeles	NHL	4	0	1	1	4	1	0	0	—	—	—	—	—
—Long Beach	IHL	59	23	28	51	14	...	...	...	17	8	9	17	4
98-99—Milwaukee	IHL	16	7	6	13	0				—	—	—	—	—
—Nashville	NHL	55	7	10	17	10	-10	0	1	—	—	—	—	—
99-00—Nashville	NHL	68	16	16	32	12	5	1	1	—	—	—	—	—
00-01—Nashville	NHL	78	15	19	34	10	-5	4	1	—	—	—	—	—
01-02—Nashville	NHL	75	11	16	27	14	-16	1	2	—	—	—	—	—
02-03—Nashville	NHL	62	5	15	20	12	7	0	0	—	—	—	—	—
NHL Totals (8 years)		487	83	133	216	88	-30	14	6					

YAKUBOV, MIKHAIL   C   BLACKHAWKS

PERSONAL: Born February 16, 1982, in Bamaul, U.S.S.R. ... 6-3/185. ... Shoots left.
TRANSACTIONS/CAREER NOTES: Selected by Chicago Blackhawks in first round (first Blackhawks pick, 10th overall) of NHL entry draft (June 24, 2000).

			REGULAR SEASON								PLAYOFFS				
Season Team	League	Gms.	G	A	Pts.	PIM	+/-	PP	SH	Gms.	G	A	Pts.	PIM
99-00—Lada Togliatti	Rus. Div. II	26	12	19	31	14	...	...	...	—	—	—	—	—
00-01—Lada Togliatti	Russian	25	0	0	0	4	...	...	...	4	0	0	0	0
01-02—Red Deer	WHL	71	32	57	89	54	...	...	...	23	14	9	23	28
02-03—Norfolk	AHL	62	6	5	11	36	...	...	...	—	—	—	—	—

YASHIN, ALEXEI   C   ISLANDERS

PERSONAL: Born November 5, 1973, in Sverdlovsk, U.S.S.R. ... 6-3/220. ... Shoots right. ... Name pronounced uh-LEK-see YA-shihn.
TRANSACTIONS/CAREER NOTES: Selected by Ottawa Senators in first round (first Senators pick, second overall) of NHL entry draft (June 20, 1992). ... Suffered strep throat (December 4, 1993); missed one game. ... Missed entire 1999-2000 season due to contract dispute. ... Traded by Senators to New York Islanders for RW Bill Muckalt, D Zdeno Chara and first-round pick (C Jason Spezza) in 2001 draft (June 23, 2001). ... Strained groin (April 6, 2002); missed final four games of season.
STATISTICAL PLATEAUS: Three-goal games: 1993-94 (1), 1994-95 (1), 1995-96 (1), 1997-98 (1), 1998-99 (1), 2000-01 (1), 2001-02 (1). Total: 7. ... Four-goal games: 2002-03 (1). ... Total hat tricks: 8.

			REGULAR SEASON								PLAYOFFS				
Season Team	League	Gms.	G	A	Pts.	PIM	+/-	PP	SH	Gms.	G	A	Pts.	PIM
90-91—Avtomo. Sverdlovsk	USSR	26	2	1	3	10	...	...	...	—	—	—	—	—
91-92—Dynamo Moscow	CIS	35	7	5	12	19	...	...	...	—	—	—	—	—
92-93—Dynamo Moscow	CIS	27	10	12	22	18	...	...	...	10	7	3	10	18
93-94—Ottawa	NHL	83	30	49	79	22	-49	11	2	—	—	—	—	—
94-95—Las Vegas	IHL	24	15	20	35	32	...	...	...	—	—	—	—	—
—Ottawa	NHL	47	21	23	44	20	-20	11	0	—	—	—	—	—
95-96—Ottawa	NHL	46	15	24	39	28	-15	8	0	—	—	—	—	—
96-97—Ottawa	NHL	82	35	40	75	44	-7	10	0	7	1	5	6	2
97-98—Ottawa	NHL	82	33	39	72	24	6	5	0	11	5	3	8	8
—Russian Oly. team	Int'l	6	3	3	6	0	...	...	...	—	—	—	—	—
98-99—Ottawa	NHL	82	44	50	94	54	16	19	0	4	0	0	0	10
99-00—Ottawa	NHL						Did not play.							
00-01—Ottawa	NHL	82	40	48	88	30	10	13	2	4	0	1	1	0
01-02—New York Islanders	NHL	78	32	43	75	25	-3	15	0	7	3	4	7	2
—Russian Oly. team	Int'l	6	1	1	2	0	...	...	...	—	—	—	—	—
02-03—New York Islanders	NHL	81	26	39	65	32	-12	14	0	5	2	2	4	2
NHL Totals (10 years)		663	276	355	631	279	-74	106	4	38	11	15	26	24

YELLE, STEPHANE   C   FLAMES

PERSONAL: Born May 9, 1974, in Ottawa ... 6-2/190. ... Shoots left. ... Name pronounced YEHL.
TRANSACTIONS/CAREER NOTES: Selected by New Jersey Devils in eighth round (ninth Devils pick, 186th overall) of NHL entry draft (June 20, 1992). ... Traded by Devils with 11th-round pick (D Stephen Low) in 1994 draft to Quebec Nordiques for 11th-round pick (C Mike Hansen) in 1994 draft (June 1, 1994). ... Nordiques franchise moved to Colorado and renamed Avalanche for 1995-96 season (June 21, 1995). ... Pulled groin (February 15, 1996); missed nine games. ... Strained hip flexor (December 14, 1996); missed three games. ... Sprained right wrist (November 28, 1998); missed nine games. ... Sprained knee (May 3, 1999); missed nine playoff games. ... Injured sternum (January 25, 2000); missed two games. ... Strained hip flexor (March 7, 2000); missed one game. ... Injured ankle (October 25, 2000); missed one game. ... Strained groin (November 18, 2000); missed three games. ... Injured back (December 20, 2000); missed three games. ... Suffered herniated disk in back (December 27, 2000); missed 10 games. ... Injured knee (February 17, 2001); missed nine games. ... Sprained knee (March 24, 2001); missed six games. ... Injured ankle (November 16, 2001); missed one game. ... Suffered from the flu (November 27, 2001); missed one game. ... Bruised foot (December 23, 2001); missed one game. ... Bruised knee (January 3, 2001); missed one game. ... Injured shoulder (March 14, 2002); missed five games. ... Traded by Avalanche with LW Chris Drury to Calgary Flames for D Derek Morris, LW Dean McAmmond and C Jeff Shantz (October 1, 2002). ... Signed by Flames (July 15, 2003).

			REGULAR SEASON								PLAYOFFS				
Season Team	League	Gms.	G	A	Pts.	PIM	+/-	PP	SH	Gms.	G	A	Pts.	PIM
91-92—Oshawa	OHL	55	12	14	26	20	...	...	...	7	2	0	2	1
92-93—Oshawa	OHL	66	24	50	74	20	...	...	...	10	2	4	6	4
93-94—Oshawa	OHL	66	35	69	104	22	...	...	...	5	1	7	8	2
94-95—Cornwall	AHL	40	18	15	33	22	...	...	...	13	7	7	14	8
95-96—Colorado	NHL	71	13	14	27	30	15	0	2	22	1	4	5	8
96-97—Colorado	NHL	79	9	17	26	38	1	0	1	12	1	6	7	2
97-98—Colorado	NHL	81	7	15	22	48	-10	0	1	7	1	0	1	12

Season Team	League	REGULAR SEASON								PLAYOFFS				
		Gms.	G	A	Pts.	PIM	+/-	PP	SH	Gms.	G	A	Pts.	PIM
98-99—Colorado	NHL	72	8	7	15	40	-8	1	0	10	0	1	1	6
99-00—Colorado	NHL	79	8	14	22	28	9	0	1	17	1	2	3	4
00-01—Colorado	NHL	50	4	10	14	20	-3	0	1	23	1	2	3	8
01-02—Colorado	NHL	73	5	12	17	48	1	0	1	20	0	2	2	14
02-03—Calgary	NHL	82	10	15	25	50	-10	3	0	—	—	—	—	—
NHL Totals (8 years)		587	64	104	168	302	-5	4	7	111	5	17	22	54

YORK, JASON D PREDATORS

PERSONAL: Born May 20, 1970, in Nepean, Ont. ... 6-1/208. ... Shoots right.

TRANSACTIONS/CAREER NOTES: Selected by Detroit Red Wings in seventh round (sixth Red Wings pick, 129th overall) of NHL entry draft (June 16, 1990). ... Traded by Red Wings with C/RW Mike Sillinger to Mighty Ducks of Anaheim for LW Stu Grimson, D Mark Ferner and sixth-round pick (LW Magnus Nilsson) in 1996 draft (April 4, 1995). ... Sprained right ankle (December 1, 1995); missed two games. ... Traded by Mighty Ducks with C Shaun Van Allen to Ottawa Senators for C Ted Drury and rights to D Marc Moro (October 1, 1996). ... Strained groin (December 4, 1996); missed six games. ... Suffered concussion (January 3, 1998); missed four games. ... Injured right eye (April 13, 1998); missed three games. ... Strained shoulder (October 1, 1998); missed first two games of season. ... Strained groin (December 8, 1999); missed three games. ... Strained shoulder (October 27, 2000); missed one game. ... Suffered from the flu (January 16, 2001); missed one game. ... Fractured leg (February 8, 2001); missed six games. ... Signed as free agent by Mighty Ducks (July 3, 2001). ... Injured right shoulder (January 9, 2002); missed five games. ... Traded by Mighty Ducks to Nashville Predators for future considerations (October 23, 2002).

Season Team	League	REGULAR SEASON								PLAYOFFS				
		Gms.	G	A	Pts.	PIM	+/-	PP	SH	Gms.	G	A	Pts.	PIM
89-90—Windsor	OHL	39	9	30	39	38	...	...	...	—	—	—	—	—
—Kitchener	OHL	25	11	25	36	17	...	...	...	17	3	19	22	10
90-91—Windsor	OHL	66	13	80	93	40	...	...	...	11	3	10	13	12
91-92—Adirondack	AHL	49	4	20	24	32	...	...	...	5	0	1	1	0
92-93—Adirondack	AHL	77	15	40	55	86	...	...	...	11	0	3	3	18
—Detroit	NHL	2	0	0	0	0	0	0	0	—	—	—	—	—
93-94—Adirondack	AHL	74	10	56	66	98	...	...	...	12	3	11	14	22
—Detroit	NHL	7	1	2	3	2	0	0	0	—	—	—	—	—
94-95—Adirondack	AHL	5	1	3	4	4	...	...	...	—	—	—	—	—
—Detroit	NHL	10	1	2	3	2	0	0	0	—	—	—	—	—
—Anaheim	NHL	15	0	8	8	12	4	0	0	—	—	—	—	—
95-96—Anaheim	NHL	79	3	21	24	88	-7	0	0	—	—	—	—	—
96-97—Ottawa	NHL	75	4	17	21	67	-8	1	0	7	0	0	0	4
97-98—Ottawa	NHL	73	3	13	16	62	8	0	0	7	1	1	2	7
98-99—Ottawa	NHL	79	4	31	35	48	17	2	0	4	1	1	2	4
99-00—Ottawa	NHL	79	8	22	30	60	-3	1	0	6	0	2	2	2
00-01—Ottawa	NHL	74	6	16	22	72	7	3	0	4	0	0	0	4
01-02—Anaheim	NHL	74	5	20	25	60	-11	3	0	—	—	—	—	—
02-03—Cincinnati	AHL	4	3	2	5	8	...	...	...	—	—	—	—	—
—Nashville	NHL	74	4	15	19	52	13	2	0	—	—	—	—	—
NHL Totals (11 years)		641	39	167	206	525	20	12	0	28	2	4	6	21

YORK, MIKE LW OILERS

PERSONAL: Born January 3, 1978, in Waterford, Mich. ... 5-10/185. ... Shoots right. ... Full Name: Michael York.

TRANSACTIONS/CAREER NOTES: Selected by New York Rangers in sixth round (seventh Rangers pick, 136th overall) of NHL entry draft (June 21, 1997). ... Bruised ribs (January 22, 2001); missed one game. ... Injured left shoulder (February 9, 2001); missed two games. ... Suffered from the flu (March 13, 2002); missed one game. ... Traded by Rangers with fourth-round pick (D Ivan Koltsov) in 2002 draft to Edmonton Oilers for D Tom Poti and LW Rem Murray (March 19, 2002).

Season Team	League	REGULAR SEASON								PLAYOFFS				
		Gms.	G	A	Pts.	PIM	+/-	PP	SH	Gms.	G	A	Pts.	PIM
95-96—Michigan State	CCHA	39	12	27	39	20	...	...	...	—	—	—	—	—
96-97—Michigan State	CCHA	37	18	29	47	42	...	...	...	—	—	—	—	—
97-98—Michigan State	CCHA	40	27	34	61	38	...	...	...	—	—	—	—	—
98-99—Michigan State	CCHA	42	22	32	*54	41	...	...	...	—	—	—	—	—
—Hartford	AHL	3	2	2	4	0	...	...	...	6	3	1	4	0
99-00—New York Rangers	NHL	82	26	24	50	18	-17	8	0	—	—	—	—	—
00-01—New York Rangers	NHL	79	14	17	31	20	1	3	2	—	—	—	—	—
01-02—New York Rangers	NHL	69	18	39	57	16	8	2	0	—	—	—	—	—
—U.S. Olympic team	Int'l	6	0	1	1	0	...	...	...	—	—	—	—	—
—Edmonton	NHL	12	2	2	4	0	-1	1	0	—	—	—	—	—
02-03—Edmonton	NHL	71	22	29	51	10	-8	7	2	6	0	2	2	2
NHL Totals (4 years)		313	82	111	193	64	-17	21	4	6	0	2	2	2

YOUNG, SCOTT RW STARS

PERSONAL: Born October 1, 1967, in Clinton, Mass. ... 6-1/200. ... Shoots right. ... Full Name: Scott Allen Young.

TRANSACTIONS/CAREER NOTES: Selected by Hartford Whalers in first round (first Whalers pick, 11th overall) of NHL entry draft (June 21, 1986). ... Suffered lacerations above right eye (October 8, 1988). ... Lacerated face (February 18, 1990). ... Traded by Whalers to Pittsburgh Penguins for RW Rob Brown (December 21, 1990). ... Traded by Penguins to Quebec Nordiques for D Bryan Fogarty (March 10, 1992). ... Injured rib (February 14, 1993); missed one game. ... Bruised ribs (February 23, 1993); missed one game. ... Sprained right ankle (October 5, 1993); missed eight games. ... Played in Europe during 1994-95 NHL lockout. ... Nordiques franchise moved to Colorado and renamed Avalanche for 1995-96 season (June 21, 1995). ... Bruised right shoulder (December 23, 1996); missed five games. ... Traded by Avalanche to Mighty Ducks of Anaheim for third-round pick (traded to Florida) in 1998 draft (September 17, 1997). ... Bruised right foot (November 22,

1997); missed two games. ... Bruised right foot (November 29, 1997); missed five games. ... Suffered eye abrasion (March 9, 1998); missed two games. ... Signed as free agent by St. Louis Blues (July 16, 1998). ... Suffered sore back (February 8, 1999); missed one game. ... Injured back (January 28, 2000); missed three games. ... Separated shoulder (April 5, 2000); missed final two games of regular season. ... Injured shoulder (December 5, 2000); missed one game. ... Suffered back spasms (October 13, 2001); missed four games. ... Injured eye (January 8, 2002); missed 11 games. ... Signed as free agent by Dallas Stars (July 5, 2002). ... Suspended two games by NHL for high-sticking incident (March 12, 2003).

STATISTICAL PLATEAUS: Three-goal games: 1992-93 (1), 1993-94 (1), 1994-95 (1), 1996-97 (1). Total: 4.

		REGULAR SEASON								PLAYOFFS				
Season Team	League	Gms.	G	A	Pts.	PIM	+/-	PP	SH	Gms.	G	A	Pts.	PIM
84-85—St. Marks H.S.	Mass. H.S.	23	28	41	69	...	...	...	...	—	—	—	—	—
85-86—Boston University	Hockey East	38	16	13	29	31	...	...	...	—	—	—	—	—
86-87—Boston University	Hockey East	33	15	21	36	24	...	...	...	—	—	—	—	—
87-88—U.S. Olympic team......	Int'l	59	13	53	66	...	...	...	...	—	—	—	—	—
—Hartford	NHL	7	0	0	0	2	-6	0	0	4	1	0	1	0
88-89—Hartford	NHL	76	19	40	59	27	-21	6	0	4	2	0	2	4
89-90—Hartford	NHL	80	24	40	64	47	-24	10	2	7	2	0	2	2
90-91—Hartford	NHL	34	6	9	15	8	-9	3	1	—	—	—	—	—
—Pittsburgh..................	NHL	43	11	16	27	33	3	3	1	17	1	6	7	2
91-92—U.S. national team	Int'l	10	2	4	6	21	...	...	...	—	—	—	—	—
—U.S. Olympic team......	Int'l	8	2	1	3	2	...	...	...	—	—	—	—	—
—Bolzano......................	Italy	18	22	17	39	6	...	...	...	—	—	—	—	—
92-93—Quebec	NHL	82	30	30	60	20	5	9	6	6	4	1	5	0
93-94—Quebec	NHL	76	26	25	51	14	-4	6	1	—	—	—	—	—
94-95—Frankfurt....................	Germany	1	1	0	1	0	...	...	...	—	—	—	—	—
—Landshut....................	Germany	4	6	1	7	6	...	...	...	—	—	—	—	—
—Quebec	NHL	48	18	21	39	14	9	3	3	6	3	3	6	2
95-96—Colorado	NHL	81	21	39	60	50	2	7	0	22	3	12	15	10
96-97—Colorado	NHL	72	18	19	37	14	-5	7	0	17	4	2	6	14
97-98—Anaheim	NHL	73	13	20	33	22	-13	4	2	—	—	—	—	—
98-99—St. Louis	NHL	75	24	28	52	27	8	8	0	13	4	7	11	10
99-00—St. Louis	NHL	75	24	15	39	18	12	6	1	6	6	2	8	8
00-01—St. Louis	NHL	81	40	33	73	30	15	14	3	15	6	7	13	2
01-02—St. Louis	NHL	67	19	22	41	26	11	5	0	10	3	0	3	2
—U.S. Olympic team......	Int'l	6	4	0	4	2	...	...	...	—	—	—	—	—
02-03—Dallas........................	NHL	79	23	19	42	30	24	5	1	10	4	3	7	6
NHL Totals (15 years).........		1049	316	376	692	382	7	96	21	137	43	43	86	62

YUSHKEVICH, DMITRY D

PERSONAL: Born November 19, 1971, in Yaroslavl, U.S.S.R. ... 5-11/215. ... Shoots right. ... Name pronounced yoosh-KAY-vihch.

TRANSACTIONS/CAREER NOTES: Selected by Philadelphia Flyers in sixth round (sixth Flyers pick, 122nd overall) of NHL entry draft (June 22, 1991). ... Sprained wrist (January 28, 1993); missed two games. ... Strained groin (February 18, 1994); missed four games. ... Played in Europe during 1994-95 NHL lockout. ... Suffered from sore back (February 23, 1995); missed three games. ... Sprained left knee (April 14, 1995); missed five games. ... Traded by Flyers with second-round pick (G Francis Larivee) in 1996 draft to Toronto Maple Leafs for first-(RW Dainius Zubrus) and fourth-round (traded to Los Angeles) picks in 1996 draft and second-round pick (G Jean-Marc Pelletier) in 1997 draft (August 30, 1995). ... Sprained knee (October 26, 1995); missed eight games. ... Bruised knee (December 30, 1995); missed two games. ... Pulled hamstring (December 14, 1996); missed four games. ... Injured knee (March 22, 1997); missed two games. ... Fractured toe (October 15, 1997); missed six games. ... Sprained knee (December 31, 1997); missed two games. ... Strained groin (December 12, 1998); missed three games. ... Suffered injury (November 30, 2000); missed one game. ... Suffered blood clot in leg (February 5, 2002); missed remainder of season. ... Traded by Maple Leafs to Florida Panthers for D Robert Svehla (July 18, 2002). ... Traded by Panthers with fifth-round pick in 2003 draft to Los Angeles Kings for RW Jaroslav Bednar and D Andreas Lilja (November 26, 2002). ... Traded by Kings to Philadelphia Flyers for fourth-round pick in 2003 and seventh-round pick in 2004 draft (March 2, 2003).

		REGULAR SEASON								PLAYOFFS				
Season Team	League	Gms.	G	A	Pts.	PIM	+/-	PP	SH	Gms.	G	A	Pts.	PIM
88-89—Torpedo Yaroslavl	USSR	23	2	1	3	8	...	...	...	—	—	—	—	—
89-90—Torpedo Yaroslavl	USSR	41	2	3	5	39	...	...	...	—	—	—	—	—
90-91—Torpedo Yaroslavl	USSR	43	10	4	14	22	...	...	...	—	—	—	—	—
91-92—Dynamo Moscow........	CIS	41	6	7	13	14	...	...	...	—	—	—	—	—
—Unif. Olympic team......	Int'l	8	1	2	3	4	...	...	...	—	—	—	—	—
92-93—Philadelphia	NHL	82	5	27	32	71	12	1	0	—	—	—	—	—
93-94—Philadelphia	NHL	75	5	25	30	86	-8	1	0	—	—	—	—	—
94-95—Torpedo Yaroslavl	CIS	10	3	4	7	8	...	...	...	—	—	—	—	—
—Philadelphia	NHL	40	5	9	14	47	-4	3	1	15	1	5	6	12
95-96—Toronto	NHL	69	1	10	11	54	-14	1	0	4	0	0	0	0
96-97—Toronto	NHL	74	4	10	14	56	-24	1	1	—	—	—	—	—
97-98—Toronto	NHL	72	0	12	12	78	-13	0	0	—	—	—	—	—
—Russian Oly. team.......	Int'l	6	0	0	0	2	...	...	...	—	—	—	—	—
98-99—Toronto	NHL	78	6	22	28	88	25	2	1	17	1	5	6	22
99-00—Toronto	NHL	77	3	24	27	55	2	2	1	12	1	1	2	4
00-01—Toronto	NHL	81	5	19	24	52	-2	1	0	11	0	4	4	12
01-02—Toronto	NHL	55	6	13	19	26	14	3	0	—	—	—	—	—
02-03—Florida	NHL	23	1	6	7	14	-12	0	0	—	—	—	—	—
—Los Angeles...............	NHL	42	0	3	3	24	-4	0	0	—	—	—	—	—
—Philadelphia	NHL	18	2	2	4	8	7	0	0	13	1	4	5	2
NHL Totals (11 years).........		786	43	182	225	659	-21	15	4	72	4	19	23	52

YZERMAN, STEVE C

PERSONAL: Born May 9, 1965, in Cranbrook, B.C. ... 5-11/185. ... Shoots right. ... Name pronounced IGH-zuhr-muhn.

TRANSACTIONS/CAREER NOTES: Selected by Detroit Red Wings in first round (first Red Wings pick, fourth overall) of NHL entry draft (June 8, 1983). ... Fractured collarbone (January 31, 1986). ... Injured ligaments of right knee (March 1, 1988) and underwent surgery. ... Injured right knee in playoff game (April 8, 1991). ... Suffered herniated disc (October 21, 1993); missed 26 games. ... Sprained knee (May 27, 1995); missed three playoff games. ... Suffered from the flu (March 17, 1996); missed one game. ... Bruised ankle (April 9, 1997); missed one game. ... Sprained medial collateral ligament in knee (January 28, 1998); missed three games. ... Strained groin (April 11, 1998); missed three games. ... Suffered lacerations to forehead and nose and fractured nose (January 21, 1999); missed one game. ... Sprained knee (March 29, 2000); missed final four games of regular season. ... Sprained knee (September 28, 2000); missed first two games of season. ... Underwent knee surgery (October 13, 2000); missed 23 games. ... Bruised ankle (December 26, 2001); missed three games. ... Underwent right knee surgery (January 27, 2002); missed six games. ... Reinjured knee (February 26, 2002); missed 19 games.

STATISTICAL PLATEAUS: Three-goal games: 1983-84 (1), 1984-85 (1), 1987-88 (2), 1988-89 (2), 1989-90 (2), 1990-91 (3), 1991-92 (3), 1992-93 (3). Total: 17. ... Four-goal games: 1989-90 (1). ... Total hat tricks: 18.

		REGULAR SEASON								PLAYOFFS				
Season Team	League	Gms.	G	A	Pts.	PIM	+/-	PP	SH	Gms.	G	A	Pts.	PIM
81-82—Peterborough..............	OHL	58	21	43	64	65	...	...	...	6	0	1	1	16
82-83—Peterborough..............	OHL	56	42	49	91	33	...	...	...	4	1	4	5	0
83-84—Detroit......................	NHL	80	39	48	87	33	-17	13	0	4	3	3	6	0
84-85—Detroit......................	NHL	80	30	59	89	58	-17	9	0	3	2	1	3	2
85-86—Detroit......................	NHL	51	14	28	42	16	-24	3	0	—	—	—	—	—
86-87—Detroit......................	NHL	80	31	59	90	43	-1	9	1	16	5	13	18	8
87-88—Detroit......................	NHL	64	50	52	102	44	30	10	6	3	1	3	4	6
88-89—Detroit......................	NHL	80	65	90	155	61	17	17	3	6	5	5	10	2
89-90—Detroit......................	NHL	79	62	65	127	79	-6	16	†7	—	—	—	—	—
90-91—Detroit......................	NHL	80	51	57	108	34	-2	12	6	7	3	3	6	4
91-92—Detroit......................	NHL	79	45	58	103	64	26	9	*8	11	3	5	8	12
92-93—Detroit......................	NHL	84	58	79	137	44	33	13	†7	7	4	3	7	4
93-94—Detroit......................	NHL	58	24	58	82	36	11	7	3	3	1	3	4	0
94-95—Detroit......................	NHL	47	12	26	38	40	6	4	0	15	4	8	12	0
95-96—Detroit......................	NHL	80	36	59	95	64	29	16	2	18	8	12	20	4
96-97—Detroit......................	NHL	81	22	63	85	78	22	8	0	20	7	6	13	4
97-98—Detroit......................	NHL	75	24	45	69	46	3	6	2	22	6	18	24	22
—Can. Olympic team	Int'l	6	1	1	2	10	...	...	...	—	—	—	—	—
98-99—Detroit......................	NHL	80	29	45	74	42	8	13	2	10	9	4	13	0
99-00—Detroit......................	NHL	78	35	44	79	34	28	15	2	8	0	4	4	0
00-01—Detroit......................	NHL	54	18	34	52	18	4	5	0	1	0	0	0	0
01-02—Detroit......................	NHL	52	13	35	48	18	11	5	1	23	6	17	23	10
—Can. Olympic team	Int'l	6	2	4	6	2	...	...	...	—	—	—	—	—
02-03—Detroit......................	NHL	16	2	6	8	8	6	1	0	4	0	1	1	2
NHL Totals (20 years).........		1378	660	1010	1670	860	167	191	50	181	67	109	176	80

ZALESAK, MIROSLAV RW SHARKS

PERSONAL: Born January 2, 1980, in Skalica, Czechoslovakia ... 6-0/200. ... Shoots left.

TRANSACTIONS/CAREER NOTES: Selected by San Jose Sharks in fourth round (fifth Sharks pick, 104th overall) of NHL entry draft (June 27, 1998). ... Signed by Sharks (July 15, 2003).

		REGULAR SEASON								PLAYOFFS				
Season Team	League	Gms.	G	A	Pts.	PIM	+/-	PP	SH	Gms.	G	A	Pts.	PIM
95-96—HC Nitra	Slovakia Jrs.	49	53	29	82	...	...	...	...	—	—	—	—	—
96-97—HC Nitra	Slovakia Jrs.	58	51	31	82	...	...	...	...	—	—	—	—	—
97-98—HC Nitra	Slovakia Jrs.	23	33	23	56	16	...	...	...	—	—	—	—	—
—Plastika Nitra	Slovakia	30	8	6	14	0	...	...	...	—	—	—	—	—
98-99—Plastika Nitra	Slovakia	15	4	3	7	10	...	...	...	—	—	—	—	—
—Drummondville	QMJHL	45	24	27	51	18	...	...	...	—	—	—	—	—
99-00—Drummondville	QMJHL	60	50	61	111	40	...	...	...	16	7	11	18	4
00-01—Kentucky	AHL	60	14	11	25	26	...	...	...	3	0	1	1	4
01-02—Cleveland	AHL	74	22	20	42	44	...	...	...	—	—	—	—	—
02-03—Cleveland	AHL	50	27	22	49	35	...	...	...	—	—	—	—	—
—San Jose	NHL	10	1	2	3	0	-2	0	0	—	—	—	—	—
NHL Totals (1 year).............		10	1	2	3	0	-2	0	0					

ZAMUNER, ROB LW BRUINS

PERSONAL: Born September 17, 1969, in Oakville, Ont. ... 6-3/203. ... Shoots left. ... Name pronounced ZAM-uh-nuhr.

TRANSACTIONS/CAREER NOTES: Selected by New York Rangers in third round (third Rangers pick, 45th overall) of NHL entry draft (June 17, 1989). ... Signed as free agent by Tampa Bay Lightning (July 14, 1992). ... Rangers awarded third-round pick in 1993 draft as compensation (July 23, 1992). ... Hyperextended elbow (March 19, 1995); missed five games. ... Sprained knee (October 4, 1995); missed 10 games. ... Suffered sore back (April 1, 1998); missed five games. ... Strained groin (October 30, 1998); missed three games. ... Strained groin (November 8, 1998); missed 18 games. ... Strained groin (February 26, 1999); missed three games. ... Traded by Lightning with conditional second-round pick in 2002 draft to Ottawa Senators for C/LW Andreas Johansson to complete deal that allowed Tampa Bay to sign general manager Rick Dudley (June 30, 1999). ... Strained groin (October 28, 1999); missed five games. ... Sprained medial collateral ligament in left knee (December 23, 1999); missed 19 games. ... Strained groin (January 25, 2001); missed three games. ... Signed as free agent by Boston Bruins (July 6, 2001). ... Injured shoulder (October 23, 2001); missed 14 games. ... Strained hip flexor (March 1, 2002); missed two games.

STATISTICAL PLATEAUS: Three-goal games: 1997-98 (1).

Season Team	League	REGULAR SEASON								PLAYOFFS				
		Gms.	G	A	Pts.	PIM	+/-	PP	SH	Gms.	G	A	Pts.	PIM
86-87—Guelph	OHL	62	6	15	21	8	...	...	...	—	—	—	—	—
87-88—Guelph	OHL	58	20	41	61	18	...	...	...	—	—	—	—	—
88-89—Guelph	OHL	66	46	65	111	38	...	...	...	7	5	5	10	9
89-90—Flint	IHL	77	44	35	79	32	...	...	...	4	1	0	1	6
90-91—Binghamton	AHL	80	25	58	83	50	...	...	...	9	7	6	13	35
91-92—Binghamton	AHL	61	19	53	72	42	...	...	...	11	8	9	17	8
—New York Rangers	NHL	9	1	2	3	2	0	0	0	—	—	—	—	—
92-93—Tampa Bay	NHL	84	15	28	43	74	-25	1	0	—	—	—	—	—
93-94—Tampa Bay	NHL	59	6	6	12	42	-9	0	0	—	—	—	—	—
94-95—Tampa Bay	NHL	43	9	6	15	24	-3	0	3	—	—	—	—	—
95-96—Tampa Bay	NHL	72	15	20	35	62	11	0	3	6	2	3	5	10
96-97—Tampa Bay	NHL	82	17	33	50	56	3	0	4	—	—	—	—	—
97-98—Tampa Bay	NHL	77	14	12	26	41	-31	0	3	—	—	—	—	—
—Can. Olympic team	Int'l	6	1	0	1	8	...	...	...	—	—	—	—	—
98-99—Tampa Bay	NHL	58	8	11	19	24	-15	1	1	—	—	—	—	—
99-00—Ottawa	NHL	57	9	12	21	32	-6	0	1	6	2	0	2	2
00-01—Ottawa	NHL	79	19	18	37	52	7	1	2	4	0	0	0	6
01-02—Boston	NHL	66	12	13	25	24	6	1	2	6	0	2	2	4
02-03—Boston	NHL	55	10	6	16	18	2	3	0	5	0	0	0	4
NHL Totals (12 years)		741	135	167	302	451	-60	7	19	27	4	5	9	26

ZEDNIK, RICHARD   RW   CANADIENS

PERSONAL: Born January 6, 1976, in Bystrica, Czechoslovakia ... 6-0/200. ... Shoots left. ... Name pronounced ZEHD-nihk.

TRANSACTIONS/CAREER NOTES: Selected by Washington Capitals in 10th round (10th Capitals pick, 249th overall) of NHL entry draft (June 29, 1994). ... Suffered from the flu (November 6, 1996); missed two games. ... Suffered from the flu (December 12, 1997); missed one game. ... Suffered concussion (March 18, 1998); missed six games. ... Strained abdominal muscle (April 2, 1998); missed final eight games of regular season and four playoff games. ... Bruised shoulder (October 21, 1998); missed 10 games. ... Suspended four games and fined $1,000 by NHL for high-sticking incident (November 20, 1998). ... Strained groin (December 19, 1998); missed 19 games. ... Suffered concussion (February 23, 2000); missed 13 games. ... Suspended four games by NHL for cross-checking incident (October 19, 2000). ... Sprained foot (January 12, 2001); missed two games. ... Traded by Capitals with C Jan Bulis and first-round pick (C Alexander Perezhogin) in 2001 draft to Montreal Canadiens for C Trevor Linden, RW Dainius Zubrus and second-round pick (traded to Tampa Bay) in 2001 draft (March 13, 2001).

STATISTICAL PLATEAUS: Three-goal games: 2000-01 (1).

Season Team	League	REGULAR SEASON								PLAYOFFS				
		Gms.	G	A	Pts.	PIM	+/-	PP	SH	Gms.	G	A	Pts.	PIM
93-94—Banska Bystrica	Slovakia	25	3	6	9	...	...	...	...	—	—	—	—	—
94-95—Portland	WHL	65	35	51	86	89	...	...	...	9	5	5	10	20
95-96—Portland	WHL	61	44	37	81	154	...	...	...	7	8	4	12	23
—Portland	AHL	1	1	1	2	0	...	...	...	21	4	5	9	26
—Washington	NHL	1	0	0	0	0	0	0	0	—	—	—	—	—
96-97—Washington	NHL	11	2	1	3	4	-5	1	0	—	—	—	—	—
—Portland	AHL	56	15	20	35	70	...	...	...	5	1	0	1	6
97-98—Washington	NHL	65	17	9	26	28	-2	2	0	17	7	3	10	16
98-99—Washington	NHL	49	9	8	17	50	-6	1	0	—	—	—	—	—
99-00—Washington	NHL	69	19	16	35	54	6	1	0	5	0	0	0	5
00-01—Washington	NHL	62	16	19	35	61	-2	4	0	—	—	—	—	—
—Montreal	NHL	12	3	6	9	10	-2	1	0	—	—	—	—	—
01-02—Montreal	NHL	82	22	22	44	59	-3	4	0	4	4	4	8	6
02-03—Montreal	NHL	80	31	19	50	79	4	9	0	—	—	—	—	—
NHL Totals (8 years)		431	119	100	219	345	-10	23	0	26	11	7	18	27

ZETTERBERG, HENRIK   LW   RED WINGS

PERSONAL: Born October 9, 1980, in Njurunda, Sweden ... 5-11/176.

TRANSACTIONS/CAREER NOTES: Selected by Detroit Red Wings in seventh round (fourth Red Wings pick, 210th overall) of NHL entry draft (June 27, 1999).

Season Team	League	REGULAR SEASON								PLAYOFFS				
		Gms.	G	A	Pts.	PIM	+/-	PP	SH	Gms.	G	A	Pts.	PIM
97-98—Timra	Sweden Jr.	18	9	5	14	4	...	...	...	—	—	—	—	—
—Timra	Sweden Dv. 2	16	1	2	3	4	...	...	...	4	0	1	1	0
98-99—Timra	Sweden Dv. 2	37	15	13	28	2	...	...	...	4	2	1	3	2
99-00—Timra	Sweden Dv. 2	11	4	6	10	0	...	...	...	10	10	4	14	4
00-01—Timra	Sweden	47	15	31	46	24	...	...	...	—	—	—	—	—
01-02—Timra	Sweden	48	10	32	42	20	...	...	...	—	—	—	—	—
—Swedish Oly. team	Int'l	4	0	1	1	0	...	...	...	—	—	—	—	—
02-03—Detroit	NHL	79	22	22	44	8	6	5	1	4	1	0	1	0
NHL Totals (1 year)		79	22	22	44	8	6	5	1	4	1	0	1	0

ZHAMNOV, ALEXEI   C   BLACKHAWKS

PERSONAL: Born October 1, 1970, in Moscow, U.S.S.R. ... 6-1/204. ... Shoots left. ... Full Name: Alex Zhamnov. ... Name pronounced ZHAM-nahf.

TRANSACTIONS/CAREER NOTES: Selected by Winnipeg Jets in fourth round (fifth Jets pick, 77th overall) of NHL entry draft (June 16, 1990). ... Suffered hip flexor (November 2, 1992); missed two games. ... Suffered back spasms (January 27, 1993); missed one game. ... Suffered back spasms (February 3, 1993); missed one game. ... Suffered back spasms (February 12, 1993); missed 12 games. ... Suffered left quad contusion (October 26, 1993); missed three games. ... Sprained back (December 27, 1993); missed eight games. ... Suffered back spasms

(March 19, 1994); missed remainder of season. ... Suffered stress fracture in leg (October 12, 1995); missed eight games. ... Suffered from the flu (January 5, 1996); missed one game. ... Bruised back (March 7, 1996); missed four games. ... Injured back (March 16, 1996); missed remainder of regular season. ... Jets franchise moved to Phoenix and renamed Coyotes for 1996-97 season; NHL approved move on January 18, 1996. ... Traded by Coyotes with RW Craig Mills and first-round pick (RW Ty Jones) in 1997 draft to Chicago Blackhawks for C Jeremy Roenick (August 16, 1996). ... Fractured toe (November 2, 1997); missed four games. ... Suffered concussion (November 29, 1997); missed one game. ... Suffered concussion (March 3, 1998); missed four games. ... Bruised back (April 4, 1998); missed one game. ... Fractured finger (April 15, 1998); missed two games. ... Bruised ankle (November 10, 1998); missed one game. ... Suffered from the flu (December 26, 1998); missed one game. ... Injured back (February 6, 1999); missed four games. ... Strained groin (November 7, 1999); missed three games. ... Strained hamstring (January 15, 2000); missed eight games. ... Fractured larynx (January 21, 2001); missed 18 games. ... Suffered hip pointer (March 3, 2002); missed four games.
STATISTICAL PLATEAUS: Three-goal games: 1993-94 (2), 1994-95 (1), 1995-96 (1), 1996-97 (1). Total: 5. ... Five-goal games: 1994-95 (1). ... Total hat tricks: 6.

			REGULAR SEASON							PLAYOFFS				
Season Team	League	Gms.	G	A	Pts.	PIM	+/-	PP	SH	Gms.	G	A	Pts.	PIM
88-89—Dynamo Moscow	USSR	4	0	0	0	0	...	...	...	—	—	—	—	—
89-90—Dynamo Moscow	USSR	43	11	6	17	23	...	...	...	—	—	—	—	—
90-91—Dynamo Moscow	USSR	46	16	12	28	24	...	...	...	—	—	—	—	—
91-92—Dynamo Moscow	CIS	39	15	21	36	28	...	...	...	—	—	—	—	—
—Unif. Olympic team	Int'l	8	0	3	3	8	...	...	...	—	—	—	—	—
92-93—Winnipeg	NHL	68	25	47	72	58	7	6	1	6	0	2	2	2
93-94—Winnipeg	NHL	61	26	45	71	62	-20	7	0	—	—	—	—	—
94-95—Winnipeg	NHL	48	30	35	65	20	5	9	0	—	—	—	—	—
95-96—Winnipeg	NHL	58	22	37	59	65	-4	5	0	6	2	1	3	8
96-97—Chicago	NHL	74	20	42	62	56	18	6	1	—	—	—	—	—
97-98—Chicago	NHL	70	21	28	49	61	16	6	2	—	—	—	—	—
—Russian Oly. team	Int'l	6	2	1	3	2	...	...	...	—	—	—	—	—
98-99—Chicago	NHL	76	20	41	61	50	-10	8	1	—	—	—	—	—
99-00—Chicago	NHL	71	23	37	60	61	7	5	0	—	—	—	—	—
00-01—Chicago	NHL	63	13	36	49	40	-12	3	1	—	—	—	—	—
01-02—Chicago	NHL	77	22	45	67	67	8	6	0	5	0	0	0	0
—Russian Oly. team	Int'l	6	1	0	1	4	...	...	...	—	—	—	—	—
02-03—Chicago	NHL	74	15	43	58	70	0	2	3	—	—	—	—	—
NHL Totals (11 years)		740	237	436	673	610	15	63	9	17	2	3	5	10

ZHITNIK, ALEXEI   D   SABRES

PERSONAL: Born October 10, 1972, in Kiev, U.S.S.R. ... 5-11/215. ... Shoots left. ... Name pronounced ZHIHT-nihk.
TRANSACTIONS/CAREER NOTES: Selected by Los Angeles Kings in fourth round (third Kings pick, 81st overall) of NHL entry draft (June 22, 1991). ... Suffered from the flu (January 12, 1993); missed five games. ... Suspended one game by NHL for cross-checking (November 30, 1993). ... Traded by Kings with D Charlie Huddy, G Robb Stauber and fifth-round pick (D Marian Menhart) in 1995 draft to Buffalo Sabres for G Grant Fuhr, D Philippe Boucher and D Denis Tsygurov (February 14, 1995). ... Fractured thumb (February 19, 1995); missed three games. ... Reinjured thumb (March 8, 1995); missed one game. ... Ruptured calf muscle (March 19, 1995); missed 11 games. ... Suspended two games and fined $1,000 by NHL for high-sticking incident (November 1, 1996). ... Missed first four games of 1997-98 season due to contract dispute. ... Bruised chest (November 29, 1998); missed one game. ... Suffered eye injury (October 17, 1999); missed one game. ... Fractured finger (March 8, 2000); missed six games. ... Suspended one playoff game by NHL for high-sticking incident (April 19, 2000). ... Suspended four games by NHL for high-sticking incident (October 18, 2000). ... Suspended one game by NHL for kneeing incident (November 8, 2002).

			REGULAR SEASON							PLAYOFFS				
Season Team	League	Gms.	G	A	Pts.	PIM	+/-	PP	SH	Gms.	G	A	Pts.	PIM
89-90—Sokol Kiev	USSR	31	3	4	7	16	...	...	...	—	—	—	—	—
90-91—Sokol Kiev	USSR	40	1	4	5	46	...	...	...	—	—	—	—	—
91-92—CSKA Moscow	CIS	36	2	7	9	48	...	...	...	—	—	—	—	—
—Unif. Olympic team	Int'l	8	1	0	1	0	...	...	...	—	—	—	—	—
92-93—Los Angeles	NHL	78	12	36	48	80	-3	5	0	24	3	9	12	26
93-94—Los Angeles	NHL	81	12	40	52	101	-11	11	0	—	—	—	—	—
94-95—Los Angeles	NHL	11	2	5	7	27	-3	2	0	—	—	—	—	—
—Buffalo	NHL	21	2	5	7	34	-3	1	0	5	0	1	1	14
95-96—Buffalo	NHL	80	6	30	36	58	-25	5	0	—	—	—	—	—*
96-97—Buffalo	NHL	80	7	28	35	95	10	3	1	12	1	0	1	16
97-98—Buffalo	NHL	78	15	30	45	102	19	2	3	15	0	3	3	36
—Russian Oly. team	Int'l	6	0	2	2	2	...	...	...	—	—	—	—	—
98-99—Buffalo	NHL	81	7	26	33	96	-6	3	1	21	4	11	15	*52
99-00—Buffalo	NHL	74	2	11	13	95	-6	1	0	4	0	0	0	8
00-01—Buffalo	NHL	78	8	29	37	75	-3	5	0	13	1	6	7	12
01-02—Buffalo	NHL	82	1	33	34	80	-1	1	0	—	—	—	—	—
02-03—Buffalo	NHL	70	3	18	21	85	-5	0	0	—	—	—	—	—
NHL Totals (11 years)		814	77	291	368	928	-37	39	5	94	9	30	39	164

ZHOLTOK, SERGEI   C   WILD

PERSONAL: Born February 12, 1972, in Riga, U.S.S.R. ... 6-1/197. ... Shoots right. ... Name pronounced SAIR-gay ZOHL-tahk.
TRANSACTIONS/CAREER NOTES: Selected by Boston Bruins in third round (second Bruins pick, 56th overall) of NHL entry draft (June 20, 1992). ... Signed as free agent by Ottawa Senators (June 25, 1996). ... Signed as free agent by Montreal Canadiens (September 9, 1998). ... Sprained knee (November 30, 1998); missed one game. ... Bruised hip (April 6, 1999); missed three games. ... Injured shoulder prior to start of 1999-2000 season; missed first 11 games of season. ... Suffered injury (December 3, 1999); missed one game. ... Traded by Canadiens to Edmonton Oilers for C Chad Kilger (December 18, 2000). ... Traded by Oilers to Minnesota Wild for future considerations (June 29, 2001). ... Bruised left shoulder (March 12, 2002); missed eight games.

Season Team	League	REGULAR SEASON								PLAYOFFS				
		Gms.	G	A	Pts.	PIM	+/-	PP	SH	Gms.	G	A	Pts.	PIM
90-91—Dynamo Riga	USSR	39	4	0	4	16	...	...	...	—	—	—	—	—
91-92—HC Riga	CIS	27	6	3	9	6	...	...	...	—	—	—	—	—
92-93—Providence	AHL	64	31	35	66	57	...	...	...	6	3	5	8	4
—Boston	NHL	1	0	1	1	0	1	0	0	—	—	—	—	—
93-94—Providence	AHL	54	29	33	62	16	...	...	...	—	—	—	—	—
—Boston	NHL	24	2	1	3	2	-7	1	0	—	—	—	—	—
94-95—Providence	AHL	78	23	35	58	42	...	...	...	13	8	5	13	6
95-96—Las Vegas	IHL	82	51	50	101	30	...	...	...	15	7	13	20	6
96-97—Las Vegas	IHL	19	13	14	27	20	...	...	...	—	—	—	—	—
—Ottawa	NHL	57	12	16	28	19	2	5	0	7	1	1	2	0
97-98—Ottawa	NHL	78	10	13	23	16	-7	7	0	11	0	2	2	0
98-99—Montreal	NHL	70	7	15	22	6	-12	2	0	—	—	—	—	—
—Fredericton	AHL	7	3	4	7	0	...	...	...	—	—	—	—	—
99-00—Quebec	AHL	1	0	1	1	2	...	...	...	—	—	—	—	—
—Montreal	NHL	68	26	12	38	28	2	9	0	—	—	—	—	—
00-01—Montreal	NHL	32	1	10	11	8	-15	0	0	—	—	—	—	—
—Edmonton	NHL	37	4	16	20	22	8	1	0	3	0	0	0	0
01-02—Minnesota	NHL	73	19	20	39	28	-10	10	0	—	—	—	—	—
02-03—Minnesota	NHL	78	16	26	42	18	1	3	0	18	2	11	13	0
NHL Totals (9 years)		518	97	130	227	147	-37	38	0	39	3	14	17	0

ZIGOMANIS, MIKE — C — HURRICANES

PERSONAL: Born January 17, 1981, in North York, Ont. ... 6-1/200. ... Shoots right. ... Full Name: Michael Zigomanis.

TRANSACTIONS/CAREER NOTES: Selected by Buffalo Sabres in second round (fourth Sabres pick, 64th overall) of NHL entry draft (June 22, 1999). ... Returned to draft pool by Sabres and selected by Carolina Hurricanes in second round (second Hurricanes pick, 46th overall) of NHL entry draft (June 23, 2001).

Season Team	League	REGULAR SEASON								PLAYOFFS				
		Gms.	G	A	Pts.	PIM	+/-	PP	SH	Gms.	G	A	Pts.	PIM
97-98—Kingston	OHL	62	23	51	74	30	...	...	...	12	1	6	7	2
98-99—Kingston	OHL	67	29	56	85	36	...	...	...	5	1	7	8	2
99-00—Kingston	OHL	59	40	54	94	49	...	...	...	5	0	4	4	0
00-01—Kingston	OHL	52	40	37	77	44	...	...	...	—	—	—	—	—
01-02—Lowell	AHL	79	18	30	48	24	...	...	...	5	1	1	2	2
02-03—Lowell	AHL	38	13	18	31	19	...	...	...	—	—	—	—	—
—Carolina	NHL	19	2	1	3	0	-4	1	1	—	—	—	—	—
NHL Totals (1 year)		19	2	1	3	0	-4	1	1					

ZIZKA, TOMAS — D — KINGS

PERSONAL: Born October 10, 1979, in Sternberk, Czechoslovakia ... 6-2/206. ... Shoots left.

TRANSACTIONS/CAREER NOTES: Selected by Los Angeles Kings in sixth round (sixth Kings pick, 163rd overall) of NHL entry draft (June 27, 1998).

Season Team	League	REGULAR SEASON								PLAYOFFS				
		Gms.	G	A	Pts.	PIM	+/-	PP	SH	Gms.	G	A	Pts.	PIM
94-95—ZPS Zlin	Czech. Jrs.	39	1	10	11	...	...	...	...	—	—	—	—	—
95-96—ZPS Zlin	Czech. Jrs.	47	2	8	10	...	...	...	...	—	—	—	—	—
96-97—ZPS Zlin	Czech. Jrs.	14	1	0	1	...	...	...	...	—	—	—	—	—
97-98—ZPS Zlin	Czech Rep.	33	0	3	3	2	...	...	...	—	—	—	—	—
—ZPS Zlin	Czech. Jrs.	11	3	4	7	...	...	...	...	—	—	—	—	—
98-99—ZPS Zlin	Czech Rep.	44	3	7	10	14	...	...	...	11	1	2	3	...
99-00—HC Barum Zlin	Czech Rep.	46	4	6	10	30	...	...	...	4	1	0	1	4
00-01—HC Continental Zlin	Czech Rep.	43	2	11	13	16	...	...	...	6	0	0	0	6
01-02—Manchester	AHL	58	4	17	21	22	...	...	...	4	1	0	1	14
02-03—Manchester	AHL	61	13	30	43	50	...	...	...	—	—	—	—	—
—Los Angeles	NHL	10	0	3	3	4	-4	0	0	—	—	—	—	—
NHL Totals (1 year)		10	0	3	3	4	-4	0	0					

ZUBOV, SERGEI — D — STARS

PERSONAL: Born July 22, 1970, in Moscow, U.S.S.R. ... 6-1/200. ... Shoots right. ... Name pronounced SAIR-gay ZOO-bahf.

TRANSACTIONS/CAREER NOTES: Selected by New York Rangers in fifth round (sixth Rangers pick, 85th overall) of NHL entry draft (June 16, 1990). ... Suffered concussion (February 26, 1993); missed one game. ... Suffered from the flu (February 4, 1995); missed one game. ... Underwent wrist surgery (February 27, 1995); missed nine games. ... Traded by Rangers with C Petr Nedved to Pittsburgh Penguins for LW Luc Robitaille and D Ulf Samuelsson (August 31, 1995). ... Fractured finger (October 9, 1995); missed nine games. ... Reinjured finger (November 11, 1995); missed seven games. ... Bruised shoulder (March 31, 1996); missed one game. ... Traded by Penguins to Dallas Stars for D Kevin Hatcher (June 22, 1996). ... Suffered from the flu (November 20, 1996); missed one game. ... Suffered back spasms (January 24, 1997); missed two games. ... Sprained neck (March 4, 1998); missed nine games. ... Bruised wrist (April 14, 1999); missed one game. ... Sprained medial collateral ligament in knee (March 29, 2000); missed final five games of season. ... Bruised shoulder (January 6, 2001); missed two games. ... Sprained shoulder (December 2, 2001); missed two games.

Season Team	League	Gms.	G	A	Pts.	PIM	+/-	PP	SH	Gms.	G	A	Pts.	PIM
		REGULAR SEASON								**PLAYOFFS**				
88-89—CSKA Moscow...........	USSR	29	1	4	5	10	...	...	...	—	—	—	—	—
89-90—CSKA Moscow...........	USSR	48	6	2	8	16	...	...	...	—	—	—	—	—
90-91—CSKA Moscow...........	USSR	41	6	5	11	12	...	...	...	—	—	—	—	—
91-92—CSKA Moscow...........	CIS	36	4	7	11	6	...	...	...	—	—	—	—	—
—Unif. Olympic team.....	Int'l	8	0	1	1	0	...	...	...	—	—	—	—	—
92-93—CSKA Moscow...........	CIS	1	0	1	1	0	...	...	...	—	—	—	—	—
—Binghamton................	AHL	30	7	29	36	14	...	...	...	11	5	5	10	2
—New York Rangers......	NHL	49	8	23	31	4	-1	3	0	—	—	—	—	—
93-94—New York Rangers......	NHL	78	12	77	89	39	20	9	0	22	5	14	19	0
—Binghamton................	AHL	2	1	2	3	0	...	...	...	—	—	—	—	—
94-95—New York Rangers......	NHL	38	10	26	36	18	-2	6	0	10	3	8	11	2
95-96—Pittsburgh...............	NHL	64	11	55	66	22	28	3	2	18	1	14	15	26
96-97—Dallas......................	NHL	78	13	30	43	24	19	1	0	7	0	3	3	2
97-98—Dallas......................	NHL	73	10	47	57	16	16	5	1	17	4	5	9	2
98-99—Dallas......................	NHL	81	10	41	51	20	9	5	0	23	1	12	13	4
99-00—Dallas......................	NHL	77	9	33	42	18	-2	3	1	18	2	7	9	6
00-01—Dallas......................	NHL	79	10	41	51	24	22	6	0	10	1	5	6	4
01-02—Dallas......................	NHL	80	12	32	44	22	-4	8	0	—	—	—	—	—
02-03—Dallas......................	NHL	82	11	44	55	26	21	8	0	12	4	10	14	4
NHL Totals (11 years).........		779	116	449	565	233	126	57	4	137	21	78	99	50

ZUBRUS, DAINIUS — RW — CAPITALS

PERSONAL: Born June 16, 1978, in Elektrenai, U.S.S.R. ... 6-4/231. ... Shoots left. ... Name pronounced DIGH-nuhz ZOO-bruhz.

TRANSACTIONS/CAREER NOTES: Selected by Philadelphia Flyers in first round (first Flyers pick, 15th overall) of NHL entry draft (June 22, 1996). ... Bruised right hand (October 8, 1997); missed two games. ... Reinjured right hand (October 15, 1997); missed five games. ... Suspended two games and fined $1,000 by NHL for slashing incident (April 2, 1998). ... Strained left hamstring (December 15, 1997); missed one game. ... Traded by Flyers with second-round pick (D Matt Carkner) in 1999 draft to Montreal Canadiens for RW Mark Recchi (March 10, 1999). ... Strained hip flexor (October 20, 1999); missed one game. ... Injured back (October 27, 1999); missed five games. ... Suffered back spasms (January 4, 2000); missed one game. ... Suffered concussion (February 27, 2000); missed six games. ... Injured ribcage (September 27, 2000); missed first two games of season. ... Suffered concussion (December 21, 2000); missed 19 games. ... Traded by Canadiens with C Trevor Linden and second-round pick (traded to Tampa Bay) in 2001 draft to Washington Capitals for F Jan Bulis, F Richard Zednik and first-round pick (C Alexander Perezhogin) in 2001 draft (March 13, 2001). ... Strained groin (December 13, 2001); missed five games. ... Injured foot (January 22, 2002); missed one game. ... Injured right arm (February 26, 2002); missed five games.

STATISTICAL PLATEAUS: Three-goal games: 2000-01 (1).

Season Team	League	Gms.	G	A	Pts.	PIM	+/-	PP	SH	Gms.	G	A	Pts.	PIM
		REGULAR SEASON								**PLAYOFFS**				
95-96—Pembroke	CJHL	28	19	13	32	73	...	...	...	—	—	—	—	—
—Caledon.....................	Jr. A	7	3	7	10	2	...	...	...	17	11	12	23	4
96-97—Philadelphia	NHL	68	8	13	21	22	3	1	0	19	5	4	9	12
97-98—Philadelphia	NHL	69	8	25	33	42	29	1	0	5	0	1	1	2
98-99—Philadelphia	NHL	63	3	5	8	25	-5	0	1	—	—	—	—	—
—Montreal	NHL	17	3	5	8	4	-3	0	0	—	—	—	—	—
99-00—Montreal	NHL	73	14	28	42	54	-1	3	0	—	—	—	—	—
00-01—Montreal	NHL	49	12	12	24	30	-7	3	0	—	—	—	—	—
—Washington	NHL	12	1	1	2	7	-4	1	0	6	0	0	0	2
01-02—Washington	NHL	71	17	26	43	38	5	4	0	—	—	—	—	—
02-03—Washington	NHL	63	13	22	35	43	15	2	0	6	2	2	4	4
NHL Totals (7 years)...........		485	79	137	216	265	32	15	1	36	7	7	14	20

ZYUZIN, ANDREI — D — WILD

PERSONAL: Born January 21, 1978, in Ufa, U.S.S.R. ... 6-1/210. ... Shoots left. ... Name pronounced ZYOO-zihn.

TRANSACTIONS/CAREER NOTES: Selected by San Jose Sharks in first round (first Sharks pick, second overall) of NHL entry draft (June 22, 1996). ... Suspended two playoff games by NHL for slashing incident (April 19, 1999). ... Traded by Sharks with D Bill Houlder, LW Shawn Burr and C Steve Guolla to Tampa Bay Lightning for LW Niklas Sundstrom and third-round pick (traded to Chicago) in 2000 draft (August 4, 1999). ... Injured shoulder (October 28, 1999); missed five games. ... Injured shoulder (January 11, 2000); missed remainder of season. ... Suffered concussion (November 20, 2000); missed five games. ... Suffered concussion (December 1, 2000); missed five games. ... Injured shoulder (January 30, 2001); missed two games. ... Sprained ankle (March 15, 2001); missed one game. ... Suffered concussion (March 21, 2001); missed three games. ... Traded by Lightning to New Jersey Devils for D Josef Boumedienne, D Sasha Goc and LW Anton But (November 9, 2001). ... Injured shoulder (December 5, 2001); missed four games. ... Bruised foot (February 27, 2002); missed three games. ... Claimed on waivers by Minnesota Wild (November 3, 2002). ... Re-signed by Wild (July 31, 2003).

Season Team	League	Gms.	G	A	Pts.	PIM	+/-	PP	SH	Gms.	G	A	Pts.	PIM
		REGULAR SEASON								**PLAYOFFS**				
94-95—Salavat Yulayev Ufa	CIS	30	3	0	3	16	...	...	...	—	—	—	—	—
95-96—Salavat Yulayev Ufa	CIS	41	6	3	9	24	...	...	...	2	0	0	0	4
96-97—Salavet Yulayev Ufa	USSR	32	7	10	17	28	...	...	...	7	1	1	2	4
97-98—San Jose....................	NHL	56	6	7	13	66	8	2	0	6	1	0	1	14
—Kentucky...................	AHL	17	4	5	9	28	...	...	...	—	—	—	—	—
98-99—San Jose....................	NHL	25	3	1	4	38	5	2	0	—	—	—	—	—
—Kentucky...................	AHL	23	2	12	14	42	...	...	...	—	—	—	—	—
99-00—Tampa Bay.................	NHL	34	2	9	11	33	-11	0	0	—	—	—	—	—
00-01—Tampa Bay.................	NHL	64	4	16	20	76	-8	2	1	—	—	—	—	—
—Detroit......................	IHL	2	0	1	1	0	...	...	...	—	—	—	—	—
01-02—Tampa Bay.................	NHL	9	0	2	2	6	-6	0	0	—	—	—	—	—
—New Jersey................	NHL	38	1	2	3	25	1	1	0	—	—	—	—	—
—Albany......................	AHL	3	0	1	1	2	...	...	...	—	—	—	—	—
02-03—New Jersey................	NHL	1	0	1	1	2	-1	0	0	—	—	—	—	—
—Minnesota.................	NHL	66	4	12	16	34	-7	2	0	18	0	1	1	14
NHL Totals (6 years)...........		293	20	50	70	280	-19	9	1	24	1	1	2	28

2003 TOP DRAFT PICKS

BERNIER, STEVE   RW   SHARKS

PERSONAL: Born March 31, 1985, in Quebec City. ... 6-2/233. ... Shoots right.

TRANSACTIONS/CAREER NOTES: Selected by San Jose Sharks in first round (second Sharks pick, 16th overall) in 2003 NHL entry draft (June 23, 2003).

Season Team	League	REGULAR SEASON					PLAYOFFS				
		Gms.	G	A	Pts.	PIM	Gms.	G	A	Pts.	PIM
01-02—Moncton	QMJHL	66	31	28	59	51	—	—	—	—	—
02-03—Moncton	QMJHL	71	49	52	101	90	—	—	—	—	—

BROWN, DUSTIN   RW   KINGS

PERSONAL: Born November 4, 1984, in Ithaca, NY ... 6-0/195. ... Shoots right.

TRANSACTIONS/CAREER NOTES: Selected by Los Angeles Kings in first round (first Kings pick, 13th overall) in 2003 NHL entry draft (June 23, 2003).

Season Team	League	REGULAR SEASON					PLAYOFFS				
		Gms.	G	A	Pts.	PIM	Gms.	G	A	Pts.	PIM
00-01—Guelph	OHL	53	23	22	45	45	4	0	0	0	10
01-02—Guelph	OHL	63	41	32	73	56	9	8	5	13	14
02-03—Guelph	OHL	58	34	42	76	89	—	—	—	—	—

BURNS, BRENT   RW   WILD

PERSONAL: Born March 9, 1985, in Ajax, Ont. ... 6-4/210. ... Shoots right.

TRANSACTIONS/CAREER NOTES: Selected by Minnesota Wild in first round (first Wild pick, 20th overall) in 2003 NHL entry draft (June 23, 2003).

Season Team	League	REGULAR SEASON					PLAYOFFS				
		Gms.	G	A	Pts.	PIM	Gms.	G	A	Pts.	PIM
02-03—Brampton	OHL	68	15	25	40	14	—	—	—	—	—

CARTER, JEFF   C   FLYERS

PERSONAL: Born January 1, 1985, in London, Ont. ... 6-3/182. ... Shoots right.

TRANSACTIONS/CAREER NOTES: Selected by Philadelphia Flyers in first round (first Flyers pick, 11th overall) in 2003 NHL entry draft (June 23, 2003).

Season Team	League	REGULAR SEASON					PLAYOFFS				
		Gms.	G	A	Pts.	PIM	Gms.	G	A	Pts.	PIM
01-02—Sault Ste. Marie	OHL	63	18	17	35	12	4	0	0	0	2
02-03—Sault Ste. Marie	OHL	61	35	36	71	55	—	—	—	—	—

COBURN, BRAYDON   D   THRASHERS

PERSONAL: Born February 27, 1985, in Calgary, Alb. ... 6-5/205. ... Shoots left.

TRANSACTIONS/CAREER NOTES: Selected by Atlanta Thrashers in first round (first Thrashers pick, eighth overall) in 2003 NHL entry draft (June 23, 2003).

Season Team	League	REGULAR SEASON					PLAYOFFS				
		Gms.	G	A	Pts.	PIM	Gms.	G	A	Pts.	PIM
01-02—Portland	WHL	68	4	33	37	100	7	1	1	2	9
02-03—Portland	WHL	53	3	16	19	147	—	—	—	—	—

FEHR, ERIC   RW   CAPITALS

PERSONAL: Born September 7, 1985, in Winkler, Man. ... 6-3/187. ... Shoots right.

TRANSACTIONS/CAREER NOTES: Selected by Washington Capitals in first round (first Capitals pick, 18th overall) in 2003 NHL entry draft (June 23, 2003).

Season Team	League	REGULAR SEASON					PLAYOFFS				
		Gms.	G	A	Pts.	PIM	Gms.	G	A	Pts.	PIM
01-02—Brandon	WHL	63	11	16	27	29	12	1	1	2	0
02-03—Brandon	WHL	70	26	29	55	76	—	—	—	—	—

FLEURY, MARC-ANDRE　　　　　　G　　　　　　PENGUINS

PERSONAL: Born November 28, 1984, in Sorel, Que. ... 6-1/172. ... Catches left.
TRANSACTIONS/CAREER NOTES: Selected by Pittsburgh Penguins in first round (first Penguins pick, 1st overall) in 2003 NHL entry draft June 23, 2003).

			REGULAR SEASON								PLAYOFFS						
Season Team	League	Gms.	Min	W	L	T	GA	SO	Avg.	SV%	Gms.	Min.	W	L	GA	SO	Avg.	SV%
00-01—Cape Breton	QMJHL	35	1705	12	13	2	115	0	4.05	.886	2	32	0	1	4	0	7.50	—
01-02—Cape Breton	QMJHL	55	3043	26	14	8	141	2	2.78	.915	16	1003	9	7	55	0	3.29	—
02-03—Cape Breton	QMJHL	51	2889	17	24	6	162	2	3.36	.910	—	—	—	—	—	—	—	—

GETZLAF, RYAN　　　　　　C　　　　　　MIGHTY DUCKS

PERSONAL: Born May 10, 1985, in Regina, Sask. ... 6-2/185. ... Shoots right.
TRANSACTIONS/CAREER NOTES: Selected by Anaheim Mighty Ducks in first round (first Mighty Ducks pick, 19th overall) in 2003 NHL entry draft (June 23, 2003).

		REGULAR SEASON					PLAYOFFS				
Season Team	League	Gms.	G	A	Pts.	PIM	Gms.	G	A	Pts.	PIM
01-02—Calgary	WHL	63	9	9	18	34	7	2	1	3	4
02-03—Calgary	WHL	70	29	39	68	121	—	—	—	—	—

HORTON, NATHAN　　　　　　C　　　　　　PANTHERS

PERSONAL: Born May 29, 1985, in Welland, Ont. ... 6-2/201. ... Shoots right.
TRANSACTIONS/CAREER NOTES: Selected by Florida Panthers in first round (first Panthers pick, third overall) in 2003 NHL entry draft (June 23, 2003).

		REGULAR SEASON					PLAYOFFS				
Season Team	League	Gms.	G	A	Pts.	PIM	Gms.	G	A	Pts.	PIM
01-02—Oshawa	OHL	64	31	36	67	84	5	1	2	3	10
02-03—Oshawa	OHL	54	33	35	68	111	—	—	—	—	—

JESSIMAN, HUGH　　　　　　RW　　　　　　RANGERS

PERSONAL: Born March 28, 1984, in New York, NY ... 6-4/200. ... Shoots right.
COLLEGE: Dartmouth College.
TRANSACTIONS/CAREER NOTES: Selected by New York Rangers in first round (first Rangers pick,12th overall) in 2003 NHL entry draft.

		REGULAR SEASON					PLAYOFFS				
Season Team	League	Gms.	G	A	Pts.	PIM	Gms.	G	A	Pts.	PIM
02-03—Dartmouth College	ECAC	34	23	24	47	48	—	—	—	—	—

KASTSITSYN, ANDREI　　　　　　LW　　　　　　CANADIENS

PERSONAL: Born February 3, 1985, in Novopolotsk, Belarus ... 6-0/189. ... Shoots left.
TRANSACTIONS/CAREER NOTES: Selected by Montreal Canadiens in first round (first Canadiens pick, 10th overall) in 2003 NHL entry draft (June 23,2003).

		REGULAR SEASON					PLAYOFFS				
Season Team	League	Gms.	G	A	Pts.	PIM	Gms.	G	A	Pts.	PIM
02-03—HC CSKA Moscow	Russian	6	0	0	0	2	—	—	—	—	—

MICHALEK, MILAN　　　　　　RW　　　　　　SHARKS

PERSONAL: Born December 7, 1984, in Jindrichuv, Czech. ... 6-2/205. ... Shoots left.
TRANSACTIONS/CAREER NOTES: Selected by San Jose Sharks in first round (first Sharks pick, sixth overall) in 2003 NHL entry draft (June 23, 2003).

		REGULAR SEASON					PLAYOFFS				
Season Team	League	Gms.	G	A	Pts.	PIM	Gms.	G	A	Pts.	PIM
00-01—Budejovice	Czech. Jr.	30	10	13	23	30	—	—	—	—	—
01-02—Budejovice	Czech.	47	6	11	17	12	—	—	—	—	—
02-03—Budejovice	Czech.	46	3	5	8	14	—	—	—	—	—

2003 TOP DRAFT PICKS

NILSSON, ROBERT   RW   ISLANDERS

PERSONAL: Born January 10, 1985, in Calgary, Alb. ... 5-11/176. ... Shoots left.
TRANSACTIONS/CAREER NOTES: Selected by New York Islanders in first round (first Islanders pick, 15th overall) in 2003 NHL entry draft (June 23, 2003).

Season Team	League	Gms.	G	A	Pts.	PIM	Gms.	G	A	Pts.	PIM
				REGULAR SEASON					PLAYOFFS		
00-01—Leksand	Sweden Jr.	18	11	25	36	20	—	—	—	—	—
01-02—Leksand	Sweden Jr.	21	13	18	31	24	—	—	—	—	—
02-03—Leksand	Sweden Dv. 2	41	8	13	21	10	—	—	—	—	—

PARISE, ZACH   C   DEVILS

PERSONAL: Born July 28, 1984, in Minneapolis, Minn. ... 5-11/186. ... Shoots left.
COLLEGE: University of North Dakota.
TRANSACTIONS/CAREER NOTES: Selected by New Jersey Devils in first round (first Devils pick, 17th overall) in 2003 NHL entry draft (June 23, 2003).

Season Team	League	Gms.	G	A	Pts.	PIM	Gms.	G	A	Pts.	PIM
				REGULAR SEASON					PLAYOFFS		
02-03—Univ. of North Dakota	WCHA	39	26	35	61	34	—	—	—	—	—

PHANEUF, DION   D   FLAMES

PERSONAL: Born April 10, 1985, in Edmonton, Alb. ... 6-2/205. ... Shoots left.
TRANSACTIONS/CAREER NOTES: Selected by Calgary Flames in first round (first Flames pick, ninth overall) in 2003 NHL entry draft (June 23, 2003).

Season Team	League	Gms.	G	A	Pts.	PIM	Gms.	G	A	Pts.	PIM
				REGULAR SEASON					PLAYOFFS		
01-02—Red Deer	WHL	67	5	12	17	170	21	0	2	2	14
02-03—Red Deer	WHL	71	16	14	30	185	—	—	—	—	—

SEABROOK, BRENT   D   BLACKHAWKS

PERSONAL: Born April 20, 1985, in Richmond, B.C. ... 6-2/225. ... Shoots right.
TRANSACTIONS/CAREER NOTES: Selected by Chicago Blackhawks in first round (first Blackhawks pick, 14th overall) in 2003 NHL entry draft (June 23, 2003).

Season Team	League	Gms.	G	A	Pts.	PIM	Gms.	G	A	Pts.	PIM
				REGULAR SEASON					PLAYOFFS		
01-02—Lethbridge	WHL	67	6	33	39	70	4	1	1	2	2
02-03—Lethbridge	WHL	69	9	33	42	113	—	—	—	—	—

STAAL, ERIC   C   HURRICANES

PERSONAL: Born October 29, 1984, in Thunder Bay, Ont. ... 6-3/182. ... Shoots left.
TRANSACTIONS/CAREER NOTES: Selected by Carolina Hurricanes in first round (first Hurricanes pick, second overall) in 2003 NHL entry draft (June 23, 2003).

Season Team	League	Gms.	G	A	Pts.	PIM	Gms.	G	A	Pts.	PIM
				REGULAR SEASON					PLAYOFFS		
00-01—Peterborough	OHL	63	19	30	49	23	7	2	5	7	4
01-02—Peterborough	OHL	56	23	39	62	40	6	3	6	9	10
02-03—Peterborough	OHL	66	39	59	98	36	—	—	—	—	—

SUTER, RYAN   D   PREDATORS

PERSONAL: Born January 21, 1985, in Madison, Wis. ... 6-1/183. ... Shoots left.
TRANSACTIONS/CAREER NOTES: Selected by Nashville Predators in first round (first Predators pick, seventh overall) in 2003 NHL entry draft (June 23, 2003).

Season Team	League	Gms.	G	A	Pts.	PIM	Gms.	G	A	Pts.	PIM
				REGULAR SEASON					PLAYOFFS		
01-02—U.S. national team	Int'l	34	2	10	12	75	—	—	—	—	—
02-03—U.S. national team	Int'l	47	8	19	27	114	—	—	—	—	—

VANEK, THOMAS   LW   SABRES

PERSONAL: Born January 19, 1984, in Vienna, Austria ... 6-2/208. ... Shoots right.
COLLEGE: University of Minnesota.
TRANSACTIONS/CAREER NOTES: Selected by Buffalo Sabres in first round (first Sabres pick, fifth overall) in 2003 NHL entry draft (June 23, 2003).

		REGULAR SEASON					PLAYOFFS				
Season Team	League	Gms.	G	A	Pts.	PIM	Gms.	G	A	Pts.	PIM
00-01—Sioux Falls	USHL	20	19	10	29	15	—	—	—	—	—
01-02—Sioux City	USHL	52	46	45	91	54	—	—	—	—	—
02-03—Univ. of Minnesota	WCHA	45	31	31	62	60	—	—	—	—	—

ZHERDEV, NIKOLAI   RW   BLUE JACKETS

PERSONAL: Born November 5, 1984, in Kiev, Ukraine ... 6-0/176. ... Shoots right.
TRANSACTIONS/CAREER NOTES: Selected by Columbus Blue Jackets in first round (first Blue Jackets pick, fourth overall) in 2003 NHL entry draft (June 23, 2003).

		REGULAR SEASON					PLAYOFFS				
Season Team	League	Gms.	G	A	Pts.	PIM	Gms.	G	A	Pts.	PIM
00-01—Elemash	Russian1	18	5	8	13	12.	—	—	—	—	—
01-02—Elemash	Russian1	53	13	15	28	60	—	—	—	—	—
02-03—HC CSKA Moscow	Russian	44	12	12	24	34	—	—	—	—	—

NHL HEAD COACHES

BABCOCK, MIKE — MIGHTY DUCKS

PERSONAL: Born April 29, 1963.

HEAD COACHING RECORD

BACKGROUND: Head coach, Red Deer (Alta.) College (1988-89 through 1990-91). ... Head coach, University of Lethbridge, Alta. (1993-94).

Season Team	League	W	L	T	OTL	Pct.	Finish	W	L	Pct.
				REGULAR SEASON				**PLAYOFFS**		
91-92—Moose Jaw	WHL	33	36	3	—	.479	6th/East Division	0	4	.000
92-93—Moose Jaw	WHL	27	42	3	—	.396	8th/East Division	—	—	—
94-95—Spokane	WHL	32	36	4	—	.472	5th/West Division	6	5	.545
95-96—Spokane	WHL	50	18	4	—	.722	1st/West Division	9	9	.500
96-97—Spokane	WHL	35	33	4	—	.514	3rd/West Division	4	5	.444
97-98—Spokane	WHL	45	23	4	—	.653	2nd/West Division	10	8	.556
98-99—Spokane	WHL	19	44	9	—	.326	7th/West Division	—	—	—
99-00—Spokane	WHL	47	21	4	—	.681	1st/West Division	10	5	.667
00-01—Cincinnati	AHL	41	26	9	4	.569	2nd/Southern Division	1	3	.250
01-02—Cincinnati	AHL	33	33	11	3	.481	3rd/Central Division	1	2	.333
02-03—Anaheim	NHL	40	27	9	6	.543	2nd/Pacific Division	15	6	.714
NHL Totals (1 year)		40	27	9	6	.543	**NHL Totals (1 year)**	15	6	.714

NOTES:
91-92—Lost to Prince Albert in East Division preliminary round.
94-95—Lost to Tri-City in West Division semifinals.
95-96—Defeated Portland in division quarterfinals; defeated Kamloops in division finals; lost to Brandon in WHL Finals.
96-97—Defeated Kelowna in division quarterfinals; lost to Prince George in division semifinals.
97-98—Defeated Kelowna in division quarterfinals; defeated Prince George in division semifinals; lost to Portland in division finals.
99-00—Defeated Tri-City in division quarterfinals; defeated Prince George in division finals; lost to Kootenay in WHL Finals.
00-01—Lost to Norfolk in conference quarterfinals of Calder Cup playoffs.
01-02—Lost to Chicago in qualifying round of Calder Cup playoffs.
02-03—Defeated Detroit in Western Conference quarterfinals; defeated Dallas in Western Conference semifinals; defeated Minnesota in Western Conference finals; lost to New Jersey in Stanley Cup Finals.

BURNS, PAT — DEVILS

PERSONAL: Born April 4, 1952, in St.-Henri, Que.

HEAD COACHING RECORD

BACKGROUND: Assistant coach, Canadian National team (1986). ... Assistant coach, Canadian Junior National team (1987).

Season Team	League	W	L	T	OTL	Pct.	Finish	W	L	Pct.
				REGULAR SEASON				**PLAYOFFS**		
83-84—Hull	QMJHL	25	45	0	—	.357	6th/LeBel Division	—	—	—
84-85—Hull	QMJHL	33	34	1	—	.493	2nd/LeBel Division	1	4	.200
85-86—Hull	QMJHL	54	18	0	—	.750	1st/LeBel Division	15	0	1.000
86-87—Hull	QMJHL	26	39	5	—	.407	4th/LeBel Division	4	4	.500
87-88—Sherbrooke	AHL	42	34	4	—	.550	3rd/North Division	2	4	.333
88-89—Montreal	NHL	53	18	9	—	.719	1st/Adams Division	14	7	.667
89-90—Montreal	NHL	41	28	11	—	.581	3rd/Adams Division	5	6	.455
90-91—Montreal	NHL	39	30	11	—	.556	2nd/Adams Division	7	6	.538
91-92—Montreal	NHL	41	28	11	—	.581	1st/Adams Division	4	7	.364
92-93—Toronto	NHL	44	29	11	—	.589	3rd/Norris Division	11	10	.524
93-94—Toronto	NHL	43	29	12	—	.583	2nd/Central Division	9	9	.500
94-95—Toronto	NHL	21	19	8	—	.521	4th/Central Division	3	4	.429
95-96—Toronto	NHL	25	30	10	—	.462		—	—	.
97-98—Boston	NHL	39	30	13	—	.555	2nd/Northeast Division	2	4	.333
98-99—Boston	NHL	39	30	13	—	.555	3rd/Northeast Division	6	6	.500
99-00—Boston	NHL	24	33	19	6	.409	5th/Northeast Division	—	—	—
00-01—Boston	NHL	3	4	1	0	.438		—	—	—
02-03—New Jersey	NHL	46	20	10	6	.622	1st/Atlantic Division	16	8	.667
NHL Totals (13 years)		458	328	139	12	.563	**NHL Totals (10 years)**	77	67	.535

NOTES:
84-85—Lost to Verdun in quarterfinals of President Cup playoffs.
85-86—Defeated Shawinigan in quarterfinals of President Cup playoffs; defeated St. Jean in semifinals of President Cup playoffs; defeated Drummondville in President Cup finals.
86-87—Eliminated in President Cup quarterfinal round-robin series.
87-88—Lost to Fredericton in quarterfinals of Calder Cup playoffs.
88-89—Defeated Hartford in Adams Division semifinals; defeated Boston in Adams Division finals; defeated Philadelphia in Wales Conference finals; lost to Calgary in Stanley Cup finals.
89-90—Defeated Buffalo in Adams Division semifinals; lost to Boston in Adams Division finals.
90-91—Defeated Buffalo in Adams Division semifinals; lost to Boston in Adams Division finals.
91-92—Defeated Hartford in Adams Division semifinals; lost to Boston in Adams Division finals.
92-93—Defeated Detroit in Norris Division semifinals; defeated St. Louis in Norris Division finals; lost to Los Angeles in Campbell Conference finals.
93-94—Defeated Chicago in Western Conference quarterfinals; defeated San Jose in Western Conference semifinals; lost to Vancouver in Western Conference finals.
94-95—Lost to Chicago in Western Conference quarterfinals.

95-96—Replaced as head coach by Nick Beverley (March 4) with club in fifth place.
97-98—Lost to Washington in Eastern Conference quarterfinals.
98-99—Defeated Carolina in Eastern Conference quarterfinals; lost to Buffalo in Eastern Conference semifinals.
00-01—Replaced as head coach by Mike Keenan (October 25).
02-03—Defeated Boston in Eastern Conference quarterfinals; defeated Tampa Bay in Eastern Conference semifinals; defeated Ottawa in Eastern Conference finals; defeated Anaheim in Stanley Cup Finals.

CASSIDY, BRUCE — CAPITALS

PERSONAL: Born May 20, 1965, in Ottawa. ... Full Name: Bruce J. Cassidy.
TRANSACTIONS/CAREER NOTES: Selected by Chicago Blackhawks in first round (first Blackhawks pick, 18th overall) of NHL entry draft (June 8, 1983).
HONORS: Won Emms Family Award (1982-83). ... Named to OHL All-Star second team (1983-84). ... Named to IHL All-Star first team (1988-89 and 1989-90).
MISCELLANEOUS: Played defense.

Season Team	League	Gms.	G	A	Pts.	PIM	+/-	PP	SH	Gms.	G	A	Pts.	PIM
				REGULAR SEASON								PLAYOFFS		
81-82—Hawkesbury	OJHL	37	13	30	43	32	...	...	...	—	—	—	—	—
82-83—Ottawa	OHL	70	25	86	111	33	...	...	...	9	3	9	12	10
83-84—Ottawa	OHL	67	27	68	95	58	...	...	...	13	6	16	22	6
—Chicago	NHL	1	0	0	0	0	0	0	0	—	—	—	—	—
84-85—Ottawa	OHL	28	13	27	40	15	...	...	...	—	—	—	—	—
85-86—Chicago	NHL	1	0	0	0	0	0	0	0	—	—	—	—	—
—Nova Scotia	AHL	4	0	0	0	0	...	...	...	—	—	—	—	—
86-87—Chicago	NHL	2	0	0	0	0	-1	0	0	—	—	—	—	—
—Nova Scotia	AHL	19	2	8	10	4	...	...	...	—	—	—	—	—
—Canadian nat'l team	Int'l	12	3	6	9	4	...	...	...	—	—	—	—	—
—Saginaw	IHL	10	2	13	15	6	...	...	...	2	1	1	2	0
87-88—Chicago	NHL	21	3	10	13	6	-3	2	0	—	—	—	—	—
—Saginaw	IHL	60	9	37	46	59	...	...	...	10	2	3	5	19
88-89—Chicago	NHL	9	0	2	2	4	-5	0	0	1	0	0	0	0
—Saginaw	IHL	72	16	64	80	80	...	...	...	6	0	2	2	6
89-90—Chicago	NHL	2	1	1	2	0	-1	1	0	—	—	—	—	—
—Indianapolis	IHL	75	11	46	57	56	...	...	...	14	1	10	11	20
90-91—Alleghe	Italy	36	23	52	75	20	...	...	...	10	7	8	15	2
91-92—Alleghe	Alpenliga	18	13	28	41	16	...	...	...	—	—	—	—	—
—Alleghe	Italy	18	11	18	29	0	...	...	...	9	3	11	14	2
92-93—Alleghe	Alpenliga	32	19	40	59	12	...	...	...	—	—	—	—	—
—Alleghe	Italy	16	6	22	28	4	...	...	...	9	6	8	14	6
93-94—Kaufbeuren	Germany	33	8	9	17	12	...	...	...	4	1	2	3	...
94-95—Indianapolis	IHL	29	2	13	15	16	...	...	...	—	—	—	—	—
95-96—Indianapolis	IHL	56	5	16	21	46	...	...	...	5	1	0	1	4
96-97—Indianapolis	IHL	10	0	4	4	11	...	...	...	—	—	—	—	—
NHL Totals (6 years)		36	4	13	17	10	-10	3	0	1	0	0	0	0

HEAD COACHING RECORD

BACKGROUND: Director of Hockey Operations, Indianapolis Ice (1998-99). ... Director of Hockey Operations, Trenton Titans (1999-2000).

Season Team	League	W	L	T	OTL	Pct.	Finish	W	L	Pct.
				REGULAR SEASON					PLAYOFFS	
96-97—Jacksonville	ECHL	15	25	10	—	.400	—	—	—	—
97-98—Jacksonville	ECHL	35	29	6	—	.543	4th/Southeast Division	—	—	—
98-99—Indianapolis	IHL	33	37	12	—	.476	3rd/Central Division	3	4	.429
99-00—Trenton	ECHL	37	29	4	—	.557	4th/Northeast Division	8	6	.571
00-01—Grand Rapids	IHL	53	22	7	—	.689	1st/East Division	6	4	.600
01-02—Grand Rapids	AHL	42	27	11	0	.594	1st/West Division	2	3	.400
02-03—Washington	NHL	39	29	8	6	.524	2nd/Southeast Division	2	4	.333
NHL Totals (1 year)		39	29	8	6	.524	**NHL Totals (1 year)**	2	4	.333

NOTES:
98-99—Defeated Cincinnati in first round of Turner Cup playoffs; lost to Detroit in conference semifinals of Turner Cup playoffs.
99-00—Defeated Richmond in conference quarterfinals of Kelly Cup playoffs; defeated Hampton Roads in conference semifinals of Kelly Cup playoffs; lost to Peoria in conference finals of Kelly Cup playoffs.
00-01—Defeated Cleveland in conference semifinals of Turner Cup playoffs; lost to Orlando in conference finals of Turner Cup playoffs.
01-02—Lost to Chicago in conference quarterfinals of Calder Cup playoffs.
02-03—Lost to Tampa Bay in Eastern Conference quarterfinals.

CRAWFORD, MARC — CANUCKS

PERSONAL: Born February 13, 1961, in Belleville, Ont. ... Shot left. ... Full Name: Marc Joseph John Crawford.
... Brother of Bob Crawford, right winger with four NHL teams (1979-80 and 1981-82 through 1986-87).
TRANSACTIONS/CAREER NOTES: Selected by Vancouver Canucks in fourth round (second Canucks pick, 70th overall) of NHL entry draft (June 11, 1980). ... Suspended three games by NHL for leaving bench to fight (February 3, 1987).
MISCELLANEOUS: Played left wing.

Season Team	League	Gms.	G	A	Pts.	PIM	+/-	PP	SH	Gms.	G	A	Pts.	PIM
				REGULAR SEASON								PLAYOFFS		
78-79—Cornwall	QMJHL	70	28	41	69	206	...	...	...	—	—	—	—	—
79-80—Cornwall	QMJHL	54	27	36	63	127	...	...	...	18	8	20	28	48
80-81—Cornwall	QMJHL	63	42	57	99	242	...	...	...	19	20	15	35	27
81-82—Dallas	CHL	34	13	21	34	71	...	...	...	—	—	—	—	—
—Vancouver	NHL	40	4	8	12	29	0	0	0	14	1	0	1	11
82-83—Vancouver	NHL	41	4	5	9	28	-3	0	0	3	0	1	1	25
—Fredericton	AHL	30	15	9	24	59	...	...	...	9	1	3	4	10

Season Team	League	REGULAR SEASON								PLAYOFFS				
		Gms.	G	A	Pts.	PIM	+/-	PP	SH	Gms.	G	A	Pts.	PIM
83-84—Vancouver	NHL	19	0	1	1	9	0	0	0	—	—	—	—	—
—Fredericton	AHL	56	9	22	31	96	...	...	...	7	4	2	6	23
84-85—Vancouver	NHL	1	0	0	0	4	-4	0	0	—	—	—	—	—
—Fredericton	AHL	26	10	14	24	55	...	...	...	—	—	—	—	—
85-86—Vancouver	NHL	54	11	14	25	92	-7	0	0	3	0	1	1	8
—Fredericton	AHL	26	10	14	24	55	...	...	...	—	—	—	—	—
86-87—Vancouver	NHL	21	0	3	3	67	-8	0	0	—	—	—	—	—
—Fredericton	AHL	25	8	11	19	21	...	...	...	—	—	—	—	—
87-88—Fredericton	AHL	43	5	13	18	90	...	...	...	2	0	0	0	14
88-89—Milwaukee	IHL	53	23	30	53	166	...	...	...	11	2	5	7	26
NHL Totals (6 years)		176	19	31	50	229	-22	0	0	20	1	2	3	44

HEAD COACHING RECORD

BACKGROUND: Player/assistant coach, Fredericton Express of AHL (1987-88). ... Nordiques franchise moved to Denver for 1995-96 season and renamed Colorado Avalanche. ... Hockey analyst, CBC television (1998-January 24, 1999).

Season Team	League	REGULAR SEASON					Finish	PLAYOFFS		
		W	L	T	OTL	Pct.		W	L	Pct.
89-90—Cornwall	OHL	24	38	4	—	.394	6th/Leyden Division	2	4	.333
90-91—Cornwall	OHL	23	42	1	—	.356	7th/Leyden Division	—	—	—
91-92—St. John's	AHL	39	29	12	—	.563	2nd/Atlantic Division	11	5	.688
92-93—St. John's	AHL	41	26	13	—	.594	1st/Atlantic Division	4	5	.444
93-94—St. John's	AHL	45	23	12	—	.638	1st/Atlantic Division	6	5	.545
94-95—Quebec	NHL	30	13	5	—	.677	1st/Northeast Division	2	4	.333
95-96—Colorado	NHL	47	25	10	—	.634	1st/Pacific Division	16	6	.727
96-97—Colorado	NHL	49	24	9	—	.652	1st/Pacific Division	10	7	.588
97-98—Colorado	NHL	39	26	17	—	.579	1st/Pacific Division	3	4	.429
98-99—Vancouver	NHL	8	23	6	—	.297	4th/Northwest Division	—	—	—
99-00—Vancouver	NHL	30	29	15	8	.457	3rd/Northwest Division	—	—	—
00-01—Vancouver	NHL	36	28	11	7	.506	3rd/Northwest Division	0	4	.000
01-02—Vancouver	NHL	42	30	7	3	.555	2nd/Northwest Division	2	4	.333
02-03—Vancouver	NHL	45	23	13	1	.628	2nd/Northwest Division	7	7	.500
NHL Totals (9 years)		326	221	93	19	.565	NHL Totals (7 years)	40	36	.526

NOTES:
89-90—Lost to Oshawa in Leyden Division quarterfinals.
91-92—Defeated Cape Breton in first round of Calder Cup playoffs; defeated Moncton in second round of Calder Cup playoffs; lost to Adirondack in Calder Cup finals.
92-93—Defeated Moncton in first round of Calder Cup playoffs; lost to Cape Breton in second round of Calder Cup playoffs.
93-94—Defeated Cape Breton in first round of Calder Cup playoffs; lost to Moncton in second round of Calder Cup playoffs.
94-95—Lost to New York Rangers in Eastern Conference quarterfinals.
95-96—Defeated Vancouver in Western Conference quarterfinals; defeated Chicago in Western Conference semifinals; defeated Detroit in Western Conference finals; defeated Florida in Stanley Cup finals.
96-97—Defeated Chicago in Western Conference quarterfinals; defeated Edmonton in Western Conference semifinals; lost to Detroit in Western Conference finals.
97-98—Lost to Edmonton in Western Conference quarterfinals.
98-99—Replaced Mike Keenan as head coach (January 24).
00-01—Lost to Colorado in Western Conference quarterfinals.
01-02—Lost to Detroit in Western Conference quarterfinals.
02-03—Defeated St. Louis in Western Conference quarterfinals; lost to Minnesota in Western Conference semifinals.

FRANCIS, BOBBY   COYOTES

PERSONAL: Born December 5, 1958, in North Battleford, Sask. ... Son of Emile Francis, goaltender with Chicago Blackhawks (1946-47 and 1947-48) and New York Rangers (1948-49 through 1951-52); and head coach with New York Rangers (1965-66 through 1974-75) and St. Louis Blues (1976-77, 1981-82 and 1982-83).
TRANSACTIONS/CAREER NOTES: Signed as non-drafted free agent by Calgary Flames (October 27, 1980). ... Traded by Flames to Detroit Red Wings for the rights to RW Yves Courteau (December 2, 1982).

Season Team	League	REGULAR SEASON								PLAYOFFS				
		Gms.	G	A	Pts.	PIM	+/-	PP	SH	Gms.	G	A	Pts.	PIM
72-73—Brooklyn	NYMHL	38	36	34	70	44	...	...	...	—	—	—	—	—
73-74—Brooklyn	NYMHL	41	41	53	94	63	...	...	...	12	17	11	28	24
74-75—Bronx	NYMHL	40	53	59	112	71	...	...	...	—	—	—	—	—
75-76—Beawick	NEJHL	40	62	74	136	61	...	...	...	—	—	—	—	—
76-77—Univ. of New Hamp.	Hockey East					Did not play.								
77-78—Univ. of New Hamp.	Hockey East	40	9	44	53	...	...	...	...	—	—	—	—	—
78-79—Univ. of New Hamp.	Hockey East	35	20	46	66	44	...	...	...	—	—	—	—	—
79-80—Univ. of New Hamp.	Hockey East	28	19	23	42	30	...	...	...	—	—	—	—	—
80-81—Birmingham	CHL	18	6	21	27	20	...	...	...	—	—	—	—	—
—Muskegon	IHL	27	16	17	33	33	...	...	...	—	—	—	—	—
81-82—Oklahoma City	CHL	80	48	66	114	76	...	...	...	4	1	2	3	11
82-83—Colorado	CHL	26	20	16	36	24	...	...	...	—	—	—	—	—
—Detroit	NHL	14	2	0	2	0	-1	0	0	—	—	—	—	—
—Adirondack	AHL	17	3	8	11	0	...	...	...	—	—	—	—	—
83-84—Colorado	CHL	68	32	50	82	53	...	...	...	1	0	1	1	0
84-85—Salt Lake City	IHL	53	24	16	40	36	...	...	...	6	1	1	2	0
85-86—Salt Lake City	IHL	82	32	44	76	163	...	...	...	5	0	4	4	10
86-87—Salt Lake City	IHL	82	29	69	98	86	...	...	...	17	9	8	17	13
NHL Totals (1 year)		14	2	0	2	0	-1	0	0					

HEAD COACHING RECORD

BACKGROUND: Assistant coach, Salt Lake City Golden Eagles of IHL (1986-87 through 1988-89). ... Assistant coach, Boston Bruins (1997-98 and 1998-99).

		REGULAR SEASON						PLAYOFFS		
Season Team	League	W	L	T	OTL	Pct.	Finish	W	L	Pct.
89-90—Salt Lake City	IHL	37	36	9	—	.506	2nd/West Division	5	6	.455
90-91—Salt Lake City	IHL	50	28	5	—	.633	2nd/West Division	0	4	.000
91-92—Salt Lake City	IHL	33	40	9	—	.457	4th/West Division	1	4	.200
92-93—Salt Lake City	IHL	38	39	5	—	.494	2nd/Pacific Division	—	—	—
93-94—Saint John	AHL	37	33	10	—	.525	2nd/Atlantic Division	3	4	.429
94-95—Saint John	AHL	27	40	13	—	.419	4th/Atlantic Division	1	4	.200
95-96—Providence	AHL	30	40	10	—	.438	4th/Northern Division	1	3	.250
96-97—Providence	AHL	35	40	5	—	.469	4th/New England Division	4	6	.400
99-00—Phoenix	NHL	39	31	8	4	.524	3rd/Pacific Division	1	4	.200
00-01—Phoenix	NHL	35	27	17	3	.530	4th/Pacific Division	—	—	—
01-02—Phoenix	NHL	40	27	9	6	.543	2nd/Pacific Division	1	4	.200
02-03—Phoenix	NHL	31	31	11	5	.468	4th/Pacific Division	—	—	—
NHL Totals (4 years)		145	116	45	18	.517	**NHL Totals (2 years)**	2	8	.200

NOTES:
89-90—Defeated Milwaukee in quarterfinals of Turner Cup playoffs; lost to Indianapolis in semifinals of Turner Cup playoffs.
90-91—Lost to Phoenix in Turner Cup quarterfinals.
91-92—Lost to Kansas City in West Division quarterfinals.
93-94—Lost to Moncton in Atlantic Division semifinals.
94-95—Lost to Prince Edward Island in Atlantic Division semifinals.
95-96—Lost to Springfield in Eastern Conference quarterfinals.
96-97—Defeated Worcester in Southern Conference quarterfinals; lost to Springfield in Southern Conference semifinals.
99-00—Lost to Colorado in Western Conference quarterfinals.
01-02—Lost to San Jose in Western Conference quarterfinals.

GRANATO, TONY · AVALANCHE

PERSONAL: Born June 25, 1964, in Downers Grove, Ill. ... Played right wing. ... Shot right. ... Full Name: Anthony Lewis Granato. ... Name pronounced gruh-NAH-toh.

TRANSACTIONS/CAREER NOTES: Selected by New York Rangers in sixth round (fifth Rangers pick, 120th overall) of NHL entry draft (June 9, 1982). ... Bruised foot (February 1989). ... Traded to Rangers with RW Tomas Sandstrom to Los Angeles Kings for C Bernie Nicholls (January 20, 1990). ... Strained groin (January 25, 1990); missed 12 games. ... Injured knee (March 20, 1990). ... Tore rib cartilage (December 18, 1990); missed 10 games. ... Strained back (October 6, 1992); missed three games. ... Strained back (December 4, 1993); missed one game. ... Strained lower back (December 13, 1993); missed nine games. ... Suspended 15 games without pay and fined $500 by NHL for slashing incident (February 16, 1994). ... Strained back (April 3, 1994); missed remainder of season. ... Strained hip flexor (March 13, 1995); missed one game. ... Fractured bone in foot (April 6, 1995); missed 13 games. ... Underwent brain surgery (February 14, 1996); missed remainder of season. ... Signed as free agent by San Jose Sharks (August 15, 1996). ... Injured back (December 21, 1996); missed one game. ... Reinjured back (January 29, 1997); missed two games. ... Suspended three games and fined $1,000 by NHL for cross-checking incident (February 5, 1997). ... Injured jaw (November 1, 1997); missed 19 games. ... Suspended two games and fined $1,000 by NHL for high-sticking incident (January 24, 1998). ... Suffered injury (November 21, 1998); missed two games. ... Injured back (December 10, 1998); missed six games. ... Tore anterior cruciate ligament in knee (January 11, 1999); missed 36 games. ... Suffered head injury (January 22, 2001); missed four games.

STATISTICAL PLATEAUS: Three-goal games: 1988-89 (2), 1991-92 (1), 1994-95 (1), 1996-97 (2). Total: 6. ... Four-goal games: 1988-89 (1). ... Total hat tricks: 7.

		REGULAR SEASON							PLAYOFFS				
Season Team	League	Gms.	G	A	Pts.	PIM	+/-	PP	SH	Gms.	G	A	Pts.	PIM
81-82—Northwood School	N.Y. H.S.					Statistics unavailable.								
82-83—Northwood School	N.Y. H.S.					Statistics unavailable.								
83-84—Univ. of Wisconsin	WCHA	35	14	17	31	48	...	...	...	—	—	—	—	—
84-85—Univ. of Wisconsin	WCHA	42	33	34	67	94	...	...	...	—	—	—	—	—
85-86—Univ. of Wisconsin	WCHA	33	25	24	49	36	...	...	...	—	—	—	—	—
86-87—Univ. of Wisconsin	WCHA	42	28	45	73	64	...	...	...	—	—	—	—	—
87-88—U.S. national team	Int'l	49	40	31	71	55	...	...	...	—	—	—	—	—
—U.S. Olympic team	Int'l	6	1	7	8	4	...	...	...	—	—	—	—	—
—Denver	IHL	22	13	14	27	36	...	...	...	8	9	4	13	16
88-89—New York Rangers	NHL	78	36	27	63	140	17	4	4	4	1	1	2	21
89-90—New York Rangers	NHL	37	7	18	25	77	1	1	0	—	—	—	—	—
—Los Angeles	NHL	19	5	6	11	45	-2	1	0	10	5	4	9	12
90-91—Los Angeles	NHL	68	30	34	64	154	22	11	1	12	1	4	5	28
91-92—Los Angeles	NHL	80	39	29	68	187	4	7	2	6	1	5	6	10
92-93—Los Angeles	NHL	81	37	45	82	171	-1	14	2	24	6	11	17	50
93-94—Los Angeles	NHL	50	7	14	21	150	-2	2	0	—	—	—	—	—
94-95—Los Angeles	NHL	33	13	11	24	68	9	2	0	—	—	—	—	—
95-96—Los Angeles	NHL	49	17	18	35	46	-5	5	0	—	—	—	—	—
96-97—San Jose	NHL	76	25	15	40	159	-7	5	1	—	—	—	—	—
97-98—San Jose	NHL	59	16	9	25	70	3	3	0	1	0	0	0	0
98-99—San Jose	NHL	35	6	6	12	54	4	0	1	6	1	1	2	2
99-00—San Jose	NHL	48	6	7	13	39	2	1	0	12	0	1	1	14
00-01—San Jose	NHL	61	4	5	9	65	-1	1	0	4	1	0	1	4
NHL Totals (13 years)		774	248	244	492	1425	44	57	11	79	16	27	43	141

HEAD COACHING RECORD

STATISTICAL PLATEAUS: Three-goal games: 1988-89 (2), 1991-92 (1), 1994-95 (1), 1996-97 (2). Total: 6. ... Four-goal games: 1988-89 (1). ... Total hat tricks: 7.

Season Team	League	REGULAR SEASON						PLAYOFFS		
		W	L	T	OTL	Pct.	Finish	W	L	Pct.
02-03—Colorado	NHL	32	11	4	4	.667	1st/Northwest Division	3	4	.429
NHL Totals (1 year)		32	11	4	4	.667	NHL Totals (1 year)....................	3	4	.429

NOTES:
02-03—Replace Bob Hartley as head coach (December 19); Lost to Minnesota in Western Conference quarterfinals.

HARTLEY, BOB — THRASHERS

PERSONAL: Born September 7, 1960, in Hawksbury, Ont. ... Full Name: Robert Hartley.

HEAD COACHING RECORD

Season Team	League	REGULAR SEASON						PLAYOFFS		
		W	L	T	OTL	Pct.	Finish	W	L	Pct.
87-88—Hawkesbury	CJHL	9	39	0	—	.188	—	1	4	.200
88-89—Hawkesbury	CJHL	35	20	1	—	.634	—	6	6	.500
89-90—Hawkesbury	CJHL	40	15	1	—	.686	—	12	3	.800
90-91—Hawkesbury	CJHL	42	10	4	—	.746	—	12	0	1.000
91-92—Laval	QMJHL	38	27	5	—	.579	—	4	6	.400
92-93—Laval	QMJHL	43	25	2	—	.629	1st/Robert Le Bel Division	12	1	.923
94-95—Cornwall	AHL	38	33	9	—	.531	2nd/Southern Division	8	6	.571
95-96—Cornwall	AHL	34	39	7	—	.469	4th/Central Division	3	5	.375
96-97—Hershey	AHL	43	22	10	—	.640	2nd/Mid-Atlantic Division	15	8	.652
97-98—Hershey	AHL	36	31	7	—	.534	2nd/Mid-Atlantic Division	3	4	.429
98-99—Colorado	NHL	44	28	10	—	.598	1st/ Northwest Division	11	8	.579
99-00—Colorado	NHL	42	28	11	1	.579	1st/Northwest Division	11	6	.647
00-01—Colorado	NHL	52	16	10	4	.695	1st/Northwest Division	16	7	.696
01-02—Colorado	NHL	45	28	8	1	.598	1st/Northwest Division	11	10	.524
02-03—Atlanta.................................	NHL	19	14	5	1	.551	3rd/Southeast Division	—	—	—
NHL Totals (5 years)		202	114	44	7	.610	NHL Totals (4 years)...................	49	31	.613

NOTES:
92-93—Defeated Verdun in quarterfinals of President Cup playoffs; defeated Drummondville in semifinals of President Cup playoffs; defeated Sherbrooke in finals of President Cup playoffs.
94-95—Defeated Hershey in division semifinals in Calder Cup playoffs; defeated Binghamton in division finals in Calder Cup playoffs; lost to Fredericton in league semifinals in Calder Cup playoffs.
95-96—Defeated Albany in conference quarterfinals in Calder Cup playoffs; lost to Rochester in conference finals in Calder Cup playoffs.
96-97—Defeated Kentucky in conference quarterfinals in Calder Cup playoffs; defeated Philadelphia in conference semifinals in Calder Cup playoffs; defeated Springfield in conference finals in Calder Cup playoffs; defeated Hamilton in Calder Cup finals.
97-98—Defeated Kentucky in conference quarterfinals in Calder Cup playoffs; lost to Philadelphia in conference semifinals in Calder Cup playoffs.
98-99—Defeated San Jose in Western Conference quarterfinals; defeated Detroit in Western Conference semifinals; lost to Dallas in Western Conference finals.
99-00—Defeated Phoenix in Western Conference quarterfinals; defeated Detroit in Western Conference semifinals; lost to Dallas in Western Conference finals.
00-01—Defeated Vancouver in Western Conference quarterfinals; defeated Los Angeles in Western Conference semifinals; defeated St. Louis in Western Conference finals; defeated New Jersey in Stanley Cup finals.
01-02—Defeated Los Angeles in Western Conference quarterfinals; defeated San Jose in Western Conference semifinals; lost to Detroit in Western Conference finals.
02-03—Replaced Curt Fraser as head coach (January 14).

HITCHCOCK, KEN — FLYERS

PERSONAL: Born December 17, 1951, in Edmonton.
COLLEGE: University of Alberta.

HEAD COACHING RECORD

BACKGROUND: Assistant coach, Philadelphia Flyers (1990-91 through 1992-93). ... Associate coach, Canadian Olympic team (2002).

Season Team	League	REGULAR SEASON						PLAYOFFS		
		W	L	T	OTL	Pct.	Finish	W	L	Pct.
84-85—Kamloops.............................	WHL	52	17	2	—	.746	1st/West Division	10	5	.667
85-86—Kamloops.............................	WHL	49	19	4	—	.708	1st/West Division	14	2	.875
86-87—Kamloops.............................	WHL	55	14	3	—	.785	1st/West Division	8	5	.615
87-88—Kamloops.............................	WHL	45	26	1	—	.632	1st/West Division	12	6	.667
88-89—Kamloops.............................	WHL	34	33	5	—	.507	3rd/West Division	8	8	.500
89-90—Kamloops.............................	WHL	56	16	0	—	.778	1st/West Division	14	3	.824
93-94—Kalamazoo	IHL	48	26	7	—	.636	1st/Atlantic Division	1	4	.200
94-95—Kalamazoo	IHL	43	24	14	—	.617	2nd/Northern Division	10	6	.625
95-96—Michigan	IHL	19	10	11	—	.613	—	—	—	—
—Dallas	NHL	15	23·	5	—	.407	6th/Central Division	—	—	—
96-97—Dallas	NHL	48	26	8	—	.634	1st/Central Division	3	4	.429
97-98—Dallas	NHL	49	22	11	—	.665	1st/Central Division	10	7	.588
98-99—Dallas	NHL	51	19	12	—	.695	1st/Pacific Division	16	7	.696
99-00—Dallas	NHL	43	23	10	6	.585	1st/Pacific Division	14	9	.609
00-01—Dallas	NHL	48	24	8	2	.634	1st/Pacific Division	4	6	.400
01-02—Dallas	NHL	23	17	6	4	.520	—	—	—	—
02-03—Philadelphia	NHL	45	20	13	4	.628	2nd/Atlantic Division	6	7	.462
NHL Totals (8 years)		322	174	73	16	.613	NHL Totals (6 years)...................	53	40	.570

NOTES:
84-85—Defeated Portland in West Division semifinals; defeated New Westminster in West Division finals; lost to Prince Albert in WHL finals.
85-86—Defeated Seattle in West Division semifinals; defeated Portland in West Division finals; defeated Medicine Hat in WHL finals.

86-87—Defeated Victoria in West Division semifinals; lost to Portland in West Division finals.
87-88—Defeated New Westminster in West Division semifinals; defeated Spokane in West Division finals; lost to Medicine Hat in WHL finals.
88-89—Defeated Victoria in West Division semifinals; lost to Portland in West Division finals.
89-90—Defeated Spokane in West Division semifinals; defeated Seattle in West Division finals; defeated Lethbridge in WHL finals.
93-94—Lost to Cincinnati in Eastern Conference quarterfinals.
94-95—Defeated Chicago in Eastern Conference quarterfinals; defeated Cincinnati in Eastern Conference semifinals; lost to Kansas City in Eastern Conference finals.
95-96—Replaced Bob Gainey as head coach (January 8).
96-97—Lost to Edmonton in Western Conference quarterfinals.
97-98—Defeated San Jose in Western Conference quarterfinals; defeated Edmonton in Western Conference semifinals; lost to Detroit in Western Conference finals.
98-99—Defeated Edmonton in Western Conference quarterfinals; defeated St. Louis in Western Conference semifinals; defeated Colorado in Western Conference finals; defeated Buffalo in Stanley Cup finals.
99-00—Defeated Edmonton in Western Conference quarterfinals; defeated San Jose in Western Conference semifinals; defeated Colorado in Western Conference finals; lost to New Jersey in Stanley Cup finals.
00-01—Defeated Edmonton in Western Conference quarterfinals; lost to St. Louis in Western Conference semifinals.
01-02—Replaced as head coach by Rick Wilson (January 25).
02-03—Defeated Toronto in Eastern Conference quarterfinals; lost to Ottawa in Eastern Conference semifinals.

JULIEN, CLAUDE — CANADIENS

PERSONAL: Born November 11, 1958, in Orleans, Ont. ... Played defense. ... Shot right.
TRANSACTIONS/CAREER NOTES: Signed as free agent by St. Louis Blues (September 1981). ... Sent with D Gordon Donnelly to Quebec Nordiques as compensation for Blues signing coach Jacques Demers (August 1983). ... Broke nose (February 1, 1986). ... Signed by Fredericton Express after completing a season in Europe (March 1987).

Season Team	League	Gms.	G	A	Pts.	PIM	+/-	PP	SH	Gms.	G	A	Pts.	PIM
				REGULAR SEASON								PLAYOFFS		
77-78—Newmarket	OHA	45	18	26	44	137	...	...	...	—	—	—	—	—
—Oshawa	OMJHL	11	0	5	5	14	...	...	...	—	—	—	—	—
78-79—						Did not play.								
79-80—Windsor	OMJHL	68	14	37	51	148	...	...	...	16	5	11	16	23
80-81—Windsor	OMJHL	3	1	2	3	21	...	...	...	—	—	—	—	—
—Port Huron	IHL	77	15	40	55	153	...	...	...	4	1	1	2	4
81-82—Salt Lake City	IHL	70	4	18	22	134	...	...	...	5	1	4	5	0
82-83—Salt Lake City	IHL	76	14	47	61	176	...	...	...	6	3	3	6	16
83-84—Milwaukee	IHL	5	0	3	3	2	...	...	...	—	—	—	—	—
—Fredericton	AHL	57	7	22	29	58	...	...	...	7	0	4	4	6
84-85—Fredericton	AHL	77	6	28	34	97	...	...	...	6	2	4	6	13
—Quebec	NHL	1	0	0	0	0	...	...	...	—	—	—	—	—
85-86—Quebec	NHL	13	0	1	1	25	...	...	...	—	—	—	—	—
—Fredericton	AHL	49	3	18	21	74	...	...	...	6	1	4	5	19
86-87—Fredericton	AHL	17	1	6	7	22	...	...	...	—	—	—	—	—
87-88—Fredericton	AHL	35	1	14	15	52	...	...	...	13	1	3	4	30
—Baltimore	AHL	30	6	14	20	22	...	...	...	—	—	—	—	—
88-89—Halifax	AHL	79	8	52	60	72	...	...	...	4	0	2	2	4
89-90—Halifax	AHL	77	6	37	43	65	...	...	...	4	0	1	1	7
90-91—Kansas City	IHL	54	7	16	23	43	...	...	...	—	—	—	—	—
91-92—Moncton	AHL	48	2	15	17	10	...	...	...	4	0	1	1	4
NHL Totals (2 years)		14	0	1	1	25	...	...	...					

HEAD COACHING RECORD

Season Team	League	W	L	T	OTL	Pct.	Finish	W	L	Pct.
				REGULAR SEASON					PLAYOFFS	
02-03—Montreal	NHL	12	16	3	5	.375	4th/Northeast Division	—	—	—
NHL Totals (1 year)		12	16	3	5	.375				

NOTES:
02-03—Replaced Michel Therrien as head coach (January 18).

KEENAN, MIKE — PANTHERS

PERSONAL: Born October 21, 1949, in Bowmanville, Ont. ... Full Name: Michael Edward Keenan.

Season Team	League	Gms.	G	A	Pts.	PIM	+/-	PP	SH	Gms.	G	A	Pts.	PIM
				REGULAR SEASON								PLAYOFFS		
69-70—St. Lawrence Univ.	ECAC	10	0	4	4	32	...	...	...	—	—	—	—	—
70-71—St. Lawrence Univ.	ECAC	22	4	12	16	35	...	...	...	—	—	—	—	—
71-72—St. Lawrence Univ.	ECAC	25	13	16	29	52	...	...	...	—	—	—	—	—

HEAD COACHING RECORD

BACKGROUND: Coach, Canadian national junior team (1980). ... Coach, NHL All-Star team (1985-86, 1987-88 and 1992-93). ... Coach, Team Canada (1987). ... General manager, Chicago Blackhawks (1989-90 through 1991-92). ... General manager/coach, Team Canada (1991). ... Coach, Canadian national team (1993). ... General manager, St. Louis Blues (1994-95 through December 18, 1996).

Season Team	League	W	L	T	OTL	Pct.	Finish	W	L	Pct.
				REGULAR SEASON					PLAYOFFS	
79-80—Peterborough	OHL	47	20	1	—	.699	1st/Leyden Division	15	3	.833
80-81—Rochester	AHL	30	42	8	—	.425	5th/Southern Division	—	—	—
81-82—Rochester	AHL	40	31	9	—	.556	2nd/Southern Division	4	5	.444
82-83—Rochester	AHL	46	25	9	—	.631	1st/Southern Division	12	4	.750
83-84—University of Toronto	OUAA	41	5	3	—	.867	1st/OUAA	9	0	1.000

Season Team	League	W	L	T	OTL	Pct.	Finish	W	L	Pct.
						REGULAR SEASON			**PLAYOFFS**	
84-85—Philadelphia	NHL	53	20	7	—	.706	1st/Patrick Division	12	7	.632
85-86—Philadelphia	NHL	53	23	4	—	.688	1st/Patrick Division	2	3	.400
86-87—Philadelphia	NHL	46	26	8	—	.625	1st/Patrick Division	15	11	.577
87-88—Philadelphia	NHL	38	33	9	—	.531	3rd/Patrick Division	3	4	.429
88-89—Chicago	NHL	27	41	12	—	.413	4th/Norris Division	9	7	.563
89-90—Chicago	NHL	41	33	6	—	.550	1st/Norris Division	10	10	.500
90-91—Chicago	NHL	49	23	8	—	.663	1st/Norris Division	2	4	.333
91-92—Chicago	NHL	36	29	15	—	.544	2nd/Norris Division	12	6	.667
92-93—Canadian nat'l team	Int'l	—	—	—	—	.000	Record unavailable.	—	—	—
93-94—New York Rangers	NHL	52	24	8	—	.667	1st/Atlantic Division	16	7	.696
94-95—St. Louis	NHL	28	15	5	—	.635	2nd/Central Division	3	4	.429
95-96—St. Louis	NHL	32	34	16	—	.488	4th/Central Division	7	6	.538
96-97—St. Louis	NHL	15	17	1	—	.470	—	—	—	—
97-98—Vancouver	NHL	21	30	12	—	.429	7th/Pacific Division	—	—	—
98-99—Vancouver	NHL	15	24	6	—	.400	—	—	—	—
00-01—Boston	NHL	33	26	7	8	.493	4th/Northeast Division	—	—	—
01-02—Florida	NHL	16	29	8	3	.357	4th/Southeast Division	—	—	—
02-03—Florida	NHL	24	36	13	9	.372	4th/Southeast Division	—	—	—
NHL Totals (17 years)		579	463	145	20	.540	**NHL Totals (11 years)**	91	69	.569

NOTES:

81-82—Defeated New Haven in Calder Cup quarterfinals; lost to Binghamton in Calder Cup semifinals.

82-83—Defeated Binghamton in Calder Cup quarterfinals; defeated New Haven in Calder Cup semifinals; defeated Maine in Calder Cup finals.

83-84—Defeated Guelph in OUAA semifinals; defeated Western Ontario in OUAA finals; defeated New Brunswick in East Regional Qualifying Round; defeated Trois-Rivieres in CIAU Championship Tournament semifinals; defeated Concordia in CIAU Championship Tournament finals.

84-85—Defeated New York Rangers in Patrick Division semifinals; defeated New York Islanders in Patrick Division finals; defeated Quebec in Wales Conference finals; lost to Edmonton in Stanley Cup finals.

85-86—Lost to New York Rangers in Patrick Division semifinals.

86-87—Defeated New York Rangers in Patrick Division semifinals; defeated New York Islanders in Patrick Division finals; defeated Montreal in Wales Conference finals; lost to Edmonton in Stanley Cup finals.

87-88—Lost to Washington in Patrick Division semifinals.

88-89—Defeated Detroit in Norris Division semifinals; defeated St. Louis in Norris Division finals; lost to Calgary in Campbell Conference finals.

89-90—Defeated Minnesota in Norris Division semifinals; defeated St. Louis in Norris Division finals; lost to Edmonton in Campbell Conference finals.

90-91—Lost to Minnesota in Norris Division semifinals.

91-92—Defeated St. Louis in Norris Division semifinals; defeated Detroit in Norris Division finals; defeated Edmonton in Campbell Conference finals; lost to Pittsburgh in Stanley Cup finals.

92-93—Finished fourth in World Championships.

93-94—Defeated New York Islanders in Eastern Conference quarterfinals; defeated Washington in Eastern Conference semifinals; defeated New Jersey in Eastern Conference finals; defeated Vancouver in Stanley Cup finals.

94-95—Lost to Vancouver in Western Conference quarterfinals.

95-96—Defeated Toronto in Western Conference quarterfinals; lost to Detroit in Western Conference semifinals.

96-97—Replaced by interim Jimmy Roberts as head coach (December 18).

97-98—Replaced Tom Renney as head coach (November 13) with club in seventh place.

98-99—Replaced as head coach by Marc Crawford (January 24) with team in third place.

00-01—Replaced Pat Burns as head coach (October 25).

01-02—Replaced Duane Sutter as head coach (December 2).

LEMAIRE, JACQUES   WILD

PERSONAL: Born September 7, 1945, in Ville LaSalle, Que. ... Full Name: Jacques Gerard Lemaire. ... Uncle of Manny Fernandez, goaltender, Minnesota Wild. ... Name pronounced luh-MAIR.

STATISTICAL PLATEAUS: Three-goal games: 1977-78 (1), 1978-79 (2). Total: 3.

Season Team	League	Gms.	G	A	Pts.	PIM	+/-	PP	SH	Gms.	G	A	Pts.	PIM
				REGULAR SEASON								**PLAYOFFS**		
62-63—Lachine	QJHL	42	41	63	104	...	...	...	...	—	—	—	—	—
63-64—Montreal Jr. Can.	OHA Jr. A	42	25	30	55	17	...	...	...	—	—	—	—	—
64-65—Montreal Jr. Can.	OHA Jr. A	56	25	47	72	52	...	...	...	—	—	—	—	—
—Quebec	AHL	1	0	0	0	0	...	...	...	—	—	—	—	—
65-66—Montreal Jr. Can.	OHA Jr. A	48	41	52	93	69	...	...	...	—	—	—	—	—
66-67—Houston	CPHL	69	19	30	49	19	...	...	...	6	0	1	1	0
67-68—Montreal	NHL	69	22	20	42	16	15	3	1	13	7	6	13	6
68-69—Montreal	NHL	75	29	34	63	29	31	5	0	14	4	2	6	6
69-70—Montreal	NHL	69	32	28	60	16	19	13	0	—	—	—	—	—
70-71—Montreal	NHL	78	28	28	56	18	0	6	0	20	9	10	19	17
71-72—Montreal	NHL	77	32	49	81	26	37	8	0	6	2	1	3	2
72-73—Montreal	NHL	77	44	51	95	16	59	9	0	17	7	13	20	2
73-74—Montreal	NHL	66	29	38	67	10	4	10	0	6	0	4	4	2
74-75—Montreal	NHL	80	36	56	92	20	25	12	0	11	5	7	12	4
75-76—Montreal	NHL	61	20	32	52	20	26	6	0	13	3	3	6	2
76-77—Montreal	NHL	75	34	41	75	22	70	5	2	14	7	12	19	6
77-78—Montreal	NHL	76	36	61	97	14	54	6	0	15	6	8	14	10
78-79—Montreal	NHL	50	24	31	55	10	9	6	1	16	11	12	23	6
NHL Totals (12 years)		853	366	469	835	217	349	89	4	145	61	78	139	63

HEAD COACHING RECORD

BACKGROUND: Assistant coach, University of Plattsburgh (1981-82). ... Assistant coach, Montreal Canadiens (October 1982-February 1983). ... Assistant to managing director/director of player personnel, Canadiens (1985-86 through 1987-88). ... Assistant to managing director of Verdun, Canadiens organization (1988-89). ... Assistant to managing director, Canadiens (1989-90 and 1990-91). ... Assistant to managing director of Fredericton, Canadiens organization (1991-92 and 1992-93). ... Served as interim coach of Montreal Canadiens while Jacques Demers was hospitalized with chest pains (March 10 and 11, 1993; team was 1-1 during that time). ... Consultant to General Manager, Canadiens (1998-99 and 1999-2000).

Season Team	League	W	L	T	OTL	Pct.	Finish	W	L	Pct.
								REGULAR SEASON						PLAYOFFS		

Season Team	League	W	L	T	OTL	Pct.	Finish	W	L	Pct.
79-80—Sierre	Switzerland	—	—	—	—	.000	—	—	—	—
80-81—Sierre	Switzerland	—	—	—	—	.000	—	—	—	—
82-83—Longueuil	QMJHL	37	29	4	—	.557	3rd/LeBel Division	8	7	.533
83-84—Montreal	NHL	7	10	0	—	.412	4th/Adams Division	9	6	.600
84-85—Montreal	NHL	41	27	12	—	.588	1st/Adams Division	6	6	.500
93-94—New Jersey	NHL	47	25	12	—	.631	2nd/Atlantic Division	11	9	.550
94-95—New Jersey	NHL	22	18	8	—	.542	2nd/Atlantic Division	16	4	.800
95-96—New Jersey	NHL	37	33	12	—	.524	6th/Atlantic Division	—	—	—
96-97—New Jersey	NHL	45	23	14	—	.634	1st/Atlantic Division	5	5	.500
97-98—New Jersey	NHL	48	23	11	—	.652	1st/Atlantic Division	2	4	.333
00-01—Minnesota	NHL	25	39	13	5	.384	5th/Northwest Division	—	—	—
01-02—Minnesota	NHL	26	35	12	9	.390	5th/Northwest Division	—	—	—
02-03—Minnesota	NHL	42	29	10	1	.573	3rd/Northwest Division	8	10	.444
NHL Totals (10 years)		340	262	104	15	.544	**NHL Totals (7 years)**	57	44	.564

NOTES:
82-83—Defeated Chicoutimi in President Cup quarterfinals; defeated Laval in President Cup semifinals; lost to Verdun in President Cup finals.
83-84—Defeated Boston in Adams Division semifinals; defeated Quebec in Adams Division finals; lost to New York Islanders in Wales Conference finals.
84-85—Defeated Boston in Adams Division semifinals; lost to Quebec in Adams Division finals.
93-94—Defeated Buffalo in Eastern Conference quarterfinals; defeated Boston in Eastern Conference semifinals; lost to New York Rangers in Eastern Conference finals.
94-95—Defeated Boston in Eastern Conference quarterfinals; defeated Pittsburgh in Eastern Conference semifinals; defeated Philadelphia in Eastern Conference finals; defeated Detroit in Stanley Cup finals.
96-97—Defeated Montreal in Eastern Conference quarterfinals; lost to New York Rangers in Eastern Conference semifinals.
97-98—Lost to Ottawa in Eastern Conference quarterfinals.
02-03—Defeated Colorado in Western Conference quarterfinals; defeated Vancouver in Western Conference semifinals; lost to Anaheim in Western Conference finals.

LEWIS, DAVE — RED WINGS

PERSONAL: Born July 3, 1953, in Kindersley, Sask. ... Full Name: David Rodney Lewis.
TRANSACTIONS/CAREER NOTES: Selected by New York Islanders in third round (second Islanders pick, 33rd overall) of 1973 NHL entry draft. ... Traded by Islanders with RW Billy Harris to Los Angeles Kings for C Butch Goring (March 10, 1980). ... Traded by Kings to Minnesota North Stars for C Steve Christoff and D Fred Barrett (October 3, 1983). ... Traded by North Stars to New Jersey Devils for LW Brent Ashton (October 3, 1983). ... Released by Devils (July 1, 1986). ... Signed as free agent by Detroit Red Wings (July 27, 1986).

Season Team	League	Gms.	G	A	Pts.	PIM	+/-	PP	SH	Gms.	G	A	Pts.	PIM
		REGULAR SEASON								PLAYOFFS				
71-72—Saskatoon	WCJHL	52	2	9	11	68	...	...	...	8	2	3	5	4
72-73—Saskatoon	WCJHL	67	10	35	45	89	...	...	...	16	3	12	15	44
73-74—New York Islanders	NHL	66	2	15	17	58	-7	1	1	—	—	—	—	—
74-75—New York Islanders	NHL	78	5	14	19	98	8	0	0	17	0	1	1	28
75-76—New York Islanders	NHL	73	0	19	19	54	29	0	0	13	0	1	1	44
76-77—New York Islanders	NHL	79	4	24	28	44	29	0	1	12	1	6	7	4
77-78—New York Islanders	NHL	77	3	11	14	58	32	0	1	7	0	1	1	11
78-79—New York Islanders	NHL	79	5	18	23	43	43	0	0	10	0	0	0	4
79-80—New York Islanders	NHL	62	5	16	21	54	10	0	0	—	—	—	—	—
—Los Angeles	NHL	11	1	1	2	12	3	0	0	4	0	1	1	2
80-81—Los Angeles	NHL	67	1	12	13	98	25	0	0	4	0	2	2	4
81-82—Los Angeles	NHL	64	1	13	14	75	-19	0	0	10	0	4	4	36
82-83—Los Angeles	NHL	79	2	10	12	53	-22	0	0	—	—	—	—	—
83-84—New Jersey	NHL	66	2	5	7	63	-19	...	...	—	—	—	—	—
84-85—New Jersey	NHL	74	3	9	12	78	-29	0	0	—	—	—	—	—
85-86—New Jersey	NHL	69	0	15	15	81	0	0	0	—	—	—	—	—
86-87—Detroit	NHL	58	2	5	7	66	12	0	0	14	0	4	4	10
87-88—Detroit	NHL	6	0	0	0	18	-3	0	0	—	—	—	—	—
NHL Totals (15 years)		1008	36	187	223	953	92	...	...	91	1	20	21	143

HEAD COACHING RECORD

BACKGROUND: Associate coach, Detroit Red Wings (1988-89 through 2001-02).

Season Team	League	W	L	T	OTL	Pct.	Finish	W	L	Pct.
		REGULAR SEASON						PLAYOFFS		
02-03—Detroit	NHL	48	20	10	4	.646	1st/Central Division	0	4	.000
NHL Totals (1 year)		48	20	10	4	.646	**NHL Totals (1 year)**	0	4	.000

NOTES:
02-03—Lost to Anaheim in Western Conference finals.

MacLEAN, DOUG — BLUE JACKETS

PERSONAL: Born April 12, 1954, in Summerside, P.E.I.
COLLEGE: Prince Edward Island, then Western Ontario (master's degree in educational psychology).

HEAD COACHING RECORD

BACKGROUND: Assistant coach, London Knights of OHL (1984-85). ... Assistant coach, St. Louis Blues (1986-87 and 1987-88). ... Assistant coach, Washington Capitals (1988-89 and 1989-1990). ... Assistant coach, Detroit Red Wings (1990-91 and 1991-92). ... Assistant general manager, Red Wings (1992-93 and 1993-94). ... General manager, Adirondack, Red Wings organization (1992-93 and 1993-94). ... Director of player development/scout, Florida Panthers (1994-95).

Season Team	League	REGULAR SEASON						PLAYOFFS		
		W	L	T	OTL	Pct.	Finish	W	L	Pct.
89-90—Baltimore	AHL	17	13	5	—	.557	3rd/Southern Division	6	6	.500
95-96—Florida	NHL	41	31	10	—	.561	3rd/Atlantic Division	12	10	.545
96-97—Florida	NHL	35	28	19	—	.543	3rd/Atlantic Division	1	4	.200
97-98—Florida	NHL	7	12	4	—	.391	—	—	—	—
02-03—Columbus	NHL	15	22	4	1	.405	5th/Central Division	—	—	—
NHL Totals (4 years)		98	93	37	1	.509	NHL Totals (2 years)	13	14	.481

NOTES:

89-90—Defeated Adirondack in quarterfinals of Calder Cup playoffs; lost to Rochester in semifinals of Calder Cup playoffs.

95-96—Defeated Boston in Eastern Conference quarterfinals; defeated Philadelphia in Eastern Conference semifinals; defeated Pittsburgh in Eastern Conference finals; lost to Colorado in Stanley Cup finals.

96-97—Lost to New York Rangers in Eastern Conference quarterfinals.

97-98—Suspended two games and fined $5,000 by NHL for confrontation with officials (November 4). Replaced by interim Bryan Murray as head coach (November 24) with club in sixth place.

02-03—Replaced Dave King as head coach (January 8).

MacTAVISH, CRAIG — OILERS

PERSONAL: Born August 15, 1958, in London, Ont.

HIGH SCHOOL: Westminster (London, Ont.).

COLLEGE: Lowell (Mass.).

TRANSACTIONS/CAREER NOTES: Selected by Boston Bruins in ninth round (ninth Bruins pick, 153rd overall) of NHL amateur draft (June 15, 1978). ... Involved in automobile accident in which another driver was killed (January 25, 1984); pleaded guilty to vehicular homicide, driving while under the influence of alcohol and reckless driving and sentenced to a year in prison (May 1984); missed 1984-85 season. ... Signed as free agent by Edmonton Oilers (February 1, 1985). ... Strained lower back (January 1993); missed one game. ... Suffered concussion (March 10, 1993); missed one game. ... Strained wrist (October 18, 1993); missed one game. ... Reinjured wrist (December 7, 1993); missed one game. ... Suffered whiplash (December 15, 1993); missed four games. ... Bruised foot (December 30, 1993); missed one game. ... Traded by Oilers to New York Rangers for C Todd Marchant (March 21, 1994). ... Signed as free agent by Philadelphia Flyers (July 6, 1994). ... Injured foot (January 24, 1995); missed one game. ... Bruised foot (April 14, 1995); missed two games. ... Underwent knee surgery (September 25, 1995); missed first eight games of season. ... Traded by Flyers to St. Louis Blues for C Dale Hawerchuk (March 15, 1996). ... Announced retirement (April 29, 1997).

STATISTICAL PLATEAUS: Three-goal games: 1985-86 (1), 1990-91 (1). Total: 2.

Season Team	League	REGULAR SEASON								PLAYOFFS				
		Gms.	G	A	Pts.	PIM	+/-	PP	SH	Gms.	G	A	Pts.	PIM
77-78—University of Lowell	ECAC-II	24	26	19	45	...	...	...	...	—	—	—	—	—
78-79—University of Lowell	ECAC-II	31	36	52	88	...	...	...	...	—	—	—	—	—
79-80—Binghamton	AHL	34	17	15	32	29	...	...	...	—	—	—	—	—
—Boston	NHL	46	11	17	28	8	...	0	0	10	2	3	5	7
80-81—Boston	NHL	24	3	5	8	13	-1	0	0	—	—	—	—	—
—Springfield	AHL	53	19	24	43	89	...	...	...	7	5	4	9	8
81-82—Erie	AHL	72	23	32	55	37	...	...	...	—	—	—	—	—
—Boston	NHL	2	0	1	1	0	...	...	...	—	—	—	—	—
82-83—Boston	NHL	75	10	20	30	18	15	0	0	17	3	1	4	18
83-84—Boston	NHL	70	20	23	43	35	9	7	0	1	0	0	0	0
84-85—Boston	NHL						Did not play.							
85-86—Edmonton	NHL	74	23	24	47	70	17	4	1	10	4	4	8	11
86-87—Edmonton	NHL	79	20	19	39	55	9	1	4	21	1	9	10	16
87-88—Edmonton	NHL	80	15	17	32	47	-3	0	3	19	0	1	1	31
88-89—Edmonton	NHL	80	21	31	52	55	10	2	4	7	0	1	1	8
89-90—Edmonton	NHL	80	21	22	43	89	13	1	6	22	2	6	8	29
90-91—Edmonton	NHL	80	17	15	32	76	-1	2	6	18	3	3	6	20
91-92—Edmonton	NHL	80	12	18	30	98	-1	0	2	16	3	0	3	28
92-93—Edmonton	NHL	82	10	20	30	110	-16	0	3	—	—	—	—	—
93-94—Edmonton	NHL	66	16	10	26	80	-20	0	0	—	—	—	—	—
—New York Rangers	NHL	12	4	2	6	11	6	1	0	23	1	4	5	22
94-95—Philadelphia	NHL	45	3	9	12	23	2	0	0	15	1	4	5	20
95-96—Philadelphia	NHL	55	5	8	13	62	-3	0	0	—	—	—	—	—
—St. Louis	NHL	13	0	1	1	8	-6	0	0	13	0	2	2	6
96-97—St. Louis	NHL	50	2	5	7	33	-12	0	0	1	0	0	0	2
NHL Totals (18 years)		1093	213	267	480	891	...	...	...	193	20	38	58	218

HEAD COACHING RECORD

BACKGROUND: Assistant coach, New York Rangers (1997-98 and 1998-99). ... Assistant coach, Edmonton Oilers (1999-2000).

STATISTICAL PLATEAUS: Three-goal games: 1985-86 (1), 1990-91 (1). Total: 2.

Season Team	League	REGULAR SEASON						PLAYOFFS		
		W	L	T	OTL	Pct.	Finish	W	L	Pct.
00-01—Edmonton	NHL	39	28	12	3	.549	2nd/Northwest Division	2	4	.333
01-02—Edmonton	NHL	38	28	12	4	.537	3rd/Northwest Division	—	—	—
02-03—Edmonton	NHL	36	26	11	9	.506	4th/Northwest Division	2	4	.333
NHL Totals (3 years)		113	82	35	16	.530	NHL Totals (2 years)	4	8	.333

NOTES:

00-01—Lost to Dallas in Western Conference quarterfinals.

02-03—Lost to Dallas in Western Conference quarterfinals.

MARTIN, JACQUES — SENATORS

PERSONAL: Born October 1, 1952, in St. Pascal, Ont.

HEAD COACHING RECORD

BACKGROUND: Assistant coach, Chicago Blackhawks (1988-89 through 1989-90). ... Assistant coach, Quebec Nordiques (1990-91 through 1992-93 and 1994-95). ... Assistant coach, Colorado Avalanche (1995 through January 24, 1996). ... Associate coach, Canadian Olympic team (2002).

Season Team	League	W	L	T	OTL	Pct.	Finish	W	L	Pct.
85-86—Guelph	OHL	41	23	2	—	.636	2nd/Emms Division	15	3	.833
86-87—St. Louis	NHL	32	33	15	—	.494	1st/Norris Division	2	4	.333
87-88—St. Louis	NHL	34	38	8	—	.475	2nd/Norris Division	5	5	.500
93-94—Cornwall	AHL	33	36	11	—	.481	T3rd/Southern Division	4	2	.667
95-96—Ottawa	NHL	10	24	4	—	.316	6th/Northeast Division	—	—	—
96-97—Ottawa	NHL	31	36	15	—	.470	T3rd/Northeast Division	3	4	.429
97-98—Ottawa	NHL	34	33	15	—	.506	5th/Northeast Division	5	6	.455
98-99—Ottawa	NHL	44	23	15	—	.628	1st/Northeast Division	0	4	.000
99-00—Ottawa	NHL	41	28	11	2	.567	2nd/Northeast Division	2	4	.333
00-01—Ottawa	NHL	48	21	9	4	.640	1st/Northeast Division	0	4	.000
01-02—Ottawa	NHL	38	26	9	7	.531	3rd/Northwest Division	7	5	.583
02-03—Ottawa	NHL	52	21	8	1	.683	1st/Northeast Division	11	7	.611
NHL Totals (10 years)		364	283	109	14	.544	**NHL Totals (9 years)**	35	43	.449

NOTES:

85-86—Defeated Sudbury in OHL quarterfinals; defeated Windsor in OHL semifinals; defeated Belleville in J. Ross Robertson Cup finals.
86-87—Lost to Toronto in Norris Division semifinals.
87-88—Defeated Chicago in Norris Division semifinals; lost to Detroit in Norris Division finals.
93-94—Defeated Hamilton in quarterfinals of Calder Cup playoffs; defeated Hershey in division finals of Calder Cup playoffs; lost to Moncton in semifinals of Calder Cup playoffs.
95-96—Replaced Rick Bowness as head coach (January 24).
96-97—Lost to Buffalo in Eastern Conference quarterfinals.
97-98—Defeated New Jersey in Eastern Conference quarterfinals; lost to Washington in Eastern Conference semifinals.
98-99—Lost to Buffalo in Eastern Conference quarterfinals.
99-00—Lost to Toronto in Eastern Conference quarterfinals.
00-01—Lost to Toronto in Eastern Conference quarterfinals.
01-02—Defeated Philadelphia in Eastern Conference quarterfinals; lost to Toronto in Eastern Conference semifinals.
02-03—Defeated New York Islanders in Eastern Conference quarterfinals; defeated Philadelphia in Eastern Conference semifinals; lost to New Jersey in Eastern Conference finals.

MAURICE, PAUL — HURRICANES

PERSONAL: Born January 30, 1967, in Sault Ste. Marie, Ont.

HEAD COACHING RECORD

BACKGROUND: Assistant coach, Hartford Whalers (June 9-November 6, 1995). ... Whalers franchise moved to North Carolina and renamed Carolina Hurricanes for 1997-98 season; NHL approved move on June 25, 1997.

Season Team	League	W	L	T	OTL	Pct.	Finish	W	L	Pct.
93-94—Detroit	OHL	42	20	4	—	.667	1st/West Division	11	6	.647
94-95—Detroit	OHL	44	18	4	—	.697	1st/West Division	16	5	.762
95-96—Hartford	NHL	29	33	8	—	.471	4th/Northeast Division	—	—	—
96-97—Hartford	NHL	32	39	11	—	.457	5th/Northeast Division	—	—	—
97-98—Carolina	NHL	33	41	8	—	.451	6th/Northeast Division	—	—	—
98-99—Carolina	NHL	34	30	18	—	.524	1st/Southeast Division	2	4	.333
99-00—Carolina	NHL	37	35	10	0	.512	3rd/Southeast Division	—	—	—
00-01—Carolina	NHL	38	32	9	3	.518	2nd/Southeast Division	2	4	.333
01-02—Carolina	NHL	35	26	16	5	.524	1st/Southeast Division	13	10	.565
02-03—Carolina	NHL	22	43	11	6	.335	5th/Southeast Division	—	—	—
NHL Totals (8 years)		260	279	91	14	.474	**NHL Totals (3 years)**	17	18	.486

NOTES:

93-94—Defeated Owen Sound in quarterfinals of OHL playoffs; defeated Sault Ste. Marie in semifinals of OHL playoffs; lost to North Bay in OHL finals.
94-95—Defeated London in first round of OHL playoffs; defeated Peterborough in second round of OHL playoffs; defeated Sudbury in third round of OHL playoffs; defeated Guelph in J. Ross Robertson Cup finals.
95-96—Replaced Paul Homgren as head coach (November 6) with club in third place.
98-99—Lost to Boston in Eastern Conference quarterfinals.
00-01—Lost to New Jersey in Eastern Conference quarterfinals.
01-02—Defeated New Jersey in Eastern Conference quarterfinals; defeated Montreal in Eastern Conference semifinals; defeated Toronto in Eastern Conference finals; lost to Detroit in Stanley Cup finals.

MURRAY, ANDY — KINGS

PERSONAL: Born March 3, 1951, in Gladstone, Man.
COLLEGE: Brandon (Man.) University (degree in political science/sociology, 1972); then University of Manitoba.

HEAD COACHING RECORD

BACKGROUND: Assistant coach, Brandon University (1973-74). ... Head coach, Brandon Travelers of Manitoba Junior A Hockey League (1974-75 through 1977-78). ... Head coach, Brandon University (1978-79 through 1980-81). ... Served as head coach for several of

NHL HEAD COACHES

Switzerland Division-A teams (1981-82 through 1987-88). ... Assistant coach, Hershey Bears of AHL (1986-87 and 1987-88). ... Assistant coach, Philadelphia Flyers (1988-89 and 1989-90). ... Assistant coach, Minnesota North Stars (1990-91 and 1991-92). ... Head coach, Lugano of Swiss League (1991-92). ... Head coach, Eisbaren Berlin of German League (1992-93). ... Assistant coach, Winnipeg Jets (1993-94 and 1994-95). ... Head coach, Canadian national team (1996-97 and 1997-98). ... Head coach, Shattuck-St. Mary's (Fairbault, Minn.) HS (1998-99). ... General Manager, Koln of German League (1998-99).

		REGULAR SEASON						PLAYOFFS		
Season Team	League	W	L	T	OTL	Pct.	Finish	W	L	Pct.
99-00—Los Angeles	NHL	39	27	12	4	.549	2nd/Pacific Division	0	4	.000
00-01—Los Angeles	NHL	38	28	13	3	.543	3rd/Pacific Division	7	6	.538
01-02—Los Angeles	NHL	40	27	11	4	.555	3rd/Pacific Division	3	4	.429
02-03—Los Angeles	NHL	33	37	6	6	.439	3rd/Pacific Division	—	—	—
NHL Totals (4 years)		150	119	42	17	.521	NHL Totals (3 years)	10	14	.417

NOTES:
99-00—Lost to Detroit in Western Conference quarterfinals.
00-01—Defeated Detroit in Western Conference quarterfinals; lost to Colorado in Western Conference semifinals.
01-02—Lost to Colorado in Western Conference quarterfinals.

OLCZYK, EDDIE — PENGUINS

PERSONAL: Born August 16, 1966, in Chicago. ... Played left wing. ... Shot left. ... Full Name: Ed Olczyk. ... Name pronounced OHL-chehk.
TRANSACTIONS/CAREER NOTES: Selected by Chicago Blackhawks in first round (first Blackhawks pick, third overall) of NHL entry draft (June 9, 1984). ... Hyperextended knee (September 3, 1984). ... Fractured bone in left foot (December 16, 1984). ... Traded by Blackhawks with LW Al Secord to Toronto Maple Leafs for RW Rick Vaive, LW Steve Thomas and D Bob McGill (September 1987). ... Pinched nerve in left knee (January 3, 1990). ... Traded by Maple Leafs with LW Mark Osborne to Winnipeg Jets for D Dave Ellett and LW Paul Fenton (November 10, 1990). ... Dislocated elbow and sprained ankle (January 8, 1992); missed 15 games. ... Sprained knee (November 24, 1992); missed nine games. ... Traded by Jets to New York Rangers for LW Kris King and RW Tie Domi (December 28, 1992). ... Fractured right thumb (January 31, 1994); missed 24 games. ... Suffered from kidney stones (January 24, 1995); missed six games. ... Suffered back spasms (March 3, 1995); missed three games. ... Traded by Rangers to Jets for fifth-round pick (D Alexei Vasiljev) in 1995 draft (April 7, 1995). ... Strained rib cage (October 28, 1995); missed four games. ... Strained back (January 3, 1996); missed four games. ... Sprained knee (March 7, 1996); missed 13 games. ... Signed as free agent by Los Angeles Kings (July 8, 1996). ... Suffered from the flu (December 12, 1996); missed two games. ... Traded by Kings to Pittsburgh Penguins for RW Glen Murray (March 18, 1997). ... Suffered concussion (October 4, 1997); missed five games. ... Suffered depressed fracture of zygomatic arch in neck (December 1, 1997); missed 18 games. ... Suffered back spasms (March 8, 1998); missed two games. ... Signed as free agent by Chicago Blackhawks (August 26, 1998). ... Suffered sore back prior to 1999-2000 season; missed first game of season. ... Suffered herniated disc in back (October 16, 1999) and underwent surgery; missed 25 games. ... Bruised ankle (January 15, 2000); missed three games. ... Strained groin (February 20, 2000); missed six games.
STATISTICAL PLATEAUS: Three-goal games: 1988-89 (1), 1989-90 (1), 1992-93 (1), 1995-96 (1), 1996-97 (1). Total: 5.

		REGULAR SEASON								PLAYOFFS				
Season Team	League	Gms.	G	A	Pts.	PIM	+/-	PP	SH	Gms.	G	A	Pts.	PIM
83-84—U.S. national team	Int'l	56	19	40	59	36	...	...	...	—	—	—	—	—
—U.S. Olympic team	Int'l	6	2	7	9	0	...	...	...	—	—	—	—	—
84-85—Chicago	NHL	70	20	30	50	67	11	1	1	15	6	5	11	11
85-86—Chicago	NHL	79	29	50	79	47	2	8	1	3	0	0	0	0
86-87—Chicago	NHL	79	16	35	51	119	-4	2	1	4	1	1	2	4
87-88—Toronto	NHL	80	42	33	75	55	-22	14	4	6	5	4	9	2
88-89—Toronto	NHL	80	38	52	90	75	0	11	2	—	—	—	—	—
89-90—Toronto	NHL	79	32	56	88	78	0	6	0	5	1	2	3	14
90-91—Toronto	NHL	18	4	10	14	13	-7	0	0	—	—	—	—	—
—Winnipeg	NHL	61	26	31	57	69	-20	14	0	—	—	—	—	—
91-92—Winnipeg	NHL	64	32	33	65	67	11	12	0	6	2	1	3	4
92-93—Winnipeg	NHL	25	8	12	20	26	-11	2	0	—	—	—	—	—
—New York Rangers	NHL	46	13	16	29	26	9	0	0	—	—	—	—	—
93-94—New York Rangers	NHL	37	3	5	8	28	-1	0	0	1	0	0	0	0
94-95—New York Rangers	NHL	20	2	1	3	4	-2	1	0	—	—	—	—	—
—Winnipeg	NHL	13	2	8	10	8	1	1	0	—	—	—	—	—
95-96—Winnipeg	NHL	51	27	22	49	65	0	16	0	6	1	2	3	6
96-97—Los Angeles	NHL	67	21	23	44	45	-22	5	1	—	—	—	—	—
—Pittsburgh	NHL	12	4	7	11	6	8	0	0	5	1	0	1	12
97-98—Pittsburgh	NHL	56	11	11	22	35	-9	5	1	6	2	0	2	4
98-99—Chicago	NHL	61	10	15	25	29	-3	2	1	—	—	—	—	—
—Chicago	IHL	7	2	2	4	6	...	...	...	—	—	—	—	—
99-00—Chicago	NHL	33	2	2	4	12	-8	0	0	—	—	—	—	—
NHL Totals (16 years)		1031	342	452	794	874	-67	100	12	57	19	15	34	57

QUENNEVILLE, JOEL — BLUES

PERSONAL: Born September 15, 1958, in Windsor, Ont. ... Full Name: Joel Norman Quenneville.
TRANSACTIONS/CAREER NOTES: Selected by Toronto Maple Leafs in second round (first Maple Leafs pick, 21st overall) of NHL amateur draft (June 15, 1978). ... Traded by Maple Leafs with RW Lanny McDonald to Colorado Rockies for RW Wilf Paiement and LW Pat Hickey (December 1979). ... Injured ribcage (March 1980). ... Underwent surgery to repair torn ligaments in ring finger of left hand (March 1980). ... Sprained ankle, twisted knee and suffered facial lacerations (January 4, 1982). ... Rockies franchise moved to New Jersey and became the Devils (June 30, 1982). ... Traded by Devils with C Steve Tambellini to Calgary Flames for C Mel Bridgman and D Phil Russell (July 1983). ... Traded by Flames with D Richie Dunn to Hartford Whalers for D Mickey Volcan and third-round pick in 1984 draft (August 1983). ... Fractured right shoulder (December 18, 1986); missed 42 games. ... Separated left shoulder (January 19, 1989); missed nine games. ... Traded by Whalers to Washington Capitals for cash (October 3, 1990). ... Signed as free agent by Maple Leafs (July 30, 1991).

Season Team	League	REGULAR SEASON								PLAYOFFS				
		Gms.	G	A	Pts.	PIM	+/-	PP	SH	Gms.	G	A	Pts.	PIM
75-76—Windsor	OHL.	66	15	33	48	61	...	...	...	—	—	—	—	—
76-77—Windsor	OHL	65	19	59	78	169	...	...	...	9	6	5	11	112
77-78—Windsor	OHL	66	27	76	103	114	...	...	...	6	2	3	5	17
78-79—Toronto	NHL	61	2	9	11	60	7	0	0	6	0	1	1	4
—New Brunswick	AHL	16	1	10	11	10	...	...	...	—	—	—	—	—
79-80—Toronto	NHL	32	1	4	5	24	-2	1	0	—	—	—	—	—
—Colorado Rockies	NHL	35	5	7	12	26	-21	1	0	—	—	—	—	—
80-81—Colorado Rockies	NHL	71	10	24	34	86	-24	3	0	—	—	—	—	—
81-82—Colorado Rockies	NHL	64	5	10	15	55	-29	0	0	—	—	—	—	—
82-83—New Jersey	NHL	74	5	12	17	46	-13	0	1	—	—	—	—	—
83-84—Hartford	NHL	80	5	8	13	95	-11	0	2	—	—	—	—	—
84-85—Hartford	NHL	79	6	16	22	96	-15	0	0	—	—	—	—	—
85-86—Hartford	NHL	71	5	20	25	83	20	1	0	10	0	2	2	12
86-87—Hartford	NHL	37	3	7	10	24	8	0	1	6	0	0	0	0
87-88—Hartford	NHL	77	1	8	9	44	-13	0	0	6	0	2	2	2
88-89—Hartford	NHL	69	4	7	11	32	3	0	0	4	0	3	3	4
89-90—Hartford	NHL	44	1	4	5	34	9	0	0	—	—	—	—	—
90-91—Washington	NHL	9	1	0	1	0	-8	0	0	—	—	—	—	—
—Baltimore	AHL	59	6	13	19	58	...	...	...	6	1	1	2	6
91-92—St. John's	AHL	73	7	23	30	58	...	...	...	16	0	1	1	10
NHL Totals (13 years)		803	54	136	190	705	-89	6	4	32	0	8	8	22

HEAD COACHING RECORD

BACKGROUND: Player/coach, St. John's of the AHL (1991-92). ... Assistant coach, St. John's (1992-93). ... Assistant coach, Quebec Nordiques (1994-95). ... Quebec franchise moved to Denver and renamed Colorado Avalanche for 1995-96 season. ... Assistant coach, Colorado Avalanche (1995-96 through January 5, 1997).

Season Team	League	REGULAR SEASON						PLAYOFFS		
		W	L	T	OTL	Pct.	Finish	W	L	Pct.
93-94—Springfield	AHL	29	38	13	—	.444	4th/Northern Division	2	4	.333
96-97—St. Louis	NHL	18	15	7	—	.538	4th/Central Division	2	4	.333
97-98—St. Louis	NHL	45	29	8	—	.598	3rd/Central Division	6	4	.600
98-99—St. Louis	NHL	37	32	13	—	.530	2nd/Central Division	6	7	.462
99-00—St. Louis	NHL	51	19	11	1	.689	1st/Central Division	3	4	.429
00-01—St. Louis	NHL	43	22	12	5	.598	2nd/Central Division	9	6	.600
01-02—St. Louis	NHL	43	27	8	4	.573	2nd/Central Division	5	5	.500
02-03—St. Louis	NHL	41	24	11	6	.567	2nd/Central Division	3	4	.429
NHL Totals (7 years)		278	168	70	16	.588	**NHL Totals (7 years)**	34	34	.500

NOTES:

93-94—Lost to Adirondack in division semifinals of Calder Cup playoffs.

96-97—Replaced Mike Keenan as coach (January 6); lost to Detroit in Western Conference quarterfinals.

97-98—Defeated Los Angeles in Western Conference quarterfinals; lost to Detroit in Western Conference semifinals.

98-99—Defeated Phoenix in Western Conference quarterfinals; lost to Dallas in Western Conference semifinals.

99-00—Lost to San Jose in Western Conference quarterfinals.

00-01—Defeated San Jose in Western Conference quarterfinals; defeated Dallas in Western Conference semifinals; lost to Colorado in Western Conference finals.

01-02—Defeated Chicago in Western Conference quarterfinals; lost to Detroit in Western Conference semifinals.

02-03—Lost to Vancouver in Western Conference quarterfinals.

QUINN, PAT | MAPLE LEAFS

PERSONAL: Born January 29, 1943, in Hamilton, Ont. ... Full Name: John Brian Patrick Quinn.

HIGH SCHOOL: Central (Hamilton, Ont.).

COLLEGE: UC San Diego, then Widener University (degree in law).

TRANSACTIONS/CAREER NOTES: Loaned by Detroit Red Wings to Tulsa Oilers for 1964-65 season. ... Fractured ankle (1965). ... Selected by Montreal Canadiens from Red Wings in intraleague draft (June 1966). ... Sold by Canadiens to St. Louis Blues (June 1967). ... Traded by Blues to Toronto Maple Leafs for rights to LW Dickie Moore (March 1968). ... Selected by Vancouver Canucks in NHL expansion draft (June 1970). ... Selected by Atlanta Flames in NHL expansion draft (June 1972). ... Fractured leg (1976).

Season Team	League	REGULAR SEASON								PLAYOFFS				
		Gms.	G	A	Pts.	PIM	+/-	PP	SH	Gms.	G	A	Pts.	PIM
58-59—Hamilton Jr. A	OHA	20	0	1	1	...	...	...	...	—	—	—	—	—
59-60—Hamilton Jr. A	OHA	27	0	1	1	...	...	...	...	—	—	—	—	—
60-61—Hamilton Jr. B	OHA					Statistics unavailable.								
61-62—						Did not play.								
62-63—Edmonton	CAHL					Statistics unavailable.								
63-64—Knoxville	EHL	72	6	31	37	217	...	...	...	8	1	3	4	34
64-65—Tulsa	CPHL	70	3	32	35	202	...	...	...	3	0	0	0	9
65-66—Memphis	CPHL	67	2	16	18	135	...	...	...	—	—	—	—	—
66-67—Houston	CPHL	15	0	3	3	66	...	...	...	—	—	—	—	—
—Seattle	WHL	35	1	3	4	49	...	...	...	5	0	0	0	2
67-68—Tulsa	CPHL	51	3	15	18	178	...	...	...	11	1	4	5	19
68-69—Tulsa	CHL	17	0	6	6	25	...	...	...	—	—	—	—	—
—Toronto	NHL	40	2	7	9	95	10	0	0	4	0	0	0	13
69-70—Tulsa	CHL	2	0	1	1	6	...	...	...	—	—	—	—	—
—Toronto	NHL	59	0	5	5	88	-14	0	0	—	—	—	—	—
70-71—Vancouver	NHL	76	2	11	13	149	2	0	0	—	—	—	—	—
71-72—Vancouver	NHL	57	2	3	5	63	-28	0	0	—	—	—	—	—
72-73—Atlanta	NHL	78	2	18	20	113	2	0	1	—	—	—	—	—
73-74—Atlanta	NHL	77	5	27	32	94	15	0	0	4	0	0	0	6
74-75—Atlanta	NHL	80	2	19	21	156	12	0	0	—	—	—	—	—
75-76—Atlanta	NHL	80	2	11	13	134	5	0	1	2	0	1	1	2
76-77—Atlanta	NHL	59	1	12	13	58	-7	0	0	1	0	0	0	0
NHL Totals (9 years)		606	18	113	131	950	-3	0	2	11	0	1	1	21

HEAD COACHING RECORD

BACKGROUND: Assistant coach, Philadelphia Flyers (1977-78). ... Coach, Team Canada (1986). ... President/general manager, Vancouver Canucks (1987-88 through November 4, 1997). ... Assistant general manager, Team Canada (1996 and 1997). ... Head coach, Canadian Olympic team (2002).

Season Team	League	REGULAR SEASON						PLAYOFFS		
		W	L	T	OTL	Pct.	Finish	W	L	Pct.
78-79—Philadelphia	NHL	18	8	4	—	.667	2nd/Patrick Division	3	5	.375
79-80—Philadelphia	NHL	48	12	20	—	.725	1st/Patrick Division	13	6	.684
80-81—Philadelphia	NHL	41	24	15	—	.606	2nd/Patrick Division	6	6	.500
81-82—Philadelphia	NHL	34	29	9	—	.535	3rd/Patrick Division	—	—	—
84-85—Los Angeles	NHL	34	32	14	—	.513	4th/Smythe Division	0	3	.000
85-86—Los Angeles	NHL	23	49	8	—	.338	5th/Smythe Division	—	—	—
86-87—Los Angeles	NHL	18	20	4	—	.476	4th/Smythe Division	—	—	—
90-91—Vancouver	NHL	9	13	4	—	.423	4th/Smythe Division	2	4	.333
91-92—Vancouver	NHL	42	26	12	—	.600	1st/Smythe Division	6	7	.462
92-93—Vancouver	NHL	46	29	9	—	.601	1st/Smythe Division	6	6	.500
93-94—Vancouver	NHL	41	40	3	—	.506	2nd/Pacific Division	15	9	.625
95-96—Vancouver	NHL	3	3	0	—	.500	3rd/Pacific Division	2	4	.333
98-99—Toronto	NHL	45	30	7	—	.591	2nd/Northeast Division	9	8	.529
99-00—Toronto	NHL	45	27	7	3	.591	1st/Northeast Division	6	6	.500
00-01—Toronto	NHL	37	29	11	5	.518	3rd/Northeast Division	7	4	.636
01-02—Toronto	NHL	43	25	10	4	.615	2nd/Northeast Division	10	10	.500
02-03—Toronto	NHL	44	28	7	3	.579	2nd/Northeast Division	3	4	.429
NHL Totals (17 years)		**571**	**424**	**144**	**15**	**.557**	**NHL Totals (14 years)**	**88**	**82**	**.518**

NOTES:

78-79—Defeated Vancouver in Stanley Cup preliminary round; lost to New York Rangers in Stanley Cup quarterfinals.

79-80—Defeated Edmonton in Stanley Cup preliminary round; defeated New York Rangers in Stanley Cup quarterfinals; defeated Minnesota in Stanley Cup semifinals; lost to New York Islanders in Stanley Cup finals.

80-81—Defeated Quebec in Stanley Cup preliminary round; lost to Calgary in Stanley Cup quarterfinals.

84-85—Lost to Edmonton in Smythe Division semifinals.

90-91—Replaced Bob McCammon as head coach (January) with club in fifth place; lost to Los Angeles in Smythe Division semifinals.

91-92—Defeated Winnipeg in Smythe Division semifinals; lost to Edmonton in Smythe Division finals.

92-93—Defeated Winnipeg in Smythe Division semifinals; lost to Los Angeles in Smythe Division finals.

93-94—Defeated Calgary in Western Conference quarterfinals; defeated Dallas in Western Conference semifinals; defeated Toronto in Western Conference finals; lost to New York Rangers in Stanley Cup finals.

95-96—Replaced Rick Ley as head coach (March 28) with club in third place; lost to Colorado in Western Conference quarterfinals.

98-99—Defeated Philadelphia in Eastern Conference quarterfinals; defeated Pittsburgh in Eastern Conference semifinals; lost to Buffalo in Eastern Conference finals.

99-00—Defeated Ottawa in Eastern Conference quarterfinals; lost to New Jersey in Eastern Conference semifinals.

00-01—Defeated Ottawa in Eastern Conference quarterfinals; lost to New Jersey in Eastern Conference semifinals.

01-02—Defeated New York Islanders in Eastern Conference quarterfinals; defeated Ottawa in Eastern Conference semifinals; lost to Carolina in Eastern Conference finals.

02-03—Lost to Philadelphia in Eastern Conference quarterfinal.

RUFF, LINDY   SABRES

PERSONAL: Born February 17, 1960, in Warburg, Alta. ... Full Name: Lindy Cameron Ruff.

TRANSACTIONS/CAREER NOTES: Selected by Buffalo Sabres in second round (second Sabres pick, 32nd overall) of NHL entry draft (August 9, 1979). ... Fractured ankle (December 1980). ... Fractured hand (March 1983). ... Injured shoulder (January 14, 1984). ... Separated shoulder (October 26, 1984). ... Fractured left clavicle (March 5, 1986). ... Sprained shoulder (November 1988). ... Traded by Sabres to New York Rangers for fifth-round pick (D Richard Smehlik) in 1990 draft (March 7, 1989). ... Fractured rib (January 23, 1990); missed seven games. ... Fractured nose (March 21, 1990). ... Bruised left thigh (April 1990). ... Signed as free agent by Sabres (September 1991).

Season Team	League	REGULAR SEASON								PLAYOFFS				
		Gms.	G	A	Pts.	PIM	+/-	PP	SH	Gms.	G	A	Pts.	PIM
76-77—Taber	AJHL	60	13	33	46	112	...	...	...	—	—	—	—	—
—Lethbridge	WCHL	2	0	2	2	0	...	...	...	—	—	—	—	—
77-78—Lethbridge	WCHL	66	9	24	33	219	...	...	...	8	2	8	10	4
78-79—Lethbridge	WHL	24	9	18	27	108	...	...	...	6	0	1	1	0
79-80—Buffalo	NHL	63	5	14	19	38	-2	1	0	8	1	1	2	19
80-81—Buffalo	NHL	65	8	18	26	121	3	1	0	6	3	1	4	23
81-82—Buffalo	NHL	79	16	32	48	194	1	3	0	4	0	0	0	28
82-83—Buffalo	NHL	60	12	17	29	130	14	2	0	10	4	2	6	47
83-84—Buffalo	NHL	58	14	31	45	101	15	3	0	3	1	0	1	9
84-85—Buffalo	NHL	39	13	11	24	45	-1	2	0	5	2	4	6	15
85-86—Buffalo	NHL	54	20	12	32	158	8	5	1	—	—	—	—	—
86-87—Buffalo	NHL	50	6	14	20	74	-12	0	0	—	—	—	—	—
87-88—Buffalo	NHL	77	2	23	25	179	-9	0	0	6	0	2	2	23
88-89—Buffalo	NHL	63	6	11	17	86	-17	0	0	—	—	—	—	—
—New York Rangers	NHL	13	0	5	5	31	-6	0	0	2	0	0	0	17
89-90—New York Rangers	NHL	56	3	6	9	80	-10	0	0	8	0	3	3	12
90-91—New York Rangers	NHL	14	0	1	1	27	-2	0	0	—	—	—	—	—
91-92—Rochester	AHL	62	10	24	34	110	...	...	...	13	0	4	4	16
92-93—San Diego	IHL	81	10	32	42	100	...	...	...	14	1	6	7	26
NHL Totals (12 years)		**691**	**105**	**195**	**300**	**1264**	**-18**	**17**	**1**	**52**	**11**	**13**	**24**	**193**

HEAD COACHING RECORD

BACKGROUND: Assistant coach, Florida Panthers (1993-94 through 1996-97).

Season Team	League	REGULAR SEASON						PLAYOFFS		
		W	L	T	OTL	Pct.	Finish	W	L	Pct.
97-98—Buffalo	NHL	36	29	17	—	.543	3rd/Northeast Division	10	5	.667
98-99—Buffalo	NHL	37	28	17	—	.555	3rd/Northeast Division	14	7	.667
99-00—Buffalo	NHL	35	32	11	4	.494	3rd/Northeast Division	1	4	.200
00-01—Buffalo	NHL	46	30	5	1	.591	2nd/Northeast Division	7	6	.538
01-02—Buffalo	NHL	35	35	11	1	.494	5th/Northeast Division	—	—	—
02-03—Buffalo	NHL	27	37	10	8	.390	5th/Northeast Division	—	—	—
NHL Totals (6 years)		216	191	71	14	.511	**NHL Totals (4 years)**	32	22	.593

NOTES:

97-98—Defeated Philadelphia in Eastern Conference quarterfinals; defeated Montreal in Eastern Conference semifinals; lost to Washington in Eastern Conference finals.

98-99—Defeated Ottawa in Eastern Conference quarterfinals; defeated Boston in Eastern Conference semifinals; defeated Toronto in Eastern Conference finals; lost to Dallas in Stanley Cup finals.
99-00—Lost to Philadelphia in Eastern Conference quarterfinals.
00-01—Defeated Philadelphia in Eastern Conference quarterfinals; lost to Pittsburgh in Eastern Conference semifinals.

SATHER, GLEN   RANGERS

PERSONAL: Born September 2, 1943, in High River, Alta. ... Full Name: Glen Cameron Sather.
TRANSACTIONS/CAREER NOTES: Selected by Boston Bruins from Detroit Red Wings (June 1965). ... Selected by Pittsburgh Penguins from Bruins (June 1969). ... Traded by Penguins to New York Rangers for C Syl Apps (January 1971). ... Traded by Rangers with player to be named later to St. Louis Blues for RW Jack Egers (October 1973); Rangers sent Rene Villemure to Blues to complete deal. ... Traded by Blues to Montreal Canadiens (June 1974) to complete deal in which Blues sent their fourth choice in 1974 draft (D Barry Legge) to Canadiens for D Rick Wilson and their fifth choice in 1974 draft (Don Wheldon) (May 27, 1974).. ... Traded by Canadiens to Minnesota North Stars for cash and future considerations (June 1975). ... Signed as free agent by Edmonton Oilers of WHA (August 1976).

Season Team	League	REGULAR SEASON								PLAYOFFS				
		Gms.	G	A	Pts.	PIM	+/-	PP	SH	Gms.	G	A	Pts.	PIM
64-65—Memphis....................	CPHL	69	19	29	48	98	...	...	...	—	—	—	—	—
65-66—Oklahoma City	CPHL	64	13	12	25	76	...	...	...	9	4	4	8	14
66-67—Boston	NHL	5	0	0	0	0	...	...	...	—	—	—	—	—
—Oklahoma City	CPHL	57	14	19	33	147	...	...	...	11	2	6	8	24
67-68—Boston	NHL	65	8	12	20	34	...	...	...	3	0	0	0	0
68-69—Boston	NHL	76	4	11	15	67	...	...	...	10	0	0	0	18
69-70—Pittsburgh................	NHL	76	12	14	26	114	...	...	...	10	0	2	2	17
70-71—Pittsburgh................	NHL	46	8	3	11	96	...	...	...	—	—	—	—	—
—New York Rangers......	NHL	31	2	0	2	52	...	...	...	13	0	1	1	18
71-72—New York Rangers......	NHL	76	5	9	14	77	...	...	...	16	0	1	1	22
72-73—New York Rangers......	NHL	77	11	15	26	64	...	...	...	9	0	0	0	7
73-74—New York Rangers......	NHL	2	0	0	0	0	...	...	...	—	—	—	—	—
—St. Louis	NHL	69	15	29	44	82	...	...	...	—	—	—	—	—
74-75—Montreal....................	NHL	63	6	10	16	44	...	...	...	11	1	1	2	4
75-76—Minnesota..................	NHL	72	9	10	19	94	...	...	...	—	—	—	—	—
76-77—Edmonton	WHA	81	19	34	53	77	...	...	...	5	1	1	2	2
WHA Totals (1 year)		81	19	34	53	77	...	...	...	5	1	1	2	2
NHL Totals (10 years).........		658	80	113	193	724	...	...	...	72	1	5	6	86

HEAD COACHING RECORD

Season Team	League	REGULAR SEASON						PLAYOFFS		
		W	L	T	OTL	Pct.	Finish	W	L	Pct.
76-77—Edmonton	WHA	9	7	2	—	.556	—	1	4	.200
77-78—Edmonton	WHA	39	38	3	—	.506	—	1	4	.200
78-79—Edmonton	WHA	48	30	2	—	.613	—	6	7	.462
79-80—Edmonton	NHL	28	39	13	—	.431	4th/Smythe Division	0	3	.000
80-81—Edmonton	NHL	25	26	11	—	.492	4th/Smythe Division	5	4	.556
81-82—Edmonton	NHL	48	17	15	—	.694	1st/Smythe Division	2	3	.400
82-83—Edmonton	NHL	47	21	12	—	.663	1st/Smythe Division	11	5	.688
83-84—Edmonton	NHL	57	18	5	—	.744	1st/Smythe Division	15	4	.789
84-85—Edmonton	NHL	49	20	11	—	.681	1st/Smythe Division	15	3	.833
85-86—Edmonton	NHL	56	17	7	—	.744	1st/Smythe Division	6	4	.600
86-87—Edmonton	NHL	50	24	6	—	.660	1st/Smythe Division	16	5	.762
87-88—Edmonton	NHL	44	25	11	—	.619	2nd/Smythe Division	16	2	.889
88-89—Edmonton	NHL	38	34	8	—	.525	3rd/Smythe Division	3	4	.429
93-94—Edmonton	NHL	22	27	11	—	.458	6th/Pacific Division	—	—	—
02-03—New York Rangers	NHL	11	10	4	3	.464	4th/Atlantic Division	—	—	—
WHA Totals (3 years)		96	75	7	0	.559				
NHL Totals (12 years)		475	278	114	3	.611	**NHL Totals (10 years)**....................	89	37	.706

NOTES:

76-77—Lost to Winnipeg in Avco Cup quarterfinals.
77-78—Lost to Houston in Avco Cup Western Division semifinals.
78-79—Defeated New England in AVCO Cup semifinals; lost to Winnipeg in AVCO Cup finals.
79-80—Lost to Philadelphia in Stanley Cup preliminary round.
80-81—Defeated Montreal in Stanley Cup preliminary round; Lost to New York Islanders in Stanley Cup quarterfinals.
81-82—Lost to Los Angeles in Stanley Cup preliminary round.
82-83—Defeated Winnipeg in Smythe Division semifinals; defeated Calgary in Smythe Division finals; defeated Chicago in Campbell Conference finals; lost to New York Islanders in Stanley Cup finals.
83-84—Defeated Winnipeg in Smythe Division semifinals; defeated Calgary in Smythe Division finals; defeated Minnesota in Campbell Conference finals; defeated New York Islanders in Stanley Cups finals.

84-85—Defeated Los Angeles in Smythe Division semifinals; defeated Winnipeg in Smythe Division finals; defeated Chicago in Campbell Conference finals; Defeated Philadelphia in Stanley Cup finals.

85-86—Defeated Vancouver in Smythe Division semifinals; lost to Calgary in Smythe Division finals.

86-87—Defeated Los Angeles in Smythe Division semifinals; defeated Winnipeg in Smythe Division finals. defeated Detroit in Campbell Conference finals; defeated Philadelphia in Stanley Cup finals.

87-88—Defeated Winnipeg in Smythe Division semifinals; defeated Calgary in Smythe Division finals; defeated Detroit in Campbell Conference finals; defeated Boston in Stanley Cup finals.

88-89—Lost to Los Angeles in Smythe Division semifinals.

02-03—Replaced Brian Trottier as head coach (January 31).

STIRLING, STEVE — ISLANDERS

PERSONAL: Born November 19, 1949, in Toronto.

TRANSACTIONS/CAREER NOTES: Played for: Boston University (1968-1971); Boston Braves of the AHL (1971-74); Rochester (AHL), Binghamton (AHL) and in Vienna, Austria (1974-1978).

HEAD COACHING RECORD
BACKGROUND: Head Coach, Babson College (1978-83 and 1985-1993). ... Head Coach, Providence College (1983-1985). ... Athletic Director, Babson College (1986-1997). ... Scout, New York Islanders (1997-98). ... Assistant coach, Lowell Lock Monsters of AHL (1998-2001). ... Assistant coach, New York Islanders (2000-01).

HONORS: Division II/III NCAA Coach of the Year (1980 and 1982). ... Won Hockey News' Minor Pro Coach of the Year (2001-02).

Season Team	League	REGULAR SEASON						PLAYOFFS		
		W	L	T	OTL	Pct.	Finish	W	L	Pct.
01-02—Bridgeport	AHL	43	25	8	4	.588	1st/East Division	12	8	.600
02-03—Bridgeport	AHL	40	26	11	3	.569	2nd/East Division	5	4	.556

NOTES:

01-02—Defeated Manitoba in conference quarterfinals; defeated St. John's in conference semifinals; defeated Hamilton in conference finals; lost to Chicago in Calder Cup Finals.

02-03—Defeated Manchester in conference quarterfinals; lost to Binghamton in conference semifinals.

SULLIVAN, MIKE — BRUINS

PERSONAL: Born February 27, 1968, in Marshfield, Mass. ... Played center. ... Shot left. ... Full Name: Michael Barry Sullivan.

TRANSACTIONS/CAREER NOTES: Selected by New York Rangers in fourth round (fourth Rangers pick, 69th overall) of NHL entry draft (June 13, 1987). ... Traded by Rangers with D Mark Tinordi, D Paul Jerrard, RW Brett Barnett and third-round pick (C Murray Garbutt) in 1989 draft to Minnesota North Stars for LW Igor Liba, C Brian Lawton and rights to LW Eric Bennett (October 11, 1988). ... Signed as free agent by San Jose Sharks (August 9, 1991). ... Sprained left knee (April 6, 1993); missed remainder of season. ... Claimed on waivers by Calgary Flames (January 6, 1994). ... Pulled groin (January 29, 1994); missed 13 games. ... Bruised knee (April 6, 1994); missed one game. ... Bruised left foot (March 17, 1995); missed two games. ... Sprained right ankle (April 13, 1995); missed final eight games of season. ... Suffered concussion (February 15, 1997); missed two games. ... Suffered back spasms (March 16, 1997); missed two games. ... Traded by Flames to Boston Bruins for seventh-round pick (RW Radek Duda) in 1998 draft (June 21, 1997). ... Injured wrist (February 4, 1998); missed two games. ... Selected by Nashville Predators in NHL expansion draft (June 26, 1998). ... Traded by Predators to Phoenix Coyotes for seventh-round pick (G Kyle Kettles) in 1999 draft (June 30, 1998). ... Fractured toe (December 17, 1998); missed three games. ... Fractured rib (January 11, 1999); missed 12 games. ... Separated shoulder (February 26, 1999); missed four games. ... Bruised ankle (January 12, 2000); missed three games. ... Strained muscle in abdomen (November 1, 2000); missed six games. ... Suffered concussion (January 23, 2001); missed three games. ... Strained groin (January 26, 2002); missed eight games. ... Injured ribs (February 26, 2002); missed 12 games.

Season Team	League	REGULAR SEASON								PLAYOFFS				
		Gms.	G	A	Pts.	PIM	+/-	PP	SH	Gms.	G	A	Pts.	PIM
85-86—Boston College H.S.	Mass. H.S.	22	26	33	59	...	...	...	...	—	—	—	—	—
86-87—Boston University	Hockey East	37	13	18	31	18	...	...	...	—	—	—	—	—
87-88—Boston University	Hockey East	30	18	22	40	30	...	...	...	—	—	—	—	—
88-89—Boston University	Hockey East	36	19	17	36	30	...	...	...	—	—	—	—	—
—Virginia	ECHL	2	0	0	0	0	...	...	...	—	—	—	—	—
89-90—Boston University	Hockey East	38	11	20	31	26	...	...	...	—	—	—	—	—
90-91—San Diego	IHL	74	12	23	35	27	...	...	...	—	—	—	—	—
91-92—Kansas City	IHL	10	2	8	10	8	...	...	...	—	—	—	—	—
—San Jose	NHL	64	8	11	19	15	-18	1	0	—	—	—	—	—
92-93—San Jose	NHL	81	6	8	14	30	-42	0	2	—	—	—	—	—
93-94—San Jose	NHL	26	2	2	4	4	-3	0	2	—	—	—	—	—
—Kansas City	IHL	6	3	3	6	0	...	...	...	—	—	—	—	—
—Saint John	AHL	5	2	0	2	4	...	...	...	—	—	—	—	—
—Calgary	NHL	19	2	3	5	6	2	0	0	7	1	1	2	8
94-95—Calgary	NHL	38	4	7	11	14	-2	0	0	7	3	5	8	2
95-96—Calgary	NHL	81	9	12	21	24	-6	0	1	4	0	0	0	0
96-97—Calgary	NHL	67	5	6	11	10	-11	0	3	—	—	—	—	—
—Adirondack	AHL	17	1	3	4	2	...	...	...	—	—	—	—	—
97-98—Boston	NHL	77	5	13	18	34	-1	0	0	6	0	1	1	2
98-99—Phoenix	NHL	63	2	4	6	24	-11	0	1	5	0	0	0	2
99-00—Phoenix	NHL	79	5	10	15	10	-4	0	2	5	0	1	1	0
00-01—Phoenix	NHL	72	5	4	9	16	-6	0	3	—	—	—	—	—
01-02—Phoenix	NHL	42	1	2	3	16	-3	0	0	—	—	—	—	—
NHL Totals (11 years)		709	54	82	136	203	-105	1	14	34	4	8	12	14

HEAD COACHING RECORD
BACKGROUND: ... Assistant coach, Boston Bruins (March 19, 2003 - April 5, 2003)

Season Team	League	REGULAR SEASON						PLAYOFFS		
		W	L	T	OTL	Pct.	Finish	W	L	Pct.
02-03—Providence	AHL	47	17	9	4	.669	—	—	—	—

PERSONAL: Born October 7, 1956, in Viking, Alta. ... Played left wing. ... Shot left. ... Full Name: Brian Louis Allen Sutter. ... Brother of Darryl Sutter, head coach, San Jose Sharks and left winger with Chicago Blackhawks (1979-80 through 1986-87); brother of Brent Sutter, center with New York Islanders (1980-81 through 1991-92) and Blackhawks (1991-92 through 1997-98); brother of Ron Sutter, center, San Jose Sharks; brother of Rich Sutter, right winger with seven NHL teams (1982-83 through 1994-95); and brother of Duane Sutter, right winger with New York Islanders (1979-80 through 1986-87) and Blackhawks (1987-88 throug

TRANSACTIONS/CAREER NOTES: Selected by St. Louis Blues from in second round (second Blues pick, 20th overall) of NHL amateur draft (June 1, 1976). ... Suffered hairline fracture of pelvis (November 3, 1983). ... Fractured left shoulder (January 16, 1986). ... Reinjured left shoulder (March 8, 1986). ... Damaged left shoulder muscle (November 1986). ... Sprained ankle (November 1987). ... Retired as player and signed as head coach of Blues (June 1988).

					REGULAR SEASON							PLAYOFFS			
Season Team	League	Gms.	G	A	Pts.	PIM	+/-	PP	SH		Gms.	G	A	Pts.	PIM
72-73—Red Deer	AJHL	51	27	40	67	54	...	...	...		—	—	—	—	—
73-74—Red Deer	AJHL	59	42	54	96	139	...	...	...		—	—	—	—	—
74-75—Lethbridge	WCHL	53	34	47	81	134	...	...	...		6	0	1	1	39
75-76—Lethbridge	WCHL	72	36	56	92	233	...	...	...		7	3	4	7	45
76-77—Kansas City	CHL	38	15	23	38	47	...	...	...		—	—	—	—	—
—St. Louis	NHL	35	4	10	14	82	-38	4	0		4	1	0	1	14
77-78—St. Louis	NHL	78	9	13	22	123	-2	12	0		—	—	—	—	—
78-79—St. Louis	NHL	77	41	39	80	165	3	6	0		—	—	—	—	—
79-80—St. Louis	NHL	71	23	35	58	156	-8	0	0		3	0	0	0	4
80-81—St. Louis	NHL	78	35	34	69	232	12	17	0		11	6	3	9	77
81-82—St. Louis	NHL	74	39	36	75	239	-2	14	0		10	8	6	14	49
82-83—St. Louis	NHL	79	46	30	76	254	-1	11	0		4	2	1	3	10
83-84—St. Louis	NHL	76	32	51	83	162	-6	14	2		11	1	5	6	22
84-85—St. Louis	NHL	77	37	37	74	121	11	14	0		3	2	1	3	2
85-86—St. Louis	NHL	44	19	23	42	87	-12	8	0		9	1	2	3	22
86-87—St. Louis	NHL	14	3	3	6	18	-5	3	0		—	—	—	—	—
87-88—St. Louis	NHL	76	15	22	37	147	-16	4	1		10	0	3	3	49
NHL Totals (12 years)		779	303	333	636	1786	-64	107	3		65	21	21	42	249

HEAD COACHING RECORD

BACKGROUND: Assistant coach, Team Canada (1991).

			REGULAR SEASON						PLAYOFFS		
Season Team	League	W	L	T	OTL	Pct.	Finish		W	L	Pct.
88-89—St. Louis	NHL	33	35	12	—	.488	2nd/Norris Division		5	5	.500
89-90—St. Louis	NHL	37	34	9	—	.519	2nd/Norris Division		7	5	.583
90-91—St. Louis	NHL	47	22	11	—	.656	2nd/Norris Division		6	7	.462
91-92—St. Louis	NHL	36	33	11	—	.519	3rd/Norris Division		2	4	.333
92-93—Boston	NHL	51	26	7	—	.649	1st/Adams Division		0	4	.000
93-94—Boston	NHL	42	29	13	—	.577	2nd/Northeast Division		6	7	.462
94-95—Boston	NHL	27	18	3	—	.594	3rd/Northeast Division		1	4	.200
97-98—Calgary	NHL	26	41	15	—	.409	5th/Pacific Division		—	—	—
98-99—Calgary	NHL	30	40	12	—	.439	3rd/Northwest Division		—	—	—
99-00—Calgary	NHL	31	36	10	5	.439	4th/Northwest Division		—	—	—
01-02—Chicago	NHL	41	27	13	1	.579	3rd/Central Division		1	4	.200
02-03—Chicago	NHL	30	33	13	6	.445	3rd/Central Division		—	—	—
NHL Totals (12 years)		431	374	129	12	.524	**NHL Totals (8 years)**		28	40	.412

NOTES:

88-89—Defeated Minnesota in Norris Division semifinals; lost to Chicago in Norris Division finals.

89-90—Defeated Toronto in Norris Division semifinals; lost to Chicago in Norris Division finals.

90-91—Defeated Detroit in Norris Division semifinals; lost to Minnesota in Norris Division finals.

91-92—Lost to Chicago in Norris Division semifinals.

92-93—Lost to Buffalo in Adams Division semifinals.

93-94—Defeated Montreal in Eastern Conference quarterfinals; lost to New Jersey in Eastern Conference semifinals.

94-95—Lost to New Jersey in Eastern Conference quarterfinals.

01-02—Lost to St. Louis in Western Conference semifinals.

SUTTER, DARRYL   FLAMES

PERSONAL: Born August 19, 1958, in Viking, Alta. ... Played left wing. ... Shot left. ... Brother of Brian Sutter, left winger with St. Louis Blues (1976-77 through 1987-88) and head coach with Blues (1988-89 through 1991-92), Boston Bruins (1992-93 through 1994-95) and Calgary Flames (1997-98 through 1999-2000); brother of Duane Sutter, right winger with New York Islanders (1979-80 through 1986-87) and Chicago Blackhawks (1987-88 through 1989-90); brother of Rich Sutter, right winger, with seven NHL teams (1982-83 through 1994-95); brother of Ron Sutter, center, San Jose Sharks; and

TRANSACTIONS/CAREER NOTES: Selected by Chicago Blackhawks in 11th round (11th Blackhawks pick, 179th overall) of NHL amateur draft (June 1978). ... Lacerated left elbow, developed infection and underwent surgery (November 27, 1981). ... Fractured nose (November 7, 1982). ... Fractured ribs (November 1983). ... Fracture left cheekbone and injured left eye (January 2, 1984). ... Underwent arthroscopic surgery to right knee (September 1984). ... Bruised ribs (October 1984). ... Fractured left ankle (December 26, 1984). ... Separated right shoulder and underwent surgery (November 13, 1985); missed 30 games. ... Injured knee (February 1987). ... Retired as player to become assistant coach of Blackhawks (June 1987).

Season Team	League	REGULAR SEASON							PLAYOFFS				
		Gms.	G	A	Pts.	PIM	+/-	PP	SH	Gms.	G	A	Pts.	PIM
74-75—Red Deer..................	AJHL	60	16	20	36	43	...	...	...	—	—	—	—	—
75-76—Red Deer..................	AJHL	60	43	93	136	82	...	...	...	—	—	—	—	—
76-77—Red Deer..................	AJHL	56	55	78	133	131	...	...	...	—	—	—	—	—
—Lethbridge	WCHL	1	1	0	1	0	...	...	...	15	3	7	10	13
77-78—Lethbridge	WCHL	68	33	48	81	119	...	...	...	8	4	9	13	2
78-79—New Brunswick..........	AHL	19	7	6	13	6	...	...	...	5	1	2	3	0
—Iwakura	Japan	20	28	13	41	0	...	...	...	—	—	—	—	—
79-80—New Brunswick..........	AHL	69	35	31	66	69	...	...	...	12	6	6	12	8
—Chicago....................	NHL	8	2	0	2	2	1	0	0	7	3	1	4	2
80-81—Chicago....................	NHL	76	40	22	62	86	-1	14	0	3	3	1	4	2
81-82—Chicago....................	NHL	40	23	12	35	31	0	4	3	3	0	1	1	2
82-83—Chicago....................	NHL	80	31	30	61	53	18	10	0	13	4	6	10	8
83-84—Chicago....................	NHL	59	20	20	40	44	-18	8	0	5	1	1	2	0
84-85—Chicago....................	NHL	49	20	18	38	12	8	2	0	15	12	7	19	12
85-86—Chicago....................	NHL	50	17	10	27	44	-15	3	0	3	1	2	3	0
86-87—Chicago....................	NHL	44	8	6	14	16	-3	1	0	2	0	0	0	0
NHL Totals (8 years)...........		406	161	118	279	288	-10	42	3	51	24	19	43	26

HEAD COACHING RECORD

BACKGROUND: Assistant coach, Chicago Blackhawks (1987-88). ... Associate coach, Blackhawks (1990-92). ... Special assistant to general manager, Blackhawks (1995-96 and 1996-97).

Season Team	League	REGULAR SEASON					Finish	PLAYOFFS		
		W	L	T	OTL	Pct.		W	L	Pct.
88-89—Saginaw	IHL	46	26	10	—	.622	2nd/East Division	2	4	.333
89-90—Indianapolis	IHL	53	21	8	—	.695	1st/West Division	12	2	.857
92-93—Chicago	NHL	47	25	12	—	.631	1st/Norris Division	0	4	.000
93-94—Chicago	NHL	39	36	9	—	.518	5th/Central Division	2	4	.333
94-95—Chicago	NHL	24	19	5	—	.552	3rd/Central Division	9	7	.563
97-98—San Jose	NHL	34	38	10	—	.476	4th/Pacific Division	2	4	.333
98-99—San Jose	NHL	31	33	18	—	.488	3rd/Pacific Division	2	4	.333
99-00—San Jose	NHL	35	30	10	7	.488	4th/Pacific Division	5	7	.417
00-01—San Jose	NHL	40	27	12	3	.561	2nd/Pacific Division	2	4	.333
01-02—San Jose	NHL	44	27	8	3	.585	1st/Pacific Division	7	5	.583
02-03—San Jose	NHL	8	12	2	2	.375	—	—	—	—
—Calgary	NHL	19	18	8	1	.500	5th/Northwest Division	—	—	—
NHL Totals (9 years)		321	265	94	16	.529	**NHL Totals (8 years)**.....................	29	39	.426

NOTES:
88-89—Lost to Fort Wayne in quarterfinals of Turner Cup playoffs.
89-90—Defeated Peoria in quarterfinals of Turner Cup playoffs; defeated Salt Lake City in semifinals of Turner Cup playoffs; defeated Muskegon in Turner Cup finals.
92-93—Lost to St. Louis in Norris Division semifinals.
93-94—Lost to Toronto in Western Conference quarterfinals.
94-95—Defeated Toronto in Western Conference quarterfinals; defeated Vancouver in Western Conference semifinals; lost to Detroit in Western Conference finals.
97-98—Lost to Dallas in Western Conference quarterfinals.
98-99—Lost to Colorado in Western Conference quarterfinals.
99-00—Defeated St. Louis in Western Conference quarterfinals; lost to Dallas in Western Conference semifinals.
00-01—Lost to St. Louis in Western Conference quarterfinals.
01-02—Defeated Phoenix in Western Conference quarterfinals; lost to Colorado in Western Conference semifinals.
02-03—Replaced as head coach (December 2, 2002); replaced Greg Gilbert as head coach (December 28, 2002).

TIPPETT, DAVE   STARS

PERSONAL: Born August 25, 1961, in Moosomin, Sask. ... Played center. ... Shot left. ... Full Name: David G. Tippett.
TRANSACTIONS/CAREER NOTES: Signed as non-drafted free agent by Hartford Whalers (February 29, 1984). ... Injured right thumb tendons (October 8, 1989). ... Traded by Whalers to Washington Capitals for sixth-round pick (C Jarret Reid) in 1992 draft (September 30, 1990). ... Separated shoulder (November 28, 1990); missed 11 games. ... Signed as free agent by Pittsburgh Penguins (August 28, 1992). ... Fractured thumb (November 20, 1992); missed six games. ... Signed as free agent by Philadelphia Flyers (August 2, 1993). ... Broke bone in left foot (November 27, 1993); missed eight games.

Season Team	League	REGULAR SEASON							PLAYOFFS				
		Gms.	G	A	Pts.	PIM	+/-	PP	SH	Gms.	G	A	Pts.	PIM
79-80—Prince Albert..............	SJHL	85	72	95	167	...	...	...	...	—	—	—	—	—
80-81—Prince Albert..............	SJHL	84	62	93	155	...	...	...	...	—	—	—	—	—
81-82—Univ. of North Dakota .	WCHA	43	13	28	41	24	...	...	...	—	—	—	—	—
82-83—Univ. of North Dakota .	WCHA	36	15	31	46	44	...	...	...	—	—	—	—	—
83-84—Can. Olympic team	Int'l	66	14	19	33	24	...	...	...	—	—	—	—	—
—Hartford	NHL	17	4	2	6	2	-1	0	1	—	—	—	—	—
84-85—Hartford	NHL	80	7	12	19	12	-24	0	0	—	—	—	—	—
85-86—Hartford	NHL	80	14	20	34	18	9	0	2	10	2	2	4	4
86-87—Hartford	NHL	80	9	22	31	42	0	0	3	6	0	2	2	4
87-88—Hartford	NHL	80	16	21	37	32	-4	1	2	6	0	0	0	2
88-89—Hartford	NHL	80	17	24	41	45	-6	1	2	4	0	1	1	0
89-90—Hartford	NHL	66	8	19	27	32	0	0	1	7	1	3	4	2
90-91—Washington	NHL	61	6	9	15	24	-13	0	0	10	2	3	5	8
91-92—Washington	NHL	30	2	10	12	16	2	0	0	7	0	1	1	0
—Canadian nat'l team	Int'l	1	0	0	0	4	...	...	...	—	—	—	—	—
—Can. Olympic team	Int'l	6	1	2	3	10	...	...	...	—	—	—	—	—
92-93—Pittsburgh..................	NHL	74	6	19	25	56	5	0	1	12	1	4	5	14
93-94—Philadelphia	NHL	73	4	11	15	38	-20	0	2	—	—	—	—	—
94-95—Houston	IHL	75	18	48	66	56	...	...	...	4	1	2	3	4
NHL Totals (11 years).........		721	93	169	262	317	-52	2	14	62	6	16	22	34

BACKGROUND: Assistant coach, Houston Aeros (1994-95). ... General manager, Aeros (1998-99). ... Assistant coach, Los Angeles Kings (1999-2000 through 2001-02).

Season Team	League	W	L	T	OTL	Pct.	Finish	W	L	Pct.
							REGULAR SEASON		PLAYOFFS	
95-96—Houston	IHL	29	45	8	—	.402	5th/Central Division	—	—	—
96-97—Houston	IHL	44	30	8	—	.585	2nd/Southwest Division	8	5	.615
97-98—Houston	IHL	50	22	10	—	.671	2nd/Southwest Division	1	3	.250
98-99—Houston	IHL	54	15	13	—	.738	1st/Southwest Division	11	8	.579
02-03—Dallas	NHL	46	17	15	4	.652	1st/Pacific Division	6	6	.500
NHL Totals (1 year)		46	17	15	4	.652	**NHL Totals (1 year)**	6	6	.500

NOTES:
96-97—Defeated Las Vegas in conference quarterfinals of Turner Cup playoffs; defeated San Antonio in conference semifinals of Turner Cup playoffs; lost to Long Beach in conference finals of Turner Cup playoffs.
97-98—Lost to Milwaukee in conference quarterfinals of Turner Cup playoffs.
98-99—Defeated Long Beach in conference semifinals of Turner Cup playoffs; defeated Chicago in conference finals of Turner Cup playoffs; defeated Orlando in Turner Cup finals.
02-03—Defeated Edmonton in Western Conference quarterfinals; lost to Anaheim in Western Conference semifinals.

TORTORELLA, JOHN   LIGHTNING

PERSONAL: Born in Boston.
COLLEGE: Salem State College, then Maine.

Season Team	League	Gms.	G	A	Pts.	PIM	+/-	PP	SH	Gms.	G	A	Pts.	PIM
			REGULAR SEASON								PLAYOFFS			
79-80—University of Maine	ECAC	31	14	22	36	71	...	...	...	—	—	—	—	—
82-83—Hampton Roads	ACHL	1	1	0	1	2	...	...	...	—	—	—	—	—
—Erie	ACHL	12	2	10	12	4	...	...	...	—	—	—	—	—
83-84—Virginia-Erie	ACHL	64	25	37	62	77	...	...	...	4	1	1	2	18
84-85—Virginia	ACHL	63	33	54	87	66	...	...	...	4	3	4	7	0
85-86—Virginia	ACHL	60	37	59	96	153	...	...	...	5	1	3	4	60

HEAD COACHING RECORD

BACKGROUND: General Manager, Virginia Lancers ACHL (1986-87 and 1987-88). ... Assistant coach, New Haven Nighthawks AHL (1988-89). ... Assistant coach, Buffalo Sabres (1989-90 through 1994-95). ... Assistant coach, Phoenix Coyotes (1997-98 and 1998-99). ... Assistant coach, New York Rangers (1999-March 28, 2000). ... Assistant coach, Tampa Bay Lightning (2000-January 6, 2001).

Season Team	League	W	L	T	OTL	Pct.	Finish	W	L	Pct.
							REGULAR SEASON		PLAYOFFS	
86-87—Virginia	ACHL	36	19	3	—	.647	1st overall	8	4	.667
87-88—Virginia	AAHL	37	5	1	—	.872	1st overall	3	5	.375
95-96—Rochester	AHL	37	38	5	—	.494	3rd/Central Division	15	4	.789
96-97—Rochester	AHL	40	30	9	—	.563	1st/Empire State Division	6	4	.600
99-00—New York Rangers	NHL	0	3	1	0	.000	4th/Atlantic Division	—	—	—
00-01—Tampa Bay	NHL	12	27	1	3	.291	5th/Southeast Division	—	—	—
01-02—Tampa Bay	NHL	27	40	11	4	.396	3rd/Southeast Division	—	—	—
02-03—Tampa Bay	NHL	36	25	16	5	.537	1st/Southeast Division	5	6	.455
NHL Totals (4 years)		75	95	29	12	.424	**NHL Totals (1 year)**	5	6	.455

NOTES:
86-87—Defeated Carolina in ACHL semifinals; defeated Mohawk Valley in ACHL finals.
87-88—Defeated Johnstown in round-robin series; lost to Carolina in AAHL finals.
95-96—Defeated Adirondack in conference quarterfinals of Calder Cup playoffs; defeated Cornwall in conference semifinals of Calder Cup playoffs; defeated Syracuse in conference finals of Calder Cup playoffs; defeated Portland in Calder Cup finals.
96-97—Defeated Syracuse in conference quarterfinals of Calder Cup playoffs; lost to Albany in conference semifinals of Calder Cup playoffs.
99-00—Replaced John Muckler as head coach on interim basis (March 28).
00-01—Replaced Steve Ludzik as head coach (January 6).
02-03—Defeated Washington in Eastern Conference quarterfinals; lost to New Jersey in Eastern Conference semifinals.

TROTZ, BARRY   PREDATORS

PERSONAL: Born July 15, 1962, in Winnipeg.

Season Team	League	Gms.	G	A	Pts.	PIM	+/-	PP	SH	Gms.	G	A	Pts.	PIM
			REGULAR SEASON								PLAYOFFS			
79-80—Regina	WHL	41	4	8	12	42	...	...	...	—	—	—	—	—
80-81—Regina	WHL	62	4	13	17	115	...	...	...	—	—	—	—	—
81-82—Regina	WHL	50	6	28	34	155	...	...	...	20	1	7	8	79

HEAD COACHING RECORD

BACKGROUND: Player/assistant coach, University of Manitoba (1983-84). ... Head coach/general manager, Dauphin Kings junior team (1984-85 through 1986-87). ... Assistant coach, University of Manitoba (1987-88). ... Scout, Washington Capitals (1988-89 through 1990-91). ... Assistant coach, Baltimore Skipjacks of the AHL (1991-92). ... Scout, Nashville Predators (1997-98).

Season Team	League	W	L	T	OTL	Pct.	Finish	W	L	Pct.
							REGULAR SEASON		PLAYOFFS	
92-93—Baltimore	AHL	28	40	12	—	.425	4th/Southern Division	3	4	.429
93-94—Portland	AHL	43	27	10	—	.600	2nd/Northern Division	12	5	.706
94-95—Portland	AHL	46	22	12	—	.650	2nd/Northern Division	3	4	.429
95-96—Portland	AHL	32	38	10	—	.463	3rd/Northern Division	14	10	.583

NHL HEAD COACHES

Season Team	League	REGULAR SEASON							PLAYOFFS		
		W	L	T	OTL	Pct.	Finish		W	L	Pct.
96-97—Portland	AHL	37	33	10	—	.525	3rd/New England Division		2	3	.400
98-99—Nashville	NHL	28	47	7	—	.384	4th/Central Division		—	—	—
99-00—Nashville	NHL	28	40	7	7	.384	4th/Central Division		—	—	—
00-01—Nashville	NHL	34	36	9	3	.470	3rd/Central Division		—	—	—
01-02—Nashville	NHL	28	41	13	0	.421	4th/Central Division		—	—	—
02-03—Nashville	NHL	27	35	13	7	.409	4th/Central Division		—	—	—
NHL Totals (5 years)		145	199	49	17	.413					

NOTES:

92-93—Lost to Binghamton in the first round of Calder Cup playoffs.

93-94—Defeated Albany in Northern Division semifinals; defeated Adirondack in Northern Division finals; defeated Moncton in Calder Cup finals.

94-95—Lost to Providence in Northern Division semifinals.

95-96—Defeated Worcester in Eastern Conference quarterfinals; defeated Springfield in Eastern Conference semifinals; defeated Saint John in Eastern Conference finals; lost to Rochester in Calder Cup finals.

96-97—Lost to Springfield in Southern Conference quarterfinals.

PERSONAL: Born May 28, 1955, in Windsor, Ont. ... Played defense. ... Shot right. ... Full Name: Ronald Lawrence Wilson. ... Son of Larry Wilson, center with Detroit Red Wings (1949-50, 1951-52 and 1952-53) and Chicago Blackhawks (1953-54 through 1955-56) and coach with Red Wings (1976-77); and nephew of Johnny Wilson, left winger with four NHL teams (1949-50 through 1961-62) and coach with four NHL teams and two WHA teams (1969-70 through 1979-80).

COLLEGE: Providence (degree in economics).

TRANSACTIONS/CAREER NOTES: Selected by Toronto Maple Leafs in seventh round (seventh Maple Leafs pick, 132nd overall) in NHL entry draft (June 3, 1975). ... Loaned by Davos HC to Minnesota North Stars for remainder of NHL season and playoffs (March 1985). ... Loaned by Davos HC to Minnesota North Stars for remainder of NHL season and playoffs (March 1986). ... Traded by Davos HC to Minnesota North Stars for D Craig Levie (May 1986). ... Separated shoulder (March 9, 1987).

Season Team	League	REGULAR SEASON									PLAYOFFS				
		Gms.	G	A	Pts.	PIM	+/-	PP	SH		Gms.	G	A	Pts.	PIM
73-74—Providence College	ECAC	26	16	22	38	...	...	...	...		—	—	—	—	—
74-75—Providence College	ECAC	27	26	61	87	12	...	...	...		—	—	—	—	—
—U.S. national team	Int'l	27	5	32	37	42	...	...	...		—	—	—	—	—
75-76—Providence College	ECAC	28	19	47	66	44	...	...	...		—	—	—	—	—
76-77—Providence College	ECAC	30	17	42	59	62	...	...	...		—	—	—	—	—
—Dallas	CHL	4	1	0	1	2	...	...	...		—	—	—	—	—
77-78—Dallas	CHL	67	31	38	69	18	...	...	...		—	—	—	—	—
—Toronto	NHL	13	2	1	3	0	-5	1	0		—	—	—	—	—
78-79—New Brunswick	AHL	31	11	21	32	13	...	...	...		—	—	—	—	—
—Toronto	NHL	46	5	12	17	4	-10	4	0		3	0	1	1	0
79-80—New Brunswick	AHL	43	20	43	63	10	...	...	...		14	3	2	5	2
—Toronto	NHL	5	0	2	2	2	-2	0	0		3	1	2	3	2
80-81—EHC Kloten	Switzerland	38	22	23	45	...	...	...	...		—	—	—	—	—
81-82—Davos HC	Switzerland	38	24	23	47	...	...	...	...		—	—	—	—	—
82-83—Davos HC	Switzerland	36	32	32	64	...	...	...	...		—	—	—	—	—
83-84—Davos HC	Switzerland	36	33	39	72	...	...	...	...		—	—	—	—	—
84-85—Davos HC	Switzerland	38	39	62	101	...	...	...	...		—	—	—	—	—
—Minnesota	NHL	13	4	8	12	2	-1	0	0		9	1	6	7	2
85-86—Davos HC	Switzerland	27	28	41	69	...	...	...	...		5	6	2	8	...
—Minnesota	NHL	11	1	3	4	8	-2	1	0		5	2	4	6	4
86-87—Minnesota	NHL	65	12	29	41	36	-9	6	0		—	—	—	—	—
87-88—Minnesota	NHL	24	2	12	14	16	-4	1	0		—	—	—	—	—
NHL Totals (7 years)		177	26	67	93	68	-33	13	0		20	4	13	17	8

HEAD COACHING RECORD

BACKGROUND: Assistant coach, Milwaukee Admirals of IHL (1989-90). ... Served as interim coach of Milwaukee while Ron Lapointe was hospitalized for cancer treatments (February and March 1990; team went 9-10). ... Assistant coach, Vancouver Canucks (1990-91 through 1992-93).

Season Team	League	REGULAR SEASON							PLAYOFFS		
		W	L	T	OTL	Pct.	Finish		W	L	Pct.
93-94—Anaheim	NHL	33	46	5	—	.423	4th/Pacific Division		—	—	—
94-95—Anaheim	NHL	16	27	5	—	.385	6th/Pacific Division		—	—	—
95-96—Anaheim	NHL	35	39	8	—	.476	4th/Pacific Division		—	—	—
96-97—Anaheim	NHL	36	33	13	—	.518	2nd/Pacific Division		4	7	.364
97-98—Washington	NHL	40	30	12	—	.561	3rd/Atlantic Division		12	9	.571
98-99—Washington	NHL	31	45	6	—	.415	3rd/Southeast Division		—	—	—
99-00—Washington	NHL	44	24	12	2	.610	1st/Southeast Division		1	4	.200
00-01—Washington	NHL	41	27	10	4	.561	1st/Southeast Division		2	4	.333
01-02—Washington	NHL	36	33	11	2	.506	2nd/Southeast Division		—	—	—
02-03—San Jose	NHL	19	25	7	6	.395	5th/Pacific		—	—	—
NHL Totals (10 years)		331	329	89	14	.492	NHL Totals (4 years)		19	24	.442

NOTES:

96-97—Defeated Phoenix in Western Conference quarterfinals; lost to Detroit in Western Conference semifinals.

97-98—Defeated Boston in Eastern Conference quarterfinals; defeated Ottawa in Eastern Conference semifinals; defeated Buffalo in Eastern Conference finals; lost to Detroit in Stanley Cup finals.

99-00—Lost to Pittsburgh in Eastern Conference quarterfinals.

00-01—Lost to Pittsburgh in Eastern Conference quarterfinals.

02-03—Replaced Darryl Sutter as head coach (Decemeber 4).

Get Inside The Game

☑ YES!

Send me 30 issues of Sporting News Magazine for just 99¢ each.
I SAVE 75% OFF the newsstand price.
For new subscribers only.

NAME (Please Print)

ADDRESS

CITY   STATE   ZIP

☐ Payment enclosed ☐ Bill me later   5GCF4

Canada add $20.80 for subscription postage (U.S. funds only). Other international rates available on request. Sporting News Magazine is published weekly, with special double issues. **www.sportingnews.com**

MAIL THIS CARD OR CALL TOLL-FREE:
1-800-238-0452

Get Inside The Game

☑ YES!

Send me 30 issues of Sporting News Magazine for just 99¢ each.
I SAVE 75% OFF the newsstand price.
For new subscribers only.

NAME (Please Print)

ADDRESS

CITY   STATE   ZIP

☐ Payment enclosed ☐ Bill me later   5GCF4

Canada add $20.80 for subscription postage (U.S. funds only). Other international rates available on request. Sporting News Magazine is published weekly, with special double issues. **www.sportingnews.com**

MAIL THIS CARD OR CALL TOLL-FREE:
1-800-238-0452

BUSINESS REPLY MAIL
FIRST-CLASS MAIL   PERMIT NO 1397   BOULDER CO

POSTAGE WILL BE PAID BY ADDRESSEE

PO BOX 51576
BOULDER CO 80323-1576

NO POSTAGE
NECESSARY
IF MAILED
IN THE
UNITED STATES

BUSINESS REPLY MAIL
FIRST-CLASS MAIL   PERMIT NO 1397   BOULDER CO

POSTAGE WILL BE PAID BY ADDRESSEE

PO BOX 51576
BOULDER CO 80323-1576